THE OLD TESTAMENT (OT)

Genesis
Exodus
Leviticus
Numbers
Deuteronomy
Joshua
Judges
Ruth
1 Samuel
2 Samuel
1 Kings
2 Kings
1 Chronicles
2 Chronicles
Ezra
Nehemiah
Esther
Job
Psalms
Proverbs
Ecclesiastes
Song of Solomon
Isaiah
Jeremiah
Lamentations
Ezekiel
Daniel
Hosea
Joel
Amos
Obadiah
Jonah
Micah
Nahum
Habakkuk
Zephaniah
Haggai
Zechariah
Malachi

THE NEW TESTAMENT (NT)

Matthew
Mark
Luke
John
Acts
Romans
1 Corinthians
2 Corinthians
Galatians
Ephesians
Philippians
Colossians
1 Thessalonians
2 Thessalonians
1 Timothy
2 Timothy
Titus
Philemon
Hebrews
James
1 Peter
2 Peter
1 John
2 John
3 John
Jude
Revelation

Deuterocanonical Books/Apocrypha: In Roman Catholic Bibles, the OT includes the following deuterocanonical books: (following Nehemiah) Tobit, Judith, Esther with the additions, 1–2 Maccabees; (following Song of Songs) Wisdom, Ecclesiasticus; (following Lamentations) Baruch including the Letter of Jeremiah; (following Ezekiel) Daniel with the additions.

In addition to these books, the Bible of the Greek Orthodox community includes 1 Esdras, the Prayer of Manasseh, Psalm 151, 3 Maccabees, with 4 Maccabees as an appendix.

Protestants regard the deuterocanonical books as not part of the OT canon and either do not include them in their Bibles, or print them in a separate section (''Apocrypha'') following the OT or at the end of the Bible.

HARPER'S BIBLE DICTIONARY

Harper's Bible Dictionary

GENERAL EDITOR

Paul J. Achtemeier

ASSOCIATE EDITORS

Roger S. Boraas

Michael Fishbane

Pheme Perkins

William O. Walker, Jr.

With the Society of Biblical Literature

HarperSanFrancisco

A Division of HarperCollins*Publishers*

Publication Staff

Editor:
John B. Shopp
Assistant Editor:
Shelley Thacher
Production Editor:
Dorian Gossy
Production Coordinator:
Steve Dietz
Copyeditor:
Ann Moru
Proofreaders:
Kathy Lee, Janine Baer, Anne Collins, Caroline Crawford,
Jean Mann, Virginia Rich, David Sweet,
Jack Whelan, Barbara Yoder
Photo research:
InfoEdit Leslye Borden, Elizabeth Ely
Jacket, cover, and text design:
Design Office Bruce Kortebein with design and production
assistance from Joy Dickinson
Color photograph insert design:
Christy Butterfield
Text illustrations:
Heather Preston, Sally Shimizu
Typesetting, page make-up:
Auto-graphics, Inc.
Text printing and binding:
The Haddon Craftsmen
Jacket printing:
Lehigh Press, Inc.
Cartography and color maps printing:
Hammond Inc.
Color photograph separation:
Color Tech Corporation
Color photograph printing:
Eastern Press

Library of Congress Cataloging-in-Publication Data
Main entry under title:

Harper's Bible dictionary.

Includes index.
1. Bible—Dictionaries. I. Achtemeier, Paul J. II. Harper & Row. III. Title: Bible dictionary. BS440.H237 1985 220.3 85-42767
ISBN 0-06-069863-2 (thumb-indexed)
ISBN 0-06-069862-4

96 97 98 99 HAD 17 16 15 14 13 12

EDITORIAL BOARD

CONTRIBUTORS

I.T.A. I. Tzvi Abusch, Ph.D.
Associate Professor of Assyriology
Brandeis University
Waltham, Massachusetts

E.R.A. Elizabeth Achtemeier, Ph.D.
Visiting Professor of Bible and Homiletics
Union Theological Seminary
Richmond, Virginia

P.R.A. Peter R. Ackroyd, Ph.D.
Professor (Emeritus) of Old Testament Studies
King's College
University of London
London, England

J.E.A. John E. Alsup, Dr. Theol.
Associate Professor of New Testament
Austin Presbyterian Theological Seminary
Austin, Texas

H.W.A. Harold W. Attridge, Ph.D.
Associate Professor of New Testament
Perkins School of Theology
Southern Methodist University
Dallas, Texas

L.R.B. Lloyd R. Bailey, Ph.D.
Associate Professor of Old Testament
Divinity School
Duke University
Durham, North Carolina

W.R.B. William Baird, Ph.D.
Professor of New Testament
Brite Divinity School
Texas Christian University
Fort Worth, Texas

D.B. Denis Baly, BA. Hons. Geog.
Emeritus Professor of Religion
Kenyon College
Gambier, Ohio

J.B. James Barr, D.D.
Regius Professor of Hebrew
Oxford University
Oxford, England

J.M.B. Jouette M. Bassler, Ph.D.
Assistant Professor
Department of Theology
Georgetown University
Washington, D.C.

R.A.B. Richard A. Batey, Ph.D.
W. J. Millard Professor of Religion
Rhodes College
Memphis, Tennessee

S.B. Stephen Benko, Ph.D.
Professor of Ancient History
California State University
Fresno, California

A.B. Adele Berlin, Ph.D.
Associate Professor of Hebrew
University of Maryland
College Park, Maryland

E.B. Ernest Best, Ph.D.
Emeritus Professor of Divinity and Biblical Criticism
University of Glasgow
Glasgow, Scotland

J.W.B. John W. Betlyon, Ph.D.
Chaplain and Assistant Professor of Religion
Smith College
Northampton, Massachusetts

H.D.B. Hans Dieter Betz, Dr. Theol.
Professor of New Testament
Divinity School
University of Chicago
Chicago, Illinois

P.A.B. Phyllis A. Bird, Th.D.
Associate Professor of Old Testament
Perkins School of Theology
Southern Methodist University
Dallas, Texas

R.B. Robert G. Boling, Ph.D.
Professor of Old Testament
McCormick Theological Seminary
Chicago, Illinois

M.E.B. M. Eugene Boring, Ph.D.
Darbeth Distinguished Professor of New Testament
Graduate Seminary, Phillips University
Enid, Oklahoma

D.R.B. Dennis R. Bratcher, Ph.D.
Adjunct Professor of Biblical Studies
Virginia Union University
Richmond, Virginia

R.G.B. Robert G. Bratcher, Th.D.
Translation Consultant
United Bible Societies
New York, New York

M.Z.B. Marc Z. Brettler, M.A.
Lecturer
Department of Religious Studies
Yale University
New Haven, Connecticut

W.B. Walter Brueggemann, Ph.D.
Evangelical Professor of Biblical Interpretation
Eden Theological Seminary
St. Louis, Missouri

G.W.B. George Wesley Buchanan, Ph.D.
Professor of New Testament
Wesley Theological Seminary
Washington, D.C.

E.F.C. Edward F. Campbell, Ph.D.
Francis A. McGaw Professor of Old Testament
McCormick Theological Seminary
Chicago, Illinois

C.E.C. Charles E. Carlston, Ph.D.
Norris Professor of New Testament Interpretation
Andover Newton Theological School
Newton Centre, Massachusetts

J.H.C. James H. Charlesworth, Ph.D.
George L. Collord Professor of New Testament Language and Literature
Princeton Theological Seminary
Princeton, New Jersey

D.L.C. Duane L. Christensen, Th.D.
Professor of Old Testament Languages and Literature
American Baptist Seminary of the West
Berkeley, California

R.J.C. Richard J. Clifford, Ph.D.
Dean and Professor of Old Testament
Weston School of Theology
Cambridge, Massachusetts

G.W.C. George W. Coats, Jr., Ph.D.
Professor of Old Testament
Lexington Theological Seminary
Lexington, Kentucky

M.C. Mordechai Cogan, Ph.D.
Professor of Bible and Ancient Near East
Ben Gurion University of the Negev
Beer-sheva, Israel

A.Y.C. Adela Y. Collins, Ph.D.
Professor of Biblical Studies
University of Notre Dame
Notre Dame, Indiana

J.J.C. John J. Collins, Ph.D.
Professor of Biblical Studies
University of Notre Dame
Notre Dame, Indiana

M.D.C. Michael D. Coogan, Ph.D.
Associate Professor of Old Testament
Harvard University
Cambridge, Massachusetts

R.A.C. Robert A. Coughenour, Ph.D.
Professor of Old Testament
Western Theological Seminary
Holland, Michigan

L.W.C. L. William Countryman, Ph.D.
Associate Professor of New Testament
Church Divinity School of the Pacific
Berkeley, California

F.B.C. Fred B. Craddock, Ph.D.
Franklin Parker Professor of Preaching and New Testament
Candler School of Theology
Emory University
Atlanta, Georgia

P.L.C. Patricia L. Crawford, B.A.
Graduate Teaching Fellow
Department of Archaeology
Boston University
Boston, Massachusetts

J.L.C. James L. Crenshaw, Ph.D.
Professor of Old Testament
Divinity School
Vanderbilt University
Nashville, Tennessee

J.D.C. John Dominic Crossan, Th.D.
Professor of Religious Studies
DePaul University
Chicago, Illinois

J.J.D. John J. Davis, Th.D.
Professor of Old Testament and Archaeology
Grace Theological Seminary
Winona Lake, Indiana

J.A.D. J. Andrew Dearman, Ph.D.
Associate Professor of Old Testament
Austin Presbyterian Theological Seminary
Austin, Texas

W.G.D. William G. Dever, Ph.D.
Professor of Near Eastern Archaeology
University of Arizona
Tucson, Arizona

J.D. Joanna Dewey, Ph.D.
Associate Professor of New Testament and Christianity and Culture
Graduate Seminary
Phillips University
Enid, Oklahoma

K.P.D. Karl Paul Donfried, Dr. Theol.
Professor of Religion and Biblical Literature
Smith College
Northampton, Massachusetts

D.A.D. David A. Dorsey, Ph.D.
Associate Professor of Old Testament
Evangelical School of Theology
Myerstown, Pennsylvania

J.F.D. Joel F. Drinkard, Jr., Ph.D.
Assistant Professor of Old Testament Interpretation
Southern Baptist Theological Seminary
Louisville, Kentucky

D.R.E. Douglas R. Edwards, M. Div.
Visiting Instructor
Department of Religion
University of Vermont
Burlington, Vermont

J.M.E. James M. Efird, Ph.D.
Associate Professor of Biblical Languages and Interpretation
Divinity School
Duke University
Durham, North Carolina

B.L.E. Barry Lee Eichler, Ph.D.
Associate Professor of Assyriology
University of Pennsylvania
Philadelphia, Pennsylvania

D.E. David Ewert, Ph.D.
President and Professor of New Testament
Mennonite Brethren Bible College
Winnipeg, Canada

J.C.E. J. Cheryl Exum, Ph.D.
Associate Professor of Old Testament
Boston College
Chestnut Hill, Massachusetts

G.D.F. Gordon D. Fee, Ph.D.
Professor of New Testament
Gordon-Conwell Theological Seminary
South Hamilton, Massachusetts

H.F. Harold Fisch, B. Litt.
Professor of English and Comparative Literature
Bar-Ilan University
Ramat-Gan, Israel

J.A.F. Joseph A. Fitzmyer, S.J., Ph.D.
Professor
Department of Biblical Studies
Catholic University of America
Washington, D.C.

E.L.F. Elisabeth L. Flynn, Ph.D.
Associate Professor of Art History
Longwood College
Farmville, Virginia

J.P.F. Jan P. Fokkelman, Dr. Phil.
Lecturer, Faculty of Arts
State University
Leiden, Holland

D.A.F. Daniel A. Foxvog, Ph.D.
Visiting Lecturer in Assyriology
University of California
Berkeley, California

F.S.F. Frank S. Frick, Ph.D.
Professor of Religious Studies
Albion College
Albion, Michigan

T.S.F. Tikva S. Frymer-Kensky, Ph.D.
Visiting Associate Professor
Program on Religion
University of Michigan
Ann Arbor, Michigan

R.H.F. Reginald H. Fuller, M.A.
Molly Laird Downs Professor of New Testament
Virginia Theological Seminary
Alexandria, Virginia

V.P.F. Victor Paul Furnish, Ph.D.
University Distinguished Professor of New Testament
Perkins School of Theology
Southern Methodist University
Dallas, Texas

J.G.G. John G. Gammie, Ph.D.
Emma A. Harwell Professor of Biblical Literature
University of Tulsa
Tulsa, Oklahoma

F.O.G. Francisco O. Garcia-Treto, Ph.D.
Professor of Religion
Trinity University
San Antonio, Texas

S.G. Stanley Gevirtz, Ph.D.
Professor of Bible and Ancient Near Eastern Civilizations
Hebrew Union College-Jewish Institute of Religion
Los Angeles, California

Y.G. Yehoshua Gitay, Ph.D.
Assistant Professor of Hebraic Studies
Wesleyan University
Middletown, Connecticut

D.A.G. David A. Glatt, M.A.
University of Pennsylvania
Philadelphia, Pennsylvania

R.M.G. Robert M. Good, Ph.D.
Assistant Professor of Religion
Dartmouth College
Hanover, New Hampshire

F.E.G. Frederick E. Greenspahn, Ph.D.
Assistant Professor of Judaic Studies
University of Denver
Denver, Colorado

E.L.G. Edward L. Greenstein, Ph.D.
Associate Professor in Bible
Jewish Theological Seminary of America
New York, New York

M.R.G. Michael R. Greenwald, M.A.H.L.
Rabbi
Temple Beth Shalom
Melrose, Massachusetts

M.I.G. Mayer I. Gruber, Ph.D.
Senior Lecturer in Bible
Ben Gurion University of the Negev
Beer-sheva, Israel

R.H.G. Robert H. Gundry, Ph.D.
Professor of New Testament and Greek
Westmont College
Santa Barbara, California

P.D.H. Paul D. Hanson, Ph.D.
Bussey Professor of Divinity
Harvard University
Cambridge, Massachusetts

J.P.H. John Paul Heil, S.S.D.
Professor of New Testament
Kenrick Seminary
St. Louis, Missouri

D.C.H. David C. Hester, Ph.D.
Assistant Professor of Religion
Berea College
Berea, Kentucky

R.H.H. Richard H. Hiers, Ph.D.
Professor, Department of Religion
University of Florida
Gainesville, Florida

R.F.H. Ronald F. Hock, Ph.D.
Associate Professor of Religion
University of Southern California
Los Angeles, California

C.R.H. Carl R. Holladay, Ph.D.
Associate Professor of New Testament
Candler School of Theology
Emory University
Atlanta, Georgia

H.B.H. Herbert B. Huffmon, Ph.D.
Professor of Old Testament Studies
Theological School
Drew University
Madison, New Jersey

A.J.H. Arland J. Hultgren, Th.D.
Associate Professor of New Testament
Luther Northwestern Theological Seminary
St. Paul, Minnesota

W.L.H. W. Lee Humphreys, Ph.D.
Professor of Religious Studies
University of Tennessee
Knoxville, Tennessee

B.S.J. Bernard S. Jackson, D. Phil.
Professor of Law
University of Kent
Canterbury, England

J.F.J. John F. Jansen, Th.D.
Professor Emeritus of New Testament Interpretation
Austin Presbyterian Theological Seminary
Austin, Texas

J.G.J. J. Gerald Janzen, Ph.D.
Professor of Old Testament
Christian Theological Seminary
Indianapolis, Indiana

R.J. Robert Jewett, Dr. Theol.
Professor of New Testament Interpretation
Garrett-Evangelical Theological Seminary
Evanston, Illinois

H.C.K. Howard C. Kee, Ph.D.
William Goodwin Aurelio
Professor of Biblical Studies
School of Theology
Boston University
Boston, Massachuetts

A.D.K. Ann Draffkorn Kilmer, Ph.D.
Professor of Assyriology
University of California
Berkeley, California

P.J.K. Philip J. King, S.T.D.
Professor of Biblical Studies
Boston College
Chestnut Hill, Massachusetts

J.D.K. Jack Dean Kingsbury, Dr. Theol.
Aubrey Lee Brooks Professor of
Biblical Theology
Union Theological Seminary
Richmond, Virginia

D.A.K. Douglas A. Knight, Dr. Theol.
Associate Professor of Hebrew
Bible
Divinity School
Vanderbilt University
Nashville, Tennessee

I.U.K. Ilse U. Köhler-Rollefson, Dr. med.vet.
Adjunct Professor
Dept. of Anthropology
San Diego State University
San Diego, California

J.S.K. John S. Kselman, Ph.D.
Associate Professor of Semitic
Languages
Catholic University of America
Washington, D.C.

J.L.K. James L. Kugel, Ph.D.
Professor of Near Eastern
Languages
Harvard University
Cambridge, Massachusetts

N.L.L. Nancy L. Lapp, M.A.
Lecturer in Biblical Hebrew and
Archaeology
Pittsburgh Theological Seminary
Pittsburgh, Pennsylvania

W.E.L. Werner E. Lemke, Th.D.
Professor of Old Testament
Interpretation
Colgate Rochester Divinity School
Rochester, New York

B.M.L. Bernard M. Levinson, M.A.
Brandeis University
Waltham, Massachusetts

B.L. Barnabas Lindars, S.S.F., D.D.
Rylands Professor of Biblical
Criticism and Exegesis
University of Manchester
Manchester, England

T.R.W.L. Thomas R. W. Longstaff, Ph.D.
Professor of Philosophy and
Religion
Colby College
Waterville, Maine

B.M. Burton MacDonald, Ph.D.
Associate Professor
St. Francis Xavier University
Antigonish, Canada

D.R.M. Dennis R. MacDonald, Ph.D.
Associate Professor of New
Testament and Christian Origins
Iliff School of Theology
Denver, Colorado

P.B.M. Peter B. Machinist, Ph.D.
Associate Professor of Ancient
Near Eastern History
University of Arizona
Tucson, Arizona

J.A.R.M. J. A. Ross Mackenzie, Ph.D.
Senior Minister
First Presbyterian Church
Gainesville, Florida

B.J.M. Bruce J. Malina, Ph.D.
Professor, Department of Theology
Creighton University
Omaha, Nebraska

F.J.M. Frank J. Matera, Ph.D.
Professor of New Testament
St. John's Seminary
Brighton, Massachusetts

G.L.M. Gerald L. Mattingly, Ph.D.
Associate Professor of Biblical
Studies
Johnson Bible College
Knoxville, Tennessee

P.K.M. P. Kyle McCarter, Jr., Ph.D.
Professor of Religious Studies
University of Virginia
Charlottesville, Virginia

T.L.M. Thomas L. McClellan, Ph.D.
Lecturer, Department of Middle
Eastern Studies
University of Melbourne
Parkville, Australia

F.R.M. Foster R. McCurley, Ph.D.
Associate in Mission Research
Lutheran Church in America
New York, New York

L.C.M. Lane C. McGaughy, Ph.D.
George H. Atkinson Professor of Religious and Ethical Studies
Willamette University
Salem, Oregon

A.J.M. Allan J. McNicol, Ph.D.
Professor of New Testament
Institute for Christian Studies
Austin, Texas

J.P.M. John P. Meier, S.S.D.
Associate Professor of Biblical Studies
Catholic University of America
Washington, D.C.

R.F.M. Roy F. Melugin, Ph.D.
Cloud Professor of Religion
Austin College
Sherman, Texas

B.M.M. Bruce M. Metzger, Ph.D.
George L. Collord Professor of New Testament Language and Literature, Emeritus
Princeton Theological Seminary
Princeton, New Jersey

C.L.M. Carol L. Meyers, Ph.D.
Associate Professor
Department of Religion
Duke University
Durham, North Carolina

E.M.M. Eric M. Meyers, Ph.D.
Professor of Religion
Duke University
Durham, North Carolina

C.H.M. Charles H. Miller, S.T.D.
Professor of Theology
St. Mary's University
San Antonio, Texas

J.M.M. J. Maxwell Miller, Ph.D.
Professor of Old Testament
Candler School of Theology
Emory University
Atlanta, Georgia

M.K.M. Mary K. Milne, M.A.
Lecturer in Graduate Theology
St. Mary's University
San Antonio, Texas

S.C.M. Stephen C. Mott, Ph.D.
Professor of Christian Social Ethics
Gordon-Conwell Theological Seminary
South Hamilton, Massachusetts

W.M. Winsome Munro, Ed.D.
Assistant Professor of Religion
Luther College
Decorah, Iowa

R.E.M. Roland E. Murphy, S.T.D.
George Washington Ivey Professor of Biblical Studies
Divinity School
Duke University
Durham, North Carolina

C.A.N. Carol A. Newsom, Ph.D.
Assistant Professor of Old Testament
Candler School of Theology
Emory University
Atlanta, Georgia

J.H.N. Jerome H. Neyrey, Ph.D.
Assistant Professor of New Testament
Weston School of Theology
Cambridge, Massachusetts

K.G.O. Kevin G. O'Connell, S.J., Ph.D.
Associate Professor
Department of Religious Studies
John Carroll University
University Heights, Ohio

S.B.P. Simon B. Parker, Ph.D.
Associate Professor of Old Testament
School of Theology
Boston University
Boston, Massachusetts

L.E.P. Laurie E. Pearce, Ph.D.
Lecturer, Department of Classical and Modern Languages
University of Connecticut
Stamford, Connecticut

L.G.P. Leo G. Perdue, Ph.D.
Associate Professor of Old Testament
Graduate Seminary
Phillips University
Enid, Oklahoma

D.M.P. Dana M. Pike, B.S.
Teaching Fellow
Department of Oriental Studies
University of Pennsylvania
Philadelphia, Pennsylvania

J.R.P. Joshua R. Porter, M.A.
Professor, Department of Theology
University of Exeter
Exeter, England

J.L.P. James L. Price, Jr., Ph.D.
Professor of Religion
Duke University
Durham, North Carolina

J.D.P. James D. Purvis, Th.D.
Professor of Religion
Boston University
Boston, Massachusetts

C.Q. Corethia Qualls, Ph.D.
Archaeological Consultant
Kuwait National Museum
Kuwait City, Kuwait

A.F.R. Anson F. Rainey, Ph.D.
Professor of Ancient Near Eastern Cultures and Semitic Linguistics
Tel Aviv University
Tel Aviv, Israel

S.R. Susan Rattray, M.A.
University of California
Berkeley, California

S.B.R. Stephen Breck Reid, Ph.D.
Assistant Professor of Hebrew Scriptures and Biblical Theology
Pacific School of Religion
Berkeley, California

H.E.R. Harold E. Remus, Ph.D.
Associate Professor, Department of Religion and Culture
Wilfrid Laurier University
Waterloo, Canada

J.H.P.R. John Reumann, Ph.D.
Professor of New Testament and Greek
Lutheran Theological Seminary
Philadelphia, Pennsylvania

S.L.R. Suzanne Richard, Ph.D.
Assistant Professor of Archaeology
Drew University
Madison, New Jersey

K.H.R. Kent Harold Richards, Ph.D.
Professor of Old Testament
Iliff School of Theology
Denver, Colorado

J.J.M.R. J. J. M. Roberts, Ph.D.
William Henry Green Professor of Old Testament Literature
Princeton Theological Seminary
Princeton, New Jersey

C.J.R. Calvin J. Roetzel, Ph.D.
Arnold Lowe Professor of Religious Studies
Macalester College
St. Paul, Minnesota

A.R. Alexander Rofé, Ph.D.
Associate Professor of Bible
Hebrew University
Jerusalem, Israel

J.W.R. Joel W. Rosenberg, Ph.D.
Associate Professor, Hebrew Literature and Judaic Studies
Tufts University
Medford, Massachusetts

A.J.S. Anthony J. Saldarini, Ph.D.
Associate Professor
Department of Theology
Boston College
Chestnut Hill, Massachusetts

J.M.S. Jack M. Sasson, Ph.D.
Professor of Religious Studies
University of North Carolina
Chapel Hill, North Carolina

M.M.S. Marilyn M. Schaub, Ph.D.
Professor of Biblical Studies
Duquesne University
Pittsburgh, Pennsylvania

B.E.S. Bruce E. Schein, Ph.D.
Associate Professor of New Testament
Trinity Lutheran Seminary
Columbus, Ohio

L.H.S. Lawrence H. Schiffman, Ph.D.
Professor of Hebrew and Judaic Studies
New York University
New York, New York

P.L.S. Philip L. Shuler, Ph.D.
Professor of Religion
McMurry College
Abilene, Texas

D.J.S. Daniel J. Simundson, Ph.D.
Professor of Old Testament
Luther Northwestern Theological Seminary
St. Paul, Minnesota

D.M.S. Dwight Moody Smith, Ph.D.
Professor of New Testament Interpretation
Divinity School
Duke University
Durham, North Carolina

R.H.S. Robert H. Stein, Ph.D.
Professor of New Testament
Bethel Theological Seminary
St. Paul, Minnesota

D.W.S. David W. Suter, Ph.D.
Associate Professor of Religious Studies
St. Martin's College
Lacey, Washington

M.A.S. Marvin A. Sweeney, Ph.D.
Assistant Professor of Religion
University of Miami
Coral Gables, Florida

C.H.T. Charles H. Talbert, Ph.D.
Professor of Religion
Wake Forest University
Winston-Salem, North Carolina

R.C.T. Robert C. Tannehill, Ph.D.
Fred D. Gealy Professor of New Testament
Methodist Theological School
Delaware, Ohio

H.M.T. Howard M. Teeple, Ph.D.
Executive Director
Religion & Ethics Institute, Inc.
Evanston, Illinois

J.W.T. James W. Thompson, Ph.D.
Professor of Bible
Institute for Christian Studies
Austin, Texas

J.H.T. Jeffrey H. Tigay, Ph.D.
A. M. Ellis Associate Professor of Hebrew and Semitic Languages and Literatures
University of Pennsylvania
Philadelphia, Pennsylvania

L.E.T. Lawrence E. Toombs, Ph.D.
Professor, Religion and Culture
Wilfrid Laurier University
Waterloo, Canada

W.S.T. W. Sibley Towner, Ph.D.
Archibald McFadyen Professor of Biblical Interpretation
Union Theological Seminary
Richmond, Virginia

P.T. Phyllis Trible, Ph.D.
Baldwin Professor of Sacred Literature
Union Theological Seminary
New York, New York

G.M.T. Gene M. Tucker, Ph.D.
Professor of Old Testament
Candler School of Theology
Emory University
Atlanta, Georgia

J.B.T. Joseph B. Tyson, Ph.D.
Professor of Religious Studies
Southern Methodist University
Dallas, Texas

J.U. Jeremiah Unterman, Ph.D.
Associate Professor, Jewish Studies
Barry University
North Miami Beach, Florida

J.M.W. James M. Weinstein, Ph.D.
Lecturer, Department of Classics
Cornell University
Ithaca, New York

D.B.W. David B. Weisberg, Ph.D.
Professor of Bible and Semitic Languages
Hebrew Union College-Jewish Institute of Religion
Cincinnati, Ohio

J.L.W. John L. White, Ph.D.
Associate Professor of Theology
Loyola University
Chicago, Illinois

R.A.W. Robert A. Wild, S.J., Ph.D.
Associate Professor
Theology Department
Marquette University
Milwaukee, Wisconsin

M.M.W. Marsha M. Wilfong, D. Min.
Union Theological Seminary
Richmond, Virginia

S.K.W. Sam K. Williams, Ph.D.
Associate Professor of Religion
Colorado College
Colorado Springs, Colorado

R.R.W. Robert R. Wilson, Ph.D.
Professor of Old Testament
Yale University
New Haven, Connecticut

D.P.W. David P. Wright, Ph.D.
Assistant Professor of Hebrew and Near Eastern Languages
Brigham Young University
Provo, Utah

ABBREVIATIONS

Akk.	Akkadian	Gk.	Greek
Arab.	Arabic	Heb.	Hebrew
Aram.	Aramaic	Lat.	Latin
Assyr.	Assyrian	Pers.	Persian
Bab.	Babylonian	Phoen.	Phoenician
Egypt.	Egyptian	Syr.	Syrian

B.C.E.	Before the Common Era	ms.	manuscript
C.E.	Common Era	mss.	manuscripts
Dt.	Deuteronomic	v.	verse
Dtr.	Deuteronomistic historian	vs.	version
EB	Early Bronze Age	vss.	versions
LB	Late Bronze Age	vv.	verses
MB	Middle Bronze Age		

DSS	Dead Sea Scrolls	ASV	American Standard Version
LXX	Septuagint	JB	Jerusalem Bible
MT	Masoretic Text	KJV	King James Version
NT	New Testament	NASB	New American Standard Bible
OT	Old Testament	NEB	New English Bible
Vg.	Vulgate	NIV	New International Version
		RSV	Revised Standard Version
		TEV	Today's English Version

BOOKS OF THE BIBLE (WITH APOCRYPHA)

Old Testament

Gen.	Genesis	Eccles.	Ecclesiastes
Exod.	Exodus	Song of Sol.	Song of Solomon
Lev.	Leviticus	Isa.	Isaiah
Num.	Numbers	Jer.	Jeremiah
Deut.	Deuteronomy	Lam.	Lamentations
Josh.	Joshua	Ezek.	Ezekiel
Judg.	Judges	Dan.	Daniel
Ruth	Ruth	Hos.	Hosea
1 Sam.	1 Samuel	Joel	Joel
2 Sam.	2 Samuel	Amos	Amos
1 Kings	1 Kings	Obad.	Obadiah
2 Kings	2 Kings	Jon.	Jonah
1 Chron.	1 Chronicles	Mic.	Micah
2 Chron.	2 Chronicles	Nah.	Nahum
Ezra	Ezra	Hab.	Habakkuk
Neh.	Nehemiah	Zeph.	Zephaniah
Esther	Esther	Hag.	Haggai
Job	Job	Zech.	Zechariah
Ps. (Pss.)	Psalms	Mal.	Malachi
Prov.	Proverbs		

Apocrypha

1 Esd.	1 Esdras	Let. Jer.	Letter of Jeremiah
2 Esd.	2 Esdras	Song of Three Children	Song of the Three Children
Tob.	Tobit	Sus.	Susanna
Jth.	Judith	Bel and Dragon	Bel and the Dragon
Rest of Esther	Rest of Esther	Pr. of Man.	Prayer of Manasseh
Wisd. of Sol.	Wisdom of Solomon	1 Macc.	1 Maccabees
Ecclus.	Ecclesiasticus	2 Macc.	2 Maccabees
Bar.	Baruch		

ABBREVIATIONS

New Testament

Matt.	Matthew	1 Tim.	1 Timothy
Mark	Mark	2 Tim.	2 Timothy
Luke	Luke	Titus	Titus
John	John	Philem.	Philemon
Acts	Acts of the Apostles	Heb.	Hebrews
Rom.	Romans	James	James
1 Cor.	1 Corinthians	1 Pet.	1 Peter
2 Cor.	2 Corinthians	2 Pet.	2 Peter
Gal.	Galatians	1 John	1 John
Eph.	Ephesians	2 John	2 John
Phil.	Philippians	3 John	3 John
Col.	Colossians	Jude	Jude
1 Thess.	1 Thessalonians	Rev.	Revelation
2 Thess.	2 Thessalonians		

PSEUDEPIGRAPHA AND EARLY PATRISTIC BOOKS

Adam and Eve	Books of Adam and Eve
2–3 Apoc. Bar.	Syriac, Greek Apocalypse of Baruch
Apoc. Mos.	Apocalypse of Moses
As. Mos.	Assumption of Moses
1–2–3 Enoch	Ethiopic, Slavonic, Hebrew Enoch
Ep. Arist.	Epistle of Aristeas
Jub.	Jubilees
Mart. Isa.	Martyrdom of Isaiah
Odes Sol.	Odes of Solomon
Pss. Sol.	Psalms of Solomon
Sib. Or.	Sibylline Oracles
T. 12 Patr.	Testaments of the Twelve Patriarchs
T. Levi	Testament of Levi
T. Benj.	Testament of Benjamin, etc.
Acts Pil.	Acts of Pilate
Apoc. Pet.	Apocalypse of Peter
Gos. Eb.	Gospel of the Ebionites
Gos. Eg.	Gospel of the Egyptians
Gos. Heb.	Gospel of the Hebrews
Gos. Naass.	Gospel of the Naassenes
Gos. Pet.	Gospel of Peter
Gos. Thom.	Gospel of Thomas
Prot. Jas.	Protevangelium of James
Barn.	Barnabas
1–2 Clem.	1–2 Clement
Did.	Didache
Diogn.	Diognetus
Herm. Man.	Hermas, Mandate
Sim.	Similitude
Vis.	Vision
Ign. Eph.	Ignatius, Letter to the Ephesians
Magn.	Ignatius, Letter to the Magnesians
Phld.	Ignatius, Letter to the Philadelphians
Pol.	Ignatius, Letter to Polycarp
Rom.	Ignatius, Letter to the Romans
Smyrn.	Ignatius, Letter to the Smyrnaeans
Trall.	Ignatius, Letter to the Trallians
Mart. Pol.	Martyrdom of Polycarp
Pol. Phil.	Polycarp to the Phillippians
Bib. Ant.	Ps.-Philo, Biblical Antiquities

DEAD SEA SCROLLS AND RELATED TEXTS

CD	Cairo (Genizah text of the) Damascus (Document)
Ḥev	Naḥal Ḥever texts
Mas	Masada texts
Mird	Khirbet Mird texts
Mur	Wadi Murabbaʿat texts
p	Pesher (commentary)
Q	Qumran
1Q, 2Q, 3Q, etc.	Numbered caves of Qumran, yielding written material; followed by abbreviation of biblical or apocryphal book
QL	Qumran literature
1QapGen	*Genesis Apocryphon of* Qumran Cave 1
1QH	*Hôdāyôt (Thanksgiving Hymns)* from Qumran Cave 1

1QIsa[a,b]	First or second copy of Isaiah from Qumran Cave 1
1QpHab	*Pesher on Habakkuk* from Qumran Cave 1
1QM	*Milḥāmāh (War Scroll)*
1QS	*Serek hayyaḥad (Rule of the Community, Manual of Discipline)*
1QSa	Appendix A *(Rule of the Congregation)* to 1QS
1QSb	Appendix B *(Blessings)* to 1QS
3Q15	Copper Scroll from Qumran Cave 3
4QFlor	*Florilegium* (or *Eschatological Midrashim*) from Qumran Cave 4
4QMess ar	Aramaic "Messianic" text from Qumran Cave 4
4QPBless	*Patriarchal Blessings* from Qumran Cave 4
4QPrNab	Prayer of Nabonidus from Qumran Cave 4
4QTestim	*Testimonia* text from Qumran Cave 4
4QTLevi	*Testament of Levi* from Qumran Cave 4
4QPhyl	Phylacteries from Qumran Cave 4
11QMelch	*Melchizedek* text from Qumran Cave 11
11QPs[a]	*Psalm Scroll a* from Qumran Cave 11
11QtgJob	*Targum of Job* from Qumran Cave 11

TARGUMIC MATERIAL

Tg. Onq.	*Targum Onqelos*	*Tg. Neof.*	*Targum Neofiti 1*
Tg. Neb.	*Targum of the Prophets*	*Tg. Ps.-J.*	*Targum Pseudo-Jonathan*
Tg. Ket.	*Targum of the Writings*	*Tg. Yer. I*	*Targum Yerušalmi I*
Frg. Tg.	*Fragmentary Targum*	*Tg. Yer. II*	*Targum Yerušalmi II*
Sam. Tg.	*Samaritan Targum*	*Yem. Tg.*	*Yemenite Targum*
Tg. Isa	*Targum of Isaiah*	*Tg. Esth I. II*	*First or Second Targum of Esther*
Pal. Tgs.	*Palestinian Targums*		

MISHNAIC AND RELATED LITERATURE

m.	Mishnah	*Meg.*	*Megilla*
t.	Tosepta	*Me'il.*	*Me'ila*
b.	Babylonian Talmud	*Menaḥ.*	*Menaḥot*
y.	Jerusalem (Palestinian) Talmud	*Mid.*	*Middot*
'Abot	*'Abot*	*Miqw.*	*Miqwa'ot*
'Arak.	*'Arakin*	*Mo'ed*	*Mo'ed*
'Abod. Zar.	*'Aboda Zara*	*Mo'ed Qat.*	*Mo'ed Qaṭan*
B. Bat.	*Baba Batra*	*Ma'as. Š.*	*Ma'aśer Šeni*
Bek.	*Bekorot*	*Našim*	*Našim*
Ber.	*Berakot*	*Nazir*	*Nazir*
Beṣa	*Beṣa* (= *Yom Ṭob*)	*Ned.*	*Nedarim*
Bik.	*Bikkurim*	*Neg.*	*Nega'im*
B. Mes.	*Baba Meṣi'a*	*Nez.*	*Neziqin*
B. Qam.	*Baba Qamma*	*Nid.*	*Niddah*
Dem.	*Demai*	*Ohol.*	*Oholot*
'Erub.	*'Erubin*	*'Or.*	*'Orla*
'Ed.	*'Eduyyot*	*Para*	*Para*
Giṭ.	*Giṭin*	*Pe'a*	*Pe'a*
Ḥag.	*Ḥagiga*	*Pesaḥ.*	*Pesaḥim*
Ḥal.	*Ḥalla*	*Qinnim*	*Qinnim*
Hor.	*Horayot*	*Qidd.*	*Qiddušin*
Ḥul.	*Ḥullin*	*Qod.*	*Qodašin*
Kelim	*Kelim*	*Roš. Haš.*	*Roš Haššana*
Ker.	*Keritot*	*Sanh.*	*Sanhedrin*
Ketub.	*Ketubot*	*Šabb.*	*Šabbat*
Kil.	*Kil'ayim*	*Šeb.*	*Šebi'it*
Ma'aś.	*Ma'aśerot*	*Šebu.*	*Šebu'ot*
Mak.	*Makkot*	*Šeqal.*	*Šeqalim*
Makš.	*Makširin* (= *Mašqin*)	*Soṭa*	*Soṭa*

Sukk.	*Sukka*	'Uq.	*'Uqṣin*
Ta'an.	*Ta'anit*	Yad.	*Yadayim*
Tamid	*Tamid*	Yebam.	*Yebamot*
Tem.	*Temura*	Yoma	*Yoma* (= *Kippurim*)
Ter.	*Terumot*	Zabim	*Zabim*
Ṭohar.	*Ṭoharot*	Zebaḥ	*Zebaḥim*
Ṭ. Yom	*Ṭebul Yom*	Zer.	*Zera'im*

OTHER RABBINIC WORKS

'Abot R. Nat.	*'Abot de Rabbi Nathan*	Pesiq. R.	*Pesiqta Rabbati*
'Ag. Ber.	*'Aggadat Berešit*	Pesiq. Rab Kah.	*Pesiqta de Rab Kahana*
Bab.	*Babylonian*	Pirqe R. El.	*Pirqe Rabbi Eleizer*
Bar.	*Baraita*	Rab.	*Rabbah* (following abbreviation for biblical book: *Gen. Rab.* [with periods] = *Genesis Rabbah*)
Der. Er. Rab.	*Derek Ereṣ Rabba*		
Der. Er. Zuṭ.	*Derek Ereṣ Zuṭa*		
Gem.	*Gemara*		
Kalla	*Kalla*	Sem.	*Ṣemaḥot*
Mek.	*Mekilta*	Sipra	*Sipra*
Midr.	*Midraš;* cited with usual abbreviation for biblical book; but *Midr. Qoh.* = Midraš Qohelet	Sipre	*Sipre*
		Sop.	*Soperim*
		S. 'Olam Rab.	*Seder 'Olam Rabbah*
		Talm.	*Talmud*
Pal.	*Palestinian*	Yal.	*Yalquṭ*

NAG HAMMADI TRACTATES

Acts Pet. 12 Apost.	*Acts of Peter and the Twelve Apostles*	Marsanes	*Marsanes*
Allogenes	*Allogenes*	Melch.	*Melchizedek*
Ap. Jas.	*Apocryphon of James*	Norea	*Thought of Norea*
Ap. John.	*Apocryphon of John*	On Bap. A	*On Baptism A*
Apoc. Adam	*Apocalypse of Adam*	On Bap. B	*On Baptism B*
1 Apoc. Jas.	*First Apocalypse of James*	On Bap. C	*On Baptism C*
2 Apoc. Jas.	*Second Apocalypse of James*	On Euch. A	*On the Eucharist A*
Apoc. Paul	*Apocalypse of Paul*	On Euch. B	*On the Eucharist B*
Apoc. Pet.	*Apocalypse of Peter*	Orig. World	*On the Origin of the World*
Asclepius	*Asclepius 21–29*	Paraph. Shem	*Paraphrase of Shem*
Auth. Teach.	*Authoritative Teaching*	Pr. Paul	*Prayer of the Apostle Paul*
Dial. Sav.	*Dialogue of the Savior*	Pr. Thanks.	*Prayer of Thanksgiving*
Disc. 8–9	*Discourse on the Eighth and Ninth*	Sent. Sextus	*Sentences of Sextus*
Ep. Pet. Phil.	*Letter of Peter to Philip*	Soph. Jes. Chr.	*Sophia of Jesus Christ*
Eugnostos	*Eugnostos the Blessed*	Steles Seth	*Three Steles of Seth*
Exeg. Soul	*Exergesis on the Soul*	Teach. Silv.	*Teachings of Silvanus*
Gos. Eg.	*Gospel of the Egyptians*	Testim. Truth	*Testimony of Truth*
Gos. Phil.	*Gospel of Philip*	Thom. Cont.	*Book of Thomas the Contender*
Gos. Thom.	*Gospel of Thomas*	Thund.	*Thunder, Perfect Mind*
Gos. Truth	*Gospel of Truth*	Treat. Res.	*Treatise on Resurrection*
Great Pow.	*Concept of our Great Power*	Treat. Seth	*Second Treatise of the Great Seth*
Hyp. Arch.	*Hypostatis of the Archons*	Tri. Trac.	*Tripartite Tractate*
Hypsiph.	*Hypisphrone*	Trim. Prot.	*Trimorphic Protennoia*
Interp. Know.	*Interpretation of Knowledge*	Val. Exp.	*A Valentinian Exposition*
		Zost.	*Zostrianos*

KEY TO PRONUNCIATION GUIDES

a	*cat*
ah	*father*
ahr	*lard*
air	*care*
aw	*jaw*
ay	*pay*
b	*bug*
ch	*chew*
d	*do*
e	*pet*
ee	*seem*
f	*fun*
g	*good*
h	*hot*
hw	*wh*ether
i	*it*
ī	*sky*
ihr	*ear*
j	*joke*
k	*king*
kh	*ch*, as in the German word *Buch*
ks	*vex*
kw	*quill*
l	*love*
m	*mat*
n	*not*
oh	*go*
o͝o	*put*
o͞o	*boot*
ou	*how*
oy	*boy*
p	*pat*
r	*run*
s	*so*
sh	*sure*
t	*toe*
th	*thin*
t͟h	*then*
uh	*cut*
uhr	*purr, teller*
v	*vow*
w	*weather*
y	*young*
z	*zone*
zh	*vision*

Preface

THE PURPOSE OF this dictionary is to make more widely available, and to an audience of nonspecialists, the results of the best of current biblical scholarship. In pursuing that goal, technical language has been avoided wherever possible, and where technical terms are used, they are carefully defined. When persons or places are mentioned, they are identified, and their dates are given with as much precision as is possible. Words in the biblical languages are defined and translated, with the result that information can be gleaned from the articles by persons of widely varying educational backgrounds. Those who know biblical history will learn here the latest results of the best scholarship; those who will here experience for the first time the thrill of the pursuit of historical knowledge will have opened up to them a whole new world of information.

This dictionary stands as the latest in the long line of Harper's Bible dictionaries that have provided help in understanding the world of Scripture. This is, however, a totally new edition. All of the articles have been newly written, illustrations newly selected, and maps newly designed. It also represents a unique venture in the field of publishing, since it is the result of a cooperative project between a major learned society, the Society of Biblical Literature (SBL), and a major publishing house, Harper & Row. In this joint effort, the Society of Biblical Literature has assumed responsibility for the content of the Dictionary, while Harper & Row has handled matters of format and editorial style. This has assured the widest circulation of what is surely the most authoritative volume in its field.

Contributors: The 179 scholars who have contributed their knowledge and skills to this volume come from some seven countries, and are acknowledged experts in the fields about which they have written here. They were chosen because of their knowledge and their ability to communicate to scholars and nonscholars alike. They span the spectrum of religious thought within the Judeo-Christian heritage, and the majority of them have published either books or articles, or both, on the subjects about which they have written for this dictionary. The authors do not, however, write from any confessional perspective, but rather from the broad perspective of expert biblical knowledge. Their intention is not to convert the reader to a particular religious point of view, but rather to provide information and to aid understanding.

The result is a highly readable, authoritative, and reliable summary of the best of contemporary knowledge about the Bible and the world from which it emerged.

The articles, while written by experts who are in the forefront of their respective fields of knowledge, are nevertheless designed to give the reader a consensus of current scholarly opinion. If novel theories are expressed, whether those of the author or of others, they are clearly identified as that. Because the articles represent great care in reaching conclusions only where the evidence will support such conclusions, much of what was once considered certain will be shown to rest on the smallest foundations of factual knowledge, while other things about which the reader may have been in confusion will be shown to have enough evidence to clear up the difficulties. Scholarship is an adventure in learning, in which new facts constantly open new horizons of information, and the pages of this dictionary reflect that adventure.

Many of the articles have been written by just those people whose discoveries in archaeology, literature, history, art, music, and language have contributed to the explosion of knowledge about the Bible and its world—discoveries that have been reported in the newspaper as well as the scholarly journals within the past two decades. Because some of the discoveries are so recent, sufficient time has not elapsed for a consensus to form on their meaning. For that reason dates for the same event may differ by a year or two in different articles, but in every case they rest on expert evaluation of the most recent evidence available. The designations B.C. and A.D. are still the most widely recognized way of identifying historical dates, and they have been used in this dictionary. They are used here as historical conventions, and are not meant to be interpreted as confessional statements.

Because the authors are experts in biblical languages as well as history, they have often made their own translations of the original languages of the Bible. When published translations have proven adequate, they have been used, most often the Revised Standard Version of the Bible, but other translations have been cited as well. When the authors give their own translations, it provides for the reader a new insight into the meaning of the published translations most frequently used.

Range of the Articles: The articles themselves represent every name used in the Bible three times or more, and those important names mentioned even less frequently have also been included. In addition to all important names of persons and places found in the Bible, there are articles on all important theological terms, on every book in the Bible, including the Apocrypha, on all major archaeological sites, and on all of the words used in the Bible in an important or unusual way. In addition, there are general articles on the impact of ancient cultures on the language and history of the biblical peoples, articles on Assyria, Babylonia, Persia, Greece, and Rome, to mention but five. There are articles on the languages of the Bible, and on the kinds of literature the Bible contains, articles on the economics of biblical times, on the music and art, and on the sociological structures of biblical and nonbiblical peoples. There are major articles on the Temple in Jerusalem, on the historical geography of the biblical lands, and on the worship practices of ancient Israel and those of its neighboring cultures. There are definitive articles on Moses, Jesus, and Paul, and on the various manuscripts of the biblical books, from which scholars must determine which most closely represent the lost original copies of those writings. There are highly informative articles on the history of the translation of the Bible into English, and on the ancient writings that reflect the Judeo-Christian heritage, but which were not included in the Bible, such as testimonies attributed to the patriarchs Abraham, Isaac, and Jacob, and writings attributed to disciples such as the Gospel of Thomas.

Of major importance are the archaeological articles, all of which are newly written, often by the people who led or participated in the expeditions that provided the latest data. There are major articles on the history of biblical archaeology, on its methods, and on its results. There are articles on major archaeological finds of the recent past: Ebla, a vast empire of the third millennium B.C. whose existence was unknown until the discovery of its archives in the recent past; Nag Hammadi, with its original writings of a kind of Christianity, Gnosticism, which had heretofore been known principally through secondary references. There are also authoritative evaluations of the best current thinking on such famous archaeological finds as the Dead Sea Scrolls, and the ancient royal correspondence from such sites as Tell el-Amarna, Nuzi, and Mari. How they affect our understanding of biblical history and the clues they give to a better knowledge of the languages of the Bible will be much clearer to the person who reads these articles carefully.

Format and Illustrations: The format of the articles is designed to yield the most information to the reader. When the article concerns a term that is unusual, or based on an ancient language, the pronunciation and derivation of the word are given, along with its meaning in the original language, if that meaning is known. The word is defined in terms of its use in the Bible, or its relevance to the biblical materials, and the body of the article then discusses the meaning that term has for our understanding of the Bible. Cross references will often be found at the end of the article, showing where to look to find more information. Longer articles also frequently have bibliographies appended to them, which inform the reader about books or articles where more information can be gained than can be included in the limited space of a dictionary. If the article concerns a book in the Bible, an outline of the book will also be given, except in the case of a few books where the contents do not lend themselves to such treatment.

In addition to providing completely new articles, the pages of this book are also filled with illustrations, both photographs and line drawings, which act as a further aid in learning about the Bible. The illustrations have been chosen with great care, many of them of ancient art and artifacts contemporary with the biblical writings themselves, and in many cases the illustrations are those recommended, or even provided, by the expert authors of the various articles they illustrate. The maps, both black and white, and color, have been carefully chosen for clarity and accuracy, and many have been commissioned especially for this dictionary. In all cases they have been brought up to date on the basis of the latest archaeological and geographical information. Such maps and illustrations will be found both in the pages of the dictionary and in special sections within and at the back of the book. In every case, the captions indicate the significance of the material, and to what article or articles it is related.

Even the tables of abbreviations contribute to the authoritative nature of this dictionary. They give the complete tables of abbreviations for all materials and texts cited by those who study and write about the Bible. Their presence alone makes this book a valuable reference tool.

Obviously, such an undertaking could not be brought to completion without the cooperation of many people. Not all of them can be named here, but some who have given special help must be cited. The names of the associate editors and the contributors, without whom of course none of this would have been possible, are listed at the beginning of this dictionary. Their willingness to share their expertise has made it possible to publish this one-volume dictionary of unparalleled authority. The people at Harper & Row have shown great patience in dealing with the eccentricities of scholars, and here John Shopp, Shelley Thacher, Dorian Gossy, and Steve Dietz must receive a special word of appreciation. The editor's tasks would have been far more difficult without the ready help of Martha Aycock, the reference librarian at Union Theological Seminary in Virginia, and the secretarial expertise of Brenda Lee. The Society of Biblical Literature, under whose scholarly supervision this dictionary was produced, has been most cooperative, under the leadership of Prof. Kent H. Richards, the executive secretary, and Dean Leander E. Keck, who was chairman of research and publications for the Society when this project began.

All of these, and many more, have contributed to this adventure in scholarship and publication. Readers will benefit from their contributions as the strange yet familiar world of the Bible parades before them from the pages of this book. Ancient customs, ancient dress, ancient gods and goddesses and the worship practices accorded them, ancient business practices with their coins and measurements, ancient cities and peoples and empires, ancient thinkers who pondered for their times the meaning of human life—all these and more will parade before the attentive reader of these articles, allowing that ancient world of the Bible to achieve a liveliness and clarity available only to those who have access to such information. A whole world awaits exploration in these pages. The scholars of the SBL invite the readers of this dictionary to share that adventure with them.

THE GENERAL EDITOR

Opposite: Assyrian slingers attacking the Judean fortress of Lachish. The Assyrian king Sennacherib's conquest of Lachish in 701 B.C. was recorded in bas-relief on the walls of his palace at Nineveh.

A

A, first letter of the alphabet, commonly used to designate Codex Alexandrinus, a fifth-century A.D. parchment manuscript of the Greek Bible. Apparently written in Egypt (Alexandria?), its presentation by the Patriarch of Constantinople to King James I of England was arranged in 1624, but because of delays, it did not arrive in England until 1627, by which time James had died and been succeeded by Charles I. It was presented as part of the Royal Library to the British Museum in 1757, where it is currently on display. It consists of 773 leaves (630 OT; 143 NT), each measuring 12-5/8 by 10-3/8 inches with two columns of writing to the page; originally it may have contained 820 leaves. At the end stand the two Epistles of Clement, with some pages missing; the table of contents indicates that these were followed by the Psalms of Solomon. ***See also*** Codex; Texts, Versions, Manuscripts, Editions. B.M.M.

Aaron (air'uhn), the brother of Moses and Miriam. The name is of uncertain meaning but may be Egyptian, as are other names among the tribe of Levi, to which Aaron belonged.

In Mic. 6:4, the only reference to him in the prophets, Aaron is said to have been sent by God, together with Moses and Miriam, to lead Israel from Egypt (cf. Josh. 24:5; 1 Sam. 12:6, 8; Pss. 77:20; 105:26) and this conforms to the representation of him in the earliest Pentateuchal strata. There he appears as Moses' helper and joint leader in the events of the Exodus, and there is no evidence of his having specifically priestly functions. Rather, he is depicted as a prophet (Exod. 7:1), particularly in the sense of one who announces the divine will (Exod. 4:16; 16:9; Num. 14:26–28). He accompanied Moses and the elders of Israel on important sacrificial occasions (Exod. 18:12; 24: 9–11). He and Hur held up Moses' hands during the battle with Amalek (Exod. 17:12), these two acted as judges when Moses was absent (Exod. 24:14), and, along with Moses, Aaron received the report of the spies (Num. 13:26).

All these, and other, references (e.g., Exod. 4: 27–31) suggest that Aaron, together with other now rather shadowy figures, such as Miriam, Hur, and the elders, once played a distinctive, even an independent role, in the Exodus events, an observation that may be confirmed by the traditions that show Aaron in an unfavorable light because of his opposition to Moses, notably Num. 12:1–16, but also by the episode of the golden calf (Exod. 32). However, in the early Pentateuchal material he is clearly subordinated to Moses as his agent and indeed is assimilated to the greater leader. Thus a miraculous rod, which originally belonged to Moses (Exod. 4: 2–5, 17), is also attributed to Aaron; with it he causes the Egyptian plagues (Exod. 7:9–12, 19; 8:5–7, 16–17). Both Aaron and Moses suffer the Israelites' hostility in the wilderness (Num. 16: 1–3; 20:2), both are denied entrance to Canaan for the sin of striking the rock (Num. 20:12), and both die on a mountain outside it (Deut. 32: 48–52).

Aaron portrayed as high priest in his robes of office on the west wall of the third-century synagogue at Dura-Europos.

In the later priestly sources of the Pentateuch (Exod. 25–31; 35–40; all Leviticus; Num. 1–10; 15–19; 25–35), Aaron is given very much greater prominence. Here he appears essentially as the ancestor of the Aaronite priesthood that finally emerged at Jerusalem after the Exile: the story of the budding of Aaron's rod (Num. 17:1–11) seems designed to establish the claims of the Jerusalem clergy over rival claimants. Aaron and his sons alone are to serve as priests (Exod. 28:1), to offer sacrifices (Num. 8: 1–7), and to bless the people (Num. 6:22–27). He fathers an everlasting priesthood (Exod. 40: 14; Num. 25:13), and his successors in his office are given supreme authority, even over the secular leader (Num. 27:21; cf. Ecclus. 45:17). In particular, the figure of Aaron represents the high priest and the position he held as the head of the Jerusalem Temple state in postexilic times, where he took over much of the role of the former king. So Aaron was anointed (Lev. 8:12), as was the Israelite king, and the special vestments that he wore were those worn by pre-exilic monarchs (Exod. 28:1–38); such seems certainly to be the case with the breastpiece (Exod. 28:15–30) and the turban and its gold plate (Exod. 28:36–38). On him centers the particular priestly concern with atonement, for it is he, and his high-priestly successors, alone who officiate on the Day of Atonement (Lev. 16:32–34).

In later Jewish thought, the picture of Aaron is still further developed. He is the most prominent figure in the list of Israel's great men, much more even than Moses, in Ecclus. 44–49 and the high-priestly vesture is endowed with symbolic and cosmic significance (Wisd. of Sol. 18:24). ***See also*** Aaronites; Leviticus; Priests; Temple, The.

Bibliography

Cody, A. *A History of Old Testament Priesthood.* Rome: Pontifical Biblical Institute, 1969.

Noth, M. *A History of Pentateuchal Traditions.* Englewood Cliffs, N.J.: Prentice-Hall, 1972. Pp. 178–182.

J.R.P.

Aaronites (air'uh-nīts), a term equivalent to "sons of Aaron" (Lev. 1:7) or "house of Aaron" (Ps. 115:10), indicating the postexilic view that the whole priesthood was descended from Aaron. It was divided into twenty-four families, each serving in the Temple for a week, sixteen claiming descent from Aaron's elder son Zadok and eight from his younger son Ithamar (1 Chron. 24:1–19). Zechariah, the father of John the Baptist, was a member of such a division of priests (Luke 1:5, 8–9). ***See also*** Aaron; Priests.

Ab (ahb; from Akkadian *abu*), the fifth month in the Jewish sacred calendar equivalent to the eleventh month in the Jewish civil calendar. It is usually parts of July and August. ***See also*** Time.

Abaddon (uh-bad'uhn; Heb., "destruction"). **1** In the OT, the dwelling place of the dead. It is used as a synonym for Sheol, the Hebrew term for the underworld (Job 26:6; Prov. 27:20) and is closely associated with death and the grave (Job 28:22; Ps. 88:10–12). **2** In the NT, the Hebrew name for the ruler of the Abyss, whose Greek name was Apollyon, "the Destroyer" (Rev. 9:11). ***See also*** Abyss; Eschatology; Gehenna; Sheol.

Abana (ah-bah'nah), a river in ancient Syria. When Elisha told the Syrian commander Naaman he could cure his leprosy by washing in the muddy Jordan, he angrily replied, "Are not Abana and Pharpar, the rivers of Damascus, better than all the waters of Israel?" (2 Kings 5:12). His complaint was justified, for the Abana (modern Barada, Hellenistic Chrysorrhoas) is a swift, clean, abundant stream descending from the snows of Mt. Hermon, "the peak of Amana" (Song of Sol. 4:8). It supplies the great oasis of Damascus through seven branches before finally disappearing in a desert marsh. The picturesque gorge provides the major route from Damascus westward into the Beqa'a Valley. ***See also*** Damascus; Elisha; Hermon; Naaman; Pharpar.

D.B.

The Abana River. The Abana descends from Mount Hermon and in biblical times, as today, it was noted for its clear, plentiful waters.

Abarim (ab'uh-reem; Heb., "parts beyond"), a mountain (Num. 27:12; Deut. 32:49) or mountains (Num. 33:47) situated to the east of the Jordan River and in the vicinity of Mt. Nebo. Jeremiah couples it with Bashan and Lebanon as locations from which the people cry in vain to God for rescue (Jer. 22:20).

Abba (ah'buh), the definite form of the Aramaic word for "father" (lit. "the father"), properly translated as "my father" or "our father." Used by Jesus (and early Christians) to address God (Mark 14:36; cf. Rom. 8:15; Gal. 4:6), the word suggests familial intimacy. Many scholars find indications of such use in ancient Judaism, but others argue that it originated with Jesus. ***See also*** Father; God.

Abdiel (ab'dee-el; Heb., "servant of El [God]"), the father of Ahi, a clan leader of the tribe of Gad (1 Chron. 5:15).

Abdon (ab'dahn; Heb., "service, servile"?). **1** A levitical town in Asherite territory (Josh. 21:30; 1 Chron. 6:74), probably modern Khirbet 'Abdeh nineteen miles south of Tyre and about three miles east of the Mediterranean coast at Achzib. **2** One of the minor judges of Israel (Judg. 12:13–15) whose eight-year work is unknown but whose family is described as both large and rich. **3** A Benjaminite son of Shashak (1 Chron. 8:23–24). **4** The firstborn son of the Gibeonite Jeiel and his wife Maacah, and an ancestor of Saul (1 Chron. 8:30; 9:36). **5** A servant of Judah's King Josiah commanded to seek the validity of the scroll found (2 Chron. 34:20; this person is named Achbor in 2 Kings 22:12).

R.S.B.

Abednego (ah-bed'nay-goh), the new name given to Azariah, one of Daniel's three companions (Dan. 1:7) who were appointed over the province of Babylon (2:40) and subsequently thrown into the fiery furnace. A lengthy prayer is ascribed to him in the Greek version of Daniel 3. *Abed-nego* in Hebrew means "servant of Nego," a pejorative variation of Nebo, a Babylonian god of wisdom. ***See also*** Azariah; Meshach; Shadrach.

Abel (ay'bel), the second son of Adam and Eve (Gen. 4:1–16). No data can be educed for an identifiable historical person, so he must be reckoned as a character in the one isolated narrative. In that narrative, Abel is the one who offers an acceptable sacrifice to God, although we are not told why it is acceptable. He is therefore murdered by his jealous brother Cain. The name Abel in Hebrew means "breath, vapor," suggesting the fragile quality of his life. Gen. 4: 1–16 has no real interest in Abel but focuses on the fate of Cain.

In the OT, it is noteworthy that Abel plays no role in Israel's faith reflections and is not again mentioned. In the NT, Abel becomes a theological reference for innocent blood (Matt. 23:35; Luke 11:51; Heb. 12:24) and an exemplar of faith (Heb. 11:4). ***See also*** Cain. W.B.

Abel-meholah (ay'bel-me-hoh'luh), a settlement in the Jordan Valley to the south or southeast of Beth-shean. Its exact location is disputed, the biblical indications being insufficiently specific or clear. The name appears as a designation of one of the boundaries of Solomon's fifth administrative district, in which Megiddo, Taanach, and Beth-shean are the chief towns (1 Kings 4:12). This reference, however, may be part of a later attempt to specify or update the precise extent of this district. Abel-meholah was one of the destinations of the Midianites fleeing from the hill of Moreh, where Gideon and his small band had routed them (Judg. 7:22). God refers to Elisha as being of the same town when he tells Elijah to go and anoint him as his successor (1 Kings 19:16). Last, Saul's daughter, Merab, was married to a man from Abel-meholah: Adriel the Meholathite (2 Sam. 21:8). It is possible, however, that more than one place is meant by these references. S.B.P.

Abel-shittim (ay'bel-shit'teem; Heb., "brook of the acacias," Num. 33:49). ***See also*** Shittim.

Abiathar (ahb-ee-ah'thahr), the son of Ahimelech, who escaped the slaughter of the priests of Nob and joined David's outlaw band (1 Sam. 22: 2–23), where he served as private chaplain (1 Sam. 23:6–11). He was rewarded by David for his loyalty with a monarchic appointment as chief priest (2 Sam. 20:25), but he was later banished by King Solomon to the family estate in Anathoth for his part in supporting Adonijah, Solomon's rival to the throne (1 Kings 2:26–27). The prophet Jeremiah may have been a descendent of the family of Abiathar (Jer. 1:1). He is incorrectly identified as high priest in David's time in Mark 2:26. ***See also*** Priests. M.C.

Abib (ah'beeb), later called Nisan, the original Canaanite name of the first month (March/April) in the Hebrew religious calendar. It is the month during which the exodus occurred and the Passover was celebrated (Exod. 13:4; 23:15; Deut. 16: 1). ***See also*** Nisan.

Abiel (ah-bee'el; Heb., "El [God] is my father"). **1** A Benjaminite, the grandfather of both King Saul (1 Sam. 9:1) and Abner, the captain of Saul's army (1 Sam. 14:50–51). **2** One of David's fighting men (1 Chron. 11:32) also called Abialbon (2 Sam. 23:31).

Abiezer (ay-bee-ee'zuhr; Heb., "my father is help"). **1** A son of Manasseh who received an inheritance in Canaan (Josh. 17:2) and who headed the clan of the Abiezerites to which Gideon belonged (Judg. 6:11). The name also occurs as Iezer (Num. 26:30). **2** A Benjaminite from Anathoth; one of David's fighting men who was given command of a division of twenty-four thousand men (2 Sam. 23:27; 1 Chron. 27:12). **3** A Manassite, the son of Gilead's sister (1 Chron. 7:18).

Abigail (ab'i-gayl). **1** Wife of Nabal, a wealthy and churlish rancher in Carmel (1 Sam. 25:2–3). Nabal refused to acknowledge David's authority and as a result David determined to have Nabal killed. Abigail, a beautiful and intelligent woman, arranged a meeting with David, unbeknownst to her husband, and persuaded him not to harm Nabal. Shortly afterward, Nabal died suddenly (apparently from shock after hearing how his wife had intervened on his behalf), and David married Abigail (1 Sam. 25:39–42). She and Ahinoam, another wife of David, accom-

Abigail at the deathbed of Nabal; detail from a thirteenth-century French miniature.

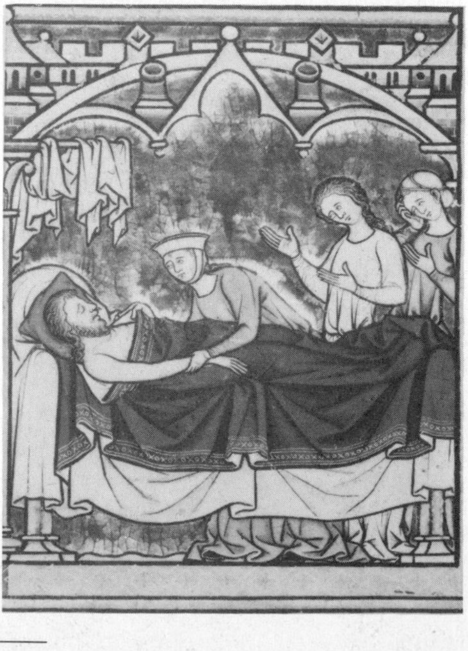

panied him when he sought refuge in the Philistine territories (1 Sam. 27:3), and the two were later captured by raiding Amalekites. David tracked down the raiders and rescued his wives (1 Sam. 30). Later, in Hebron, Abigail bore David a son named Chileab (2 Sam. 3:3; 1 Chron. 3:1 records the son's name as Daniel). **2** According to 2 Sam. 17:25 Abigail was the mother of Amasa, whom Absalom appointed commander in place of Joab (cf. also 2 Sam. 19:13), the wife of Ithra the Israelite (Jether the Ishmaelite according to 1 Chron. 2:17), the daughter of Nahash, and the sister of Joab's mother, Zeruiah. According to 1 Chron. 2:16 Abigail and Zeruiah were the daughters of Jesse and the sisters of David. A.B.

Abihu (ah-bee'hōō; Heb., "he [Yahweh] is father"), one of Aaron's priestly sons who ascended the mountain of God (Exod. 24:1, 9). He later died for offering a sacrifice incorrectly (Lev. 10:1). ***See also*** Nadab.

Abijah (ah-bī'jah; Heb., "Yah[weh] is my father"). **1** The son of Becher, grandson of Benjamin (1 Chron. 7:8). **2** The son of Samuel, who served as judge in Beer-sheba (1 Sam. 8:2). **3** The son of Rehoboam, king of Judah (911–908 B.C.), during whose reign the border wars between Judah and Israel continued unabated (1 Kings 15:7). Though seen as a religious miscreant by the editor of Kings, later tradition portrays Abijah as a pious king who, trusting in the Lord, successfully routed his Israelite attackers and captured Bethel, Jeshana, and Ephron (2 Chron. 13). **4** The son of Jeroboam, son of Nebat, who failed to recover from a childhood illness; his death was interpreted as a sign of divine displeasure (1 Kings 14). M.C.

Abijam (ah-bī'jem). ***See*** Abijah.

Abilene (ab-uh-lee'nee), tetrarchy around Abila, some nineteen miles northwest of Damascus in the Baroda Valley. According to Luke 3:1 and an inscription at Abila, dating from the reign of Tiberius, it was governed by Lysanias at the time of Jesus' public life. In A.D. 34 it was given to Agrippa I. ***See also*** Agrippa I; Lysanias.

Abimael (ah-bim'uh-el; Heb., "El [God] is my father"), the son of Joktan, a descendant of Noah's son Shem (Gen. 10:28).

Abimelech (ah-bim'e-lek; Heb., "my father is king"). **1** King of Gerar (Tell Jemmeh?, ten miles south of Gaza), before whom Abraham posed as Sarah's brother (Gen. 20; cf. Gen. 12:10–20). Elsewhere, Abimelech is "King of the Philistines," whom Isaac, living at Gerar, similarly deceives (Gen. 26). **2** The son of the judge Jerubbaal (Gideon) and a Shechemite concubine (Judg. 8:29–9:57). Abimelech accepted seventy "pieces of silver" from the Shechem temple treasury, slew seventy "brothers," and became local king for three years while commanding the Israel tribal militia. When monarchical support collapsed, Abimelech used the militia to destroy Shechem, and he died in the course of besieging Thebez. Excavations have uncovered the fortress-temple along with massive evidence of Shechem's destruction ca. 1150–1125 B.C. ***See also*** Judges, The Book of; Shechem. R.B.

Abinadab (ah-bin'uh-dab; Heb., "father of generosity"). **1** A prominent man from Kireath-jearim, who had custody of the Ark after its return from the Philistines until David moved it to Jerusalem (1 Sam. 7:1; 1 Chron. 13:7). **2** The second son of Jesse (1 Sam. 16:8; 17:13; 1 Chron. 2:13).

Abinoam (ah-bin'oh-am; Heb., "my father is delight"), the father of Barak, a military leader in the period of the judges (Judg. 4:6; 5:1).

Abiram (ah-bī'ruhm; Heb., "my father is exalted" or "the Exalted One is my father"). **1** A Reubenite who, along with his brother Dathan, a fellow Reubenite named On, and the Levite Korah, conspired with some two hundred and fifty tribal leaders to challenge the authority of Moses and the priestly leadership of Aaron. After Abiram and Dathan defied a summons from Moses, Korah led the rebels in an attempt to offer incense to God. Abiram, along with Korah and Dathan as well as their families and possessions, perished when the ground opened and swallowed them. The rest of the rebels were consumed by fire from God (Num. 16:1–40; Ps. 106:16–18). **2** The firstborn son of Hiel the Bethelite (1 Kings 16:34). His death is attributed to the operation of the curse pronounced by Joshua upon anyone who rebuilt Jericho (Josh. 6:26), although the Canaanite practice of child sacrifice may also have been involved. ***See also*** Hiel; Korah. D.R.B.

Abishag (ab'i-shag), a Shunamite maiden brought to minister to the dying King David (1 Kings 1:4, 15). Although David did not have sexual relations with her (v. 4), Solomon chose to view her as one of David's wives; when Adonijah requested to marry her, Solomon had him executed for treason (1 Kings 2:13–25).

Abishai (ah-bee'shī), the son of Zeruiah, David's sister, and the brother of Joab and Asahel (1 Chron. 2:16). His reputation as a belligerent warrior and defender of David is attested by his desire to kill the sleeping Saul (1 Sam. 26:6–9) and also Shimei of Saul's house (2 Sam. 16:9–11), by his killing the Philistine giant Ishbibenob (2 Sam. 21:17), and by his leading a portion of David's army into a battle that resulted in the death of eighteen thousand Edomites in the Valley of Salt (1 Chron. 18:12). Perhaps he is best known for the story in which he avenged the death of his brother Asahel by murdering Abner in Hebron (see 2 Sam. 2:12–28; 3:26–30). ***See also*** Abner; Asahel; Joab; Zeruiah. F.R.M.

Abishua (ab-i-sho͞o'uh; Heb., "my father is deliverance" or "my father is prosperity"). **1** A Levite, the son of Phineas and descendant of Aaron; he served as a priest (1 Chron. 6:4–5, 50) and was an ancestor of Ezra (Ezra 7:5). **2** A Benjaminite, the son of Bela and descendant of Jacob (1 Chron. 8:4).

Abner (ab'nuhr), the son of Ner, grandson of Abiel, cousin of Saul, and Saul's army commander (1 Sam. 14:50–51). After the Philistine defeat of Israel at Mt. Gilboa, Abner kept the remnant of Saul's kingdom together, ostensibly in the service of Eshbaal, Saul's son (2 Sam. 2:8–9). Abner led operations against David, but eventually abandoned Saul's followers to negotiate a private compact with David for the transfer of the North to him. Nevertheless Abner was cut down by Joab, his personal rival and commander of Judah's militia; he was buried with royal honors in Hebron (2 Sam. 3:12–39). ***See also*** David; Saul. M.C.

abomination, usually something contrary to proper religion. The Hebrew term recurring in Leviticus 11 designates "unclean" creatures that are not to be eaten. Two other Hebrew terms typically refer to foreign gods, their images, or related worship practices (e.g., Deut. 27:15; 29:17, RSV: "detestable things," NIV: "detestable images"; 1 Kings 11:7; 2 Kings 23:13). They also denote improper ways of worshiping God (Deut. 12:31; 17:1) and wicked or unlawful conduct (e.g., Lev. 18:22; Deut. 22:5; Prov. 20:23). One of these terms is typically rendered in the Septuagint by a Greek word that, in the NT, means evil acts or attitudes (e.g., Luke 16:15; Rev. 21:27). ***See also*** Abomination that Makes Desolate, The. R.H.H.

abomination that makes desolate, the, an act desecrating the Jerusalem Temple. While attempting to ban Jewish religious practices, Syrian authorities under Antiochus IV erected an altar to Zeus in the Temple (ca. 167 B.C.). 1 Macc. 1:54 characterizes this as "a desolating sacrilege" (cf. 2 Macc. 6:1–5). The book of Daniel, probably written to encourage hope among Jews persecuted by these authorities for keeping the traditions, twice mentions "the abomination that makes desolate" (11:31; 12:11; cf. 9:27), probably meaning this altar to Zeus. The author of Daniel assured his contemporaries that supernatural deliverance would occur within a relatively short time (Dan. 12:7: "a time, two times, and half a time," probably meaning three and one-half years; cf. vv. 11–12) from the time the altar was erected. Later, Daniel was read as a book of prophecy, and the abomination that makes desolate was viewed as one of the final signs that must take place before the end (Matt. 24:15; Mark 13:14: "the desolating sacrilege," KJV: "abomination of desolation"; cf. also 2 Thess. 2:3–4). The emperor Caligula's plan to erect a statue of himself in the Temple (ca. A.D. 40) may have been seen by some as at least a partial fulfillment of this "prophecy," but the Gospels of Matthew and Mark, both written more than twenty years later, associate the abomination with the events to precede the expected return of Jesus as "Son of man" and evidently regard it as yet to be fulfilled (Matt. 24:15–21; Mark 13:14–19). Some may have seen its fulfillment in the destruction of the Temple by the Romans in A.D. 70. ***See also*** Abomination; Antiochus; Apocalyptic Literature; Daniel, The Book of; Eschatology; Maccabees; Parousia; Temple, The. R.H.H.

Abraham (ay'brah-ham; Heb., "father of a multitude"), a Hebrew patriarch and an important figure in three living religions: Judaism, Christianity, and Islam. Earlier known as Abram (Heb., "exalted father") he is perceived as the patriarch of several peoples from the regions of

Abraham and the binding of his son Isaac. This illuminated page from a fifteenth-century Armenian Gospel depicts an episode in the story of Abraham told in Genesis 22.

Palestine. He is called "the father of many nations" (Gen. 17:5) and the friend of God (2 Chron. 20:7).

The biblical account moves from Mesopotamia to Palestine (as is shown on Map 2 in the section of color maps). The genealogy of Abraham (Gen. 11:10–32) places him in Ur. He then receives divine instructions to leave (Gen. 12: 1–8). This is followed by the story of Sarah and Abraham in jeopardy (Gen. 12:10–13:1). Next follows the tale contrasting Abraham and Lot (an ethnological story, meant to demonstrate the character and origin of the Moabites and Edomites; Gen. 13:2–18). The story then moves to an enigmatic episode about an alliance of eastern kings (Gen. 14:1–24). The subsequent birth of Ishmael, the son of Abraham by his wife's servant, Hagar, is followed by a story about the origin of circumcision (Gen. 17:27). The ethnological tale that began in Gen. 13 continues (Gen. 18–19). Another story of Abraham and Sarah in jeopardy in Gerar occurs in Gen. 20:1–18. The birth of Isaac (Gen. 21:1–21) is told next, followed closely by the story of the substitution of a ram for the sacrifice of Isaac (Gen. 22). The story of Abraham's purchase of burial property (Gen. 23:1–20) is then followed by an account of his death (Gen. 25:1–18).

The place of Abraham in the history of the ancient Near East is difficult to assess. The stories are by their nature family tales with little material that would have been included in the public records. Some scholars maintain that there was a historical Abraham; others generally maintain that Abraham is an eponymous figure, a person whose name is taken for a people. However, there has been an attempt to date the material and uncover the historical Abraham by locating a time when the culture and customs presumed in the stories in Genesis prevailed in the ancient Near East. Several alternatives have been proposed.

One of these is that the patriarchs date from the Early Bronze Age (3000–2000 B.C.) as evidenced by the appearance of similar names in the Ebla material which originates in that period. A more popular alternative has been to date the material to the Middle Bronze Age (2000–1500 B.C.), "the Patriarchal Age." This theory is based on several factors: there is correspondence between the biblical names and Amorite personal names of that period; Middle Bronze Age I (2000–1900 B.C.) represents a nonurban period that would make the types of migrations recounted in the Genesis text more plausible; there are references to *khapiru* and Benjamin in the Mari texts which also come from this period; and the customs in the Abraham story are found in the Mari texts as well.

John Van Seters argues that all of the above, with the exception of the Mari material, can be found much later, hence the stories could be Late Bronze Age (1500–1200 B.C.) or Iron Age I (1200–900 B.C.). Thomas Thompson argues that, because of the nature of the document (i.e., the Bible) in which the accounts of Abraham appear, the historical issues cannot be satisfactorily resolved. Albrecht Alt maintains that in the growth of Hebrew religion the relationship between Abraham and God could be construed under the general theme of the "God of the Fathers" (see Exod. 2:24; 3:6, 13, 15; 4:5; 6:3, 8; Lev. 26:42; Deut. 30:20). Abraham becomes that person who is both the advocate with God and the pioneer in faith.

The early Christian writings represent Abraham as the patriarch (Matt. 1:1, 2, 17; 3:9). Abraham as patriarch becomes a symbol of compassion (Luke 16:19–31) and the one who legitimates (John 8:33–38). However, the most prominent theme in the NT with regard to Abraham depicts him as the pioneer of trust in God (Acts 7:2–50; Rom. 4:1–25; Gal. 3:1–29; Heb. 7: 1–10; 6:13–14; 11:8, 11). ***See also*** Genesis; Khapiru; Mari; Patriarch. S.B.R.

Abraham's bosom, a metaphor in Jesus' parable about the rich man and Lazarus (Luke 16: 19–31). To be in or at someone's bosom means to recline to the right of the host (the place of honor) at a meal (cf. John 13:23). Various ideas and images were current in Jesus' time to describe the state of the dead, especially those special to God; these included references to Abraham (cf. *1 Enoch* 22; 4 Macc. 13:17; 2 Esd. 7:36, 38, 88–99). Christians later used this metaphor as another designation for Paradise. ***See also*** Abraham; Heaven; Hell; Immortality; Paradise; Resurrection; Sheol.

Abram (ayb'ruhm). ***See*** Abraham.

Absalom (ab'suh-lohm), one of the sons of Israel's greatest king, David. Because he was handsome and ambitious, Absalom was the most conspicuous of David's sons; his mother was Maachah, princess of the neighboring vassal state of Geshur. The story of Absalom is told in 2 Samuel 13–20. When his half-brother Amnon raped his full sister Tamar and David took no action, Absalom took the law in his own hands and killed Amnon, after which he spent three years in exile in Geshur. Laborious mediation on the part of Joab brought Absalom back to the court, but David refused to see him for another two years. This filled Absalom with such anger and resentment that he harbored the idea of a coup d'état. It took him four years to prepare for an uprising that stood a good chance of success. He directed and capitalized upon the resistance felt by many people who saw the spectacular growth of David's empire, court, and administrative machinery, but who could not accept or keep up with the concomitant changes that took place in social patterns and values. In his rebellion Absalom won the support of the royal counselor Ahithophel, whose authority was above all criticism.

Absalom gave the signal for the revolt from Hebron, the selfsame town in central Judah where David himself had risen to national power. His march to Jerusalem forced David to leave the country. Ahithophel advised Absalom to pursue and isolate David forthwith, but Absalom was deceived by the flattery of Husai who acted as a spy for David and who gave the opposite advice. Thus, David was able to escape across the Jordan and start the organization of a military comeback. A few weeks later the dramatic denouement followed in the Transjordan, not far from Mahanaim. Aided by the rough terrain, David's experienced regular army, which had remained loyal to him, defeated Absalom's militia. Though David had ordered his generals to spare the prince, Joab, who found Absalom entangled in the branches of an oak, had him slaughtered as an archrebel —a realistic military choice but one that cost him a good relationship with the mourning father. In the end, it was intemperate ambition that became fatal for Absalom and brought him down. ***See also*** David; Joab. J.P.F.

abyss, the watery deep as contrasted with sky and earth (Ps. 77:16). It is the abode of the dead (Rom. 10:7), the place where evil spirits are confined (Luke 8:31; Rev. 9:1–11; 20:1–3), and the place from which the Antichrist will ascend (Rev. 11:7; 17:8). ***See also*** Antichrist, The; Hades; Heaven; Hell; Sheol.

Accad (ah'kahd; also found as Agade, Akkad), a city of Nimrod's kingdom in the land of Shinar (Gen. 10:10). The association with cities in Genesis 10 named Babel and Erech establishes the Mesopotamian location known from numerous extrabiblical textual, artistic, and literary sources. The precise location of the city Accad is not known, but it likely lay around modern Baghdad, Iraq, or the terrain between Baghdad and Babylon.

The language known as Akkadian was written in cuneiform script, is Semitic in character, and has been found in a large collection of economic, administrative, legal, and religious texts that give us clues to the nature and location of a third-millennium B.C. culture of rich resources and diverse strengths.

The territory known as Accad (Akkad) began at the narrowest proximity of the Tigris and Euphrates rivers, just north of the confluence of the Diyala tributary to the Tigris. It stretched south to reach ancient Babylon and Kish, a distance of some hundred miles. As with the older Sumerian culture farther south, the city-states comprising the Akkadian empire (Old Babylonia) were sustained by the agriculture and trade provided by the rivers and the flood-nourished agriculture in the plain between the rivers.

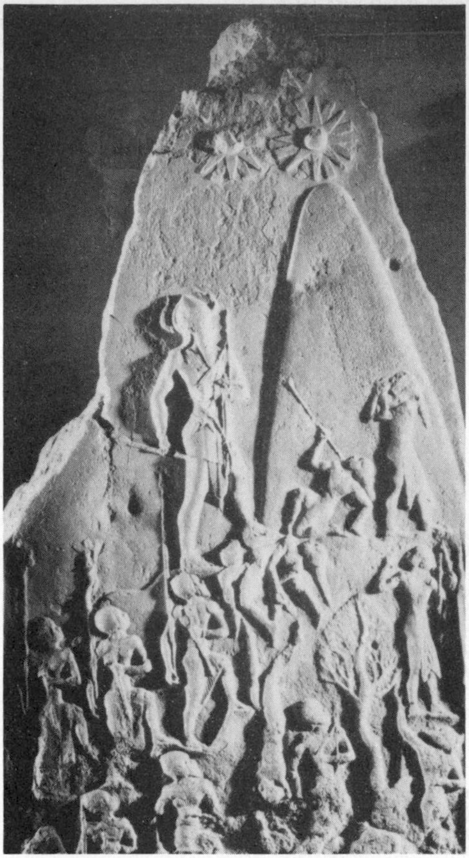

Stele of Naram-Sin, grandson of "Sargon of Agade," commemorating his victory over the Lullubians; third millennium B.C.

Little is known about Akkadian political life. A "Sargon's Chronicle" and a "Sargon of Agade," found on portions of tablets, tell of the expansion by Sargon, king of the city Kish, to the northwest and southeast, establishing an "empire" lasting only four generations. His sons Rimush and Manishtusu succeeded him, but his grandson Naram-sin is better known. The expansion and control of this dynasty was probably established primarily to secure supplies of metal and other goods. Ships brought traders from the Indus Valley, and overland connections were made with Iran's plateau. Booty of conquest and trade goods found include metals, timber, and precious stones. An occupation army was stationed at Susa, and construction of storage, temple, and town facilities indicate control of parts of Syria and the upper reaches of the Tigris Valley. All this ranged from 2350 to 2200 B.C.

Of most interest to biblical students is a rich literary heritage from Akkadian authors. Frequently using earlier Sumerian materials, they have given us rich comparative sources. Specifically of interest for their bearing on biblical ideas are "The Creation Epic" *(Enuma Elish)*, "The Epic of Gilgamesh," "Descent of Ishtar to the Nether World," numerous hymns, wisdom speculations, rituals, and law codes. These texts may be found in James B. Pritchard, ed., *Ancient Near Eastern Texts*, 3d ed. (Princeton, NJ: Princeton University Press, 1974). R.S.B.

Acco (ak'koh; also Accho, Acre), one of the great port cities of antiquity located along the eastern Mediterranean Littoral. Acco (modern Tell el-Fukhkhar) has in modern times been superseded by the important harbor city of Haifa, directly to the south. Numerous textual references and archaeological discoveries of Minoan, Mycenaean, and Egyptian imports bear witness to Acco as a flourishing commercial center with ties throughout the Mediterranean and Near East for over twenty-five hundred years (Middle Bronze Age through the Roman period; ca. 2000 B.C.–A.D. 324). Its maritime influence receded after the Arab conquest in A.D. 636 but was regained during the Crusader occupation, when the city was known as St. Jean d'Acre. Biblical references provide insights into the political and religious strife during the Hellenistic period when battles erupted between the Maccabaeans and the Greek citizens of Acco, then known as Ptolemais (1 Macc. 5:14–15, 20–23). The city was clearly very hostile to the Jews (1 Macc. 12: 45, 48). On his third voyage, Paul visited this city whose inhabitants had early on converted to Christianity (Acts 21:7; there called Ptolemais). Recent findings of characteristic Philistine pottery corroborate the biblical text that cites the inability of the Israelite tribes to conquer this city or any other coastal city under the dominion of the Philistines (Judg. 1:31). S.L.R.

Aceldama. ***See*** Akeldama.

Achaia (uh-kay'yuh), the Roman province consisting of the southern half of the Greek peninsula. The name is derived from the designation for the Greeks in Hittite and Egyptian sources. In Homer the Achaeans are Achilles' men and the followers of Agamemnon. In historical times, the name referred to southeastern Thessaly and the northern coast of the Peloponnesus. In the division of provinces in 27 B.C., the Roman province of Achaia comprised the lower half of Greece. In the NT the term is connected with Paul's preaching in its capital, Corinth (Acts 18: 27; 1 Cor. 16:15; 2 Cor. 1:1).

Achaicus (uh-kay'uh-kuhs), a Christian from Corinth who, with Stephanas and Fortunatus, was with Paul in Ephesus when he wrote 1 Corinthians (1 Cor. 16:17). The three apparently brought information to Paul concerning the condition of the church in Corinth and perhaps were the bearers of the letter mentioned in 1 Cor. 7:1. They may also have carried 1 Corinthians back to Corinth. ***See also*** Fortunatus; Stephanas.

Achan (ah'khahn), the son of Carmi (RSV: "Achar") (1 Chron. 2:7), who stole some of the "devoted things" after the victory of Joshua over Jericho (Josh. 7). For this breach of the "ban," God punished Israel with a military setback at Ai, and Achan and his family were stoned to death. ***See also*** Ai.

Achbor (ahkh'bohr; Heb., "mouse"). **1** The father of the Edomite king Baal-hanan (Gen. 36: 38). **2** The son of Micaiah; he was one of those sent by Josiah to inquire of Hulda the prophetess concerning the significance of the book of the law discovered in the Temple (2 Kings 22:12–14). He is possibly the same person mentioned by Jeremiah (26:22; 36:12) as the father of Elnathan, a courtier of Jehoiakim.

Achish (ay'kish), the ruler of the Philistine city of Gath from whom David sought asylum when he fled from Saul. At first David was distrustful of Achish and feigned madness to escape when he was recognized as a successful military leader (1 Sam. 21:10–15); but later Achish accepted David and his men as mercenaries and gave David the city of Ziklag in exchange for his raids on southern tribes hostile to the Philistines (1 Sam. 27:1–12). However, because of the suspicions of some of his commanders, Achish excused David from raids on Israel (1 Sam. 29: 1–11). ***See also*** David; Philistines.

Achor (ay'kohr; Heb., "trouble"), **Valley of,** part of the north border of Judah (Josh. 15:7) and the location of the execution of Achan (Josh. 7: 24–26) after his profiteering in a holy war. In Hos. 2:15 and Isa. 65:10 its reputation for that former "trouble" is reversed and the prophets use it as a symbol of better times to come. It is probably modern el-Buqei'ah between Jericho and the north end of the Dead Sea.

Achsah (ak'suh), the daughter of Caleb whom he gave to his kinsman Othneil as a wife for capturing the city of Kiraith-sepher (Debir; Josh. 15:16–17; Judg. 1:12–13). The dowry Caleb gave her consisted of two springs located near Hebron (Josh. 15:18–19). ***See also*** Caleb; Debir; Kiriath-sepher.

Achshaph (ahkh'shaf), an ancient city in northern Canaan along the border of the territory of Asher. The king of Achshaph joined the coalition led by Jabin of Hazor against the Israelites, but the city was eventually captured by Joshua (Josh. 11:1; 12:20). It is thought to be located near modern Acco, although the exact site has not been positively identified.

Achzib (ahkh'zib). **1** A city in northern Canaan located near the coast north of Acco. Although on the border of the territory of Asher, the Canaanites were never totally expelled from the city (Josh. 19:29; Judg. 1:31). It is tentatively identified as the present ez-Zib or Tel Akhziv. **2** A city in the lowlands of Judah, tentatively identified as Tel el-Beida, northwest of Lachish (Josh. 15:44; probably also Mic. 1:14).

acropolis (uh-krahp'uh-lis; Gk., "high city"), the nucleus of many ancient cities. It was a walled stronghold built on a hill that overlooked the town on its slopes. Often the temples and shrines would be within the walls of the acropolis, as was the case with ancient Athens.

Acts of the Apostles, the, the fifth book in the NT. The book of Acts deals with the history of the earliest Christian church and includes a major section on the career of Paul.

Authorship and Date: There are certain indications that the author of Acts was a companion of Paul, who traveled with him on some occasions. These indications are found in the "we" sections, i.e., those places in Acts in which the author writes in the first person plural instead of the usual third person. These sections are found in Acts 16:10–17; 20:5–15; 21:1–18; and 27:1–28:16. The author may, in these sections, be using a travel diary that he himself wrote at an earlier time, drawing on a diary written by a companion of Paul, or using the first-person pronoun as a subtle way to add verisimilitude to the narrative by identifying himself as a participant. Scholars evaluate the "we" passages differently. Some think that the author was indeed a companion of Paul, while others are more cautious about such claims. The major point of agreement among NT scholars is that the book of Acts and the Gospel According to Luke were written by the same person, whom we call Luke. Most would tend to date the two books ca. A.D. 80–85.

Contents: The book of Acts begins precisely at the point where the Gospel of Luke left off, with the ascension of Jesus. The author then describes the history of Christianity in general conformity with the geographical outline given in Acts 1:8. According to this verse, the Christian movement begins in Jerusalem, then spreads into Judea and Samaria, and then to "the end of the earth." Thus, Luke begins his narrative by describing the situation of the followers of Jesus in Jerusalem (Acts 1:4–8:3). In Acts 8:4–12:25, the movement begins to spread into other parts of Judea and Samaria. Then, in Acts 13:1–21:16, the author concentrates almost exclusively on Paul, whose missionary activity takes him into Asia Minor and Greece. In Acts 21:17–22:30, Paul is back in Jerusalem, and he undergoes four trials there and in Caesarea (Acts 23:1–26:32). In the final section, Acts 27:1–28:31, Paul is on his way to Rome as a prisoner, preparing to face his final trial before the Roman emperor. The voyage to Rome is described in the first person and in great detail.

The acropolis of Athens. Surmounting the hill is the Parthenon, fifth century B.C. Paul preached to the court that met on the hill of Areopagus close by.

Main Themes: One of the notable themes in Acts is the relationship of Christianity to Judaism. Luke makes it clear that the Christian movement began in Jerusalem among the Jewish followers of Jesus. After a period of amazing growth among Jews, the Christian message came to Gentiles. Peter baptized the first Gentile convert, Cornelius, but it was through the efforts of Paul that large numbers of Gentiles were brought into the movement. Luke also is aware that there were some problems with the incorporation of Gentiles into the Christian movement. In his story, the conversion of Cornelius was made possible only after Peter had received a vision in which a voice from heaven declared all foods clean, i.e., dietary regulations that Jews had heretofore been bound to observe were abolished (Acts 10:1–11:18). Later in Acts, we read that some Jewish Christians wanted to require circumcision for Gentile converts but that Paul and the apostles agreed that no such requirements were to be imposed (Acts 15:1–29). As Luke describes the missionary activity of Paul, he stresses Paul's habit of going first to Jewish synagogues to present the Christian message. Almost invariably, Paul has little success among Jews and is forced to preach to Gentiles, who respond favorably and in large numbers (e.g., Acts 14:1–7; 17:1–9, 10–15; 18:1–17; 19:8–20). On three occasions, Paul announces his intention not to preach to Jews any longer but rather to go only to Gentiles (Acts 13:46–47; 18:6; 28:28). Here, there is a parallel between the geographical structure of Acts and a fundamental theological theme: geographically, Christianity, which started in Jerusalem among Jews, moved out into the wider world among Gentiles; theologically, Christianity increasingly grew distinct from and independent of Judaism.

Other themes that have been detected in the book of Acts include: Christianity as the legitimate fulfillment of Judaism; the nonrevolutionary and nonsubversive nature of the Christian movement in relation to Roman authority; and the divine impetus and legitimation of the Christian movement in the form of the Holy Spirit.

Estimates differ regarding the essential historical reliability of Acts. Most scholars agree, however, that, whatever the source materials available to the author, the narrative has been shaped in a deliberate manner to express the author's own particular concerns and purposes. The various speeches in the book (e.g., 2:14–36; 3:12–26; 7:2–53; 13:16–41), at least in their present form, appear to be compositions of the author. As a source for the career of Paul, it is generally recognized that Acts must be subordinated to the statements in Paul's own Letters. ***See also*** Holy Spirit, The; Luke; Luke, The Gospel According to; Paul; Pentecost; Theophilus; Tongues as of Fire; Tongues, Speaking with.

Pentecost: "And there appeared to them tongues as of fire, distributed and resting on each one of them" (Acts 2:3). Detail from the Pala D'Oro, a twelfth-century altar in St. Mark's Cathedral, Venice.

Bibliography

Haenchen, Ernst. *The Acts of the Apostles: A Commentary*. Philadelphia: Westminster, 1971.

Hengel, Martin. *Acts and the History of Earliest Christianity*. Philadelphia: Fortress, 1980.

Jervell, Jacob. *Luke and the People of God*. Minneapolis, MN: Augsburg, 1972. J.B.T.

OUTLINE OF CONTENTS

The Book of Acts

I. Prologue (1:1–3)
II. Christianity in Jerusalem (1:4–8:3)
III. Christianity in Judea and Samaria (8:4–12:25)
IV. Paul's activity in Gentile lands (13:1–21:16)
V. Paul's activity in Jerusalem (21:17–22:30)
VI. Paul's trials (23:1–26:32)
VII. Paul's trip to Rome (27:1–28:31)

Adah (ay'duh; Heb., "ornament"). **1** Lamech's first wife, the mother of Jabal and Jubal (Gen. 4:19–20, 23). **2** The Hittite wife of Esau, the mother of Eliphaz (Gen. 36:2, 4; cf. 26:34).

Adaiah (ah-dī'uh; Heb., "Yah [God] has ornamented himself"). **1** The maternal grandfather of King Josiah (2 Kings 22:1). **2** A Levite in the ancestry of Asaph (1 Chron. 6:41). **3** A clan leader in the tribe of Benjamin (1 Chron. 8:21). **4** The father of the Judean military captain Maaseiah (2 Chron. 23:1). **5** A member of the family of Bani; he was condemned by Ezra for marriage to a foreign woman (Ezra 10:29). **6** Another man, likewise condemned for taking a foreign wife (Ezra 10:39). **7** A Judahite of the clan of Perez who lived in postexilic Jerusalem (Neh. 11:5). **8** A priest who lived in postexilic Jerusalem (1 Chron. 9:12), probably the same one mentioned in Nehemiah (11:12) as serving in the Temple.
D.R.B.

Adam (Heb., "[hu]man"), a proper noun rarely appearing outside of Genesis 1–5. In Gen. 1:1–2:4a, God creates man and woman in his image, separating them from the animals, to rule the earth. In Gen. 2:4b–4:26, Yahweh forms Adam (Heb. *'adam)* from the "earth" (Heb. *'adamah*), sets him over the Garden, and allows him to name the animals. Tranquility rules until Adam and Eve break Yahweh's rule, eat the forbidden fruit, and suffer expulsion from the Garden and the curse of a life of sweat, pain, and death.

According to some Jewish writings, Adam's sin disrupted the cosmos, robbed the earth of fruitfulness, made animals wild and vicious, and stripped humankind of its height, beauty, and immortality (*Jubilees*, Baruch, and 4 Ezra). Other authors, however, exalt Adam above all creatures (Ecclus. 49:16) as a wise man, "king," or "angel" (3 *Enoch* 30:11–12) who remained uncompromised even though Eve was seduced

(*Vita Adae* 12–15). Philo found two Adams in Genesis 1–2: a "heavenly" Adam in God's image, who was wise, virtuous, and perfect, and an "earthly" Adam who sinned, becoming the father of all people of a lower nature.

In the NT, Luke carries Jesus' genealogy back to God through Adam (3:38), and 1 Timothy elevates Adam over Eve because of her sin (2: 13–14), but most references to Adam occur in Paul's Letters. Rom. 5:12–21 contrasts the first (earthly) Adam, who was disobedient, with Christ, the last (heavenly) Adam, who was obedient, thus reversing Philo's order. Those who are in the first Adam suffer corruption; those in the last experience grace and life (see 1 Cor. 15:20–28, 45–49). Note, however, that for Paul sin was not transmitted biologically.

According to many scholars, 1 Cor. 11:2–16 deals with origins, not the subordination of woman. The hierarchy God, Christ, man (Adam), woman (Eve) treats the source (head) of each rather than the rule of one over the other; unlike 1 Timothy, this passage assumes a mutuality, though distinctiveness, between man and woman. ***See also*** Creation; Eden; Eve; Fall, The; Human Being; Paradise; Serpent; Sin; Women.

C.J.R.

adamah (ah-dah-mah'), a Hebrew word that occurs 225 times in the OT and means arable, cultivable land. That meaning can be seen in the expression "man of the *adamah*" meaning "farmer" (Gen. 9:20; Zech. 13:5). *Adamah* and its synonym *afar* ("dust, ground") are the material from which God forms the first man (Heb. *adam;* Gen. 2:7; 3:19; Ps. 90:3; Job 10:9; 34:15). In addition to this primary meaning, *adamah* can signify the inhabited world (Gen. 12:3; 28: 14; Deut. 7:6; 14:2; Isa. 24:21; Amos 3:2), the land God gives to Israel in fulfillment of his oath to the patriarchs (esp. Deut. 5:6; 7:13; 11:9; 26: 10, 15), from which they are exiled (2 Kings 17: 23; 25:21) and to which they return (Isa. 14:1; Jer. 16:15; 23:8; Ezek. 28:25). A number of scholars have proposed that the noun *adam*, "man," does not only indicate "humankind" but, in a number of instances, is a masculine variant (or a miswriting) of the feminine form *adamah*. Among the possible texts are Gen. 16:12; Jer. 32: 20; Zech. 9:1; 13:5; Job 36:28; and Prov. 30:14. ***See also*** Adam. J.S.K.

adamant (ad'uh-muhnt), an impenetrable hard substance, at one time identified with the diamond. It is used of Judah's sinful heart (Zech. 7:12) and of Ezekiel's forehead (3:9).

Adar (ay'dahr), the twelfth month of the post-exilic Jewish lunar calendar (February–March; Ezra 6:15).

adder, a poisonous snake. The KJV translates four different Hebrew words for species of serpents that cannot be precisely identified with the word "adder" (e.g., Gen. 49:17; Ps. 140:3; cf. Rom. 3:13, where the RSV has "asp"). The words cluster as parallel terms in poetry where the snakes symbolize moral venom (e.g., Ps. 58:3–5; Prov. 23:30–33).

Additions to Daniel, the. ***See*** Daniel, The Additions to.

Adiel (ad'ee-el; Heb., "El [God] is an ornament"). **1** A clan leader in the tribe of Simeon (1 Chron. 4:36). **2** A priest who lived in postexilic Jerusalem (1 Chron. 9:12). **3** The father of Azmaveth, overseer of the royal storehouses of King David (1 Chron. 27:25).

Adin (ay'din; Heb., meaning uncertain, possibly "luxury" or "delight"). **1** A family group ("sons of Adin") who returned with Zerubbabel from the Babylonian captivity (Ezra 2:15). **2** A second group led by Ebed who returned with Ezra (Ezra 8:6). **3** A member of the postexilic community in Judah who signed the covenant to keep the law (Neh. 10:16).

Adlai (ad'lī), the father of Shaphat (1 Chron. 27: 29): Shaphat served David as a supervising herdsman.

Admah (ad'muh), one of the five cities of the plain in the Valley of Siddim at the southern end of the Dead Sea (Gen. 10:19; 14:2). The city was destroyed, along with Sodom, Gomorrah, and Zeboiim, while the fifth city, Zoar, was spared. Admah and Zeboiim became proverbial examples of God's wrath (Deut. 29:23; Hos. 11:8). The exact site is unknown. ***See also*** Sodom; Zoar.

Adonijah (ad'oh-nī'jah; Heb., "Yahweh is the Lord"). **1** The son of David and Haggith and apparent heir to the throne in Jerusalem after the death of Absalom. Though supported by the priest Abiathar and Joab the army commander (1 Kings 1–2), Adonijah's ambitions were frustrated by the secret anointing of Solomon at the spring of Gihon by the priest Zadok. Adonijah's subsequent request to marry the beautiful Abishag, David's nurse, was the occasion of his execution by Solomon. **2** Two other men in the OT (2 Chron. 17:8; Neh. 10:17).

Adonikam (ad-uh-nī'kuhm; Heb., "my lord has arisen"). **1** A family group ("sons of Adonikam") who returned with Zerubbabel from the Babylonian captivity (Ezra 2:13). **2** A smaller group who returned later with Ezra (Ezra 8:13).

Adoniram (ad-uh-nī'ruhm; Heb., "my lord is exalted"), an official in the service of King Solomon who supervised the conscripted labor force in the construction of the Temple (1 Kings 5: 13–14). He is probably the same person who served a similar role later under King Rehoboam and was stoned to death by the people of the Northern Kingdom of Israel when he attempted to enforce the harsh policies of Rehoboam (1 Kings 12:18). In the Hebrew text of 1 Kings 12: 18 he is called Adoram, a shortened form of Adoniram, although the Greek text (Septuagint) reads Adoniram. It is less likely that he is to be identified as the same official elsewhere called Adoram (2 Sam. 20:24). ***See also*** Adoram.

D.R.B.

Adonizedek (a-doh'ni-ze'dek; Heb., meaning uncertain, either "my lord is righteous" or "my god is Zedek [a deity]"), the Amorite king of Jerusalem who, fearing the strength of the invading Israelites, organized a coalition with four other kings to attack the city of Gibeon because its inhabitants had formed an alliance with Joshua. The attack failed and he and the other kings were put to death by Joshua (Josh. 10: 1–26). ***See also*** Amorites; Gibeon.

adoption, a NT term that functions in the context of specialized salvation language, usually translated "sonship." It draws meaning from the theological realities of belonging, connectedness, relationship, and inheritance established by God's promise to human beings. The frame of reference is that of the family and foundational membership; its affirmations are derived from the "sonship" of Christ, and its scope is inclusive of both men and women. Adopted relationships among humans are found in the OT (e.g., Gen. 15:1–3; Exod. 2:10; Esther 2:7, 15; cf. also the system of levirate marriage, Deut. 25:5–10) and elsewhere in Semitic cultures, but the focal point upon which the NT builds is the declared "adoption-sonship" ("election") relationship between God and Israel (e.g., Hos. 11:1; Exod. 4: 22).

In the NT, Jesus himself is not adopted (see the hymnic christological formulations in Phil. 2:6–11; Col. 1:15–20; also Heb. 1:5–7; cf. also, however, Rom. 1:3–4). By virtue of the mediation of the Son (resurrected Lord) and the Spirit, people become (ingrafted) heirs in "sonship" through faith and are thus enabled to utter "Abba, Father" (Rom. 8:15; Gal. 4:6; cf. Eph. 1:5; Mark 14:36; Luke 11:2; Matt. 6:9). Other probable backgrounds for NT thought on adoption are the manumission and adoption of slaves and other Greco-Roman customs regarding property and birthright (cf. the "household tables" of Col. 3:18–4:1; Eph. 5:21–6:9; 1 Pet. 2: 18–3:7; also cf. Philemon). ***See also*** Abba; Election; Family, The; Father; Salvation; Slavery; Sons of God, Children of God.

J.E.A.

Adoraim (ad-uh-rī'im; Heb., meaning uncertain, possibly "two hills"), one of the fifteen cities in Judah fortified and provisioned by Rehoboam as defensive strongholds (2 Chron. 11:9). Its location has been identified as modern Dura, about six miles west of Hebron in southern Judah.

Adoram (a-dohr'uhm; a shortened form of Adoniram, Heb., "my lord is exalted"), a name apparently identifying one administrative official who served under both David and Rehoboam, although some scholars believe that there were, in fact, two different persons bearing this name. If so, the first (Adoram, 2 Sam. 20:24) supervised conscripted labor under King David while the second served a similar role under Solomon and Rehoboam (Adoniram, 2 Kings 4: 6; Adoram, Heb. text of 12:18, but Adoniram in the Greek text). However, it is possible that Adoram came into office near the end of David's reign and continued to serve in the same position through successive reigns until his untimely death at Shechem (1 Kings 12:18). ***See also*** Adoniram; Hadoram.

D.R.B.

Adrammelech (a-dram'muh-lek). **1** A deity to whom human sacrifices were offered. He was one of the gods worshiped by the Sepharvites who were resettled in Samaria by the Assyrian ruler Sargon around 720 B.C. (2 Kings 17:31). **2** One of the sons of the Assyrian ruler Sennacherib who, with the help of his brother Sharezer, assassinated his father in 681 B.C. and fled to Ararat (2 Kings 19:37; Isa. 37:38). ***See also*** Molech.

Adramyttium (ad-ruh-mit'ee-uhm), modern Edremit, a port on the northwest coast of Turkey opposite Lesbos; in Roman times, it was in the province of Asia. According to Acts 27:2–5, Paul sailed from Caesarea to Myra, en route to Rome, aboard a ship of Adramyttium.

Adria (ay'dree-uh), **Sea of,** in Acts 27:27 denotes the body of water in the central Mediterranean Sea between Crete and Sicily through which Paul's ship, en route to Rome, drifted for fourteen days before breaking up in the surf of Malta. The name derives from the town of Adria on the lower Po River and originally designated the sea between Italy and the Balkan Peninsula, the modern Adriatic. In NT times, it also designated the Ionian Gulf and the waters between the Peloponnesus and Sicily.

Adullam (ah-duhl'ahm), an ancient settlement most likely Tell esh-Sheikh Madkur in the Judean hills ca. five miles south of Beth-shemesh. Nearby is a cave where David and his early followers camped (1 Sam. 22:1). The site was fortified by Rehoboam to strengthen Judah during the early years of the Divided Kingdom (2 Chron. 11:7). ***See also*** Divided Kingdom, Divided Monarchy.

adultery, illicit sexual relations with someone other than one's marriage partner. In the OT adultery had a precise and limited definition: sexual relations between a married (or betrothed) woman and any man other than her husband. Adultery, therefore, was committed only against a husband, never against a wife. It was considered a most grievous transgression (Exod. 20:14; Deut. 5:18; Lev. 18:20), to be punished by the death of both parties (Deut. 22: 22–24). There is no actual evidence that this punishment was ever carried out, but it may have been in certain instances, and the threat of execution still existed in the first century (cf. John 7:53–8:11). The law was probably intended to ensure that any child born to the wife was really the husband's child, since it was considered crucial for the husband to have offspring, so that the family name could be perpetuated.

In the NT period, it appears that the definition of adultery was extended in its scope. For example, the teaching of Jesus was understood to mean that a husband could now be held responsible for committing adultery against his wife (Matt. 5:32; Mark 10:11; Luke 16:18). Adultery was forbidden by various NT writers (Rom. 13:9; Gal. 5:19; James 2:11).

Adultery was sometimes used as a symbol of the unfaithfulness of the people toward God (e.g., Hos. 9:1; Matt. 12:39). ***See also*** Family, The; Fornication; Harlot; Law; Marriage; Women.

J.M.E.

Adummim (ad-yo͞o'meem), a name referring both to a pass (RSV: "ascent"; Josh. 18:17) and to an area used to distinguish the border between the tribal inheritance of Benjamin and that of Judah (Josh. 15:7). Following that border constituted the shortest way to go down from Jerusalem to Jericho, and then on to Transjordan.

adversary, in the OT, anyone (or anything) standing in the way of the completion of God's will or opposing God's people either collectively or individually (e.g., 2 Sam. 19:22; 1 Kings 5: 4; 11:25; Ezra 4:1). "Adversary" is the literal meaning of the Hebrew word *satan*, and the idea eventually developed that Satan was *the* adversary (see Job 1:6–2:7). In certain NT passages, the term is also used with this connotation (e.g., 1 Pet. 5:8; cf. 1 Tim. 5:14–15). ***See also*** Devil; Satan.

Advocate. ***See*** Paraclete.

Aeneas (e-nee'uhs), a paralytic at Lydda, otherwise unknown, who was healed by Peter (Acts 9:33–35).

Aenon (ee'nuhn), a well-watered site, the scene of baptism by John the Baptist, in the vicinity of Salim (John 3:23). The exact location is unknown. A fourth-century reference by Eusebius situated Aenon in the Beth-shean valley, some six miles south of Beth-shean. A mosaic floor map discovered in a sixth-century church in Madeba, Jordan, represents Aenon on the eastern side of the Jordan River. Recent speculation places it near Nablus, not far from the abundant water of Wadi Far'-ah.

Agabus (ag'uh-buhs), a Christian prophet from Jerusalem who, in Antioch, predicted a widespread famine during the reign of the emperor Claudius (Acts 11:27–28); later, at Caesarea, he foresaw Paul's arrest in Jerusalem and subsequent imprisonment by the Gentiles (Acts 21: 10–11). ***See also*** Prophet.

Agag (ay'gag), the name (or perhaps the royal title) of the king of the Amalekites whom Saul defeated but spared, contrary to divine command. After rebuking Saul bitterly, Samuel hewed Agag to pieces in Gilgal "before the Lord" (1 Sam. 15).

agape (ah-gah'pay), the principal Greek word used for "love" in the NT. Of the three words for love in the Hellenistic world, it was the least common. The other two words were *eros*, which meant sexual love, and *philos*, which meant friendship, although their meanings could vary according to the context in which they appeared. Agape, because it was used so seldom and was so unspecific in meaning, could be used in the NT to designate the unmerited love God shows to humankind in sending his son as suffering redeemer. When used of human love, it means selfless and self-giving love. ***See also*** Love.

agate. ***See*** Chalcedony.

agora (ag'uh-ruh), the center of the lower part

The agora at Corinth: remains of shops and the Temple of Athena.

of a Greek town. The usual translation "marketplace" does not do justice to its function as the place where people gathered for social and political as well as commercial business. In the early phases of Greek city development, the agora was a natural open space near the main entrance to the acropolis. As the government of Greek cities changed from monarchy to democracy, the citadel, or fortified area, lost its importance as a vital nucleus of the town to the agora, which served as the place in which the citizens gathered to transact public business. A good deal of early Christian evangelizing will have taken place in the agora. Little more than a platform for the speakers was required. Athens was unusual in having a building, the Pynx, designed for large public assemblies. In later periods the theater was often used as the place for assembly (cf. Acts 19:29). P.P.

agriculture. ***See*** Farming.

Agrippa (uh-grip'uh) **I,** Herod Agrippa I, son of Aristobulus and Bernice and grandson of Herod the Great. He was born ca. 10 B.C. and sent to Rome when he was six, shortly before the death of his grandfather, to be educated in the company of Drusus, son of the emperor Tiberius, and Claudius. Herod Agrippa (or, as he styled himself later, Julius Agrippa) became a close associate of Caius, who was to become the emperor Caligula. Grown accustomed to luxury and extravagance, Agrippa became a notorious spendthrift, constantly in debt for ever increasing amounts. At the urging of his sister Herodias, his brother-in-law Herod Antipas helped him with money and a position in Tiberias, but they soon quarreled and Agrippa found himself back in Rome, where he remained in debt and his incautious speech led to a brief imprisonment by Tiberius. When Tiberius died, only months later, and Caligula became emperor, Agrippa's fortunes suddenly improved. Caligula bestowed many honors and much wealth upon him, settling upon him, in A.D. 37, the former tetrarchies of Lysanias in Abilene and of Philip and, in 40, the territories of the exiled Herod Antipas. When Caligula was assassinated in 41, Claudius, his successor, also rewarded his old friend, giving him Judea and Samaria (his territory now comprised the kingdom formerly ruled by Herod the Great) and raising him to consular rank. From 41 to 44, Agrippa ruled Palestine with a pious, scrupulous, and apparently sincere adherence to the Jewish law that brought him the warm praise of the Pharisees. He also persecuted the early Christians and, according to Acts 12, was responsible for the beheading of James the son of Zebedee and the imprisonment of Peter (Acts 12:1–4). Agrippa's death in A.D. 44 was sudden and unexpected; Acts and Josephus agree that it came at Caesarea and that he suffered an attack while dressed in splendid robes after having been acclaimed by the crowd (Acts 12:20–23). ***See also*** Herod. F.O.G.

A coin of Herod Agrippa I, ruler over Palestine from A.D. 41 to 44, with the ruler's image. A human image on a Jewish coin, in light of the biblical prohibition against images, is unusual (see Exod. 20:4).

Agrippa (uh-grip'uh) **II,** Herod Agrippa II or Marcus Julius Agrippa, the last of the Herodian house to hold a kingdom. When his father, Agrippa I, died suddenly in A.D. 44, Agrippa II was only seventeen and was being educated in Rome. The emperor Claudius, though well disposed toward him, did not immediately grant him the rights of succession because of his youth. By 50, however, he had been given the small territory of his deceased uncle, Herod of Chalcis, and in 53, he was permitted to exchange this for rule over the former tetrarchy of Philip and certain territories in the Lebanon. Nero added parts of Galilee and Perea to this realm, and Agrippa renamed his capital, Caesarea Philippi, Neronia in the emperor's honor. Agrippa's sister, Bernice, had been the wife of Herod of Chalcis, and she came to live with her brother after her husband's death. Their relationship became notorious as an incestuous affair, which apparently lasted throughout their lives in spite of her brief marriage to Polemon of Cilicia and her scandalous affair with Titus. The relationship between Agrippa and Bernice adds a poignant note to the account, in Acts 25:13–26:32, of Paul's appearance before them as a prisoner. Agrippa retained important rights having to do with the Temple in Jerusalem and was directly involved in its completion and the subsequent paving of the streets of Jerusalem with white marble. He attempted, insofar as possible, to support and promote Judaism. His true loyalty to Rome never wavered, however, even when put to the ultimate test provided by the

Jewish revolt of A.D. 66 and its subsequent suppression by the Romans. Agrippa, after futile efforts to forestall revolt, joined the Roman side and not only regained his kingdom with Roman help but was closely associated with Titus, the conqueror of Jerusalem. Agrippa moved to Rome, and there he died after A.D. 93. ***See also*** Herod. F.O.G.

Ahab (ay'hab; Heb., "father's brother"[?]). **1** The son and successor of Omri, king of Israel (ca. 869–850 B.C.). His queen was Jezebel, daughter of Ethbaal, king of Tyre. Ahab inherited his father's military virtues and maintained a strong and stable government. He successfully defended his country against the powerful Aramean kingdom of Damascus, which he defeated in several battles. Ahab is the first king of Israel to come into conflict with Assyria. He is also the first whose name is recorded on the Assyrian monuments where we learn that he put two thousand chariots and ten thousand soldiers on the battlefield against Shalmaneser III at Qarqar in 853 B.C.

In the biblical account the point of interest lies not in the king himself, but in his four encounters with the prophets, especially Elijah. The first encounter concerns the great drought predicted by Elijah (1 Kings 17:1), which culminated in the contest between Elijah and the prophets of Baal on Mt. Carmel (1 Kings 18:17–40), at which Ahab was present. The second involved two unnamed prophets, one of whom encouraged Ahab in his resistance against Ben-hadad of Damascus (1 Kings 20:22). The third was the episode of Naboth's vineyard. After Naboth had refused Ahab's offer to buy his vineyard, Jezebel had Naboth executed so that Ahab could take possession of the coveted vineyard. When Ahab did so, he was confronted by Elijah who threatened the total destruction of his house. As a result Ahab did penance for his part in the crime (1 Kings 21). The fourth encounter occurred during Ahab's campaign against the Arameans, a campaign that led to his death (1 Kings 22). When Ahab's court prophets predicted success, his ally Jehoshaphat of Judah asked for the word of another prophet of the Lord. The man summoned was Micaiah ben Imlah, who at first predicted success but, when pressed, uttered his fateful prediction.

The judgment of the Deuteronomic historian who gave 1 Kings its final form is extremely harsh on Ahab, primarily because he permitted Jezebel to patronize the cult of Baal. Excavations at Samaria have revealed the magnificence of his buildings (1 Kings 22:39). The dominance of Ahab over Judah is shown by his treatment of Jehoshaphat in the campaign of Ramoth-gilead (1 Kings 22:29–31). Ahab's daughter Athaliah was married to Jehoram, king of Judah, and held the throne herself for six years after Jehoram's death. **2** The son of Kolaiah, a false prophet among the Babylonian exiles. Jeremiah accused him of adultery and impiety and threatened him with death by fire at the hands of Nebuchadnezzar (Jer. 29:21–23). ***See also*** Elijah; Omri; Samaria, City of. D.L.C.

Ahasuerus (ah-hahz-yo͞o-ay'ruhs), king generally identified as Xerxes I (485–464 B.C.) and described in the book of Esther as ruling from India to Ethiopia (Esther 1:1). After banishing his queen, Vashti, he sought a replacement, selecting Esther. In the story of Esther and Mordecai, Ahasuerus appears as malleable and prone to extreme actions, first manipulated by Haman to allow the destruction of all Jews and then later by Esther and Mordecai to permit the Jews to defend themselves at the cost of many Gentile lives.

King Ahasuerus and Queen Esther (right) as depicted in the wall paintings of the third-century A.D. synagogue at Dura-Europos.

The historical Xerxes I ruled over twenty satrapies (Herodotus, Hist. III, 89), and his queen was Amestris from a noble Persian family (Hist. VII, 61).

According to Daniel 9:1, Ahasuerus was the father of Darius the Mede, and in Tobit 14:15 Ahasuerus joins Nebuchadnezzar in the destruction of Nineveh. Both notices pose severe chronological and historical problems. ***See also*** Esther; Persia; Xerxes. W.L.H.

Ahava (ah-hah'vah), a river or canal in Babylonia (Ezra 8:15, 21, 31), location unknown, the rallying point for Ezra's journey to Jerusalem, where a preparatory fast was celebrated. Some Greek texts and 1 Esd. 8:41 call the river/canal Thera(s). In Ezra 8:15, Ahava could be a place name, perhaps a settlement, but this is less probable.

Ahaz (ay'haz; Heb., "he [Yahweh] has grasped"), son of Jotham and the father of Hezekiah. Ahaz was the eleventh king of Judah, reigning between 735 and 715 B.C. Only twenty years old at his succession, Ahaz is judged by the Hebrew historians as having committed such abominable Canaanite practices as sacrificing his son and worshiping at high places (2 Kings 16:1–4).

During the reign of Ahaz, the Assyrian Empire advanced to new heights, causing the entire region west of Mesopotamia to fight or pay tribute. Rezin, King of Syria, and Pekah, King of Israel, joined forces to stop the advance of Assyria. When Judah would not join their alliance, those two kings sought ways to replace Ahaz with a man named Tabeel, apparently an Aramean (see 2 Kings 16:5; Isa. 7:1–25). Ahaz sought to rescue himself from this threat by appealing to Assyria's King Tiglath-pileser, even giving him portions of the temple treasury. Perhaps it was this vassalage to Tiglath-pileser that led to Ahaz's replacement of the Lord's altar in the Jerusalem Temple with one modeled after an altar in Damascus (2 Kings 16:10–16). ***See also*** Hezekiah; Jotham; Pekah; Rezin; Tabeel.
F.R.M.

Ahaziah (ay-huh-zī'uh; Heb., "Yahweh holds firm"), the name of two biblical kings. **1** The son of Ahab, king of Israel (ca. 850–849 B.C.). Ahaziah permitted his mother, Jezebel, to maintain and even strengthen the Baal cult (1 Kings 22: 52–53). He apparently joined Jehoshaphat of Judah in a naval expedition which was wrecked at Ezion-geber, the port of departure (2 Chron. 20:35–37; but cf. 2 Kings 22:48–49). The country of Moab rebelled under Ahaziah (2 Kings 1:1); and apparently the Ammonites also gained their freedom at that time (2 Chron. 20:1). In his second year Ahaziah was severely injured in a fall from a window and sent for an oracle from Baalzebub, the god of Ekron. He was reproved by Elijah, who threatened him with death, which followed shortly (2 Kings 1:2–18). **2** The son of Jehoram and Athaliah, king of Judah (ca. 842 B.C.). He was allied with Jehoram of Israel in an unsuccessful campaign to recover Ramoth-gilead from Hazael of Damascus (2 Kings 8:28). When Jehoram was wounded in battle, Ahaziah visited him in Jezreel. Because of this kinship and friendship, Jehu, the king of Israel, assassinated him along with Jehoram (2 Kings 9:27–28). ***See also*** Ahab; Elijah; Ezion-geber; Jehu.
D.L.C.

Ahiezer (ay-hī-ee'zuhr; Heb., "my brother is help"). **1** The head of the tribe of Dan during the wilderness wanderings (Num. 1:12), who also served as their military commander (10:25). **2** The leader of a group of Benjaminites who were kinsmen of Saul, yet joined David's fighting men at Ziklag (1 Chron. 12:3).

Ahijah (ah-hī'jah; Heb., "Yah is brother"). **1** A prophet from Shiloh who tore his garment into twelve pieces in order to demonstrate visually the coming dissolution of the United Monarchy. The prophet from Shiloh also foretold Jeroboam's (ca. 924–903 B.C.) rise to power (1 Kings 11:29–31; 12:15; 2 Chron. 10:15). This same prophet later predicted the death of Jeroboam's son (1 Kings 14:2–18; 15:29). **2** The father of Baasha, who conspired against Nadab, son of Jeroboam, and reigned in his stead (1 Kings 15: 27–33). **3** The son of Jerahmeel, brother of Caleb of the tribe of Judah (1 Chron. 2:25). **4** One of David's mighty men (1 Chron. 11:36). **5** A Levite, overseer of the treasures of the house of God in David's time (1 Chron. 26:20). **6** A Levite, who with Nehemiah sealed the covenant (Neh. 10: 26).
S.B.R.

Ahikam (ah-hī'kuhm; Heb., "my brother has arisen"), the son of Shaphan who served as a courtier of King Josiah. He was among those who went to enquire of Hulda the prophetess concerning the significance of the book of the law found in the Temple (2 Kings 22:12–14). He later helped protect Jeremiah from King Jehoiakim (Jer. 26:24) and is often mentioned as the father of Gedaliah, the governor of Judah appointed by Nebuchadnezzar of Babylon around 587 B.C. and later assassinated (Jer. 40).

Ahilud (ah-hī'luhd), the father of two royal officials: Jehoshaphat, who served both David and Solomon as record keeper (1 Chron. 18:15; 1 Kings 4:3), and Baana, who was a district administrator charged with provisioning Solomon for one month of the year (1 Kings 4:12).

Ahimaaz (ah-him'ah-ahz), a name whose derivation has not been satisfactorily explained, borne by two men in the OT. **1** The father of Ahinoam, wife of Saul (1 Sam. 14:50). **2** Son of Zadok the priest, who was active during Absalom's revolt. He was loyal to David and remained in Jerusalem as a secret agent when David fled the city (2 Sam. 15:27–36; 17:15–22). He later was anxious to inform David about the suppression of the revolt, but he did not himself report that Absalom had been killed (2 Sam. 18: 19–32). He may have been King Solomon's son-in-law, married to Basemath, Solomon's daughter (1 Kings 4:15), and stationed in Naphtali as the king's administrator. **3** An abbreviation, Maaz, occurs in 1 Chron. 2:27.
J.G.G.

Ahimelech (ah-hi'me-lek; Heb., "my brother [or kin] is king"). **1** The son of Ahitub and priest of Nob to whom David fled from the wrath of Saul (1 Sam. 21:1–15). Falling victim to David's story of a secret mission from King Saul, Ahimelech provided David and his men with "holy bread" (see Matt. 12:3–4). He also gave to David the sword of Goliath whom David had killed years earlier in the valley of Elah (1 Sam. 22: 9–10). For so assisting David, Ahimelech and most of his family were killed by Doeg the Edomite at the command of Saul (2 Sam. 22: 18–19). **2** A Hittite officer in the service of David (1 Sam. 26:6). ***See also*** Doeg; Goliath. F.R.M.

Ahinoam (ah-hin'oh-ahm; Heb., "good is my brother," or "my brother (God) is good"). **1** The daugher of Ahimaaz who became King Saul's wife (1 Sam. 14:50). She was the mother of Jonathan, Ishvi, Malchishua, Merab, and Michael (1 Sam. 14:49). **2** A native of Jezreel of south Judah, who was married to David, and who was the mother of his eldest son, Amnon (2 Sam. 3:2; 1 Chron. 3:1).

Ahiram (ah-hī'ruhm). **1** Perhaps another name for Hiram, the king of Phoenicia. The capital city under Hiram was Byblos (Gebal). The excavation of his sarcophagus, dating from the eleventh century B.C., gives an example of Phoenician script that illuminates an important link in the development of the alphabet. He is not to be confused with Hiram of Tyre who was a trading ally of Solomon. Tyre is south of Byblos. **2** One of the sons of Benjamin (Num. 26:38). ***See also*** Gebal.

Ahithophel (ah-hith'oh-fel), one of David's advisors, noted for his wisdom (2 Sam. 16:23; 1 Chron. 27:33–34). He proved disloyal to David during the revolt of Absalom (2 Sam. 15:17) and became the latter's chief counselor. When his advice was ignored he committed suicide (2 Sam. 17:23). Bathsheba, David's wife and Solomon's mother, may have been his granddaughter (2 Sam. 11:3; 23:34). His house was in Giloh, a town in Judah (2 Sam. 15:12). ***See also*** David.

Ahola (ah-hoh'lah). ***See*** Oholah, Oholibah.

Aholibah (ah-hohl'i-bah). ***See*** Oholah, Oholibah.

Ai (ay'ī), a Canaanite town near and to the east of Bethel (Gen. 12:8; 13:3), generally identified with the modern site of et-Tell. The name "Ai" means "ruin" in Hebrew, paralleling the modern Arabic name "et-Tell," "heap, mound." Et-Tell, about one and a half miles east of Bethel (modern Beitin), was excavated by Judith Marquet-Krause from 1933 to 1935 and again by Dr. Joseph A. Callaway from 1964 to 1970. Ai was an important urban center of about 27.5 acres during the Early Bronze Age from approximately 3000 to 2400 B.C. (this size may be compared with that of OT Jericho, which was only about 10 acres).

In the Early Bronze Age, Ai had a temple and a royal quarter. Its inhabitants apparently came originally from Syria and Anatolia. Egyptian influence is evident from the temple of this period and imported alabaster and stone vessels. The city had a massive stone-lined reservoir of 480,000 gallon capacity. The Early Bronze Age city was destroyed about 2400 B.C. and remained a ruin until about 1200 B.C. Thus throughout the period of the OT patriarchs (ca. 2000–1300 B.C.), Ai was a ruin.

A small unwalled village was found on about 2.5 acres of the mound, dating from about 1220 B.C. The village was abandoned a final time about 1050 B.C.

Joshua 8 describes the capture and destruction of Ai by Israelites. However, at the time commonly accepted for the Israelite conquest of Canaan, about 1250 B.C., Ai was uninhabited. One explanation suggests the account in Joshua 8 is etiological (i.e., explanatory) rather than historical, ascribing a well-known ruin to the conquest by Joshua. Callaway has proposed instead that the Israelite capture of Ai fits well with the evidence of the unwalled Iron Age village. The Israelites may have captured and resettled that village. The conquest of Ai would then date to about 1125 B.C. An alternative view favored by W. F. Albright suggests that the biblical story of Joshua 8 originally referred to the capture of Bethel and was later transferred to the nearby ruins of Ai. Callaway's reconstruction does preserve the biblical account, though admittedly suggesting that the biblical account greatly exaggerated the size of Ai at the time the Israelites took it. ***See also*** Bethel; Conquest of Canaan. J.F.D.

Aijeleth hash-Shahar (ay'je-leth hash-shah' hahr); Heb., part of the superscription of Psalm 22, meaning "Hind of (*or* A Hind is) the Dawn." These were perhaps the first words of a popular song whose tune accompanied this psalm.

Ajalon (aj'uh-lahn), the valley in Josh. 10:12 where the moon was to stop in its course (along with that of the sun over Gibeon to the east), so that Joshua and the troops could defeat the Canaanites. The valley proceeds west past the ascent to Beth-horon and turns north toward Lod.

'Ajjul (aj'uhl), **Tell el-,** a large tell located four miles southwest of Gaza on the northern bank of the wadi Ghuzzeh. The site was densely populated ca. 2000–1500 B.C., producing a large number of inscribed seals and an impressive quantity of gold and jewelry. Perhaps the site is the Beth Eglayim mentioned by Eusebius (*Onamasticon* 48:19). ***See also*** Tell; Wadi.

Akeldama (ah-kel'duh-muh; "Field of Blood," transliterated from Aramaic), field in Acts 1:18–19 (see Matt. 27:3–10) that Judas Iscariot is said to have purchased with the blood money he received for betraying Jesus. He died there; hence the name. ***See also*** Judas; Potter's Field.

Akhenaton (ahkh-uh-nah'tuhn) or Amenophis (ah-men'oh-fis) or Amenhotep (ah-men'hoh-tep) IV, the "heretic" king of Egypt (ca. 1364–1347 B.C.) and one of the most controversial figures of antiquity. A pharaoh of the powerful eighteenth dynasty (1546–1319 B.C.), he is best known for his promotion of the exclusive cult of the sun disk, the Aten. Early in his reign he changed his name from Amenophis, honoring the god Amun of Thebes (and thereby Amun's powerful priesthood), to Akhenaton (Egyptian, "It is well with the Aten"). By the eighth year of his reign he moved the capital from Thebes to the new settlement of Akhetaten (Tell el-Amarna), a site in Middle Egypt unconnected with the cult of any other deity. Under his predecessor Amenophis III (ca. 1402–1364) the Aten had become more prominent, but now the Aten was celebrated as the sole god, creator of all lands and peoples, mother and father of all creation. The "Great Hymn to the Aten" has some striking parallels with Psalm 104. In many reliefs the Aten is represented as a radiating sun disk, the rays terminating in hands holding out the symbol of life. To some extent Akhenaten and the royal family worshiped the Aten, and the rest of the people worshiped the royal family. His queen, Nefertiti, played an unusually prominent part in the court rituals. It is not clear whether Akhenaton or others were the prime movers behind this monotheistic reform.

Attempts were made to suppress other cults, and the king did not partake in the usual festivals in honor of other gods. In spite of the fundamental changes, Akhenaton was quite secure in his unwalled capital and Egypt remained strong at home and abroad. Egypt was intensively involved politically in Syria and Palestine. Akhenaton's successor, the young Tutankhamun, switched his allegiance to Amun and moved the capital back to Thebes. About fifty years later the attempt to eradicate the memory of Akhenaton and his Aten reform was underway. It did not succeed. ***See also*** Amarna, Tell el-; Egypt; Re. H.B.H.

Akkad (a'kad). ***See*** Accad.

alabaster, compact, translucent gypsum often carved into vases. In the NT a globular perfume flask carved from alabaster is mentioned. Made without handles it had a long neck that was broken to pour out the perfume (Mark 14:3; Matt. 26:7).

Alabaster vessels from Dir el-Balah, 1500–1200 B.C.

Alamoth (ah'lah-mohth; Heb., "young maidens"), a musical direction of unknown origin and meaning. Its derivation has led some to suggest it may mean "to be sung by young women" (Ps. 46), but its use as a direction for playing the harp (1 Chron. 15:20) implies a musical theme or rhythm. ***See also*** Psalms, The.

Alcimus (al'si-muhs), a Jew installed by the Seleucids as high priest ca. 161–159 B.C. in opposition to the Maccabees (1 Macc. 7:5–25; cf. 2 Macc. 14:3–26). He was hated for such acts as treacherously slaughtering a group of Hasideans and giving orders to destroy the inner wall of the Temple (1 Macc. 9:54–57). ***See also*** Maccabees; Seleucids, The.

א

aleph (ah'lef), the first letter of the Hebrew alphabet, often used to designate a fourth-century A.D. parchment manuscript of the Greek Bible. The manuscript was discovered during the nineteenth century by Konstantin von Tischendorf at the Monastery of St. Catherine on Mount Sinai and hence called Codex Sinaiticus. Originally containing about 720 leaves, each measuring 15 by 13½ inches with four columns to the page, today the OT portion consists of 43 leaves at Leipzig, fragments of three leaves at Leningrad, and 199 leaves, together with the entire NT portion of 148 leaves, in the Royal Library of the British Museum in London. At the close of the NT stand *The Epistle of Barnabas* and part of *The Shepherd of Hermas*. In 1980, a dozen more leaves of the manuscript were reported found at St. Catherine's. ***See also*** Codex; Texts, Versions, Manuscripts, Editions. B.M.M.

Alexander. 1 Alexander III (356–323 B.C.),

known as "Alexander the Great," one of the greatest leaders of all time. In 336 B.C. he succeeded to the throne as king of Macedon and the Greek city-states conquered by his father, Philip II.

In 334 B.C. Alexander began the conquest of the Perisan Empire in the east. The first phase of his conquest occupied the period 334–330 B.C., during which time the Persian king, Darius III, was still alive and able to offer resistance to Alexander. During the first years of this campaign, Alexander marched through Anatolia, Phoenicia, Palestine, Egypt, and Mesopotamia. Though the Greek naval fleet had been disbanded in 334 B.C., Alexander was able to neutralize the Persian navy by controlling its bases. In 331 the oracle of Amun Re in Egypt proclaimed Alexander divine. At some point, Alexander may even have demanded that he be paid divine honors. In April of 331, Alexander founded the city of Alexandria on the western edge of Egypt's Nile delta. Alexander was able to obtain wealth from captured Persian capitals. He burned Persepolis in 330 and in July of that year Darius was murdered. Alexander concluded this phase of his conquest by disbanding his Greek allies.

The second phase (330–327 B.C.) involved putting down nationalist uprisings in the empire. It saw an increasing orientalization of the court and Alexander's marriage to the Bactrian princess Roxanne. During this period a number of cities called "Alexandria" were founded throughout the empire.

In 327 B.C. Alexander undertook his famous march through Afghanistan into India. His eastward progress was stopped when the troops refused to go any further. He marched down the Indus River, but plans to coordinate the army and fleet fell through when the ships were delayed by monsoons. Only twenty-five percent of the army survived the western crossing of the Gedrosian desert (southern coast of modern Iran and Pakistan). Upon his return, Alexander removed officials whose loyalty had proved questionable while he was in India.

The final eighteen months brought the disbanding of Alexander's Macedonian veterans. The army and the court were increasingly staffed by Iranians. Alexander ordered the repatriation of Greek exiles in the empire. He appears to have come to insist on being paid divine honors by having those entering his presence prostrate themselves. Finally, while preparing for a campaign into Arabia, Alexander died on June 10, 323. His body was a prize at the funeral games and won by Ptolemy I, who took it to Egypt. Though he retained the Persian administrative system of satrapies, Alexander established garrisons and Greek-style cities throughout the area, which led to an "orientalized Greek culture" among the educated of the entire region. The Hellenistic period (ca. 300 B.C.–A.D. 300) that resulted and saw Greek culture dominate the greater Mediterranean basin owes its impetus to Alexander's victories and it began with his death. The results of that dominance by Greek culture, and especially the Greek language, led to the translation of the OT in Greek (the LXX), and to the writing of the NT in that same language. Disputes over the degree to which Greek culture might be admitted into Jewish life also led to disputes between those who favored its adoption and those who opposed it altogether.

2 The son of Simon of Cyrene (Mark 15:21).

3 A member of the high-priestly family (Acts 4:6).

4 A Jew from Ephesus (Acts 19:33).

5 An apostate in 1 Tim. 1:20. ***See also*** Alexandria; Persepolis; Persia. P.P.

Head of Alexander the Great. Alexander is pictured as a youthful Herakles with lionskin cap on this silver tetradrachma minted after his death in the second century B.C. in Greece.

Alexandra, the wife of the Hasmonean king Alexander Jannaeus. She ruled over the Jewish state from her husband's death in 76 B.C. until 69 B.C. The Pharisees enjoyed considerable influence during her reign, which was a peaceful time for the Macabbean kingdom. At her death, her two sons, Hyrcannus II, who had served as high priest during his mother's rule, and Aristobulus II, began a bitter struggle for the kingdom. ***See also*** Hasmoneans; Maccabees.

Alexandria, an Egyptian city on the Mediterranean coast near the Nile delta, founded in 332 B.C. by Alexander the Great; under Ptolemy, his successor, it became Egypt's capital. Alexandria was one of the largest cities of the Hellenistic world, a major shipping port (Acts 27:6; 28:11)

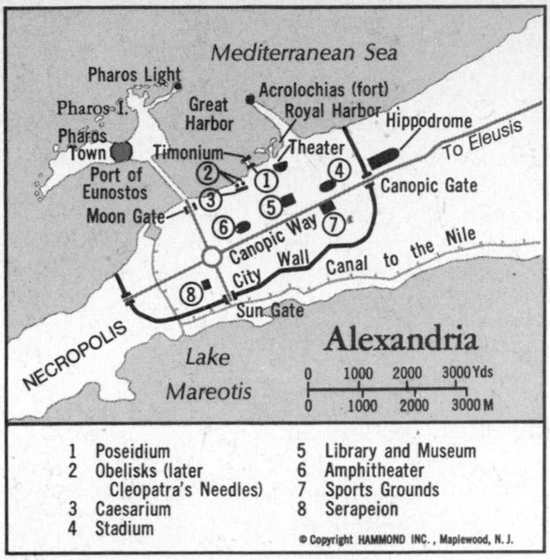

famed for its 445-foot-high lighthouse, and the focal point of Hellenistic intellectual and cultural life with an unrivaled four-hundred-thousand-volume library and museum.

Alexandria's population of nearly one million included a large Jewish component, which by the first century A.D. was the largest Diaspora (i.e., Jews living outside Palestine) community in the world. Relations between groups in the city were tense, however, erupting during that period into bloody riots and pogroms and producing the first known Jewish ghetto. The violence was quelled in A.D. 41 by an edict from the Roman Emperor Claudius that directly confirmed the religious liberty of the Jews in Alexandria and throughout the Empire and indirectly contributed to the period of relative calm that allowed the new Christian church to expand.

The literary flowering in Alexandria left a direct impact on the Bible. There the Greek translation of the Hebrew Bible, the Septuagint, was made; the Wisdom of Solomon, 3 and perhaps 2 and 4 Maccabees were written; and the allegorical method of interpretation was refined, a method that is found in the writings of Philo, a Jewish philosopher-theologian, the Letter to the Hebrews, *The Epistle of Barnabas*, and the later writings of church teachers like Clement of Alexandria and Origen.

Although Alexandria had Jewish inhabitants from its inception, the beginnings of Christianity there are shrouded in mystery. Apollos (Acts 18:24), a co-worker of Paul, was an Alexandrian, but he converted to Christianity only after he left that city. Legend attributes the initial Christian mission there to Mark, but the first firm evidence for Alexandrian Christianity derives from the second century A.D. The story of Christianity in Alexandria is intimately bound up with the struggle against Gnosticism, which also flourished on Egyptian soil. ***See also*** Apollos; Gnosticism; Philo; Septuagint; Wisdom of Solomon, The. J.M.B.

Alexandrinus. ***See*** A.

algum (al'guhm), a sumptuous wood imported by Solomon for the Temple (2 Chron. 2:8; 9:10–11). ***See also*** Almug.

almond *(Amagdalus communis)*, a fruit tree, in Palestine growing as high as twenty-five feet. It flowers toward the end of January, the color of its blooms ranging from pink to pure white. According to Gen. 30:37 Jacob used rods of almond, poplar, and plane in his plan against Laban. In Gen. 43:11 almonds are among the choice fruits of the land. According to Num. 17:8, Aaron's rod put forth buds, blossoms, and ripe almonds, thus demonstrating he was divinely chosen. Jeremiah's vision of the rod of almond (Heb. *shaqed*) is the occasion for God to say he is watching over (Heb. *shoqed*) his word (Jer. 1:11). Koheleth uses the almond blossom to illustrate declining old age (Eccles. 12:5). In Exod. 25:33–34 and 37:19–20, the cup on each

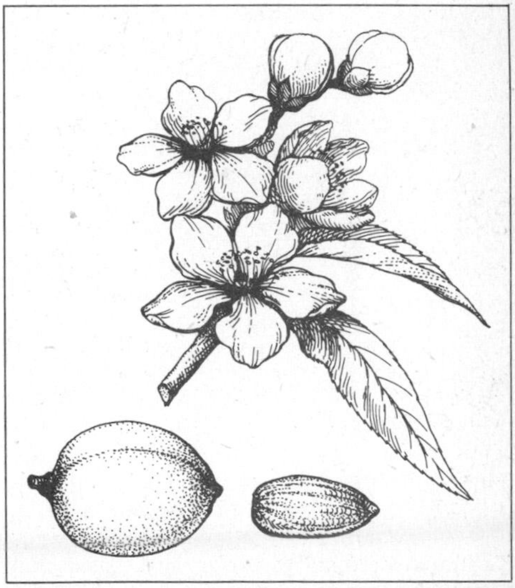

Almond.

of the six branches and main stand of the candlestick (menorah; RSV: "lampstand") were shaped like almonds; the almonds and other vegetal shapes suggest an original connection with fertility rites. ***See also*** Lampstand. R.J.C.

alms, gifts to the needy. Almsgiving is a common practice in the Bible that recognizes God's blessings and maintains proper community relations. In the OT care for the poor is recommended (Prov. 14:21, 31; Isa. 58:6–8) as just behavior, required by the tithe for the poor every three years (Deut. 14:28–29) and the leaving of fallen produce at harvest for the poor (Deut. 24: 19–22). The NT also recommends the traditional Jewish practice of almsgiving (Matt. 6:1–4), calling it by a word that comes from the Greek word for "mercy." The early Christian community cared for its poor (Acts 6; 2 Cor. 8–9) and the parable of the sheep and the goats (Matt. 25: 31–46) makes final judgment depend on care given to the needy. ***See also*** Love; Poor.

A.J.S.

almug (al'muhg), a special kind of wood, perhaps red sandalwood *(Pterocarpus santalinus)*. Almug was imported from Ophir (southwest Arabia) by Hiram of Tyre and used in the construction of Solomon's Temple and for musical

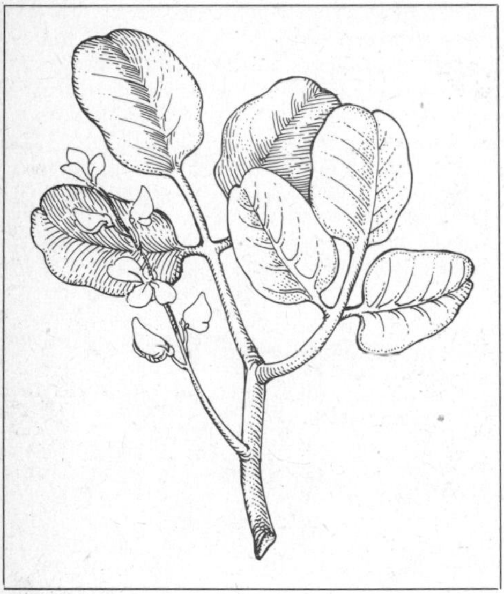

Traditional almug.

instruments (1 Kings 10:11–12). The parallels in 2 Chron. 2:7 and 9:10–11 have *algum*, perhaps by transposition of two letters. The occurrence of a similar word in Ugaritic *(almg)* suggests that the spelling in Kings is correct.

aloes, any plant of the genus *Aloe*. The aloes mentioned in the Bible are not the bitter, medicinal plant with which we are familiar, but a fragrant wood of either an eaglewood or sandalwood tree used as perfume. In Ps. 45:8 and Song of Sol. 4:14, it is listed along with other fragrant spices such as myrrh and cassia. Some scholars think that the aloes brought for Jesus' burial in John 19:39 do refer to the medicinal aloes, which were used by the Egyptians in embalming. However, others point out that the passage may just as easily refer to the valuable, fragrant perfume, perhaps used to soak the linen wrappings.

P.P.

alpha (al'fuh), the first letter of the Greek alphabet. In Revelation, God (1:8; 21:6) and Jesus (22:13) are called "the Alpha and the Omega," meaning the first and the last (omega is the last letter in the Greek alphabet; cf. Isa. 44:6 for God as "first" and "last"). God was present at the first (Gen. 1:1–2:24; Ps. 90:2), and Jesus was also from the beginning (John 1:1–3). Both God and Jesus were expected to reign in the last days. ***See also*** Creation; Eschatology; Kingdom of God; Millennium; Omega; Parousia; Son of Man; Symbol.

alphabet. ***See*** Writing.

Alphaeus (al-fee'uhs). **1** Father of James, one of Jesus' twelve disciples who is not to be identified with James the son of Zebedee (Matt. 10:3; Mark 3:18; Luke 6:15; Acts 1:13). **2** Father of Levi (Matthew?) the tax collector (Mark 2:14; see Matt. 9:9; Luke 5:27). ***See also*** James; Levi; Matthew.

altar, the translation of a Hebrew word denoting "place of sacrifice." Because it is formed from a verbal root that means "to slaughter" or, more specifically, "to slaughter and cut up for the purpose of sacrifice," the term "altar" obviously is derived from the ancient, prebiblical practice of animal sacrifice. However, by the time of its usage in connection with biblical ritual, its early association with animal slaughter had been extended. Altars mentioned in the Bible were used for oblations in general: for a variety of foodstuffs, including grain mixed with oil and/or salt and incense, wine, fruits, four-legged animals, birds; and for incense alone. In addition, the probability that the prebiblical sacrifices or ritual killings took place on the altar itself appears remote. While offerings of all types were deposited and burnt on the altar, the actual slaughtering of sacrificial animals took place at a specially designated spot adjacent to the altar itself.

The word for altar *(mizbayahkh)* is found approximately four hundred times in the Hebrew Bible. In addition, most English versions use "altar" to render another Hebrew term *(hahrel)*, which literally means "mountain of God" and may refer to Syro-Mesopotamian altar constructions, since Ezekiel (43:15) probably uses it in reference to an altar built by King Ahaz in emulation of an altar he had seen in Damascus (2 Kings 11:10–16).

Virtually half of the OT usages appear in the Pentateuch, as might be expected, because of the concentration of priestly texts in the first section of the Hebrew Bible. Other biblical books with frequent mentions of the altar are 1 and 2 Kings, which include the description of the Solomonic Temple altar, 2 Chronicles,

Incense burners from Tel Zafit and Tel Amal and a small altar, first millennium B.C.

which has a decidedly priestly interest, and Ezekiel, a prophet whose visions are highly influenced by Temple imagery.

In the NT the word for "altar" (Gk. *thusiastērion)* is used in twenty-four places. In one instance, in reference to a pagan structure (Acts 17:23), another Greek word *(bōmos,* "high place') is translated "altar." Older English versions render a third word *(thumiatērion)* "censer" in one other place, Heb. 9:4, although the usage probably denotes the golden incense altar, as the RSV understands it. The NT references exhibit concentrations in Matthew (seven times), with only two mentions in Luke and none in Mark or John, and in Revelation (eight times), as might be expected because of the Temple visions of that book.

The construction of sacrificial altars was not necessarily limited to the Jerusalem Temple or to any temple for that matter, at least not before the time of the centralization of the cult in Jerusalem in Josiah's time (639–609 B.C.). By their very nature, involving as they did the processing of animal carcasses and the burning of various foodstuffs, altars (except for incense altars) were open-air structures. Therefore, altars could in fact exist and function independently of temple buildings. This fact is especially apparent in the reference to altars in the patriarchal narratives of Genesis (e.g., Gen. 13:18; 33: 20). However, the converse is apparently not true, and temple buildings were always accompanied by altars in their courtyards. In addition, the somewhat enigmatic shrines known as "high places" were perhaps a category of altar.

Biblical altars can be classified according to the material from which they were fabricated, namely, stone, earth, or metal. The first two kinds of material are associated with altars that could exist apart from sanctuaries. The third type of altar with respect to material (but not form) is mentioned only in connection with the central sanctuary of Israel, the tabernacle or Temple. A fourth type of altar, made of brick, is mentioned only once in the Bible, in Isa. 65:3, where a word *(lebaynah)* different from the normal Hebrew term is employed.

Stone Altars: These consisted of both natural and man-made forms. Evidently any large stone could be used in its original position and condition, as in the story of Gideon's offering of bread and meat upon a rock (Judg. 6:19–23; cf. 13: 19–20). In other cases, a large stone might be moved from its existing position into a more convenient place, as for example when Saul insisted that a stone be brought to where he stood for the slaughter, presumably as an altar sacrifice, of sheep and oxen captured from the Philistines (1 Sam. 14:31–35). Simple stone altars apparently could be enhanced somewhat by the hollowing out of depressions in the rock to contain liquids. The evidence for such altars is archaeological rather than biblical, however, and the identification of large rocks with "cup holes" or shallow depressions as altars remains tentative. In addition to isolated stones, unhewn stones, as commanded in Exod. 20:25, could be formed into altars, either as irregular heaps (e.g., Gen. 31:46) or as dry-laid masonry structures. The latter seems to be the case for the carefully arranged stones of Elijah's altar on Mt. Carmel (1 Kings 18:30–35).

It is obvious that any of these stone altars could be established with relative ease, a consideration no doubt related to the fact that, until Josiah's reform, all slaughtering of animals for meat was to be considered a sacrificial act, at least according to the tradition preserved in Lev. 17:3–5 and altered by the proscriptions in Deut. 12:15–28.

Earthen Altars: These could also be erected anywhere, according to Exod. 20:24, for the sacrifice of various kinds of offerings. Simplicity and availability to all the people characterize both earth and stone altars; neither technical competence nor craft specialization were associated with the construction of these altars. Brick altars, although hardly in evidence in Palestine in contrast with Mesopotamian practice, were technically earthen structures but would have required somewhat more skill in their fabrication.

Metal Altars: Altars of metal are mentioned in the Bible only in connection with the central sanctuary of ancient Israel. Several biblical sources provide descriptive materials: the tabernacle texts of Exodus, the Solomonic Temple description in 1 Kings, Ezekiel's Temple vision, and to a lesser extent the Temple vision in the

Two altars pictured *in situ* in the Holy of Holies of the Israelite temple at Arad, ninth century B.C.

book of Revelation. These texts contain a number of discrepancies, omissions, or contradictions in their presentation of the altars, as might be expected since they deal with sanctuaries that existed over a wide period of time, from a premonarchical tent shrine through the First Temple with its subsequent alterations and perhaps even the postexilic Temple. Nonetheless, a fairly accurate understanding of the two metal altars, the golden altar of incense and the bronze altar of burnt offerings, of the main cultic center can be acquired from these sources.

The *altar of incense* was placed inside the sanctuary, directly in front of the inner sanctum and flanked, according to the Exodus texts (Exod. 30:1–10; 37:25–28; cf. 1 Kings 7:20–21, 48), by two other appurtenances, the menorah and the table of the Bread of the Presence. (The latter may functionally be an altar, but it is not technically designated as such.) It was made of wood and, like everything within the sanctuary, was covered with the precious metal gold. An upright pillar measuring 1 × 1 × 2 cubits (perhaps 18″ × 18″ × 36″), the incense altar featured, in addition to rings and staves for carrying, horns on its four upper corners. For this reason it has been compared to various horned incense altars recovered from Iron Age levels at such sites as Megiddo and Shechem as well as to small stone altars without horns from Arad, even though these excavated examples are notably different in size and material from the biblical incense altar. Twice daily incense was burned in the tabernacle or Temple on the golden altar.

The *altar of burnt offering* stood in the courtyard of the tabernacle (Exod. 27:1–8; 38:1–7) and occupied a special "holy place," akin to the holiness within the sanctuary, which could be approached only by priests even though nonpriests could be present in the courtyard. The Temple description in 1 Kings omits a description of this altar, perhaps because Ahaz had moved it or because Solomon had used one made by David; but 2 Chron. 4:1 does describe a courtyard altar (20 × 20 × 20 cubits or about 30 × 30 × 30 feet), and 1 Kings 8:64 also mentions it. Thus there can be no doubt that the Jerusalem Temple featured a courtyard altar as the focus of its sacrificial cult. Although larger than the tabernacle altar, which was 5 × 5 × 3 cubits (about 7½ × 7½ × 4½ feet), it was also made, or perhaps overlaid, with bronze, like the other courtyard appurtenances. An even larger courtyard altar, in the Syrian style, was introduced by Ahaz and probably continued to be used until the Temple was destroyed. The information in Ezekiel, while not mentioning the material from which it was constructed, emphasizes the altar's great size (12 cubits high and 18 × 18 cubits at its base or about 18 feet high and about 27 × 27 feet at the base) and tiered shape and most likely reflects the altar Ahaz commissioned. Both the tabernacle courtyard altar and that of Ezekiel's vision had horns at their four upper corners, a feature that perhaps can be associated with the large horned altar made of hewn sandstone blocks discovered at Beersheba.

The important role of sacrificial altars in ancient Israel is clearly derived from common Near Eastern practices. However, non-Israelite sacrificial systems were rooted in the idea of providing sustenance and pleasing odors for the gods in their earthly residences. Israelite altars, while technically hearths for God's dwelling, did not preserve that concept. Rather they functioned to bring humanity close to heaven and not vice versa. The consecration of altars, that is the establishment of their holiness, was linked to a divine theophany (appearance); hence, altars were installations that enabled people to draw near to God's presence. This concept of altar holiness underlies both the sacrificial aspect and also the testimony (cf. Josh. 22:26–29) and asylum (e.g., 1 Kings 2:28; cf. Exod. 21:14) functions of biblical altars. The NT continues the OT traditions; its references to altars are mainly to the courtyard altar of the Jerusalem Temple, either in pre-exilic or post-exilic (chiefly Herodian) times. In one significant development of this pattern, the Christian altar of Heb. 13:10 appears to be a metaphor for human self-offering which, like its Hebraic precursor, brings the offerant close to God. ***See also*** Bethel; Tabernacle; Temple, The; Temples; Worship.

Bibliography

Aharoni, Yohanan. "The Horned Altar of Beersheba." *Biblical Archaeologist* 37 (1979):2–6.

Haran, Menahem. *Temples and Temple Service in Ancient Israel.* Oxford: Clarendon, 1970.

de Vaux, Roland. "Altars." In *Ancient Israel.* New York: McGraw-Hill, 1961. Pp. 406–14.

C.L.M.

Altashheth (ahl-tahsh'eth; Heb., "do not destroy"), a Hebrew word found at the beginning of Psalms 57–59, 75, translated in the RSV "Do Not Destroy." It may have been a musical notation of some sort, designating a familiar tune or rhythm pattern, although its meaning remains unknown. ***See also*** Psalms, The.

Amalekites (uh-mal'uh-kīts), descendants of Amalek, who was a grandson of Esau according to the OT (Gen. 36:15–16). As a people, the Amalekites inhabited territory assigned to Israel, Judah, and the Transjordanian states. They were probably nomadic, but even if they were not, they were certainly mobile. Often they are mentioned as inhabiting the fringe of settled territory or associated with the desert regions.

The Amalekites attacked Israel on its wilderness journeys from Egypt (Exod. 17:8–16), a report that highlights an antipathy between the two peoples. Other references to them suggest that they were proficient raiders of village and agrarian communities (1 Sam. 30:1–20; Judg. 6: 1–6).

As Israel solidified its territorial hold during the period of the judges and the United Monarchy (ca. 1225–926 B.C.), the Amalekite threat gradually lessened (see 2 Sam. 8:12; 1 Chron. 18: 11). There are no more OT references to the Amalekites after the narratives about David except for a summary reference in 1 Chron. 4:43.

J.A.D.

Amariah (am-uh-rī'uh; Heb., "Yah [God] has spoken" or "Yah has promised"). **1** A Levite, an ancestor of Zadok and Ezra. There are two men in one genealogical list (1 Chron. 6:7, 11) bearing this name: the first is the son of Meraioth and the second the son of Azariah. However, other lists omit one of these (1 Chron. 6:52, the first; Ezra 7:3, the second). It is possible that these latter lists were abbreviated, a practice not uncommon in the Bible. It is also possible that parts of the longer list were accidently duplicated by scribes. **2** A Levite, the second son of Hebron of the clan of Kohath (1 Chron. 23:19). **3** The chief priest in Jerusalem during the reign of Jehoshaphat (2 Chron. 19:11). **4** A Levite who shared the responsibility for distributing the Levites' portion of the offerings to the levitical cities during the reign of Hezekiah (2 Chron. 31:15). **5** A Levite who returned from the Babylonian captivity with Zerubbabel (Neh. 12:2), possibly the same one who signed the covenant to keep the law (Neh. 10:3) and was condemned by Ezra for marriage to a foreign woman (Ezra 10:42), although this identification is not certain. **6** A Judahite who lived in postexilic Jerusalem (Neh. 11:4). **7** A family group in postexilic Jerusalem whose leader was Jehohanan (Neh. 12:13). **8** A son of (King?) Hezekiah in the lineage of the prophet Zephaniah (Zeph. 1:1).

D.R.B.

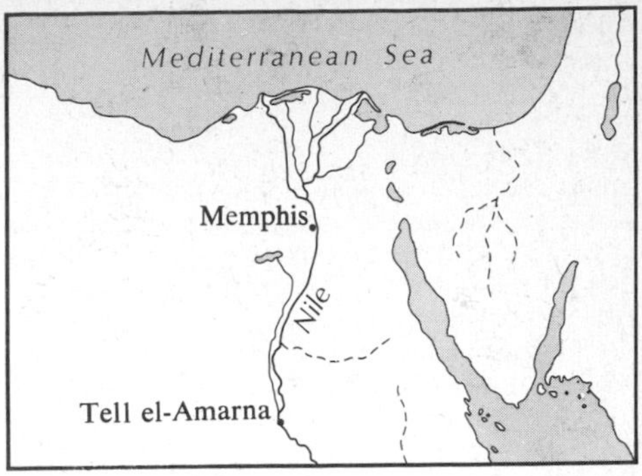

Amarna (uh-mahr'nuh), **Tell el-** (tel el-), the modern name for the ruins of ancient Akhetaten (Egyptian, "The Horizon of the Sun Disk/Aten"), briefly the capital of Egypt during the later years of Akhenaton (Amenophis IV) and his immediate successors. Settled ca. 1356 B.C., Akhetaten is in middle Egypt, at a wide plain on the east bank of the Nile about midway between Thebes and Memphis. When Akhenaton founded the city he dedicated it to the cult of the Aten, honored as the sole god. Since the city was abandoned within fifteen to twenty years of its founding—the young Tutankhamun moved the court back to Thebes—it is a unique, one-period city. The city plan features a separate complex for the royal residence and extensive structures for the ceremonial and ritual acts of the royal family. The exaggerated, naturalistic style of the sculptures, reliefs, and paintings, together with the uniquely intimate scenes of Akhenaton, his queen, Nefertiti, and their daughters, has made Amarna art world famous. From adjacent tombs come the hymns to the sole god, the Aten (or to the Aten and the king), who is also celebrated on the city's boundary stelae. Another major discovery involved tablets in cuneiform Akkadian including both literary texts and over three hundred and fifty letters exchanged between the Egyptian court and the kings of western Asia Minor. The bulk of these letters came from kings of Syria and Palestine, including rulers of Jerusalem, Shechem, and Megiddo among other biblical cities. These texts demonstrate the international character of the age and the socially and politically disturbed situation in Palestine. Prominent in the letters are the *Khapiru*, a marginal people reminiscent of the later Hebrews. ***See also*** Akhenaton; Hebrews; Khapiru. H.B.H.

Amasa (ahm'ah-suh; Heb., "to support, defend, protect" [cf. Isa. 46:3]). **1** The son of Abigail, David's half-sister, and Jether (1 Chron. 2: 17). He was the cousin of Joab and his successor as military commander-in-chief, despite his defection to the rebelling Absalom (2 Sam. 17:25; 19:14). During the revolt of Sheba, he failed to take prompt action and was therefore murdered by Joab (2 Sam. 20:1–13). He can probably be identified with Amasai, the leader of the thirty "mighty men" (1 Chron. 12:19). **2** The son of

Haldai and a prince of Ephraim (2 Chron. 28:12) who helped the prisoners of Judah (2 Chron. 28: 12–15). J.G.G.

Amaziah (am-ah-zī'ah; Heb., "Yahweh is mighty"). **1** The king of Judah ca. 800–783 B.C. Amaziah was the son of Joash; he succeeded his father as king when he was twenty-five years old (see 2 Kings 14:1–20). According to 2 Kings 14: 2 he ruled twenty-nine years, but the chronological problems posed by his synchronism with Jehoash, king of Israel (2 Kings 14:17), can only be resolved by supposing that he actually reigned only ca. eighteen years, being regent for the balance. Upon ascending the throne at his father's murder, Amaziah consolidated his power by annihilating the assassins but sparing their sons. He is said to have slaughtered ten thousand Edomites in a battle in the "Valley of Salt," but that and the site of Sela (Petra?) have not been positively located. Emboldened by his success against Edom, he made overtures to his rival Jehoash, king of Israel (2 Kings 14:8–14), only to be challenged and defeated at the battle of Beth-shemesh, after which Judah was reduced to Israel's vassal state. Later a conspiracy was mounted against him, and he was pursued to Lachish, where he was murdered. **2** A Simeonite (1 Chron. 4:34). **3** A Levite of the family of Merari (1 Chron. 6:45). **4** A priest of Bethel (Amos 7:10, 12, 14). W.G.D.

amen, a Hebrew word meaning certainty, truthfulness, and faithfulness. Both the OT and NT use it as a liturgical response at the end of Psalms and doxologies in which the congregation affirms what has been prayed by saying Amen, "So be it." In the Gospels Jesus often prefaces his teachings with "Amen I say to you," a solemn affirmation which the RSV translates "Truly I say to you."

Amminadab (ah-min'uh-dab; Heb., "my kinsman is noble"). **1** The father of both Elisheba, Aaron's wife (Exod. 6:23), and Nahshan, a tribal leader of Judah during the wilderness wanderings (Num. 2:3). He is named in the lineage of King David (Ruth 4:19–20) and in the ancestry of Jesus through Joseph (Luke 3:33). **2** A Levite of the clan of Kohath (1 Chron. 6:22), probably the same one who, as leader of the clan of Uzziel (Kohath's son), helped bring the Ark of the Covenant from the house of Obed-edom to Jerusalem (1 Chron. 15:10).

Ammishaddai (ah-mi'sha-dī; Heb., "my kinsman is Shaddai [divine name translated 'Almighty']"), the father of Ahiezar, leader of the tribe of Dan during the wilderness wanderings (Num. 1:12).

Ammonites (am'uh-nīts), a people who lived east of the Jordan River, in the area of the modern state of Jordan. According to Gen. 19:30–38, a son was born to Lot, Abraham's nephew, named Ben Ammi. This child is reputed to be the progenitor of the Ammonites. According to historical research, the rise of the kingdom of Ammon east of the Jordan coincided with the rise of several states in the greater Syro-Palestinian area during the Late Bronze and Early Iron Ages (ca. 1500–1000 B.C.). Additional peoples who also emerged in that area at that time were the Moabites, the Edomites, Israel, and several Aramean states. Ammon's capital, Rabbah, was centered at the headwaters of the Jabbok River (modern-day Amman).

Conflicts between Ammon and Israel arose early in Israel's history. Sometime after the Israelites had entered the land of Canaan, they were defeated by a coalition of Ammonites and Philistines. Jephthah, the son of Gilead and a harlot, rallied Israel to battle against them. To ensure success, Jephthah vowed to sacrifice to God the first one to meet him if he returned home victorious. His subsequent victory was marred when his only child, a daughter, was first to greet him (Judg. 10:6–11:40). In subsequent battles, the Ammonites were defeated by Saul at Jabesh-gilead (1 Sam. 11) and then by David at Rabbah (2 Sam. 12:26–31). Much that happened to the Ammonites after those defeats is obscure, but the defeats by Israel did not subdue them permanently. As the political fortunes of both Israel and Judah waned in the eighth and seventh centuries B.C., Ammonite culture continued to develop, a conclusion substantiated by both epigraphic and artifactual evidence.

Limestone statue of an Ammonite king from the ninth century B.C.

The capital city of Ammon, Rabbah, was rebuilt and enlarged in the third century B.C. by Ptolemy Philadelphus, a descendant of one of the generals of Alexander the Great who, on his death, had divided among themselves the lands he had conquered. Ptolemy renamed the new city Philadelphia in his own honor. The eventual reappearance of the name of the Ammonites in the name of the modern Jordanian city of Amman is an indication of the long-standing association of the area with that ancient people. ***See also*** Jephthah. J.A.D.

Amnon (am'nahn; Heb., "faithful"). **1** The eldest son of David and Ahinoam and the half-brother of Absalom. He fell in love with his half-sister Tamar, daughter of David and Maacah and full sister of Absalom. Acting on the advice of his cousin Jonadab, he pretended to be ill, asked David for Tamar to attend him, and then raped her when they were alone. His action infuriated Absalom, who waited patiently for his revenge. After two years had passed Absalom, who had persuaded David to send his sons with him, Absalom, to the sheepshearing, arranged with his retainers for the murder of Amnon. His death at the hand of Absalom precipitated a rift between David and Absalom (2 Sam. 13). **2** A Judahite, son of Shimon (1 Chron. 4:20). ***See also*** Absalom; David; Tamar. D.R.B.

Amon (ah'muhn). **1** A governor of the city of Samaria in the reign of Ahab (1 Kings 22:10, 26). **2** A king of Judah, the son of and successor to Manasseh. He was the father of Josiah. He became king at age twenty-two and ruled for two years (642–640 B.C.), when he was murdered in his palace by servants (2 Kings 21:19–26; 2 Chron. 33:21–25). The conspirators were apparently opponents of his and his father's pro-Assyrian policies. The author of Chronicles considers the guilt of Amon to have exceeded even that of his father, Manasseh.

Amorites (am'uh-rīts), according to biblical tradition one of the primary peoples in the land of Canaan before the rise of Israel, the others being the Canaanites and the Hittites (see Ezek. 16:3). The term "Amorite" can refer to the basic population of the whole area (e.g., Gen. 15:16; Deut. 1:7). In particular, the Amorites are associated with Transjordan and the kingdoms of Sihon, centered at Heshbon, and Og, centered at Ashtaroth and Edrei. These "two kings of the Amorites" appear as opponents of Israel prior to the settlement of Palestine. Og, with his famous "iron bedstead," is cited as the last of the celebrated giants. From the perspective of the Israelites, the Amorites were idolators and doers of iniquity (e.g., Josh. 24:15; Judg. 6:10). Accordingly, God drove them out of the land.

The Semitic-speaking Amorites appear in cuneiform (and Egyptian) sources as an early population group, associated especially with the west (including areas connected with the patriarchs of Israel, Abraham, Isaac, and Jacob), and as politically dominant in Mesopotamia in the early second millennium B.C. There was also a territory of Amurru in western Syria. At times, such as in the two centuries prior to the Exodus (fifteenth–fourteenth centuries B.C.), there was a specific kingdom of Amurru; in earlier times the area had several kings.

The antiquity of Amorites in the land of Canaan is unclear. Linguistic evidence indicates their presence as a settled population by ca. 1900 B.C., to judge from personal names, but that evidence is not decisive. The archaeological evidence is also unclear. The coming of the Amorites has been correlated by some scholars with the archaeological discontinuity at the end of Early Bronze Age III, ca. 2350 B.C. (and a transition to seminomadic pastoralism), or with the emergence of Middle Bronze I, ca. 2000 B.C. (and a transition to a more urbanized society). The problem is not settled. The patterns of population shift in the larger area are complex and precise correlations of literary and archaeological evidence are difficult. ***See also*** Og; Sihon. H.B.H.

Amos (ay'muhs), **the Book of,** one of the twelve Minor Prophets in the OT (Hosea through Malachi). The Hebrew prophet of the eighth century B.C., Amos, to whom it is attributed, was a native of Tekoa in Judah and was active in the northern kingdom of Israel. He identifies himself as a shepherd and "a dresser of sycamore trees" (Amos 7:14; cf. also 1:1), who was called to prophesy against Israel. On the basis of the superscription to the book (1:1), which places him in the reigns of Uzziah and Jeroboam, and historical allusions among his speeches, his work can be dated ca. 750 B.C. Thus he is the earliest of the prophets whose words have been handed down in writing.

OUTLINE OF CONTENTS

The Book of Amos

I. Superscription and motto (1:1–2)
II. Prophetic speeches (1:3–6:14)
   A. Prophecies against the nations and Israel (1:3–2:16)
   B. Prophecies of punishment (3:1–6:14)
III. Vision reports and prophecies (7:1–9:15)
   A. Three vision reports (7:1–9)
   B. Story of prophetic conflict (7:10–17)
   C. Two vision reports and prophecies of punishment (8:1–9:8)
   D. Prophecies of salvation (9:9–15)

The book of Amos is the third of the twelve so-called Minor Prophets. Its nine chapters consist mainly of short prophetic speeches, most of them addressed to the people of Israel as a whole. There are, however, other genres, including vision reports, an account of the prophet's encounter with Amaziah, the priest of Bethel (7:10–17), and three hymnic passages (4:13; 5:8–9; 9:5–6). Following the introductory superscription and the book's motto (1:1–2), the first major section of the book is a collection of prophetic speeches (1:3–6:14). The first part of that section (1:3–2:16) is a series of very similar prophecies of punishment, first against Israel's neighbors and then against Israel itself. The remainder of that section (3:1–6:14) is a collection of various prophecies of punishment. The second major section of the book (7:1–9:15) is organized around a series of five vision reports, which are filled out with other prophetic announcements and into which the report of Amos's encounter with Amaziah is inserted.

Most of the material in the book seems to stem from an authentic Amos tradition, handed down and eventually written down by those who succeeded the prophet. However, the concluding announcements in 9:8c–15 and the hymnic passages (4:13; 5:8–9; 9:5–6) were probably added later, during the time of the Babylonian exile. A few other verses, including 2:4–5 and 3:7, probably also are secondary.

Thc form and style of the prophet's speeches reveal his understanding of the prophetic role and message. While there are a few well-known sayings in which he calls for change on the part of the addressees (5:4–7, 14–15, 21–24), virtually all of the speeches are announcements of judgment or prophecies of punishment. They are very brief addresses in which Amos speaks in the name of God to announce that Israel's God is about to intervene to punish the people, an individual, or a group for their sins. His message is a simple one: God will soon bring disaster in the form of military defeat and exile upon Israel. The sins that have led to this judgment are social injustice, such as depriving the poor of their rights, and religious arrogance. There is, in fact, relatively little in his message that had not been known before through the religious traditions of Israel. Distinctive are his message that the end has now come, his stress on the obligations of a people elected by God (cf. 3:1–2), and his assumption that other nations have both been the objects of divine care (9:7) and are subject to God's punishment (1:3–2:3). ***See also*** Prophet.

G.M.T.

Amoz (ay'mooz; Heb., "he is strong"). The father of Isaiah (Isa. 1:1). The name, to be distinguished from Amos, is a shortened form of Amaziah.

Amphipolis (am-fip'oh-lis), a city situated inland above the Gulf of Strymon in northeastern Macedonia. The Strymon River, which formed a loop around part of the city, seems to have been the source of its Greek name, "double city." In the first century A.D., Amphipolis was a military post and station along the main east–west Roman road from Asia to Italy, the Egnatian Way. After leaving Philippi, Paul passed through Amphipolis on his way to Thessalonica (Acts 17:1).

Amram (am'ram). **1** The grandson of Levi, son of Kohath, father of Aaron and Moses (Exod. 6:16–20). **2** A son of Bani (Ezra 10:34).

amulet, a small object believed charged with divine potency and thus effective in warding off evil and inviting the protection of beneficial powers. Amulets were integral to belief in magic

A tiny silver amulet found in Jerusalem is inscribed with ancient Hebrew characters that spell out the divine name, YHWH, and which are drawn here. Originally the amulet—3.82 inches long, unrolled—was rolled and a string was threaded through it so that a person could wear it around the neck. From the writing, it may be dated to ca. sixth century B.C.

and derived their efficacy from close physical contact with a holy person or object. Frontlets and phylacteries served similar purposes (Exod. 13:9, 16; Deut. 6:8; 11:18; Matt. 23:5), as did Paul's handkerchiefs (Acts 19:12). ***See also*** Magic and Divination.

Anah (an'uh). **1** One of the eight sons of Seir the Horite; he was a tribal chieftain of the Horites, ancient inhabitants of the area of Edom (Gen. 36:20; 1 Chron. 1:38). **2** A nephew of 1 above and the father-in-law of Esau (Gen. 36:2). He was known for his discovery of a hot spring in the desert (Gen. 36:24). ***See also*** Horites; Seir.

Anakims (an'ah-keems), the plural the KJV uses for a pre-Israelite Canaanite tribe feared as gigantic (Num. 13:22, 28, 33; Deut. 1:28; 9:2; Josh. 11:21–22; 15:14; 21:11; Judg. 1:20). The RSV translates the word as "descendants of Anak." ***See also*** Canaan, Canaanites; Nephilim.

Anani (a-nay'nī), a Davidic descendant (1 Chron. 3:24).

Ananiah (an-ah-nī'ah). **1** One of the rebuilders of Jerusalem's walls under Nehemiah (Neh. 3: 23). **2** A postexilic Benjaminite city probably to be identified with Bethany (Neh. 11:32).

Ananias (an'uh-nī'uhs). **1** According to Acts 5: 1–11, an early Christian in Jerusalem who, with his wife Sapphira, fell dead shortly after falsely claiming to have given the entire proceeds of the sale of their property to the community's common fund (see Acts 4:32–37). Their death was interpreted as divine judgment, and they were seen as the opposite of the model wealthy believer, Barnabas (Acts 4:36–37). **2** According to Acts 9:10–20 and 22:12–16, an early Christian in Damascus who, after a vision from God, reluctantly received Saul (Paul) after the latter's vision on the road to Damascus, laying his hands upon him and baptizing him. **3** According to the historian Josephus, the son of Nedebaeus who was Jewish high priest ca. A.D. 47–58. In Acts 22: 30–23:10 and 24:1, he is the high priest at the time of Paul's trials in Jerusalem and Caesarea.

A.J.M.

Anat (ah'naht), a Canaanite goddess of fertility with a thirst for violence. No proposed explanation of the name "Anat" is convincing. The Ugaritic literature gives the best evidence of her character and exploits. Place names (Anathoth, Beth-anath) and a personal name (Shamgar ben Anath) reveal that she was once worshiped in the land of Israel, while the divine name Anatyahu in an Aramaic papyrus from Elephantine (an island in the upper Nile) suggests the arrival of her cult among Jews of the fifth century B.C.

anathema (ah-nah'thay-mah; Gk., "something placed or set up"), a term referring both to a votive offering to God in a temple (Luke 21:5) and then most often in the NT to its opposite, something accursed. Paul's imprecation, "Let him be accursed (Gk. *anathema*) who preaches anything contrary to the gospel" (Gal. 1:9), served as a model for church councils pronouncing anathemas against heretics. ***See also*** Curse and Blessing.

Anathoth (an'uh-thohth), a levitical town in the tribal territory of Benjamin (Josh. 21:18; 1 Chron. 6:60). Located less than three miles northeast of Jerusalem along a secondary road connecting the latter with Bethel, Anathoth was the hometown of Jeremiah (Jer. 1:1; cf. 11:21–23; 29:27; 32:7–9). Two of David's warriors, Abiezer (2 Sam. 23:27; 1 Chron. 11:28; 27:12) and Jehu (1 Chron. 12:3), were also from the town; and David's high priest, Abiathar, was banished there by Solomon (1 Kings 2:26). Men of Anathoth were among those who returned from the Babylonian exile (Ezra 2:23; Neh. 7:27), at which time the town was resettled (Neh. 11:32). The town's ancient name is preserved in the modern village of Anata; the actual Iron Age ruins of the site are located ca. a half mile to the southwest, at Ras el Kharuba. ***See also*** Benjamin; Jeremiah, The Book of; Priests.

D.A.D.

ancestor (Heb. *'ab*, "father"), the one from whom a person or group is descended, either literally or figuratively. The ancient Israelites felt a close sense of kinship with their ancestors and often thought of their families as including not only living kin but also earlier generations all the way back to the founders of the line. Before the rise of the monarchy (ca. 1020 B.C.), the members of Israel's various social groups expressed their unity by claiming descent from a common ancestor. These links to the ancestors were often expressed in a segmented or branched genealogy (e.g., Num. 26).

The OT also uses the term "ancestor" more generally to refer to earlier generations of Israelites (Exod. 3:15; 20:5; Num. 20:15; 1 Kings 14:15; Jer. 7:22; 16:11). Especially important were the founders of the nation: Abraham and Sarah; Isaac and Rebekah; Jacob, Leah, and Rachel. Particularly in Deuteronomy, God's faithfulness to Israel and the gift of the land were often thought to be motivated by the divine promise that had originally been made to the ancestors (Deut. 1:8; 6:10; 9:5; 29:13; 30:20; cf. Gen. 12:7; 17:1–8; 28:13–15). On the other hand, the sins of the ancestors were sometimes thought to bring God's wrath on their children (Exod. 20:5; 34:7; Num. 14:18). Israel's historians imply that the destruction of Samaria and Jerusalem was due to a history of accumulating ancestral sin that finally had to be punished (2 Kings 17:7–18; Ezek. 20). Such understandings were explicitly rejected by Jeremiah and Ezekiel, who stressed that individuals are punished for their own sin, not the sins of their ancestors (Jer. 31:29–30; Ezek. 18). ***See also*** Child, Children; Family, The; Genealogy.

R.R.W.

Ancient of Days, an expression used three times (Dan. 7:9, 13, 22) to designate the divine judge in Daniel's eschatological vision of the four beasts. The expression in Aramaic literally means "advanced in days" but is not intended to suggest that God ages. Instead, it conveys the qualities of wisdom and venerability which one who is "advanced in days" would possess. A parallel expression in the Ugaritic epic of Aqhat (3.6.48) describes the chief Canaanite god, El, as "the king, father of years." ***See also*** Apocalyptic Literature; Daniel, The Book of.

Andrew, one of the twelve apostles, identified as the brother of Simon Peter (Matt. 4:18; Mark 1:16; John 1:40) and son of Jona (Matt. 16:17) or John (John 1:42). Originally from Bethsaida (John 1:44), he was living in Capernaum at the time of his "call" (Mark 1:21, 29). According to Matthew and Mark, Andrew and Peter were fishing when called to follow Jesus. In John's account, Andrew, originally a disciple of John the Baptist, followed Jesus after hearing John say, "Behold, the Lamb of God!" Andrew then found his brother, Simon, and brought him to Jesus saying, "We have found the Messiah" (John 1:35–41). Andrew is among the first persons named in the apostolic lists (Matt. 10:2–4; Mark 3:16–19; Luke 6:14–16; Acts 1:13), perhaps an indication of his early selection to Jesus' inner circle of disciples. Elsewhere, Andrew appears only in Mark 13:3 and John 6:8–9; 12: 20–22. Extracanonical traditions credit him with preaching in Scythia and suffering martyrdom (crucifixion) in Achaia. ***See also*** Apostle; Disciple; John the Baptist; Peter; Twelve, The.

P.L.S.

angel (Gk. *angelos*, "messenger"), a spiritual being, subordinate to God, who serves at God's command and pleasure to deliver his messages, help his people, and punish his enemies. In the OT, angels appear in the stories of the patriarchs (e.g., Gen. 16:7–14; 19:1–22; 22:11, 15–18; 28: 12; 31:11–13; 32:1–2) and elsewhere (e.g., Exod. 3:2; 23:20–23; 33:2; Judg. 13:3–5; 1 Kings 19: 5–7; 2 Kings 19:35; Isa. 37:36; Pss. 34:7; 35:5–6; 91:11). There is some ambiguity, however, about what form these messengers take, exactly what type of beings they are, and just what their relation to God is, especially in the earlier materials. Since God frequently confronts humans directly in the OT texts, the appearance of angels is somewhat sporadic.

As religious thinking developed, and as God came to be understood as increasingly transcendent, the perceptions about angels also began to change. Ideas developed about good and bad angels, a hierarchy of angels before God, and specific duties assigned to each angel or group of angels. Many of these ideas can be found in the apocryphal and pseudepigraphical writings (e.g., Tobit, 2 Esdras, *1 Enoch*, and *The Testaments of the Twelve Patriarchs*). By the NT period, angels were understood as suprahuman or spiritual beings who were allied with God in opposition to Satan and his "angels," the demons.

Angels had many functions. They praised God (Ps. 103:20), served as his messengers to the world (Luke 1:11–20, 26–38; 2:9–14), watched over God's people (Ps. 91:11–12), and were sometimes instruments of God's judgment (Matt. 13:49–50). ***See also*** Apocalyptic Literature; Cherub; Demon; Devil; God; Seraphim.

J.M.E.

angel of the Lord (or angel of Yahweh), a figure appearing frequently in the OT (Gen. 16: 7–13; 22:11; Exod. 3:2; Num. 22:22; Judg. 13:3; Zech. 1:11; 3:1, to cite only a few references) and also in the NT (Luke 2:9–15). References to this figure usually occur when something dramatic and meaningful is about to happen, generally with serious consequences, either good or ill, for God's people. The angel of the Lord seems to have been understood as distinct from other angels and, in the earlier OT literature, appears to be almost another designation for God. In most cases, however, the angel of the Lord served primarily as a messenger from God to the people to prepare the way for God's appearance and activity. In some passages, the term probably only designates "an" angel of God (e.g., 1 Kings 19:4–8). ***See also*** Angel.

J.M.E.

anger. ***See*** Wrath.

animals. The OT describes vividly the animals that were known to the ancient Hebrews and thereby provides a comprehensive overview of the former animal life in Palestine. Anecdotes depict how animals ranging from the camel to the flea affected the life of the Hebrews, whether as domestic animals providing food, wool, or transport, as game animals, or preying carnivores, or as parasites or as a disease vector. Apart from this secular importance, animals figured prominently in Hebrew religious ritual as sacrifices. In addition, the Bible uses animals to illustrate certain abstract concepts; for instance, the lion symbolizes danger, the horse signifies warfare, and the ass signifies peace.

While we commonly use the word "animals" to mean all living creatures that are not plants, the OT seems to use it usually in the sense of "mammals," since "animals" are distinguished from birds, reptiles, and fish. For instance, in Gen. 1:24–25 God creates the animals on the sixth day of his work, the fishes and birds having been called into life the day before (Gen. 1: 20–23).

Clean and Unclean: A distinction is sometimes made between wild and domestic animals (see Gen. 3:14), but there is a crucial separation into ritually clean (and therefore also edible) and unclean animals, as specified in Lev. 11:1–47 and Deut. 14:3–21a. Gen. 7:2–3 implies the difference in status between these two categories: Noah is ordered to take into the ark seven pairs each of the animals that are chosen for sacrifice and eating, while of all the others a single pair suffices (but see Gen. 6:19–20). Animals allowed as food in the OT are all those that both chew the cud (or ruminate) and have cloven hooves (Lev. 11:2–3; Deut. 14:6). They are enumerated in Deut. 14:4–5 and include cattle, sheep, goats, deer, gazelles, roedeer, wild goats, ibex, antelope, and mountain sheep. All these species were once extant in or around Palestine

Heron and snake; detail from a floor mosaic in the Church of the Multiplication of Loaves, Tabgah, fifth–sixth century A.D.

and in zoological terms are all members of the suborder Ruminantia of the order Artiodactyla. In the NT, however, such provisions for identifying "clean" and "unclean" animals were understood to have been set aside with the coming of Jesus (Mark 7:19; see also Acts 10:10–16).

Specifically mentioned as unclean in Lev. 11:4–7 are the camel, the coney ("rock badger"), the hare, and the pig ("swine"). The first three (as it was thought) all ruminate but do not have cloven hooves; the opposite applies to the swine. Of all aquatic and marine animals only those that have scales and fins are declared clean (Lev. 11:9–10). Unclean birds are listed in Lev. 11:13–19. Also forbidden to the Hebrews to be eaten were all flying insects (with the exception of locusts and the like; see Matt. 3:4), animals that walk on paws (i.e., carnivores), and the mole, the rat, the lizard, the gecko, the mouse, the snail, and the chameleon (Lev. 11:29–30). Not only was it forbidden to eat unclean animals, one was not supposed to even touch them (Lev. 11:8). Leviticus issues regulations about every creature or item that has touched a dead body, for these were also considered unclean (Lev. 11:31–40). Even clean animals that died a natural death were taboo (Deut. 14:21).

In Israelite Religious Ritual: As mentioned above, animals also played a fundamental role in Israelite ritual sacrifices, and detailed instructions about the procedures to be followed and the types of animals to be offered were given (Deut. 16:1–4; 17:1; Lev. 1:1–7:38). In general it is the animals "from the herd or from the flock" that are asked for (Lev. 1:2)—cattle, goats, and sheep. To the Israelites as herdsmen whose wealth was measured in numbers of such animals, these were especially precious. All firstborn male animals were to be sacrificed (Deut. 15:19) in an annual ceremonial feast unless something was wrong with them (Deut.15:21). However, just as the NT understood the coming of Jesus to have abolished the categories of "clean" and "unclean" animals, so the NT also viewed Christ's death on the cross as a sacrifice that brought to an end all need for further sacrifices (e.g., Heb. 7:27; 9:12; 10:10).

The equation of the OT references to animals with the animal species we recognize today has always presented a formidable problem, and as a consequence there is great variation in the different translations. For example, one term (Heb. *beth ya'anah*) is translated "ostrich," "owl," and "eagle owl" in the various versions of the Bible. There are several reasons for these difficulties. First, the Hebrews did not necessarily distinguish between similar species and sometimes they lumped two or more together under one term. One word (*nesher*), for instance, seems to identify both the eagle and the vulture. Second, the early European interpreters of the Bible had little knowledge of zoology and much less of the wildlife of Palestine. As they were not familiar with gazelles, they translated the Hebrew for gazelle (*tsebi*) as "roedeer," which was better known to Europeans. Matters were further complicated by the fact that many animal species that were common in Palestine when the Bible was written have since become extinct in that location, for instance, the lion, the ostrich, the fallow deer, the onager, and some antelope species. As a consequence, there are still several animal terms that cannot be translated with certainty. ***See also*** Birds. I.U.K.

anise. ***See*** Dill.

Anna (an'uh), a Jewish prophetess who, together with the prophet Simeon, witnessed the dedication of the infant Jesus in the Temple and spoke of him and the expected redemption of Israel (Luke 2:22–38). ***See also*** Simeon.

Annas (an'uhs) or Ananus, son of Seth, installed as high priest by Quirinius in A.D. 6, after the latter deposed Joazar. Annas held the post until A.D. 15, when he was deposed by Valerius Gratus. Annas's family was wealthy and influential, and five of his sons, as well as his son-in-law Joseph Caiaphas, attained the office of high priest. References in Luke 3:2 and Acts 4:6, where he is anachronistically called "high priest" (in the former passage a joint high-priesthood with Caiaphas is suggested), present a problem not soluble with present evidence. ***See also*** Caiaphas; Priests; Quirinius, P. Sulpicius.

annunciation, the, the announcement to Mary by the angel Gabriel that she would bear a son who would be "holy, the Son of God," found only in Luke's account of the birth of Jesus (Luke 1:26–38). In the development of the Christian calendar, this event came to have significant status, and March 25 was set aside to commemorate the annunciation. The medieval church developed the prayer "Ave Maria" partly from this Lucan passage. There have been numerous artistic depictions of the annunciation. ***See also*** Gabriel; Jesus Christ; Mary, The Virgin; Virgin Birth.

anoint, to cover the body or an object with oil or ointment. In the ancient Near East, it was a sign of luxury or festivity to anoint oneself with aromatic oils, usually after bathing. For this reason, mourners abstained from anointing (Isa. 61:3). Anointing was a means of investing someone with power, such as the anointment of King Solomon upon his ascent to the throne (1 Kings 1:39), perhaps to signify divine sanctification and approval. It could also signify the consecration of someone or something for a holy purpose. Jacob anointed a pillar at Bethel, calling the place a house of God (Gen. 28:18). Aaron was anointed for the priesthood (Exod. 29:7), and, hence, the high priest is often called the "anointed priest" (Lev. 4:3–15). In Second Temple times (ca. 538 B.C.–A.D. 70), however, the priests were no longer anointed. The tabernacle and its furnishings were likewise anointed (Exod. 40:9–15). 1 Sam. 24:6 refers to the king as "the Lord's anointed," which eventually became the Hebrew term *mashiah*, "Messiah," and Greek *christos*, "Christ," signifying the king who would rule in the end of days. Peter testifies "how God anointed Jesus of Nazareth with the Holy Spirit and with power" (Acts 10:38). ***See also*** Priests. L.H.S.

ant, a small insect. The ant appears in the OT as a homiletic model of wisdom and industry (Prov. 6:6; 30:25).

antelope, a ruminant, deerlike mammal. Antelope are mentioned in Deut. 14:5, and in Isa. 51:20 as being caught with nets. Today the only antelopes in Palestine are gazelles, but the ancient Hebrews also knew the Arabian oryx (*Oryx leucoryx*), a large white antelope with black markings on legs and face and very long, nearly straight horns, living in the Arabian desert and Jordan.

anthropomorphism, the description of God in terms that are literally appropriate for human beings. References to God's hands or ears, or to his evening walk in a garden (Gen. 3:8), or to his being moved by passion, irritation, or regret are typical examples. Traditional religion has tended to regard most such expressions as figurative, inexact, or improper, because they provide in inadequate "human" form expressions of a divine reality that is itself far removed from these inadequacies.

Within the Bible anthropomorphic expressions appear to be more concentrated in earlier sources than in later, in the OT rather than in the NT, and in narrative or prophetic rather than in priestly or wisdom materials. When God appears to Abraham, he seems to be one of three "men" (Gen. 18–19). He speaks with people in articulate human speech. He smells sacrifice. He regrets what he has done. On the other hand, many passages emphasize the great difference between God and humans, his consistency and lack of change (1 Sam. 15:29, interestingly a passage where God has in fact just changed his mind, rejecting Saul whom he himself had chosen).

Important elements of biblical thought seek to deal with these problems. The "image of God" in humans may establish a proper relation between God and humans while avoiding the suggestion that God is a larger man. Speech through intermediaries like prophets reduces the difficulties presented by direct speech by God. In the NT the centrality of Jesus leaves the "Father" more transcendent and yet makes God "appear" in human form.

Later exegesis relates these ideas to the Greco-Roman philosophical tradition, which had also sought to reconcile anthropomorphic depictions with the universal and eternally consistent being of deity. J.B.

Antichrist, the, the final opponent of Christ and thus of God. This designation is found only in the Letters of John. The author supposes that his audience has heard the term before (1 John 2:18), and he suggests that it now refers to individuals ("antichrists") whose religious influence is already a danger to the church (1 John 2:18–29; 4:1–6; 2 John 1:7–11). It is unclear whether such leaders, whose errors are both Christological and moral, are to be identified with Gnostics or with some other group.

Earlier, Jewish thinkers, amidst persecution by the Greeks (second century B.C.), believed that the blasphemous "little horn" (Antiochus IV) would be vanquished by the sudden rule of "the saints of the Most High" (Dan. 7). Soon thereafter it was believed that a coming Messiah would terminate persecution, whether it was inflicted by Greece or Rome. The hostile empire was often given the name Belial/Beliar (Heb., "worthless one").

Early Christianity continued the practice of depicting the enemy as an individual or beast who would be defeated at the Messiah's (Christ's) return. The enemy is variously referred to as "the lawless one" (2 Thess. 2:8), Belial (2 Cor. 6:15), and Gog and Magog (Rev. 20:8). A final attack upon the church is sometimes identified with the reappearance of the emperor Nero.

This may be the background for the expected "antichrist," which the author of 1 John redefines in religious terms. The church has continued to use this designation for its enemies in every age, both within and outside of its membership. ***See also*** Apocalyptic Literature; Belial; John, The Letters of; Man of Lawlessness.

L.R.B.

Anti-Lebanon, the name sometimes given to the range of mountains running north-south and located east of the Litani Valley in Lebanon, between that valley and the eastern desert. It is parallel to (hence "anti-") the Lebanon range standing west of the valley, between the valley and the Mediterranean Sea. The height of the Anti-Lebanon range is anchored on the south by Mount Hermon (elevation 9,332 feet above sea level) and drops as the ridge runs northward. Its crevices hold snow well into May on northward slopes.

Antioch (an'tee-ahk) (Syrian), a city (modern Antakya in Turkey) founded by Seleucus Nicator in 300 B.C. and conquered by Rome in 64 B.C. Located on the Orontes River in the northwestern corner of the Roman province of Syria, it was the province's capital, the third largest city of the empire, a center of Greek culture, and a commercial hub. Jews inhabited Antioch from its foundation and enjoyed the right to observe their own customs. The various synagogues of the city sent representatives to a council of elders presided over by a "ruler." Large numbers of Antiochene Gentiles were attracted to Jewish worship. Nicolaus of Antioch, one of the seven Hellenist leaders in Jerusalem (Acts 6:5), was among those Gentiles who became Jewish proselytes. The first Jewish war (A.D. 66–73) occasioned anti-Jewish riots in Antioch, but on the whole Judaism enjoyed a peaceful life at Antioch and thus provided early Christians a stable matrix. Public order, a prosperous urban culture, a Judaism used to contacts with Gentiles, an intellectual and religious milieu open to many currents, interest in mystery cults, fine roads and lines of communication—all these factors favored Antioch as an energetic center for Christian missionary outreach.

Christianity at Antioch: Christianity was brought to Antioch ca. A.D. 40 by Hellenists who fled from Jerusalem after the martyrdom of Stephen (Acts 11:19–20). Thus began the first Christian generation at Antioch (A.D. 40–70). At Antioch Hellenists from Cyprus and Cyrene made the momentous decision to begin, as a matter of policy, to convert Gentiles without circumcision. This striking difference from Jewish proselytism set these believers apart, and so it was at Antioch that they received a new name, "Christians" (Acts 11:26). The Jerusalem church sought to control this new development by sending Barnabas, a fellow Cypriote, to guide the Antiochene community. To aid him in teaching this "large company" of believers, Barnabas brought Saul (Paul) from Tarsus to Antioch, where "for a whole year they met with the church" (Acts 11:22–26). Along with Symeon Niger, Lucius of Cyrene, and Manaen (a childhood companion of Herod Antipas), they formed a leadership group of "prophets and teachers" (Acts 13:1). This group sent Barnabas and Saul on their first missionary journey (Acts 13:2–14:28).

Around A.D. 49, objections to Antioch's circumcision-free mission were raised by some Jerusalemite Christians. Paul, Barnabas, and Titus went to Jerusalem for a meeting with Peter, James, John, and other leaders. This "Council of Jerusalem" decided that Gentiles did not have to be circumcised (Acts 15:1–19; Gal. 2: 1–10). Some time after this meeting, Peter visited Antioch. At first he practiced table fellowship with Gentile Christians, but then withdrew under pressure from members of the James party, recently arrived from Jerusalem. Paul, fearing that Gentile converts would think that circumcision was necessary to be fully Christian, publicly rebuked Peter for hypocrisy (Gal. 2:11–21). Since Paul soon left Antioch without Barnabas (who sided with Peter), and since Paul never mentions Antioch again in his letters, returning there only briefly, it may be that Paul lost the argument. Luke smooths over this painful incident by omitting all reference to Paul's clash with Peter. He assigns Paul's break with Barnabas to a squabble over Barnabas' cousin, John Mark (Acts 15:36–40). After Paul's departure, the tension within the Antiochene church may have been relieved by

Plan of ancient Antioch that highlights the city in the early Christian period.

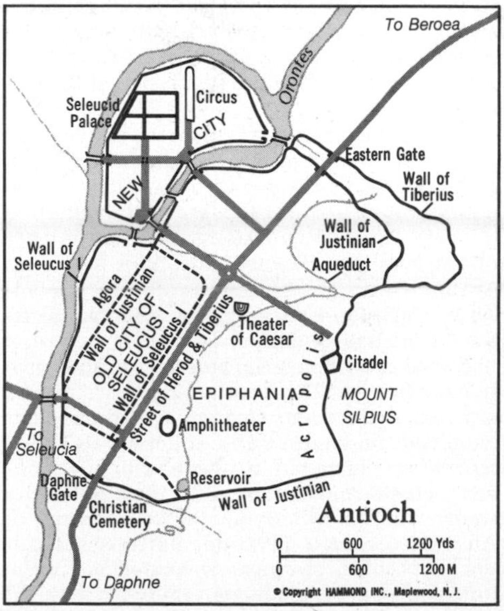

the compromise enshrined in the "Apostolic Letter" of Acts 15:23–29. The circumcision-free mission was confirmed, but the Gentiles had to observe certain "kosher laws" mentioned in Leviticus 17–18, laws considered incumbent on Gentiles living in the Holy Land. Such observance would make possible common life with Jewish Christians. Amid the tensions between the Hellenist left and the Jamesian right, Peter probably represented a centrist position around which various groups could rally; but the James party had the upper hand.

Second Christian Generation at Antioch: There is practically no source of information for the second Christian generation at Antioch (A.D. 70–100), with the possible exception of Matthew's Gospel. If, as many think, Matthew does come from Antioch, we may gather that the Antiochene church continued to feel strains between the Jamesian right and the Hellenist left. However, the Jewish war, the martyrdom of James, the destruction of Jerusalem, and the eventual break with the local synagogue(s) had weakened the conservative Jewish element in the Antiochene church. Meanwhile, the success of the Gentile mission both pointed the way to the church's future and created new problems for the Christian reformation of pagans. It was Matthew's task to reinterpret and synthesize the competing traditions at Antioch to provide a smooth transition from a Jewish past to a Gentile future. Matthew's Gospel takes the form of a "foundation story," to give a pastoral answer to the crisis of identity the Antiochene church faced in the second generation as it strove to define itself over against both Judaism and paganism. Jewish roots, fulfillment of prophecy, and large blocks of Jewish moral teaching serve to anchor an increasingly Gentile church in the sacred past. But the norm of morality, the center of faith, is now Jesus Christ, who validates a universal, circumcision-free mission at the end of the Gospel (Matt. 28:16–20). This balancing act allows Matthew to preserve both "new and old" (Matt. 13:52). Hence he extols Peter, Antioch's centrist figure, as the "chief rabbi" of the church (Matt. 16:18–19). Yet, while admitting the need for Christian leaders, Matthew is wary of the trappings of power and titles (Matt. 23: 1–12).

Third Christian Generation at Antioch: In the third Christian generation (after A.D. 100), the new pressures of imperial persecution and gnosticising tendencies overrode Matthew's dislike of titles. The need for clearer church structures to defend church discipline and teaching called forth the triple hierarchy of one bishop, a council of elders, and deacons. The first testimony we have of this development is from Ignatius of Antioch (d. ca. A.D. 117). Ignatius inherited Antioch's problem of opposing tendencies in the form of a weak Judaizing movement on the right and a more dangerous Docetism on the left. Like Matthew, Ignatius sought unity through balance. He synthesized strains of Matthean, Pauline, and Johannine traditions to strengthen the emerging "catholic church"—a phrase first used by Ignatius. Matthew's Gospel and the triple hierarchy were Antioch's twin gifts to this catholic church. ***See also*** Barnabas; James; Matthew, The Gospel According to; Paul; Peter.

Bibliography

Brown, R., and J. Meier. *Antioch and Rome.* New York: Paulist Press, 1983.

Downey, G. *A History of Antioch in Syria from Seleucus to the Arab Conquest.* Princeton, NJ: Princeton University Press, 1961.

Meeks, W., and R. Wilken. *Jews and Christians in Antioch.* Missoula, MT: Scholars Press, 1978.

J.P.M.

Antiochus (an-tī'uh-kuhs), a name borne by thirteen kings or pretenders of the Seleucid dynasty (Hellenistic inheritors of Syria, southern Asia Minor, and other portions of the empire of Alexander the Great). The land of Israel fell under Seleucid rule in 198 B.C., when Antiochus III (the Great) defeated the Ptolemies of Egypt. Antiochus IV (Epiphanes) ruled from 175 until 164 B.C. (see 1 Macc. 1:10). The Maccabean revolt was the response of pious and nationalistic Jews to Antiochus Epiphanes' efforts to hellenize them and to suppress Judaism. ***See also*** Alexander; Maccabees; Ptolemy; Seleucids, The.

Antipas (an'ti-puhs). **1** See Antipater. **2** Herod Antipas, tetrarch of Galilee and Perea (4 B.C.–A.D. 39) after the death of his father, Herod the Great. See also Herod. **3** Christian martyr from Pergamum (Rev. 2:13).

Antipater (an-tip'uh-tuhr), also known as Antipas, an Idumean with strong connections to Rome who, as procurator of Judea (55–43 B.C.), governed most of Palestine; father of Phasaelus and Herod the Great. ***See also*** Herod; Idumaea; Phasaelus.

Antipatris (an-tip'uh-tris), a town on the coast-

View of Antipatris; OT Aphek during the time of the Philistines, rebuilt by Herod the Great in 9 B.C.

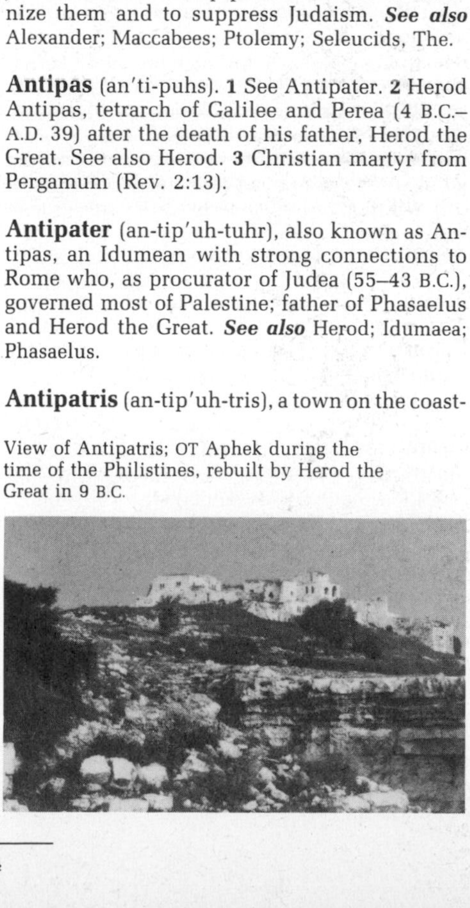

al plain along the principal international highway of Palestine, the Via Maris, guarding the pass between the mountains to the east and the Yarkon River to the west. The site has been identified with OT Aphek (Josh. 12:18; 1 Sam 4:1; 29: 1), where the Philistines were encamped when they captured the Ark of the Covenant, and with Pegae (Gk., "springs") of the Hellenistic period. The town was rebuilt by Herod in 9 B.C. midway between his new capital, Caesarea, and the old Jewish capital, Jerusalem, and named after Herod's father, Antipater. Here Paul stayed overnight during his trip from Jerusalem to Caesarea to stand trial before Felix (Acts 23:31).

M.K.M.

Antonia (an-toh'nee-uh), **Tower of,** a Hasmonean fortress (known as Baris) on the rocky scarp at the northwest end of the Temple in Jerusalem, luxuriously rebuilt in the late first century B.C. by Herod the Great and named for his friend Mark Antony. In it were kept the high priest's vestments between festivals, under the seal of Herod and later of the Roman procurators. It was taken and destroyed by Titus in the revolt of the Jews against Rome in A.D. 70. Once thought to be the site of Jesus' trial (John 19:13), a pavement below the present-day convent of Notre Dame de Sion has now been shown to date from Hadrian's Aelia Capitolina (the name he gave to Jersualem when he rebuilt it) of the second century A.D. The Antonia is, however, referred to in Acts 21:34–37; 22:24; and 23:10, 16, 32 (RSV: "barracks") as the scene of Paul's arrest and consequent imprisonment after a riot provoked by Asian Jews who accused him of bringing a Gentile into the Temple (Acts 21:27–36). ***See also*** Baris; Herod; Temple, The. C.H.M.

Antonius Felix. ***See*** Felix, Antonius.

ape, a semierect primate resembling a monkey. The apes mentioned in 1 Kings 10:22 and 2 Chron. 9:21 are probably monkeys, possibly *Papio hamadryas*, a baboon once common in Egypt and Somalia.

Apharsachites (ah-far'sah-kīts), a word used by the KJV to translate a Persian loan word (a word from one language taken into another) found in the Aramaic text of Ezra (5:6; 6:6) that denotes some type of official. These officials are among those who complain to Darius about the Jews who rebuilt the Temple in Jerusalem. The RSV and NIV translate the word as "governor," indicating uncertainty about the precise meaning of the Persian *frasaka*, although the meaning "investigator" has been proposed.

Aphek (ay'fek; Heb., "fortress"?; also Aphik, Judg. 1:31). **1** A city-state on the coastal plain captured by Joshua (Josh. 12:18). Its strategic value was used by the Philistines against hill-based Israelites both at Ebenezer (1 Sam. 4:1) and at Jezreel (1 Sam. 29:1). It is modern Ras el'Ain some ten miles east of the Mediterranean coast and west and slightly north of Shiloh. The Herodian-Roman city Antipatris was built there as well. **2** A border town with the Amorites (Josh. 13:4), probably modern Afqa about fifteen miles east of ancient Byblos in Lebanon. **3** A town of the tribe of Asher (Josh. 19:30), possibly modern Tell Kerdanah three miles from Haifa and about six miles southeast of Acco. **4** A site some three miles from the eastern shore of the Sea of Galilee in the Transjordan, modern Fiq. It marked the location of Ahab's victories against Syria's Ben-hadad (1 Kings 20:26–30) and Joash's defeat of Syria under Elisha's instruction (2 Kings 13:14–25). ***See also*** Antipatris.

R.S.B.

Apocalypse. ***See*** Revelation to John, The.

apocalyptic literature, literature taking its name from the Revelation (Gk. *apokalypsis*) to John in the NT. The genre is represented in the Hebrew Bible by the book of Daniel, but the main corpus lies outside the Bible in such books as *1* and *2 Enoch*, *4 Ezra*, *2* and *3 Baruch*, *Jubilees*, and the *Apocalypse of Abraham*. These writings have been preserved in various translations—Ethiopic, Latin, Syriac, Greek, Slavonic. Fragments of *1 Enoch* have been discovered in Aramaic among the Dead Sea Scrolls and are the oldest extant apocalyptic literature (third century B.C.). The genre generally declined in Judaism after the first century A.D. but flourished in Christianity down to the Middle Ages.

The apocalyptic books report mysterious revelations that are mediated by angels and disclose a supernatural world. They are characterized by a focus on eschatology, which often entails cosmic transformation and always involves the judgment of the dead. The apocalypses are usually pseudonymous—the revelations are attributed to ancient heroes such as Enoch or Abraham, not to the real authors. A few early Christian apocalypses, notably the book of Revelation and *The Shepherd of Hermas*, are exceptions to this rule.

In general, apocalypses are of two types. The more familiar "historical" apocalypses, exemplified by Daniel and Revelation, are concerned with great historical crises. History is often divided into a set number of periods, and the course of history is "prophesied" from the time of the supposed author down to the actual time of composition. The period before the end is marked by catastrophic upheavals. Salvation may include the restoration of the land of Israel, but the emphasis is on a transition to a radically different world order. In the second type of apocalypse, exemplified in the *Enoch* books and the *Apocalypse of Abraham*, the visionary ascends through the heavens. Seven is the classical number of heavens but three and five are also attested. These journeys, guided by an angel, usually include a vision of the abodes of the dead.

Many themes of the "historical" apocalypses are anticipated in the Prophets, notably in Isaiah 24–27. The genre is attested independently in Persian sources, but the date of the Persian material is notoriously uncertain. The Jewish apocalypses were a new development drawing on various sources—the Hebrew scriptures, ancient myths, Persian and Hellenistic materials.

Some apocalypses were written in times of distress: Daniel in the persecution of 168 B.C., *4 Ezra* and *2 Baruch* in the aftermath of the destruction of Jerusalem. Others responded to less specific problems, but all reflect some kind of dissatisfaction with the present world and seek salvation either in a new world to come or in another world beyond. Apocalyptic ideas played a crucial role in the formation of early Christian beliefs in the resurrection and Second Coming of Christ.

Closely related material can be found in the Dead Sea Scrolls, *The Sibylline Oracles*, and *The Testaments of the Twelve Patriarchs*. The genre was also adapted by the Gnostics, who tended, however, to place greater stress on salvation in the present. ***See also*** Daniel; Enoch; Eschatology; Revelation to John, The; Scrolls, The Dead Sea. J.J.C.

Apocrypha (uh-pahk'rif-uh), **Old Testament,** a group of books or parts of books not part of the Jewish canon of the Hebrew Scriptures but found in early Christian versions of the OT. "Apocrypha" is from the Greek for "concealed" or "hidden" (cf. 2 Esd. 12:37–38; 14:45–46), although in current Christian usage it has the sense of "set aside" or "withdrawn" from full canonical status as Scripture. The Christian scholar Jerome (ca. 331–420) labeled most of these books as apocryphal and did not include them in his translation of the Bible, the Vulgate (Vg). During the Reformation, Protestants gathered the books of that kind then current in Western Bibles into a separate section following the OT under the title "Apocrypha." Works so treated usually include:

- 1 Esdras
- 2 Esdras (4 Ezra)
- Tobit
- Judith
- The Rest of the Book of Esther
- The Wisdom of Solomon
- Ecclesiasticus (Sirach)
- Baruch
- A Letter of Jeremiah
- The Additions to the Book of Daniel:
    - The Song of the Three Children (with the Prayer of Azariah)
    - Susanna
    - Bel and the Dragon
- The Prayer of Manasseh
- 1 Maccabees
- 2 Maccabees

While there is no universal agreement on which books properly belong to the Apocryphal OT, most scholars would agree that the list just given is to be considered standard. Similarly, these fifteen books also go by various titles. Occasionally the Rest of the Book of Esther is identified as Additions to the Book of Esther; or Bel and the Dragon, Susanna, and the Song of the Three Children (with or without the Prayer of Azariah) will be identified as the Rest of (or Additions to) the Book of Daniel; or Ecclesiasticus, because it was written by Jesus ben Sirach, will be called the Wisdom of Sirach, or even the Wisdom of Jesus the Son of Sirach. For the most part, the titles of the OT apocryphal books will be referred to in this Dictionary as they are given in the list above, but occasionally another form of their name may be used.

In English-speaking countries, Protestant practice has been to omit the Apocrypha from editions of the Bible. Catholics consider most of these books authoritative and use the term "deuterocanonical," meaning books recognized as canonical at a later date, to distinguish them from the "protocanonical" books found in the Jewish canon of Scripture. In Catholic usage, the term "Apocrypha" is applied to the Pseudepigrapha, a group of Jewish writings other than those included in the OT Apocrypha, which have been preserved and used by various groups of Christians but, with some exceptions (Ethiopia, for example), not included in the Bible.

The Jewish Background of the Apocrypha: The books of the Apocrypha are largely of Jewish origin, produced for the most part during the period preceding the destruction of the Temple by the Romans in A.D. 70. With the exception of 2 Esdras, they are interspersed among the other books of the OT in early Christian copies of the Septuagint (LXX), the Greek version of the Hebrew Scriptures derived from Alexandrian Judaism and adopted by early Christians as their first Bible. While the *source* of these books is the literature that circulated in the Hellenistic synagogue, their *status* among Jews in Alexandria or elsewhere is not so certain.

In Palestine, the rabbis after A.D. 70 recognized a Palestinian canon of twenty-four books (according to their system of enumeration) divided into Law (Torah), Prophets, and Writings and reflecting the principle that revelation begins with Moses and ends with Ezra. The Apocrypha originated some time after Ezra, some of them having been composed in Greek, and thus did not have a claim to be included in this definition of Scripture. Rabbinic debate after A.D. 70 is over Ezekiel, Proverbs, the Song of Solomon, and Ecclesiastes, which are retained in the Palestinian canon, rather than over the inclusion or rejection of books later found among the Apocrypha. The rabbis claim that the person who brings together more than twenty-four books creates confusion (*Midr. Qoh.* 12:12) and that one who reads in the outside books will have no place in the world to come (*b. Sanh.* 100b). Ecclesiasticus was read and quoted by the rabbis for several centuries and then was dropped from use; however, whether they meant to include other books of the Apocrypha than simply Ecclesiasticus among the "outside books" is not certain.

Scholars have traditionally assumed that the Writings were a fluid collection prior to A.D. 70, that the Alexandrian Jewish community had an expanded version of this collection that included the books of the Apocrypha, and that this expanded collection of the Writings is the reason for the greater extent of the Christian LXX as compared to the Jewish Palestinian canon. The Alexandrian Jewish community, however, appears to have accepted only the Torah (in Christian terms, the Pentateuch—Genesis through Deuteronomy) as Scripture. Philo of Alexandria, a Jewish commentator (late first century B.C. to early first century A.D.) quotes almost exclusively from the Torah when citing Scripture, while the translation of that section in the LXX is done with far greater care and attention to the literal text. There is thus little evidence for the existence of an expanded Alexandrian canon that would explain the extent of the LXX in Christian circles. (The Additions to Daniel and The Rest of Esther require separate treatment. Instead of the problem of the editing of collections of books into canonical Scripture, we encounter here the internal expansion of a book through the accretion of stories, legends, and appropriate prayers and letters—a process that must have taken place within Judaism.)

The Apocrypha in Early Christianity: It would appear more likely that the extent of the Christian LXX was determined by Christians themselves. This determination could have been haphazard, as the result of the combination of a larger selection of Jewish literature in Greek, which presumably would have been preserved as individual books in scroll form, into the codex, or "book" form. The latter was pioneered by Christians because it permitted the inclusion of a number of books in one more easily managed volume. This process of editing could have taken place with minimal regard to what was considered canonical within the library of the Hellenistic synagogue. The extent of the LXX could also be the result of the conscious selection by the early church in the late first and early second centuries of a distinctively Christian canon of Scripture. In either case, Christians came to include in their OT a wider selection of books than was considered authoritative in Judaism and to arrange them more along the lines of chronology and genre than according to the tripartite division into Law, Prophets, and Writings.

Even so, copies of the LXX do not suggest a rigidly fixed Christian canon, since some manuscripts omit the Prayer of Manasseh and others include Psalm 151 and 3 and 4 Maccabees. 2 Esdras, a Jewish apocalyptic writing stemming from the end of the first century A.D. and no longer extant in Greek, appears in some manuscripts of the Old Latin (OL) version, the initial Bible of Western Christianity translated from the LXX, and thus has also come to be included among the Apocrypha.

Jerome and the Vulgate: Early Christians tended to cite from the whole of the LXX, although, as time passed, scholars and theologians in the East became aware of the extent of the Jewish canon, and some began to limit their use of the OT to the books preserved by the Jews. In Western Christianity, the books of the Apocrypha retained their status. As the result of dissatisfaction with the OL version of the Bible, however, Jerome began a new translation (fourth century A.D.). His initial intention was to translate the LXX anew, but studies of the text of that version convinced him that, in order to establish a secure text, he would need to return to the Hebrew original. Journeying to Bethlehem, he studied Hebrew with a Jewish teacher and produced a new Latin version of the OT, the Vg, based on the Hebrew text and essentially limited to the extent of the Jewish canon. He treated the apocryphal works as edifying but not to be used for the purpose of establishing doctrine. His Vg does include the additions to Esther and Daniel, clearly marked to indicate their absence from the Hebrew text, and, as the result of a request from two friends among the Western bishops, he hastily produced versions of Judith and Tobit.

The Vg became the standard Bible of the Western church, and the writings that Jerome set aside as apocryphal were added to its text from the OL version. Right up to the Reformation, however, an awareness of Jerome's position persisted in the West.

The Reformation and the Apocrypha: In the Protestant Reformation, the question of the canonical status of the Apocrypha became involved in disputes over doctrine. 2 Macc. 12:43–45 was used to support the idea of purgatory and masses for the dead, while Tob. 12:9; Ecclus. 3:30; and 2 Esd. 8:33 claim that good deeds bring merit, counter to Martin Luther's emphasis upon grace. Under the influence of Jerome, and perhaps also of Renaissance scholarship (which preferred texts in the original languages), Luther gathered the apocryphal books into one section at the end of the OT in his 1534 edition of the whole Bible and gave this section the title "Apocrypha." He indicated that these books were not of the status of Holy Scripture but could be read profitably.

The Reformed tradition came to accord an even lower status to the Apocrypha, particularly in England, where editions of the Geneva Bible began in 1599 to omit it and the Westminster Confession of Faith (1646–48) equated it with secular literature. The Church of England, on the other hand, resisted this tendency and included readings from the Apocrypha in its lectionary. In 1827, after a decade of particularly acrimonious debate, the British and Foreign Bible Society refused to support continental societies that circulated Bibles containing the Apocrypha.

As in Christian use of the codex in an earlier age, the technology and economics of publishing may have had an impact upon the Apocrypha. English language editors have sought to fill a demand for lighter and perhaps more economical Bibles by omitting it from their editions. Such a measure, however, is only possible as a result of its devaluation in status.

Catholic response to the Protestant treatment of the Apocrypha was to affirm their canonical status. On April 8, 1546, the Council of Trent declared anathema anyone who did not accept the whole of the Vg as canonical. The edition of the Vg intended includes all of the disputed works with the exception of 1 and 2 Esdras and the Prayer of Manasseh. In later Catholic editions of the Bible, these three books are sometimes printed in an appendix.

Orthodox Christianity shows a greater latitude in its treatment of the canon of the OT. Bibles approved by the Holy Synod of the Greek Orthodox Church currently include what Catholics term the deuterocanonical books plus 1 Esdras, the Prayer of Manasseh, 3 and 4 Maccabees and Psalm 151. In 1977, with the Orthodox Bible in mind, the Revised Standard Version Bible Committee expanded its translation of the Apocrypha to include the last three books in an effort to produce an ecumenical Bible.

The Importance of the Apocrypha: Along with the Pseudepigrapha, the Dead Sea Scrolls, and the writings of Josephus and Philo, the Apocrypha are of immense importance for historical research into Judaism during the period of the Second Temple (515 B.C.–A.D. 70). Their content reflects the struggle of the Jewish people to maintain faith as they encountered religious, political, and military oppression under foreign rule in Palestine and attempted to preserve their way of life in the face of the power of Hellenistic culture both at home and in the Diaspora (i.e., those lands other than Palestine where Jews lived). Strikingly absent from this body of literature is the prophetic voice, which was now associated with the previous age. The books, on the other hand, give abundant evidence of the continued importance of narrative in Jewish culture.

The Apocrypha exist as a group, however, primarily because of their role in Christian discussions of the extent of the canon of the OT. As a result of their place in the Christian OT, the Apocrypha have a potential role in the ecumenical movement as groups of Christians seek for the means of communication with one another. In including 3 and 4 Maccabees and Psalm 151 among the Apocrypha, the Revised Standard Version Bible Committee seemed to be reaching for an inclusive rather than an exclusive understanding of the canon of the OT, in which the extent of Scripture is defined as broadly as possible to permit the interests of as many groups as possible to intersect in one body of Scripture. This principle has been absent from discussions of the canon of the OT but was of importance in the final determination of the extent of the NT. ***See also*** Canon; Pseudepigrapha; Septuagint; Vulgate; listings under the individual titles of the Apocrypha.

Bibliography

Anderson, G. W. "Canonical and Non-canonical." In *The Cambridge History of the Bible.* 3 vols. Cambridge: At the University Press, 1963–70. Vol. 1. *From the Beginnings to Jerome.* Edited by P. R. Ackroyd and C. F. Davis, 1970. Pp. 113–59.

De Lange, Nicholas. *Apocrypha: Jewish Literature of the Hellenistic Age.* The Jewish Heritage Classics. New York: Viking, 1978.

Metzger, Bruce M. *An Introduction to the Apocrypha.* New York: Oxford University Press, 1957.

Nickelsburg, George W. E. *Jewish Literature Between the Bible and the Mishnah: A Historical and Literary Introduction.* Philadelphia: Fortress, 1981.

D.W.S.

Apocryphal New Testament, a vast body of literature that, generally speaking, refers to extracanonical Christian writings that claim to preserve memories of Jesus and the apostles and that frequently imitate the major genres of NT literature: gospel, acts, epistle, and apocalypse. Most of this literature was written from the second to the ninth centuries A.D. and comes to us in Greek, Latin, Syriac, Coptic, Arabic, Slavonic, and Anglo-Saxon. The recent discovery at Nag Hammadi, Egypt, of many previously unknown apocryphal documents has revitalized interest in this area, but much of the NT Apocrypha still requires the most basic scholarly attention, such as critical editions and translations.

Even though this literature in general tells us little that is reliable about Christian origins, it is indispensable for understanding the piety of Christians in late antiquity. Here we find their liturgies, prayers, dreams, and their attitudes toward martyrdom, money, and sex. Analysis of this literature also reveals much concerning the canonizing of the NT and the theological diversity of the early church.

Gospels: Apocryphal Gospels reshaped the memory of Jesus to meet contemporary needs and satisfied pious imaginations by supplying information about the life of Jesus not found in the NT—most notably, details of his birth, youth, and postresurrection revelations. Unlike the canonical Gospels few of these contain stories of Jesus' death.

Apocryphal Gospels have generated much scholarly attention, largely because of the possibility of finding in them dominical *agrapha*, or authentic sayings of Jesus not found in the Bible. Study of *The Gospel of Thomas* has proven particularly helpful for understanding the oral transmission and literary collection of Jesus' teachings. Some of the more important representatives of the genre are:

The Protoevangelium of James
The Infancy Gospel of Thomas
The Gospel of Peter
The Gospel of Nicodemus
The Gospel of the Nazoreans
The Gospel of the Ebionites
The Gospel of the Hebrews
The Gospel of the Egyptians
The Gospel of Thomas
The Gospel of Philip
The Gospel of Mary

Acts: Scholars customarily divide the apocryphal Acts into two groups: (1) those in antiquity sometimes attributed to Leucius Charinus, a collection of five books used in certain heretical circles, and (2) those outside this group. Of the two, the first group has attracted the most attention, in part because of their probable earlier dating, and in part because they stimulated considerable opposition from ecclesiastical authors. These five Acts, though interrelated, seem to have come from different locations and theological circles, some of which were Gnostic. They share an insistence on sexual asceticism, a fascination with fantastic tales (e.g., those about obedient bed bugs, talking colts, and a baptized lion), and a curiosity concerning the apostles' deaths. Though some of them indicate their authors knew the canonical Acts, the literary genre of these Acts seems more similar to contemporary Greek romances. The "Leucian Acts" are:

The Acts of John
The Acts of Peter
The Acts of Paul
The Acts of Andrew
The Acts of Thomas

Other Acts include:

The Acts of Andrew and Matthias (originally part of *The Acts of Andrew?*)
The Acts of Philip
The Acts of Thaddaeus
The Acts of Peter and Paul
The Acts of Peter and Andrew
The Martyrdom of Matthew
The Slavonic Act of Peter
The Acts of Peter and the Twelve Apostles

Epistles: Of the four apocryphal genres here discussed, the pseudonymous Epistle apparently was the least popular, even though several such Epistles appear already in the NT (e.g., the pastoral and the Petrine Epistles). The apocryphal Epistles include:

Third Corinthians
The Epistle to the Laodiceans
The Letters of Paul and Seneca
The Letters of Jesus and Abgar
The Letter of Lentulus
The Epistle of Titus

Apocalypses: All of the Christian representatives of this genre, apart from the canonical book of Revelation, are pseudonymous; that is, all of them claim to be divine revelations to a biblical hero. Their favorite themes are the means of salvation, ethics, historical destiny, and graphic depictions of heaven and hell. They are:

The Apocalypse of Peter
The Coptic Apocalypse of Peter
The Apocalypse of Paul
The First Apocalypse of James
The Second Apocalypse of James
The Apocryphon of John
The Sophia of Jesus Christ
The Letter of Peter to Philip
The Apocalypse of Mary

See also Canon; Gnosticism; Gospel of Thomas; Nag Hammadi.

Bibliography

Hennecke, E., and W. Schneemelcher, eds. *New Testament Apocrypha.* 2 vols. Philadelphia: Westminster, 1963, 1965.

James, M. R. *The Apocryphal New Testament.* Oxford: Oxford University Press, 1924.

Robinson, James M., ed. *The Nag Hammadi Library in English.* San Francisco: Harper & Row, 1977.

D.R.M.

Apollonia (ap-uh-loh'nee-uh) of Macedonia, one among many Greek cities named for the Greek god Apollo. It was a station on the main east–west Roman road from Asia to Italy, the Egnatian Way, and was visited by Paul en route from Philippi to Thessalonica (Acts 17:1).

Apollos (uh-pahl'uhs), a Jewish Christian from Alexandria who appears in the narrative of Acts (18:24–19:1) and in 1 Corinthians. According to Acts, he possessed great skills in Greek rhetoric and had already learned much about Jesus when he arrived in Ephesus and began speaking in the synagogue. His abilities soon brought him to the attention of the Christians Priscilla (Prisca) and Aquila, who gave him further instruction in the Christian faith ("he knew only the baptism of

John"; Acts 18:25). Apollos then left Ephesus to go to Corinth. According to one ancient text (Codex Bezae), he was received with enthusiasm in Corinth (Acts 18:27). While in Corinth, he became acquainted with Paul. When divisions arose in the church at Corinth, Apollos was admired by some Christians as a greater authority than Paul, perhaps because of his reputation as an orator (1 Cor. 1:11–4:6). Apollos apparently did not encourage this sentiment: after going back to Ephesus, he resisted Paul's invitation to pay another visit to Corinth (1 Cor. 16:12). Brief mention of Apollos is made in Titus 3:13. ***See also*** Aquila; Corinthians, The First Letter of Paul to the; John the Baptist; Paul; Prisca, Priscilla. A.J.M.

Apollyon (a-pahl'ee-uhn; Gk., "the Destroyer"), a possible allusion to the Greek god Apollo or to the angel of death (Rev. 9:11).

apostasy, rebellion or abandonment of faith. It refers in the OT to Israel's unfaithfulness to God (Jer. 2:19; 5:6; cf. Josh. 22:22; 2 Chron. 33:19) and in the NT to the abandonment of Christian faith (Heb. 6:6). In Acts 21:21, the Greek root of the word "apostasy" is used for Paul's alleged rejection of Moses and, in 2 Thess. 2:3, for an expected rebellion before the end.

apostle (uh-pahs'uhl), the English transliteration of a Greek word meaning "one who is sent out." An apostle is a personal messenger or envoy, commissioned to transmit the message or otherwise carry out the instructions of the commissioning agent.

In the NT Gospels, the term is commonly associated with the special inner circle of Jesus' disciples, chosen and commissioned by him to accompany him during his ministry, to receive his teachings and observe his actions, and to follow his instructions. Thus, they are uniquely qualified both to authenticate his message and to carry on his work through the ministry of the church.

Apostolic lists appear in Matt. 10:2–4; Mark 3:16–19; Luke 6:13–16; and Acts 1:13. Each of the lists contains twelve names, but not always the same twelve. The number twelve probably refers to God's elect, the twelve tribes of Israel, who settled Canaan after the Exodus. If so, then twelve is a symbolic number, signifying God's saving activity in Jesus and his followers.

The exact nature of "apostleship" in the early church is obscure. In Acts 1:21–26, the qualification for Matthias, chosen an apostle after Judas's death, is that of being an eyewitness: he was present with Jesus from the time of John the Baptist through the death and resurrection of Jesus. "Peter and the apostles," centered in Jerusalem, are the recognized leaders and guiding force of the development of the church according to the early chapters of Acts. Paul the apostle is also an eyewitness (1 Cor. 9:1), but probably only of the risen, not the earthly, Jesus (see 1 Cor. 15:8). Further proof of his apostleship was derived from the nature and role he occupied in the mission and expansion of the church among the Gentiles (Acts 9:15–16; 15:1–35; Gal. 2:1–10). Although Acts is hesitant to refer to Paul as an apostle (but see 14:14), he himself, in his Letters, insists on the title (esp. Gal. 1:1; cf. vv. 11–12). The designation of Barnabas (Acts 14:14) and Andronicus and Junias (Rom. 16:7) as apostles is more difficult to explain except in more general etymological terms. By the second century, the term no longer identifies an office of the church.

In Heb. 3:1, Jesus is the "apostle," the one sent by God. ***See also*** Barnabas; Church; Disciple; John the Baptist; Judas; Junias; Matthias; Paul; Peter; Twelve, The. P.L.S.

apothecaries. ***See*** Perfumers.

apparel. ***See*** Dress.

Apphia (af'ee-uh), a Christian woman addressed by Paul in Philemon (Philem. 2), possibly Philemon's wife. ***See also*** Archippus; Philemon.

Appian (ap'ee-uhn) **Way,** one of the main roads out of ancient Rome. One branch, the Via

Jesus at the head of a procession of the twelve apostles as depicted in a tenth-century Byzantine illuminated manuscript.

Domitiana, led through Cumae to Puteoli, which lay just west of modern Naples. Puteoli was the great port for trade with the east during the first century. The Egyptian grain fleet put in there. It declined after the emperor Trajan built a new harbor for sea-going vessels off the mouth of the Tiber (Ostia). The Forum of Appius mentioned in Acts 28:15 was a market town on the Appian Way south of Rome.

Appius (ap'ee-uhs), **Forum of** (KJV: "Market of Appius"), a town about forty miles south of Rome on the Appian Way where Paul was met by Christians from Rome as he was being led prisoner from the port of Puteoli (Acts 28:15). ***See also*** Taverns, The Three.

apple, a tree-grown fruit with wide geographic distribution. Although traditionally considered the fruit from the tree of knowledge in the Garden of Eden, the apple is never mentioned by name (Gen. 2:9, 17; Gen. 3:6). The fruit of Eden is referred to in Hebrew as *tappuaḥ*. The apple (*Pyrus malus*) may not have been originally native to the Levant although it grows commonly there now. Consequently, many specialists agree that the "apples of gold" in Prov. 25:11 were apricots (*Prunus armeniaca*), trees that provide both abundant shade and golden fruit, sweet and refreshing to the taste (Song of Sol. 2:3, 5). Also considered as the "apple" of the Scriptures are the citron, orange, and quince. ***See also*** Mandrake; Vine of Sodom. P.L.C.

apron, a minimal item of clothing, perhaps an undergarment, probably formed originally by wrapping material around the lower trunk. In the Eden story, the primeval couple fashions such garments as the first human apparel (Gen. 3:7). Elsewhere the term, sometimes rendered "girdle," denotes a sash wrapped over the tunic or outer garment and sometimes serving a decorative as well as a functional purpose.

Aqabah (ah'kah-bah), **Gulf of,** a northern arm of the Red Sea, east of the Sinai Peninsula. At its head were located Ezion-geber (1 Kings 9:26) and Elath (Deut. 2:8). Trade from the south came through the Gulf and continued north via the King's Highway. As political fortunes shifted, so did control of the Gulf (2 Kings 14:22, 16:6).

Aquila (ak'wi-luh), according to Acts 18:2–3, a Jewish Christian from Pontus in Asia Minor who, like Paul, was a tentmaker (or leatherworker) by trade. Along with his wife Prisca (in Paul's Letters) or Priscilla (in Acts), he was expelled from Rome by the edict of the emperor Claudius, probably in A.D. 49/50. Being of the same faith and occupation, Paul lodged with Aquila and Priscilla during his stay in Corinth, and they became among the most trusted of his co-workers. As owners of property and giving evidence of an ability to travel widely, Aquila and Priscilla apparently had considerable financial means. For the writer of Acts, they are models of the ideal Christian: friendly, hospitable, and generous with their wealth. According to Acts (18:18–19), Aquila and Priscilla left Corinth with Paul, accompanied him to Ephesus, apparently established a house-church there (see 1 Cor. 16:19), and later instructed Apollos when he came to Ephesus (Acts 18:24–26). If Romans 16 is an integral part of Paul's Roman Letter (which is doubted by some), they apparently returned to Rome after the revocation of Claudius' edict in A.D. 54; otherwise, they likely remained in Ephesus (Rom. 16:3–5a). ***See also*** Apollos; Claudius; Paul; Prisca, Priscilla; Romans, The Letter of Paul to the. A.J.M.

Arabah (ahr'ah-bah; Heb., "desert plain or steppe"), a term variously translated as "plain," "desert," or "wilderness" (Job 24:5; Ps. 68:7; Isa. 33:9). "The Arabah" means the Palestinian rift valley south of the Lake of Galilee, with three divisions: the Jordan valley north of the Dead Sea; the area of the Dead Sea, the "Sea of the Arabah" (2 Kings 14:25); and the area from the Dead Sea to the Red Sea, about one hundred miles (160 km.) in length. This last area is "the Arabah" in modern terminology. This third region has an average annual rainfall of only 2 inches (50 mm.) and rises gradually from 1,298 feet (366 m.) below sea level to 655 feet (200 m.) above sea level in the center before descending gradually to the Gulf of Aqabah. Underground water from the highlands on both sides makes possible a fair amount of desert scrub, though it has been shockingly overgrazed in modern times. A very important north-south route in biblical times, the Arabah contained valuable copper mines at Feinan (biblical Punon), probably the place where Moses raised the bronze serpent (Num. 21:4–10; 33:42–43), modern Khirbet an-Nahas, Khirbet al-Maqteh on the

The Arabah in modern terminology is the name given to the desert region of the Palestinian rift valley that extends from the Dead Sea to the Red Sea. It has an average annual rainfall of only two inches.

east, and to the southwest Mikhrot Timna. This last location, once called "Solomon's mines," was worked by the Egyptians and Kenites but abandoned before Solomon's time. ***See also*** Dead Sea; Jordan; Red Sea. D.B.

Arabia, a vast, largely desert peninsula between Iraq and the Persian Gulf on the east, the Indian Ocean on the south, and the Red Sea on the west. The peninsula is sixteen hundred miles (2,600 km.) long by nearly fourteen hundred miles (2,300 km.) wide. The mountainous western escarpment along the Red Sea reaches a height of 12,336 feet (3,760 m.) in the southeast in Yemen, where the general altitude exceeds 9,840 feet (3,000 m.). From the great western wall the plateau slopes gently northeast toward the Persian Gulf, although in Oman, the southeastern corner, a spur of the Iranian mountain chain attains a height of 9,774 feet (2,979 m.). The main areas of true sand desert are the vast Ruba' el-Khali (Arabic, "the Empty Quarter") in the southern part of the peninsula and the smaller Nefud in the northwest. Elsewhere it is largely stony desert, although a great semicircle of sand dunes curving around eastward joins the Nefud to the Ruba' el-Khali.

The climate is severe. Winters can be bitterly cold on the plateau, frost being common everywhere except in the low-lying coastal areas. Summers are blindingly hot and, near the coast, extremely humid. Except for rare storms, rain is confined to the mountains, occurring in winter in Oman and northwest of Mecca and in summer on the high ranges of Asir and Yemen southeast of Mecca. This alternation of winter and summer rain on the Red Sea mountains made possible the trading caravans between north and south, for in the south the wells were full in summer and autumn, and in the north during winter and spring.

As early as 6000 B.C., and perhaps even before, products seem to have been exchanged along this route by means of donkey transport, and after the taming of the camel about 1500 B.C. (or possibly as early as 2000) this trade vastly increased. The visit of the Queen of Sheba (Saba in the Yemen) was almost certainly concerned with it (1 Kings 10:1–10). The gifts of the three Wise Men (Matt. 2:1–12) must surely have come along this road: frankincense and myrrh from Yemen and the Hadhramaut in the south (Heb. *Hazarmaweth*, Gen. 10:26) and gold probably from Mahad adh-Dhahab, southeast of Medina. The gold the ships of Hiram brought to King Solomon (1 Kings 10:11) may have come from the same source via the port of Jiddah, or perhaps from East Africa, whence came certainly the more exotic "ivory, apes and peacocks" (1 Kings 10:22). This trade became of enormous importance with the development of the vast empires of the Persians, Alexander and his successors, and the Romans and Parthians; it even included commodities from India and China.

Biblical mention of Arabia is rare and often vague, and for the biblical writers in Jerusalem the name seems to have connoted all the general desert area to the east, including Sinai. Thus, Paul's sojourn in Arabia (Gal. 1:17) was probably in some small settlement east of Damascus, and the Arabians who were present at Pentecost (Acts 2:11) may have come from no further than eastern Transjordan, although perhaps from a Jewish oasis community such as the one at Medina. "Geshem the Arab" (Neh. 2:19; 4–7; 6:1) is of uncertain provenance. Some identify him with the ruler of Kedar mentioned in a fifth-century B.C. Egyptian inscription and also an Arabian inscription at Dedan (Arabic, *el-Ula*,) but others believe he was the governor of Edom under the Persians.

Refugees from Assyrian invasions in the eighth century B.C. and Babylonian in the sixth century fled to northwestern Arabia (Isa. 21:13–15, where "thickets" [Heb. *ya'ar*] may perhaps refer to oasis vegetation). Close to the end of the Babylonian Empire northwest Arabia achieved unusual importance for about ten years when Nabonidus, the last Babylonian ruler, captured Tema (modern Teima) on the Medina-Damascus route, about two hundred and fifty miles (400 km.) southeast of Aqabah, and made it his capital. ***See also*** Alexander; Damascus; Dedan; Geshem; Hiram; Kedar; Paul; Pentecost; Sheba. D.B.

Arad (air'ad), or Tel Arad, a Canaanite city and important archaeological site in the eastern Negev, located about eighteen miles east-northeast of Beer-sheba. The site consists of an upper mound or acropolis, where excavation has revealed an Iron Age (post thirteenth century B.C.) Israelite citadel, and a lower city, where extremely important Early Bronze I–II (third millennium B.C.) habitation has come to light. Fourteen seasons of excavation in the lower city have provided us with the most comprehensive view of an early Canaanite city to date. Due to the broad horizontal exposure achieved, we know that Arad was a well-planned urban center of 22 acres encompassed by substantial fortifications including semicircular towers. The residential areas consist of clusters or blocks of houses disposed within a concentric system of streets running parallel to the city wall. Intersecting streets appear to radiate toward the focal point of the city, the reservoir; it is in this vicinity where the public district was found. The excavators uncovered what appears to be a sacred precinct comprising large and small twin temples, a large ceremonial building, altars, cult basins, and courtyards. Arad appears to have flourished in this peripheral, semiarid region as a result of its commercial relations with Egypt and the Sinai, although agriculture and animal husbandry were also important factors. Its height of prosperity was the EB II period (mid-third millennium B.C.), after which it was abandoned along with most other sites in this marginal area.

Arad was likewise an important site in the Iron Age (beginning in the twelfth century B.C.), as reflected by its fortified citadel and biblical references. It is the Canaanite king of Arad who "fought against Israel, and took some of them captive" (Num. 21:1; 33:40). Rebuilt throughout the first millennium B.C., the citadel is mentioned in the list of the conquered cities of Joshua (Josh. 12:14) and of the Egyptian pharaoh Shishak. The site was a strategically important frontier fortress guarding the eastern Negev. The citadel contained storerooms, dwellings, industrial installations, and a sanctuary. Of special import are the "Arad Letters," epigraphic materials including lists of merchandise and historically important correspondence written in ink on ostraca (broken pieces of pottery). Smaller forts from the Persian, Hellenistic, and Roman periods (ca. 538 B.C.–A.D. 324) were also discovered. S.L.R.

Aram (ay'ruhm). **1** The son of Shem and grandson of Noah (Gen. 10:22–23; 1 Chron. 1:17). **2** The grandson of Nahor, Abraham's brother (Gen. 22:21). **3** A descendant of Asher (1 Chron. 7:34). In Matt. 1:3, 4, and Luke 3:33 (KJV), "Aram" represents the OT name "Ram." **4** A powerful state (or confederation of states) that rose to ascendancy during the early first millennium B.C. and vied with Israel for control over their region of the Levant. Saul was Israel's first king to clash with the Arameans (1 Sam. 14:47). David defeated Hadadezer, king of Zobah (the Aramean state whose center was north of Damascus), and gained control of the Aramean lands from Damascus to Hammath (2 Sam. 8: 5–12). Solomon apparently had to crush a revolt in "Hamath-zobah" early in his reign (2 Chron. 8:3–4); but in the latter part of Solomon's reign Rezon gained control of Damascus and established an Aramean kingdom that was hostile to Solomon (1 Kings 11:23–25). At Rezon's death Hezion seized the throne of Aram and established a dynasty that lasted a century. Members of this dynasty, especially Ben-hadad I and Ben-hadad II, frequently led Aram against the northern kingdom of Israel (1 Kings 15:18; 1 Kings 20; etc.). In ca. 843 B.C. Hazael usurped the Aramean throne and continued the opposition against Israel (2 Kings 8:28–29; 9:15; 10:32–33; 13:22). Jeroboam II of Israel finally overpowered Aram, and the latter declined in importance thereafter, with one short-lived rally during the reign of Ahaz, king of Israel. The kingdom was brought to an end in 732 B.C. by Tiglath-pileser III of Assyria. ***See also*** Isaiah, The Book of. D.A.D.

Aramaic (air-uh-may'ik), a Semitic language closely related to Hebrew. It has been spoken in the Levant from the ninth century B.C. until the present in a variety of dialects. It originated among the Arameans of northern Syria, said to be among the ancestors of Abraham (Gen. 28: 2–5; Deut. 26:5). When the Assyrians conquered the Arameans, Aramean scribes within the bureaucracy of the empire made Aramaic into a universal language of the Near East, which endured from the eighth to fourth centuries B.C. Aramaic then continued in widespread use in a number of dialects through the NT period until the Arab conquest (seventh century A.D.). Several passages in the OT are written in Official Aramaic (Ezra 4:8–6:18; 7:12–26; Dan. 2:4–7:28; Jer. 10:10–11; Gen. 31:47). Jesus probably spoke a dialect of Western Aramaic and some words in the NT come from Aramaic, e.g., "Talitha Cumi," "Maranatha," and "Golgotha." The Dead Sea Scrolls, inscriptions, and many documents show that Aramaic was in common use during the first century A.D. In succeeding centuries Aramaic split into several dialects. Syriac, a form of Aramaic, was used by the Christians in Syria; Jewish Palestinian Aramaic was used in the composition of the Palestinian Talmud and Babylonian Aramaic in the Babylonian Talmud. Targums are Jewish translations of the OT into Aramaic for the common people in the synagogue. ***See also*** Calvary; Maranatha; Talitha Cumi; Talmud; Targums. A.J.S.

Ararat (air'uh-rat), the biblical name (Assyrian *Urartu*) for the region around Lake Van (southeast Turkey, extending into northwest Iran) and the people and state established there from the ninth through the early sixth centuries B.C. Best known from Assyrian records, Urartu constantly hindered Assyria's advances northward. The assassins of Sennacherib fled there from Nineveh (2 Kings 19:37; Isa. 37:38). Later, after the collapse of Assyria, Ararat and other northern nations are summoned in Jer. 51:27–28 to attack Babylon. In Gen. 8:4 the ark settles on the mountains of Ararat, here evidently conceived as the highest part of the world. The modern "Mt. Ararat" is a later appellation. S.B.P.

Aratus (ah'ruh-tuhs), a Stoic poet of the mid-third century B.C. whose work *Phainomena* is quoted in Paul's Areopagus speech (Acts 17:28: "for we are indeed his offspring"). ***See also*** Areopagus; Stoics.

Araunah (ah-roh'nah), a Jebusite, also named Ornan (1 Chron. 21). God's plague against the Israelites during David's reign ceased at Araunah's granary (2 Sam. 24). David purchased this granary, and according to 1 Chron. 22:1 and 2 Chron. 3:1 it was the site of the Temple in Jerusalem. Araunah may be a Hurrian title "noble" rather than a personal name.

Archaeology, History, and the Bible

ARCHAEOLOGY generally is the study of antiquity; technically it is the scientific study of the material remains of past human life and activities. Like many other disciplines, the passage of time and the explosion of knowledge have made archaeology quite complex; consequently no one definition is adequate. Until recently Near Eastern archaeology had been principally inductive, emphasizing description; now it is more deductive, stressing explanation. An interplay of induction and deduction would be ideal.

Because archaeology touches upon the natural and social sciences as well as the humanities, it is not easy to categorize. The nature of archaeology and its relation to other sciences are still matters of discussion. Is archaeology an autonomous discipline or is it a subdiscipline of history or anthropology? Some say archaeology is a social science; others maintain it is anthropology. Some see archaeology as a tool of history; others claim it is a discipline in its own right. Meaningful archaeology must relate to history and it is especially useful in reconstructing cultural history.

Archaeology and the Bible are closely related; they inform each other. The process of correlating archaeological evidence and the biblical record is traditionally called biblical archaeology. From the perspective of the biblical scholar this process is a biblical discipline because it is applied for the benefit of biblical studies. Near Eastern archaeologists whose discoveries impinge upon the Bible prefer a geographical or regional designation such as Syro-Palestinian archaeology or the archaeology of the Fertile Crescent as a more accurate description of their discipline. Whatever the nomenclature, archaeological research and biblical studies are best understood as independent but certainly interrelated disciplines.

Archaeology is comprehensive, embracing both the prehistorical and historical periods and encompassing both written (epigraphical) and

Some of the more than seventeen thousand cuneiform tablets as they were discovered in the archive room of the royal palace at Ebla, dating from ca. 2500 B.C.

artifactual or unwritten (nonepigraphical) discoveries. Although literary remains in the form of texts, inscriptions, ostraca, and seals are the subject of epigraphy and paleography, archaeological investigation is usually responsible for their initial discovery. Without archaeology much written evidence would remain buried forever in the ground. Ancient Near Eastern texts recovered at sites such as Mari, Ugarit, and Ebla in Syria, although only indirectly related to the Bible, can shed valuable light on the biblical record and on the history and religion of ancient Palestine. Unwritten materials include everything made by human craft, such as fortifications, pottery, tools, jewelry, and weapons.

Syro-Palestinian Archaeology, Beginnings to World War II: Archaeology knows no geographical limitations; archaeologists work everywhere. The archaeology of the Bible is concerned principally with the region of ancient Syro-Palestine, including today Syria, Lebanon, Jordan, and Israel. As a discipline Syro-Palestinian archaeology has a short history, dating only to the nineteenth century. In the rediscovery of the Holy Land during the past century few scholars contributed as much as the American Edward Robinson. A distinguished geographer and explorer, he was also a leading biblical scholar. In 1838 Robinson, accompanied by the Arabist Eli Smith, undertook a historic trip to the Holy Land. Although unable to date the ruins, they succeeded in identifying over a hundred biblical sites and thus laid the foundations for biblical archaeology and geography. Robinson is rightly called the first scientific explorer of Palestine.

A direct result of Robinson's topographical investigations was the establishment of the British Palestine Exploration Fund in 1865 for the purpose of exploring Palestine systematically and scientifically. The Palestine Exploration Fund of London sponsored several of the great geographical surveys of western Palestine and Transjordan, as well as major excavations of biblical sites.

Beginnings of Systematic Excavations. The first quasi-systematic excavation in Palestine took place in 1890 when the British Egyptologist W. M. Flinders Petrie came from Egypt to Tell el-Hesi in the northern Negev. The word *tell* designates a land formation common in Palestine. Shaped like truncated cones, these tells or mounds are sites of ancient settlements. Successive human occupation over a long period of time is responsible for the conical shape of these tells. In

Tell Dotha, viewed from the west, illustrates the truncated conical shape of tells. Identified as the biblical town of Dothan, excavations there reveal continuous occupation from 3200 to 700 B.C.

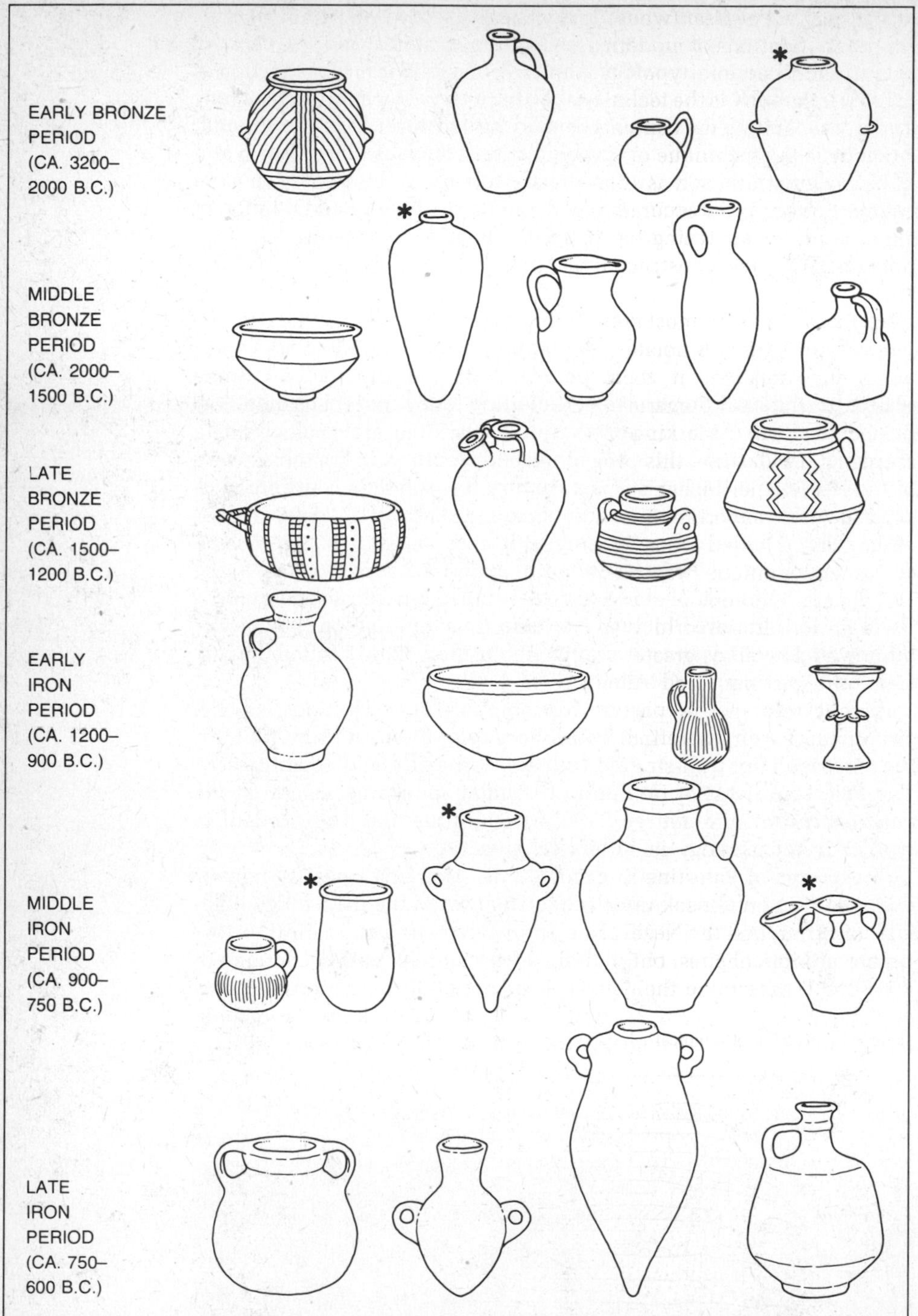

Profiles of characteristic pottery types from the principal archaeological periods in Palestine. Such a chart is an outgrowth of the pioneering work of Petrie and Albright on ceramic typology. (Pots marked with an asterisk are drawn to half-scale relative to the other pots.)

excavating Tell el-Hesi (whose identification is still uncertain) Petrie laid the foundations of modern archaeology by his application of stratigraphy and ceramic typology, the twin principles of field archaeology. Stratigraphy is the technique of digging a tell layer by layer while carefully separating the contents of each occupational layer or stratum. Typology is the technique of classifying artifacts on the basis of external characteristics, such as shape, ware, and decoration in the case of pottery. Pottery is an accurate tool for dating the occupational levels of a mound. By analyzing the potsherds lying within the successive strata at Hesi Petrie constructed a chronological framework for Palestine.

Before World War I most archaeological projects in Palestine resembled treasure hunts. A notable exception was the first American excavation in Palestine; it took place between 1908 and 1910 at Sebastiyeh (biblical Samaria) under George A. Reisner and architect Clarence S. Fisher. Marking the beginning of systematic digging and recording in Palestine, this project revolutionized Palestinian archaeology. The Reisner-Fisher method consisted in separation of occupational layers of superimposed strata, accompanied by careful analysis of typology, detailed recording, and study of architecture. The Reisner-Fisher technique was far more comprehensive and meticulous than Petrie's method.

The period after World War I marked a notable advance in field techniques as well as greater accuracy in dating sites. William F. Albright, the distinguished American biblical archaeologist, played a prominent role in the postwar era. Building on Petrie's pioneer achievements Albright refined the pottery chronology of Palestine. His dig at the small but well-stratified site of Tell Beit Mirsim (identity still disputed), southwest of Hebron in the foothills, shed much light on Bronze and Iron Age pottery. Without question Albright established Palestinian archaeology as a discipline in its own right.

An explorer of Palestine in the tradition of Edward Robinson, the American Nelson Glueck undertook extensive topographical surveys in Transjordan and the Negev. Not only was he able to identify a large number of biblical sites, but with his knowledge of pottery chronology he could determine their periods of occupation. Although recent

A schematic drawing of a typical tell shows the various levels of occupation.

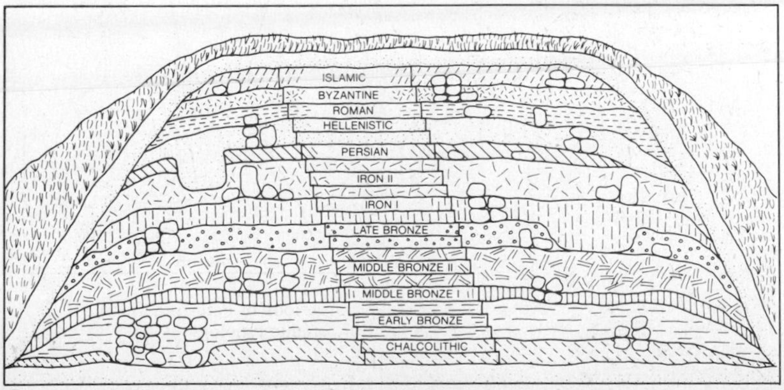

surveys have revised some of Glueck's conclusions, they also support many of them. Glueck had posited a gap in the population of southern Jordan between 1900 and 1200 B.C. Subsequent surveys have produced pottery evidence from every period, including the Middle Bronze and Late Bronze Ages (1900–1200 B.C.). In addition to Glueck, several other scholars, including the German Albrecht Alt, contributed to the topographical history of Palestine.

After World War II: After World War II the archaeology of Palestine advanced rapidly, with significant improvements in the techniques of digging and recording as well as in the interpretation of remains. Three archaeologists contributed meaningfully to this development: Kathleen Kenyon of England, Yigael Yadin of Israel, and G. Ernest Wright of the United States.

Kenyon's dig at Tell es-Sultan, identified with OT Jericho, was the most important excavation of this period. Before working in Palestine Kenyon had trained under Mortimer Wheeler at the Romano-British town of Verulamium in England. There they developed the famous Wheeler-Kenyon method. Emphasizing debris analysis, this system is characterized by stratigraphical control and careful recording in measured sections. This procedure is quite similar to the Reisner-Fisher method utilized at Sebastiyeh. No one has had a greater influence on archaeological method than Kenyon; today all excavators employ the stratigraphical method of Kenyon with adaptations to suit their own sites.

The first large-scale dig in modern Israel took place at Tell el-Qedah, site of biblical Hazor in upper Galilee. Yadin directed this project, which was very well organized and functioned by teamwork. Previously almost all digs proceeded autocratically—the director made all decisions. Many members of Yadin's team at Hazor have become leading achaeologists in Israel.

Since the establishment of the state of Israel the archaeologists of

A defensive wall constructed of stone blocks from the excavation in Galilee of Tell el-Quedah, biblical Hazor, is evidence of the Assyrian conquest ca. 725 B.C.

that country have been busy recovering their national history. Israelis show a preference for sites containing monumental architecture that have not been dug previously. The British and Americans, on the other hand, are inclined to reexcavate mounds dug earlier in order to clarify their occupational history.

G. Ernest Wright, distinguished student of Albright, conducted a major excavation at Tell Balatah, site of biblical Shechem in central Palestine. Following the Wheeler-Kenyon method, Wright also emphasized pottery chronology in the tradition of the Albright school. More important, Shechem was the training ground for American archaeologists; at Shechem Wright created a new school of field archaeology. Several of Wright's staff went on to direct their own archaeological projects.

The Tell Gezer dig in Israel was an important offshoot of Shechem. After launching the Gezer project Wright relinquished it to William G. Dever and H. Darrell Lance, who developed it into a long-term excavation. In turn, Gezer became the training ground for hundreds of American volunteers. In exchange for academic credits these students not only moved dirt but also learned the art of digging and recording. Their in-service training was supplemented by lectures and seminars at the Gezer field school.

The pace of archaeological activity since the Arab-Israeli war of 1967 has accelerated so rapidly on both sides of the Jordan River that it is difficult even to name all the field projects underway in Israel and Jordan, as well as in the adjacent countries such as Syria, Iraq, Egypt, and Saudi Arabia. American, British, French, German, and other archaeologists continue to excavate in the Near East, but native archaeologists are doing much of the work in their own countries.

The most important excavations in Israel since the Six-Day War focus on Jerusalem. Although Jerusalem has been the most excavated city in the world, the recent digs in the Old City have revolutionized the traditional understanding of Jerusalem's history. The three major projects are Benjamin Mazar's at the Temple Mount, Nahman Avigad's in the Jewish Quarter, and Yigal Shiloh's in the City of David.

Syro-Palestinian Archaeology Today: Instead of a list of excavations and surveys since 1967, a description of the state of the art would seem to be more informative. Almost every aspect of Near Eastern archaeology has changed radically in the last two decades. The temporal and geographical horizons of Near Eastern archaeology have broadened appreciably. Now chronological studies begin as early as the Paleolithic period (ca. 100,000 B.C.) and extend to the Ottoman era (A.D. 1918). Archaeology has begun to pay attention to the previously neglected periods of Judaism and early Christianity. American archaeologist Eric M. Meyers, through excavations of synagogues and regional surveys, is reconstructing life in upper Galilee during the Talmudic period (A.D. 200–500). At the same time excavations at Pella in Jordan and Caesara Maritima in Israel are illuminating early Christianity. N.T. archaeology has not advanced nearly so rapidly as the archaeology of the O.T. By studying the remains of the Hellenistic, Imperial Roman, and Byzantine periods in countries surrounding the Aegean sea, archaeologists and historians will be able to shed additional light on early Christianity.

Geographically surveys and excavations encompass Carthage and Cyprus to the west and the Arabian peninsula and the Gulf states to the southeast. Yemen's archaeology is just coming of age. As the center of two successive and famous civilizations, the Sabean and the Himyarite, Yemen was known for its frankincense trade and impressive irrigation and storage systems, especially the monumental dam at Marib, the capital of the ancient Sabean kingdom. To supplement earlier field projects an interdisciplinary reconnaissance is underway in the area around Zafar, the ancient Himyarite capital, as well as an archaeological and epigraphical survey in the Wadi al-Jubah to the southwest of Marib, to solve the vexing problems of South Arabian chronology and other aspects of the pre-Islamic cultures of Yemen.

Interdisciplinary Emphasis at Excavations. The composition of the dig staff is perhaps the most striking development in field archaeology; all staffs are interdisciplinary. The field archaeologists are supported by specialists from the natural and social sciences, including geologists, physical and cultural anthropologists, paleoethnobotanists and zoologists, hydrologists, and ethnographers. Stratigraphy and typology continue to be the backbone of field archaeology, but many other processes are being carried out in the attempt to recover the total environment of a past society and the human impact upon it. The Tell Hesban expedition in Jordan is a model of interdisciplinary research. The comprehensive environmental studies at Hesban included work on climate, geology, soil, hydrology, phytogeography, and zoogeography.

Not long ago on the typical dig floral and faunal remains were ignored. The current concern for the environment renders the ecofacts as important as the artifacts. In paleoenvironmental studies organic materials such as seeds, pollen, animal bones, fish bones, insects, and mollusks illuminate the ancient environment and the human response to it. Organic evidence helps to define the economic base of a settlement. Ethnoarchaeology makes it possible to determine from modern use of the environment how it may have been utilized in antiquity.

Archaeology benefits substantially from the improved techniques of retrieval, recording, and analysis of data. These are procedures developed by the natural sciences to date and identify archaeological materials and artifacts. For example, the new photogrammetry and computer graphics not only provide plans, elevations, and three-dimensional images of standing architecture but also are revolutionizing the recording, analysis, and storage of inscriptional evidence and ancient texts. Low-altitude aerial photography is preserving vital data in visual form and can present a synoptic view of structures and habitations for comparative study.

Chronometric dating has revolutionized archaeology. Among the most useful dating techniques are radiocarbon, potassium argon, thermoluminescence, and dendrochronology. While thermoluminescence is useful in dating pottery and other fired clay artifacts, neutron activation analysis can determine the provenance of the clay used in making the pottery. Likewise, atomic absorption spectrometry and other techniques can determine the sources of the stones used in ancient construction and the metals employed in ancient tools and weapons. These analytical techniques can shed light on ancient crafts, patterns of trade, and the economy.

Until recently Near Eastern archaeology focused almost exclusively on history, particularly political history. Stratigraphical sequences revealed in deep trenches of large tells helped to establish the chronology of the site. In view of the current emphasis on anthropology, horizontal exposure, providing a picture of the physical layout, is important. By exposing broad areas archaeologists can begin to reconstruct the daily life of ancient peoples as well as their social organizations. The deep, narrow trenches at Kenyon's dig at Jericho could not provide the kinds of data that interest social scientists. New World archaeology with its stress on anthropology has stimulated Near Eastern archaeology to take an interest in social change, ancient economies, trade patterns, population shifts, and so on.

Archaeological reconnaissance is less interested in single tells and more concerned with whole regions. Instead of concentrating exclusively on an isolated mound, archaeologists are combining the excavation of the multiperiod tell with a study of its surroundings. Regional study is invaluable in understanding the economic and demographic relationships of an urban center with the territory under its control. By studying a homogeneous district as an ecological unit archaeologists learn a great deal about the relationship among settlements, town planning, economic development, industrial growth, and population expansion. Israeli archaeologist Yohanan Aharoni's regional surveys in upper Galilee and the Negev earned for him the title of father of systematic surveys in Israel.

Archaeology and Biblical Studies: Archaeology has much to contribute to biblical studies. In the first place, it supplies the material evidence needed to elucidate the biblical text. Archaeology makes it possible to place the Bible in its original setting by providing a physical context in time and place. By furnishing also the cultural context of the

Aerial view of Tel Halif (biblical Rimmon?). It shows the tell itself, with its grids of excavation areas and the major digging areas: the north slope, the Persian area, and the field behind the firebreak at the far right. In the foreground is the field camp—the tent kitchen and camp headquarters housed in trucks and buses.

Bible archaeology liberates modern students from the constrictions of their own thought patterns and traditional categories of analysis and allows them to grasp the biblical mentality. Archaeology is especially useful in topography, specifically in establishing the location of ancient sites mentioned in the biblical literature, as Edward Robinson and Eli Smith demonstrated a century and a half ago. By illuminating the ambient cultures of the ancient Near East archaeology contributes to a better understanding of the social, economic, and religious environment of which ancient Israel was a part.

How does one reconstruct the history of ancient Israel? There are several approaches: the Albright school would utilize archaeology; the German school would follow a tradition-history approach; and sociologists would try to understand early Israelite life in socioeconomical categories.

In accordance with the Albright-school view archaeology is a source of history; it recovers the written data for the study of ancient history, as well as provides other material evidence to illuminate the text. Archaeology can be of great value to the historian in reconstructing the history of ancient Israel. With the written documents as a framework historians can interpret the archaeological data. Each of these sources offers a different but valuable point of view. Interpretation, however, is fraught with danger because the artifacts are always mute and the literary sources often ambiguous. All ancient documents, including the Bible, must be subjected to literary-critical analysis.

Historical interpretations are not to be made on the results of limited excavation. Geographical, stratigraphical, and chronological evidence must be well established. The archaeological data must be controlled and unambiguous. The correlation of archaeological evidence and written sources must be based on many sites, never on a single site. Such correlation must be founded on multiple cultural traits, such as pottery, art, and architecture, never on a single cultural trait. Archaeology may be said to support a position only when sufficient distinctive archaeological evidence is available for making a judgment.

The Bible itself must be approached critically. Its historical claims are not always to be taken at face value. As a book of faith the Bible is not always free of bias; it presents historical events from a confessional point of view. On the other hand, if it were not for the Bible the Israelites would be as little known as the Moabites, the Edomites, and the Philistines.

Despite the limitations inherent in archaeology, history, and the Bible by reason of ambiguity or tendentiousness, these three disciplines together can furnish valuable insights into the life, culture, and religion of ancient Israel. Archaeology, history, and the Bible are vibrant disciplines today. Archaeology is generating so much material that it is almost impossible for any one person to encompass it. Archaeological activity is the source of new insights into biblical life and times; it is also the guarantee that the Bible will never be a dead letter, but always a living word.

Bibliography

Sauer, J. A. "Syro-Palestinian Archaeology, History, and Biblical Studies." *Biblical Archaeologist* 45 (1982): 205.

P.J.K.

archaeology, methods of, the procedure by which ancient artifacts are recovered, identified, and interpreted. There is no single "proper" approach to archaeological method, any more than there can be an all-embracing theoretical definition. Archaeology is what the majority of competent archaeologists do. However, since what one learns in archaeological research is the direct result of what one is trying to find out and how one goes about it, theory is not only important, but theory and method are inextricably entwined.

This article traces theory and method in biblical and Syro-Palestinian archaeology from the classic period of its early development in the 1920s until the present.

Between the Two World Wars, 1920–1940: Although modern archaeology in Palestine began late in the nineteenth century with Sir William M. F. Petrie at Tell el-Hesi (1890), it was not until after World War I that large-scale work, particularly American, got underway.

The 1920s and 1930s constituted a "golden age," with numerous well-financed and competently staffed field excavations—many of them at biblical sites such as Ai, Bethel, Beth-shan, Beth-shemesh, Beth-zur, Debir, Gerasa, Gibeah, Jericho, Mizpah, Samaria, Shechem, and others. The British Mandate Department of Antiquities promulgated new antiquities laws in 1919, and the various foreign schools flourished in the following period. Particularly prominent was the role of the American School of Oriental Research in Jerusalem, directed first by the prominent orientalist W. F. Albright, and later by the rabbi and biblical scholar-explorer Nelson Glueck.

"Biblical Archaeology": It was in this period that the movement popularly known as "biblical archaeology" came to full flower. Interest in the Bible had, of course, motivated much of Western participation in exploration and discovery in the Holy Land from the early nineteenth century. But among European archaeologists, especially the British, there also developed a parallel "secular" tradition (see below). Among Americans working in Palestine, this secular approach was also seen in the University of Chicago's excavations at Megiddo (1925–1939), as well as in the work of the University of Pennsylvania at Beth-shan (1921–1933) and of Yale University at Gerasa (1928–1934).

It was Albright and the American school in Jerusalem who dominated the scene in the formative phase in the 1920s and 1930s. Grouped around them were a number of consortia of church schools and seminaries, with staff and financial support drawn from religious circles, digging at biblical sites. Albright, a formidable scholar of extraordinary breadth in the whole of ancient Near Eastern studies, was the mentor of this group. In his view, archaeology was a promising new tool of biblical studies. It alone could produce *external* evidence to illuminate the biblical text—often dramatically—thereby cutting through what he regarded as the sterile debates of textual and literary criticism, especially of the skeptical variety then in vogue in both European and American liberalism. It was Albright who coined the phrase "the archaeological revolution." By that he meant the opening up of the lands, peoples, and lost sites of the ancient Near East, so that the Bible no longer stood merely as a lone monument from the past without a cultural and historical context. The Bible now had a historicity, and thus a new "credibility."

A reconstructed pottery serving bowl found at Tel Halif (biblical Rimmon?) is important because its form, design, and method of construction allowed the archaeologists who found it to date it and other structures in the area to 750–700 B.C.

Albright was reacting in part to the temper of his times. This was "conservatism" in the best sense, but Albright the scholar was certainly no "fundamentalist." Yet, the *popular* notion of archaeology that grew out of this approach—and continues to prevail among much of the American public—was that archaelogy's primary function is to "prove the Bible true."

Methods of "Biblical Archaeology": In order to perfect this new tool one obviously had to be able to correlate the material remains of the past, brought to light now by archaeology, with the biblical texts one sought to clarify. Two basic methods were pioneered by the first generation of the school of "biblical archaeology." Both were highly technical and had little to do with theology, but they were necessary to the task at hand.

Stratigraphy. The first method was stratigraphy. A typical Middle Eastern *tell* (or artificial mound) is the result of an extraordinarily complex series of man-made and natural deposits, often laid down in a continuous sequence stretching over thousands of years. Occupational activities, repeated disturbances, constant rebuilding, and frequent destructions have churned up the debris from as many as thirty strata, or successive cities, superimposed one on another. The first challenge of modern archaeology was therefore simply to learn how to dig stratigraphically—that is, to untangle these layers precisely in the reverse order of their deposition, and thus to reconstruct the history of a site, period by period. This was to prove very difficult, and indeed its accomplishment was not to be fully achieved until the next period.

The developing techniques of stratigraphy, however, were particularly crucial for "biblical archaeologists," who were fundamentally historians and whose primary aim was to reconstruct the broad course of what we may call "political history" in the biblical period. It was thought that this history of great events—the formation and collapse of states, the conflict of political ideologies and institutions, the activities of prominent kings and public figures—was what the Bible dealt with primarily, and what archaeology could uniquely confirm. For these early "biblical archaeologists" the focus was on such great historical epochs as the patriarchal period (ca. 2000–1700 B.C.) and the Israelite exodus and conquest (ca. 1300–1200 B.C.).

Ceramic Typology. A second challenge, however, grew inevitably out of stratigraphy, which could at best provide only a relative sequence of events, and that was the problem of absolute chronology (i.e., dating events). Here it was pottery that could provide the clue, as Petrie had long ago said. If the characteristic pottery from each layer could be separated precisely, and if that pottery could then be placed along a "time line" of developments in form and decoration, one could provide fixed dates for each stratum and its contents. In practice this meant developing ceramic typology, the art of charting changes in local pottery styles and then correlating these through comparative studies with similar styles in neighboring areas such as Egypt and Mesopotamia, which unlike Palestine in the early periods possessed both written records and an astronomically fixed chronology.

Albright himself was in the vanguard of the development of both these methods, especially in his excavations from 1926 to 1932 at Tell Beit Mirsim (biblical Debir?). The publication of the results of his work at this site provided the framework for the history, teminology, and chronology of ancient Palestine that is still used today. In particular, Albright's mastery of the common pottery of Palestine, handed on to his second and third generations of students, determined the course of archaeological research almost until the present time. This was one of the greatest achievements of "biblical archaeology."

The Postwar Period, 1950–1970: After the Second World War, when fieldwork resumed in the Middle East, especially in Israel and Jordan, stratigraphic methods came to the fore again. Despite the attempts of the earlier generation, it

Gridding the field. Archaeologists at Tel Halif pound in stakes and stretch string, dividing the area to be excavated into squares. They then study the "balks" of undisturbed debris between the squares as excavation proceeds downwards.

became obvious that much of the material previously unearthed was so poorly excavated that it could not be adequately dated, much less interpreted. It was therefore largely useless for historical reconstruction. Thus problems high on the agenda of "biblical archaeology," such as the historicity of the patriarchs or the Israelite conquest of Palestine, had not been resolved, despite the accumulation of much new data.

The "Balk-Debris Layer" Method. The impetus for improved field methods came, however, from secular quarters, especially in the work of the eminent British archaeologist Dame Kathleen M. Kenyon at Jericho in 1952–1958. Kenyon had learned more sophisticated and precise stratigraphic techniques on Romano-British sites under the tutelage of Sir Mortimer Wheeler (thus the popular designation of her method as "Wheeler-Kenyon"). At Jericho she adapted the basic principles of this method to the peculiar problems of a Middle Eastern mound. The essence of the system was the gridding of each field into squares (usually 5 by 5 m.), then leaving standing "balks" of undisturbed debris (1 m. wide) between the squares as excavation proceeded downward. Careful, smaller probe trenches guided the digging level by level. The focus of attention was not architecture per se, but the debris layers that made up most of the contents of a mound. The assumption was that the debris, if meticulously separated and analyzed, would reveal the story of successive human activity, including the smaller inner changes in the architecture, often previously overlooked. Further, the analysis and drawing of the sections visible in the balks would aid in interpreting and presenting the evidence in "three dimensions," so necessary in complex Palestinian sites.

The Kenyon system (nowadays more commonly termed the "balk-debris layer" method) was difficult, expensive, and confined to small areas. But it produced obviously superior results in digging, analyzing, and presenting the data, particularly in re-excavating old and badly dug sites, where meticulous examination of the scant material left was essential. Thus it was soon adopted and coupled with Albrightian ceramic analysis by most Americans working in Jordan, including G. E. Wright at Shechem (1956–1969), P. W. Lapp at Ta'anach (1963–1968) and elsewhere, J. A. Callaway at 'Ai (1964–1969), and others. Current excavations in Jordan, foreign as well as local, follow this system.

Archaeological "Field Schools." The system was also introduced in Israel by Wright, followed by his students W. G. Dever, H. D. Lance, and J. D. Seger, in the well-known Gezer project (1964–1973), the largest and longest-running American excavation of this period in Israel. Here the combined British-American approach was supplemented by a "field school" that trained hundreds of student volunteers and others in field methods, as well as pioneering in the "new archaeology" (see below). By the 1970s, all American excavations in Israel were organized along similar lines, such as those at Tell el-Ḥesi, Shema-meiron, Caesarea, Tel Anafa, Tell Jemmeh, and many others. The Israeli archaeologists, while still preferring larger exposures at virgin sites and a more architectural orientation, have gradually adopted most aspects of the new stratigraphic methods, despite the controversy that continued throughout the 1970s (particularly over the use of sections and section-drawing).

The "New Archaeology," 1970 – : It is now commonly recognized that just as earlier "revolutions" in the archaeological method can be distinguished, so a new and potentially revolutionary phase can be said to have begun about 1970, called the advent of the "new archaeology." It may be helpful to sketch briefly the reasons for this shift in theory and method.

Before listing various factors in the current revolution, we must acknowledge that all the newer thinking grew out of frustration that old questions had not been answered satisfactorily, as well as from the desire to raise what were regarded as new and more exciting, more relevant questions. Now archaeologists could date pottery and architecture fairly accurately and could compare Palestine with neighboring cultures. But what did the data mean? Archaeologists could describe the dry dust and bones of the past, but could they explain how people really lived and thought? What could archaeology tell us that the biblical and other texts could not? Was ancient Israel unique, and if so how? What relevance did archaeology as a developing science actually have for biblical studies?

One of the dissatisfactions that precipitated change was a certain decline of interest in the older-style "biblical archaeology" due to pessimism about its prospects. Even a cursory survey of recent literature by archaeologists and biblical historians will demonstrate that after nearly a hundred years of active research on early Israelite origins we are further than ever from a consensus of scholarly opinion. We cannot yet explain, at least in human and historical terms, the ultimate sources of the Yahwistic movement that appeared so dramatically in ancient Canaan with such devastating effects. The same is true for the patriarchs of Genesis—the "fathers" of the faith of later Israel—who remain figures as shadowy as ever. If the "biblical archaeology" movement had as its aim a convincing reconstruction of an actual historical setting for these formative events, then it must be confessed that it failed. Perhaps the failure was the result of unrealistic expectations. Archaeology can answer such questions as "what," "who," "when," and "how"—but not "why."

An arch with keystone from what was probably the stable of a house at Ai. From the eighth century B.C., it is one of the earliest such structures found in Israel.

Multi-Disciplinary Archaeology: The first real signs of change, however, came in the multi-disciplinary approach. Earlier archaeologists, especially of the "biblical archaeology" school, had concentrated on stratigraphy, pottery chronology, and major architecture such as temples, palaces, and defense works. These categories of evidence were subjected to minute examination because they were pertinent to the basic orientation of that generation toward what we have termed above "political history." But what about social and even individual history?

In the late 1960s archaeologists began to realize that in their rather parochial approach much data of potential significance had been overlooked, and in many cases vital evidence had even been discarded. Individual sites had been excavated with no consideration of environmental factors. But why were those sites located there in the first place? How had defensible position, water supply, rainfall, climate, and the availability of arable land and raw materials shaped the culture that developed in a particular time and place? And what could bones, seeds, and other organic remains tell us of economic strategies, social differentiation, diet, disease, longevity, and the like? Archaeologists began to see that if total retrieval of the material remains were possible, and if they were studied in both natural and cultural context, they could begin to discern social, economic, ethnic, and perhaps even religious groupings. Moreover, they might then get at what they had really sought all along (now defined as the true objective of archaeology): an understanding of the phenomenon of cultural process and change.

Prompted by these broader theoretical interests and research objectives, both biblical and Syro-Palestinian archaeologists began about 1970 to employ larger, multi-disciplinary excavation staffs. The trend began at Gezer, which was experimenting self-consciously in methodology, as early as 1966; but within a few years most digs in Israel and Jordan exhibited the "new look." Now, alongside the traditional biblical scholars, historians, stratigraphers, and ceramic experts, one increasingly found on staff such specialists as geologists, geomorphologists, climatologists, paleo-ethnobotanists and zoologists, physical and cultural anthropologists, ethnographers, historians of technology, and, more recently, statisticians and computer programmers. Data of every sort now had to be retrieved: living-surface deposits were sifted and put through froth-flotation machines for seeds; all bone fragments were saved; soil and pollen samples were taken; extensive regional and environmental surveys were carried out; material culture samples and artifacts were submitted for laboratory analysis.

It was obviously expensive and laborious to coordinate the fieldwork and research of so many specialists. And, since this approach was so novel, few final results are yet available in a published form that would seem to realize the full potential of the newer approach. Finally, some discounted the "revolution" as nothing more than a passing fad. It could be argued that no far-reaching philosophical or disciplinary changes were in evidence, only a pragmatic borrowing from the natural sciences. Yet other scientific techniques had long been accepted in archaeology, such as radiocarbon dating, neutron activation analysis to "fingerprint" clays and pinpoint the source of pottery, electrical resistivity surveying to plot underground structures, and many other techniques whose value was obvious. Modern technology had already made its contribution in the form of aerial and satellite photography, laser-beam transits for rapid and accurate mapping—and especially in the computer, potentially the most powerful new tool in archaeology. It may safely be said that no single innovation has done as much to transform this branch of archaeology as the new alignment with the natural sciences and the multi-disciplinary orientation, that is clearly here to stay.

The "Secularization" of "Biblical Archaeology": Another factor influencing archaeology, beginning in the late 1960s, was changing sources of support, both personal and financial, which led to the secularization of "biblical archaeology." This had two aspects, the first of which was the advent of digs done exclusively with student volunteers in the wake of rising costs and the shortage of labor in the Middle East.

This approach was pioneered at Gezer, beginning in 1964, with the first dig structured entirely around a "field school" offering practical experience and academic credit. At first this was also a strategy born of necessity, but before long archaeologists everywhere in Israel were responding to the exhilaration of teaching while doing fieldwork. What archaeologists did not anticipate was that students' persistent and often impertinent questions (always "why?") would force them to rethink their own motivations and presuppositions, sometimes painfully. These students—some Christians, many Jewish, mostly secularists, all adventurers of one sort or another—completely transformed life on a typical dig with a staff of former "biblical archaeologists" in transition.

The second aspect of secularization brought even more profound and long-lasting changes. As the costs of doing fieldwork rapidly outstripped the resources of private and church-related sources, it became necessary to turn to federal and public sources of support. A typical six-week season with a diversified staff and workforce of a hundred now cost $100,000 or more. Beginning in 1966, Gezer was supported almost wholly by U.S. government funds channeled through the Smithsonian Institution, with some help from the Ford and Rockefeller foundations.

The newly found sources of support were timely and salutary. But they forced "biblical archaeologists" to distance themselves somewhat from theological and religious studies, to develop credentials as professional (rather than amateur or part-time) archaeologists, and to broaden their research designs into the kind of proposals that could withstand the peer review process common in American anthropology and archaeology. That trend was intensified as the National Endowment for the Humanities became the major source of funds by the mid-1970s, and as the American Schools of Oriental Research (historically the sponsoring agency of many American excavations in the Middle East) adopted its standards by the end of the decade.

One response to financial pressure and the need to produce more deliberate research designs to justify public funding was a shift away from the large, expensive tell-site excavation, with its more generalized objectives. Newer projects now tended toward "problem-solving" archaeology designed to focus specifically on a neglected area, site, or topic, as well as the excavation of one-period sites and regional surveys to study settlement patterns from surface remains. This was attractive both because these projects appeared to produce more results for the investment, and also because the complex newer methods appeared to be more manageable for projects on this scale. In Israel, new excavations of the 1970s included an investigation of upper Galilean synagogue sites (Eric Meyers et al., 1971–1979) and a study of late third-millennium arid lands settlement sites in the Negev (W. G. Dever and Rudolph Cohen, 1978–1980). In many areas of Jordan previously almost completely unworked by archaeologists survey work became very popular.

Another factor strengthening the growth of secularism was the ascendency of the various "national schools" in the Middle East. The colonial powers had long dominated archaeology, but by 1970 the initiative in Israel had long since passed to the state-supported and well-staffed Israeli school with all its natural advantages, and this was rapidly becoming the case in Jordan and Syria as well. Each of these schools had its own independent rationale, agenda, and objectives, all of which differed considerably from those of the foreign schools, especially those of the former "biblical archaeologists." Even in Israel, where archaeology still remains somewhat "bibliocentric," the Bible is used not so much as theological or confessional literature, but rather as a document of national history. In any case, Israeli archaeology is strongly secular, never having been clerically dominated as in America. This had always been true of several of the European schools, especially the British, where from Petrie to the present one could scarcely have found a "biblical archaeologist."

It must be stressed that all agreed that it was not a question of *whether* to use the Bible, but *how*. What was the proper relationship of archaeology and history, as the "new archaeology" began to move away from the traditional alignment solely with biblical history? Could archaeology any longer be simply the "handmaiden" of history, as it was so often described? Recently W. G. Dever has argued that "biblical archaeology" of the classic style of the 1920s–1960s was uniquely American, largely an aspect of biblical studies and the theological climate of that period rather than a part of the mainstream development of archaeology. The continued flourishing of the secular schools in other countries showed unmistakably that there were other valid approaches to the archaeology of this region of the Middle East. Indeed, beginning about 1970 there was a rather strong reaction against the term and even the concept of "biblical archaeology," in preference for Albright's old alternate term (which had remained in use nearly everywhere else), the "archaeology of Syria-Palestine." In this view Syro-Palestinian archaeology was a professional and academic discipline *independent* of biblical studies, with its own appropriate aims and methods, a branch of Near Eastern archaeology far broader in scope than the biblical periods and peoples. The term "biblical archaeology" would thus be retained for the dialogue between some aspects of this discipline and biblical studies, for example, between Iron Age specialists and OT scholars. Ironically, the new "secular archaeology," while demanding autonomy, promised to contribute even more to biblical studies as it grew in sophistication, precision, and confidence.

Oven and stone for food preparation excavated at Gezer, from the late second millennium B.C.

The Impact of New World Archaeology: Finally, somewhat belatedly, Syro-Palestinian, as well as biblical, archaeology was affected by New World archaeology, where the more scientific and anthropological thrust of the "new archaeology" had been strongly felt already during the early 1960s. Among the concepts younger archaeologists in this field borrowed (sometimes rather naïvely) were: first, the "holistic" view of culture as consisting of a number of interacting, adaptive economic and social subsystems, most of which leave traces that must be sought in the archaeological record; second, the notion that archaeology must not only describe artifacts but must explain the human behavior they express, and that the goal of this enterprise is to discern universal "laws" of the cultural process; and third, the insistence that material culture remains must be not only well excavated but must be quantified and statistically manipulated (usually with computers) so as to analyze a number of independent variables that may help to account for culture difference and culture change.

Obviously this more anthropological approach was a long way from the older historical archaeology, especially that devoted exclusively to concerns of biblical history. Many questioned whether in this the new archaeology is not too specialized, too radical a departure from the venerable traditions of humanistic archaeology. But graduate programs in North American universities (Toronto, Chicago, Pennsylvania, Arizona) have rapidly taken up the new archaeology. The current projects of the American Schools of Oriental Research, its publications, and its program at the annual meetings all reveal its strong hold. The younger generation is firmly committed to it, partly because it seems more intellectually challenging, more in the mainstream of archaeology today, and partly because on the academic scene this is where the action is perceived in terms of financial support, professional development, and career opportunities. As had long been observed, American archaeology is anthropology or it is nothing.

Again, the newer approach, despite controversy, is here to stay. This does not obviate the need for the Syro-Palestinian archaeologist to be fully competent at the same time in biblical languages, literature, and history, as well as in the traditional skills of stratigraphy and ceramic typology. Yet because it becomes increasingly difficult for one individual to master all that is required, we will likely see some division of labor. Alongside the new "secular archaeology" one may safely predict that there will be a revival of a new and more sophisticated style of "biblical archaeology," for as the pace of discovery quickens, popular interest in archaeology and the Bible has reached an all-time high. There is room for both Syro-Palestinian and biblical archaeology, as long as archaeology remains an honest inquiry, marked by scholarship rather than by sensationalism.

Three cisterns in the courtyard of a typical house excavated at Ai, seventh century B.C.

To sum up this review of recent developments of method, archaeology in the Middle East today is still related to biblical studies, but it is also related increasingly to the social and natural sciences, especially anthropology. Its future in America may lie as much in the university and in the public forum as in the seminary. To use a figure of speech, the archaeology of the Holy Land has come out of the cloister, into the academy and the marketplace.

Prospects for the Future: It remains only to suggest some examples that may illustrate how the methods of the "new archaeology" may enable it to do what the old could not.

The first example is the *patriarchal period*. Earlier "biblical archaeologists" like Albright and Glueck had confidently connected the narratives of Genesis concerning the patriarchal migrations directly to the Middle Bronze I (MB I) period in Palestine, ca. 2200–2000 B.C., and related them further to "Amorite" movements from upper Syria. That was possible because MB I is an archaeological phase when nomadism temporarily eclipsed town life, and some elements in the material culture appear to be derived from Syria. But today no scholar supports that correlation, largely because we now know that pastoral nomads constituted one aspect of the society and economy in every period in ancient Palestine. In addition, further study of the Akkadian texts demonstrates that the Amorites mentioned there were not an ethnic but a socioeconomic group, only some of whom were pastoral nomads. The "Amorite"–MB I–patriarchal equation was intriguing, but too simplistic. As a result, biblical historians like T. L. Thompson, J. Van Seters, and others, reacting against Albright's overevaluation of archaeological evidence, dismiss the patriarchs as entirely fictitious.

A more fruitful approach would be to continue to apply the newer archaeological methods so as to reconstruct the entire social history of the Levant in the second millennium B.C. with greater precision and confidence. The study of pastoral nomadism—in the Mari and other texts, in the archaeological record, and in modern ethnographic parallels—has been particularly rewarding. Current research thus indicates that while the stories in Genesis cannot be fixed in any one particular archaeological phase, they do generally reflect economic and social conditions in Syro-Palestine in the second millennium B.C. and may therefore rest on a genuine historical memory. In this sense, archaeology may yet provide a convincing background against which to view the biblical narratives—in itself a worthy and challenging, if modest, goal.

Another example is the *Israelite settlement in Canaan*. Again, earlier archaeologists tended to jump directly from the pages of Joshua into the

ARCHAEOLOGY, METHODS OF

archaeological trenches, where destruction levels seemed to confirm and date a rapid Israelite military conquest of greater Canaan around 1200 B.C. Today, however, with the accumulation of much new and varied data, that view is also regarded as too simplistic. Some of the destructions prove to be only localized disturbances; others are due to the "Sea Peoples" or Philistines; and many sites show no destruction at all (including those such as Jericho, 'Ai, Gibeon, and others that the Israelites claimed to have destroyed). Again, some biblical scholars reacted quite negatively, claiming that there was no statistically significant appearance of a new people known as the Israelites at the beginning of the Iron Age and that what occurred was simply a "peasant's revolt" against the late Bronze Age Canaanite city states.

A better starting point than Joshua may be the book of Judges, which freely acknowledges that the settlement was a long and at first only sporadically successful struggle against the Canaanite city states. It is the more realistic account, and certainly the more amenable to investigation and confirmation using the newer techniques, especially survey and settlement archaeology. Indeed, recent survey work in the Negev, the central hills, and upper Galilee has brought to light dozens of small unfortified villages founded on virgin soil. These new settlements, mostly one-period sites, exhibit a new style of courtyard house suitable for peasant agriculture and an egalitarian social structure, while the pottery and other aspects of the material culture are still in the Late Bronze tradition. These new villages are established in marginal areas, rather than on the ruins of Canaanite sites, but they are not entirely culturally isolated. Those excavated so far ('Ai, Radannah, Giloh, Izbet Ṣarṭeh, and Tel Masos) are the first truly "Israelite" villages archaeologists have been able to recognize, and they reflect almost exactly the conditions portrayed in the book of Judges. A study by L. E. Stager on early highland villages of Israel seeks to demonstrate how the new, multi-disciplinary archaeology illuminates the actual process of Israelite settlement, using textual studies, settlement history, archaeology, ecology, sociology, and ethnoarchaeology.

A final example is the *ancient cult and religion*. Earlier "biblical archaeologists" thought that almost everything otherwise inexplicable was "cultic," i.e., had some religious significance. Further and more sophisticated research has demolished most of these cultic explanations on the one hand, while on the other hand it has brought to light a number of genuinely cultic installations and artifacts. Among these are early Israelite shrines at Dan, Megiddo, Ta'anach, Tell el-Farah (Tirzah), Lachish, Beersheba, and Arad. The most spectacular is the eighth-century B.C. sanctuary at Kuntillet 'Ajrûd

Canaanite altar at Megiddo from the Early Bronze III period.

in the eastern Sinai, where a plastered shrine yielded many votive offerings and Hebrew dedicatory and blessing formulae. One fascinating inscription on a storejar reads, in part, "Yahweh of Samaria and his Asherah," and above it is painted an enthroned, half-nude female—possibly Asherah, the mother goddess of Canaan. Perhaps in overreaction against the excesses of earlier archaeologists' interpretation, biblical scholars have paid scant attention to these recent discoveries, but they are uniquely capable of complementing the biblical texts, which are often elitist and thus portray the normative religion of temple, priests, and king. Archaeology today, however, is capable of documenting "folk religion," or actual religious practice, and setting it in the larger context of social behavior.

The above examples are all preliminary, drawn as they are from the current horizon of archaeological research which is still experimental. But they do illustrate the exciting prospects of the newer archaeology, which is only beginning to realize its full potential. It is sometimes supposed that the "archaeological revolution" is over. In reality, it has scarcely begun.

Bibliography

Brothwell, D. and E. S. Higgs, eds. *Science in Archaeology*. 2d ed. New York: Praeger, 1970.

Dever, W. G. "Archaeological Method in Israel: A Continuing Revolution." *The Biblical Archaeologist* 43 (1980): 41–48.

______. "The Impact of the 'New Archaeology' on Syro-Palestinian Archaeology." *Bulletin of The American Schools of Oriental Research* 242 (1981): 15–29.

______. "Syro-Palestinian and Biblical Archaeology, ca. 1945–1980." In D. A. Knight and G. M. Tucker, eds. *The Hebrew Bible and Its Modern Interpreters*. Philadelphia: Westminster, 1984.

Wright, G. E. "The Phenomenon of American Archaeology in the Near East." *Near Eastern Archaeology in the Twentieth Century*. Edited by J. A. Sanders. Garden City, NY: Doubleday, 1970. Pp. 3–40.

W.G.D.

Archelaus (ahr-kuh-lay'uhs), Herod Archelaus, son of Herod the Great who became ethnarch of Judea, Samaria, and Idumea when his father died in 4 B.C. (see Matt. 2:22). His rule was relatively short and disastrous. Both Jews and Samaritans petitioned Rome for his removal because of his brutal and insensitive rule. Augustus banished him to Gaul in A.D. 6, and his territory became a Roman province under the prefect Coponius. ***See also*** Ethnarch; Herod.

archers, warriors armed with bows and arrows. Archers played an important role in ancient Near Eastern warfare since they could strike accurately from a distance while being protected by a full-length shield. Their importance was so significant that in the Bible a bow may metonymically represent general military strength (Hos. 1:5). Although individual archers and even target practice are mentioned in the Bible (e.g., 1 Sam. 20:35–36), no organized Israelite archery corps is ever described. Perhaps Israel lacked the materials needed to produce composite bows and therefore never established a large archery corps. Alternately, the Bible may never have mentioned an Israelite archery corps, even though it existed. Small groups of Israelite archers are portrayed in the Assyrian reliefs of the siege of Lachish, where several Israelite archers try unsuccessfully to stave off the Assyrian army, which incorporated a large organized corps of archers. M.Z.B.

Archippus (ahr-kip'uhs), perhaps a member of Philemon's household, greeted by Paul in Philemon 2 (cf. Col. 4:17). ***See also*** Apphia; Philemon; Philemon, The Letter of Paul to.

architecture, the art of designing and building structures for various human activities. This article discusses major features of architectural remains as they relate to biblical texts and highlights the archaeological and artistic record of Syro-Palestine and the cultures with which it had historical contact.

The Bible does not use the term "architecture." It speaks rather of specific constructions, sometimes giving remarkable details, but always incidental in narratives composed for other purposes. Furthermore, the archaeological evidence for architecture seldom survives in more than the form of building foundations. Efforts at rebuilding, the redesign of city layouts, damage due to earthquakes or military destruction, or quarrying for reusable stone, and the vagaries of time and weather have all diminished the evidence drastically. Artistic representations such as the four-column facade of the Roman temple on the Esbus coin found in its proper Roman context at Hesban or the stairway up the mountainside toward Tell er-Ras on a coin found at Shechem are frequently helpful, but usually they are of so small a scale as to give only hints of the architecture represented. There is the further problem, shared with all artistic representations, of uncertainty about the accuracy of the artist, whether for reasons of propaganda or artistic license.

With these acknowledged limits one must claim at the outset that the architectural achievements in Syro-Palestine were at their best relatively minor compared to the massive gates, palaces, ziggurats, and gardens of Mesopotamian centers such as Ur, Babylon, Asshur, and Nineveh. Similarly, examination shows very minor achievement in tombs, temples, canals, and palaces compared to those of Old, Middle, and New Kingdom Egypt as even a quick glance at the design of the pyramids of Giza, the temples of Luxor and Karnak, and palaces such as Tell el-Amarna will show. It is an elementary but true observation that biblical period architecture reflects in part the geophysical and geopolitical place of the biblical peoples: they inhabited a narrow corridor on which larger societies played out their histories, often leaving little or no room for truly indigenous development, and frequently stifling emerging native life before it had much chance to flower. One result of this feature is a largely eclectic and reflective architecture in many periods. Clear Egyptian influence on temple design and furnishing at Byblos on the Lebanese coast in pre-Phoenician life is paralleled by obvious Canaanite patterns of city defenses, temples, and palaces and later Hellenistic and Roman motifs in everything from city plans (Jerash) to city features (theaters, aqueducts, hippodromes, living quarters, tomb design, temple construction and layout) on both sides of the Jordan Valley.

Canaanite Architecture: The architecture of Middle and Late Bronze Age Palestine (2000–1500 B.C.) was predominantly Canaanite. Although Palestine in that period was nominally under Egyptian control, the Amarna letters from Canaanite city-state monarchs to headquarters in Egypt show that local autonomy was extensive. The main features architecturally were defense walls comprising substantial stone and rubble-filled ramparts, sometimes with an external *glacis* to increase defensive efficiency. Examples are evident at Hazor and Dan as well as Shechem and Megiddo. Gateways were the most vulnerable point in such constructions and so were reinforced with towers or elaborate entrance routes, putting assaulting forces at an additional disadvantage. All of this was successor to some of the massive mudbrick defense walls and gates of the Early Bronze Age (3000–2000 B.C.), such as at Tirzah, though use of stone for major defense construction had been known in the country since Neolithic times in Jericho (ca. 8000 B.C.).

Within the defense perimeter, dominant public buildings tended to be the royal residence and a temple for the local Baal. As with the defenses themselves, construction was usually of large uncut stone, yielding the term "Cyclopean" from the assumption that only a giant like the mythical Cyclops could have maneuvered such rock into place. Palaces tended to be multiroomed with storage and servants' quarters attached. Compared to a structure like the palace at Mari, palaces in the Holy Land were very modest in size and complexity. Debate over the nature of a structure such as the open-court temple (really a palace?) excavated at Shechem indicates a large degree of diagnostic uncertainty as to function for some of these public buildings.

Temples were similarly elementary and seem to be modeled on north Syria designs. The extensive uncut stone altar of Level XIX at Megiddo was rigged with stairs on the east, presumably to allow priestly access for rites, possibly of sacrifice. The unmortared but carefully built stone walls of the Early Bronze Age temple at Ai (et Tell), its plastered interior wall faces, and the saw-cut pillar bases down the center of the nave for roof support all indicate that construction and decorative technique, while elaborate for Palestine, was yet far removed from the upper reaches of the skills of neighboring lands. The Late Bronze Age temple at Shechem, with its fragment of a sacred pillar and mount, and its use of walls the stone foundations of which were 17 feet thick, attests the utilitarian mind that in later biblical tradition attributed the local use of the building to that of treasury as well as shrine (Judg. 9:4), and possibly even of haven (Judg. 9:46).

Housing for ordinary folk was modest in most periods. One or two courses of stone used as foundations for single or two-storied mudbrick structures may have been one-room units or two- to four-room units incorporating an open or partly roofed courtyard in which the cooking hearth, storage vessels for water, and sometimes other goods were placed. Decoration of such dwellings was modest or nonexistent. Roofs were flat layered earth or crude plaster supported by a framework of timbers sometimes with vertical posts of stone or wood for excessively long spans. The walls may have been faced with mud plaster which, as the roofs, needed annual refacing due to weathering and other wear and tear.

Fragment of a sacred pillar from the temple at Shechem, Late Bronze Age (1500–1200 B.C.).

Israelite Achievements: The rise of the Israelites to dominance in the early Iron Age reflects their adoption of Canaanite architecture in reuse of defenses and extremely modest indigenous construction. With the rise of a United Monarchy (tenth century B.C.) and its brief divided survival prior to invasion by Assyria in the eighth century, the flower of Israelite architectural achievement was reached. Credit for this in the biblical record is given to Solomon. His touted achievements include the construction of store-cities (1 Kings 9:19), rebuilt cities (1 Kings 9:17), chariot cities (1 Kings 9:19), special palaces for his wives (1 Kings 9:24) and for himself (1 Kings 7:1), special units like the House of the Forest of Lebanon (1 Kings 7:2–5), the Hall of Pillars (1 Kings 7:6), and the Hall of the Throne (1 Kings 7:7), fortifications for cities (1 Kings 9:15), and most famously the Temple of Yahweh in Jerusalem (1 Kings 6:1–38), reportedly a seven-year project in the construction phase. Of this vast enterprise, nothing has survived archaeologically of the Temple or palace materials, but evidences of the fortifications of cities, both those mentioned (Megiddo, Hazor, and Gezer) and others (like Shechem) have been abundant and are impressive.

Solomonic gateways were constructed of cut stone, usually paved, and rigged with interior step barriers allowing the packing of defenders at each of as many as four internal partitions to keep people from reaching the interior access gate. The gates were flanked with towers allowing three-way crossfire against intruders. The width of the gate was sufficient only to allow one chariot, or in peacetime one cart, abreast. The skilled stonecutting evident in some of these structures suggests that the lessons learned from the Phoenician craftsmen brought in to build the Temple were applied well and broadly throughout the construction program.

The best example of an Israelite temple is that excavated at Arad. Threefold separation of internal space, an altar of uncut stone and earth, bases of sacred pillars, and two incense altars match numerous biblical descriptions for such design and furnishing.

The palace tradition survived in the facilities built by northern monarchs Omri (885–873 B.C.) and Ahab (873–851 B.C.) at Samaria. Because it was the earliest architecture on the summit and has been overlaid by extensive later construction of Hellenistic and Herodian buildings, little of the palace walls survived. Eloquent testimony to the affluence of the court is given by extensive inlaid ivory decora-

West guardroom of the gate fortification at Gezer, dating from the time of Solomon.

Painted plaster wall and imitation fluted columns in Herod's northern palace at Masada.

tions, over five hundred fragments of which were recovered. Header-stretcher masonry typical of the Solomonic period was still used extensively, and casemate defense wall foundations illustrate that such a design (found also as widely spread as from Hazor to Tell Beit Mirsim) had been found helpful. It proved insufficient, however, against Assyria's forces at Samaria as well as Hazor and elsewhere.

While the land suffered the ravages of Assyria and then of the Neo-Babylonians under Nebuchadnezzar in the eighth and seventh centuries B.C., architecture declined. The destruction of Jerusalem in 587 B.C. was matched by destructions elsewhere in the land (such as depicted on Assyrian reliefs concerning Lachish). Even under Persia's permissive attitudes toward local societies, in the light of which the Jewish return from Exile and the efforts to reconstitute both state and national shrine took place (late sixth–early fifth centuries B.C.), Israel's struggle was simply to survive.

Herod's Construction: With the Hellenistic influences brought in first by Alexander's conquests, then by the successive domination of the Ptolemies, the Seleucids, and the briefly independent Maccabees, new styles became apparent, made most firmly felt by Roman implementation and those who followed such ideological footprints as Herod the Great (40–4 B.C.). Herodian construction was thoroughly Hellenistic, vividly apparent not only in the surviving foundations of the rebuilt Jerusalem Temple compound, but in port cities like Caesarea and Herod's numerous hideaways, notably at Masada. The painted plaster interior walls, fake fluted column faces (plaster laid over stone plinth cores), extensive water cisterns, and other storage buildings serving his three-level, north-point accommodations at Masada bespoke his love of Roman adaptations of Hellenistic motifs, whether in column capitals or decorative affluence.

Palestine's suffering the defeat of the first (A.D. 66–70) and second (A.D. 132–135) Jewish revolts resulted in more distinguished Roman architecture being visible elsewhere in the region. Cities of the Decapolis, such as Gadara (modern Um Qeis), Philadelphia (modern Amman), or other sites such as Jerash and Baalbek are rich with Roman temples, fora, colonnades, theaters, and domestic installations of a wide variety. Tombs of the Roman period are the most lavish both in exterior and interior design, including sealing doors of both swinging and rolling stone types.

A final word pertains to the distinctive architecture of the Nabateans, found not only at their major headquarters of Petra, with the elaborate cave facades, amphitheater, and the distinctive Robinson High Place shrine, but also at other sites. Their mastery of cantilevered roof and stair construction is most evident at modern Umm al-Jimal in the Transjordan desert, giving vivid proof of a unique interior genius. ***See also*** House; Temple, The; Temples. R.S.B.

Arcturus (ahrk-to͞or'uhs), the third brightest star of the Northern Hemisphere (magnitude 0.2). In place of Arcturus (LXX, KJV), RSV translates "Bear" (Job 9:9; 38:32). It is part of constellation Boötes and is in line with the tail of Ursa Major (Great Bear), whence the associated name. Orange colored, it is about forty light-years from the sun.

Ard (ahrd). **1** One of the sons of Benjamin (Gen. 46:21). **2** The son of Bela and grandson of Benjamin (Num. 26:40), called (erroneously?) Adar in 1 Chron. 8:3.

Areopagus (air'ee-ahp'uh-guhs; Gk., "hill of Ares"), a low hill in Athens northwest of the acropolis. The hill had stone seats for the council that met there, the origins of which went back to the advisory council of Athenian kings.

Though the council's political power had declined by the fifth century B.C., it retained jurisdiction over cases of homicide. Paul is said to have spoken on the Areopagus (Acts 17:19, 22) and converted a member of the council, Dionysius (Acts 17:34).

Aretas (ah'ruh-tuhs) **IV,** Nabatean king who greatly expanded his kingdom (9 B.C.–A.D. 40). His governor attempted to seize Paul in Damascus (2 Cor. 11:32). ***See also*** Nabatea, Nabateans.

Argob (ahr'guhb; Heb., "a mound [clod] of earth" or possibly "an area of hills"). **1** A specified region east of the Jordan, either an area within Bashan or simply another name for it. Its precise location is not known. It was identified as the kingdom of Og containing sixty cities and captured by the Israelites before crossing the Jordan (Deut. 3:4). The territory was given to the half-tribe of Manasseh whose leader, Jair, renamed it Havvoth-Jair ("the cities of Jair"; Heb., Deut. 3:13–14). **2** In the Masoretic Text of 2 Kings 15:25, Argob and Arieh are given as coconspirators with Pekah in the assassination of King Pekahiah of Samaria. But since these are both place names, they are probably misplaced from the listing of territories captured by Tiglath-pileser in the following verses (2 Kings 15: 29). ***See also*** Bashan. D.R.B.

Ariel (ahr'e-el). **1** One of the leading men summoned by Ezra (Ezra 8:16). **2** In 2 Sam. 23:20 (1 Chron. 11:22), either a personal name or a common name meaning "heroes" or "altar hearths." **3** A word correctly translated "altar hearth" in the unambiguous context of Ezek. 43:15–16; it probably has the same meaning in the Moabite inscription of king Mesha. **4** A poetic designation for Jerusalem, apparently derived from the presence of Yahweh's main altar there (Isa. 29: 1–2). The plural, translated "valiant ones" in the RSV (Isa. 33:7), probably means "inhabitants of Ariel." J.J.M.R.

Arimathea (air-uh-muh-thee'uh), a hellenized form of the Hebrew *Ramathaim, Ramoth, Ramah;* home of Joseph who buried Jesus in his own tomb (Matt. 27:57–60; Mark 15:42–46; Luke 23:50–53; John 19:38–42). Arimathea is variously identified with modern Rentis (fifteen miles east of Jaffa), er-Ram (five miles north of Jerusalem), or el-Birah-Ramallah (eight miles north of Jerusalem). ***See also*** Joseph.

Arioch (ahr'ee-ahkh). **1** The king of Ellasar who, in alliance with the kings of Shinar, Elam, and Goiim, raided the area around the Dead Sea, including Sodom and the Cities of the Plain, and took Lot prisoner. He and the other kings were defeated by Abram and his allies (Gen. 14:1–16). **2** The captain of King Nebuchadnezzar's guard who was instructed to kill all the wise men of Babylon because they could not interpret the king's dream. He later brought Daniel before the king (Dan. 2:14–15; 24–25).

Aristarchus (air-is-tahr'kuhs), according to Acts a native of Thessalonica and a companion of Paul in Ephesus, on the final trip to Jerusalem, and on the voyage to Rome (Acts 19:29; 20:4–5; 27:2). It was very probably the same Aristarchus who was Paul's fellow prisoner, perhaps in Ephesus (Philem. 24; cf. Col. 4:10).

ark, a container of indeterminate size. In the OT, "ark" translates two Hebrew words, *tebah* and *aron,* both of which mean "box" or "chest." The former is used only for Noah's ark (Gen. 6–9) and for the ark of bulrushes in which Moses was placed (Exod. 2:3, 5). The latter designates a coffin (Gen. 50:26) and a chest (2 Kings 12:9), but it is usually employed for a religious object, called the Ark of Yahweh or the Ark of God in early sources, the Ark of the covenant in typically Deuteronomic language (Deut. 10:8), and the Ark of the testimony in priestly material (Num. 4:5).

Originally, the characteristic feature of the Ark was that it could be carried about. Portable shrines are known from Egypt and Mesopotamia and also from Canaan, where examples have been found decorated with cherubim, like those that eventually sheltered the Israelite Ark (1 Kings 8:6–7). The pre-Islamic Arabs had a portable tent-shrine, the *qubba,* which contained two sacred stones, was in the charge of a religious officiant, was used for divination, and was taken into battle. The Israelite Ark led the people in the desert (Num. 10:33), was carried round the walls of Jericho (Josh. 6), and was brought into the camp during military operations (1 Sam. 4:2–4). It was kept in a tent (2 Sam. 6:17) with an attendant (1 Sam. 7:1) and used for oracular enquiries (1 Sam. 14:18). According to biblical tradition, the Ark contained the two tablets of the law (Deut. 10:2, 5), but the wording of 1 Kings 8:9 suggests that it may once have held something else, perhaps the two stones that formed the sacred lots, Urim and Thummim.

The most striking fact about the Ark at an early period was that it was a direct manifestation of God's presence and was virtually identified with him. Moses addressed the Ark as God (Num. 10:35–36), the Philistines equated the Ark with a god (1 Sam. 4:6–8), and those who desecrated the Ark were struck down by its divine power (1 Sam. 6:19; 2 Sam. 6:6–7). When we find the expression "before God" in a sanctuary context, this often seems to refer to the Ark.

It is possible that at one time various sanctuaries each had their own Arks, but the one that becomes central in the OT is that of the Shiloh temple, where it had probably already become a national symbol of the tribal confederacy. From the so-called history of the Ark (1 Sam. 4:1–7:2), we learn of its capture by the Philistines, its devastating power in their territory, its triumphant return to Israel, and its concealment at Kiriath-jearim for some twenty years of Philistine occupation. After defeating the Philistines, David brought it from there and installed it in his new capital, Jerusalem, as part of his policy of uniting the tribes under his rule (2 Sam. 6). This event was probably reenacted annually, with Psalm 132 as the liturgy of the festival.

A decisive step in the story of the Ark came when it was transferred into the Holy of Holies of Solomon's new Temple (1 Kings 8:4–7). From this time onward, it remains stationary and is viewed as a throne, on which God sits as an invisible deity above the two guardian cherubim (2 Kings 19:15). The belief that God resided permanently in the darkness of the Holy of Holies (1 Kings 8:12–13) led to the doctrine of the inviolability of the Temple and Jerusalem.

The Ark was destroyed or captured in the Babylonian sack of Jerusalem in 586 B.C. Whether there was one in the second Temple is uncertain. In Jer. 3:15, which may well be postexilic and is the only reference to the Ark in all the prophetic literature, Jerusalem replaces the Ark as God's throne. There is no mention of the Ark in the detailed vision of the new temple in Ezekiel 40–48, and a later Jewish legend tells of its being hidden until a remote future at the time of the Exile (2 Macc. 2:4–8). On the other hand, there is an Ark in the Priestly account of the tabernacle, which is in many respects an image of the Second Temple; in any case, the Ark holds an important place in Priestly theology. By now it has become an elaborate, gold-plated object (Exod. 25:10–15). But it is only a container for the "testimony," the tablets of the law (Exod. 25:16), and interest is focused on the gold "mercy seat" or cover on top of it. This is now God's throne, where he appears in a cloud (Lev. 16:2) to communicate his will (Exod. 25:17–22). As the Hebrew term *kapporeth* suggests, this was also the place where atonement was made, supremely by the sprinkling of blood on the Day of Atonement (Lev. 16:14–16). It is this representation of the ark that is found in Heb. 9:3–5 (cf. Rom. 3:25), which also reflects later Jewish tradition that, as well as the tablets of the law, it contained the manna (Exod. 16:33–34) and Aaron's miraculous rod (Num. 17:10). ***See also*** Cherub; Tabernacle; Urim and Thummim.

Wagon, which may be a depiction of the Holy Ark, carved in a lintel at the late second–early third century synagogue at Capernaum.

Bibliography

de Vaux, R. *Ancient Israel: Its Life and Institutions.* New York: McGraw-Hill, 1961. Pp. 297–302.

von Rad, G. *Old Testament Theology.* New York: Harper & Row, 1962. Pp. 234–241.

Woudstra, M. H. *The Ark of the Covenant from Conquest to Kingship.* Philadelphia: Presbyterian and Reformed Publishing Co., 1965. J.R.P.

Armageddon (ahr-muh-ged'duhn; Heb., "Mount Megiddo"). The word occurs only in Rev. 16:16 as a Greek transliteration of the term claimed to be Hebrew. It represents the location of the final cosmic battle of the forces of good and of evil, according to the apocalyptic view of the writer. However, no such term appears elsewhere in Hebrew, and there is no mountain known to ancient or modern geographers by that name. The spelling of the term differs in various manuscripts (Harmagedon, Armagedon, Maged[d]on). Translations suggested therefore have included "city of Megiddo," "land of Megiddo," "mount of assembly," "city of desire," and "his fruitful mountain."

Megiddo, situated at the north end of the major pass through the Mount Carmel range where the coastal road moved up from the south into the Plain of Esdraelon, was the site of many well-known ancient battles (Deborah and Barak versus the Canaanite king Sisera, Judg. 5:19; Jehu versus Ahaziah, 2 Kings 9:27; Josiah versus Neco, 2 Kings 23:29). The archaeological data reinforce the literary portrait in showing frequent extremely heavy defense facilities at the site. It may have appeared, therefore, an excellent symbol to the apocalyptic writer for the ultimate conflict he saw as the culmination of history. R.S.B.

arms, armor, implements for war. The vocabulary for arms in the Bible is used in contexts ranging from literal description to metaphor. Already in Gen. 14:13–16 there is an account of Abraham's retainers, or trained men, whose success in battle presupposes their efficient use of arms. In tribal societies like that of early Israel arms consisted of spears, swords, sling stones, and bows and arrows. Armor is known from Egyptian reliefs from the mid-second millennium B.C., but it is first referred to in

Israel when Saul offered David his armor to use in the upcoming combat with Goliath. The Philistine's own armor was considerable: a bronze helmet, a bronze coat of mail, and bronze leglets or greaves. In addition, he carried a sword and a spear and was accompanied by a shield bearer (1 Sam. 17:5–7).

All of Goliath's armor except the greaves was paralleled among Israelite forces. Ahab had a coat of scales (mail) according to 1 Kings 22:34, and apparently construction workers rebuilding Jerusalem during Nehemiah's governorship wore protective armor (Neh. 4:16). To protect themselves these workers also had spears, shields, and bows. Bronze armor was used for royalty, but leather for shields and perhaps body armor was more common for foot soldiers.

Armor is mentioned often in contexts other than war or narrative description. It can be the subject of a proverbial saying (1 Kings 20:11), the object of God's power (Ps. 46:9), and arms transformed can be the basis for a new social order (Isa. 2:1–4; Mic. 4:1–5). Thus NT writers had some precedent for such metaphorical language as the "full armor of God," which includes such things as the "breastplate of righteousness" and the "helmet of salvation" (Eph. 6:13–17), and the word of God being "sharper than any two-edged sword" (Heb. 4: 12).

Jesus' references to arms are few but not without surprises, as evidenced by his somber proverb concerning those who wield swords (Matt. 26:52), the nature of his mission (Matt. 10:34), or his sarcasm over the sword's effectiveness (Luke 22:38). In Rev. 1:16 the risen Christ is described as one from whose mouth extends a sword, a metaphor for his role in carrying out divine vengeance and judgment.

J.A.D.

army, an organized fighting force. Although there was no standing army in ancient Israel until the monarchy, Abraham rallied 318 followers to rescue his relatives who had been captured by a coalition of kings (Gen. 14). Loosely bonded clans also cooperated against a common foe (Exod. 17:8–13). In the tribal federation a people's militia served the Lord of Hosts (Heb. "Yahweh Sabaoth") on call by a leader, judge, or field commander. The local muster unit (as few as six men) was, in Hebrew, the *'aleph* (easily confused with the word for "thousand," which has the same spelling). God was commander-in-chief of the army; his divine will was ascertained by oracles.

Saul added a bodyguard of "three thousand" (three exceptionally large units?) responsible to himself and Jonathan, and later to Abner, as commander (1 Sam. 13:2; 17:55). Abner's counterpart under the reign of David was Joab. Mercenaries in David's bodyguard (2 Sam. 8: 18; 15:19–22) supported the southern throne, in contrast with a tumultuous dynastic sequence in the north. Solomon introduced chariotry. Under the monarchy the army became highly organized, and warfare was greatly routinized.

After the fall of the two kingdoms (Israel in 721 B.C., Judah in 587 B.C.), only foreign armies appear in the OT, until guerrilla warfare (Maccabees) achieved national independence ca. 165 B.C. The new standing army included Jewish and non-Jewish soldiers. Herod the Great patterned his organization on Roman models, with mercenaries from as far away as Germany and Gaul. Roman features are also evident in the description of the army found in an apocalyptic text from the Dead Sea sectarians, the so-called *Scroll of the War of the Sons of Light against the Sons of Darkness*. Although the NT recalls OT feats of arms (Heb. 11:34), the armies mentioned are either Roman (Luke 21:20; see Acts 23:27) or supernatural (Rev. 9:16; 19:14, 19). R.B.

Arnon, the River (modern name Wadi el-Mojib), a river whose water flows from the east into the Dead Sea at about the midpoint of its eastern shore. As a deep gorge, it made north–south travel difficult in Transjordan. The river has a substantial northern tributary that flows southwesterly and feeds into the main artery of the river just before the main channel empties into the Dead Sea. Dibon, the Moabite capital under Mesha, is located north of the main branch but south of the northern tributary. On several occasions the Arnon is mentioned as a boundary (Num. 21:24; Judg. 11:18; Deut. 3:8, 16; Josh. 13:16). It is also mentioned in line 26 of the Mesha Inscription. ***See also*** Moabite Stone, The. J.A.D.

Aroer (ah-roh'uhr). **1** A fortress on the Arnon River's northern rim, the southern limit of Amorite (Deut. 2:36), Reubenite-Gadite (Deut. 3:12), Davidic (2 Sam. 24:5), and Syrian (2 Kings 10: 33) activities in Transjordan. Excavations at modern Khirbet Ara'ir have uncovered fortifications from Mesha's day (mid-ninth century B.C.; cf. Moabite Stone). The last reference to Aroer identifies it as Moabite (Jer. 48:19–20). **2** A town in southern Judah (1 Sam. 30:28), modern Khirbet Ar'areh. **3** An Ammonite settlement near Rabbah (Josh. 13:25). ***See also*** Arnon, The River; Gad; Mesha; Moab; Moabite Stone, The; Reuben.

Arpachshad (ahr-pak'shad), the name of the son of Shem born after the Flood and grandfather of Eber, in the line of Abraham (Gen. 11: 10). The term is probably geographic in origin. Context suggests it was in Mesopotamia, and later tradition locates it near Babylon; however, the exact reference is not known.

Arphaxad (ahr'pax-ad). ***See*** Arpachshad.

Artaxerxes (ahr-tuh-zerk'sees; Heb. *Ar-takhshast*), the name of four known Achaemenid (Persian) kings: Artaxerxes I (Longimanus), 465–424 B.C.; Artaxerxes II (Arsakes), 405/4–359/58; Artaxerxes III (Ochos), 359/58–338/37; Artaxerxes IV (Arses), 338/37–36. Identifications of these kings in the OT text depend on historical probability. The name appears in Ezra 4:7, 8, 11, and 23, in a composite passage that is out of chronological context (4:6–23); 4:8–23 refers to appeals to Artaxerxes against Jewish activity in Jerusalem. The usual assumption is that all these refer to Artaxerxes I. Ezra 6:14 adds Artaxerxes after Cyrus and Darius in a list of Persian rulers. Ezra 7:1–8:1 has several references, all to the period of Ezra's activity. Scholarly opinion is divided between Artaxerxes I and II. Neh. 2:1; 5:14; and 13:6, connected with Nehemiah's two periods as governor, are most often held to refer to Artaxerxes I, though Artaxerxes II cannot be ruled out. Persian desire to control Egypt may have provided the political context for the appointment of both Ezra and Nehemiah regardless of which Persian ruler was responsible. ***See also*** Ezra; Nehemiah, The Book of. P.R.A.

Artemas (ahr'tuh-muhs), a companion of Paul mentioned only in Titus 3:12. ***See also*** Tychicus.

Artemis (ahr'tuh-muhs) **of the Ephesians** (KJV: "Diana"), a goddess widely worshiped in antiquity throughout the Hellenistic and Roman world. Although identified with the Greek Artemis (and the Roman Diana), the sister of Apollo, the Ephesian Artemis had little in common with those deities of classical mythology. Rather, she was more the ancient Anatolian and Asian mother goddess known also as Cybele, Atargatis, and Ashtoreth—a patroness of nature and fertility.

The cult of the mother goddess in a primitive shrine near the mouth of the Cayster River at the northern foot of Mt. Pion in western Asia Minor long antedated the settlement of the first Greeks in the area ca. 1000 B.C. Acts 19:35 refers to a "sacred stone that fell from the sky," possibly a meteorite, but the image of the goddess known in NT times appears to date only from the fourth century B.C. The goddess is portrayed with numerous breasts (eggs?) as symbols of fertility, a turret crown, and a long skirt with bands of animals and birds in relief. She is often accompanied by dogs or stags on either side, probably due to the syncretism with the original Greek Artemis.

The earliest Greek shrine, consisting of two platforms, was eclipsed ca. 600 B.C. with the construction of the Archaic Artemision, or Temple of Artemis, over the site. The Cretan architect Chersiphron constructed a massive temple (375 × 180 feet) with 60-foot marble columns, the work being completed ca. 500 B.C.

Ancient cultic statute of Artemis of the Ephesians.

This temple burned on the night of Alexander the Great's birth in 356 B.C., but a new Artemision was soon begun by the architect Dinocrates and completed ca. 250 B.C., one of the Seven Wonders of the World. It was destroyed by the Goths in A.D. 263 and practically nothing of it remains today.

Opinion varies concerning the miniature shrines that provided the livelihood of Demetrius and his fellow silversmiths (see Acts 19:23–41), as to whether they represented the original primitive shrine or the Hellenistic Artemision. The struggle between the followers of Christ and of Artemis continued even after the destruction of the Artemision, according to a fifth-century inscription mentioning the replacement of a statue of the goddess by a cross. ***See also*** Asherah; Demetrius; Ephesus; Paul; Shrine; Smith; Syncretism. M.K.M.

artificer. ***See*** Craftsman.

Art in the Biblical Period

WHILE THE BIBLICAL PERIOD properly extends from at least the Middle Bronze Age (2000–1500 B.C.) to the Greco-Roman period of the first century A.D., the artistic influence that affected Palestine was fundamentally Eastern, not Western. Therefore, this article focuses on ancient Near Eastern art, especially that of Egypt and Assyria–Babylonia. Just as these major civilizations dominated the economics and politics of Syro-Palestine, they provide the backdrop against which Israel's art and that of its neighbors must be seen.

Egyptian Art: Egyptian theology determined the style and content, as well as setting, for Egyptian art. The major repositories of art from the Old Kingdom (ca. 2700 B.C.) to the eve of the Hellenistic period (ca. 350 B.C.) are tombs and temples. Art and architecture served the needs of the afterlife, primarily for the pharaoh, the divine king, and his family, but also for nobles and ordinary citizens. The earliest tombs, from which the later step pyramids probably developed, were low, squat mastabas, rectangular brick structures comprised of many internal compartments built over the actual subterranean burial chamber. Since these tombs were also temples, the structure provided for a chapel and niche for a statue of the deceased and offering tables upon which gifts for the spirit of the deceased could be placed. The walls of the tomb-temple were covered with bas-reliefs and paintings depicting scenes

Ancient Egyptian banquet scene. Female musicians with harp and stringed instruments, from the tomb of Rekhmera, Thebes.

Bust of monumental statue of the ancient Egyptian pharaoh Akhenaton, from Karnak, fourteenth century B.C.

from the life of the deceased. By the New Kingdom (1550–1100 B.C.) rock-cut chambers had been adopted as burial places for kings and commoners, and the kings were buried, for security reasons, at some distance from their mortuary buildings, which were now magnificent temples dedicated to the memory of the divine king and the supreme god, Amon.

Like the buildings, the bas-reliefs and paintings that adorn the New Kingdom tombs had developed from the rather austere scenes of the Old Kingdom, in which the deceased was depicted receiving offerings from the devout who paraded before him on horizontal registers in rather lifeless, frozen form. The New Kingdom scenes depict luxurious living; the offering scene has become a banquet. By contrast with themes painted elsewhere in the ancient Near East, Egyptian artists rendered events from the private and family life of the deceased, including fishing or hunting trips, dances, and games. Boldly the artists projected these scenes of enjoyment and pleasure, drawn from this life, into the next life, so that past and future were fully merged on the tomb walls.

Statuary, like painting, also served the cause of the next life. In the Old Kingdom, the statues were designed to represent the deceased, providing a perpetual image with which the spirit of the deceased could be identified. This task gave the statuary its distinctive character: it had to offer an ideal representation, since the pharaoh was also a god, and yet the image had to be personal, identifiable with the dead king whose memory it preserved. Egyptian artists succeeded to a remarkable degree in this effort to create individuality and personality within rather rigid formal constraints. By the New Kingdom, statuary had become merely monumental, official memorials to the deceased. Style was basically continuous with the Old Kingdom until the reign of Akhenaton (1369–1353 B.C.), whose radical concern for realism broke the tension with the ideal form, resulting in a kind of caricature that went beyond the limits of "realism," exemplified in some thirty statues of this apostate pharaoh found at Karnak. Akhenaton's successors returned to the classical style, yet the effect of the brief revolution in style was not altogether lost. The return to the classical style, however, was more characteristically marked by a penchant for elegance, often devoid of inspiration.

Minor arts from Egypt, of which we have some fine examples, include wood furniture from as early as the Old Kingdom, glassware from the Middle Kingdom onward, and well-modeled bronzes, and fine jewelry.

Bronze head of a king, possibly Sargon of Akkad, from Nineveh, third millennium B.C.

Assyrian and Babylonian Art: Assyrian art is the heir of Sumerian invention from the third millennium B.C. The sense of struggle against a hostile environment, fraught with threats both natural and supernatural, from which protection must be sought by placating the gods and fielding an army dominates artistic style and content. The confident celebration of life so prominent in Egyptian art is absent from that of Mesopotamia. Here one senses the significant distance between the gods and humankind. The king is not divine but can only hope for the favor of the gods, before whom he, as all others, must bow.

Ziggurats or "temple towers" continued in the Assyrian period to exemplify the distance between earth and heaven. They were at-

Ashurbanipal hunting lions from his chariot; bas-reliefs at Nineveh.

tached to a number of temples, though not all, and graphically represented the mountain home of the Assyrian storm god. The Assyrian architecture seems to have modified the earlier forms by removing the open, external stairways to the top in favor of a less obvious means of approach, in some cases directly from a neighboring temple roof.

At the center of Assyrian cities, however, stood the royal palace. Again developing a Sumerian model, the palaces of the great kings multiplied the courtyards and adjoining buildings enclosed within the complex. The palace at Mari, for example, dated to the beginning of the second millennium B.C., included more than two hundred and sixty rooms and courtyards spread over some 6 acres.

The palace provided the setting for the type of art most characteristic of Assyria: the low relief. Beginning in the ninth century B.C., when Ashurnasirpal II moved the capital from Assur to Nimrud, Assyrian artists began to fill the walls of the palace rooms with reliefs. Authorities generally regard this innovation as the greatest and most original achievement of Assyrian art. The subject of these carved friezes was the king and his exploits, particularly his victories over ever rebelling vassals. The power of the king was conveyed by the sheer overpowering experience of being completely surrounded by reliefs depicting the unending accomplishments of the monarch. In the beginning, these friezes were usually about 7 feet high, sometimes the whole surface being covered in a single design. More often, however, the wall was divided into two registers, separated by a band of cuneiform inscriptions. In later buildings, for example, Sargon's palace at Khorsabad (late eighth century B.C.), individual sculptured figures even reach a height of 9 feet. These huge figures are more representational than narrative, as they march in awesome procession —the king and his courtiers—defying any challenge to authority and disparaging any doubt about the stability of the throne. For the most part, however, the wall reliefs were intended to function as narrative art, depicting in stone what the annals attested in writing. The work was highly detailed and skillfully planned, marked by stylistic vitality, especially in the depiction of animals where musculature and a sense of motion was well developed.

Winged sphinx. Carved ivory and gold from Nimrud, eighth–seventh century B.C.

During the reign of Shalmaneser III (858–24 B.C.) this new relief style was applied to metal work. The huge doors of a palace near Nimrud were covered with horizontal bands of bronze, each 11 inches in height

Ishtar Gate, two mythical creatures. Enameled tile and ceramic brick reconstruction of the processional entrance to Babylon during the time of Nebuchadnezzar, sixth century B.C.

and 8 feet in length. The subjects of these reliefs, like their stone counterparts, were historical; processional scenes were particularly well suited to the narrow registers.

Not all the themes of the Assyrian mural reliefs were military. From the time of Assurbanipal (668–627 B.C.) we have magnificent hunting scenes, vividly portraying dramatic action, with full, sensitive expression of the suffering and death of the victims as well as the power and prowess of the hunter. A comparison of the "Lion Hunt" scenes of Ashurbanipal at the end of the Assyrian period with a similar portrayal of Ashurnasirpal II at the beginning of the period reveals just how well developed and mature the art of relief sculpture had become over two centuries of refinement.

Statuary in Assyria was relatively insignificant, continuing the cylindrical style and impersonal features of Sumerian sculpture. The exception is a kind of statuary that is neither relief nor 'in the round." Stone slabs, called "orthostats," were set in the entry way to Sargon's palace and the citadel at Khorsabad and carved into winged, human-headed bulls. Those at the citadel were 13 feet high and 14 feet long, and they stared menacingly at all who approached the precincts. They were protective guardians, like their much earlier Hittite predecessors, the lion orthostats at Boghazköy.

Among the minor arts represented in Assyria, most notable are cylinder seals, which show the same care for detail and preference for animals and landscape as the reliefs. In the late period, stamps were also molded, but their designs offer nothing new. Cylinder seals remained dominant, providing rich opportunity for personal design and expression. Finally, there are ivories, sculptured and engraved, reflecting exquisite skill and precision. The Nimrud ivories are perhaps the best-known examples. Their style and content, however, raises a difficult question concerning whether they really represent

Lion orthostat from the temple at Hazor, probably Late Bronze Age (1500–1200 B.C.).

Assyrian art or, as appears more likely, the distribution throughout the empire of Phoenician ivory.

Babylonian art from the sixth century B.C. did not continue the Assyrian style. Instead, it appears to return to the style of pre-Assyrian days, reviving the southern Mesopotamian traditions. Buildings were mudbrick, ornamented with glazed bricks upon which huge bulls and dragons were depicted in bright colors. These beasts, however, by contrast with the gate-guardians of the Assyrians, were purely decorative, as their profile images attest, for example, on the Ishtar Gate. Notably, too, Babylonians provide us with an example of figures in true profile, as seen on the boundary stone of Marduk-apalaiddina (714 B.C.). Finally, we have cylinder seals and a number of rather artless terracottas from the period of Nebuchadnezzar.

Syrian and Palestinian Art: The style and content we met in Egypt or Mesopotamia occurs again in Syria and Palestine. Since the area provided the corridor for trade and warfare between East and West, it should come as no surprise to find that the art of the region betrays the influence of the dominant cultures. To be sure, artistic efforts did not merely ape their sources. For example, figurines are more narrow-shouldered than their Egyptian counterparts and generally less substantial. A stele portraying the weather god found at Ras-Shamra (Ugarit) shows the figure with raised arm in a gesture depicting victory, typical of Egyptian reliefs, yet the god wears typical Syrian garb, including a horned cap symbolic of his divinity.

Large statuary of human figures is rare, but statuettes depicting fertility figures are numerous. These are typically nude female figures with exaggerated breasts and, often, hands raised toward the breasts. The orthostat animal sculptures of the Hittites have already been mentioned. Stone carving of excellent quality has also been found in the Late Bronze Age temple at Hazor. Relief carving is also plentiful,

Judean royal stamp-seal impression with symbol of a solar disk with wings, seventh century B.C. At top are the letters *lmlk* and below, the place name *zp*, "Ziph."

Golden dish from Ras-Shamra, detail of a hunter in his chariot pursuing a wild bull, fourteenth century B.C.

and especially noteworthy is a finely worked golden dish from Ras-Shamra bearing a hammered design of a hunter riding his chariot in pursuit of wild bulls and gazelles.

Finally we may speak briefly of Israelite art. Like the rest of Syro-Palestine, Israel drew her artistic efforts from Egyptian and Mesopotamian models. As elsewhere in the ancient Near East, religious conviction determined the character and extent of Israelite artistic enterprise. Since the Torah expressly forbade the shaping of images and idols, the subjects that dominated sculpture and painting among its neighbors were not available to Israel. All that remains that may be described as Israelite, in fact, are minor arts, namely, ivories and stamp seals. Seals were particularly numerous and clearly show Egyptian influence in subject matter, being decorated with griffons, sphinxes, scarabs, and solar disks with wings. These seals were purely decorative, as the frequent inclusion of the owner's name indicates. They were mostly scarab in shape, in imitation of the Egyptian beetle, and made of semiprecious stones. Name seals, without any pictorial representation, have been found almost exclusively in Judah.

Ivories have been found at Megiddo, Samaria, and Hazor. The dominant influence on these pieces, too, was Egyptian, as the examples from Samaria showing a cherub astride a plant and the child-god Horus crouching upon a lotus indicate. The style of these ivories is Phoenician, and we may be sure that they have come to Israel through that well attested channel of trade and technical expertise (see 1 Kings 5–10).

The discovery of Astarte figurines in sites as separated as Megiddo and Hebron confirms the prophets' protest against the popularity of the "Queen of Heaven" as a fertility figure in Israel (Jer. 7:18; 44:17–19, 25). Some statuettes show influence from Egypt, with Astarte holding lotus flowers; others reflect a Babylonian style represented by the inclusion of a tiara.

Though nothing remains of Solomon's Temple, a detailed description of its floor-plan and furniture is provided by biblical tradition. Moreover, the tradition makes no claims to originality in this architectural effort; Solomon relied on Phoenician expertise. The resulting rectangular, tripartite plan was already well known in Egypt.

Bibliography

Frankfort, Henri. *The Art and Architecture of the Ancient Orient*. 4th impression. London: Penguin Books, 1969.

Lloyd, Seton. *The Art of the Ancient Near East*. New York: Praeger, 1961.

Moscati, Sabatino. *The Face of the Ancient Orient*. Garden City, NY: Doubleday, Anchor Books, 1962.

D.C.H.

Two winged genii with Horus in the center on a lotus. Ivory plaque from Arslan Tash, northern Syria, eighth century B.C.

Arumah (ah-ro͞o'mah), the town where Abimelech, temporary king of Shechem, resided (Judg. 9:31, 41). It was probably modern Khirbet el-Ormeh, about five miles south and slightly east of Shechem and about seven miles north and slightly east of Shiloh.

Arvad (ahr'vad), a north Phoenician island city located two miles from shore about 125 miles north of Tyre, known today as Ruad. Its inhabitants are listed among the pre-Israelite descendants of Canaan (Gen. 10:18) and are mentioned in Ezek. 27:8, 11 as having served under Tyre. The city is also known to have existed in Hasmonean times (1 Macc. 15:23).

Asa (ay'suh), the fifth king of the Davidic dynasty. Asa ruled Judah for a comparatively long period, ca. 913–873 B.C. In the beginning, his grandmother Maacha (a daughter of Absalom) probably acted as regent. The continual border conflicts between the Northern Kingdom, Israel, and Judah in the region of the tribe Benjamin, which are clear evidence of the extent to which the disruption of Judah and Israel after Solomon constituted a national trauma, did not come to an end. Asa's main opponent was Baasha, who ruled in Tirzah ca. 909–886. When this king of Israel fortified the strategically situated Ramah (only five miles north of Jerusalem) and thus tried to impose a blockade on the Judean capital, Asa decided to have recourse to the treasury and to call upon the help of Ben-hadad I, the king of Damascus. The plan succeeded, for Ben-hadad's army played havoc in Galilee and Baasha was forced to retreat. In his turn, Asa enlarged the villages of Gebah and Mizpah (a few miles east and north of Ramah, respectively) and rebuilt them as fortifications. The editor of the book of Kings appreciated Asa as a strict worshiper of Yahweh who forbade the fertility cults of Asherah and Baal (see 1 Kings 15:9–24). ***See also*** Baasha; Ramah. J.P.F.

Asahel (as'uh-hel). **1** David's nephew (1 Chron. 1:13–16), killed by Abner (2 Sam. 2:18–23), buried in Bethlehem (2:32). He served in David's royal bodyguard (23:24). **2** Judean Levite under Jehoshaphat (2 Chron. 17:8). **3** Temple overseer under Hezekiah (2 Chron. 31:13). **4** Jonathan's father during Ezra's administration (Ezra 10:15).

Asaph (ay'saf; Heb., "collector"). **1** The father of the Joah who was recorder in the court of King Hezekiah of Judah (727–698 B.C.; 2 Kings 18:18). **2** A musician who was among those whom David appointed to oversee music in worship (1 Chron. 6:39), and who sang at the dedication of Solomon's Temple (2 Chron. 5:12). A number of psalms were also attributed to him (Pss. 50, 73–83). **3** A Levite whose descendants lived in Judah after the Exile (1 Chron. 9:15). **4** A Levite whose descendants served as gatekeepers in the Temple (1 Chron. 26:1). **5** The keeper of the forests of King Artaxerxes of Persia, who was comanded by royal letter to furnish timber for Nehemiah's restoration of the Temple (mid to late sixth century B.C.; Neh. 2:8).

ascension of Christ, the, the risen Jesus' departure into heaven after his final appearance to his disciples. It is described only in Acts 1:2–11, although there may be a different and shorter version in Luke 24:50–51 and allusions to it elsewhere in the NT (e.g., John 6:62; 20:17; Eph. 4:8–10). In the setting of Acts, the ascension is preparatory to the sending of the Spirit at Pentecost (2:1–4). The forty-day interval (1:3) is probably symbolic, as this number is frequently used to denote indefinite periods of time. The setting for the ascension has traditionally been regarded as the Mount of Olives. For possible OT precedents, note the "translation" of Enoch (Gen. 5:24) and the "assumption" of Elijah (2 Kings 2:1–14); in the intertestamental period, similar stories appeared regarding other ancient figures. ***See also*** Elijah; Enoch; Holy Spirit, The; Olives, Mount of; Pentecost; Resurrection.

J.M.E.

Asenath (as'en-ath), the daughter of Potipherah, priest of On (Heliopolis) in Egypt. Pharaoh gave her in marriage to Joseph (Gen. 41:45). Their two sons were Manasseh and Ephraim (Gen. 41:50–52; 46:20).

Ashan (ay'shuhn), a city in the southern lowlands of Judah, first given to the tribe of Judah (Josh. 15:42) and later reassigned to the tribe of Simeon because they were unable to conquer the territory originally given to them (Josh. 19:7). It is possibly the same city listed as a city of refuge and given to the Levites (1 Chron. 6:59), although it is elsewhere called Ain (Josh. 21:16). The site is not known.

Ashbel (ash-bel), the (second?) son of Benjamin (Gen. 46:21; 1 Chron. 8:1).

Ashdod (ash'dahd), a town in northern Judah two and a half miles inland from the Mediterranean coast. We know from the Ugaritic material that Ashdod, Accho, and Ashkelon dealt with Ugarit (Ras-Shamra) and hence existed as a city as early as the fourteenth century B.C. The city is supposed to have been allotted to Judah (Josh. 15:47); however, it was also one of the cities in the Philistine Pentapolis (Josh. 11:22; 13:3) and hence may never have come under Judah's control. The Ark of the Covenant was brought to the temple of Dagon in Ashdod when it was taken by the Philistines. The Ark was later sent away (1 Sam. 5:1–8; 6:17).

The city was broken down by King Uzziah (ca. 783–742 B.C.) of Judah (2 Chron. 26:6).

Ashdod later fell to Sargon, king of Assyria (Isa. 20:1). Subsequently Azuri, the reigning king of Ashdod, was dethroned and replaced by his brother in 712 B.C. due to the revolt of Ashdod against the Assyrian domination. Nevertheless, a year later Iammi and Sargon had to suppress another Ashdod rebellion. This time the town was annexed to the Assyrian Empire. According to the Greek historian Herodotus (2.157) the Egyptian pharaoh Psamtik attacked the city after the demise of the Assyrian Empire in the west. Ashdod worked to keep Jerusalem a weak power in the Persian period (ca. 538–333 B.C.; Neh. 13:23–24). During the Hellenistic period (333–63 B.C.) the name was changed to Azotus. Jonathan the Hasmonean destroyed the temple of Dagon (1 Macc. 10:84). Azotus subsequently came under the control of John Hyrcanus still later and it was held by Alexander Jannaeus (Josephus *Antiquities* 13.395). Pompey and Galbinius partitioned it from Judea (Josephus *Wars* 1.156, 165–66).

Augustus gave the city to Herod, who in turn gave it to his sister Salome (ca. A.D. 38). Vespasian marched on the city in the first Jewish revolt (A.D. 66–70). The evangelist Philip is reported to have passsed through the city on his missionary travels (Acts 8:40). S.B.R.

Asher (ash'uhr; Heb., "happy"). **1** Son of Jacob and Zilpah (Gen. 30:12–13) and the eponymous ancestor of the tribe Asher. The name may derive from that of a god, the male counterpart of Asherah or a variant of Ashar, a divine name element in Old Akkadian and Amorite names. **2** The western highlands of Galilee, which constituted the ninth Solomonic district (1 Kings 4:16). The Blessings of Jacob (Gen. 49:20) and of Moses (Deut. 33:24–25) allude to the fertility of Asher's land. Asher failed to participate in the battle against Sisera (Judg. 5:17), but responded to Gideon's calls to expel the Midianites (Judg. 6:35; 7:23).

Asherah (ah'sher-ah), a Canaanite goddess, the wife of El according to Ugaritic tradition, but the consort of Baal in Palestine. In the Ugaritic literature she is called "Lady Asherah of the Sea," a title that may signify "she who treads on the sea." Apart from her name, she has other connections with the sea. Her servant is called "fisherman of Lady Asherah of the Sea." A drinking cup from Ras-Shamra seems to portray her underwater.

The cult of Asherah was ancient. Tyre seems to have been a major center for her veneration. Her cult was widely diffused, but combinations with the figures Anat and Astarte and other factors have made its identification problematic. She was called, in addition to Asherah, Elat ("Goddess") and Qudshu ("Holy"). Asherah

A life-size statue, possibly of the Canaanite goddess Asherah, from the ninth century B.C. The OT prophets denounced the cult of Asherah, blaming its following in Israel on the influence of Jezebel.

probably stands behind the Punic goddess Tanit ("She of the Serpent"?).

Asherah plays an important role in the mythological texts from Ras-Shamra in modern northern Syria. The gods are regarded as the children of Asherah and El. As the wife of El, Asherah is called on to intercede with her husband on behalf of the project of building a palace for Baal. Her relationship with Baal is perplexing. Baal's assault on the offspring of Asherah is once narrated, yet Asherah advocates for Baal the role of king and judge among the gods. A Canaanite myth that survives only in a Hittite version ("El, Ashertu, and the Storm God") reveals that Asherah once sought the storm god (Baal) as a lover, a quest achieved with El's approval but to the eventual humiliation of Asherah. In the Ugaritic legend of Kirta (Keret), Asherah receives a vow from Kirta, but when he fails to fulfill his vow, she brings sickness upon him. Asherah is a mother figure, and it is announced that the offspring of Kirta will take nourishment at her breasts.

In the Bible, the noun "Asherah" is used with more than one meaning. Asherah remains a Canaanite goddess whose veneration in Israel is blamed on Jezebel (see 1 Kings 18:19). Jezebel's Asherah had four hundred prophets. Asherah was also worshiped in the south, and the Deuteronomistic historian praises Asa for destroying a detestable image made for Asherah (1 Kings 15:13). Manasseh, by contrast, is blamed for erecting a statue of Asherah (2 Kings 21:7). Vessels sacred to Asherah were also deposited in the Jerusalem Temple (2 Kings 23:4).

The name of Asherah is associated with that of Baal, and these were evidently a divine couple; but Baal is also linked to Astarte. Hebrew jar inscriptions from Kuntillet 'Ajrud raise the problem of Yahweh's relationship with Asherah. These inscriptions permit a reading that associates Yahweh of Samaria with his Asherah. If correct, these readings would demonstrate that in popular religion Yahweh was associated with a consort, Asherah, an eventuality that can cause no surprise in light of all we know about other religions of this period and area. But the noun "Asherah" may also signify "sanctuary" or refer to a cult object, and so the interpretation of the Kuntillet 'Ajrud inscriptions can be disputed.

Asherah can also refer to a cult object or objects. A high place might have an asherah (1 Kings 14:23; 2 Kings 18:4), but an asherah could equally be found outside a high place. The Baal temple at Samaria had an asherah (1 Kings 16:33), and they were, in general, common in places of worship in ancient Israel. The asherah is thought to have represented the goddess; it may have been carved from wood (Judg. 6:25) or it may have been a living tree planted to serve as an asherah (Deut. 16:21). Deuteronomy commands the destruction of the asherah by burning (Deut. 12:3). It can be guessed that an asherah was formed as a pole, but descriptions of the object are wanting.

The cult of the goddess Asherah and the use of the cultic object called asherah are persistently opposed in Israel's literature (Mic. 5:12–13; Deut. 16:21). Israel's faith did not admit the worship of gods other than Yahweh. However, since the worship of Yahweh owed much to the cults of El and Baal, the danger constantly existed that the exaltation of a divine couple modeled on the association of El and Asherah or Baal and Asherah would take root in Israel. The Canaanite divine couples lived with a sexual endowment. The Yahweh of the Bible, however, was not to be thought of as a sexual being. ***See also*** Anat; Baal; El; High Place; Ras-Shamrah.

R.M.G.

ashes, what is left after a fire, similar in appearance to dust, with which they are often mentioned. Ashes signify destruction (Ezek. 28:18; Mal. 4:3; Heb. 3:21; 2 Pet. 2:6) and are contrasted with glory (Isa. 61:3). Sitting on them or putting them on one's head were rituals of mourning and repentance (2 Sam. 13:19; Isa. 58:5; Jer. 6:26). Ashes are also mentioned as symbolic of insignificance (Gen. 18:27).

Ashkelon (ash'ke-lahn; variously spelled Askalon, Askelon, Eshkalon, Ascalon in NT times), a city located about twelve miles north of Gaza. It is mentioned in the Tell el-Amarna texts (ca. 1400–1360 B.C.) as being loyal to Egypt. The Merneptah stele (ca. 1230 B.C.) indicates Ashkelon with Gezer and Yanoam as cities conquered by pharaoh Merueptah. When Ashkelon rebelled Ramesses II reconquered it (ca. 1280 B.C.). It was one of the Philistine Pentapolis cities (Josh. 13:3; 1 Sam. 6:4, 17; Judg. 14:19). Elsewhere (Judg. 1:18), it is designated as a city conquered by the tribe of Judah. Tiglath-pileser III invaded Ashkelon (ca. 734 B.C.). Hezekiah of Judah and Sidqa of Ashkelon revolted against Assyria, but Sennacherib (701 B.C.) reconquered it for Assyria. Psamtik I (664–609 B.C.) of Egypt took Ashkelon. The city was destroyed by Nebuchadnezzar (609 B.C.; Jer. 47:5–7; Zeph. 2:4–7). It was a Tyrian possession during the Persian period (587–333 B.C.) and a Ptolemaic possession during the Hellenistic period (301–198 B.C.).

S.B.R.

Ashkenaz (ash'ke-naz). **1** Noah's great-grandson (Gen. 10:3). **2** A nation near Armenia (Jer. 51:27), generally identified with the Ashkuza, an Indo-European people mentioned in seventh-century Assyrian inscriptions, and the Scythians mentioned by Herodotus.

Ashtaroth (ash'tuh-rohth), the capital city of Og, king of Bashan, whom the Israelites under Moses defeated in battle (Deut. 1:4; cf. Josh. 9:10; 12:4). It is later mentioned as a city of refuge given to the Gershomites, a levitical group, from the territory of the half-tribe of Manasseh (1 Chron. 6:71). It was located to the east of the Sea of Galilee. Because the name is the plural form in Hebrew of Ashtoreth, the Canaanite goddess of fertility, it is probable that the city was once a special place of her worship. ***See also*** Asherah; Og.

Ashtoreth (ash'tuh-reth), the female consort of the Caananite deity El. ***See also*** Asherah.

Ashurbanipal (ash-uhr-bahn'i-pahl). ***See*** Assyria, Empire of.

Ashurnasirpal (ash'uhr-naz'uhr-pahl) **II,** the king of Assyria from 883 to 859 B.C., who by means of regular military campaigns to the four quarters of the Near East, forged a new Assyrian empire. In the West, he reached as far as Beth-eden (Amos 1:5) and Carchemish (Isa. 10:9). The royal inscriptions depict him as a valiant warrior, mercilessly punishing all resisters. Calah (modern Nimrud), completely rebuilt and repopulated with captives, served as his main administrative center. ***See also*** Assyria, Empire of.

M.C.

Ash Wednesday, the first day of Lent and the seventh Wednesday before Easter. It derives its name from the early ecclesiastical custom of putting ashes on the heads of believers on that day, as a sign of penitence.

Asia, a term occasionally referring to the old Persian Empire, but generally the Seleucid kingdoms, whose rulers were called "the kings of Asia" (1 Macc. 8:6). When Attalus III died (133 B.C.), he willed his kingdom to Rome, who called the new province "Asia" from the ruler's title. Asia was evangelized quickly by Christian missionaries (Acts 13–16). Paul sent his Letter to the Galatians to the many churches in that region of Asia. The Revelation to John was addressed to "the seven churches of Asia," the coastal cities of Ephesus, Smyrna, Pergamum, Thyatira, Sardis, Philadelphia, and Laodicea (1: 4, 11), and some of those to whom 1 Peter was addressed also lived in Asia (1:1). From Asia Pliny wrote to Rome about persecuting the Christian churches. J.H.N.

Asiarchs (ay'zi-ahrks), Roman administrative officials selected by a league of cities in the province of Asia. Their duties included overseeing local patriotic cultic activities on behalf of Rome and the emperor. Acts 19:31 represents some of them in Ephesus as friendly toward Paul.

Asnapper (as-nap'uhr), the name in KJV for Osnappar. ***See also*** Esarhaddon; Osnappar.

asp, a poisonous snake *(Naja haja)*, depicted in bronze at Gezer; it is employed by several biblical poets as a metaphor to convey deadly anger or poison (e.g., Deut. 32:33; Rom. 3:13).

Asriel (as'ree-el), a son of Manasseh by his Aramean concubine (1 Chron. 7:14), probably the same person (erroneously?) identified elsewhere as his great-grandson (Num. 26:31), although there is uncertainty over which genealogy is correct. It is possible these are different persons.

ass, a four-footed mammal related to the horse, common both in the wild and domesticated state in biblical times. The wild ass is portrayed most vividly in Job 39:5–8: it enjoys the freedom of the desert and finds its own pasture, scornful of the bustle of the city and heedless of the animal driver. It represents the presence of the desert where once there were bustling cities (Isa. 32:14). Ishmael is characterized as a wild ass (Gen. 16:12). The domesticated ass was very common in Israel. It appears as a basic item of a person's property (e.g. Exod. 22:8, 9; 23:4, 5; Job 24:3; Luke 13:15), and the number of asses was one of the measures of a patriarch's wealth or an army's booty. The domestic ass is most

Wild asses being hunted. On the upper register, two men hold a captured wild ass with ropes. On the bottom, two of the animals flee. Bas-reliefs from Ashurbanipal's palace at Nineveh, seventh century B.C.

frequently referred to as a means of transport for goods or people (e.g., 2 Sam. 16:1–2), but occasionally it appears as a draft animal (e.g., Isa. 30:24). Issachar is called an ass because his life is hard labor (Gen. 49:14; cf. Ecclus. 33:24). Though they usually knew where they were kept (Isa. 1:3), asses would not infrequently wander off and get lost (Exod. 23:4; Deut. 22: 1–3; 1 Sam. 9–10). Under siege conditions starvation might lead people to pay eighty shekels of silver for an ass's head, according to 2 Kings 6:25. Normally a dead ass was simply dragged outside the city and thrown away (Jer. 22:19). Samson used an ass's jawbone, which he found lying on the ground, to slay a thousand Philistines. Balaam's ass, which shows greater insight and loyalty than her master (Num. 22:21–35), is probably the most famous ass in the Bible (cf. 2 Pet. 2:16). In the ancient Near East gods and kings rode on asses. So in the prophecy of Zech. 9:9 the new king of Jerusalem comes to the city riding on an ass—as then does Jesus (Matt. 21: 1–11; Mark 11:1–11; Luke 19:28–38; John 12: 12–19). S.B.P.

Assassins (KJV: "murderers"; Gk. *sikarioi;* Lat. *sicarii,* from *sica,* "dagger"), according to Josephus a Jewish revolutionary group operating against the Romans and their collaborators prior to the revolt of A.D. 66. In Acts 21:38, Paul is mistakenly thought to be one of their leaders. ***See also*** Zealot.

Assir (as'sir; Heb., "bondman" or "captive"), the name of three Levites. **1** The son of Korah and great-grandson of Uzziel (Exod. 6:24). **2** The son of Ebiasaph and great-grandson of 1 above (1 Chron. 6:23). **3** The son of a second Ebiasaph and the great-grandson of Izhar the brother of Uzziel (1 Chron. 6:37). Because of the repetition of names some scholars think scribal errors have confused the proper order of these lists; it is therefore possible that these are all the same person. Some versions also understand Jeconiah to have had a son named Assir (1 Chron. 3:17), but the RSV properly translates "Jeconiah the captive." ***See also*** Ebiasaph; Korah. D.R.B.

Assos (as'ohs), seaport on the northwest coast of Asia Minor, visited by Paul (Acts 20:13–14).

Assur (ah'suhr), ancient Assyria. In Mesopotamia, Assur designates the nation and land of Assyria, its oldest capital city, and its god. Originally, the name was associated with just the city and god; its national significance was added in Middle Assyrian times (1500–900 B.C.), when the city expanded into a state.

The city itself, modern Qala'at Sharqat (in Iraq) lies on a promontory overlooking the Tigris River. Its history, as revealed especially in the German excavations of 1903–14, stretches from ca. 3000 to 614 B.C., during which it developed from a satellite of southern Mesopotamia (3000–2000), through an independent city-state (2000–1500), to the capital of the territorial state and empire of Middle Assyria (1500–900), finally to one of several centers of the enlarged Neo-Assyrian Empire (900–614). There was, in addition, a revival in the Parthian period, ca. 100 B.C.–A.D. 250.

Paralleling this history was that of Assur the god, who is first attested as the patron of the city ca. 2000 B.C. and thereafter grew into the principal deity of the Assyrian state and empire, taking on characteristics of many other gods, particularly the Babylonian gods Enlil and Marduk.

In the OT, Assur refers only to the nation or land (e.g., Isa. 10:5) or, by extension, to its eponymous ancestor (Gen. 10:22; 1 Chron. 1:17). There is no mention of the city (Gen. 10:11 and Ezek. 27:23 likely indicate the land) nor of the god (except obliquely, as an element in the royal name Esarhaddon: 2 Kings 19:37; Isa. 37:38; Ezra 4:2). In the NT, Parthians are mentioned among those who heard the disciples speaking in various languages at Pentecost (Acts 2:9). ***See also*** Assyria, Empire of. P.B.M.

assurance, the theological concept of certainty and persuasion communicated in the gospel to the eyes of faith about God and God's utter trustworthiness as the faithful Promiser. Implying neither personal tranquility nor robust confidence, neither blanket security nor rosy optimism, this assurance is created by God's self-witness and is sustained by the experience of the repeated righteous fidelity of God (Rom. 5–7; 2 Cor. 1:3–11; 1 Thess. 1; 2:13–16; 2 Tim. 1:12; Heb. 11:1–2; cf. Isa. 32:17). Assurance takes shape in the form of a conscience bound to God (Rom. 2:15; 12:2; 13:5; 1 Cor. 8:10; 2 Cor. 4:2; 5:11; 1 Pet. 2:19), of an awareness in the arena of doubting and decision making, of conduct and behavior (Heb. 10:19–24; 1 John 3:11–24). It motivates, activates, and enables discernment both reactively *and* proactively in matters of responsible living. It is closely connected to the work of the Spirit (John 14:16, 26; 15:26; 16:7) and represents finally the verification that God's new creation in the resurrection of Jesus is the ultimate reality upon which one stakes one's life (Acts 17:31; 1 Cor. 15). ***See also*** Conscience; Faith; Holy Spirit, The; Promise. J.E.A.

Assyria (uh-seer'ee-uh), **Empire of,** one of the major empires in the ancient Near East. The heartland of Assyria lay in what is now northern Iraq around the Upper Tigris River. Its initial development as a territorial state and empire came in the second millennium B.C., in the Old and Middle Assyrian periods. But its greatest period—and the only one involving direct contact with Israel—was its last: the Neo-Assyrian period of the first millennium B.C. (911–609). The triumphant achievement of Neo-Assyria was the creation of an empire that went far beyond earlier models to become the largest political configuration the Near East had yet seen. Four phases marked the course of this achievement.

In the first phase (911–824 B.C.), Adad-nirari II, Tukulti-ninurta II, Ashurnasirpal II, and Shalmaneser III finally halted the Aramaean attacks that had plagued Assyria for the preceding three centuries and counterattacked through Syria, the best known of their battles occurring at Qarqar in 853 between Shalmaneser and a Syro-Palestinian coalition that included Ahab of Israel (1 Kings 22). In these as in other campaigns to the north, east, and Babylonian south, the Assyrians wanted not so much permanent conquest as the neutralization of external threats and the acquisition of booty and prisoners, which could then be used in building projects such as Ashurnasirpal's grandiose reconstruction of the city of Calah.

The death of Shalmaneser III (824) initiated the second phase, which continued until 744 B.C. Its first decades saw more military activity against the Aramaeans, of which one beneficiary was Israel (2 Kings 13:5). But in the main, this was a time of Assyrian retreat, brought on by the growing power of its northern neighbor, Urartu, and by the growing challenge to royal authority by various Assyrian officials. With Assyria and the Aramaeans thus weak, it is no surprise that in the latter years of this phase Israel and Judah were able to expand their territories significantly, under their kings Jeroboam II (2 Kings 14:23–29) and Uzziah (2 Chron. 26) (770–744 B.C.).

Assyria's troubles were reversed in the third and climactic phase of the Neo-Assyrian period, the century (744–627) of Tiglath-pileser III, Shalmaneser V, Sargon II, Sennacherib,

Ashurbanipal, king of Assyria, carrying a basket for the rebuilding of the temple of Esagila in Babylon, seventh century B.C.

Esarhaddon, and Ashurbanipal. Under the standard set by Tiglath-pileser, they restored royal power and established a standing army, whose constant campaigning eventually brought under Assyrian sway almost all of the Near East. The aim now was not simply spoil, but permanent conquest—an empire of provinces and vassal states backed by an increased use of deportation to control the conquered. To administer this, the bureaucracy became more complex and more dependent on non-Assyrian deportees, especially Aramaeans, whose language and culture gradually pervaded the whole. To display the new-found power, the imperial cities, especially the heartland capitals of Ashur, Calah, Nineveh, and the short-lived Dur-Sharrukin, were made larger and more splendid.

This empire had serious flaws, however. Its heartland became increasingly dependent on tribute and deportees from the conquered areas, who, being increasingly burdened, revolted whenever they could. Israel, for example, joined revolts against Tiglath-pileser, Shalmaneser, and Sargon and paid for its "disobedience" by dismemberment into provinces and deportation (732–720 B.C.; 2 Kings 17:1–6). Judah, fearing the consequences, remained a loyal vassal through these revolts; but eventually it too yielded, joining the outbreak against Sennacherib (704–701 B.C.), who responded harshly but allowed Judah to resume its vassal status (2 Kings 18:13–20:21).

These recurring revolts strained Assyrian resources and organization and exacerbated latent tensions within the ruling elite, which resurfaced in the assassination of Sennacherib (681) and especially in the civil war between Ashurbanipal and his brother, who was regent of Babylonia, a constantly troublesome vassal (652–648 B.C.). Ashurbanipal won, but the ensuing military and political exhaustion began a loosening of imperial authority.

The process accelerated after Ashurbanipal's death (627), in the fourth and final phase of Neo-Assyrian history. Now many subjects openly asserted their independence—Judah under King Josiah (2 Kings 21:24–23:34), Babylonia under its new Neo-Babylonian/Chaldean dynasty, the Medes—and conflict broke out again among the Assyrian elite for what power remained. Exploiting this conflict, the Medes and Chaldeans began attacking the Assyrian heartland, and between 614 and 612 the capital cities fell into their hands. The Assyrian army, always a kind of state within the state, held out a little longer in Harran to the west, apparently with Egyptian support. But in 610–609, a Chaldean army dislodged it, helped by Josiah of Judah, who at the cost of his life (2 Kings 23:29–30) delayed the arrival of Egyptian forces. With that, the Assyrian state disappeared, and the bulk of its territories were taken by the Chaldeans. ***See also*** Aram; Babylon; Chaldea; Esarhaddon; Nineveh; Sargon II; Sennacherib; Shalmaneser; Tiglath-pileser III; Uzziah. P.B.M.

Astarte (ah-stahr'te). ***See*** Asherah.

astrologer, a person who reads the influence of the stars on human and terrestrial affairs, supposedly foretelling events by the positions of the planets and stars. Clay tablets show that astrology flourished among the ancient Assyrians and Babylonians (ca. 1000–500 B.C.). Belief that the stars influence human affairs appears occasionally in the OT (Judg. 5:20; Job 38:33). It is generally associated with apostasy (Isa. 47:13–14) or with the gentile nations (Dan. 1:20; 2:2, 10). Combined with Greek mathematics, astrology came into the Greco-Roman world during the Hellenistic period (325–63 B.C.). Fragments of what appears to be a horoscope of the messiah were found among the Dead Sea Scrolls. The Magi (Matt. 2:1–12) were led to Jesus by observation of an unusual astronomical phenomenon at the time of his birth. P.P.

Atad (ah-tahd'; from Akkadian *etidu*), translated "thorns" (Ps. 58:9) and "bramble" (Judg. 9:14–15) and transliterated (Gen. 50:10, 11). In Genesis it refers to a threshing floor east of the Jordan where Jacob's family mourned his death, causing a renaming of the place.

Ataroth (a'tah-rohth). **1** Khirbet Attarus, eight miles northwest of Dibon (Num. 32:3, 34) associated with the tribe of Gad. **2** Tell el-Mazar, an east border town of Ephraim (Josh. 16:7). **3** KJV for RSV Atroth-beth-joab (1 Chron. 2:54). **4** It appears as part of the compound name Ataroth-addar (Josh. 16:5; 18:13), a border town between Ephraim and Benjamin, modern day Kefer 'Aqab.

Ater (ay'tuhr). **1** A family group ("sons of Ater") who returned with Zerubbabel from the Babylonian captivity (Ezra 2:16). **2** A family group of gatekeepers who also returned (Ezra 2: 42). **3** A member of the postexilic community who signed the covenant to keep the law (Neh. 10:17); he could be associated with either of the families identified above.

Athaliah (ath-uh-lī'yah; Heb., "Jah is strong"), the only ruling queen of Judah. She was the daughter of Jezebel and Ahab of Israel, and the wife of Jehoram, king of Judah (ca. 849–843 B.C.). She ruled (ca. 843–837 B.C.) upon the death of Ahaziah at the hands of Jehu (2 Kings 9:29). She instigated a purge of the male heirs. After six years, Jehoida, one of the priests, mounted a successful coup by producing Joash, a male who escaped the purge, and Athaliah was murdered (2 Kings 11:1–20).

Athens, the capital of the ancient Greek province of Attica (2 Macc. 9:15; Acts 17:15–18; 18: 1; 1 Thess. 3:1). The name "Athens" antedates the arrival of the Indo-European peoples in Greece (ca. 2000 B.C.). The city stands on a site that has been continuously inhabited since the fourth millennium B.C. In Mycenaean times (ca. 1300–1225 B.C.) it was a fortified citadel with a palace and cult sanctuary to Eros/Aphrodite. What would later become the agora was at that time a burial site.

The Classical Period: The glory of classical Athens belongs to the fifth century B.C. Tribute money from the vast Athenian empire and its commerce paid for the beautiful buildings erected on the acropolis (454–414 B.C.). The Parthenon, whose marble friezes are now displayed in the British Museum, was built in honor of the goddess Athena. Its architects had mastered the details of perspective and curvature so that they could make its rows of columns appear straight even when viewed along the building's longitudinal axis. The figures sculpted for the processional frieze are completely finished on all sides as though they were to have been viewed straight on and not from 39 feet below. Some four hundred people and two hundred animals are shown participating in the Panathenaic procession, which brought the goddess a new sacred robe every fourth year. The great statue of Athena is known to us from copies. Clothed in a gold robe, the goddess had ivory limbs and an ivory face. She wore gold earrings, necklace, and bracelet, and a military helmet with the sphinx and winged Pegasoi. One hand held a spear. Her shield portrayed the gods and giants. The sacred snake, Erichthonius, was ent-

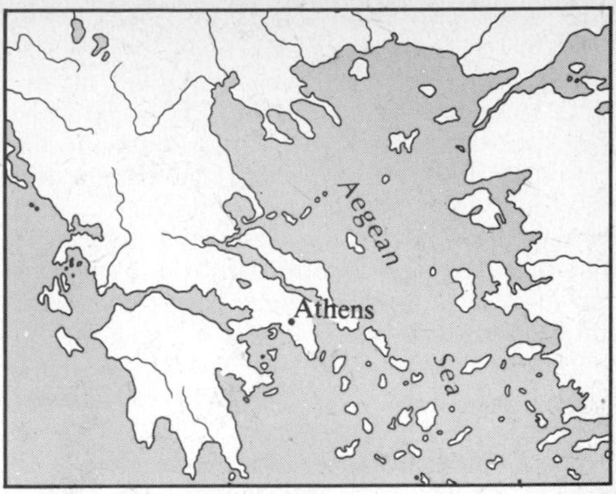

wined around her left leg while her right hand held an image of a winged victory.

The Hephaisteion temple overlooking the agora is the most perfectly preserved temple of the era. The Erechtheum, built on the site of the Mycenaean palace, was begun in 421 B.C. but interrupted by the Peloponnesian War in 415 B.C. and not resumed until 409 B.C. It was thought to stand on a holy spot where Poseidon had stuck his trident in the ground and Athena had caused the sacred olive tree to spring up. Its innovative caryatid porch had the six maidens, all different, supporting the roof. Hadrian had a complete copy made for his villa at Tivoli.

This period also saw considerable building in the agora, including a prison, a council house, a building for semipublic meetings, and several colonnaded porches *(stoa)*, the Painted Stoa, the Stoa of Zeus, and the long double-aisled stoa to the south. The theater of Dionysus was built on the south slope of the acropolis during the fourth century B.C. The theater as seen today comes from the last part of that century. It seated between fourteen and seventeen thousand. The scene building may have had a temporary stage. The permanent stage was added during the Hellenistic period. The Romans added a marble barrier around the orchestra to protect spectators at beast fights and gladiator shows. In the second century B.C. the Stoa of Attalos, which has been reconstructed to house the agora museum, was built.

The Augustan Age and After: The Augustan age (31 B.C.–A.D. 14) saw a flurry of Roman building. Julius Caesar had planned a Roman forum for Athens. A small round temple to Rome and the emperor Augustus modeled after the Vesta in Rome was built on the acropolis east of the Parthenon. In the center of the old orchestra in the Greek agora Agrippa built an auditorium for about one thousand persons. The Romans also dismantled and brought to the agora a temple to Ares, which was built in fifth-century B.C. style.

There is little evidence of any building in the agora during the first century A.D. By the second century, Athens was a university town. The inscription from an early second-century A.D. library reads, "No books circulate. Open 6 A.M. to noon." The middle of the second century saw a new building spree under the emperor Hadrian (A.D. 117–138) including a huge temple to Olympian Zeus, a gymnasium, and a library north of the Roman agora. Agrippa's Odeon, used as a lecture hall, was remodeled in A.D. 150 to hold 500 persons and was decorated with pairs of statues representing the various philosophical schools in the city. ***See also*** Acropolis; Agora; Areopagus; Stoa; Theater.

Bibliography

MacKendrick, P. *The Greek Stones Speak.* 2d ed. rev. New York: Norton, 1981.

Wycherley, R. E. *How the Greeks Built Cities.* 2d ed. Garden City, NY: Doubleday, 1969. P.P.

Athlit (ath'lit), an impressive site on the Mediterranean shore ca. twelve and a half miles south of Haifa. It appears to have been occupied from the Late Bronze period (1500–1200 B.C.) until the Hellenistic period (333–63 B.C.). It is situated on the main travel thoroughfare of antiquity in western Palestine, the *Via Maris* (Lat., "the way of the sea"). Its most impressive feature is a Crusader castle *(Castellum Peregrinorum).* The city has been identified with Kartah of Zebulun (Josh. 21:34).

atonement, the means by which the guilt-punishment chain produced by violation of God's will is broken, as well as the resulting state of reconciliation ("at-onement") with God. For most ancients, violation of the world order led to punishment by divine powers; only atonement could prevent or end such punishment. The character of atonement varied greatly, however, depending on concepts of the deity, human existence, and the order of violation.

The English word "atonement" does not occur in the RSV (cf. Rom. 5:11: "atonement" in the KJV, "reconciliation" in the RSV). The Hebrew word with which the concept of atonement is associated in the OT can be translated variously as "purge," "cleanse," "expiate," "purify," "wipe on or off," "cover," etc. The Septuagint (LXX) Greek equivalent was of influence for the language and thought of the NT.

The OT viewed a number of offerings and sacrifices as atoning. The best known were the elaborate sacrificial/priestly rites of atonement developed mainly in the postexilic period. Basic to their development was the OT view of God: God was the faithful, holy covenant partner to his people; he provided the means of atonement when the sanctuary or the land became defiled, or when the people were unfaithful. God did not need appeasement; rather, atonement removed the sinful barrier to the covenantal relationship. The rites of atonement were carried out by the high priest through prescribed sacrifices in the Temple. Covenant renewal and restoration were connected to the Day of Atonement (Lev. 16). Atonement was anything but routine and automatic (Pss. 40; 51:15–17). For early Judaism, the atonement base was broadened to include the sacrifice of martyrs whose achievements were calculated and deemed meritorious for others (e.g., 4 Macc. 6:28–29; 17:20–24).

In the NT, atonement is linked conclusively to the ministry, death, and resurrection of Jesus. According to early traditions in the first three ("synoptic") gospels, Jesus may have understood his destiny in atoning terms (Mark 10:45b; 14:24; cf. Isa. 53; Exod. 32:30–32). Early Christian thought developed this and other OT backgrounds. For Paul, for example, the location and source of God's mercy, namely Jesus Christ, was central (KJV: "mercy seat," RSV: "expiation"; Rom. 3:25). For Hebrews, the central image was that of the high priest (Heb. 2:17; 4:14–5:10; 10:19–21; cf. Lev. 16; Ps. 110:1–4). Early appropriation of an intercessory "on-our-behalf" traditional formula enhanced this development of seeing in Jesus the locus of atonement (1 Cor. 15:3). Atonement as "redemption" (1 Cor. 6:20; 7:23; Gal. 3:13; 4:5) may have other backgrounds beside those of the OT (Exod. 4:22–23; 21:30; 30:16; Num. 35:31–33). Unlike other NT writings, Luke-Acts makes little use of atonement concepts. ***See also*** Atonement, Day of; Blood; Covenant; Expiation; Pardon; Priests; Reconciliation; Redemption; Salvation; Sin; Worship. J.E.A.

Atonement, Day of (Heb. *Yom Kippur),* a fast day on which no work was done, observed in Israel ten days after the fall new year (Lev. 23:27–32) to atone for the sins of the past year. An offering of incense was made by the high priest in the innermost chamber of the Temple, the Holy of Holies, the only time in the year he entered there. The sins of the people were symbolically placed upon the "scapegoat," which was driven into the wilderness. Hebrews 8–9 draw heavily on the Day of Atonement to explain Christ's sacrifice. ***See also*** Azazel.

A.J.S.

Attalia (at-uh-lī'uh), a seaport on the southern coast of Asia Minor. From here, Paul and Barnabas sailed to Antioch at the end of their first journey (Acts 14:25).

Augustus (Lat., "august, revered"), a title granted to Octavian (63 B.C.–A.D. 14), the grandnephew and adopted heir of Julius Caesar, by the Roman senate in 27 B.C., when it confirmed his powers to rule (Lat. *iperium).* He was the Roman ruler when Jesus was born in a province of the empire (Luke 2:1). Though Augustus was in fact the sole ruler of the empire, he ostensibly contented himself with only the necessary powers of rule, the supreme command of most of the army *(imperium proconsulare)* and the consular powers over the city of Rome *(imperium consulare)*. When Augustus ceased to stand for annual election to the consulate he was granted new tribunician powers. These included powers he already possessed such as personal immunity from prosecution and appellate jurisdiction and added powers to convene the senate and popular assembly and to submit measures to either at any time. He could also veto any item of public business or the action of any other magistrate.

Administration of provinces requiring military presence was entrusted to legates who were personal emissaries of the emperor. Augustus created the foundations of Roman imperial power. As the title *augustus*, which was derived from a word associated with sanctuaries, suggests, he initiated the process by which the emperor and his family were identified with the majesty of the Roman state and in later times were deified. ***See also*** Roman Empire; Rome. P.P.

Authorized Version (AV), an early seventeenth-century translation of the Bible into English, more commonly known as the King James Version (KJV). ***See also*** English Bible, The.

AV. ***See*** Authorized Version; English Bible, The.

Avaris (uh-vah'ris), the capital of the Asiatic Hyksos in the eastern Nile delta. It was overrun by Egyptian forces in the resurgence beginning the New Kingdom (ca. 1530 B.C.). Avaris may be modern Tell el-Dab'a or possibly San el-Hagar, ancient Tanis, both of which have impressive remains. ***See also*** Hyksos; Zoan.

Aven (ah'ven; Heb., "evil power"). **1** Term used to describe Bethel (Hos. 10:9) in Hosea's indictment. **2** KJV for RSV "On," Egyptian city of Heliopolis (Ezek. 30:17). **3** A frequent element in compound names; it is used for Canaanite [hence evil] deities (Josh. 7:2; 18:12; 1 Sam. 13:5; 14:23).

avenger, one who extracts satisfaction from or punishes a wrongdoer, usually the next of kin of the wronged person. In the ancient Near East, this method of seeking justice was used whenever strong governmental authority was lacking. Blood vengeance, the execution of a murderer by the avenger, was recognized by the Hebrew people as a custom sanctioned by God (Gen. 9:5–6; Num. 35:16–21), although this custom was limited by a sense of compassion and mercy (Gen. 4:10–16; Num. 35:9–15, 22–28). Unlimited vengeance is presented as part of the lawlessness that led to the Flood (Gen. 4:23–24).

The Hebrews thought of God as the avenger on the wicked and on their enemies (Ps. 94), and thought God exercised his vengeance through their activities (Judg. 12:3–6; 2 Kings 9:7; Jos. 10:13). They were forbidden to take vengeance upon one another (Lev. 19:18).

Believers in Jesus as the Christ are taught not to execute vengeance themselves (Matt. 5:38–42; Rom. 12:17–19). God will punish the evildoer (1 Thess. 4:6; Rom. 12:19). The state executes vengeance on God's behalf (Rom. 13:4). God is portrayed as one who avenges the suffering of the faithful (Rev. 6:10; 19:2). ***See also*** Blood; Justice; Mercy; Vengeance. A.Y.C.

ax, battle-ax. ***See*** Weapons.

Ayin (ī'yin; Heb., "eye," "spring"). **1** The sixteenth letter of the Hebrew alphabet. It may have originated from the pictogram outline of the human eye. It has the numerical value of seventy. **2** A village near Riblah on the northern boundary of Palestine (Num. 34:11). **3** A town near Rimmon (Josh. 15:32; 1 Chron. 4:32).

Azarel (az'uh-rel; Heb., "God has helped"). **1** A Korahite, one of David's warriors (1 Chron. 12:6, Hebrew v. 7). **2** The son of Jeroham, a Danite leader in the time of David (1 Chron. 27:22). **3** A levitical musician in the time of David (1 Chron. 25:18; often identified with Uzziel in v. 4). **4** A postexilic Israelite who divorced his foreign wife in response to Ezra's proclamation (Ezra 10:41). **5** A postexilic priest living in Jerusalem (Neh. 11:13). **6** A postexilic priest who participated in the dedication of the wall at the time of Nehemiah (Neh. 12:36, possibly the same as 5).

Azariah (az-uh-rī'uh; Heb., "Yah[weh] has helped"), a name appearing in the OT as Azaryah and Azaryahu. This is the name of a number of men, primarily Judeans, from the time of Solomon through the return from Babylonian exile. **1** The king of Judah (2 Kings 14:21; 15:1, 7, 17, 23, 27; 1 Chron. 3:12), otherwise named Uzziah. **2** The two sons of the Judean king Jehoshaphat (2 Chron. 21:2). **3** The royal governor and army officer (1 Kings 4:5; 2 Chron. 23:1). **4** A prophet (2 Chron. 15:1). **5** Several priests (1 Kings 4:2; 1 Chron. 6:9, 10 [the second, Ezra 7:3], 13–14 [Ezra 7:1]; 9:11; 2 Chron. 6:36 [Uzziah in 1 Chron. 6:24]; 2 Chron. 29:12; Neh. 8:7 [1 Esd. 9:48]). **6** Various tribal or other leaders (Jer. 42:1 [with Septuagint]; 43:1; 1 Chron. 2:8, 38–39; 2 Chron. 28:12; Neh. 3:23–24; 7:17; 12:33). **7** The original name (Azzariah) of Abednego (Dan. 1:6–7, 11, 19; 2:17; 1 Macc. 2:59; Song of Three Children 1:65). ***See also*** Uzziah. P.B.M.

Azazel (ah-zay'zel), a demonic figure to whom the sin-laden scapegoat was sent on the Day of Atonement (Lev. 16:8, 10, 26). The Hebrew word has been traditionally understood as a phrase meaning "the goat that escapes," giving us the word "scapegoat." But in light of modern re-

search, both this interpretation and those that understand it as a place name are incorrect. The word is a proper name and means something like "angry god." Yet, though Azazel is a demon, he does not play an active role in the rite as corresponding figures do in similar rituals of the ancient Near East. ***See also*** Atonement, Day of.
D.P.W.

Azaziah (az-uh-zī'uh; Heb., "Yah [God] is mighty"). **1** A Levite musician during the reign of King David (1 Chron. 15:21). **2** The father of Hoshea, the military commander of the tribe of Benjamin (1 Chron. 27:20). **3** A Levite Temple official during the reign of King Hezekiah who helped collect the tithes (2 Chron. 31:13).

Azekah (ah-zee'kah), a city (modern Tell ez-Zahariyeh) in Judah occupied prior to Israel's entering Canaan (Josh. 10:10–11; 15:35). It lies a short distance northeast of Lachish. The Philistines and Goliath camped between Succoth and Azekah (1 Sam. 17:1). Rehoboam fortified this city (2 Chron. 11:9). Only Azekah and Lachish were left in the Judean countryside (Jer. 34:7) when Nebuchadnezzar attacked Jerusalem and the fortified cities of Judah. Not only is Azekah tied to Lachish in the biblical text, but they are corresponding towns in the Lachish letters. After the Exile Azekah existed between Eleutheropolis (Heb. Beth Govrin) and Jerusalem. This may be Khirbet al-'Almi east of Tell ez-Zahariyeh, according to Eusebius (early fourth century A.D.). However, the mound Tell ez-Zahariyeh shows occupation from pre-Israelite through the Byzantine periods. S.B.R.

Azel (ay'zel), a Benjaminite, a descendant of Saul's son Jonathan (1 Chron. 8:37).

Azgad (az'gad; Heb., "Gad is mighty"). **1** A family group ("sons of Azgad") who returned with Zerubbabel from the Babylonian captivity (Ezra 2:12). **2** Another group who returned with Ezra (Ezra 8:12). **3** A member of the postexilic community in Judah who signed the covenant to keep the law (Neh. 10:15) and could be associated with either of the families named above.

Azmaveth (az'muh-veth; Heb., "death is strong"). **1** One of David's fighting men (2 Sam. 23:31). **2** A Benjaminite, descendant of Saul's son Jonathan (1 Chron. 8:36). **3** The father of Jaziel and Pelet, two of Saul's kinsmen from Benjamin who joined David at Ziklag (1 Chron. 12:3). **4** The son of Adiel; overseer of the royal storehouses under King David (1 Chron. 27:25). **5** A small family group ("sons of Azmaveth") who returned with Zerubbabel from the Babylonian captivity (Ezra 2:24). Some scholars see the variant Beth-azmaveth in a parallel list (Neh. 7:28) as indicating a town where the returning exiles settled rather than a family group (see 6 below), the result of a confusion of a place name with a family. But since Beth-azmaveth means "the house of Azmaveth," it could as easily refer to the family group. **6** A village of the postexilic community; identified with the modern Ras-Dhukeir or El-Hizma, about five miles northeast of Jerusalem (Neh. 12:29). D.R.B.

Azmon (az'muhn), a settlement along the southernmost border of the Canaanite land claimed by Israel (Num. 34:4–5) and part of the southern boundary of Judah (Josh. 15:4); it is possibly identical with Ezem (Josh. 15:29). The site is unknown, although thought to lie slightly northwest of Kadesh-barnea.

Azotus. ***See*** Ashdod.

Azriel (az'ree-el; Heb., "El [God] is my help"). **1** The head of a family in the tribe of Manasseh (1 Chron. 5:24). **2** The father of Jeremoth, a military commander of the tribe of Naphtali (1 Chron. 27:19). **3** The father of Seraiah, a courtier of King Jehoiakim (Jer. 36:26).

Azrikam (az-rī'kuhm; Heb., "my help arises"). **1** A descendant of Zerubbabel and in the lineage of the kings of Judah through David (1 Chron. 3:23). **2** The son of Azel and descendant of Saul's son Jonathan (1 Chron. 8:38). **3** A Levite, the grandfather of Shemaiah, a resident of postexilic Jerusalem (1 Chron. 9:14). **4** The overseer of the royal household of King Ahaz of Judah; he was assassinated along with the king's son and his chief of state by Zichri in conjunction with a coordinated attack against Judah by King Pekah of the Northern Kingdom of Israel and Rezin, king of Syria (2 Chron. 28:7). ***See also*** Pekah.
D.R.B.

Azubah (ah-zo͞o'buh; Heb., "forsaken"). **1** The daughter of Shilhi; she was a wife of King Asa of Judah and mother of Jehoshaphat (1 Kings 22:42). **2** One of the wives of Caleb, son of Hezron (1 Chron. 2:18).

Azzur (az'zuhr; Heb., "helped"). **1** One of those who signed the postexilic covenant to keep the law (Neh. 10:17). **2** The father of Hananiah, the false prophet who challenged Jeremiah (Jer. 28:1). **3** The father of Jaazariah, a corrupt leader seen by Ezekiel in a vision (Ezek. 11:1).

Opposite: The weather god Baal holding a lance in his left hand with branches that may represent lightning; from a fourteenth-century B.C. stele from the Temple of Baal at Ras-Shamra. Opposition to the worship of Baal is a persistent theme in the OT.

B

B, the second letter of the alphabet, commonly used to designate Codex Vaticanus, a fourth-century A.D. parchment manuscript of the Greek Bible, now in the Vatican Library. It consists of 759 leaves (out of an original total of about 820), each measuring 10-5/8 by 10-5/8 inches with three columns to the page. The OT is complete, but all of the NT after Heb. 9:14 is lost (including the Pastoral Epistles and Revelation). Vaticanus is the leading representative of the type of text that scholars identify as Alexandrian. ***See also*** Codex; Texts, Versions, Manuscripts, Editions.

Baal (bay'al), a Canaanite god. The Semitic word "baal" means "owner," "husband," "lord." It can be used as a common noun or as a proper noun. In the latter case it refers to the god Baal. In the Bible it is not always clear which use is intended. There is an additional complication in using "Baal" as a proper noun. Baal is, in one sense, a specific deity with characteristic attributes and functions. But gods other than this specific Baal may be called Baal. The Carthaginian god Baal Hamon seems to manifest the character of El. In the Bible, El of the Covenant (Judg. 9:46) and Baal of the Covenant (Judg. 8:33) denote the same deity.

Canaanite Background: These problems notwithstanding, the identity of Baal is clear. Baal is a weather god associated with thunderstorms. He is best known from the literature of Ras-Shamra (fifteenth century B.C.); Philo of Byblos, a Greek historian (ca. A.D. 63–141), collected additional valuable information about Baal, whom Philo called Zeus. At Ras-Shamra, Baal was called the son of Dagan, a fact not easily harmonized with the more general notion that El was sire of the pantheon. Also known as Hadd (Hadad), Baal was called "the Prince," "the Powerful," "Rider of the Clouds" (an epithet once predicated of Yahweh in the Bible, Ps. 68:4). At Ras-Shamra, Baal's consort, evidently also his sister, was Anat.

The phenomena associated with thunderstorms were closely linked to Baal. Baal was said to appoint the season of rains. Clouds were thought to be part of his entourage. Lightning was his weapon, and it may have been his invention. The windows of Baal's palace were thought to correspond to openings in the clouds through which rain flowed. Rain was important to Canaanite agriculture, and Baal was consequently a god of fertility—a prodigious lover as well as the giver of abundance.

The Ugaritic literature preserves a cycle of myths in which Baal is the protagonist. They link Baal to Mount Zaphon. They tell of his battle against Lotan (Leviathan) and of his struggles against other adversaries called Yamm (Sea) and Mot (Death). The struggle between Baal and Yamm has left its mark on Israelite literature in the form of stories about and allusions to Yahweh's encounters with watery enemies (e.g., Isa. 51:9b–10; Ps. 74:13). Through his struggles, Baal achieves the first rank among the gods. Along the way Baal perishes and revives, providing the Ugaritic literature with stirring themes and dramatic moments.

The relationship between El and Baal in Canaanite mythology has been a matter of dispute. There is some indirect evidence of antagonism between these important gods, inasmuch as they were competitors for the highest position in the pantheon. Yet there is also evidence of concord between them. Philo of Byblos reported an accommodation whereby Baal ruled on earth with the permission of El; many have seen in this arrangement the pattern of relations between the two most important gods of the Canaanites.

Baal and Ancient Israel: The cult of Baal was widespread in the Syro-Palestinian world and became the focus of Israelite religious animosity. Baal's consort in Palestine was not Anat, but Asherah (Judg. 3:7) or Astarte (Judg. 2:13; 10:6). Syncretism had blurred distinctions between Asherah, Astarte, and Anat, while for Israelite writers such distinctions were not of interest. We hear of the cult of Baal in a number of local manifestations: Baal of the Covenant at Shechem (Judg. 9:4); Baal of Peor at Shittim (Num. 25:3); Baal "Zebub" ("of the flies"; but should Zebul, "Prince," be read?) of Philistia (2 Kings 1:2–3); and perhaps Baal of Hamon (Song of Sol. 8:11). Jezebel introduced to Samaria the worship of Tyre's god Baal (1 Kings 18:19). It is not altogether clear whether these local baals were taken to manifest the single great god Baal or whether they were imagined as discrete deities.

Opposition to the worship of Baal is a persistent theme of the Israelite literature. The Deuteronomic corpus repeatedly condemns the veneration of Baal, speaking sometimes of "the Baals." The Deuteronomistic historian applauds the destruction of the Baal temple at Jerusalem in the revolution against Athaliah (2 Kings 11:18) and transmits old stories of conflict between the worshipers of Yahweh and the followers of Baal (Judg. 6:25–32; 1 Kings 18:16–40). The struggle against Baal worship was carried on forcefully by Israel's prophets, especially in the ninth century B.C. and later. There was much at stake. The worship of Baal was popular. Many Israelite names were composed with the element "Baal" (e.g., Beeliada). Although the word "Baal" in such names may refer to Yahweh as "lord," on the whole such names can be taken as evidence of the erosion of strict devotion to Yahweh. Some Israelite writers changed the name Baal in personal names to the word *bosheth* ("shame"), as in the name Ishbosheth. Since Yahweh could be called "lord," baal, the danger existed that Israel's God would take on the characteristics of the Canaanite weather god. In part this could occur without compromise to the character of Yahweh. The majesty of a thunderstorm and the gift of fertility in nature could be construed as the evidence of Yahweh's work. But Baal was a god of sexual congress whose cult sported erotic acts that offended Israelite sensitivities, and the full identification of Yahweh and Baal was not a possibility. Israel's prophets fought to preserve a vision of transcendent Yahweh over against the Canaanite concept of Baal the nature god. ***See also*** Anat; Asherah; Ras-Shamra. R.M.G.

Baalah (bay'uh-luh), a feminine form of the word *baal* (Heb., "master"), the name of the Semitic fertility god; it is used to mean "the place of Baal." **1** Another name for Kiriath-jearim, a city on the northern border of Judah (Josh. 15: 9–10) where David kept the Ark of the Covenant before moving it to Jerusalem (1 Chron. 13: 6).The site is identified as modern Deir el-Azar or Tel Qiryat Yearim, about eight miles west and slightly north of Jerusalem. Baalah is also called Kiriath-baal (Heb., "the city of Baal," Josh. 15: 60) and Baale-Judah (2 Sam. 6:2). **2** A city on the southern border of Judah, possibly the same one elsewhere called Balah (Josh. 19:3) and Bilhah (1 Chron. 4:29) and given to the tribe of Simeon. The site is not known. **3** A mountain on the northern border of Judah near Ekron (Josh. 15: 11). ***See also*** Kiriath-jearim. D.R.B.

Baalath (bay'uh-lath), a place name that is a feminine form of the word *baal* (Heb., "master"), the name of a Semitic deity. It is the name of a city in northern Canaan assigned to the tribe of Dan (Josh. 19:44), whose site is unknown. It is also given as one of the cities later rebuilt by Solomon (1 Kings 9:18), but it is not certain that it is the same city. The city rebuilt by Solomon may have been further south in Judah, perhaps identified with Bealoth (Josh. 15:24) or Baalath-beer (Josh. 19:8), although these identifications are also questionable.

Baalbek (bahl'bek), a city located in the Beqaa Valley of Lebanon. It is the site of Roman Heliopolis and the ruins of temples for the triad of Jupiter, Mercury, and Venus (this is not the Heliopolis of Jer. 43:13, which was the Egyptian city of On). The Heliopolitan cult of Jupiter, Venus, and Mercury at Baalbek, which was an adaptation of one of the older Semitic gods Hadad, Atargatis, and Baal, became widespread throughout the Roman Empire.

The Temple of Bacchus at Baalbek, a city in the Beqaa Valley of Lebanon and site of the Roman city of Heliopolis. The architecture is of typical second-century A.D. Roman design.

Baal-gad (bay'uhl-gad), probably modern Hasbaiya in Lebanon's Beqaa Valley (Josh. 11:17; 12: 7; 13:5).

Baal-hamon (bay'uhl-hay'muhn; Heb., "Lord of abundance, wealth"), a town, location unknown (Song of Sol. 8:11).

Baalhanan (bay'uhl-hay'nan; Heb., "Baal [deity] is gracious"). **1** The son of Achbor, and a pre-Israelite king of Edom (Gen. 36:38–39). **2** A regional overseer of olive and sycamore trees during the reign of King David (1 Chron. 27:28).

Baal-hazor (bay'uhl-hay'zohr; Heb., "Baal of Hazor"), Absalom's location for shearing sheep (2 Sam. 13:23). It is not to be confused with the city of Hazor. It was probably modern Tell Azur, some six miles northeast of Bethel and about five miles south and slightly west of Shiloh.

Baal-hermon (bay'uhl-huhr'muhn; Heb., "Baal of Hermon"), a Hivite town (Judg. 3:3) on the north border of Manasseh's tribal land (1 Chron. 5:23). Some scholars consider it identical to Baal-gad (Josh. 11:17; 12:7; 13:5). If so, it was situated somewhere on the western side of Mount Hermon about equidistant from Tyre and Sidon on the Mediterranean coast. The precise location is unknown.

Baal-meon (bay'uhl-mee'uhn; Heb., "lord of habitation"), an area assigned to the tribe of Reuben (Num. 32:3, 38; Josh. 13:17; 1 Chron. 5:8). It was Moabite in the ninth century B.C. when the Moabite king Mesha built a reservoir there. It may have been in Israelite hands again in the eighth century, but it reverted to Moabite control later (Jer. 48:23; Ezek. 25:9). It was probably at modern Ma'in about four miles southwest of Medeba and nine miles southwest of Hesban in central Transjordan.

Baal-peor (bay'uhl-pee'ohr; Heb., "Baal of Peor"), the scene of an Israelite idolatrous episode with the god "Baal of Peor" (Num. 25:3–5) which was long remembered (Hos. 9:10; Deut. 4: 3; Ps. 106:28). The site was probably modern Khirbet esh-Sheikh Jayil some eight miles west of Hesban in the Transjordan hills leading down to the Jordan Valley.

Baal-perazim (bay'uhl-pair-ah-zeem'), modern Sheikh Bedr northwest of Jerusalem. David defeated Philistines there (2 Sam. 5:20; 1 Chron. 14:11).

Baal-shalisha (bay'uhl-shah'lee-shah), modern Kefr Thilth southwest of Shechem, from which a man came bringing bread to Elijah (2 Kings 4:42–44).

Baal-tamar (bay'uhl-tay'mahr; Heb., "lord of the palm"), the staging area for the successful Israelite assault on Gibeah (Judg. 20:33–48). Its location must have been near Gibeah, but it is yet uncertain. One possibility is modern Ras et-Tawil just north of Jerusalem.

Baal-zebub (bay'uhl-zee'buhb; also Beelzebub [bee-el'zi-buhb]), a god worshiped by the Philistines at Ekron (2 Kings 1:2–16). The original form and meaning of the term are unclear. Originally, it may have meant "lord of the lofty abode"; then, because this god was considered by the Hebrews to be an unworthy rival to Yahweh, it may have been revised to "lord of flies" (Baal-zebub). Later, it was altered even further to Beel-zebul, meaning "lord of dung." In the intertestamental period, when numerous names were used to designate the leader of the forces of evil, one of the names selected was Baal-zebub (or the alternative form Beel-zebul). In the Gospels, Jesus denies that he casts out demons by Beel-zebul, "the prince of demons" (Matt. 12: 24–27; Mark 3:22–26; Luke 11:15–19; cf. Matt. 10:25). ***See also*** Baal; Devil; Satan. J.M.E.

Baal-zephon (bay'uhl-ze'fahn), possibly Tell Defenneh (Egyptian Tahpanhes) in the eastern Nile delta; a point on the Exodus route (Exod. 14:2; Num. 33:7).

Baana (bay'uh-nuh). **1** The son of Ahilud and a district administrator under King Solomon. He was responsible for provisioning the king for one month of the year from the district around Megiddo and in the Jezreel Valley in north-central Israel (1 Kings 4:12). **2** The son of Hushai and another official with similar duties in Asher, the coastal area of far northern Israel (1 Kings 4:16). **3** The father of Zadok, one who helped repair the Fish Gate in Jerusalem under Nehemiah (Neh. 3:4); he is possibly the same person called Baanah listed as one of those who returned from Babylon with Zerubbabel (Ezra 2:2; Neh. 10:27). ***See also*** Baanah. D.R.B.

Baanah (bay'uh-nuh). **1** A Benjaminite commander of a group of soldiers under Ishbosheth, Saul's son. He and his brother Rechab killed Ishbosheth and took his head to David, thinking David would be pleased at the removal of this threat to his newly established rule. Instead, David was angry at their treachery and ordered them both killed, mutilated, and publicly displayed (2 Sam. 4). **2** The father of Heleb (Heled), one of David's fighting men (2 Sam. 23:29). **3** One who returned with Zerubbabel from the Babylonian captivity (Neh. 7:7), probably the same one who signed the covenant to keep the law (Neh. 10:27); he is possibly the same person elsewhere called Baana whose son helped rebuild the Fish Gate in Jerusalem (Neh. 3:4). ***See also*** Baana; Ishbosheth. D.R.B.

Baasha (bah'eh-sheh), the third king of Israel who gained the throne by murdering his predecessor Nadab (1 Kings 15:27–28). He later exterminated the house of Jeroboam (1 Kings 15:29). His long rule (twenty-four years) was labeled wicked and rebellious (1 Kings 15:34) and his own house was brought to a violent end when Zimri, an Israelite military commander, murdered Baasha's son Elah, in accordance with the prophecy of Jehu (1 Kings 16:1–4) Baasha's contemporary in Judah was Asa, with whom he battled throughout his reign. The main recorded incident was Baasha's attempt to fortify Ramah, resulting in Syrian intervention by Ben-hadad the Syrian king at the request and bribe of Asa (1 Kings 15:16–20). D.L.C.

Babel (ba'buhl), the Hebrew name for Babylon. It was the site of the episode in Gen. 11:1–9, which recounts the origin of separate languages. Once humankind spoke one language, but when people settled in Shinar (understood by most modern scholars as Sumer), they purposed to make bricks and building materials and build a city and tower "with its top in the heavens, and . . . make a name for [themselves], lest [they] be scattered abroad upon the face of the whole earth" (Gen. 11:4). God, beholding this, concluded that with a single common language humankind could do anything it wished, so he confounded human speech, creating linguistic havoc and scattering the people over the earth. The story is thus perhaps a variant on the spread of nations recounted in Genesis 10.

The story neatly divides into two parts: vv. 1–4 recount the proposals of the builders, 5–9 the counter-purposes of the deity. Throughout, plays on the letters "b" and "l" occur: "let us make bricks" (Heb. *nilbenah),* "for stone" (Heb. *le'eben*), and "let us . . . confuse" (Heb. *nabelah*). The place is called "Babel" because "there the Lord confused [Heb. *balal*] the language of all the earth."

The unfinished tower may have been of the common spiral or terraced type known in the Akkadian language as a *ziggurat*. Babylon's own ziggurat, the Marduk temple known as Entemenanki, was not built until the seventh/sixth centuries B.C. The biblical episode has been compared to the building of Esagila in the Babylonian creation epic *Enuma elish* 6. 60–62. But whereas the Babylonian tradition reflects deep pride in the building of cities, as an art of civilization, the biblical author characteristically expresses a more negative view. ***See also*** Babylon; Mesopotamia; Sumer; Ziggurat. J.W.R.

Babylon (bab'uh-lahn; from Akkadian *bāb īli,* "the gate of the god"), the Akkadian name of a Mesopotamian city. In the Hebrew Bible, Babylon (Heb. *bavel*) refers both to Babylonia and Babylon, the region and its capital. Babylon covered over two thousand acres, making it one of the largest ancient Mesopotamian sites. It is located along the Euphrates River in the area where it most closely approaches the Tigris River, in what is now Iraq. Its location at the northern end of the Euphrates flood plain gave Babylon potential control of major trade routes.

The German archaeologist Robert Koldewey conducted excavations at Babylon between 1899 and 1917. The Iraq Directorate General of Antiquities began further excavation and restoration in 1958.

Babylonia has supported settled life from as early as the sixth millennium B.C. Babylon is first mentioned in a date formula of the Sargonic king Shar-kali-sharri (2217–2193 B.C.). By this time, there were already two temples on the site. **Under Hammurabi:** The city achieved little notoriety, however, until the nineteenth century B.C., when the Amorites, under Sumu-abum, founded their dynasty at Babylon. The previously weak political position of Babylon strengthened during the reign of that city's and dynasty's most famous king, Hammurabi (1792–1750 B.C.). The influence of Babylon spread to the Palestine region; Hammurabi had ambassadors residing at Hazor. Hammurabi's political acumen and charismatic personality enabled him to unify Babylonia, which had heretofore been dotted with independent petty states. Several generations later, in 1595 B.C., his successors lost the city when the Hittites, under Murshili I, sacked Babylon.

Plan of the ancient city of Babylon as envisioned by a modern mapmaker, highlighting the city of the sixth century B.C.

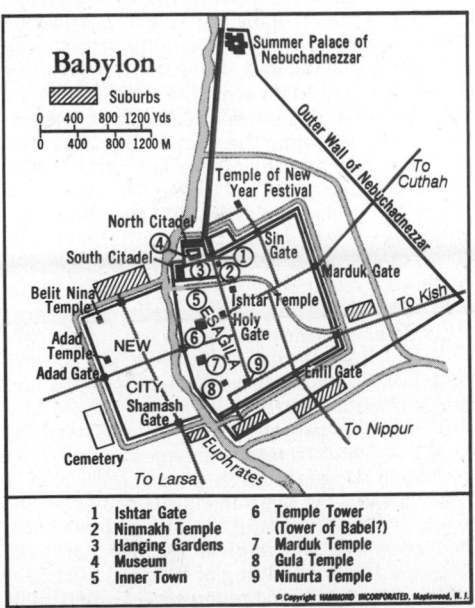

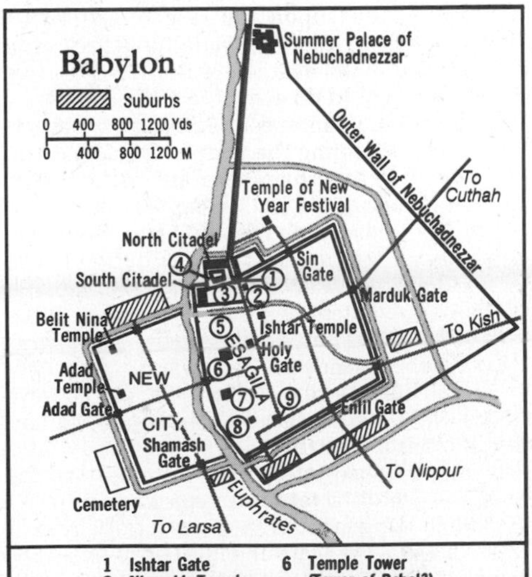

The social and cultural climate in Babylon at the time of the Amorite dynasty laid the foundation for spectacular cultural developments. The Law Code of Hammurabi, formulated in conditional clauses, contributed the principle of *lex talionis,* the law of exact retributions. This is expressed in the biblical legal material (Exod. 21:23–25), although its force is qualified by the subsequent formulations that call for the liberation of a slave to compensate for the loss of an eye or tooth (Exod. 21:26–27).

Another legal development in Babylonia at this time was the oral promulgation of acts of justice (Akkadian *mesharum*), which were designed to alleviate short-term social and economic ills. In the Bible this institution is preserved (Heb. *mesharim*) in Pss. 9:9; 58:2; 75:3; 96:10; 98:9; and 99:4.

The scribal school flourished during this Old Babylonian period and gave rise to Babylon's claim to being a literary and scholarly center. Its voluminous output was no less important than the longevity of the school. The latest known cuneiform text, dated to A.D. 79, is from Babylon. Scribes in this city, along with those in Uruk, employed the cumbersome cuneiform writing system long after alphabetic scripts had taken hold throughout the Near East. At the end of the first millennium B.C., the scribal school at Babylon produced almost exclusively astronomical and astrological reports. The biblical tradition was aware of this and Isaiah (47:13) reported on astrological readings there.

Succeeding Dynasties and Kings: During the still poorly understood Kassite dynasty (ca. 1570–1150 B.C.), Babylon conducted extensive trade with Egypt during Egypt's Amarna Age. Documents treating the relations between these two regions have been recovered at either end of the Fertile Crescent. Dynastic marriages, such as those between Solomon and Egyptian princesses (1 Kings 9:16), occurred between ruling houses of Egypt and Babylonia.

Babylon did not experience another golden age until the reign of Nabonassar (747–734 B.C.). This period was so significant that the Babylonian Chronicle (a contemporary historical record) began its account with it and later Ptolemaic records assign an exact date and time to its beginning. It is a period marked by a curious blend of cultural achievement and political unrest, a time in which the fortunes of the Israelite nation are intertwined with those of Mesopotamia.

Tiglath-pileser III reigned as king of Assyria from 744–727 B.C. and simultaneously as regent of Babylonia from 728–727 B.C. Known in the Hebrew Bible as Pul, he collected tribute from Menahem of Israel (2 Kings 15:19) and carried off captives from the tribes of Reuben, Gad, and the half-tribe of Manasseh (1 Chron. 5:26). Isaiah (66:19) includes Pul among the rulers to whom God will send a sign of his glory.

During the less glorious reign of his successor, Shalmaneser V (726–722 B.C.), events with great ramifications for the biblical world occurred. Shalmaneser V besieged King Hoshea in Samaria after the Israelite king engaged in intrigue with Egypt against the Babylonian king (2 Kings 18:9–10). Shalmaneser died before the siege of Samaria was completed; credit for this task is claimed by his successor, Sargon II (722–705 B.C.). 2 Kings 18:10–11 records the completion of this siege, although it does not mention Sargon. The author's understanding of the fine points of the chronology seems to have been confused.

Sennacherib, who reigned as king of Assyria (704–681 B.C.) and of Babylon (704–703 B.C.), attempted to take Jerusalem from Hezekiah but failed. He received Temple treasures as tribute but was forced to retreat to Nineveh.

Merodach-Baladan II (721–710 and 703 B.C.) sent envoys to Jerusalem, after which the prophet Isaiah warned that all that was in Hezekiah's house would be carried to Babylon (2 Kings 20:12). In 2 Kings 20:12 this Babylonian king is rightly called Merodach-Baladan; but in Isa. 39:1, he is called Berodach-Baladan.

The next major contact between Babylon and the biblical kings came during the reign of the Babylonian Nebuchadrezzar II (605–562 B.C.). He carried King Jehoiachin of Judah and his family into exile. Records from the palace in Babylon list the rations the Israelite monarch and his family received. Nebuchadrezzar installed Jehoiachin's uncle, Zedekiah, as governor of Jerusalem. When Zedekiah rebelled, Nebuchadrezzar laid siege to the city, destroyed the Temple and carried the remnant of the population off to exile in Babylonia (2 Kings 24:10–25:21).

In the Mesopotamian record, Nebuchadrezzar is remembered for his expansion and restoration of Babylon. Three palaces date to this time period. The Southern Palace, Nebuchadrezzar's principal palace, may have been the site of Belshazzar's feast (Daniel 5). The inner city was divided by a magnificent processional way. At one end stood the Ishtar Gate, decorated wth glazed bricks. The hanging gardens of Babylon were also the creation of

The Chronicle of the Babylonian king Nebuchadnezzar II (605–562 B.C.; his name is alternately spelled Nebuchadrezzar) mentions the removal of Jehoiachin of Judah as king of Israel and the appointment of his uncle, Zedekiah, in his place. It also records the siege and destruction of Jerusalem when Zedekiah rebelled in 586.

Nebuchadrezzar. After these, the most famous architectural remain in Babylon was the ziggurat to Marduk who was there called Entemenanki, Akkadian "the lord of the foundation of heaven and earth." Such a stepped tower may have been the prototype for the Tower of Babel (Gen. 11:9). In Genesis the city's name is said to derive from the Hebrew verb *balal*, "to confuse," thus connecting the city of Babylon with the story of the confusion of tongues. There is only one additional reference to Babylon in the Pentateuch: in Gen. 10:10, it is included among the cities in the kingdom of Nimrod.

Political intrigue and domestic unrest plagued Babylonia again. The final Babylonian king, Nabonidus (555–539), exhibited personality flaws severe enough to receive mention in Daniel 4, although there they are ascribed to Nebuchadrezzar. Nabonidus absented himself from Babylon at the time of the New Year's Feast, making its observance impossible, and sequestered himself for ten years in the Arabian caravan city of Teima. A Qumran fragment speaks of this incident.

The weakening of Babylonia left the door open for rule by a new, non-Mesopotamian dynasty. The Persian or Achaemenid dynasty, of which Cyrus (538–530 B.C.) was the first important ruler, restored not only the fortunes of Babylon, but of the cities and regions Babylon had conquered. In 538, Cyrus granted permission for the Jews exiled in Babylonia to return to Jerusalem. Among the Jewish community Cyrus enjoyed a good reputation. Isaiah called him God's anointed (45:1). Restoration of the Temple was interrupted and not resumed until the reign of the Achaemenid king Darius I (522–486 B.C.).

The Jewish Community in Babylon: In Babylonia, the exilic and postexilic Jewish community developed its own character and left a legacy still felt today. It is clear that the community felt the burden of its position (Ps. 137), but they had the resources to overcome this hardship. Jeremiah strongly encouraged the participation of the Jewish population in the commercial, agricultural, and cultural life of Babylonia. He depicts the well-being of the community (Jer. 29: 7).

The prophetic writings in the Bible, heavily concerned with the exilic experience, naturally present several viewpoints about Babylon. In oracles against Babylon, the city is seen as the instrument of divine judgment against Judah. Babylon itself is brought for judgment in Jer. 51:59–64. The mixed feelings toward Babylon and the Exile are seen in the fact that the writings of Ezekiel contain no anti-Babylon strands.

Babylon continued to figure prominently in world and Jewish history. Alexander the Great died there in 323 B.C.

The increasingly powerful and independent Jewish community of Babylonia separated itself from events in Palestine. Following the Roman destruction of the Second Temple (A.D. 70), Babylonian financial support of the Palestinian community stopped. Babylonia's Jews supported neither the war against Rome (A.D. 66–70), nor the Bar-Kochba revolt of A.D. 132–135. It was in Babylon during the subsequent centuries that many of the legal and religious institutions of Judaism developed. The massive Babylonian Talmud is witness and monument to the legal and biblical issues discussed in the academies, to the theological concerns and formulations of the rabbis, and to the folkways and beliefs of the common people. This major Jewish center thrived for centuries, only to be eclipsed with the fall of the Bagdad Caliphate in the eleventh century.

Parts of the city of Babylon itself lay in ruins sometime in the second century A.D., as evidenced by the reports of the satirist Lucian of Samosata. ***See also*** Babel; Mesopotamia. L.E.P.

Baca (bay'kuh), unidentified valley associated with weeping or balsam (Ps. 84:6). The term is derived from the verb "to drip," hence its association with weeping.

badger, a medium-sized burrowing mammal. The Hebrew word *(shaphan)* translated "badger" in Ps. 104:18 and Prov. 30:26 and "rock badger" in Lev. 11:5 and Deut. 14:7 more likely refers to the coney or hyrax *(Procavia capensis)*, a hare-sized, rock-dwelling ungulate. The true badger *(Meles meles)* also lives in Palestine but is rarely to be seen.

bag (KJV: "scrip"), a knapsacklike bag, usually of leather, for carrying goods and provisions (Jth. 10:5; 13:10, 15). It is distinguished from a purse (Luke 10:4; 22:35–36) and belt for carrying money (Matt. 10:9–10; Mark 6:8). It was not a beggar's bag. The disciples during Jesus' ministry were not to carry such a bag of provisions on their mission but to trust in God's provision.

Bahurim (buh-hōō'rim), modern Ras et-Tmin east of Mount Scopus by Jerusalem. It is mentioned most frequently in the David stories (2 Sam. 3:16; 16:5; 17:18; 19:16; 23:31; 1 Kings 2: 8).

baker, one engaged in the process of baking. While baking (Heb. *'aphah*) was a normal daily activity of women engaged in the preparation of meals, the specialized profession of baker *('opheh)* developed in urban centers. Jer. 37:21 speaks of a "street of the bakers," where those engaged in this trade must have had their shops. Baked products included bread (*lekhem,* Lev. 26:26; Isa. 44:15, 19), leavened and unleavened *(matsah)*, for ordinary meals (Gen. 19:3; 1 Sam. 28:24) and ritual purposes (Exod. 12:8; Lev. 6: 10; 24:5). Several passages wherein bakers appear are worthy of note. In Genesis 40, the chief baker and cupbearer of Pharaoh, important functionaries at court, are imprisoned with Joseph, who interprets the dreams that preview their fate. Another important text is 1 Sam. 8:13,

Woman kneading dough; pottery figurine from a Phoenician cemetery at Achziv, eighth–sixth century B.C.

which is part of the famous passage in which Samuel details the abuses of royal power that will obtain in monarchical Israel. One of these abuses is the corvée, or the impressing of Israelite men and women into royal service: "He [the king] will take your daughters to be perfumers and cooks and bakers." In the futility curse of Lev. 26:26, the scarcity of food is underlined by the statement that ten women will need only one oven for baking bread. A baker appears in Hos. 7:4, 6, but the text and the role of the baker in it are both obscure. J.S.K.

Balaam (bay'luhm), a non-Israelite prophet known from both biblical and extrabiblical sources as a person from the region of Transjordan skilled not only in divination but also in performative acts. His fame in the culture of the ancient world places him alongside Noah, Daniel, and Job as a folk hero in the repertoire of the storyteller.

Balaam appears commonly in the OT and regularly in the NT as an example of an evil artist, a prophet who would sell his skill for the proper price without reference to the Word of God supposedly represented by his words (Deut. 23:4, 5; Josh. 13:22; 24:9, 10; Neh. 13:2; Mic. 6:5; 2 Pet. 2:15; Jude 11; Rev. 2:14). The fable in Num. 22:21–35 constitutes a narrative from this facet of the tradition. In the fable, Balaam, known to tradition as a *seer of the gods* cannot see as well as his ass. Moreover, Balaam carries the responsibility for causing Israel to sin at Baal-peor (Num. 31:8, 16).

In contrast, the legend in Num. 22–24 holds Balaam in a favorable light. When the antagonist, Balak, hires Balaam to curse the armies of Israel so that his defense against the Israelite threat would be manageable, Balaam responds with an appeal to his prophetic virtue. He can offer Balak only the word given him by God for the occasion. Balaam finishes the scene with an affirmation of his prophetic virtue: "Did I not tell your messengers whom you sent to me, 'If Balak should give me his house full of silver and gold, I would not be able to go beyond the word of the Lord, to do either good or bad of my own will; what the Lord speaks, that will I speak'?" (Num. 24:12–13). ***See also*** Prophet. G.W.C.

Balak (bay'lak), the king of Moab and principal antagonist in the Balaam story (Num. 22–24). His pathetic plea for a curse against Israel casts him as a tragic figure, yet places him in comic contrast to the prophet who blesses Israel. ***See also*** Balaam.

balances, instruments devised for weighing. They consisted of a central support and crossbeam from which two equally weighted pans were suspended by cords. From earliest times balances, probably at first hand held, must have been in use for the purpose of commercial transactions. Indeed the balance is a symbol known from the earliest writing and from many illustrations. The weight of an object was determined by its relationship to an accepted standard, at first grain, then stones of various shapes and sizes. Biblical references to balances are numerous, both to false or deceitful scales (Prov. 11:1; 20:23; Hos. 12:7; Amos 8:5) and to just balances (Lev. 19:36; Job 31:6; Prov. 16:11; Ezek. 45:10). Metaphorically the balance was used to judge a person's righteousness (Dan. 5:27; cf. Rev. 6:5), a parallel to the Egyptian religious belief of balancing before the gods the deceased's heart against the *ma'at,* or emblem of truth and justice. S.L.R.

balm, the resin or gum of the balsam tree *(Commiphora gileadensis)* which was used as a scent for oils and perfumes as well as a medicine to heal wounds (Jer. 8:22). The resin is collected naturally or by incision, and it hardens into small nodules. Often referred to as a "spice," it

Balsam, the source of balm.

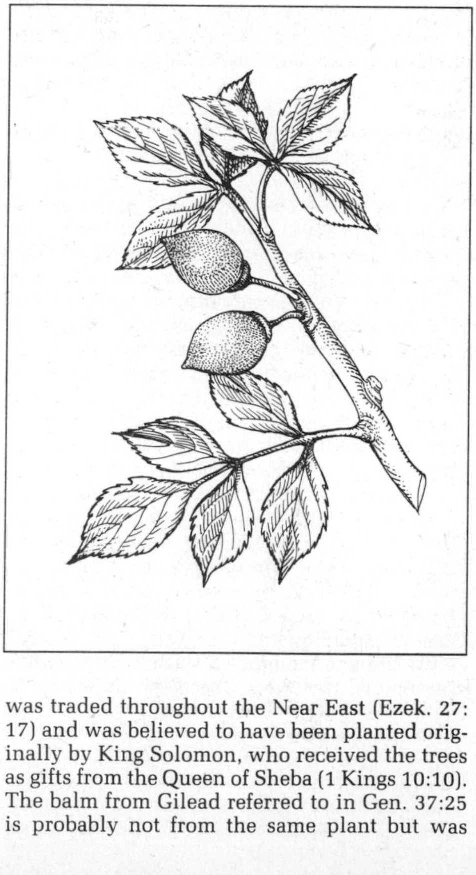

was traded throughout the Near East (Ezek. 27:17) and was believed to have been planted originally by King Solomon, who received the trees as gifts from the Queen of Sheba (1 Kings 10:10). The balm from Gilead referred to in Gen. 37:25 is probably not from the same plant but was gathered instead from the mastic tree *(Pistachia lentiscus)*. ***See also*** Spices. P.L.C.

ban (Heb. *ḥerem*), dedication of persons or materials to God. References to the total destruction of towns or persons and their possessions, generally by fire, in consequence of such a dedication are concentrated in the "conquest" era. The ban is connected (though not synonymous) with the taking of booty after battle and warriors' compensation. Items collected under the ban are reserved for the priestly cadre (Lev. 27: 21–22; Num. 18:14; Ezek. 44:29), although it is uncertain that the goods "donated" to the Lord in these texts were necessarily obtained in battle. Of cities taken in conquest, Jericho alone is placed off limits for Israelite occupation (Josh. 6). Also under the ban were Ai (Josh. 8), Makkedah, Lachish, Eglon, Hebron, Debir (Josh. 10), and Hazor (Josh. 11). Early practice was regulated, presumably by oracle (Num. 21:1–3; cf. contradictory claims within Josh. 11:12–13).

It may be speculated that the ban originated in order to control pestilential disease, especially bubonic plague, in the wake of warfare. Because Achan had taken as booty items that were under the ban (contaminated), he and all who might be infected by contact were burned with the goods (Josh. 7; cf. Lev. 27:28). Alternatively, the ban may have had its origins in the religious sphere, as part of votary offerings to the Lord of battles—possibly in connection with vows (Num. 21:1–3)—and was later extended in scope.

In the book of Judges the ban is mentioned only in the editorial frame rather than in the older traditions (Judg. 1:17; 21:11). The story of Gideon's ephod seems to caricature the misuse of booty (Judg. 8:22–28).

Under the Israelite monarchy, distribution of booty became the king's prerogative (1 Sam. 30: 23–25), and the ban was presented as a comprehensive commandment from antiquity, applicable to all cities within the "promised" land that refused the invaders' offer of peace (Deut. 20:10–18). The most extreme claim, "the whole land . . . all that breathed" (Josh. 10:40), is presumably editorial rather than historical.

Some scholars have compared the *ḥerem* to the *asakkum*, known from cuneiform texts from the city of Mari (eighteenth century B.C.). In these documents, the phrase "to eat the *asakkum*" of god or king refers to a violation of a decree regarding spoils of war. Contemporary with Israelite monarchy, Mesha, king of Moab (ninth century B.C.), boasts of imposing the *ḥerem* on captured Israelites.

In prophetic texts, the ban remained the prerogative of God alone, whether for weal (Zech. 14:11; Isa. 34:5) or for woe (Isa. 43:28; Mal. 3:24). In the postexilic period, a shift seems to have occurred, for the ban mentioned in Ezra 10:8 seems to refer to the confiscation of property due to noncompliance with an administrative decree. R.B.

Bani (bay'nī). **1** One of David's "mighty men," i.e., warriors (2 Sam. 23:36). **2** The head of a family of returned exiles (Ezra 2:10; 10:29; Neh. 10:14). **3** The founder of a family (Ezra 10:38). **4** A descendant of Judah (1 Chron. 9:4). **5** The name of four Levites (1 Chron. 6:46; Neh. 3:17; 9:4; 11:22).

bank, a repository for funds. Temple treasuries served such a purpose. Requirements of trade led to money changing and moneylending. Though the Torah forbade loaning money at interest to a fellow Israelite (Exod. 22:25; Lev. 25: 37), such activity was common (Luke 19:11–27; Josephus *Antiquities* 18.157). It constituted a burden for those who fell behind in payments of rent or taxes or needed seed to plant a crop (Luke 16:1–8a). Debtors were punished by imprisonment (Matt. 18:25–34). Josephus reports that at the start of the Jewish revolt in A.D. 66 the records of the moneylenders were destroyed so that debts could not be collected (*War* 2.247). P.P.

banner, a cloth ensign used for identification of a group. The Hebrew term, sometimes translated "ensign," can indicate a cloth object (Isa. 33:23; Ezek. 27:7) used as a rallying point (Isa. 5:26; 11:10; 13:2, hence its use for tribal standards in Num. 2:2), apparently because it could be easily seen. Another term sometimes translated "banner" is formed from a root that means "see." Most often used by an army (see Song of Sol. 6:4, 10), banners are sometimes mentioned symbolically (Exod. 17:15; Song of Sol. 2:4).

banquet, an elaborate meal, often called a feast. People in the Bible use food and drink both as nourishment and as ways of saying something to each other. A meal to which others are invited is a form of communication, with important social messages being exchanged between the host and those invited, those who should or might have been invited but were not, and those who declined the invitation (cf. Matt. 22:1–10). Just as the material used for communication in speech is language, so the material used for communication in a festive meal is food and drink and their setting. Thus the type of food and drink chosen, their mode of preparation, method of service, and seating or reclining arrangements all say something about the inviter's assessment of those invited (cf. Luke 14:7–11). A banquet differs from simply sharing a meal with other persons much like a formal speech differs from casual conversation. A banquet is formal communication, usually with messages of great importance (cf. John 13:2–30).

A royal banquet at which the king (probably Ashurbanipal) and queen are served in a garden by attendants with fans; from the reliefs at Nineveh, seventh century B.C.

There are two general types of banquets: ceremonial and ritual. A ceremonial banquet is a festive meal at which the inviter and the invited celebrate their mutual solidarity, their belonging to each other, their oneness. The festive meals of Israel's appointed feasts (see Lev. 23:2–44), much like the national and personal celebrations in the story of Esther (banquet for Persian elites, nonelites, and women, Esther 1:3–9; in honor of Esther, Esther 2:18; and of the king and, by ruse, of Mordecai, Esther 5:1–7:10) were such ceremonial banquets. The same is true of the gathering of Christians described by Paul in 1 Cor. 11:17–33.

A ritual banquet is one that marks some personal or interpersonal transition or transformation, held to give honor to those undergoing the important social change. As a ritual feature of hospitality, banquets indicate the transformation of a stranger into a guest (Gen. 19:3–14; Luke 5:29) or of an enemy into a covenant partner (Gen. 26:26–31; 2 Sam. 3:20). Banquets mark important transitional points in a person's life, e.g., Isaac's weaning day (Gen. 21:8); the weddings of Jacob (Gen. 29:22), Samson (Judg. 14: 10), the Lamb (Rev. 19:9), and in the parable of Matt. 22:2–10; the birthdays of Pharaoh (Gen. 40:20), of Herod (Mark 6:21); or the victory banquet hosted by God in Rev. 19:17. At the Last Supper Jesus changes the ceremonial banquet of the Jewish Passover into a ritual banquet effectively symbolizing the meaning of his impending death (Mark 14:12–25 and parallels).

B.J.M.

baptism, rite involving water. The term is derived from a Greek word meaning "to immerse in or wash with water" (Mark 7:4). Washing rites characterize priestly preparation for offering sacrifice in the OT (Exod. 40:12–15). On the Day of Atonement, the high priest bathes both before and after his offering (Lev. 16:4, 24). Visitors to the Temple should not enter the inner courts without washing hands and feet (*t. Kelim* I.6). Water washings are linked not only with religious purity but also with concern for sinfulness and moral purity (see Isa. 1:16–17; Jer. 4:14; Ezek. 36:25). More domestic versions of these concerns are found in Jewish ablutions in Jesus' time. John 2:6 speaks of large stone jars that hold water "for purification" (see Mark 7: 2–4). John's baptism and the ablutions of the Qumran covenanters belong to this tradition of cultic and moral ablutions. Jews also apparently performed baptisms of proselytes as part of the purification of new covenant members (*m. Pesahim* VIII.7; *Eduyyot* V.2).

Baptism in the NT begins with John's baptism, which was a prophetic call to repentance and forgiveness of sins (Mark 1:4). When Jesus is baptized, however, it is understood quite differently: it is *not* for sin (Matt. 3:13–15); rather it is a theophany (i.e., a self-revealing of God) in which Jesus is identified as "Beloved Son" and commissioned as the herald of God's kingdom (Mark 1:10–11; see Isa. 42:1–9). Christian baptism of converts retained the sense of rites of purification (1 Peter 3:21) as well as adoption as God's children. Paul speaks of God pouring his Holy Spirit into converts' hearts, enabling them to say "Abba, Father" (Gal. 4:6; Rom. 8:15–17). This baptism was in some sense to Christianity what circumcision was to Judaism. John 3:3–5, in fact, makes baptism—not circumcision—the formal entrance rite into the covenant community (see Col. 2:11–12).

The interpretation of Christian baptism was fluid in the first century. At Corinth it was compared to Israel's exodus through the sea and its eating of the manna in the desert (1 Cor. 10:1–4). In other places it was compared with Noah's escape from God's wrath on sinners (1 Pet. 3:21). It was also compared with Jesus' death and resurrection; Christians symbolically die to their sins and former lives, a death they share with Christ, and are buried with him; as they rise from baptism in purity, they share the new life brought by Jesus' resurrection (Rom. 6:

1–4). Hence baptism may be compared to a new birth (John 3:4–5).

Although adults were generally baptized, there is a suggestion in Mark 10:13–16 that infants were also baptized. The argument rests on the term "hinder" (Gk. *kōlyō*), which may have been part of the technical terminology of baptism: Jesus tells his disciples not to "*hinder*" the children from coming to him; compare the language of the eunuch in Acts 8:36 who asks, "what is to prevent (GK. *kōlyō*) my being baptized?" ***See also*** John the Baptist; Proselyte; Purity; Sacraments. J.H.N.

bar (bahr), the Aramaic word for "son," equivalent to the Hebrew *ben*, occurring in phrases such as *bar enash* ("human being"; lit., "son of man," Dan. 7:13) and *bar elahin* ("divine being"; lit., "son of [the] god[s]," Dan. 3: 25). It occurs also in personal names, generally as part of a patronymic, such as Barabbas, Bar Jesus, Simon (Peter) Bar-Jona, Barnabas, Bartholomew, Barqos, Barsabbas, and Bartimaeus; in the epithet of the leader of the Second Jewish Revolt Bar Kochba; and in the Jewish ritual Bar Mitzvah (lit., "son of the commandment").

Barabbas (buh-rab'uhs; Heb., "son of Abba"), a person imprisoned for being a bandit or, perhaps, for stirring up rebellion against Roman rule, who tradition holds was released from jail at the time Jesus was crucified (Matt. 27:16; Mark 15:11; Luke 23:18; John 18:40). Roman law treated rebellious subjects as bandits and crucified them at the site of their crimes or near a busy highway as a warning to others. Mark and Matthew report that Pilate had a custom of releasing a prisoner at Passover. John reports that Pilate calls it a Jewish custom when he releases Barabbas. Lack of any evidence for the custom from other sources makes it impossible to evaluate the Gospel tradition. ***See also*** Cross; Trial of Jesus, The. P.P.

Barak (bay'rak; Heb., "lightning"), the son of Abinoam. Commander of Israelite militia and subordinate to Deborah in Ephraim in Judges 4 (prose) and 5 (victory song), Barak was among the deliverers of Israel (1 Sam. 12:11 LXX; cf. Heb. 11:32).

The opposition ("kings of Canaan," Judg. 5: 19), headed by Jabin "king of Canaan at Hazor" (4:2, 23) and led by the nine hundred chariots of Sisera (a non-Semitic name) from Harosheth "of the nations," represents domination by other newcomers (Sea Peoples).

When the people sought Deborah's "judgment," she recalled Barak from Kedesh (in Naphtali) and outlined her strategy, after which she returned to Kedesh with Barak (Judg. 4:4–9). Barak mustered ten units (not ten thousand!) from Zebulun and Naphtali. Other tribes also responded, according to Judg. 5. At the waters of Megiddo, Barak routed and destroyed the opposition. Sisera fled far north and was slain by another woman, Jael (Judg. 4:17–22).

This account shows how new Israelite settlements throughout the hill country (late twelfth century) had so disrupted commerce that Israel could challenge, with help of a cloudburst, sophisticated armaments of the plains (i.e., chariots). ***See also*** Army; Judges, The Book of; Sisera. R.B.

barbarian, a term originally referring to one who spoke a foreign language. Herodotus, the Greek historian who lived in the fifth century B.C., called Egyptians "barbarians," i.e., alien speakers. 1 Cor. 14:11 and Ps. 113:1 in the Septuagint (LXX; 114:1 in Hebrew) carry the same nuance. From "alien tongue," barbarian came to mean "alien race, region, or people," i.e., non-Greeks (see, e.g., Acts 28:2, 4).

Used pejoratively, "barbarian" demeaned those lacking Hellenistic culture as crude, coarse, boorish, savage, or bestial (see, e.g., Ezek. 21:36 in the LXX [21:31 in Hebrew]; 2 Macc. 4:25; 15:2). Somewhat milder is Paul's reference to "barbarians" as "backward" or "ignorant" (Rom. 1:14).

Paul and Philo combine "Greek and barbarian" to mean the entire world (excluding Jews). Whereas Philo believed that Judaism united all peoples through Law, Paul foresaw a union forged by Christ (Rom. 1:5, 14). A late Paulinist summarized this view nicely in Col. 3:11. ***See also*** Gentile; Greeks; Nations. C.J.R.

barefoot, unshod, not wearing shoes or sandals. In the OT, it is a sign of reverence in obedience to the divine command, as in the theophanies to Moses (Exod. 3:5) and Joshua (Josh. 5:15). David's going barefoot is probably part of a ritual of penitence (2 Sam. 15:30). In a prophetic symbolic action, Isaiah goes about naked and barefoot for three years as a sign to Judah of the coming defeat by Assyria of Egypt and Ethiopia, Judah's allies, who will be led away naked and barefoot as prisoners of war and exiles (Isa. 20:2–4).

Baris (bair'is; from Heb. *birah*), name given by Flavius Josephus for the Temple fortress of Jerusalem built by Nehemiah (Neh. 2:8; 7:2), later renovated by the Hasmoneans. According to 2 Macc. 4:12, Jason founded a gymnasium "under the citadel." Sostratus was captain of the citadel (4:28), and Menelaus took refuge there during Jason's siege of Jerusalem (5:5). ***See also*** Antonia, Tower of.

Bar-Jesus. ***See*** Elymas.

Bar-Jona (bahr-joh'nah), an Aramaic surname of Simon Peter meaning "Son of Jona" or "Son of John" (Matt. 16:17; cf. John 1:42; 21:15).

barley, one of the two staple grain crops in the biblical period (wheat was the other). Bread made of barley was the food of lower-income people (Ezek. 4:12; John 6:9). Seven weeks elapsed from the beginning of the barley harvest in late April until the completion of the wheat harvest at the beginning of June (Deut. 16:9–12; Ruth 2:23). The harvest culminated at the feast of Pentecost. Since barley was the staple of the lower classes, failure of the barley harvest or absurdly high prices for barley served as a judgment oracle against the nation (Job 31:40; Rev. 6:6). Real devastation is indicated in Ezek. 4:9 when the prophet is instructed to eat bread composed of all kinds of grains, since there is not enough of any one kind to make a loaf. Ezek. 13:19 may refer to use of barley in connection with divination. Num. 5:15 mandates a barley offering as part of the "test" by which a jealous husband determines the fidelity of his wife.
P.P.

Barnabas (bahr'nuh-buhs), according to Acts 4:36–37 a Levite from Cyprus whose cognomen was Joseph and who became a member of the early Christian community in Jerusalem and was surnamed "Barnabas" (Heb., "Son of encouragement") by the apostles. A Diaspora Jew (i.e., one born in a country outside Palestine) who may have come to Jerusalem because of his priestly connections, Barnabas was a cousin of John Mark (Col. 4:10) and soon became a leader in the church. According to Acts, he introduced Saul (Paul), a fellow Greek-speaking Jewish believer in Jesus, to the apostles in Jerusalem (Acts 9:27); this suggests that Acts knew Barnabas to be well versed in the activities of the Christian movement in Syria, where Saul had become a Christian.

After the persecution of the Hellenists (Jewish Christians whose native language was Greek) in Jerusalem, Barnabas appeared in Antioch-on-the-Orontes as a representative of the Jerusalem church (Acts 11:19–26). There, he affirmed the mission to the Gentiles and worked with Saul as senior partner or supervisor of a Christian mission in Syria-Cilicia. Acts reports that he and Saul took the famine offering from Antioch to Jerusalem (Acts 11:27–30; 12:25). If the reports in Acts are accurate, Barnabas must have had a formative role in the development of Saul's theological outlook (but see Gal. 1:13–17). Paul does imply that Barnabas was a fellow apostle (1 Cor. 9:3–6; cf. Acts 14:4, 14). Acts also records that both Paul and Barnabas chose to work with their hands as tradesmen, even though their families had financial means (cf. Acts 4:36; 23:16).

According to Acts, Paul and Barnabas worked together on a mission tour to Cyprus and the Iconium region of Asia Minor (Acts 13:1–14:28), appeared together at the Jerusalem conference (Acts 15:1–35), but then disagreed and separated over the question of allowing John Mark to accompany them on a second tour (Acts 15:36–41) after he had cut short his participation in an earlier tour (13:13). Barnabas' role in the dispute in Antioch over whether circumcised and uncircumcised believers should eat together is obscure (Gal. 2:11–14). According to Acts 15:1–35, Barnabas was a strong defender of not binding circumcision on Gentile converts. Yet he apparently had great respect for Peter and sided with him (and Mark) in the dispute with Paul.

Acts speaks of Barnabas as "a good man, full of the Holy Spirit and of faith" (11:24). Some traditions beyond the canonical writings regard him as the author of the Letter to the Hebrews. Likewise, *The Epistle of Barnabas* is attributed to him, although it actually comes from the second century. ***See also*** Antioch; Apostle; Circumcision; Cyprus; Gentile; Hellenists; Levites; Mark; Paul; Peter; Syria.
A.J.M.

barracks. ***See*** Antonia, Tower of.

Barsabbas (bahr-sab'uhs; KJV: "Barsabas," bahr'suh-buhs). **1** According to Acts 1:23–26, "Joseph called Barsabbas, who was surnamed Justus," along with Matthias, was put forward as a candidate to replace Judas Iscariot among the twelve apostles after the latter's death; Matthias was chosen. **2** According to Acts 15:22–34, "Judas called Barsabbas," a prophet and a leader in the Jerusalem church, was given the task, along with Silas, of announcing the decision of the Jerusalem conference to the churches in Antioch, Syria, and Cilicia. They accompanied Paul and Barnabas to Antioch, later returning to Jerusalem. ***See also*** Apostle; Judas; Matthias; Paul; Silas, Silvanus.
A.J.M.

Bartholomew, one of the twelve apostles about whom little is known. His name appears in all of the NT apostolic lists (Matt. 10:2–4; Mark 3:16–19; Luke 6:14–16; Acts 1:13) but nowhere else in the NT. Because "Bartholomew" follows "Philip" in three of the lists (Matthew, Mark, and Luke), some scholars have identified him with the "Nathanael" whom Philip brought to Jesus (John 1:45–51; Bartholomew is never mentioned in John, nor is Nathanael in Matthew, Mark, or Luke). This identification lacks conclusive evidence, however, and reflects harmonizing tendencies. Later Christian traditions identify Bartholomew as a missionary in India (Eusebius) and author of an apocryphal gospel (Jerome). ***See also*** Apostle; Disciple; Nathanael; Philip; Twelve, The.
P.L.S.

Bartimaeus (bahr'ti-may'uhs; translated in Mark 10:46 as "son of Timaeus"), a blind beggar healed by Jesus on leaving Jericho (Mark 10:46–52). The other accounts report Jesus healed two (unnamed) blind men on leaving Jericho (Matt. 20:29–34) or one (unnamed) blind man on entering Jericho (Luke 18:35–43). ***See also*** Blindness; Disease and Healing; Miracles.

Baruch, Jeremiah's friend and secretary. Baruch, son of Neriah, son of Mahseiah, belonged to a respected Jerusalemite family and his brother, Seraiah, was minister to King Zedekiah (Jer. 51: 59). Bullae (seals) of the two brothers, Baruch and Seraiah, have been recently found and published. The bulla of Baruch reads "to/from Baruch // son of Neriah // the scribe" (Heb. *lbrkyhw // bn nryhw // hspr;* plausibly then the biblical name is a hypocoristicon from which the divine name has been removed). The title *hspr*, present also in Jer. 36:32, indicates Baruch's position as a royal clerk, like other people called "scribe" (Heb. *sopher*) in records of his age (e.g., Jer. 36: 10, 20).

Baruch's supposed employment may explain his rather sporadic association with Jeremiah—three times only. In the years 605–604 B.C. Jeremiah dictated his prophecies to Baruch, who bravely read the scroll to the people in the Temple and again to the ministers of Jehoiakim (608–598 B.C.). The scroll was then read to the king, who burned it, ordering the seizure of Jeremiah and Baruch. Both went into hiding and rewrote their scroll (Jer. 36). Jeremiah's high opinion of his secretary at that time is illustrated by his dedicating to Baruch a special prophecy that attests (Jer. 45) to the latter's ambitions either in his professional field or as the prophet's disciple who may have been enticed by the hope of attaining prophetic inspiration.

Baruch is mentioned a second time when Jeremiah redeems Hanamel's field in Anathoth (Jer. 32:12–16). The deeds, however, were written by Jeremiah himself, the role of Baruch being limited to their proper preservation. It appears that Jeremiah, detained alone in prison, took advantage of a visit of Baruch in order to entrust him with the legal deeds.

Baruch is mentioned a third and last time (43:3) when "the captains of the forces" inquired of the Lord by Jeremiah in Geruth Chimham (cf. 41:17). However, they refused to follow his advice, charging that Baruch had incited the prophet against them. This confirms Baruch's origins from an influential family known for its pro-Babylonian orientation (51: 59). For this reason, the captains, having participated in Zedekiah's revolt and not yet having officially submitted to the Chaldeans, were afraid of the acrimony of the sons of Neriah. In spite of Jeremiah's warnings, the captains opted for fleeing to Egypt and took along both Jeremiah and Baruch. Nothing more is said about the latter, but the records left from this late "Egyptian" period (43:8–13; 44; 46:13–26) prove that the two friends did not perish violently.

The story in Jeremiah 36 attributes to Baruch the first lasting record of Jeremiah's words (vv.

An Egyptian scribe, from the fifth dynasty, ca. 2400 B.C. Baruch's profession was similar; he was a royal clerk, or "scribe."

27–32). Probably a good deal of the extant original words of Jeremiah were contained in that scroll. Yet, internal analysis of the collections of prophecies (chaps. 1–24; 30–31; 33; 46–51) proves that they underwent various transformations before reaching their present form: they were first expanded and reworked by Deuteronomistic and later writers, then they were partly reorganized in collections organized by content. It is therefore no longer possible to reconstruct the scroll of Baruch from the received book of Jeremiah.

According to some modern scholars, the authorship of the biographical chapters in Jeremiah is to be attributed to Baruch. This material consists of two distinct parts: a series of nine independent speeches and episodes (25–29; 32; 34–36), and a continuous story of Jeremiah from the siege of Jerusalem to his captivity in Egypt (37–44). Both portions underwent Deuteronomistic reworking and expansion, but a certain contribution of Baruch is possible for the independent episodes, because these do not start with the beginning of the prophet's career in 627 B.C., but rather "in the beginning of the reign of Jehoiakim" (26:1), nearly when Baruch first appeared at Jeremiah's side.

On the other hand, one cannot credit Baruch with the composition of the continuous story in 37–44, for the following reasons: first, 37:12–21 and 38:1–13 are two versions of one episode, where Jeremiah is thrown into a pit and taken thence to the court of the Guard. This joining of doublets presumes a long period of oral traditions, and Baruch, a contemporary, did not need to depend on such traditions. Second, the liberation of Jeremiah after the fall of Jerusalem is also told in two versions (39:3, 14 and 39:11–12 + 40: 1–6), the second of them being a legendary recasting that makes the archenemy Nebuzaradan confess before Jeremiah the supremacy of the Lord. This tendency reveals the story's affinity with the late Daniel legends (chaps. 2–4; 6). Third, in 40:7–41:18 the author incorporated a source, a chronicle that described the rise and fall of Gedaliah. If Baruch were its author, he would not have passed over in silence his own and his master's fate in that eventful period. That chronicle, then, originated in the court circles and was reused in later times by the compiler of Jeremiah's biography. Fourth, chaps. 42 and 44 have been transmitted, not merely reedited, by a Deuteronomistic writer.

In conclusion, one cannot credit Baruch with the present composition of Jeremiah's words and deeds, but only with the beginning of their recording—a role that well befits this gallant and ambitious but also brave and faithful friend of the prophet. Postexilic Judaism elaborated on his character, attributing to him the composition of one apocryphal book and two apocalypses. ***See also*** Jeremiah, The Book of.

Bibliography

Avigad, N. "Baruch the Scribe and Jerahmeel the King's Son." *Israel Exploration Journal* 28 (1978):52–56.

A.R.

Baruch, the Book of, a short collection of prayers and poems from diverse sources, attributed to Baruch, Jeremiah's scribe (Jer. 36:4), and found in the Septuagint (LXX). It is sometimes termed 1 Baruch to distinguish it from two pseudepigraphical writings, *The Syriac Apocalypse of Baruch (2 Baruch)*, and *The Greek Apocalypse of Baruch (3 Baruch)*. While difficult to date, Baruch seems to have been composed in Hebrew, possibly early in the second century B.C. The occasional affinities to the language of Jeremiah and Deuteronomy are more likely an indication that the authors have steeped themselves in Scripture than evidence for composition by the historical Baruch. The book has not survived in Hebrew and seems to have been largely ignored by early Christians. The Latin Vulgate and some manuscripts of the LXX include with it the Letter of Jeremiah, although elsewhere the latter appears as a separate work. Protestants treat Baruch as part of the Apocrypha, while Catholics classify it as deuterocanonical. It is composed of four distinct parts.

The narrative introduction (1:1–14) sets the writing in Babylonia during the Exile. Baruch returns the Temple vessels to Jehoiakim, the high priest in Jerusalem, along with funds for burnt and sin offerings and a request that the accompanying prayer of confession be read in the Temple on feast days. The introduction also reflects an attitude of accommodation to gentile authorities in that it requests prayers on behalf of Nebuchadnezzar and Belshazzar, his son. Baruch agrees with *2 Baruch* 6 in associating Jeremiah's scribe with traditions concerning the preservation of the Temple vessels (contrast Ezra 1:7–11).

A prayer of confession (1:15–3:8) is the second part of Baruch. It is a penitential prose prayer on behalf of the inhabitants of Judah as well as the exiles. It addresses God as "Lord" (probably Heb. *Yahweh*) and reflects the point of view of Deuteronomy 28–32 as well as the phraseology of the prayer in Dan. 9:4–19.

A hymn to Wisdom personified (3:9–4:4) is a poem echoing both Job 28, in speaking of a search for Wisdom, and Ecclesiasticus 24, in identifying her as the Torah, the law of God. The personification of Wisdom and the identification with the Torah point to a period late in the development of the wisdom tradition when concern had shifted from practical instruction to revelation as the primary mode of knowledge. This section and the next use the generic term "God" (probably Heb. *Elohim*) rather than "Lord."

A psalm of comfort (4:5–5:9) is the concluding section of Baruch. It is composed primarily of the lament of Zion over her lost children (cf. Lamentations). The tone is one of comfort and hope for the return of the exiles, and in achieving it the psalm frequently echoes Isaiah 40–66.

Since the precise date of Baruch is unknown, it is not clear why its writers, who lived long after the sixth century B.C., chose to appropriate the memory of the Exile. Either the book is intended to express a hope for the end of the Diaspora, or it is related in some way to the desecration of the Temple by the Syrian king Antiochus IV Epiphanes. While it is not highly regarded as Scripture, it provides a valuable look into the development of Jewish traditions during what is essentially a dark age. ***See also*** Apocrypha, Old Testament; Exile; Jeremiah, The Book of; Letter of Jeremiah, The.

D.W.S.

Barzillai (bahr-zil'ī), one of three wealthy individuals from the region of Gilead who sent food and other supplies to David and his followers when they were at Mahanaim during the rebellion of David's son Absalom (2 Sam. 17: 27–29). Invited to become a part of David's court at Jerusalem, Barzillai refused the honor because of his advanced age (eighty years; 2 Sam. 19:31–40).

Basemath (bas'e-math). **1** A wife of Esau (Gen. 26:34; 36:2–17). **2** Wife of Ahimaaz (1 Kings 4: 15—here identified as one of Solomon's daughters).

Bashan (bay'shuhn; Heb., "smooth, soft earth"), the fairly level, very fertile, grain-producing plateau of south Syria extending across the Yarmuq to the foothills of Gilead. The name also included the Jebel Druze, the "many-peaked mountain of Bashan" (Ps. 68:15) as far as Salecah (Heb. *Salkeh;* Deut. 3:10; Josh. 12:5; 13:11; 1 Chron. 5:11). In pre-Israelite days (prior to ca. 1250 B.C.) as the territory of King Og (Num. 21:33; 32:33; Deut. 1:4; 3:4; Josh. 9:10; Neh. 9:22), Bashan included the indeterminate region of Argob (1 Kings 4:13), apparently in the southeast. The fat bulls and cows of Bashan were proverbial (Ps. 22:12; Amos 4:1), as were rams, lambs, and goats, "all of them fatlings of Bashan" (Ezek. 39:18). The great trees of Bashan (Isa. 2:13; Ezek. 27:6) may have come from the mountain. ***See also*** Gilead; Og; Salecah.

D.R.B.

basin, a shallow receptacle for liquids. In the OT there are several Hebrew words that mean "basin," "bowl," "laver," or the like. One such word *(mizrak)* describes a utensil used in both cultic (Exod. 27:2; Num. 7) and noncultic settings (Amos 6:6; Zech. 9:15). Another common word *(kiyyor)* also identifies a vessel used in both cultic (Exod. 30:18) and secular settings (Zech. 12:6). Other kinds of basins or bowls were used to catch the blood of sacrificial victims (Exod. 12:22; 24:6), or were temple vessels made of gold (1 Chron. 28:17; Ezra 1:10; 8:27).

bath, a liquid measure, approximately 22 liters, equal to the ephah of dry measure (Ezek. 45:11, 14).

bathing, the immersion of the body, in part or whole, for hygienic, cultic, or recreational purposes. As a normal human activity, bathing includes such instances as Pharaoh's daughter bathing (Exod. 2:5), David washing after mourning the death of Bathsheba's child (2 Sam. 12:20), or the washing of an infant after birth (Ezek. 16:4). A common gesture of hospitality is providing guests with water to wash their feet (Gen. 18:4; 19:2; Judg. 19:21; John 13:4–17; 1 Tim. 5:10). As a ritual act, bathing to remove ritual pollution is part of the priestly consecration ceremony for Aaron and his sons (Exod. 29:4; 30:17–21; 40:30–32; Lev. 8:6; 16:4, 24). Nonpriestly ritual bathings include purification from leprosy (Lev. 14:8–9) and other kinds of personal uncleanness or pollution (Lev. 15, Num. 19), washings that perhaps serve hygienic as well as ritual purposes. Similarly, bathing and the cleanliness of the camp mandated for holy war (Deut. 23:9–14) may be hygienic as well as cultic. The washing of the hands is part of the ritual of absolution from the bloodshed of an unsolved murder (Deut. 21:6–9).

Figuratively, washing or bathing is a universal symbol of moral cleanness, for instance the cleansing of the hands (Pss. 26:6; 73:13; Isa. 1:15–18) or the heart (Ps. 51:17; Jer. 4:14). Also to be classed as figurative are the washings associated with healing miracles, such as the curing of Naaman's leprosy (2 Kings 5:10–14) or the restoration of sight to the man born blind (John 9:7). A gruesome example of such figurative usage is the picture in Ps. 58:10 of the victor bathing his feet in the blood of his enemies (a description parallel to the picture of the goddess Anat in Canaanite literature wading through the blood of those she has slaughtered). Finally, it has been suggested that the Flood in Genesis 6–8 is to be understood not simply as punishment for sin, but as a means of cleansing the earth of pollution. In the NT, many of these figurative uses are taken up into the symbolism of baptism.

J.S.K.

Pharaoh's daughter retrieving the infant Moses from his basket (cf. Exod. 2:5); a panel from the third-century A.D. synagogue at Dura-Europos.

Bathsheba (bath-shee'bah), daughter of Eliam, the son of Ahitophel, one of David's advisors (2 Sam. 11:3; 23:34). The wife of Uriah the Hittite, she was coveted and seduced by David while her husband was with Joab, fighting against the Ammonites at Rabbath, east of the Jordan (2 Sam. 11:1–4). After David had ordered Uriah sent into the forefront of the battle where he was killed, he married Bathsheba. The Bathsheba adultery was rebuked by Nathan the prophet. Bathsheba became the mother of Solomon (2 Sam. 12:24) and begged the elderly David for Solomon's succession to the throne (1 Kings 1:15–17). In another instance, she interceded for Adonijah, Solomon's half-brother, who had requested to be given Abishag the Shunammite (1 Kings 2:13, 22). The name "Sheba" ("Shua" in 1 Chron. 3:5) probably refers to a foreign god, which may indicate the family of Bathsheba was of non-Israelite origin. ***See also*** David. Y.G.

battering ram, a war engine that usually consisted of a heavy wooden ramrod, probably metal-tipped, suspended within a wooden tower in a fashion that allowed it to be worked back and forth. The tower was wheeled so as to move the ram up an earthen ramp and position it at the base of the walls of a city under siege, and it was also armored to afford protection to those within it who were manning the ram.

The earliest examples of battering rams attested in the ancient Near East are those mentioned in the eighteenth-century B.C. letters of Išme-Dagan and Shamši-Adad of Mari, on the Upper Euphrates, and in seventeenth- and sixteenth-century B.C. documents from Boghazkoy, the Hittite capital. The modern Israeli scholar and statesman Yigael Yadin has argued persuasively that the massive earthen embankments and plastered slopes *(terre pisé* and *glacis)* that first appeared in the Middle Bronze IIB–C period and surrounded nearly all of the city-states of Palestine in the eighteenth to sixteenth centuries B.C. were developed precisely as a defense against these new machines of war.

In the Iron Age (1200 B.C. on) the Assyrians used these formidable weapons against the cities of Israel and Judah. A relief of Tiglath-pileser III (ca. 745–728 B.C.) depicts a battering ram working against a tower of the city wall at Gezer, where archaeological evidence shows a destruction ca. 734 B.C. In 1977–1983, excavations by D. Ussishkin at Lachish uncovered part of the Assyrian siege ramp at the southwest of the mound, vividly corroborating the famous reliefs from the palace of Sennacherib that show, among other details of the battle of 701 B.C., typical Assyrian ramps and battering rams (see 2 Kings 18:13–14).

Biblical references to battering rams include possibly 2 Sam. 20:15, which speaks of Joab "battering" the walls of Abel of Beth-maacah. The prophesies of Ezek. 4:2; 21:22; and 26:9 depict the siege of Jerusalem and Tyre with a surrounding ramp topped with battering rams (see Isa. 22:5). ***See also*** Assyria, Empire of; Gezer; Lachish; Walls; War. W.G.D.

battle, a military engagement between individuals or armies. War is an almost universal experience and it was certainly not missing in the Palestine of biblical times. According to the book of Genesis human beings have struggled violently among themselves from the very beginning (cf. Gen. 4:23–24) and the Revelation to John depicts this struggle as continuing until the creation of a new heaven and a new earth (cf. Rev. 19:11).

In the Bible there are many references to battles both on a large scale where national armies struggle and in individual combat where each combatant represents his comrades (1 Sam. 17: 8–10). In the description of some battles may come hints of strategy (Josh. 8:1–25) or the claim that divine activity is more important than the strength of the soldiers (Exod. 15:1–18).

Israel's own testimony is that its land was gained and subsequently maintained through armed struggle. Battles are recorded with various Canaanite cities and with neighboring countries. From a purely political viewpoint some of these battles were offensive (cf. Josh. 1–12) and some were defensive (Judg. 6:1–8:21).

Nations such as Israel or Judah were often forced into battle by complex forces outside their control. One reason for this was geography: the Israelite tribal inheritance lay between the two great civilization centers of Egypt and Mesopotamia. Political tensions between the two civilizations almost always involved Israel as well. Furthermore, two main traveling routes passed through the area, a north-south route along the Mediterranean coast known as

The "Smiting of Dabigu," a city in northern Syria. The top row shows the town under attack by archers with a sapper and scaler on the right. The bottom row shows the impaled bodies of six vanquished inhabitants; ornamental gates to a palace of Shalmaneser III (858–824 B.C.).

the Way of the Sea (Lat. *Via Maris)* and another north-south route in Transjordan known as the King's Highway. These two routes were linked by a road through the Jezreel Valley in northern Israel. The imposing site of Megiddo guarded the western end of the valley and was itself the site of several battles. In fact, the last battle of human history is symbolically depicted as taking place at Armageddon (Rev. 16:16), a name that is a Greek version of the Hebrew phrase "Mountain of Megiddo."

In addition to the many battles mentioned in the Bible, archaeological research has produced evidence of yet more battles involving Israel. The Moabite Stone narrates various struggles between the Omride dynasty in Israel and Moab (ninth century B.C.), and both the annals and palace reliefs of the Assyrian king Sennacherib (ca. 705–681 B.C.) depict battles between the Assyrian forces and Judah under Hezekiah's leadership (727–698 B.C.).

In the NT, Paul uses battle as a metaphor for the Christian life (cf. 1 Cor. 14:8), and the conflict between God and evil is also depicted in the Revelation to John as a battle (Rev. 9:7, 9; 16:14; 20:8). J.A.D.

battle-ax. *See* Weapons.

battlement, often called "parapet," probably a guard rail on a roof. According to Deut. 22:8 persons who owned a house without a guard rail were criminally negligent if someone fell from their roof. An ornate example of a porch railing was found in the excavations at Ramat Rahel, probably the Beth-hacherem of the OT. The railing was made from limestone. Fortified areas, including towers, on the walls of cities were also called battlements, and they were depicted in some of the artwork from the ancient Near East.

bay tree (KJV, Ps. 37:35; RSV: "cedar of Lebanon"), the laurel *(Lauris nobilis)*, whose fragrant evergreen leaves are symbols of prosperity and distinction.

beam, a shaped piece of wood whose length far exceeds its girth. In the Bible, beam refers to part of a loom and to timbers for construction, the latter used in both buildings and gates. The "weaver's beam" was the large bar on which the warp cords were wound. It served as the model for a huge spear handle in biblical tradition (1 Sam. 17:7; 2 Sam. 21:19; 1 Chron. 11:23; 20:5). Any wood could be used, but the best was cedar (1 Kings 6:36; Song of Sol. 1:17). Construction beams were used to support walls and ceilings (1 Kings 6:6, 9) and could level stone courses (1 Kings 6:36). They could also be used in gates (Neh. 2:8; 3:3, 6) either as swing pivots or bars for locking against intrusion. Symbolic beams of God's chambers are mentioned in Ps. 104:3. On Persian authority, a beam from a seditious man's house could be used to impale him (Ezra 6:11) and the beams of his house would cry out against an evildoer (Hab. 2:11). The KJV uses the word "beam" (RSV: "log") in Jesus' saying about tending other peoples' minor faults while ignoring the major weakness in oneself (Matt. 7:3–5; Luke 6:41–42). R.S.B.

beards, hair left growing on the lower male face. Beards were worn in a wide variety of styles among ancient Near Eastern peoples. Judging from ancient reliefs, Egyptians were generally clean shaven, Syrians were bearded, while in Mesopotamia the fashion changed several times. The Israelites depicted in the Black Obelisk of Shalmaneser III (mid-ninth century B.C.) and the Israelite delegation standing before Sennacherib in the Lachish reliefs (late eighth century B.C.) are bearded. This fits what we know from the Bible, which prohibits a specific type of beard trim (Lev. 19:27) and where men like David and Ezra are depicted as bearded (1 Sam. 21:13; Ezra 9:3). The lack of a full beard was cause for embarrassment (2 Sam. 10:4–5; cf. Isa. 7:20; Jer 48:37), though occasionally beardlessness was a sign of mourning (Jer. 41:5). M.Z.B.

beasts, large, often dangerous animals. In the Bible the word has several uses. **1** As a general term for animals (Gen. 1:24). **2** As a term for wild, dangerous animals (Rev. 6:8). **3** As a pejorative term for human beings (Titus 1:12). **4** As a term for mythical beings or allegorical symbols. In Daniel 7 four different beasts symbolize four kingdoms. In Revelation a beast from the

Green bay *(Lauris nobilis)*.

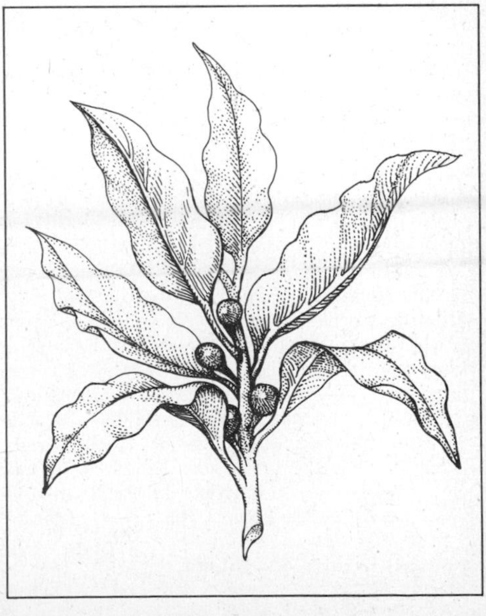

sea symbolizes the Roman Empire (13:1), a beast from the earth represents the leaders of the province of Asia (13:11), and a beast from the abyss portrays the Antichrist (11:7; 17:8). ***See also*** Abyss; Antichrist, The; Behemoth; Dragon; Leviathan; Rahab; Serpent.

Beatitudes (Lat., "blesseds"), declarations typically associated with the Sermon on the Mount in Matthew (5:3–12) and the Sermon on the Plain in Luke (6:20–23). They are pronouncements that confer an end-time blessing upon persons who are characterized by what they are (e.g., the poor) or do (e.g., the peacemakers). The blessing assures the addressees of the vindication and reward that attend the salvation of God's end-time Rule and thus provides encouragement in time of difficulty. Luke has four Beatitudes balanced by four woes (6:20–26), and all take the form of direct address in the second person plural ("Blessed are you . . ."). Matthew has nine Beatitudes and no woes (5:3–12), and all but the last are in the third person plural ("Blessed are the . . ." or "Blessed are those who . . ."). Beatitudes of both types are found in Hebrew and Greek literature.

Many scholars believe that Luke's Beatitudes, with their more direct reference to socioeconomic circumstances (e.g., "Blessed are you poor"), are more nearly original than are Matthew's, which appear to represent a later, "spiritualizing" tendency on the part of the church (e.g., "Blessed are the poor in spirit"); others, however, disagree. Since the four Beatitudes of Luke reappear, with some modification, in Matthew, this interpretation concentrates on the latter. "The poor (in spirit)" are those who are not only economically deprived but who also stand before God with no illusions of self-righteousness or self-sufficiency. "Those who mourn" are those who grieve over sin and evil in the world. "The meek" are those who are lowly and powerless, whose only hope is God. "Those who hunger and thirst for righteousness" are those who yearn for the final salvation that only God can effect. "The merciful" are those who eschew judgment and forgive. "The pure in heart" are those who are undivided in their allegiance to God. "The peacemakers" are those who work for the wholeness and well-being that God wills for a broken world. "Those who are persecuted for righteousness' sake" are those who incur tribulation because, as disciples of Jesus, they serve God. What is promised these various persons is essentially the same benefit, the end-time salvation that attends God's kingly Rule (Matt. 5:3, 10). ***See also*** Kingdom of God; Mercy; Peace; Persecution; Poor; Purity; Righteousness; Sermon on the Mount, The. J.D.K.

Beautiful Gate. ***See*** Nicanor.

Bebai (bee'bī). **1** A large family group ("sons of Bebai") who returned from the Babylonian captivity with Zerubbabel (Ezra 2:11). **2** A second, smaller group led by Zechariah, Bebai's son, who returned from Exile with Ezra (Ezra 8:11). **3** A member of the postexilic community who signed the covenant to keep the law (Neh. 10:15). He could be the head of the family groups above or simply a member of the group.

bed (couch), a place to recline. A variety of terms are used with little distinction in meaning. A wooden bed frame (ninth century B.C.) still showing signs of stringing has been found in a tomb in Jericho and is perhaps the type of bed mentioned in 2 Kings 4:10 and 2 Chron. 16:14. Most people slept on the floor or a mud-brick bench (1 Sam. 28:23; Mark 4:21) using garments for mattress and blankets (Exod. 22:27).

The well-to-do often had a separate bedchamber (2 Sam. 4:7; 2 Kings 11:2) with elaborate furnishings (Esther 1:6). Excavations at the palace of Ahab (871–852 B.C.) revealed large numbers of small ivory pieces which were probably inlaid in furniture (1 Kings 22:39; Amos 6:4). Decorated with colored insets of glass, paste, or gold leaf, the ivories reflect Egyptian influence and show motifs of sphinxes and the child Horus sitting on a lotus plant. These indicate the foreign influence and great wealth that Amos vehemently condemns (Amos 3:15; 6:1–4). The Greco-Roman period saw the addition of banqueting couches in many homes of the wealthy (John 13:23).

The bed functions in a number of ways in the Bible: it is a place to sleep or relax (Ps. 132:3; Luke 17:34); a sign of wealth (Song of Sol. 3:7–10); the location of dreams and visions (Job 7:13; Dan. 2:28); good or evil meditation (Ps. 63:6; Mic. 2:1); a pallet for the sick or disabled (2 Sam. 3:31; Matt. 9:2); the deathbed for the aged (Gen. 49:33) or one who has been murdered (2 Sam. 4:11); a metaphor for death (Job 17:13; Isa. 57:2), life (Exod. 21:18), apostasy (Ezek. 23:17), and marital fidelity (Heb. 13:4); the site of lovemaking (Song of Sol. 5:13), adultery (Gen. 49:4), and sexual participation in a foreign cult (Isa. 57:7–9); and an area that can receive or transmit contamination (Lev. 15:4, 5, 21–26). D.R.E.

Beelzebub (bee-el'zay-buhb). ***See*** Baal-zebub.

Beelzebul (bee-el'zay-buhl; Heb., "Baal Prince"). ***See*** Baal-zebub.

Beer (bee'air; Heb., "well"). **1** A location where the Israelites dug a well in the Transjordan (Num. 21:16–18). Its exact location is unknown. **2** The place to which Jotham fled for refuge after implicitly attacking the kingship of Abimelech (Judg. 9:21). This was probably modern el-Bireh north of the Plain of Esdraelon and about ten miles south of the southern tip of the Sea of Galilee.

Beeri (bee-ay'rī). **1** The Hittite father of Esau's wife Judith (Gen. 26:34), possibly a Canaanite. **2** The name of the father of the Israelite prophet Hosea (Hos. 1:1).

Beeroth (buh-ee'rohth; Heb., "wells"; cf. Beirut), a Gibeonite city in Benjamin (Josh. 9:17; 18:25). It was the home of the murderers of Ishbosheth (2 Sam. 4:2–3), and of Naharai, Joab's armor-bearer and one of David's mighty men (2 Sam. 23:37; 1 Chron. 11:39). Seven hundred and forty-three exiles from Beeroth are included in the census of the first return (Ezra 2:25; see also Neh. 7:29; 1 Esd. 5:19). The site has not been conclusively identified, but the most likely location is modern Khirbet el-Burj; note the nearby site Khirbet el-Biyar, which was occupied only in later periods but which may preserve the name of Beeroth. Other suggestions for its location include Nebi Samwil and el-Bireh (east of Ramallah; this may be Berea or Bereth, 1 Macc. 9:4). M.D.C.

Beer-sheba (beer-shee'bah), the major city in the northern Negev desert, in the territory of the tribe of Simeon (Josh. 19:2). The Beer-sheba plain with its ample winter pasturage is well suited for seminomadic living; thus it served as the principal homestead of Israel's patriarchs.

A double tradition explains the derivation of the name Beer-sheba; both stories concern the question of water rights. Abraham and Abimelech, king of Gerar, settled their dispute over a well (Heb. *beer)* by concluding a treaty "sworn" (Heb. *nishbe'u)* ceremoniously with an offering of "seven" (Heb. *sheba')* ewes; the site was thereafter named Beer-sheba, i.e., "the well of swearing seven" (Gen. 21:22–32). A generation later, renewed contention between the shepherds of Isaac and Abimelech was resolved by another oath at Beer-sheba (Gen. 26:26–33).

Reconstructed altar made of hewn stones (cf. Joshua 8:31) found at Beer-sheba, from the eighth century B.C.

An early tradition records that Samuel's two sons were judges at Beer-sheba (1 Sam. 8:2) and it is likely that the city served as a regional administrative center during the monarchy (ca. 1004–586 B.C.). David's realm stretched "from Dan to Beer-sheba"; this geographical description became the standard term of the limits of Israelite settlement in the Promised Land (2 Sam. 17:11; 24:2; 1 Kings 5:5).

The prophet Amos makes critical reference to the sanctity of this southern city (Amos 5:5; 8:14), which could claim Abraham as the founder of its local religious site. The patriarch had planted a tamarisk and "invoked the name of the Lord, God of the Universe" in Beer-sheba (Gen. 21:33).

The Negev was lost to the Edomites in the late seventh century B.C.; Beer-sheba and its environs were temporarily regained during the governorship of Nehemiah (sixth century B.C.; Neh. 11:26).

Archaeological excavations at the mound of Tell es-Saba', three miles east of the modern city, have uncovered five occupation levels in a walled fortress that date to the Israelite period. A large ashlar stone altar, disassembled and reused in secondary construction, was recovered at the site. The altar's profanation may be evidence for the cultic reform undertaken by King Josiah who centralized worship in Jerusalem (2 Kings 23:8). M.C.

beggar, one who is poor and needy, who begs for food or asks for alms. Frequently the beggar was lame (Acts 3:10), blind (Mark 10:46–52; John 9), or afflicted with sores (Luke 16:19–20). The most famous beggar of the Bible is Lazarus, who, upon death, was received into the bosom of Abraham in contrast to the rich man who went to the torments of Hades (Luke 16:19–30). In Mark (10:46–52) the blind beggar whose sight is restored by Jesus outside Jericho is identified as Bartimaeus, son of Timaeus. In the parallel accounts he is left unnamed (Matt. 20:29–34; Luke 18:35–43). J.G.G.

Behemoth (be-hay'muth), a mighty, mortal beast (Job 40:15) valued by God and celebrated for reproductive organs (v. 16). Behemoth served as an object lesson for Job (vv. 19–24). It was probably originally the hippopotamus, but intertestamental authors and later rabbis understood it to be of mythic significance. ***See also*** Leviathan.

beka(h) (be-kah'), a unit of weight averaging 6.2 grams in the inscribed specimens of balance weights recovered to date. Exod. 38:26 identifies it as half a shekel "by the shekel of the sanctuary" (RSV). See also Gen. 24:22 and Exod. 30:13,

15 for its use as gift and offering. Matt. 17:24 indicates the unit was used as the amount for the Temple tax. ***See also*** Weights and Measures.

Bel (bayl), one of the names of Marduk, the leading god of Babylon (Isa. 46:1; Jer. 50:2). In the apocryphal book Bel and the Dragon, Bel is the name of the idol.

Bel and the Dragon, one of the Additions to Daniel found at the end of that book in both the Septuagint and Theodotion, Greek translations of the Hebrew OT. It was probably composed in Hebrew and added to some manuscripts of the Hebrew-Aramaic version of Daniel during the course of the second century B.C. It includes:

I. Daniel and the statue of Bel (vv. 1–22)
II. Daniel and the dragon (vv. 23–27)
III. A second story of Daniel in a lions' den (vv. 28–42).

The narrative is a mixture of folklore and Jewish satire directed against idolatry. It centers around the act of eating, becoming more fantastic and humorous as it goes along. The food offered to the "dead" god, Bel, is eaten by his living priests, who are put to death by the king, Cyrus, for their deception after Daniel exposes them as frauds. The dragon, a living "god," eats Daniel's concoction and dies. Angered, the Babylonians force the king to cast Daniel into the lions' den. The lions' daily ration of two human bodies and two sheep is suspended, but they do not eat Daniel. In the meantime, God transports the prophet Habakkuk from Judea—suspended by his hair—with boiled pottage and bread to feed Daniel while in the lions' den. After a week, Daniel is discovered alive by the king, who comes to mourn him. He orders Daniel's enemies cast into the den, where they are immediately eaten. All of this is designed to prove that only God is God, a theme explored in a more serious vein by the stories in Daniel 1–6.

Protestants include Bel and the Dragon among the Apocrypha, while Catholics print it with the canonical text of Daniel. ***See also*** Apocrypha, Old Testament; Daniel, The Additions to; Idol. D.W.S.

Belial (bee'lee-uhl; Heb., "wickedness," "worthlessness"), a popular name for Satan in the Qumran literature. A variant form of the name, Beliar, appears frequently in the Jewish intertestamental literature (*Jubilees, Sibylline Oracles, Testaments of the Twelve Patriarchs*) as well as in the NT (2 Cor. 6:15) and in the rabbinic literature. Following scholarly consensus on the root meaning of the word, the RSV often translates as "worthless fellows" what the KJV more literally renders as "sons of Belial" (see 1 Sam. 10:27).

bells (Heb., *pa'amon,* "striker"), ringing objects, made of gold attached to Aaron's vestments (Exod. 28:33–34; 39:25, 26) as part of a complex of six ritual acts, embracing all human senses, performed inside the tabernacle. Another Hebrew word (*metzilot,* "that which tinkles") refers to bells used in equine trappings (Zech. 14:20). ***See also*** Aaron; Tabernacle.

Beloved Disciple, the, a disciple mentioned only in the Gospel of John and never identified by name. Appearing first at the Last Supper, reclining at Jesus' bosom, at Peter's bidding he asks the identity of Jesus' betrayer (13:23–25). At the crucifixion, standing beneath the cross with Jesus' mother, he is entrusted with her care (19:25–27). On Easter morning, he outruns Peter to Jesus' tomb and finds it empty (20:2–10). Later, in Galilee, he identifies for Peter a figure standing on the shore as the risen Jesus (21:7). Finally, Jesus parries Peter's question about whether the Beloved Disciple will live until Jesus' return (21:20–23), after which—at the end of the narrative—he is identified as the witness behind, and apparently the author of, the Gospel of John (21:24). References to this disciple have also been seen in the "other disciple" who gains for Peter admittance to the courtyard of the high priest (18:15–16) and the trusted witness of 19:35 (cf. 21:24), although in these instances the person is not named. In every case except 19:25–27, 35, the Beloved Disciple appears alongside Peter.

The assumption that the Beloved Disciple must have been one of the Twelve led to the traditional view that he was John the son of Zebedee. Yet that identification is never made in the Gospel. The sons of Zebedee are mentioned only once (21:2) and John never by name. Moreover, the Gospel of John contains none of the episodes in which the sons of Zebedee figure according to the accounts of Mark and the other synoptic Gospels (cf. Mark 1:19–20; 1:29; 3:17; 5:37; 9:2; 10:35–45; 13:3; 14:33). ***See also*** John the Apostle; John, The Gospel According to; John, The Letters of. D.M.S.

Belshazzar (bel-shaz'uhr; neo-Babylonian *Bel-shar-utzur,* "bel protect the king"), in Dan. 5:2 the son of Nebuchadnezzar and the last king of Babylon (vv. 30–31). He gives a feast that is interrupted by the mysterious appearance of fingers writing on the wall. Daniel interprets the writing and denounces Belshazzar, who is slain that very night.

The historical Belshazzar was the son not of Nebuchadnezzar but of Nabonidus the last king (556–539 B.C.) of Babylon. Nabonidus was at odds with the Babylonian clergy and withdrew to Teima in the Arabian desert for a period of ten years. In his absence Belshazzar was regent in Babylon, but he did not have the authority to take the king's place in the New Year Festival, so the ceremonies were omitted. Nabonidus had returned to Babylon but fled before its capture by the Persians in 539 B.C. He was later captured but his life was spared. Xenophon, the ancient Greek historian, claims (*Cyropaedia* 7.5) that the Babylonian king was killed when the city fell. This has sometimes been taken as support for Daniel's statement that Belshazzar was killed, but Xenophon's reliability is very doubtful. ***See also*** Daniel, The Book of; Nabonidus; Nebuchadnezzar. J.J.C.

Belteshazzar (bel'te-shaz'uhr), the Babylonian name given to Daniel at the royal court (Dan. 1:7). The underlying form was probably neo-Babylonian *balatshu-utzur*, "protect his life," which in turn was probably abbreviated from *Bel-* (or *Marduk-*) *balatshu-utzur*—an invocation of a Babylonian god for protection. ***See also*** Daniel, The Book of.

Benaiah (ben-ī'uh; Heb., "Yahweh has built"). **1** The son of Jehoiada, a priest (1 Chron. 27:5) from Kabzeel (2 Sam. 23:20) and one of David's mighty men (1 Chron. 27:6) who supervised the Cherethites and Pelethites (2 Sam. 8:18) and was renowned for his heroic exploits (2 Sam. 23: 20–23). With Zadok and Nathan, he supported Solomon, whose opponents he executed at Solomon's instruction, after which he was appointed chief of the army (1 Kings 1). **2** An Ephraimite commander in David's army (1 Chron. 27:14). **3** A priest who participated in the celebration of the Ark's arrival in Jerusalem during the reign of David (1 Chron. 15:24; 16:6). **4** A levitical musician appointed by David (1 Chron. 15:20; 16:5). **5** The grandfather of Jahaziel, an Asaphite from the time of King Jehoshaphat (2 Chron. 20:14, perhaps to be identified with one of the preceding). **6** A Simeonite leader who settled in rich pastureland near Gedor in the time of Hezekiah (1 Chron. 4:36). **7** A levitical Temple official in the time of Hezekiah (2 Chron. 31:13). **8** The father of Pelatiah, a Jerusalemite leader who died after Ezekiel's condemnation (Ezek. 11:1, 13). **9** The name of several postexilic Israelites who divorced their foreign wives in response to Ezra's proclamation (Ezra 10:25, 30, 35, 43; 1 Esd. 9 gives different names). F.E.G.

Ben-ammi (ben-am'ee; Heb., "son of my kin"), the name given by Lot's daughter to the offspring of her incestuous union with her father; the ancestor of the Ammonites (Gen. 19: 38).

benediction, a prayer for God's blessing on someone or a prayer recognizing that blessing has been given. The great priestly blessing (Num. 6:24–26), the beatitudes (Matt. 5:2–12) and the ending of some letters (e.g., Rom. 15:13; 2 Cor. 13:14; Heb. 13:20–21) are prominent examples.

Benedictus, the (Latin for "blessed"), the poetic oracle attributed to Zechariah the father of John the Baptist in Luke 1:68–79, named for the first word in the Latin translation. According to the account, Zechariah was struck dumb when he disbelieved the angelic promise of John's birth (Luke 1:5–25); then, when John was born and Zechariah indicated that his name should be "John," his tongue was loosed and he delivered the oracle (vv. 57–67). His psalm praises God for the mighty act of salvation about to be accomplished and emphasizes that John will be the forerunner for *the one* who is to be the instrument of this salvation. As the "Benedictus," Zechariah's psalm entered the liturgy of the church. ***See also*** Elizabeth; Hymn; John the Baptist; Music; Oracle; Zechariah. J.M.E.

Ben-hadad (ben hay'dad; Heb., "son of Hadad"), the name of several kings of Damascus. Scholars disagree as to whether biblical references to a king of Damascus by this name refer to two or three separate individuals. In addition, Assyrian texts mention Adad-idri (Hadadezer) and Mari (an Aramaic title meaning "my lord"), which may be alternate names for some of the same rulers. The available information indicates the following: **1** The son of Tabrimmon, who was bribed by Judah's King Asa (early ninth century B.C.) to break his alliance with Israel, after which he conquered several cities and the territory of Naphtali (1 Kings 15:18–21). **2** In the ninth century, a king who erected a stele near Aleppo in honor of the Tyrian god Melqart. **3** The king who attacked Israel several times during the reign of Ahab (mid-ninth century B.C.), who was able to defeat him. Although Ben-hadad fled, he was forced to restore cities he had taken from Ahab's father, Omri, and grant Ahab commercial privileges in Damascus (1 Kings 20). **4** Hazadezer, who participated with Ahab in a coalition of Syrian kings who resisted the army of the Assyrian emperor Shalmaneser III at Qarqar in 853. **5** One who besieged Samaria during the time of Elisha (mid-ninth century B.C.) (2 Kings 6:24). This Ben-hadad was murdered by Hazael, one of his officers (2 Kings 8:7–15), after receiving a prophecy from Elisha. **6** A king who led an unsuccessful coalition of several north Syrian kings against King Zakir of Hamath early in the eighth century B.C. **7** The son of Hazael, who took several cities from Jehoahaz, king of Israel, and whose son Jehoash recaptured them (2 Kings 13:24–25). **8** Mari, who paid tribute to the Assyrian king Adad-nirari III after being besieged in Damascus. It is from such data that one must reconstruct careers and names of the Syrian kings. F.E.G.

Benjamin (Heb., "son of the right hand," hence "southern"; similar to the name of a nomadic group mentioned in eighteenth-century B.C. documents from the upper Euphrates kingdom of Mari), Jacob's last son, born after his return from Mesopotamia. Benjamin was named

Ben-oni (Heb., "son of my suffering") by his mother, Rachel, who died in childbirth, although Jacob preferred "Benjamin" (Gen. 35: 18). He is mentioned often in association with Joseph, his only full brother. These facts imply that the tribe of Benjamin, which occupied the central ridge between Jerusalem and Bethel (Josh. 18:11–20) and traced its ancestry back to Benjamin, was originally associated with the northern tribes and may have formed as a separate entity relatively late, after arriving in Canaan. An atrocity in Benjaminite territory created friction with other Israelite tribes (Judges 19–21). The judge Ehud came from the tribe of Benjamin as did Saul, Israel's first king. The tribe also recognized Saul's son Eshbaal (Ishbosheth) rather than David until Abner insisted otherwise (2 Sam. 2:8–9; 3:17–21). The tribe, which constituted one of Solomon's administrative districts (1 Kings 4:18), produced two opponents to the Davidic dynasty, Shimei and Sheba (2 Sam 16:5; 19:16; 20:1), but was incorporated into the Southern Kingdom by Solomon's successor, presumably to provide a buffer for Jerusalem. ***See also*** David; Joseph; Rachel; Tribes, The. F.E.G.

Beracah (bair'uh-kah; Heb., "blessing" or "praise"). **1** A kinsman of Saul from the tribe of Benjamin who joined David's fighting men at Ziklag (1 Chron. 12:3). **2** A valley in central Judah near Tekoa. During the reign of Jehoshaphat an alliance was formed by Edom, Ammon, and Moab and they invaded Judah. But, as promised by the prophet Jahaziel, the army was destroyed when they began fighting among themselves; the people "blessed" God for the victory, because of the spoils taken and the peace that would follow, and named the site accordingly (2 Chron. 20:26). The location has not been identified. ***See also*** Jahaziel. D.R.B.

Berea (be-ree'uh). ***See*** Beroea.

Berechiah (ber-e-khī'ah; Heb., "Yah[weh] has blessed"). **1** A son of Zerubbabel (1 Chron. 3:20). **2** The father of Asaph and son of Shimea; a Levite (1 Chron. 6:39; 15:17). **3** A son of Asa; a Levite and a gatekeeper for the Ark (1 Chron. 9: 16; 15:23). **4** A son of Meshillemoth; an Ephraimite chief (2 Chron. 28:12). **5** The father of Meshullam (Neh. 3:4, 30; 6:18). **6** The father of the prophet Zechariah, a son of Iddo (Zech. 1: 1, 7). **7** The full name of Jeremiah's scribe Baruch, occurring on a late seventh-century B.C. seal impression from Judah that reads "Belonging to Berechiah son of Neriah the scribe." **8** Beracah, a Benjaminite follower of David (1 Chron. 12:3), whose name is often emended to Berechiah (cf. LXX). ***See also*** Baruch. M.D.C.

Beriah (be-rī'uh; Heb., "in misery" or "in misfortune"; see 1 Chron. 7:23). **1** A son of Asher; he was among those who went with Jacob to Egypt at Joseph's invitation (Gen. 46:17). He became the head of a family group (Beriites) who later left Egypt in the Exodus with Moses (Num. 26:44). **2** A son of Ephraim, born after two other sons, Ezer and Elead, were killed by the Philistines in a livestock raid against Gath; his name reflects the mourning for those killed (1 Chron. 7:23). **3** A Benjaminite clan leader who lived at Aijalon and was successful in fighting the Philistines at Gath (1 Chron. 8:13, 16). Some scholars think he may be the same as 2, reflecting a family group of mixed Ephraimite and Benjaminite origins. **4** A Levite, the son of Shimei of the Gershonite clan (1 Chron. 23:10–11). D.R.B.

Bernice (buhr-nees'), daughter of Herod Agrippa I and sister of Herod Agrippa II. She was married to Herod of Chalcis, her father's brother. After his death, in A.D. 48, she apparently carried on an incestuous relationship with her brother, with whom she listened to Paul while he was a prisoner in Caesarea (Acts 25: 13–26:32). In A.D. 64, she married Polomon of Cilicia but then abandoned him to continue her incestuous affair. When Titus Flavius Vespasianus came to Palestine, she became his mistress and later followed him to Rome, causing a scandal. ***See also*** Agrippa I; Agrippa II; Herod.

Berodach-baladan, KJV spelling at 2 Kings 20: 12 for Merodach-baladan. ***See*** Merodach-baladan.

Beroea (be-ree'uh; KJV: "Berea"), a Macedonian city located twenty-four miles inland from the Aegean Sea in the plain below Mt. Bermion. Springs in the area gave the city its name, "place of many waters." After leaving Thessalonica during the second journey, Paul and Silas probably traveled the main east–west Roman road, the Egnatian Way, to Beroea, where the people were receptive to Paul's message and escorted him safely to Athens (Acts 17:10–15). El-Bireh in Palestine is sometimes referred to as Berea (1 Macc. 9:4).

beryl, a precious stone of a sea-green color. Emerald and aquamarine are two types of beryl. It was one of the twelve stones on the high priest's breastplate (Exod. 28:20), one of the jewels worn by the king of Tyre (Ezek. 28:13), and the eighth foundation of the wall of the heavenly Jerusalem (Rev. 21:20).

beth (bayth), the second letter of the Hebrew alphabet. It has a numeric value of two. It has been proposed that the letter was originally a crude pictogram of a house. The use of this term as "house" or "dwelling" resulted in its use as a portion of compound place names such as Bethlehem, Bethel, Bethphage, Bethsaida, and the like. The term can also be used to indicate a dynasty such as the "house of David," a reference to the heirs of the Davidic line.

Bethabara (beth-ah'buh-ruh; Heb., "house of the ford"), where John was baptizing (John 1:28 KJV, favored by Origen; the best manuscripts, however, and now the RSV read "Bethany"). John 1:28 describes the place of baptizing as "beyond the Jordan," but a sixth-century mosaic floor map discovered in Madeba, Jordan, shows Bethabara on the west side of the river, near the present traditional site of Jesus' baptism. ***See also*** Bethany.

Beth-anath (beth-ah'nath; Heb., "temple of Anat [a deity]"), a walled Canaanite city in the territory of Naphtali in upper Galilee (Josh. 19:38) whose inhabitants the Israelites could not expel but subjugated as servants (Judg. 1:33). Its location is not certain, although it is sometimes identified with modern Safed el-Battikh, about fifteen miles east and slightly south of Tyre.

Bethany (beth'uh-nee). **1** A village on the lower eastern slope of the Mount of Olives (Mark 11:1; Luke 19:29), about fifteen stadia (approximately two miles) east of Jerusalem (John 11:18), where Jesus visited his friends, Mary, Martha, and Lazarus (Luke 10:38–42; John 12:1–8; cf. Matt. 21:17; Mark 11:11), raised Lazarus from the dead (John 11:1–44), and was anointed in the home of Simon the Leper (Matt. 26:6–13; Mark 14:3–9; cf. Luke 7:36–50). Jesus' triumphal entry into Jerusalem began here (Mark 11:1–11; Luke 19:28–38). The name of the present-day village, El-Azarieh, is the Arabic form of Lazarion, the fourth-century name of the village and the church that was built over the traditional site of Lazarus' tomb. Excavations revealed that the first church, probably destroyed by an earthquake, was replaced by a fifth-century structure which underwent modifications through the centuries. In the 1950s, a new church was built on the foundations of earlier ones. Within the church's precincts are numerous rock-cut tombs. One particularly impressive tomb, below the adjacent mosque, with a vestibule and vaulted inner chamber, is the traditional tomb of Lazarus. **2** Bethany beyond the Jordan, where John the Baptist baptized (John 1:28); it is Bethabara in some manuscripts. Its location is unknown. ***See also*** Bethabara; Lazarus; Martha; Mary.

M.K.M.

Beth-arabah (beth-ahr'uh-bah), a town on the northern border of Judah (Josh. 15:6, 61) and the southern border of Benjamin (Josh. 18:18, 22), possibly modern 'Ain el-Gharbah southeast of Jericho.

Beth-eglaim (beth eg-lah'eem), a place not mentioned in the Bible but included in the *Onomasticon* of Eusebius, bishop of Caesarea, in the early fourth century A.D. It was formerly identified with Tell el-'Ajjul, located about four miles southwest of modern Gaza, but this *tell* is now thought to be the site of ancient Sharuhen. The location of Beth-eglaim thus remains unknown. ***See also*** Sharuhen.

Bethel (beth'uhl), an important biblical city (modern Beitin) on the north-south mountain road north of Jerusalem. Bethel had few natural defenses, but it did have plentiful water from nearby springs. It also stood at the intersection of the north-south road that passed through the central hill country and the main east-west road that led from Jericho to the Mediterranean Sea.

W. F. Albright made a trial excavation at Bethel in 1927. Albright then mounted a full excavation in 1934. His assistant that year, J. L. Kelso, continued the excavation in 1954, 1957, and 1960. Their excavations revealed a thriving town of the Middle Bronze Age (2000–1500 B.C.), the period of the biblical patriarchs. Remains included a stone sanctuary with many cultic objects.

Bethel, formerly named Luz (Gen. 28:19), was conquered by the Joseph tribes (late thirteenth century B.C.; Judg. 1:22–25) and became a part of the tribe of Ephraim. The religious heritage of Bethel for the Hebrews went back to Jacob (eighteenth century B.C.). When Jacob was going to Aram, he spent the night at Bethel and had a dream. As a result he built a shrine there and named the place Bethel (Heb., "house of God"; Gen. 28:19; 35:1–7).

Surprisingly, the conquest of Bethel is not mentioned in the book of Joshua. However, the men of Bethel are said to have aided the men of Ai against the Hebrews (Josh. 8:17). This makes the omission of the conquest of Bethel even more striking. The site of Beitin does show a massive destruction by fire at the end of the Late Bronze Age, the time usually ascribed to the conquest (late thirteenth century B.C.). W. F. Albright has suggested that the biblical account of the fall of Ai was transferred from the capture and destruction of Bethel. It should be noted that Ai (modern et-Tell, southeast of Bethel) was not inhabited at the time of the conquest; it was only an impressive ruin.

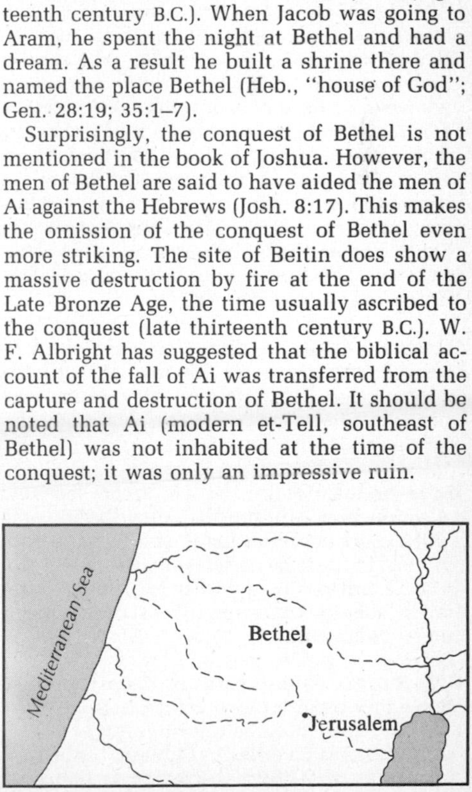

In addition to the discoveries dating from the Middle Bronze Age, several fine houses were excavated dating to the Late Bronze Age (1500–1200 B.C.). Also belonging to this period were flagstone pavements and a drainage system.

In the period of the judges (1200–1000 B.C.), Bethel was an important town. The Ark of the Covenant was located there for a time (Judg. 20: 18–28), and it was a center of the tribal confederacy. Samuel made regular visits to Bethel on his annual circuit while he was a judge. But the town was not mentioned during the reigns of David and Solomon, its role as a sanctuary apparently being usurped by Jerusalem, the capital city. With the division of the kingdoms during the reign of Rehoboam, Bethel again rose to prominence (late tenth century B.C.). Jeroboam I made it a chief sanctuary and set up a golden calf there (1 Kings 12:26–33). Bethel was a royal sanctuary at the time of Amos (Amos 7:12–13). From the evidence of excavation, Bethel was apparently destroyed by the Assyrians (722–721 B.C.). During the resurgence of Judah's power at the time of Josiah (ca. 639–609 B.C.), Bethel's sanctuary was destroyed and its priests killed (2 Kings 23:15–20), but the city was spared. Bethel was not destroyed by the Babylonians under Nebuchadrezzar but was destroyed either by the Babylonian ruler Nabonidus or the Persians.

The town was soon rebuilt and showed continued growth through the Hellenistic and Roman periods (333 B.C.–A.D. 324). The Roman town shows the first use of cisterns, suggesting an increased population or water use beyond the capacity of the springs. The city reached its greatest extent during the Byzantine period (early Middle Ages). A reservoir just below the mound supplemented the water supply for this age. A main street of the Byzantine city is still in use. The ancient city was abandoned about the time of the Arab conquest. ***See also*** Ai; Luz.

J.F.D.

Bethesda (beh-thes'duh), a name found in later NT manuscripts for the original Bethzatha in John 5:2. It is the Hebrew name of the pool near the "sheep gate" in Jerusalem. ***See also*** Bethzatha.

Beth-hoglah (beth-hahg'lah; Heb., meaning uncertain, possibly "the place of the partridge"), a city on the border of Judah and Benjamin but assigned to the tribe of Benjamin (Josh. 15:6; 18: 21). It is tentatively identified with modern Ein Hajlah, about six miles northwest of the mouth of the Jordan River.

Beth-horon (beth-hohr'uhn; Heb., "house of [the god] Horon"), a city of refuge assigned to the levitical family of Kohath (Josh. 21:22; 1 Chron. 6:68), one of twin cities in Ephraim (Josh. 16:3, 5; 1 Chron. 7:24) near the border of Benjamin (Josh. 18:13, 14). "Upper" and "Lower" Beth-horon are frequently distinguished; these designations survive in the modern Arabic names Beit Ur el-Foqa and Beit Ur el-Tachta. They guarded a major pass on the road from the coast by way of the Valley of Aijalon to the hill country and Jerusalem (see 2 Sam. 13:34, Septuagint); because of this strategic location, Beth-horon was the site of frequent military activity. Joshua chased the Amorite kings from Gibeon "by way of the ascent of Beth-horon" (Josh. 10:10–11; cf. *Jubilees* 34:4); it was attacked by Philistine raiders (1 Sam. 13:18) and Amaziah's northern mercenaries (2 Chron. 25:13); Solomon fortified it (1 Kings 9:17; 2 Chron. 8:5), but the pharaoh Shishak captured it in ca. 925 B.C. Judas Maccabeus defeated Seron there (1 Macc. 3:16, 24); Nicanor's army camped there (1 Macc. 7:39); later Bacchides refortified it (1 Macc. 9:50; see also Jth. 4:4). ***See also*** Shishak. M.D.C.

Beth-jeshimoth (beth-jesh'i-muhth), a settlement east of the Jordan in the plains of Moab opposite Jericho, the area of one of the encampments of the Israelites (Num. 33:49). It was captured by Joshua and assigned to the tribe of Reuben (Josh. 12:3; 13:20), although by the time of the Exile it was again under Moabite control (Ezek. 25:9). The site is usually identified as modern Tell el 'Azeima, about two and a half miles northeast of the north end of the Dead Sea. ***See also*** Jeshimon.

Bethlehem (beth'le-hem; Heb. *beth leḥem*, "house of bread"; Arabic *beit lahm*, "house of meat"). **1** A small town of approximately fifteen thousand inhabitants, about five miles south of Jerusalem, but now forming part of the modern Jerusalem-Bethlehem conurbation. Perched 2,460 feet (750 m.) above sea level on the north-south ridge road along the central highlands, it looks westward to the fertile cultivated slopes around Beit Jala and eastward to the desolate wilderness of Judah, in which is the ancient monastery of Mar Saba in the Wadi en-Nar. Close outside to the north is the traditional site of the tomb of Rachel (Gen. 35:19; 48:7), profoundly sacred to the Jewish people, although it is possible that the true site is north of Jerusalem near Ramah (1 Sam. 10:2).

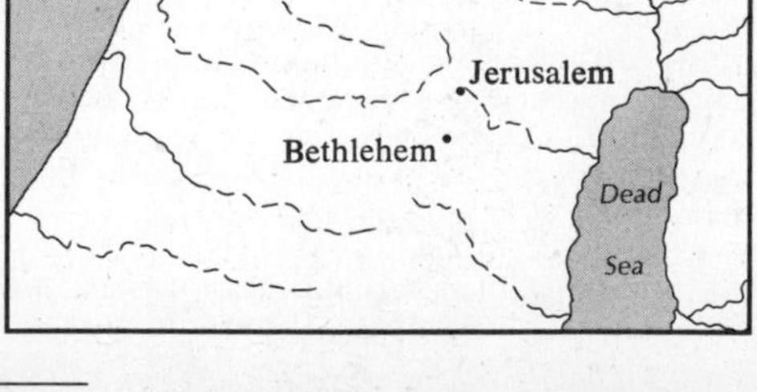

View of modern Bethlehem from the west.

Bethlehem was first mentioned in one of the Amarna letters (letters written to Egyptian pharaohs by local kings of Palestine and Syria prior to ca. 1250 B.C.) in the fourteenth century B.C., in which the Jerusalem ruler complained that *Bit-Lahmi* had deserted to the side of the *Apiru* people (perhaps "Hebrew" people). Prior to the period of the Israelite monarchy, Bethlehem was the home of the Levite who went to act as priest for a man named Micah in Ephraim (Judg. 17:7–13) and of the unfortunate concubine, whose murder caused the tragic massacre of the people of Gibeah (Judg. 19–20). Bethlehem figures prominently also in the story of Ruth, the great-grandmother of David (Ruth 1; 2: 4; 4:11). Its greatest importance in the OT, however, is its relation to King David. It was his family home (1 Sam. 16:1; 17:12) and the place of his anointment as king (1 Sam. 16:4–13). At one time under Philistine control (2 Sam. 23: 13–17) Bethlehem was also the home of Elhanan, one of the thirty mighty men who formed David's bodyguard. It was the home also of Asahel, another of the thirty (2 Sam. 23:24), who was later buried there (2 Sam. 2:32).

After the division of the Hebrew kingdom into Israel (north) and Judah (south) following Solomon's death, Bethlehem was one of the fifteen cities in Benjamin and Judah fortified by Rehoboam (2 Chron. 11:5–12). Following the murder of Gedaliah the governor of Judah under the Babylonians in 582 B.C. some of the Judean refugees stayed near Bethlehem on their way to Egypt. Subsequently, over a hundred Bethlehemites were among those who returned from Babylon (Ezra 2:21; Neh. 7:26).

The great importance of Bethlehem for Christians throughout the centuries is that the Gospels record the birth of Jesus as having taken place there, in fulfillment of a prophecy of Micah (Mic. 5:2; Matt. 2; Luke 2; John 7:42). The traditional site of the manger in which the infant Jesus was laid (Luke 2:7) is a cave under the great Church of the Nativity, the place of the manger being marked by a star with the Latin inscription *Hic De Virgine Maria Jesus Christus Natus Est*, "Here Jesus Christ Was Born of the Virgin Mary." A bitter dispute between the Orthodox and Roman Catholics about this star (1847–53) was one of the causes of the Crimean War (1853–56). The tombs of Jerome (d. 420) and his friends Paula (d. 404) and Eusebius of Cremona (d. ca. 423) are in neighboring grottoes.

Bethlehem was destroyed by the emperor Hadrian in the second century A.D., but in about 325, after the empire had become Christian, Queen Helena, the mother of Constantine, promoted the building of the great church. Badly damaged during the Samaritan revolt of 521–528, the church was rebuilt in the sixth century in very much its present form by the emperor Justinian. It was spared during the savage Persian invasion of 614 because the soldiers saw the mosaic portrayal of the three Magi in Persian costume.

2 A small town in the hill country of Zebulun (Josh. 19:15) about seven miles northwest of Nazareth, probably (though this is not certain) the home and burial place of Ibzan, one of the minor judges (Judg. 12:8–10).

3 In 1 Chronicles a personal name, once of a descendant of Caleb (2:51, 54), and once of the son of Ephrathah, a descendant of Hur (4:4). Since Ephrath is identified with the Bethlehem in Judah (Gen. 35:19; Ruth 4:11; Mic. 5:2), the names here are probably tribal rather than personal. ***See also*** Benjamin; Gibeah; Judah; Rachel; Ramah; Rehoboam. D.B.

Bethlehem, Star of. ***See*** Stars, Star of Bethlehem.

Beth-pelet (bayth-pel'et; Heb., "house of refuge"; KJV: "Beth-palet"), a town of the tribe of Judah at the southern extremity of its territory (Josh. 15:27). Also settled in postexilic times (Neh. 11:26), its location is still in dispute.

Beth-peor (beth-pay'ohr; Heb., "temple of Peor"), a settlement on the western edge of the Moabite plateau, part of the territory assigned to the tribe of Reuben (Josh. 13:20). The site is undoubtedly near Mount Nebo, but its exact location remains unknown. Its name probably indicates that Beth-peor was a religious center of the god Baal-peor.

Just before their invasion of Canaan, the Israelites camped "in the valley opposite Beth-peor," where Moses recounted their long journey and repeated Israel's covenant obligations (Deut. 3:29; 4:46). Shortly thereafter, Moses viewed the promised land from Mount Pisgah, died, and was buried in the vicinity of Beth-peor (Deut. 34:1–6). ***See also*** Baal-peor; Peor.

G.L.M.

Bethphage (beth'fuh-jee; Heb., "house of unripe figs"), a village apparently on the Mount of Olives, near Bethany, where Jesus sent his disciples to procure an ass for his triumphal entry into Jerusalem (Matt. 21:1; Mark 11:1; Luke 19:29). Its exact location has never been determined.

Bethsaida (beth-say'uh-duh; Heb., "house of the fisherman"), a town situated probably at the northeast corner of the Sea of Galilee near where the Jordan River flows into it. The exact site, however, is uncertain. Apparently a small fishing village, it was raised to the dignity of a "city" by the tetrarch Philip and renamed "Bethsaida-Julias" in honor of the daughter of Caesar Augustus sometime before 2 B.C. The tetrarch died here in A.D. 34. The apostles Peter, Andrew, and Philip were born here (John 1:44; 12:21). Jesus fed the five thousand in the area (Mark 6:45; Luke 9:10–17), healed a blind man (Mark 8:22–26), but cursed the town for not accepting him (Matt. 11:21–22; Luke 10:13–14). ***See also*** Andrew; Peter; Philip.

C.H.M.

Beth-shan (beth-shan'; RSV: also "Beth-shean" [beth-shee'uhn]), an important biblical city (modern Tell el-Husn), located between the Jezreel and Jordan valleys. Beth-shan protected the branch of the Via Maris that passed near the tell (mound). The site of Tell el-Husn was occupied almost continuously from the Chalcolithic period, about 3500 B.C., to the time of the Crusaders.

Some Neolithic pottery related to Neolithic (10,000–4000 B.C.) pottery at Jericho has been found at Beth-shan. The first permanent structures belong to the Chalcolithic period (4000–3000 B.C.). A few houses and copper tools belonging to this era have been recovered.

Two scenes of a dog and lion in combat, from the Amarna period (fourteenth century B.C.) at Beth-shan.

The first real town at Beth-shan belongs to the Early Bronze Age, ca. 3000–2400 B.C. In addition to private houses, public buildings and intersecting streets of this period have been found. Limited remains also indicate that Beth-shan was inhabited during the Middle Bronze Age (2000–1500 B.C.), the time of the biblical patriarchs.

Beth-shan is definitely mentioned for the first time historically in the list of conquered cities of Pharaoh Thutmose III, 1468 B.C. Belonging to this Late Bronze Age city (1500–1200 B.C.) is a temple complex close to the city gate. The temple, and the city of this time, shows much Egyptian influence. Among the finds at this level is a cartouche containing the name of Thutmose III. From the Amarna age (ca. 1400 B.C.) at Beth-shan have been found a temple, a granary, and an inner fortress (Heb. *migdol*) that served as the final defense for the city. Strong Egyptian influence is evident in the temple. Also belonging to this period is a stele (an inscribed stone slab) dedicated to Ashtoreth, a Canaanite goddess. At the time of the conquest (late thirteenth century B.C.), Beth-shan was listed among the cities of Manasseh. However, the Israelites were unable to conquer the city because of the strength of the Canaanites living in it (Josh. 17:11–12; Judg. 1:27).

Apparently Beth-shan was taken by the Philistines at the beginning of the Iron Age (ca. 1200 B.C.). The plan of the upper city changed completely at this time. Two temples of the Iron Age have been found. Both of these temples have a basilica shape, with two rows of columns along the length of the temple and a holy of holies of the broad-room type (i.e., a room that, on the building's long axis, is wider than it is long). The two temples are connected by a complex of anterooms and storerooms. The smaller of the two temples is dedicated to the Canaanite goddess Anat. 1 Sam. 31:12 relates that the bodies of Saul and his sons were exposed on the walls of Beth-shan by the Philistines. By implication, Beth-shan was conquered by David, because it appears in a list of towns in the fifth administrative district of Solomon. After this reference, Beth-shan is not mentioned again in the OT.

In the Hellenistic (333–63 B.C.), Roman (63 B.C.–A.D. 324), and Byzantine (A.D. 324–632) periods, the town was known as Scythopolis. It was frequently mentioned in the literature of the period. Scythopolis was for a time the chief city of the Decapolis, an area traversed by Jesus (Mark 7:31), and the only city of the Decapolis west of the Jordan River. In this later period, the main portion of the city moved off the mound down into the valley. The city was described as a city of many churches and monasteries in the Byzantine era. On the mound, remains of a Roman temple and a Byzantine church have been excavated. Also two synagogues of the fifth and sixth centuries A.D. have been found. Following the Arab conquest, the name reverted to the original name, Beth-shan, or Beisan in Arabic. J.F.D.

Beth-shean (beth-shee'uhn). ***See*** Beth-shan.

Beth-shemesh (beth-she'mesh; Heb., "house of sun"), a name borne by four cities that appear to have been centers for a sun cult. **1** A city in the Valley of Sorek, sixteen miles southwest of Jerusalem, modern Tell er-Rumeileh (Ain Shems), on the highway to Ashdod and the Mediterranean. The city was established in the late Bronze Age (ca. 1500–1200 B.C.) and had continuous occupation through the Byzantine period. It is not mentioned in nonbiblical sources. The town was part of the allotment for the tribe of Dan (Josh. 19:41).

Its location, name, and history would indicate that Beth-shemesh was a transitional community that was related to the Philistines (Philistine pottery has been found there) as well as the Hebrews. When the Ark of the Covenant was taken by the Philistines, it was finally returned to the people of Beth-shemesh (1 Sam. 6:1–16). The city was destroyed violently, a destruction that may be connected to the raid of Pharaoh Shishak I (940–919 B.C.) of Egypt (1 Kings 14:25–28). Joash, king of Israel (800–785 B.C.) captured Amaziah, king of Judah, at Beth-shemesh (2 Kings 14:11–14; 2 Chron. 25:21). During the war between Syria and Ephraim, the Philistines were able to get control once again of Beth-shemesh (2 Chron. 28:18). The kings of Israel and Damascus (Syria) put pressure on Ahaz, king of Judah, to join a coalition with them against the Assyrians. While Ahaz decided instead to become a willing vassal of the Assyrians, however, this moment of instability was all that the Philistines needed to make substantial advances into the holdings of Judah, including Beth-shemesh. The city was destroyed in the sixth century B.C., probably by Nebuchadnezzar. Occupation of the area continued but it never regained status as a city.

2 A city mentioned in Josh. 19:22, possibly modern Khirbet Shemsin or el-'Abeidiyeh, south of the Sea of Galilee along the Jordan.

3 A town in the allotment of Naphtali (Josh. 19:38).

4 A center for the sun cult in Egypt, possibly the city On (Heliopolis; Jer. 43:13). S.B.R.

Bethuel (beth-yo͞o'el; Heb., "house of God"). **1** The son of Nahor, nephew of Abraham, father of Laban and Rebekah (Gen. 22:22, 23; 24:15, 24, 47, 50). In Gen. 25:20 he is identified as an Aramean of Paddan-aram. **2** In 1 Chron. 4:30, a town in Simeonite territory west of the Dead Sea (Bethel in Josh. 19:4).

Bethzatha (beth-zay'thuh; Heb., "house of olives"), a name appearing only in John 5:2 (RSV; some manuscripts read Bethesda, "house of mercy," as in the KJV, while others have Bethsaida, "house of the fisherman"). A similar name, Beth Eshdatayin, "house of poured-out waters," appears in the Copper Scroll from Qumran. All seem to refer to a pool (or twin pools) just north of the Temple in Jerusalem, near the district of Bezetha. The pools, rediscovered in 1871, had five porticoes, one on each side and one between them (John 5:2). It was here, according to John 5:2–9, that Jesus healed the man who had been sick for thirty-eight years. ***See also*** Bethesda. C.H.M.

Excavations at the Bethzatha pool (John 5:2) in Jerusalem.

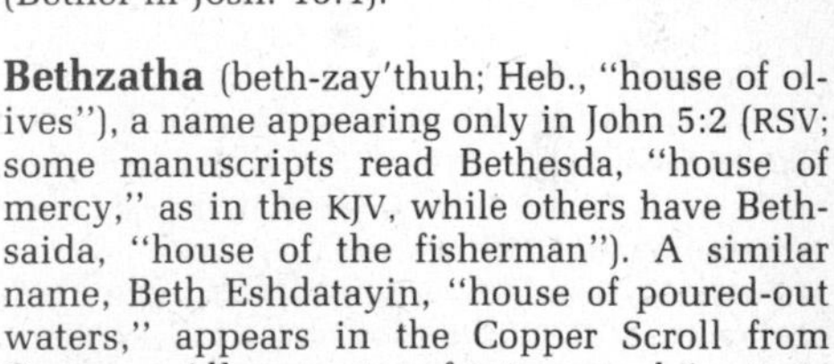

Beth-zur (beth-zo͞or'; Heb., "house of the [divine] Rock"), a town (modern Khirbet et-Tubeiqah) on the Jerusalem road four miles north of Hebron. A Judean town (Josh. 15:58) of Calebite descent (1 Chron. 2:45), it was fortified by Rehoboam as one of fifteen outposts south and west of Jerusalem (2 Chron. 11:5–10). Neh. 3:16 suggests it was a district center in the fifth century. It changed hands often in the Maccabean struggles (1 Macc. 4–11).

Archaeology attests a fortified settlement ca. 1700–1550 B.C. abandoned until reoccupied in the eleventh century B.C. There is, however, no town or fortification for Rehoboam's time (tenth century). A succession of citadels and settlements illustrate the strategic importance during the Maccabean clashes. ***See also*** Maccabees; Rehoboam. E.F.C.

Beulah (byo͞o'luh; Heb., "married"; see Gen. 20:3; Deut. 22:22), according to Isa. 62:4 (cf. 54:1), one of the new names to be given to Jerusalem after the Exile, when it will be "remarried" to God.

Bezai (bee'zī). **1** A family group ("sons of Bezai") who returned with Zerubbabel from the Babylonian captivity (Ezra 2:17). **2** A leader of the postexilic community in Judah who signed the covenant to keep the law (Neh. 10:18); he was probably the leader of the family group.

Bezaleel, (bez'uh-leel; Heb., "in the shadow [i.e., under the protection] of God"). **1** The craftsman of the tribe of Judah who, assisted by Oholiah, was chosen by God to construct the desert Tabernacle and its furnishings, including the Ark, the lampstand, and the altars. His commissioning and the instructions given him are reported in Exod. 31:1–10 (God to Moses) and 35:30–35 (Moses to the people). The execution of these instructions is reported in Exod. 36–39. Bezaleel is mentioned in the genealogy of Judah in 1 Chron. 2:20, and in 2 Chron. 1:5. **2** One of those mentioned in the book of Ezra, in the list of those who had taken foreign wives (10:30). J.S.K.

Bezek (bee'zek). **1** A Canaanite city also occupied by the Perizzites, ruled by Adoni-bezek and defeated by the tribes of Judah and Simeon shortly after Joshua's death (Judg. 1:1–7). There is debate over its exact location. It is most often located in north-central Canaan (see 2 below), but that site is in the territory of Manasseh. Since the tribes of Judah and Simeon were allied to take possession of their own lands in the far southern part of Canaan (Judg. 1:3) and the next battles recorded are in the south (Jerusalem, Hebron; Judg. 1:8–10), it is more probable that Bezek lay between Shechem and Jerusalem, probably nearer Jerusalem (Judg. 1:7). **2** A city in north-central Canaan used by Saul as the assembly point for his rally of men to rescue the besieged city of Jabesh-gilead from the Ammonites (1 Sam. 11:8). It is identified as modern Khirbet Ibziq, about twelve miles northeast of Shechem (Nablus) and some sixteen miles west of Jabesh-gilead. ***See also*** Perizzites. D.R.B.

Bezer (bee'zuhr; Heb., "gold ore,"? "fortress"?). **1** A descendant of Asher (1 Chron. 7:37). **2** A city of refuge in Reuben, assigned to the levitical family of Merari (Deut. 4:43; Josh. 20:8; 21:36; 1 Chron. 6:63); it is probably the same as Bozrah in Moab (Jer. 48:24). According to the Mesha Stele, it was restored by Mesha, the king of Moab. It was probably located on the site of modern Umm el-Amad, ca. eight miles northeast of Madaba. ***See also*** Bozrah; Mesha.

Bezetha (bee'zeth-uh, KJV for Beth-zaith; Heb., "house of the olive"), modern Beit Zeita, located about three miles north of Beth-zur. 1 Macc. 7:19 records that the Syrian general Bacchides camped there after his violence in Jerusalem.

Bible. The English word "Bible" is derived from the Old French *bible,* which is in turn based on Latin *biblia* and Greek *biblia* ("books"), plural of *biblion,* diminutive from *biblos.* Most commonly the term refers to the Scriptures of the Christian church, but it may also denote the canon of Jewish scriptures.

The Bible has been handed down to us in more than one form. *The Hebrew Bible,* often called the Masoretic Text (MT), is a collection of twenty-four books written in Hebrew (but including also a few passages in Aramaic). Its form is as follows:

The Law (Heb. *torah):* Genesis, Exodus, Leviticus, Numbers, Deuteronomy (the Pentateuch)

The Prophets (Heb. *nebi'im):* Former Prophets: Joshua, Judges, Samuel, Kings; Latter Prophets: Isaiah, Jeremiah, Ezekiel; the twelve minor prophets

The Writings (Heb. *ketubim):* Psalms, Job, Proverbs, Ruth, Song of Solomon, Ecclesiastes, Lamentations, Esther, Daniel, Ezra-Nehemiah, Chronicles

A translation of the Jewish scriptures into Greek, commonly called the *Septuagint* (LXX), probably had its earliest form as a translation of the Pentateuch into Greek in the third century B.C. This collection came to contain, not only the books of the Hebrew Bible listed above, but also a number of other writings (although there are variations in the manuscripts): 1 Esdras, the Wisdom of Solomon, the Wisdom of Jesus, the Son of Sirach (Ecclesiasticus), Judith, Tobit, Baruch, the Letter of Jeremiah, the four books of Maccabees, plus certain additions to books in the MT, notably the additions to Daniel (Susan-

Detail of page from the Pentateuch of a Hebrew Bible (MT), 1310. The left-hand column is a commentary on the text.

na, Bel and the Dragon, the Prayer of Azariah, and the Song of the Three Young Men) and to the book of Esther.

The Christian Bible consists of the Old Testament (OT) and the New Testament (NT). In the Roman Catholic and Eastern Christian communities (e.g., Greek, Syriac, Armenian), the OT is based on the LXX, while most Protestant churches accept only the books of the Hebrew Bible as their OT canon. The NT canon we have inherited now consists of twenty-seven books: the Gospels of Matthew, Mark, Luke, John; Acts of the Apostles; Romans, 1 and 2 Corinthians, Galatians, Ephesians, Philippians, Colossians, 1 and 2 Thessalonians, 1 and 2 Timothy, Titus, Philemon (all attributed to Paul); Hebrews, James, 1 and 2 Peter, 1, 2, and 3 John, Jude, and Revelation.

Development of the Biblical Canons: The development of the various biblical canons was a long and complex process. Prior to the fall of Jerusalem in A.D. 70, the working canon of Jewish scriptures in Palestine seems to have been rather open-ended and inclusive. After 70, however, there was a narrowing tendency, so that by about the time of the Council of Jamnia (ca. A.D. 90) the rabbis had rejected the larger canon that continued in the LXX in favor of the twenty-four-book collection we have labeled the Hebrew Bible. Ultimately this Jamnian canon became the canon for Judaism as a whole.

We are unable to reconstruct with confidence precisely which lists of books were considered authoritative by Jesus and his earliest followers. By the second century, it was not uncommon to find church fathers using books found in the LXX but not in the Jamnian canon. Yet a few writers (e.g., Origen, Jerome) distinguished between the books of the Hebrew Bible and the remainder in the LXX tradition; indeed, the latter group they labeled "Apocrypha" ("hidden" or "outside" books), a group they considered edifying but not authoritative. On the whole, however, Eastern and Roman Catholic tradition generally considered the OT "apocryphal" books to be canonical. It was not until the Protestant Reformation that these books were clearly denied canonical status (in Protestant circles). The Roman church, however, continues to affirm their place in the canon of Scripture.

The NT canon also has an uneven and complex history. Each of the books of our presently accepted NT achieved early recognition in some circles, but no canonical lists appear before around A.D. 150, when the heretic Marcion proclaimed a canon consisting of his version of Luke and ten Letters of Paul. By the end of the century, more inclusive lists of authoritative NT writings were advanced, e.g., the Muratorian Canon (listing at least twenty-two of our present twenty-seven), Irenaeus, a bishop of Lyon in the mid-second century A.D. (clearly naming twenty-one), and Tertullian, a North African presbyter of the same period (twenty-two). The inclusion of Revelation was a matter of considerable disagreement. The second and third Letters of John, 2 Peter, and Jude were often not included, and Hebrews was sometimes omitted. At the same time, writings not found presently in our canon of twenty-seven were sometimes cited. The twenty-seven-book Latin Vulgate (Vg.) of Jerome (late fourth century) exerted considerable influence upon what books were generally recognized; moreover, provincial church councils held at Hippo (393) and Carthage (397) recognized a twenty-seven-book NT canon. Unanimity in the Western church was not fully achieved, but the twenty-seven-book canon was predominant. In the east, the Syrian church achieved a twenty-two-book canon by the fifth century, although later christological controversies created division, resulting in some erosion of the fifth-century consensus.

Formation of the Hebrew Scriptures: The question of which *books* were to be considered canonical represents only the later stages of the formation of the canonical collections. The oral and literary process by means of which the biblical literature was formed took well over a thousand years, according to the best estimates of biblical research.

Scholars have argued that the Pentateuch is the final product of the interweaving of several literary sources, called J, E, D, and P. The Yahwist source (J) is generally considered to be the earliest, dating from the period of the early monarchy (ca. 1000 B.C.). It is a narrative source that contains tales of the patriarchs, the Exodus, Sinai, and wilderness wanderings. Its most distinctive characteristic is its use of the divine name Yahweh (or Jahweh), from which comes the designation J or Yahwist. The Elohist source (E), which is characterized by its use of Elohim for the divine name prior to the theophany at the burning bush (Exod. 3), is a narrative strand in many respects quite similar to J. Its portrayal of God is less anthropomorphic than that of J, however, and it betrays special theological concerns, such as an interest in prophecy and a belief that the name Yahweh was first known when revealed to Moses at the burning bush. Scholars generally date E about a century later than J. The Deuteronomic source (D), dating from the period of the late monarchy (ca. seventh century B.C.) is confined largely to the book of Deuteronomy. Its concerns lie chiefly in its radical opposition to the worship of Baal; indeed, its program of restricting sacrifice to the Jerusalem Temple was developed for the purpose of stamping out Baal worship by outlawing sacrifice anywhere but Jerusalem. The Priestly source (P), dating from the period of the Babylonian exile (late sixth to early fourth centuries B.C.) emphasizes the cultic institutions of Israel: the Sabbath, circumcision, the role of Aaron (and, by implication, his priestly line), and the detailed legislation about cultic matters reportedly received at Sinai.

Attached to Deuteronomy was a Deuteronomistic edition of Joshua, Judges, Samuel, and Kings. This narrative of Israelite experience from the conquest of the land to the Babylonian exile reflects the Baal polemic and the program of centralization of sacrifice characteristic of Deuteronomistic theologians.

By the early postexilic period (late sixth century B.C.), the first two parts of the Hebrew Bible, the Torah and the Prophets, were almost complete. The section of the canon called the Writings was not finally completed until the second century B.C. The books of the Apocrypha (so-called) were written during the first two centuries B.C. and the first century A.D.

Formation of the Christian New Testament: The NT also underwent a complex history of development. Scholars generally agree that much of the material in the synoptic Gospels (Matthew, Mark, and Luke) originated in oral traditions, only later finding its way into written Gospels. Most scholars believe that Mark was the first of the Gospels to be written. The compilers of Matthew and Luke used both Mark and what may have been a source of Jesus' teachings labeled Q, according to the prevailing view. A minority of scholars, however, doubt the priority of Mark and the existence of Q. It is widely accepted that John is the latest of the four Gospels, though early traditions may be contained within it. The synoptic Gospels were probably written between A.D. 70 and 100, with John coming in the late first or early second century.

The Letters of Paul were probably written in the 50s and 60s. Many scholars doubt that Paul wrote Ephesians (some doubt Colossians and 2 Thessalonians also), and there is a widespread belief that the pastoral Letters (1 and 2 Timothy, Titus) were written perhaps after the turn of the second century by someone speaking in the name of the revered apostle Paul. The "catholic (or general) epistles" (James, 1 and 2 Peter, Jude, 1, 2, and 3 John) probably emerged in the late first and early second centuries. It is likely that Hebrews and Revelation stem from the late first century. ***See also*** Apocrypha, Old Testament; Aramaic; Biblical Criticism; Canon; English Bible, The; Greek, New Testament; Hebrew; Hermeneutics; New Testament; Old Testament; Oral Materials, Sources, and Traditions; Pentateuch; Septuagint; Sources of the Pentateuch; Synoptic Problem, The; Texts, Versions, Manuscripts, Editions. R.F.M.

The Bible and Western Art

THE INHERENT NEED in human nature to express itself in visual images is the essential reason art and religion have been inseparable since earliest times. From the great cave paintings of the prehistoric age to the Parthenon of Athena (432 B.C.), Western civilization has stated its religious tenets through the creative talents of artists. The early Christians began to illustrate their beliefs in the same manner as their contemporaries. The rapid spread of Christianity was based on the appeal of its message of salvation and the efficient communication system of the Roman Empire. From the outset, Christians made no political attempt to separate themselves from Rome. Rather, they accepted their world and were quick to adopt and adapt Roman practices into the Christian life. Art in the Roman Empire was a major means of communication, and Imperial architecture and sculpture expressed the religion, power, and stability of Rome. The early Christians assumed this creative mode of expression and communication.

Iconography: Christian iconography, or the system of using signs and symbols, began and developed quickly in the first three centuries, when the cross and the fish were the most popular symbols for Christ. Problems of subject and the suitability of images arose but were resolved in favor of the need to relate the episodes of both the OT and the NT as a means of teaching history and doctrine. Artists used signs and symbols not only to enhance their compositions but as allusions to deeper meanings. Over the centuries, fruit, animals, vegetation, colors, and objects have become part of the vocabulary of both the artists and the viewers. The apple (Lat. *malum*) of the tree of knowledge (Gen. 3:3) signifies the evil (*malum*) of temptation when in the hands of Eve, but in pictures of Mary it is a symbol of salvation. The palm leaf of Roman victory was adopted as the symbol of the martyr's victorious death. The lily, symbolizing purity, is found in paintings of the Virgin, and the iris was used by fifteenth-century Flemish artists as a reference to her sorrows. The gourd represented the pilgrim's flask and the holly with its thorns was symbolic of the Passion of Christ. The snuffed-out candle in the Annunciation panel of the *Mérode Altarpiece* (ca. 1434) by Robert Campin is indicative of the end of the OT and the dove of the Holy Spirit is the beginning of the NT (John 1:32).

The baptism of Jesus. In John 1:32 the dove of the Holy Spirit descends upon Jesus as he is baptized by John the Baptist. Detail from the Florence Baptistry doors by Andrea Pisano, ca. 1336.

The four Evangelists—Matthew, Mark, Luke, and John—are represented by the angel, lion, ox, and eagle, respectively, from Ezek. 1:5 and Rev. 4:7. These creatures are depicted with wings symbolic of their divine mission. Medieval manuscripts often used the symbol instead of the name to signify the author of the Gospel. The eagle on lecterns supporting the Sacred Books refers to the flight of prayer to God. The lamb is the symbol of Christ: "Behold the Lamb of God" (John 1:29). In medieval times the pelican was recognized as a symbol of Christ because in legend it was held to open its breast to feed its young with its own blood. The book held by Christ in most Byzantine mosaics, with the Alpha and the Omega, represents him as "the Word." As Pantocrator, Christ the Redeemer holds his right hand with the two index fingers extended to symbolize his two natures, divine and human. The goldfinch, which eats thorns and thistles, is symbolic of the Passion of Christ. The *Madonna of the Goldfinch* by Raphael (1483–1520) represents the incarnation and the Passion. The tree is symbolic of life and is seen as such in the iconography of many religions. Water is also symbolic of life.

Geometric figures such as the circle (symbolic of eternity and God, with no beginning and no end), the triangle (the Trinity), the pentagon (the five wounds of Christ), and the square (the four elements of earth, fire, air and water) are all used as individual objects and as the basis of compositional development. Each of the numbers from one to ten has one or more biblical references, such as the nine choirs of angels and the seven times Jacob bowed in submission. Thirteen refers to faithlessness and betrayal. Colors too have symbolic meaning. The white of the Virgin's veil is innocence and purity. Green is the sign of hope and blue means heaven and truth. Purple signifies royalty or sorrow, and in paintings of the Passion, Christ wears a red robe indicating his sacrifice. Yellow is either the sun and divinity or jealousy and treason. Judas usually wears a dirty yellow cloak. Black represents death and hopelessness. Most of the symbols—numbers, colors, animals, and objects—have more than one biblical reference.

Early Christian and Byzantine Art: During the first three centuries of Christianity, the struggle for freedom of worship gave no opportunity for monumental or permanent artistic expression. The catacombs, underground cemeteries, were decorated with signs and symbols of varying artistic quality. On the ceiling of a cubicula, a small chapel or gallery, in the Catacomb of Sts. Peter and Marcellino in Rome of the fourth century is a late fresco work of the story of Jonah. Through visual images Christianity expressed its justification as the fulfillment of the OT Law. Jonah as the prefiguration of Christ is one example of an OT figure used by the artists from early Christian times through to the Renaissance (Michelangelo [1475–1564] painted his powerful figure of Jonah on the Sistine Chapel ceiling [1508–1512]).

Adam and Eve, from the fourth-century sarcophagus of Junius Bassus.

Following the edict of A.D. 325 in which Constantine gave freedom to the Christians to practice their religion openly, the public artistic expression of the new religion developed in a way that was essentially Roman in style and Christian in concept. The Roman tradition of burial in sarcophagi was continued, and in such works as the marble sarcophagus of the Roman prefect Junius Bassus of A.D. 359 scenes from the OT and the NT are intermingled, with Adam and Eve, Daniel in the lions' den, Christ's entry into Jerusalem, and Christ among the doctors included among them. The ornate style and deep carving are essentially fourth-century Imperial. The Roman determination to announce itself to the world was expressed in clear monumental forms. This syle was found to be exactly suited to the message of Christianity.

By the end of the fourth century, Christianity was established and prayerful praise of God and eloquent explanation of his divine love through artistic expression was not only accepted, but required. Immediately after the edict of 325, Christians considered sites for the construction of places of worship. The early builders were faced with a formidable task that involved technical as well as philosophical changes from the kind of buildings that went before. The Greco-Roman rectangular temple form was not suitable to Christianity. Essentially, this traditional temple was designed to be appreciated from the exterior and rites and rituals were conducted for the public on outside altars. Christianity demanded the inclusion of the faithful in the house of God. The solution came early in A.D. 333 with the construction of Old St. Peter's basilica (destroyed in the fifteenth century) supposedly on the site of the burial place of St. Peter in Rome. The Christian architects redesigned the Roman basilica, which was a rectangular structure of a nave and side aisles with an apse, or a large niche, at either end. They replaced the apse on the west end with the atrium or colonnaded forecourt of the Roman house and established the basic form of Christian ecclesiastical architecture. Over the centuries the plan evolved into the Latin cross plan, with the focal point at the main altar within the apse at the east end of the nave. Christian churches were oriented on an east-west axis, with the main entrance at the west, from which the sound of the trumpets of judgment and salvation would come. The interior altar was at the east end so the faithful could face the heavenly city of Jerusalem.

Artist's reconstruction of Old St. Peter's.

The Roman temple tradition of brick construction with marble facing was altered to suit the spiritual and economic needs of the Christian community. The comparatively plain brickwork was retained on the outside and attention was directed to the interior, which was meant to be the house of God. Artists were to decorate this heavenly space in keeping with the atmosphere created by the Divine Presence. The walls of the nave above the columns and the Christian adoption of the triumphal arch at the crossing of the bema (an early form of the transept) and nave provided ample space and opportunity for the development of art programs in mosaics and fresco.

Mosaic programs were the most expensive but the longest lasting. Those of Santa Maria Maggiore in Rome (early fifth century) are an example of the union of technique, medium, and subject, where the light of the clerestory windows illuminates the brilliant glass mosaics and creates an atmosphere of spiritual splendor and heavenly protection. These programs of OT and NT subjects, but principally of the life of the Virgin and Christ, became the accepted and standard mode of church decoration. The mosaics of Santa Maria Maggiore in Rome are considered to be among the most beautiful stylistically and the most complete programmatically.

The walls of Jericho fall. Mosaic scene from Santa Maria Maggiore in Rome, early fifth century.

The Roman mosaic tradition was adapted not only for decoration but also for theological and didactic purposes. As the Christian church developed and eventually equaled or replaced civil influence on and control of everyday life, the styles of art and the media of mosaic or fresco reflected the social, political, and religious philosophy of the Roman Christian world. The political life of imperial Rome and the division of the Empire in A.D. 395 led to new interpretations of the role of the emperor and concomitantly of that of Christ.

The Greco-Roman interpretation of Christ as Apollo in the classical style of sculpture gave way to the influence of the Eastern Empire with the emphasis on Christ as Pantocrator (lord over all reality—abstract, conceptual, formal, and regal). Sixth-century mosaic programs in Ravenna, Justinian's capital of the Eastern Empire in Italy, show Christ in royal purple, seated on a Byzantine throne and holding the scepter as a symbol of his authority. These mosaic programs, in structures such as the Mausoleum of Galla Placidia, the Arian Baptistry, and the Church of San Vitale (ca. A.D. 547), combine OT and NT stories in the Imperial style. The gold background signifying the paradise of the future accentuates the formal patterns of rich color and dazzling light. Visually, the authority and power of the reign of Christ is both temporal and eternal.

The Virgin enthroned as Queen of Heaven and Earth. Beside her, emperors Justinian (left) and Constantine offer her the Hagia Sophia church that each built during his reign; tenth century.

The sixth-century building and decoration programs of emperor Justinian and his empress, Theodora, led to the construction in Constantinople of one of the largest and most imperial structures in the history of architecture, the basilica of Hagia Sophia, the Church of Holy Wisdom, A.D. 532–537. Two geometricians, Anthemius of Tralles and Isidorus of Miletus, designed the dome on pendentives (curving triangular segments of vaulting) formed at the intersections of the arches at the tops of the four walls. They changed the square of earth into the circle of eternity and equated spiritual and imperial space. The Christian believer was overcome by the power and majesty of Christ and his representative, Justinian. Shimmering gold mosaics of the four archangels on the pendentives held the dome of heaven above the imperial throne and the faithful. This interpretation of Christ in majesty with the Virgin enthroned as Queen of Heaven and Earth became basic to the faithful and to the artistic expression of the theology of the Western church through to the Renaissance. In the East, this style developed into the rich tradition of the icon as seen in Andrei Rublev's *Old Testament Trinity* (ca. 1410–20).

Medieval Art: Neither the church hierarchy nor the artists overlooked any opportunity to express the teachings of Christ. One of the most obvious places for the depiction of the OT and NT was the door to the church. Bronze doors with their double leaves provided the most immediate format for typological or symbolic programs. The great bronze doors at St. Michael's in Hildesheim, Germany (ca. 1015) have scenes such as the "Expulsion of Adam and Eve" of the OT matched with the "Annunciation" of the NT. The scenes on these doors are typical of the medieval expression of faith. They are graphically direct: God points to Adam who points to Eve who points to the serpent. Each one blames the other. The clarity of the design tells the story and its meaning to those who cannot read.

Other doors, such as the north and south doors of the Baptistry in Florence (1330–36) by Andrea Pisano (ca. 1290–1348), tell the stories in clear logical sequence. Each scene is framed by a quatrefoil, an ornamental frame of four lobes, symbolic of the four Evangelists. Included on the north doors are the Evangelists with their symbols. But the style of Pisano appears old-fashioned when compared with that of the east doors of 1425–53, familiarly known by Michelangelo's appellation as the "Gates of Paradise," by Lorenzo Ghiberti (ca. 1378–1455). Ghiberti's program was totally modern in its concept and execution. No longer did both leaves match OT to NT; the ten panels were all OT episodes. The quatrefoils were discarded and in their place Ghiberti presented the new style of perspective space and logical placement of figures within the picture frame. The clarity of the composition illustrated the OT stories and proclaimed the advent of the Renaissance.

Before printing, the arts of painting, sculpture, architecture, and the preaching of the Word were the means by which the church taught the stories of the Bible and the lessons people were to learn that would lead them to salvation. Oratory and the reading of the sacred Scripture demanded a visible separate platform from which the Word could be explained. The pulpit, or ambo, was the stage from which preachers promulgated the teachings of Christ. As its role was of major importance, it received special attention both in placement and in execution. It was positioned in the nave near the crossing of the transept in full view of the congregation. Usually octagonal in shape, symbolic of the resurrection of Christ eight days after his entry into Jerusalem, pulpits became both architectural and sculptural expressions of faith. In the Siena pulpit (1265–68), Nicola Pisano (ca. 1220–1284?) combined the architectural elements with an iconographic program that included a central column supporting the superstructure with the personifications of music and the seven liberal arts on the base. Plastic (modeled) forms were crowded together in seven panels of the visitation, the birth of Christ, and the Last Judgment. Nicola united Roman classical forms in surface compositions that denied real (earthly) space in favor of the abstract Gothic expression of heavenly space.

The marble pulpit in the Pisa Baptistry, executed by Nicola Pisano in 1260 prior to his Sienna pulpit.

Manuscript illumination is perhaps the best example of art directly connected with the publication of the Bible. The papyrus scrolls of ancient biblical texts were copied onto vellum or parchment sheets and bound, and the Roman tradition was adapted to illustrations of OT and NT stories in these reproductions. The *Vienna Genesis* of the early sixth century gives an example of the continuous pictorial narration of an OT subject in a style of the Hellenistic tradition. Text and illustrations are unified in a single composition on purple vellum. The *Utrecht Psalter* (ca. 820–832) from Reims combines pen illustrations and text in a fully developed program presenting David and his songs. *The Book of Kells*, considered by some to be among the greatest works of art, is the compilation of the four Gospels. The exquisite colors and detailed designs, the influence of the Viking abstract animal forms, and the obvious delight and tender loving care in execution of this manuscript make it the outstanding work of the eighth century. The development of the palace schools of manuscript painting under the aegis of Charlemagne (742?–814) was one of the unique expressions of the marriage of Christian and barbaric thoughts and techniques. In the *Coronation Gospels* (790–800), made of vellum soaked in purple dye, the Gospel According to John uses the Imperial Roman style of ages past in an inventive design and golden letters.

Cover of the *Imperial Book of Gospels* from the Palace School at Aachen; gilded silver, eighth century.

Medieval manuscripts became progressively more elaborate in decoration, script, and cover. These portable works of art were—especially in the less stable Western world—a major artistic expression. Separate books of the Bible and other writings were copied in monasteries, and individuals and groups took three to four years to complete one manuscript. Books were expensive, treasured gifts and the medieval manuscript is one of the great glories of the art of the Christian world.

"The Bible in Stone" is an oft-quoted phrase describing Romanesque and Gothic cathedrals. The sculptural programs express both the religious and the secular life of the period. Often over the portals or on capitals of columns we find signs of the zodiac, some of which have biblical references, scenes of the life of the Virgin, the Last Judgment, the Passion, and lives of the saints free-standing or in relief. On the tympanum (space beneath an arch, usually over a doorway) and capitals of Autun Cathedral (1130–35), the sculptor Giselbertus mixed OT and NT themes. Noah's ark still balances precariously on top of the mountain while the animals march in. The splendor and light of the stained glass of the medieval cathedral, even today, translates the historical events of the Bible into spiritual illumination.

Renaissance and Baroque Art: Christian doctrine became the stabilizing force of Western civilization through to the Enlightenment of the eighteenth century and the Industrial Revolution of the nineteenth century. Art was always used wherever and whenever possible for the glorification of God and the instruction and edification of the faithful. The church assumed the role of patron of the arts and the church officials considered this to be part of their religious duties. Bishops had resident artists in their household and talented craftspeople such as goldsmiths and weavers were rarely without work. The furnishings for the altar, the vestments, chalices, candlesticks, reliquaries, and choir stalls, demanded the inventiveness of the artists. Civil leaders, kings, lords, and ladies also took upon themselves the financial and intellectual support of the arts and religion. Biblical and apocryphal topics were the major subjects of these arts and crafts until the late fifteenth century.

Pope Julius II's patronage of Michelangelo, Raphael, and Bramante (1444–1514) exemplifies the role of the patron and the church in us-

Jesus hands the keys to the Kingdom of Heaven to St. Peter (cf. Matt. 16:19) in this fifteenth-century fresco by Perugino in the Sistine Chapel.

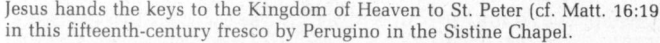

ing the talents of the artists to illustrate and defend the teachings of Christ. In the Sistine Chapel, Michelangelo in 1508–12 painted the ceiling program of the genealogy and prefiguration of Christ in the OT. The harmony and clarity of Renaissance composition was expressed by Pietro Vannucci (called Perugino, ca. 1445–1523?) in his *Delivery of the Keys* in 1482. This fresco is an example of the use of negative space as the positive element in expressing the significance of Christ's statement "I will give you the keys of the kingdom of heaven" (Matt. 16:19). Fifteenth-century Humanism and Neo-Platonism were reconciled in Perugino's classically balanced composition of geometric perspective, mathematical proportions, sculptural forms, and rational spirituality. In 1541, on the altar wall, Michelangelo completed *The Last Judgment.* It is an extraordinary statement of contemporary thought in terms of biblical subjects. The diverse fresco styles, stories, and interpretations in the Sistine Chapel achieve unity through their subject matter, which is drawn from the Bible.

The Renaissance was characterized by the study of classical ideas and their reconciliation with the theology of Christianity. This study centered on the understanding of ancient philosophers' comprehensions of the universe as mathematical harmony. The textual sources for this intellectual, aesthetic, and spiritual harmony were the writings of the ancient philosophers, the church fathers, and the Bible. This perception of perfect harmony, that is, God, was stated visually and materially not only in painting and sculpture but, most importantly, in architecture. A centrally planned church, that is, one with a longitudinal axis, which starts at the main entrance, of equal length as the transverse axis (they bisect each other at their centers), expressed the understanding of God as the center and circumference of the universe. From the centrally planned church, architects developed either a Greek cross plan such as Bramante's first plan for the new St. Peter's in Rome (1506) or a circular plan such as the one for S. Eligio degli Orefici (1511–12) by Raphael.

Also during the Renaissance in the fifteenth century, religious art began to lose its primary role—secular art occupied the artists' and patrons' time as well, and often the two realms clashed. The great religious reformers Savanarola, Martin Luther, John Calvin, St. Charles Borromeo, and St. Ignatius of Loyola all, directly or indirectly, influenced the artistic and religious expression of their ages. Savanarola, a Franciscan monk of the late fifteenth century, demanded that artworks on nonreligious subjects be burned. Followers of Luther destroyed works in churches as "idolatrous," and Calvinists tended to eschew all expressions of religious art. The Council of Trent of 1563 declared that no nude figures could appear in churches. Therefore fig leaves were added to paintings and sculptures of Adam and Eve and even Michelangelo's *Last Judgment* did not escape the decision. Artists were to be historically correct in their paintings and famous patrons like the Medici in their own magnificent brocades could no longer be included as the Magi. The Spanish painter Francisco de Zurbaran (1598–1664) got around the problem of painting his self-portrait in his *Crucifixion* by using his face as the model for St. Luke, the patron of artists.

The preaching of reformers such as St. Ignatius led the Catholic

David, by the sculptor Bernini, 1625.

church into an age of spiritual renewal and fervor that required new patronage of the arts. The Baroque Age, the seventeenth century, was one of the greatest splendor—religious and secular. Elements of the OT and NT were restated in works such as Bernini's (1598–1680) *David* (1625) and Rubens's (1577–1640) triptych of the *Descent from the Cross* (ca. 1614). Patronage of the arts remained part of the church's role until the nineteenth century. Art requires inspiration, creativity, time, and money. Twentieth-century mass-production methods and the general lack of critical ecclesiastical patronage have forced the artists to rely on themselves to communicate the aesthetic and spiritual interpretations of the Bible in modern styles.

The artist, never a clearly definable character in any circumstance, is sometimes ignored or misunderstood by the general public. Stories of Michelangelo's arguments with Pope Julius II have led some to believe that artists often played only a craftsman's role, i.e., they did what they were told. A careful study of art reveals that the artists as people of their times also believed in the stories and doctrines they were illustrating. The quality of the artists' spiritual life is sometimes, but not always, reflected in their work, such as Fra Angelico's (ca. 1400–1455) tender love of the Virgin. Michelangelo Caravaggio (1573–1610) was an example of an artist whose spiritual life seems at odds with the quality and intensity of religious understanding found in his

Descent from the Cross, Rubens, ca. 1614.

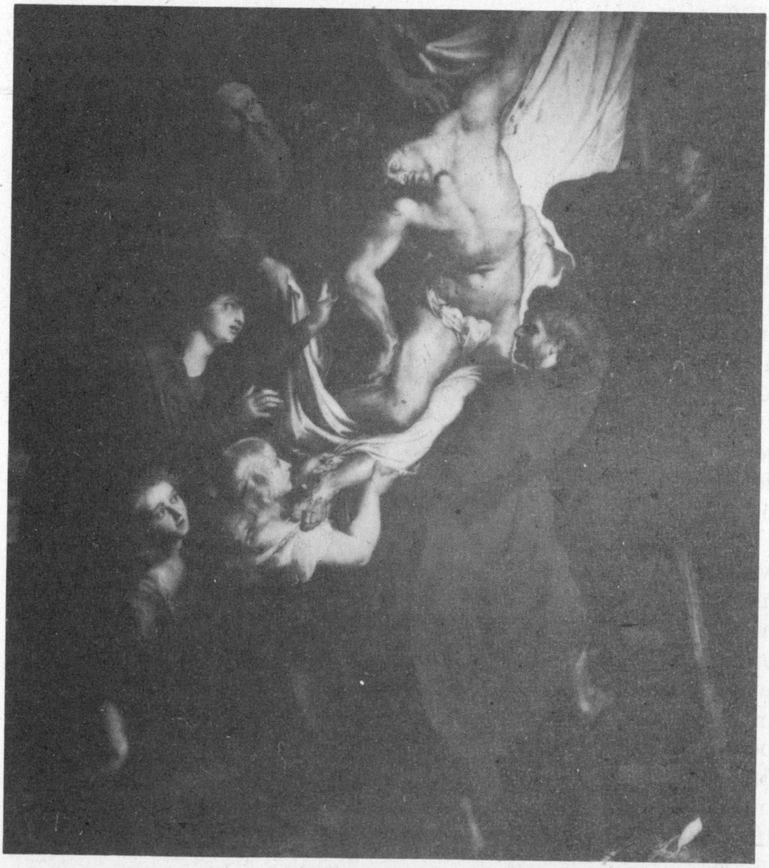

work. (In the twentieth century, the French artist Georges Rouault [1871–1958] said, "All my work is a prayer for those who know how to look at it." Henri Matisse [1869–1954] said that to him Paradise was a place where he could paint frescoes.) The creative force or genius is never completely understood by either the artist or the public. The gift of aesthetic expression has regularly been used by artists to make the Bible visible and inspirational.

For example, in the Arena Chapel, Padua (1305–6), a small structure of barrel vaulting, Giotto (ca. 1266–1337) enlarged theologically and spatially his interpretation of the personal and human qualities of the biblical subjects. His technical use of color and light made visible the psychological and spiritual responses of the characters.

The three registers of scenes from the life of the Virgin, the public life of Christ, and his Passion are united by the *Annunciation* on the triumphal arch before the sanctuary and the *Last Judgment* over the wall of the entrance. Within the biblical tradition Giotto maintained the narrative with succeeding scenes and stylistic unity. Prophets with their scrolls frame the individual scenes. The blue in the barrel vaulting and in the background of the separate scenes relates Paradise to earth. Space is rationally defined by balanced groupings of figures in landscape and architectural settings. Giotto's consistent use of narration, iconography, and composition within separate but related scenes expresses the human psychological and spiritual depth of the scene.

In the *Kiss of Judas,* Giotto filled the background with the confusion of the soldiers and their lances. In the foreground to the left, Peter is seen cutting off the ear of the servant of Pilate. Christ and Judas occupy the center foreground plane, and even though Judas' dirty yellow cloak covers most of Christ, the lines of the garment lead directly to the Savior's face. Here, in profile, Christ gazes directly into Judas's eyes with quiet understanding, acceptance, and compassion. Giotto's humanistic interpretation was made possible by his exploration into the technical aspects of fresco paint. For the artist, the development of new techniques is necessary for the full expression of the subject. Space, color, light, modeling, organization of masses, and iconography are used in simple, straightforward designs leading the family to contemplation and prayer. In the *Last Judgment,* below the cross and the resurrected dead, is the patron, Enrico Scrovegni, presenting to an angel a model of the Arena Chapel, one of the supreme achievements in Christian and Western art and one of the most complete programs of biblical exposition.

Another example is the Brancacci Chapel in Florence, where Masaccio (1401–1428?) painted the fresco *The Expulsion of Adam and Eve from Paradise* (1424–28). Masaccio accomplished one of the most significant breakthroughs in the history of art. Through his observation of the world about him he realized that light is the vehicle by which forms are perceived. The technical and philosophical achievement of the use of light enabled him to realize the forms of the human beings and their psychological and spiritual understanding of the loss of their relationship with God. The anguish on Eve's face and the humiliation of Adam, expressed through the modeling of the figures by light, is not only a major step in the technical world of art, but a visual statement of the result of the sin of disobedience. Masaccio's scientific and aesthetic experiment opened the way for the Renaissance study of the human response to the spiritual life.

Such biblical topics as *The Feast of Herod* (ca. 1425) and the *Mary Magdalen* (ca. 1453) were sculpted by Donatello (ca. 1386–1466) in his search for an understanding of the classical heritage and its reconciliation with that of Christianity. In *The Feast of Herod*, a bronze panel on the font in the Baptistry of Seina, Donatello used the new science of linear perspective to plan his three-dimensional relief composition on a two-dimensional surface and expressed rationally and realistically the moment when Herod realized the horror of his actions. Visually, *The Feast of Herod* was transformed into a contemporary experience for all who saw it. *Mary Magdalen* is carved in wood. Her scraggly unkempt hair, emaciated sagging skin, deep-set hollow eyes, and skeletal frailty are the visual evidence of the reality of sin and atonement, for which Mary Magdalen is a biblical example.

Perhaps the most famous of religious and biblical paintings is *The Last Supper* (ca. 1495–98) by Leonardo da Vinci (1452–1519) on the refectory wall of Santa Maria delle Grazie in Milan. This traditional subject and its artistic problems had plagued artists since the beginning of Christianity: how does one place on a two-dimensional surface a composition of thirteen three-dimensional people and at the same time express the psychological and spiritual intensity of the specific moment when Christ says "One of you will betray me"? Leonardo, because he had pursued Renaissance studies of mathematics and paintings, solved the problem. His logical organization of the apostles in two groups of three on each side of Christ in the center, his use of individual gestures and glances leading the viewers' eyes toward Christ, and his understanding of geometric and atmospheric perspective make the event appear alive, real, and immediately comprehensible. Leonardo's *Last Supper* is popular precisely because it seems real. Renaissance concepts of logic and harmony in the spiritual and temporal worlds are visually realized in this NT event.

With the invention of movable-type printing in 1455 by Johannes Gutenberg, the Bible began to become accessible to the educated classes. Woodcuts and etchings were popular techniques of illustration for the new and less expensive editions of the Bible. In 1509, Albrecht Dürer (1471–1528) published the *Small Woodcut Passion*, a pocket-sized book with thirty-seven plates measuring about 5 × 3 inches. Dürer's Germanic expressionism interpreted in black and white an intense personal and spiritual understanding of the Passion. Continuity of story and individuality of episodes were treated with consistent technical skill and creative awareness.

Christ at Emmaus (cf. Luke 24:13–31), Rembrandt, 1629.

The Rembrandt Edition of the Bible, first published in 1959, is an example of the artistic productivity of a man who over a long career (1606–1669) never traveled more than a hundred miles in any direction. Rembrandt painted portraits, landscapes, and mythological stories, but it was his love and study of biblical themes, people, and events that led him to his profound psychological and spiritual masterpieces. Rembrandt explored his subjects technically, historically, and emotionally. His *Christ at Emmaus* (1629) is both a homage to Leonardo and a reenactment of an event that appears in the Gospel According to Luke (24:13–31).

Caravaggio's *Deposition* (1602), one of the great treasures of the Vatican collection and a masterpiece of realism and intense spirituality, presents Christ as the cornerstone of salvation. The religious fervor of the late sixteenth and early seventeenth centuries was expressed in numerous canvasses by this man, notorious in Rome for his scandalous public life. Caravaggio's dramatic light, his solid plastic forms, his detailed realism, and his placement of his figures in the foreground plane give his works the power to attract their viewers and draw them into mystical contemplation of the event.

Religious Art in the Twentieth Century: Modern artists are less restrained than their predecessors in expressing personal insights and interpretations of biblical themes. One may consider as an example the German artist Emile Nolde (1867–1956), who returned to the Bible as a source of inspiration. His use of raw color as an emotional force makes him one of the most romantic and mystical artists of the twentieth century. His *Pentecost* (1909), *Doubting Thomas* (1912), and *Holy Night* (1912) are modern expressions of traditional biblical and German subjects. Color provided for Nolde a vocabulary of ideas and interpretations with which to contemplate the mystical experience. His uncompromising and expressive use of color makes his work stark and compelling. Another example is Salvadore Dali (1904–), who has used in his paintings such biblical events as the Last Supper and the Crucifixion to express the conflict between reality and the subconscious. His surrealistic device of dissolving images into unmeasurable space takes the viewer from the historical, factual world into the spiritual and contemplative realm of the soul. Barnett Newman (1905–71) in 1965–66 did a series called *Stations of the Cross* in a style called Abstract Expressionism. This nonrepresentational style demands that the viewers explore their own spiritual depth and the mystical reality of the Passion. Henri Matisse's Chapel of the Rosary at Vence, France, of 1947 is an expression of the spiritual life in a complete exposition of architecture, painting, sculpture, furniture, and vestments. The light of the stained glass *Tree of Life* is a modern statement of the medieval tradition of light as spiritual illumination.

Head of Christ by Georges Rouault, who said, "All my work is a prayer for those who know how to look at it"; detail from *Ecce Dolor*, 1936.

A concordance of all biblical themes, events, characters, objects, animals, flora, fauna and all their visual interpretations in painting, sculpture, architecture, and the minor arts is an impossibility. The subjects of the Bible have been and continue to be interpreted in the styles and techniques of their artists' times and localities. Artistic expression is limited only by the creative talents of the artists who are free to explore any subject and any medium in any style that will communicate the understanding of reality they share with their contemporaries. As art and religion are inseparable, it should not be surprising that the Bible and art are united in the expression of reality both human and divine.

Bibliography

Cahn, Walter. *Romanesque Bible Illumination.* Ithaca, NY: Cornell University Press, 1982.

Christe, Yves, Tania Velmans, Hanna Losouska, and Roland Recht. *Art of the Christian World: A.D. 200–1500. A Handbook of Styles and Forms.* New York: Rizzoli, 1982.

Janson, H. W. *History of Art.* Englewood Cliffs, NJ: Prentice-Hall, 1978.

E.L.F.

Bible and Western literature, the. The Bible has permeated the literature of the Western world to a degree that cannot easily be measured. More than any other single body of writing, ancient or modern, it has provided writers from the Middle Ages on with a store of symbols, ideas, and ways of perceiving reality. This influence can be traced not only in texts that deal directly with biblical characters or topics, but also in a vast number of poems, plays, and other writings that are not overtly biblical in theme but that testify to a biblical view of humankind and the world. Moreover, the Bible has had a profound effect in shaping the very language writers use. This is especially true of the English language which, as Tyndale and later Addison perceived, was particularly adaptable to the pattern and idiom of Hebrew speech. The cadences and phraseology of the English Bible, especially as found in the King James Version (1611), have entered the English language to become, according to the historian J. R. Green, "the standard of our language." Martin Luther's German translation (1522) had a similarly formative influence on German literature and language. The presence of the Bible is indeed so pervasive in all periods of Western literature that it will only be possible here to indicate some of the more striking examples of its presence.

The Medieval Period: The *Divine Comedy* (begun about 1300) by Dante (1265–1321) represents a unique synthesis: it follows classical models to a great extent (the Roman poet Vergil accompanies Dante on his imaginary voyage through Hell and Purgatory), but in its overarching vision of salvation it is thoroughly biblical. Characters from the Bible mingle with figures from Greek and Roman antiquity and with characters living and dead from Dante's native Florence.

The most characteristic influence of the Bible in this period, however, is not in "high" literature as represented by Dante's great poem, but in homelier, more everyday forms of writing. Earlier, in the fourth century, Augustine had viewed the Bible as a model of the "humble style" (Lat. *sermo humilis*), especially noticeable in the Psalms, the OT narratives, and the Gospels. The Bible's style came as a counterweight to the more rhetorical verse and prose inherited from Greek and Roman antiquity. A simplified form of discourse is thus found not only in sermons and moral discourses written during the time but even in the tales of Giovanni Boccaccio (1313–75) and Geoffrey Chaucer (ca. 1340–1400). This simplified discourse goes hand in hand with a more democratic view of what constitutes the material of literature. While ancient epic and drama were generally about kings and noblemen, writers of the Christian Middle Ages discovered significance in the lives of ordinary people.

The effect of the "humble style" is best shown in the religious drama of the period. The anonymous miracle or mystery plays, found in France, Germany, Spain, and elsewhere, but reaching their fullest development in England in the fifteenth and sixteenth centuries, were a popular dramatization of the biblical record. They were arranged in cycles of several episodes culminating in the Passion and acted by artisans belonging to the different guilds on the principal days of the Christian year, especially Easter, Whitsun, and Corpus Christi Day. The Wakefield Cycle (ca. 1450) is particularly notable; in the Noah episode we witness a bout of fisticuffs between Noah and his wife; in the *Second Shepherds' Play (Secunda Pastorum)*, the Wakefield dramatist does not hesitate to set the scene of the nativity in the perspective of a comic (indeed, farcical) story of sheep-stealing in a rustic English community.

The Renaissance: The flowering of secular learning and the new humanist emphasis led to a noticeable shift in the sixteenth and seventeenth centuries from concern with Gospel stories (which dominated the medieval miracle plays) to concern with the OT. The human aspects of the stories are emphasized, in line with what J. C. Powys perceives as "the human wisdom, the human sensuality, . . . the human magnanimity, the human triumph" of the OT (*The Enjoyment of Literature*, 1938). These human aspects are to the fore in George Peele's romantic drama *The Love of King David and Fair Bethsabe* (1599). In Holland a little later, Joost van den Vondel wrote a number of plays on topics such as Adam in exile, Joseph and his brothers, and Jeptha and King Solomon. In Italy, the great actor Giambattista Andreini wrote and produced an Adam play (1613).

William Shakespeare (1564–1616) wrote no play directly on a biblical theme, but his writing everywhere bears witness to his preoccupation with the Bible, its images, and language. *Measure for Measure* (1604) has been correctly interpreted as a gloss on Matt. 7:1. Behind *King Lear* (1605) are intimations of the crucifixion and it has also been termed a "pantomime version of Job" (Jan Kott, *Shakespeare Our Contemporary*, 1967). *The Tempest* (1611) frequently seems to echo the stories of Genesis, e.g., Prospero appears to act the part of Joseph who, by means of various deceptions and trials, teaches his brothers the error of their ways. Macbeth's imagination (*Macbeth*, 1605) is saturated with biblical imagery. The famous lines from his final soliloquy,

> And all our yesterdays have lighted fools
> The way to dusty death. Out, out, brief
> candle!
> Life's but a walking shadow . . .

echo two passages from Job (KJV). "For we are

 BIBLE AND WESTERN LITERATURE

When the Morning Stars sang together, and all the Sons of God shouted for Joy; illustration for the Book of Job (38:7) by William Blake.

PARADISE
LOST.

BOOK I.

OF Mans Firſt Diſobedience, and the Fruit
Of that Forbidden Tree, whoſe mortal taſt
Brought Death into the World, and all our woe,
With loſs of *Eden*, till one greater Man
Reſtore us, and regain the bliſsful Seat,
Sing Heav'nly Muſe, that on the ſecret top
Of *Oreb*, or of *Sinai*, didſt inſpire
That Shepherd, who firſt taught the choſen Seed,
In the Beginning how the Heav'ns and Earth
Roſe out of *Chaos*: Or if *Sion* Hill
Delight thee more, and *Siloa's* Brook that flow'd
Faſt by the Oracle of God; I thence
Invoke thy aid to my adventrous Song,
That with no middle flight intends to ſoar
A Above

Opening page of Milton's biblical epic poem, *Paradise Lost*, 1667.

but of yesterday, and know nothing, because our days upon earth are but a shadow" (8:9) and "The light shall be dark in his tabernacle, and his candle shall be put out with him" (18:6). *Hamlet* (1602) is perhaps the best example of all. Hamlet, like Moses, is summoned to receive a "commandment," which he then inscribes on "tables" (Act 1, scene 5); in this he functions in a kind of covenant drama. Like many OT characters, he is elected to a moral task: that of cleansing the realm of evil.

A little later in the same century, the Italian tragedian Frederico della Valle dramatized the stories of Esther (1628) and Judith (1628), inspiring many imitators to follow his example. Before the seventeenth century was over, the greatest of French tragedians, Jean Racine (1639–99), produced his two plays on OT subjects, *Esther* (1689) and *Athalie* (1691). The latter, based on 2 Kings 11, is probably the finest example of the adaptation of biblical materials to the forms of classical tragedy. In England, *Samson Agonistes* (1671) by John Milton (1608–74) was a less successful attempt to apply the canons of classical tragedy to a biblical story.

Biblical Epic Poems: Epic poems on biblical subjects became popular in the sixteenth century. There are many biblical reminiscences in Torquato Tasso's *Jerusalem Delivered* (1575) on the subject of the Crusaders' conquest of the Holy City. In France, Guillaume du Bartas, a Huguenot, devoted his gifts to an epic poem on Judith (1574) and later (in 1578) produced his more famous *La Semaine*, translated into English by J. Sylvester as *Divine Weeks and Works*. This latter poem is based on the biblical account of the creation and the subsequent history of humanity. John Milton may have had this work in mind when he came to write his two great epics, *Paradise Lost* (1667) and *Paradise Regained* (1671). Like du Bartas and his own English predecessor Edmund Spenser, Milton refers to the muse who inspires him in the composition of his biblical poems under the name of Urania, whom he links with the figure of Wisdom in Prov. 8:30.

Wisdom thy Sister, and with her didst play
In presence of th' Almighty Father, pleas'd
With thy Celestial Song.
(*Paradise Lost*, 7.10–12).

Milton brought to bear on his biblical epics the whole weight of his vast classical and patristic learning. Indeed, the baroque richness and epic superstructure of the first six books of *Paradise Lost* make it difficult for readers to recognize the simple outlines of the Genesis story of Adam and Eve in the Garden. But with

BIBLE AND WESTERN LITERATURE

the seventh book, Milton leaves aside the grand synods in Heaven and Hell and the battles between the good and bad angels and concentrates on the drama of the human pair, their frailties and strengths. In doing so, he comes much closer to the language and story line of Genesis. Though a Calvinist by upbringing, Milton, in humanist fashion, sees Adam as free and morally responsible, his sin not predestined. He was "sufficient to have stood, though free to fall" (3.99). When he eats the forbidden fruit, he does it out of love for Eve and with full knowledge of the consequences.

In *Paradise Regained*, the "mortal sin original" will be made good by Christ, not as in the normative Christian tradition through his death on the cross, but rather through his successful resistance to Satan in the temptation in the wilderness (Luke 4). This makes him into a neat counterpart to the important figure of Adam. We know from Milton's posthumous theological work *De Doctrina Christiana* that he questioned the divinity of Christ and leaned toward the Arian heresy, which understood Christ to be more human than divine. John Dryden's *Absalom and Achitophel* (1681) and Abraham Cowley's *Davideis* (1668) veered away from the epic prayer toward something less elevated. In these works the heroic stories of the Bible are applied wittily to political and social issues of the authors' time.

The Biblical Strain in Romantic Poetry: Christopher Smart's *Song to David* (1763) in praise of David's psalms is a work of lyrical intensity that broke with the more restrained neoclassical tradition of its time. In Germany, Friedrich Klopstock's *Messias (The Messiah*, 1751–6), a poem of nearly twenty thousand lines on the theme of the redemption offered by Christ, was inspired by both Milton and the Bible. At about the same time the Swiss writer Salomon Gessner wrote an epic prose poem, *Der Tod Abels (The Death of Abel*, 1758) on the Garden of Eden and the Fall. In it he romanticized the figure of Cain. Later Romantic poets likewise tended to identify themselves with Cain as a wanderer and an outcast. Samuel Taylor Coleridge's fragmentary prose poem "The Wanderings of Cain" is an example of this. Lord Byron (1788–1824) in his verse play *Cain* (1821) gives us a bold and defiant hero who refuses to bow down to divine tyranny. His Cain embodies something of the author's own rebellion against tradition, as well as his own sense of himself as a guilt-laden figure. Abel, a Christ figure who forgives his murderer, attracts less of the audience's sympathy. This inverted use of the Bible becomes more frequent from the Romantic period (which in England began at the end of the eighteenth century) onward. Byron's "Hebrew Melodies" (1815), a group of a dozen or so short lyrics, have a nonecclesiastical immediateness. They express a direct personal sympathy for Saul and Jepthah's daughter as well as for the exiled Jews of modern times.

The forms of poetry in the Hebrew Bible were being seriously explored at this time. In 1753 Bishop Robert Lowth published his *Lectures on the Sacred Poetry of the Hebrews*, defining the parallelistic structure of Hebrew verse. Poetry based on this principle was, he said, elegant and symmetrical but also vehement and impetuous. In Germany, Johann Gottfried von Herder (1744–1803) in *The Spirit of Hebrew Poetry* (1783) followed Lowth in urging that Hebrew forms and subject matter be used as models by modern poets. He also put his ideas into practice and disseminated them by translating specimens of Hebrew poetry into unrhymed German verse himself.

The work of William Blake (1757–1827) in England represents the culmination of this trend both in theory and practice. Blake held that "the Sublime of the Bible" was the true standard of poetry and was far preferable to "the Stolen and Perverted Writings of Homer and Ovid, of Plato and Cicero" *(Preface to Milton*, 1803). He adopted in his own longer compositions a loose, flowing kind of rhapsodic verse expressive of what he felt to be the prophetic strain of Hebrew poetry. The imagery of the Song of Solomon is an especially powerful influence in his writings; Beulah (from Isa. 62: 4) becomes the state of fulfilled desire in his system of symbolism; the ultimate spiritual state, that of the enlightened Imagination, is identified with Eden; and the final redemption of the world and of history will be achieved with the union of Albion (the Divine Humanity) with his "Emanation," Jerusalem, representing biblical liberty and inspiration. He believed *(The Marriage of Heaven and Hell*, ca. 1790) that Isaiah and Ezekiel dined with him. Nevertheless, in the spirit of the French writer Voltaire, he violently rejected the OT code: in "The Everlasting Gospel" (1818), Jesus, who stands for pride and free love, tears aside and overthrows the evil laws of Moses. Blake's use of the Bible is thus highly revisionary.

Among the greater poets of this period, special significance attaches to the writings of the German Johann Wolfgang von Goethe (1749–1832). His youthful projects included a prose epic poem on Joseph and his brothers as well as dramas about Jezebel and Belshazzar. The "Prologue in Heaven," with which his great dramatic poem *Faust* (1770–1832) begins, is fashioned on the first chapters of Job, where God is persuaded by Satan to put his favorite to the test. The example of Job also seems to have provided Goethe with the notion of salvation for his hero. Instead of the devils dragging Faust to Hell as in the established form of the legend, he is saved and rewarded, like Job, at the end of the

BIBLE AND WESTERN LITERATURE

play. C. Friedrich Hebbel, a later Romantic dramatist, offered the German public two biblical dramas of violence and passion, *Judith* (1840) and *Herodes and Mariamne* (1850).

Among the French Romantic poets, Alfred de Vigny wrote something like one-fifth of his poems on biblical themes. "Moise" (in *Poems*, 1826) projects his own sensual and spiritual longings onto the figure of Moses, while "La Fille de Jephté" ("Jepthah's Daughter") also expresses his own doubts about and complaints against divine providence. The subjectivity of the Romantic poets in their use of the Bible reaches a climax in the French writer Victor Hugo (1802–85) on many biblical themes.

The Genre of the Novel: The novel, which came into prominence with the rise of the Protestant middle classes, was always particularly hospitable to biblical themes and patterns. John Bunyan's *The Pilgrim's Progress* (1678), sometimes regarded as the first English novel, is a religious allegory, the key to which is provided by the biblical proof-texts to which readers are directed. A biblical seriousness enters into Daniel Defoe's *Robinson Crusoe* (1719), whose trials by sea and desert recall those of Jonah the prophet and whose sins against his father explicitly recall the parable of the prodigal son. Henry Fielding's *Joseph Andrews* (1742) humorously tells of the resistance of a latter-day Joseph to the seductions of his mistress. But the effect of the biblical patterning is not entirely parodic; we are supposed to see Joseph and his mentor, Abraham Adams (likewise modeled on the example of the biblical Abraham), as the heroes of a moral fable. Fielding shows us how the Bible's influence can work in the new, secular setting. The standard of behavior it comes to support is goodness of heart and charity rather than holiness. In the nineteenth century an example such as George Eliot's *Silas Marner* (1861) stands out. This is a moral, pastoral novel in which the child heroine's decision to abandon her natural family and stay with her foster father strongly echoes the story of Ruth.

In America, Herman Melville (1819–91) gives us in *Moby Dick* (1851) a symbolic novel of epic scope in which the story of Jonah and the great fish provides a controlling metaphor: the ending of the novel with the survival of the mariner-narrator Ishmael explicitly echoes Job. Remarkably, all the main characters have biblical names. In Melville's shorter work *Billy Budd* (posthumous, 1924), he combines the motifs of the Fall and the crucifixion. Billy, the hero who is put to death at the behest of a "Father," Captain Vere, functions both as a Christ figure and as Adam betrayed by the serpent (the wicked Claggart). In general, the strong compulsion of biblical ideas and motifs is very evident among American writers—perhaps the effect of their Puritan past. William Faulkner combines a realistic perception of the life of a decaying society in the South with a biblically conditioned view of the relations between his characters. *Light in August* (1932) is clearly based on the NT; its hero, Joe Christmas, is a killer but also a savior. And, like Christ, he dies at the age of thirty-three. *Absalom, Absalom* (1936) is, as the title implies, related to an OT vision of sin and retribution; the familial pattern in the book recalls that of David and his children. His favorite Bible story was the binding of Isaac. Faulkner's English contemporary, D. H. Lawrence, shows an equally strong biblical tendency. *The Rainbow* (1915) evokes the imagery of Genesis 9. In *The Man Who Died* (1931) the story of the resurrection is given a sexual interpretation.

Though it may be assumed that the vernacular text of the Bible was less widely diffused in Russian society than in the Protestant countries of the West, the Russian novelists Leo Tolstoy (1828–1910) and Fyodor Dostoyevsky (1821–81) show themselves remarkably sensitive to biblical sources and images. Dostoyevsky's hero in *Crime and Punishment* (1886), Raskolnikoff, is patterned on a Christian view of sin and redemption; Alyosha in *The Brothers Karamazov* (1880) is likewise something of a Christ figure. Tolstoy in his later writings accepted the Sermon on the Mount as the fundamental law of life (for example, in *Life*, 1888). In his highly unconventional treatise *What is Art?* (1898) he even tried to apply a Christian standard, based on a biblical spareness and simplicity, to the writing of novels. The moral tales of his last period (including the novel *Resurrection*, 1899) are an attempt to apply these principles in the actual work of composition. *The Master and Margarita* (posthumous, 1967) by a more recent Russian writer, Mikhail Bulgakov, is a marvelously complex and fantastic tissue of mythological motifs; it has as one of its central threads a rereading of the story of Pontius Pilate and his part in the trial and execution of Jesus.

The Bible in the Modern Theater: While there has been no great flowering of biblical drama in the modern period, modern dramatists have shown a strong interest in certain biblical themes. Abraham's sacrifice of Isaac, which seems to have haunted the Norwegian dramatist Henrik Ibsen (see *Brand*, 1866), reappears as a central motif in Arthur Miller's *All My Sons* (1947), where the binding of Isaac seems to combine with the story of the crucifixion. Joe Keller sacrifices his son Larry; the other son, Chris, as his name implies, has the role of savior.

In the twentieth century Job has been a compelling presence (as Franz Kafka's *The Trial*, 1914, illustrates outside of the theater). Archibald MacLeish's *J. B.* (1956) spoke powerfully to a generation that had survived the horrors of World War II. In that play the biblical story of Job becomes an image for human endurance in

BIBLE AND WESTERN LITERATURE

the face of radical suffering and loss. But Mac Leish, a modern secular poet, had difficulty in reaffirming the category of dialogue with God. Deviating from his biblical model, he discovered a salvation for his hero in the restoration of human love, that between Job and his wife. The Dutch writer H. de Bruin likewise published a dramatic adaptation of Job after World War II. The Catalan poet Salvador Espriu has shown a fine sensitivity to biblical themes. His dramatic work *First History of Esther* (1948) finds a parallel between the exiled Jews of Shushan threatened with destruction and his own fellow Catalonians in the aftermath of the Spanish Civil War.

Modern dramatists have shown themselves adept in discovering the humorous possibilities of the biblical narratives. G. B. Shaw's *Back to Methuselah* (1921), while it undoubtedly provided a vehicle for a serious discussion of creation and evolution, did so primarily through comedy. André Obey, the French dramatist, in his Noah play (1929), likewise set out to debunk or demythologize; the Bible story loses its gravity as God becomes a venerable, if somewhat irritable, gentleman. In a series of plays on biblical subjects (*Jonah and the Whale*, 1932; *Tobias and the Angel*, 1931; *Susannah and the Elders*, 1937) the British dramatist James Bridie likewise offered a light-hearted and occasionally fantastic treatment of the Bible stories, especially the stories of miracles. But a moral message often comes through just the same. More gravity was achieved by Christopher Fry's *The Firstborn* (1956), on the subject of Moses and the Exodus, and *A Sleep of Prisoners* (1951), which explores a number of biblical episodes through the medium of a dream.

The Jewish Contribution: Not surprisingly, Jewish writers have shown themselves particularly responsive to biblical motifs and images, though their work only entered the mainstream of Western literature in relatively recent times. Heinrich Heine (1797–1856) often compares himself to various figures from the Bible, including (rather wryly) Nebuchadnezzar, but his way of handling these topics is often irreverent. There is a feeling that God himself belongs to his own Jewish world and can hence be treated with "a degree of ironic familiarity" (S. S. Prawer, *Heine's Jewish Comedy*, 1983). In his "Hebrew Melodies" (1851)—the title was taken from Byron—he features several biblical characters, including Moses, Job, and Jeremiah. In later years, during his long, fatal illness, he was to find a special meaning in the sufferings of Job.

In the nineteenth century Jews also developed a secular literature in the Jewish languages, Yiddish and Hebrew, as part of the so-called *Haskalah* ("Enlightenment"). From the beginning of that movement, the exploration of the literary possibilities of the Bible was a major preoccupation. An early example from Germany is Naftali Hirz Wessely's *Shirei Tiferet* ("Songs of Glory," posthumous, 1829), a long epic poem in Hebrew on the life of Moses. In Lithuania, the Hebrew poet "Mikhal" (Micah Joseph Lebensohn) later on published (1851) a group of remarkable lyrics including "Jael and Sisera," "Samson's Revenge," and "Moses on Mount Abarim." Abraham Mapu, the first modern Hebrew novelist, wrote *Ahavat Zion* (1853; trans. A. M. Schapiro as "In the Days of Isaiah"), based on the stories of the kings of Judah. Later on we note a series of biblical novels by the Yiddish writer Sholem Asch, including his NT trilogy (*The Nazarene, The Apostle,* and *Mary*; 1939–49) and *The Prophet* (1955), which concerns the author of the second part of Isaiah.

Yet the great flowering of Jewish writing on biblical themes has taken place in Israel and a full account of it would be virtually a history of modern Hebrew literature. Particular mention should be made of the novelist S. Y. Agnon, whose writings, often set in the background of the Jewish townships of Eastern Europe, invariably have a biblical resonance. *A Simple Tale* (1935), a novel of love and separation, shows how the story of the lover and the Shulamite of the Song of Solomon continues to create meaning for the modern writer. Leah Goldberg in her poem "Love of Samson" (1968) enters sympathetically into the passional life of Samson; the honey he finds in the carcass of the lion becomes the symbol for the tragic passion of love between Samson and Delilah. Many of the new poets did not so much summon up images of episodes from the past as achieve a new contemporary awareness of the meaning of the biblical source. In Amir Gilboa's poems on such figures as Isaac, Moses, Saul, and Rahab, the Bible figures are newly interiorized to express the anxieties and traumas of present-day humanity. Often the Bible serves to express national as well as private dilemmas. An example is Abba Kovner's *A Canopy in the Desert* (1970), a long poem of twelve "Gates" that brings to life the notion of a marriage between God and Israel originally contracted in the desert (see Jer. 2:2; Song of Sol. 8:5). The theme gains agonizing actuality in the light of modern Jewish history spanning the Nazi holocaust and the rise of the state of Israel down to the return to the desert of Sinai in the Six-Day War of 1967—a history of tragedy and triumph that only biblical metaphors seem capable of adequately rendering.

Modern Criticism and the Bible: Modern literary criticism has shown itself increasingly aware of the importance of the biblical dimension in texts of all kinds. Studies of Milton, Blake, Shakespeare, and many others have stressed this. The novels of the nineteenth-century French writer Emile Zola have revealed a mythological patterning drawn from Genesis. Yet the Bible has been seen as a source of more than particular motifs—it has been seen as the embodiment of a "definitive myth, a single archetypal structure extending from creation to apocalypse," which is everywhere present as a shaping influence in Western literature (Northrop Frye, *Anatomy of Criticism*, 1957). As such, its images will shape literary symbolism even when not overtly acknowledged. Special attention has also been paid to the way in which novels are structured. The biblical mode of apocalypse seems to shape the genre as a whole by creating in readers the sense of a desired historical consummation, something quite fundamental to the dynamics of the novel (Frank Kermode, *The Sense of an Ending*, 1967). The tension of history, especially the history of salvation, is very much the theme of the Bible. From the Bible, this awareness has deeply penetrated modern literature from Shakespeare to the present day (Tom F. Driver, *The Sense of History in Greek and Shakespearian Drama*, 1960).

Bibliography

Auerbach, E. *Mimesis: The Representation of Reality in Western Literature*. Translated by W. Trask. Princeton, NJ: Princeton University Press, 1953.

Brown, D. C. *The Enduring Legacy: Biblical Dimensions in Modern Literature*. New York: Scribner, 1975.

Frye, N. *The Great Code: The Bible and Literature*. New York: Harcourt Brace Jovanovich, 1982.

H.F.

Bible lands, the territories that provided a geographic setting for the narratives of the Bible. They include the modern state of Israel (with the West Bank and Gaza), Jordan, Lebanon, Syria, Iraq, Turkey, Egypt, Ethiopia, Greece, Cyprus, and the Aegean islands.

biblical criticism, the study and investigation of biblical writings that seeks to make discerning and discriminating judgments about these writings. The term "criticism" is derived from the Greek word *krinō*, which means "to judge," "to discern," or to be discriminating in making an evaluation or forming a judgment. It has come to refer to a form of inquiry whose purpose is to make discriminating judgments about literary and artistic productions. Thus, we speak of literary criticism, art criticism, music criticism, or film criticism as disciplines or fields of inquiry whose purpose is to review productions in their respective areas in order to discuss and appraise their significant features and judge their lasting worth.

Generally speaking, the questions asked in biblical criticism have to do with the preservation and transmission of the biblical text, including in what manuscripts the text has been preserved, their date, setting, and relationship to each other, and what the most reliable form of the text is; the origin and composition of the text, including when and where it originated, how, why, by whom, for whom, and in what circumstances it was produced, what influences were at work in its production, and what sources were used in its composition; and the message of the text as expressed in its language, including the meaning of the words as well as the way in which they are arranged in meaningful forms of expression.

Textual Criticism: The aim of this field of biblical criticism is to establish the original wording or form of the biblical text insofar as this is possible. Even with modern printing technology, what an author sends to the printer and what is actually printed may differ. When we recognize a typographical error on a printed page, or note an obvious omission or transposition of a word or phrase, realize that this could not have been the author's intention, and mentally correct the text, we are engaging in textual criticism.

In dealing with ancient texts, it is more difficult to determine what an author actually wrote for several reasons. First, ancient texts were written and copied by hand, and this increased the likelihood that changes in the text could occur. As ancient scribes copied these manuscripts, either by transcribing a written text or by copying a text as it was read aloud by a reader, they sometimes copied the same word or phrase twice, omitted words or phrases, misspelled words, heard one thing and wrote another, heard incorrectly what was read, or made changes they thought would improve the text in some way. As a result, the various copies of surviving texts differ in their actual wording.

Second, whereas with modern texts it is usually possible to check the printed copy against the author's manuscript, this is not possible with ancient biblical texts. In no case has the author's original text, the autograph copy, been preserved. What have survived are copies of the original (or, more accurately, copies of copies), translations of the original into other languages, and quotations of the original by later authors. Quite often, these were written many years, even centuries, later. During this intervening period, numerous changes occurred, not only in the wording but also in the form of the text. In some cases, entire sections of the original have been lost, and thus what remains is incomplete. Or, in other cases, perhaps only portions of the original text have been preserved, often because only certain passages have been quoted by other authors.

It is the task of textual criticism to collect and study these various writings in which a text has been preserved, determine the changes that have occurred in the wording and arrangement of the text, assess the significance of such changes, and restore, if possible, the original wording or form of the text. If this is not possible, one must decide on the best or most reliable wording and try to account for the historical process through which the text has been changed. In every case, textual criticism seeks to establish a reliable text that can serve as the basis for serious study and reflection.

Sometimes textual criticism is referred to as "lower criticism," as opposed to other fields of inquiry concerning the text that are called "higher criticism." It is "lower" not because it is less important but because it is foundational to other forms of inquiry.

Historical Criticism: Every biblical writing arose in a particular historical setting or perhaps even developed over time in one or more historical settings. Consequently, a biblical writing may be said to have a history of its own, which includes its time and place of composition, the circumstances in which it was produced or written, its author or authors (whether an actual author, editor, or group of editors), how it came to be written, and the audience(s) to which it was addressed. The process through which one attempts to reconstruct the historical situation out of which a writing arose and how it came to be written is one of the main tasks of historical criticism.

A crucial part of determining the history of a text is to establish its date of composition. Sometimes, this is possible because of explicit references in the text itself (e.g., Isa. 1:1; 6:1; Jer. 1:1–3). More often, the text contains no clear indication of its date and this must be determined indirectly, usually through the use of external sources, such as archaeological evidence or nonbiblical writings from the same period that provide reliable evidence for dating persons or events mentioned in the text. For example, the discovery of an inscription that mentions Gallio, the proconsul of Achaia (Acts 18:12–17), has made it possible to date Paul's first visit to Corinth in A.D. 51–52 (Acts 18:1–18; 1 Cor. 2:1–5). This has provided valuable evidence not only for dating 1 and 2 Corinthians, but also for establishing NT chronology as a whole.

Historical criticism has also made it possible to see that some biblical writings were written much later than the time of the events depicted in the work. The book of Daniel describes events in Israel's history that occurred as early as the sixth century B.C., but the book was actually composed much later, during the Hellenistic period (mid-second century B.C.). Through historical critical analysis, the book of Isaiah is now seen to reflect at least two historical periods, the first part (chaps. 1–39) stemming from an eighth-century pre-exilic situation, the second part (chaps. 40–66) a sixth-century exilic or even postexilic situation.

The place of composition, or provenance of the writing, also figures prominently in historical criticism. The general provenance of all the biblical writings is the Mediterranean basin, especially the eastern part, including Egypt, Palestine, Babylon, Syria, and Asia Minor. In some cases, it may even be possible to locate a writing in a given region or city (e.g., Ezek. 1:1–3; Rev. 1:9–11). Knowing the geographical region in which a writing arose may help in understanding the political and social situation better and thereby serve to clarify certain features of the text.

Another major concern of historical criticism is authorship, including both the identity of the author and the author's method of composition. A writing may be anonymous (e.g., Genesis, the Gospels, Hebrews), but quite often within the text itself the writing is attributed to a named person (e.g., Deut. 1:1–3; Isa. 1:1; Jer. 1:1; Ezek. 1:3; Hos. 1:1; Joel 1:1; Amos 1:1; the Pauline Letters [e.g., Rom. 1:1]; James 1:1; 1 Pet. 1:1; 2 Pet. 1:1; Rev. 1:1, 4, 9). Some biblical writings are pseudonymous, that is, they were written in one period but attributed to an illustrious figure of an earlier period (e.g., Ecclestiastes, Song of Solomon, Isa. 40–66; the pastoral Letters).

Many biblical writings are composite works, either because various sayings or writings of a single author have been collected and edited into a single work (e.g., most of the shorter prophetic books perhaps; John, Romans, 2 Corinthians, Philippians) or because the works of several authors or editors have been edited together into a single work (e.g., the Pentateuch, Isaiah). To be sure, some writings were written by a single author in one particular time and place (e.g., Philemon).

Closely related to authorship is the question of the sources that have been employed in the composition of a biblical work. So important has this stage of investigation been that it has emerged as a subdiscipline of historical criticism in its own right and is referred to as source criticism.

Biblical source criticism was first systematically employed in the eighteenth century, when it was discovered that the Pentateuch was based on at least two separate documentary sources (J and E), distinguishable by their consistent use of separate divine names, *Yahweh* (*Jahveh* in German) and *Elohim*. Further investigation eventually led to the detection of two additional sources, one reflecting a priestly outlook (P), the other a Deuteronomic outlook (D). From this emerged the consensus view that the Pentateuch, rather than being of Mosaic authorship or even the work of a single individual, such as Joshua, was actually a composite work based on at least four separate literary sources.

Once it was established that biblical writings had their own history of composition, source criticism was extended to other books. One of the clearest instances of this is the way in which the Chronicler, the editor of 1 and 2

BIBLICAL CRITICISM

Chronicles, utilized the earlier biblical writings of 1 and 2 Samuel and 1 and 2 Kings as sources for his work.

Similar methods of historical analysis came to be applied to the NT writings as well, especially the Gospels. In the nineteenth century, the Gospel of Mark came to be generally regarded as the earliest written Gospel and was seen as a literary source upon which the Gospels of Matthew and Luke were based. This led to the proposal that Matthew and Luke had used a second source, designated as Q (German *Quelle*, "source"), which contained material common to them but absent in Mark. This became known as the Two-Source Hypothesis and is still widely used to explain the interrelationship of the synoptic Gospels. Source analysis was also extended to other parts of the NT, most notably John and Acts, but with less assured results.

Also closely related to authorship is audience: to whom was the work addressed? This may be clearly stated (e.g., Deut. 1:1; Luke 1: 1–4; Acts 1:1; the Pauline Letters; Rev. 1:4, 11) or remain unstated (e.g., Genesis, the other Gospels, Hebrews). It is not simply a matter of identifying the addressees but trying to determine the circumstances that existed between them and the author that prompted the writing.

Literary Criticism: If historical criticism is concerned with the historical circumstances in which a text was written, literary criticism is concerned with the text as a finished piece of writing. The questions here are not so much how the text came to be written or what we can know from outside the text to account for what is in it, but what we can learn from what is said in the text itself. In this sense, the text constitutes a "world" in its own right and as such serves as an object of investigation in all its aspects.

The study of the language of a text includes looking at the words of the text and their various meanings or shades of meaning. Various disciplines of learning, such as philology and lexicography, provide essential tools for such analysis. Individual words, however, are not the sole vehicles through which meaning is expressed. Words are arranged in larger units or patterns of meaning ranging from phrases to sentences, paragraphs, chapters, and sections. To analyze these, it is often necessary to examine the grammar of a language, which includes the arrangement of words (syntax) and how their forms are changed (inflection or accidence). At this level of investigation, literary criticism is helpful in noting various patterns of sentence structure, such as parallelism (a b a′ b′) or chiasm (a b b′ a′).

Closely related to the use of language is the literary style reflected in the text. Quite obviously, the vocabulary used in the text reflects this, whether the words are simple, well-known words or whether they are more complex, less familiar words. Not only the choice of words but how they are arranged and the effect they achieve contributes to literary style. In judging a text, one might ask whether the style is sophisticated or ordinary, calm or excited, narrative or argumentative.

Literary criticism also recognizes the existence of a variety of literary forms or genres in which a biblical text may be written. In some instances, entire books belong to a single genre, such as historical narrative (1 Samuel), poetry (Psalms), wisdom (Job), prophetic oracle (Amos), Gospel (Matthew), letter (Romans), or apocalypse (Revelation). Yet within these larger works are found smaller literary forms: creation myths; genealogies; narratives relating the stories of individual figures, such as Abraham or Joseph; legal codes; testaments; psalms; proverbs; prophetic oracles; miracle stories; parables; prayers; hymns; exhortations; and warnings. This list is not comprehensive, but it does suggest that the Bible, rather than being a single literary genre, contains many genres and subgenres.

Why is it important to classify biblical texts according to their literary form? First, the literary form of a text is often a clue to its meaning. For example, how we interpret Genesis 1–3 depends on whether it is read as a creation myth, allegory, or scientific history. The meaning we see in a text often derives from our prior judgment about its literary form. Second, the literary form is often a clue to its life setting. If we recognize that a text is in the form of a hymn, this allows us to relate it to the liturgical setting out of which it arose. Third, properly recognizing a literary form enables us to compare the text with similar literary forms in both biblical and nonbiblical writings. Such comparison often enables us to see things in a text we would otherwise miss.

Another area of study is the unity and integrity of a text. As noted earlier, historical criticism often investigates this question, but it is also an important concern of literary criticism. In looking at a finished piece of writing, the literary critic must often judge whether it is a unified whole or a composite work, whether certain portions (interpolations) were added earlier or later, and whether they all stem from the original author.

Literary criticism also asks questions that would be appropriate to interpreting any literary work, especially narrative. These would include questions about character, such as how characters are portrayed in the text, how they interact with each other, how they develop through the narrative. One may also analyze the plot, asking how the plot or story line is developed, how tension is introduced into the narrative, and how it is resolved, if at all. Another concern is the literary mood of the text, and one might ask what emotions the text is intended to elicit from readers. Literary critics have also analyzed biblical texts in terms of the literary perspective of the writing: whether the writing, especially narrative, is written by a participant in the story or by an outside observer; or whether the author is sympathetic, unsympathetic, or neutral with respect to the story that is told.

Form Criticism: This is a hybrid of historical and literary criticism. It begins with the recognition that a particular biblical text, or a portion of that text, may have a history of its own, independent of the larger work in which it is located. This "prehistory" may include both oral and written stages. The text may have originally circulated in oral form and may have gone through several stages of oral development. Then it may have been written down and possibly have gone through several written versions before it finally appeared in the biblical text.

Reconstructing this process of development is known as tradition history. This is possible because in some instances the same biblical text occurs in different parts of the Bible in different forms (e.g., the Decalogue in Exod. 20: 1–17; Deut. 5:6–21; cf. Exod. 34:17–26). We may surmise that these different forms reflect different stages of use and development within the communities in which they were used.

Form criticism also employs literary criticism as well. Combined with this recognition of the prehistory of a text is literary analysis, which classifies various parts of the biblical writings into literary forms, or literary genres. Usually, the focus here is on smaller literary units within a larger writing rather than on the entire book itself. This type of literary analysis was first systematically applied to the Psalms, which were classified according to distinct literary forms, such as enthronement psalms (e.g., Pss. 2, 110) or individual laments (e.g., Pss. 22, 130). But along with this literary classification (what is the literary form of the text?) went historical analysis (in what life setting did the Psalm originate?). This close connection between the form of the text and its life setting led to a completely new way of interpreting the Psalms as well as understanding the worship of Israel.

Similar methods of analysis were later applied to the Gospels, beginning in the early part of the twentieth century. Here, too, literary and historical analysis were combined in examining the smaller literary units of the Gospels. Systematic efforts were made to classify the Gospels into literary forms. Basically, two types of material were detected: narrative material and sayings material. Narrative material includes those passages that relate stories about Jesus, including the entire Passion narrative, but also individual stories in which he performs a miracle (miracle stories), makes a pronouncement (pronouncement stories), or in which he is the center of a divine action (legends). The sayings material includes all the words and sayings attributed to Jesus, such as one-line pronouncements, parables, prayers, sermons, proverbs, and wisdom sayings.

Closely related to this literary classification of the Gospel materials was historical analysis. As was the case in the form-critical analysis of the Psalms, here too it was recognized that any particular saying or story might have had its own prehistory in which it originated and circulated in oral form and was transmitted through several oral and written stages until it reached its final written form in the Gospel text. As with the Psalms, a central concern is to determine the particular circumstances in which the story or saying originated, whether its "life setting" had to do with preaching, worship, teaching, or polemical argument.

Here again, we see the close correlation between historical and literary analysis. In form criticism, one determines the literary form of the text, tries to reconstruct the historical process or stages of development through which it passed before it reached its final literary form, and in doing so attempts to correlate it with a particular life setting. As this is done, our understanding of the text increases and various aspects of its meaning become clearer.

Eventually, form-critical analysis was also applied to other parts of the NT, most notably the Letters. Here too, smaller units were analyzed with a view to reconstructing their prehistory, but because it is not so easy to establish a clear chronological sequence for tracing stages of development, as is the case with the synoptic Gospels, the results have been less successful.

The overall effect of form criticism was to focus on the smaller units of the biblical writings. Less attention was given to individual authors or editors who compiled the final literary edition, and more emphasis was placed on the community as a formative influence in shaping and preserving the material. For the Gospels, this meant that they were seen as collections of smaller units, and the authors came to be regarded as editors who collected the materials together into a rather loose narrative framework.

Redaction Criticism: This was a direct outgrowth of form criticism and provided an important corrective. As a further refinement of form criticism, it too combines both literary and historical criticism and proceeds on many of the same assumptions. The crucial word here is "redaction," which applies to the way in which a text or tradition has been redacted or edited. To engage in redaction criticism, one must be able to separate at least two stages of development in the use of a text. This is clearly the case in 1 and 2 Chronicles, where materials from 1 and 2 Samuel and 1 and 2 Kings have been appropriated and re-edited by the Chronicler. The redaction critic's task is to analyze the individual instances where the editor has redacted an earlier text or tradition, assess the overall significance of such changes, and interpret these in the light of the editor's literary and theological purpose.

Redaction criticism has also been fruitfully applied to the Gospels, because of the possibility of arranging them in chronological order and positing stages of development. With Mark serving as the earliest Gospel and as the source upon which Matthew and Luke draw, the redaction critic can analyze the points at which Matthew and Luke have redacted Mark. The particular emphasis of the redaction critic is to isolate the precise points at which the tradition or text has undergone changes at the hands of an editor, or redactor, and from these to try to determine the theological motivations for the changes.

If such analysis is carried out for a Gospel as a whole, it is possible to establish theological tendencies that occur repeatedly enough to be seen as major themes or preoccupations of the author. For this reason, redaction criticism is less concerned with the smaller literary units and the role of the community in shaping these units, but more concerned with the total effect achieved through the cumulative redaction of the materials at the Evangelist's disposal. Accordingly, redaction criticism has resulted in a renewed appreciation of the individual authors as theologians in their own right rather than as simply scissors-and-paste editors who loosely stitched together individual literary units into a narrative framework.

Canonical Criticism: This more recent type of biblical criticism builds on the results of earlier methods. Unlike them, however, it places greater emphasis on the final form of the canonical text. It is less interested in the stages of development that led up to the writing of the text or even the various literary aspects of a writing. It seeks to take more seriously the fact that the Bible is a collection of canonical writings regarded as sacred and normative in two communities of faith, Israel and the church.

This emphasis on the canonical form of the bibical text implies several things. First, the biblical writings possess another dimension, one that may not have been there when the text was originally composed but one it has acquired nevertheless. Even if a writing was composed without the initial intention or expectation that it would eventually become normative for Israel or the church, the fact that it acquired this status means that it must be read from this added perspective. In interpreting the text, readers must not only ask historical and literary questions about the text, but also how and why the text has addressed communities of faith. Their canonical status means that the texts have acquired a universal audience—communities of faith in every age and place who read them not simply to ask what their original authors intended but what they are saying to the living community of faith in the present.

Second, as part of a collection of biblical writings, a book acquires a canonical context. It is no longer read in isolation but along with the other biblical witnesses in all their variety. As such, it is no longer a single voice to be heard alone but stands as part of a chorus of voices to be heard along with the rest. Interpreters can no longer inquire solely into the message of a single text but must investigate this message as part of the entire canonical message, the sum total of all the canonical witnesses heard together. ***See also*** Bible; Canon; Hermeneutics; New Testament; Old Testament; Oral Materials, Sources, and Traditions; Pentateuch; Sources of the Pentateuch; Synoptic Problem, The; Texts, Versions, Manuscripts, Editions.

Bibliography

Ackroyd, P. R., et al., eds. *The Cambridge History of the Bible*. 3 vols. Cambridge: Cambridge University Press, 1963–70.

Hahn, Herbert F. *Old Testament in Modern Research*. Philadelphia: Fortress, 1966.

Henry, Patrick. *New Directions in New Testament Study*. Philadelphia: Westminster, 1979.

C.R.H.

Bichri (bik'rī; Heb., meaning uncertain, either "youthful" or "of [the clan of] Becher"; see Gen. 46:21), a Benjaminite, the father of Sheba and the leader of an unsuccessful northern rebellion against the kingship of David (2 Sam. 20:1–22). ***See also*** Sheba.

Bigvai (big'vī). **1** A large family group ("sons of Bigvai") who returned with Zerubbabel from the Babylonian captivity (Ezra 2:14). **2** A smaller family group led by Uthai and Zabbud who returned later with Ezra (Ezra 8:14). **3** A leader of the postexilic community who returned from the Exile with Zerubbabel (Ezra 2:2); he is possibly the same person who later signed the covenant to keep the law (Neh. 10:16). He could be the head of the family groups above or simply a member of the group.

Bildad (bil'dad), a Shuhite, one of Job's three friends (Job 2:11). In the cycle of speeches he is the second speaker with three separate discourses (chaps. 8, 18, 25). The meaning of the name is obscure, but may be related to the Edomite king Bedad (Gen. 36:36). The name is compounded with the theophoric element *dad* (after the Edomite god of that name).

Bilhah (bil'hah). **1** The servant of Laban's daughter Rachel and mother of Dan and Naphtali (Gen. 29:29; 30:4–7). Rachel's childlessness led her to give Bilhah as concubine to Jacob; in an adoption ritual (Gen. 30:4), Bilhah's children would legally be Rachel's. **2** In 1 Chron. 4:29, a location in Simeonite territory (Balah, Josh. 19: 4).

Bilhan (bil'han). **1** The son of Ezer and grandson of Seir the Horite (Gen. 36:27). **2** The son of Jediael and grandson of Benjamin (1 Chron. 7: 10).

Binnui (bin'nōō-ī; Heb., "built" or "building"). **1** A family group ("sons of Binnui") who returned with Zerubbabel from the Babylonian captivity (Neh. 7:15), also called the "sons of Bani" (Ezra 2:10). Since the name Bani and Binnui are elsewhere associated (Ezra 10:38; see 2 below), it is possible that the clans were closely related or were the same family. **2** A member of the clan of Bani who was condemned by Ezra for taking a foreign wife (Ezra 10:38). **3** A member of the clan of Pahath-moab who was likewise condemned (Ezra 10:30). **4** A Levite of the clan of Henadad who helped repair the walls of Jerusalem and signed the covenant to keep the law (Neh. 3:24; 10:9); he is possibly the same Levite who returned from the Exile with Zerubbabel (Neh. 12:8). Perhaps he is also the father of Noradiah, an assistant in the inventory of valuables brought by Ezra from Babylon (Ezra 8: 33). The identity of these latter two is not clear. ***See also*** Bani. D.R.B.

birds, feathered, winged vertebrates. Palestine is blessed with an extremely rich bird life and, due to its geographical location, it witnesses twice yearly the great bird migrations between Africa and Europe. Unfortunately, due to ruthless hunting, the numbers have been greatly declining in the last few years.

Of the three collective terms for birds used in the Bible, one is translated as "flier" (Heb. *'oph*), another means literally "owner of a wing" (Heb. *ba'al kanap*), and a third means "winged" or "flying" (Gk. *peteinon*). Furthermore, birds in the OT were classified either as "screamers" (Heb. *'ayit*) or as "twitterers" (Heb. *tsippor*). To the former belonged most of the raptorial birds, such as birds of prey and owllike birds, and to the latter the passerine (sparrowlike) birds.

Important for Jewish ritual in the OT is the distinction between clean and unclean birds, although such distinctions no longer held for the NT. There are twenty unclean "birds" listed in Lev. 11:13–19 and in Deut. 14:11–20. These are: the eagle, metire ("vulture"), osprey, falcon, kite, raven, ostrich, nighthawk, seagull, hawk, owl, cormorant, ibis, marsh hen ("water hen"), pelican, vulture, stork, heron, hoopoe, and bat. Most of these are raptors. The bat of course is not a bird, but a mammal. Some have speculated that the reason behind the taboo on all these is that they are considered carnivor-

Mosaic floor depicting various birds. Below the two peacocks are, from left to right, a crane, a pheasant, and a goose, and below them, a partridge, a bird of prey, and a quail; sixth century A.D., excavated at Beth-govrin.

ous or at least partly so, and therefore might have had contact with a corpse or with blood. The inclusion of the strictly vegetarian hoopoe, however, calls such speculation into question.

The clean birds, which are not specifically listed but are mentioned throughout the OT, are, for instance, the pigeon, the partridge, the quail, and the passerines, which are all vegetarians. All of them feature as important sources of food in different circumstances (cf. Matt. 10:29; Luke 12:6). Concerning birds as sacrifices, Lev. 1:14 specifies that turtledoves or young pigeons should be chosen for burnt offerings (see Luke 2: 24).

In the Gospels, birds are used by Jesus as illustrations of God's providence (Matt. 6:26) or as examples of items of very little value (Luke 12:6–7, 24). Yet even they have a security denied the Son of man (Matt. 8:20). I.U.K.

birth, new. ***See*** Conversion; Regeneration.

birthright (Heb. *bekorah*) or primogeniture, the practice whereby the eldest son receives a larger (double) share of the inheritance than do his younger brothers. This preferential treatment of the eldest son is known throughout the ancient Near East (Mari, Nuzi, Alalakh, Ugarit, Assyria), although the law codes of Lipit-Ishtar (twentieth century B.C.) and Hammurabi (eighteenth century B.C.) both legislate an equal sharing of the inheritance by all the male heirs. In the OT, the law of Deut. 21:15–17 protects the birthright of the eldest son, although the sale of the birthright to a younger son is known from Nuzi as well as from the OT (Gen. 25:27–34). The disregarding of primogeniture by the choice of a younger rather than the eldest son is witnessed both in the OT (Gen. 48:12–20; cf. Rom. 9:12) and in texts from Nuzi, Alalakh, and Ugarit. J.S.K.

bishop (Gk. *episcopos*, "overseer," "guardian"), early Christian office mentioned first in Phil. 1:1, qualifications for which are stated in 1 Tim. 3:1–7; Titus 1:5–9 (cf. 1 Tim. 5:17–22). Titus equates bishop and elder (Gk. *presbyteros*; cf. Acts 20:17, 28). It is possible that in the older church referred to in 1 Timothy (Ephesus) bishops evolved from a larger group of elders, gaining pre-eminence as apt teachers (1 Tim. 3:1; 5: 17), while in the younger churches mentioned in Titus (Crete) insufficient time had elapsed for such functional distinctions to appear. ***See also*** Presbyter, Presbytery.

Bithynia (buh-thin'ee-uh), a Roman province in northwest Asia Minor containing Christian communities by the time 1 Peter was written. The NT records no mission there. According to Acts 16:7, Paul and his companions "attempted to go into Bithynia, but the Spirit of Jesus did not allow them." Early legends attribute the evange-

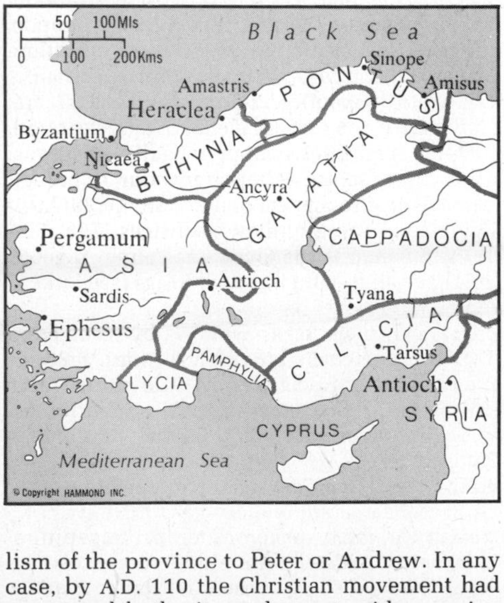

lism of the province to Peter or Andrew. In any case, by A.D. 110 the Christian movement had permeated both city and countryside, causing neglect of pagan temples and social unrest.

bitter herbs (Heb. *maror*), vegetables with characteristically bitter taste. Exod. 12:8 states, "They shall eat the flesh [of the paschal lamb] that night, roasted; with unleavened bread and bitter herbs they shall eat it." The herbs have been variously identified as certain types of lettuce, endive, and chervil. From tannaitic times (first century A.D.), these herbs have been eaten at the Passover seder to represent the bitterness of the lives of the Israelites under Egyptian slavery.

bittern. ***See*** Hedgehog.

bitumen, a type of asphalt or mineral pitch, either occurring naturally or found as a by-product of burning coal or wood. The KJV translates it as "slime." Throughout antiquity this black sticky substance was used as an adhesive or a caulk. For example, flint knife blades were set into a sickle haft filled with bitumen as a mortar; likewise bitumen held in place inlays of shell and stone. It could also be used for waterproofing, as in the construction of Noah's ark (Gen. 6: 14) and the bulrush basket of Moses (Exod. 2:3). References are made to pitch oozing from the earth (Gen. 14:10) near the Dead Sea, where it occurs naturally. Metaphorically, Isaiah uses the image of these slime pits to evoke the Day of the Lord when the land and streams shall be turned into burning pitch (Isa. 34:9). S.L.R.

blasphemy, a term derived from a Greek word meaning to injure the reputation of another. In the Bible it means showing contempt or a lack of reverence for God (Lev. 24:16; Mark 2:7) or something sacred (Matt. 26:65), including claiming for oneself divine attributes by word or deed (Mark 14:64; John 10:33).

blessing. ***See*** Curse and Blessing.

blindness, sightlessness. It is God who has the power to make people blind (Exod. 4:11) as well as to restore them to sight (Ps. 146:8). In Gen. 19: 11 the angels of God who visited Lot struck the evil men of Sodom with blindness. Through Elisha's prayer God struck the Syrian army with blindness (2 Kings 6:18). In Isa. 42:7 God commissions his servant "to open the eyes that are blind."

Blindness was one of the blemishes disqualifying descendants of Aaron from performing sacrifice to God (Lev. 21:16–24). Likewise, it was forbidden to offer blind animals in sacrifice (Lev. 22:22; Deut. 15:21; Mal. 1:8). The blind were to be protected in accord with God's covenantal instructions: no stumbling block was to be placed in their way (Lev. 19:14); and anyone who misled a blind person was cursed (Deut. 21:18). Isaac (Gen. 27:1), Eli (1 Sam. 3:2), and Ahijah (1 Kings 14:4) suffered the blindness of old age. One of the expectations of the eschatological age was the opening of the eyes of the blind by God (Isa. 29:18; 35:5; LXX 61:1).

In the NT Jesus' healing of blindness was one of the "deeds of the Christ" illustrating and bringing about the Kingdom of God (Matt. 11: 2–6; 15:29–31; Luke 4:16–19; 7:18–23). There are several examples in which the blind had their sight restored by Jesus: the faith of two blind men enabled them to be healed by Jesus (Matt. 9:27–31); he healed a blind and dumb demoniac (Matt. 12:22); by healing the blind in the Temple Jesus restored them to the worshiping community (Matt. 21:10–17).

Some of Jesus' healings of the blind may function as symbolic characterizations of the revelation and recognition of Jesus' profound identity. That may be the case in the healing of the blind man at Bethsaida in Mark 8:22–26. The painstaking, step-by-step manner in which Jesus performs this healing characterizes the way he is trying to bring his disciples to understand and "see" his profound identity. This healing serves as a symbolic anticipation and transition to the confession of Jesus as "the Christ" in Mark 8:29. Similarly, Bartimaeus, healed of his blindness, represents the insightful disciple who follows Jesus to Jerusalem, the place of his suffering and death (Mark 10:46–52). The healing of the man born blind in John 9 characterizes the spiritual "blindness" of the Jews and indicates how Jesus is the "light of the world."

The concept of blindness was particularly appropriate for metaphorical use; it often characterized spiritual "blindness" or lack of insight into the revelation of God (Isa. 6:9–10; 42:16–19; 59:10; Matt. 15:14; Acts 28:26–27; Rom. 2:19; 11: 8–10). J.P.H.

blood, a term understood in biblical writings not only as that which is essential to life but also as the seat of life's power. Though sometimes used simply to designate mortal life (usually in conjunction with flesh), it was often connected with God, the life-giver. Injunctions existed against consuming blood (Gen. 9:4; Lev. 17:10–16; Deut.12:15–18; 1 Sam. 14:32–35; Acts 15: 23–29); spilling it was forbidden under penalty of death (Gen. 9:4–7; Exod. 20:13; 21:23–24; Lev. 24:20–21; Deut. 19:21; cf. Matt. 5:21–26, 38–42).

Blood plays an important role in the theology of the OT, the institution of sacrificial atonement, and the work of the priests. Applied to the altar, blood becomes a powerful expiatory agent as sin offering, especially on the annual Day of Atonement (Lev. 16). The priest, who is himself set apart by blood consecration (Exod. 29:19–21), alone is qualified to apply the blood (Lev. 1–7). The Passover celebration remembers the blood on the doorposts of Hebrew houses in Egypt (Exod. 12:7) and the deliverance accomplished by the God of the Covenant (see blood of the Covenant in Exod. 24:6–8; Ps. 50:5; Zech. 9:11). Blood can also symbolize woes and terrors (e.g., 1 Chron. 22:8; 28:3; Exod. 7:14–24; Joel 2:30–31).

The NT writings vary in the degree of development of the image of blood, but where the image appears it focuses on the shed blood of Jesus and its atoning character. Interpreted in terms of his obedient surrender of his life to God, it becomes the foundation for God's new covenant of grace. The people of faith celebrate this grace at the Lord's Supper; the cup of blessing is the new covenant in Christ's blood (Mark 14:24; 1 Cor. 11:23–29). The most extensive development of the image is found in Hebrews 9–10 (see also John 6:53–56; 19:34–37; 1 John 5:6–8; Rom. 3: 24–25; 1 Cor. 5:6–8; 1 Pet. 1:18–19; Rev. 5:6–14; 7:14). ***See also*** Atonement; Atonement, Day of; Expiation; Flesh; Life; Lord's Supper, The; Passover, The; Worship. J.E.A.

Boanerges (boh'uh-nuhr'jeez), the name given by Jesus to James and John, sons of Zebedee (Mark 3:17). The derivation and meaning are uncertain though perhaps the word comes from a Hebrew phrase meaning "sons of rage" or "sons of thunder." Mark's definition, "sons of thunder," could refer to tempestuous dispositions or to manner of speech, but most likely to the former. ***See also*** James; John.

boats, watertight vessels for traveling on water. **In the Bible:** Noah's ark (Gen. 6:14–16) aside, the inland origin of the ancient Hebrews is apparent in the infrequent OT references to boats and sailing. Certainly they knew of traders and seafaring (e.g., 2 Chron. 8:17–18; 9:21; Pss. 104:26; 107: 23–30; Prov. 31:14; Ezek. 27; 1 Macc. 8:23, 26, 28) and were acquainted with travel by ship for peaceful purposes (the Egyptian ambassadors, Isa. 18:2; the Chaldeans rejoicing in their ships, Isa. 43:14 [Hebrew text unclear]; Jonah fleeing God's will, Jon. 1) or for making war (the Sea Peoples, Num. 24:24; a galley that cannot attack a town, Isa. 33:21, 23a; Roman warcraft to destroy Antiochus IV Epiphanes, Dan. 11:30; the Egyptian army supported by ships, 1 Macc. 11: 1; the Seleucid army landed at Tripoli, 2 Macc. 14:1).

Solomon relied on the expertise of the sailors employed in the commercial fleet of Hiram of Tyre for transporting the materials for the Temple (1 Kings 5:9; 2 Chron. 2:16) and on Hiram's sailors for navigating the fleet supplied by him at Ezion-geber near Elath on the Red Sea (1 Kings 9:26–28; 2 Chron. 8:17; 9:21). These seagoing ships traded at faraway Tarshish and Ophir for large amounts of gold for Solomon's treasury. Jehoshaphat's attempt to emulate Solomon's achievement ended disastrously (1 Kings 22:47–49; 2 Chron. 20:35–37). Inland waters were the home of craft like the ferryboat

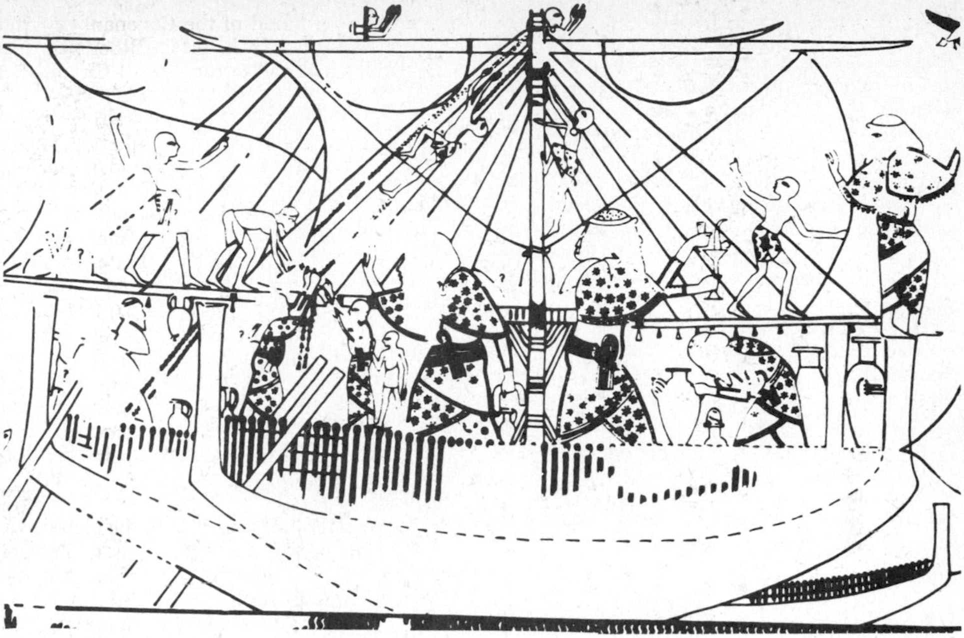

A boat carrying Syrians approaching an Egyptian port. Two Syrians stand in the middle, one giving orders and the other making an offering. Sketch of an ancient Egyptian tomb painting, Thebes.

that carried King David, newly crowned, across the river Jordan at Gilgal (2 Sam. 19:18).

In NT times, fishing and travel across Lake Tiberias (the Sea of Galilee) are commonly reported (Matt. 8:23, 9:1; Mark 4:36, 38; Luke 8: 22–23; John 6:16, 22, 23; 21:4–14). On one occasion, Jesus used a fishing boat as pulpit (Luke 5: 1–11). The Mediterranean travels of Paul were beset by shipwrecks and becalmed seas (2 Cor. 11:25), especially his final voyage to Rome (Acts 27). His trips were made on trading vessels such as the grain boat running between Alexandria, Egypt, and Peutoli, Italy (Acts 28:13).

Evidence from the Ancient World: Artifacts recovered by archaeologists in the area occupied by the ancient Hebrews, and the history of water transport in the ancient Near East corroborate this picture of the Hebrews as land lovers. Other peoples, however, plied rivers and seas in boats from earliest times. The oldest known model boat, from as early as 5000 B.C., was found broken and left on a floor below a series of seventeen temples at Eridu in southern Mesopotamia. By about 4000 B.C. there is evidence from southern Iraq and southwest Iran for cargo-carrying boats, small boats for local passenger traffic with little freight, and an intermediate type that could carry both passengers and some freight; the sail was probably in use and trade by sea was under way. The earliest certain representation of a sail comes from Egypt and belongs to the end of the pre-Dynastic period, ca. 3200 B.C. No doubt the Egyptians did invent their sail quite early, because a boat carried downstream on the Nile could always take advantage of the prevailing wind from the north to sail back upstream.

Whether the Egyptians built the sea-going "Byblos ships" mentioned in their inscriptions is still debated; the phrase could mean that the ships were made in Byblos or that their route was between Egypt and Byblos. Egypt lacked wood suitable for building ships, but wood was plentiful near Byblos. Whether the Egyptians themselves sailed these boats is another question: a sailor in a tomb painting from about 2000 B.C. wears a distinctly foreign coiffure. Neither question can be answered definitely on evidence available now.

Inhabitants of the coastal cities like Byblos and Ugarit were the chief traders in the eastern Mediterranean after 2000 B.C.; eventually the size of the navy of Ugarit far surpassed that of the Greeks at Troy. One Ugaritic boat used for carrying grain had a capacity estimated at four hundred and fifty metric tons, roughly twice the size of the flagship in which Columbus discovered the New World. Two models recovered from Byblos may depict these ships, as may a Syrian merchant ship in an Egyptian tomb painting. Similar to the models from Byblos is the Egyptian hieroglyph for boat found in inscriptions at Abydos (thirteenth century B.C.).

The models and the hieroglyph are contemporary with a Syrian boat found off the coast of Turkey. These boats are the direct formal ancestors of the merchant ships seen in Assyrian reliefs of the late eighth and early seventh centuries B.C., especially those showing the escape of Luli of Tyre from Assyrian troops. The remainder of the ancient history of boats in the eastern Mediterranean is fully documented in Greek and Roman sources. ***See also*** Egypt; Ezion-geber; Hiram; Jonah, The Book of; Jordan River, The; Mesopotamia; Noah; Ophir; Ras-Shamra; Red Sea; Solomon; Tyre.

Bibliography

Casson, Lionel. *Ships and Seamanship in the Ancient World.* Princeton: Princeton University Press, 1971.

Johnstone, Paul. *The Sea-craft of Prehistory.* Prepared for publication by Sean McGrail. London: Routledge & Kegan Paul, 1980.

Rougé, Jean. *Ships and Fleets of the Ancient Mediterranean.* Translated by Susan Frazer. Middletown, CT: Wesleyan University Press, 1981.

C.Q.

Boaz (boh'az). **1** A land owner in Bethlehem in Judah who lived "when the judges ruled" (twelfth century B.C.) Israel and whose story is told in the book named after his wife, Ruth. He was kind to Ruth, a Moabite widow of his kinsman Mahlon, whose mother, Naomi, was the sole survivor of an Ephrathite family. Boaz extended protection to Ruth, a foreigner, allowing her privileges normally extended only to female clan members. When Boaz celebrated the conclusion of the harvest by consuming a nightly meal on the threshing floor, Ruth asked him to accept her into his immediate family and to redeem Naomi's land. Boaz, however, agreed to take her as his primary wife. After a brilliant legal maneuver at the city gate, Boaz also succeeded in obtaining the right to redeem Naomi's land. Boaz's first son by Ruth, Obed, was pledged as Mahlon's, thus perpetuating the memory of the deceased upon his estate. Obed was also deemed Boaz's first son and thus served to link Boaz's ancestry in the tribe of Judah to Obed's grandson, David the king. The book of Ruth took pains to give Boaz favorite status by placing his name in the seventh slot of David's genealogy (4:18–20; 1 Chron. 2:9–15; cf. Matt. 1:3–6; Luke 3:31–33). **2** One of two bronze pillars placed at the entrance to Solomon's Temple. ***See also*** Jachin and Boaz; Mahlon; Ruth.

J.M.S.

body, the physical side of human beings and animals. Slaves are "bodies" when considered good only for physical labor (Rev. 18:13, "slaves" in the RSV). The term occurs almost exclusively as a translation in the NT for the Greek *sōma*. It can refer to a dead body, i.e., a corpse or carcass (Mark 15:43; Luke 17:37; 24:3, 23; Acts 9:40; Heb. 13:11; Jude 9), but usually refers to a living body. Because God created the human body (Gen. 2:7), the Bible portrays it favorably as integral to human being, a means of concrete activity in the world (1 Cor. 6:20; 2 Cor. 5:10), rather than unfavorably as a drag on the soul (but cf. Wisd. of Sol. 9:15). Yet the Bible does not glorify the body as an artistic ideal of human strength and beauty.

The body may stand for the whole human being. For some interpreters, this usage approaches the meaning "person" (see the alternation of "bodies" and "selves" in Rom. 6:12–13). Others see this usage as a simple figure of speech (synecdoche), where the context makes a physical emphasis appropriate (see the emphasis on the "members" of the body as the apparently physical "instruments" of human activity in Rom. 6:12–13). The body contrasts with the soul (Matt. 10:28), spirit (1 Cor. 5:3), and mind (Rom. 7:23–24). Paul speaks of the possibility that he was outside his body in a visionary state (2 Cor. 12:2–3). To be dead is to be away from the body (2 Cor. 5:6–10; Phil. 1:20–24). The physical meaning of body makes it stand for solid reality in contrast with unsubstantial shadow (Col. 2:17, "substance" in the RSV).

The body is composed of materials and parts, by which the OT normally refers to it, most often by the material term "flesh." The NT term "members" refers to limbs and organs and stresses the body as the instrument of human activity (Rom. 6:12–13). Sin, one's own or that of others, has brought suffering, persecution, and death of the body (Rom. 5:12–6:23; 2 Cor. 4:7–12; Heb. 13:3). But God has created the body as integral to human being, and this, joined with his purpose to save human beings, spells the resurrection of the body. In the NT, Christ's bodily death and resurrection make possible the bodily resurrection of human beings (Rom. 6:5; 1 Cor. 15:3–26; 1 Pet. 2:24; cf. 3:18–22). Therefore, also, "the body of Christ" comes to mean the church, its limbs and organs made up of individual believers united in Christ and functioning for mutual benefit (1 Cor. 12:12–31). ***See also*** Flesh; Flesh and Spirit; Human Being; Mind; Resurrection; Soul.

R.H.G.

book, a term applied in the Bible to a wide range of writings but generally to a written document in which events, poems, or prophecies are recorded or in which persons or objects are enumerated. Various materials were used for early records, such as the clay hexagonal prism on which was inscribed the "Annals of Sennacherib" (probably clay tablets are referred to in Jer. 32:10–14), the stone tablets of the Ten Commandments (Exod. 24:12), the metal plaques or scrolls of the Qumran community, and the wax tablets discovered in the Roman city of Pompeii (cf. Luke 1:63).

This octagonal prism, used for keeping historical records, is from the reign of the Assyrian king Esarhaddon (680–669 B.C.).

The earliest form of books was the scroll made either of papyrus or animal skins (later vellum or parchment was used). The scroll was made by joining sheets of papyrus or leather together into a continuous strip which was then rolled. The average size of the scroll was about 10–12 inches high and 20–30 feet long. Although much longer scrolls exist, they were awkward to use and individual passages were difficult to find. Scholars have suggested that some of the divisions of the Bible, such as the division of the Torah (Gen.–Deut.) into five books, were dictated by the length of scroll that could be handled easily. Beginning about the second century A.D. the bulky scrolls were replaced by the codex, composed of single or folded sheets of writing stacked and sewn together in the manner of the modern book. However, the use of handwritten scrolls in the Jewish synagogue has continued to the present.

There were many other books in the historical and religious literature of the Israelites and the early Christian community than the sixty-six books preserved in the modern Bible. Many of these exist today, but there are also books mentioned in the Bible that are otherwise unknown and lost. The majority of these were official court records of the Israelite kings, such as the "Book of the Acts of Solomon" (1 Kings 11:41), the "Chronicles of King David" (1 Chron. 27:24), and other court records of the Divided Kingdom (1 Kings 14:19; 1 Chron. 9:1; 2 Chron. 16:11; 24:27; Neh. 12:23) as well as of Persia (Esther 2:23; 6:1; 10:2). Historical accounts by the prophets Shemaiah and Iddo are also mentioned (2 Chron. 12:15). Quotations from two books of poetry also occur: David's elegy for Saul and Jonathan (2 Sam. 1:17–27) and the song of Joshua (Josh. 10:12–13) are taken from the "Book of Jashar" and fragments of the victory song (Num. 21:14–15; possibly also vv. 17–18, 27–30) are taken from the "Book of the Wars of the Lord." Luke (1:1) possibly alludes to now lost narratives of the life of Jesus.

It is likely that portions of other books were incorporated into the present biblical books, such as the account of the defeat of the Amalekites (Exod. 17:14), the record of the cities surveyed in Canaan (Josh. 18:9) and various genealogical records (Neh. 7:5). Similarly, the "Book of the Covenant" (Exod. 24:7) is thought by scholars to refer to the laws attributed to Moses and preserved in Exodus (specifically 20:22–23:33) and various references to the "Book of the Law" or the "Book of Moses" (Josh. 1:8; 8:34; 2 Chron. 17:9) allude to the law codes contained in the Pentateuch, especially as summarized in Deuteronomy (2 Chron. 25:4; cf. Deut. 28:61). The law book found in the Temple by the high priest Hilkiah in the time of Josiah (ca. 622 B.C.; 2 Kings 22:8–23:25) was probably a portion of Deuteronomy, while the "Book of the Law of Moses" read by Ezra after the return from Exile was probably much of the present Pentateuch. An account of the writing of a book of prophecy is recorded in Jeremiah (36:1–32; cf. 25:13; 30:2); there are other references to prophetic books (2 Chron. 12:15; Nahum 1:1; Luke 4:17–20).

The concept of a record book kept by God appears in several places in the OT. In it are recorded God's plans (Ps. 139:16) and the record of the sufferings of his people (Ps. 56:8; cf. Job 19:23). There also developed the idea of the "Book of Life," God's register of righteous persons from which the wicked would be erased, an action that meant death (Exod. 32:32–33; Ps. 69:28). Malachi begins to fuse the two concepts of a record of deeds and a list of names by connecting God's "Book of Remembrance" with a future vindication of the righteous (Mal. 3:16–18). Daniel understands God's book to contain the names of the inhabitants of the coming messianic kingdom, but he also portrays God as Judge (Dan. 7:10;12:1). The NT writers combine the concepts and understand the "Book of Life" to be both a record of deeds that required judgment (Rev. 20:12–14) and a register of the citizenship of the heavenly kingdom (v. 15; cf. Luke 10:20; Phil. 4:3; Rev. 21:27).

Several examples of ancient Egyptian "books" survive, including the "Book of the Dead" and the "Pyramid Texts" dealing with the afterlife and the "Instruction of Amen-em-ope," a collection of proverbial sayings some scholars believe to be the model for parts of Proverbs (esp. 22:17–23:22). "Books" discovered in the ruins of Nineveh include the *Enuma elish*, a mythical creation epic in which the god Marduk subdues the dragon of chaos, and the "Gilgamish Epic," which tells of a legendary king's quest for immortality and includes an account of a flood sent by the gods to destroy humanity. ***See also*** Clay; Codex; Papyrus; Scroll; Scrolls, The Dead Sea; Writing.
D.R.B.

Book of the Covenant. ***See*** Law.

booth. ***See*** Tabernacles, Festival of.

Booths, Feast of. ***See*** Tabernacles, Festival of.

bottles, containers for liquids, usually made of goatskin, clay, or glass. Dried skins of goats in particular made quite functional vessels, once sewed up with the hair on the outside (Gen. 21:14–19). In antiquity, as is still done in the Near East today, animal skins filled with milk were hung from trees, then shaken until the contents thickened to the consistency of butter. A related process turned fermented milk into yoghurt (Heb. *leban*) (Judg. 4:19). Similar skins were also used to carry water (Josh. 9:4, 13; Judg. 4:19; 1 Sam. 16:20).

The same word seems to refer to a skin container used to hold wine. The parable concerning new wine in old skins (Matt. 9:17; Mark 2:22; Luke 5:37) reflects the condition that arises when skins become old and dried out: they cannot be used to hold new wine, which produces gas as it ferments, because they will burst (Job 32:19). Terra-cotta bottles are well known from every period, and although what their contents were is not always certain, it is clear that tiny vessels were used as unguentaria and perfume containers. Their fragility is used as a figure of speech by Jeremiah to depict the destruction of Jerusalem (19:1–11). Yet another type of bottle is referred to in Psalm 56:8: "put thou my tears in thy bottle." Such small "tear vases," either of terra-cotta, faience, or highly decorated glass, are known especially from Egyptian tombs.
S.L.R.

boundary stones, stones erected to delineate boundaries between nations or between private individuals, the latter type frequently also registering special tax exemptions. The many royal stelae found throughout the ancient Near East also served as indications of national boundaries. Although written testimony amply attests to the existence of markings for private property, examples beginning from the Late Bronze Age (1500–1200 B.C.) have been excavated almost exclusively in Mesopotamia. In Israel where theoretically all property was deemed inalienable, because God-given, boundary stones were set "by the ancestors" (Deut. 19:14) to guarantee the demarcation of private fields (cf. also Prov. 22:28). Allusions to implicit abuse of such rights are found, however (cf. Deut. 27:17; Hos. 5:10; Prov. 23:10; Job 24:2).
J.M.S.

Boundary inscription from Gezer, first century B.C.–first century A.D. It reads, "The boundary of Gezer" on top with the name of the owner of the area, "Alkios," below.

bow. ***See*** Archers; Weapons.

bowl, an open vessel that is wider than it is deep. Biblical references to bowls are numerous and, on the basis of vocabulary and context, indicate a wide variety of types. There were large bowls that served as banquet dishes for wine (Amos 6:6) and craters out of which the food of the main meal was apparently lifted by hand (Prov. 19:24; Matt. 26:23). Temple equipment included a wide range of bowls, often of precious metal, for usage in sacrifices and offerings (Exod. 25:29; Num. 7:79; Zech. 14:20). The bowl was an important element of the menorah, or seven-branched lampstand (Zech. 4:2), as well as part of the capitals of the Temple pillars (1 Kings 7:41).

Archaeological excavation has shown the bowl to be ubiquitous in antiquity, ranging widely in size and in material. Leather, basketry, wood, stone, ceramic, glass, and metal were all used; ceramic was the most common and metal and alabaster were the most precious. Except for obvious cases, e.g., cooking pots, lamps, incense or other cultic equipment, attempts to correlate specific excavated vessel types with terms and usages in the biblical text remain highly speculative.
S.L.R.

bowstring, the lanyard spanning the two ends of a bow (KJV: "withe"). Delilah used a bowstring to bind Samson, but he broke it easily (Judg. 16:7, 9). The exact composition of that bowstring is not clear from the text.

Bozrah (bahz'rah; Heb., "fortress, enclosure"). **1** The chief city of northern Edom, 3,608 ft. (1,100 m.) above sea level, overlooking the Wadi el-Hamayida, eight miles (13 km.) south of modern Tafileh and five miles (8 km.) northwest of the highest point on the plateau. Excavations by Crystal-M. Bennett reveal that it flourished in the seventh and sixth centuries B.C. and probably continued into the fourth. As is the case with other Edomite sites, it does not appear to have existed before the eighth century B.C., which raises serious questions about the historical accuracy of the Edomite king lists in which it is mentioned (Gen. 36:33; 1 Chron. 1:44). Evidently famous for its strong fortifications, Bozrah symbolizes in the prophetic oracles the whole of Edom (Isa. 34:6; Jer. 49:13, 22; Amos 1:12). The suggestion by some scholars, on the basis of Isa. 63:1–3, that it was celebrated for dyeing seems highly speculative. **2** A town in Moab (Jer. 48:24), perhaps the same as modern Bezer. **3** A city close to the southern frontier of Syria, known today as Busra eski-Sham. Captured by Judas Maccabeus (165–160 B.C.), it became a century later the northernmost stronghold of the Nabatean Empire and continued to be a vital caravan center through the Umayyad period (A.D. 661–750). It contains today impressive Roman and Byzantine ruins. ***See also*** Bezer; Edom; Moab; Nabatea, Nabateans. D.B.

bracelets, a common form of personal adornment in the biblical world. Found with some frequency in archaeological excavations, they were usually made of bronze or precious metals, although iron examples are known and glass bracelets abound in the Roman period. Both males and females wore bracelets, which were placed at or near the wrist, in contrast to armlets which adorned the upper arm. In addition to being decorative items, bracelets could serve, as did jewelry in general, as a repository of wealth. The story of Rebekah (Gen. 24:22, 30, 47) demonstrates their use as items of monetary value, as does the fact that bracelets were among the valuables donated to the tent of meeting (Num. 31:50). C.L.M.

brambles, various spiny bushes often forming impenetrable thickets (Judg. 14–15; Song of Sol. 2:2). The bramble of Luke 6:44 is probably a fruit-bearing bush such as the blackberry (*Rubus sanguineus*). ***See also*** Thorns.

branch, a growth from the main stem or root of a plant. Various Hebrew words are translated as branch or shoot. The most common one (*tsemahkh*) can be defined as any sprout of vegetation (Gen. 19:25; Ezek. 16:7; Ps. 85:11). "Branch" or "shoot" is used metaphorically in prophecies of redemption to refer to the future glory of the Israelites (Isa. 60:21) and, more commonly, to the divinely appointed ruler. In Isa. 11:1–5, the future son of David will be imbued with the divine spirit of wisdom, power, and God's will in order to judge humankind in righteousness. God will establish a "righteous branch" of David whose way will be just (in contradistinction to that of Jeremiah's contemporary, Zedekiah; Jer. 23:5; 33:15; cf. Ps. 132:17). His days will be characterized by security (Jer. 23:6; 33:16), and the Israelites shall always be ruled by descendants of David (Jer. 33:17–26). In Zech. 3:8 and 6:12 (cf. Hag. 2:21–23) Zechariah points to two messianic figures, Joshua, the high priest, and Zerubbabel, governor of Judah and the descendant of David. In their time, the people shall dwell securely (Zech. 3:6–10) and the Temple will be rebuilt (Zech. 4:5–14; 6:9–15). ***See also*** Eschatology. J.U.

brass, an alloy of copper and zinc that is malleable and durable. The KJV translates the Hebrew word *neḥoshet* (meaning "copper" or "bronze") as "brass." Except for several metaphorical references (Lev. 26:19; Deut. 28:23; Isa. 48:4), the RSV uses the term "bronze." Other modern translations tend to omit the word "brass" altogether, since brass was unknown in biblical times.

bray. 1 A term used in the KJV where the RSV has "crush," as is done in a mortar and pestle (Prov. 27:22). **2** The sound made by the wild ass (Job 6:5) or by worthless men (Job 30:7).

brazier, a container for fire used for warming a living area. Jehoiakim sat before a fire burning in a brazier (Heb. *'aḥ*) and threw in pieces of Jeremiah's scroll of prophecy as it was read to him (Jer. 36:22, 23). It was probably made of clay, although in the palace of a king it could possibly be of metal. ***See also*** Oven.

bread, the staff of life (Lev. 26:26; Ezek. 5:16; 14:13); bread and water make up life's two basic staples (Num. 21:5; Isa. 3:1). It is frequently used as a metaphor for food in general (Judg. 13:16; Luke 15:17).

Bread was made primarily from wheat or barley (2 Kings 4:42; John 6:9, 13), the latter being eaten primarily by the poor. At times any mixture of grains, such as beans, lentils, millet, etc., might be ground up and made into bread (Ezek. 4:9). Grain was usually ground and used in coarse form (Lev. 2:14, 16), but at times it was ground more finely (Gen. 18:6; Lev. 2:2; 6:15). The best bread was made from wheat in which only the grain, not the bran, was ground (Deut. 32:14; 2 Kings 7:1). Upon being ground, grain was mixed with water, salt, and old dough. The mixture was then kneaded in a bowl (Exod. 8:3; 12:34), allowed to rise, and baked. Bread was baked either by setting it on hot stones and covering with hot ashes (1 Kings 19:6; Isa. 44:19), by cooking on an iron griddle

(Lev. 2:5; 6:21; 7:9), or by baking in an oven (Lev. 2:4; 7:9; 26:26) that was heated by stubble (Mal. 4:1), grass (Matt. 6:30), or twigs (1 Kings 17:12).

The term "bread" is used metaphorically in various ways to refer to earning a living (2 Thess. 3:12); sharing in the future kingdom (Luke 14: 15); the word of God (Isa. 55:2); an enemy about to be consumed (Num. 14:9); and Christ as the true food from heaven (John 6:31–51).

Bread is also associated with various religious rites: the Passover and Feast of Unleavened Bread (Exod. 12:8, 14–20; 13:3–10); the bread of the Presence (Exod. 25:23–30; 40:22–23; Lev. 24:5–9; Heb. 9:2); various cereal offerings (Exod. 29:2, 23–25; Lev. 2:4–16; 7:9; 1 Sam. 10:3–8); the manna in the wilderness (Exod. 16:14–30); and the Lord's Supper (Matt. 26:26–29; Mark 14:22–25; Luke 22:14–23; 1 Cor. 11:23–26). The latter was also called the "breaking of bread" (Acts 2:42, 46; 20:7, 11). ***See also*** Lord's Supper, The; Manna; Passover, The. R.H.S.

breastpiece (KJV: "breastplate"), an item of Aaron's ceremonial garb (Exod. 28:15, 22–30; 39:8–21; Lev. 8:8). A kind of pouch, it was a square (about 9 × 9 inches) made by folding in half a rectangular piece of material. Attached to the ephod by two chains, two frames, and three pairs of rings, all of gold, the breastpiece was like the Aaronide ephod in being a mixed fabric of linen and wool woven with gold, in using the same brilliant colors (purple, blue, and scarlet), and in exhibiting a special kind of workmanship (Heb. *khoshev*, "figured weaving"). These features, like the details of Aaron's robe and diadem, link the breastpiece to the materials and workmanship of the vessels and curtains inside the tabernacle, thereby giving concrete expression to the unique role of Aaron, to the exclusion of other cultic personnel, within the sanctuary.

The symbolic nature of the breastpiece emerges further from the assemblage of precious stones attached to it in four rows of three each. Twelve different gemstones, set in gold filigree, were used, each one inscribed like a signet with the name of an Israelite tribe. While only Aaron ministered inside the tabernacle before the Holy of Holies, he symbolically and regularly brought all Israel in with him, in the form of the tribal names that served as "a reminder before the Lord." In addition, the Urim and Thummim, by means of which Aaron exercised his divinatory function of bearing "the judgment of the people of Israel on his heart" (Exod. 28:30), were attached to the breastpiece.

"Breastpiece" is also used to translate a term that refers to a military garment, a cuirass or plate of metal or mail worn on the chest (1 Kings 22:34; cf. KJV: "habergeon"). The metaphoric use of breastpiece in Isa. 59:17 and in the NT (Eph. 6:14; 1 Thess. 5:8; Rev. 9:9, 17) probably stems from the military, protective sense rather than from the ritual-priestly usage. ***See also*** Aaron; Ephod; Tabernacle; Urim and Thummim. C.L.M.

breastplate. ***See*** Breastpiece.

brick, a square or oblong block made of mud or clay used principally for construction of buildings and walls. Mudbrick construction is well known from ancient times in spite of the fact that stones were plentiful in Palestine and well used in building projects. Bricks were normally made of a mixture of clay and water, and sometimes straw was included to prevent cracking. Bricks could be sun-dried or fired in a kiln, though the former practice was habitual in Palestine.

Brickmakers at work; a wooden model from an ancient Egyptian tomb. The Israelites in Egypt were brickmakers (Exod. 5:6–9).

Mudbrick could be used for either walls or buildings. Good examples of mudbrick architecture have come from such diverse sites as Jericho, Gezer, and Ezion-geber. After the conclusion of excavations at modern Tel Sheva, the probable site of biblical Beer-sheba, the Israeli government partially reconstructed some houses and walls using modern mudbrick made locally and sun-dried.

The governing authorities of other nations in antiquity who made bricks sometimes had them stamped with royal seals. The best-known example of a royal building project using bricks is that of the pharaoh who oppressed the Israelites in Egypt by forcing them to make the bricks (Exod. 1:13–14; 5:6–9).

Apparently sacred altars could be constructed of bricks, although their use in such activity was not in accord with Hebrew law. A postexilic prophet protested against such activity in Isa. 65:3. Bricks are not mentioned in the NT. J.A.D.

bride, bridegroom. ***See*** Marriage; Wedding.

bridge, a device providing access between two points. The term is not used in the Bible, but archaeological remains and literary texts show use of such devices in the biblical period both in and out of Palestine. Technically it is a construction to provide a level path for foot or vehicle traffic over deep cuts in the earth, frequently riverbeds. Bridges were superior to fords or ferries in eliminating the water hazard. The best surviving examples of bridges are those built by Greek or Roman engineers, many in the time prior to the NT period. They helped make passable the Roman roads used by Paul and other early Christian missionaries who carried their message around the Mediterranean world. R.S.B.

brigandine. ***See*** Coat of Mail.

brimstone, sulphur, a greenish-yellow nonmetallic substance that is highly flammable. It is used in the modern manufacturing of matches and gunpowder. Sulphur is associated in popular belief with divine punishment by fire (Gen. 19:24; Rev. 14:10). ***See also*** Fire; Hell; Sodom.

broad place, a large and level area, usually with a connotation of goodness. Figuratively, it describes the place to which one is brought by God's deliverance from straits of various kinds (Job 36:16; 2 Sam. 22:20=Ps. 18:19; Ps. 31:8), perhaps in reference to the open spaces in cities used for assemblies, with a connotation of restoration to community.

bronze, an alloy of copper and tin. The Middle Bronze Age (2000–1500 B.C.) saw the replacement of copper by bronze in the production of metal weapons, tools, jewelry, and vessels, since bronze was harder than the copper that had been used earlier. Because of its qualities, bronze was used not only for weapons of war but also for decorations, since it could be burnished to a bright, smooth surface. Both qualities, hardness and brightness, are reflected in the many biblical references to bronze, both literal (e.g., Job 20:24; Exod. 25–38; 1 Kings 7) and figurative (e.g., Job 40:18; Rev. 1:15). S.L.R.

Bronze Age, the era spanning roughly the third and second millennia (ca. 3200–1200 B.C.) in the biblical lands of Palestine and Transjordan. There are three major subdivisions: the Early Bronze Age (EB; 3200–2000), the Middle Bronze Age (MB; 2000–1500), and the Late Bronze Age (LB; 1500–1200). These are roughly coterminous with the Old, Middle, and New Kingdoms in Egypt and the Sumerian, Old Babylonian, and Middle Babylonian periods in Mesopotamia.

Bronze Age civilization is a witness to the beginnings of urbanization, the consolidation of urban centers into powerful city-states, and their eventual decline. Around 1200 B.C., the arrival of new peoples in Palestine, among them Israelites and Philistines, and the consequent break in the archaeological record mark the inception of a new era, the Iron Age. The history of the Bronze Age, however, is essentially the history of the biblical people known as Canaanites. Although this ethnic designation does not appear in the literary record until the second millennium, Canaanite culture, as we know it from both textual and archaeological remains, has its antecedents in the Early Bronze Age.

With few exceptions, attempts to correlate early pre-Israelite biblical traditions with Bronze Age civilization have not elicited a consensus of scholarly opinion. Exemplifying this state of affairs are the attempts by scholars to situate the patriarchal narratives in their proper historical and cultural milieu. Suggested contexts range from the end of the Early Bronze Age through successive periods up to and including the early Iron Age. This divergence of scholarly opinion reflects the virtual nonexistence of firm historical data in the biblical text prior to the period of the Israelite Monarchy (ca. 1025–587 B.C.).

Early Bronze Age: The Early Bronze Age represents the first period of urbanization in the area, as attested at sites such as Arad, Megiddo, Lachish, Jericho, Hesi, Ai, and Bâb edh-Dhra. Except for writing, which is found in neighboring countries, the elements of a nucleated urban culture are present: substantial cities surrounded by fortifications, town planning, distinct domestic quarters, monumental public buildings (e.g., palaces and temples), sophisticated water retrieval and storage facilities, an established cult, and an economy based on agriculture, animal husbandry, and trade. Still shrouded in mystery are the reasons for the abrupt cessation of urban life about 2400 at the end of the EB III period. In the EB IV (2400–2000) period, we find a society of virtual pastoral nomads in western Palestine. In Transjordan current excavations at Bâb edh-Dhra and Khirbet Iskander suggest a less drastic cultural break at 2400; indeed sedentary life continues, although on a reduced scale.

Middle Bronze Age: The Middle Bronze Age marks a return to urban life in Palestine and Transjordan. Following upon the "Dark Age" of the EB IV period, related peoples from Syria, carrying with them the traditions of a highly sophisticated culture, spurred the area into what is generally considered the zenith of Canaanite civilization. Vast city-states arose that were characterized by massive fortifications that included a glacis, a huge earthen rampart, thought to serve as a defense against the battering ram. Cities such as Dan, Hazor, Shechem, Gezer, and Megiddo reflected this new prosperity and wealth in their material culture; excavations have revealed beautiful wheel-made pottery, bronze weapons and tools, and numerous imports from the eastern Mediterranean Littoral. It is this period that is most often cited as the milieu for the patriarchs, based on comparisons of customs and traditions as known from texts of Syro-Mesopotamia. The American archaeologist G. Ernest Wright has connected the open-air shrine at Shechem with biblical traditions (Gen. 33:18–20).

Late Bronze Age: The Late Bronze Age was ushered in by a series of campaigns by eighteenth-dynasty pharaohs who overthrew their Hyksos overlords and made Syro-Palestine part of the Egyptian Empire. As the cities were rebuilt, a high level of prosperity returned. Indeed the period is rightly termed the "age of internationalism," for imports from Mycenaea, Cyprus, Syria, and Egypt are found at almost every site. A large body of cultic artifacts, temples, and texts (from Ugarit) found in this period provides a basis for comparative studies between Canaanite religion and later Israelite traditions. It is generally agreed that the events of the Egyptian bondage, Exodus, and early Israelite conquest traditions are probably to be situated in this period. The break-up of empires throughout the Mediterranean area before 1200 is the context in which the Israelites made their first historical appearance in "the promised land." S.L.R.

brook (Heb. *nahal*), the bed of a stream or river (Arabic, *wadi*) generally dry or nearly dry during the summer months but sporadically or continuously filled with water from the rains during the winter. The land of Canaan had numerous such watercourses (Deut. 8:7; 10:7; cf. Lev. 11: 9–10). They are mentioned over a hundred and twenty times in the OT. Well-known brooks of the Bible include: the Zered (Num. 21:12), the Arnon (Deut. 2:24), the Jabbok (Deut. 2:37), the Kanah (Josh. 17:9), the Kishon (Judg. 4:7), the Sorek (Judg. 16:4), the Besor (1 Sam. 30:9), the Kidron (1 Kings 2:37; cf. John 18:1), the Cherith (1 Kings 17:3), and the Brook of Egypt, Canaan's southern boundary (Num. 34:5). D.A.D.

brothers, blood relatives, especially one's siblings; can also be used of one's close male associates. Cain and Abel are blood brothers (Gen. 4: 9), as are Jacob and Esau (Gen. 25:26) and Simon and Andrew (Mark 1:16). Much is made of the pattern of the younger brother superseding the elder; Abel is preferred over Cain, Jacob over Esau, David over Jesse's sons. Gentile election is seen as part of this pattern in Rom. 9:10–13. "Brother" also embraces clans, compatriots, and allies. David calls Jonathan his "brother" (2 Sam. 1:26). Allied kings (Solomon and Hiram of Tyre) are "brothers" (1 Kings 9:13); Amos 1:9 laments the breaking of this "covenant of brotherhood." Israelite priests constitute a brotherhood (2 Chron. 29:34); they must marry within the brotherhood, thus cementing the bonds. Finally we find "brother" used to express the spiritual relationship of coreligionists. Essenes act as "brothers" (Josephus, *Bella Judaica* II.122). Jesus calls brothers those "who hear the word of God and do it" (Luke 8:20). Paul regularly speaks of his coreligionists as "brothers" (1 Cor. 1:10) and as "beloved brothers" (1 Thess. 1:4). ***See also*** Sister. J.H.N.

Bukki (buhk'ī). **1** A leader of the tribe of Dan who was in charge of apportioning the land within the tribe (Num. 34:22). **2** A Levite, a descendant of Aaron and ancestor of Ezra (1 Chron. 6:5; Ezra 7:4).

Bul (bo͞ol; Heb., "produce"?), a term designating the old Canaanite name for the eighth month of the year (1 Kings 6:38, approximately October-November). After the Exile, this month was called *Markheshvan* by the Hebrews.

bull, an animal important in ancient Near Eastern religions, including the religion found in the Bible. In Egypt, Apis the bull was thought to impart fertility; in one ritual a bull was driven over fields to increase their yield. Apis also came to be the herald of the national god Ptah and occasionally his earthly manifestation, an instance of the Egyptian tendency to ascribe sacral significance to animals. In Mesopotamia, the bull of heaven was given by Anu to Inanna to execute wrath against Gilgamesh and the land of Uruk. "Bull of heaven," "bull," and "great bull" are also designations of the storm god Ishkur/Adad as god of fertility. Among the Canaanites, Israel's immediate neighbors, El, the president of the divine assembly, was called Bull for his strength and procreative power. To praise gods and heroes one often gave them the names of animals whose virtues they were thought to display: bull, cow, boar, gazelle, ram. A designation for Israel's God in Genesis, commonly translated "Mighty One of Jacob," was originally in Hebrew "Bull of Jacob" (Gen. 49: 24).

Israel was forbidden to make any image through which its God might present himself to the worshiper (Exod. 20:4–5; Deut. 4:15–19); hence images of animals could not be the means of divine-human encounter. An animal

Statue of the Apis bull representing the Egyptian god Ptah.

could however be the throne of the Lord, like the cherubim (composite winged animals) of the Jerusalem Temple (cf. 1 Kings 6:23–28); God was "enthroned upon the cherubim." Israel's neighbors also knew of the animal as the throne of the deity. Statues of bulls have been found, some of which have a god astride the back; those without the god presumably were seen as animal thrones for the invisible deity. There was always the danger that the animal throne of the Lord would itself become the object of worship. This danger was actually realized, according to the biblical writer, in the two young bulls that Jeroboam I set up in Bethel and Dan in the tenth century B.C. He called to the people, "Behold your gods, O Israel, who brought you up out of the land of Egypt" (1 Kings 12:28, cf. Exod. 32:4). Bulls were too much a part of the iconography of the East not to play a part in the Temple; the most famous example was the molten sea, a huge bowl supported by twelve oxen, three facing in each direction. Bulls, like other animals of dignity and value, were often sacrificed in the Temple. ***See also*** Cults; Jeroboam I. R.J.C.

bulrush. ***See*** Rush.

Bunni (buhn'ī). **1** A Levite, an ancestor of some postexilic inhabitants of Jerusalem (Neh. 11:15). **2** A leader of the postexilic community who signed the covenant to keep the law (Neh. 10:15). **3** A Levite who participated in the dedication ceremony of the returning exiles (Neh. 9:4); perhaps he is the same person as 2, although here the word may not be a name at all since there is some textual evidence to read both Bani and Bunni in this verse (Neh. 9:4) as Heb. *bene*, "sons of." ***See also*** Bani.

burden, a heavy load, but also psychological and spiritual anxiety (Deut. 1:12; Gal. 6:2, 5). Certain superscriptions in prophetic books use a term meaning "that which is lifted up" as a technical designation for a weighty proclamation of judgment (Nah. 1:1; Hab. 1:1; Mal. 1:1; Zech. 9:1; cf. Isa. 13:1; Ezek. 12:10). A conscious reflection on this term occurs in Jer. 23:33–40, where Jeremiah accuses opposition prophets of becoming a burden to the deity, although they claimed to possess the burden of the Lord. Since God alone could break the yoke of oppression (Isa. 9:4; 10:27; 14:25), hope arose that the burden would eventually diminish. Jesus thus described his burden as light (Matt. 11:30).

J.L.C.

burial, the disposition of a human corpse to prevent its desecration. The Hebrew word *(qeburah)* and the Greek word *(entaphiazō)* meaning "burial" describe either the act of burying (Eccles. 6:3; Isa. 14:20; Jer. 22:19; Matt. 26:12) or the burial place (Gen. 47:30; Deut. 34:6; 2 Kings 9:28; 21:26: 23:30).

Burial customs among the Hebrews consisted of two important elements: the mortuary ritual, which accompanied the burial, and the physical preparation of the body and its final resting place.

Because of the warm climate of Palestine and the popular belief that a dead body was ritually impure, burial usually took place as soon after death as possible (Deut. 21:23), usually within twenty-four hours (Acts 5:5–6, 10). Among the Jews interment or burial of the body was the common practice, and to allow the body to decay above ground or be subject to destruction by vultures or dogs was the greatest of dishonors (1 Kings 14:10–14; 2 Kings 9:34–37). Anyone who discovered a corpse by the roadside was required to bury it (2 Sam. 21:10–14).

Preparation for Burial: While the complete mortuary rituals among the Hebrews are not described in the Bible, most elements are represented in a variety of passages. As soon as the individual expired, the eldest son or nearest relative present would close the eyes of the deceased (Gen. 46:4), which is simply explained by the resemblance of death to sleep. The mouth was bound shut (John 11:44), the body washed (Acts 9:37) and then anointed with aromatic ointments (John 12:7; 19:39; Mark 16:1; Luke 24:1). The body was then wrapped in cloth (usually linen, Matt. 27:59; John 11:44), although indi-

Cover of a pottery sarcophagus from Beth-shan, twelfth–tenth century B.C.

viduals of high rank would frequently be clothed in fine garments.

Both archaeological and biblical data indicate that individuals of wealth or political rank enjoyed burials with elaborate funerary assemblages that included robes, jewelry, furniture, weapons, and pottery (1 Sam. 28:14; Isa. 14:11; Ezek. 32:27).

While cremation was widely practiced among the later Greeks and Romans along with the Canaanites, it was the Hebrew custom to inter the body. The only exceptions to this practice occurred when the bodies were in an advanced state of decay after mutilation (1 Sam. 31:12) or there was the threat of a plague (Amos 6:10).

Embalming was not a part of Hebrew burial practice, but because Jacob and Joseph died in Egypt, they were mummified after the local custom by physicians (Gen. 50:2–3, 26). A coffin (Heb. *'ārôn*, "portable box" or "chest") was used for the burial of Joseph (Gen. 50:26), but this was not generally the case among the Hebrews. In NT times bones were often collected and placed in small boxes called ossuaries.

After preparations of the body were complete, the procession to the grave or tomb began with the corpse being carried on a wooden bier, usually by friends, servants, or relatives (2 Sam. 3:31). The procession was led by professional mourners, followed by family members who filled the air with cries of sadness and agony (2 Sam. 3:31; 2 Sam. 3:32; Job 21:33; Eccles. 12:5; Jer. 9:17; Amos 5:16; Matt. 9:23). Among the Canaanites the mourning ritual included cutting or mutilating one's flesh, but this was expressly forbidden by Jewish law (Lev. 19:27–28; 21:5; Deut. 14:1).

The period of mourning varied among the ancient Hebrews. Mourning for Jacob lasted for seventy days (but this also included the embalming period, Gen. 50:3) while Aaron (Num. 20:29) and Moses (Deut. 34:5–8) were mourned for a period of thirty days after burial.

Burial Sites: A variety of burial sites were utilized by the ancient Hebrews depending on the occasion of death, the time allotted for burial, and the geological characteristics of the area. The most common type of burial arrangement was the simple shaft or trench grave, which was often lined with mats, wood, or stone slabs. These simple graves were sometimes marked by a tree (Gen. 35:8), although in the case of infamous individuals, the burial plot was identified by a pile of stones placed over it (Josh. 7:26; 2 Sam. 18:17).

The Bible does not mention the use of pits for burials, but some have been discovered at various sites in Palestine. Some were designed for a single contracted burial while others were large enough to accommodate several cinerary urns (for ashes) or storage jars.

Caves were frequently utilized for burials either for their convenience or because time or money did not permit the cutting of a tomb from rock. Sarah (Gen. 23:19) and other members of Abraham's family (Gen. 25:9; 49:31; 50:13) were buried in the cave of Machpelah at Hebron.

Rock-cut tombs are the best documented burial sites known today and they display a wide variety of forms. Some were designed for a single interment, but most were designed for multiple burials, usually by one family (Isa. 22:16). The tombs of the wealthy were frequently located in gardens (2 Kings 21:18, 26; Matt. 27:57; John 19:41–42). Some tombs were marked by monuments or pillars (2 Kings 23:17) or whitewashed on the outside (Matt. 23:27) to prevent Jews from accidently touching them and being rendered ceremonially defiled.

Rock-cut tombs were sealed with square slabs of stone or, as was common in the Roman period, with rolling stones (Matt. 27:60). Excavations have revealed sixty such tombs west of the Jordan River while two have been discovered at Tell Hesban, east of the Jordan. J.J.D.

burnt offerings. ***See*** Worship.

business. ***See*** Trade and Transportation.

butter. ***See*** Bottles; Food.

Byblos (bib'luhs). ***See*** Gebal.

Opposite: The Muiredach cross from County Louth, Ireland, dates from the first quarter of the tenth century.

C

cab (KJV; RSV: "kab"), a unit of measure. ***See*** Kab; Weights and Measures.

Caesar, Gaius Julius (100–44 B.C.), Roman general and author. He conquered Gaul (58–51 B.C.) and then in the civil wars of 49–45 B.C. he dispersed the supporters of his rival Pompey and the Roman senate and emerged as a virtual dictator. He was assassinated March 15, 44 B.C. After more civil wars, his grand-nephew and adopted heir, Octavian (Augustus) who had taken the name "Caesar," emerged as sole ruler of Rome. "Caesar" then came to be used as a title for the emperor (e.g., Matt. 22:21; Mark 12:14; Luke 20:22). ***See also*** Augustus.

Caesarea (ses-uh-ree'uh), a seaport on the eastern coast of the Mediterranean between the ancient cities of Dor and Jaffa, originally a small fortified Phoenician anchorage named Strabo's Tower. In the year 63 B.C., Pompey added the area, together with other towns on the seashore, to the Roman province of Syria. Mark Antony gave it to Cleopatra VII, but when Octavian (Augustus) won the battle of Actium, he gave the small town to Herod the Great (30 B.C.). Herod built a magnificent new city and port on the site and named it Caesarea Maritima in honor of Octavian, now Caesar Augustus. The harbor

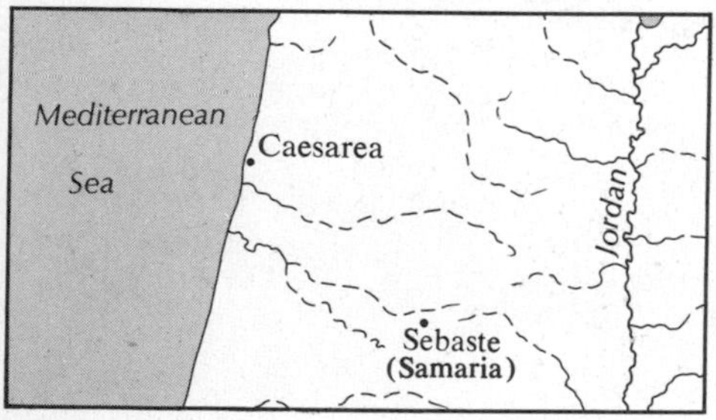

complex was given the name Limen Sebastos by Herod (Sebastos being the Greek form of Augustus).

Caesarea was the capital of Roman government in Palestine for over six hundred years, serving as the seat of the Roman governors of the province of Judea and headquarters for the Roman legions stationed in the province. The great Jewish war against Rome began here with an uprising by the Jews in A.D. 66, and "Judaea Capta" coins were minted here to commemorate their defeat. Vespasian (A.D. 69–79), proclaimed emperor by his legions while at Caesarea, raised the city to the rank of a Roman colony.

According to Acts, Christianity was preached in Caesarea by Philip (8:40) and Peter (10:1–11:18; cf. 15:7–9), the latter being responsible for the conversion of the Roman centurion Cornelius. Limen Sebastos was the port of arrival and departure for several of Paul's journeys according to Acts (Acts 9:30; 18:22; 21:8; 27:1–2). Paul was brought to Caesarea in custody from Jerusalem (Acts 23:23–35) to stand trial before Felix, Festus, and Agrippa II (Acts 24–26).

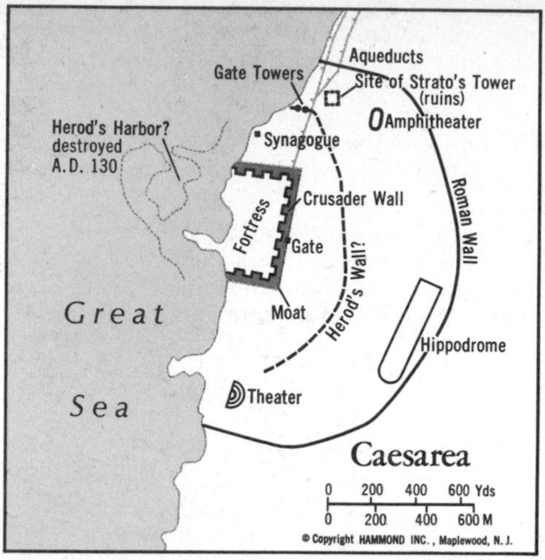

Based on available evidence, this plan of Caesarea highlights the city of Herod the Great and also includes building of other periods.

Excavations at Caesarea Maritima have revealed streets, palaces, public buildings, a temple, a hippodrome, a theater, and a spacious sewer system from the Roman and Byzantine periods. Marine archaeologists exploring the port have discovered the immense size of the harbor and some of the Roman mole forming the ancient breakwater.

Following the Islamic invasion of the seventh century, Caesarea declined rapidly, but Louis IX of France built a short-lived Crusader fortress at the site of the ancient harbor. ***See also*** Cornelius; Herod; Paul; Peter; Philip. M.K.M.

Caesarea Philippi (ses-uh-ree'uh fi-lip'ī), a Gentile frontier town located on the southern slope of Mt. Hermon at one of the sources of the Jordan River. The site was known in antiquity as a shrine of the Greek and Roman nature god, Pan. According to the Jewish historian Jose-

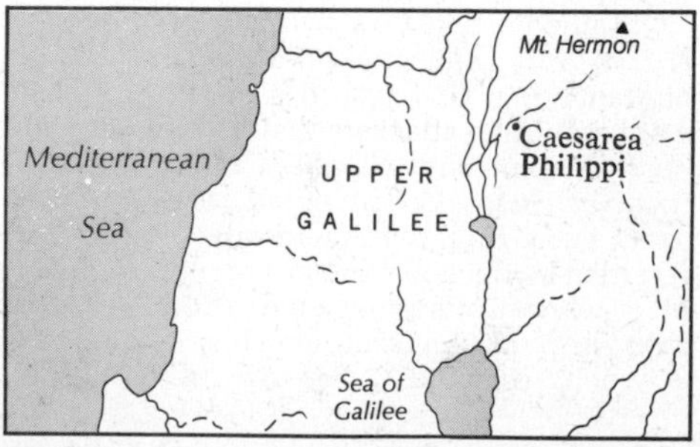

phus, Caesar Augustus gave the city, under the name of Panion, to Herod the Great. When Herod's son Philip became tetrarch of the region, he rebuilt the city and renamed it after the emperor and himself. In or near the city of Caesarea Philippi was the scene of Peter's great confession (Matt. 16:13–19; Mark 8:27–29). M.K.M.

Caesar's household, a collective designation for the thousands of slaves and freedmen of the ruling Roman emperor who typically performed various lower-level governmental functions. Because even the freedmen retained fixed obligations of service, these individuals formed a stable corps of civil administrators and workers, and they labored in every part of the Empire. If certain freedmen attained to exceptional power (Pallas [brother of Felix, Acts 23–24] and Narcissus under Claudius, Nymphidius under Nero), most kept their same tasks throughout their lives. Phil. 4:22 refers to members of Caesar's household found either at Rome or, more probably, at Ephesus. Since such people were debarred from military service, Phil. 1:13 very likely refers to a different group of people. ***See also*** Felix, Antonius; Philippians, The Letter of Paul to the. R.A.W.

Caiaphas (kay'uh-fuhs), Joseph, son-in-law and eventual successor of Annas as high priest, attaining the position in A.D. 18 and holding it until he was deposed by Vitellius, Pontius Pilate's successor, in the year 36–37. He was, therefore, high priest at the time of the trial of Jesus (Matt. 26:3, 57; John 18:13, 24). On the other hand, Luke 3:2 and Acts 4:6 raise a difficult problem regarding his relation to Annas. John 11:49–52 and 18:14 ascribe to him the judgment that it was "expedient . . . that one man should die for the people," with reference to Jesus. ***See also*** Annas; Pilate, Pontius; Priests; Trial of Jesus, The. F.O.G.

Cain (kayn; Heb., "metalworker," although Gen. 4:1 connects it with a verb meaning "to acquire" or "create"). **1** Adam and Eve's first son, a farmer whose offering God rejected in favor of the firstlings brought by his brother Abel. Angered, Cain killed Abel and subsequently denied knowledge of his whereabouts. As a punishment, God withheld the ground's fertility from Cain, who was condemned to a life of wandering. God placed a mark on Cain to warn would-be attackers that he remained under God's protection (Gen. 4). Cain later built the first city. He was the father of Enoch and ancestor of Tubal-cain, the first metalworker. Cain is regarded as the eponymous ancestor of the Kenites, who are often considered to have originated as a tribe of wandering metalworkers. **2** A city in Judah (Josh. 15:57). ***See also*** Abel; Smith. F.E.G.

Calah (kay'luh; Akkadian *Kalkhu;* Arabic *Birs Nimrud*), a city on the eastern bank of the Tigris River, about twenty miles south of modern Mosul and ancient Nineveh in northern Iraq. Since the first excavations in 1849 by A. H. Layard, further excavations, including those directed by M. E. L. Mallowan, have been carried out intermittently until 1974. Layard wrongly identified the site as Nineveh, perhaps due to the biblical attribution of the building of Nineveh to the hunter Nimrod as well as Calah (Gen. 10:11–12). Nimrod is listed as a descendant of Cush (Gen. 10:8; 1 Chron. 1:10). In Mic. 5:5, the geographic term "Nimrod" appears in parallelism with Assyria. The city was founded in the thirteenth century B.C. by Shalmaneser I (1274–1245 B.C.) during a period of extensive building and expansion in Assyria.

At the beginning of his reign, Ashurnasirpal II (883–859 B.C.) moved his capital to Calah from Nineveh. His rebuilding program included a partially subterranean canal, a city wall, a palace of brick faced with stone, and elaborate low-reliefs depicting religious ceremonies and battle and hunting scenes. At this time, the palace covered about 6 acres. From the northwest section of the palace were found numerous fragments of ivory furniture inlay and decorative plaques carved in the Phoenician style.

The Black Obelisk of Shalmaneser III (858–824 B.C.), which depicts Jehu, son of Omri, submitting to the Assyrian king, was found at Calah. Other important records include the governor's archives, dealing with provincial administration during the reign of Tiglath-pileser III (747–727 B.C.), and from the southeastern area, called Fort Shalmaneser, were also recovered many ivory fragments. L.E.P.

Caleb (kay'leb), the founding father of the Calebites, a distinct group of people in Judah, perhaps extra-Israelite in origin. As a representative of Judah, Caleb functions in the spy tradition (Num. 14) as the person who, along with Joshua, brought a positive report to the Israelites about the land available for conquest. In contrast to the other spies whose reports were negative, Caleb won the right to enter God's land and to inherit space in the vicinity of Hebron in the south. The tradition about Caleb reflects the special interests of Judah, the southern tribe. In contrast to Caleb's reward, the representatives of the northern tribes were denied entry into the land. The construction of this tradition doubtless mirrors the political struggles between the north and the south after the conquest. ***See also*** Hebron; Joshua; Judah. G.W.C.

calendar. ***See*** Time.

calf, a young offspring of a cow. The calf can be used in the Bible as a general symbol for heathen idol worship, as in the story of the Golden Calf in Exodus 32. While Moses received the Ten Commandments on Mount Sinai, the Israelites asked Aaron to provide them with a god to lead them. He collected their gold and shaped it into the form of a calf, which, mounted on an altar, induced them to a wild orgy. Moses, on his return, melted the calf down, ground it to powder, and scattered it on water he then forced the idolatrous Israelites to drink. In addition, God punished the Israelites with a plague.

A long tradition of a cattle cult exists in the Near East, dating back to Neolithic times (8000–4500 B.C.). Best known is the sixth millennium B.C. cattle shrine at Catal Huyük in Anatolia. There is also evidence for cattle worship from early Crete. A large number of bovine clay figurines found at the seventh-millennium village of Ain Ghazal in Jordan may reflect a similar tradition.

In Israel the calf was an appropriate sacrifice (Lev. 9:2, 8) as a sin offering. It served as food for special occasions as well (see Luke 15:22–24). I.U.K.

call, a common word acquiring theological significance when God or Christ is the one who calls, implying divine election or commission. Sometimes individuals are called to special vocations in God's plan of salvation: God called Moses (Exod. 3:4), the judges (Judg. 3:9), the prophets (Jer. 1:5), and Jesus (Matt. 2:15), and Jesus called the apostles (Matt. 4:21; Rom. 1:1). When the call is a general summons to repentance and salvation, every Israelite or Christian is viewed as its recipient and hence Israel and the church are collectively designated God's "called" or "elect" (Isa. 41:9; Heb. 3:1). Frequently individuals call on God for succor (Pss. 99:6; 116:1). ***See also*** Apostle; Election; Moses; Prophet. J.M.B.

Calneh (kal'ne). **1** A north Syrian city referred to by Amos (Amos 6:2) and Isaiah (Isa. 10:9, Calno) as an example and warning: Israel's fate would be like that of Calneh; despite power and self-confidence, it would not be able to withstand the onslaught of the Assyrian armies. Located in the plain of Antioch, Calneh was capital of the Neo-Hittite state of Unqi. It was tributary to Assyria in the ninth century B.C., and it was conquered and annexed to Assyria by Tiglath-pileser III in 738 B.C. **2** A city in southern Babylonia founded by Nimrod (Gen. 10:10, KJV) that has not been identified. M.C.

Calvary (kal'vuh-ree), the site of Jesus' crucifixion. Three Gospels record both the Semitic name of this site, "Golgotha," and a translation, "Place of the Skull" (Matt. 27:33; Mark 15:22; John 19:17). Luke 23:33 records only a shorter and more accurate translation, "Skull." The name "Calvary" derives from the Vulgate's Latin translation of this word *(calvaria)*. It is likely that the site was so named because of its habitual use for executions. Less likely is an explanation rooted in the physical appearance of the place.

Apart from the name very little is confidently known about Calvary. John 19:20 and Jewish and Roman execution customs indicate that it was located outside Jerusalem's city walls. Roman crucifixion customs and the reference to passers-by (Matt. 27:39) also suggest it was near a thoroughfare, while the fact that the cross was visible from afar (Matt. 27:55) could indicate an elevated location. Nevertheless its precise location remains in dispute.

Since the fourth century the site now marked by the Church of the Holy Sepulchre has been revered as the location of Calvary. Objections that this church is *inside* the presumed location of the ancient city walls, and thus incompatible with the Gospel account, have been challenged by recent archaeological excavations defining more clearly the location of the walls. A rival hypothesis locating Calvary on a vaguely skull-shaped rise northeast of the Damascus Gate ("Gordon's Calvary," named after the main proponent of this location), advanced since the nineteenth century, has somewhat fewer advocates. ***See also*** Cross; Jerusalem; Vulgate. J.M.B.

camel, a large, humped ruminant. The camel (Heb. *gamal)* is frequently described in the Bible as a beast of burden and as a riding animal, often in association with nomadic tribes. There are two types of domesticated camels: the one-humped dromedary *(Camelus dromedarius)* and the two-humped Bactrian camel *(Camelus bactrianus)*. The dromedary as a proverbial desert animal is distributed throughout Arabia, northern Africa, the Near East, Pakistan, and India, whereas the longer-haired and heavier-built Bactrian camel is better adapted to a colder climate and is at home in central Asia, Afghanistan, and Iran. Usually it is the dromedary that is alluded to in the Bible, but the Bactrian camel may be referred to in Tob. 9:2.

The time and locale of the earliest camel domestication have long been an enigma, but recent finds from Shahr-i Sokhta in Iran and several sites in Turkmenistan suggest that the Bactrian camel came under human control here during the third millennium B.C. Archaeological evidence, consisting of camel bones and reference to a camel on a stele, also indicate that the dromedary was domesticated in Oman and eastern Arabia at about the same time.

There is however no archaeological corroboration for the camel being known in Palestine or Egypt at the beginning of the second millennium B.C., as the seventeen references to the camel in Genesis might suggest, and those references are therefore considered anachronisms. Abraham,

Camel carrying desert raiders in battle against Ashurbanipal's forces, as depicted in the Nineveh reliefs, seventh century B.C.

for example, is said to have been given camels by Pharaoh (Gen. 12:16) and to have supplied his servant with ten camels to search for Rebekah in Mesopotamia (Gen. 24:10). Again, Jacob is supposed to have ridden a camel to Canaan (Gen. 31:17) and to have presented Esau with camels (Gen. 32:15). Genesis 24 also furnishes information on the care of camels, including watering them (24:14, 19–20), feeding them (24:25, 32), and making them kneel (24:11).

Only at the end of the second millennium B.C. did the Israelites make the acquaintance of the camel, when they were invaded in the twelfth or eleventh century B.C. by nomadic Arab tribes ("Midianites") riding on camels (Judg. 6:5). But the Israelites soon started keeping camels themselves and used them (1 Chron. 12:40) to take gifts to King David, who himself employed an Ishmaelite to take care of his camels (1 Chron. 27:30).

Camels were also instrumental for the establishment of long-distance trade; they carried spices and incense all the way from southern Arabia to the Mediterranean and goods from Palestine to Egypt (Gen. 37:25). When the queen of Sheba visited King Solomon, her luggage was transported by camels (1 Kings 10:2).

But camels were not only used as beasts of burden; they were also raised as livestock. The nomadic Arabs kept camels on a large scale; the Hagarites are reported to have owned fifty thousand camels (1 Chron. 5:21), and Job (Job 1:3; 42:12) first had three thousand camels and later six thousand. Camels were also raised for their milk, which may be alluded to in Gen. 32:15. Although camels chew the cud, they do not have cloven hooves, so their meat was forbidden to the Israelites to eat (Lev. 11:4; Deut. 14:7).

In NT times the camel continued to be used as a beast of burden. Jesus noted that "it is easier for a camel to go through the eye of a needle than for a rich man to enter the kingdom of God" (Matt. 19:24; Luke 18:25). Jesus condemned and belittled the Pharisees for striving to strain out a gnat yet being willing to swallow a camel (Matt. 23:24). I.U.K.

camel's hair, type of material for clothing mentioned only in Matt. 3:4 and Mark 1:6. John the Baptist wore clothing made of camel's hair, a common form of dress in the Middle East even today. Because these passages refer to John's austere lifestyle, scholars have debated whether the apparel was the more expensive woven cloak, a less expensive girdle or loincloth, or a garment of dressed camel skin; probably, it was the last (cf. Matt. 11:8; Luke 7:25). Some scholars link Elijah's "garment of haircloth" (2 Kings 1:8), a sign of his prophetic office (Zech. 13:4), with John's camel's-hair garment, thereby identifying Elijah as John's prototype. ***See also*** Elijah; John the Baptist. P.L.S.

Cana (cay'nuh), a village of Galilee, mentioned only in the Gospel of John as the site of Jesus' wedding feast miracle (2:1–11), of the long-distance healing of the Capernaum official's son (4:46–54), and as the home of Nathanael (21:2). Latin and Orthodox churches at Kefr Kenna, about four miles northeast of Nazareth, claim to mark the spot of the wedding, but most scholars agree that the much more likely site of the ancient village is the unexcavated Khirbet Qana on a hill about nine miles north-by-northwest of Nazareth. ***See also*** Galilee; Nathanael.

Canaan (kay'nan), **Canaanites** (kay'nuh-nīts), the ancient name of a territory and its inhabitants that included parts of what is now Israel (with occupied territories) and Lebanon. The origin and etymology of the name "Canaan" remain obscure. It is presumably a Semitic term, but the effort to link Canaan with the Akkadian word *kinahhu*, referring to the redness of a wool dye, is problematic. The word "Canaanite" occurs already in third millennium B.C. texts from Ebla.

Sphere of Influence: In proper usage, the term "Canaan" seems to have referred to a discrete region whose precise boundaries cannot at present be determined. At Ugarit on the Syrian coast of the Mediterranean Sea, Canaan was regarded as a region lying to the south. Late Bronze Age letters from the Amarna archives often refer to Canaan and sometimes give the impression of a discriminating use of the term. Rib-Addi, a king of Byblos, situated Byblos in Canaan. The affairs of Sidon and Hazor were reckoned Canaanite matters. At other times, however, Amarna letters use the word "Canaan" broadly, and so a letter from Tyre implies that Ugarit was a Canaanite city, contradicting the native view at Ugarit itself. Uses of the word "Canaan" in the Bible reflect both the precision and the looseness of the term. The Genesis "Table of Nations" sets the boundaries of Canaan as follows: from Sidon to Gerar near Gaza, and eastward as far as Sodom, Gomorrah, Admah, and Zeboiim to Lasha (Gen. 10:19). The Bible elsewhere speaks of Canaan with a less precise referent in view.

The distinctiveness of the term "Canaan" has been blurred in modern writings. "Canaanite" now serves as an adjective for any aspect of the pre-Israelite, Semitic culture of the Holy Land. Thus the Canaanite languages include not only the dialects of Canaan proper, but by extension all members of a family of languages closely related to Phoenician and Hebrew, a family that is sometimes said to include Ugaritic. Since Canaanite culture blended with the culture of surrounding regions, Canaanite civilization is studied not only from the records and evidence of Canaan proper, but also from the (more abundant) evidence of the larger Syro-Palestinian world.

Society and Religion: Before the emergence of Israel (late thirteenth century B.C.), Canaan was organized politically into small principalities centered around the major towns of Palestine. The Amarna correspondence between Egyptian pharaohs and the kings of Canaanite states gives a vivid picture of petty strife and political intrigue in the land. Concerted action of Canaan's rulers was rare, leaving the countryside vulnerable to Philistine invasion and permitting in the end the development of the ancient state of Israel. There are stories in the Bible about Canaanite alliances against Israel (Josh. 9:1–2; 10:1–5), but such incidents must have been exceptional. The extent of the problem of Canaanite fragmentation is suggested by the list of kings and kingdoms that fell to Joshua (Josh. 12:7–24): thirty-one rulers and principalities are accounted for in this small region.

Canaan's major towns were located for the most part in agricultural regions, especially on the fertile plains of the countryside. The Canaanites enjoyed a reputation as traders and the Phoenicians and other coastal inhabitants as seafarers. The word "Canaanite" itself came to mean "merchant" (Zech. 14:21). Nevertheless, agriculture was a vital preoccupation of Canaan.

The religious festivals of Canaan were, insofar as they are known or inferred, devoted to the concerns of the farmer and the vintager. Israel probably inherited its cycle of harvest festivals from the Canaanite population of Palestine (Exod. 23:14–17). Canaanite religion seems to have placed emphasis on fertility in the natural world. Sexuality in the cult, a feature of Canaanite religion despised by Israel, may have been linked to the task of maintaining plant and animal fecundity. The gods of the Canaanites were in various ways involved in the life cycles of nature. The powerful storm god Baal was a giver of rain. His adversary, Mot, was a god of death and sterility. The ability of gods and goddesses to mate and their whereabouts in the cosmos were tied directly to the fate of human beings and their crops and animals. Palestinian agriculture relied on rain, and so the quality of autumn and winter rains was a central religious concern of the Canaanites.

Canaanite society was stratified. We are left with the impression of a small advantaged class surrounded by a larger population subjected to various controls and under the burden of a variety of taxes and other impositions. Samuel's description of the ways of a king (1 Sam. 8:11–18) is generally taken as a good account of the pattern of Canaanite kingship, even though its inspiration was kingship in Israel.

Canaan and the Biblical Israelites: In the Bible, Canaan is the son of Ham and the grandson of Noah. He is first encountered in the story of Noah's drunkenness (Gen. 9:18–27). Here Canaan's father, Ham, incites the anger of Noah by "looking on the nakedness" of inebriate Noah, and in retribution for this impropriety, Noah curses Ham's son Canaan. Canaan is to be a slave, a curse that may reflect the fate of some elements of the Canaanite population in Israel (Judg. 1:28). Since "to look on the nakedness" of someone suggests a sexual offense, the story may express Israel's disdain for the sexual morality of the Canaanite world.

Canaan next appears in the "Table of Nations" (Gen. 10:6; 15–20) as brother of Put (Libya), Cush (Ethiopia), and Egypt. He is reckoned the father of Sidon, Heth, the Jebusites and a host of other peoples living in the land of Israel. This expresses in the form of genealogy the human geography of early Israel: the Canaanites were the recent inhabitants of much of the land that became Israel. This fact is expressed in more than one fashion in the OT. Canaan's name together with the names of certain of his "sons" can be combined in what has been called the "Deuteronomistic name formula" (Deut. 7:1) to denote the native popula-

Canaanite dignitary with arm raised in salute; bronze plaque from Hazor, fifteenth century B.C.

tion of the land. The Yahwist calls the native inhabitants of the land simply the "Canaanites" (Gen. 12:6), while the Elohist prefers the term "Amorites" (Num. 21:13).

Israel was hostile to Canaan. It loathed much that was associated with Canaanite religion and regarded Canaanite life ways as abominable. Israel's literature urges the eradication of Canaanite religion together with the Canaanite people (Deut. 20:16–18). Nevertheless, one can recognize that Israel owed much to the legacy of Canaan. Canaanite enclaves were incorporated into the population of Israel. Canaanite religious language and thought influenced the religion of Israel. These positive sides of the relationship between Israel and Canaan need to be appreciated alongside recognition of the clash between Canaanite and Israelite cultures. ***See also*** Amarna, Tell el-; Baal; Gebal; Hazor; Sidon; Sources of the Pentateuch; Tyre.

Bibliography

Gray, John. *The Legacy of Canaan.* Leiden: E. J. Brill, 1957.

R.M.G.

Cananaean (kay-nuh-nee'uhn), epithet of the disciple Simon in Mark 3:18 and Matt. 10:4, derived from Aramaic *qan'an'*, "zealous." In Luke 6:15 and Acts 1:13, he is called a Zealot, one who opposed Roman rule. ***See also*** Zealot.

Candace (kan'duh-see), the queen of the Ethiopians (Acts 8:27), mentioned because Philip baptized her treasury minister, an Ethiopian eunuch. Her name is actually a title, presumably "queen," or "queen mother," so she cannot be identified with any of the otherwise known queens of the Nubian realm of Meroe, along the upper Nile (modern Sudan). ***See also*** Philip.

candle. ***See*** Lamp.

candlestick. ***See*** Lampstand.

canon, English term derived from a Greek word meaning "rule" or "standard." Among the meanings it acquired early in Christian history was "list of religious writings deemed authoritative." When such lists first originated, they had the function of helping believers distinguish among the great variety of religious writings available and identify those titles approved within their own religious community for such purposes as reading at services of worship, exposition, or establishing moral or doctrinal norms. Only in about the fourth century A.D. were efforts made to assemble all "canonical" texts into a single volume or uniform format that one might call a "Bible."

The Hebrew Canon: Among Jews, the oldest canon appears to have been the one defining the Torah (the first five books of modern Bibles), which was not only the central document of Jewish faith but also the fundamental law of the Jewish nation. These five books reached final form and were set apart not earlier than the mid-sixth and not later than the fourth century B.C. It is the one canon upon which all Jewish groups, and also Samaritans and Christians, have usually agreed.

Alongside the Torah, most Jews of the first century A.D. appear also to have accepted a second canon of somewhat less authority, called the "Prophets." This included historical books (Joshua through 2 Kings, but not Ruth), as well as the more strictly prophetic books of Isaiah, Jeremiah, Ezekiel, and the Twelve Prophets (Hosea through Malachi in the Protestant order). The remaining titles of the Hebrew Bible —the total list corresponding to the canon of the Protestant OT—are known as the "Writings" (Ruth, Esther through Song of Solomon).

The canon of Prophets may be almost as old as that of Torah, but neither it nor the Writings was accepted by Samaritans or, perhaps, by Sadducees. The canon of Writings probably reached final form only after the first Jewish war against Rome (A.D. 66–70), under the leadership of the rabbinic courts at Jabneh (Jamnia). In the Dead Sea Scrolls, which were hidden away during that war, a wide variety of writings is found, with no obvious canonical distinctions among them.

The Hebrew canon was developed among Jews who spoke Hebrew or Aramaic. Many Jews of late antiquity, however, spoke only Greek. As early as the third century B.C., Greek versions of the Hebrew books were being made for their use. Some of these Greek books have rather different forms from those they took in the Hebrew canon (e.g., Jeremiah and Daniel); others were ultimately excluded from the Hebrew canon (e.g., Ecclesiasticus). There were also original works written in Greek, such as the Wisdom of Solomon, which came to be canonical only in the Greek language realm. The result was a larger, but somewhat ill-defined, canon of writings revered among Greek-speaking Jews.

The early Christian church achieved its greatest successes in the Greek-speaking world and inherited these Greek-language scriptures (often called, collectively, the Septuagint). Christians never fully agreed, however, on the exact boundaries of the canon. Eastern and Western churches used somewhat different lists. St. Jerome (d. A.D. 420) attempted to introduce the Hebrew canon into the West through his Latin translation, the Vulgate, but failed to win assent. The Ethiopian Church continued to revere books such as *1 Enoch* that disappeared elsewhere. During the Reformation, Protestants on the European continent used the Hebrew canon to define their OT, while Anglicans granted a "deutero" or secondary canonical status to books not found in the Hebrew canon but long accepted among Western Christians (the so-called OT Apocrypha).

The Christian Canon: While the church of the first century A.D. accepted the existing Jewish scriptures in varying forms, it had, at first, no distinctively Christian canon. In the second century, however, it began to set apart specifically Christian writings and treat them as equal to the older scriptures (for example, by reading from them in worship). The process of making a NT canon (and thus of identifying the Jewish scriptures as an "Old" Testament) was not clearly defined in advance, and the results were consolidated only gradually.

In the early second century, the "heretic" Marcion created a canon consisting solely of edited versions of Luke and of some of Paul's Letters; he rejected the OT entirely. The first such canons or collections among the "orthodox" were probably those of the four Gospels and ten Letters of Paul (not including 1 and 2 Timothy and Titus). They date from about the time of Marcion, and scholars debate whether the "orthodox" NT canon was more a reaction to Marcion or an independent development. Not until A.D. 367 does one encounter a canon identical to the modern one (in a "Festal Letter" of Bishop Athanasius), and even thereafter the status of several books (e.g., Hebrews, Revelation, and *1 Clement*) continued uncertain for some time. To the present day, there is no universal agreement on the boundary of the Christian canon of Scripture; the Apocrypha which Roman Catholics include is excluded by Protestants from their canon. ***See also*** Apocrypha, Old Testament; Bible; Hagiographa; Pentateuch; Sadducees; Septuagint; Texts, Versions, Manuscripts, Editions; Torah; Vulgate. L.W.C.

canonical criticism. ***See*** Biblical Criticism; Canon.

Canticles. ***See*** Song of Solomon, The.

Capernaum (cah-puhr'nay-uhm; from the Heb. for "village of Nahum"), a town on the northwest shore of the Sea of Galilee, about two and one-half miles from the mouth of the Jordan River. Capernaum was the center of Jesus' Galilean ministry (Matt. 4:13). Here he healed the centurion's son (Matt. 8:5–13; Luke 7:1–10; cf. John 4:46–54) and engaged in other healing, teaching, and exorcising (Matt. 17:24; Mark 2:1; Luke 4:23, 31; John 2:12; 6:17, 24). In particular, Jesus was active in the synagogue (Mark 1:21; John 6:59) and in "the house" (Peter's?; Matt. 8: 14–17; Mark 1:29–34; 9:33). In spite of all his work there, however, Jesus apparently felt rejected by the people of Capernaum and cursed the town (Matt.11:23–24; Luke 10:15). Outside the Gospels, Capernaum is mentioned by the historian Josephus and by Talmudic sources, as well as in pilgrim accounts from the Byzantine period.

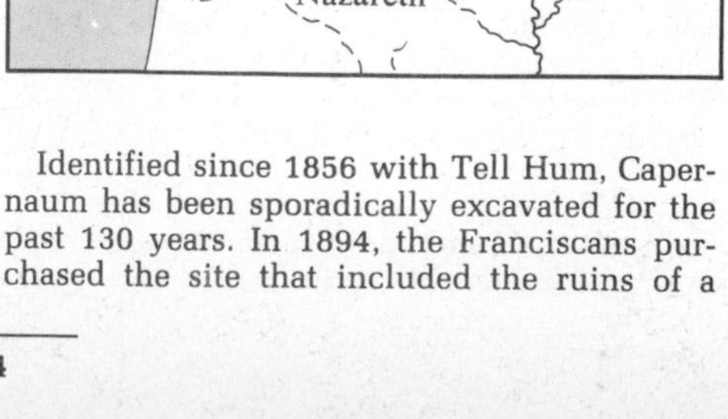

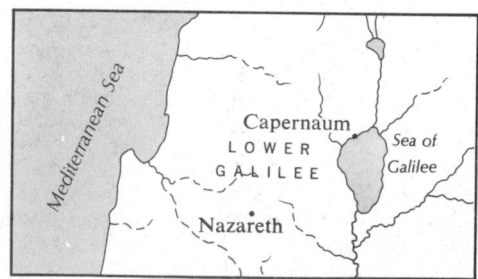

Identified since 1856 with Tell Hum, Capernaum has been sporadically excavated for the past 130 years. In 1894, the Franciscans purchased the site that included the ruins of a white limestone building already identified in 1838 as a synagogue. First excavated by a German team in 1905, the synagogue continued to be the object of work by the Franciscans into the 1920s and again in the 1950s, 1960s, and 1980s. Opinion concerning the dating of this synagogue varies from the late second century to the fifth century A.D., but the 1981 excavations have confirmed the ruins of a basalt first-century synagogue, possibly the very synagogue in which Jesus preached, immediately beneath the limestone one.

A few yards to the south are the remains of a triple octagonal fifth-century church, constructed over a fourth-century "house-church," itself incorporating and preserving the remains of a first-century home similar to the many surrounding houses of the same period. The Franciscans identify this structure as "Peter's House" on the basis of inscriptions and of early pilgrim accounts.

Other recent excavations to the east of the Franciscan site have uncovered late Byzantine and early Arab dwellings of the seventh and eighth centuries. This was apparently a time of prosperity for Capernaum, as witnessed by a hoard of 282 gold Umayyad dinars (about $250,000) found under a courtyard pavement in 1982. ***See also*** Peter; Synagogue. C.H.M.

Caph (kaf) or kaph, the eleventh letter in the Hebrew alphabet. ***See also*** Writing.

Caphtor (kaf'tohr), a place referred to by Amos (9:7) as the home of the Philistines who are called the "remnant of the coastland of Caphtor" (Jer. 47:4) and "the Caphtorim" (Deut. 2:23). Scholars have offered various suggestions for its location. The most widely accepted is the Aegean island of Crete; some Philistine names suggest an origin in the Aegean basin. Other scholars see a connection between Caphtor and Kafto, an Egyptian designation for the southern coast of Asia Minor and propose Cilicia on the southeast coast as the location. The Septuagint translates Caphtor as Cappadocia, a region in Asia Minor, although this probably is not correct. ***See also*** Caphtorim; Philistines. D.R.B.

Caphtorim (kaf'tuh-rim), the designation of a group of people described in the Table of Nations (Gen. 10:14; 1 Chron. 1:12) as the "sons of Mizraim [Egypt]" and connected with the descendants of Ham, although this list is more a record of political and historical relationships than a genealogical list. They are elsewhere identified with the Philistines who inhabited the southern coastland of Canaan north of Egypt (Deut. 3:23; Amos 9:7). ***See also*** Caphtor; Philistines.

Cappadocia (kap-uh-doh'shee-uh), an isolated interior region of eastern Asia Minor lying

north of the Taurus Mountains, east of Lake Tatta, south of Pontus, and west of the Euphrates River. Although possessing some urban centers —Mazaca/Caesarea and Tyana were the most important—much of Cappadocia remained rural and was divided as early as Hittite times into immense royal and temple estates. After 585 B.C. Cappadocia came under Persian rule, then passed to Seleucid control, and then after ca. 255 B.C. was ruled by its own kings. Roman influence in Cappadocian affairs became strong during the late second and first centuries B.C., and Tiberius finally made Cappadocia a Roman province in A.D. 17. A Jewish community may have existed in Cappadocia as early as the second century B.C. (see 1 Macc. 15:22; Acts 2:9 offers somewhat later evidence). Among those who received 1 Peter were Christians in Cappadocia (1 Pet. 1:1). References in the LXX to Cappadocia represent a mistranslation of the name "Caphtor" (Deut. 2:23; Amos 9:7). ***See also*** Asia; Peter, The First Letter of; Persia; Pontus; Seleucids, The; Tiberius. R.A.W.

captain, a leader, usually of a military detachment. Several different Hebrew and Greek words can be translated as "captain," "officer," "ruler," or "leader." Such persons could be in charge of specified groups ranging from tens to thousands (Exod. 18:21) and their duties included military authority, civil administration, and judicial responsibilities. The NT contains several references to such officers (Mark 6:21; Luke 22:4; Acts 4:1; 5:26; 27:11), some of whom may have had military or police duties and some of whom may have been Levites. Jesus is termed in early preaching a "leader" (Gk. *archēgon*) unto salvation (Acts 3:15, RSV: "author"; 5:31; Heb. 2:10; 12:2, RSV: "pioneer").

Captivity. ***See*** Exile.

caravan, a mixed company of travelers, usually fairly large for the purpose of safety, that included merchants and their pack animals who regularly traversed the trade routes to oversee the transport of their goods. The pack animals were usually the ass and, less commonly, the camel, after the latter was domesticated ca. 1100 B.C. Accordingly, before the camel came into common use the range and movement of caravans was limited. The earliest biblical reference to domesticated camels, which were probably used in caravan trade in the Transjordan, is to the camels of the Midianites in Judg. 6:5. Camels are also mentioned in connection with the spice and incense caravan traffic with Arabia (1 Kings 10:2; Isa. 60:6). Other biblical references to caravans includes a caravan of Ishmaelites in Gen. 37:25 (KJV: "company"); the endangered caravan traffic due to the unstable political conditions in the period of the judges in Judg. 5:6a (KJV: "highways"); the caravan trade in Edom in Job 6:18 (KJV: "paths"; 6:19, KJV: "troops"); and the caravans of Dedanites in Arabia in Isa. 21:13 (KJV: "traveling companies"). As these references suggest, there was both internal caravan trade and the more significant caravan activity with the Transjordan and Arabia. Caravan cities, including caravansaries, developed along the principal routes to provide support for the caravan trade. ***See also*** Ass; Camel; Trade and Transportation. F.S.F.

Carchemish (kahr'kuh-mish), a city on the Euphrates River in northern Syria, about sixty miles northeast of Aleppo. It appears in the Akkadian sources of the eighteenth century B.C. as an ally of Shamshi-adad I against Yahdun-lim of Mari. Carchemish also participated in the struggle against the Hittite king Hattushili I.

Carchemish allied itself with the Hittites in the battle against Egypt at Kadesh, 1286 B.C. Although reduced in size and power by the Sea Peoples at the end of the thirteenth century B.C., Carchemish reemerged in the first millennium B.C. as a center of Neo-Hittite culture. Mesopotamian interest in Carchemish culminated in the transformation of the city into an Assyrian province under Sargon II (Isa. 10: 9).

In the sixteenth century B.C., Egypt extended its influence into southwestern Asia. Pharaoh Ahmosis (ca. 1565) claimed to have reached the city of Carchemish, and Pharaoh Thutmose III to have conquered it. In the first millennium B.C., Pharaoh Neco encountered Josiah at Carchemish before the two engaged in battle on the plain of Megiddo (2 Chron. 35:20, 22). Carchemish figured in the struggle between Egypt and Babylonia for hegemony over Syria. In 605 B.C., Nebuchadnezzar defeated Egypt there and Babylonia assumed control of the region (Jer. 46:2). This event was a turning point in the prophecies of Jeremiah (see Jer. 25:1–13a). L.E.P.

Carmel (kahr'muhl; Heb., "garden," "orchard"). **1** A range of fertile, forested hills (Amos 1:2; Isa. 33:9; Nah. 1:4) about fifteen miles long on the west border of the land allotted to the tribe of Asher (Josh. 19:26). It extends from the Samaritan hill country west to the Mediterranean and south to the Mount Carmel headland. Mount Carmel, which is the entrance of the Jezreel Valley (Esdraelon), commands an excellent view of the shoreline and rises 556 feet above the harbor of modern Haifa. Because of its height it provided an important strategic position for the control of the fertile valley land. Mt. Carmel was the scene of the contest between Elijah and the four hundred and fifty prophets of Baal and the four hundred prophets of Asherah (1 Kings 18:19). However, the most important archaeological find in the area is prehistoric. The famous Carmel caves are from this region, along modern Wadi el-Mugharah overlooking the Plain of Sharon.

2 An ancient city identified as modern Khirbet el-Kirmel (or Kermel) eight miles southeast of Hebron. The city was allotted to the tribe of Judah (Josh. 15:55). It was here that Saul commemorated his victory over the Amalekites by erecting a monument (1 Sam. 15:12). Also, near Carmel the events told in the story of Abigail, David, and Nabal took place. In this story the prosperous but ill-mannered Nabal insulted David, and David's wrath was averted only by the intercession of Abigail on Nabal's behalf. However, God struck Nabal down and Abigail was then free to marry David who acquired by that marriage Nabal's wealth, power and prestige (1 Sam. 25). ***See also*** Mughara, Wadi el-. S.B.R.

carpenter, an artisan skilled in working with wood. The Israelites were apparently lacking great skills in this area in the time of David and Solomon (ca. 1050–975 B.C.), since carpenters had to be imported from Tyre to aid the construction of David's palace (2 Sam. 5:11) and Solomon's Temple (1 Kings 5:6). Among the returnees from the Exile in the sixth century B.C., however, there were native craftsmen able to aid in the restoration of Jerusalem and the Temple (Jer. 24:1; 29:2). A description of a carpenter's tools and procedures is given in Isaiah's account of the manufacture of an idol (Isa. 44: 13–17): a "line" for measuring, a pencil for marking, planes for shaping, and a compass for designing. The carpenter there described also plants, tends, and cuts down the trees with which he works.

In the Gospels, Jesus is reported to be a carpenter (Mark 6:3) or the son of one (Matt. 13: 55), indicating his common birth, since learned men did not pursue that profession. A tradition from the mid-second century A.D. says Jesus made yokes and ploughs, and some legendary stories of the young Jesus picture him helping his father build a house and fashion a bed, but they are of doubtful historical value. While the Greek word usually rendered "carpenter" can also mean "craftsman" or "builder," there is no clue in the Gospels as to how the term is to be understood other than as one who worked with wood for a living. R.S.B.

Carpus (cahr'puhs), person in Troas with whom Paul left his cloak and other items. Timothy is asked to fetch them in 2 Tim. 4:13.

carriage, a term that in the KJV translates several terms that refer to baggage or burdens, not to a vehicle of transport (Judg. 18:21, RSV: "goods"; 1 Sam. 17:22, RSV: "things" and "baggage"; Isa. 10:28, RSV: "baggage"; Isa. 46:1, RSV: "things you carry"; Acts 21:5, RSV: "made ready," where the reference is to preparing the necessary baggage for a journey).

cart, or wagon, a term denoting either a two- or four-wheeled vehicle drawn by oxen or other animals (rarely horses). It was used for transporting people and things. The particular meaning of "cart" is derived from the biblical context. The function of a cart was different from that of the chariot, however. In Gen. 45:19, 21, 27; 46:5; Num. 7:3–8 (RSV: "wagon"); and Jth. 15:11 no special function is indicated. In 1 Sam. 6:7–14; 2 Sam. 6:3; and 1 Chron. 13:7 a cart that had not been used for "secular" purposes and cows that had never been under a yoke are used to transport the Ark of the Covenant into Jerusalem. Several passages (Isa. 28:27, 28; Amos 2:13) refer to the cart in its agricultural uses. ***See also*** Carriage; Chariots. F.S.F.

cassia *(Cinnamomum cassia)*, a tree native to India and the Far East, whose bark is easily peeled into long hollow rolls. The bark, buds, leaves, and twigs of the cassia tree, having a cinnamon smell, were imported for use in making spices, perfumes, and oils (Ezek. 27:19; Exod. 30:24; Ps. 45:8). The leaves and pods also have medicinal properties. ***See also*** Spices.

castle. ***See*** Architecture.

Castor and Pollux. ***See*** Twin Brothers, The.

caterpillar (KJV; RSV: "destroying locust" [Joel 1:4] and "destroyer" [Joel 2:25]), the worm-shaped larva of a moth, butterfly, or other insect, considered destructive because of its voracious appetite for growing plants. It is viewed as one of the forms of punishment or judgment God uses (1 Kings 8:37; 2 Chron. 6:28; Ps. 78:46; Isa. 33:4).

catholic Epistles. ***See*** General Letters.

cattle, a generic term for ruminant animals. There is a generic term for domesticated cattle in the OT (Heb. *baqar*), but a variety of terms are used in the Bible to describe the different types of cattle. Domesticated cattle were used by the Hebrews in many ways: as a food source (in 1 Kings 4:23 Solomon's daily household ration included thirty cattle and oxen), as sacrificial offerings (Solomon offered twenty-two thousand oxen in 1 Kings 8:63), to pull carts (Num. 7:3), as pack animals (1 Chron. 12:40), for threshing (Deut. 25:4) and, together with sheep and goats, for milk products and dung. The wild ancestor of domesticated cattle, the aurochs (Heb. *re'em)*, was extant in Palestine until the Bronze Age (2000–1500 B.C.). I.U.K.

Cauda (kou'duh; KJV: "Clauda"), a small island (modern Gavdos) southwest of Crete, by which Paul sailed toward Malta, en route to Rome (Acts 27:16).

caulkers (KJV: "calkers"), men from Byblos (Gebal, Ezek. 27:9) or Tyre (Ezek. 27:27) whose work was making ships watertight. Materials used may have been bitumen and some fiber binder to plug seams between planks.

cave, a natural opening in a hillside. There are two Hebrew terms designating a cave *(meā'rāh* and *ḥôr);* the latter term literally means "hole" but is also translated "cavern."

Natural caves are abundant in Syro-Palestine due to the presence of chalk, limestone, and sandstone formations in the hills and moun-

Cassia.

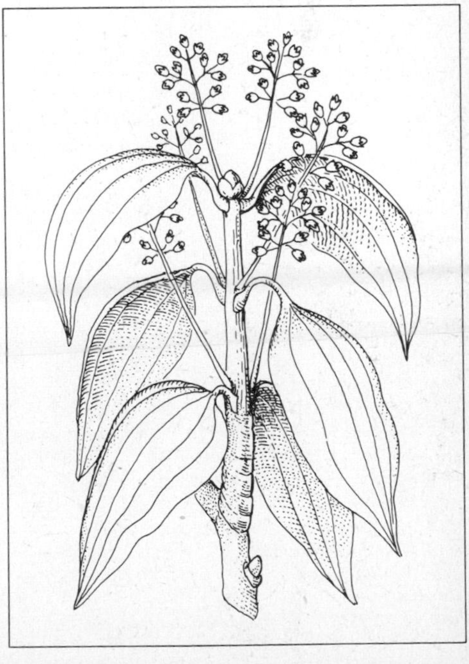

tains. Because of the soft qualities of these materials, man-made tombs and caves are also abundant.

Not only are the caves in this region abundant, but they are frequently massive in size. One cave complex near Damascus in modern Syria was capable of holding four thousand men, according to Strabo, a Greek geographer who wrote in the late first century B.C. That complex of caves is still visible today. Palestine also had large caves as indicated by the fact that David could conceal four hundred men in the cave of Adullam (1 Sam. 22:1–2).

A number of caves are mentioned in Scripture and some are given specific names, further attesting to their importance. The first cave mentioned is the one to which Lot and his daughters fled after the destruction of Sodom and Gomorrah (Gen. 19:30). Abraham purchased the cave of Machpelah from the Hittites who were living in the region of Hebron (Gen. 23:1–20). Another cave mentioned by name is the cave at Makkedah to which the defeated kings of the Amorites fled after the battle of Beth-horon (Josh. 10:16–27).

The cave of Adullam, located in the region of Bethlehem, enabled David and his men to escape from King Saul (1 Sam. 22:1–2). En-gedi was the place to which David fled with his men from Saul and they were able to utilize there a large cave for protection (1 Sam. 23:29; 24:3). It was there that David also cut off part of Saul's garment (1 Sam. 24:4).

Caves were utilized in a variety of ways by the inhabitants of Syro-Palestine. Archaeological discoveries indicate that one of the earliest and most common uses was as a domestic dwelling. Lot and his daughters utilized a cave for that purpose (Gen. 19:30; see also Num. 24:21; Song of Sol. 2:14; Jer. 49:16; Obad. 3). During times of political unrest or warfare, caves were frequently sought out as a place of refuge (Judg. 6:2; 1 Sam. 13:6; 22:1). The tradition that Jesus was born in a cave is of post-NT origin.

Archaeological and biblical data also point to the widespread use of caves as tombs. Abraham bought a cave for that purpose (Gen. 23:17–18; 49:29) and Lazarus was buried in a cave (John 11:38).

Numerous caves were employed for the purpose of worship. During the Roman persecution of Christians in the first century A.D. and following, many utilized the protection of the cave to worship their God.

Excavations in the caves at Wadi en-Natuf (northwest of Jerusalem), Mugharet ez-Zuttiyeh (northwest of the Sea of Galilee), Wadi Khareitun (east of Bethlehem) and Wadi el-Mugharah (in the Carmel mountain range) have provided important information on the prehistoric cultures of Palestine.

During the second Jewish revolt under Bar-Kokhba, hundreds fled to the caves west of the Dead Sea and their remains have been discovered by explorations in Wadi Muraba'at. The approach of the Roman army in the first century A.D. caused the Essenes at Qumran to hide their valuable manuscripts in caves, and since 1947 these have been coming to light through excavation and trade. J.J.D.

Caves located in the area of Tel Halif (biblical Rimmon?) were probably created in the third millennium B.C.

cedar *(Cedrus libani*; Heb. *'ereṣ*), a tree mentioned frequently in the Bible. It is a magnificent deep-rooted coniferous tree of the Holy Land, especially Lebanon, where its distinctive pyramidal image adorns the modern flag of that country. The cedar lives to a great age, as many as two thousand years, therefore attaining great heights and diameters. Consequently, it is often referred to as a symbol of strength and power (Ezek. 31; Ps. 92:12). Its fragrant, gum-exuding wood is red in color and is especially durable and resistant to insects and decay. These properties made it a popular choice for the construction of items such as musical instruments, chests, and various household furnishings. Cedar was also preferred for the construction of buildings, as attested by the numerous references in the book of Kings (1 Kings 6, 7). Its superlative qualities made it an important trade item in antiquity. Solomon's Temple and palace in Jerusalem had timbers and panels of cedar sent by the king of Tyre (1 Kings 5:6–10; 9:11; 2 Chron. 2:3). The Egyptians are said to have imported the cedars of Lebanon for the tall straight masts of their ships and for the durable coffins of their dead. The great demand for and the subsequent overuse of cedar in both ancient and recent times has severely depleted this important resource. Consequently, programs for replanting are currently underway in suitable areas of the Levant. ***See also*** Forest; Woods.

P.L.C.

Cenchreae (sen'kree-uh), a harbor seven miles east of Corinth on the Saronic Gulf, used for trade with Asia. Here, prior to sailing to Ephesus during his second journey, Paul shaved his head (Acts 18:18–20). Cenchreae was the home of Phoebe (Rom. 16:1). ***See also*** Phoebe.

censer, a small hand-sized vessel containing hot coals on which incense was sprinkled. Brass censers (RSV: "firepans") were used in the tabernacle (Exod. 27:3) and in the First Temple (1 Kings 7:50), while gold censers were among the Temple vessels carried off to Babylon when Nebuchadnezzar overthrew Israel, burned the Temple, and carried the people into exile in Babylon (2 Kings 25:15). Several censers have been excavated, suggesting that incense offerings played an important role in popular religion (cf. Ezek. 8:11).

census. ***See*** Enrollment.

centurion, the commander of a hundred men in a Roman legion. The centurion held a position similar to that of a company commander. There were grades among the sixty centurions serving in a legion, with the highest ranking centurion achieving a position similar to that of a "knight" (Lat. *equites)* among the Roman nobility. Such men were prestigious members of a relatively small class governing the military. They received substantial pensions upon retirement and would easily count among the local notables of a town (cf. Luke 7:2; Acts 10:1). A centurion supervised the soldiers who crucified Jesus (Mark 15:19).

Cephas (see'fuhs; from Aramaic *kay fah*, "rock" or "crag"), a surname equivalent to the Greek name "Peter" (John 1:42; cf. Matt. 16:17–18). ***See also*** Peter.

chaff, the covering of the grain removed during the process of winnowing. Nearly all references in the Hebrew Bible are to chaff blown in the wind (Job 13:25; 21:18; Pss. 1:4; 35:5; 83:13; Isa. 17:13; 29:5; 33:11; 41:15; Jer. 13:24; Dan. 2:35; Hos. 13:3; Zeph. 2:2). In the NT it is what is burned as worthless "with unquenchable fire" after the one who baptizes with the Holy Spirit has gathered the wheat into the granary (Matt. 3: 12; Luke 3:17).

chains, metal rings connected in series. Made of various metals both base and precious, they were used in ancient Israel for decorative purposes, as jewelry (e.g. Ezek. 16:11), for architectural ornamentation (1 Kings 7:17), and in assembling the priestly vestments (e.g., Exod. 28:14). Chains were not used to bind prisoners, though they were occasionally used as leashes, as depicted in the Black Obelisk of Shalmaneser III. Later, chains were used to bind people (cf. Mark 5:3–4), replacing the fetters and ropes typically used earlier.

chalcedony (kal-sed'uh-nee; KJV; RSV: "agate"), third of the precious stones in Rev. 21: 19. Pliny *(Natural History* 37, 7, 92ff) designates a kind of jasper and a kind of emerald "Chalcedonian." Which gem Revelation refers to is uncertain.

Chalcolithic (kal'koh-lith'ik) **Age.** ***See*** Copper.

Chaldea (kal-dee'uh), a region at the head of the Persian Gulf, home to a loose confederation of Semitic- (possibly Aramaic-) speaking peoples, organized along tribal lines. It includes the birthplace and ancestral home of Abraham (Gen. 11:28, 31; 15:7). The Aramaic sections of the book of Daniel (2:5, 10; 4:4; 5:7, 11) include Chaldeans among the learned magicians and conjurers. Detailed astronomical cuneiform records provide information valuable for reconstructing historical events and confirm the Chaldeans' reputation as astrologers and astronomers. Merodach-baladan and Nebuchadnezzar, prominent Chaldean kings, figure in biblical accounts (especially in 2 Kings and Jer.) which reflect the political prowess of this last native Mesopotamian dynasty, which ruled during the time known as the Neo-Babylonian

period. Chaldea joined with Median forces to conquer Assur in 614 B.C. Heavy political unrest characterized the internal affairs of this dynasty.
L.E.P.

chapman (KJV; RSV: "traders" [2 Chron. 9:14]), an archaic term for merchant.

charge. ***See*** Superscription.

charger, term used in the KJV for a shallow platter (RSV: "plate," "platter," or "basin"). It is not a common domestic utensil, but rather a vessel used in cultic rituals (Num. 7:13–85; Ezra 1:9; Exod. 25:29). The head of John the Baptist was carried on such a vessel (Matt. 14:8, 11).

chariots, vehicles of various types with two wheels (commonly of four, six, or eight spokes) normally drawn by two horses. Horse-drawn chariots were introduced into Canaan by the Hyksos (ca. 1800–1600 B.C.), who were major innovators in the development of instruments of warfare. Chariots in Egypt and early Assyria were characteristically manned by two men, a driver (1 Kings 22:34; 2 Chron. 18:33; Jer. 51:21), who did not carry a weapon, and an archer. The Hittites, and later the Assyrians and Syrians, introduced a third man, a shield bearer, into the chariot. The three-man chariot seems to have been used by the Hebrews since the military specialist (RSV: "officer"; Heb. *shalish*, "third man") was probably the third man in the chariot (Exod. 14:7; 15:4; 1 Kings 9:22; 2 Kings 9:21–25).

Assyrian war chariot with armed charioteers; detail from the bas-reliefs at the palace of Ashurbanipal at Nineveh, seventh century B.C.

The principal use of the chariot was a military one, especially for rapid flanking movements in open country. As military equipment the chariot was used by the Canaanites against the Israelites (Josh. 17:16; Judg. 1:19, where "chariots of iron" probably refers to metal [bronze?] plates that were used to reinforce the wood chariot bodies; Judg. 4:3, 13; Josh. 11:4–9). Similarly, the Philistines employed chariots against the Israelites in the time of Samuel and Saul (1 Sam. 13:5). Since chariots were of limited use in the central highlands, the principal area of early Israelite settlement, they were not used by the Israelites until the time of David (eleventh century B.C.) in his successful campaigns against the Philistines (2 Sam. 8:4; 1 Chron. 18:4). The chariot became a highly developed regular part of the military equipment of the state under Solomon (1 Kings 10:26), under whom there was considerable building activity and trade in connection with horses and chariots (1 Kings 4:26; 9:19; 10:29).

In addition to their use in warfare, chariots were a symbol of power as the vehicle of kings and their court (Gen. 41:43; 2 Sam. 15:1; 1 Kings 1:5). The chariot of the Ethiopian whom Philip addressed (Acts 8:26–38) was a sign of his rank as Queen's minister. ***See also*** Horse; War.
F.S.F.

charismatic. ***See*** Spiritual Gifts.

charity, the term used in the KJV to translate one of the NT words for "love" (Gk. *agape*) in 26 of its 116 occurrences. Charity (from Lat. *caritas*, "costliness, esteem, affection") has acquired connotations that make it unsuitable for modern readers as the bearer of the biblical writers' meaning. Nevertheless, modern connotations of the word do coincide with the biblical ideal of caring for the neediest members of the covenant community of Israel (Deut. 15:7–9; 24:19–22; Job 31:16–23; Ps. 82:2–4; Prov. 14:21, 31; Isa. 1:16–17) and the Christian church (Matt. 25:31–46; James 1:27). ***See also*** Love.

Chebar (ke'bahr), a water course in Babylonia. The Chebar canal was the scene of Ezekiel's vision and of a Jewish settlement in sixth century B.C. Babylonia (Ezek. 1:13; 3:15, 23; 10:15, 20, 22; 43:3). The Jewish settlement of Tel Aviv (Akkadian *til abubi*) was located on this canal (Ezek. 3:15), an important irrigation channel near the city of Nippur. ***See also*** Ezekiel, The Book of.

Chedorlaomer (ked'uhr-lay-oh'muhr), "king of Elam" and one of four kings from the East who joined forces to attack five kings in the Dead Sea Valley, according to Genesis 14. The five kings were conquered and remained subject to Chedorlaomer for twelve years. In the thirteenth they rebelled. In the fourteenth Chedorlaomer and his allies marched against them, conquering widely in Canaan, and finally routing the rebels. He plundered Sodom and Gomorrah and took Lot captive. Abraham gave chase, attacked, and retrieved all the booty and captives. The name "Chedorlaomer" reflects authentic elements of Elamite personal names—*kuter* or *kutir*, as in the royal names Kutir/Kuternakkhunte, and *Lagamar*, the name of a deity—but neither the specific name nor the general events are attested or alluded to elsewhere. S.B.P.

Chemosh (kee'mohsh), the national god of Moab. Although he was worshiped at Ugarit and perhaps also at Ebla, little is known about this god before the first millennium B.C. Biblical evidence is scanty: the Moabites were "the people of Chemosh" (Num. 21:29; Jer. 48:46; cf. also Jer. 48:7), and Solomon built a high place for Chemosh "the abomination of Moab" (1 Kings 11:7; cf. 11:33), which Josiah destroyed (2 Kings 23: 13). In Judg. 11:24 he seems to have been the chief Ammonite deity, although this may be an error. More information is found in the victory stele of Mesha, the king of Moab (ca. 840 B.C.). Its language indicates that the Moabite theology of Chemosh was close to that of Yahweh in Israel. ***See also*** Mesha; Moab. M.D.C.

Chenoboskion (ken'aw-bahs'kee-uhn). ***See*** Nag Hammadi.

Cherethites (ker'uh-thīts), a people, probably Cretans, who lived in the area to the southeast of Philistia ("the Negeb of the Cherethites," 1 Sam. 30:14). As mercenaries, they constituted a section of David's personal army under the leadership of Benaiah, son of Jehoiada (2 Sam. 8:18; 20:23).

Cherith (kay'rith), a brook or *wadi* (i.e., river bed with water only in the rainy season) east of the Jordan, near Jericho. It could be a wadi that empties into the Jabesh River. On the basis of the exploration of Transjordan, the archaeologist Nelson Glueck argued that present day Wadi Qelt (which runs down to Jericho) appears to be the best candidate. However, no firm designation can as yet be made. We are told that Elijah sought refuge there (1 Kings 17:3, 5) from Ahab and Jezebel. On the basis of that story some have identified Cherith as Yabis, which empties into the Jordan approximately five miles south of Pella. S.B.R.

cherub (chair'uhb; pl. cherubim [chair'yo͞o-bim]), a Hebrew term denoting an unnatural, composite being associated with sacral contexts in the Bible. Although cherubim are mentioned 92 times (91 in the OT, and in Heb. 9:5), no single type of creature is referred to in all cases. Rather the term represents a variety of fanciful beings. The only feature found in many of the biblical usages (particularly in connection with the Arks of the tabernacle and of the Solomonic Temple and also with the visions of Ezekiel 1 and 10) and not contradicted by other usages is that the cherubim were winged. Otherwise, specific details are either absent or contradictory. For example, the Ark cherubim apparently have a single face, whereas the Ezekiel Temple cherubim have two faces and the Ezekiel vision cherubim have four. The character of the faces ranges from human through bovine, leonine, and aquiline; and the body is sometimes biped and in other instances quadruped. Such variations confirm the underlying principle that the cherub was a hybrid, and hence unnatural, creature.

As unnatural beings, cherubim are always connected with the deity. They appear in direct association with a mobile God, as his steed (e.g., 2 Sam. 22:1; Ps. 18:11) or parts of his chariot, or as components of his throne (the Ark passages). They are indirectly associated with God when they are guardian figures (as in Gen. 3:24; Ezek. 28:14, 16) amidst sacred vegetation. As both actual beasts and plastic representations of such beasts, the biblical cherubim share in the contemporary iconographic repertoire of composite beasts well known from ancient Near Eastern art. The biblical cherub is thus totally different from the chubby children often depicted in religious art in the West. ***See also*** Ark; Tabernacle; Temple, The. C.L.M.

chest. 1 A large container, usually square with a hinged lid. King Jehoash (Joash; 837–800 B.C.) circumvented prior priestly laggardliness in repairing the Temple by commanding the priest Jehoida to build a chest into which worshipers would directly deposit religious donations and from which professional craftsmen would be paid (2 Kings 12:10–11; 2 Chron. 24:8–11). **2** The KJV translation of a rare word that RSV renders as "carpets" (Ezek. 27:24), contextually, a precious commodity brought to Tyre by traders.

cheth (kheth), the eighth letter in the Hebrew alphabet. The letter is placed by the KJV as a heading to the eighth section of the acrostic Psalm 119, vv. 57–64. Each of those verses begins with this consonant.

child, children, offspring, which were highly valued by Israelites as gracious gifts of God (Pss. 113:9; 127:3; 128:5–6). Having large numbers of children was considered a divine blessing (Gen. 24:60; Ruth 4:11–12), and the multiplication of descendants was part of God's promise to Israel's ancestors (Gen. 12:2; 15:5; 16:10; 17:2; 22: 17; 26:4). Barrenness was considered at best a vexation (Gen. 16:2; 30:2; 1 Sam. 1:3–8) and at worst a divine punishment (Gen. 20:18). Children often received symbolic names (Gen. 4:1; 25:25–26; 29:32, 35; 30:6, 8, 11, 13, 18, 24; 41: 51–52; Isa. 8:3; Hos. 1:2–9) and were educated by their parents, particularly in Israel's faith (Prov. 1:8; 6:20; Exod. 12:26–27; Deut. 4:9; 6:7, 20–25; 32:46). Children received an inheritance from their parents, with the eldest son receiving a double portion (Num. 36; Deut. 21:15–17). Firstborn sons were thought to belong to God but were to be redeemed (Exod. 13:11–15; 22:29; 34:20; Num. 18:15). However, the privileges of firstborn children did not extend into the religious sphere, and the OT contains many stories of God's blessing going to a younger child (Gen. 28:13–14; cf. Gen. 27:1–40; 47:8–20; 49:1–27).

Because Israel organized its society on the model of a family, members of the covenant community sometimes described themselves as children of their ancestor Jacob/Israel (Isa. 17:3, 9; 29:22–23; Ezek. 37:16). From their ancestor the children inherited both the blessings and obligations of the covenant.

This practice is also found in the NT, where church members are seen as children of the same mother or father (2 John 1, 4, 13). Christians were sometimes addressed as children by church authorities, a practice the church traced to Jesus (Gal. 4:19; 2 Tim. 1:2; Philem. 10; 1 John 2:1, 12, 18, 28; Matt. 9:2; Mark 2:5; 10:24; John 13:33). ***See also*** Ancestor; Family, The. R.R.W.

children of God, a term used by early Christians to mark their special relationship as "adopted" heirs of the promises made by God to Israel (Rom. 8:16–17, 21; Phil. 2:15; John 1:12; and ironically in John 11:52). It may have been the common designation for Christians in the Johannine community (1 John 3:1, 2, 10; 5:2).

Chileab (kil'ee-ahb), the second son of David, born in Hebron to Abigail, former wife of Nabal of Carmel (2 Sam. 3:3). In 1 Chron. 3:1, however, Daniel is given as the name of David's second son.

Chilion (kil'ee-ohn), the second son born to Elimelech and Naomi, an Ephrathite couple who emigrated to Moab when famine struck the region of Bethlehem (Ruth 1:2; 4:9). As told in the book of Ruth, Chilion married a Moabite woman, Orpah. Upon his death, his widow returned to her own people, unlike his brother's widow, Ruth. The name "Chilion" may mean "weakness" in Hebrew.

Chimham (kim'ham), a man taken to Jerusalem, apparently as a royal pensioner, at the insistence of Barzillai, a Gileadite who had assisted David during Absalom's revolt, and who was presumably Chimham's father (2 Sam. 19:31–40: see 1 Kings 2:7; Jer. 41:17).

Chinnereth (kin'e-reth; Heb., "harp"), a fortified city on the northwest side of the Sea of Galilee in the territory of Naphtali (Josh. 19:35) which overlooks a fertile valley and the Via Maris. Now known as Khirbet el-Oreime, the city's name was applied to the region as well as to the adjacent lake.

Chios (kī'ohs), a large mountainous island of volcanic origin in the Aegean Sea five miles west of Asia Minor, claimed to have been the home of Homer. Paul and his companions passed Chios on the final voyage to Jerusalem (Acts 20:15).

Chislev (kiz'lev), the postexilic Hebrew name for the ninth month of the year (Zech. 7:1, approximately November-December). The name was borrowed from the Akkadian month-name *Kisliwu (or Kislimu).*

Chittim (ki'tim). ***See*** Kittim.

Chloe (kloh'ee), a woman from Corinth or Ephesus whose slaves, employees, or household members told Paul, in Ephesus, about problems in the Corinthian church (1 Cor. 1:11). ***See also*** Corinthians, First Letter of Paul to the; Corinthians, Second Letter of Paul to the.

Chorazin (koh-ray'zin), a first-century A.D. Jewish town in upper Galilee two miles north of Capernaum. Along with Bethsaida and Capernaum, Chorazin was reproached by Jesus (Matt. 11:20–24; Luke 10:13–15). Excavations of the now deserted town indicate that it once covered an area of twelve acres and was built on a series of terraces with the basalt stone local to this mountainous region. The synagogue was one of the earliest in the area.

Ruins of a post-NT synagogue at Chorazin, third–sixth centuries A.D.

Christ (Gk. *Christos*, "anointed one"). ***See*** Jesus Christ; Messiah.

Christian, a term that, although eventually the accepted name for the followers of Jesus the Christ, occurs only three times in the NT (Acts 11:26; 26:28; 1 Pet. 4:16). According to Acts 11: 26, it was in Antioch of Syria that the term was first used, but it appears that the Greek word was derived from a Latin original. Some have argued that the designation was at first a term of derision; others, that it simply denoted a group loyal to "Christ" (*Christos* in Greek). Although certainty is not possible, the term was likely coined by non-Christians. Whatever the origin, "Christian" is the term that was increasingly applied to Jesus' followers in the late first and early second centuries. J.M.E.

Christmas, the annual festival commemorating the birth of Jesus, celebrated on December 25 in all churches except the Church of Armenia, for which it is January 6. The term appears as early as A.D. 1123 in Old English as "Cristes maesse" (and variations) and "Christmas" by 1568, meaning Mass of Christ. The actual date of Jesus' birth is unknown. There is no evidence of celebrating the nativity before the third century. January 6 became widely observed in the third century to commemorate the "manifestation" ("epiphany") of Christ on earth, including his birth, baptism, and the visit of the Magi, with varying local emphases. The celebration of the nativity is attested in Rome in A.D. 336 (where Epiphany, January 6, commemorated the visit of the Magi), and this became widespread in the fifth and sixth centuries. Although there are various theories on the selection of December 25, the most widely accepted is that this date had already been a major pagan festival, that of *Sol Invictus*, the "birth" of the "Unconquerable Sun," marking the winter solstice (the sun's triumph over darkness). With the triumph of Christianity, Christmas replaced the pagan festival, Christians having applied "Sun of Righteousness" (Mal. 4:2) to Christ. ***See also*** Epiphany; Jesus Christ; Sun; Wise Men. A.J.H.

Christology, the study of Jesus' self-understanding and of the titles, concepts, and conceptual patterns in which the NT church expressed its faith in him. ***See also*** Jesus Christ; Messiah; Son of God; Son of Man.

Chronicler, the name given the writer or school responsible for 1 and 2 Chronicles, Ezra, and Nehemiah. Scholars have suggested a variety of dates for this activity, with the most commonly held date around 400 B.C. These four books are considered a single historical work because of similar literary features and theological interests. Some scholars propose more than one period of literary activity, e.g., multiple chroniclers from two or three distinct historical periods. A growing number of scholars attribute Ezra and Nehemiah to an independent source because of inconsistencies between those books and 1 and 2 Chronicles, thematic differences such as the lack of importance of the house of David in Ezra and Nehemiah, and the manuscript evidence, which rarely finds these four books in our present OT order. ***See also*** Chronicles, The First and Second Books of the; Ezra; Nehemiah, The Book of. K.H.R.

Chronicles, the First and Second Books of the, the thirteenth and fourteenth books in the OT containing the compilation of data on Israel's history made by the "Chronicler."

Title: The Hebrew (as one book) is entitled "acts of the days," meaning "annals," while the Greek (as two books) is called "the things left out." This latter represents a serious misunderstanding of the work, namely, that it is designed to supplement the books of Samuel and Kings. Rather, the work must be understood as another presentation of the story of Israel from creation to the end of the monarchy.

Content: The books may be divided into four sections: 1 Chronicles 1–9, by genealogies and lists, the story from Adam to the period of restoration after the exile; 1 Chronicles 10–29, the reign of David, prefaced by a presentation of Saul's failure and culminating in Solomon's commission to build the Temple; 2 Chronicles 1–9, the reign of Solomon centered on the building of the Temple; and 2 Chronicles 10–36, the monarchy of the Davidic line to its downfall in the exilic period.

The Relation of 1 and 2 Chronicles to Other OT Writings: The closest parallels are in Samuel and Kings and there are numerous points where the text is almost word for word that of Samuel and Kings. This suggests direct dependence on

Unloading timber from a ship. Solomon imported timber from Lebanon for the building of the Temple (cf. 2 Chron. 2:16). Relief from the palace of Sargon II at Khorsabad, eighth century B.C.

those books or on a similar form of their text. Textual evidence from Qumran suggests that the text used by Chronicles was closer to that form. However, large sections of Samuel and Kings do not appear in Chronicles—for example, almost the whole of the David narratives in 2 Sam. 9–20—and the Northern Kingdom is virtually ignored. In some instances, on the other hand, it is assumed that readers are familiar with material not included, as, for example, in the Hezekiah narratives of 2 Chronicles 32. Also, there is much material in Chronicles not found in Samuel and Kings, for example, the accounts of David's preparations for the building of the Temple and information about his organization of Temple worship. Numerous narratives concerning the kings of Judah contain substantial unparalleled material, often of a homiletic nature. Detailed differences between the two texts (1 and 2 Chron. and 1 Sam.–2 Kings) may reflect changes made in the interests of the particular interpretation and the logical viewpoint of Chronicles. Some modifications may result from changes in the language by the time Chronicles was composed. Use is made in 1 Chronicles 1–9 of genealogies and lists found in Genesis and elsewhere. Small narrative fragments appear within the lists. Various theories of additions to earlier forms of the text have been proposed.

Position in the Canon: In the Greek and hence in the Latin and English, Chronicles appears, with Ezra and Nehemiah, among the narrative books—after Kings and before Esther. This is understandable, since these books are clearly designed to tell the story of Israel; all the narrative books offer interpretations of that story or parts of it.

In the Hebrew, Chronicles stands at the end of the third part of the canon, the Writings. Some manuscripts place it first in this part of the canon, before Psalms, associating Chronicles' presentation of David as establisher of worship with the psalms as Davidic. Much of the third part of the Hebrew canon is associated with worship, and hence with David and Solomon as the royal founders of worship and the Temple.

The present division between Chronicles and Ezra-Nehemiah shows an overlap: 2 Chron. 36:22–23 are repeated in Ezra 1:1–3a. These verses could have been added to Chronicles to give a hopeful ending to the book (and indeed to the canon) or could point toward the sequel in Ezra-Nehemiah, whether or not this is regarded as a continuation of Chronicles.

The Relation between Chronicles and Ezra-Nehemiah: The textual traditions all separate these two works, but they have often been regarded as belonging to the same author or at least to the same school of thought. Chronicles-Ezra-Nehemiah may be treated as a single work, even without complete consistency of language or outlook. Arguments for separation based on linguistic use are not conclusive, partly because of the use of source material in all parts of the work. Arguments based on content and outlook are more significant. The stress on the Davidic monarchy in Chronicles contrasts with the relative absence of Davidic allusion in Ezra-Nehemiah, but the underlying concern of both is with the Temple, its foundation, and its rebuilding. The Davidic dynasty in Chronicles is of interest virtually only in relation to that Temple activity. Ezra-Nehemiah offers an interpretation of the authenticity of the rebuilt Temple as continuing the original one when Davidic rule has gone forever. The conciliatory attitude to the north, traceable in some passages (e.g., in 2 Chron. 28 and 31) contrasts with the exclusivism expressed in Ezra and Nehemiah. But the true Israel is in both limited to the areas of Judah and Benjamin (cf. Ezra 4:1), to which any loyal believer must adhere; the north is outside that orbit. The final decision is one of balance; whether the points of difference weigh too heavily against unity or against the concept of a school in which both works belong, or whether, considering the diversity that appears in many biblical writings, the differences here are no greater than in other instances. The earliest form of the text known to us invites us to read them together; and the Greek form in 1 Esdras in the Apocrypha reads the narratives through from 2 Chronicles 35 to Nehemiah 8 without a break, leaving out the main part of the clearly distinguishable Nehemiah material.

The Viewpoint of Chronicles: The central interest lies in the place of David as founder of the worship at the Jerusalem Temple and in Solomon as the builder of that Temple. Interest in the later kings concentrates largely on their loyalty to that Temple, approves their reforms (especially Hezekiah, Manasseh, and Josiah) and condemns their failures (especially Ahaz). The people involved in this are the true Israel, consisting of Judah and Benjamin, which remained loyal to the Davidic house. An appeal is made to the apostate north to rejoin the true Israel, but the response is meager, and association with the apostates is condemned (e.g. Jehoshaphat). The successes and failures of the true Israel are measured in terms of obedience and loyalty. Wars lost are judgments on disloyalty, whereas victories are won by faith. In those victories God himself is the victor, responding to the appeals of his faithful and giving them success. The ultimate verdict of disloyalty and disregard of prophetic warning brings the disaster of the conquest by Babylon, and an exile that leaves the land totally empty. But the prospect of restoration is present not only in the final two verses (2 Chron. 36:22–23, possibly a later addition), but also in the lists of returned exiles in 1 Chronicles 9. The theology may be seen as representing a continuation and refinement of

Deuteronomic thought, combined with a concern for holiness and purity that resembles the thought of the Priestly writers and Ezekiel. Yet Chronicles offers its own particular variant on these other theological viewpoints. The date of the work is uncertain, but probably fourth century B.C.; the authorship unknown. ***See also*** Chronicler; Ezra; Nehemiah, The Book of.

Bibliography

Myers, J. M. *I and II Chronicles*. Anchor Bible, 12, 13. Garden City, NY: Doubleday, 1965.

Williamson, H. G. M. *Israel in the Books of Chronicles*. Cambridge: Cambridge University Press, 1977.

______. *1 and 2 Chronicles*. New Century Bible. London: Marshall, Morgan & Scott, 1982.

P.R.A.

chronology, New Testament, the dating of the books and of certain events of the NT. Several kinds of evidence are used to determine the chronology of NT writings. References in the Pauline Letters concerning travel plans and historical events and persons make them the most reliably datable of the writings. A few references to datable historical events and persons provide a framework for the chronology of the Gospels, but estimates in this area remain tentative. Efforts to reconstruct the historical setting of other writings are highly subjective and produce only probable ranges of dates. Recent scholarship indicates decreasing certainty and agreement in such reconstructions. Thus, Revelation and 1 Peter are dated A.D. 64–95; James and Hebrews, 55–95; and Luke-Acts, 64–90. Disagreements regarding authenticity produce dates for the pastoral Letters in the early 60s or the 90s, Ephesians and Colossians in 55–60 or 80–90, and 2 Peter and Jude in the 60s or 100–135. Those accepting the hypothesis of a "Q" source for the synoptic Gospels date it ca. 50–60, while scholars accepting the priority of Mark debate whether to place it just before or just after the fall of Jerusalem in A.D. 70. Matthew is dated ca. 85 by most scholars, though some still argue for the mid-60s. There is more agreement in placing John's Gospel ca. 90–100 and the Johannine Epistles around 100, but the arguments are not conclusive. Only the Pauline Letters can be dated with a high measure of certainty, with 1 Thessalonians (and 2 Thessalonians if authentic) around 49–50, Galatians in 53–54, 1 and 2 Corinthians and Philemon in 55–56, and Romans in 56–57. If Philippians was written from an Ephesian imprisonment, as is most probable, it can be placed in 54–55; otherwise, a few years later.

OUTLINE OF CONTENTS

The First and Second Books of the Chronicles

- I. Genealogies from Adam to Saul (1 Chron. 1:1–9:44)
  - A. Adam to the sons of Israel (Jacob; 1 Chron. 1:1–2:2)
  - B. Genealogies of the twelve tribes (2 Chron. 2:3–8:40)
  - C. List of returned exiles dwelling in Jerusalem (1 Chron. 9:1–34)
  - D. Repetition of Saul's genealogy (1 Chron. 9:35–44)
- II. The reign of David (1 Chron. 10:1–29:30)
  - A. Saul's demise and David's accession (1 Chron. 10:1–11:3)
  - B. Military events and religious concerns characterizing David's reign (1 Chron. 11:4–20:8)
  - C. David's preparations for building the Temple (1 Chron. 21:1–28:21)
  - D. Solomon's accession and David's death (1 Chron. 29:1–30)
- III. The reign of Solomon (2 Chron. 1:1–9:31)
  - A. Solomon's endowment with wisdom (2 Chron. 1:1–17)
  - B. Building and dedication of the Temple (2 Chron. 2:1–7:22)
  - C. Other activities of Solomon; his death (2 Chron. 8:1–9:31)
- IV. The Davidic monarchy to the Exile (2 Chron. 10:1–36:23)
  - A. Division of the kingdom and reign of Rehoboam (2 Chron. 10:1–12:16)
  - B. Abijah, Asa, Jehoshaphat, and Jehoram (2 Chron. 13:1–21:20)
  - C. Ahaziah, Athaliah, and Joash (2 Chron. 22:1–24:27)
  - D. Amaziah, Uzziah, Jotham, and Ahaz (2 Chron. 25:2–28:27)
  - E. Hezekiah: reform and Assyrian invasion (2 Chron. 29:1–32:33)
  - F. Manasseh and Amon (2 Chron. 33:1–25)
  - G. Josiah: reform and discovery of the lawbook (2 Chron. 34:1–35:27)
  - H. The last kings of Judah: Jehoahaz, Jehoiakim, Jehoiachin, and Zedekiah (2 Chron. 36:1–21)

The principal events of NT history provide some uncertainties difficult to resolve, with Jesus' birth placed between 5 B.C. and A.D. 4, the opening of his ministry between 26 and 32, the length of his ministry between one and three years, and the date of the crucifixion probably April 7, 30, or April 3, 33. There is greater agreement in setting Paul's conversion ca. 33–35, but dates for the Jerusalem conference (Acts 15; Gal. 2:1–10) range from 47 to 51 and of Paul's execution in Rome from 62 to 64, with 51 more likely for the former and 62 for the latter. The historical details on which such events rest are more reliably determined in the case of Paul's Letters than in that of the Gospels, though disagreements still remain in assessing the chronological implications of Paul's escape from Aretas (A.D. 37–39; 2 Cor. 11:32–33; cf. Acts 9:23–25), his encounter with Gallio in Corinth (A.D. 50–51; Acts 18:12–17), and the Claudius Edict that banned Prisca and Aquila from Rome, whom Paul met in Corinth (A.D. 41 or 49, the latter more likely; Acts 18:1–3). ***See also*** Aquila; Aretas IV; Claudius; Gallio; Jesus Christ; Paul; Prisca, Priscilla; Q; Synoptic Problem, The. R.J.

chronology, Old Testament, the historical dating of persons and events in the OT. The biblical books Genesis through 2 Kings, our primary source of information for the history of ancient Israel and Judah, provide a continuous chronology of generations, key persons, and events from creation to the Babylonian exile (see Gen. 5; 11:10–26; 21:5; 25:7; 26; 35:28; 47:9; 28; Exod. 12:40; 1 Kings 6:1; 11:42; 14:21; and so on). Further chronological information may be derived from other biblical books, such as 1 and 2 Chronicles, and occasionally from ancient nonbiblical documents. The Assyrian and Babylonian records are especially useful in this regard, since they provide absolute dates that can be calculated in terms of present-day calendars. It can be established from the Babylonian records, for example, that Jerusalem fell to the Babylonians on March 16, 597 B.C. Theoretically one might begin with this latter "benchmark" date and, utilizing the chronological information provided in Genesis through 2 Kings, figure backwards to creation.

Unfortunately, the situation is not that simple. First, the chronological data provided in Genesis for the beginnings of the universe and human civilization (a seven-day creation, people who lived over nine hundred years) do not square with the perspectives of modern science. Second, many of the numbers recorded throughout Genesis through 2 Kings appear to be symbolic or schematic. Note the constant recurrence of twenty, forty, and multiples of forty. Third, different manuscripts and versions of the biblical books often provide differing readings, especially where numbers are involved. Finally, there is no way to verify the biblical chronology, or even to verify the historicity of the early biblical characters and events. Abraham, Isaac, Jacob, Joseph, Moses, Joshua, the Israelite sojourn in Egypt, the Israelite conquest of Canaan, Saul, David, Solomon —none of these are mentioned in any of the ancient nonbibical documents recovered thus far. Indeed, with one exception, nothing has turned up in either the nonbiblical documents or the ancient city ruins that points to a specifically Israelite presence in any area before the ninth century B.C. This exception is an Egyptian inscription from the reign of Merneptah that seems to refer to a group known as "Israel" on the scene in Palestine during the late thirteenth century B.C.

While the problematic nature of the evidence warns against assigning specific dates to any of the individual characters in the book of Judges, a case can be made for associating the "period of the judges" in general with the opening centuries of the Iron Age, that is, roughly 1200 to 1000 B.C. The stories about the judges presuppose village life in the central Palestinian hill country, for example, a phenomenon characteristic of the Iron Age rather than of the preceding Bronze Age. Beginning with chronological information available for later kings (see below) and figuring backward, one arrives at 925 B.C. as an approximate date for Solomon's death. Both David and Solomon are credited with forty-year reigns, a number probably not to be taken literally. 1 Sam. 13:1, on the other hand, which reports the length of Saul's reign, is obscure. Thus the most we can say with any degree of certainty is that Saul, David, and Solomon lived sometime around 1000 B.C.

The books of 1 and 2 Kings provide for each of the kings of Israel and Judah (the two kingdoms of the Divided Monarchy) a "synchronism," the year of the king's accession to the throne dated in terms of the regnal year of his contemporary on the throne of the other kingdom, and a "regnal period," the length of the king's own reign (e.g., 1 Kings 15:1–2, 9–10, 25, 33). Further chronological notations are provided for some kings (e.g., 1 Kings 14:25; 16:23–24; 2 Kings 18:13). While it cannot be proved, scholars generally believe that these data were derived originally from official records. Occasionally the Chronicler adds similar notations not found in 1 and 2 Kings, material probably less authentic. Finally, beginning with Omri and Ahab, there are occasional references to Israelite and Judean kings in the royal inscriptions of Moab, Assyria, and Babylon.

This abundance of chronological information renders it possible to calculate dates more closely for the period of the separate kingdoms (ca. 925–597 B.C.) than for the earlier periods. Nevertheless, problems still preclude exact dates before the fall of Jerusalem in 597 B.C. For example, variant readings for the synchronisms and regnal periods in different manuscripts and versions of 1 and 2 Kings warn against overconfident use of this information. And there are internal discrepancies in all of the manuscripts. In none of them, for example, do the regnal periods square completely with the synchronisms. Also, the biblical figures require more time than certain "benchmark" dates derived from Assyrian records allow. Finally, there are several crucial unknowns. Did both Israel and Judah use the same calendar—that is, did they both begin the new year at the same time? What method(s) was (were) used for reckoning the length of each king's reign? When a king died in mid-year, for example, was the incomplete year ascribed to his reign, to his successor's reign, or to both? Were there co-regencies other than the one recorded for Uzziah (Azariah) and Jotham in 2 Kings 15:5? If so, how are they calculated in the biblical figures?

The chronology provided here is based primarily on the regnal periods recorded in the Hebrew (Masoretic) version of 1 and 2 Kings and calculated in accordance with an "antedating" reckoning system; that is, the length of reign recorded for each king is presumed to include the year in which he ascended the throne and, in some cases where the figures seem to require it, the year in which his successor ascended the throne as well. In a few places, where the biblical figures interpreted in the above fashion still do not "add up" or where the Mesopotamian records seem to require it, more extensive "adjustments" have been made. Thus all of the dates for the period prior to the Babylonian conquest of Jerusalem in 597 B.C. are to be regarded as approximate.

2 Kings and Jeremiah date certain events associated with the final fall of Jerusalem in terms of the regnal years of both Zedekiah and the contemporary Babylonian rulers (Nebuchadnezzar and Amel-Marduk; see 2 Kings 25:8, 27; Jer. 52:

CHRONOLOGY
OF THE RULERS OF THE DIVIDED KINGDOM

Judah	*Israel*
Rehoboam (924–907 B.C.)	Jeroboam I (924–903 B.C.)
Abijah (907–906)	
Asa (905–874)	
	Nadab (903–902)
	Baasha (902–886)
	Elah (886)
	Zimri (885)
	Omri (885–873)
Jehoshaphat (874–850)	
	Ahab (873–851)
Jehoram (850–843)	Ahaziah (851–849)
	Jehoram (849–843)
Ahaziah (843)	
Athaliah (843–837)	Jehu (843–816)
Jehoash (Joash) (837–?)	Jehoahaz (816–800)
Amaziah (?–?)	
Azariah/Uzziah (?–?)	Joash (800–785)
Jotham (?–742)	Jeroboam II (785–745)
	Zechariah (745)
	Shallum (745)
Ahaz (742–727)	Menahem (745–736)
	Pekahiah (736–735)
	Pekah (735–732)
Hezekiah (727–698)	Hoshea (732–723)
	Fall of Israel (Samaria; 722 B.C.)
Manasseh (697–642)	
Amon (642–640)	
Josiah (639–609)	
Jehoahaz (609)	
Jehoiakim (608–598)	
Jehoiachin (597)	
Babylonian Conquest of Jerusalem (597)	
Zedekiah (597–586)	
Destruction of Jerusalem (586 B.C.)	

12, 31–34). Although there are some minor difficulties in the interpretation of even these passages, it seems clear that Jerusalem fell the second time in 586 B.C.

Biblical books pertaining to the postexilic period, when Persia dominated the Middle East, often date events in terms of the regnal years of the Persian rulers. Thus the decree that allowed the exiles to return to Judah is recorded in Ezra 1:1 as occurring in Cyrus's first regnal year (538 B.C.). Several dates are provided in connection with the beginning of construction of the Temple, all between Darius' second and sixth year (520–515 B.C.; see Ezra 4:24; 6: 15, 19; Hag. 1:1, 15; 2:1, 10; Zech 1:1, 7, 7:1). Unfortunately, it is not entirely clear how these dates relate to each other.

Perhaps the most tantalizing chronological problem in biblical history has to do with the dating of Ezra and Nehemiah. We are told precisely that Ezra returned from exile in the fifth month of the seventh year of Artaxerxes (Ezra 7: 1–10) and that Nehemiah returned soon after the month of Nisan in the twentieth year of Artaxerxes (Neh. 1:1). Unfortunately we are not told whether it was Artaxerxes I (464–423 B.C.) or Artaxerxes II (404–358 B.C.). Possibly it was not even the same Artaxerxes in both cases.

Bibliography

Miller, J. M. *The Old Testament and the Historian*. Philadelphia: Fortress, 1976.

Shenkel, J. D. *Chronology and Recensional Development in the Greek Text of Kings*. Harvard Semitic Monographs 1. Cambridge, MA: Harvard University Press, 1968.

Thiele, E. R. *The Mysterious Numbers of the Hebrew Kings: A Reconstruction of the Chronology of the Kingdoms of Israel and Judah*. Grand Rapids, MI: Eerdmans, 1965.

J.M.M.

church, the English translation of a Greek word *(ekklēsia)* meaning "assembly" or "gathering." The word does not normally appear in English translations of the OT. In the Greek translation of the OT (the Septuagint), two main words are used for the People of God: assembly *(ekklēsia)* and synagogue *(synagogē)*. Since Jews in the first century used the latter term, the first Greek-speaking Christians selected the former in order to show that their roots lay in the OT and that they continued the OT People of God. They affirmed the same by applying other terms from the OT to themselves: 1 Pet. 2:9 uses Exod. 19: 5–6; in Gal. 3:29 Christians are called Abraham's offspring; in Rom. 11:17–24 the Gentiles are grafted into Israel, the true olive tree. In the NT, "church" always denotes a group of people, either all the Christians in a city (Acts 14:23; 1 Cor. 1:2; 2 Cor. 1:1) or those gathered for worship in a particular house (Rom. 16:5; 1 Cor. 16: 19) or all Christians in all the churches, the whole church (Matt. 16:18; Eph. 1:22). It never signifies a building or a "denomination."

The baptism of a child depicted on a Roman sarcophagus (cf. Mark 10:13–16).

Its Identity: If there was continuity between the NT church and the OT People of God, there was also discontinuity brought about by the Christian belief that Jesus was the expected Jewish Messiah. Thus, a new set of terms to describe the church appeared, terms involving Christ. This was natural, for the first Christians had all been his personal followers. He had gathered a group of disciples (Matt. 10:1–4; Mark 3:13–19; Luke 6: 13–16) who went about with him and whom he sent to preach and heal as he himself did (Matt. 10:1; 5:15; Mark 6:7–13; Luke 9:1–6). The People of God is thus explicitly related to Christ. It is his body, he is its head (1 Cor. 12:12, 27; Rom. 12: 4–5; Eph. 1:22–23; 4:15–16; Col. 1:18; 2:19). Believers are members of that body with particular functions within it (1 Cor. 12:12–31; Rom. 12: 4–8). They became part of it at baptism, being baptized into Christ (Rom. 6:3–4; Gal. 3:27), and are consequently "in Christ" (Phil. 1:1; Rom. 8: 1). They are a building of which Christ is the cornerstone (Eph. 2:20). The church is the bride of Christ (Eph. 5:22–33), taking up another OT image in which Israel is the wife or bride of God (Hos. 1–3; Ezek. 16, 23). Christ is the vine; they are the branches (John 15:1–11). All of these phrases draw Christians closely together and closely to Christ, giving them a deep sense of identity with him and with other Christians.

Ministry: From the beginning, there was some kind of ministry in the church. Two disciples of Jesus, Peter and John, and his brother James occupied leading positions and exercised responsibility (Acts 3:1; 15:6–22; Gal. 2:9). Paul, who had no connection with the historical Jesus, was eventually regarded as their equal. Ministry is described both in quite general terms (1 Thess. 5:12; Heb. 13:7) and with a variety of more specific titles (e.g., deacon, 1 Tim. 3:8–13; bishop, 1 Tim. 3:1–7; elder, 1 Tim. 4:17–20; pastor, Eph. 4:11; teacher, 1 Cor. 12:28; evangelist, Eph. 4:11; and prophet, 1 Cor. 12:28). Ministers exercising the same function may have been given different titles in various areas of the church. It is not clear what function each title included. The functions of prophets and teachers are, of course, indicated by the titles. Baptism was administered, the Eucharist celebrated, and sermons preached, but the NT writings do not state which "officials" presided in these activities. Those who held office were believed to be endowed by the Spirit (1 Cor. 12:4–11). Their ministry was a gift from God (Rom. 12:4–8; Eph. 4: 7–11). Such gifts and endowments of the Spirit were not confined to "officials," however, and were many in type, including healing, speaking in tongues, and administration; all Christians were expected to be endowed with them and to use them to benefit the whole church.

Not only did specified individuals exercise a ministry within the church, but the church as a whole had a ministry. The church is the light of the world, the salt of the earth, and the leaven that leavens the whole lump (Matt. 5:13–16; 13:33). The members are a royal priesthood, set to declare to the world the wonderful deeds of God (1 Pet. 2:9). Since the NT covers a period of rapid development, more formal structures appear in some of the later writings (1 and 2 Timothy and Titus), and instructions are given on continuing the ministry (e.g., 1 Tim. 3:1–13), so that the church may be preserved from error (2 Tim. 1:13–14).

Problems Within and Without: The NT church was not a perfect body. In 1 Corinthians, Paul rebukes a man who has committed incest (5:1), believers take one another to court (6:1–11), some members think it a matter of indifference if they sleep with prostitutes (6:12–20), and some are drunk during the Eucharist (11:21). Early on, one serious problem threatened to split the church: the terms on which Gentiles could become Christians. Did they need to keep the OT Law in whole or in part (Acts 10:1–11:18; 15: 1–35; Gal. 2:1–10)? In the end, they were accepted without condition because both Jew and Gentile had been reconciled to one another through the death of Christ (Eph. 2:13–18). To assist their growing together, the mainly Gentile churches established by Paul sent a collection of money to the poor "saints" (the normal word for "Christian" in Paul's letters) in Jerusalem (Gal. 2:10; 1 Cor. 16:1–4; 2 Cor. 8–9; Rom. 15:25–27). Further divisions appeared later in the church, mainly over "false teaching" and behavior (1 John 4:1–6; 2 John 9–11; 1 Tim. 4:1–5; 2 Tim. 3: 1–9).

In the NT period, the church was always a small body in the midst of what it regarded as a largely hostile world. While there was no systematic state persecution, hatred was shown to the Christians in an isolated and sporadic fashion (1 Thess. 2:14–16; 1 Pet. 1:6; 3:17; 4:13–14; Heb. 10:32–34; Rev. 2:10; Acts 17:5–9). Their faith forced them to withdraw from many accepted everyday practices connected with the worship of other deities. They became a closely knit group separated from others. At the beginning, they shared their possessions (Acts 2:44–45; 4:32–5:11), but this practice soon disappeared. Although Jesus had taught his followers to love all people (Luke 10:25–37), there were times when more emphasis was laid on loving other Christians (Rom. 12:10; 1 Thess. 4: 9; 1 John 3:23; Heb. 13:1; 1 Pet. 1:22; 2:17; 4:8) than those outside the church. The Christians exhibited many of the qualities of a "sect." They attempted to preserve the purity of church life and disciplined those whom they thought transgressed too far in behavior or rejected orthodox views (1 Cor. 5:3–5; 2 Cor. 13: 2; Acts 5:1–11; 20:29–31; 1 Tim. 1:20; 4:7; 2 Tim. 2:16–17; 3:5; 2 John 10; Rev. 2:14–15).

At the same time, Christians were active in preaching Christ to others and sought to draw into their fellowship those outside it. The actual procedures of evangelism are not clear apart from the great missionary work of Paul, who went to the main centers of population in the northern Mediterranean area. Strong churches are also found in the early second century in Egypt, Babylonia, and North Africa, however. Other missionaries must have evangelized these areas in the first century. Much evangelism must also have been carried out quietly in the home or at work (1 Pet. 3:1–2).

Worship: Within the church, the social and other distinctions of the ancient world were abolished at worship (Gal. 3:28; 1 Cor. 11:5; Philem. 16), although there was apparently no advocacy of the liberation of slaves, and women were given a position below men in at least some of the churches (1 Cor. 14:34; 1 Tim. 2:11–12). There were no special church buildings, worship taking place in private homes (see 1 Cor. 16: 19). Admission to the church was by baptism. The Eucharist distinguished Christian worship from that of the Jews and of other religions. A number of people, including women (1 Cor. 11: 5), might participate in a service (1 Cor. 14:26–33). As well as readings from the OT, which was their only Scripture, letters from leaders like Paul would be read (1 Thess. 5:27; Col. 4:16). There would be singing (Col. 3:16; Phil. 2:6–11 was probably originally a hymn) and teaching or preaching (1 Tim. 4:11–16). Worship took place on the first day of the week (1 Cor. 16:2), if not also on other days.

The members of the church were drawn from all levels of society. Some were wealthy enough to own slaves (Philem. 15–16), to have positions of importance in the secular community (Acts 13:12; 17:12, 34; Rom. 16:23), and to have houses large enough for meetings to be held in them (Acts 18:7; Rom. 16:5; 1 Cor. 16:19; Col. 4:15). These were a minority, however (1 Cor. 1:26). Many Christians were slaves (1 Cor. 7:20–24; Col. 3:22–25; Eph. 6:5–9; 1 Pet. 2:18–25), but it would be wrong to assume the majority were. The first churches were all in cities; it was some time before Christianity spread into rural areas. Although Jesus' disciples had all been Jews, by the end of the first century the vast majority in the churches were Gentiles.

It is important to keep in mind that the development of the church proceeded differently in different places and that the NT writings provide a highly selective and incomplete picture of this development. ***See also*** Apostle; Bishop; Elders; Evangelist; Gentile; Holy Spirit, The; Lord's Supper, The; Minister; Paul; Persecution; Peter; Prophet; Sociology of the New Testament; Spiritual Gifts; Teaching; Worship. E.B.

Chuza (kyōō'zuh), a steward (property manager?) of Herod Antipas and the husband of Joanna, one of several women who followed and ministered to Jesus (Luke 8:3). ***See also*** Antipas; Joanna.

Cilicia (si-lish'yuh), a Roman province along the southeastern coast of Asia Minor, divided into two sections: the mountainous western section ("Rugged Cilicia"), into which Cyprus was politically incorporated in 58 B.C., and the fertile, well-watered eastern plain ("Level Cilicia"). The province was bounded by the Taurus Mountains on the north. The pass through these mountains to Cappadocia was known as the Cilician Gates. On the east, the Amanus Mountains separated Cilicia from Syria; the ancient

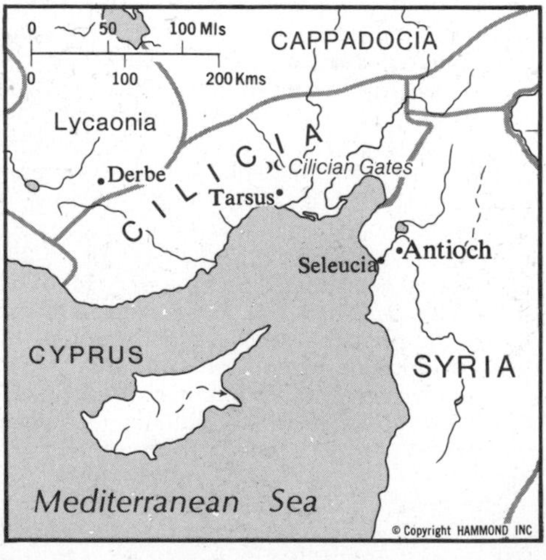

pass through these mountains was known as the Syrian Gates. Tarsus, the hometown of Paul (Acts 21:39; 22:3), was located on the eastern plain. Acts records that Paul passed through the area during his second journey (Acts 15:40–41) and also later when he departed from Antioch for Galatia and Phrygia (Acts 18:23). ***See also*** Tarsus. M.K.M.

circumcision, the removal of the foreskin (prepuce) of the male penis. In the ancient Near East, the practice varied. Some societies, including the Hebrews, completely amputated the prepuce, while other cultures (e.g., the Egyptians) made dorsal incisions upon the foreskin. In ancient Israel and in Judaism, circumcision was routinely performed upon infants of eight days (Gen. 17:12; Lev. 12:3; Luke 1:59; 2:21; Phil. 3:5), though circumstances might permit or require performance upon adolescents (cf. Gen. 17:25) or even upon grooms (cf. Gen. 34:14–24). Having lost all memory of the origins of the rite, the Hebrews attributed different aspects of the practice to divine injunction to Abraham (Gen. 17:9–27), to Joshua (Josh. 5:2–7), and to Israel (Lev. 12:1–5; cf. Exod. 12:44, 48). In one obscure passage (Exod. 4:24–26) reflecting an ancient stratum of tradition, Zipporah, Moses' wife, is credited with saving her husband's life by circumcising her son. Apparently the ancient ritual had an apotropaic dimension: it served to ward off evil. Against that background, the significant theological reinterpretation of the rite in Gen. 17:11, where circumcision serves as a "sign" of God's covenant with Israel, may be appreciated. This theological revaluation has remained a basic explanation of the symbolism of the rite.

According to Jeremiah (9:25–26), many of Israel's neighbors practiced circumcision, notably the Egyptians, Edomites, Ammonites, Moabites, and Arabs. The Philistines, who probably came from Aegean stock, never practiced circumcision and for this earned Israel's contempt (cf. Judg. 14:3; 15:18; 1 Sam. 14:6; 17:26). Ezekiel (32:21–30) also placed many nations among the uncircumcised.

During the Hellenistic period, circumcision became a central issue between assimilationists or pro-Greek factions and nationalists or neoorthodox groups. To avoid scorn (cf. Horace *Satires* I,v,95; ix,70; Martial *Epigrams* vii, lxxii, 5, 6 etc.), Hellenized Jews underwent painful surgery to restore the foreskin (1 Macc. 1:15; 1 Cor. 7:18; Josephus *Antiquities* XII.v.1). Probably reflecting this situation, *Jubilees* (15:6) regards circumcision as necessary to distinguish the children of the covenant from those of destruction. Antiochus Epiphanes played into the hands of the pro-Hellenic Jews when he forbade circumcision on pain of death (1 Macc. 1:48, 60). During the Hasmonean period (second to mid-first centuries B.C.), circumcision was forced upon the Edomites and the Ituraeans (Josephus *Wars* XIII.ix.1; xi.3). In the Roman period (63 B.C. on), the emperor Hadrian also forbade circumcision, and this helped trigger the Bar-Kochba revolt (132–35 A.D.).

Among Jews of the ancient rabbinic period (late first century B.C.–first century A.D.), circumcision was a joyous occasion, celebrated with blessing and a festive meal. The importance of this occasion, when the male child entered the "covenant of Abraham," is further indicated by the fact that the ceremony could occur even on the Sabbath. In Jewish tradition, the symbolism of Elijah and the messianic advent play a particularly strong role. In early Christianity, the merits of continuing the ritual of circumcision were debated. Spiritual circumcision was eventually deemed sufficient (cf. Acts 15 and Rom. 2:29; Col. 2:11; 1 Cor. 7: 19; Gal. 6:15). Among the Copts (Christians of Egypt), the practice of circumcision continued. A "spiritual" interpretation can already be found in Hebrew Scriptures. Thus persons who are deemed "uncircumcised of ear" (Jer. 6:10) are considered to be unreceptive, haughty, and proud, while those who have an "uncircumcised heart" (Lev. 26:41; cf. Ezek. 44:7, 9) are considered to be stubborn. Conversely, when the verb "to circumcise" has "heart" as its direct object (cf. Deut. 10:16; 30:6; Jer. 4:4; Rom. 2:28–29), the sense of spiritual dedication is indicated.

Bibliography

de Vaux, Roland. *Ancient Israel.* New York: McGraw-Hill, 1961. Pp. 46–48.

Isaac, E. *Anthropos* 59 (1964): 444–456.

Schauss, Hayyim. *The Lifetime of a Jew.* New York: Union of American Hebrew Congregations, 1950. Pp. 31–76.

J.M.S.

cisterns, underground chambers for storing water. In the dry climate of the Near East they were used to catch natural rain runoff during rainy seasons and retain it through the months of dry weather to allow people and animals to survive. As such they were precious and considered inviolable.

Biblical references to cisterns include declaration of their ritual purity (Lev. 11:36) and mention of normal private use (2 Kings 18:31; Prov. 5:15; Isa. 36:16) and of special construction to allow a city to survive a siege (Jer. 41:9). They were a form of prison (Jer. 38:7), an intended instrument of death (Jer. 38:6–9) from which rescue was sometimes possible (Jer. 38: 10–13); a burial site (Jer. 41:9); a symbol of unearned grace (Deut. 6:11); hiding places (1 Sam. 13:6); a symbol of wealth (2 Chron. 26:10) or rich booty (Neh. 9:25); and a symbol of unfaithfulness leading to futility (Jer. 2:13) and destruction (Jer. 14:3).

Archaeological discovery of cisterns is frequent and varied in the Near East. In Palestine most cisterns are cut into rock or adapted from natural cave formations in the rock. The porous nature of the native limestone and chert made a form of waterproofing essential to avoid tragedy (see Jer. 2:13). Use of such waterproofing in the form of a limestone plaster became widespread at the end of the Late Bronze Age (thirteenth century B.C.), and the number of cisterns increased substantially thereafter.

Most cisterns were protected from unwanted rubbish by being cut in a bottle shape or having a rim that narrowed the mouth, frequently blocked with a cover stone. Water would thus be drawn by lowering a vessel through the mouth by rope, filling it, and raising it for transfer to a carrying vessel or an animal trough. Some cisterns were open by design, and some were even stepped to allow access to water at low levels, as at Qumran. Mud in the bottom (Jer. 38:6) and degeneration of the plaster required periodic cleaning and repair.

R.S.B.

citadel. *See* Architecture.

cities, large areas of high population density. In modern usage several terms are used to describe the size or population of communities. Typical terms in ascending order are "village," "town," "city," and "metropolis." In OT usage, the two terms "city" (Heb. *'ir, qrya)* and "village" (Heb. *ḥaṭser)* did not refer directly to size, but to the presence or absence of a defensive wall. Cities were walled; villages were unwalled. Generally villages, being unwalled, were smaller and less important than cities, but this was not always the case.

A number of factors led to the location of a city or village at a particular site. Initially, the presence of food and water nearby, the raw materials for tools and shelter, and ease of defense were critical in site selection. Secondary factors such as proximity to trade routes or to sanctuaries and shrines were also considered.

The earliest city yet excavated in Palestine is OT Jericho, Tell es-Sultan. The pre-pottery Neolithic city there dates to between 8000 and 7000 B.C. This walled city was built before the introduction of pottery. The city had a strong defensive wall with a huge round watch tower inside the wall. The tower was 28 feet in diameter at its base and still stands 19 feet high. Evidently, even at this early period, enough city organization existed to plan, build, and maintain such defenses.

None of the cities in Palestine compare in size to the great cities of Mesopotamia. Nineveh covered approximately 1,720 acres or over 2.5 square miles. Calah (ancient Nimrud) covered over 875 acres or 1.4 square miles. Jerusalem at the time of Solomon, by comparison, covered only 33 acres, and even at the time of Jesus covered less than 200 acres.

The Canaanite moat, tower, and fortification wall at Tell es-Sultan, OT Jericho, the earliest city yet excavated in Palestine. Though built before the introduction of pottery (8000–7000 B.C.), enough city organization existed to plan, build, and maintain the defenses.

In the OT, we find that often the larger cities of Palestine were associated with smaller villages around them. The OT speaks of cities "with their villages" (Josh. 19:16; Neh. 11:30) or a city literally "with its daughters" (Num. 21:25; 2 Chron. 13:19). The two phrases appear to be synonymous. In much the same pattern as our large cities today, with their suburbs and satellite towns, the Palestinian city was the hub of most activity for the surrounding villages and rural area. Most of the trade and commerce for the region took place in the city. The city sat on or near the main highway and trade route. The chief shrine or sanctuary for the region was most often located in the city. When warfare threatened, the people of the surrounding villages would flee to the walled city for protection. From archaeological excavations of the Israelite cities of the monarchy (1025–587 B.C.) we find a number of common features that suggest a relatively high degree of city planning.

Walls: The walls of cities during the early monarchy were regularly casemates, consisting of two parallel walls reinforced by perpendicular walls at regular intervals. Usually the outer wall was somewhat stronger. The space between the two walls was often used for living space. Later a single massive wall, often as much as 16 feet thick, replaced the casemates. The development of the battering ram is usually cited as the cause for this new defensive wall. A sloping glacis, or plastered embankment, was frequently added to the outside of the wall to prevent easy access to its foundations and to impede the use of a battering ram.

Gate: The weakest point in the defense of the city was the gate. Massive defensive towers usually guarded either side of the gate. The gate opening itself was 12 to 15 feet wide and had two heavy wooden doors that could be shut and braced with bars. The gate complex had two, four, or six rooms that served as guard rooms. The walls of these inner rooms could support additional wooden doors in time of war. Inside and outside the gate were open squares where much of the business of the city was carried on. The city gate was also the courtroom for the OT city (Josh. 20:4; Ruth 4:1–6). It is noteworthy that a fully preserved gate structure from the Middle Bronze Age has recently been excavated at Tell Dan. Dating to the eighteenth century B.C., this mudbrick gate was fully preserved and has the earliest example of an arch known in Palestine. An Early Bronze IV (2500–2000 B.C.) entrance gate with stone benches along both sides has been found at Khirbet Iskander, Jordan.

Water Supply: The water supply was another necessity for a city. A protected water supply available from within the walls of the city was required for it to endure an extensive siege. Most cities were located near springs, and many had cisterns dug in individual houses. The spring was usually at the foot of the tell (mound) outside the city wall. Hezekiah's tunnel in Jerusalem (cf. 2 Kings 20:20) is but one example of a well-developed system for bringing water into the city. At Hazor, Megiddo, and other sites, great water tunnel and pool systems were constructed by cutting down through the bedrock of the tell to reach the level of the supply.

Acropolis: Many cities of the OT had an upper city or acropolis. This area was located on the highest part of the tell and often served as an inner citadel with its own defense wall. The aristocracy or royalty usually occupied this area and the sanctuary was most often located here. Houses here were large and made of the finest masonry.

Public Buildings: Public buildings were usually located near the city gate or on major streets of the city. The city gate area was a favorite location because of easy access and the presence of heavy fortifications. Public buildings were often clustered together in one section of the city.

Street Plan: Israelite cities of the period of the monarchy had a regular street plan. Immediately inside the city gate was an open court or plaza. From this point, a circular street enclosed the city. A row of houses or public buildings were built between the circular street and the city wall. This street gave easy access to all sections of the city. Other streets branched off this circular street into the core of the city.

Israelite cities were neither large nor heavily populated. Recent projections suggest that most cities could support 160 to 200 persons per acre. Thus Shechem might have had a population of 2,000 to 2,500; Jerusalem in Solomon's time (tenth century B.C.) could have supported 5,000 to 6,500. Even when Jerusalem expanded in Josiah's time (late seventh century B.C.) it would have had no more than 25,000 inhabitants.

Cities changed drastically in the Hellenistic (333–63 B.C.) and Roman (63 B.C.–A.D. 324) periods. Herod (40–4 B.C.) brought the Roman city to Palestine. Roman cities are noted for their broad streets paved with flagstones. Usually the Roman city was rectangular with a main north-south road, the *cardo*, and a main east-west road, the *decumanus*. Recent excavations in the old Jewish quarter of Jerusalem have uncovered an extensive section of the *cardo* there (although this section of the *cardo* dates to the Byzantine period). This street was 39 feet wide and was flanked by colonnaded, covered sidewalks, each an additional 17 feet wide. The street even had a covered drainage system. From these same excavations, a palatial house of the Roman period was discovered overlooking the Temple Mount. This house has several baths and numerous mosaics. Decorated with frescoes, plastered walls, and ceilings, this house must have belonged to a priestly or aristocratic family. Many of the Roman cities in Palestine had the theaters, hippodromes, forums, baths, aqueducts, and villas which brought a bit of Rome to the provinces.

Bibliography

Kenyon, Kathleen. *Royal Cities of the Old Testament*. New York: Schocken Books, 1971.

Shiloh, Yigal. "Elements in the Development of Town Planning in the Israelite City." *Israel Exploration Journal* 28 (1978): 36–51.

Yadin, Yigael. *Hazor*. 4 vols. Oxford: Oxford University Press, 1972. J.F.D.

Clauda. ***See*** Cauda.

Claudia (klaw'dee-uh), woman sending greetings to Timothy, along with Linus and Pudens (2 Tim. 4:21); legends abound concerning their relationships. ***See also*** Eubulus; Linus; Pudens.

Claudius (klaw'dee-uhs; 10 B.C.–A.D. 54), the fourth Roman emperor; he assumed power following Gaius Caligula's assassination (A.D. 41). His weak constitution and ill health contributed to the emergence of rich and powerful freedmen. Though generally conciliatory toward the Jews, he expelled some from Rome because of rioting (Acts 18:3).

Claudius Lysias (klaw'dee-uhs lis'ee-uhs), according to Acts 21:30–23:35, the Roman military tribune who commanded the Roman garrison at the fortress (probably the Tower of Antonia) adjacent to the Jerusalem Temple and who arrested Paul for protective custody to prevent his being lynched by a mob. Afterward, he sent Paul to Caesarea with a letter to Felix, the procurator of Judea, telling about the circumstances of Paul's problems in Jerusalem. The cognomen Lysias indicates that Claudius was of Greek birth. His Roman name would probably have been obtained after he purchased Roman citizenship (Acts 22:28). ***See also*** Antonia, Tower of; Felix, Antonius; Paul. A.J.M.

clay, a plastic (pliable) material composed of various types of earth combined with moisture. The earliest and most widespread use of clay by human beings appears to have been for the production of pottery. That fact has made the identification of the age of various types of pottery a useful tool for dating archaeological discoveries. Clay was also formed into brick for the construction of houses and other buildings (e.g., Exod. 5:6–9). Clay tablets were used in ancient Meosopotamia as the medium on which to preserve writing. Discoveries of libraries of such tablets have added much to our knowledge of ancient cultures. Clay figurines have also been discovered which appear to have served purposes ranging from childrens' toys to cultic images of idols. In the NT, clay functions as a therapeutic agent in an account of Jesus healing a blind man (John 9:11). ***See also*** Amarna, Tell el-; Cuneiform Writing; Ebla; Mari; Nuzi.

P.J.A.

clay tablets. ***See*** Clay; Cuneiform Writing.

clean. ***See*** Animals; Purity.

Clement, Letters of, two letters from the late first and early second century A.D. that early tradition attributed to an author named Clement. 1 Clement was written in the late first or early second century from Rome to the church in Corinth, seeking to quell certain disputes that had arisen there over leadership. Regarded as authoritative in the second century, it was finally not included in the canonical NT. Its attribution to a Clement who was an early Pope is uncertain. 2 Clement is more a homily than a letter and appears to have been composed sometime in the mid-second century A.D. Despite its association with the name "Clement," it is not clear to whom the letter was addressed, or from where.

P.J.A.

Cleopas (klay'oh-puhs), a disciple who with an unnamed companion encountered the resurrected Jesus as they traveled to Emmaus (Luke 24:18–35).

Cleophas (klee'uh-fuhs). ***See*** Clopas.

cloak. ***See*** Dress.

Clopas (kloh'puhs; KJV: "Cleophas"), husband of one of the Marys present at Jesus' crucifixion (John 19:25). ***See also*** Mary.

clothing. ***See*** Dress.

clouds, masses of water vapor suspended in the air. Seasonally limited and encountered as harbingers of life-giving rains in winter, clouds were experienced and perceived as an awesome manifestation of divine power by the Canaanites and ancient Israelites. The Ugaritic texts call the storm god Baal "Cloud Rider." Israel applied the same title to God (Ps. 68:5). The Yahwist reports that by day a cloud pillar represented Yahweh and guided the wilderness march of Israel. A cloud at the Jerusalem Temple manifests the presence of Yahweh (1 Kings 8:10–11). In the NT the voice of God comes from a cloud (Mark 9:7), and a cloud masks the departure from earth of Jesus (Acts 1:9). ***See also*** Baal; Yahwist.

R.M.G.

Cnidus (nī'duhs), a city near Cape Krio in southwest Turkey; it received a letter from the Roman consul Lucius (Calpurnius Piso) ca. 140 B.C. backing Simon's rule over the Jews (1 Macc. 15:23). Paul's ship sailed past Cnidus en route to Rome (Acts 27:7).

coat. ***See*** Dress.

coat of mail (KJV: "brigandine"), defensive armor consisting of overlapping plates of metal strung on leather or cloth. Cavalrymen and archers are identified as the warriors who wore it (Jer. 46:4; 51:3).

cock, fowl whose crowing highlights the story of Peter's denial of Jesus in all four Gospels (Matt. 26:34, 74–75; Mark 14:30, 72; Luke 22:34, 60–61; John 13:38; 18:27). Prov. 30:31 so translates a word of uncertain meaning. ***See also*** Fowl.

code. ***See*** Law.

codex, one of the two formats in which ancient manuscripts were written, the other being the scroll. The codex or leaf-book soon came to be used by Christians to differentiate their sacred books from the synagogue scrolls of the OT. A codex was made by placing sheets of papyrus or parchment on top of one another and folding them down the middle, producing a quire. Such a single-quire codex tended to be clumsier, the larger the number of sheets used in its manufacture. Scribes soon saw the advantage of utilizing smaller quires, each comprising four sheets folded in half three successive times so as to make eight pages, and then stitching the several quires together at the back.

Some of the most famous parchment codices of the Bible are Codex Alexandrinus, a fifth-century manuscript of the whole Bible, with some lacunae; Codex Vaticanus, dating from the fourth century; Codex Sinaiticus, also from the fourth century; Codex Bezae, a fifth-century manuscript containing the Gospels and Acts in Greek and Latin; Codex Washingtonianus, a fourth- or fifth-century manuscript of the Gospels; the Vienna Genesis, a deluxe purple parchment Greek manuscript of the fifth or sixth century A.D. with forty-eight watercolor miniatures; and the Khludov Psalter of the ninth century A.D., containing more than two hundred miniatures illustrating the LXX text of the Psalms.

For noteworthy papyrus codices of biblical books, ***see*** Papyrus. ***See also*** A; Aleph; B; Texts, Versions, Manuscripts, Editions.

B.M.M.

Coele Syria (se'law sihr'ee-uh; Lat., from Gk: lit., "hollow" Syria), the valley between the Lebanon and Anti-Lebanon ranges ("Beka'a," Josh. 11:17). In the Apocrypha, it also refers to the Seleucid province in that valley, or to southwestern Syria (2 Macc. 3:5; 4:4; 8:8).

coins. ***See*** Money.

collection. ***See*** Contribution for the Saints.

college (KJV; RSV: "Second Quarter" [2 Kings 22:14; 2 Chron. 34:22]), that part of Jerusalem in which Huldah the prophetess lived; the western hill. ***See also*** Huldah; Jerusalem.

collop (KJV; RSV: "fat" in Job 15:27), a roll or flap of fatty tissue.

Colossae (kuh-lahs'ay), a city in Asia Minor located in the upper Lycus River valley about 110 miles east of Ephesus, ten miles east of Laodicea, and twelve miles southeast of Hierapolis. In the fifth century B.C. and later, Colossae was an important center. Herodotus called it "a large city of Phrygia" and Xenophon described it as "a populous city, large and well off." This prominence derived especially from its wool-working and cloth-dying industries; the dark red wool cloth known as *colossinum* was widely known. However, by the late first century B.C. Colossae had been outstripped by both Laodicea and Hierapolis, and Strabo lists it among a group of smaller towns. A severe earthquake in A.D. 60 or 61 may have further accelerated Colossae's decline. A significant number of Jews probably resided at Colossae; a statement made by Cicero (*Pro Flacco* 68) permits the estimate that over ten thousand Jewish males lived in the Laodicea-Hierapolis-Colossae area. A Christian community, perhaps founded by Epaphras (Col. 1:7–8), existed here in the mid-first century A.D. and was the recipient of a Pauline letter. Colossae passed into oblivion in later Roman times—only a few coins survive from this period—and its site, rediscovered in 1835 and still unexcavated, became a quarry in the Byzantine era. ***See also*** Asia; Colossians, The Letter of Paul to the; Epaphras; Ephesus; Hierapolis; Laodicea; Phrygia. R.A.W.

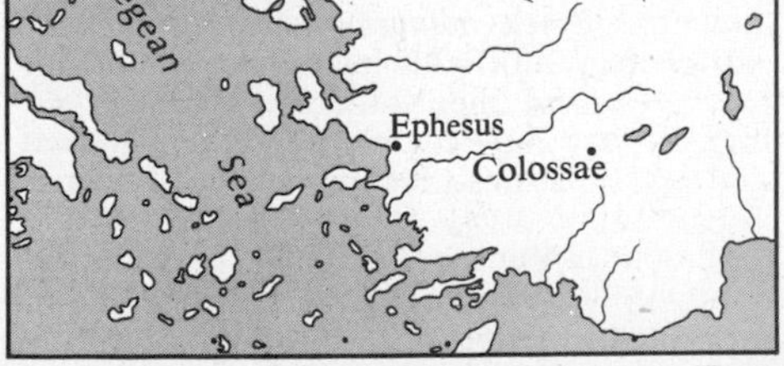

Colossians (kuh-lahsh'uhnz), **the Letter of Paul to the,** a letter written either by the apostle Paul or, more probably, by one of his early followers to the Christian community at Colossae and included subsequently in the NT canon.

Background: The immediate cause for this letter was the appearance at Colossae of Christian teachers announcing a "philosophy" or "tradition" (Col. 2:8) to which the author of Colossians took strong exception. The exact identity of this so-called Colossian heresy is much debated. There are links with Judaism: the teachers demanded circumcision (Col. 2:11), the observance of festivals, new moons, and sabbaths (2:16), dietary restrictions (2:16, 21), and what the author terms the "worship of angels" (2:18). This last, clearly alien to more traditional Judaism, probably represented an effort to propitiate the heavenly powers or "elemental spirits" (2:8, 20)—in Judaism these could be called "angels"—who were thought to control the movements of the stars and planets and thereby to influence human destiny. Those who observed the ascetical and ritual practices advocated by the teachers sought harmony with God and with the ruling spirits of the cosmos, a harmony perhaps confirmed by visionary experiences (Col. 2:18). While some have ascribed these teachings to Gnostic or Essene sources, they more likely derive from a form of Jewish Christianity modified by influences from Hellenistic astrology and perhaps from the pagan mystery cults. The reference in Col. 4:11 to the few Jewish Christians who remain as co-workers of Paul perhaps reflects this situation.

Content: In reply to such teachings the author of Colossians emphasizes the unique and all-powerful role of Christ and the present, saved existence of the Christian community. Christ, the "image" of God (1:15) in whom "the whole fulness of deity dwells bodily" (2:9; see 1:19), cre-

OUTLINE OF CONTENTS

The Letter of Paul to the Colossians

- I. Salutation (1:1–2)
- II. Thanksgiving for the community's faith and love (1:3–8)
- III. Prayer that the community may hold fast to its life in Christ (1:9–20)
- IV. Summation and warning: do not depart from this Gospel (1:21–23)
- V. The teaching authority of Paul (1:24–2:5)
- VI. The false teaching contrasted with the authentic way of Christ (2:6–3:4)
- VII. A proper understanding of Christian ethics (3:5–4:6)
- VIII. Concluding greetings and instructions (4:7–18)

ates (1:16), gives coherence to (1:17), and has absolute power over (1:18–20) all beings whether earthly or heavenly. Indeed, the cosmic "principalities and powers" have no independent authority but are mere captives in Christ's triumphal procession (2:15). The community does not need some new form of protection or deliverance; it already has been "delivered" and "transferred" to the kingdom of the Son (1:13), even resurrected with Christ (2:12). The author stresses that "forgiveness of sins" (1:14; 2:13; 3:13) is a present reality; perhaps some had viewed the rigorous new teaching as a solution for moral imperfection. Men and women, insists Colossians, need not retreat from the world in order to live upright lives; they have power here and now from Christ through baptism to act morally. Indeed, for Colossians the family household is a privileged locus for ethical activity (3:18–4:1).

Style and Authorship: In style and diction Colossians differs markedly from the clearly genuine Letters of Paul. Many of its sentences are long and involved, e.g., 1:9–20 and 2:8–15. Everywhere synonyms and parallel expressions appear in abundance, and the author delighted in stringing together without clear subordination various types of modifying phrases. Colossians has 34 words found nowhere else in the NT (Galatians, however, has 31 and Philippians 36) and 53 other words not found in the clearly genuine Pauline Letters. More importantly, a number of connective words and particles frequently utilized by Paul do not appear in Colossians. Certain theological themes in Colossians seem at variance with Paul's usual perspectives. The cosmic rule of Christ, the "headship" of Christ over the body (now viewed as the *worldwide* Church), and the present existence of Christians as "risen with Christ" (i.e., a "realized" rather than a "future" eschatology) are stressed; and Christ's death is mentioned but rarely (1:20; 2:14).

Those who defend Paul's authorship of Colossians argue that the particular situation faced by the apostle evoked these stylistic divergencies and trace the theological shifts to natural developments in his thought. Accordingly, Paul would have written Colossians toward the end of his life (ca. A.D. 58–60) during his imprisonment at Rome or, less likely, at Caesarea.

However, the accumulated force of the above arguments suggests that someone other than Paul composed Colossians. Epaphras (Col. 1:7–8; 4:12), Onesimus (4:9), and, more plausibly, Timothy (1:1) have all been proposed as authors but no candidate is a clear favorite. Authorship was, nonetheless, attributed to Paul (1:1) because the actual writer wished to indicate firm adherence to his teachings. Colossians almost certainly does not describe a fictional situation but was written to an actual community that presumably knew many of the Pauline followers mentioned in 4:7–17. Further, its author refers clearly to Philemon but to none other of the Pauline Letters. Colossians must therefore be early (ca. A.D. 65–70), and its author probably lived in some city in Asia Minor not too far from Colossae. ***See also*** Colossae; Eschatology; Gnosticism; Paul; Pseudonym.

Bibliography

Francis, F. O., and W. A. Meeks, eds. *Conflict at Colossae*. 2d ed. SBL Sources for Biblical Studies 4. Missoula, MT: Scholars Press, 1975.

Lohse, Eduard. *Colossians and Philemon. Hermeneia*. Philadelphia: Fortress, 1971.

O'Brien, Peter T. *Colossians, Philemon*. Word Biblical Commentary 44. Waco, TX: Word Books, 1982.

R.A.W.

Comforter. ***See*** Paraclete.

Coming of Christ, Second. ***See*** Eschatology; Millennium; Parousia.

commandment (Heb. *mitzvah*), a verbal or written requirement or order. This important term appears over a hundred and eighty times in the OT. Over ninety percent of these refer to God's requirements of Israel as stipulated in the Pentateuch. The religious usage of "commandment" may be tied to the secular ones of king-subject (e.g., 2 Kings 18:36) and parent-child (e.g., Jer. 35:14; Prov. 6:20). The term appears often in conjunction with *torah* and laws (e.g., Gen. 26:5; Exod. 24:12; Deut. 6:1). The people are enjoined to "keep" (lit., "guard") the commandments (e.g., Lev. 26:3). Far from being burdensome, the commandments are the psalmist's "delight" (Ps. 119:47, 143) and "love" (vs. 127). Indeed, in the Ten Commandments, God calls those who observe his commandments "those who love me" (Exod. 20:6; Deut. 5:10).

For Jesus, the two greatest commandments are love of God and neighbor (Matt. 22:35–40; Mark 12:28–34; Luke 10:25–28, based upon Deut. 6:5 and Lev. 19:18)—a perspective rooted in Jewish tradition contemporary with Jesus. ***See also*** Covenant; Law. J.U.

communion. ***See*** Lord's Supper, The.

Complutensian Polyglot, the. ***See*** Texts, Versions, Manuscripts, Editions.

concubine, a marital associate of a man secondary to his wife. When barren wives such as Sarah, Leah, and Rachel gave their handmaidens as surrogates to their husbands to bear children (Gen. 16:1–3; 30:3–13), they were following a practice known from Babylonia (*Code of Hammurabi*, 144–145). Similarly, that the children Sarah and Rachel later bore inherited more than those of the handmaidens (Gen. 21:10–13; 48; 49:22–26) is also reflected in the

Code of Hammurabi (170–171). The Torah legally guaranteed the rights of a Hebrew girl sold into concubinage (Exod. 21:7–11).

For another to engage in sexual intercourse with a man's concubine was perceived as usurption of the latter's authority and was a blatant act of rebellion (Gen. 35:22; 49:4; 2 Sam. 3:7; 1 Kings 2:13–25). It was for this reason that Absalom lay with his father's concubines "in the sight of all Israel" (2 Sam. 16: 20–22)! ***See also*** Genesis; Marriage. J.U.

conduit (channel, aqueduct, trench), term translated "streams" in Ezek. 31:4 (RSV), but more likely a reference to channels for irrigation (Job 38:25). It is rendered "trench" in 1 Kings 18: 32–38, the channel Elijah dug around the stone altar to retain water he poured over his sacrifice.

The more common use of this term is to describe an artificial channel or aqueduct designed to carry water from its source to a particular location, usually inside a city. One such channel is referred to as "the conduit of the upper pool" and it brought water from the Gihon spring down along the side of the Kidron Valley to the lower, "old pool" (Isa. 22:9, 11) or "King's Pool" (Neh. 2:14). It was along this conduit that Isaiah met Ahaz (Isa. 7:3), and that the officers of Sennacherib taunted Hezekiah (2 Kings 18:17; Isa. 36:2).

When it appeared that Sennacherib was about to conquer Jerusalem, Hezekiah ordered that the openings of these conduits be closed, including those associated with the Brook Kidron (2 Chron. 32:1–4). Later Hezekiah had a 1,780-foot tunnel cut through solid rock to bring water from the Gihon into the city (2 Kings 20:20).

Many believe that it was an underground conduit or "water shaft" that David's men used to enter Jerusalem and bring an end to Jebusite control of that city (2 Sam. 5:8). Similar conduits or water tunnels have been discovered at Gezer, Megiddo, Gibeon, and Hazor.

Water conduit systems were varied in their construction. Some were underground tunnels cut through rock while others consisted of plastered troughs or tiled pipes.

Much to the distress of the citizens of Jerusalem Herod the Great and Pontius Pilate used Temple funds to finance the construction of an elaborate system of aqueducts to bring water from pools south of Bethlehem to Jerusalem, a distance of about fifteen miles. J.J.D.

A water gallery excavated at Megiddo. The narrow tunnel cut through the Solomonic casemate wall (tenth century B.C.) and carried water to the city from a spring outside the wall.

coney. ***See*** Hedgehog.

confection (KJV; RSV: "blended"), something put together (Exod. 30:35). ***See also*** Food.

confectioner. ***See*** Food.

congregation, a gathering, usually of people who share common interests or ancestry. Two basically synonymous Hebrew terms denote "congregation": *'aydah* (from the root "to appoint") and *kahhahl* (the corollary verbal root is "to convoke"; Prov. 5:14).

The antiquity of *'aydah* is seen in its appearance in Ugarit in the phrase "assembly of the gods" (cf. Ps. 82:1). *'Aydah* can refer to gatherings of animals (Judg. 14:8; Ps. 68:30), the nations (Ps. 7:7), and sinners (Ps. 22:16). However, the vast majority of occurrences signify the official Israelite socioreligious body (particularly in Exodus–Numbers) during the period of the desert sojourn and the conquest—an appropriate designation since *'aydah* may indicate the assembly of Israel at the tent of "meeting" (Heb. *mo'ayd;* Lev. 8:3–4).

Although *kahhahl* also signifies official Israel in Exodus–Numbers (as well as Deuteronomy, Ezra, Nehemiah, and Chronicles), it refers elsewhere in the Bible to both Israelite and other human gatherings (with a military connotation in Ezek. 17:17; 38:15). The Christians may have chosen the Greek word *ekklēsia* for church because its first two consonants (k, l) are the same as this Hebrew word. J.U.

Coniah (koh-nī'uh; a shortened form of Jehoiachin, Heb., "Yahweh has appointed"), the son of Jehoiakim and grandson of Josiah who began his reign as king in Judah about 598 B.C. (Jer. 22:24, 28; 37:1). He was the last king of Judah before it fell to Babylon and was deported to Babylon by

Nebuchadnezzar. He is also called Jeconiah (Jer. 24:1; Matt. 1:11). ***See also*** Jehoiachin.

Conquest Era, the time during which Israel invaded Canaan and subdued the peoples living there. The biblical accounts of conquest and settlement occur in the following texts: Numbers 13–14; 21:1–3, 21–32; 22–24; 32; Joshua 1–24; and Judg. 1:1–2:5. These represent different understandings of what occurred during the thirteenth and twelfth centuries B.C. The archaeological evidence is similarly diverse. The issues are twofold: to what extent was Israel's possession of the Promised Land sudden and decisive, and to what extent was possession accomplished through a unified effort of all the tribes or individual tribal efforts? While the answers to these questions are complicated, the predominant remembrance throughout the Hebrew canon is that a unified Israel led by Moses and then Joshua produced sweeping victories that gave Israel unquestioned possession of the land. ***See also*** Joshua; Joshua, The Book of; Moses. K.H.R.

Conquest of Canaan, a term used with reference to the forceful occupation of Canaan by the Hebrews after the Exodus. This historical process can be defined in broad or narrow terms. One can speak broadly about the conquest beginning with Moses' military victories in Transjordan (thirteenth century B.C.) and continuing until the consolidation of the Israelite monarchy under David and Solomon (tenth century B.C.). A more restricted use of the term focuses upon the period between the Israelite attack on Jericho and their occupation of the land according to tribal allotments (i.e., from shortly after Moses' death until the death of Joshua). This article recognizes the Israelite conquests in Transjordan as necessary antecedents to the invasion of Canaan proper and defines the conquest as a more gradual process that extended beyond the brief series of campaigns described in the book of Joshua.

After forty years of wandering in the wilderness, the Hebrews launched their invasion by securing the Transjordanian territories of Sihon and Og (Num. 21:21–35). Since Moses had been prohibited by God from entering Canaan (Deut. 32:48–52), the conquest was under Joshua's leadership (Josh. 1:1–6). Spies were sent to reconnoiter the land, the Jordan River was crossed, and the Israelites established their base of operations at Gilgal (Josh. 2–4).

Although the Amorites and Canaanites were demoralized by the reputation that preceded the Hebrews (Josh. 5:1), the conquest was not accomplished without opposition (cf. Josh. 9:1–2). After an unconventional siege and divinely assisted victory over Jericho (Josh. 5–6), the Israelites attacked Ai, which fell after Achan had been punished for appropriating to himself some of the booty that had been dedicated to God (Josh. 7:1–8:29). The Hivites of Gibeon avoided defeat by tricking Joshua into forming an alliance (Josh. 9), and the Hebrews were called upon almost immediately to protect their new alies. When a coalition of five Amorite kings planned to attack the Hivite league to discourage others from making treaties with Israel, the Lord's hailstorm and Joshua's army defeated this powerful force (Josh. 10:1–39). In its final comment on the battle at Beth-horon, the theological motif of the book of Joshua becomes explicit in the author's assertion that "the Lord fought for Israel" (Josh. 10:14). These major victories allowed the Hebrews to consolidate their hold on central and southern Canaan (Josh. 10:40–42).

When an alliance of Canaanite city-states was formed by Jabin, king of Hazor, Joshua led a surprise attack against this army at the Waters of Merom. Israel's enemies were gathered there in large number, "like the sand that is upon the seashore, with very many horses and chariots" (Josh. 11:4), but Joshua's army was still victorious. The city of Hazor, "the head of all those kingdoms," was burned, and the other towns were looted by the Hebrews (Josh. 11:10–15). Hazor's fall led to a consolidation of Israelite power in the north. This ended the first phase of the conquest of Canaan, a major military offensive with campaigns against the central, southern, and northern sections of Palestine (Josh. 11:16–23). Joshua 12 lists thirty-one towns that fell to Israel in this major offensive; it is important to note that not all of these victories are described in the preceding chapters of Joshua, a clear indication that the first eleven chapters were not intended to provide an exhaustive narration of the conquest. Indeed, a careful examination of Joshua and Judges (esp. Judg. 1:1–2:5) allows one to see that the occupation of Canaan was not as swift and comprehensive as a superficial reading of the texts may suggest.

Following its account of the initial campaigns, the book of Joshua describes the division of the land among Israel's tribes (chaps. 13–19), the establishment of six cities of refuge (chap. 20), and the assignment of forty-eight cities to the Levites (chap. 21). This does not mean, however, that the conquest of Canaan was completed in a period of five or six years (cf. Josh. 14:7–10). Indeed, Josh. 13:2–6 says that large portions of Canaan remained unconquered (e.g., "all the regions of the Philistines"). In other words, Joshua's victories provided the Israelites with footholds in their respective allotments, but the individual tribes were responsible for completing the conquest (cf. Judg. 1:3). Furthermore, some towns had to be recaptured (e.g., Hebron; cf. Josh. 10:36–37; 15:13–14).

Since the historical, archaeological, and biblical data are open to different interpretations, scholars continue to debate the nature and date of the Israelite occupation. There is more agreement on the theological themes of the narratives; central among these is the belief that the Lord's promise to Abraham (Gen. 12:1) was fulfilled when the Hebrews took possession of the land of Canaan (Josh. 21:43–45; 23:14). ***See also*** Amorites; Canaan, Canaanites; Israel; Joshua, The Book of. G.L.M.

conscience, the English translation of a word that, in classical Greek, referred to knowledge, especially the knowledge derived from reflection on one's past deeds. The appraisal of these deeds determined whether the conscience was "good" or "bad." The focus of OT faith is primarily on Israel's relation to God, and the Greek idea of conscience as self-reflection finds little place. Something similar to the concern for a "clear conscience" before God is expressed, however, in the OT desire for a "clean heart" (e.g., Ps. 51:10), and a usage similar to that in the Hellenistic world is found in the Wisdom of Solomon 17:11.

In the NT, which appears to be influenced by Hellenistic usage, the term occurs some thirty times, primarily in Paul's Letters (Romans and 1 and 2 Corinthians) and in other writings traditionally associated with Paul (the pastoral Letters), although it also occurs twice in Acts (23:1; 24:16, both times on the lips of Paul), five times in Hebrews (9:9, 14; 10:2, 22; 13:18), and three times in 1 Peter (2:19; 3:16, 21). In a few instances, the meaning apparently is something like "consciousness" or "awareness" (Heb. 10:2; 1 Pet. 2:19, RSV: "mindful"). Elsewhere, the writers can speak of a "good" or "bad" conscience (Acts 23:1; 24:16; 1 Tim. 1:5, 19; 3:9; 4:2; 2 Tim. 1:3; Titus 1:15; Heb. 10:22; 13:18; 1 Pet. 3:16, 21) or of "perfecting" or "purifying" the conscience (Heb. 9:9, 14).

Paul's use of the term is somewhat more difficult to characterize. In Rom. 2:15; 9:1 and 2 Cor. 1:12, he apparently uses it in the sense of one's knowledge or awareness of the nature of one's own thoughts, motives, and actions. In 2 Cor. 4:2 and 5:11, it appears to refer to one's judgments regarding the motives and actions of another. The exact meaning in Rom. 13:5 is unclear. Paul's understanding of the role of conscience is most fully expressed in his correspondence with the Corinthians concerning eating food offered to idols (1 Cor. 8–10). Some Corinthians apparently decided to let their conscience be their guide in this matter. Paul responds that conscience alone is an inadequate guide for Christian ethics. In an extremely sensitive or weak Christian, conscience may become too critical and oppressive. The stronger Christian, on the other hand, may be inconsiderate of the scruples of the weaker Christian. Paul does not think additional knowledge per se will be a sufficient guide for behavior in such a situation; rather, he admonishes that conscience follow the love ethic. ***See also*** Food Offered to Idols; Heart; Love; Mind. R.A.B.

contribution for the saints, an offering from Gentile to Jewish Christians. In 1 Cor. 16:1–2, Paul the apostle gives instructions to the Corinthian Christians about a fund that he is intent on raising for the Jewish Christians in Jerusalem. His churches in Galatia (1 Cor. 16:1) and Macedonia (2 Cor. 8:1–5; 9:1–2) had also been urged to make contributions, and the latter, at least, seem to have responded generously (2 Cor. 8:3–5). The Corinthians, however, while quick to pledge their support, apparently were slow to follow through with any gifts (2 Cor. 8:6; 9:1–5). It may be that opponents of Paul, intruders who were seeking to gain control over the Corinthian congregation, had caused the Christians there to suspect Paul's motives in soliciting their money (2 Cor. 12:14–18).

At least two factors account for the high priority Paul seems to have placed on the collection project over a several-year period: first, he considered it a needed act of charity (2 Cor. 8:4; Rom. 15:26), perhaps an extension of the relief fund he and Barnabas had delivered to the Jerusalem church on behalf of the Christians in Antioch (Acts 11:27–30); second, he had committed himself to it as a part of the agreement reached when the Jewish-Christian leaders in Jerusalem approved his mission to the Gentiles (Gal. 2:1–10); it therefore symbolized the partnership of Jews and Gentiles in the gospel. Perhaps he also associated it with the prophets' expectation of an ultimate Gentile pilgrimage to Mount Zion (Isa. 2:2–3; 60:4–7; Mic. 4:1–2), but the Gentiles would come with the gospel, not in order to embrace the law (Rom. 11:25–26). About the actual completion and delivery of the collection, however, the sources provide little information (Rom. 15:25–31; cf. 1 Cor. 16:3–4; Acts 20:24; 24:17). ***See also*** Paul; Poor. V.P.F.

conversion, a concept whose biblical meaning is especially difficult to understand because of the many connotations associated with the term as a rallying point for various contemporary religious groups. The difficulty is compounded by the fact that the realities associated with the concept in the biblical writings cannot be subsumed adequately under a single lexicographical entry. The basic meaning is that of "turning," "turning to," or "returning," and it can be applied either to God or to human beings in relation to God (e.g., Deut. 13:17; Josh. 24:20; Pss. 51:13; 85:3; Isa. 6:10—note Mark 4:12 and parallels; John 12:40; Acts 28:27—Isa. 44:22; 51:11; 55:7; Jer. 3:14; 8:4–6; Ezek. 33:10–16; Acts 9:35; 15:3, 19; James 5:19–20). Implied in these passages is a change of course or direction, not merely an attitudinal change or altering of one's opinion.

Because the religion of Israel was national in scope and was hence a matter of birth, individual conversion plays a minor role in the OT. While individuals of other nationalities did occasionally become worshipers of Yahweh (e.g., Ruth 1:16–18), a large-scale conversion of Gentiles to Yahweh was anticipated only as part of end-time events (Isa. 2:2–4; 66:18–21; Zech. 14: 16–17).

At least three larger complexes in the NT are important for the concept of conversion. First are the traditions associated with John the Baptist and his call to repentance (Matt. 3:1–12; Mark 1:1–8; Luke 3:1–20). Second, the Gospels as a whole present "conversion" as the goal of Jesus' life and ministry. He summons people to repent (change direction); people accept his summons as God's turning to them in forgiveness and healing; they respond in faith and follow in discipleship (e.g., Matt. 8:8, 10; Mark 10: 46–52; 10:17–22 and parallels; Luke 7:47–50; 15:7, 10, 18–19; 19:1–10; 22:32). The third complex is the Damascus Road "conversion" of Paul (Acts 9:1–19; 22:3–16; 26:9–18; 1 Cor. 9:1; 15:8; Gal. 1:13–17). While this combined form of "conversion/appearance and commissioning" is atypical in the NT, the life-redirection element is constitutive for the early church (e.g., Acts 2:41, 47; 3:19; 8:5–8; 11:21; 14:15–17; 26:17–29; 2 Cor. 3:16–18; 1 Thess. 1:9–10; 4:1–8). ***See also*** Repentance.

J.E.A.

convocation (Heb. *mikrah*, "declaration"), a calling together or a summons to meet. The term appears primarily in the phrase "holy convocation" and signifies the call to assembly at the sanctuary of the Israelite congregation on a holy day. The days decreed as "holy convocation" were: the weekly Sabbath (Lev. 23:3); the first and seventh days of Passover (Lev. 23:5–8; Num. 28:18–25); the Festival of Weeks (Lev. 23:21; Num. 28:26); the first day of the month Tishrei (Lev. 23:24; Num. 29:1); the Day of Atonement (Lev. 23:27; Num. 29:7); and the first and eighth days of the Festival of Booths (Lev. 23:35–36; Num. 29:12–35). Characteristic of these days was the prohibition of work. The convocation was called by the blowing of special trumpets (Num. 10:2, 10). ***See also*** Feasts, Festivals, and Fasts.

J.U.

Copper jug with incised zig-zag pattern and copper ibex scepter (right) from the fourth millennium B.C., found at the "Cave of the Treasure," attest to a sophisticated metallurgy industry.

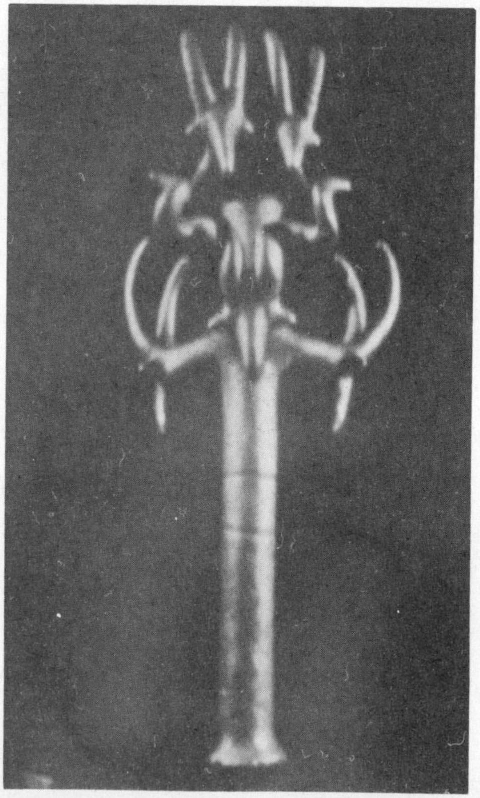

copper, a malleable, metallic element of reddish brown color. The word "copper" (Lat. *cuprum*) derives from "Cyprus," the island renowned in antiquity for its copper industry. The utilization of copper led to the science of metallurgy. The exact origins of metallurgy have recently been the subject of intensive scholarly research (and debate), with the proposed sites of origination stretching from Europe to the Near East and the Far East, in particular Thailand. Though arguments have been advanced in support of independent origins of metallurgy in these three areas, the total evidence still strongly suggests that the Near East was the homeland of metallurgy. The development of this technology must be seen against the larger cultural backdrop of the origins of agriculture, domestication of animals and urbanization, all of which occurred first in the Near East.

The earliest metal finds come from Shanidar Cave in Iraq and Cayönü in Turkey, dated respectively to the ninth and eighth millennia B.C. These objects are of pure copper, that is, copper in its native state, and were worked by cold hammering. The growing demand for copper gradually led to the utilization of copper ores, far more abundant, but requiring a process for extracting the copper from the ore. Thus began true metallurgy, the discovery of smelting techniques, in the fifth millennium B.C. (Chalcolithic period). By the fourth millennium copper metallurgy appeared widespread throughout the ancient world.

In the biblical lands, the discovery of a smelting complex, including remains of ore, slag, and crucibles, at the Chalcolithic site of Tell Abu Matar near Beer-sheba attests a sophisticated industry. In one of the more spectacular discoveries of the same period, a hoard of 416 copper objects from the "Cave of the Treasure" came to light in the Nahal Mishmar in southern Palestine. This Judean desert find comprised a cache of chisels, axes, maceheads, wands or standards, and crowns, all apparently ritual objects used in the temple cult. From the Early Bronze Age (3000–2000 B.C.) there are copper daggers, pins, awls, axes, spearheads, and jewelry found at nearly every site. About 2000 B.C., the beginning of the Middle Bronze Age, bronze, an alloy of tin and copper, began to supersede copper in the production of metal objects.

According to biblical tradition, the first metallurgist was a figure named Tubal-cain, "the forger of all instruments of bronze [read copper] and iron" (Gen. 4:22). "Cain" means "smith" in Hebrew and the tradition probably derives from the Kenites, a tribe of smiths in the Wadi Arabah region (Gen. 15:19; Num. 24:21; Judg. 1:16). In fact this area, south of the Dead Sea, was and is a principal copper mining area (Deut. 8:9; Job 28:1–5), as is evident from excavations at Fenan and Timna. Timna may have been worked as early as the Chalcolithic period. There is no evidence for "Solomon's copper mines" at Ezion-geber (1 Kings 9:26–28) as formerly thought. The Wadi Arabah copper industry predates the Solomonic period (ca. 965–926). ***See also*** Metals.

S.L.R.

cor, a measure of capacity. A cor comprised thirty-five to possibly sixty gallons, wet, or about fourteen bushels, dry (Ezek. 45:14). ***See also*** Weights and Measures.

coral, salt-water submarine growth composed of the calcareous remains of anthozoan polyps. Pieces of coral were considered precious (Job 28:18). They were considered the epitomy of the color red (Lam. 4:7, KJV: "rubies") and were important trade goods (Ezek. 27:16). Found in both Mediterranean and Red Sea coastal waters, coral was a popular material for beads and various forms of jewelry. ***See also*** Jewelry.

corban (kawr'ban), the Hebrew word for an offering dedicated to God (Lev. 1:2; Num. 7:13); it was used of the Nazirites in reference to their life style (Josephus *Antiquities* 4.73). Mark 7:11–13 claims that property declared to be "corban" did not have to be used in support of one's parents. No other evidence of such a ruling exists. The Mishnah, codified after the Gospels were written, appears to hold that a person is to break a vow, if that vow leaves one without enough to support one's parents.

coriander (*Coriandrum sativum*), an herb whose leaves and aromatic seeds were used medicinally and for flavoring breads and other dishes. The round white seeds are likened to the manna found in the desert (Exod. 16:31).

Coriander.

Corinth

The "street" connecting ancient Corinth with the port at Lechaion. In the background is the Acrocorinth.

A MAJOR CITY OF ANTIQUITY, Corinth controlled the isthmus between mainland Greece and the Peloponnesus. Situated at the foot of the Acrocorinth (altitude 1,886 feet) and later including it within its fortification walls, the city was founded by Dorian Greeks in the tenth century B.C. and had established colonies at Corfu and Syracuse (Sicily) by the eighth century B.C. The Acrocorinth was fortified by the sixth century, but most extant remains there date only from the fourth century B.C. Corinth controlled the ports at Lechaion on the Gulf of Corinth and at Cenchreae on the Saronic Gulf, drawing much of its wealth from the commerce that passed between the Adriatic and the Aegean seas. The five-foot-wide rock-cut track (Gk. *diolkos*) for wheeling ships across the isthmus was constructed by the tyrant Periander (ca. 625–585 B.C.). By 400 B.C., long walls connected Corinth to Lechaion and the population may have approached 100,000. The leader of the Achaian League when Rome demanded its dissolution in 147 B.C., Corinth resisted, but was sacked and utterly destroyed in 146 B.C. by the consul Lucius Mummius, who slaughtered the men and sold the women and children into slavery. For a hundred years, its appears that only a handful of squatters occupied the site.

In 44 B.C., Julius Caesar undertook to refound the city, naming it Colonia Laus Julia Corinthiensis and populating it with Italian freedmen. Latin, indeed, continued to dominate public inscriptions until well into the second century A.D., although most of the citizens must have spoken Greek by the time of Paul's arrival ca. A.D. 50, due to the influx of Greeks from neighboring areas. Approximately half of the names of people in Corinth mentioned in the NT are Greek, half Latin. In 27 B.C., Corinth was named capital of the senatorial province of Achaia, seat of the ruling proconsul. In spite of earthquakes and de-

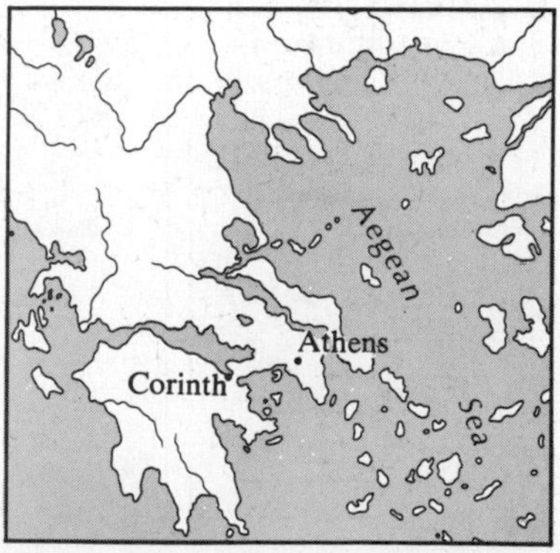

Corinth, located on the isthmus between mainland Greece and the Peloponnesus, had two ports for commerce passing between the Aegean and Adriatic seas.

structions by Goths and Herulians in the third and fourth centuries A.D., the city remained an important commercial center through the Middle Ages. The present village at the site was rebuilt after a 1928 earthquake.

In the First Century: Many commentators on the NT describe the Corinth of Paul's time as a city of unbridled sexual orgies, basing their view on certain remarks of ancient, mostly Athenian, writers and on a passage of Strabo's *Geography* referring to a thousand temple prostitutes of Aphrodite on the Acrocorinth. More recent scholarship has pointed out, however, both that the Athenian references were snobbish disparagements of the pre-146 B.C. city and that sacred prostitution was a Middle Eastern custom, not a Greek one at all. Corinth was probably no more or less virtuous than any other cosmopolitan port city of the Mediterranean in the first century A.D.

Part of a colonnade still stands in the agora at the ruins of Corinth.

Jewish communities were well established in the Hellenistic world and throughout the Roman Empire by the first century A.D., and, according to Acts 18:1–3, Paul encountered the Christians Aquila and Priscilla (Prisca) on his first visit to Corinth ca. A.D. 50. Paul remained there, preaching in the synagogue, in spite of a suit brought against him by some Jews before the proconsul Gallio, probably in the fall of A.D. 51 or the spring of A.D. 52 (Acts 18:4–18). Apollos also visited Corinth (Acts 18:27–19:1; 1 Cor. 1:12; 3:4–9; 4:6), possibly contributing to the factionalism and difficulties Paul addresses in 1 and 2 Corinthians. Paul's Letter to the Romans was probably written from Corinth (Rom. 15:25–27; cf. Acts 20:3).

The ongoing twentieth-century excavations by the American School of Classical Studies at Athens have revealed much about first-century Corinth. One inscription mentions the name of Erastus the aedile, an official in charge of public works (possibly the "city treasurer" of Rom. 16:23; cf. 2 Tim. 4:20). In the center of the forum was found a platform (Gk. *bēma*) constructed ca. A.D. 44, probably Gallio's "tribunal" at Paul's trial (Acts 18:12, 17). In the Lerna Asclepium and in other temples of the city can be seen the ruins of sacral dining halls that illuminate 1 Corinthians 8 and 10. An early first-century Latin inscription refers to a *macellum*, as Paul uses the Greek *makellon* in speaking of the "meat market" (1 Cor. 10:25). And a crude, undatable Greek inscription on a broken lintel stone seems to announce the "Synagogue

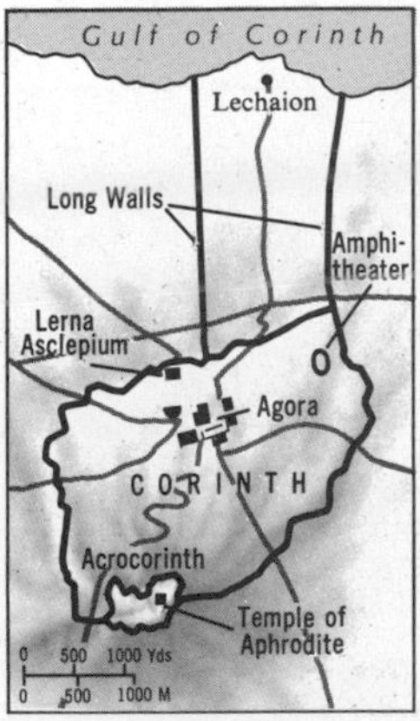

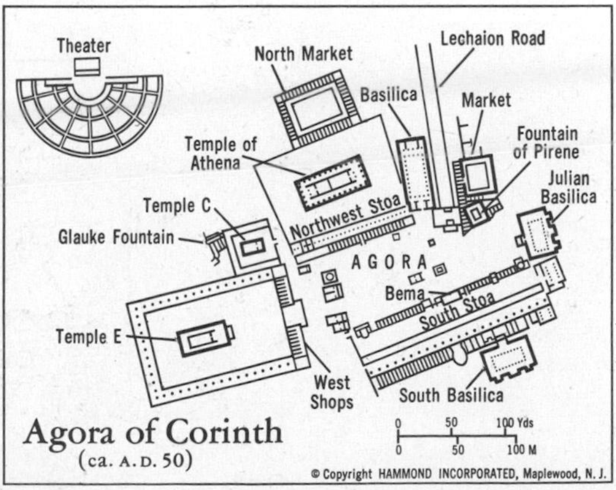

Agora of Corinth (ca. A.D. 50)

The *bēma* at Corinth constructed ca. A.D. 44. The Roman proconsul Gallio may have tried Paul from this platform.

of the Hebrews." Again, in the forum have been excavated rows of shops of the type Paul would have shared with his fellow tentmaker Aquila. A contemporary villa gives a good understanding of the limitations on the size of "house-churches," perhaps explaining why factions arose in Corinth (several house-churches) and why there was discrimination in the communal meals of the general assembly (the dining room could only accommodate a select few, according to a Roman custom of ranking guests).

See also Apollos; Aquila; Cenchreae; Corinthians, The First Letter of Paul to the; Corinthians, The Second Letter of Paul to the; Erastus; Food Offered to Idols; Gallio; Paul; Prisca, Priscilla; Tribunal.

Bibliography

Meeks, Wayne A. *The First Urban Christians: the Social World of the Apostle Paul.* New Haven, CT: Yale University Press, 1983.

Murphy-O'Connor, Jerome. *St. Paul's Corinth: Texts and Archaeology.* Wilmington, DE: Michael Glazier, 1983.

C.H.M.

An inscription at Corinth (shown here in part) mentioning the name of Erastus, who may have been the "city treasurer" mentioned in Rom. 16:23.

Corinthians, the First Letter of Paul to the, one of two canonical Letters addressed to Corinth and one of the five letters Paul is known to have written to his congregation there. An earlier letter is described below; three later letters are discussed in the article on 2 Corinthians. A so-called 3 Corinthians, which has been incorporated into the apocryphal *Acts of Paul*, dates only from the end of the second century.

The Church in Corinth: It is probable that Paul's first visit to Corinth, and therefore his founding of a congregation there, took place in A.D. 50–51, although a date nearly ten years earlier has also been suggested. Silvanus and Timothy were active along with Paul in this venture (2 Cor. 1:19). Apollos is not mentioned as one of the founders, but since he was well known to the Corinthians (1 Cor. 1:12; 3:4–6; 4:6; 16:12) he must have exercised some kind of responsibility in the congregation between the time of its founding and the writing of 1 Corinthians. Peter, referred to as "Cephas" in 1 Cor. 1:12, was most likely known to the Corinthians only by reputation, however.

Paul's earliest converts in the city were Stephanas and his household (1 Cor. 1:16; 16:15). Other prominent converts included Crispus (1 Cor. 1:14) who, according to Acts 18:8, had been president of the local synagogue, Gaius (1 Cor. 1:14; cf. Rom. 16:23a), and (if chap. 16 of Romans was written from Corinth) Lucius, Jason, Erastus (a public official), Quartus, and perhaps Tertius the scribe (Rom. 16:21–23). While the Corinthian Christians were primarily Gentile, it is clear that some were of Jewish background; and while they belonged primarily to the lower socioeconomic class (1 Cor. 1:26), it is clear that some were persons of higher social and economic standing.

The religious beliefs and activities of the congregation, as these developed between its founding and the writing of 1 Corinthians, have often been described as "Gnostic," since there is evidence that the Corinthian Christians attached great importance to the acquisition and display of special religious knowledge (*gnōsis*, e.g., 1 Cor. 1:5; 8:1, 10) and wisdom (e.g., 1 Cor. 1:20–2:13; 3:18–19), that they tended to equate spirituality with possession of the more spectacular kinds of spiritual gifts (1 Cor. 12–14), and that they dissolved the Christian hope for resurrection from the dead into pretentious claims about the believer's present life (see esp. 1 Cor. 4:8; 15:12–19). Whether these tendencies be called Gnostic, proto-Gnostic, or simply Hellenistic, it is clear that they led to serious divisions within the congregation and were a matter of serious concern to Paul.

The "Previous Letter": The first letter Paul is known to have written to Corinth is not the canonical 1 Corinthians but a letter referred to by the apostle himself as one sent previously (1 Cor. 5:9–11). According to 1 Cor. 5:9, this previous letter contained instructions "not to associate with immoral persons," and some scholars believe that part (or most) of that letter has been preserved in 2 Cor. 6:14–7:1. Other parts of that letter may also have been inserted later into 1 Corinthians (6:12–20; 10:1–22 or 10:1–23; and 11:2–34 are among passages scholars have suggested). If so, it would appear that, contrary to Paul's comments in 1 Cor. 5:10–11, the Corinthians had in fact understood the earlier letter, and that it is the apostle who is changing his mind when he now says that he had only immoral Christians in view. Such a conclusion is, however, based on scholarly speculation. Where this "previous" letter was written from and how much else it may have contained is not known. It would have been sent sometime between A.D. 51 and 54.

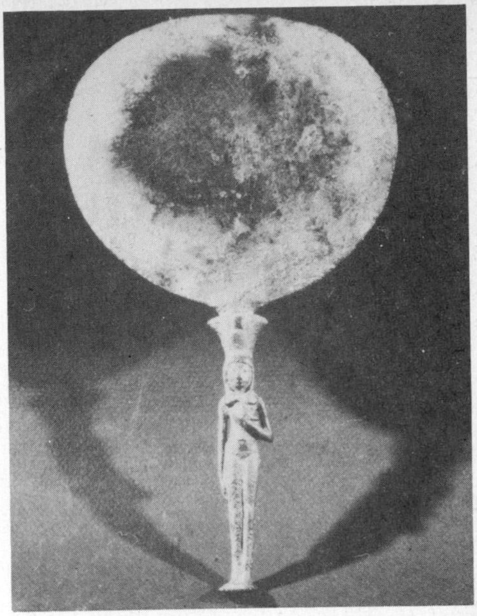

A bronze mirror of Egyptian origin found near Acco. The words of 1 Cor. 13:12, "For now we see in a mirror dimly," may refer to the imperfect image reflected in the mirrors of polished metal of that time.

Authenticity and Literary Integrity: No serious question can be raised about the authenticity of 1 Corinthians as a whole, although certain passages are sometimes held to be later, non-Pauline additions (e.g., 11:3–16; chap. 13; 14:34–35). Various interpreters question its literary integrity, however, maintaining that in its canonical form it is a composite of parts of two or more originally distinct Pauline letters. In particular, passages such as 6:12–20; 9:1–18; 10:1–22 or 10:1–23; and 11:2–34 are sometimes regarded as intrusive where they stand, and so are assigned to some other letter. Most scholars, however, do not find the alleged difficulties serious enough

1 CORINTHIANS

to warrant the kinds of partition hypotheses that have been proposed and continue to accept 1 Corinthians as an integral whole.

Occasion and Purpose: As Paul writes 1 Corinthians, he is in Ephesus where he intends to remain until Pentecost (16:8). Sosthenes is with him (1:1), but Timothy seems to be en route to Corinth (4:17; 16:10). Stephanas, Fortunatus, and Achaicus are also with Paul, apparently as representatives of the Corinthian congregation (16:17–18). There is no indication that the apostle has been back to Corinth since the conclusion of his initial, extended period of evangelization (see Acts 18:1–18). The present Letter has been dated as early as A.D. 49 and as late as A.D. 56, but the most likely year is 54.

The purpose of 1 Corinthians is to deal with a number of specific problems the apostle has learned are endangering the Christian life and witness of his Christian congregation. From "Chloe's people" he has learned of the emergence of various factions threatening the church's unity (1:11–12), and perhaps from the same source he has heard an alarming report about one of the brethren whose incestuous relationship with his stepmother has gone undisciplined by the congregation (5:1–13). These matters are addressed in chaps. 1–6. Beginning in chap. 7, Paul takes up several topics raised by the Corinthians themselves in a letter he has received from them (see 7:1). These apparently included questions about the appropriateness for Christians of sexual relationships, marriage, and divorce (chap. 7); about eating food sacrificed to idols (chaps. 8–10); about various matters pertaining to Christian worship, including speaking in tongues (chaps. 11–14); about the resurrection of the dead (chap. 15); and about the collection for the Jerusalem church which Paul had solicited from them earlier (chap. 16).

OUTLINE OF CONTENTS

The First Letter of Paul to the Corinthians

This Letter follows the general pattern exhibited by virtually all of the Pauline Letters (opening, with address and blessing; thanksgiving; body of the letter; and closing, with greetings and benediction).

- I. Letter opening (1:1–9)
  - A. Address and apostolic blessing (1:1–3)
  - B. Thanksgiving (1:4–9)
- II. Letter body (1:10–16:4)
  - A. Appeal to adhere to Paul's "ways in Christ" (1:10–6:20)
    1. On true and false wisdom (1:10–3:20)
    2. On spiritual pretentiousness (3:21–4:21)
    3. On immorality (5:1–6:20)
  - B. Replies to questions (7:1–16:4)
    1. About sex, marriage, and divorce (7:1–40)
    2. About food offered to idols (8:1–11:1)
    3. About public worship and spiritual gifts (11:2–14:40)
    4. About the resurrection of the dead (15:1–58)
    5. About the collection for the saints (16:1–4)
- III. Letter closing (16:5–24)
  - A. Itineraries (16:5–12)
  - B. Final admonitions (16:13–18)
  - C. Greetings (16:19–20)
  - D. Apostolic attestation and benediction (16:21–24)

Major Themes: The conviction that underlies and finds expression in all of the specific apostolic appeals of chaps. 1–6 is articulated in 2:5—that faith should "not rest in the wisdom of men but in the power of God." In opposition to those who would attach themselves to particular apostolic leaders in the quest for special religious knowledge and spiritual power, Paul insists that it is only in the apparent foolishness and weakness of the cross that salvation is to be found (1:18–25). Presupposed here is the apostle's "theology of the cross," which finds expression in other Letters: that in Christ's obedience unto death God's saving love is disclosed and operative (Rom. 5:6–11; Gal. 2:20), and that those who by faith in Christ "die" to their old selves are drawn under the rule of Christ's love and find new life in him (2 Cor. 5:14–15; cf. Rom. 6:3–11). It is in this saving love, according to Paul, that the power of the cross consists, and that is why he urges the Corinthians to give up their boasting in human wisdom, be it their own or that of their apostles (see, e.g., 1 Cor. 1:28–31; 2:13; 3:5–9, 18–23; 4:6–7). That Paul believes the Corinthians' spiritual arrogance has also eroded their sense of right and wrong is clear from chaps. 5 and 6, where he reminds them that Christ's death involves a claim as well as a gift (e.g., 5:6–8; 6:19–20).

Paul's theology of the cross is also apparent as the apostle responds to the topics his correspondents have raised with him (1 Cor. 7:1–16:4), although it is expressed in various ways. In chap. 7, the Corinthians are reminded that a high price was paid to bring them out of slavery to their old way of life, and that they were called thereby to a new life of devotion to the Lord (e.g., 7:23–24, 35). The fundamental concern of 8:1–11:1 is for the "building up" in love of those who, because they share the common salvation bestowed in Christ's death, have been incorporated into his "body" (see esp. 8:1–13; 10:14–24; 11:1). The idea of the community of faith as Christ's body is reiterated in 11:23–32 and subsequently elaborated in chaps. 12–14, love is identified as its life-force and the criterion by which every spiritual gift is to be evaluated. Finally, echoing in part the themes of earlier chapters, Paul summarizes his whole gospel by citing a creedal statement about Christ's saving death and the power of his resurrection life (15:1–11), and urges his readers to abound "in the work of the Lord," confident that it is God's future that gives meaning to the present (15:58). ***See also*** Corinth; Corinthians, The Second Letter of Paul to the; Food Offered to Idols; Gnosticism; Love; Marriage; Paul; Resurrection; Spiritual Gifts; Tongues, Speaking with; Wisdom; Worship.

Bibliography

Barrett, C. K. *A Commentary on the First Epistle to the Corinthians.* New York and Evanston: Harper & Row, 1968.

Conzelmann, Hans. *I Corinthians. Hermeneia.* Philadelphia: Fortress, 1975.

Murphy-O'Connor, Jerome. *1 Corinthians.* New Testament Message, 10. Wilmington, DE: Michael Glazier, 1979.

V.P.F.

Corinthians, the Second Letter of Paul to the, one of two canonical Letters addressed to Corinth, although it may be a composite of two or more letters or parts thereof. The church in Corinth and the two earliest letters Paul is known to have addressed to it are discussed in the article on 1 Corinthians. The correspondence with the congregation represented by 2 Corinthians is of somewhat later date.

The "Tearful Letter": In 2 Corinthians chaps. 2 and 7 the apostle refers to an earlier letter he had dispatched to Corinth, written "out of much affliction and anguish of heart and with many tears" (2:4). Paul explains that he had chosen to send it rather than to make another personal visit, which he feared would have turned out like the last one—painful for all parties concerned (2:1–3). The traditional view is that 1 Corinthians was that "tearful letter," but there are serious difficulties with this identification. First, since 1 Corinthians seems to presuppose no presence of Paul in Corinth other than during his initial period of evangelization there, the "painful visit" referred to in 2 Cor. 2:1 would have to be the visit on which he made his first converts and established a Christian congregation, which is unlikely. Second, if 1 Corinthians is the "tearful letter," then the errant brother with whose case that letter was concerned (see 2 Cor. 2:5–11; 7:8–12) would have to be the incestuous man mentioned in 1 Cor. 5:1–5. Yet there is no convincing way to reconcile Paul's instructions about that man with the apostle's instructions about the brother who is in view in 2 Cor. 2:5–11. As a result, many interpreters hypothesize that sometime between the writing of 1 and 2 Corinthians Paul had paid a second ("painful") visit to Corinth. Then, in the wake of that he had sent off a "tearful letter" to his congregation sharply critical of it for failing to take any disciplinary action against a brother with whom, apparently, Paul himself had had some kind of serious confrontation. Unless an early editor of the Corinthian correspondence incorporated part (or most) of the "tearful letter" into canonical 2 Corinthians (discussed below), it—like the "previous letter" mentioned in 1 Cor. 5: 9–11—no longer survives.

Authenticity and Literary Integrity: The authenticity of 2 Corinthians, taken as a whole, is not seriously in doubt, but many scholars believe that there are good reasons to regard 2 Cor. 6:14–7:1 as a later, non-Pauline addition to the text. For example, the passage seems to disrupt an otherwise clear flow of thought from 6:11–13 to 7:2–3 (or 4). A number of words in the passage are found nowhere else in the Letters of certainly Pauline authorship, or else are used very differently in those other Letters. Also, several of the most important ideas of the passage (e.g., the exhortations to separate oneself from unbelievers and to cleanse oneself "from every defilement of body and spirit") are hardly compatible with Pauline thought as it is known from authentic materials. And finally there are numerous parallels between this passage and the Dead Sea Scrolls, which originated within a Jewish sectarian movement at Qumran about two hundred years before Paul. It is not clear why anyone would have wanted to add this material to a letter of Paul—or why Paul himself would have incorporated some preformulated material into it as he wrote, as a few have suggested. Yet these problems do not lessen the seriousness of the difficulties faced by those who defend the authenticity of the passage.

A broader and more fundamental question about 2 Corinthians is whether, as it stands, it is a composite of two or more originally separate Pauline letters to Corinth. There is considerable evidence to suggest that this is the case, including the following general points: First, chaps. 1–9 do not entirely cohere with chaps. 10–13 in either form or content. While in chaps. 1–9 Paul seems generally confident about his readers and his mood is conciliatory, in chaps. 10–13 he is clearly upset and does not hesitate to criticize and threaten them. Moreover, as he writes chaps. 1–9 he seeks to explain why his plans for a visit had to be cancelled, but as he writes chaps. 10–13 he is on the verge of another visit. Again, one would not expect the appeal on behalf of his collection for Jerusalem (chaps. 8 and 9) to be followed immediately by the kind of impassioned invective one finds in chaps. 10–13. Second, since chaps. 8 and 9, both devoted to the matter of the collection, can be read independently, some scholars doubt whether these chapters would have stood in the same letter. Third, if

2 CORINTHIANS

the long discussion of apostleship in 2:14–7:4 were removed from its present position, then the references to Titus and to Paul's journey into Macedonia (2:12–13) would connect up meaningfully with 7:5–16, where the apostle describes his meeting with Titus in Macedonia.

One widely held partition theory finds parts of four or five letters in 2 Corinthians, identifying 2:14–7:4 (excluding 6:14–7:1) as the earliest, followed by chaps. 10–13 (the "tearful letter"); 1:1–2:13 plus 7:5–16; chap. 8 (unless it goes with chap. 7); and chap. 9. Some who are willing to accept 6:14–7:1 as authentic regard it as part of the "previous letter" referred to in 1 Cor. 5: 9–11; and a few have devised even more complex partition hypotheses. A division of canonical 2 Corinthians into at least two originally distinct letters, represented by chaps. 1–9 and 10–13 respectively, does indeed seem warranted, whatever one thinks about the alleged redundancy of chaps. 8 and 9. However, there are serious difficulties with the identification of chaps. 10–13 as part of the "tearful letter," and some very good reasons for regarding these

OUTLINE OF CONTENTS

The Second Letter of Paul to the Corinthians

If 2 Corinthians is a composite of two or more originally separate letters, then its present structure is due to the work of some early editor. Thus, if one distinguishes chaps. 1–9 from chaps. 10–13, the former has lost its closing section and the latter has lost its opening. As it stands in its canonical form, however, the Letter may be outlined as follows:

- I. Letter opening (1:1–11)
  - A. Address (1:1–2)
  - B. Blessing (Thanksgiving) (1:3–11)
- II. Letter body (1:12–13:10)
  - A. Assurances of concern (1:12–2:13)
  - B. Comments on apostolic service (2:14–5:19)
  - C. Appeals (5:20–10:18)
    1. About reconciliation with God (5: 20–6:10)
    2. About reconciliation with the Pauline apostolate (6:11–7:3)
    3. About the collection for Jerusalem (7:4–9:15)
    4. About obedience (10:1–18)
  - D. A "fool's speech" (11:1–12:13)
  - E. Renewal and conclusion of the appeals (12:14–13:10)
- III. Letter closing (13:11–14)
  - A. Final admonitions and greetings (13: 11–13)
  - B. Apostolic benediction (13:14)

chapters as written after the letter(s) represented by chaps. 1–9. Some scholars continue to defend the noncomposite nature of the entire Letter.

Occasion(s) and Purpose(s): Assuming, with a number of interpreters, that 2 Corinthians is a composite of two originally separate letters, the earlier represented by chaps. 1–9 and the later by chaps. 10–13, one must take account of two distinct occasions for writing. Chaps. 1–9 were sent from Macedonia (perhaps Philippi) not long after Paul had been met there by Titus, on the way back from Corinth with generally encouraging news about the congregation (7:5–7). Chaps. 10–13, also sent from Macedonia, were written shortly after Paul's receipt of some alarming news about the congregation, and not long before his own departure for a third visit to the city (e.g., 10:1–2; 12:14, 20–21; 13:1–2). Chaps. 1–9 may be dated tentatively in the summer or fall of A.D. 55 and chaps. 10–13 about one year later.

The letter represented by chaps. 1–9 was written to assure the Corinthians of their apostle's continuing care for them, despite his "tearful letter" which had upset them, and despite his apparent vacillation in the matter of a promised return visit (1:12–2:13); to clarify the apostolic commission he had sought to discharge in his dealings with them (2:14–5:19); and to appeal to them on behalf of his gospel, his ministry, and his collection for the church in Jerusalem (5:20–9:15). The letter represented by chaps. 10–13 was written to warn and admonish the Corinthian congregation in advance of Paul's forthcoming visit (see esp. 13:10). Rival apostles had intruded themselves and their teachings into the congregation, seeking to displace Paul and his gospel. Chaps. 10–13 are dominated by Paul's attack on these intruders, whom he describes as "false apostles, deceitful workmen," and ministers of Satan in disguise (11:13–15).

Theme: The theme that pervades the whole of 2 Corinthians, however many letters be represented there, is the meaning of apostleship—and, by extension, the meaning of Christian ministry in general. Throughout, Paul emphasizes that Christian ministry is the service of the gospel of God's reconciling love as present in Christ (see especially 5:11–19), and that ministers are made adequate for this service by God alone (2:14–3: 6). Against the rival apostles who would have the Corinthians believe otherwise, Paul insists that special religious knowledge, ecstatic experiences, or miraculous powers do not certify one as a true apostle. The important question is whether, in one's serving of the gospel, the saving death and resurrection life of Jesus are evident (see esp. 4:10–12). For this reason, Paul repeatedly lists the hardships he has experienced as an apostle (4:8–9; 6:4b–5; 11:23b–29; 12:10), not in order to boast of the strength with which he has endured them, but in order to "boast" of his weaknesses (the "fool's speech," 11:1–12:13), and thus of the transcendent power of God (see esp. 4:7; 13:4). ***See also*** Corinth; Corinthians, The First Letter of Paul to the; Paul; Reconciliation; Scrolls, The Dead Sea.

Bibliography

Barrett, C. K. A. *Commentary on the Second Epistle to the Corinthians.* New York: Harper & Row, 1973.

Fallon, Francis T. *2 Corinthians.* New Testament Message, 11. Wilmington, DE: Michael Glazier, 1980).

Furnish, Victor Paul. *II Corinthians.* Anchor Bible 32A. Garden City: Doubleday & Co., 1984.

V.P.F.

cormorant, any of about thirty species of birds that live near water and feed mainly on fish. It is listed among birds prohibited as food (Lev. 11:17; Deut. 14:17) for the Jews. In Isa. 34:11 the KJV uses it for a term the RSV translates "hawk." The KJV also uses it for an uncertain reading in Zeph. 2:14 (RSV: "vulture").

corn, a term used generically in the KJV and NEB for cereal crops in the OT (RSV: "grain"). An ancient poem designates the Promised Land a place of "corn and new wine" (Deut. 33:28). The noun phrase "corn, new wine, and oil" occurs frequently in the OT and denotes the range of native agricultural produce: cereal farming, viticulture, and olive cultivation.

The development of cereal agriculture antedated the settlement of Israel's tribes (beginning in the thirteenth century B.C.). Israel inherited from Canaan the techniques of farming and a cycle of agricultural festivals: Unleavened Bread; Weeks (Pentecost); and Ingathering (Tabernacles). ***See also*** Pentecost; Tabernacles, Festival of; Unleavened Bread, Feast of the. R.M.G.

Cornelius (kor-neel'yuhs), a Roman centurion stationed in Caesarea. The story of his conversion to Christianity is told at length in Acts 10 and he is defended by Peter in Acts 11:1–18. A further allusion to him is made in Acts 15:5–7. The repetition of his story indicates his significance for Acts as the model Gentile convert. Before his conversion, Cornelius was apparently associated with the synagogue as a "god-fearer." He gave alms and dedicated himself to prayer. While he and his friends listened to Peter present the gospel, the Holy Spirit came upon them. For the writer of Acts, this was divine attestation that Gentiles should be accepted into the Christian community on the same basis (i.e., faith) as Jewish converts to belief in Jesus as the Messiah. It is significant that, in Acts, it is Peter who opens the door of faith to the Gentiles, but he does so only after having received a vision from God. ***See also*** Caesarea; Gentile; Peter. A.J.M.

cornerstone, most often the large stone placed in the foundation at the principal corner of a building but occasionally (e.g., *Testament of Solomon* 22:7–23:4 [ca. A.D. 200]) the top or final stone of a building. Most biblical occurrences of this term are metaphorical. Job 38:6, for example, imagines God as creator laying a cornerstone upon which to "construct" the world. The cornerstone of Ps. 118:22 is either Israel or its king, rejected as "insignificant" by the nations but exalted by God. In Isa. 28:16 God lays a cornerstone in Zion. This much debated image possibly refers to God's announcement of salvation or to the faith of the renewed Israel. *Targum Jonathan* (Christian era) interprets the "cornerstone" of this text as a king. In the NT both Ps. 118:22 and Isa. 28:16 are applied to Jesus as Messiah (Matt. 21:42; Mark 12:10; Luke 20:17 [Ps. 118:22 used in a saying of Jesus]; Acts 4:11; Rom. 9:33; Eph. 2:20; and 1 Pet. 2:4–8). The passages from Romans and 1 Peter (also Luke 20:18?) allude as well to the "stone of stumbling" of Isa. 8:14, and the various authors may have drawn this "stone" imagery from an early Christian biblical testimony collection not unlike the Qumran text *4Q Florilegium*. R.A.W.

Cornerstone of an unfinished house from the time of the Israelite king Omri, ca. 885–873 B.C.

cornet, a term used by the KJV (RSV: "horn") to translate the Hebrew *qeren* (Dan. 3:5, 7, 10, 15) and *shophar* (1 Chron. 15:28; 2 Chron. 15:14; Ps. 98:6; Hos. 5:8). In 2 Sam. 6:5 the KJV has "cornets" for a different word better translated "castanets," as in the RSV.

Cos (kohs), an island with a city of the same name in the Aegean Sea, southwest of Asia Minor, where Paul spent one night on his final journey to Jerusalem (Acts 21:1). Known for its ointment, purple dye, and excellent wine, it was a major shipping port. Under Ptolemaic rule in the third century B.C., it developed an outstanding library. Several Ptolemaic princes were educated there.

A cult of Asklepios as well as hot springs probably influenced Hippocrates, the father of medicine, to found a medical school on Cos. It was a Coan physician who convinced Claudius to grant Cos immunity from taxation.

Because it was an important Jewish center (1 Macc. 15:23), Herod the Great gave large sums for building purposes. A dedicatory statue to his son has also been found there. D.R.E.

cosmetics, any of a number of products used to dress the hair or beautify the skin. Cosmetics were used by men and women throughout the ancient Near East, although Egyptian paintings and objects illuminate this practice best. The Egyptians, as well as other nations, imported a variety of cosmetics, balms, gums, and myrrh from Palestine (Gen. 43:11; Ezek. 27:17). The most common cosmetics were kohl, henna, rouge, powder, ointments, and perfumes. Kohl was used to line the eyes in black, so clearly illustrated in Egyptian paintings. It appears to have served as protection against light reflected from the bright sun as well as to beautify the eyes. In Israel, women who "painted their eyes" were not held in high regard (2 Kings 9:30; Jer. 4:30; Ezek. 23:40). Henna was used for dying the hair and also for painting the toenails and fingernails. Archaeological finds corroborate the importance of cosmetics in daily life: cosmetic palettes, kohl tubes and sticks, spoons, rods, rouge pots, hairpins, combs, cosmetic dishes, tweezers, ear picks, and mirrors have all been found. S.L.R.

couch. ***See*** Bed.

coulter. ***See*** Plowshare.

council, the English translation given in some contexts to the Greek word *synedrion*. In the kind of ancient villages or ethnic communities described in the biblical materials, rules were often made and enforced by a council of community leaders and elders. The Gospels occasionally refer to local councils that render justice (Matt. 5:22) or persecute Christians (Matt. 10:17; Mark 13:9). Paul speaks of a council of elders (Acts 22:5); most other references are to the Sanhedrin of chief priests and leaders in Jerusalem. ***See also*** Sanhedrin.

counsel, advice, human or divine. The city of Abel had a reputation for sound counsel (2 Sam. 20:18). Although private individuals gave advice, professional advisors also existed. They included diviners like Balaam, courtiers (Joseph, Daniel), parents, and teachers. In wisdom literature, the word for counsel became a technical term (Jer. 18:18; Prov. 8:14).

counselor, an advisor to kings. David's court had two counselors, Ahithophel and Hushai. Ahithophel's advice was likened to an oracle from heaven, but even that could not stand when the deity interfered. Disgraced, Ahithophel committed suicide. Late OT texts mention seven counselors of Artaxerxes (Ezra. 7:14) and counselors to the king (Dan. 3:24, 27). Royal ritual gave birth to messianic hope concerning a wondrous counselor (Isa. 9:6).

courage, the resolve to meet danger with strength, daring, and confidence; it is manifested by Israel's "men of valor" (or "men of courage," Josh. 1:14; 8:3). Other expressions for courage are found in the OT (e.g., Deut. 31:7; Josh. 2:11; 1 Sam. 17:32; 2 Sam. 10:12; Dan. 11:25) and in the NT (Acts 28:15; Phil. 1:20). Christians are summoned to courage on the basis of Christ's victory over death and worldly powers (John 16:33; Acts 23:11; 2 Cor. 5:6, 8).

covenant (Heb. *berith),* a formal agreement or treaty between two parties with each assuming some obligation. In the Hebrew Bible, a covenant might be a pact of mutuality concerning individuals, such as Laban and Jacob (Gen. 31:44–54) or David and Jonathan (1 Sam. 18:3; 23:18); states or other political units, such as Abraham and the Amorites (Gen. 14:13), Abraham and Abimelech, king of Gerar (Gen. 21:22–32), Abner and David (2 Sam. 3:12–13, 21), David and the people (2 Sam. 5:3), Solomon and Hiram (1 Kings 5:26), and Asa and Ben-hadad (1 Kings 15:18–19); husband and wife (cf. Mal. 2:14; Ezek. 16:8).

A covenant also might be imposed by a greater power upon a lesser one. The greater power demands loyalty and obligates itself to the protection of the lesser one, such as Israel and the Gibeonites (Josh. 9) and the request by Jabesh-gilead of the king of Ammon (1 Sam. 11:1–2). The vast majority of the references to covenant in the Bible are to such a treaty—the covenant that God makes with Israel at Sinai. This covenant must be understood on the basis of political and judicial categories.

The Sinai Covenant: The framework of the Sinai Covenant has significant affinities with suzerain-vassal treaties from the ancient Near East, specifically, the Hittite treaties of the fourteenth and thirteenth centuries B.C. and the Assyrian treaties of the seventh and sixth centuries B.C. In these documents a suzerain makes a treaty with a lesser kingship. The main elements of the Hittite treaty, for example, are: the identification of the treaty-maker (i.e., the great king); a historical introduction (prior beneficial acts done by the great power on behalf of the smaller one); the stipulations (the primary demand is for loyalty); a list of divine witnesses; and blessings and curses. The treaty was recited, a ceremonial meal eaten, and the treaty deposited at the feet of the idol.

The narrative concerning the Sinai Covenant

COVENANT

in Exod. 19–24 has similar elements: the identification of God and his saving acts for Israel (Exod. 19:4–6; 20:2); the stipulations (Exod. 20: 3–23:33); the treaty recital (Exod. 24:7); and the ceremonial meal (Exod. 24:9–11). The other elements appear particularly in Deuteronomy. The deposit of the treaty in the Ark of the Covenant is mentioned in Exod. 25:16; 40:21; Deut. 10:1–5; and 31:25–26 (the Ark elsewhere is called the footstool of God, Pss. 99:5; 132:7–8; 1 Chron. 28:2). Witnesses appear in the form of "heaven and earth" (Deut. 4:26; 30:19; 31:28), in "this book of the Torah" (Deut. 31:26), and the "Song of Moses" (Deut. 31:19, 21). Blessings and curses are listed in Leviticus 26 and Deut. 27:11–28:68 (cf. 29:17–27). This political structure emphasizes the seriousness of the relationship between God and Israel and ipso facto eliminates the possibility of foreign alliances (e.g., Isa. 31:1–3; Jer. 2:18, 36).

The judicial element of the Sinai Covenant is manifested in the stipulations, which are the law of the nation. Now, any crime committed is against God, whether it be ritual or civil. Israel is apparently unique in its perception that all its law is divinely given.

A further social element contained in the Sinai Covenant is the familial one. The Israelites are called God's children in Deut. 14:1 (see also Exod. 4:22 and Deut. 32:9–12, 18 with Exod. 19:4). Furthermore, the stipulations and even the covenant are called *Torah* (Deut. 31: 25–26), which originally means "teaching" or "instruction." Within the context of the covenant it is equivalent to law, but if Proverbs (e.g., 3:1; 4:2; 7:2) uses *torah* in its original social context—as parent instructing child—then its usage in the covenant may suggest the analogy of God instructing Israel.

Covenants with Abraham and David: The Sinai Covenant is depicted as conditional; Israel must keep the stipulations (familial, societal, dietary, ritual, agricultural, etc.) or suffer severe punishment. The two other primary divine covenants, those with Abraham (Gen. 15) and David (2 Sam. 7; Ps. 89:1–38), were originally perceived as unconditional. These two covenants are patterned after the promissory royal grant of the ancient Near East as, also, attested in Hittite and Assyrian documents. Under this kind of covenant, fiefs are granted to loyal servants by the king and require no further action on behalf of the grantee. Gen. 17:1–14 does demand circumcision of Abraham and his descendants, but this is only a sign of the covenant, and therefore of a loyalty that is to be expected.

The Davidic covenant assures David of a permanent dynasty in which the Davidic king is depicted metaphorically as the son of God (2 Sam. 7:14; Pss. 2:7–8; 89:27–28) in terminology reminiscent of other ancient Near Eastern documents. There is, however, a tendency to view the Davidic covenant as conditional and dependent on obedience to the Sinai Covenant (1 Kings 2:4; 8:25; 9:4–9; Ps. 132:12). This view was that of the minority and reflects the ideology of the editor of 1 and 2 Kings.

The Davidic covenant captivated the popular imagination, which saw in it a promise of permanent security in the continued stability of government, worship (centered in the Temple), and life of the people. As such, it ran contrary to the conditionality of the Sinai Covenant taught in the Pentateuch and understood by the prophets as dominant. The prophets did believe in the ultimate validity of the Davidic covenant, though, as expressed in their prophecies of messianic expectation.

Obedience to the stipulations of the Sinai Covenant was perceived by the prophets as necessary for the continued existence of Israel on its land. The covenant in its strict sense of a suzerain-vassal treaty, did not, however, totally define the relationship between God and Israel. It only served as a prevalent image of that relationship. When Israel broke the covenant, therefore, the relationship was not destroyed. According to the prophets, the relationship was permanent and the breaking of the cov-

Treaty between Esarhaddon of Assyria and Ramataia, a Medean vassal king (672 B.C.). A typical suzerain-vassal treaty of the ancient Near East, it ends with a sequence of curses against treaty violators and has affinities with the Sinai Covenant.

enant once it had taken place was viewed only as a momentary setback. Thus, Jer. 31:27–37 (building upon Hos. 2) predicts the people's return, growth, and prosperity followed by God's establishing a new covenant with Israel. The uniqueness of this covenant lies not in its content, which is identical to the Sinai Covenant (the Torah, v. 33), but in its form—it will be given internally. The covenant will become part of the nature of each individual, so that obedience is guaranteed (v. 34). Thus, it is unbreakable, and its eternality is assured (vv. 35–37; cf. Jer. 32:36–44). Thereby, Jeremiah was able to depict a future in which by an act of God's mercy, sin, the lack of repentance, and the consequent catastrophic punishment would no longer exist.

In the NT: NT authors, influenced by the idea of a new covenant, saw in the death of Jesus of Nazareth the beginning of it (Mark 14:24; 1 Cor. 11:25) and saw his followers as members of that new covenant (cf. 2 Cor. 3:6), although that did not annul the first covenant given to Israel (Luke 1:72; Acts 3:25; Gal. 3:17). The Letter to the Hebrews makes the greatest use of covenant language in the NT (e.g., Heb. 7:22; 8:8–13; 9:15; 12:24). ***See also*** Abraham; David; Sinai; Torah.

Bibliography

Hillers, D. R. *Covenant: The History of a Biblical Idea.* Baltimore, MD: Johns Hopkins University Press, 1969.

McCarthy, D. J. *Treaty and Covenant.* Analecta Biblica 21. Rome: PBI, 1963.

Mendenhall, George E. *Law and Covenant in Israel and the Ancient Near East.* Pittsburgh, PA: The Biblical Colloquium, 1955. J.U.

Covenant, Book of the. ***See*** Law.

Covenant, New. ***See*** New Testament.

cow. ***See*** Cattle.

cracknel, a term in the KJV for a hard and brittle biscuit (1 Kings 14:3; RSV and NASB: "cakes").

crafts. ***See*** individual entries.

craftsman, a smith or carpenter whose work is mentioned with the building of the Temple and often in idol making (Acts 19:24; Isa. 40:19 ["workman"]; 44:12; Neh. 3:8; 1 Kings 7:14). ***See also*** Refining; Smith; Tubal-cain.

crane, a bird of the *Gruidae* family of the *Gruiformes* order. Cranes are tall wading birds similar in appearance to herons. Isa. 38:14 indicates its noisy character, although the Hebrew is uncertain. Jer. 8:7, similarly uncertain, focuses on its nesting habits.

creation, the act of God by which the universe came into being. The Bible's chief account of creation is that in Gen. 1:1–2:3 (or 2:4a). This text is generally attributed to a sixth-century B.C. Priestly author (P), who radically changed (demythologized) the origin of the cosmos depicted in the poetic accounts current in the ancient Near East (esp. the Ugaritic Baal epic and Babylonian *Enuma Elish).* Instead of divine combat and struggle with a willful primordial matter—motifs otherwise abundant in biblical poetry—we find a sole, sovereign master of the universe directing the work of creation by verbal command and a freely determined plan. God is here shown making the world in six days and resting on the seventh (cf. Exod. 20:11).

The creation story as depicted in a thirteenth-century mosaic from the dome of St. Mark's Basilica, Venice. The inner circle portrays the creation of light and dark; the next, that of the seas, plants, animals, and Adam; the outer circle (partial view) shows the expulsion from paradise.

On the first day God created light and darkness, night and day; on the second, the firmament separating earthly and heavenly waters; on the third, dry land and vegetation; on the fourth, the heavenly luminaries of the sun ("greater luminary") for ruling the day and the moon (chief "lesser luminary") for ruling the night; on the fifth, sea creatures and birds; and on the sixth, land creatures and humans. The first three days present frameworks of the cosmos, the last three their respective inhabitants. God names the works of the first three days, the humans presumably (cf. 2:19–20) the rest.

The creation story's verbal structure is artful. The verb "created" (Heb. *bara'*) appears in poetic parallel to the verb "made" (Heb. *'asah*) in 2:4 (the verse's two halves are usually ascribed to separate authors), and the two alternate throughout 1:1–2:3: "created" generally on odd-numbered days (1:1, 21), "made" generally on even-numbered (1:7, 16, 25); both are together in the creation of man and woman (1:26–27) and sanctification of the Sabbath (2:3). Creation by verbal command occurs throughout the six days but seems to alternate with more physical and artisanlike depictions reflecting older poetic conceptions about divine activities.

The first half of the Garden story (Gen. 2) presents another, probably older, view of creation. The order of creation is here reversed: man appears first (2:7), plants and animals later (19–20). Woman is created separately (2: 22), instead of simultaneously with the male as in 1:26–27. Whereas 1:26–28 places humans as rulers over earthly creation (cf. Ps. 8:5–9), 2: 15–17 makes man a cloistered servant of divinity, assigned menial labors and token responsibilities—though the underlying story is probably one of royal investiture.

Canaanite and Babylonian creation accounts, often associated with New Year festivals, depicted a divine struggle with primordial foes, culminating in the protagonist's victory, triumphal procession, enthronement, promulgation of law, and dedication of a sanctuary. Often, as in Marduk's battle (*Enuma Elish* 4. 28ff.) with Tiamat (cf. Heb. *Tehom*, "the Deep," Gen. 1:2), the protagonist struggles to contain and delimit primordial waters. Divine struggle with waters, victory over chaos, and cosmogonic promulgation of law/wisdom are found throughout biblical poetry (cf. Exod. 15; Isa. 40–42; 45; Heb. 3: 8; Pss. 18; 19; 24; 29; 33; 68; 93; 95; 104; Prov. 8:22–33; Job 38–41), and are closely associated with God's saving actions on behalf of Israel and its leaders. Creation accounts also occur in apocryphal sources (2 Esd. 6; Ecclus. 43). Christian authors introduced the idea of Christ as mediator and agent of creation (e.g., Col. 1:15–16). In doing this they were drawing on earlier traditions that said that divine Wisdom was the agent of creation, a tradition that appears both in the OT (e.g., Prov. 8:25–27) and in apocryphal writings (e.g., Wisd. of Sol. 7:24–25; Ecclus. 24:3, 9). Jewish and Christian apocalyptic (esp. *1 Enoch*; Revelation) also project creation motifs onto end time. ***See also*** Firmament; Genesis. J.W.R.

creature, any animate being whose existence is dependent upon God (see Gen. 1:20, 24; Ps. 104:24; Rev. 5:13). Despite some translations of 2 Cor. 5:17, Paul's reference there is probably to "a new creation" inclusively, not specifically to "a new creature." ***See also*** Creation; Life; Soul.

creeping things, a general term for various forms of reptile, insect, or worm life. Gen. 1: 24–26 uses it as a generic term. It is similarly used in the Flood story (Gen. 6:7, 20; 7:14, 23; 8:17,19). Such creatures are considered unclean (Lev. 22:5), but they join in praise of God (Ps. 148:10). They are associated with corruption and evil (Ezek. 8:10) and express awe at God's wrath (Ezek. 38:20), but they will participate in God's promised covenant (Hos. 2:18). It appears to be a general term for creatures that are neither birds, fish, nor wild or domesticated animals. R.S.B.

Crescens (kres'uhnz), a person who, when 2 Timothy was written, had left the writer for Galatia (Gaul?; 2 Tim. 4:10). Nothing more is known about him.

Crete (Caphtor in the OT), the fifth largest Mediterranean island, 152 miles long (243 km.) from west to east, 7.5-35 miles wide (12-56 km.) and 3,189 square miles in area (8,259 sq. km.). Crete forms the southern boundary of the Aegean Sea. While maintaining a resolute identity and culture of its own, its primary relationship is with Greece, rather than with Anatolia, Egypt, or the Levant, although there has been constant communication between them. Structurally related to the mountain ranges of the Peloponnesus and southwest Turkey, Crete is composed of four limestone massifs, reaching an altitude of 8,058 ft. (2,456 m.) in the center, almost that in the west, but only 4,757 ft. (1,450 m.) further east. In the south the mountains drop steeply into the sea, leaving little room for settlement, Kali Limenes (Gk., "Fair Havens," Acts 27:8) being the only good anchorage. The northern coast is less precipitous, with better harbors, and is consequently the most populated region.

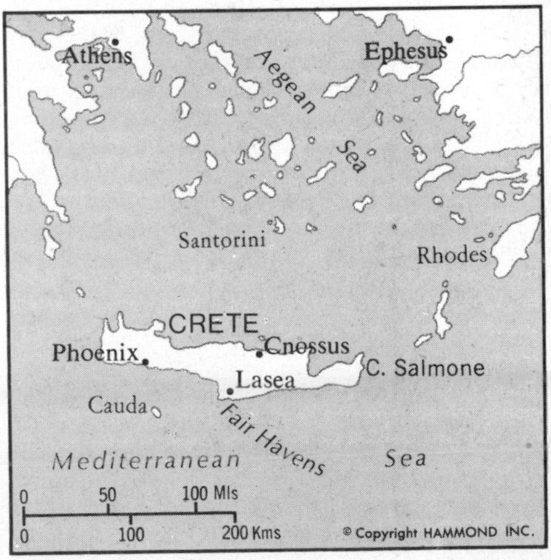

The island has winter rainfall (about 20 inches [500 mm.] on the north coast) and heavy snow on the mountains. Summers are dry and hot, especially when the "Libyan wind" sweeps across from the Sahara to the south, but the mountains may have thunderstorms. Winter gales can be severe, especially on the south coast, where northeast winds can pour tempestuously down the steep mountainsides (Acts 27:14–15). The now bare highlands were once thickly clothed with oak, cypress, juniper, pine, and Spanish chestnut. Grapes, olives, barley, and oats have always been the main crops; today citrus is also grown. Sheep and goats are reared on the mountain slopes.

Crete was first settled between 6000 and 5000 B.C., and gradually the brilliant Bronze Age Minoan culture developed. Large palaces were first built around 2000, and, after a severe earthquake about 1700 B.C., the even more splendid "New Palace" culture arose, with superb frescoes and sculpture as well as intricate ceremonial activity and widespread trade throughout the Mediterranean. The language of this period was Greek, written in "Linear B" script, and by 1500 Mycenaean Greek was becoming dominant. About 1450 a disastrous earthquake, related to the gigantic eruption of the volcanic island of Santorini, initiated a cultural decline, and Crete thereafter acted as "middleman" in the development of Mediterranean culture rather than as leader.

Biblical references to Caphtor or Crete are few. The Israelites, who played no active role at all on the Mediterranean Sea, knew the remote island chiefly as the home of the Philistines (Deut. 2:23; Jer. 47:4; Amos 9:7; see also Gen. 10:14; 1 Chron. 1:12), part of the great movement of the "Sea Peoples." Among these Philistine immigrants were the Cherethites and Pelethites, who formed an important part of David's army (2 Sam. 8:18; 15:18; 20:23).

The Letter to Titus speaks of a visit to Crete by the apostle Paul. Paul subsequently left Titus in Crete "to amend what was defective and appoint elders" (Titus 1:5). His derogatory, and probably unjustified, quotation about the Cretans being "always liars, evil beasts, lazy gluttons" (cf. Titus 1:10) comes from the same poem of the Cretan poet Epimenides that Paul had quoted in Athens (Acts 17:28). ***See also*** Fair Havens; Pelethites; Philistines. D.B.

crib. ***See*** Manger.

crimes and punishments. ***See*** Law.

Crispus (kris'puhs), according to Acts 18:8 the ruler of the synagogue in Corinth who became a Christian; he was baptized by Paul himself (1 Cor. 1:14). His conversion indicates that the Corinthian church was not entirely Gentile. ***See also*** Synagogue.

criticism, biblical. ***See*** Biblical Criticism.

cross, an ancient instrument of execution. Originally the "cross" was an upright stake to which the corpse of an executed criminal was bound for public display or on which the living body of a condemned person was affixed to await death. During Roman times a crossbar was sometimes added across the top of the stake forming a T (later known as St. Anthony's cross) or intersecting it to form the familiar Christian shape. Later an X-shaped form (St. Andrew's cross) was also employed.

This mode of execution is unknown in the OT, which only reports the practice of exposing the corpse (Deut. 21:22–23). It seems to have originated as an instrument of execution with the Persians, from whom it passed to the Greeks and Romans. Among the latter it was widely employed for its deterrent value, especially against rebellious slaves and seditious provincials.

Though the procedure was subject to wide variation according to the whim and sadism of the executioner, by the Roman period several features were fairly standard. With a placard proclaiming the crime hung around the neck, the condemned prisoner carried the crossbar, not the whole cross, to the place of execution where the upright stake was already in place. There the offender was stripped and flogged. The prisoner's arms were affixed to the crossbar with ropes or nails, and the crossbar was then raised and attached to the upright stake. A small wooden block attached to the stake beneath the buttocks supported the weight of the suspended body, which was bound to the stake with ropes. Often the feet were also affixed to the stake with ropes or nails. Because deterrence was a primary objective, the cross was always erected in a public place. Death came slowly, often only after several days, and resulted from the cumulative impact of thirst, hunger, exhaustion, exposure, and the traumatic effects of the scourging. After death the body was usually left hanging on the cross. Because of the protracted suffering and the extreme ignominy of this manner of execution, it was viewed by the Romans as the supreme penalty, the "most wretched of deaths" (Josephus), and generally reserved for the lowest classes and the most heinous crimes.

The Crucifixion of Jesus: The biblical account of Jesus' crucifixion reveals few variants from the usual procedure. The fact that Jesus was crucified confirms that his condemnation was pronounced by the Roman procurator (Pilate), who alone had the authority to impose *this* death sentence. Further, the wording on the placard ("The King of the Jews") reveals that the crime for which Jesus was condemned was not the Sanhedrin's charge of blasphemy, but the political crime of high treason, generated by messianic claims, which to Roman ears sounded like a threat to Caesar's sovereignty. Thus Pilate pronounced the death sentence reserved for treason, and Jesus was flogged (Mark 15:19) and led away to be crucified. Perhaps because Jesus was scourged *before* being led away and was thus too weak to carry the crossbar, a bystander was pressed into service (Mark 15:21).

Crosses: *(left to right, top)* Greek; St. Andrew's; Tau; *(bottom)* Latin; Celtic; Slavic or Russian.

The crucifixion took place outside the city near a thoroughfare (Mark 15:29). Jesus was stripped (Mark 15:24) and nailed hand and foot (Luke 24:39) to the cross, with the placard affixed above his head (Matt. 27:37). Following Jewish custom, Jesus was offered an opiate to dull the pain (Mark 15:23), but he rejected it. Death came rather quickly, after only six hours. Jesus' body was not left on the cross; a disciple, Joseph of Arimathea, appealed to Pilate for the body in accordance with the injunction of Deut. 21:23 (Mark 15:43–45).

In Theology: When Christians hailed as Messiah and worshiped as Lord one who died on a cross, a central theological problem was posed. How could such high status be accorded to one who died under the vilest death sentence, condemned as a criminal according to Roman law and cursed by God according to Jewish law (Deut. 21:23)? Paul's Letters reveal how foolish and scandalous this seemed to both Jews and Gentiles (1 Cor. 1:18–25) and also what an impetus it was to Christian theological reflection.

Quite early, Jesus' death was interpreted as an atonement, a sacrifice to deal with sin. Paul takes over this interpretation (Rom. 3:25) but expands it into a full theology of the cross that stresses its further significance. Thus Jesus' death on the cross, condemned by the Jewish law, marks the end of this law (Gal. 3:13), and participation in the cross through baptism means death to sin (Rom. 6:6) and to this world (Gal. 6:14). Along with the victory over these old forces, baptismal participation in the cross marks the beginning of a new life of grace (Gal. 2:19–21). Because these forces were defeated through a means that the world deemed scandalous and weak, judgment is leveled through the cross against the wisdom of the world while God shows through it that divine strength is paradoxically revealed in weakness (1 Cor. 1:18–25). Finally, the cross is not only a comfort to the oppressed, whose sufferings imitate the crucifixion and who can hope to share in the resurrection, but it also becomes a behavioral model as it symbolizes obedience and other-regarding love (Phil. 2:5–11).

The first three Gospels also use the cross to signify the life of self-renunciation demanded of believers (Mark 8:34). The fourth Gospel emphasizes instead the resurrection, which is paradoxically symbolized there by the raising of Jesus' body onto the cross (John 12:32). ***See also*** Blasphemy; Calvary; Joseph; Messiah; Pilate, Pontius; Sanhedrin.

Bibliography

Dahl, Nils A. *The Crucified Messiah.* Minneapolis, MN: Augsburg, 1974.

Hengel, Martin. *Crucifixion.* Philadelphia: Fortress, 1977.

Moltmann, Jürgen. *The Crucified God.* New York: Harper & Row, 1974. J.M.B.

crown, the translation for several Hebrew and Greek words designating special headpieces worn in biblical times. Among all items of apparel, a person's headgear was perhaps most significant in designating social, religious, and/or political status. The different words for "crown" probably reflect important nuances in the official, royal, or priestly position of those wearing such headdresses. Since crowns recovered from excavations or recognized on ancient monuments cannot be identified with the biblical terms, the specific characteristics of the words for "crown" remain unclear, although surely they represent such headpieces as circlets, diadems, turbans, and mitres, worn individually or in combination.

The most general Hebrew word for crown *('atarah)* is found frequently in poetic contexts. Another term *(nezer)* tends to have priestly associations, though such a distinction is imprecise because royal and priestly authorities were often closely linked (cf. Zech. 6:11–14). A third term *(keter)* appears only in Esther; and a related term *(koteret)* has architectural significance and is usually translated "capital." In the KJV "crown" renders another architectural term (Heb. *zayr;* "molding" in the RSV; e.g., Exod. 25: 11); and the top of the head *(kadkod)* also appears in English as "crown" (Job 2:7). In the NT the royal aspect is frequent in the use of Gk. *stephanos,* even when it denotes the "crown of thorns," but the word is also used to symbolize the final reward of faithful Christians (e.g. 2 Tim. 4:8; James 1:12; 1 Pet. 5:4; Rev. 2:10).

C.L.M.

crucible, a vessel, usually ceramic, employed for heating substances to high temperatures. It was used mainly for the refining of silver (Prov. 17:3; 27:21). It also designates the bottom of a small furnace where a bloom of metal gathers in the refining process. ***See also*** Refining; Silver; Smith.

crucifixion. ***See*** Cross; Jesus Christ.

cruse, a small oil jar. Mentioned in the story of the widow of Zarephath (1 Kings 17:12, 14, 16), such ceramic vessels are common in Iron Age archaeological finds.

crystal, a form of mineral with flat, symmetrical surfaces. The Greek word can mean ice or rock crystal, namely, pure silica or quartz in a transparent and colorless form (Rev. 4:6; 22:1; see also Job 28:17; Ezek 1:22).

cubit, the standard ancient Near Eastern linear measure. Theoretically it encompassed the distance from the elbow to the tip of the middle finger, about 17.5 to 20 inches. ***See also*** Weights and Measures.

cucumber *(Cucumis sativus)*, the familiar cool, water-filled, slender, fleshy "fruit" growing on a vine. It was commonly cultivated in Egypt (Num. 11:5) and Palestine as a staple of the diet. During the growing season, in order to discourage theft, the cucumber fields were guarded (Isa. 1:8).

Cucumber.

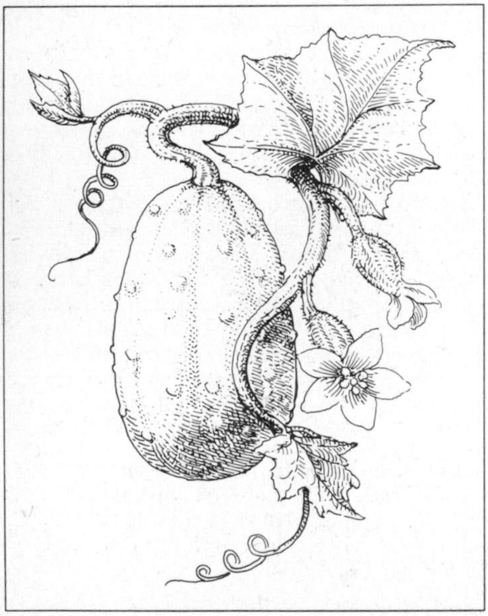

cults, illicit non-Israelite forms of worship. Throughout the history of ancient Israel, there were those who participated in and fostered the growth of cults (cf. 2 Kings 21). These cults arose from Canaanite influence in the land of Israel itself and from the influence of neighboring countries. One of the main tasks of the prophets was to return the people to the proper worship of God and to eliminate these competing cults (1 Kings 18:20–40). ***See also*** Asherah; Baal; Chemosh; Harlot; High Place; Idol; Milcom; Molech; Queen of Heaven; Tammuz; Topheth; Worship; Zeus.

cummin *(Cuminum cyminum)*, a cultivated herb whose tiny aromatic seeds were harvested by beating the stalks with a rod (Isa. 28:25, 27). It was used medicinally, as a perfume oil, and as a seasoning. Jesus uses the tithing even of those tiny seeds while not observing the Law's requirements to act justly and mercifully as an example of hypocrisy (Matt. 23:23).

Cummin.

cuneiform writing, a form of written communication done in wedge-shaped marks. A massive body of writings in cuneiform script has been unearthed during the past hundred and forty years. Most of these texts come from Mesopotamia, are impressed on clay tablets, and are written in the Sumerian or Akkadian languages of Mesopotamia. Writing was first invented in Mesopotamia. The cuneiform ideographic script was devised in the late fourth millennium B.C. in order to facilitate the administration of the large economic complexes that the southern Mesopotamian Sumerian temples had become. Originally the script was largely pictographic/ideographic. Increasingly, it developed a phonetic dimension, and in addition to representing concepts it could now also represent sounds. Moreover, elements began to be written in the order in which they occurred in speech. Even with phonetization, Mesopotamian cuneiform writing never surrendered its ideographic (some prefer logographic) quality and remained a mixed logographic-syllabic system of linguistic representation.

The Earliest Texts: The earliest texts were administrative accounts and sign lists for scribes. With increased phonetization, the script began to convey complex statements in Sumerian as well as words in a foreign language, namely, Akkadian. Narrations and utterances were now recorded, though initially writing served as an aid to memory rather than a full record. Alongside administrative and lexical texts, we witness the appearance of votive inscriptions, narratives, incantations, hymns, myths, and proverbial instructions. Accordingly, a distinction may be drawn between two types of texts: those that have no existence except in writing and require writing as their medium (these come into existence alongside and consequent to the invention of writing, e.g., administrative accounts, lexical lists, collections of omens) and texts that exist independently of writing and are set down as the cultural importance of writing is discovered (e.g., epics, incantations, hymns). The recording of this latter type becomes fuller and more explicit in the course of time and new texts of this type may eventually be composed originally in writing.

With the development of phonetization came the adaptation of the script by Semitic speakers for the representation of Akkadian. The system of writing was eventually adopted and adapted for the rendering of Elamite, Hurrian, Urartian, Hittite, and others. The Mesopotamian writing system was not borrowed in a vacuum; those who borrowed the writing were themselves influenced by the literary forms and, in turn, became bearers of the culture. In this manner, Mesopotamia influenced biblical literature and Greek mythology. And cuneiform forms became the point of origin and model for a developed Near Eastern legal tradition.

Writings in Sumerian and Akkadian: The balance of this article focuses on Mesopotamian writings in Sumerian and Akkadian. The classification of texts according to whether they are canonical, archival, or monumental provides a convenient arrangement for purposes of schematic presentation.

Canonical texts include those literary, religious, technical, and scholastic texts that were copied, transmitted, revised, edited, and occasionally even preserved in ancient institutions and private collections. One such institutional collection was the famous library of Assurbanipal. The discovery of this collection in Nineveh in the mid-nineteenth century served as the starting point for the recovery and reconstruction of Akkadian literature. While Sumerian texts were also found in the library, it was the discarded remains of the Old Babylonian schools of Nippur that served as the basis for the reconstruction of Sumerian literature. Canonical literature is normally sorted into four major temporal clusters: Sumerian texts from the third millennium (Fara, Abu-Salabikh, etc.); Sumerian texts from the Ur III and Old Babylonian periods (Nippur, Ur); Akkadian texts from the Old Babylonian period (e.g., *Gilgamesh, Atrahasis, Anzu);* and standard Babylonian Akkadian texts from the end of the second and the first millennium. Prior to ca. 1250 B.C. in the post–Old Babylonian period, canonical texts are found mainly outside of Mesopotamia (e.g., Amarna, Ugarit, Boghazkoi). It is often assumed that almost all major works of Akkadian literature were composed and stan-

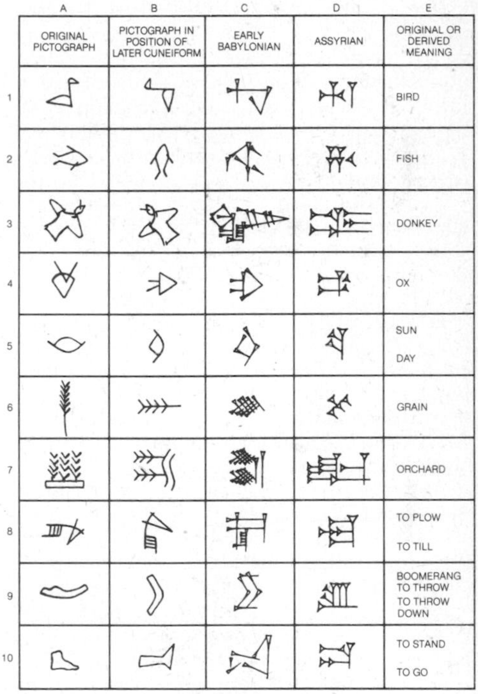
A
B
C
D
E
ORIGINAL PICTOGRAPH
PICTOGRAPH IN POSITION OF LATER CUNEIFORM
EARLY BABYLONIAN
ASSYRIAN
ORIGINAL OR DERIVED MEANING
1
BIRD
2
FISH
3
DONKEY
4
OX
5
SUN
DAY
6
GRAIN
7
ORCHARD
8
TO PLOW
TO TILL
9
BOOMERANG
TO THROW
TO THROW DOWN
10
TO STAND
TO GO

Diagram showing pictorial origin of ten Early Babylonian and Assyrian cuneiform signs.

dardized by the latter half of the second millennium, and that the first millennium was relatively impoverished as regards the creation of traditional religious literature. A more reasoned judgment seems to be that also Mesopotamia of the first millennium was religiously and literarily creative, certainly far more creative than is normally assumed, and that some classics (e.g., perhaps *Enuma elish* and *Maqlû)* were actually composed during the several centuries prior to their attestation in the libraries and collections of Assyria and Babylonia of the eighth century B.C. and later. By the same token, the oft-repeated statement that the religious poetry of the post–Old Babylonian period is characterized in the main by stock phrases combined to create stereotyped forms is to be modified and perhaps disregarded. Because of the small number of workers in the field, the need to sort and decipher tablets, and the concentration by twentieth-century scholars on the literature of the earlier periods, much more penetrating and sophisticated study remains to be done concerning the creative and editorial activities of literati and theologians in the centers of ancient Babylonia and Assyria.

The reader of the Bible as well as all humanists will find particular pleasure in reading such Akkadian texts as the creation epic *(Enuma elish)*, the *Epic of Gilgamesh*, prayers of the individual supplicant, sequences of incantations and their accompanying ritual, wisdom compositions, and the humorous *Poor Man of Nippur*. Of no little interest, also, are the scholarly collections of such items as medical prescriptions, omens, and lexical equations. In these scribal handbooks, both the individual entry as well as the pattern of arrangement of units merit attention.

The masses of archival texts and numerous monumental texts allow us to study government administration, international diplomacy, economic enterprises, military organization, and the like. Not always are we able to integrate or even harmonize the contemporary evidence of these texts with the information embedded in the traditional canonical literature. Here the reader of the Bible may be particularly drawn to examine such diverse bodies of texts as the Akkadian Amarna letters written to Egypt from Canaan in the fourteenth century B.C., collections of laws such as the code of Hammurabi, and Neo-Assyrian and Neo-Babylonian royal inscriptions and historiography. Particularly during these last mentioned periods (750 B.C. on) there was direct contact between Israelites on the one hand and Assyrians/Babylonians on the other, and during these periods Mesopotamian literary forms and intellectual life began to have a profound impact on the Bible and rabbinic Judaism.

Bibliography

Hallo, W. W., and W. K. Simpson. *The Ancient Near East: A History*. New York: Harcourt Brace Jovanovich, 1971. Pp. 151–169, 178–183.

Jacobsen, T. "Mesopotamia: Literature." *Encyclopedia Judaica*. Vol. 16. Cols. 1505k–1505aa.

Oppenheim, A. L. *Ancient Mesopotamia*. Chicago: University of Chicago Press, 1977. Pp. 228–287.

I.T.A.

cup, a utensil for holding a limited amount of liquid for individual consumption. Cups were made of precious metal (Gen. 44:1–34; Jer. 51:7; Rev. 17:4; cf. the cuplike oil holder of the Temple lamp, Exod. 25:31–35). The world of the Bible is a world of limited good; everything that exists is perceived to exist in limited amounts, in amounts that cannot be augmented without depriving others. In this perspective, all persons can be said to have their "cup," i.e., the limited and fixed amount of whatever God has to offer them in life, either in entirety, such as a lifetime of devotedness to God (Pss. 11:6; 16:5) or a life of abundance (overflowing cup, Ps. 23:5), or in part, such as rescue (cup of salvation, Ps. 111:13; cup of consolation, Jer. 16:7), or punishment (cup of wrath, Isa. 51:17; Hab. 2:15; cup of staggering or reeling, Isa. 51:22; Zech. 12:2). The cup then symbolizes a person's lot or fate (Jer. 49:12; Ezek. 23:31–33; Mark 10:38–39 and parallels; 14:36 and parallels), with a cup of wine serving as a prophetic symbol of the significance of one's fate (Jer. 15:15–28; at the Lord's Supper, Mark 14:23–25 and parallels; 1 Cor. 11:25–29). At a formal meal there was a cup of blessing (1 Cor. 10:16) marking a new stage in the meal and symbolizing the unity of meal participants (1 Cor. 10:21).

B.J.M.

cupbearer, a confidant in a royal entourage (1 Kings 10:5). The cupbearer could exercise influence on a king's policies (Neh. 1:11–2:8). The first servant of the Pharaoh imprisoned with Joseph had held the Pharaoh's cup "in my hand . . ." (Gen. 40:11), suggesting that the cupbearer carried responsibility for nurturing (giving food and drink to) those in his care. The term also refers to God in his nurturing relationship with creation (Ps. 104:13). ***See also*** Joseph; Nehemiah, The Book of.

curse and blessing, oral pronouncements for harm or good.

Terminology: The three most frequently used words for "curse" in the Hebrew Bible are *alah*, *arar*, and *killel*. The first *(alah)*, meaning curse as imprecation, describes curse from the point of view of its pronouncement or utterance (hence, properly "malediction"). It is used in oath or adjuration, as a conditional curse to achieve a desired result or to preclude an undesirable one, or as a conditional imprecation or prayer for the punishment of an evildoer whose guilt cannot be proved. The second term *(arar*, especially in its passive participial form *arur*, "cursed") describes curse from an operational point of view, as effecting a ban or barrier to exclude or anathematize (hence roughly equivalent to "spell"). It is a decree rather than an imprecation or prayer. The third term *(killel)* describes a wide range of injurious activity, from verbal abuse to material harm. Its basic meaning is "to treat lightly," i.e., to treat with disrespect, to repudiate, to abuse. In those locutions where the Deity is the object of this verb, it suggests the lack of respect for the ethical standards sanctioned by God. Its opposite is not "bless" so much as "to fear God," i.e., to show respect for the standards ordained by God. The related noun *(kelalah)* describes the result of curse or abusive treatment, i.e., "misfortune, harm, calamity" or the like.

Over against this variety of words for "curse," there is only a single word for "bless" (*berek*, and its related noun *berakah*, "blessing, good fortune," along with the passive participle *baruk*, "blessed," analogous to *arur*, "cursed"). The content of "blessing" includes such goods as vitality, health, longevity, fertility, and numerous progeny; "curse," on the other hand, results in death, illness, childlessness, and such disasters as drought, famine, and war.

Theological Considerations: Curse and blessing are among the basic organizing concepts of the book of Genesis, concepts that link the primeval history of Genesis 1–11 to the history of the Patriarchs in Genesis 12–50. The Priestly author of Genesis 1 places the divine blessing on humankind at the beginning of his work (1:28); but the Yahwist chapters that follow are a narrative dominated by God's curse, from the man and woman (Gen. 3:16–19) to Cain (4:11) to the Flood and the renewal of the divine blessing to its survivors (9:1). The cycle of sin and curse begins again, climaxing in the hybris of the Tower of Babel (11:1–9), but it is countered now by a new act of God, the blessing of Abram (12:1–3). This is the beginning of a history of blessing (22:15–18; 24:60; 26:2–4) that culminates in the blessing of Jacob by Isaac (27:27–29) and by God (32:27).

Balancing this history of blessing is the history of salvation in Exodus, Leviticus, and Numbers. These two alternative modes of divine activity, blessing and salvation, have been studied especially by C. Westermann. In Deuteronomy curse and blessing are structured after the model of the suzerainty treaty. Deuteronomy brings the Torah to a close on the note of covenant, with blessings promised for covenant obedience and curse for covenant breach (Deut. 28). "I have set before you life and death, blessing and curse" (Deut. 30:19); the history that follows (Joshua–2 Kings) demonstrates the tragic consequences of choosing death and curse, a theme fundamental to the pre-exilic prophets. The relationship between blessing and curse in Deuteronomy and the Prophets can be seen by comparing such traditional curses as Deut. 28:30–40; Amos 5:11; Mic. 6:15; Zeph. 1:13; and Hag. 1:6 to corresponding formulations of blessing (Deut. 6:11; Josh. 24:13; Amos 9:14–15; Isa. 62:8–9; 65:21–23). In the NT, blessings are frequent (e.g., Matt. 5:3–11; Rom. 1:25; Eph. 1:3) but Jesus commanded his followers not to curse (Luke 6:28; cf. Rom. 12:14).

Bibliography

Brichto, H. C. *The Problem of "Curse" in the Hebrew Bible*. Journal of Biblical Literature Monograph Series 13. Philadelphia: Society of Biblical Literature, 1963.

Hillers, D. R. *Treaty-Curses and the Old Testament Prophets*. Biblica et orientalia 15. Rome: Pontifical Biblical Institute, 1964.

Westermann, C. *Blessing in the Bible and the Life of the Life of the Church*. Overtures to Biblical Theology Series. Philadelphia: Fortress, 1978.

J.S.K.

Cush (ko͝osh). ***See*** Ethiopia.

Cushan-rishathaim (ko͞o'shan ri-shah-thay'im), the name of a king by whom the Israelites were oppressed until delivered under the leadership of the judge Othniel (twelfth century B.C.; Judg. 3:8–10).

cylinder seals. ***See*** Seal.

cymbal. ***See*** Music.

cypress *(Cupressus sempervirens)*, a kind of tall evergreen found among stands of cedar and oak. Because of their beauty, cypresses were used as ornamentals in gardens and cemeteries. The hard fragrant wood was preferred for buildings and furniture (Isa. 44:14, RSV: "holm tree"). The fir trees supplied by Hiram of Tyre to Solomon for his Temple and palace (1 Kings 9:11) were cypress, as was also the "gopher wood" of Noah's ark (Gen. 6:14). ***See also*** Fir Tree; Woods.

Cypress.

Cyprus (sī'pruhs), an island lying in the eastern Mediterranean about sixty miles west of the Syrian coast and about the same distance from the coast of Turkey. Approximately a hundred and forty miles long and sixty miles wide (about the same size as ancient Israel), the island was known as Alashia in the cuneiform literature, and Elishah in the OT (Ezek. 27:7; cf. Gen. 10:4;

1 Chron. 1:7). Some also equate the island with the biblical name Kittim (Jer. 1:10), although others identify the latter with Crete. By NT times the island was called *Kypros*, a Greek word from which the word "copper" comes. Cyprus was famous throughout the ancient world for its copper, a metal whose importance made the island a center of seafaring commerce. The island's active participation in world trade is evidenced by the discovery of great quantities of Cypriot imports in ancient Mesopotamia, the Levant, Egypt, Asia Minor, and the Aegean world. Apparently an independent state during the second half of the second millennium B.C., Cyprus was colonized and ruled by Phoenicia in the tenth–eighth centuries, then subjugated by the Assyrians in the late eighth and seventh centuries.

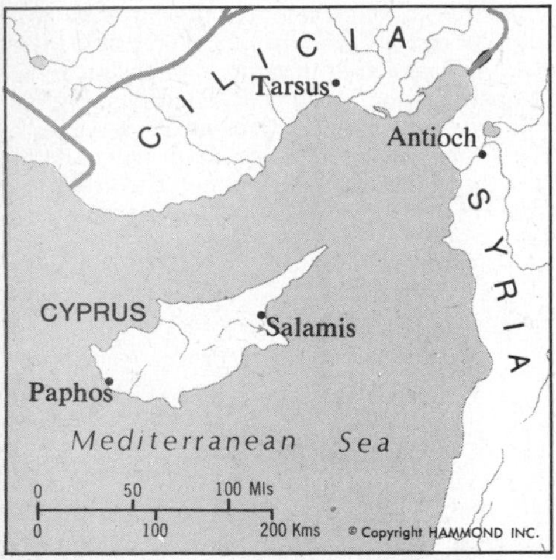

Cyprus subsequently became part of the Greek and Roman empires. A Jewish population is attested on the island as early as Ptolemy I (cf. 1 Macc. 15:23; 2 Macc. 12:2), and by the Roman period (63 B.C.–A.D. 325) that population was significant. A Jew named Barnabas, an early convert to Christianity, was a native of Cyprus (Acts 4:36), as were some of the other early disciples (Acts 11:19–20; 21:16). Acts reports that Paul and Barnabas traveled across the island, from Salamis to Paphos, on their first missionary journey (Acts 13:4–13). At Paphos they encountered the sorcerer Bar-Jesus and the proconsol Sergius Paulus. Barnabas and Mark later returned to Cyprus during Paul's second missionary journey (Acts 15:39). D.A.D.

Cyrene (sī-reen'uh), city in Cyrenaica (modern Libya) which had a thriving Jewish community of settlers from Egypt from Ptolemaic times (late fourth century B.C.). Two noted Hellenistic Jewish writers, Jason, whose history was abbreviated in 2 Maccabees, and Ezekiel, the tragedian, came from Cyrene. People from Cyrene were known for their patriotism and their ties to Palestine (Acts 6:9). Simon of Cyrene is said to have carried Jesus' cross (Mark 15:21). Cyrenian Christians were prominent in Antioch (Acts 11:20; 13:1).

Cyrenius. ***See*** Quirinius, P. Sulpicius.

Cyrus II (sī'ruhs; Heb. *kōreš*, Akkadian *kuraš*, Persian *kuruš*; etymology unknown), a Persian emperor and founder of the Achaemenid dynasty (ruled Babylonia 539–530 B.C.). His name occurs twenty-two times in the Bible, in the books of Daniel, Ezra, 1 and 2 Chronicles, and Isaiah. Extrabiblical evidence comes from the classical Greek authors Herodotus and Xenophon (though their reports are often encrusted with legend) as well as cuneiform records. From the latter we learn that Cyrus's ancestor was Teispes of Anshan. Cyrus's grandfather was named Cyrus (I); his father, Cambyses (I); his mother, Mandane, was the daughter of Median king Astyages. Cyrus is therefore known to moderns as Cyrus II; Cyrus II's son, who ruled Babylonia from 530 to 522 B.C., was Cambyses II. Cyrus's capital was Pasargadae, in what is now southern Iran.

Cyrus's military victories eventually put him in possession of the largest empire the world at that time had yet seen. They began with the conquest of Media (549), followed by Lydia (546) and Babylonia (539). It would seem that the Babylonian provinces of Eber nāri (today's Syria, Lebanon, and Israel) fell to him after the conquest of Babylonia, although no specific mention of them is extant in contemporary records.

Cyrus's policy toward the peoples of his empire was one of tolerance and understanding. His authorization of the rebuilding of the Jerusalem Temple by returning Judeans (end of 2 Chronicles; beginning of Ezra) accords well with what we know from contemporaneous documents. Isaiah (45:1–3) speaks with enthusiasm of Cyrus as the anointed one (messiah) of the Lord. Because of these achievements, Cyrus II's reign has been characterized as "a great turning point in ancient history" by the modern historian Richard N. Frye.

A co-regency with his son, Cambyses, ran for a short while in 530 and ended in the same year with the death of Cyrus in battle. Achaemenid rule in Babylonia continued for two hundred years until another "great turning point in ancient history," the coming of Alexander III, the Great. ***See also*** Persia. D.B.W.

Opposite: David, the most powerful king of biblical Israel, is depicted as a Byzantine emperor in a sixth-century A.D. mosaic at the Monastery of St. Catherine, Sinai.

D

D, the siglum for the Deuteronomist, one of the sources of the Pentateuch. ***See also*** Deuteronomist; Deuteronomistic Framework; Deuteronomistic Historian; Sources of the Pentateuch.

dagger. ***See*** Sword; Weapons.

Dagon (day'gahn), an ancient Semitic deity attested in the northern Mesopotamian area from the late third millennium and in the entire West Semitic area through biblical times. The etymology of the name is disputed; Jerome's derivation of it from Hebrew *dag*, "fish," is farfetched. More probable is the root attested in Arabic *dagana*, "to be cloudy, rainy," appropriate to a god of rain and fertility. The common Northwest Semitic word for grain, *dagan*, is to be derived from the fertility god, like Latin *ceres*, "bread, grain," from the god Ceres. The texts from Ugarit give no information about the god except that he is the father of Baal Haddu, the major god of fertility at Ugarit; Dagon does have a temple at Ugarit so he must have been honored in public worship.

The Philistines, after they settled on the coast of Palestine in the twelfth century B.C., honored Dagon. The Bible sees the god as the chief god of the Philistines, at least as the god to whom thanks were given after a victory. In 1 Sam. 5:2–7, God represented by the captured Ark in the temple at Ashdod causes the statue of Dagon to fall before him; the second fall destroys the statue. In Judg. 16:23, the imprisoned Samson pulls down around his head the temple of Dagon with the help of God. According to 1 Chron. 10:10, the Philistines hung up the head of Saul as a trophy in the temple of Dagon, presumably at Beth-shean (cf. 1 Sam. 31:12). 1 Macc. 10:83 and 11:4 mention a temple of Dagon in Ashdod. The place names, Beth-dagon in Judah (Josh. 15:41) and Beth-dagon in Asher (Josh. 19:27) preserve the name of the deity. R.J.C.

dainties, delicious sweets, delicacies, and confections generally served at the tables of kings (Gen. 49:20). While such foods were not viewed as inherently unfavorable just because they appeal to one's appetite (Job 33:20; Rev. 18:14), the prudent Israelite was to avoid eating them at the table of unscrupulous persons whose intentions might be harmful (Ps. 141:4; Prov. 23:3, 6).

daleth (dah'leth), the fourth letter of the Hebrew alphabet; its numerical value is four. The earliest form of the letter in proto-Sinaitic inscriptions resembles a fish. The later early Phoenician form became a triangle, which has survived in the Greek letter delta. Later Phoenician and early Hebrew forms of the ד

The Ark of God being returned by the Philistines (left; cf. 1 Sam. 6:7–8) after it has caused the statue of Dagon to break in front of his temple (right; cf. 1 Sam. 5:2–5); wall painting from the synagogue at Dura-Europos, third century A.D.

letter add a downward stroke to the triangle. It was this form that eventually developed into the letter found in the classical Hebrew square script. In Judaism this letter is often used as an abbreviation of the divine name (tetragrammaton). ***See also*** Writing.

Dalmanutha (dal-muh-nōō'thuh; etymology uncertain), unidentified site to which Jesus sailed across the Sea of Galilee after feeding the four thousand (Mark 8:10; various manuscripts read "Magadan," "Magedan," "Magdala," and the parallel in Matt. 15:39 has "Magadan"). It probably refers to the vicinity of Magdala. ***See also*** Magdala.

Dalmatia (dal-may'shee-uh), the southwestern part of Illyricum along the modern Yugoslav coast of the Adriatic Sea. Illyricum was established as a Roman province in A.D. 9–10. The name Dalmatia dates from the period of the Flavian emperors (ca. A.D. 70) and came to be used interchangeably with the name of the province as a whole. In 2 Tim. 4:10 Titus leaves Paul to go to Dalmatia. ***See also*** Illyricum.

Damaris (dam'uh-ris), a woman who was one of Paul's few converts in Athens (Acts 17:34).

Damascus (duh-mas'kuhs), the capital city of modern Syria, located about sixty miles east of the Mediterranean coast almost directly east of Sidon. On a plateau about 2,300 feet above sea level, the city had the waters of the oasis Ghuta, which was nourished by the twin rivers draining eastward from the Anti-Lebanon range: the Nahr Barada (Abana), which subdivides into numerous branches after a course through a narrow gorge out of the hills; and the Nahr el-'Awaj (Pharpar), just south of the town. Both rivers dissipate into the eastern desert. The quality of its water sources was compared by Naaman with the Jordan (2 Kings 5:12). The "River" (Euphrates) was a political metaphor used by Isaiah to signal Assyria's destruction of the Damascus-based Aramaean kingdom under Rezin (Isa. 8:5–8).

Damascus, one of the oldest continuously inhabited sites known to archaeologists, figured long and often in biblical awareness. It was a reference place for Abraham's rescue of his kinsmen (Gen. 14:15). David brought it within Israelite control (2 Sam. 8:5–6), but during Solomon's reign the first of a series of Aramaean kings made Damascus his capital city, continuing to intervene in the life of Israel and Judah until the Assyrian conquest in 732 B.C. In this series of local dynastic politics, biblical traces occur of the founder Rezon (1 Kings 11:23–25); Tabrimmon, ally of the Judean Abijam against Israel (1 Kings 15:19); his father Hezion (same verse); his son Ben-hadad (I, 900–875 B.C.), who was allied with Baasha of Israel, but later with Asa of Judah (1 Kings 15:18–19); Ben-hadad II (1 Kings 20) and his son Hadadezer who fought Ahab of Israel; and Ben-hadad III who was killed by Hazael (843–797 B.C.; 2 Kings 8:7–15) who then succeeded him. The deepest penetration into Israel was under Ben-hadad IV, who even laid siege to the capital city, Samaria (2 Kings 6:24). Only under Israel's Jeroboam II was Damascus restored to Israel's earlier borders (2 Kings 14:28). When Assyria's pressure worked west, the effort of Rezin of Damascus with Pekah of Israel to bring Judah's king Ahaz into the alliance against Assyria (known as the Syro-Ephraimite War) in 734 B.C. failed (Isaiah's counsel of Judah [7:14] on the occasion is the "young woman shall conceive and bear a son" passage used in Matthew's birth narrative in 1:23), Assyria's success brought the destruction of Damascus in 732 B.C., including Rezin's death.

Damascus became an administrative zone under Assyria, but not until it was made a Nabatean capital under Roman policy (85 B.C.) did any real power revive. The conquest of Aretas III by Rome in 65 B.C. led to Nabatean rule by governors, including Aretas IV who was in charge when Paul came to Damascus (Acts 9:2–30).

As reflected in the names of several monarchs, the chief deity of the city was the storm god Hadad on whose temple site the Roman emperor Theodosius (A.D. 379–395) built the church of Saint John Baptist. Under the Umayyad Muslims (A.D. eighth century) this was destroyed except for the perimeter wall and the towers at the four corners when al-Walīd built the famous Great Mosque there.

R.S.B.

Dan. 1 One of the twelve sons of Jacob, by Bilhah, handmaiden of Rachel (Gen. 30:1–6); he is the ancestor of the tribe of Dan.

2 One of the twelve tribes of Israel assigned a small piece of land west of Benjamin; when they

A Greek and Aramaic inscription found at Tel Dan from the late third–early second century B.C. contains the word "Dan" (second line) and helps to identify the site.

were crowded out, however, they migrated north (Josh. 19:40–48; Judg. 18).

3 A city on the northern border of Israel ("Dan to Beer-sheba" expresses the northern and southern limits of Israel). Formerly called Laish, it is mentioned in the execration texts, the eighteenth-century B.C. Mari tablets, and the records of the Egyptian pharaoh Thutmose III. It is identified with Tel Dan (modern Tell el-Qadi) covering about 50 acres in the center of a fertile valley near one of the principal springs feeding the Jordan River.

Tel Dan has been excavated by A. Biran since 1966. The earliest occupation, probably the full extent of the *tell*, goes back to about the middle of the third millennium B.C. A Middle Bronze II rampart (1900–1700 B.C.) surrounds the city and on the southeast a mud-brick gateway with two towers joined by an intact arch of three courses is preserved to a height of 20 feet. A Late Bronze Age tomb with quantities of Mycenaean pottery, gold and silver jewelry, bronze swords, and ivory boxes indicates a prosperous fourteenth–thirteenth century occupation in the vicinity.

A ninth-century B.C. gate and fortifications have been revealed, and biblical sources claim Jeroboam set up a golden calf at Dan to provide the Northern Kingdom with a sanctuary (1 Kings 12:26–30). Archaeologists have uncovered a sacred area, perhaps a *bamah* (Heb., "high place") on the northwest. Within three phases related to Jeroboam I, Ahab's rebuilding, and Jeroboam II's prosperity, cultic incense burners and stands, figurines, and a horned altar have been uncovered. The area continued in use down to Hellenistic and Roman times. A bilingual Greek and Aramaic votive inscription of the late third or early second century B.C. to the "god who is in Dan" identifies the site. An elaborate water installation existed near the spring in Roman times, and the latest coins belong to the time of Constantine the Great (ca. A.D. 325). N.L.L.

dancing, rhythmic bodily movement, often to music. As a sign of rejoicing, dance had a place in the secular and religious life of ancient Israel. Dance could be accompanied by song and instrumental music. Women customarily greeted the return of victorious soldiers with music and dance (1 Sam. 18:6), a practice akin to recent bedouin custom. Dancing had a role at the old harvest festival at Shiloh (Judg. 21:21). Dance could be performed in the worship of God (Ps. 149:3). When he led the Ark of the Covenant to Jerusalem, David danced before the Lord (2 Sam. 6:14), a performance his wife Michal thought unseemly. The Song of Songs celebrates the dance of the Shulammite (Song of Sol. 6:13).

Dance also played a role in the religions of Israel's neighbors. Dance before the golden calf (Exod. 32:19) represents a pagan practice. Cul-

Terra-cotta plate with dancers, musicians, and singers (2000–1600 B.C.).

tic dance can be inferred from a Ugaritic text. Egyptian reliefs portray both male and female dancers. Cultic dancers are known to have existed in Mesopotamia.

In the NT, dance is a natural part of the celebration of the return of the prodigal son (Luke 15:25). Dancers were sometimes engaged for entertainment at royal courts in the Hellenistic and Roman worlds (cf. Matt. 14:6). ***See also*** David; Gebal; Michal; Shiloh. R.M.G.

Daniel, the hero of the Book of Daniel, represented as a Jew in the Babylonian exile who is skilled in the interpretation of dreams and is miraculously preserved in the lions' den. Daniel

Daniel as depicted in a sixth-century A.D. mosaic at the Monastery of St. Catherine, Sinai.

was already the name of a legendary wise man in Ezek. 28:3 and was linked with Noah and Job (Ezek. 14:14). This legendary figure is probably related to the *Dnil* of the Ugaritic Aqhat legend (from about 1500 B.C.). *Dnil* was a judge who defended the fatherless and the widow. The function of judge is suggested by the name Daniel (Heb., "my judge is God" or possibly "judge of God") and appears again in the story of Susanna. The author of the biblical book probably took over the legendary name for his fictional hero. ***See also*** Daniel, The Book of. J.J.C.

Daniel, the Additions to, several stories, a prayer, and a hymn not found in the Masoretic (Hebrew) Text (MT) of Daniel, but present in both the Septuagint (LXX) and Theodotion, two distinct Greek versions of the OT. These passages are the Song of the Three Children, Susanna, and Bel and the Dragon. The Song of the Three Children is included between Dan. 3:23 and 3:24. In Theodotion, Susanna stands at the beginning of Daniel, and Bel and the Dragon at its end, while the LXX version places both additions at the end. Protestants have relegated the Additions to the Apocrypha, while Catholics retain them as part of Daniel.

It is difficult to disentangle the history of the text of Daniel, and the role of the Additions in it is only one of a series of thorny problems. Daniel seems to have grown by accretion, beginning with the stories of chaps. 2–6. The Additions are only the final stage in that process. Susanna and Bel and the Dragon may represent part of a larger cycle of stories associated with the legendary figure of Daniel, similar to the ones found in chaps. 1–6 of the NT. The prayer (vv. 1–22) and the hymn (vv. 28–68) in the Song of the Three Children are probably independent liturgical compositions. All of these passages seem to have been added to the Hebrew-Aramaic archetypes of the versions of Daniel in the LXX and Theodotion sometime between the composition of Daniel during the Maccabean revolt (167–164 B.C.) and 100 B.C., the probable date of the LXX translation of Daniel. Along with 1 Esdras and the Rest of Esther, the Additions are evidence of the fluidity of the texts of some parts of the OT prior to the end of the first century A.D. ***See also*** Bel and the Dragon; Daniel, The Book of; Song of the Three Children; Susanna; Texts, Versions, Manuscripts, Editions. D.W.S.

Daniel, the Book of, an OT Bible book placed with the Writings in the Hebrew Bible but with the Prophets in the ancient collections of Scripture. Chaps. 1–6 are stories set at the Babylonian and Persian courts, narrated in the third person. Chaps. 7–12 are apocalyptic revelations, narrated in the first person. The Greek translations include certain additions accepted as canonical by the Roman Catholic Church: the Prayer of Azariah and the Song of the Three Young Men in chap. 3 and the stories of Susanna and Bel and the Dragon in additional chapters. Even within the twelve chapters of Daniel in the Hebrew Bible there are signs of composite authorship. Chaps. 1:1–2:4a and chaps. 8–12 are in Hebrew; chaps. 2:4b–7:28 are in Aramaic.

The stories in Daniel 1–6 bristle with historical problems. Chap. 4 tells of the transformation of Nebuchadnezzar into a beast. This story seems to have its origin in an episode in the life of Nabonidus, the last Babylonian king. A variant of the tradition has been found in the "Prayer of Nabonidus" among the Dead Sea Scrolls. Chap. 5 represents Belshazzar as king of Babylon at the time of its destruction, although he was never actually king. Chap. 6 speaks of a wholly unhistorical Darius the Mede who is said to have been the conqueror of Babylon. Darius was the name of later Persian monarchs. In view of these problems, the stories in chaps. 1–6 must have been written a considerable time after the Babylonian exile.

The apocalyptic section of the book, chaps. 7–12, can be dated more precisely. Chap. 11 contains a lengthy prophecy of history, communicated to Daniel by an angel. No names are mentioned, but persons and events can be easily identified down to Antiochus IV Epiphanes of Syria and his persecution of the Jews, which began in 168 B.C. The prophecy goes on to predict, incorrectly, that the king would die in the

OUTLINE OF CONTENTS

The Book of Daniel

I. The tales (chaps. 1–6)
   A. Training and testing of youths (chap. 1)
   B. Nebuchadnezzar's dream (chap. 2)
   C. The fiery furnace (chap. 3)
   D. Nebuchadnezzar's madness (chap. 4)
   E. Belshazzar's feast (chap. 5)
   F. The lions' den (chap. 6)
II. The visions (chaps. 7–12)
   A. The beasts from the sea and the son of man (chap. 7)
   B. The ram and the he-goat (chap. 8)
   C. The interpretation of Jeremiah's prophecy (chap. 9)
   D. The angel's revelation (chaps. 10–12)
      1. The apparition of the angel (chap. 10)
      2. The angel's prophecy of the course of history (chap. 11)
      3. The resurrection (12:1–4)
      4. Concluding material (12:5–13)

land of Israel. We must infer that the accurate "prophecy" was written after the fact and that the actual time of composition was during the persecution, but prior to the king's death in 164 B.C. The persecution is also the focal point of the other apocalyptic revelations in chaps. 7–12. By contrast, there is no clear allusion to it in chaps. 1–6.

The composition of the book, then, can be reconstructed as follows: the Aramaic stories were traditional tales that probably took shape in the third century B.C. Chap. 7 was added in Aramaic after the outbreak of the persecution. Chaps. 8–12 were then added in Hebrew, perhaps for nationalistic reasons. Chap. 1 was either translated from the Aramaic or composed as an introduction to the book, in Hebrew. Scholarly opinions vary on the details of this reconstruction but there is a consensus on its main outline. Many conservative Christians however continue to defend the view that the whole book was composed in the sixth century B.C. and that Daniel was a historical person.

In its final form the book of Daniel was intended to offer hope and consolation to the persecuted Jews. It shows no sympathy for the armed revolt of the Maccabees. Instead it advocates a stance of piety and acceptance of martyrdom. The victory is in the hands of Michael the Archangel. The martyrs will be rewarded in the resurrection, when they will "shine like the stars." Daniel is the only book in the Hebrew Bible that clearly attests a belief in resurrection. It is also the only OT example of the apocalyptic genre. Daniel's visions are interpreted by an angel. The division of history into a set number of periods, which is characteristic of apocalyptic writings, is found in the four-kingdom prophecy in chap. 2 and again in chap. 7. The prophecy of Jer. 25:11–12 and 29:10, that the Jews would be restored after seventy years, is reinterpreted in Dan. 9 as seventy weeks of years. The most influential part of the book, however, is the vision in chap. 7 of "one like a son of man coming with the clouds of heaven" (v. 13). This figure is variously interpreted as a collective representation of the Jewish people, or, more probably, as their angelic representative, Michael. In the NT the phrase "son of man" from Dan. 7:13 was adapted so that Son of man became a title for Jesus (see Mark 14:62). ***See also*** Apocalyptic Literature; Daniel; Darius; Dreams.

Bibliography

Collins, John J. *The Apocalyptic Vision of the Book of Daniel*. Missoula, MT: Scholars Press, 1977.

Hartman, L. F., and A. A. DiLella. *The Book of Daniel*. Garden City, NY: Doubleday, 1978.

Lacocque, A. *The Book of Daniel*. Atlanta, GA: John Knox, 1979.

J.J.C.

Darda (dahr'duh; probably Heb., "thistle"), the son of Mahol, and one of the four sages of 1 Kings 4:31 whose wisdom was exceeded by Solomon.

daric (dair'ik; Heb. *adarkon;* Ezra 8:27; 1 Chron. 29:7; Heb. *darkemon* [drachma?]: Ezra 2:69; Neh. 7:70, 72), a gold coin, probably introduced by Darius I. The Greek term *dareikos stater* denotes a stater of Darius. The word "daric" was originally used as an adjective to modify stater; later the term was shortened to "daric." It is used of Temple building contributions in Ezra 8:27 and anachronistically in 1 Chron. 29:7. ***See also*** Darius; Money.

Darius (dah-rī'uhs). **1** Darius I (the Great, 522–486 B.C.), the first of three Persian (Achaemenid) rulers. This Darius is intended in Ezra 4–6, Haggai, and Zechariah 1–8. He established himself on the throne in a power struggle in the years 522–520 B.C. The account of this appears on the trilingual inscriptions at Behistun in the Zagros mountains in northern Mesopotamia. While they contain important information, allowance must be made for Darius' desire to establish his legitimacy as ruler; his relationship to the royal house is not clear. The upheavals of his accession suggest a background to the prophecies of Hag. 2:6–7 and 2:21–22, with their reference to the overthrow of kingdoms, and to the complaint in Zech. 1:11–12 that peace has been restored without the expected outcome of the reestablishment of Judah and Jerusalem. However, the precise interpretation of these passages is not certain. Ezra 5–6 shows Darius reaffirming Cyrus's authorization for the rebuilding of the Jerusalem Temple, in response to an inquiry by the governor of the province "Beyond the River" and his associates. 1 Esd. 4:42–5:3 credits Darius

Darics, mentioned in 1 Chron. 29:7, were coins issued by the Persian king Darius I (522–486 B.C.). The monarch had his own likeness stamped on the coins showing himself running swiftly, holding a spear and bow.

directly with the appointment of Zerubbabel to restore Judah. Darius' conquests, his organization of the Persian Empire, his successful control of it over a period of nearly forty years, and his building achievements, especially at Susa and Persepolis, point to great administrative and military ability. The later years of his reign mark the development of conflict with Greece and his army's defeat at Marathon in 490 B.C. This conflict was dramatically to affect subsequent Persian history. The records suggest a mixture of extreme cruelty and generosity. He is credited, probably rightly, with the introduction of the coin known as the daric. **2** Darius II (Pers., Okhos, Nothos, 423–405/4 B.C.), who is described in the Elephantine papyri as responsible for a rescript to the Persian satrap in Egypt about religious observance at the Jewish shrine there. **3** Darius III (Pers., Kodomannos, 336–330 B.C.), the last ruler of the Empire, who was murdered shortly after Alexander's final defeat of the Persian army. The reference to Darius the Persian in Neh. 12:22 in relation to high priestly genealogy could be to either Darius II or Darius III. **4** Darius the Mede (Dan. 5:31; 6; 9:1; 11:1), person identified as a Median ruler after Belshazzar but before Cyrus. There is no satisfactory historical explanation for this reference. It might derive from prophecies speaking of the conquest of Babylon by the Medes (e.g., Isa. 13:17) since a Median Empire is placed between the Babylonian and Persian empires (cf. Dan. 8:20; also the interpretation of the dream in Dan. 2:31–45 and of the vision in 7:3–7; 15–18). ***See also*** Cyrus II; Daniel; Daric; Ezra; Media, Medes; Persia.

P.R.A.

darkness, quality regarded as less valuable than light (Eccles. 2:13). Imagery based on darkness is especially prominent in the poetic books where it represents destruction, death, and the underworld (Isa. 5:30; 47:5; Ps. 143:3; Job 17:13; cf. Mark 15:33) in a manner similar to that known in other ancient Near Eastern cultures. Conceived as a curse or punishment (Deut. 28:29; Ps. 35:6), darkness characterizes the coming Day of the Lord (Joel 2:2; Amos 5:18). God's appearance is often accompanied by darkness (1 Kings 8:12), which, according to Gen. 1:2, prevailed prior to creation, although Isa. 45:7 and Ps. 104:20 assert that it was created by God. The Dead Sea Scrolls contrast light and darkness as representing the forces of good and evil, both metaphysically and psychologically; a similar view has been noted in the Gospel of John.

F.E.G.

dark saying. ***See*** Parable.

dart. ***See*** Weapons.

date, the sweet fruit of the date palm (*Phoenix dactylifera*). The trees grow as separate male and female plants and must be wind- or hand-pollinated in order to bear fruit five years after reaching maturity. The fruits hang in clusters from the top of the trees and are collected when they ripen in the late summer and early fall.

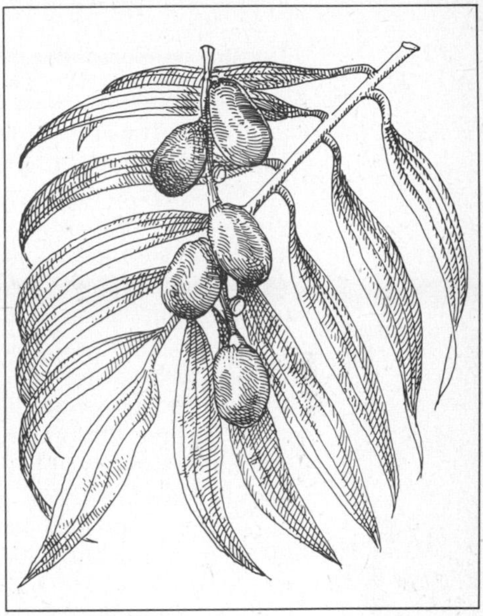

Date palm.

Since the date palm is characteristic of oases and watered places, the fruit is especially valued by the desert traveler. It not only provides a quick, high-energy source when fresh, but also becomes a storable, easily portable food when dried or made into small cakes. The ground and soaked seeds provide a nutritious fodder for camels and other animals. A sweet wine is made from the fermented juice of the terminal buds. The date has been valued as a trade item since early times. ***See also*** Palm.

P.L.C.

Dathan (day'than), a Reubenite who, with his brother Abiram, rebelled against Moses, claiming he had led the Exodus in order to rule over the Israelites (Num. 16). The earth swallowed Dathan and Abiram alive (Deut. 11:6).

David

THE MOST POWERFUL KING of biblical Israel, David ruled from ca. 1010 to 970 B.C. The story of David is recorded in 1 Sam. 16:13–1 Kings 2:12. David belonged to the tribe of Judah and was born in Bethlehem, youngest son of Jesse. He started his career at King Saul's court as player of the lyre, and subsequently became his squire. His courage and leadership in regular skirmishes with the Philistines and the immense popularity he gained as a commander soon earned him great notoriety and caused Saul to feel threatened. A long and complicated process of attraction and repulsion between the two men followed. The psychological scale was turned in favor of David when the old prophet Samuel, who had himself conducted Saul to the first kingship, became disappointed with Saul for theocratical reasons and anointed David as the new favorite of God.

King David playing a harp; from a thirteenth-century Hebrew manuscript.

Path to Kingship: David survived attempts on his life made by Saul in bursts of rage and fled the court. In the south he became a war lord with his own army of outlaws and performed services of protection. He also fought the enemies of Judah in the west and southwest. Although Saul found no way of eliminating him, the pressure he exerted became so strong that David decided to take refuge in Gath, where he became a vassal of the Philistine king Achish. Playing a double game, David maintained good relations with the tribes in the south: Judah, Cain, Jerachmeel, and Simeon. Because of the Philistine generals' mistrust, David was not called upon to perform his duties as a vassal in the final war against Saul. At this time, Israel was defeated on Mt. Gilboa, Saul and three princes were killed in battle, and the Philistines were left a free hand in Ephraim and Galilee. Saul's tribe, Benjamin, emerged to temporarily fill the power vacuum with the impotent kingship of Esbaal in the Transjordan, but the strong man of this rump state, Abner, soon found out that he could not win the civil war that threatened Judah and concluded a pact with David. Retarded by the base political murders of Abner and Esbaal, this development eventually led to the subjection of the northern tribes to David's rule and to their acceptance of him as a king. David ruled Judah from Hebron for seven years and ruled over the whole of Israel for thirty-three years. David created a unified state which would, however, disintegrate after Solomon. The numbers found in 2 Sam. 5:5 for David's reign are, admittedly, typological (seven and forty are holy numbers), but they nevertheless seem to approximate the historical reality as we know it.

Diplomatically, David chose a neutral city for the new capital of his kingdom: Jerusalem. His conquest of this non-Israelite city-state alarmed the Philistine city confederation, but David was able to repel their attacks and settle matters with this enemy for good. During his reign, David increased the status of "the city of David" by bringing to it the ancient Ark, once the mobile palladium of the wandering Israelite tribes. His son, Solomon, subsequently carried on this policy by building the central state sanctuary, the famous Temple of Solomon. (Three centuries later the Temple became the only legitimate worship center on account of the religious reforms of Josiah; after the Exile the so-called Second Temple, fifth century B.C.–A.D. 70, was its successor.)

Israel an Empire: In the phase of consolidation following his coronation, David triumphed over nearly all the then neighboring nations in a series of military campaigns. In the north he encountered the Aramaic states, and Damascus, Hamath, and Zobah rendered him tribute; in the east and southeast, David subjected the Ammonites and Moab; in the south he took over Edom; in the southwest he subjected small desert tribes like the Amalekites; and in the west he defeated the Philistines. With the Phoenician states and ports, however, he maintained friendly and noncombative relations. David's great power and military effectiveness were internally founded on good organization and the presence of an experienced standing army consisting mainly of mercenaries under the command of the competent military strategist Joab, while externally his power and effectiveness rested on the impotence of the great powers. In the eleventh century B.C. the civilizations along the Nile and between the Euphrates and Tigris passed through a period of weakness that temporarily spared Palestine (a strategic buffer region and zone of passage for trade routes) their meddling influence. Thus, under David and Solomon, Israel was (for a brief century) a powerful empire—for the first and last time.

A soldier using a sling similar to the type David used in the story of his encounter with Goliath (1 Sam. 17); relief from an orthostat at the palace at Gozan, tenth–ninth century B.C.

Faced with Rebellion: This formation of power also had its repercussions. David himself became an absolute ruler after the model of the region, and his place above the law ran counter to the sense of justice and the religious beliefs of many of his subjects. Much discontent was fomented as people viewed the grand court with its predilection for international mores and literature, and especially for its tight administrative grip put on the community in the form of heavy taxes and conscription for purposes hardly understood. The decay of the older tribal and theocratical values and patterns also frightened people. Thus, already during David's lifetime, these growing feelings of discomfort came to a head during Absalom's revolt. This prince made shrewd use of the mood of resistance, suggested political alternatives, and, after thorough preparation, seized power so that David was even forced to leave his own country. When the usurper, however, failed to isolate David at once, the latter gained time to re-align himself with those of his standing army who had remained loyal to him and subsequently to effect a political reversal through a hard battle in the Transjordan. Upon his return to Jerusalem, David discriminated against the northern tribes in favor of his own tribe of Judah and for this he immediately had to pay a high price: a secession of the north under the leadership of Sheba ben Bichri. Once more Joab, who as a statesman had already intervened twice in David's policy toward Absalom, had to save the throne by means of a swift campaign that eliminated Sheba.

Like many great men David omitted arranging for his succession, so that even before his death a vehement struggle broke out at the court. The group around Solomon, headed by his mother, Bathsheba, and the prophet Nathan, appeared to be the strongest and shortly after David's death eliminated the rival prince Adonijah who was supported by Joab. Joab was subsequently eliminated as well.

David was not only a very powerful leader and personality as both soldier and statesman, he was also a first-class poet. He was the author of the poignant dirge in 2 Samuel 1 as well as many of the compositions the book of Psalms ascribed to him. The court established by him and extended by Solomon gave a tremendous spiritual and literary impulse to the literature of biblical Israel, to its many genres, and to the values conveyed by them. The dynasty David founded survived the disruption after Solomon and kept on ruling in Judah until the Exile, which began in 586 B.C. Its prestige inspired later poets to messianic prophecies; and in the NT his royal line is extended to include Jesus of Nazareth, "the Anointed" (*Christos* in Gk.) as a descendant of David (Matt. 2:6; 21:9; Luke 3:31; 18:38–39). The effect of David's choice of Jerusalem as his city is felt to the present time: in the eyes of the Jews, Christians, and Muslims the city is holy. And the poems of David live on in the liturgy of Jewish and Christian communities, sung to this very day.

The Story of David—the Zenith of Hebrew Narrative: The portrait of David presented here is grounded on the estimate that its only source, 1–2 Samuel, is in outline historically reliable. In any case, the figure of David inspired the narrator(s) to such an extent that this text has

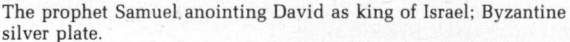

The prophet Samuel anointing David as king of Israel; Byzantine silver plate.

David slaying Goliath and cutting off his head (top) and Abner bringing David with Goliath's head to Saul (bottom). Jonathan, overcome with love for David, gives him his own garments (1 Sam. 17:45–18:4); page from a thirteenth-century French illumination.

become the zenith of Hebrew narrative art. It not only draws a picture of the rise of the untouchable favorite of God, but also of the David who, as a king, yielded to the luxury of absolute power and who, as a father, failed toward his overambitious sons Amnon, Absalom, and Adonijah. Thus a detached, highly critical, but certainly not relentless portrait of profound psychological insight and spiritual depth has come down to us.

See also Absalom; Jerusalem; Messiah; Saul; Solomon.

Bibliography

Bright, John. *A History of Israel*. 3d ed. Philadelphia: Westminster, 1981.

Fokkelman, J. P. *Narrative Art and Poetry in the Books of Samuel*. Vol. 1, *King David*. Vol. 2, *The Crossing Fates*. Assen: Van Gorsum, 1981, 1985.

Hallo, William W., and William Kelly Simpson. *The Ancient Near East, A History*. New York: Harcourt Brace, 1971.

J.P.F.

David, City of, the name given to the part of Jerusalem that was the Jebusite city, after its capture by David (2 Sam. 5). This oldest part of Jerusalem, which had been an urban site since the early third millennium B.C., was located in the southeastern part of present-day Jerusalem on a land peninsula that is formed by the Kidron Valley on the east and the Tyropoeon Valley (Gk., "Valley of the Cheese-makers") on the west. In area the City of David comprised no more than 7.5 to 10 acres and was thus no more than a medium-sized village.

As a fortified city surrounded by valleys, it was vulnerable only at two points: at its principal water source on the east and at the highest part of the ridge on the north, a part of the city's fortifications that received continuing attention. The city's principal water source was the Gihon spring (Heb., "gusher"), which flowed at the foot of the ridge on the Kidron side, below and outside the city walls. Excavations have shown that the spring was made accessible to the Jebusites by means of a shaft that connected the spring to a point just inside the city walls, about midway down the slope of the valley. The narrative of David's conquest of the city in 2 Sam. 5:7–8 suggests that he took the city by stealthily gaining entry to it through this water shaft. Soon after he took the city, David undertook to secure its strategic weak point on the north. He repaired the walls and the *Millo* (2 Sam. 5:9; Heb., "filling"), which is probably to be identified with the stone retaining walls of the terraces on the slopes, which enabled the expansion of the habitable area of the city. That the spring remained a strategic weak point is attested by the construction of a water tunnel by Hezekiah in the late eighth century B.C. Its purpose was to secure the city's water source against siege by the Assyrians (2 Kings 20:20; 2 Chron. 32:30), a feat recorded in the Siloam Inscription.

Other than the Jebusite water shaft and some of the walls of the Jebusite-Davidic city, almost nothing survives in Jerusalem today from the period of David or Solomon. Neither David's palace nor his tomb have been found. The structure on Mount Zion today called "David's Tomb" has neither archaeological nor historical claim to authenticity.

David's son and successor, Solomon, expanded the city to the north, where he constructed a large platform on which he built the Temple and other elaborate royal buildings (1 Kings 6–7). After Solomon the city grew farther to the north and to the west on the hill today identified as Mount Zion, a hill that is protected on the south and west by the Valley of Hinnom. This identification of Mount Zion, which in 2 Sam. 5:7 is applied to David's city, derives from the Jewish historian Josephus, who identified all of the Jerusalem of his day (the first century A.D.) with the city of David. ***See also*** Hezekiah; Jerusalem; Kidron; Siloam Inscription. F.S.F.

day. ***See*** Time.

Day of Atonement. ***See*** Atonement, Day of.

Day of Judgment, Day of the Lord. ***See*** Eschatology; Judgment, Day of.

daysman, a term in the KJV where the RSV has "umpire" in Job. 9:33.

dayspring, the rising of the sun, used as an image for the coming of the Messiah (Luke 1:78).

Daystar. ***See*** Lucifer.

deacon, deaconess. ***See*** Church.

Dead Sea, the lake into which the Jordan River flows. The lake is fifty miles (80 km.) long by ten miles (16 km.) wide. The biblical names vary: "Salt Sea" (Gen. 14:3; Num. 34:3, 12; Deut. 3:17; Josh. 3:16; 12:3; 15:2, 5; 18:19), "Sea of the Arabah" (Deut. 3:17; 4:49; Josh. 3:16; 12:3), "Eastern Sea" (Ezek. 47:18; Joel 2:20; Zech. 14:8), and

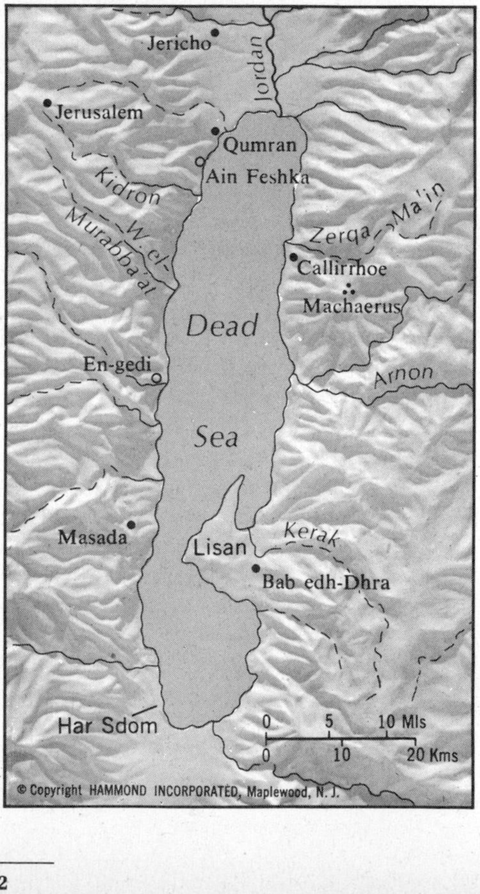

"Sea of Sodom" (2 Esd. 5:7). The shoreline is 1,294 feet (394 m.) below sea level, with the greatest depth about 1,300 feet (396 m.) below that, and it has a twenty-five percent mineral content, entirely the result of evaporation. In ancient times it was valued for its salt and for the asphalt that occasionally floats to the surface. The water is usually calm because of its great density, but dangerous storms can develop.

The average annual rainfall is only 2 inches (50 mm.), with occasional severe thunderstorms. The steep, desolate western slopes leave sufficient room for a north-south road, and there are two important springs, one at modern 'Ain Feshka close to Qumran in the north and the other at En-gedi in the center. An important feature of later prophecy is the promise that living water would flow in both summer and winter from the Jerusalem Temple down these arid slopes into the Dead Sea, making it fresh and productive (Ezek. 47:1–12; Zech. 14:8). In the extreme southwest is the remarkable salt dome of Har Sdom. Most of the eastern shore is formed of forbidding sandstone precipices, cleft by the narrow gorges of the Zerqa Ma 'in and the Arnon, but in the southeast, behind the Lisan peninsula, there is a coastal plain where winter crops are grown. At the exit of the Kerak wadi (probably the OT Ascent of Horonaim; cf. Jer. 48:5) is the important Bronze Age site of Bab edh-Dhra'. The whereabouts of Sodom and Gomorrah (Gen. 13:10; 19:24) remain a total mystery. ***See also*** En-gedi; Qumran, Khirbet; Sodom. D.B.

Dead Sea Scrolls, the. ***See*** Scrolls, The Dead Sea; Texts, Versions, Manuscripts, Editions.

death, the end of physical and/or spiritual life. Ancient Israel's official response to mortality was, first, to accept it as God's original design and, second, to forbid worship that was concerned with the dead (Lev. 19:28; 20:1–11). Neighboring cultures believed that the dead lived on in the underworld in a communicative state (Deut. 18:9–14), but Israel's theologians taught that they were, for practical purposes, nonexistent (Eccles. 9:5–6). Nonetheless, foreign ideas and practices continued (1 Sam. 28; Isa. 8:19).

Mortality must be distinguished from other concepts of death. Biologically, death is the end of every creature's existence; God alone is immortal (Ps. 90:1–6). Metaphorically, "death" is a value judgment upon those things that detract from life as the Creator intended it (1 Sam. 2:6–7). Mythologically, death is a power that acts independently (Job 18:13; Jer. 9:21).

The last usage is a rare vestige of polytheism, since orthodox religion denied the existence of more than one divine force. Thus death was reduced to a natural process and no Devil was acknowledged to exist. The second usage (metaphorical), contrasts "life" with psychological, sociological, and spiritual "death," which holds the world in its grip. "Life" was mediated through Israel's sociology, ethics, and worship.

The first usage (biological) consists of narrative observations that so-and-so died. This reality did not lead to the belief that life was therefore meaningless. Nonetheless, a death that was premature (Isa. 38:1–12), or violent (1 Sam. 15:32), or that left no heir (2 Sam. 18:18) produced anxiety.

Death and the Divine Plan: Mortality, within the divine plan, is outlined in Gen. 2–3. The first humans rebelled against their Creator and were denied further access to the Tree of Life. Their status as creatures thus proceeded to its natural conclusion. This is the understanding of human destiny in the OT and Jewish literature. However, another reading of the text was to become evident in the intertestamental literature and the NT. Since death might have been delayed indefinitely through obedience, perhaps the intent was that the couple live forever! Death could then be understood as an evil intrusion into the divine plan.

This new understanding was suggested by several realities. First, internal conflict within the religious group and external persecution led to a new religious outlook (Apocalypticism). God's assumed desire for a world like that at creation must produce a sudden transformation of the earth (Daniel)—perhaps a return to the paradise of Eden. Second, Greek culture introduced a new view of humans. In traditional biblical thought, death was total (there is no distinction between body and soul). In Greek thought, a "soul" was thought to exist and to be detachable from the corpse. Thus the dead live on, somewhere, and to a Semite (though not to a Greek) they would be available for bodily reconstruction (resurrection). Bodily death, then, came to be seen a temporary evil. Third, if one's lifespan could be shortened by sin (Prov. 10:21; 11:19; Job 36: 13–14), could that also be the cause of mortality?

Therefore, in some of the intertestamental literature, mortality is decried as the creation of a "devil" rather than as the Creator's design (Wisd. of Sol. 1:12–13; 2:23–24).

In the NT: The NT writers accept this new perspective. Paul thus depicts death as an unintended fate unleashed as a consequence of primeval disobedience (Rom. 5:18–19). However, since death came about within history (rather than from the Creator's design), it is subject to a historical solution: if sin can be overcome, mortality can be countered. This has been done through the appearance of a new "Adam" (Christ) who empowers his followers, just as the old "Adam" affected those who came after him

(1 Cor. 15:45–49). His resurrection demonstrated that death has lost its power.

In the synoptic Gospels, little attention is given to mortality. It serves primarily as an incentive to obey Jesus while there is yet time (Matt. 3:1–10; Luke 12:16–20). In the Gospel of John, mortality is even less an issue. Rather, it is "death" and "life" in the metaphoric sense that are crucial. It is not so much that Jesus will return and the dead will be resurrected (as in Apocalypticism) as it is that Jesus is already present, mediating "eternal life" (1:4; 3:36; 5: 24).

The Bible's final word on the matter is that of Apocalypticism: mortality and martyrdom, as the goal of Satan and his instrument Rome, will shortly come to an end. The paradise the Creator intended will then be restored and "death will be no more" (Rev. 21:4). ***See also*** Devil; Eternal Life; Hades; Resurrection; Soul. L.R.B.

Debir (de-bihr'; Heb., "back part"?). **1** A king of Eglon who joined the Amorite confederation trying to stop Joshua (Josh. 10:3). **2** Part of the north border of Judah (Josh. 15:7), probably Thoghret ed-Debr, "pass of Debir," ten miles east of Jerusalem and about eight miles southwest of Jericho. **3** A city of Gad (Josh. 13:26), probably modern Umm el-Dabar about twelve miles north of Pella. It may be the same as "Lodebar" (Amos 6:13; 2 Sam. 9:4–13; 17:27), a refuge for Jonathan's son Mephibosheth, and later a source of assistance for David. Amos used it as a sarcastic reference to insignificant business by changing the vowels of the word to make it mean "a thing of no value." **4** A Canaanite city in Judah about eleven miles southwest of Hebron (Josh. 10:36–39; 12:13). Inhabited by Anakim (Josh. 11:21), it was assaulted by Joshua or by Calebites (Josh. 15:15–17; Judg. 1:11–15) or both, and became an administrative district headquarters (Josh. 15:49). It was assigned as a levitical city (Josh. 21:15; 1 Chron. 6:58) and is twice mentioned as having another earlier name: Kiriath-sepher, Heb., "city of the scribe" (Josh. 15:15; Judg. 1:11); Kiriath-sannah (Josh. 15:49) is a probable misspelling of that name. The site location is debated. Proposals have included modern Khirbet Rabud (M. S. Astour, M. Noth), but the general weight of opinion has favored modern Tell Beit Mirsim over other possible tells in the vicinity. The excavation of Tell Beit Mirsim by W. F. Albright in four seasons (1926–1932) set a new mark in Palestinian archaeology. The separation of strata and their ceramic contents from each other allowed the first development of a decisive ceramic chronology for the periods from Early Bronze (3000–2000 B.C.) through Iron Age II (900–600 B.C.).

Bibliography

Albright, W. F. *The Excavation of Tell Beit Mirsim.* The Annual of The American Schools of Oriental Research. New Haven, CT: American Schools of Oriental Research. Vol. 12 (1930–31); vol. 13 (1931–32); vol. 17 (1936–37); vols. 21–22 (1941–43). R.S.B.

Deborah (deb'aw-ruh; Heb., "bee"). **1** Rebekah's nurse (Gen. 35:8; 24:59). **2** An Israelite judge and prophet. Though the exact duties of the judges are not clear, some appear to have exercised legal functions while others were purely military leaders. Deborah combined these two important offices in addition to holding a third one, that of prophet (Judg. 4:4). She rendered legal decisions to Israelites who came to her in the hill country of Ephraim (Judg. 4:5), and she led an Israelite coalition to victory over the militarily superior Canaanite forces of Sisera in the plain of Esdraelon. This was a strategic battle in the struggle for control of central and northern Palestine. Deborah's victory is recorded in prose (Judg. 4) and poetry (Judg. 5). In the prose version, her general, Barak, refused to go into battle unless Deborah accompanied him. She agreed, declaring that "the Lord will sell Sisera into the hand of a woman." That woman, we discover later on, is not Deborah, but another courageous woman, Jael.

The poem, known as the "Song of Deborah," is one of the oldest examples of biblical literature, dating ca. 1125 B.C. and roughly contemporaneous with the events it describes. Vivid and fast-paced, with a repetitive style akin to older, Canaanite poetry from Ugarit, it is widely acclaimed for its literary qualities. It graphically portrays the excitement of the battle in which God comes from the South (Edom, Sinai) to lead the Israelite troops as well as the cosmic forces against the enemy ("From heaven fought the stars/from their courses they fought against Sisera," Judg. 5:20). The poem concludes with a striking juxtaposition of two "domestic" scenes: Jael's assassination of Sisera (5:24–27) and Sisera's mother waiting anxiously for the return of her spoil-laden son (5: 28–30). Whereas the prose version mentions only the tribes of Naphtali and Zebulun, the poem praises Ephraim, Benjamin, Machir, Zebulun, Issachar, and Naphtali for their brave participation in the battle, while censuring Reuben, Gilead, Dan, Asher, and Meroz (otherwise unknown) for not responding to the muster. Though more tribes are mentioned as cooperating in this crucial battle than any other in Judges, the traditional twelve tribes are not all enumerated. Judah, Simeon, and Levi are missing, while Machir and Gilead appear instead of Manasseh and Gad.

Judges 4:4 identifies Deborah in Hebrew as an *'eshet lappidot*, usually translated "wife of Lappidoth" but perhaps meaning "spirited woman." No Lappidoth is known to us. **3** The grandmother of Tobit (Tob. 1:8). ***See also*** Barak; Jael; Judges, The Book of. Poetry. J.C.E.

debt, owing money or property of some kind to another person. Israelite law forbade charging fellow Israelites interest on loans (Exod. 22:24; Deut. 23:20; Lev. 25:35–38). Though it was considered a good deed to lend money to the poor (Ps. 37:21; Ecclus. 29:1–2; Matt. 5:42), many refused to do so because they would not be paid back (Ecclus. 29:3–7).

The prohibition against charging interest was not observed (Prov. 28:8; Ezek. 18:8, 13, 17; 22: 12; Matt. 25:27; Luke 19:23). Neh. 5:1–13 speaks of the people as burdened with debts. The annual interest rate among Jews at Elephantine in the fifth century B.C. was 12 percent.

Movable goods might be taken as a pledge to repay, though the law forbade taking a person's means of livelihood (Deut. 24:6–13). Such goods may have represented persons who stood to guarantee a pledge, often the debtor's children, who would become enslaved to the creditor if the debt was not paid (2 Kings 4:1–7; Neh. 5:2–7; Exod. 22:24; Isa. 50:1). Other persons could intervene as surety on behalf of an insolvent debtor and assume the responsibility for getting the debtor to pay or be liable to seizure themselves (Prov. 6:3–5; 20:16; Ecclus. 29:14–20).

Sabbatical year legislation requiring that slaves be set free was aimed at the problem of persons who had become enslaved because they were unable to pay debts. Approach of the sabbatical year then became an excuse for the refusal to grant a loan (Exod. 21:2–6; Deut. 15: 1–11). In the time of Herod the Great, Hillel permitted contracts to contain a *prosbol* (Gk.), a clause by which the debtor renounced the sabbatical privilege. ***See also*** Bank; Sabbatical Year.
P.P.

debt, remission of. ***See*** Loan.

Decalogue. ***See*** Ten Commandments, The.

Decapolis (de-kap'oh-lis), a federation of ten cities of Hellenistic culture in an area east of Samaria and Galilee. The Roman scholar Pliny the Elder (ca. A.D. 77) lists them as Damascus, Philadelphia, Raphana, Scythopolis, Gadara, Hippos, Dion, Pella, Gerasa, and Canatha. ***See also*** Cities.

Decision, Valley of, the name given in Joel 3: 14 to the place where God will execute judgment on the Day of the Lord against the nations gathered for the eschatological assault against Jerusalem. The valley is also called "Valley of Jehoshaphat" in Joel 3:2, 12. Traditional interpretation identifies the Valley of Jehoshaphat/ Decision with the Kidron Valley, east of Jerusalem, where the pious kings Asa and Josiah are reported to have destroyed pagan idols (1 Kings 15:13; 2 Kings 23:4, 6, 12; 2 Chron. 15:16; 29:16; 30:14).

decrees, in the ancient world, declarations (usually in written form) by rulers or other persons in authority directing the conduct of especially significant matters for communities or individuals. The decree of Cyrus calling for the rebuilding of the Temple in Jerusalem (Ezra 5: 13, 17) and the decree of Caesar Augustus for a census (Luke 2:1) are but two examples of such decrees in the OT and NT (see also, e.g., Isa. 10: 1; 2 Chron. 30:5; Ezra 6:1, 3; Esther 1:20; Dan. 3: 10; Acts 17:7). Apparently, God's will and purposes were also considered "decrees," although these did not have to be written to be in force. God exercises these decrees in areas of human conduct and destiny (Dan. 4:17, 24), in the development of human history (Ps. 2:7), and in the founding and ordering of the created universe (Job 28:26). The community of Israel also understood the laws of the covenant, as established initially by Moses, to be God's decrees. ***See also*** Commandment; Covenant; Law. J.M.E.

Dedan (dee'duhn), the city and kingdom of the Dedanites, an Arabian people of unclear origin (Gen. 10:6–7; 25:1–3). Al-'Ula, an oasis ca. fifty miles southwest of Tema, was central to Dedan's far-reaching commercial activities, which included trade with Tyre (Ezek. 27:20). The prophets denounced Dedan (Isa. 21:13; Jer. 25:23; 49:8; Ezek. 25:13). ***See also*** Arabia.

dedication, setting something apart, or marking new use or practice. The Hebrew root *khnk* and its Aramaic cognate appear seventeen times in the Bible, sixteen of which are in the sense of dedication (the one exception is Prov. 22:6 where the verb is used in the sense of instruction or training).

A man who had not dedicated the new house he built was ordered to return home from the mobilized army in order to dedicate it (Deut. 20:5). No ceremony is mentioned, however. According to Num. 7:10–88, the dedication of the sacrificial altar in the desert occurred on the day of its anointing and sanctification (v. 1). The dedication consisted of lavish offerings —silver plates, basins, gold spoons full of incense, bulls, rams, lambs with their meal offerings, and goats—all presented by the tribal princes. The dedication of the altar of Solomon's Temple took seven days (2 Chron. 7:9). Solomon's Temple was dedicated with a multitude of sacrifices (1 Kings 8:63; 2 Chron. 7:5). The relative paucity of offerings at the dedication of the rebuilt Temple of the returned exiles from Babylon indicates their meager resources (Ezra 6:16–17). The words "song of dedication of the Temple" appear to be an editorial interpolation in Ps. 30:1 that assigns that Psalm to the festival of Hanukkah (see *Soperim* 18:2). The dedication of the rebuilt wall of Jerusalem during the days of Ezra and Nehemiah was accompanied by music, song, thanksgiving offerings, and joy (Neh. 12:27–45). The pagan dedication of Nebuchadnezzar's idol was accompanied by music and worship (Dan. 3:2–5).

It appears that a dedication differed from a sanctification (or consecration) in that the community as a whole participated in the former, while the latter was performed only by those responsible for the sanctified object(s) (e.g., the priests). ***See also*** Altar; Dedication, Feast of; Temple, The. J.U.

Dedication, Feast of, or Hanukkah (hahn′uh-kuh), a Jewish festival celebrating the purification of the Temple in the time of the Maccabean revolt. On the 25th of Kislev (December), 167 B.C., during the religious persecution of the Jews by the Seleucid Antiochus Epiphanes, the altar of the Temple was polluted with pagan sacrifices. Observant Jews, under the leadership of Mattathias (a priest) and his five sons, rebelled against the Seleucids. Upon Mattathias' death, his son Judas Maccabee took command of the revolt, won several victories over the Seleucid army, and reconquered Jerusalem. After cleansing the Temple, rebuilding the sanctuary, consecrating the courts, and making a new sacrificial altar and holy vessels, "they burned incense on the [incense] altar and lighted the lamps on the lampstand, and these gave light in the Temple. They placed bread on the table and hung up the curtains . . ." (1 Macc. 4:50–51). Then, on the 25th of Kislev, 164 B.C., three years to the day after the pollution of the altar, the new altar was dedicated with sacrifices, song, music, and joyous worship for eight days (vv. 52–58). Judas and the people determined that those eight days of dedication should be celebrated annually beginning with the 25th of Kislev (December; v. 59). Hanukkah thus became the only Jewish festival not ordained in the Hebrew Bible.

It has been suggested that the eight days of celebration copy Solomon's consecration of the Temple (2 Macc. 2:12) or Hezekiah's (2 Chron. 29:17). However, all the testimony points to the intention to celebrate Hanukkah as a second Feast of Tabernacles. "And they celebrated it for eight days with rejoicing in the manner of the Feast of Booths, remembering how not long before, during the Feast of Booths, they had been wandering in the mountains and caves like wild animals" (2 Macc. 10:6, also vv. 7–8 and 1:9, 18). It was for this reason that Hanukkah was tied to Solomon's consecration, which was held at the time of the Feast of Booths (1 Kings 8:2). Furthermore, as during the Feast of Tabernacles, Jews recite the entire Hallel (Pss. 113–118) daily.

It was apparently the relighting of the Temple candelabras that led to the festival also taking the name "lights" (Josephus *Antiquities* 12:7:7). Eventually it became customary for Jews to light a special Hanukkah candelabra in the home, adding one light each night during the festival. A legendary story (*t. Sabb.* 21b) of a small cruse of holy oil discovered at the cleansing of the Temple that was miraculously able to light the Temple lamp for eight days until more oil could be supplied has supplanted the origins of the festival rites.

Hanukkah's ongoing significance lies in its commemoration of the victory of the few whose desire for freedom to practice their religion impelled them to battle against far greater forces. Indeed, were it not for the Maccabees, the Jewish people and their monotheistic faith might have perished. ***See also*** Dedication; Tabernacles, Festival of. J.U.

defense, protection against hostile acts mounted against an individual, a city, or a nation. The requirements for defense in the ancient world were factors in city planning and in national policy. Regarding the former, the "defensibility" of a city and a protected water supply were of paramount importance. One of the oldest known urban structures in Palestine is the neolithic tower at Jericho. Its purpose was defense against assault, among other things. Major cities from the Early Bronze Age (3000–2000 B.C.) had walls, with some cities surrounded by two of them. This pattern continued through the period of the kings in Israel. To protect the water supply at key sites, water tunnels or shafts were dug from inside the city's walls to the water table or spring located outside the walls. Examples of these can be found at the ancient sites of Gibeon, Jerusalem, Hazor, and Megiddo.

Israel's location at a crossroads in the ancient Near East between Mesopotamia to the north and Egypt to the south required a strategic policy for defense. This requirement was one reason the kings in Israel or Judah maintained a standing army. According to 2 Chron. 11:5–12, Rehoboam fortified key sites in Judah for defensive purposes, perhaps in response to a campaign in Palestine by Pharaoh Shishak (ca. 922 B.C.). According to the annals of the Assyrian king Shalmaneser III (859–824 B.C.), Ahab of Israel was involved in a coalition with neighboring states to oppose Assyrian control of Syro-Palestine and the Mediterranean coast.

In the Sermon on the Mount, Jesus taught an ethic that placed concern for an enemy or opponent above one's personal defense (cf. Matt. 5:23–26, 43–48). J.A.D.

deity, the divine quality that distinguishes God from other entities (Rom. 1:20; Col. 2:9); therefore God cannot be likened to any created thing, however precious (Acts 17:29). ***See also*** God.

Delaiah (de-lī′yah; Heb., "God draws up"). **1** The head of one of the twenty-four divisions of priests organized by David (1 Chron. 24:18). **2** A royal official who urged Jehoiakim not to burn Jeremiah's scroll (Jer. 36:12, 25). **3** The head of a family that returned from exile with Zerubbabel (Ezra 2:60; Neh. 7:62; 1 Esd. 5:37). **4** A descendant of David through Zerubbabel (1 Chron. 3:24). **5** The father of a contemporary of Nehemiah (Neh. 6:10).

Delilah (de-lī'lah), a woman, probably Philistine, who was loved by Samson. After three unsuccessful attempts to discover the secret of his strength, she succeeded and betrayed him to the Philistines for money (Judg. 16:4–22). Her name (perhaps meaning "loose hair" or "small, slight") is a pun on the Hebrew word for "night" *(laylah)* while Samson's is related to "sun" *(shemesh)*. ***See also*** Philistines; Samson.

deluge, an excessive amount of rain (Ezek. 13: 11, 13; 2 Pet. 3:6). ***See also*** Flood, The.

Demas (dee'muhs), originally one of Paul's "fellow workers" who joins Paul in sending greetings to Philemon, Apphia, and Archippus (Philem. 24; cf. Col. 4:14). According to 2 Tim. 4:10, Demas, "in love with this present world," deserted Paul and went to Thessalonica.

Demetrius (di-mee'tree-uhs). **1** A silversmith in Ephesus who instigated a riot against Paul because Paul's missionary activities threatened the business of making silver statuettes of the goddess Artemis (Acts 19:24–41). ***See also*** Artemis. **2** A Christian who was commended by the author of 3 John (v. 12).

democracy, a system of government in which sovereignty rests with the people themselves, although not always with all the people; women and slaves are often excluded (see 1 Cor. 7:20–31; Col. 3:22; 4:1). A primitive kind of democracy, in which an assembly of the eligible controlled basic decision making, is thought to have preceded Mesopotamian aristocracies (late fourth-early third millennium B.C.). It has occasionally been suggested that a similar system may have existed in early Israel, with power resting in groups such as the elders. The tribal structure that this reflects may even have persisted after the creation of a monarchy and the increased social stratification that followed, although many passages cited in this regard, particularly those alluding to "all Israel" or "all the people," are probably schematic or anachronistic. Some scholars have seen what they call an "economic democracy" in early Israelite tribalism. Others have pointed to a kind of "social democracy," in which the worth of each individual is stressed (see Acts 10:34–35; 2 Chron. 19:7). More to the point, perhaps, are the types of biblical literature like Deuteronomy and the prophetic writings that emphasize just treatment for those in the lower social strata, "the stranger, the widow, and the orphan," (Deut. 24: 19–21) and Jesus' habit of disregarding social rank in choosing those with whom he associated (e.g., Matt. 9:10; Mark 2:15–17; Luke 7:34).

F.E.G.

demon, the English transliteration of a Greek term *(daimōn)* originally referring to any one of numerous, vaguely defined spirit beings, either good or bad. In the NT they are understood as evil spirits, opposed to God and God's people. In the KJV, the term is regularly translated "devil," a word that appears in the RSV only as the translation of a different Greek term meaning "accuser" or "slanderer" *(diabolos)*. It is used as a virtual synonym for "Satan."

In the ancient world, there was widespread belief in spiritual powers or beings that existed in addition to the well-known gods and goddesses. These beings were not understood as necessarily evil, though some might be. The idea that many or even all such beings were allied with the forces of darkness and wickedness only came into focus, probably under the influence of Persian thought, during the intertestamental period of Judaism.

There are traces of the belief in harmful spirits in the OT writings (e.g., Gen. 6:1–4; Lev. 16: 6–10, 26; Isa. 34:14; Job 6:4; Ps. 91:5), but little was made of this idea in Hebrew thought until the late postexilic period. Then, the belief developed that there existed not only numerous evil spirits or demons but also a leader for these evil forces. This leader came to be known in Jewish thought by several titles, though the most common designation was Satan (the Greek title "the devil" was then used as a virtual synonym for Satan, as, e.g., in John 8:44). As a result of this type of thinking, the idea developed that there were armies of demons, under the leadership of Satan or the devil, doing battle with God and God's allies.

The idea then developed that demons could invade human bodies and personalities and cause mental illness, physical disease, or other specific problems such as deafness or blindness. Some even believed that demons could take control of nature and cause natural calamities and disasters. Such ideology is clearly reflected in the synoptic Gospels of the NT, where Jesus is known as one who characteristically exorcises demons (e.g., Matt. 8:28–34; Mark 5:1–20; Luke 8:26–39; Matt. 12:22–32; Mark 3:22–27; Luke 11:14–23).

The apostle Paul understood the "principalities" and "powers" to be evil forces in this world (Rom. 8:38; cf. Col. 1:16; 2:15; Eph. 3:10; also 1 Cor. 10:20). In some of the later NT writings, however, the place of the demons began to give way to the centrality of the leader of the demonic forces, namely, Satan or the devil (who is sometimes referred to as "the evil one"). Thus, in the Fourth Gospel, there are no references to demon possession or exorcism. The devil has become *the* instigator of evil (e.g., John 13:2), though the charges fly back and forth between the religious authorities and Jesus as to who "has a demon" (John 7:20; 8:48–49; 10:20–21), probably meaning, in the Fourth Gospel, who was thoroughly evil and opposed to God.

The idea that there are evil forces in the world that manifest themselves in various ways is still valid. How one articulates this idea may change from one culture to another, however. Demonology was a part of the culture of the NT world and should be interpreted and understood against that background. ***See also*** Angel; Belial; Devil; Magic and Divination; Satan.
J.M.E.

demonology. ***See*** Demon; Devil.

denarius (KJV: "penny"; pl. denarii), Roman silver coin representing a worker's daily wage (Matt. 18:28; 20:2, 9, 13; 22:19; Mark 6:37; 12:15; 14:5; Luke 7:41; 10:35; 20:24; John 6:7; 12:5; Rev. 6:6). Devaluation under Nero early in the second half of the first century A.D. cut the value of the denarius in half.

deputy, an official of secondary rank (1 Kings 22:47); the same term is commonly translated "officer" or the like in 1 Kings 4:5. Elsewhere, Greek and Hebrew words that the KJV renders "deputy" are now more commonly regarded as indicating specific officials (hence "proconsul," "governor," etc.).

Derbe (duhr'bee), a city in the region of Lycaonia in central Asia Minor where Paul and Barnabas won believers at the end of their first journey through the Roman province of Galatia (Acts 14:20–21). Paul returned here during his second journey (Acts 16:1). Paul's companion Gaius was from Derbe (Acts 20:4). ***See also*** Gaius; Lycaonia.

desert, an area inhospitable to human habitation. Absolute desert, i.e., a region where rain almost never falls, is in the Middle East to be found only in the Sahara, the peninsula of Arabia, and Iran. The deserts of Palestine, Syria, Transjordan, and Sinai are all "tame deserts," with a little rain every winter, often in sudden storms causing dangerous flash floods. Such rain as occurs tends to fall in March and April, or even early May, when the high-pressure system over Arabia is breaking up. Occasionally heavy rain can occur more frequently during the winter, and then the desert does indeed "blossom abundantly" (Isa. 35:2).

The character of the desert varies greatly. On the Transjordan plateau it is mainly a level area carpeted with millions of small stones (Arabic *hamada*), and further east is the formidable and desolate region of black basalt (Arabic *harrah*). In the south the plateau has been broken by a complicated network of geological faults, and the desert here consists of broad sandy corridors between towering cliffs. In Palestine the southern desert contains much *hamada*, with some sandy areas on the west and precipitous slopes to the rift valley on the east. The Sinai desert is low in the northern basin but rises to a towering granite massif in the south, reaching 8,671 feet (2,637 m.) in Jebel Katarina, close to Jebel Musa, the traditional site of Mt. Sinai. Sand dunes exist in only very few places, e.g., parts of north Sinai and the extreme south of Transjordan, and are always extremely small and restricted in area.

In the OT four Hebrew words are used for desert: "desolate land" (*midbar*), which is by far the most common; *'arabah*, normally used for the dry plain of the rift valley, especially south of the Dead Sea; "wasteland" (*yeshimon*), used especially for the barren dissected slopes of Judah overlooking the Dead Sea; and "dry, deserted area" (*ḥarbah*). With the exception of the last all these are also translated as "wilderness," and the two words "desert" and "wilderness" are really interchangeable.

In biblical times, although no longer the case today, the desert, especially in Transjordan and Sinai, was the home of a multitude of wild animals, e.g., gazelles, onagers, wolves, foxes, leopards, hyenas, and ostrich. In the NT period the Transjordan and Palestine deserts had been largely "tamed" by the Nabateans to promote their far-flung trade, and they managed to cultivate patches of ground that had never been farmed before. True deserts, of course, are nowhere to be found in Jesus' homeland in Galilee. The words translated "wilderness" (Gk. *erēmos, erēmia*) refer to uninhabited areas (Matt. 4:1; 14:13; 15:33; Mark 1:12–13; 6:31; Luke 4:2), but the writers certainly also had in mind parallels with Israel's testing and feeding in the desert during the Exodus. ***See also*** Nabatea, Nabateans; Sinai, Transjordan. D.B.

desolating sacrilege. ***See*** Abomination That Makes Desolate, The.

deuterocanonical (dōō-tuh-roh-kuh-nahn'i-kuhl) **literature,** those books or parts of books of the OT that are found in the Greek Septuagint (LXX) translation but not in the Hebrew text. These books are accepted as Scripture by the Roman Catholic and Orthodox communions but rejected by the reformation churches, which confined themselves to the Hebrew Scriptures. They are also referred to as the apocryphal ("hidden") books, but "deuterocanonical" is perhaps to be preferred because "apocryphal" has the pejorative connotation of "spurious" or "heretical." Deuterocanonical means secondarily canonical or added later to the canon and is a more descriptive and neutral term introduced by Sixtus of Sienna in 1566. The books recognized as deuterocanonical and authoritative by Roman Catholics are: Tobit, Judith, Wisdom of Solomon, Ecclesiasticus (also called Sirach or Ben Sira), Baruch (including the Letter of Jeremiah), 1 and 2 Maccabees, and additions to the books of Esther and Daniel. The canon of the Greek Orthodox community also includes 1 Esdras, the Prayer of Manasseh, Psalm 151, and 3 Maccabees, with 4 Maccabees as an appendix. ***See also*** Apocrypha, Old Testament; Septuagint; Vulgate. A.J.S.

Deuteronomist, the term for the person(s) responsible for a specific view of God's relationship to human beings incorporated in the OT books from Deuteronomy to 2 Kings. The nomenclature used by scholars to describe the book of Deuteronomy and the history writing that emerged from that tradition is complicated and diverse. The term "Deuteronomist" refers to the history writer(s) who shaped the material in those books (Deut.–2 Kings) to explain that the judgment of Israel by God was due to the grave sins of the people. This judgment was justified and was explained to those who were suffering in order to get them to change their ways and return to obedience to God's law. The view of the relationship between this history writer and the author of Deuteronomy varies among contemporary scholars. The origins and date of the traditions that are included in Deuteronomy have contributed to the nomenclature problems. Therefore it may be best to refer to the historian, irrespective of the dating, as the Deuteronomistic historian (usually abbreviated Dtr.). Deuteronomic (usually abbreviated Dt.) may then be used to refer to the core of materials in the book of Deuteronomy. ***See also*** Deuteronomy; Sources of the Pentateuch. K.H.R.

Deuteronomistic framework, the framework that shapes the telling of the story of Israel's judges and kings (Judg.–2 Kings). The stories of the judges repeat a four-part pattern: apostasy, punishment often in the form of oppression by the enemy, a cry for help or conversion, and deliverance or liberation. This pattern can most easily be observed by reading the account of Othniel (Judg. 3:7–11). The accounts of the kings not only give an evaluation based upon the degree to which the Deuteronomic laws concerning the centralization of worship in Jerusalem were followed but also introduce the king by such items as dating in relation to kings in the other Israelite kingdom, residence, length of reign, age of the king at accession, and occasionally his mother's name. The account is concluded by reference to other sources, place of burial, and the name of the successor. A good example is the framework used in the account of Manasseh's reign in 2 Kings 21:1–26. ***See also*** Deuteronomist; Judges, The Book of; King; Law. K.H.R.

Deuteronomistic historian, the person(s) responsible for the history that runs from Deuteronomy through 2 Kings. They combined the old covenant theology that saw the destruction of Israel as due to apostasy and the promise given David as a sign of continuing hope. Scholars differ regarding the date and number of editions of the work. There is considerable agreement on the creative work of this historian, which may be contrasted with the Priestly work and that of the Chronicler. Each of these in differing ways combined diverse traditions to interpret their meanings to a later generation. ***See also*** Chronicler; Deuteronomy; Priestly Writer(s); Sources of the Pentateuch.

Deuteronomy (Gk., "the second law"), the fifth and final book of the Torah or Pentateuch (Gen. through Deut.). It is presented as a speech of Moses given to the Israelites in Moab as they prepare to cross the Jordan to take possession of Canaan.

Authorship: Traditionally, the authorship of Deuteronomy has been attributed to Moses the lawgiver and prophet, although the book itself never makes such a claim and it is obvious from even a superficial reading of the book that parts of it (e.g., the account of Moses' death, chap. 34) came from another source. Modern scholarship generally agrees that while Deuteronomy contains a core of material from ancient Mosaic traditions or writings, the book in its present form reflects a highly complex history. Although some still propose Mosaic authorship for the entire book, most scholars, based on a variety of evidence, agree that the basic form of the book was first composed during the later part of Manasseh's reign or in the early part of Josiah's reign (ca. 650–640 B.C.). And while no direct evidence exists, it is thought that a group of prophets or priests in Jerusalem was responsible for the collection and ordering of the material of that first edition. It was that early form of Deuteronomy that Hilkiah the high priest found in the Temple in the eighteenth year of Josiah's reign (ca. 621 B.C.). Josiah, who had already begun religious reforms early in his reign (2 Kings 22:1–7; 2 Chron. 34:1–7) used the newly discovered law book to guide further his sweeping program of reform and national renewal (2 Kings 22:8–23:25; 2 Chron. 34:8–35:19). The book reached basically its present form during or immediately following the Exile (587–539 B.C.) when additions were made to the original book in the form of theological interpretations of the crisis of the Exile (eg., 29:28; cf. 29:29–30:5; 28:49–57, 64–68).

However, the recognition of diverse strands of tradition within the book is no indication that parts of the book should be considered inferior or of less value. The long and complex history of the Mosaic legal traditions and their later incorporation along with commentary into the present setting of Deuteronomy demonstrates an ongoing process of reinterpretation of the old traditions in light of new historical circumstances. The authors, whether prophets or priests, were attempting to revitalize the nation's religion by making the old traditions alive and relevant for their own time. Because of this vitality and the basically theological nature of the book (as opposed to primarily historical content) Deuteronomy should be seen, at least in its theological communication, as a unity.

Style and Content: One of the most important distinguishing features of the book is its homiletical style; that is, the laws are not presented in a static legal format but are interwoven with exhortations and pleas of a more personal nature, similar to the style of a sermon. While there is still emphasis on the laws and legal provisions, there is an overriding emphasis on obedience, not simply to a code of laws written in a book, but obedience as the proper attitude of humanity in response to God's will (e.g., 6:20–25; 7:7–11; 11:1–7; 28:45–47). In this, Deuteronomy moves toward more responsibility for the individual (e.g., 30:11–14) and a subsequent emphasis on motive and intention, a concern that was shared by the prophets, most of whom were active during the time the book was reaching its basic form (see, e.g., Jer. 7:21–23). This fusing of obedience to law and proper intentions is reflected in the *Shema* (Deut. 6:4–9), one of the creedal cornerstones of Jewish faith. In fact, it was this blending of legal and prophetic concerns that allowed the book to be organized as a speech of Moses who was the model of both lawgiver (Exod. 24:12) and prophet (Deut. 34:10).

Other characteristics of the book are closely related to this emphasis on proper obedience. Total loyalty to God is demanded. While this is most often connected with obedience to the commandments, there is always an underlying demand to forsake the worship of false gods (6:13–15; 8:19; 9:7–12; 30:15–20). There is reflected throughout the book a concern with equality and justice (1:16–17; 25:13–16), especially toward the weaker members of society (10:18–19; 14:28–29; 15:1–18; 24:14–15). God's love for his people and a desire for a mutual loving relationship are also prominent (6:5; 7:13–14; 10:12–15; 23:5; 30:6, 19–20). There is in the book a development of a view that equates obedience with blessing and life, and disobedience with curse and death (11:26–28; 30:15–20). While such a view would later be distorted into a wooden legalism, Deuteronomy itself stresses obedience on the level of proper love (10:12–13; cf. Mic. 6:8).

Influence: The influence of Deuteronomy could hardly be exaggerated. Its perspectives provided the criteria by which Israel examined and judged itself; so much so that scholars can refer to the history of Israel recorded in the Former Prophets (Joshua–2 Kings) as the "Deuteronomic History." Deuteronomy also represents the first step toward the development of a canon of Scripture that would become binding upon the people in matters of faith and practice.

Deuteronomy is one of the books most frequently quoted in the NT. Jesus quoted part of the *Shema* (6:4–5) as the summary of both legal and prophetic teachings (Matt. 22:37; Mark 12:30; cf. Luke 10:27). The Gospels also record that Jesus quoted from Deuteronomy in facing the three temptations (Matt. 4:1–10; Luke 4:1–13; from Deut. 8:3; 6:13, 16). ***See also*** Canon; Hexateuch; Josiah; Shema; Sources of the Pentateuch.

D.R.B.

OUTLINE OF CONTENTS

Deuteronomy

- I. Introductory address (1:1–4:43)
  - A. The setting (1:1–5)
  - B. Historical review (1:6–3:29)
  - C. Exhortations (4:1–40)
  - D. Cities of refuge (4:41–43)
- II. The Law of Moses (4:44–26:19)
  - A. The setting (4:44–49)
  - B. The Ten Commandments and commentary (5–11)
  - C. Other laws (12–26)
- III. The covenant of obedience (27:1–30:20)
  - A. The ceremony (27)
  - B. The provisions (28)
  - C. The oath (29–30)
- IV. Moses' final words (31:1–33:29)
  - A. Words of encouragement (31:1–8)
  - B. Final concerns (31:9–29)
  - C. The song of Moses (31:30–32:47)
  - D. The trip to Nebo (32:48–52)
  - E. The blessing of Moses (33)
- V. Moses' death (34:1–12)

devil, the English translation of a Greek word (*diabolos*) meaning "accuser" or "slanderer," used in the Septuagint to translate the Hebrew "Satan" and in the NT as a virtual synonym for the same term. In the KJV, it is also regularly employed as a translation of another Greek word (*daimōn*), which, however, in the RSV is transliterated as "demon." The idea that Satan was an angel put out of heaven because of his rebellion against God and his desire to assume the prerogatives of divinity seems to be reflected in

Luke 10:18. Jesus' ability to expel the demons who were Satan's minions was understood to be the result of his having conquered and "bound" Satan (see Mark 3:27). ***See also*** Demon; Satan.
J.M.E.

devoted thing, something irredeemably dedicated to God (Lev. 27:28; cf. Mark 7:11). Such items could be dedicated by an individual (Lev. 27:28), but more commonly they were items proscribed in war. People and cities under the status of a devoted thing were destroyed lest they be profaned by human use or contact (Lev. 27:29; Deut. 2:34), while war spoils could become the property of the sanctuary (Josh. 6: 24).

dew, water from the air condensed on a cool surface, usually overnight. Its presence is of prime importance if plants are to survive the hot dry months (May–August) in Palestine when no rain falls. It is thus a sign of blessing (Gen. 27: 28), nourishment (Deut. 32:2), peace (Ps. 133:3), royal favor (Prov. 19:12), relief from heat (Isa. 18:4), life for the dead (Isa. 26:19), the environment of animals (Dan. 4:25), short-term loyalty (Hos. 6:4), or the promise of good life (Mic. 5:7).

dial, a flat disk with numbers or other symbols around its edge. Though the sundial was known in antiquity, the word in the story of Hezekiah's healing (2 Kings 20:11; Isa. 38:8) probably refers only to a stairway whose steps were gradually shaded by a nearby object as the day progressed.

Diana of the Ephesians. ***See*** Artemis of the Ephesians.

Diaspora (dī-as'paw-rah; Gk., "scattered abroad"), the Jews who lived outside the land of Palestine after the Babylonian Exile (586 B.C.). They exercised a significant influence on the Jewish faith, ranging from the translation of the Hebrew Bible into Greek (LXX) to the formulation of the Babylonian Talmud, a collection of materials on Jewish religious interpretation and customs. In 1 Peter, the term (RSV: "Dispersion") is applied to Christians who lived in some Roman provinces in Asia Minor (1:1), although it is not clear if the scattering away from the homeland is understood there in a physical or a spiritual sense.
P.J.A.

Dibon (dī'bahn). **1** An important settlement located on the King's Highway, thirteen miles east of the Dead Sea and three miles north of the Arnon River. Dibon's ruins are located adjacent to and are partially covered by modern Dhiban. Before the arrival of the Hebrews in Transjordan (thirteenth century B.C.) the Amorite king Sihon took possession of northern Moab. This same region, including Dibon, was captured by the Israelites (Num. 21:21–31). Because the Moabite plateau was good pasturage, the territory surrounding Dibon was allotted to the Israelite tribes Reuben and Gad (Num. 32:3; Josh. 13:9). Although it was ultimately assigned to Reuben (Josh. 13:17), Dibon was rebuilt by Gad (Num. 32:34), hence the town was also called Dibongad (Num. 33:45–46).

The Moabite Stone, which was discovered at Dhiban in 1868, describes King Mesha's rebellion against Israel and the reestablishment of Moabite independence (ca. 840 B.C.). Line one of this inscription refers to Mesha as "the Dibonite." It is clear that ninth-century Dibon was important for military, political, and religious reasons. The site's continuing importance is confirmed by later references to Dibon in Isa. 15:2, 9 and Jer. 48:18, 22.

Excavations were conducted at Dibon between 1950 and 1956; these investigations recovered material from the Early Bronze, Iron Ages I–II, Nabatean, Roman, Byzantine, and Arab periods (3000 B.C.–A.D. 1500), but there is a notable absence of Middle and Late Bronze Age remains.

2 A village in the northern Negeb that was reoccupied by Jews in the postexilic period (Neh. 11:25). This Dibon, whose location remains uncertain, is probably identical with Dimonah (Josh. 15:22). ***See also*** Gad; Mesha; Moabite Stone, The; Reuben; Sihon.
G.L.M.

Didymus (did'uh-muhs, KJV; RSV: "twin"), a Greek name for Thomas (John 11:16; 20:24; 21: 2). ***See also*** Thomas.

dill (KJV: "anise"), an aromatic plant used in cooking as a condiment and medicinally as a

Dill.

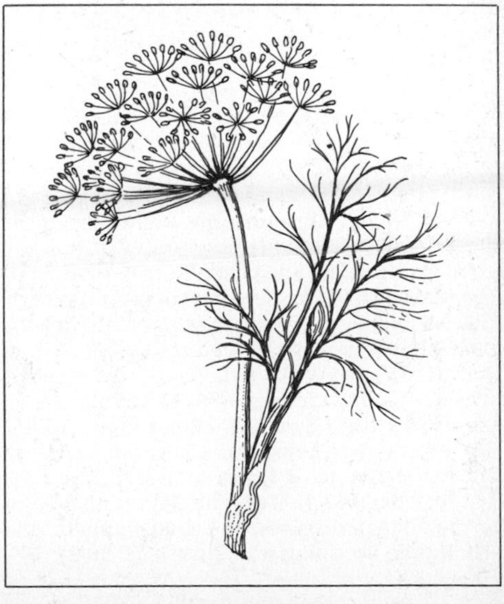

carminative and breath-freshener. Paying a tithe on dill (Matt. 23:23) symbolizes scrupulous attention to details of ritual law.

Dinah, Jacob's daughter by Leah (Gen. 34). That account, which relates her problematic relationship with Shechem, apparently reflects the Israelite struggle to establish proper social boundaries for marital unions. ***See also*** Jacob; Shechem.

Dionysius (dī-uh-nee'suhs), a member of the Areopagite council in Athens who is said to have been converted by Paul's preaching there (Acts 17:34).

Diotrephes (dī-ah'truh-feez), church leader mentioned (unfavorably) only in 3 John 9–10. He "likes to put himself first," rejects the authority of the Letter's author, and refuses to receive the latter's emissaries, ejecting from the church those who do. ***See also*** John, The Letters of.

disciple (translates the Gk. for "learner"), an apprentice or pupil attached to a teacher or movement; one whose allegiance is to the instruction and commitments of the teacher or movement. Closely paralleling rabbinic custom, most NT references to "disciple" designate "followers" of Jesus, often a large group including both his closest associates (the Twelve) and a larger number who followed with varying positive response (Luke 6:17). For disciples of other persons, see Luke 11:1 and John 1:35 (John the Baptist), Matt. 22:16 and Mark 2:18 (Pharisees), John 9:28 (Moses), and Acts 6:1–7 (Christians); cf. also Isa. 8:16 (Isaiah). ***See also*** Apostle; Twelve, The. P.L.S.

Disciple whom Jesus loved. ***See*** Beloved Disciple, The.

discus. ***See*** Games.

disease and healing, physical illness and its cure. The diseases recorded in the Bible are many and varied, but imprecise description of them often makes their identification in today's terms difficult. Since disease could have grave social and economic consequences in the ancient Near Eastern and Greco-Roman worlds, its causes and cures were matters of great moment. **Causes:** Some passages dealing with disease name no cause (Lev. 13; 1 Kings 17:17; 2 Kings 5:1; Mark 1:30; 5:25). Others specify a cause, whether natural (2 Kings 4:38–40) or, more commonly, divine (1 Sam. 5:6–12; 2 Kings 6:18; Ps. 38), especially when disease is connected with sin (Num. 12; cf. 2 Kings 5:20–27; Num. 16: 41–50; 2 Sam. 12:15–18). The Deuteronomic interpretation of disease is the most emphatic and detailed in ascribing it to sin (Deut. 28:22, 27–28, 35, 59–61). Such an interpretation, or its application to specific instances, is questioned in the book of Job and in the account of the healing of the blind man in John 9:1–3. Ascribing all—both good and evil, disease and healing—to the Lord (Deut. 32:39) posed problems. Why should God torment Saul with an "evil spirit" (1 Sam. 16:14–15) or incite David to a census of Israel for which he then punishes Israel with a plague (2 Sam. 24)? Later OT writings mitigated such problems by reference to "a/the Satan" (lit. "a/the adversary") who, in bringing on disease, is depicted as acting either independently (*he* incited David, 1 Chron. 21:1) or as one of "the sons of God" who report regularly to the Lord (Job 1:6–12; 2:1–6). In 2 Cor. 12:7–8 Satan (now a proper name) retains this functionary role, but in other passages disease is seen as caused by Satan/the devil and his demonic minions acting independently (e.g., Mark 1:35; 3: 22–26; 7:25; Luke 13:16, 32). At the same time the theme of disease as divine retribution is retained (1 Cor. 11:29–30; Acts 12:21–23).
Cures: In the biblical writings, as well as in ancient Near Eastern and Greco-Roman sources generally, diseased persons are seen as having recourse to several means of treatment. One is folk medicine (balm, Jer. 8:22; 46:11; 51:8; wine, 2 Tim. 5:23; oil and wine, Luke 10:34; music, 2 Sam. 16:23). The sick might also turn to physicians for help (2 Chron. 16:12; Mark 5:25–26; note the mention of physicians in Job 13:4; Jer. 8:22; Matt. 9:12; Mark 2:17; Luke 4:23; 5:31; Col. 4:14), or they might appeal to a deity. These various means of healing were generally not sharply distinguished and might, in fact, be conjoined: a fig cake was applied to Hezekiah's boil at the command of the prophet Isaiah (2 Kings 20:7); oil was used by early Christian elders in a healing ritual (James 5:14; cf. Mark 6:13). Sometimes, however, religion and physicians are seen in opposition, explicitly (2 Chron. 16: 12) or implicitly: a woman with a chronic hemorrhage turns from physicians to Jesus for relief (Mark 5:25–26).

This theme—the failure of medical science—is common in healing accounts in the Greco-Roman world. As a result of such failure, the sufferer then turns to a healer. These accounts follow a common pattern, both in the Bible and outside it: the sickness is described as incurable by ordinary means; the sufferer (or a representative) approaches the healer, who effects a sudden healing; proof of the healing is followed by acclamation of the healer and/or deity (see 1 Kings 17:17–24; 2 Kings 5:25–37; Mark 5:25–34; 7:32–37). Biblical portraits of certain holy men as healers (Elijah, Elisha, Jesus, Peter, Paul) also have affinities with those of healers in extrabiblical sources, for example, in the use of gestures and material means (1 Kings 17:21; 2 Kings 5:10–11; Mark 7:

33; 8:23, 25; Acts 19:12; 28:8) and foreign words (Mark 5:41; 7:34).

Healing in the NT: The NT evidence on healing is ambivalent. The book of Acts presents Paul as a healer (Acts 14:8–10; 16:18; 19:11–12; 28:8–9), and Paul's mention of his apostolic "signs and wonders" (Rom. 15:19; 2 Cor. 12:12) may refer to healings; yet he himself reports that his prayers for his own healing were rejected (2 Cor. 12:7–9). The NT accounts of Jesus as healer are in contrast to the story of his helplessness in the face of his own suffering and death (cf. Matt. 27:42; Mark 15:31; Luke 23:35). Nor is Jesus able to heal consistently where faith in him is lacking (Mark 6:5–6; cf. Matt. 13:58). Belief in healers and their procedures—by sick persons and their social groups—has been shown by modern investigators to be crucial in healing. It presumably figures into some of the wondrous healings reported for the Greek god of healing, Asclepius, with whom the risen Jesus as healer comes into rivalry as early Christians performed healing rituals in Jesus' name. Early followers of Jesus, who are reported as healing by the command of Jesus (Mark 6:13; Matt. 10:8) or in his name (Acts 3:7; 16:18), may well have recounted and recorded some of the stories of Jesus as healer to inspire confidence and as warrant for their healing rituals. In those cases, the details of procedures in these accounts (use of gestures, material means, foreign words) may have served as guides for their own procedures (cf. esp. Mark 9:29). ***See also*** Devil; Leprosy; Magic and Divination; Miracles. H.E.R.

Dispersion (Gk. *diaspora* from *diaspeirein*, "to scatter"), terms referring to the exile or emigration of Jews from Israel to other countries. When the northern kingdom of Israel was conquered by the Assyrians in 721 B.C., many Israelites were taken into exile in Mesopotamia. When the southern kingdom of Judah was conquered in 597 and again in 587 many of its leaders and people were exiled to Babylon, laying the foundation of a community that flourished until A.D. 1000. During the Persian (539–332 B.C.) and Hellenistic (332 B.C.–A.D. 63) periods Jews moved to all major population centers in the eastern Mediterranean. Jewish mercenaries settled in upper Egypt and southern Asia Minor. In NT times, under the Romans, Jews were a recognized ethnic group with legal rights. Vigorous communities existed in Rome, Alexandria, Cyprus, the cities of Greece and Asia Minor, Antioch in Syria, and beyond the Empire in Mesopotamia. Acts 2:9–11 names the diverse origins of pilgrims to Jerusalem. Greek was the most common language of the eastern Roman Empire and the Septuagint, the Greek translation of the OT, was made to serve the large Greek-speaking Jewish community. In John 7:35 people speculate whether Jesus will go among the Jews (called Greeks) of the Dispersion. ***See also*** Babylon; Israel; Septuagint. A.J.S.

distaff. ***See*** Spinning and Weaving.

Dives (dī'vees; from the Lat. for "wealth"), a term that became attached as a name to the rich man in the parable of Lazarus and the rich man (Luke 16:19–31) because of its use in the Vulgate, a Latin translation of the Bible.

Divided Kingdom, Divided Monarchy, the two-hundred year period in ancient Judah and Israel from 922 to 722 B.C. Following Solomon's reign, his son Rehoboam was unable to retain leadership in the northern state of Israel. Judah, the southern state, was much more at ease with the dynastic succession (son following father), but Israel did not follow suit. Therefore when Rehoboam went to Shechem to be confirmed as king over Israel as was the custom (1 Kings 12:1–20), his trip ended in failure. As a result Jeroboam I became king of the northern state and the Divided Kingdom was begun. Israel during this time had no fewer than eighteen kings and Judah twelve kings. While political leadership during the Divided Kingdom lacked distinction, included in the period are great eighth-century B.C. prophets such as Amos, Hosea, and Isaiah. ***See also*** Jeroboam I; Prophet; Rehoboam; Solomon. K.H.R.

divination. ***See*** Magic and Divination.

divinity of Jesus. ***See*** Jesus Christ.

divorce. ***See*** Marriage.

doctor. ***See*** Disease and Healing.

document. ***See*** Acts of the Apostles, The; New Testament; Q; Sources of the Pentateuch.

Dodanim (doh'duh-neem), a term in Gen. 10:4 that should rather be read Rodanim, as in 1 Chron. 1:7. In both texts the name is that of the fourth and last son of Javan (Ionia), who was the fourth son of Japheth. As reflected in the Greek (LXX) version of the name—*Rhodioi*—it refers to the people of Rhodes, the large island off the southwest coast of Asia Minor.

Dodo (doh'doh; Heb., "his beloved"). **1** A member of the tribe of Issachar and the grandfather of Tola, one of the judges of Israel (Judg. 10:1). **2** An Ahohite, father of Eleazer, one of the three chief leaders of David's fighting men (2 Sam. 23:9). He is probably the same person referred to as Dodai the Ahohite (1 Chron. 27:4), although it is probable that due to an inadvertent omission in the text it was his son Eleazer who commanded the division of twenty-four thousand men under

David and not Dodai himself. **3** A man from Bethlehem, the father of Elhanan, one of David's warriors (2 Sam. 23:9). D.R.B.

Doeg (doh'eg), "the Edomite," unscrupulous henchman of Saul (1 Sam. 21–22). He witnessed Ahimelech, a priest in Nob, giving assistance to David. Doeg reported Ahimelech's action to Saul, who, ignoring Ahimelech's protestation of faith in David's loyalty, ordered all the priests of Nob slain. While most of Saul's servants refused to strike God's priests, Doeg proceeded to kill them, their families, and their livestock.

dog, a domesticated member of the canine family. Dogs were highly esteemed and possibly even worshiped in Egypt, and they were popular in Mesopotamia as hunting companions; dogs are depicted on Assyrian reliefs from the seventh century B.C. The Hebrews, however, viewed them with utter disgust. In the Bible the dog (Heb. *keleb*; Gk. *kyōn*) is usually described as a scavenger. An exception is obviously the dog that followed at the heels of Tobias (Tob. 5:16; 11:4). The little dogs (Gk. *kynarion*) that ate the proverbial bread "crumbs that fall from their master's table" at least had access to the house and may have been pets (Matt. 15:27; Mark 7:28).

The dog *(Canis familiaris)*, whose wild ancestor was the wolf *(Canis lupus)*, is held to be the earliest domesticated animal. This assumption rests on remains of a presumably domesticated dog found at Palegawra Cave in Iraq and dated to 10,000 B.C. Recently a puppy skeleton buried with a human and ascribed to the Natufian period (ca. 12,000–4500 B.C.) was unearthed at Ein Mallaha in northern Israel. This find testifies to the existence of a close relationship between humans and dogs for the same time in Palestine (ca. 10,000 B.C.).

Dogs were useful as watchdogs and because they cleared away refuse, carcasses (Exod. 22:31), and vermin. But they are also said to eat human flesh (e.g., 1 Kings 14:11; 16:4) and to lick human blood (1 Kings 21:19). 2 Kings 9:30–36 tells the gruesome story of Jezebel, who was eaten by dogs after being thrown over the city wall.

Hunting dog and Assyrian hunter;
seventh-century B.C. relief from Nineveh.

When applied to a person "dog" becomes a term of disregard and humiliation and in Ps. 22:16 enemies are called "dogs." In 1 Sam. 17:43 Goliath ridicules David's weapons by saying "Am I a dog, that you come to me with sticks?" Considering this attitude of the Hebrews one wonders why in Eccles. 9:4 "a living dog is better than a dead lion." I.U.K.

dominion, rule or lordship, referring to political authority exercised by human beings (Gen. 37:8; Judg. 14:4; Ps. 72:8) or the realm in which such authority is exercised (2 Kings 20:13). Humanity also rules over creation, though under God (Gen. 1:26, 28; Ps. 8:6). Oppressive rule is condemned (Lev. 25:43, 53; Matt. 20:25). Ultimate and eternal dominion over all things belongs to God (Pss. 22:28; 145:13; Dan. 4:3; Rev. 1:6). In the NT, dominion may also refer to certain angelic or cosmic powers (Col. 1:16; Rom. 8:38), which, however, are subordinated to the power of God (Eph. 1:21; Col. 2:15).

doorkeepers, people who guard access to important or restricted places. Doorkeepers were appointed in the Temple as "keepers of the threshold" to collect money from the people (2 Kings 22:4). Levites were appointed as gatekeepers for the Ark (1 Chron. 15:23–24). Eunuchs were doorkeepers at the palace of the Persian king (Esther 2:21) and a woman was doorkeeper at the house of King Ishbosheth (2 Sam. 4:6; cf. John 18:16–17; Acts 12:13).

doors, floor-level breaches in a wall with openable barriers. The biblical use of the term is both literal and symbolic, with shrine doors used in both ways.

Among the literal uses, one finds doors to houses (Gen. 19:6), which could be broken in during assault (Gen. 19:9); doors used for signs for deliverance (Exod. 12:23) or bondage (Deut. 15:17) or work zones (Neh. 3:20); doors used for assignations (Job 31:9); and doors built unwisely (Prov. 17:19), closed for privacy (Matt. 6:6; Luke 11:7), and pounded upon to rouse occupants (Luke 13:25).

Symbolically, doors were places where sin lay in wait (Gen. 4:7), the apertures through which speech made its exit (Ps. 141:3), the model of sluggish action (Prov. 26:14), an access route for hope (Hos. 2:15), the narrow passage to eternal life (Luke 13:24), the right access to the human community of the church (John 10:1), the access route of faith among the Gentiles (Acts 14:27), opportunity to proclaim the gospel (2 Cor. 2:12), and the route of access to one's life (Rev. 3:12).

In references to shrines, the Bible uses the word "door" in the case of tents, buildings, and parts of buildings. Applied to tents and the tabernacle in the wilderness, it is slightly misused, meaning rather the flap or entrance opening which usually had no construction as its support (Gen. 18:1; Exod. 26:36; Lev. 14:11). Elaborate doors were part of the Temple, being described as built of two swinging leaves each (1 Kings 6:34; Ezek. 41:24), and there were numerous doors throughout the structure (Ezek. 40:13–47:1).

Archaeological evidence in numerous locations supports the suggestion that doors were hung from a pivot post set in a socket. They could be bolted shut, both with horizontal and vertical bolt locks. They were sometimes reinforced with iron, carved or otherwise decorated, and, as with gates in city walls, were the most vulnerable point in the building's perimeter when under assault. Stone doors (swinging and rolling type) have been found for both tombs and buildings (especially in the Roman and Nabatean remains in Palestine and the Transjordan; cf. Matt. 27:65–28:2). R.S.B.

Dor, a well-situated natural seaport on the coast of the Mediterranean Sea south of Mt. Carmel. Dor is first mentioned in an Egyptian inscription of the thirteenth century B.C. Tel Dor (modern Khirbet el-Burj) is one of the largest tells in Israel (ca. 35 acres). It was excavated in the 1920s by John Garstang and G. M. Fitzgerald for the British School of Archaeology and in the 1980s by E. Stern for the Israel Exploration Society. The king of Dor was one of a coalition of Canaanite kings defeated by Joshua (mid- or late thirteenth century B.C.; Josh. 11:2; 12:23). The city was included in the territorial allotment of Manasseh (Josh. 17:7–13; 1 Chron. 7:29), although the Joshua text notes that the Canaanites continued to occupy Dor. Indeed, it is known from the Egyptian *Tale of Wen-Amon* (ca. 1100 B.C.) that the city was occupied by the Tjeker, a sea people related to the Philistines. The city was under Israelite control by the tenth century (Solomon's son-in-law Ben-abinadab was governor of the district of Dor, 1 Kings 4:11) but it became the center of an Assyrian administrative district in the eighth century (probably the "Way of the Sea" of Isa. 9:1–2). It was subsequently controlled by the Persians and the Phoenicians and during the Hellenistic period was a large, well-fortified independent city. The Hasmonean Simon fought against Trypho of Dor in an alliance with Antiochus Sidetes (1 Macc. 15:1–14) and the city was later taken by Alexander Jannaeus. Pompey restored independence to the citizens in 63 B.C. J.D.P.

Dorcas (dor'kuhs), a Christian woman in Joppa whose Aramaic name was Tabitha ("gazelle"). Well known for her works of generosity and charity, she died and was restored to life by Peter (Acts 9:36–42).

dot, a projection or hook as part of a letter of the alphabet (serif) or of a stroke to mark accents and breathing, hence a metaphor for something insignificant (Matt. 5:18; Luke 16:17).

Dothan (doh'than), a town in central Palestine where Joseph and his brothers pastured their flocks (Gen. 37:17). It was there also that the king of Syria sought out the prophet Elisha (2 Kings 6:13). Ancient Dothan is identified with modern Tell Dotha, ten miles north of Samaria/Sebaste and near the southern edge of the Esdraelon plain. In antiquity as well as today Dothan was close to the main commercial route and in the midst of pasture lands.

Tell Dotha was excavated by Joseph Free from 1953 to 1960. Thirty feet of debris represent rather continuous occupation from Late Chalcolithic times (ca. 3200 B.C.) through Iron Age II (to 700 B.C.) and included a Hellenistic acropolis, some slight Roman remains, and a Mamluk palace. Widespread Middle Bronze occupation and several Iron Age II levels can be related to the biblical accounts. N.L.L.

dove, a small bird of the Columbidae family. Three varieties of the small species of pigeon identified as a "turtledove" are known in Palestine. Noah, following a custom of ancient mariners, uses doves to determine if the Flood has subsided (Gen. 8:8–12). Lev. 12:8 prescribed the offering of a pair of doves or two young pigeons to purify the mother after childbirth if the family could not afford a lamb. Doves for such offerings were sold in the Temple court (Mark 11:15; John 2:14). Mary makes this offering after the birth of Jesus (Luke 2:4).

The stories of Jesus' baptism all describe the descent of the Holy Spirit on Jesus "like a dove" (Mark 1:10; Matt. 3:16; Luke 3:22; John 1:32). Although the tradition presumably derives from the early Palestinian community, no early Jewish parallel for the use of a dove to represent the Spirit has yet been found. Some scholars think that the hovering Spirit of Gen. 1:2 might have suggested the image. Others point to the "dove" of Gen. 8:8 or to the comparison of the Spirit of God to an eagle in Deut. 32:11. P.P.

dowry. *See* Marriage.

drachma (drak'mah). *See* Money.

dragon, a reptilian monster well known in the mythology and iconography of the ancient Near East. In the Babylonian creation myth, *Enuma*

This composite creature, with the head of a serpent, body of a lion, and hind feet of an eagle, is a reconstruction of the original that decorated the Ishtar Gate at Babylon during the reign of Nebuchadnezzar II, seventh century B.C.

elish, the dragon Tiamat is slain by the god Marduk and her supporters taken captive. In a Hattic myth, the dragon Illuyankas defeated the storm god and later was slain by him. The Ugaritic myths from Ras-Shamra refer to various monsters defeated by the storm god Baal or his sister Anat. In the Bible the dragon appears as the primeval enemy of God, killed or subjected in conjunction with creation (Pss. 74:13–14; 89:10; Isa. 51:9; Job 26:12–13), but appearing again at the end of the world, when God will finally dispose of it (Isa. 27:1, using traditional language attested in the Baal myths of Ras-Shamra). The book of Revelation takes up the latter theme. The dragon (identified now with the Devil) and its agents campaign against God and his forces but are finally defeated (Rev. 12–13; 16:13–14; 20:2–3, 7–10). For now, however, it is kept under guard (Job 7:12), its supporters lying prostrate beneath God (Job 9:13). Referred to variously as Tannin, Rahab, or Leviathan, it is usually conceived of as a sea monster, as in the *Enuma elish* and sometimes at Ras-Shamra. As a great opponent of God's people, Egypt was known as Rahab. The oracle of Isa. 30:7 gives Egypt the name "Rahab [is] put down," alluding to the dragon's defeat by God, and Ps. 87:4 simply assumes Rahab as an accepted name for Egypt. The king of Egypt was portrayed as a sea monster lurking in the Nile, whom God would catch and kill (Ezek. 29:3; 32:2). There may be no mythological allusion here, and there is certainly none when the words *tannin* and *leviathan* are used to refer to the monsters of the deep created by God (Gen. 1:21; Ps. 104:26), summoned to praise God (Ps. 148:7), and beyond human capture (Job 41:1). The apocryphal Bel and the Dragon (23–27) relates Daniel's unorthodox disposal of a dragon worshipped by the Babylonians. ***See also*** Leviathan; Rahab. S.B.P.

dreams, visions widely attested in the early books of the Bible (e.g., Jacob's dream, Gen. 28:12; Joseph's dreams, Gen. 37), yet often viewed with distrust in the later tradition, as in Jer. 23:28: "Let the prophet who has a dream tell the dream, but let him who has my word speak my word faithfully" (see also Deut. 13:2–6; Jer. 27:9–10; 29:8–9; Sir. 34:1–8). Dreams are rehabilitated as a mode of revelation in the apocalyptic literature. Daniel interprets the dreams of the Gentile king and receives his own revelations in dream-visions (also cf. Zech. 1:8 with the prophecy of Joel 2:28). In the NT dreams figure most prominently in the nativity story of Matthew. ***See also*** Daniel, The Book of; Joseph; Magic and Divination. J.J.C.

dress, clothing worn for utility as well as decoration. The biblical terms for dress, garments, clothes, robes, and various items of garb are general and exchangeable in translation, and the clothes they represent are difficult to describe from them. Artistic representations from the Near East are very helpful, and some forms of dress are defined by function, as with a soldier's helmet (1 Sam. 17:5), which is used metaphorically as well (Isa. 59:17; Eph. 6:17).

The earliest forms of clothing were generally made from animal skins, a practice never really given up to this day (witness the popularity of furs, hides for shoes and gloves, leather for belts, tool carriers, decorative items [watchbands or bracelets and hair fasteners], and billfolds). The beginnings of fabric weaving are lost in the advancing centuries of the Stone Age (ended ca. 4500 B.C.), and the use of straw and reeds for mats and houses probably preceded adaptation of plant fiber for clothing. Linen (from flax) and cotton cloth were apparently distinctively Egyptian developments, whereas the use of wool for fabric seems to have become popular sometime between the Sumerian use of lapped leaves (of leather or metal) for skirts evident in their statuary and the draped robes of Gudea, the king of Lagash in the later Sumerian period. Weaving cloth of wool or hair (for tents), stitching fabric pieces together, and dyeing fabric to allow variation in color are known throughout the biblical period. The tomb paintings from Egypt at Beni-hasan give representations of both styles and colors in use there.

Biblical styles and materials were those shared throughout the Near East from the Early Bronze Age (3000–2000 B.C.) into the Roman period (63 B.C.–A.D. 324). Characteristic references to Israelite garments used by both men and women indicate that the cultural habits in dress changed as different peoples invaded and dominated Syro-Palestine, but there were always certain exceptions for traditional and distinctive official dress.

It is immediately clear that dress was geared to climate and necessities of movement rather than simply to appearance or aesthetic appeal.

Ancient Styles of Dress: **1a.** One type of loincloth (Semite, ca. 1800 B.C.); **1b.** Animal skin; **2.** Men's tunic or coat; **3.** Men's mantle; **4.** *Himation;* **5.** First-century cloak or cape; **6.** Women's dress; **7.** High priest; **8.** Type of prayer shawl; **9.** Hebrew royal attire; **10.** Persian; **11.** Roman toga; **12.** Roman *stola* and *pallium;* **13.** Egyptian loincloth (ca. 1300 B.C.); **14.** Egyptian sheath-like dress (ca. 2000 B.C.); **15.** Babylonian (ca. 2000 B.C.); **16.** Assyrian (ca. 900 B.C.).

Again there were exceptions. The notorious dress of the harlot (Prov. 7:10) was probably as much a public advertisement as was her conduct toward the young and unsuspecting prospect. Soldiers' dress was geared to battle efficiency, priestly garments included many symbolic representations (as with some modern clerical garb), and there were special dress arrangements for special occasions, such as a wedding, mourning, or a planned deceit (Josh. 9:5).

Men's Clothing: The term translated "clothes" in 1 Sam. 4:12 and Judg. 3:16 was apparently a long robe of some sort (2 Sam. 10:4) since it could be cut off "in the middle, at their hips." A term for any whole garment could also mean a cover cloth for the Ark (Num. 4:6–9, "a cloth") or a bed (1 Sam. 19:13, "the clothes"), royal robes (2 Sam. 13:31, "garments"), war prisoners' clothing (Jer. 52:33, "prison garments"), mourning garb (2 Sam. 14:2, "mourning garments" worn in this case by a woman), and priestly garments (Exod. 28:2, "holy garments"). Such clothing might be made of either linen or wool, but in the codes in Deuteronomy and Leviticus they were not to be mixed (Deut. 22:11; Lev. 19: 19).

The "wrap-around" garment usually called a mantle could cover nakedness (Noah's in Gen. 9:23), a sword (1 Sam. 21:9), or dress clothing while moving incognito (Ruth 3:3), or serve as an offering basket (Judg. 8:25). It was the clothing of wanderers (Deut. 8:4), the strangers (Deut. 10:18), and the poor (Exod. 22:26–27), who used it as a sleeping cover. For that reason it was not to serve as collateral for more than the part of a day remaining until sundown, when the owner would need it for the night. As with all clothing, it could be ripped (1 Kings 11:30). To be without such garments was the extremity of poverty or neglect (Job 24:7). Ezek. 27:23–24 indicates that clothing was a trading item when it was distinctively rich or finely worked goods. NT language for general clothing items includes reference to an oblong outer garment (Matt. 17:2; 27:31) worn over a coat (Matt. 5:40; Luke 6:29, "shirt").

With the outer clothing mentioned above were worn certain items as undergarments. A long or half-sleeved, ankle-length shirt in white or in colors was used by both men and women (Gen. 37:3, 31–33). Gen. 3:21 reports that God made such garments for Adam and Eve out of skins. They were usually anchored over one if not both shoulders. Men's sometimes reached only to the knees. The collared tunic of Job 30: 18 was also used by women (2 Sam. 13:18–19; Song of Sol. 5:3), as by priests (Exod. 28:4). Usually made of wool, it was specified to be of linen for priests. The seamless tunic of Jesus (John 19: 23) for which the soldiers cast lots was such an item, as was the garment torn by the high priest (Mark 14:63). A linen undergarment (Jud. 14: 12–13) is identified by the same term as that for the shroud (Mark 15:46) for the dead. The young man who lost his "linen cloth" (Mark 14:51–52) in a scuffle was probably dressed only in a wraparound of some sort. The "girdle," whether of leather (as Elijah's, 2 Kings 1:8) or cloth (Jer. 13: 1), was in effect a loincloth, and while it was loosened at night, it was not necessarily removed. Linen breeches covering "from the loins to the thighs" were part of priestly vestments (Exod. 28:42). A true belt, sash, or girdle tying one's clothes together at the waist and serving to suspend a soldier's sword was also normal. If made of folded cloth, it could hold money or other valuables (Mark 6:8).

Footwear in the form of sandals or shoes was essential, given the thistle and thorn growth in the countryside. They could be removed in holy places (Exod. 3:5), for mourning, or for repair (Josh. 9:5). Artistic representation shows them attached to the foot by straps around the ankle or, in some periods, even up the calf of the leg.

Head covering was vital for shade from the sun in summer as well as for warmth during the rainy season. A simple cloth might be draped, folded, or wrapped (as a turban) and be held in place by a headband in the fashion still used as *egal* and *kaffiyeh*. The use of lightweight cloth was remarkably suited to the climate, providing a shade penetrable by breeze in the heat of the summer, but allowing multiple folds in which to wrap both face and head as protection against cold, wind, or dust. Specific headgear with certain decorations were designated for priests and their ceremonial duties.

Women's Clothing: The same general terms for clothing mentioned above applied to the garments women wore. The same divisions of outerwear, undergarments, girdles, footwear, and headgear are appropriate, with the addition of the veil in some situations. Outerwear consisted of a long robe, possibly decorated with fringes, or in later periods, with embroidery. It was fastened at the waist with a belt or girdle (Isa. 3:24, even a rope in hard times). Such a mantle or cloak could enfold goods (Ruth 3:15, grain) as well as the wearer. The undergarments of women included the wool or linen shoulder-suspended shift used by men (2 Sam. 13:18), and artistic representations of them show greater variety of colors than those used by men. For footwear, sandals were normal, and might be made especially attractive (Song of Sol. 7:1; Jth. 10:4; 16:9), with special enhancements appropriate at the time of a woman's marriage (Ezek. 16:10). The most distinctive items of dress for women pertain to the head. The "turban" (Isa. 3:23) or "headdress" (Isa. 3:20) was supplemented at least in certain circumstances by a veil for the face (Gen. 24:65, in the presence of a stranger; 38:14, to allow a ruse) or for the body (Isa. 3:23).

Special Occasions: Aside from the special dress for priests in service and soldiers on duty, there was also a customary dress for mourning, whether for the dead, tragedy, or danger from war, usually referred to as sackcloth (a coarse burlap) and ashes (Isa. 58:5; Jer. 6:26; Luke 10: 13). Special adornments were also appropriate for weddings, although they may have comprised unusually ornate garments or headdresses rather than special additional items. Additional jewelry was surely appropriate for any number of celebrations, and the removal of such adornments as signs of repentance was most apparent with the donning of sackcloth and ashes.

Garments were also a symbol of rank and station, especially during the Roman period, when government officials such as kings, legates, and procurators were each marked by distinctive insignia, much in the way the military uses different uniforms for different units, duties, and stations. As in all societies, the poorest folk were most poorly clothed, the wealthiest most ornately dressed. Pretentiousness could show in dress as in manners. Parades tended to draw finery into public view and add color, variety, and festivity, whether to religious, civil, or private ceremonies of celebration. Dress could also be a means of protest, as with the shedding of clothes by Isaiah as a warning to Egypt (Isa. 20:1–6). ***See also*** Jewelry; Priests. R.S.B.

drink, liquid nourishment. In the womb the fetus derives food and shelter from the mother without differentiation between physical and spiritual dimensions. Postnatal liquid foods are milk, water, and wine. Physically milk and water are essential; wine gives superabundance and elation. Used figuratively, all bespeak a consciousness that one does not live by physical elements alone but by intangible realities of which they are symbols. Drinking together connotes fellowship; giving drink to the thirsty connotes compassion. Israel eats and drinks before God at Sinai (Exod. 24:9–11). God's wisdom for the exiles is water, milk, and wine (Isa. 55:1–5). Jesus' teaching is living water (John 4:10, 13–14), his death for others covenanting wine. Paul warns that the Kingdom of God is not food and drink but righteousness and peace and joy in the Holy Spirit (Rom. 14:17); James (2:14–17) and John (1 John 3:16–18) warn that the Kingdom of God is not known apart from compassionate sharing of the physical elements. J.G.J.

dromedary. ***See*** Camel.

dropsy. ***See*** Disease and Healing.

drunkenness, the state of inebriation induced by the ingestion of too much alcohol, in the Bible, principally wine. On the one hand, wine was enjoyed in Israel as a divinely given fruit of the ground. Used in cultic meals (Deut. 14:26), it was a figure for divine wisdom (Isa. 55:1–2; Prov. 9:1–6) as well as human love (Song of Sol. 7:9). It bespeaks superabundance, connoting the elative sense of life heightened above the ordinary.

On the other hand, drunkenness was persistently condemned (e.g., Gen. 9:20–27; Gal. 5: 21). It rendered one insensible and imperceptive, a social nuisance, an economic ruin, and a moral and spiritual reprobate. This it caused through its power to deceive, conveying a false sense of clear perception, intelligence, and power. As wine could symbolize divine wisdom, drunkenness could symbolize human folly and the deceitfulness of false gods. Hence it characterized also general moral and spiritual practices of habitual injustice and idolatry.

Sobriety and wine in moderation come to represent a religion opposed to the false consciousness arising from intoxication with false values and practices sponsored by other gods. Similarly, in the NT the wisdom of the cross (1 Cor. 1–2) is offered in the covenanting wine, conveying moral and spiritual insight and enhancing the elative sense (Eucharist), in contrast to the occluded consciousness of the wisdom of the world. J.G.J.

Drusilla (droo-sil'uh), the wife of Antonius Felix who was procurator of Judea (ca. A.D. 52–59) while Paul was imprisoned in Caesarea. A Jewess, she was the daughter of Herod Agrippa I and great-granddaughter of Herod the Great. Originally given in marriage to the Syrian Azizus of Emesa, she was apparently persuaded to leave him for Felix. In Acts 24:24–27, she is present when Paul speaks about Jesus to her husband. Codex Bezae (an ancient manuscript containing the text of Acts) reports that she instigated the session but adds that when Felix was not responsive to Paul's message, it was Drusilla's wish that Paul remain in prison. ***See also*** Agrippa I; Felix, Antonius; Herod; Paul. A.J.M.

dulcimer. ***See*** Music.

Dumah (doo'mah; Heb., "silence"). **1** A son of Ishmael (Gen. 25:14; 1 Chron. 1:30), possibly resident in south central Arabia at modern Dumat al-Ghandal (el-Jof). **2** A city in the south-central hills of Palestine, probably modern ed-Dome, six miles southwest of Hebron (Josh. 15: 52). **3** The subject of an oracle in Isa. 21:11–12, where it may be a scribal error for Edom, or its meaning, "silence," may indicate the uncertain sense of the oracle.

dumbness. ***See*** Disease and Healing.

dung, human or animal feces. While dried

bricks of human and animal dung were used in Egypt to fuel ovens, the Israelite concept of purity (plus the alternative fuel of Canaan's trees) made this practice obnoxious (Ezek. 4:12, 15). Dung was used as fertilizer (Isa. 25:10; Luke 13: 8) and continues to be so used in the modern Middle East. There are several references to the scarcities of a military siege constraining a city's inhabitants to consume their own excrement (2 Kings 18:27; Isa. 36:12; cf. Lev. 26:29; Deut. 28: 53–57) or "dove's dung" (2 Kings 6:25), which may designate a plant.

Cultic legal texts require that human voiding (Deut. 23:12–14) occur outside of the camp perimeter and the fecal matter in the intestines of sacrificial animals be burned outside of the camp (Exod. 29:14; Lev. 4:11; 8:17; 16:27; Num. 19:5) because of the impurity of excreta (Mal. 2:3). Dung may also refer to an unburied human corpse left as offal (2 Kings 9:37; Jer. 8: 2; 9:21; 16:4; 25:33; Ps. 83:12) or to the worthless impious (Zeph. 1:17; Job 20:7).

The "Dung Gate" of Jerusalem's south wall (Neh. 2:13; 3:13–14; 12:31), a still-current appellation, is probably the exit through which the city's refuse was removed. Paul regarded as dung his religious accomplishments and rank achieved prior to his Christian conversion (Phil. 3:8). B.M.L.

Dura (dōōr-uh), a plain "in the province of Babylon" (Dan. 3:1) where King Nebuchadnezzar set up the golden image for all to worship. Because of the refusal of Daniel and his friends to heed that decree, they were cast into the fiery furnace. The location of the plain is uncertain. ***See also*** Daniel, The Book of.

dyeing, the practice of coloring cloth by adding pigment through hot or cold treatment. Dyeing is discussed only by implication in the Bible. Three references occur in one verse of the poetic version of the defeat of Sisera. In an ironic hypothetical chant of the mother of the dead Canaanite king, she imagines him taking the spoils of the victor, which would include dyed and embroidered cloth, two pieces of which would be for her neck (Judg. 5:30). In a corrected reading of Job 38:14 (where the text has been distorted by transcriptional errors) the poet likens divine control of the dawn to the changes in a garment when it is dyed or clay when it is rolled or stamped with a signatory seal.

A dyed cloth, known in Ugarit by 1500 B.C., became famous throughout the ancient Near East for its distinctive color, "royal purple." It was long a practical monopoly of the Syro-Phoenician coastal people, but Ezekiel (27:7) was apparently impressed that it was available from Cyprus. Jesus was covered with a "purple cloak" during his incarceration for a time (Mark 15:17–20), and the goods continued to be traded into Roman times (Acts 16:14).

Dye vats excavated at Tell Beit Mirsim, seventh century B.C.

Archaeological evidence of a local dyeing industry in Palestine has been found at Gezer, Beth-zur, Beth-shemesh, Tell en-Nasbeh, and most notably at Tell Beit Mirsim in housed installations numbering about thirty. A 10-by-30-foot room was fitted with two vats with small cover openings and draining rims. Basins and benches were placed near or between the vats. Additional vessels for fixing agents, lime or potash, were nearby. From the vat capacities (cavities about a foot and a half across) and the small openings in the covers, the equipment was apparently intended to dye thread rather than whole cloth. The Hellenistic installation at Gezer included a three-vat room, and vat design was now open-topped in the mode of a tub. A basement furnace here suggested use of hot dyes.

The basis of the coveted royal purple was a coloring agent extracted from two primary gastropods of the Muricidae family, especially *Murex brandaris* and *Murex trunculus*, extensive shell beds of which have been found on the Mediterranean coast of north Lebanon and Syria. The dye derived from the secretion of the hypobranchial gland of the mollusk and the small quantity extractable from each shell contributed to the high cost and value of goods treated with the product. ***See also*** Purple. R.S.B.

dysentery. ***See*** Disease and Healing.

Opposite: Head of Ramesses II (1279–1212 B.C.), the Egyptian king who may have been the pharaoh of the oppression (Exod. 1–2) or the pharaoh of the Exodus (Exod. 5–12).

E

E, in modern biblical source criticism the letter that refers to materials presumed to derive from a northern Israelite milieu. The letter E itself is an abbreviation of the divine name *Elohim*, the use of which is taken to be one of the characteristics of this source in the patriarchal narratives. ***See also*** Sources of the Pentateuch.

Ea (ee'ah), an early and important Mesopotamian god. Akkadian Ea, a variant of which may perhaps be Haia, corresponds to the Sumerian Enki(k). He was the god of fresh water and its sources. He was a creator god who formed and engendered life. He was a master of crafts and wisdom. Furthermore, he possessed the knowledge and power of magic and was the god of the magician. As flowing water, he both washed away and received evil; as a body of water, he encompassed and controlled monsters and demons.

In origin, he was the local god of Eridu and made his home there. He also shared the direction and rule of the universe with An, Enlil, and the mother goddess Ninhursag. While it is possible that he was secondarily attached to this triad, he is undoubtedly primary to and dominated the gods of Eridu and its environs and this region's tradition of creation myths of irrigation. He appears in myths revolving around figures of his own circle, e.g., "Enki and Ninmah." Here he seems to disappear and then to reappear and (enter into an incestuous relationship with his mother Nammu in order to) create humankind thereby, relieving the gods of their toil. Ea reappears in pan-Mesopotamian myths originating and centering in Nippur. Thus in the "Story of Atrahasis," a probable source of the biblical account of the Flood, the discontent of the gods recurs and it is again Ea who assists in the creation of humankind in order to relieve the gods. The rescue of humanity from utter destruction in the Flood is due to Ea's intervention. I.T.A.

eagle, a large predatory bird. The Hebrew word (*nesher*) that has traditionally been translated "eagle" seems more likely to refer to the griffon vulture. Vultures and eagles are difficult to distinguish from a distance, and perhaps for that reason the same term is applied to both birds. The context determines which one is meant. The passage in Prov. 23:5 where a large bird (Heb. *nesher*) flies toward heaven is thought to refer to the imperial eagle (*Aquila heliaca*), as this bird was believed able to see into the sun. Where the same word depicts a bird as a symbol for swiftness, it may be the golden eagle (*Aquila chrysaetos*) that is alluded to, as this bird possesses great speed (cf. 2 Sam. 1:23; Jer. 4:13).

A number of other eagle species also nest in Palestine or pass through during migration, such as the booted eagle (*Hieraaetus pennatus*), Bonelli's eagle (*Hieraaetus fasciatus*), and the tawny eagle (*Aquila rapax*), some or all of which may also have been present in biblical times. While the kind of "eagle" referred to by Jesus as collecting where a body is to be found (Matt. 24:28; Luke 17:37) probably refers to a vulture, the great bird of Rev. 4:7 may well refer to an eagle. I.U.K.

earrings, jewelry worn at the ear. Earrings were listed together with brooches, signet rings, and armlets (bracelets) as gifts brought to the tabernacle in the wilderness (Exod. 35:22). They were offered with beads and other items as atonement for defiling the dead (Num. 31:50), and Ishmaelite men gave them as material from which Gideon made an ephod (Judg. 8:24–26). They were viewed by Ezekiel as part of the garb of the exquisitely clothed woman (Ezek. 16:12) and reflected God's treatment of Jerusalem.

In archaeological evidence, earrings are most commonly found in burials, and the forms of single and multiple pendant designs frequently incorporated the lunar motif as a most popular expression. Materials used included silver and gold, as with rings and bracelets. Filigreed gold is sometimes extremely fine work in these examples, and the numerous burials with single earrings reflect the practice of Roman times. R.S.B.

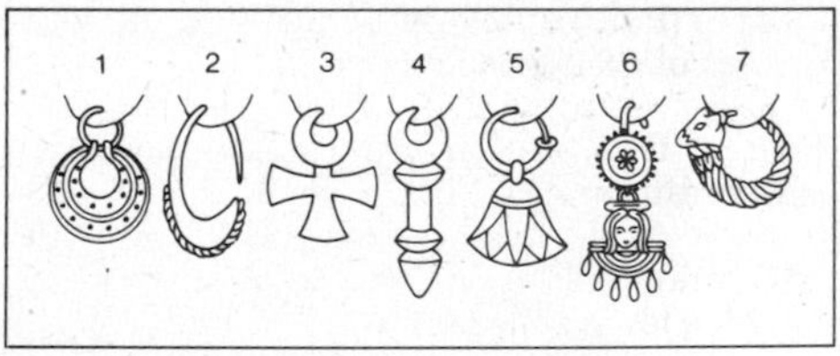

Earrings: 1. From Tell el-'Ajjul (1600 B.C.); 2. From the period of the Judges (1100 B.C.), gold; 3. and 4. Assyrian (900–800 B.C.); 5. Egyptian (800 B.C.); 6. Egyptian (100 B.C.); 7. Greek (100 B.C.).

earthquake, a shaking or trembling of the earth's surface, fairly frequent in geologically active Syro-Palestine. Specific earthquakes within the biblical period include one in 31 B.C. reported by the Jewish historian Josephus, which left clear marks in Qumran's ruins, and one in Uzziah's days (ca. 760 B.C.) cited in Amos 1:1 and remembered in Zech. 14:5. The excavators of Hazor assign the destruction of Stratum VI to this latter earthquake. In legendary but graphically realistic description, earthquakes related to the swallowing up of Dathan and Abiram in Num. 16:30–34, to Elijah's experiences at Sinai (1 Kings 19:11–12), to the destruction of Sodom and Gomorrah (Gen. 19:24–29), to the Holy War panic among the Philistines (1 Sam. 14:15), and to the divine theophany in Exod. 19:18. On virtually every occasion that an earthquake appears in the Bible, it has figurative dimensions of God's intervention; note especially the earthquakes at Jesus' death (Matt. 27:51) and his resurrection (Matt. 28:2). It was readily projected, then, as attending the judgment at the final days (see Isa. 29:6; Matt. 24:7; Rev. 6:12–17; among many others.) ***See also*** Amos, The Book of; Dathan; Eschatology; Hazor; Qumran, Khirbet; Sodom. E.F.C.

east, the, one of the four cardinal points of the compass. The OT terminology for "east" is derived chiefly from two sources. First, it is drawn from language associated with sunrise (Heb. *mizrakh*, "rising, shining," Josh. 4:19), sometimes with sun (*shemesh*, Judg. 21:19) or going forth (*motsah*, Ps. 75:7) with the sun (Ps. 19:5–7), and morning (*boker*, Ps. 65:9). Second, it is drawn from derivatives from the root meaning "before, in front" (*kdm*). Since one orients oneself by facing east, the east is what is before or in front of one. Several derivatives of the root meaning "east" are found in Gen. 11:2; Ezek. 40:6; Gen. 2:14; and Ezek. 10:19. A common use of "east" in the OT, especially in poetry, is in the listing of the four cardinal points to express totality ("everywhere," Joel 2:20; Ps. 75:7; Job 23:8–9). In the NT, "east" (Gk. *anatole*) is similarly used (Matt. 8:11; Luke 13:29). The east is the source of such OT wisdom figures as Job (Job 1:3), Agur (Prov. 30:1), and Lemuel (Prov. 31:1), as well as of the NT Magi (Matt. 2:1). J.S.K.

Easter, the Christian festival that celebrates Jesus' resurrection. The name "Easter" derives from the Anglo-Saxon goddess of Spring (Eostre or Ostara), but the Christian festival developed from the Jewish Passover (Heb. *pesech*, Gk. *pascha*), because according to the Gospels the events of Jesus' last days took place at the time of Passover. Easter was originally observed on the day following the end of the Passover fast (14 Nisan), regardless of the day of the week on which it fell. In the mid-second century, however, some Gentile Christians began to celebrate it on the Sunday after 14 Nisan, with the preceding Friday observed as the day of Christ's crucifixion, regardless of the date on which it fell. The resulting controversy over the correct time for observing the Easter festival reached a head in A.D. 197, when Victor of Rome excommunicated those Christians who insisted on celebrating Easter on 14 Nisan. The dispute continued until the early fourth century, when the Quarto-decimans (from Latin for "14") were required by Emperor Constantine to conform to the empire-wide practice of observing Easter on the Sunday following 14 Nisan, rather than on that date itelf.

Currently celebrated on the first Sunday after the first full moon following the vernal equinox, Easter falls differently for Orthodox Christianity which, unlike Western Christianity, did not accept the Gregorian calendar reform in 1582.

Originally a unitary feast celebrating the Exodus and the Christian redemption, Easter was split up in the fourth century into its component parts, Easter Day becoming a separate commemoration of Christ's resurrection. For a long time it was also the preeminent occasion for Christian initiation (baptism), understood as a participation in the paschal mystery. ***See also*** Passover, The; Resurrection. R.H.F.

Ebal (ee'bahl). **1** The ancestral name of a Horite clan in Edom (Gen. 36:23; 1 Chron. 1:40). **2** A variant spelling of Obal (1 Chron. 1:22; cf. Gen. 10:28). ***See also*** Horites.

Ebal (ee'bahl), **Mount,** the salient peak, 3,109 feet above sea level, forming the north side of the Shechem pass opposite Mount Gerizim, in the Samaritan hills. On or at Ebal, Joshua was to erect an altar and memorial stones (Josh. 8:30–35; Deut. 27:1–8), features of an ancient covenant ceremony noted in Deut. 11:29 and 27:11–26. Altar and stones probably relate to the sacred precinct of Shechem on Ebal's lowest slopes, 1,400 feet below the summit near the valley floor. Alternatively they may relate to structures on the heights such as the one on the far side of the summit ridge, found in 1983 to date to the twelfth century B.C. ***See also*** Gerizim; Shechem. E.F.C.

Ebed (e'bed; Heb., "servant"). **1** The father of Gaal, the leader of a group who settled in Shechem and attempted an ill-fated rebellion against Abimelech (Judg. 9:26–45). **2** The leader of the clan of Adin, a family group who returned from exile in Babylon with Ezra (Ezra 8:6).

Ebedmelech (ebed-me'lek; Heb., "servant of the king"), the Ethiopian eunuch and Jerusalem palace official who was responsible for rescuing Jeremiah out of an empty cistern into which the latter had been thrown by the Judeans, who found offensive Jeremiah's advice to surrender to the Babylonians (Jer. 38:1–13).

Ebenezer (eb-uh-nee'zuhr; Heb., "stone of help"), a site near Aphek, four miles south of Gilgal, according to 1 Samuel. In the account of the double defeat of the Israelites and capture of the Ark by the Philistines (1 Sam. 4:1–11; 5:1), the name has an ironic ring. In 1 Sam. 7:2–12 Samuel names a stone Ebenezer to commemorate God's help in Israel's recovery of the same territory.

Eber (ee'buhr). **1** The great-grandson of Shem, father of Peleg and Joktan (Gen. 10:24–25; 11:14–17; 1 Chron. 1:18–19, 25), ancestor of Abram (Gen. 11:17–26) and Jesus (Luke 3:35). Eber would appear to be the eponymous ancestor of the Hebrews (cf. Israel), but nothing is made of this beyond the placing of the name in Abram's ancestral line. **2** Beside Asshur (Assyria) in Num. 24:24, probably the region and population "beyond" (the literal meaning of *eber* in Heb.) the river (Euphrates; cf. e.g., Josh. 24:2, 3, 14, 15). **3** The head of the priestly family of Amok in the generation following that of those who returned to Jerusalem with Joshua and Zerubbabel (Neh. 12:20). **4** A Gadite (1 Chron. 5:13). **5** A Benjaminite, son of Elpaal (1 Chron. 8:12). **6** A Benjaminite, son of Shashak (1 Chron. 8:22).

S.B.P.

Ebiasaph (e-bī'uh-saf; Heb., "my father has gathered"; more properly Abiasaph, Exod. 6: 24), the name of three Levites in the genealogical lists. **1** The son of Korah through Izhar and either the father (1 Chron. 6:23) or the brother (Exod. 6:24) of Assir. **2** The son of Elkanah and great-grandson of a second Korah through Uzziel (1 Chron. 6:37), also the father of Assir. Because of the repetition of names in these lists it is possible that they have been disordered through scribal errors and that these two are the same person. **3** A Levite, the son of Korah and the father of Shallum, the chief gatekeeper of the Levites (1 Chron. 9:19; also called Asaph, 1 Chron. 26:1). Some scholars understand this passage (1 Chron. 9:17–27) to be a postexilic record (corresponding to Neh. 11:1–19); however, other scholars see at least part of this chapter to be adapted from a record of pre-exilic Israel, an introduction to the narratives of Saul and David that follow. If it is pre-exilic, this Ebiasaph may be identified with the first two above; otherwise he is a much later descendant of the clan of Korah. ***See also*** Assir; Korah.

D.R.B.

Ebla (eb'luh), modern Tell Mardikh, a large mound of some 140 acres, located in Syria about forty-two miles south of Aleppo, astride major routes of east-west and north-south communication. Systematic excavation of the site began in 1964 by an Italian team under the direction of Paolo Matthiae; and it is their finds, especially the statue with the inscription of Ibbit-Lim and the tablets of level IIB1, that have established the identification of the site as ancient Ebla.

The history of Ebla, as revealed by the still ongoing work of Matthiae and his team, stretches over fourteen levels, from ca. 3500 B.C. (Chalcolithic) to the third through seventh centuries A.D. (Roman-Byzantine), with perhaps later, and briefer, occupations in Islamic and Crusader times. Within this range, it is only the four levels IIB1, IIB2, IIIA, and IIIB that cover the whole site, acropolis and lower city, and represent, it appears, Ebla's most prosperous period. The four collectively spanned ca. 2600–1600 B.C., and all but IIB2 have been intensively explored by Matthiae's group.

Cuneiform tablets as they were discovered at Ebla, fallen from their original shelving arrangement ca. 2600–2250 B.C.

Level IIB1 (ca. 2600–2250 B.C.): This is the best known and most widely discussed level. Debate continues about its exact date. Matthiae's group argues for ca. 2400–2250 B.C. (Early Bronze IVA/ Mesopotamian Early Dynastic IIIB and Sargonic), with a final destruction by the Sargonic ruler of Mesopotamia, Naram-sin, as the latter boasted in his own inscriptions. G. Pettinato and others, however, suppose a somewhat earlier date of ca. 2600–2400 B.C. (Early Bronze III/Mesopotamian Early Dynastic IIIA–B).

The main building so far uncovered is Palace G, on the west and southwest acropolis slopes. Its central element is a large porticoed audience hall, north of which are a massive tower with stone-inlay stairway, a second stairway, and (storage) rooms, while on its east and south are the monumental gateway to the palace and the administrative quarters.

The objects found in this building include wooden furniture decorated with friezes, seal impressions, and small sculptures—all showing local adaptation of Mesopotamian art of the mid-third millennium B.C. Especially important are the tablets: more than seventeen thousand pieces, recovered largely during the 1974–1976 excavations, which, allowing for a number of fragments, comprise about four thousand com-

Large sacrificial basin found at Tell Mardikh (Ebla). The short side shows warriors marching over lions, the long side a banquet scene; Middle Bronze Age.

plete texts. Most tablets were found fallen in the debris of two rooms, though in a way that made it possible to reconstruct the original shelving arrangements. All are in cuneiform scripts, like that of mid-third-millennium B.C. Mesopotamia, and, apparently, in two languages: Sumerian, the principal written language of southern Mesopotamia in the third millennium, and a hitherto unknown Semitic language labeled conveniently "Eblaite," whose precise linguistic affiliations are still under discussion. As for content, the tablets represent at least four categories, again with Mesopotamian parallels: administrative records involving the palace; lexical texts for the scribes; literary and religious texts; and texts bearing on the events of the day, such as a commercial treaty with the city of Ashur (some scholars read as Abarsal).

Together, these texts reveal that Ebla in the IIB1 period was presided over by rulers called EN (Sumerian)/*malikum* (Eblaite), who worked with the city "elders" (Sumerian AB × ÁŠ). Under their authority were a variety of officials and workers, who functioned in the upper city or acropolis, the administrative center, or in the lower city, consisting of four quarters each associated with one of the city gates, or in the outlying network of dependent settlements. This complex urban structure was large as well, for one text, according to Pettinato, puts the population at about 260,000.

The religious picture was also complex. Attested are Sumerian deities from Mesopotamia, like Enki, Enlil, and Utu; local Canaanite deities, like Baal, Hadad, Rasap (Resheph), and, most important, Dagan; and a couple of Hurrian gods. In addition, we hear of DINGIR.A.MU (Sumerian, "the god of my father"; cf. Gen. 43: 23) and DINGIR.EN (Sumerian, "the [personal] god of the ruler").

Finally, the texts inform us about a range of localities in contact with Ebla. Most prominent, of course, are those in the city's immediate environs: along the Syrian coast and in the hinterland (e.g., Ugarit, Tilum, Byblos) and along the middle and upper Euphrates (e.g., Carchemish, Emar, Mari). Mentioned as well are sites in northern Mesopotamia (Gasur, perhaps Ashur) and southern (e.g., Kish, Lagash, Nippur, Shuruppak), and in Iran (Hamazi) and perhaps Anatolia (Kanish). Egypt also is known, from the imported stone vases excavated at Ebla. The contacts in evidence here are of several kinds: commercial, especially textile trading; diplomatic and military, especially with Mari; and cultural, most visibly with Mesopotamia, from which, as noted, Ebla adopted and adapted the cuneiform script, the Sumerian language, and various textual traditions and art forms.

In this range of contacts, however, references to Palestine seem at best insignificant and often uncertain. For example, the claims made when the first tablets were deciphered that they mentioned such cities as Hazor, Jerusalem, Sodom, and Gomorrah have yet to be demonstrated. Indeed, the initial enthusiasm about the light the tablets would shed on the early stages of biblical culture is now mostly seen as exaggerated. Clearly, no biblical personages can be identified in the tablets; and while personal names can be found there similar to those in the Bible, e.g., Ishmael, such names are not exclusive to Ebla; they also appear in other areas of the Near East. Moreover, Eblaite, though a Semitic language, does not look specifically close to biblical Hebrew, as originally thought; and the proposal to find the Israelite god Yahweh in the Ebla texts cannot be supported: the supposed form *ya*, which occurs as an element in Eblaite personal names, is ambiguous in reading and interpretation. The major contribution, thus, of the tablets of Ebla IIB1 is in understanding Syria and Mesopotamia of the third millennium B.C., especially in showing that the complex city-state system attested for Syria in the second millennium had an honorable precedent in the third.

Level IIB2 (ca. 2250–2000 B.C.): Level IIB1 was destroyed, and the new occupation, IIB2, belonged to the Early Bronze IVB period, correlating with the post-Akkadian and Ur III periods in Mesopotamia. IIB2 seems to have been reasonably prosperous, to judge by its mention in contemporary Mesopotamian sources; but this cannot be fully confirmed, as the Italian excavations have so far barely touched this level.

Level IIIA–B (ca. 2000–1600 B.C.): These two succeeding levels, however, have been well explored. IIIA, following soon after the destruction of IIB2, fits into the Middle Bronze I/Mesopotamian Isin-Larsa and Old Babylonian periods (ca. 2000–1800 B.C.), when Amorites were gaining political power in many parts of the Near East.

Although outside references to Ebla are now less plentiful than formerly, what is available suggests the city's continuing prominence in trade, bespeaking a prosperity that archaeologists have confirmed. Among their findings: a *terre pisée* city rampart, with towers, a small arsenal (M), and a monumental gate (one of four); two quarters of private houses in the lower city; two new palaces on the acropolis (E) and the lower city west (western palace); and four temples (B1, B2, D, N), which, like the palaces and city gate, have parallels elsewhere in Syro-Palestine.

The following IIIB level (ca. 1800–1600 B.C., Middle Bronze II/Mesopotamian Old Babylonian periods) saw a loss of Ebla's political sovereignty to the neighboring state of Yamhad (Aleppo), which became dominant now in Syria. But the prosperity of the city seems not to have suffered. All the buildings of level IIIA continued, without noticeable decline; and a royal burial ground appeared now in full form, constructed out of the natural caves beneath the western palace. Of the three excavated tombs (Tombs of the Princess, Lord of the Goats, and Cisterns), two (Princess and Lord of the Goats) yielded treasures of significant wealth; and the complex as a whole attests to the development of a royal cult of the dead at Ebla, as is known elsewhere in Syria and Mesopotamia during this period and later. Level IIIB was destroyed probably in the Hittite invasion of Syria, of Hattushili I or Murshili I.

Bibliography

Biggs, Robert. "The Ebla Tablets: An Interim Perspective." *Biblical Archaeologist* 43 (1980): 76–87.

Matthiae, Paolo. *Ebla: An Empire Rediscovered.* Garden City, NY: Doubleday, 1981.

______. "New Discoveries at Ebla: The Excavation of the Western Palace and the Royal Necropolis of the Amorite Period." *Biblical Archaeologist* 47 (1984): 18–32.

Pettinato, Giovanni. *The Archives of Ebla: An Empire Inscribed in Clay.* Garden City, NY: Doubleday, 1981.

Viganò, Lorenzo, with Dennis Pardee. "Literary Sources for the History of Palestine and Syria: The Ebla Tablets." *Biblical Archaeologist* 47 (1984): 6–16.

P.B.M.

Ecclesiastes (ee-klee'-zee-ast'eez), the twenty-first book in the OT. This book, one of the most often quoted of the Hebrew Bible, is also one of the most mysterious; scholars still do not agree about its provenance, language, literary genre, unity, or overall message.

Name: The name of the book in Hebrew, *Qohelet,* is itself something of a mystery. This word occurs nowhere else outside of the book. It appears to be related, however, to the term *qahal* ("assembly"), which is why the Greek translators of the Bible rendered it as *ekklesiastes,* "assemblyman" (hence, in some translations, "the

Eccles. 2:5–6 describes a garden similar to this one with a pond filled with fish, ducks, and plants surrounded by palm and pomegranate trees; Egyptian wall painting, fourteenth century B.C.

Preacher" or "Speaker"). *Qohelet,* then, would appear to be some sort of title or office, a supposition supported by the use of this term with the definite article in 12:8 (and possibly 7:27). Some modern scholars, dissatisfied with this explanation, have sought to view *qohelet* as the proper name or nickname of an actual figure or, alternately, as wisdom personified, a walking assembly *(qohelet)* of wise sayings. Perhaps the most promising of recent suggestions connects the word *qohelet* with the rare, but chronologically appropriate, biblical word *qehillah* (Neh. 5:7), which in context seems to mean "harangue" or "argumentative speech." Ecclesiastes may simply be the "arguer" or "haranguer."

Language: The Hebrew in which the book is written shows definite signs of lateness, e.g., by the use of the Persian loan words *pardes* ("garden") in 2:5 and *pitgam* ("decree") in 8:11 (these words must certainly mean that the book was written after the end of the sixth century B.C., when the Jewish homeland became part of the Persian Empire). Apart from this, the language of the book is somewhat strange, with features of grammar, syntax, and vocabulary not paralleled elsewhere in the OT. In the past, scholars have suggested that the book is actually a poor translation of an Aramaic original, but that hypothesis is now largely and justly rejected. More recently, it has been argued that the original language was Phoenician, a dialect closely related to Hebrew but with distinctive features. Yet some of these very features are absent or only intermittently present in Ecclesiastes; this hypothesis too is to be rejected. Most likely, the language of Ecclesiastes is a late brand of Hebrew, with many northern (or at least non-Jerusalemite) features, a language thus situated somewhere between the artificial, "literary" Hebrew of other postexilic writings and the dialect known as Mishnaic Hebrew that was to become a literary language only after the close of the biblical period in the writings of rabbinic Judaism. That is to say, the author of Ecclesiastes did not consistently frame his words, as other late authors did, in a literary, official Hebrew; on the contrary, he seems at times to have relished the brassy sound of contemporary, colloquial speech, especially when debunking accepted ideas.

Content: This view of his language as often consciously down-to-earth and unliterary is in keeping with his message. For although concerned with ultimate issues, Qohelet never loses his focus on the day-to-day life "under the sun." His book is peppered with allusions to the world of commerce and other daily pursuits. Surprisingly, despite the ingenuity of commentators, only a single allusion to Israel's sacred writings or traditions has been convincingly demonstrated to exist in this book (Eccles. 5:3; cf. Deut. 23:22).

The literary form of Ecclesiastes is also unique. Its basic unit of expression is the *mashal*, the two-part proverb or saying. Yet it is not merely a collection of sayings (like, for example, the book of Proverbs). Instead, the sayings seem to frame a life history. The first-person speaker of the book, Qohelet, describes himself as having been "king over Israel in Jerusalem" (1:12). In the opening chapters he describes his experiment in investigating both Wisdom (i.e., the path of patience and restraint) and Folly (hedonism and reckless abandon), an experiment that the resources of a king or ruler make him especially well suited to undertake (2:12). The pursuit of pleasure, with wine, rich living, and concubines—and indeed, the very project of this "scientific" (2:3) inquiry into enjoyment—seems a young man's quest; but Qohelet finds no answer in dissoluteness. He continues to try to grasp the totality of human existence, seeking to embrace it all in the propounding of wise sayings, but it eludes him; everything is "vanity." (The Hebrew *hebel* actually means not "vanity" but something fleeting and futile, utterly insubstantial.) Again and again he tempers his previous observations with "But I returned and saw . . ." or "I saw further . . ." and some of his earlier observations are expressly contradicted by later ones. Some commentators have tried to shape Qohelet's observations into a logical step-by-step argument, but the text resists such an approach as it does any attempt to outline its contents in orderly progression. Instead, what one can say is that Qohelet presents bits and pieces of the truth as he has seen it in his life, and the presence of that life is an all-important framing device. If a youthful inquisitiveness shines through the opening two chapters, the mood then switches to something more somber, resigned, and later, reconciled. The speaker himself seems to age, and by chap. 12, one can feel the weight of his many years and the expectation of death. At the book's end, Qohelet is no more: we get his epitaph (12:9–10).

The book's basic argument seems to be that human existence, like so many things in the natural world (chap. 1), is round, circular; different activities and desires fit at one moment, when their time comes around, but not at another (chap. 3). Like a sphere, the whole of life's surface cannot be described from any one angle; one must travel around it in order to account for all, and truths apparent from one standpoint prove to be *hebel* from another.

Author: At some point after it was written, Ecclesiastes came to be attributed to King Solomon, the exemplar of wisdom in the Bible; no doubt this attribution helped to preserve its place in the sacred corpus of Jewish writings (for Solomon's wisdom was of divine provenance, 1 Kings 3:12) despite its heterodox, and potentially heretical, teachings. Obviously, for the linguistic reasons cited above, this attribution is impossible; most likely, the book was written in the fourth or fifth century B.C. Its author may indeed have been named or nicknamed Qohelet, and if he was a (Davidide?) governor or administrator appointed by the Persian powers, his self-description as "king over Israel [the Jews] in Jerusalem" may be no literary persona but a statement of fact. J.L.K.

Ecclesiasticus (ee-klee'zee-as'ti-kuhs), or the Wisdom of Jesus the Son of Sirach, a book of instruction and proverbs, written in Hebrew around 180 B.C. in Jerusalem by an instructor of wealthy youths. It was translated into Greek in Alexandria by the author's grandson sometime after 132 B.C. The work is of value because it provides extensive evidence for the character of Judaism and Jewish society in Palestine just prior to the Maccabean revolt (167–64 B.C.). We gain a picture of a social order highly polarized between rich and poor, powerful and weak, male and female, pious and nonobservant, and Jew and Gentile, as well as a look into the development of the way of Torah—life centered around the Mosaic law—which will become the central characteristic of Judaism when the Temple is no more.

Much of the Hebrew of Ecclesiasticus has survived in manuscripts found in the Genizah (an attic where badly worn Torah scrolls were "treasured" away when retired from service) of the Ezra Synagogue in Cairo, as well as in a few fragments from the Dead Sea Scrolls. Although not considered canonical, the book remained in use within Judaism as late as the eleventh century A.D. The complete version has survived in Greek translation as a part of the Septuagint. In western Christianity it came to be known as Ecclesiasticus, "the Church's Book," probably because it was the most important of the writings not found in the Hebrew Bible to be preserved in the Vulgate. Protestants relegate it to the Apocrypha, while Catholics classify it as deuterocanonical.

Ecclesiasticus defies outline in any detail, since much of it consists of short passages on a variety of topics, from how to give and attend a party to exhortations to care for the poor. The predominant types of language are the art proverb and the instruction genre, the latter of which is characterized by imperatives followed by reasons for fulfilling the command. The outline which accompanies this article gives some idea of its contents.

Jesus, the son of Sirach, were he alive today, would be a professor of public administration. In some ways, his book reads like a modern-day text on business ethics, although he prefers the public sector to the private and assumes that all merchants are corrupt (26:29). His goal is to instruct the young in the art of living well, in the best sense of the phrase. His students will seek careers in public service as scribes, the class from which public administrators, civil servants, and diplomats were drawn (see 39:1–11). Frugality, hard work, compassion for the poor, honesty, and independence rather than riches are the true measure of character, although wealth is preferable to poverty. The goal of instruction is to learn self-control and correct management techniques in both private and public life in order to enjoy the good life, under the guidance of the Law of God. The major problem for modern readers in his advice is in the treatment of women. He characterizes the wickedness of a wife as the highest of all evil (25:13) and claims that sin and death had their origin from a woman (25:24). The good wife, he asserts, is silent, while one must remain eternally vigilant in caring for a daughter to preserve her purity (26:10–12, 14). While the attitudes are undoubtedly those of the age, the tone with which they are expressed seems more personal in character.

While Ecclesiasticus stands in the wisdom tradition of Proverbs, an important transformation has taken place. Where once there had been a clear separation between the responsibility of the priest for Torah, or Law, and the sage for counsel (Jer. 18:18), the two have come together in Ecclesiasticus. Wisdom is now to be found in the Temple in Jerusalem (24:10) and is identified with "the book of the covenant of the Most High God, the law which Moses commanded us" (24:23). Ecclesiasticus settles the debate in postbiblical Judaism over the dwelling place of wisdom, like Baruch 3:9–4:4, by declaring that it has been revealed to Israel by God in the moral instruction of the Law, rather than reserved in the heavens where only the specially initiated receive instruction in the secrets of the cosmos (cf. Wisd. of Sol. 8:15–22; 9:4, 9–10; *1 Enoch* 42). According to Ecclesiasticus, the sage must be satisfied with the limitations of the human intellect (3:21–24).

The marriage of Torah and counsel is also reflected in the models for the good life offered in the praise of the famous in chaps. 44–50. The highest praise is reserved for Moses, Aaron, and Phinehas the son of Eleazar, priestly heroes important for their work as public administrators and leaders of worship, each of whom, in the son of Sirach's eyes, was the recipient of a covenant with God (chap. 45). Next in rank comes David. He is pictured as an effective ruler concerned for the administration of public worship, who was given a covenant of kingship (45:25; 47:2–11). In his own time, the son of Sirach offers the model of Simon the Just, the high priest who was the theocratic ruler of his people from about 219 to 196 B.C. and as such combined the offices of priest and king (thus wedding Torah and counsel). Simon is pictured both as an effective public administrator and leader of worship in a passage important for its information about the worship of the Temple in the Second Temple period (50:1–21). Ecclesiasticus' praise of the famous also makes it clear that by 200 B.C. both the Torah and the Prophets are fixed divisions of Scripture in Palestinian Judaism. ***See also*** Apocrypha, Old Testament; Education; Proverb; Temple, The; Torah; Wisdom; Women. D.W.S.

OUTLINE OF CONTENTS

Ecclesiasticus

I. The prologue (by the author's grandson)
II. In praise of wisdom (1:1–20)
III. A collection of instructions and proverbs concerning the good life (1:22–23:27), including passages on fearing God (chap. 2), honoring parents (3:1–16), meekness (3:17–31), caring for the poor (4:1–10), friendship (6:5–17), enemies (12:8–18), dealing with the powerful (13:1–26), and sin (21:1–28)
IV. In praise of wisdom (24:1–34)
V. More instruction and proverbs (25:1–37:31), including advice on wives and daughters (25:16–26:18), giving and attending banquets (31:12–32:13), and sacrifice and prayer (chap. 35), as well as a prayer for deliverance from the Gentiles (36:1–17)
VI. A discourse on honorable professions, including the physician, farmer, artisan, smith, potter, and scribe (38:1–39:11)
VII. More proverbs and instruction (39:12–42:25)
VIII. The cosmic order (chap. 43; cf. Psalm 148; Song of the Three Children 35–68)
IX. In praise of the famous (44:1–50:21)
X. Conclusion (50:22–51:30)

ECONOMICS IN NT TIMES

Overview of the ancient agora in Athens. The agora was a center of economic activity in cities in NT times.

economics in New Testament times. A passage in Mark's Gospel about John the Baptist, while not itself an economic text, nevertheless contains the language with which to begin an analysis of economics in NT times. The author of this Gospel describes John as preaching "in the wilderness" and as drawing people to him "from the whole Judean countryside and the city of Jerusalem" (Mark 1:4–5, NEB). These three terms—"city," "countryside," and "wilderness"—can be used as general analytic categories for classifying and organizing the NT data into a coherent description of the ancient economy.

The City: NT cities, from Jerusalem and Rome to the seven cities of Revelation 2–3, were the scene of many economic institutions and roles. An obvious example is the marketplace, whose economic functions included not only buying and selling but also hiring. Thus it is to the marketplace that the foolish virgins go to buy oil (Matt. 25:9) and where Mary Magdalene and the other women go to buy spices (Mark 16:1), and it is in the marketplace where men gathered to be hired for occasional or seasonal labor (Matt. 20:3; cf. Acts 17:5).

Also in cities were the workshops of various artisans. Paul made tents from leather in Thessalonica, Corinth, Ephesus, and elsewhere (1 Thess. 2:9; 1 Cor. 4:12; Acts 18:3). References to other artisans—a tanner (Acts 9:43), a silversmith (Acts 19:24), a potter (Rom. 9:21), and a metal-worker (2 Tim. 4:14)—at least hint at the variety of crafts in an ancient city, as do references to manufactured products: jewelry (Luke 15:22), fine linen (Luke 16:19), gold and silver utensils (2 Tim. 2:20), and carriages (Rev. 18:13).

The range of economic activity is not limited, however, to retailers and artisans. Other activities, sometimes less widespread and sometimes less reputable, also had their place in the urban economic scene. For example, port cities were involved in shipping (Acts 21:2–3), though especially important was the Roman grain trade which receives incidental notice in the course of Paul's journey to Rome for trial (Acts 27:2, 6, 38; 28:11). Grain, of course, was not the only import to Rome, as the long list in Rev. 18:12–13 shows. A sample of the list includes gold and silver, jewels and pearls, purple cloth, silks and fine linen, scented woods, ivory, cinnamon, incense, perfumes, wine, oil, horses, and slaves.

In addition to trading, others engaged in construction that formed a part of the economic activity of all cities, at least to some degree (cf. Mark 12:10; 1 Cor. 3:10; Eph. 2:20; Heb. 3:3). Equally ubiquitous, though less reputable, were the economic activities of various marginals: thieves breaking into strong boxes (Luke 12:33) or stealing clothes (Rev. 16:21; cf. in general Matt. 24:43; Rom. 2:22; Eph. 4:28; 1 Thess. 5:2; 1 Pet. 4:15); the blind, lame, or sick begging outside houses (Luke 16:20) or temples (Acts 3:2; cf. also Mark 10:46; Luke 16:3; 1 John 3:17); and prostitutes taking the money of prodigal youths (Luke 15:30) and merchants (Rev. 18:3; cf. also Matt. 21:31; 1 Cor. 6:16; Heb. 13:4).

Economic activity even characterized some urban settings that today are seldom associated so explicitly with the economy. For example, temples were places of buying and selling sacrificial animals (Mark 11:15; John 2:14). Priests were entitled to their share of these sacrifices (1 Cor. 9:13), and temples became receptacles of many offerings, large and small (Mark 12:41–43; Acts 21:24). When such other economic activi-

ECONOMICS IN NT TIMES

ties as collecting the temple tax and money-changing are included, it becomes plausible why Jesus used an economic metaphor when denouncing the Jerusalem Temple as an "emporium" (John 2:16) or, less directly but no less economically, as "a cave for brigands' [booty]" (Mark 11:17).

And yet, in addition to the urban settings already mentioned—marketplace, workshops, harbors, construction sites, and temples—the principal locus of economic activity and power was a place not associated today with economic functions. That place was the urban household, especially the "great households [s]" (2 Tim. 2:20). These households were large, complex, and economically important institutions and so deserve extended discussion. At this point, however, only the urban side of these households will be in view; their rural side will be treated below.

The great urban households were large. They included not only the householder and his wife and children, but also numerous slaves—a social pattern familiar from the household codes of Eph. 5:22–6:9 and Col. 3:18–4:1 in which moral instruction is given to husbands and wives, parents and children, and masters and slaves. But these households might also contain other persons on occasion or even for extended periods of time: other rich friends and neighbors invited in for a banquet (Mark 6:21–28; Luke 14:12; 1 Cor. 11:17–34); more formal groups, or associations, provided with room and resources for religious and social meetings (Rom. 16:1–2, 23; 1 Thess. 5:12; Philem. 1–2); travelers given room and board and perhaps provisions for the next leg of their journey (Acts 21:8; Philem. 22; 3 John 5–8); and still others, such as teachers and workers, admitted into the household for indefinite periods (1 Cor. 9:5–6; cf. Acts 18:3).

The large numbers of people that could belong to a great household suggest its complexity, especially given the many roles one person may have played in it or the variety of roles distributed throughout it. Thus the householder had many roles—husband, father, master, friend, patron, and host—whereas slaves were assigned to a variety of roles and tasks. Loyal and dependable slaves had positions of responsibility as stewards, overseeing the householder's accounts (Luke 16:1), paying his occasional hired help (Matt. 20:6), or being put in charge of the other slaves (Luke 12:42–45). These other slaves, in turn, might wait on tables (Luke 17:8), take down dictation for a letter (Rom. 16:22), deliver messages (Luke 14:17), answer the door (Mark 13:34), or work as artisans, a role not attested in the NT but probably implicit, for example, in Paul's perception of his working as slavish, as something associated with slaves (1 Cor. 9:1, 19). At any rate, older slaves might become tutors of the householders' children (1 Cor. 4:15), and infant slaves might be raised as playmates of their householders' children, again a role only hinted at in the NT (cf. Acts 13:1).

The economic role and importance of the great urban households are apparent to some extent from their size and complexity. As economic institutions, for example, these households required considerable wealth for their operations: to purchase and maintain slaves, to host banquets, and to provide hospitality. The principal consequence of this wealth for the householder (and his immediate family) was a life of leisure. With slaves to serve food, answer the door, run errands, work at various trades, and watch over or amuse the children, it is clear that the householder did not have to work and otherwise had little to do. As a further consequence, the leisurely rich had only contempt for workers and work itself, a contempt Paul felt directed at him, as is clear from the inclusion of his working with his hands in a list of experiences that put him among "the dregs of humanity" (1 Cor. 4:12–13).

But if householders remained aloof from work on a day-to-day basis and in fact were restrained from working by their aristocratic ideas, it does not follow that they had no active economic role. On occasion, and particularly in times of trouble, the householder assumed responsibility and intervened. He might have to inspect a new parcel of land in the countryside (Luke 14:18), decide what to do in wake of sabotaged fields (Matt. 13:27–30), deal personally with rebellious tenants (Mark 12:9), dismiss a steward suspected of mismanagement (Luke 16:2), or decide how to treat a returning runaway slave who may have stolen something (Philem. 10–18).

And yet, this intervention in household management notwithstanding, householders are probably more appropriately viewed economically as users or consumers of wealth. They (or their families) typically used their considerable wealth for public display or for personal enjoyment, for impressing one another or for distancing themselves from everyone else. Thus there is the display of wealth in jewelry and fine clothing (Matt. 7:6; Luke 7:25; 16:19; Acts 20:33; James 5:2–3), but especially at banquets with their gold and silver serving dishes (2 Tim. 2:20), extravagant menus (Luke 16:19), and costly entertainment. Indeed, how impressed Herod Antipas' rich Galilean friends must have been when he is said to have offered to pay the dancing girl up to one half of his kingdom (Mark 6:22). Likewise impressed must have been the poor who filled the places of a banquet originally planned for the rich (Luke 14:21–23), or those who saw the rich placing much money in the Temple boxes (Mark 12:41), or those who witnessed the public contributions to the poor (Matt. 6:2; cf. Luke 19:12; Acts 10:2).

In any case, the use of wealth for personal

ECONOMICS IN NT TIMES

enjoyment is also easily documented: in the hedonistic motto of one householder to eat, drink, and enjoy himself (Luke 12:19), in the depiction of another householder's son as feasting in great magnificence every day (Luke 16:19), and in the general characterization of the rich as always full and sated or otherwise satisfying their desires (Luke 6:25; 1 Thess. 5:6–8; 1 Tim. 6:9–10; James 5:5).

Finally, it may not be apparent what the sources of householders' wealth were that they used so freely. Some wealth originated in the household itself through the work of slave artisans. But there were other sources: loans (Matt. 18:23; 25:20–23), savings (Luke 19:23), tax collections (Luke 3:13; 19:2), not to mention confiscation (Matt. 25:24) and hoarding (Luke 12:18). Still, these sources of wealth leave out the principal one: land. The rich householders of the city were largely a landed aristocracy. Their wealth ultimately came from the agricultural produce of extensive—and growing (Mark 12:1; Luke 14:18)—holdings beyond the city walls in the countryside.

The Countryside: The word "countryside" (Gk. *chora)* is a technical term with a decidedly economic usage. The term refers to the land, plains and hills, around a city that was agriculturally productive—for example, the countryside of Gadara where a large herd of pigs is to be pictured feeding in the hills (Mark 5:11; cf. also John 11:55; Acts 10:39; James 5:4).

In addition, there were villages scattered throughout the countryside where the vast majority of people in ancient society lived. These villages had their craftsmen (Mark 6:3), shopkeepers (Luke 9:12; cf. 11:5–6), perhaps an innkeeper (Luke 10:35; cf. 9:12; 24:28–29), and certainly various economic marginals: seasonally hired workers (Luke 15:17), the sick or handicapped (Mark 6:56; 8:23; Luke 17:12), and beggars (Mark 10:46).

Most villagers, however, were engaged in agriculture, and as the principal producers of wealth in the ancient economy their roles, activities, and lives are of particular importance. Some agricultural workers, of course, were independent, working their own land (Mark 4:3; Matt. 21:28), but many others worked on land owned by urban householders, whether as tenants (Mark 12: 1, 9) or as slaves (Luke 17:7). In either case they worked for their absentee landlords and in effect became rural members of the landlords' already sizable households. Accordingly, the surplus of their produce went to them (Mark 12:2; Luke 12:16–19; 13:7).

The produce of the countryside was varied and hence required a variety of agricultural roles, or at least a variety of agricultural tasks. Farmers and herders are the basic categories, though fishermen, particularly in light of the Gospel accounts, cannot be ignored. At any rate, farmers, of course, grew grain (Matt. 13:24–25; Mark 4:26–29) but could also take care of a vineyard (Matt. 21:28; Mark 12:1; 1 Cor. 9:7), fig trees (Luke 13:7; James 3:12), olive trees (Rom. 11:17–18), not to mention a garden for planting mustard (Luke 13:19) or vegetables (Matt. 13:32; cf. Rom. 14:2). Likewise, herders obviously tended their livestock, cattle (Luke 15:23) or, more likely, sheep (Matt. 18:12; Luke 2:8; 1 Cor. 9:7), goats (Matt. 25:33; Luke 15:29), or pigs (Mark 5:11). And yet, herders might also join unskilled idlers from the village (or city) in helping farmers with the vintage (Matt. 20:17) or the harvest of grain (Matt. 9:37; 13:30). And all might, on occasion, engage in such other tasks as hunting (Luke 21:34) or cutting timber (cf. 1 Cor. 3:12; Rev. 18:12).

These various agricultural tasks can be classified further into specific tasks that give a rather detailed picture of daily life in the countryside. Farmers, for example, had much to do: plowing the fields (Luke 9:62; 17:7; 1 Cor. 9:10), sowing (Matt. 13:24; Mark 4:3, 26), perhaps weeding (Matt. 13:27–28), harvesting (Matt. 13:30; Mark 4:29), winnowing (Luke 3:17), storing the grain (Matt. 6:26; Luke 12:18), and burning the chaff (Matt. 3:12); or they might set out vines (1 Cor. 9:7), or cultivate, water, and prune them (Luke 13:7; 1 Cor. 3:8; John 15:2), or they might spread manure (Luke 13:8), make olive grafts (Rom. 11:17–18), water the oxen (Luke 13:15), or burn pruned branches (Matt. 7:19).

Similarly, herders had to watch their flocks, chasing after strays (Luke 15:4), digging pits to trap marauding wolves (Matt. 12:11), and separating sheep and goats at nightfall (Matt. 25:32), whereas fishermen could be found throwing their nets into the water (Mark 1:16), hauling in fish (Luke 5:6–7), sorting fish (Matt. 13:48), washing and mending nets (Luke 5:2; Matt. 4:21), or cooking fish on the shore (John 21:9). And, finally, at home there were the tasks of spinning (Matt. 6:28), grinding (Luke 17:35), making bread (Matt. 13:33), and cleaning (Luke 15:8).

Not only the number of tasks but many other details about them make it plain that the lives of farmers, herders, and fishermen were hard indeed—a far cry from the leisure and luxury of their urban masters. At any rate, many tasks were physically demanding, such as digging (Luke 16:3). And there was the scorching sun (Matt. 20:12; Rev. 7:16) or, in the case of fishermen, working the whole night through (Luke 5:5; John 21:3).

What is more, these workers toiled on diets near subsistence level. Even when fields produced abundantly, the surplus went to the householders (Luke 12:16–19). At other times, the land might produce thorns (Heb. 6:8; cf. Matt. 7:16) and the nets come up empty (Luke 5:5). Even sparrows could become a meal (Matt. 10:29), and famine was always a specter (Luke 15:14; Acts 11:28; Rev. 6:8).

Agricultural workers had more to face than hard work, long hours, and little food, however. Herders had to contend with wolves and brigands (Matt. 7:15; John 10:8, 10), fishermen with squalls (Mark 4:37), and everyone with fraudulent tax collectors and their brutal soldiers (Luke 3:11; 19:8). Finally, a householder might withhold the wages of those who had harvested his crops (James 5:4), and when those from the countryside went to the city they could fall prey to prostitutes (Luke 15:30), or be identified by and ridiculed for their speech (Matt. 26:73), be compelled to do some task (Mark 15:21; cf. Matt. 5:41), or even be regarded as a brigand (cf. Luke 22:52) and summarily executed.

To be sure, the life of farmers and herders was not totally grim and unyielding. There was a simple joy and celebration at finding a lost sheep (Luke 15:5–6) or the greater joy or hope of finding a buried treasure (Matt. 13:44). Still, the overall impression must be of most people toiling incessantly in the countryside in order that a few householders and their families might live in the ease and extravagance to which they thought they were entitled.

The Wilderness: The third of the general categories for analyzing the ancient economy is the "wilderness" (Gk. *eremos).* This word is often invested with religious meaning—as a place for repentance and renewal (Mark 1:2–6) or retreat (Mark 1:35), but it also has economic significance in connection with the city and the countryside.

If the countryside is the immediate and productive land that surrounds and supplies the city, then the wilderness is the more distant and nonproductive land that extends beyond the countryside in all directions. As nonproductive land the wilderness could consist of desert, such as the wilderness of barren land in the Jordan valley near the Dead Sea (Mark 1:4; cf. John 11:54) or the Arabian desert (1 Cor. 10: 5). Yet wilderness is not usually desert. It is simply any nonproductive area, such as very hilly, mountainous, or otherwise isolated land (Matt. 15:33; 2 Cor. 11:26). It can even refer to once productive and populated areas (Matt. 12: 25; Luke 21:20).

Yet to say that wilderness is economically unproductive land (or at best economically marginal land in the sense of accommodating an occasional herder [Luke 15:4]) is not to exhaust its economic roles. A wilderness might be traversed by roads on which traders and other travelers moved (Luke 10:30–33). Here they were exposed to attack by brigands who operated at will in these distant and isolated areas (Luke 10: 30; 2 Cor. 11:26). Indeed, from the safety of their wilderness hideouts brigands might make forays into the countryside to attack, say, the flocks of herders (John 10:1) and, if numerous enough and rapacious enough, they might even pose a political threat (Acts 5:36–37; 21:38).

Summary and Conclusion: The economics of NT times was essentially agricultural. The vast majority of people lived as farmers and herders in the countryside that surrounded a city and worked on land that was usually owned by an urban aristocracy who lived off its surplus. The two groups—the one producers of wealth, the other consumers of it—were related socially through the institution of the household and surrounded geographically by economically marginal hills, mountains, or deserts—all lumped together as wilderness.

In NT times there was some, perhaps considerable, commercialization, but the economy remained fundamentally tied to agriculture. There were also the activities of free artisans and shopkeepers in the city (and rural villages) and of brigand gangs in the caves of the wilderness and along its trade routes. This pattern, repeated hundreds of times throughout the ancient Mediterranean, thus constitutes an economic model of NT times.

The evidence for this description of the ancient economy has been drawn exclusively from the NT itself. This evidence, which is scattered from Matthew to Revelation, yields a remarkably detailed and coherent account. Nevertheless, even if the main features of the ancient economy are relatively clear, the description is hardly complete. It is possible to point to some other sources and indicate their value for a study of the ancient economy.

For example, among the literary sources is Longus's *Daphnis and Chloe,* which, despite some pastoral flights of fancy, provides a lengthy and coherent account of the lives of herders in the countryside. Complementing Longus are the *Letters* of Alciphron, which give many experiences of farmers and fishermen. For the life of hunters on the edge of the countryside and wilderness there is the seventh *Oration* of Dio Chrysostom, and for considerable attention to brigands there is the *Ephesian Tale* by Xenophon. Lastly, the lives of householders, artisans, and other urban characters find detailed, if humorous, treatment in the *Satires* of Lucian.

Evidence on papyrus and stone is the staple of historians of the ancient world and among this evidence are many documents such as apprentice contracts, receipts, and records of gifts to temples that detail virtually every aspect of ancient economic life.

Bibliography

Finley, M. I. *The Ancient Economy.* Berkeley and Los Angeles: University of California Press, 1973.

MacMullen, R. *Roman Social Relations 50 B.C. to A.D. 284.* New Haven, CT: Yale University Press, 1974.

Rickman, G. *The Corn Supply of Ancient Rome.* Oxford: Clarendon, 1980. R.F.H.

economics in Old Testament times. Eco-

ECONOMICS IN OT TIMES

The queen of Sheba's visit to Solomon may be seen as an effort to establish trade agreements for incense and spices from Arabia; detail from the Gates of Paradise, Florence, ca. 1425.

nomics in the ancient world, like the modern, was a function of three interacting elements: climate and geography, social structures of people living in the land, and historical circumstances affecting the ability of residents to maximize the potential of their locality. Of these three elements, climate and geography remain relatively constant, except insofar as territory may be gained or lost, especially by war or conquest. Social structures must be able to adapt to historical exigencies, arranging and rearranging economic relationships for the continuance of the community. Ancient Israel's socioeconomic history reflects three major stages, marked by radical change in response to communal threat: the early settlement period (1250–1020 B.C.), the period of the monarchy (1020–586 B.C.), and the period of restoration (538–416 B.C.).

Climate and Geography: The designation of Israel's homeland as a "land flowing with milk and honey" offers an idyllic and partial picture of ancient Palestine. Lush, richly producing areas like the central hill country and the eastern hills of the Transjordan provide diverse products, including wheat, barley, grapes, figs, olives, and honey. Here the annual rainfall ranges from 20 to 40 inches. But to the south and east this green belt fades rapidly to desert, where rainfall is less than 10 inches per year and sheep, cattle, and other livestock provide a living. Between the western and eastern hills lies the Rift Valley, stretching from the Orontes River in the far north to the Dead Sea in the south. Through this valley courses the Jordan River, which winds its way from the Sea of Galilee to the Dead Sea, dropping from 695 feet below sea level to 1,285 feet below sea level. Along the narrow floodplain of the valley, called the Ghor, grows the "jungle of the Jordan" (Jer. 12:5), dense thickets of thorn scrub and tamarisk. This "good broad land" (Exod. 3:8) where Israel made a home is a land of sharp geographic contrasts, which mirror equally sharp seasonal changes. The year is divided into two seasons: a rainy winter season and a dry summer season. The winter season begins in autumn with the "early rains" that mark the beginning of the agricultural season and extends to the "latter rains" of March and April, so important for ripening crops. Mean temperatures in January range from 42 degrees Fahrenheit in the hill country to 58 degrees in the coastal plain and on the desert's edge. The summer season is virtually rainless, and temperatures rise to an August mean of between 71 and 93 degrees Fahrenheit. Available rainfall and temperatures tend to decrease from west to east and from north to south, effecting marked differences in the type and amount of agricultural products available to sustain communities.

The Early Settlement Period (1250–1020 B.C.): In this early period, Israel consisted of a federation of tribes bound together by loyalty to their God who had delivered them from slavery in Egypt and given them the land in which they now dwelt, thus changing their social status from slaves to settlers. Economically, each tribe was autonomous, consisting, in turn, of a collection of extended families organized into protective associations (usually called "clans"). The land—initially the central hill country and later northern and southern territories—was divided into tribal allotments, which were subdivided for family use. According to the federation's view, the land belonged to God and was granted to the tribes in trust for their use and benefit. The land could be inherited, ordinarily transferred from father to son, but it was not to be sold outside the association of families since God had given it to the tribe in perpetuity. Each family lived off the land, growing or raising what it needed and bartering for the few craft items it could not produce. Life was village based and agriculture intensive, producing wine, oil, fruits, and vegetables, supplemented by small cattle herds and larger flocks of sheep and goats.

While pastoral nomadism was likely practiced, especially in regions where rainfall and climate varied greatly, necessitating the relocation of animals for winter and summer pastur-

ECONOMICS IN OT TIMES

age, recent studies indicate that nomadism never played a significant role in the tribal life of ancient Israel. Indeed, where pastoral nomadism occurred, it was probably only a specialization of some herdsmen within the dominant agricultural enterprise of the extended family and certainly not the lifestyle of whole tribes, either before or after settlement in the land.

In this period, Israelite society was structured in an egalitarian fashion, each tribe with its families having the rights to production from its own land. Tribes were self-governed and largely patriarchal, and they were united only for the purpose of mutual self-defense and common religious practices. By the middle of the twelfth century B.C., the force that would lead to a radical change in Israel's way of life was already beginning to grow along the coast of Palestine, as the Philistines expanded their reach into Israelite territory, their presence attested by pottery finds in the Negev (south) and Shephelah (west) regions from ca. 1150 B.C. on. By the middle of the eleventh century, the superior military organization and armaments of the Philistines encouraged their encroachment into the Judean hill country. The tribal federation's military leadership, in an effort to stem the threat from the Philistines, transformed Israelite society into a monarchy.

The Monarchy (1020–586 B.C.): Once the Philistines were defeated by David at the beginning of the tenth century, the modest and limited kingship initiated by Saul and David was transformed by Solomon into a complex, bureaucratic, and expansive royal domain. A process of urbanization had begun, focused especially on the royal city, Jerusalem, and a growing class of courtiers and royal officials, whose increasing wealth and control over the land dominated socioeconomic structures. The royal appetite for expenditures during Solomon's reign was seemingly insatiable, whether for new construction, fortifying towns, or maintaining an increasingly expensive standing army. Solomon resorted to direct taxation for the first time in Israelite history and established a levy of compulsory military and civil service from the population. Population remained largely rural, but socioeconomic power shifted to the cities, favored by royal monopoly over exports and imports. Increasingly, means of production became state owned or state influenced, as family properties were broken up and taken over by rich landlords. These large estates (Lat. *latifundia*) were worked by slave labor or by wage labor. The cities became marketplaces where surplus agricultural commodities could be exchanged for urban-based crafts, with various specialties located on specific streets or in specific quarters of the city. Exchange took place "in the gate," where rural and urban population met, together with traders and caravaners passing through the city en route to foreign markets.

A Hebrew inscription on an eighth-century B.C. ostracon reads: "gold from Ophir to Beth-horon—30 shekels." Solomon had earlier introduced foreign trade to Israel and built ships to carry goods from Ophir to Israel.

Solomon introduced Israel to foreign trade. Located in the crossroads of trade from Mesopotamia to Egypt or Asia Minor and from Egypt to Asia Minor and Assyria/Babylonia and from southern Arabia to points north, east, or west, Israel was in a most enviable position to broker goods from all over the region. It is not coincidental that the three cities Solomon is credited with refortifying, Gezer, Megiddo, and Hazor (1 Kings 9:15–18), are all on important trade routes. Indeed, Solomon seems to have established a network of storage cities that enabled him to take full advantage of his control over caravan trade coming overland and maritime trade coming from Phoenicia, Egypt, or southern Arabia. Moreover, he built a fleet of ships to carry goods, including ivory, silver, gold, and apes (1 Kings 10:11, 22), from Ophir to Ezion-geber, whence they continued the journey to market overland. One may fairly see in the queen of Sheba's fabled visit to Solomon an effort to establish trade agreements for incense and spice from Arabia. Finally, we are told that Solomon imported and exported horses from Cilicia (biblical Kue) and chariots from Egypt, playing the lucrative role of middleman (1 Kings 10:28–29). In all these commercial ventures, Solomon was aided by a close relationship with Tyre, the most important Phoenician port city, which supplied not only building materials for Solomon's projects but expert technical assistance for the Ezion-geber fleet operations.

Whatever the economic benefits of Solomon's activity, especially for the new urban aristocracy and merchant class, his reign transformed Israelite society remarkably, imposing a highly structured, bureaucratic, state-monopolized system on a formerly tribal, village, largely rural, and self-sufficient population. At Solomon's death, the monarchy splintered over the economic demands of the court and the hardships imposed on the common people. Nevertheless, the monarchic model stayed in place, both in the northern kingdom of Israel and the southern kingdom of Judah. These two kingdoms now found themselves dependent on one another if control of the international trade routes and the export and import efforts initiated under Solomon were to continue. However, the division of the kingdom was fatal, since each kingdom now had to fend for itself in the maelstrom of international politics created by the imperialistic designs of Egypt, Assyria, and Babylonia. While marked by a few brief periods of prosperity, Israel and Judah's economic history was characterized until the end of Israel in 722 B.C. and Judah in 586 B.C. by exploitation at the hands of foreign overlords and widening disparity at home between the beneficiaries of royal monopolies and the common people. To both these crises the prophets of Israel addressed themselves, holding up as standard the memory of earlier, more egalitarian social structures and calling for justice for those exploited by the new system.

The Restoration (538–416 B.C.): With Cyrus of Persia's decree of 538 B.C. granting permission, Israelites began to return to their land from exile. Those returning found others who had never left living on the land, scraping out a subsistence livelihood much as their ancestors had done when the land was first settled. Still under the tutelage of Persia, for whose economic benefit Israel was expected to labor, those returning attempted to set up a semi-autonomous state, with a priestly class and Judean elite at the helm. Despite the efforts of some of the new leaders, like Ezra and Nehemiah, to establish a more equitable relationship between the upper and lower classes (see Neh. 5:1–13), the egalitarian ideal of earlier days was never realized. Israel's economic welfare remained tied to the winds of international politics and the whims successively of Persian, Ptolemaic, Seleucid, and Roman overlords. ***See also*** Ownership.

Bibliography

De Vaux, Roland. *Ancient Israel: Social Institutions.* Vol. 1. New York: McGraw-Hill, 1965.

Gottwald, Norman. *The Tribes of Yahweh: A Sociology of the Religion of Liberated Israel, 1250–1050 B.C.E.* New York: Orbis Books, 1979.

May, H. G., ed. *Oxford Bible Atlas.* 3d ed. New York: Oxford University Press, 1984. D.C.H.

Eden, the garden in which the first man and woman were placed and from which they were driven because of their breach of divine law. Although traditionally identified with the Hebrew word meaning "luxury, pleasure, delight" *(eden),* Eden is more probably to be related to a Sumerian word meaning "plain, steppe" or the like *(edin).* Its location "in the east" (Gen. 2:8) probably places it, for the author of Genesis 2–3, in the area at the head of the Persian Gulf; this location may relate Eden to Dilmun of Sumerian myth—the idyllic land where old age, sickness, and death are unknown to its blessed inhabitants.

In Genesis 2–3, Eden is mentioned in 2:8 ("garden in Eden"), 2:10 (simply "Eden"), and 2:14; 3:23, 24 ("garden of Eden"). In Gen. 2:9, 16 and 3:1, 2, 3, it is referred to as "the garden." It is the source of four great rivers (Gen. 2:10–14) and the site of the Tree of Life and the Tree of Knowledge, both of which are "in the middle of the garden" (Gen. 2:9; 3:3). In Genesis, Eden is a garden created by God for human beings, to provide for human needs.

After Genesis, the most important source of references to Eden is the book of Ezekiel. In Ezek. 28:11–19, a variant of the Eden story in Genesis, the prophet describes Eden as the "garden of God" (28:13) situated on God's holy mountain from which primal man was expelled by the cherub because of his iniquity. While sharing many motifs with Genesis 2–3 (including the abundance of precious stones in Eden, Gen. 2:12; Ezek. 28:13), Ezekiel differs from Genesis in describing Eden as the "garden of God," recalling Sumerian Dilmun, over against the character of Eden in Genesis as a garden created for human beings to till and keep (Gen. 2:15). The account in Ezekiel also differs in having only one inhabitant. Eden as the garden of God also occurs in Ezekiel 31, a complex allegory of a tree that in grandeur and beauty surpassed even the trees in Eden (31:8, 9, 16, 18). The garden of Eden is a metaphor for the renewal of the land of Israel by God after the Exile (Ezek. 36:35; Isa. 51:3, where "Eden" is paralleled by "garden of Yahweh"). In Joel 2:3, the transformation of the land from garden of Eden to devastated wilderness is part of an oracle forecasting the Day of Yahweh. J.S.K.

Eder (ee'der; Heb., "flock" or "herd"). **1** A clan leader in the tribe of Benjamin (1 Chron. 8:15). **2** A Levite family leader in the clan of Merari (1 Chron. 25:23). **3** A settlement in southern Judah near the border with Edom, probably in the vicinity of Beer-sheba (Josh. 15:21); the site is unknown. **4** A site called Migdol-eder (Heb., "the tower of Eder" or "the flock tower") near which Jacob camped following the burial of Rachel in Bethlehem (Ramah? Gen. 35:21), probably located somewhere between Jerusalem and Hebron.

Edom (ee'duhm), a name derived from the Semitic root meaning "red," "ruddy" and given to the area situated south of the Dead Sea on both sides of the Wadi Arabah because of the reddish color of the sandstone of that district.

Edom's northern boundary on the east was the Wadi el-Ḥasā. West of the Arabah the northern border was the south border of Israel, which was a line running from the Dead Sea southward to the Ascent of Akrabbim to Zin and Kadesh-barnea (Num. 34:3–4; cf. Josh. 15:1–3). Num. 20:16 placed Kadesh-barnea on the edge of Edom (cf. Num. 20:23; Josh. 15:1, 21). The eastern border was probably very poorly defined but lay somewhere in the desert. The northern shore of the Gulf of Aqabah was its southern border (Deut. 2:8). There was probably no fixed western boundary. The eastern region of Edom appears more frequently in biblical references. All the Edomite kings and chiefs listed in Gen. 36:31–43 appear to reside east of the Arabah. The country of Edom stands in apposition to the land of Seir (Gen. 32:3; 36:8; Judg. 5:4).

The earliest reference to Edom is in an Egyptian letter from the end of the thirteenth century B.C. Here permission is granted to the nomadic Shasu tribes of Edom to enter the eastern Nile delta.

Edom is said to be a descendant of Esau (Gen. 36:1, 8), the brother of Jacob-Israel, and the elder of the twin sons of Isaac and Rebekah (Gen. 25: 19–26). Esau-Seir is the ancestor of the Edomites in the same way that Jacob-Israel is the eponym of the Israelites. Edom was probably first identified with Esau in the period after David's conquest.

Recent archaeological surveys in the eastern segment of Edom have collected evidence of occupation dating back to at least five hundred thousand years ago. Population appears to have been especially dense during the Middle Paleolithic (ca. 30,000 B.C.), Iron II (ca. 900–600 B.C.), Nabatean (ca. 330 B.C.–A.D. 106), and Byzantine (ca. A.D. 324–640) periods.

An important highway, namely the King's Highway (Num. 20:17), passed through the eastern segment of Edom in a north to south direction. Later on the Roman road *Via Nova Triana* passed through Edom joining Bosra in the north to Aqabah in the south. Other routes traversed the territory in an east-west direction.

Agricultural activity and grazing are possible in Edom, especially the eastern segment. In antiquity copper was mined in Edom. ***See also*** Aqabah, Gulf of; Arabah; Edomites; Esau; Idumaea; Isaac; Jacob; Kadesh; Rebekah; Seir. B.M.

Edomites (ee'duhm-īts), the inhabitants of the land of Edom (Seir) located south of the Dead Sea. The Bible emphasizes the close relationship between the Edomites and the Israelites.

The Edomite "kings" of Gen. 36:31–39 were probably tribal chiefs. The Edomites refused permission to the group led by Moses to pass through their territory (Num. 20:14–21). Saul fought successfully with the Edomites (1 Sam. 14:47). Doeg, an Edomite, appears among Saul's servants (1 Sam. 21:7; 22:9, 18, 22). David conquered the Edomites (2 Sam. 8:12–14). Solomon appears to have had access to the port of Ezion-geber in the land of Edom (1 Kings 9: 26). Pharaoh Shishak's invasion (1 Kings 14:25; 2 Chron. 12:2–9) possibly gave the Edomites a chance to regain their independence. In the time of Jehoshaphat (ca. 874–850 B.C.), Judah expanded southward, ruled Edom (1 Kings 22: 47), and used the port of Ezion-geber (1 Kings 22:48–49; 2 Chron. 20:35–37). The Edomites successfully revolted when Jehoram was king of Judah (ca. 850–843 B.C.), set up a king of their own (2 Kings 8:20–22), and maintained their independence for about fifty or sixty years until the middle of Amaziah's reign (ca. 800–785 B.C.; 2 Kings 14:7; 2 Chron. 25:11–12). Amaziah's son, Uzziah (Azariah) recaptured Edom and built Elath (2 Kings 14:22; 2 Chron. 26:1–2). At the time of Ahaz (ca. 742–725 B.C.), the Edomites defeated Judah (2 Chron. 28:17) and recovered Elath (2 Kings 16:6). From this time onward Judah was not able to exercise control over them.

Edom was known and recognized by Assyria as a clearly identifiable and even important kingdom from the beginning of the eighth century B.C. onward. This is substantiated by the excavations of C.-M. Bennett at Umm el-Biyara, Tawilan, and Buseirah (probably Bozrah, the chief royal Edomite city, cf. Gen. 36:33) in central Edom.

It is difficult to say whether the Edomites participated in the destruction of Jerusalem in 587 B.C. They seem to be the subject of destruction by the Babylonians in the sixth century B.C. (Jer. 27:2–3, 6; 49:7–22; Ezek. 32:29). The oracle of Mal. 1:2–4 indicates that by the time of its writing Edom was in ruin. By the fourth century B.C., the Nabateans replaced the Edomites, many of whom went westward to southern Judea, later to become Idumaea, while others were absorbed by the newcomers.

Except for some seventh-century B.C. jar stamps from Tell el-Kheleifeh, no Edomite writing has come down to us. It is assumed that it was not very different from Moabite and Hebrew.

The Edomites were known for their wisdom (Jer. 49:7; Obad. 1:8; Bar. 3:22). It is believed that they were devoted to the gods and goddesses of fertility. Qaus was the deity peculiar to the Edomites. Another divine name perhaps known to the Edomites was Eloah (Hab. 3:3).

The economy of the Edomites was based on agriculture and commerce rather than on the control of the copper mines of the Wadi Arabah. The Edomites, however, depended for their prosperity on the caravan routes. When they could no longer control these routes, their civilization declined. ***See also*** Bozrah; David; Edom; Ezion-geber; Idumaea; Moab; Nabatea, Nabateans; Saul; Seir. B.M.

Edrei (ed'ree-ī; Heb.). **1** An ancient Transjordanian site, a royal residence of Og, King of Bashan, whose land, following his defeat by the Israelites, was allocated to Manasseh (Num. 21:33; Deut. 1:4; 3:10; Josh. 12:4; 13:12, 31); in Roman times it was called Adraene and today is called Dar'a. **2** A town in Naphtali (Josh. 19:37).

education, the process of handing on acquired knowledge and wisdom.

In Ancient Israel: The Hebrew Bible does not provide a clear picture of education in ancient Israel. A few texts have generally been understood as references to formal education (e.g., Isa. 28:9–13; 50:4–9; Prov. 22:17–21), but the evidence is highly problematic. The first refers specifically to infants who have just been weaned, and the second merely indicates that eloquence was taught somewhere, presumably in the home. The third text pertains to a foreign setting, inasmuch as it reflects an indebtedness to the Egyptian Instruction of Amen-em-opet, an Egyptian sage. Other biblical references have seemed to support a thesis of an Israelite school; the main ones are the existence of a city named Qiriath Sepher (City of the Book; Josh. 15:15–16; Judg. 1:11–12), the mention of a youth who could write in Judg. 8:13–17, Isaiah's allusion to his disciples ("the taught ones," 8:16), references in Prov. 4:5 and 17:16 to buying wisdom, and the inscription about the men of Hezekiah who copied earlier proverbs. The earliest specific reference to an Israelite school occurs in Ecclus. 51:23, which invites students to Ben Sira's *beth hammidrash* (Heb., "house of study").

Extra-Biblical Evidence: The paucity of evidence for schools in the Hebrew Bible has been supplemented from two different sources: ancient Near Eastern parallels to the OT materials and Palestinian inscriptions. Knowledge of education in ancient Egypt is quite extensive, thanks to instructional texts and scribal controversies that have survived. Similarly, several school texts from Sumer exist today, allowing scholars to paint a reasonably clear picture of education in Mesopotamia. The same is true for Ugarit, where scribes played a significant role in society. The temptation therefore is to draw upon this combined picture to clarify the situation in Israel. Such a procedure is risky, given the relative simplicity of the Hebrew language and of the Israelite society even during the monarchy. If a school existed in Solomon's time, one wonders why the list of governmental officials does not include the equivalent of a superintendent of education.

Recent evidence from Palestinian inscriptions has elicited differing interpretations. Some critics have used the following data to argue for schools in early Israel: lists, abecedaries (i.e., alphabet lists), transposition of similar letters, repeated words, large letters, poorly formed figures, and evidence of beginnings in a foreign language. None of these requires a school, inasmuch as parental instruction adequately explains all of the above features that might point to the activity of children. Many of the features may be explained otherwise; for

A teacher sits between two students who hold open scrolls; third-century tomb relief.

example, large letters may indicate poor eyesight and an aged writer, just as less than perfect drawings may suggest a shaky hand or meagre ability as an artist. Perhaps the evidence would be stronger if it had been found in a single site, rather than scattered hither and yon throughout Palestine.

Types of Instruction: While differences of opinion exist about the pertinence of these Palestinian inscriptions and parallels from neighboring cultures to Israel's education, consensus seems to have formed with regard to the centrality of the family in early instruction. As a matter of fact, even the references to "my son" and to "father" in Proverbs, which are usually interpreted as technical language for student and teacher, may be taken literally. That is certainly true where the mother is mentioned alongside the father, although one critic has sought to explain that occurrence as the result of the demands of literary parallelism in the text of Proverbs.

It seems likely that many youngsters acquired training in guilds. We hear of prophetic and priestly guilds, and it is probable that other skills like pottery making, metallurgy, and the like were acquired in various guilds. A decisive shift in the direction of official bureaucracy may have taken place under King Hezekiah (725–697 B.C.), if it had not already occurred in Solomon's reign. In any event, young men now received instruction in the scribal art at the royal court. With the author of Ecclesiastes, it seems that a conscious effort was made to instruct "the people," if that expression really implies a democratization of learning. A different sort of teaching is reported in 2 Chron. 17:7–9, in this instance continuing the earlier religious instruction that assumed such importance in Deuteronomy, but with a decisive difference. In Chronicles official priests, Levites, and princes are said to have instructed the people in the Book of the Law. As is well known, the author of Chronicles was less faithful to historical events than his predecessors, and this report must be viewed cautiously.

It may be easier to describe Israelite education than to determine exactly where it took place, but even here much conjecture is necessary. It seems that education was restricted to boys, for the most part, if the canonical proverbs actually functioned as textbooks, as many scholars think. The constant reference in Prov. 1–8 to the adulteress as the villain was directed at male audiences, as was also true of specific instructions that without exception are aimed at men. Furthermore, teaching was often reinforced by punishment, an unhappy feature of education throughout Egypt and Mesopotamia as well. In Israel the actual subject matter of instruction may have consisted of religious traditions and proverbial sayings, if Ben Sira's writing (i.e., Ecclus.) reflects the curriculum in his school. Under Hellenistic influence, the author of Wisdom of Solomon adopted a much different curriculum (7:17–22). It follows that education in ancient Israel was remarkably diverse, with respect both to the actual place of instruction and the curriculum.

In the NT: While no formal education is described in the NT, Jesus is pictured as educating ("teaching") large crowds (Mark 4:1–2; 14:49) as well as his disciples (lit. "learners"; cf. Matt. 5:1b–2). The risen Christ commands his disciples to continue such activity (Matt. 28:20). Paul reports he was educated in the law by the famous teacher Gamaliel (Acts 22:3), having left his home to go to Jerusalem for that purpose, thus giving evidence that the rabbinic schools much in evidence in the later traditions of the Mishnah were already highly developed. There is no evidence in the NT of formal education in the Christian faith; at that point it appears to have been a matter of family instruction (1 Tim. 1:5; cf. Deut. 11:19). J.L.C.

Eglon (eg'lahn). **1** The fat king of Moab who together with the Ammonites and Amalekites, invaded Israelite territory during the period of the judges and ruled over the people from "the city of palms" (Jericho) for eighteen years. According to Judges 3:12–30, Eglon's rule ended when Ehud, the left-handed judge, concealed a dagger under his cloak and assassinated Eglon when they were alone. **2** A Canaanite city allied with Jerusalem, Hebron, Jarmuth, and Lachish in an unsuccessful attempt to oppose Joshua's invasion of the land of Canaan (Josh. 10:3–5). Joshua captured the city (Josh. 10:34–35; cf. 12:12), which was later included among the cities of Judah (Josh. 15:39). Modern Tell Aitun is currently identified as the site of Eglon. ***See also*** Judges, The Book of. M.A.S.

Egypt, one of the great civilizations of the ancient world, centered along the Nile River in northeast Africa. Egypt was already an ancient civilization by the time of the biblical patriarchs, and its delta settlements reached to within two hundred miles of Israel's territory, yet Egyptian cultural influence on Palestine was modest. The Egyptians were not very interested in settlement abroad, partly because there were many possibilities for expansion at home, though Egypt did dominate Palestine politically during many periods. Egypt's influence was greater in the Phoenician coastal cities, with which it had important cultural and commercial ties. This article emphasizes Egypt's relationships with biblical history.

Geographical Setting: As the "gift of the Nile," Egypt is geographically somewhat isolated. The Nile has no tributaries in Egypt proper and the land receives little rain. Even the delta has at best 8 inches of rainfall annually, whereas the

An Asiatic tribe in traditional costume asking permission to enter Egypt, as Abraham and Jacob may have done; copy of a mural from the tomb at Beni-Hassan, nineteenth century B.C.

Nile Valley has virtually none. The settled area of Egypt therefore resembles a flower bending in the breeze. The delta (Lower Egypt), which spreads out north of Cairo for a hundred miles to the Mediterranean and is more than a hundred and fifty miles wide, is the blossom, and the Nile Valley (Upper Egypt) is the long, slender stalk, between six and nine miles wide and extending five hundred and seventy-five miles from Cairo to Aswan. The one exception to this picture is the Faiyum, a well-watered area about fifty miles south of Cairo that reaches fifty miles into the desert west of the Nile.

Egypt had a strong sense of duality: there were "Two Lands," the delta and the valley, and together they constituted the "Black Land," in contrast to the neighboring desert, the "Red Land." Bordered by the Mediterranean on the north with desert on the remaining sides, Egypt was fairly secure from major movements of people. The overland route to Palestine led through the Sinai wilderness and along the Mediterranean coast before moving up into the hill country and cities such as Hebron and Jerusalem (ca. two hundred and fifteen miles from the easternmost settlements of the delta). Accordingly, only small groups of people from Syro-Palestine were continuously going into Egypt, prompted by drought, commerce, and other concerns (cf. Gen. 12:10; 42–43; Matt. 2:14). Asiatics and Libyans came into the delta, usually peacefully, and Nubians into the Nile Valley.

Predynastic and Early Dynastic Periods: Predynastic Egypt (ca. 3400–3100 B.C.) featured regional cultures and village society. Constellations were forming in Upper and Lower Egypt, but with considerable conflict. In dynasties I–II (ca. 3000–2686), the "Two Lands" experienced the formation and consolidation of a unified government, centered at Memphis. Key elements were the development of court culture and royal bureaucracy. An enduring pattern of division into provinces (nomes) was established.

Old Kingdom Period: Dynasties III–VI (ca. 2686–2181 B.C.) represented a period of immense cultural and political achievement. Building on the accomplishments of the Early Dynastic period, a remarkable level of culture and organization was reached. The third dynasty (ca. 2686–2613) was still a period of some innovation, leading up to the climactic development of the fourth dynasty (ca. 2613–2498 B.C.), whose impressive scale was symbolized by the great pyramids. A pattern of rule developed that served with variations and adaptation for over two thousand years. The divine king had absolute power filtered through an efficient civil service. In dynasties V and VI (ca. 2498–2181) the king's power was more widely dispersed. The royal center remained in the Memphis area, where the "Two Lands" joined. During the Old Kingdom Egypt engaged in extensive commercial interchange with Phoenicia, especially Byblos, and also sent many expeditions to Sinai in search of raw materials like copper and turquoise.

First Intermediate and Middle Kingdom Periods: When the system of the Old Kingdom broke down, it was followed by about a hundred and fifty years of civil war and assertiveness by local provinces (dynasties VII–XI, ca. 2181–2060 B.C.). The last kings of dynasty XI (ca. 2060–1991) managed to unify Egypt again, and during the twelfth dynasty (ca. 1991–1782) the central organization was furthered, though the king was less absolute than in the Old Kingdom. Southern Egypt, with its center in Thebes, became more prominent, though the kings still ruled from the Memphis area. During the Middle Kingdom Egypt asserted itself in southern Syro-Palestine in more than a commercial relationship. The term "empire" is probably inappropriate, but there was at least a claim to hegemony. The "Execration" Texts list princes and peoples of the area, many specifically from Palestine, Transjordan, and Phoenicia, who owed some kind of allegiance to Egypt. The names of many Palestinian locations first appear in these texts. The earlier patriarchal traditions concerning Egypt may relate to this period.

Second Intermediate (Hyksos) Period: The forces for decentralization again triumphed (dynasties XIV–XVII, ca. 1782–1570), and there were various separatist movements. For the first time pharaonic Egypt experienced a major influx of foreigners, as the Asiatic Hyksos, with superior military technology and organization in spite of their varied backgrounds, gained control of the delta (dynasty XV, ca. 1663–1555). Also, Nubia broke away, so native Egyptian rulers were restricted to the Nile Valley and at that were under Hyksos domination. This was a period of considerable interchange between Egyptian and Syro-Palestinian culture, though it is not well documented. Many scholars regard this period as the time of Joseph's rise in Egypt. The native traditions endured most effectively in Thebes. Eventually the Theban rulers prevailed against the Nubian-Hyksos tandem and their Egyptian allies.

New Kingdom Period: Theban success against the outsiders ushered in the New Kingdom (dynasties XVIII–XX, ca. 1550–1070 B.C.). Ahmose I (ca. 1550–1525) captured the Hyksos capital of Avaris, drove the Hyksos back into Syro-Palestine, and unified again the "Two Lands." Indeed, from the time of Thutmose I (ca. 1504–1492) to Ramesses II (ca. 1279–1213) Egypt was politically powerful also in much of Syro-Palestine as well as Nubia and it is possible to refer to an Egyptian Empire. In Egypt, an effective administration endured during the whole of the New Kingdom, surviving crises such as the Amarna "revolution" and the changes in dynasties. Noteworthy was the power conflict between the royal court and the evergrowing priesthoods, especially that of Amun-Re (Thebes), which reached a climax during Akhenaton's reign. Noteworthy also was the level of cultural interchange with Syro-Palestine. Many Semitic gods had a following in Egypt, and the Asiatic population in Egypt continued to be significant, especially in Lower Egypt. In the time of the long-lived and powerful Ramesses II a group of oppressed Hebrew slaves working on building projects in the delta staged a mass escape into the Sinai wilderness under the leadership of Moses. The pursuing Egyptian forces were miraculously stopped. In the "Victory Stele" of Pharaoh Merneptah, the immediate successor of Ramesses II, there occurs the first extrabiblical reference to Israel. Nonetheless Egypt's power was waning. Though Ramesses III (ca. 1185–1154) could still repel the Sea Peoples and Libyans, the effort was the last sign of real strength and Egypt began a period of depression and disorder.

Third Intermediate Period: By this period (dynasties XXI–XXV, ca. 1100–664) Egypt's political and cultural greatness now was in the past. In this period Egypt was weakened by regionalism and factionalism. One of the pharaohs of this period even gave a daughter in marriage to Solomon, something formerly unheard of. At times descendants of former Libyan prisoners and mercenaries were in power. One Libyan ruler, Shishak (Shoshenq I, ca. 945–924), gave refuge to the future king of Israel Jeroboam I and even campaigned successfully against Jerusalem and other Palestinian cities. Nubian princes succeeded in extending control into Upper Egypt. In the twenty-fifth dynasty (ca. 772–664 B.C.), Nubian pharaohs came to control a united Nubia and Egypt, partly by allowing Thebes practical independence. But the Nubian kings were not able to restrain Assyria, and again, in the early seventh century B.C., Asiatic forces controlled much of Egypt. The Assyrians sacked Memphis and Thebes but had only temporary power.

Late Period: This period covers dynasties XXVI–XXXI, ca. 664–332. The twenty-sixth, Saite Dynasty (ca. 664–525), based in the western delta and aided by Greek and Carian mercenaries, led Egypt in its last period of independence and unity. Neco II even campaigned in north Syria—Josiah of Judah died in opposing him—and dominated Palestine for four years. The Saite period formally imitated the artistic style of the Old Kingdom, but not its grandeur. The Saites did enlarge Egypt's commercial contacts and absorbed sizable foreign colonies, including many Greeks. They managed to stop the Babylonian army short of Egypt proper, but subsequently Persian strength proved too great. The invasion of Cambyses (525 B.C.) brought Egypt into the Persian domain. Although Egypt regained some independence between 404 and 342, it was precariously involved with Greek mercenaries. The Persians enjoyed a brief but troubled period of power again (342–332) prior to their collapse in the face of Alexander's armies.

Hellenistic-Roman Period (332 B.C.–A.D. 324): Alexander stayed only a short while in Egypt. He assigned Ptolemy Soter, one of his generals, to rule Egypt, thus founding the Ptolemaic dynasty (305–30). He also founded the port city of Alexandria, which became one of the major cities of the Mediterranean world, but much more a Hellenistic than an Egyptian center. (Alexandria had a prominent Jewish population within a few decades.) The Ptolemies hellenized the Egyptian administration and exploited the country while also identifying with the pharaonic tradition and sponsoring major building projects. For much of the period the Ptolemies contended with the Seleucid rulers of Syria for control of Palestine. The Ptolemies ruled Palestine throughout the third century B.C., but little is known of Jewish history under them. In Egypt the Ptolemies had much internal strife and became increasingly subordinate to Rome. Rome assumed direct rule from 30 B.C. to A.D. 324 but continued the Ptolemaic administration. Many Egyptian cults, such as that of the goddess Isis, gained a wide following in the Hellenistic-Roman world. The Christian community in Egypt, which began quite early, developed into the Coptic church.

Egypt and the Bible: Egypt's influence on the people of Palestine involved serving as a refuge area or place of exile, military and political domination, and cultural influence. As the great granary of the eastern Mediterranean, Egypt attracted many people to its abundant agricultural resources. The biblical patriarchs, from Abra-

Captive Asiatics, with arms upraised in a gesture of submissive greeting to Pharaoh Sahure, being taken by ship to Egypt; stone relief ca. 2446 B.C.

ham to Jacob and his sons, are described as going to Egypt for survival. Similarly, following the fall of Jerusalem to the Babylonians, a group from Judah took refuge in Egypt. The great Exodus from Egypt under Moses of Hebrews who had become oppressed was a continuing model for liberation and a return to Egypt was a commonly threatened punishment.

In the few centuries prior to Moses, Egypt had been a dominant power in Palestine, ruling basically through local princes. During the Israelite monarchy and the subsequent periods of foreign control, Egypt was generally restricted to brief raids and involvements in various alliances against the great Asiatic powers. Significant control by Egypt occurred again only in the time of the Ptolemies. In connection with the military campaigns, many people from Palestine were taken as captives to Egypt, basically to work for the king and the gods. During the fifth century B.C. there was a Jewish military colony at the southern border of Egypt (Elephantine), and in Ptolemaic times there were many Jewish settlers. From ca. 163 B.C. until A.D. 73 there was even a Jewish temple at Leontopolis in the eastern delta.

Egypt's cultural influence in Palestine was modest, considering the proximity. Egypt sought raw materials, especially metals and wood, from Syro-Palestine and was not bent on cultural dominance. There is a modest number of Egyptian loan words in the Hebrew Bible (Egyptian is a distantly related language). Moses was "instructed in all the wisdom of the Egyptians" (Acts 7:22), and indeed he and many of the priestly class in Israel bore Egyptian names. Yet although Akhenaton's "monotheism" antedated Moses by a century, the contrast is considerable and Egyptian religion had little, if any, specific influence on that of Israel. The most direct sign of literary borrowing is in Prov. 22: 17–24:22, which apparently utilized the Egyptian "Instruction of Amenemope." Other literary influence is found in novellas and love poetry. The political organization under David and Solomon seemed to draw upon Egyptian models, but presumably through Phoenician intermediaries. Above all, Egypt served as a model of idolatry and arrogant power, Israel's redemption from which in the Exodus proved to be a lasting, central motif. ***See also*** Akhenaton; Amarna, Tell el-; Exodus; Hyksos; Neco II; Nile; Pharaoh; Sea Peoples.

Bibliography

Morenz, S. *Egyptian Religion*. Ithaca, NY: Cornell University Press, 1973.

Trigger, B. G., B. J. Kemp, D. O'Connor, and A. B. Lloyd. *Ancient Egypt: A Social History*. Cambridge: Cambridge University Press, 1983.

Wilson, J. A. *The Culture of Ancient Egypt*. Chicago: University of Chicago Press, 1951. H.B.H.

Egypt, Brook of (KJV: "Egypt, River of"), the Wadi el-Arish, a valley in the Sinai Peninsula of Egypt with a seasonal stream that flows into the Mediterranean (Num. 34:5; Josh. 15:4; 1 Kings 8: 65; 2 Kings 24:7; 2 Chron. 7:8; Isa. 27:12). It marked the traditional southwestern border of the land of Canaan (and of the claims of Judah or, in Ezek. 48:28, Gad), the northern border being either the Entrance of Hamath or the Euphrates. The River of Egypt in Gen. 15:18 was apparently the same, as was probably Shihor (1 Chron. 13:5) and the Brook of the Arabah (Amos 6:14). ***See also*** Arabah; Shihor. H.B.H.

Ehud (ee'ho͞od), a left-handed Benjaminite who through a clever ruse killed Eglon, the fat Moabite king, and subsequently led the Israelites to victory over the Moabites (Judg. 3:12–4: 1). ***See also*** Eglon.

Ekron (ek'rahn; Heb., "barren place"? or "fertile place"?; Gk. *Akkarōn)*, the northernmost city of the Philistine Pentapolis. It is most commonly identified as modern Khirbet el-Muqanna about twenty-two miles west of Jerusalem. It was assigned to the territory of Judah (Josh. 15: 11) or to Dan (Josh. 19:43) but was reported to be in Philistine hands when the Ark was taken there (1 Sam. 5:10). The town received defeated forces of the Philistines (1 Sam. 17:52) as David's gains brought compression of Philistine territory.

In prophetic traditions Elijah was called to challenge the authority of Ekron's god, Baalzebub (Heb., "lord of the flies"?) to indicate Israelite King Amaziah's fate (2 Kings 1:2–16). Amos (1:8), Jeremiah (25:20), Zephaniah (2:4), and Zechariah (9:5, 7) denounced Ekron as a symbol of evil power to be destroyed.

Captured by Assyria's Sennacherib (ca. 705–681 B.C.), as it had earlier been taken by Egypt's Shishak (last quarter of tenth century B.C.), it was later given by Alexander Balas to Jonathan Maccabeus (ca. 160–142 B.C.; 1 Macc. 10:89) and had its Greek name at least into the fourth century A.D. R.S.B.

El, the chief god of the Canaanite pantheon, raises his hand in benediction to a king or high priest before him; relief from Ugarit, thirteenth century B.C.

El, a word for "God" in the ancient Semitic languages. The word could be used as either a proper noun or a common noun. As a proper noun, El refers to a god in the pantheons of the Canaanite world. In the Bible the word occurs often in personal names (e.g., *El*iab, *El*ijah). *Elohim* (Heb.) and not El is the most common biblical word for God, but El occurs frequently in the Bible referring to God, particularly in the book of Job and other works of poetry.

In Ugaritic Literature: The Ugaritic literature produced in the north Canaanite city-state of Ugarit (second millennium B.C.) reveals much of what we know about the Canaanite god El. El is the king, regarded as ruler among the gods. In the assembly of the gods, El holds the highest position. Permission to build a palace for Baal must come from El, and it is El who surrenders Baal to Baal's enemy Yamm. To judge from his epithets, El is a creator. At Ugarit he was called the "Builder of Things Built," and elsewhere he held the title "Creator of the Earth." El has other epithets in the Ugaritic literature. He is called the "Father of Years," a title that recalls his epithet "Eternal" on a Sinaitic inscription. El is an aged god. Ugaritic texts refer to his gray beard and speak of his wisdom. El is called "Compassionate," "The Bull," "Beneficent," and the "Father of Humankind." El lives at the source of two rivers amid the fountains of the (world-encompassing) Deep (cf. Gen. 1:1). This is a localization that lies beyond the boundaries of terrestrial space.

Although in title chief among the gods, El does not always play a forceful role in the Ugaritic myths and legends. His daughter Anat coerces him with threats of violence. His surrender of Baal has the character of submission to Yamm. In one short text, El is portrayed drinking himself into a stupor and wallowing in his own excrement and urine. Such behavior has led to questions concerning El's status in the Ugaritic pantheon. Some have suggested that El at Ugarit was in his twilight, and others believe that Baal was in the process of supplanting El in Ugaritic religion. Yet there are times in the Ugaritic literature when El acts effectively, and this puts the issue in doubt. It is El who brings about the healing of Kirta (Keret) when all other gods fail, and it is the threat of El's intervention that silences a fractious Athtar. It should be noted that while the Ugaritic literature presents a variegated picture of El, other sources are more consistently flattering of the god. Philo of Byblos (ca. A.D. 64–141), a Greek historian who collected Phoenician lore, identified El with Kronos, told of El's marriage to Astarte, Rhea, and Dione, and reported that Zeus (Baal) ruled the earth with the permission of El. Here there is no hint of a declining El or of conflict between El and Baal.

At Ugarit, El's consort was Asherah, a goddess whom the Bible links with Baal. A Canaanite myth "El, Ashertu, and the Storm God" (surviving in a Hittite version) tells of how Asherah was faithless to her consort El and sought the affection of the storm god (Baal).

In Ancient Israel: The cult of El was widely diffused in the Syro-Palestinian world and spread from there to the Phoenician colonies of the central and western Mediterranean basin. El was worshiped in the Holy Land at an early date. The Bible reveals many local manifestations of El. At Beer-lahairoi Hagar encounters El Roi (Heb., "God of Seeing," Gen. 16:7–14). At Beersheba Abraham worships El Olam (Heb., "Eternal God," Gen. 21:33). The name El Elyon (Heb., "God Most High") was associated with Jerusalem (Gen. 14:18–20). Jacob has a revelation of El Bethel (Heb., "God of Bethel") at Bethel (Gen. 35:7). El Berith (Heb., "God of the Covenant") is linked to Shechem (Judg. 9:46), but the same god appears to be called Baal-berith elsewhere (Judg. 9:4). Many if not all of these local manifestations of El go back to pre-Israelite times (pre-thirteenth century B.C.). The worship of El at local Palestinian sanctuaries provided a setting for the transmission of aspects of the cult of El to the religion of Israel. During its settlement in Canaan, Israel adopted for itself the veneration of El.

Israelite tradition recognized the primacy of

El worship. When the Priestly writer introduces the divine name Yahweh into his narrative (Exod. 6:2–8), he shows that Yahweh was known at first as El Shaddai. The Priestly writer often uses the name El Shaddai for Israel's God. The Bible speaks of "El, the God of Israel" (Gen. 33:20), and when it is recognized that the name Israel is a compound including the divine name El, the importance of El in the early religion of Israel becomes clear.

Some elements from the Canaanite cult of El made their way into the worship of Israel's God Yahweh. Yahweh took over the leading role in the council of the gods (Ps. 89:6–7). He may have taken the title "King" from El. Notions of the compassion and mercy of Yahweh may stem from the image of "Benevolent El." Yahweh as creator and father is reminiscent of El.

In one instance at least, the image of Canaanite El has made its way directly into the Bible. The figure of the Ancient of Days in the book of Daniel is inspired by the aged El (Dan. 7:9–14).

The accommodation of El worship by Yahwism was a remarkable occurrence, for Israel was as a rule hostile to the cults of Canaanite gods and goddesses. Israel identified Yahweh as El. The supremacy of El in the native religions of Palestine made this identification attractive. It has even been proposed that Yahweh was no more than a special name of El. Whatever the cause of the identification, it provides a striking contrast to the general conflict between Israelite religion and that of its neighbors. ***See also*** Baal; God; Ras-Shamra. R.M.G.

Elah (ee'lah). **1** The valley in Judah where David is reported to have killed Goliath (1 Sam. 17: 2, 19; 21:9); it was protected by the cities of Libnah and Azekah (modern Wadi es-Sant). **2** The son and successor of Baasha, king of Israel. He ruled for less than two years (ca. 886 B.C.). While he was intoxicated, he was murdered by Zimri in Tirzah (1 Kings 16:6–14). **3** The father of Hoshea, the last king of Israel (ca. 732–723 B.C.; 2 Kings 15:30; 17:1; 18:1, 9).

Elam (ee'lahm), the region east of the Tigris River, which provided Mesopotamia with a rich source of raw materials; hence the continuing Mesopotamian interest in Elam. Three rivers water the region, making it especially fertile. The unification of Anshan, the mountainous eastern region, with the southeastern plain of Shushan meant independence for Elam. The diverse areas of Elam were always organized into a federal state. Elamite pictographs first appear around 2900 B.C., whereas writing begins in Mesopotamia around 3100 B.C. A linear Elamite script, known from only eighteen inscriptions, dates from the twenty-third century B.C. Carved seals from the third millennium B.C. depict various activities of the Elamite economy: hunting, fishing, herding, and agriculture. A female deity, Pinikir, headed the Elamite pantheon until the middle of the second millennium B.C., when the male Humban replaced her.

Contact between Mesopotamia and Elam appears as early as 2550 B.C., when Enmebaragesi of Kish records carrying off "as booty the weapons of the land of Elam." Elam remained under Mesopotamian control until Ibbi-Sin, the last ruler of the Ur III dynasty, was carried off to exile in Elam, where he died. The early Sumerian view of the Elamites as undesirables prevailed throughout the second millennium B.C. Conflict between these two regions continued until the thirteenth century B.C., the floruit of Elamite civilization, when Elam freed itself of Babylon's control.

In the Bible: In the Bible, Elam is best known from Genesis 14, which details the coalition of several kings, including the Elamite Chedorlaomer, against the kings of the Dead Sea region. The coalition captured Lot, who was rescued by his uncle, Abram. The Hebrew name (*Chedorlaomer*) may reflect an actual Elamite name; *Kuter-Lagamar* would mean "the goddess Lagamar is protection." The name, however, is not yet attested in native inscriptions. In the Table of Nations, Elam is listed as a descendant of Shem (Gen. 10:22).

Shushan (Susa), the capital of Elam, is called "the castle" in Neh. 1:1, Dan. 8:2, and Esther 1: 2. During the reign of Darius, Susa became the winter palace of the Persian Empire.

In the eighth and seventh centuries B.C., Elam

A tablet from Susa, ca. 2900 B.C., showing early Elamite "writing."

alternatively showed its last independence and joined Chaldean and Aramean coalitions against Assyria. The Assyrians prevailed, and in 646 B.C. Ashurbanipal sacked Susa. Ezek. 32:24 describes the destruction of Elam. Isaiah (11:11; 21:2; 22:6) records Elamite help in Assyrian attacks on Judah. In all of these instances, Elam is depicted as a fierce nation, whose warriors are adept at the use of the bow and arrow as well as chariotry. During the reign of Zedekiah, Jeremiah (49:35–39) prophesied God's promise of a total victory over Elam and a return from the captivity.

Jews from Elam are counted among the returnees from the Babylonian captivity in Ezra 2:7, 31 and 8:7. The chiefs of the Jewish tribes in Elam were among those who set their seals to the reform covenant upon their return (Neh. 10:14). Neh. 12:42 records the participation of a priest named Elam in the rededication of the walls of Jerusalem.

The one mention of Elamites in the NT (Acts 2:9) records their presence in Jerusalem at the feast of Pentecost. ***See also*** Chedorlaomer.

L.E.P.

Elath (ee'lath). ***See*** Ezion-geber.

El Bethel, probably a deity. Among the many El epithets in the OT, El Bethel occurs twice (Gen. 31:13; 35:7). These Hebrew phrases may be understood as either "the El [i.e., god] Bethel" or "the El [i.e., god] of Bethel." Jer. 48:13 and Amos 5:4–6 seem to indicate the existence of a god named Bethel, but other ancient sources refer to the god of Bethel. ***See also*** Bethel; El; God; Names.

Eldad (el'dad; Heb., "El [god] has loved"?), an Israelite elder. With his companion Medad, Eldad was chosen with sixty-eight others to receive God's spirit around the Tent of Meeting. The two tarried in the camp and prophesied there. When Joshua learned of their unauthorized activity, he urged Moses to restrain them, but Moses rebuffed the complaint, saying: "Would that all the Lord's people were prophets!" (Num. 11:16, 26–30). ***See also*** Prophet; Tabernacle.

elders, senior tribesmen of Israel. The elders performed tasks of local government and justice throughout the biblical period. Aspects of their function and historical importance can be seen in Exod. 18:13–17; 24:1–11; Num. 11:16–30; Judg. 21:16–24; and 1 Sam. 8:1–9. In the NT, elders were either important Jewish leaders (e.g., Matt. 15:2; Mark 14:43; Luke 7:3; Acts 4:8) or leaders in the nascent Christian communities (Acts 15:2; 21:18; Titus 1:5; James 5:14) although the word can also mean simply an elderly person (1 Tim. 5:1).

Elealeh (el-uh-ay'leh), a Moabite city east of the Jordan River that, along with Heshbon and surrounding cities, was given to the tribe of Reuben after they and the tribe of Gad requested that Moses allow them to settle there (Num. 32:1–5). The city was rebuilt by the Reubenites (Num. 32: 33–38), although by the time of Isaiah and Jeremiah it was back in Moabite hands (ca. 700–625 B.C.; Isa. 15:4; Jer. 48:34). The city is identified as modern el-Al, a ruin about two miles northeast of Tell Heshban and about fifteen miles east and slightly north of the north end of the Dead Sea.

D.R.B.

Eleasah (el-ee-ay'suh; Heb., "El [God] has made" or "El has acted"). **1** A descendant of Judah (1 Chron. 2:39–40). **2** A Benjaminite descendant of Saul's son Jonathan (1 Chron. 8:37).

Eleazar (el-ee-ay'zer; Heb., "God has helped"), the name of seven different persons in the OT, the foremost being the third son of Aaron. He, with his brothers, became a priest (Exod. 29; Lev. 8) and later became high priest when Aaron died (Num. 20:25–28). He served as high priest during the remaining years of Moses' leadership and through Joshua's tenure as leader. An Eleazar is also mentioned in the list of Joseph's ancestors in Matt. 1:15.

election, a technical theological term in the Bible having nothing to do with the democratic political process. The subject of election is God, who chooses on the basis of his sovereign will for his creation. Associated with election are theological terms such as "predestination," "providence," and "covenant."

In the OT, God elects a people (Israel), its king (David), and the city of Jerusalem. His free choice is not based on the previous accomplishment or on the natural superiority of those he chooses; yet, the chosen are under obligation to live by God's will and to be his servants (e.g., Deut. 7:6–11; 1 Chron. 16:9–13; Jer. 33: 19–26; Amos 3:2).

In the NT, election is focused on Jesus Christ as the elect one (often with a reference to the OT) through whom God ultimately accomplishes his purpose (e.g., Matt. 12:18; Luke 9:35; 23:35; 11 Pet. 2:4, 6). Through faith and discipleship, his followers are called "elect" (e.g., Mark 13:20–27; Matt. 22:14; Titus 1:1; 1 Pet. 1:2; 2:9–10). Although this elect group is made up of people from all nations, Paul also expects that God's election of Israel will be fulfilled in the end (Rom. 11:2, 28). ***See also*** Covenant; Grace; Predestination; Providence.

J.E.A.

Elephantine. ***See*** Egypt; Passover, The; Syene; Temple, The.

Eleusis (el-yo͞o'sis). ***See*** Mystery.

Eleven, the, the disciples or apostles of Jesus (originally twelve) during a brief period after the death of Judas Iscariot and before the choice of Matthias (Acts 1:23–26). The Eleven are mentioned in Matt. 28:16; Mark 16:14 (in some manuscripts); Luke 24:9, 33; Acts 1:26; 2:14 (in some manuscripts); 1 Cor. 15:5 (in some manuscripts). ***See also*** Apostle; Disciple; Judas; Matthias; Twelve, The.

Elhanan (el-hay'nuhn; Heb., "God is gracious"). **1** The son of Dodo from Bethlehem; one of David's thirty mighty men (2 Sam. 23:24). **2** The son of Jair (or Jaareoregim) of Bethlehem, who killed Goliath (2 Sam. 21:19) or Goliath's brother Lahmi (1 Chron. 20:5). The apparent confusion as to his victim may be the result of an attempt to harmonize the contradiction that resulted when David was credited with Elhanan's accomplishment (1 Sam. 17). Some scholars, however, consider Elhanan to be David's personal name.

Eli (ee'lī; Heb., "[God] is exalted"), judge of Israel (1 Sam. 4:18) and priest in Shiloh where the Ark was located during the period of the Judges. On observing Hannah praying silently for children, he first thought she was drunk, but then assured her that her prayer would be fulfilled. Samuel, the offspring of this promise, was later brought to Shiloh where he was devoted to divine service and subsequently succeeded Eli, whose sons Hophni and Phinehas were both wicked. When Eli learned of their deaths at the battle of Aphek and the loss of the Ark, he fell, broke his neck, and died (1 Sam. 4). F.E.G.

Eli, Eli, lema sabachthani (ay'lee, ay'lee, luh-mah' sah-bakh'thah-nee, Matt. 27:46; RSV transliterates "lama") and *"Eloi, Eloi, lama sabachthani"* (Mark 15:34), mixed Hebrew and Aramaic renderings of the first verse of Psalm 22, "My God, my God, why hast thou forsaken me." *Eli* and *Lama* are Hebrew; the other words are Aramaic. Psalm 22 is quoted and alluded to several times in the passion accounts of Mark and Matthew (e.g., Matt. 27:35, 43) and seems to have been used to interpret the meaning and manner of Jesus' death. The desolation or despair of Jesus' cry has long intrigued and shocked commentators, especially those concerned with the relationship of Jesus' divinity to his humanity. Reformation theologians associated this verse with Jesus being forsaken by the Father as an atonement for sin; in reaction, other theologians suggested that Jesus recited the whole psalm, which ends in hopeful confidence in God. Contemporary interpretations link these words with an existentialist analysis of human experience. In context the citation of Ps. 22:1 (Heb. 22:2) communicates Jesus' sense of human separation from God in the face of sin and death. In the light of the resurrection it functions literarily as part of a sharp contrast between Jesus' apparent powerlessness and ultimate victory. Theologically the Psalm, which is part of God's revealed word, argues that Jesus' suffering and death were planned with a purpose by God. ***See also*** Atonement; Passion. A.J.S.

Eliab (e-lī'ab; Heb., "God is father"). **1** Reubenite father of Dathan and Abiram who rebelled against Moses (Num. 16:1). **2** Son of Helon, leader of Zebulun in the generation prior to the conquest of Canaan (Num. 10:16). **3** A Levite in the line of Kohath (1 Chron. 6:27). **4** David's oldest brother (1 Sam. 17:28) whose stature and appearance impressed Samuel when he sought a king from among Jesse's sons (1 Sam. 6:6–7). **5** A Gaddite who served David in the desert (1 Chron. 12:9). **6** A levitical musician in the time of David (1 Chron. 15:18, 20; 16:5).

Eliada (e-lī'uh-duh; Heb., "El [God] knows"). **1** One of David's sons born in Jerusalem (2 Sam. 5:16), also called Beeliada (Heb., "Baal knows," 1 Chron. 14:7). Although Baal was originally another name for the deity, names that contained "Baal" were sometimes changed to avoid any association with the Canaanite fertility god of that name. **2** The father of Rezon, the ruler of Syria and enemy of David (1 Kings 11:23). **3** A Benjaminite commander of two hundred thousand bowmen under King Jehoshaphat (2 Chron. 17:17).

Eliakim (e-lī'a-kim; Heb., "God raises up"). **1** The son of Hilkiah and royal steward under King Hezekiah. He had replaced Shebna in that office in accordance with the prophecy of Isaiah, but he later fell into disfavor with the prophet or with his disciples (Isa. 22:20–25). Together with Shebna, now royal secretary, and Joah, royal herald, Eliakim played an important role in the negotiations with the Assyrian Rabshakeh during Sennacherib's siege of Jerusalem (2 Kings 18: 18–19:7). **2** The king of Judah from 609 to 598 B.C. When Pharaoh Neco killed Eliakim's father, King Josiah, the Judean gentry chose a younger son, Jehoahaz, as the new king, but three months later the Egyptian replaced Jehoahaz with Eliakim, whom he renamed Jehoiakim (2 Kings 23: 34; 2 Chron. 36:44). **3** A priest who took part in the dedication of the wall of Jerusalem rebuilt by Nehemiah (Neh. 12:41). **4** The son of Abiud, listed in the postexilic genealogy of Jesus (Matt. 1:13). **5** The son of Melea, in Luke's genealogy of Jesus (Luke 3:30). ***See also*** Jehoiakim; Shebna. J.J.M.R.

Eliam (ee'lee-uhm; Heb., "God is kin" or "uncle"). **1** One of David's mighty men, the son of the Gilonite Ahithophel (2 Sam. 23:34). **2** The father of Bathsheba (2 Sam. 11:3), called Ammiel in 1 Chron. 3:5 (both names include the same components, but in reversed order).

Elias (ee-lī'uhs). ***See*** Elijah.

Eliasaph (e-lī'uh-saf; Heb., "El [God] has added"). **1** The head of the tribe of Gad during the wilderness wandering (Num. 1:14; 2:14). **2** A Levite, the head of the Gershonite clan who were in charge of carrying the fabrics of the tabernacle (Num. 3:24).

Eliashib (el-ī'uh-shib; Heb., "God restores"). **1** The head of a priestly division in the time of David (1 Chron. 24:12). **2** The son of Eshyahu and a high-ranking official at the late sixth-century B.C. fortress at Arad, where documents written to him have been found. **3** The name of three postexilic Israelites, including one levitical singer, who divorced their foreign wives in response to Ezra's proclamation (Ezra 10:24, 27, 36). **4** The father of Jehohanan in whose chamber Ezra spent a night (Ezra 10:6). **5** The Jerusalemite high priest in the time of Nehemiah who assisted in rebuilding a northwest section of the city wall (Neh. 3:1) and whose grandson married the daughter of Sanballat (Neh. 13:28; this may be the same as 3 and 4). **6** A priest responsible for the Temple chambers, who permitted an Ammonite to dwell there until he was expelled by Nehemiah (Neh. 13:4–8). **7** A late postexilic descendant of David through the line of Zerubbabel (1 Chron. 3:24). F.E.G.

Eliel (ee-lī'el; Heb., "God is my god"). **1** A Korahite ancestor of Samuel (1 Chron. 6:34, called Elihu in 1 Sam. 1:1 and perhaps Eliab in 1 Chron. 6:27). **2** A Levite from the family of Hebron whom David assigned to assist in bringing the Ark to Jerusalem (1 Chron. 15:4–15). **3** A Gaddite who joined David in the desert (1 Chron. 12:11, Hebrew v. 12). **4** The name of two of David's mighty men, one of them a Mahavite (1 Chron. 11:46–47). **5** A Temple official who assisted in the supervision of offerings during the reign of Hezekiah (2 Chron. 31:13). **6** The name of two Benjaminites, one the son of Shimei (1 Chron. 8:20), the other of Shashak (1 Chron. 8:22). **7** The head of a Transjordanian Manassite household deported by the Assyrian king Tiglath-pileser III (1 Chron. 5:24). F.E.G.

Eliezer (el-ee-ay'zuhr; Heb., "my God is help"). **1** Abraham's servant, who would have been his heir in place of a son (Gen. 15:2). Presumably, it is Eliezer who finds a wife for Isaac in Genesis 24. **2** Moses' second son, the founder of a levitical family (Exod. 18:4; 1 Chron. 23: 15–17; 26:25). **3** The son of Dodavahu, and a prophet who spoke against King Jehoshaphat's naval alliance with Ahaziah (2 Chron. 20:35–37). **4** The son of Becher (1 Chron. 7:8). **5** A priest (1 Chron. 15:24). **6** The son of Zichri, and a Reubenite chief (1 Chron. 27:16). **7** A leading man sent by Ezra to seek Levites for Temple service (Ezra 8:16). **8** Three men who divorced foreign wives (Ezra 10:18; 10:23; 10:31). **9** An ancestor of Jesus (Luke 3:29). M.A.S.

Elihu (ee-lī'hyo͞o), a young man who speaks to Job just prior to God's speeches from the whirlwind (Job 32–37). Claiming divine inspiration, Elihu merely repeats in other words the views of Job's three friends. Some scholars take Elihu's speeches as interpolations designed to provide the baffling book of Job with a more satisfactory answer. Assessment of these speeches generally turns on one's reading of the book as a whole. ***See also*** Job, The Book of.

Elijah (ee-lī'juh), an Israelite prophet in the times of kings Ahab and Ahaziah, during the first half of the ninth century B.C. Elijah is the protagonist of four stories in the book of Kings. **The Four Stories:** In the first story, 1 Kings 16: 29–19:18, Elijah declared a drought to punish the nation for its idolatry. At this time, Elijah himself hid and miraculously survived the famine. The drought ended in a contest between Elijah and the Baal prophets: the god who would answer his prophet's call with fire from heaven would be vindicated as the true god. Elijah won, Yahweh was vindicated, and Elijah's Baalite antagonists were slaughtered. Pursued by Queen Jezebel who sought vengeance for her protegés, Elijah fled to Horeb, reported to the Lord, and was commanded to anoint Hazael, Jehu, and Elisha, three new protagonists in the fight against Baal. This story, which is often considered one of the masterpieces of biblical narrative, was probably written in Judah during the reign of Manasseh, some two hundred years after the events portrayed. Its late composition is indicated by the adoption of a legend from Elisha's cycle (1 Kings 17:8–16, cf. 2 Kings 4:1–7), the adaptation of the royal annals of Samaria to the present plot (1 Kings 16:29–17:1, to which the end, 19:16–18, corresponds), the incorporation of Isaiah's concept of "the remnant" (1 Kings 19: 18) and the anachronistic detail about the persecution of prophets (1 Kings 18:4, 13, 22; 19:10, 14).

The second story involving Elijah, in 1 Kings 21, tells about the judicial murder of Naboth. The royal consort, who coveted his vineyard, had him judged and executed for blasphemy. Ahab then went to inherit the vineyard and was confronted by Elijah with a terrible prophecy of doom. It may be suggested that the present story was composed in the postexilic age, on the basis of its late diction and its being acquainted with all the legal corpora found in the Torah (cf. Exod. 22:27; Lev. 24:13–16; Num. 36:7–9; Deut. 19:15). An older, certainly more original, version is hinted at in 2 Kings 9:

Elijah (center) receives a dead child from his mourning mother (in black), revives the child, and returns it to his mother (right), who is now clad in the bright clothing of happiness (1 Kings 17:17–24); panel from the third-century A.D. synagogue at Dura-Europos.

25–26, 36–37. In spite of the many variations, the older version seems to confirm Elijah's important role in the Naboth affair.

In the third story (2 Kings 1:2–2:17) Ahaziah fell ill and sent to inquire of Baal-zebub of Ekron if he would recover. Elijah intervened and sent the messengers back to the king with a prophecy of doom that he himself reiterated when summoned to the king's presence. The derivative character of this prophetic legend, which twice let fire down from heaven in order to save Elijah, although he was in no danger at all, indicates late composition. This is confirmed by its late diction.

The fourth story dealing with Elijah (1 Kings 19:19–21; 2 Kings 2:1–18) relates how Elisha became Elijah's servant, followed him until his ascension to heaven, and then inherited two-thirds of his master's spirit. This story belongs to the Elisha cycle and contains a spurious tradition aimed at binding together two great prophets of the past. Originally, however, the two were quite distinct: while Elijah was a zealot of the Lord fighting against idolatry and injustice, Elisha was a wonder worker who saved Israel during the Aramean crisis. This story should therefore not be taken into account in the assessment of the tradition about Elijah.

Interpretation: The three reliable stories of the Elijah cycle, being all late, contain many of the theological concepts, historical notions, and literary tastes of the latest biblical writers. Nevertheless the traditions preserved in these stories are not altogether spurious, as proved by the comparison of the two versions of the Naboth incident and by the coherent description of Elijah as a zealot of the Lord fighting against Baal in the other two accounts. At the root of the present stories stood older ones, now lost. Due to the popularity of Elijah, stories about him were retold by each new generation so that only the later accounts were incorporated in the book of Kings.

Elijah came from the town of Tosabe in Gilead. His leather attire and his nomadic habits make it plausible that he belonged to a family of shepherds in Transjordan. This may explain his zeal in fighting Baal in both manifestations —Baal as god of the Israelite peasants, who credited him with the land's fertility, and Baal as god of the Phoenicians who was imported into Israel at that age.

The introduction of the Tyrian Baal into Israel during the Omride dynasty (882–842 B.C.) is a historical fact; it was brought about by the marriage of Ahab, son of Omri, to the Tyrian princess Jezebel. From its center in Samaria Baal worship spread out to the provincial towns, given impetus by the syncretistic concept of the Lord to whom the name of Baal and his attributes had been applied from old. In declaring a drought, Elijah challenged Baal in his very quality as a fertility god. A second challenge was contained in the contest with the Baal prophets, for here the real issue was who the true god of the storm was. The story in 2 Kings dwells on related matters: who is the right god to inquire oracles of? Who strikes and heals, gives death and life?

The outcome of the contest on Mt. Carmel is a monotheistic creed: the Lord is God! (1 Kings

18:39). This explicit belief of the seventh-century B.C. author was already intrinsic in the contest, because at first Israelite monotheism did not dwell on the otiose question of the mere existence of gods. The relevant questions were: who besides the Lord is judge (Ps. 82), savior (Deut. 32), bestower of rain and dew (1 Kings 17)? Who is able to answer invocation and prayer (1 Kings 18)? Thus Elijah's zeal for the Lord was the genuine expression of a well-rooted ancient monotheism.

The older version of the Naboth story, reflected in 2 Kings 9:25–26, 36–37, presents some significant variations also regarding the role of the prophet in the story. Elijah is mentioned only in v. 36, which makes his participation plausible, but not beyond doubt. The prophet did not use the messenger formula "Thus says the Lord," but pronounced an oath in the Lord's name, making the verdict irrevocable. Rebuke and doom were not independent of each other as in 1 Kings 21:19 but integrated together (2 Kings 9:26). The doom was expressed in more general terms—"I will requite you in this field"—which were later adapted to history (1 Kings 21:19b, 21–24). However, the most essential part of the prophet's message has been left unaltered: in both stories the prophet proclaims the verdict of the Lord, a supreme, omniscient judge who will requite in due time.

Elijah's role as fighter against Baal and injustice is taken up in 2 Chron. 21:12–15. The historicity of the letter mentioned there is doubtful. It is more appropriate to the time of the Second Temple (ca. fifth century B.C.), when pseudepigraphic prophecies were circulated. The mention of Elijah at the conclusion of the Torah-Prophets canon in Mal. 3:22–24 identifies him with the Lord's messenger (Heb. *mal'akh)* of Mal. 3:1, expected to purify the priesthood (vv. 2–3) and himself described as a priest and a teacher of Torah (Mal. 2:7). These relationships may thus help explain Elijah's role in connection with the observation of the Torah (3:22–23). As supreme teacher, he is expected to "reconcile fathers and sons." In the light of *Jubilees* 23:16–31, this expression must be understood as referring to the various religious sects emerging in Judaism at the beginning of the Hellenistic age.

In the NT, Elijah is identified in the popular mind with Jesus (Mark 6:15; 8:28) but Jesus identified John the Baptist as Elijah who was to return and restore all things (Mark 9:12). ***See also*** Elisha; Prophet. A.R.

Elim (ee'lim), the second stopping place (after Marah) of the Israelites after they crossed the "sea of reeds" (Heb., *yam suph;* Exod. 15:27; Num. 33:9). This oasis was reported to have twelve springs and seventy palm trees. Because Exod. 15:22–27 and Num. 33:8–9 suggest that the Israelites camped there soon after leaving Egypt but prior to reaching the Wilderness of Sin (Exod. 16:1; Num. 33:10–11), Elim is frequently identified with the Wadi Gharandel, about sixty-three miles southeast of Suez in the western Sinai, which today has fresh water, palm trees, and tamarisks. ***See also*** Exodus. J.M.W.

Elimelech (e-lim'e-lek), an Ephrathite clan member who emigrated to Moab when a great famine broke out in Bethlehem of Judah during the period of the judges (Ruth 1:2–3; 2:1, 3; 4:3, 9). After his death, his two sons married local women. The ensuing story is narrated in the book named after Ruth, one of Elimelech's daughters-in-law. The story tells how, despite the death of all male members of his family, Elimelech's estate in Bethlehem remained in the family's hands through Ruth's brilliant maneuvering. The name in Hebrew may mean either "my God is sovereign," "the Divine King," or "my God is Milku." J.M.S.

Elioenai (el-ee-oh-ee'nī; a shortened form of Eliehoenai, Heb., "my eyes are toward God"). **1** A Judahite, descendant of the kings of Judah through David (1 Chron. 3:23–24). **2** A family leader in the tribe of Simeon (1 Chron. 4:36). **3** A Benjaminite of the clan of Becher (1 Chron. 7:8). **4** A Levite of the priestly clan of Pashur. He was condemned by Ezra for taking a foreign wife (Ezra 10:22) and may be the same priest who served in postexilic Jerusalem (Neh. 12:41). **5** A member of the clan of Zattu, likewise condemned by Ezra (Ezra 10:27).

Eliphaz (el'i-faz). **1** The eldest son of Esau and father of several Edomite clans, including Teman (Gen. 36:15–16). **2** The first and, presumably, oldest of Job's three friends (Job 2:11; 4:1; 15:1; 22:1; 42:7, 9). Assuming Job's basic piety, he urged submission. Eliphaz's designation, the Temanite, suggests he was from the area settled by the Edomite clan mentioned above. ***See also*** Job, The Book of.

Eliphelet (e-lif'e-let; Heb., possibly "God's deliverance" or "the divine deliverer"). **1** David's last son, born in Jerusalem to a nameless wife or concubine (2 Sam. 5:16). The repetition of the name in 1 Chron. 3:6 and 8 is difficult to explain (cf. 1 Chron. 14:5, 7). **2** One of David's strong men, son of Ahasbai (2 Sam. 23:34). The author of Chronicles may have named him Eliphal, son of Ur (1 Chron. 11:35). **3** A descendant of Saul and Jonathan, the third son of Eshek (1 Chron. 8:39). **4** The son of Adonikam, a leader returned from the Babylonian exile (Ezra 8:13; 1 Esd. 8:39). **5** The son of Hashum, husband of a foreign woman (Ezra 10:33; 1 Esd. 9:33). J.M.S.

Elisha (ee-lī'shuh; Heb., "El [God] is salvation"), a prophet of the northern kingdom of

Israel who was active for a period of some fifty years (ca. 850–800 B.C.) during the reigns of Joram, Jehu, Jehoahaz, and Jehoash (Joash). The successor and disciple of Elijah, Elisha is remembered in the biblical stories as a man of wisdom and a worker of miracles both on behalf of his nation in times of crisis and in the lives of individuals in time of need.

Elisha was a farmer who lived with his parents at Abel-meholah (location uncertain; 1 Kings 19:16–21). Since he was plowing with twelve pairs of oxen when Elijah met him, scholars have suggested that his father was a wealthy landowner. Elisha was bald (2 Kings 2: 23) and carried a staff, which was common to rural residents and aided travel in the rugged hills of Palestine (2 Kings 4:29). However, unlike Elijah who lived in caves in the desert, Elisha stayed in the cities (2 Kings 6:13, 19, 32). He was provided comfortable guest quarters by a wealthy woman of Shunem (2 Kings 4:8–10) and apparently maintained his own house at Samaria (2 Kings 6:32; cf. 2:25; 5:3). He often appears in the company of groups of prophets ("the sons of the prophets"; 2 Kings 2:3–15; 4: 1; 5:22; 9:1), and he frequented religious centers such as Bethel (2 Kings 2:23), Gilgal (2:1; 4: 38), and Mount Carmel (2:25; 4:25). His actions, notably using his staff as an instrument of activity (2 Kings 4:29; cf. Exod. 4:2–5) and using music to induce a prophetic trance (2 Kings 3:15; cf. 1 Sam. 10:5–7), recall an older era of prophets represented by Moses and Samuel.

Elisha, in the dark robe, with Naaman, captain of the king of Aram's host (cf. 2 Kings 5); from the Amiens Picture Bible, Spain, 1197.

Since Elisha left no written works of his own, the Elisha narratives (2 Kings 2–9; 13:14–21) reflect oral traditions about the prophet that first circulated independently among the people and were later (700 B.C.?) reduced to written records. Because of their roots in oral tradition, these narratives (and those of Elijah) are concerned not so much with a static presentation of historical facts as with a retelling of the significance of events that swirled around this prophetic figure in relation to the faith of Israel. In their present form, the narratives consist of loosely collected anecdotes about the prophet interwoven with historical sketches of the period. Taken together, these on one level portray a figure who, through the telling and retelling of his story among the people, has been cast in near legendary terms; but on another level they demonstrate the sovereignty and power of God at work in spite of the political schemings and the personal crises of a nation.

Personal and Political Dimensions: Elisha's work within Israel involved two areas: personal and political. As a man easily accessible to the people, he frequently interceded in the ordinary events of life that bring anguish and crisis. The purification of a vital spring (2 Kings 2:19–22), the raising of the Shunammite's only son (4: 18–37), the provision of an antidote for the poisonous stew (4:38–41), the healing of Naaman's leprosy (5:1–19; cf. Luke 4:27), and the recovery of a borrowed axe head (6:1–7) not only demonstrate Elisha's ministry on a personal level but also show the power of God over all aspects of nature, an indirect challenge to the worship of Baal. Similarly, the increase of the widow's oil (2 Kings 4:1–7), the multiplication of grain (4: 42–44), and the restoration of the Shunammite's land (8:1–6) demonstrate God's power in the economic and social spheres.

But Elisha's greatest work was on a political level. In accepting the hairy mantle of Elijah, Elisha also accepted the commission of Elijah. As his master had been deeply involved in the politics of his day, so Elisha went on to complete the tasks assigned to Elijah (1 Kings 19: 15–16; 2 Kings 8:7–15; 9:1–10) and became constantly involved in the affairs of the nation. He provided water to a thirsty army (2 Kings 3: 4–20), was instrumental in routing the Moabites (3:21–27), warned the king of enemy plans more than once (6:8–12), helped avert disaster at the hands of the Syrians (6:13–7:23), was involved in the overthrow of Ben-hadad of Damascus (8:7–15) and Jehu of Israel (9:1–13; see also 9:14–36), and from his deathbed prophesied Joash's defeat of the Syrians (13:14 –19).

While Elisha was often termed a patriot, like

Elijah, much of his political involvement was directed at bringing the apostate monarchy back to a recognition of God's sovereignty in the world. While some of the Elisha narratives are often challenged from a modern ethical and theological perspective as not in harmony with true Israelite belief (e.g., 2 Kings 2:23–25), together they fill an important theological role within the framework of the book of Kings in demonstrating that every facet of life is subject to God's control. ***See also*** Abel-meholah; Baal; Elijah; Kings, The First and Second Books of the; Prophet. D.R.B.

Elishah (el'ee-shah). **1** The son of Javan (Greece) in Gen. 10:4 and 1 Chron. 1:7. **2** An island producing valuable dyed goods in Ezek. 27:7. This suggests that Elishah is Cyprus, which was known as *Alashia* in cuneiform (i.e., Babylonian and Assyrian) sources.

Elishama (e-lish'uh-muh; Heb., "El [God] has heard"). **1** The son of Ammihud; the leader of the tribe of Ephraim during the wilderness wandering (Num. 1:10; 10:22). **2** A son of David born in Jerusalem (2 Sam. 5:16). Another list of David's sons gives a second son named Elishama (1 Chron. 3:5–8), but comparison with a third list (1 Chron. 14:4–7) reveals that the repeated name in 1 Chron. 3:6 is probably a scribal error for Elishua, otherwise omitted. **3** A descendant of David and the grandfather of Ishmael, the leader of a group who assassinated Gedeliah (2 Kings 25:25; Jer. 41:1–3). **4** A descendant of Judah (1 Chron. 2:41). **5** A priest during the reign of Jehoshaphat who taught the people about the law (2 Chron. 17:8). **6** The royal scribe of King Jehoiakim of Judah (Jer. 36:12). D.R.B.

Elizabeth (KJV: "Elisabeth"), according to Luke 1:5–80, the wife of Zechariah and mother of John the Baptist. Luke describes her as coming from a priestly family. Her long period of barrenness connects her with earlier women in Israel such as Sarah (Gen. 17:15–21; 18:9–15; 21: 1–7) and Hannah (1 Sam. 1:1–20), who gave birth to children who would be important for new eras in Israel's history.

After Elizabeth's five-month period of seclusion, the news that she would have a child was given to her "kinswoman" Mary at the annunciation. Mary then visited Elizabeth. Although, according to Luke, it was Mary who visited Elizabeth, it was also Mary who was honored by Elizabeth's prophecy that she would be the mother of the Lord. Thus, for Luke, just as John the Baptist would be subordinate to Jesus, so also was John's mother subordinate to Mary. ***See also*** Annunciation; Hannah; John the Baptist; Mary, The Virgin; Sarah; Zechariah. A.J.M.

Elizaphan (el-ee-zay'fuhn; Heb., "El [God] protects"). **1** A Levite, the son of Uzziel; a clan leader of the Kohathites who were in charge of the utensils of the tabernacle (Num. 3:30); he is probably the same person referred to elsewhere as Elzaphan (Exod. 6:22; Lev. 10:4). **2** A levitical family group ("sons of Elizaphan") headed by Shemaiah who helped bring the Ark of the Covenant to Jerusalem during the reign of King David (1 Chron. 15:8). The same family group later took part in the cleansing of the Temple during the reforms of Hezekiah (2 Chron. 29:13). **3** The son of Parnach; a leader of the tribe of Zebulun who supervised the apportionment of land within the tribe (Num. 34:25). D.R.B.

Elizur (e-lī'zuhr; Heb., "El [God] is Rock"), the leader of the tribe of Reuben during the wilderness wanderings (Num. 1:5; 10:18).

Elkanah (el-kay'nah; Heb., "God created [the fetus]"), the name of five men in the Bible. The best known is Samuel's father, who favored his infertile wife Hannah, whom God eventually pitied and allowed to bear a son (1 Sam. 1–2).

Ellasar (el-lah'suhr), the home country or city of King Arioch (Gen. 14:1, 9). The identification of Ellasar is uncertain but there are three major claimants. **1** Larsa, a city in southern Babylonia that flourished ca. 2025–1763 B.C. **2** A city in middle Mesopotamia: either Til-Asurri, located about twenty-five miles south-southeast of the junction of the Euphrates and Chabur rivers or Al-Assur located on the Tigris River. **3** A district in eastern Asia Minor: either Cappadocia (as in the Qumran *Genesis Apocryphon* 21:23) or its northern neighbor, Pontus (as in the Greek translation by Symmachus and the Vulgate). The first identification seems likely if Shinar, the home of Amraphel (Gen. 14:1, 9), ultimately derives from the Sinjar Mountains of middle Mesopotamia. J.G.G.

Elnathan (el-nay'thuhn; Heb., "God has given"). **1** A Judean royal official who was sent to Egypt to fetch the prophet Uriah (Jer. 26:22) and later protested the king's burning of Jeremiah's scroll (Jer. 36:25); he may also have been the same as **2** The father of Nehushta, whose son Jehoiachin became king of Judah (2 Kings 24:8). **3** Several leading figures in the time of Ezra (Ezra 8:16).

Elohim (e-loh-heem'). ***See*** El; Names of God in the Old Testament.

Elohist (el'oh-ist), the name given one of the sources found in the books of Genesis through Numbers. The siglum given the source is "E," which is derived from its use of the name Elohim for God prior to the revealing of the name Yahweh to Moses (Exod. 3:13–15). While it is more difficult, compared to the case of other sources discerned in the Pentateuch, to recognize this as a continuous and independent source, most scholars at least see in it expansions and revisions of the Yahwistic passages (the "J" source). An eighth- or ninth-century B.C. date is usually suggested. The locale for this source is undoubtedly prophetic circles in the north since there is considerable concern with idolatry, worship, and charismatic leadership. The source begins with the call of Abraham (Gen. 12) and therefore does not have a primeval history. Among the passages most prominently mentioned as Elohistic are Gen. 22:1–19; 40:1–23; and Exod. 20:1–26. ***See also*** Abraham; E; El; Sources of the Pentateuch. K.H.R.

eloi, eloi, lama sabachthani. ***See*** Eli, Eli, Lema Sabachthani.

Elon (ee'lahn; Heb., "oak," "terebinth"). **1** A Hittite, father of Basemath, a wife of Esau (Gen. 26:34). **2** A "minor judge" for ten years, of the tribe of Zebulun, buried at Aijalon (Judg. 12:11, 12). **3** A town of the tribe of Dan (Josh. 19:43). **4** A son of Zebulun in the clan lists of Gen. 46:14 and Num. 26:26.

Eloth (ee'luhth), a place name that means in Hebrew "a grove of large trees," usually referring to the terebinth tree or the palm. It is also another name for Elath, an important port city located at the end of the northeast arm of the Red Sea, the modern Gulf of Aqabah. The site was passed by the Israelites as they left Egypt (Deut. 2:8) and later expanded by Solomon into a trading port (1 Kings 9:26–28). It was apparently destroyed by Edom (2 Kings 8:20–21), later rebuilt by Uzziah (2 Chron. 26:2), and again lost permanently to Edom (or Syria?) during the reign of Ahaz (2 Kings 16:6). Some scholars identify Eloth/Elath as a later name for Ezion-geber, while others maintain that they are two distinct sites (2 Chron. 8:17). ***See also*** Ezion-geber. D.R.B.

El Shaddai (el shad'ī), a name that God used to reveal himself to the patriarchs in the Priestly source of the Pentateuch. Outside of the passages Gen. 17:1; 28:3; 35:11; 43:14; 48:3; and Exod. 6:3, it occurs only in Ezek. 10:5. El Shaddai is like other Hebrew names of God in Genesis beginning with the element *el*, "God," plus a substantive or adjective, e.g., El Olam ("the Everlasting God"), El Elyon ("God most High"), El Elohe Yisrael ("El the God of Israel"). The etymology of *Shaddai* is not certain; "God, the One of the mountain" is plausible, the mountain being the divine residence. R.J.C.

Elul (e-lo͞ol'), the postexilic (late sixth century B.C. on) name of the sixth month of the year (August/September), which is the twelfth month of the older civil calendar, when vintage begins. ***See also*** Time.

Elymas (el'i-muhs), a Jewish magician (also called Bar-Jesus) associated with Sergius Paulus, the Roman proconsul of Cyprus. He opposed Paul's preaching, but he was blinded, and the proconsul believed (Acts 13:6–12). ***See also*** Magic and Divination; Paulus, Sergius.

embalming, a technique used by the Egyptians to preserve the bodies of humans and certain animals. The most important steps in the procedure were removing the visceral organs, dehydrating the body by immersing it for up to seventy days in a "bath" of dry natron salt, applying various spices and unguents, and wrapping the body in clean linen. Both Jacob (Gen. 50:2–3) and Joseph (Gen. 50:26) were embalmed; the treatment for Jacob is said to have taken forty days (the number forty being one of the symbolic numbers in the OT). ***See also*** Numbers.

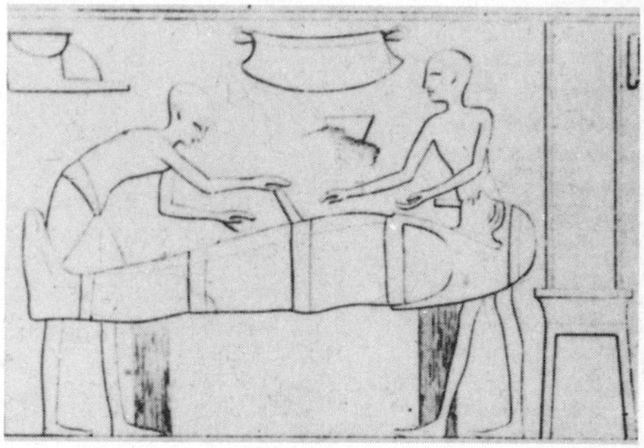

Embalmers wrapping a body in linen bandages; detail from an Egyptian tomb painting (ca. 1350–1200 B.C.).

embroidery. ***See*** Needlework.

emerods (em'uhr-awds), an archaic term for hemorrhoids. It is used in the KJV where RSV has "tumors" (1 Sam. 6:11, 17) or "boils" (Deut. 28:27). This illness afflicted the Philistines while they held the Ark of the Covenant (1 Sam. 5:6–6:5).

Emmanuel (em-man'yo͞o-el). ***See*** Immanuel.

Emmaus (eh-may'uhs; Heb., "warm wells"), a town of disputed location that figures in the postresurrection story of Luke 24:13–35. Most manuscripts place it about seven miles (sixty *stadia*) from Jerusalem, but others and the ancient Palestinian tradition prefer about twenty miles (160 *stadia*). A town named Emmaus stood at the latter distance in the Valley of Ajalon in the time of the Maccabees (1 Macc. 3:40, 57; 4:1–15), where Judas defeated Gorgias. Bacchides, a Syrian general, later fortified the site (1 Macc. 9:50). A Roman villa, two Byzantine churches and a baptistry, and a Crusader church

have been excavated there. Other sites closer to the shorter distance that have been identified with Emmaus since Crusader times are Abu-Ghosh, Qaloniyeh, and Motsa west of Jerusalem, as well as el-Qubeibeh to its northwest. None of these sites, however, has any ancient literary attestation of the name of Emmaus. Anyone familiar with Palestinian bedouin or Arabs in a pre-automotive culture would not doubt the disciples' ability to walk forty miles in a day.
C.H.M.

encampment, or camp, apart from references in the Pentateuch, a military enclosure (Josh. 8: 13; 1 Sam. 13:1; 17:20, KJV: "trench"; 26:5). The Hebrew term translated camp *(maḥaneh)* derives from a verb meaning "to bend, to curve" *(ḥnh)*, suggesting an encampment's circular form, a meaning mirrored in the Greek *parembolē*, which translates *maḥaneh* in the Septuagint (LXX) and is used in reference to the Roman garrison in Jerusalem (e.g., Acts 21:34). The term is used symbolically once in the NT (Rev. 20:9) in reference to the church militant. In the Pentateuch the noun translated is *ṭîrâh*, which suggests a tribal encampment protected by stone walls (Gen. 25:16; Num. 31:10, KJV: "castle"). Outside the Pentateuch this noun appears in 1 Chron. 6:54 (KJV: "castle"); Ps. 69:25 (KJV: "habitation"); and Ezek. 25:4 (KJV: "palaces").
F.S.F.

enchantment. ***See*** Magic and Divination.

En-dor (ayn-dohr'; Heb., "spring of circle," "habitation," or "generation"), a Canaanite city belonging to Manasseh (according to Josh. 17: 11–12). It was situated about three miles southwest of Mt. Tabor. In a famous episode (1 Sam. 28:3–25) on the eve of King Saul's fatal defeat by the Philistines at Gilboa, he journeyed there to enjoin its medium to raise up Samuel from the dead. En-dor is also mentioned as the site of the defeat of Midian by Gideon (Ps. 83:10). ***See also*** Magic and Divination; Saul.
J.U.

En-gannim (en-gahn-eem'; Heb., "fountain of gardens"). **1** A town belonging to the allotment of Judah, located in the lowlands (Josh. 15:34). The literary context would indicate that it is in the region near Azekah and Jarmuth. **2** A border town between Issachar and Manasseh (Josh. 19: 21; 21:29). It may be the "garden house" of 2 Kings 9:27. However, in both circumstances, the specific location of the site is undetermined.

En-gedi (en-gee'dee; Heb., "spring of the young goat"), an important oasis, with fresh water and hot springs, on the west shore of the Dead Sea near its center, about eighteen miles southeast of Hebron. It was part of the allotment of Judah (Josh. 15:62). Archaeological interest in En-gedi began in 1949 with a trial dig at Tell el Jurn.

The spring that feeds the pool at En-gedi, an oasis near the Dead Sea.

More recently the work of Hebrew University excavations in 1961–64 has yielded some interesting finds. The earliest settlement (Stratum V) appears to be from the period of Josiah up to the destruction of Jerusalem (ca. 639–587 B.C.). The settlement was completely destroyed and a new settlement built in the Persian period, probably in the time of Zerubbabel (mid sixth century B.C.) (Stratum VI). The romance and beauty of the site, which is a modern-day tourist attraction, is evident in Hebrew Scriptures (Song of Sol. 1:14; cf. Ecclus. 24:14).
S.B.R.

engines of war, the machinery for warfare, which could be used for either offensive or defensive purposes. Offensively, battering rams were used quite effectively by armies campaigning in Palestine. Graphic examples of fortified battering rams are given in the Assyrian king Sennacherib's palace reliefs depicting the siege of Lachish (701 B.C.; 2 Kings 18:13–14). Variations of this siege machine were used by the Babylonians and the Romans. Defensively, catapults were used to hurl stones from battlements on city walls. According to the Chronicler, King Uzziah had catapults in some of his fortified cities for hurling stones and for shooting arrows (2 Chron. 26:15). In open-field warfare chariots were well known and extensively used. Like the battering ram, they required support troops for maximum effectiveness.
J.A.D.

English Bible, the. The earliest written translation of any part of the Bible into English may have been made by the Venerable Bede, who died in 735, but none of his translation has survived. The *Wessex Gospels*, of the tenth century, are the oldest surviving Old English translation of the Gospels. The first translation of the whole Bible, in 1382, is credited to John Wycliffe (1324–1384), "The Morning Star of the Reformation." His translation work was part of his larger task of reforming the church. It is not certain, however, how great a part Wycliffe himself played in this version or in the second one, which appeared after his death in 1384. Both were made from the Vulgate (Vg), but the second one was less a word-for-word equivalent of the Latin than the first one. Wycliffe was denounced as a heretic; in 1415 his Bible was condemned and burned, and in 1428 his body was exhumed and burned.

From Tyndale to King James: William Tyndale (1484–1536), "The Father of the English Bible," wanted to make the Scriptures available to all: "I had perceived by experience how that it was impossible to establish the lay people in any truth, except that the scriptures were plainly laid before their eyes in their mother tongue, that they might see the process, order, and meaning of the text." Unable to get permission from church or Parliament to do his translation in England, he went to the Continent, where in February 1526 his NT, translated from the Greek, was printed. Copies of it soon arrived in England, where they were publicly burned by Cuthbert Tunstall, bishop of London. Tyndale continued his work of translating the OT from the Hebrew; the Pentateuch (Gen. through Deut.) was published in 1530, and Jonah followed. Tyndale was arrested in May 1535 and imprisoned in a fortress in Vilvorde, six miles north of Brussels. In August 1536 he was tried and found guilty of heresy, and on October 6, 1536, he was strangled and burned at the stake. His last words were, "Lord, open the King of England's eyes." The king was Henry VIII.

Readers of the English Bible owe more to Tyndale than to any other person in history. It is estimated that eighty percent of the King James (KJV) NT is Tyndale's work, and his influence is seen also in the OT. "Tyndale's honesty, sincerity, and scrupulous integrity, his simple directness, his magical simplicity of phrase, his modest music, have given authority to his wording that has imposed itself on all later versions" (J. Isaacs, "The Sixteenth-Century English Versions," in H. W. Robinson, ed., *The Bible in Its Ancient and English Versions*, p. 180).

Before Tyndale's death a complete Bible in English, edited by Miles Coverdale (1488–1569), was published on the Continent. It was dedicated to Henry VIII, and the NT was essen-

A manuscript copy, ca. 1420, of the NT of Wycliffe's Bible. John Wycliffe (1324–1384) is credited with the first translation of the whole Bible into English.

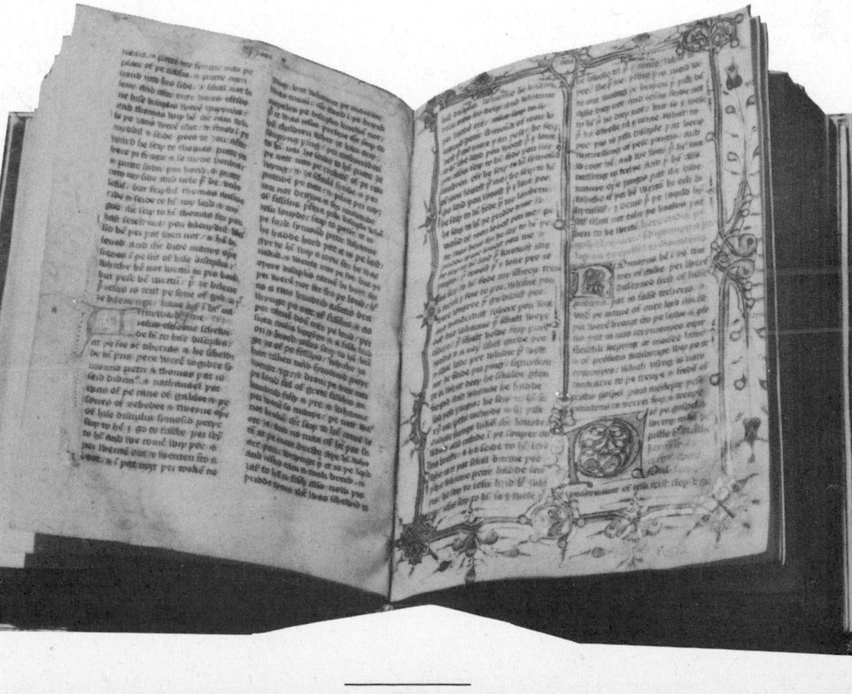

THE ENGLISH BIBLE: FROM THE EARLIEST TRANSLATIONS TO TODAY

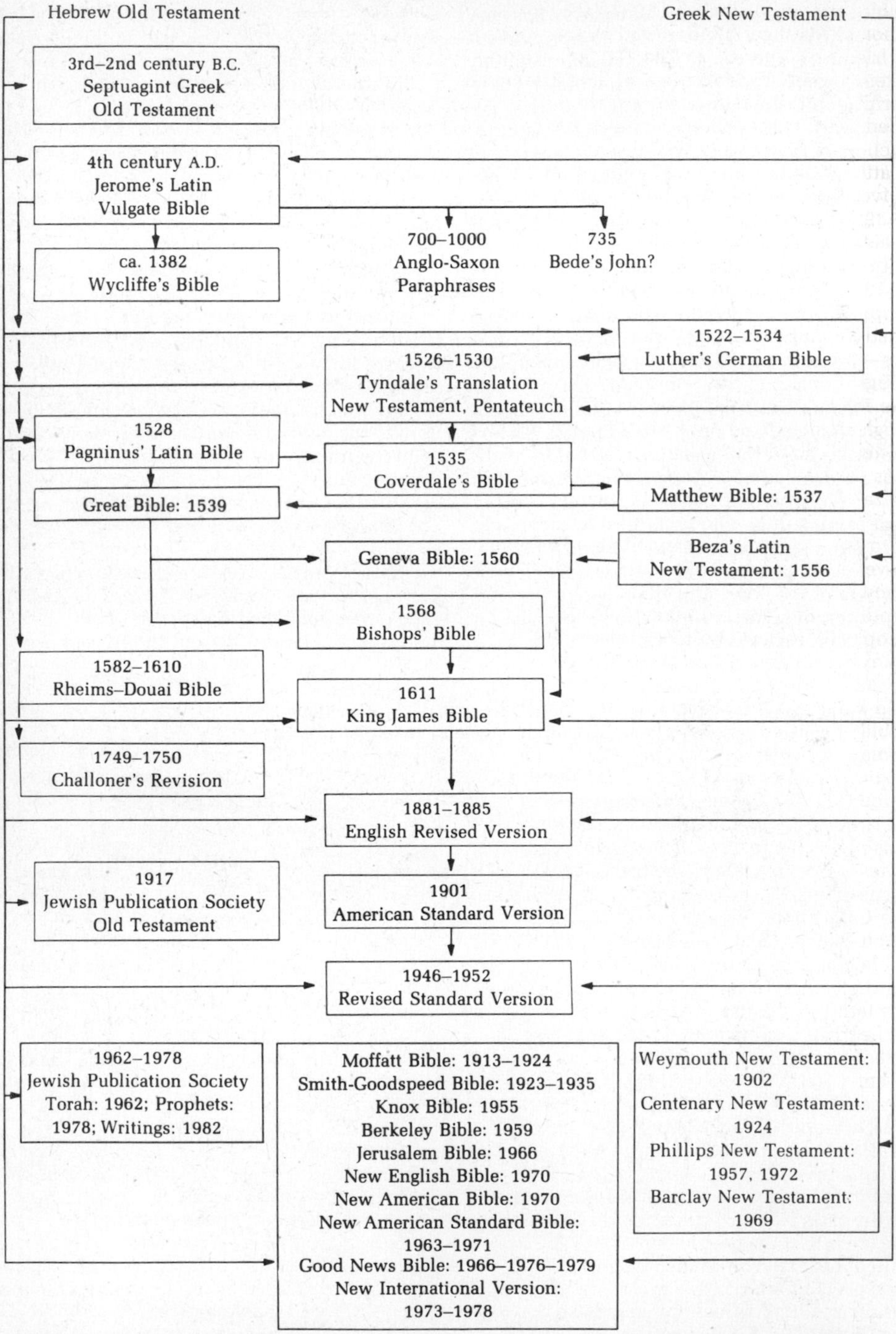
Hebrew Old Testament
Greek New Testament
3rd–2nd century B.C. Septuagint Greek Old Testament
4th century A.D. Jerome's Latin Vulgate Bible
ca. 1382 Wycliffe's Bible
700–1000 Anglo-Saxon Paraphrases
735 Bede's John?
1522–1534 Luther's German Bible
1526–1530 Tyndale's Translation New Testament, Pentateuch
1528 Pagninus' Latin Bible
1535 Coverdale's Bible
Matthew Bible: 1537
Great Bible: 1539
Geneva Bible: 1560
Beza's Latin New Testament: 1556
1568 Bishops' Bible
1582–1610 Rheims–Douai Bible
1611 King James Bible
1749–1750 Challoner's Revision
1881–1885 English Revised Version
1917 Jewish Publication Society Old Testament
1901 American Standard Version
1946–1952 Revised Standard Version
1962–1978 Jewish Publication Society Torah: 1962; Prophets: 1978; Writings: 1982
Moffatt Bible: 1913–1924
Smith-Goodspeed Bible: 1923–1935
Knox Bible: 1955
Berkeley Bible: 1959
Jerusalem Bible: 1966
New English Bible: 1970
New American Bible: 1970
New American Standard Bible: 1963–1971
Good News Bible: 1966–1976–1979
New International Version: 1973–1978
Weymouth New Testament: 1902
Centenary New Testament: 1924
Phillips New Testament: 1957, 1972
Barclay New Testament: 1969

Source: American Bible Society

tially a revision of Tyndale's translation; Coverdale made use also of Tyndale's translation of portions of the OT. The first authorized Bible was published in 1537, the so-called Thomas Matthew Bible, edited by John Rogers, a friend of Tyndale's. The NT and the Pentateuch were Tyndale's work, and his manuscripts of Joshua through 2 Chronicles were used. The "Great Bible" (its pages were 9 × 15 inches) of 1539 was Coverdale's revision of the Matthew Bible, and it was enthusiastically received by Tunstall, now bishop of Durham. In 1539 a lawyer, Richard Taverner, published a revision of the Matthew Bible.

In the reign of "Bloody Mary" Tudor (1553–1558) all printing of English Bibles in England stopped, and the English Bible could not be used in church services. Many Protestant leaders—perhaps as many as eight hundred—sought refuge on the Continent. The pastor of the English Church in Geneva, William Whittingham, translated the NT (1557) and served as editor of the OT translation. The whole Bible was published in 1560 and dedicated to Queen Elizabeth, who had begun to reign in 1558. It was printed in Roman type, bound in small octavo size, and was the first Bible in English to have verse numbers. The Geneva Bible (also known as the "Breeches Bible," because of its rendition of Gen. 3:7) became the Bible of the people: it was the Bible of Shakespeare and of Bunyan; of the pilgrims to the New World, and of the Mayflower Compact; of Oliver Cromwell and his army, for whom the "Soldier's Pocket Bible" was published in 1643. It was the first Bible published in Scotland (1579) and was dedicated to James VI, King of Scotland. It ran through 140 editions, and remained popular for nearly a hundred years. The last edition was published in 1644. Its extremely Protestant notes were offensive to the bishops, but its immense success showed up the inadequacy of the Great Bible. A revision of the Great Bible, published in 1568, was named "The Bishops' Bible" because of the great number of bishops on the committee. In 1570 the Convocation of Canterbury ordered it to be placed in all the cathedrals, thus making it the second Authorized Version in England. It went through twenty editions before 1606, but did not replace the Geneva Bible in popular esteem.

The KJV and Its Revisions: When James VI of Scotland ascended to the throne of England as James I in 1603, there were two competing Bibles in the realm: the Bishops' Bible, preferred by the church authorities, and the Geneva Bible, the favorite of the people. In January 1604 James called a conference of theologians and churchmen at Hampton Court "for the hearing, and for the determining, things pretended to be amiss in the Church." A Puritan leader, John Reynolds, president of Corpus Christi College of Oxford, proposed that a new translation be made, to replace the two Bibles. The King, who had an amateur's interest in Bible translation, gave his approval, and on February 10, 1604, he ordered that "a translation be made of the whole Bible, as consonant as can be to the original Hebrew and Greek, and this is to be set out and printed without any marginal notes and only to be used in all Churches of England in time of Divine Service." Fifty-four "learned men" were organized into six panels: three for the OT, two for the NT, and one for the Apocrypha. Fifteen rules were drawn up to guide their work, the first one of which was: "The ordinary Bible read in the Church, commonly called the *Bishops' Bible*, to be followed, and as little altered as the truth of the original will permit." Rule 6 stipulated that no marginal notes be affixed "but only for the Explanation of the *Hebrew* or *Greek Words*, which cannot without some circumlocution, so briefly and fitly be express'd in the text." Rule 14 specified that "when they agree better with the Text than the Bishops' Bible" the following translations were to be used: Tyndale, Matthew, Coverdale, Whitchurch (that is, the Great Bible), and Geneva.

The translation was published in 1611 and very rapidly went through several editions, nearly all of which had some changes in the text. The most careful and comprehensive revision was published in 1769, the work of Benjamin Blayney, of Oxford, who spent nearly fourteen years on the task. Although never formally authorized by King or Parliament, the name "The Authorized Version" became attached to it, and that is how it is known in Great Britain.

There were some fierce critics of the new Bible, notably the eminent Hebrew scholar Hugh Broughton, who had not been invited to work on it. He himself was preparing a Bible, based on the Geneva Bible, but did not live long enough to see it published. It took nearly forty years for the KJV to replace the Geneva Bible in the affection of the people; once established, however, it became the Bible of English-speaking peoples for over 350 years, down to the present time.

In 1870 the Church of England authorized a revision of the KJV. Fifty-four scholars were appointed, most of them Anglicans, but including Methodists, Presbyterians, Congregationalists, Baptists, and one Unitarian. Americans were invited to participate, by correspondence, with the proviso that an American edition not be published until fourteen years after the publication of the British edition. The work was carefully, not to say pedantically, done, and in the NT alone about 30,000 changes were made, over 5,000 of them on the basis of a better Greek text. The NT, published in May 1881, was greeted with wild enthusiasm. The complete text was published in special Sunday supplements (May 22) of the Chicago *Tribune* and the Chicago *Times*. The complete Bible appeared in 1885, with an appendix which listed the changes preferred by the American scholars. The *American Standard Edition* of the Revised Version was published in 1901. Neither the English nor the American Version replaced the KJV in church and private usage.

The latest, and probably the last, Bible in the Tyndale–King James tradition, is the *Revised Standard Version* (RSV), authorized in 1937 by the International Council of Religious Education. The NT was published in 1946, the OT in 1952, and the Apocrypha in 1957. In 1977 an Expanded Edition appeared: in addition to the books considered deuterocanonical by Roman Catholics, it includes also 3 and 4 Maccabees and Psalm 151, from the canon of the Septuagint (LXX), thus making this Bible acceptable to Eastern Orthodox Churches. The RSV is not so much a new translation as it is a revision which sought to preserve the language of the KJV where that language could still be understood by modern readers. Where it could not, the RSV expresses the thought in contemporary language. The "Preface" published in most copies of the RSV gives an extensive account of these matters.

Mention should be made of John Wesley's revision of the KJV NT (1755) "for plain unlettered men who understand only their Mother Tongue." In 1833 Noah Webster published a complete KJV in which he corrected some 150 words and phrases that were either misleading or wrong. In Matt. 23:24 he correctly identified "strain at a gnat" as a printer's error and corrected it to "strain out a gnat." *The New King James Bible* (Thomas Nelson, 1982), falsely claiming to be "the first major revision of the KJV since 1867," claims to "unlock the spiritual treasures found uniquely in the King James Version of the Holy Scriptures."

Versions Independent of the KJV: Many Bibles and perhaps as many as 250 NTs in English have appeared since 1611. Only a few can be mentioned here. In 1862 Robert Young, an Edinburgh bookseller best known for his exhaustive *Analytical Concordance to the Bible,* produced a literal translation, which is practically a word-for-word equivalent of the original. Charles Thomson, Secretary of the Continental Congress, began his work of translating the LXX and the NT after retiring at age sixty from politics and business. It took him almost twenty years to complete his work (1808) and he holds the distinction of producing the first English NT to be translated and published in America, as well as the first English translation of the LXX (see John H. P. Reumann, *The Romance of Bible Scripts and Scholars,* pp. 122–144). Ferrar Fenton, an English businessman, translated the NT in 1895 and the whole Bible in 1903; his translation enjoyed considerable success, and as late as 1944 a new edition was published. He claimed his translation was the most accurate ever made, "not only in words, but in editing, spirit, and sense."

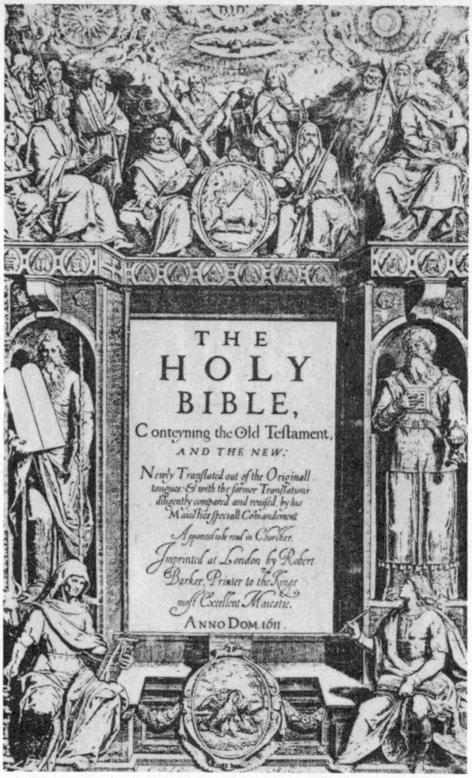

Title page from the first edition of the King James Bible, 1611.

Modern Translations: The modern era in Bible translation began with the *Twentieth Century* NT of 1901–2. The translators—mostly laymen and laywomen—did a remarkable job of producing a scholarly and faithful translation into clear and idiomatic English. One of the consultants of the group was Richard Francis Weymouth, a London classical scholar who in 1866 published an edition of the Greek NT. His translation of this text was published posthumously in 1902. But it was the Scottish scholar James Moffatt whose *New Testament: A New Translation* (1913) had the greatest impact upon the reading public. His translation of the OT appeared in 1924, and the whole Bible was revised in 1935. Moffatt was at work translating the Apocrypha when he died in 1944. Ernest J. Goodspeed was the American counterpart of Moffatt. His NT was published in 1923; the OT, translated by a panel headed by J. M. Powis Smith, was published with the Goodspeed NT in 1935 as *The Bible, an American Translation.* In 1938 Goodspeed translated the deuterocanonicals, and *The Complete Bible: an American Translation* came out in 1939.

Many major translations of the Bible into English have appeared in the United States and Great Britain in the last thirty years: Monsignor

Ronald Knox's translation of the Bible from the Vg (1955); the Jehovah's Witnesses' *New World Translation of the Holy Scriptures* (1961); *The Jerusalem Bible*, the English version of *La Bible de Jérusalem* (1966), which has the most comprehensive and scholarly readers' helps of any Bible in English at this time; the *New American Bible* (1970), the first Catholic Bible in English translated from the original Hebrew and Greek texts; *The New English Bible* (1970), a new translation, rather than a revision of earlier translations, produced by a group of scholars from the British Isles that included experts in both Bible and English literature; the *Good News Bible* (1976), sponsored by the American Bible Society (edition with deuterocanonicals, 1979); and the *New Jewish Version*, a translation of the Hebrew Scriptures by American Jewish scholars (1982).

The RSV was condemned as unfaithful by the vast majority of American conservatives, and several translations have been made with the purpose of providing conservatives a translation they would accept, such as the *Amplified Bible* (1965), the *Modern Language Bible* (1969), and the *New American Standard Version* (1971). The culmination of this process was reached in 1978 with the publication of the *New International Version*, produced by an international team of conservative Protestant scholars "with a high view of Scripture," as they described themselves. Although it is not a translation, Taylor's *The Living Bible, a Paraphrase* (1971) may also be mentioned.

Future Translations: Although "the rage to translate" seems to have abated, the translation of the Bible into English will continue, because we have or will have better Hebrew and Greek texts from which to translate, a greater knowledge of the meaning of the original, a better understanding of the translator's task, and the need to keep up with changes in the English language. As Goodspeed said, any translation of a masterpiece must be a failure. Consequently, no one translation should become *the* Bible for all readers, and a major revision, if not a new translation, should appear at least every thirty years. Perhaps the greatest current need for the American Bible-reading public is a translation that will use the full resources of the language and achieve a level of style, grace, and beauty not yet reached by any American Bible. No translation can ever be perfect, but better translations can help achieve Tyndale's goal of enabling readers to "see the process, order, and meaning of the text."

Bibliography

Bailey, Lloyd R., ed. *The Word of God*. Atlanta, GA: John Knox, 1982.

Bratcher, R. G. "Englishing the Bible." *Review and Expositor* 76.3 (1979): 299–314.

Bruce, F. F. *The English Bible*. New York: Oxford University Press, 1961.

Kubo, Sake, and Walter F. Specht. *So Many Versions?* Grand Rapids, MI: Zondervan, 1983.

Lewis, Jack P. *The English Bible from KJV to NIV*. Grand Rapids, MI: Baker, 1981. R.G.B.

Enlil (en-lil'; Akkadian, "Lord Wind"), an ancient and important god of Mesopotamia. He was associated with agriculture and was the god of the wind, of the destructive storm and the beneficent breeze of spring. Enlil was the creator of the primitive farming tool, the hoe, and his wife Ninlil was a grain goddess. The god of the city Nippur, Enlil's main temple there was Ekur ("House-mountain"). In a mythological tradition originating in Nippur, Enlil separated heaven from earth, and humankind sprouted forth—was created—at the place of the division.

Like Ea and the Canaanite El, Enlil is a creator god; like these, he also appears as a patriarchal ruler on whose behalf a young god takes up arms and organizes natural and political structures. In a developed form of the pantheon, he shares control of the world with An, Ea, and a mother goddess. He is the head of the gods and master of the land. In early Mesopotamia, he was the primary executive of the gods, and he bestowed and legitimated divine and human kingship. Assur, the god of the Assyrians, was later identified with Enlil.

In Mesopotamian accounts of the creation of humankind and human order (the Atrahasis Epic; Gilgamesh Epic, Tablet XI), Enlil brought the Flood to destroy humankind; the present order emerged as an adjustment necessary to allow humanity to exist without distressing Enlil. The biblical story of the flood in Genesis 6 may be dependent upon these accounts. ***See also*** Ninlil; Nippur. I.T.A.

Enoch, seventh patriarch from creation in Gen. 5:18–24; he was the son of Jared and the father of Methuselah. He lived 365 years, walked with God, and God took him (*Elohim*, the Heb. word usually rendered as "God" may, in the first instance, be more appropriately translated as "angels"). The figure is modeled in part on ancient Mesopotamian heroes, especially Enmeduranki, the seventh king. In the Hellenistic age (300 B.C.–A.D. 300) a corpus of apocalyptic writings was attributed to Enoch (*1 Enoch, 2 Enoch*). In later Jewish mysticism he was identified with Metatron, the "Little Yahweh," or angel closest to God himself. ***See also*** Apocalyptic Literature. J.J.C.

Enoch, Books of. ***See*** Pseudepigrapha.

Enosh (ee'nush; Heb., "humanity" or "the human race"), a name used to identify the son of Adam through whom the genealogies to Noah, to Abraham, and eventually to Christ are traced (Gen. 4:26; 1 Chron. 1:1). He is called Enos in Greek (Septuagint; Luke 3:38).

En-rogel (ayn roh'gel; Heb., "spring of a treader or fuller"), the name of a spring near Jerusalem that served as the boundary line between the tribes of Judah and Benjamin (Josh. 15:7; 18:16). During the rebellion of Absalom against his father David, this spring was the place where information was passed by a maidservant to David's men (2 Sam. 17:17). Later, when David was near death, his other son, Adonijah, prematurely declared himself king while sacrificing animals and celebrating with his friends by the Serpent's Stone, which was beside En-rogel (1 Kings 1:5–10). ***See also*** Absalom; Adonijah. F.R.M.

enrollment, a census that identifies, locates, and numbers the people in a particular group or area, usually for purposes of taxation but also at times for other ends such as conscription or forced labor. Several such enrollments are mentioned in the OT (e.g., Exod. 30:11–16; Num. 1: 1–49; 26; 2 Sam. 24:1–9; cf. 1 Chron. 21:1–5; 1 Chron. 7:40; 2 Chron. 2:17; 25:5; Ezra 2:2b–67). In the Roman Empire, it appears that periodic enrollments were common (in Egypt, for example, every fourteen years). The most famous of the enrollments is that mentioned in Luke 2:1–5 (cf. Acts 5:37) in connection with the birth of Jesus. The association of this enrollment with the governorship of Quirinius, however, raises a problem. Most scholars agree that Jesus was born about 6 B.C., but the available evidence indicates that Quirinius was governor of Syria about eleven years later and that he did, at this later date, supervise an enrollment. Some believe that Quirinius held a military position in Syria at the earlier date and, since he was more widely known, the historical connection was made with him rather than with the lesser known governor in 6 B.C., a Sentius Saturnius. In the story, the enrollment is apparently carried out in accordance with Jewish, not Roman, custom, since Joseph goes back to his ancestral home. It has also been suggested that Joseph perhaps owned some property in Bethlehem, which necessitated the journey from Galilee to Judea. It has been conjectured that the entire story represents an attempt to reconcile Jesus' Galilean (Nazareth) background with traditions of the Messiah's birth in Bethlehem. ***See also*** Bethlehem; Messiah; Nazareth; Quirinius, P. Sulpicius; Tribute, Tax, Toll. J.M.E.

En-shemesh (ayn she'mesh; Heb., "spring of the sun [god]"), a spring located east of Jerusalem and Bethany. Known as the "Spring of the Apostles" in the first century A.D. and known today as Ain el-Hod, it is the last spring on the road between Jerusalem and the Jordan Valley. In premonarchical Israel it served as the boundary between Judah and Benjamin (Josh. 15:7; 18: 17).

Epaphras (ep'uh-fras), person mentioned in Philem. 23 and Col. 1:7; 4:12–13 as an associate of Paul ("fellow prisoner" in Philemon). Apparently a native of the Lycus Valley in Asia Minor, he may have been Paul's personal representative to such cities as Colossae, Laodicea, and Hierapolis in that area. His being named before Mark, Luke, and others (Philem. 23–24) perhaps indicates the high esteem in which Paul held him. There is no evidence that Epaphras is a short form of Epaphroditus, the name of another co-worker of Paul mentioned in Phil. 2:25–30 and 4:18. ***See also*** Colossae; Colossians, The Letter of Paul to the. A.J.M.

Epaphroditus (e-paf'roh-dī'tuhs), a Philippian Christian who brought gifts from Philippi to Paul in prison (Phil. 4:18). Epaphroditus had been seriously ill but had recovered. Because of anxiety in Philippi concerning the illness of Epaphroditus, and because Paul himself was unable to go, he sent Epaphroditus back to Philippi (Phil. 2:25–30). ***See also*** Philippians, The Letter of Paul to the.

ephah (ee'fah), a dry measure equal to the liquid *bath* and approximately the equivalent of three-eighths to two-thirds of a U.S. bushel. It may also represent the container for such a quantity (see Zech. 5:6–11). ***See also*** Weights and Measures.

Epher (ee'fuhr; Heb., "fawn" or "kid [of mountain goat]"). **1** A son of Midian and grandson of Abraham and his concubine Keturah (Gen. 25: 4). **2** The son of Ezrah, a descendant of Judah (1 Chron. 4:17). **3** A clan leader of the eastern half-tribe of Manasseh (1 Chron. 5:24).

Ephesians, the Letter of Paul to the, the tenth book in the NT. The earliest and most reliable Greek manuscripts of Ephesians have nothing where later manuscripts read "in Ephesus" (Eph. 1:1). If originally present, "in Ephesus" is unlikely to have later disappeared. The Letter is also very general, lacking any personal references to the readers. The author has never visited these readers, and they do not know him (1: 15; 3:2–3; 4:21). Yet, according to Acts, Paul founded the church in Ephesus (Acts 18:19–20; 19:8–10). Ephesians was probably written, therefore, to a group of churches, one of which may have been Ephesus, or it may have been written from Ephesus. Thus, "in Ephesus" was inserted later when this Letter required identification distinguishing it from other Pauline writings.

Style and Authorship: There are good grounds for doubting whether Paul was the author of Ephesians. Much of it is written in an elevated or liturgical style, and, though Paul writes brief passages in this manner, he never sustains it for long. The sentences are longer and more complex than those Paul normally writes (e.g., 1:3–14, 15–23; 2:1–7; 3:1–7); their length is often disguised in English, since translators break them up for easier understanding. Words and ideas are used in ways foreign to Paul. In this and other respects, Ephesians is closely related to Colossians, though it is unlikely that the same person wrote both. The dispute about the admission of Gentiles into the church is no longer a living issue as in the genuine Pauline Letters. The apostles belong to a former generation (2:20; 3:5). While none of these reasons by itself would be an insuperable obstacle to Pauline authorship, their cumulative effect makes it unlikely.

A disciple of Paul probably wrote the letter about A.D. 80–90, wishing to continue his master's teaching and apply it to changing circumstances. He directed it to churches in Asia Minor, most of whose members were Gentiles (1:11–14; 2:1–3, 11–22; 3:1; 4:17–19; 5:8). The Letter itself affords no clue as to why it was written. Though employing Gnostic terms, the writer does so not directly to oppose Gnostic teaching but to interpret Christianity for those familiar with such terms. The rich style reflects liturgical material in use in the church. A hymn is quoted in 5:14, and a *Haustafel* (a code for social behavior) is taken and amplified in 5:22–6:9 (cf. Col. 3:18–4:1; 1 Pet. 2:13–3:7 for similar material). The Letter may also incorporate portions of hymns and creeds used in the contemporary church.

Theme and Content: The author meditates on a number of interrelated themes centering on the church and its relation to Christ and on Christian behavior. A divine plan, in God's mind since before the creation of the world (1:4), has now been revealed to the apostles and prophets (3:5) and is being accomplished through the death, resurrection, and ascension of Christ. He is Lord not only of humanity but also of all supernatural powers, both good and evil (1:20–23), and in him all things will finally be united (1:10). Thus God redeems the whole universe as well as humanity. Prior to Jesus, Jews alone were central to God's plan. Now Gentiles are also included, for both have been delivered from sin and reconciled to one another through Christ's death (2:13–18). Jewish and Gentile Christians form a third group, the church, which is neither Jewish nor Gentile but Christian. Like a building, the church has a chief cornerstone, Christ, and a foundation, the apostles and prophets (2:20). As a body with various members (4:7–11), its head is Christ, by whom it is continuously nourished (4:15–16). As a bride, its groom is Christ who died for it (5:22–33). It brings God's salvation to the supernatural powers (3:9–10) as well as to humanity. Paul himself has a special place in this in relation to the Gentiles (3:2, 3, 8).

The church is involved in the full accomplishment of God's plan. Christians must therefore stand firm in love (3:17) and display love in daily living (chaps. 4–6). Since the readers are ex-Gentiles, detailed guidance is given in respect of behavior. Christian behavior reflects, in its turn, the cosmic dimension since it is a struggle against supernatural powers (6:10–18). ***See also*** Ephesus; Paul; Pseudonym. E.B.

OUTLINE OF CONTENTS

The Letter of Paul to the Ephesians

I. Address (1:1–2)
II. The church as fellowship of the redeemed (1:3–3:21)
  A. Praise of God (1:3–14)
  B. Intercession (1:15–23)
  C. Life from death (2:1–10)
  D. Jew and gentile reconciled (2:11–22)
  E. Paul's ministry in revelation (3:1–13)
  F. Intercession (3:14–21)
III. The church in the world (4:1–6:20)
  A. Unity and diversity in service (4:1–16)
  B. The old life and the new (4:17–24)
  C. Christians in the world (4:25–5:14)
  D. How Christians should live together (5:15–6:9)
  E. The Christian's armor (6:10–20)
IV. Closing greetings (6:21–24)

Ephesus

A PORT CITY of western Asia Minor at the mouth of the Cayster River, Ephesus (ef'uh-suhs) lay between Smyrna and Miletus. Site of an immemorial primitive shrine to the Anatolian mother goddess and peopled by Carians and Lelegians, the area was first colonized by Ionian

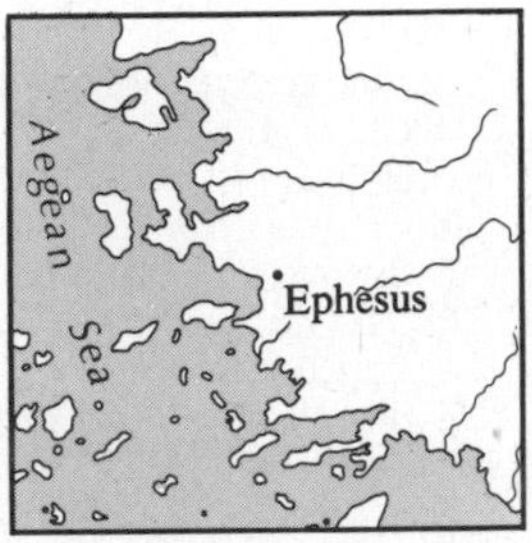

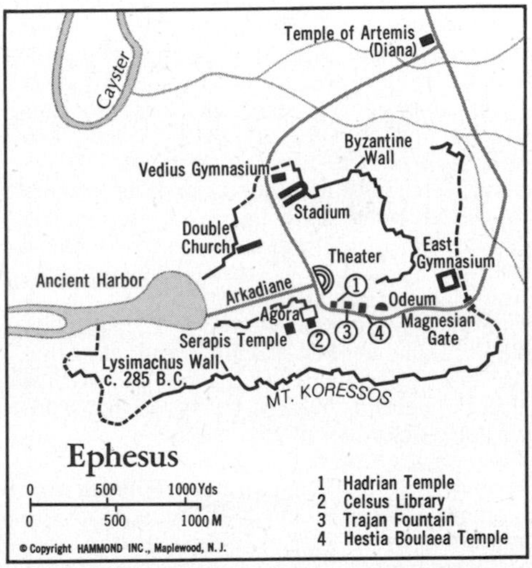

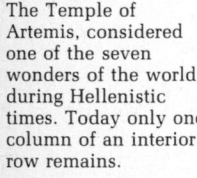

The city plan (right) shows buildings and walls over several centuries before, during, and after Paul's time in the mid-first century A.D.

The Temple of Artemis, considered one of the seven wonders of the world during Hellenistic times. Today only one column of an interior row remains.

Greeks under the leadership of Androclus of Athens in the tenth century B.C. The Greeks identified the deity with their own Artemis, but the attributes remained those of the ancient fertility goddess. A new phase of the city began with its conquest ca. 560 B.C. by Croesus of Lydia, who erected the Archaic Artemision and moved the city from the northern slopes of Mt. Pion to the plain south of the Artemision. After the Persian king Cyrus defeated Croesus in 547 B.C., Ephesus remained subject to Persian rule until Alexander's arrival in 334 B.C. In the meantime, the Artemision had burned (356 B.C.), and a new temple had been begun, the classical structure that was known as one of the Seven Wonders of the World in Hellenistic times.

Lysimachus, a general and successor of Alexander, moved the city to higher ground in 287 B.C. between Mt. Pion and Mt. Koressos because of the danger of flooding. A new five-mile-long wall, much of it still visible, was built at this time, as were a new harbor and streets. From 281 B.C., the Seleucids held Ephesus until Antiochus III's defeat by the Romans entrusted the city to the kings of Pergamum, but Rome took it back at the death of Attalos III in 133 B.C. An abortive revolt, linked to Mithradates VI of Pontus in 88 B.C., was put down by the Roman general Sulla, and the city remained peacefully Roman and then Byzantine for the rest of its history. Having dedicated a sacred precinct to Rome and

Caesar in 29 B.C., Ephesus enjoyed the height of its prosperity in the first and second centuries A.D. as the fourth largest city in the Empire. As the harbor silted up, the city declined in the Byzantine period (ca. fifth to tenth centuries A.D.), but a new wall and churches were built. The Turkish town of Seljuk today is the sixth city on the site.

Paul in Ephesus: In the NT, Ephesus and Ephesians are mentioned more than twenty times. According to Acts 18:19–21, Paul sailed from Corinth to Ephesus with Priscilla (Prisca) and Aquila for his first visit there. The latter couple instructed Apollos in Ephesus (Acts 18:24–26). Paul returned on his "third" missionary journey (Acts 19:1–20:1) to stay for more than two years, preaching and exorcising. The silversmiths in the commercial agora finally rioted at the threat of Paul's monotheism against their income from miniatures of the Artemision and dragged Paul's companions, Gaius and Aristarchus, into the theater before the town clerk was able to calm the mob (Acts 19:23–41). Later, on his way back to Jerusalem, Paul met with the elders of Ephesus at Miletus (Acts 20:16–38). The presence of Paul's companion Trophimus, an Ephesian, was the reason for a riot of Jews in the Jerusalem Temple and the arrest of Paul (Acts 21:27–22:30).

Portion of the Ephesus city wall built by Lysimachus, ca. 285 B.C.

Remains of the Temple of Hadrian at Ephesus.

A silver denarius depicting the Artemision and the fertility goddess Artemis of the Ephesians, here called Diana, whose adherents had rioted at the threat of Paul's monotheism; from the time of Emperor Hadrian (117–138).

In 1 Cor. 15:32, Paul writes that he "fought with beasts at Ephesus," but whether this is meant figuratively or literally is uncertain. 1 Tim. 1:3 charges Timothy to remain at Ephesus. 2 Tim. 1:18 refers to service rendered by Onesiphorus at Ephesus, and 4:12 to the sending there of Tychicus. The church of Ephesus is the first of the seven churches of Revelation (1:11; 2:1–7). Ephesus as the location of the "saints" addressed in Eph. 1:1 occurs in some manuscripts, but not in the best ancient witnesses (see note in the RSV).

Austrian archaeologists in this century have excavated the 24,000-seat theater and the commercial agora, as well as many other public buildings and streets of the first and second centuries A.D., so that the modern visitor can gain some impression of the city as known by Paul.

In postbiblical tradition, Ephesus was associated with John the Apostle, to whose memory a Byzantine basilica was built, and with the Virgin Mary, particularly at the Council of Ephesus (A.D. 431).

See also Apollos; Aquila; Artemis of the Ephesians; Ephesians, The Letter of Paul to the; John the Apostle; Mary, The Virgin; Paul; Prisca, Priscilla; Shrine; Smith.

Bibliography

Finegan, Jack. *The Archaeology of the New Testament: The Mediterranean World of the Early Christian Apostles.* Boulder, CO: Westview, 1981.

Yamauchi, E. *The Archaeology of New Testament Cities in Western Asia Minor.* Grand Rapids, MI: Baker, 1980.

C.H.M.

The remains of the theater at Ephesus, which may be the one into which Paul's companions Gaius and Aristarchus were dragged, as told in Acts 19:23–41.

ephod (ee'fahd), the most prominent of the elaborate Aaronide garments described in the tabernacle texts (Exod. 28; 39), it designates the only article of priestly apparel that plays a significant role outside the priestly writings contained in the Pentateuch. A "linen" ephod appears in stories of Samuel (1 Sam. 2:18; 22:18) and David (2 Sam. 6:14; 1 Chron. 15:27), and an ephod linked with teraphim is found in Judges 17–18 (cf. Hos. 3:4; Isa. 30:22). Not simply a ceremonial garment or a divination device, the ephod can best be understood in relation to the special trappings that adorned cult statues in Mesopotamian or Egyptian temples and that, in Israelite religion as priestly garments or objects, similarly helped bring human beings into contact with the deity. ***See also*** Priests; Tabernacle.
C.L.M.

ephphatha (ef'fah-thah), the contraction of an Aramaic verb meaning "Let it be opened." In Mark 7:34 Jesus gives this command while curing a man who is deaf and unable to speak.

Ephraim (ee'free-uhm; Heb., probably "fruitful place"; note Gen. 41:52 for a popular etymology).

1 Joseph's younger son born in Egypt to Asenath. Ephraim was blessed by Jacob (Gen. 48:1–20) designedly ahead of his brother Manasseh, portending tribal Ephraim's ascendancy.

2 An increasingly prominent Israelite tribe (unit of social organization and the territory it occupied). Joshua 16 and 17:14–18 show Joseph, one tribe and territory, replaced by two: note how Josh. 16:4 shifts abruptly from defining Joseph's territory to defining Ephraim's and then Manasseh's. Josh. 16:5–10 with 17:7–12 gives Ephraim's boundaries from premonarchical times (prior to tenth century B.C.); here Shechem with its fertile vale belonged to Manasseh. Even so, Ephraim's lands had better soil and were more easily protected than were Manasseh's. Probably with the definition of districts under Solomon (1 Kings 4:7–19), Shechem became part of *Mount* Ephraim (RSV: "the hill country of Ephraim"; see Josh. 20:7; 21:15, 20–21). Possibly 1 Chron. 7:28–29 retains an authentic memory of the further expansion of Ephraim. Clearly, by the mid-eighth century B.C., Ephraim could become for Isaiah and Hosea a designation for the whole Northern Kingdom; in Isaiah, it is allied with Syria in the "Syro-Ephraimite war" (Isa. 7:1–17; cf. 2 Kings 16: 5–9), and throughout Hosea it is the disloyal covenant partner of God (Hos. 5:3–14). Ephraim's immensely important role in Israel was partially veiled by the Jerusalem focus of our sources, but a large number of indicators point to it: Bethel, Shiloh, and at some point Shechem, all ancient worship centers, were in Ephraim. Joshua was an Ephraimite (Num. 13:8; cf. Deut. 34:9); he and Eleazar, who allotted the land (Num. 34:17; Josh. 14:1), were buried in Ephraimite towns (Josh. 24:29, 33). Samuel (1 Sam. 1:1) was an Ephraimite, as was Jeroboam (1 Kings 11:26), men who embodied the northern attitude toward monarchy, which urged its severe limitation in view of God's identification as Israel's true king. The "judges" Tola, Abdon, and Deborah were all connected to Ephraim (Judg. 4:5; 10:1; 12:15).

3 A town in 2 Sam. 13:23 where Absalom avenged Tamar upon Amnon. It was most likely located near Bethel in Ephraimite territory (see also John 11:54; 1 Macc. 11:34) but may have derived its name simply from being a "fruitful place." Similarly, the forest of Ephraim, in Transjordan near Mahanaim, where Absalom met his death, may be so named because of its fruitfulness; otherwise it may be evidence along with Judg. 12:4 (a difficult verse) that Ephraimites controlled this portion of Manasseh's eastern holdings at some time. ***See also*** Abdon; Absalom; Bethel; Deborah; Hosea, The Book of; Isaiah, The Book of; Jeroboam I; Joseph; Joshua; Mahanaim; Manasseh; Samuel; Shechem; Shiloh; Tola; Tribes, The.
E.F.C.

Ephraimite (ef'rah-im-īt), the term for a person of the tribe of Ephraim (translating Heb. *'eprātî*, in Judg. 12:5; 1 Sam. 1:1; and 1 Kings 11: 26, which is elsewhere translated "Ephrathite").

Ephrath (ef'rath). **1** A place on the way to which Rachel was buried (Gen. 35:16). It was located in the territory of Benjamin (1 Sam. 10: 2) near Ramah (Jer. 31:15), and thus it was not Bethlehem. **2** A place identified with Bethlehem (Gen. 35:19; 48:7) and spelled Ephrathah in Ruth 4:11; Ps. 132:6; and Mic. 5:1. **3** The wife of Caleb (1 Chron. 2:9) spelled with feminine ending in 1 Chron. 2:50 and 4:4. **4** A Hebrew word the adjectival form of which, Ephrathite (1 Sam. 17:12), also designates an Ephraimite (Judg. 12: 5; 1 Sam. 1:1; 1 Kings 11:26).

Ephrathah (ef'ruh-thuh; Heb., "fertility"). **1** The wife of Caleb, a descendant of Judah; the mother of Hur, the ancestor of Bethlehem, Kiriath-jearim, and Beth-gader (1 Chron. 2:50; 4: 4). She is also called Ephrath (1 Chron. 2:19). **2** Another name for Bethlehem or the area immediately surrounding it (Ruth 4:11; Mic. 5: 2). Jesse, David's father, is called an Ephrathite of Bethlehem (1 Sam. 17:12) as are Naomi's sons (Ruth 1:2). There seems to be some relationship between the persons in the genealogical lists (see 1 above) and the name of Ephrathah applied to the area of Bethlehem, although the exact nature of that relationship is not evident. The families could have given their names to various sites or the clans could have taken their names from the localities since some of the sites predate Israelite settlement. Some scholars suggest that the genealogies were composed to account for the place names. The identity of Ephrathah in Ps. 132:6 is uncertain. Some scholars understand "field of Jaar" to be Kiriath-jearim west of Jerusalem on the border between Judah and Benjamin. Ephrathah would then refer to the district around it, perhaps including the area around Bethlehem some ten miles to the southeast. Other scholars simply equate Ephrathah here with Bethlehem. ***See also*** Bethlehem; Ephrath; Kiriath-jearim. D.R.B.

Ephron (ef'rohn). **1** A Hittite, the son of Zohar, who sold Abraham the cave of Machpelah as a burial place for Sarah (Gen. 23; 25:9; 49:30–31; 50:13). **2** A city near Bethel mentioned in 2 Chron. 13:19. The place is not mentioned elsewhere, and there have been various attempts to correct the text. The Masoretic Text (MT) with the vowels "Ephrain" and others take it to be the Ophrah of Benjamin mentioned in Josh. 18:23. **3** A major fortified city east of the Jordan between Karnaim and Beth-shean, captured by Judas Maccabeus (1 Macc. 5:45–51; 2 Macc. 12: 27–28; Josephus *Antiquities* 12.8.5). **4** Mount Ephron, a hill on the Judean boundary (Josh. 15: 9; cf. Josh. 18:15 RSV). ***See also*** Hittites; Machpelah. G.M.T.

Epicureans (ep-i-kyuhr-ree'uhns), followers of the philosopher Epicurus (342–270 B.C.). Members of the Epicurean school of philosophy established in Athens are mentioned in Acts 17: 18. Epicurean teaching was expounded in a lengthy poem by the first-century B.C. Latin writer Lucretius. Epicureans were often attacked as atheists, since they held that sense perception was the only basis for knowledge. Everything had come into being out of atoms and the void. A random "swerve" in the path of the atoms caused the world to come into being and provided the material basis for free will, since no god had created or ruled over human beings, according to the Epicureans.

Epicureans argued against fear of death, since in their view death was merely the dissolution of the atoms entangled to make up the human, and against fear of the gods, who would enjoy their own blessedness without troublesome concern for human affairs. Free from these fears, they counseled, one should seek to live a peaceful life in which the body is free from pain and the mind peaceful and undisturbed. Consequently, one should choose a private life, pursuing this ideal in the pleasant company of friends. Some Epicurean philosophers in Athens discussed Paul's religious beliefs with him (Acts 17:18). P.P.

Epiphany, or the manifestation of Christ to the world (January 6), a Christian observance originally commemorating Jesus' baptism (Mark 1: 9) and his changing water into wine at Cana (John 2:1–11). Later, the visit of the Magi (Matt. 2:1–12) from Christmas was added. ***See also*** Christmas.

epistle, written communication, letter. The English word is derived from the Greek *epistolē*, a common word in the NT world for all kinds of letters. In modern times, the German biblical scholar Adolf Deissmann (1866–1937) distinguished between the letter and the epistle. He suggested that the letter was unliterary and intended only for the person(s) to whom it was addressed. Because it was personal and transitory, it was a "real" letter. By contrast, the epistle was literary and intended for circulation or publication. The epistle was both more impersonal and permanent and the most essential features of the "real" letter, its address and its confidential/spontaneous message, were only a stylistic device in the epistle.

Though Deissmann's use of the term "epistle" is useful in identifying writings that are in the form of a letter but that are actually intended for a broader public, a genuine letter is not to be determined merely by whether it is unliterary or transient. Personal letters were often written by masters of style. In fact, the more unpracticed and hurried the letter, the more likely it is that it will be dependent on conventions and be impersonal.

In the NT, all of the undisputed Letters of Paul (Rom., 1, 2 Cor., Gal., Phil., 1 Thess., Philem.), as well as 2 and 3 John, are genuine letters in Deissmann's sense: they are personal and are actually intended for the recipients identified in the opening address. However, this does not mean that they are written in an unliterary manner. Most, if not all, of the remaining NT documents that are in letter form are to be classified as epistles, often belonging more to the classification of sermon or theological essay than to letter. Thus, Hebrews and 1 John are sermons; James is a treatise on moral teaching and wisdom; 1 Timothy and Titus contain a body of instructions on church offices; 2 Timothy and 2 Peter are literary testaments. ***See also*** Letter; Salutations. J.L.W.

Epistles, Johannine. ***See*** John, The Letters of.

Epistles, pastoral. ***See*** Timothy, The First and Second Letters of Paul to, and Titus, The Letter of Paul to.

Erastus (e-ras'tuhs), a common name (Gk., "beloved") designating one or more men associated with Paul. **1** City treasurer (superintendent of public works?), probably of Corinth, among Paul's "fellow workers" sending greetings (Rom. 16:23). **2** Paul's colleague sent with Timothy from Ephesus into Macedonia (Acts 19:22). **3** An associate who remained in Corinth (2 Tim. 4:20).

Erech (ee'rek; Akkadian, *Uruk;* Gk., *Orchoi),* the ancient name of a southern Babylonian city situated near the Euphrates River, now know as Warka. Shortly after its founding in the fourth millennium B.C., it covered approximately two hundred acres. German archaeologists have been excavating Warka since 1912.

The first evidence of pictographic writing and numerical notation on clay tablets appears at Uruk around 3100 B.C., lending support to mythological speculation that the place to which the goddess Inanna brought the arts of civilization is in fact Uruk.

Holy to Inanna and to Anu, head of the Sumerian pantheon, Uruk housed two major temple complexes. Eanna, Inanna's temple, preserves eighteen archaic levels. The "White Temple" of Anu is the best example of the Sumerian "high temple." The Uruk Vase depicts components of the Sumerian cultic practices. Uruk housed an important cuneiform scribal school and astronomical observatory until the last century of the first millennium B.C.

The Table of Nations in Gen. 10 includes Erech in the kingdom of Nimrod. Ezra 4:9 mentions Ashurbanipal's seventh-century deportation of Uruk citizens to Samaria. L.E.P.

Esaias (e-zay'uhs). ***See*** Isaiah, The Book of.

Esarhaddon (es-ahr-had'duhn; Assyrian *Assur-aha-iddina),* king of Assyria, 681–669 B.C. Esarhaddon came to the throne after the murder of his father Sennacherib by his brothers. He was not an accomplice to the murder. Still, he seems to have reverted to earlier imperial policy as regards the management of the Assyrian Empire. He rebuilt Babylon and became king of Babylonia; he defended the northern borders against Cimmerian and Scythian incursions; he reasserted and strengthened imperial control, especially in the west, in part for the purposes of controlling mercantile centers (e.g., Phoenicia), and expanded the borders of the empire into Egypt. Some of the cultural and religious policies of King Manasseh of Judah (2 Kings 21: 1–18) may have been due to the constant presence of, and Manasseh's involvement with, Assyrians in the west, although the Assyrians did not require vassals to accept Assyrian religious practices. In Esarhaddon's reign, diviners and exorcists exercised particular influence in the royal court—their activities are known from a large body of correspondence—in part perhaps because of the king's chronic ailments. It is likely that he suffered from a skin disease, systemic lupus erythematosus. His health was failing especially during the last years of his reign, and most of the letters date to the last three or four years of the reign (the numerous letters are a rich source of information on Mesopotamian religion and medicine). At the beginning of this period (672), Esarhaddon established the succession: Ashurbanipal was to be king of Assyria, and Shamashshumukin, king of Babylonia. A treaty binding governors and vassals to abide by and support the succession was drawn up. The vassal treaties show points of similarity to Deuteronomy and have contributed to its understanding. ***See also*** Manasseh. I.T.A.

Esau (ee'saw), the older son of Isaac and Rebekah (Gen. 25–36). As such, he was entitled to the primary blessing and birthright of his family. He forfeited both, either because of his own foolishness (25:27–34) or by Jacob's trickery (27:1–45). He was the rejected son displaced by the younger Jacob, who became the bearer of the promise. Esau is portrayed as a gracious older brother (33:1–17) and the tradition continues to have a positive regard for him (36). Some have argued that he is to be understood as a folk figure in tradition stories, i.e., a literary construct.

In the ongoing Hebrew tradition, Esau was linked to the territory of Edom, Israel's rival and threat for territory (Deut. 2:4–29; Jer. 49: 8–10; Obad. 6–21). Through this linkage Esau, the folk hero, became the focus of great hostility, an attitude absent from the original Genesis narrative, and was enmeshed in a deep political conflict. Esau's portrait in the later tradition is rooted in the Genesis narrative but is handled with great imagination. Esau is also mentioned in two NT writings, once in a favorable context (Heb. 11:20), twice in an unfavorable one (Rom. 9:13; 12:16). ***See also*** Edom; Jacob. W.B.

eschatology (es-kuh-tahl'uh-jee), a nonbiblical term meaning ideas about the end or "last" (Gk. *eschatos*) period of history or existence. A variety of such ideas appear in biblical and intertestamental literature.

In Genesis, God tells Abraham, Isaac, and Jacob that he will bring them to a land—later popularly called the "promised land" (12:1; 26: 3; 28:13). Subsequently, God promises Moses that he will bring the people of Israel "to a good and broad land, a land flowing with milk and honey" (Exod. 3:8). The book of Joshua reports that God did give Israel the land as their "inheritance" (11:23), thereby fulfilling "all the good promises" he had made to Israel (21:43–45). But then came a series of oppressors and conquerors. In 721 B.C., the Assyrians totally defeated Israel, and, in 586 B.C., the Babylonians overcame the surviving kingdom of Judah, destroying Jerusalem and the Temple, and carrying most of the Jews into exile. Preexilic prophets interpreted these disasters as

God's judgment against his people for worshiping other gods and failing to do justice and mercy (e.g., Amos 4–8; Hos. 4–10; Jer. 2–8). Generally, these prophets also expected God to punish foreign nations for their false religion, pride, and wickedness (e.g., Isa. 13; Jer. 46; Ezek. 30). Most of them promised that God would restore the fortunes of Israel and Judah afterwards. Oracles of future redemption envisioned not only the restoration of national strength and status but also the establishment of an era of everlasting peace and blessing (e.g., Hos. 2:14–23; Isa. 2:2–4; 11; 35; Jer. 31:1–37; Ezek. 16:53–63). This promised era did not materialize after the Exile, but later prophets hinted that it might yet do so if the Jewish people would rebuild the Temple (Hag. 2; Zech. 3:6–4:14) or offer right sacrifices (Mal. 3: 10–12).

Prophetic vs. Apocalyptic: No clear line distinguishes this prophetic eschatology from apocalyptic eschatology. Many similar motifs appear in each. One major difference is that the apocalyptic writers no longer believed that other nations oppressed the Jews because God was thereby punishing them for breaking the covenant. Instead, the oppressing nations were seen as evil, linked, perhaps, with cosmic powers opposed to God (e.g., Isa. 24:17–23; Dan. 7:1–8). Thus, in apocalyptic thought, God is not directly in control of history. His sovereignty is affirmed, however, in that he has known the future all along and has revealed (Gk. *apokalyptein*) it to a prophet or seer. Through imaginative visions and images, apocalyptic writers rehearse earlier history up to the time for which they write, showing that everything predicted so far has come true, thereby adding conviction to their assurances that God will soon intervene in history to make things right. Then, the faithful will be vindicated (Dan. 7:13–27; cf. Isa. 26:1–19) and their oppressors destroyed (Dan. 2:44–45; 7: 11). (It should be noted that passages expressing apocalyptic eschatology have apparently been added to the earlier prophetic writings in some instances.)

Late prophetic eschatology sometimes anticipated certain preliminary occurrences or "signs." According to Mal. 4:5–6, the prophet Elijah would return to preach repentance "before the great and terrible day of the Lord comes." This expectation appears later in Ecclus. 48:10 and in the synoptic Gospels of the NT. Joel 2:30–31 depicts various cosmic phenomena, e.g., the turning of the sun to darkness and the moon to blood, expected "before the great and terrible day of the Lord comes." Like the preaching of the eschatological Elijah, these portents were to prompt people of the last times to repent (Joel 2:32). Such signs and wonders became common features of later apocalyptic eschatology (e.g., 2 Esd. 5:4–5; *1 Enoch* 80:4–5; Mark 13:24–25; Rev. 6:12–14).

The apocalypses usually predict a time of intense persecution or tribulation just before the moment of divine intervention (e.g., Dan. 12:1; Rest of Esther 11:5–9). Additionally or alternatively, they look for a time of cosmic conflict between God's people and their enemies (e.g., Ezek. 38:1–39:20; Joel 3:9–12; 2 Esd. 13:31–34; and the Qumran *War Scroll*). The faithful who perish may hope to be raised from the dead (Isa. 26:19; Dan. 12:2; 2 Esd. 7:32–35; 2 Bar. 30:1–5). In some of these accounts, only the righteous will be raised; in others, righteous and wicked alike will be raised to stand before the judgment seat of God or his Messiah. The wicked will be condemned to eternal torment (Isa. 66:24; *1 Enoch* 103:7–8) or extinction (2 Esd. 7:61). Those finding favor will experience life together with God in a land of preternatural fertility and abundance (e.g., Joel 3:18; *2 Enoch* 8; 2 Bar. 29: 3–8; cf. Isa. 25:6 and Ezek. 47:6–14, which do not mention prior judgment).

In the final era of peace and justice, Israel will either share God's blessings with other peoples (e.g., Isa. 19:24–25; Jer. 48:47; Ezek. 47: 21–23) or acquire "the wealth of the nations" as tribute (Isa. 60:11–12; 61:6; Hag. 2:6–7; Zech. 14:14). Dan 7:18–27 contemplates a future in which righteous Jews will govern all other nations forever.

In some passages, the advent of the final era was to be marked by the appearance of a messiah or king (e.g., Isa. 11:1–5; Jer. 30:9; Zech. 3:8; 9: 9), usually described as a descendant of David. Other visions of future restoration contain no mention of such a figure (e.g., Isa. 2:2–4; Jer. 31: 1–37; Zech. 14:1–21); here, God alone will act or be manifested. *1 Enoch* (e.g., 69:27) anticipates the appearance of a "Son of man" (cf. Dan. 7:13: "one like a son of man") as eschatological judge.

Wisdom Writings: The wisdom of writings focused primarily on the situation in individuals. Their basic doctrine was that the righteous are rewarded (by wealth and long life) and the wicked punished (by the converse) *in this life* (e.g., Ps. 37; Prov. 12:7; 13:21; but cf. Eccles. 7: 15, which challenges this doctrine). Generally in the OT, there was no expectation of individual resurrection or future life. The end of life was "the pit" or Sheol (Ps. 6:5; Eccles. 9:10). Offerings of food could be left for the dead (Deut. 26: 14; Tob. 4:17), but clear references to resurrection (2 Macc. 7:9–14) or immortality (Wisd. of Sol. 3:1–4) are rare outside apocalyptic contexts.

Synoptic Gospels: According to the synoptic Gospels (Matthew, Mark, and Luke), Jesus believed that the coming of the Kingdom of God, Son of man, and time of judgment were near (Matt. 4:17; Mark 1:15; Matt. 16:27–28; Mark 8: 39–9:1; Luke 9:26–27). He preached repentance and dispatched his followers to do likewise, so that others might repent beforehand (Matt. 10: 5–23; Luke 10:1–12). Likewise, he and his disciples exorcised (cast out) demons to overcome the power of Satan and prepare for God's rule on earth (Matt. 12:25–29; Mark 3:22–27; Luke 11: 17–22; Luke 10:17–20). Jesus may have shared the belief that Elijah would come first and may have seen John the Baptist in that role (Matt. 11: 11–14; 17:10–13). He may also have expected a time of tribulation (Mark 13:19) if not warfare (Mark 13:8) and certain cosmic phenomena (Mark 13:24) before the final events occurred. Yet he urged his followers to pray God to bring his Kingdom without their first having to endure temptation (Matt. 6:13; Mark 14:38), meaning, perhaps, eschatological tribulation (cf. Rev. 3: 10); and Jesus summoned his hearers to be ready at all times, since the Kingdom of God and Son of man could come without further signs or warnings (Matt. 24:42–44; Luke 12:39–40; Mark 13:33–37; Luke 21:34–36; cf. Luke 17:20–21). Those still alive, along with the dead of previous generations, would be judged before the Son of man (Matt. 12:41–42; Luke 11:31–32; Matt. 25: 31–46). The unrighteous would be condemned to eternal punishment (Matt. 25:46; Mark 9:43–49), but the righteous would enter or "inherit" eternal life in the Kingdom of God (Matt. 25:34, 46) and sit at table with Abraham, Isaac, Jacob, and other righteous ancients (Matt. 8:11–12; Luke 13:28–29) and with Jesus himself (Matt. 26:29; cf. Rev. 2:7; 3:20). Many contemporary interpreters suggest that certain eschatological occurrences were already "realized" or in process of actualization during Jesus' lifetime. Thus, some suggest that Jesus' appearance itself was a manifestation of the Kingdom of God or that the "powers" of the Kingdom were at work in his exorcising of demons.

The term "eschatology" is ambiguous in that it may refer to events during the last days of the present age, events occurring at the Parousia (return of Christ), or conditions of life in the new world or age. The expression "last day(s)" is used in the NT in at least two of these senses: John 6:40; 12:48; 2 Tim. 3:1; Heb. 1:2; James 5: 3; and 2 Pet. 3:3. Paul held that those "in Christ" were already a new creation (2 Cor. 5: 17) but cautioned against believing that the day of the Lord had come (1 Cor. 4:5; cf. 2 Thess. 2: 1–2). Paul expected to be alive when Jesus came as Lord. Then, the dead in Christ would be raised incorruptible, while those still alive would be given new ("spiritual") bodies in order to "inherit" the Kingdom of God, visualized as a heavenly community up "in the air" (1 Cor. 15:35–53; Phil. 3:20–21; 1 Thess. 4:13–18). Like Jesus, Paul believed that the Parousia events might occur at any time (Phil. 4:5; 1 Thess. 5:1–7). As Jesus taught his followers to pray, "Thy kingdom come!" (Matt. 6:10), Paul prayed, "Our Lord, come!" (1 Cor. 16:22; cf. Rev. 22:20).

Johannine Writings: Like Paul, the writer of John's Gospel looked for eternal life in the heavenly mansions (John 14:1–3). In Revelation, however, the final dwelling place of the righteous would be new Jerusalem, come down from heaven to earth (21:2–22:5), but only after a thousand-year interregnum (chap. 20). Several NT writings share Jesus' and Paul's belief that the events marking the beginning of the new age are about to occur (James 5:7–9; 1 Pet. 4:7; 1 John 2:18; Rev. 1:3), and most reveal their authors' understanding that the decisive eschatological events were yet to come (Acts 17:30–31; Eph. 5: 3–16; Col. 3:1–25; 2 Thess. 1:5–10; 1 Tim. 6: 11–16; 2 Pet. 3:11–13). Nevertheless, according to John, eternal life with God was already a present possibility, at least for Christians who had died (5:25–29; 6:40) and perhaps for all others who believed in Jesus (e.g., John 3:36; 1 John 5:13). ***See also*** Apocalyptic Literature; Devil; Eternal Life; Heaven; Hell; Judgment, Day of; Judgment, The Last; Kingdom of God; Messiah; Millennium; Parousia; Resurrection; Satan; Son of Man.

Bibliography

Burrows, Millar. *An Outline of Biblical Theology*. Philadelphia: Westminster, 1946. Chap. 11.

Hiers, Richard H. *Jesus and the Future: Unresolved Questions for Understanding and Faith*. Atlanta, GA: John Knox, 1981.

Koch, Klaus. *The Rediscovery of Apocalyptic*. London: SCM, 1972.

R.H.H.

Esdraelon (es'dray-lahn; Gk. for "Jezreel"), the western section of the valleys and plains that separate Galilee from Samaria. The smaller eastern section is the Valley of Jezreel; sometimes this name is used for the whole area. Esdraelon itself is not mentioned in the OT, but includes the Plain of Megiddo, stretching along the northern slopes of Mt. Carmel to the Plain of Acco, to En-gammin (modern Jenin) on the south, and northeast to the slopes of Mt. Tabor. The river Kishon wanders through the plain and alluvium has left the valley rich and fertile.

Roads north and south, east and west pass through the plain. The "Way of the Sea" (Isa. 9: 1) connecting Egypt with the north led from the Philistine coast through the Carmel pass at Megiddo, then either crossed the Esdraelon plain northwest around Mt. Tabor to Hazor and on to Damascus, or led between Moreh and Mt. Gilboa descending the Valley of Jezreel to Beth-shan, crossing the Jordan and then northward to Damascus. To the northwest one could reach the Plain of Acco, and traveling south through Ibleam enter the Dothan Plain, then go into the hills of Samaria or west to the Plain of Sharon.

The strategic site during OT times was Megiddo, guarding the Carmel pass. It was controlled by the Canaanites probably until the time of David (Judg. 1:27), but Taanach and the river Kishon were the scene of Deborah's victory (Judg. 4:7; 5:19). ***See also*** Acco; Carmel; Deborah; Ibleam; Jezreel; Kishon; Megiddo; Taanach; Tabor.

N.L.L.

Esdras (ez'druhs), **the First Book of,** an alternative version of 2 Chron. 35:1–36:23, all of Ezra, and Neh. 7:38–8:12. It is included in the Septuagint (LXX), the Greek version of the OT in use in the early church. The LXX also includes the primary translation of the works of the Chronicler (1 and 2 Chronicles, Ezra, and Nehemiah). The book is called 3 Esdras in the Vulgate. Since the sixteenth century, it sometimes appears in Catholic Bibles with 2 Esdras and the Prayer of Manasseh in an appendix following the NT. Protestants treat it as one of the Apocrypha.

The work is either the remnant of a distinct Greek translation of Chronicles, Ezra, and Nehemiah or a selection of parts of these books edited and translated into Greek sometime late in the second century B.C. Its Greek reflects greater freedom and style than that of the more extensive version of Chronicles, Ezra, and Nehemiah in the LXX. Along with the Rest of Esther and the additions to Daniel, the existence of 1 Esdras suggests that the format and content of some of the latest books in the OT were still in flux in the second and first centuries B.C.

What the purpose of 1 Esdras was is not certain, although concentration on the Temple, its worship, and leaders who reformed or restored its worship suggests that it may have been intended to make a statement of some sort concerning the Temple cult or its leadership. The book begins with the Passover celebrated at the culmination of Josiah's reform of the Temple (ca. 621 B.C.), then moves swiftly to the restoration of the Temple and its worship under Jeshua and Zerubbabel (516 B.C.), and concludes with Ezra's reform a generation or so later. It builds up the role of Zerubbabel at the expense of Sheshbazzar, the leader of the first group of returned exiles in 538 B.C., and minimizes that of Nehemiah in relation to Ezra, whom it calls the "high priest" (1 Esd. 9:40, 49). Unique to the OT is its fanciful account of the three bodyguards in the court of Darius (1 Esd. 3:1–5:6), an account told in order to honor the wisdom of Zerubbabel and to explain how Darius came to commission him to return to Jerusalem and restore the Temple. The history of the restoration is confused in 1 Esdras, although the first-century A.D. Jewish historian Josephus used this book as his primary source for the period when he wrote his *Antiquities*. ***See also*** Apocrypha, Old Testament; Exile; Josephus; Septuagint; Temple, The.

D.W.S.

OUTLINE OF CONTENTS

The First Book of Esdras

I. Josiah's Passover and the account of his death (1:1–33; cf. 2 Chron. 35:1–27)
II. The fall of Jerusalem (1:34–58; cf. 2 Chron. 36:1–21)
III. Cyrus the Great's edict permitting Jews to return and restore the Temple (2:1–30; cf. Ezra 1:1–11; 4:7–24)
IV. The contest of the three bodyguards in the court of Darius (3:1–5:6)
V. Lists of the exiles returning under Zerubbabel and their efforts to reconstruct the Temple (5:7–73; cf. Ezra 2:1–70; 3:1–5:5)
VI. The completion of the Temple under Haggai and Zechariah (6:1–7:15; cf. Ezra 4:24–6:22)
VII. Ezra's reforms (8:1–9:55; cf. Ezra 7:1–10:44 and Neh. 7:73–8:12)

Esdras (ez'druhs), **the Second Book of,** a Jewish apocalypse dating from the very end of the first century A.D. The material was written under the pseudonym of Ezra in order to use the

OUTLINE OF CONTENTS

The Second Book of Esdras

I. 5 Ezra: an apocalypse of Christian composition concerned with the rejection of Israel and the announcement of the rewards of the coming kingdom to all of the nations (chaps. 1–2)
II. 4 Ezra: a Jewish apocalypse of seven visions (chaps. 3–14)
   A. Vision 1: a dialogue between Ezra and Uriel concerning God's justice and the seed of evil sown in Adam (3:1–5:20)
   B. Vision 2: a dialogue concerning the mystery of God's choice of Israel in light of the people's subsequent suffering (5:21–6:34)
   C. Vision 3: a dialogue concerning creation, the messianic age, and the subsequent judgment (6:35–9:25)
   D. Vision 4: Ezra encounters Zion as a woman mourning for her dead son (9:26–10:59)
   E. Vision 5: an allegorical vision of an eagle (cf. Dan. 7:3–8), representing the Roman Empire (chaps. 11–12)
   F. Vision 6: an allegorical vision of a man from the sea (chap. 13; cf. Dan. 7:13–14)
   G. Vision 7: the legend of Ezra and the restoration of the Scriptures (chap. 14)
III. 6 Ezra: an apocalypse of Christian origin describing the tribulations of the end of history (chaps. 15–16)

conquest of Jerusalem by the Babylonians a century prior to Ezra as a means of reflecting upon the intense suffering occasioned by the destruction of Jerusalem by Rome in A.D. 70. The work is at times designated 4 Esdras or 4 Ezra (chaps. 3–14). It is included among the Apocrypha by Protestants and is sometimes printed by Catholics along with 1 Esdras and the Prayer of Manasseh in an appendix following the NT. The original language was probably Hebrew, which was then translated into Greek. Neither the Hebrew nor the Greek is extant, but the book survives in a number of versions made from the Greek, including Latin, Syriac, Ethiopic, and Armenian. Chaps. 1–2 and 15–16 represent Christian additions to the original Jewish apocalypse and are occasionally designated 5 and 6 Ezra, respectively.

The apocalypse in chaps. 3–14 is divided into seven visions, some of which contain dialogues between Ezra and the angel Uriel concerning God's justice in permitting his chosen people to suffer at the hands of the unrighteous Babylonians, others of which deal allegorically with history, the sufferings of the present, and the coming of the messianic age. In this they are similar to the visions of Revelation. The seventh vision, chap. 14, parallels Ezra to Moses and has Ezra dictate while in a trance the twenty-four books of the Hebrew Scriptures lost in the burning of Jerusalem. The book thus reflects the Palestinian or rabbinic definition of the canon of Scripture, which implicitly treats Moses and Ezra as the beginning and end of revelation.

While chaps. 3–14 ultimately conclude that the mysteries of sin and suffering are unfathomable, they do develop a theology of history that claims that the whole of the human race from Adam on is sinful, subject to the evil inclination, and therefore deserving God's punishment. After the fashion of the wisdom tradition, various analogies are drawn from nature and human life to deal with the limits of human knowledge and to justify the suffering of the righteous and God's slow pace in setting things right. The goal of history is a four-hundred-year messianic age, following which the messiah will die and all things will be returned to a seven-day primeval silence. Then will come the resurrection and last judgment. The sixth vision of the man from the sea in chap. 13 is remarkable in that it is based on Dan. 7:13–14 and thus plays an important role in scholarly discussions of the christological title "Son of man" in the NT. ***See also*** Apocalypse; Apocrypha, Old Testament; Eschatology; Messiah; Pseudonym; Son of Man.

D.W.S.

Eshbaal (esh'bay'al). ***See*** Ishbosheth.

Eshcol (esh'kohl; Heb., "cluster"). **1** The name of the valley near Hebron, in south-central Judea, from which spies sent by Moses brought back on a pole a cluster of grapes and some pomegranates and figs (Num. 13:23–24). Although this fruit indicated a good land, their report of giants discouraged the people of Israel from entering the land (Num. 32:9). **2** The brother of Mamre and Aner, Amorite allies of Abram, who helped the patriarch rescue Lot (Gen. 14:13, 24). ***See also*** Mamre.

Eshtaol (esh'tay-ahl), a city in the lowlands of Judah counted as belonging to both Judah and Dan (Josh. 15:33; 19:41). It was probably originally occupied by Danites (Judg. 13:25; 18:2–11) and then later occupied by Judah when the Danites were forced to move to the north (Judg. 18:11). Evidence of this is seen in 1 Chron. 2:53 where Eshtaolites are regarded as descendants of Judah. It is also possible that the camp of Dan at Kiriath-jearim (Judg. 18:12) led to a mixing of the two tribes in this region. Eshtaol is tentatively located near modern Ishwa, about fourteen miles west of Jerusalem and about six miles slightly southwest of Kiriath-jearim. D.R.B.

Eshtemoa (esh-te-moh'uh). **1** A city in the hill country of Judah that was given to the Levites (Josh. 21:14). David shared his booty with the city following his defeat of the Amalekites (1 Sam. 30:28). It is also called Eshtemoh (Josh. 15:50) and is tentatively identified as modern es-Samu, about ten miles south and slightly east of Hebron. **2** A son of Ishbah, descendant of Simeon (1 Chron. 4:17). It is not clear whether Eshtemoa the Maacathite (4:19) is the same person or of a different family since the text is disordered in these verses.

Essenes (eh-seenz'), a sect of Judaism from the middle of the second century B.C. until the war with Rome in A.D. 66–70. They are described by the first-century A.D. authors Josephus and Philo and mentioned by some non-Jewish writers. They have been convincingly identified with the inhabitants of Qumran who wrote the Dead Sea Scrolls. The meaning of the Greek name "Essenes" is unclear; it may come from the Aramaic for "pious" or "healers."

Archaeological research at Qumran, data from ancient sources, and cryptic allusions to the sect's history in its writings suggest that the group, whose members were probably some of the Hasideans who supported the Maccabees, withdrew from Jerusalem and active participation in the Temple because Jonathan Maccabee assumed the high-priesthood in 152 B.C. though he was not from the correct, hereditary priestly family. The group was led by a prominent priest whose identity is hidden behind the designation "Teacher of Righteousness." The community built a complex of buildings on the cliffs around the Dead Sea at Qumran, between Jericho and En-gedi, and went through

Aerial view of Qumran showing cave number four. Qumran is at the northwest edge of the Dead Sea.

several stages of development there, including a refounding of the community after an earthquake in 31 B.C. The community was persecuted and attacked by Jonathan Maccabee, survived other pressures, but was finally destroyed by the Romans in A.D. 68. Some Essenes also lived in towns and cities, probably in small communities, and a few are mentioned by name in Josephus as playing a political role.

The Qumran community was sharply divided into hereditary priests and nonpriests. They were ruled by an elaborate hierarchy of officers and councils and guided by a detailed set of rules based on biblical law. Numerous practices were peculiar to this sect. Property was held in common, celibacy was practiced, a high state of ritual purity was maintained, economic and social relations with nonmembers were greatly restricted, admission to full membership was preceded by three years probation, solemn ritual meals were held regularly, participation in the ritual of the Jerusalem Temple was forbidden for as long as the Temple was improperly run, and detailed rules of behavior supported a rigorous ethic that was sanctioned by judges and punishments, including excommunication. The Essenes who lived outside the Qumran community seem to have married, had private property, and engaged in some social relations with outsiders.

Besides some OT books and other Jewish pseudepigraphical writings the Essenes had their own biblical commentaries, hymns, rules, and apocalyptic writings. Though Josephus compares them to the Greco-Roman Stoics, the Essenes were apocalyptic in their thought and orientation, maintaining ritual purity, ethical probity, and spiritual readiness for the intervention of God to destroy evil. No convincing evidence has been produced to demonstrate any dependence on Essene thought by John the Baptist, Jesus, or other early Christian leaders. The similarities that exist are more likely due to their common Jewish background than to any direct relationship. ***See also*** Qumran, Khirbet; Scrolls, The Dead Sea; Teacher of Righteousness.

Bibliography

Vermes, G. *The Dead Sea Scrolls: Qumran in Perspective*. London: Collins, 1977.

______. *The Dead Sea Scrolls in English*. 2d ed. New York: Penguin, 1975. A.J.S.

Esther, the name both of the biblical book and of its heroine; it is derived from the Persian *stara* ("star") and has a prototype in the name of the Babylonian deity Ishtar. The book serves as a festal legend for Purim, the celebration of the deliverance of Jews of the eastern Diaspora from persecution. Some scholars suggest that the link between the story of Esther and Mordecai and Purim is secondary, the story serving to legitimize a popular festival that originated in Persian New Year celebrations. The book probably dates from the later Persian period (400–322 B.C.).

In the story suspense is built and held, a series of delightful coincidences and juxtapositions climax a fateful night as the king cannot sleep, Mordecai's past service is recalled, and the failure to reward him noted. Haman, coming to the court for permission to hang Mordecai, is asked to advise on how the king might reward "the man whom the king delights to honor." Haman fatally misreads the situation, and the tables turn on him.

The book is best described as a novella. Some suggest it is a "historical novella," but while a historical core is possible, the events cannot be verified, and the central figures of Esther, Mordecai, Haman, and Vashti have left no historical trace elsewhere. The novella is designed to entertain and show how humans act under certain circumstances. It is striking that God is not mentioned in Esther. The story unfolds on the human level and deals with typical human deeds. Yet it seems probable that an allusion to a divine design is found in Esther 4:14. Any theological tones in the story are muted, however, and do not transform it into a vehicle for an overt religious message.

Esther (whose Jewish name is Hadassah) first

appears as a quite passive heroine, acted upon rather than actor and under the guidance of Mordecai. Yet once she resolves to appear unsummoned before the king (Esther 4:15–18), she becomes the primary instigator of action that leads to Haman's fall and the Jews' deliverance.

In time, additions were made to the book of Esther, which are found in the Apocrypha (Rest of Esther). They serve to enhance the drama of the story (Esther's appearance unbidden before the king provokes first rage and then, as she swoons, compassion), to bring the book into line with forms of Jewish piety (Esther and Mordecai pray for divine aid and lament that they must violate certain practices involving diet and intercourse with pagans), to further villainize Haman ("copies" of the edicts are provided), and to underscore divine knowledge and control of events (Mordecai has a dream at the outset that predicts the course of events and realizes in the end that all happened as predicted).

The book's place in the Jewish and Christian canons was challenged by some, even as late as Luther; others have been lavish in their praise of the book. Maimonides, the great medieval Jewish scholar, placed it just after the Torah in

Events in the story of Esther: Ahasuerus selects Esther, Haman and Mordecai, and Haman hangs from the gallows; nineteenth-century embroidered sheet.

OUTLINE OF CONTENTS

The Book of Esther

While sometimes criticized as harsh and vengeful, the story is nevertheless artfully told and rarely fails to delight, as the following outline suggests.

I. Introduction to the Persian court and king (chap. 1)
  A. Ahasuerus' feast (1:1–4)
  B. A special feast and the king's command to Vashti (1:5–11)
  C. Vashti's disobedience and banishment (1:12–22)

II. Esther becomes Ahasuerus' queen (chap. 2)
  A. A search for Vashti's replacement (2:1–5)
  B. Mordecai's instructions to Esther (2:6–11)
  C. Esther becomes queen (2:12–18)
  D. Mordecai uncovers a plot to assassinate the king (2:19–23)

III. Elevation of Haman and his plans to destroy the Jews (chaps. 3–4)
  A. Conflict between Haman and Mordecai (3:1–6)
  B. Royal approval for and determination of the day of Jewish destruction (3:7–15)
  C. Mordecai enlists the aid of Esther (4:1–17)

IV. Haman's plot thwarted (5:1–8:2)
  A. Esther's appearance unbidden before the king and the first soirée (5:1–8)
  B. Events of a fateful night (5:9–6:14)
    1. Haman's plot to hang Mordecai (5:9–14)
    2. Royal insomnia (6:1–6)
    3. Advice on how to rectify an oversight (6:7–9)
    4. Mordecai's reward and Haman's shame (6:10–14)
  C. Esther's second soirée (7:1–10)
    1. Haman's plot uncovered (7:1–6)
    2. Haman is hanged (7:7–10)
    3. Mordecai assumes Haman's office and estate (8:1–2)

V. The pogrom prevented (8:3–10:3)
  A. An edict allowing Jews to defend themselves (8:3–17)
  B. The Jews are victorious (9:1–15)
  C. Letters fixing the celebration of Purim (9:16–23)
  D. Summary of a happy resolution (10:1–3)

importance. ***See also*** Ahasuerus; Haman; Lot, Lots; Mordecai; Persia.

Bibliography

Moore, Carey A. "Esther." In *The Anchor Bible*. Garden City, NY: Doubleday, 1971.

Berg, Sandra Beth. *The Book of Esther*. Missoula, MT: Scholars Press, 1979. W.L.H.

Esther, the Rest of the Book of, five additions found in the Septuagint (LXX), or Greek, version of Esther but not in the original Hebrew. Jerome, in making his Vulgate translation of Esther, removed all but one of these passages and placed them at the end of the book, so that chapter and verse numbers in modern editions treat them as though they were an ending to Esther.

The purpose of the additions is to give a more specifically religious cast to the book as well as to the festival of Purim associated with

OUTLINE OF CONTENTS

The Rest of the Book of Esther

The following outline shows the way in which the LXX intersperses the *additions* with the original text of the book (italics indicate additions). The LXX also embellishes the passages it translates from the Hebrew version, adding references to God and altering the plot at several points.

I. *Mordecai's dream* (11:2–12:6)
   A. An apocalyptic vision (11:2–12)
   B. Mordecai foils a plot against the king (12:1–6)
II. Esther 1:1–3:13 (the beginning of the Hebrew version)
III. *Artaxerxes' decree enjoining the persecution of the Jews* (13:1–7)
IV. Esther 3:14–4:17 (part of the Hebrew version)
V. *The prayers of Mordecai and Esther* (13:8–15:16)
   A. Mordecai's prayer (13:8–18)
   B. Esther's prayer (14:1–19)
   C. Esther appears before the king (15:1–16; replaces 5:1–2 in the Hebrew version)
VI. Esther 5:3–8:12 (part of the Hebrew version)
VII. *Artaxerxes' decree rescinding the persecution* (16:1–24)
VIII. Esther 8:13–10:3 (the ending of the Hebrew version)
IX. *Mordecai's dream interpreted* (10:4–11:1)
   A. The apocalyptic vision explained with reference to the story of Esther (10:4–13)
   B. The colophon (11:1)

it. Since the Hebrew version of Esther never mentions God, its canonical status within Judaism was sometimes a matter of dispute. The additions attribute to God the deliverance of his people through the device of the apocalyptic vision and its interpretation, which now begin and end the book, as well as through the composition of prayers for Mordecai and Esther. Salvation now comes not as a consequence of Esther's courage and beauty, but as a result of her piety, in order to show that God answers prayer and protects his people. The vision draws upon the genre of the apocalypse current in Judaism of the Hellenistic age to suggest that God is in control of history, while the addition of prayers at appropriate places is another device used in the period to expand a text (cf. Jon. 2). The two decrees of Artaxerxes may have been composed in Greek with the intention of adding authenticity to the story. The other passages were probably written first in Hebrew. Along with 1 Esdras and the Additions to Daniel, the Rest of Esther suggests the fluidity of the biblical text within Judaism of the Hellenistic era.

The colophon of the Greek version attributes translation of the book to a certain Lysimachus, apparently a Hellenistic Jew, and suggests that it was brought to Egypt in the fourth year of Ptolemy and Cleopatra (either 114 B.C., 77 B.C., or 44 B.C., depending upon which royal pair is intended) possibly in an effort to introduce Purim to the Alexandrian Jewish community. For Protestants, the Rest of Esther is included among the Apocrypha, isolated from the translation of the Hebrew version. Catholics consider it deuterocanonical and print it either at the end of Esther or, following the order of the LXX, interspersed with the passages of the Hebrew version. ***See also*** Apocrypha, Old Testament; Daniel, The Additions to; Esdras, The First Book of; Esther, The Book of; Purim, The Feast of. D.W.S.

Etam (ee'tam). **1** The place where Samson defeated the Philistines and was subsequently delivered to them by the people of Judah (Judg. 15:8, 11). **2** A village in the territory of Simeon (1 Chron. 4:32), possibly identified with **3** A city near Bethlehem fortified by Rehoboam (2 Chron. 11:6). **4** The Israelites' first desert stop before turning back after they had left Sukkot (Exod. 13:20). It was located on the edge of the wilderness (Num. 33:6).

eternal life, a life uninterrupted by death. It is surprising to learn that in ancient Israel there was no belief in a life after death. Ezekiel 37 speaks of life returning to dry bones, but that should be understood only as a metaphor for the restoration of Israel after the Exile.

The Idea of an Afterlife: The idea of an afterlife or eternal life came late in postexilic times and is attributed to Jewish contact with Persian doctrines. Dan. 12:1–2 is conceded to be the first biblical reference to an afterlife (ca. 175 B.C.); it speaks of a time of terrible persecution of Jews by Antiochus IV Epiphanes who ordered loyal Jews to give up their ancestral faith or face death. He martyred many of them. Their survival of death is announced in Dan. 12 in terms of their resurrection, which is God's radical vindication of his faithful ones. The same historical background illuminates 2 Macc. 7 where the seven brothers die in defense of the Torah, confident that "the King of the universe will raise us up to an everlasting renewal of life, because we have died for his laws" (7:11).

In the Wisdom of Solomon we are told that God created Adam deathless: "God created man for incorruption and made him in the image of his own eternity" (2:23). Death came because of sin: "The day you eat of it you shall die" (Gen. 2:17; 3:19). Yet the Wisdom of Solomon is unusual in Jewish literature for it speaks not of resurrection from death but of the immortality of the soul by which humankind survives after death: "Their hope is full of immortality" (3:4). The wicked would seem to vanish at death, while "the righteous live for ever" (5:15).

Despite Daniel, 2 Maccabees, and the Wisdom of Solomon, however, not all Jews believed in life after death, whether by resurrection or through immortality. In describing the Sadducees and the Pharisees, the Jewish historian Josephus contrasted their views on postmortem existence. The Sadducees did not believe in the afterlife; God does not reward or punish and certainly not in the afterlife. The Pharisees believed in "an immortal soul," and so in an afterlife when God rewards the righteous and punishes the wicked (*Bella Judaica* II.162–166; *Antiquities* XVIII.11–22). Acts 23:6–9 records a dispute between Sadducees and Pharisees over the resurrection (see also Mark 12:18–27). The Sadducean position is not so implausible when one recalls that until Daniel, there was no notion of an afterlife in the Hebrew scriptures. We know, moreover, from the targumic discussions of Gen. 4:8 (see Tgs. Yer. I, II Gen. 4:8), that the issue continued to be debated in Jewish circles.

Eternal Life in Early Christian Preaching: Afterlife and eternal life become an essential part of Christian preaching in virtue of Jesus' resurrection from the dead. That survival of death enjoyed a variety of interpretations: it was the vindication of the Son of man (Mark 14:62), echoing God's vindication of the Maccabean martyrs in Dan. 7; it was a new creation in which the new Adam, who is sinless, is restored to deathlessness (Rom. 5:12–21); and it was a heavenly exaltation, an ascent like that predicted in Ps. 68:18 (see Eph. 4:6–8). NT authors regularly speak of the prophecy of the resurrection in the Scriptures (see Luke 24:44–46), alluding to Psalms 110 and 16 as well as Hos. 6:1–3. But this is surely Christian commentary (midrash) on those texts.

In Christian preaching, Jesus is said to offer his followers eternal life, not just in the future, but now: "he who hears my word . . . has eternal life; he does not come into judgment, but has passed from death to life" (John 5:24). In John, this mode of discourse is related to the claim that Jesus' truth, sacraments, and rites are superior to those of the synagogue: "This is the bread which came down from heaven, not such as the fathers ate and died; he who eats this bread will live for ever" (John 6:58). Thus, Christian baptism allows one to "have eternal life" (John 3:15); unlike Jacob's well, Jesus' waters will become a spring welling up to eternal life (John 4:14); unlike those who ate Moses' manna, those who eat Jesus' bread of life "have eternal life" (John 6:40, 47).

This type of discourse, while understandable in its dialectical context in John, nevertheless led to problems. Some took the preaching literally and considered themselves already beyond death and in the resurrection (see 2 Tim. 2:17–18; perhaps also 1 Cor. 4:8). Some who took this literally were shocked by the death of a beloved disciple such as Lazarus (John 11). These problems led to adjustments in the understanding of eternal life. The importance of present conversion to Jesus' group is still underscored by the assertion that one has passed from death to life (1 Pet. 1:3); but this is balanced with other statements that remind converts that, while there is a realized aspect to this eternal life, it remains a promise to be realized fully in the future. Converts may have crossed from death to life in baptism, but it is also affirmed that Jesus "raises them on the last day" (John 6:40; 11:25). ***See also*** Death; Immortality; Resurrection; Soul.

Bibliography

Nickelsburg, George W. E. *Resurrection, Immortality, and Eternal Life in Intertestamental Judaism.* Cambridge: Harvard University Press, 1972.

Stendahl, Krister. *Immortality and Resurrection.* New York: Macmillan, 1965.

J.H.N.

Ethan (ee'thuhn; Heb., "enduring," hence "long-lived"). **1** A wise "Ezrahite" (meaning uncertain), credited with Psalm 89 (see 1 Kings 4:31). **2** Grandson of Judah and Tamar through the line of Perez (1 Chron. 2:6–8). **3** A levitical musician from the Merarites in the time of David, possibly to be identified with Jeduthun (1 Chron. 15:17, 19; see 16:41–42; 25:1–2). **4** A levitical attendant from the line of Gershom (1 Chron. 6:42).

ethics, human moral conduct according to principles of what is good or right to do. Ethical concerns occupy a central position throughout the Bible with respect to the actions of individuals as well as the whole community. At points this is presented in terms of general and absolute norms (as in the Ten Commandments), and in other places it can be discerned in the actions of people and the customs of the society.

In the OT: It is clear from the OT that the people of Israel faced a full range of moral problems as well as dilemmas in which they had to make moral choices. Marriage and the family form one such sphere of morality, and here the cohesiveness and continuation of this basic unit are the highest values. Israelite society was structured on a patriarchal base, with primary power and legal rights vested in the male as head of the household. This colored marital and familial morality, as is often evident in laws and stories. A woman's legal rights were restricted in areas of property ownership, inheritance (Num. 27:1–11), and oath taking (Num. 30); essentially every female was under the protection and authority of some male, first her father and then later her husband. Divorce could be initiated only by the husband, but the law did attempt to ensure against unjust cause (e.g., Deut. 22:13–21) and required a "bill of divorce" (Deut. 24:1). Children were also under the authority of their parents, especially the father. A harsh law prescribing death for a stubborn child is mentioned in Deut. 21:18–21 (see also Exod. 21:15, 17), although there is no evidence that such a penalty was ever enforced. The fifth commandment (Exod. 20:12) may actually be directed toward adult children, charging them to "honor" their parents by, among other things, caring for them in their old age.

Sexual Ethics. Sexual ethics in the OT is also affected by the patriarchal nature of that ancient society. Sexual license was granted much more to males than to females. Polygyny and concubinage were allowed, and going to prostitutes was apparently condoned for men (e.g., Gen. 38:12–26; Josh. 2), although prostitutes themselves were often stigmatized and prostitution became a prophetic metaphor for apostasy (Hos. 1–3; Ezek. 16; 23). Adultery, which in the OT refers to intercourse between a married or betrothed (engaged) woman and any man who is not her husband or her betrothed, is strictly prohibited and punishable by death (Deut. 22:20–27) or ordeal (Num. 5:11–31). However, by no means is the sexual ethics of the OT only negative and restrictive. Gen. 2:24–25 declares the intimate bond between a husband and wife to be completely appropriate and good. The Song of Solomon amounts to a virtual sexual reverie, with the male and the female as equal partners reveling in the delights of each other's bodies.

Justice. Justice is one of the most important aspects of OT ethics. Individuals as well as the society as a whole are expected to act justly, promoting proper relationships within the community (Mic. 6:8; Ps. 112; Job 31). God's great release of the Israelites from slavery in Egypt serves often as the basis for other efforts to overcome oppression and exploitation within the Israelite society. With no catalogue of an individual's inalienable rights, the OT focuses more on the moral responsibility that persons should have for each other. There are persons who are especially vulnerable and defenseless in society, such as the poor, the widow, the orphan, the slave, and the stranger, and protecting them is not just a moral requirement but also a religious duty as a reflection of God's compassion for the world. The problem was especially severe in the eighth century B.C. when the country experienced a fair degree of affluence, and prophets like Amos, Isaiah, and Micah were quick to criticize the wealthy who had no regard for the plight of those suffering economically. God, they maintain, is the guarantor of justice and will intercede on behalf of the poor by punishing the powerful if the community itself does not act morally in correcting the injustice.

OT ethics is thus geared toward creating and maintaining right relationships—in the family, in the larger society, in business dealings, in government, and in other arenas. The covenant between God and Israel is a symbol of proper relations among humans, and because of the covenant God can command the people to practice a life of obedience and responsibility. At the base of this also is a fundamental affirmation of the goodness of life in this world (Gen. 1), a stance that means that it is urgent that persons act morally here and now, making this a just world rather than pinning all hopes on a world to come.

In the NT; Jesus: In OT ethics morality is fundamentally interwoven with religion: that which is good and right to do has been commanded by God. The same is true in the NT. In preaching the coming of the Kingdom of God and the future hope, Jesus also teaches the importance of acting mercifully and responsibly to others in the present. At points it may seem that Jesus is thinking mostly about the future: he makes moral acts a strict requirement for admission to the Kingdom (e.g., Mark 10:24–25; Matt. 25:31–46), threatens persons with the final judgment (Mark 9:42–48; 12:40; Matt. 5:22), and promises final reward to those who act rightly (Mark 10:21; Matt. 6:19–21). However, it is clear from the range of Jesus' teachings that one's primary motivation for morality should be the desire to live in conformity to God's standards, not simply for one's own benefit and not merely in accord with common practices (Matt. 5:43–48).

Jesus' view of the OT law is positive, upholding it generally and departing from it usually only to make it more radical, as in his teachings on murder, adultery, divorce, oath taking, and retaliation (Matt. 5:21–42). Most fundamental in Jesus' ethic is the two-fold love commandment taken from the OT law—to love God and to love one's neighbor (Mark 12:29–31; from Deut. 6:4–5 and Lev. 19:18). With this as the primary principle Jesus proceeds, in his teachings and parables, to indicate concrete ways in which love should affect moral behavior: affirming marriage and discouraging divorce (Mark 10:2–9), granting women equality with men (note the role of women in Jesus' ministry, e.g., Luke 23:55–56), using wealth to benefit the poor (Luke 19:8), caring for anyone in need (the parable of the good Samaritan, which broadens the OT understanding of "neighbor"), loving one's enemies and avoiding violence (Matt. 26:52), giving proper support to the state (Mark 12:13–17), and living a life of service (Luke 22:26–27).

Paul. For Paul the Christ event is fundamental to the Christian ethic in that it has direct implications for the understanding of human nature, the Law, and sin. Paul discusses this with considerable care in Romans 5–8. He maintains that the Christian is transformed by Christ, is free from the Law as a means of salvation, and yet still remains subject to the commandments of God (1 Cor. 7:19). Paul especially emphasizes Jesus' love commandment, "the law of Christ" (Gal. 6:2), as the basis for morality (Rom. 13: 8–10; Gal. 5:14). In his letters to the churches Paul often responds to specific problems that must have existed among the early Christians, including relationships between men and women, the use of possessions, the issue of slavery, and the claims of the state. It is also apparent to him that Christians must search in harmony for God's will and for the specific ways to fulfill it (Rom. 15:5–6; Phil. 2:1–4). ***See also*** Ancestor; Covenant; Family, The; Women.

Bibliography

Harrelson, Walter. *The Ten Commandments and Human Rights.* Philadelphia: Fortress, 1980.

Houlden, J. L. *Ethics and the New Testament.* New York: Oxford University Press, 1977.

Sanders, Jack T. *Ethics in the New Testament: Change and Development.* Philadelphia: Fortress, 1975.

Zimmerli, Walther. *The Old Testament and the World.* Atlanta, GA: John Knox, 1976. D.A.K.

Ethiopia (or Nubia), the ancient name of the Nile valley region between the first and second cataracts south of Aswan. At the height of Ethiopian power, however, the name denoted an area reaching as far as the junction of the Blue Nile and White Nile at Khartoum (not to be confused with modern Ethiopia, i.e., Abyssinia). The Hebrew term is *Cush,* which the KJV keeps, but some translations use the Greek word *Aithiopia* (for "Cush" in Gen. 2:13, ***see*** Gihon).

For two hundred years, from about 1971 to 1786 B.C., Egyptian control and trading ventures penetrated farther and farther up the Nile but were then forced to withdraw. After expelling the Hyksos invaders (ca. 1550) the Egyptian rulers once more controlled Nubia, but during the period of the Israelite monarchy Nubia became the independent kingdom of Nabatea, which dominated Egypt. The Nubian ruler Taharka (RSV: "Tirhaka"; 690–664 B.C.) appears in both Assyrian and Judean records (Isa. 37:9) as the ally of Hezekiah, despite protestations from the prophet Isaiah (Isa. 18: 1–2; 20:1–6). Egypt fell to the Assyrians in 670, but Nubia remained independent until it became part of the Persian Empire in the sixth century B.C. In Acts 8:26–40 the Ethiopian eunuch was probably a high official in the court of "the Candace," i.e., the queen mother. ***See also*** Hezekiah; Hyksos. D.B.

Ethnarch (eth'nahrk), a title whose Greek etymology ("leader" or "ruler of a people") is clear but whose application and significance in the Hasmonean and Roman periods remain unclear. It occurs only once in the NT (2 Cor. 11: 32), where the RSV, TEV, and NIV render it "governor." From other sources, it is known to be a title given to Simon Maccabeus, Hyrcanus II, and Archelaus. Perhaps it was a title given to rulers over their own people (e.g., the Jews) while under the overall rule of a foreign power (e.g., Rome), ranking somewhat lower than "king." ***See also*** Governor; Tetrarch.

Eubulus (yo͞o-byo͞o'luhs), a Christian who, according to 2 Tim. 4:21, was with Paul during one of Paul's imprisonments. ***See also*** Claudia; Linus; Pudens.

Eucharist. ***See*** Lord's Supper, The.

Eunice (yo͞o'nis), Timothy's mother, who was born Jewish but became a Christian, the wife of a Gentile (Acts 16:1). Influenced by her mother, Lois, Eunice gave Timothy religious instruction (2 Tim. 1:5; 3:14–15), but he was not circumcised until he joined Paul's mission (Acts 16:3; cf. 2 Tim. 3:10–11). ***See also*** Timothy.

eunuch, a male who has been castrated. Eunuchs were in demand as guards of royal harems. Consequently, most biblical references to these persons who by accident or design had lost their capacity to procreate come from narratives about the kings and their courts. Although excluded from the sacred assembly (Deut. 23:1), eunuchs often received favorable report (one rescued Jeremiah; cf. the Ethiopian eunuch in Acts 8:27). Becoming a eunuch for religious reasons is mentioned in Matt. 19:12, although the exact meaning of that verse is unclear. It is probably metaphorical for remaining celibate to serve God better (cf. 1 Cor. 7:32–34).

Euodia (yo͞o-oh'dee-uh; KJV: "Euodias," yo͞o-oh'dee-uhs), a woman in the church at Philippi who was urged by Paul to settle her dispute with

Syntyche (Phil. 4:2). The dispute apparently troubled Paul, because, uncharacteristically, he opened the hortatory portion of his letter to the Philippians by referring to it. ***See also*** Philippians, The Letter of Paul to the; Syntyche.

Euodias (yōō-oh'dee-uhs). ***See*** Euodia.

Euphrates (yōō-fray'teez) **River,** the largest river in western Asia. It was one of four rivers flowing from Eden (Gen. 2:14) in biblical tradition. It served as the northern boundary of Israelite territory under David (2 Sam. 8:3) but was terrain usually under Aramaean control.

The headwaters of the system are two branches that originate in Armenia in eastern Turkey. The western branch (Kara Su) runs first westward from its source in a pond. The eastern branch (Murat Suyu) similarly runs westward, then both join north of Malatiya from which the course runs southeast and southwest into the Syrian plain. The Hellenistic city of Somasata was built near an important ford. Running south, the Euphrates passed Carchemish where Nebuchadrezzar decisively beat the Egyptian-Assyrian alliance in which Neco of Egypt participated (Jer. 46; 2 Kings 24: 7). Main tributaries from the north are the Belikh and the Khabur. Farther downstream were Dura-Europos, famous for a synagogue with Hellenistic painted scenes, and Mari, notable for its palace and library of texts. Continuing its southeast course the river divides just above Babylon. It reunites and then joins the Tigris for the last hundred miles before emptying into the Persian Gulf.

The bed of the river ran somewhat higher than that of the Tigris, and this allowed ancient irrigation canals to carry Euphrates water across the land between the two rivers for agriculture and transport. The lower reaches provided some ten thousand square miles of land for such reclamation, allowing the foundations of cities and city-states in what we know as one of the earliest centers of civilization, Sumer. ***See also*** Damascus; Tigris River. R.S.B.

Eurakylon (yōō-rah-kee'lohn). ***See*** Euroclydon.

Euroclydon (yōō-rahk'lee-dohn), in the RSV, JB, and NIV (Acts 27:14) "the northeaster," a violent, springtime, northeast wind that blew Paul's ship, en route to Rome, south of Crete. The best manuscripts read *eurakylōn* (from Gk. *euros*, "east wind," and Lat. *aquilo*, "northeast wind").

Eutychus (yōō'tuh-kuhs), a youth who dozed during a long discourse by Paul, fell from a third-story window, and was presumed dead; Paul intervened and the youth lived (Acts 20: 7–12).

evangelist (Gk., "one who proclaims good news"), a noun occurring only three times in the NT (Acts 21:8; Eph. 4:11; 2 Tim. 4:5); the idea of proclaiming the good news about God's Kingdom and about Jesus the Christ, however, is found throughout the NT writings. The cognate verb, evangelize (lit. "to proclaim good news"), is frequent, as is the Greek noun translated "gospel" or "good news," which comes directly into English as "evangel." In the earliest days of the church, the work of evangelism, that is, proclaiming the Christian gospel to those who had not heard, was carried out by the apostles and others (Philip is specifically labeled an evangelist in Acts 21:8). Later, as the church grew and spread and as time passed, "evangelist" came to designate a specific office (cf. Eph. 4:11).

By the third century, the authors of the four canonical Gospels ("evangels") had come to be known as "Evangelists." Earlier, an identification was made between the Gospels and their authors, and the four living creatures of Rev. 4: 7 (an identification not intended, however, by the author of Revelation). On that basis, the lion came to symbolize Matthew, the ox to symbolize Mark, the man to symbolize Luke, and the eagle, John. ***See also*** Apostle; Church; Gospel, Gospels; Philip. J.M.E.

Eve, the first woman, created by God (Gen. 2: 21–22). The meaning of the name is uncertain. In sound, but not in derivation, the name resembles the Hebrew word "life." The association pertains in Gen. 3:20, where the primal woman is designated "the mother of all living." Scholars speculate whether mythological images such

Eve spins while Adam digs; thirteenth-century stone relief, Sainte Chapelle, Paris.

as Earth Mother or Mother Goddess lie behind the figure. The story may suggest that by naming the woman Eve, the man rules over her and so corrupts their God-given relationship of equality (Gen. 2:23). In this context the name may be ironic. It suggests life even as life for the woman is diminished. Eve also appears in Gen. 4:1, 2 Cor. 11:3, and 1 Tim. 2:13. P.T.

everlasting life. ***See*** Eternal Life.

evil, a term with several nuances of meaning in the biblical writings. At base, the primary understanding evolves from a religious perspective, since all forms of evil are regarded as ultimately occasioned by the disobedience and rebellion of the human race with regard to God and God's will. Evil occurs where and when God's will is hindered by human sin. Bad situations or natural calamities were sometimes referred to as "evil," and such occurrences were frequently interpreted as having been sent by God as a punishment for sin (e.g., Deut. 31:17; Amos 3:6; Jer. 26:19). Moreover, if something did not function properly or could not be understood, this too was seen to be "evil" (e.g., Eccles. 6:1–2).

Quite early in the development of Israel's religious understanding, evil came to be concretized in specific persons or events. Later, it came to be understood as a separate and pervasive power in the created order. This system of evil had a leader (Satan, the devil) who exercised control over numerous underlings (demons). However it was seen to be manifested in human experience, evil was interpreted as rebellion against God or the thwarting of God's will through actions (by humans or others) that were at odds with God's plans and purposes for the world.

Various biblical passages locate evil in different places: the human will (e.g., 1 Sam. 24:13; Mark 7:20–23; cf. also Gen. 6:5), the desire for worldly wealth (e.g., 1 Tim. 6:10), or demonic powers that take control of human lives (cf. the stories of demon possession in the synoptic Gospels). Wherever evil originated, however, it was understood to be effective only as it took human form. It was clear from observation, if nothing else, that human beings are inclined toward, open to, and perpetrators of evil and that evil always has tragic consequences for the human race. ***See also*** Demon; Devil; Satan; Sin.

J.M.E.

Evil-merodach (ee'vil-mair'oh-dahk), a Neo-Babylonian (Chaldean) king (561–560 B.C.) and the immediate successor of Nebuchadnezzar II. Evil-merodach released King Jehoiachin from imprisonment; the Judean king was given an allowance, and for the remainder of his life he dined at the Babylonian king's table (2 Kings 25: 27–30; Jer. 52:31–34). Evil-merodach may have been trying to modify his father's policies; he was killed in a revolution.

evil spirits. ***See*** Demon; Devil.

ewe, a female sheep (Heb. *raḥel*). Ewes are mentioned, for example, in Gen. 32:14, where Jacob presents Esau with two hundred ewes, and in Lev. 22:28, where it is forbidden to kill a ewe on the same day that her lamb is killed.

excavation. ***See*** Archaeology, Methods of.

Exile, a term used, often synonymously with "captivity," to refer to the period in the sixth century B.C. when part of the Judaean population was exiled to Babylonia. The term is not historically satisfactory, since it is too easily taken to suggest that the whole population was deported.

Deportation as a policy was practiced by various ancient powers: Assyria deported part of the population of the Northern Kingdom (Israel) in 722 B.C. 2 Kings 17:6 and 18:11 list places to which they were taken; their subsequent history is unknown. Sennacherib's siege of Lachish (701 B.C.) resulted in deportation of captives. Babylon deported Jehoiachin and other members of the royal family in 597 B.C., together with leading military men, military personnel, and craftsmen (2 Kings 24:15–16); a second deportation followed in 587 B.C. consisting of survivors in Jerusalem and deserters (2 Kings 25:11). Jer. 52:30 records a third deportation in 582 B.C. The numbers are differently computed: Jer. 52:30 gives a total for all three deportations of 4,600; 2 Kings 25:14 has 10,000 for 597 B.C. alone. Similar policies are attested for the Persians and for later Greek and Roman rulers.

The Assyrians brought deportees from elsewhere to Samaria (2 Kings 17); the Babylonians appointed a Judaean notable, Gedaliah, to control the area (2 Kings 25:22–24). The parallel in Jeremiah 40 implies a considerable population in Judah; 2 Kings 24:14 and 25:12 know only of "some of the poorest of the land" left to tend crops. 2 Chron. 36:21, taking up prophecies of total desolation (e.g., Jer. 7:34, cf. Lam. 1:3), clearly envisages a land emptied of population. This theological motif reflects the view that restoration came only from the exiles in Babylonia (cf. Jer. 24:5–7; 29:4–14; Ezek. 11).

The biblical account provides no direct information about Judah during the exilic age. Jeremiah 41–44 implies that no population was left in Judah after Gedaliah's death. The accounts of restoration in Ezra are problematic, but hints appear of local inhabitants in addition to returned exiles (cf. also Hag. 2:4). Some continuity of population in Judah must be assumed.

Conditions in Babylon are also poorly attested. Jer. 29:5–6 envisages settlement and

Two Judean captives of Sennacherib's conquest of Lachish, 701 B.C.; Nineveh.

some independence of life. Ezek. 8:1 and 20:1 refer to elders of the community meeting with the prophet. Ezek. 1:1; Ezra 1:4; and 8:15–17 suggest various settlements at which Jews were to be found; both Ezek. 11:16 and Ezra 8:17 may imply the existence of temples. That Jews continued to live in Babylonia is clear from renewed movements to Judah with Ezra and Nehemiah, the presence of some Jewish names in Babylonian documents of the fifth century B.C. (e.g., those of the firm of Murashu), and the later importance of Babylonian Jewry. Impetus to renewed faithfulness of Jewish customs evidently came from there on more than one occasion.

Exile as a theological theme becomes clear in later writings. Thus, the sins for which the Exile is punishment are variously assessed and theologically justified; and various preconditions are given for the termination of the Exile, like divine grace, human repentance, or a combination of the two (cf. Jer. 24; 31; Ezek. 18; Lam. 5). In Jer. 25:11–12 and 29:10 (cf. Zech. 1: 12) a seventy-year figure is used for the Exile; Ezek. 4:5–6 has a forty-year scheme, as well as 390 (or 150 or 190) for the Northern Kingdom. Dan. 9:2, 24–27 reinterprets the seventy-year period as 490 years, seeing the end of Exile as sequel to the desecration of the Temple in 167 B.C. The theme reappears in various intertestamental writings. Psalm 137 offers an interpretation of the experience in terms of desolation and hope. It would also appear that the Exile was a time when national traditions were consolidated and cadres of interpreters of Scriptures were trained (see Neh. 8).

Bibliography

Ackroyd, P. R. *Exile and Restoration*. Philadelphia: Westminister Press, 1968.

Bickermann, E. "The Babylonian Captivity." *Cambridge History of Judaism*. Vol. 1. Edited by L. Finkelstein and W. D. Davis. Cambridge: Cambridge University Press, 1984. Pp. 342–358.

Klein, R. W. *Israel in Exile*. Philadelphia: Fortress, 1979.

P.R.A.

Exodus, the second book of the Hebrew Bible and the story of Moses' call by God to rescue his people from oppression in Egypt. After encountering God and entering into a convenant in the wilderness at Sinai, the Israelites constructed a portable shrine (tabernacle) and set out on a journey toward Canaan, the land promised by God to their ancestors as an inheritance. Exodus is the book's Greek title in the Septuagint (LXX); in Hebrew it is called (from its opening words) *ve'elleh sh^{e}moth*, "And these [are] the names," or simply *Sh^{e}moth*, "Names."

The Event: The event was the successful escape of Semitic residents from hardship and forced labor in northern Egypt. According to the Joseph stories (Gen. 37; 39–50) they had entered the country considerably earlier to avoid famine in Canaan (perhaps as part of a larger population movement). The underlying historical events are now obscure. Later Israelites frequently retold their past and reenacted it in worship, but they inevitably expanded and modified the very traditions they preserved. The resulting narratives contained the people's self-understanding and gave it unity and cohesion, but the narratives did not always record past events with historical accuracy.

Like the biblical accounts in their time, modern reconstructions of the exodus event cannot avoid being partially subjective. Judgments about content or tone, about what is possible or likely depend on the evaluator's training, attitudes, and experiences of God's presence in (or apparent absence from) human life. Different experiences or different perceptions may lead to different evaluations of the biblical record. No reassessment of historical likelihood can be compulsory, but such reassessment may lead to new insights or better understanding.

The movement of Israel's ancestors into Egypt and out again is hard to reconstruct. Some groups may have gone there as early as the late eighteenth century B.C., at the start of foreign (Hyksos) rule; others may have arrived in the late fourteenth or early thirteenth century, only a few years before the oppression reflected in Exodus 1. Similarly, groups of these ancestors may have left Egypt at different times, separated by many years, and under varied circumstances. The later Israelites preserved few stories from the period of their ancestors' earliest movements into Egypt until the oppression and exodus, but they knew it had been very long (430 years, Exod. 12:40; 400 years, Gen. 15:13). If there were repeated departures from Egypt, surviving traditions merged them into one complex movement. That simplification, the distance in time between even the latest departures

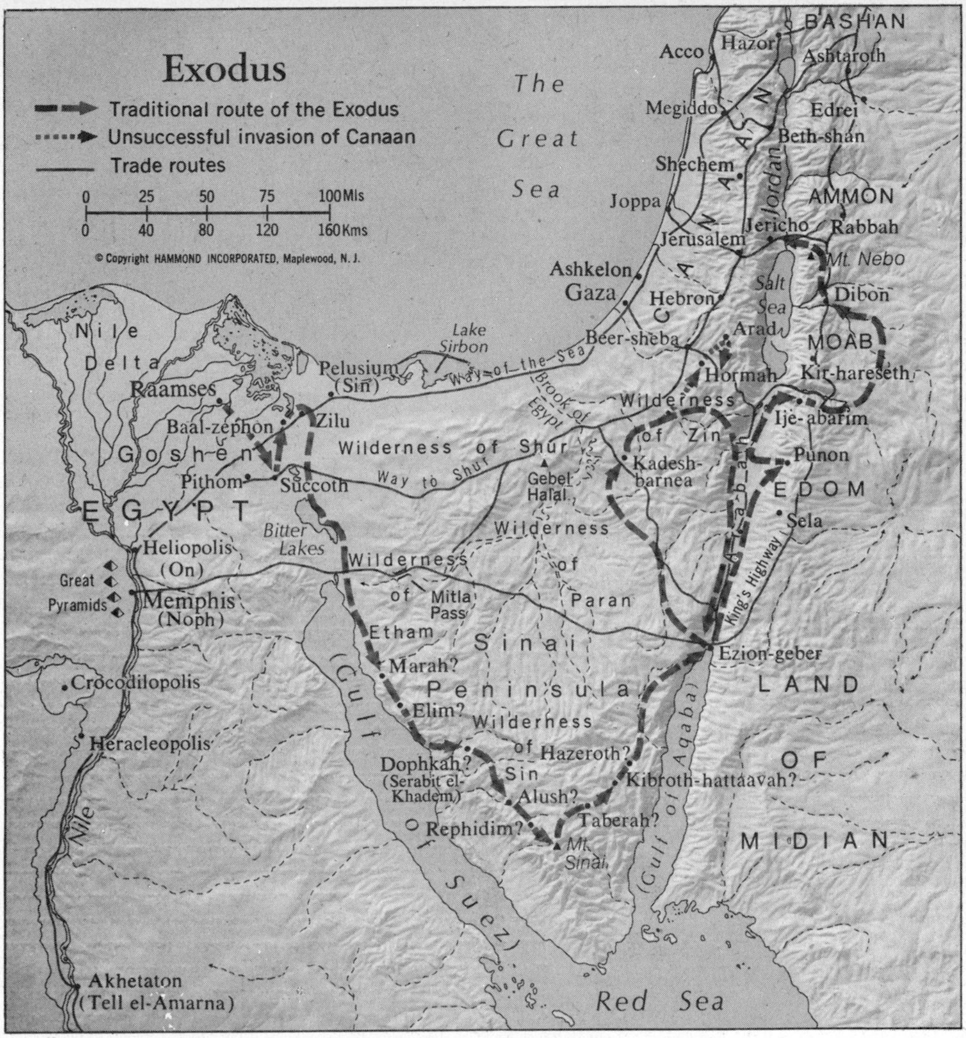

The map outlines the traditional route of the Exodus and also shows ancient routes of travel across the Sinai that Israelites may have used between Egypt and Canaan.

from Egypt (thirteenth century B.C.) and the composition of the major literary sources for Exodus (tenth to sixth centuries or later), and the likelihood that the biblical authors knew nothing of the geography of the exodus events make it unwise to propose one route for the exodus or to expect that all the exodus stories will form a fully consistent narrative.

The exodus traditions are marked by humor and lively imagination (especially in the repeated confrontations between Moses and Pharaoh). The accounts of the covenant at Sinai represent varied theological understandings of its consequences for the people's life. The wilderness traditions have been shaped by later writers to provide useful perspectives on Israel's subsequent experiences in the land. Emphasis on the miraculous serves to highlight God's involvement in the people's deliverance. The traditions also record many individual episodes.

Most scholars tend to date the (final) Exodus from Egypt early in the reign of Pharaoh Ramesses II (ca. 1290 B.C.), so that the oppression would have begun not long after the nineteenth dynasty took power (ca. 1350 B.C.), and the invasion of Canaan would have started some years before the end of Ramesses' reign (ca. 1230 B.C.). Another view is that the Hebrew tribes entered Egypt from Canaan at the time of the Hyksos, that the rise of the eighteenth dynasty (ca. 1580 B.C.) began the oppression, and that the Exodus occurred during the reign of Thutmose III (ca. 1450 B.C.). This is in harmony with the statement (1 Kings 6:1) that the construction of Solomon's Temple (ca. 970 B.C.) began 480 years after the Israelites left Egypt. This figure (twelve generations of forty years) is too exact and probably secondary.

Different routes have been proposed for the Exodus, as well. One route turns south after crossing the line of the modern Suez Canal (near the Bitter Lakes), parallels the eastern coast of the Gulf of Suez to the vicinity of the turquoise mines at Serabit el-Khadem, and continues inland to the traditional site of Mount Sinai at Gebel Musa. After the stay at Sinai, the people would have journeyed in a northeasterly direction to the northern tip of the Gulf of Aqaba, then around Edom and Moab, and on to Transjordan. While this route locates Mount Sinai at the place accepted since Byzantine times, it lacks earlier support and conflicts with the biblical view that the people first headed for Canaan and were only condemned to wander after they had been at Sinai and had rejected the report of the spies sent into the land from Kadesh in the wilderness of Paran (Num. 13–14).

Another route runs north (a little east of the present Suez Canal), turns east along the Mediterranean coast, and follows the narrow strip of land that divides Lake Sirbon from the sea. This allows Lake Sirbon to be identified as the sea where Israel was delivered and the Egyptian pursuers were drowned (Exod. 14–15). Unfortunately, there is no obvious route from Lake Sirbon to Kadesh nor any easy access across the sand dunes to Sinai proper. Consequently this route also has little to recommend it.

At least three trails extend east-west across the northern half of Sinai: a coastal road just south of Lake Sirbon and on past Gaza and Megiddo toward Damascus; a central route from Lake Timsah through Khatmia Pass, south of Gebel el Maghara, north around Gebel Halal, then southeast to Ain Qudeirat and Kadesh, and northeast toward Beer-sheba, Hebron, and

OUTLINE OF CONTENTS

The Book of Exodus

I. Introduction: the new threat (1:1–22)
II. Moses (2:1–7:7)
 A. A child is found (2:1–10)
 B. Escape to Midian (2:11–22)
 C. Transition (2:23–25)
 D. Call and commission (3:1–12)
 E. Development of commission (3:13–22)
 F. Fruitless objections (4:1–17)
 G. Return to Egypt (4:18–31)
 H. Initial encounter with Pharaoh (5:1–6:1)
 I. Covenant promises and commission (6:2–13)
 J. Genealogy (6:14–25)
 K. Summary and transition (6:26–27)
 L. Renewed commission (6:28–7:7)
III. Contest with Pharaoh (7:8–12:32)
 A. Rod to serpent (7:8–13)
 B. Spoiling of water (7:14–24)
 C. Frogs (7:25–8:11; RSV 7:25–8:15)
 D. Gnats (8:12–15; RSV vv. 16–19)
 E. Flies (8:16–28; RSV vv. 20–32)
 F. Plague on cattle (9:1–7)
 G. Boils (9:8–12)
 H. Hail (9:13–35)
 I. Locusts (10:1–20)
 J. Darkness (10:21–29)
 K. Death of firstborn I (11:1–10)
 L. Interlude: Passover observance (12:1–28)
 M. Death of firstborn II (12:29–32)
IV. Departure from Egypt (12:33–15:21)
 A. Initial haste (12:33–42)
 B. Regulations for Passover I (12:43–49)
 C. Summary (12:50–51)
 D. Regulations for Passover II (13:1–16)
 E. Divine guidance (13:17–22)
 F. Pharaoh's pursuit (14:1–9)
 G. Fear and protection (14:10–20)
 H. Defeat of Egyptians (14:21–31)
 I. Victory song (15:1–21)
V. In the wilderness (15:22–18:27)
 A. Water at Marah and Elim (15:22–27)
 B. Manna and quail (16:1–36)
 C. Water at Massah and Meribah (17:1–7)
 D. Victory over Amalek (17:8–16)
 E. Jethro's visit (18:1–27)
VI. At the mountain (19:1–40:38)
 A. Preparations I (19:1–25)
 B. Decalogue (20:1–17)
 C. Preparations II (20:18–21)
 D. Covenantal law (20:22–23:19)
 E. Threat and blessings (23:20–33)
 F. Covenant ceremonies (24:1–11)
 G. Moses and God (24:12–18)
 H. Prescriptions for the tabernacle and its service (25:1–31:11)
 I. Sabbath observance I (31:12–17)
 J. Transition (31:18)
 K. Sin and punishment (32:1–35)
 L. Repentance, intercession, and divine mercy (33:1–23)
 M. Renewed covenant and Moses' mediation (34:1–35)
 N. Sabbath observance II (35:1–3)
 O. Preparing the tabernacle and its service (35:4–39:42)
 P. Setting up the tabernacle and its furnishings (40:1–33)
 Q. God's Presence in the tabernacle (40:34–38)

Shechem; a southern road (the Darb el-Hajj or "Pilgrim's Road" to Mecca) from the northern end of the Gulf of Suez eastward through Mitla Pass and then southeast toward the northern end of the Gulf of Aqaba. Three other routes across Sinai connect those roads: one branching northeast off the road from Suez to Aqaba and extending to Kadesh; another heading southeast from Kadesh to Aqaba; and a third north from Aqaba to the southern end of the Dead Sea. The different Pentateuchal sources may have put the route of the Exodus on different combinations of these trails, but all apparently located it in the northern half of Sinai with a stop at Kadesh-barnea and an approach to the northern end of the Gulf of Aqaba.

The Book: The book of Exodus is based on the unified J (Yahwist) source, supplemented by a number of E (Elohist) passages and a few from D (Deuteronomist), with a new outline and a great deal more material from P (Priestly writer). While the details of source division are often disputed, and some scholars question the main lines of the analysis, the general validity of the Pentateuchal sources may be assumed.

J's version of Exodus, part of a longer narrative extending from the creation account in Genesis 2 to the Balaam stories in Numbers 22–24, presents a general theology of human life in covenant with God. People can on occasion acknowledge their weakness and their need of divine assistance, but more often they respond inappropriately to God and to the challenges of human life. Consequently, God appears as the dominant agent in J, Moses is more of a witness or messenger than a primary actor, and the people's role is to "stand firm, and see the salvation of the Lord, which he will work" (Exod. 14:13). The human propensity for failure or inappropriate response finds expression in disbelief, murmuring, even open rebellion against the Lord and his chosen representatives. The incident of the golden calf (Exod. 32) is an integral part of the J narrative and has been shaped to make two related points: first, the people's failure was present from the earliest moments of the Sinai covenant (but God's care for them continued); and, second, the Northern Kingdom's departure from the Davidic covenant after the death of Solomon is not the collapse of the divine plan, but another instance of the constant human tendency to reject the good. God's care will continue even now, and the divine assistance will be available for those who do not walk away (or who return). Even when the Exodus generation failed to trust the Lord's help and were excluded from entry into the Promised Land, God's promises remained in effect for their descendants (cf. Num. 13–14).

The intent of the J narrative in Exodus (and generally) was to encourage and support faithful members of the covenant community discouraged at that covenant's apparent collapse in Jeroboam's (ca. 924 B.C.) revolt and the split between north (Israel) and south (Judah) by suggesting that the crisis was neither unique nor definitive. Only God's reaction really matters, and God can be trusted to be faithful to the chosen ones.

The elements from E are hard to detect, at least in Exodus, and no clear statement can be made about their nature and purpose. The D materials in Exodus are also too limited for analysis here.

P expanded the available J traditions and recast them into a new work with an entirely different intention. Thus the plague narratives (Exod. 7–12) become a dramatic contest between God's champions (Aaron and Moses) and those of Pharaoh (the magicians). Bit by bit the magicians are defeated, and finally they disappear from view. Somewhat earlier, in Exod. 6:14–25, P's genealogy of Moses and Aaron is carried down an extra generation to culminate in the birth of Aaron's grandson Phinehas; he will have a decisive role in the climactic incident where "a covenant of eternal priesthood" is promised to him and his descendants after him (Num. 25:6–13). The Sinai events are important to P primarily because they provide a context for the revelation of instructions for the proper performance of worship. That is, Temple worship can be the continuation and completion of what was begun at Sinai, and consequently the absence of a Davidic ruler in the Exile or after the return is not particularly important for P or for the audience to which the P version is directed.

Deliverance from bondage, protection in the wilderness, and covenant at Sinai all find their deepest meaning and abiding value, for P, in the proper performance of the worship whose regulations were communicated through Moses at Sinai. This narrowing of focus stands in some tension with the J materials, and that tension is itself a part of the biblical challenge for readers of the present book of Exodus. Discovering how to respond to that challenge is the task that beckons each person who reads Exodus with care. ***See also*** Baal-peor; Canaan, Canaanites; Covenant; Hebrews; Hyksos; Jethro; Korah; Law; Manna; Moses; Pentateuch; Plagues; Quail; Sinai; Ten Commandments; Yam Suph.

K.G.O.

exorcism. ***See*** Magic and Divination.

expiation, a term associated with the removal, cleansing, or forgiveness of sin; it is often confused with "propitiation" (cf. Rom. 3:25; 1 John 2:2; 4:10 [KJV: "propitiation"; RSV: "expiation"]). Both terms create confusion for many modern readers because of their infrequent occurrence in contemporary usage (even in translations of the Bible) or because of their apparent synonymity. They are to be differentiated, however, and their categorical distinction is of considerable importance.

The root meanings in Latin (expiate: "to make satisfaction"; propitiate: "to cause someone to become favorably inclined") are of some help initially when translated into the context of atonement texts in the OT and the NT and the content of their practices and concepts. Both terms presuppose a common starting point as fundamental: God has established a covenant with his people; he is faithful to that covenant; the covenant people, on the other hand, are not faithful and sin against God corporately or individually, ritually or personally; but God provides a means for restoration to the right covenantal relationship, i.e., atonement is possible. The need for interpreting the atonement creates the occasion for use of the terms "expiation" and "propitiation."

Expiation and propitiation provide two angles of vision: the former looks at the object causing the broken covenantal relationship (sin), while the latter looks at the subject initiating and sustaining the covenant (God). Propitiation as a category of interpretation tends to think in forensic, legal terms; i.e., it thinks of God as the injured party in a liability case. It adds to this perspective the theological dimension of the divinely instituted order. The human being has transgressed that order and the injured deity is justifiably angry with the transgressor. Punishment is to be expected. The fundamental notion is that God is going to remain angry until he is suitably appeased or placated. Propitiations ward off, or turn away, the divine wrath; they are apotropaic in function. Expiation, on the other hand, tends to concentrate on the transgression itself and the issue of how it is to be removed, cleansed, and forgiven. It does not specifically counter the notions associated with propitiation as though they were groundless, but as a matter of choice it declines to speculate about the degrees of divine anger or to calculate the proportions necessary to appease or satisfy God's wrath.

On the whole, expiation as a category of interpretation is far more in keeping with the angle of vision taken by biblical writers of both Testaments (though not always for the theories of atonement in modern theological textbooks) than is propitiation. This judgment is based largely on the following consideration: the provision of a means for atonement is itself a strong indication that, while God's wrath over the transgression of his order and his covenant is real and justified, it is important to concentrate on the initiative taken to remove the transgression. This angle of vision seeks to honor the perspective of God who makes forgiveness possible because of his mercy, love, and grace.

For the OT levitical sacrificial system, there were basically two types of expiatory offerings: the sin offering and the guilt offering (Lev. 4:1–6:7; 6:24–7:1). The former purified or cleansed in the area of ceremonial offenses, while the latter involved offenses in social intercourse (broken pledges, property violations, etc). As a rule, the object of the verb "to expiate" is not God; thus, the notion of appeasement should be avoided. In a few cases, an apotropaic, propitiatory notion is likely, however (Gen. 32:20; Num. 16:47–48; 25:11; 1 Sam. 26:19; 2 Sam. 21:3–4; 24:25; Prov. 16:14). Hence, propitiation may not be a useless category altogether; yet, as pertains to God it is an interpretive possibility where words are few and inadequate.

In the NT, the Greek term variously translated as "expiation" or "propitiation" is applied to the work of Christ in four passages (Rom. 3:25; Heb. 2:17; 1 John 2:2; 4:10). In all of these passages, the RSV reads "expiation"; in all except the second, where it has "reconciliation," the KJV reads "propitiation." Taking Paul's theology of the cross as our angle of vision, we sense that there is something about the crucifixion of Jesus that is awe-inspiring, cosmic drama. What exactly happened there with regard to God's holy nature, his wrath at the presence of sin, and his will to destroy it is something into which human eyes cannot penetrate and human reason cannot discern (Rom. 3:21–26; 2 Cor. 5:21). It is perhaps not entirely inappropriate to leave open the possibility that a propitiatory moment is present in the atoning sacrifice of Christ, while mortals choose by necessity to focus their attention on expiation.
See also Atonement; Blood; Forgiveness; Grace; Justification; Pardon; Reconciliation; Redemption; Salvation; Sin; Worship.

Bibliography

Goppelt, Leonard. *Theology of the New Testament*, Vol. 1. Grand Rapids, MI: Eerdmans, 1981. Pp. 193–199. Vol. 2, 1983. Pp. 87–106.

Hengel, Martin. *The Atonement: The Origins of the Doctrine in the New Testament*. Philadelphia: Fortress, 1981.

von Rad, Gerhard. *Old Testament Theology*, Vol. 1. New York: Harper & Row, 1962. Pp. 254–279. Vol. 2, 1965. Pp. 275–292. J.E.A.

eye, an organ adapted to perceive light and darkness. In the Bible, the word can refer to the eyes of humans and animals (Gen. 27:1; Job 21:20) and appears in a number of combinations such as "raising one's eyes" (Gen. 18:2). "Eye" may also be used to refer to a person's look or appearance (Lev. 13:55). "Eye" also appears in a number of metaphorical senses. A person whose eye is "evil" is one consumed with jealousy, envy, or malice toward another (Ecclus. 14:10; Matt. 6:23; Mark 7:22). "Eye" can be used in connection with the heart or mind (Ecclus. 17:8; Eph. 1:18; Luke 19:42). Therefore, those who are without understanding can be spoken of as having their eyes blinded (Isa. 6:10; Mark 8:18; Matt. 13:15; John 12:40; Acts 28:27). God is often pictured with multiple eyes (Zech. 4:

10). They rove over the world like the agents of the great king (cf. Job 1:6). A figurine of the goddess Ishtar shows multiple eyes on top of the goddess's head vanishing toward infinity. "Eye" also appears in the names of springs or fountains in the OT (Gen. 16:7; Num. 33:9).

P.P.

eye of a needle, the. *See* Needle's Eye.

Ezekiel (ee-zee'kee-uhl), **the Book of,** an OT book of prophecies attributed to the sixth-century prophet Ezekiel (Heb., "God strengthens").

The Prophet: When King Nebuchadnezzar of Babylon captured Jerusalem in 597 B.C., he took many of the leading citizens of Jerusalem as hostages to Babylon, among whom was Ezekiel the priest, the son of Buzi (1:3). They were resettled at a place called Tel Abib (Heb. "mound of the flood") on the river Chebar, one of the tributary canals of the Euphrates River southeast of Babylon, near the ancient city of Nippur. It was there that Ezekiel received his call as a prophet of the Lord in 593 B.C. From then on, he prophesied intermittently until 571 B.C.

Ezekiel seems to have been deeply affected by the message he was called upon to deliver. Following his initial call, he sat overwhelmed for seven days (3:15). He was given to extraordinary visions and engaged in prophetic symbolic acts, which must have appeared strange to many of his contemporaries (3:1–3; 4:1–17; 5:1–3). From the time of his call and until the final fall of Jerusalem in 586 B.C., he was a virtual recluse in his house and afflicted with fits of dumbness and immobility (3:24–27; 24:25–27; 33:21–22). The sudden death of his wife and his inability to mourn for her according to custom become a symbol of the sudden destruction of God's sanctuary in Jerusalem (24:15–18). His contemporaries viewed him as somewhat of a curiosity (33:30–33). Only in retrospect was his true greatness recognized and his words were preserved for posterity. We do not know when or under what circumstances Ezekiel died, though presumably it was in exile.

The Book: Ezekiel gives evidence of having been shaped editorially by a school of disciples, who, however, were not far removed in time from the prophet himself. Its outline exhibits a clear threefold structure. Chaps. 1–24 consist chiefly of oracles of judgment against Judah and Jerusalem prior to the fall of the city. This is followed in chaps. 25–32 by oracles against various foreign nations. After a transitional chapter (33) that links the first and third sections, there follow in chaps. 34–48 prophecies about the future restoration of the people in the promised land.

The Message: Ezekiel was called to be a watchman in the service of God, whose chief task it was to warn his people in accordance with the words God had given him (3:16–21; 33:1–9). This he did faithfully throughout his ministry, irrespective of whether his compatriots heeded him or not. Ezekiel's message is imbued with a

Ezekiel's vision of dry bones; a detail from a panel at the third-century synagogue at Dura-Europos. Ezekiel, touched by the hand of the Lord, stands among disjointed human remains; he is told to prophesy that the bones would live again (Ezek. 37:1–14).

strong sense of the sovereignty of God and the self-directed purposefulness of God's activity in history, which cannot be thwarted by human failure. This divine activity in history involves both judgment and salvation and is designed to bring Israel and the nations to the true knowledge of God. Because of Israel's repeated failure and sin, God had resolved to destroy the nation. This decision was irrevocable (14:12–20; 21:1–7). Unlike Hosea and Jeremiah, who viewed Israel's history as one of initial faithfulness followed by disobedience, Ezekiel describes Israel's entire existence from Egypt on as one of disobedience and rebellion (20:1–38). The harlotry metaphor, already used by Hosea and Jeremiah to describe Israel's waywardness, is elaborated to the extreme by Ezekiel in chaps. 16 and 23. Ezekiel also attacks all false human hopes (12:21–28; 33:23–29), thereby preparing the ground for a hope based not on human merit or potential, but on God's own character and purpose (36:16–38).

With the destruction of Jerusalem in 586 B.C., Ezekiel's message of judgment received its ultimate validation. From that point on, the prophet's message increasingly focuses on the theme of hope and salvation. Ezekiel reminds those who felt cut off from God in a pagan and unclean land that the glory of the Lord was not tied to the Temple in Jerusalem but had traveled with them into exile (chaps. 1 and 10). God himself had even become their sanctuary for a while, until he would bring them back to their own land (11:16–17). Ezekiel gently reminds those crushed by a sense of guilt and despair (33:10) that the Lord takes no pleasure in the death of the wicked, but that he is more than willing and able to forgive penitent sinners and restore them to life even in exile (33:11–20). The sins of past generations could not prevent the present generation from making life-affirming choices (18:1–20); and the same truth was operative even within the lifespan of one human being or generation (18:21–32). God's intentions for humanity are fundamentally salvific (18:32; 33:11). Ezekiel goes on to speak of the future restoration of his people in their own land, where they would live in peace and security, under righteous rulers, and with God as their good shepherd (34; 35:1–36:15; 37:1–28). God's sanctuary would be restored in their midst and the glory of the Lord would return to the place from which it once had departed (40:1–43:5). Not only would the nation be restored outwardly, but God would also renew them inwardly through the gracious bestowal of his spirit and the renewal of the human heart (36:26–27; 37:14; 11:19–20).

OUTLINE OF CONTENTS

The Book of Ezekiel

I. Oracles of judgment against Judah and Jerusalem (1:1–24:27)
   - A. Vision of God's glory and call of Ezekiel (1:1–3:21)
   - B. Symbolic acts: the coming siege of Jerusalem (3:22–5:17)
   - C. Oracles of judgment and announcement of its imminence (6:1–7:27)
   - D. Abominations in the Temple: God's glory departs (8:1–11:25)
   - E. Symbolic acts describing the Exile and sayings against unresponsive people and false prophets (12:1–14:23)
   - F. Historical allegories and sermons: against the people, their kings, and individual wickedness (15:1–20:49)
   - G. Further oracles of judgment (21:1–32:49)
   - H. Symbolic acts: the siege begins (24:1–27)

II. Oracles against foreign nations (25:1–32:32)
   - A. Judah's immediate neighbors: Ammon, Moab, Edom, the Philistines (25:1–17)
   - B. Tyre (26:1–28:26)
   - C. Egypt (29:1–32:32)

III. Prophecies of future restoration (33:1–39:29)
   - A. Announcement of Jerusalem's fall: Ezekiel's role as watchman and importance of individual responsibility (33:1–33)
   - B. Promises of deliverance from exile and restoration in the land (34:1–37:28)
   - C. God and Magog: the enemy's ultimate defeat (38:1–39:29)

IV. Program for reorganization of the restored community (40:1–48:35)
   - A. Plans for new Temple: God's glory returns (40:1–43:12)
   - B. Temple regulations and personnel (43:13–46:24)
   - C. The healing waters of the Temple spring (47:1–12)
   - D. Division of the land (47:13–48:35)

Bibliography

Greenberg, M. *Ezekiel 1–20*. Garden City: Doubleday, 1983.

Zimmerli, W. *Ezekiel*, vols. 1 and 2. Philadelphia: Fortress, 1979, 1983.

W.E.L.

Ezem (ee'zem; Heb., "bone"), a town in southern Judah counted as belonging to both Judah (Josh. 15:29) and Simeon (Josh. 19:3). Since the tribe of Simeon was early assimilated into Judah, the town was probably originally assigned to Simeon but was absorbed into Judah as Simeon lost its identity (note Gen. 49:5–7). The site is unknown.

Ezer (ee'zuhr), the English translation of two OT words. As a translation of the Hebrew word *'etser* ("treasure") it is the name of a son of Seir and chieftain of the Horites, ancient inhabitants of Edom (Gen. 36:21). As a translation of the Hebrew word *'ezer* ("help") it names the following: **1** A descendant of Judah in the clan of Hur (1 Chron. 4:4). **2** A Manassehite, the son of Ephraim; he was killed with his brother Elead in a raid against Philistine livestock at Gath (1 Chron. 7:21). **3** A Gadite who joined David's fighting men at Ziklag (1 Chron. 12:9). **4** The son of Jeshua; he helped rebuild the walls of Jerusalem under Nehemiah (Neh. 3:19). **5** A priest who took part in the dedication of the rebuilt walls in postexilic Jerusalem (Neh. 12:42); he is possibly the same as 4. ***See also*** Horites. D.R.B.

Ezion-geber (ee'zee-ahn-gay'buhr), a town in Edom on the Gulf of Aqabah. It is listed in Num. 33:35–36 as a stopping place during the Exodus. Solomon "built a fleet of ships at Ezion-geber" and sent them on profitable journeys to southern Arabia and East Africa (1 Kings 9:26–28; 10:11; 2 Chron. 8:17; 9:10–11). After Solomon's death (ca. 976 B.C.) the region reverted to Edomite control. It was reconquered by Jehoshaphat of Judah, who also built a fleet of ships that were, however, "wrecked at Ezion-geber" (1 Kings 22:48; 2 Chron. 20:36). They may have been destroyed by the Edomites, or quite probably by a tempest, for although the average rainfall is only 2 inches (50 mm.), savage winter storms can bring floods from the Edomite mountains and, along the Arabah, howling gales stirring the sea to fury.

The exact site of Ezion-geber is far from certain. Some authorities equate it with Elath (although Deut. 2:8; 1 Kings 9:26 [RSV: "Eloth"]; and 2 Chron. 8:17 [RSV: "Eloth"] speak of two separate places, suggesting that Ezion-geber was the Israelite name and Elath the Edomite), and identify the site with the oasis of Aqabah at the northeast corner of the gulf, an area with a good water supply and easy access to the Edomite plateau via the Wadi Ytem. Unquestionably, this is the obvious place for settlement, but there is, unfortunately, absolutely no evidence of Iron Age (1200–334 B.C.) occupation in this area, although it is possible that all vestiges of a settlement could have been washed away by flash floods. Those who believe that there were two distinct settlements usually place Elath at Aqabah and Ezion-geber at modern Tell el-Kheleifeh, which is located almost in the center of the northern tip of the gulf and 550 yards (457 m.) from the shore.

This site was excavated by the American archaeologist Nelson Glueck between 1938 and 1940 and revealed five periods of occupation. The earliest structure, probably erected in the reign of Solomon, was a small well-built mudbrick building with a courtyard and massive southern gate. Glueck first equated this with Solomon's copper refinery, but the modern archaeologist B. Rothenburg has shown that the nearby copper mines are in fact some centuries earlier, and he suggests that the building was a Solomonic fort or caravanserai. Since the site is completely exposed to the occasional furious winter storms, it can hardly have served as an important anchorage for shipping; a military outpost to guard the south end of the Arabah seems far more probable.

The second period had a much stronger building, with double mudbrick wall and massive four-chambered gate, probably belonging to the reign of Jehoshaphat. The last biblical mention of Ezion-geber occurs in connection with Jehoshaphat's rule (1 Kings 22:48), but Elath was recaptured for Judah either by Amaziah (2 Kings 14:22) or more probably by Uzziah (2 Chron. 26:2, RSV: "Eloth"), whose son Jotham appears to be mentioned on a seal found in the third period of Tell el-Kheleifeh. In about 733 B.C. Elath fell to the Edomites (2 Kings 16:6), who evidently rebuilt Tell el-Kheleifeh, for some Edomite jar handles have been found at the fourth level. The fifth and final occupation was sometime in the sixth century B.C. during the Babylonian and early Persian empires, but the site was abandoned in the early fifth century B.C.. ***See also*** Amaziah; Edom; Jehoshaphat; Solomon. D.B.

Ezra (Heb., "help"), an OT book and the priest to whom it is ascribed.

The Book of Ezra: The material in the first part of the book of Ezra in Hebrew is what the English Bible has as Ezra and Nehemiah. The English book of Ezra also appears as part of 1 Esdras in the Apocrypha. The first part (chaps. 1–6) concerns the restoration of the Jewish community after the Exile and the second part (chaps. 7–10) the account of Ezra's mission (continued in Neh. 8–9).

Chaps. 1–6 provide several different elements, mainly concerned with the early years of the restoration of Israel under Darius and Cyrus (late sixth century B.C.). Chap. 1 relates a decree authorizing the rebuilding of the Temple and the handing of the sacred Temple vessels to Sheshbazzar. 2:1–3:1 interrupts the narrative with a list, found also in Nehemiah 7, of those who returned to Judah; the list is composite and clearly includes material belonging to quite different stages. It ends in a narrative fragment which in its present form provides a lead-in to chap. 3 (2:70–3:1). 3:2–13 relates the restoring of the altar (2–7) and Temple (8–13), both attributed to Zerubbabel and Jeshua. The sequel appears to be in 4:1–5, which relates an attempt by "adversaries" to collaborate in the building of the Temple, a collaboration rejected by the leaders of the returned exiles. As a result, further building was prevented by the "people of the land" (4:4, local inhabitants). More probably the real sequel is in the Passover ceremony of 6:19–22. The intervening material is almost entirely in Aramaic, though the first two verses 4:6 and 7 (in Hebrew) report two further initiatives against the returned exiles, addressed to Xerxes and Artaxerxes. 4:8–23 has a fuller account of opposition, particularly associated with the authorities in Samaria—there is no hint here of religious opposition—and concerned with the rebuilding of the city, not the Temple. 4:24 provides a link to 5:1–6:18, where another account of the Temple is given, in which the main activity is attributed to the elders supported by the prophets Haggai and Zechariah. An inquiry to Darius brings renewed authority to rebuild the Temple, work that is described as having continued without interruption from the days of Cyrus. It is clear that the various elements in these chapters do not provide a fully harmonized account of the restoration; distinct elements stand side by side, with some linkages between the various themes. For the relation between Chronicles, Ezra, and Nehemiah, ***See*** Chronicles, The First and Second Books of the.

The Man Ezra: The story of Ezra, priest and scribe (secretary), appears in Ezra 7–10 and Nehemiah 8–9. The setting is the time of Artaxerxes (7:1), but it is not clear which king of this name is intended. As the narratives now stand, the activities of Ezra and Nehemiah overlap, but there is no real contact between them and it is most often believed that they worked entirely separately. This has led to the proposal that Ezra should be placed later than Nehemiah, Nehemiah in the reign of Artaxerxes I and Ezra in that of Artaxerxes II, but there is no certainty here. Ezra 7 describes his commissioning and sets out (in Aramaic, 7:11–26) his authority to impose the law within the Persian province "Beyond the River." Ezra 8 provides a list of those who went with him and gives an account of the journey. Ezra 9 and 10 deal with the problems created by marriages with women of foreign origin, and the action taken by Ezra to eliminate this religious danger. It incorporates a poetic prayer in 9:6–15. 7:27–9:15 is a first person narrative, while the remainder of the Ezra material is in the third person. The story continues in Nehemiah 8, though this passage, dealing with the proclaiming and acceptance of the law, would more logically precede the material of Ezra 9–10. Nehemiah 9 has a short opening narrative (vv. 1–6), which appears to be a duplicate or summary of what precedes, followed by a long psalm-prayer that the Greek translators of the Septuagint (so too RSV) attribute to Ezra.

Ezra is also mentioned in Neh. 12:26 and 36, probably as a harmonizing addition to the Nehemiah narrative. The name appears also in lists in Neh. 12:13 and 33. In 12:1 and 12:13 he is named as a priestly leader.

Ezra occupies a prominent place in later Jewish tradition, particularly in connection with the writing of the Scriptures; this tradition is evident in 2 Esdras (4 Ezra) 14, where he has become a prophet (2 Esd. 1:1) and is described as dictating the whole of ninety-four books, to replace what had been lost in Exile. Of these, twenty-four are the canonical books, to be made public: the remaining seventy, presumably works like 2 Esdras itself, were to be kept secret for the "wise." Ezra thus becomes the preserver of the religious tradition from its earlier stages through to the forerunners of the great rabbis, and thus occupies a place in some respects similar to that of Moses. A markedly hostile view of Ezra is to be found in Samaritan tradition, which reflects the views of those who opposed the returned exiles and their attempt to assume the religious leadership of Palestine. ***See also*** Artaxerxes; Law; Nehemiah, The Book of.

Bibliography

Finshaw, F. C. *The Books of Ezra and Nehemiah.* Grand Rapids, MI: Eerdmans, 1982.

Myers, J. M. *Ezra-Nehemiah.* Anchor Bible 14. Garden City, NY: Doubleday, 1965.

P.R.A.

OUTLINE OF CONTENTS

The Book of Ezra

- I. Restoration of the community (1:1–6:22)
  - A. Decree authorizing rebuilding (1:1–11)
  - B. List of returnees (2:1–70)
  - C. Restoration (3:1–13)
    - 1. Altar (3:2–7)
    - 2. Temple (3:8–13)
  - D. Opposition to restoration (4:1–24)
  - E. Restoration completed (5:1–6:22)
    - 1. Temple completed (5:1–6:18)
      - a. Work begun (5:1–2)
      - b. Official reports (5:3–6:12)
      - c. Work completed (6:13–18)
    - 2. Completion celebrated (6:19–22)
- II. Ezra's mission (7:1–10:44)
  - A. Ezra introduced (7:1–10)
  - B. Ezra's commission (7:11–26)
  - C. Ezra's departure (8:1–36)
    - 1. Preparations (8:1–30)
    - 2. Departure (8:31–36)
  - D. The purity of God's people (9:1–10:44)
    - 1. Mixed marriages: problem (9:1–2)
    - 2. Mixed marriages: reaction (9:3–10:6)
    - 3. Mixed marriages: action (10:7–19)
    - 4. Mixed marriages: result (10:20–44)

Opposite: Fisherman with basket of fish; decorated pottery oil lamp, first century A.D.

F

fable, a short fictitious story that usually uses animals, plants, or inanimate objects as characters to teach a moral lesson. There are two clear examples of this form in the Bible: Jotham's fable of the thorn tree (Abimelech) that was chosen king instead of more worthy trees (Jerubbaal's sons; Judg. 9:7–15) and Jehoash's fable of the thorn bush (Amaziah) that arrogantly challenged the cedar of Lebanon (Jehoash) and was trampled (2 Kings 14:9; 1 Chron. 25:18). In some older English translations (e.g., KJV) "fables" (Gk. *mythos*) refer to false teachings that were being urged upon the early church (1 Tim. 1:4; 2 Tim. 4:4; 2 Pet. 1:16). Most newer translations use the word "myths." D.R.B.

Fair Havens, a bay on the south-central coast of Crete, where Paul's ship put in on his journey to Rome (Acts 27:8); it is still known by the same name in Greek. The nearby town of Lasea flourished in Roman times. The bay itself is protected by some small islands, the second largest of which is today known as St. Paul's Island. Weighing anchor here in the fall, Paul's ship, against his advice, made a run for the safer harbor of Phoenix to the west but was driven off course by a sudden northeast wind, the Euraquilo (KJV: "Euroclydon"; RSV: "northeaster"; Acts 27:9–15). ***See also*** Crete; Euroclydon; Paul; Phoenix. C.H.M.

faith, in the Bible trust in, or reliance on, God who is himself trustworthy. The NT and the Greek OT express the understanding of faith primarily with two terms (*pistis, pisteuein*), which are related to the primary OT verb "to be true" or "be trustworthy" (*'aman*). The OT concept is considerably broader than this term and its cognates, yet *'aman* remains the most profound expression to describe faith in the OT.

Faith in the OT: It is important to recognize the context in which the concept of faith functions in the OT. God stands at the center; it is his initiative and faithfulness as described by the OT writers in creation, in the Exodus event, in the covenant and the subsequent history of Israel that allow his people to respond to his fidelity. Since God's promises are intended for his people, the emphasis of faith is not focused primarily on the individual, but on the relationship of the people of Israel to God. However, in the Psalms, and to a limited extent in Deutero-Isaiah (i.e., Isa. 40–55) and elsewhere, the individual expression of faith is given attention. The prophets intensify the covenant dimension of faith and in Isaiah the imagery of faith is given a new and creative impulse. Throughout the OT the focus of faith is exclusively on the God of Abraham, Isaac, and Jacob: "And Israel saw the great work which the Lord did against the Egyptians, and the people feared the Lord; and they believed in the Lord and in his servant Moses" (Exod. 14:31). God's mighty acts allow and call for trust and belief in him.

The Hebrew verb means, for the most part, "to be true"; lying behind this is the root meaning "solid," "firm." This sense of "to be true" is intensified in the passive (Niphal) form of the verb so that one can speak of a person as "trustworthy" or "reliable." The causative (Hiphil) form of the verb suggests the acceptance of someone as trustworthy or dependable. Thus, one accepts God as trustworthy and believes his word (Deut. 9:23) and his promises, as is the case with Abraham in Gen. 15:1–6: "And he believed the Lord; and he reckoned it to him as righteousness." It has been argued that it is the use of the verb in the causative form that encompasses the most personal relationship of faith between God and the believer.

The primary nouns derived from the verb "to trust" (*'aman*) are "firmness, stability" (*'emunah*; Isa. 33:6: "and he will be the stability of your times . . .") and "truthfulness, fidelity, faithfulness" (*'emet*; Ps. 71:22: "I will also praise thee with the harp for thy faithfulness, O my God"). Throughout the OT stability results in security and together they are signs of God's fidelity to his people. Another term used in this connection refers to Yahweh's loving-kindness in a covenant context (*ḥesed*; Ps. 33:18: "Behold, the eye of the Lord is on those who fear him, on those who hope in his steadfast *love*"). God chose Israel (Deut. 7:6–7: "the Lord your God has chosen you to be a people for his own possession . . .") and his loving-kindness is demonstrated by the many blessings they have received. This covenant relationship presupposes a mutuality of obligation (Deut. 7:9: "Know therefore that the Lord your God is God, the faithful God who keeps covenant and steadfast love with those who love him and keep his commandments . . ."); Israel's response of faith is possible only because of God's prior and con-

God ordering Noah to build the ark (Gen. 6: 14–22) exemplifies the exclusive demand of obedience of the covenant relationship; ninth-century ivory plaque, Italy.

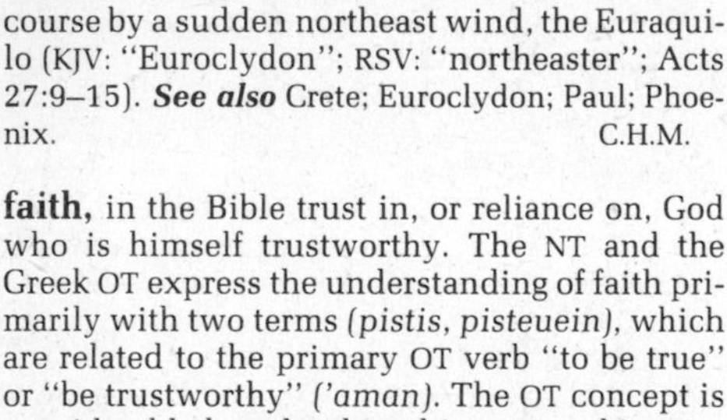

tinued faithfulness. Out of this mutuality of obligation the paradoxical relationship between faith and fear in the OT (Exod. 14:31 above) becomes more intelligible. The covenant relationship between God and his people results in an exclusive demand (Exod. 20:3; Deut. 6:5; 18:13; 1 Kings 8:61; Isa. 38:3) of obedience (Noah in Gen. 6:9, 22; 7:5; Abraham in Gen. 22:1–18; Joshua in 1:7–8; 24:22–31; Samuel in 1 Sam. 15:17–33) in which idols must be totally rejected (Isa. 42:17). In fact, the opposite of faithfulness is apostasy, as, for example, in Deut. 32:20, in which the phrase "children in whom is no faithfulness" is synonymous with idolatry. Since the faith of Israel is always reflective of God's fidelity and loving-kindness, it must be expressed not only in obedience but also in praise (Pss. 5:11; 9:10; 13:5; 18:1–3; 22:1–5; 27:14; 62:1, 5–8; 141:8).

The prophets deepen the meaning of faith in several ways. For Isaiah (7:1–9) security does not rest in political power but in utter trust in God; in fact, the totality of life must be based on such trust in him (Isa. 7:9: "If you will not believe, surely you shall not be established"). This point is also stressed in Isa. 28:16, a verse of importance for the NT: "Therefore thus says the Lord God, 'Behold, I am laying in Zion for a foundation a stone, a tested stone, a precious cornerstone, of a sure foundation: "He who believes will not be in haste." ' " Deutero-Isaiah broadens the concept of faith in the direction of hope and knowledge. Typical of the former is Isa. 40:31: "But they who wait for the Lord shall renew their strength, they shall mount up with wings like eagles, they shall run and not be weary, they shall walk and not faint." Faced with difficult predicaments, the energy of faith results not in despair, but in hope. The broadening of faith in the direction of knowledge is particularly evident in Isa. 43:10: " 'You are my witnesses,' says the Lord, 'and my servant whom I have chosen, that you may know and believe and understand that I am He.' " Knowledge is not used here in a speculative sense; the reference is to the knowledge of God's fidelity and loving-kindness experienced in history.

Faith in the NT: For the NT understanding of faith, Hab. 2:4 is an important reference: "Behold, he whose soul is not upright in him shall fail, but the righteous shall live by his faithfulness." Here the characteristic meaning of trust (*'emunah*) is well summarized: fidelity to God as the sign of the righteous person. God alone can be the object of trust and faithfulness because he "is my rock, and my fortress, and my deliverer, my God, my rock, in whom I take refuge, my shield, and the horn of my salvation, my stronghold" (Ps. 18:2).

In the NT the noun and verb denoting faith (*pistis/pisteuein*) appear frequently. In the synoptic Gospels, they are used least frequently, and among them it is used with least precision in the Gospel of Mark. Faith for Mark can have as its object God (Mark 11:22: "And Jesus answered them, 'Have faith in God' ") or faith in Jesus as the manifestation of God's power (Mark 5:36; 9:23–24). Closely related to this last usage are the direct references of Jesus to the faith of his audience (Mark 2:5: "And when Jesus saw their faith, he said to the paralytic, 'My son, your sins are forgiven' "; Mark 5:34: "And he said to her, 'Daughter, your faith has made you well; go in peace, and be healed of your disease' "; Mark 10:52: "And Jesus said to him [the blind man], 'Go your way; your faith has made you well' "). Finally, Mark can have the gospel, in a way not dissimilar to Paul, as the object of faith (Mark 1:15: "Jesus came . . . saying, 'The time is fulfilled, and the kingdom of God is at hand; repent, and believe in the gospel' "). Lack of faith can be referred to in a similar way (Mark 4:40: "He [Jesus] said to them, 'Why are you afraid? Have you no faith?' "). In the Gospel of Luke faith is often used in the most general sense of faithfulness (Luke 16:10–12; see also 1:20, 45: "And blessed is she who believed that there would be a fulfillment of what was spoken to her from the Lord"). In addition, faith is used with the verb "to save" (7:50: "And he said to the woman, 'Your faith has saved you; go in peace' "; 8:12: "believe and be saved").

The Gospel of Matthew further intensifies the theme of faith. At the conclusion of the story about the healing of the centurion's slave, Matthew adds the words: "And to the centurion Jesus said, 'Go; be it done for you as you have believed' " (Matt. 8:13). Similarly, Matthew modifies the Marcan and Lucan account of the healing of two blind men by inserting the question from Jesus: " 'Do you believe that I am able to do this?' They said to him, 'Yes, Lord' " (Matt. 9:28). Other Matthean passages also emphasize faith. In the account of the Canaanite woman Matthew alters the Marcan account precisely for this purpose: "Then Jesus answered her, 'O woman, great is your faith! Be it done for you as you desire.' And her daughter was healed instantly" (Matt. 15:28). Similarly, in an encounter with the chief priests and the elders Matthew elevates the issue of faith: "Jesus said to them, 'Truly, I say to you, the tax collectors and the harlots go into the kingdom of God before you. For John came to you in the way of righteousness, and you did not believe him, but the tax collectors and the harlots believed him; and even when you saw it, you did not afterward repent and believe him' " (Matt. 21:31b–32; cf. Luke 7:29–30). In a polemical passage dealing with scribes and Pharisees Matthew accuses them of neglecting the weightier matters of "the law, justice and mercy and faith" (Matt. 23:23; Luke 11:42 does not contain the reference to faith). In the passage dealing with the false christs and false prophets Matthew twice uses the verb "to believe" while Luke does not (Matt. 24:23–25; Luke 17:23–24). This same pattern can be found in Matt. 17:19–20 and in Matt. 21:21. The former is an account of the boy possessed by a spirit who was healed by Jesus. Of the three evangelists, only Matthew adds this statement of Jesus by way of response to the disciples' question, "Why could we not cast it out?": "Because of your little faith." In Matt. 21:21 there is a clear intensification over against Mark 11:22. In Mark Jesus answers, "Have faith in God"; in Matthew Jesus answers, "Truly, I say to you, if you have faith and never doubt . . ."

Paul's Concept of Faith: In the apostle Paul one finds the broadest and profoundest articulation of the concept of faith in early Christianity. Faith has as its object God (1 Thess. 1:8), specifically God's salvific manifestation through the death and resurrection of Jesus Christ (1 Thess. 4:14). This act of God in Christ is preached (Rom. 10:17: "So faith comes from what is heard, and what is heard comes by the preaching of Christ") and is received by faith (Rom. 3:25), a faith that rests "in the power of God" (1 Cor. 2:5). Those who have received the good news of God's act in Christ, namely, the gospel, are called "believers" (1 Thess. 1:7). There is only one gospel (1 Cor. 15:11) and its goal is salvation (1 Cor. 1:21).

For Paul the concept of faith is a dynamic one. Thus, he can refer to the "activity of faith" (1 Thess. 1:23), an activity that manifests itself in love (Gal. 5:6: "faith working through love"). Faith involves "progress" (Phil. 1:25); it is not something static, captured once for all, but involves striving (Phil. 1:27: "with one mind striving side by side for the faith of the gospel . . .") and it increases (2 Cor. 10:15) and it is an energy at work in believers (1 Thess. 2:13). Since faith is not a static possession, Paul urges that faith be established (1 Thess. 3:2) and made firm (1 Cor. 16:13; 2 Cor. 1:24), for it is possible not only to have deficiencies in faith (1 Thess. 3:10; Rom. 14:1) but also to believe in vain (1 Cor. 15:2; Rom. 11:20). Essential for Paul's understanding of faith is the conviction that God assigns to each the measure of faith he wishes (Rom. 12:3, 6; 1 Cor. 12:9). Yet no matter what that measure of faith is, the obedience of faith is expected from all (Rom. 1:5; 16:16).

Paul on several occasions uses the triadic formulation "faith, love and hope" (1 Thess. 1:3; 5:8; 1 Cor. 13:13). On the one hand, as noted above, faith must be active in love; without love faith is empty. On the other hand, faith must be grounded in hope so that it recognizes that the first-fruits of God's promises manifested in the death and resurrection of Christ will be fulfilled on the last day (Gal. 5:5; Rom. 6:8; Rom. 15:13: "May the God of hope fill you with all joy and peace in believing, so that by the power of the Holy Spirit you may abound in hope"). The specific hope of faith is rooted in the resurrection of Christ as an anticipation of the fulfillment of the last day (1 Cor. 15:14, 17; 2 Cor. 4:14: "knowing that he who raised the Lord Jesus will raise us also with Jesus and bring us with you into his presence"). Yet this faith that is received in baptism (Gal. 3:27–28) and allows one entrance into the body of Christ, the church, is a faith that has as its model the suffering and death of Jesus and so during this earthly sojourn faith may well be called to a cruciform existence (Rom. 8:18; Phil. 1:29: "For it has been granted to you that for the sake of Christ you should not only believe in him but also suffer for his sake . . ."). Further, this new act of God in Christ received by faith involves not only new existence for the believer but for the world itself (Rom. 8:18–25).

Particularly in Galatians and Romans Paul links his concept of faith to terms like the righteousness of God and justification and to a negative attitude toward the works of the law. This development of his thought is brought about, on the one hand, by his conflict with certain Judaizers, and, on the other hand, his reflections of the relation of Jews and Gentiles. Thus, in Gal. 2:16 he can write that "a man is not justified by works of the law but through faith in Jesus Christ . . ." and in Rom. 10:4 that "Christ is the end of the law, that every one who has faith may be justified." These points are articulated at length with much use of the OT, including Gen. 15:6, in such chapters as Galatians 3 and Romans 4. For Paul the villain is not the law, but sin, which renders its usefulness ineffective. Thus the basic dilemma of the human situation is captivity to sin (Rom. 3:9–18). Christ has come to free humanity from this captivity; whether Jew or Greek, all have sinned and all can come to God in Christ only through faith (Rom. 3:21). Thus Paul can ask rhetorically: "Wretched man that I am! Who will deliver me from this body of death? Thanks be to God through Jesus Christ our Lord!" (Rom. 7:24–25a).

The same dynamic of faith is evident when Paul links faith with righteousness/justification language, as, for example, in Rom. 1:16–17: "For I am not ashamed of the gospel: it is the power of God for salvation to every one who has faith, to the Jew first and also to the Greek. For in it the righteousness of God is revealed through faith for faith; as it is written, 'He who through faith is righteous shall live.'" The righteousness of God, which faith receives as God's gift, is viewed as part of a much broader historical and eschatological context. It is for Paul God's sovereignty over the world that reveals itself eschatologically in Jesus. When Paul speaks of the "gift of righteousness" in Rom. 5:17 he is referring to a gift that is both present and future, already received and still expected. It is a gift that recognizes God's sovereign power and the fact that the believer is placed under that power in obedient service. For the person who is justified, who has received the gift in faith, salvation is not yet completed in the present; it has still to be consummated and fulfilled on the last day. Only as Christians wait and hope are they saved (Rom. 8:23–25; Gal. 5:5). It is precisely for this reason that the apostle is so careful in his language about present and future as, for example, in Rom. 6:8 ("But if we have died with Christ, we believe that we shall also live with him") and Rom. 5:9 ("Since, therefore, we are now justified by his blood, much more shall we be saved by him from the wrath of God"). This process of the Christian life is similarly emphasized in Philippians (2:12–13; 3:9–14). While the Christian life is for Paul a single process, he does stress three different nuances of the process: justification, an initiating event that is actualized and made concrete through sanctification; sanctification, a present process, dependent upon justification, that has future implications, namely, consummated salvation; and salvation, a gift to be consummated in the future, already anticipated and partially experienced in justification and sanctification and definitely dependent upon them. **Other NT Writings:** Other NT writings that stress the concept of faith include the Gospel of John, where only the verb form is found. The author describes his Gospel as intended to produce faith: "Now Jesus did many other signs in the presence of the disciples, which are not written in this book, but these are written that you may believe that Jesus is the Christ, the Son of God, and that believing you may have life in his name" (John 20:30–31). This Evangelist's view of faith is very much linked to the contingency of his situation, especially his dialogue and polemic with Judaism, many of whom do not believe (9:18) and reject faith in Jesus (5:38) despite the signs performed (4:48) and the testimony of Scripture, Abraham, and Moses. The view of faith found in the Fourth Gospel is also closely linked to its understanding of Christology, namely, Jesus as the one sent by the Father as his revealer (John 6:29: "Jesus answered them, 'This is the work of God, that you believe in him whom he has sent' "). The Acts of the Apostles is also a rich witness to the NT concept of faith. Here the term "believer" is used with frequency (e.g., Acts 2:44) and the object of belief is the preaching of the apostles (Acts 4:1–4). In James 2:14–20, the view of faith that insists that faith without works is useless is most likely not a criticism of Paul, but of those who have lost sight of the Pauline relationship between the activity of faith and its expression in and through love. The oft-quoted verse from Hebrews, "Now faith is the assurance of things hoped for, the conviction of things not seen" (11:1), has no specific Christian emphasis as it stands; the entire chapter serves as a model for the purposes of exhortation and reaches its culmination and Christian interpretation in chapter 12: "Therefore . . . let us run with perserverance the race that is set before us, looking to Jesus the pioneer and perfecter of our faith, who for the joy that was set before him endured the cross . . ." (12:1–2). This reference to Jesus as "the pioneer and perfecter" of faith expresses concisely the dynamic conception of faith found in much of the NT. ***See also*** Hope; Love; Righteousness.

K.P.D.

Fall, the, the original disobedience of Adam and Eve and the results of this disobedience, as depicted in Genesis 3. There are two different accounts of creation in Genesis 1–3. The second, found in 2:4b–3:24, is the older of the two and is considered part of an ancient history of Israel known as the Yahwistic history (dating from perhaps as far back as 950 B.C.). This history, designated "J," was one of the various collections of traditions later combined and edited to form the Torah or Pentateuch. The J creation story depicts God forming a male human being, placing him in a garden, and eventually creating a suitable mate for him. The subsequent disobedience of this human pair and their expulsion from the garden is usually designated as "the Fall."

According to the story, the serpent (*not* Satan or the devil, as assumed by later interpreters) deceived the woman into eating the fruit of the forbidden tree, that is, the Tree of the Knowledge of Good and Evil, and she, in turn, gave the fruit to the man. The meaning of "knowing good and evil" may indicate the ability to make moral judgments, as some interpret it, but it more like-

Serpent around the forbidden tree, Eve with hand outstretched, and Adam beside her; fifteenth-century relief, Italy.

ly carries the connotation of "knowing everything." The central idea, however, is that human sin is rooted in the desire to "be like God," to usurp God's rightful place as Creator, and for humans to have life revolve around themselves and their own desires.

Because of the Fall, the positive relationship the humans had with God was broken, and all evil and tragedy in the created order were explained as a result of this rebellion and disobedience. The Fall resulted in humanity being trapped in its sinful state, which issued in death, not simply (or primarily) physical death but rather spiritual separation from God.

The doctrine of the Fall is never worked out in any systematic manner in the OT, but, in the NT, Paul alludes to the story, setting up a parallel between "the first Adam" and Christ as "the last Adam" (Rom. 5:12–21; 1 Cor. 15:21–22, 45–49). In later Christian theology, the doctrine of the Fall is developed in great detail. ***See also*** Adam; Atonement; Creation; Death; Devil; Eden; Eve; J; Redemption; Salvation; Satan; Serpent; Sin; Sources of the Pentateuch. J.M.E.

familiar spirit. ***See*** Magic and Divination.

family, the (Heb. *bayit*, "house"; *bet 'ab*, "father's house"; *mishpaḥah*, "clan"), the basic social unit in Israel during the biblical period.

The Nuclear Family: The smallest family unit was the nuclear family (the "house"), which usually occupied its own dwelling. The nuclear family normally consisted of parents and their unmarried children, although occasionally nonkin such as slaves or long-term visitors also shared the family's living quarters. Archaeological evidence suggests that no more than six or seven people occupied the average house on a regular basis. Within the nuclear family children were socialized by being taught the customs and lore of their people (Prov. 1:8; 6:20), including the story of God's dealings with Israel (Exod. 10:2; 12:26, 13:8; Deut. 4:9; 6:7, 20–25; 32:7, 46). Well into the monarchical period (ca. 1020–586 B.C.) each nuclear family was also a self-sustaining economic unit. Agricultural products grown by the family were stored in the house, and any animals that the family might own were quartered there. Living arrangements may have been different in the period before Israel's settlement in Canaan (thirteenth–twelfth centuries B.C.), but there is little firm evidence on this point.

Most of the authority in the nuclear family belonged to the father, who exercised legal control over his children and wife, although his power was not absolute (Exod. 21:7–11; Deut. 21:15–21). Children were expected to honor and obey their parents, and failure to do so was considered a serious matter (Exod. 20:12; 21:15, 17; Lev. 20:9; Deut. 27:16; Prov. 30:17). The integrity of the family was further protected by harsh laws against adultery and incest (Exod. 20:14; Lev. 18:20; 20:10–21; Deut. 5:18; 22:22). However, families could be dissolved through divorce (Deut. 24:1–4).

Children remained under their father's control until they were married, when they left home to start a new family unit. Marriages were carefully regulated (Lev. 18). In early Israel polygyny was common (Gen. 4:19; 16:1–2; 22:20–24; 25:1, 6; 29:15–30), although by monarchical times it was limited primarily to the royal family. Even after marriage children were expected to honor their parents and were exhorted to care for them in their old age (Prov. 23:22).

The Extended Family: The extended family (the "father's house") was composed of two or more nuclear families that claimed descent from the same ancestor. Members of the extended family sometimes lived together in adjoining houses, although this does not seem to have been common, and occasionally worked at the same trade or profession (1 Chron. 4:14, 21, 23). The extended family acted as a corporate entity and was granted certain legal rights in order to maintain its solidarity. When one of its nuclear families was forced to sell property, the extended family had the right to redeem the property in order to keep it from leaving the family (Lev. 25:25; Jer. 32:6–15). Individuals threatened with being sold into slavery could be redeemed by a member of their extended family, and, at least in the early period, the family was allowed to avenge a wrong done to one of its members (Lev. 25:47–49). Power in the extended family was exercised by the ancestor from whom all of its constituent nuclear families were descended. If this individual was not living, then questions of authority were negotiated among the heads of the nuclear families.

Clan and Tribe: Several extended families were sometimes linked together to form a clan. In this case they traced their genealogies to a single ancestor, although at the level of the clan factors other than genuine consanguinity often played a role in establishing group unity. Clan members usually lived in the same geographical area and sometimes made up an entire village (Judg. 18:11–13). Clans may have helped to protect their members against outside attack but otherwise seem to have had few social functions.

The family metaphor was extended beyond the clan to include the tribe and the nation of Israel itself, so that the whole people could be seen as one enormous family represented by a complex segmented or branched genealogy (Gen. 46:8–27; Num. 26:5–62; 1 Chron. 1–9). Because of the large numbers of people involved in these groups, it is difficult to know how effectively they functioned as social units.

Although some of the power of the tribes and

clans was taken away by the monarchy, the nuclear and extended families seem to have survived intact throughout Israel's history. After the Exile caused many changes in Israel's structure, the family played an even greater role in maintaining the people's stability.

In the NT: NT views of the family are somewhat different from those found in the OT. On the one hand, some of Jesus' sayings subordinate family loyalty to loyalty to the gospel (Matt. 10: 34–39; 12:46–50; Mark 3:31–35; Luke 12:49–53). On the other hand, Jesus quoted approvingly the command to honor parents and thus supported the traditional Jewish family structure (Matt. 19:16–22; Luke 18:18–30). In the early church support of one's family was seen as a virtue (1 Tim. 5:8), but the traditional view of family was transformed by seeing the Christian community as a new family (Gal. 6:10; Eph. 2: 19). ***See also*** Genealogy; Sociology of the Old Testament. R.R.W.

famine, a prolonged scarcity of food, accompanied by extreme hunger. It is listed as one of God's "four sore acts of judgment" along with the sword (war), evil beasts, and pestilence (Ezek. 14:21). It is also a divine judgment in Jeremiah, along with the sword (fourteen times), and with the sword and pestilence (fifteen times). In Deuteronomy 28, hunger (v. 48) is one of the many curses God will send for disobedience.

Perhaps the most widely-known famine in the Bible is the one predicted by Joseph in his interpretation of Pharoah's dream (Gen. 41). It, too, was sent by God (v. 25). Other periods of severe famine are recorded during the days of Abraham (Gen. 12:10), Isaac (Gen. 26:1), Elisha (1 Kings 7; 8:16), and Zedekiah after the siege of Jerusalem (2 Kings 25:3; cf. Lam. 5:10). Philistia was threatened with famine in an oracle from Isaiah (Isa. 14:30).

Famine may lead to disease (Jer. 14:18) and, most gruesome of all, cannibalism of one's own offspring (Deut. 28:47–57). Other attendant judgments may be captivity (Jer. 15:2), exile (Ezek. 5:12), nakedness (Deut. 28:47), and earthquakes (Matt. 24:7). The prophet Amos speaks of a famine not of bread, nor of thirst for water, but "of hearing the words of the Lord" (Amos 8:11).

Famine is symbolized by the third horseman of the Apocalypse who announces exorbitant prices for food and precedes the horseman named Death (Rev. 6:5–8). Paul affirms that famine will not be able to separate believers from the love of God in Christ (Rom. 8:35–38). J.G.G.

fan. ***See*** Winnowing Fork.

Far'ah, Tell el-. ***See*** Sharuhen; Tirzah.

farming, the whole process of cultivating land

A farm near Jerusalem, dating to ancient times, is still under cultivation.

and raising crops, from soil preparation to the storage and transport of crops to market. Archaeologists have discovered that farming has been practiced in Palestine for almost ten thousand years. If one includes the breeding of livestock, it is clear that agriculture has always been the basis of Palestine's economy. No human activity is as prevalent in the Bible as farming. Agricultural pursuits are mentioned in the opening pages of Genesis (2:15; 4:2; 9:20), and farming activities were important enough to be regulated by Mosaic law (e.g., Lev. 19:9; 25:3–5; Deut. 22:9–10). The orderly system used in working the land was attributed to God (Isa. 28:26), and Jesus used figures derived from farming to picture the coming of God's Kingdom (Mark 4:3–8, 26–29).

The most important crops were wheat, grapes, and olives (Ps. 104:15; Joel 2:19); other crops included barley, flax, lentils, chick-peas, cucumbers, onions, melons, dates, figs, and spices. Because of variations in soil productivity, temperature, and rainfall, certain areas of the country were better suited than others for specific crops, but a wide range of crops and trading and pastoral activities enabled farmers to provide for their families.

Unlike their Egyptian and Mesopotamian counterparts, Palestinian farmers were not dependent upon irrigation to water crops; rainfall and dew usually sufficed (Deut. 11:10–11; 1 Kings 17:1). Naturally, ancient farmers contended with the elements, pests, and warfare, but the major enemy was drought (cf. Jer. 14:1–6).

Farmers were occupied throughout the year with animal husbandry, and heavy field work never ended. Land was marked off with boundary stones (Prov. 22:28); ground was cleared of rocks and thorns (Isa. 5:2); fields, vineyards, and orchards were hedged and walled (Isa. 5:5; cf. Mark 12:1); and hillsides were terraced. Most farming activities, however, were controlled by the seasons.

Plowing for winter crops did not begin until after the "early" or "former" rains of autumn (Prov. 20:4); only then could lightweight plows scratch the surface of sun-baked fields. Once the plowman and his team of draft animals had broken the soil, clods were pulverized and the surface flattened with hoes or harrows (Isa. 28:24–25).

Sowing, which was usually accomplished by broadcasting seed, could precede or follow plowing. Fields or individual plants were fertilized with dung (Jer. 9:22; Luke 13:8), and the rain and sun brought different crops to maturity at different times. Following the winter rains and the "latter" rains of March-April, barley was ready to be harvested in April and May, and wheat matured three or four weeks later. Grain was pulled up by the roots or cut with flint-bladed or iron sickles (Deut. 16:9).

The harvested sheaves were spread out on a threshing-floor (i.e., a rock outcropping or a hard-packed earthen surface), and the stalk, chaff, and grain were cut apart by animal hooves (Deut. 25:4), flails (Ruth 2:17), or threshing sledges (Isa. 41:15). Grain was separated from the chaff by winnowing (Isa. 41:16), and the kernels were sifted to remove bits of straw (Luke 22:31). After a bumper crop, the threshing and winnowing process could last all summer. The finished product was bagged, hauled away for storage or sale, and the chaff was burned (Matt. 3:12).

Meanwhile, summer crops had been planted after the winter rains; these plants were cultivated throughout the dry summer months. The harvesting of fruit, including olives and grapes, began in late summer and continued into fall.

The Bible demonstrates that almost every aspect of agricultural work assumed a figurative meaning in the minds of ancient speakers and writers (e.g., Isa. 21:10; Amos 9:13; Mic. 4:12–13; Matt. 9:37–38; 13:3–32; Luke 9:62; 1 Cor. 9:9–11; Gal. 6:7; Rev. 14:14–20). ***See also*** Plow; Sowing; Winnowing. G.L.M.

farthing. ***See*** Money.

fasting, abstention from food. In the OT there are two kinds of fasting, public and private. Public fasts were periodically proclaimed (2 Chron. 20:3; Ezra 8:21–23; Neh. 1:4–11; Jer. 36:9). The fasts were always accompanied by prayer and supplication and frequently by wearing sackcloth as a sign of penance and mourning (Neh. 9:1; Dan. 9:3; 1 Macc. 3:47). In the tragic days surrounding the fall of Jerusalem, four fast days were proclaimed (Zech. 7:5; 8:19). "Humbling or afflicting oneself," synonymous with "fasting," is required on the Day of Atonement (Lev. 16:31–34). Public fasts ordinarily lasted a day, and offerings of various sorts were made (Lev. 16:1–5; Judg. 20:26; Jer. 14:11–12). The prophetic writings contain strong warnings against abusing the fasting rituals (Isa. 58:1–9; Jer. 14:11–12; Zech. 7:3–5; 8:18–19). The prophet Joel, however, unhesitatingly calls for a public fast and communal lamentation (Joel 1:8–2:17). Private fasts were observed as acts of penance (2 Sam. 12:15–23; 1 Kings 21:27; Ps. 69:1–15), when others became sick (Ps. 35:13–14), and when one was accused and scorned (Ps. 109:4–21).

In the NT Jesus stresses that there should be joy in fasting (Matt. 6:16–18; cf. Zech. 8:19), and he fasted at the outset of his ministry (Matt. 4:2). He does not, however, enjoin his disciples to fast as did John the Baptist (Mark 2:18–20). Later textual tradition adds "and fasting" to Jesus' assertion that certain kinds of demons could not be "driven out by anything but prayer" (Mark 9:29). In the early church fasting accompanied prayer prior to the consecration of teachers and elders (Acts 13:2–3; 14:23) and during times of severe trial (Acts 27:1–38).

J.G.G.

fat (Heb. *ḥelev),* greasy tissue of sacrificial animals burnt on the altar as an offering. Specifically, *ḥelev* refers to the fat covering and surrounding the entrails and the fat on the kidneys (Lev. 3:3–4), but it also has a more general sense that includes the kidneys, liver appendage, and tail (of a sheep; Lev. 4:31; 7:3–4). The fat of sacrificial animals must not be eaten (Lev. 7:23–25; cf. 3:17).

The word is also used of human fat or fat in general (Judg. 3:22, 2 Sam. 1:22; Ps. 119:70) and can also be used to mean "best of" (Num. 18:12, 29–32; Pss. 81:16; 147:14). D.P.W.

father, in the OT the immediate male progenitor, the head of a people or tribe (Gen. 19:37), the grandfather (32:9), or the founder of a town (1 Chron. 2:41–52) or a profession (Gen. 4:20, 21). The plural "fathers" refers to previous generations (Jer. 31:32; Ps. 22:4; Lam. 5:7). "Father" can be an appellation for advisors to the king or high governmental officials (Gen. 45:8; Isa. 22:21) or an honorary title given to prophets and priests (Judg. 17:10; 2 Kings 2:11; 6:21; 13:14).

A father was permitted to arrange his daughter's marriage and receive her bride-price (Gen. 34:12; 1 Sam. 18:25), the fine of the seducer (Exod. 22:17; Deut. 22:19, 29), and the compensation of a gored child (Exod. 21:31). However, the patriarchal narratives indicate that it was the custom to ask the daughter if she agreed to a marriage (Gen. 24:57–58). The father also had the right to cancel his daughter's vows (Num. 30:4–6). Although the Torah forbade selling one's daughter into prostitution (Lev. 19:29), it did permit the selling of a daughter into servitude on the condition that she become the wife of her master or his son; if the condition was not met, she would be freed (Exod. 21:7–9). As in the ancient Near East, the father apparently could sell his sons into servitude for his debts (Isa. 50:1; cf. 2 Kings 4:1). But this practice was condemned by Nehemiah (Neh. 5:1–9).

Deut. 24:16 decrees that children may not be punished for the sins of the parents (cf. 2 Kings 14:6) and vice versa, which was upheld by the prophets (Jer. 31:29–30; Ezek. 18:20). Whether or not Exod. 20:5–6 (Deut. 5:9–10) acknowledges such vicarious punishment by God is problematic; the text may refer to successive generations that continue to sin (but see Josh. 7:15, 24–25; 2 Sam. 21:6–9).

The father was obligated to circumcise his sons (Gen. 17:12, 23; 21:4; Lev. 12:3), to redeem his firstborn son (Exod. 13:13), and to educate the children in the Torah (Exod. 13:8; Deut. 4:9; 6:7, 20–25; also Prov. 3:12; 4:1). The children were to revere and obey the father equally with the mother (Exod. 20:12; Lev. 19:3; Deut. 21:18, 20; cf. Exod. 21:15; Lev. 20:9). The father's love and blessing (Gen. 27:27–40; 49) is the basis for the image of God the Father of Israel (Exod. 4:22; Deut. 14:1; 32:6; Hos. 11:1; Jer. 3:4, 19; 31:9; Ps. 103:13) and David (2 Sam. 7: 14; Pss. 2:7; 89:27–28).

In the NT, "father" can refer to the male progenitor (e.g., Matt. 1:1–16; Mark 1:20; Acts 28:8), but in most instances it is used to refer to God. This Christian practice probably derives from the intimate term for father that Jesus used to address God (Heb. and Aram. *abba;* Mark 14:36; cf. Rom. 8:15; Gal. 4:6). "Father" is also the term for God Jesus used in the prayer he taught his followers (Luke 11:2). Rather than being derived from a human analogy, the term "Father" for God represents the ideal by whom every human father is to be judged (Eph. 3:14–15). ***See also*** Curse and Blessing; Family, The.

J.U.

fear of the Lord, the awe that a person ought to have before God (Prov. 5:7; Eccles. 12:13). As such it can be said to constitute "true religion" (Ps. 34:11). This "fear of the Lord" is represented by the "fear and trembling" with which Paul exhorts the Philippians to work out their salvation (Phil. 2:12). It describes the piety of the growing church in Acts 9:31. However, it may also carry overtones of judgment (2 Cor. 5:11; 1 Pet. 1:17).

feasts, festivals, and fasts, activities that, in the Bible, are observed to commemorate or emphasize events in the relationship between God and human beings. In the OT, feasts and festivals were occasions of joy. They were times for thanking God for blessings and granting relief to the poor and oppressed. They were often accompanied by singing, instrumental music, dancing, elaborate meals, and sacrifices. Depending on the nature and the requirements of the occasion, they were celebrated either at a sanctuary or at a person's home.

OT Feasts and Festivals: The Pentateuch prescribes the observance of several recurring festal or otherwise positive religious occasions: every seventh day was to be set apart as a Sabbath on which no work was to be performed (Exod. 20: 8–11; Deut. 5:12–15). In every seventh year (Sabbatical Year), Israelite slaves were to be released (Exod. 21:2–6; Deut. 15:12–18), land was to lie fallow (Exod. 23:10–11; Lev. 25:1–7), and debts of Israelites were to be suspended or cancelled (Deut. 15:1–6). In every fiftieth year (Jubilee Year), property was to return to its original owner, Israelite slaves were to be freed, and the land was to lie fallow (Lev. 25:8–17, 23–55). On the first day of each lunar month, a special series of sacrifices was to be made (Num. 28:11–15; cf. Ezek. 46:6–7). These new-moon festivals were days of feasting (1 Sam. 20:5, 18, 24, 27) and apparently days of rest (Amos 8:5). Of the new-moon festivals, that in the seventh month (the Feast of Trumpets) was the most important (Lev. 23:23–25; Num. 29:1–6). Three festivals, called pilgrimage festivals, required the participation of Israelite males at the sanctuary (Exod. 23:14, 17; 34:23; Deut. 16:16–17): (a) the Passover and Feast of Unleavened Bread, which were celebrated from the sunset of the fourteenth to the twenty-first day of the first month (Exod. 12; 23: 15; 34:18, 25; Lev. 23:5–8; Num. 9:1–14; 28:16–25; Deut. 16:1–8; Ezek. 45:21–24); (b) the Feast of Weeks, which occurred at the beginning of the wheat harvest seven weeks after the presentation of the barley omer (Exod. 23:16; 34:22; Lev. 23:15–21; Num. 28:26–31; Deut. 16:9–10); and (c) the Feast of Booths, which was celebrated on the fifteenth through the twenty-second days of the seventh month when the harvest and produce were gathered in (Exod. 23:16; 34: 22; Lev. 23:33–36; Num. 28:12–39; Deut. 16:13–18; Ezek. 45:25).

Beside the foregoing prescribed festivals, there are descriptions of other types of festivals and feasts in ancient Israel. Judg. 21:19–24 tells of a yearly festival in Shiloh. This may have been Shiloh's version of the Feast of Booths or it may have been a separate festival celebrating the new vintage. According to 1 Samuel 1 and 2, Elkanah and his family made yearly visits to the sanctuary at Shiloh to offer sacrifice and worship God. These visits may have been connected with the yearly festival mentioned in Judges 21, but more probably they were separate family or clan celebrations in the sanctuary city (cf. 1 Sam. 20:5–6, 24–39).

The joyous festivities marking the occasion when David brought the Ark of the Lord to Jerusalem; from a thirteenth-century French miniature.

Public celebrations accompanied dedication or renovation of temples (1 Kings 8; 2 Chron. 29) and the coronation of kings (1 Kings 1:39–40; 2 Kings 11:12, 13, 20). Military victories were occasions of celebrations (1 Sam. 18:6–7; cf. 30: 16). Families celebrated major events in the lives of their members such as the weaning of children (Gen. 21:8) or marriages (Gen. 29:22; Judg. 14:10–11; Tob. 10:7; Mark 2:19; John 2:1–2). Sheepherders, with families and friends, held festivals when flocks were sheared (1 Sam. 25; 2 Sam. 13:23–29; cf. Gen. 31:19; 38:12). Finally, sharing a sacrifice made to celebrate one's well-being with invited guests was a joyful festive occasion (cf. Lev. 3; 7:11–18; Deut. 12:6–7, 11–12, 17–18; 1 Sam. 9:22–24; 16:2–5; Job 1:4).

There were certainly festal observances in biblical times about which the Bible says little or nothing. The *Temple Scroll* from Qumran (columns 19–25) prescribes new-wine, new-oil, and wood-offering (cf. Neh. 10:35; 13:31) festivals in addition to the three pilgrimage festivals in the Pentateuch. These are probably not inventions but reflect ancient practice that was never codified in the Bible.

Later Jewish religious victories gave rise to celebrations that have remained part of Judaism to this day. Hanukkah (the Feast of Dedication) commemorates the rededication of the Temple altar by Judas Maccabeus on the 25th of Kislev (December) in 164 B.C. (1 Macc. 4:36–59; 2 Macc. 10:6–8; John 10:22). Purim, celebrated on the fourteenth and fifteenth of Adar (Feb.–March), commemorates the deliverance from the persecutions of Haman as described in the book of Esther (cf. 9:19–28).

Fasts: In contrast to feasts and festivals, fasts were times of mourning and self-denial arising from misfortune and sin. They could be single spontaneous responses of individuals, single spontaneous responses of the public, or recurring annual public observances.

Individuals fasted to obtain divine aid (2 Sam. 12:16–23; Dan. 9:3), to repent (1 Kings 21:27), to mourn (Neh. 1:4), to obtain revelation (Exod. 34:28), or to express devotion to God (Ps. 35:13; Luke 18:12). Similarly, the community often undertook a single fast to obtain God's help or protection (Judg. 20:26; 1 Sam. 14:24; Joel 1:14; Esther 4:3; Ezra 8:21–23), to express repentance (1 Sam. 7:6; Jon. 3:5–10), or to mourn the death of leaders (1 Sam. 31:13; 2 Sam. 1:12).

The only prescribed annual fast is that on the Day of Atonement (Lev. 16:29–34; 23:26–32; Num. 29:7). It occurred on the tenth day of the seventh month. The people were to "afflict themselves," meaning they were to abstain from food and drink and other bodily gratifications (cf. 2 Sam. 12:16–20; Dan. 10:2–3).

After the destruction of Jerusalem and the Temple by the Babylonians (580 B.C.), fasts were annually held in the fourth, fifth, seventh, and tenth months to mourn this calamity

(Zech. 7:3, 5; 8:19). A public fast preceded the festival of Purim on the thirteenth of Adar; Esther 9:31 apparently refers to this (cf. 4:16).

In the NT: In the NT, the Gospels report that Jesus observed Jewish feasts (John 5:1; 7:2, 10; Matt. 26:17–18), and a tradition recorded by Paul reports that Jesus transformed Passover for his followers into a ritual remembrance of his death (1 Cor. 11:24). Aside from that, however, the NT contains few regulations pertaining either to fasts (Matt. 6:16–18 does not prescribe fasts, it simply gives advice to those fasting; but see Mark 2:20) or to festivals. Those that are observed by Christians have grown out of the traditions of the life and practices of Jesus and the experiences of the church: for example, Christmas, to celebrate Jesus' birth (Luke 2:1–20); Epiphany, the appearance of the Magi (Matt. 2:1–12); Lent, Jesus' temptation in the wilderness (Matt. 4:1–11; Luke 4:1–12); Easter, Jesus' resurrection (Mark 16:1–8); Ascension Day, his ascent into heaven (Acts 2:9–10); and Pentecost, the gift of the Holy Spirit (Acts 2:1–11). Because the cardinal event of the Christian faith, the resurrection of Jesus, occurred on a Sunday, Christians turned to that day, rather than the Sabbath (Saturday), for their regular worship. ***See also*** Atonement, Day of; Easter; Esther; Fasting; Jubilee; Lord's Supper, The; Passover, The; Pentecost; Purim, The Feast of; Sabbath; Sabbatical Year; Tabernacles, Festival of; Trumpets, Feast of; Worship.

Bibliography

de Vaux, Roland. *Ancient Israel*. New York and Toronto: McGraw-Hill, 1965. Pp. 468–517.

Milgrom, Jacob. "The Temple Scroll." *Biblical Archaeologist* 41 (1978): 105–120.

D.P.W.

Felix, Antonius (fee'liks, an-tohn'ee-uhs), Roman procurator of Judea (ca. A.D. 52–59). According to the historians Tacitus and Josephus, he was brutal in his rule. He owed his position to his influential brother Pallas, but, because of immorality and incompetence, he was eventually replaced.

According to Acts 23:23–24:27, Felix became involved with Paul when the apostle was sent to Caesarea for trial upon recommendation of Claudius Lysias, the tribune in Jerusalem. The writer of Acts indicates that Felix followed appropriate judicial procedure during Paul's hearing. After listening to Paul speak on matters pertaining to faith in Jesus Christ, however, he is pictured in unfavorable terms. Hoping for a bribe, which was not forthcoming, and "desiring to do the Jews a favor," he allowed Paul to languish in prison for the remainder of his term in office. ***See also*** Claudius Lysias; Paul.

A.J.M.

felloe (fel'oh; KJV; RSV: "rim"), the edge of a wheel on the portable water stands in the Jerusalem Temple (1 Kings 7:33).

fellowship, communal association for the mutual benefit of those involved. In the OT the Sinai covenant binds together all Israelites into what is, ideally, a grand fellowship of mutual obligation and concern. Furthermore, covenant images clearly suggest a kind of fellowship between God and his people. For example, Israel is the wife of God (Hos. 1–3; Jer. 2:2; Ezek. 16); God has "known" (chosen) Israel (Amos 3:2), and Israel is to "know" (acknowledge, obey) God. God's election of Israel is motivated by his love (Deut. 7:7), and Israel is to be his own possession among all peoples (Exod. 19:5). The language of petition and worship often reflects the close bond between ancient Israel and its God (e.g., Pss. 42, 46, 63), as do the rituals of sacrifice.

Occasionally the Bible presents instances of a special fellowship with God enjoyed by individual persons. Enoch "walked with God" (Gen. 5:24); Abraham is called the "friend" of God (2 Chron. 20:7; Isa. 41:8); and Moses talks with God "face to face" (Exod. 33:11; cf. Deut. 34:10). The prophets' experience of being commissioned by God suggests a special bond between the deity and his spokesmen (Isa. 6; Jer. 1; Ezek. 1), and the Davidic king is called God's son (2 Sam. 7:14; Ps. 2:7). In spite of all this, however, the Hebrew equivalent of the word "fellowship" is remarkably rare in the OT.

In the NT, fellowship is the bond among Christians created by their common confession that Jesus is Lord. In Paul's Letters this fellowship is marked by the spiritual oneness effected by baptism and bestowal of the Spirit (Gal. 3:27–28; 1 Cor. 12). It is manifested by the gathered community at the Lord's Supper (1 Cor. 11:17–34) and characterized above all by self-giving love (1 Cor. 13). This fellowship of believers is dependent on—and an expression of—their fellowship with Christ. Eating the one loaf of the Lord's Supper makes the many into one body even as it enables the participants to commune with the Crucified One (1 Cor. 10:16–17).

Fellowship with Christ means that believers share his death and experience the new life that corresponds to his resurrection (Rom. 6:1–11; Phil. 3:8–11), sustained by the hope that at his coming they will forever be with him (1 Thess. 4:13–17). The apostle stresses, further, that communion with Christ excludes other types of fellowship, for example, fellowship with prostitutes or demons (1 Cor. 6:15–17; 10:19–21).

In the Gospel of John Christian fellowship is characterized by a perfect oneness grounded in the closest of relationships with the Father and the Son (17:11, 21–23; see also 1 John 1:3, 6, 7). Jesus is the true vine in which believers must "remain" if they would bear fruit—which is, above all, love for one another (John 15). ***See also*** Covenant; Friendship; Lord's Supper, The.

S.K.W.

fenced cities, a term used by the KJV where the RSV has "fortified cities" (Josh. 14:12; 2 Kings 18:13; 2 Chron. 8:5). ***See also*** Forts; Walls.

Fertile Crescent, a term coined by the modern scholar J. H. Breasted to describe the crescent-shaped area of fertile land extending from the

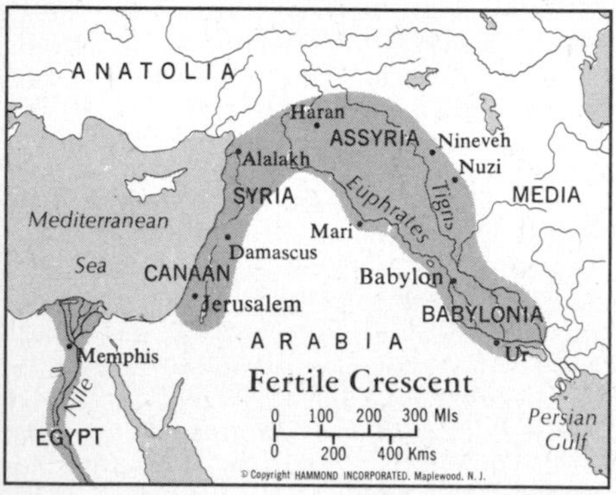

Tigris and Euphrates rivers, commonly known as Mesopotamia, westward over Syria to the Mediterranean and southward through Palestine and the Nile Valley of Egypt. While the term does not appear in the Bible and is used less frequently today, it is a convenient term to use for this important strip of land in which some of the earliest sedentary cultures emerged. The ancient cities in this region included Ur, Mari, Nuzi, and Alalakh. Sumerians, Assyrians, and Hittites passed through this land. Hebrew tradition developed here. The region also provided a bridge between Africa, Asia, and Europe for armies, merchants, and pilgrims and continues to do so in the twentieth century. ***See also*** Hittites; Mari; Mesopotamia; Nuzi; Sumer; Ur. K.H.R.

fertility cult. ***See*** Worship.

Festus, Porcius (fes'tuhs, pohr'shuhs), the Roman procurator over Judea who replaced Antonius Felix (ca. A.D. 59). According to the historian Josephus, he was a competent public official. He died in office several years after his appointment.

According to Acts 25:1–26:32, Festus encountered Paul, a prisoner in Caesarea, when Festus arrived as procurator. He was bewildered by Paul's religious convictions. After Paul appealed his case to Caesar in Rome, Festus arranged for a hearing in the presence of the visiting King Agrippa II and Bernice, where Paul again gave a defense of his belief in Jesus. Again, while Festus was incapable of perceiving anything worthwhile in Paul's preaching and declared him mad, neither could he find any reason to imprison him or put him to death (26:30–32). Nevertheless, because Paul had appealed to Caesar, he was sent, under guard, to Rome (Acts 27–28). ***See also*** Agrippa II; Bernice; Felix, Antonius; Paul. A.J.M.

fig *(Ficus carica)*, a fruit tree common in both wild and cultivated forms throughout the Near East since ancient times. It is a beautiful shade tree whose large palm-shaped leaves were said to have been used to cover the nakedness of Adam and Eve in the Garden of Eden (Gen. 3:7). The pear-shaped fruit, which is produced more than once during the year, has a high sugar content and is very sweet when ripe. It is eaten fresh or dried into cakes, which like those made from dates are storable and thus an ideal food for travelers (1 Sam. 25:18).

The fertilization of the fruit is dependent on a tiny wasp, which carries pollen into the inner parts by boring into the center of the fruit. The fig tree therefore will not bear fruit if the wasp is absent and may even require hand-fertilization by incision.

The fig also has medicinal properties as a poultice applied to wounds and boils (2 Kings 20:7; Isa. 38:21). The beauty and shade quality of the fig tree, as well as the popularity of the fruit, make it a favorite even today in house gardens and orchards where it is often planted alone in a corner. The fig is often associated with the grape vine as a symbol of peace and prosperity, providing shade and sustenance for the family it protects (1 Kings 4:25). A fig tree that failed to bear figs was cursed by Jesus (Matt. 21:18–19) perhaps as a metaphor for the destruction of the Temple that similarly failed to

Fig.

bear proper religious fruit (cf. Mark 11:12–25). ***See also*** Mulberry; Sycamore. P.L.C.

figurines, small carved or molded figures that function in ornamental or symbolic fashion. The *teraphim* (Gen. 31:19, 34; Lev. 26:1) is an example. Probably small representations of divinities, they were a form of protection in the Greco-Roman world (Acts 19:24), as well as in more ancient Palestine (Jer. 10:24). They have been found in almost every era of occupation in a number of archaeological sites.

fine, a verb (KJV) that designates the process by which impurities are removed from precious metals (RSV: "refine," Job 28:1; see also Prov. 25:4; 27:1). As an adjective it means of good and delicate or firm quality (Gen. 41:42) or composed of extremely small particles (Exod. 9:9).

finer (KJV; RSV: "smith"), one who processes metals by purifying ore (Prov. 25:4).

fining-pot. ***See*** Crucible.

fire, combustion giving off light, flame, and heat. Besides normal domestic uses (cooking, heating, lighting), it was used in the refining of metals, in various crafts, in the waging of war, and in sending messages. Fire also had specialized uses in worship. A perpetual fire burned in the Temple, and fire was used both for roasting sacrifices for human consumption and for burning incense. Of much greater importance in the Bible, however, is its symbolic meaning.

Fire is a common symbol of holiness and in some cases of protection (cf. Zech. 2:5). It represents divine action, with God himself presented as "a consuming fire" (Heb. 12:29; cf. Deut. 4:24). Fire is God's servant (Ps. 104:4; Heb. 1:7), and his word is like fire (Jer. 23:29). In reference to God's action, fire is most frequently a symbol of destruction associated with the wrath of God and his jealousy. As a metaphor of God's holiness, however, it may also purge or purify. The Babylonian exile is described as purification by fire (Ps. 66:12; Isa. 43:2), and certainly the Day of the Lord will purify Israel (Zech. 13:9; cf. 1 Cor. 3:13–15).

Fire is a central element of the description of theophany throughout biblical literature. God's appearance for covenant with Abraham (Gen. 15:17), the appearance in the burning bush (Exod. 3:2), the leading of Israel with the pillar of fire by night (Exod. 13:21–22), and the appearance in fire on Mount Sinai (Exod. 19:18) are central elements in Israel's faith. Such fiery theophanies continue in the NT as well. Christ's appearance in the vision of John is with "eyes of fire" (Rev. 1:14; 2:18), and the descent of the Holy Spirit is accompanied by "tongues of fire" (Acts 2:3). ***See also*** Theophany. D.L.C.

fire, tongues of. ***See*** Tongues as of Fire.

firebrands, usually pieces of wood set on fire. They were used by Samson in his revenge against the Philistines (Judg. 15:4); they were tossed over the city wall in time of military siege, as were the olive boughs during the attack of Lachish; or they were hurled as missiles by madmen (Prov. 26:18). Plucked by God "from the burning," they symbolized individuals rescued by the Lord (Amos 4:11).

firepan, a portable metal pan for carrying hot coals on which incense was placed as an offering (Lev. 16:12–13; Num. 16:46). Firepans were made for use with the lampstand and the burnt offering altar (Exod. 25:38; 27:3).

firkin. ***See*** Gallon.

firmament, God's division between cosmic waters on the second day of creation (Gen. 1: 6–8), forming the sky. One must here imagine a flat earth and a domed expanse of heavens holding back celestial waters from terrestrial. The Hebrew term *raqia'* suggests a thin sheet of beaten metal (cf. Exod. 39:3; Num. 17:3; Jer. 10:9; also Job 37:18). Similar metaphors for sky are

The Hebrew universe. The ancient Hebrews imagined the world as flat and round, covered by the great solid dome of the firmament which was held up by mountain pillars (Job 26:11; 37:18). Above the firmament and under the earth was water, divided by God at creation (Gen. 1:6, 7; cf. Pss. 24:2; 148:4). The upper waters were joined with the waters of the primordial deep during the Flood; the rains were believed to fall through windows in the firmament (Gen. 7:11; 8:2). The sun, moon, and stars moved across or were fixed in the firmament (Gen. 1:14–19; Ps. 19:4, 6). Within the earth lay Sheol, the realm of the dead (Num. 16:30–33; Isa. 14:9, 15).

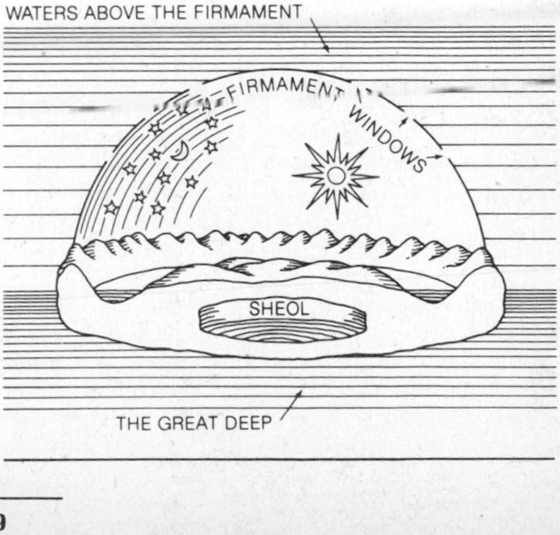

found in Homer and Pindar. Job 26:13 depicts God's breath as the force that calmed (or "spread," "smoothed" or "carpeted") the heavens. Luminaries were set in the firmament on the fourth day of creation (Gen. 1:14–19). Rains were believed to fall through sluices or windows in its surface (cf. Gen. 7:11). During the Flood, the upper waters joined with the waters of the primordial deep (Heb. *tehom).* In more pacific contexts, the firmament, or its pattern of luminaries, is said to declare the praises of God (Ps. 19:1; cf. 150:1). In Ezekiel's "chariot" vision, a crystal firmament supports the divine throne (Ezek. 1:22, 25, 26), just as something resembling a pavement of lapis lazuli is said to lie at the feet of Yahweh's throne in Exod. 24:10. Dan. 12:3 alludes to the "radiance" (Heb. *zohar)* of the firmament. Rabbinic sources regarded the firmament as the chief source of light for heavenly denizens. ***See also*** Creation; Genesis.

J.W.R.

firstborn, first fruits, firstling, the firstborn male child (Exod. 13:12–15; Num. 18:15–16), the seasonal initial produce of agriculture (Exod. 23:19; Lev. 23:10; Num. 15:20–21; Deut. 26:1–11) and food products (Num. 18:12–13; Deut. 18:4; Ezek. 44:30), and the first offspring of domesticated pure and impure animals (Exod. 13:12–13; Lev. 27:26–27; Num. 18:16–18; Deut. 15:19–23). These three "firsts" are all accorded a sanctified status in the Hebrew Bible (and were also often similarly regarded in other cultures of the ancient Near East). The first fruits of agriculture are given to God in religious ritual in acknowledgment of his ownership of the earth (Ps. 24:1), upon which humans are mere tenants (thus, Abel's offering is preferable to Cain's, Gen. 4:3–5). This transfer invokes God's blessing on the rest of the produce (Lev. 19:24–25; Prov. 3:9–10). The male firstborn of humans and beasts in Israel become dedicated to God because he saved them from the slaughter of the firstborn of Egypt (Exod. 13:14–15). This plague, in turn, was brought upon the Egyptians for enslaving Israel, God's own appointed firstborn (Exod. 4:22; cf. Jer. 2:3; 31:9). Israel's firstborn status is reflective of sociolegal realities. The firstborn son inherits a double portion of his father's estate (Deut. 21:15–17; Isa. 61:7), the paternal blessing (Gen. 27), and succession to authority (Gen. 27:29, 37; 37:21–22; 2 Kings 2:9). The Davidic king is also viewed metaphorically as God's firstborn (Ps. 89:28), an appellation the NT applies to Jesus (Heb. 1:6). ***See also*** Curse and Blessing; Priests; Worship.

J.U.

fir tree, a general term often mentioned in the book of Isaiah in reference to coniferous evergreens, such as the cypress, juniper, and pine. Specifically, "fir tree" most likely refers to the stately Aleppo pine *(Pinus halepensis),* a tree common to the arid hilly regions of Palestine

Fir (Aleppo pine).

and Lebanon. It is often found growing mixed with cedars (Isa. 60:13; 2 Kings 19:23 KJV; RSV: "cypress") and was one of the trees sent by Hiram to Solomon for the construction of his Temple (1 Kings 5:10; 2 Chron. 2:8; RSV: "cypress"). Aside from its use in architecture, the fir tree was also cut into planks for shipbuilding (Ezek. 27:5) and made into some musical instruments (2 Sam. 6:5). ***See also*** Cypress; Forest; Pine; Woods.

P.L.C.

fish, aquatic gilled animals. The Bible takes fish and fishing for granted and makes no distinction between fresh- and salt-water fish, access to both of which was readily available in certain parts of the country. The major salt-water fish sources were the long coast of the Mediterranean Sea and the waters of the Gulf of Aqaba. The primary source of fresh-water fish was the Sea of Galilee and some of the reaches of the Jordan River. Archaeological recovery of both salt- and fresh-water fish bones used as food, jewelry, or both indicates that they were shipped considerable distances, illustrated for instance by both Mediterranean and Red Sea (Gulf of Aqaba) species recovered at Tell Hesban in Moabite Transjordan, east of the Dead Sea. The main fresh-water species available in the Sea of Galilee included the mouth breeding Cichlidae, of which two varieties of Tilapia *(Tilapia galilaea* and *Tilapia nilotoca)* were common, Cypinidae, including two common carp *(Barbus canis* and *Barbus longiceps),* and Siluridae, the catfish *Clarias lazera.*

Levitical law considered fish with fins and scales to be clean, but others unclean (Lev. 11:9–12). Catfish were thus spurned among the fresh-water species, but salt-water eels, sharks, rays, and lampreys were also shunned. In addition to the "fish of the sea" (Gen. 1:26), the Bible recognized the habitats of fish to include the Nile (Exod. 7:18; Num. 11:5), streams (Ezek. 29:4), the Mediterranean ("Great Sea," Ezek. 47:10) and the Sea of Galilee (Luke 5:1–11, "Gennesaret"). Methods of catching fish mentioned include dragnet (John 21:8), angling with hook (Job 41:1; Amos 4:2; Matt. 17:27), harpoons and spears (Job 41:7), and thrown hand-nets (Matt. 4:18).

While the primary use of fish was for food (Luke 11:11; Mark 6:41), preparation of which included broiling (John 21:9), the symbolism of fish included the death of the plagues (Exod. 7:21) and the death of drought (Isa. 50:2) as well as untimely death (Eccles. 9:12). Fish being caught symbolized the helplessness of humans before the power of God (Hab. 1:14–16). The techniques of fishing became a model for the work of Jesus' disciples as "fishers of men" (Mark 1:17; Matt. 4:19). One of the gates of Jerusalem was named the "Fish Gate" (2 Chron. 33:14; Neh. 3:3; 12:39; Zeph. 1:10) in postexilic reconstruction, possibly in the north wall of the Mishneh or Second Quarter of the city.

Sometime in early church life, the figure of a fish took symbolic value as the sign of the Christ. The acrostic derived from the Greek letters of the word "fish" *(ichthys)* were understood to stand for the Greek words for "Jesus *[i]* Christ *[ch]*, God's *[th]* Son *[y]*, Savior *[s]*" and the use of the symbol persists to this day in Christian iconography. R.S.B.

fitch, a designation (KJV) for two plants. In Ezek. 4:9 it designates an inferior species of wheat (RSV: "spelt"), either *Triticum spelta* or *Triticum dicoccoides*. In Isa. 28:25, 27 it probably designates black cumin (RSV: "dill") or "nutmeg flower" *(Nigella sativa)* rather than the true cumin with which it is paired. True dill, *Anethum graveolens*, and true cumin, *Cuminum cyminum*, were both cultivated as condiments. Fitch is also an archaic term for "vetch," a group of plants in the *Vicia* genus.

flags (KJV; RSV: "reeds" in Exod. 2:3, 5; Job 8:11 or "rushes" in Isa. 19:6), a variety of plants growing in marshy or river bank locations, such as iris or cattails. The Hebrew term *suph* ("soof") is used for the reeds or rushes at the edge of the Nile in the story of Moses' infancy (Exod. 2:3, 5) and is the name of the "Sea of Reeds" through which Moses led the Israelites out of Egypt (Exod. 13:18), although the latter is translated by the Septuagint as "Red Sea." In Job 8:11 the watery matrix needed by the plants is cited, and in Isa. 19:6 the decay of the plants is a sign of desolation and destruction. R.S.B.

flax *(Linum usitatissimum)*, a delicate plant

Flax.

with beautiful blue flowers. It has been known since prehistoric times in the Near East. It is the earliest known cultivated fiber plant and was used to make linen. Linen of varying quality was used for Temple vestments (Exod. 25:4) as well as for ordinary garments, sails, nets, and even twine. It was also the wrapping cloth used for the dead (Matt. 27:59). The harvested flax plants were soaked in water in order to separate the fibers and then spread to dry, the hot exposed rooftops being an ideal place for such activity (Josh. 2:6). Linseed oil is extracted from the seeds, and the dregs are then given to the animals as fodder. ***See also*** Linen. P.L.C.

flesh, the soft material of the body (Job 10:11). More narrowly, it can refer to the penis (Exod. 28:42), foreskin (Gen. 17:9–14), and hence sexual union (Gen. 2:24) and generation (John 1:13). More broadly, it refers to the whole body or person as represented by the body (John 1:14), to one's kin (Rom. 9:3), to humanity and therefore what is human (Isa. 40:5; Phil. 3:3–4), and to humans and animals (Gen. 6:17–20). Animal flesh is "meat" (Dan. 10:3) or the meaty part of a sacrifice (Lev. 6:24–27). "Flesh" connotes sensitivity (Ezek. 11:19), superficiality (John 8:15), weakness (2 Chron. 32:8), and mortality (Ps. 78:39). Paul uses "flesh" for the urge to sin (Gal. 5:19–21). ***See also*** Body; Flesh and Spirit; Human Being. R.H.G.

flesh and spirit, complementary and contrastive terms whose meaning must be derived from the context in which they are used. The phrase "the spirits of all flesh" (Num. 16:22; 27:16) refers to human beings as animated physical bodies. Their spirit, or breath, comes from God. He can withdraw it from flesh so as to produce death (Gen. 6:3) or grant it to flesh so as to produce life, even life after death (Ezek. 37:1–14). Thus, in the NT, Jesus' resurrection by the Spirit is more impressive than his fleshly descent from David (Rom. 1:3–4; cf. 1 Tim. 3:16).

Since flesh connotes weakness (Ps. 56:4; Rom. 8:3) and spirit connotes power (Zech. 4:6; Luke 24:49; Acts 1:8), the two stand side by side for the contrast between weak human beings and Almighty God (Isa. 31:3). Similarly, acceptable worship of God in the Spirit contrasts with unacceptable attempts to please God in the flesh (Phil. 3:3). But the weakness of flesh (simple tiredness) can prove stronger than the human spirit's will to pray (Mark 14:38, a will some people think refers to the Holy Spirit's desire).

According to 2 Cor. 7:1, sin may defile both the flesh (in the sense "body," as in the RSV) and the spirit (not the Holy Spirit, which is hardly the object of defilement). One can be absent in flesh (again in the sense "body," as in the RSV) but present in spirit (Col. 2:5). At the last day, the spirit may be saved even though the flesh (presumably the present mortal body, though some think the sinful urge) has to be destroyed prematurely in punishment for a heinous and unrepented sin (1 Cor. 5:5).

In Paul's writings, the contrast between the Holy Spirit and flesh (often as the sinful urge) looms larger than the distinction between the human spirit and the physical flesh it animates (in some passages, however, it is unclear whether God's Spirit or the human spirit is intended). Paul associates the Spirit favorably with faith, the flesh unfavorably with the works of the law (Gal. 3:2–3). Isaac, freeborn according to the Spirit, represents God's gracious promise; Ishmael, slaveborn according to the flesh, represents the law, which brings a curse (Gal. 4:21–31). The spiritual person is determined by God's Spirit; the fleshly person behaves like unbelievers, who do not have the Spirit (1 Cor. 2:12–3:4). Vices (nonphysical as well as physical) are the works of the flesh; virtues are the fruit of the Spirit (Gal. 5:16–25). Fleshly behavior leads to death; behavior according to the Spirit leads to eternal life (Gal. 6:7–8; Rom. 8:1–17).

In the Gospel of John, the gift of the divine Spirit makes up for what is lacking in merely human (but not evil) flesh (John 3:3–8; 6:52–63). ***See also*** Flesh; Holy Spirit, The; Human Being.

R.H.G.

fleshhooks, forklike implements used by priests for sacrifices (Num. 4:14; 1 Sam. 2:13–14, which speaks of their having three prongs), now usually translated "forks." Those in use at the Jerusalem Temple were made of gold (1 Chron. 28:17) and bronze (2 Chron. 4:16).

flint, an impure quartz rock, usually gray, brown, or black, abundant in Palestine. It fractures on conchoidal lines, and holds an extremely sharp edge, either smooth or serrated. It was used for a variety of tools from the earliest toolmaking period and continues in use to the present. It was especially efficient for awls, axes, knives, picks, scrapers, sickles, and weapons (arrowheads and spear points).

Knives used for circumcision were made of flint (Exod. 4:25; Josh. 5:2, 3). Flint serves as a metaphor for sharp-cutting destructive power (Isa. 5:28) and stubborn faithfulness (Isa. 50:7) and is a dubious source of water (Ps. 114:8; Deut. 8:15). It can be manipulated by humans (Job 28:9) but is a most unlikely source of any nourishment (Deut. 32:13).

Flint tool technology is an increasingly helpful datum for dating prehistoric cultures, and archaeological research is adding constantly to such resources and their precise use in identifying historical epochs.

R.S.B.

flock. ***See*** Sheep.

Flood, the, the catastrophic excess of water described in Genesis 6–8. The biblical story of the Flood relates how God destroyed the existing world but saved Noah and his family and representatives of each animal species in an ark. After the waters subsided and the ark rested on Mount Ararat (8:4), Noah sent out a raven and then a dove (which brought back an olive branch); seven days later he sent out another dove, which did not return (8:6–12). Noah disembarked, offered sacrifices, and formally rebegan the world by a contract (covenant) in which Noah and his sons received instructions and God promised not to bring a flood again (8:13–22; 9:8–17), a promise signaled by the appearance of the rainbow.

The OT word for the cosmic flood is *mabbul*, which also refers to the heavenly ocean (cf. e.g., Ps. 29:10). The Flood was an undoing of creation: the cosmic waters overwhelmed the earth, coming through the windows of the sky and the fountains of the great deep beneath the earth (7:11; cf. 8:2). Thus, return to the primeval watery condition set the stage for a new beginning for the world (cf. Gen. 1:2, 9).

Mesopotamian Flood Stories: The meaning of the Flood story is illuminated by comparative studies. Although there are many Flood legends throughout the world, particularly in America, Australia, and the Pacific Islands, the many parallels between the biblical and Mesopotamian Flood stories (most strikingly the sending of the birds) indicate that these stories come from the

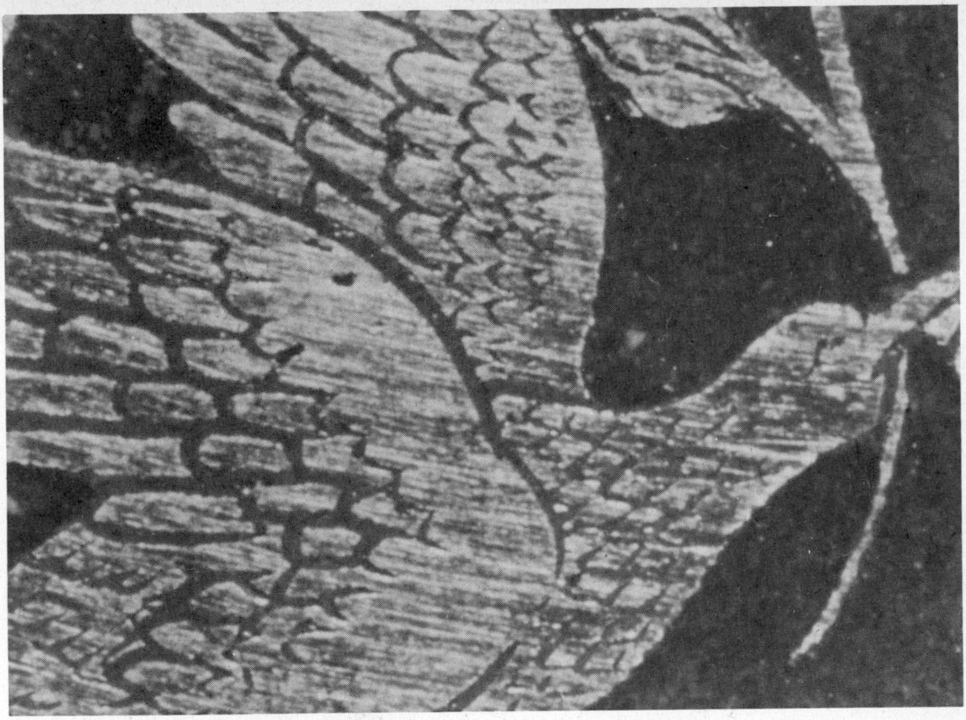

Dove with olive leaf, which indicated to Noah that the waters had subsided from the earth (Gen. 8:11); panel from the Verdun Altar, 1180.

same literary tradition. There are three major cuneiform retellings of the Flood: the Sumerian Flood story (which is somewhat fragmentary), the Gilgamesh Epic, and the Atrahasis Epic. In the Gilgamesh Epic, the survivor of the Flood, Utnapishtim, tells Gilgamesh about the Flood in order to show him how his own attainment of immortality was unique. Although this tale tells little about the significance of the Flood, it shows a contrast in the concept of the survivor. In the Gilgamesh Epic and the Sumerian Flood story (Atrahasis is broken at this point), the hero-survivor is rewarded with immortality. In the Bible, by contrast, Noah has a more human fate: he becomes drunk, is sexually embarrassed or abused by his own son, and ultimately dies (9:20–28).

The Atrahasis Epic presents the Flood in the context of a primeval history of humanity. In this story, the creation of humanity caused a problem that prompted Enlil and the gods to send plague, drought, saline soil, famine, and ultimately a Flood to destroy humankind. One god, Enki, helped people escape the early problems and then had Atrahasis build an ark; after the Flood he created barrenness, miscarriage, and stillbirth in women, celibate women, and additional provisions that are now lost. It seems that the Flood was seen as the result of an overpopulation problem that could not be permanently solved by the "natural disasters" but that could be controlled by the permanent population safeguards initiated by Enki after the Flood.

The Biblical Story and Its Meaning: The biblical story is emphatically not about overpopulation, for people are strongly commanded to be fruitful, multiply, and fill the earth (8:1). As in Atrahasis, however, the biblical Flood came because of a problem for which God provided a remedy after the Flood. In the Bible, the problem was the progressive pollution of the earth by the misdeeds of humanity (6:5–7). Immediately after the Flood, therefore, God gave Noah and his sons several laws. The difference between the ante- and postdiluvian worlds is in these laws, for laws are considered the *sine qua non* of humanity's ability to continue to live on the earth. There are three laws presented in Genesis 9: an iteration and reiteration of the commandment to multiply (vv. 2, 7); permission to eat meat accompanied by an injunction not to eat blood or eat from a living animal (vv. 3–4); and a demand for capital punishment for murderers (vv. 5–6). These are important principles in biblical law: the Pentateuch prohibits eating the blood of animals six times (Gen. 9:4; Lev. 3:17; 7:26; 17:10–14; Deut. 12:16; 12:23–24). The reason is that blood is the life of the animal; the penalty was death (Heb. *karet*, "to be cut off"). The inviolability and incomparability of human life is one of the fundamental axioms of Israelite religious law. Capital punishment was never invoked for property offenses, and homicide could not be compensated for by the payment of a monetary fine—it could only be rectified by the execution of the murderer, even if the murderer were an animal (for example, a goring ox, Exod. 21:29). Despite its importance, this demand for execution of murderers was a postdiluvian provision, for both Cain (Gen. 4:8–16) and Lemech (4:23–24) were kept alive under divine protection. This had disastrous consequences for the earth. The ground on which Abel was killed became barren (Gen. 4:10–12), and by the time Noah was born the barrenness had become widespread. Noah was to bring relief (LXX: "give rest") from human toil on the land that God had cursed (Gen. 5:29), for by the time of the Flood the whole earth had become polluted (Gen. 6:11–12). The Flood was a means of getting rid of a polluted world and starting again with a well-washed one. Then, since God had recognized humanity's evil impulses, he gave Noah the basic laws, particularly the strict instructions about the shedding of blood in order to prevent the earth's becoming so polluted again.

The idea that moral misdeeds can contaminate the earth is an important idea in biblical thought, for Israel believed that it had inherited the land after the previous inhabitants had polluted it and it had "vomited them out," and that it too might lose its land for the same reason (Lev. 18:24–28). Israel worried that it might contaminate the land because of unsolved murders (Deut. 21:7–8), the failure to execute murderers (Num. 35:31–34) or sexual impropriety (Jer. 3:1). Ultimately, the prophets came to believe that Israel had polluted its land (Jer. 2:7) and was therefore exiled (Ezek. 36:18). Israel's retelling of the flood story showed a cosmic parallel to Israel's pollution, purgation, and ultimate restoration. There are several allusive references to the Flood in the first nine chapters of Ezekiel, which portray Israel just before the destruction, and the one explicit biblical reference to the Flood outside of Genesis (Isa. 54:9) promises that like the Flood, Israel's exile was a unique occurrence, not to be repeated.

Despite numerous attempts to find archaeological evidence for a universal deluge, one has not been found, although localized flood levels have been discovered in various Mesopotamian cities. The tradition of the flood, which may have been very old, was retold in Mesopotamia to illustrate Mesopotamia's concern with overpopulation and was retold in the Bible as a dramatic portrayal of Israel's concern with misdeeds, pollution, and the destruction they can bring.

Bibliography

Frymer-Kensky, Tikva. "Pollution, Purification and Purgation in Biblical Israel." *The Word of the Lord Shall Go Forth*. Ed. C. Meyers and M. O'Connor. Winona Lake, IN: Eisenbranus, 1983. Pp. 399–414.

______. "The Atrahasis Epic and its Significance for Our Understanding of Genesis 1–9." *Biblical Archaeologist* 40 (1977): 147–155.

Lambert, W. G., and A. Millard. *Atrahasis: The Babylonian Story of the Flood*. Oxford: The University Press, 1969.

T.S.F.

floor, a flat, sometimes enclosed area. In biblical usage the term designated primarily the "threshing floor" (Gen. 50:10; Judg. 6:37; Ruth 3:14; 2 Sam. 24:21; Hos. 13:3; Matt. 3:12; Luke 3:17). In ancient as in modern times, it was usually a flat rock surface large enough to accommodate piles of grain from individual farmers with sufficient space to allow each farmer to drive a threshing sledge over the grain at the edge of his harvested pile to shred it prior to winnowing. It was usually a communal installation, although individual farmers may have had their own spots for their operations.

Of the references to floors of structures, those included are of the tabernacle (Num. 5:17, evidently an earthen floor), a roof chamber (Judg. 3:25, possibly a rolled earthen or plastered floor), Solomon's Temple (1 Kings 6:15, described as partly overlaid with gold [6:30]), and the Temple in Ezekiel's specifications (Ezek. 41:16, 20).

Archaeological evidence indicates that floors were built of various materials, from plain tamped or rolled earth, to pebble, cobble, unfitted and fitted slab stone paving (see John 19:13), to plain, geometric, and elaborately decorated and inscribed mosaic tile. Floors and the artifacts associated with their construction and use form part of the data most helpful to archaeologists for dating the construction and use of a building. R.S.B.

flour. ***See*** Bread; Mill.

flowers (Heb. *nitṣanum*), a general term referring to the colorful array of blossoms that abound in the Holy Land, especially when the rains of winter and the warmth of spring combine to bring new life to the land (Song of Sol. 2:12). The previously arid and parched fields, waste places, and desert areas burst into a showy display of color that persists until the summer droughts again desiccate the landscape.

The earliest flowers of spring are diverse in form and color. The pink, white, and lilac blossoms of the cyclamen appear as early as January. The various shades of reds and pinks of the abundant crown anemones, poppies, and mountain tulips successively dominate the landscape. The flowers of the diverse tuberous plants of the lily family also add their array of colors to the mosaic. As the summer progresses, the short-lived delicate blossoms of spring are replaced by fields of yellow and white daisylike flowers of chamomile and chrysanthemums. The less showy yellow, blue, white, pink, and purple flowers of the various hardy thorny shrubs and plants remain through the summer to decorate the dry hills, rocky terrain, and waste places (Hos. 10:8).

Since flowers are referred to in general terms in the Bible, the specific identity of individual species is difficult to ascertain. Although context often may elucidate which flowers are indicated, it is not enough to identify a specific plant. Even in those cases where specific flowers such as lilies or roses are named they are not necessarily botanically correct designations.

In general, the term "lily" applies to the family of plants that have bulbs, tubers, or rhizomes as roots *(Liliaceae)*. Such plants commonly found in the Holy Land are the true lilies, such as the white Madonna lily and the deep red Martagon lily. The tulip, asphodel, Star of Bethlehem, hyacinth, and related narcissus, daffodil, crocus, and iris inhabit the rocky ground and dry places of the hill country. The "lily of the valleys" of the Song of Sol. 2:1–2 is probably the blue hyacinth. The lilies of the field of Matt. 6:28–30, however, are most likely not true lilies but rather one of the numerous showy spring flowers such as the crown anemone.

As is the case with the lily, the specific references to the rose do not necessarily indicate a true rose, but rather a showy, colorful, flower. The true roses of the Holy Land, such as the wild Phoenician rose, may have been the "rose plants in Jericho" (Ecclus. 24:14). Fruit-bearing shrubs such as raspberry and blackberry blossom along watercourses. Fruit trees such as the apple, plum, cherry, apricot, and almond (genus *Prunus)* are also of the rose family and display light pink and white clouds of blossoms in the spring time. The rose of Sharon (Song of Sol. 2:1) may also have been one of these or one of the more common flowers such as the tulip or narcissus, both of which grow profusely on the plains of Sharon. The showy roselike flowers of the woody shrubs of the rock rose family *(Cistaceae)*, which adorn the rocky and dry areas in the spring and early summer, may also be candidates.

Flowers enter many aspects of life in the Holy Land. The flowering trees and shrubs, the flowers of the fields, and the less showy blossoms of various herbaceous plants such as mints and mustards provide nectar for the bees in this land of milk and honey (Isa. 7:22; Num. 13:37). Their fragrances are extracted as essential oils to form the basis for various perfumes and unguents. Their scents freshen homes and garments, and their colors decorate in garlands of blossoms. The forms of the flowers provide inspiration for decorative motifs as well. The columns of King Solomon's Temple are capped by lilies, probably the lotus seen in Egyptian design (1 Kings 7:19, 26).

Various references to flowers in the Bible are symbolic as well as literal. The flowers of spring signify renewal (Song of Sol. 2:12) as well as the fragility and transience of life (Isa. 40:6–7; 1 Pet. 1:24; Job 14:2). The qualities of beauty, purity, and sweetness are also likened to flowers (Song of Sol. 2:1–5, 5:13; Isa. 28:4). ***See also*** Lily; Rose; and such individual entries for plants and trees as Almond; Fig; Flax; Mustard. P.L.C.

flute. ***See*** Music.

fly, a small flying insect. Many species of flies are known in Palestine and Egypt. In the Bible two Hebrew words mean "fly." **1** *'arōb*, the flies visited on the Egyptians as the fourth plague (Exod. 8:20–32; alluded to in Pss. 78:45; 105:31). The species of fly involved in this plague is uncertain; it may have been the Tabanid fly *(Stomoxys calcitrans)*. **2** *zebūb* (Eccles. 10:1; Isa. 7:18), probably the ordinary housefly *(Musca domestica)*. Baal-zebub, "lord of flies," was a deity worshipped at Ekron, whom King Ahaziah wanted to ask whether or not he would recover from his final illness (2 Kings 1:2–6, 16). ***See also*** Plagues. J.M.W.

food, one of the necessities for the sustenance of life. The chief staple in biblical times was bread, as suggested by the fact that the Hebrew word for bread *(lekhem)* can also designate food in general. Barley, wheat, and emmer were the most common varieties of grain from which bread was baked. Besides their use in flour, these cereals were also eaten in roasted form, either whole or crushed (Josh. 5:11; Lev. 2:14). Next to bread, fruits, vegetables, and dairy products were the most important staples of the Israelites. Common fruits were grapes, olives (used mostly in the form of oil), figs, dates, apples, and pomegranates. Among the vegetables, beans, cucumbers, lentils, onions, leeks, and garlic were most commonly grown. Dairy products, derived more from goats than cows, were consumed chiefly in the form of cheese, curds, and butter. Meat was also part of the diet, but for the ordinary Israelite only on special occasions, since it was too expensive for daily fare. Both domesticated and wild animals, such as deer, gazelle, fish, and fowl, were used for food. Boiling or roasting were the preferred methods of preparing meat, from which all blood had to be drained carefully, since blood was considered sacred as the seat of life which belonged to God alone (Gen. 9:4–6; Lev. 17:10–11; Deut. 12:23–25; Acts 15:19). Certain animals considered ritually unclean could not be consumed (see Lev. 11:1–47). The Israelite diet was rounded out by spices and other natural products such as salt and honey. Those Christians who lived in the Holy Land will have had similar food available, although the category of "unclean" was eliminated (Mark 7:14–20; Acts 10:9–15; Rom. 14:20). Because Christians were of all nationalities and were scattered throughout Europe and the Mediterranean basin, their eating habits reflected those of their respective native lands.

Availability: While the food supply was generally adequate, famines, caused either by natural calamities, such as drought and locusts, or by human warfare, were not infrequent in biblical times (Gen. 26:1; 43:1; Amos 4:6–9). Some regions of the country were more fertile and productive than others. Thus, for instance, the tribe of Asher, situated on the northern coast of Palestine, was known for its abundance of food (Gen. 49:20); and the Transjordanian region of Bashan was blessed with very fertile soil, which made possible the raising of herds of cattle known for their sleekness (Amos 4:1). The adequacy of one's diet also depended to a large extent upon one's wealth and social status. Kings and nobles usually ate better than peasants. The quantity of food consumed at Solomon's court was enormous, as suggested by the following list of daily provisions: "And Solomon's provision for one day was thirty cors [ca. 330 bushels] of fine flour, and sixty cors [ca. 660 bushels] of meal, ten fat oxen, and twenty pasture-fed cattle, a hundred sheep, besides harts, gazelles, roebucks, and fatted fowl" (1 Kings 4:22–23).

Significance: Besides its obvious function for the maintenance of physical life, food had other functions and uses in the Bible. It was a means of bonding social relationships and of establishing covenants (Gen. 31:54; Exod. 24:11). Food was also used as presents or as tribute (Gen. 32:13–18; 1 Sam. 25:18; 2 Sam. 16:1; 1 Kings 14:1–3). It was also used for making loans (Deut. 23:19) and as wages or payments for goods and services rendered (1 Sam. 2:5; 1 Kings 5:9–11; Ezra 3:7; Matt. 10:10). Not eating was a sign of grief (1 Sam. 1:7), scant rations were a means of punishment (1 Kings 22:27; Amos 4:6), and feasting on an abundance of food was a sign of joy and celebration (Isa. 25:6; Luke 15:23). Food was also used for religious purposes, such as the bringing of offerings (Lev. 1–7; 1 Sam. 2:12–17; 1 Cor. 8) and in sacred communal meals (Exod. 12; 1 Sam. 1:4–5; Matt. 26:17–29; Acts 2:46). God, however, does not need or partake of food (Ps. 50:12–13).

Because food was of such fundamental significance, it could easily be misused or be given undue importance. Consequently, the Bible also warns against the misuse of food and reminds us that there is more to life than food and drink. While humans may produce bread from the earth, God is seen as the ultimate source of all food (Pss. 104:14; 136:25; 147:9; 2 Cor. 9:10). Furthermore, human beings do not live by bread alone, but by everything that proceeds out of the mouth of the Lord (Deut. 8:3; Luke 4:1–4). The absence of God's life-giving word may cause a famine as severe as any lack of food (Amos 8:11–12). Life consists of more than food (Matt. 6:25), and the kingdom of God does not consist of food and drink, but of righteousness and peace and joy in the Holy Spirit (Rom. 14:17). In the kingdom of God, one's food is to do the will of God (John 4:34; 6:27), and citizens of that kingdom are enjoined to progress from simpler to more solid forms of spiritual food (1 Cor. 3:2; Heb. 5:12–14). ***See also*** Bread; Meals. W.E.L.

Geese being presented, possibly as payment of taxes; ivory from Megiddo, thirteenth–twelfth century B.C.

food offered to idols, the English translation of one Greek word that was used first by Greek-speaking Jews to refer to the sacrifices (often of animals, thus the reference to "meat" in 1 Cor. 8:13) that were regularly a part of pagan cultic observances (see 4 Macc. 5:2). The classical Greek term for such sacrifices meant, literally, "(something) offered to a deity," and in later Greek a related term meant, simply, "(something) offered to a divinity." The latter occurs in 1 Cor. 10:28, where Paul quotes what someone might say to a Christian dinner guest about the food being served. Sacrificial offerings were customarily divided into three portions: part was burned on the altar, part was placed on a special table for the deity, and part was allotted to the worshipers for their consumption within the temple precincts. What was left was sold in the public market.

According to Acts, when a special Jerusalem meeting of apostles and elders agreed to endorse the preaching of the gospel to the Gentiles, several restrictive provisions were laid down. One was that Gentile converts to Christianity should abstain from eating anything that had been offered in sacrifice to idols (Acts 15:29; cf. 21:25). The Nicolaitans opposed in Rev. 2:14–15 (cf. Num. 25:1–2; 31:16) and the Christian prophetess (perhaps their leader) opposed in Rev. 2:20 are accused of laxity in exactly this regard.

Despite what Acts reports about Christian strictures on eating food that had been sacrificed in pagan rites (Paul never mentions the decree of the Jerusalem leaders in his letters), some members of Paul's Corinthian congregation saw nothing wrong in doing so. They apparently reasoned that, because the only true God is the one known in Jesus Christ, other "so-called gods" had no real existence and sacrifices made to them had no real significance (1 Cor. 8:4–6). Perhaps these folk occasionally ate in pagan temples (see 1 Cor. 8:10), or their eating of sacrificial food could have been done at the quasi-religious dinners of fraternal associations or at meals hosted by pagan friends or relatives who had offered some special sacrifice. Whatever the particular setting(s) may have been, they seem to have participated with a certain bravado, alleging their possession of a superior "knowledge" (1 Cor. 8:1b) and criticizing those brothers and sisters as persons "weak" in conscience (1 Cor. 8:7) who declined to eat what had been offered in sacrifice.

In 1 Cor. 8:1–11:1, Paul responds to this situation without either appealing or alluding to the prohibition reported in Acts 15:29. Instead, the apostle insists that neither eating nor abstaining from food offered to idols is in itself consequential (8:8). Thus, he thinks it unnecessary that Christians inquire about the origin of the meat they are considering purchasing in the market or that pagan friends serve at a private dinner (10:25–27). Paul also insists, however, that this Christian freedom must always be exercised in love (note 8:1c; 10:23–24) and without endangering one's partnership in the body of Christ (note 10:18–22). He understands this to exclude a Christian's participation in any pagan sacrificial meals (10:14–22) and to require abstention from what has been sacrificed previously whenever eating it might be injurious to other Christians or confusing to nonbelievers (8:7–13; 10:28–29a). It may be that Romans 14 refers to the same problem, although the reference to "meat" is more general. ***See also*** Idol; Jezebel; Love; Worship. V.P.F.

fool, foolishness, folly, terms referring to the lack of wisdom. Since wisdom, however, has so many different connotations and nuances, there are numerous characteristics of a life of foolishness or folly. In general, a fool in the Bible is a person who lives life as if God and God's will were of no consequence: "The fool says in his heart, 'There is no God' " (Pss. 14:1; 53:1; cf. Prov. 1:7).

A fool can be recognized by various characteristics: lack of intelligence or experience, sometimes without being aware of it (Prov. 12:15; Eccles. 5:1; Luke 12:20); an inability to be cautious in speech (Prov. 18:6–7); or pursuing courses of conduct or action that ultimately prove to be harmful (2 Sam. 24:10). There is another aspect of foolishness or folly that is even more insidious: the actions of one who deliberately sins against God's laws (Jer. 29:23; Deut. 22:21; 2 Sam. 13:11–14). A fool is one who, either by ignorance or by deliberate and calculated premeditation, follows a lifestyle or commits specific acts that are detrimental for the person or for society. Such actions and lifestyles can be described as foolishness or folly. In the Bible these characteristics stem from the lack of a proper relationship with God.

In Matt. 5:22, Jesus warns that anyone who calls another person a "fool" is in danger of eternal punishment. ***See also*** Wisdom. J.M.E.

foot, a body part used in a variety of figurative ways in the Bible. God required Moses to go barefoot on the holy ground of Horeb (Exod. 3:5). Barefootedness was part of David's mourning (2 Sam. 15:30). God commanded Isaiah to walk barefoot as a symbol of future captivity (Isa. 20:2–4). Placing the foot on the neck of the vanquished enemy indicated victory (Josh. 10:24; Ps. 110:1; Matt. 22:44); God's placing all things "under the feet" expresses absolute dominion (Ps. 8:7; 1 Cor. 15:27; Eph. 1:22; Heb. 2:8). Listeners and pupils sat at their master's feet: Mary at Jesus' feet (Luke 10:39); Paul at Gamaliel's feet (Acts 22:3). Love is shown Jesus by the washing, kissing, and anointing of his feet (Luke 7:38,

44–47; John 12:3). Jesus washed his disciples' feet as an example of humble service (John 13: 5–17). Homage is shown Jesus by falling down at his feet (Mark 5:22; Luke 8:41). Jesus heals those placed at his feet (Matt. 15:30). The disciples are to shake the dust from their feet to reject inhospitality (Matt. 10:14; Mark 6:11; Luke 9:5; 10:11). J.P.H.

footman (KJV), an infantry soldier. The RSV has variously men "on foot" (Num. 11:21), "foot soldiers" (1 Sam. 4:10), "footmen" (2 Kings 13: 7), or "guard" (1 Sam. 22:17).

footstool, a royal symbol (see 2 Chron. 9:18), most often used figuratively for the Ark (1 Chron. 28:2), the Temple (see Isa. 60:13), or even Zion (Lam. 2:1). Elsewhere and in response to this view, the entire earth is described as God's footstool (Isa. 66:1; cf. Matt. 5:35; Acts 7:49). The term is also used to represent vanquished enemies in Ps. 110:1 (cf. Matt. 22:44; Acts 2:35; Heb. 10:13).

forehead, the portion of the face between eyebrows and hairline. The Bible depicts the forehead or brow as a significant spot due to its location and visibility. As represented in ancient Near Eastern art, the upper portion of the

Armed Lagashite warriors wearing tight-fitting helmets that nearly cover, but reveal the shape of, their foreheads; detail from Eannatum's stele, ca. 2450 B.C.

forehead was often covered by hair, a headband, or some type of head covering; but the lower portion was generally visible. Even soldiers' helmets sometimes left the lower brow somewhat vulnerable (which is also evident from the story of Goliath, 1 Sam. 17:49).

The following passages illustrate the visual prominence of the forehead. The phrase "Holy to the Lord" was to appear over the high priest's forehead (Exod. 28:36–38). God struck Uzziah with leprosy on his forehead (2 Chron. 26:19, 20; see also Lev. 13:41–43). A frontlet or phylactery was to be worn "between the eyes," a phrase referring to the forehead (Exod. 13:9, 16; Deut. 6:8). In visions of the future, allegiance to God was often represented by a mark or seal on the forehead (Ezek. 9:4; Rev. 7:3; 9:4; 14:1; 22:4); association with "the beast" was likewise depicted in such a manner (Rev. 13: 16; 14:9; cf. Rev. 20:4).

The term "forehead" was also used figuratively to represent persistent obstinancy (Isa. 48:4; Ezek. 3:7–9) and shamelessness (Jer. 3:3; this allusion probably derived from an actual mark; cf. Rev. 17:5). ***See also*** Phylacteries. D.M.P.

foreigner, one not native to a land. Any non-Israelite having temporary contact with Israel was considered a "foreigner" and if friendly was entitled to hospitable treatment. In contrast, a "sojourner" was resident alien who enjoyed some social and religious privileges. This distinction is frequently blurred in translation. For example, the KJV rarely uses the word "foreigner," but often translates the Hebrew terms for both "foreigner" and "sojourner" as "stranger." The RSV, while delineating more clearly, occasionally uses "stranger" to render both terms. Another Hebrew term with the general meaning of "stranger" adds to this confusion.

Israelites were frequently warned that extended contact with foreigners would lead to religious corruption (Exod. 23:31–33; Isa. 2:6–8); thus the directive against foreign wives (1 Kings 11:1–4; Neh. 13:26–27). Also, foreigners were not permitted to participate in ritual festivities (Exod. 12:43; Neh. 9:1–3), nor could their animals be used for Israelite sacrifices (Lev. 22:25). In economic dealings, interest was chargeable on loans to foreigners, but not on those to fellow Israelites (Deut. 23:19. 20), and a foreigner's debt was not remitted in a year of release (Deut. 15:2, 3). References to foreigners as enemies occur in passages such as Obadiah 11 and Lam. 5:2 (RSV: "aliens"; NEB and NIV: "foreigners").

NT writings continued the OT usage of "foreigner" (Luke 17:18; Acts 26:11). However, as nationality became less of a guide to religious affiliation, terms such as "foreigner" and "sojourner" developed a theological orientation as well. Eph. 2:19, for example, states that those accepting Jesus as Christ are "no longer strangers and sojourners, but . . . fellow citizens with the saints" (RSV; KJV: "strangers and foreigners"). ***See also*** Gentile; Stranger. D.M.P.

forerunner (translates the Gk. for "one who goes before"), in antiquity a military term for soldiers who ran ahead of the regular army either to announce (herald) or to prepare for (scout) its arrival (cf. Wisd. of Sol. 12:8). Heb.

6:20 refers to Jesus entering the Holy of Holies as forerunner, thereby preparing for the access of others to God's presence. John the Baptist serves as forerunner (although the term itself is not used) to Jesus by announcing and preparing for God's kingdom (Matt. 3:1–12; 11:10; Mark 1:2–8; Luke 3:1–18; 7:27; John 1:6–8, 19–34; cf. Isa. 40:3–11; Mal. 3:1). ***See also*** John the Baptist.

forest, a general term for the once extensive wooded areas of the Levant. In ancient times forests were a source of timber for both local use and foreign export. Wood was important for a wide range of uses such as domestic and industrial fuels, the construction of buildings, and the manufacture of furniture and household items. The highlands of Lebanon boasted forests of majestic cedars, while oak and pistachio, the characteristic trees of the Mediterranean region, were especially common in the northern hill country. Stands of Aleppo pine, mixed with components of the oak forest, existed in Galilee, Samaria, and Judea. Scrub forests in the foothills, composed of mixed evergreens, once provided shelter for wild animals such as boar and lions (Ps. 80:13; Amos 3:4).

Biblical references to specific stands of trees such as the forest of Hereth (1 Sam. 22:5), the forests of the south (Negeb; Ezek. 20:46–47), the forests of Arabia (Isa. 21:13), the king's forest (Neh. 2:8) and the forest (wood) of Ephraim (2 Sam. 18:6), indicate the importance of these natural resource areas.

In modern times little evidence remains of the past luxuriant tree growth. Centuries of overgrazing by sheep and goats, decimation for timber and fuel, the clearing of land for agriculture (Josh. 17:17–18), and the modern felling of timber for railroad ties have depleted the once prevalent forests. Recent replanting schemes have been unable to replenish the original tree cover but have nevertheless once again brought areas of green to the hills and plains of the Holy Land. ***See also*** Woods. P.L.C.

forgiveness, a term denoted in the OT by words that mean "send away," "cover," "remove," and "wipe away." In the NT "send away" is used most often; forgiveness is also communicated by words which mean "loose" (Luke 6:37), "be gracious to" (Luke 7:43; 2 Cor. 2:7), and "pass over" (Rom. 3:25). The Bible records human sinfulness, God's eagerness to forgive, and frequent calls by the prophets, Jesus, and Jesus' followers for repentance from sin and return to God.

The OT system of worship provides sacrifices for expiating the guilt of those who have sinned unwittingly or repented of their sins (Lev. 4–5), but sacrifice must always be accompanied by a proper disposition (1 Sam. 15:22; Hos. 6:6). The prophets testify repeatedly that God desires to forgive human sins and asks for repentance (Isa. 1:18–19; Hos. 12:2–3; Joel 2:13) as a prerequisite for a renewed relationship between God and Israel.

The NT continues the tradition of God's mercy shown in forgiveness of sins. God initiates contact with humans (Gal. 1:4; 2 Cor. 5:19; Rom. 9:23–26) and forgives sins through the death of Jesus (Rom. 3:21–26; 4:25; Mark 10:45; Gal. 1:4; Acts 13:38). God's forgiveness is variously described as justification, salvation, and reconciliation. It is associated with the celebration of the Lord's Supper (Matt. 26:28) and in some passages Jesus himself forgives sins (Mark 2:5–6; Acts 5:31). Members of the Christian community also have a role in the forgiveness of each other's sins (John 20:23; James 5:13–16). Community relations depend on members forgiving one another (Matt. 18:21–35; Luke 17:3). The Lord's Prayer makes divine forgiveness dependent on forgiveness of others (Matt. 6:12, 14–15; Luke 11:4) and another Gospel saying instructs early Christians to be reconciled before offering sacrifice to God (Matt. 5:23–24; Mark 11:25). ***See also*** Justification; Mercy; Repentance; Salvation; Sin. A.J.S.

forks. ***See*** Fleshhooks.

form criticism. ***See*** Biblical Criticism; Oral Materials, Sources, and Traditions.

fornication, any type of illicit sexual activity. Included in the realm of sexual misconduct in the OT are seduction, rape, sodomy, bestiality, certain forms of incest, prostitution (male or female), and homosexual relations (cf. Lev. 18; 19:20–22, 29; 20:10–21). The specific sin of adultery, related to marriage, was considered more serious than the others, however, so that a special set of laws governed it.

In the NT, almost any form of sexual misconduct (that is, sexual activity outside the marriage relationship) could be designated as fornication or "immorality" (cf. 1 Cor. 6:9; 2 Cor. 12:21; Eph. 5:5; Col. 3:5; 1 Thess. 4:3; 1 Tim. 1:10; Heb. 13:4; Jude 7). ***See also*** Adultery; Family, The; Harlot; Homosexuality; Marriage; Sodomy. J.M.E.

fortification. ***See*** Defense; Fenced Cities; Forts; Walls.

forts, fortified locations, often towns. A series of forts usually implies a regional if not a state authority. A fortress system did not appear in Israel until the monarchy (eleventh-tenth centuries B.C.), although individual forts were known in the period of the judges. According to the OT, David garrisoned troops in outlying areas to ensure his political control (2 Sam. 8:6). Solomon had cities for his chariots (1 Kings 9:19), and archaeological investigations have dated several forts in the Sinai to the period of David and

Battered brick tower of ancient fortification system excavated at Tell el-Hesi, biblical Eglon(?), in the district of Lachish.

Solomon. The presence of trade routes in the Sinai required some kind of military watch and control, and whenever the fortunes of Judah increased, parts of both the Sinai and the Negev were under Judean control.

The fortress of Arad is a good example of a Judean site used for regional control and administration. Originally constructed under David or Solomon's rule, its successive strata give a good indication of the type of fortifications used throughout the history of the monarchy in Judah. A number of fortified cities guarded important passes into the heartland of either Israel or Judah. In addition to Arad, which guarded the southern approach to Jerusalem, Judah was defended by several other fortresses (2 Chron. 11:5–11), including the imposing site of Lachish, which guarded an approach into the Judean hill country from the southwest. Israel possessed several highly fortified sites, including Megiddo and Hazor. Megiddo guarded the western entrance into the Jezreel Valley and Hazor guarded the approach from southern Syria into Israelite territory.

In the Transjordanian kingdoms of Ammon, Moab, and Edom, archaeologists have discovered various fort systems ranging from watchtowers and what could be termed police outposts to regional garrisons and even double-walled fortresses. Because of the trade routes running north-south through these kingdoms and the agrarian, pastoral nature of their economies, these different types of forts were necessary for what little security they could ensure. J.A.D.

Fortunatus (for-chuh-nah'tuhs), one who with Achaicus and Stephanas brought information to Paul in Ephesus about troubles in the church at Corinth (1 Cor. 16:17). Perhaps they came as emissaries, bearing a letter from some in the Corinthian church (1 Cor. 7:1). ***See also*** Achaicus; Stephanas.

forum. ***See*** Architecture.

foundations, constructions providing a stable base for any superstructure. Translating a variety of biblical terms, the word is used both literally and figuratively. Thus it occurs referring to natural formations (Deut. 32:32) or humanly prepared anchorages for buildings (Solomon's Temple, 1 Kings 5:17; its rebuilding, Ezra 3:10; a house, Luke 6:48; a prison, Acts 16:26; and city walls, Rev. 21:19 [where it refers to the new Jerusalem but reflects real construction procedures]). Such foundations could be elaborate and costly (1 Kings 7:10–11) or dust (Job 4:19), each yielding its appropriate durability (Luke 6:48–49).

Among the figurative uses, the word refers to universal stability (2 Sam. 22:16; Pss. 18:15; 82:5), the righteousness and justice of God (Ps. 89:14), God's redemption (Isa. 28:16), the beginning of things (Matt. 13:35; John 17:44), prior Christian work (Rom. 15:20), Jesus Christ (1 Cor. 3:11), the apostles, prophets, and Jesus (Eph. 1:4), God's work (2 Tim. 2:19), and a permanent basis of life because it is crafted by God (Heb. 11:10).

Archaeological evidence shows that bedrock was preferred for major construction, but if such were not available the next best was a solid stone platform constructed of layers of blocks of stone closely fitted. As references to the cornerstone indicate, it was important to all wall foundations, and frequently served as a repository for inscriptions or other commemorative goods. To improve a cornerstone's stability, it would frequently be worked even in a wall of unworked stone. For storage buildings foundations were made rodent tight by use of plaster in the chinks. For more modest housing, stone foundations one course high and one or two courses thick were minimal. Leveling in the foundation trenches was frequent, using gravel or small rock. ***See also*** Cornerstone. R.S.B.

founder, the KJV's archaic word for a "smelter" or "refiner," i.e., a metal-smith (Judg. 17:4; Jer. 6:29; 10:9, 14; 51:17).

fountain, a spring or source of flowing water. The RSV uses "spring" and "fountain" in an indiscriminate way to translate a number of Hebrew and Greek terms. It is clear, however, that the ancients distinguished between a natural outflow of water, an artificial water-storage system (i.e., cisterns and reservoirs), and a man-made well. Palestine's geological structure is conducive to the formation of springs (Deut. 8:7). Campsites and permanent settlements were often located in close proximity to springs; this situation is reflected in place names beginning with the syllable en, a prefix derived from a Hebrew word translated as "fountain" (e.g., En-gedi).

Springs represent divinely bestowed security and bounty (Ps. 104:10–13; Isa. 41:17–18; Ezek. 34:13), especially when water symbolizes eschatological blessings (e.g., Ezek. 47:1–12; Joel 3:18; Zech. 14:8; Rev. 21:6; 22:1–2). The Lord is described as "the fountain of living waters" (Jer. 2:13), a symbol that Jesus later applied to himself (John 4:10–15).

While copious springs symbolize God's favor, reference is still made to water that quenches thirst, physically or spiritually. The fountain also symbolizes the source of something besides water, e.g., descendants (Deut. 33:28), wisdom (Prov. 18:4), and forgiveness (Zech. 13:1). God was praised as "the fountain of life" (Ps. 36:9). ***See also*** Cisterns; Water. G.L.M.

Fountain Gate (RSV; KJV: "Gate of the Fountain"), a city gate in the southeast sector of Jerusalem opening either to Gihon or to En-rogel spring (Neh. 2:14; 3:15; 12:47). It was repaired by Nehemiah. It may be identical to the "gate between the two walls"(2 Kings 25:4).

A seal found in a grave at Tell en Nasbeh depicts a fighting cock; sixth century B.C.

fowl, in its wider sense a collective term for edible birds. Fowls are represented by the Hebrew word meaning "flyers" (*'oph*; see Lev. 7:26; Neh. 5:18). Fowl in the narrower sense of domesticated poultry is mentioned in the NT, either referring to the hen gathering her young (Matt. 23:37) or the crowing of the cock (Matt. 26:34). When the chicken first appeared in Palestine is unknown, but a Hebrew seal from Tell en Nasbeh from the sixth century B.C. depicts a fighting cock.

fowler, a person who hunts birds. Hunting birds may be done by bait, lure, or snare for food or sport. Biblical usage sees it as a metaphor for danger (Prov. 6:5; Pss. 91:3; 124:7), even from fellow humans (Jer. 5:26).

fox, a carnivorous doglike mammal. Three species of fox live in Palestine: the European fox (*Vulpes vulpes*) dwells in temperate zones, and the desert fox (*Vulpes rüppeli*) and the fenek (*Fennecus zerda*) are desert-adapted species; any one or all three may have been there in biblical times as well. In the NT the fox is mentioned in connection with its habit of burrowing holes (Matt. 8:20; Luke 9:58). It is also used in the Bible as a symbol for slyness; in Luke 13:32 Jesus calls Herod Antipas, the ruler of Galilee, a fox. Similarly, in Ezek. 13:4, false prophets are termed foxes.

frankincense, a fragrant gum resin exuded in large, light yellowish-brown tears from Boswellia trees *(Boswellia Carterii, Boswellia Papyrifera, Boswellia Thurifera)* which grow in South Arabia, Ethiopia, Somaliland, and India. Frankincense was imported into Judah by camel caravan from Sheba (Isa. 60:6; Jer. 6:20), a trade connection that originated with the queen of Sheba's visit to Jerusalem in the reign of Solomon (1 Kings 10:10; 2 Chron. 9:9).

Frankincense could be used for secular purposes as a perfume (Song of Sol. 3:6; 4:6, 14), but it appears most frequently in the Bible in a religious context. Exod. 30:34–38 contains the recipe for a frankincense-based incense dedicated for ritual use. No other incense was permitted on the altar (Exod. 30:9) and secular use of the sacred recipe was absolutely forbidden (Exod. 30:38).

Boswellia Thurifera, a source of frankincense.

Offerings of frankincense were made at the Temple (Isa. 43:23; 66:3; Jer. 17:26; 41:5) where it was stored for later use (Neh. 13:5, 9; 1 Chron. 9:29). Frankincense was set beside the Bread of the Presence (Lev. 24:7) and accompanied cereal offerings (Lev. 2:1–2, 14–16; 6: 14–18). It was prohibited with a sin offering (Lev. 5:11) or a cereal offering of jealousy (Num. 5:15). Frankincense was among the gifts offered to the infant Jesus by the Wise Men (Matt. 2:11). Rev. 18:13 lists frankincense as part of the cargo of the merchants who weep for the fallen city. ***See also*** Sheba, Queen of; Worship. M.A.S.

freedman (KJV: "libertine"), a person in the Greco-Roman world who had been a slave but had secured release from that status by purchasing freedom or working to achieve it. When Jewish slaves in the world of that time, especially from the city of Rome, won their freedom, many of them went to Jerusalem. Consequently, a synagogue was established there for them. Acts 6:9 reports that "some of those who belonged to the synagogue of the Freedmen" argued with Stephen. ***See also*** Freeman, Freewoman; Liberty; Slavery; Stephen.

freeman, freewoman, a person who had been born free. One of the most fundamental distinctions of status (and hence of rights and duties) in the Roman world was that of slave or free. Those who were free persons might either be free by birth (Lat. *ingenui*), that is, freemen or freewomen, or free because they had received a grant of freedom from slavery, that is, freedmen or freedwomen (Lat. *liberati*). The latter remained bound to their former masters (see 1 Cor. 7:22). If they died without an heir, their property was given to the master. They were not eligible for the higher ranks in the army or free to embark upon an official career of public office holding, though there were influential freedmen at the imperial court. However, children born after a slave had been freed were considered to be free born. Paul enunciated a major tenet of the early Christian faith when he declared that in Christ all such differences among people had been nullified (Gal. 3:28). P.P.

fret, an act of causing unease, used in the Bible as a reflexive imperative verb: "fret not yourself" (Ps. 37:1, 7, 8; Prov. 24:19).

friendship, a relationship of mutual trust and congeniality. While many biblical writers realized that friendship enriches human life, as a subject of serious reflection the theme of friendship is not developed in the Bible—in sharp contrast to the Greek and Roman traditions. Thus, although Deuteronomy characterizes a friend as a person "who is as your own soul" (13:6), the mutual affection and devotion of David and Jonathan strike the readers of the OT as extraordinary (see 1 Sam. 18:1; 19:1; 20:17; 2 Sam. 1:26). Where the covenant concept prevails, natural attraction and personal preference appear to be less important than covenant obligations as the bases of relationships between persons.

The benefits and requirements of friendship are among the subjects addressed by Israel's wise men, especially in Proverbs and Ecclesiasticus. The sage stresses loyalty and steadfastness as marks of the true friend (Prov. 17:17; 18:24; Ecclus. 6:14–16) but warns that poverty or adversity often reveals people to be friends in name only (Prov. 19:4, 6–7; Ecclus. 12:9; 13:21;

37:4–5). An irony of the book of Job is that Job's three friends, in their frenetic attempts to effect his repentance, intensify rather than relieve his suffering. Because they are more loyal to their theological certainties than to Job, they are unable to attain the genuine sympathy that marks real friendship.

The special bond between God and a person chosen as his instrument is occasionally described as friendship. God spoke to Moses face to face, "as a man speaks to his friend" (Exod. 33:11), and Abraham is called God's friend (2 Chron. 20:7; Isa. 41:8; see also James 2:23).

In the NT, Jesus' effort to mirror God's love and mercy even to religious outcasts earns him the epithet "a friend of tax collectors and sinners" (Matt. 9:11; Luke 7:34). In the Gospel of John, two persons, Lazarus and the unnamed "beloved disciple," are the objects of Jesus' special affection (11:3, 36; 13:23; 19:26; 20:2; 21:7, 20). Jesus says that his disciples are his friends if they do what he commands; he calls them friends because he has revealed to them what he heard from his Father (15:14–15). To be Jesus' friend is to love one another (cf. 15:12–14). In a saying highly reminiscent of the Greek tradition, Jesus declares that the supreme manifestation of love is a person's willingness to give his life for his friends (15:13).
S.K.W.

fringes (tassels, borders, hems), a common decoration on Near Eastern garments. The oldest rule about fringes in the OT says simply, "You shall make yourself tassels on the four corners of your cloak with which you cover yourself" (Deut. 22:12). The more elaborate command in Num. 15:38–40 says that the tassels shall be of blue cord and function as a reminder to obey the commandments. In the Gospels the woman with the hemorrhage touches the fringe of Jesus' garment (Matt. 9:20; Luke 8:44) and other sick wish to do likewise (Mark 6:56; Matt. 14:36). Jesus criticizes Pharisees for hypocrisy in wearing ostentatious fringes (Matt. 23:5). The Talmud commands the wearing of fringes as part of its devotion to God through Torah (observing God's teachings, and thus obeying his will). The Talmud allows white threads to be used, specifies that each tassel have eight threads, and describes the knots that must be tied. Over the centuries tassels were transferred to the prayer shawl and to a linen vest worn under the outer garments.
A.J.S.

frog, a tailless amphibian especially of the family Ranidae, common in Egypt and Palestine. As a second plague on the Egyptians, God threatened to send hoards of frogs out of the water and into their homes, even into Pharaoh's bedroom (Exod. 8:1–15; alluded to in Pss. 78:45; 105:30). When the frogs came, Pharaoh appealed to Moses and Aaron and promised to let the Israelites go if the frogs were removed. However, after the frogs died, Pharaoh refused to let the Israelites leave. ***See also*** Plagues.

frontlet, a headband, the most common form of headdress worn in Syria and Palestine in OT times. The Torah enjoins that certain of God's teachings (Deut. 6:8; 11:18) and rites commemorating the Exodus (Exod. 13:16, cf. v. 9) are to "be as frontlets between [the Israelites'] eyes" (i.e., on their foreheads, cf. Deut. 14:1). ***See also*** Phylacteries.

fruit. ***See*** Food; also such individual entries as Fig; Pomegranate.

fuels, materials used to start and maintain fires. Wood and charcoal were the most common fuels in antiquity, the latter becoming more important with the advent of metallurgy and other crafts because of its higher burning temperature. Other fuels were thorny shrubs (Nah. 1:10), withered sticks and twigs, straw or stubble from the fields (Exod. 15:7), fat remains, date kernels, dung of cattle, bones of fishes, birds, and animals (Ezek. 24:5–10), logs (Gen. 22:3; Lev. 1:7) and chips from the carpenter's shop (Wisd. of Sol. 13:12). Figuratively, "the fuel for the fire" in Ezek. 21:32 is Israel. The NT knows braziers with charcoal or charcoal fires on the ground (John 18:18; 21:9).
R.A.C.

fuller, a person whose occupation it is to clean, whiten, bleach, thicken, shrink, or dye cloth. The fuller cared for newly shorn wool or woven garments. The process varied but generally included washing with lye (Mal. 3:2) and cleansing by pressure, usually the treading of feet, as the Hebrew word implies (Exod. 19:10; 2 Sam. 19:24). The cloth was then spread out on the ground to be bleached by the sun. There were areas outside the city, the fuller's field (2 Kings 18:17; Isa. 7:3), designated for these professional laundering and cleaning services. A fuller apparently was also one who traded in textiles (2 Kings 18:17; Isa. 7:3; 36:2). Biblical writers found the fuller's profession to be an apt metaphor for purity (Ps. 51:7; Jer. 2:22; 4:14; Zech. 3:3; Rev. 4:4). Christ's transfiguration garments were whiter than any fuller could bleach them (Mark 9:3).
S.L.R.

funeral. ***See*** Burial.

furlong, one-tenth of a mile. Used only once in the RSV (Matt. 14:24) in a phrase of uncertain textual origin, it is a measurement no longer in common use except in horseracing. ***See also*** Weights and Measures.

furnace, an installation for containing fire, whether for domestic or industrial purposes. The word is used in the Bible for various installations employed in daily life, and metaphorically for God's presence (Gen. 15:17), for the judgment or redemption of his people (Deut. 4:20; 1 Kings 8:51; Isa. 48:10; Jer. 11:4; Ps. 102:3; Isa. 33:14), for the refining of God's word as silver is worked in a crucible (Ps. 12:6), and in the NT for the fires of hell (Matt. 13:42, 50; Rev. 9:2) and the appearance of Christ's feet (Rev. 1:15).

Six words in Hebrew and one in Greek lie behind the word "furnace." The most common OT term (Heb. *tannûr)* is an oven, often of the kind used for baking bread (Ps. 21:9; Dan. 3:6). Other terms refer to a pottery or lime kiln (Gen. 19:28; Exod. 9:8; 18:18) or a smelter or refining installation for metals (Prov. 17:3; 27:21; Ezek. 22:20).

Archaeological and metallurgical researchers in Palestine have uncovered numerous furnaces of antiquity from the Chalcolithic period (fourth millennium B.C.) at Teleilat et-Ghassul in the southeast Jordan rift, across the valley from Jericho, and at Abu Matar near Beer-sheba (ca. 3500 B.C.), to the late medieval period (A.D. 1450) at Mugharat Wardeh in the Gilead mountains (Ajlun district) of Jordan. Perhaps the best examples of early copper furnaces are from Timna in the southern Negeb.

Iron-smelting furnaces were used in Palestine in the twelfth and eleventh centuries B.C. The furnace site at modern Tell el-Kheleifeh excavated by Nelson Glueck and once thought to be "the Pittsburgh of ancient Palestine" is now known to have been used as early as the Chalcolithic period (4000–3000 B.C.) and as late as the Roman (63 B.C.–A.D. 324) but is not likely to be Solomonic in origin. A number of smithing furnaces dating from twelfth century to 870 B.C. were found at Gerar (modern Tell Jemmeh). ***See also*** Metals. R.A.C.

furnishings. ***See*** Furniture.

furniture, equipment for basic human actions such as sitting, lying, eating, worshiping, and the like. In the Bible, it usually describes the equipment (also called "furnishings") of the tabernacle (Exod. 25:9; 40:9; Num. 1:50; 3:8; 4:15; 7:1) or a person's dwelling (tent, Num. 19:18; or house, Neh. 13:8). "Furniture" applies to the equipment of the Temple (1 Chron. 9:29) as well. The KJV also uses it (RSV: "utensils") when speaking of the tabernacle table (Exod. 31:8), lampstand (Exod. 35:14), or altar of burnt offering (Exod. 31:9).

Archaeological and artistic evidence indicates that the most common furnishings in wealthy homes were tables, beds, chairs, and storage chests. Royal tomb fittings from Ur in Mesopotamia and from Egypt show that such items of wood were frequently inlaid, carved, gilded, and otherwise embellished with ivory, precious metal, and precious stones. That such opulence was imitated by Solomon may be reflected in the records concerning his palace (1 Kings 7:1–11; see also Amos 6:4a). The largely intact materials of the tomb of Tutankhamen of Egypt excavated by Howard Carter beginning in 1922 have given us spectacular samples of such furniture in remarkable states of preservation.

The ordinary family furniture in a typical Palestine home is less clearly evident. Such a room as Jesus directed the disciples to locate (Mark 14:15; Luke 22:12) may have had a table and some stools, but it also may have had only mats for seating, a lamp, and serving vessels for bread and wine. Other contexts suggest that furnishings in such a home included sleeping mats or rolls (Mark 2:9), grinding equipment (Matt. 24:41), a broom (Luke 15:8), a niche or stand for a lamp (Matt. 5:15), and water storage vessels (John 2:6). Special accommodations for a guest might include a bed, table, chair, and lamp (2 Kings 4:10). Because wood and cloth decay rapidly, they seldom survive in archaeological ruins. The most commonly recovered furnishings are cookpots, lamps, bowls, and grinding stones. R.S.B.

future life. ***See*** Eschatology; Eternal Life; Hades; Heaven; Hell.

Clay model of a bed; found at Gezer, from ca. 3000 B.C.

Opposite: The traditional symbols of the four Gospels: (clockwise) the winged human (or angel), Matthew; the winged lion, Mark; the eagle, John; the winged ox, Luke; from the eighth-century *Book of Kells.*

G

A gaming board scratched into the flagstone pavement of the courtyard of Herod's Antonia fortress, excavated in Jerusalem.

Gabbatha (gab'ah-thah), a term that appears but once in the NT in John 19:13 as the Hebrew (actually Aramaic) equivalent of the Greek term *lithostrōton*, "the pavement" (which does appear in the other Gospels) where the hearing of Jesus before Pontius Pilate was held. The first-century Jewish historian Josephus (*Wars* 2.14.8) refers to a paved yard adjacent to Herod's palace where court was held, but no paved court has yet been discovered there, even though some still hold this area, today part of the citadel adjacent to Jaffa Gate, to be the most likely site of Jesus' trial.

The other probable location of the *lithostrōton* is what would have constituted the courtyard of the fortress Antonia, a garrison Herod constructed on the northwest corner of the Temple Mount, a site that is today visible in the basement of the Convent of the Sisters of Zion on the Via Dolorosa. Some 2,500 square yards of pavement made of large flagstones, averaging 4 feet by 3.5 feet by 2 feet thick, and having incised treads to prevent animals from slipping, have been excavated here, together with a Roman gaming board that illustrates the narrative about Roman soldiers on capital punishment details in the Gospels (e.g., Matt. 27:35), and large Herodian cisterns. ***See also*** Antonia, Tower of. F.S.F.

Gabriel, one of the archangels in Jewish and early Christian thought. In the OT, Gabriel appears only in Dan. 8:15–26 and 9:21–27, and, in the NT, only in Luke 1:11–20, 26–38. In these passages, Gabriel appears as a messenger ("angel") from God and an interpreter for the people to whom he is sent. In the apocryphal and pseudepigraphical writings, angels were organized into categories with specific duties and status before God. In Tob. 12:15, for example, "Raphael" is mentioned as "one of the seven holy angels who present the prayers of the saints and enter into the presence of the glory of the Holy One" (cf. also Rev. 8:2). In *1 Enoch* 40, Gabriel is considered one of the top four in rank, perhaps second only to Michael. Gabriel's duties included intercession on behalf of God's people (*1 Enoch* 9:1; 40:6) as well as being the instrument for destruction of the wicked (*1 Enoch* 9:9–10). Tradition associated Gabriel with the archangel whose trumpet blast would announce the return of Christ (cf. 1 Thess. 4:16; Matt. 24:31). ***See also*** Angel; Michael. J.M.E.

Gad (Heb., "luck"). **1** Canaanite god of fortune (Isa. 65:11). **2** Son of Jacob and Zilpah (Gen. 30:9–11); eponymous ancestor of the Israelite tribe of that name. Gad occupied territory between the Jabbok and Arnon rivers, which it shared with the tribe of Reuben. The Jabbok served as the boundary between Gad and the half-tribe of Manasseh. Mesha, king of Moab, ca. 830 B.C., conquered Ataroth, which "the men of Gad inhabited from of old." Sometime afterward the territory of Gad was overrun by Hazael of Damascus (2 Kings 10:32–33). The region may have been restored to Israel by Jeroboam II (2 Kings 14:25), but it was lost again to the Assyrian conqueror Tiglath-pileser, who deported its population (1 Chron. 5:26). **3** A prophet-seer of David (2 Sam. 24:11).

In Poetry: In the Blessing of Jacob (Gen. 49:19), by means of an alliterative play on the name "Gad," the poet alludes to military tactics of the tribe. In the Blessing of Moses (Deut. 33:20–21) Gad is described as a lioness who tears both arm and head and is praised for having performed the righteous ordinances of Yahweh. In the Song of Deborah (Judg. 5:17) Gad, under the designation Gilead (cf. Judg. 12:7), is listed among those tribes that failed to participate in the war against Sisera and is chided for having remained across the Jordan. ***See also*** Mesha; Tribes, The.

S.G.

Gadara (gad'uh-rah; inhabitants: Gadarenes [gad'uh-reenz]), site (modern Umm Qeis) of Jesus' healing a demoniac (Mark 5:1–10); one of the hellenized cities of the Decapolis in which Jesus is reported to have ministered (Matt. 4:23–25; Mark 7:31). It lies about six miles southeast of the Sea of Galilee. A number of Cynic philosophers, orators, and poets are associated with the city. One of the love poems of Meleager of Gadara (first century B.C.) mentions the Jewish Sabbath: "If your love is a 'sabbath-keeper,' no great wonder. Not even love burns on cold Sabbaths." The city was granted to Herod by Augustus. In an inscription from the Hellenistic period it calls itself "cultivator of the arts." There seems to have been only a small Jewish population in the city. P.P.

Gaius (gay'yuhs), a common masculine name (a Latin praenomen) in NT times, apparently used to refer to several people in the NT. **1** A person in Corinth baptized by Paul (1 Cor. 1:14); he likely was partial to Paul's position in the church disputes in Corinth. He may be the same Gaius identified as "host to me and to the whole church" in Rom. 16:23. **2** A traveling companion, with Aristarchus, of Paul mentioned in Acts (19:29). Coming from Macedonia, they were caught up in a riot provoked by Paul's missionary work in Ephesus. This may be the same Gaius mentioned as a traveling companion of Paul in Acts 20:4, although this Gaius is identified as being from Derbe (in Asia Minor). **3** A recipient of 3 John (v. 1). His leadership is favored over that of a certain Diotrephes (vv. 9–10). ***See also*** Aristarchus; Diotrephes; Paul. A.J.M.

Galatia (gah-lay'shee-ah). **1** Territory located in north central Asia Minor dominated by the Gauls, a Celtic tribe famed for warcraft and cunning, from the third to the first century B.C. **2** Roman province after the first century B.C. that included the traditional Galatian territory plus portions of other ethnic territories, especially to the south.

Because Galatia can refer both to the territory and to the province, it is difficult to know in which sense the word is used in the NT. 1 Pet. 1:1 and 2 Tim. 4:10 (if one prefers the reading "Galatia" to the variant "Gaul") surely refer to the province, but there remains doubt concerning the other four references (Acts 16:6; 18:23; 1 Cor. 16:1; and Gal. 1:2), all of which relate to Paul's ministry. Some think they refer to the province (the "south Galatian hypothesis"), arguing that Acts records no mission to north central Asia Minor but does record Paul's visits to Antioch, Iconium, Lystra, and Derbe, cities outside the Galatian territory but inside the province. Those who think the texts in question refer to the territory (the "north Galatian hypothesis") argue that Acts 16:6 should be read "Phrygia and the Galatian region" (cf. 18:23), thereby referring to territories, since there was no Phrygian province. The issue may be insoluble. Paul's letter to the Galatians is silent about their ethnic composition and location, and scholars reasonably doubt the reliability of Acts for reconstructing Paul's itinerary. ***See also*** Galatians, The Letter of Paul to the. D.R.M.

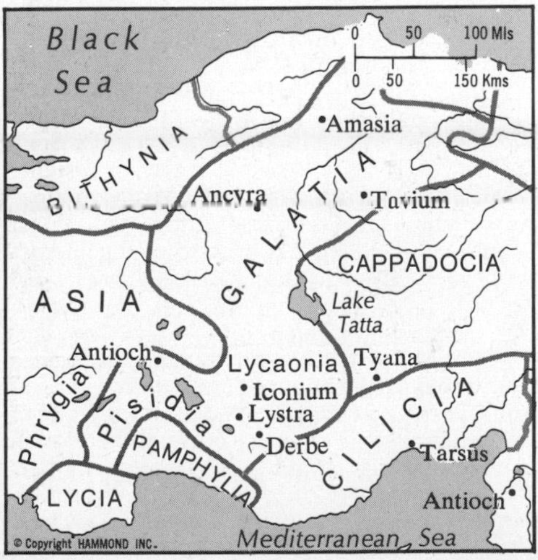

Galatians, the Letter of Paul to the, the ninth book in the NT and one of the most important historical and theological documents from early Christianity. Chaps. 1 and 2 especially are the only extant primary source of information concerning the earliest period of primitive Christian history. Theologically, the Letter is the first complete statement of Gentile Christian theology and thus its oldest self-definition, in which the new Christian religion is separated (as far as we can tell, for the first time) from Judaism.

Written by Paul (1:1; 6:11–18), the Letter is addressed to a group of congregations, "the churches of Galatia" (1:2). Scholars are still debating whether these churches were located in central Anatolia (the so-called North Galatian hypothesis) or, as seems less likely, further to the south (the so-called South Galatian hypothesis, by which the churches may be connected with the cities of Antioch, Lystra, Derbe, and Iconium mentioned in Acts 13–14).

Paul himself names the cause for writing his Letter (1:6–7): the newly founded churches are about to shift their allegiance away from their apostle and founder to his opponents, who are competing Jewish Christian missionaries. Paul's Letter is designed to prevent such a shift. Its thoroughgoing argument amounts to a defense of the gospel as he preached it and as Gentile Christianity had accepted it. In order to understand the Letter, today's readers must comprehend the rather complicated theological arguments made and presupposed in the text. Paul's *explicit* argument attempts to reassure the Galatian readers that the gospel they received from Paul is fully sufficient for their salvation. After hearing this gospel (3:2–5), they received the Holy Spirit (3:2–3, 14; 4:6) and became partakers "in Christ" (3:26–28). Equipped with the benefits of justification by faith in Christ (1:4; 2: 15–16), Paul assures them that they can look forward with confidence to their eternal inheritance, the Kingdom of God (3:29; 5:5; 6:8, 16–18). Embedded in the Letter we also discover an *implicit* argument being used by the Jewish-Christian missionaries against Paul, according to which the Galatians have come to doubt Paul's message when they were faced with "transgressions" in their midst (6:1). Apparently, Paul's opponents have helped them understand these transgressions as evidence that they were still "sinners" outside salvation (2:15–17, 21), and these opponents have almost persuaded them to accept circumcision (2:3; 5:2–3, 6; 6: 12–13, 15) and the Jewish Torah (3:2, 5; 4:9–10, 21; 5:2–4, 18).

The Opposition to Paul: The problem of who Paul's opponents were has been the subject of much discussion for almost two centuries. Were there two oppositional fronts (W. Lütgert) or just one? Were they Christian or non-Christian Jews, or were they Gentiles attracted to Judaism ("Judaizers")? Were they resident Galatians or outside intruders? J. R. Crownfield held them to be Jewish-Christian syncretists (those who took elements from one religion into another) interested in circumcision as a symbolic ritual. J. Munck took them to be Gentiles who had recently become converts of a Judaizing Christian movement in Galatia, a "heretic" offshoot of Paulinism. W. Schmithals advanced the hypothesis that they were (Christian or non-Christian) Jewish Gnostics who practiced circumcision as a magically potent ritual but were otherwise "libertines." Schmithals's hypothesis was later modified by G. Bornkamm, K. Wegenast, H. Koester, and D. Georgi, all of them assuming that the opponents were Jewish-Christian missionaries representing some kind of Asia Minor syncretism.

A further problem is the connection between Paul's opponents and the "men from James" and Jerusalem (2:11). Were they agitators moved by political nationalism in Jerusalem (D. B. Bronson)? Did they try to ease the pressures the church in Jerusalem suffered from the hands of the Zealots by organizing a campaign to "judaize" Gentile Christians in Asia Minor (R. Jewett)? H. D. Betz proposed that 2 Cor. 6: 14–7:1, a section that had long been identified as *non*-Pauline, be regarded as a piece of *anti*-Pauline theology compatible or even identical with that of Paul's opponents in Galatia. G. Lüdemann has shown that these opponents must be seen in connection with the history of anti-Paulinism in Asia Minor in the first two centuries of the Christian era.

Composition: Galatians is an apologetic Letter, the epistolary "frame" consisting of the prescript (1:1–5) and the postscript (6:11–18). The prescript follows the basic Pauline pattern with the superscription (Lat. *superscriptio*, i.e., opening words; 1:1–2a: the name of the principal sender, his official title and the definition of the title, and stating the [unnamed] co-senders), the ascription (Lat. *adscriptio*, i.e., those to whom the letter was addressed; 1:2b), and the greetings, or salutation (Lat. *salutatio;* 1:3–4), expanded by christological and soteriological formulae indicating the major concerns of the Letter and ending in a doxology with the concluding "amen" (1:5). The postscript, written in Paul's own hand (6:11), presupposes that the preceding parts of the letter (1:1–6:10) show the hand of an amanuensis or scribe (cf. Rom. 16: 22). The postscript authenticates the Letter and sums up its major points, thus serving as the *recapitulatio* (summary) and *peroratio* (conclusion).

The body of the Letter (1:6–6:10) is composed as an apologetic speech with its traditional rhetorical parts. The introductory statement (Lat. *exordium;* 1:6–9) names the

OUTLINE OF CONTENTS

The Letter of Paul to the Galatians

I. The epistolary prescript (1:1–5)
II. The introduction *(exordium)* (1:6–11)
III. The statement of facts *(narratio)* (1:12–2:14)
  A. Thesis (1:12)
  B. First part: from Paul's birth to the mission in Asia Minor (1:13–24)
  C. Second part: Paul's second visit to Jerusalem (the Jerusalem conference) (2:1–10)
  D. Third part: the conflict at Antioch (2: 11–14)
IV. The proposition *(propositio)* (2:15–21)
V. The proofs *(probatio)* (3:1–4:31)
  A. First argument: the Galatians' experience of the Spirit (3:1–5)
  B. Second argument: God's promise to Abraham (3:6–14)
  C. Third argument: common human practice of law (3:15–18)
  D. Digression: the Jewish Torah (3:19–25)
  E. Fourth argument: Christian tradition (3:26–4:11)
  F. Fifth argument: friendship (4:12–20)
  G. Sixth argument: an allegory of Sarah and Hagar (4:21–31)
VI. The exhortation *(exhortatio)* (5:1–6:10)
  A. Warning against acceptance of the Jewish Torah (5:1–12)
  B. Warning against corruption of the "flesh" (5:13–24)
  C. Recommendations for the Christian life (5:25–6:10)
VII. The epistolary postscript (6:11–18)

problem (Lat. *causa;* 1:6–7) and presents Paul's immediate response, the reissuing of a previously issued curse against apostates (1:8–9). The defense arguments are presented in four major sections: first, the narrative (Lat. *narratio;* 1:12–2:14) recites the events preceding and leading up to the present situation. These events are of course told with a partisan slant so as to assist the defense; they end with the dilemma the Galatians are now facing (2:14). Second, the statement of the problem (Lat. *propositio;* 2:15–21) sets forth the major points of agreement and disagreement between the author and his readers. Third, the demonstration, or proof (Lat. *probatio;* 3:1–4:31) includes an interrogation (3:1–5) and arguments from Scripture and tradition. The final section is exhortation, with three subsections, each of which begins with the restatement of the doctrinal presupposition (5:1a, 13a, 25a).

Reading the Letter Today: Modern readers will have to learn how to read Galatians as a piece of ancient epistolary literature. In those terms, the Letter represents the author, Paul, who is physically absent and must communicate despite the limits of a written text (cf. 4:18–20). His Letter carries his entire defense speech to the readers, who, reading it aloud, transpose it into oral speech. They then have to make up their minds whether Paul's line of argument is convincing. Whatever they decide will activate the conditional curse and blessing (1:8–9; 6:16) that is also carried to them by the Letter. The same situation must be faced by modern readers: the letter again confronts readers in every age by arguing the central points of Paul's theology and by presenting to them the fateful choice between salvation and condemnation. ***See also*** Circumcision; Faith; Flesh and Spirit; Galatia; Gentile; Gnosticism; Holy Spirit, The; Justification; Kingdom of God; Law; Paul; Syncretism.

Bibliography

Betz, H. D. *Galatians: A Commentary on Paul's Letter to the Churches in Galatia.* Hermeneia: A Critical and Historical Commentary on the Bible. Philadelphia: Fortress, 1979.

Bruce, F. F. *The Epistle to the Galatians: A Commentary on the Greek Text.* The New International Greek Commentary. Grand Rapids, MI: Eerdmans, 1982.

Ebeling, G. *The Truth of the Gospel.* Philadelphia: Fortress, 1984.

Lüdemann, G. *Paul, Apostle to the Gentiles: Studies in Chronology.* Philadelphia: Fortress, 1984.

H.D.B.

galbanum (gal'buh-nuhm), a gum resin derived from several plants (such as *Ferula galbaniflua).* It is an ingredient in incense (Exod. 30:34) for use in worship. Yellow or greenish brown, it had a prominent aroma and a bitter taste. In Ecclus. 24:15 it is one of a list of sweet spices that symbolize wisdom.

Galilean (gal-uh-lee'uhn), inhabitant of Galilee (Matt. 26:69; Acts 1:11; 2:7; Mark 14:70; Luke 13:1, 22:59; 23:6; John 4:45; 7:52). The term appears as an epithet for the insurrectionist Judas (Acts 5:37). The regional accent of Galilean speech apparently enabled others to identify their origin by it (Matt. 26:73).

Galilee (gal'i-lee; Heb. *galil),* the region of northern Palestine that is situated between the Litani River in modern Lebanon and the Jezreel Valley in modern Israel. The designation "Galilee" first occurs as a proper name in Joshua (20:7; 21:32) and in Chronicles (1 Chron. 6:76) in reference to the site of Qadesh of Naphtali. It occurs with the definite article in 1 Kings 9:11, "in the land of Galilee." From Isa. 9:1 we learn it was known as a land of foreigners. The proper name occurs regularly in the writings of the first century historian Josephus and the NT (Gk. *galilaia).*

This tiny region, approximately forty-five miles long north to south, is first mentioned by Pharaoh Thutmose III in 1468 B.C. when he captured twenty-three Canaanite cities there. From the time of the Israelite settlement (late thirteenth–early twelfth century B.C.) Galilee is associated with the tribes of Naphtali, Asher, Issachar, and Zebulun; the tribe of Dan eventually moved there. The reorganization into administrative districts under King David saw a consolidation of Israelite presence there. King Solomon, however, returned some twenty Galilean cities to Hiram, king of Tyre, in payment for building materials (1 Kings 9:10–11).

During the period of the Divided Monarchy (924–586 B.C.) Galilee was invaded by Pharaoh Shishak in 924 B.C. in the fifth year of Rehoboam. In ca. 885 during the reign of Israel's King Baasha, Ben-hadad of Damascus captured Ijon, Dan, Able-beth-maacah, and "all the land of Naphtali" (1 Kings 15:18–20). The confrontation of Ahab, king of Israel, with Shalmaneser III of Assyria at Qarqar in 853 B.C. ultimately led to the confrontation at Mt. Carmel in 841. Tiglath-pileser III, also of Assyria, however, took much of Galilee in 732 B.C. when he captured thirteen of its cities (2 Kings 15:29) and united it to Assyria as a province. From then on Galilee as a region became known as the Assyrian province of Megiddo. Galilee's history remains obscure until the Greek conquest by Alexander the Great in 332 B.C.

Jewish settlement in Galilee followed the Maccabean revolt in 164 B.C. Galilee was annexed by Judah Aristobolus I in 104 B.C. His brother and successor Alexander Jannaeus further extended the borders of Galilee during his reign. With the Roman conquest of Palestine in 63 B.C. Pompey recaptured many Galilean cities and incorporated them into a new Roman administration. Under Herod the Great (40–4 B.C.), Galilee, together with Judea and Perea, formed a large portion of the new Judea. Upon Herod's death in 4 B.C. Galilee and Perea were made part of the tetrarchy of Herod Antipas, his son.

Galilee constitutes the area in which Jesus conducted the major part of his ministry. His youth and early ministry took place in Nazareth in Lower Galilee; much of his public ministry was located at the northwestern end of the Sea of Galilee, at Capernaum, which was known as Jesus' own city (Matt. 9:1). Galilee is also the area in which Judaism assumed its definitive form, ultimately producing the Mishnah and Palestinian Talmud there.

The first-century historian Josephus (*Life* 45.235) maintains that there were 204 villages in all Galilee. Archaeology has shown that that figure is not improbable. In Lower Galilee the major centers in the first centuries A.D. were Tiberias and Sepphoris. In Upper Galilee, called Tetracomia ("Four Villages") by Josephus, Gush Halav (Gischala) and Meiron were certainly among the largest villages. Jewish population in both areas of Galilee, however, did not fully accelerate till after the two devastating wars with Rome in A.D. 66–73 and 132–135. It was in the aftermath of these debacles that Jews as well as Christians relocated themselves there.

E.M.M.

Galilee (gal'uh-lee), **Sea of,** a harp-shaped fresh-water lake in the district of Galilee in northern Palestine, given various names throughout history: "the Sea of Chinnereth" (or "Chinneroth"), from the Hebrew word for a harp-like instrument (Num. 34:11; Josh. 12:3; 13:27); "the Sea of Tiberias" (John 6:1; 21:1);

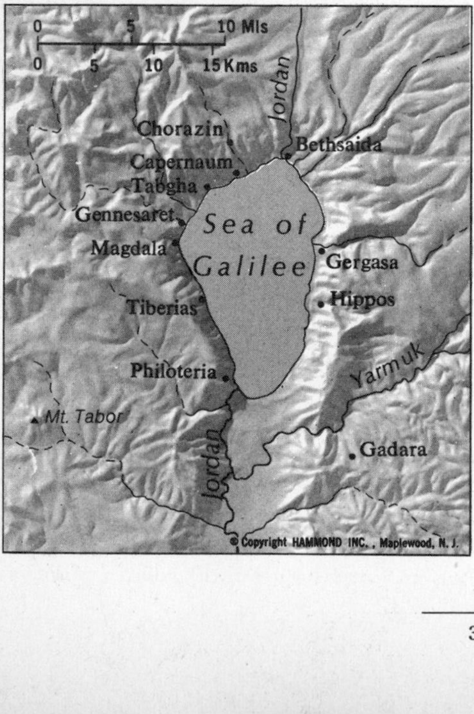

"the Lake of Gennesaret" (Luke 5:1); and "the waters of Gennesaret" (1 Macc. 11:67). Elsewhere, it is referred to simply as "the lake" (Luke 5:2; 8:22–33) or "the sea" (John 6:16–25). It appears as "the Sea of Galilee" in Matt. 4:18; 15:29 and Mark 1:16; 7:31.

Along with the Jordan River and the Dead Sea, this body of water is an integral part of the Syro-African rift, a geological fault that extends from Syria in the north to the northeastern part of Africa in the south. The lake is approximately 700 feet below sea level and has a maximum depth of 150 feet. The Jordan River, carrying the melted snows of Mt. Hermon, enters the lake from the north, flows through its thirteen-mile length, and continues its course after leaving the lake along the southwestern shoreline. The water surface of the lake varies according to the season and the amount of rainfall. At its widest part, the lake measures about eight miles, and its circumference is about thirty-two miles.

Due to the height of the hills (1,200 to 1,500 feet) surrounding the below-sea-level lake, abrupt temperature shifts occur, causing sudden and violent storms, as the NT accounts indicate (Matt. 8:23–27; Mark 4:35–41; Luke 8:22–25; Matt. 14:22–33; Mark 6:45–52; John 6:16–21). The northern end of the lake has little protection and remains subject to strong winds. Nevertheless, the natural features of climate, fertile soil, and abundance of water attracted inhabitants from prehistoric times to the present day to settle along the shores of the lake.

The main route of an international highway known as the *Via Maris* followed a portion of the western coast of the lake, helping the area to develop as one of the larger population centers in NT Palestine. Fishing, agriculture, and fruit growing added to the attraction of the area. Some forty different species of fish inhabit the waters, and salted fish were exported widely throughout the Roman Empire. Fishing remains an important occupation of the region today. Some of the towns and areas near the Sea of Galilee that are mentioned in the Gospels are Bethsaida, Capernaum, Chorazin, Gadara, Gennesaret, Magdala, and Tiberias. Numerous hot mineral springs near Tiberias, Gadara, and Tabgha, combined with the tropical climate around the lake, have made the area a natural health spa throughout the centuries. ***See also*** Bethsaida; Capernaum; Chorazin; Gadara; Galilee; Magdala; Tiberias; Winds.

M.K.M.

gall, liver bile (Job 16:13) or venom ("gall of asps," Job 20:14). It is used as a metaphor for bitter punishment for evil (Job 20:25). It is also an herb both bitter (Matt. 27:34) and poisonous (Ps. 69:21). It stood for bitterness (Acts 8:23) and in Lam. 3:19 it is paired with wormwood as the extremity of bitter experience. The "poisonous

1

2

3

1 In 701 B.C. Assyrian king Sennacherib conquered most of Judah including the fortress-city of Lachish. The victory was recorded in remarkable detail on bas-reliefs at his Nineveh palace. This scene is poignant testimony to the plight of his victims, who were deported with only what they could carry on their backs.

2 Tell ed-Duweir, the site of ancient Lachish viewed from the air, appears as an imposing mound in the foothills of Judah. The Judahite palace-fort, razed by Sennacherib, is the rectangular raised area on the far side of the top of the mound. **3** The storming of the Lachish gate-tower. On a track of logs a siege engine equipped with a spearlike beam batters the city gate. One of the Assyrian soldiers within the engine pours water on its front from a long-handled ladle to extinguish firebrands thrown by the Lachish defenders atop the walls. From a door in the tower emerge men and women fleeing the doomed city.

1

2

3

1 The Black Obelisk of Shalmaneser III (858–824 B.C.). This detail shows King Jehu of Omri—the name the Assyrians gave to ancient Israel—prostrate in obeisance before Shalmaneser. **2** A copper crown, one of 416 copper objects found in the "Cave of the Treasure," in the Nahal Mishmar in southern Palestine; fourth millennium B.C. **3** Hill of Shemer. Strategically located beside major routes to Jerusalem on the south, Megiddo and the Jezreel Valley on the north, the Mediterranean Sea and coastal plain on the west, and Shechem and the Jordan Valley on the east, it is here that King Omri built the city of Samaria, capital of the northern kingdom of Israel, in the early ninth century B.C.

1

2

3

1 The stele of Hammurabi. From the reign of the Babylonian king, 1728–1686 B.C., it is inscribed with the "Code of Hammurabi," a prologue, 282 laws, and an epilogue, which parallels in some respects the ancient Hebrew Covenant Code. In the scene at top, Hammurabi worships the enthroned sun god Shamash.
2 Statue head of Gudea, *ensi* or local governor of the city-state of Lagash from 2141 to 2122 B.C. Lagash was close to Ur, traditional home of the biblical Abraham.
3 Section of the wall of the Old City of Jerusalem. The tower, today called the Tower of David, rises from the foundations of the original Phasael Tower, constructed by Herod the Great after 40 B.C. to protect his palace at the vulnerable northwestern corner of the city.

1

2a

1, 2a, 2b Fresco paintings from the western wall of the third-century A.D. synagogue at Dura-Europos, a city on the Euphrates River in Syria. The top panel, "The Consecration of the Tabernacle and Its Priests," is dominated by the figure of Aaron, portrayed as high priest in his robes of office. Beside him is a templelike structure, the Tabernacle, with the *menorah*, an altar, and incense burners aflame in front. At his feet is a stone wall representing the synagogue courtyard with its three entrances (cf. Exod. 40:2–8). To his left are two trumpeters (cf. Num. 10:2–3) and sacrificial animals—a humped bullock and a white, fat-tailed ram. The bottom "Exodus" panel, which begins its narrative at the right (2b), depicts Moses three times, from far right to left: Moses strides toward the Red Sea with staff upraised leading the ancient Israelites out of Egypt, represented by the wall with the red and black columns in front, which symbolize the pillars of fire and cloud that led the Israelites through the wilderness by

(Continued on facing page)

1

2b

(Continued from previous page) night and day (Exod. 13:21–22). In the middle Moses holds back the sea while the people cross. Finally, on the left side, under the protective hands and forearms of God appearing at the top of the panel, Moses holds his staff down to touch the pool of Marah (Exod. 15:23–25a). The twelve figures to his right represent the numbering of the tribes of Israel (Num. 1).

1 Part of the limestone gable of the oldest known Holy Ark (third century A.D.), which sheltered a wooden Torah shrine at the synagogue of Nabratein in Upper Galilee. Shows two rampant lions surmounting the decorated gable. A hole is pierced in the center for a chain from which to hang the eternal light. The pediment weighs one thousand pounds and was toppled to the ground by an earthquake; it was reused, upside down and unrecognized by excavators until 1981, in the foundation of a later synagogue prayer platform.

1

2

1 Jesus washing Peter's feet (John 13:3–11). Manuscript page from *The Four Gospels*, twelfth century. **2** White limestone remains of the synagogue at Capernaum, late second to fifth century A.D. Beneath it has been excavated an earlier synagogue of black basalt—contemporaneous with the ruins of the first-century houses seen in the foreground—in which Jesus may have preached (cf. Mark 1:21; John 6:59).

1

2

3

1 Jesus as the Good Shepherd was a favorite symbol in the catacombs and on the sarcophagi of early Christians (cf. Ps. 23; Luke 15:4 – 6). This wall painting is from the third-century catacomb of St. Priscilla, Rome. **2** Jerusalem, view of the Temple Mount (site of the ancient Temple) from the Mount of Olives. From the time of its capture by the Israelites under David nearly three thousand years ago, Jerusalem was the key city in biblical history. According to the NT, Jesus entered Jerusalem from the Mount of Olives in the climactic final week of his ministry.
3 The river Jordan just above where it empties into the Dead Sea. The Moabite hills rise in the background. The NT tells that Jesus was baptized by John in the Jordan (Mark 1:9).

1

2

3

1 Aerial view of ancient Ephesus from the southwest. The agora (foreground) and theater seating twenty-four thousand behind it date from the first and second centuries A.D. when Ephesus was the fourth largest city of the Roman Empire. In this or an earlier theater, Paul's opponents in Ephesus gathered to defend their worship of Artemis (Acts 19:28–41). **2** Corinth, first founded in the tenth century B.C., was an important city in the NT. In the foreground is the *bema*, or platform, situated in the center of the city forum and probably Gallio's "tribunal" before which Paul was brought (Acts 18:12–17). Behind the *bema* rises the Acrocorinth. **3** Paul, as depicted in the sepulcher of the child Asellus, ca. 313, Rome.

weeds" of Hos. 10:4 (KJV: "hemlock") may possibly be *Conium maculatum*, such as Socrates reportedly drank.

Gallio (gal'lee-oh), the son of the Roman rhetorician Seneca, brother of Seneca the philosopher, and holder of several important civil positions in the Roman Empire. His full name was Lucius Junius Gallio Annaeus. According to Acts 18:12–17, Paul was brought before Gallio's judgment seat in Corinth (discovered in recent times in the old city) when Gallio was proconsul in Achaia. After a perfunctory hearing, Gallio perceived that the dispute between Paul and his Jewish accusers was over an internal religious matter and refused to proceed with the case. In this account, Gallio is characterized as one possessing no inclination, in the case either of Paul or of the subsequent beating of Sosthenes, to make official intervention in what he perceived as strictly internal Jewish issues.

There are no further references to Gallio in the NT. Roman sources indicate that, after spending time in Achaia and Egypt, he returned to Rome to take an official position. After his brother Seneca's death in a conspiracy against Nero in the early 60s, Gallio fell into disgrace and ultimately committed suicide.

Gallio is important to biblical studies because his stay in Corinth is generally regarded as providing important extrabiblical evidence for establishing the chronology of Paul's activities. An inscription discovered at Delphi mentions Gallio as proconsul of Achaia at the time of the twenty-sixth accolade (an honor given to Roman officials) of the Emperor Claudius. It is not clear whether this was A.D. 52/53 or 51/52, but most scholars prefer the earlier date. Thus, according to Acts 18:12–17, the inscription, and Paul's own writings (1 Cor. 3:5–15), it would appear that Paul was in Corinth ca. A.D. 51/52 and that he founded the church there.

If Acts 18:1–17 is read as an accurate account of Paul's first visit to Corinth, it could be concluded that Paul founded the church there ca. A.D. 51–53. It is possible, however, that the text has condensed the accounts of several visits of Paul to Corinth, and thus the links between the Gallio inscription and Paul's activities in Corinth may not be as sure an indicator as some suppose regarding the date when Paul founded the church in Corinth. ***See also*** Achaia; Chronology, New Testament; Corinth; Paul; Tribunal. A.J.M.

An inscription discovered at Delphi mentions Gallio as proconsul of Achaia during the reign of the emperor Claudius, important extrabiblical evidence for establishing the date of Paul's presence in Corinth.

gallon, a word appearing only in John 2:6, where the RSV converts a Greek term (translated "firkins" in the KJV) into an approximate equivalent in gallons. The Greek term equals about nine gallons. ***See also*** Weights and Measures.

Gamaliel (gah-may'lee-uhl; Heb., "recompense of God"). **1** The son of Pedahzur, a prince of Manasseh on the march through the wilderness (Num. 1:10; 2:20). **2** A Pharisee in the Sanhedrin, honored by all the people, who counseled letting the apostles out of prison (Acts 5:34–39) and a teacher of the law who instructed Paul (Acts 22:3). In rabbinic literature Gamaliel is identified as Gamaliel I or the Elder, who flourished in the mid-first century. Little is known of him reliably; the list of princes or patriarchs of Judaism in *Pirke Abot* (part of the Mishnah) lists him after Hillel. **3** Gamaliel II (late first and early second century), the leader of the rabbinic assembly which gathered after the destruction of the Temple in A.D. 70. To him and his predecessor or colleague, Johanan ben Zakkai, are credited many of the adaptations made by Judaism in response to the loss of Temple and priesthood in A.D. 70. A.J.S.

game, the meat of any of a variety of wild animals hunted for food. Jacob prepared a dish of game (KJV: "venison") for his father Isaac as part of his plot to gain the birthright of his brother Esau by trickery (Gen. 25:28; 27:3–33).

games, activities of varying degrees of structure and organization that are pursued for pleasure. Games in biblical times may be categorized as mental exercises, sporting events, or board games.

The riddle proposed by Samson (Judg. 14:12–14) is an instance of a mental exercise. Riddles were widely known in the ancient Near East but were supposed to deal with common experience or knowledge.

One reference to a sporting event in the OT,

A game board decorated with shells found in a tomb at Ur. Although not specifically mentioned in the Bible, game boards date as far back as the twenty-sixth century B.C.

described in 2 Sam. 2:12–17, set twelve of Joab's men against twelve of Abner's men. The contest, which was probably intended to be wrestling, had, however, a fatal outcome.

The NT shows the influence of Greek culture and Greek games on Palestine. These games included foot races, horse races, chariot races, boxing, wrestling, the discus throw, and the javelin throw, among others. Paul frequently uses the metaphor of sporting events. He speaks of running a race (1 Cor. 9:24–27; Gal. 2: 2; 5:7; Phil. 3:14) and of fighting a good fight (1 Tim. 1:18; 2 Tim. 4:7).

Board games, though not mentioned specifically in the Bible, have been found in a number of archaeological excavations. In the NT, the soldiers cast lots for Jesus' garments, probably gambling with dice (Matt. 27:35). Inlaid gaming boards were known from Ur as early as the twenty-sixth century B.C. Likewise, game boards and boxes have been uncovered from Egypt dating to the third and second millennia B.C. One Egyptian set is fully preserved. Of the ten ivory playing pieces five were carved with dogs' heads and five with jackals' heads. These pieces were apparently moved around a playing board with numerous holes for the pieces. Three astragali (animal knuckle bones) served as the dice to determine moves.

Game boards have also been found in Palestine. An ivory board from Megiddo is largely circular with fifty-eight holes for pieces to move along. A limestone game board from Tell Beit Mirsim has fifteen ruled squares and ten playing pieces of blue faience, five cone-shaped and five tetrahedrons. It also has a small die in the shape of a truncated pyramid, with numbers on the four sides. Unfortunately, no evidence remains to indicate how these games were played. However, games must have been enjoyed as much in biblical times as checkers, chess, backgammon, and similar games are today. J.F.D.

garden, a plot of cultivated land enclosed by walls made of stones, mudbrick, or hedges. Entrance was normally through a gate which could be locked (Song of Sol. 4:12; 2 Kings 25:4). Located near ample supplies of water, gardens were lush and desirable pieces of property used both for decorative and utilitarian purposes (Gen. 13:10; Num. 24:6; Jer. 31:12). Vegetables, spices, fruit trees, and flowers were grown in them (1 Kings 21:2; Jer. 29:5; Song of Sol. 4: 12–16; Luke 13:19). Gardens were also used as meeting places for social occasions and for meditation and prayer (Esther 1:5; John 18:1). Occasionally, idolatrous religious practices were carried on in gardens (Isa. 65:3; 66:17). Ancestral tombs were often located in gardens. Thus, many Judean kings were buried in garden tombs (2 Kings 21:18, 26), and the body of Jesus was placed to rest in a garden tomb belonging to Joseph of Arimathea (John 19:41–42). The care of gardens might require the employ of a gardener (John 20:15).

The word "garden" is also used metaphorically and symbolically in the Bible. Thus, in the Song of Solomon, the word refers to the young woman or bride whom the lover comes to court (Song of Sol. 4:12; 5:1; 6:2). Elsewhere, the word refers to the mythical "garden of God" or "garden of the Lord," also known as "Eden," where God walked among the trees in the cool of the day and from which the primordial human beings were banished (Gen. 2:15; 3: 1, 2, 3, 8, 10, 23, 24; Ezek. 28:13; 31:8–9). In this latter sense it is also used as a simile to describe the eschatological restoration of the land of Israel (Isa. 51:3; 58:11; Ezek. 36:35). ***See also*** Eden; Paradise. W.E.L.

garment. ***See*** Dress.

gate. ***See*** Walls.

Gate, Beautiful. ***See*** Nicanor.

Gath, one of the Philistine Pentapolis cities located on the coastal plain in southern Palestine (Josh. 13:3). It, like Ashdod, was one of the remaining homes of the Anakim (giants; see Josh. 11:22; 2 Sam. 21:22). The city is mentioned twice in conjunction with the stories about the Ark of the Covenant (1 Sam. 4–6; 2 Sam. 6). The Philistine inhabitants of Ashdod sent the Ark to Gath (1 Sam. 5:8; 6:17; 7:14). Gath was also the home of Goliath the Philistine (1 Sam. 17:4, 23). David befriended Achish, the king of Gath, during his period of social banditry (1 Sam. 27: 2–11). However Gath continued as a center of opposition to the Hebrews, and it provided fighting men who opposed the Hebrews (2 Sam. 15:18; 21:20). During the reign of Joash (ca. 800–785 B.C.) Hazael, king of Damascus/Syria, took the city (2 Kings 12:17). According to the Chronicler, the city was captured by David (2 Chron. 26:6) and recaptured by Uzziah (ca. 783–742 B.C.). However, there is no corroboration of those conquests in the Deuteronomistic history (Joshua–2 Kings). We know from ancient Near Eastern sources that Sargon II of Assyria destroyed the city (ca. 712 B.C.).

Gath is a common place name. The biblical references given do not make for an easy or certain determination as to which site was ancient Gath. W. F. Albright identified it with Tell esh-Sheikh Ahmed el-Areini, but this has not received much support in recent years. Some have argued in favor of Tell en-Nagileh. Y. Aharoni and A. Rainey have proposed Tell es-Safi as the correct site. S.B.R.

Gathrimmon (gath-rim'ahn; Heb., "the winepress of Rimmon"), a city originally assigned to Dan but later given to the Levites (Josh. 19:45; 21:24). In a parallel account it is listed as being given to the Levites from the tribe of Ephraim (1 Chron. 6:69), but the Chronicles account omits a verse preserved in Joshua (21:23) that specifies that the city is in Dan. A second Gathrimmon given to the Levites from the half-tribe of Manasseh is also recorded (Josh. 21:25), but in the parallel account (1 Chron. 6:70) the city is called Bileam. There is probably only one Gathrimmon and the confusion in the accounts is usually attributed by scholars to scribal errors. The city is thought to be located northeast of Joppa, although the exact site is not known. Perhaps the fact that this area is near the borders of Dan, Ephraim, and Manasseh contributed to the confusion in the accounts. D.R.B.

Gaza (gah'zah), a settlement about three miles from the Mediterranean coast, marking the southern border of Canaan. It was captured by pharaoh Thutmose III (ca. 1469 B.C.). It is also mentioned in the Tell el-Amarna tablets and Taanach tablets as an Egyptian administrative center. It was captured by men of the tribe of Judah (Judg. 1:18) and was included in the allotment given to that tribe (Josh. 15:47). It was part of the Philistine Pentapolis, the southernmost city in that league of five cities (Josh. 13:3; 1 Sam. 6:17; Jer. 25:20). The city was later taken by Tiglath-pileser III, king of Assyria. We also have an account of Hezekiah's conquest of the city (2 Kings 18:9). Pharaoh Neco II occupied the city briefly in 609 B.C. It was a royal fortress under the Persian control of the area, according to the Greek historian Herodotus (2.159); it was called Kadytis.

It was the only city in its area to oppose Alexander the Great (332 B.C.). Later on, it was an outpost of the Ptolemies, who were the ruling power in Egypt during the Hellenistic period, until its capture in 198 by Antiochus III, the Seleucid king who was in control of Syria. The Seleucid city was subsequently attacked by Jonathan the Hasmonean (145 B.C.; see 1 Macc. 11:61–62). During the Hasmonean civil war, the city was taken by Alexander Jannaeus in 96 B.C. The Roman Pompey restored the city and Galbinius, also a Roman official, rebuilt the city (ca. 57 B.C.). King Herod the Great held the city for a short time, but after his death it came under the authority of the Roman proconsul of Syria. It flourished as a Roman city and remained a center for the Jewish community and the emerging Christian community throughout the Roman era (63 B.C.–A.D. 324) and continuing into the Byzantine period (324–1453).

As part of the Philistine Pentapolis, Gaza played an important role in the Samson saga (Judg. 13–16). Modern Tell Harube has been identified as ancient Gaza. It was excavated by W. J. Phythian-Adams in 1922 for the Palestine Exploration Fund. In 1965, a mosaic pavement was discovered by the Egyptian Department of Antiquities. In 1967 A. Ovadiah excavated the area and discovered a synagogue from the sixth century A.D. There appears to have been continuous occupation from the Late Bronze era until the Byzantine period (ca. 1500 B.C.–A.D. 632). S.B.R.

gazelle, an antelope-like creature. Three species of these antelope lived in Palestine: the Dorcas gazelle (*Gazella dorcas*) in the deserts, the mountain gazelle (*Gazella gazella*) in the hillier areas, and the goitred gazelle (*Gazella subgutturosa*) east of the Jordan. They were symbols of

A gazelle tended by a western Asiatic; detail of a wall painting from a tomb at Beni-Hasan, Egypt, second millennium B.C.

love and beauty for the Hebrews (Song of Sol. 2: 9, 17). They were also a major game animal, regularly supplied at Solomon's table (1 Kings 4: 23), though they were difficult to catch because of their swiftness (2 Sam. 2:18; 1 Chron. 12:8).

Geba (gee'buh), a town to the northwest of the Dead Sea given to the Levites from the tribe of Benjamin (Josh. 21:17). It guarded the Michmash pass and was the scene of Israelite battles with the Philistines (1 Sam. 13:3). It is sometimes confused with Gibeah and Gibeon in the Hebrew text. Geba was later fortified by Asa (1 Kings 15:22) and was repopulated in the postexilic period (after mid-sixth century B.C.) (Neh. 11:31). ***See also*** Gibeah; Gibeon; Michmash; Philistines.

Gebal (gee'bahl; Heb., "mountain"). **1** A Canaanite and Phoenician port about twenty miles (32 km.) north of Beirut, known to the Greeks as Byblos, from which comes our word "bible," and today called Jebail. Mentioned in Josh. 13: 5 as part of "the land that yet remains" to be conquered, it was famous for its craftsmen: stonemasons and carpenters who helped construct Solomon's Temple (1 Kings 5:18), and shipwrights (Ezek. 27:9) who used cedar, spruce, and cypress from the high mountains immediately east of the city.

Excavations by P. Montet (1921–1924) and M. Dunand (since 1925) reveal a long and fascinating history. First settled in the pre-pottery Neolithic period as early as ca. 8000 B.C., it was already important during the Chalcolithic period (ca. 3500–3100 B.C.). In the Bronze Age (ca. 3000–1200 B.C.) Gebal traded as far afield as Anatolia, Mesopotamia, and the Sudan, not only in lumber, but also in such goods as wine, leather and oil. So important was the wood for Egypt, which had none of its own, that whenever strong enough it maintained control there. However, between ca. 1800 and 1500 B.C. Gebal fell to the Hyksos, who fortified it strongly. Egypt regained control after 1500 but never attained its earlier authority. The Tell el-Amarna Letters indicate that Rib-Addi of Gebal alone remained faithful to Egypt, but his repeated appeals for help apparently evoked no Egyptian response. Despite the defeat of the Sea Peoples by the pharaoh Rameses III (ca. 1175 B.C.) Egyptian dominance came to an end, and an account of how an Egyptian official, Wen-Amon, was rudely received in ca. 1000 B.C. vividly reveals Gebal's complete freedom of action.

To the following century belongs the fine sarcophagus of King Ahiram, bearing the earliest known Phoenician alphabetic inscription. In fact, almost all early Phoenician inscriptions so far discovered come from Gebal. Although the city strongly supported the coalition against the Assyrian invasion at Qarqar in 853 B.C., it was already being supplanted by Tyre and was never again so powerful. It remained an important trading center until the Byzantine period (A.D. 324–632), but suffered a sudden eclipse after the Muslim conquest in A.D. 636. In 1103 it was captured by the Crusaders, whose strong citadel still stands, but it fell to Saladin in 1189.

2 A tribal area south of the Dead Sea mentioned in Ps. 83:7 in connection with Moab and Edom; some modern scholars equate it with 1 above. ***See also*** Egypt; Hyksos; Mesopotamia; Temple, The. D.B.

Geber (gay'buhr; Heb., "vigorous"), the son of Uri; he was Solomon's provisions procurement officer in Gilead (1 Kings 4:19).

Gedaliah (ged-uh-lī'uh), the son of Ahikam son of Shaphan, who was appointed by the Babylonian king Nebuchadnezzar as governor of

Judah after its capture in 586 B.C. (1 Kings 25: 22). Gedaliah was a member of a prominent Jerusalem family; his father and grandfather had served in Josiah's court (2 Kings 22:3, 14). He, too, may have been a royal official, if he is identical with "Gedaliah, the royal steward" whose name appears on a stamp seal discovered at Lachish.

Though viewed with suspicion by his contemporaries as being a Babylonian collaborator, Gedaliah succeeded in restoring order to the countryside with the support of former army officers and the prophet Jeremiah. But his tenure at Mizpah, the provincial capital, was cut short by a conspiracy led by Ishmael, son of Nataniah, of the royal line. Despite prior warnings, Gedaliah and his entourage were slaughtered; the conspirators escaped across the Jordan to Ammon (Jer. 40–41). A national day of fasting and mourning was inaugurated among the exiles to mark his tragic murder (Zech. 7:5). ***See also*** Nebuzaradan. M.C.

Gederah (ge-dee'ruh; Heb., "a wall"), a city in the lowlands of Judah noted for its royal potters (Josh. 15:36; 1 Chron. 4:23). It was also the home of Jozabad, one of David's warriors (1 Chron. 12: 4) and of Baal-hanan, an agricultural official under David (1 Chron. 27:28). The site is unknown.

Gehazi (ge-hay'zī; Heb., "valley of vision"), the servant or younger associate of Elisha the prophet. In the story of the wealthy Shunammite woman (2 Kings 4:8–37), Gehazi is portrayed as Elisha's faithful messenger and perhaps overzealous protector (v. 27). Some time later Gehazi is in conversation with the king of Israel when this same woman appears seeking recovery of her property after a sojourn in Philistia (2 Kings 8:1–6). In the story of Naaman (2 Kings 5) Gehazi is portrayed as greedy and deceitful and is cursed with Naaman's leprosy by Elisha. A rabbinic tradition suggests the identification of the four lepers at the gate who discover the mysterious rout of the Syrians (2 Kings 7:3–8) with Gehazi and his three sons. D.L.C.

Gehenna (ge-hen'nah), hell or hellfire. The word is derived from Hebrew *ge-hinnom*, meaning "valley of Hinnom," also known in the OT as "the valley of the son(s) of Hinnom." Located west and south of Jerusalem and running into the Kidron Valley at a point opposite the modern village of Silwan, the valley of Hinnom once formed part of the boundary between the tribes of Judah and Benjamin (Josh. 15:8; 18:16; Neh. 11:30). During the monarchical period, it became the site of an infamous high place (called "Topheth" and derived from an Aramaic word meaning "fireplace"), where some of the kings of Judah engaged in forbidden religious practices, including human sacrifice by fire (2 Chron. 28:3; 33:6; Jer. 7:31; 32:35). Because of this, Jeremiah spoke of its impending judgment and destruction (Jer. 7:32; 19:6). King Josiah put an end to these practices by destroying and defiling the high place in the valley of Hinnom (2 Kings 23:10).

Probably because of these associations with fiery destruction and judgment, the word "Gehenna" came to be used metaphorically during the intertestamental period as a designation for hell or eternal damnation. In the NT, the word is used only in this way and never as a geographic place name. As such, Gehenna is to be distinguished from Hades, which is either the abode of all the dead in general (Acts 2:27, 31; Rev. 20:13–14) or the place where the wicked await the final judgment. By contrast, the righteous enter paradise, or a state of bliss, immediately upon death (Luke 16:19–31; 23: 43; 2 Cor. 12:3). Jesus warned his disciples of committing sins that would lead to Gehenna (Matt. 5:22, 29–30; 23:33; Mark 9:45; Luke 12: 5). In the NT, Gehenna designates the place or state of the final punishment of the wicked. It is variously described as a fiery furnace (Matt. 13:42, 50), an unquenchable fire (Mark 9:43), or an eternal fire prepared for the devil and his angels (Matt. 25:41). ***See also*** Hell, Sheol. W.E.L.

Gemariah (gem-uh-rī'uh). **1** The son of Shaphan, of an influential Jerusalem family of scribes in the early sixth century B.C. The scroll of Jeremiah's collected prophecies was first read in Gemariah's chamber in the Temple precinct (Jer. 36:10). Later, Gemariah appears among the prophet's supporters at the court of Jehoiakim. **2** The son of Hilkiah, who carried Jeremiah's letter to the exiles in Babylonia (Jer. 29:3).

genealogy, a history of the descent of a person or group (family, tribe, or nation) from an ancestor. The term appears in both the OT and the NT (1 Chron. 5:1, 7, 17; 2 Chron. 31:16; Ezra 2:62; Neh. 7:5, 64; 1 Tim. 1:4; Titus 3:9; also Matt. 1: 1 RSV [KJV: "origins"]).

The OT contains about two dozen genealogical lists. The first is at Gen. 4:17–22 (from Cain through seven generations). Other prominent lists are the generations from Adam to Noah (Gen. 5:1–32), the descendants of Noah (Gen. 10:1–32), the generations from Shem to Abraham (Gen. 11:10–26), the descendants of Jacob (Gen. 46:8–27) and Levi (Exod. 6:16–25), and the list of persons and families of the postexilic community who continue the line from pre-exilic times (Ezra 2:2b–61). The most extensive genealogy is in 1 Chron. 1:1–9:44 (Adam to the descendants of Saul).

These genealogies vary in historical value and purposes. The aim of constructing genealogies was to establish descent and thereby one's identity. Certain generations and individuals, however, were omitted. For example, Exod. 6:16–20 identifies Moses as the great-grandson of Levi, which is hardly possible in a strict sense, since the time span is over four hundred years (cf. Exod. 12:40).

The earliest sources of the Pentateuch (J and E) contain relatively little genealogical material (Gen. 4:1, 19–24; 9:20–27). These serve chiefly to account for differences among peoples and cultures. The impetus for genealogies arises above all after the Deuteronomic reform (seventh century B.C.), which stressed purity of the community (Deut. 7:1–4; 23:1–8). This was intensified in the postexilic era when ethnic purity had to be documented and foreign influence had to be removed (Ezra 2:59–63; 10: 9–44; Neh. 13:23–28). Moreover, genealogies were constructed for the Aaronic priesthood (restricted to descendants of Levi; Exod. 28:1–29:44).

Since royal succession in the Southern Kingdom was determined by Davidic descent, a royal genealogical record had to be kept. Furthermore, it was expected (although not in all circles) that the Messiah would be a descendant of David (Isa. 11:1–5), whose "house" and "throne" had been established forever by divine promise (2 Sam. 7:16; Ps. 89:3–4).

The NT genealogies of Jesus in Matt. 1:1–17 and Luke 3:23–38 seek to establish above all his Davidic descent (Matt. 1:1, 6, 17; Luke 3: 31). Matthew's also establishes his descent from Abraham (1:1–2, 17), while Luke's traces his descent to "Adam, the Son of God" (3:38). Although both genealogies cover the span from Abraham to Jesus, they cannot be harmonized. Matthew computes three groups of fourteen generations each for this span (1:17), although only forty-one (not forty-two) names actually appear (inclusive of Abraham and Jesus), while Luke lists fifty-seven names. The names are mostly the same from Abraham to David in both (Luke 3:33 adds Arni and Admin), but thereafter only three names appear in common (Shealtiel, Zerubbabel, and Joseph). In spite of attempts to explain the discrepancies, these genealogies should be seen as containing some historical information but designed primarily in light of the intent of the Evangelists: to establish that Jesus fulfills the messianic hopes of Israel. ***See also*** David; King; Messiah; Priests.

A.J.H.

general Letters, the seven NT Letters attributed to James, Peter (2), John (3), and Jude, also known as "catholic Epistles." The Letters are written either to a general audience or to an individual not otherwise identifiable (2 and 3 John). ***See also*** Epistle; Letter.

generation (Heb. *dor*), the period of time between the birth of parents and the birth of their children; all of the people alive during that time. The OT uses "generation" only loosely as a measure of time, and it is therefore difficult to use the term in exact chronological calculations. Although a generation sometimes covers up to a hundred years (Gen. 15:13, 16; Exod. 12:40), most biblical writers seem to consider thirty to forty years to be a normal generation (Deut. 2:14; Job 42:16; Ps. 95:10). Usually "generation" simply refers to all of the people at a given time (Gen. 6:9; Pss. 14:5; 24:6; 49:19; 24:6; 112:2; Jer. 2:3).

Some English translations use "generations" to translate the Hebrew word *toledot*, a term that refers to a sequence of people or events and that might better be translated "genealogy" or "story." In Genesis the formula "these are the generations of X" is used to give structure to the book. Sometimes the formula introduces genealogies that summarize a history of events, trace the transmission of something from one generation to another, or relate characters to each other (Gen. 5:1; 10:1; 11:10; 25:12; 36:1). Elsewhere the formula introduces a new block of narrative (Gen. 2:4; 6:9; 11:27; 25:19; 37:2). Outside of Genesis, the word "generations" usually introduces or concludes a genealogy (e.g., Exod. 6:16, 19; 28:10; Num. 3:1; 1 Chron. 5:7; Matt. 1:17). ***See also*** Genealogy. R.R.W.

Genesis, the first book in the Bible; it is the narrative account of beginnings—of the world, of the community of Israel, of faith. It is a theological statement, claiming that all real beginnings are wrought by the purpose and speech of Yahweh, the God of Israel.

Content: The beginnings concern the theological ground of the created world and the origin of Israel among the peoples of the world. Gen. 1–11 is a collection of materials presenting a particular notion of the character of the cosmos. It is clear that while Israel borrows and utilizes the common deposit of ancient Near Eastern traditions in this material, Israel has shaped these appropriated materials to make a particular statement about the character of the world in relation to God. This statement does not concern scientific origins. It asserts that the world is formed by, accountable to, and destined for Yahweh's purposes but is recalcitrant, refusing to be God's obedient creature. The narrative concerns the theological issues of fidelity and disobedience.

The remainder of the book concerns Abraham and Sarah (Gen. 12–25), Isaac and Rebekah (Gen. 25–26), Jacob and Rachel (Gen. 25–36), and Joseph (Gen. 37–50). Again diverse materials are used. The completed tradition makes a theological claim that Israel is formed by Yahweh's summoning, promising purpose to be a vehicle for God's way in the world. Israel becomes the arena in which God's remarkable deeds of fidelity are enacted.

The origin of the world and the origin of Israel are expressed in different modes and different textures. The connection of the two is decisive for understanding the intent of the book. On the one hand, it is frequently suggested that Gen. 12: 1–4a (with its mention of "blessing for the nations") is the key link that looks back to a created world under curse and looks forward to Israel as a source of blessing among the nations. On the other hand, the goodness of the world (1:31) and Joseph's verdict on God's good providence (50: 20) provide a way of holding together both origins under God's promise.

Critical Study: The critical study of Genesis has included three approaches in the last several centuries: work on the oral tradition, the written sources, and the history behind the text. There is no doubt that Genesis includes many materials that were shaped and transmitted orally. A study of Genesis thus attends to oral narrative, the forms and modes of such transmission. Reference to Hermann Gunkel's work is of crucial importance, as well as more recent studies in literary and rhetorical analysis.

Extensive study has been given to the editorial work done on the written sources. The

OUTLINE OF CONTENTS

Genesis

- I. Creation and the history of the nations (1:1–11:32)
  - A. Traditions of creation (1:1–2:25)
    - 1. Creation deemed good (1:1–2:4a)
    - 2. Creation of man and woman (2:4b–25)
  - B. Traditions of creation troubled (3: 1–4:16)
    - 1. Trouble in the garden (3:1–24)
    - 2. Trouble with the brothers (4:1–16)
  - C. Materials before the Flood (4:17–6:4)
  - D. The Flood narrative (6:5–9:29)
    - 1. Corruption and God's resolve (6:5–22)
    - 2. The coming of the Flood (7:1–24)
    - 3. The resolution of the Flood (8:1–22)
    - 4. The covenant of rainbow (9:1–17)
    - 5. The family of Noah (9:18–29)
  - E. The generations of the sons of Noah (10:1–32)
  - F. The Tower of Babel (11:1–9)
  - G. The generations of Shem (11:10–32)
- II. The Traditions of Abraham (12:1–25:18)
  - A. The initial summons (12:1–9)
  - B. A sojourn in Egypt (12:10–20)
  - C. Division of the land with Lot (13:1–18)
  - D. Tradition of the kings (14:1–24)
  - E. Covenanting with Abraham (15:1–21)
  - F. Sarah and Hagar (16:1–16)
  - G. Covenant and circumcision (17:1–27)
  - H. The impossible promise (18:1–15)
  - I. Sodom and Gomorrah (18:16–19:38)
  - J. Abraham, Sarah, and Abimelech (20: 1–18)
  - K. Abraham, Sarah, and their sons (21: 1–21)
  - L. Traditions of Beer-sheba (21:22–34)
  - M. The testing of Abraham (22:1–24)
  - N. The death of Sarah (23:1–20)
  - O. The marriage of Isaac and Rebekah (24:1–67)
  - P. Abraham's genealogy and death (25: 1–18)
- III. Traditions of Isaac and Jacob (25:19–36: 43)
  - A. The birth of Jacob and Esau (25:19–34)
  - B. Traditions of Isaac (26:1–30)
  - C. The blessing of Jacob and Esau (27:1–28:22)
    - 1. The blessing by Isaac (27:1–45)
    - 2. The warning against foreign women (27:46–28:9)
    - 3. The dream at Bethel (28:10–22)
  - D. Jacob, Rachel, and their sons (29:1–31:55)
  - E. Jacob and Esau reconciled (32:1–23: 20)
    - 1. Preparation for meeting (32:1–21)
    - 2. The meeting at Penuel (32:22–32)
    - 3. The meeting with Esau (33:1–17)
    - 4. Jacob at Shechem (33:18–20)
  - F. Jacob's sons at Shechem (34:1–31)
  - G. Various Jacob traditions (35:1–29)
  - H. The descendants of Esau (36:1–43)
- IV. The story of Joseph and his brothers (37:1–50:26)
  - A. The initial dream (37:1–36)
  - B. A Judah tradition (38:1–30)
  - C. Joseph and the way to power (39:1–41:57)
    - 1. Joseph and Potiphar's wife (39:1–23)
    - 2. Joseph as dream interpreter (40: 11–23)
    - 3. Joseph raised to power (41:1–57)
  - D. Joseph meets his brothers (42:1–44: 34)
  - E. Joseph discloses himself (45:1–28)
  - F. Israel settles in Egypt (46:1–47:26)
  - G. The death of Jacob (47:27–50:14)
  - H. Joseph meets his brothers again (50: 15–26)

The frontispiece to Genesis from the first Bible of Charles the Bald (ninth century) shows (top) the creation of man and woman, (middle) eating the fruit of the forbidden tree, and (bottom) the banishment of Adam and Eve from the Garden of Eden.

scholarly consensus (associated with the name of Julius Wellhausen) is the four-document hypothesis (the Pentateuch is composed of four sources J, E, D, and P), which is an attempt to deal with problems discerned in the text. That hypothesis is now under severe attack from several quarters, but so far no compelling alternative has been proposed.

Historical study (using linguistic and archaeological methods, with particular reference to the work of W. F. Albright) has sought to establish the historical realities behind the text. While important gains have been made, there is currently a great reticence about claiming too much. Whatever there is that is historical, it is now available to us only in a form that is the result of an inventive, constructive literary process.

Theological Statement: For the communities of faith that have valued the book of Genesis, it is finally a theological statement. The world and Israel belong to God, exist because of God's intention, and are called to live toward God's hope. Every scientific, historical, or literary analysis that misses this claim misunderstands the text.

For Jews, the book of Genesis asserts the decisive vocation of Israel among the nations as a people under promise. For Christians, the book of Genesis is understood as the source of a promissory process that leads from this community to the community gathered around Jesus. For both Jews and Christians, Genesis functions to keep the world open for God's hope against every ideological and technological effort to close the world and end the historical process. ***See also*** Patriarch; Pentateuch.

Bibliography

Brueggemann, Walter. *Genesis.* Atlanta, GA: John Knox, 1982.

Brueggemann, Walter, and Hans Walter Wolff. *The Vitality of Old Testament Traditions.* 2nd edition. Atlanta, GA: John Knox, 1982.

Coats, George W. *Genesis with an Introduction to Narrative Literature.* Grand Rapids, MI: Eerdmans, 1983.

Hayes, John H. *An Introduction to Old Testament Study.* Nashville, TN: Abingdon, 1979. Chap. 5.

W.B.

Gennesaret (ge-nes'uh-ret). ***See*** Galilee, Sea of.

gentile (from Latin *gens,* "nation"), a non-Jew. The distinction has its roots in the OT in the seven nations (Heb. *goyim*) not driven completely from the land (Josh. 24:11). According to several traditions, the Israelite was enjoined to maintain strict separation from them in matters of religion, marriage, and politics (Exod. 23:28–33; Deut. 7:1–5; Josh. 23:4–13), although, historically speaking, the amount of interchange between Israel and the peoples of the land seems to have been considerable. Only in postbiblical Hebrew did it become possible to speak of an individual "Gentile" *(goy)* as, after Ezra, the Jewish community began to close ranks in the wake of the Exile.

Jew and Gentile: The distinction between Jew and Gentile is related to a tension between universalism and particularism. The Isaianic tradition spoke of Israel as "a light to the nations" (Isa. 42:6; cf. 60:3). In the latter days, the nations would flow to Jerusalem to learn Torah (Isa. 2: 2–4) or to participate in the coming reign of God (45:22–24; 51:4–5). On the other hand, in an effort to establish a separation between Jew and Gentile, Ezra and Nehemiah commanded Jews in Jerusalem to divorce their non-Jewish wives —not just those of the seven nations (Ezra 9–10; Neh. 10:30; 13:23–31). Ruth and Jonah seem to be parables written to protest this action in the name of a more universal understanding of God's care for his human creation.

The Apocrypha and Pseudepigrapha give evidence of a wall being erected between Jew and Gentile (see 2 Macc. 14:38), although expressions of universalism are still found. The claim that the world was created for Israel alone *(T. Moses* 1:12; 2 Esd. 6:56) contrasts sharply with echoes of the Isaianic "light to the nations" *(T. Levi* 2:11; 14:4; Tob. 13:11; *T. Judah*

24:5–6; 1 *Enoch* 10:21). Ecclus. 11:34 warns against receiving a stranger into your household, lest your way of life become alienated. The prohibition of mixed marriages became a central concern (Tob. 4:12–13; *T. Levi* 9:10; 14:6). Other areas in which separateness was particularly apparent include food (Dan. 1:8–15; Tob. 1:10–12), circumcision (1 Macc. 1:11–15), and avoidance of the idolatry characteristic of Gentile society (1 Macc. 3:48). 1 Maccabees 1 presents in bold relief the contrast between life according to Jewish and Gentile law and custom. While it was possible for a Gentile to become a proselyte, many of those attracted to Jewish monotheism became "God-fearers" (Acts 10:2; 13:16) rather than undergo circumcision and keep the food laws required of full converts.

Rabbinic attitudes toward Gentiles vary depending upon the conditions of Jewish life. The righteous Gentile was expected to keep the seven Noachian laws (*Gen. Rab.*, Noah, 34:8) and, according to some, would be given a place in the world to come (*t. Sanh.* 13:2). The Jew was to deal honestly with Gentiles in order to avoid profanation of the name of God (*Abod. Zar.* 26a) and was obligated to relieve their poor (*Gittin* 61a). The charging of interest to Gentile as well as Jew was prohibited (*B. Mes.* 70b–71a). On the other hand, one finds polemics directed against Gentiles for their idolatry and immorality as well as regulations designed to maintain Jewish separateness—for example, prohibitions against wines and cooked foods prepared by Gentiles.

In the Early Christian Community: The development of Christianity, which began as a Jewish movement, was profoundly affected by the success of the Gentile mission undertaken by the apostle Paul and others. The Jerusalem conference of about the year A.D. 49 determined that Gentile converts to Christianity did not have to become Jewish proselytes (Gal. 2:1–10; Acts 15: 1–35), thus opening membership in the Christian community to those who might otherwise have remained "God-fearers." Paul fought efforts to distinguish between Jew and Gentile in the Christian community (Rom. 3:29–30; Gal. 2: 11–21; 3:26–29). He was opposed by the Judaizers or "circumcision party" (Gal. 2:12), Christians who insisted that Gentile converts become Jewish proselytes. Paul's practice furthered the success of Christianity within the empire and led to its emergence as a distinct religion by the end of the first century.

An inscription forbidding non-Jews (i.e., Gentiles) from entering the Temple in Jerusalem; cast of the original stone, which dates to 20 B.C.

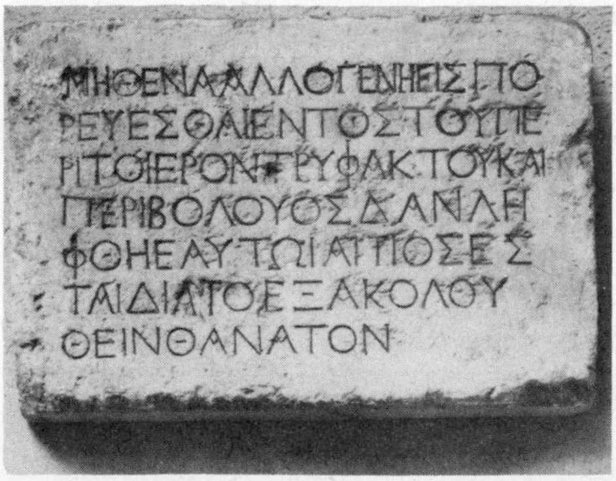

As a result of the controversy over the role of Gentiles in the church, it is difficult to determine the attitude of Jesus himself, since both sides seem to have affected the preservation of the Jesus tradition. Some scholars suggest that Jesus understood the activity of the Messiah in traditional terms as directed toward the Jewish people (Matt. 10:5–6; 15:24) with, perhaps, the inclusion of the Gentiles in the final rule of God. On the other hand, Jesus does not seem to have been a supporter of Jewish nationalism, and some of his more radical sayings and actions (Matt. 21:31; Mark 11:15; Luke 10:30–35) suggest that he proclaimed a kingdom that confronted men and women rather than Jew and Gentile. ***See also*** Monotheism; Paul; Proselyte; Stranger.

Bibliography

Jeremias, Joachim. *Jesus' Promise to the Nations*. Translated by S. H. Hooke. Naperville, IL: Allenson, 1958.

Manson, Thomas Walter. *Jesus and the Non-Jews*. London: Athlone, 1955.

Montefiore, Claude G., and Herbert Loewe. *A Rabbinic Anthology*. New York: Schocken, 1974.

D.W.S.

Gentiles, Court of the. ***See*** Temple, The.

Gera (gee'ruh). **1** A son of Benjamin (Gen. 46: 21). **2** A son of Bela and grandson of Benjamin (1 Chron. 8:3). **3** A second son of Bela and grandson of Benjamin (1 Chron. 8:5). **4** A Benjaminite, the father of Ehud (Judg. 3:15). **5** A Benjaminite, son of Ehud (1 Chron. 8:7). It is difficult to separate these names and assign them to specific persons. They may all represent the same person whose ancestry has become confused in the records; or the name may represent an ancient clan within the tribe of Benjamin whose exact genealogy was not known. **6** A member of Saul's family and father of Shimei, the man who pronounced a curse on David (2 Sam. 16:5; 19:16).

D.R.B.

gerah (geer'uh), measure of weight comprising one twentieth of a shekel (Exod. 30:13; Lev. 27: 25; Num. 3:47; 18:16; Ezek. 45:12). Recovered samples to date indicate an average weight of 0.565 grams. ***See also*** Weights and Measures.

Gerar (ge'rahr), a town in the Negev whose exact location remains undetermined. Abraham visited the town and entered into some type of agreement with the king of Gerar, Abimelech (Gen. 20:1–2). However, the bulk of episodes in the OT involving Gerar are in the Isaac stories (Gen. 26). This has led some scholars to argue that the Isaac stories originated in that region.

The only other references to the town are in 2 Chronicles (14:9–14). Here we have a story of Asa's (905–874 B.C.) defeat of Zerah, an invading Ethiopian.

The stories about Gerar are of such a sort that it is difficult, if not impossible, to discern its location with any certainty. W. M. F. Petrie identified modern Tell Jennah as Gerar during his 1927 excavation. W. J. Phythian-Adams had excavated the site in 1922 for the Palestine Exploration Fund. This site has been by and large discarded as a possible candidate for Gerar. Y. Aharoni argued in 1956 that modern Tell Abu Huweirah was ancient Gerar. The fact is that the excavation of the site by D. Alon, which turned up Middle Bronze material, does not clearly demonstrate that Tell Abu Huweirah is Gerar. S.B.R.

Gerasa (ge'rah-sah; modern Jerash), one of the three greatest cities of Roman Arabia. It is thirty-three miles southeast of the Sea of Galilee in the mountains of Gilead. Hence Luke's identification of it with Jesus' healing of the demoniac (8: 26) cannot be correct. The city was administered by an appointee of the legate of Syria and officially known as "Antioch on the Chrysorrhoas." Excavations have revealed extensive remains of public buildings from the first and second centuries A.D. The city wall, gates, and towers, several main streets, the forum, as well as remains of the hippodrome, theaters, triumphal arch, and temples of Zeus and Artemis have been found. A coin from the reign of Commodus attests that the city was founded by Alexander the Great. The earliest dates for the city come from the second century B.C. Josephus, a Jewish historian, reports that the Jews living in the town were spared by the Gentile population when the city was attacked by Jewish rebels during the Jewish revolt (*War* 2.480). P.P.

Gergesenes (guhr'ge-seenz). ***See*** Gadara; Gerasa.

Gerizim (gair'uh-zeem), the bulky mountain 2,890 feet above sea level opposite Ebal in the central highlands; in the pass between Ebal and Gerizim lies Shechem, at the intersection of main east-west and north-south roads. Deut. 11: 29; 27:12; and Josh. 8:33 portray a ceremony of blessings shouted from Gerizim, curses from Ebal: the consequences of covenantal loyalty or disloyalty. In Judg. 9:7 Jotham speaks his fable from Gerizim, perhaps from the ruined seventeenth- or sixteenth-century B.C. sanctuary on a knoll one-quarter mile from Shechem, 300 feet above it. Judg. 9:37 mentions the "center of the

Remains of public buildings from the first and second centuries A.D. excavated at Gerasa, one of the three greatest cities of Roman Arabia.

land," which may mean that Gerizim was thought of as meeting place of heaven and earth by early Israelites. For Samaritans, it is the highest of all mountains, *the* place to worship God (John 4:20). They built a temple there in the fourth century B.C., says the first century A.D. Jewish historian Josephus. In the second and third centuries A.D., coins and literature depict a temple built by Hadrian (ca. A.D. 130) on Gerizim. Excavation at modern Tell er-Ras, the Gerizim spur nearest Shechem, has found Hadrian's temple foundations, resting on what probably constitutes the podium for the Samaritan sanctuary. On the main summit, a half-mile south, are remains of a church built by Zeno ca. A.D. 484 and fortified by Justinian ca. A.D. 532. Nearby is the Samaritan celebration site, still in use by modern descendants. ***See also*** Covenant; Ebal; Samaritans; Shechem. E.F.C.

Gershom (geer'shuhm). **1** Moses' eldest son, born to Zipporah in Midian (Exod. 2:22). The name, popularly explained as "sojourner there" (Heb. *ger sham*), may be based on the verb *garash* ("drive away"), used for Pharaoh's release of Israel from Egypt (Exod. 6:1; 11:1) and for the expulsion of earlier inhabitants from Canaan (Exod. 23:28–31 and elsewhere). It also recalls Moses' rescue of Zipporah and her sisters from the shepherds who "drove them away" from the well (Exod. 2:17). This Gershom is the ancestor of the priest at Dan (Judg. 18:30). **2** A descendant of Phinehas (Ezra 8:2). The Gershom of 1 Chronicles 6 (cf. 15:7) is a scribal error. ***See also*** Gershon. K.G.O.

Gershon (geer'shuhn), the first son of Levi, followed by Kohath and Merari (Gen. 46:11 and elsewhere). The name appears as Gershom several times in 1 Chronicles 6 (cf. 15:7), but this is an error. Numbers 4 and Joshua 21 list Gershon's descendants between Kohath's and Merari's, while 1 Chron. 15:5–7 and 2 Chron. 29:12 put them third. Num. 7:7–9 allocates two wagons to Gershon's sons and four to Merari's (for carrying sections of the tabernacle), but none to the sons of Kohath (for the smaller tabernacle furnishings). Gershon's two sons are Libni (Exod. 6:17; Num. 3:18) or Ladan (1 Chron. 23:7; 26:21) and Shimei. ***See also*** Gershom. K.G.O.

Geshem (gee'shem), an Arab opponent of Nehemiah who ridiculed the plan to rebuild Jerusalem's walls and subsequently plotted against him (Neh. 2:19; 6:1–9). We may assume that he was the ruler of the Persian province of Arabia, south of Judah. This position may explain his motivation to interfere in Judah's domestic affairs.

Geshur (gesh'uhr). **1** A small ancient kingdom whose territory formed part of southern Golan, east of the Sea of Galilee (Josh. 12:5; 13:11). During the wars of conquest (late thirteenth-early twelfth centuries B.C.) it proved difficult for Israel to win (Josh. 13:11, 13), and it remained an independent Aramean kingdom in the time of David. Seeking to establish political relationships with this kingdom, David married Maacah, the daughter of Geshur's king, Talmai (2 Sam. 3:3). She bore him Absalom who, after killing Amnon, fled to his grandfather's territory (2 Sam. 13:37–38). **2** A region in the south of Palestine, mentioned in Josh. 13:2 as yet to be won and in 1 Sam. 27:8–11 as conquered by David while he was with the Philistines. Y.G.

gestures, movements of the hands and other parts of the body by which humans and other primates consciously or unconsciously express attitudes or feelings.

The Bible, like other literatures from the earliest antiquity to the present day, employs words and phrases to enable readers to visualize gestures, postures, and facial expressions. In many cases the words and phrases in the Bible that refer to gestures can be correlated with specific gestures illustrated in sculptures, seals, reliefs, and tomb paintings from the ancient Near East.

The analysis of gestures, postures, and facial expressions and the systematic investigation of their role in the conscious or unconscious expression of emotions and ideas are today referred to under the rubrics of body language, kinesics, nonverbal communication, and semiotics. Research in these fields has demonstrated, among other things, that gesticulation is universal among humans; that no gesture has precisely the same meaning in every culture; and that the pattern of gesticulation within a given culture operates in consonance with the spoken language to effect a two-channel communication. These findings have put to rest the assumption, widely held until recently, that the Bible frequently refers to gestures, postures, and facial expressions because the Bible is a product of the Middle East, whose inhabitants, it was alleged, being less civilized than the peoples of northern Europe, exert less control over the spontaneous physical expression of their emotions.

Prayer Gestures: The prayer gesture most frequently mentioned in the OT is "spreading the palms" (Exod. 9:29, 33; 1 Kings 8:22, 38, 54; 2 Chron. 6:12, 13, 29; Ezra 9:5; Job 11:13; Ps. 44:21; Isa. 1:15; Jer. 4:31). Apparently this gesture was employed with prayers of petition to suggest that God fill the hands of the petitioner with the requested benefit. This gesture is probably to be distinguished from "lifting up the hands" toward the holy place or sanctuary (Pss. 28:2; 134:2). While in both its attestations the latter gesture was directed toward an earthly sanctuary, Akkadian, Ugaritic, Greek, and Roman parallels suggest that it originated as a salute to God in his heavenly temple.

Kneeling figure, probably Hammurabi, in a gesture of prayer; from Larsa, ca. 1750 B.C.

Prayer Postures: Bending over is the posture of worship prescribed for one who presents the first fruits of the harvest in Deut. 26:10 and for one who approaches any of the gates of the Temple in Ezekiel 46, but bending over is associated with idolatrous worship in Lev. 26:1 and Ezek. 8:16. Other OT references to bending over in the worship of the Lord include 2 Kings 18:22; Pss. 5:8; 22:28; 86:9; 132:7; 138:2; and Isa. 66:23. Other postures of worship mentioned in the Bible include stooping (1 Kings 8:54; 19:18; 2 Chron. 29:29; Ezra 9:5; Ps. 22:30; Isa. 45:23), falling on the face (Gen. 24:26, 48; Exod. 4:31; 12:27; 34:8; 2 Chron. 29:30; Neh. 8:6; Ezek. 44:4; Matt. 26:39; Mark 14:35; Rev. 1:17), throwing oneself down (Deut. 9:18, 25; Ezra 10:1), and bowing the head (Isa. 58:5; Mic. 6:6). Kneeling, to be distinguished from stooping, is mentioned as a posture of prayer in 2 Chron. 6:13; Ps. 95:6; Dan. 6:11; and Luke 22:41. Standing is attested as a posture of prayer to God in Neh. 9:2; Ps. 106:30; Jer. 18:20; Matt. 6:5; and Mark 11:25 and as a posture of idolatrous worship in Dan. 2:3. King David is portrayed as praying to God in a seated position in 2 Sam. 7:18.
Reading and Teaching Scripture: While no specific posture is prescribed for the septennial reading of the Torah in Deut. 31:10–13 (contrast *m. Sota* 7:8), Nehemiah 8–9 states that when Ezra read from the Torah both he and the congregation were standing. Luke 4:17–20 informs us that Jesus stood to read from the book of Isaiah in the synagogue at Nazareth but that he afterward sat down to teach. According to Matt. 5:1, Jesus was seated while preaching the Sermon on the Mount, while Luke 6:17 asserts that Jesus stood on that occasion. Matt. 26:55 and Luke 2:46 both refer to Jesus' sitting while teaching in the Temple.
Postures of Entreating Jesus for Healing: According to Matt. 8:2 and Mark 1:40 the leper kneels in supplication before Jesus while in Luke 5:12 the leper falls on his face in entreaty. According to Matt. 15:25 the Phoenician woman kneels when asking Jesus to exorcise the demon from her daughter, while in Mark 7:25 she falls at Jesus' feet. Entreating Jesus for healing in a kneeling posture is attested also in Matt. 17:14 and Matt. 20:20, while falling on the face while supplicating Jesus for healing is mentioned in Mark 5:22; Luke 8:41; and Luke 8:28.
Obeisance: One bends over (Gen. 23:7, 12; 33:3, 6, 7; 37:10; 2 Sam. 9:6; 14:22; Isa. 49:23, stoops (Esther 3:2, 5), or falls down (Gen. 50:18; Esther 6:13) before sovereigns or grasps their feet (2 Kings 4:27) in order to acknowledge that one is beneath them in rank.
Greeting: Lev. 19:32 prescribes that when younger persons encounter their elders the former should stand. In 1 Kings 2:19 King Solomon stands up to greet his mother. Job tells us that before disaster befell him he was so highly esteemed in the community that even the elderly when encountering him "rose and stood" (Job 29:8). An alternative posture for greeting high-status persons is bending over (Gen. 19:1; 43:28; 1 Sam. 25:41; 2 Kings 2:15).
Kissing: While 1 Sam. 20:41 and 2 Sam. 19:40 show that close friends might kiss upon taking leave of each other, kissing is generally reserved in the OT for greeting close relatives (Gen. 29:11, 13; 33:4; 45:15; 48:10; Exod. 4:27) or taking leave (Gen. 31:28; 32:1; 50:1; Ruth 1:9, 14). The purely erotic kiss is mentioned in the Bible only in

A courtier kisses the ground in a gesture of obeisance; bas-relief from Hermopolis, Egypt.

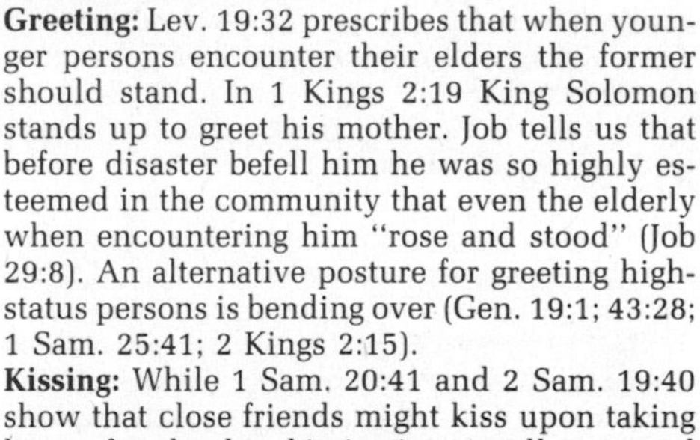

Prov. 7:13 and Song of Sol. 1:2; 8:1. The kiss of betrayal is attested only in 2 Sam. 20:9 and Matt. 26:49 (parallels, Mark 14:45; Luke 22:47). In the NT the kiss is a greeting exchanged between Christians (see Acts 20:37; Rom. 16:16; 1 Cor. 16:20; 2 Cor. 13:12; 1 Thess. 5:26; 1 Pet. 5:14).
Sadness: Sadness is expressed by the fallen face (Gen. 4:5–6; Mark 10:22), the "changed countenance," i.e., the gloomy face (Job 14:20; Eccles. 8:1; Dan. 5:6, 9, 10; 7:28), and darkened eyes (Lam. 5:17). "The face is bad," i.e., "the face is gloomy" (Gen. 40:7; Neh. 2:2; Eccles. 7:3) and weeping (Gen. 27:38; 42:24; 50:17; Ezra 3:12; Ps. 126:6) also show sadness.
Happiness: Contentment, joy, and kind disposition to others is associated with one's face being lit up (Job 29:24; Isa. 60:1), the head (Pss. 3:4; 110:7) or face (Num. 6:26; Deut. 28:50) being lifted up, and shining eyes (1 Sam. 14:27, 29; Pss. 13:4; 19:9; Prov. 29:13; Ezek. 9:8).
Anger: One of the most common expressions for being angry in the OT Hebrew is a phrase that means literally "the face burns." This expression reflects the well-known reddening of the face of angry persons. It is applied to persons (Gen. 39:19; Judg. 9:30; 14:19; 1 Sam. 11:6) and, by extension, to God (Exod. 4:14; Num. 11:10; 12:9; 25:3; 32:10, 13; Deut. 29:26; 2 Sam. 6:7). Descriptions of divine anger that reflect the angry person's increase in body temperature include Isa. 30:27: "Behold, the name of the Lord comes from far, burning with his anger, and in thick rising smoke; his lips are full of indignation, and his tongue is like a devouring fire" (see also Deut. 32:22). Frowning is referred to as "stiffening the face" in Mic. 7:18 and as "hardening of the face" in Ps. 90:11. Fuming in anger is referred to in 2 Sam. 22:9 (Ps. 18:9); Ps. 74:1; and Isa. 65:5.
Patience: Just as anger is referred to in the OT primarily by reference to its manifestation on the countenance, so is patience referred to primarily by a phrase whose literal meaning is "broadness of face." Examples include Exod. 34:6; Num. 14:18; Ps. 86:15; Prov. 14:29; Joel 2:13; and Jon. 4:2.
Judicial Postures and Gestures: Because one lifted one's hand, thereby pointing to God's heavenly throne, when taking an oath (Deut. 32:40), swearing came to be referred to simply as "lifting the hand" (see Gen. 14:22; Exod. 6:8; Ezek. 20:5, 6, 15, 23, 28, 42). That the judge was seated while hearing cases is reflected in Exod. 18:13, which also informs us that the litigants stood during the legal proceeding (see also Judg. 4:4; Ruth 4:2; Ps. 9:8; John 19:13). ***See also*** Dancing; Mourning Rites; Prayer.

Bibliography

Gruber, M. I. *Aspects of Nonverbal Communication in the Ancient Near East.* Studia Pohl, no. 12. 2 vols. Rome: Biblical Institute Press, 1980.

M.I.G.

Gethsemane (geth-sem'ah-nee; Heb., "oil press"), the site mentioned twice (Mark 14:32, Matt. 26:36) where Jesus prayed in lonely anguish just before his public betrayal and subsequent arrest there. Its precise location is not known. Mark and Matthew refer to a "place" called Gethsemane and imply it was near the Mount of Olives. Luke does not mention Gethsemane, suggesting instead that these events took place on the mount itself. Though John records neither name nor anguished prayer, he locates the betrayal in a "garden," which he locates across the Kidron Valley from Jerusalem and thus on the western slopes of the Mount of Olives. Today authenticity is claimed for several sites on or near this mountain, but none can trace their claim back earlier than the fourth century. Heb. 5:7–8 interprets the events in Gethsemane as proof of the "godly fear" and "obedience" that formed a prelude to Jesus' perfection. ***See also*** Jerusalem; Olives, Mount of.

J.M.B.

Gezer (ge'zuhr; also *Tell Jezer, Gazru*), a 33-acre mound, five miles south-southeast of Ramleh, one of the largest Bronze and Iron Age sites in ancient Palestine. It is situated on the last of the central foothills sloping down to the northern Shephelah, guarding the crossroads of the Via Maris and the trunk road to Jerusalem, at the entrance of the Valley of Aijalon.

Identified with biblical Gezer by C. Clermont-Ganneau in 1871, the site was the scene of the first modern excavations in Palestine, directed by R. A. S. Macalister for the Palestine Exploration Fund from 1902 to 1909. It was dug again briefly by A. Rowe in 1934. From 1964 to 1973 the first large-scale American excavations in the state of Israel were directed at Gezer by G. E. Wright, W. G. Dever, and J. D. Seger. These excavations, sponsored by the Hebrew Union College, Harvard University, and the Smithsonian Institution, pioneered in new stratigraphic and scientific methods.

Occupation began ca. 3500 B.C. in the Late Chalcolithic period, and Gezer continued as a small village throughout most of the Early Bronze Age until a gap ca. 2400–2000 B.C. Beginning in the subsequent Middle Bronze Age, Ge-

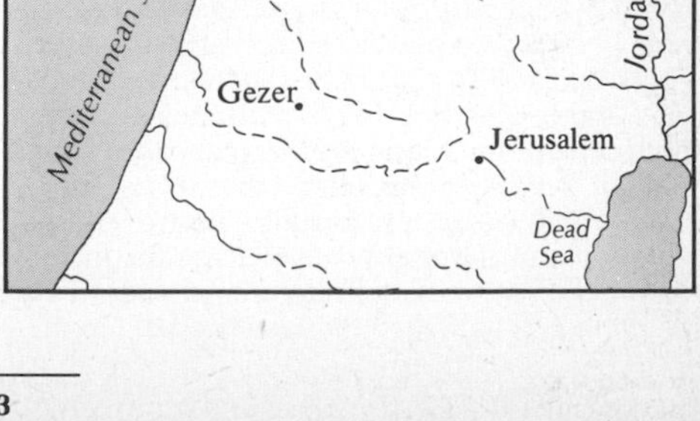

The six-chambered gate at Gezer with the entrance at the far end. Solomon similarly fortified Hazor and Megiddo (cf. 1 Kings 9:15–17).

zer gradually grew into the most massively fortified site in Palestine, with a three-entryway, two-story gate and an inner stone and mudbrick city wall more than 50 feet thick at one point. An outdoor alignment of ten large stelae may be a Canaanite "high place" of the type recalled in the Bible (e.g., 2 Kings 18:4; Jer. 32:35). Gezer was finally destroyed ca. 1482 B.C. by Pharaoh Thutmose III, whose inscription on the walls of the Temple of Karnak records this victory.

In the late Bronze Age, ca. 1500–1200 B.C., Gezer was largely under Egyptian domination. Ten letters from three successive kings of Gezer, written to the pharaohs of Egypt, were found in the famous archives at el-Amarna in Egypt. The outer city wall was built in the fourteenth century B.C., enclosing an even larger area, but Gezer declined toward the end of the thirteenth century B.C. It seems to have been partially destroyed in 1208 B.C. by Pharaoh Merneptah, whose well-known "Victory Stela" mentions both Israel and Gezer.

In the twelfth and eleventh centuries B.C. Gezer remained a Canaanite outpost. It was not taken by the incoming Israelites, although the king of Gezer was killed at the battle of Lachish (Josh. 10:31–33). Philistines, possibly Egyptian mercenaries, are attested by Philistine bichrome pottery, a granary, and several patrician houses.

After several destructions within the Philistine period, Gezer was partially destroyed in an Egyptian punitive raid ca. 950 B.C. The pharaoh then ceded it to King Solomon as a dowry in giving his daughter to the Israelite king in marriage. The historical note in 1 Kings 9:15–17, recording these events and Solomon's subsequent fortification of "Jerusalem and Hazor and Megiddo and Gezer," has been dramatically confirmed by archaeology. A magnificent four-entryway city gate and a double wall—identical to those at Megiddo and Hazor—have been brought to light immediately above a destruction layer.

Gezer remained an Israelite site, albeit rather unimportant, until its destruction by the Assyrians ca. 734 B.C., attested both by archaeological remains and a relief of Tiglath-pileser III (ca. 745–728 B.C.) depicting the siege of "Gazru." The site recovered, as several Neo-Assyrian cuneiform inscriptions found there indicate, but it was destroyed again by the Babylonians ca. 587 B.C.

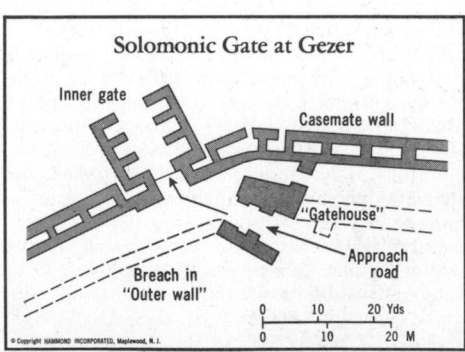

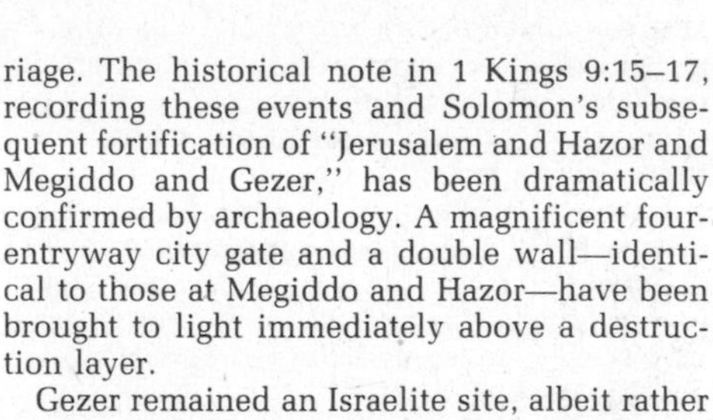

There are only scant remains from the Persian and early Hellenistic periods. In the Maccabean wars of the second century B.C., however, Gezer became the residence of Simon Maccabeus (RSV: "Gazara," 1 Macc. 13:43–48), and the city gate and walls were repaired for the last time. Gezer then fell into decline, and by the first century A.D. its lands had become a private holding of a certain "Alkios," as a series of boundary inscriptions shows. The Muslim *wêli* (shrine) was built in the sixteenth century A.D., and the modern Arab village of Abu Shusheh (now destroyed) was established in the nineteenth century A.D.

Bibliography

Dever, W. G. et al. "Excavations at Gezer." *The Biblical Archaeologist* 30 (1967): 47–62.

———. "Further Excavations at Gezer, 1967–71." *The Biblical Archaeologist* 34 (1971): 94–132.

———. *Gezer I. Preliminary Report of the 1964–66 Seasons.* Jerusalem: Hebrew Union College, 1974.

———. *Gezer IV. The 1969–71 Seasons in Field VI, the "Acropolis."* Jerusalem: Hebrew Union College, 1985.

W.G.D.

Ghor, the. ***See*** Jordan River, The.

ghost, a disembodied spirit. Belief in disembodied "shades" is attested both in biblical writings and in their cultural contexts. "Shades" (Heb. *rephaīm*) inhabit Sheol (Job 26:5; Ps. 88:10; Prov. 2:18; 9:18; 21:16; Isa. 14:9; 26:19; cf. 29:4, "a ghost [Heb. *ohb*] from the ground"). Samuel's shade is summoned up (1 Sam. 28:12–14). A nocturnal "spirit" (*ruach*) terrifies Eliphaz and he sees a "form" (Heb. *temunah*) (Job 4:15–16). Jesus' disciples, seeing him walking on water (Mark 6:49; Matt. 14:26) or risen (Luke 24:37), think it is a "ghost" (Gk. *phantasma*). ***See also*** Death; Magic and Divination; Sheol.

giant, a term used by the Greek translators of the LXX in the third and second centuries B.C. and by English translators until recently to render several different Hebrew words. Hebrew *gibbor*, one of the words translated "giant," is more accurately "mighty man, warrior," in Gen. 10:8, 9 and in Job 16:14, with the RSV and other modern translations. The RSV is cautious with another term, *Nephilim*, transliterating rather than translating it in its only two occurrences (Gen. 6:4; Num. 13:33). In Gen. 6:4 the Nephilim are the offspring of the sons of God and the daughters of men, part of the formidable race of humans before the Flood. Num. 13:33 says that the sons of Anak, ancient inhabitants of Canaan so huge that the Israelite spies felt like grasshoppers in comparison, were part of the Nephilim of olden times. Other passages also speak of the ancient inhabitants of Canaan, traditionally rendered as "giants" (Deut. 2:11, 20; 3:11, 13; Josh. 12:4; 13:12; 15:8; 17:15; 18:16). Another Hebrew word often rendered "giants" is *rephaim*. The precise meaning of the word is uncertain; it has been suggested that it means "the hale ones" and describes a group of gods, and sometimes humans, who are related to "The Hale One," El, the high god of Canaanite mythology. Biblical *rephaim* may well have been an elite group of warriors, men with sufficient wealth to provide chariots and other weapons of war for themselves; there is some evidence that the *rephaim* met together for feasting. The Israelites might have encountered these military guilds and attributed to them great size and power. At any rate it is clear that the people of the Bible, like many of their neighbors, believed that there were giants of old in the land. There is no archaeological evidence to support the view that the pre-Israelite inhabitants were giants; to attribute great size to them was probably a narrative way of expressing their military prowess.

R.J.C.

Gibbethon (gib'buh-thuhn; Heb., "mound" or "height"), a city originally assigned to Dan and later given to the Levites (Josh. 19:44; 21:23), although by the time of King Asa of Judah (ca. 900 B.C.) it was in Philistine hands (1 Kings 15:27). It was the site of the assassination of Nadab, king of Israel (Northern Kingdom) by his general Baasha during an attempt to take the city from the Philistines (1 Kings 15:27). It was also the site twenty-four years later of a revolt against Zimri by his general Omni during another siege of the city (1 Kings 16:15). It is identified with modern Tel el-Malat, about four miles northeast of Joppa, although the location is not certain.

D.R.B.

Gibeah (gib'ee-ah), a Hebrew word meaning "hill," in contrast to "mountain." As a name it is attached in OT tradition to a site in Benjamin, the home of Saul and center for his career as king (1 Sam. 10:26). Under the modern name Tell el Ful the site, located about five miles north of Jerusalem, reveals a succession of occupations that, at least in part, corresponds with the OT's account of Saul's residence. The earliest relevant level, destroyed by fire in the twelfth century B.C., provides the context for a more extensive and fortified construction from the Early Iron Age. The most important building from this level is an eleventh-century structure, a fortress with casemate wall and corner tower, perhaps the "rustic palace" of King Saul. Successive constructions suggest that some violent destruction occurred, with rebuilding in more modest quality. The site was finally abandoned.

In the biblical tradition, Gibeah was the location for Saul's association with a band of prophets (1 Sam. 10:1–10), an event related to selection of Saul as king. From this site Saul engineered a liberation of Jabesh-gilead from the Ammonites (1 Sam. 11:1–11) as well as a contest of strength with the Philistines (1 Sam. 14). From this site, Saul sought help in his search for David. Ironically, some of David's associates were from this site (2 Sam. 23:29).

The most important tradition about Gibeah unrelated to Saul is the account of inhospitable reception for an Ephraimite, including the rape and murder of his concubine, and the ensuing war between Ephraim and Benjamin (Judg. 19–20). Perhaps the parallel between this violation of the rules of hospitality and the notorious violation of the same principle in Sodom (Gen. 19) points to a folk tradition about the evil quality of Gibeah's residents (including Saul?). Perhaps use of the word in reference to the site where David discovered the Ark, in preparation for establishing Jerusalem as the religious center of his kingdom, should be taken as a place name, not simply a noun (2 Sam. 6:3). Such a combination would reflect an attempt in tradition to unify David and the circles associated with Saul. It could also suggest that the Ark functions as a symbol of unity between the traditions about Saul and those about David. ***See also*** Saul.

G.W.C.

Gibeath (gib'ee-ath), the KJV term for Hebrew spelling of Gibeah in Josh. 18:28.

Gibeon (gib'ee-uhn), a town identified with modern el-Jib, five and a half miles (9 km.) northwest of Jerusalem. The identification was made when excavations there from 1956 to 1962 by J. Pritchard uncovered over fifty jar handles of the seventh and sixth centuries B.C., many of which were inscribed with the name Gibeon. Towns associated with the Gibeonite enclave were Chephirah, Beeroth, and Kiriath-jearim (Josh. 9:17).

During the conquest of Canaan the Gibeonites, who are described as Hivites (Josh. 9:7) or Amorites (2 Sam. 21:2), tricked the Israelites into making a treaty not to harm them. It was upheld, but the Gibeonites were reduced to becoming hewers of wood and drawers of water (Josh. 9:3–27). In an ensuing battle near Gibeon (Josh. 10:1–14), the Israelites defeated a coalition of Canaanite kings led by Adoni-zedek of Jerusalem. Although Gibeon figures prominently in these narratives of the conquest, an event often dated to the thirteenth century B.C. (the Late Bronze Age), no evidence for a settlement at el-Jib during that period has been found.

Later (eleventh century B.C.) King Saul broke the treaty with the Gibeonites when he attempted to annihilate them, an act that caused famine during David's reign. The Gibeonites gained revenge by impaling seven of Saul's sons on the mountain of Yahweh (2 Sam. 21:1–15), possibly the high place at Gibeon. At the beginning of his reign Solomon traveled to Gibeon to sacrifice at what was called the great high place (1 Kings 3:4–15). The great stone at Gibeon (2 Sam. 20:8) may be associated with this high place.

The spiral staircase cut along the edge of the shaft of the pool of Gibeon becomes a tunnel at the bottom and provided access to the water table during times of siege.

In the time of King David young warriors led by Joab and Abner fought on the edge of a pool at Gibeon (2 Sam. 2:12–17). A circular shaft identified as the pool was found cut into bedrock at a point immediately inside the city wall. It is approximately 36 feet (11 m.) in diameter and 36 feet (11 m.) deep. Cut along its edge is a stairway that spirals down to the bottom of the shaft. Thereafter the stairway continues to descend in the form of a tunnel, to a room whose floor is 1.5 feet (.5 m.) below the modern water level. The purpose of such shafts was to provide access to the water table or springs from inside the city during times of siege. It was still a landmark in the early sixth century B.C. (Jer. 41:12).

During the eighth and seventh centuries B.C. there was a winery, attested by inscribed and stamped handles of wine jars and clusters of rock-cut pits that functioned as wine cellars. Over fifty tombs were found dating from the third to the first millennia B.C., attesting to the length of time there were settlements on this site.

T.L.M.

Gideon (gid'ee-uhn; from the Heb. root meaning "to cut off"; also called Jerubaal, Judg. 6:32), the son of Joash the Abiezrite of the town of Ophrah in the tribal area of Manasseh. Gideon is counted among the major judges although the narrative describing his exploits (Judg. 6:11–8:32) does not refer to him as such.

There is scholarly disagreement concerning the sources of the Gideon story and their dates of composition. Nonetheless, the placement of Gideon after Deborah appears logical, since Deborah's victory over the Canaanites may have opened the door to incursions by desert nomads. These incursions were common in times of political and military weakness. The story of Gideon is prefaced by the camel-mounted invasions of the Midianites, Amalekites, and "children of the East" who looted the Israelite crops and animals (6:1–6).

It is at this time of dire circumstances and impoverishment (6:2, 6, 11) that Gideon receives his call to action by an angel (6:11–23). His hesitancy (6:15–21) is reminiscent of the call to Moses (Exod. 3–4), while his confrontation of the divine "face-to-face" (6:22) recalls Jacob's wrestling with the angel (Gen. 32:30; thereby, the author indicates to the reader that Gideon will be one of the great heroes of Israel). The building of the altar (6:24) indicates Gideon's preparedness. His first act is a religious revolt—an attack on the local Baal-Asherah cult (6:25–32), which is deemed to be at the root of Israel's suffering (6:1, 7–10).

Battle Against the Midianites: After the initial success, Gideon began preparation for his battle against the Midianites, which occupies the main body of the story (6:34–8:21). He gathered together men from the tribes of Manasseh, Asher, Zebulun, and Naphtali (6:36–40). In order to emphasize God's might (and not the people's), Gideon's army was pared down from thirty-three thousand (7:3) to ultimately only three hundred—the most courageous and able warriors (7:2–8). That night Gideon and a servant gathered intelligence information (by way of a dream interpretation, 7:8–15) at the Midianite camp at En-dor between the hill of Moreh and Mt. Tabor (7:1; Ps. 83:11). That same night, using psychological warfare, surprise, and darkness, Gideon and his band attacked the Midianites with maximum effect, causing them to flee toward the Jordan Valley (7:16–22). Soldiers from the tribes of Naphtali, Ephraim, Asher, and Manasseh (the thousands sent back to lie in ambush?) cut the Midianites down at the Jordan fords and two Midianite princes, Oreb and Zeeb, were killed (7:23–25; Ps. 83:12–13). After calming down the Ephraimites who complained of not being included in the initial preparations (8:1–3), Gideon and his three hundred pursued the kings of Midian, Zebah, and Zalmunna beyond the Jordan. On the way, Gideon requested food for his men from Succoth and Penuel but was rebuffed (8:4–9). At Karkor, once again using stealth and surprise, Gideon fell upon the remnants of the Midianites (8:10, fifteen thousand out of a hundred and twenty thousand!) and captured the two kings (8:10–13). After exacting punishment upon Succoth and Penuel (8:14–17), Gideon, acting as the blood-avenger for his brothers' deaths, killed Zebah and Zalmunna (8:15–21). The fame of this victory over the Midianites is attested by its reference in other Biblical sources (Isa. 9:3; 10:26; Ps. 83:10–12; cf. 1 Sam. 12:11; Heb. 11:12).

Gideon's humility (cf. 6:15) and religiosity are evinced by his refusal to accept hereditary rulership over Israel with the immortal words, "I will not rule over you, and my son will not rule over you; the Lord will rule over you" (8:23). This incident illustrates the need for a stable leadership that eventually culminated in the monarchy as well as the view of the religious elite during the period of the judges that Israel could have only one king who was the permanent ruler—God; any attempt to create a human kingship was perceived as a revolt and rejection of God (1 Sam. 8:7). Despite Gideon's rejection, after his death his son Abimelech tried to take the kingship for himself (Judg. 9).

One element of Gideon's religiosity is criticized: his fashioning of an ephod out of the spoil of the golden earrings (cf. Exod. 32:2–3), which became the people's fetish (8:24–27). The editor's conclusion mentions Gideon's seventy sons and his burial in the crypt of his father (8:29–32). ***See also*** Abimelech; Chronology, Old Testament; Jotham; Judges, The Book of; Midianites. J.U.

gier (gī′uhr) **eagle** (KJV; RSV: "vulture," Lev. 11:18, or "carrion vulture," Deut. 14:17), a bird considered unclean by the Hebrews.

gifts of the Spirit. ***See*** Spiritual Gifts.

Gihon (gī′hahn; Heb., "a bursting forth"). **1** The second of the four rivers flowing "out of Eden to water the garden. . . . it is the one which flows around the whole land of Cush" (Gen. 2:10, 13). Once Gihon was equated with the Nile on the assumption that Cush meant Abyssinia, but it almost certainly indicates a now unidentifiable irrigation channel in southern Iraq, "Cush" being the land of the Kassites.

2 A pulsating spring in Jerusalem, south of the temple area on the west side of the Kidron Valley, called in Arabic by the Muslims Ain Umm el-Daraj, "spring of the steps," and by Christians Ain Sitti Maryam, "the Virgin's Fountain." Because of the steepness of the slope the spring was outside the town walls at the summit, and although water was normally obtained by carrying jars down to it, perhaps using donkeys, in times of siege the jars could apparently be lowered down a vertical shaft ("Warren's Shaft"). Another, less deep, shaft exists, which was perhaps used at an earlier date when the water table may have been higher. Probably Warren's Shaft was the one by which David was able to capture Jerusalem (2 Sam. 5:8).

Gihon is Jerusalem's only immediate source of water and could support a population of about twenty-five hundred. As were a great many other springs in a land where water is often scarce, the Gihon fountain was evidently a sacred place, and for this reason Solomon (and probably also later rulers) was anointed king there (1 Kings 1:32–40). That anointing was accomplished to thwart Adonijah, who had offered a sacrifice at En-rogel, a spring somewhat further down the valley (1 Kings 1:

9–10). Later in the monarchy the supply of water from Gihon seems to have been supplemented by water brought from a greater distance along a conduit, perhaps to the "upper pool," where Isaiah met and rebuked King Ahaz (Isa. 7:3).

Hezekiah, who succeeded Ahaz, was confronted by the danger of Assyrian invasion and therefore sought not only to prevent the invaders from obtaining water in the vicinity of Jerusalem (2 Chron. 32:4) but to ensure the security of the city's own supply. This he did by means of his celebrated tunnel, 1,750 feet (533 m.) long, leading from Gihon to the Pool of Solomon, then possibly an underground cistern. The tunnel was carved from both ends simultaneously and follows a curiously winding course, perhaps to permit cutting a vertical shaft from inside the city to reach the water in a crisis. ***See also*** Adonijah; Ahaz; En-rogel; Hezekiah; Kidron; Siloam Inscription; Solomon. D.B.

Gilboa (gil'boh-uh), modern Jebel Fuqu'ah, a hill opposite the Hill of Moreh. Together Gilboa and Moreh guard the eastern pass from the Plain of Esdraelon into the Valley of Jezreel, the main access from the coastal plain to the Jordan Valley. Gilboa rises to a height of 1,696 feet above sea level, but plunges abruptly 2,000 feet below on the east to the Jordan. Its more gradual western slopes are probably where Saul fought his last battle with the Philistines: his three sons were killed and Saul took his own life after he was seriously wounded (1 Sam. 31). In his lament over Jonathan David levels a curse upon the scene of his death (2 Sam. 1:22). ***See also*** Esdraelon; Jezreel; Moreh. N.L.L.

Gilead (gil'ee-ad), a region in Transjordan (modern Jordan) from the Arnon to the Yarmuk rivers, between Bashan and Moab. Its name, which in Hebrew means "rugged," describes it well: it is mountainous, and in antiquity was densely forested (see Jer. 22:6). The major trade route in Transjordan, the King's Highway, which went from the Gulf of Aqaba to Damascus, passed through Gilead, and the inhabitants of the region thus controlled this important thoroughfare. Southern Gilead (from the Arnon to the Jabbok) was under the control of Sihon, the king of the Amorites in the Mosaic period (thirteenth century B.C.). It was assigned to the Israelite tribes of Reuben and Gad in the division of the land, and later corresponded approximately to the kingdoms of the Ammonites, with their capital at Rabbath-ammon (modern Amman), and Moab. This area was especially well suited for herding (Num. 32:1; Song of Sol. 6:5). Northern Gilead (from the Jabbok to the Yarmuk) was assigned to Manasseh, and remained under Israelite control until the Assyrian conquest (721 B.C.), although both the Ammonites to the south and the Aramaeans to the north occupied it at times (see Judg. 10:8; 1 Kings 22:3; Amos 1:3). In the Persian period (ca. 538–333 B.C.) Gilead was a separate province, and in the Roman period Gilead was subdivided into the districts of Perea and the area controlled by the Decapolis. Major cities in Gilead include Heshbon and Rabbath-ammon (later Philadelphia) in the south, and Pella, Gerasa, Gadara, Abila, Jabesh-gilead, and Ramoth-gilead in the north. The exact composition of the proverbial "balm of Gilead" (Jer. 8:22; cf. Gen. 37:25) has not been definitely established. ***See also*** Cities; Perea. M.D.C.

Gilgal (gil'gahl; Heb., "circle," probably of stones), the name of several towns in the OT, at least three of which have been identified with some certainty. **1** Gilgal between Jericho and the Jordan, the Israelites' first encampment after crossing the Jordan (Josh. 3–4), which became Joshua's base of operations. This Gilgal is probably modern Khirbet el-Mafjir, about one and a quarter miles from ancient Jericho, or possibly Khirbet en-Nitleh about two miles southeast of Jericho. In the tribal period and the early monarchy (thirteenth-eleventh centuries B.C.) it became an important political, religious, and military center, especially for the tribe of Benjamin. It was one of the places visited by Samuel on his yearly circuit (1 Sam. 7:16). A number of the early traditions about Saul are set here. It was a rallying point in Saul's campaigns against the Philistines (1 Sam. 13:4–7). It is here that he was affirmed by the people as king (1 Sam. 11:14–15) and it was here also that the kingship was taken from him (1 Sam. 13:8–15) for presuming on Samuel's priestly prerogatives. This Gilgal is denounced by the eighth-century prophets as the site of a national sanctuary under royal patronage with a corrupt sacrificial cult (Hos. 4:15; 9:15; 12:11; Amos 4:4; 5:5; Mic. 6:5). **2** Gilgal of Elijah and Elisha (2 Kings 2:1–4; 4:38), probably the present village of Khirbet 'Alyata about seven miles north of Bethel. **3** Gilgal near Dor mentioned in a list of conquered Canaanite kings in Josh. 12:23 (RSV: "Galilii"). Probably the modern village of Jiljulieh, about five miles north of Antipatris *(Ras el-'Ain)*. F.S.F.

girdle. ***See*** Apron; Dress.

Girgashites (gihr'gush-īts), one of the peoples whom God displaced for the Israelites at the time of Joshua (Gen. 15:21; Josh. 3:10). According to the genealogy in Gen. 10:16 these nations are the offspring of Canaan. The personal name Girgishi is also known from Ugarit. Some texts of the NT include a reference to the Gergesenes at Mark 5:1 and its parallels.

Gittite (git'tīt), someone who lives in or is from Gath. Gath was one of the five major cities of the Philistines located in the coastal plain of southwestern Judah. The giant Goliath and his brother Lahmi were Gittites (2 Sam. 21:19; 1 Chron. 20:5), as were Obed-edom, whose house was the temporary resting place of the Ark of the Covenant (2 Sam. 6:10–11; 1 Chron. 13:13), and Ittai, the refugee who joined David and became one of his military commanders (2 Sam. 15:19–22; 18:2). ***See also*** Gath; Philistines.

Gittith, a Hebrew word appearing in the phrase *al ha-gittith.* Of uncertain significance, it appears at the beginning of Psalms 8, 81, and 84. It is often left untranslated ("according to the Gittith"), though some translators have sought to explain the term via the Hebrew *gath* "(wine) press" or the Philistine city of Gath. Like the similar (and equally mysterious) phrase *al hasheminith* ("on the eighth"), this phrase has been taken to refer to a musical mode, such as exist in traditional Arabic music, or to a particular musical instrument, or even to a particular well-known song that served as a contrafact for the psalms in question. ***See also*** Psalms, The.
J.L.K.

glass. ***See*** Mirrors.

gleaning. ***See*** Farming.

glede (gleed; KJV; RSV: "buzzard," Deut. 14:13), a word derived from an Old English root meaning "to glide," it applies especially to the red kite, *Milvus milvus.*

glory, an important theological term in both the OT and the NT. The most important Hebrew word for glory, *kabod,* means "weight" or "importance." Thus, to have glory is to be weighty or important to oneself or others. In the OT, glory is applied to humans, showing their significance in the world (Job 19:9; Prov. 16:31; 20:29; Isa. 8:7). Frequently, it is also applied to God. God's glory is particularly God's visible manifestation to humans (Num. 16:19, 42; Ps. 102:16; Ezek. 10:4). At the giving of the law at Mount Sinai, God's glory appears as or in a cloud and as fire (Exod. 16:10; 24:16–17). It is associated with the tabernacle and the Temple (Exod. 40:34; Num. 20:6; Pss. 24:7–10; 78:60–61). God's glory frequently appears in Ezekiel's visions (Ezek. 10:4; 28:22; 43:2–5). Finally, glory may refer to God's future eschatological appearance (Isa. 4:5; 60:1–2). The appropriate human response to God is to ascribe glory to him (Pss. 22:23; 29:2; 86:9; Isa. 66:5).

The NT continues OT meanings of glory. Occasionally, it is applied to humans (Luke 12:27; John 7:18). More often, it is applied to God: God's glory is seen (Luke 2:9; John 11:40; Acts 7:55; Rev. 15:8). People are to give glory to God (Acts 12:23; 1 Cor. 10:31). The NT also extends OT usages referring to God to include Christ: glory is applied to the risen Christ (1 Cor. 2:8; Heb. 2:7, 9; 1 Pet. 1:11; Rev. 5:12–13) and to Christ's Second Coming as Son of man (Matt. 25:31; Mark 8:38; cf. Titus 2:13). The latter often draws on the OT image of clouds (Matt. 24:30; Luke 21:27).

The Gospel of John develops furthest the notion of glory as applied to Christ's human existence. God's glory appears in Jesus (John 13:31; 17:5). Christ is the Word incarnate: "we have beheld his glory, glory as of the only Son from the Father" (John 1:14). Glory is revealed through Christ's miracles (John 2:11; 11:4). It is also closely associated with his death as his hour of glorification (John 12:23; 17:1). Finally, both the Gospel of John and Paul extend the OT eschatological hope of seeing God's glory to the hope of participating in it (John 17:22; Rom. 5:2). ***See also*** Shekinah.
J.D.

glossolalia. ***See*** Tongues, Speaking with.

gnat, a nonspecific term referring to gnats, lice, mosquitos, or sand flies. It probably includes all such blood-sucking, two-winged insects. In Exod. 8:16–18 gnats are the third plague upon the Egyptians. In Matt. 23:24 scribes and Pharisees are charged with straining out the gnat and swallowing the camel, that is, paying close scrutiny to details of ritual impurity while neglecting the ethical demands of justice, mercy, and faith.

Gnosticism, a generic term for a variety of religious movements of the first centuries of the Christian era. Although the theology, ritual practice, and ethics of these groups differed considerably, all purported to offer salvation from the oppressive bonds of material existence through *gnōsis,* or "knowledge." Such knowledge was diverse, although it regularly dealt with the intimate relationship of the self to the transcendent source of all being, and this knowledge was often conveyed by a revealer figure.

What is known about Gnosticism traditionally depended upon reports in the church fathers such as Irenaeus, Hippolytus, Tertullian, Origen, and Epiphanius, who were opponents of Christian Gnostic teachers. Since the eighteenth century, several original Gnostic works have been discovered, including Codex Askew, Codex Bruce, the Berlin Gnostic Codes and, most recently, the Nag Hammadi collection.

The relationship between Gnosticism and early Christianity has been a controversial issue. Against the patristic view that Gnosticism was a Christian heresy begun by Simon Magus, many modern scholars have held that it was originally an independent movement. Earlier expressions of this opinion, which posited at the core of Gnosticism a redeemed-redeemer myth of possible Iranian origin, have proven questionable.

Primarily on the basis of the Nag Hammadi evidence, many today hold that Gnosticism first emerged in the late Hellenistic or early Imperial period among speculative and syncretistic Jews.

By the second century, Gnosticism achieved its classical form among both Christian and non-Christian exponents. One example is found in the teachings of the Valentinians, Christian Gnostics who held that the world emerged from a primordial pair, or "syzygy," Depth and Silence, from which emanated a complex spiritual world or "Pleroma." One element or "aeon" in that world, Sophia, fell and produced from her passion and repentance the psychic and material realms of existence. In a movement that typifies the whole soteriological process, Christ came to restore her to her original condition. Humanity is composed of the results of this process, having spiritual, psychic, and material components. The *gnōsis* provided by Jesus, a being separate from Christ, awakens the awareness of the spiritual component of humanity about its essential identity with the Godhead and leads to ultimate restoration.

Despite its suppression by ecclesiastical authorities in the third and fourth centuries, Gnosticism continued in the guise of Manichaeism and Mandaeism and in various medieval speculative movements. ***See also*** Gospel of Thomas, The; Nag Hammadi; Simon Magus.

H.W.A.

goad, an implement used to control oxen. Acquaintance with ox goads in daily life (1 Sam. 13:21) gave rise to figurative speech, where the teachings of the wise were said to stimulate thought in others (Eccles. 12:11), although these words of wisdom prodded thoughtful persons. Refusing to acknowledge the obvious or to act on one's insight constituted kicking against the goads (KJV: "pricks"; Acts 26:14). At least one judge, Shamgar, is reputed to have used an ox goad as a weapon (Judg. 3:31).

goat, a ruminant mammal related to the sheep. The goat *(Capra hircus)* is one of the most versatile of domestic livestock animals. It has always been of special importance in the Near East, to whose arid climate it is excellently adapted. Goat bones attributed to domesticated animals are the most frequently found faunal remains on the Early Neolithic sites of the southern Levant, as at Jericho, Beidha, and Ain Ghazal. They testify that humans started herding goats in this area about 9,000 years ago. At the beginning goats were kept mainly for their meat, but it is thought that by the Chalcolithic period (ca. 4000 B.C.) they were also used for milk, with hair and skin being useful by-products.

Goats are very hardy beasts that can live off shrubs and the scanty vegetation of the desert, thereby utilizing areas that are useless for agriculture. Even today they form the basis for the nomadic existence of many bedouins, who live in tents woven from black goat hair, eat goat milk, butter, yoghurt, and cheese, sell goat meat, and use goat skins as containers. It seems that the bedouin life style has hardly changed since biblical times, since numerous references are made in the Bible to the same usages of the goat. Lev. 7:23 and Deut. 14:4 mention its meat, while Deut. 32:14 and Prov. 27:27 report that it provided milk. Gen. 21:14 and Josh 9:4 refer to goatskin bottles. 1 Sam. 19:13 implies that goat hair was processed into fabric. The roof of the tabernacle was made of goat hair (Exod. 26:7; 36:14–15).

The goat was also of importance as a sacrificial animal. Male animals were preferred (Lev. 1:10; 22:19), but sometimes female goats were demanded (Lev. 4:28; 5:6). The efficacy of such sacrifices was rejected by the early Christian community, however (Heb. 9:12–13, 19; 10:4). That they were nevertheless common in Palestine at that time is attested by Jesus' reference to them in one of his parables (Matt. 25:32–33).

I.U.K.

God, a general term for the deity (or, in the plural, deities). In the Bible, the word is used to refer both to the deity worshiped in the Judeo-Christian tradition (God) and to deities worshiped by other peoples (god or gods).

In the OT: In the OT, the word "God" most often translates the Hebrew *El* (or the plural form, *Elohim*), the general Semitic term for deity which is probably derived from a root denoting power or strength. Although Israel's faith apparently emerged from a polytheistic environment as a strong henotheism (i.e., worship of only one among a plurality of deities) and evolved into a highly developed ethical monotheism, the frequently used plural form should not be understood as a residue from an earlier period. The form is the plural of majesty (magnitude) and a sign of honor paid to the Deity.

The authors of the Bible do not concern themselves with abstract questions of definition (i.e., about the existence or nature of God) but rather portray God through a series of images or incidents in which God becomes the subject of the narrative rather than an object of thought. In the OT God is presented as the Creator and Sustainer of the world, who enters into covenantal relationship with a chosen people, Israel, and who guides the history of that people toward a redemptive goal. Although masculine images for God dominate (e.g., king, judge, father, brother, shepherd, etc.), it must be recognized that feminine images are also frequently used to describe God's activity. Among these are images related to feminine anatomy (e.g., womb and breasts) and feminine function (e.g., conception, pregnancy, childbirth, maternal nurture, etc.).

It may be suggested, therefore, that any comprehensive understanding of the way in which God is portrayed in the OT must be grounded in an equally comprehensive understanding of Israel's history, since history is seen as the primary locus of God's self-revelation. In that history, the events surrounding the revelation of the divine name, the Exodus, and the establishment of the covenant at Sinai occupy a special place. In these incidents, many characteristics of God, more fully developed in other narratives, are illustrated. For example, the transcendent Deity, who controls both nature and history, draws near to Israel in a highly personal, even intimate, way. In the covenant, the past beneficence of God and a concern for all people are connected with an emphasis on the holiness, justice, righteousness, and wrath of a Deity who alone is to be worshiped. It is, indeed, the story of this Deity, first known only partially, then by name (Yahweh) as the God of Israel (henotheism), and ultimately as the one true God (radical monotheism), that unfolds in the pages of the OT.

In the NT: In the NT, the word "God" translates the Greek *theos*, also a general term for deity and used in the Septuagint to translate *El* and *Elohim*. Since much has been written drawing sharp contrasts between "the God of the OT" and "the God of the NT," it may be well to comment that in most respects there is a remarkable consistency in the portrayal of God throughout the Bible. Certainly, there is no solid ground for contrasting a God of wrath (OT) with a God of mercy (NT), for mercy and judgment are among the characteristics of God in both Testaments. The major difference is that the NT reflects the conceptual world of the late Hellenistic and early Roman periods (i.e., 100 B.C. to A.D. 100), a later stage in intellectual history than that of the OT. Further, belief in the incarnation substantially changes the understanding of God presented in the NT. For Christian thought, the primary locus of God's self-revelation is not in the events of the history of a people but rather in the person of Jesus Christ (e.g., Matt. 1:23; John 14:9; 20:28–29). For this reason, the dominant image used to refer to God is the language of familial intimacy: *Abba*, Father.

Although reference to God as Father is not unique to Christianity (it is found in the OT, in late Judaism, and in other religions), it may be suggested that the doctrine of the incarnation brought new meaning to this familiar terminology. It seems likely that Christian use of this image originated in the teaching and practice of Jesus and was enriched as the first stages of trinitarian thought developed during the first century A.D. In the NT, although there are passages stressing the unity of Father and Son, a clear distinction is also drawn between the two. As in the OT, there is a balance between immanence and transcendence. While drawing near in the incarnation, God remains the Deity who alone is worshiped as Creator and Ruler of the world. ***See also*** Abba; El; El Shaddai; Holy Spirit, The; Incarnation; Jesus Christ; Names of God in the New Testament; Names of God in the Old Testament; Revelation; Son of God; Trinity, The.

T.R.W.L.

God, Kingdom of. ***See*** Kingdom of God.

God, names of in the New Testament. ***See*** Names of God in the New Testament.

God, names of in the Old Testament. ***See*** Names of God in the Old Testament.

godlessness, a mode of thinking or being that excludes God from life and ignores or perhaps even deliberately violates God's laws and commandments. There are, of course, numerous characteristics that can demonstrate the godlessness of a person, including worthlessness, ruthlessness, wickedness, pride, impiety, and the like.

In the KJV, the various Hebrew and Greek designations for "godless" or "ungodly" are frequently translated as "hypocrite." Hypocrisy was, indeed, one of the manifestations of godlessness, but the state should not be understood as identical only with hypocrisy. Basically, the godless or ungodly person is one who lives, acts, and thinks as though God could be ignored or spurned. For some illustrations of the varieties of godlessness, see Deut. 8:11–20; Job 8:13; Ps. 119:51; Rom. 1:18–32; 4:5; 5:6; 1 Tim. 1:9; 4:7; 6:20; 2 Tim. 2:16; 2 Pet. 2:5–6; and Jude 4, 15. ***See also*** Evil; Fool, Foolishness, Folly; Hypocrisy; Sin.

J.M.E.

godliness, godly, the English translation of a Greek root (also translated as "religion, religious," "piety, pious," "devotion, devout," or "worship, worshipper") common in the NT world to describe respect for Greek and Roman gods and for the orders of society. This may be why the term seldom appears either in the Septuagint (LXX) or in the NT. Biblical writers prefer such words as "righteousness," "faith," "steadfastness," "holiness," etc., to describe the faith and life pleasing to God. In the OT, true godliness or piety usually finds expression as covenant loyalty, steadfastness, faithfulness, kindness, goodness, or holiness: "Help, LORD, for there is no longer any that is godly; for the faithful have vanished . . ." (Ps. 12:1); "But know that the LORD has set apart the godly for himself" (Ps. 4:3); God desires "godly offspring" (Mal. 2:15). Faithfulness to God is expressed in faithfulness to covenant partners.

In Acts 3:12, Peter denies that "our own power and godliness" (RSV: "piety") healed a lame man. Only in the later Letters of the NT (the Pastorals and 2 Peter) does the term occur as a description of Christian life, and then it is linked with such characteristic biblical words as "righteousness," "faith," "love," "steadfastness," and "gentleness" (1 Tim. 6:11). Similarly, 2 Pet. 1:5–7 links godliness with "faith," "virtue," "knowledge," "self-control," "steadfastness," "brotherly affection," and "love." The adjectival form of the root, sometimes rendered as "devout" (e.g., Acts 10:2, 7), is, at times, linked more specifically with Christian behavior: "the grace of God has appeared . . . training us . . . to live sober, upright, and godly lives in this world, awaiting our blessed hope" (Titus 2:11–13). Godliness is more than correct behavior; it is possible to have "a form of godliness" (RSV: "form of religion") while denying its power (2 Tim. 3:5). That power is found in Christ; thus, 1 Tim. 3:16 calls an early confession of faith "the mystery of godliness" (RSV: "the mystery of our religion"). Only through Christ is true godliness possible, for God's power "has granted to us all things that pertain to life and godliness" (2 Pet. 1:3). ***See also*** Religion, Religious; Worship. J.F.J.

Gog, historically probably Gyges, a seventh-century B.C. king of Lydia. Whatever his origin, he has been transformed in Ezekiel 38–39 into an apocalyptic figure who marches from the north (Ezek. 38:6, 15; 39:2) and ravages Israel before being destroyed by God (Ezek. 38:19–22; 39:3–5). The sources for the description of Gog's attack and defeat include Jeremiah's "enemy from the north" (Jer. 1:14; 4:6; 6:1, 22; 10:22; 13:20) and the Isaianic motif of the destruction of Israel's foes on the mountains of Israel (Isa. 14:24–25; 17:12–14; 31:8–9). Gog reappears in the NT (Rev. 20:18–20), paired with Magog; in Ezek. 38:2 Magog is probably equivalent to a phrase in the Akkadian language, *mat Gog* ("land of Gog"). ***See also*** Ezekiel, The Book of. J.S.K.

Golan (goh'lahn; Heb., "circuit"?), part of the plateau of Bashan between Mt. Hermon and the Wadi el-Yarmuk east of the Jordan River. It was called Gaulanitis by the historian Josephus. Golan is also the name of a city of refuge in Manasseh assigned to the levitical family of Gershon (Deut. 4:43; Josh. 20:8; 21:27; 1 Chron. 6:71) in this region. ***See also*** Bashan.

gold, the precious metal most often named in the Bible (385 times). It was imported from the yet to be located sites named Uphaz (Jer. 10:9), Raamah (Ezek. 27:22), Sheba (1 Kings 10:2), Havilah (Gen. 2:11), and Ophir (1 Chron. 29:4; 2 Chron. 8:18). Occasionally gold was acquired as booty (Exod. 12:35; Judg. 8:26) but more often through commercial enterprises (1 Kings 10:14–24).

Ancient sites outside Palestine proper knew of gold and early learned to work it beautifully,

Above: A gold-leaf figurine, probably of the Canaanite goddess Astarte, found at the excavations at Gezer dates to the sixteenth century B.C. *Below:* Gold cup from the royal tomb at Ur, third millennium B.C.

as the excavations at Ur in ancient Sumer demonstrate (ca. 2500 B.C.). There the archaeologist Woolley found fluted vases, bowls of pure gold, intricately fashioned ornaments, and 9 yards of gold ribbon in a headdress. At Ebla (modern Tell Mardikh; ca. 3200 B.C.) in Syria excavators found objects of gold such as a ceremonial hammer and wooden frames overlaid with gold. Also at Ebla commercial texts report a caste or guild of smiths including goldsmiths. Precious metals measured in bars with specific weights given in minas (a mina equaled 47 grams) were held in an Eblaite storehouse. One text showed the tribute paid by the kingdom of Mari to include 134.26 minas of gold. More well-known and much later is the golden treasure of Egypt's Tutankhamen (mid-fourteenth century B.C.).

The Bible employs thirteen different words for gold in a variety of forms and usages. Jewelry made of gold includes necklaces (Song of Sol. 1: 11), rings (James 2:2), and other unspecified items (Exod. 3:22).

In public worship gold played a part in both idolatry such as the calf fashioned by Aaron (Exod. 32:2–4; cf. Deut. 29:17; 1 Kings 12:28; Isa. 2:20; Rev. 9:20), and in the worship of God in both the tabernacle and later in the Solomonic Temple in Jerusalem. The Ark was covered with gold (Exod. 25:11). Most of the furniture was gold-plated, while the vessels and other articles of pure gold included the high priest's clothing, crown, ephod, and breastplate (Exod. 39:2–30). In Solomon's Temple the entire inner sanctuary was overlaid with gold, as were the cherubim, carved palm trees, and flowers (1 Kings 6:14–31).

While valued as a standard of importance (Isa. 60:17; Hos. 2:8; 1 Pet. 1:18), gold is less worthy than wisdom (Job 28:15, 17; Prov. 3:14; 8:10; 16: 16), faith (1 Pet. 1:7), and knowledge (Pss. 19:10; 119:72; Prov. 20:15). One should not put one's trust in gold (Job 31:24) for it can become a stumbling block (Ezek. 7:19) and finally is of no value at all (Isa. 46:6; Ps. 135:15; 1 Tim. 6:9). Nevertheless, the Bible recognizes its value as a gift since one of the Wise Men laid gold before the infant Jesus (Matt. 2:11); elders will wear golden crowns (Rev. 4:4); metaphorically gold is spiritual wealth (Rev. 3:18); and the new Jerusalem will be constructed of pure gold (Rev. 21:18).
R.A.C.

Golden Rule, a modern term (first attested in English in the seventeenth century as "golden law") for a saying of Jesus regarded as of inestimable ("golden") and universal importance: "Whatever you wish that persons would do to you, do so to them" (Matt. 7:12; Luke 6:31). Similar statements, in negative form, are found in Judaism and Confucianism.

Golgotha (gahl'guh-thuh). ***See*** Calvary.

Goliath (guh-lī'eth), a Philistine champion from Gath. He was defeated by David in single combat in the Valley of Elah according to 1 Samuel 17, where the might of the seasoned Philistine warrior is contrasted with the vulnerability of the callow Israelite shepherd, who fells his heavily armed opponent with a sling stone. According to 2 Sam. 21:19, however, Goliath was defeated by Elhanan, one of David's warriors. Perhaps the name of the Philistine slain by David was not given in an older tradition, and the name of Elhanan's victim was substituted for the anonymous adversary of the better-known David. According to an old textual tradition of 1 Sam. 17:4 (preserved at Qumran, in Josephus, and some LXX versions), Goliath was a giant "four cubits and a span" (6 feet, 9 inches) in height. An exaggerated figure is found in the received Hebrew text (MT) where Goliath's height is recorded as "*six* cubits and a span" (9 feet, 9 inches)! ***See also*** David. P.K.M.

Gomer (goh'muhr). **1** A son of Japheth (Gen. 10:2) and the ancestor of a people from southern Russia called Gimirrai by the Assyrians and Cimmerians. **2** The harlot wife of Hosea (Hos. 1: 3), who bore him three children.

Gomorrah (guh-mor'ah). ***See*** Sodom.

Good Friday, the Friday immediately before Easter on which Christians memorialize the day Jesus was crucified (see Mark 15:42).

Good Samaritan, the man who, by aiding a Jew who had been wounded by thieves, proved neighbor in Jesus' famous parable (Luke 10:29–37). A "good Samaritan" would have been a contradiction in terms for most Jews of Jesus' day, because of the centuries-long mutual hatred between Jews and Samaritans. ***See also*** Samaritans.

gopher wood, the material Noah was instructed to use in building the ark (Gen. 6:14). Its identification is uncertain.

Goshen (goh'shuhn). **1** The fertile region in the eastern Nile delta of Egypt (modern Wadi Tumilat) where the family of Jacob was allowed to settle (Gen. 47:28–29, 34). Also known as "the land of Rameses" (Gen. 47:11), this territory was well suited for grazing, as evidenced both in the Egyptian sources and in the Bible (Gen. 47:3–6). Goshen (evidently not called by that name except in the Bible) was apparently somewhat of a hinterland to the Egyptians, perhaps because of its distance from the network of Nile irrigation canals (cf. Gen. 46:34). The Hebrews were still dwelling in the region at the time of the plagues (Exod. 8:22; 9:26). From this territory Moses led the Israelites out of Egypt (Exod. 4–13). **2** A geographical region between the southern hill country of Judah and the Negev, mentioned only in Josh. 10:41 and 11:16. Its precise delineations are unknown. Possibly it should be related to 3. **3** A city in the southern hill country of Judah, in the same district as Debir (modern Khirbet Rabud), Anab, Socoh, and Eshtamoh (Josh. 15:41). Its identification is unknown. Proposals include such modern locations as Tell Beit Mirsim, Dhahariya, and, more recently, Tell el-Kheleifeh, all sites near the southeast edge of the Judean hill country. ***See also*** Egypt; Exodus; Patriarch. D.A.D.

gospel, Gospels, the English translation of the Greek *euangelion*, which means "good news." In the NT it refers to the good news preached by Jesus that the Kingdom of God is at hand (Mark 1:15) and the good news of what God has done on behalf of humanity in Jesus (Rom. 1:3–5). The background for the noun is found in the OT where the verbal form "to bring good news" or "to announce good news" appears rather than the noun. So in Isa. 40:9; 41:27; 52:7; and 61:1 the messenger announces the good news of Israel's redemption from Exile. In Luke 4:18–19 Jesus takes up the words of Isa. 61:1–2 to announce his glad tidings. And in Matt. 11:5 and Luke 7:22 Jesus' response to the messengers of John, that the poor have the good news preached to them, is a way of affirming his messiahship. In addition to this background the NT also reflects Hellenistic usage. The Roman proconsul Paulus Fabius Maximus, for example, honored Caesar Augustus by reckoning Caesar's birthday as the beginning of the new year. In doing so, he called Caesar's birthday "good news" (*euangelion*) for the whole world.

Although the word "gospel" is commonly associated with the writings of Matthew, Mark, Luke, and John, it is Paul who uses the noun more than any other writer of the NT. On several occasions he employs it without further qualification (Rom. 10:16; 11:28; 1 Cor. 4:15; 9:14, 18), thereby showing that his audience readily understood its content. At other times he offers a description of the gospel as "the gospel of God" (Rom. 1:1; 15:16; 2 Cor. 11:7), "the gospel of Christ" (Rom. 15:19; 1 Cor. 9:12; 2 Cor. 2:12; 9:13; 10:14; Phil. 1:27; 1 Thess. 3:2), and "the gospel of his Son" (Rom. 1:9). The first phrase usually refers to the origin of the gospel, which is in God, while the last two point to the content of the gospel, which is Jesus Christ. In Rom. 1:1–6 and 1 Cor. 15:1–8 Paul gives his most detailed descriptions of the gospel. It comes from God. It was promised through the prophets. Its content is Jesus, a descendant of David according to the flesh, designated Son of God by the resurrection. Paul bears witness to this resurrection.

Although Paul can speak of "my gospel" (Rom. 2:16; 16:25) and "our gospel" (2 Cor. 4:3) there is no other gospel (Gal. 1:7). There is only

The four Evangelists as represented by their symbols in one of two Evangelist pages from the eighth-century *Book of Kells*.

one gospel and it was disclosed to Paul when God revealed his Son to him (Gal. 1:16). Paul's gospel, then, is not a human affair; it has its origins in God (Gal. 1:11). The apostle strives to prevent his audience from turning to false versions of the gospel (2 Cor. 11:4; Gal. 1:6). The true gospel demands obedience (Rom. 10:16) and Paul does everything for the sake of it (1 Cor. 9:23), even surrendering his legitimate rights so that the gospel can be preached free of charge (1 Cor. 9:18).

Among the Evangelists only Mark and Matthew employ the noun "gospel." Mark begins his account, "The beginning of the Gospel of Jesus Christ, the Son of God." Here gospel does not describe the literary genre of Mark's work but the content of his message, i.e., Jesus Christ is the Son of God. In this regard Mark is similar to Paul. For Mark, the gospel is the message Jesus preached, the arrival of the Kingdom of God (1:14–15), and the present proclamation about Jesus. The latter point is evident in Mark 8:35 and 10:29 where Mark equates the gospel with the person of Jesus, and in Mark 13:10 and 14:9 where the gospel is equated with the story of Jesus.

Matthew, unlike Mark, always qualifies the noun "gospel." Thus he speaks about "the gospel of the Kingdom" (4:23; 9:35; 24:14) by which he means the gospel whose content is the Kingdom of God, preached first by Jesus and now by the church. He also speaks of "this gospel" (26:13) and so emphasizes the message preached by the church. Luke does not employ the noun "gospel" except in Acts 15:7 and 20:24. Instead he uses the verbal form "to preach." Thus in the Acts of the Apostles preaching the gospel becomes the dominant activity of the church.

In the NT period the noun "gospel" did not refer to a genre of written literature as it does today. Instead it denoted the oral message that encapsulates God's salvific activity in Jesus Christ on behalf of humankind. It was only in the middle of the second century that the plural form "Gospels" was employed. Thus Justin Martyr (ca. 100–165) writes that the "memoirs composed by the apostles" are called "Gospels" (*First Apology* 66). Yet even in this period it was recognized that there is only one gospel as can be seen from the titles applied to these works, "The Gospel According to Matthew," "The Gospel According to Mark," etc.

The formation of the Gospels encompassed three stages. The first is the life and the teaching of Jesus. During this period Jesus gathered disciples who heard his teaching and witnessed his deeds. The second was that of the oral tradition, the time between the death of Jesus and the first written Gospel, approximately A.D. 33–70. In this period the church assembled collections of Jesus' words and deeds, e.g., his sayings, parables, miracles, and the passion narrative. The collections were employed for liturgical, catechetical, apologetical, and missionary purposes. In the third stage the Evangelists gathered these diverse collections to form their gospels. The first to do so was probably Mark about the year 70. Fifteen to twenty years later Matthew and Luke, independently of each other, undertook a revision of Mark. In making their revisions they appear to have had access to a collection of Jesus' sayings unknown to Mark. In addition each had special material such as is found in their infancy narratives. The diagram indicates the probable literary relationships among the first three Gospels. Because Matthew and Luke depend upon Mark as their primary source, there is a striking similarity between the first three Gospels and they are given the name "the synoptic Gospels."

The Gospel of John was composed toward the end of the first century. Although it may show knowledge of the synoptic Gospels, it is strikingly different in style, tone, and theology, with its strong emphasis on a Jesus with much fuller consciousness of his divinity. Set in a three-year rather than a one-year time span as in the synoptic Gospels, the career of Jesus moves regularly between Galilee and Jerusalem. Written in a unique and deceptively simple style, John nevertheless makes many theological points explicit that in the other gospels remain only implicit. ***See also*** John, The Gospel According to; Kingdom of God; Luke, The Gospel According to; Mark, The Gospel According to; Matthew, The Gospel According to; Synoptic Problem, The.

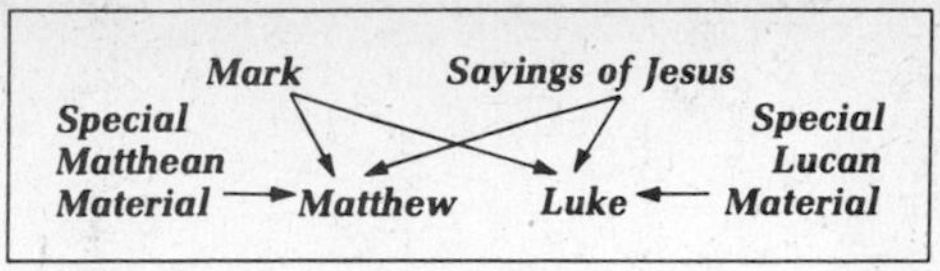

Literary relationships between the synoptic gospels.

Bibliography

Fitzmyer, Joseph A. *A Christological Catechism: New Testament Answers*. New York: Paulist Press, 1982.

Harrington, Daniel J. *Interpreting the New Testament: A Practical Guide*. Wilmington, DE: Michael Glazier, 1979.

Kee, H. C. *Understanding the New Testament*. 4th ed. Englewood Cliffs, NJ: Prentice-Hall, 1983.

F.J.M.

Gospel of Thomas, a collection of 114 sayings purportedly dictated by the "Living Jesus" to Judas Thomas, "the Twin," discovered as part of the Nag Hammadi library. The work is not a Gospel in the genre of the canonical Gospels, since it contains no narrative about the birth, ministry, or passion of Jesus. It resembles the probable form of the hypothetical sayings collection ("Q") generally presumed to be a source of the synoptic Gospels. The Nag Hammadi version is a translation from Greek into Coptic. Three Greek fragments of the work were found at Oxyrhynchus in Egypt in 1898 and 1903 but were not identified as parts of the Gospel until the Coptic version was discovered. It is possible that the Greek version was itself a translation from an Aramaic text. The earliest of the Greek fragments can be dated to the early third century. Hence the gospel must have been composed prior to A.D. 200. The date of the original composition is difficult to determine more precisely. A date of approximately A.D. 140 has often been conjectured, but a first-century date cannot be excluded. The place of composition was probably Syria, where traditions about the apostle Judas Thomas, identified as the twin brother of Jesus, were common and where the ascetic ("Encratite") and heterodox form of Christianity advocated in the Gospel was at home from an early period.

Content: Many of the sayings, parables, proverbs, and brief dialogues in the Gospel parallel sayings attributed to Jesus in the synoptic Gospels, but appear for the most part to be independent of the canonical versions. The parables, for example, lack the allegorical features found in the Synoptics, features that are generally recognized to be secondary accretions. Thus *The Gospel of Thomas* provides an important resource for the investigation of the earliest forms of the sayings of Jesus. Among the sayings in the Gos-

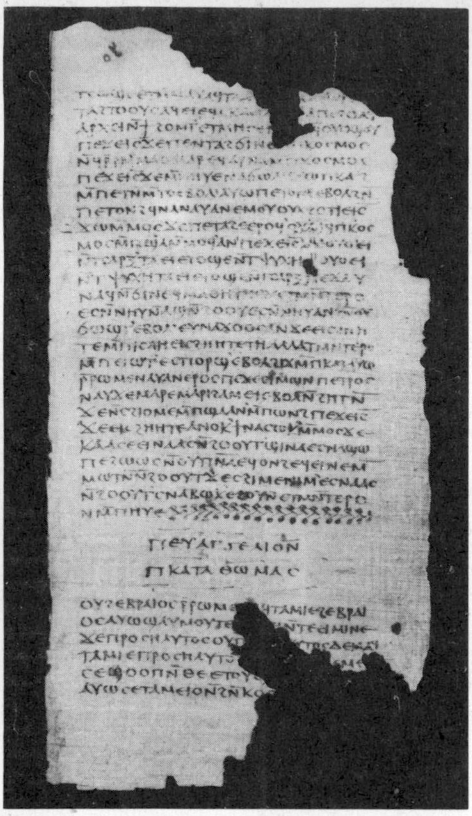

The closing page of the Coptic *Gospel of Thomas*, with title; second century A.D.

pel not paralleled in the Synoptics, some are found in the NT apocrypha, such as *The Gospel of the Egyptians* (Saying 22), and others in patristic reports about Jesus. Many of the sayings, however, were unknown before the discovery of the text. Some are probably compositions by Christian circles developing the traditions of Israel's wisdom literature, although some are as likely to be authentic sayings of Jesus as those in many canonical texts. The sayings of Jesus in *The Gospel of Thomas* that are paralleled in the canonical tradition have little of the Gospel's distinctive theology, although that theology was probably meant to be read allegorically in those familiar sayings.

Gnostic Influence: *The Gospel of Thomas* clearly reflects Gnostic theology. In formal terms, it claims to afford an esoteric *gnōsis*, or knowledge, that guarantees immortality (Saying 1). The contents of this troubling yet marvelous knowledge (Saying 2) involve an understanding of one's true self, which is superior to any other knowledge (Saying 67). Through this knowledge, one recognizes the origin of the essential self in the world of light (Sayings 49, 50), where the self pre-existed (Saying 19) and to which it is destined to return (Saying 18) to enjoy a state of final rest (Saying 60). Recipients of this knowledge thus realize that they are sons of the Living Father (Sayings 4, 50).

A sharp dichotomy between flesh and spirit and an anticosmic dualism are evident in the Gospel's description of the human condition. Without the saving *gnōsis* provided by Jesus, the Revealer from the world of light (Sayings 13, 61, 77), people are in a state of drunken blindness (Saying 28), spiritual beings whose true wealth is ensnared in a poverty-ridden body (Saying 29). When one understands the world, it becomes clear that it is a corpse (Saying 56). The soul content with a state of dependence on the body is wretched (Sayings 87, 112). The illuminated disciple is exhorted to reject the world. Such recommendations are sometimes offered in the form of paradoxical metaphors. On the one hand, the disciple is urged to "fast" from the world (Saying 27); on the other, the disciple will "consume" the world, imaged as both carnivorous lion (Saying 70) and sacrificial lamb (Saying 60), before the disciple is consumed as a corpse by the inimical forces of matter.

The disciple who receives the saving knowledge is enabled to overcome the problems of life in this world and to achieve a unitary state (Saying 11), wherein the differentiations of inner and outer or male and female are overcome (Sayings 22, 114). The illumined disciple enters the "bridal chamber" (Saying 75), where duality is dissolved, and becomes a *monachos* or "solitary one" (Sayings 4, 16, 23, 49). The disciple thus enters into the Kingdom of God, which for this Gospel is not an eschatological manifestation of divine sovereignty, but an inner, spiritual reality (Sayings 3, 49, 113, 114).

Although the Gnostic orientation of the work is clear, the text incorporates materials that are not Gnostic in origin. Thus, one saying that exalts the importance of James the Just (Saying 12) is probably of Jewish-Christian origin. The collection probably went through various editorial stages where different theological perspectives were incorporated. ***See also*** Apocryphal New Testament; Gnosticism; Nag Hammadi.

Bibliography

Davies, Stevan L. *The Gospel of Thomas and Christian Wisdom*. New York: Seabury, 1983.

Koester, Helmut, and James M. Robinson. *Trajectories Through Early Christianity*. Philadelphia: Fortress, 1971.

Koester, Helmut, and Thomas O. Lambdin. "The Gospel of Thomas," in James M. Robinson, ed., *The Nag Hammadi Library in English*. San Francisco: Harper & Row, 1977. Pp. 117–130.

H.W.A.

gossip. ***See*** Talebearing.

gourd, a hard-rinded inedible fruit of the genus *Lagenaria* (large) or of the species *Cucurbita pepo* (small), used both as utensils (dippers, cups, storage vessels) and for ornamentation. In Jon. 4:4–10 the KJV has "gourd" where the RSV has "plant" due to uncertain identification. Gourd motifs decorated the Temple interior (1 Kings 6:18) and the bronze sea in the Temple (1 Kings 7:24; 2 Chron. 4:3). A "wild gourd" (only in 2 Kings 4:39) had poisonous fruit.

government, the administration of society by those in power. The form varies greatly with village assemblies, heads of familial and tribal associations, intertribal judges, theocratic kings, and worldly emperors with their representatives (procurator or subordinate king) and local council (Sanhedrin). The purpose and dangers of government, however, receive attention, particularly in relationship to the king. Government, uniquely representing God, the ultimate source of justice (Ps. 72:1–4; cf. Rom. 13:1, 4), is responsible for justice for the weak (1 Kings 10:9; Prov. 31:8–9; Ezek. 34:1–6, 23; even secular governments: Dan. 4:27). Executing justice requires power (Ps. 101:1, 5, 8; conversely, Isa. 3:4–5). Government needs limits; rule is a function, not a status or class (Deut. 17:14–20). The people are not mere subjects but are also participants, even in the covenantal aspects of kingship (2 Kings 11:17; 23:1–3). ***See also*** King; Law; Procurator; Sanhedrin. S.C.M.

governor, the ruler of a Roman province, usually a former consul. Pilate was governor over the province of Judea when Jesus was crucified (Matt. 27:2). In the larger senatorial provinces a governor would usually serve for three years. Governors of provinces in which two to four legions were stationed held an important military command. Entrusted with the responsibility of maintaining peace, they would investigate any potential source of difficulty, such as the dispute between Paul and his enemies (Acts 24:1; 25:1–4).

Gozan (goh'zan; Akkadian *Guzana*), a city (modern Tell Halaf) on the Habor (Heb. *Khabur*) River, the city and its surrounding region which became part of the Assyrian Empire in the ninth century B.C. (alluded to in 2 Kings 19:12; see Isa. 37:12). Gozan was one of the places to which the Israelites were deported after the capture of Samaria (2 Kings 17:6; 18:11; 1 Chron. 5:26); texts from Tell Halaf mention some of the exiles' descendants. ***See also*** Habor.

grace, the English translation of a Greek word meaning concretely "that which brings delight, joy, happiness, or good fortune." Grace in classical Greek applied to art, persons, speech, or athletics, as well as to the good fortune, kindness, and power bestowed by the gods upon divine men, moving them to miraculous deeds.

The LXX employs this word to translate the Hebrew root meaning "favor." Thus, Noah found favor before the Lord (Gen. 6:8); Jacob sought favor in the eyes of Esau (Gen. 32:5). Similarly, those showing favor do gracious deeds. For example, showing kindness to the poor (Prov. 14:31) or generosity to all living (Ecclus. 7:33) was an act of grace. Likewise, the Psalms speak confidently of God's graciousness in hearing prayers, healing (6:2; 41:4), rescuing the oppressed (9:13), giving the Law (119:29), forgiving sin, rescuing the weak, and the like.

Even where the vocabulary of grace is absent, God's actions are suffused with grace. God loved Israel in spite of its puny numbers (Deut. 7:6–9) and rescued the community from the howling wilderness, encircling it with care (Deut. 32:10). God kept covenant with Israel even when the covenant was violated by the people (Ezek. 16:8) and brought the captives home from Babylon (Isa. 49:14–18). Promises abound in the OT that flow from God's graciousness.

In the Apocrypha and Pseudepigrapha, grace was synonymous with divine mercy on the elect (Wisd. of Sol. 3:9). For deliverance from the flood, Noah prayed: "For Thy *grace* has been great towards me, And great has been Thy *mercy* to my soul" (*Jubilees* 10:3). The Qumran community used "covenant loyalty" synonymously with grace: "Behold you have begun to show covenant loyalty to your servant. You are gracious to me with your mercies" (*Thanksgiving Hymn* 16:8–9). Even while relying on God's grace, the community strictly hued to the Law with no sense of contradiction. The way of grace and the demand of the Law were integral to the *one* path to salvation.

Except for its emphasis on Jesus, the NT understanding of grace resembles that just surveyed. In Luke and Acts, power from the divine realm infuses god-like men, moving them to perform miraculous deeds. The divine grace rests on the infant Jesus (Luke 2:40), who subsequently grows in grace (2:52), speaks gracious words (4:22), and, like a divine man, passes unharmed through a hostile mob (4:30). Followers of Jesus, such as Stephen, full of "grace," do signs and wonders (Acts 6:8; cf. 14:3). Likewise, Paul assumes that recipients of God's grace will perform deeds of grace. The gracious gift he received is apostleship (Rom. 1:5; 12:6–8); the range of gifts ("graces") others receive runs from esoteric, ecstatic speech to mundane, administrative skills, but all are deemed important (1 Cor. 12:4–31).

Elsewhere, grace connotes God's favor shown sinners through Jesus Christ. Historically condemned as "sinners," Gentiles gain entrance to the messianic community through the "gift" (Rom. 3:24) or "free gift" (Rom. 5:15) of grace

(Gal. 2:17–21; Rom. 4:16). While Paul forbade no Jewish Christian to observe the Law, Christ revalued the Law. Although he disassociated grace and Law observance for Gentiles (Galatians), Paul, like the Qumraners, expected obedience to accompany the life of grace. Repeatedly, Paul cautioned against using grace as a license to sin, lest believers "accept the grace of God in vain" (2 Cor. 6:1).

Paul also used grace to mean "thanks to God" (Rom. 6:17; 7:25; 1 Cor. 15:57), a thank offering, or an acknowledgment of God's good gifts. In the opening of his Letters, Paul offers the traditional Greek greeting, "grace" (coupled with the Hebrew "peace" wish), expressing delight at touching the addressee's world. The letters characteristically close with a petition for divine favor, "grace," on the recipients. ***See also*** Covenant; Forgiveness; Love; Mercy; Promise; Spiritual Gifts. C.J.R.

gracious, to be kindly disposed or to show favor and mercy to someone, usually by a person of superior position and power to a person of inferior position and power. Thus, Potiphar dealt graciously with Joseph (Gen. 39:4), Ruth found favor in the eyes of Boaz (Ruth 2:10), and Esther was treated graciously by King Ahasuerus (Esther 2:17; 5:2). In the Bible, it is above all God who is gracious toward human beings, as stated in the ancient liturgical formula: "The Lord, the Lord, a God merciful and gracious, slow to anger, and abounding in steadfast love and faithfulness" (Exod. 34:6; see also Pss. 86:15; 103:8; 145:8). This is one of the few doctrinal statements about God in the OT in adjectival form. In the NT, the adjective "gracious" is virtually absent; the noun "grace," however, is used frequently in salutations (Rom. 1:7; Eph. 1:20), but most often to describe what God has done in Christ for humanity (Rom. 5:2, 15, 17; 1 Cor. 15:10; Eph. 2:8). ***See also*** Grace; Mercy. W.E.L.

graft. ***See*** Olive.

grain, a general term used throughout the Bible to indicate the seed of cultivated cereal grasses such as wheat, barley, millet, and sorghum. Ground into flour, it was the major component of breads and other cooked foods. ***See also*** Barley; Corn; Millet; Rye; Spelt; Wheat.

granary, a storage facility for threshed and winnowed grains such as wheat and barley. The facility ranged in size and format from an entire building of rooms or compartments to plastered or unplastered pits or silos to individual jars or containers. The presence of large granary structures in the ancient Near East implies a surplus production of wheat to guard against famine years as well as some type of organized system for redistribution of the grain (see Jer. 50:26; Joel 1:17; Matt. 3:12; Luke 3:17).

grape. ***See*** Vine.

grasshopper. ***See*** Locust.

grave. ***See*** Architecture; Burial.

graven images. ***See*** Idol.

graving, engraving, incising, the practice of impressing deeply in metal, clay tablets, or stone with an iron tool or stylus. The OT mentions an engraver who did work for the Temple (2 Chron. 2:7), one Huramabi by name (2 Chron. 2:13–14), but the OT also contains a prohibition against making graven images (Exod. 20:4). Engraving was done on a gold plate for Aaron's turban with the inscription, "Holy to the Lord" (Exod. 28:36; 39:30). On bronze stands in the Temple cherubim, lions, palm trees and wreaths were engraved (1 Kings 7:36; 2 Chron. 3:7). Isa. 8:1 mentions clay tablets and Jer. 17:1 engraving

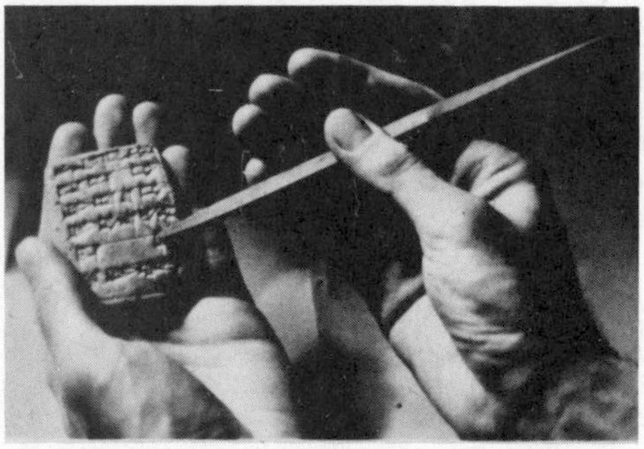

A reed stylus ready to engrave a clay tablet typifies those used widely throughout the ancient Near East.

with a pen of iron with a diamond point. Exod. 28:9, 11 and 39:6, 14 refer to two onyx stones with six Israelite tribal names incised on each. Job 19:24 mentions an incised tablet with lead-filled letters. Zech. 3:9 speaks of a seven-faceted stone engraved with an inscription. Artifacts such as seal cylinders and stamps for impressions on documents are relatively frequent. Inscribed Egyptian and Hyksos scarabs can be used for dating archaeological finds. Paul assures his listeners they can learn nothing about God from the result of the engraver's technique (Acts 17:29). R.A.C.

Great Assembly, a succession of Jewish scholars in the sixth to the third centuries B.C. The chain of tradition in the Mishah tractate Abot (also called Pirke Abot and the Chapter of the Fathers) traces the handing on of Torah from Moses to the rabbis of the second and third centuries. The gap in the chain between the traditional last prophets (Haggai, Zechariah, and Malachi) and Simeon the Just, high priest ca. 200 B.C., is filled by the "men of the Great Assembly" (Heb. *keneset*), sometimes referred to as the Great Synagogue. Talmudic authors (third century A.D. on) identified this group with the assembly in Nehemiah 8–9 and attributed various legal and ritual enactments to it. Though scholars have argued about the nature of this institution, it is unlikely that any historical institution is remembered here. Organs of community leadership probably varied considerably from 500 to 200 B.C. ***See also*** Sanhedrin.

A.J.S.

greave, armor protecting the lower leg. The ones Goliath wore were made of bronze (RSV; KJV: "brass," 1 Sam. 17:6).

Grecia (gree'shee-uh), an archaic form of "Greece," found in the KJV (e.g., Dan. 8:21; Zech. 9:13; Acts 20:2). Similarly "Grecians" is the archaic form to describe the inhabitants of Greece (KJV, Joel 3:6; Acts 9:29), in modern parlance "Greeks." ***See also*** Greece.

Greece, a country that lies at the terminus of the central mountain structure of southern Europe. By the eighth century B.C. city-states built around a fortress on the acropolis (Gk., "high city") had replaced the older tribal states or villages. Between 750 and 500 B.C. Greeks, pressed for land, founded numerous colonies in the Aegean, along the Black Sea, in Cyrenaica, Sicily and southern Italy as well as Asia Minor. By 500 B.C. Sparta had united most of the Peloponnesus. After defeating the Persians, the Athenians united most of the Greeks in the Aegean as well as those along the coast of Asia Minor. Athens' defeat by Sparta ended this league, though attempts would be made to form new leagues around prominent cities. In the north, Greece had remained divided into weak tribal monarchies until Philip II of Macedon consolidated power in the region. Philip defeated Athens and a weak coalition of cities at Chaeronea in 338 B.C. The Romans gained control of Greece in 146 B.C. Greece is mentioned only in two later OT books (Dan. 8:21; 10:20; 11:2; Zech. 9:13). It figures prominently in the NT, however. Three of the cities to which Paul addressed letters were in Greece (Corinth, Philippi, Thessalonika), and he visited other cities there as well (see Acts 16:9–18:18; 2 Cor. 2:12).

P.P.

Greek, New Testament.

Historical Context: The twenty-seven books of the NT were written in a dialect of the ancient Greek language called Koine or Hellenistic Greek. All living languages are historically contingent: their vocabulary and syntax are constantly changing in response to cultural pressures and internal social developments. The historical roots of ancient Greek can be traced to the arrival in Greece of Indo-European peoples referred to as Achaeans in the *Iliad*. Their migration is usually dated to the beginning of the Middle Helladic period (ca. 1900 B.C.) and credited with producing the dialects of Aeolic and Ionic. At the beginning of the Iron Age (ca. 1100 B.C.) a second major wave of Indo-European invaders introduced the Doric dialect and forced many of the Achaeans to resettle on the western coast of Turkey, referred to in ancient history as Ionia. Because the Homeric bards were centered on the island of Chios, the *Iliad* (ca. 750 B.C.) and the *Odyssey* (ca. 700 B.C.) were written in an early form of Ionic. The *Histories* of Herodotus, a native of Halicarnassus, were composed in new Ionic ca. 460–425 B.C. The dialect spoken in Athens during the golden age of Periclean democracy (ca. 500–350 B.C.) was Attic, which resulted from the impact of Doric on the old Ionic of the Greek mainland. The writings of Plato, Thucydides, Euripides, and Demosthenes, to name a few, were all composed in Attic, which is therefore the "standard" form of the language still taught in classical Greek courses.

The next major shift in the history of the Greek language occurred during the Hellenistic period (ca. 325–63 B.C.). After Alexander the Great and his armies conquered the Persian Empire, numerous Greek colonies were established throughout the Near East to spread Greek culture and fuse the two traditions. As a result of this forced syncretism, Attic Greek was transformed into the Koine dialect in which the NT writings were composed. The term *koine* is thus used in both senses of its definition, "common": it became the *universal* language of late antiquity (dominating until the sixth century A.D.) and it was simplified into a *colloquial* idiom by nonnative Greek speakers in the process of its geographical diffusion. Some literary "purists" like Dionysius of Halicarnassus and his circle resisted this transformation of Attic into Koine and, especially in the second century A.D., consciously imitated the Attic of the classical period in their writings. A major boon to the study of NT Greek has been the discovery during the past century of tens of thousands of papyrus documents in Egypt, as well as inscriptions and ostraca unearthed during archaeological excavations. Scholars now possess a wide spectrum of written materials from late antiquity, thus permitting a comparative analysis of NT Greek with other Greek writings of the time.

Description: The earliest extant Greek texts were written in a script called Linear B and are dated to the Late Helladic period (1400–1200 B.C.). This script was adapted from a Minoan form of writing, Linear A, which is evidently based on a syllabic system employed by West Semitic language groups of the Levant. Sometime after 1000 B.C., this form of writing was transformed into an alphabetic system, which Herodotus (5.58) attributes to Phoenician influence. The alphabets of most European languages were, in turn, derived from the Greek alphabet. Several of the original letters were lost during the Archaic period so that the official alphabet [*alphabet* (a)] adopted in Athens at the end of the Peloponnesian War (404 B.C.) contained twenty-four letters with the English equivalents indicated in the accompanying table.

In addition to the vowels *alpha (a)*, *iota (i)*, and *üpsilon (u)*, the Greek alphabet has separate letters for long *ē (ēta)* and *ō (ōmega)* and for short *e (epsilon)* and *o (omicron)*, thus totaling seven vowels. The exact pronunciation of ancient Greek sounds is no longer known. The examples listed in the table therefore represent a more or less arbitrary pronunciation for each letter sound as adopted by modern scholars. Two guidelines are helpful in pronouncing ancient Greek words: first, every letter is vocalized and second, words should be divided into the same number of syllables as there are separate vowels or diphthongs, e.g., *a*-pĕ-cri-thē, *a*-lē-thei-*a*, prŏ-phē-tēs, with the consonant(s) beginning the next syllable.

Linguists divide languages into three major types: *isolating* (all words are separate roots), *agglutinative* (word formation via the combination of separate morphemes), and *inflectional* (word formation via modification of stems or word bases with prefixes, suffixes, or internal changes). Greek is an example of a highly inflected language like Latin and German. There are three major inflectional patterns (called declensions) in the nominal system, divided according to stem endings: nominal stems ending in *a* or ē belong to the first declension, those ending in *o* to the second declension, and those ending in consonants to the third declension. Suffixes are added to nominal stems according to regular patterns in each declension and signal the following grammatical information: *gender* (each nominal word is masculine, feminine, or neuter and is so indicated by the corresponding article in a Greek dictionary), *number* (singular or plural; the dual number of classical Greek has disappeared in Hellenistic Greek), and *case* (in general, the nominative case signals the subject, the accusative the direct object, the dative the indirect object, and the genitive the possessive case; separate case endings for the vocative of direct address, ablative signaling origins, and instrumental and locative functions have become almost fully assimilated to the nominative, genitive, and dative cases respectively in Hellenistic Greek).

Greek verbs are also divided into inflectional patterns (called conjugations) according to which vowel or consonant occurs at the end of the verb base. By the presence or absence of a variety of prefixes, infixes, and suffixes, each verb form signals the following grammatical information: *person* (first, second, or third), *number* (singular or plural), *voice* (active, middle, or passive), *mood* (indicative, subjunctive, optative, imperative, infinitive, or participle), and *tense* (both as *time*—past, present, or future—and as *type of action*—punctiliar, durative, or completive). Since Greek is so highly inflected, there is the possibility that each verb can occur in more than six hundred separate forms.

While at first encounter this may seem an insurmountable number of variables to master, the advantage is soon apparent: because there is a separate form to indicate each nuance of meaning in the nominal and verbal systems, translation from Greek to English, for example, is relatively free from ambiguity and far "easier" than from a less fully inflected language. Second, since the grammatical function of words in Greek is indicated by their inflectional signals rather than by word order, subjects, verbs, and predicates can occur in a variety of sequences in Greek texts, reflecting compositional style and emphasis. Third, the full contours of a highly inflected language began to erode in the Koine, so that modern Greek is far less inflected than its ancestor dialects.

The following modifications of the inflectional patterns described above can already be observed in the Koine: the substitution of

THE GREEK ALPHABET

Greek Form Capital	Small	*Name*	*Translit-eration*	*Approximate Pronunciation*
Α	α	alpha	a	*drama*
Β	β	bēta	b	*bible*
Γ	γ	gamma	g	*glucose*
Δ	δ	delta	d	*decalogue*
Ε	ε	epsīlon	e	*ego*
Ζ	ζ	zēta	z	*Zeus*
Η	η	ēta	ē	*they*
Θ	θ	thēta	th	*theist*
Ι	ι	iōta	i	*intrigue*
Κ	κ	kappa	k, c	*crisis*
Λ	λ	lambda	l	*logic*
Μ	μ	mu	m	*mother*
Ν	ν	nu	n	*anti*
Ξ	ξ	xī	x	*axiom*
Ο	ο	omīcron	o	*apology*
Π	π	pi	p	*poet*
Ρ	ρ	rhō	r	*catarrh*
Σ	σ, ς	sigma	s	*syntax*
Τ	τ	tau	t	*topic*
Υ	υ	üpsīlon	u, y	*tu* (French), *Tür* (German)
Φ	φ	phī	ph	*phonetic*
Χ	χ	chī	ch	*chasm*
Ψ	ψ	psī	ps	*apse*
Ω	ω	ōmega	ō	*ode*

prepositional phrases for oblique (genitive, dative, and accusative) case endings to indicate syntactical relationships within the predicate; a decline in the use of the middle voice to indicate that the object of the verb is the same as the subject, and its replacement with the active voice and a reflexive pronoun; the gradual domination of regular over irregular conjugation patterns; the loss of distinction in the protasis ("if" clause) of a conditional sentence between probable (subjunctive mood) and doubtful (optative mood) conditions so that the optative is very rare in the NT; an increase in the use of periphrastic constructions (auxiliary verb plus participle) in place of the appropriate tense stem; a decline in the use of the imperfect and pluperfect tenses to distinguish different kinds of action in the past; and confusion among subordinating conjunctions and prepositions so that syntactical distinctions between contrasting pairs are blurred. In sum, the historical changes in the Greek world after Alexander the Great, despite the archaizing efforts of the Atticists, produced a movement away from the intricate structure of classical Greek toward simpler phonological, morphological, and syntactical forms of expression in the Hellenistic period.

Implications for the Study of the NT: Study of the Greek language is helpful, if not crucial, for the interpretation of the NT at a variety of points. First, knowledge of Greek enables the scholar or preacher to compare the variant readings contained in the multitude of manuscripts of the NT books and to establish the text that will serve as the basis for a commentary or sermon. Second, attention to an author's compositional style often illuminates the strategy and purpose in writing. The Pauline Letters, for example, while presumably composed with some urgency and in a conversational style to reflect Paul's apostolic presence, contain arguments and rhetorical conventions reminiscent of contemporary Stoic-Cynic preachers and orators like Seneca. The author of the Gospel of John, on the other hand, employs a very different compositional strategy only fully evident in the Greek text. He frequently strings together simple sentences with the conjunction *kai* ("and"): "After these things Jesus and his disciples went into the land of Judea *and* he stayed there with them *and* he baptized. *And* John was also baptizing at Aenon near Salim because there was much water there, *and* they [people] came *and* they were baptized" (John 3:22–23). As a result of this paratactic style, the Greek of the Fourth Gospel is often judged to be the closest to the vernacular and NT Greek textbooks usually begin with passages from John. But the author sprinkles his work with double entendres and symbolic terms that can trap those who, like Nicodemus in John 3, take the simple style literally, i.e., as an indication of conceptual simplicity.

Whether Jesus taught in Aramaic or Greek is another critical issue relating to the language of the NT. Since Aramaic was the native language of Palestine in the Persian and Hellenistic periods, many nineteenth-century scholars assumed that the four canonical Gospels are Greek translations of a primitive Aramaic Gospel. While most twentieth-century scholars have abandoned this hypothesis, there is still considerable debate over the extent to which the gospels reflect Hebrew expressions via the Septuagint translation of the OT and Aramaic influences from the oral tradition. Some scholars, on the basis of inscriptional evidence from first century Palestine that show how common Greek was, have recently argued that Jesus was bilingual and may even have taught in Greek and they claim that the parables must have been composed in Greek. These three examples illustrate how a study of the language of the NT can illuminate key issues in the interpretation of its contents.

Bibliography

Blass, F., and A. Debrunner. *A Greek Grammar of the New Testament and Other Early Christian Literature*. Translated by R. W. Funk. Chicago: University of Chicago Press, 1961.

Voelz, J. W. "The Language of the New Testament." In *Aufstieg und Niedergang der Römischen Welt*. Vol. 2.25.2. *Principat*. Edited by W. Haase. Berlin & New York: Walter de Gruyter, 1984. Pp. 893–977.

L.C.M.

Greeks, persons of Greek descent, language, and culture as opposed to non-Greek "barbarians." In a broader sense, persons, whatever their origins, who had come under the influence of Greek culture and who lived in the hellenized cities of the Roman Empire as opposed to the rustic, rural population could be called Greek. In the Bible, "Greeks" may refer to pagans in contrast to Jews (2 Macc. 4:36; Acts 9:29). From a Jewish standpoint the expression "Jews and Greeks" embraces all of humanity (Acts 14:1; Rom. 2:9–10; Gal. 3:28; Col. 3:11; 1 Cor. 12:13). The expression "pious Greeks" can be used for proselytes or God-fearers, Greeks who converted to Judaism or were interested in it (Acts 17:4). P.P.

grisled ("grizzled"), a term meaning "gray streaked" or "roan," the archaic KJV translation for "mottled" (Gen. 31:10,12) or "dappled" (Zech. 6:3, 6).

grove, a cluster of trees or a resting spot such as an orchard or an oasis. The sacred places referred to in the Scriptures are probably groves of oaks (Josh. 24:26). Often designated as "high places," they are the places of worship of the pagan gods Baal and Astarte (Deut. 12:2–3; 2 Kings 17:10, 16). The grove planted by Abraham in Beer-sheba was of tamarisk trees (Gen. 21:33). ***See also*** Oak; Trees; Woods.

grudge, a feeling of anger, prohibited by Lev. 19:18, although elsewhere God is said to maintain his anger (Nah. 1:2), albeit not forever (Jer. 3:5, 12; Ps. 103:9). Ungrudging behavior is encouraged in Deut. 15:10 and 1 Pet. 4:9. The word translated "grudge" in the KJV of Ps. 59:15 and James 5:9 is better understood as "grumble" or "complain."

guard, bodyguard, a person or persons assigned to the protection of an important person or group of persons. Both OT and NT give evidence of persons who functioned in these capacities. In the OT various royal figures are depicted as having guards (Gen. 37:36; Dan. 2:14; 2 Kings 25:8–21). David had an elite troop of Cherethites and Pelethites who served as his bodyguard (2 Sam. 8:18; 23:23). As "foreigners" these soldiers would have personal loyalty to their employer and would be less likely to be influenced by competing internal political factions. The Temple area in Jerusalem also required guards (1 Kings 14:27–28; 2 Kings 11:19).

During the Roman occupation of Palestine the Temple area had at least two different sets of guards. One set of Roman soldiers was stationed in the fortress of Antonia (see Acts 21: 30–34) and the priestly officials had levitical "security officers" as well. Roman guards watched the tomb of Jesus (Matt. 27:65–28:4) and supervised the house arrest of the apostle Paul (Acts 28:16). J.A.D.

guest, one invited to a feast (1 Kings 1:41; Matt. 22:10–11) or to lodge overnight (Luke 19:7). In the ancient Mediterranean world, it was considered obligatory to lodge travelers and strangers (Judg. 19:15–21; Heb. 73:2).

guilt, a concept that is difficult to define precisely and with every nuance present in the various writings of the Bible. For the biblical writers, guilt is not understood primarily as an inward feeling of remorse or a bad conscience, but rather as involving a situation that has arisen because of sin committed against God or one's neighbor (sin either of commission or of omission). Thus, in the Bible, guilt appears to have two primary presuppositions for its existence: first, human beings are responsible and accountable for their actions, thoughts, and attitudes; and second, these actions, thoughts, and attitudes constitute a state of guilt when relationships between human beings and God or other human beings have been broken because of sin.
Responsibility: The principal ingredient in the biblical concept of guilt appears to be the dimension of responsibility. Human beings are accountable for what they do and for the consequences of what they do. This accountability lies at the center of the biblical understanding of guilt. So great was this sense of responsibility that people could be guilty without even being aware that they had done anything wrong (e.g., Lev. 5:17–19). When a person sinned, guilt was the natural consequence. Often guilt was depicted in the OT as a burden or weight that could crush a person (e.g., Ps. 38: 4, 6), or as a cancer that could destroy a person from within (e.g., Ps. 32:3–4), or as a debt that must be paid (e.g., Lev. 5:1–6:7; Num. 5:5–8).
Reconciliation: Because of these understandings that all people were guilty before God and each other, there developed in Israel a system of sacrifices and rituals that were designed to "purify" the people involved by their paying a penalty for the wrong done. This ritual was not designed simply to relieve the conscience of the guilty party but rather to make restitution, to lay aside the burden of guilt, and to restore the broken relationship caused by the guilt. The system was designed, in part at least, to establish a reconciliation between the guilty party and the party sinned against. In the NT, Paul makes frequent use of this idea (e.g., Rom. 5:6–11; 2 Cor. 5:16–21; cf. Col. 1:19–20).
Collective and Individual: Because of the biblical understanding of the importance of the community, i.e., the people of God, guilt could be both collective and individual. What one person did could cause guilt to come upon an entire group of people (cf. esp. the story of Achan, Josh. 7). The basis for this view was the Hebrew belief in corporate solidarity, the essential importance of the people as a whole, not just as an aggregate of individuals. Individuals might sin, however, and bring guilt and the consequences of sin upon themselves. The famous lament and confession of sin in Psalm 51 points to such a situation, as does the well-known challenge of Ezekiel to the people in Exile (chap. 18).

Guilt brought with it serious consequences, such as separation from God and one's neighbors and specific penalties for sins committed. The NT writers used a particular word (Gk. *enochos*) with regard to guilt, which usually means "deserving of punishment" (e.g., Matt. 26:66; 1 Cor. 11:27; James 2:10). According to Paul, all human beings are guilty before God (e.g., Rom. 1:18–3:20). In both the OT and the NT, it is only because of God's grace that guilt can be set aside through God's forgiveness. ***See also*** Atonement; Evil; Expiation; Justification; Reconciliation; Sanctification; Sin; Worship. J.M.E.

guilt offerings. ***See*** Worship.

Guni (gōō'nī). **1** A son of Naphtali who settled with Jacob's family in Egypt (Gen. 46:24) and became the head of the Gunite clan (Num. 26: 48). **2** A descendant of Gad (1 Chron. 5:15).

Opposite: Hittite warrior taken prisoner by the Egyptians at the battle of Kadesh; from a relief ca. thirteenth century B.C.

H

H, the siglum for the "Holiness Code," a modern term for the material contained in Leviticus 17–26, which consists of regulations Israel is to observe so it may separate itself from those practices not pleasing to God. To be separated for God in that way is what "holy" means. ***See also*** Holiness.

Habakkuk (huh-bak'kuhk), **the Book of,** the thirty-fifth book in the Christian OT and one of the twelve Minor Prophets. Nothing is known about the prophet Habakkuk except what can be deduced from his oracles. The book consists of two distinct parts (chaps. 1–2 and chap. 3), each with its own heading. After the title in 1:1 there is a lament concerning the success of the wicked (1:2–4). God responds in 1:5–11 that he is raising up the Chaldeans (i.e., Babylonians) whose cruel power is irresistible. In 1:12–17 the prophet renews his complaint, acknowledging the success of the Babylonians as an act of God's judgment, but asking when their excesses will be judged. God responds a second time in 2:1–5. Despite the apparent delay, the fulfillment of the vision will be accomplished in its proper time, and the righteous who remain faithful will be preserved. (Paul quotes Hab. 2:4b with an altered sense in Rom. 1:17 and Gal. 3:11.) A series of five threats against the wicked (each introduced by "woe to") follows in 2:6–19. A liturgical summons to keep silence before God introduces the prayer of Habakkuk in chap. 3. The prayer is actually a hymn with strong mythological overtones, describing God's appearance to do battle with his enemies (cf. Judg. 5; Deut. 33; Ps. 68). The hymn contains technical notes concerning its (musical?) performance such as one finds in the book of Psalms.

The reference to the coming of the Chaldeans in 1:6 makes it likely that Habakkuk was active in the last quarter of the seventh century B.C. It is unclear, however, to whom Habakkuk refers as "the wicked." It may be the Assyrians who ruled Judah until their defeat by the Babylonians in 612 B.C. (an event referred to in the book of Nahum, written at about this time). On the other hand, Habakkuk may have been referring to corrupt Judean nobles whom he expected the Babylonians to overthrow before being themselves destroyed by God's power (a point stressed by Jeremiah, also a contemporary of Habakkuk). The lament-response form of chaps. 1–2 and the psalmlike hymn in chap. 3 may indicate that the book took shape as a liturgy for use in the Temple. Other prophets whose work is probably to be related to the Temple worship are Nahum, Obadiah, and Joel. In the first century B.C. the Qumran community (authors of the Dead Sea Scrolls) produced a commentary on Habakkuk 1–2, relating it to historical events in their own time.

This short book (it contains only fifty-six verses) may be outlined as follows:

- I. Title (1:1)
- II. Dialogue-lament (1:2–2:19)
  - A. Lament on the success of the wicked (1:2–4)
  - B. God's response (1:5–11)
  - C. Lament on the success of Babylon (1:12–17)
  - D. God's response (2:1–5)
  - E. Five woes against the wicked (2:6–19)
- III. Hymn on God's victory over his enemies (2:20–3:19).

See also Chaldea; Jeremiah, The Book of; Nahum, The Book of; Scrolls, The Dead Sea.

C.A.N.

habergeon (hab'uhr-jun), the KJV's term for the RSV's "garment" (Exod. 28:32; 39:23), "javelin" (Job 41:26), and "coat of mail" (2 Chron. 26:14; Neh. 4:16). It was a short coat of mail, part of defensive armor.

Habiru (khah-bee'ro͞o). ***See*** Khapiru.

Habor (hah'bohr), ancient and modern Habur (Khabur), a major tributary of the Euphrates River, which it enters from the northeast below modern Deir ez-Zor. The Habor was a major route in antiquity and was densely settled, as the many tells that dot its banks show. In the OT the Habor is called the river of Gozan and is named as one of the places to which the Israelites were exiled in 722 B.C. (see 2 Kings 17:6; 18:11; 1 Chron. 5:26). ***See also*** Gozan.

Hachilah (ha-kee'luh), an unidentified hill in southern Judah in the wilderness of Ziph not far from Hebron. David hid there from Saul (1 Sam. 23:19; 26:1), and Saul encamped on that very hill in his search for David (26:3). ***See also*** Ziph.

Hadad (hay'dad), a Semitic storm god, also known as Haddu, Adad, and Addu. The meaning of the name is unclear, but it may be connected with the noise of a storm. A late folk etymology erroneously took the name to signify "the unique."

The veneration of Hadad is attested by some of the earliest Mesopotamian texts. Apparently of West Semitic origin, the god found a following in Assyria (both early and late) and among the Aramaeans. At Ras-Shamra (Ugarit), Hadad (Haddu) passes as the storm deity Baal and is once called "the shepherd." An Aramaic inscription from Zinjirli dedicates a statue of the god, to whom the local king Panammuwa owed personal thanks. Lucian, a Greek author of the second century A.D. (or Pseudo-Lucian), treats the cult of Hadad in his work on the Syrian goddess Atargatis; at Hierapolis Hadad was coupled with Atargatis (Anat?), just as earlier at Ras-Shamra Baal (Haddu) was coupled with Anat.

In the Bible, "Hadad" survives chiefly in personal names (Gen. 36:35, 39; 1 Kings 11:14–22; 1 Chron. 1:30). The book of Zechariah once condemns the practice of offering lamentations for Hadad-rimmon, a god behind whose name we recognize the storm deity (Zech. 12:11). ***See also*** Anat; Baal; Ras-Shamra. R.M.G.

Hadadezer (had-ad-ay'zuhr; Heb., "Hadad is help"), the king of Zobah who was defeated by David in various campaigns against Aramaean resistance (2 Sam. 8:3–12; 10:15–19; 1 Chron. 18:3–11; 19:16–19). David's victory consolidated his control over both southern Syria and the Transjordan. His tactics included hamstringing his enemy's horses to cripple their defensive power (1 Chron. 18:4).

Hadad-rimmon (hay'dad-rim'uhn), a name, probably a combination of the names for the Syrian gods Hadad and Rimmon. Hadad was the storm god Baal of the Ugaritic texts. Rimmon, an alternate name for Hadad, was worshiped in Damascus (2 Kings 5:18). The mourning to come in Jerusalem is compared to the ritual mourning for Hadad-rimmon at Megiddo (Zech. 12:11). ***See also*** Baal; Hadad; Ras-Shamra; Rimmon.

Hadar (hay'dahr). ***See*** Hadad.

Hadassah (ha-da'sah), another name for Esther (Esther 2:7), probably her given Hebrew name. "Esther" is a Babylonian or Persian name (the goddess Ishtar or "star"), which may have been the name given her in the royal court (see Esther 2:8–9) or a name adopted in conformity with Persian style.

Hades (hay'deez), a Greek god whose name means "The Unseen." He was lord of the underworld, the abode of the dead. The Greek word "Hades" was used to translate several Hebrew words in the Bible, namely, "the pit," "stillness," "death," "those who bring death," "deep darkness," and, most commonly, "Sheol." "Sheol" probably derives from the verb "to ask or inquire" and thus refers to the realm of the dead as the place from which oracles were sought. The seeking of such oracles was forbidden by the Torah (Deut. 18:11) but was apparently practiced (1 Sam. 28:3–25).

Sheol sometimes refers to a place (Gen. 37:35) and sometimes to a being (Job 26:6). As a place, Sheol was a watery abyss (Job 26:5; 2 Sam. 22:5), the waters of chaos confined beneath the earth that corresponded to the waters of chaos above the firmament. As a being Sheol is portrayed with an immense, devouring mouth and as insatiable (Isa. 5:14; Prov. 30:15–16). This imagery derives from Canaanite myths about Baal, Anath, and Mot (Death). Mot reigns over the underworld and swallows Baal and all who die.

The dead are referred to as "shades," pale reflections of the men and women they had once been (Isa. 14:10; Eccles. 9:10). Existence in Sheol is characterized by forgetfulness and inactivity (Ps. 88:12; Eccles. 9:10). Sheol is not a place of punishment in the OT.

In the NT likewise, Hades appears both as a place (Acts 2:31) and as a being (Rev. 6:8). As a place it is the abode of the dead (Acts 2:27, 31). The notion that the realm of the dead had one or more gates controlling movement into and out of it is a very ancient one. It appears in the OT (Isa. 38:10) and in the NT (Matt. 16:18). In Rev. 1:18 the risen Christ says that he has "the keys of Death and Hades." The saying implies that Christ is able to unlock and lock the gates of Hades, that he has power over life and death. The saying in Matt. 16:18 means that the powers of death and other God-opposing forces will not triumph over the church (the community of believers in Jesus as the Christ).

Gehenna is the word most commonly used in the NT for the place where sinners will be punished after death (Matt. 5:22). In one passage Hades is presented as a place of torment (Luke 16:23). ***See also*** Abyss; Death; Gehenna; Heaven; Hell; Sheol. A.Y.C.

Hadoram (ha-doh'ruhm). **1** A son of Joktan, descendant of Shem (Gen. 10:27). **2** The son of Tou (Toi), king of Hamath; he was sent with gifts to congratulate David on his victory over Hadadezer (1 Chron. 18:10). He is also called Joram (2 Sam. 8:10). **3** An official of King Rehoboam (926–910 B.C.) of Judah; he supervised the conscripted labor force and was stoned to death by the people of Israel (the Northern Kingdom) when he attempted to enforce the harsh policies of Rehoboam (2 Chron. 10:18). He is called Adoram in the Hebrew text of 1 Kings 12:18, but Adoniram in the Greek text (Septuagint), and he may be identical with persons of both these names (1 Kings 4:6; 5:13–14). ***See also*** Adoniram; Adoram. D.R.B.

Hagar (hay'gahr), the Egyptian maidservant whom Sarah gave to Abraham as his concubine; she bore him Ishmael. There are two stories concerning Hagar, both showing the rivalry between her and Sarah. In the first (Gen. 16:1–16) Sarai (Sarah) was barren and, in accordance with custom, gave her maidservant to her husband so that she could bear a child in place of her mistress. When Hagar became pregnant, she acted arrogantly towards Sarah and so Sarah, with Abraham's permission, dealt so harshly with her that Hagar fled into the Wilderness of Shur. There she met an angel who announced that she should return to her mistress and that she would bear a son, to be named Ishmael, from whom would spring many descendants.

In Gen. 21:8–21 Hagar is back in Abraham's household. Some time has passed and Sarah has given birth to Isaac. Sarah felt that Ishmael threatened Isaac's position as heir, so she urged Abraham to expel Hagar and Ishmael. He acquiesced only after God assured him that he should heed Sarah, for Abraham's main line of descent was to be through Isaac, although God would also make a nation from Ishmael's descendants. Hagar was sent away with some bread and water and her child. When the provisions were used up and the child's death seemed imminent, an angel appeared and reassured Hagar that the child would produce a great nation. A well of water appeared and she gave her son water to drink. Ishmael grew up and became an archer in the Wilderness of Paran and married an Egyptian woman.

These stories show that Ishmael's descendants, the bedouins living to the south of the Israelites, were of the same stock as the Hebrews but from a religiously less important branch of the family. The inferiority of Hagar and Ishmael is used allegorically in the NT by Paul (Gal. 4:21–31). A.B.

Haggadah (hah-gah-dah'; Palestinian Talmud: "Aggadah"), the interpretation of the historical and religious passages of Jewish Scripture that are not legal in character. Haggadic texts often supplement the biblical narrative. A rich variety of Jewish "retelling" of the tradition comes under the category "Haggadah." Chronicles is sometimes described as a "historical midrash" (i.e., commentary) on the earlier historical writings. Hellenistic Jewish historians such as Josephus and Philo and writings such as the Apocrypha, the Pseudepigrapha, and the Dead Sea Scrolls all contain a wealth of haggadic material. Many stories and legends came to be told about such central figures in Israel's history as Adam, Enoch, Abraham, Joseph, and Moses.

Some NT examples of haggadic material about Moses show that its writers were familiar with such traditions. 2 Tim. 3:8 gives the names of the Egyptian sorcerers defeated by Moses, namely, Jannes and Jambres. Several writers refer to a tradition that the Law was given by angels rather than God (Gal. 3:19; Acts 7:53; Heb. 12:2). The water-giving rock is said to have accompanied the children of Israel on their journey (1 Cor. 10:4). Jude 9 refers to a legend that the archangel Michael and Satan struggled over the body of Moses.

Unlike the strict logic of legal interpretation, Haggadah could give free play to the imagination. Haggadic expositions are not bound to the previous tradition. However, the story had to remain within the bounds of what was acceptable to the religious community. ***See also*** Halakah. P.P.

Haggai (hag'ay-ī; Heb., "festal," "of a festival"), an OT prophetic book and the prophet named in that book who, with Zechariah, is also mentioned in Ezra 5:1 and 6:14; he is one of the twelve so-called minor prophets. There is no biographical material given in either book and, as a result, we know little more than the prophet's name. The framework to the book associates the message with dates in the second year of Darius I (about 520 B.C.). The similarity of this material to elements in the Priestly Code, the last of the four Pentateuchal sources, and also to Chronicles, suggests that this framework may be of later, editorial, origin.

The message is given to Zerubbabel and Joshua the high priest, and (in 1:12; 2:2) to the "remnant of the people." The first section (1:2–11) associates failure to rebuild the Temple with drought and agricultural disaster which has its origin in divine judgment. The second section (1:12–14) tells of the rebuilding as the response of leaders and people to the divine messenger (v. 13). The date in 1:15 is fragmentary and does not enable us to date the material with any accuracy. The next section (2:2–9) develops the Temple theme. The contrast between the glorious former Temple and the modest restored Temple will be reversed in the splendor of the new building. Both 2:6–7 and 2:21–22, with their picture of upheavals among the nations, may reflect the political uncertainties in Darius I's struggle to achieve supremacy. They also suggest a theophany, a divine intervention in human affairs. 2:10–14 use a priestly decision to comment on the people's life. While these verses can be interpreted in a variety of ways the most probable interpretation is that they criticize false trust in the rebuilt shrine. 2:15–19 speaks again of former disasters and present blessings (see 1:2–11). The book concludes (2:20–23) with a strongly worded hope centered on Zerubbabel as the divinely chosen Davidic leader, the "servant,"

OUTLINE OF CONTENTS

The Book of Haggai

I. God's call to repair the Temple (1:1–11)
   A. The need to repair it (1:2–6)
   B. Problems caused by failure to repair it (1:7–11)
II. Response to God's call (1:12–15)
III. Future glory of the Temple (2:1–9)
   A. God will fulfill his promise (2:1–5)
   B. Future splendor of the Temple (2:6–9)
IV. God's promise of blessing to come with Temple repair (2:10–19)
   A. Former misery (2:10–17)
   B. Future blessing (2:18–19)
V. God's confidence in Zerubbabel (2:20–23)

the "signet ring," royal executive of God.

Central to Haggai's message is a concern for the priority of the rebuilt Temple and for a purified and faithful community. This message is set in the framework of this community as the true remnant of God's chosen people and as the recipient of glorious hopes for the future. Because Haggai emphasizes that God will keep his promises, later readers can also find a message of hope for their own day. ***See also*** Darius; Sources of the Pentateuch; Temple, The; Zechariah; Zerubbabel. P.R.A.

Haggith (hag'ith; Heb., "festive"), one of David's wives and the mother of his fourth son, Adonijah (2 Sam. 3:4).

Hagiographa (hag-ee-ah'grah-fah; Gk., "sacred writings"), the final section of the Hebrew Bible in the tripartite arrangement attested before the rise of Christianity and maintained in Jewish versions to this day. This arrangement apparently reflects the three stages whereby the canon came into being. The Greek-derived name corresponds to the Hebrew *Kethubim* ("writings"), reflecting the miscellaneous character of these books, which include what the early rabbis called the "three big writings" (Psalms, Proverbs, Job), the later collection of "five scrolls" (Heb. *megillot)* arranged in order of the holidays at which they are read in the synagogue (Song of Songs, Ruth, Lamentations, Ecclesiastes, and Esther), and historical-narrative books (Daniel, Ezra-Nehemiah, and Chronicles). The section is called by a variety of names in the earliest sources, including "wisdom of the ancients" (Ecclus. 39:1), "writings of David" (2 Macc. 2:13), "Psalms" (Luke 24:44), and "other books" (introduction to Ecclus.; see also Josephus *Against Apion* 1:8 and Philo *On the Contemplative Life* 3), reflecting its still fluid contents, a condition that may also be mirrored in rabbinic uncertainty as to the canonicity of Song of Songs, Ecclesiastes, and Esther. The sequence of this group of eleven books, which does not exist as a discrete entity in the Christian canon where the books are arranged generically, was still not fixed in the Middle Ages. ***See also*** Bible; Canon; Old Testament. F.E.G.

Hagrites (hag'rīts), the name of a tribe with whom the eastern Israelite tribes of Reuben, Gad, and the eastern half-tribe of Manasseh fought and whom they eventually defeated in the time of Saul (ca. 1000 B.C.). Their territory lay east of the Jordan beyond Gilead in northern Arabia (1 Chron. 5:10, 19–20). The similarity of the names Hagrite and Hagar, Sarai's handmaid who bore Ishmael to Abraham (Gen. 16:1, 15), suggests to some scholars that the early Jewish historians saw some connection between this tribe and the Ishmaelites; however, such a connection is not certain. The Hagrites are listed with the traditional enemies of Israel, including the Ishmaelites (Ps. 83:6), although Jaziz the Hagrite was the overseer of the royal flocks under David (1 Chron. 27:30 [v. 31 in some versions]), and another Hagrite may have fought with David (1 Chron. 11:38, although "Gadite" in 2 Sam. 23:36). ***See also*** Ishmaelites. D.R.B.

Hai (hay'ī). ***See*** Ai.

hail, ice pellets formed when raindrops are thrown through alternating warm and cold air currents. Usually destructive to plants, hail is seen as a plague (Exod. 9:18–34; 10:5–15), as divine judgment (Hag. 2:17), as a destroying power (Isa. 28:2, 17), and always as part of violent storms (Pss. 148:8; 105:32; 78:47–48; cf. Rev. 8:7; 11:19).

hair, outgrowth from the head or elsewhere on the body. Several men in the Bible are known for their hairiness or their long hair. Esau's hirsuteness (Gen. 25:25; 27:11) contrasts with Jacob's smoothness and also links him phonetically with the place in which he ultimately settled: Se'ir (Gen. 36:8) has the same consonants as *se'ar*, "hair." The prophet Elijah was apparently identified by his hairiness (or perhaps his mantle, 2 Kings 1:8). Absalom's long, thick hair is a mark of handsomeness (2 Sam. 14:26) and also figures in his death—he was caught by the "head" in a terebinth (2 Sam. 18:9). Samson's long hair was the source of his strength. When it was shaved he was helpless (Judg. 16:17), but when it grew back (Judg. 16:22) he was able to pull the temple of Dagon down upon the Philistines.

Samson had long hair because he was a Nazirite (Judg. 13:5), a group whose vows included the injunction that "no razor shall come upon his head" (Num. 6:5; cf. 1 Sam. 1:11). The hair of the Nazirite was left uncut for the duration of his vow; when the period of Nazir-ship came to an end, either because the vow was fulfilled or through defilement (accidental contact with a corpse), his head was shaved and the hair offered as a sacrifice (Num. 6:9–18).

Shaving of the body was part of the purification of Levites (Num. 8:5–7), but a priest was not to make his head bald or shave the corners of his beard (Lev. 21:5). Priests in Ezekiel's description of the Temple were not to shave their heads or let their hair grow long (Ezek. 44:20). According to another priestly rule, lay Israelites were forbidden to cut the hair of their temples or beard (Lev. 19:27). Shaving was connected with the cure from leprosy (Lev. 13:33; 14:8–9), and shaving is also mentioned in various contexts in connection with mourning (Job 1:20; Isa. 15:2; Jer. 41:5; 47:5; 48:37; Ezek. 7:18). It is likely that the shaving of captive women (Deut. 21:12–13) is a sign of their mourning.

Disheveled hair was a sign of public shame.

From left to right: Head of one of the "Sea Peoples" (Philistines) captured by Ramesses III. He is beardless and wears a high feathered helmet; Medinet Habu, twelfth century B.C. Life-sized head of the Persian king Darius. His elaborately curled beard extends to his chest, his hair is arranged in ringlets in front and hangs in a bun at the back, and his mustache is curled at the tip; Behistun, fifth century B.C. The Assyrian king Tiglath-pileser III with long flowing hair and beard; copy of a wall painting from Tell 'Ahmar, eighth century B.C. Head of a Mede with pointed beard, mustache, and hair bunched at the neck—all elaborately curled; Persepolis, fifth century B.C.

Thus the leper's hair was loosened (Lev. 13: 45), as was the hair of a woman accused of infidelity (Num. 5:18). A priest's hair could not be let loose (Lev. 21:10, cf. Lev. 10:6).

One from whose head not one hair shall fall is one who is safe from harm (1 Sam. 14:45; 2 Sam. 14:11; 1 Kings 1:52; cf. Luke 21:18; Acts 27: 34). The hairs of the head may be used to represent a large number (Pss. 40:13; 69:5); that their number is known to God Jesus cites as a sign of his care (Matt. 10:30; Luke 12:7). Wiping Jesus' feet with their hair was a way two women showed him their devotion (Luke 7:38; John 12: 3). A.B.

Halah (hay'luh), a region in Assyria to which Israelite exiles were deported by the triumphant Assyrian kings (Pul, Tilgath-pilneser, 1 Chron. 5:26) who overthrew Samaria in 722 B.C (2 Kings 17:6; 18:11; Obad. 20). Its exact location in Mesopotamia is still a matter of dispute among scholars, though a location in the north, near Nineveh, seems most likely.

halakah (hahl-ah-kah'; from Heb. *halak*, "to walk, go, follow"), in Judaism the teaching one is to follow, the rules or statutes that are to guide a person's life. In the first instance, the ancient interpretation of the legal texts of the Torah (the first five books of the OT) sought to expound the consequences of individual commandments, the cases in practical life to which they applied, and how they might be accurately observed. However, halakic interpretation had to solve a number of difficulties: it had to eliminate discrepancies within the Law itself by determining an authoritative interpretation; in cases where the changed conditions of life made literal observance impossible or extremely inconvenient it had to show how one could "obey" yet not violate the wording of the Torah; and in cases where the written (and oral) tradition was incomplete, it had to establish a tradition. A considerable portion of Jewish Law was not directly connected with the Torah but has been established by custom, habit, or long-standing legal tradition. However, halakah is always understood to be a restatement of the Torah.

Hillel, a late first century B.C. rabbi, is said to have given seven rules for providing evidence in reaching a halakic decision: (1) arguing from a lesser case to a greater; (2) using an inference based on analogy; (3) deriving a legal principle from one text in the Torah; (4) deriving a principle from two texts; (5) making a general case more precise using a particular instance or defining a general case on the basis of a particular; (6) using similarities between two passages to provide one passage with a more precise definition; and (7) understanding the matter from its subject. These rules were later expanded into thirteen by dividing the fifth rule into eight more specific applications and dropping the sixth rule.

Since the Torah was to be the foundation of all Jewish life, halakic interpretation was in principle unending. The rabbis devoted much of their effort to religious matters such as precepts about sacrifices, about the Sabbath and other festivals, about dues to the Temple, and about tithes, offerings for firstborn, first fruits, vows, and other voluntary offerings. In the area of civil law, marriage receives the most attention. Criminal law is least developed in Talmudic sources, since it was frequently in the hands of those who ruled over the Jewish people, e.g., the Romans.

Examples of halakic debate between Jesus and the Pharisees are found in such NT passages as the story of plucking grain on the Sabbath (Matt. 12:1–8), the healing of the man with the withered hand (Matt. 12:9–12), and Jesus' teaching about divorce (Matt. 19:1–9). ***See also*** Haggadah. P.P.

hallel (hah-layl'; Heb., "praise"). ***See*** Hallelujah.

hallelujah (hah-lay-lo͞o'yah; Heb., "[let us] praise the Lord"), in the Hebrew Bible, a word restricted to Psalms, where it occurs only in Pss. 104–150. It is used twenty-three times as the introduction or conclusion of a psalm and, contrary to the rules of Hebrew grammar, is written as one word, though this practice was not universally accepted in the Talmudic period. Only in Psalm 135:3, where "hallelujah" is an intrinsic part of a verse rather than an introduction or conclusion of a psalm, is it written as two words. Both the Septuagint and Vulgate transliterate the word rather than translate it. These factors suggest that "hallelujah" was a religious cry, probably used to encourage audience participation in the liturgical recitation of psalms. Later, "hallelujah" became a stereotyped cry of joy; the Jews of Alexandria sang it after being saved from annihilation by the Egyptians (3 Macc. 7:13) and it introduces the angelic praise of God in Rev. 19:1–8. The recitation of the word "(h)allelujah" played an important role within the early church liturgy. M.Z.B.

hallow, to make holy or to set apart for special service. In the OT hallow is used to render a form of the Hebrew word *qādēsh*, the primary meaning of which is "separation" or "setting apart." In its various forms the Hebrew word is also translated as "holy," "holiness," "consecrate," "sanctify," "dedicate," "purify," or something similar. Thus, a "hallowed thing" was something set apart for a special use or purpose, such as the gifts Israel dedicated to God (Exod. 28:38) or the Jubilee Year (Lev. 25:10), and "to hallow" (consecrate, sanctify) persons or things was to remove them from the realm of ordinary profane labor or use to that of the sacred, such as the consecration of Aaron's sons as priests (Exod. 29:1; cf. 20:11). Associated with this appointment for special use was a sense of respect and reverence, clearly seen in the application of the term "hallowed" to God's name, which was understood to be in the sacred realm and therefore deserving of special reverence (Matt. 6:9; Luke 11:2). ***See also*** Holiness; Sanctification. D.R.B.

Ham. 1 In the Priestly notices of Gen. 5–10, Noah's second son (between Shem and Japheth) and the father of Cush, Egypt, Put, and Canaan. In Gen. 9:20–27 (attributed to J), disrespect for Noah by Ham, there his youngest son, earns Noah's curse on Canaan. Since the curse subordinates Canaan to both Shem and Japheth, perhaps the narrative was originally about Canaan, too. Occasionally Ham is a synonym for Egypt, one of Ham's sons. **2** A city of the Zuzim in Transjordan (Gen. 14:5).

Haman (hay'muhn), the villain in the book of Esther, who was appointed prime minister by the Persian ruler Ahasuerus. He plotted to destroy all Jews when Mordecai the Jew refused to prostrate himself before him. Esther and Mordecai collaborated to defeat Haman, and the tables were turned when he was hanged on the gallows he had erected for Mordecai; Mordecai then assumed Haman's office and estate.

Haman is called an Agagite (Esther 3:1) and Mordecai is placed in the line of Kish (Esther 2:5), linking their enmity with that of Agag the Amalakite and Saul son of Kish (1 Sam. 15). ***See also*** Esther; Mordecai; Purim, The Feast of. W.L.H.

Hamath (hay'muth), a city (modern Hama) on the Orontes River in Syria between Damascus and Aleppo; it also designated the district of which Hamath was the capital. Excavations have shown that the city was inhabited almost continually from the Neolithic period (ca. 8000 B.C.) to the present. Because of its strategic location and political importance it is mentioned frequently in extrabiblical sources (including a number found at Hamath itself) beginning in the first millennium as well as in the Bible. The first known ruler of Hamath was Toi (2 Sam. 8:9), who sent David gifts after the latter's victory over Zobah. Acccording to 2 Chron. 8:3–4 Solomon captured Hamath-zobah, probably an inaccurate designation of Zobah loosely based on David's campaign, and built store-cities in Hamath, which is historically questionable. During the Assyrian period Hamath figured prominently in the Assyrian annals; Sargon II (ca. 722–705 B.C.) describes himself as "the destroyer of Hamath." Following usual Assyrian practice, inhabitants of Hamath were deported to Samaria after its capture (2 Kings 17:24), and apparently Israelites were exiled to Hamath (Isa. 11:11). The phrase *lebō'-ḥamāt* (RSV: "the entrance of Hamath," Num. 13:21; Josh. 13:5) refers to a town (modern Lebweh) within the jurisdiction of Hamath but considerably to its south; it was the traditional northern limit of Israel's territory (see Num. 34:8; Ezek. 47:15). ***See also*** Zobah. M.D.C.

Hammath (ham'uhth). **1** A town on the west shore of the Sea of Galilee, a mile south of Tiberias where there are hot springs. It was part of Naphtali (Josh. 19:35) and perhaps the same as Hammoth-Dor (Josh. 21:32) and Hammon (1 Chron. 6:76). The springs are claimed to be the earliest known thermal baths in Palestine; Herod Antipas was probably the first to exploit them. **2** The proper name of the father of the house of Rechab (1 Chron. 2:55), or, as recently interpreted by some scholars, the "family (in-law)" of the father of the house of Rechab.

Hammedatha (ham-uh-day'thuh), the father of Haman, the Persian official of King Ahasuerus who attempted to exterminate the Jews (early fifth century B.C.; Esther 3:1; 8:5).

hammer, a striking tool used to fracture or to transmit force to a spike or other object. It could be used for murder (Judg. 4:21; 5:26, RSV: "mallet"), stonecutting (1 Kings 6:7), jewel-working (Isa. 41:7), woodworking (Jer. 10:4), or breaking rock (Jer. 23:29). It is a symbol of power (Jer. 51:20); when broken, it becomes a figure for helplessness or weakness (Jer. 50:23).

Hammon (ham'uhn; Heb., "hot spring"?). **1** An Asherite town (Josh. 19:28), probably modern Umm el-'Awamid near the Mediterranean coast fifteen miles north of Acco. **2** A yet unidentified levitical town of the Gershomites (1 Chron. 6:76) in Naphtali.

Hammoth-dor (ham'ahth-dawr). ***See*** Hammath.

Hammurabi (Hahm-ōō-rahb'ee; alternate spelling, Hammurapi), the most famous member of the first dynasty of Babylon. The members of the dynasty were of Amorite stock. Under this Old Babylonian dynasty (1894–1595 B.C.) the once unimportant city of Babylon became a new, major center for the first time and started taking on the appearance of a national capital.

Hammurabi (left), king of Babylon (1792–1750 B.C.), worships the god Shamash in a detail from the upper part of Hammurabi's stele found at Susa. (A full view is included with the color photographs.)

Hammurabi ruled for forty-three years (1792–1750) and eventually unified the country under the rule of Babylon. Though his military and diplomatic achievements do not seem to have lasted much beyond his reign, he transformed a small city-state into a large territorial state, created the prototype or even the pattern of the country of Babylonia with its capital in Babylon, and shifted the balance of activity and power to the north. Babylon now began to gain the power and prestige that allowed it to eclipse the southern centers as well as Nippur; and in later periods of Assyrian domination, the Assyrian conquerors found themselves compelled to work out various plans of accommodation with the city and the political, cultural, and religious forces that it came to represent.

Hammurabi's activities and times are known to us from year names, royal inscriptions, administrative and legal texts, literary texts, and, most of all, numerous letters and the rightly famous "Code of Hammurabi." The letters and the code have become the standard for what is now treated as the classic form of the Akkadian language.

Letters from Mari inform us of diplomatic and political events; letters from such centers as Larsa reveal the intricacies of local administration under Hammurabi and of Hammurabi's personal involvement. He seems to have devoted much attention and energy to administrative and judicial details. His style of government was similar to that of other successful contemporaries. His involvement in the execution of justice and in matters of routine administration seems to indicate a concern for an effective and just governance and for the public perception of such concern. His concerns conform to and continue the earlier tradition and ideal of the king as the one responsible for the peace, well-being, and justice of the land and its inhabitants.

Hammurabi's concern for justice finds its finest expression in what is the single most important document of his period, the Code of Hammurabi. Written near the end of his reign, the code is attested on stelae and tablets from the Old Babylonian and later periods. The most important witness is the stele found in Susa, where it had been moved by Elamites in the twelfth century B.C. The code comprises a prologue that catalogues Hammurabi's conquests of the various cities and his care of their cults, 282 paragraphs—the paragraph divisions are modern—presenting the laws in casuistic or case form, and an epilogue emphasizing the significance of this promulgation of justice. However, the term "code" is a misnomer; the document is neither a code in the accepted sense of the word nor even a collection of actual laws. The format of the code is not new with Hammurabi. This type of document, as well as individual representatives, derives from *misharum* edicts (adjustment of prices and wages, remission of debts and obligations) promulgated at the beginning of a reign in order to alleviate distress and create a new socioeconomic balance. Yet the code is a literary document whose publication was intended to mark Hammurabi as a good shepherd of his people and a model of a just king, for his generation and for generations to come. In part, the text takes the form of a royal inscription encasing laws rather than campaigns. Incorporating *misharum* materials as well as legal formulations of earlier collections, the code may perhaps also include examples of customary law, outstanding precedents, and innovations.

Most of all, however, it is a work of legal and literary scholarship. And certainly the code of Hammurabi is fuller and more elegantly articulated and arranged than earlier texts. It is a monument to the legal speculation of the period. Scribal scholarship is here seen at work: the legal mind plays out various possibilities, including the theoretical and/or the unlikely, and thereby examines cases that are extreme or unusual but logical alternatives to previously stipulated situations in order to explore, exemplify, and even invent principles. The code is not binding and does not necessarily reflect actual practice; it is, however, a literary and intellectual construct that gives expression to legal thinking and moral values. The importance of the Code of Hammurabi for the interpretation of such biblical collections as the Covenant Code (Exod. 21–23) can hardly be exaggerated. ***See also*** Babylon.

Bibliography

Driver, G. R., and J. C. Miles. *The Babylonian Laws*. Vols. 1–2. Oxford: Clarendon, 1952–55.

Edzard, D. O. "The Old Babylonian Period." In *The Near East: The Early Civilizations*. Ed. J. Bottéro,et al. New York: Delacorte, 1967. Pp. 177–231.

Oates, J. *Babylon*. New York: Thames & Hudson, 1979. Pp. 60–82.

I.T.A.

Hamor (hay'mohr), the Hivite ruler of Shechem (Gen. 34:2) from whom Jacob bought a piece of land (Gen. 33:19) where Joseph's remains were later buried (Josh. 24:32; cf. Acts 7: 16). Hamor died when his son Shechem raped Dinah, the daughter of Jacob and Leah, and her brothers attacked the city in revenge (Gen. 34).

hamstring (KJV: "hough"), to cut the tarsal joint tendons, preventing an animal from being able to walk (Josh. 11:6, 9; 2 Sam. 8:4; 1 Chron. 18:4).

Hamul (hay'muhl; Heb., "spared"), the son of Perez and grandson of Judah (Gen. 46:12); he was the head of the clan of the Hamulites (Num. 26:21).

Hanamel (han'uh-mel), the son of Shallum and the cousin of the prophet Jeremiah. Hanamel sold a field to Jeremiah according to the laws of redemption. Its purchase at the time the Babylonians were laying siege to Jerusalem (ca. 588 B.C.) became a symbol to Jeremiah of God's promised restoration of Israel (Jer. 32:7–15). The transaction is also of interest because it sheds light on the legal system then in operation.

Hanan (hay'nuhn). **1** One of David's warriors (1 Chron. 11:43). **2** A Benjaminite (1 Chron. 8:23). **3** A descendant of Saul (1 Chron. 8:38; 9:44). **4** The head of a prophetic guild in the time of Jeremiah (Jer. 35:4). **5** The head of one of the families of "Temple servants" after the Exile (Ezra 2:49; Neh. 7:49). **6** A Levite who interpreted the law (Neh. 8:7) and subscribed to Ezra's covenant (Neh. 10:10). **7** The assistant to the Levites appointed by Nehemiah as Temple treasurers (Neh. 13:13). **8** Two of "the chiefs of the people" who subscribed to Ezra's covenant (Neh. 10:22, 26). P.K.M.

Hananel (huh-nan'uhl; Heb., "God is gracious"; KJV: "Hananeel"), a tower repaired by Nehemiah (Neh. 3:1; 12:39) in the north wall around Jerusalem near the northeast corner (Jer. 31:38; Zech. 14:10). It flanked an approach to the Temple and is named for an unknown person.

Hanani (hah-nay'nee; Heb., a shortened form of Hananiah, "God has favored me [with a child]"). **1** A musician, the son of Heman, a contemporary of David (1 Chron. 25:4). **2** A prophet who rebuked the Judean kings Asa (2 Chron. 16: 7) and Jehoshaphat (2 Chron. 19:2) and whose son Jehu rebuked the Northern king Basha (1 Kings 16:1). **3** A postexilic priest who married a foreign wife (Ezra 10:20). **4** Nehemiah's brother or kinsman (Neh. 1:2). **5** A musician who helped Nehemiah restore Jerusalem's wall (Neh. 12:36). Perhaps the sentiment which the name conveyed made it so popular among the Israelites.

M.Z.B.

Hananiah (ha-nah-nī'ah; Heb., "God has favored me [with a child]"), a name borne by at least ten biblical personages. Two are well known. **1** Hananiah, the son of Azur, who died for falsely prophesying against Jeremiah (Jer. 28). **2** Hananiah, also called Shadrach, one of Daniel's three friends who was miraculously saved from the fiery furnace (Dan. 1–3).

hand (Heb. *yadh;* Gk. *cheir*), a term occurring approximately fifteen hundred times in the Bible meaning, among other things, hand, side, and power. It can operate on behalf of the whole person, frequently as a substitute for an individual's activities, dealings, and even spiritual impulses. Offering one's hand indicates a token of sincerity and willingness to help another (2 Kings 10:15). Conversely, the hand is the means of murder (Gen. 4:11) and retaliation (Exod. 21:24; Deut. 25:11). The hand's ability to seize, control, or manipulate explains its association with strength or power. The hand of God, a prominent Jewish symbol and popular motif for later Christian iconography, symbolizes God's sovereign power (Deut. 3:24; Job 19:21; Heb. 10:31; 1 Peter 5:6). God's hand governs the forces of history (Exod. 13:3, 14; 1 Sam. 5:9; Ps. 8:7) and strengthens believers (Mark 6:2; Acts 5:12). The NT places Jesus at the right hand of God, the side of authority and power (Mark 12:36; Acts 2:25; Heb. 1:3; cf. Ps. 110:1, 5; Dan. 7:13).

The hand's equation with power or strength helps explain such phrases as "the hand of the tongue" (Prov. 18:21 [RSV: "power of the tongue"]; cf. Josh. 8:21) and "to raise the hand," meaning a revolutionary uprising (1 Kings 11:26). Job is placed in Satan's hand, i.e., under his domain and authority (Job 2:6; cf. Jer. 22:3; Matt. 26:45). "Hand" can also substitute for a personal pronoun (Lev. 8:36; Isa. 35:3).

As a ritual the "laying on of hands" occurs frequently in the sacrificial cult (Lev. 16; Num. 8) and serves as a form of ordination (Num. 27:18; Deut. 34:9; 1 Tim. 4:14). It may also impart a blessing (Gen. 48:18; Isa. 44:3; Matt. 19:13). Healing the sick is closely associated with the hand in the NT, indicating the transference of spiritual and physical wholeness (Mark 5:23; Luke 13:13). The hand transmitted power, authority, and the Holy Spirit after baptism (Acts 8:7; 19:6; Heb. 6:2). It symbolizes betrayal (Matt. 26:23), apocalyptic power (Mark 1:31), ritual purity (Mark 7:2), and persecution (Luke 21:12; Acts 13:3). D.R.E.

handkerchief, a small piece of cloth used by the Romans primarily for wiping the face and hands. The Jewish community also used the handkerchief for this purpose, but several examples in the NT show that the cloth could serve other functions as well. In Luke 19:20, this word is used for a cloth in which money is stored (KJV and RSV: "napkin"). In John 11:44 and 20:7, the same word refers to a cloth that is placed over the face of a dead person (KJV: "napkin"; RSV: "cloth" in 11:44 and "napkin" in 20:7). In a different vein, handkerchiefs that had come into contact with Paul were believed to have healing power (Acts 19:11–12). ***See also*** Napkin.

J.M.E.

hanging, a method of execution in which the victim is suspended from a rope around the neck. Hanging was not a method of execution in the Bible; rather, executed people were hung after death. Thus Joshua hung the corpse of the king of Ai (Josh. 8:29) and of the five anti-Gibeonite kings (Josh. 10:26), and David hung the corpses of Rechab and Baanah (2 Sam. 4:12). The custom was also known among the Egyptians, for Joseph predicted that Pharaoh would hang the baker (Gen. 40:19). Later on Persians were impaled (Herodotus 3. 115, 159), and we do not know whether the hangings in the book of Esther (Esther 2:23; 5:14; 7:9, 10; 9:13–14) were hangings or impalings. Hanging is permitted in the book of Deuteronomy (Deut. 21:22–23) with the proviso that the corpse be taken down before evening to avoid contaminating the land; the corpses hung by Joshua were left only until evening (cf. the removal of Jesus from the cross, Matt. 27:57). There is a second Hebrew verb *(yoqi'a)* that may refer to either hanging or impaling; the procedure was used by the Philistines (1 Sam. 31:10) and the Gibeonites (2 Sam. 21:10–14). According to Mishnah *Sanhedrin* 6:4, in later Israel only those criminals executed by stoning were hanged; according to the first-century historian Josephus *(Antiquities* IV viii 24), all executed criminals were. T.S.F.

hangings, the usual translation of a Hebrew term for the fabric forming the walls of the tabernacle court (Exod. 27:9–18; 35:9; 38:12–18; 39:40). Stretched along the perimeter of the 100 × 50 cubit enclosure (about 150 × 75 feet), the hangings were attached at intervals to pillars 5 cubits (about 7.5 feet) in height. Additional hangings flanked the courtyard gate. Like the material enclosing the tabernacle itself (RSV: "curtains") and that of the embroidered "screens" (RSV; cf. KJV: "hangings") at the door of the tent and at the courtyard gate, the hangings were made of a fine-twined linen (Heb. *shaysh)* which bespeaks an Egyptian origin; but the brilliant colors (blue, purple, and scarlet) of the hangings are more akin to color words and preferences of the Syro-Mesopotamian world.

Two other examples of hangings, for which the Hebrew word differs, occur in the Bible: in 2 Kings 23:7, women weave hangings for the Asherah, presumably to drape the goddess's cult image or pole; and Esther 1:6 describes blue hangings that adorn the royal garden for a magnificent banquet. ***See also*** Tabernacle.

C.L.M.

Hannah (Heb., "grace"), wife of Elkanah and mother of the prophet Samuel (1 Sam. 1:2, 20). On an annual pilgrimage to God's shrine at Shiloh, Hannah vowed that if she bore a son, she would dedicate him to God. This granted, she named him Samuel, and when she had weaned him, she fulfilled her vow. Hannah later bore three sons and two daughters (1 Sam. 2:21). To Hannah is attributed a prayer (1 Sam. 2:1–10) whose words constitute a song of praise to God, who metes out justice to all the world in accordance with his unique wisdom: abasement of the mighty and exaltation of the lowly, death and life God alone dispenses; his enemies are doomed, but his faithful ones are protected. The theme, the reversal of human fortunes, is encountered in other Psalms and in Wisdom literature (e.g., Ps. 113:5–9; Eccles. 10:5–7; cf. Luke 1: 51–53). S.G.

Hanoch (hay'nahkh). **1** The son of Midian and grandson of Keturah and Abraham (Gen. 25:4; 1 Chron. 1:33). **2** The son of Reuben who went with Jacob to Egypt (Gen. 46:9; Exod. 6:14). **3** The head of the clan of the Hanochites who left Egypt with Moses (Num. 26:5).

Hanukkah (hahn'uh-kuh). ***See*** Dedication, Feast of.

Hanun (hay'nuhn; Heb., "gracious"). **1** The Ammonite king whose insult to David's servants led to war and defeat resulting in slavery (2 Sam. 10:1–19; 1 Chron. 19:1–19; 2 Sam. 11:1; 12:26–31). **2** A man of Zanoah who repaired the Jerusalem city wall and gate (Neh. 3:13, 30).

Haran (hay'ruhn), a city located in northern Mesopotamia about sixty miles above the confluence of the Balikh and Euphrates rivers. Haran was an important center of religious and political activity for the Hurrians, who dominated this region in the middle of the second millennium B.C. Haran is well attested in the archives from Nuzi, which provide an ample picture of Hurrian life at this time. Haran becomes an important commercial center in the first millennium B.C. Activity there is mentioned in Ezek. 27:23. The city, sacred to the moon god, may have been the king's residence in the last decades of Assyrian rule, when the moon god's term was assumed to have begun.

In the period of Assyrian domination, the governor of Haran was a powerful official. He was the commander-in-chief of the Assyrian forces and was appointed by the king. In the practice of naming years after officials in the kingdom, the rotation of the commander-in-chief followed that of the king.

Following the fall of Nineveh in 612 B.C., the remaining Assyrians fled to Haran for refuge. In spite of support from the advancing forces of Pharaoh Neco, the Assyrians, under Ashuruballit (611–610 B.C.), were unable to stave off the attack from a coalition of Medes, Scyths, and Babylonians who were under the leadership of Nabopolassar. 2 Kings 19:12 mentions the destruction of Haran by this coalition.

Haran was an important center for the worship of the moon god, Sin. Two dedicatory stelae report the rebuilding of the Sin temple, Ehulhul, by Nabonidus (555–539 B.C.), the last native Babylonian king. This follows Nabonidus' ten-year absence from Babylon, reported in these stelae, at the command of Sin after the god decimated the populations of urban centers that had sinned against him. At the order of Sin, Nabonidus installed the cult figures of Sin and other lunar deities in Haran on a permanent dais. The biographical text of Adad-guppi, Nabonidus' mother, reports how Sin abandoned Haran. Her report includes a record of her devotion to the moon god's cult, in spite of his decline, and her procurement for Nabonidus of the right and distinction to return Ehulhul to its former glory and to restore the cult images to their proper places.

Haran figures prominently in the patriarchal narratives and in the attempts at historical reconstruction of the patriarchal period. In addition to Haran, the father of Lot and brother of Abram (Gen. 11:31), the names of several of Abram's relatives are the names of cities or towns in the region of Haran: Peleg, a distant ancestor (Gen. 11:18); Serug, Abram's great-grandfather; Nahor, his grandfather and his brother; and Terah, his father (Gen. 11:22–29). Terah took his household to Haran after leaving Ur of the Chaldees (Gen. 11:31–32) and died in Haran. Abram left Haran for Canaan at God's instruction (Gen. 12:1), gathering with him his sizable household and considerable wealth, amassed while in Haran (Gen. 12:4–5). Abraham sent his servant back to the region of Haran to procure a wife for his son Isaac (Gen. 24:10).

Jacob is instructed by Rebecca to return to Haran as a place of refuge following his appropriation of Esau's birthright (Gen. 27:43; 28:10). In Haran, he took his wives and fathered the sons who would become the fathers of Israel's tribes. Laban (Heb., "white"), the name of Jacob's uncle, is attested in Mesopotamian texts of the sixteenth century B.C. as an epithet of the moon god.

The association of Haran with Ur of the Chaldees has fueled scholarly debate about the actual location of Ur. Some would locate Ur in the region of Haran, arguing that Ur does not become a Chaldean outpost until the late first millennium B.C., long after the patriarchal narratives occurred, and that Ur, in southern Mesopotamia, is too far from Haran. However, Ur, an important urban center in Sumerian times, was the center of worship of the moon god in southern Mesopotamia. Its ziggurat (temple with each higher level stepped in from the lower) to the moon god was built at the end of the third millennium B.C. The destruction of Ur by the Elamites in the early second millennium B.C. would have provided impetus for Terah's departure for Haran around this time along an established trade route. ***See also*** Abraham; Ur. L.E.P.

hare, any herbivorous rodent of the family *Leporidae,* in Palestine either *Lepus europaeus judaeus* or *Lepus syriacus.* It was considered unclean (Lev. 11:6; Deut. 14:7) for an inaccurate reason, namely, the assumption that a hare chews the cud.

Harim (hay'rim; Heb., "consecrated" or "dedicated"). **1** A priest, descendant of Aaron and head of the third group of priests (1 Chron. 24:

8). Any of the following could be descendants of his family. **2** A family group ("sons of Harim") who returned from the Babylonian captivity with Zerubbabel (Ezra 2:32); this is probably the same family who had eight members condemned by Ezra for taking foreign wives (Ezra 10:31). **3** A much larger priestly family group who returned with Zerubbabel (Ezra 2:39); five members of this family took foreign wives (Ezra 10:21). The family group headed by Adna could be this group or 2 above (Neh. 12:15). **4** A member of the postexilic community who signed the covenant to keep the law (Neh. 10:5). **5** A leader of the people who also signed the covenant (Neh. 10:27). **6** The father (ancestor?) of Malchijah, one who helped repair the walls of postexilic Jerusalem (Neh. 3:11). He could be either one of the men above (4 or 5) or "son of Harim" may simply designate Malchijah as a member of the larger family group (1). D.R.B.

harlot, a prostitute, one who accepted money for the performance of sex. Several important characters in Israelite history were connected to harlots. The Jericho harlot Rahab sheltered Joshua's spies (Josh. 2), Jephthah was the son of a harlot (Judg. 11:1), and Tamar pretended to be a harlot to induce Judah to have sex with her (Gen. 38:14–18). None of these women were stigmatized, but prostitutes in general were considered an underclass. Priests could not marry harlots (Lev. 21:7), Israelites should not make their daughters harlots (Lev. 19:29), and a priest's daughter who became a harlot should be burned (Lev. 21:9). The payment a prostitute received was considered like the price of a dog: neither could be used to fulfill vows (Deut. 23:18). Like the death of children in battle, the turning of wives into harlots was considered a tragedy of destruction (Amos 7:17).

We know little of how harlots worked. Tamar waited at a crossroads, Rahab had a house. Tamar was veiled for her meeting with Judah, but this was more probably to conceal her identity than to indicate harlotry (note that in Assyria harlots were forbidden the veil). The phrases "act like a harlot" or "treat as a harlot" are not always literal: when Dinah's brothers complained that Shechem treated Dinah like a harlot (Gen. 34:31), they refer to the lack of proprieties rather than an offer of money. The point of the Deuteronomic order to stone a nonvirgin bride is that she acted wantonly while in her father's house (Deut. 22:20–21), not that she accepted money. Similarly, the personified Israel is called a "harlot" to indicate wanton, rather than mercenary behavior (Hos. 1:2); furthermore, such passages as Jer. 5:7 refer to the faithlessness of the nation rather than to rampant sex among the people.

The OT uses another term (Heb. *qedeshah*) to refer to sacred prostitutes. These were part of the fertility cult that Israel was trying to suppress (e.g., Judg. 8:33; Ezek. 16). In the NT, when Rome is designated harlot (e.g., Rev. 17:1, 15) it is a term of general moral opprobrium and does not mean harlots were more common in Rome than elsewhere in the Greco-Roman world. T.S.F.

Harod (hay'ruhd). **1** A rushing, copious spring, now 'Ain Jalud, on the northwesternmost spur of Mount Gilboa where the Jezreel Plain narrows to run down to Beth-shan and the Jordan—a crucial military location. Here Gideon's militia camped opposite the Midianites under Mount Moreh (Judg. 7:1). It is also "the spring in Jezreel," where Saul camped (1 Sam. 29:1). **2** The home of Shammah and Elika, two of David's "thirty" (2 Sam. 23:25; the name "Shammoth the Harorite" in 1 Chron. 11:27 is probably a corruption). ***See also*** Gilboa; Jezreel; Moreh. E.F.C.

Harosheth-ha-goiim (ha-roh'sheth-ha-gaw-yeem'; Heb., "Harosheth of the Gentiles"), the home base of Sisera, the commander of the army of the Canaanite king Jabin (Judg. 4:2). There Sisera gathered his men and chariots and was defeated by Barak and Deborah (4:13–16). Harosheth-ha-goiim was strategically located near the Plain of Esdraelon southeast of Mt. Carmel, but its exact location remains unknown. It has been identified with modern Tell Amr or Tell Harbaj on the Kishon River, or with that general region, on the assumption that the name is related to the Hebrew root *hrsh* ("wooded height").

harp. ***See*** Music.

hart, the male (female, hind) of the red deer *Cervus elaphus*, viewed as clean (Deut. 12:15, 22; 14:5; 15:22). Its need for water is a metaphor for human longing for God (Ps. 42:1) and its jumps are a model of healthy life (Isa. 35:6), but without pasture it symbolizes hopeless confusion (Lam. 1:6).

harvest. ***See*** Farming.

Hashabiah (hahsh-uh-bee'uh; Heb., "Yah/Yahu [God] has considered/regarded"), a male personal name. It occurs in the OT principally in lists of names (1 Chron. 6:45; 9:14; Neh. 11:15; 1 Chron. 25:3, 19; 26:30; 27:17; 2 Chron. 35:9; 1 Esd. 1:9; Ezra 8:19, 24; 10:25; 1 Esd. 9:26; Neh. 3:17; 10:11; 11:22; 12:21, 24).

Hasmoneans (has-muh-nee'uhnz), derived from (Heb.) Hashmon, meaning "descendants of Hashmon," a Jewish family that included the Maccabees and the high priests and kings who ruled Judea from 142 to 63 B.C. ***See also*** Maccabees.

Hattin (hah-teen'), **Horns of,** a prominent hill

about 5 miles west of the Sea of Galilee. This extinct volcano was identified by the Crusaders —with little justification—as the Mount of the Beatitudes. The site controls a strategic segment of the ancient road from Egypt to northern Syria, near the point where the highway begins its descent to the Sea of Galilee. The remains of the important Canaanite city found on top of the hill have been identified with biblical Adamah (Josh. 19:36) or, alternately, with Madon (Josh. 11:1; 12:19).

Hattush (hat'to͞osh). **1** A son of Shemaiah, and a descendant of David (1 Chron. 3:22). **2** The head of a house that accompanied Ezra on the return from the Babylonian exile, perhaps the same person as 1 (Ezra 8:2). **3** A son of Hashabneiah, who took part in restoring the walls of Jerusalem (Neh. 3:10). **4** One of the priests who sealed the covenant after the return from the Exile (Neh. 10:4). **5** A prominent priest who returned from the Exile in Babylon with Zerubbabel (Neh. 12:2).

Hauran (hawr'an), the northeast limit of Ezekiel's vision of the restored Israel, mentioned only in Ezek. 47:16, 18. Hauran was the broad Syrian plateau country south of Damascus, east of Jaulan (Golan Heights), west of the Jebel Druze, and north of the Yarmuk River. Ancient Egyptian texts speak of it as *Huruna*, and Assyrian records as *Haurana*. Easily invaded from the north, it was devastated by the Assyrian kings more than once: Shalmaneser III in 842 B.C., Tiglath-pileser III ten years later, and Ashurbanipal in his ninth campaign against the Arabians. The Maccabeans conquered it in the second century B.C. and in the early first century it became part of the Nabatean Empire. The Roman name for the fertile southern region (OT Bashan, modern Hauran) was Auranitis. ***See also*** Assyria, Empire of; Bashan; Nabatea, Nabateans; Syria. D.B.

Havilah (hah'vee-lah; Heb., perhaps "sandy area"), the name given to more than one district east of Palestine. Gen. 2:11 places it in Eden, surrounded by the river Pishon; Gen. 10:7 and 1 Chron. 1:9 relate Havilah to Cush, suggesting a region in southern Mesopotamia. However, in Gen. 10:26–29 and 1 Chron. 1:20–23 Hazarmaveth, Sheba, Ophir, and Havilah are closely related as descendants of Shem, indicating an area somewhere in the east or southeast of Arabia. Gen. 25:18 places it in northeast Arabia, saying the Ishmaelites "dwelt from Havilah to Shur, which is opposite Egypt." In 1 Sam. 15:7 "Havilah" should probably read "Hachilah." ***See also*** Ethiopia; Hachilah; Ophir; Sheba. D.B.

Havvoth-jair (hay-vuhth-jay'ihr; Heb., "villages of Jair"), sixty (Deut. 3:14) or thirty (Judg. 10:4) villages in Bashan in Gilead.

hawk, a common bird of prey in Palestine. The Hebrew term *nēṣ* applied to the sparrowhawk or the small but swift kestrel. As carnivorous birds, hawks were considered unclean and therefore inedible for the Hebrews (Deut. 14:11–18). Their raptorial habits make hawks valuable hunters of rodents and other small pests.

A symbol of speed and freedom, hawks are still seen soaring on updrafts above the Jordan Valley, a route of the fall southward migration (Job. 39:26). They frequent desolate areas, nesting in the rocky crags and cliffs of gorges. P.L.C.

Hazael (ha'zah-el; Heb., "God has seen"), an Aramean king of Damascus during the latter half of the eighth century B.C. According to the Bible, he was to have been anointed by Elijah (1 Kings 19:15). An officer of King Ben-hadad, he was sent to learn from Elisha whether his master would recover from an illness, at which time the prophet foresaw the troubles Hazael would bring to Israel (2 Kings 8). Hazael returned and murdered Ben-hadad, then ascended the throne (v. 15). Assyrian sources, which call him "son of nobody" because of his nonroyal background, note his unsuccessful confrontations with Shalmaneser III in 841 and again in 837. He was able to conquer Ramoth-gilead in the Transjordan (2 Kings 10:32; see also Amos 1:3), leaving the son of Israel's King Jehu with only limited forces (2 Kings 13:7). After conquering Gath, his attention turned to Jerusalem, which bought its freedom with tribute (2 Kings 12:17–18). He was succeeded by his son Ben-hadad, who lost to Israel's King Jehoash the cities Hazael had conquered (2 Kings 13:25). ***See also*** Aram; Ben-hadad. F.E.G.

Hazarshual (hay-zahr-sho͞o'uhl; Heb., meaning uncertain, possibly "the haunt of the fox"), a settlement in southern Judah counted as belonging to both the tribes of Judah (Josh. 15:28) and Simeon (Josh. 19:3). It was probably originally occupied by Simeon and then later occupied by Judah as the tribe of Simeon lost its identity and was absorbed into Judah (1 Chron. 4:28–31; note Gen. 49:5–7). It was later occupied by returning exiles (Neh. 11:27). Its exact location is unknown.

Hazeroth (hah-zee'ruhth), one of the camping places of the Israelites as they left Egypt. According to the OT narrative it was located between Kibroth-hattaavah and Rithmah in the Wilderness of Paran (Num. 11:35; 33:17–18). At this site Aaron and Miriam criticized Moses' actions and leadership, which resulted in Miriam being struck with leprosy (Num. 12:1–16). The site is unknown although several locations in the northeastern Sinai have been suggested.

Hazor (hay'zohr; Heb., "enclosed"). **1** A city in

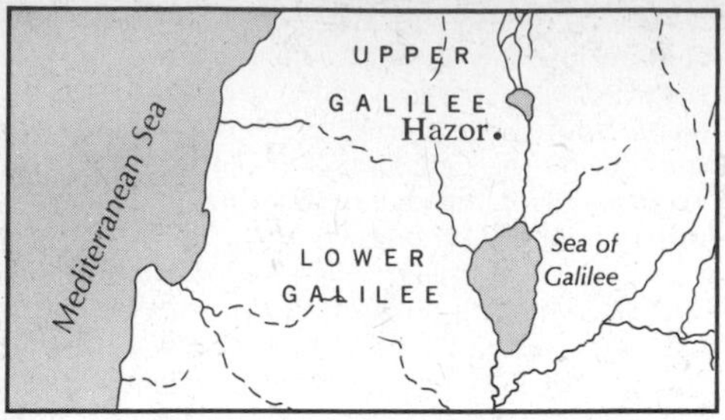

the northern reaches of the Holy Land. The main city had two components: an upper tell and a lower rectangular plateau (modern Tell el-Qedah or Tell Waqqas) both located four miles southwest of Lake Huleh, ten miles north of the Sea of Galilee, and covering 175 acres.

It was a major fortified Canaanite city that first figures in biblical stories of Joshua's battles. According to Joshua 11, Jabin, King of Hazor, responded to news of the Israelite presence by marshaling allies to meet the intruders. By hamstringing the horses and burning the chariots of the allies, Joshua defeated Jabin and burned the city of Hazor as well as defeating the allies (Josh. 11:6–15; 12:19).

According to Judg. 4:2–24, Jabin's commander, Sisera, fought Israelites under Deborah and Barak but was defeated by them (see also Judg. 5 for a poetic version of the encounter), an episode remembered as an act of divine deliverance, though sometimes in error (1 Sam. 12:9).

Solomon fortified Hazor (1 Kings 9:15), but

Reconstruction of the citadel gate at Hazor from the time of King Ahab, ninth century B.C.

Assyria captured it under Tiglath-pileser III (ca. 745–727 B.C.; 2 Kings 15:29), an event vividly evident in destroyed brick blockage of doors in the casemate defense walls of the upper city. If the territory under the city's control extended to Arab tribes east of the city, it may have been the subject of Jeremiah's oracle of warning (Jer. 49:28–33) in Neo-Babylonian times (sixth century B.C.).

Hazor was excavated extensively by Yigael Yadin from 1955 to 1972. It had been sounded by J. Garstang in 1928, but Yadin's reports are the definitive archaeological record of the site. Occupied first in the Early Bronze Age (3000–2000 B.C.; strata XXI–XIX), there was sparse architecture surviving, as there was for stratum XVIII (Middle Bronze I). Extensive architecture was recovered in both upper and lower cities for remaining Middle (2000–1500 B.C.) and Late Bronze periods (1500–1200 B.C.), and a thirteenth-century B.C. destruction by fire was attested. Minor construction marked the early Iron Age city (post 1200 B.C.), but Solomonic construction of defenses, both walls and gates, was massive, as at Gezer and Megiddo. Following another destruction by fire, major building again occurred. Public structures built in Iron Age II (900–600 B.C.) subsequently became living quarters (stratum VI) that were rebuilt (stratum V) after destruction by earthquake. The fiery destruction of this rebuilt city was attributed by Yadin to Assyria's Tiglath-pileser. A major water system comprising an entrance pit and horizontal tunnel to the source was also cleared and dated as a ninth century B.C. construction.

From both the extensive archaeological and topographical evidence, the literary records (eighteenth-century B.C. Mari Letters; fourteenth-century Amarna Letters; nineteenth-century execration texts; Egyptian topographical lists; thirteenth-century Papyrus Anastasi I) attesting its major importance in trade and politics of the Ancient Near East are confirmed.

2 A city in the territory of Judah, modern el-Jebariyeh (Josh. 15:23).

3 A city in the territory of Benjamin, modern Khirbet Hazzur, some four miles north and slightly west of Jerusalem (Neh. 11:33). ***See also*** Assyria, Empire of; Solomon. R.S.B.

ה

he (hay), the fifth letter of the Hebrew alphabet; its numerical value is five. The earliest proto-Canaanite form of the letter is a pictograph of a calling man. Phoenician and early Hebrew forms developed from this. The old form is still recognized in the Latin "E" and Greek epsilon. The classical Hebrew square script adapted a form of the Aramaic variant of this letter. In Judaism this letter is often used as an abbreviation of the divine name (the tetragrammaton). ***See also*** Writing.

head, the first or foremost; anatomically the topmost part of the human body. The biblical words for "head" are employed in a variety of usages. "Head" can refer to an anatomical part of the body. Israel laid his hand "upon the head of Ephraim" (Gen. 48:14). Wagging the head in scorn or derision is decribed in Ps. 109:25 and Mark 15:29.

"Head" can also have transferred meanings. It can refer to a leader, such as the head of a family (Josh. 22:14) or province (Neh. 11:3). In Eph. 4:15, Jesus is described as the head of the church. In a phrase such as "on the top (Heb. *rosh*, 'head') of the hill" (Exod. 17:9) it refers to a topographical feature. It can be used with an opposite noun to designate a limit: "from the sole of the foot even to the head" (Isa. 1:6); "from the beginning (Heb. *rosh*) to the end" (Eccles. 3: 11). ***See also*** Anoint; Beards; Gestures; Hair.

D.B.W.

heart, probably the most important anthropological word in the Hebrew scriptures, referring almost exclusively to the human heart (814 times; cf. "the heart of God," 26 times; "heart of the sea," 11 times). The physical activity of the heart, though rarely mentioned, is what caused the limbs to move. A stopped heart indicated paralysis, not death (1 Sam. 25:37; 2 Sam. 18: 14). Eating strengthened one's heart (Gen. 18:5 [RSV: "refresh yourselves"]; Judg. 19:5) and was associated with its recovery (1 Kings 21:7; Acts 14:17; James 5:5). The inaccessibility of the heart helps explain "heart of the sea" (Ezek. 27: 25–27) and "heart of heaven" (Deut. 4:11), i.e., those areas incapable of exploration.

The heart is the center of emotions, feelings, moods, and passions. Equated with the heart are joy (Deut. 28:47; Acts 2:26), grief (Ps. 13:2; Lam. 2:11), ill-temper (Deut. 15:10), love (Phil. 1:7), courage (2 Sam. 17:10; Ps. 27:14), and fear (Gen. 42:28). A swollen heart breeds arrogance (Isa. 9:9), which is in marked contrast to the gentle and lowly heart of Jesus (Matt. 11:29).

The heart's function as the source of thought and reflection highlights its intellectual capacities (Isa. 6:10; Mark 7:21–23). The heart understands (Deut. 8:5; Isa. 42:25), provides wisdom to rule justly and wisely (1 Kings 3:12; 10:24), and discerns good and evil (1 Kings 2:49).

The heart also represents the idea of volition and conscience (1 Sam. 24:5; 2 Sam. 24:10). The request for a pure heart is the desire for a new and more perfect conscience (Ps. 51:10; Matt. 5:8). Since the heart is the center for decisions (2 Sam. 7:21), obedience, devotion, and intentionality, it represents the total human person. Within the heart, human beings meet God's word (1 Sam. 12:24; Jer. 32:40) and thus it is the location where conversion takes place (Ps. 51:10; Joel 2:12; Acts 2:37).

D.R.E.

heathen. ***See*** Gentile; People, Peoples.

heaven, the firmament, the massive transparent dome that covers the earth in the world view of the ancient Hebrews. The blue color of the sky was attributed to the chaotic waters that the firmament separated from the earth (Gen. 1:7). The earth was thus surrounded by waters above and below (Deut. 5:8). The firmament was thought to be substantial; it had pillars (Job 26:11) and foundations (2 Sam. 22:8). When the windows of the firmament were opened, rain fell (Gen. 7: 11–12).

In biblical Hebrew the word for heaven is always plural. Under that influence, the Greek word for heaven in the NT also frequently appears in the plural. The use of the plural probably does not mean that the ancient Hebrews conceived of more than one heaven. Heaven was the place of the stars, sun, and moon (Gen. 1:14–16) and of the birds (Gen. 1:20; Deut. 4: 17). It is also the abode of God (1 Kings 8:30) and where God is enthroned (Isa. 66:1; Exod. 24:9–11). The prophet Elijah, doer of mighty deeds, was taken up to heaven in a whirlwind, according to 2 Kings 2:1–12.

In the myths of many ancient Near Eastern peoples, heaven appears as a god. The gods were called upon as witnesses of international treaties (covenants). Heaven and earth were often included in the list of divine witnesses. Heaven was apparently called upon to witness the covenant between God and the Israelites (Deut. 32:1). When the covenant was broken, God accused Israel before heaven (Isa. 2:1; Jer. 2: 12).

The prophets of Israel claimed to have access to the heavenly court (1 Kings 22:19–23). In later Jewish writings, prophets and visionaries were granted visions of the heavenly world and even the opportunity to ascend to heaven, contemplate God, and travel about in the heavenly regions observing heavenly secrets, including the abodes of the righteous and the wicked dead and their respective rewards and punishments. Dreams and visions of the heavenly world and the future were attributed to Daniel (Dan. 7–12). Enoch, who had been taken up to heaven like Elijah (Gen. 5:24), is the subject and reputed author of a large body of revelatory literature dating from the third century B.C. to the third century A.D. (*1 Enoch, 2 Enoch,* and *3 Enoch*). The NT book of Revelation stands in this tradition. An open door appears in heaven so that the early Christian prophet John may see heavenly secrets (Rev. 4:1). Apocryphal Christian apocalypses are especially concerned with the punishment of the wicked (*The Apocalypse of Peter, The Apocalypse of Paul*).

The pseudepigraphical Jewish and apocryphal Christian literatures contain many references to multiple heavens. Seven heavens is the most common notion (*2 Enoch, The Ascension of Isaiah*). ***See also*** Elijah; Enoch; Firmament; Hell; Vision.

A.Y.C.

Heaven, Kingdom of. *See* Kingdom of God.

heave offering (Heb. *teruma*), an incorrect translation in the KJV whose proper meaning is "dedication" or "dedicated gift." It is used of the animal thigh of the well-being offering (Lev. 7:32–34), the tithe (Num. 18:24–29), sanctuary building materials (Exod. 25:2), land (Ezek. 48: 8–21) and several other sacred donations. Dedication indicates the transference of an object from the owner to God. Unlike the so-called wave offering (more accurately "elevation offering"), dedication is not a ritual act done at the sanctuary but is a simple dedication effected outside its precincts. In Second Temple times the dedication offering became a definite ritual act, hence the translation "heave offering."
D.P.W.

Heber (hee'buhr; Heb., "enclave"), a name occurring in several tribes. **1** The eponym of a clan in Asher (Gen. 46:17; Num. 26:45; 1 Chron. 7: 31–32). **2** The father or founder of Soco in Judah (1 Chron. 4:18). **3** A family in Benjamin (1 Chron. 8:17; cf. Eber in v. 12). **4** In an early narrative, the Kenite ("smith") husband of Jael; Jael killed Sisera in her tent at The Oak in Zaananim, in north Galilee (Judg. 4:21; 5:24). This Heber had migrated to the territory of Naphtali, which had a common border with Asher, and had settled in peace with Jabin, king of Canaan at Hazor (Judg. 4:11, 17). ***See also*** Barak; Judges, The Book of; Sisera.
R.B.

Hebrew, the original language of the OT. It was the tongue spoken by the ancient Israelites. In the OT it is known as "Judean," "[language of the] Jews" (2 Kings 18:26, 28; Isa. 36:11, 13; 2 Chron. 32:18; Neh. 12:24). Once it is apparently called the "language [lit., lip] of Canaan" (Isa. 19:18).

Ancient Hebrew is a member of the Canaanite family of languages. Canaanite is known from the second millennium B.C. only in transcriptions into Egyptian hieroglyphs or in the cuneiform of the el-Amarna Tablets. Other Canaanite dialects (from the first millennium) are Phoenician and Moabite and probably also Edomite and Ammonite. The Canaanite tongues are part of the Northwest Semitic branch of the Semitic language family (so called after Shem, the father of the Semitic peoples, Gen. 10:1). Some of the other Northwest Semitic languages are Ugaritic (classed by some scholars as Canaanite because of certain similarities with Hebrew), Aramaic (in which a few passages of the OT are written), and Amorite (known only from personal names in Egyptian and cuneiform documents).

During postexilic times (mid-sixth century B.C. and later) the Jews used Aramaic in their contacts with the society around them because it was the international language of the Persian Empire. But Hebrew continued to be used even into the Greco-Roman period (333 B.C.–A.D. 325). It was especially important for the discussion of religious matters. The name "Hebrew" denoting the language first appears in the introduction to the Wisdom of Jesus the Son of Sirach (Ecclesiasticus). It is debated whether all the references to "Hebrew" in the Apocrypha and the NT (4 Macc. 12:7; 16:15; Acts 21:40; 22:2; 26: 14) always mean Hebrew. In some cases, Aramaic may be meant. The Dead Sea Scrolls and the Bar-Kochba (A.D. 135) correspondence show that Hebrew was still in use for other than rabbinic discussions. The opinions of the rabbis, i.e., the Mishnah, is in late Hebrew and its Talmudic commentary (Gemara) is in Aramaic with some Hebrew parables. ***See also*** Aramaic; Hebrews; Israel; Old Testament.
A.F.R.

THE HEBREW ALPHABET

Form	*Name*	*Translit-eration*	*Approximate Pronun-ciation*
א	aleph	ʼ	ah'lef
ב	beth	b	bayth
ג	gimel	g	gim'mel
ד	daleth	d	dah'leth
ה	he	h	hay
ו	waw	w	wou
ז	zayin	z	za'yin
ח	heth	ḥ/kh	cheth
ט	teth	t	teth
י	yod	y	yohd
כ	kaph	k	kaf
ל	lamed	l	lah'med
מ	mem	m	mayim
נ	nun	n	no͞on
ס	samekh	s	sahm'ek
ע	ayin	ʻ	a'yin
פ	pe	p	pay
צ	tsadhe	ts	tsah'de
ק	qoph	q	kawf
ר	resh	r	raysh
שׂ	sin	s	seen
שׁ	shin	sh	sheen
ת	taw	t	tou

The forms shown on this table are those of Hebrew square script, which is the script used in printing today. The Old Hebrew of the biblical period can be seen on ancient inscriptions, such as the Siloam inscription, a photograph of which is included with the article "Siloam inscription."

Hebrews, an alternate designation for the people of Israel, the descendants of Abraham. **The Term:** The Hebrew form translated "Hebrew" is *ʻiḇrî*, grammatically an adjective created by the addition of the suffix *-iy*, which becomes long *i*, to a base presumed to be *'ibr-*. Without the suffix this base would take the form *'eber*, a form that is in fact the personal name Eber, an ancestor of several Semitic peoples (Gen. 10:24–25; 11:14–15; 1 Chron. 1:18–19). If the term "Hebrew" is derived from Eber, then one might expect it to be applied to some of the other peoples descended from him, e.g., the Aramaeans, but this does not necessarily follow from the biblical genealogies in which Eber is mentioned. All that is required is the assumption that in the specific contexts where "Hebrew" is employed in the Bible, e.g., vis-à-vis Egyptians or Philistines, it is intended to designate the particular ethnic or national group Israel.

Other suggestions have been based on the assumption that the root word *'eber* goes back to a form meaning, "one who has passed over." Such is the reasoning behind the Septuagint (LXX) rendering of "Abram the Hebrew" in Gen. 14:13. The Greek translation is, literally, "Abram, the one who crossed over." An ancient rabbinic view took it to mean that the Israelites were those who had crossed the Red Sea. Some scholars in modern times have linked the term to the statement that Abraham came from *across* the Euphrates (Josh. 24:2–3). Various other, mostly quite implausible, interpretations have been made, such as the nineteenth-century view that the "Hebrews" were those who had crossed the River Jordan.

As Ethnic Designation: Whatever the etymological derivation, the term "Hebrews" was clearly meant to be the designation of an ethnic or national group. This is clearly seen by its usage in juxtaposition to another such ethnic appellative, "Egyptian" (Heb. *miṣrî*). Genesis records that "the Egyptians might not eat bread with the Hebrews" (Gen. 43:32). Moses "saw an Egyptian beating a Hebrew" (Exod. 2:11), and elsewhere it was reported to Pharaoh that "the Hebrew women are not like the Egyptian women" (Exod. 1:19). A further indication that the term is an ethnicon is its parallelism with "Israel." "The Lord, the God of Israel" (Exod. 5:1) is equated with "the God of the Hebrews" (Exod. 5:3). The biblical writers use the term "Hebrew" to designate the direct ethnic progenitors of the people who can later be called "Israel," or "the sons of Israel." The most striking example of this usage is its application to Abram. It was necessary to give him an ethnic designation to distinguish him from the other personages mentioned in the same context. Thus, we find "Abram the Hebrew" together with "Mamre the Amorite" (Gen. 14:13) and his brothers, Eshcol and Aner. Attempts to read into this passage a militaristic flavor to the term "Hebrew" because Abram had a fighting force (Gen. 14:14) ignore the fact that the other three heroes play a similar role in the story. "Abram the Hebrew" is purely an ethnic definition.

This latter example is the classic usage by a narrator wishing to distinguish between the Israelites or their forebears and some other nationality. Other cases are Gen. 43:32 cited above, where the reference is to the sons of Jacob, and the allusions to their own descendants who have grown into a numerous people in Egypt (Exod. 1:15; 2:11, 13). Even more specific is the usage with regard to the Israelites already settled in the land by the time of Saul's leadership. "The Hebrews who had been with the Philistines . . . turned to be with the Israelites who were with Saul and Jonathan" (1 Sam. 14:21). Attention is often called to this passage as proof that "Hebrews" can apply to people other than the Israelites, but, in fact, the very qualification of those with Saul and his son demonstrates that all of them were from the same nationality.

On other occasions, Israelites or their ancestors refer to themselves as Hebrews in discussions with foreigners. Joseph defines his country of origin as "the land of the Hebrews" (Gen. 40:15); the "land of Israel" is only applicable after the settlement of the tribes. Incidentally, Joseph's reference is to the land of Canaan and not to some special reserve to which the Hebrews were confined. Therefore, it is not legitimate to compare Joseph's expression with the "territory [lit., field] of the *'apirū*" mentioned in an ancient treaty between the king of the Hittites and the king of Ugarit. The latter is really a "reserve" where stateless persons were being allowed to live. The Hebrew midwives speak to Pharaoh of "Hebrew women" (Exod. 1: 19), as does the sister of Moses when speaking to Pharaoh's daughter (Exod. 2:7). In the same semantic context one must understand Jonah's reply to the query of the sailors, "I am a Hebrew" (Jon. 1:9). The fact that Jonah adds, "and I fear the Lord, the God of heaven, who made the sea and the dry land," demonstrates that his ethnic reference is to the Israelite nation.

The same nuance prevails in the speech of foreigners referring to Israelites. Note, for example, Potiphar's wife in speaking of Joseph (Gen. 39:14, 17); likewise the chief butler (Gen. 41:12). The king of Egypt himself makes reference to the "Hebrew women" (Exod. 1:16) and his daughter recognizes the infant Moses as "one of the Hebrews' children" (Exod. 2:6). Such usage is prominent in 1 Samuel where the Philistines are often quoted as referring to the Israelites as Hebrews. There can be no doubt that the book of Samuel intends for the reader to understand that Hebrews means the people of Israel, e.g., in 1 Sam. 4:5–9 where the Philistines speak about "the gods who smote the Egyptians with every sort of plague" as having come (in the form of the Ark) to the camp of the Hebrews (v. 6; also v. 9). In like manner one must understand 1 Sam. 13:3 on the basis of comparison with the reading in

LXX, "... and the Philistines heard of it saying, 'The Hebrews have rebelled.' And Saul blew the trumpet throughout all the land," which is then naturally followed by the next verse: "And all Israel heard ..."(1 Sam. 13:4). The present Hebrew text, followed by RSV, ignores the LXX and would have Saul calling to the Hebrews, not the Israelites. The equation of Hebrews with Israelites is further confirmed by the reference to the Philistine monopoly on metal smithing, "Lest the Hebrews make themselves swords or spears" (1 Sam. 13:19), because it goes on to say that "every one of the Israelites went down to the Philistines to sharpen his plowshare ..." (v. 20). So there can be no doubt that the Philistines are speaking of the Israelites when they notice Jonathan coming toward them, "Look, Hebrews are coming out of the holes ..." (1 Sam. 14:11).

Finally, the last such Philistine allusion to the Hebrews must be taken in the same way. When David and his fighting men appeared at Aphek, the Philistine commanders said, "What are these Hebrews doing here?" (1 Sam. 29:3). Just because David's band was composed of all sorts of renegades (1 Sam. 22:2), it has been assumed that the Philistines are using the term "Hebrew" as one would use the term *'apiru* in the Late Bronze Age. Though the sociological parallel between David's men and the outcasts and freebooters called *'apiru* during the second millennium B.C. is cogent, there is no justification for violating the clear semantic usage of the ethnicon, "Hebrew, Hebrews," in the book of 1 Samuel.

The Hebrew Slave: Special notice must be taken of the law pertaining to the "Hebrew slave" (Exod. 21:2). The rules for release of slaves in the seventh year and the special rules for female slaves (Exod. 21:7–11) were clearly predicated on the fact that they were truly Israelites. In Deut. 15:12 it is stressed that the slave referred to is "a Hebrew man, or a Hebrew woman." Jeremiah comments on this same law, and he makes it clear that the intention is the defense of native Israelites. He defines the "Hebrew slaves, male and female" as a Judean (RSV: "Jew") brother (Jer. 34:9, 14). Again, comparison has been made with the *'apiru* who sold themselves into servitude to the Hurrian residents of Nuzi on the Tigris. In fact, the *'apiru* there are clearly foreigners, not from the local population at all. The situation is the direct opposite of the Hebrew slave.

In the Apocrypha: The usage of the term is the same in the Apocrypha as in the OT: in the mouths of foreigners (Jth. 12:11; 14:18); by Jews speaking to non-Jews (Jth. 10:12; 2 Macc. 7:31); in narration, to distinguish the Jews from foreigners (2 Macc. 11:13; 15:37).

In the NT: The term "Hebrew" is used by the NT writers to denote those Jews who continued to maintain their traditional Judaic heritage, including their Hebrew (and Aramaic) language, in contrast to the hellenizing Jews who had adopted the Greek language and culture (Acts 6: 1; 2 Cor. 11:22; Phil. 3:5).

Summary: There is nothing pejorative about the term "Hebrew" in the OT, the Apocrypha or the NT. It was adopted by the OT writers as the designation of their pre-Israelite forebears. Linguistically, the form is an ethnic appellative, built on a base that may go back to Eber as the eponymous ancestor or else reflect the tradition that the ancestors had come from "beyond" the Euphrates. ***See also*** Khapiru.

Bibliography

Greenberg, M. "Hab/piru and Hebrews." In B. Mazar, ed. *Patriarchs*, Vol. 2 of *World History of the Jewish People*. Tel Aviv: Massada Publishing Co., 1970. Chap. 10. Full bibliographic references.

A.F.R.

Hebrews, the Letter to the, an anonymous book appearing in the NT following the Letters attributed to Paul. Although the book came to be attributed to Paul and has been entitled "to the Hebrews" from very early times, the identities of the author and of the readers are unknown. The actual text of the book does not identify the readers. The title, "to the Hebrews," is probably based on inferences derived from the book. The argument of the book, which is developed from extensive use of the OT, might suggest that the readers were Jewish Christians. This conclusion is plausible but not certain. Gentile audiences also acquired familiarity with OT themes.

Although Hebrews came to be attributed to Paul in the ancient church, this view is precluded by the author's indication that he belongs to a subsequent generation (2:3–4). Furthermore, the excellent Greek style is to be distinguished from the style of Paul's Letters. Among the NT books, only Luke and Acts equal Hebrews in style. Although many suggestions have been offered in attempts to identify the author, both the author and the readers remain unknown. In part because of this uncertainty, the inclusion of Hebrews in the NT was debated within the early church.

The literary form of Hebrews is to be distinguished from that of other NT books. Although commonly referred to as an "epistle," it has few of the epistolary characteristics. It lacks the normal epistolary introduction, opening rather with a theological discussion that serves as an "overture" to the major theme of the book: the finality of the Christian revelation. In the following chapters, the author proceeds with a series of arguments derived from the OT. Each argument is followed by a practical exhortation to the readers. At the conclusion of the book, the author refers to the document as a "word of exhortation" (13:22), a term that elsewhere refers to a sermon (Acts 13:15). Thus, Hebrews is a sermon to an early Christian community. A traditional epistolary conclusion is given to the sermon in 13:24–25.

The exhortations that appear between the theological arguments provide a portrait of the situation of the readers who are addressed. The readers, who probably live in the closing decades of the first century, are tempted to give up their salvation (2:3). Their capacity to "hold fast" (3:6), to hold "firm to the end" (3:14), and to endure (10:36–39) is now in doubt. They have "drooping hands" and "weak knees" (12: 12), and some have the habit of neglecting to meet together (10:25). The readers appear, therefore, to be afflicted with a general weariness. It is possible that the threat of persecution is also involved (12:3–11).

Although the theological arguments appear to be unrelated treatments of various passages from the OT, an underlying unity emerges out of the separate essays. The prologue in 1:1–4 introduces the dominant motif that is to be found throughout this sermon. Christ is introduced as the one who, as a result of his sacrifice and exaltation, is now "superior" to angels or any other object of comparison (1:3–4). Consequently, he is God's ultimate word to his people. The prologue, written with extraordinary rhetorical artistry, reminds the readers of the incomparable Christian revelation. The word "superior" which occurs in 1:4 is used thirteen times in Hebrews. Christ is superior to angels and earthly high priests (1:4; 7:7, 19, 22). His sacrifice, his covenant, and the hope he provides are also superior to any alternatives (8:6; 9:23; 10:34). Thus, the separate units employ various objects of comparison from the OT to show that the word addressed to "us" (1:2) is without equal.

The purpose of the theological sections is to provide the basis for the author's appeal to his audience. Because of the magnificence of the Christian revelation, readers are reminded of the greatness of their hope (10:19–25; 11:1; 6: 13–20) and the terrible consequences of neglecting the "great salvation" (2:3; cf. 6:4–8; 10: 26–31). ***See also*** Angel; Apostasy; Covenant; Epistle; Faith; Melchizedek; Persecution; Preaching; Priests; Worship. J.W.T.

OUTLINE OF CONTENTS

The Letter to the Hebrews

I. Prologue (1:1–4)
II. Christ the Son (1:5–4:16)
  A. Christ and angels (1:5–2:18)
  B. Christ and Moses (3:1–6)
  C. Christ and Joshua (3:7–4:11)
  D. Exhortation (4:12–16)
III. Christ the high priest (5:1–10:39)
  A. Christ and the high priests (5:1–10)
  B. Exhortation (5:11–6:12)
  C. Christ and Melchizedek (6:13–7:28)
  D. Sanctuary and sacrifice (8:1–10:18)
  E. Exhortation (10:19–39)
IV. Major exhortation (11:1–12:29)
  A. Faith and endurance (11:1–12:17)
  B. Sinai and Zion (12:18–29)
V. Concluding exhortations (13:1–25)

Hebron (hee'bruhn), one of the "central" cities in the southern hill country of Judah some twenty miles south-southwest of Jerusalem. It is situated at one of the highest points (ca. 3,040 feet above sea level) on the central mountainous ridge and is one of the oldest continually inhabited cities in Palestine. It is in an area with an abundant water supply in the form of wells and springs and is a regional center of grape and olive production. A reference to its antiquity is found in Num. 13:22, where it is said to have been founded seven years before Zoan (Avaris, later Rameses) in Egypt, probably in the seventeenth century B.C. Hebron's original name (Gen. 23:2; Josh. 20:7) was Kiriath-arba (Heb., "four-fold city").

The city's current name, *el-Khalil* (Arabic, "the friend"), is an indication of its close connections with the traditions about Abraham (Gen. 13:18; 18:1), who is known as "the friend of God" (2 Chron. 20:7; Isa. 41:8; James 2:23). It was at Hebron that Sarah died and it was there that Abraham purchased the cave of Machpelah from Hittites in the area for use as a family tomb (Gen. 23:7–16), a site over which the current Haram el-Khalil (Arabic, "the sacred area of the friend") traditionally stands.

At the time of the entry of the Israelites, Hebron was held by three of the legendary Anakim, "the giants" (Num. 13:22), who apparently reestablished themselves there after the conquest (Josh. 14:12). After falling to Joshua (Josh. 10:1–27; 36–39; 11:21–23) and having been secured again by Caleb (Josh. 15: 13–14) Hebron was allotted to Caleb (Josh. 14: 12) and subsequently became a city of the Kohathite Levites and one of the six cities of refuge (Josh. 20:7).

Hebron also played a prominent role in the early years of David (ca. 1004–998 B.C.). It was one of the cities that aided him in his refugee years (1 Sam. 30:31), and it was there that he was anointed "king of Judah" (2 Sam. 2:11) and reigned for seven and a half years (2 Sam. 5:5), while Saul's son Ishbosheth ruled in the north. David's son Absalom began his revolt against his father at Hebron (2 Sam. 15:7–10).

In the period of the Divided Monarchy (924–586 B.C.) Rehoboam strengthened Hebron's defenses (2 Chron. 11:5, 10). A number of stamped jar handles from storage jars of uniform capacity (2 baths, equal to about 10 gallons) dating to the eighth century B.C. bear the name of Hebron, where these jars were apparently made in a royal pottery.

Beginning in the Exile (586–ca. 538 B.C.), Hebron was occupied by the Edomites (Idumeans) until it was recaptured in 164 B.C. by Judas Maccabeus (1 Macc. 5:65). Although it is not mentioned in the NT, Hebron was the site of building by Herod the Great, some of whose characteristic construction can be seen today at the Haram el-Khalil. ***See also*** David; Machpelah; Mamre. F.S.F.

hedge, a barrier or boundary, sometimes of live plants such as thorny bush (Mic. 7:4; Hos. 2:6), used to protect vineyards (Mark 12:1; Matt. 21:33) or to mark off roads and fields (Luke 14:23). It symbolizes God's protection (Job 1:10) or his restriction (Job 3:23).

hedgehog (KJV: "bittern"), a small mammal, also designated as "porcupine." The Hebrew word (*qippōd*) is used for the hedgehogs *Erinaceus auritus* or *Erinaceus sacer*. In Isa. 14:23 it is a metaphor for the desolation of a place under divine judgment that a city is the "possession of" such an animal. The same is true in an oracle against the nations in Isa. 34:11. Similar negative desolation is involved in Zeph. 2:14, where Nineveh's destruction is described.

Hegai (heg'ī), a eunuch of King Ahasuerus of Persia; he was in charge of the royal harem and Esther was placed in his custody before she was called before the king (Esther 2:3, 8, 15).

heifer, a young cow; it was used for ploughing (Judg. 14:18), trained to thresh grain (Hos. 10:11; Jer. 50:11; Deut. 21:3), and valued for its milk (Isa. 7:21).

It was one of the sacrificial animals (1 Sam. 16:2) and appears in three significant rites: it was divided to ratify a covenant (Gen. 15:9); it was killed to expiate murder by an unknown person (Deut. 21:1–9); and it was burned and its ashes used to counteract uncleanness caused by contact with a corpse (Num. 19:1–10; cf. Heb. 9:13). Although a different Hebrew word is used here, a young cow seems to be intended.

The heifer's beauty was much appreciated, so the word could be used figuratively of a woman (Judg. 14:18; the female name Eglah, 2 Sam. 3:5, is the same word) and of the splendor of Egypt (Jer. 46:20). Obedient Ephraim is compared to a trained heifer (Hos. 10:11), disobedient Israel to a stubborn one (Hos. 4:16, though again the Hebrew word is different). J.R.P.

heir. ***See*** Inheritance.

Heldai (hel'dī). **1** David's captain for the twelfth month (1 Chron. 27:15). **2** A Jew who returned from Babylon (Zech. 6:10).

Helez (hee'lez; Heb., "vigor" or "strength"). **1** An Ephraimite, one of David's fighting men who later served him as the commander of a division of twenty-four thousand men (2 Sam. 23:26; 1 Chron. 27:10). **2** A descendant of Judah (1 Chron. 2:39).

Heli (hay'lee; Gk. form of the Heb. *Eli* [ee'lī], "[the Lord is] exalted"). **1** In the OT, the priest (Eli) before whom Samuel ministered at Shiloh (1 Sam. 1–4). **2** In the NT, Heli is the name of the father of Joseph in Luke's genealogy of Jesus (Luke 3:23).

Heliopolis (hay-lee-ah'poh-lis). ***See*** On.

hell, an English word used to translate Heb., Sheol; Gk., Hades; and Heb., Gehenna. In Christian tradition it is usually associated with the notion of eternal punishment, especially by fire. This idea appears in Isa. 66:24, but it is not clearly associated with a place. Jewish writings from the third century B.C. onward speak of places of punishment by fire for evil spirits and the wicked dead (*1 Enoch* 18:11–16; 108:3–7, 15; 2 Esd. 7:36–38). The book of Revelation describes a lake that burns with fire and brimstone in which the wicked will be eternally punished (Rev. 19:20; 20:14–15; 21:8). ***See also*** Gehenna; Hades; Punishment, Everlasting; Sheol.

Hellenists (hel'in-ists; KJV: "Grecians"), a term found in Acts 6:1 and 9:29, probably denoting Greek-speaking Jewish Christians in the early church in Jerusalem. The Hellenists probably interpreted the Torah less stringently than did the "Hebrews," the Aramaic-speaking Jewish Christians in the Jerusalem church. The presence of these Hellenists may have served as an intermediate point of transition for the Christian movement in its spread into the Greek-speaking Gentile world. ***See also*** Greeks; Hebrews.

helmet, a leather or metal protective covering for the head worn by soldiers. The word used in the OT for "helmet" is of foreign origin, and foreigners attacking Israel are often reported as wearing helmets (1 Sam. 17:5 [Goliath]; Jer. 46:4; Ezek. 23:24). Later Israel's armies were similarly equipped (2 Chron. 26:14), but the reference to Saul's helmet in 1 Sam. 17:38 may be an anachronism. The helmet worn by God as he marches against his enemies (Isa. 59:17) is envisioned as part of the armor given to Christians to protect themselves against evil (1 Thess. 5:8; Eph. 6:17).

hem, the edge, border, or "skirts" of a garment. Pomegranates of blue, purple, and scarlet stuff were placed between bells of pure gold all around the hem of the blue priestly robe of Aaron (Exod. 28:31–35; 39:22–26). So great was the healing power of Jesus that the mere touching of the hem of his garment resulted in the immediate and miraculous healing of the hemorrhaging woman (Matt. 9:20; Luke 8:44) and the crowds of sick people at Gennesaret (Matt. 14:36; Mark 6:56). ***See also*** Fringes.

Heman (hee'muhn; Heb., "faithful"). **1** A grandson of Jacob and son of Zerah (1 Chron. 2:6). **2** A wise man in the time of Solomon (1 Kings 4:31). **3** A grandson of Samuel and son of Joel, whom David put in charge of the service of song (1 Chron. 6:31–33). He is identified as the "singer" and as the first in the list of three appointed by David may have been the chief musician. Psalm 88 is probably attributed to him.

Hemath. ***See*** Hamath; Hammath.

hemlock. ***See*** Gall.

hen, common fowl mentioned in the Bible only in Matt. 23:37 and Luke 13:34. ***See also*** Fowl.

Henadad (hen'uh-dad; Heb., "Hadad [a deity] is gracious"); a shortened form of Henhadad. **1** The "father" of two postexilic inhabitants of Jerusalem, Bavvai and Binnui, who helped repair the city walls. It is almost certain that the ancestral head of the family group is meant here rather than the actual father, with "son" of Henadad meaning "descendant" (Neh. 3:18, 24; 10:9); possibly the head of the family group in 2. **2** A levitical family group ("sons of Henadad") who helped supervise the workmen in the rebuilding of the Temple following the Exile (Ezra 3:9).

Bronze helmet of the type worn by Roman soldiers stationed in Judea; first century A.D.

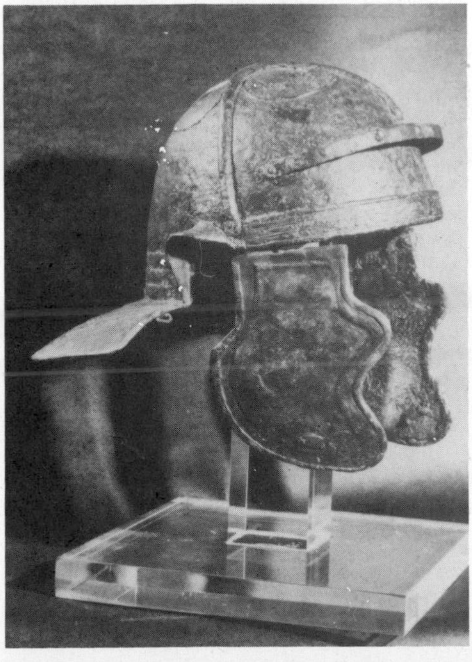

henotheism. ***See*** Polytheism.

Hepher (hee'fuhr). **1** A town west of the Jordan (Josh. 12:17). **2** A son of Gilead (Num. 26:32; 27:1; Josh. 17:2, 3). **3** A man of Judah (1 Chron. 4:6). **4** One of David's mighty men (1 Chron. 11:36).

Hephzibah (hef'zi-bah; Heb., "my delight rests in her," said by the delighted parent). **1** A wife of Hezekiah, king of Judah (715–687 B.C.), and the mother of Manasseh (687–642 B.C.; 2 Kings 21:1). **2** The name given by the Lord to restored Jerusalem in Isa. 62:4.

Heptateuch, the first seven books (Genesis through Judges) in the OT, which carry the story of Israel through the time of the conquest of Canaan. ***See also*** Hexateuch; Pentateuch.

herbs, plants gathered for flavor, aroma, or medicinal value (2 Kings 4:39). Used at Passover, they were a symbol of suffering (Exod. 12:8; Num. 9:11), but they could comprise a modest meal (Prov. 15:17).

herd. ***See*** Cattle; Sheep.

hereafter, the. ***See*** Eschatology; Glory; Hades; Heaven; Hell; Paradise.

heresy, a term derived from the Greek word *hairesis,* originally an opinion or way of thinking. It was used as a designation of a sect, party, or philosophical school. It is used in this sense of the Sadducees and Pharisees in Acts 5:17 and 15:5. Later Christian usage (from late second century A.D.) understood "heresy" to indicate deviation from the accepted teaching or practice of the dominant Christian community. Something of this sense may be found in the treatment of Christians as a "sect of the Nazarenes" in Acts 24:5, 14 and 28:22, where Christianity is opposed by Jewish religious authorities. Paul used the word for an internal faction within the Christian community (Gal. 5:20; 1 Cor. 11:19).

P.P.

Hermas (huhr'muhs), a Christian to whom, along with others, Paul sends greetings in Rom. 16:14. Perhaps the added words, "and the brethren who are with them," refer to a small house-church.

hermeneutics (huhr-muh-n$\bar{oo}$'tiks), an English transliteration, based on a family of Greek words which, in its broadest sense, means "interpretation." Other shades of meaning include "explanation," "exposition," "expression," "intelligible rendition," or even "translation." This range of uses is reflected in classical Greek as well as in the Greek OT, or Septuagint, and in the NT, where the word family designates the act of explaining difficult or unfamiliar terms or even translating from one language into another (e.g., Gen. 42:23; Ezra 4:7; 2 Macc. 1:36; John 1: 38, 42; 9:7; Heb. 7:2; cf. Acts 9:36). It can also mean "interpretation" as making sense of an otherwise unintelligible utterance (e.g., 1 Cor. 12:10, 30; 14:5, 13, 26, 27, 28) or explaining an obscure saying (Eccles. 47:17). It may also refer specifically to the act of interpreting a sacred text in the sense of unfolding hidden, obscure meanings in Scripture or expounding its full significance (e.g., Luke 24:27).

In the broadest sense, hermeneutics is the field of theological study that deals with the interpretation of Scripture. Often, it is characterized as being primarily concerned with the theory or theories of interpretation, and in this respect it can be distinguished from exegesis, which may be thought of as the practical application of hermeneutical principles. As compared with exegesis, hermeneutics is more comprehensive in its scope as well as more theoretical in its orientation. It encompasses both the study of the principles of biblical interpretation and the process through which such interpretation is carried out.

In the ancient and medieval periods, a primary concern was to articulate proper principles or rules for biblical interpretation. In the Jewish tradition, rabbis devised sets of rules for interpretation, such as the seven rules of Rabbi Hillel or the thirteen rules of Rabbi Ishmael. Among Christians, two fundamentally different hermeneutical approaches emerged in the late second and early third centuries A.D., one associated with Alexandria (Clement, Origen), which gave primacy to allegory as the fundamental hermeneutical principle, and another associated with Antioch (Theodore of Mopsuestia, John Chrysostom), which attached greater importance to typology and the literal meaning of Scripture.

Through the medieval period, the dominant hermeneutical approach was the fourfold meaning of Scripture, a scheme allowing a text to be understood in at least four senses: literal, allegorical, moral, and heavenly. The Reformation saw a shift in emphasis but still continued to debate principles of interpretation, such as whether Scripture is its own best interpreter or whether it must be interpreted in light of the church's received tradition.

The modern period became less concerned with devising rules, norms, and principles of interpretation and more concerned with rethinking, clarifying, and making explicit the process of interpretation itself. In the nineteenth century, philosophical analysis was applied to hermeneutics, resulting in new questions: what is involved in the process of understanding an ancient text from another time and culture? How are a single passage and a whole work interrelated? How does a written text reveal the psychological personality of the writer? In what sense is a text an "expression" of human experience? In the twentieth century, other questions were pressed: how is the essential biblical message (Gk. *kerygma*, "proclamation") mediated through Scripture? How is this understood and appropriated by modern readers or hearers? What is the relationship between language as a vehicle through which communication occurs and language as a communicative act itself, a "word-event"? The hermeneutical process has also been visualized as the fusion of two horizons, that of the interpreter and that of the text itself. In more recent times, the hermeneutical process has been explored from a variety of other perspectives, such as modern literary criticism, structuralism, and the social sciences. ***See also*** Bible; Biblical Criticism; Canon; New Testament; Old Testament. C.R.H.

Hermes (huhr'meez). **1** The divine messenger of the Greek gods. Originally a demon that haunted the piles of stones set up as roadside markers, Hermes was the messenger of the greater gods, especially Zeus. He was also a trickster who stole Apollo's cattle and was thought to have invented the lyre. Paul and Barnabas are mistaken for Hermes and Zeus when they visit Lystra and Paul heals a cripple there (Acts 14:12). **2** A Christian greeted in Rom. 16: 14.

Hermogenes (huhr - mah' juh - neez), Asian Christian known only as one who deserted Paul (2 Tim. 1:15). ***See also*** Phygelus.

Hermon (huhr'muhn; Heb., "sacred" or "forbidden"), the three-peaked summit at the southern end of the Anti-Lebanon range. It rises 9,230 feet (2,814 m.) above sea level and is the highest point in the entire Levant, 1,968 feet (600 m.) higher than any part of the Lebanon mountains and towering above the Bashan plateau and upper Jordan valley. According to Deut. 3:9, "the Sidonians call Hermon Sirion, while the Amorites call it Senir," and these three names are sometimes used together in the OT (Deut. 4:48; 1 Chron. 5:23). Ps. 42:6 speaks of the "Hermons," which may refer to the three peaks.

Heavy precipitation, well over 40 inches (1,000 mm.), mainly in the form of snow, falls on the summit and western slopes and sinks through the porous sandstone to supply the powerful sources of the Jordan and Litani rivers and the oasis of Damascus. Snow covers the upper regions during the entire winter and early spring and in sheltered crevices may persist even as late as the end of October. Villages

Mt. Hermon rises 9,230 feet above sea level and towers above the upper Jordan Valley.

with vineyards and orchards are plentiful on the western slope up to about 3,300 feet (1,000 m.). In the ancient past these slopes were thickly forested (Ezek. 27:5) and the home of lions and leopards (Song of Sol. 4:8). Earlier in this century the Syrian bear was still to be found here. Evidently a sacred mountain (Judg. 3:3 calls it "Baal-hermon"), it formed the northernmost limit of Joshua's conquests (Josh. 11:3, 17; 12:1, 5; 13:5, 11). Some have speculated that it may have been the scene of the transfiguration of Jesus, since Caesarea Philippi lies at its foot. ***See also*** Anti-Lebanon; Bashan; Caesarea Philippi; Damascus; Jordan River, The; Transfiguration, The; Transjordan. D.B.

Herod (hair'uhd), name of a family of Idumean origin with strong connections with the Roman government who, from the time of Queen Alexandra (76–67 B.C.), became centrally involved in the affairs of the Jewish state. Members of the family, under a variety of titles, governed Palestine and adjacent areas from ca. 55 B.C. until near the close of the first century A.D. The name "Herod" is Greek and originated with a shadowy ancestor about whom, even in antiquity, little was known. Two ancient traditions make him either a descendant of a notable Jewish family with a lineage traceable to the Babylonian exile or a slave in the temple of Apollo in the Philistine city of Ashkelon. Neither can be proved.

The first Antipater, the grandfather of Herod the Great, rose to the position of military commander of his native Idumea under the Hasmonean rulers Alexander Jannaeus (103–76 B.C.) and Alexandra. The Idumeans had been forcibly converted to Judaism by John Hyrcanus (134–104 B.C.), and thus the family of Herod was, at least technically, Jewish. Herod's father, also named Antipater (or Antipas), was by all accounts not only a skilled soldier but also a shrewd politician and diplomat. His successful intervention in favor of Hyrcanus II in the latter's struggle for supremacy with his brother Aristobulus, coupled with the outstanding services he rendered to Pompey and Julius Caesar in their campaigns, earned him Roman citizenship and the post of procurator of Judea, granted by Caesar in 47 B.C. Antipater and his Nabatean wife, Cypros, had four sons and a daughter, and the two eldest, Phasaelus and Herod, were nominated by their father as governors (Gk. *stratēgoi*), the former of Judea and the latter of Galilee. The following members of the family appear in the NT:

1 Herod I (Herod the Great), king of the Jews. He was probably about twenty-five years old when, as governor of Galilee, he successfully campaigned against Galilean bandits, executing the leaders and coming out of the subsequent showdown with the Jewish Sanhedrin in Jerusalem not only politically stronger but also with enhanced status in the eyes of Rome. When, in 40 B.C., the Roman Senate appointed Herod King of the Jews, he was given a prize still requiring conquest, for on the throne of Judea sat Antigonus II, the last of the Hasmonean rulers, newly placed there by Rome's enemies, the Parthians. Herod succeeded, with the backing provided by his friend Mark Antony, in taking Jerusalem in 37 B.C. Antigonus was executed by the Romans at Herod's request, and, in the same year, Herod married Mariamne I, a Hasmonean (one of ten wives). From 37 until his death in 4 B.C., Herod ruled as king of the Jews, a reign marked by his total loyalty to Rome, his grandiose and sometimes magnificent building programs, his family strife, and his harsh repression of any opposition. Herod showed an uncanny ability to maintain favor with the Roman leadership, managing, for example, to switch his allegiance from Antony to Octavian (later Augustus) after the Battle of Actium in 31 B.C.

In honor of Augustus, Herod rebuilt ancient Samaria into the Hellenistic city of Sebaste (Gk., "Augustus"), and he constructed, on the site of a minor anchorage on the Mediterranean coast called Strato's Tower, the magnificently planned and constructed city of Caesarea Maritima, a major port and the Roman administrative center for Palestine. There is much to admire in Caesarea, including the enormous blocks of stone with which a breakwater was constructed to make a harbor, the sewers that were designed to be flushed out by the sea, and the theaters and temples of the city. The crown of Herod's constructions, however, was the Temple in Jerusalem, which he rebuilt on a grandiose scale. The project, begun in 20 B.C., was not completed until A.D. 62, and it is this Temple that Jesus and his disciples knew. Recent excavations along the south and southwest walls of the Temple Mount have revealed the broad stairways leading up to the two wide gates on the southern wall, as well as many details of the construction of the walls and of the streets around them.

The Kingdom of Herod the Great
(Late first century B.C.)
Boundary of Herod's kingdom
Other boundaries
Cities of the Decapolis
Fortresses
0 5 10 15 20 25 30 35 Mls
0 10 20 30 40 50 60 Kms
© Copyright HAMMOND INCORPORATED, Maplewood, N. J.
Chalcis
ABILENE
Abila
Sidon
MT. LEBANON
Iturea
Damascus
SYRIA
Phoenicia
Leontes
Paneas
Paneas
Tyre
Ulatha
Cadasa
Gischala
Gaulanitis
Batanea
Raphana
Ptolemais
Bethsaida
GALILEE
Sea of Galilee
Taricheae
(Magadan)
Hippos
Dion ?
Mt. Carmel
Gabae
Sepphoris
Abila
Nazareth
Mediterranean
Gadara
Dora
Caesarea
(Strato's Tower)
Scythopolis
Pella
DECAPOLIS
Narbata
Sea
Plain of Sharon
SAMARIA
Sebaste
(Samaria)
Gerasa
Jordan
Amathus
Apollonia
Mt. Gerizim
Jabbok
Antipatris
Alexandrium
Joppa
Gadara
Phasaelis
PEREA
Philadelphia
Gophna
Lydda
Jericho
Jamnia
Emmaus
Betharamphtha
Cyprus
Esbus
Jerusalem
Bethany
Qumran
Azotus
Medeba
Bethlehem
Hyrcania
Ascalon
(free city)
JUDEA
Herodium
Callirrhoe
Agrippias
(Anthedon)
Machaerus
Hebron
Gaza
Adora
Engaddi
Lake Asphaltitis
(Dead Sea)
Arnon
IDUMEA
Masada
Raphia
Bersabe
Malatha
Elusa
Khirbet Tannur
Nabatean sanctuary
NABATEA

Herod also fortified his realm with a string of impressive wilderness fortresses, the major ones being Masada, Machaerus, the Herodium in Perea, the Alexandrium, Cypros, Hyrcania, and the Herodium southeast of Bethlehem (the only one built on a previously unfortified site and also the place where Herod was buried). These fortresses served as prisons and, given the internal strife that marked Herod's relations with his family, occasionally as places of imprisonment and execution for members of the family. Eventually, Herod ordered the execution of his Hasmonean wife, Mariamne, of their two sons, Alexander and Aristobulus, of other members of the Hasmonean family, and of his son Antipater.

According to Matt. 2:1–18 (cf. Luke 1:5), the birth of Jesus occurred while Herod was king, probably no earlier than 6 B.C. The king's well-known ruthlessness in defending his throne against any threat forms the background for the story of the massacre of Bethlehem's children (Matt. 2:16–17).

After Herod's death in 4 B.C., Augustus Caesar resolved the dispute that broke out among three of Herod's surviving sons by dividing the kingdom but withholding the royal title from the heirs. To Archelaus, son of Malthace, went the title "ethnarch" and half of the territory (Judea, Idumea, and Samaria). The other half was split into two tetrarchies: Antipas, younger brother of Archelaus, received Galilee and Perea; Philip, son of Cleopatra, received Batanea, Trachonitis, and Auranitis. ***See also*** Augustus; Caesarea; Ethnarch; Idumea; Maccabees; Phasael; Samaria, City of; Temple, The; Tetrarch.

2 Herod Archelaus, son of Herod the Great and ethnarch of Judea, Samaria, and Idumea (4 B.C.–A.D. 6). ***See also*** Archelaus.

3 Herod Philip, son of Herod the Great and tetrarch of Batanea, Trachonitis, and Auranitis (4 B.C.–A.D. 33/34). He ruled uneventfully and apparently successfully in his northern domains. His name is remembered in that of Caesarea Philippi (see Matt. 16:33; Mark 8:27), which was his rebuilding of the ancient Panias near the springs of the Jordan River. Philip apparently married his niece Salome, daughter of Herodias and of Philip's half-brother Herod the son of Mariamne (Mark 6:17 and Matt. 14:3 apparently confuse Philip and Herod). ***See also*** Caesarea Philippi; Herodias; Salome.

4 Herod Antipas, son of Herod the Great and tetrarch of Galilee and Perea (4 B.C.–A.D. 39). He is "that fox" of Luke 13:31–32 and the Herod most frequently mentioned in the NT. Both Jesus and John the Baptist were his subjects and carried out their public careers mostly in his territories (Matt. 14:1–12; Mark 6:14–29; Luke 3: 19–20; 9:7–9; Mark 8:15; Luke 13:31–32; 23:6–16; Acts 4:27). His career was dominated by his relationship to Herodias, whom he married in spite of the fact that she was his niece and married to his half-brother Herod when they met and that he was compelled to divorce a daughter

THE HERODS: A SIMPLIFIED FAMILY TREE

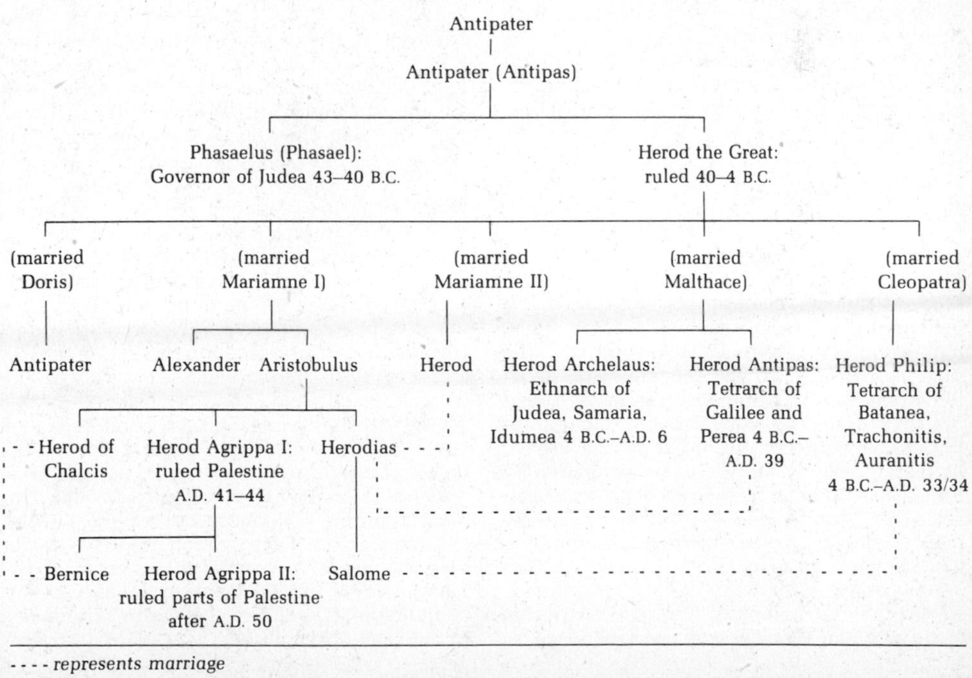

---- represents marriage

of Aretas, the powerful king of the Nabateans, in order to marry her. John, who, according to the Gospels, had criticized this marriage, was imprisoned and later executed by Antipas at Machaerus (Matt. 14:1–12; Mark 6:14–29; Luke 3:19–20; 9:7–9). According to the Gospel of Luke, Antipas also played a role in the trial of Jesus (Luke 23:6–16; Acts 4:27).

Antipas' capital was Tiberias, characteristically named after the Roman emperor, which Antipas built on the shore of the Sea of Galilee and which was later to play a central role in the history of Judaism. Antipas' star set as that of his nephew and brother-in-law Agrippa was rising. When Gaius Caligula became emperor, he granted to Agrippa Philip's former territories, but with the title of king. Under Herodias' prodding, Antipas went to Rome to seek royal status. Not only did he fail, but the agents of Agrippa accused him of crimes against Rome, and the outcome for him was deportation to Gaul and the grant of his territories to Agrippa. Herodias, to her credit, followed him into exile. ***See also*** Herodias; John the Baptist; Tiberias.

5 Herod Agrippa I. ***See*** Agrippa I.

6 Herod Agrippa II. ***See*** Agrippa II. F.O.G.

Herodians (her-oh'dee-uhnz), a term found twice in Mark (3:6; 12:13; also 8:15 in some manuscripts) and once in Matthew (22:16 = Mark 12:13) but never in Luke or John, designating a group who, together with the Pharisees, opposed Jesus. If the name refers to an actual party or faction, it may have been the supporters of the rule and policies of Herod Antipas. Both Matthew and Mark associate them with the Pharisees in putting before Jesus the difficult question regarding paying taxes to Caesar (Matt. 22:15–22; Mark 12:13–17). ***See also*** Herod; Pharisees.

Herodias (her-oh'dee-uhs), the daughter of Aristobulus and Bernice and thus a granddaughter of Herod the Great and sister of Herod Agrippa I. She was married twice: first, to her paternal half-uncle Herod (erroneously called Philip in Matt. 14:3, not all manuscripts, and Mark 6:17), to whom she bore a daughter, Salome; then, once again to a half-uncle, Herod Antipas. The second marriage, carried out after she abandoned her first husband and Antipas divorced his royal Nabatean wife, brought about their public condemnation, according to the Gospels, by John the Baptist and Herodias' retaliation by having her daughter Salome ask for John's head as a prize (Matt. 14:3–12; Mark 6:17–29; cf. Luke 3:19–20; 9:7–9). ***See also*** Herod; John the Baptist; Salome. F.O.G.

heron, any of the family *Ardeidae* of wading birds with long thin legs and necks who feed on fish and other marine life. The Hebrews considered them unclean (Lev. 11:19; Deut. 14:18).

Heshbon (hesh'buhn), a city of northern Moab captured by the Amorite king Sihon, who made it his capital (Num. 21:26–30). The Israelites defeated Sihon in their first battle in Transjordan (Num. 21:21–24; Josh. 12:2) and distributed his territory to Reuben and Gad, assigning Heshbon to Reuben (Num. 32:37). Later, Heshbon was considered Gad's inheritance (Josh. 13:27) and allotted to the Levites (Josh. 21:39). Prophetic oracles against Moab mention Heshbon (probably restored by Mesha, ca. 830 B.C.) falling before unnamed enemies. Heshbon reappears (as Esbus) in documents of the Hellenistic and Roman periods, but it is not mentioned in the NT.

Excavations undertaken by Andrews University (1968–1976) at the tell near the modern Jordanian village of Hesban reveal successive occupations from the early Iron Age through Late Mamluk (ca. 1200 B.C.–A.D. 1456) with a gap from ca. 500 to 250 B.C. Lack of Bronze Age remains and sparse evidence for early Iron Age settlement suggest necessary reassessment either of the site identification or of the historical reliability of the Sihon tradition. ***See also*** Gad; Moab; Moabite Stone, The; Reuben; Sihon. P.A.B.

Heth (heth), in the Table of Nations (Gen. 10:15; 1 Chron. 1:13) the son of Canaan and great-grandson of Noah, and the eponymous ancestor of the Hittites. The "sons of Heth" witnessed Abraham's purchase of the Cave of Machpelah from Ephron (Gen. 23:6, 16, 18). Rebekah was annoyed by Esau's marriage to a "daughter of Heth" (Gen. 27:46). Ezekiel describes Jerusalem's ancestry with the words "your father was an Amorite, and your mother a Hittite" (Ezek. 16:3, 45). ***See also*** Canaan, Canaanites; Hittites; Noah.

Hexateuch (heks'uh-to͞ok), the first six books of the OT. The term connotes a theological unity, exposed by a specialized method of biblical study (form criticism), in contrast to the canonical unity defined by the term Pentateuch (the first five books of the OT). The structure of the Hexateuch corresponds to the structure of several brief, credo-like speeches set in a context of worship (e.g., Deut. 26:5–11; Josh. 24:1–28). These speeches recite God's acts on behalf of Israel in four units: promise for progeny and land in Canaan to the patriarchs, exodus from oppression in Egypt, leadership through the dangers of the wilderness, and conquest of the land in Canaan. Each section begins with its own theologically oriented introduction. Each narrates a span of traditions in order to show the completion of the theological theme introduced at the head of the unit.

The four units in the credo speeches exclude reference to God's gift of the law at Sinai, suggesting that the Sinai traditions were originally distinct from the credo traditions. They belonged perhaps to a different group of people whose sacred traditions became a part of the OT story when they became a part of the people who remembered a common past. It is also possible to explain the absence of the Sinai tradition from the credo speeches in other ways, however. Perhaps Sinai was not included in the recitation of God's deeds because the events at Sinai were conceived in a totally different way from the patterns of the other four. Perhaps the Sinai narratives, not attached to a special introduction as the other four are, were conceived as part of the wilderness theme of traditions rather than as a distinct theme or an independent narrative. In that case, the structure of the Hexateuch would reveal its theological connections, not simply in the patterns of the cultic credo with their confessions about God's acts on Israel's behalf, but in its alternation between stories about God's acts on behalf of Israel and stories about God's gift of the law that defines Israel's response to those acts. The alternation, intrinsic for the character of the Hexateuch, depicts interaction between grace and law. To isolate the law (Sinai) from the grace (the credo traditions) violates the present structure of the Hexateuch.

The relationship between law and grace in these traditions is, moreover, of greater importance than would be implied by a simple juxtaposition of narratives about God's acts and narratives about the gift of the law. The acts of God described by the traditions about the patriarchs, exodus, wilderness, and conquest already imply the law defined by the Sinai narratives. To be redeemed from the house of bondage is to hear the imperative from God to respond in particular ways. To receive the grace resident in the descriptions of God's acts without receiving the law that follows is to deny the grace and its claims on its audience.

The theological structure of the Hexateuch focuses not only on God's mighty acts but also on the critical leadership of the people chosen by God to stand at the head of his flock. For the theology of the Hexateuch, to believe in God, to draw identity as the people of God from the covenant relationship established for the people by God, is at the same time to believe in Moses (Exod. 14:31), or with other particular traditions, to believe in Abraham or Joshua. The Hexateuch reveals a dual character in both its theological affirmations and its literary structure: God redeems his people; his chosen servants contribute substantively to the process.

The contrast between Hexateuch and Pentateuch can be defined in another manner. The Pentateuch comprises the Moses saga in relationship to the sagas about the patriarchs and the primeval period. A critical problem in defining the structure of the Pentateuch/Hexateuch lies in the relationship between the Moses traditions and the patriarchal traditions, between stories about Israel in Egypt and the stories about the fathers of Israel in Canaan. The Hexateuch comprises the Moses saga in relationship to the sagas about the patriarchal age, thus encompassing the same problem in the history of the traditions as found in the Pentateuch, plus the Moses saga in relationship to the Joshua saga. The Hexateuch thus unites a broader range of traditions than does the Pentateuch by including in its history the traditions about the conquest of the Promised Land. ***See also*** Sources of the Pentateuch.

Bibliography

Coats, George W. *Genesis. The Forms of* OT *Literature* 1. Grand Rapids: Eerdmans, 1983. Pp. 13–26.

Noth, Martin. *A History of Pentateuchal Traditions.* Englewood Cliffs, NJ: Prentice-Hall, 1972.

von Rad, Gerhard. "The Form-Critical Problem of the Hexateuch." In *The Problem of the Hexateuch and Other Essays.* London: Oliver and Boyd, 1966. Pp. 1–78.

G.W.C.

Hezekiah (hez-e-kī'uh; Heb. "God strengthens"), the son of Ahaz and king of Judah (727–698 B.C.). He was considered by the author of the book of Kings to have been utterly loyal to the Lord, God of Israel; "there was no one like him among all the kings of Judah after him, nor among those who were before him" (2 Kings 18: 3–6). This commendation is based on Hezekiah's attention to ritual matters in his kingdom: he closed down all rural cult sites ("high places") throughout Judah, thereby centralizing sacrifice at the altar of the Temple in Jerusalem (cf. 2 Kings 18:22). He also banned many fetishes that had become common practice: the use of sacred pillars and trees (asherah) and the reverencing of the "bronze serpent" (Heb. *nehushtan)* associated with Moses and the miraculous healing of the people attacked by scorpions in the desert (Num. 21:4–10).

Hezekiah's Reign: Hezekiah's reign fell during the age of major Assyrian military and commercial activity in Phoenicia and the Philistian coast. Shalmaneser V campaigned twice in the area and in 722 conquered Samaria. His successor, Sargon II, reconquered Samaria in 720 and marched as far as Rapiah, where he engaged an Egyptian force supporting the local rulers in their rebellion against Assyria. Four years later, Sargon appeared again, this time founding a trading colony south of Gaza, based in part on cooperation with local Arab tribes of the western Negev. The rebellion in Gaza in 713 was quelled by Sargon's commander-in-chief ("Tar-

A section of the tunnel that brought water from the Gihon spring to the Pool of Siloam, built during the reign of King Hezekiah (727–698 B.C.) to ensure Jerusalem's water supply during a siege.

tan," see Isa. 20:1, KJV) in 712 and the city was annexed to the Assyrian Empire.

Throughout this decade, Hezekiah remained a vassal of Assyria, a status he inherited from his father Ahaz and accepted as the prudent course of state. But in his fourteenth year as king, in 713, Hezekiah received the Babylonian delegation of Merodach-baladan (2 Kings 18: 13; 20:12–13) and this diplomatic dealing with the sworn enemy of Sargon is indicative of an anti-Assyrian undercurrent in Judah. Hezekiah was likely involved in the political stirrings in Philistia. Although Sargon does not claim to have engaged Judah outright, several fortresses in the Judean Shephelah (Ekron, Gibbethon and perhaps Azekah) did fall to the Assyrian armies.

Rebellion Against Assyria: Hezekiah openly broke with Assyria in 705; the death of Sargon had been the signal for rebellion throughout the empire. In the west, Hezekiah was the driving force behind the military coalition that was to face the new monarch Sennacherib. Hezekiah moved into the coastal plain with force (2 Kings 18:8) and he ousted rulers who were hostile to his policies. As part of his plans for preparedness, Hezekiah secured Jerusalem's water supply in the event of siege by the drilling of the Siloam tunnel (2 Kings 20:20; 2 Chron. 32:3–4). But Hezekiah's efforts were no match for Sennacherib's superior forces. In 701, Sennacherib campaigned in the west. The Phoenician cities succumbed quickly and the allies in Philistia were defeated, despite the support lent them by an Egyptian expeditionary force (2 Kings 19:9). A biblical chronistic extract reports: "Sennacherib king of Assyria came up against all the fortified cities of Judah and took them" (2 Kings 18: 13). Sennacherib's inscription concurs: "As for Hezekiah of Judah, who did not submit to my yoke, I laid siege to 46 of his strong cities, walled forts and to the countless small villages in their vicinity, and conquered them. . . . I drove out 200,150 people, young and old, male and female, horses, mules, donkeys, camels, big and small cattle, beyond counting and considered them booty."

Jerusalem came under siege and negotiations were conducted by a high-level Assyrian team and Hezekiah's advisors for Hezekiah's total surrender. Sennacherib claims that he "made him a prisoner in Jerusalem, his royal residence, like a bird in a cage." Though the prophet Isaiah counseled holding out, for the Lord "will defend this city to save it" (2 Kings 19:34), Hezekiah submitted to the Assyrian demands and paid a heavy indemnity (2 Kings 18:14–16). Jerusalem did not, however, become prey to the Assyrians and in prophetic circles this "salvation" was celebrated as vindication of Isaiah's prophecy of divine intervention. It was told: "That night an angel of the Lord went forth, and slew one hundred and eighty-five thousand in the camp of the Assyrians, and . . . early in the morning, behold, these were all dead bodies" (2 Kings 19:35). Much of Judah's territory was transferred to the coastal city-states loyal to Assyria and Hezekiah resumed his vassal status as king of Jerusalem and its immediate environs.

Though Hezekiah is highly praised in the book of Kings, a later generation criticized him for his Babylonian entanglements; they saw in these moves the seed of the Babylonian exile over a century later (2 Kings 20:16–19). In the NT, Hezekiah is listed in the genealogy of Jesus (Matt. 1:9–10). ***See also*** Isaiah, The Book of; Kings, The First and Second Books of the; Sennacherib.

M.C.

Hezron (hez'ruhn). **1** The father of a Reubenite tribe (Gen. 49:6; Exod. 6:14; Num. 26:6; 1 Chron. 5:3). **2** The father of a Judean tribe (Gen. 46:12; Ruth 4:18–19; Matt. 1:3; Luke 3:33). **3** A city on the south border of Judah (Josh. 15:3).

Hiddekel (hid'ek-kel), the term in the KJV for the RSV's "Tigris," the major eastern river in Mesopotamia (modern Iraq; Dan. 10:4; Gen. 2: 14). ***See also*** Tigris River.

Hiel (hī'el; Heb., "God is brother"), a man from Bethel whose two sons died when he violated Joshua's curse (Josh. 6:26) by rebuilding Jericho (1 Kings 16:34).

Hierapolis (hī-uh-rap'uh-lis), a city of Asia Minor located in the upper Lycus valley close to the hot springs of Pamukkale. It is one hundred miles east of Ephesus, twelve miles from Colossae, and six miles from Laodicea. Although originating probably as the village center of a temple estate dedicated to the Phrygian mother goddess, Hierapolis grew and finally received formal status as a city from the King of Pergamum in the early second century B.C. In 133 B.C. Rome took control of Hierapolis and made it part of the province of Asia. Its subsequent prosperity was largely based on its famous textile and cloth dyeing industry. Both grave inscriptions and literary evidence (Cicero, *Pro Flacco* 68; see Josephus, *Antiquities* 12.147–53) indicate a substantial Jewish presence around Hierapolis. Col. 4:13, the sole NT reference, reports that Epaphras "labored much" for the Christians in Colossae, Laodicea, and Hierapolis. Hierapolis' extensive remains include a Roman theater (now restored), baths, city walls, and a necropolis. ***See also*** Asia; Colossae; Epaphras; Ephesus; Laodicea; Pergamum. R.A.W.

higgaion (hi-gay'yuhn), a Hebrew word that appears in three Psalms. In two of them it seems to have some sort of musical connotation: in Ps. 9:16, where it occurs with the unknown word *Selah* and is simply transliterated, and in Ps. 92:3, where it is translated "melody" (KJV: "solemn sound"). In Ps. 19:14, it is translated "meditation."

high place, an elevated location used for religious rites. "High place" in the OT translates the Hebrew *bamah*, pl. *bamoth*, a rendering deriving from the Septuagint and Vulgate. The plural means "heights" (of the earth) in a number of passages (e.g., Deut. 32:13; Isa. 58:14; Amos 4:13) and usually *bamoth* were situated on high ground, as in the regular Deuteronomic description of them as "upon the high mountains and upon the hills and under every green tree" (Deut. 12:2). But there were also *bamoth* within towns (2 Kings 17:9) and in valleys (Jer. 7:31; 32:35; Ezek. 6:3), and they are commonly spoken of as being "built" (e.g., 1 Kings 14:23) and, when removed, "broken down" (e.g., 2 Chron. 31:1). Thus the *bamah* was not simply a natural shrine and it is now generally agreed that, in its religious sense, the word means an artificially constructed platform on which sacrifices were offered and cultic objects placed, though it always seems to have been in the open air.

The high place was a common feature in the religions of the small states surrounding Israel, such as Moab (Jer. 49:35), where the word occurs in line 3 of the victory stele of the ninth-century B.C. Moabite king Mesha, and Ammon (1 Kings 11:7), and its use appears to be confined to this area. In the OT, it is characteristic of the Canaanite fertility religion and the worship of Baal (Jer. 19:5; 32:35), so it is generally strongly condemned, especially in Deuteronomic passages in the book of Kings, in Chronicles, and in the Prophets, and reforming kings destroyed the high places (2 Kings 18:4; 23:8, 13, 15, 19). The rites practiced at the high places and the cultic objects found there are typically Canaanite: ritual prostitution (1 Kings 14:23–24; Ezek. 16:16), child sacrifice (Jer. 7:31; 19:5; 32:35; Ezek. 16:20), sacrifices and the burning of incense (1 Kings 22:43; 2 Kings 12:3), the stone pillar symbolizing Baal, and the wooden pole symbolizing the goddess Asherah (1 Kings 14:23; 2 Kings 17:10). It has been suggested that the *bamah* was a burial mound and that the high place was where rites of the dead were celebrated, but there is no real evidence for this.

Role in Popular Religion: From the OT denunciations, it is clear that the high places had a central part in popular religion and, before the Deuteronomic demand for their destruction and the centralization of worship at a single sanctuary, they were considered a legitimate feature of the worship of Yahweh. In 1 Sam. 9:12–24, we find Samuel sacrificing and presiding at the attendant meal at the high place of Ramah, which was situated above the town, and in 1 Sam. 10:5 a band of prophets has clearly been worshiping at the high place of Gibeath-elohim. Cultic platforms, either circular or rectangular in shape, which were used for sacrifice, have been recognized as *bamoth* by archaeologists at several Palestinian sites during the period of Israelite occupation, among them Hazor and Arad; the one discovered at Dan was almost certainly built by Jeroboam I (1 Kings 13:32).

The word *bamah*, however, is also used in the OT in a wider sense to denote the whole of a sanctuary or shrine and the complex of buildings it contained, such as the hall of Ramah (1 Sam. 9:22) or other cultic structures. (1 Kings 13:32). Before the Deuteronomic reform (ca. 630 B.C.), a number of these sanctuaries, such as Shechem, Bethel, Gilgal, Shiloh, and above all Jerusalem, achieved a far greater importance than the small local high places, and their individual traditions are very significant for Israel's religion in the period of the monarchy (ca. 1025–586 B.C.). Characteristic of these are stories that ascribe their foundation to great figures of the past, who are often said to have erected an altar or some other cultic object at the place and to inaugurate the worship of Yahweh there. So Abraham founded Hebron (Gen. 13:18); both he and Isaac are said to have founded Beer-sheba (Gen. 21:33; 26:23–25). Jacob founded Bethel

A bronze model of an Elamite sanctuary, or "high place," found at Susa, twelfth century B.C.

(Gen. 28:18–22; 35:7, 14–15) and Shechem (Gen. 33:18–20), with which Joshua is also associated (Josh. 8:30–35). Joshua erected the twelve stones marking the shrine at Gilgal (Josh. 4:20–24), while 2 Samuel 24 is the sacred legend of the Jerusalem sanctuary, telling how it was inaugurated by David.

Importance: However, the real reason for the great attention paid to these sanctuaries is that they were originally important Canaanite centers, both before and after the first arrival of the Israelites. The stories of their founding by the patriarchs and other heroes are intended to legitimize their adoption by Israel, to claim that they had always been Israelite. The details of Gen. 28:10–22, especially v. 19, show that Bethel was not a deserted spot but an ancient Canaanite city and sanctuary. Shechem remained Canaanite long after the time of Jacob and the center of a non-Yahwistic religion (Judg. 9:4, 27, 46), and the pillar and the tree in the sanctuary there are the regular features of a Canaanite high place (Josh. 24:26; Judg. 9:6). Again, it should be noted how often the patriarchs invoke Yahweh by titles of the great Canaanite deity El, by which he was known at different sanctuaries (El Elyon, Gen. 14:22; El Olam, Gen. 21:33; El Bethel, Gen. 31:13; cf. Jer. 48:13). Inevitably, this brought about a degree of fusion between Yahwism and Canaanite religion and even worship by Israelites of the fertility deity Baal, which incurred the condemnation of Deuteronomists and prophets (Hos. 2:2–20). But the influence of Canaan through the sanctuaries was not wholly negative: Shechem's deity was called the "god of the covenant" and this encouraged the development there of a great Israelite celebration of the renewal of the Sinai covenant and the reading of the law (Deut. 27). And Israel's three great annual pilgrimage feasts (Exod. 23:14–18) were agricultural occasions originally held at the Canaanite shrines.

Ten large stelae at Gezer may have been a Canaanite "high place" (cf. 2 Kings 18:4); Middle Bronze Age.

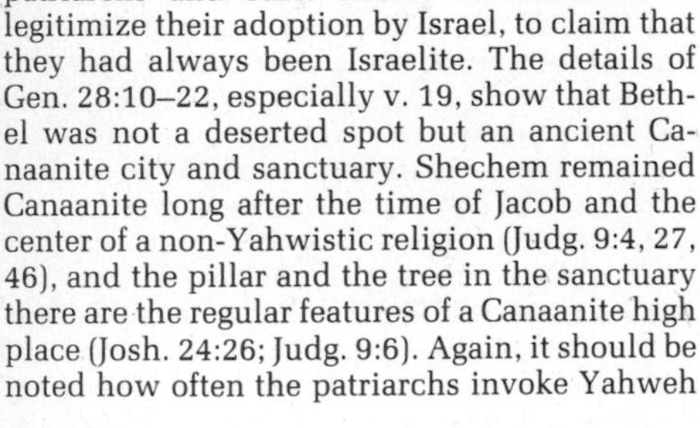

Another reason for the importance of certain high places was that they were the sanctuaries of particular tribes, as may be seen in the case of the one founded by the tribe of Dan, though again on an old Canaanite site (Judg. 18:27–31). It is possible that, in the premonarchical period, a sanctuary like Shiloh functioned as a center for the whole tribal confederation, marked by the presence of the Ark as a national symbol (1 Sam. 4:1–4). With the establishment of the monarchy, the sanctuaries that enjoyed royal patronage achieved outstanding importance. This was particularly the case with Jerusalem in the south and with Bethel in the Northern Kingdom (Amos 7:13).

It was the great prestige of Jerusalem that enabled the implementation of Deuteronomy's program by Josiah, who destroyed all the numerous high places in both the south and north (2 Kings 23:4–20) and left the Temple at Jerusalem as the sole place where Yahweh could be worshiped. The Babylonian invasion a few years later (early sixth century B.C.) probably brought about the destruction of any high places that may have lingered on. From this time on, nothing further is heard of them, and on the return from Exile it was only the Jerusalem sanctuary that was reestablished (Ezra 3). ***See also*** Ark; Covenant; Deuteronomy; Josiah.

Bibliography

de Vaux, R. *Ancient Israel: Its Life and Institutions.* New York: McGraw-Hill, 1961. Pp. 284–311.

Kraus, H.-J. *Worship in Israel.* Oxford: Blackwell, 1966. Pp. 134–178.

Vaughan, P. H. *The Meaning of 'Bāma' in the Old Testament.* London: Cambridge University Press, 1974. J.R.P.

high priests. ***See*** Priests.

Hilkiah (hil-kī'uh; Heb., "God is my portion"). **1** A Levite from the line of Merari (1 Chron. 6: 45). **2** The son of Hosah, a Merarite Levite in the time of David (1 Chron. 26:11). **3** The father of Eliakim, a royal official in the time of King Hezekiah (2 Kings 18:18; see Isa. 22:20). **4** The father of Jeremiah, a priest (Jer. 1:1). **5** A high priest in the late seventh century B.C. who reported that a book of the law had been found at the Temple (2 Kings 22–23; see 2 Chron. 35:8). He appears to have been an ancestor of Ezra (Ezra 7:1, see 1 Chron. 6:13–15). **6** The name of several other OT figures (see Jer. 29:3; Neh. 8:4; 12:7; Bar. 1:1; Sus. 2). F.E.G.

hill country, a general designation in the Bible for those parts of the Holy Land that are hilly rather than flat. Since the land of Palestine has a mountainous spine running its length between the Jordan River to the east and the Mediterranean Sea to the west, any area along that spine can be designated "hill country." In addition, the hills found along the east bank of the Jordan River also constitute an upland area, any part of which can be termed "hill country."

Among the areas identified as "hill country" are parts of Seir, south of the Dead Sea (Gen. 36:8); the area of the Jebusites (Josh. 11:3); the dwelling place of the Anakim (Josh. 11:21); areas in both Judah and Israel (Josh. 11:21); and the tribal areas of Naphtali and Ephraim (Josh. 20:7), among many others. Indeed, hill country could be identified from as far south as the Wilderness (1 Sam. 23:14) to as far north as the land of the Amorites, near the head of the Euphrates River (Num. 13:29). In the NT, the story of Jesus begins in the hill country of Judah (Luke 1:39, 65). D.B.

hin. ***See*** Weights and Measures.

hind, the female adult red deer, a symbol of beauty (Prov. 5:19) and desperate loyalty (Jer. 14:5). ***See also*** Hart.

Hinnom (hin'uhm), **Valley of,** a valley known also as the "Valley of the Son, or Sons, of Hinnom." It was probably the Wadi er-Rababi, beginning west of Jerusalem near the present Jaffa Gate, and curving round south of the Old City to join the Kidron Valley. It was entered from the "Potsherd Gate" (Jer. 19:2, 6) and formed part of the boundary between Judah and Benjamin (Josh. 15:8; 18:16; Neh. 11:30). It is notorious in the OT as the scene of much idolatry, including the sacrifice of children, especially under Ahaz and Manasseh (mid-eighth to mid-seventh century B.C.; 2 Chron. 28:3; 33:6) and again in Jeremiah's day (Jer. 7:30–34; 32:35), despite the abolition of such practices by Josiah (2 Kings 23: 10). Such evil associations caused its Hebrew name *ge-hinnom* (hence "Gehenna") to be identified with hell (e.g., Matt. 5:22, 29; 23:15, 33; Mark 9:43, 47; James 3:6). ***See also*** Ahaz; Gehenna; Josiah; Manasseh. D.B.

Hiram (hī'rem; shortened from Heb. *Ahiram*, "my brother [god] is exalted" or "brother of the exalted one"; alternatively Huram [Chronicles]). **1** The king of Tyre, and a contemporary of David and Solomon. Hiram I, son of Abibaal, was nineteen years old when he ascended the throne, and he reigned thirty-four years (ca. 969–935 B.C.). The kingdom he established is vividly pictured by Ezekiel (chaps. 26–27). Under Hiram's rule Tyre became the leading city of Phoenicia, which launched a colonial empire that spread over the whole of the Mediterranean. He enlarged the island city of Tyre by uniting it with a smaller island and undertook extensive building programs.

The power of the Philistines was apparently broken by an alliance between the Tyrian kings Abibaal and Hiram on the one hand (at sea) and David on the other (on land). David traded with Hiram for materials and craftsmen to build his royal palace in Jerusalem (2 Sam. 5: 11; 1 Chron. 14:1). David established a treaty with Hiram, which was renewed by Solomon who also traded with him for materials and craftsmen, particularly in the building of the Temple in Jerusalem (1 Kings 5:12–18; 2 Chron. 2:3–12). Hiram supplied cedar and other building materials, along with craftsmen, in exchange for wheat and olive oil. Some years later Hiram gave Solomon gold and another larger shipment of cedar and other woods and received in exchange twenty towns in Galilee known collectively as Cabul (1 Kings 9:10–13). Hiram also aided Solomon in his commercial ventures by supplying both ships and sailors for a merchant fleet that operated out of the port of Ezion-geber (1 Kings 9:26–28).

Some scholars have suggested the possibility of a relationship between this Hiram of Tyre and the famous King Ahiram of Phoenician Byblos (ca. 1000 B.C.). There is also an eighth-century King Hiram of Tyre mentioned in an inscription of Tiglath-pileser III. **2** An artisan sent by King Hiram of Tyre to do the bronze work for the Temple in Jerusalem (1 Kings 7:13–14). The son of a woman of the tribe of Naphthali (1 Kings 7: 14) or of Dan (2 Chron. 2:14) and a man of Tyre, he was responsible for casting the bronze pillars, the molten sea, and other Temple furnishings in a specially suited clay which was found between Succoth and Zarethan (1 Kings 7:40–46). ***See also*** David; Solomon; Tyre. D.L.C.

hireling, a servant who is paid wages (Job 7:2; Mal. 3:5; Luke 15:17). The Law protected their rights (Deut. 24:14–15), and terms of service might be specified (Isa. 16:14; Job 7:1). John 10: 12–13 contrasts the cowardice of a hired shepherd with the owner's concern for the sheep. The Mishnah stipulated that a hired servant had to compensate the owner for any loss due to negligence. "Hireling" could sometimes be used to imply "inferior" (Plutarch *Moralia* 37C). It is also used of hired fishermen (Mark 1:20).

historical criticism. ***See*** Biblical Criticism.

historical geography of the Bible, the study of historical events and peoples in their geographical and ecological environment, and the reconstruction of sociological and economic patterns in antiquity on the basis of geographical data.

Of all the sacred books of the world religions, the Bible is the most closely linked to geographical settings. It recounts the experience of a historical people in its physical environment and biblical faith sees in all of nature, particularly the weather and other ecological phenomena, the expression of divine power. Both Jews and Christians have a profound concern for the physical setting of biblical history. In traditional Judaism, many commandments are predicated on one's very presence in the land of Israel. Christians down through the ages have always sought to deepen their experience by seeing the true landscape of biblical events. Modern research utilizes many disciplines of the physical and social sciences as well as the humanities to reconstruct the ancient ecological milieu of the Bible's historical peoples.

Physiography: Since the first modern map of Palestine by the engineers who came with Napoleon in 1799 (the Jacotin Map, 1810), significant advances have been made. The explorations by Edward Robinson in 1838 and 1853 brought to Western scholarship a large body of geographical information, especially the location of dozens of biblical towns. Other explorers added further details, and the culmination of nineteenth-century research was the thorough mapping conducted by the team of British military engineers sponsored by the Palestine Exploration Society during 1870–76. That expedition, called the Survey of Western Palestine, produced a detailed map in twenty-two sheets with accompanying commentary and name lists. Their maps were still used by both sides in World War I and only under the subsequent British mandate was the process of remapping the country taken up again. This has continued under the Israeli and Jordanian survey departments to the present time. All the tools of modern cartography, including aerial photogrammetry, computers, and even satellite pictures are used. A special grid was also established for locating sites and features.

The terrain of the ancient land of Israel consists of "brooks of water, of fountains and springs, flowing forth in valleys and hills" (Deut. 8:7). It is the contrast between hill regions and plains that has determined the fragmented nature of the societies that lived there in antiquity. For example, in the Canaanite period, the small city-states were located on the plains, usually at the foot of the adjacent hills where springs of water come forth from the porous limestone layers that make up the ranges of Palestine (cf. Josh. 17:16). The initial area open to the tribes of Israel was mainly in the hilly areas (Josh. 17:18). The deep Jordan Valley gave a north-south orientation to the mountain ranges of both Cisjordan and Transjordan; the former coastlines of the eastern Mediterranean basin have shaped the coastal plains. East-west faulting has created some prominent valleys (such as the Jezreel Valley) and thus broken up the central hill country into smaller units such as Galilee, Mt. Ephraim, and Mt. Judah. On the south, the zone of aeolic sand deposits form the biblical Negeb.

The study of the physical environment in biblical times is facilitated by analysis of the present geological morphology of the land and the processes that have brought it into being. For example, the coastal sands brought by the currents are later than the Byzantine period (mid-fourth century A.D.–1453) because they cover ancient sites from that era. But the coastal sandstone ridges are much earlier, being the petrified sand dunes of more ancient times. The level of erosion from the hills onto the plains can be dated by the age of the sites from antiquity still on the surface. The flora of prehistoric and historic periods can be determined by pollen studies from cores bored in lake and river bottoms. The organic remains, including plant and animal (bone) remains from archaeological digs, can tell the botanist and the zoologist about the ecology of more closely dated ages in the historical record. Thus, they reveal the ways in which

Map opposite: Solomon's twelve districts; from 1 Kings 4:7–19, an "administrative text," it is possible to derive the approximate territories of Solomon's "district commissioners," but the boundaries between the districts can only be drawn in a general way.

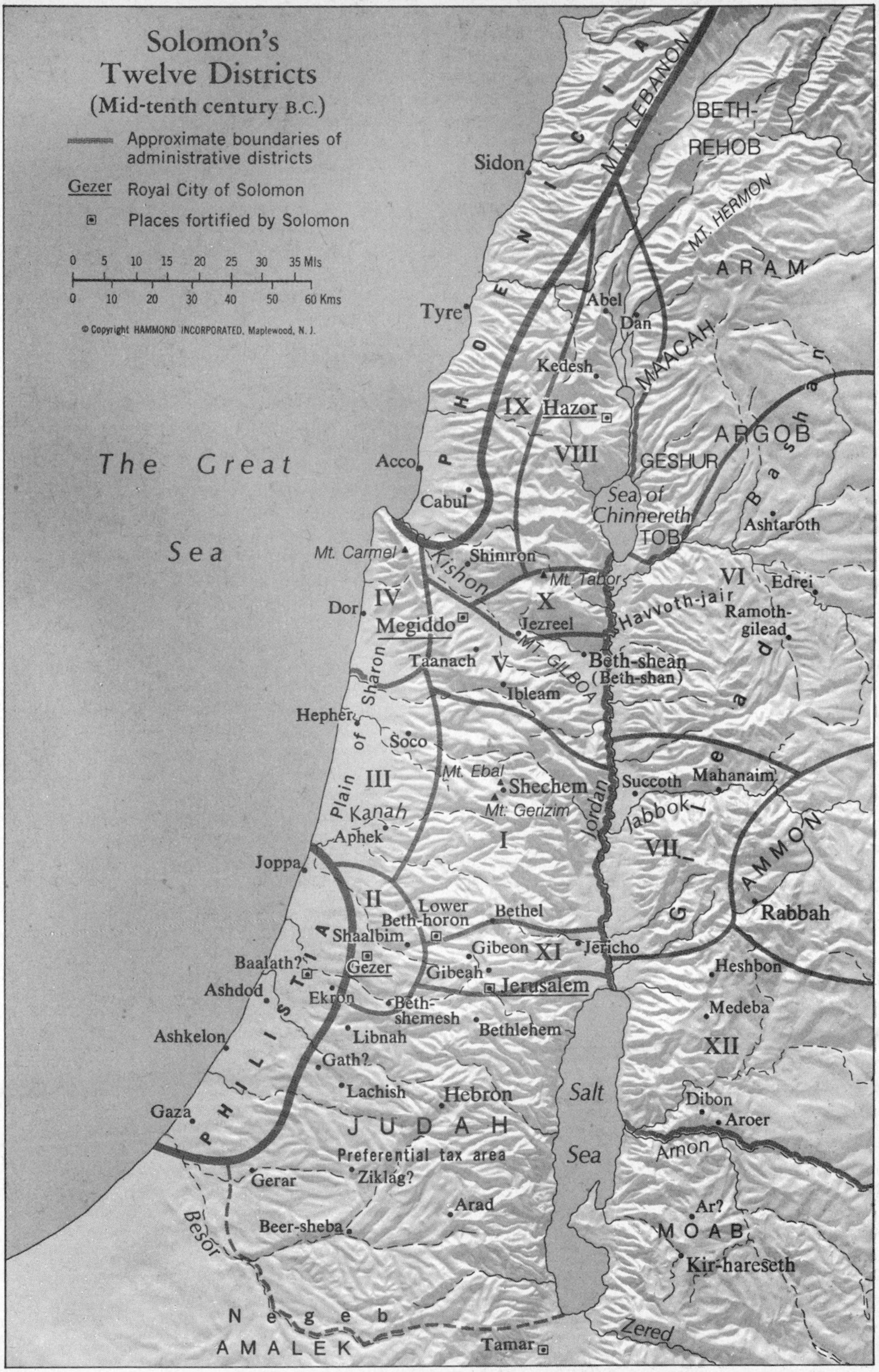
Solomon's
Twelve Districts
(Mid-tenth century B.C.)
Approximate boundaries of administrative districts
Gezer Royal City of Solomon
Places fortified by Solomon
0 5 10 15 20 25 30 35 Mls
0 10 20 30 40 50 60 Kms
© Copyright HAMMOND INCORPORATED, Maplewood, N. J.
The Great Sea
PHOENICIA
MT. LEBANON
BETH-REHOB
MT. HERMON
ARAM
Sidon
Tyre
Abel
Dan
MAACAH
Kedesh
IX
Hazor
VIII
ARGOB
Bashan
GESHUR
Acco
Cabul
Sea of Chinnereth
TOB
Ashtaroth
Mt. Carmel
Shimron
Kishon
Mt. Tabor
VI
Edrei
IV
X
Havvoth-jair
Ramoth-gilead
Dor
Megiddo
Jezreel
MT. GILBOA
Beth-shean
(Beth-shan)
Taanach
V
Ibleam
Gilead
Plain of Sharon
Hepher
Soco
III
Mt. Ebal
Shechem
Succoth
Mahanaim
Kanah
Mt. Gerizim
Jordan
Jabbok
Aphek
I
VII
AMMON
Joppa
II
Lower Beth-horon
Bethel
Rabbah
Shaalbim
Gibeon
XI
Jericho
Baalath?
Gezer
Gibeah
Jerusalem
Heshbon
Ashdod
Ekron
Beth-shemesh
Medeba
PHILISTIA
Ashkelon
Libnah
Bethlehem
XII
Gath?
Lachish
Hebron
Salt Sea
Gaza
JUDAH
Dibon
Aroer
Arnon
Preferential tax area
Gerar
Ziklag?
Arad
Ar?
Besor
Beer-sheba
MOAB
Kir-hareseth
Negeb
AMALEK
Tamar
Zered

ancient people provided food for their communities. Patterns in the flora, compared with similar regimes in modern times, help to define the weather patterns for the ancient periods.

Generally speaking, the grain crops, wheat and barley, were cultivated on the plains: the Jezreel Valley, the Philistine plain, the table land of Moab, and the plateau of Bashan. The hilly slopes were especially good for the development of orchards and vineyards, often by means of terraces built on the natural limestone strata. The Judean steppe land (the so-called "wilderness," Josh. 15:61) was good for grazing, as was the Negeb and the central Sharon Plain. Vineyards were often cultivated on the sandstone coastal ridges. Fishing was possible both in the Mediterranean and in the fresh-water Sea of Chinnereth (Sea of Galilee). The grain crops were dependent upon the rains of the winter season while the vineyards and orchards were dependent upon the dews of the summer months. There was never a sterile season in the annual cycle. The real fear of the ancient farmer was of a prolonged drought (1 Kings 17:1; 18:1–5). In years of good rain even the semi-arid Negeb could bring forth abundant crops (Gen. 26:12). A proper curse on the land meant the cessation of both the dew and the rain (2 Sam. 1:21).

A major task of historical geography is to establish the proper biblical names of the physical features on the terrain. Since the beginning of modern research there has been considerable looseness in the application of ancient terms. Modern maps of Israel include the "wilderness of Beer-sheba" (Gen. 21:14) and the "wilderness of Zin" (Num. 13:21) in the Negev (Israeli Hebrew spelling). The biblical Negeb was actually limited to its northern zone (cf. Num. 13:22, 29). Such features as the brook Besor (1 Sam. 30:10), now identified with the Wadi Ghazzeh, and the "waters of the Jarkon" (RSV: "Me-jarkon," Josh. 19:46), now equated with the Wadi el-'Aujeh, are based on the interpretation of their biblical contexts, sometimes with the help of later Jewish or Christian sources. In the case of the Jarkon, the Septuagint (LXX) version of Josh. 19: 46 suggests that another stream is meant, Wadi Musrarah, now called Nahal Ayalon on Israeli maps. The study of physical geography will have little meaning for the Bible student if ancient regional names are not applied to their original terrain.

Philology: Geographical details in the ancient narratives can usually be counted on for reliability. Many geographical texts are of an administrative nature reflecting true-to-life situations. Even in hero stories such as 1 Sam. 17, the details regarding features and towns in the vicinity of the action must derive from the local population.

An interest in historical geography is as old as the Bible itself. A chapter such as Genesis 14 reveals that the author knew of a pre-Israelite tradition of place names (Bela, Enmishpat, etc.); he keeps them in the narrative with updated glosses so the reader will know the proper locations in the Israelite period.

The Masoretic Text (MT) must be compared with the LXX and sometimes other versions to get the most accurate text of any geographical passage being studied. The decision as to which version is more ancient may even be made on the basis of which one makes the best sense in the relevant landscape (cf. the problem of the Jarkon in Josh. 19:46 discussed above).

Some examples of administrative texts are the town lists in the book of Joshua and the genealogical tables of the various tribes in 1 Chronicles. The most explicit document of this type is the roster of Solomon's district commissioners and their respective territories (1 Kings 4:7–19). The enumeration of towns fortified by Solomon (1 Kings 9:15–19; also 2 Chron. 8:1–6) and by Rehoboam (2 Chron. 11:5–12) may also derive from the administrative archives that were later incorporated into the royal Chronicles. Other passages are more purely historiographical in nature, e.g., the unconquered Canaanite cities (Judg. 1:21, 27–35) or the "land that yet remains" (Josh. 13:1–6). The itinerary of the wandering Israelites (Num. 33) probably is based on itineraries for caravans operating across the Sinai deserts during the monarchical period (mid-eleventh century to 586 B.C.). Even prophetic oracles were sometimes geographic in nature: Isaiah's "march through Benjamin" (Isa. 10:28–32); Micah's lament over his homeland, the Shephelah (Mic. 1:10–15); the denunciations of Philistia (Amos 1:6–8; Jer. 47:1–7), of Moab (Isa. 15–16; Jer. 48) and of Edom (Jer. 49:7–22). The "Table of Nations" (Gen. 10) records a geographical world view (cf. Ezek. 27:1–25).

In the Greco-Roman period (333 B.C.–A.D. 324) the Hellenistic spirit of inquiry about the world we live in led to the composition of many geographical works such as those of Strabo, Ptolemy, and Pliny. But within the rabbinic literature of Judaism there are many detailed geographic references to OT sites and their Roman period equivalents. This was because of the need to determine the exact extent of the land of Israel so as to know where the commandments pertaining to life on the land were in force. A new copy of such a Judaic geographical text has been found on the mosaic floor of a synagogue near Beth-shean. The Gospels, Acts, and many of the Letters make reference to places in Palestine and the rest of the Roman Empire but no passages occur with a purely geographical intent. The church fathers, particularly the research center at Caesarea (Origin, Eusebius), produced works of major geographical import because of their deep interest in Bible study. Their surviving works are essential tools for locating sites from

 HISTORICAL GEOGRAPHY

The lower Jordan River on the mosaic Madeba Map; it flows south (right) into the Dead Sea.

the biblical period. The Madeba Map, a mosaic in the floor of a church in Transjordan, exemplifies the Christian interest in sites where the events of sacred history took place. It also provides abundant details about the size and status of various towns in the Byzantine period.

The accounts of later pilgrims and of the Crusaders are less reliable. Accurate sources for Palestinian geography are the works of the Arab geographers but their interest was mainly descriptive and not biblical. Eshtori Haparhi, a Jewish scholar of the early thirteenth century, came to Palestine and made extensive geographical inquiries in search of OT sites. His work remained in obscurity for centuries until Edward Robinson discovered that Eshtori had preceded him in many discoveries.

Today, scholars have at their disposal a corpus of geographical texts from Egyptian records, on papyrus and stone, and also from cuneiform inscriptions. The Palestinian epigraphic finds (i.e., inscriptions) have been few and mostly of less geographical import. The Mesha stele and the Samaria ostraca are notable exceptions. Of the outside sources for the Canaanite period, the most detailed are the topographic lists of Pharaoh Thutmose III and the letters in cuneiform from the archive from the site of Tell el-Amarna in Egypt. For the age of the Israelite monarchy, the records of the kings of Assyria and Babylon are of major importance.

Toponymics: The primary link between our times and antiquity is the corpus of Arabic place names in Palestine that still preserves the forms, albeit with some linguistic shifts, of names in the Bible. By the end of the nineteenth century, scholars had succeeded in recording most, if not all, of the surviving Arabic names and the rules of transmission had been formulated. One could usually trace the transformation of a Hebrew name to the Arabic form still used by Palestinian peasants.

The study of the ancient names from the Bible and contemporary sources, including the spellings in the MT and LXX, is a special branch of research that can shed light on the society and psychology of the Canaanites and the people of Israel. Greek and cuneiform spellings may contribute to the linguistic history of the Hebrew language.

The search for biblical towns is seldom easy unless the Arabic name is a true reflex of the ancient one. In areas where there was a fairly continuous sedentary population, the geographical nomenclature may be reasonably preserved. Some of the Arabic and biblical equations are obvious, e.g., Esdud is Ashdod, Yafa is Joppa (Heb. *Yafo*), 'Arad is Arad, and so on. In other instances the change is only slight, e.g., Beisan for Beth-shean. The ancient name may, however, have become transformed into an entirely different Arabic phrase such as *'Eid el-Ma*, "Festival of the Water," which has developed from the Hebrew *Adullam*. A special case of religious modification is the alteration of the theophoric component *-el* into the pseudo plural *-in* (from

HISTORICAL GEOGRAPHY

Arabic); thus Bethel became Beitin, Jezreel became Zer'in and even a valley named after Ishmael became the Wadi Isma'in. Names having as their root the three consonants *ayin, pe*, and *resh*, such as Ophrah, or Ephraim (2 Sam. 13:23) were changed because they were too close to the Arabic *'ifrit*, "demon." The new name given was just the opposite, et-Tayibeh, "The Favored." Place names with the consonants *heth, pe*, and *resh* also underwent this same process, probably because the Hebrew guttural consonants such as *ayin* and *heth* were not being pronounced properly by the late Talmudic period when the Arab conquest took place (seventh-eighth centuries A.D.).

When a biblical town with a biblical name was given a new Greco-Roman name, e.g., when Aphek became Antipatris (Acts 23:31) or Acco became Ptolemais (Acts 21:7), the local population usually continued to speak their own Semitic language and called their town by its old name. When the Byzantines left, the people at a town like Lod/Lydda no longer used the imperial name Diospolis; so in Arabic, the name became Ludd. In contrast, the Herodian name Sebastia survived as Sebastiyeh while the Semitic name, Samaria (Heb. *Shomron*), was lost; the real Semitic-speaking Samaritans had been expelled or killed during the reign of Alexander the Great, so the non-Semitic population preserved the Greek name given by Herod. Caesarea was a new foundation, as was Tiberias; thus, their Greco-Roman names also survived in Arabic. On occasion, the biblical name underwent a transformation, becoming the name of a Moslem saint whose grave is venerated on or near the site, e.g., ancient Rehob south of Beth-shean survives as the tomb of Sheikh Rihab on the site.

Archaeology: The older explorers were often fooled by the fact that the biblical name had been moved from the mound of the OT town to a nearby site where the Roman and/or Byzantine town was located. Therefore, it became imperative to devise some means of identifying the debris and ruins of an OT city as against those of a Greco-Roman or Byzantine one. It was Sir William Flinders Petrie who demonstrated in 1890 at Tell el-Hesi that the artificial mounds were built up by successive building and destruction of settlements. The artifacts and structures in the respective layers of debris (strata) were seen to reflect typological features that developed through time. Eventually, archaeologists were able to give relative dates and sometimes more absolute dates to the finds in particular strata. Field archaeology became another discipline contributing to reconstruction of the ancient way of life in the various periods of antiquity.

Very seldom has an epigraphic discovery confirmed an identification. Usually it is a case of a site where the Arabic name had already pointed to the proper equation, e.g., Arad, Gezer. The name of Beth-shean found in an Egyptian text on a stele at the mound of Tell el-Husn proved what scholars had already deduced, namely, that this was the site of OT Beth-shean, the name of which was preserved in the adjacent town of Beisan (with a slight corruption already evident in Talmudic times). The Mesha stele mentions Dibon; its find spot was the Arabic town of Dhiban and the equation was not difficult to make. Doubts about the identification of el-Jib with ancient Gibeon were dispelled when jar handles with *gb'n* incised on them were found there in a great water shaft. The name of Arad appears on some of the ostraca found at Tell 'Arad. In the case of Lachish, the name also showed up in an ostracon from Tell ed-Duweir, which site was already assumed by the excavators to be Lachish, but without an Arabic name. The same can be said for the cuneiform tablet found by a tourist in the plowed field on Tell Waqqaṣ. It contained the name of Hazor, and thus it confirmed the identification of that huge site with the most prominent city of Galilee (Josh. 11:10). There are still many sites from antiquity for whom the ancient name is still unknown in spite of modern excavations, e.g., Tell Kisan in the plain of Acco, Tell Jerisheh in north Tel Aviv, and Tell el-Hesi in the southern coastal plain.

At least from excavations, a proper idea of the size, function, and importance of a site can be obtained, that is, if the excavations are not confined to a narrow trench. The successive layers of occupation can show when the site was occupied. Of course, some chapters in a city's history may accidentally not be mentioned in the written sources while some documented periods may not be represented in the archaeological stratigraphy. One cannot necessarily expect a perfect correlation between the two kinds of evidence.

Archaeological survey, the examination of as many sites as possible on the surface of a well-defined geographical region, is now contributing even more to the reconstruction of the ancient life of Israel in its ecological environment. The plotting of the sites reveals their pattern of distribution in relation to the types of rock and soil and the local water sources. The use of collected pottery to date the sites and the accurate description of their physical shape (high mound, low circle of debris, and so forth) can tell much about the density of population centers in a given area and during particular historical periods. Ecological factors, including the nature of the terrain, water sources, and the evidence of organic remains from excavation can be synthesized to give a clear picture of the quality of life in the region being studied. Coupled with an analysis of the historical sources, this information serves to illumine the role of the individual regions in both the political and the economic history of the country. ***See also*** Archaeology, History, and the Bible.

Bibliography

Aharoni, Y. *The Land of the Bible*. Philadelphia: Westminster, 1979.

Avi-Yonah, M. *The Holy Land*. Grand Rapids, MI: Baker, 1977.

A.F.R.

Hittites (hit'tīts), an Indo-European people who established a strong kingdom in east central Anatolia in the second millennium B.C. The Hittites, named after the non-Indo-European Hattians whom they displaced, spoke several different Indo-European languages. The official language of the kingdom, written in a cuneiform (i.e., wedge-shaped) script adapted from Akkadian, is called Cuneiform Hittite. In the outlying regions a hieroglyphic system was used to write a related language, referred to as Hieroglyphic Hittite. Luwian, which is very close to Hieroglyphic Hittite, and Palaic were also spoken within the kingdom.

History: The history of the Hittites can be divided into three periods: the Old Kingdom, the New Kingdom, and the Neo-Hittite kingdoms. Sometime around 1650 B.C. Hattusilis I pushed out of Anatolia into north Syria and captured Aleppo, and his successor, Mursilis I, sacked Babylon. Following these two great rulers of the Old Kingdom, the Hittite empire declined, due both to internal difficulties and to the growing power of the Hurrians under the rulers of Mitanni.

The revival of the New Kingdom began in the fifteenth century B.C., but it was Suppiluliuma (1375–1335 B.C.) who made it a major power by his conquest of Mitanni and northern Syria. All the small states of north and central Syria, including most of Lebanon, became vassals of the Hittites. This area became a battleground between the Egyptians and the Hittites until the peace treaty between Ramesses II and Hattusilis III (ca. 1280 B.C.), but the Hittites remained in control of the region. After this treaty, the main threat to Hittite hegemony in Syria came from Assyria, and Carchemish, the capital of the Hittite vice-regent in the east, gained in importance. It was the Sea Peoples (i.e., people from the Greek islands, including Crete) from the west, however, who destroyed the Hittite empire. The Hittite homeland collapsed first, and then the coastal areas under its control, from Ugarit to Amurru, fell to these invaders about 1200 B.C.

The devastation did not reach too far inland, however, and the remnants of the Hittite empire formed Neo-Hittite kingdoms in Carchemish, Hamath, and a number of other inland sites, particularly in the Taurus region and in northern Syria. Hieroglyphic Hittite and Neo-Hittite culture continued in many of these sites even after the Aramean influx at the end of the second millennium led to Aramean dynasties gaining power.

The Assyrians continued to refer to the inhabitants of these new kingdoms as Hittites. From the time of Tiglath-pileser I (1115–1070 B.C.) onward, the Assyrians called all the territory between the Euphrates and northern Lebanon the Land of Hatti. With Assyrian expansion into southern Syria and Palestine, the term was expanded to include those regions. Shalmaneser III (858–824 B.C.) lists Ahab among the Hittite kings, and Esarhaddon (680–669 B.C.) includes the kings of Judah, Edom, Moab, Ammon, and a couple of Philistine rulers among the kings of Hatti. The term "Hatti" continued to be used into the Neo-Babylonian period (sixth century B.C.) as a geographical designation that included Palestine.

In the Bible: The biblical use of the term "Hittite" is probably dependent, at least in part, on this cuneiform usage. Canaan is listed as the father of Heth in the Table of Nations (Gen. 10:15), and many texts (e.g., Gen. 15:20; Exod. 23:28) list the Hittites among the pre-Israelite inhabitants of Canaan, but there is no evidence that the Hittites of the empire ever penetrated that far south, much less settled there. Ezekiel makes the mother of Jerusalem a Hittite (16:3, 45), and the Priestly writer mentions Hittites in his accounts of the patriarchs (Gen. 23; 25:9; 26:34; 27:46), but both were probably just following the Neo-Babylonian geographical terminology of their time when they designated these inhabitants of Canaan as Hittites.

The attempt to prove that Abraham's purchase of the cave of Machpelah (Gen. 23) followed imperial Hittite law is not compelling, and all of the Hittites mentioned by name in the OT—Ephron, Zohar, Beeri, Elon, Ahimelech, and Uriah—bear Semitic, not Hittite, names. If they were of Hittite or Neo-Hittite stock, they had assimilated into the dominant Semitic culture of the region. On the other hand, Ahimelech (1 Sam. 26:6) and Uriah (2 Sam. 11:3) are both designated Hittites in written sources that antedate strong Assyrian influence on Judah. That suggests that they may indeed have been assimilated descendants of Hittite or, more likely, Neo-Hittite stock. The references to the land of the Hittites (Judg. 1:26) and the kings of the Hittites (1 Kings 10:29; 2 Kings 7:6) probably refer specifically to the Neo-Hittite states of Hamath and northern Syria, and thus also reflect an earlier usage than that of the Priestly writer (P) or Ezekiel (sixth century B.C.). ***See also*** Horites; Mitanni.

J.J.M.R.

Hivites (hi'vīts). ***See*** Horites.

Hobab (hoh'bab), one of three names for Moses'

father-in-law (Judg. 4:11). With Jethro (Exod. 3:1; 18:1) and Reuel (Exod. 2:18), the name belongs to a complex tradition about Moses' family. Num. 10:29 defines Hobab as the son of Reuel, the founding father of the Kenites.

Hodaviah (hahd-uh-vī'uh; Heb., "praise Yahweh"). **1** A son of Elioenai; a descendant of Judah and the royal lineage through Zerubbabel (1 Chron. 3:24). **2** A clan leader of the eastern half-tribe of Manasseh (1 Chron. 5:24). **3** A descendant of Benjamin (1 Chron. 9:7). **4** A levitical family group ("sons of Hodaviah") who returned from the Babylonian captivity with Zerubbabel (Ezra 2:40); a corresponding passage (erroneously?) reads "sons of Judah" (Ezra 3:9). The family group is also called Hodevah, a variant spelling of the same name (Neh. 7:43).

Hodiah (hoh-dī'uh; Heb., "Yah [god] is my splendor"). **1** A descendant of Judah (1 Chron. 4:19). **2** A Levite who helped explain to the people the law read by Ezra (Neh. 8:7); this is probably the same Levite who took part in the covenant renewal ceremonies and signed the covenant to keep the law (Neh. 9:5; 10:10). **3** A second Levite who signed the renewed covenant (Neh. 10:13). **4** A leader of the people who also signed the covenant (Neh. 10:18).

holiness, a term in Hebrew probably meaning separate from the ordinary or profane. Also in Hebrew and in Greek "holy" implies connection with God or the divine. Thus, God is holy and people, things, and actions may be holy by association with God. Holiness may also include the ideas of consecration to God and purity from what is evil or improper.

In the OT: In the OT God is the Holy One par excellence. Israel's earliest hymn praises God as "majestic in holiness" (Exod. 15:11). Both Psalms and Isaiah frequently refer to God as the Holy One (Isa. 1:4; 5:19; Ps. 99) and in Isaiah's vision of the heavenly court the angels sing praise to God as "Holy, holy, holy" (Isa. 6:3). Places where God appeared and was customarily worshiped were also holy. At the burning bush (Exod. 3:5) Moses is instructed to remove his shoes because he stands on holy ground. After Jacob receives a vision at Bethel, he consecrates it as a holy place (Gen. 28:11–22). Other ancient Israelite shrines were consecrated by similar contact with God. The Temple in Jerusalem was the most holy place in Israel because God's presence dwelled there (1 Kings 8:10–11). The equipment used in the Temple, including the jars, altars, candleholders, musical instruments, and vestments, were especially set aside and thus holy. The sacrificial animals and other food had to meet stringent requirements and once designated holy could not be returned to secular use. They were either burned on the altar or consumed by the priests in the Temple. The priests and other personnel of the Temple were holy and only they could enter certain parts of the Temple and perform the sacrifices and other ritual acts. Holiness extended to the rituals and the words used at the Temple, to the name of God (Lev. 20:3), to the Sabbath (Gen. 2:3), and to the other feasts (Lev. 23).

In addition to God and to Israel's worship practices, Israel itself is a holy nation (Exod. 19:4; Deut. 7:6). Israel's holiness depends on its adherence to God's commandments and avoidance of sin. The Holiness Code, a comprehensive series of ethical and ritual laws in Lev. 18–26, demands observance because of holiness: "You shall be holy; for I the Lord your God am holy" (Lev. 19:2).

The Pharisees and the latter rabbis extended the ritual holiness of the Temple and its food to the ordinary people who were urged to observe ritual purity in eating, sex, and celebration of festivals. The text of the Bible, which became a central symbol for a life consecrated to God and obedience to God's commandments, became holy (cf. Rom. 7:12), as did "every action done for the sake of Heaven."

In the NT: The NT reaffirms the ideas of holiness found in Judaism. God, the Temple, and the law are all holy. The physical Temple is deemphasized because Gentile Christians had moved away from the practice of Judaism and because the Temple was destroyed in A.D. 70. But the Temple occurs as a metaphor for Christian holiness (1 Cor. 3:17; 6:19). God is addressed as "Holy Father" by Jesus (John 17:11), praised in heaven by the threefold "Holy" of Isaiah (Rev. 4:6–10), and addressed by the petition of the Lord's Prayer, "Hallowed be thy name." Jesus is also called holy on numerous occasions because of his closeness to God. The unclean spirit recognizes Jesus as the Holy One of God (Mark 1:24), as does Peter (John 6:69). The angel announcing Jesus' birth to Mary says that the Holy Spirit and God's power will make the child holy (Luke 1:35) and the disciples preaching after Jesus' death refer to him as holy (Acts 3:14; 4:27, 30), as does the book of Revelation (3:7).

The Holy Spirit plays a special role in the NT. The Spirit of God in the OT guided the prophets and other servants of God and was a manifestation of God's active power. However, in the NT the Holy Spirit acts as the continuing power and presence of Jesus in Luke and Acts, especially in the early days of the Jerusalem community. The Holy Spirit comes upon those who have believed in Jesus as a sign of God's power. In Paul's Letters the Holy Spirit is God's presence, which sanctifies and teaches (Rom. 15:13, 16; 1 Cor. 2:13). In John the Holy Spirit and Paraclete play a special role in strengthening and guiding the community in times of trouble (John 14:26).

Like Israel in the OT, the Christian community is holy. Paul addresses his communities as "the saints," that is, "the holy ones" (Rom. 1:7; 1 Cor. 1:2), and argues that believers consecrate one another holy (1 Cor. 7:14). The First Letter of Peter repeats the OT in calling the community a holy nation (2:9) and demanding that it be holy because God is holy (1:16). The Letter to the Ephesians compares the Gentiles to Israel and reaches a climax with the metaphor of the community as a holy temple in which God dwells in the Spirit (Eph. 2:19–22). In general, the Christian way of life derives from God and so is holy. Consequently, the community must avoid sin and evil and anything that would compromise its holiness and closeness to God. ***See also*** Holy Spirit, The; Purity; Sanctification; Worship.

A.J.S.

Holy of Holies. ***See*** Tabernacle; Temple, The.

Holy One of Israel, the, a term for God. In the OT the phrase is used frequently by the Hebrew prophets, especially Isaiah, as a title for Yahweh, Israel's God (Isa. 1:4; 5:19, 24; 10:17, 20; 40: 25; 41:14, 16, 20; 43:3, 14–15). The phrase also appears in the Psalms (71:22; 78:41; 89:18). In the NT, "Holy One of God" is applied to Jesus in Mark 1:24; Luke 4:34; and Acts 3:14 (cf. 1 John 2:20). ***See also*** Names of God in the New Testament; Names of God in the Old Testament.

Holy Sepulcher (of Jesus). ***See*** Burial; Calvary; Jerusalem.

Holy Spirit, the, the mysterious power or presence of God in nature or with individuals and communities, inspiring or empowering them with qualities they would not otherwise possess. The term "spirit" translates Hebrew *(ruach)* and Greek *(pneuma)* words denoting "wind," "breath," and, by extension, a life-giving element. With the adjective "holy," the reference is to the divine spirit, i.e., the Spirit of God.

Emphases in the OT: In the OT, three major emphases may be identified, the first of which is the Holy Spirit as an agent in creation. This is an almost impersonal representation of the Spirit by which the awesome power of God is depicted (e.g., Gen. 1:2; Ps. 33:6; Ezek. 37:1–10). The second is the Holy Spirit as a source of inspiration and power. In these instances (particularly evident in the stories of the judges, kings, and prophets), the Holy Spirit becomes a vehicle of God's revelation and activity. Israel's leaders—from Moses to Joshua, to the judges, to David and Solomon, to the enigmatic "Servant of God" of Isaiah 42—all receive their wisdom, courage, and power as gifts resulting from the possession of God's Spirit. The primary example, however, is surely the inspiration of the prophets, who, because they possess (or are possessed by) this Spirit, speak and act with an authority and power not their own (an element also illustrated by the occurrence of ecstatic phenomena, cf. 1 Sam. 10:9–13). In this connection, it should be noted that the Spirit can be conveyed from one person to another, as with Moses and Joshua, Saul and David, Elijah and Elisha. The third emphasis is the Holy Spirit as God's presence in the convenantal community. To some degree connected with eschatological hope and expectations of the sanctification of Israel, this aspect is a significant, if less frequently found, understanding of the Holy Spirit (see esp. Ezek. 11: 14–21; 36:22–32).

In the NT: In the NT, a more diverse range of meaning for this term is to be seen. Although the earlier usage continues (it is the Spirit of God that endows Jesus with power as the Messiah [Matt. 3:13–17; Mark 1:9–11; Luke 3:21–22; Matt. 12:28; Luke 4:16–21] and that empowers the church for its mission [Acts 2]), the close relationship of Jesus to God (the incarnation) expands and significantly transforms the understanding of the Holy Spirit in Christianity (cf. the related expressions, "Spirit of Christ," "Spirit of the Lord," "Spirit of Jesus," and especially passages such as Gal. 4:6, where God sends "the Spirit of his Son" to the followers of Jesus). Indeed, although the doctrine of the Trinity is a later development, a number of NT passages suggest that the Holy Spirit is sent jointly from God and the Risen Christ (i.e., from the Father and the Son; cf. Acts 2:33). In keeping with this, the Holy Spirit comes to represent both the presence and activity of God and the continuing presence of Jesus Christ in the church. While not uniquely Johannine, this idea comes to fullest expression in John 14, where the Holy Spirit is described as a "Counselor" (Paraclete) who represents both divine presence and guidance for the disciples.

Since this term is found in nearly every book of the NT, other nuances can, of course, be mentioned. In Acts, there is a close connection among four elements: the proclamation of the gospel, baptism, the laying on of hands, and the reception of the Holy Spirit. In both Acts and Paul's Letters, reception of the Holy Spirit brings the "gifts" needed for Christian ministry (as well as the gift of ecstatic speech) and extends the presence and power of Christ to each new generation of Christians. In Pauline thought, however, there is an additional dimension seen in the contrast of "flesh" with "spirit" as characteristic of life in the old age and the new age, respectively. The Spirit makes Christians one "in Christ" and empowers them, not only for the mission of the church, but also for the moral and ethical life appropriate to those who understand themselves to be people of the new age. ***See also***

Baptism; Creation; Flesh and Spirit; God; Incarnation; Inspiration; Jesus Christ; Laying On of Hands; Paraclete; Pentecost; Revelation; Sanctification; Spiritual Gifts; Tongues as of Fire; Tongues, Speaking with; Trinity, The. T.R.W.L.

home. ***See*** House.

homer. ***See*** Weights and Measures.

homosexuality, a word for which there is no specific equivalent in the Hebrew OT or the Greek NT, since the concept itself, as well as the English word, originated only in the nineteenth century. Nevertheless, there are a few biblical references to persons of the same sex who engage in sexual intercourse.

The most explicit OT references to such a practice are in the "Holiness Code" of Leviticus, where, under penalty of death, a male is strictly prohibited from lying with another male as a woman does (Lev. 18:22; 20:13). This and other provisions in the code may have been prompted by a concern that Israel not adopt the ways of Egypt and Canaan (see Lev. 18:3–4). Neither here nor elsewhere in the OT is female homosexuality mentioned. Despite the fact that from postbiblical times up to the present the terms "sodomy" and "sodomite" have been used of homosexual practices in general, the story in Gen. 19:1–29 involves only the more specific case of intended gang rape—of Lot's angelic visitors by the men of Sodom (cf. a parallel incident in Judges 19). Elsewhere in the OT, Sodom symbolizes not "homosexuality" but immorality in general, as in Ezek. 16:49–50 (gluttony and various forms of social injustice). If there is any identification of Sodom with homosexuality in the NT, it is in Jude 7 (cf. 2 Pet. 2:6–8), but it is more likely that the "unnatural lust" mentioned there is that of mortals for angels (Lot's visitors).

That the female and male cultic prostitution proscribed in Deut. 23:17–18 involved homosexuality is doubtful. It is difficult to understand how homosexual prostitution could have had any symbolic function in the Canaanite fertility religion, against the practices of which this legislation was directed. The same may be said of the cultic prostitution mentioned elsewhere (e.g., 1 Kings 14:22–24).

Two of the three relatively clear NT references to homosexual practice occur in more or less traditional lists of vices. The noun listed after "adulterers" in 1 Cor. 6:9 literally means "soft" and was sometimes applied to the male who remained passive during homosexual intercourse. The following word in the list was perhaps coined in Hellenistic Judaism on the basis of the Greek text of Lev. 18:22 and 20:13 and literally means "(a male) lying with a male," as the one who takes the active role in homosexual intercourse. This second term is also among the vices listed in 1 Tim. 1:10.

The most extensive biblical reference, and the only one to female homosexuality, is in Rom. 1: 26–27. There, such activity is mentioned as one example of the perversions that follow when humankind refuses to give glory and thanks to the one sovereign God (see Rom. 1:18–25, 28–32). The prevailing model for homosexuality in Paul's day involved the sexual exploitation of a preadolescent youth by an adult male for the purposes of the adult's own gratification. This practice was widely condemned by the apostle's non-Christian contemporaries, often with remarks similar to his in Rom. 1:26–27, where it is likely that the same kind of practice is in mind. ***See also*** Harlot; Law; Leviticus; Sodomy.

V.P.F.

honey, viscid sweetener produced by several bees of *Apis* genus. Biblical references include those to domestic or cultivated honey (2 Chron. 31:5); wild honey recovered from among rocks (Deut. 32:13), from trees (1 Sam. 14:25–26), or even from an animal carcass (Judg. 14:8–9); and honey from grapes or dates (Arabic *dibs).* It was basic fare in the wilderness ("locusts and wild honey," Mark 1:6), and it symbolizes both rich productive land (Exod. 3:17), deceitful enticement (Prov. 5:3), and the ultimate in sweetness (Ps. 119:103). Though frequently used as a sacrifice material, it was forbidden as part of burnt offerings (Lev. 2:11).

hope, in the Bible the expectation of a favorable future under God's direction.

Hope in the Old Testament: In the OT there is no easy correspondence between the NT words for hope (Gk. *elpis/elpizein*) and any specific Hebrew word, although the most frequent expression of the concept may lie with the Hebrew verbs "to wait, to expect" *(kawah)*, and "to be full of confidence, to trust" *(batah)*. The present survey is limited to this word group and does not include the larger area of eschatology in general.

The prophet Jeremiah speaks for much of the OT tradition when he utters: "O Lord, the hope of Israel, all who forsake thee shall be put to shame; those who turn away from thee shall be written in the earth, for they have forsaken the Lord, the fountain of living water" (17:13; see also 14:8). This text asserts that God is not only the hope of the nation but of the individual as well, a thought also echoed in Ps. 71:5: "For thou, O Lord, art my hope, my trust, O Lord, from my youth." God's loving-kindness (Heb. *hesed*), revealed in repeated deeds of fidelity (Exod. 6:4–8), gives the people of Israel confidence that he will fulfill his promises in the future; thus, he is the basis of all hope. God will continue to pour out his loving-kindness as long as Israel places its hope in him (Ps. 33:18: "Behold, the eye of the Lord is on those who fear him, on those who hope in his steadfast love . . ."). Thus he is the source of Israel's true hope and can be called upon as their rock (Isa. 26:4; Ps. 18:2) and the refuge of the poor and righteous (Ps. 94:22). False hope, that is, hope in anyone or anything other than God, leads to chaos and disaster. Neither weapons of war (Hos. 10:13) nor wealth (Ps. 49:5–9) nor idols (Isa. 44:9–11) can give lasting security.

When Israel was destroyed by the Assyrians in 721 B.C. and Judah destroyed by Babylonians in 587 B.C., there were a variety of prophetic responses and warnings. Perhaps the most negative is that of Amos who warned his people that their hope was misguided: "Woe to you who desire the day of the Lord! Why would you have the day of the Lord? It is darkness, and not light . . ." (5:18). Isaiah sternly warned against foreign alliances (31:1–9) as an avenue of hope, and Ezekiel revealed a vision in which it is said, "Son of man, these bones are the whole house of Israel. Behold, they say, 'Our bones are dried up, and our hope is lost; we are clean cut off' " (37:11). Even in Ezekiel this hopelessness was balanced by a glimmer of hope, as the succeeding verses show (see also the theme of the new remembrance of the covenant in Ezek. 16:59–63 and 36:25–32) and the Deuteronomic editor of Amos could not resist adding prophecies of restoration at the very end of the book (9:11–15). This positive vision of restoration and hope in God despite the destruction is found in Hosea under the theme of the new covenant (2:17–20). It is well articulated by Jeremiah: "For I know the plans I have for you, says the Lord, plans for welfare and not for evil, to give you a future and a hope" (29:11). The classic formulation of this new covenant theme is found in Jer. 31:31–34 and mentioned in Isa. 55:3 as well. As in Israel's youth, so now in its period of destruction and exile, only hope in God and his loving-kindness can give it true security.

Hope in the New Testament: In the NT, the words for hope (Gk. *elpis/elpizein*) have no unique significance in either the synoptic Gospels or the Gospel of John. Only the verb form occurs. It is used in a purely secular sense (Luke 6:34; 23:8) or with specific regard to the OT and Israel. Thus Matt. 12:41 quotes Isa. 42:1–2; Luke 24:21 refers to the two disciples on the road to Emmaus lamenting that "we had hoped that he [Jesus] was the one to redeem Israel"; and in John 5:45 Jesus replies to the Jews that "it is Moses who accuses you, on whom you set your hope." In Acts the concept of hope, other than its purely secular use (16:19; 24:26; 27:20), always refers to the hope of Israel as culminating in "the resurrection of the Christ" (2:26; 23:6; 24:15; 26:6, 7; 28:20).

Paul's Letters: The broadest use of the words for hope and the most developed concept of hope is found in the Pauline Letters. Already in Paul's brief and earliest Letter, known as 1 Thessalonians, hope is referred to four times (1:3; 2:19; 4:13; 5:8), twice in the triadic formula of "faith, love, and hope" (1:3; 5:8). Paul, who is so affectionately bonded to this community of Christians (2:19: "For what is our hope or joy or crown of boasting before our Lord Jesus at his coming? Is it not you?"), warns them not to grieve "as others do who have no hope" (4:13; see also the deutero-Pauline text in Eph. 2:12) and then proceeds to relate their belief that Jesus died and rose to the problem of those among them who had just recently died.

The fact that hope appears as part of the triadic formula "faith, love, and hope" not only in 1 Thessalonians but also in 1 Cor. 13:13, and somewhat more loosely in Gal. 5:5–6, suggests that it belongs to that process of new life in Christ that begins with faith and is fulfilled at the consummated salvation event of the last day. Thus hope emanates from faith and it reflects the guarantee (Gk. *arrabōn;* 2 Cor. 5:5) that what God has begun in Christ will be brought to consummation on the last day. The "good courage" (2 Cor. 5:6) nurtured by hope as a gift of the Spirit allows the believer to actualize faith through love (Gal. 5:6). Basic for Paul is the understanding that hope provides the essential linkage between the already/not-yet of the salvation event in Christ; hope assures the believers, provided they remain faithful to the kindness of Christ (Rom. 11:22; 1 Cor. 15:2), that what was begun in baptism will be completed at their resurrection.

Fundamental for Paul's concept of hope is the differentiation between justification and salvation; justification marks the beginning of the new life in Christ and sustains it to the end; salvation is the consummation of the gifts already experienced as a foretaste in baptism and in the living of the new life in Christ. This is precisely the point in Rom. 5:1–3, a most crucial text. What the Christian has obtained in this life is "access," not completed entrance, to God's grace, and the apostle rejoices in the "hope of sharing the glory of God" at the future consummation. The sign that the believer has access to this grace now is that "God's love has been poured into our hearts through the Holy Spirit which has been given to us." Thus Paul can assert that the ones in Christ who have "the first fruits of the Spirit, groan inwardly as we wait for adoption as sons, the redemption of our bodies. For in this hope we were saved" (Rom. 8:23–24). Rom. 8:18–25 is also an important text, for it shows, as all the authentic Pauline references to salvation do, that salvation has a future orientation and is not yet complete (see Rom. 5:9–10; Phil. 3:7–14). It further shows that God's revelation in Jesus Christ affects not only individuals, but creation itself, which God has subjected in hope "because the creation itself will be set free from its bondage to decay and obtain the glorious liberty of the children of God" (Rom. 8:19–21).

One of the important components in Paul's dynamic understanding of faith is hope. Since strong hope leads to strong faith rather than weak faith, Paul uses Abraham as an example in his exhortation in Romans 4, because in "hope he believed against hope, that he should become the father of many nations. . . . He did not weaken in faith. . . . No distrust made him waver concerning the promise of God, but he grew strong in his faith as he gave glory to God, fully convinced that God was able to do what he had promised" (Rom. 4:18–21; see also the deutero-Pauline text in Col. 1:23). The apostle can refer and point to this deeper understanding of hope by using a number of shorter formulations, such as "the God of hope" (Rom. 15:13), "abound in hope" (Rom. 15:13), and "rejoice in your hope" (Rom. 12:12). Also important to Paul is the relationship of the hope given in Christ to the hope expressed in the OT. Paul can write to the Christians in Rome that "whatever was written in former days was written for our instruction, that by steadfastness and by the encouragement of the scriptures we might have hope" (Rom. 15:4). For the believers in Christ that dimension of hope already present in the OT is made even more apparent in Christ, because in him the veil has been removed from the old covenant and thus the believers have become very bold in hope (2 Cor. 3:12–17; for a similar idea see also Heb. 7:19).

Other New Testament Writings: In other NT texts, the deutero-Pauline references stand relatively close to the Pauline usage (see in addition to the texts already cited Eph. 1:18; Col. 1:15 and 1 Tim. 4:10). Hebrews, with its theme that the church is the wandering people of God in sojourn between their earthly and heavenly home, also shapes the NT concept of hope. Thus, Christians must hold fast to their confidence until the end (3:6; 6:11; 10:23). Heb. 11:1 summarizes in a broader way the statements on hope in that writing, and Heb. 6:19, with its analogy of the anchor, concretizes the author's intention: "We have this as a sure and steadfast anchor of the soul, a hope that enters into the inner shrine behind the curtain, where Jesus has gone as a forerunner on our behalf, having become a high priest for ever after the order of Melchizedek." The theme of confidence in relationship to hope also appears in 1 Pet. 1:21. The congregation represented in 1 Peter lives in the midst of enormous difficulty, probably persecution, and the author urges them to "set your hope fully upon the grace that is coming to you at the revelation of Jesus Christ" (1:13). In the midst of their difficulties they should not fear their persecutors or be troubled by them, but they must always "be prepared to make a defense to any one who calls you to account for the hope that is in you . . ." (3:15). ***See also*** Faith; Love. K.P.D.

Hophni (hawf'nee; Egyptian, "tadpole"), the brother of Phinehas, and the son of Eli, the priest at the tabernacle of the Lord in Shiloh in the days of Samuel. Hophni and his brother also served as priests at Shiloh, but they disgraced themselves. Even Eli was accused of honoring his sons more than the Lord, so they were all condemned (1 Sam. 1–2). Their leadership gave way to Samuel's as the two sons were killed when the Ark of God was captured and Eli died upon hearing the news (1 Sam. 4). ***See also*** Eli; Phinehas; Samuel.

Hor (hohr), **Mount,** the mountain on which Aaron died and on which the Israelites gathered and camped on the border of Edom (Num. 20: 22–29; 33:37–39). Traditionally it has been identified with modern Jebel Harun, overlooking Petra where there is a Muslim shrine. But this is unlikely because Jebel Harun is in the midst of Edom, and its high peaks are not conducive to the gathering of people. It is also identified as the northern boundary of Israel's inheritance (Num. 34:7, 8); perhaps Mt. Hermon is indicated.

Horeb (hoh'reb), **Mount,** the name for Mt. Sinai used by the E and D writers of the Pentateuch, probably stemming from different tribal traditions. Here Moses was called (Exod. 3:1–12) and here he obtained water from the rock (Exod. 17:6–7). Here the Israelites made a covenant with Yahweh (Deut. 5:2), and from there they set out for Kadesh-barnea and Canaan (Deut. 1:19). Elijah fled to Horeb because of Jezebel's wrath. Since early Christian times Mt. Horeb/Sinai has been identified with modern Jebel Musa in southern Sinai, but there are no certain geographical data for this identity. ***See also*** Sinai. N.L.L.

Horites (hoh'rītes), the pre-Edomite inhabitants of Seir (Gen. 14:6; 36:20–30; Deut. 2:12, 22), the chief mountain of Edom. The name was traditionally derived from Hebrew *khor,* "hole," and interpreted as meaning "cave dwellers," though there is little archaeological evidence for cave dwelling in Edom. Thus when nonbiblical texts revealed the important role the Hurrians played in Syria during the second millennium B.C., scholars attempted to connect the biblical Horites with the Hurrians of the Akkadian, Hittite, and Egyptian texts. Phonetically the names are identical, but two difficulties make the historical equation doubtful: first, the names of the Horites listed in Genesis 36 are all Semitic, not Hurrian; and, second, while the Hurrians, who first appeared in northern Mesopotamia around

1800 B.C. and were later organized under the empire of Mitanni, did expand into Cisjordan (i.e., the land west of the Jordan River), where there were Hurrian garrisons in the early 15th century B.C., they did not enter southern Transjordan (i.e., the land east of the Jordan River).

The Hivites, however, do appear in regions where the nonbiblical texts make the presence of Hurrians plausible—at Schechem (Gen. 34: 2), at Gibeon (Josh. 9:7, 19), at the foot of Mount Hermon (Josh. 11:3), and on Mount Lebanon (Judg. 3:3)—and there is some evidence for the identification of Hivites and Horites. Zibeon the Hivite (Gen. 36:2) is listed among the Horites in Gen. 36:20, 29, and some texts of the Septuagint read "Horite" for "Hivite" in Gen. 34:2 and Josh. 9:7. Thus some scholars suggest that the biblical tradition has simply switched the terms "Horite" and "Hivite." Others identify the Hivites with the Hurrians of Cisjordan, assume there was a distinct people in Edom with a homophonous name, and explain the use of "Hivite" to designate the Hurrians of Cisjordan as a gradual development to avoid confusion between the two different Hurrian people.

A more likely reason for the identity in name between the biblical Horites and the nonbiblical Hurrians lies in the peculiar Israelite use of earlier nomenclature. Canaan and Hor were both traditional names for Cisjordan. Israel used the term "Canaan" for that region, and since they had no traditional designation for southern Transjordan, they adopted the superfluous term "Hor." Thus the inhabitants of this region became Horites, but with little historical basis. ***See also*** Mitanni. J.J.M.R.

Hormah (hohr'mah; Heb., "destruction" or "accursed"), a city in the region of Judea, close to the border with Edom. In their first attempt to take the city the Israelites were defeated by the Canaanites and Amalek (Num. 14:45; Deut. 1: 44). It was later subdued by Joshua in the conquest and was initially allotted to the tribe of Judah (Josh. 15:30). Later it was considered the land of the tribe of Simeon (Josh. 19:4; 1 Chron. 4:30; Josh. 12:14). It was a center of Davidic sympathizers and thus received some of the spoils of his activity (1 Sam. 30:30). The location of the site remains uncertain. Further, since Hormah means "destruction" and the place is unclear, modern OT scholars such as Martin Noth and Albrecht Alt argue that the Joshua accounts concerning Hormah are etiological (i.e., explain the nature of what they name). S.B.R.

horn, a word used both literally and symbolically in the Bible. **1** The bony projection from the head of various animals: for example, of a ram (Gen. 22:13); of a bull (Ps. 69:31). **2** A musical instrument made from a ram's horn (Heb. *shophar*); it was used in worship (e.g., 2 Chron. 15:14) as well as in war (e.g., Josh. 6:4–13; since the two terms for such musical instruments used in this passage both mean "horn," the RSV translation "trumpets" in v. 5 is misleading). **3** The projection at each of the four corners of an altar (Exod. 27:2; Rev. 9:13); the precise significance of the symbolism here is not known, however. The instruction to put some blood of a sacrificed bull on the altar horns (Lev. 4:7) attests to their importance in Israel's religious ritual of animal sacrifice. People desiring asylum symbolized that desire by clinging to the altar's horns (1 Kings 1:50–51; 2:28–34). Persons accused of manslaughter may have sought such asylum at the altar (Exod. 21:14 says it is to be denied), but specific provision for such places of safety was made by means of cities of refuge (e.g., Num. 35: 9–28) rather than by means of altars. Altars as places of sanctuary are nowhere specifically mentioned. **4** A receptacle for liquids: for the oil kept in the shrine (1 Kings 1:39) and used for anointing kings (1 Sam. 16:1, 13); perhaps for eye make-up ("horn of paint" is the literal meaning of the name of Job's third daughter, Job 42: 14); and for ink (Ezek. 9:2–11). **5** A symbol of power, whether in animals (e.g., wild ox, Num. 23:22; Deut. 33:17) or human beings (iron horns symbolize a king's victory in war, 1 Kings 22: 11). The term "horn of salvation" denotes royal saving power (e.g., Ps. 18:2; Ecclus. 49:5; cf. Luke 1:69). A further development of this theme is found in the use of "horn" for "king" in the visions in Daniel 7–8, where the horns refer to specific rulers. In the Revelation to John horn signifies supernatural power: the power of the lamb (5:6), of the dragon (12:13), of the beast from the sea (13:1), of the beast from the earth (13:11), and of the scarlet beast upon which a woman sits (17:3–16). Moses' shining face when he descended from Sinai and the presence of God (Exod. 34:29–35) is described in Hab. 3:4 ("rays of light") with a word that could be connected with the word for "horn" (Heb. *qeren*). That led the Latin Vulgate translation to assume Moses had "horns of light," a figure given literal representation in Michelangelo's statue of Moses. **6** The crown of a hill, or the hill itself (e.g., Isa. 5:1). P.R.A.

hornet, an insect of the order *Hymenoptera*, larger and more dangerous than a wasp, probably *Vespa orientalis*. The Hebrew term for hornet also means "depression, discouragement." In Josh. 24:12; Exod. 23:28; and Deut. 7:20 the term could have a literal meaning or it may symbolize God's intervention on Israel's behalf.

Horonaim (hohr-oh-nay'im), a Moabite city mentioned by both Isaiah (15:5) and Jeremiah (48:3, 5, 34); from the other place names mentioned in these passages, it was probably located in the southern part of Moab and has been identified by some scholars as modern el-Iraq, about nine miles east of the southeast corner of the Dead Sea, although this identification is questionable. The city appears in the Mesha Inscription (Moabite Stone) as being recaptured by King Mesha of Moab from an unidentified enemy (the tablet is damaged here), most likely the Israelites who are mentioned elsewhere in the inscription (see 1 Kings 3:4). ***See also*** Mesha; Moab; Moabite Stone, The. D.R.B.

horse, a large solid-hoofed mammal. The horse *(Equus caballus)* was first domesticated in the Eurasian steppes, probably around 3000 B.C. Horses were introduced into Palestine by the Hyksos in the first half of the second millennium B.C. With their horse-drawn chariots the Hyksos managed to besiege the whole Near East. Horse burials, probably sacrificial, were found at Tell el-'Ajjul some four miles southwest of Gaza, and attributed to this period.

The first biblical reference to the horse is in Gen. 47:17, where Joseph trades horses and other livestock for food for his starving people in Egypt. In the Bible the horse is a symbol of power and most often associated with war. Even the heavenly armies are equipped with war horses (Rev. 19:11, 14). In contrast, the ass seems to signify peace (Zech. 9:9; Matt. 21:1–7). It appears that for this reason the Hebrews were forbidden to keep horses on a large scale. In Deut. 17:14–16 Moses tells the Israelites that if they elect a king, they should make sure that he does not "multiply horses for himself" or buy horses from Egypt, in other words, build up an army. Samuel (1 Sam. 8:11–17) repeats this warning and impresses on them that, should they insist on a king, their sons will be needed to equip the war chariots. For a while this warning seems to have been observed, as Joshua killed the horses he had taken from the Canaanites (Josh. 11:9) and David disposed of the horses he had captured, except for a hundred chariot teams (2 Sam. 8:4). King Solomon, on the other hand, is reported to have had stables for four thousand horses (2 Chron. 9:25) or even forty thousand (1 Kings 4:26). He also imported horses from Egypt and other places (2 Chron. 9:28) and fed them on straw and barley (1 Kings 4:28). Later King Hezekiah was offered two thousand horses by the general of the Assyrian king Sennacherib (2 Kings 18:23).

Horse-drawn chariots were not only used for warfare but also constituted a very noble and honorable means of transport. Joseph was provided with a chariot by Pharaoh as a special sign of honor (Gen. 41:43) and Jacob's dead body was brought back to Canaan accompanied by horses and chariots (Gen. 50:9). Similarly the body of King Amaziah of Judah was returned to Jerusalem in a war chariot (2 Kings 14:20), and the eunuch, a royal minister with whom Philip spoke, was traveling by chariot (Acts 8:27–28).

In later times horses must have been quite common in Palestine, for a so-called Horse Gate existed in Jerusalem and the royal palace was equipped with a special entrance for horses (2 Chron. 23:15). The exiles on their return from Babylon brought with them 736 horses (Neh. 7:68) and according to Ezek. 27:14 horses were also imported from Togarmah (Armenia).

A galloping horse bearing a Scythian rider served as a handle on the lid of a copper jar dating to the fifth century B.C.

A very vivid description of how the horse acts on the battlefield is given in Job 39:19–25. The fear inspired by the war horse is reflected when supernatural afflictions are pictured as being brought by horsemen (Rev. 6:2–8). Ps. 32:9 demands, "Be not like a horse or a mule without understanding, which must be curbed with bit and bridle" (cf. James 3:3).

Equines other than the horse are also featured in the Bible. The ass or donkey *(Equus asinus)* reached Palestine in the fourth millennium B.C. from Egypt, where it had been domesticated. It was used as a riding animal not only for the poor, but also for the well-to-do (Judg. 1:14) and even kings (Zech. 9:9; cf. Matt. 21:5).

The onager *(Equus hemionus)* or semi-ass roamed the Syrian steppes until the nineteenth century. The Sumerians used these animals, which were tamed but not domesticated, to pull four-wheeled chariots. This is evidenced by the famous standard from the third millennium B.C. found at the Royal Cemetery at Ur.

The mule, a cross between a horse mare and a donkey stallion, was the beast of burden par excellence. As the Hebrews were forbidden to crossbreed animals (Lev. 19:19), they probably imported mules. I.U.K.

horseleach. ***See*** Leech.

Hosah (hoh'sah; Heb., "refuge" or "protection"). **1** A porter (gatekeeper) in the time of

David (1 Chron. 16:38; 26:10). **2** A village of Asher (Josh. 19:29), possibly the same as Uzu near Tyre.

hosanna (hoh-zan'uh), a Hebrew expression of two words meaning "Save, I [we] pray" (Ps. 118: 25) but transliterated as one word in Greek and then English. Ps. 118:25 was recited once daily for six days in the liturgy of the Feast of Tabernacles (Booths) but seven times on the seventh day as branches were waved (*M. Sukka* 4.5). The Psalm became associated with messianic expectations (vv. 25–26: "Hosanna . . . blessed be he who enters in the name of the Lord"). In the gospels, Jesus is hailed as Messiah by use of the words of Ps. 118:25–26 as he enters Jerusalem (John 12:13; with variations in Matt. 21:9, 15; Mark 11:9–10; Luke 19:38). ***See also*** Feasts, Festivals, and Fasts; Palm Sunday; Tabernacles, Festival of. A.J.H.

Hosea (hoh-zay'uh), **the Book of,** the twenty-eighth book in the OT. Hosea (Heb., "[God] has saved"), the prophet to whom it is attributed, was the son of Beeri and was active in the last years of the Northern Kingdom. His Hebrew name is the same as that of the Northern Kingdom's last king (usually spelled Hoshea in English; the Hoshea of Num. 13:8 is a reference to Joshua).

Date: It has been difficult for scholars to pinpoint the exact dates of Hosea's prophetic career, although most agree that it extended from about 745 B.C., when Zechariah, the son of Jeroboam II, was killed, to the end of this king's reign. Whether Hosea lived to the fall of Samaria in 721 B.C. is not known. Moreover, while this temporal range makes good historical sense, it must be noted that explicit textual references for precisely dating specific prophecies are lacking —though scholars have made bold attempts to concretize the prophecies. Thus, texts like Hos. 7:11; 9:13; and 12:2 have been interpreted as reflecting the attempt of King Hoshea to seek out the support of Egypt against Assyria; and 13:10, 15 have been taken, correspondingly, as referring to Assyria's subsequent punishment.

Author: Even as the precise dates of Hosea's prophecies are in question, so are the details of his life. Thus, even the opening unit (chaps. 1–3), which deals with a marriage between the prophet and one Gomer and their subsequent divorce and remarriage (an episode symbolizing the relationship between God and Israel), is contradictory (cf. chaps. 1–2 with 3) and subject to various interpretations—including nonhistorical ones (i.e., the episode is a dream or parable). Further, the details of the abominations and sins described in chaps. 4–9 cannot be precisely fixed with respect to Israelite history or the prophet's life. Chaps. 10–13 deal with God's oracles of judgment on Israel and express other aspects of the complex relationship between God and Israel. Chap. 14 concludes the book with an appeal for repentance and hope in restoration. Because of divergences in tone, voice, and content, some modern scholars have separated Hosea 1–3 from 4–14 and seen the latter as a deutero-Hosean anthology. But this position has not won wide support, and most scholars prefer to treat the entire work as the prophecies of one prophet.

Themes: Hosea shares many themes with other classical prophets and, like them, uses symbolic names and actions. Three of his children are called Jezreel, Lo Rukhama (Heb., "unloved"), and Lo Ammi (Heb., "not my people"), indicating God's warning to Israel. He describes God's anger at Israel's sins, which include ethical misbehavior (4:2; 10:13) and overreliance on both cultic activity (8:13) and military capability (10: 13). Because of this, he warns, God will punish the nation, bringing destruction to the land (10: 7–8) and removing its inhabitants (9:3).

As the only native of the northern kingdom of Israel among the literary prophets, Hosea's linguistic idiosyncrasies may reflect a northern dialect of Hebrew. His prophecy is characterized by its extensive use of Israelite historical traditions (see, e.g., 12:3–4, which refer to the patriarch Jacob). Primary among these are references to the Exodus and wanderings: God brought Israel out of Egypt (11:1), but the people proved unfaithful even before reaching the promised land (9:10). Once there, they failed to recognize the true source of success (13:1–6), ascribing it to Baal, the local god (11: 1–2). The past is important not only for its theological implications, but also as prefiguring the future. As a punishment, Israel will return to Egypt (8:13; 9:3). God will seduce them back into the wilderness, where Israel will answer "as in the days of her youth" (2:14–15). Chap. 2 suggests that God will make the desert bloom so that Israel cannot again make the mistake of thinking that the land's produce comes from Baal (see also 13:4–8).

Israelite apostasy, manifest particularly through idolatry, forms of divination, and various fertility rituals (cf. 4:12–19), constitutes the major concern of Hosea, whose marriage to a prostitute named Gomer is used to symbolize God's problem with Israel. Although scholars differ in their understanding of the relationship between the accounts in chaps. 1 and 3, and whether they are to be understood as factual or visionary, in both Israel's lack of fidelity to God is described as adultery. In keeping with this marital imagery, Hosea looks forward to a new honeymoon in the desert (2:14–15, Hebrew vv. 16–17) and a time when Israel will no longer speak of God as her master (Heb. *baal*), but as her husband (Heb. *ish*), a hint that at one time it may have been acceptable to speak of God as *baal*, a usage that became unacceptable once it was associated with a Canaanite god as well. Hosea's apparent condemnation of those who idolize the golden calves at Bethel and Dan (8:5–6) suggests a similar development, whereby a once legitimate cultic object came to be used for idolatrous purposes. (A similar process took place with regard to the bronze serpent, originally made by Moses at God's command [Num. 21:8–9], but destroyed by Judah's King Hezekiah after it had become an object of worship [2 Kings 18:4].) In addition to the marital imagery, Hosea also portrays the divine-human relationship in such images as father-son (11:1–3), physician-patient (7:1), and fowler-birds (7:12).

OUTLINE OF CONTENTS

The Book of Hosea

I. Hosea's marriage: symbol of God's relationship with Israel (1:1–3:5)
   A. Hosea's family: God's judgment (1:1–2:1)
   B. God and Israel: warnings of judgment and promise of restoration (2:2–23)
   C. The husband's love (Hosea and God; 3:1–5)
II. Details and consequences of Israel's unfaithfulness to God (4:1–13:16)
   A. Charges of infidelity against people and leaders (4:1–5:7)
   B. Warnings of judgment unless repentance occurs (5:8–6:6)
   C. Pervasiveness of Israel's transgressions: geographical, ethical, political, cultic (6:7–9:9)
   D. Judgment in light of Israel's history with God (9:10–13:16)
III. Life beyond judgment (14:1–9)
   A. Call to repentance and promise of restoration (14:1–8)
   B. Instruction for reader to take heed (14:9)

Some scholars have thought that hopeful passages, such as 11:8–11, could not be authentic, given the prophet's generally negative tone; others, however, see this rejection as without basis. Hosea's use of the past to prefigure the future and his repeated use of Exodus imagery would seem to support the latter position. ***See also*** Amos, The Book of; Prophet.

Bibliography

Wolff, H. W. *Hosea*. Hermeneia. Philadelphia: Fortress, 1974. F.E.G.

hosen, a dialect plural of "hose," a form of leg clothing. In Dan. 3:21 the KJV translates the Aramaic *paṭîš* as "hosen." The RSV translates "tunics" based on the garment series there.

Hoshea (hoh-shee'uh; Heb., "salvation"). **1** The original name of Joshua (Num. 13:8; cf. Deut. 32:44). **2** The last king of Israel (ca. 732–724 B.C.), the son of Elah (2 Kings 15:30), and a contemporary of Ahaz and Hezekiah. Hoshea usurped the throne by murdering Pekah and served as a vassal ruler to Tiglath-pileser III and, after his death (727), to Shalmaneser V of Assyria. Shalmaneser "found treachery" in Hoshea, however, when he withheld tribute and instead turned for aid to the Egyptian king "So" (probably Tefnakhte I of Sais, 2 Kings 17:4). Egyptian aid never materialized and Samaria was taken by Sargon II after a siege of three years. The ultimate fate of Hoshea is not known. **3** The prophet whose Hebrew name has been commonly spelled in English as Hosea. **4** An Ephraimite chief in David's bureaucracy (1 Chron. 27:20). **5** A Levite who with others set his seal to the covenant in the time of Nehemiah (Neh. 10:23). D.L.C.

hospitality, the act of friendship shown a visitor. Hospitality in the ancient Near East was tightly bound up in customs and practices which all were expected to observe. As in an intricately choreographed dance, where any participant who does not observe his or her role must either learn it, or leave the dance if the whole is not to be jeopardized, so it was with the customs of ancient hospitality. One ignored the customs at one's own peril. To try to understand those carefully structured and rigidly observed practices in terms of the relative informality of modern Western practices of hospitality would be completely to misunderstand them.

In the ancient Near East, hospitality was the process of "receiving" outsiders and changing them from strangers to guests. Hospitality thus differed from entertaining family and friends. If strangers were not to be entirely ignored (or worse) either physically or socially (see Matt. 10:14–23), the reception occurred in three stages:

Testing the Stranger: Strangers pose a threat to any community since they are potentially harmful. Hence they must be tested both on how they may fit in and whether they will subscribe to the community's norms. Officials (Josh. 2:2) or concerned citizenry (Gen. 19:5) could conduct such tests; an invading outsider must be repelled (Mark 5:17; the Gerasenes ask the "stranger" Jesus to leave). An invitation to speak can be a test (Acts 13:14–15), while letters of recommendation can excuse from a test, although not always (e.g., 2 and 3 John; Rom. 16:3–16; 1 Thess. 5:12–13). The ritual of foot washing marks the movement from stranger to guest (see Gen. 18:4; 19:2; 24:32; lacking in Luke 7:36–50).

The Stranger as Guest: Since transient strangers lacked customary or legal standing within the visited community, it was imperative that they be under the protection of a patron, a host, who was an established community member.

Through a personal bond with the host (something inns could not offer), strangers were incorporated as guests or clients/protegés. To offend the stranger become guest was to offend the host, who was protector and patron of the guest (poignantly underscored in the case of Lot, Gen. 19:1–10). Yet such patronage could yield more trouble than honor (e.g., Prov. 6:1).

A guest could infringe the requirements of hospitality by insulting the host or by any show of hostility or rivalry either toward the host or other guests; a guest must honor the host (when Jesus eats with sinners he neither accuses them of being sinners nor asks them to change, Matt. 9:10; Luke 5:29). The guest must not usurp the role of the host, e.g., make oneself at home when not yet invited to do so (in the home of another, Jesus heals only when asked, Mark 1:30), or take precedence (see Luke 14:8), or give orders to the dependents of the host, or demand or take what is not offered (see Luke 7:36–50, where Jesus is the perfect guest; Mark 6:10 and parallels with its rules for traveling disciples). By refusing what has been offered, the guest infringes the role of guest. The guest is above all bound to accept food (see Luke 10:18); the directives to disciples for their travels in Mark 6:8 require them to accept patronage (see 1 Cor. 9:4).

On the other hand, a host could infringe the requirements of hospitality by insulting the guests or by any show of hostility or rivalry, or by neglecting to protect the guests and their honor, for guests individually are the responsibility of the host. Thus while fellow guests have no explicit relationship, they were bound to forego hostilities, since they offended their host in the act of offending one another. The host had to defend each against the other since both were his guests (thus Paul's problem at the Lord's supper in 1 Cor. 11:17–34). The host could not fail to attend to the guests, to grant them the precedence that was their due or to show concern for their needs and wishes, or in general to earn the good will guests were supposed to show. Thus in Luke 7:36–50, Simon the Pharisee fails on all counts with his guest, Jesus: no foot washing; no kiss; no anointing; no keeping away the sinful woman; the parable in Luke 7: 40–41 represents Jesus' defense of his honor as guest. Finally, failure to offer the best is to denigrate the guest (John 2:10).

A host's infringing these requirements assures that a stranger will rarely, if ever, reciprocate hospitality. Hence the necessity and value of observing rules of hospitality (Matt. 25:38) and avoiding their infringement (Matt. 25:43).

While hospitality entails reciprocity between individuals, it can also be viewed as a reciprocal relationship between communities. Such hospitality to traveling Christians was both urged (see Rom. 12:13; 1 Pet. 4:9) and much practiced (e.g., Acts 17:7; 21:17; 28:7; Rom. 16:23).

From Guest to Transformed Stranger: The stranger-guest will leave the host either as friend or enemy. If as friend, the guest will spread the praises of the host (e.g., 1 Thess. 1:9; Phil. 5:16), notably to those sending the stranger (e.g., Mark 9:37). If as enemy, the one aggrieved will have to get satisfaction (e.g., 3 John).

It is probably in this context of the practice of hospitality that the meaning of John 1:10, "his own received him not," may best be understood. B.J.M.

host, a term referring to multitudes or armies. A title given the God of Israel is the "Lord of Hosts" (1 Sam. 17:45). The armies may be those of Israel or those of heaven, the latter made up of angels and other beings depicted in God's retinue or court (1 Kings 22:19; Isa. 6:1–5). Associated with the heavenly hosts are heavenly bodies (Judg. 5:20) and the forces of nature (Amos 4:13).

hough. *See* Hamstring.

hour. *See* Time.

house. **1** The ordinary dwelling unit of the settled population. The Bible offers numerous references to specific parts of houses, such as roofs, upper rooms, doors, courtyards, but it gives no full description of a typical house. The supplementary evidence provided by archaeology makes it possible to trace at least the general development and characteristics of the house in Palestine, although information is not complete for every period and is based essentially upon preserved foundations and partial walls.

The Mesolithic peoples were the pioneering settlers who built the first houses in Palestine in the eighth millennium B.C. Beidha and Jericho furnish a good sequence of progress in building, from the earliest semisubterranean houses through periods of free-standing round houses to the fully evolved rectangular architecture of the Neolithic period (8000–4500 B.C.). Differences in style were influenced by a combination of factors: environment, which determined both materials and available space; new ideas and techniques spreading along with trade; and migrations of newcomers.

In the Early Bronze Age (3000–2000 B.C.) distinctive types of houses appear. The earlier ones feature solid walls and rooms with one rounded or apsidal end. The form that came to dominate the period was a rectangular house with the entrance on one of the longer sides. Stone benches, the "furnishings" of the house, extended around the length of the walls, and there was usually a flat stone slab serving as a table in the center. The size of the houses varied considerably. It is difficult to ascertain the general appearance of the houses since usually only the foundations remain. A terra-cotta model of a rectangular

Four-room house discovered in the Iron Age II (1000–701 B.C.) ruins at Beer-sheba.

house discovered at Arad (about thirty-five miles south of Jerusalem) has therefore special value. It has no windows, indicating that the door was the only source of light, and the doorway itself reaches almost to the roof, suggesting that the height of the house was about that of a person.

The prosperity of the Middle Bronze Age (2000–1500 B.C.) is reflected in its architecture. Courtyard houses appear, ranging from single-room, one-story houses to multiple-room, two-story houses with an outer stairway rising to the second floor. All faced a courtyard, which contained a baking oven and a well. The courtyard house with its various arrangements of rooms seems to have continued throughout the Late Bronze Age (1500–1200 B.C.).

The nomadic Israelite tribes who settled in Palestine in the thirteenth and twelfth centuries B.C. at first copied this type of construction but in the course of time developed a distinctive Israelite style of building. This is known as the four-room house. Its principal feature was a back room the width of the building with three long rooms stemming forward from it. This form, with varied expansions and elaborations, continued from the end of the eleventh century B.C. to the destruction of Judah (586 B.C.). Most houses were two stories high, although two- and three-room, one-story houses are also found. The lower part of the wall was constructed of stone and the upper part of adobe brick or wood and was plastered with lime. The flat roofs were made of wooden beams filled in with dried mud and brushwood and, in the larger houses, were supported by rows of stone columns. The inhabitants generally lived in the upper story, although in the hot weather the roofs were used for sleeping. According to Deut. 22:8, a parapet was to be built around the roof as a safety precaution. The four-room plan has been found at numerous Iron Age (beginning in 1200 B.C.) sites, including Tell Beit Mirsim, Ai, Hazor, and Beer-sheba.

The growing social inequality between rich and poor, which was vehemently denounced by the eighth century prophets (e.g., Amos 6: 4–6), seems to receive archaeological confirmation in certain excavations such as Tell el-Farah. In the tenth century B.C. all the houses were of the same size and arrangement. In the eighth century B.C. at the same site, the rich houses are larger, better built, and in a different quarter from the smaller, simpler houses of the poor, which were huddled together.

In the Hellenistic (333–63 B.C.) and Roman (63 B.C.–A.D. 324) periods marked changes in architecture occurred under Western influence. As yet there is little information about the houses of the common people, but recent excavations in Jerusalem have provided a good picture of how the wealthy lived in the days of Herod the Great (40–4 B.C.), with their homes resembling the magnificent mansions well known from the ruins in Pompeii (destroyed A.D. 79). One huge house, covering over 2000 square feet, has a series of rooms arranged around a central courtyard that contained four sunken ovens. Some houses have frescoed walls with ornamentation done in the decorative style of Pompeii. All of the excavated houses contained at least one cistern hewn into the bedrock, with the larger ones having many such water installations.

2 A term (Heb. *bêt;* Gk. *oikos, oikia)* with many extended uses in both the OT and NT. It can signify a family line, like "house of Levi" (Exod. 2:1) or a tribal group, like Israel (Num. 1: 2). It is also used in a wider sense of domain, as in the house of slavery (Egypt in Exod. 13:3). By the "house of God" is meant an Israelite place of worship (Mark 2:26), sometimes called a house of prayer (Mark 11:17). In Heb. 3:3–6 the expression "house of God" is applied to the Christian community. ***See also*** Towns.

Bibliography

Beebe, H. K. "Ancient Palestinian Dwellings." *Biblical Archaeologist* 31 (1968):38–58. M.M.S.

Huldah (huhl'duh), a Jerusalemite prophetess. She was the wife of Shallum, keeper of the (king's) wardrobes during the reign of Josiah (639–609 B.C.). Consulted by Josiah's officials after discovery of a "scroll of Moses" in the Temple, Huldah prophesied the destruction of Jerusalem, adding that Josiah would die before the catastrophe. Huldah's prophecy helped spur vast religious reforms (2 Kings 22; 2 Chron. 34). ***See also*** Josiah; Prophet.

human being, a term traditionally translated by the generic "man." The Genesis creation accounts portray humans as part of the natural world but also specially related to God. As created, they are not divine but stand under God's authority. As uniquely created in his image, however, they are his agents in ruling other creatures and caring for the earth. Thus, the sexuality necessary to populate, rule, and care for the earth is not base but represents God's intention. Human superiority is also seen in Adam's naming the other creatures.

Human subordination to God appears both in God's creating Adam and Eve and in his command not to eat from the tree of the knowledge of good and evil. Eating would be deciding for themselves, apart from and against God, what constitutes good and evil. Disobedience broke fellowship with God and damaged relations between humans, with other creatures, and with the earth (Gen. 3). God's barring the way to the tree of life brought the penalty of death and averted the moral disaster of immortality in a state of sin.

In the OT, increasing sin brought increasing judgment (Gen. 6–7, 11, and throughout). But humans kept their superior dignity (Ps. 8), and God still valued them so highly that he acted to restore them to fellowship with himself. He sought Adam and Eve, called Abraham, initiated a covenant with Israel, sent prophets, and, in the NT gave his Son as a sacrifice for sin, raised him from death, and promised eternal life and the fullness of his Spirit to the faithful. Nevertheless, humans remain creatures. The ultimate aim of salvation is the glory of God the Creator and (now) Redeemer (Rom. 11:36; 1 Cor. 15:28). Paul presents Christ as the last Adam who perfectly exhibits God's glory (2 Cor. 4:4; cf. Col. 1:15) and heads up a new humanity of the faithful in Christ (Rom. 5:12–21).

As needed, regulations governing the relations of humans with God, one another, and the whole creation are prescribed throughout the Bible (e.g., Mosaic Law, messages of OT prophets, the Sermon on the Mount, and practical exhortations in NT Letters). Shifting circumstances produce changes, deletions, and additions designed to enhance the human condition with justice, love, and mercy. The emphasis falls on interrelations in family, clan, tribe, nation, and religious community, with little of the modern psychological stress on relationship to oneself. Individualism tends to grow somewhat from early to late in the Bible, but not at the expense of social units.

The Bible offers no systematic view of the individual human constitution. Indications that do appear are incidental to the interrelationships that entail thinking, feeling, and willing. Generally, the Bible suggests that humans have visible and invisible sides. The terminology, however, is mixed: on the one side, "flesh," "body," "members," "outer person"; on the other, "soul," "spirit," "mind," "inner person." And the two suit and interpenetrate each other, so that physical organs such as the heart, liver, kidneys, and bowels function on behalf of the inner consciousness. The brain does not get the credit modern science gives it, and clean distinctions among thinking, feeling, and willing are absent (e.g., the heart thinks and wills, as well as feels).

When the breath of life departs, the body returns to dust and the person survives only as an unsubstantial shade. Because of Greek influence, distinctions between the visible and invisible sides of human beings and their separability become more explicit in the NT. But no denigration of physicality follows. Doctrines of Christ's incarnation and of bodily resurrection reaffirm the psychosomatic wholeness of human beings first indicated at creation. ***See also*** Body; Conscience; Flesh; Flesh and Spirit; Heart; Mind; Soul.

Bibliography

Eichrodt, W. *Man in the Old Testament.* London: SCM, 1951.

Jewett, R. *Paul's Anthropological Terms.* Leiden: Brill, 1971.

Wolff, H. W. *Anthropology in the Old Testament.* Philadelphia: Fortress, 1974. R.H.G.

humility, in the biblical world a value that directs persons to stay within their inherited social status, specifically by not presuming on others and avoiding even the appearance of lording over another. Humble persons do not threaten or challenge another's rights, nor do they claim more for themselves than has been duly allotted them in life. They even stay a step below or behind their rightful status (e.g., the "unworthy" John the Baptist, Mark 1:7). Thus humility is a socially acknowledged claim to neutrality in the competition of life. Conversely, to attempt to better oneself at the expense of others, to acquire more than others, to strive for honors others currently enjoy are all instances of proud and arrogant behavior. God humbles such proud people (Matt. 23:12; Luke 18:14; see Deut. 8:2, 16), while he exalts the humble (Luke 1:52; 14:7–11); hence humility has precedence over honor (Prov. 15:33; 18:12). To humble or humiliate others is to shame them (e.g., Dinah in Gen. 34:2; Isa. 2:9, 11, 17). To humble or humiliate oneself is to declare oneself powerless to defend one's status (e.g., Phil. 2:9) and then to act accordingly—either factually by becoming powerless, like the lowborn, or ritually, by a rite in which the use of power is set aside, symbolized by behavior typical of the lowborn: fasting, rending garments, weeping, lamenting, confession (e.g., Lev. 26:41; 1 Kings 21:29; 2 Kings 22: 8–20; Ps. 69:10). Such self-humiliation before God is praiseworthy (e.g., Prov. 3:34; James 4:10; 1 Pet. 5:5–6; 2 Cor. 12:21) and obtains God's help. While Jesus is no arrogant teacher (Matt. 11:29), he does not exhort to traditional self-humiliation but simply to avoid challenging the honor of others (Matt. 23:12; Luke 14:11; 18:14), in that way acting as though one were as power-

less to do so as a child (Matt. 18:4). Such humility is highly valued (Eph. 4:2; Col. 3:12).
B.J.M.

hunting, an activity seldom mentioned in the Bible and apparently not a common occupation among the Israelites. Neither of the two men in the OT specifically designated as hunters, Nimrod (Gen. 10:9) and Esau (Gen. 25:27), were Israelites. Much more common for the Hebrews was the killing of game encountered by chance (Judg. 14:6) or the killing of wild animals that attacked the shepherd's flocks (lions and bears are mentioned specifically in 1 Sam. 17:34–37).

The typical weapons used for hunting included bow and arrow (Gen. 27:3), the sling and slingstone (1 Sam. 17:40, 49–50), and the shepherd's staff (1 Sam. 17:40). Egyptian paintings depict the use of hunting dogs, while Assyrian reliefs show noblemen in chariots hunting lions. The first-century A.D. Jewish historian Josephus tells us that Herod the Great enjoyed hunting on horseback (*Wars* 1.21.13).

Along with hunting, fishing (Isa. 19:8) and trapping birds with nets (Amos 3:5; Prov. 6:5; Pss. 91:3; 124:7) are mentioned.

Spear hunting desert animals, including a lion and an ostrich, as depicted on an Assyrian cylinder seal; twelfth–tenth century B.C.

Wild animals considered acceptable for food and thus apparently hunted included the hart, the gazelle, the roebuck, the wild goat, the ibex, the antelope, and the mountain sheep (all listed in Deut. 14:5). Forbidden to the Hebrews, but apparently acceptable to the Canaanites, were the hare and the wild pig (Lev. 11:6–7). ***See also*** Animals; Fish.
J.F.D.

Hur (huhr), a name of uncertain derivation. **1** One of Israel's leaders during the wilderness sojourn, who helped govern the people at Sinai in Moses' absence (Exod. 24:14) and supported Moses' arms during the battle with the Amalekites (Exod. 17:10, 12). He evidently was the same Hur who was a descendant of Judah and grandfather of Bezalel, the craftsman who built the tabernacle (Exod. 31:2; 1 Chron. 2:19). **2** One of the five Midianite kings killed by Moses in Transjordan (Num. 31:8). **3** The father of Rephaiah, an official contemporary with Nehemiah (Neh. 3:9).

Huram (hōō'rahm). ***See*** Hiram.

Hurrians. (hōōr'ree-uhns). ***See*** Horites.

husband. ***See*** Family, The.

husbandman, an archaic term used in the KJV to refer to farmers as distinct from vinedressers (2 Chron. 26:10; 2 Kings 25:12; Jer. 52:16; Joel 1:11; Amos 5:16) and shepherds (Jer. 31:24; 51:23), but also sometimes to vinedressers (Gen. 9:20; Mark 12:1–9 and parallels; John 15:1f.). In Mark 12:1–9 the term is used metaphorically for the Jewish leadership.

Hushai (hōō'shī), an Archite who is called the "friend of David" (2 Sam. 15:32; 1 Chron. 23:33), although this is a technical term for an official of the king who served as a personal advisor (1 Kings 4:5; for the feminine counterpart, see Ps. 45:14). He remained loyal to David during Absalom's attempt to seize the throne and was sent by David back to Absalom as a spy (2 Sam. 15:32–37). He convinced Absalom of his loyalty and persuaded Absalom to take his counsel over the advice of Ahithophel, another advisor of David's who had joined Absalom's conspiracy. He then sent word to David of Absalom's plans, allowing David and his men to escape (2 Sam. 16:16–18; 17:5–22). He is probably the same person mentioned as the father of Baana, an official of King Solomon (1 Kings 4:16). ***See also*** Absalom; Ahithophel; David.
D.R.B.

Husham (hōō'sham), a pre-Israelite king of Edom, either from the area or the tribe of Teman (Gen. 36:34–35).

Hushim (hōō'shim). **1** A son of Dan who went to Egypt with Jacob (Gen. 46:23), although by a reversal of letters the name is Shuham in Numbers (26:42) and the clan of which he is the ancestral head is called the Shuhamites. Many scholars consider the passage in Numbers to be more accurate. **2** The son of Aher; a descendant of Benjamin (1 Chron. 7:12). **3** The wife of Shaharaim, a Benjaminite, and mother of Ahitub and Elpaal (1 Chron. 8:8, 11). ***See also*** Shuham.

husks. ***See*** Pods.

Huz. ***See*** Uz.

Hyksos (hik'sohs), the Greek name given by the third-century B.C. Egyptian priest Manetho to the Asiatic princes who ruled in Egypt as the fifteenth and sixteenth dynasties (ca. 1667–1559 B.C.). The contemporary Egyptians called them *Heqau khasut*, "rulers of foreign hill-countries." These Asiatics were largely Semitic in origin. They were evidently sufficiently well organized to be able to take advantage of a period of weakness in Egypt and gain control of much of the Nile valley. They had previously consolidated their power in the eastern delta, where Asiatics had been living in increasing numbers since the early second millennium B.C. Their principal deity was the Egyptian god Seth, whom they equated with one of their own Semitic deities.

In 1667 B.C. the Hyksos captured the Egyptian administrative capital of Memphis; this event inaugurates the fifteenth dynasty. Monuments bearing the names of Hyksos kings are rare; many of the Hyksos rulers are known only from the occurrence of their names on scarabs (beetle-shaped, semiprecious stones). These scarabs have been found in both Egypt and southern Palestine; in the latter area, the majority of these royal-name scarabs have been found at Tell el-'Ajjul, probably to be identified with the ancient Hyksos stronghold of Sharuhen. Eventually the Hyksos were defeated and thrown out of Egypt by King Kamose (ca. 1576–1570 B.C.) and his successor, King Ahmose (ca. 1570–1546 B.C.).

The two principal cities associated with the Hyksos were Avaris and Sharuhen. Avaris, their Egyptian capital, is identified with Tell el-Dabaa in the area of Khatana-Qantir in the eastern Nile delta. Manfred Bietak of the Austrian Archaeological Institute in Cairo excavated this site beginning in 1966; he found there extensive town remains that date to the Second Intermediate Period (thirteenth through seventeenth dynasties, ca. 1786–1570 B.C.). The finds at Tell el-Dabaa include a series of temples of Syro-Palestinian form as well as tombs of Asiatics who were interred with a variety of Levantine burial goods.

Sharuhen was evidently the principal Hyksos stronghold in southwestern Palestine. Tell el-'Ajjul, an enormous mound about four miles southwest of modern Gaza, which was excavated by the British Egyptologist W. M. Flinders Petrie and his staff during the 1930s, is the most probable site for Sharuhen.

Some scholars connect the Hyksos with the biblical patriarchs by viewing the patriarchal migration to Egypt and sojourn in the delta as the movement of Asiatics into Egypt before and during the Hyksos period. The story of Joseph and his rise to authority would certainly be understandable during a period when Asiatics were in power in Egypt. Moreover, Flavius Josephus, a first-century A.D. Jewish historian, actually equates the expulsion of the Hyksos from Egypt with the Exodus of the Hebrews, but this may be a later attempt to give a great antiquity to the Jews. This theory remains highly speculative, and nothing in the patriarchal narrative need necessarily be dated to the Hyksos period in Egypt. ***See also*** Sharuhen. J.M.W.

Hymenaeus (hī-muh-nee'uhs), opponent of Paul, associated with Alexander (1 Tim. 1:18–20; cf. 2 Tim. 4:14) and Philetus (2 Tim. 2:14–18). With Philetus, Hymenaeus held that the general resurrection was already past (cf. 2 Thess. 2:1–2). Gnostic dualistic assumptions probably supported an anti-Pauline spiritualizing of the Christian hope and a denial of bodily resurrection. ***See also*** Alexander; Gnosticism; Philetus.

hymn, broadly speaking, any poetical composition in honor of God or suitable for use in a liturgical setting, i.e., in worship. Such poetical pieces could be sung or chanted or recited antiphonally as in a responsive reading. With this understanding, many of the Psalms in the OT fall into the category of "hymn," but there are passages incorporated into other OT writings that can also be understood as hymns. There are the Song of Moses (Exod. 15:1–18), the Song of Miriam (Exod. 15:21), and the Song of Hannah (1 Sam. 2:1–10), to cite only three. The Psalms, as well as other hymns not included in the canon (such as psalms discovered at Qumran), were used in the worship of the postexilic Jewish synagogues.

The early Christian church incorporated hymns in its liturgies (see, e.g., Acts 16:25; 1 Cor. 14:26; Col. 3:16), perhaps following the example of Jesus and the disciples at the Last Supper (Matt. 26:30; Mark 14:26). Some of the best-known poetical compositions in the Gospels are found in Luke: the Benedictus (1:68–79), the Magnificat (1:46–55), the Gloria of the Angels (2:10–14), and the Nunc Dimittis (2:29–32). Some scholars affirm that there are short compositions or perhaps fragments from early Christian hymnody embodied in Eph. 5:14; 1 Tim. 1:17; 3:16; 6:16; 2 Tim. 4:18; Rev. 4:11; 5:9–10; 11:17–18; and 15:3–4. One collection of early Christian hymns has survived outside the traditional NT canon; it is known by the title *The Odes of Solomon*.

Many NT scholars believe that hymns were an essential part of the early Christian worship and life, especially hymns in honor of Jesus and hymns used in connection with the rite of baptism. One of the most widely acknowledged examples of a hymn in honor of Christ is found in Phil. 2:6–11. This poem has been discussed at length in NT scholarly circles, and the general consensus is that the hymn was a pre-Pauline liturgical piece, adapted and used by Paul in Philippians because it was appropriate to his exhortation in that context. Another possible hymn in honor of Christ may be found in Col. 1:15–20, but this is more debatable than the Philippians example. The prologue to

John's Gospel (1:1–18) may have been structured around a Christ hymn. The second use for hymns in liturgy seems to have been in the baptismal initiation of new members into the Christian community. Some have even argued that such a background was the setting for the poem in Col. 1:15–20, and it is also possible that part of Romans 6 and of 1 Peter may have served a similar function.

It is probable that the OT Psalms continued to be used in the worship of the early church and that new hymns were composed or made from the reworking of OT passages and poetic odes from the Greco-Roman world. These hymns could take the form of doxologies or creedal statements in addition to the baptismal and Christ hymns. Hymnody has been a recurring phenomenon throughout the history of the Christian church. ***See also*** Baptism; Benedictus, The; Magnificat; Music; Nunc Dimittis; Poetry; Psalms, The; Worship. J.M.E.

hypocrisy, a term and idea that are primarily limited in the Bible to the NT writings. The Greek word transliterated into English as "hypocrite" was used to denote an actor, one who performed behind a mask. Thus the popular understanding came to be that of persons who pretended to be something that they were not. It is interesting to note, however, that hypocrisy does not appear to be so limited in meaning in the NT. The term can sometimes denote general wickedness or evil, self-righteousness, pretense, or breach of "contract."

The best-known passage in the NT describing hypocrisy is Matthew 23, where self-righteousness and pretense are both in evidence (cf. also Matt. 6:2, 5, 16; 7:5; 15:7; 22:18; 24:51; Mark 7:6; Luke 6:42; 12:56; 13:15).

In Gal. 2:13, Paul accuses Peter, Barnabas, and other Jewish Christians of hypocrisy (RSV: "insincerity"). Although the term does not occur in Acts 5:1–11, the story reflects the seriousness with which the early church regarded hypocritical behavior. Perhaps the most frightening aspect of this sin is that one can enter the state of hypocrisy and not realize it (Matt. 7:21–23). J.M.E.

Hyrcanus (huhr-ka'nuhs), a name borne by two of the Hasmoneans. **1** John Hyrcanus I, son of Simon Maccabeus, who inherited the offices of high priest and ethnarch when his father and two brothers were murdered by a pretender. He ruled for thirty years (135/34–104 B.C.), during which time he consolidated the territorial and political status of Judea, forced the conversion to Judaism of the Idumeans, and destroyed the rival Samaritan temple of Mount Gerizim. **2** Hyrcanus II, son of Alexander Jannaeus and Alexandra Salome, who, as a pawn of Antipater the Idumean, fought with his brother Aristobulus II for the kingship. He served as high priest during his mother's reign (76–66 B.C.) and after the Roman conquest (63–40 B.C.) and was eventually executed by Herod the Great in 30 B.C. ***See also*** Antipater; Herod; Maccabees. **3** Hyrcanus son of Tobias, a wealthy depositor in the Temple treasury, not otherwise mentioned (2 Macc. 3:11). F.O.G.

Hyssop.

hyssop *(Origanum Syriacum),* in the Bible Syrian Hyssop, a small shrub about 27 in. high with small white flowers in bunches at the end of the stem. A bunch of hyssop was used to apply blood to doorposts at Passover (Exod. 12:22). Hyssop was also used to sprinkle a blood and water mixture on a healed leper or a renovated house (Lev. 14:4, 6, 49, 51–52). In the view of Hebrews (9:19), Moses sprinkled blood on the people in the ceremony of Exod. 24:6–8 using hyssop. The use of hyssop to purify is used metaphorically in Ps. 51:7. John 19:29 says that hyssop was used to put a vinegar-soaked sponge to Jesus' lips (cf. Matt. 27:48; Mark 15:36). D.P.W.

Opposite: Ivory head of a woman; Megiddo, fourteenth–twelfth century B.C. Carved ivory pieces from as early as the Mesolithic Period (ca. 12,000–8,000 B.C.) help reconstruct aspects of life in the ancient Near East.

I

Ibleam (ib'leem), a strongly fortified town near one of the southern passes into the Esdraelon Plain. It is to be identified with modern Khirbet Bel'ameh located a quarter mile south of Jenin. Ibleam is mentioned in the fifteenth-century list of Canaanite towns Pharaoh Thutmose III brought under his control. The tribe of Manasseh was unable to drive the Canaanites out of Ibleam (Josh. 17:11, 12; Judg. 1:27), and it probably remained in Canaanite hands until the time of David. Bileam of 1 Chron. 6:70 is probably identical with Ibleam; it is listed there as a levitical town of Manasseh, while the Septuagint of the parallel passage, Josh. 21:25, lists Ibleam. Ahaziah, king of Judah, was wounded by Jehu near Ibleam (2 Kings 9:27), and according to a Greek text it was at Ibleam that Shallum murdered Zechariah, king of Israel (2 Kings 15:10). ***See also*** Esdraelon. N.L.L.

Ichabod (ik'uh-bahd), a child born to Phinehas, son of Eli, the priest of Shiloh, at the time of the battle of Ebenezer. The Hebrew name, which means "Alas, the Glory!" belongs to a category of names expressing mourning for an absent deity (cf. Jezebel). According to 1 Sam. 4: 19–21 Ichabod's mother gave him the name in grief over the capture of the Ark.

Iconium (ī-koh'nee-uhm), a city (modern Konya) in south-central Asia Minor in a rich oasis at the edge of the central Anatolian plain. According to Greek mythology, Perseus decapitated Medusa here.

The area was apparently settled by Phrygians who spoke an Indo-European language and who came from Thrace or Macedonia ca. 1200 B.C., following the collapse of the Hittite Empire. In an area of shifting political boundaries, however, Iconium was sometimes considered part of Phrygia to the west, sometimes of Lycaonia to the east. Xenophon's *Anabasis* (ca. 399 B.C.) mentions the Persian king Cyrus's march eastward through Iconium as the last city of Phrygia, but Cicero, Strabo, and Pliny refer to it as in Lycaonia. Linguistically and ethnically, nonetheless, Iconium remained Phrygian.

Iconium was rarely independent, being subject to Lydia and Persia before its hellenization under the Seleucids in the third century B.C. It came under the sway of the invading Gauls after 278 B.C., when the entire central region of Asia Minor became known as Galatia, and was ruled by them until ceded to Pontus in 129 B.C. In 36 B.C., Mark Antony returned control of Iconium to the Galatian king Antymas, upon whose death in 25 B.C. all of Galatia (including Iconium) became a Roman province. Under Claudius (A.D. 41–54), Iconium received the honorary name of Claudiconium.

At the time of Paul's first missionary journey as reported in Acts 13:1–14:26 (ca. A.D. 47–48), Iconium, Lystra, Pisidian Antioch, and Derbe were all considered part of Galatia. Coming from Cyprus to Antioch, Paul and Barnabas were driven from the city by jealous members of the local Jewish community. They moved on to Iconium, where they remained for some time preaching successfully but causing division among the inhabitants, both Jews and Gentiles (Acts 13:51–14:7). Expelled in turn from Iconium, Paul and Barnabas went on to Lystra, some eighteen miles south, but were hounded down even there by Antiochian and Iconian Jews. They managed, nonetheless, to return to Iconium in order to encourage the fledgling church they had begun there (Acts 14:21–23).

On his second missionary journey as reported in Acts 15:40–18:21 (ca. A.D. 49–51), Paul visited Iconium again (Acts 16:1–6), when he recruited as his companion Timothy of Lystra, who was well known and respected in Iconium. A third journey (ca. A.D. 51–54) to Galatia and Phrygia (Acts 18:23) may well have included a stop in Iconium.

The church in Iconium may have been among the addressees of Paul's Letter to the Galatians and of 1 Peter (Gal. 1:2; 3:1; 1 Pet. 1:1). 2 Tim. 3:11 later recalled the persecutions of Paul's first visit to the city.

In the second century, Iconium was raised to the status of a Roman colony, and it provided the setting for the apocryphal romance of *The Acts of Paul and Thecla*. ***See also*** Antioch; Derbe; Galatia; Galatians, The Letter of Paul to the; Lycaonia; Lystra; Phrygia; Timothy. C.H.M.

iconography. ***See*** Symbol.

Iddo (id'oh), the English form of several different Hebrew names. **1** The father of Abinadab, one of Solomon's twelve district administrators (1 Kings 4:14). This is the only occurrence in pre-exilic literature. **2** The fifth-named son of Gershom, son of Levi (1 Chron. 6:21). **3** An officer responsible for the Gileadite half of Manasseh under David (1 Chron. 27:21). **4** A prophet and writer recording activities of Solomon, Rehoboam, and Abijah (2 Chron. 9:29; 12: 15; 13:22). **5** The father (Ezra 5:1; 6:14) or grandfather (Zech. 1:1, 7) of the prophet Zechariah. **6** One of the priests and Levites who returned to Jerusalem with Zerubbabel and Joshua (Neh. 12: 4, 16). **7** The head of a Jewish settlement in Casiphia, to whom Ezra sent for ministers to serve in the Temple. **8** A Jew who had married a foreign woman (Ezra 10:43). S.B.P.

idol, an image or statue of a deity fashioned to be an object of worship. The English word, which has a pejorative meaning, reflects several different Hebrew words. Some of these are neutral terms describing the manufacture, e.g., *pasil* or *pesel*, "(carved) image," and *masseka*, "(cast) image." For these the pejorative "idol" is not

Clay "idol" from the second millennium B.C. found in northern Syria.

always appropriate; "image" or "statue" is sometimes better. Other Hebrew words for statues of deities are intentionally contemptuous and therefore are appropriately translated "idols," e.g., *'elilim*, "powerless ones," *gillulim*, "pellets of dung," and *shiqqutsim*, "shameful things."

Statues of deities are a common feature of ancient Near Eastern religions. Exactly how the ancients imagined their gods to be present in the statues is not easy to discern. Sometimes they treated the image itself as if it were the god; they bathed, clothed, and fed it. One may not conclude from this practice that they believed the image itself was the god. It seems rather that they believed the image imitated, however sketchily and impressionistically, the heavenly reality; the likeness made it possible for the god to encounter the worshiper. Statues are but one instance of the general religious phenomenon of earthly imitations of heavenly realities. Temples, for example, reproduce the heavenly palaces of the gods; their rites and liturgies imitate the elaborate ceremonies of the heavenly court and enable the earthly worshiper to participate in the honoring of the god. Israel was not prohibited from adapting this feature of Near Eastern religion. The Temple in Jerusalem was the center of worship where God "placed his name" and met the people; it is contrasted in some texts with heaven where he "dwelt" (e.g., 1 Kings 8:27–53). The predecessor of the Temple, the desert tabernacle, was constructed according to the pattern that was shown to Moses on Sinai; it is a copy of the heavenly tent dwelling (Exod. 25:9).

Prohibition Against Idols: Statues of God, however, were strictly forbidden to Israel according to the Bible, a prohibition that sets Israel apart from its neighbors. The aniconic tradition appears to be ancient and effective. No male image that has been certainly identified as Yahweh has so far been found at an Israelite site. The second commandment, generally considered to be early, connects the prohibition against images with monotheism: "You shall have no other gods before me. You shall not make for yourself a graven image . . . for I the Lord your God am a jealous God . . ." (Exod. 20:3–5; cf. Deut. 5:7–9; Roman Catholics and Lutherans count the prohibition as the first commandment; other traditions see in them two commands). The phrase "no other gods before me" was originally at home in the ancient Near Eastern sanctuary where images of different deities confronted worshipers. In contrast, the Bible imagines God as reigning invisibly upon a single visible throne in the Holy of Holies.

The prohibition against idols is most decisively stated in the book of Exodus, in which God liberates the Hebrews from bondage to Pharaoh in Egypt and makes them his people at his mountain, Sinai. Israel agrees to worship him alone (Exod. 19–24, esp. 19:1–8). The people's apostasy from their fundamental commitment is depicted as worship of the golden calf (Exod. 32), which the text interprets as an idol (32:8). 1 Kings 12:28 relates Jeroboam's founding of countershrines outside Jerusalem to that original apostasy. Many scholars believe that the calf in the Exodus passage originally meant the animal as the throne of the deity rather than the deity itself. Statues have been excavated from West Semitic sites, some of which show the god astride an animal and some of which show the animal only. In the latter, the god was imagined as invisibly enthroned upon the animal. The Exodus and Kings passages may have interpreted the animal as a god rather than a throne in order to make the point that the worship was false.

Joshua, in his great speech, eloquently exhorts all Israel, which has just received its land, to "put away the gods which your fathers served beyond the River, and in Egypt, and serve the Lord" (Josh. 24:14). Much of the power of biblical preaching from Moses to the time of the Exile comes from its stark either-or choice between Yahweh and the "other gods." The great ninth-century B.C. contest at Carmel in 1 Kings 18 between Yahweh and Baal regarding control of the rain, hence of deity, contains the challenge of Elijah: "If the Lord is God, follow him, but if Baal, then follow him" (v. 21). To choose the other gods would have meant embracing an idol. In the great period of apostasy in Judah under Manasseh in the seventh century, 2 Kings 21:7 mentions a graven Asherah, a sacred pole by the altar, which the king put up in the sanctuary.

In the Exile and After: The Exile of the sixth century B.C. seems to mark a turning point in the biblical attitude toward idols, a result perhaps of the Babylonian Jewish community's ability to distance itself from the utterly strange Babylonian culture and worship system. Second Isaiah several times parodies the idols of Babylon (40: 18–20; 41:5–7, 21–29; 44:6–20; 46; cf. Jer. 10: 1–16; Pss. 115; 135). In his eyes the idols represented the deities only too well. A passive and inert statue cannot move itself, nor can it hear, speak, or act; the god is correspondingly lifeless and helpless. Made by humans of earthly material, the image shows forth nothing divine. The prophet's chief interest in the idols is to contrast them with Israel, which by its faithful action truly images forth, and witnesses to, the vitality of its God, Yahweh. Another text from the same period, Gen. 1:26–27, speaks of humans in their divinely ordained activity as the image and likeness of God. From perhaps the same period, Deut. 4:15–18 shows a similarly reflective awareness of the relationship between the statue and God: "Since you saw no form on the day that the Lord spoke to you at Horeb out of the midst of the fire, beware lest you act corruptly by making a graven image for yourselves." With the Exile, the theoretical foundation of monotheism seems sure; postexilic literature does not show the same urgent concern with idolatry as do the earlier, pre-exilic sources.

Early Christianity likewise does not inveigh strenuously against idolatry, to judge from the teachings of Jesus. Paul does, it is true, forbid Christians to take part in rites honoring other gods; civic feasts in the Roman Empire could be so interpreted (1 Cor. 10:14). Pauline theology's radical devaluation of the present age in view of the coming of the new age led it to brand excessive concern with the wealth of this age as idolatry (Col. 3:5). R.J.C.

Idumaea (id-yo͞o-mee'uh), the Greek name for Edom as found in the Septuagint. After the Exile (586 B.C.) the name designated the region in Judea from Beth-zur to south of Beer-sheba, an area occupied in part by Edomites (Idumaeans; Ezek. 36:5). Throughout the Seleucid, Hasmonean, and Herodian periods (ca. 198 B.C.–A.D. 44) Idumaea changed hands frequently. Herod the Great was an Idumaean, and people from Idumaea came to hear Jesus (Mark 3:8). ***See also*** Beer-sheba; Beth-zur; Edom; Edomites; Exile; Hasmoneans; Herodians; Judea; Seleucids, The.

Igal (ī'gal; Heb., "[God] redeems"). **1** The spy from Issachar sent by Moses to scout the promised land (Num. 13:7). **2** One of David's mighty men from Zobah (2 Sam. 23:36); apparently named as Joel in 1 Chron. 11:38. **3** A postexilic descendant of David (1 Chron. 3:22).

Ignatius, Letters of, letters written in the late first or early second century by a bishop of Antioch in Syria to cities in Asia Minor through which he passed on his way to be killed by wild beasts in the amphitheater in Rome. The cities to which letters are addressed are Smyrna, Ephesus, Magnesia, Tralles, Philadelphia, and Rome. He also wrote a letter to Polycarp, the bishop of Smyrna. While the letters are basically thank-you notes to the churches that had shown him kindness during his trip, Ignatius was also anxious to see a single bishop (a "monarchial episcopate") established over the churches in a given area, and he urged such a form of church government on the recipients of his letters. His letter to Rome, with its prohibition of any activity that might keep him from a martyr's death, shows the high regard in which martyrdom was held in the early church. P.J.A.

Illyricum (i-lir'i-kuhm), land of the Illyrians, a Roman province on the eastern coast of the Adriatic, today's Yugoslavia and Albania. Ancient writers speak of the Illyrians as wild and given to piracy. It took the Romans about two hundred and fifty years to subjugate the area completely and to integrate it fully into the Empire early in the first century A.D. under Tiberius (A.D. 14–37). Paul speaks of having preached from Jerusalem to Illyricum in Rom. 15:19, but it is not clear whether he was actually in Illyricum or merely considered it the eastern boundary of his apostolic activity up to the time of writing Romans. There were Christian communities in Illyricum by the second century, and Jerome, translator of the Bible into Latin (the Vulgate), was born there ca. 342. ***See also*** Dalmatia. C.H.M.

image. ***See*** Idol; Symbol.

image of God, a key term for understanding the divine-human relationship in biblical thought. The exact meaning of the phrase in Gen. 1:26–27 and 9:6 is problematic, and numerous suggestions have been proposed. To speak of human beings ("Adam") as created in the image of God apparently refers primarily to the bodily form (the Hebrew term for "image" usually denotes a concrete likeness) but also to the spiritual attributes the physical body symbolizes. The plural pronouns of Gen. 1:27–28 indicate that male and female share equally in the image of God and connect this idea to the twofold commandment ("Be fruitful and multiply

... and have dominion over ..."), so that both in nature and in function human beings are understood to reflect their Creator.

In the NT, vestiges of the OT meaning survive (1 Cor. 11:7–12; James 3:9), but the emphasis shifts and it becomes Christ who embodies the image of God (2 Cor. 4:4; Phil. 2:6; Col. 1:15). This reflects the Christian view (most evident in John 14 and 15) in which Christ becomes the mediator between God and human beings.

T.R.W.L.

Imlah (im'luh; Heb., "he fills"), the father of Micaiah the prophet. Micaiah challenged four hundred other prophets and predicted the defeat of King Ahab (1 Kings 22:8–29). ***See also*** Micaiah.

Immanuel (im-man'yōō-el; Heb., "God is with us"), the name of a child whose birth is symbolic of God's guiding and protecting presence among his people (Isa. 7:14; 8:8; Matt. 1:23). The name was first used by the prophet Isaiah as a sign given to King Ahaz of Judah during the Syro-Ephraimitic war (ca. 734 B.C.). At that time, Syria and Israel declared war on Judah because of her refusal to join their alliance against Assyria. Ahaz in turn appealed to Assyria for help. During his preparations for the impending conflict, Ahaz was warned by Isaiah not to rely upon the military might of Assyria, but instead to put his trust in the Lord (Isa. 7:1–9). Ahaz, however, did not heed Isaiah's advice. Shortly after, Isaiah encouraged Ahaz to ask a sign of the Lord that would assure him of God's presence and protection. Ahaz refused, taking recourse in a religious subterfuge in order to mask his lack of faith (Isa. 7:12). Despite that refusal, the prophet Isaiah gave him a sign in the form of the Immanuel prophecy (Isa. 7:13–17).

While this text is beset with a number of problems about its exact interpretation, its essential meaning appears to be something as follows. A young woman, who either already was or soon would be pregnant, would give birth to a son who would be named Immanuel. Before the child was old enough to know the difference between good and evil, the two nations of whom Ahaz was afraid would be destroyed. But in their stead, a much more formidable threat against Judah would materialize in the rising power of Assyria (Isa. 7:17; 8:1–10).

In the NT, Isa. 7:14 was used by Matthew as scriptural support for his belief in the virginal conception of Jesus, a conviction arrived at independently on other grounds. It is clear, however, that in its own eighth-century B.C. context, Isa. 7:14 did not speak of the miraculous birth of Jesus centuries later. Neither the virginity of the woman, nor the miraculous birth of the child received any special emphasis. The sign of Immanuel offered by the prophet to Ahaz had to do with the imminent birth of a child, of a mother known to Ahaz and Isaiah, and signified God's presence with his people and the royal Davidic line during the turbulent years of the Assyrian invasions that were soon to engulf the kingdom of Judah. As such it did not so much initiate a novel theological insight, as it gave symbolic expression to a conviction widely held in the OT, namely, that God was present with his people, guiding their destiny (Gen. 28:15; Num. 23:21; Deut. 31:8; Isa. 43:5) and protecting them from danger (Deut. 20:1, 4; 1 Sam. 18:14; 2 Chron. 32:8; Ps. 46:7, 11). ***See also*** Isaiah, The Book of.

W.E.L.

immortality, immunity to death, endless existence. Two Greek words express the idea of immortality. One *(athanasia)* is translated literally as deathlessness (1 Cor. 15:53); the other *(aphtharsia)* as imperishability (Rom. 2:7). It is significant that the only passages in the Greek version of the Jewish Bible that contain these words are in writings originally composed in Greek, the Wisdom of Solomon and the fourth book of the Maccabees. The notion of immortality is a Hellenistic idea. The Hebrews accepted death as a limit ordained by God (Gen. 3:19). Blessedness consisted in a peaceful death at an old age and in having posterity to carry on in one's place (Gen. 15).

Certain elements, however, in the Jewish Bible press beyond the notion of death as a limit. For example, the song of Hannah proclaims, "The Lord kills and brings to life; he brings down to Sheol and raises up" (1 Sam. 2:6). Bringing to life probably refers to conception and birth rather than to raising from the dead. "Bringing down to Sheol" and "raising up" are probably not meant literally. These phrases are images for experiences of catastrophe and well being, respectively. The vivid language of overcoming death in such OT passages, however, may have played a role in the later development of the idea of resurrection (see also Pss. 16:10–11; 49:15; 73:24).

The people of Israel and the Jews at a later time were familiar with myths in neighboring cultures of dying and rising gods, such as Baal and Osiris. These myths reflect the rhythms of night and day, summer and winter, dormancy and fertility. The Israelites did not conceive of God as dying and rising but apparently made use of these myths to understand their own destiny as a people (Hos. 6:1–3; Ezek. 37:1–14). This language about the people rising from death to life as a nation may have influenced the emergence of the notion of individual resurrection.

The idea of individual resurrection appears first in Dan. 12:2–3, written about 167 B.C. According to Daniel, many, but not all, people will rise from the dead. The wise will rise, not to bodily existence on earth, but to a new form of life, "like the stars." Many ancients believed that the stars were divine beings. Resurrection in Daniel for the wise means a kind of angelic existence. The wicked will rise to shame and everlasting contempt.

In the Hellenistic and early Roman periods (325 B.C.–A.D. 325) some Jews held to the old idea of death as a limit (Ecclus. 30:4–6; 1 Macc. 2:49–70). Some looked forward to the resurrection (*Pss. Sol.* 3:16; 2 Macc. 7:9). Others believed in the immortality of the soul (*Jub.* 23:31; Wisd. of Sol. 3:1–4).

As Jesus is pictured in the Gospels, he shares the Hebrew notion of resurrection, rather than the notion of an immortal soul (e.g., John 11: 23–25; cf. Mark 12:18–27). Indeed, the word "immortal" does not appear in the Gospels. In the Fourth Gospel, eternal life also describes the quality of life in the new age, rather than exclusively a future, unending life, since such eternal life can be enjoyed prior to death (e.g., 3:16).

In a few passages Paul appears to speak of a personal afterlife apart from and prior to resurrection (2 Cor. 5:1–15; Phil. 1:23). Resurrection is a more common image in his letters, however. Immortality for Paul is not the continuing existence of the soul apart from the body, but is rather the new heavenly existence of those who, clothed in "spiritual bodies," share in Jesus' resurrection in the new age (1 Cor. 15:42–50, 53–54). ***See also*** Eternal Life; Flesh and Spirit; Resurrection; Soul. A.Y.C.

Imnah (im'nuh; Heb., either "right-hand" or "south" [on the right facing east]). **1** A son of Asher who went with Jacob to Egypt (Gen. 46: 17); he is considered the head of the clan of the Imnites (Num. 26:44). **2** A Levite, the father of Kore, a Temple official during the reign of Hezekiah (2 Chron. 31:14).

incarnation (Lat. *incarnatio*), a term meaning "to enter into or become flesh." It refers to the Christian doctrine that the pre-existent Son of God became man in Jesus. The term does not appear in the NT, but the elements of the doctrine are present in different stages of development.

The resurrection was the most important event for identifying Jesus in the earliest Christian proclamation. According to that proclamation, it was at the resurrection that God made Jesus Lord and Messiah (Acts 2:32–36) and begot and designated him as Son (Acts 13:32–33; Rom. 1:3–4). This preaching, however, does not exclude the reality that Jesus was already Son of God during his lifetime. Thus Mark attests that God addressed Jesus as his "beloved Son" at the baptism (1:11) and transfiguration (9:7). Matthew and Luke, through their infancy narratives, push the origins of Jesus' divine sonship further back when they speak of the virgin birth (Matt. 1:18–23; Luke 1:26–38). Moreover, all three Evangelists refer to Jesus as the Son of man who will return from heaven as God's final judge (Matt. 25:31–46; Mark 13:24–27; Luke 21:25–28). None of these writers, however, deals with the question of Jesus' pre-existence.

Paul does not directly address the question of the incarnation, but there are several passages that seem to imply the pre-existence of God's Son. Thus he speaks of God who "sent forth his Son" (Gal. 4:4; Rom. 8:3) and of Jesus Christ as the one Lord "through whom are all things and through whom we exist" (1 Cor. 8:6). In addition, he writes of Christ as "the wisdom of God" (1 Cor. 1:24), thereby recalling the OT motif of pre-existent wisdom. The most important and disputed texts, however, are those found in the hymns of Phil. 2:6–11 and Col. 1:15–20. The first seems to imply a period of divine pre-existence, whereas the second speaks of Christ as "the image of the invisible God, the firstborn of all creation . . . for in him all the fullness of God was pleased to dwell" (Col. 1:15, 19; cf. 2:9).

The notion of pre-existence becomes clearer in Hebrews where the author writes of the Son as the one through whom God created the world (1:1–3a). In addition, the author describes the Son as superior to the angels (1:5–2: 8) and as sinless (4:15; 7:26). But it is in the Gospel of John that the notion of pre-existence flowers. The Gospel begins with a hymn (1:1–17) that proclaims that the pre-existent Word of God "became flesh and dwelt among us" (1: 14). The background for this thought is found in the wisdom speculation of the OT, which saw wisdom as residing with God from eternity (Prov. 8; Ecclus. 24; Wisd. of Sol. 8). In addition, the Gospel speaks of Jesus' prior existence (6:62; 8:38), his descent from heaven (3:13; 6: 33), his coming from God (16:27; 17:8), and his coming into the world (10:36; 12:46). Moreover it is only in John's Gospel that Jesus says, "before Abraham was, I am" (8:58). By the time of John the notion of pre-existence is so strong that the Johannine Letters must combat a tendency to deny the humanity of Jesus (1 John 4: 2–3). It is only with the fathers of the church in the third and fourth centuries, however, that a full-fledged theory of the incarnation develops. ***See also*** Lord; Savior; Son of God; Son of Man; Wisdom; Word.

F.J.M.

incense, a compound of aromatic gums and spices, of which the ingredients, apparently made by skilled perfumers (Exod. 37:29), are detailed in Exod. 30:34–35. In this sense, the use of incense in Israelite worship is reported only in late priestly material (e.g., Lev. 1, 2, 16). This has led to the view that it was a postexilic introduction (mid to late sixth century B.C.). How-

Incense burner, bowl and stand, found in a house at Tell Qiri, twelfth–eleventh century B.C.

ever, the golden altar in Solomon's Temple (1 Kings 7:48) was probably for the burning of incense, and two incense altars stood in the Yahweh shrine at Arad, which was in use from the tenth to the eighth centuries. Incense was regularly offered in Canaanite religion (Jer. 7:9; 44:17) and is frequently condemned as part of Israelite worship of other gods (Jer. 1:16; Ezek. 8:11). It had a secular use as a costly adornment (Song of Sol. 3:6; 4:6, 14), but the incense employed in worship was clearly distinguished and considered as specially holy (Exod. 30:37–38). Originally this was burned in portable censers (Lev. 10:1; 16:12; Num. 16:17–18) but later also on the altar of incense that stood before the veil of the Holy of Holies in the Temple (Exod. 40:26).

Because of its very sacred character, the offering of incense was confined to the high priest, who burned it morning and evening (Exod. 30:7–8), although Luke 1:8–9 indicates that this duty was later transferred to ordinary priests. Those not duly authorized (Num. 16:1–35, 40; 2 Chron. 26:16–21) or those who offered incense improperly made (Lev. 10:1–2) were struck down.

In Israel's postexilic ritual, the primary concept of incense was that the burning of it made atonement by propitiating the divine wrath. This idea is expressed in the episode of Aaron's action in Num. 16:46–48 and in the reason given for the high priest's bringing of incense into the Holy of Holies on the Day of Atonement (Lev. 16:12–13). Similarly, incense was added to the cereal offering (Lev. 2:1), to make the propitiatory "pleasing odor," provided by the burning fat in the case of animal sacrifices (Lev. 1:9). Hence, the offering of incense can be paralleled to the offering of prayer (Ps. 141:2), a link that is also developed in the NT (Luke 1:10; Rev. 5:8; 8:3–4). ***See also*** Altar; Worship. J.R.P.

India, the subcontinent lying east of Africa and south of Asia. It is mentioned in the phrase "from India [Heb. *hodu*, the Indus Valley] to Ethiopia" in Esther 1:1 and 8:9 as the eastern boundary of the Persian Empire under Ahasuerus (perhaps fifth century B.C.). In 1 Macc. 6:37 a reference to an "Indian driver" of each war elephant of Antiochus (second century B.C.) occurs. India is not otherwise attested in the biblical record. Nevertheless, widespread trade between ancient Mesopotamia and Indus Valley civilizations existed from as early as the Early Dynastic III through the Old Akkadian periods (ca. 2500–2200 B.C.), as evidenced by vases, carnelian beads and seals. There is an Aramaic inscription from Taxila (near Rawalpindi, Pakistan) from the third century B.C. that illustrates the contact between India and the biblical lands. D.B.W.

infidel. ***See*** Unbeliever.

inheritance, the passing of property at the owner's death to those entitled to succeed. Unlike ancient Near Eastern society, which bestowed the legal status of son or daughter with rights to inherit upon a stranger through adoption, Israelite law recognized only family relationships of blood kinship. Furthermore, the patriarchal structure of Israelite society was based on the agnatic family in which only blood relatives on the father's side were considered family and hence entitled to inherit. Most of the scant biblical legislation governing inheritance is imbedded in the material dealing with the territorial division of the land of Canaan according to tribes and families at the time of the conquest (thirteenth–twelfth centuries B.C.).

The major rule states that if a man died without leaving a son, his property was transferred to his daughter. If he had no daughter, his property was assigned to his brothers. If he had no brothers, it was assigned to his father's brothers. If there were none, the property was assigned to the nearest relative in his own clan (Num. 27:8–11). There is a supplementary rule that required the daughter who inherited to marry into a family of her father's tribe, preferably into the family of her father's brothers (Num. 36:6, 11). By recognizing only the father's kin as family and by requiring the daughter who was heir to marry within the clan, no transfer of real property to another family or tribe was possible upon the death of the father. Thus the primary aim of the biblical inheritance legislation was to preserve the territorial integrity of the clans and tribes established at the time of the settlement of Canaan (cf. Num. 36:7). This right to inherit and transmit one's patrimony was strongly advocated in the monarchical period (ca. 1025–586 B.C.; 1 Kings 21:3).

Biblical legislation also established the right

of the firstborn to inherit a double portion of his father's possessions, i.e., twice as much as that received by each of his brothers (Deut. 21:17). It furthermore prohibited the father from conferring the right of the firstborn upon a younger son (Deut. 21:16), which had been a prevalent practice in the patriarchal period (ca. 2000–1700 B.C.; Gen. 21:10; 27:37; cf. Gen. 48:18–20; 1 Chron. 5:1).

There are other scattered references to inheritance customs in the nonlegal literature of the Bible. It is not clear how the status of the mother affected her son's right to inherit. On the one hand, there is evidence that the sons of a concubine did not inherit (Gen. 21:10; 25: 5–6; cf. Judg. 11:1–2); yet at times, such sons seem to have been considered equal to the sons of the primary wife (Gen. 35:23–26). Perhaps the right of the sons of a concubine to inherit was dependent upon the wishes of the father. This would accord well with the Laws of Hammurabi (§§170–171), which state that if a father legally recognized as his sons the children borne to him by a slave girl, they were to be counted among his heirs; but if he failed to acknowledge them, they had no claim to his estate. The right of daughters to inherit along with their brothers is mentioned only in the book of Job (42:15) whose setting is non-Israelite.

In addition to its legalistic usage, the term "inheritance" is used in theological contexts to affirm the relationship between God and his people (Deut. 9:26, 29; Jer. 10:16; Ps. 28:9; Gal. 3:7–14).

In the NT Jesus on one occasion refused to judge the rectitude of an unequal inheritance (Luke 12:13). He also told parables involving such bequests (Matt. 21:38; Luke 15:12). The Pauline Letters speak of God's Kingdom or of salvation as inheritance (e.g., Eph. 5:5; Col. 3: 24; cf. Heb. 9:15; 1 Pet. 1:4). ***See also*** Law; Marriage. B.L.E.

iniquity. ***See*** Sin.

ink, in antiquity a liquid material used for writing on papyrus, made from soot, gum arabic, and water. Since this kind of ink does not stick well to leather or parchment, scribes also employed ink made with tannic acid derived from nut galls (oak galls). These were pulverized and then mixed with sulphate of iron and water. The ingredients for making ink were kept in an inkhorn, made of metal or wood, which the scribe carried at his belt (Ezek. 9:2–3, 11).

Besides black ink, other colors of ink were sometimes used. Titles might be written with red ink, which was made from either cinnabar or miniam. Purple ink was made from a liquid secreted by two kinds of gastropods, the murex and the purpura. For deluxe parchment or vellum manuscripts, scribes occasionally employed silver and gold inks.

The Bible refers to the use of ink in Jer. 36:18; 2 Cor. 3:3; 2 John 12; and 3 John 13. ***See also*** Writing. B.M.M.

inn. ***See*** Architecture; Caravan.

inscription. ***See*** Superscription, Title.

insincerity. ***See*** Hypocrisy.

inspiration, the filling with or domination by spirit. This concept first appears in biblical materials as a way of describing and understanding certain types of oral discourse. In ancient Israel, prophecy was understood as being uttered under the influence of God's Spirit (e.g., Num. 24: 2) or spirits (1 Kings 22:19–23). Sometimes this was evident in peculiar behavior by the prophets (e.g., 1 Sam. 10:6); at other times, it appears simply as a claim to divine authorization (e.g., Isa. 61:1).

The experience of prophetic inspiration apparently declined in Israel along with the prophetic institution itself (see Zech. 13:2–6), and the early rabbis did not approve of claims to special inspiration on the part of their contemporaries. Such claims were revived, however, among the early Christians. They understood the giving of the Spirit as a sign of the last times (Acts 2:16–18), as a mark of full assimilation into the Christian community (e.g., Heb. 6: 4), and as a source not only of prophecy but of other functions vital to or common in the life of the churches (1 Cor. 12:4–11). As in the earlier tradition, the NT writings are not uniform as to whether there is one spirit involved or several (1 John 4:1–3; 1 Cor. 14:32).

The concept of inspiration is applied to written documents in 2 Tim. 3:16. The same idea may also be implied in Heb. 3:7 and 9:8, which describe the Spirit as speaking through the words or provisions of Scripture. As in earlier references to the inspiration of oral discourse, the inspiration of written works is seen as evidenced in the authority and utility of the results.

The idea of an inspired text was perhaps implicit even earlier. Some of the translators who produced the Old Greek Version of the Jewish scriptures (the LXX) made an effort to find an equivalent Greek term for every Hebrew word, even at the expense of making sense in Greek. This tendency was carried still further by a later redactor, Aquila—sometimes to the point of complete absurdity. Ancient commentators also proceeded at times as if the most minute details of the biblical text were fraught with meaning. On the other hand, the Dead Sea Scrolls, the oldest library of biblical manuscripts we have, show a certain indifference to exact preservation of texts, and biblical interpreters at Qumran and in the NT sometimes cite their texts very loosely.

Speculation about modes and effects of inspiration continued and expanded in later Christianity. The Spirit's work has been described by a variety of metaphors, such as playing on a musical instrument or giving dictation to a secretary. Inspiration was understood to constitute the inspired utterance, even in its written form, as the Word of God, but this expression could mean a variety of things to different interpreters. There has often been a sense that the biblical interpreter as well as the original author stands in need of inspiration, and this continues the original oral context of the whole notion of inspiration. ***See also*** Holy Spirit, The; Prophet; Revelation; Scrolls, The Dead Sea; Septuagint; Spiritual Gifts. L.W.C.

instruction. ***See*** Education; Family, The; Rabbi, Rabboni; School; Synagogue.

instrument, a term used in the KJV that connotes tools, utensils, weapons, or implements. The Hebrew term *kelî* can refer to weapons ("instruments of war"; Gen. 49:5; 1 Chron. 12:33, 37), musical instruments (1 Chron. 15:16; 16:42; 23:5) or utensils (1 Chron. 28). In the RSV the term is normally translated with a word identifying the specific type of utensil; the word "instrument" is reserved for musical devices. The use of utensils is one of the aspects of technology that is attributed to the "fallen angels" (*1 Enoch* 6–11). This story accents the potential for either good or evil of technology and instruments. S.B.R.

intercession. ***See*** Prayer.

interest. ***See*** Loan.

interpretation. ***See*** Hermeneutics.

Ira (ī'rah; Heb., "a male ass"), name of three officials of the Davidic period. **1** A (nonlevitical) priest (2 Sam. 20:26). **2** Two others were among David's warriors (2 Sam. 23:26, 28; 1 Chron. 11: 28, 40; 27:9). **3** Some of the ancient biblical translations identify the priest Ira with one of David's warriors.

Iran (ihr-ahn'), the modern name for the territory of biblical Media or Persia, extending from the Zagros mountains east to Baluchistan and from the Caspian Sea south to the Persian Gulf and Indian Ocean.

iron, a metal whose hardness and malleability made it ideal for implements of war as well as of more peaceful pursuits.

Biblical References: Biblical references to iron occur in all parts of the Hebrew Bible. The NT mentions iron once in Acts and five times in the Revelation to John.

Pentateuchal references include the attribution of iron working to Tubal-cain (Gen. 4:22), the traditional "father of metallurgy." Moses uses iron in a simile, stressing its hard and unyielding property (Lev. 26:19). Iron taken as booty in the defeat of Midian was required to be purified (Num. 31:22). Og, king of Bashan, had an iron bedstead (Deut. 3:11). Captivity in Egypt is likened to being in an iron furnace (Deut. 4:20). The land of Palestine is described as a land whose "stones are iron" (Deut. 8:9). Moses threatens the disobedient with a "yoke of iron" (Deut. 28:48).

The historical books reflect the use of iron by Israel and its enemies. Canaanites had chariots of iron (Josh. 17:16). The Canaanite Sisera was said to have had nine hundred war chariots plated or studded with iron. Much has been made of the Philistines' two-hundred-year local monopoly of the metal industry (1 Sam. 13:19–21), which was broken when David came to power. Goliath's spear is described as weighing six hundred shekels of iron (1 Sam. 17:7). David was familiar with iron. The city of Mahanaim in the Jabbok Valley, well known to David, may have been the administrative center of the iron industry of his day, located as it is only about two miles from the largest and best iron mine of the Gilead mountains. An axe head was found at Gibead (modern Tell el-Ful), the capital of Saul's kingdom. Barzillai, whose name in Hebrew means "man of iron," was a Gileadite who helped David and was properly rewarded (2 Sam. 17:27–29; 19:31–39). The suggestion is that he was David's chief metallurgist. The floating axe head recovered by Elisha (2 Kings 6:6) shows evidence of a ninth-century iron implement. Iron furnaces were known in the early monarchy (1 Kings 8:51). Solomon had iron workers (2 Chron. 2:7), and by the reign of Joash (800–785 B.C.), Israel had craftsmen in iron (2 Kings 24:14; see also 2 Chron. 24:12). In prepara-

Dagger with iron blade and other implements from ca. 1200 B.C., found at Tell el-Far'ah (Tirzah) and Beth-shan.

tion for building, David gathered materials including "great stores of iron for nails for the doors of the gates and for clamps" (1 Chron. 22:3), but iron was prohibited in the Temple (1 Kings 6:7). Later rabbinic interpreters gave the reason: It is not right to use instruments of death in the creation of an instrument of life. After David's farewell speech, heads of households gave free-will offerings that included "a hundred thousand talents of iron" (1 Chron. 29:7).

Prophetic references to iron include the most descriptive passages of the ironsmith's craft (Isa. 44:12; 54:16), as well as the metaphoric use of iron as a symbol of strength and toughness (Isa. 48:4; Jer. 1:18); servitude (Jer. 28:13–14; see also Deut. 4:20); and judgment (Isa. 1:25; Jer. 6:29–30; Ezek. 22:20–31).

In Psalms, Proverbs, and Daniel, iron is referred to in historical allusion (Ps. 105:18 tells that Joseph's neck was put in an iron collar when he was sold as a slave), proverbially (Prov. 27:17, "iron sharpens iron, and one man sharpens another") and in apocalyptic dream and vision (Dan. 2:35, where the image of Nebuchadnezzar's dream had feet of iron and clay; and Dan. 2:40–45, where one of the successive kingdoms is of iron).

NT references describe objects made of iron (e.g., an iron gate, Acts 12:10; breastplates of iron, Rev. 9:9; and vessels of iron, Rev. 18:12) and someone ruling "with a rod of iron" (Rev. 2:27; 12:5; 19:15).

Historical and Archaeological Data: The importance of iron in antiquity is attested by its use in pre-Iron Age periods. Meteoric iron, known by the name "metal of heaven" in Egyptian texts, was used for ornaments, jewelry, and dagger blades as early as 2000 B.C. The beginnings of iron metallurgy (smelting and forging) are linked generally to the Hittites of Asia Minor, ca. 1400 B.C. The Iron Age in Palestine is separated into three time periods: Iron I (1200–1000 B.C., biblically the era of judges and the United Monarchy); Iron II (1000–586 B.C., Divided Monarchy); and Iron III (or Persian, ca. 587–332 B.C., the Exile and Restoration).

Iron ore sources in ancient Palestine are very limited. Minor deposits are detected in the area southwest of the Dead Sea, in Galilee and in the Arabah, south of the Dead Sea. The largest ore source of antiquity is a mine at modern Mugharat Wardeh in the Southern Ajlun mountains (biblical Gilead), a site about twenty-two miles north-northwest of Amman, Jordan, about two miles north of the Zerqa (biblical Jabbok) River. The hypothesis of Philistine and Israelite use of this mine has strong circumstantial evidence, but to date no material evidence of Iron Age use has been found at the site. Medieval exploitation of Wardeh was carried out in A.D. 1185–1450 by the Islamic rulers of the Ayyubid-Mamluk period. The ore body at Wardeh is approximately 980 feet in length by 650 feet wide and some 30 meters in thickness. The ore reserve at the Wardeh mine is estimated at some 561,000 metric tons.

Numerous ancient literary texts yield evidence of iron. Documents from Mesopotamia's eighteenth century B.C. (the time of Hammurabi) mention iron implements. The Hittite king Hattusilis (1289–1265 B.C.) shows Hittite territory as the source of Assyrian iron in the thirteenth century B.C. Papyrus Anastasi I, ca. 1250 B.C. in Jaffa, tells of Canaanite craftsmen repairing iron chariots. Assyrian texts from Sargon II (722–705 B.C.) mention tribute in iron bars received from various vassals. Several suras of the Koran make reference to iron, e.g., in Sura 34:10, the Arabs give David a gift of iron, and in Sura 57:25, "We made iron soft for him."

Some archaeological artifacts of Near Eastern antiquity are an iron dagger found in Tutankhamen's tomb (ca. 1350 B.C.), some 160 tons of iron bars from Sargon II's palace at Khorsabad, an axe head from Ugarit (ca. 1300 B.C.), a miner's pick from the eleventh century B.C. in Israel, and an iron-tipped plow point from Gibeah of Saul (modern Tell el-Ful). The Philistine sites of modern Tell el Far'ah (Sharuhen), Tell Jemmeh, Tell Qasileh, and Ashdod yielded furnaces and implements; Gezer produced wedge-shaped lumps of iron; and Beth-shemesh (Ain Shems) had forges.

The most recent research of Robert Maddin and colleagues of the University of Pennsylvania suggests that early iron was carburized and perhaps the Iron Age should have been called the Steel Age. Further archaeo-metallurgical study by researchers from the Museum of the University of Pennsylvania and by Britain's Institute of Archaeo-metallurgy may revolutionize the understanding of iron and other metals from the ancient world.

Bibliography

Coughenour, R. A. "Preliminary Report on Mugharat Wardeh." *Annual of the Department of Antiquities of Jordan* (1976): 71–77.

Muhly, J. D. "How Iron Technology Changed the Ancient World." *Biblical Archaeology Review* (Nov.-Dec. 1982): 42–54.

Wertime, T. A., and J. D. Muhly, eds. *The Coming of the Iron Age*. New Haven, CT: Yale University Press, 1980.

R.A.C.

Iron Age, the designation of an archaeological period during which iron artifacts began to come into common use. In Palestine the Iron Age began around 1200 B.C. Iron had been utilized as early as 2700 B.C. in Mesopotamia and Egypt but only came into Israel at this later period because of the slower development of the necessary technology there. Biblical references in Josh. 6:24; 17:16; 22:8; 1 Sam. 13:19–22; and 1 Sam. 17 tend to corroborate the archaeological evidence of the relatively late entry of Israel into the Iron Age. The Iron Age is normally divided into these subdivisions:

Iron I or Early Iron: 1200–900 B.C.

Iron II or Middle Iron: 900–600 B.C.

Iron III, Late Iron or Persian: 600–300 B.C.

See also Archaeology, History, and the Bible; Egypt; Iron; Mesopotamia; Palestine. K.H.R.

irrigation. ***See*** Farming; Water.

Isaac (ī'zuhk), the second of the three patriarchs of the Israelites (Exod. 2:24; 3:6; Jer. 33: 26). Born to the hundred-year-old Abraham (Gen. 21:5) and the ninety-year-old Sarah (17: 17), Isaac was the fulfillment of the Divine promise of an heir to Abraham with whom God would establish his eternal covenant (17:15–21; 18:10–15; 26:2–5, 24).

The word "Isaac" comes from the Hebrew word for "laughter" (cf. 17:19 with 18:12, 13, 15; 21:3, 6–7), which was Sarah's reaction when she heard the prediction that she would bear a son even though she was well past the age of childbearing (18:10–11). Sarah and Isaac, thus, form the first and most extreme example in the Bible of the motif of the barren woman who finally bears a son due to divine intervention (see also Rebekah and her sons Esau and Jacob, Gen. 25:21–26; Rachel and Joseph, Gen. 30:22–24; Samson and his mother, Judg. 13:2–25; Hannah and Samuel, 1 Sam. 1:1–20). Isaac is even named by God (Gen. 17:19). He was the first to be circumcised at eight days as commanded by God (21:4; cf. 17:12). Isaac's birth resulted in the expulsion of his half-brother by Abraham and Hagar, Ishmael. This was accomplished after the feast of Isaac's weaning at Sarah's insistence, since she perceived Ishmael to be a threat to Isaac's future as Abraham's heir (21:8–14).

The major event of Isaac's life in the biblical narration must surely have been "the binding of Isaac" (Gen. 22). Abraham's loyalty to God above all else was tested by a divine command to sacrifice his beloved son and sole heir (after the expulsion of Ishmael) on a mountain in the land of Moriah (vv. 1–2). At the time, Isaac is depicted as a lad of indeterminate age (v. 5). After leaving the servants and donkey behind (v. 5), Abraham gives the wood for the sacrifice to Isaac to carry, while he himself takes the firestone and knife (v. 6). Isaac, surprised at the lack of a sacrificial animal, asks his father ". . . where is the lamb for a burnt offering?" (v. 7). Abraham's enigmatic reply, "God will provide himself the lamb for a burnt offering, my son" may have confirmed Isaac's fears, but that the two walk on together (v. 8) may indicate that Isaac is prepared for whatever destiny awaits him. Indeed, for the rest of the story, Isaac plays a passive role—he is bound and placed upon the altar Abraham makes, and only when Abraham has already taken hold of the knife to slaughter him, is Isaac's fate resolved. An angel cries out from heaven and a ram is substituted for Isaac. Thus, God's promise to Abraham is reaffirmed.

For Isaac, this traumatic experience seems to have shaped his character and life. His passivity reappears with the choosing of Rebekah as wife for him, without consulting him (Gen. 24; at the age of forty! 25:20). He is the only patriarch to be monogamous and without concu-

The angel staying Abraham's hand as he is about to sacrifice Isaac (cf. Gen. 22); detail from the twelfth-century Lambeth Bible.

bines. It appears that Isaac had been bound to God in a special way, for of all the husbands of barren wives in the Hebrew Bible, only his prayer for a child by such a wife is mentioned as being answered by God (25:21). Isaac always remained the passive naïve innocent who was unaware of the intention of others—he does not know of God's plan for his sons, Jacob and Esau (25:23), nor of Rebekah's and Jacob's conspiracy to get his blessing transferred from Esau (Gen. 27). On the other hand, he is protected by God and all his doings are greatly blessed by God, and he attains great wealth and power (26:1–33). Isaac died at the age of one hundred and eighty, attended by his sons (35:27–29).

There is far less biblical material concerning Isaac than either Abraham or Jacob (or, for that matter, Joseph), which may indicate that many traditions have been lost. For instance, the origin of the phrase "Fear of Isaac" (31:42, 53) is unknown. His individual importance is attested by Amos (7:9, 16), who equates the name "Isaac" with the northern state of Israel. Isaac is frequently mentioned in the NT, along with Abraham and Jacob, as one of the three patriarchs (e.g., Matt. 1:2; Luke 3:39; Acts 7:8). The binding of Isaac is mentioned in James 2: 21, and Paul emphasizes his wondrous birth (Rom. 9:7, 10) and the promise of God associated with him (Gal. 4:28). ***See also*** Genesis; Patriarch. J.U.

Isaiah (ī-zay'uh), **the Book of** (Heb., "salvation of God" or "God is salvation"). Isaiah is a common name which appears especially in the postexilic period (Ezra 8:7, 19; Neh. 11:7; 1 Chron. 3:21; 25:3, 15; 26:25) but is most widely known as the name of the longest prophetic book in the Hebrew Bible.

Two almost complete manuscripts of the entire book of Isaiah were found in 1947 in a remote cave above the north end of the Dead Sea. This discovery is, in the American archaeologist W. F. Albright's words, "one of the greatest manuscript finds of modern times." The text is dated to the second or first century B.C. Significantly, in spite of various corrections and interlineations, there are no important differences between the Masoretic text of Isaiah and that of the Dead Sea Scrolls.

Biographical Sketch: It appears that the prophet Isaiah was from Jerusalem (in contrast to Amos and Jeremiah who grew up on the periphery), which was the center of his activity. He was married to a woman whom he calls prophetess (8:3) and they had at least two sons: *Shearjashub* (Heb., "a remnant shall return") and *Mahershalal-hashbaz* (Heb., "the spoil speeds, the prey hastes"). Their names are associated with prophetic pronouncements (7:3; 8:3). He may also have had a third son, *Immanuel* (Heb., "God is with us"; cf. 7:14; 8:18), who also bears a symbolic name. Isaiah is mentioned outside of his book in 2 Kings 19:20; 2 Chron. 26:22; and 32:20, 32. He was the son of Amoz. According to a Talmudic tradition (*Meg.* 10b), Amoz was the brother of Amaziah, king of Judah. Isaiah was a contemporary of the prophet Micah and was preceded slightly by Amos and Hosea who were active in the Northern Kingdom of Israel. Isaiah prophesied in Judah during the reigns of kings Uzziah, Jotham, Ahaz, and Hezekiah, in the second half of the eighth century approximately between 740 and 701 B.C. He had access to the king (7:1 ff) and was his counselor (37: 1–7). Due to his frequent references to wisdom forms and vocabulary there is a tendency to regard him as a member of the wisdom school, or as a wisdom teacher, but this is unclear. However, 30:8 may indicate that he studied in a school of scribes (cf. 2 Chron. 26:22).

The Book: The present book contains sixty-six chapters, a form that had already appeared in the beginning of the second century B.C. Ben-Sira, the author of Ecclesiasticus, refers to Isaiah (Ecclus. 48:17–25) as a single work. The Dead Sea Scrolls as well as the NT regard the entire

OUTLINE OF CONTENTS

The Book of Isaiah

I. First Isaiah (1–39)
  A. Prophecies against Judah and Jerusalem (1–12)
  B. Oracles against foreign nations (13–23)
  C. Prophecies of universal judgment and Zion's subsequent role (24–27)
  D. Oracles of woe against Judah and Jerusalem (28–33)
  E. Prophecies of Zion's restoration after judgment (34–35)
  F. Historical account concerning Isaiah and Hezekiah (36–39)
II. Second Isaiah (40–55)
  A. The coming salvation of Yahweh, the only God; Babylon's fall and Cyrus as God's anointed (40–48)
  B. Promises of restoration for Zion/Jerusalem (49–55)
III. Third Isaiah (56–66)
  A. Prophecies of judgment against the restoration community (56–58)
  B. Call to repentance and community response (59)
  C. Promises of salvation (60–62)
  D. Community lament and God's response (63–64)
  E. Further prophecies of judgment and promises of final salvation (65–66)

sixty-six chapters as a single book. However, the present structure does not mirror the original book. As a rule, modern prophetic scholarship distinguishes between two major "books": chaps. 1–39 and 40–66, called First Isaiah and Second Isaiah (Deutero-Isaiah), respectively. The two compositions reflect two distinct historical periods. The first relates to the second half of the eighth century B.C., the Assyrian period, while chaps. 40–66 are a product of the sixth–fifth centuries B.C., the Persian period. The distinction has been recently confirmed by a computer analysis of the language (Y. T. Radday). (Many scholars call chaps. 56–66 of the second composition a third "book," Third Isaiah; first suggested by B. Duhm in 1892.) In contrast to First Isaiah, Second Isaiah does not bear any historical superscriptions, and it is attached to First Isaiah without any external reference. The distinction between the two compositions (first suggested in modern research in 1783 by Eichhorn and in 1789 by Döderlein) is based therefore on historical, thematic, and philological criteria.

The prophet of Second Isaiah prophesied to the exilic community in Babylonia, witnessing the collapse of Babylon (539 B.C.) and the triumph of Cyrus, the founder of the great Persian Empire. Second Isaiah knows about the destruction of the Temple of Jerusalem and assigns Cyrus to build the new Temple (44:28; 45:1; cf. 52:5, 11), which dates the work to the sixth century B.C. In contrast, First Isaiah refers to political events that took place prior to the fall of the Northern Kingdom of Israel (722/1 B.C.) and deals with Assyria's threat to invade Judah during the second half of the eighth century. The distinct periods reflect different subjects and prophetic themes in the books. First Isaiah deals with social problems of the moral-ethical misbehavior of the elite of Judah, while Second Isaiah responds to the national-religious crisis of the exiles that followed the fall of Jerusalem and the destruction of the Temple (586 B.C.). Hence, speeches of judgment distinguish First Isaiah while words of comfort and encouragement characterize Second Isaiah.

On the other hand, we find specific linguistic usages common to both parts of the book. Thus, for instance, the combination "Holy One of Israel," which is characteristic of First Isaiah, appears as well in Second Isaiah (41:14, 16, 20; 43: 3, 14; 45:11; 47:4; 48:17; 49:7; 54:5; 55:5; 60:9, 14). Also, the expression "Thus says the Lord," an imperfect tense, appears in both books instead of the regular perfect, "said" (1:11, 18; 33: 10; 41:21; 66:9; cf. 40:1, 25). Such linguistic similarities do not question, however, the distinction between the books, which was already recognized in the twelfth century A.D. by the commentator Abraham Ibn Ezra (in his comments on Isa. 40:1).

An inscription quoting Isa. 66:14 carved on the western wall of the Temple Mount in Jerusalem during the reign of the Roman emperor Julian, who, in the fourth century, promised the resettlement of Jerusalem by Jews.

The question remains: how did the two distinct books get tied together? We can only speculate. Perhaps it was just a technical matter, and a shorter scroll was attached to a longer one for preservation. It was then forgotten over the years that originally two separate manuscripts had been put together. Or, perhaps the combination was intentional, and this combination was the product of a specific theological school that intended to create a continuous work. Thus, the period of judgment, which had been fulfilled, paved the way for the new period of comfort and consolation. We may assume that the author of Second Isaiah considered himself Isaiah's disciple. This may explain the similarities in idiom and phrases. Thus, in a rare passage where the author of Second Isaiah refers to himself, he describes God's words as teaching (50:4), using words resembling Isaiah's (8:16). Isaiah, in the difficult hour of "distress and darkness" (8:22), decided to seal his testimony (8:16–17). His spiritual disciple, who feels that the times have changed, notices that God has revealed himself to everyone (40:5) and considers himself as the one who carries on the master's testimony.

The Unity of First Isaiah: The material is divided into two major sections: prophecies (chaps. 1–35) and a historical account (chaps. 36–39). The prose material parallels the narrative of the book of Kings (2 Kings 18:3, 17–20: 19). There are close similarities between Kings and Isaiah in spite of certain differences. It is assumed that Isaiah relied on Kings. Thus, for instance, Isa. 36:1 is parallel to 2 Kings 18:13. The text from Kings that follows (vv. 14–16), describing Hezekiah's surrender to Assyria and detailing the heavy taxation Hezekiah had to pay on account of the Temple, is missing from Isaiah. This may be understood as an intentional omission and the longer detailed text is assumed to be the original (notice, however, the addition of Hezekiah's psalm in Isa. 38:9–20). In any case, Isaiah 36–39 is a prose appendix.

The portrayal of Isaiah in the appendix is significant. Here he appears as a healer (2 Kings 20:1–7), an image that differs from his prophetic activities as depicted in his speeches. The image of the healer fits that of earlier prophets, such as Elisha's healing actions described, for example, in 2 Kings 4–5. One should note, however, that even in chaps. 1–35 Isaiah does not confine himself to the characteristic role of the classical prophet, as God's verbal messenger; he also acts in a symbolically significant manner. Thus, he walked barefoot and naked in Jerusalem for three years as a symbol of the fate that would overtake Egypt and its ally, Ethiopia, at the hands of Assyria (chap. 20). The book of Isaiah the prophet ends in chap. 35. The book of Isaiah appears to have a long literary history. The Talmud (*B. Bat.* 15a) hints at the editorial process, which indicates that it was not Isaiah himself who wrote this book, but later scribes, Hezekiah and his school.

The Literary Shape of First Isaiah: The structure is complex. Even a brief glance at the chapters reveals several superscriptions (1:1; 2:1; 13:1). Isaiah himself states that he ceased his activity and sealed his prophecies as a testimony (8:16–17; see also 30:8). Furthermore, Isaiah's deeds sometimes are described indirectly in the third person (7:1–9; 20, for example). All this hints to the possibility that First Isaiah, even chaps. 1–35, is not a single composition.

Are there any indications of a certain development or a specific literary pattern for the arrangement of the book? A comparison with the book of Ezekiel and the Septuagint version of Jeremiah suggests a literary pattern:

1. Prophecies against Judah and Jerusalem: chaps. 1–12
2. Oracles against foreign nations: chaps. 13–23
3. Prophecies of hope and salvation: chaps. 24–35.

The preceding arrangement may reflect a late editorial process that had the specific theological intention of concluding the prophecies of judgment with words of hope and comfort. The arrangement of the prophetic books of Amos (9:7–15) and Zephaniah (3:14–20) reveals a similar theological pattern. We should realize, however, that this literary scheme is rather forced. Prophecies of judgment are found in other than the first collection (chaps. 28–29). The oracles against the nations include prophecies against Judah's leaders as well (22:15–25); another oracle directed against foreign nations is located in chap. 34 (cf. 30:6–7). Prophecies of hope are found in the first collection as well (2:1–5; 11:1–10). It appears that we have to find a better explanation for the arrangement of the book.

According to many scholars, the various superscriptions and the prose material indicate the existence of a number of independent scrolls. In addition, several pieces (5:25–30; 9:7–17, 18–21) are connected on the basis of a refrain, "For all this his anger is not turned away and his hand is stretched out still," and a key word "woe" (Heb. *hoy;* see also chaps. 28–33). Are these repeated stylistic formulae revealed in other literary collections? Based on literary patterns, many scholars suggest that First Isaiah is a construction of various literary fragments. Scholars are attempting to reconstruct the literary building blocks and thus to discover the original Isaiah. Two major theories are proposed: that at the beginning there were a number of independent short collections; or that there was an original text to which certain additions have been made.

Concerning such editorial processes and the additions, the assumption is that the original Isaianic speeches are the poetic pieces that relate to the concrete issues of the political times. The original prophecies in which Isaiah appears as God's messenger were collected as scrolls by the prophet himself. The prose texts and sermons that are not restricted to concrete historical events (as 2:1–[4]5, or 11:1–10) were added by Isaiah's disciples. Likewise, the oracles against foreign nations were edited by the disciples. To these collections new material was added, usually prophecies of comfort and salvation, which supplements the original prophetic utterance of judgment. The explanation is that Isaiah's speeches were recited repeatedly in later periods when the prophetic word was a spiritual essential. The recitation of fulfilled prophecies of judgment confirmed the power of the prophetic word. Later, when under new conditions the audience needed a new message, it was added to the original prophecies. Thus, for example, 9:1–6 is an optimistic addition to a series of prophecies of judgment.

Recently a new proposal has been suggested (H. Barth) in regard to the prophecies of salvation, which are considered unauthentic and are found throughout the book. Many of these prophecies deal with the collapse of the Assyrian Empire (10:24–26; 30:27–31, for instance). The explanation is that the Assyrian pieces were added during Josiah's reign (639–609 B.C.), a period in which the great Assyrian Empire was collapsing. This impressive political development was understood by certain religious schools in Jerusalem as God's interference and punishment. The poems and oracles of salvation were added as fresh commentaries to Isaiah's original speeches. There is also a socio-psychological explanation for the additions (R. P. Carroll). The issue concerns what happens to a community of believers when specific prophecies are not fulfilled. To release the believers' frustrations new prophecies adjusted to the new reality are added, thus keeping Isaiah's prophecy alive and meaningful.

The editorial theories are not free of criticism. The major problem lies in the literary-thematic criteria for the distinction between authentic speeches and the additions.

The Period and First Isaiah's Speeches: Isaiah provides a series of responses to specific political and domestic situations. These developments and his speeches are related. Isaiah has a broad view of world events and offers his specific prophetic interpretations of the political situation. His prophecies and visions must be studied not just as individual speeches but in light of the prophet's thematic way of thinking. Oracles of judgment do not have to contradict prophecies of comfort and salvation, as both may be integrated in Isaiah's prophetic view. The book deals with the two major political events that shocked Judah: the Syro-Ephraimite war (734–733/2), and the Assyrian threats on Jerusalem (734–701).

Isaiah's prophecy does not reflect these events merely as political-military developments; they are presented within a broader prophetic understanding. Chaps. 1–9 reflect the Syro-Ephraimite war, which threatened the house of David (see 7:6). This political and religious trauma that brought the danger of breaking the sacred promise of God to David (2 Sam. 7) motivates Isaiah's response. The prophet tries to calm the frightened King Ahaz (Isa. 7:2) by reporting the near collapse of his enemies (7:5–9). Isaiah opposes Ahaz's inclination to use foreign aid from Assyria or Egypt (7:18–25). Since the king rejects Isaiah's advice, the prophet seals his words and awaits the future (8:16–18). The threat of replacing the house of David is answered by prophecies about the continuity of David's throne (9:1–6; 11:1–10).

Isaiah does not restrict himself to the political situation, however. He deals in depth with the cause of the problem and points out the domestic issues such as the social-ethical misbehavior of the people (1:4–5, 10–17, 21–23; 3:16–26; 5:1–30). The war is God's punishment for the people's misbehavior. The punishment, however, is not final; Jerusalem will be purified and justice will be restored (1:26–27; 2:2–[4]5). Concerning chap. 6, regarded by many as Isaiah's call, his "inaugural vision," note should be taken of the message—to harden the hearts of the people (vv. 9–10). This response refers to the people's stubbornness and denial of Isaiah's previous criticism (chaps. 1–5). The vision is therefore in its appropriate setting and reflects the prophet's feelings.

Chaps. 10–11 should be read in light of the implications of Assyria's threat. Ephraim and Aram had collapsed, and Judah was powerless against the Assyrians' military machine. This new political development invited a prophetic interpretation. Isaiah delivered a series of speeches that shed light on the meaning of the events and pointed out the causes of the catastrophe. He again indicated moral-ethical misbehavior as a cause (10:1–4). God's response is direct: Assyria is his means of punishment (10:5–6). However, Assyria exaggerates its self-reliance, and will be punished (10:7–11). Isaiah is not pessimistic. He believes in the restoration of Judah and the house of David. He anticipates a new spiritual period of justice and peace (11:1–16).

The collection of oracles against the nations in

Cyrus's clay cylinder text, 538 B.C., recording that he "liberated those who dwelt in Babylon from the yoke that chafed them."

chaps. 13–23 includes prophecies that are not Isaianic (chaps. 13–14 and perhaps also chap. 23). However, the collection includes a prophecy against Judah that concludes with a personal attack on two high officials (22:1–8). It appears that this collection is also integrated in Isaiah's thematic understanding. The structure of this collection resembles that of Amos, who starts with a series of prophecies against foreign nations, and climaxes with a specific prophecy against Israel (1:2–2:16), which was the object of Amos's prophecy. The common theme in Isaiah's prophecies against other nations is the military defeats of the various nations. Hence, Isaiah repeatedly reveals his basic religious-political conception. Read against Isaiah's prophetic understanding, this collection reveals his belief that the international political situation does not take place in a vacuum but is determined by God and does not exclude Judah. Consequently, all Judah's military efforts to protect itself will fail (22:1–11).

The visions of chaps. 24–35 again abstractly summarize Isaiah's general prophetic view: God's absolute universal domination and his punishment in the form of military defeat for misbehavior (24:1–5, 21–23; 28:14–22; 29:13–14; 30:1–3; 34:1). Isaiah, a master of language, moves from a visionary to a more concrete style. We should realize that he attempts to deliver his message effectively, using various styles and modes of speech, including poetry, as his means of communication. Characteristically, Isaiah concludes with an optimistic vision of the future (35:1–10). It is not necessary, therefore, to regard chaps. 34–35 with their enthusiastic tone as part of Second Isaiah's prophecy (C. C. Torrey, Y. Kaufmann).

First Isaiah; Conclusion: Isaiah's speeches are not developed methodologically in a specific thematic order. His speeches are responses to specific situations. Isaiah's major effort is to discover and present to his audience the relationship between cause and effect, sin and punishment—the connection between the people's moral-ethical misbehavior and the wars. He provides a general overview of his vision of Jerusalem and the house of David. Thus, reality and eschatology are mixed, creating Isaiah's profound political-religious viewpoint.

The Context of Second Isaiah; Time, Place, Political and Religious Conditions: The social and political elite of Judah were in Babylon in exile (2 Kings 24:12–16; Jer. 52:16–30). Evidence suggests that the exiles enjoyed political and religious autonomy to a limited degree. Many of the Jews in exile preserved their national and religious identity. Increased emphasis on the Sabbath as the expression of the covenant between God and his people has distinguished the Jews since this period (Isa. 56; 58:13–14). The exilic period is also noted for its national-religious literary activity. The masterpiece of biblical historiography, the Deuteronomistic work (Deuteronomy–Judges), was developed and crystallized in this period. Nevertheless, there was a feeling of dissatisfaction among the exiles. The exiled prophet Ezekiel asks desperately: "How are we to go on living?" (33:10; see also 37:11). This pessimism was also expressed by the repeated phrase in Lamentations: "There is none to comfort me" (1:2, 16, 17, 21). It is reflected also in Ps. 137 and is presented by Second Isaiah (40:6–7). The exiles understood their pessimistic spiritual-religious condition to be a sign of neglect by God, and even as a sign of God's disappearance from the historical stage. This is the background of conditions faced by the author of Second Isaiah.

The unknown prophet was aroused by the momentous events occurring on the international political scene and was led to persuade the exiles that the immediate future held great promise and new hope. The sensational victories of Cyrus, king of Persia, and the threat to Babylon itself motivated Isaiah to consider Cyrus as God's agent (44:28; 45:12–23) who would change Israel's present hopeless national-religious condition. Against the background of the spiritual crisis and the emergence of Cyrus, the prophet struggled with two main themes: the claim that God was not hidden from his people, and the insistence that the new political events were directed by God and that, consequently, they had direct implications for the exiles' future. These themes mainly underlie chapters 40–48.

The Historical Development of Second Isaiah: In 539 Babylon surrendered to Cyrus. In 538 Cyrus published his famous declaration allowing the exiled Jews of Babylon to return to Jerusalem and restore the Temple (Ezra 1:3–5; 2 Chron. 36:23; Ezra 6:3–5). An important issue in the interpretation of Second Isaiah's prophecy is whether the author addressed the exiles before Babylon's fall or following it. Do the main themes of the prophet's work fit the period preceding the fall of Babylon? Chaps. 40–66 do not reflect Cyrus's edict. One of the main themes of Second Isaiah is the people's skepticism about God's control over contemporary political events. Second Isaiah's argument would be inappropriate if Cyrus had already publicly granted permission to rebuild the Temple in Jerusalem. Furthermore, Second Isaiah's descriptions of the fall of Babylon are not realistic. In contrast to inscriptions that report that the city fell peacefully without a battle, Second Isaiah describes Marduk, Babylon's god, as being carried into captivity (46:1–2). It appears, therefore, that the author of Second Isaiah prophesied prior to 539. We may assume that he was active in the period following Cyrus's conquest of Lydia in 547, which made it obvious that Babylon's days were numbered.

The Structure of Second Isaiah: Formally, a

concluding phrase, "There is no peace, says the Lord, for the wicked" (48:22; 57:21), divides chaps. 40–66 into three major parts. This division is close to the divisions concluded by modern research: 40–48, 49–55, and 56–66. It is commonly argued that chap. 56 starts a new book called Third Isaiah (or Trito-Isaiah), which is dated to the fifth century B.C. (see above). Only a few scholars maintain that the entire twenty-seven chapters of Second Isaiah are a single book (C. C. Torrey, Y. Kaufmann). Another view holds that chaps. 49–66 are distinguished from 40–48 in location but not in authorship (M. Haran). This view holds that following Cyrus's edict the prophet returned to Jerusalem and continued his prophetic activity there. Zion is the background for this material (49:14–18; 51:17–23; 54:1ff; 60:1–7; 62:1–9). In any case there is a certain thematic and stylistic difference between chaps. 40–48 and the remainder. Only in 40–48 is Cyrus mentioned, and only here are there arguments against the foreign gods, stressing Yahweh as the only God (40:12–31; 41:6–7; 43:8–13; 44:9–20; 46:5–11). The tone and mood of enthusiasm and encouragement of 40–48 are changed mainly in 56–66 to a stronger criticism of the people of Israel (56:9–57:12; 58; 59:1–18; 65:1–15; 66:1–10, 15, 17).

Second Isaiah's Literary Units: The composition of the book is the pivotal issue of the literary study of Second Isaiah. The questions involved are the determination of the literary units and the organization of the book as a whole. In general, two approaches have been taken with regard to these questions. The first considers the book to be a product of planned writing activity and sees the book as composed of large units. The second approach argues that the prophet delivered his addresses orally; hence the book is a collection of small units that once existed independently. The point of departure for the first approach is basically the issue of the content, supported at times by stylistic or structural analysis. On the other hand, the starting point of the second approach, i.e., the small independent units, is the formal formulae of opening and concluding speeches ("form criticism").

Another question involving the approach of independent prophetic units concerns the arrangement of the material. It has been argued (S. Mowinckel) that the small independent units were arranged mechanically according to key words or similarities in themes. Thus, each speech was placed on the basis of its association with the preceding speech. While form criticism concentrates on the external form of each speech and regards each one separately, the approaches that look at the book as a unified composition (J. Muilenburg, E. Hessler, C. Westermann) discuss the whole in relation to the individual components. Hence, they are able to explore the work's overall compositional techniques and are not restricted to the separate small units. The question of the structure of the individual unit and the arrangement of the book as a whole depends on the function of the prophecies.

The author of Second Isaiah sought to change his audience's religious attitude. In order to accomplish this goal, he appealed to his audience employing numerous means of persuasion. Contrary to the earlier prophets, Second Isaiah (esp. in chaps. 40–48) did not announce judgment and punishment, nor did he threaten. Rather, he sought to appeal to his audience through the effectiveness of his arguments and the impact of the style and expression of his proclamations. Such means of persuasion are rhetorical in nature. To present his argument persuasively, the prophet paid close attention to the organization of each address. Each address emerges from and is a response to a particular situation.

An analysis of the book from this approach that focuses our attention on Second Isaiah's major efforts to affect his audience in chaps. 40–48 reveals that the material is composed of ten units: 40:1–11; 40:12–31; 41:1–29; 42:1–13; 42:14–43:13; 43:14–44:23; 44:24–45:13; 45:14–46:13; 47:1–15; 48:1–22. Another division based on stylistic-literary assumptions (e.g., J. Muilenburg) is: 40:1–11, 12–31; 41:1–42:4; 42:5–17; 42:18–43:7; 43:8–13; 43:14–44:5; 44:6–8, 21–23; 44:9–20; 44:24–45:13; 45:14–25; 46:1–13; 47:1–15; 48:1–22. (See also E. Hessler's and C. Westermann's divisions.)

The Songs of the Servant of the Lord (*Ebed Yahweh* Songs): There are four poems spoken by the servant of the Lord: 42:1–4; 42:5–7; 49:1–6; and 50:4–9, and two poems that speak about the servant: 50:10–11; and 52:13–53:12. The poems share a common theme: the servant suffers, ignored by the people around him, but he will be recognized in the future as God's servant and his mission to restore justice will be fulfilled. The poems occupy a special place in the history of interpretation and have significant theological meaning in the histories of Jewish and Christian interpretation (cf. Matt. 12:18–21; 1 Pet. 1:24–25). Scholars have debated whether to isolate the poems from their context or to consider them to be an integral part of Second Isaiah's message. Mention should also be made of Second Isaiah's other references to God's servant (41:8–10, 13; 42:19; 44:1–2).

The major question is the identity of the servant. Scholars are divided in understanding the servant as an individual or in a collective sense. There are many attempts to identify the servant as a specific public or historical figure (such as Jeremiah, Josiah, or Zerubbabel), including the prophet himself (61:1–2). In light of the frequent references to Israel as God's servant (see also 49:3) some scholars regard the servant as the people of Israel, sympathetically portrayed by Second Isaiah in order to arouse hope and feelings of mission. Another view holds that the servant is neither a particular figure nor a group, but a combination that represents a mythological-cultic and royal figure.

Third Isaiah: The opinion has already been stated that chaps. 56–66 comprise a separate collection of another anonymous prophet who was active during the period of Ezra and Nehemiah in the fifth century B.C. (see above). The distinction, however, is not readily obvious and the portrayal of Zion may represent a shift in location but not necessarily a change in authorship. Chaps. 56–66 emphasize ritual requirements (56:2, 7; cf. 57:3–13; 65:1–7), the Sabbath (58: 13–14), and the law. On the other hand, chaps. 60–62 convey optimistic expectations similar to those of Second Isaiah and may hint at Second Isaiah's influence. 66:1–4 rejects the building of the Temple, which reflects a view opposite of the cultic conception of Haggai and Zechariah, other prophets of the period, who enthusiastically supported the rebuilding of the Temple around the year 520 B.C. ***See also*** Babylon; Cyrus II; Hezekiah; Jerusalem; Scrolls, The Dead Sea. Y.G.

Iscariot (is-kair'ee-uht), the surname of Judas, the disciple who betrayed Jesus (Matt. 26:14–16; 47–49). ***See also*** Judas.

Ishbosheth (ish-boh'sheth; Heb., "man of shame"), the fourth son of Saul (2 Sam. 3:14–15). This version of his name appears in the book of Samuel and is, according to most modern scholars a theologically corrected reading of the original name Eshbaal (which is preserved in 1 Chron. 8:33 and 9:39; the noun *ish* may, in fact, mean "gift," on the basis of Ugaritic; hence "gift of Baal"). The name was changed in order to avoid use of "Baal" in proper names (cf. Hos. 2:16–17). Upon the death of Saul, Ishbosheth attempted to rule all of the tribes. The tribe of Judah refused allegiance. With Abner as general, Ishbosheth set up his capital east of the Jordan River at Mahanaim (2 Sam. 2:8–10). After a stormy career, during which Abner deserted him, Ishbosheth was murdered by two of his own henchmen, Rechab and Baanah, who took his head to David at Hebron, expecting a reward. However, David's sense of justice led to the execution of the two criminals and the burial of the head of Ishbosheth at Hebron (2 Sam. 4). This event marked the end of Saul's brief dynasty. ***See also*** Abner; David. M.A.F.

Ishi (ish'ī; Heb., "[God has] saved [me]"). The name of members of the Judean (1 Chron. 4:20), Simeonite (1 Chron. 4:42), and Yerahmeelite (1 Chron. 2:31) branches of the Calebites as well as a leader of the Transjordanian Manassites (1 Chron. 5:24). It is also a term used by the KJV to transliterate the Hebrew term "my husband," which, according to Hos. 2:16 (Hebrew v. 18), is to be used instead of "my master" (Heb. *baali)* for God.

Ishmael (ish'may-uhl; Heb., "God has heard"). **1** The son of Abraham by the Egyptian handmaiden of Sarah whose name was Hagar (Gen. 16; 17; 21:1–21). He is especially celebrated in the Priestly source as one whom God would bless, multiply and make fruitful: "he shall be the father of twelve princes, and I will make him a great nation" (Gen. 17:20). Ishmael is circumcised (Gen. 17:25) at the age of thirteen and thus brought into the covenant of circumcision (v. 10), but not into the "everlasting covenant," as Isaac is (v. 19). The latter covenant evidently pertains to possession of the land (v. 8). The high standing of Ishmael in the Priestly source is seen not only in his genealogy, but also in his comparative age, since old age is worthy of honor: Abraham is 175 years old (Gen. 25:7); Isaac is 180 years old (Gen. 35:28); Jacob is 147 years old (Gen. 47:28); Ishmael is 137 years old (Gen. 25:7); Sarah is 127 years old (Gen. 23:1); and Joseph is 110 years old (Gen. 50:26).

Also in the Yahwistic and Elohistic sources, Ishmael is favored of God. The angel of the Lord who guarded Isaac (Gen. 22:11–13), Lot (Gen. 16:16–19:28), and Joseph (Gen. 48:16) also protected Ishmael's mother in her pregnancy (Gen. 16:6–14), and then protected both Hagar and Ishmael (Gen. 21:15–21). These sources reiterate that God will make Ishmael "a great nation" (Gen. 21:18). But a great difference remains between the father and this son: compare the favorable promise to Abraham (Gen. 12:3) with the statement about Ishmael: "his hand [shall be] against every man and every man's hand against him" (Gen. 16:12). According to the Elohistic source Ishmael dwelt in the Wilderness of Paran (Gen. 21:21) and became an expert bowman (v. 20).

2 The son of Nethananiah, a man of royal blood and the assassin of Gedaliah, whom the Babylonians appointed ruler of Judah after the fall of Jerusalem (2 Kings 25:25).

3 Other royal, courtly, and priestly figures (1 Chron. 8:38; 2 Chron. 19:11; 23:1; Ezra 10:22). ***See also*** Ishmaelites; Sources of the Pentateuch. J.G.G.

Ishmaelites (ish'may-uhl-īts), those who are related to Ishmael. **1** The descendants of Ishmael, who are listed by name (Gen. 25:13–16; 1 Chron. 1:28–31). The genealogy in Genesis 25 is probably from the Priestly source as evidenced by the common phrase "twelve princes" (Gen. 17:20; 25:16). The names indicate some affinities with the Edomites (see Gen. 36) with whom they intermarried (Gen. 28:9) and with the descendants of Keturah (Gen. 25:1–4; 1 Chron. 1: 32–33). Root meanings of the patronymics reveal they were darkened (Kedar), perfumers (Mibsam), fierce (Hadad), settlers in Tema (Tema) or in encampments protected by stone walls (Jetur), "very wealthy" (Naphish), and ones who traveled "eastward" (Kedmah). **2** A synonym for traders between Gilead and Egypt to whom Joseph was sold (Gen. 37:25–28). They are also called Midianites (v. 28). The latter reference may reflect a second (Elohistic) version of the story. Scholars today, however, are more inclined to see in the variation of names a stylistic preference of a single author or editor. ***See also*** Ishmael. J.G.G.

Ishtar (ish'tahr), a goddess in the Akkadian pantheon. Ishtar was widely worshiped in Mesopotamia from earliest times until at least the first century B.C. The etymology of her name is uncertain, although the relationship between the name "Ishtar" and the names of other Semitic goddesses and gods is clear (Astarte, Athtar). In the Akkadian language, "Ishtar" came to mean "goddess" and could be used as a common noun.

The cult of Ishtar was prominent at Nineveh, Arbela, and especially at Uruk (biblical Erech). Ishtar's famous temple, the Eanna, stood in Uruk, and because the Mesopotamian *Epic of Gilgamesh* was set in that city, she played an important role in that literary masterpiece. In the religion of Mesopotamia, Ishtar acceded to the position of the Sumerian goddess Inanna (Innin), with whom she was identified. In part the cult of the Semitic goddess Ishtar owed its prominence to the ascendancy of Semitic peoples in Mesopotamia.

Stele of Ishtar of Arbela standing on a lion. She is armed with a sword and quiver and her right hand is extended in benediction; from Tell 'Ahmar, eighth century B.C.

Associated with the planet Venus, Ishtar was reckoned the child of the moon god Sin; her brother was the sun god Shamash (Sumerian Utu), and she had as her consort the sky god Anu, although she was sometimes reckoned the paramour of Tammuz (Sumerian Dumuzi). The cult of Ishtar and Tammuz, reflected in the myth "The Descent of Ishtar to the Nether World," enjoyed widespread popularity and made its way to Israel (Ezek. 8:14). It is often assumed that the "Queen of Heaven" (Jer. 7:18; 44:17–19) refers to Ishtar. The Bible preserves the name of Ishtar only in the personal name Esther.

Two aspects of the character of Ishtar were prominent: eroticism and belligerence. She was celebrated as a goddess of war, but at the same time she was vitally involved in the realm of sexuality and fecundity. When she descends to the nether world, mating and procreation cease on earth. She was not viewed with universal admiration. Her role in the *Epic of Gilgamesh* is undignified, and she is taunted by the hero Gilgamesh as a faithless lover. ***See also*** Erech; Tammuz. R.M.G.

Ishvi (ish'vī). **1** A son of Asher who went with Jacob to Egypt (Gen. 46:17); he is considered the ancestral head of the clan of the Ishvites (Num. 26:44). The name Ishvah, which is given as another son of Asher (Gen. 46:17; 1 Chron. 7:30; but omitted in Num. 26:44), probably identifies the same person and is a variant spelling of Ishvi that is (erroneously?) repeated in the text. **2** A son of King Saul and brother of Jonathan (1 Sam. 14:49); he is probably the same person elsewhere called Eshbaal (1 Chron. 8:33) and Ishbosheth (2 Sam. 2:8). ***See also*** Ishbosheth. D.R.B.

island, a body of land surrounded on all sides by water. The word, translated in the KJV as "isles" or "islands" (Heb. *'iyim*), means "regions with borders on the sea." Hence the word is frequently translated in the RSV as "coastlands" or "coasts."

A number of specific islands are referred to in the Bible. **1** "Isles of the sea" (KJV), which are Mediterranean islands (RSV coastlands) in general (Isa. 11:11; 24:15; 1 Macc. 14:5; cf. Ezek. 26:18). **2** Arvad, in northern Phoenicia, an island-city located two miles off shore (Ezek. 27: 8, 11). **3** Cauda, a small island south of Crete where, Acts records, Paul took refuge during a storm (Acts 27:13–17). **4** Chios, an island off the northern coast of Ionia (Acts 20:15). **5** Cos, an island off the southwest coast of Asia Minor, fifty miles northwest of Rhodes, to which Paul sailed on his way back to Jerusalem (Acts 21:1). **6** Crete (biblical Caphtor), a famous island, 160 miles long, reputed to be the place of origin of the Philistines (Jer. 47:4; Amos 9:7). Paul sailed along its coast (Acts 27:7–21). It is also the area for which Titus was appointed as supervisor (Titus 1:5–14). **7** Cyprus (KJV: " 'isles' of the Kittim"), a large island located seventy-five miles off the northern Levant coast (Jer. 2:10; Ezek. 27: 6; Acts 4:36; 11:19–20; 13:4; 15:39; 21:3; 16; 27: 4). **8** Malta, a small island fifty miles south of Sicily, on which Paul, according to Acts, was shipwrecked (Acts 27:39–28:10). **9** Patmos, a small island off the Ionian coast, west of the island of Samos, on which John received his revelation (Rev. 1:9). **10** Rhodes, an island off the southwest coast of Asia Minor visited in the course of Paul's return to Jerusalem (Acts 21:1). **11** Samos, located off the Ionian coast, twelve miles southwest of ancient Ephesus (Acts 20: 14). **12** Sicily, the largest of the Mediterranean islands. Although it is not mentioned by name, it was visited by Paul when he landed and stayed for three days at Syracuse, its leading city (Acts 28:12). **13** Tarshish, possibly Sardinia (Ps. 72:10; Ezek. 27:25). **14** Tyre, an island-city of the Phoenicians that was famous for its trade and wealth (Ezek. 26–28). It was conquered by Alexander the Great after he built a half-mile long mole from the coast to the island. Thereafter it remained connected to the mainland.

The word "island" is used as a synonym for the nation(s) of the Gentiles (Gen. 10:5; Isa. 41: 1; 42:4; 51:5). As a noun "island" is used to indicate nation(s) afar off (Isa. 41:5; 49:1; 66:19; Jer. 31:10). An island is a symbol of that which is taken to be permanent, but which at the end of time will be removed and flee away (Rev. 6: 14; 16:20). J.G.G.

Israel, the collective name of the twelve tribes descended from Jacob, whose name was also "Israel" (Gen. 32:28; 35:10). In the Bible the people are called "the children of Israel" (usually rendered "the people of Israel" by the RSV) or simply "Israel." As a political designation "Israel" refers either to the nation as a whole or, during the period of the Divided Monarchy (924–721 B.C.), to the Northern Kingdom in particular, as distinct from Judah, the Southern Kingdom.

The Origin of the Name: According to biblical tradition "Israel" was the name of the ancestor of the people as well as the people themselves. We might conclude from this that the patriarchal name was the retrojection onto a common ancestor of the collective name of the people, who were called "the children of Israel" (KJV) just as the Ammonites were called "the children of Ammon" or the Edomites "the children of Edom." Modern analysis, however, shows that Hebrew *yisra'el*, "Israel," has the form of a personal name rather than a tribal or national name. It belongs to a well-known type of name and means "May God contend" or possibly "May God rule." This suggests that the patriarchal name has historical priority.

In Gen. 32:28 Jacob is given the name "Israel" after a struggle with a divine being on the bank of the Jabbok (the name *yisra'el* being understood there to mean "he strives *[yisra]* with God *['el]*" [cf. Hos. 12:4]), and there is another account of Jacob's renaming in Gen. 35:10. The ancestor of the Israelites, therefore, was known by two names, a fact that suggests to many scholars that two patriarchs lie behind the figure of Jacob-Israel. Traditions about an originally distinct ancestor named Israel, in other words, were merged with those about Jacob as a consequence of an early process of tribal affiliation. If this hypothesis is correct, it seems likely that the "Israel" traditions belonged first to the people who occupied the central part of the country, i.e., the two half-tribes of Joseph (Ephraim and Manasseh [cf. Gen. 48]) and the tribe of Benjamin. These people traced their origin to a common ancestor, Israel. After the formation of the larger tribal organization, Israel was identified with Jacob, the patriarch of another group, and the name "children of Israel" was extended to apply to members of the new alliance as a whole.

The People of Israel: The earliest occurrence of the name outside the Bible is in a hymn celebrating the victories of the Egyptian king Merneptah, composed about 1230 B.C. The poem, which lists numerous enemies defeated in Palestine, contains the boast that "Israel has perished: its seed is no more." In the Egyptian text "Israel" is marked with the hieroglyphic determinative signifying "foreign people," not "foreign land." This is usually taken to mean that a group called Israel was present in Palestine at this time, but that they had not yet settled in the land and claimed territory for themselves.

Exactly what this group might have been, however, is impossible to determine. It is not likely that it was the fully developed twelve-tribe entity of biblical tradition. Although the Bible presents "all Israel" as a unified people, comprising the ancestors of all later Israelites, who acted in concert from the earliest times, it is improbable that any such unification was achieved before the time of David. We should probably think of a small group of tribes that gradually evolved into a political unit of national scope.

This is not to say, however, that Israel had no formal organization before the establishment of the kingdom. The biblical account of the premonarchical period and the rise of kingship (thirteenth–eleventh centuries B.C.) suggests that the monarchy was imposed on some kind of antecedent tribal order, which modern scholars have attempted to reconstruct from the biblical evidence on the basis of analogies with other tribal organizations. The term "amphictyony," which properly refers to certain twelve-tribe groups in early Greece and Italy, has frequently been applied to premonarchical Israel on the basis of supposed parallels of structure and function. Evidence for many of the distinctive features of the Aegean institution, however, is lacking in the case of Israel, and most scholars now prefer to speak more generally of a tribal league or confederation. There are also better analogies available: intertribal associations united by treaties and bonds of kinship were characteristic of Near Eastern nomadic society, as attested, for example, by the Mari archive, which provides information about the nomadic tribes of northwestern Mesopotamia in the second millennium B.C.

Thus the "Israel" of the Song of Deborah (Judg. 5), an ancient song celebrating a victory over the forces of Canaanite Hazor, was probably a loose confederation of tribes, perhaps ten in number (cf. vv. 14–18) and including some of the later tribes (Benjamin, Zebulun, Issachar, Reuben, Dan, Asher, Naphtali, and the half-tribe Ephraim) along with others (Machir, Gilead). The account of Joshua's covenant ceremony in Joshua 24 is often thought to preserve a memory of the establishment of this institution. It is impossible, however, to trace its history in the premonarchical period with any confidence. The various episodes of the book of Judges have been set in an "all Israel" framework by their editors, as if the ancestors of all the later Israelites were involved in every event, but a reading of the stories themselves shows that originally they were strictly local in character. The most we can say is that some kind of intertribal organization called "Israel" existed in Palestine from at least the last half of the thirteenth century B.C. until the time of the early monarchy, when the full twelve-tribe structure became the established ideal. Thereafter Israel's memories of its own premonarchical history were interpreted in light of this ideal structure, which was reinforced by the development of a genealogical scheme linking the twelve tribes together in a tradition of common origin.

The Nation of Israel: Sometime near the end of the first millennium B.C. Israel became a nation. The political ties that had bound the tribes together previously were routinized, and the group as a whole came to recognize the authority of a king. We should not, however, think of this transition as the replacement of the people

The stele of the Egyptian king Merneptah (ca. 1230 B.C.) contains the earliest mention of the name "Israel" (detail, bottom) outside the Bible. As used on the stele, the name signifies a "foreign people" rather than a "foreign land."

Israel with the nation Israel. The concept of the people Israel, with its basis in kinship ties, remained as viable as ever during the monarchy and, indeed, provided the starting point for a new understanding of Israel after the fall of the state. During the period of the Israel and Judean monarchies (924–721 B.C.), therefore, Israel was both a people and a nation.

Saul's Kingdom: Saul was Israel's first king, and it was under his rule that the old tribal alliance became a nation (late eleventh century B.C.). He came from a prominent family in Gibeah of Benjamin (1 Sam. 9:1–2), and after demonstrating his military leadership by a victory over the Ammonites (1 Sam. 11), he was able to command the allegiance of a fairly extensive region in the central hills and Transjordan. We cannot be sure exactly how much territory Saul controlled, but the domains he passed on to his heir at his death included "Gilead and the Ashurites [so RSV, but probably read 'Geshurites,' inhabitants of northeastern Palestine in the region of the present-day Golan Heights] and Jezreel and Ephraim and Benjamin and all Israel" (2 Sam. 2:9). In this case "all Israel" is probably a summary reference to the preceding list of territories. In the time of Saul, then, "Israel" was a state in central Palestine bounded on the west by the coastal plain and on the east by the Transjordanian plateau; it ran along both banks of the Jordan from the Jezreel Valley south to Benjamin.

The United Monarchy: Before David became king of Israel, he was king of his native Judah (2 Sam. 2:4). His former alliance to the house of Saul, however, gave him a claim to Saul's throne, and eventually he united the two kingdoms under his rule (late eleventh century B.C.; 2 Sam. 5:1–3). It was the personal achievement of David, therefore, that joined Judah with Israel, creating the basis for the biblical view of a greater Israel encompassing both northern and southern Palestine. According to this view, which the biblical writers retrojected to the time of the conquest, Israel extended "from Dan to Beer-sheba," that is, from the southern wash of Mount Hermon in the north to the northern Negev in the south.

The Divided Monarchy: In fact, however, the historical Israel attained to the boundaries of the ideal Israel only for a brief period. The union of Israel and Judah did not survive the death of David's son Solomon (924 B.C.). The northern tribes refused to acknowledge the sovereignty of the king in Jerusalem, and Judah was left as a separate state. Nor were the two kingdoms together as extensive as the United Kingdom that preceded them. For only two short periods, during the reigns of Omri and Ahab in the first half of the ninth century B.C. and Jeroboam II a century later, did Israel expand to its Davidic-Solomonic borders to the north and east.

This history accounts for the ambivalence of the use "Israel" as a political designation in the historical books of the Bible. In the stories of the reigns of David and Solomon, when Israel and Judah were united under a single king, "Israel" is often used to refer to the larger nation (2 Sam. 8:15; 1 Kings 4:1). In the same materials, however, it can be used to designate the northern tribes as distinct from Judah (2 Sam. 19:41). In the account of the Divided Monarchy in 1 and 2 Kings "Israel" is ordinarily the Northern Kingdom as distinct from "Judah," the Southern Kingdom. Nevertheless, the ideal of a greater Israel persists in the literature after the account of the secession of the northern tribes, so that in 1 Kings 12:17, for example, we find reference to "the people of Israel who dwelt in the cities of Judah" (1 Kings 12:17). Even before the fall of Samaria (721 B.C.), therefore, "Israel" is sometimes used in reference to Judah (Isa. 1:3; 8:18), and after the destruction of the Northern Kingdom this usage becomes common (Ezek. 2:3).

The Idea of Israel: "Israel" is not only an ethnic and political designation in the Bible; it is also a central theological term. The idea of Israel as the chosen people of God pervaded the religious thought not only of the ancient Israelite community but of early Judaism and Christianity as well. We can discern two major phases in the early development of this idea.

First, there was the concept of Israel as the people chosen to live in the promised land. Fundamental to this concept was the notion that the land inhabited by the Israelite nation belonged to God. It was his land, and he chose one people to live in it to the exclusion of all others. This concept receives its primary articulation in the Hexateuchal narrative, i.e., the story that extends from Genesis through Joshua. There we are told that God summoned Abram to Canaan, promising that his descendants would take possession of the land and become a great nation there. From the twelve sons of Abram's grandson Jacob, whose name was also Israel, were descended twelve tribes. These "children of Israel" became enslaved in Egypt, but God rescued them, guided them through the desert, and brought them into Canaan. They conquered the land, eliminating its previous inhabitants, and settled in it, growing eventually into the great nation promised to Abram. This concept of Israel seems to have been a basic component of the theology of the pre-exilic community. Its most conspicuous feature is the centrality of the land.

Second was the concept of Israel as the people chosen to receive the Torah. This concept is expressed in the same biblical narrative, but in this case the climax of the story is the gift of the Torah at Sinai rather than the conquest of the land. In other words, our attention here is upon the Tetrateuchal narrative, i.e., the story that extends from Genesis through Numbers, and, more specifically, upon the Priestly materials ("P") within that narrative. God (*Elohim,* as he is usually called in this part of the story) is the universal creator, and it was his will that his human creatures should be blessed (Gen. 1:28). Because of their inclination towards error, however, it seemed impossible for human beings to live safely in the divinely created world. They tended to pervert the blessing into a curse. The divine solution was the election of one people through whom the other "families of the earth" could receive their blessing (cf. Gen. 12:3). God would give this people a set of instructions by which it would be possible for them to live safely in the world and receive the divine blessing as intended. This, then, was the reason for the call of Abram. From his grandson Jacob or Israel, the children of Israel were descended. After their escape from Egypt, they came to Mount Sinai, where God gave them the rules by which they were to lead their lives. This concept of Israel probably reflects the theology of the exilic (mid-sixth century B.C.) and postexilic (late sixth century and later) communities. Emphasis on the land, the chief characteristic of the pre-exilic concept (pre-586 B.C.), has been replaced by emphasis on the Torah.

Exilic and Postexilic Literature: A related idea, which receives its first clear expression in exilic literature, conceives of Israel as a vehicle by which the other nations would come to recognize and acknowledge the greatness of God. In the oracles of Ezekiel, for example, God explains his dealings with Israel as a means of vindicating himself in the sight of the nations (Ezek. 36: 22–23). Israel, he says, will suffer the calamity of exile, "and all the nations shall see my judgment which I have executed" (39:21; cf. v. 23). Also, however, Israel will be resanctified, and "the nations will know that I the Lord sanctify Israel" (37:28; cf. 36:36). In short, God's purpose in the destruction and restoration of Israel is to demonstrate his justice and power to the nations. "So I will show my greatness and my holiness and make myself known in the eyes of many nations. Then they will know that I am the Lord" (38:23).

The same idea is expressed in Deutero-Isaiah's presentation of Israel as "witnesses" to the incomparability of God (Isa. 43:10, 12; 44: 8). Eventually, we are told, the other nations will come to Israel in supplication, saying, "God is with you only, and there is no other, no god besides him" (45:14). This passage is sometimes cited as evidence that Deutero-Isaiah understood Israel to have a "mission to the Gentiles," whereby other nations were to be converted to the worship of God. The result envisioned, however, seems not to be the universal worship of God but rather the universal recognition of God's uniqueness. Accordingly, Israel's role is that of a witness, not a missionary.

Apocalyptic Judaism: In later Judaism the biblical concept of Israel as a people chosen by God to receive the Torah was combined with the apocalyptic expectation of the advent of the universal rule of God. The belief was that only when Israel was truly living according to the precepts of the Torah could the kingdom of God arrive. Apocalyptic groups dissented from the authority of those in power in Jerusalem, whom they regarded as corrupt and illegitimate. They believed themselves to be the true Israel and structured their lives accordingly in the conviction that by doing so they would make possible the final realization of the divine plan.

One such group was the Essene community at Qumran. They understood themselves as the "precious cornerstone" of Isa. 28:16, laid by God as "a sure foundation" (1QS 8.7–8). Their community organization into twelve tribes led by twelve tribal chiefs (1QSa 1.27–2.1), including both laity and priests, shows that they regarded themselves as the true Israel.

The Early Church: Likewise the early church, which also emerged from apocalyptic Judaism, understood itself as the legitimate heir to the ancient promises. Paul argued that the Jews had forfeited these promises, which had come to Abraham through faith, not the law (Rom. 4:13). Because "it is men of faith who are the [true] sons of Abraham" (Gal. 3:7), Christians, not Jews, could now claim to be descended from the Israelite patriarchs. The church was, in fact, "the twelve tribes in the Dispersion" (James 1: 1). It follows that the early Christian community, like the Qumran community, regarded itself as the true Israel, that is, "the Israel of God" (Gal. 6:16). Appropriating for the church language applicable to ancient Israel, the author of the First Letter of Peter addressed his audience as "a chosen race, a royal priesthood, a holy nation, God's own people" (1 Pet. 2:9).

Rabbinic Judaism: Paul, then, taught that the true Israel was descended from Abraham through faith, not the Mosaic law, which had served a temporary purpose that was now past (Gal. 3:17–26). By contrast, the Judaism of that time regarded the Torah as the one thing that distinguished Israel from the other nations. Although it was no longer possible to claim that the written Torah was the possession of Jews alone, this was still true of the oral Torah, which had been passed down alongside the written Torah and was now known and discussed by the rabbis. The oral Torah, though its authority was denied by the Sadducees, survived with the support of the Pharisees to find expression in the Mishnah, the Talmud, the midrashim, and other works based on them. There we find the rabbinic teaching that the Torah had been made available to the other nations, who were unwilling to live by such a restrictive code. The reason for Israel's special election, then, was precisely their willingness to accept and obey the Torah (*Abod. Zar.* 2b–3a; *Num. Rab.* 14:10; *Sipre Deut.* 343). ***See also*** Hebrews; Sources of the Pentateuch.

Bibliography

Danell, G. A. *Studies in the Name of Israel in the Old Testament*. Uppsala: Appelbergs boktryckeri, 1946.

de Vaux, R. *The Early History of Israel*. Philadelphia: Westminster, 1978.

Sandmel, S. *The Several Israels*. The James A. Gray Lectures, 1968. New York: Ktav, 1971.

P.K.M.

Israel, Kingdom of. ***See*** Samaria, District of.

Israelite, a descendant of Jacob. Before the Davidic empire split into two separate kingdoms in the tenth century B.C., the term "Israelite" signified every Hebrew. After that event, it properly connoted an Ephraimite as opposed to an inhabitant of Judah. The Israelite (i.e., the Northern) kingdom had its capital at Shechem, then at Tirzah, and finally at Samaria. The latter was destroyed by the Assyrians in 722 B.C., and Israelites were deported, only to become assimilated into the alien culture. Hopes that a remnant from the two kingdoms would some day come together again seem to have arisen in some circles (cf. Ezek. 37:15–22). In the NT, discussion took place over who actually could lay claim to the title "Israelite." Paul made a distinction between an Israelite by physical lineage and one forged through religious bonds (Rom. 2: 28–29). J.L.C.

Issachar (is'uh-kahr; Heb., "hire"). **1** The ninth son of Jacob, his fifth by Leah (Gen. 30: 14–18), and the eponymous ancestor of one of the twelve tribes of Israel. His name is evidently a verbal form from *sakar*, "hire, wages" (cf. Gen. 30:16–18). Issachar and his four sons immigrated to Egypt with Jacob's family (Gen. 46:13; Exod. 1:3; Num. 26:23–24; 1 Chron. 7:1). Jacob's blessing of Issachar seems to imply that the tribe would hire itself out to bear the burdens of others (Gen. 49:14–15). The tribe of Issachar was allotted the fertile territory between the eastern Jezreel Valley and the Jordan Valley (Josh. 19: 17–23), i.e., the region known today as the Heights of Issachar. Its allotment extended from Mt. Tabor on the north to the edge of the hill country of Samaria on the south and included such towns as Jezreel (the winter palace of Ahab and Jezebel), Kesullot (modern Iksal, in the Jezreel Valley below Nazareth), Shunem (modern Solem), the home of the elderly couple who were hospitable to the prophet Elisha (2 Kings 4), and En-gannim (evidently the Beth-haggan of 2 Kings 9:27 and the Gina of the El Amarna Letters; modern Jenin). Issachar was an important factor in the battle of Deborah and Barak (Judg. 5:15). In fact, the territory of Issachar was the scene of a number of battles in ancient times, including those of Gideon (Judg. 7) and Saul (1 Sam. 28). **2** The son of Obed-edom, a Korahite gatekeeper during the reign of David (1 Chron. 26:5). D.A.D.

Isshiah (i-shī'ah). **1** A descendant of Issachar (1 Chron. 7:3). **2** One of David's mighty men (1 Chron. 12:6). **3** A leading member of the descendants of Rehabiah, possibly descended from Moses (1 Chron. 24:21; see 23:15–17). **4** A son of Uzziel from the tribe of Levi (1 Chron. 24: 25). **5** A postexilic Israelite who divorced his foreign wife in response to Ezra's proclamation (Ezra 10:31).

issue, a term used in KJV to translate words referring to a male's bodily discharge (sore or venereal; Lev. 15:1–15), female bleeding (nonmenstrual; Lev. 15:25–30; Matt. 9:20), and a person's offspring (Gen. 48:6).

Italian Band. ***See*** Italy.

Italy, the boot-shaped peninsula extending about 750 miles from the Alps into the western part of the Mediterranean Sea. The name, according to ancient Greek writers, derives from a King Italos, who ruled the southern part in the late second millennium B.C. By the first century A.D., it had come to designate the entire peninsula.

Settled in remote antiquity by various tribes, Italy was in contact with Mycenaean traders in the second millennium B.C. By the middle of the first millennium, the north was organized into Etruscan city-states, while the south was so heavily colonized by Greeks that it eventually became known to the Romans as Magna Graecia ("Great Greece"). Through the three Punic Wars (264–146 B.C.), Rome mastered the entire peninsula and began its expansion throughout the Mediterranean.

The earliest account of Jews in Italy is 1 Maccabees 8, which recounts the accomplishments of the Romans and a treaty with Rome made by Judas Maccabeus ca. 160 B.C. His brother Jonathan renewed the treaty some years later (1 Macc.12:1–4), and Simon sent a third delegation in 139 B.C. after Jonathan's death (1 Macc. 14: 16–19, 24). After 63 B.C., Palestine was under either direct or indirect control of Rome.

By NT times, there were Jews living in Rome and elsewhere in Italy. Among those banished by a decree of Claudius (ca. A.D. 49) were Aquila and Priscilla (Acts 18:2). On his way to Rome, Paul sailed up the west coast from Rhegium to Puteoli, where he encountered fellow Christians, and others came out from Rome to welcome him along the Appian Way (Acts 27:1; 28:13–16).

"Those who come from Italy" sent greetings to the addressees of Hebrews (13:24). In Acts 10:1, Cornelius is identified as a centurion of the "Italian Cohort" (KJV: "centurion of the band called Italian"), stationed in Caesarea. ***See also*** Aquila; Claudius; Cornelius; Maccabees; Paul; Prisca, Priscilla; Puteoli; Rhegium; Roman Empire; Rome. C.H.M.

Ithai (ith'ī; Heb., abbreviation of "God is with me"; according to others, "God exists"), the son of the Benjaminite Ribai and one of David's mighty men (1 Chron. 11:31). His name is given as Ittai in 2 Sam. 23:29. ***See also*** Ittai.

Ithamar (ith'uh-mahr), the fourth and youngest son of Aaron (Exod. 6:23). Ithamar's priestly line continued to enjoy prominence, but not dominance, according to biblical writers, even after the fall of Jerusalem (1 Chron. 24:1–18). The two elder sons of Aaron died when presumptuously offering incense before the Lord, and the priestly succession thus devolved upon Eleazar and Ithamar (Lev. 10:1–7). Kohathites who carried the Ark were subservient to Eleazar; Gershonites and Merarites who performed more menial duties were subservient to Ithamar (Num. 4:1–33). The line of Eleazar is traced through Zadok, the line of Ithamar through Abiathar of Shiloh. Ezekiel recognized only the succession through Zadok, but the Chronicler recognized the validity of both priestly lines. ***See also*** Aaronites; Zadok. J.G.G.

Ithmah (ith'mah), a Moabite mercenary in David's employ (1 Chron. 11:46), one of the sixteen mighty men added by the Chronicler to David's thirty.

Ithnan (ith'nuhn), a city in the list of Canaanite cities assigned to Judah whose site in the south (Josh. 15:23) is as yet unidentified.

Ithra (ith'ruh), the father of Joab's cousin Amasa who served as chief of staff for Absalom in his rebellion against his father, David. Ithra is called an Israelite in 2 Sam. 17:25 (see RSV note), but an Ishmaelite in 1 Chron. 2:17, where the RSV translates his name as "Jether." ***See also*** Jether.

Ithran (ith'ruhn). **1** The son of Dishon and descendant of Seir the Horite (Gen. 36:26; 1 Chron. 1:41). **2** The son of Zophah; descendant of Asher (1 Chron. 7:37).

Ithream (ith'ree-uhm; Heb., "the kinsman is abundance"), the sixth son of David, born at Hebron by Eglah (2 Sam. 3:5; 1 Chron. 3:3).

Ithrite (ith'rīt), the designation of Ira and Gareb, two of David's "thirty" soldiers (2 Sam. 23:38; 1 Chron. 11:40). The word occurs as the name of a family listed in a genealogy and located in the town of Kiriath-jearim (1 Chron. 2:53). However, the name originally may have signified that David's two heroes were from the town of Jattir in the hill country of Judah (Josh. 15:48; 21:14).

Ittai (it'tī; Heb., "with God"?). **1** "The Gittite" who swore an oath of loyalty to David during Absalom's revolt (2 Sam. 15:19–23). He was a commander of one-third of David's army, thus ranking with Joab and his brother Abishai (2 Sam. 18:2–12). His loyalty to David is remarkable because he was a foreigner, only recently arrived in Judah. The epithet "the Gittite" indicates that he was from the Philistine city of Gath. **2** The son of Ribai of Gibeah in the territory of the tribe of Benjamin; he was one of David's "thirty" soldiers (2 Sam. 23:29; 1 Chron. 11:31). ***See also*** Philistines.

Ituraea (i'tōō-ree'ah), an area northeast of the Sea of Galilee. Mentioned only once in the Bible as being, together with Trachonitis, the territory ruled over by Philip, son of Herod the Great and brother of Herod Antipas (Luke 3:1), Ituraea was the region occupied by the tribe descended from Jetur, son of Ishmael (Gen. 25:13–16; 1 Chron. 1:31). In 1 Chron. 5:9–10 the tribe is described as the enemy of Reuben, Gad, and Manasseh, i.e., as seeking to penetrate Bashan and north Transjordan. The exact position of their homeland is not altogether clear, but it was probably the western slopes of Mt. Hermon, from which they expanded into the southern Beqa'a area between Lebanon and Anti-Lebanon. In the second century B.C. they dominated the entire Beqa'a region and were regarded by the Romans as skilled and dangerous marauders. Pompey subdued them in the mid-first century B.C., though they remained troublesome. After the death of their ruler Lysanias I in 36 B.C. the territory was divided and part was given to Cleopatra. In 20 B.C. the emperor Augustus transferred part, or perhaps all, of this area to Herod the Great. ***See also*** Bashan; Hermon; Herod; Philip; Syria; Trachonitis; Transjordan. D.B.

ivory, a costly material in ancient times, derived from the tusks of elephants (or sometimes hippopotami) and used for jewelry and various other luxury items. The Hebrew name, *shen*, means "tooth." The ivory used in the land of Canaan may have come from elephants of Syria, the so-called Asiatic elephant, which was well known in the upper Euphrates area until it became extinct in the first millennium B.C. Egyptian ivory was procured from African elephants. A third source of ivory for the ancient Near East was India. The use of ivory is attested as early as the Neolithic period (8000–4500 B.C.) in Egypt, where it was employed for making harpoons. In Palestine, from the Mesolithic period (12,000–8000 B.C.) on ivory is attested, and it becomes quite common during the Chalcolithic period (4500–3000 B.C.). Ivory was also in use in Mesopotamia during the early periods. In the excavations at Alalakh, in northern Syria, a storeroom full of elephant tusks was discovered in the eighteenth-century B.C. palace of King Yamrilim. Large collections of ivory wares dating from the Late Bronze Age (1550–1200 B.C.) have been found in excavations of Syrian and Palestinian sites.

At Ugarit ivories were discovered in the royal palace, including both figurines and ivory plaques carved in relief. At Megiddo similar ivories were found in the city's palace. In addi-

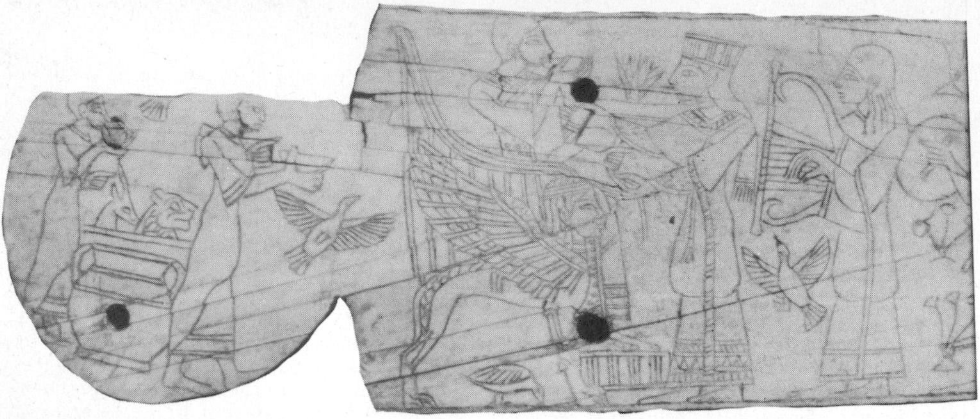

Detail of an ivory knife from Megiddo that depicts a scene from the royal court, twelfth century B.C.

tion, 380 items of ivory were found in a storeroom adjacent to the palace. One of the most famous pieces is an ivory knife engraved with a scene from the royal court, portraying the king seated on his throne, which is supported by cherubim. He is drinking from a cup while one girl (a princess?) presents him with a lotus flower and another girl serenades him with a harp. A procession is approaching the throne, headed by a soldier followed by two naked male captives and a horse-drawn chariot. From behind the throne two cup-bearers are bringing refreshments to the king. Such ivories aid in reconstructing everyday life in ancient Canaanite palaces.

During the Iron Age (1200–586 B.C.) ivory continued to enjoy popularity as a luxury item. The Assyrian kings often list ivory alongside the precious metals and stones received as tribute. Sennacherib (ca. 705–681 B.C.), for example, mentions tribute that included beds of ivory, chairs of ivory, and tusks. Collections of ivories from this period have been found in Egypt, Palestine, Syria, and Mesopotamia. Those of Nineveh, Arslan Tash, and Samaria are the most famous. The Samaria ivories are carved in high relief and exhibit a decorative repertoire taken from Egyptian art. They were probably carved by Phoenician or Syrian artisans. On the back they are inscribed with Hebrew letters, presumably to facilitate their mounting on furniture.

Ivory is mentioned a number of times in the OT. Solomon's fleet of ships, on its three-year voyages, brought back ivory along with gold, apes, peacocks, and other exotic items (1 Kings 10:22; 2 Chron. 9:21). Solomon had his "great throne" inlaid with ivory (1 Kings 10:18). "Palaces adorned with ivory" are mentioned in Ps. 45:8; and in Song of Sol. 5:14 the exquisite body of the lover is compared to polished ivory. Amos prophesies against the "palaces of ivory" of the Northern Kingdom (Amos 3:15); and he scornfully refers to the "beds of ivory" (i.e., beds inlaid with ivory) upon which the aristocratic women of Samaria lie (6:4). ***See also*** Amos, The Book of; Samaria, City of.

D.A.D.

Izhar (iz'hahr; Heb., "fresh [olive] oil"). **1** The son of Kohath and grandson of Levi (Exod. 6:18) and the ancestral head of one of the major subdivisions of the Kohathite clan of Levites, the Izharites (Num. 3:27). He was the father of Korah, the leader of the wilderness rebellion against Moses and Aaron (Num. 16:1). **2** The son of Ashur and Helah; a descendant of Judah (1 Chron. 4:7).

Opposite: Judas's kiss of betrayal (Matt. 26:49); fresco at the fourteenth-century St. Clement Church, Ohrid, Yugoslavia.

J

J, the siglum for the Yahwist (from the German form *Jahvist),* one of the sources of the material in the Pentateuch. ***See also*** Sources of the Pentateuch; Yahwist.

Jaazaniah (jay-az-uh-nī'uh; Heb., "the Lord hears"). **1** The son of Maacathi, or the Maacathite who remained with Gedaliah, the governor of Judah, after the destruction of Jerusalem by the Babylonians (2 Kings 25:23; Jer. 40:8). **2** The son of Jeremiah (not the prophet) who was a Rechabite whose religious principles were tested by the prophet Jeremiah (Jer. 35:3). **3** The son of Shaphan; he appears in Ezekiel's vision of the idolatrous elders in the Temple (Ezek. 8:11). **4** The son of Azzur; one of the twenty-five evil leaders in another of Ezekiel's visions (Ezek. 11: 1).

Jabal (jay'buhl), the first son of Lamech by Adah. According to the tradition preserved in Gen. 4:20, Jabal is credited with being the founder (or "culture hero") of nomadism in the seventh generation after Adam. With his brothers, Jubal and Tubal-cain, he was thus considered an originator of ancient social patterns. The meaning of the name is not certain, although it may derive from a Semitic word indicating "ram."

Jabbok (jab'buhk), modern Nahr es-Zerqa (Arabic, "the blue river"), one of the four major eastern tributaries of the Jordan. The Jabbok rises in Amman, flows northeast to modern Zerqa, and then west until it joins the Jordan twenty-five miles north of the Dead Sea. In Gen. 32:22–32 Jacob fights with his divine adversary (who in an older form of the story may have been the river demon) at Penuel on the Jabbok; there is word play here on the names: Jacob (Heb. *y'aqōb)* wrestled *(wayyē'ābēq)* at the Jabbok *(yabbōq).* The Jabbok was a natural boundary, forming a border of Sihon's kingdom (Num. 21:24; Josh. 12:2; Judg. 11:13, 22), the Ammonites (Num. 21: 24; Deut. 2:37; 3:16; Josh. 12:2), and Reuben and Gad (Deut. 3:16). It was a thoroughfare from the Jordan Valley to the Transjordanian plateau; cf. Judg. 8:4–9, where Gideon pursued the Midianites up the Jabbok passing Succoth and Penuel. Other sites on the Jabbok and its tributaries are Gerasa (modern Jerash), Adam, and Tulul edh-Dhahab. M.D.C.

Jabesh, Jabesh-gilead (jay'besh, jay'besh gil'ee-ad; Heb., "dried"). **1** The father of King Shallum of Israel (2 Kings 15:10, 13–14). The name may, however, represent a place rather than a person, meaning that Shallum's family lived at Jabesh.

2 A town east of the Jordan River, frequently called Jabesh-gilead. The name is evidently related to that of the Wadi Yabis, rising at Mihna north of Ajlun in the Gilead highlands. Scholars now usually accept the identification with the joint site of modern Tell el-Meqbereh (apparently the residential area) and Tell Abu Kharaz (a powerful fortress overlooking it) on the north bank of the *wadi* where it enters the Jordan Valley about five miles (8 km.) south of Pella. Others, however, place it at Tell el-Maqlub somewhat further up the valley on the basis of Eusebius' statement that in the early fourth-century A.D. Jabesh-gilead was still a great city "at the sixth milestone from the city of Pella" on the road to Gerasa.

Jabesh-gilead first appears in Israelite history in the strange story of how all the men and married women were killed because no one from the town had come to the assembly at Mizpah, but four hundred young virgins were given to the men of Benjamin (Judg. 21:8–15). Later, when Nahash the Ammonite threatened to gouge out the right eye of every man in Jabesh-gilead, Saul, who had only recently been anointed king, came to their rescue and utterly routed the Ammonites. This victory is said to have convinced even his detractors that he was fit to rule Israel (1 Sam. 11). The people of Jabesh-gilead remained profoundly grateful and when, some years later, Saul and his sons died fighting against the Philistines on Mt. Gilboa, "all the valiant men arose, and went all night" to rescue their bodies from the walls of Beth-shan, where the victorious Philistines had triumphantly hung them. The bodies were then ceremonially burned and the bones buried under a tamarisk tree (1 Sam. 31:8–13). As soon as he heard of this, David, now accepted as king in Judah, with his usual generosity sent messengers praising the men of Jabesh for what they had done for his erstwhile enemy (2 Sam. 2:4–7). He also indicated that he had now become king in Saul's place, but it seems probable that their strong loyalty to the family of Saul kept the people of Jabesh faithful to Saul's ineffective son Ishbosheth, whom Abner had made king over Gilead and northern Palestine (2 Sam. 2:8–10). ***See also*** Abner; Ammonites; Benjamin; David; Gerasa; Gilboa; Mizpah; Nahash; Pella; Philistines; Saul. D.B.

Jabin (jay'bin), the king of the Canaanites (ca. 1100 B.C.), who fought against the Israelites according to Joshua 11 and Judges 4. In Joshua 11, Jabin, who led a coalition of Canaanite petty princes, was defeated at the Waters of Merom and was executed (Josh. 11:10). In Judges 4:2, Jabin is called "king of Canaan who reigned in Hazor" and his army commander Sisera was defeated by the Hebrew leaders Deborah and Barak near the Brook Kishon (cf. Ps. 83:9). Scholars debate whether these two accounts from Joshua and Judges refer to a single battle, whether the same Jabin is mentioned in both stories, and whether the name Jabin is original to the traditions of both books. M.Z.B.

Jabneel (jab'nay-el; Heb., "God is builder"). **1** A city in northwest Judah (Josh. 15:11). Jabneel is the Jabneh of 2 Chron. 26:6 and Jamnia of the Apocrypha (1 Macc. 4:15; 5:58; 2 Macc. 12:8, 9). This was the site of the Jamnia council of A.D. 90. It is believed by some that at this council the Jewish Sanhedrin established the canon of Hebrew Scriptures. **2** A northern border city of the tribal allotment of Naphtali, west of the south end of the Sea of Galilee (Josh. 19:33).

S.B.R.

Jachin (jay'kin; Heb., "he establishes"). **1** The son of Simeon (Gen. 46:10; Exod. 6:15) and ancestor of the "Jachinite family" (Num. 26:12). **2** A priest (1 Chron. 24:17; cf. 9:10; Neh. 11:10). **3** The name of the pillar on the right of the entrance to the Temple in Jerusalem. ***See also*** Jachin and Boaz.

Jachin (jay'kin) **and Boaz** (boh'az), the names of the pillars standing to the right and left of the entrance to the Temple in Jerusalem (1 Kings 7: 21; 2 Chron. 3:15–17). These were cast of bronze/copper. According to 1 Kings 7:15 and Jer. 52:21 each pillar stood 18 cubits high (ca. 26.5 feet), had a circumference of 12 cubits (ca. 17.5 feet), and was hollow, with a thickness of 4 fingers (ca. 3 inches). Each was surmounted by a bowl-shaped capital 5 cubits high (ca. 7.5 feet), ornamented with checkerwork, wreathed with chainwork, and bedecked with lily leaves 4 cubits high (ca. 6 feet). Varying dimensions for the height of the pillars and of the capitals are provided in 2 Chron. 3:15 and 2 Kings 25:17, respectively. From the description in 1 Kings 7:21 the location of the pillars is not entirely clear, but according to 2 Chron. 3:15 they were free-standing at the Temple's entrance. Similar items flanking temple entrances have been noted at Khorsabad, are graphically depicted on coins from Cyprus, Sardis, Pergamum, and Sidon, on a clay model of a temple from Idalion (Cyprus), on a relief from Quyunjiq, and are described by Herodotus as having flanked the entrance to the sanctuary of Herakles at Tyre. The presence of such pillars may also be indicated by pillar bases at the entrances of the temples at Canaanite Hazor and Tell Tainat.

The function these pillars may have served is uncertain, but the suggestion of the scholar W. Robertson Smith that these may have been fire altars, i.e., that the bowl-shaped capitals served as huge cressets in which the fat of sacrificial animals was burned, finds support in the employment of the term *gullot* (Heb.) to designate the bowl-shaped capitals (1 Kings 7:41), for the noun in singular number, *gullah*, denotes the bowl atop the lampstand in Zechariah's vision (Zech. 4:2).

The meaning of the name "Jachin" is "he establishes," but that of Boaz, which is the same as that of David's great-grandfather (Ruth 4:17, 21–22), is unknown.

At the time of the destruction of Jerusalem in 586 B.C., the pillars were dismantled, and, along with other metal objects from the Temple, were removed as booty to Babylon (2 Kings 25:13).

S.G.

jackal (*Canis aureus*; Heb. *tannoth*), a member of the dog family similar in looks to the wolf, though considerably smaller in size, with a relatively shorter tail and smaller ears. A nocturnal carrion eater, the jackal also devours fruit and crops and kills chickens and other small animals. Its distribution range includes southeast Europe, southern Asia and northern Africa and it is still fairly common in Palestine and Jordan today. Its preference for a dry habitat is alluded to in Isa. 35:7 and 43:20. Numerous passages in the OT refer to the jackal prowling around settlements and in Mic. 1:8 its characteristic wailing howl is mentioned. According to Neh. 2:13 a well named after the jackal existed outside Jerusalem. Its lair could symbolize a destroyed or deserted settlement (Jer. 9:11). I.U.K.

Jacob (Heb., "heel grabber" [Gen. 25:26] or "supplanter" [Gen. 27:36]). **1** An OT patriarch. He is the brother of Esau, the son of Isaac and Rebekah, the father of Dinah and of twelve sons whose names are those of tribes. Jacob's own name was changed to "Israel" (Gen. 32:28; 35: 10). The name "Jacob" was probably a shortened form of Jacob-el (Heb., "may God supplant") and hence originally bore witness to a divine, rather than a human, action. Jacob not only embodies and represents the nation, Israel, but also typifies the settler-farmer, the trickster, the reverent worshiper of God, the man of gallantry, the successful emigré and herder, the penitent brother, and the benevolent father.

Because the traditions concerning Jacob feature sites in northern Israel (Bethel, Shechem) and in northern Transjordan (Mahanaim, Penuel), it is generally agreed that Jacob was a northerner. Many authorities favor placing Jacob in the Middle Bronze Age (ca. 1950–1550 B.C.) and see an association between Jacob and the Hyksos movement in Egypt (ca. 1720–1570 B.C.). Because of the Aramaean presence in northern Mesopotamia, other authorities are inclined to place the historic Jacob at the beginning of the early Iron Age (ca. 1200–900 B.C.) when a sizable incursion of Aramaeans into northern Mesopotamia took place. Regardless of date, the diversity of style in the traditions about Jacob give evidence of their having come into being over a long period of time.

Pattern of Arrangement of the Jacob Traditions: Recent investigations, however, have brought to light the fact that these traditions have been arranged with an order and sophistication previously unsuspected, in that the first element corresponds to the last, the second element to the second from last, etc. This pattern of arrangement has been variously called concentric, mirrorlike, or chiastic (from the Greek letter chi, which is shaped like an X).

Genealogical framework (Gen. 25:1–11)

A. Death of Abraham; burial by two sons (Isaac, Ishmael); genealogy and death of Ishmael; birth and youth of Esau and Jacob (Gen. 25:12–34)

B. Regional strife (in southern Israel): Isaac vs. the Philistines; honorable covenant (chap. 26)

C. Beginnings of fraternal strife in Cisjordan (Jacob vs. Esau: settler-farmer vs. hunter); Isaac blesses Jacob not Esau (chap. 27)

D. Departure of Jacob alone to northeast with theophany enroute at Bethel (chap. 28)

E. Arrival alone at the northeast (Haran in Upper Mesopotamia); marriage to Leah and Rachel; acquisition and naming of sons by Leah; commencement of strife with Laban (chap. 29)

F. Acquisition and naming of sons by handmaidens and of first son (Joseph) by Rachel (Gen. 30:1–24)

F′ Preparation to leave the northeast; acquisition of herds (Gen. 30:25–43)

E′ Departure from the northeast with flocks, progeny, and two wives; conclusion of strife with Laban in a covenant in Gilead (Gen. 31:1–32:2)

D′ Return from the northeast with theophany enroute at Penuel; change of name to Israel (Gen. 32:3–32)

C′ Conclusion of fraternal strife in Transjordan (Jacob vs. Esau: herder vs. herder); Jacob blesses Esau (Gen. 33:1–17)

B′ Regional strife (in northern Israel): Jacob's sons vs. Shechemites; deceitful covenant; putting away of foreign gods (Gen. 33:18–35:5); theophany at Bethel; change of name to Israel (Gen. 35:6–7, 9–15); combines parts of E and E′

A′ Birth of second son by Rachel (Benjamin); death of Rachel; genealogy of Israel; death of Isaac; burial by two sons (Esau, Jacob; Gen. 35:8, 16–29)

Genealogical framework (chap. 36)

Because the Priestly material in 35:6–7, 9–15 is disruptive of the chiastic pattern, it is clear that the one responsible for the chiastic ar-

In his dream (Gen. 28:12) Jacob sees angels ascending and descending a ladder to heaven; from the twelfth-century Lambeth Bible. (The binding of Isaac appears on the right.)

rangement (possibly the one who combined the Yahwistic and Elohistic sources) worked independently from the Priestly source. It is widely agreed that the genealogical relationship of Jacob to his sons is a literary construct, but one that accurately reflects tribal, sociological realities; the genealogical relationship to Abraham and Isaac is also a literary construct but of less certain sociological significance.

Theologically Jacob, like Abraham and Isaac, is the recipient of the divine promise of land and plentiful progeny (Gen. 28:13–15). Divine manifestations are made to Jacob (Gen. 28:10–22; 32:3–22) despite the fact that he engages in deception (Gen. 27). This biblical agent of blessing (see Gen. 48–49), like others, is not flawless. Jacob's death and burial is described in Gen. 49:28–50:14.

2 The father of Joseph, the husband of Mary (Matt. 1:15–16). ***See also*** Esau; Genesis; Isaac; Israel; Patriarch; Sources of the Pentateuch.

Bibliography

Brueggemann, Walter. *Genesis.* Atlanta, GA: John Knox, 1982.

Fishbane, Michael. "Genesis 25:19–35:22: The Jacob Cycle." In *Text and Texture: Close Readings of Selected Biblical Texts.* New York: Schocken, 1979. Pp. 40–62.

Gammie, John G. "Theological Interpretation by Way of Literary and Tradition Analysis: Genesis 25–36." In *Encounter With the Text.* Edited by Martin J. Buss. Philadelphia: Fortress, 1979. Pp. 117–134.

J.G.G.

Jacob, the blessing of, the title accorded the poem of Gen. 49:1–27; it derives from the poem's postscript, Gen. 49:28b. Ostensibly the death-bed observations in Egypt of Jacob-Israel regarding his sons, the evaluations are of the Israelite tribes as they were settled in Canaan (Gen. 49:28a). The figure through whom the poet speaks, the patriarch Jacob, who is now at the point of death, is the eponymous ancestor of the federated tribes of Israel. Of the component poems, those on Judah (Gen. 49:8–12) and Joseph (Gen. 49:22–26) predominate and pertain to the kingdoms of Judah and Israel. The poem was composed, then, not much earlier than the inauguration of the Divided Monarchy, and Jacob's evaluations of the tribes have reference to their roles in the disintegration of the federation. Because Joseph alone is unequivocally blessed, the perspective of the poet is that of one sympathetic to the Northern Kingdom. ***See also*** Poetry. S.G.

Jacob's Well, the setting for Jesus' encounter with a Samaritan woman in John 4. Of considerable depth, its still waters contrasted with Jesus' "living [i.e., flowing or bubbling] water . . . welling up to eternal life" (John 4:14). Its location is fixed by reference in v. 20 to "this mountain," Gerizim, revered by Samaritans, and in v. 5 to the field Jacob gave Joseph (Gen. 33:18–20 with 48:22; see the RSV margin: "*Shekem*, shoulder"). Shechem is thus the correct context; Sychar in v. 5 is probably a corrupted form of Shechem.

Early Christian tradition correctly connected Jacob's Well to one a quarter-mile southeast of ancient Shechem's edge, now sheltered in the old crypt beneath the unfinished Greek Orthodox church in modern Balatah. Measurements of its depth to the water table fluctuate between 105 and 75 feet. Much of the shaft was hewn through the soft chalk of the valley floor. From it one could see the ruined Samaritan sanctuary on the spur of Gerizim now called Tell er-Ras, 1,950 feet above it. ***See also*** Gerizim; Samaritans; Shechem; Sychar. E.F.C.

Jael (jay'el; Heb., "mountain goat"), the wife of Heber the Kenite, who is celebrated in the Song of Deborah (Judges 5) and in the prose version of Judges 4 for her part in the aftermath of the miraculous victory of the Israelite militia over a superior Canaanite army during the period of the judges. Since the Kenites, a semi-nomadic group with longstanding ties with the Israelites, evidently were not threatened by Canaanite expansionism and thus were on good terms with the chief Canaanite king in the north, Jabin of Hazor (Judg. 4:17), the Canaanite general Sisera sought refuge among them when he fled following the defeat of his forces. Jael offered him refreshment and then, probably while he rested, smote him with a tent peg. As a heroine acting on behalf of the Israelites, Jael is an example of the way in which, during this pioneering period, unlikely figures served the Israelite cause. ***See also*** Deborah. C.L.M.

Jah (yah), a shortened, archaic form of the sacred name of God (KJV, Ps. 68:4). It is also found in theophoric names, as Jerem*iah*, Isa*iah*, where the person's name contains the divine name.

Jahath (jay'hath). **1** A Levite, the son of Gershom and father of Shimei (1 Chron. 6:43). **2** A Levite, the son of Libni (Ladan) and grandson of Gershom (1 Chron. 6:20); but elsewhere called Jehiel (1 Chron. 23:7). **3** A Levite, the son of Shimei and grandson of Gershom (1 Chron. 23:10–11). Because of the repetition of names in these lists it is possible that the names have become disordered through scribal errors and that these all represent the same person. **4** A Levite member of the Shelomoth family of the Izharite clan (1 Chron. 24:22). **5** A Levite of the clan of Merari who helped repair the Temple during King Josiah's reforms (ca. 621 B.C.; 2 Chron. 34:12). **6** A descendant of Judah of the clan of the Zorathites (1 Chron. 4:2). D.R.B.

Jahaz (jay'haz), a Moabite city that had been taken by the Amorite king Sihon and made a part of his kingdom. It was the site of the battle between the Amorites and the Israelites in which Sihon was killed and the Israelites took possession of a large part of the land east of the Jordan (Num. 21:23–26). The city was among those assigned to the tribe of Reuben and later given to the Merarite clan of Levites (Josh. 13:18; 21:36; called Jahzah in 1 Chron. 6:78). It appears in the Mesha inscription (Moabite Stone) as being fortified by Israel but captured by the Moabite king Mesha and two hundred men (ca. 850 B.C.; see 2 Kings 3:4–5). It was still in Moabite hands in the time of Isaiah (ca. 742–701 B.C.; Isa. 15:4; Jer. 48:34). From the place names that occur with Jahaz, one can infer that it was located in the vicinity of Heshbon northeast of the Dead Sea. It has sometimes been identified as modern Khirbet el-Medeiyina about eleven miles northeast of Heshbon, although the site is not certain. ***See also*** Amorites; Moab; Moabite Stone, The. D.R.B.

Jahaziel (ja-hay'zī-el; Heb., "El [God] sees"). **1** One of Saul's kinsmen who joined David's fighting men at Ziklag (1 Chron. 12:4). **2** A priest who was appointed by King David as musician to celebrate the arrival of the Ark of the Covenant at the tabernacle in Jerusalem (1 Chron. 16:6). **3** A Levite, the third son of Hebron of the clan of Kohath (1 Chron. 23:19). **4** A Levite who was a descendant of Asaph. He prophesied to King Jehoshaphat (ca. 874–850 B.C.) that he would not need to fight the invading allied armies of Edom, Moab, and Ammon because God would fight for him. The armies were destroyed in the Valley of Beracah after they began fighting with each

other (2 Chron. 20:1–30). **5** The father of an unnamed (Ben-jahaziel?) member of the clan of Shecaniah who returned with Ezra from the Babylonian captivity (Ezra 8:5). ***See also*** Berachah.
D.R.B.

Jahweh, an alternate transcription of Yahweh, the unpronounced name of God. ***See also*** God.

Jair (jay-eer'). **1** A son of the tribe of Manasseh who conquered the region of Argob in Gilead (Num. 32:41; Deut. 3:14). The captured cities were called Havvoth-jair, and were sixty in number (Josh. 13:30; 1 Kings 4:13). In 1 Chron. 2:22, Segub of Judah is the father of Jair and his mother is from Manasseh. Possibly, one of the descendants of Jair is appointed David's priest (2 Sam. 20:26). **2** According to another tradition (Judg. 10:3–4), a judge, also of Gilead, whose thirty sons possessed thirty cities, also called Havvoth-jair. **3** The father of Mordecai, a descendant of King Saul (Esther 2:5; see 1 Sam. 9:1). **4** The father of Elhanan (2 Sam. 21:19; 1 Chron. 20:5). ***See also*** Judges, The Book of.
J.U.

Jairus, the synagogue ruler who fell before the feet of Jesus and begged him to heal his only daughter who was at the point of death. When it was learned that the daughter had already died, Jairus was advised not to trouble Jesus further. Jesus encouraged Jairus with the words, "Do not fear, only believe," in contrast to the mourners whose lack of faith in Jesus led to derisive laughter. Jesus, by raising the young girl, manifested his power to overcome death (Mark 5:21–43; Luke 8:40–56).

Jesus raising Jairus's daughter (Mark 5:21–43); from a fourth-century sarcophagus, Rome.

Jalam (jay'luhm), the son of Esau and Oholibamah the Hivite. He was a clan chieftain of the Edomites (Gen. 36:5, 18).

James, the English equivalent of the Greek *Jacobus*, apparently a common name in the first century. **1** James, the son of Zebedee (Matt. 4:21; 10:2; Mark 1:19; 3:17) and brother of John (Matt. 17:1; Mark 3:17; 5:37; Acts 12:2), with whom he was called by Jesus to be one of the Twelve (Matt. 4:21; Mark 1:19–20; Luke 5:10–11). Jesus nicknamed James and John "Boanerges," meaning "sons of thunder" (Mark 3:17). The two are prominent in the various lists of the Twelve (Matt. 10:2–4; Mark 3:16–19; Luke 6:14–16; Acts 1:13). With Peter, they were present when Jesus raised Jairus's daughter (Mark 5:37; Luke 8:51), at the transfiguration (Matt. 17:1; Mark 9:2; Luke 9:28), and in the Garden of Gethsemane (Matt. 26:37; Mark 14:33). The brothers (or their mother) request special places beside Jesus at the time of the messianic kingdom (Matt. 20:20–23; Mark 10:35–40). They are clearly very close associates of Jesus. Acts 12:2 reports James's martyrdom by decapitation at the command of Herod Agrippa I. **2** James, the son of Alphaeus. Identified in the apostolic lists as one of the Twelve (Matt. 10:3; Mark 3:18; Luke 6:15; Acts 1:13), little else is known about him. He is sometimes identified with the "James the younger" of Mark 15:40. **3** James, the brother of Jesus. The relationship of Jesus to "the brothers of the Lord" (1 Cor. 9:5; cf. Matt. 13:55; Mark 6:3; Acts 1:14; Gal. 1:19) is much debated. Possibilities include literal brothers (or half-brothers or stepbrothers) of Jesus, more distant relations of Jesus (e.g., cousins), or close friends and associates of Jesus. Though apparently not followers during Jesus' ministry (Matt. 12:46–50; Mark 3:31–35; Luke 8:19–21; John 7:3–5), the brothers are reportedly with the Twelve and others after Jesus' resurrection and ascension (Acts 1:14), and James is identified as one to whom Jesus appeared (1 Cor. 15:7). Eventually, James emerges as the recognized successor (along with the elders) to the leadership role originally exercised by Peter and the apostles (Acts 15 and following). Paul acknowledges James's role of leadership (Gal. 2:1–12), and Acts 15 reports his persuasive defense of the Gentile mission. Both the Jewish historian Josephus and the Christian Hegesippus (according to the fourth century church historian Eusebius) report that James was put to death by the priestly authorities in Jerusalem a few years before the destruction of the Temple in A.D. 70. **4** James, the father (KJV: "brother") of Judas (one of the Twelve; Luke 6:16), otherwise apparently not mentioned in the NT. ***See also*** Agrippa I; Alphaeus; Apostle; Boanerges; Disciple; Jacob; John the Apostle; Judas; Twelve, The; Zebedee.
P.L.S.

James, the Letter of, the first of the "catholic" or "general" Epistles in the NT. The Letter, addressed to "the twelve tribes in the dispersion" (1:1), is intended as a response to the problems of the church at large. The primary recipients appear to be Jewish Christians.

Form and Content: Although it has the common

epistolary introduction (1:1), the book lacks the other characteristics of an epistle. It is composed primarily of self-contained sections that appear to be connected only loosely by catchwords (e.g., 1:4–5). Little sequence or development can be detected, as the author speaks authoritatively on a variety of subjects. The "epistle" is similar in form to such Jewish documents as Proverbs, Ecclesiasticus, and *The Testaments of the Twelve Patriarchs*. It is also similar to the Sermon on the Mount at significant points (cf. e.g., Matt. 5:33; James 5:12).

OUTLINE OF CONTENTS

The Letter of James

I. Epistolary introduction (1:1)
II. Introduction of major themes (1:2–27)
  A. Testing, wisdom, wealth (1:2–11)
  B. Testing, speech, good deeds (1:12–27)
III. Neighbor love (2:1–26)
  A. Impartiality (2:1–13)
  B. Compassion (2:14–26)
IV. Proper speech (3:1–12)
V. On envy (3:13–4:12)
  A. Earthly and heavenly wisdom (3:13–18)
  B. Worldly desire (4:1–10)
  C. Slanderous speech (4:11–12)
VI. Testing and wealth (4:13–5:6)
VII. Patience and prayer (5:7–20)

Several recurring themes within the epistle suggest that the author has provided more than a random collection of exhortations. The themes of testing, wisdom, wealth, and generosity, which are introduced in the first chapter, are developed in the remainder of the book. What holds the disparate chapters together is the author's intention to encourage an emphasis on deeds or "works," whereby one becomes a "doer of the word" (1:22) and "perfect and complete" (1:4).

The works envisioned in James primarily involve social obligations within the community. Christian behavior is demonstrated in the keeping of the law (4:11), which is known also as the "perfect law of liberty" (1:25) and the "royal law" (2:8). The law that Christians keep is the fulfillment of the love command, "You shall love your neighbor as yourself" (2:8), not the ritual requirements of the OT. Observance of the love command precludes the show of partiality (2:1–13), lack of compassion on the poor (2:14–26), and slanderous speech against a brother (4:11–12; cf. 3:1–12). "Pure religion" involves concern for the helpless (1:27). Christian behavior includes a pattern of life that is not controlled by desire (4:13–5:6) or worldliness (4:1–6) but that manifests submission to God (4:7–10; 5:7–11).

The apparent sharp contrast between James and Paul on the question of faith and works (James 2:24; cf. Rom. 3:28) suggests that James was written in direct opposition to Paul. The language in Paul and James is so similar that some relation between the two writers is probable. The "works of the law," against which Paul argues, however, include primarily the ritual requirements such as circumcision, while the "works" insisted upon by James are deeds of compassion. Furthermore, James appears to have a more "static" concept of "faith" than does Paul; it is a content rather than an act of trust (e.g., 2:19). Thus, James is not to be taken as a direct polemic against Paul but against a misuse of Paul's teaching on justification by faith. The insistence in James on deeds of compassion and on the love commandment bears a close resemblance to the teaching of Jesus, particularly in the Gospel of Matthew, and to the exhortations of Paul (e.g., Rom. 12:9–13).

Authorship: The author identifies himself only as "James, a servant of God and of the Lord Jesus Christ" (1:1). The traditional view is that the author is James, the brother of Jesus. Indeed, the book apparently purports to be written by the brother of Jesus, inasmuch as only one James in the latter part of the first century was of such stature as to speak with authority without further identification. Nevertheless, serious difficulties with the traditional view have been raised. The excellent Greek of the epistle has been mentioned as an argument against Jesus' brother as the author who would not be likely to have had the kind of education presumed by such stylistic skill. Furthermore, the fact that 2:14–26 appears to be a reaction to an abuse of Paul's Letters poses difficulties for the traditonal view, inasmuch as James's death prior to A.D. 66 would allow little time for the collection and use of Paul's Letters. In addition, the debate within the ancient church regarding authorship is an argument against authorship by the brother of Jesus. While none of these objections against the traditional view is conclusive, collectively they make this view improbable. The epistle is probably a collection of exhortations preserved in Palestinian Christianity under the name of the brother of Jesus.

Little can be inferred about the situation of the original readers. The author's focus on the themes of poverty, generosity, and worldly desires may suggest that the book was addressed to communities that were experiencing severe economic difficulties. ***See also*** Faith; General Letters; James; Justification; Law; Love; Poor; Religion, Religious; Tongue; Wealth; Wisdom.

J.W.T.

Jamin (jay'min; Heb., either "right-hand" or "south" [on the right facing east]). **1** A son of Simeon who went with Jacob to Egypt (Gen. 46:10); he became the head of the clan of the Jaminites who left Egypt with Moses (Exod. 6:15; Num. 26:12). **2** The son of Ram, a descendant of Judah (1 Chron. 2:27). **3** A son of Simeon (1 Chron. 4:24). **4** One, probably a Levite, who explained to the people the law read by Ezra (Neh. 8:7).

Japheth (jay'feth), one of the three sons of Noah (Gen. 5:32; 6:10; 7:13; 9:18, 23, 27; 1 Chron. 1:4), evidently either the youngest (he is normally listed third) or the second son (cf. Gen. 9:22, 24). According to the Table of Nations in Genesis 10, Japheth was the ancestor of a number of widespread ethnic groups known to ancient Israel, including: Gomer (the Cimmerians, who inhabited the Black Sea region, and later, Asia Minor; perhaps related to the Scythians); Magog (possibly the Scythians); Madai (the Medes of the Iranian Plateau); Javan (the Ionians, representing the Hellenic group); Tubal and Meshech (in Akkadian, Tabal and Mushku, two peoples of Asia Minor); Tiras (often identified with the Etruscans, but this is uncertain); Ashkenaz (the Ashguza of Assyrian inscriptions, a Scythian country); Riphath (unknown); Togarmah (Hittite Tagarma, between Asia Minor and the Upper Euphrates); Elishah (Cyprus); Tarshish (the identification of this famous toponym is disputed); Kittim (the Cretians, or a Hellenic people on Cyprus); and the Dodamin (possibly to be read "Rodanim," referring to the inhabitants of Rhodes). ***See also*** Noah. D.A.D.

Japhia (juh-fī'uh). **1** A king of Lachish in southern Judea, allied against Gibeon (Josh. 10:3), and executed by Joshua at a Makkedah cave (vv. 22–26). **2** A son of David (2 Sam. 5:15; 1 Chron. 3:7 14:6). **3** A town on the southern edge of the territory of Zebulun (Josh. 19:12), a short distance southwest of the Nazareth of Jesus' day.

Jareb (jay'reb), an Assyrian king. References to a King Jareb (KJV: Hos. 5:13; 10:6) are now usually understood as a Hebrew form of the standard Assyrian title *malku rabu*, known also in Aramaic, which means "great king," although other translations (e.g., "patron") are possible. The prophet refers thus to an Assyrian king of the second half of the eighth century B.C., perhaps Tiglath-pileser III.

Jarmuth (jahr'muhth; Heb., "a height"). **1** A city belonging to the tribe of Judah formerly controlled by the Amorites whose king was killed and the city taken by Joshua (Josh. 10:3–23; 12:11; 15:35; Neh. 11:29). It is probably modern Khirbet Yarmuk, ca. eight miles from Beit Jibrîn, south of Beth-shemesh. **2** A levitical city located in the tribal area of Issachar (Josh. 21:29). The archaeological remains from this site are predominantly Early Bronze Age (ca. 3000–2000 B.C.).

Jashar (jah'sher; Heb., "upright, righteous"; KJV: "Jasher"), **the Book of,** a source apparently containing heroic songs, cited twice in the OT: in the account of Joshua's battle at Gibeon, when "the sun stood still" (Josh. 10:13), and again in David's lamentation for Saul and Jonathan (2 Sam. 1:18). A third possible citation from this source is 1 Kings 8:12–13, where the Septuagint (LXX) adds, "is it not written in the book of songs," a reading that is perhaps due to a simple transposition of two Hebrew consonants. The nature of the "book" has been a matter of discussion from pre-Christian times. It was apparently a collection of archaic poetry which, though well known in ancient Israel, has not survived, perhaps because it was transmitted primarily in oral form by professional singers. D.L.C.

Jashobeam (juh-shoh'bee-uhm; Heb., "the people will return"). **1** The son of Zabdiel the Hachmonite. He was the commander of David's elite group of thirty fighting men (1 Chron. 11:11), a position apparently also held at one time by Abishai and Amasai (1 Chron. 11:20; 12:18). Jashobeam is credited with killing three hundred men in one battle and later became the commander of a division of twenty-four thousand men under King David (1 Chron. 27:2). Some scholars understand Josheb-basshebeth the Tahchemonite as a textual variant of the same name (2 Sam. 23:8), while others think he is an entirely different member of David's group. **2** A Levite of the clan of Korah who joined David's fighting men at Ziklag (1 Chron. 12:6); he may be the same as 1. D.R.B.

Jason (jay'suhn), a famous Greek name often utilized as a family name by Hellenistic (i.e., Greek-speaking) Jews for such Hebrew names as Joshua or Jeshua. **1** A Jewish high priest, ca. 174–171 B.C., who obtained the priesthood by bribery, fostered a policy of Hellenization, was deposed, and, after unsuccessful attempts to regain the priesthood, died in exile (2 Macc. 4:7–5:10). **2** According to Acts 17:5–9, Paul's host while the latter was establishing a Christian community in Thessalonica. After a riot occasioned by Paul's missionary work, Jason was required, as part of his role as patron, to accept legal responsibility for the future activity of Paul. It may be the same Jason who sends greetings in Rom. 16:21. A.J.M.

jasper. ***See*** Breastpiece; Jewelry.

Jaulan (joh'luhn). ***See*** Golan.

Javan (jay'vuhn). **1** The fourth son of Japheth (Gen. 10:2; 1 Chron. 1:15). His name, like the names of the fifth son (Tubal) and the sixth son (Meshech), also became the name for the area he settled, 2 below. **2** A region in Asia Minor (Gk.

Ionia; Isa. 66:19; Ezek. 27:13). In the passage in Isaiah, Javan and Tubal are specifically referred to as "coastlands." In the latter passage, a famous lament, Ezekiel states that Javan, Tubal, and Meshech trafficked with Tyre in slaves and vessels of bronze. Ionia was located between Aeolia and Doria. Famous cities of Javan (Ionia) were Miletus, Ephesus, Smyrna (Rev. 2:8–11), and Magnesia. **3** A name for Greece overall, hence in Joel 3:6 "Greeks" is literally "sons of Javan," and in Daniel 8:21 "the king of Javan" is clearly Alexander the Great. "Javan" also means "Greece" in Zech. 9:13; Dan. 10:20; and 11:2.

J.G.G.

javelin. ***See*** Weapons.

Jazer (jay'zer), a site in modern Jordan. References to this site in the OT are to a settled place and in two instances to the territory around the settlement (Num. 32:1–3; Josh. 13:25; 21:39). At various times the site belonged to Amorites, Israelites, Ammonites, and apparently Moabites (Num. 21:24, 32; Josh. 13:25; Isa. 16:8; Jer. 48:32; 1 Macc. 5:8). References to the site are also found in the writings of the Jewish historian Josephus and the Christian scholar Jerome. It is probably located a few kilometers west of present day Amman, with several places as likely candidates.

jealousy. 1 A term used of God to refer to the unique relationship between God and his people (Exod. 20:5; Deut. 5:9; Josh. 24:19; 1 Kings 14:22). They are not to provoke God's "jealousy"/wrath by idolatry or sinful behavior (Deut. 32:16; 1 Cor. 10:22). **2** What humans show as zeal or ardor (2 Cor. 9:2; 11:2; Rom. 10:2). **3** Envy, a negative quality in humans (Gen. 26:14; Ecclus. 30:24; 1 Cor. 3:3; Rom. 13:13; 2 Cor. 12:20; Gal. 5:20; Jas. 3:14, 16).

Jebus (jay'buhs), a Canaanite village in central Palestine. The Jebusites were children of Canaan (Gen. 10:16). Three passages equate Jebus with Jerusalem (Josh. 15:8; 18:28; Judg. 19:10), leading many to propose that Jebus was the pre-Davidic name for Jerusalem. The data are not plentiful, however; the E source refers to Jebusites only once (Num. 13:29).

Such an identification of Jebus as Jerusalem is contained in 2 Sam. 5:6–9 and 24:18–25, however. Those passages argue that since the Jebusites were in Jerusalem then Jebus was the same as Jerusalem. This theory is problematic in light of the reference to Jerusalem in the Tell el-Amarna tablets. One could argue that Jebus and Jerusalem are two different names for the same city used simultaneously, but it is no longer possible to argue that Jebus was the name for pre-Davidic Jerusalem in light of those Tell el-Amarna texts.

Identifying the exact location of Jebus involves a number of problems. The term occurs in the boundary lists of both the tribe of Judah and the tribe of Benjamin (Josh. 15:5b–11; 18:15–19). If one accepts the parenthetical comment in Josh. 15:8 that Jebus is Jerusalem, then the other geographical designations in Josh. 15:5b–11 do not fit. Another problem is that Jebus is not listed as being on the Benjaminite side of the tribal allotment (Josh 18:15–19). The tribal history on the contrary recounts that the men of Judah took Jebus (Judg. 1:8–9). Yet Benjamin is mentioned with regard to Jebus (Judg. 1:21; see also Josh. 15:63). Some scholars argue that the Benjaminite material that mentions Jebus in connection with the Benjaminites is older and that the material that places Jebus in Judah later, was written in light of the assumed identification of Jebus with Jerusalem.

Moreover, topographically Jebus as Jerusalem is an awkward place for a boundary line. However, if modern Wadi Beit Hanina, which is opposite ‘Ain el-Madauwerah in the Wadi Beit Hanina system, is what is meant by "the valley of the son of Hinnom," then the "shoulder of the Jebusite" (Josh. 15:8) would be the prominent ridge just north of present day Sha‘fat. Again, the account of the tribal war with Benjamin in Judges 19–21 presents problems related to Gibeah only if one posits that Jebus is Jerusalem. If, on the other hand, one posits that Jebus is Sha‘fat, just north of Jerusalem, the places mentioned do make sense. It appears therefore that Sha‘fat may work better as the site of Jebus than does Jerusalem in such passages as Josh. 15:5b–11; 18:15–19; Judg. 19–21.

Jebus is not mentioned in other ancient Near Eastern texts. The origin of the city remains obscure. Nevertheless, it is clear from the references to the Jebusites that they were a powerful force in the hill country (see Exod. 3:8; 13:5; 23:23; 33:2; 34:11; Josh. 12:8; 24:11). During the pre-monarchical period and later (ca. 1200–1000 B.C.), the Jebusites remained a force in the area (Judg. 1:21). Whether one accepts Jerusalem or Sha‘fat as the site of Jebus, it is clear that the Jebusites were in control of Jerusalem in the period just prior to David's conquest of it as his royal city (2 Sam. 5:6–9). The Jebusite control of Jerusalem is presupposed in the story of David's purchase of land for the Jerusalem Temple; David bought the land from the absentee landlord who was a Jebusite (2 Sam. 24:18–25).

Jebus is not referred to in the postexilic period (after ca. 538 B.C.) with the exception of references in the Chronicler's work that are based on the interpretation of 2 Sam. 5:6–9 and 24:18–25, which, as we saw, construed Jebus as Jerusalem. It seems that the name "Jebus" was no longer used to refer to any contemporary city but only an ancient name for a city, in this case Jerusalem. Therefore, if one can argue that

Jebus is Sha'fat and not Jerusalem it seems likely that either the town was destroyed or had a name change prior to the postexilic material, since that material does not seem to be aware of Jebus's existence. It was this lack of awareness that probably led to the conclusion that since Jebus was close to Jerusalem and the Jebusites had control of Jerusalem that Jebus was in fact Jerusalem. None of this is conclusive; on the contrary, it merely demonstrates that there is a lack of clarity about the location of Jebus in OT references that has yet to be explained away. S.B.R.

Jeconiah (jek'oh-nī'uh). ***See*** Jehoiachin.

Jedaiah (je-dī'uh), an OT name derived from two Hebrew words, *yeda' yah* ("Yah [God] knows"); it was borne by several Levites mostly in postexilic Judah. It is difficult to separate these names since some may refer to the same person or family group. **1** A descendant of Aaron and head of the second group of priests (1 Chron. 24:7); he was probably the ancestral head of one or more of the family groups below. **2** A priest and postexilic inhabitant of Jerusalem; he is called the "son of Joiarib" (Neh. 11:10), but in 1 Chronicles (9:10) "son of" is omitted and Joiarib (Jehoiarib) is simply another priest. **3** A Levite who returned from the Babylonian captivity with Zerubbabel (Neh. 12:6); however, this verse probably refers to a family group who returned, since Uzzi is given as a family head of Jedaiah (Neh. 12:19). **4** A second Levite who returned with Zerubbabel (Neh. 12:7); also probably a family group with Nethanel as the leader (Neh. 12:21). **5** A family group ("sons of Jedaiah") of the clan of Jeshua who returned with Zerubbabel (Ezra 2:36; Neh. 7:39). This group could be related to either 3 or 4. **6** One of the representative exiles named in a prophecy of Zechariah (Zech. 6:10, 14).

The name Jedaiah may also be derived from Hebrew *yedayah*, a name of uncertain meaning, possibly "Yah [God] is praise." **7** The son of Shimri; a descendant of Simeon (1 Chron. 4:37). **8** One who helped repair the walls of postexilic Jerusalem (Neh. 3:10). D.R.B.

Jediael (je-dī'yuh-el; Heb., meaning uncertain, possibly "El [God] knows"). **1** A son of Benjamin and head of a large family group (1 Chron. 7:6, 10, 11). **2** The son of Shimri; he and his brother Joha were members of David's fighting band (1 Chron. 11:45); he may be the same one who defected to David at Ziklag from the tribe of Manasseh (1 Chron. 12:20). **3** A Levite of the clan of Korah, the second son of the eastern gatekeeper Meshelemiah (Shelemiah; 1 Chron. 26:2).

Jeduthun (je-dōō'thuhn), member of a levitical family (1 Chron. 9:16) who is associated with the Judean village Netophah, and distinguished from "gatekeepers," although in another place (1 Chron. 16:42) "the sons of Jeduthun" apparently fulfilled that occupation (so MT) at the Gibeon shrine (cf. 1 Chron. 16:38 for the family as gatekeepers at Jerusalem). Jeduthun and Heman are mentioned as concerned with Temple music, instrumental alone and associated with song (1 Chron. 16:41–42). In 1 Chron. 25:1, 3, and 6 Jeduthun and his family are included among Temple musicians, prophesying with musical accompaniment (cf. 2 Kings 2:15) and offering praise. 2 Chron. 5:12 specifies in addition their fine linen garments and their station to the east of the altar. The Jeduthun family appears among the Levites who consecrated themselves and cleansed the Temple at Hezekiah's reform (2 Chron. 29:13–15; cf. a similar list in Neh. 11:15–17). 2 Chron. 35:15, in the account of Josiah's reform, describes Jeduthun as "the king's seer" (one form of text has a plural to include Heman, so designated in 1 Chron. 25:5).

The name Jeduthun also appears in the titles of Psalms 39, 62, and 77, perhaps indicating a musical or liturgical tradition. The association of this levitical family with prophetic activity (1 Chron. 25:1–6; 2 Chron. 35:15) is important for the understanding of the function of prophecy in the later OT writings. ***See also*** Music; Psalms, The. P.R.A.

Jehiel (je-hī'uhl; Heb., "God lives"). **1** The son of Ladan (1 Chron. 23:8). He founded a priestly family called the Jehieli (1 Chron. 26:21–22) and had charge of the Temple treasury under King David (1 Chron. 29:8). **2** A Levite musician who served before the Ark (1 Chron. 15:18, 20; 16:5). **3** An attendant of King David's sons (1 Chron. 27:32). **4** A son of King Jehoshaphat (2 Chron. 21:2). **5** Two Temple officers (2 Chron. 31:13; 35:8). **6** The father of Obadiah who returned from exile with Ezra (Ezra 8:9). **7** The father of Shecaniah who agreed to Ezra's marriage reforms (Ezra 10:2). **8** Two men who divorced foreign wives in the time of Ezra (Ezra 10:21, 26).

Jehoahaz (je-hoh'ah-haz; Heb., "God has grasped"). **1** The eleventh king of Israel, the son of Jehu, he ruled 816–800 B.C. He continued to suffer from the depredations of Hazael, king of Syria (2 Kings 13:3, 22) which had already begun in the reign of his father, Jehu. Hazael's son Ben-Hadad apparently led the victorious armies of Syria (2 Kings 13:3), which faced little opposition from the decimated army of Jehoahaz (2 Kings 13:7). Although Jehoahaz sought God's deliverance from the divine wrath against Israel due to the worship of Asherah practiced there (2 Kings 13:6), and received the promise of a savior (2 Kings 13:4–5), the promise was not fulfilled during his reign. He was succeeded by his son, Joash. **2** The seventeenth king of Judah, the son of Josiah, he reigned for a short time, perhaps only three months (2 Kings 23:31; 609 B.C.). After his father's death at the hands of Pharaoh Neco at the battle of Megiddo, Jehoahaz was made king by the people even though he was not the oldest son of Josiah. Pharaoh Neco deposed him in favor of his brother Eliakim, whom Neco renamed Jehoiakim (2 Kings 23:34). Jehoahaz was taken to Egypt as a captive, and died there. Although he was adjudged an evil king (2 Kings 23:32), neither Jeremiah (who calls him Shallum; 22:10–12) nor Ezekiel (19:2–4) refer to him in such terms. **3** The twelfth king of Judah, who is better known as Ahaz. ***See also*** Ahaz; Asherah; Ben-hadad; Chronology, Old Testament; Hazael; Syria. P.J.A.

Jehoash (je-hoh'ash). ***See*** Joash.

Jehohanan (jee-hoh-hay'nuhn; Heb., "God is gracious"). **1** One of the gatekeepers in David's tabernacle (1 Chron. 26:3). **2** A captain under the Judean king Jehoshaphat (2 Chron. 17:15). **3** The son of Bebai; he was one of the men who had married a foreign woman (Ezra 10:28). **4** A son of Eliashib (Ezra 10:6). **5** A son of Tobiah (Neh. 6:18). **6** A priest in the time of the Judean king Jehoiakim (Neh. 12:13). **7** A priest who was a contemporary of Nehemiah (Neh. 12:42).

Jehoiachin (je-hoy'ah-kin; also called Joiachin, Jeconiah, Jechoniah, and Coniah), one of the last two kings of Judah. He came to the throne in 597 B.C. at the age of eighteen after the death of his father, Jehoiakim (2 Kings 24:8). At that time, Babylon besieged Jerusalem, and, after he had reigned only three months, he, his mother, wives, servants, princes, and officers surrendered themselves captive to Nebuchadnezzar (2 Kings 24:12; reflected in the prophecy of Jer. 22:24–30). The Babylonians also exiled ten thousand soldiers, officers, craftsmen, and smiths, leaving the land impoverished of skilled labor and administrators (2 Kings 24:14, 16; Jer. 24:1; 29:2). The Temple and palace treasures were also looted. According to Daniel, this exile included Daniel, Hananiah, Mishael, and Azariah (Dan. 1:1–7), and, according to Esther 2:6, it included Mordecai. Ezekiel was also among the captives (Ezek. 1:1–21; cf. Jer. 29:1).

Jeremiah prophesied the divine redemption of these captives of the first Babylonian exile (Jer. 24:4–7), but this would only come after a hiatus of seventy years (29:10–14; cf. vv. 1–7). Thus, he was at odds with Hananiah the son of Azzur, who predicted the immediate return of Jehoiachin and the exiles (28:1–4).

Several Babylonian food-rationing lists mention Jehoiachin's name or call him "King of Judah." Since he apparently surrendered quickly (2 Kings 24:12), he may have been treated fairly well. The Bible tells us (2 Kings 25: 27–30; Jer. 52:31–34) that in the thirty-seventh

Babylonian cuneiform text that refers to Nebuchadnezzar's siege of Jerusalem and the exile of Jehoiachin to Babylon in 597 B.C.

year of Jehoiachin's captivity (561 B.C.), Nebuchadnezzar's successor, Evil-merodach, raised his status to that of a valued court retainer. For a people then wholly exiled, this fact served to provide hope that the tide had turned, and that the promised redemption would not long be delayed. ***See also*** Jeremiah, The Book of.

J.U.

Jehoiada (je-hoy'ah-dah). **1** The chief priest in the days of Athaliah and Joash of Judah (early eighth century B.C.). His wife was Jehosheba, daughter of King Jehoram and sister of King Ahaziah, Jehoram's son (2 Chron. 22:11). After Ahaziah died, his mother, Athaliah (Ahab's daughter), took the throne and had Ahaziah's children murdered. Jehosheba saved the youngest, Joash, and, with Jehoiada, hid him in the Temple for six years (vv. 11–12). In the seventh year Jehoiada formed a conspiracy of the commanders of the royal guard, the Levites, and chiefs of clans to restore the crown to the house of David (2 Chron. 23:1–7, 20). With the citizenry in attendance, Jehoiada crowned and anointed Joash and had Athaliah killed (vv. 8–15). He then renewed the covenant between God, the king, and the people (v. 16) which resulted in the destruction of the Tyrian Baal cult (v. 17). Jehoiada restored proper administration in the Temple (vv. 18–19), and exerted significant influence over Joash (2 Chron. 24:2–3). With the king's avid cooperation, Jehoiada collected a tax for the Temple's maintenance and effected repairs (vv. 4–14). The Chronicler relates that he lived to be one hundred thirty and that he was buried in the tombs of the kings in the city of David—a sign of the great respect in which he was held (vv. 15–16). Jehoiada's fame may be remembered in Jer. 29:26. He was the father of Zechariah, who prophesied against Judah's apostasy. **2** A chief priest (1 Chron. 12:27; 27:5), the father of Benaiah, the chief of David's elite mercenaries (2 Sam. 8:18) and the head of the army under Solomon (1 Kings 2:35). **3** A high priest in the time of Nehemiah (Neh. 13:28). J.U.

Jehoiakim (je-hoy'ah-kim), king of Judah (609–598 B.C.; 2 Kings 23:36). He was installed as king at the age of twenty-five by Pharaoh Neco after Neco had deposed his younger brother Jehoahaz (2 Kings 23:33–34). A son of Josiah, Jehoiakim's given name was Eliakim before Neco changed it. The Pharaoh executed a tribute of a hundred talents of silver and a talent of gold upon Judah (v. 33), which Jehoiakim raised by tax (v. 35).

In 605 B.C., Babylon defeated Egypt decisively at Carchemish (Jer. 46:2; cf. 2 Kings 24:7) and captured Syria and the land of Israel (cf. Jer. 36:9). When the king's officers and princes tried to present the scroll of Jeremiah's prophecies to Jehoiakim, he burned it because of the prophet's prediction of the coming Babylonian destruction (Jer. 36:29). Jehoiakim became Babylon's vassal for three years, and then rebelled (2 Kings 24:1). Nebuchadnezzar responded with an invasion of troops from Moab, Ammon, and Aram (v. 2; cf. Jer. 35:11), but Judah was able to maintain its sovereignty for a few more years. The prophet who dared to oppose Jehoiakim risked his life: Jehoiakim had Uriah killed, and Jeremiah was put on trial for his life (Jer. 26). Although Jeremiah predicted that Jehoiakim would die an undignified death due to his murderous behavior (Jer. 22:17–19; cf. 2 Kings 24:4), 2 Kings 24:6 relates that he was buried in the tomb of the king of Judah. ***See also*** Jeremiah, The Book of; Josiah; Nebuchadnezzar. J.U.

Jehonadab (je-hahn'uh-dab), the son of Rechab and spiritual father of the Rechabite sect, whose members were distinguished by their abstinence from drinking wine, planting vineyards, sowing the land, and building houses (Jer. 35:6–7; RSV: "Jonadab"). Jeremiah praises them for their unswerving loyalty to their ancestral code of asceticism. Such symbolic clinging to Israel's nomadic past suits the role of Jehonadab in historical literature as the protagonist of native Israelite tradition. He was partner to Jehu in the mid-ninth century B.C. in the bloody overthrow of the Omride dynasty in Samaria and in eradicating the cult of the Tyrian Baal introduced by the Phoenician princess Jezebel (2 Kings 10:15–29). ***See also*** Jehu. M.C.

Jehonathan (je-hoh'nuh-thuhn; Heb., "Yahweh has given"), name of some sixteen different OT characters. The names Jehonathan and Jonathan appear to be used interchangeably. ***See also*** Jonathan.

Jehoram (je-hoh'rem; Heb., "Yahweh is exalted"), alternately Joram (joh'rem), the name of two contemporary kings in Judah and Israel who were also brothers-in-law. **1** A king of Judah (ca. 849–842 B.C.), son and successor of Jehoshaphat, and husband of the Omride Princess Athaliah. According to the account in 2 Chronicles 21 he murdered his six brothers upon succession to the throne. There was a close alliance between Judah and Israel during his reign and the subsequent reign of Athaliah. Edom rebelled during Jehoram's reign, thus gaining its independence from Judah. According to the Chronicler the Philistines also attacked Judah, and Libnah was taken (2 Chron. 21:16–17; 2 Kings 8:22). The Chronicler also reports that Jehoram suffered an incurable disease, predicted by Elijah, and was not buried in the tombs of the kings. **2** A king of Israel (ca. 849–842 B.C.) and brother and successor of Ahaziah. This Jehoram was probably coregent with his father Jehoshaphat with the result that his independent rule was less than the twelve years recorded in 2 Kings 3:1. He was unable to put down the rebellion of King Mesha of Moab. The prophet Elisha accompanied the armies of Jehoram when Mesha, in desperate straits, "offered up his eldest son as a burnt offering" on the city wall in full view of the attackers. Israel and Aram were apparently allies early in Jehoram's reign, while Ben-hadad II was alive. In the reign of his successor, Hazael, however, Jehoram was wounded in battle against Aram. He was subsequently assassinated in Jezreel by his commander-in-chief, Jehu, who cast Jehoram's body into the field of Naboth, this destroying the Omride dynasty (2 Kings 9:23–24). ***See also*** Jehoshaphat. D.L.C.

Jehoshabeath (jay-hoh-shah-bee'ath; Jehoshaba, 2 Kings 11:2; Heb., "Yahweh is an oath"), the daughter of King Jehoram, and wife of the priest Jehoiada. She saved her young nephew Joash (Jehoash) from the murderous wrath of Athaliah, the wicked queen, mother of the slain Ahaziah, by hiding him during her six-year reign (2 Chron. 22:10–12).

Jehoshaphat (je-hoh'shuh-fat; Heb., "Yahweh establishes justice"; also Joshaphat). **1** The son of Ahilud, "recorder" under David (2 Sam. 8:16; 20:24; 1 Chron. 18:15) and Solomon (1 Kings 4:3). **2** The son of Paruah, an officer in Issachar under Solomon (1 Kings 4:17). **3** King of Judah (cf. 1 Chron. 3:10; Matt. 1:8). He succeeded his father Asa on the throne (1 Kings 15:24; 22:41–46) and reigned twenty-five years, ca. 873–848 B.C. He is shown in 1 Kings 22 as the subordinate ally with the Israelite king who is named as Ahab only in 1 Kings 22:20 (cf. 39–40), whereas 2 Chronicles 18 introduces both names in vv. 1–3 to give a clearer identification. Jehoshaphat, by his insistence on consulting the prophets and specifically Micaiah, is contrasted with the Northern ruler, Ahab; he is delivered in battle in spite of being mistaken for his ally, whereas the doom pronounced by Micaiah brings death to the disguised king of Israel. 2 Kings 3:4–27 describes another such alliance with Jehoram of Israel and the king of Edom. This too uses the motif of the prophet, here Elisha, who promises victory; but the eventual outcome is disaster for Israel.

2 Chronicles 18 tells the same story as 1 Kings 22, noting the marriage alliance with Ahab in v. 1 and elaborating the welcome given to Samaria (18:2). This is prefaced in 2 Chronicles 17 with an account of Jehoshaphat's strengthening the position of Judah against Israel, commenting also on his obedience to God and his prosperity. Priests and Levites were sent to teach the law in the cities of Judah (cf. also 19:4–11). The surrounding nations honor Jehoshaphat and some send tribute. Details are given of fortresses, store cities, and military forces. The sequel (19:1–3) is a prophetic judgment against Jehoshaphat by Jehu, son of Hanani the seer, for allying himself with the wicked apostates of the North, a judgment alleviated by reference to Jehoshaphat's pious actions, and 19:4–11 repeats the theme of justice. Hence, so 20:1–30 relates, an attack by Moabites, Ammonites, and others is met by fasting and prayer. The prayer is set out in 20:6–12 and expresses the powerlessness of Judah and its trust in God. Divinely inspired, a Levite preacher proclaims divine help and coming victory. An act of praise follows, led by the Levites. Before the battle, Jehoshaphat further exhorts the people, using words close to those of Isa. 7:9. The singers offer praise, and the result is a divinely arranged victory that leaves the Judean army only the task of despoiling the totally destroyed enemy forces. Peace and prosperity are restored. This story may represent a reworking of 2 Kings 3.

A supplement in 2 Chron. 20:35–37 elaborates 1 Kings 22:47–49, showing another alliance with the Israelite king Ahaziah; a trading expedition to Tarshish is condemned by a prophet Eliezer, and the ships are wrecked. The accounts in Chronicles are clearly pious elaborations of the earlier narratives, partly linked with interpretation of the king's name—the theme of justice—and partly sermons on the relation between obedience and divine help. **4** The father of Jehu, king of Israel (2 Kings 9:2, 14), and son of Nimshi, elsewhere described as Jehu's father (1 Kings 19:16; 2 Kings 9:20; 2 Chron. 22:7). **5** The Valley of Jehoshaphat, place of divine judgment on the nations (Joel 3:2, 12). Its location is unknown; it is almost certainly a symbolic rather than a real place. P.R.A.

Jehoshaphat (je-hoh'shuh-fat), **Valley of,** the site where the nations surrounding Israel will be judged by God for transgressions committed against Israel according to Joel 3:2, 12. Some scholars claim that the Valley of Jehoshaphat was known before Joel's time and that it was named for Jehoshaphat, king of Judah. Most scholars, however, believe that it was Joel who symbolically named a valley in Jerusalem, possibly the Kidron Valley or Gehinom, Jehoshaphat, namely "Yahweh judges." Whether or not this name originated with Joel, it is appropriate for the place where Yahweh "will enter into judgment" (Joel 3:2) and "will sit to judge" (3:12), a place also called "the valley of decision" (3:14). M.Z.B.

Jehovah (juh-hoh'vuh). *See* Tetragrammaton, The Sacred.

Jehovah-jireh (je-hoh'vah-jee'reh; KJV; RSV: Heb., "The Lord will provide [or see]"), the name given by Abraham to the site where he found a ram to be offered in place of his son Isaac (Gen. 22:14).

Jehovah-nissi (je-hoh'vah-nis'se; KJV; RSV: Heb., "The Lord is my banner"), the name given by Moses to the altar he built (Exod. 17:15) to commemorate the victory over the Amalekites at Rephidim on the way to Canaan (see Exod. 17: 8–16).

Jehovah-shalom (je-hoh'vah-shah-lohm'; KJV; RSV: Heb., "The Lord is peace"), the name given by Gideon to commemorate the appearance of the Lord to him and his commission to deliver Israel from the Midianites (Judg. 6:24).

Jehovah-shamma (je-hoh'vah-shahm'mah; KJV; RSV: Heb., "The Lord is there"), the name of Jerusalem in the restoration envisioned by Ezekiel, emphasizing the divine presence in the holy city (Ezek. 48:35; cf. Isa. 60:14–22; Rev. 21: 2–22:5).

Jehovah-tsidkenu (je-hoh'vah-tsid-ken'o͞o; KJV; RSV: Heb., "The Lord is our righteousness"), the name given by Jeremiah to the future king through whom God would save the people (Jer. 23:6; 33:16). The name may be a play on the name of Zedekiah, regent in Jerusalem from 597 to 587 B.C.

Jehozabad (je-hoh'zuh-bad; Heb., "Yahweh is a gift" or "Yahweh has given"). **1** A retainer of

King Joash of Judah who, with another retainer, Jozacar, assassinated the king (2 Kings 12:21; 2 Chron. 24:26); he was executed by Joash's son Amaziah shortly after Amaziah took the throne (ca. 800? B.C.; 2 Kings 14:5). **2** The son of Obed-edom; a Levite of the clan of Korah who shared responsibility for the south storehouse of the Temple during the reign of King David (1 Chron. 26:4, 16). **3** A Benjaminite commander of a hundred and eighty thousand troops under King Jehoshaphat (2 Chron. 17:18).

Jehozadak (je-hahz'uh-dak; Heb., "Yahweh is righteous"), a priestly descendant of Aaron who was exiled to Babylon by Nebuchadnezzar (1 Chron. 6:14–15). He was the father of Joshua (Jeshua) who was the high priest in Jerusalem following the Exile (586–490 B.C.; Hag. 1:1; Zech. 6:11). He is also called Jozadak, a shortened form of the same name (Ezra 3:8; 5:2). In some versions the name also occurs as Josedech. ***See also*** Jozadak.

Jehu (jay'hōō). **1** The son of Jehoshaphat; he was king of Israel for twenty-eight years (ca. 843–816 B.C.) and established a dynasty that lasted five generations and ninety years (2 Kings 9–10; 15:12).

Jehu's reign and his war against the worship of Baal was set forth in God's speech to the prophet Elijah on Mt. Horeb (1 Kings 19:16–18). Although Elijah was given the task of anointing Jehu as king, it was finally carried out by a member of a prophetic band at the command of Elisha (2 Kings 9:1–6). In a bloody coup, Jehu killed Jehoram, king of Israel (849–843 B.C.; v. 24) and directed the killings of Jehu's confederate King Ahaziah of Judah (843; v. 27), Jezebel (vv. 30–37), Ahab's seventy sons (10:1–10), all members and associates of the house of Ahab (vv. 11, 17), Ahaziah's forty-two brothers (vv. 13–14), all the worshipers of Baal in Israel (vv. 18–25). Jehu also ordered the destruction of the temple and the idols of Baal (vv. 26–28). Thus, Jehu eliminated the worship of the Tyrian Baal. The bloodiness of the coup was still remembered a hundred years later by Hosea (1:4).

Although Jehu's coup and religious reforms ended the political alliance of Tyre, Israel, and Judah, it consolidated the military, the populace, and the prophetic movement in Israel behind him. The army looked to him as a strong leader to combat the Aramaeans. The poor needed him to reverse their fortunes after the economic hardships brought upon them by the dynasty of Omri (Jehonadab, son of Rechab, was one of these, 2 Kings 10:15–16).

In order to counter the Aramaeans, Jehu made himself vassal to the king of Assyria in 841 B.C. (as is inscribed in the annals of Shalmaneser III and the Black Obelisk). Shalmaneser III campaigned against Aram from 841 to 838. Afterward, however, the Aramaeans reasserted their military supremacy and conquered all of Ramoth-gilead (2 Kings 10:32–33).

2 The son of Hanani, and a prophet who prophesied against Baasha (902–886 B.C.), king of Israel (1 Kings 16:1–4, 7, 12), and both rebuked and praised Jehoshaphat (874–850 B.C.), king of Judah (2 Chron. 19:2–3). 2 Chron. 20:34 attributes authorship of the history of Jehoshaphat to him.

3 The son of Joshibiah, and a prince of the tribe of Simeon (1 Chron. 4:35).

4 One of David's mighty men from Anathoth (1 Chron. 12:3).

5 A Judahite, a descendant of Jarha, an Egyptian slave (1 Chron. 2:38). ***See also*** Elijah; Jehoshaphat; Omri; Shalmaneser. J.U.

Jehudi (je-hōō'dee), a servant of the court of Jehoiakim. He was sent by the nobles to order Baruch to bring them the scroll of Jeremiah's prophecies and then was ordered by the king to read the scroll before the court (Jer. 36:14, 21–23).

Jeiel (je-ī'el; Heb., "El [God] takes away"). **1** A clan chieftain in the tribe of Reuben (1 Chron. 5:7). **2** A Benjaminite, the father of Gibeon and great-grandfather of Saul (1 Chron. 8:29; 9:35). **3** The son of Hotham the Aroerite; one of David's fighting men (1 Chron. 11:44). **4** A Levite musician of the Merarite clan who helped celebrate the transfer of the Ark of the Covenant to Jerusalem (1 Chron. 15:18, 21). A second Jeiel is also listed among the group of musicians (1 Chron. 16:5), but he is elsewhere called Jaaziel (1 Chron. 15:18) or Aziel (1 Chron. 15:20). It is possible that Jeuel, a variant spelling of Jeiel, refers to the same person (2 Chron. 29:13), although he is from the clan of Elizaphan. **5** A Levite associated with the musical clan of Asaph; an ancestor of Jehaziel, the prophesier of deliverance for King Jehoshaphat (2 Chron. 20:14), he is possibly the same as 4. **6** A scribe during the reign of Uzziah (Azariah) in Judah (2 Chron. 26:11). **7** A leader of the Levites who contributed animals for the celebration of the Passover reinstated by Josiah (2 Chron. 35:9). **8** A member of the clan of Nebo who took a foreign wife (Ezra 10:43). D.R.B.

Jemimah (je-mī'mah), the first of Job's three daughters born when God restored his fortunes. All of these daughters were exceptional for their beauty and their receiving an inheritance from their father (Job 42:13–15).

Jephthah (jef'thuh; Heb., "he opens"; cf. the place name Iptahel, "God opens [the womb?]," Josh. 19:14, 27), a Gileadite who delivered Israel from Ammonite domination. Jephthah sacrificed his daughter to fulfill a vow, suppressed an Ephraimite force in Gilead, and judged Israel six years (Judg. 10:6–12:7).

Born the son of a harlot, Jephthah was disowned and driven out from his family. In the district of Tob near the modern Jordan-Syria border, he gathered a band of mercenaries and was later recalled by the elders of Gilead. Ammonite forces had invaded Gilead and penetrated across the Jordan into Judah, Benjamin, and Ephraim. The elders of Gilead made Jephthah head and ruler, negotiations culminating in Jephthah's vows before Yahweh, at Mizpeh (in the vicinity of Jebel Jal'ad, south of the River Jabbok).

The territory disputed in the negotiations had belonged earlier to the Amorite kingdoms north of the Arnon River, which were defeated by Israel under Moses (Judg. 11:14–28; Num. 21). The territory was subsequently taken by Moab (Judg. 3:12–30). When Ammon became strong enough to press its own claims against Israel, the Ammonite king made claims and charges in the name of Moabite sovereignty over the disputed territory (perhaps claiming to hold it in trust). Jephthah recognized the jurisdiction of Chemosh, god of Moab, for diplomatic purposes, but argued that because God's gift to Israel was far older, Israel had not seized Ammonite land. When negotiations failed, Jephthah toured Gilead and Manasseh, presumably to muster the army, and returned to Mizpeh. From Mizpeh Israel moved to meet the Ammonites, defeating them along a line from southern Aroer (the northern edge of the Arnon gorge) to Abel-keramim (probably Tell el-Umeiri at the northern end of the Madeba plain). As a result, Ammon was pushed back to the desert fringe.

Upon accepting his commission, Jephthah made a vow that if he were to return victorious, he would sacrifice whatever emerged first from his house (Judg. 11:30–31; Iron Age dwellings, like many Palestinian village houses today, incorporated space for small cattle). The first creature to emerge was his only child, a daughter, who refused to let Jephthah break his vow. She requested two months to wander the hills with her dear friends, lamenting her virginity (childlessness; Judg. 11:39–40). The story serves to explain the otherwise obscure four-day rite observed annually by the daughters of Israel. Human sacrifice, a horror neither condoned nor unknown in ancient Israel, is here secondary to the irrevocability of the vow.

In the final story of the Jephthah cycle, Ephraimites crossed into Gilead, complaining that Jephthah had not summoned them to the Ammonite war and threatening to burn his house (Judg. 12:1). Again negotiations failed and Jephthah was victorious in the fighting. Gileadites used a password, *shibboleth*, to betray dialect differences, and many Ephraimites were slain at the Jordan fords (Judg. 12:5–6). Joshua 22 describes an earlier confrontation of Israelite tribes in the same area. ***See also*** Judges, The Book of; Shibboleth. R.B.

Jephunneh (je-fuhn'nuh). **1** A Kenizzite, the father of Caleb, one of the twelve spies sent to Canaan by Moses (Num. 13:6; 32:12). **2** The son of Jether; descendant of Asher (1 Chron. 7:38).

Jerah (jihr'ah; Heb., "moon"), a son of Joktan (Gen. 10:26; 1 Chron. 1:20), and the member of a tribe whose territories were probably located in the south Arabian coastland.

Jerahmeel (je-rah'mee-el; Heb., "may God have compassion"). **1** The ancestor who gave his name to a group of non-Israelites, the Jerahmeelites, who lived in the extreme southern part of the land of Judah. David came into contact with them there after his flight from Saul (1 Sam. 27:10; 30:29). **2** The son of Kish, and a Levite (1 Chron. 24:29). **3** One of the three men sent by the Judean king Jehoiakim to arrest Jeremiah and

Jephthah, returning home from battle victorious, meets his daughter first (left); after a period of mourning (center), she is sacrificed according to Jephthah's irrevocable vow to God (right; Judg. 11:30–40); from a thirteenth-century French miniature.

Baruch (Jer. 36:26). Although Jerahmeel is called "the king's son," that may be an official title, and hence does not necessarily mean he was Jehoiakim's son. M.A.F.

Jerash (jair'ash). ***See*** Gerasa.

Jeremiah (jair-uh-mī'uh), **the Book of,** an OT book of prophetic oracles attributed to the Judean prophet Jeremiah (seventh–sixth century B.C.).

The Prophet: Jeremiah of Anathoth was the son of Hilkiah. He was of priestly extraction, perhaps descending from David's priest, Abiathar, who was expelled by Solomon to Anathoth where he owned a field (1 Kings 2:26–27). This may explain the vivid memory of the fall of Shiloh in Jeremiah (7:12, 14; 26:6, 9), because Abiathar himself was the great-grandson of the Shilonite priest Phinehas, son of Eli.

Still young, Jeremiah was appointed prophet in the thirteenth year of Josiah (627/6 B.C.). Hence he was born sometime between 645 and 640. He first prophesied in Anathoth, provoking the anger of his villagers and family (11:21; 12:6). He then moved to Jerusalem, a one-hour walk from home. Some of his prophecies against the nations (e.g., 49:1–5) and those of restoration to Ephraim (31:1–21) as well as his indictment of the Judean policy of alliance with Egypt against Assyria (2:14–19, 36–37) certainly belong to his first period, up to the fall of Nineveh in 612 and the death of Josiah in 609.

In those early years, Jeremiah perhaps belonged to a guild of professional prophets. He repeatedly mentions such a group alongside the priests as connected with the Temple (23:11) and as vindicating its sanctity (26:7–16) and integrity (27:16–18; 28:3). In time Jeremiah broke away from them, but his early prophecies of salvation and victory, and his prayers against the drought (14:2–10; 14:19–15:1) attest to the legacy of traditional prophecy embedded in his message.

In the reign of Jehoiakim (608–598 B.C.), Jeremiah was already a mature man and prophet, well versed in the international events that led to the battle of Carchemish in 605 (46:2–12). He collected his previous sayings into one scroll (chap. 36) and dared to assault the king (22: 13–19) and the Temple (26:1–19) with it. At that time he found friends and protectors within the noble families of Jerusalem, the sons of Shaphan (26:24; 36:10, 25) and of Neriah (36: 4).

Jeremiah's stature grew even more in Zedekiah's reign (597–587 B.C.). Repeatedly, he warned the king from revolting against Babylon (27:12–15). The revolt broke out, yet the king kept consulting him, either by messengers (37: 3–10) or personally (37:17–20). The ministers wanted Jeremiah dead but did not dare kill him. Charging him with desertion to the enemy, they jailed him in a pit-house where he would starve to death (37:11–16), but the king moved him to a better prison, "the court of Guard," where he received food until the fall of Jerusalem (586 B.C.; 37:21).

The Chaldeans freed Jeremiah from prison, committing him to the care of their Judean governor, Gedaliah, son of Ahikam (39:14). After the latter's assassination, the remnants decided, against Jeremiah's oracle, to flee to Egypt, taking along the prophet and his secretary Baruch. The presence in the book of Jeremiah of several oracles from this "Egyptian" period (43:8–44:30; 46:13–26) proves that Jeremiah and Baruch did not die a violent death after the exile. The legend about their being lynched by the Jewish mob originated in the late Jewish interpretation of the prophets as martyrs who died for their faith's sake.

The Book: The book of Jeremiah is the only reliable source about the prophet and his message, but a critical-historical examination of this source reveals its many textual and historical difficulties. The structure is relatively clear: Chaps. 1–24 contain visions and prophecies of judgment as well as personal laments. Chaps. 25–45 contain speeches of Jeremiah and stories about him, all dated. Within this section there is a further definable subunit, chaps. 30–33, which contain prophecies of restoration and comfort arranged around the consolation story of chap. 32. Chaps. 46–51 contain prophecies against the nations. Finally, chap. 52 is a historical appendix.

Within these collections, the arrangement was apparently determined by a concentric principle, sometimes referred to as *inclusio*, according to which similar material was set at both edges of one corpus. The first collection, chaps. 1–24—apart from the consecration (1:4–10)—starts and ends with visions (almond rod, baskets of figs), each of them followed by "And the word of the Lord came to me, saying, 'Jeremiah, what do you see?' And I said . . ." (1:11; 24:3). The second collection, chaps. 25–45, is enclosed by two stories of the fourth year of Jehoiakim (25:1; 45:1). This collection is composed of single episodes (chaps. 25–29; 32; 34–36) and a continuous biography (chaps. 37–44). The single episodes also reflect a concentric pattern, starting and ending in the fourth year of Jehoiakim (25; 36). They are arranged as following: five episodes from Zedekiah's reign (27; 28; 29; 32; 34) are enclosed by four from the time of Jerusalem (25; 26; 35; 36). The restoration collection surrounds chap. 32, as noted. The collection of the oracles against the nations (46–51) begins and ends with major powers; it begins with Egypt, which was defeated by Babylon, and ends with the latter.

A different order obtains in the Septuagint. In this version, the oracles against the nations

JEREMIAH, THE BOOK OF

come between 25:13 and 25:15. This order is secondary, as it follows a pattern by which later scribes arranged other prophetical books (Isaiah, Ezekiel, Zephaniah): rebuke and doom against Israel; rebuke and doom against the nations; restoration. Yet another arrangement, a chronological one, is manifest in 1:2–3 and 40:1. According to it, chaps. 1–39 contain prophecies up to the fall of Judah, while chaps. 40–44 contain prophecies from the fall on.

Single sayings of Jeremiah were often arranged together due to the association of key words. For instance, the two laments of 20:7–9, 10–12, first joined because of the similar expressions "entice . . . prevail" (vv. 7, 10), were then added to the Pashhur incident (19:1–20:6), because of the common key word "terror all around" (20:3, 10).

The growth and formation of the book can be reconstructed as follows. Single sayings of the prophet and episodes from his life were at first recorded on relatively short scrolls. The sayings, from one to ten verses, were generally abstracts of longer oral pronunciations. The recording of both genres is plausibly attributed to Jeremiah's scribe, Baruch, son of Neriah. This point is sufficiently proved for the sayings by Jer. 36:2, 4, 18, 28, 32. As for the episodes, the fact that the oldest is from the beginning of the reign of Jehoiakim (26:1), shortly before Baruch first appeared at Jeremiah's side (36:1–4; 45:1), indicates Baruch as a very probable author.

In the next stage these original records were transmitted by Deuteronomistic disciples who reworked them according to their literary and religious concepts. Both episodes and sayings were reworked into speeches, as with 37:3–10 which was reshaped in 21:1–7, or 21:11–12a which was rephrased in 22:1–5. Other times the Deuteronomist contributions were rather limited, adding half a verse, as in 21:12b, or a few words, as in 22:17. But all in all the Deuteronomist reworking is ubiquitous, changing as it did the whole aspect of the book. The aims of these editors were the following: the interpretation and updating of prophecies, as in 22:25, 27 which expand 22:24, 26; theodicy as in 22:8–9, added for that end to 22:6–7; unequivocal support of the Josiah covenant (11:1–14); the bestowal of a preferential status to the exiles of 597 B.C. as against those who were left in the country or who emigrated to Egypt (24:6–7, 9–10; 29:10–14, 16–20); and the emphasis on human free will, the opportunity to repent, and an ever readapting divine retribution—tenets common to most Deuteronomist sermons in Jeremiah (e.g., 7:1–15 which expand 7:4, 9–14). The Deuteronomist editing of Jeremiah extended over a long period, its apex being in the early fifth century.

The book was open to expansions during the entire Persian period (late sixth–early fifth centuries B.C.). Jewish religious propaganda of the Second Temple period is extant in 10:1–16. The expectation of a David *redivivus* in 30:8–9 is typical of an editorial stratum of other prophetical books (cf. Ezek. 34:23–24; 37:24–25; Hos. 3:5). The liberation of Jeremiah by the Chaldeans in 39:14 has been reworked into a martyrological legend (39:11–12; 40:1–6) where the prophet attains an international status while the archenemy Nabuzaradan confesses the supremacy of the Lord's word (cf. Dan. 2–4; 6).

Finally the book was organized into the collections identified above. The lateness of this operation is proved by the fact that all layers—

OUTLINE OF CONTENTS

The Book of Jeremiah

- I. Visions, prophecies of judgment, and personal laments (chaps. 1–24)
  - A. Jeremiah's consecration as prophet (1:1–10)
  - B. Vision of almond rod and prophecies of judgment (1:11–15:21)
  - C. Jeremiah's vocation (16:1–21)
  - D. Judgment against Judah (17:1–27)
  - E. Sayings about potters and judgment (18:1–19:15)
  - F. Personal lament of Jeremiah (20:1–18)
  - G. Judgment against Judah (21:1–23:40)
  - H. Vision of baskets of figs and prophecies of judgment (24:1–10)
- II. Speeches of and stories about Jeremiah (chaps. 25–45)
  - A. Speeches against Judah and against the nations (25:1–29:32)
    1. Episodes from the time of Jehoiakim (25:1–26:24)
    2. Episodes from the time of Zedekiah (27:1–29:32)
  - B. Prophecies of restoration and comfort (30:1–33:26)
  - C. Episode from the time of Zedekiah (34:1–22)
  - D. Episodes from the time of Johoiakim (35:1–36:32)
  - E. Biographical materials (37:1–45:5)
- III. Prophecies against the nations (chaps. 46–51)
  - A. Oracles against Egypt (46:1–28)
  - B. Oracles against the Philistines (47:1–7)
  - C. Oracles against Moab (48:1–47)
  - D. Oracles against the Ammonites (49:1–39)
  - E. Oracles against other peoples (50:1–46)
  - F. Oracles against Babylon (51:1–64)
- IV. Historical appendix (chap. 52)

original elements, secondary expansions, reedited pieces, and late additions—are represented in every collection. At that final stage some small topical collections were put together: droughts (14:1–15:4), kings (21:11–23:8), prophets (23:9–40), restoration (chaps. 30–33), and a partial biography of Jeremiah during and after the fall of Jerusalem (chaps. 37–44).

Interpretation: Jeremiah's message is difficult to assess even after the recovery of his original words. In the course of his career, which extended for more than forty years, Jeremiah's political attitudes certainly changed more than once. While at first he criticized the alliance of Josiah with Egypt in the revolt against Assyria (2:14–19, 36–37), he later joined in the enthusiasm of the renewed conquests, announcing revenge to the neighbors-inheritors of Israel (49:1–5) and the return of the Israelite exiles (31:1–21). The death of Josiah, whom he esteemed (22:15–16), must have been a traumatic event for Jeremiah. He sought and found the reason for this event—sin in the land—and his political outlook conformed to this perception. There are many indications in chaps. 25; 26; 36; and 45 that Jeremiah expected a total destruction to come upon Judah in the wake of the first campaign of Nebuchadrezzar to the west (604), following his victory at Carchemish. But the disaster was averted by the prompt submission of Jehoiakim—an event that again affected the prophet's views: from now on Jeremiah constantly predicated submission in order to prevent destruction (27; 29; 34; 37–38; 42). Thus, his definition as a Judean Cassandra (i.e., a prophet of evil who is not believed), due to his early visions (chap. 4), is ironically improper. Jeremiah realistically understood the necessity of submitting to the rule of the Babylonian Empire. This line was continued by Deutero-Isaiah, who expected the restoration to occur in the frame of another world power: the Persians.

Embedded in Jeremiah's diatribes there is much of permanent value about concepts and institutions. Jeremiah denounces piety when its object is a syncretistic worship in the open (2:23–25; 14:10) and stigmatizes bravery and dispatch, if their end is adultery (23:10). For him royalty is not expressed by luxurious palaces, but by timely justice to the oppressed (22:14–16; cf. 21:11–12). Sanctity does not grant immunity to transgressors (7:4, 9–14), and not even to buildings dedicated to God. Prophecy is tested by the personal conduct of its bearers (23:14) and their faculty of turning people back from evil (23:17, 22), because this is God's will. Revelation does not come in a state of torpor, because the word of the Lord "is like fire, . . . and like a hammer which breaks the rock in pieces"; it stirs the whole of the prophet's being (23:29). Most important of all, Jeremiah deepens the concept of repentance (2:33–35; 3:1–5, 12b–13, 19–20—all one piece). He rejects the easy, elegant recantation that confides in God's mercy and rather looks for true contrition, for the pains of remorse, and their outcome—tears of despair (3:21–4:1).

Jeremiah's concept of repentance plausibly explains his attitude to the great religious revolution that occurred in his time, the unification of worship in Jerusalem. If he condemned the syncretistic worship in nature (2:20, 23; 3:2; 13:27), he certainly could only welcome a reform forbidding all sacrifice outside of a single temple in Jerusalem. But Jeremiah could not be satisfied with that. Ceremonies, conventions, processions, headed by the old establishment of elders, priests, and prophets (2 Kings 23:1–2) were for him a parody of repentance, and therefore unacceptable. His exacting moral demands could not be easily grasped by the Deuteronomist editors of the book who therefore coined them in a more formal way: "the men of Judah and the inhabitants of Jerusalem . . . have turned back to the iniquities of their forefathers" and broken the covenant (11:10). On the other hand Jeremiah's legacy was fully realized by a later prophet: "rend your heart and not your garments," says Joel (2:13), and his call was echoed and made normative in the rabbinic teaching (*m. Ta'an* 2:1). Jeremiah is cited twice in the Gospel of Matthew (2:17; 27:9); some people had also identified Jesus with Jeremiah the prophet. ***See also*** Baruch; Prophet. A.R.

Jeremiah, the Letter of. ***See*** Letter of Jeremiah, The.

Jeremoth (jer'e-muhth). **1** A son of Becher and grandson of Benjamin (1 Chron. 7:8). **2** A descendant of Benjamin of the clan of Elpaal (1 Chron. 8:14). **3** A Levite, the son of Mushai of the clan of Merari (1 Chron. 23:23); he is also called Jerimoth (1 Chron. 24:30). **4** A Levite, head of the fifteenth course of musicians (1 Chron. 25:22); he is probably the same person earlier called Jerimoth (a variant spelling; 1 Chron. 25:4). **5** The son of Azriel, head of the tribe of Naphtali during the reign of David (1 Chron. 27:19). **6** A member of the clan of Elam who took a foreign wife (Ezra 10:26). **7** Another, of the clan of Zattu, who took a foreign wife (Ezra 10:27). **8** A third, from the clan of Bani, who took a foreign wife (Ezra 10:29). ***See also*** Jerimoth. D.R.B.

Jericho (jair'i-koh), a city in the Jordan Valley, six miles north of the Dead Sea. Its broad plain, irrigated from the copious spring of modern 'Ein es-Sultan, just east of the ancient city, is extremely fertile. A ford near the city carries an important east-west road and makes Jericho a strategic entrance point from Transjordan into the highlands of Judah. The city of OT times is represented today by a mound 70 feet high and 10 acres in area. The tropical climate and vegetation of the Jordan Valley earned Jericho the title

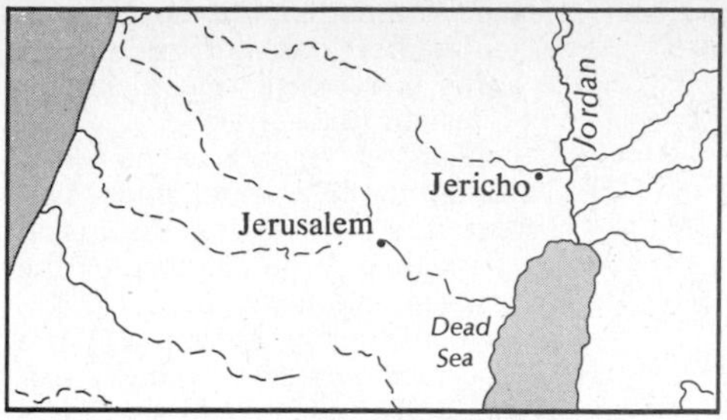

"city of palm trees" (Deut. 34:3). The ancient city was excavated by C. Warren (1867), E. Sellin and C. Watzinger (1907–09), J. Garstang (1930–36), and K. Kenyon (1952–58).

After the Babylonian invasions (early sixth century B.C.) the mound was abandoned and settlement concentrated in the irrigated oasis where modern Jericho is located. During the Hasmonean (167–63 B.C.) and Herodian (40 B.C.–A.D. 44) periods a complex of royal buildings grew up on the banks of the Wadi Qelt one and a quarter miles south of the ancient city. This site (modern Tulūl Abu el-'Alâiq) is commonly called New Testament Jericho. It was excavated by C. Warren (1868); A. Nöldeke, C. Watzinger, and E. Sellin (1909–11); J. L. Kelso and D. C. Baramki (1950); J. Pritchard (1951); and E. Netzer (after 1973).

The earliest occupation at Jericho (ca. 9000 B.C.) was a small Mesolithic shrine near the spring. The next phase (the Neolithic, ca. 8000–4000 B.C.) has given Jericho the description "the oldest walled town in the world." In the earliest Neolithic phase (ca. 8000–7000 B.C.), before the invention of pottery, the town, which was then as large as at any later time, was surrounded by a stone wall into which was set a circular stone tower 25 feet high. From the second Pre-pottery Neolithic phase we have ten human skulls, molded over with plaster to produce portrait heads. The city then passed through two pottery-bearing Neolithic phases and, after a period of inoccupancy, a Proto-Urban phase, represented only by rock-cut tombs (ca. 4000–3000 B.C.).

With the urbanization of Palestine in the Early Bronze Age (ca. 3200–2000 B.C.) Jericho again became a walled city. It flourished for several centuries before being destroyed by nomadic intruders. Little trace of their occupation (Middle Bronze I, ca. 2000–1900 B.C.) remains on the mound itself. The culture is known principally by its distinctive shaft tombs which often contain the remains of only one individual.

The Middle Bronze Age (ca. 1900–1500 B.C.), the era of the biblical patriarchs, saw Jericho a flourishing city, defended by powerful walls mounted on a high earthen embankment. A feature of this period of special interest to students of the Bible is a series of burial caves in which much of the grave furniture was preserved. The mats, baskets, tables, stools, beds, boxes, bowls, combs, and beads give a unique sampling of the objects in daily use during the time of the patriarchs.

In the Bible: Jericho first appears in the biblical record in connection with the Israelite conquest of Canaan at the end of the Late Bronze Age (ca. 1500–1200 B.C.). The wide plain on both sides of the Jordan near Jericho provided an ideal campground from which to launch an attack on Canaan. According to the Priestly document the invading tribes were encamped in the Transjordanian portion of the plain when they defeated Sihon, Og (Num. 22:1), and the forces of Midian (Num. 31:12). At the camp a census was taken (Num. 26:3, 63) and the main provisions for the division and settlement of Canaan were made (Num. 33–36). When two spies, who were saved from death in Jericho by Rahab (Josh. 2), reported favorably, Joshua's army crossed the river, aided by a miraculous division of its waters (Josh. 3:14–17), and laid siege to Jericho.

If it could be established archaeologically, the date of the fall of Jericho would fix the beginning of the Israelite invasion of Canaan. This would require the identification of a layer of destruction debris that could reasonably be attributed to Joshua's total devastation of the city, and the identification of the city walls

A human skull molded in plaster, excavated at Jericho from the Pre-pottery Neolithic phase (ca. 7000–4000 B.C.).

A clay oven with a juglet nearby (foreground) inside a house wall: scanty evidence of Late Bronze Age occupation of Jericho excavated by Kathleen Kenyon and dated by her to ca. 1350 B.C.

that, according to biblical tradition, collapsed under the spectacular conditions described in Joshua 6. J. Garstang believed that the ruin of a massive mudbrick wall, the destruction of which he dated to about 1400 B.C., was the wall in question. Dr. Kenyon's later excavation showed that this "wall" was in fact part of two Early Bronze Age walls, many centuries older than the time of Joshua. Kenyon found no trace of Late Bronze Age city walls, and only one fragment of a house floor belonging to the period. The forces of erosion had removed all the vital evidence. Principally on the basis of the pottery from five Late Bronze Age tombs, Dr. Kenyon suggested a date in the last half of the fourteenth century B.C. for the Israelite conquest of Jericho, but the more commonly accepted date of around 1200 B.C. is not ruled out on the basis of the Jericho evidence.

After its destruction by the Israelites Jericho lay unoccupied for about four centuries. It was uninhabited during the time of the prophets Elijah and Elisha, who were both active in the region (2 Kings 2:4). The long period of abandonment accounts for the almost complete erosion of the Late Bronze Age walls and buildings. Jericho was rebuilt by Hiel of Bethel during the reign of Ahab (873–851 B.C.). In the loss of his eldest and youngest sons (1 Kings 16:35) Hiel suffered the consequences predicted in the curse that Joshua laid on anyone who reestablished the city (Josh. 6:26).

Archaeologically, little is known about Israelite Jericho. Its remains have been completely eroded from the summit of the mound. It probably began as a small-scale settlement, but by the seventh century B.C. it had expanded so that impressive buildings occupied the slopes of the mound outside the line of the earlier walls. After the Babylonian invasions the site of the ancient city was abandoned.

Jericho figured in a minor way in the ministry of Jesus. He was baptized in the Jordan near the city (Matt. 3:5–17). His temptation probably took place on a mountain west of the city (Matt. 4:1–11). He came from Galilee to Jerusalem by way of the Jordan Valley and Jericho (Matt. 20). At Jericho he healed blind Bartimaeus (Mark 10: 46–52), had his encounter with the tax collector Zacchaeus (Luke 19:1–11), and told the parable of the pounds (Luke 19:12–28).

Jesus' activity in Jericho was probably confined to the poorer quarter of the city and did not take him into Herod's magnificent winter capital on the banks of the Wadi Qelt, where archaeological excavations have produced spectacular results.

The Hasmonean structures, all on the north

side of the wadi, were probably built by Alexander Jannaeus (103–76 B.C.). They consist in part of a palatial building (164 by 230 feet) and a swimming pool (65 by 115 feet) associated with a large courtyard. Herod renovated and extended the site on a grand scale. South of the wadi stood his earliest palace, and along the wadi's southern edge lay a magnificent sunken garden with columned porticoes at either end and a monumental facade of ornamental brickwork. On the north bank of the wadi, opposite the sunken garden, was a building designed primarily for guests. It had a columned facade 285 feet long and contained a paved reception hall; two courts, one with Ionic and one with Corinthian columns; a luxurious Roman-style bath; and numerous other rooms. Herod's private palace with adjoining swimming pool, gardens, pavilions, and ritual baths was at some distance to the west of the audience building. ***See also*** Archaeology, History, and the Bible; Conquest of Canaan; Joshua.

Bibliography

Kenyon, K. M. *Digging up Jericho.* New York: Praeger, 1957.

Kenyon, K. M., G. Foerster, G. Bacchi, and E. Nezer. "Jericho." In *Encyclopedia of Archaeological Excavations in the Holy Land.* Vol. 2. Jerusalem: Masada, 1970. Pp. 550–575. L.E.T.

Jerimoth (jer'i-muhth). **1** A son of Bela and grandson of Benjamin (1 Chron. 7:7). **2** One who joined David's fighting men at Ziklag (1 Chron. 12:5). **3** A Levite, son of Mushai of the clan of Merari (1 Chron. 24:30); he is also called Jeremoth (a variant spelling; 1 Chron. 23:23). **4** A Levite musician of the clan of Heman (1 Chron. 25:4); probably the same person also called Jeremoth who was head of the fifteenth course of musicians (1 Chron. 25:22). **5** A son of King David and father of Mahalath, a wife of King Rehoboam (2 Chron. 11:18). **6** A Levite Temple official during the reign of King Hezekiah (2 Chron. 31:13). ***See also*** Jeremoth. D.R.B.

Jeroboam I (jair-uh-boh'uhm; meaning uncertain; possibly Heb., "may the people multiply" or "he who contends for the people"), the first king of the Northern Kingdom (Israel), who reigned from ca. 922 to 901 B.C. Jeroboam, the son of Nebat and Zeruah, was an Ephraimite from Zeredah who began his rise to power when Solomon appointed him to oversee the forced labor in Ephraim and Manasseh (1 Kings 11: 26–28). The precise circumstances of his becoming king are unclear, since the Masoretic Text (MT) and the Septuagint (LXX) preserve conflicting accounts of the event. According to the MT, Jeroboam rebelled against Solomon, although the details of the revolt are not given (1 Kings 11: 26). Jeroboam was promised kingship over the northern tribes by the prophet Ahijah of Shiloh, who interpreted the later revolt of the north as a judgment on the house of David because of the sins of Solomon (1 Kings 11:29–39). Solomon then sought to kill Jeroboam, who was forced to flee to Egypt until the king's death. Jeroboam then returned and played a leading role in the events that led to the secession of the northern tribes.

The LXX amplifies the picture of Jeroboam's rebellion by stating that he fortified the city of Sarira and gathered three hundred chariots in an attempt to overthrow Solomon (LXX, 1 Kings 12:24). When this attempt failed, Jeroboam fled to Egypt, where he married into the royal family (cf. MT, 1 Kings 11:14–22). After he returned home, he again fortified Sarira, but before he could pursue the revolt further, his son became ill. When he asked Ahijah about the fate of the child, the prophet predicted the end of Jeroboam's dynasty (cf. MT, 1 Kings 14). No matter which of these two accounts is accurate, it is probable that Jeroboam did not become king until after the northern tribes had withdrawn their support from Solomon's son and successor Rehoboam because of the latter's refusal to lighten the burdens that Solomon had placed on them (1 Kings 12:1–20).

After becoming king, Jeroboam fortified Shechem and Penuel (1 Kings 12:25) and may have used them as his capital before he established his residence in Tirzah (1 Kings 14:17). In order to discourage his Ephraimite subjects from traveling to Jerusalem for worship, he set up gold bull images ("calves") at Bethel and Dan, an act he probably understood as a revival of an older form of the worship of God (see Exod. 32:1–6). At the same time, he revised the cultic calendar, instituted a non-levitical priesthood, built shrines on the high places, and served as a priest himself, at least on certain occasions (1 Kings 12:26–33).

These religious reforms earned him the condemnation of the writers of the books of Kings, for whom he became the paradigm of the evil king. According to their interpretation of Israelite history, Jeroboam's cultic sins immediately led to the condemnation of the altar at Bethel by an unnamed prophet from Judah (1 Kings 13:1–10) and later provoked Ahijah to prophesy the destruction of Jeroboam's royal line (1 Kings 14:7–11; 15:27–30). Throughout their account of the history of the Northern Kingdom, the writers of Kings claim that all subsequent Ephraimite kings "did what was evil in the sight of the Lord and walked in the way of Jeroboam" (e.g., 1 Kings 15:26). The pattern of sin established by Jeroboam continued until the Northern Kingdom itself was finally destroyed (2 Kings 17:21–23).

When the Egyptian pharaoh Shishak invaded Palestine (ca. 918 B.C.), he made raids into Israel and destroyed a number of cities. This incursion may have weakened Jeroboam's control over his kingdom and encouraged the neighboring Philistines and Aramaeans to seize Israelite territory. The Chronicler also reports extensive warfare with Judah during Jeroboam's reign, although the outcome of these battles is unclear (2 Chron. 12:15; 13:2–20; cf. 1 Kings 14:30; 15:6–7). R.R.W.

Jeroboam II (jair-uh-boh'uhm; meaning uncertain; possibly Heb., "may the people multiply" or "he who contends for the people"), the son of Joash and his successor as king of Israel. Although the writers of the books of Kings say little about Jeroboam's forty-one-year reign (ca. 786–746 B.C.) except that "he did what was evil in the sight of the Lord [and] did not depart from all the sins of Jeroboam son of Nebat" (2 Kings 14:24), a more complete account of his relatively prosperous kingship can be reconstructed on the basis of extrabiblical sources.

As the penultimate king of the Jehu dynasty, Jeroboam inherited a more favorable set of political circumstances than did his predecessors. Effective Assyrian intervention in Palestine ended with the campaigns of Adad-nirari III (809–782 B.C.), who at the end of the ninth century moved west and defeated the Aramaeans of Damascus, who had been harassing Israel since the end of Jehu's reign (ca. 816 B.C.; cf. 2 Kings 13:5). The Assyrian king exacted tribute from several rulers in the area, including Jeroboam's father, Joash, but the heaviest blows fell on the Aramaeans, whose political power was severely restricted. During the first half of the eighth century Adad-nirari III and his successors were occupied with internal strife at home, and the resulting power vacuum in Palestine allowed Jeroboam to expand his borders from the Sea of the Arabah (the Dead Sea) to the "entrance of Hamath" (2 Kings 14:25) and to reclaim territory lost during the reign of Jehu and Jehoahaz (2 Kings 10:32–33; 13:1–9). He may also have moved into Transjordan and gained control over Damascus, thus restoring the boundaries of the old Davidic Empire (2 Kings 14:28; Amos 6:13), but the texts that describe these events are difficult to interpret.

Jeroboam's expansionist activities, which were supported by the prophet Jonah, the son of Amittai (2 Kings 14:25), brought prosperity to Israel, particularly in the larger cities. The new land was presumably assigned to the king's supporters, who became part of a new class of wealthy landowners. Increased agriculture and trade brought more tax revenue into the royal court. This redistribution of land and money increased the number of poor people in the land and created a class of servants and slaves, who were exploited by the rich. These social and economic abuses, together with a continuation of Baal worship, provoked sharp judgment oracles from the prophet Amos, whose words dramatize the negative aspects of Jeroboam's economic prosperity (Amos 2:6–8; 4:1–3; 5:10–12; 6:4–7, 11–14; 8:4–6). ***See also*** Amos, The Book of. R.R.W.

Bronze copy of a seal inscribed, "Belonging to Shema, the servant of Jeroboam"; Megiddo, from the reign of Jeroboam II, 786–746 B.C.

Jeroham (je-roh'huhm; Heb., "may he be loved" or "may he have compassion"). **1** A Levite, the father of Elkanah and grandfather of Samuel (1 Sam. 1:1; 1 Chron. 6:34). **2** A family group ("sons of Jeroham") in the tribe of Benjamin (1 Chron. 8:27). **3** A Benjaminite, the father of Ibneiah, an inhabitant of postexilic Jerusalem (1 Chron. 9:8). **4** A priest, the father of Adaiah, another inhabitant of postexilic Jerusalem (1 Chron. 9:12; Neh. 11:12). **5** A man from Gedor whose two sons, Joelah and Zebadiah, joined David's fighting men at Ziklag (1 Chron. 12:7). **6** The father of Azarel, the leader of the tribe of Dan during David's reign (1 Chron. 27:22). **7** The father of Azariah, a military leader under the high priest Jehoida (2 Chron. 23:1). D.R.B.

Jerubbaal (jair-yo͞o-bah'ahl). ***See*** Gideon.

Jerusalem

THE CENTRAL CITY of ancient Israel.

Topography: Jerusalem does not derive its importance from natural endowments except for a perennial spring. Situated at the edge of the Judean desert, it has an arid climate. Its land is agriculturally poor and its limestone base has no minerals of value. Strabo, a Greek geographer of the first century A.D., described it as a place that would not be envied, one for which no one would fight.

The area over which the city has spread lies between the divided watershed of the highlands, the ridge road, and the Mount of Olives. The Kidron Valley separates it from the Mount of Olives on the east and the north, and the Hinnom Valley from the ridge on the west and south. Its terrain is rugged. Running through the middle of the area is a north-south valley called the Tyropoeon (Heb., "cheese makers"). Between the Tyropoeon and the Kidron the short Beth-zatha Valley further divides this section. The resulting hill between the Tyropoeon and Kidron valleys is squeezed to a narrow land bridge at its center. The steeply sloping area south of this was called originally Mount Zion or the Ophel hill; the flatter area to its north, where the Dome of the Rock is now located, Mount Moriah or the Temple Mount. "Zion" eventually was used to refer to both areas as well as the city as a whole. A still higher section lies north of the Temple Mount, known as Beth-zatha in the first century and now as the Moslem Quarter. The hill formed between the Hinnom and Tyropoeon valleys is divided by two east-west depressions. The southern one runs along the line of the present Old City wall forming an area to its south now wrongly called Mount Zion. The one to the north borders the present David Street. The Jewish and Armenian quarters now cover the area between the depressions. The entire area south of this depression is also called the western hill. The area to the north of it is the present Christian Quarter. The entire western section slopes downward from west to east. The location of Jerusalem was not suited for a well laid-out city plan.

The word "Jerusalem" incised on a wall of a rock-cut burial cave near Laḥish; early sixth century B.C.

Nor was Jerusalem blessed with an abundant water supply. Only one

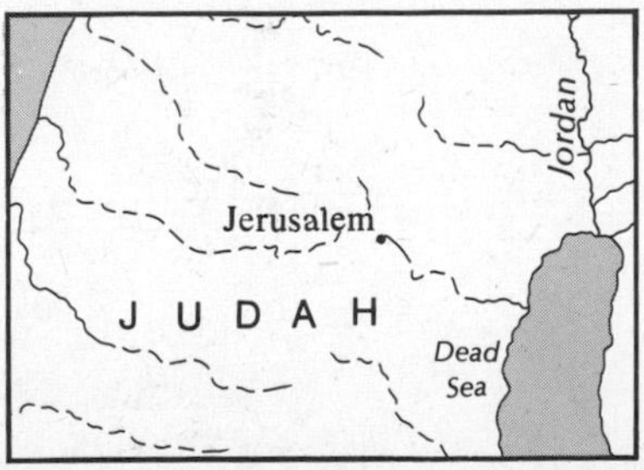

Situated in the central hill country, Jerusalem became, under David, the key city of ancient Israel, and thus it remained. (In addition to the three plans of Jerusalem included later in this article, three more plans of the city at different historical periods are included in the section of color maps [15, 16, 17].)

spring was located in the area, the Gihon. Being on the level of the Kidron Valley it was not naturally a protected site. A second spring, En-rogel, located in the middle of the Kidron but south of the city was even more exposed.

In later tradition Jerusalem's poor setting would be understood as the result of the loss of paradise, which was thought to have been located here. The Gihon spring was described as the remnant of one of the rivers of Eden (Gen. 2:13). Mount Moriah, the Temple Mount, was seen as the foundation or navel of the earth.

Jerusalem was not an important natural commercial center. It did not straddle a major trade crossroad as did Shechem or Bethel. The natural east-west axis of trade was eight miles north of this area on the Beth-horon Road and the Way of Bethel-Ai.

Jerusalem was initially important for its control of traffic along the north-south ridge road as it enters a broad, comparatively level section of the highlands to its north. This area was the territory of the tribe of Benjamin to which Jerusalem belonged. It also served to protect against any aggression from the west through the Sorek-Rephaim valley system and to prevent surprise attack from the Judean desert.

Early History: In the Paleolithic period (prior to ca. 25,000 B.C.) the broad area where the Rephaim Valley meets the north-south ridge, not the rugged terrain east of the ridge, was the location of the first known settlement in the area. This site overlooked the Rephaim Valley to the west and the Hinnom to the east as it rested on the ridge. It flourished ca. 120,000 B.C. In historic times this area was too vulnerable and lacked a sufficient water supply for any substantial settlement. People migrated to the Gihon spring area.

Aerial view of Jerusalem showing, in the center, the site of the ancient city. The Dome of the Rock stands in the area that was the Temple Mount, to the right of which is the Kidron Valley, which continues into the foreground. Above the steep slope of the Kidron is the Ophel hill, site of the City of David.

Mount Zion (Heb., "dry place") above the spring is well protected by the Kidron and the Tyropoeon valleys. The western hill is sufficiently distant and steeply sloped to keep archers at a safe range, although it blocks the view of the ridge road. The north side, in all times the most exposed part of the city, was defended by a high "bulge," Ophel, and the easily protected land bridge to the Temple Mount.

Entrance to Hezekiah's tunnel cut beneath the City of David in the eighth century B.C. It brought water from the Gihon spring to the west side of the Ophel hill.

The earliest indication of settlement so far discovered on the Ophel hill was in the Early Bronze Age (3000–2000 B.C.). No walls or buildings have been found. Ophel hill may simply have supported an encampment around the Gihon spring.

The early records of Jerusalem's name, which appears only in lists, underscore its unexceptional nature. Its earliest appearance, called "Salim," may be in commercial documents from Ebla in Syria ca. 2400 B.C. Egyptian execration texts from the nineteenth century B.C. call the city "Rushalimum," and those from el-Amarna in Syria in the fourteenth century "Urusalim." The name probably meant "the foundation of the god, Salem." "Salem" became its shortened form (Ps. 76:2; and Gen. 14:18, if this originally referred to Jerusalem, not Salem in Samaria). Jerusalem was understood in rabbinic and Christian writings to mean "Seeing of Peace." The interpretation "City of Peace" became popular after the biblical period.

Excavations on Ophel hill confirm that during the Middle Bronze Age (2000–1500 B.C.) there was a walled city. The wall followed the edge of the hill on the west side but enclosed most of the slope on the east. A tower of the eastern gate was uncovered near the Gihon spring. The entrance to the spring, which remained outside the city walls on the valley floor, was covered and shafts were dug to it from just inside the city walls. In order to make use of the slope above the city walls, terraces were built called *millo* (Heb., "filling"), which were often in need of repair (2 Sam. 5:9). By the Late Bronze Age (1500–1200 B.C.) the Jebusites occupied this excellent stronghold, which they boasted the lame and blind could defend (2 Sam. 5:6). The 11-acre city with a crowded population of no more than 1000 was called Jebus during this period. Jebus's strength is indicated by its being the last major city on the ridge to resist settlement by the people under Joshua. Although located within Benjaminite borders, it was never occupied by this tribe for any significant period (Josh. 18:16; Judg.1:21). Its king, Adonizedek, led the Amorite kings of the south against Joshua (Josh. 10:1).

Under David and Solomon: Jerusalem was elevated to its place of central importance by David ca. 1000 B.C. He turned Jerusalem into a religious and political symbol of the unity of the people of God. David needed a neutral place, located at the boundary between the northern and southern groups of the Israelites, to establish his monarchy. He took the city by utilizing the steep shaft of the Gihon spring, through which his commander, Joab, entered the city. Joab then opened the gates to David's forces (2 Sam. 5:8). The city was now also called the City of David. Judah occupied it (Josh. 15:63). There was no need to alter the size or defenses of the city. David's palace was built on the north end of the city.

Mount Moriah, or the Temple Mount, is 130 feet above the City of

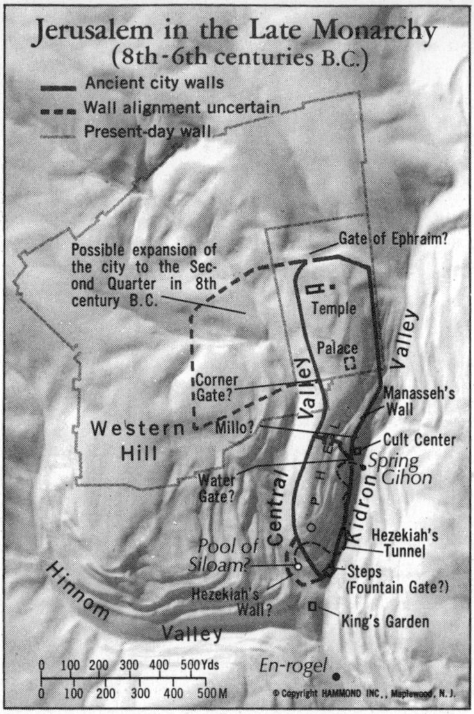

Ahaz, Hezekiah, Manasseh, Josiah, and Jehoiakim are among the kings of Judah who reigned in Jerusalem in the eighth to sixth centuries B.C. The prophets Isaiah of Jerusalem and Jeremiah were active in this period.

David and provides for a central holy place. This was the "threshing floor of Arauna" (2 Sam. 24) and probably had been a Jebusite holy area as well. The tabernacle was set here and the Ark brought to rest in its Holy of Holies. Given its dual function as administrative center and holy place for the entire nation, Jerusalem prospered. The resulting symbol of unity was paradoxical. A poorly endowed village had become a crucial religious and political center. Its central holy place was even lower than the hills about it. God's exaltation of this common place became an important motif in Israelite theology (Ps. 68: 15–16; Ezek. 16:1–10).

Although forbidden by the Torah to bury in a city, David may have followed foreign custom by having a tomb prepared in the middle of the city (1 Kings 2:10). The kings of Judah continued to follow this custom. A series of horizontal shaft tombs have been uncovered in the center of Ophel. It is not certain that these belong to the kings of Judah. Some claim that "in" Jerusalem refers to the area around the city and doubt that David's tomb was within its walls. In the first century, however, David's tomb was thought to be in this part of the city.

Solomon (ca. 962–922) increased the symbolic importance of Jerusalem. It was no longer central for just the hill country, but for the entire kingdom. His building program in Jerusalem paralleled his consolidation of David's kingdom. He extended the walls from the Ophel to enclose the Temple Mount (1 Kings 3:1). Jerusalem became a 32-acre city. Administrative buildings and palaces filled this area and the Temple replaced the tabernacle. No traces of his building activity have been uncovered. Reconstructions of Solomon's Temple and palaces based on the biblical accounts show Phoenician influence (cf. 1 Kings 6:18; 7:13–14). The city was becoming cosmopolitan. Solomon needed international support for his policies. Pagan shrines were built on the hill facing Ophel on the east (1 Kings 11:7). The symbolic unity of the people expressed in a central city with one shrine began to erode.

The Divided Monarchy to the Fall of Judah (587 B.C.): The additional walled space did not provide for normal housing growth. The population spread to the western hill, which was heavily populated by the eighth century. Tombs from the ninth century found in the Tyropoeon Valley side of the Temple Mount may indicate sparse settlement in the area prior to the eighth century. The western hill was known as *Mishneh*, "second." A wall was built to enclose the *Mishneh* in the eighth century. A 128-foot section of this wall has been found in the middle of the Jewish Quarter. It is 22.5 feet thick and is preserved in places to a height of 10 feet. The extent of the walled area is not clear. Some would limit the walled area to three-quarters of the present Jewish Quarter with the southern limit being the Old City walls. Others would extend it farther south.

The need for strengthening Jerusalem's defense system became acute when Assyria threatened Judah after taking the Northern Kingdom in 722 B.C. Hezekiah strengthened the city walls. A tower and gate were built just north of the wall segment at the edge of the northern east-west depression, evidently to provide a double entrance at the vulnerable north side of the city. The tower still stands to a height of 25.5 feet. Some claim the wall was then extended to the top of the western hill, passing through the present citadel area and along the line of the Old City wall, then continuing around the western hill until it reached the City of David. No remains have been found.

Hezekiah sealed the Gihon spring and cut a 1,750-foot tunnel beneath the City of David to bring the water into the Tyropoeon Valley on the west side of Ophel, where it could be better protected (2 Chron. 32:2–4). The Pool of Siloam was constructed to collect the water (John 8:7). This was eventually divided into upper and lower basins. One of the earliest inscriptions found in Jerusalem is the "Siloam Inscription," which was chiseled near the tunnel's mouth. It describes the meeting of the workers who dug from both ends of the tunnel. The pool was either protected by the newly constructed city wall or enclosed in a cistern.

The huge retaining wall at the southwestern corner of the Temple Mount from the time of Herod the Great.

Some of the stone for Hezekiah's building projects was probably taken from a quarry located north of the Temple Mount near the present-day Damascus Gate, now called Solomon's Quarry or Zedekiah's Cave. This quarry was used through the Roman period (63 B.C.–A.D. 324).

When the messengers of Sennacherib, king of Assyria, approached the secured city, their offers for peaceful submission were rebuffed. Soon after, Assyria was forced to depart the land, never testing the defense preparations (2 Kings 18–19). Sennacherib's view of the city is reflected in his description of Hezekiah as a prisoner in Jerusalem like a bird in a cage.

Jerusalem under the succeeding kings of Judah did not continue its trust in God as it had under Hezekiah. The image of the prostitute and widow became prophetic ways of describing the city as more pagan practices entered its life (Isa. 1:21; Lam. 1; Ezek. 16). Jesus would continue to use this female imagery when addressing the city (Luke 23:28). Evidence of the decadence of the city is seen in the number of fertility goddesses found in excavations. The city was warned that it would be returned to its lowly origin if it did not reform. Zion would be plowed as a field (Mic. 3:12).

A century later this prophecy was fulfilled. Excavations on the Ophel and *Mishneh* indicate how devastating was Babylon's plundering of the city in 598 B.C. and its leveling of it in 587 B.C. (2 Kings 25:10). Spearheads still litter the *Mishneh* wall area. Building walls are charred and their basements filled with ash and rubble. The supports of the *millo* were removed and the terraces left to erode. So complete was the destruction on the eastern slopes of the Ophel that that area would never be part of the city again. Jerusalem's population was taken into exile.

The Restoration to the Hasmoneans: In 538 B.C. Cyrus of Persia gave permission for a group of exiles to return and rebuild the city (Ezra 1). Only a fraction of the former population returned and the city was confined to Ophel. No evidence of occupation during this period has been found on the western hills. The lack of artifacts or pottery from this period outside of Ophel further indicates how small the population was. The city walls built by Nehemiah (mid-sixth century B.C.) only circled the crest of the Ophel, the slopes above Gihon spring being left outside of the city. Zerubbabel rebuilt the Temple. The city no longer was a symbol of the unity of the north and south but was reduced to a center for preserving Judean purity (Neh. 13:28–30). Jerusalem would retain this understanding of its role into the Roman period (John 4:20–22).

Persian marble head, perhaps of Cyrus II, sixth century B.C.

During the Persian period (538–333 B.C.) a different picture of Jerusalem was developed by those opposed to the city's becoming so exclusive in its political and religious life. They lost hope in the establishment of the symbol of unity of a united Israel by political means, and in apocalyptic visions they dreamed of a transformed city established by God at the end of time. This Jerusalem no longer is located in a poor setting. Its geography is totally altered to exalt the city. The surrounding hills are leveled and the city is raised to the highest of mountains (Zech. 14:16–19; Isa. 40:4). It returns to its state before the loss of paradise (Ezek. 47). From this center of the world God rules as a victorious king. The nations come as pilgrims to central Jerusalem to worship (Isa. 56:1–8; Zech. 14:16–19). This apocalyptic vision of Jerusalem continues into NT times (Rev. 21–22).

In the Hellenistic period (333–63 B.C.) the attempt to establish a religiously pure Jerusalem resulted in conflict among Judeans themselves. Part of the inhabitants wanted to follow the Hellenistic culture brought to the east by Alexander the Great. A stadium and gymnasium were built in the city (1 Macc. 1:14). Some of its inhabitants were granted Antiochean (Greek) citizenship (2 Macc. 4:9). This has been understood by some to mean that the name of the city was changed to Antioch, an opinion that is now generally doubted. In order for their party to control the city, the Hellenists built a fortress by the Temple Mount called the Akra. No traces of this building have been found. It is possible it was located north of the Temple Mount in the area of the present Via Dolorosa.

As Jerusalem again gained in importance as a religious and political center, the western hill again was used by the growing population. The city wall of the *Mishneh* was rebuilt after the anti-Hellenistic Hasmoneans finally took control of the city in the second century B.C. This was probably part of the building program completed by the Hasmonean (Maccabean) Simon in 140 B.C. (1 Macc. 14:37). The city wall definitely encircled the entire western hill. Portions of the wall have been found on all sides of this area. A defense tower was built in the center of the northern part of the wall beside that of Hezekiah's day.

Under Rome: After the Romans conquered the city in 63 B.C. under Pompey, Jerusalem reached its pinnacle of grandeur and strength as a result of the building program of Herod the Great, whom Rome appointed king of Judea in 40 B.C. He strengthened the Hasmonean walls. At the top of the western hill he built a huge palace complex for himself. Its two sections were named after his Roman benefactors, Caesar and Agrippa: the Caesarium and Agrippium. This later became the *praetorium* (quarters) for the prefect or procurator of Judea. Three monumental towers built into the Hasmonean wall as it curved to the south protected the palace from attacks from the north at this vulnerable corner of the city. The towers were named Mariamne (after Herod's wife), Phaesalis (after his brother), and Hippicus (after his friend). The base of Phaesalis tower, now called "The Tower of David," is still standing in the citadel area of the Old City.

The northern section of the Hasmonean wall was also vulnerable

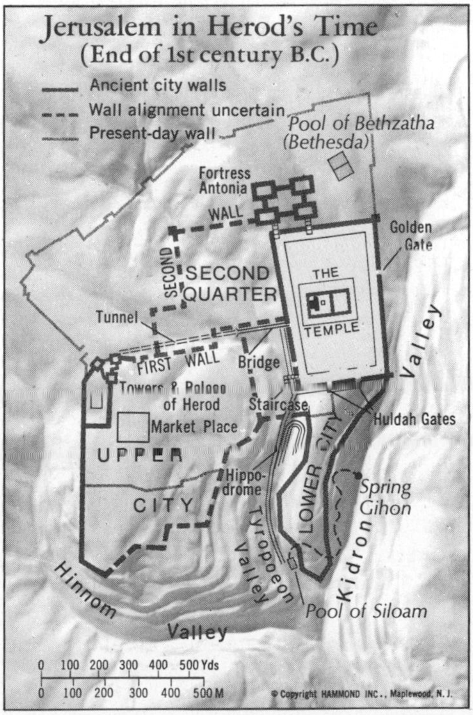

Herod the Great (40–4 B.C.) undertook a massive building program in Jerusalem that included extending the Temple Mount to the south and constructing a new Temple edifice.

Excavations in front of the southern wall of the Temple Mount have revealed significant remains from the Umayyad, Byzantine, Herodian, Hasmonean, and First Temple periods.

where the ridge created by the northern east-west depression disappears along its eastern half. To strengthen this and include more of the western area in the city, Herod built a second wall that circled from the middle of the first, or Hasmonean wall, to a fortress north of the Temple Mount called the Antonia. Some trace this wall as far north as the present-day Damascus Gate, where it is claimed part of the wall has been found. Others describe the wall as turning to the Antonia just east of the Church of the Resurrection. To further strengthen this second wall, which was open to attack from the west, a quarry was opened in front of it that served as a defense moat. Excavations in the area of the Lutheran Church of the Redeemer have uncovered parts of this quarry. The entrance to the quarry cut into the sloping western hill. A section of this was not worth quarrying and it was left standing as a mound of limestone. It was called Golgotha, Aramaic and Heb., "skull" (John 19:17). This part of the quarry belonged to Joseph of Arimathea, who cut his family tomb into the exposed hill of the quarry adjacent to Golgotha (John 19:41). This is now part of the Church of the Resurrection and probably was the burial place of Jesus.

Herod's most spectacular building project in the city was on the Temple Mount. He extended the level top of the Temple Mount to the south by a huge platform at places reaching a height of 180 feet. Access to the Temple Mount from the western hill was by bridge over the Tyropoeon Valley in the area of the present Wailing Wall and by a magnificent staircase from the market that was southwest of the Temple Mount. Access from the Ophel was by two subterranean passages.

North of the Temple Mount a huge fortress, called the Antonia after Herod's first Roman patron, controlled activity on the Temple Mount as well as provided further protection from the district of Beth-zatha, which sloped to the Temple Mount from the north. This was also called "the Barracks" (Acts 21:37). As with the second wall built by

The Mount of Olives (upper left) and the traditional site of the Garden of Gethsemane (center, to the left of the church).

Herod, this defense was strengthened by a moat called the Struthion Pool. The political administrative centers of the Antonia, Caesarium, and Agrippium dominated the Temple, visually reminding the city of the strength of its occupiers. The Pool of Siloam, En-rogel, the Struthion Pool, and cisterns in homes were not enough to meet the demands for water in this administrative and pilgrim center whose population had grown to about twenty-five thousand and may have supported an additional seventy-five thousand during major festivals. The Hinnom Valley was dammed on the west side of the city to provide reservoirs. This had already been done to the Beth-zatha Valley at the northeast corner of the Temple Mount before Herod. This double reservoir was called the Sheep Pool (John 5:2). The reservoirs have been excavated near St. Anne's Church. When these did not suffice, Herod built aqueducts from a spring area south of Bethlehem, now called the Pools of Solomon, to Jerusalem. By the first third of the first century A.D. this also had to be expanded by building an aqueduct from springs even further south in the Valley of Baraka. This was a project of Pontius Pilate.

The discovery of a shrine to the god of healing, Aesculapius or Serapis, by Beth-zatha's Sheep Pool, evidences the continuing Hellenistic influence in Jerusalem. Shallow pools and votives from this healing center have been found. Jesus demonstrated God's superiority to pagan gods by healing a person here (John 5:2–9).

Roman cultural influence is reflected in the homes of the wealthy on the western hill, now called the Upper City. In its mansions one found fine imported pottery, frescoes made according to the most advanced techniques, and fine glassware. As did other cities of the Roman Empire, Jerusalem had places of entertainment such as a stadium to the north of the city and a theater, probably located in the Kidron Valley.

Tension under Roman domination grew as did appreciation of that culture. The attempt by Herod Agrippa in A.D. 42 to bring the northern suburbs of the city within a third wall was halted before completion of the wall, so that the city would not become even more difficult for Rome to control in the event of a rebellion. Some claim that the line of this third wall follows that of the present-day northern Old City wall. Wall fragments from this period have been found in the Damascus Gate area of the present Old City. Others place the wall 400 yards north of Damascus Gate, where sections of wall or monumental building stones have been found. If this was the third wall, it had no foundation.

Tension between Jerusalem and Rome reached its climax during the rebellion begun in A.D. 66. In A.D. 70 three legions were sent to bring the city again under Roman control. The line of blocks found north of the city may be evidence of their siege wall. Jerusalem was captured and destroyed in August of A.D. 70 on the same day, according to tradition, that it had fallen to the Babylonians. Excavations show that the destruction was equally devastating. Only the Temple platform and Phaesalis Tower were left standing. The city's walls were torn down and the buildings fired. Citizens were slaughtered in their homes. As the OT prophets had warned of the destruction of Jerusalem because of the derogation of its symbol of political and

KEY TO EVENTS OF SIEGE

1. Romans breach Third Wall May 25 and capture New City.
2. Romans enter Second Quarter. Jews withdraw behind First Wall. May 30-June 2.
3. Titus' divided attack on First Wall and the Antonia fails.
4. Romans build siege wall around city.
5. Romans renew assault on the Antonia. Fortress falls to Titus July 22.
6. Romans burn gates and enter Temple courtyards. On August 29 Temple destroyed by fire.
7. Romans burn Lower City. September 2?
8. Romans assault Herod's Palace and enter the Upper City. Resistance ends on September 26.

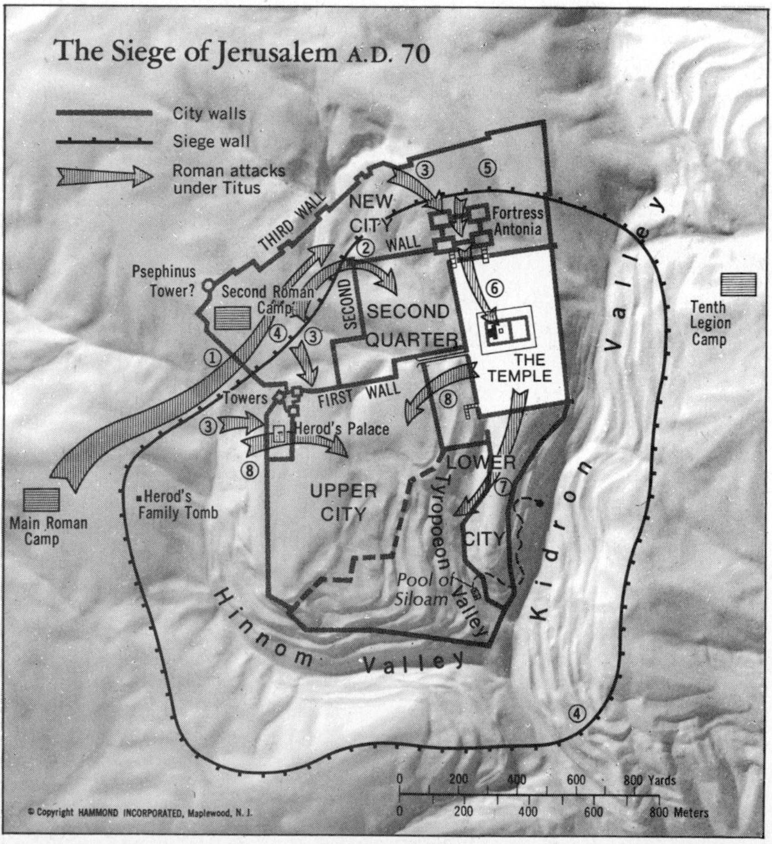

The base of "the Tower of David" dates to the time of Herod the Great, when it was part of the Phaesalis tower.

religious unity under God's law, so Jesus had warned of the city's destruction during his ministry (Luke 19:41–44; 21:20–24).

Through the last third of the first century most of the city remained in ruins. Jamnia (Yavneh) on the coastal plain became the religious center of the country as the Pharisaic party was appointed by Rome to represent the Judeans. There is little evidence that the Temple's altar was restored for worship. None of the fine homes or administrative centers were rebuilt. Tensions with Jerusalem's occupying power were not reduced, however. This resulted in a second revolt against Rome in A.D. 130 led by Bar-Kochba. The immediate cause of the war was Rome's decision to build a temple to Jupiter on the Temple Mount. It is not clear whether this was completed before or after the revolt. After the revolt was crushed all Judeans were banned from the city. The temple to Jupiter on the Temple Mount was completed. Jesus had predicted that such a pagan center would be set up in the Temple area (Mark 13:14).

The twin arches of the now walled-up Golden Gate in the eastern wall of Jerusalem's old city, originally built in the Byzantine period.

The city was rebuilt as a Roman military camp called Aelia Capitolina. Aelia was the family name of Hadrian, the emperor who crushed the revolt, and Capitolina referred to Jupiter. This small city was concentrated on the western hill in the area of the present Jewish Quarter. The area just north of the city became its forum. Remains of the second wall were leveled and the quarry in the area was filled when the forum was laid out. Golgotha on the north edge of the forum was rejoined by fill to the western slope and served as the acropolis for the forum. A temple to Aphrodite was constructed here. A fine monumental arch was built at the site of the present Damascus Gate and in the area where the Struthion Pool had been located. This was the extent of the city until the rise of Constantine (early fourth century A.D.), who made Jerusalem a Christian center. Golgotha and the tomb of Jesus now became part of a church that was the center of a Jerusalem whose walls extended around the western hill, the City of David, the Temple Mount and the suburbs north of the city as far as the present city walls. Byzantine Jerusalem reached its greatest size as a walled city.

See also Assyria, Empire of; David, City of; Gihon; Hasmoneans; Hezekiah; Hinnom, Valley of; Jesus Christ; Kidron; Moriah; Olives, Mount of; Ophel; Siloam Inscription; Temple, The; Zion. B.E.S.

Jeshaiah (je-shī'yuh; Heb., "Yah [God] saves" or "Yah is salvation"). **1** A Judahite, the grandson of Zerubbabel and in the royal lineage of the kings of Judah (1 Chron. 3:21). **2** A Levite musician of the clan of Jeduthun; head of the eighth course of musicians (1 Chron. 25:3, 15). **3** A Levite who shared the responsibility of keeping the Temple treasures (1 Chron. 26:25). **4** The son of Athaliah; a leader of the clan of Elam who returned from the Babylonian captivity with Ezra (Ezra 8:7). **5** A Levite of the Merarite clan who joined Ezra at the Ahava River to return to Jerusalem from Babylon (Ezra 8:19). **6** A descendant of Benjamin (Neh. 11:7). D.R.B.

Jeshanah (jesh'ah-nah; Heb., "old"), a city on the border of Judah and Israel, probably modern Burj el-Isaneh about six miles southeast of Shiloh. 2 Chron. 13:19 relates its capture by Abijah in his war with Jeroboam I.

Jeshimon (je-shī'muhn; Heb., "desert" or "barren waste"). While the word is used simply to mean "barren wilderness" (Deut. 32:10; Ps. 107:4), there are several places where it seems to indicate a specific geographical location. **1** A region in the hill country of Judah into which David fled from Saul (1 Sam. 23:19, 24; 26:1–3). Other place names mentioned (Maon, Ziph, En-gedi) identify Jeshimon as the eastern section of the Judean hill country, an area between Hebron and the Dead Sea generally called the Wilderness of Judah. **2** In Numbers (21:20; 23:28) Jeshimon is an area of the Jordan Valley northeast of the Dead Sea (the Plains of Moab) overlooked by Mount Pisgah (Nebo?) and Mount Peor. There may be some connection between the name Jeshimon for this area and the Moabite settlement of Beth-jeshimoth (Num. 33:49). It is possible that the word simply means "desert" in both instances above. ***See also*** Beth-jeshimoth; Maon.

Jeshua (jesh'o͞o-uh; Heb., "Yahweh is salvation"), the Aramaic form of Joshua. **1** A Levite, the head of the ninth division of priests (1 Chron. 24:11); he is probably the ancestral head of the family groups below. **2** A priest who shared the responsibility for distributing the Levites' portion of the offerings to the levitical cities during the reign of Hezekiah (2 Chron. 31:15). **3** The son of Jozadak (Jehozadak) and a priest and clan leader who, along with Zerubbabel, led the return of a group of exiles from the Babylonian captivity (ca. 521 B.C.; Ezra 2:2; Neh. 7:7). He worked closely with Zerubbabel in reestablishing the worship of God in Jerusalem, first building an altar and reinstating sacrificial worship (Ezra 3:1–5) and then, with the encouragement of the prophet Haggai (Hag. 1:1–11) helping organize the rebuilding of the Temple (Ezra 3:8–9; 5:2). He is referred to as the high priest by Haggai (1:1) and Zechariah (6:11) and was the father of Joiakim who probably succeeded him as high priest (Neh. 12:10–12). In one of Zechariah's visions (Zech. 3:1–10) Jeshua is the representative of Israel whose exchange of "filthy garments" for "rich apparel" symbolizes not only the cleansing and reinstatement of the priesthood (v. 7), but also the atonement of the people's sins through the suffering of the captivity (v. 4; see Jer. 32:36–44). To him was given the messianic announcement of the coming of "My Servant" and the "Branch" who would finally remove the people's sin (vv. 8–9). In another vision (Zech. 6:10–15), Jeshua is given a crown and equated with the Branch; however, most scholars recognize a textual error here (v. 11) and read Zerubbabel for Jeshua. The Hebrew form of the name, Joshua, is used by the prophets (Hag. 1:1; Zech. 3:1). **4** A clan ("house of Jeshua") of which the family group of Jedaiah returned from the Exile with Zerubbabel (Ezra 2:36). **5** A family group of the clan of Pahath-moab who also returned from Exile (Ezra 2:6). **6** A priestly family of the clan of Hodaviah who returned from Exile (Ezra 2:40). **7** A Levite, the father of Jozabad, one who helped inventory the valuables brought back by the returning exiles (Ezra 8:33). **8** An official of the district of Mizpah who helped rebuild the walls of postexilic Jerusalem (Neh. 3:19). **9** One who helped explain to the people the law read by Ezra (Neh. 8:7); he is probably the same Levite who returned from the Exile with Zerubbabel (Neh. 12:8), took part in the covenant renewal ceremonies (Neh. 9:4–5) and signed the covenant (Neh. 10:9). He is possibly also the same as the son of Kadmiel who was a levitical leader under the priest Joiakim (Neh. 12:24). **10** A name occurring once for Joshua the son of Nun (Neh. 8:17). **11** A town settled by Judahites following the Exile (Neh. 11:26). Its location is suggested by some as modern Tel es-Sawa, about nine miles east of Beersheba. ***See also*** Branch; Haggai; Joshua; Zechariah, The Book of; Zerubbabel.

Jeshurun (jesh'uh-ruhn), a poetic title in Hebrew for the people of Israel (Deut. 32:15; 33:5, 26), with the symbolic meaning of "upright one" (Isa. 44:2).

Jesse, the father of King David. According to the tradition of the book of Ruth (4:17–22; see also Matt. 1:5) Jesse was the grandson of Boaz and Ruth. He was a prosperous farmer who could afford to send gifts to Saul (1 Sam. 16:20). His social position is stressed in 1 Sam. 17:12, where the Hebrew indicates that he was "an old man ... who came among men of standing." This reference suggests that, like comparable references to Akkadian noblemen, Jesse was a distinguished elder of the community.

Jesse is mentioned in the messianic prophecy of Isaiah (11:1,10), which refers to the house of David, and also in the genealogies of Jesus (Matt. 1:5–6; Luke 3:22). Y.G.

Jesus Christ

THE CENTRAL FIGURE OF THE NT, whose life, death, and resurrection represent for Christians God's saving act for sinful humanity. His name (Jesus) and his title (Christ) bear witness to that saving act. The name "Jesus" is derived from a Hebrew word that means "savior" (see Matt. 1:21), and the title "Christ" (Heb., "messiah") means "anointed," and refers to one commissioned by God for a special task. The attempt to write an account of Jesus' life and teachings has long commanded the attention of religious scholars. That attempt must take numerous items into account.

Jesus' face as depicted in a sixth-century mosaic at the Monastery of St. Catherine, Sinai.

Method: It is generally recognized today that our four NT Gospels were written "from faith for faith," that is, that they come from and are intended for the believing community. Christians with a high view of Scripture, therefore, will read them to see how the Christian communities behind the Gospels understood Jesus of Nazareth to be their Lord, so that they may nourish and correct their own views in the light of that understanding. It is also generally held that the earliest developments in the Jesus tradition are best understood by a patient analysis of the first three ("synoptic") Gospels, though NT theology as a whole includes all four Gospels and the rest of the NT as well, while a broader, more systematic understanding of all early Christian movements uses not only our canonical books but all surviving early Christian literature, as well as fragments of Hellenistic literary works, papyri, archaeological remains, etc.

The synoptic Gospels—Matthew, Mark, and Luke—are universally recognized as standing in a close literary relationship, the most commonly accepted view of which is that Matthew and Luke both composed their Gospels by reading earlier sources (Luke 1:1–4) that included our Gospel of Mark and another brief document, now lost, usually designated "Q." The study of each of these documents and of the traditions behind them is important in its own right. But a genuinely historical picture of Jesus of Nazareth can only be obtained by a critical winnowing of all these materials and setting aside (not as an irrelevance but as a key aspect of early Christian theology) those materials that seem to have been shaped in the light of the experience of the early church. The following picture of the career of Jesus rests on such a critical winnowing.

The World at Jesus' Birth: The conquests of Alexander the Great (332–323 B.C.) had the effect of exposing almost the entire Mediterranean basin (as well as the region east of it to the borders of India) to some degree to Greek culture and, more importantly, to the Greek language. Thus most educated people in the area read Greek, whatever their family tongue, and were at least partially familiar with Greek thought and customs. Jews shared in this general atmosphere. Their Scriptures were available in Greek centuries before the time of Jesus, and hence the earliest documents of the Christian movement were composed in that language. In addition, however, Jews also retained (to some degree, in some places) the use of Aramaic and (especially for the reading of the Scriptures) Hebrew. Jewish inhabitants of rural areas with a less cosmopolitan culture probably spoke almost entirely in Aramaic and used Greek rarely if at all. Latin, which became the official language of the Roman Empire shortly before Jesus' birth, was hardly known in many far-flung areas and almost certainly did not affect the places of Jesus' ministry. Greek (and, to a lesser degree, Roman) customs and religious practices were thus close by, even to those areas largely untouched by Greek culture.

This explains the fact that although Jesus and practically all of his earliest disciples spoke Aramaic rather than Greek and the traditions about Jesus at first circulated in Aramaic, those traditions gradually and increasingly came to be known primarily in Greek forms. Hence not only our surviving Gospels but, as far as we can tell, most of the traditions behind them were already in Greek. (Extant Aramaic versions of the NT are late retranslations from the Greek and thus of no significance for early Christian history.) Inevitably, therefore, both Semitic and Greek culture and habits of thought (which are not to be sharply distinguished in any case) influenced the understanding and transmission of the ongoing Jesus tradition in the apostolic age (i.e., the period during which the apostles remained alive).

The slaughter of the innocents—part of the account of Jesus' birth in Matthew—as portrayed by P. Brueghel (1525–1569).

Jesus' Life Before His Public Ministry: Very little is known about Jesus' life before the time of John the Baptist. The birth stories of Matthew provide no chronological information, and themes of Matthean theology are so deeply interwoven with the introductory genealogy (1:1–17) and the various recorded incidents (the appearance to Joseph, 1:18–25; the Wise Men, 2:1–12; the flight to Egypt, 2:13–15; the slaughter of the innocents, 2:16–18; the return to Israel, domicile in Nazareth, 2:19–23) that it is not possible to separate out the historical from the theological data in the accounts.

The study of Lucan birth stories is somewhat more rewarding. The birth of Jesus is implicitly correlated with the birth of John the Baptist (1:36, 41–42); several political figures we know are named (Herod, king of Judea, 1:5; Caesar Augustus, 2:1; Quirinius, governor of Syria, 2:2); and Caesar's enrollment is specifically said to be the "first," taken under Quirinius' rule in Syria (2:1). Yet these data are only broadly helpful: Herod's death (in 4 B.C.) may be a year or two after Jesus' birth if Jesus' public ministry began when he was "about thirty" (3:23); and Augustus' reign (27 B.C.–A.D. 14) surely includes Jesus' birth in any case. The only census for which we have clear evidence took place in Judea, not Galilee, in A.D. 6/7, which is too late for Jesus' birth no matter how loosely one understands "about thirty." The other elements of the birth stories (including especially the relationships with John the Baptist and the five hymns in 1:32–35, 46–55, 68–79; 2:29–32, 34–35) may include old traditions (possibly from circles that revered John the Baptist), but they are more certainly related to the theology of the Evangelist than to early historical developments as such.

Not much is known, in other words, of the circumstances of Jesus' birth and early life, though many theological themes from the birth stories (among them his virginal conception, his Davidic descent, and his mission as Savior of the world) are essential elements in the NT Christology (i.e., the theological understanding of Jesus) as a whole.

Rugged hillside in the vicinity of Nazareth.

Our canonical Gospels contain no information about Jesus' youth except the story of Jesus in the Temple (Luke 2:41–52), which probably represents the attempt to fill in the chronological gaps in the Jesus tradition, as the incidents in such noncanonical Gospels as the Greek/Latin *Infancy Gospel of Thomas* surely do.

It is probable that Jesus' family had some connection with Nazareth (Matt. 2:23; Luke 2:39) and quite certain that his ministry began in and was largely confined to Galilee. While the Greek text of Mark 6:3 is uncertain—it could suggest either that Jesus was a carpenter or that Joseph was—there is no reason to doubt that Jesus was familiar with the crafts and economy of Galilean village life. Nothing can be known from our texts of his psychological development and little of his education, though it is clear that he knew and had reflected deeply on the Hebrew Scriptures. His unusually close association with women (not ordinarily characteristic of Jewish teachers) and favorable attitude toward them in his later life and teaching both point toward a normal home and social life during his formative years.

The Beginnings of Jesus' Public Ministry: The beginnings of Jesus' public ministry are obscure. It is virtually certain that he was baptized by John the Baptist, probably as an indication of his desire to share in John's calling of the people of God to repentance (Matt. 3:2; Luke 3:3). In our Gospels John is understood as a forerunner, a pointer to Jesus, implicitly in Mark (1:7), explicitly in the other Gospels (Matt. 3:14; Luke 1:43–44; John 1:29–34). While Jesus' message is more complex than John's (see below), he shares with John the view that the people of God must "repent," that is, return from their erring ways to God.

While the message is addressed to the Jewish nation as a whole by both John and Jesus, those individuals who heeded the call remained at first a comparatively small group within Judaism and no doubt continued to mix for some time with other Jews. Of John's disciples we know very little (e.g., Mark 2:18; Matt. 11:2), though groups appealing to him continue down to the Mandeans of our own day.

Jesus' disciples, however, were called by him during his lifetime to share his teaching and healing ministry (see esp. Matt. 10). Varying lists (Matt. 10:2–4; Mark 3:16–19; Luke 6:14–16; Acts 1:13) suggest that

Galilee, the region where Jesus' ministry began and was centered.

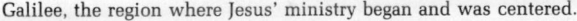

The Samaritan woman meeting Jesus at the well (John 4:1–42); sixth-century mosaic at San Apollinare in Classe, Ravenna, Italy.

twelve of them may have been selected to represent the twelve tribes of Israel, a renewed people of God (Luke 22:30; Matt. 19:28). This, rather than some theory about male leadership, is almost certainly the reason only men were chosen. Jesus, unlike the rabbis, had women disciples, and, as Romans 16 and other texts show, women exercised leadership in many early Christian congregations.

Jesus' Teaching: Although a very close connection exists between Jesus' actions, especially the miracles and his fellowship with the poor and the rejected, and his teaching, it is convenient to analyze them separately.

The Kingdom of God: The central emphasis of Jesus' teaching is the Kingdom (or Reign) of God (see esp. Mark 1:14–15; Matt. 4:2; Luke 4:43). Though this symbol has enormous implications for human life and conduct, its central concern lies elsewhere, namely, in God. It evokes all that is implied in the divine activity, e.g., God's action for the deliverance of the people of God, the righting of wrongs, and the establishment of a reign of justice and peace. It includes, like the message of John the Baptist (see esp. Luke 3:7–9; Matt. 3:7–10), a note of judgment (see, e.g., Matt. 5:22, 30; 7:2, 13–14; 10:15, 28; 11:20–24; 16:27), but it emphasizes, far more than John seems to have done, the divine purpose to save.

It is striking that Jesus' teaching about the end of human history (his eschatology) includes three elements that are not easily harmonized and yet that must be kept together if his teaching is not to be distorted: the presence of the Kingdom, the futurity of the Kingdom, and a close connection between the coming of the Kingdom and Jesus' own ministry. (The Kingdom itself is never defined.)

The futurity of the Kingdom is expressed in many ways. Jesus' teaching as a whole is summarized by Mark in these words: "The time is fulfilled, and the kingdom of God has drawn near. Repent and believe in the gospel" (1:15). For our purposes, it is important to note that the Kingdom is here expected in the near future; it is neither simply present nor distant. The same must be said of Mark 13:28–29, where similar language is used. Neither text, to be sure, represents a verbatim account of the teaching of Jesus. Yet what they imply is attested in many other passages. In the Lord's Prayer the disciples pray for the Kingdom to come (Matt. 6:10; Luke 11:2). Jesus speaks of the "coming" of a day of judgment with a variety of symbols (see, e.g., Mark 13:2; Matt. 10:14–15; Luke 10:10–12; Matt. 11:20–24; Luke 10:13–15). In these texts it is presumed to be yet future (see also Matt. 7:1–2; Luke 6:37–38; Matt. 7:13–14; Luke 13:23–24; Matt. 12:36, 41–42; Luke 11:31–32). The words at the Last Supper, Mark 14:25, surely represent very ancient tradition; there is little reason to doubt that Jesus spoke of a future day when fellowship with the disciples would be restored.

In addition, the theme of future judgment is inherent in many of Jesus' most significant parables; see, for example, the adversary (Matt. 5:25–26; Luke 12:57–59), the two houses (Matt. 7:24–27; Luke 6:47–49), the seed growing secretly (Mark 4:26–29), the laborers in the vineyard (Matt. 20:1–16), the friend at midnight (Luke 11:5–8), the rich fool (Luke 12:16–21), the rich man and Lazarus (Luke 16:19–31), and the importunate widow (Luke 18:1–6). While it may be the case that all or part of some of these parables were created in the light of conditions in the early church—and such judgments can never achieve certainty—methodologically, it cannot be too strongly emphasized that such "inauthentic" materials often represent some degree of continuity with the teaching and situation of Jesus. For example, the "cherry tree" incident of early American history is certainly "inauthentic." Yet it is historically significant that it is told of George Washington, a man of utmost integrity, not of some other president in American history.

On these grounds, such "inauthentic" parables as the thief in the night (Matt. 24:43–44; Luke 12:39–40), the faithful or unfaithful servant (Matt. 24:45–51; Luke 12:42–48), and the wicked husbandmen (Mark 12:1–12) also represent developments of a theme clearly rooted in Jesus' own teaching. The same may be said also of the large number of texts that speak of the coming in judgment of the Son of man, a technical term that probably arose in early Christian apocalyptic thought (Mark 8:38; cf. Luke 9:26; 12:8–9 with Matt. 10:32–33; Luke 17:24, 26, 30; Matt. 24:27; Luke 17:24; Matt. 19:28; Luke 22:30).

It is thus clear that Jesus' call for repentance (i.e., conversion, namely, a change of heart, mind, and direction) is based on warnings of an imminent, not a distant, judgment.

What is unusual about Jesus' teaching is that this thoroughly Jewish motif is inextricably connected with another theme much less well attested in Jewish writings of the period (though there are hints of it at Qumran), namely, the insistence that the coming judgment has in some way already begun. The most explicit statement of this view is the saying in Luke 11:20 (and Matt. 12:28): "But if [i.e., because] by the finger [Matt.: Spirit] of God I cast out demons, then the Kindgom of God has come upon you." But many sayings and parables reflect the same conviction. The strong man (Mark 3:27), the wedding guests (Mark 2:19), and the so-called parables of growth—which do not really stress growth so much as beginning and harvest—(see the sower, Mark 4:3–8; the seed growing secretly, Mark 4:26–29; and the mustard seed and the leaven, Matt. 13:31–33 and parallels) all indicate that the promised time of the end has begun. Several sayings point in the same direction; e.g., Luke 10:23–24 (Matt. 13:16–17); Luke 11:31–32 (Matt. 12:41–42); Matt. 11:12–13 (Luke 16:16); and the very difficult comment in Luke 17:20, which must mean "the Kingdom of God is in your midst," i.e., in the presence of Jesus. This latter motif is important (see below); here it can only be noted that it lies as a presupposition behind Jesus' answer to John's disciples in Matt. 11:2–6 (Luke 7:22–23).

In other words, side by side with an insistence on an imminent judgment, in the light of which repentance is required, lies a "note of fulfillment" explaining the significance of Jesus' ministry in God's plan of salvation.

Many of the texts cited, as well as others, point toward a resolution of this difficult "already/not-yet" paradox: the future Kingdom is present, not in world history as a whole, but in the ministry of Jesus. Its presence is christologically defined. This is particularly clear in the "finger of God" statement (Luke 11:20; "Spirit of God," Matt. 12:28), in which, to be sure, the "I" is unemphatic but still a pointer to the locus of God's eschatological activity: God's victory over the power of the Evil One (so also Mark 3:23–27) is evidence of the Kingdom's presence in Jesus' ministry. Since exorcisms are clearly an integral part of Jesus' activity, this motif can hardly be overemphasized.

Since the judgment, then, is not simply a far-off event but a reality beginning already in the present, the response to Jesus' message is one of eternal importance: see Luke 12:8–9 and parallels and Matt. 7: 24–27 (Luke 6:47–49). Jesus understands both his words and his works as decisive, as "God's last word to humanity."

It should also be noted, however, that while Jesus' teaching is characterized by an urgent call to repentance, not every element of that teaching must be forced into this same framework. Some of the "wisdom" elements in his proclamation prevent us from seeing too radical

"And he went about all Galilee, teaching in their synagogues" (Matt. 4:23). *Below:* Aramaic inscription in the floor mosaic of the late third–early fourth-century synagogue at Hammath-Tiberias. It reads, in part, "Peace be upon everyone who has fulfilled the commandment in this holy place."

a discontinuity between the world as it has been and the world as it is beginning to be. If Jesus challenges his hearers to "leave the dead to bury their own dead" (Luke 9:60; Matt. 8:22; a radical break with traditional obligations) and notes that no one who puts his hand to the plow and then looks back is fit for the Kingdom of God (Luke 9:62), he also uses parables and proverbs that, like the wisdom materials of the OT, presume continuing structures in the ethical basis of the universe.

This motif may be seen in ethical demands like the so-called Golden Rule (Luke 6:31; Matt. 7:12) and turning the other cheek (Luke 6:29; Matt. 5:39), in questions like the blind leading the blind (Luke 6:39; Matt. 15:14), and in various generalizations about life or nature (see Luke 6:40, 45; 10:7; 12:34; 16:13; 17:37 with the parallels in Matt.). It is also presumed in little parables like the speck and the log (KJV: mote and the beam, Luke 6:41; Matt. 7:3), the lamp and the bushel (Luke 11:33; Matt. 5:15), the measure (Luke 6:38; Matt. 7:2), the tree and its fruit (Luke 6:44; Matt. 12:33), and such metaphors as the fish and the serpent (Luke 11:11; Matt. 7:9–10) and treasures on earth (Luke 12:33; Matt. 6:19).

Sometimes, to be sure, these wisdom sayings can be fitted easily into the context of eschatological urgency (so, e.g., Luke 9:60 and Matt. 8: 22; or the weather proverb behind Matt. 16:2–3 and Luke 12:54–55) that lies behind Jesus' teaching as a whole. But the God who is coming in judgment in Jesus' ministry is not different from the God who created the world and called a people into being, so the demands of the new world, though often different in form, are similar to those of the world that is passing away.

Jesus' Ethics: We turn, then, to Jesus' ethics. Three factors are of special importance: repentance as the basis of the ethical life, the radical nature of God's ethical demand, and the centrality of the love commandment. All are related.

Jesus' call to repentance, like that of the OT prophets, presupposes an immense distance between God's will for the people and their daily lives (see Isa. 6:10; 45:22; 55:7; Jer. 3:12–14, 22; 4:1; 8:5; 15:19; 18:8–11; 35:15; 36:3, 7; Ezek. 14:6; 18:30; 33:11; Hos. 6:1; 14:1). What is required, therefore, is not so much the correction of a number of individual sins as a fundamental change, a redirection of life, a change of mind and heart (Gk. *metanoia;* cf. Heb. *shub,* "to turn, return"—the Heb. noun *teshubah* is first used for repentance in post-biblical Judaism, in the Dead Sea Scrolls and in prayers). Unlike the prophets, Jesus seems to have little interest in the worship practices of Israel or in the keeping of the Law as evidence of one's seriousness about God's will. It is thus possible for Jesus, as it is not for his rabbinic contemporaries, for the Law or sincere religious activity to become a barrier to God; see, e.g., the elder brother in Luke 15:11–32. Repentance, whatever else it may involve, implies primarily a turning to God. Jesus' ethics are theologically based; they are not autonomous (i.e., derived from the needs of human individuals or society).

This does not mean that they are new or even, in most cases, different. One who would do the will of God is still called upon to be humble, merciful, compassionate, selfless, honest, and pure, to avoid strife and violence, to serve the poor and outcast, and to go beyond the merely external demands of the Law (see Mark 4:19; 6:34; 8:2; 10:

23; 43:44; Matt. 5:3–9, 21–47; 6:12, 24; 7:1–5; 10:16; 12:35; 18:21–22; Luke 6:24–26; 12:13–21; 14:11; 18:9–14; 19:8). Further, the wisdom elements in Jesus' teaching, which cannot be eliminated, show that most people of good will, especially among the covenant people, are capable of both knowing and doing what is good. From time to time Jesus even accepts without challenge the notion that God rewards the good and punishes the wicked (see Mark 10:29–30; Matt. 6:1–6, 16–18, 19–21; 10:40–42).

What is different in the ethical teaching of Jesus is the central place occupied by God, who not only will come in judgment (so also the prophets and apocalyptists) but who also is beginning already, in the ministry of Jesus, to establish the Kingdom, in which good and evil are to be separated, so that the concept of "reward" is rendered trivial. Both the twofold (already/not-yet) nature of Jesus' eschatology and its christological conditioning are critical for Jesus' ethics.

Thus alongside the more or less traditional portrait of the will of God there lies another, more absolute strain: God wills not approximate but radical obedience. What is demanded is not one's best, but everything. A man does not build a tower unless he is sure he has enough money to finish (Luke 14:28–30); a king does not go to war unless he is certain of victory and willing to pay the price (Luke 14: 31–32). The so-called Antitheses of the Sermon on the Mount ("you have heard that it was said . . . , but I say to you . . . ," Matt. 5:21–47), the command to the rich man to sell all (Mark 10:21), the gentle judgment on the elder brother (Luke 15:31–32), and the paradoxical command to take up the cross (i.e., to die in order to live; Mark 8:34–35) all point in the same direction: God is concerned not for what is practicable, but for what is right. Jesus' God always calls to perfection, not merely to improvement. At the same time, to make of this demand, or any aspect of it, a law (as the Russian novelist Tolstoy did, e.g., with the call to nonviolence) is to accept and attempt to live by precisely what Jesus rejected—a legalistic understanding of the will of God.

Such a legalistic understanding is invalid, for the overarching context of the will of God is the love commandment (Mark 12:28–31). This is not new. Love of God and neighbor are ancient biblical requirements (see Deut. 6:5; Lev. 19:18). Even love of enemies (Matt. 5:44; Luke 6: 27), though rejected at Qumran and unknown in Judaism until more than a century after Jesus' death, is not incompatible with a high spiritual legalism. What is new in Jesus' teaching is that the love commandment is not merely a way of adjudicating conflicting requirements of the Law (as, e.g., the obligation both to provide for one's parents and to keep one's oaths—Jesus' judgment in Mark 7:9–13 is the same as that given by most rabbis) but a way of transcending even such solemn obligations as familial responsibilities (Mark 3:35; Luke 14:26; Matt. 10:37) and keeping the Sabbath (Mark 2:23–29; 3:1–5; Luke 13: 10–17). Love will always express itself in concrete actions for my neighbor's good; but no action can exhaust the love commandment.

It should be emphasized that affection as such is not implied (this is a modern misunderstanding), and neither are such matters as one's own or one's neighbor's dignity. The God who sends rain indifferently upon the just and the unjust (Matt. 5:45) can be relied upon to be concerned for the concrete good of the whole Creation. What God loves, I too must love. It is thus apparent that the disciple of Jesus can never substitute ethics for God, on the one hand, or define belief or trust in God apart from action, on the other. The God who wants not simply my effort but *me* is genuinely loved and trusted only by those who, in Matthew's words, acknowledge Jesus as Lord by doing "the will of my Father who is in heaven" (7:21).

How Jesus Taught: Finally, it should be noted that although the above summary is stated propositionally by necessity, Jesus' public proclamation must not be reduced to "teaching" in the didactic sense. His use of metaphor and parable is so extensive—more than one-third of his words are in parabolic form—that it is evidently impossible to separate the form from the content of those words. Simple metaphors and similes like "that fox" Herod (Luke 13:32) or "Be wise as serpents and innocent as doves" (Matt. 10:16) as well as colorful gnomic (i.e., proverbial) sayings ("Where the body [carcass] is, there the vultures will be gathered together," Luke 17:37 and Matt. 24:28) abound; they serve

Christ as Pantocrator; a fourteenth-century mosaic in the Kariye Church, Istanbul, attempts to represent the resurrected and glorified Christ of faith.

to sharpen, to illuminate what is said, to direct it not only to the hearers' minds but in some way to their wills and affections as well. This is even more evident in the parables.

It is customary to categorize Jesus' parables in three groups: similitudes, parables proper, and exemplary stories. A similitude is general and tends to have a few verbs in the present tense (see, e.g., the scribe trained for the Kingdom, Matt. 13:52; or the unclean spirit seeking rest, Matt. 12:43–45 and Luke 11:24–16). A parable, on the other hand, may involve quite an extensive narrative and speaks of a particular occurrence, with verbs in the past tense (see the sower, Mark 4:2–8; the two sons, Matt. 21:28–32; the importunate widow, Luke 18: 2–8). A few Lucan stories (e.g., the good Samaritan, 10:29–37; or the rich man and Lazarus, 16:1–9) are classified as exemplary stories because they seem to include no metaphorical elements but rather serve merely as illustrations of a certain kind of conduct. This latter classification is an unfortunate one, however, especially in the case of the good Samaritan, where the use of "Samaritan" involves an unexpected category shift (from a normally despised heretic to the hero of the parable) and thus provides a stimulus to the hearer's normal thought-world.

It is not easy to spell out exactly how such parables function. Clearly, as both metaphor and narrative, they appeal to something innate in the human psyche that involves the hearer more profoundly than either statements or imperatives do. This appeal depends on an emotional and aesthetic stimulus, possibly to confront (so, e.g., the two sons, Matt. 21:28–32), perhaps to amuse (so the speck and the log, Matt. 7: 4–5), to provoke thought (the dishonest steward, Luke 16:1–9), to en-

The healed paralytic walks away with his bed (cf. Matt. 9:2–8); seventh-century ivory.

courage (the sower, Mark 4:1–20), to challenge (the hidden treasure, Matt. 13:44), and so on. So parables serve to make the Kingdom available, to call disciples into it, to illuminate its demands and rewards, rather than to define or illustrate it. Like the call to repentance, Jesus' use of parable and metaphor portrays the human problem and divine grace as far more than merely intellectual. And, again, like the call to repentance and its eschatological warrants, it combines the threat of judgment and the promise of grace in a single call, opening the hearer to God by telling stories about the ordinary world, where the divine Lordship is to be acknowledged.

Jesus' Actions: In all the Gospels Jesus is portrayed as a teacher, miracle worker, and friend of sinners. His association with the poor and outcast, with tax collectors and sinners (Mark 2:15–17; Matt. 9:9; Luke 1:53; 4:18; 14:12–14; 15:1–32; 18:10–14) is an important aspect of his ministry. Such people, not the righteous, are the special objects of God's love and care. The Kingdom is thus directly related to Jesus' choice of friends and table companions.

The proclamation of the Kingdom and the miracles are also inextricably related. It is customary to categorize Jesus' miracles in three groups: exorcisms, healings, and nature miracles. All three reflect current first-century conceptions, and all three are told (with some important exceptions) in the same stock ways as the miracles performed by other, especially Hellenistic, healers in the period.

In a healing miracle, for example, it is customary to describe the illness, often with vivid details (its extreme consequences; the failure of other healers); then to portray the healing itself (usually out of public view, involving use of words or even names, gestures, instruments, and so on); and finally to offer some concrete evidence of the healing (activity of the person healed, awe and wonder of the onlookers; see, e.g., Mark 5:1–20, 21–43). An early emphasis on exorcisms, especially in Mark, gradually is broadened to include—as indeed it does already in the earliest traditions—illnesses of many kinds as well (so esp. Matthew; see, e.g., 8:16). It must be noted that in critical ways Jesus' miracles are portrayed differently from those of his surrounding culture: he rarely makes use of instruments (but see Mark 7:33; 8:23); he heals with a touch (Mark 1:31; 3:10) or a mere word (Mark 1:25; 2:11; 3:5; 5:13; 7:29; 10:52; cf. 5:41; 9:25–27; and the parallels in Matthew and Luke). He never uses foreign languages (Mark 5:41 and 7:34 are "foreign" only to Greek readers, since Aramaic was Jesus' mother tongue) or magical formulas, charms, drugs, or techniques. In many cases, though by no means all, faith is presupposed or required (see Matt. 8:10; Luke 7:9; Mark 2:5; 5:36; 9:23; 10:52; cf. 4:40, and esp. 5:34, which Matt. 9:22 rearranges to show that faith comes before healing). And the miracles are done for someone's concrete benefit, not for display. Quite evidently, the early testimony (no doubt in full accord with Jesus' own practice) wishes to reflect two not easily compatible things: Jesus is fully capable of performing mighty acts by the power of God, but, unlike contemporary miracle workers, he has no connection with demonic (see Mark 3:22–27) or magical forces.

Jesus entering Jerusalem (the traditional "Palm Sunday"); enamel panel from the Pala d'Oro, twelfth century.

The same emphasis can be seen in the nature miracles. On the one hand, Jesus is master of the elements (Mark 4:35–41; 6:45–52). On the

The Last Supper (Matt. 26:20–29, Mark 14:17–25, Luke 22:14–38) from the twelfth-century *Four Gospels* illuminated manuscript.

other, his miracles benefit others rather than enhance his own reputation (Mark 6:30–44; 8:1–21; one possible exception to this generalization is the cursing of the fig tree, Mark 11:12–14, 20–22, but note v. 22). They are (esp. in Matthew; see 9:35–38) tokens of his compassion. When confronted with the demand to work miracles as a sign (Mark 8:11–13) or for selfish or frivolous reasons (Matt. 4:1–7), he refuses. God is to be worshiped, not used.

It is fully compatible with these motifs that some miracles are wrought, so to speak, *on* rather than *by* Jesus: his baptism (Mark 1: 9–13), the transfiguration (Mark 9:2–9), and, most significant of all, the resurrection. From the very beginnings of his public ministry (Matthew and Luke: from birth) the Son of God is accompanied by the power of God.

It is thus of no great importance that the honorific titles for Jesus such as Messiah, Christ, Son of God, Son of man, Lord, and the like probably arose in early Palestinian Christianity rather than during the ministry of Jesus. To be sure, they reflect to a considerable degree a concentration on the person of Jesus that goes beyond Jesus' own understanding. But they make explicit what is clearly implicit in Jesus' claim to be God's final messenger, to offer in his own person and teaching (see esp. Luke 12:8–9 and parallels) exclusive access to

God's saving Reign. That the Proclaimer became the Proclaimed is thus a token of the very heart of Jesus' message: God is active in history for the salvation of the people of God.

Jesus' Final Days: It was perhaps inevitable that Jesus' person and teaching should be accepted by some, rejected or ignored by many, and misunderstood by the most powerful political authorities in his region, the Romans. The details of Jesus' final days or of the political processes that led to his crucifixion are no longer recoverable. But two groups in particular—his Jewish co-religionists and the occupying Romans—had different reasons for failing to sympathize with him. On Jewish grounds, his teaching represented a challenge to the hegemony of the Law, and the "messianic" elements, though hardly punishable (Jews did not persecute their errant religious teachers), were clearly dangerous in first-century Palestine. Thus there was no particular reason for them to defend Jesus' cause when the political authorities, no doubt misunderstanding his teaching about the Kingdom and mistrusting his popularity, decided that Jesus should be put to death. Pontius Pilate, the Roman procurator, showed no inclination whatsoever to take any personal risks in defending Jesus' innocence. So Jesus was arrested and, after a brief examination by both Jewish (Mark 14:53–65) and Roman (Mark 15:1–15) authorities, was taken to Golgotha, outside the city of Jerusalem, and put to death in the presence of other criminals.

The Crucifixion, by Hubert and Jan Van Eyck, early fifteenth century.

So ends the life of Jesus of Nazareth. But both our earliest traditions (1 Cor. 15:3–7, which reflects beliefs current no more than a few years after A.D. 30, the most probable date of the crucifixion) and all the canonical Gospels (Matt. 28; Mark 16; Luke 24; John 20–21) agree not only that Jesus rose from the dead but that he was seen by many of his followers to have done so. The difficulty of the details (a solid body, Luke 24:36–43, with real wounds, John 20:24–29, that can pass through walls, John 20:19; recognizability, Matt. 28:9 and Luke 24: 36–38, combined with unrecognizability, Luke 24:16 and John 20:14) shows that the resurrection is no easily demonstrable phenomenon. Yet faith and trust in Jesus and his message, properly understood and obeyed, open a new and living way to God. The resurrection was, for the earliest Christians, no mere natural wonder; it was God's great act for the redemption of the world. The gospel of the Crucified One is "God's power for salvation to everyone who believes" (Rom. 1:16). And thus the Jesus of history is seen, by the eyes of disciples in every age, to be the Christ of faith.

See also Cross; Disease and Healing; Easter; Gospel, Gospels; John the Baptist; Kingdom of God; Lord; Messiah; Miracles; Parables; Resurrection; Son of God; Son of Man; Tomb, Jesus'; Transfiguration, The; Trial of Jesus, The.

Bibliography

Fuller, Reginald. *The Foundations of New Testament Christology*. London: Lutterworth, 1965.

Jeremias, Joachim. *The Parables of Jesus*. Rev. ed. Translated by S. H. Hooke. New York: Scribner, 1963.

Kee, Howard Clark. *Jesus in History*. 2d ed. New York: Harcourt, Brace, Jovanovich, 1977.

Kingsbury, Jack Dean. *Jesus Christ in Matthew, Mark, and Luke*. Philadelphia: Fortress, 1981.

Saunders, Ernest W. *Jesus in the Gospels*. Englewood Cliffs, NJ: Prentice-Hall, 1967.

C.E.C.

Jether (jeth'uhr; also translated "Ithra"). **1** The father of Amasa (1 Kings 2:5, 32; 1 Chron. 2:17; he is called "Ithra" in 2 Sam. 17:25). **2** The son of Jeder: he died childless (1 Chron. 2:32). **3** One of the four sons of Ezrah (1 Chron. 4:17). **4** A member of the tribe of Asher, and the father of Jephunneh, Pispa, and Ara (1 Chron. 7:38). ***See also*** Ithra.

Jethro (jeth'roh), Moses' father-in-law, "the priest of Midian" (Exod. 3:1). The Hebrew form is *ytrw* in the Masoretic Text (except for Exod. 4:18, *ytr*, Jether) and in the Samaritan Pentateuch; the Septuagint has *Iothor* throughout. Jether occurs elsewhere for the father of Amasa and for sons of Gideon, Jada, Ezrah, and Zophah; related names include Jattir, Jithrite (Ithrite), Jithran (Ithran), and Jithream (Ithream). Jethro, however, is reserved for Moses' Midianite father-in-law. He cared for Moses' wife and sons during the Exodus; afterwards, he suggested a more effective structure for Moses' governance of the people (Exod. 18). His relationships with Reuel (Exod. 2:18) and with Hobab (Num. 10:29; Judg. 4:11) are unclear. If Reuel were Jethro's father and Zipporah's *grand*father, Hobab could either be Reuel's son, Jethro's (half-)brother, and Zipporah's uncle, or Reuel's grandson, Zipporah's (half-)brother, and Jethro's son or nephew. Less likely is the suggestion that Reuel is the clan name of both Jethro and Hobab.

K.G.O.

Jeush (jee'uhsh; Heb., "he will come to help"). **1** The son of Esau and Oholibama; he was a chief of the Edomites (Gen. 36:5; 1 Chron. 1:35). **2** The son of Bilhan; he was a descendant of Benjamin (1 Chron. 7:10). **3** A Benjaminite, son of Eshek and descendant of Saul (1 Chron. 8:39). **4** A son of Shemei, of the Gershonite clan of Levites (1 Chron. 23:10–11). **5** The son of King Rehoboam and David's granddaughter Mahalath (2 Chron. 11:19).

jewelry, body ornaments, usually made of metal and/or precious stones. As with other generic terms (like "tools"), biblical usage tends to favor specific designations of jewel material or artifacts over use of the general word. References to the general term include both figurative ("lips of knowledge are a precious jewel" in parallel with "costly stones" [Prov. 20:15]; the "imperishable jewel of a gentle and quiet spirit" [1 Pet. 3:4]; wisdom is "more precious than jewels" [Prov. 3:15] or "better than jewels" [8:11]; a good wife is "far more precious than jewels" [Prov. 31:10]; and the erotic comparison of the beloved's "rounded thighs" as "like jewels, the work of a master hand" [Song of Sol. 7:1]) and literal applications.

Items of jewelry specifically mentioned include the necklace (Song of Sol. 4:9), ring (Hos. 2:13), strings of jewels (Song of Sol. 1:10), and gold and pearls (Rev. 17:4; 18:16). Specific materials from which jewelry was made include silver and gold (Gen. 24:53), including fine gold (Job 28:17).

Certain passages are especially helpful in identifying particular types of jewelry characteristic of the biblical period. One of these is Exod. 35:22 which describes gifts brought for the equipping of the shrine. Included here are brooches, earrings, signet rings, and armlets. In addition, Num. 31:50 mentions bracelets and beads. In Ezekiel's description of the exquisitely garbed woman (metaphoric of Jerusalem) are included bracelets on the arms, a chain on the neck, a ring in the nose, earrings, and a crown on the head (16:11–12). Ezekiel also describes some of the stones found on royal garb, properly considered jewel material (28:13): "carnelian, topaz, and jasper, chrysolite, beryl, and onyx, sapphire [probably lapis lazuli], carbuncle, and emerald" in addition to gold settings. While it described his sense of the royal garb of the king of Tyre, the similarities to the stones used as jewels in the garb of the high priest are striking. In Exod. 28:17–21 for the breastpiece are specified sardius, topaz, and carbuncle (first row); emerald, sapphire, and diamond (probably jasper; second row); jacinth, agate, and amethyst (third row); and beryl, onyx, and jasper (fourth row); all set in gold filigree. The difficulties in identifying the ancient names with accurate modern equivalents are considerable, leading some to suggest that what the translations reflect are the stones precious to the translators. There is some of the same uncertainty about additional items considered precious in Job 28:12–19: glass, coral, and crystal as well as gold from Ophir and topaz of Ethiopia. In this passage wisdom is judged to be more valuable than all these things—it can't be bought with them or its source discovered. Eschatological visions include precious metals and stones embellishing the holy city of Jerusalem (Isa. 54:12; Rev. 21:19–21) and often involve highly imaginative speculations (a city gate of a single pearl, Rev. 21:21).

Archaeological investigations have recovered

Gold jewelry found at Tell el-'Ajjul dates to the second millennium B.C.

samples of all forms of personal jewelry mentioned from a variety of periods in Near East history. Furthermore they are amply represented in the art of Egypt, Mesopotamia, Persia, Greece, and Rome, giving further evidence that they were commonly used throughout the biblical period. On the other hand, the finds pertaining to Israelite history are remarkably restrained, but include finger rings; seals and scarabs; bracelets of copper, bronze, silver, and gold; bracelets and necklaces of drilled beads in a dozen shapes; earrings of single and multiple pendant designs; inscribed and carved brooches; multilayered necklaces; leg bracelets and carved plaques; decorative pins of bone or ivory; amulets rigged for pendant use; and shell and carved bone pendants. But the level of craftsmanship, intricacy of designs, and volume of precious materials involved suggest modest economic means rather than extravagant wealth. Lavish decorative hoards are rare and are usually associated with royalty, as with the Royal Cemetery materials from Ur and pharaonic burials like that of Tutankhamen in Egypt, or with the belongings of wealthy nobles such as occur in Greek and Roman period finds.

A glimpse of the jeweler's craft is given in Exod. 28:9–11 where the names of the Israelite tribal ancestors are to be inscribed on two onyx stones. "As a jeweler engraves signets" describes one of the most distinctive Near East achievements: inscribing stones as stamp or cylinder seal signature devices. The practice of using a small stone cylinder, drilled through the long axis to allow suspension on a cord from one's arm or neck, was first developed into fine art in Mesopotamia. From the older, simpler models, the art developed some of the most exquisite miniature representations of figures, animals, trees, and action scenes (from hunting to votive offerings) ever crafted. Their small size and durability have allowed their survival in archaeological debris to a remarkable extent, and the collections of such items in museums such as the Archaeological Museum in Istanbul, the Yale Babylonian Collection, and the University of Pennsylvania Museum are outstanding. They were used extensively by the Romans as well and, together with stamp seals and seal-bearing rings, provide helpful insights into trends in art, religion, and even commerce (stamped handles on wine jars shipped from Rhodes are a late commercial adaptation of an earlier practice of rolling a seal over the soft clay envelope of an inscribed tablet). R.S.B.

A gold bracelet inset with glass, pearls, and semiprecious stones, from the first century B.C.

Jews, a national-ethnic and, subsequently, religious designation for the people of the Judean state or province and their Diaspora. The title became common only after the Babylonian exile (586 B.C.). In the NT it is frequently used to distinguish the descendants of Israel from proselytes, Samaritans, and Gentiles.

Jezebel (jez'uh-bel; Heb., "Where is the Prince?"). **1** A Phoenician princess (daughter of Ethbaal, king of Sidon), who married King Ahab of Israel and incited him to sin (1 Kings 16:31; 21:25). A devotee of the Phoenician god Baal and a zealous missionary, she supported some 850 prophets of Baal and Asherah (1 Kings 18: 19) and sought to suppress worship of Yahweh (1 Kings 18:4, 13). Thus she became the formidable adversary of the prophet Elijah, able to instill fear even in him (1 Kings 19:1–3). Her influence in Israel was strong during the reigns of her husband Ahab and her two sons Ahaziah and Jehoram and extended to the southern kingdom of Judah, where her daughter Athaliah became queen (2 Kings 8:18). The story of the appropriation of Naboth's vineyard (1 Kings 21) illustrates Jezebel's disregard for Israelite custom and ruthless use of royal power. Elijah's prophecy, "The dogs shall eat Jezebel within the bounds of Jezreel" (1 Kings 21:23), was fulfilled when Jehu seized power (2 Kings 9–10; cf. Hosea's later prophecy regarding the bloodshed at Jezreel, 1: 4). Jezebel met her death with characteristic audacity: she painted her eyes, adorned her head, and greeted Jehu from her window with a caustic insult (2 Kings 9:30–31). Jezebel was pushed out the window at Jehu's command, and when they later went to bury her, only her skull, feet, and palms remained. **2** In Rev. 2:20 the name applied to a false prophet. ***See also*** Ahab; Asherah; Baal; Elijah; Jehu. J.C.E.

Jezreel (jez'ray-uhl; Heb., "God sows"). **1** A town on the southern border of Issachar, commanding the Valley of Jezreel, identified with modern Zer'in at the foot of Mt. Gilboa. Here the Israelites encamped before battling the Philistines (1 Sam. 29), and this was one of the towns over which Ishbosheth, son of Saul, briefly reigned (2 Sam. 2:9). Ahab had a royal residence here (1 Kings 18:45, 46), and Naboth's vineyard which Jezebel plotted to obtain was beside the palace (1 Kings 21). At Jezreel Jezebel met her

The fertile valley of Jezreel. A modern highway marks the route of the Via Maris, which connected Egypt and Syro-Palestine.

bloody death (2 Kings 9:30–37), as did the remainder of the house of Ahab (2 Kings 10: 1–11).

2 The Valley of Jezreel, the eastern section of the broad valley separating Galilee from Samaria. From the pass between the Hill of Moreh and Mt. Gilboa, where the town of Jezreel was located, the valley descends eastward along the Jalud River to the Jordan, with Beth-shan commanding its eastern entrance. The broader plain to the west, known as Esdraelon, is included as a part of the Valley of Jezreel by some scholars.

The Valley of Jezreel, in addition to providing a fertile growing area, provided one of the few ways of access to the Jordan Valley and the east. Traders and armies from Egypt and the Palestinian coast as well as invaders from the east used this pass from earliest times. From Beth-shan and the Jordan a road passed through the Yarmuk Valley to Damascus to the north and east.

The Canaanites controlled the valley with chariots of iron when the Israelites entered the land (Josh. 17:16) and here Gideon met the Midianites and Amalekites in battle (Judg. 6:33–7: 23). According to Hosea (1:5) it was in this valley that the battle would take place which would bring an end to the kingdom of Israel.

3 A town of Judah, location unknown, but probably southwest of Hebron in the vicinity of Ziph and Juttah (Josh. 15:56). A wife of David, Ahinoam, was from there.

4 The son of Etam, a descendant of Judah (1 Chron. 4:3).

5 The first son of Hosea (1:4), named symbolically for the acts that were to befall Israel because of the blood shed by Jehu at Jezreel. ***See also*** Beth-shan; Esdraelon; Gilboa. N.L.L.

Joab (joh'ab). **1** A Kenizzite, the son of Seraiah, and ancestor of a group of craftsmen called Geharashim (1 Chron. 4:14). **2** The second and most prominent of the three sons of David's sister Zeruiah (1 Chron. 2:16). Joab was the commander of David's army during much of his reign (2 Sam. 8:16; 20:23; 1 Chron. 18:15). He seems already to have held this position at the time of the struggle for power between David and Saul's son Ishbaal (cf. 2 Sam. 2:13), but according to 1 Chron. 11:6 he was awarded his command in consequence of his valor and leadership during David's conquest of Jerusalem. He led the army to its first victory in the war against the Ammonite-Aramean coalition (2 Sam. 10: 7–14), and he was in charge of the subsequent siege of Rabbath-ammon, the Ammonite capital (2 Sam. 11:1, 26–31). He conducted the census described in 2 Samuel 24. Everywhere he is presented as a skilled and courageous soldier and a shrewd politician, fiercely loyal to his king and people. At the same time, however, he is shown to be unscrupulous, calculating, and occasionally brutal. Indeed the callous belligerence of the sons of Zeruiah is an important theme in the stories of David's reign, in which Joab and his brothers serve as foils to the gentle, vacillating king (cf. 2 Sam. 3:39). On occasions when David's excessive sentimentality seemed to threaten the stability of his throne, Joab's cold pragmatism was beneficial. He arranged a reconciliation between David and Absalom after the murder of Amnon (2 Sam. 14:1–24), and he intervened when David's extreme grief at the death of Absalom provoked a crisis in the army (2 Sam. 19:1–8). More often, though, he was a violent, disruptive force. He assassinated Abner, the strongman of Ishbaal's rump government in Gilead (2 Sam. 3:27), who had slain Asahel, Joab's youngest brother, in battle (2 Sam. 2:18–23), and he ordered the execution of Absalom during the civil war (2 Sam. 18:9–15). Both of these killings were without David's knowledge, and the second was against his explicit orders (2 Sam. 18:5; cf. 18:12). Joab also slew Amasa (2 Sam. 20:8), with whom David had replaced him as commander of the army after Absalom's revolt. In the contest over the succession to David's throne Joab sided with Adonijah against Solomon (1 Kings 1:7), a mistake that cost him his life. Solomon charged him with the deaths of Abner and Amasa, and he was executed by Benaiah (1 Kings 2:38–34), who became commander of the army under Solomon (1 Kings 2:35). **3** The ancestor of a group of Israelites from the clan of Pahath-moab listed in the census of the first return from exile (late sixth century B.C.) in the time of Zerubbabel (Ezra 2:6; 8:9; Neh. 7:11). ***See also*** Abner; Absalom; Adonijah; Amasa; David. P.K.M.

Joah (joh'uh; Heb., "Yah [God] is a brother"). **1** The son of Asaph; he was the record keeper of King Hezekiah who, with Eliakim the palace steward and Shebnah the scribe, met with the envoy of the Assyrian ruler Sennacherib who was demanding the surrender of Jerusalem (2 Kings 18:17–37; Isa. 36). **2** A Levite of the Gershonite clan (1 Chron. 6:21). **3** The son of Obed-edom, of the Korahite clan of gatekeepers (1 Chron. 26:4). **4** The son of Zimmnah; he was a Levite of the Gershonite clan who, with his son Eden, participated in the cleansing of the Temple during Hezekiah's reforms (2 Chron. 29:12). **5** The son of Joahaz; he was sent by King Josiah to effect repairs on the Temple (2 Chron. 34:8). D.R.B.

Joanna (joh-an'uh). **1** According to Luke 8:3, the wife of Chuza, Herod's (i.e., Herod Antipas) steward, and one of the women who accompanied Jesus. Along with Mary Magdalene, Susanna, and others who "had been healed of evil spirits and infirmities," Joanna gave assistance ("out of their means") to Jesus and the Twelve. In Luke 24:10, she is one of the women (with Mary Magdalene, Mary the mother of James, and others) who, having gone to anoint Jesus' body, find the tomb empty. **2** One of the ancestors of Jesus in Luke 3:27 (KJV; RSV: "Joanan"). ***See also*** Chuza; Herod; Mary; Steward; Susanna; Twelve, The. P.L.S.

Joannan (joh-an'uhn; RSV: "John"), **1** Father of Mattathias Hashmon, whose resistance to the Syrian officials began the Maccabean revolt. **2** Also, the first son of Mattathias (1 Macc. 2:1–2, KJV). ***See also*** John; Maccabees.

Joash (joh'ash). **1** The youngest son of Ahaziah, king of Judah (835–796[8?] B.C.). After Ahaziah's death, his mother, Athaliah, had all his children killed. However, Joash, an infant, was saved by Jehosheba, Ahaziah's sister and the wife of the chief priest Jehoiada (2 Kings 11:2), who hid Joash in the temple for six years (v. 3; 2 Chron. 22:11–12). In the seventh year, Jehoiada conspired against Athaliah, crowned and anointed Joash, and had Athaliah slain (2 Chron. 23:1–15). Next Jehoiada renewed the covenant of God with the king and the people, which resulted in the destruction of the Tyrian Baal cult in Judah (2 Kings 11:17–18) as well as the repair of the Temple (12:7–17). Afterward, Hazael, king of Aram, attacked Israel, taking Gath, and threatened Jerusalem (v. 18). Joash was forced to buy him off with the gold of the temple and palace, and other gifts (v. 19).

The late narrative of 2 Chron. 24:15–27 (the veracity of which is debated by scholars) relates that after Jehoiada's death, Judah lapsed into paganism, provoking a prophecy by Jehoiada's son Zechariah, who was killed at the command of Joash. Another Aramaean campaign despoiled Judah, wounding Joash in the battle. Joash was murdered by two of his servants. He was succeeded on the throne by his son Amaziah.

2 The son of Jehoahaz, king of Israel (801–785 B.C.). During his reign, Assyria, under Adad-nirari III, resumed its domination of Aram by attacking Damascus and defeating its armies. This allowed Israel to regain its captured cities (2 Kings 13:25). These events are reflected in the prophecy to Jehoash of the dying Elisha (vv. 14–19). An Assyrian inscription names Jehoash as one of those paying tribute to Adad-nirari and includes Israel as one of the countries subdued in the campaign.

The late narrative of 2 Chron. 25:6–13 relates that Jehoash's contemporary, Amaziah, king of Judah, hired one hundred thousand soldiers of Israel (which could hardly have been done without the agreement of Jehoash) for one hundred talents of silver to help him against Edom. However, after a prophecy condemning this hiring, Amaziah sent them home before the battle was joined. On the way back, the Israelites raided Judean cities. These raids may have been the reason for Amaziah challenging Jehoash to battle, which ended disastrously for Judah—Amaziah was captured, although not killed, and "the wall of Jerusalem for four hundred cubits from the Ephraim Gate to the Corner Gate" was dismantled, and the temple and palace treasures were looted (2 Kings 14:8–14).

3 An Abiezrite, the father of Gideon the judge, who defended his son's destruction of the Baal altar (Judg. 6:11, 29–31).

4 The son of Ahab, king of Israel, in whose co-custody the prophet Micaiah's imprisonment was entrusted (1 Kings 22:26).

5 A son of Shelah, the son of Judah (1 Chron. 4:21–22).

6 One of David's mighty men, ambidextrous with bow or sling, who came to David at Ziklag. They were relatives of Saul. Joash was the brother of their chief Ahiezer and the son of Shemaah of Gibeah (1 Chron. 12:1–3). J.U.

Job, the Book of, the eighteenth book in the OT, and a major example, along with Proverbs, of wisdom literature. The Hebrew name "Job" may mean "where is the [divine] father?" or it may mean "hated/persecuted one"; or it may combine both meanings to pose the book's question. The date, place, and identity of authorship are still debated. Commonly proposed dates fall between the seventh and the fourth centuries B.C.; an exilic date (after 586 B.C.) is here assumed.

Various sections of the book have been identified as secondary: chap. 28; chaps. 32–37; one or another part of chaps. 38–41; and the prologue and/or the epilogue. Such judgments rest largely on one's interpretation of the book as a whole. The unity of the book is not without its proponents, and that view is here adopted.

Background: The book has its background in the history of Israel's religion up to the Exile and in Canaanite and Mesopotamian religious traditions (as reflected in the book's many allusions to common ancient mythic motifs). In Mesopotamia and Canaan, the gods were viewed as divine creators and rulers of the world, with humans as subjects. Majestic in wisdom and power, they acted at times beneficently and at times with inscrutable arbitrariness. In second-millennium Mesopotamia a form of "personal religion" arose within which a god (as divine parent) endowed the human devotee (as child) with generativity, nurture, guidance, and protection. This "personal religion" was important for Israel's ancestors beginning with Abram (Heb. "the [divine] father is exalted") and for the birth of Israel in the Exodus and the covenanting at Sinai (see Exod. 2:23–25; 3:6, 13–15; 4:22–23; 19:3–6). The latter enactments displayed God as compassionate to the innocent oppressed and just in the establishment of Israelite life upon a basis of law. Israel's Eden story (Gen. 2–3) universalized this vision of God as beneficent creator and covenanter; and the creation account of Genesis 1, with its portrayal of humankind as made in God's image, affirmed the deepest affinity between human and divine within a context of creation as good.

In Mesopotamia this "personal religion" crumbled before the experience of persistent evils, and older views prevailed portraying the gods as inscrutably arbitrary. In Israel the numerous Psalms of complaint (e.g., Pss. 3–6; 22; 30), together with other voices such as the prophet Habakkuk, attest to the challenge that Israel's experience of evil posed to their self-understanding and their vision of God, a challenge that became excruciating with the Exile.

The Question of Undeserved Suffering: Israel's question, posed through Job, concerned the meaning of undeserved suffering before the silence and inactivity of God: what is one to make of the tradition, of oneself, and of divine character and purpose in view of such experience (chaps. 3–37)? This human question is presented as arising out of, and therefore as em-

"The torment of Job" (lying on his back in the center) as imagined by the twelfth-century artists of Chartres Cathedral.

bedded in, a narratively prior question in the divine realm concerning the character and purpose of human piety (1:6–12; 2:1–6). These two complementary questions, asked and explored with painstaking honesty on both sides, may be viewed as a transformed exposition of the traditional Israelite themes of divine-human covenanting and of the viability and possible significance of humankind as dust in God's image, as human child of divine parent.

Job's friends have learned well the lessons of Sinai—perhaps too well. Observation and folk wisdom, reinforced by centuries of teaching concerning the claims of the covenant and its conditional blessings and curses (see Deut. 30: 15–20), produced a sensibility ingrained with a strict calculus of retribution: reward for uprightness, punishment for wickedness. Job shared this theology, but now his experience calls it in question. As voiced by his friends, this theology would force him to deny his experience and to confess a wickedness that his conscience could not in truth attest. He therefore explores alternative possibilities. God must after all be no benevolent creator, compassionate father, or just covenanter, but merely a brutally insensitive power acting in a grotesque parody of wisdom and purpose. Yet from time to time Job imaginatively entertains a vision in which God is, somehow, on his side (8:33 [with RSV note]; 14:13–17; 16:19–21; 19: 25–27). He displays covenanting loyalty in his refusal to stop addressing God, if only with stormy questions. This loyalty comes to a first climax in his oath of a clear conscience, sworn in the name of the very God responsible for his condition. Then, after a soliloquy in which (unlike chap. 3) he affirms the worthwhileness of his past life (chap. 29) alongside his present condition (chap. 30), he utters an extended oath of conscience (chap. 31), appealing to divine conscience (31:35–37) and leaving himself in the hands of God so appealed to (31:38–40).

The three friends and Job have based their views largely on observation, experience, and tradition, although in 4:17–5:7 Eliphaz briefly invokes the authority of a nocturnal revelation. Now Elihu appears (chaps. 32–37), filled with inspiration, to settle the issue with his revelation. But he only repeats the views of the three friends, thereby unwittingly betraying himself as a false prophet (cf. 1 Kings 22:13–23). Finally, God breaks the long, divine silence and speaks directly to Job (chaps. 38–41).

The Divine Speeches: The divine speeches are generally acknowledged to hold the key to the meaning of the book of Job. Yet they themselves require a key, and interpretations vary widely. Do they reinforce some aspect of the friends' theology? Or Elihu's? Do they shout Job down by reference to cosmic mysteries beyond Job's possible fathoming? Do they confirm his fear that heaven is indifferent to human concerns? Perhaps the genius of this climax to the book lies in the way it requires each reader to construe the resolution for him- or herself, thereby placing the reader in the shoes of Job who hears God's words and responds (42:1–6).

Two prominent features appearing throughout the book may offer keys for one's hearing of the divine speeches. These features are the use of irony and of questions. Ironic speech abounds, in which the obvious sense is subverted and another implicit sense emerges through them. Often the device serves to mask and reveal dissenting views in the garb of conventional wisdom, which is thereby left intact for the imperceptive but exploded for the keen listener. As for questions, where they address existential concerns they can serve to draw the one who entertains them into new contexts of understanding and existence. Repeatedly in Job, irony and question combine to mutually intensifying effect. One or another speaker poses questions that appear merely rhetorical, assuming common assent to conventional wisdom; yet the context shows that these supposedly rhetorical questions in fact function as genuine questions opening alternative possibilities.

The divine address to Job (chaps. 38–41) is composed almost entirely of questions ostensibly rhetorical and thereby serves to throw him back into a conventional wisdom according to

OUTLINE OF CONTENTS

The Book of Job

- I. Prose prologue: Job's calamity (chaps. 1–2)
- II. Job's opening soliloquy (chap. 3)
- III. Dialogues with friends (chaps. 4–27)
  - A. First cycle of dialogues (chaps. 4–14)
  - B. Second cycle of dialogues (chaps. 15–21)
  - C. Third cycle of dialogues (chaps. 22–27)
- IV. Monologues (chaps. 28–37)
  - A. Meditation on the inaccessibility of wisdom (chap. 28)
  - B. Job's concluding soliloquy and oath (chaps. 29–31)
  - C. The "inspired" utterance of Elihu (chaps. 32–37)
- V. Dialogues with God (38:1–42:6)
  - A. God's first answer from the whirlwind (38:1–40:2)
  - B. Job's first response (40:3–5)
  - C. God's second answer (40:6–41:34)
  - D. Job's second response (42:1–6)
- VI. Prose epilogue: Job's restoration (42:7–17)

which the experience of suffering conveys a baffling revelation of the incomprehensibility of life and the dissolution of the human understandings that are articulated in those traditions that focus on the Exodus, the Sinai covenant, and the good creation including humankind as in God's image. But when these divine questions are reread in the context of Job's own words and experience, in the context of Israelite tradition generally, and in the context of the use of questions and irony throughout Job, the suspicion may arise that they function ironically, so that their supposedly rhetorical character masks and reveals their genuine indication of a positive possibility for Job's self-understanding. So read, these questions become a re-presentation of the two voices heard in the divine realm (1:6–12; 2: 1–6), similar to the two voices heard in the Garden (Gen. 2:16–17; 3:1–5), calling for discerning hearing and decision. So read, the divine questions become a restatement of vocation and divine-human covenanting hitherto only latent in Israel's tradition. (That vocation will emerge more explicitly in connection with the figure of the Servant in Isaiah 40–55 and, later, e.g., in Mark 10:35–45. In the latter instance, interestingly, apparently rhetorical questions supposedly functioning as a rebuke to pretension are subsequently disclosed to function as genuine vocational solicitations.)

Job's Response: Job's response (42:1–6) comes as a confession, a speaking in agreement with God. It comes to a climax in 42:6, the Hebrew text of which (as already the twelfth-century Jewish scholar Maimonides in part recognized, and recently has come to be noted by several scholars) may be translated, "Therefore I recant and change my mind concerning dust and ashes." In his last soliloquy (30:19) Job had taken his sufferings as God's arbitrary action to put him in his proper place as "dust and ashes." Now, as a result of what God has said to him, he repents of that dour interpretation of God and of himself. He comes to a new understanding of his experience as suffering dust, suffering human. But that new understanding is undisclosed. As with the divine speeches, readers must come to such an understanding for themselves, through self-involvement in the story. In any case, neither Job's earlier fears concerning divine arbitrariness and indifference nor the friends' doctrine of strict retribution is established; and the book implies an opening out onto other possibilities.

Restoration: The book ends with a brief but densely textured portrayal of restoration. Some have felt that it rehabilitates the doctrine of retribution so painstakingly dismantled in the dialogues and therefore must be a secondary, and uncomprehendingly misleading, addition to the book. Read in full view of the dialogues, however, the epilogue should not be interpreted as though it followed immediately after the prologue. Rather, it may be taken to bring the rare insights of the existential mountaintop down to the plain of ordinary life, where it now identifies divine and human transactions, not in conventional *quid pro quo* terms, but as suffused with freedom, spontaneity, and loyalty. The covenant is renewed with each partner acting, not out of necessity or duty, but out of freedom, felicity, and loyalty, thereby with the other bringing into being a world of worth in the face of all that can and does go wrong.

So read, the book of Job presents a vindication of the portrayal of humankind as divine image and an exploration of what such a status implies for human vocation. Far from being an anthropomorphic domestication of the divine in accordance with human wishes, it presents a call to leave the homeland of one's settled human self-understanding and to follow God in the manner in which the mystery of evil is engaged.

Bibliography

Glatzer, N., ed. *The Dimensions of Job*. New York: Schocken Books, 1969.

Pope, M. *The Anchor Bible: Job*. 3d ed. Garden City: Doubleday, 1973.

Sanders, P., ed. *Twentieth Century Interpretations of the Book of Job*. Englewood Cliffs: Prentice-Hall, 1968.

J.G.J.

Jobab (joh'bab). **1** A "son" of Joktan, descendant of Shem, and representative of an Arabian tribe (Gen. 10:29; 1 Chron. 1:23). **2** An Edomite king (Gen. 36:33–34; 1 Chron. 1:44–45). **3** A king allied with Jabin of Canaanite Hazor who fought against Joshua (Josh. 11:1). **4** Two men of Benjamin's tribe (1 Chron. 8:9, 18).

Jochebed (joh'kee-buhd), the name of Moses' mother. According to priestly traditions, she and her husband, Amram, both descendants of Levi, were the parents of Aaron, Moses (Exod. 6: 20), and Miriam (Num. 26:59). This is a conflation of earlier statements in Exodus (2:1–10; 4: 14; 15:20).

Joda (joh'duh; RSV; KJV: "Juda"), an ancestor of Jesus (Luke 3:26).

Joel (joh'el), a common name in the Hebrew Bible, meaning "Yah[weh] is God," the inverse form of the name Elijah. Joel is thus a polemical name, proclaiming that Yahweh, and not another party, is God. It is used of a number of people in the OT. **1** One of the sons of Samuel who became a judge but perverted justice (1 Sam. 8:2). **2** A Simeonite whose name appears in early genealogical records (1 Chron. 4:35). **3** A member of the tribe of Reuben, and the father of Shemaiah (1 Chron. 5:8). **4** The father of Shema (1 Chron. 5:12), he may be the same person mentioned in 3. **5** The father of Heman, a Koathite singer (1 Chron. 6:33). **6** The son of Azariah and

JOEL, THE BOOK OF

the father of Elkanah (1 Chron. 6:36). **7** One of the five sons of Izrahiah, all of them chief men (1 Chron. 7:3). He may be the same person as 6. **8** The brother of Nathan and one of David's mighty men (1 Chron. 11:38). **9** The chief of 130 Levites, descendants of Gershom, who was included among the Levites appointed by David to accompany the Ark to Jerusalem (1 Chron. 15:7, 11). **10** The father of one of the Levites, Heman, appointed by David to sing as the Ark was brought to Jerusalem (1 Chron. 15:17). He may be the same as 5. **11** One of the three sons of the Levite Ladan (1 Chron. 23:8). **12** One of the two sons of Jehieli who were in charge of the treasuries of the house of the Lord (1 Chron. 26:22). **13** The son of Pedaiah; he was one of the officers from the half-tribe of Manasseh in David's kingdom (1 Chron. 27:20). **14** A Levite in the reign of King Hezekiah (ca. 725–697 B.C.); he helped in the resanctification of the Temple (2 Chron. 29:12). **15** One of seven sons of Nebo; he put aside his foreign wife and his children at the behest of Ezra (Ezra 10:43). **16** A Benjaminite, the son of Zichri, who was a leader among those who lived in Jerusalem at the time of its restoration under Nehemiah (sixth century B.C.; Neh. 11:9). **17** The son of Pethuel and the prophet of the book of Joel (Joel 1:1; cf. Acts 2:16). ***See also*** Joel, The Book of. M.Z.B.

Joel, the Book of, an OT book, the second of the Minor Prophets. This book depicts a locust plague that is perceived as the onset of the Day of the Lord, and narrates the future fortunes of Israel and the other nations. The Hebrew text contains four chapters, but its chapters two and three are combined in most English editions, following the Septuagint (LXX) and the Vulgate.

OUTLINE OF CONTENTS

The Book of Joel

- I. National lament in response to a locust plague (1:1–20)
  - A. Superscription (1:1)
  - B. Description of the locust plague (1: 2–4)
  - C. Call to lament (1:5–14)
  - D. A lament (1:15–20)
- II. The Day of the Lord as judgment on Judah (2:1–29)
  - A. The locust plague as harbinger of the day of the Lord (2:1–11)
  - B. Call to repentance (2:12–17)
  - C. God's positive response: promise of deliverance (2:18–29)
- III. The Day of the Lord as judgment on Judah's enemies (2:30–3:21)
  - A. Signs of the Day of the Lord (2:30–32)
  - B. Judgment on the nations (3:1–17)
  - C. Summary: prosperity for Zion and destruction for enemies (3:18–21)

Four issues must be addressed before the book is interpreted: whether the locusts are real or symbolic; the repetitions and inconsistencies in the book; the meaning of the Day of the Lord; and the book's date. Many medieval exegetes understood the locusts allegorically, usually as representing foreign forces. This interpretation strains 2:7 and 2:18–27 and has been rejected by critical scholarship. Thus, it is now held that an actual locust plague motivated Joel to write this book.

The unity of the book of Joel is often questioned. Some scholars think all of the references to the Day of the Lord in chaps. 1 and 2 are later additions to the text of Joel; others claim that 3: 4–8 is a late addition. Joel incorporates several inconsistencies—1:1–18 describes a locust plague while 1:19–20 describes a drought. The book contains several repetitions—there are many calls to lament and several descriptions of the locust plague. These inconsistencies and repetitions however probably reflect the book's poetic style rather than implying multiple authorship. The phrase "You shall know . . . that I, the Lord, am your God" (2:27; 3:17) and the depictions of the darkness of the Day of the Lord (2:2, 10, 30–31; 3:15) unify the book.

The Day of the Lord is an important theme in prophetic literature, first appearing in Amos 5: 18. It is a "great and terrible day" (Mal. 4:5), a dark day (Amos 5:18; Zeph. 1:15), when God manifests himself in war against his enemies (Isa. 13). Joel could thus recognize the locusts' great destruction as the harbinger of the more destructive Day of the Lord.

Although Joel contains no explicit chronological references, it was composed after a great national tragedy (3:2), but when the Temple was standing (1:14; 2:17). A date in the late sixth or early fifth century B.C. is likely. This is consistent with Joel's use and adaptation of traditional material (e.g., 2:13; cf. 3:10 and Isa. 2:4 and Mic. 4:3).

Interpretation: In light of these conclusions, the following interpretation of Joel may therefore be suggested. In its first section (1:1–10), Joel describes the locust plague. He opens in general terms (1:2–4) and then calls upon the drunkards (1:5–7), the populace at large (1:8–10; 1:9 foreshadows 1:13–14) and the farmers (1:11–12) to lament. The chapter ends with a call to the priests to lament (1:13–14) and incorporates a lament (1:15–20) that begins with a reference to the Day of the Lord (1:15).

The second section opens and closes with a description of the locust plague as a harbinger of the Day of the Lord (2:1–3, 10–11), emphasizing its darkness and God's power. These verses frame a poetic description of the locusts (2:4–9).

The third and fourth sections are a call to repentance (2:12–17) and God's positive response (2:18–29). God's reversal of the locusts' damage is a natural motif in this context (2:18–27), but his bestowal of prophetic power "on all flesh" (2:28–29) is unparalleled in prophecy (but cf. Num. 11:24–30).

The fifth section (2:30–3:17) is framed by descriptions of the darkness of the Day of the Lord and references to Zion (2:30–32; 3:15–17). The frame encloses the destruction of Israel's enemies at the Valley of Jehoshaphat in return for the crimes committed against Israel (3:1–14).

The book concludes with a summary of the fourth and fifth sections. 3:18–21 oscillates between Israel's prosperity and the demise of its enemies. God's role in this reversal of fortunes is emphasized—the book ends with "For the Lord dwells in Zion."

Bibliography

Allen, Leslie. *The Books of Joel, Obadiah, Jonah and Micah.* Grand Rapids, MI: Eerdmans, 1976.

Driver, S. R. *Joel and Amos.* Cambridge: Cambridge University Press, 1915.

Wolff, Hans Walter. *Joel and Amos.* Philadelphia: Fortress, 1977. M.Z.B.

Johanan (joh-hay'nan; Heb., "God shows favor"; cf. John). **1** The eldest son of Josiah (1 Chron. 3:15). **2** A descendant of the Davidic family, son of Elioenai (1 Chron. 3:24). **3** A member of the priestly line of Zadok (1 Chron. 6: 9–10). **4** One of David's "mighty men" (1 Chron. 12:4), possibly the same as a Gadite in 1 Chron. 12:12. **5** Father of an Ephraimite chief, Azariah, in the time of king Ahaz (2 Chron. 28:12). **6** The son of Kareah (2 Kings 25:33; Jer. 40:8–43:5), a leader in Judah after the destruction of Jerusalem (587 B.C.) under Gedaliah, who refused him permission to kill Ishmael who subsequently assassinated Gedaliah. He was a leader in rescuing the captives taken by Ishmael and in asking for divine guidance from Jeremiah. But Jeremiah's message to stay in Judah was repudiated by Johanan and his associates and they took refuge in Egypt. **7** The son of Hakkatan of the Azgad family who brought 110 men to Ezra's company (Ezra 8:12). **8** The son (possibly grandson) of Eliashib, priest or high priest contemporary with Nehemiah (Neh. 12:22–23; cf. Jonathan in 12:11). ***See also*** Gedaliah; Jeremiah, The Book of.

P.R.A.

Johannine Epistles. ***See*** John, The Letters of.

Johannine literature, the, a name given by modern scholars to the five books of the NT that are attributed to an author named John. Of the five—the Gospel According to John, 1, 2, and 3 John, the Revelation to John—only Revelation carries the name of its author in the text (1:4). The remaining four owe the attribution of authorship to post-NT tradition. That the "John" is the disciple John of Zebedee is an early tradition, but it was disputed as early as the early third century A.D. by Origen. Along with the similarities in content and style that have caused scholars to link these five books, there are also enough differences to call into question their authorship by one individual. Some have suggested they were written by followers of John of Zebedee (the "Johannine School"), whence the similarities and the attribution to John.

P.J.A.

John (short for Johanan or Jehohanan), a common name among Jews and in the NT. **1** The father of Mattathias and grandfather of Judas Maccabeus (1 Macc. 2:1). **2** The oldest son of Mattathias and brother of Judas Maccabeus (1 Macc. 2:2; 9:35–42). **3** John the Baptist (Matt. 3: 1). **4** John the son of Zebedee (Mark 10:35). **5** John Mark (Acts 16:37). **6** The father of Peter (John 1:42; 21:15–17). **7** A member of the high-priestly family (Acts 4:6). **8** The author of Revelation (Rev. 1:1, 4, 9; 22:8). ***See also*** John the Apostle; John the Baptist; Maccabees; Mark; Peter; Revelation to John, The.

John, the Gospel According to, the fourth canonical Gospel in the NT. It is traditionally ascribed to John, the son of Zebedee, one of the Twelve and the brother of James. Yet Zebedee's sons are mentioned only in 21:2 and then not by name. Although the Beloved Disciple, who figures prominently in the latter part of the narrative, is traditionally identified as John, that equation is not made in the Gospel. For reasons that will be given below, most modern scholars do not think that the Gospel is apostolic in origin.

The Distinctiveness of the Fourth Gospel: In the Gospel of John, Jesus delivers no Sermon on the Mount (or Plain). He tells no parables, heals no lepers, does not instruct his disciples to pray the Lord's Prayer, and does not institute the Lord's Supper on the night of his betrayal and arrest. In short, the kinds of moral teaching and religious instruction associated with the Jesus of the synoptic Gospels are almost completely absent from John, as are his typically brief and epigrammatic sayings (e.g., Mark 2:27; 12:17).

Jesus delivers discourses and carries on debates with his opponents in the Fourth Gospel up to the point (chap. 12) at which he withdraws from the world to be with his disciples, whom he commands to love one another (13: 34). These discourses and debates do not, however, concern the interpretation of the Law and related practical moral issues, as in the Synoptics; rather, they dwell upon the claim to messiahship and divine sonship that Jesus makes for himself. The prologue's (1:1–18) description of him as the "Word" (Gk. *logos)* sent from God is borne out in his appearance and dis-

JOHN, THE GOSPEL ACCORDING TO

courses. His opponents are often categorized simply as "the Jews," even though the Gospel presents Jesus himself as a Jew, a native of Nazareth (1:45–46; 4:22; 18:33–35). The distinction between Jesus and his disciples, on the one hand, and the Jews, on the other, is altogether characteristic of the Gospel of John but not of the other Gospels, where Jesus appears as a figure within Judaism. (The other authors and their communities are, of course, also convinced that Jesus is not only Christ but Son of God.) This difference may afford some indication of the reasons for the distinctiveness of the Fourth Gospel: it arises out of a sharp conflict between Jews who accept the messiahship of Jesus and those who do not.

Jesus performs healing and other miracles in the Fourth Gospel, as in the Synoptics, but John has accounts of different episodes. Yet, like the others, John recounts how Jesus fed a multitude, apparently miraculously, and soon thereafter was seen walking on the water by his disciples, who were in a boat on the lake. Typically, John portrays Jesus performing a healing, then debating with Jews (or Pharisees) about its significance (cf. chaps. 5 and 9). In this Gospel, the miracles are "signs" signifying who Jesus is and they are intended to evoke faith on the part of those who witness them, beginning with the disciples (2:11). Yet one can see signs and, even without rejecting them, fail to attain adequate faith (2:23–25). Nevertheless, Jesus' miracles, like his message, are in John's Gospel fundamentally testimonies to who he is (see 20:30–31). They are not acts of mercy or signs of the Kingdom of God, as in the Synoptics, but serve to convey John's message about Jesus Christ (i.e., Christology).

Although John's narrative of the events leading from Jesus' arrest to his death and burial is remarkably similar to the Synoptics', the role and demeanor of Jesus are again distinctive. Jesus seems above, or aloof from, the maelstrom of events. He is not silent before the Roman procurator Pilate, however, but virtually turns the tables on him. In the Johannine trial scene, Pilate shuttles back and forth between Jesus and the accusing Jews, seeming to wish to release Jesus but not having the fortitude to do so. When Jesus goes to his execution, it is as if by his own initiative. In death, he shows no pain or emotion (cf. Mark 14:33–39) but says, "It is finished," as if he remained in control of events until the very end (19:30). And that is precisely the picture this Gospel encourages its readers to form.

The rather different and contrasting portrayal of Jesus, his message, and his ministry in the Fourth Gospel raises questions about the causes or conditions that produced the Gospel, as well as its historical validity. The latter question is perhaps less complex, although both are difficult enough.

In an earlier, uncritical era, John was used to supplement the Synoptics, as though each were a straightforward historical account. But this is true of none of them. They are all "gospels." The gospel is an almost uniquely Christian literary genre, albeit with affinities with late Hellenistic (i.e., 100 B.C. to A.D. 100) biography as well as OT narratives. The Gospels undeniably intend to

OUTLINE OF CONTENTS

The Gospel According to John

- I. Introduction (1:1–51)
  - A. Prologue (1:1–18)
  - B. Encounter with John the Baptist and call of disciples (1:19–51)
- II. Jesus' manifestation of God's glory before the world (2:1–12:50)
  - A. Wine miracle (2:1–11)
  - B. Cleansing of the Temple (2:12–22)
  - C. Discussion with Nicodemus on birth from above (2:23–3:21)
  - D. The second appearance of the Baptist (3:22–36)
  - E. Conversation with Samaritan woman (4:1–42)
  - F. Healing of official's son (4:43–54)
  - G. Healing at Pool of Bethzatha and related discourse (5:1–47)
  - H. Feeding of five thousand and related incidents and discussions (6:1–71)
  - I. Jesus at Feast of Tabernacles (7:1–52) (Woman taken in adultery—7:53–8:11—a later addition to the Gospel)
  - J. Jesus the Light of the World (8:12–59)
  - K. Restoration of sight to blind man (9:1–41)
  - L. Jesus the Good Shepherd (10:1–42)
  - M. Raising of Lazarus from the dead (11:1–44)
  - N. Condemnation of Jesus (11:45–57)
  - O. Triumphal entry and related events (12:1–50)
- III. Jesus' manifestation of God's glory to his disciples (13:1–20:31)
  - A. The Last Supper; Jesus washes disciples' feet (13:1–38)
  - B. First farewell discourse to disciples (14:1–31)
  - C. Second farewell discourse to disciples (15:1–16:33)
  - D. Jesus' final prayer (17:1–26)
  - E. The Passion narrative: Jesus' arrest, trial, crucifixion, and burial (18:1–19:42)
  - F. Discovery of empty tomb and resurrection appearances in Jerusalem (20:1–31)
- IV. Appendix: Jesus' appearance by Sea of Galilee to Peter and others (21:1–25)

report historical events, but in the overall framework or context of a distinctly Christian theological interpretation. Because the Synoptics do not generally present Jesus as proclaiming himself, i.e., presenting christological doctrine, and because the issues they portray him dealing with are largely indigenous to early first-century Palestinian Judaism, historians have rightly preferred their renditions of Jesus' teaching particularly, but also his healing activity and his death. Yet in all probability John contains some valid historical data peculiar to itself (e.g., the dating of Jesus' execution on the afternoon before the beginning of Passover rather than during the feast), as well as authentic sayings of Jesus. Whether John knew the synoptic Gospels is a debated question. Obviously, he did not feel constrained to agree with them or conform to them.

Language and Style: The style and language of even Jesus' speech in the Fourth Gospel are in many respects closer to the three Letters of John than to the other Gospels. Not surprisingly, tradition has held and many scholars have agreed that all are the work of the same author.

Although the book of Revelation is in language and style quite different from the Gospel of John, the two nevertheless have certain features in common. In both, Jesus is described as the "Word" and "Lamb (of God)," and in both heavy emphasis is laid on witnessing to Jesus and the gospel. Strikingly, in Revelation, the crucified and risen Jesus delivers the initial revelation (Rev. 1–3), and his words are not unlike those of the Johannine Jesus (cf. Rev. 3:20). Several seemingly diverse factors may also be pertinent here: the author of Revelation is a prophet (1:3), through whom words of the living Jesus are conveyed; 1 John 4:1–6 apparently deals with Spirit-inspired prophets; and in the farewell discourses of the Gospel of John (chaps. 14–16), Jesus promises the disciples that he will send them the Counselor, the Holy Spirit, who will somehow mediate his further teaching to them. Quite possibly, the activity of Spirit-inspiration among Christians who produced such books as the Gospel of John, as well as the other Johannine writings, is related to the distinctiveness of the Johannine style and particularly to the unique framing and content of the discourses of Jesus in the Fourth Gospel. However that may be, the very distinctiveness of the Johannine emphases, language, and store of concepts suggests that the circumstances and influences that helped produce the Gospel of John were distinctively different from those affecting the Synoptics.

Influences: The concept of the "word," prominent in Greek philosophy since Heraclitus and important to the Stoic philosophers, dominates the prologue of John's Gospel. Interpreters once took this as a clue to the Greek character and origin of John. Analogies to this hellenization

John the Evangelist with his symbol, the eagle, behind him; page from the seventh-century *Lindisfarne Gospels.*

(i.e., adaptation to Greek ways of thinking) of the Christian gospel were seen in the work of the Alexandrian Jew Philo and the apocryphal Wisdom of Solomon, and such affinities are real. But soon after World War II, they were overshadowed by the Qumran Scrolls. Of Jewish origin and discovered in Palestine near the Dead Sea, they share significant theological vocabulary and dualistic thought patterns (e.g., light/darkness, truth/lie) with the Fourth Gospel. Earlier suggestions of a profoundly Jewish substratum of the Gospel seemed to be confirmed.

In the meantime, a number of scholars came to believe that John was influenced by, or written to refute, an earlier form of the so-called Gnostic heresy that flourished during the second century and threatened for a while to become the dominant form of Christianity. Gnosticism tended to equate Creation with the Fall, to regard the material world as evil, and to see in Jesus the emissary from an alien God who had descended into this world to save his kindred spirits, the elect. Some elements of this view, especially its Christology and concept of salvation seemed to find an echo in the Fourth Gospel. On the other hand, the Gospel's assertion that all things were made through Christ (1:3), its positive use of the OT, and 1 John's denunciation of those who deny the fleshliness (i.e., humanity) of Jesus (4:2–3) could be construed as directly opposed to Gnosticism. Significantly, however, the earliest known commentary on the Fourth Gospel was

JOHN, THE LETTERS OF

written by a mid-second-century Gnostic named Heracleon. Perhaps because it was used by Gnostic Christians who came to be regarded as heretics, and also because it was so obviously different from the Synoptics, John was looked upon with suspicion by some orthodox churchmen. When, in the last quarter of the second century, Bishop Irenaeus argued for the necessity of four Gospels, he may have been defending the authority of the Gospel of John in particular.

Authorship and Date: As we push back into the middle and first half of the second century, there is some evidence that John was known among orthodox churchmen (Ignatius, Justin Martyr), but no connection is made either with John the son of Zebedee or with Ephesus in Asia Minor, the traditional place of origin. Statements that the Gospel of John was written by the son of Zebedee in Ephesus appear at about the time when the four-Gospel canon was emerging in the general usage of the church, that is, the end of the second century. It was said that John was a "spiritual" Gospel, written after the other Gospels and with knowledge of them (Clement of Alexandria, at the end of the second century). The implication that John was the last of the four canonical Gospels was thus willingly accepted. Therefore, the widely held critical opinion that John could not have been composed much before the end of the first century has ancient roots. Such a date accommodates the distinct possibility that the manifest hostility between Jesus and his disciples and the authorities, called Jews, is a reflection of a conflict, which began within the synagogue (cf. John 9:22; 12:42), between those Jews who believed Jesus was the Messiah and those (the precursors of rabbinic Judaism) who did not. The latter, after the Jewish-Roman war (A.D. 66–70), oversaw the retrenchment of Judaism associated with the town of Jamnia. ***See also*** Beloved Disciple, The; Gnosticism; Gospel, Gospels; Holy Spirit, The; John the Apostle; John, The Letters of; Logos; Paraclete; Philo; Revelation to John, The; Sign.

Bibliography

Brown, Raymond E. *The Community of the Beloved Disciple*. New York: Paulist Press, 1979.

______. *The Gospel According to John*. 2 vols. The Anchor Bible. Garden City, NY: Doubleday, 1966, 1970.

Kysar, Robert. *The Fourth Evangelist and His Gospel: An Examination of Contemporary Scholarship*. Minneapolis, MN: Augsburg, 1975.

______. *John's Story of Jesus*. Philadelphia: Fortress, 1984.

Smith, D. Moody. *John*. Proclamation Commentaries. Philadelphia: Fortress, 1976.

D.M.S.

John, the Letters of, three brief writings at the end of the NT before Jude and Revelation. 2 and 3 John are in epistolary form. The longest, 1 John, has neither salutation nor conclusion but is clearly a written communication to a group of Christians. The author of 2 and 3 John refers to himself in the salutation as "the Elder." The author of 1 John does not identify himself at all, although presumably he is an authoritative figure.

Traditionally, these Letters have been ascribed to the same John, the son of Zebedee, who is said to have written the Gospel of John and Revelation. Since 1 John, in its prologue and elsewhere, seems to presuppose the Gospel, the Letters were probably written later. As in the case of the Gospel, the area around Ephesus is the traditional place of origin. The documents themselves, however, give no clues to their geographical provenance or date. Only the relation to the Gospel of John enables us to assign them a probable date near the end of the first century or even a little later.

Consideration of language and style lends some support to the traditional view that the Gospel and Letters (not Revelation) are by the same author. Terms such as "life," "light," "love," "Son," "Spirit," "word," "world," and "truth" play an important role in the Gospel and in 1 John particularly. The same can be said for a number of grammatical constructions. The New Commandment to love one another, which Jesus gives in the Gospel (13:34), is said to be both old and new in 1 John 2:7–8 (cf. 2 John 5–6), but the context reveals that it is still the same commandment of love.

OUTLINE OF CONTENTS

The First Letter of John

1 John has no clearly defined structure, but its essential content can be represented in the following way:

I. Prologue: the grounds of the testimony (1:1–4)
II. The true message of Jesus (1:5–3:24)
  A. Fellowship, obedience, and forgiveness (1:5–2:17)
  B. Warnings against false teaching (2:18–28)
  C. The marks of life in the community (3:1–24)
III. Testing the claims of those who testify (4:1–5:12)
  A. Testing the spirits (4:1–6)
  B. Love as the essential test (4:7–21)
  C. Obedience to the commandments (5:1–5)
  D. The true testimony (5:6–12)
IV. Postscript: sins, forgiveness, and certain knowledge (5:13–21)

The question of the identity of the author is not satisfactorily resolved by the tradition that identifies him with John, the son of Zebedee. If 2 and 3 John are his work, it is curious that he refers to himself only as an elder and not as an apostle. 1 John remains anonymous. Although considerations of language, style, and theology may favor common authorship of the Gospel and Letters, modern critics have observed some significant differences between the Gospel and 1 John. For example, the concept of Jesus' death as expiation for sin is more important in 1 John than in the Gospel, and the expectation of Jesus' return is very much alive in 1 John (2: 18; 3:2) but is being revised or reinterpreted in the Gospel. While the close relationship of the Gospel and Letters is not in dispute, the same cannot be said of the identity of their author(s).

To a considerable extent, 1 and 2 John address a specific set of problems in the life of Christian communities. Some members, or former members (1 John 2:19), while claiming not to sin (cf. 1:8), fail to obey Jesus' commandments (2:3) and hate rather than love their brothers and sisters (2:9–11). Presumably these same people claim to possess God's Spirit but deny that Jesus was really human, i.e., "has come in the flesh" (4:2). Thus, in his prologue, the author of 1 John emphasizes the visibility and tangibility of what he proclaims, namely, Jesus Christ, while he later insists that Jesus has come "not with the water only but with the water and the blood" (5:6), an allusion to the historical baptism and death of Jesus. 2 John also emphasizes the importance of obeying the love commandment and confessing that Jesus has come in the flesh.

Given this emphasis on Jesus' humanity, we can more easily understand why in 1 John "the beginning," which in the prologue of the Gospel means primordial time, means the beginning or source of the Christian tradition, namely, Jesus himself. The beginning and source of Christianity is Jesus, and a proper understanding of who he was and what he commanded is of prime importance in the first Johannine Letter.

The other two Johannine Letters, each no more than a page long, are similar to 1 John and to each other, but they also betray some striking differences. While 3 John names the recipient, Gaius, 2 John is addressed only to "the elect lady and her children." In the conclusion, the "children" of her "elect sister" are said to send greetings. Probably this is a symbolic reference to churches. While the issues in 2 John are similar to those in 1 John, 3 John deals with hospitality offered by churches to visiting emissaries of the Elder and upbraids the ambitious Diotrephes, possibly the head of a house-church, who has refused to extend such hospitality. Interestingly enough, 2 John instructs its readers not to extend hospitality to those who do not adhere to true doctrine.

2 John can be outlined as follows:

I. Salutation (1–3)
II. The love commandment and the true doctrine of Christ (4–11)
III. Conclusion (12–13).

3 John can be outlined as follows:

I. Salutation (1–4)
II. Hospitality to emissaries (5–12)
III. Conclusion (13–15).

In the earliest canonical lists, dating from the end of the second century, 1 John already appears. Indeed, 1 John is quoted as authoritative by Bishop Polycarp of Smyrna before the middle of the second century. The attestation of 2 John is almost as good. There is no second-century reference to 3 John, but that is not surprising, since it deals with a specific, local issue. Probably it was eventually included with 1 and 2 John because it was known to be the work of a notable authority in the church. ***See also*** Beloved Disciple, The; Diotrephes; John the Apostle; John, The Gospel According to; Revelation to John, The.

Bibliography

Brown, Raymond E. *The Community of the Beloved Disciple.* New York: Paulist Press, 1979.

———. *The Epistles of John.* The Anchor Bible. Garden City, NY: Doubleday, 1982.

D.M.S.

John the Apostle, the son of Zebedee and brother of James. Along with James, John was called by Jesus to be one of the Twelve (Matt. 4: 21–22; Mark 1:19–20; Luke 5:10–11) while they were fishing. His name appears in each of the apostolic lists (Matt. 10:2; Mark 3:17; Luke 6:14; Acts 1:13). Some think that Mark's reference to "hired servants" indicates a prosperous family background (Mark 1:20). John and James receive from Jesus the nickname "Boanerges," meaning "sons of thunder" (Mark 3:17). Their prominence among the Twelve is indicated by their presence, along with Peter, at the raising of Jairus's daughter by Jesus (Mark 5:37; Luke 8: 51), at the transfiguration of Jesus (Matt. 17:1; Mark 9:2; Luke 9:28), and with Jesus in the Garden of Gethsemane (Matt. 26:37; Mark 14:33). According to Luke 22:8, John and Peter are instructed by Jesus to make the preparations for the Passover. James and John (or their mother) ask special consideration upon the advent of the messianic kingdom (Matt. 20:20–23; Mark 10: 35–40). All of this indicates that John was close to Jesus. It is John who complains about the exorcist (Mark 9:38; Luke 9:49), and James and John request that the unresponsive Samaritan village be destroyed (Luke 9:54). Paul attests to John's prominence by referring to him as one of the "pillars" of the Jerusalem church (Gal. 2: 6–10). In spite of these and a few other references to John in the NT, the data necessary for a fuller sketch of his life, character, and activities do not exist.

JOHN THE BAPTIST

Further attestation to John's prominence among the apostles is evidenced by the fact that he is traditionally regarded as the author of the Fourth Gospel, of the three canonical letters bearing his name, and of the book of Revelation. That John the Apostle wrote the Fourth Gospel is by no means certain. Patristic evidence tends to identify John with the Fourth Gospel beginning with the church father Irenaeus (late second century), who adopts the view of his teacher, Polycarp. This tradition, coupled with recent studies on the early dating of the superscriptions (titles) of the Gospels, lends some support to the view that the Fourth Gospel was written by John the Apostle or by his disciple(s). Even so, one must still proceed cautiously, because the Gospel bears no signature, nor is the author identified therein. Furthermore, significant differences between the portrayals of Jesus in the Fourth Gospel and in the Synoptics must be kept in mind. Attempts to link John the Apostle with "the beloved disciple" (John 13:23; 19:26; 20:2; 21:7, 20–24), though not impossible, are nevertheless conjectural. The situation is further complicated by the relationship between "the beloved disciple" and the unnamed "other" disciple in John 1:40 and 18:15–16. Similar difficulties surround attempts to link the author of the three Letters of John (particularly 2 and 3 John) to John the Apostle. Although tradition has identified the John of Revelation (1:1, 4, 9) with John the Apostle, many scholars seriously question this association.

According to some traditions, John survived until ca. A.D. 100 in Ephesus, but it is also possible that he was martyred much earlier, along with his brother James. ***See also*** Apostle; Beloved Disciple, The; Boanerges; Disciple; Jairus; James; John, The Gospel According to; John, The Letters of; Revelation to John, The; Twelve, The; Zebedee. P.L.S.

John the Baptist, from a pulpit plaque, Ravenna, Italy.

John the Baptist, or John the Baptizer, an important figure in each of the four NT Gospels. He is identified with the beginning of Jesus' ministry and understood as the forerunner to Jesus the Messiah. Reference to John is the first point of convergence among the canonical Gospels, all of which give a somewhat similar account of his person, preaching, and activity, though varying in detail.

John's Ministry: Historically, the account of John in each of the Gospels indicates that his was apparently an effective and successful ministry in its own right (Matt. 3:5–6; Mark 1:5). Considerable care is taken to maintain the distinctive character of Jesus' activity in relation to that of John. In Matthew, Mark, and Luke, John is arrested and imprisoned before Jesus' public ministry begins (Matt. 4:12; Mark 1:14; Luke 3: 20). In the Fourth Gospel, although Jesus begins his ministry before John's arrest (John 3:23–24), the relationship between the two is clarified in the prologue (1:6–9) and elsewhere (1:19–23). In each case, John's words convey his recognition of the one greater than himself who is to come baptizing not with water but with the Spirit (Matt. 3:11–12; Mark 1:7–8; Luke 3:16–17; John 1:26–27). In Matt. 3:13–15, John is reluctant to baptize Jesus and must be encouraged by Jesus to do so. The care with which the authors seek to clarify the roles of and relationship between these two figures suggests that, because of the impact of John's ministry and the close proximity of John and Jesus, there was a distinct possibility of the readers confusing the two men and their ministries. Indeed, when Herod, after having had John beheaded, is informed of Jesus' ministry, his first thought is that John has come back to life (Matt. 14:1–12; Mark 6:14–29; Luke 9:7–9). Further attestation to the effectiveness of the ministry of John the Baptist is found in Acts, where on two occasions Christians encounter disciples of John who, after being further instructed, are received into the church (Priscilla and Aquila meet Apollos in Acts 18:24–28, and Paul meets twelve such disciples, perhaps associated with Apollos, in Acts 19:1–7). Thus, the prominence of John's ministry is attested by the care with which the Gospel writers compose their accounts of him, the fact that Herod deemed it necessary to have him killed (the historian Josephus also reports, with somewhat different details, that John was executed by Herod in the fortress of Machaerus near the Dead Sea), and the fact that some years after Jesus' death Christians still encountered people (in Asia Minor!) who knew only "the baptism of John."

Prophet: The portrayal of John in the canonical Gospels is that of a prophet who came out of the desert to proclaim the advent of the Kingdom of God and issue a call to repentance (Matt. 3:1–12; Mark 1:4–8; Luke 3:1–20). According to Luke, he was of priestly descent, the son of Zechariah and Elizabeth (1:5–80; 3:2), and John and Jesus were related (1:36). Matthew and Mark describe John's appearance and diet: he wore a camel-hair cloak with a waist belt made of leather and he dined on locusts and wild honey (Matt. 3:4; Mark 1:6). He baptized those who repented of their sins and announced the coming of one after him who would be greater than he and would baptize with the Spirit. Thus, John is cast into a role like Elijah's (Matt. 17:10–13; Mark 9:11–13; Matt. 11:7–15; cf. Mal. 4:5–6; Ecclus. 48:10), that is, he is the austere one who prepares for and announces the advent of the Messiah (John 1: 6–8, 19–36). Luke 1–2 most clearly balances John's role with that of Jesus by his presentation of John traditions in parallel with Jesus traditions, a parallelism that echoes the story of Abraham and Sarah (Gen. 17:15–21; 18:1–15; 21:1–8).

Scholars have noted the possibility that John knew of and perhaps was even associated with the Qumran community (which produced the Dead Sea Scrolls). The location of his ministry, content of his preaching, interest in water purification, and lifestyle all point to similarities between John and the Essenes. It has also been suggested that, prior to the beginning of his own ministry, Jesus may have been among the followers of John. All such conclusions remain speculative, however. ***See also*** Elijah; Elizabeth; Essenes; Forerunner; Herod; Machaerus; Salome; Scrolls, The Dead Sea; Wilderness; Zechariah. P.L.S.

Joiada (joy'ah-dah; Heb., "Yahweh knows"). **1** The son of Paseah and one of the builders of the wall of Jerusalem under Nehemiah (Neh. 3:6; KJV "Jehoiada"). **2** A postexilic high priest, the son of Eliashib and the father of Jonathan (Neb. 12:10–11, 22), also called Jehoiada in Neh. 13: 28.

Joiakim (joy'uh-kim; Heb., "Yahweh will raise up"), a shortened form of Jehoiakim, the son of Jeshua, the high priest in Jerusalem following the return from the Exile; he succeeded his father as high priest (ca. 500–450 B.C.?; Neh. 12:10, 12, 26).

Joiarib (joy'uh-rib; Heb., "Yahweh will contend"), a shortened form of Jehoiarib. **1** A Levite teacher who met Ezra at the Ahava River and was commanded to return to Jerusalem from Babylon (Ezra 8:16). **2** A Judahite ancestor of Maaseiah, a postexilic inhabitant of Jerusalem (Neh. 11:5). **3** Apparently the father of Jedaiah, a priest who lived in postexilic Jerusalem (Neh. 11:10). However, a parallel passage (1 Chron. 9: 10) omits "son of" and lists Joiarib (Jehoiarib) as one of the priests along with Jedaiah. **4** A priest who returned from the Babylonian captivity with Zerubbabel (Neh. 12:6); possibly the same as 3 above. **5** A postexilic family group headed by Mattenai (Neh.12:19). D.R.B.

Jokneam (juhk'nee-uhm), a Canaanite city in Carmel (Josh. 12:22). It was located in the territory of Zebulun and marked its limits (Josh. 19: 11). It was assigned to the Levites from among the cities in Zebulun according to Joshua (21: 34); according to 1 Chronicles, where it is spelled Jokmeam, it was among the cities in Ephraim (6:68). The toponym Jokmeam also occurs in 1 Kings 4:12. It is located six miles northwest of Megiddo at modern Tel Qaimun.

Joktan (jawk'tan), a descendant of Shem and the brother of Peleg, whose thirteen sons are generally to be identified with various Arabian tribes (Gen. 10:25–30).

Jonadab (joh'nuh-dab; Heb., meaning uncertain, perhaps "Yahweh is noble"), a shortened form of Jehonadab. **1** The son of Shimeah (Shimea), David's brother, and cousin of Amnon, David's son. He gave Amnon the plan that led to Amnon's rape of Tamar, his half-sister (2 Sam. 13:3–5). It is possible that he is the same nephew of David elsewhere (erroneously?) called Jonathan (2 Sam. 21:21; 1 Chron. 20:7). **2** The son of Rechab, the founder of the Rechabites, a strict religious sect characterized by adherence to traditions, abstinence from wine, and nomadic life style. Since Jonadab is referred to as the authority for the rules of this group (Jer. 35:6), he probably effectively organized the sect. Jeremiah praised the strictness with which the later descendants of the group followed the traditions established by Jonadab in contrast to the infidelity that Judah and Jerusalem had shown to God (Jer. 35:1–19). The religious zeal characteristic of the group is perhaps reflected in Jonadab's (here Jehonadab) accompaniment of Jehu in his chariot as he killed those loyal to the apostate Ahab (2 Kings 10:15–17) and then attempted to exterminate the worshipers of Baal (2 Kings 10:18–25). ***See also*** Amnon; Jehonadab; Jonathan; Rechab. D.R.B.

Jonah (joh'nuh), **the Book of,** an OT book, fifth of the Minor Prophets. Jonah, the son of Amittai, was an eighth-century B.C. Israelite prophet. He is mentioned in 2 Kings 14:25 as God's "servant" from Gath-hepher in Galilean Zebulun, who prophesied Israel's expansion under Jeroboam II (785–745 B.C.). The same prophet is also mentioned in the book of Jonah; however, it is generally regarded that the protagonist of the work placed among the twelve Minor Prophets retains only the loosest connection to the historical Jonah. Rather, the book of Jonah has the character of a parable, dealing with the role and purpose of the prophet. Often dated to postexilic times (late sixth century B.C. and beyond), the work nevertheless bears thematic affinities to Genesis, the Deuteronomistic history, and to pre-exilic prophets such as Micah, Nahum, and Jeremiah.

Content: According to the story, Jonah was commanded by God (1:1–2) to warn Nineveh in Assyria of its great evil. Jonah, however, fled, boarding a ship to Tarshish that God then assailed with a storm. The sailors called upon their gods and desperately cast lots to learn who was responsible for the divine wrath. Jonah, slumbering in the hold, was singled out. He instructed the crew to cast him overboard, which, once done, quieted the sea—whereupon the sailors offered thanks to God (chap. 1). God then appointed a great fish to swallow Jonah. Inside the fish, Jonah burst into prayer, expressing partly lament, partly thanksgiving for God's (future?) deliverance. The fish then vomited Jonah alive onto dry land (chap. 2).

After these episodes, God again commanded Jonah to warn Nineveh. Jonah now complied, with spectacular results—bringing the Ninevites and their animals (!) to total repentance in sackcloth and ashes by a single brief oracle (chap. 3). But Jonah brooded angrily, apparently disappointed that divine mercy left his oracle of judgment unfulfilled. God grew a castor plant (Heb. *kikayon)* over Jonah, providing him shade from the sun's heat, but turned Jonah's comfort to distress by withering the plant (chap. 4). "You pity the plant," said God, "for which you did not labor . . . should I not pity Nineveh, that great city, in which there are more than a hundred and twenty thousand persons who do not know their right hand from left, and also much cattle?"

Interpretation: Modern investigators differ on the story's meaning. Some hold it to deal with Israel's mission, reluctantly embraced by Jonah, to preach God's universal mercy to non-Israelite nations. The book would thereby represent a polemic against the alleged narrow nationalism of Ezra's postexilic community. Others, with perhaps more justice, see an intra-Israelite message concerned with divine mercy and the power of repentance. The book also stresses a change in a prophet's role from a deliverer of oracles to a persuader—since God's decrees can be reversed by repentance, the prophet must preach to arouse change of heart. Literary interpreters note the story's intensive wordplays and thematic coherence, despite its composite character. Chaps. 1 and 3 portray Jonah's interaction with uncommonly repentant Gentiles; chaps. 2 and 4, his own experience of God's providence. Jonah's prayer, echoing both psalm themes and certain Ugaritic motifs of sacred enclaves and personal redemption, satirically underscores Jonah's apparent narcissism and isolation.

The work was interpreted allegorically by Jewish and Christian readers. It is read publicly by Jews on the Day of Atonement to mirror the experience of the repentant worshipers. In Matt. 12:39–41, Jonah 2 is cited to prefigure Jesus' death and resurrection. Medieval Jewish Cabala saw it as a paradigm of general resurrection. ***See also*** Prophet. J.W.R.

OUTLINE OF CONTENTS

The Book of Jonah

I. Jonah's call and his reaction (1:1–17)
   A. God tells Jonah to preach repentance to Nineveh (1:1–2)
   B. Jonah takes a ship in the opposite direction (1:3)
   C. Jonah is cast from the storm-wracked ship (1:4–16)
   D. Jonah is swallowed by the great fish (1:17)

II. Jonah in the great fish (2:1–10)
   A. Jonah's prayer (2:1–9)
   B. Jonah is put on dry land by fish (2:10)

III. Jonah as preacher of repentance (3:1–4:5)
   A. Jonah preaches repentance to Nineveh (3:1–5)
   B. Nineveh repents and God has mercy on the city (3:6–10)
   C. Jonah disappointed by God's mercy (4:1–5)

IV. The castor plant (4:6–11)
   A. Growth and death of plant; Jonah's reaction (4:6–8)
   B. God's word to Jonah (4:9–11)

Jonas (joh'nuhs). ***See*** Jonah, The Book of.

Jonathan, the most important son of the first king of Israel, Saul, and David's bosom friend. Jonathan lived in the second half of the eleventh century B.C. This prince figures in 1 Sam. 13–31, and first appears in chaps. 13–14 as a grownup and commander-in-chief directly under Saul. In his military capacity, Jonathan provoked war with the Philistines, the enemy on the coast, though Israel was weak and badly armed at that time (the Philistines had a monopoly on forged iron). With the outbreak of hostilities, the enemy swept over central Palestine and, to make matters worse, Saul came into conflict with Samuel, the prophet who had anointed him king. However, inspired by the courage of his exceptional trust in God, Jonathan managed to climb what was considered an impregnable rocky mount and eliminated a Philistine watchpost. The psychological shock of this success brought with it a reversal in the battle. Saul, however, became jealous, forfeited the victory on account of excessive religious zeal, and made a scapegoat of his son Jonathan who had severely criticized him. Saul hoped to have his son executed; but at the last moment the soldiers intervened to save Jonathan.

As soon as Jonathan, one round of war later, saw the military prowess of David (who slew Goliath), he acknowledged him as his peer, grew affectionate toward him, and symbolically assigned to him his own rights to the throne. Furthermore, he demonstrated deep friendship and loyalty to David: twice he tried to mediate on his behalf with Saul, the king, and to protect his friend against his father's jealousy. In so doing, Jonathan risked a breach with his own father. In addition, when David was forced to flee the court, Jonathan concluded a special covenant-pact with him, whom he recognized as God's chosen one.

In the final battle on Mt. Gilboa where the Philistines settled accounts with Saul's army, Jonathan did his duty as a warrior and died together with his father. David honored him as a hero and celebrated his noble character and selfless behavior by dedicating the climax of his dirge in 2 Samuel 1 to his friend: "Your love to me was wonderful, / passing the love of women." ***See also*** David; Saul. J.P.F.

Joppa (jah'puh; Heb., "beauty"), an important harbor in ancient Palestine. Today it is a suburb of modern Tel Aviv. Occupation began as early as the Middle Bronze Age (1900–1500 B.C.), with a large fortified enclosure with a beaten earth rampart found on the site. It was first mentioned in the victory list of Pharaoh Thutmose III (ca. 1468 B.C.). The city is subsequently characterized as an Egyptian stronghold in the Tell el-Amarna tablets. During excavations of the site of ancient Joppa a thirteenth-century B.C. citadel gate was uncovered, which had dressed stones with titles and an inscription mentioning Pharaoh Rameses II (ca. 1304–1237). The city is mentioned along with Azor, Bene-berak and Beth-dagon as having been under the influence of Sennacherib in the "prism stele" (701 B.C.).

According to the OT, this city was allotted to the tribe of Dan (Josh. 19:46). It was also the port through which the cedars of Lebanon came for the construction of both the First and Second Temples (2 Chron. 2:16; Ezra 3:7). It was from this port that the prophet Jonah sailed in his attempt to evade God's command to him (Jon. 1:3). It was also in Joppa that Peter raised the dead Dorcas (Acts 9:36–43).

This city also has a place in Greek mythology. The Greek legend of Perseus and Andromeda was supposed to have taken place in the Sea of Jaffa. The inscription of Eshmunazar of Sidon (probably fifth century B.C.) would indicate that the city was under the control of the king of Persia during that time. The city was colonized by the Greeks in the Hellenistic period (333–63 B.C.). The Zenon papyri, a travel diary of an Egyptian treasury official who visited Palestine (ca. 259/58 B.C.) during the reign of Pharaoh Ptolemy II, makes reference to the city. The Seleucids captured the city in the Hasmonean period (ca. 175–63 B.C.). It was destroyed by the Romans on more than one occasion, first by Cestius Gallus and then by Vespasian.

The site was excavated in 1948–50 by P. L. O. Guy for the Palestine Exploration Fund and later, in 1952, J. Bowman and B. S. J. Isserlin did additional work in the area on behalf of the University of Leeds. In 1955 J. Kaplan excavated the site in an expedition sponsored by the Museum of Antiquities, Tel Aviv-Jaffa.

S.B.R.

Joram (joh'rem; Heb., "[Yah] God is high"). **1** The son of King Toi of Hamath (2 Sam. 8:10). **2** A Levite (1 Chron. 26:5). **3** A short form of the name Jehoram. ***See also*** Jehoram.

Jordan River, the (Heb. *ha-yarden*), a river that runs from north of the Sea of Galilee to the Dead Sea. Occupying two-thirds of the deep rift valley between Israel and Jordan, i.e., the Pales-

Waterfall at the headwaters of the Jordan River.

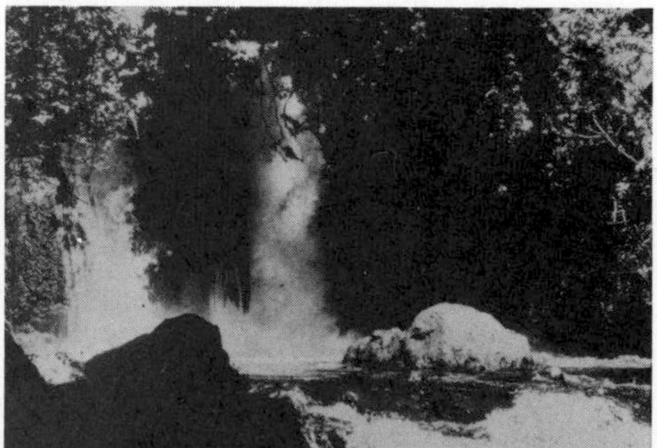

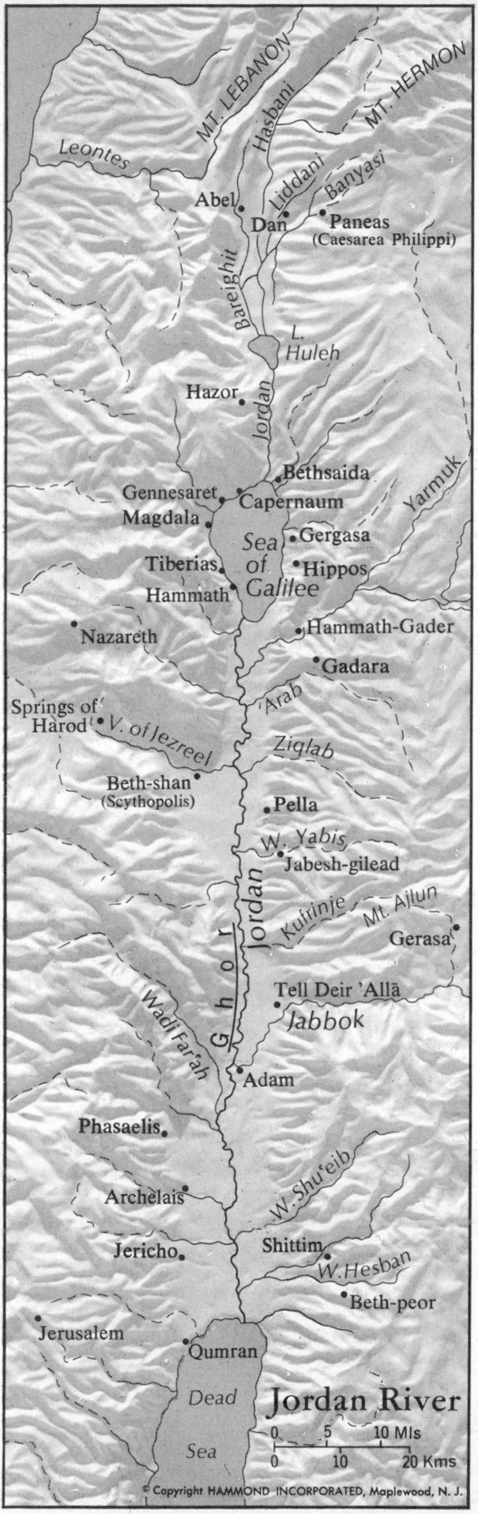

tinian section of the rift valley system that extends from southern Turkey about thirty-five hundred miles (5,600 km.) to the Zambesi in southeast Africa, it is the world's lowest river, flowing mainly well below sea level. Except just north of the Sea of Galilee, the valley is enclosed between steep mountain walls; the eastern side is usually higher and more precipitous and provides most of the tributaries, since the plateau edge receives heavier rainfall than the Palestine highlands. The whole valley is in a rain shadow, since the rain-bearing westerly winds in winter are warmed and dried by their rapid descent. Average annual rainfall at Dan in the north is 24 inches (600 mm.), at the Sea of Galilee 16 inches (400 mm.), and at Jericho 5 inches (125 mm.). Heavy rain can sometimes occur, even far south, causing the desolate wastes to blossom amazingly. Summers are exhaustingly hot, but the winters pleasantly warm.

The major headwaters come from the slopes of Mount Hermon, the Hasbani being the most northerly, and the Liddani, near Dan (modern Tell el-Qadi), and Banyasi at Paneas (Banyas), both at the southern foot, being the strongest. The smallest, the Bareighit, rises just north of modern Metullah. Cut off from the north by a sudden change in height, the Bareighit was usually a political frontier, and its sanctuaries amidst the rich forest were renowned. The oracle at Abel (modern Tell Abil; 2 Sam. 20:18), the royal high place at Dan (1 Kings 12:29; Amos 8:14), the sacred cavern at Paneas, and NT Caesarea Philippi, where Peter first recognized Jesus as the Christ (Mark 8:27–29), are all located along it.

The streams once meandered through a papyrus marsh, with fauna and flora often similar to those of the Sudan, to the shallow Lake Huleh, 250 feet (76 m.) above sea level. All this, however, is now drained. Crossing was possible only just south of the lake, where the Damascus road came to join the north-south route that passed further to the west. Guarding the junction was the great Bronze Age city of Haẓor, which "formerly was the head of all those kingdoms" (Josh. 11:10), destroyed by Joshua, but fortified again by Solomon (1 Kings 9:15), and even more strongly by Ahab. South of Huleh the river descends 945 feet (290 m.) through a narrow gorge, sometimes 1,000 feet (300 m.) deep, cut through a basalt outflow. Beyond the basalt is the Sea of Galilee (Lake Tiberias), 695 feet (212 m.) below sea level, roughly heart-shaped and twelve miles long by seven wide (18 by 12 km.). The encircling hills leave room for a shoreline track, widest at the little plain of Gennesaret in the northwest.

Mentioned in the OT only as a border (Num. 34:11; [Heb. *kinneret*] Josh. 11:2), the lake bustled with life in Roman times, exporting lake fish and grain from the eastern plateau. Capernaum, the center of Jesus' activity, is in the northwest, with Bethsaida, the birthplace of Philip, Andrew, and Peter (John 1:44) located at modern al-'Araj, just across the Jordan mouth. Tiberias, then a busy Gentile city with famous hot springs, was apparently never visited by Jesus. On the basalt plateau northward are the ruins of Chorazin, one of the cities condemned by Jesus (Matt. 11:21), and east of the lake was Gergasa and the Decapolis city of Hippos. The scene of the healing of the Gadarene demoniac is unknown but may be on the southeastern shore.

The Jordan then meanders for about two hundred miles (320 km.) to the Dead Sea, though the direct distance is only sixty-five miles (105 km.). Twenty miles (32 km.) south of the lake the mountains close in from both sides, creating a narrow "waist" to the valley. Immediately south of the lake the river is joined by the Yarmuq from the east, as large as the Jordan itself, with the fine Roman baths at Hammamat Gader a few miles above the confluence. Then further southward come the 'Arab, the Taiyebeh, the Ziqlab, and the Yabis, just north of which is the Decapolis city of Pella (Khirbet Fahil) with impressive early Christian and Muslim ruins. Jabesh-gilead, famous in the saga of Saul (1 Sam. 11:1–11; 31:8–13), was either at the entrance to the Wadi Yabis or at Tell Miqlab further upstream. At the narrow "waist" the Kufrinje descends from the Ajlun mountains, towering 4,000 feet (1,220 m.) above the valley. Westward the Harod comes from Jezreel, the only lowland breach in the Palestine mountains, the entrance guarded by Beth-shan (Arabic Beit Shean), later called Scythopolis.

Immediately south of the "waist" the 'Faria joins the Jordan from the west, and the much larger Jabbok (Gen. 32:22; modern Zerqa) from the east. Close to the confluence is Adam (modern Tell ed-Damiyeh; Josh. 3:16). Just north of the Jabbok is Tell Deir 'Alla, an important Bronze Age (3000–1250 B.C.) sanctuary, perhaps the site of the "altar of great size" (Josh. 22:10). A desert climate now prevails, and the river wanders in a thick jungle of tamarisk and other shrubs through the Zor, the "pride" (RSV: "jungle") of Jordan (Jer. 12:5; Zech. 11:3). On either side are the grey, desolate badlands of the Qattara, and beyond them the downward sloping plain of the Ghor. The base of the highlands was intensely cultivated wherever there were springs. On the west was Jericho (modern Tell es-Sultan) with striking early Neolithic (ca. 8000–4000 B.C.) defenses, but apparently not a walled city in the time of Joshua, and also the Roman settlements of Phasaelis (Khirbet Fasayil) and Archelais (Auja et-Tahta). The site of Gilgal is, alas, still obscure. On the eastern springline are the well-watered "plains of Moab" (Num. 22:1). The "waters of Nimrim" (Isa. 15:6) flow down the Wadi Shu'eib. The Wadi Kufrein supplied Abel-shittim (modern Tell el-Hammam; Num. 33:49; Josh. 2:1 [Shittim]; Mic. 6:5), and the Wadi Hesban fed Beth-peor (or Baal-peor; Deut. 3:29; Josh. 13:20; Hos. 9:10). The location of "Bethany beyond Jordan," where John baptized Jesus (John 1:28), is unknown, but the traditional site is modern el-Mughtas, six and a half miles (10 km.) north of the Dead Sea. ***See also*** Abel; Adam; Ahab; Bethany; Bethsaida; Beth-shan; Caesarea Philippi; Capernaum; Chorazin; Dan; Gilgal; Hazor; Hermon; Jabbok; Jabesh, Jabesh-gilead; Jericho; Pella; Solomon. D.B.

Joseph, the name of several men who figure prominently in the biblical narrative. **1** The oldest son of Rachel, favorite wife of the patriarch Jacob. Joseph appears in the tradition as one of the fathers of the tribes of Israel (Gen. 49:22–26). The tribe of Joseph divided into Ephraim and Manasseh when, in the history of the tribal league, Levi left the tribal structure (Gen. 48:8–22).

Joseph plays the central role in a novella, Gen. 37:1–47:27, and in a collection of narrative traditions in Gen. 47:28–50:26. One problem in the history of Pentateuchal traditions is the relationship between the saga tradition about the patriarchs in Genesis (Jacob in Canaan) and the saga tradition about Moses in Exodus (the sons of Israel in Egypt). The Joseph novella constitutes a link between those two saga traditions.

As is typical for the tradition about the patriarchs in Canaan, the Joseph novella builds its plot around a problem created by strife in the patriarchal family. The narrative characterizes each member of the family as a party to the strife. Joseph appears initially as a spoiled son, favored by his doting father, proud of his pre-eminence. The father adds to the explosive atmosphere of the family by giving his favorite son a piece of clothing that marks his pre-eminence and by freeing him from the responsibility carried by the other sons for work with the family flocks. The brothers succumb to sibling jealousy and seek an occasion to rid the family of their troublemaker. Their resolve increases when Joseph reports dreams that confirm his pre-eminence. Their anger breaks into open violence when Joseph leaves the protection of the father in order to seek out the brothers' condition. Their initial plan to kill him changes to a more economically advantageous plan to sell him to passing merchants; yet the sale is tantamount to killing him.

The narrator alerts the audience that the issue has not yet been resolved, however. The merchants sell Joseph in Egypt. Genesis 39–41 constitutes a self-contained story about Joseph as the wise and prudent administrator who rises from servant in a private household to vizier in Pharaoh's court. As second in command over the entire kingdom, Joseph receives responsibility from Pharaoh to administer grain reserves in a time of famine. But specifically, the story depicts the standards for judging an effective administration in the king's court. All administrators should be as wise and prudent as Joseph. This story about the ideal administrator derives from royal wisdom tradition, a guide for developing effective court officials. As a distinct story, it was available for use by the author of the Joseph novella as an explanation of Joseph's transition from brother at the mercy of jealous brothers to brother with power over jealous brothers.

Joseph administers the grain reserves during the famine for the benefit of the Egyptians and, indeed, for all the people of the world. Ironically, the famine forces Joseph's brothers to travel to Egypt in order to buy enough grain to sustain their families. In Egypt they stand at the mercy of Joseph whom they do not recognize but who recognizes them. After two accounts depicting the brothers as subject to the whim of Joseph, Joseph finally reveals his true identity. Reconciliation between the brothers occurs, and Jacob with all the families in Canaan comes to Egypt. The family reunion effects reconciliation of a family once at war within itself.

The storyteller affirms that the reconciliation occurs by the hand of God (45:7, 8, 9). God led Joseph to Egypt, to his place of power, so that the family might live through the famine. Now, brothers who once hated Joseph embrace him and share news of their father. Joseph, who lost his position in the family because of the brothers' jealousy, provides for the entire family and, indeed, saves them from death in the famine. If the strife in Israel characteristic for an entire history is represented by the strife in the family at the beginning of the Joseph story, then the reconciliation at the denouement represents a reconciliation for the striving brothers of Israel. In the view of the theologian who composed the novella, God intends his people to be together, a single family. Joseph, the ancestral father of the leading tribe in the north, effects that reconciliation.

The narrative framework for the Joseph story, however, suggests that the reconciliation effected by the Joseph transaction did not work. The narrative from the end of the Joseph novella to the end of Genesis depicts the family as deceptive and distrusting, indeed, as untrustworthy. When the father dies, the brothers approach Joseph with a plea for pardon based on a request of the father before he died. The tradition, of course, contains no such request from Jacob and clearly asserts that the brothers have manufactured their story to Joseph just as earlier they manufactured their story to Jacob. The author of the framework argues that reconciliation has not yet occurred, that the family is as broken as it ever was. Reconciliation cannot be found, ac-

Harvesting grain with sickles. (In the Genesis narrative Joseph administers the grain reserves for Pharaoh.) From the tomb of Mennah, scribe of Thutmose IV, ca. 1390 B.C.

cording to the larger context, in the patriarchal traditions.

2 The father of the Igal who was one of the spies Moses sent into Canaan (Num. 13:7).

3 A musician in the service of David (1 Chron. 25:2, 9).

4 A priest in the time of Joiakim (Neh. 12:14).

5 One of the sons of priests who in the time of Ezra put away the foreign women they had married (Ezra 10:42).

6 The son of Jacob (Matt. 1:16) or Heli (Luke 3:23), the husband of Mary (Matt. 1:16), and, in the eyes of his compatriots, the father of Jesus (Luke 4:22; John 1:45; 6:42). A descendant of David (Matt. 1:20), his unwillingness publicly to set aside his pregnant betrothed showed him to be a just man (Matt. 1:19). The notion that he was an older man when he married Mary has no basis in the Gospel accounts—this tradition probably arose to account for Joseph's absence in the Gospel narratives about the mature Jesus.

7 A high-ranking (Luke 23:50), rich (Matt. 27: 57), and honorable (Mark 15:34) Jew who wrapped the body of the crucified Jesus in a linen shroud and buried him in a tomb newly cut from rock (Luke 23:53), perhaps the tomb he had had prepared for himself (Matt. 27:60). That he was a disciple of Jesus (Matt. 27:57; John 19: 38) is not mentioned by either Luke or Mark.

8 The name of three ancestors of Joseph, the husband of Mary (Luke 3:26, 30, 34).

9 A follower of Jesus, also called Barsabbas, surnamed Justus, who was not chosen to replace Judas as one of the twelve disciples when he, along with Matthias, was put forward for that position (Acts 1:23).

10 An early Christian, surnamed Barnabas (Acts 4:36), who along with Saul (Paul) was sent on a missionary journey by the church in Antioch (Acts 13:2). A later dispute over a traveling companion led them to go their separate ways (Acts 15:36–39).

11 One of the sons of Mary and a brother of Jesus (Matt. 13:55) who bore the Greek rather than the Hebrew form of the name (Joses; Mark 6:3). Perhaps the Joses mentioned as a son of Mary in Matt. 27:56 and Mark 15:40, 47 is the same brother of Jesus. ***See also*** Genesis; Hexateuch; Jacob; Patriarch.

Bibliography

Coats, George W. *Genesis*. Vol. 1 of *Forms of Old Testament Literature*. Grand Rapids, MI: Eerdmans, 1983. Pp. 259–266.

von Rad, Gerhard. "The Joseph Narrative and Ancient Wisdom." In *The Problem of the Hexateuch and Other Essays*. London: Oliver and Boyd, 1966. Pp. 292–300.

G.W.C./P.J.A.

Josephus (joh-see'fuhs), Flavius Josephus or Joseph ben Matthias, the single most important Jewish historian in the early Roman period. He was born of a priestly family in the first year of the emperor Gaius (A.D. 37–38) and also claimed descent from the Hasmoneans. In his twenty-sixth year (A.D. 63–64) he served on an embassy to Rome. During the revolt against Rome that began in 66, he led the revolutionary forces in Galilee until he was captured by the Roman general Vespasian at Jotapata (A.D. 67). After his capture, he predicted that Vespasian would become emperor. When the prophecy was fulfilled, he was released. For the remainder of the war he served as an interpreter for the Romans. He spent the rest of his life in Rome, engaged in literary activity under imperial patronage. He died ca. A.D. 100.

While in Rome Josephus produced works, four of which have survived. *The Jewish War* is an account in seven books of the Jewish revolt, prefaced with a brief survey of Jewish history from the second century B.C. *The Antiquities of the Jews* is a twenty-volume work, the first half of which paraphrases the Jewish scriptures, while the second half records, in greater detail than in the *War*, the postbiblical history of the Jews. *Against Apion* is an apologetic work in two books refuting slanders leveled against the Jews during the Hellenistic period. The brief *Life*, an appendix to the *Antiquities*, provides general autobiographical information but focuses on Josephus' period of revolutionary leadership in Galilee. Josephus also composed an Aramaic account of the Jewish revolt which has not survived.

Throughout his works, Josephus strove to elicit sympathy for his people, and to make Jewish traditions comprehensible to the Greco-Roman world. At the same time he attempted to blame the revolt on a fanatical minority of the Jewish people. H.W.A.

Joses (joh'ses; Gk., "Joseph"). **1** One of Jesus' brothers (Mark 6:3; cf. Matt. 13:53, "Joseph"). The meaning of "brothers" is debated. One view includes cousins and perhaps others, maintaining that Jesus was Mary's only child; other views hold that Jesus did have (half or even full) brothers and sisters. **2** A brother of James the younger (Mark 14:40, 47; cf. Matt. 27:56, "Joseph"), perhaps identical with 1. **3** The original name of Barnabas, Paul's co-worker (Acts 4:36). ***See also*** Barnabas; Brothers; James; Joseph.

Joshaphat (josh'uh-fat). ***See*** Jehoshaphat.

Joshua. **1** The dominant figure in the book of Joshua: the successor of Moses and the supervisor of Israel's conquest of Canaan and of the allotment of the land to the tribes. According to Num. 13:16, Joshua was an Ephraimite, originally called Hoshea and renamed by Moses. An Ephraimite genealogy is provided for him in 1 Chron. 7:20–27. He first appears in Exod. 17: 8–13, where Moses appoints him to lead the battle against Amalek, which he does successfully. In Exod. 33:11 he appears as a young man serving as Moses' assistant in the tent of meeting. He urges Moses to restrict spirit-inspired behavior but is overruled by Moses (Num. 11: 28–29). As one of the twelve spies sent to reconnoiter Canaan, he agrees with Caleb; Joshua and Caleb constitute the minority who recommend confidence in God and a direct assault (Num. 14: 6–10). For this God exempts them from the general condemnation of that generation to death in the wilderness. God then tells Moses to lay his hands on Joshua and designate him a leader like Moses, who will be obeyed fully by all the people (Num. 27:18–23; cf. Deut. 34:9). In Num. 34:17 God tells Moses that Joshua, along with Eleazer and an officer from each tribe, will be responsible for allotting the land to the people. Moses publicly encourages Joshua and recognizes his future role in Deut. 31:7–8 (cf. 3:28; 31: 3). Joshua is commissioned by God himself in Deut. 31:14, 23 and Josh. 1:1–9. The book of Joshua then relates how Joshua fulfilled his dual role as conqueror and distributor of the promised land, concluding with a notice of Joshua's death at the age of one hundred and ten and his burial in his allotted territory (Josh. 24:29–30; Judg. 2:8–9).

Many of Joshua's deeds are analogous to those of Moses, and the text says that God was with Joshua as with Moses (Josh. 3:9) and that Israel revered Joshua as they had Moses (4:14). Like Moses, the original Joshua probably would have had a much more restricted historical role. But the present, developed literary figure is of greater theological significance than any historical antecedent—as an archetypal leader, who by his faith and obedience to God accomplished his mission effectively and completely. He has some of the characteristics of a monarch and may have been modeled on or served as a model for such kings as Josiah. In later tradition Joshua is remembered for his great deeds (Ecclus. 46:1–8) and cited specifically for his obedience to the law (1 Macc. 2: 55) and his intercession for Israel (2 Esd. 7: 107). **2** A resident of Beth-shemesh on whose land the cows bringing the Ark from its Philistine captivity came to a standstill (1 Sam. 6:14, 18). **3** A governor of Jerusalem, after whom a gate was named during the late monarchical period (2 Kings 23:8). **4** An alternate form of the name Jeshua. ***See also*** Joshua, The Book of. S.B.P.

Joshua, the Book of, the sixth book of the OT, the first of the Former Prophets (i.e., the historical books, which conclude with Nehemiah). In broad outline, the book tells of Israel's conquest of Canaan under Joshua after the death of Moses (chaps. 1–12) and Joshua's subsequent distribution of the land among the tribes (chaps. 13–19). Six cities are then designated places of asylum (chap. 20), and forty-eight are reserved for Levites (chap. 21). The east Jordan tribes then return to their Transjordanian territory (chap. 22). In his old age, Joshua delivers a valedictory address (chap. 23). In another address, he challenges the tribes to commit themselves to God alone (chap. 24). The book ends with notices of Joshua's death, the interment of Joshua's remains and Israel's faithfulness to God until Joshua's contemporaries died (24:29–33).

OUTLINE OF CONTENTS

The Book of Joshua

I. Introduction: transfer of leadership to Joshua (1:1–18)
   A. God's instructions and promises to Joshua (1:1–9)
   B. Joshua's instructions to the people (1:10–18)
II. The conquest of Canaan (2:1–12:24)
   A. In central Palestine; the crossing of the Jordan (2:1–9:27)
   B. In the south (10:1–43)
   C. In the north (11:1–23)
   D. Summary list of defeated kings (12:1–24)
III. Distribution of the land (13:1–22:34)
   A. God's instructions to Joshua (13:1–7)
   B. Moses' allotments to Transjordanian tribes (13:8–33)
   C. Tribal allotments made by Joshua (14:1–19:51)
   D. Designation of cities of refuge and levitical cities (20:1–21:42)
   E. Summary of conquest: promises fulfilled (21:43–45)
   F. Dismissal of Transjordanian tribes (22:1–34)
IV. Concluding speech and historical notices (23:1–24:33)
   A. Farewell address of Joshua (23:1–16)
   B. Covenant at Shechem (24:1–28)
   C. Death and burial notices: Joshua, Joseph, Eleazar (24:29–33)

The present book contains some old traditions of historical value. The remains of premonarchical tribal accounts of local conflicts are scattered through the book, the first third of which depends on Benjaminite traditions (perhaps shaped by the worship practices carried on at Gilgal), which have been combined, generalized, and extended to create a single, national epic of a march of miraculous conquest under a single leader. The lists of boundary markers, cities, and territorial units perhaps go back to administrative reorganization during the early monarchy (late eleventh century B.C.). The book owes its present character to the Deuteronomists (see esp. 1; 8:30–35; 11:10–23; 21:43–22:6; 23–24), who distinguish the conquest from the subsequent cycles of apostasy and deliverance (Judges) and from the formation of Israel under Moses (Pentateuch). For them it is through Joshua's faithfulness to the law of Moses, especially as recorded in Deuteronomy, that Israel is able to possess the promised land. ***See also*** Conquest of Canaan; Joshua. S.B.P.

Josiah (joh-sī'uh; Heb., "Yahweh gives," "cures," or "brings forth"). **1** The son of King Amon by Jedidah, whom the people of the land made king of Judah at the age of eight after his father's assassination (639 B.C.). Josiah's reign during the last half of the seventh century B.C. lasted thirty-one years. The Assyrian Empire, which had previously dominated the region, was in its final decline, making the expansion and religious reform that characterized Josiah's reign possible. According to 2 Kings 23, the reform (ca. 620) was motivated by discovery of "the book of the law," generally considered some form of Deuteronomy; Chronicles, however, suggests that the reform had already started six years before. The relationship of Josiah's reform to that of Hezekiah almost a century earlier is also uncertain.

Josiah's religious actions included the removal of all traces of foreign worship and the elimination of all outlying places of worship, including those in Assyrian-controlled sections of what had been the Northern Kingdom (v. 15), thereby effectively centralizing all officially sanctioned religious practice in Jerusalem. Josiah entered into a covenant with God and observed a unique Passover in Jerusalem. His political accomplishments are manifest in the evidence of the kingdom's expansion, perhaps the result of an attempt to recreate the kingdom of David, an attempt made possible by Assyria's weakened condition. Not only did Josiah remove shrines in Samaria (2 Kings 23:19) and Galilee (2 Chron. 34:6) as foretold in 1 Kings 13:2, but he apparently also expanded in other directions, as shown by the discovery of a Hebrew letter from this period at Yavneh Yam, a Judean fort on the Philistine coast of the Mediterranean Sea.

Josiah was killed in 609 B.C. at Megiddo while trying to block Pharaoh Neco II from helping the last remnant of the Assyrian Empire against the rising power of Babylonia (2 Kings 23:29). Whether this action was coordinated with Babylonia or undertaken on Josiah's own initiative is unknown. According to 1 Chron. 35:20–24, he was merely wounded at Megiddo and taken from there to Jerusalem where he died. He was succeeded by his sons Jehoahaz (2 Kings 23:30, called Shallum in Jer. 22:11), who was installed by the people, and Jehoiakim (Jer. 22:18, previously Eliakim according to 2 Kings 23:34), who was installed by Neco. Later his son Zedekiah (or grandson according to 2 Chron. 36:10), whose original name was Mattaniah, became Judah's last king (2 Kings 24:17).

Josiah's reign was a time of Judean national resurgence. The king was highly regarded by Jeremiah (Jer. 22:15), who lived during his reign as did the prophet Zephaniah (Zeph. 1:1; see also Jer. 1:2; 25:3; 36:2). Josiah was considered by the author of Kings to have been Judah's outstanding monarch (2 Kings 23:25).

2 The son of Zephaniah, a Jerusalemite homeowner who lived immediately after the Exile (mid-sixth century B.C.) (Zech. 6:10). ***See also*** Deuteronomy. F.E.G.

jot (KJV; RSV: "iota"), in Matt. 5:18 representing the equivalent of "i," the smallest letter in the Greek alphabet. In the KJV, it is combined with "tittle" (RSV, dot), which means a small part of a letter. The phrase as used by Jesus emphasizes that nothing will be removed from the law, not a letter, not even part of a letter, as long as heaven and earth endure.

Jotham (joh'thuhm; Heb., "Yah[weh] is perfect"). **1** The youngest of seventy sons of Jerubbaal (Gideon). He alone escaped when his brother Abimelech conspired to be crowned king at Shechem and killed the remaining sons of Jerubbaal (Judg. 8:29–9:5). After hearing that the men of Shechem had made Abimelech king (9:6) Jotham went to the top of Mount Gerizim near Shechem and, speaking loudly enough to be heard in the valley below, denounced the selection of Abimelech as king by telling the fable of the trees who foolishly selected a thorn bush as their king instead of a more worthy tree (9:7–21). The curse pronounced against the city of Shechem and Abimelech was fulfilled three years later by a civil war in which Shechem was leveled and Abimelech was killed by a millstone thrown from a wall (Judg. 9:22–57). **2** The son of Uzziah (Azariah), and king of Judah (ca. 750–734 B.C.). The sixteen years of his reign included about eight years in which he served as regent for his father, who was struck with leprosy (2 Kings 15:5, 7; 2 Chron. 26:16–27:1). Jotham was given a rather mediocre evaluation as king by the writer of the book of Kings and a slightly better rating by the Chronicler. He is credited with several building projects as well as subjugating the Ammonites, and he prospered because "he ordered his ways before the Lord" (2 Chron. 27:4–6; cf. 2 Kings 15:34). However, he failed to remove the high places on which the people offered sacrifice to Baal (2 Kings 15:35; cf. 2 Chron. 27:2). Late in his reign an alliance of Pekah of Israel (the Northern Kingdom) and Rezin of Syria threatened Judah with invasion, but Jotham died before the threat could be carried out. His son Ahaz bore the force of the invasion (2 Kings 15:37; 16:5). Jotham was contemporary with the prophets Hosea (1:1),

Isaiah (1:1), and Micah (1:1). **3** The son of Jahdai, a Judahite of the clan of Caleb (1 Chron. 2:47). ***See also*** Fable; Gideon. D.R.B.

journey, Sabbath. ***See*** Sabbath Day's Journey.

joy, an expression pervading both OT and NT. Scattered throughout the OT are references to the happiness derived from sexual love (Song of Sol. 1:4), married life (Prov. 5:18), the birth of children (Ps. 113:9), and especially the pleasures of harvest (Deut. 26:1–11) and feasting (Eccles. 8:15). These, however, merely form the backdrop and establish the metaphors for the far more pervasive exultation in God's actions on behalf of Israel. Nature itself is invited to join in this joyous mood of thanksgiving (Ps. 98), which often had a cultic setting as Israel celebrated in her feasts and liturgy God's past acts of deliverance. The righteous especially are summoned to look with joy upon acts of divine redemption and vengeance, in which the wicked receive just recompense for their deeds (Ps. 58:10). In a similar vein, wisdom literature rejoices in the law, which leads Israel in the paths of obedience and righteousness that are pleasing to God (Ps. 1).

Under circumstances of oppression, however, the mood became more anticipatory as Israel looked ahead to the joy that would accompany their future deliverance by God (Isa. 65:17–19). God's own joy over this event is also anticipated (Zeph. 3:17) and thus joy emerges as a dominant aspect of Israel's eschatological hope.

Because the early Christians believed that the advent of Jesus marked the inbreaking of God's final redemptive act, all the eschatological joy that Israel had anticipated was now associated with Jesus. This motif is particularly strong in Luke's Gospel, where the birth of the infant Jesus occasions an outpouring of human and heavenly joy (Luke 1–2) and his ministry (10:17) and resurrection (24:52) evoke the same response. Acts describes the early church sustaining this mood of rejoicing and spreading it beyond the borders of Judea (Acts 8:8).

John's Gospel employs the familiar metaphors of marriage and harvest joy to suggest the exultant mood accompanying Jesus' ministry of salvation (John 3:29; 4:36). Even more characteristic of this Gospel, however, is the explicit association of joy with the person of Jesus and the perfect joy of those secure in their fellowship with him (John 15–17).

The Pauline Letters are filled with the mood of rejoicing, for eschatological joy, closely linked with the Holy Spirit, is both the impetus (1 Thess. 2:19–20) and the goal (2 Cor. 1:24) of Paul's apostolic ministry. Paul, however, also stresses the paradox that this joy can be experienced in the midst of temporal afflictions. Not only are afflictions viewed as transitory and thus unable to dampen the joy of the believer, they also suggest the imminent fulfillment of the believers' hopes and thus heighten rather than diminish the mood of exultation (Rom. 5:3). Paul also suggests that affliction, even martyrdom, could be viewed as a reflection of Jesus' own suffering, and thus it becomes a sign of the true disciple or apostle and a further basis for rejoicing (2 Cor. 11:23–12:10). Thus Paul's Letter to the Philippians, written under circumstances of severe apostolic suffering, is also the most joyous of all his Letters. J.M.B.

Jozabad (johz'uh-bad; Heb., "Yahweh is a gift" or "Yahweh has given"), a shortened form of Jehozabad. **1** A Gederathite who joined David's fighting men at Ziklag (1 Chron. 12:4). **2** One from the tribe of Manasseh who defected from Saul to join David (1 Chron. 12:20). **3** A Levite who helped oversee the collection of the Temple offerings during the reign of Hezekiah (2 Chron. 31:13). **4** A Levite leader who contributed animals for the Passover celebration during King Josiah's reforms (2 Chron. 35:9). **5** A Levite who helped inventory the valuables brought back by the exiles who returned with Ezra (Ezra 8:33). **6** A member of the clan of Pashur who took a foreign wife (Ezra 10:22). **7** A Levite who took a foreign wife (Ezra 10:23). **8** One, probably a Levite, who helped explain to the people the law read by Ezra (Neh. 8:7). **9** A Levite leader who helped supervise the rebuilding of the Temple following the return from the Exile (Neh. 11:16). He may be the same as 8 above. D.R.B.

Jozadak (joh'zuh-dak; Heb., "Yahweh is righteous"), a shortened form of Jehozadak. He was a priest, the father of Jeshua, the high priest in Jerusalem following the return from the Babylonian captivity (Ezra 3:2; 10:18). He is most often called Jehozadak (1 Chron. 16:14; Hag. 1:12). ***See also*** Jehozadak.

Jubal (jōō'bal), "father" (i.e., ancestral patron) of musicians playing the lyre and pipe, according to the early tradition of Gen. 4:21. One of two sons of Lamech by Adah, he is linked through his brother Jabal with herdsmen.

Jubilee, the fiftieth year occurring at the end of seven Sabbatical cycles of seven years each, in which all land was returned to its ancestral owners and all Israelite slaves were freed. The Jubilee is described in Lev. 25:8–17, 23–55; 27:16–25; and Num. 36:4. It was proclaimed with the blowing of the shophar (trumpet made from a ram's horn) on the Day of Atonement. (Hebrew *yovel,* "Jubilee," takes its name from the ram's horn.) The land was also left fallow in the Jubilee Year. The Jubilee was observed in the seventh Sabbatical in Second Temple times, so that there was a forty-nine-year cycle. ***See also*** Feasts, Festivals, and Fasts; Sabbatical Year; Shophar. L.H.S.

Jubilees, Book of. ***See*** Pseudepigrapha.

Judaea (jōō-dee'uh). ***See*** Judea.

Judah, the name of a region in Palestine, of a tribe, and of an individual, who is the eponymous ancestor of the tribe. In Genesis, Judah is introduced as the fourth son born to Jacob and his first wife, Leah (Gen. 29:35; 37:26; 43:3, 8; 44:14, 16, 18; 46:28). The tribal name "Judah" may have derived from the geographical area in which clans settled in the highlands approximately between Jerusalem and Hebron (i.e., the mountains of Judah), the greater part of southern Palestine. The twelve-tribe scheme includes under Judah a number of other tribal groups that settled in the area from Hebron southward into the Negeb—i.e., the Calebites (in the territory around Hebron; Josh. 14:13–15; Judg. 1:20), Kenites (in the area around Arad; Judg. 1:16), Kennizzites (in the environs of Debir; Josh. 15: 15–19; Judg. 1:11–15), Simeonites (near Zepath-hormah; Judg. 1:17), Jerahmeelites, and Othnielites. Of these groups, Simeon alone is given autonomous tribal status among the southern tribes and represented as a partner to Judah in Judges 1. The fact that Judah is not mentioned in the ancient Song of Deborah (Judg. 5) is probably due to its firm association with the south from a very early period. Judah's position in the Blessing of Moses (Deut. 33:7), which stems from a relatively early period, is that of a rather insignificant tribe. The Blessing of Jacob (Gen. 49:8–12), however, makes Judah the ruler and displaces the older Reuben. This probably reflects the situation of the tribes in the time of David (late eleventh century B.C.). The tribe of Judah became the state of Judah in the time of David. In Hebron, the capital of Judah, David was anointed king by "the men of Judah" (2 Sam. 2:4) to rule over what was apparently a loose confederation of southern tribes.

In the NT, Judah is ranked at the head of "the sealed" (Rev. 7:5) and Jesus' descent is from Judah, a nonpriestly tribe in Heb. 7:14. ***See also*** Caleb; Judah, Kingdom of; Kenaz; Kenites; Simeon. F.S.F.

Judah, Kingdom of, a kingdom in southern Palestine consisting of the tribal areas of Judah and Benjamin that was created by the dissolution of the United Monarchy at the death of Solomon (922 B.C.). Following this division there was a period of civil war between Judah (the Southern Kingdom) and Israel (the Northern Kingdom) that finally terminated in the time of Jehoshaphat, king of Judah (868–847 B.C.). Although Judah was considerably less populous than its sister kingdom, it enjoyed greater political stability due to the presence of Jerusalem and the Davidic monarchy. Because of its relatively secluded geographic location, it was somewhat less vulnerable to external aggression.

The population of Judah, from the time of David on, had incorporated considerable numbers of non-Israelites, leading to an alternation between pro-Canaanite, non-Yahwist religious policies on the part of some kings and the reversal of such policies in periodic religious reforms. Thus, Rehoboam (ca. 926–907 B.C.), the first king of Judah, adopted pro-Canaanite policies (1 Kings 14:21–24), but his policies were reversed by his grandson Asa (ca. 905–874; 1 Kings 15:9–13). Asa's pro-Yahwist reforms were continued by his son Jehoshaphat, but they were again reversed by the extremely anti-Yahwist policies of Queen Athaliah (843–837 B.C.; 2 Kings 8:26; 11:2; 2 Chron. 24:7), a daughter or sister of Ahab of Israel, who seized the throne violently, causing a break in what had been Judah's orderly succession to the throne. She ruled as Judah's only queen until she was ousted by the Jerusalem priesthood acting in concert with the Judean rural nobility. The Davidic succession was renewed with Athaliah's ouster (2 Kings 11:17) and the installation of her seven-year-old grandson Jehoash (837–801 B.C.) on the throne.

Jehoash's son Amaziah (ca. 801–787) campaigned against Edom (2 Kings 14:7) and was involved in costly hostilities with Joash of Israel (2 Kings 14:8–14). He fell victim to a conspiracy mounted by pro-Yahwists, who assassinated him and placed his sixteen-year-old son, Uzziah (ca. 787–747), on the throne. The reign of Uzziah (or Azariah in 2 Kings 14:21; 15:1, 6, 7, 8) was marked by territorial expansion, an increase in population, strengthening of defenses, advancement of agriculture with the cultivation of semiarid areas, and the development of commerce. Uzziah pursued Yahwist policies but was afflicted with leprosy, leading the Chronicler (2 Chron. 26:16–21) to blame his illness on the fact that he had usurped a priestly prerogative by sacrificing incense in the Temple. His son Jotham (ca. 756–742), who began his reign before his father's death, continued Uzziah's successful policies, but Judah suffered losses under Jotham's son, Ahaz (ca. 742–727), losing territory to the Philistines and to Edom and being attacked by an Israel-Syrian alliance. These losses drove Ahaz to Assyria for help, and he instituted pro-Assyrian, anti-Yahwist practices, including even the human sacrifice of his own son (2 Kings 16:2–4).

Early in the reign of Ahaz's son Hezekiah (ca. 727–698), the Assyrians conquered Israel, leaving Judah as the sole surviving independent state in the area. The Judean state was one of the few in the region that avoided the catastrophe that befell the other states of the area in the latter part of the eighth century in the reigns of the Assyrian kings Tiglath-pileser III (745–727 B.C.) and Sargon II (722–705).

The fall of the Northern Kingdom encouraged Judean kings to pursue nationalistic policies aimed at recovering a united Davidic monarchy. Accordingly, Hezekiah pursued thorough-going religious reforms (2 Kings 18; 2 Chron. 29–31). He revolted against the Assyrians after the death of Sargon II in 705, and Sargon's successor, Sennacherib, responded with an invasion in 701, in which he conquered the fortified cities of Judah and besieged Jerusalem (2 Kings 19). Jerusalem, however, escaped destruction when "The angel of the Lord went forth, and slew a hundred and eighty-five thousand in the camp of the Assyrians" (2 Kings 19:35), causing the Assyrians to withdraw.

The extensive reforms of Hezekiah, in a now familiar pattern, were completely reversed by his son Manasseh (ca. 697–642; 2 Kings 21:1–18; 2 Chron. 33:1–20), who submitted to the Assyrians and "seduced [his people] to do more evil than the nations had done whom the Lord destroyed before the people of Israel" (2 Kings 21:9). His son Amon (ca. 641–640) was assassinated by pro-Yahwist elements, who installed his eight-year-old son Josiah on the throne (ca. 639–609; 2 Kings 21:24). When he came of age, Josiah instituted strongly nationalistic, pro-Yahwist policies in a time when Assyria had begun to be severely threatened by the Babylonians and the Medes (2 Kings 22:3–20; 23:8, 15, 19). Josiah purified religious practices and centralized them in Jerusalem. After the Assyrian capital Nineveh fell in 612, Josiah exploited the situation by seeking to expand his territory. The Egyptian pharaoh Neco, at the same time, sought to go to the aid of the Assyrians. Josiah attempted to stop Neco in 609 at the pass of Megiddo and lost his life in the failed attempt (2 Kings 23:29). The disastrous death of such a reformer king put to rest any visions of a restored Davidic empire and marked the end of an independent Judean state.

Josiah's son, Jehoahaz, reigned for only three months and was then deposed by the pharaoh and deported to Egypt. The Egyptians installed Jehoiakim (Eliakim) on the throne of Judah (608–598); Jehoiakim was hated by his people, both because of his pro-Egyptian policies and the heavy tribute he exacted from them to send to Egypt. There was also a religious decline under his rule (2 Kings 24:2–4).

The last years of Judah saw a struggle between Egypt and Babylon for hegemony over Palestine. The Babylonians, under the leadership of Nebuchadrezzar (or Nebuchadnezzar), decisively defeated the Egyptians at Carchemish in 605 (2 Kings 24:1). It was this Nebuchadrezzar, as king of the newly ascendant Babylonian Empire, that Jehoiakim rebelled against three years later. Responding to this rebellion, Nebuchadrezzar moved against Judah (2 Kings 24:2). Thus Jerusalem fell into Babylonian hands on March 15/16, 597 B.C., as reported in the Babylonian Chronicles. Jehoiakim died during the siege of Jerusalem and was succeeded by his son Jehoiachin, who surrendered to Nebuchadrezzar (2 Kings 24:12). The upper classes and skilled artisans were exiled to Babylon (2 Kings 24:14–16). The Babylonians appointed Zedekiah as their puppet on the throne. After nine years he rebelled against the Babylonians, bringing Nebuchadrezzar to Jerusalem again, which suffered under a two-year siege. Jerusalem fell in 587 and more people were sent into exile (2 Kings 25:11).

The kingdom of Judah outlasted the kingdom of Israel by some 135 years, but it too fell to a foreign power, bringing to an end a period of national independence that had lasted nearly a half millennium. ***See also*** Rehoboam. F.S.F.

Judaism, the religion of the Jewish people from the Sinai theophany through the present day. Up to and including modern times, Judaism professes the belief in the one, asexual, eternal, creator God, righteous and compassionate judge, king, and parent, who entered into a permanent historical relationship with "the children of Israel" that would culminate in eschatological redemption. The written and oral Torah perpetually obligated the people to a detailed code of ethical and ritual behavior. The term appears (in Greek) in 2 Macc. 2:21; 8:1; 14:38; and Gal. 1:13–14.

Judas (jo͞o-duhs; Gk. for the Heb. *Judah*). **1** Judas, the son of Jacob (Matt. 1:2–3). **2** Judas, an ancestor of Jesus (Luke 3:30). **3** Judas Maccabeus, the third of the five sons of Mattathias. After Antiochus IV Epiphanes polluted the Temple in 167 B.C. ("the abomination that

Judas kisses Jesus, identifying him for Roman soldiers; from the *Winchester Psalter*, ca. 1160.

makes desolate") Mattathias moved with his family to Modein (1 Macc. 2:1–14). When officers of Antiochus sought to force Mattathias and his family to apostasize, Mattathias rose up in defense of the law and the covenant, killed an officer, and led his sons into the wilderness in revolt (1 Macc. 2:15–48). Upon the death of his father, Judas successfully led Israel in numerous battles against the Syrians. He defeated a combined army of Syrians and Samaritans (1 Macc. 2:49–4:35), the Syrians led by Seron, the Syrians led by Gorgias, and the Syrians led by Lysias, after which the Temple was purified (1 Macc. 4: 36–61; cf. John 10:22). Judas continued to lead Israel in battle with great success, liberating Jews from surrounding territories and even making a treaty with Rome. Finally, against a Syrian army led by Bacchides, Judas fell in battle in 160 B.C. (1 Macc. 9:1–18). **4** Judas, the son of Chalphi, an officer of Jonathan Maccabeus (1 Macc. 11:70). **5** Judas, the son of Simon Maccabeus and nephew of Judas Maccabeus who with his brother John successfully led the forces of Israel against Candebeus (1 Macc. 16:2–10). **6** Judas, one of the senders of a letter to Aristobolus (2 Macc. 1:10). **7** Judas of Galilee, a Jewish leader who led a revolt against Rome during the census of Quirinius (Acts 5:37). Josephus credits him with founding the "sect" of the zealots. **8** Judas Iscariot, one of the twelve apostles, the son of Simon Iscariot. He is to be distinguished from the other apostle called Judas (John 14:22). The origin of the name Iscariot is debated. Some suggestions are: man (Heb., *ish*) of Karioth; the assassin (from Gk. *sikarios*); man from Issachar. Certainty is impossible, but if the first is correct, Judas was the only apostle from Judea.

Judas possessed a privileged position among the apostles as treasurer of the group (John 12: 5–6; 13:29). His proximity to Jesus at the Lord's Supper (John 13:21–26) also suggests this. Why he betrayed Jesus is uncertain. Some suggestions are that he did it (Mark 14:10–11) after being convinced that Jesus truly planned to die (Mark 14:3–9); that he did it for money (Matt. 26:14–16); or that he did it to help Jesus fulfill his purpose of dying! The last suggestion, however, is at odds with Jesus' words in Mark 14: 21. Despite a loving gesture by Jesus (John 13: 26–27), Judas proceeded to betray his Lord.

What Judas betrayed is easier to answer. One suggestion is that he betrayed Jesus' claim to be the Messiah, but his absence at the trial, when such witnesses were sought, refutes this. What he betrayed was how Jesus could be arrested privately (Mark 14:1–2). This he did in Gethsemane by singling him out at night with a kiss.

Upon reflecting over what he had done, Judas experienced remorse and sought to undo his evil deed (Matt. 27:3–4), but it was not possible. In sorrow he hanged himself (Matt. 27:5) and, falling headlong, his body split open and his bowels fell out (Acts 1:18). **9** Judas, the son of James and one of the apostles (Luke 6:16; Acts 1:13; John 14:22). This is probably the Thaddaeus of Matt. 10:3; Mark 3:18. The qualification of Judas in these latter two passages only makes sense if there were another Judas in the group. **10** Judas, one of the four brothers of Jesus (Mark 6:3) whom tradition associated with the author of Jude. **11** Judas, a man in whose home in Damascus the blind Saul was brought (Acts 9: 11). **12** Judas Barsabbas, a leader in the Jerusalem church chosen along with Silas to accompany Paul and Barnabus back to Antioch in order to announce the apostolic decree (Acts 15: 22–23). It is possible that he and Joseph (Acts 1: 23) were brothers. ***See also*** Apostle; Maccabees.

R.H.S.

Jude, a shortened form of "Judas," a person described as "a servant of Jesus Christ and brother of James" and identified as the author of the Letter of Jude (v. 1), which many scholars, however, regard as pseudonymous. It is generally agreed that this is not the Judas, son (or brother) of James, identified in Luke 6:16 and Acts 1:13 as one of the Twelve (in Matt. 10:2–4; Mark 3:16–19, however, "Thaddaeus" occurs rather than "Judas"). Traditionally, Jude is identified with Judas, one of the "brothers of the Lord" (Matt. 13:55; Mark 6:3; cf. Acts 1:14; 1 Cor. 9:5). His identification with the disciple "Judas" of John 14:22 is questionable. ***See also*** Apostle; Brothers; Disciple; James; Judas; Jude, The Letter of; Thaddaeus; Twelve, The.

P.L.S.

Jude, the Letter of, one of the "catholic" or "general" Epistles of the NT. The author, who describes himself as "Jude, a servant of Jesus Christ and brother of James" (v. 1), has traditionally been identified with Judas, one of the brothers of Jesus (Matt. 13:55; Mark 6:3). The internal evidence of the book, however, makes such an identification unlikely. The author's purpose is to challenge his readers to contend for the faith "once for all delivered to the saints" (v. 3) and to summon his readers to "remember" the words of the apostles (v. 17). These appeals to the readers suggest that the author is not a contemporary of the apostles.

The book lacks the common characteristics of an epistle, including the identification of the readers and the closing greetings. Thus, it should be regarded as a tract addressed to Christians generally about the inroads being made by heretical groups who endanger the faith "once for all delivered to the saints."

Because the heretics are described as those who "set up divisions" (v. 19), they are frequently identified by scholars as an early sect of Gnostics. The author's description of their licentious behavior (vv. 4, 6–8, 12–13, 16) makes such an identification plausible but not certain. Behavior that might be characterized as wanton is a characteristic of some Gnostic groups but not of all, nor is it limited to Gnostic groups.

The denunciations are accompanied by warnings of severe punishment awaiting heretics. The warnings are derived from the OT (v. 7) and from two later Jewish apocalyptic writings, 1 *Enoch* (vv. 6–15) and *The Assumption of Moses* (v. 9). Similar material is found in 2 Pet. 2:1–18, suggesting that Jude may be a source for 2 Peter.

The book may be outlined as follows:

I. Salutation (1–2)
II. Purpose for writing (3–4)
III. Judgment on false teachers (5–16)
  A. Examples of punishment on unbelievers (5–13)
  B. Enoch's prophecy of judgment (14–16)
IV. Warnings and exhortations (17–23)
V. Doxology (24–25).

See also Epistle; General Letters; Gnosticism; Heresy; Judas; Pseudepigrapha. J.W.T.

Judea (jōō-dee'uh; KJV: "Judaea," except in Ezra 5:8), the Greco-Latin form of Judah. The geographical term "Judea" is introduced in Ezra-Nehemiah to designate the area of the Jewish state under the Persians, which included only a relatively small area around Jerusalem, smaller in extent than the former area of Judah. Following the Persian period (ca. 538–333 B.C.), Judea is spoken of in the Maccabbean era (ca. 167–63 B.C.) as a greatly expanded, independent Jewish state (1 Macc. 5:45; 7:10; 11:28, 34; 12:38). In its most comprehensive political sense, Judea comes to include all of Palestine (with the exception of some Hellenistic cities), although in its more limited sense it continues to refer to the region around Jerusalem and one of the three main divisions of the country: Judea, Samaria, and Galilee. In its extended political sense it is the territory over which Herod the Great (37–4 B.C.) ruled. His son Archelaus (4 B.C.–A.D. 6) however, as ethnarch of Judea, ruled from Jerusalem over the more limited area of Judea-Idumea-Samaria, not over Galilee and Perea.

After Archelaus, Judea became part of the Roman province of Syria and was ruled by procurators appointed by Rome. These procurators presided over the same limited area as Archelaus, but from Caesarea. The first-century A.D. Jewish historian Josephus often uses the term "Judea" in its broad political sense, as does the NT (Matt. 19:1; Luke 1:5; 4:44; 7:17; 23:5; Acts 10:37; 11:1, 29; 26:20). Throughout Jesus' lifetime (after the banishment of Archelaus in A.D. 6), Judea continued to be ruled by a Roman procurator who served under the proconsul, or president, of Syria who resided in Antioch (Luke 3:1; Josephus *Antiquities* 17.13.5; 18.1.1); among them was Pontius Pilate (A.D. 26–36).

Judea was not traversed by major trade routes. The land included a sizeable desert area in the Wilderness of Judea and had a pastoral economy supplemented by olives and grapes, the principal crops of the highlands. Economically, however, Judea was always dependent upon the revenues generated by Jerusalem, and its population tended to be concentrated around Jerusalem. ***See also*** Jerusalem; Judah. F.S.F.

Judges, the Book of, OT Bible book containing stories of the period between Joshua and Samuel, which were collected early in the monarchy, later edited into a national history (late seventh century B.C.), and finally re-edited after the destruction of Jerusalem (in 587 B.C.).

OUTLINE OF CONTENTS

The Book of Judges

I. Introduction: from invasion to stalemate (1:1–3:6)
II. Ideal and office (3:7–16:31)
  A. Othniel, Ehud, Shamgar (3:7–31)
  B. Deborah and Barak versus royal coalition (4:1–5:31)
  C. Gideon (chaps. 6–8) and Abimelech (chap. 9)
  D. "Minor" judges and Jephthah (10:1–12:15)
  E. Samson: unexemplary (13:1–16:31)
III. Supplements: more lessons from the past (17:1–21:25)

The book begins with Israel united for offensive war (chap. 1) and recapitulates materials reported earlier in Joshua chaps. 14–15, though with several significant changes in detail and orientation. Through these changes the historian of Judges 1 could present a different view of the nature of the conquest and Israel's role in it. The editorial prologue attributed to a deuteronomic redactor (2:11–23) articulates the evaluation of the period that pervades the book: cycles of idolatry, divine punishments, the appeal for divine aid, the emergence of a "savior" figure, and a period of rest when the people were ruled or judged by the heroic savior. This pattern is also found as a connective element between the various traditions of the book (for another evaluation, see 3:1–5). The Hebrew verb used in connection with the military judge, *shaphat*, has the broader sense "to rule." From notices about "minor" judges (10:1–5; 12:8–15) it appears that such influence rarely extended beyond the Judge's neighboring tribes. The stories, however, laud exploits of saviors in time of crisis for the federation, "major" judges. There then appears to be an overlap of semantic uses for the verb, which includes military and administrative-legal functions. The "major" judges seem to have performed both tasks; the "minor" ones only the latter.

The body of the book is arranged didactically, alternating between good and not-so-good examples of leadership. Othniel is presented as an ideal leader. He is followed by Cushanrishathaim who may be Irsu, a Syrian usurper in Egypt (late thirteenth century B.C.). The next judge is Ehud, whose "left-handed" dagger diplomacy dealt with Eglon, king of Moab (3:15–23).

The story of the prophetess Deborah and the commander Barak (chap. 4), followed by a virtual eyewitness poem (Song of Deborah and Barak, chap. 5), recounts a war for the fertile plains, especially Esdraelon. The Israelite population was concentrated in upland villages founded after ca. 1200 B.C. Forces of the "kings of Canaan" (5:19) were led by Sisera (a non-Semitic name) from Harosheth "of the nations." Sisera's overlord was "Jabin king of Canaan" at Hazor (4: 2, 24; cf. Josh. 11). Possibly (but not necessarily) two battle accounts are conflated. Victory "at Taanach, by the waters of Megiddo" may be dated to ca. 1125 B.C., when Megiddo was unoccupied and Taanach violently destroyed.

Gideon (Jerubbaal), who led the rout of the Midianites (camel-riding raiders), piously declined the offer of kingship and requested instead the trappings of diviner-judge.

Abimelech, the son of Gideon by a Shechemite concubine, accepted funds from the covenant sanctuary at Shechem and became king of Shechem, while serving as commander of the tribal militia. When local support collapsed, he used the militia to destroy Shechem; after his victory he sowed the city with salt. Massive mid-twelfth-century destruction at Tell Balata witnesses to the violence.

Jephthah, the Gileadite son of a harlot, gathered a band of mercenaries in the north and was later recalled by the elders of Gilead to lead Israel against the Ammonites. He sacrificed his daughter to fulfill a vow and turned back an Ephraimite force using the password *shibboleth*.

Samson appears as a tragic figure who opposed the Philistines, the eleventh-century successors to the earlier Sea Peoples. A cycle of adventures of this hero have been artfully gathered and crafted in chaps. 13–16. As against other judges, Samson appears less as a national savior figure than as a person with private exploits and vendettas. The account may draw from old folk motifs.

With examples of charismatic leadership inconclusive, stories of escalating internal chaos follow. Micah (chap. 17) was proprietor of a free-lance shrine (probably Bethel) and a maker of graven images, whose young levitical priest from Bethlehem was taken by migrating Danites to become founder of the far northern priesthood. "In those days there was no king in Israel; every man did what was right in his own eye" (17:6).

The southern polemic against northern sanctuaries is countered in the sequel (chaps. 18–21). A northern Levite rallied the militia to avenge the rape and murder of his southern concubine, glossing over his own responsibility in the affair (chaps. 19–20). A tragic civil war is recounted with grim humor, "all Israel" versus Benjamin. Finally, to secure wives for the six hundred Benjaminite survivors, the elders recommend one more massacre and then authorize the kidnapping of Shiloh maidens. "In those days ... right in his own eyes" becomes the last word (21:25), lamenting such behaviors and commending the establishment of the monarchy. The negative example of the Benjaminites in the last section may have been deliberately arranged so as to climax the chaotic period and serve as an anti-Saulid polemic (Saul was a Benjaminite) by pro-Judean monarchists. ***See also*** Abimelech; Barak; Jephthah; Shibboleth; Sisera. R.B.

judgment, day of, a term found mainly in the NT referring to the time when God or his Messiah (or the Son of man) is to punish the wicked and redeem the righteous. Related terms and concepts appear frequently in the OT, intertestamental writings, and the NT.

In the OT: In the OT, God is regarded as the Judge of all the earth (Gen. 18:25; Ps. 9:7–8). His judgment is often invoked on individuals (Gen. 16: 5) or nations (Judg. 11:27). Psalm writers, particularly, looked for God to reward the righteous, whether individuals (Ps. 1:5–6), nations (Ps. 110:6), the needy and oppressed (Pss. 72:2–4; 103:6), or the whole world (Ps. 96:13). Many prophets spoke of the "day of the Lord" when, because of their wickedness, God would punish other nations (Obad. 15), Israel (Amos 5:18–20), Judah (Joel 1:15), or all the inhabitants of the earth (Zeph. 1:14–18). Joel 2:30–32 and Mal. 4: 5–6 suggest that those who repent beforehand may be spared. Other OT expressions likewise refer to the coming of God's judgment against the wicked: "on that day" (Isa. 24:21), "the days are coming when ..." (Jer. 9:25–26; Amos 4:2), or simply "then" (Mal. 3:5). The second expression frequently points toward the time when God is to restore his people (Jer. 23:7–8; Amos 9:13). Related phrases, notably "in that day" (Amos 9:11), "in those days" (Jer. 33:16), and "in the latter days" (Hos. 3:5), typically connote the coming era of redemption.

Generally, the OT writers expected God's judgment to occur in history: in the little histories of individuals or the larger history of nations and the world. A few passages hint that the righteous might hope for redemption beyond this life or this world (Job 19:25–27; Isa. 26:19; Ezek. 37:1–14). Dan. 12:1–3 promises that many who have died will awake, some to everlasting life, some to everlasting contempt. Isa. 66:24 and Jth. 16:17 contemplate the eternal torment of the wicked. Wisd. of Sol. 3:1–9, on the other hand, offers assurance that "the souls of the righteous are in the hand of God"; thus, if the righteous are not vindicated and the wicked punished in this life, they will be in the next. 2 Esd. 14:34–35 looks for judgment after death.

The term "day of judgment" appears in several intertestamental writings (e.g., Jth. 16:17; Wisd. of Sol. 3:18, "day of decision"; 2 Esd. 12:34; 2 *Enoch* 51:3). The emerging idea is that people will be judged individually in the new age, or, perhaps, after death, and consigned to their respective destinies. The "day of judgment" and related expressions in the NT often have similar meaning.

In the NT: According to the first three Gospels, Jesus spoke frequently of the coming judgment. The term "day of judgment" appears in Matt. 10:15; 11:22, 24; and 12:36. Often, reference is simply to "the judgment" (Matt. 12:41, 42; Luke 10:14). Related expressions include "that day" (Luke 21:34–35), "on that day" (Matt. 7:22; Luke 17:31), and "in those days" (Mark 13:17, 19, 24). Sometimes, these terms also refer to the expected time of tribulation. Many of Jesus' parables (e.g., Matt. 18:23–35) and other sayings (e.g., Mark 10:17–25) called his hearers to repentance and responsive neighbor-love, so that they might, at the judgment, be found fit to enter the Kingdom of God. The classic passage is Matt. 25:31–46, where the Son of man or "king" sits in judgment, separating the "sheep from the goats." According to Matt. 19:28, the twelve disciples are to join in judging Israel. In John's Gospel, Jesus speaks of a future judgment (5:28–29; 12:48), but more often emphasizes his own authority as judge (5:22, 30) and suggests that judgment is already taking place (9:39; 12:31).

The term "day of judgment" also appears in 2 Pet. 2:9; 3:7; and 1 John 4:17. That God will judge the world on a certain future day, often designated as "that day" or the "day of the Lord," is also stated (Acts 17:31; Rom. 2:16; 1 Thess. 5:2–4; 2 Thess. 2:2; 2 Tim. 1:18; 4:1–8; 2 Pet. 3:10–12; Jude 6). Paul alternatively refers to the coming "day of our Lord Jesus Christ" (1 Cor. 1:8), "the day of the Lord Jesus" (2 Cor. 1:14), "the day of Jesus Christ" (Phil. 1:6), and "the day of Christ" (Phil. 1:10; 2:16). Rev. 14:7 looks for the "hour" of God's judgment. In some of these passages, God is the expected judge; in others, it is Christ. Paul thought that "the saints" (faithful Christians) would also judge the world (1 Cor. 6:2; cf. Matt. 19:28). Only those who lived rightly could hope for a favorable decision at the judgment (Rom. 2:1–8; 2 Cor. 5:6–10; cf. Gal. 5:16–21; so also Rev. 20:12–13). Exactly how Paul's ideas about the coming judgment are to be reconciled with his doctrine of "justification through faith" (e.g., Gal. 2:15–16; 3:1–14; Rom. 3:21–4:25) is not completely clear (but cf. 1 Cor. 3:10–15).

Christ as judge; sixth-century mosaic in San Apollinare Nuovo, Ravenna, Italy.

Many NT traditions urge that the time of judgment, along with the coming of the Kingdom of God (or the Son of man), is so near that it may happen at any time (e.g., 1 Thess. 5:1–3; James 5:8–9; 1 Pet. 4:5, 7, 17). One writer, perhaps Paul, had to oppose certain enthusiasts who thought the day of the Lord already present (2 Thess. 2:1–12; cf. 1 Cor. 4:5). A few NT passages hint that judgment takes place directly after death (Luke 16:1–9, 19–31; Heb. 9:27; cf. 2 Esd. 14:34–35). ***See also*** Apocalyptic Literature; Eschatology; Heaven; Hell; Judgment, The Last; Parousia; Resurrection; Son of Man. R.H.H.

judgment, the last, a nonbiblical term commonly meaning the future trial of nations or individuals before God or Christ, especially as in Matt. 25:31–46 (the Son of man). ***See also*** Eschatology; Heaven; Hell; Judgment, Day of; Kingdom of God; Parousia; Son of Man.

judgment hall. ***See*** Architecture; Gabbatha.

judgment seat, one translation of the Greek word referring to the judicial bench of a city court in the Roman Empire (Gk. *bēma;* also translated as "tribunal" and once as "throne") Jesus was put on trial before Pilate "while he was sitting on the judgment seat" (Matt. 27:19). The Gospel of John locates Pilate's judgment seat "at a place called The Pavement, and in Hebrew, Gabbatha" (19:13). Since the Middle Ages, the trial of Jesus was thought to have been at the Tower of Antonia, a belief reinforced in the nineteenth century by the discovery of a Roman pavement under the convent of the Sisters of Sion in the Via Dolorosa of Jerusalem. The pavement is now known to be of the second century A.D., however, and most scholars today would place Jesus' trial before Pilate at the site of Herod's palace, the Citadel of Jerusalem today.

The term "judgment seat" is used as an eschatological symbol by Paul in Rom. 14:10 ("the judgment seat of God") and 2 Cor. 5:10 ("the judgment seat of Christ"). ***See also*** Antonia, Tower of; Gabbatha; Judgment, Day of; Judgment, The Last; Throne; Tribunal. C.H.M.

Judith (jo͞o′dith), a Hebrew name meaning female Judean or Jewess. **1** The daughter of Beeri the Hittite (despite her Hebrew name) and wife of Esau. **2** The heroine of the book of Judith, a widow of Bethulia, who killed the Assyrian Holofernes and saved her city from destruction.

Judith, a book in the Apocrypha. It is a tale of faith and horror in which Judith, the beautiful and pious widow, entices and brutally assassinates Holofernes, the Assyrian general besieging her hometown, Bethulia. The story may have been written in Hebrew in the Maccabean era and possibly reflects the defeat of the Seleucid general Nicanor by Judah the Maccabee (161 B.C.). The deliberate confusion of names and events from the Persian, Babylonian, and Assyrian eras, however, is probably a device on the part of the author to indicate that the work is intended as fiction. The name "Judith" means "the Jewess," and like a good hero from the period of the judges she returns to her home after delivering her people from the enemy (cf. 16:21). Judah the Maccabee and his brothers, on the other hand, seek continuing political power. The story thus may be, in part, a comment by the Ḥasidim, the forerunners of the Pharisees and Essenes and, initially, the allies of the Maccabees, on Maccabean political ambitions.

Judith, portrayed by Bernardo Cavallino (1616–1656), with the head of the Assyrian general Holofernes.

OUTLINE OF CONTENTS

Judith

I. Holofernes' invasion (chaps. 1–7)
   A. The western nations, including the Jews, refuse to help Nebuchadnezzar, king of the "Assyrians," in defeating Arphaxad, king of the Medes (chap. 1)
   B. Nebuchadnezzar commissions Holofernes to invade the western nations (chap. 2)
   C. Except for the Jews, all sue for peace and are accepted as vassals (chap. 3)
   D. The Jews are alarmed and cry out to God (chap. 4)
   E. Holofernes prepares to invade Judea; Achior the Ammonite is turned over to the Jews; he is not to see Holofernes' face again until the general has dealt with them (chaps. 5–6)
   F. Holofernes besieges Bethulia, and its terrified leaders prepare to surrender (chap. 7)

II. The story of Judith (chaps. 8–16)
   A. Judith is introduced as a beautiful, virtuous, and pious widow with a plan to deliver her people; she asks the leaders to postpone surrender, noting that, in addition to their town, the sanctuary in Jerusalem is in danger (chap. 8)
   B. Judith's prayer (chap. 9)
   C. She arrays herself in beautiful clothes, provisions herself with kosher foods, and with her maidservant seeks asylum in Holofernes' camp; he is captivated by her great beauty (chaps. 10–11)
   D. For three nights, Judith goes out to pray and bathe in a spring; on the fourth evening, Holofernes throws a banquet at which he plans to seduce her (chap. 12)
   E. Alone in the chambers with the general, Judith decapitates him and, pretending to go out again to bathe, carries his head away to Bethulia in her food bag (chap. 13)
   F. Achior looks upon Holofernes' face and becomes a proselyte, as the Assyrians discover his body (chap. 14)
   G. The Assyrians flee while Judith is honored by the high priest (chap. 15)
   H. The song of Judith (16:1–17)
   I. The spoil is dedicated to the Temple and Judith returns home (16:18–25)

Like its prototype, the story and song of Deborah (Judg. 4–5), Judith carries a message of faith in the deliverance of God's people in the face of political and military oppression. In particular, the feminism of the book is deliberate. The point seems to be not so much that God chooses a woman to prove his strength—Judith is no weakling—but that a woman is the appropriate instrument of a God who is the helper of the oppressed (9:11). Judith may be also a personification of "Judea" and, in her final song of triumph, speak as the mother of the Jewish people.

The story has had an influence on Western literature and art. It was one of the two apocryphal books with sufficient popularity in the West to convince Jerome to include it in his Vulgate translation of the Bible. For Catholics, it is one of the deuterocanonical books, while, for Protestants, it is included among the Apocrypha. ***See also*** Apocrypha, Old Testament; Deborah; Deuterocanonical Literature; Maccabees; Women. D.W.S.

Julia (jo͞ol'yuh), a woman to whom Paul sends greetings in Rom. 16:15. Philologus, mentioned first in the verse, is perhaps her husband, and "Nereus and his sister" are possibly their children. "All the saints who are with them" may have formed a house-church in their home.

Julius (jo͞ol'yuhs), a Roman centurion mentioned by name only in Acts 27:1, 3. He is probably the same centurion who was helpful to Paul throughout his eventful sea voyage as a prisoner from Caesarea to Rome (Acts 27:6, 11, 31, 43). According to Acts 27:1, Julius was a member of the "Augustan Cohort." This may have been an honorary title (named after the Emperor Augustus) given to Julius's regiment. Julius represents another example of the favorable attitude toward the Gentiles found in Acts. Unlike Cornelius, however, there is no evidence that Julius became a Christian. ***See also*** Cornelius; Gentile; Paul. A.J.M.

Junias (jo͞o'nee-uhs; KJV: "Junia"), a Christian to whom Paul sends greetings in Rom. 16:7. It is unclear whether a masculine (Junias) or a feminine name (Junia) is intended (the masculine is not found elsewhere). If a woman, Junia may be the wife of Andronicus. It is significant that the two are perhaps referred to as "apostles." ***See also*** Apostle.

Jupiter, a Roman sky god of agricultural origins. Jupiter was head of the Roman pantheon, and is the god most frequently mentioned in Latin inscriptions. Jupiter formed a powerful triad with Juno, protectress of women, and Minerva, the goddess of craftsmen, in Roman religion. Even in Egypt, one finds a temple dedicated to Jupiter Capitolinus. In the moral and political sphere, Jupiter was associated with wars, treaties, and oaths. He was identified with the sky gods of other peoples, especially with Zeus. ***See also*** Zeus.

justice, the standard by which the benefits and penalties of living in society are distributed. The same basic meaning of justice is found throughout the different books and types of writing of the Bible despite the differing spheres to which it is applied. The pervasiveness of the concept of justice in the Bible can be veiled from the English reader by the fact that the original terms most approximating justice have been frequently translated in English as "righteousness" and "judgment." A rule of thumb can be that when these terms appear in a context of social distribution or social conflict, "justice" would be a better translation.

Foundation: Justice is founded in the being of God, for whom it is a chief attribute. As such, God is the sure defender of the poor and the oppressed (Jer. 9:23–24; Ps. 10:17–18). This care of God is universal (Pss. 76:8–9; 103:6). The Psalms ground it in God's role as the sovereign creator of the universe (Ps. 99:1–4). The demands of God's justice thus extend beyond the nation of Israel (Ps. 9:7–9; cf. Dan. 4:27).

Since the justice of God is characterized by special regard for the poor and the weak, a corresponding quality is demanded of God's people (Deut. 10:18–19). When they properly carry out justice, they are agents of the divine will (Isa. 59:15–16). Paul presents God's justice as a grace flowing into and through the believers to the needy (2 Cor. 9:8–10). The demand of God for justice is so central that other responses to God are empty or diminished if they exist without it (Amos 5:21–24; Mic. 6:6–8; Matt. 23:23). Justice is demanded of all the people, but particularly of the political authorities (Jer. 21:11–12; Isa. 1:10, 17).

Focus: Justice is closely related to love and grace (Deut. 10:18–19; Hos. 10:12) rather than being a contrasting principle. It thus provides vindication, deliverance, and creation of community in addition to retribution. Need is the criterion for distributing benefits although the provisions do not exclude ability as a criterion once this priority is met. Thus the focus is upon the oppressed with particular attention given to specific groups, such as the poor, widows, the fatherless, slaves, resident aliens, wage earners, and those with physical infirmities (Job 29:12–17; Ps. 146:7–9; Mal. 3:5). Justice is associated with the basic requirements of life in community. Basic needs are basic rights. Thus what is literally "the justice belonging to the needy" is properly translated as "the rights of the needy" (Jer. 5:28, RSV). These rights, found by observing what matters are involved in the context of passages mentioning justice (cf. Job 24:1–12; 22:6–9, 23; 31:6, 17–19), include land (Ezek. 45:9), food and clothing (Deut. 10:18), and shelter (Job 8:6). While due process is not omitted (Exod. 23:1–3, 6–8), the dominating concerns are substantive, material, and benefit oriented. The context for the carrying out of justice is the creation of community and the preservation of people in it (Lev. 25:35–36; Job 24:5; Ps. 107:36; Luke 7:29–30).

Justice is a deliverance, rectifying the gross social inequities of the disadvantaged (Ps. 76:9). It puts an end to the conditions that produce the injustice (Ps. 10:18). Such redress will not be to the advantage of everyone in the community. The oppressed are raised; the oppressors are judged (1 Sam. 2:7–10; cf. Luke 1:51–53; 6:20–26).

Paul uses the language and meaning of justice to describe God's work of salvation in his theme of "the righteousness of God." It occurs primarily in Romans, where he treats the inclusion of the Gentiles in the new order of redemption. By justice, God brings into community the Gentiles, who previously had no rights in the commonwealth of Israel. ***See also*** Justification; Law; Righteousness.

Bibliography

Mott, Stephen Charles. *Biblical Ethics and Social Change.* New York: Oxford University Press, 1982. Chap. 4.

Snaith, Norman H. *The Distinctive Ideas of the Old Testament.* London: Epworth, 1944. Chap. 3.

S.C.M.

justification, the exculpation of guilt or the demonstration of the correctness of an act or statement. "Justification" and its related terms "just," "justly," "justify" help to render the Hebrew *ṣdq* and the Greek *dikaioō* (altogether the two words occur in the Bible about seven hundred and fifty times). These concepts are more frequently expressed in English Bibles by the term "righteousness" and its related forms. Translation by means of the English word "justification" comes through the Vulgate's *justitia.* The Latin verb *justificare* added the sense of "*make* just," though the Hebrew regularly meant "*declare* just." The two concepts relate, as at Rom. 3:26 where Christ's death demonstrates that God "is righteous and that he justifies" one who believes in Jesus.

OT uses reflect the human desire to justify oneself (Job 32:2; 33:32; Isa. 43:9) or show one is "in the right." When applied to God (Job 32:2; Ps. 51:4), they raise the question of theodicy or justifying the ways of God to human beings. The OT insists God "is just in all his ways" (Ps. 145:17) and asks, "How can a person be just before God?" (Job 9:2). It knows the complaint that "the way of the Lord is not just" (Ezek. 18:25, 29) but replies God will judge nonetheless (33:17, 20). The eventual answer is not that love or mercy triumphs over righteousness but that righteousness is seen as having a saving dimension (Isa. 51:1, 5, 6, 8, RSV: "deliverance"). God who saves is the one who justifies (Rom. 8:33; cf. Isa. 50:8, "vindicates").

Early Jewish Christians confessed that Jesus was put to death "for our trespasses" and raised "for our justification" (Rom. 4:25) and that we are "justified . . . in Christ Jesus . . . by his blood" (Rom. 3:24–25). They further confessed that when "the Son was made sin" (perhaps a "sin offering," 2 Cor. 5:21) it demonstrated God's righteousness while at the same time showing that sinners are justified by faith in Jesus (Rom. 3:26).

Paul deepened this idea of justification through faith "apart from works of the law" (Rom. 3:28) and applied it to non-Jews (Gal. 3:8) as well as Jews (Rom. 3:30), on the basis of Abraham's experience (Rom. 4). The universality of justification is shown by comparing Christ with Adam: Adam's trespass brought condemnation for all, whereas Christ's act of "righteousness" brings justification or acquittal and life to all. Thus sinners are "made [declared, established as] righteous" (Rom. 5:16–21). God "justifies the ungodly" who trust him (Rom. 4:5); they receive peace and life in the Spirit (Rom. 5:1; 8:4). The ethical aspects of justification emphasize "whatever is just" (Phil. 4:8).

James speaks of justification (2:24–25), not in opposition to Paul but against people who fail to understand that faith includes obedience (Rom. 1:5) to God beyond creedal assent. ***See also*** Righteousness. J.H.P.R.

Justus (juhs'tuhs). **1** A Latin praenomen for Joseph Barsabbas, who lost out by lot in an appointment to the Twelve to replace Judas Iscariot after his suicide (Acts 1:15–26). **2** A "worshiper of God" (Gentile attracted to Judaism?) in Corinth who, according to Acts 18:7, offered hospitality to Paul after the latter was forced to leave the synagogue. He probably hosted a house-church. Some manuscripts give his name as Titus Justus, but the strongest evidence points to Titius Justus. **3** A Jewish-Christian coworker with Paul, mentioned with respect in Col. 4:11. On the precarious basis of different punctuation and the changing of several letters of the text, Philem. 23–24 could be translated: "Epaphras my fellow prisoner in Christ sends greetings to you, and so do Justus (not Jesus), Mark, Aristarchus, Demas, and Luke, my fellow workers." Thus, the same greeters would appear in both Col. 4:10–14 and Philem. 23–24. ***See also*** Barsabbas; Paul; Titus. A.J.M.

Opposite: Samuel anoints David (far right) king (1 Sam. 16:11–13); from a panel at the third-century A.D. synagogue at Dura-Europos.

K

kab (KJV: "cab"), a measure of capacity in 2 Kings 6:25. From rabbinic information it was 1/18 of an ephah which is 1 1/16 of a quart. ***See also*** Weights and Measures.

Kabzeel (kab'zay-el; Heb., "may God gather"), a town of Judah near the Edomite border (Josh. 15:21), the home of Benaiah (2 Sam. 23:20; 1 Chron. 11:22). Modern Khirbet Hora, about ten miles northeast of Beer-sheba, may be the site of ancient Kabzeel. The city is called Jekabzeel in Neb. 11:25.

Kadesh (kay'desh), a city in ancient Palestine. **1** Kadesh-barnea (kay'desh-bahr-nee'ah) or Qadesh, 'Ain Kadeis, 'Ain el-Qudeirat or Gedeirat, a place in the wilderness of Paran between Shur and Edom, or alternatively in the Wilderness of Zin, where it formed the south border of Canaan and the west border with Edom. Abraham dwelt in the area (Gen. 20:1). It was the camp for the failed invasion of Canaan from the south (Num. 13–14), after which the Israelites left the area (Num. 20:1–29). At this time Kadesh became an important symbol in the early history of Israel (see Num. 32:8; 33:36–37; Deut. 1:2, 19, 46; 2:14; 9:23; 32:51; Josh. 10:41; 14:6–7; 15:3; Judg. 11: 16–17). The name En-mishpat is based on a geographical origin (etiology) story about the decisions made there (Gen. 14:7) and is another name for Kadesh. Miriam died there (Num. 20: 1). It was there that the Hebrews were camped when they were denied permission to traverse Edom by the king of Edom (Num. 20:14–21). Modern 'Ain-Gedeirat, the location of ancient Kadesh, has a tenth-century B.C. fortress as well as a reservoir 75 feet square and 9 feet deep dating from the pre-Roman era. **2** Kadesh-on-the-Orontes, where Rameses II fought with the Hittites (ca. 1286 B.C.). While the Hittites were able to prevail in the battle, they were unable to press the advantage. S.B.R.

The oasis at 'Ain-Gedeirat in southern Israel, the location of the biblical Kadesh-barnea.

Kadmiel (kad'mee-el; Heb., "God is of old" or "God goes before"), the father of a Levite family (Ezra 2:40; Neh. 7:43) who supervised reconstruction in the Jerusalem Temple in the late sixth century B.C. (Ezra 3:9) and participated in various services there (repentance, Neh. 9:4, 5; sealing the covenant, 10:9; thanksgiving, 12:8; praise and thanks, 12:24).

Kadmonites (kad'muh-nīts; Heb., "easterners"), a tribe or people living in terrain west of the Euphrates River. In Gen. 15:19 they are paired with other nomadic people, the Kenites and Kenizzites, whose lands were promised to Abraham's descendants. The name may reflect simply the direction of their territory from the standpoint of the biblical writer in Palestine.

Kain (kayn). **1** An alternative name for the clan called Kenites (Num. 24:22, KJV: "the Kenite"). **2** A city of Judah (Josh. 15:57, KJV: "Cain"), whose location may be modern Khirbet Yaqin, about seven miles southeast of Hebron, traditionally viewed as a Kenite city. Arab tradition associates it with Abraham's seeing Sodom and Gomorrah destroyed (Gen. 19:24–28).

Kallai (kal'ī), the head of a priestly family in postexilic Judah under the high priest Joiakim (Neh. 12:20).

Kanah (kay'nah; Heb., "reed"). **1** A small brook, the modern Wadi Qanah, that forms part of the boundary between the tribes of Ephraim and Manasseh (Josh. 16:8; 17:9). It flows generally west and southwest, joining the Yarkon before emptying into the Mediterranean Sea north of present-day Arsuf. **2** The north border town of the tribe of Asher (Josh. 19:28), modern Qana (not NT Cana) about six miles southeast of Tyre.

kaph (kaf). ***See*** Caph.

Kareah (kuh-ree'uh; Heb., "bald"), the father of Johanan, a military commander in Judah at the beginning of the Exile (2 Kings 25:23; Jer. 40:8).

Kattath (kat'ath), a town of the tribe of Zebulun (Josh. 19:15) whose location is unknown. It may be identical to Kitron (Judg. 1:30).

Kedar (kee'duhr; Heb., "dark"), a confederation of Arab tribes based in the north Arabian desert. In Gen. 25:13 and 1 Chron. 1:29 Kedar is one of the twelve sons of Ishmael. The Kedarites were a major force from the late eighth century B.C. until the rise of the Nabateans in the fourth century B.C. and are frequently mentioned in Assyrian and Neo-Babylonian sources. They raided lands on their eastern and western borders and controlled the eastern trade route from Arabia to the Fertile Crescent. The later extent of their influence is illustrated by a silver bowl dated to the fifth century B.C. from modern Tell el-Maskhuta in the eastern Nile delta dedicated to the goddess Han-Ilat by "Qaynu the son of Gashmu the king of Kedar"; this Gashmu is the same as "Geshem the Arab" of Neh. 2:19 and 6:1.

In the Bible the military might of the Kedarites is indicated by reference to their archers and warriors (Isa. 21:16–17). Thus, although they dwelt in the eastern desert in dark tents (Isa. 42:11; Jer. 2:10; 49:28; Ps. 120:5; Song of Sol. 1:5) and were herders (Isa. 60:7; Jer. 49:29), their "princes" traded with Tyre, which lay on the coast of the Mediterranean Sea far to the north and east (Ezek. 27:21). Their being singled out in Isaiah and Jeremiah as objects of oracles shows their importance and corresponds to what we know of them from nonbiblical sources. ***See also*** Geshem. M.D.C.

Kedemah (ked'e-mah; Heb., "eastern[er]" from the root *qdm* meaning "front"), the "front" or "beginning" of the day is in the east, hence the sense of the word. It is the name of one of Ishmael's sons, and thus of an Arabian tribe (Gen. 25:15; 1 Chron. 1:31).

Kedemoth (ked'e-mohth), the wilderness area east of Jordan from which Moses sent a message to Sihon requesting permission to pass through his land (Deut. 2:26). Later it appears as a levitical city within the territory of Reuben (Josh. 13:18) assigned to the Merarite families (Josh. 21:37; 1 Chron. 6:79). Among the modern places identified as the location of Kedemoth are Kasr ez-Za'faran, Khirbet er-Rumeil or 'Aleiyan northeast of Dibon, and es-Saliyeh southeast of Dibon. However, the location of the site remains uncertain. ***See also*** Dibon; Merari; Reuben; Sihon.

Kedes (kay'desh). ***See*** Kadesh.

Kedesh (kay'desh; Heb., "to be holy"), a name for several places with ancient sanctuaries; they are often difficult to distinguish from one another. **1** Kedesh-naphtali, a place allotted to the tribe of Naphtali (Josh. 19:37); it is the town from which Barak was called (Judg. 4:6) and where he gathered his forces (4:10). Modern Khirbet Qedish in southeastern Galilee is a more likely site for the Israelite forces to assemble than 2 below. **2** Kedesh in Galilee, a site identified with modern Tell Qadis northwest of Lake Huleh. It was set apart as a city of refuge and levitical town (Josh. 20:7; 21:32; 1 Chron. 6:76). The Kedesh where Heber pitched his tent and Sisera escaped (Judg. 4:11, 17) was probably this northern site, near Canaanite Hazor and away from the center of Israelite strength. It was captured by Tiglath-pileser III in the reign of Pekah (ca. 735–732 B.C.), king of Israel (2 Kings 15:29). **3** Kedesh in Issachar, the levitical city of Issachar according to 1 Chron. 6:72, although the parallel Joshua passage (21:28) identifies it as Kishion, as does Josh. 19:20. This may be the town listed after Taanach and Megiddo whose king was taken by Joshua (Josh. 12:22); perhaps it is to be identified with modern Tell Abu Qudeis, which lies between the two sites. **4** Kedesh in Judah, a city near the southern border (Josh. 15:23). ***See also*** Kadesh. N.L.L.

Keilah (kee-ī'lah), a town of Judah (Josh. 15:44; 1 Chron. 4:19) identified as modern Khirbet Qila, located eight and a half miles northwest of Hebron. It was repaired by postexilic Levites (Neh. 3:17–18), but it is more prominent as a town rescued by David from Philistine assault during threshing season (1 Sam. 23:1–5) and used by David as a haven from Saul until fear of betrayal by the local people moved him to seek safety in the hills (1 Sam. 23:6–14).

Kemuel (kem'yoo͞-el), a name of uncertain derivation or meaning. **1** A cousin of Abraham and ancestor of the Aramaeans (Gen. 22:21). **2** A leader of the tribe of Ephraim, appointed by Moses to assist in dividing the land of Canaan into tribal territories (Num. 34:24). **3** A Levite whose son was that tribe's official representative in David's government (1 Chron. 27:17).

Kenath (kee'nath), an important city of Bashan guarding the desert highway from Rabbath-ammon to Damascus, located about 50 miles south-southeast of the latter. Mentioned in the Egyptian Execration Texts, the annals of Thutmose III, and the Amarna correspondence, the city was conquered by Nobah of Manasseh and renamed after him (Num. 32:42). Subsequently the city fell under Aramaean control (1 Chron. 2:23) and by NT times was one of the Decapolis cities (Canatha). It has been identified with the extensive ruins of Qanawat.

Kenaz (kee'naz). **1** The grandson of Esau and the Edomite clan chief (Gen. 36:11, 42; 1 Chron. 1:36). **2** The father of Othniel and younger brother of Caleb (Josh. 15:17; Judg. 1:13; 3:9; 1 Chron. 4:13). **3** The grandson of Caleb (1 Chron. 4:15).

An ethnic group known as the "Kenizzites" were one of the pre-Israelite peoples of Canaan, mentioned once in the OT (Gen. 15:19).

Whether they should be connected with the Kenaz of Gen. 36:11, however, is uncertain.

Three times (Num. 32:12; Josh. 14:6, 14) Caleb is referred to as "Caleb the son of Jephunah the Kenizzite." Presumably this designation should be related to the Kenizzites of Gen. 15:19.

D.A.D.

Kenites (ke'nīts), an ethnic group listed among the pre-Israelite inhabitants of the land of Canaan (Gen. 15:19). Their name is popularly derived from "smith" (Heb. *qayin*), a theory supported, but not proven, by the fact that the Kenites lived in northern Sinai, a region of copper mining and smelting in ancient times (cf. Num. 24:17–22). Moses' father-in-law, Jethro (or Hobab), a priest of Midian (Exod. 2:15–16; 3:1; 18:1; Num. 10:29), is identified in Judg. 1:16 and 4:11 as a Kenite. In view of the fact that Moses first encountered Yahweh in the service of the priest Jethro, and since Jethro later blessed Moses, offered sacrifice to Yahweh, and instructed Moses regarding delegation of authority (Exod. 18:17–27), it has been speculated by some scholars that Moses learned Yahwism from the Kenites (the so-called Kenite Hypothesis). The evidence, however, is not adequate to support this view.

Some Kenite families evidently accompanied the Israelites to the Plains of Moab, for the descendants of Moses' father-in-law, the Kenite, went up from the city of palms (presumably Jericho) with the men of Judah to live among the people of the wilderness of Judah, in the Negeb near Arad (see Judg. 1:16). One Kenite family from this Negeb community, Heber and his wife Jael, migrated north to settle in Zaanannim, near Kedesh (probably just northeast of Mt. Tabor), and Jael subsequently killed Israel's enemy Sisera in her tent (Judg. 4:11, 17–22; 5:24–27). In Saul's campaign against the Amalekites of northern Sinai, he sent word to the Kenites to separate themselves from the Amalekites; Saul wanted to spare the Kenites, since they had shown "kindness to all the people of Israel when they came up out of Egypt" (1 Sam. 15:6). During Saul's reign (late eleventh century B.C.) a section of the Negeb, evidently in the Arad area (cf. Judg. 1:16), was known as "the Negeb of the Kenites" (1 Sam. 27:10). David, while living in Ziklag, sent gifts of spoil to some of the "cities of the Kenites" in southern Judah (1 Sam. 30:29). The tent-dwelling Rechabites (Jer. 35) were evidently Kenites (1 Chron. 2:55). ***See also*** Cain; Jethro. D.A.D.

Kennizites (ke'niz-īts), Kenezzites (kee'nez-īts). ***See*** Kenaz.

Keren-happuch (kair'uhn-hap'uhk; Heb., "horn of antimony" [black eye-shadow]), the third of Job's latter-day daughters, along with Jemimah and Keziah (in Hebrew Jemimah means "dove" and Keziah means "cassia" [a perfume]). While the three earlier daughters (Job 1:2) were unnamed, like the sons in both prologue and epilogue of the book of Job, these daughters are named, and, uncharacteristically for the time, they receive inheritances along with their brothers. Thus the epilogue in part resembles, yet transforms, the scene presented in the prologue, reflecting the transformation of vision effected through the dialogues of 3:1–42:6. ***See also*** Job, The Book of.

Kerioth (kee'ree-ohth; Kirioth, Amos 2:2). **1** A town in the mountains of Idumea, west of the southern shore of the Dead Sea, the Kirioth-hezron of Josh. 15:25. **2** A city in Moab (Jer. 48:24, 41). Numerous sites have been proposed by modern archaeologists. It may have been a royal city of some sort, as Amos 2:2 refers to its royal palaces. Line 13 of the Moabite Stone refers to its having a principal sanctuary of the god Chemosh. ***See also*** Moabite Stone, The.

kerygma (kay-rig'muh), the transliteration of a Greek noun usually translated "preaching" but indicating the content of the preaching more than the act. In the NT, that content is the "gospel," i.e., the "good news" of God's redemptive activity in the life, death, and resurrection of Jesus (Matt. 12:41; Luke 11:32; Rom. 16:25; 1 Cor. 1:21; 15:14; Titus 1:3). ***See also*** Preaching.

kesitah (kes'i-tah), a Hebrew unit of value, equivalent unknown. Jacob bought land from the Shechemites for a hundred kesitahs (Gen. 33:19; see also Josh. 24:32). Here the kesitah is connected with God's promises and fulfillments to Israel. Job's kin, as instruments of God's restoration, each present him with a kesitah and a gold ring (Job 42:11). In each instance, the kesitah figures in fullness of fortunes under God's aegis.

Keturah (ke-tōō'rah), a wife or concubine of Abraham, after the death of Sarah, who bore him six sons: Zimran, Jokshan, Medan, Midian, Ishbak, and Shuah (Gen. 25:1–6; 1 Chron. 1:32–33). This genealogy links these six tribes and their descendants, who settled to the south and east of the Hebrews, with the descendants of Abraham. It also marks the partial fulfillment of God's promise to Abraham that his offspring would be like "the stars of the sky" (Gen. 15:5).

key, a device to open a lock. In the Bible it is often a symbol of the steward's authority over his master's household and of who gains entry to his master's presence. In the OT, God promises to raise up a new "steward" over Israel and to give him the "key of the house of David" so that what he opens no one will shut and what he shuts no one will open (Isa. 22:22). A similar image in the NT is used of the authority Peter is

Peter receiving "the keys of the Kingdom of Heaven" (cf. Matt. 16:19), as depicted on an eleventh-century enamel plaque.

to have in the emerging Christian community (Matt. 16:19). The "keys" of the kingdom suggest the image of the steward with the keys to the rooms and storechambers of the house. Not only does the bearer of the "key" have authority to determine who is admitted, the chief steward also has responsibility for overseeing all that takes place in the master's house. Rev. 3:7 presents Jesus as the one who possesses the "key of David." Some interpreters hold that this passage contrasts Jesus' "opening and shutting" with Jewish exclusion of Christians from their synagogue (called "synagogue of Satan," 3:9). Others think that the image is meant to encourage Christians to continue in their attempts to evangelize the Jews, since in other contexts Paul often speaks of missionary activity as an "open door" (1 Cor. 16:9; 2 Cor. 2:12).

Other uses of "key" in Revelation refer to the keys of Hades and death held by Jesus (1:18). Rabbinic tradition held that God reserved three keys to himself, the power over rain, the womb, and the tomb (*b. Sanh.* 113a). Heavenly angels wield the keys to the abyss from which the plague of locusts is released (Rev. 9:1) and in which Satan is to be bound (20:1). P.P.

Keziah (ke-zī'uh). ***See*** Keren-happuch.

Khapiru (khah-pee'ro͞o), an Amorite term meaning "outcast," once thought to be the source of the word "Hebrew." The correct form of this pejorative social term was *'apiru*, probably with a long vowel in the first syllable. It appears in cuneiform texts, often written with a Sumerian ideogram, *SA.GAZ*, from the Ur III period (end of the third millennium B.C.) through the Late Bronze Age in the Levant (to 1200 B.C.). Cuneiform has only signs with ḫ (= kh) for representing the West Semitic *'ayin;* thus the pseudo-form Khapiru, or Habiru, is found in many books.

The *'apiru/SA.GAZ* are "outcasts, outlaws," or "displaced persons, renegades." They served as mercenaries throughout the Fertile Crescent from Anatolia to southern Mesopotamia and Egypt. They were from many races and ethnic groups, and they never had a tribal social organization. At Nuzi on the Tigris, homeless refugees called *'apiru* sold themselves into servitude. In the Hittite Empire they were hired troops. They often sought refuge in hilly regions away from the urban Canaanite centers from which they had fled. They came from the upper class and had often been trained as charioteers. They were recruited by Canaanite leaders who were seeking to seize neighboring territories.

The dynastic state of Amurru was founded with the help of *'apiru* troops. The rulers of Shechem in the Amarna tablets (fourteenth century B.C.), Lab'ayu and his sons, used *'apiru* when trying to conquer the principal towns on the main caravan route. References to them in the Jerusalem Amarna letters led scholars to think that there was some connection between them and the Hebrews in the book of Joshua.

Many theories have been promulgated to explain the connection between the *'apiru* and the Hebrews (the patriarchs and the invading tribes). None of them are sound, but because of the strong desire to find some extrabiblical allusions to the patriarchs and to Joshua's campaigns, the theories continue to have their appeal. Actually, the proto-Israelites probably stem from another group, the tribal pastoralists called Sutu in cuneiform and *Shasu/Shosu* in Egyptian; these latter are never confused with the *'apiru*. A new theory, that the *'apiru* were revolting peasants, has no textual support, either in the Bible or in extrabiblical documents. ***See also*** Hebrew; Hebrews. A.F.R.

Kheleifeh, Tell (kel-ay'fuh). ***See*** Ezion-geber.

Khirbet et-Tannur (keer'bet et-tahn'uhr), the ruins of a Nabatean temple on top of a prominent mountain that rises from the floor of Wadi el-Hesa (the biblical River Zered). The archaeologist Nelson Glueck excavated this isolated and elaborately decorated temple complex in 1937. Built at the end of the second century B.C., the temple was used into the second century A.D. A variety of artistic and architectural styles are represented here, along with a host of deities, including the fertility goddess Atargatis. ***See also*** Nabatea, Nabateans.

Khirbet Kerak (kihr'bet kair'ak; Arabic, "ruins of the fortress"), a location not mentioned in biblical texts, presumably because it stood unoccupied in the periods from the end of Middle Bronze Age II (1600 B.C.) until Persian occupation (after 538 B.C.). The 60-acre site was occupied from Chalcolithic times (4000–3000 B.C.) until its abandonment and from the Persian through late Roman times (A.D. fifth century). It is best known for a large quantity of Early Bronze III (2500 B.C.) pottery carrying its name

(Khirbet Kerak Ware), and its strategic value lay in its location just west of the start of the Jordan River at the south end of the Sea of Galilee. A nearby ford allowed traffic heading toward Damascus and other points north and east to cross the Jordan. The site was also known as Beth-yerah (Heb., "house of the moon") and Philoteria (named for a sister of Ptolemy Philadelphus [285–246 B.C.] in the Hellenistic period).
R.S.B.

Khirbet Qumran (kihr'bet qo͞om'rahn). ***See*** Qumran, Khirbet; Scrolls, The Dead Sea.

Kibbroth-hattavah (kib'rohth-haht'ah-vah; Heb., "graves of lust"), a locale between Mount Sinai and Hazeroth (identified with modern Rueis el-Ebeirij). It was there that the Israelites died by plague as they consumed quail rained down upon them by Yahweh in answer to their complaints. The plague punished their lusting after the meat, fish, and other delicacies they had enjoyed in Egypt (Num. 11:31–34; cf. 1–6; 33:16–17; Deut. 9:22).

kid, a young goat, regarded as a delicacy when prepared for food (cf. Luke 15:29). In the OT it is also a symbol for helplessness (Judg. 14:6); in God's kingdom even such an animal will be safe from its natural enemies (Isa. 11:6). ***See also*** Goat.

kidney, part of the group of fat pieces burnt on the altar as the well-being, purification, reparation, and priestly consecration offerings (Exod. 29:22; Lev. 3:4; 4:9; 7:4). The Bible also uses the term to refer to the human organ (Job 16:13; Lam. 3:13). Metaphorically, the term can denote the mind or conscience (Jer. 11:20; 20:12; Ps. 139:13). Once it refers to wheat of high quality (Deut. 32:14; lit., "the kidney fat of wheat"). ***See also*** Fat.

Kidron (kid'ruhn), the valley that lies east of Jerusalem between the Temple Mount and the Mount of Olives. The valley runs on a north-south axis, joining the Tyropoeon and Hinnom valleys south of the Jebusite and Davidic city of Jerusalem. Originally the Gihon spring flowed into the Kidron, but Hezekiah's tunnel brought the water of Gihon to the Pool of Siloam inside the city. From Jerusalem, the Kidron Valley extends southeastward through the Wilderness of Judah to the Dead Sea.

The Kidron Valley lay just beyond the eastern boundary of Jerusalem during the monarchy (1025–586 B.C.). David fled from Jerusalem across the Kidron during Absalom's rebellion (2 Sam. 15:23). Nearly a thousand years later, Jesus, with his disciples, crossed the Kidron after the Last Supper on the way to Gethsemane (John 18:1).

The Kidron was also the place where idols and cult objects from pagan shrines were destroyed by the reformer kings Asa (1 Kings 15:13), Hezekiah (2 Chron. 29:16; 30:14), and Josiah (2 Kings 23:4–6). Kidron may have been chosen because it was just outside the boundaries of the city and convenient to the Temple.

Aerial view of the Kidron Valley, which separates the Temple Mount area in Jerusalem from the Mount of Olives to the east (left).

On the east side of Kidron are a number of ancient tombs along with a modern Jewish cemetery. Most notable of the ancient tombs are the Pillar of Absalom, the Cave of Jehoshaphat, the Tomb of Bene Hezir, and the Tomb of Zachariah. Each of these monuments appears to belong to the Hellenistic period of the third and second centuries B.C.

The Gihon spring is on the west side of the Kidron. Recent excavation has uncovered a Jebusite water shaft that led to this spring centuries before Hezekiah constructed his famous tunnel. Remains of a water channel, cut into the bedrock of the hillside, have also been recovered. This water channel brought water from Kidron to the Pool of Shelah, below the Pool of Siloam, during the early monarchy (eleventh–tenth centuries B.C.).

Kidron is often identified as the site of the king's garden (Neh. 3:15). Similarly Kidron is frequently identified with the "King's Valley" where Absalom built his monument, which later became his tomb (2 Sam. 18:18). Despite these popular identifications of Kidron, however, there is no definite evidence linking it either to the King's Valley or to the king's garden. The tombs popularly ascribed to Absalom and other kings also belong to a later era. ***See also*** Gihon; Jerusalem; Olives, Mount of.
J.F.D.

king, in both the OT and the NT a term designating a male sovereign who exercised ultimate political authority over a city-state, a nation-state, or an empire. A king generally held office for life, and monarchies in the biblical world were generally hereditary.

In the OT, the Israelite king may also be referred to as "prince" (1 Sam. 9:16; 13:14), a title that may point to one who is so designated by God, while "king" is a designation given by people. The king in Israel is also called the "anointed one" (1 Sam. 2:35; Ps. 132:17), from which the term Messiah is derived.

In Ancient Israel: The place of the king in the OT is different from that of the monarch in Egypt and Mesopotamia, where kingship was regarded as a divinely ordained political order that had existed from nearly the beginning of time. In Israel, by contrast, kingship was a relatively late institution. Before the institution of the monarchy, early Israel was ruled by what were essentially charismatic clan chieftains. Kingship developed in response to both internal pressures and external threats, the principal of which came from the Philistines (1 Sam. 13: 19–21), which called forth greater political unity. Kingship was not instituted, however, without serious reservations, misgivings reflected in the assessment of the role and function of the king, especially in his relationship to divine authority. Jotham's fable (Judg. 9:7–15) reflects opposition to the institution of kingship in Israel with its moral that only a useless person (symbolized by the bramble) would ever accept the office.

The accounts of the institution of the monarchy in 1 Sam. 1–12 evidence both anti- and promonarchical tendencies. The so-called antimonarchic source (1 Sam. 7:3–8:22; 10:17–27; 12) brands Israel's attempt to set up a stable political government by imitating nations around her as a rejection of the Lord's rule over his people Israel (1 Sam. 8:7). In this source, God is pictured as reluctantly conceding to the initiative of his people. Samuel warns the people of the "ways of the king" (1 Sam. 8:10–19) in a passage that lists monarchic excesses. In the promonarchic source (1 Sam. 9:1–10:16; 11), however, there is nothing about divine disapproval, and in fact Samuel, as God's prophet, takes the initiative in finding and anointing Saul as the first king, who then is further distinguished by being possessed by "the spirit of God." But even when the objection to the monarchy waned in Israel, the king's power was not unrestrained and was repeatedly checked by the terms of God's covenant with his people. The king in Israel, even David who was later regarded as the ideal king, was never an absolute lord over his subjects. He could not expropriate land with impunity (2 Sam. 24:24; 1 Kings 16:24; 21:4), nor was he exempt from moral and civil law generally (Deut. 17:14–20). Even with these restraints, however, Israel did know some despotic monarchs who were guilty of apostasy and lawlessness, chief among them being Manasseh (2 Kings 21:1–18). Excesses in monarchical power were one of the main things to call forth prophetic rebuke, and there is recorded a whole series of prophet–king encounters, beginning with Nathan–David and continuing until the dissolution of the monarchy with the fall of the two nation-states of Israel and Judah.

God as King: The prophetic critique of kingship is based upon the conviction that God was the original and only king of Israel and, later by extension, of all peoples (Jer. 10:7–10). The formula introducing a prophetic oracle, "Thus says the Lord," was in fact originally a formula announcing a message from a monarch. Thus the form of God's covenant with Israel resembles that of a suzerainty treaty between king and people. The king in Israel was one of the people and, as such, Yahweh's vassal and servant. Even though the southern kingdom of Judah believed that God's covenant included an everlasting covenant guaranteeing the perpetuity of the Davidic line, there was never the accompanying belief in the divinity of the king.

A mythically enlarged or spiritualized conception of kingship is found in the Psalms (Pss. 47; 96–99). For all people to know and worship God who was "a great King above all gods" (Ps. 95:3) became a goal of Jewish apocalyptic and later Christian thought, a goal that is reflected in Jesus' teachings in the synoptic Gospels about the Kingdom of God (Mark 1:14–15; Luke 22:18–30). That this was primarily a religious concept for Jesus, rather than a political or economic one, is reflected in the fact that although Jesus is in the Davidic line (Matt. 4:8–16) and is accused of royal pretensions (Luke 23:2; John 18:33), he repudiated all popular attempts to make him king (Matt. 4:8–10). In the NT apocalyptic book, Revelation, Jesus is described with royal terminology (Rev. 2:5; 3:21; 14:14; 17:14; 19:15–16). ***See also*** God; Kingdom of God; Messiah; Prince; Psalms, The. F.S.F.

Kingdom of God, the sovereignty, reign, or rule of God. The term "Kingdom of God" occurs only in the NT, but similar expressions are found in the OT.

OT Background: Numerous biblical traditions hail God as King of Israel (e.g., Deut. 33:5; Judg. 8:23; Isa. 43:15). The author of the books of Chronicles refers to the Davidic throne as God's kingdom (1 Chron. 17:14; 28:5; 29:11). Various Psalms also acclaim God as the one who reigns over all nations (e.g., Pss. 22:28; 47:2, 7–8). The "Enthronement Psalms" (93; 95–99) emphasize his present sovereignty over all creation, as well as his future coming to judge the earth (96:13; 98:9; cf. Psalm 94).

The prophets likewise saw God as ruler over nations. He would devastate foreign nations for violating the covenant of brotherhood (Amos 1: 3–2:3), but he would also punish Israel and Judah for breaking covenant (Amos 2:4–3:2; Isa. 10:1–11). God also would use another nation to restore Israel (Isa. 45:1–13); then, Israel would become "a light to the nations," that God's redeeming rule might reach to the ends of the earth (Isa. 49:6).

Many of the prophets looked for the "day" when God would not only restore the fortunes of

KINGDOM OF GOD

his people Israel and Judah but also establish an everlasting era of peace, justice, and mercy. Then, Israel and Judah would again become one kingdom (Jer. 30:3; Ezek. 37:15–22), ruled, perhaps, by a descendant of David (Isa. 9:7; Jer. 30:9; Ezek. 37:24–26). There would be a new covenant between God and his people (Hos. 2:16–20; Jer. 31:31–34), and peace would obtain not only among all nations (Isa. 2:2–4; 19:19–25) but throughout the whole creation, among all living things (Hos. 2:18; Isa. 11:6–9; 65:17–25). Such hopes, however, were not fulfilled during the biblical period.

Even before the Exile (ca. 586–538 B.C.), a king of Judah called on God to reassert his sovereignty over the kingdoms of the earth (2 Kings 19:15–19). Jeremiah (e.g., chaps. 1–11) and Ezekiel (e.g., chaps. 12–16) viewed the Exile as God's punishment of his people for forsaking him and his covenant; near its end, Second Isaiah (Isa. 40–55) sought to comfort the exiles by assuring them that their time of punishment was over since they had received double for their sins (Isa. 40:2). Yet, for centuries afterward, foreign nations continued to dominate the Jewish people and their homeland. No longer was it clear that God ruled the kingdoms of the earth. Prophets and others promised and longed for the future coming of God's kingdom or rule on earth (e.g., Dan. 2:44; 4:17; cf. 7:27; Obad. 21; Hag. 2:20–23; Zech. 14:9; Tob. 13).

In the NT period, Jews and the emerging Christian communities lived under Roman rule. Moreover, NT writings attest to Satan's present rule on earth. In the temptation scene, the devil declares that he has authority over "all the kingdoms of the world" (Luke 4:5–6). Satan's minions, the demons, still afflict humankind. Paul understood that the world was subjugated to Satan or evil powers (1 Cor. 2:8; 15:24–27; 2 Cor. 4:4), while the Fourth Gospel considers Satan "the ruler of this world" (John 12:31; 14:30). The most explicit expression of this understanding is in 1 John 5:19: "the whole world is in the power of the evil one." The author of Revelation identified the evil ruler of the present age as Rome (chaps. 13; 17–18), linked, perhaps, with Satan, who was to continue his reign of terror on earth a while longer (chaps. 12; 20).

In the NT: The great majority of references to the Kingdom of God in the NT are in the first three Gospels. Here, the basic message of Jesus (Matt. 4:17; Mark 1:15) and his disciples (Matt. 10:7; Luke 10:9, 11) was that the Kingdom of God had come near. Jesus taught his followers to pray for its coming (Matt. 6:10; Luke 11:2). When it came, God's will would be done on earth (Matt. 6:10). Only those who, in the meantime, lived in accordance with God's will might hope to enter it (Matt. 5:3–10; 7:21–23). (Matthew's Gospel frequently uses the term "Kingdom of *Heaven*," while Mark and Luke always use "Kingdom of *God*." "Heaven" in these instances is a circumlocution—a way of referring to God without using his name, which Jews and Jewish Christians believed too holy to pronounce or even write. Thus, "Kingdom of Heaven" and "Kingdom of God" are identical in meaning. We do not know which expression Jesus himself may have used.) According to the synoptic Gospels, Jesus declared that the Kingdom of God and the Son of man would come within the lifetime of some who heard him (Matt. 16:28; Mark 9:1; Luke 9:27; Matt. 24:32–36; Mark 13:28–32; Luke 21:29–33), and, at the Last Supper, he vowed not to drink wine again until he did so in the coming kingdom (Matt. 26:29; Mark 14:25; Luke 22:18). Nevertheless, many interpreters read certain of the parables (e.g., Mark 4:30–32; Matt. 13:33; Luke 13:20–21) and other sayings (e.g., Matt. 12:28; Luke 11:20; Luke 17:20–21) to mean that Jesus believed the Kingdom of God was already present in some way: in his person, as the one who would be Messiah in the coming kingdom, in his power to exorcise demons, or perhaps, in the response of faith by those who repented and changed their lives.

The Kingdom of God was a central topic of apostolic preaching in Acts (e.g., 8:12; 19:8) and is mentioned frequently in Paul's Letters. Paul writes of inheriting the Kingdom of God in the future (1 Cor. 6:9; Gal. 5:21), but also hints that it might somehow be present in the life of Christian communities (Rom. 14:17; 1 Cor. 4:20). Those "in Christ" are already new creatures (2 Cor. 5:17), yet both Christians still alive and those who will have died when Christ comes must then be transformed, since "flesh and blood cannot inherit the Kingdom of God" (1 Cor. 15:42–54). Like the Jesus of John's Gospel who promised believers eternal life in the heavenly mansions (John 14:1–3), Paul looked for the new life of the transformed in a heavenly commonwealth (Phil. 3:20–21). The author of Revelation looked for the establishment of God's kingdom both in heaven and on earth (11:15; 12:10), albeit a new heaven and a new earth (21:1). In the end, new Jerusalem would come down from heaven (Rev. 21:2, 10), and God and the Lamb would "reign for ever and ever" (22:5). All this, the writer promised his contemporaries, would take place soon, "for the time is near" (22:6–7, 10, 12).

It is noteworthy that the term "Kingdom of God" is almost totally absent from the Gospel of John, occurring only in 3:3, 5; apparently, the author reinterpreted the concept in terms of his own interest in "eternal life." ***See also*** Eschatology; Eternal Life; Jesus Christ; Judgment, Day of; Judgment, The Last; King; Messiah; Millennium; Parables; Parousia; Resurrection; Satan; Son of Man.

Bibliography

Dodd, C. H. *The Parables of the Kingdom*. Rev. ed. New York: Scribner, 1961.

Hiers, Richard H. *The Kingdom of God in the Synoptic Tradition.* Gainesville, FL: University of Florida Press, 1970.

Schweitzer, Albert. *The Mystery of the Kingdom of God: The Secret of Jesus' Messiahship and Passion.* New York: Schocken, 1964. R.H.H.

Kingdom of Heaven. ***See*** Kingdom of God.

King James Version (KJV). ***See*** English Bible, The.

Kings, the First and Second Books of the, the eleventh and twelfth books of the OT.

Name and Contents: These two narratives, the fifth and sixth books of the second division of the Hebrew Bible, the Prophets, were originally considered one book in Jewish sources (*t. B. Bat.* 14a). The Greek tradition, which is followed by the Vulgate, treated 1 and 2 Kings together with 1 and 2 Samuel as a single composition and divided the whole into the "four books of Reigns/Kingdoms" (Gk. *Basileion).*

1 and 2 Kings is the major history of the Israelite monarchy, covering the four centuries from the death of David and the succession of Solomon (ca. 965 B.C.) until the destruction of Jerusalem and the Exile (586 B.C.). It is an eclectic work, whose editors(s) drew upon a variety of earlier sources, all of which have been subsumed under a single point of view. The tragic series of events in the history of Israel—the breakup of the United Kingdom into the separate states of Judah and Israel, the fall of Samaria and ultimately of Jerusalem and its Temple—are explained as the Lord's just punishment of the violators of his law.

Structure: 1 Kings 1–11 covers the death of David, the reign of Solomon, and the building of the Temple. 1 Kings 12–2 Kings 17 concerns the Divided Monarchy, from the founding of the kingdom of Israel by Jeroboam I until the Assyrian conquest, and the kingdom of Judah from Rehoboam until Ahaz. 2 Kings 18–25 is about the kingdom of Judah from Hezekiah until the Babylonian conquest. Uniting the whole is a fixed, schematic framework, particularly evident in the history of the Divided Monarchy. The editor provided an opening and closing formula for each king in which he noted: the date of accession according to the years of the reigning king in the neighboring kingdom; the age of the king at accession (only for the kings of Judah); the length of his reign; the name of his

Elijah, with raised arm, as the fire of the Lord falls upon the bull offering, in the contest with the prophets of Baal (1 Kings 18:30–39); panel at the third-century A.D. synagogue at Dura-Europos.

mother (only for kings of Judah); an evaluation; a reference to "Annals" (e.g., "Book of the Chronicles of the Kings of Israel"); the death of the king and his burial; and the succession of his son.

Sources: The editor referred his original readers to three works available to them for further details that he did not include in his book: the "Book of the Annals of Solomon" (1 Kings 11:41); the "Books of the Annals (or Chronicles) of the Kings of Israel" (1 Kings 14:19; 15:31; and fifteen other references); the "Books of the Annals of the Kings of Judah" (1 Kings 14:29; 15:7; and thirteen other references). These works, which are otherwise unknown to us, contained information on the political and military exploits as well as building projects accomplished by the kings. In addition, the "Annals of Solomon" highlighted that king's wisdom, which "was greater than the wisdom of the Kedemites [easterners] and than all the wisdom of the Egyptians" (cf. 1 Kings 4:29–34; 5:1–14; 10:1–13, 23–24; 11:41) and was likely the product of the wisdom circle at court. It, too, has been lost.

In addition to the books specifically mentioned by name, other unacknowledged sources fill out the editorial frame. Temple archives in Jerusalem supplied data on Temple affairs; e.g., architectural plans and materials used in its construction (1 Kings 6–7); alterations and innovations in structure and service (2 Kings 12:5–17; 16:10–16; 22:3–9); and the looting of the Temple treasury (1 Kings 14:26; 15:18; 2 Kings 12:19; 16:17–18; 18:15–16). Prophetic stories extend the history of the Northern Kingdom; they center, for the most part, around the lives of Elijah the Tishbite (1 Kings 17–19; 21; 2 Kings 1–2:18) and his disciple Elisha (1 Kings 19:15–21; 2 Kings 2:9–25; 13:14–21), as well as other prophetic individuals (e.g., Micaiah, 1 Kings 22; cf. 1 Kings 20). The peculiar diction and the unique social setting depicted in these narrative cycles suggest that a northern prophetic document—dated to the mid-eighth century B.C. (?)—was utilized by the editor of Kings.

Historiography: The editorial judgments, their spirit, and their distinctive language, conform with the ideals articulated in the book of Deuteronomy (esp. Deut. 12), and so the editor can be conveniently labeled a member of the Deuteronomistic school. This Deuteronomist's evaluation of each king is phrased: "he did what was pleasing/what was not pleasing to the Lord." This judgment is based upon a single criterion: religious loyalty to the God of Israel as specified in the teaching of Moses. Thus all worship was to be concentrated at one chosen site and care taken not to imitate the practices of other nations in service of the Lord. The northern kingdom of Israel, born in revolution against the house of David, was condemned from the start; its first king, Jeroboam son of Nebat, had founded royal shrines outside Jerusalem at Bethel and Dan, where golden calves symbolized the Lord's presence (1 Kings 12:25–32). The Deuteronomist adjudged every king of Israel sinful because he followed the ways of Jeroboam (cf. e.g., 1 Kings 15:25–26, 33–34).

As for the kings of Judah, all but two were sinful, for instead of checking the worship at the rural shrines ("high places") in favor of the

OUTLINE OF CONTENTS

The First and Second Books of the Kings

I. The reign of Solomon (1 Kings 1:1–11:43)
   A. Solomon's appointment as king, and David's death (1 Kings 1:1–2:46)
   B. Solomon's endowment with wisdom (3:1–28)
   C. Organization of the Kingdom (4:1–34)
   D. Building and dedication of the Temple (5:1–8:66)
   E. Solomon's vision: eternal dynasty conditional on obedience (9:1–9)
   F. Other activities of Solomon (9:10–10:29)
   G. Solomon's apostasy, adversaries, and death (11:1–43)

II. The Divided Monarchy (1 Kings 12:1–2 Kings 17:41)
   A. Division of the kingdom: Rehoboam in Judah and Jeroboam in Israel (1 Kings 12:1–32)
   B. Prophetic activity during Jeroboam's reign (12:33–14:18)
   C. Synchronized history of Israel and Judah (14:19–16:34)
   D. Reign of Ahab and fall of the house of Omri: the prophets Elijah and Elisha (1 Kings 17:1–2 Kings 10:31)
   E. Synchronized history of Israel and Judah (2 Kings 10:32–16:20)
   F. The end of the northern Kingdom of Israel (17:1–41)

III. The Kingdom of Judah (2 Kings 18:1–25:30)
   A. Hezekiah: reform and Assyrian invasion (18:1–20:21)
   B. Manasseh and Amon (21:1–26)
   C. Josiah: discovery of lawbook and reform (22:1–23:30)
   D. Jehoahaz and Jehoiakim (23:31–24:7)
   E. The end of the kingdom of Judah (24:8–25:21)
   F. Gedaliah as governor (25:22–26)
   G. Jehoiachin in exile: release from prison (25:27–30)

Jerusalem Temple, they allowed the nation to continue worshiping as they had done in the pre-Solomonic era. Only Hezekiah and Josiah come in for praise, for their wholehearted trust in the Lord, just as David their ancestor had done, and for their religious reforms, i.e., abolishing the "high places" and purifying Temple rites (2 Kings 18:1–8; 22:1–2; 23:24–25).

The inclusion in the book of Kings of the Northern prophetic document exemplifies another principle in the Deuteronomistic world view: the word of the Lord, uttered by his prophets, does not go unfulfilled (cf. 1 Kings 8:20; 12: 15; 15:29; 16:12, 34; 2 Kings 1:17; 23:16–18; 24: 2). Elijah put a curse on the royal sponsors of the cult of the Tyrian Baal (1 Kings 18; 21:20–24), justifying Jehu's execution of the house of Ahab (2 Kings 10:10–11, 30). In similar fashion, the prophetic tradition of Isaiah's prediction that the Lord "will defend this city [i.e., Jerusalem] to save it for my own sake and for the sake of my servant David" (Isa. 37:35) and its fulfillment was grafted on to the history of Hezekiah (2 Kings 18:17–19:37).

Date of Composition: The OT scholar M. Noth proposes seeing Kings as part of a larger historical work, including Deuteronomy, Joshua, Judges, and Samuel, dated ca. 550 B.C. This Deuteronomistic composition sought to explain to an exilic audience the reason for Israel's failure to possess the Promised Land and maintain its national existence. Generation after generation broke with the Lord's covenant, inextricably leading to punishment through exile.

Another OT scholar, F. M. Cross, argues for a double redaction of Kings: a first edition at the time of King Josiah's cultic reform (ca. 620 B.C.), which held out hope for salvation through a renewed Davidic monarchy, and a second edition, which attributed the destruction and Exile to the inexpiable sin of Manasseh.

There is also reason to believe that a pre-Deuteronomistic work treating the history of the Northern Kingdom has been incorporated in Kings. The signs for this early book, which contravene the general tendencies of the total work, are the sympathetic approach to certain Israelite kings (e.g., 2 Kings 13:4–5, 23; 14:25–27), the preservation of the Elijah-Elisha cycles, the contradictory chronological data. ***See also*** Judah, Kingdom of; Samaria, District of.

Bibliography

Cross, F. M. *Canaanite Myth and Hebrew Epic.* Cambridge: Harvard University Press, 1973. Esp. pp. 274–289.

Eissfeldt, O. *The Old Testament, An Introduction.* Translated by P. Ackroyd. New York: Harper & Row, 1965. Esp. pp. 281–301.

Noth, M. *The Deuteronomistic History.* Sheffield, England: University of Sheffield, 1981.

M.C.

King's Garden, the royal gardens in Jerusalem, situated in the tract before the confluence of the Kidron and Hinnom valleys and irrigated by the Siloam Pool and En-rogel. From the City of David, the gardens were reached by descending the steps from the Fountain Gate (Neh. 3:15). Through this exit, King Zedekiah fled besieged Jerusalem in 586 B.C. (2 Kings 25:4).

King's Highway, the (Heb. *derek hammelek,* "the royal way"), a route by which Moses sought to lead the Hebrews through Edom and Moab (Num. 20:17; 21:22; cf. Deut. 2:17). Although it is possible that *derek hammelek* was nothing more than the common designation for a public road that ran through a particular region, most scholars use "King's Highway" as a proper name for the major international route that traversed the entire length of Transjordan's plateau. Specifically, this roadway ran from Damascus to the Gulf of Aqaba, connecting many important towns in between (e.g., Ashtaroth, Rabbath-ammon, Dibon, Kir-hareseth, Bozra). The antiquity of this route is evident in the itinerary recorded in Gen. 14:5–6. The *Via Nova* of the Roman emperor Trajan (A.D. 98–117), which was constructed early in the second century A.D., and one of Jordan's modern highways follow closely the line of the ancient road. ***See also*** Road.

G.L.M.

Kings of Judea and Israel. ***See*** Chronology, Old Testament.

King's Pool, a reservoir in the royal gardens at Jerusalem (Neh. 2:14), probably the Pool of Shelah receiving water from the Gihon spring. It may be identical with the Upper Pool (Isa. 7:3).

King's Vale, the (KJV: "King's Dale"), the valley of Shaveh (RSV: "King's Valley") in Gen. 14: 17–18 where Abraham met the king of Sodom and also Melchizedek. In 2 Sam. 18:18 it is the location of Absalom's monument near Jerusalem. It is probably the Kidron Valley just east of that city.

Kir (kihr). **1** The place to which Assyria's king Tiglath-pileser (ca. 745–727 B.C. took his Damascus captives (2 Kings 16:9). It was remembered by Amos (9:7) as the ancestral home of the Syrians, to which they were condemned to return (1:5). It may also have been the source of allies in the action Isaiah anticipated against Judah (Isa. 22:6). The precise location is unknown. **2** The Moabite city Kir-hareseth, a Moabite capital (Isa. 15:1), identified with modern el-Kerak. It is the site of a magnificent Crusader castle and is located on a promontory eleven miles east of the Dead Sea and about seventeen miles south of the Arnon gorge. The site was protected by 300-foot drops on all sides of its

2,500 foot-long salient, and stood 3,110 feet above sea level, 4,400 feet above the surface of the Dead Sea. R.S.B.

Kiriath (kihr'ee-ath; Heb., "city of"; KJV: "Kirjath"), a frequently used prefix of compound names for places, such as Kiriath-arba, Kiriath-arim, Kiriath-baal, Kiriath-huzzoth, Kiriath-jearim, Kiriath-sannah, or Kiriath-sepher.

Kiriathaim (kihr-ee-uh-thay'em; Heb., "two cities"; KJV: "Kirjathaim"). **1** A city in Moab assigned to the tribe of Reuben (Num. 32:37; Josh. 13:19). It is thought to be in the area of modern el-Qereiyat in the Transjordan five and a half miles north-northwest of Dibon, but the identity is uncertain. It was in Moabite hands (Jer. 48:1, 23; Ezek. 25:9) and is mentioned in the Moabite Stone inscription. **2** A levitical city in the territory of Naphtali (1 Chron. 6:76) given to Gershomites, probably modern Khirbet el-Qureiyeh, likely identical with Kartan (Josh. 21:32). ***See also*** Moabite Stone, The.

Kiriath-jearim (kihr'ee-ath-jee'ahr-em; Heb., "city of forests"; KJV: "Kirjath-jearim"), a city of the tribe of Judah (Josh. 18:14), modern Deir al 'Azhar about eight and a quarter miles north of Jerusalem and just west of Abu Ghosh. Subject of an Israelite treaty with Gibeonites (Josh. 9:17), it carried the earlier name "Kiriath-baal," meaning "city of the god Baal" (Josh. 15:60), and was a border town of the tribes of Judah, Dan, and Benjamin (Josh. 18:14). It had excellent water for which it was sought as a bivouac (Josh. 18:12). The Philistines returned the Ark to this city (1 Sam. 7:2), where it remained until David moved it to Jerusalem (1 Sam. 6:20–7:2 and 2 Sam. 6:1–19, as corrected from 1 Chron. 13:5–14). Jeremiah's contemporary, the prophet Uriah, came from this city (Jer. 26:20–23), and some of the citizens returned to it from exile in Babylon (Ezra 2:25, "Kiriath-arim"; Neh. 7:29). Later it was the site of a Roman fort and a Byzantine church. R.S.B.

Kiriath-sepher (kihr'ee-ath-see'fuhr), the earlier name for Debir (Josh. 15:15; Judg. 1:11). ***See also*** Debir.

Kish, a Mesopotamian city, eight miles east of Babylon, which dominated the history of the Early Dynastic (ED) I period (2900–2700 B.C.). Excavations reveal extensive remains of the first palace known from this time. Although fragmentary, remains of two ziggurats are visible. According to the Sumerian King List, Kish is the place to which kingship is restored following the Flood. Evidence of a flood appears at Kish, but it is too limited in scope and too late (between ED II, 2700–2500 B.C., and ED III, 2500–2300 B.C.) to support native and biblical traditions of a universal flood presumed to antedate the historical ED I period.

The story of *Gilgamesh* (king of Uruk) *and Agga* (king of Kish) reflects tensions between these two early political centers. In the ED period, use of the title "King of Kish" indicated hegemony over Sumer and Akkad. Kish declined in political importance with the northward shift of power under Sargon of Akkad, ca. 2350 B.C., and his creation of the first Semitic empire.

As a personal name, Kish appears several times in the Bible. **1** The father of Saul (1 Sam. 9:1, 3; 10:11, 21; 14:51; 2 Sam. 21:14; 1 Chron. 8:30, 33; 12:1; 26:28). **2** Levites (1 Chron. 23:21, 22; 24:29; 2 Chron. 29:12). **3** An ancestor of Mordecai (Esther 2:5). ***See also*** Flood, The; Noah; Saul. L.E.P.

Kishon (kee'shahn), a stream bed in which much of the year water flows westward through the Esdraelon (Megiddo) Plain. One major source rises in the springs west of Mt. Tabor and the Galilean hills south of Nazareth and flows to the south. The other major source rises in several springs in the vicinity of Megiddo and flows to the north from near Mt. Gilboa. They join in the Esdraelon Plain, and from there the river winds its way northwestward through the narrow pass between Mt. Carmel and the Galilean hills and enters the Plain of Acco. It empties into the Mediterranean by the excavated site of modern Tell Abu Hawam.

Most of the year the Kishon is a sluggish brook. During the rainy season it can be swampy through the Megiddo Plain, as when in Deborah's defeat of the Canaanites the "torrent Kishon swept them away" (Judg. 5:21). Although the exact location of that battle cannot be determined, Sisera's chariots and troops were drawn out to meet Barak at the river Kishon (Judg. 4:7) and the Song of Deborah suggests a place near Taanach (Judg. 5:19). The recent excavations at Taanach indicate it was destroyed about 1125 B.C., and the destruction may be associated with these events. This victory at the river Kishon is recalled in Ps. 83:9.

It was near the brook Kishon that Elijah killed the prophets of Baal when they could not call down fire on their offering on Mt. Carmel (1 Kings 18:40). ***See also*** Esdraelon; Taanach. N.L.L.

kiss. ***See*** Gestures.

Kittim (kit'tim). **1** The descendant of Javan, the fourth son of Japheth who was a son of Noah, and Elishah's brother (Gen. 10:4; 1 Chron. 1:7). **2** A place the first-century A.D. historian Josephus (*Antiquities* 1:28) identifies with Kition, or Kitti, a Phoenician city on the island of Cyprus, later known as Larnaka. Apparently the term

Kittim in the OT included all islands of the Aegean Sea. Jeremiah (2:10) mentions isles of Kittim as the symbol of the western extremity of the world. Kittim is mentioned in connection with Tyre and Sidon as the mother of western maritime colonies (Ezek. 27:6). Various passages indicate a connection between Kittim and Assyria (see Num. 24:24). **3** A figurative name for Rome in the apocalyptic book of Daniel (11: 30). **4** Macedonia in 1 Maccabees (1:1). **5** A people mentioned briefly in the pseudepigraphal books *The Testament of Simeon* (6:3) and the book of *Jubilees* (24:28). In a number of Qumran texts the Kittim appear as the last gentile world power to oppress the people of God. In the Habakkuk commentary (from Cave 1 at Qumran) the "Chaldeans," sent by God to execute his judgment, were understood to be the Kittim. In a fragmentary commentary on Isaiah (from Cave 4 at Qumran) the downfall of the Assyrians was interpreted as the war of the Kittim. The war of the Kittim is described in the *War Scroll:* the Sons of Light take the field against the enemy of Israel, the Kittim, "those who deal wickedly against the covenant" (1QM 1:2; 15:2). The author of the scroll believed that Isaiah's prophecy against Assyria (Isa. 31:8) will be fulfilled after the victory over the Kittim. Many scholars identify the Kittim with the Syrians, but there are others who associate them with the Romans. However, the Kittim in the references in the Qumran commentaries resemble the Romans, even though the evidence is not decisive. Y.G.

KJV, the common abbreviation for the King James Version of the Bible. ***See*** English Bible, The.

kneading bowl, a container for mixing ingredients in preparing bread (Exod. 8:3 and 12: 34, KJV: "kneading troughs"; Deut. 28:5, 17). It could be made of wood, bronze, or pottery and was important enough to be taken along when traveling (Exod. 12:34). While shallow, it could be round or irregularly shaped. Kneading was done usually by hand, but it could be done by foot also. As an Israelite possession it could be blessed or cursed (see Deut. texts above).

kneel. ***See*** Gestures.

knife, a tool used for cutting or stabbing. A knife was used for a variety of purposes in antiquity. Abraham raised one to carry out the act of sacrificially slaying his son, only to have his hand stayed (Gen. 22:9–14). The knife was used in the ritual slaughter of animals for sacrifice. It was also used for the circumcision ceremony, where at least some of the knives were made of flint rather than metal (Josh. 5:2–3). Yet another ritual use is recorded by the prophets of Baal, who cut themselves to receive their god's attention (1 Kings 18:28). Such activity is forbidden in the levitical law (Lev. 19:28).

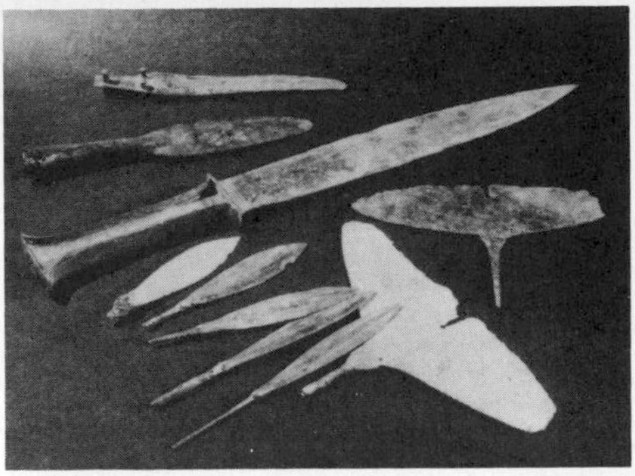

Bronze implements, including a knife, from a fourteenth-century B.C. cemetery near Acre.

The equivalent of the razor was probably a sharpened blade. It could be used for shaving or trimming a beard or other body hair (Ezek. 5: 1; Isa. 7:20).

There is some overlap in biblical references to knives and swords. The account of Joab's murder of Amasa, where the latter is stabbed as the two men embraced, probably presupposes a knife or dagger rather than a sword.

Knives also had a ceremonial role to play in the ancient world as did other implements of war. Archaeological excavations have found a number of them from different historical periods partially constructed with inlaid ivory or with precious metals. The royal treasury of Judah had fine enough ceremonial knives that Nebuchadnezzar confiscated them when Jerusalem fell to his siege (Ezra 1:9). Knives are not mentioned in the NT. J.A.D.

knop (nawp), the KJV's term for the RSV's "capitals" as a part of the lampstands in the tabernacle (Exod. 25:31–36; 37:17–22), probably a knob-shaped ornament. It is also the term in the KJV for the RSV's "gourd" (1 Kings 6:18) as part of the cedar decorations in the Temple (see also 1 Kings 7:24 where it adorned the bronze [molten] sea in the Temple furnishings).

knowledge, a term in the OT that includes experience, emotion, and personal relationship along with intellectual understanding. In Greek "knowledge" refers primarily to intelligent apprehension, but the NT use of the word usually includes OT connotations. Individual books of the Bible develop particular meanings for "knowledge."

In the OT God is known because of self-revelation and humans know by acknowledging and accepting God (Deut. 11:2–7; Isa. 11:2; 41: 20; Jer. 2:8; 9:6). The nations do not know God

(Jer. 10:25), but God's saving of Israel makes them know God's power (Isa. 37:20). Conversely, God knows humans and gives them support. God knew Jeremiah before he was born (Jer. 1:5) and appointed him a prophet. Human knowledge implies involvement and commitment. In the garden Adam and Eve ate of the tree of the knowledge of good and evil and gained personal knowledge of good and evil that changed their relationship with God (Gen. 3). The prophets describe sinners as those who know not the way of peace (Isa. 59:8). Knowing also implies experience; sexual relations are spoken of as "knowing" (Gen. 4:1; Luke 1:34).

In rabbinic writings that stress the study of Torah, the knowledge of God's word that issues from study results in acceptance of God with consequent obedience to his commandments.

The NT continues the OT tradition of knowledge as a relationship. According to Paul the believer who knows and loves God is known by God (Gal. 4:9; 1 Cor. 8:3). God can only be known by the Spirit and believers who have the Spirit (1 Cor. 2:11). God reveals the mystery of salvation in Jesus Christ (1 Cor. 2:7, 12–13; cf. Col. 2:2–3). In the Gospel of John both God and Jesus are known through signs and humans come to know the Father through the sign par excellence, Jesus (8:14; 14:7–9). Jesus knows the Father (16:30; 17:25; cf. 1:18) and the disciples know through him (17:7–8, 26). This view is also presumed by the thanksgiving formula in Matt. 11:25–27 where Jesus asserts that the Father and Son know each other, along with those to whom the Son reveals the Father. In the NT, knowledge of God comes through Jesus and concerns the saving work that God does in Jesus. Knowledge assumes faith in God and Jesus as well as obedience to them: "And by this we may be sure that we know him [Christ], if we keep his commandments" (1 John 2:3).

The later syncretistic religious movement Gnosticism (from the Greek word for "knowledge") stressed special illumination about the divine and cosmic realities and a special revelation beyond and superior to the Bible. ***See also*** Faith; Obedience; Revelation. A.J.S.

Kohath (koh'hath), the second of Levi's three sons (Gen. 46:11), grandfather of Moses and Aaron (Exod. 6:16–20), and, according to 1 Chron. 6:22–28, the ancestor of Samuel. Although Gershon was Levi's firstborn, the narrative sections (e.g., Num. 3–4) often treat Kohath and his descendants as the most important levitical family. Kohath's descendants are sometimes mentioned before Gershon's descendants (Num. 4:34–45; 1 Chron. 15:5). The Kohathites had the most important function in the tabernacle—disassembling and transporting the Holy of Holies (Num. 4:4–20). According to 1 Chronicles, they also prepared the showbread (9:32) and their descendants included Asaph and Heman, two important Temple singers (6:31–43). M.Z.B.

Koheleth (koh-hell'eth). ***See*** Ecclesiastes.

koph (kohf), the nineteenth letter of the Hebrew alphabet; its numerical value is one hundred. The letter is preserved in proto-Sinaitic inscriptions, where it resembles the number eight. The form developed in the Phoenician and early Hebrew script. The form of the letter in the classical Hebrew square script resembles the later Phoenician and early Aramaic script. ***See also*** Writing.

ק

Korah (koh'rah). **1** The chief of a clan of Edom (Gen. 36:16, 18). He is listed as both the son of Esau (Gen. 36:5, 14; 1 Chron. 1:35) and the grandson of Esau, son of Eliphaz (Gen. 36:16). **2** A son of Hebron (1 Chron. 2:43). possibly a Judean geographical site or clan name (cf. 1 Chron. 12:6). **3** A Levite family of the clan of Kohath (Exod. 6:21, 24; 1 Chron. 6:22 [Hebrew 6:7]). The Korahites were one of the major guilds of Temple singers (2 Chron. 20:19) whose name appears in the superscriptions of Pss. 42; 44–49; 84–85; 87–88. They were also Temple gatekeepers (1 Chron. 9:19; 26:1, 19) and bakers (1 Chron. 9:31). Numbers 16 reports that the eponymous ancestor of the family, Korah, together with two hundred and fifty leaders of the people, led a revolt against Moses and Aaron in the wilderness. Most scholars agree that this account was conflated with an originally independent account of a lay revolt against levitical authority led by Dothan and Abiram (cf. Deut. 11:6; Ps. 106:7). Korah's revolt indicates a conflict between priestly houses over Aaron's exclusive right to offer incense before the Lord. He died when fire came forth from the Lord, consuming the rebels. Num. 26:9–11 states that Korah and his cohorts died when the earth swallowed Dothan and Abiram, but the sons of Korah survived. ***See also*** Abiram; Dothan; Levites. M.A.S.

Kore (koh'reh), the name of a bird alternatively identified with *Ammoperdix heyi* or the slightly larger *Alectoris graeca;* both are types of partridge. It is the name of two men in the OT. **1** The father of Shallum, a member of the tabernacle gatekeepers' guild (1 Chron. 9:19). **2** A Levite contemporary with Hezekiah (2 Chron. 31:14).

Opposite: A seven-branched holy lampstand with other ritual objects—*lulav* (palm frond), shofar, and incense shovel—as depicted on the late third- or early fourth-century A.D. mosaic floor of the synagogue at Hammath-Tiberias.

L

L, a symbol designating material found only in the Gospel of Luke; it also designates the hypothetical source of this material. The Lucan narratives dealing with Jesus' birth and post-resurrection appearances are included in this material. ***See also*** Synoptic Problem, The.

Laban (lay'buhn; Heb., "white" or "pale"). **1** An unknown location east of the Jordan connected with the Israelites' wilderness wandering (Deut. 1:1); some scholars identify it with Libnah (Num. 33:20).

2 A member of Abraham's ancestral family through Nahor, Abraham's brother; he was the brother of Rebekah and father of Leah and Rachel (Gen. 24:24, 29; 29:16). His home was near Haran in Paddan-aram (or Aram-naharaim, "the river country"), the upper region of the land lying between the Tigris and Euphrates rivers (upper Mesopotamia); he and his father are both called Aramaeans ("Syrians" in some versions; Gen. 24:10; 25:20; 27:43).

Laban's greedy nature and subsequent role in the patriarchal narratives are aptly foreshadowed in his first introduction into the story where his lavish and servile greeting of Abraham's servant was prompted by the sight of the gifts (Gen. 24:29–32). Laban is encountered later in the narrative as Rebekah sends Jacob to the ancestral home at Haran to escape the anger of Esau and to find a wife from among the family clan group of Laban (Gen. 27:43–28:5). Laban's covetous nature is fully revealed in his rather uneven bargain with Jacob of seven years labor for Rachel and his subsequent deception in tricking Jacob into another seven years labor (Gen. 29:1–30). However, he finally outwitted himself in agreeing to give Jacob the oddly marked livestock; thinking to take advantage of Jacob again, he found himself with dwindling herds as Jacob shrewdly used his knowledge of animal husbandry to carry out the poetic justice of God (Gen. 30:25–43).

Laban's anger at Jacob's secret departure for Canaan was, no doubt, partly caused by the prospect of losing his daughters, much of what he considered to be his flocks, and the cheap labor of Jacob, all of which amounted to a breaking up of the family unit to which Jacob had willingly attached himself. But Laban was also concerned over the theft of the household idols (teraphim). These were more than just pagan images; they were tribal or clan symbols of ownership whose possession gave title to the family inheritance. Tablets found at the Hurrian city of Nuzi illustrate and confirm much of the legal and social background of this narrative. According to the customs portrayed in these tablets, Laban adopted his son-in-law as legal heir since, at that time, he had no male children. Jacob then had a right to the teraphim and the family inheritance, unless Laban had sons of his own who would then have precedence. Sons were later born to Laban, so neither Jacob nor Rachel had a legal right to the idols or inheritance and Laban was understandably upset over their disappearance (Gen. 31:22–30). The final parting of Laban and Jacob at Mizpah symbolizes the break between the Hebrews and their ancestral homeland in Aram and probably also reflects an ancient treaty of nonaggression between the two peoples (Gen. 31:43–55).

In the entire narrative Laban is characterized as greedy and devious and many scholars see the development of his character in the story as a satire aimed at the Aramaeans. On another level, the defeat of Laban, who seemed to have the upper hand initially, is attributed to the action of God, who used even the devious Aramaean to fulfill his divine purpose for his people (Gen. 31:5–13, 24, 42). ***See also*** Aram; Jacob; Mizpah; Nuzi; Rachel; Teraphim. D.R.B.

labor, a term mentioned in a variety of contexts in the Bible meaning manual labor or great effort. Near Eastern society knew several types of work and workers: the farmer, shepherd, craftsman, day laborer (Matt. 20:1–15), forced labor for the monarchy (1 Sam. 8:11–17), native slave (Exod. 21:2–11), and foreign slave (Deut. 21:10–14). Women generally worked in the home and field (cf. Prov. 31:10–31). Work is natural to humans (Gen. 2:15) and labor is honored and appreciated (Prov. 22:29; 10:4; Eccles. 5:12). God is pictured as working at creation (Gen. 1–2) and God brings labor to a successful conclusion (Gen. 26:12; Prov. 10:16; Eccles. 2:24; Isa. 65:21–23). Biblical laws protect the wages of laborers as part of an orderly society (Lev. 19:13; Deut. 24:14–15). Hard work is also presented as a punishment for sin (Gen. 3:17–19) and generally as a wearisome part of the human condition.

In the NT Paul speaks most often about labor. Paul himself worked as a tentmaker or leatherworker to earn his living while preaching the gospel (Acts 18:3; 1 Cor. 4:12; 1 Thess. 2:9), even though Christian preachers have a right to the support of the community (1 Cor. 9:4–18; Mark 6:10–11). Paul's emphasis on his gainful employment makes it likely that his work was part of his missionary strategy for meeting and influencing people. Work is also part of an orderly Christian life, even in the face of expectation of the end (1 Thess. 4:12; 2 Thess. 3:10–12). Ephesians affirms that slaves are to continue honest labor for their masters (6:5–8).

Paul also speaks of his labor on behalf of his missionary work (2 Cor. 11:23–29) as a sign of his genuineness. All Christians are exhorted to labor at the Lord's work (1 Cor. 15:58) and references to work for the community are frequent. In John 5:17 Jesus identifies his work with God's work, specifically his curing of a man on the Sabbath and, more generally, all God's dealings with humans. ***See also*** Sabbath. A.J.S.

Lachish

AN IMPORTANT Canaanite and Israelite city, Lachish (lay'kish) is mentioned both in biblical and nonbiblical texts. It appears in the Amarna correspondence (fourteenth century B.C.) of Pharaoh Amenophis IV (Akhenaton), as well as in Assyrian records. The OT contains many references to Lachish. When Japhia, king of Lachish, joined an anti-Gibeonite coalition to resist the Israelite invasion, Joshua put him to death and captured Lachish (Josh. 10:1–32). King Amaziah of Judah (ca. 800–783 B.C.) was killed at Lachish, where he took refuge from a palace revolt in Jerusalem (2 Kings 14:17–20).

History: The location of Lachish was uncertain until the American archaeologist William F. Albright in 1929 proposed Tell ed-Duweir as the site of Lachish, an identification generally accepted. An imposing mound in the foothills of Judah, Tell ed-Duweir lies about thirty miles southwest of Jerusalem and fifteen miles west of Hebron. This nearly rectangular tell is relatively large, measuring 18 acres at the summit and 30 acres at the base. This site had been occupied with some interruptions from Chalcolithic times (fourth millennium), when the inhabitants lived in caves, to the Persian period (ca. 538–333 B.C.); Tell ed-Duweir was abandoned finally about 150 B.C. The mound is secured by deep valleys all around except on the southwestern corner where

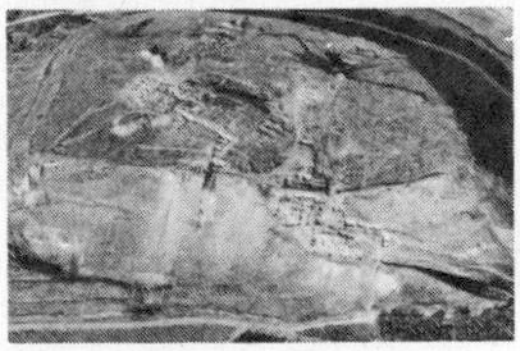

Tell ed-Duweir (above); aerial view from the southwest. William F. Albright identified this mound as the site of ancient Lachish.

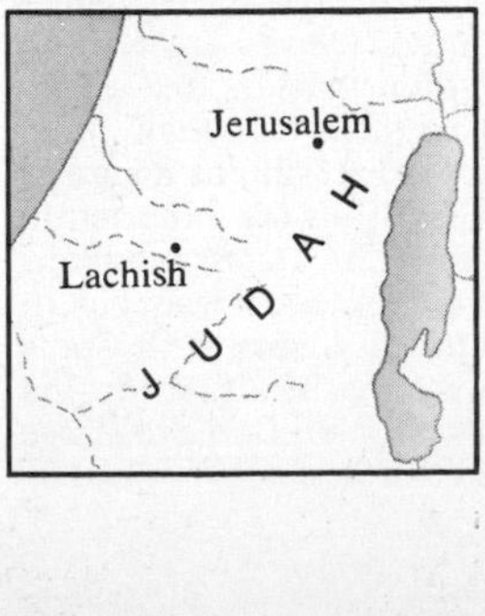

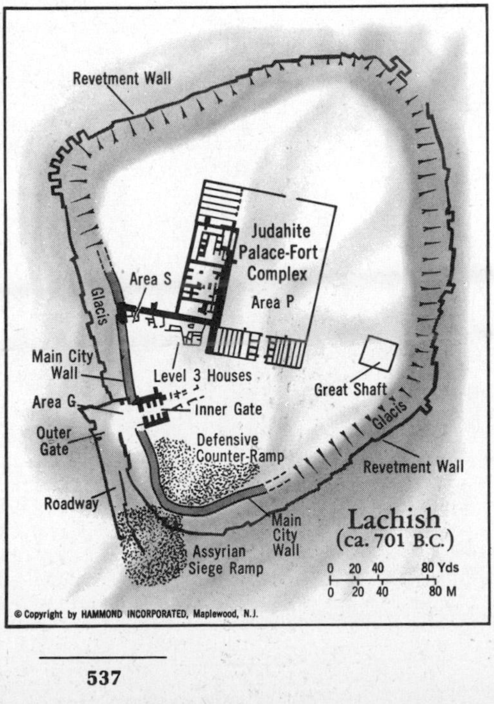

the city gate was located. This vulnerable access required strong fortifications to ward off enemy attacks.

After Joshua's conquest of Lachish the city was deserted and partially in ruins from the twelfth to the tenth centuries B.C. Then Lachish was rebuilt as a garrison city and became second in importance to Jerusalem. To protect his southern border against Egyptian and Philistine attack, King Rehoboam (924–907 B.C.) of Judah, according to 2 Chron. 11:5–12, fortified Lachish.

In 705 B.C. Sennacherib acceded to the imperial throne of Assyria. At that time Egypt, some Philistine cities, and Judah formed an alliance against Assyria; Sennacherib responded by invading Palestine in 701 B.C. After demolishing the Egyptian forces and the Philistines, he conquered most of Judah including the fortress-city of Lachish; only Jerusalem was spared. According to Sennacherib's annals forty-six of King Hezekiah's fortified cities were conquered. Despite its strong defenses—two massive city walls and a gate complex composed of an outer and inner gate—Lachish succumbed to Sennacherib who was personally present at the city at the time of its demise. The Assyrians

The Assyrian king Sennacherib conquered most of Judah, including the fortress-city of Lachish in 701 B.C. The victory was commemorated in a group of reliefs at his palace at Nineveh. In this detail, according to the inscription, "Sennacherib, king of the world, king of Assyria, sat upon a *nîmedu*-throne and passed in review the booty [taken] from Lachish [*La-ki-su*]."

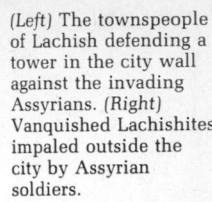

(Left) The townspeople of Lachish defending a tower in the city wall against the invading Assyrians. *(Right)* Vanquished Lachishites impaled outside the city by Assyrian soldiers.

(Left) Assyrian soldiers carrying away booty from their victory. *(Above)* Judahite families with baggage and cattle are deported after their defeat.

made their assault on the vulnerable gate complex at the southwest corner of the city; there they threw up a siege ramp against the outer side of the wall to mobilize their siege machines equipped with battering rams. The Judahites countered with a ramp of their own on the inside to support the wall, but to no avail. After his stunning victory Sennacherib reestablished his imperial rule in Palestine.

Sennacherib's devastation of Lachish is not only documented in the Bible (2 Kings 18:13) but was also memorialized in relief on the palace walls of the Assyrian royal city at Nineveh (modern Kuyunjik) opposite modern Mosul in northern Iraq. These elaborate bas-reliefs, housed in the British Museum, were uncovered in the middle of the nineteenth century by Austen H. Layard, pioneer excavator in Assyria. They depict realistically the siege and conquest of Lachish. Their detail and prominence suggest that Sennacherib viewed his conquest of Lachish as especially significant.

Archaeological Excavations: British archaeologist James L. Starkey, who trained under W. M. Flinders Petrie in Egypt and southern Pales-

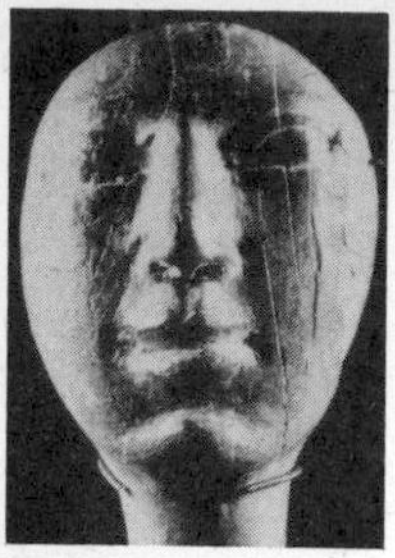

An ivory head from Lachish, ca. sixteenth–fifteenth century B.C.

tine, began a long-term, systematic excavation of Tell ed-Duweir in 1932. Paying close attention to architectural units in the course of his digging, Starkey maintained high standards of field technique. However, the project ended abruptly in 1938 when Starkey was killed in an ambush. His associates continued the project for a time, but the impetus was gone.

Starkey concentrated on the city gate complex, the Judahite palace-fort, and the west sector of the mound. Although he did not complete the investigation of the gate area, which revealed superimposed city gates, he did distinguish and date levels 2 and 3. To level 2 Starkey ascribed the conflagration of Lachish at the hands of Nebuchadnezzar of Babylon in 588/6 B.C., as most archaeologists would agree. He dated the destruction of level 3 to the first campaign of Nebuchadnezzar in 597 B.C. against King Jehoiakin of Judah. Detecting little difference in pottery types between levels 2 and 3, Starkey was satisfied that only a short time had elapsed between the two destructions.

Starkey's dating of level 3 occasioned controversy from the beginning. While preparing the results of the investigation of the gate area for publication, Olga Tufnell, who had dug with Starkey, discerned a noticeable variance in pottery typology between levels 2 and 3. Consequently she attributed to level 3 Sennacherib's conquest in 701 B.C. She also observed two phases in the gate area of level 2, dating them respectively to 597 B.C. and 588/6 B.C.

Among the outstanding epigraphical discoveries at Tell ed-Duweir are twenty-one ostraca or storage-jar fragments inscribed in black ink. Known as the Lachish Letters (most were letters, while others were lists of names), these ostraca date to ca. 590 B.C., during the reign of Zedekiah, the last king of Judah. Eighteen of the inscribed potsherds, found in 1935, lay on the floor among the ashes in a guardroom adjacent to the city gate. The remaining three, unearthed in 1938, were in the vicinity of the palace-fort. Hoshaiah, who was stationed in a garrison somewhere between Lachish and Jerusalem, had sent these letters to Yaosh, the military commander of Lachish. Written in classical

One of the ostraca, or Lachish Letters, from Hoshaiah to the Lachish military commander Yaosh, dating to ca. 590 B.C.

Hebrew prose, these ostraca not only shed light on Hebrew philology and epigraphy but also provide valuable information about the times of the prophet Jeremiah, who was speaking to King Zedekiah, "while the armies of the king of Babylon were attacking Jerusalem and the remaining cities of Judah, Lachish and Azekah; since these alone were left of the fortified cities of Judah" (Jer. 34:7).

To complete the unfinished work of Starkey and to study in greater depth the history of Lachish and its material culture, Israeli archaeologist David Ussishkin undertook in 1973 a long-term project at Lachish. In the interest of continuity he concentrated on the areas Starkey had dug. He excavated the palace-fort, as well as the monumental Canaanite buildings beneath it, situated on the summit of the mound (area P). On the western edge of the tell he dug a narrow trench to the lower slope in order to view all the strata to bedrock (area S). In this sector the excavators uncovered sections of three superimposed city walls. Ussishkin's most critical undertaking was the city gate complex (area G). In addition, the archaeological team conducted a regional survey around Tell ed-Duweir.

(Top) Ivory figurine of a crouching cat. From the excavations of the temple at Lachish, it dates to ca. the fifteenth century B.C. *(Bottom)* Ivory stopper carved in the shape of a male ibex, found in a Level-4 house at Lachish. It is perforated so that liquid, possibly perfume, could be poured through the mouth of the ibex.

As a policy Ussishkin has limited his digging to certain parts of the tell; other areas he has left untouched so future archaeologists can test his conclusions afresh. With respect to field technique Ussishkin in the spirit of Kathleen Kenyon, Britain's great archaeologist, has emphasized the vertical section; he has also attended to the restoration of pottery forms and has utilized specialists in the applied sciences, such as botany, osteology, palynology, and metallurgy.

Ussishkin concurs with Starkey that six strata lay between the Late Bronze Age (1500–1200 B.C.) and the Persian-Hellenistic period (ca. 538–63 B.C.) at Tell ed-Duweir. The levels are the following: Level 1 pertains to the postexilic period, including the Babylonian, Persian, and Hellenistic eras (from the sixth to the first century B.C.). In the time of Nehemiah, following the Babylonian captivity, Jews settled in Lachish. Level 2 represents the Babylonian destruction by fire of Lachish in 588/6 B.C. The city at this level may have been built by King Josiah (639–609 B.C.). The Lachish Letters pertain to this level. Level 3 marks the Assyrian conquest of Lachish in 701 B.C., according to Ussishkin, Tufnell, and several other scholars. At the time of this conflagration Lachish was a densely populated city. Level 4 represents the royal Judahite fortified city, composed of two city walls, the gate complex, and the palace-fort. An earthquake may have been responsible for the destruction of this level. Level 5 pertains to the late tenth century B.C., the period of the United Monarchy when Judahites began to resettle Lachish. This level was destroyed by fire. Level 6 marks the conflagration of the final Late Bronze Age III city in the twelfth century, perhaps in 1163 B.C. Canaanite Lachish was under Egyptian control at the time of the Israelite invasion.

Level 3 is key to the dating of a significant corpus of pottery in Palestine. On the basis of stratigraphy and a comparison of the pottery typology of levels 2 and 3 at Tell ed-Duweir Ussishkin is confident in dating level 3 to Sennacherib's conquest in 701 B.C. John S. Holladay and other archaeologists disagree. Some counter Ussishkin's internal evidence with external evidence from other sites, such as Samaria, the capital of the Northern Kingdom. Until scholars reach

Moundlike formation that was probably part of the Assyrian siege ramp thrown up against the Lachish city wall. A depiction of an Assyrian siege machine is with the color photographs.

consensus, a variance of more than one hundred years in the dating of a significant corpus of Palestinian pottery continues to be a problem.

In addition to the excavated areas of Tell ed-Duweir already described, two other structures were investigated: the fosse temple and the solar shrine. The fosse temple, so called because it was constructed in a moat that had been part of the Middle Bronze Age II fortifications, is situated near the northwest corner of the mound, outside the city. The original building was built of unhewn stone in the sixteenth century B.C. Rebuilt and enlarged more than once, this temple was destroyed by fire about 1200 B.C. The nature of the temple's cult is unknown.

The solar shrine, so called by Starkey because of its orientation and the presence of an altar with an adoring human figure, is situated in the eastern sector of Tell ed-Duweir. Yohanan Aharoni excavated the structure in 1966 and 1968 in an effort to clarify the chronology and history of Lachish. This solar shrine, composed of two main rooms and a court, dates to about 200 B.C. Starkey and Aharoni identified the ruins as a Jewish temple or sanctuary. Albright and Frank M. Cross disagreed because of lack of evidence.

Ussishkin's work is still in progress. Further study may render definitive several interpretations which are still tentative. What the archaeologists have already accomplished is a significant contribution to biblical history.

P.J.K.

Ladan (lay'duhn). **1** An Ephraimite, the father of Ammihud and ancestor of Joshua (1 Chron. 7: 26). **2** The head of the Gershonite clan of Levites (1 Chron. 23:7–9; 26:21); he is also called Libni (Exod. 6:17; Num. 3:18). ***See also*** Libni.

ladder, the term that translates Hebrew *sullām* in the story of Jacob's dream in Gen. 28:12 where it describes a means of ascent from earth to heaven (cf. John 1:51). Normal devices for ascending heights included rock-cut steps and constructed ladders of wood, metal, or rope. Archaeological evidences for cut and constructed stone stairways are abundant, and the most frequent uses of constructed ladders were to enter storerooms without doorways, reach rooftops without stairways, or scale defense walls as part of attack weaponry in wartime.

Lagash (lah'gahsh; Arabic *Telloh,* "tablet hill"), a Sumerian city about fifty miles north of Ur whose ruins have yielded the largest number of cuneiform tablets of the third millennium Sumerian cities. Girsu is the oldest mound of the group of sites comprising Lagash.

Lagash flourished in the Early Dynastic III period (2500–2300 B.C.). Just prior to this time, Enhegal bought several parcels of land and asserted Lagashite independence at a time when all other city governors were subject to the ruler claiming hegemony over Sumer. Lagash and Umma, its neighbor and rival, served as political buffers as well as vehicles of cultural transmission between Sumer and Elam. Tensions developed between these two cities over the question of control of a rich stretch of agricultural land called the *edin.* Eannatum of Lagash commissioned the monument "The Stele of Vultures" to commemorate his campaign for this land. He also subdued Elam.

Urukagina of Lagash promulgated the first legal reforms. Unfortunately, they and his reign were short lived. The city was already deteriorating under the weight of administrative excesses and was soon conquered by Lugalzagesi of Umma.

As city governor, Gudea ruled Lagash during the Gutian domination following the collapse of the Akkadian empire around 2168 B.C. The Ur III period of Sumerian renaissance produced artistic and textual witnesses to the final flowering of Lagashite power. Among the surviving texts are those that record the instructions Gudea received in a dream for building a temple to the city gods.

L.E.P.

Diorite statue of Gudea, ruler of Lagash, seated; ca. 2168 B.C.

Lahmi (lah'mee), a brother of Goliath, who, according to 1 Chron. 20:5, was slain by David's hero Elhanan. "Lahmi," however, is probably part of a textual error with the effect of harmonizing 2 Sam. 21:19 with 1 Sam. 17.

Laish (lay'ish; Heb., "lion"). **1** The father of Palti(el), to whom Saul gave his daughter (who was David's wife) Michal (1 Sam. 25:44) and for whose return David bargained (2 Sam. 3:12–16). **2** A Canaanite city, modern Tell el-Qadi, which was subsequently occupied by Israelites and named Dan (Judg. 18:7–31). It is located ten and a half miles north of Lake Huleh. ***See also*** Dan.

lamb. ***See*** Sheep.

Lamb of God, the title with which John the Baptist twice greets Jesus at the beginning of the Gospel of John (1:29, 35). In Revelation, the lamb also appears a number of times as a symbol for Christ, although a different Greek word is used than that found in the Gospel.

In Revelation, the lamb has clearly been slain as a ransom for sin (5:6–14). Probably the idea of the lamb as sacrificial offering lies behind John 1:29, 35 as well ("the Lamb of God, who takes away the sin of the world"), although this way of speaking of the saving work of Christ is not common in the Fourth Gospel (but cf. 1 John 1:7). It is also possible that the Suffering Servant of Isaiah 53, who is likened to "a lamb that is led to slaughter," has influenced this description of Jesus (cf. 1 Pet. 1:18–19). In the Gospel of John, Jesus died on the afternoon before the Feast of Passover began, as the Passover lambs were slain. Thus the possibility that Jesus is to be understood as the lamb of the Passover sacrifice suggests itself, even though that lamb was not technically a sin offering. The designation of Jesus as the Lamb of God, then, suggests a wide range of images from the OT, mostly having to do with expiatory sacrifice. ***See also*** Expiation; John the Baptist; John, The Gospel According to; Passover, The; Revelation to John, The; Sin. D.M.S.

Lamech (lay'mek; Heb., meaning uncertain; cf. the Old Akkadian names *Lamkium* and *Lamki-Mari).* **1** The son of Methushael, husband of Adah and Zillah, and father of three sons (Jabal, Jubal, and Tubal-Cain, the progenitors respectively of nomads, musicians, and smiths) and a daughter (Naamah; Gen. 4:18–22). The Song of Lamech (Gen. 4:23–24) is composed of three couplets, in the first of which Lamech exhorts his wives to attend his words; in the second he vaunts his prowess in having slain a man/boy for merely wounding/bruising him; and in the third he boasts: "If Cain be avenged seven-fold, then Lamech seventy and seven." Lamech thus expresses disdain for the law of retaliation, according to which a wound may be avenged with a wound, a bruise with a bruise (Exod. 21:25), and boasts that he has instead exacted the penalty of death for the hurt done him. That the object of his vengeance, as he states, was a boy, reflects the fact that warriors in the ancient world were often young boys (Judg. 8:20; 1 Sam. 17:33). The parallelism of the numbers, "sevenfold" (lit., twice seven, i.e., fourteen) and "seventy-seven," is unique, but it finds explanation in the numeral construction based upon the sum of three consecutive squared numbers; thus, $14 = 1^2 + 2^2 + 3^2$, and $77 = 4^2 + 5^2 + 6^2$. **2** The son of Methuselah and father of Noah. He lived 777 years (Gen. 5:25–29). S.G.

lamed (lah'muhd), the twelfth letter of the Hebrew alphabet; its numerical value is thirty. The earliest form of the letter is a pictograph of an ox-goad. In Phoenician script the position of the form changed, and in later Phoenician and early Aramaic forms a tail was added. It was from this form that the classical Hebrew square form developed. ***See also*** Writing.

ל

lameness, one of the blemishes disqualifying descendants of Aaron from their priestly prerogative of approaching the altar of God's sanctuary to offer bread to God (Lev. 21:16–24). It was not appropriate to sacrifice lame animals to God (Deut. 15:21; Mal. 1:8, 13). Jesus' healing of the lame was one of the "deeds of the Christ" illustrating and bringing about the Kingdom of God (Matt. 11:2–6; 15:29–31; Luke 7:18–23). By healing the lame in the Temple Jesus restored them to the worshiping community (Matt. 21:10–17). Jesus' healing of lameness was continued by Peter and John in the Temple (Acts 3:2–13) and Philip in Samaria (Acts 8:4–8).

Lamentations of Jeremiah, the, an OT book consisting of five elegies bewailing the destruction of Jerusalem and the Temple in 587 B.C. The name "Lamentations" reflects the Greek *Threnoi* and the Latin *Threni,* both of which are a translation of the Hebrew title *Qinoth* meaning "dirges" *(b. B. Bat.* 14b). The more prevalent Hebrew name, however, is *Eikhah* ("Ah, how"), the book's opening word. In the Hebrew Bible, Lamentations is one of the five scrolls in the Hagiographa. In the Septuagint and the Latin versions, however, Lamentations appears as an appendix to the book of Jeremiah.

Authorship: Tradition holds that the prophet Jeremiah was the author of Lamentations. This tradition is based on Jeremiah's central role as prophet of the destruction as well as on other verses associating him with the composition of dirges (Jer. 7:29; 9:9, 19; 2 Chron. 35:25). Modern scholarship has generally been skeptical of assigning the book to Jeremiah. Verses expressing the crushed hopes pinned on the king or on foreign alliances (4:17, 20) appear to be out of character with Jeremiah's thinking (cf. Jer. 2:18, 36; 24:8–10). Furthermore, the standard prophetic indictments against the generation of the destruction (such as practice of idol worship and socio-moral offenses, cf. Jer. 5:7–8; 7:9–10; 9:1–5, 11–13) go practically unmentioned in Lamentations. With the exception of 4:13, the book refers to Jerusalem's sins only in the most general terms (1:5, 8, 14, 18; 2:14; 4:6), and even seems to bespeak a certain measure of perplexity regarding the severity of God's judgment (3:43–44; 5:7). In these respects, Lamentations may be said to reflect the popular (i.e., nonprophetic) ideology current during the period of the monarchy (ca. 1020–587 B.C.). The spirit of the book can be traced more precisely to upper-class circles who were versed in the wisdom tradition. The concern for the fate of the king and noblemen (1:6; 2:9; 4:5, 7, 8, 20) as well as the conception of suffering expressed in chap. 3 (see below) tend to support this conclusion.

Content: Chaps. 1 and 5 provide a general description of Jerusalem's desolation in the wake of the destruction. Chaps. 2 and 4 give a more vivid account of the actual events, with chap. 2 emphasizing God's enmity on the day of his fury and chap. 4 cataloguing the terrible conditions prevailing at the time of the catastrophe. Chap. 3 departs from the general pattern of the book by focusing on the fate of a suffering individual. This individual recounts his own feeling of abandonment by God (vv. 1–18), but then proceeds to reflect on the meaning of his suffering. As in many passages associated with the wisdom tradition, God's justness in bringing on punishment as well as his ultimate kindness is accepted axiomatically (vv. 21–25, 31–38). With the recognition that his suffering is not a capricious occurrence, but rather a result of his own sins, the author accepts it willingly, mindful that a sincere change of heart will evoke God's mercy (vv. 26–30, 39–41). Significantly, the poet's call to repentance in vv. 40–41 is formulated in the first person plural, thus indicating that the message of chap. 3 indeed forms the ideological core of the entire book.

While each chapter has its individual character, certain themes are repeated throughout the book. The general conditions of famine in besieged and destroyed Jerusalem are described in 1:11, 19; 2:11–12, 19–20; 4:3–10; and 5:9–10. Another common theme is Jerusalem's isolation and disgrace in the face of jeering enemies and former allies who had abandoned it (1:2, 7, 21; 2:16; 3:46, 63; 4:17). At the end of three of the five chapters, a vengeful wish is expressed for those foes (1:22; 3:64–66; 4:21–22). Paramount in Lamentations is the attributing of the destruction to God's wrath, which is best understood as resulting from the people's sins (1:5, 14–15, 17–18; 2:1–9, 17, 21–22; 3:42–43; 4:11–13). However, despite the feeling of guilt, there is an ongoing hope in God's salvation even in the moments of greatest despair (1: 9, 11, 20–22; 2:18–20; 3:21–25, 31–32, 55–66; 4:21–22; 5:19–22).

Style: All of the book's five chapters are composed in poetic style. Chaps. 1–4 are alphabetical acrostics, with chaps. 1, 2, and 4 containing one verse for each letter of the Hebrew alphabet, and chap. 3 containing three verses for each letter. Chap. 5 is not an acrostic, but like chaps. 1, 2, and 4 it contains twenty-two metrical verses, corresponding to the number of letters in the Hebrew alphabet. Another striking poetic device is the personification of Zion as a distraught female figure (1:1–9, 17; 2:13, 18–19). In addition to these literary features, many linguistic elements run like a red thread through the book (e.g., *eikhah* in 1:1; 2:1; 4:1–2; "days of old" in 1:7; 2:17; 5:21; "sucklings" in 1:5; 2:11, 19–20; 4:4). ***See also*** Jeremiah, The Book of; Poetry.

Bibliography

Hillers, D. R. *Lamentations*. Garden City, NY: Doubleday, 1972.

Tigay, J. H. "Lamentations, Book of." *Encyclopaedia Judaica*. Vol. 10. Pp. 1368–1375.

D.A.G./J.H.T.

lamp, a vessel used to keep and control fire as a source of light. The development of such a vessel was a major achievement of early human history. This vessel, known as the oil lamp, had two basic parts: a receptacle for the oil and a wick inserted into the oil whose protruding end would burn. Olives provided the main source of oil in Palestine; various materials, including flax, served as wicks. Because the oil lamp was in everyday use and has been found in abundance in excavated sites, its typological and historical development is relatively easy to establish and indicates that the lamps in Palestine were, with few exceptions, similar to those in use all over the Mediterranean world.

Five terra-cotta oil lamps that date to the first century B.C.

In the Neolithic period (prior to fourth millennium B.C.) ordinary stone bowls were used to contain and burn oil; in the fourth millennium B.C. ordinary pottery bowls were used. Early in the third millennium the first adaptations were made for the specific placement of the wick. This vessel, a round saucer with four slight depressions on its rim, eventually developed into a square saucer with four pronounced open spouts at the corners. In the second millennium the dominant shape became a saucer with only one pinched corner. This single-spouted, open form remained in use for over fifteen hundred years while undergoing only slight utilitarian improvements affecting the base, spout, and rim. By the Late Bronze Age (1500–1200 B.C.) the oil lamp had generally assumed a triangular shape. In the Iron Age I period (1200–900 B.C.) variations on this basic form included multi-spouted, saucers and lamps with tall pedestal bases. In the Iron Age II period (900–600 B.C.) the form of the oil lamp developed somewhat differently in the two politically and culturally divided areas of Israel and Judah. In Israel the tradition of the single-spouted, open shape continued with only slight modifications, but in Judah marked changes occurred as the base became high and heavy and the rim wide. The Israel-type lamp has frequently been found in Judah but the Judah-type rarely in Israel. With the Babylonian conquest (597 B.C.) the Judah-type lamp disappeared and throughout Palestine a broad shallow lamp with wide rim came into use, the last in the long line of open oil lamps that had originated in the second millennium.

The Hellenistic lamp, which developed from a fifth-century B.C. Greek form, was a closed vessel with a long nozzle for the wick and a broad circular opening in the cover to receive the oil. Many such lamps were imported into Palestine during Hellenistic times (332–63 B.C.), but most lamps in use were made locally. These were generally of the closed type, although the older open-type saucer was also made. During the early Roman period in Palestine (63 B.C.–A.D. 135) Hellenistic forms continued to be used and the Roman round discus lamp was introduced and copied. However, new forms, distinctively Palestinian, appeared. One, the "Herodian" lamp, had a round, wheel-made body, a flat base, a large filling hole, and a separately attached nozzle. Unlike the highly decorated Roman lamps, which featured scenes from mythology, most "Herodian" lamps were unadorned, although some had simple incision marks. Sometime in the first century A.D. a different type evolved, influenced by a technical innovation already common in the Roman world—the mold-made lamp. It had a handle and its rim and nozzle were decorated with geometric and floral designs, with or without Jewish symbols. Both forms have most commonly been found in southern Palestine.

In houses and public buildings lamps were placed in niches, on shelves jutting out from the walls, or on lampstands; in later times, they were hung from the ceiling. In addition to their chief function of illumination, lamps played a central role in religious practices. The tending of the "eternal light" in the Jerusalem Temple was a sacred duty. In later Jewish tradition, Jews lit special oil lamps on Friday evening and on the eve of every holiday. The abundance of oil lamps found in tombs suggests that besides illuminating the dark interiors they may have been used as a symbolic rekindling of the spirit of the deceased, as a remedy against "evil spirits," and as subsequent memorial offerings.

An easily understandable and powerful symbol of the importance of light, the oil lamp (Heb. *nîr*; Gk. *lychnos, lampas*) is referred to frequently in the Bible in a wide range of contexts. In the OT it conveys, for example, the illuminating power of God (2 Sam. 22:29; Job 29:3) and of his precepts (Ps. 119:105); a father's instructions to his dutiful son (Prov. 6:23); and the lasting existence of the Davidic dynasty (1 Kings 11:36; 15:4). In the NT it is a symbol of the eye of the body (Matt. 6:22); the vigilance of the faithful servant (Luke 12:35); and the function of the disciples in the world (Matt. 5:14–16). ***See also*** Lampstand.

Bibliography

Smith, Robert Houston. "The Household Lamps of Palestine in Old Testament Times." *Biblical Archaeologist* 27 (1964):1–31.

______. "The Household Lamps of Palestine in Intertestamental Times." *Biblical Archaeologist* 27 (1964):101–124.

______. "The Household Lamps of Palestine in New Testament Times." *Biblical Archaeologist* 29 (1966):2–27.

Sussman, Varda. *Ornamented Jewish Oil-Lamps*. Warminster, England: Aris and Phillips, 1982. Chap. 1.

M.M.S.

lampstand (Heb., *menorah*), the term for an object that supported one or more oil lamps. Although such stands could be made of stone, pottery, or wood, the biblical passages dealing with lampstands, with one exception (2 Kings 4:10), present golden lampstands intended for cultic usage.

Four successive lampstand traditions can be identified. First, the tabernacle texts describe a single golden lampstand composed of a central, cylindrical stand with three pairs of branches and elaborate floral decorations (Exod. 25:31–40; 37:17–24). The unattached lamp or lamps were apparently grouped on the central stand rather than on the ends of the branches (cf. Lev. 24:1–4). The origins of the tabernacle lampstand in the premonarchical period can be discerned in the floral and technical vocabulary used to describe it; this vocabulary also suggests the symbolic value of the lampstand as a sacred tree form representing God's unseen presence in his earthly shrine.

Second, ten golden lampstands (1 Kings 7:49), for which no branches are specified, stood in the Solomonic Temple. These were probably cylindrical stands holding multispouted lamps similar to those known, archaeologically, from cultic contexts spanning the Middle Bronze through the Iron ages.

Third, the rebuilt Temple of the late sixth century, using the tabernacle texts as a guideline for cultic appurtenances, evidently resumed the single lampstand tradition, as Zechariah's fourth vision indicates (Zech. 4:1–6, 11–14). The second Temple was repeatedly looted and restored or rebuilt (cf. 1 Macc. 1:21; 4:49); and by the end of its existence, the single Temple lampstand with branches was fashioned according to techniques and traditions current in the Roman world. It is the last Temple lampstand, of the first century A.D., with its characteristic seven lamp-holding branches and tripodal or stepped base, that appears in the earliest artistic renderings of the holy lampstand and dominates its use as a paramount Jewish symbol, reprsenting light and life eternal.

Fourth, the apocalyptic vision in the book of Revelation expands the single golden lampstand to seven, in keeping with the other symbolic usages of that sacred Semitic number, although in one place (Rev. 11:4), building upon the Zechariah vision, two lampstands are suggested to match the two trees that flank the stands in Zech. 4:11. ***See also*** Lamp; Temple, The; Tree of Life, The. C.L.M.

landmarks, indications of property boundaries, whether erected (as boundary stones) or natural and recognized by mutual agreement. They were not to be moved (Deut. 19:14; 27:17) and doing so was a symbol of irresponsible deceit (Hos. 5:10), greed (Job 24:2), and abuse (Prov. 23:10). This biblical respect for ancestral property reflected similar concern in Babylonian, Egyptian, and later, Greek and Roman law. International markers were frequently elaborately inscribed stones.

Language of the New Testament. ***See*** Greek, New Testament.

Language of the Old Testament. ***See*** Aramaic; Hebrew.

Laodicea (lay-ahd-i-see'uh), a prosperous, commercial city in the region of Phrygia in northwest Asia Minor. It was named after his wife, Laodice, by Antiochus II of the Seleucid dynasty, which ruled Syria after the death of Alexander the Great. Situated on a plateau in the south of the Lycus River valley, Laodicea was adjacent to one of the ancient trade routes from the east. Two neighboring cities with Christian communities, Colossae and Hierapolis (Col. 2:1; 4:13–16), were in this same river valley. Epaphras, portrayed as one of Paul's companions, apparently worked in all three cities (Col. 4:12–13). According to Col. 4:16, Laodicea received a letter from Paul, and it was to exchange letters with the neighboring community at Colossae. The Laodicean letter is no longer extant, although various attempts to trace or identify it have been made over the centuries. The church of Laodicea was one of the seven rebuked in Revelation (Rev. 3:14–22), and the image used in the reprimand may reflect a natural occurrence (Rev. 3:15–16). Laodicea received its water through an aqueduct coming from a spring four miles to the south; the waters of neighboring Hierapolis, however, were famous as hot springs and would have provided a contrast with the tepid aqueduct water in Laodicea. The accusation against the community may also be a reference to an arrogant self-sufficiency reflected in the fact that, after the earthquake of A.D. 60, the Laodiceans did not wish any help from Rome in rebuilding their city. ***See also*** Colossae; Colossians, The Letter of Paul to the; Epaphras; Hierapolis; Philemon, The Letter of Paul to; Phrygia. M.K.M.

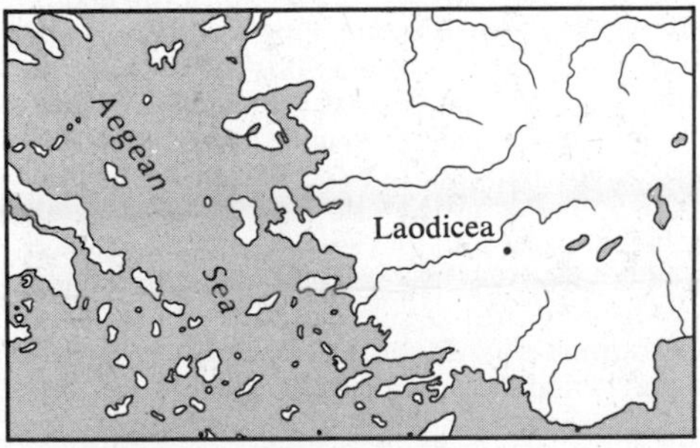

Lappidoth (lah'pee-dohth; Heb., "flash"), husband of the prophetess Deborah (Judg. 4:4). He is mentioned only once in a narrative especially concerned with commander Barak (Heb., "lightning"). ***See also*** Barak.

Lasea (lah-see'ah), a city on the south coast of Crete. It is mentioned in Acts 27:8 as a point beyond which the dangers of proceeding by sea increased dramatically, especially in winter. The coast turns sharply north at that point, bringing open sea winds to bear full force, heightening danger. Lasea is near Fair Havens, modern Limenes Kali.

Last Judgment, the. ***See*** Judgment, the Last.

Last Supper, the. ***See*** Lord's Supper, The; Sacraments.

latchet, the leather strap or thong that secures the sole of a sandal to the foot (Gen. 14:23; Isa. 5:27; Mark 1:7; Luke 3:16).

Latin, a word originally referring to peoples surrounding Rome in the area of Latium. In the second century B.C. Rome's Latin allies had a "second class" citizenship, though they might become full citizens of Rome upon moving to the city. Such a class of "Latin" citizens continued to exist in the Imperial period.

Latin was the language spoken by these people and the primary language used among the educated and romanized populace in the western part of the Roman Empire. It had developed considerable flexibility under the influence of Greek. However, Greek remained the primary language for the eastern part of the Empire, even among educated Romans. There Latin was limited to Roman military affairs. According to John 19:20, the official reason for Jesus' crucifixion was written in Latin, the official language, as well as the local Hebrew and the widely used Greek. P.P.

laughter, an expression of rejoicing (Ps. 126:2), contrasted with weeping (Eccles. 3:4; Luke 6:21) or mourning (James 4:9) or both (Luke 6:25). Laughter may mean "laughter for pleasure, merrymaking, fun, enjoyment." The contexts of Exod. 32:6 and 1 Sam. 18:7 suggest specifically religious celebrations. The reference in Gen. 26:8 seems to be explicitly sexual. Laughter is also used of the play of children (Gen. 21:9; Zech. 8:5). Prov. 26:19 condemns a deception subsequently claimed to be for a laugh. Laughter may also denote "laughter at, mockery, ridicule, derision." Job complains that his juniors laugh at him (Job 30:1), and Jerusalem recalls how its enemies laughed at its downfall (Lam. 1:7). God, who can see the fate of wrongdoers (Ps. 37:13; cf. 52:6), laughs at the futile presumptions of earthly rulers (Ps. 2:4). Laughter at God, however, is reprimanded. On the occasion of Abraham's (Gen. 17:17) and Sarah's (Gen. 18:12) laughter God directs them to call the promised son "He laughs [at]" (Heb. *yitzkhaq*, "Isaac"; Gen. 17:19). Laughter at threats or dangers is an expression of confidence and security (Job 5:22; 39:22; 41:29). Ecclesiasticus tends to deprecate laughter (Ecclus. 21:20; 31:10), while recognizing that one's laughter may reveal one's character (Ecclus. 19:30). Rarely mentioned in the NT, laughter may express either joy (Luke 6:21) or derision (Matt. 9:24).

laver (lay'vuhr), a large copper or bronze vessel used for priestly ablutions in the tabernacle (Exod. 30:17–21) and in the Temple. It stood near the altar (Exod. 40:7), and, according to Exod. 38:8, was fashioned from the mirrors of women ministering at the door of the Tent of Meeting. Solomon's Temple had ten lavers (1 Kings 7:30, 38, 40) made by Hiram of Tyre.

law, an official set of rules governing the behavior of individuals in society. Judaism divides the Bible into the Law, the Prophets, and the Writings, "Law" reflecting the Greek understanding of the Hebrew word *torah* (here used with reference to the Pentateuch) as law (Gk. *nomos*). But *torah* is more properly translated "instruction," and the content of the Pentateuch differs significantly from "law" as we usually understand it. There is little evidence that biblical Law was the law applied by the courts before the Babylonian exile. "Law" was not yet identified with the idea of a statutory text. Even in Babylonia, where we have considerable evidence of court practice, the "Codes" (the Laws of Hammurabi, and earlier the Codes of Ur Nammu, Lipit Ishtar, and Eshnunna) are never quoted in the judicial records. Rather, they are royal statements of ideal justice.

Moses receiving a scroll from God that contains the law by which the ancient Israelites are to live; a mosaic at the Monastery of St. Catherine, Sinai, sixth century A.D.

A similar pattern is evidenced from the Bible. When courts are instituted, they are charged simply to apply justice and avoid corruption (Deut. 16:18–20); in cases of difficulty they are to resort to higher authority (Deut. 17: 8–13). Jehoshaphat's reform charges the judges in similar fashion (2 Chron. 19:5–11). Quite separately, Jehoshaphat sent officers to teach from "the book of the law of the Lord" in the cities of Judah (2 Chron. 17:17–19)—a practice also found in Assyrian sources. The particular association of the book of the law (Heb. *sefer torah)* with the king, and with didactic rather than judicial functions, is found also in Deut. 17:18–20. The actual administration of justice was largely conducted by city elders sitting at the city gate, on the basis of customary rules tempered by occasional royal ordinance and determined in cases of difficulty by recourse to oracular procedures conducted in local shrines. With the centralization of the worship of God such difficult cases were transferred to Jerusalem.

The Role of the King: The role of the king in law is much disputed. Some scholars deny him any genuine legislative role. But the legal powers he claims are characteristic of kings in states where central authority is only beginning to consolidate: he could require conscription; establish military, judicial, and administrative structures; commandeer labor for his estates, the production of munitions, and the servicing of his household; and confiscate land and levy taxation (1 Sam. 8:11–17). In the last days of the kingdom of Judah, King Zedekiah (597–586 B.C.) is said to have enforced an economic reform to relieve debt-slavery (Jer. 34); but there are grounds to believe that the motivation was more concerned with recruitment into the army than the regulation of purely private law matters. Such practical ordinances as these, unlike the *torah* whose teaching the king sponsored, were not designed to establish rules that would continue in force unless repealed. Nevertheless, there is one royal ordinance that is reported to have subsisted: David's law on the distribution of booty, which the author of 1 Sam. 30:25 tells us remained "a statute and an ordinance for Israel to this day." By contrast, God's instructions to Moses regarding the distribution of the booty taken from the Midianites are not presented as establishing a general rule (Num. 31).

Moses, though not given the title of a king, frequently acted like one. On occasion, he issued commands for which no divine mandate was claimed. For example, he organized the judicial system along military lines (Exod. 18). He dictated the monuments to be raised and the ceremonies to be performed after the crossing of the Jordan (Deut. 27). He required a septennial reading of the Law at the festival of

Sukkoth (Deut. 31:10–13)—but the law of Sukkoth was itself then neglected from the time of Joshua until rediscovered in the written law by Ezra (Neh. 8:13). At Marah, before the Israelites reached Sinai, he issued a "statute and an ordinance" (Heb. *khok umishpat,* Exod. 15:25, the same term as is used of David's booty law).

Some law was produced in the course of adjudication; here too there are parallels between the narratives of Moses and later kings. In the wilderness, the case of the daughters of Zelophehad (Num. 27, 36) is presented as a dispute, its resolution by Moses is through an oracular consultation of God, and there is a statement of general rules (going beyond the situation of the dispute) that are to have abiding force. David's booty law is the product of a similar sequence: a dispute between sections of the army regarding the distribution of booty after the campaign. But not all adjudication produced precedents for the future (e.g., Solomon's judgment, 1 Kings 3:16–28); a precedent required a new act of authoritative enunciation.

Narrative sources, both inside and outside the Pentateuch, present a picture of piecemeal lawgiving, albeit divinely inspired, often springing from concrete events. Given the central role of the king in both the promulgation of law and ordinances and the king's capacity to act as supreme judge, it is not appropriate to differentiate strictly between precedent and legislation. The king's power over and responsibility for the cult and his patronage of court prophets and court scribes also contributed to the institutionalization of divine law and its consolidation into the codes we find in the Pentateuch.

The Institutionalization of Divine Law: Four narratives cast light on the process. When Samuel is asked to authorize the appointment of a king, he—a prophet—acting under divine command issues a formulation of royal privileges which he writes in a "book" (Heb. *sefer,* meaning writing on leather) and deposits in a sanctuary. If the account we have in 1 Samuel 8 is a guide, the text cannot have been long. More substantial was the text God commanded Jeremiah to have read in the Temple (Jer. 36:23), a scroll that was deposited in the Temple with the connivance of the Temple officials. The story may well cast light on the circumstances leading to the discovery of the "book of the covenant" found in the Temple in the time of Josiah (ca. 620 B.C.; 2 Kings 23), a text whose authenticity is validated by a prophetess, Huldah, who consults God probably by means of an oracle (2 Kings 22:13, 18). We have no means of identifying positively the text found on that occasion, although scholarly opinion most commonly takes it to have been the bulk of Deuteronomy. After the Exile (late sixth century B.C.), Ezra is sent to Jerusalem with the authority of King Artaxerxes to guide the restoration of Israel in its own land. He is described as a scribe learned in the *torah* of Moses, and he comes prepared to "study the law of the Lord, and to do it, and to teach his statutes and ordinances in Israel" (Ezra 7:10). The two traditions kept separate by Jehoshaphat are here combined: the teaching of divine law is now to be accompanied by implementation measures characteristic of royal ordinance. At the same time, the text of the *torah* comes to acquire the kind of force we associate with statute, so that verbal interpretation becomes necessary (Neh. 8:7–8).

The Covenant Code, the Priestly Code, and Deuteronomy: It is not easy to ascertain the place of the Pentateuchal laws in the history of the legal institutions of ancient Israel. The "Covenant Code" (Exod. 21–23, deriving its conventional title from Exod. 24:7) is generally regarded as the oldest. It falls into two halves, the first of which (Exod. 21:1–22:17) is formulated mainly in conditional sentences (known as the "casuistic form") wherein the protasis ("if" clause) states circumstances and the apodosis ("then" clause) the legal consequences. This is also the predominant (though not exclusive) form used in the ancient Near Eastern codes. The subject matter and tone (secular and without rhetorical ornamentation) also make it the most similar to its ancient counterpart. Parallels in content are found between all the biblical codes and those of the ancient Near East, but the Covenant Code includes one that is particularly striking in both form and content (Exod. 21:35; cf. *Laws of Eshnunna* 53), despite the impossibility of a direct literary connection. It perhaps serves as indirect evidence of the existence of Canaanite codes (thus far undiscovered), which may have served as intermediaries before the Israelites became familiar at first hand, as a result of conquest, with the legal traditions of Babylon and Assyria. The "Covenant Code" contains rules on slavery, homicide, various types of assault, death caused by animals, cattle theft, agricultural damage, deposit of property, shepherding, loan of animals, and seduction of a virgin. The rule "an eye for an eye . . ." is found earlier in the Laws of Hammurabi.

The second half of the Code (Exod. 22:18–23:19), expressed largely in the "apodictic" form (direct, second-person commands, unaccompanied by any statement of sanction), combines sacral offenses, humanitarian injunctions, standards for the administration of justice, the laws of the seventh year, the Sabbath, and the three pilgrimage festivals (see Exod. 23:14–17) and regulations regarding sacrifice; it may be significant that the ban on seething (boiling) a kid in its mother's milk is found in this latter context. It is likely that the Code as a whole was compiled from discrete sources, and it is widely believed not to have formed an original part of the Sinaitic narrative, to which it now belongs.

Much of the rest of Exodus, Leviticus, and

Numbers is called the "Priestly Code," associated with the literary source "P" of traditional biblical criticism. There is increasing recognition of the existence within it of early materials, and some contemporary scholars date the source as a whole earlier than Deuteronomy, thus well before the Exile. Very generally, the Priestly Code emphasizes religious and ritual concerns, while the Covenant Code deals with civil law and Deuteronomy shows special interest in matters of public law. But these characteristics are by no means exclusive: both the Priestly Code and Deuteronomy also deal with slavery and homicide; Deuteronomy alone deals with remarriage. Within the Priestly corpus, there is a distinguishable text in Leviticus 17–26, known as the "Holiness Code" in view of the reiterated motive for obedience to its laws: "Be Holy."

Narrative in Biblical Law: Biblical law has traditionally been studied much like modern statutory sources, with concentration on the wording of the individual legal provisions. For some, the biblical mixture of legal, ritual, and moral rules, together with the intermingling of law and narrative in the Pentateuch, is a matter to be ignored, or even explained away as representing a "primitive" stage of legal development. Today, these literary characteristics of the text are themselves the object of study and are increasingly seen as integral to the understanding of the laws themselves. One example is the "law of the altar" in Exod. 20:22–26, which some have regarded as misplaced, belonging properly to the Covenant Code (which is introduced only in Exod. 21:1). More likely, this law forms an essential part of the narrative that links the revelation of the law on Sinai with the sin of the golden calf (Exod. 32–34). The very arrangement of the Covenant Code may itself require explanation in terms of its narrative context, commencing with the theme of slavery (as does the Decalogue, which immediately precedes).

Attention to the narrative context is particularly important for the understanding of Deuteronomy, formulated as a speech made by Moses in the plains of Moab before the entry to the promised land. Whereas divine law is presented in Exodus–Numbers as the words of God to Moses, which he is commanded to transmit to the children of Israel, Deuteronomy recounts Moses' performance of that task: it is Moses telling the children of Israel what God has told him. Deuteronomy refers to itself (in the context of the law of the king, though the verses in question may well be secondary) as "a copy of this law" (Heb. *mishneh hatorah hazot*, 17:18), understood by the Septuagint as "this second law," rather than "a copy of this law" (RSV). The Greek rendering accords with the later Hebrew usage of the term and with what we find in the text. Moses does not proclaim a "copy" of Exodus–Numbers; though many of the themes of the latter are taken up, he provides in effect a supplementary revelation. The narrative confirms the status of this supplementary revelation: at the conclusion of the book, God commands the making of a further covenant in the plains of Moab "besides the covenant which he had made with them at Horeb" (Deut. 29:1). The strong association of law with covenant, wherein the observance of law becomes a term of the covenant, is characteristic of Deuteronomy and is thought by some to have been imposed by Deuteronomic editors on the Sinai narrative in Exodus: originally, it is argued, Sinai was understood as a reiteration of the patriarchal covenant to those descendants of the patriarchs who had escaped from Egypt, combined with the revelation of the Decalogue but not the Covenant Code or the Priestly laws.

Later Biblical Law: In the Persian, Hellenistic, and Roman periods (539 B.C.–A.D. 325), biblical law was the object of increasing restatement and elaboration. Deuteronomy itself had indicated the continuation of prophetic revelation of the law, in promising the coming of a prophet like Moses, who would perform the same function as Moses in mediating the transmission of divine commands (Deut. 18:15–22). Rabbinic tradition regarded this figure not as a single eschatological prophet, but as a sequence of prophets operating through history: Micah was one, Abraham (anachronistically) another. This Deuteronomic tradition was used by the Qumran community to validate its own restatement of scriptural rules. There is evidence of a similar association of Jesus with the prophet like Moses (as well as with other OT figures) in the NT; the Sermon on the Mount (where Jesus claims not to change an iota of the law, despite the antitheses; Matt. 5:18) may be viewed as a compilation of teachings claiming this same status of revealed restatement.

Judaism by the first century A.D. had become a highly diversified phenomenon, with different groups interpreting the OT in their own ways and for their own purposes. This pluralism went far beyond the content of the interpretation of particular passages. Given the different audiences being addressed, the very style of interpretation differed. Thus Philo (late first century B.C. to early first century A.D.) addresses an intellectual Greek audience in terms of allegory and philosophy; the Qumran community addresses itself as a group dissentient from the Temple establishment and viewing its redemption in terms of separation and purity; the rabbis after the destruction of the Second Temple in A.D. 70 seek to unify the people around the synagogue, the study-house, and the traditions of the pharisaic fellowships (Heb. *khavurot*). First, however, they needed to supplement the written law with an "Oral Law" that would really regulate the details of everyday existence, thus providing a focus for both unity and the concentration of religious (and other) energies.

Jesus spoke to a popular and unsophisticated audience moved by none of these considerations. His target was not the law, but rather any style of interpretation of the law that removed its immediacy as teaching to the people. There is no hint of an antithesis between law and grace in the teachings of Jesus. In some of the Pauline writings, the matter stands differently. But Pauline antinomianism was not an opposition to law per se (e.g., Rom. 7:12), rather an opposition to observance of the law as the route to divine redemption (e.g., Gal. 5:4). Paul's approach, too, was a function of his aims and his audience. Unlike Jesus, his audience was mainly gentile and his mission to convert them was likely to be impeded by insistence upon observance of the Mosaic law. ***See also*** Covenant; Jesus Christ; Moses; Paul; Pentateuch; Prophet.

Bibliography

Blenkinsopp, J. *Wisdom and Law in the Old Testament*. Oxford: Oxford University Press, 1983.

Boecker, H. J. *Law and the Administration of Justice in the Old Testament and Ancient Near East*. London: SPCK, 1980.

Carmichael, C. M. *The Laws of Deuteronomy*. Ithaca, NY: Cornell University Press, 1974.

Falk, Z. W. *Hebrew Law in Biblical Times*. Jerusalem: Wahrmann Books, 1964.

Kaye, B. N. and G. J. Wenham, eds. *Law, Morality and the Bible*. Leicester: Inter-Varsity Press, 1978.

B.S.J./P.J.A.

lawgiver. ***See*** Moses.

lawlessness, man of. ***See*** Man of Lawlessness.

lawyer. ***See*** Scribe.

laying on of hands, concretely, the activity of exerting force or doing physical violence (e.g., Gen. 22:12; Exod. 7:9; Luke 20:19; 21:12; Acts 21:17). Because of this concrete usage, the placing of one's hands on someone or something becomes a natural symbol of the transfer of physical activity and force, i.e., as a symbol of a person's past deeds and their effects, or of present power, or of both. Thus, by laying hands on the head of an animal to be sacrificed, people transfer their past deeds and the effects of those deeds on the beast to have them annihilated and/or transformed with the destruction of the animal (e.g., Exod. 29:10, 15, 19; Lev. 3:2, 8, 13; Num. 8:12). Laying hands on the sick effects the transference of the power of the healer to them (Mark 5:23; 7:23; Acts 9:12, 17), just as laying hands on children wards off negative influence, a protection due to the imparted power of the one laying on hands (Gen. 48:14; Mark 10:16). Finally, people can hand over their power and have another exercise it on their behalf, effecting this by the laying on of hands (Num. 8:10; Acts 6:6; 8:17; 1 Tim. 4:14). Those already wielding power over a group can hand that power on to others by laying on their hands (Num. 27:23; Deut. 34:9; 1 Tim. 5:22; 2 Tim. 1:6). B.J.M.

Lazarus (laz'uh-ruhs), a figure in two different passages in the Gospels. In Luke 16:19–31, Jesus tells the parable of the rich man and Lazarus; in John 11:1–44, Jesus raises his friend Lazarus from the dead. It is uncertain whether the same individual is intended in both cases, but there are apparent connections.

In the Lucan parable, Lazarus dies a poor man and is carried by angels to Abraham's bosom, while the rich man dies and is tormented in Hades. When the rich man seeks relief and is denied it, he asks Abraham to send Lazarus back to warn his five brothers, lest they meet a similar fate. But Abraham replies, "If they do not hear Moses and the prophets, neither will they be convinced if some one should rise from the dead" (Luke 16:31).

In John 11, a Lazarus does rise from the dead at the command of Jesus, and his resurrection precipitates Jesus' own death (11:45–53). But it does not result in general repentance or salvation. Seemingly, Abraham's prediction is fulfilled. Yet there is no explicit connection between the Lucan parable and the Johannine account.

The web of relationship does not, however, end there. In John, Lazarus is the brother of Mary and Martha of Bethany, a village near Jerusalem (11:1–2). In Luke (10:38–42), Jesus enters an unnamed village (hardly Bethany, however, for Jesus is presumably still in Galilee) and is entertained by the sisters, Mary and Martha, as he is also in John (12:2). In Luke, Mary sits at Jesus' feet, while Martha serves; in John, Mary anoints Jesus' feet (12:1–8; cf. Luke 7:36–50), and again Martha serves (12:2). Although Luke does not link Mary and Martha to

Jesus raises Lazarus from the dead (John 11:1–44); sixth-century mosaic at San Apollinare in Classe, Ravenna, Italy.

Lazarus, and though all the episodes are different, these sisters and a Lazarus who dies and whose resurrection is either suggested or recounted are encountered only in the Gospels of Luke and John. ***See also*** Martha; Mary.

D.M.S.

lead, a heavy, malleable, bluish-gray metal. It was Midianite booty (Num. 31:22), used for weights (Zech. 5:7) and for sinkers on fishing lines (British Museum examples, from ca. 1200 B.C.). Ezek. 22:18–20 mentions lead with other metals; 27:12 indicates the existence of Israelite trade in lead with Tarshish. Job 19:24 describes engraved tablets whose letters are lead-filled for reading clarity and permanence. Exod. 15:10 employs lead figuratively: Pharaoh's armies sink "as lead" into the waters. First-century lead sarcophagi are known from examples in Beirut's American University.

Leah (lee'uh), one of the two wives of Jacob. Little is known of her personally other than the fact that she was "weak-eyed" (Gen. 29:17, Heb. *rakkot,* possibly "tender"). She was clearly less favored than her beautiful sister and co-wife, Rachel, for whom Jacob had contracted with their father, Laban, to work seven years as a bride price (Gen. 29:18). At the bridal feast, Leah, the elder, was substituted for Rachel, and Jacob then married her. He married Rachel a week later and worked for Laban for another seven years (Gen. 29:23–30). Leah bore Jacob's first four children, Reuben, Simeon, Levi, and Judah, and ceased bearing (Gen. 29:31–35). Then childless Rachel gave her servant Bilhah to Jacob as surrogate mother, so she might have children "through her." Leah also gave her own servant Zilpah, and the two surrogates bore four sons—Bilbah bore Dan and Naphtali and Zilpah bore Gad and Asher. Rachel was clearly the dominant wife, for Leah had to give Rachel mandrakes (a fertility charm) in return for sleeping with Jacob (Gen. 30:14–16). Leah then bore two more sons, Issachar and Zebulun, and a daughter, Dinah. Rachel and Leah both agreed to accompany Jacob back to his homeland, and Leah was ultimately buried in the cave of Machpelah (Gen. 49:31).

In Ruth 4:11 Leah and Rachel are mentioned together as matriarchs of Israel. The name Leah means "cow" (and she was "cow-eyed") and Rachel means "ewe," so it is possible to speculate that the tale of the two wives of Jacob reflects the jockeying for position of sheep herders and cattle herders in the early tribes of Israel. An alternate hypothesis is that these animals were totemic insignia of groups of early tribes. We are certain only that the sons of Leah and Rachel were considered the ancestors of the tribes who constituted the members of the tribal federation (sometimes called the amphictyony) of Israel during the period of the judges. ***See also*** Rachel.

T.S.F.

leather, processed animal hides suitable as rough clothing (Elijah's girdle, 2 Kings 1:8; John the Baptist's girdle, Matt. 3:4; Mark 1:6) or as fine accouterments (the shoes of Ezek. 16:10 were of the material [KJV: "badger's skin"]). Leather was also employed in covering the tabernacle (Exod. 25:5, RSV: "goatskins"). While the variety of animal hides usable was large, preparation involved scraping the hair and flesh from the material, then treating it for durability, flexibility, and even fluid-proofing. It degenerates readily once discarded, so finds of intact ancient leather are archaeologically rare and important. Some of the Dead Sea Scrolls were written on leather.

R.S.B.

leaven, a fermenting agent (like yeast), which in biblical times was normally added to a batch of bread dough by using an unbaked portion of dough from the previous batch. However, the custom of nomads was to eat unleavened bread and evidence of this is found in the OT (Gen. 19:3; Judg. 6:19; 1 Sam. 28:24, which perhaps represent occasions of special bedouin hospitality).

Leavened bread was prohibited in sacrifices that went on the altar (Lev. 2:4). The reason for this was that no leaven could be burned, nor could honey (Lev. 2:11). These both caused fermentation and thus appeared to have a life of their own that must not be destroyed. So leaven is the vital force of the vegetable world as blood is of the animal, which also was forbidden to be burnt. Leavened bread was permitted for the thank offering (Lev. 7:13) and for the first fruits of the wheat harvest (Lev. 23:7), but these were not burned on the altar (Lev. 7:14). To understand Amos 4:5, it should be noted that the word there commonly translated "offer" properly means "burn."

The Feast of Unleavened Bread owes its name to the fact that all leaven was avoided during its seven days (Exod. 12:15). Scholars believe that originally this feast was distinct from Passover. It was an agricultural celebration, first observed in Palestine (Josh. 5:11–12) and probably adopted from the Canaanites. It marked the gathering of the first crop and so a new beginning. Therefore only the newly reaped grain was eaten, with no leaven from the previous year's harvest in it. Later, however, when Passover and the Feast of Unleavened Bread had been combined, the eating of unleavened bread was interpreted as a memorial of what had happened at the Exodus (Exod. 13:7–8).

In rabbinical literature, leaven was viewed as causing decay and so became a symbol of evil and the corruption of human nature. This idea is reflected in the NT in Jesus' sayings about the leaven of Pharisees, Sadducees, and Herod (Mark 8:15 and parallels) and in Paul's attack on Corinthian laxity and Galatian circumcising (1 Cor. 5:68; Gal. 5:9). But the positive concept of leaven as a powerful life-force also appears in Jesus' parable of the growth of the kingdom (Matt. 13:33; Luke 13:20–21). ***See also*** Feasts, Festivals, and Fasts; Passover, The. J.R.P.

Lebanon, the name of a mountain range parallel to the eastern Mediterranean coast. It has also given its name to the modern Republic of Lebanon, created during the French mandate of Syria between World Wars I and II. In antiquity Lebanon was populated by Canaanites and was the homeland of the Phoenicians. The name derives from a Hebrew word for "white" and refers to the snow-capped peaks of the range (Jer. 18:14). The Lebanon mountains begin at the northern border of Palestine and extend northward approximately a hundred miles. The highest peak of this rugged range is over 9,850 feet high. On the western slope of the range the coastal zone is narrow and the mountains make communications inland difficult at best. Narrow, steep valleys and small rivers run down to the sea. The northernmost river is Nahr el-Kabir, in antiquity the Eleutherus, and in the south is the Litani River. They and others are fed by heavy annual precipitation (between 40 and 60 inches in the mountains).

The Lebanon mountains were famous not only for their beautiful white peaks but for their cedar forests (1 Kings 4:33; 2 Kings 14:9; Pss. 92:12; 104:16). These tall and beautiful trees were sought by many peoples in the ancient world. The Egyptians imported cedar wood as early as the third millennium B.C. and Byblos became the primary port where timber was obtained. Consequently it was under strong Egyptian cultural influence during the third and second millennia B.C. Rulers from Mesopotamia also took timber from Lebanon for their temples. King Solomon used cedars of Lebanon in the construction of the Temple in Jerusalem (1 Kings 5:6–10; 6:15–20) and in his palace (1 Kings 7:2–3). Today only a few stands of cedars remain.

To the east, running parallel to the Lebanon mountains is the Biqa‘ Valley, classical Coelesyria (Lat., "hollow Syria"), and beyond, the Anti-Lebanon mountain range, dominated by Mount Hermon at its southern end. The high Biqa‘ is a fertile and well-watered river valley

The cedars of the Lebanon mountain range provided abundant timber for the ancient Near East; few remain today.

drained by two main streams: the Orontes that runs from Baalbek to northern Syria and the Litani that flows down the center of the southern Biqaʻ and then cuts westward to empty into the Mediterranean Sea.

In antiquity the two main areas of human settlement were the coastal plain and the Biqaʻ Valley. Paleolithic (to ca. 25,000–12,000 B.C.) remains have been found at a number of sites along the coast, the most important being modern Kasir Akil. Neolithic (10,000–4000 B.C.) settlement is well represented at Byblos and sites along the banks of the Litani River in the Biqaʻ valley. Along the coast in the Bronze and Iron Ages (ca. 3000–333 B.C.), numerous cities are known from ancient texts and archaeological excavations. Byblos is the best known, and other port cities include Tyre, Zarephath, Sidon, Beirut, Batrum, and Tripoli. At the beginning of the Iron Age the population became known as Phoenicians and their cities emerged as the leading maritime centers of the Mediterranean in the wake of the collapse of the Late Bronze Age trade. But the coastal cities never successfully united except when Tyre controlled Sidon and southern Phoenicia in the ninth and eighth centuries B.C.

Despite its renown for fruitfulness, relatively small portions of the Biqaʻ valley are profitably farmed even today, and settlement was never very dense. Partly as a result of the great diversity of farming conditions, agriculture was filled with risks and insecurity, and there were periods when sheep and goat nomadism increased. After a peak of settlement in the Early Bronze Age (third millennium B.C.) there was a gradual rural decline. In the Bronze Age about a dozen small towns were strung out the length of the valley in the rich flood plains and by springs; none were much larger than 12 acres. Political and cultural fragmentation was common. Two cities known from Egyptian sources were Kadesh in the north and Kumidi in the south. Kadesh, identified as modern Tell Nebi Mend, is on the bank of the Orontes River and was the site of the famous battle between Rameses II and the Hittites in the thirteenth century B.C. Kumidi is modern Kamid el-Loz, located a few miles east of the Litani River. Cuneiform tablets and public buildings from the Late Bronze Age have been discovered there. In Roman times Baalbek was the important sanctuary of Heliopolis in the Biqaʻ.

Significant settlement of the highlands of the Lebanon mountains only began in Roman times when deforestation went hand in hand with population increases. In a system of intensive terrace farming, a variety of cash crops were planted at different elevations and harvested sequentially. Grapes, olives, apples and other orchard crops were most important. This type of agriculture required investments of capital, time, and labor, and encouraged the development of stable but closed communities. In the early modern era mulberry orchards became important as part of silk production but the industry collapsed in the early nineteenth century. The mountains have become a home for two minority groups, the Christian Maronites and the Druse. Other prominent groups in modern Lebanon are Sunni and Shiʻite Muslims.

Bibliography

Brown, J. P. *The Lebanon and Phoencia. Vol. 1: The Physical Setting and the Forest.* Beirut: American University of Beirut, 1969.

Marfoe, L. "The Integrative Transformation: Patterns of Sociopolitical Organization in Southern Syria." *Bulletin of the American Schools of Oriental Research* 234 (1979): 1–42. T.L.M.

Lebbaeus (le-bee'us), an alternate name in some texts for Thaddeus (Matt. 10:3). ***See also*** Judas; Thaddeus.

leech (KJV: "horseleach"), a bloodsucking parasite of the class *Hirudinea* of which several varieties are common in Palestine. It is used as a symbol of insatiable appetite in Prov. 30:15.

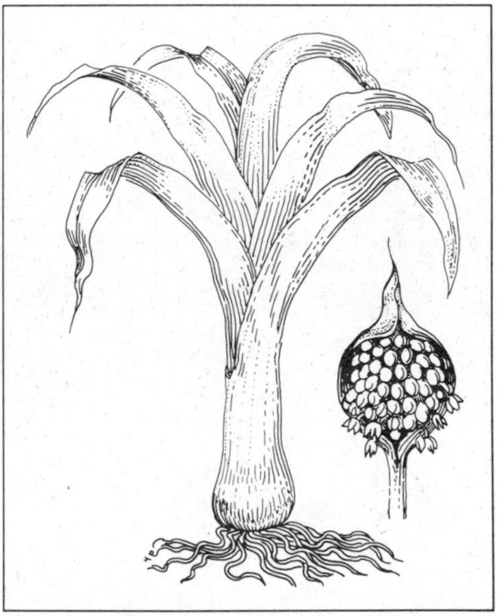

Leek.

leeks, the biennial herb *Allium porrum*, similar to garlic and onion. A staple in the ancient Near Eastern diet, leeks were reportedly yearned for by the Hebrews while in the wilderness (Num. 11:5) as a symbol of more abundant life.

lees, the residue left in a wine container during fermentation and aging. Wine with the lees in it was considered a preferable product to new wine (Isa. 25:6) and was also used as a metaphor for sluggish richness (Jer. 48:11; Zeph. 1:12) which deserved to be disturbed.

legion, a large unit of soldiers in the Roman army. With Augustus' reorganization of the Roman army a legion was composed of 5,400 to 6,000 men and a like number of auxiliary troops. The standing army comprised twenty-eight legions until A.D. 9 when three were lost. They were not replaced until two new legions were raised at the end of Caligula's reign (A.D. 37–41) in preparation for the invasion of Britain. Tacitus (*Annals* 4.5) gives the following deployment of the legions for A.D. 23: eight along the Rhine; six in the Balkans and along the Danube; three in Spain; two in Africa; and two in Egypt and four in Syria to watch over the eastern frontiers.

The auxiliary regiments consisted of infantry cohorts and cavalry recruited from among the subject peoples. Sometimes they were commanded by Roman officers and sometimes by their own tribal leaders. Trajan increased the strength of the Roman army to thirty legions.

"Legion" ("for we are many") appears as the name of a demon exorcised by Jesus in Mark 5:9 (cf. Luke 8:30). Jesus at his capture claimed God would send more than twelve legions of angels to rescue him if he so desired (Matt. 26:53). P.P.

Lehi (lee'hī; Heb., "jawbone"), a place name, the site where the Philistines camped as they sought Samson after he had burned their grain (Judg. 15:9). Samson was bound and brought to the Philistines at Lehi but broke free and killed 1,000 Philistines with the jawbone of a donkey. To mark the occasion, the place was named Ramath-lehi meaning the "height, or high place, of the jawbone" (Judg. 15:14–17). The name probably refers more to the area where the exploit occurred, including the spring named En-hakkore, rather than to a specific settlement (note Judg. 15:9, 19). It was probably located somewhere in the lowlands of southwestern Judah. The occurrence of the name in 2 Samuel (23:11) is textually uncertain and some translators read "in a troop" for "Lehi." ***See also*** Samson. D.R.B.

Lemuel (lem'yo͞o-el; Heb., "belonging to God"), the king of Massa and the addressee of his mother's wisdom in Prov. 31:1–9. The Septuagint understands "Lemuel" and "Massa" as common nouns; thus the RSV margin translates the latter in 31:1 as "oracle" ("the words of King Lemuel, the oracle which his mother taught him").

lending. ***See*** Debt; Loan.

Lent, among Christians originally the period of prebaptismal preparation, later of public penance. Finally it became a forty-day devotional preparation for Easter traditionally based on Jesus' wilderness fast (Mark 1:13).

Lentil.

lentil *(Lens culinaris)*, a plant of the legume family cultivated widely in the Near East since prehistoric times. The small lens-shaped seeds are an especially nutritious food providing both protein and carbohydrates. It was a common component of soups and stews (Gen. 25:34) as well as a flour base for breads (Ezek. 4:9).

leopard *(Panthera pardus)*, a large cat with characteristic spots. The leopard represents a great danger to shepherds and their flocks. It is at home in mountainous terrain, especially Mount Hermon and Lebanon (Song of Sol. 4:8). A few leopards are still to be found in Israel and Jordan. Hab. 1:8 mentions horses that are swifter than the leopard, but this probably refers instead to the cheetah *(Acionyx jubatus)*, another large cat once present in the area and trained for use in hunting.

leprosy, in the OT a disorder affecting humans, fabrics, and houses. There are different types of leprosy that afflict persons (Lev. 13). Though it is not clear what these skin diseases are, it is certain that they are not modern leprosy (Hansen's disease). The plague in fabrics and houses is described as greenish or reddish spots (Lev. 13:49; 14:37), thus indicating a type of mold or mildew.

Persons or objects afflicted with leprosy can pollute others. Anyone who enters a leprous house must bathe. If a person tarries there by eating or lying down, both bathing and laundering are necessary (Lev. 14:46–47). Surprisingly, the Bible says nothing about the effect of a leper's impurity. The leper certainly polluted at least like a polluted house and probably like one who has an abnormal bodily discharge (Lev. 15:2–12; cf. *m. Zabim* 5:6).

A leper is to be excluded from habitations (Lev. 13:45–46; cf. Num. 12:15; 2 Kings 7:3–4). When the person recovers from the affliction, purification rites are performed (Lev. 14:2–20, 21–32). Similar rites are performed for a renovated house (14:48–53; note that these rites are not as extensive as the healed leper's). These purification rites are not for the removal of leprosy, but only for the removal of residual ritual impurity (see Mark 1:44). A rite for the curing of leprosy is found in the case of Naaman immersing in the Jordan seven times (2 Kings 5: 10, 14).

Fabrics incorrigibly infected with leprosy are to be burned (Lev. 13:52, 55, 57) and building materials so infected must be discarded outside the habitation (14:40, 41, 45). There is some evidence that leprosy was considered a punishment from God for sin (cf. Num. 12:10–15; 2 Kings 5:27; 15:5; 2 Chron. 26:20–21).

The Gospels report that Jesus healed people afflicted with leprosy (e.g., Matt. 8:1–4; Luke 17:11–19) and he commissioned his disciples to do the same (Matt. 10:8). Jesus is also reported to have visited the home of Simon the leper (Mark 14:3), perhaps one of those he had healed. The data do not enable one to determine if this "leprosy" was Hansen's disease.

D.P.W.

Lesbos (lez′bohs), a northeastern Aegean island. Paul stopped at Mitylene on Lesbos en route to Jerusalem (Acts 20:14). ***See also*** Mitylene.

letter, a form of literary communication. The number of letters discovered in the Middle East and the Mediterranean basin within the last century shows that the letter was one of the most ancient and common forms of communication. Even these discoveries do not reflect how extensive letter writing was, because only letters written on decay-resistant materials or those preserved by a dry climate, such as papyrus letters in Egypt, have survived. Though many were written by professional scribes, the percentage written by common people indicates that illiteracy was not as prevalent in the Hellenistic culture as scholars once imagined.

There was an organized postal system as early as the Persian Empire (sixth century B.C.), but it existed only for government business and not for private correspondence. Wealthy families used slaves or couriers and common people relied on caravans, friends, or passing strangers who were traveling in the direction of the recipient of the letter.

Clay tablets from Ras-Shamra, El-Amarna, Lachish, Babylon, Mari, etc., throw light on letter writing in the OT period. Jewish letters found at Elephantine, an island in the Nile River near the first cataract on which there was a Jewish colony in the fifth century B.C., as well as other Aramaic letters on skins and potsherds, show what letter writing was like in the period immediately following that of the OT. Of the OT letters, all are embedded in OT documents and only their message is actually quoted.

Since no OT document is written in letter form, it is surprising that the letter became the largest literary category in the NT, i.e., twenty-one of the twenty-seven documents are written in epistolary form. A partial explanation of the prominence of letters in the NT is the way in which Christian leaders such as Paul employed letters as a means of instructing communities under their supervision when the leaders could not be present in person.

Greek papyrus letters, which have been discovered in great number in Egypt, help us understand Greek letter writing at the time of the NT. By comparison with these letters, NT letters tend to be longer and somewhat more literary. In the case of Paul, for example, the religious nature of his correspondence colored the manner in which he wrote letters and contributed to the creation of his recognizable style. He intended that his letters be read aloud to his communities when they were at worship. This is indicated by the manner in which he substitutes prayers of thanksgiving and/or blessing for conventional epistolary phrases at the beginning and end of the letter, and by the citation of hymns, creeds, Scripture, and catechetical instruction in the body. ***See also*** Epistle; Ostraca; Salutations; Writing.

J.L.W.

Letter of Jeremiah, the, a writing attributed to Jeremiah (late seventh–early sixth centuries B.C.) but composed most likely in the fourth century B.C. in order to provide Jews with arguments to counter their gentile neighbors' belief in the reality of idols. It is more of a homily than a letter, arising from Jeremiah's advice to the exiles concerning idolatry—"Thus shall you say to them: 'The gods who did not make the heavens and the earth shall perish from the earth and from under the heavens' " (Jer. 10:11)—as well as from his correspondence with them in Jeremiah 29. The work defies organization or outline. It is punctuated with the refrain, "Since you know by these things that they are not gods, do not fear them" (see vv. 16, 23, 29, 40, 44, 52, 56, 65, and 69), and includes all of the stock polemics that Jews directed against idols (see Jer. 10:2–16; Pss. 115:4–8; 135:15–18; Isa. 40: 18–20; 41:6–7; 46:1–7; Bel and the Dragon). They are helpless, fabricated by human beings out of wood, stone, and metal, subject to decay, rust, and rot, powerless to deliver anyone from danger, and served by impure and dishonest priests and priestesses who engage in immoral activities like cultic prostitution and theft of offerings.

The Letter was probably composed in Hebrew but has been preserved only in Greek. Its place of composition may have been Babylonia, since it is well informed concerning Mesopotamian religious practices. Some manuscripts of the Septuagint (LXX) treat it as a separate book following Lamentations, while others, along with the Vulgate, include it at the end of Baruch. For Protestants, it is part of the Apocrypha, while Catholics number it among the deuterocanonical books as a part of Baruch. ***See also*** Apocrypha, Old Testament; Baruch; Idol; Jeremiah, The Book of. D.W.S.

Letters, Johannine. ***See*** John, The Letters of.

Letters, pastoral. ***See*** Timothy, The First and Second Letters of Paul to, and Titus, The Letter of Paul to.

Letters of Clement. ***See*** Clement, Letters of.

Letters of Ignatius. ***See*** Ignatius, Letters of.

Levant (le-vant'), a term coined by early travelers to the Holy Land and more frequently used today in geological discussions to designate the lands of the eastern Mediterranean. The Levant Rift Valley, sometimes referred to as the Jordan rift, is part of an extensive fault system which was formed over a long period of time. This rift shaped the topography of the region and serves as a reminder of geography's influence on the life of a region. ***See also*** Historical Geography of the Bible; Jordan River, The.

Levi (lee'vī; Heb., "joined"). **1** The third son of Jacob (Gen. 29:34). **2** The tribe descended from 1. Together with Reuben, Simeon, Judah, Issachar, and Zebulun it formed a group of six tribes whose special relationship was expressed by their common descent from Jacob's wife Leah (Gen. 35:23). Originally, Levi must have been a full tribe, since it appears in some lists of the twelve tribes; but in others it has disappeared and, unlike all the other tribes, nowhere in the OT is it given any allocation of territory (Josh. 13–19). On the contrary, it is said that its members have no share in the land, because they have been chosen by God to serve him as priests (Josh. 18:7). So the Levites are viewed as the tribe of Levi (Deut. 18:1) who are given a number of towns to live in (Josh. 21), but also, when later priests and Levites come to be distinguished, all the cultic personnel are considered to be descended from Levi.

It seems likely that, early in its history, some disaster overtook the tribe of Levi. This is perhaps reflected in Genesis 34, which tells of an attack by Simeon and Levi on Shechem, in the neighborhood in which they may have originally settled. But Jacob is depicted as fearing that their action will cause his destruction (Gen. 34:30), and in Genesis 49, apparently referring to the same episode, Jacob is shown as promising them that they will be divided and scattered in Israel (Gen. 49:7). As a result of this, Levi lost its "secular" character and became the priestly tribe of the later Blessing of Moses (Deut. 33:8–11; it is noteworthy that v. 11 speaks of violent hostility to the tribe). However, this reconstruction remains hypothetical, and whether such an evolution of the tribe of Levi is historically correct and how far there is any factual connection between it and the Levites is still disputed. ***See also*** Levites. J.R.P.

Leviathan, a great, mythological monster. In Ugaritic mythology, Leviathan (appearing by the name "Lothan") is one of the primeval sea monsters who battles against Baal on the side of Mot (the god of the underworld) and who is ultimately defeated. This mythological tradition was adopted and transformed in the Bible where God appears as the victor over the sea monsters, Ps. 74:13–14: ". . . thou didst break the heads of the dragons on the waters. Thou didst crush the heads of Leviathan, thou didst give him as food for the creatures of the wilderness" (cf. Job 3:8; 26:12–13; 41:1–34; Ps. 104:26). The references to God "playing" with Leviathan (Ps. 104:26; Job 41:5) are explainable on the basis of God's omnipotence which reduces this mighty rebellious dragon to a plaything. The mythological pagan drama is ultimately transposed in Israel into a moral lesson. The future and final destruction of Leviathan becomes a symbol in Isaiah (27:1) for the death of the wicked, to be succeeded by the redemption of Israel (26:20–21; 27:2–13). ***See also*** Baal; Tiamat; Ugarit. J.U.

levirate law. ***See*** Marriage.

Levites (lee'vīts), generally, those belonging to the tribe of Levi, although this may not be the original meaning of the term. In some passages, Levite seems to be a description rather than a tribal name. A Levite is mentioned who was a Judahite (Judg. 17:7) and who appears as a kind of priest (Judg. 17:13); we may compare the designation of Aaron as "the Levite" and a spokesman for God (Exod. 4:14–16). The term may be from the Hebrew root meaning "to join" (Num. 18:2, 4), denoting originally a group whose members were particularly closely attached to God (Num. 3:12; 8:16). The Levites' zeal for God's cause is stressed in Exod. 32:25–28 (cf. Deut. 33:9), which tells how they were ordained for it (Exod. 32:29). Perhaps, then, Levites and the tribe of Levi were once two different groups, but, when the tribe disappeared, the

Levites were confused with them because of the similarity of the name.

In any case, wherever the Levites appear they are solely priests, whose function was not only to sacrifice but also to transmit and administer the divine law (Deut. 17:18; 33:10). In Deuteronomy, they comprise the whole priesthood and live in various towns in the country, perhaps in special levitical cities (Josh. 21:1–42). Because of its demand for the centralization of worship, Deuteronomy makes provision for the Levites to come to the central sanctuary and to join the priesthood there (Deut. 18:6–8). However, it would seem that the Jerusalem authorities would not accept them as true priests and they were reduced to a subordinate position in the cultic staff (2 Kings 23:8–9). This was because the country Levites were considered to have become tainted with Canaanite idolatry, for which they are condemned in Ezek. 44:10–14, where the priesthood is confined to the sons of Zadok, the Jerusalem hierarchy, and the Levites are demoted to Temple servants, looking after the Temple, maintaining order in it, acting as doorkeepers, and being responsible for slaying the sacrificial animals. Here for the first time we meet the clear division between priests and Levites that became normative after the Exile (late sixth century B.C. on) and that, in the postexilic priestly tradition, was attributed to the time of Moses (Num. 18:2–6).

Postexilic developments, however, greatly increased the role of the Levites and restored much of their former importance. Both they and the priests proper were now given a common descent from Levi, and the levitical order came to include all the Temple personnel other than the priests. Our fullest information about the Levites at this period comes from 1 and 2 Chronicles, which emphasize their high position and the importance of their duties, sometimes even over against the priests (2 Chron. 29:34). They alone may carry the Ark, the Temple's holiest object (1 Chron. 15:11–15). In addition, they provided the music for the services (1 Chron. 16:4–37), and two collections of psalms in the Psalter are attributed to groups into which the Levites were divided, Asaph (Pss. 50, 70–83) and Korah (Pss. 42–49). They retained their ancient functions of administering the law (1 Chron. 23:4; 2 Chron. 19:8–11) and of teaching it to the people (2 Chron. 17:7–9; 35:3); many of the speeches in 1 and 2 Chronicles may reflect the form of contemporary levitical sermons. The Levites retained their high status until the end of the Temple (A.D. 70), as Luke 10:32 indicates. ***See also*** Ark; Deuteronomy; Levi; Zadok.

J.R.P.

Levitical cities. ***See*** Priests; Levites.

Leviticus (luh-vit'i-kuhs), the third book in the Pentateuch of the OT. It gets its name from the title of the work, *Liber Leviticus*, in the Vulgate, which in turn is a translation of the name given to it in the Septuagint. So the name is descriptive, "the levitical book," that is, concerned with the Temple personnel, all of whom were supposed to be descended from Levi.

Leviticus was not originally a self-contained unity but formed part of a continuous whole comprising what are now the first four books of the OT. Its kernel is chaps. 8–10, which continue the narrative from Exod. 29:35. These chapters are mainly concerned with the consecration of the priests, so chaps. 1–7 were inserted to provide the ritual directions for the sacrifices offered on this occasion. The distinctive mark of the worshiping community thus constituted was its "holiness," that is, its being set apart from all other peoples to belong solely to God. Hence there follows in chaps. 11–15 a set of laws to maintain the purity of the nation, culminating in the description in chap. 16 of the Day of Atonement, which removed every trace of uncleanness. Finally, the remaining chapters consist largely of the so-called Holiness Code, because of the repeated refrain "you shall be holy; for I the Lord your God am holy" (Lev. 19:2), in which what being the holy nation involves is spelled out for ordinary life.

Present Form: In its present form, the work represents a priestly compilation made in Jerusalem from about 500 B.C. onward, reflecting the ritual practice of the Second Temple, built in 515, but it contains much earlier material. Not only are the sacrificial regulations of chaps. 1–7 and the Holiness Code older, independent entities that the final editors took over, but the whole book is made up of previously existing legal collections, which probably represent the traditions of various Israelite sanctuaries during the monarchical period (ca. 1050–586 B.C.). But much of the material in these collections is very old, sometimes going back to Israel's earliest days and preserving concepts and

OUTLINE OF CONTENTS

Leviticus

I. Sacrifices from the people (1:1–7:38)
  A. Burnt offerings (1:1–17)
  B. Cereal offerings (2:1–16)
  C. Sin offerings (3:1–6:30)
  D. Guilt offerings (7:1–27)
  E. Peace offerings (7:28–38)
II. Consecration of Aaron (8:1–10:20)
III. Laws of purity (11:1–16:34)
  A. Individual purity (11:1–15:33)
  B. Atonement ritual (16:1–34)
IV. Laws of holiness (17:1–27:34)

practices different from the dominant postexilic priestly outlook.

Its Nature and Purpose: Its relation to the historical situation in which it was produced is the key for understanding the nature and purpose of Leviticus. According to many scholars, it is a response to the destructions of the kingdoms of Israel (721 B.C.) and Judah (586 B.C.) and the subsequent Exile. Its priestly authors wanted to provide a program for the reconstruction of the restored community and they did this in several ways.

First, they collected and preserved the fundamental laws that were the basis of the people's life but were in danger of being lost because of the disruption caused by foreign invasions. All law was now represented as the direct commandment of God himself given for all time at Mount Sinai at the very beginning of Israel's existence as a nation (Lev. 27:34).

Second, they explained to the people the reasons for the tragedy that had befallen them. Here they adopted and developed the teaching of the great pre-exilic prophets, which had largely gone unheeded. The disaster had been sent by God himself, as a just punishment for Israel's constant disobedience to the terms of the Sinai covenant they had once accepted (Lev. 26:44–45). The distinctive way in which the priestly school presented this message was by setting out the covenant laws, to bring home the number of ways the Israelites had failed to observe them.

Third, the priestly school aimed to ensure that the laws were faithfully kept for the future, as the only guarantee of national and religious survival (Lev. 26:3–13). So reiterated teaching and exhortation, aimed to bring this about, is a marked feature of the priestly source; the Holiness Code in particular has the form of an extended sermon on this theme. Further, ancient regulations were given a new interpretation as the basis of a community under priestly direction. Great importance was now attached to the Sabbath (Lev. 23:3), the Sabbath and Jubilee years (Lev. 25:1–22), and the purity laws (Lev. 11–15) as distinctive marks of the nation. Above all, a new interpretation was given to the whole sacrificial system and the one sanctuary where it is carried out. The purpose of all sacrifices was now to make atonement, to nullify the disastrous effects of sin on both individual and community, and so there is a much greater emphasis than before on the sacrifices that primarily achieve this, the sin offering and the guilt offering (Lev. 4:1–6:7).

The levitical code regulated national life until the destruction of the Temple and the cessation of actual sacrifices (A.D. 70). But the view in Leviticus of sin, guilt, and sacrifice lived on as the mould in which the NT writers, especially the author of the Letter to the Hebrews, understood the death of Christ as the one all-sufficient, atoning sacrifice. In later Judaism, attention focused primarily on the laws of cleanliness and uncleanliness, which were much developed in rabbinic literature, as the key to the life of purity. ***See also*** Pentateuch; Purity.

Bibliography

Noth, M. *Leviticus*. Philadelphia: Westminster, 1977.

Porter, J. R. *Leviticus*. Cambridge: Cambridge University Press, 1976.

Wenham, G. J. *The Book of Leviticus*. Grand Rapids, MI: Wm. B. Eerdmans, 1979. J.R.P.

Libertines. ***See*** Freedman.

liberty, the theme of the story of the Exodus, God's liberation of the people of Israel out of Egyptian bondage; it is a central feature of the OT and a dominant biblical theme. During the Exile the language of political liberation (deliver, redeem, bring out, lead forth) became normative for describing God's saving purposes for Israel, especially in Deuteronomy and Deutero-Isaiah (Isa. 61:1).

Liberation from bondage also shaped the social consciousness of the people through laws insisting that Israel translate her own experience into a concern for the poor, the oppressed, the weak, and the enslaved (Deut. 15:12–18). This concern was formalized in the concept of the Sabbatical Year (Exod. 21:2–6) and later in the Jubilee Year, the "Year of Liberty" (Ezek. 46:17). Though perhaps only a theoretical ideal, every fiftieth or Jubilee Year liberty was proclaimed throughout the land (Lev. 25:10) and enslaved Jews and foreclosed property were emancipated from masters and creditors.

The concept of liberty became more individual in the psalms of lament, where God is called on to liberate the psalmist from the tyranny of oppression (Ps. 69) or sin (Ps. 51). The religious significance of liberty deepens in Ps. 119:45, where it is associated with obedience to the law, and in Deutero-Isaiah, where Israel, newly emancipated from the Exile, is commissioned to liberate those imprisoned in ignorance of the one true God (Isa. 42:6–7).

In the NT, John's Gospel often describes salvation in terms of freedom (John 8:32), but it is in the Pauline Letters that liberty becomes a central theological motif. For Paul, the human predicament is defined by bondage to sin (Rom. 6:20) and consequently by bondage to the law (Rom. 7:6) and to decay (Rom. 8:21). Though the law is holy, the person who encounters it is enslaved to sin. Human nature is so corrupt that even when the law is embraced as a means of escaping from sin and achieving salvation, the effort is doomed to fail (Rom. 7:7–20). The only result is a new, futile slavery to the law and death remains the inevitable outcome (Rom. 7:24). This cycle is broken by God's redemptive act in Christ. Through the atoning death on the cross, sin is remitted. Divine grace then replaces legal demand and the tyranny of the law is broken as well as the finality of death.

This new liberty, however, is not merely freedom *from* past masters; it is also freedom *for* new obedience to God so complete that Paul can paradoxically speak of a new bondage replacing the old, bondage to righteousness and God (Rom. 6:18–22), which has as its consequence life, not death. Elsewhere Paul uses a different metaphor, suggesting that the baptismal gift of the Holy Spirit indicates that the believer is no longer a slave, but fully a child of God, and the law can be fulfilled out of responsive love instead of enslaving necessity (Gal. 4:1–7). Thus the Spirit becomes a sign of liberty (2 Cor. 3:17). ***See also*** Cross; Exile, Exodus; Feasts, Festivals, and Fasts; Holy Spirit, The; Isaiah, The Book of; Law; Paul. J.M.B.

Libnah (lib'nah). **1** One of the Israelite camps in the wilderness after the Israelites left Egypt (Num. 33:20, 21). Its location is unknown.

2 A city of Judah that Joshua took during his southern campaign when he besieged Lachish, Eglon, Hebron, and Debir (Josh. 10:29–39; 12:15). It was named as one of the levitical cities (Josh. 21:13; 1 Chron. 6:57). Hamutal, one of Josiah's wives and the mother of Jehoahaz (2 Kings 23:31) and Zedekiah (2 Kings 24:18; Jer. 52:1), was the daughter of Jeremiah of Libnah.

After F. J. Bliss and R. A. S. Macalister excavated the northwestern Judean site Tell es-Safi in 1899, it was identified with Libnah. There was heavy Iron Age occupation on the mound, especially 1000–587 B.C., and Libnah (Heb., "white"), Tell es-Safi (Arabic, "white mound"), and the crusader fortress Blanche Garde (French, "white citadel") could all be associated with the white cliffs in the area. But as early as 1924 the American archaeologist and biblical scholar W. F. Albright placed Libnah at modern Tell Bornat, the preferred site today. Tell Bornat is not as far north as Tell es-Safi and is closer to the towns of Judah named as being located in the same district (Josh. 15:42). Its position near the western border may have made possible a revolt against King Jehoram while he was dealing with the rebellious Edomites to the east (2 Kings 8:22; 2 Chron. 21:10). Tell Bornat lies about five miles north of the most important city in the area, Lachish, and the Assyrian king Sennacherib turned to Libnah after the siege of Lachish in 701 B.C. (2 Kings 19:8; Isa. 37:8). ***See also*** Lachish; Sennacherib. N.L.L.

Libni (lib'nī; Heb., "white"). **1** The son of Gershon (Gershom) and the grandson of Levi (Exod. 6:17; 1 Chron. 6:20); he was the ancestral head of a major subdivision of the Gershonite clan of Levites, the Libnites (Num. 3:21; 26:58). He is also called Ladan (1 Chron. 23:7–9). **2** A Levite, the son of Mahli and the grandson of Merari (1 Chron. 6:29). ***See also*** Ladan.

Libya (lib'ee-uh), the portion of the north African coast of the Mediterranean Sea just west of Egypt. Ezekiel expected its destruction (Ezek. 30:5) together with Egypt and its neighbors. Its language was heard at Pentecost (Acts 2:10). Its people participated in the invasion of Judah led by Pharaoh Shishak of Egypt (2 Chron. 2:12) against Rehoboam about 918 B.C. Similar forces were later defeated by Asa of Judah (2 Chron. 16:8). Daniel (11:43) saw Libyans serving the "king of the north" together with Egyptians and Ethiopians, and Nahum recalled their alliance with Egypt against Assyria's invasion (3:9). Frequently associated with Put, Lud, Ethiopia, and Egypt, they figured directly in the defense against the Sea Peoples mounted by Egypt and were at times a dominant influence in Egyptian politics. ***See also*** Lubim; Sea Peoples. R.S.B.

life, in the OT a term generally meaning life on this earth. It frequently refers to one's lifespan (Deut. 4:9; Jer. 52:33) and is often contrasted to death (Gen. 47:19). Death is understood as the end of life; no soul or part of a person lives on after death. Ezekiel speaks of resurrection of the nation to renewed existence on this earth (Ezek. 37), but individual life after death is mentioned only very rarely and in late writings (e.g., Dan. 12:2).

God is the living God (Jer. 10:10), who alone creates human existence on earth and brings life and death to individuals (Gen. 2:7; 1 Sam. 2:6). Life is God's basic blessing (Deut. 30:19). Sometimes life means not only survival but health and well-being (Prov. 3:13–18). In Deuteronomy and wisdom literature, life is associated with keeping the commandments of God (Deut. 30:15–20; Prov. 4:4).

In the NT, life generally means life after death, eternal life, but otherwise the NT continues OT understandings of the term. In the synoptic Gospels, eternal life is associated with living a moral life and helping those in need (Matt. 19:16–19 and parallels; 25:31–46). Receiving eternal life is not easy and may cost a great deal (Matt. 7:14; Mark 9:42–48). It is associated with following Jesus (Mark 10:28–31).

For Paul, keeping the commandments brings not life but death (Rom. 7:10). Eternal life comes through Christ; baptism into Christ's death and resurrection enables the Christian to walk in newness of life (Rom. 6:4). "I have been crucified with Christ; it is no longer I who live, but Christ who lives in me" (Gal. 2:20). Eternal life begins in the present—the Christian lives to God by the Spirit—and will continue after death (Rom. 6:13; Gal. 5:25).

"Life" occurs particularly frequently in the Gospel of John. As God is the living God, so God has granted Jesus to have life in himself (John 5:

26) and to bring life to humanity (John 6:33, 51; 10:10). Jesus is "the bread of life," "the light of life," "the resurrection and the life," "the way, and the truth, and the life" (John 6:48; 8:12; 11:25; 14:6). The one believing in Jesus receives eternal life both in the present ("has passed from death to life," John 5:24) and in the future ("I will raise him up at the last day," John 6:40). ***See also*** Death; Eternal Life; Immortality; Resurrection. J.D.

Life, Book of, a roster of names kept in heaven of those who will survive the manifestation of God's wrath (Mal. 3:16–4:3). In the book of Revelation (21:27), only those whose names are in the Book of Life will enter the new Jerusalem.

life, eternal. ***See*** Eternal Life.

life, everlasting. ***See*** Eternal Life.

life, future. ***See*** Eschatology; Eternal Life; Hades; Heaven; Hell.

light, in most religions and cultures a symbol of God, godliness, or supernatural illumination. The Bible is no exception. God is described as covering himself with light as with a garment (Ps. 104:2). His countenance is light (Ps. 4:6), and even the darkness is not night to him (Ps. 139:12). In the beginning, God says, "Let there be light" (Gen. 1:3); there was light, and the creation narrative is underway. At the end of Revelation, the Lord God is said to be the light of his servants (Rev. 22:5).

Inasmuch as walking is used as a metaphor for life (Pss. 1:1; 15:2; 23:3–4; Prov. 4:11–14), God is fittingly implored to provide light (Ps. 43:3). "I will turn the darkness before them into light," says the Lord (Isa. 42:16). It follows that the law of God, his word, is described as "a lamp to my feet and a light to my path" (Ps. 119:105). The longed-for "day of the Lord" is expected to be light (Zech. 14:7); thus, the prophet Amos can astound his hearers by announcing it will instead be darkness (5:18, 20).

In the literature of postbiblical Judaism (after mid-second century B.C.), the imagery of light and darkness continues along the same lines. In the Qumran Scrolls, the opposition between them is quite sharp and fits a general pattern known as dualism. Such dualism appears in the antithesis between light and darkness in the NT, especially the Johannine literature (e.g., 1 John 1:5–7).

The NT use of "light" is both literal (Matt. 17:2) and symbolic (Matt. 4:16, quoting Isa. 9:2), and against the OT and Jewish background becomes clearly intelligible. In view of the Christian message, the light imagery understandably centers about Jesus. Paul speaks of "the light of the gospel of the glory of Christ" (2 Cor. 4:4) and refers to the language of the Genesis creation narrative (4:6). Believers can be described as enlightened (Heb. 6:4; 10:32). Moreover, disciples are called "the light of the world" (Matt. 5:14). Ultimately, the basis for such statements is the belief that Christ is the light of the world (John 8:12; cf. 1:4–5, 9), for he is the emissary of God, who is light (1 John 1:5) and who calls people "out of darkness into his marvelous light" (1 Pet. 2:9). D.M.S.

lightning, an electrical discharge triggered by a build-up of static electricity. This frightening natural phenomenon, always identified in ancient mythology with divine power and wrath, is also associated solely with God in the OT. It is routinely associated with theophany (the appearance of God) in such events as the revelation at Mt. Sinai (Exod. 19:16; 20:18), and in Ezekiel's inaugural vision (Ezek. 1:13–14; cf. Dan. 10:6). Lightning is a mark of God's wisdom as the creator and the giver of life (Pss. 77:18; 97:4; Jer. 10:13; 51:16; Job 28:26; 37:3; 38:25, 35). In poetic descriptions of God as the Divine Warrior, lightning is presented as one of the weapons God uses against both earthly foes (2 Sam. 22:15; cf. Neh. 2:4) and the powers of chaos itself (cf. Pss. 18:14; 77:18; 144:6; also Zech. 9:14 for a setting in the future).

Lightning as a feature of the end of the age is almost the only use made of the imagery in the NT (see Matt. 24:27; Luke 17:24; and esp. Rev. 4:5; 8:5; 11:19; 16:18), although the association with theophany is also reutilized (Matt. 28:3). Once it refers to power other than that of God. When the disciples joyously recount their discovery that they possessed power to exorcise demons in Jesus' name, Jesus cryptically remarks, "I saw Satan fall like lightning from heaven" (Luke 10:18; hints of the same tradition can be seen in its metaphorical application to the king of Babylon in Isa. 14:12–15; and in Rev. 12:7–9). W.S.T.

Lights, Feast of. ***See*** Dedication, Feast of.

lign aloes (līn al'ohs; Lat., "wood of aloes"; KJV; RSV: "aloes," in Num. 24:6), an archaic term designating the wood of any of a family of plants *Liliaceae*, genus *Aloe* or *Furcraea*.

lily, a flower such as the hyacinth or tulip that grows from a bulb (true lily). Similar groups include the iris, crocus, and narcissus. The reference to "lilies of the field" in Matt. 6:28–30 and Luke 12:27–28 implies an impressive showing of blossoms and variety of colors and therefore may be identified as the common crown anemone or windflower (*Anemone coronaria*). This poppylike flower, which is not a true lily, blooms brightly and profusely in the spring throughout the hilly country of the Holy Land. The lilies mentioned in the Song of Sol. 2:1–2

Martagon lily.

and 5:13 are referred to as symbols of beauty. The "lily of the valleys" of Song of Sol. 2:1–2 is not our common lily-of-the-valley, but most likely the sweet smelling blue hyacinth *(Hyacinth orientalis)* common in fields and rocky places. The lilies gathered in the gardens (Song of Sol. 6:2) may be true lilies such as the distinctive white Madonna lily *(Lilium candidum)* and the scarlet Martagon lily *(Lilium chalcedonicum)*, both of which are native to the Holy Land. The white Madonna lily is often traditionally depicted in representations of the annunciation as a symbol of the purity of the Virgin. The lilies that form the decorative floral motif of Solomon's Temple (1 Kings 7:19, 26) are probably water lilies or the lotus (genus *Nymphaea*). This flower is commonly represented in Egyptian architecture as well. ***See also*** Flowers.

P.L.C.

limestone, sedimentary rock formed from large concentrations of marine shell life, hence composed largely of calcium carbonate or magnesium carbonate. It is the dominant rock in the central hills of Palestine and in the heights of Transjordan. When treated with heat and water, the resulting slaked (hydrated) lime could be used for plaster, providing a smooth base for decoration. In its natural state, limestone was the primary construction material for stone walls, foundations, door sockets, lintels, and even decorative work such as stelae, friezes, bas-reliefs, and statuary in Palestine. Only basalt was in sufficient supply in some sectors to rival limestone's popularity. Most of the frequent biblical references to stone are thus to limestone (e.g., 1 Kings 5:5; 6:36; 2 Kings 12:12; Amos 5:11; Matt. 24:2). The Hebrews knew the treatment of heating it (Isa. 33:12) and the consequences on human bone (Amos 2:1). Decomposed limestone comprises the bulk of Palestine's soil. It was the matrix of modest iron and copper deposits on both sides of the Arabah. R.S.B.

linen, a fabric woven from flax yarn. Flax appears to have been the first vegetable fiber cultivated by early agriculturalists. Flax was also cultivated for its seeds, called linseeds, which contain oil and protein. As archaeologists today routinely collect paleobotanical samples, the origins and development of agriculture are slowly being pieced together. It is well known from Neolithic sites (ca. 8000–4500 B.C.), such as Jericho, that cereal production was coeval with a surge toward settled life. Domesticated flax seeds begin to make their appearance in archaeological contexts as early as the sixth millennium B.C. in Mesopotamia, a correlate apparently of the introduction of irrigation technology.

In the biblical lands, linseeds have been recorded as early as the Pre-pottery Neolithic period (eighth millennium B.C.) at the oasis site of Jericho and from Early Bronze Age (ca. 3000–2000 B.C.) sites such as Arad, Bab edh-Dhra, Numeira, and Jericho. Of exceptional interest and significance are the remains of linen cloth recovered at Bab edh-Dhra, for they are the earliest dated occurrence of flax fiber in the Syro-Palestinian region (ca. 3100 B.C.), and they reflect a local industry and a commodity that could have been a trade item even at this early period. The cloth was of a simple weave, consisting of single warps and wefts, clear evidence of loom weaving technology.

Later biblical tradition documents the cultivation of flax and the production of linen cloth (Josh. 2:6; Judg. 15:14; Prov. 31:13; Isa. 15:9). Also, the tenth-century B.C. Gezer Calendar mentions "the month of the harvest of flax." Lamp wicks were made of flax (Isa. 42:3; Matt. 12:20). It is Palestinian linen in which the Dead Sea Scrolls were wrapped.

The coolness, luster, and strength of linen made it a luxury item (Isa. 3:23), graphically illustrated by Samson's wager of thirty linen garments (Judg. 14:12–13). The long fiber of Egyptian flax lent itself to the weaver's art. Egyptian linen was considered to be the finest and most desirable; the words "fine linen" usually referred to Egyptian cloth. Pharaoh dressed Joseph in garments of "fine linen" (Gen. 41:42); Ezekiel describes the sail of a ship of Tyre as made "of fine embroidered linen from Egypt" (Ezek. 27:7); Lazarus wore "fine linen" and royal purple (Luke 16:19); and the harlot possessed as bed coverings "colored spreads of Egyptian linen" (Prov. 7:16). Extant

A monolith lintel from the synagague at Horvat Shema', ca. A.D. 284–306, bearing a *menorah* relief almost a meter wide, the largest such depiction from an ancient synagogue.

pieces of linen from royal Egyptian burials testify to its superior quality.

Flax is a plant requiring a great amount of moisture and thus is best suited to areas with fertile silty clays as in Egypt, where it grew abundantly. Elsewhere in dryer climates irrigation was necessary for cultivation. The fine linen of Egypt was produced by soaking or steeping the flax in water to loosen the fibers of the woody stem, a process called retting; compare Rahab's method of spreading flax on the roof to be moistened by the dew (Josh. 2:6), a method rendering rough, coarse fibers. Once cleaned, the stems were beaten and combed into strands, a process called hackling, then sent to the spinner.

Fine linen was a symbol of purity so it was particularly fitting for Egyptian, Greek, and Jewish priests. Thus it is again fine Egyptian linen that is called for by the Lord in his instructions to Moses concerning the construction of the tabernacle and the proper priestly vestments. Of fine linen were: the tabernacle curtains (Exod. 26:1); the veil (Exod. 26:31); the screen (Exod. 26:36); the court hangings (Exod. 27:9); the priestly garments: the ephod (Exod. 28:6), the girdle (Exod. 28:8), the breastpiece of judgment (Exod. 28:15), the coat and turban (Exod. 28:39), and the breeches (Exod. 28:42). One of the ordinances of God regarding cloth was a prohibition: "nor shall there come upon you a garment of cloth made of two kinds of stuff" (e.g., linen and wool, Lev. 19:19; Deut. 22:11; Ezek. 44:17–18).

From excavations of royal tombs in Egypt, we know that linen was used to wrap mummies in bandages sometimes hundreds of yards long. This practice very likely influenced Jewish burial traditions (John 19:39); the body of Jesus was wrapped in "linen shroud" (Matt. 27:59; Mark 15:46; Luke 23:53). S.L.R.

lintel, any solid beam, whether wood or stone, set horizontally over a doorway. Anchored on both ends, it supports the construction above the doorway and prevents its collapse into the doorway's open space. Biblical usage prescribed that blood be placed on both doorposts and the lintel as part of Passover ritual (Exod. 12:7, 22–23). The obscure Hebrew in 1 Kings 6:31 may describe a lintel shaped like an inverted "V" over the door of the inner sanctuary of Solomon's Temple. Archaeological evidence of lintels of stone, sometimes elaborately decorated, is extensive, while the more readily degenerated wooden beams used as lintels are found less frequently. R.S.B.

Linus (lī'nuhs), according to Irenaeus, successor to Peter and Paul as first bishop of Rome. Fanciful traditions relate Linus to Eubulus, Pudens, and Claudia, who, with Linus, send greetings to Timothy in 2 Tim. 4:21. ***See also*** Claudia; Eubulus; Pudens.

lion, a large predatory feline. The lion (Heb. *ari*; Gk. *leōn*) is frequently depicted in the Bible, often as a symbol of danger, but also one of strength. Today lions are more or less restricted to Africa, but an Asian subspecies, *Panthera leo persica,* once inhabited Asia Minor, Syria, Palestine, Mesopotamia, and Iran. The Asian lion is distinguishable from its African cousin by its scantier mane, thicker coat, and longer tail tassle. It became extinct in Palestine in the fourteenth century A.D., when the last specimen was killed near Megiddo, but in Syria and Mesopotamia, the marshes of the Orontes, Euphrates, and Tigris rivers provided cover, and lions survived until the nineteenth century. The lion's preference for river thickets is mentioned in Jer. 50:44.

In antiquity lion hunting was a sport favored by nobility, as is mentioned in the Assyrian records and evidenced by the famous lion hunt relief at Ashurbanipal's palace in Nineveh. Lions were also kept in captivity. The Egyptian pharaoh Rameses II is said to have owned a pet lion and Ashurnasirpal II of Assyria even succeeded in breeding them at Nimrud. With all its popularity among the ruling classes it is not surprising that the lion is a popular motif in ancient art. Well-known examples are the lions on the Processional Way in Babylon, a street used for royal celebrations, and the lion orthostat (i.e., standing erect) from the thirteenth century B.C. cemetery at Hazor (five miles southwest of Lake Huleh). The famous Samaria ivories dating to the ninth century B.C. include many lion representations. In Jordan stone-carved lions flank some of the Nabatean tombs in Petra and decorate the palace at Araq el Emir.

The Bible mentions numerous encounters between humans and lions, which usually end fatally for one of the parties. Benaiah (2 Sam. 23:20), David (1 Sam. 17:34–36), Samson (Judg. 14:6), and Paul (2 Tim. 4:17) manage to overcome their aggressors. In some cases, however, the lions tear their victims apart (1 Kings 13:24, 26), but Daniel (Dan. 6:16–24) escapes unharmed from the lion den. Lions also constituted a major threat to herdsmen and their stock. Amos (3:12) describes how a shepherd rescued a lamb from the mouth of a lion.

Some OT proverbs deal with the lion. In Eccles. 9:4 "a living dog is better than a dead lion" and in Judg. 14:18 Samson is asked, "What is stronger than a lion?" Prov. 26:13 tells the story of the lazy man, who does not want to go to work, because there "is a lion in the road! . . . a lion in the streets!" In the NT, the ferocity of the predatory lion makes it an apt simile for Satan (1 Pet. 5:8) and the fearsome nature of the apocalyptic beasts is due in large part to the resemblance of some of their characteristics to those of the lion: teeth (Rev. 9:8), head (9:17), mouth (13:2), and roar (10:3).

I.U.K.

literary criticism. *See* Biblical Criticism.

literature, the New Testament as. The appreciation of the NT as literature requires acquaintance with the traditional literary forms that appear in it and sensitivity to the ways in

A dying lion, part of Assyrian ruler Ashurbanipal's "Lion Hunt" relief from his palace at Nineveh, seventh century B.C.

LITERATURE, THE NT

which such forms can be creatively used in religious discourse.

Narrative Works: At the beginning we must distinguish between the narrative works of the NT, the four Gospels and Acts, and the remaining works, which are mostly in the form of Letters, the Revelation to John being an important exception. The first three Gospels form a special group within the narrative works, not only because of considerable shared content but also because of the predominance within these works of brief episodes that often seem to be loosely connected. These brief episodes tend to follow certain literary forms that may be derived from previous oral tradition. The vigor of these brief forms is evidently due to their rhetorical power: the stories and sayings about Jesus have been shaped to make a strong impact on hearers or readers.

The Pronouncement Story. Consideration of the pronouncement story, the parable, and the aphorism will illustrate the nature of these brief forms. The pronouncement story (a form common in Greco-Roman literature) is a brief narrative scene in which the central figure (Jesus in the Gospels) responds to something observed or said with a decisive pronouncement (sometimes accompanied by an action). The scene usually ends with the pronouncement, which is often striking in its expression, and everything else leads up to the pronouncement as climax. Because of its brief setting the pronouncement appears in a situation of dramatic interaction that highlights it. In responding to the situation, Jesus often corrects the views of others or interprets the situation in a remarkable way. The scene in Matt. 9:10–13; Mark 2:15–17; and Luke 5:29–32, in which Jesus responds to criticism by justifying his meals with tax collectors and sinners, is an example of a pronouncement story.

The Parables of Jesus. The parables of Jesus vary from brief comparisons, such as the parable of the leaven (Matt. 13:33; Luke 13:20–21), to well-developed stories of several scenes, such as the parable of the prodigal son (Luke 15:11–32). The longer parables focus on scenes involving dramatic interaction and often use contrasting characters. The parables rely on the power of a simile or an extended metaphor to change the way in which people perceive and respond. Instead of looking at situations or persons directly, hearers are invited to look at them through the metaphorical story. This new perspective on the matter can bring with it a new set of attitudes and evaluations. The strangeness of the metaphor, compared to ordinary ways of speaking about the subject matter, helps to give the metaphor imaginative power to provoke new insight.

Aphorisms. In the Gospels Jesus also speaks in aphorisms, a succinct and pointed mode of speech that presents a perspective on life or a guide to action in a striking sentence. While these aphorisms may be related to proverbs, they tend to present extreme or even paradoxical challenges to ordinary views rather than to express the wisdom arising from observation of regular patterns of life. Thus the saying about saving and losing one's life (Matt. 16:25; Mark 8:35; Luke 9:24) uses antithetical terms to convey a paradoxical vision of a disciple's existence, while the command to turn the other cheek (Matt. 5:39; Luke 6:29) focuses on a very specific situation and requires a very unusual response to it. The purpose of this command is not to provide a clear general rule to regulate behavior but to awaken the imagination of hearers to possibilities of a response that breaks out of the usual patterns of attack and counterattack.

We see, then, that the Gospels present Jesus with forceful and imaginative language. We find such language in the words attributed to Jesus. We also find it in the shaping of the stories about him. Forceful and imaginative language is important in the Gospels because the early witnesses to Jesus wanted their Master to make an impression on the imaginations of hearers and readers. The language of the Gospels is less concerned to produce an aesthetic response, a fascination with creative form as interesting and beautiful in itself, than to move hearers and readers to belief and action. It has a rhetorical purpose, and scholars who tend to distinguish literary art from rhetoric might give the Gospels an inferior rating because of this. However, a clear distinction between art and rhetoric cannot be drawn. Furthermore, the Gospels do not simply appeal to established views and prejudices in order to control behavior, the way much modern advertising does, but use language that appeals to the imagination to invite new perspectives on life that conflict with established views. Such revolutions in perspective may be produced by literary art, which has the power to awaken the imagination to view the world differently, changing the images by which we apprehend the world and thereby changing the way we act. The forceful and imaginative language of Jesus and the Gospel writers is necessary to their purpose of creating repentance and faith, for the transformation of persons requires a restructuring of the self and its life-world in which the active imagination must participate.

In the first three Gospels the brief forms discussed so far have a place within larger literary forms. Some of the parables and sayings are gathered into large, speechlike discourses of Jesus, with various literary patterns unifying segments of the discourses. Thus a major section of the Sermon on the Mount is called the "antitheses" because sayings are united in a series by a repeated antithetical introduction, "You have heard that it was said . . . But I say to you . . ." (Matt. 5:21–48). Presentation of Jesus' words in rather lengthy discourses is especially characteristic of Matthew. Matthew also shows the strongest tendency to use literary patterns that show exact repetition of words and careful balance of elements. Pronouncement stories and miracle stories can also be gathered into larger formal groups. In Mark 2:1–3:6 we find a series of five pronouncement stories in which the first and second are related thematically (they concern forgiveness of sins), as are the fourth and fifth (they concern work on the Sabbath), but there is also a chiastic (or concentric) pattern, for the first and fifth stories, as well as the second and fourth, also have similarities.

The literary units already mentioned have a place within one of the Gospels, and they may take on special significance through their particular place and function within this encompassing narrative. Like other narratives, the Gospels can be studied in terms of plot, settings, characterization, the role of the narrator, etc. Readers' experience of the story is influenced by many prior decisions concerning what to include in the story, when to pause for a detailed scene and when to summarize, how to evaluate persons and events in light of implied standards of judgment, how to connect material into a developing plot, etc. In the Gospels we experience Jesus as he is presented in the story by narrators who have (consciously or unconsciously) made such decisions and who use particular literary techniques to convey their views of Jesus. An understanding of these literary techniques is a necessary part of the interpretation of the Gospels and of Jesus as presented in them.

The Gospel writers do not simply compile traditional material; they use literary patterns to shape this material into a continuous plot. Thus in Mark 8:14–21 we find a remarkable scene in which Jesus, who is with his disciples in a boat, accuses his followers of deafness and blindness. In doing so, he refers to two previous scenes in which multitudes of people were fed (see Mark 6:30–44; 8:1–9). Following the first of these feedings, there was another scene in which the disciples were in a boat on the lake, and this scene ended with the statement that the disciples "did not understand about the loaves, but their hearts were hardened" (Mark 6:52), an accusation Jesus develops later in 8:14–21. All these scenes, and probably also the boat scene in Mark 4:35–41, are part of a developing plot line that builds up to a crisis in 8:14–21, where the failure of the disciples to understand is so vividly portrayed that it cries out for some resolution in the rest of the story. When judged by modern standards, the first three Gospels may seem to lack clear connections among the episodes within them. Nevertheless, they were meant to be read as continuous stories that have significant plot development.

The Gospel of Luke shares with Matthew and Mark characteristics we have already discussed, but it is unique in being part of a larger work that continues in Acts. The preface to the work (Luke 1:1–4) shows both the author's reflection on his literary task and awareness of the literary forms used by cultured writers of the period. The narrator takes special care to disclose to readers the overall plot of the story, which is understood to be the realization of God's plan. These disclosures are made in key scenes that are meant to provide interpretive previews and reviews of events in the narrative. The description of Jesus' mission in the Nazareth synagogue (Luke 4:16–30) and the report of the risen Jesus' commission to his apostles (Luke 24:44–49) are examples. Acts departs from the literary style of the first three Gospels in its tendency to develop longer dramatic scenes. These scenes often contain carefully composed speeches that summarize central themes in light of which events of the narrative should be understood. A similar tendency is apparent in Luke 1–2 (the birth narrative) and in Luke 24:13–35 (the Emmaus scene), parts of the Gospel independent of the traditions Luke shares with Matthew and Mark. In general, Acts has tighter narrative continuity than the Gospels; that is, a greater proportion of events can be understood as resulting from events already presented. Acts (along with Luke 1–2) also demonstrates the author's mastery of various Greek styles. Scenes with a Jewish setting and Jewish characters often use Greek influenced by the Semitic Greek of the Septuagint, while scenes in which cultured Greeks and Romans are being addressed use a cultured Greek appropriate to the audience.

The Gospel of John has its own literary form, which is strongly influenced by its interest in symbolism. An event may be narrated, followed by a dialogue and/or monologue by Jesus that uncovers the deeper symbolic significance of the event. This sometimes involves reflection on the significance of an elemental religious symbol, such as water (4:7–30) or bread (6:1–59), relating these symbols to Jesus. Words with double meanings are used (e.g., 3:3, *anōthen,* either "anew" or "from above"), resulting in misunderstanding. This emphasizes the difference between Jesus' insight and the limited perceptions of ordinary people. Some of the lengthy monologues seem to lose touch with the narrative settings in which they are placed. However, the narrator of John is also capable of presenting a dramatic series of events that has both narrative interest and symbolic meaning, as in the story of the blind man in John 9. The solemn and repetitious language of Jesus in John seems to emphasize the importance and many-sided meaning of the central concepts and symbols used in this Gospel.

Other Works: The Letters of Paul follow a traditional letter form as modified by Paul. This is most obvious at the beginning of the Letters, where we find this structure: "Paul [often with additional description] to . . . [with additional description]. Grace to you and peace . . . " This is normally followed by a section of thanksgiving for the church being addressed. In the body of the Letter Paul shapes his writing more freely. However, just as the Gospels make use of traditional forms, Paul incorporates established forms derived from the church's worship and exhortation into his Letters. The hymnlike confession of faith in Jesus Christ that we find in Phil. 2:6–11 is an example.

There is renewed interest in analyzing the Letters of Paul in light of patterns used in Greco-Roman rhetoric for the composition of speeches and letters. This may prove to be a fruitful approach, if there is proper attention to both similarities and differences. It is clear that Paul is a vigorous writer with a well-developed rhetoric that he can use to speak powerfully to the problems he must address. His methods include lively dialogue as he puts objections into the mouth of an opponent (Rom. 3:1–8), appeal to authoritative writings (the OT; Gal. 3:6–9), the string of balanced phrases with repetitive emphasis (1 Cor. 13:7), the string of antitheses (1 Cor. 15:42–44), and the like. Furthermore, his versatility is apparent from his shifting style as he approaches particular congregations and particular issues.

Letters by authors other than Paul often show the same traditional letter form (e.g., 1 Peter, 2 John, 3 John, Jude), while other letters omit all such formal elements (e.g., 1 John) or have them only at the beginning (e.g., James, 2 Peter) or at the end (e.g., Hebrews). That may be due to early mutilation of the manuscripts, or perhaps to the fact that they assumed a letter form only as a literary device and were not intended as direct communications to a specific audience.

The strange symbolism of the Revelation to John comes to a large extent from a tradition of prophetic and apocalyptic imagery that this writing reuses to address churches in a time of crisis. The complex symbolic language of Revelation suggests that events and persons, perhaps already familiar from ordinary life, have a different and deeper meaning as part of a cosmic drama. The symbolic language helps to clarify the roles of particular events and persons in this drama, partly through linking these events and persons with scriptural and apocalyptic types. This symbolic redescription of the world also involves evaluation, for it divides the world into good and evil, with appropriate emotional overtones. The symbolic visions of Revelation have been formed into literary patterns that tie these visions together in larger unities. The series of seven that builds up to a point of climax is especially common.

The Greek used by NT authors varies greatly in sophistication and elegance. Hebrews and parts of Luke-Acts contain relatively sophisticated language with complex sentences and a rich vocabulary. Many other NT writings prefer relatively simple sentences. The book of Revelation departs so far from elegant Greek as to violate basic rules of Greek grammar. ***See also*** Bible and Western Literature, The; Literature, The Old Testament as; Parables; Proverb.

Bibliography

Beardslee, William A. *Literary Criticism of the New Testament*. Philadelphia: Fortress, 1970.

Tannehill, Robert C. *The Sword of His Mouth: Forceful and Imaginative Language in Synoptic Sayings*. Missoula, MT: Scholars Press; Philadelphia: Fortress, 1975.

Wilder, Amos. *Early Christian Rhetoric: The Language of the Gospel*. Cambridge, MA: Harvard University Press, 1971.

R.C.T.

literature, the Old Testament as. To read and study the Bible as literature means to read the Bible in the ways we read texts we regard as literature—to apply the same methods of analysis that we apply to literature in general to the Bible, too. This is not to say that the Bible need be taken *only* as literature, only that it can be seen as literature—art in language. As such, to the extent that we draw meaning from figurations of language, uses of words, style, formal organization, and other linguistic aspects of a text, an approach to the Bible as literature enhances the meaning we find in the text.

The Hebrew Bible does not define its own form, be it literary or any other. It does, however, describe certain lines or passages with respect to their genre or performance style using terms such as "judgment" (Heb. *mishpat*), "law" (*ḥok*), "song" (*shir*), "chant" (*mizmor*), "psalm" (*tehilla*), "fiction" (*mashal*), "riddle" (*ḥidda*), "figure of speech" (*melitsa*), "dissertation" (*massa*), and "elegy" (*kina*). The importance of good rhetoric, of shaping a message in an effective literary form, seems to inform the powerful, emotional appeal of Judah in Gen. 44:18–34 and other passages, and the fact that the form of a message has an aesthetic side apart from its content is acknowledged in Ezek. 33:30–33, where the Lord tells Ezekiel that his audience appreciates his verse but eschews his message. When Prov. 16:21 says that "pleasant speech increases persuasiveness," it may be celebrating the value of good rhetoric, though it may, alternatively, be referring to the efficacy of a smooth delivery.

But whether the OT actually reflects upon literary art or not, its evident control of a variety of literary forms impresses critics and other readers with its quality as literature. Indeed, since classical times authors have paid tribute to the literary art of the Hebrew Bible and have compared it favorably to other great works of literature. OT style, images, story patterns, and themes continue to serve as sources and materials for literary artists.

Historical and Literary Criticism: Broadly speaking, there are two models for studying the OT as literature, each with its own methods and purposes. The historical, or diachronic, traces the history of composition of the OT literature. It endeavors to identify the sources of the present composition, describe the process by which the present composition was made, and explain the intention behind the final arrangement. The other literary model is synchronic, dealing with the text in more or less its present form and finding its meaning in that form. For the sake of clarity, only the synchronic approach will here be considered "literary criticism."

What Makes a Text Literary: Reading the OT as literature implies at least two important claims: that the OT is, at least in part, literary; and that the experience of reading or hearing the OT is, again at least in part, aesthetic.

What it is that makes a text literary or artistic is, in general, the subject of widespread theoretical discussion and controversy. Traditionally, the literary text possesses two special properties. On the one hand, the form and style of the text do not merely shape its message but comprise an integral part of the message. Form and semantic content merge to produce meaning. To take a simple example, in 1 Sam. 3:5 we read that Samuel "ran to Eli." Later, in v. 6, we read "And Samuel arose and went to Eli." The slower movement is conveyed by considerably longer wording. The literary text "does," as it were, what it "says." Similarly, the contrast between Isaac's love of Esau and Rebekah's love for Jacob in Gen. 25:28 is underscored by the usage of different Hebrew verb forms and word order for each (a fact that is rarely reproduced in translation).

On the other hand, we find a literary text to be allusive, connoting associations beyond its immediate sense and pointing to references beyond its immediate context. The literary text proliferates meaning, signifying more than it explicitly says. For example, before the Lord commissions Moses at the burning bush to lead the Israelites out of Egypt, the text presents Moses in the act of leading a flock of sheep (Exod. 3:1). This activity not only brings Moses to the site of the next scene, the image of Moses as shepherd suggests his destiny to lead his people, as the shepherd was a widespread metaphor for a king or leader (see, e.g., Num. 27:17). Through a metaphorical association, the audience considers Moses a leader before Moses does.

Literary Criticism: The theory and practice of literary criticism have increasingly diversified and specialized, so that numerous ways have developed for reading the OT as literature. Despite widely differing procedures, literary critics tend to hold in common certain fundamental assumptions about literature and the aims of criticism. Literature is created to communicate verbally with an audience that shares a language certain literary conventions, and certain frames of reference with the author. The author manipulates language and literary conventions in order to convey meaning. As in routine conversation the audience does not have to analyze what it hears or reads; it automatically perceives some message. The literary critic seeks to expose the various ways by which we make sense of a text.

Literary criticism of the OT takes many different forms, reflecting various modes of making sense of the text. Many critics will want first to ascertain the genre of a text, holding that our presuppositions about the function and literary category of a particular text affect the way in which we read it. Whether, for example, we read Esther as farce or as history or the Song of Songs as erotic poems or as religious allegory affects our responses throughout.

Critics customarily try to define the literary conventions of a text—its patterns of organization and its poetic devices—in order to follow those conventions in interpreting a text. How we determine what the conventions of ancient OT literature were depends ultimately upon what we look for in the OT. While all critics will seek out conventions that are familiar from other literatures, some will emphasize those literary features that are, on the one hand, widespread within the OT itself and, on the other, common among other texts from the ancient Near East. (The trouble with this latter criterion is that critics typically find that, although the OT shares many genres and poetic devices with other ancient literatures, it is often more richly textured and more finely nuanced than those other literatures. Thus, one might subject the OT to a more intensive and sophisticated analysis than other ancient Near Eastern texts.)

Among the many literary conventions identified in diverse OT passages are: first, the use of traditional source material, imagery, formulations, and lines of text. It would seem that wherever possible OT authors adapted or recombined earlier materials rather than created entirely novel stories or poems. Second, there are typical genre forms, story patterns, or scene types—i.e., creating stories or poems within the framework of standard structures. Other conventions include extensive repetition, within which variations receive special attention; repetition of key words within a unit or between units; wordplay, i.e., the text's attachment of special significance to certain words by repeating their sounds or to certain names by interpreting their meaning explicitly or implicitly; the use of metaphor, simile, and personification; concentric structures, in which the focal or turning point of a unit appears in the center; and, especially in OT verse, parallelism—the formation of couplets and longer series of lines through repetitions in syntactic construction and/or semantic sense from line to line.

Close Reading: The first chapter of Jonah may serve to illustrate some of the conventions just cited. The book opens with a traditional formula, leading us to expect the delivery of an oracle: "Now the word of the Lord came to Jonah the son of Amittai, saying . . ." (v. 1). The oracle, however—"Arise, go to Nineveh . . ."—is addressed to Jonah alone (v. 2). We expected a book of prophecies, but instead we get a story: "But Jonah rose to flee to Tarshish . . ." (v. 3). The description of the prophet's response, "But Jonah rose . . . ," repeats the first verb of the Lord's command—"Arise." We are set, at this point, to find the prophet fulfilling his mission, but the next word, "to flee," deviates both in form and sense from the command. The destination, "to Tarshish," exacerbates Jonah's deviation, for wherever Tarshish is, it is west and overseas, whereas Nineveh is northeast and overland.

The name the prophet bears is ironic. "Jonah," which means "dove," the symbol of peace, here designates a mean-spirited harbinger of doom, and his patronymic, "son of Amittai," connotes "son of the faithful one" —hardly apt for this rebellious prophet.

Jonah's withdrawal from his mission is delineated as a series of descents through the repetition of a key word: "He *went down* to Joppa" (v. 3), "he *went down* into the ship" (v. 3), "he *went down* into the hold of the ship" (v. 5), and "he went into a deep sleep" (v. 5). The fourth verb *(wayeradam)* derives from a different stem but sounds like the verb "he went down" *(wayered)*. The wordplay suggests that Jonah's sleep is the ultimate phase in his withdrawal.

A "close" literary reading of a text capitalizes on the sorts of observations we have just made. It reads the text at close range and follows shades of meaning in words and phrases and subtleties of word order, too, in interpreting a text. A useful procedure in such a reading is continually to ask: What difference would it have made had the text said something other than what it says? By thereby creating a "countertext" one perceives the sense of the present text more finely. If, for example, the text had only said "Jonah fled" and had not repeated the verb "he rose" (1:2), we would not experience the same surprise. If the narrative in Jonah 1 had described the ship, the sea, the activities of the sailors, and the storm in greater details, as we might find in the Homeric epics, we would be more impressed with the conflict of people against nature than with the opposition of human will and thinking to God's. In a close reading we draw significance out of what the text says and doesn't say and the way it says what it does say.

Comparative Criticism: Just as in close reading one contrasts what the text says with what it might have said, one may also contrast what one text says with what another text says. One may better appreciate and understand what is special about one text by comparing it with others. Ps. 1:3–4 and Jer. 17:5–6, for example, each compare the righteous man to a well-watered tree; yet they imagine the wicked differently. In the psalm, the wicked are pictured as chaff that is swept away in the wind; in Jeremiah, the wicked are depicted, preceding the image of the righteous, as a shrub in a parched desert. Observing this contrast leads to interpreting the nature of righteousness differently in the two passages. One may further compare different stories that relate to a common theme or subject, such as the story of Jephthah and his daughter in Judges 11, or the story of Hagar's flight from Sarah in Genesis 16 and that of the expulsion of Hagar by Abraham in Genesis 21. Because the narratives hold several elements in common, observing their differences throws the distinctive qualities of each into relief.

Since it is the goal of comparative literature to learn about individual texts by contrasting them with one another, as well as to learn about the phenomenon of literature in general by sampling a wide variety of texts, one may compare texts within the OT literature to texts from diverse places and periods. One may, for example, discern distinctive ideas of OT and Mesopotamian civilization by contrasting the Flood story in Genesis 6–9 with the account in the Epic of Gilgamesh, tablet 11. Or one may appreciate the nature of the OT's poetry and storytelling art by comparing its style, sensibilities, and themes with those of other literatures. A justly famous comparison of an OT narrative (Gen. 22) with a Homeric episode *(Odyssey*, book 19), for example, has shown that biblical narrative tends to relate the action taking place in center stage, so to speak, to the general exclusion of visual description and background as it narrates, while the Homeric epic tends to place in the foreground both description and background as it narrates. It has been widely remarked, too, that whereas epic literatures narrate in poetic form, OT poetry rarely narrates, and never at length.

On the other hand, by applying what we have learned from diverse literatures about literary art in general to the OT, we may better analyze the conventions of OT literature. Without in any way assuming that the OT's poetic and narrative devices are the same as those of another literature, we may investigate the particular ways that OT literature achieves what other literatures do, such as narration, characterization, formal organization, imagery, coherence, point of view, allusion, and thematic development. The study of literature should sensitize one to be a more perceptive reader of the Bible.

Similarly, although the literary genres and

categories of other literatures may not find precise equivalents in the OT, one's awareness of the characteristics of various genres and categories may lend one a helpful perspective on an OT text. Comparison of the narrative of Israel's exodus from Egypt to a classical comedy or of the story of King Saul to a classical tragedy, for example, may not demonstrate the identity of the OT texts with those genres. It may, however, illuminate certain significant effects of those stories and suggest the ways by which those effects have been achieved.

Literary Theory and the OT: Comparing the OT to other literatures assumes, of course, that its text is interpretable in ways similar to the interpretation of other texts. If so, one can apply to the OT the methods of analysis that have been found to be effective when applied to literature in general. Among the various approaches or theories that critics have begun to implement in recent years in analyzing the literature of the OT are: formalism, structuralism, reception or reader-response criticism, and deconstruction.

Formalism. The analysis of folk tales, in particular, has led to the impression that each tale comprises a limited series of obligatory and optional action sequences, or "functions." Many diverse stories have been found to build around a finite set of components. Identifying similar series of "functions" in biblical narratives, such as episodes in the life of Jacob and the story of Ruth, may, on the one hand, highlight significant elements of the stories and, on the other, fix the genre and literary history of the tales.

Structuralism. Structuralism is a theory of knowledge holding that communication translates underlying abstract messages into the forms that actually occur and that what we immediately perceive are these surface occurrences; our minds automatically decode surface appearances into "deep-level" messages. The phenomenon we perceive, be it an image, a sound sequence such as a musical work, or a linguistic discourse such as a conversation or a written text, is taken as a system of interdependent components. The message is primarily encoded within the various components' relations with one another. A structuralist will accordingly look for patterns and relationships, especially ones that recur, rather than single actions or utterances, in interpreting a text. Traditionally, structuralists have tended to seek relationships in which two polar opposite concepts are set into conflict and are mediated by some crucial factor. The mediation may resolve the opposition or hold it in tension.

For example, in Psalm 19 the opposition between the awesome God of a seemingly perfect natural order and the routine imperfection of God's human creature is mediated through language—God's *torah* ("teaching") and human reflection and confession. Or, in the narrative of Ruth, the opposition of potential fertility and actual barrenness of both the land of Judah and the family of Naomi is resolved through the parallel kindness of God toward the land and of Ruth and Boaz toward Naomi.

Reception or Reader-response Criticism. Reception theory holds that the meaning of a text does not inhere in the internal structure of the text itself but rather in the effects the text has on its various readers. A reader's responses to the text constitute the meaning of the text for that particular reader. In the course of reading (or hearing) a text, one forms a variety of impressions, senses the beginnings and ends of units, develops hypotheses about the text, tests the hypotheses and sustains or dismisses them, raises questions, resolves problems, and more. One's total experience of the text, rather than merely the conclusions one makes at the end of the experience, comprise the text's meaning. Reception, or "affective," criticism endeavors to explain how texts produce the effects they do.

The episode concerning how Joseph got down to Egypt in Genesis 37, for example, produces confusion as to the manner in which his conveyance took place. Was he sold by his brothers, was he kidnapped from the pit, or what? The question remains unresolved, for the text provides support for either reading (contrast Gen. 39:1 and 45:4, from which one may gather Joseph was sold to the Ishmaelites, with Gen. 37:36 and 40:15, from which one may infer he was kidnapped by Midianites). The ambiguity surrounding the physical conveyance, it has been suggested, contrasts with the unequivocal explanation by Joseph himself concerning how he came to Egypt: the Lord sent him (Gen. 45:5, 7–8). Remaining confused about the physical course of events, the reader is receptive to the unequivocal theological explanation.

Deconstruction. Deconstruction is a philosophy that has barely begun to make an impact on the literary study of the OT. It maintains that the text can only be perceived by a reader who brings an array of personal associations and interpretive strategies to the act of reading. Consequently, every reading of a text creates, so to speak, a new text, and no text can exist except in a one-time, more or less idiosyncratic version. Because each re-creation of the text is different, the act of deciding the meaning of the text must continually be held in abeyance or deferred. To fix a reading of a text would be to falsify the text's nature as open and indeterminate.

The best case for deconstruction is made by texts such as the episode of David and Bathsheba in 2 Samuel 11, which have been contrarily interpreted. The question of whether Uriah the Hittite knew that David had slept with his wife Bathsheba remains moot and undecidable because one can construe the text either way. Uriah may have refused to visit his wife (v. 11) because he suspected the adultery or because he was an extraordinarily conscientious soldier.

Conclusion: While the historian reads the OT in order to reconstruct from it part of the world of ancient Israel, the literary critic or reader understands that the text conceives its own world. Literary approaches to the OT seek to perceive that world ever more finely and to explain how it is created. ***See also*** Biblical Criticism; Hermeneutics.

Bibliography

Alter, Robert. *The Art of Biblical Narrative.* New York: Basic Books, 1981.

Henn, T. R. *The Bible as Literature.* New York: Oxford University Press, 1970.

Polzin, Robert. *Biblical Structuralism.* Philadelphia/Missoula, MT: Fortress Press/Scholars Press, 1977.

Robertson, David. *The Old Testament and the Literary Critic.* Philadelphia: Fortress, 1977.

Schneidau, Herbert N. *Sacred Discontent: The Bible and Western Tradition.* Berkeley and Los Angeles, CA: University of California Press, 1976.

E.L.G.

lizard, a four-footed reptile. Lev. 11:30 lists six types of lizards or reptiles as unclean animals: the great lizard, the gecko, the land crocodile, the lizard, the sand lizard, and the chameleon. The great lizard is probably the Negev dabb lizard *(Uromastyx).* There are a number of varieties of the gecko lizard. The term "land crocodile" seems to apply to the large carnivorous desert monitor or varan, and "lizard" could relate to the numerous lacertids ("European lizards"). The sand lizard may correspond to the burrowing skink, and the translation of the Hebrew *tinshemeth* as "chameleon" is disputable, although chameleons are quite common throughout the Holy Land.

loan, something lent or furnished on condition of being returned. Biblical legislation concerning the lending of fungibles must be understood against the background of a noncommercial agricultural society with strong tribal roots. The primary motivation of borrowers was to obtain relief from need rather than to further their economic enterprises. Furthermore, the poor and needy were deemed fellow kin of all Israelites (Deut. 15:11). Hence, biblical law considers the lending of fungibles to be a philanthropic act and thus restricts severely the rights of the lender or creditor.

Interest: According to the Mesopotamian law codes and private contracts to which OT law may be compared, Mesopotamian creditors commonly charged an annual interest rate of 20 percent for loans of silver and 33-1/3 percent for loans of grain. Biblical law, however, prohibits creditors from exercising this right over their needy brethren (Exod. 22:24; Lev. 25:35–37; Deut. 23:20), although it does allow the taking of interest from non-Israelites (Deut. 23:21). The nonlegal biblical references depicting the difficult plight of debtors in ancient Israel (e.g., 1 Sam. 22:2; Jer. 15:10) would seem to attest to the violation of this prohibition. Ezekiel brands creditors who take interest as wicked, while praising those who refrain as pious (Ezek. 18:8, 13, 17; 22:12; cf. Ps. 15:5). The wisdom literature further cautions that wealth augmented by interest is fleeting (Prov. 28:8). According to the NT, as inferred from the parable of the talents, it is proper to invest one's money with bankers for the sake of receiving interest (Luke 19:23; Matt. 25:27).

The two terms for "interest" in biblical Hebrew are *neshek* (derived from the verb "to bite") and *tarbith* (lit., "increase"), which are translated in the RSV as "interest." Scholars differ in their understanding of the two Hebrew terms. Some view the terms as a fixed pair denoting a single concept. Others attempt to distinguish them as referring to two different types of interest: advanced interest, which is "bitten" off the principal at the onset of the loan, and accrued interest resulting in an "increase" at the time of repaying the loan.

Pledges and Surety: Ancient Near Eastern law acknowledged as means of protecting the lender against loss due to default of payment both the pledge whereby chattel, real estate, or persons were surrendered as security for a loan and the surety whereby a person assumed liability for the obligation of the borrower. Limited knowledge of ancient Near Eastern pledge law, however, does not allow for clear differentiation between pledge and mortgage found in modern law. Today a mortgage is defined as a conditional conveyance of property bestowing legal title upon the mortgagee who need not have physical possession of the property. In contrast, a pledge is a bailment of property to be in the physical possession of the pledgee who does not have legal title to the property. Thus, upon default, the mortgaged property passes wholly to the mortgagee while the pledged property must be sold and only as much of the proceeds as will satisfy the debt passes to the pledgee. Similarly, limited knowledge of ancient Near Eastern suretyship does not always allow clear definition as to whether the surety becomes a co-debtor or whether he only ensures the presence of the defaulting debtor for personal prosecution by the creditor.

Biblical law recognizes the right of lenders to take a pledge. However, the law places the following restrictions upon creditors: they may not enter the debtor's home to seize a pledge but must wait outside (Deut. 24:10–11); they may not seize what is needed for one's daily living (Deut. 24:6; cf. Job 24:3); they may not seize the garment of a widow (Deut. 24:17); and the pledged garment of the poor must be returned by nightfall (Deut. 24:12–13; Exod. 22: 25–26; cf. Amos 2:8). The nonlegal literature of the Bible attests to the seizing of members of the defaulting debtor's family and to the taking of real estate to secure and satisfy a loan (2 Kings 4:1; Isa. 50:1; Neh. 5:3–5; Matt. 18:25).

Laws governing surety do not occur in the corpus of biblical law. References to the institution, however, are found in the nonlegal literature of the Bible, especially in the wisdom literature. The book of Proverbs is replete with advice against standing surety for another (6:1; 11:15; 17:18; 22:26–27; 27:13). The references reveal that the assumption of surety was accompanied by the symbolic gesture of "giving one's hand" perhaps as a type of handshake (Prov. 6: 1; 17:18; Job 17:3). Judah's assumption of surety for Benjamin (Gen. 44:32) seems to indicate that at times a surety would only ensure the physical presence of the debtor for personal prosecution by the creditor, while Prov. 22:26–27 clearly indicates that a surety often became a co-debtor. The concept of surety is used also metaphorically in prayer (Isa. 38:14; Ps. 119:122; Job 17:3; cf. Heb. 7:22).

Remission of Debt: Mesopotamian kings are known to have issued edicts designed to restore some measure of equilibrium in the economic life of the society. These edicts entailed cancellation of certain types of debts, release from certain kinds of tenant obligations, and freedom from debt servitude. Biblical law instituted a cyclical cancellation of debts by decreeing the remission of all outstanding loans in the Sabbatical (i.e., seventh) Year (Deut. 15:1–11). ***See also*** Law; Ownership. B.L.E.

loaves. ***See*** Baker; Bread; Miracles.

locks. 1 Devices on doors (Song of Sol. 5:5; Neh. 3:3, 13–15; see also Judg. 3:23–24). **2** Strands of hair, mentioned with regard to Nazirites (Num. 6:5), Samson (Judg. 16:13, 19), and levitical priests (Ezek. 44:20), all of whom were not to have their hair cut (see also Ezek. 8:3; Song of Sol. 5:2, 11).

locust, a small insect resembling a cricket or grasshopper that seasonally migrates in great swarms, causing damage to all vegetation in its path. This insect is therefore a serious pest, especially to crops, and as a major pest of the Bible it was associated with the canker worm, palmer worm, and caterpillar (Joel 1:4; 2:25). The migrating swarms of locusts were one of the "plagues" of the OT (Exod. 10:12–20) imposed by the Lord on the people of Egypt as punishment for the enslavement of the Israelites. This form of punishment was not reserved for foreigners alone, but was also extended to the Israelites as a curse for disobedience to the commandments and statutes of the Lord (Deut. 28:42).

Locust may also refer to the carob (*Ceratonia siliqua*), a common tree in the Holy Land that bears large edible beanlike pods. It is perhaps mistakenly identified as the food that provided John the Baptist with sustenance in the wilderness (Matt. 3:4; Mark 1:6). However, since the passage in Lev. 11:22 that sets out dietary guidelines refers to locusts in the same context as beetles and grasshoppers, these insects are the more likely candidates for items of diet indicated in the NT. Locusts are a cheap, though time-costly, form of protein that may be heavily exploited during a swarming event. They are even consumed by the natives of the Holy Land today as an emergency food. P.L.C.

Lod (lahd). ***See*** Lydda.

Lo-debar (loh-de-bahr'), a city in Gilead, east of the Jordan, where Jonathan's son Mephibosheth lived after his father's death (2 Sam. 9:4–5). Machir of Lo-debar gave aid to David during his flight from Absalom (2 Sam. 17:27). If one reads *lo debar* in Josh. 13:26 instead of *lodebir* in the Masoretic Text (as does the NEB; RSV: "Debir"), then the city was assigned to the tribe of Gad and probably was located near the northern edge of Gilead (see also Amos 6:13).

log. 1 the smallest Hebrew measure of capacity, about two-thirds of a pint. **2** A piece of wood, usually the trunk portion of a tree (cf. Matt. 7:3). ***See also*** Weights and Measures.

logos (law'gaws), the Greek term usually translated "word" (especially word of God) when it occurs in the NT. *Logos* has a wide range of meaning, e.g., reckoning or accounting, explanation or reason, statement or discourse. In English, it frequently appears in the names of scientific or other disciplines, e.g., bio*logy*, psycho*logy*, theo*logy*.

Originally employed as a technical philosophical term by the Greek philosopher Heraclitus (sixth century B.C.), *logos* became a particularly important concept for the Stoics (third century B.C. and later). In Stoicism, *logos* was the principle and pattern that gave the world or cosmos its character and coherence. The term was taken over by Philo, the Alexandrian philosophical theologian of Judaism, who was roughly a contemporary of the apostle Paul. By means of the *logos*, Philo sought to reconcile Greek philosophical theories about the universe (cosmology) with the biblical accounts of God's creating the world by his spoken word. God's *logos* became a clearly identifiable entity, mediating between God and the world, the mode of the divine creativity and revelation.

Already before Philo, *logos* had been used in

the Greek translation of the OT (Septuagint or LXX) to render the Hebrew term *(dabar)* usually translated into English as "word"—a term frequently used of God's speaking. Just the use of this Greek term, with its rich associations, to translate the equally pregnant Hebrew word (which could mean "word," "thing," or "event') was a significant development in the growth of the biblical tradition. At the same time, in the later OT and apocryphal books, "wisdom" (Gk. *sophia*) was beginning to play a mediatorial role between God and creation not unlike that of *logos* in Philo (cf. Prov. 8:22–31; Wisd. of Sol. 9: 1–2). The idea that God's relation to his creation was mediated through a subordinate being or mode of manifestation was thus developing in a variety of ways.

In the NT, Jesus is described as preaching the word (Mark 2:2) or word of God (Luke 5:1). In both cases, *logos* is used, as it most often is in the NT where the English has "word." The gospel message about Jesus can also be described as the word or word of God (Acts 4:31; 8:4; 1 Cor. 14:36).

Not surprisingly, in the Johannine literature, Jesus himself is called *logos* (John 1:14: "the Word became flesh"). In Rev. 19:13, Jesus is called "Word of God" *(logos* of God). Elsewhere, in the prologue of 1 John, he is referred to as "the word of life" (1:1).

Particularly significant is the role in creation assigned to the *logos*, who is incarnate in Jesus (John 1:14) in the prologue of the Fourth Gospel. It is not immediately obvious why a man sent from God, even the Messiah of Israel, should have played such a role. Yet Jesus Christ figures as the mediator in creation not only in John, but also in such NT books as 1 Corinthians (8:6), Colossians (1:15–17), and Hebrews (1:2), although the term *logos* is not used. (Interestingly enough, in 1 Cor. 1:24, Paul calls Christ "the wisdom of God," using the Greek term *sophia*, mentioned above, that has close connections with *logos*.) This development in the doctrine of Christ becomes immediately intelligible in light of the use of *logos* as God's creating and revealing mediator in Philo and the role played by "wisdom" in ancient Jewish wisdom literature. Yet an unprecedented step is taken by NT writers, especially the Fourth Evangelist, when it is claimed that the one who has played this role can be identified with a historic figure, Jesus of Nazareth. ***See also*** Christology; Creation; Jesus Christ; Philo; Septuagint; Stoics; Wisdom; Word.

D.M.S.

loincloth. ***See*** Dress.

Lois, Timothy's maternal grandmother, a woman of faith (2 Tim. 1:5). ***See also*** Eunice; Timothy.

loom. ***See*** Spinning and Weaving.

Lord, a title of dignity and honor acknowledging the power and authority of the one so addressed. In the OT "Lord" is used to translate various titles for God (e.g., *Adonai, El Shaddai*). It can also be used in a secular sense for a master or owner. In Aramaic these words are translated by *mārā*, with possessive suffixes ("my" or "our" Lord), and in Greek by *kyrios*. In the Septuagint the sacred name "Yahweh" was left untranslated in Hebrew characters but was read *kyrios*.

In Jesus' time the Aramaic word *mari*, "my Lord," was coming into use as a title of respect (not of divinity) in addressing human beings with authority, e.g., a rabbi, and it would appear that Jesus was so addressed (e.g., Matt. 7:21). Jesus insists that recognition of his authority requires obedience to the demands of God enunciated by him. Mark 7:28 suggests that a Greek-speaking woman could address Jesus as *kyrie*, "Lord" or "Sir." Thus, Jesus during his earthly life could be addressed as "Lord" in recognition of his authority as a teacher (rabbi) and as a charismatic prophet.

After Easter one of the most important OT texts to be applied to the Risen One was Psalm 110:1. Here the word "Lord" is used both for God and for the messianic king (Acts 2:34). The application of this text to Jesus meant that the title *mari*, "my Lord," addressed to him during his earthly life in recognition of his unusual authority was upgraded as a messianic address. Thus, we get the liturgical acclamation in Aramaic *marana tha*, "our Lord, come" (1 Cor. 16:22; Rev. 22:20).

Scholars once thought that use of the term "Lord" *(mārā)* in the absolute sense was not possible in Aramaic, but new evidence from the Dead Sea Scrolls shows that it was possible to refer to God as "Lord" or "*the* Lord," not only as "my Lord" or "our Lord." Consequently, it is possible that the formula from early Christian preaching, "God has made him both Lord and Christ" (Acts 2:36), goes back to the earliest Aramaic-speaking church. The title "Lord," while not connoting divinity in the metaphysical sense, means that at his exaltation Jesus entered upon a new function as the representative of God's Lordship in the world and over the church (Phil. 2:11). It is henceforth through the exalted Jesus that God exercises Lordship or kingly rule. The two "Lords" God and Jesus are distinguished from each other but not separated. We may assume that the Christology of Acts 2: 36 was shared by both the Aramaic- and Greek-speaking sections of the earliest Jerusalem community.

With the mission to the Gentiles, which began in Antioch (Acts 11:20), Christianity entered a milieu in which the title "Lord" was already given to the deities of various religious cults. They were "lords" (the feminine, *kyria*, was used for the goddess Isis) of their religious communities. Scholars used to hold that this pagan usage was the source for the application of the title *kyrios* to Jesus, but that theory has been ruled out by the Aramaic evidence for the use of "Lord." Moreover, Christianity did not regard Jesus as a cult deity. Christian worship was directed to the Father through the Son in the power of the Holy Spirit. At the same time Paul can assert the Lordship of Christ polemically against the pagan cults. "There are many 'gods' and many 'lords'—yet for us there is one God, the Father . . . and one Lord, Jesus Christ" (1 Cor. 8:6).

The title "Lord" *(kyrios)* was also coming into use in the eastern part of the Roman Empire for the emperor (Acts 25:26, here with the possessive pronoun, "my Lord"). It is doubtful, however, whether this usage had any direct effect on early Christian usage, although Luke's birth narratives polemically assert the Lordship of Christ over against the claims of Caesar (Luke 2:11).

Paul is the one NT author to develop the Lordship of Christ theologically. The authority of Jesus as teacher during his earthly life is projected into the present life of the believing community. Thus Paul uses the title "Lord" when he appeals to the teaching of the earthly Jesus (1 Cor. 7:10; 9:14; 11:21). Those who have been justified have been brought under the authority of the Lord Jesus and are now committed to obedience to him (Rom. 14:8; cf. Rom. 6: 3–11; 7:4–6). To be "in the Lord" is much the same as to be "in Christ," though the emphasis in the formula "in Christ" is primarily soteriological (having to do with salvation), whereas the emphasis of being "in the Lord" is primarily ethical. Thus, for example, Christians are to marry "in the Lord" (1 Cor. 7:39). "In the Lord" is also used in contexts concerned with ministerial activity: note how frequently the phrase occurs in Romans 16, where Paul is greeting those who shared his apostolic labors (Rom. 16:2). Finally, Paul uses "Lord" in contexts that speak of Christ's second coming. Those who are still alive at that time will be caught up in the air to meet "the Lord" (1 Thess. 4:17). That will happen "on the day of the Lord," not the day of Yahweh but the day of Christ (1 Thess. 5:12). ***See also*** Jesus Christ; Maranatha.

Bibliography

Fitzmyer, J. A. "New Testament *Kyrios* and *Maranatha* and Their Aramaic Background." *To Advance the Gospel.* New York: Crossroad, 1981. Pp. 218–35.

Fuller, R., and P. Perkins. *Who Is This Christ? Gospel Christology and Contemporary Faith.* Philadelphia: Fortress, 1983. Pp. 41–52.

Kramer, W. *Christ, Lord, Son of God.* Studies in Biblical Theology 50. London: SCM, 1966.

R.H.F.

lord, one who wields authority. When used to address some individual and not as a title for God or the Christ, this term conveys esteem to a leader from his people (e.g., Num. 32:25; cf. Acts 25:26), or a master from a slave (so the brothers to Joseph, Gen. 44:6–17; see also Jesus' parable of the wicked servant, Matt. 18:23–35). It can refer to secular heads of tribes or nations (e.g., "the five lords of the Philistines," Judg. 3: 3; Judg. 16; 1 Sam. 5:8; Isa. 16:8 ["The lords of the heights of the Arnon," Num. 21:28, may refer to idols]) or even an entire class of nobles (Dan. 1:10). In Dan. 5:1, Belshazzar gives a feast for a thousand of his lords or courtiers. It is over human lords such as these that God is "King of kings and Lord of lords" (1 Tim. 6:15; Rev. 19: 16). That lordship can be demonstrated even against the corrupt elite of Judah (cf. Jer. 22:8; 25:35; 34:5).

In one NT instance, Jesus uses the term to establish his authority over ancient custom: "The Son of man is lord even of the sabbath" (Mark 2:28; Matt. 12:8; Luke 6:5). As a verb ("to lord it over") the term is used occasionally to describe high-handed behavior (Neh. 5:15; Eccles. 8:9), the very antithesis of the style Jesus commands of his disciples (Luke 22:24–27; cf. 2 Cor. 1:24). W.S.T.

Lord of Hosts (KJV: "Lord of Sabaoth"), a term describing all the forces that operate at God's command throughout his whole creation (e.g., Ps. 89:6–8). It is an old title for God who, in the role of divine warrior, was the leader of the armies of Israel. He was believed to be enthroned upon the cherubim on the Ark of the covenant. For that reason, when the Israelites were preparing to go to war against the Philistines, they sent to the shrine at Shiloh in order to get the Ark, so that God, who was enthroned on the cherubim, might accompany them into battle, thus ensuring, they thought, their success (1 Sam. 4:4). In the NT, the term occurs in Rom. 9:29 and James 5:4. ***See also*** Names of God in the Old Testament.

M.A.F.

Lord of Sabaoth. ***See*** Lord of Hosts.

Lord's Day, the day of Jesus' resurrection, the first day of the week, Sunday. The phrase "the Lord's Day" occurs first in Rev. 1:10, the only occurrence of it in the NT. A similar phrase appears in *The Teaching of the Twelve Apostles,* also known as the *Didache* (Gk., "teaching"), a work written toward the end of the first century, probably in Syria. The readers of this work are instructed to gather on the Lord's Day to break bread and to give thanks *(Did.* 14:1). A similar practice is presupposed in Acts 20:7. When Paul instructed the Corinthians each to contribute to the collection for the saints in Judea on the first day of every week, he presupposed a gathering for worship on that day (1 Cor. 16:2). Each of the Gospels emphasizes the tradition that Jesus was raised on the first day of the week. That emphasis probably reflects liturgical practice. This association is especially clear in Luke, where the Emmaus story links the first day of the week, Jesus' resurrection, and the breaking of bread (Luke 24:13–35).

It is likely that many early Christians observed both the Sabbath, the seventh day of the week, Saturday, and the Lord's Day. Paul may have objected to Gentile Christians' adopting of Sabbath observance (Gal. 4:10). The Letter to the Colossians instructed its readers that Sabbath observance was not required (Col. 2:16). Ignatius, bishop of Antioch, wrote in the early part of the second century that the Lord's Day should be observed in place of the Sabbath (Ign. *Magn.* 9:1). ***See also*** Sabbath. A.Y.C.

Lord's Prayer, the, a prayer given by Jesus to his followers. It is found in different versions in Matt. 6:9–13 and Luke 11:2–4. The version in Matthew is longer, consisting of an address and seven petitions. It is embedded in the Sermon on the Mount (5:1–7:29), where Jesus instructs his followers (5:3–16) in doing the "greater" righteousness (5:20), which means to be wholehearted in doing God's will as interpreted by Jesus (5:48; 7:21). Acts of piety that express the greater righteousness are alms giving, prayer, and fasting (6:1–18). Such acts are to be performed in worship of God, however, and not for public show (6:1). As an example of how his disciples should pray (6:9a), Jesus recites the Lord's Prayer, which is devoid of the "empty phrases" and "many words" that characterize the prayers of the Gentiles (6:7). Here, the Lord's Prayer is a model that the disciples are to approximate in formulating their own prayers.

In Luke, the Lord's Prayer appears in a section that one scholar has termed a "catechism of prayer" (11:1–13). Jesus is on his way to Jerusalem in the company of his disciples (9:51; 13:22). Having observed Jesus at prayer, one of his disciples asks him to teach them to pray, just as John the Baptist taught his disciples (11:1). In response, Jesus recites the Lord's Prayer (11:2–4). This version, perhaps closer to the original, is shorter than the one in Matthew, consisting of an address and only five petitions. It, too, is a model prayer, but one intended for habitual use by the disciples (11:2a).

In its original form, the Lord's Prayer probably comes from the earthly Jesus himself. One indication of this is that the version in Luke essentially reappears in Matthew. Another is the Jewish and Aramaic character of the prayer. Here, two points are important: first, in form and content, the Lord's Prayer parallels in important respects the Kaddish and the Eighteen Benedictions—Jewish prayers apparently in use, in their oldest forms, in the synagogue worship of Jesus' time; second, behind the Greek word for "Father" is the Aramaic *abba*, and behind the Greek for "debts" and "sins" is *choba*. Jesus himself apparently addressed God as *abba* (cf. Mark 14:36), thus establishing a custom that was continued even by Greek-speaking Christians (Gal. 4:6; Rom. 8:15). *Choba* means "debt" or, in a religious context, "sin" or "guilt"; thus, in Aramaic, forgiveness of "debts" (Matt. 6:12) is the same as forgiveness of "sins" (Luke 11:4).

The Lord's Prayer divides itself into four parts: the address, "thou" petitions, "we" petitions, and doxology. In the address, Jesus instructs his disciples to call upon God as "Father." In the OT and intertestamental Jewish literature, God is described variously as the Father of his covenant people, Israel (Deut. 32:6), of the Davidic king (2 Sam. 7:14; Ps. 89:26), of righteous Israelites (Ps. 103:13; Ecclus. 51:10;

THE LORD'S PRAYER IN MATTHEW AND LUKE

	Matthew 6:9–13	***Luke 11:2–4***
Address:	Our **Father** who art in heaven,	**Father**,
"Thou	**Hallowed be thy name**.	**Hallowed be thy name**.
Petitions:	**Thy kingdom come**,	**Thy kingdom come**.
	Thy will be done,	
	on earth as it is in heaven.	
"We"	*Give us today*	*Give us each day*
Petitions:	**our bread for the morrow**;	**our bread for the morrow**;
	And forgive us our *debts*,	**And forgive us our** *sins*,
	as we also have forgiven	*for we ourselves forgive*
	our debtors;	*everyone who is indebted*
		to us;
	And lead us not into temptation,	**And lead us not into temptation.**
	But deliver us from evil.	
Doxology:	[For thine is the kingdom and the	
	power and the glory forever. Amen.]	

Boldface and italic indicate, respectively, exact and approximate parallels. Where translation departs from RSV it is that of J. D. Kingsbury.

Jubilees 1:24), and as the one who will act in the future to deliver his people (Isa. 63:16; Mal. 3:17). When Jesus addresses God as Father in the Gospels, however, he gives expression to his awareness of his own unique filial relationship to God (Mark 14:36). In Jesus' person and words and deeds, God's Kingdom, or end-time Rule, is a present, albeit hidden, reality (Matt. 12:28; Luke 17:20–21). Jesus is the one through whom God reveals himself to humankind (Matt. 11:27; Luke 10:22) and the one who is God's supreme agent of salvation (Matt. 1:21; Luke 2:11). In calling persons to become his disciples, Jesus, the Son of God, makes of them sons of God who do the will of God and live in the sphere of God's end-time Rule (Matt. 5:45; Luke 6:35). Still, in speaking of God to his disciples, Jesus distinguishes between God as "my Father" and God as "your Father." "Our Father" is the corporate expression employed by the disciples, exclusive of Jesus (Matt. 6:9). Nonetheless, through Jesus, who is uniquely the Son of God, the disciples are given to know God as a gracious and loving Father and are invited to approach him as such in prayer.

The words, "who art in heaven," found only in Matthew, characterize God as the heavenly Father of the disciples in contradistinction to their earthly fathers. More importantly, "heaven" is also seen as that indeterminate place from which God exercises his Rule and, through Jesus, effects his purposes on earth.

The "thou" petitions of the Lord's Prayer focus on God and implore God to act so as to achieve his purposes in the world. The first petition (hallowing God's name) is further explicated by the second (coming of God's Kingdom) and the third, found only in Matthew (doing God's will). God's "name" is synonymous with God himself; the first petition invokes God to make his holiness manifest to the world by ushering in the final day of salvation. To concretize this, the disciples pray, "Thy kingdom come," and, "Thy will be done, on earth as it is in heaven." Here, God is called upon, as part and parcel of his holiness, to establish his kingly Rule in splendor over all nations and (in Matthew) to exercise his will here on earth with as much freedom from opposition as he presently exercises it in the sphere of his heavenly abode.

The "we" petitions focus on the physical and spiritual needs of the disciples. The petition for bread is a request for the necessities of life. Traditionally translated (in Matthew), "Give us this day our daily bread," it is more accurately rendered, "Give us today our bread for the morrow." At the basis of this petition is the notion that the disciples pray for the necessities of life that they require "today" in view of the fact that "tomorrow" God's splendid Kingdom will come. The petition for the forgiveness of debts, or sins, is an appeal that God, as Father of the disciples, will graciously forgive them their sins and so enable them to forgive one another. The final petition in Luke (not being led into temptation), which is supplemented in Matthew by the petition for deliverance from evil, is a plea that God so guide the disciples through life that their relationship to him as Father may never come into jeopardy and that they may be preserved from Satanic evil of every kind.

The doxology, though missing in the oldest and best manuscripts of Matthew and not original to the Lord's Prayer, is a fitting conclusion to the prayer. Here, the disciples praise God for the unmerited privilege of knowing him as Father and assert their confidence that he will give an ear to their petition. ***See also*** Abba; God; Heaven; Kingdom of God; Prayer; Sermon on the Mount, The; Sin; Temptation.

J.D.K.

Lord's Supper, the, the last meal Jesus shared with his disciples prior to his death. The early Christian celebration known as the Lord's Supper receives this name from Paul's reference to "the supper of the Lord" in 1 Cor. 11:20. Its origin is Jesus' last meal with his disciples. Even if the synoptic Gospels are correct in describing this "last supper" as a Passover meal (in John, Jesus' last meal is eaten *before* Passover), that meal should still be viewed in the context of the table fellowship that was a distinctive feature of Jesus' ministry.

The words "after supper" in the tradition quoted by Paul in 1 Cor. 11:23–25 indicate that the Lord's Supper was originally a full meal, introduced by the blessing and breaking of the bread and concluded by the blessing and passing of the cup. Today, however, it is widely assumed that by the time 1 Corinthians was written the bread and cup were taken together at the *end* of the common meal, as a special sacramental act.

In earliest Christianity the Lord's Supper was pervaded by intense eschatological expectation. Fervent hope for the new age, to be inaugurated by the risen and exalted Jesus upon his return to earth, is obvious in Mark 14:25 and Luke 22:18 and is echoed in 1 Cor. 11:26.

Most scholars think that the words spoken over bread and cup were a crucial part of the Lord's Supper liturgy from the beginning. Nevertheless, it is not possible to determine what the original "words of institution" were, for, as even a cursory comparison shows, the different versions are by no means identical in their details (Matt. 26:26–29; Mark 14:22–25; Luke 22:14–22; 1 Cor. 11:23–26; cf. John 6:35–59). In all the Gospels, as in 1 Corinthians, the bread and wine are connected with Jesus' redemptive death, but the different writings reflect distinctive understandings of the Lord's Supper.

Jesus' last meal with his disciples, as depicted by Nicholas of Verdun on a panel from the altar at Klosterneuberg Abbey, 1180.

1 Corinthians, in fact, reveals two views of the Supper—that of Paul's "opponents" and that of the apostle himself. Apparently some of the Corinthian Christians thought that they could participate in pagan cults at will because the bread and wine of the Lord's Supper ensured salvation. Paul, in response, draws a parallel between the eucharistic bread and wine and the spiritual food and drink (manna and water from the rock) that nourished the ancestors in the wilderness (1 Cor. 10:1–4). He argues that as the ancient "sacrament" did not protect the ancestors from God's judgment when they committed idolatry, so the Lord's Supper will not magically protect Christians who partake of the cup of demons (1 Cor. 10: 6–22). The cup of blessing is rather a "*koinonia* of the blood of Christ," and the bread is a "*koinonia* of the body of Christ." The Greek word *koinonia* can be translated "fellowship," "communion," or "sharing." Some think that Paul's emphasis is on partaking of bread and wine as a means of communing with the Crucified and Risen One; others see partaking as a means of securing the benefits of Jesus' saving death. In either case, playing on a second sense of "body of Christ," Paul affirms that those who share bread and cup are bound together with each other: the many are made one by partaking of the one loaf (1 Cor. 10:17).

The apostle's emphasis is similar in 1 Corinthians 11, where he excoriates the Corinthians for the class consciousness and insensitivity to the poor that keeps the common meal from being the *Lord's* Supper. The tradition he quotes in 11:23–25 reminds the Corinthians of the meaning of Christ's death: the bread re-presents the body "for you"; the shared cup actualizes the new covenant effected through Jesus' death (see Jer. 31:31–34). If the Supper is truly to "proclaim the Lord's death until he comes," it must be marked by loving concern for every member of the body. To eat and drink without "discerning the body" is to incur divine judgment (11: 29).

In Mark's words of institution (14:22–25) the phrase "my blood of the covenant" probably echoes Exod. 24:8, and "poured out for many" stresses the atoning efficacy of Jesus' death. Matthew makes the point even more explicit by adding "for the forgiveness of sins" to Mark's cup formula (Matt. 26:28). Among the Gospels and 1 Corinthians, Luke's cup-bread-cup order is unique. Many scholars think that Luke's "long text" (that is, 22:19b–20—not included in all ancient manuscripts—as well as 22:17–19a) is dependent on Mark plus a tradition similar to that quoted by Paul. Luke (long text) is the only Gospel that, like 1 Corinthians 11, includes Jesus' command "Do this in remembrance of me."

In the Gospel of John Jesus does not institute the Lord's Supper during the last meal with his disciples, but the "bread of life" discourse in John 6 (vv. 25–59) likely reflects the understanding of the Lord's Supper in the Johannine community. Scholars disagree, however, about what that understanding was. Jesus speaks of eating his flesh and drinking his blood as the means of attaining eternal life (6:53–58). At least three interpretations of these words are possible. First, the language is sacramental: when believers eat the bread and drink the wine they are partaking of sacred food and drink that gives eternal life. (Compare the view of Ignatius of Antioch, who in the second century described the eucharistic bread as "a medicine of immortality" [Ign. *Eph.* 20:2].) Second, the language of eating Jesus' flesh and drinking his blood dramatically suggests that one must *appropriate* God's salvation, made available through Jesus' death, by being spiritually united with the Crucified and Risen One. Third, in light of the emphasis at John 6:63, the shocking and offensive language in John 6 (e.g., vv. 51, 52–57; cf. v. 60) points to the scandal of the incarnation: to have eternal life one must commit oneself to Jesus as the revealer sent from God, the Word become flesh (John 1:14). ***See also*** Jesus Christ; Passover, The; Sacraments; Worship.

Bibliography

Bornkamm, G. "Lord's Supper and Church in Paul." *Early Christian Experience.* New York: Harper & Row, 1969. Chap. 9.

Jeremias, J. *The Eucharistic Words of Jesus.* New York: Scribner, 1966.

Schweizer, E. *The Lord's Supper According to the New Testament.* Philadelphia: Fortress, 1967.

S.K.W.

Lot (laht), the son of Abraham's brother Haran. Lot is first mentioned in Gen. 11:31 as migrating with his uncle Abraham and grandfather Terah from Ur of the Chaldeans toward Canaan. After Terah's death in the Syrian locale of Haran, Lot accompanied Abraham on his journey into Canaan (12:1–9) and to and from Egypt (12:10–20; 13:1). Upon their return, a quarrel between Lot's and Abraham's herdsmen (13:7) prompted Abraham to propose an amicable separation, offering Lot his choice of where to settle. Lot preferred the well-watered Jordan plain and its prosperous towns. Abraham settled in Hebron.

Lot appears in Genesis 14 as a captive in a battle between five kings of the Jordan plain and four invading Mesopotamian kings. Abraham, with only 318 men, defeated and pursued the invaders beyond Damascus, recovering Lot and his possessions. Abraham indirectly aided Lot a second time (18:23–33) when he pleaded with God to spare Sodom and Gomorrah from destruction because of the few righteous among its inhabitants. God nevertheless destroyed the cities but first sent divine emissaries to rescue Lot and his family (19:1–29). The emissaries appeared as wayfarers and reluctantly accepted Lot's hospitality. When rowdy townsmen sought to harm the newcomers, Lot pleaded with them, offering his daughters instead. But the emissaries blinded the mob, and, with some difficulty, persuaded Lot and his wife and daughter to leave. Lot pleaded for a refuge in the nearby town of Zoar (Heb., "trifle"), which the emissaries, pressed for time, granted. On departing, Lot's wife, looking back at the destruction, turned into a pillar of salt. Lot's daughters, believing themselves the world's sole survivors, plied Lot with liquor and cohabited with him, conceiving Moab (Heb., "of the same father") and Ben-ammi (Heb., "son of paternal kin"), ancestors of Israel's Transjordanian neighbors, the Moabites and Ammonites (Gen. 19:30–38). ***See also*** Abraham; Ammonites; Moab; Sodom. J.W.R.

lot, lots, objects the casting or drawing of which was a common method for determining the divine will in ancient Israel and in NT times. A range of questions, usually posed or subdivided so that a yes or no would suffice, were dealt with in this manner. The Hebrew word *goral*, the standard term for "lot," has the additional meaning of "destiny" in certain biblical texts (Isa. 17:14; Jer. 13:25; Dan. 12:13) and in the Dead Sea Scrolls comes to mean "fate." In addition, the noun *pur*, related to the Akkadian *puru*, is found in the book of Esther; hence the name of the festival, Purim. The word *pur* denotes the instrument Haman used to fix the day for the pogrom. In Esther 3:7, *pur* is specifically identified with *goral*.

Various notable events recorded in the Bible were determined by the choosing or casting of lots. Saul, Israel's first king, was selected in this manner (1 Sam. 10:16–26), the conquered land was apportioned among the tribes by lot (Num. 26:55; Josh. 14:2), the identity of Achen as the thief of the spoil from Jericho was discovered by lot (Josh. 7:14), and by this means Jonathan was found to be the (unwitting) violator of his father's oath (1 Sam. 14:42). The ranks of Temple personnel were also determined by lot (1 Chron. 24:5; 25:8; 26:13; cf. Luke 1:9). The soldiers who crucified Jesus divided up his possessions by lot (Matt. 27:35; Mark 15:24; Luke 23:34; John 19:24 mentions Jesus' seamless robe as the object of a special casting of lots), and Matthias was chosen in this way to replace Judas among the twelve apostles (Acts 1:26).

Lots found at Masada, a mountaintop fortress on the western shore of the Dead Sea and final holdout of Jews in the rebellion against Rome, A.D. 66–73. Each is inscribed with a name and may have been used to determine who would slay the others in order to avoid capture by the Romans.

References to the use of lots abound, and the legitimacy of this means of determining the divine will was never questioned. Yet no detailed description of the actual procedures involved or of the precise nature of the instrument(s) used is offered in the Bible. ***See also*** Purim, The Feast of; Saul; Urim and Thummim. W.L.H.

Lotan (loh'tan), a son of Seir the Horite and chieftain of the Horites who inhabited the hill country of Seir (Edom) in patriarchal times (Gen. 36:20, 29). ***See also*** Horites; Seir.

love, in the Bible a relationship of self-giving. **Love in the Old Testament:** In the OT the verb "to love" (Heb. *'ahab*) and its cognates cover the full range of meanings the English word "love" has, including love for God (Exod. 20:6; Ps. 40:17) and the love God has for his people (Hos. 3:1; Deut. 7:13). This latter sense of love, God's love for his people in the covenant context, is often expressed by the term "steadfast love" (Heb. *ḥesed*). God's steadfast love is a sign of his fidelity.

A review of some texts will indicate the wide range of meaning "love" has. It can be used to describe physical love between the sexes, as well as sexual concupiscence (Gen. 34:3; Judg. 16:4, 15; 2 Sam. 13:4, 15; see also Song of Sol.). The description of love between the sexes transcending the purely physical is also common (Gen. 24:67; 29:20: "So Jacob served seven years for Rachel, and they seemed to him but a few days because of the love he had for her"). The Hebrew word can refer to love within a family (Gen. 22:2; 25:28; Ruth 4:15); among friends (Ps. 38:12; Jer. 20:4–6); and between superior and inferior or slave and master (Deut. 15:16). Especially significant is the command that Israel love the foreigner or stranger, and the rationale for such action (Lev. 19:34: "The stranger who sojourns with you shall be to you as the native among you, and you shall love him as yourself; for you were strangers in the land of Egypt: I am the Lord your God"; also Deut. 10:19). Additionally, Israel is instructed to love the neighbor, namely, the fellow Israelite (Lev. 19:18).

With the prophecy of Hosea (mid-eighth century B.C.), a profound theological conception of love is introduced into the literature of Israel. Hosea was speaking prior to the fall of Samaria to the Assyrians in 721 B.C., and he used the imagery of love and marriage to describe the faithlessness of Israel to its God. The problem is described in Hos. 6:4–6: "What shall I do with you, O Ephraim? What shall I do with you, O Judah? Your love is like a morning cloud, like the dew that goes early away.... For I desire steadfast love and not sacrifice, the knowledge of God, rather than burnt offerings" (see also 9:15; 11:1–7). The depth of God's compassionate love is manifested in his directive to Hosea to buy back again his adulterous wife, a directive that broke with legal custom and revealed the freedom by which only the Holy One of Israel can act: "Go again, love a woman who is beloved of a paramour and is an adulteress ..." (3:1). Similarly God will restore Israel, a theme expressed throughout this OT book, as, for example, in 11:8–9: "How can I give you up, O Ephraim! How can I hand you over, O Israel! How can I make you like Admah! How can I treat you like Zeboiim! My heart recoils within me, my compassion grows warm and tender. I will not execute my fierce anger, I will not again destroy Ephraim; for I am God and not man, the Holy One in your midst, and I will not come to destroy." As God initiated the covenant (11:1: "When Israel was a child, I loved him, and out of Egypt I called my son") so now, because he is the Holy One, he invites Israel once again to respond to the depth of his love for it. Similar language is found occasionally in Jeremiah (2:2; 3:2) and in Deutero-Isaiah (i.e., Isa. 40–55), but without the harlot motif. Isaiah can describe God as "your husband" (54:5–8) and can have God proclaim his love for Israel by using feminine language and imagery: "Can a woman forget her sucking child, that she should have no compassion on the son of her womb? Even these may forget, yet I will not forget you" (49:15). The metaphor is similar to Hosea's, but the roles are reversed.

In Deuteronomy the concept of love is systematically included, but its tone is considerably less passionate than that found in Hosea. The essential function of love is to undergird the concepts of election and covenant and thus the freedom of God as observed in Hosea is restrained as, for example, in Deut. 7:12–13: "And because you hearken to these ordinances, and keep and do them, the Lord your God will keep with you the covenant and the steadfast love which he swore to your fathers to keep; he will love you, bless you, and multiply you ..." (note also 4:37; 7:8; 10:15). To love God is to keep his commandments (5:10; 7:9); love is now a requirement (10:12; 11:1, 11, 13) and it is in this sense that one must understand the great *shema* (Heb., "hear") in Deut. 6:4–6: "Hear, O Israel: The Lord our God is one Lord; and you shall love the Lord your God with all your heart, and with all your soul, and with all your might. And these words which I command you this day shall be upon your heart...."

Love in the New Testament: In the NT the primary Greek words used to express the concept of love are *agapan/agape* and *philein/philia*; *eros*, signifying sexual love in Greek, is not used in the NT. Although the NT much prefers the use of *agapan*, in contrast to normal Greek usage, it is difficult to draw any precise distinctions between the NT use of *agapan* and the use of *philein*.

In the synoptic Gospels, one notes that the primary use of "love" is with regard to the great commandment (Mark 12:28–34; Matt. 22:34–40; Luke 20:39–40). In Mark a scribe approaches Jesus and asks, " 'Which commandment is the first of all?' Jesus answered, 'The first is "Hear, O Israel: The Lord our God, the Lord is one; and you shall love the Lord your God with all your heart, and with all your soul, and with all your mind, and with all your strength." The second is this, "You shall love your neighbor as yourself." There is no other commandment greater than these' " (Mark 12:28–31). The answer Jesus gives (in Matthew and Luke it is the lawyer who gives the answer) is derived from Deut. 6:5 and Lev. 19:8. God expects to be loved with the totality of one's being; the neighbor is to be loved with the same love as one has for oneself (see also Matt. 19:19).

In Matt. 5:43–46 (see Luke 6:27–35) the theme "love your enemies" is emphasized. While this is hinted at in Exod. 23:4–5 and Prov. 25:21–22 (note Paul's expansion of this in Rom. 12:16–21), the texts in both these Gospels certainly intensify this motif. Matt. 6:24 (see Luke 16:13) makes clear that God expects total response and commitment from those who claim to love him (Luke 16:13: "No servant can serve two masters; for either he will hate the one and love the other, or he will be devoted to the one and despise the other. You cannot serve God and mammon"). In Matthew, Jesus emphasizes a similar point in the context of discipleship; the disciple must love Jesus more than any family member (10: 37–38). Another reference to love found only in Matthew is in the final, eschatological narrative of the Gospel: "And because wickedness is multiplied, most men's love will grow cold. But he who endures to the end will be saved" (24:12–13). This emphasis fits in well with Matthew's emphasis on ethics, particularly in view of the delayed Parousia (24:48). Luke, too, has a passage dealing with the concept of love that is unique to his Gospel: the woman with the ointment (7:36–50). "To love" appears specifically in 7:42 and 47: "Therefore I tell you, her sins, which are many, are forgiven, for she loved much; but he who is forgiven little, loves little." Love is not the cause of her forgiveness; rather her repentance and forgiveness are the reason she is able to love.

Paul's Perspective on Love: In order to understand Paul's perspective on love, it is important to note that it is often linked with faith and hope (1 Cor. 13:13: "So faith, hope, love abide, these three; but the greatest of these is love"; see 1 Thess. 1:3; 5:8; Gal. 5:5–6). Love is a possibility only because the believer has responded to God's salvific act in the death and resurrection of Christ with faith (Rom. 5:8: "But God shows his love for us in that while we were yet sinners Christ died for us"; see Gal. 2:20). Love is given to the believer by the Holy Spirit as a gift to be exercised now and as a sign of the future consummation of that new creation which God has begun in Christ, a fulfillment that is expected in hope. In fact, hope "does not disappoint us, because God's love has been poured into our hearts through the Holy Spirit which has been given us" (Rom. 5:5).

Love as a virtue personified; bronze relief by Andrea Pisano, South Doors, Baptistry, Florence, 1336.

Love is the primary term describing the result of faith both for the believer and the community in Christ. Because Christ has died and the Holy Spirit has given the believer the gift of love, Paul can write the Corinthians that the "love of Christ controls us . . ." (2 Cor. 2:4). Paul is emphatic that love does not originate in the human heart. It is not a human possibility, it is a divine gift. It is Christ who now lives in the believer (Gal. 2:20); therefore the believer must actualize this love of Christ. Faith works through love (Gal. 5:6) and it must increase and abound (1 Thess. 1:12). The one in Christ must walk in love (Rom. 14:15). For this reason the apostle always gives a priority to love (1 Cor. 13:13), especially over knowledge. " 'Knowledge' puffs up, but love builds up" (1 Cor. 8:1). Paul is careful to note that a person can love God, but not know him; rather one is known by God. Love must be concerned not with self-elevation and boasting, but with the needs of the weak members of the body of Christ. Love is considerate of this weak brother or sister, otherwise "this weak man is destroyed, the brother for whom Christ died. Thus, sinning against your brethren and wounding their conscience when it is weak, you sin against Christ" (1 Cor. 8:11–12; note also Matt. 25:31–46). To emphasize this primary nature of love in the life of the new Christian community, Paul devotes an entire chapter to the theme in his magnificent description of love in 1 Cor. 13. That this hymn of love appears in a letter to Corinth is hardly accidental when it is remembered that one of the cult centers of Aphrodite (the Greek goddess of love who often appears together with Eros) was in Corinth.

Paul is careful to root his concept of love not only in the Christ event, but in the OT as well, undoubtedly as a way to prevent love from becoming a coverall for selfishness and self-desire. This tendency is clear in Gal. 5:14 and in response Paul cites Lev. 19:18: "For the whole law is fulfilled in one word, 'You shall love your neighbor as yourself.' " Similarly, we find such a usage of the OT in Rom. 13:8–10. Here Paul asserts that the one exception to obedience to the authorities is when they prohibit the love of neighbor; he then proceeds to articulate that theme. Additionally, love can also give great personal assurance. Among such lines the apostle writes to the Romans: "we know that in everything God works for good with those who love him. . . . For I am sure that neither death, nor life, nor angels, nor principalities, nor things present, nor things to come, nor powers, nor height, nor depth, nor anything else in all creation will be able to separate us from the love of God in Christ Jesus our Lord" (8:28–39).

The Johannine Writings: In the Johannine school (the Gospel of John; 1, 2, 3 John; and perhaps Revelation) the concept of love plays a central role, and it is here that we find an apparently synonymous usage between *agapan* and *philein*. In the first half of the Gospel (chaps. 1–12) there is no consistent usage. Jesus loves Lazarus (11:3, 36; *philein*) and Martha and her sister (11:5; *agapan*). In a debate with Jews, Jesus responds, "If God were your Father, you would love me . . ." (8:42; *agapan*). Even though "God so loved the world that he gave his only son" (3:16; *agapan*), "men loved darkness rather than light . . ." (3:19; *agapan*). John 10:17 is a direct allusion to the death, resurrection, and glorification of Jesus: "For this reason the Father loves *(agapan)* me, because I lay down my life, that I may take it again." The aspect of the Father loving the Son is also found in 3:35 *(agapan)* and 5:20 *(philein)*. In the second half of the Gospel a more consistent ethical dimension of love within the community is stressed. The key text is 13:34–35: "A new commandment I give to you, that you love one another; even as I have loved you, that you also love one another. By this all men will know that you are my disciples, if you have love for one another." This key verse is emphasized over and over again as essential to the existence of the Christian community (14: 15, 21, 23, 24; 15:9, 12, 17). Another series of texts revolve around the enigmatic "beloved disciple," someone who is without question deeply loved and respected in this Johannine community and, perhaps, is the apostle John himself. This disciple whom Jesus loved is discussed in 13:23; 19:26; 20:2; 21:7; and 21:15, 16, 17. In John 17, which contains the high priestly prayer of Jesus for the unity of his disciples, the desire is expressed "that the love with which thou has loved me may be in them, and I in them" (v. 26), because the oneness of the disciples is necessary if the world is to believe that the Father has sent the Son and loves the believers as much as the Son. Finally, the threefold questioning of Peter in the final edition of the Gospel (21:15–17) with the repeated "Do you love me?" suggests that the authority given to Peter must always be exercised in the context of love (note the similar theme in 1 Pet. 5:1–5).

The basic pattern of love defined in John 13: 34 and further articulated there, continues in the three Letters and the book of Revelation. The obvious connection with John 13 is evident in 1 John 2:7 ("Beloved, I am writing you no new commandment, but an old commandment which you had from the beginning . . ."), 1 John 3:23 ("And this is his commandment, that we should believe in the name of his Son Jesus Christ and love one another, just as he had commanded us"), 2 John 6 ("And this is love, that we follow his commandments; this is the commandment, as you have heard from the beginning, that you follow love"), and Rev. 2:4 ("But I have this against you, that you have abandoned the love you had at first"). The author of 1 John is intent on making clear the ethical implications of love and to eradicate any hypocrisy. An essential text in this writing is 3: 18: "Little children, let us not love in word or speech but in deed and in truth." Thus, the person "who says he is in the light and hates his brother is in the darkness still" (1 John 2:9); "whoever does not do right is not of God, nor he who does not love his brother" (1 John 3: 10); "If any one says, 'I love God,' and hates his brother, he is a liar; for he who does not love his brother whom he has seen, cannot love God whom he has not seen" (1 John 4:20). It is 1 John that has given us the well-known verse, "He who does not love does not know God; for God is love" (4:8). In this context the writer stresses again the priority of God's love in Christ in response to which the believers are permitted and encouraged to love one another. Thus, the Johannine authors as a whole are quite close to the Pauline understanding of love and are sophisticated interpreters of the purpose and ministry of Jesus. ***See also*** Faith; Hope.

K.P.D.

loving-kindness, a characteristic of God in the OT. The Hebrew word *khesed,* which is rendered by the KJV as "loving-kindness" (30 times), as "kindness" (38 times), and as "mercy" (145 times), is translated in the RSV chiefly as "steadfast love" (182 times) and "kindness" (21 times), but occasionally as "great kindness" (Gen. 19:19) or "loyal love" (1 Sam. 20:14). In its preference for "mercy" the KJV was obviously influenced by the Septuagint (LXX) which in 168 instances renders *khesed* as "mercy" or "compassion" (Gk. *eleos).*

All renderings in English only approximate the richness of the original. It contains the idea of devotion, loyalty, and covenant faithfulness (see Exod. 34:6; Neh. 9:32). Thus one who was *ḥasēed* (Ps. 18:25) was a "loyal" (RSV) "devout person." The plural *ḥasidim* is used frequently by historians to describe the pious and devout predecessors of the Pharisees at the time of the Maccabean revolt (167 B.C.).

This word is used chiefly, but not exclusively, of God. The "kindness" the prophet Micah enjoins humankind to love includes both its human and divine aspects (Mic. 6:1–6). It is thus a metonym for covenantal loyalty and performance.

J.G.G.

Lubim (lo͞o'bim), the Hebrew word for Libya and Libyans in the KJV, the equivalent of Egyptian *Rebu*, "Libu." These North African people settled in Egypt and served as mercenaries in the Egyptian army in the latter part of the second millennium B.C. A Libyan dynasty (the twenty-second dynasty) ruled Egypt from ca. 945 to 715 B.C. In 925 B.C. Libyans served with Shishak (Shoshenq I) when he campaigned in Palestine (2 Chron. 12:3). Subsequently (ca. 897 B.C.), they formed an important element in the army led by the Ethiopian general Zerah, who fought unsuccessfully against King Asa of Judah (2 Chron. 14:9; 16:8). Libyans also served on the side of the Ethiopians when the Assyrians captured No-amon (Thebes) in 663 B.C. (Nah. 3:9). ***See also*** Shishak; Zerah. J.M.W.

Lucifer (lo͞o'si-fuhr), the English translation in the KJV (Isa. 14:12) of the Hebrew word meaning "light bringer" or "shining one," sometimes designating the morning (or day) star, that is, Venus (cf. RSV: "Day Star"). The English word "Lucifer" comes from the Latin for "light bearer." In Isa. 14:12, the King of Babylon, in an apparent reference to Canaanite mythology, is tauntingly called "Day Star, son of Dawn" because he has fallen from his lofty but temporary position of power. In the Christian church, this passage from Isaiah came to be connected with Jesus' saying in Luke 10:18: "I saw Satan fall like lightning from heaven." Thus the connection was made (erroneously) between Lucifer and Satan, and Lucifer was popularly understood as another name for Satan. ***See also*** Canaan, Canaanites; Devil; Satan; Stars, Star of Bethlehem. J.M.E.

Lucius (lo͞o'shuhs). **1** A Roman consul who sent a letter supporting Simon Maccabeus in his struggle against the Seleucids (1 Macc. 15:15–24). ***See also*** Maccabees; Seleucids, The. **2** A prophet and teacher from Cyrene in the church at Antioch (Acts 13:1). ***See also*** Antioch; Cyrene; Prophet. **3** An associate of Paul who sends greetings in Rom. 16:21. There is no evidence that he is the Lucius of Cyrene or Luke the reputed author of the Gospel of Luke and Acts.

Lud (luhd), a name given to the son of Shem (Gen. 10:22). In its plural form, Ludim (lo͞o'dim), it designates a group of people (Isa. 66:19; Ezek. 30:5; it is now widely recognized that the Table of Nations in Genesis 10 is a record of historical and geographical relationships rather than strictly a genealogicial record). Their identification is difficult and various proposals have been made, none entirely satisfactory. There are apparently two groups designated by the name. One group is associated with peoples in Asia Minor (Isa. 66:19; possibly also Ezek. 27:10) and would probably include the "sons" of Shem (Gen. 10:22) who were Semitic people. They are often identified with the kingdom of Lydia on the western coast of Asia Minor. However the Lydians were not Semitic peoples and have little connection with other OT groups, so this identification is questionable. The second group appears to be centered in North Africa (Ezek. 30:5; Jer. 46:9) and is probably to be connected with the Ludim (Gen. 10:13) who are said to be "sons" of Mizraim (Egypt). Various conjectures are offered for their identification but none is supported by textual evidence. It is possible that the two groups are of the same origin and settled in various places. The fact that they appear in the biblical record as mercenary soldiers in the army of Tyre (Ezek. 27:10; see also 30:5) and as skilled bowmen (Jer. 46:9) might account for their wide dispersion. ***See also*** Put; Sardis. D.R.B.

Luke, the transliteration of the Greek *Loukas*, probably an affectionate form of the Latin name Lucius (Gk. *Loukios*). The name appears three times in the NT, all in Letters attributed to Paul: Philem. 24; Col. 4:14; 2 Tim. 4:11.

In Philem. 23–24, Luke, along with Epaphras, Mark, Aristarchus, and Demas, is said to be with Paul, and they join him in sending greetings to Philemon, Apphia, and Archippus (v. 2). Epaphras is called Paul's fellow prisoner (v. 23), while Luke and the others are called his fellow workers, as is Philemon (v. 2). In Col. 4:10–14, Luke, along with Demas, Aristarchus, Mark, Epaphras, and others, joins Paul in sending greetings. Here, Luke is called "the beloved physician." In 2 Tim. 4:10–12, Paul is said to have been deserted by or to have sent to other places most of his former associates (Demas, Crescens, Titus, and Tychicus). Only Luke is with him, and Paul asks Timothy to join him with Mark.

It seems clear that all three passages are intended to refer to the same person. Since, however, two of the references appear in Letters that may not have been written by Paul himself (Colossians and 2 Timothy), Philemon must be regarded as the most important reference. We should therefore put more weight on the image of Luke as a fellow worker with Paul than upon that of Luke as the beloved physician.

It is possible that the Lucius referred to in Rom. 16:21 is the same as the Luke of Philem. 24 and the other references. In Romans, however, Lucius, Jason, and Sosipater are called Paul's kinsmen and distinguished from Timothy, who is called "my fellow worker." Although the third-century scholar Origen identified the two, most modern scholars do not agree. Another Lucius is mentioned in Acts 13:1, as one of the prophets in the church at Antioch. There is little to suggest, however, that this is the person referred to in the Pauline Letters.

Irenaeus (late second century bishop of Lyons) appears to have been the first to identify the author of the third Gospel as Luke, "the companion of Paul." The Muratorian Canon, a late second century list of authoritative Christian writings, agrees and adds that this Luke was a physician, not an eyewitness of the events narrated in the Gospel but a participant in some of those in Acts, which he also wrote (presumably, a reference to the "We Passages" in Acts, in which the author uses the first-person plural pronoun, thus appearing to identify himself as a participant in the narrative). Luke, the companion of Paul, has traditionally been identified as the author of both the Gospel of Luke and the book of Acts. Modern critical scholars agree that the same author wrote both books but are more cautious about the identification of this author. ***See also*** Acts of the Apostles, The; Colossians, The Letter of Paul to the; Lucius; Luke, The Gospel According to; Timothy, The First and Second Letters of Paul to, and Titus, The Letter of Paul to.

J.B.T.

Luke, the Gospel According to, the third book in the NT, frequently called the Third Gospel. Although the author is not identified in the text of the Gospel, Irenaeus, a Christian bishop who lived and wrote near the end of the second century, claimed that the author was a companion of Paul. Presumably, Irenaeus was thinking of the Luke who is mentioned in Col. 4:14; Philem. 24; and 2 Tim. 4:11. After the time of Irenaeus, it became traditional to refer to the author of the Third Gospel, as well as the author of the book of Acts, as Luke, the companion of Paul.

Authorship and Date: The tradition that both this Gospel and the book of Acts were written by the same person is almost certainly correct. The two books have a similar literary style, and certain themes can be traced through both. Both books begin with prologues and dedications to one Theophilus (Luke 1:1–4; Acts 1:1–3), and the prologue in Acts has a brief but fitting description of the contents of what is there called "the first book" (Acts 1:1), surely a reference to the Gospel of Luke.

Although most modern scholars agree with the tradition that one author wrote both Luke and Acts, many do not agree with the traditional identification of this author as a companion of Paul. They point out that the author of Acts shows no acquaintance with Paul's literary activity or his major theological views as these may be discerned in the apostle's genuine Letters. It is felt that a companion of Paul would have known him better and would have described him in closer conformity with the image that emerges from reading the Letters. It should be noted, however, that not all scholars agree with these judgments and that many accept the traditional identification of the author of Luke-Acts as indeed a companion of Paul. The divergences with the Letters are explained on the assumption that Luke was not with Paul at every moment and that he was writing at a time when the issues that engaged Paul's attention were no longer of such great importance. Thus, the question of the authorship of Luke-Acts has not finally been settled.

The date at which Luke and Acts were written is usually set at ca. A.D. 80–85. In the prologue to the Gospel, the author implies that he was not an eyewitness to the things described and that he had consulted other documents. Similarities among the Gospels of Luke, Matthew, and Mark (the synoptic Gospels) suggest that there are certain literary relationships among these three Gospels and that Luke likely consulted one or both of the others. The Synoptic Problem is the problem of sorting out these relationships.

According to the Two-Source Hypothesis, Luke used Mark as one of his sources (Q was the other); according to the Griesbach Hypothesis, he used only Matthew. Thus, the relative date that one sets for the writing of Luke depends largely on the hypothesis one uses to solve the Synoptic Problem and the dates one assigns to the composition of Matthew and Mark. In one place, however, Luke appears to be in possession of some knowledge about the fall of Jerusalem to the Romans, an event that occurred in the year A.D. 70. Luke 21, which has parallels in Matthew 24 and Mark 13, contains some specific and detailed information about the Roman conquest and thus appears to have been written from a post-70 perspective (see esp. Luke 21:20–24). It is possible, however, that the same can be said for one or both of the other two synoptic Gospels.

How long after the year 70 did Luke write? The earliest references to Luke and Acts come from about A.D. 140. But it may be possible to narrow this range if we assume that the differences between the picture of Paul in Acts and that in Paul's Letters may be partially explained by the fact that the Letters were not available to Luke at the time he wrote. It is likely that Paul's Letters were not collected, copied, and distributed before the year A.D. 90. If Luke wrote before that time, he may not have known about the Letters. Thus, the outside chronological range for the writing of Luke-Acts would be ca. 70–90, and the dates 80–85 would probably be close to correct.

Theme and Style: As an author, Luke is usually highly regarded. His literary ability, in comparison with that of other NT writers, is frequently said to be second only to that of the author of the Letter to the Hebrews. He appears to be aware of the power of rhetorical style in the use of the Greek language; he is careful in the structuring of his narrative as a whole, and he is consistent in his characterizations and use of themes.

Probably because he is the only Evangelist to pair his Gospel with a narrative about the early history of the church, Luke is often called a historian. The German scholar Hans Conzelmann refers to Luke's writing as a history of salvation. He claims that Luke thought of world history as made up of three periods: the time of Israel, the time of Jesus, and the time of the church. The time of Israel extends to John the Baptist (see Luke 16:16), and the period of the church begins with the descent of the Spirit in Acts 2. In between is the period of Jesus, a special time of salvation according to Conzelmann, marked by the absence of the devil, who departed in Luke 4:13 and did not return until Luke 22:3. Throughout both the Gospel and Acts, the author emphasizes the theme of divine necessity, a theme that expresses the belief that God is working out a plan of salvation within world history.

Although Luke includes several statements about the consummation of history, he does not impart a sense of urgency about these matters. His Gospel has less eschatological fervor than either Matthew or Mark. He cautions against people who proclaim that the end has arrived (Luke 21:8). According to Luke, Jesus told the parable of the pounds because some people wrongly felt that the Kingdom of God was to come almost immediately (Luke 19:11–27). The Lucan Jesus emphasizes patience, a necessary quality for persons who are waiting for something that is not to be immediate.

Luke's interest in oppressed people, especially women and the poor, is frequently noted. His interest is not simply expressed, however, in terms of sympathy. In this Gospel, Jesus has as many words about the duties of the rich toward the poor as he has words of assurance to the poor. There is also a strong note of optimism in Luke. Jesus' birth is greeted by the joyful songs of angels and the hopeful praises of pious people. The teaching of Jesus is filled with hope and assurance for the future. The Kingdom of God is pictured as God's gracious gift. Jesus himself is portrayed as loving, kind, and a doer of good deeds.

Distinctiveness of Luke's Gospel: Despite the extensive similarity between Luke and the other two synoptic Gospels, there is a great deal of material in Luke that is distinctive. Only Luke has such narratives as that of the boy Jesus in the Temple (2:41–52), the raising of the widow's son at Nain (7:11–17), the dialogue with Mary and Martha (10:38–42), and Jesus' visit to the home of Zacchaeus (19:1–10). Some of the best known parables appear only in Luke: for example, the good Samaritan (10:29–37), the lost coin (15: 8–10), the prodigal son (15:11–32), the rich man and Lazarus (16:19–31), and the Pharisee and the publican (18:9–14).

Moreover, although there are similarities between Luke's birth narratives and Matthew's, the actual stories in Luke are distinctive. Only he gives us the story of the birth of John the Baptist (1:5–25, 57–80), the annunciation of Jesus' birth to Mary (1:26–38), the birth of Jesus in a manger (2:1–7), the angelic announcement and the visit of the shepherds (2:8–20), and the prayers of Simeon and Anna (2:25–38).

Finally, Luke's account of the postresurrection appearances of Jesus is distinctive. In contrast to Matthew, he locates all the appearances in the vicinity of Jerusalem, includes an especially meaningful narrative about the appearance of Jesus to two disciples on the way to Emmaus (24:13–35), and concludes his Gospel with the ascension of Jesus and the return of the disciples to Jerusalem (24:50–53). In the final

Evangelist page of the Gospel According to Luke from the *Lindisfarne Gospels* (ca. 700) shows Luke writing. Behind him is his symbol, the winged ox.

OUTLINE OF CONTENTS

The Gospel According to Luke

I. Prologue (1:1–4)
II. Infancy narratives (1:5–2:52)
III. Narratives about John the Baptist, Jesus' baptism and temptation (3:1–4:13)
IV. Jesus in and around Galilee (4:14–9:50)
V. Jesus' trip to Jerusalem (9:51–19:44)
VI. Jesus in Jerusalem (19:45–21:38)
VII. The Last Supper, trial, and death of Jesus (22:1–23:56)
VIII. Resurrection narratives (24:1–53)

verse, we find the disciples "continually in the temple blessing God" (24:53). ***See also*** Acts of the Apostles, The; Chronology, New Testament; Gospel, Gospels; L; Luke; Synoptic Problem, The; Theophilus.

Bibliography

Cadbury, Henry J. *The Making of Luke-Acts.* London: S.P.C.K., 1921; 2nd ed., 1958.

Conzelmann, Hans. *The Theology of St. Luke.* New York: Harper & Row, 1960.

Fitzmyer, Joseph A. *The Gospel According to Luke (I-XI): Introduction, Translation, and Notes.* The Anchor Bible, 28. Garden City, NY: Doubleday, 1981. Vol. 2 (chaps. 12–24) forthcoming.

Talbert, Charles H. *Literary Patterns, Theological Themes and the Genre of Luke-Acts.* SBL Monograph Series, 20. Missoula, MT: Scholars Press, 1974. J.B.T.

lute. ***See*** Music.

Luz (lo͞oz). **1** The Canaanite name of the city Bethel, renamed by Jacob (Gen. 28:19; 35:6). Luz/Bethel was on the border between Benjamin and Ephraim (Josh. 16:2; 18:13; Judg. 1:23). Josh. 16:2 implies that Luz and Bethel are distinct places. Nevertheless on the basis of all other references, Luz and Bethel are more likely two names for the same place. Similar double names are frequently found (e.g., Jebus/Jerusalem, Kiriath-arba/Hebron). **2** The name of a town in the land of the Hittites built by a refugee from the Canaanite town of Luz (Judg. 1:22–26). ***See also*** Bethel. J.F.D.

LXX, the symbol for the Greek translation of the OT called the "Septuagint." ***See also*** Septuagint.

Lycaonia (lik-uh-oh'nee-uh), a district in central Asia Minor located on a plateau north of the Taurus Mountains and bounded by the districts of Cappadocia, Cilicia, Pisidia, Phrygia, and Galatia. Annexed to the district of Galatia ca. 35 B.C., it became, with Galatia, part of the Roman Empire ca. 25 B.C. Three cities of Lycaonia were visited by Paul during his first and second journeys, Lystra, Derbe, and Iconium (Acts 13:51–14:21; 16:1–3). Paul's letter to the Galatians, which reflects the conflict between Gentile and Jewish Christians, could well have been addressed to the people residing in the district of Lycaonia. ***See also*** Derbe; Iconium; Galatia; Galatians, The Letter of Paul to the; Lystra. M.K.M.

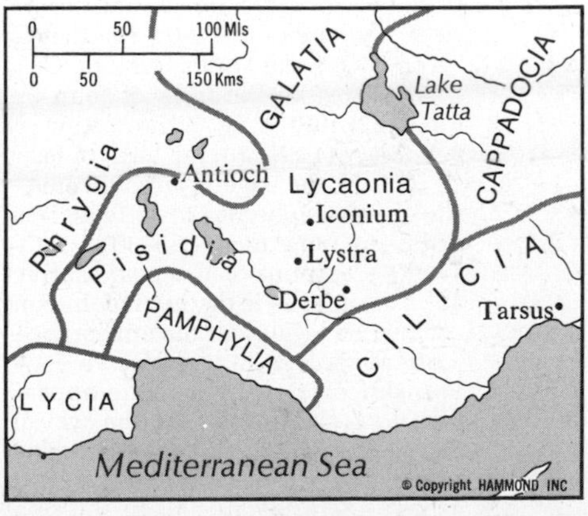

Lycia (lish'ee-uh), a coastal district in southwestern Asia Minor, bounded to the west by Lydia, to the north by Pisidia, and to the east by Pamphylia. Its principal city, Xanthus (modern Günük), headed a federation of cities and towns populated by a people possibly of Hittite origin, at least from the sixth century B.C. The central sanctuary of the federation was the Letoön, sacred to Apollo.

Ruled successively by the Persians, Alexander the Great, the Seleucids and Ptolemies, and the Romans, the area progressively abandoned the Lycian language and merged into the general Hellenistic culture of the times. According to 1 Macc. 15:23, Lycia was among the recipients of the letter concerning the Romans' alliance with the Jews sent out by the consul Lucius Calpurnius Piso in the second century B.C. The Roman generals Brutus and Cassius sacked Xanthus for money in 42 B.C., but the Roman emperor Claudius made Lycia a province in A.D. 43, and the emperor Vespasian joined it to Pamphylia in A.D. 74.

Paul changed ships at the Lycian port of Patara en route to Jerusalem (Acts 21:1) and again at Myra on his final journey to Rome (Acts 27:5–6). ***See also*** Myra; Paul. C.H.M.

Lydda (lid'uh), a town (Lod in the OT) in the fertile plain of Sharon along an eastern branch of the ancient international highway, the *Via Maris.* This location gave Lydda a certain strategic and commercial importance. First mentioned as Lydda in a Late Bronze Age list of towns in Canaan conquered by Thutmose III of Egypt (1490–1435 B.C.), the town was rebuilt by the Benjaminites (1 Chron. 8:12) and, after the return from Exile, was one of the places resettled (Ezra 2:33; Neh. 7:37; 11:35). At first outside the boundaries of Judea in the Hellenistic period, it was given to Jonathan the Hasmonean as a purely Jewish town ca. 145 B.C. (1 Macc. 11:34). In the A.D. 66–70 war of the Jews against the Romans, the city was burned by Cestius Gallus's contingent on their way to attack and destroy Jerusalem. An early Christian community lived in Lydda, and there Peter healed the paralyzed man Aeneas (Acts 9:32–35). ***See also*** Aeneas. M.K.M.

Lydia (lid'ee-uh). **1** An area in south-central Asia Minor, whose most famous king was Croesus (sixth century B.C.). Successively occupied by the Persians, Alexander the Great and his successors, and the Romans who incorporated it into the province of Asia, it is mentioned in 1 Macc. 8:8. Thyatira, Sardis, and Philadelphia (see Rev. 2:18–3:13) were located in Lydia. **2** According to Acts 16:12–15, Paul's first convert in Europe (at Philippi in Macedonia). Lydia was apparently a traveling merchant who sold luxurious purple-dyed cloth for a living. Perhaps she was a freedwoman and her name was given because she came from Thyatira, in the district of Lydia. As a Gentile, Lydia apparently had been attracted to the Jewish way of life in the synagogue, perhaps while she lived in Thyatira. She had a kind of "associate" status with the Jews as a "worshiper of God," and her attachment to Judaism was strong enough that she maintained the ties even when in Philippi, where Judaism appears to have been weak (the account in Acts suggests that there were not enough Jews to form a synagogue, since they met by the river outside the city). Lydia met Paul and, along with her household, was converted to Christianity. According to Acts, she had sufficient means to give extended hospitality to Paul and Silas in her home (see Acts 16:15, 40), even though she may have been a widow. The Philippian church perhaps initially met in her home. Lydia's stay in Philippi may not have been permanent; she is not mentioned in Paul's Philippian correspondence. ***See also*** Paul; Philippi; Purple; Thyatira. A.J.M.

lying, the act of telling falsehoods as truth. Israel is exhorted against using God's name for false oaths and lying on the witness stand in the Ten Commandments (Exod. 20:7, 16; Deut. 5:11, 20). Witnesses who testify falsely will receive the punishment that would have been meted out to their accused (Deut. 19:15–21). Indeed, all falsehoods are prohibited by the Torah (Exod. 23:7; Lev. 19:11). Persons who lie, and thereby defraud their neighbor, must pay restitution for the property loss plus a fine to the owner as well as bring a sacrificial offering before they are forgiven by God (Lev. 6:1–7). Lying is thus an abomination to God and his faithful (Prov. 12:22; Ps. 119:163), for God never lies (Num. 23:19; 1 Sam. 15:29).

False prophets are singled out for particular condemnation (Isa. 9:15; Jer. 23:9–32; Ezek. 13) since their lies may influence the people to oppose God's will. The penalty for false prophecy is death (Deut. 18:20–22; Jer. 28).

In the NT, the "father of lies" is the devil (John 8:44), and Paul condemns those who worship idols because they have exchanged the truth about God for a lie (Rom. 1:25). ***See also*** Perjury. J.U.

lyre. ***See*** Music.

Lysanias (li-say'nee-uhs), identified in Luke 3:1 as tetrarch of Abilene in the days of John the Baptist. Luke gives the date as the fifteenth year of Tiberius (i.e., A.D. 28 or 29), but the only Lysanias otherwise known as a ruler in the region died in 36 B.C. Thus, unless there was another Lysanias, Luke is in error. ***See also*** Abilene.

Lysias Claudius. ***See*** Claudius Lysias.

Lystra (lis'truh), a city in the region of Lycaonia, about twenty-five miles south-by-southwest of Iconium in central Asia Minor. Its location was unknown until 1885, when a Roman altar was found, still in place, inscribed with the city's Latin name ("Lustra") indicating that it was a Roman colony. Lystra remains unexcavated, but surface finds indicate settlement as early as 3000 B.C. Ca. 6 B.C., Augustus made the city a Roman stronghold against mountain tribes in the region. The Lycaonians had a district language, and a temple to Zeus graced the city of Lystra (Acts 14:11–13). Paul and Barnabas stopped here during the first journey and were mistaken for gods (Acts 14:6–23), and Paul returned later with Silas, when he recruited Timothy as a companion (Acts 15:40–16:4). ***See also*** Lycaonia; Timothy. M.K.M.

Opposite: The Virgin Mary and Child; Greek icon, ca. 1600.

M

M, a symbol designating material found only in the Gospel of Matthew; it also designates the hypothetical source of this material. The Matthean narratives dealing with Jesus' birth and postresurrection appearances are included in this material. ***See also*** Synoptic Problem, The.

Maacah (may'ah-kuh; sometimes Maachah in the KJV; meaning uncertain). **1** A small state south of Mt. Hermon, apparently encompassing the northern half of the Golan Heights, bounded by the other non-Israelite state of the Golan, Geshur, on its south. The Transjordanian tribes of Israel (Reuben, Gad, the half-tribe of Manasseh) failed to conquer Maacah and Geshur (Josh. 13: 11, 13; cf. 12:5; Deut. 3:14). Subsequently, the king of Maacah joined the Ammonites and Arameans in their unsuccessful war against David (2 Sam. 10:6, 8; 1 Chron. 19:7). Following its defeat, Maacah probably became tributary to David (2 Sam. 10:19). Maacah and Geshur were evidently absorbed into the expanding Aramean kingdom of Damascus after the time of Solomon. **2** The concubine of Caleb (1 Chron. 2:48). **3** The wife of Machir, Manasseh's son (1 Chron. 7:15–16). **4** The wife of Gibeon, or Jehiel, one of Saul's ancestors (1 Chron. 8:29; 9:35). **5** A princess of Geshur who married David and was the mother of Absalom and Tamar (2 Sam. 3:3). **6** The daughter of Absalom, who became the favorite wife of King Rehoboam and mother of Abijah (1 Kings 15:2; 2 Chron. 11:20–22), whom Asa finally deposed from her position of queen mother because of her involvement in idolatry (2 Chron. 15:16). **7** A son of Nahor, Abraham's brother (Gen. 22:24). **8** The father of Achish, king of Gath (1 Kings 2:39). **9** The father of Hanun who was one of David's mighty men (1 Chron. 11:43). **10** The father of Shephatiah, one of David's officials (1 Chron. 27:16). D.A.D.

Maaseiah (may'a-see'ya; Heb., "the work of Yahweh"), a very popular Israelite name. More than a dozen Maaseiahs are mentioned in the Bible.

From the pre-exilic period: **1** One of David's levitical musicians (1 Chron. 15:18, 20). **2** A commander who joined Jehoida's temple conspiracy to make Joash king (2 Chron. 23:1). **3** An officer under King Uzziah (2 Chron. 26:11). **4** King Ahaz's son who was killed in the war with Israel (2 Chron. 28:7). **5** The governor of Jerusalem commissioned by Josiah to repair the Temple (2 Chron. 28:7). **6** The father of the priest Zephaniah (Jer. 21:1; 29:25; 37:3); he may be the same as 5. **7** The father of the false prophet Zedekiah (Jer. 29:21); he may be the same as 5. **8** The son of Shallum and keeper of the threshold (Jer. 35:4).

From the postexilic period: **9** Four Israelites, three of whom were priests, who agreed to put away their foreign wives (Ezra 10:18, 21, 22, 30). Two of these are probably the priests who participated in the dedication of Nehemiah's wall (Neh. 12:41–42). **10** Six other persons mentioned in Nehemiah, some of whom may be identical (3:23; 8:4, 7; 10:25; 11:5, 7). J.J.M.R.

Maccabees (mak'uh-beez), a family (properly the Hasmoneans) that provided military, political, and religious leaders for Judea during much of the second and first centuries B.C. The events leading to their rise to prominence were related to attempts by Antiochus IV Epiphanes, Seleucid king of Syria, to foster Hellenism in Judea by tyranically suppressing Judaism (see 1 Macc. 1–2; 2 Macc. 5–7). While many Jews, primarily members of the urban upper classes and including members of the Temple priesthood, supported hellenization, many others opposed it, and some, such as the group called "Hasideans" (1 Macc. 2:42; 7:13; 2 Macc. 14:6), fought actively against it.

Antiochus decreed that sacrifice to the Greek deities be offered in every Judean city and village, and, on the fifteenth day of the month Kislev (November/December) in the year 167 B.C., caused a pagan altar to be built on the Temple altar at Jerusalem, where, on the twenty-fifth of the same month, the first sacrifice to Zeus was made. (This was the "abomination that makes desolate" of Dan. 11:31; 12: 11; see also 1 Macc. 1:54; 2 Macc. 6:1–5.) The arrival of officers to carry out Antiochus' decrees at the village of Modein, where an aged priest named Mattathias lived with his five sons, gave occasion for the outbreak of a spontaneous revolt that was to turn into a full-scale war. When Mattathias, in an act of anger, killed both the first Jew who approached the pagan altar to offer sacrifice and the royal official who presided, he and his sons (John "Gaddi," Simon "Thassi," Judas "Maccabeus," Eleazar

The earliest known representation of the Jewish menorah is depicted on a bronze coin minted during the reign of the Maccabean king Antigonus II, 40–37 B.C.

"Avaran," and Jonathan "Apphus") were forced to flee to the hills. There they became the nucleus of a growing band of rebels against Antiochus. Mattathias died soon after the beginning of the revolt, leaving military leadership in the hands of Judas, whose surname "Maccabeus" (probably from the Aramaic word *Maqqabah*, meaning "hammer") became the source of the popular name given to the family and its followers.

Under Judas's brilliant leadership, what had begun as a guerrilla war turned into full-scale military engagements in which smaller Jewish forces managed to defeat much more powerful Syrian armies. Among Judas's most notable achievements were the recapture of Jerusalem (except for the Akra fortress, where the Syrian garrison continued to hold out) and the rededication of the Temple, after the defiled altar had been demolished and rebuilt. The date of the rededication, 25 Kislev of 164 B.C., with the attendant eight-day festivities, has since that time been celebrated annually as Hanukkah or the "Feast of Dedication" (see John 10:22). Antiochus Epiphanes' death also took place in 164, and, for a time, Judas continued successfully to press what was now a war for independence. His last great victory was over the forces of Nicanor at Beth-horon, on 13 Adar (Feb./March) of 161 B.C. In the autumn of the same year, Judas was killed in battle against the vastly superior army of Bacchides, under whose occupation the "pro-Greek" party gained ascendancy in Jerusalem.

The Maccabees, although set back by Judas's defeat and death, continued to fight under Jonathan, who sided with Alexander Balas against Demetrius in the ongoing struggle for succession to the Seleucid throne. While Jonathan succeeded for a time in reestablishing the ascendancy of his party in Judea, he was treacherously captured and later murdered by Tryphon in 143 or 142 B.C., leaving the leadership to Simon, who, by this time, was the only remaining son of Mattathias.

From the Syrians, Simon gained *de jure* recognition of the *de facto* independence of Judea achieved by his brothers. From the Jews, he received legitimation of the Hasmonean house as their political and religious leaders. On 18 Elul (September) of 140 B.C., in decrees that were publicly displayed on bronze tablets in the Temple, Simon was granted the hereditary titles of high priest, commander-in-chief, and ethnarch of the Jews. The Hasmonean dynasty had officially begun. In 134 B.C., Simon was murdered, along with his sons Judas and Mattathias, by his son-in-law Ptolemy, in a bid for power by Ptolemy.

Simon's remaining son, John Hyrcanus, after

THE MACCABEES: A FAMILY TREE

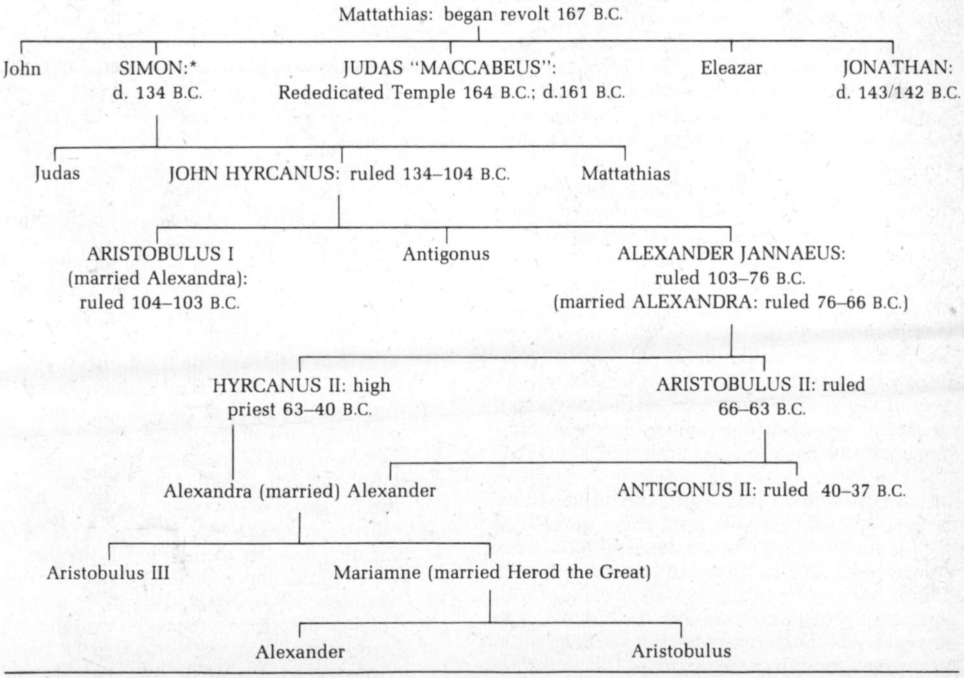

**Leaders'/Rulers' names are in capital letters.*

foiling Ptolemy's plan, was confirmed as high priest and ruled with distinction for thirty years (134–104 B.C.). During his rule, the Hasmonean state achieved its greatest territorial expansion and political power. At this time, the names "Pharisees" and "Sadducees" make their first appearance, designating rival parties within the Jewish community, and Hyrcanus' break with the former and support of the latter caused much acrimony.

Apparently, the first of the dynasty to assume the title of king was Aristobulus I (104–103 B.C.), who is reported, upon the death of John Hyrcanus his father, to have imprisoned three of his brothers, allowed his mother to starve in prison, and, later, to have caused the death of another brother. All of this was in order that he might assume sole power, contrary to the wishes of his father.

After the death of Aristobulus of a painful illness, his widow, Alexandra, freed the brothers and married one of them, Alexander Jannaeus, whose twenty-seven years of rule (103–76 B.C.) were marred externally by war and internally by conflict. Alexandra herself took the throne in 76, making her son Hyrcanus II high priest. Reversing the position of her husbands and father-in-law, she was favorable to the Pharisees, who now gained the upper hand over the Sadducees.

After Alexandra's death in 66 B.C., her sons, Aristobulus II and Hyrcanus II, became engaged in a struggle for power, in which Antipater, the military commander of Idumea, played a central role. Rome finally intervened in 63 B.C., when Pompey's legions captured Jerusalem. Aristobulus was taken to Rome as a prisoner to be paraded in Pompey's triumph, and Hyrcanus was left to rule in Jerusalem, no longer as king but as high priest, over a reduced territory (63–40 B.C.).

In a period of frequent intrigues and political upheavals, in which Antipater the Idumean and his son Herod played major roles, the Maccabean family came to an end with the execution of Antigonus II, who had ruled briefly (40–37 B.C.) with Parthian support. The future was with Rome and with Herod, who married Mariamne (granddaughter of both of Alexandra's sons) and later put her sons, other members of the family, and even Mariamne herself to death. ***See also*** Antiochus; Antipater; Hasmoneans; Herod; Seleucids, The. F.O.G.

Maccabees, the First Book of the, a history of the Maccabean revolt from the accession of Antiochus IV Epiphanes to the Seleucid (Syrian) throne in 175 B.C. until the death of Simon, one of the leaders of the Jewish resistance and then high priest and ethnarch, in 132 B.C. The struggle is the point of a clash between Hellenistic culture and the exclusivism of Judaism. The book was composed in Hebrew, sometime after the death of John Hyrcanus, Simon's son, in 104 B.C. but before the beginning of Roman rule in Palestine in 63 B.C. It is the primary source for the history of the period. The original Hebrew is no longer extant; however, the book has been preserved in Greek as a part of the Septuagint. It is considered one of the Apocrypha by Protestants, while Catholics classify it as one of the deuterocanonical writings.

The purpose of 1 Maccabees seems to be to legitimate the Hasmoneans (Maccabees) as rulers of Palestine in consequence of the contribution made to the liberation of Judea from Seleucid rule by the founders of the dynasty, Judas, Jonathan, and Simon, the sons of Mattathias. Maccabee means "the hammer" in Hebrew and is the nickname of Judas, possibly because of the hammerlike blows he dealt the enemy. It is applied more generally to the three brothers as well as to the revolt they led.

The story begins with the Hellenistic "reforms" instituted by the Hellenizers, members of the Jewish aristocracy (the "lawless men" of 1 Macc.), in association with Antiochus IV. These reforms turn Jerusalem into a Greek city-state under Greek law and lead to opposition by a large segment of the Jewish population. Antiochus responds by desecrating the Temple and attempting to extirpate Judaism in Palestine through violence. 1 Maccabees represents his motive as a desire to create a state religion rather

OUTLINE OF CONTENTS

The First Book of the Maccabees

I. Antiochus IV Epiphanes and the desecration of the Temple (175–167 B.C.; chap. 1)
II. Mattathias initiates the resistance (166 B.C.; chap. 2)
III. The struggle under Judas, who liberates the Temple but eventually perishes as a result of renewed efforts by Demetrius I to install Alcimus, one of the Hellenizers, as high priest (166–160 B.C.; 1 Macc. 3:1–9:22)
IV. Jonathan takes up the fight, driving the Syrians from the country, then becoming high priest (150 B.C.) as he takes various sides in the politics of the empire, and finally perishing as a captive (160–143 B.C.; 1 Macc. 9:23–13:30)
V. Simon follows Jonathan, becoming both ethnarch and high priest as the result of the acclamation of the Jewish people, securing virtual independence from the Syrians, and finally falling to an assassin's sword to be succeeded by John Hyrcanus, his son (143–134 B.C.; 1 Macc. 13:31–16:24)

than the need to suppress resistance to the new form of government, as in 2 Maccabees. At the forefront of the initial opposition are the *Hasidim* or "pious ones" (the Hasideans in 1 Macc.), the forerunners of the Essenes and the Pharisees. 1 Maccabees plays down their role in the revolt in favor of the Maccabees—in fact, according to 1 Maccabees it would appear that all efforts not led by Judas, Jonathan, or Simon are automatically doomed to failure. On the other hand, the book of Daniel, which seems to have been produced by the Hasidim during this revolt, plays down the role of the Maccabees (see Dan. 11:34). The Hasidim would have been satisfied with religious freedom, while the Maccabees seek political independence and power. 1 Maccabees seems to be designed to justify their choice, possibly in the face of conflict between the Pharisees and the Hasmoneans in the first years of the following century.

First Mattathias, and then his sons, one after another, lead the resistance to the Syrians with their Greek ways. The Temple is liberated and cleansed in 164 B.C. under Judas, while Jonathan later becomes high priest. Simon finally secures liberty and becomes both high priest and ethnarch before his assassination by Ptolemy, the governor of Jericho, in 132 B.C. Aiding in the fight for independence is a protracted power struggle within the Seleucid Empire after the death of Antiochus IV in 163 B.C. as well as the emergence of Rome as a major power in the near east. These factors are apparent between the lines, although 1 Maccabees attributes the victory to the leaders' reliance on the power of God. The book is filled with allusions to the older biblical histories of Israel, going back to the period of the judges, in order to develop this interpretation. ***See also*** Apocrypha, Old Testament; Daniel, The Book of; Judith; Maccabees; Maccabees, The Second Book of the.

D.W.S.

Maccabees, the Second Book of the, a second history of the Maccabean revolt, written from a different perspective than 1 Maccabees. Where the latter is concerned to praise Judas, Jonathan, and Simon for their role in the liberation of the Jewish people from Seleucid oppression, 2 Maccabees focuses upon the insult to the Temple and its cult, for which it holds the Jewish Hellenizers primarily responsible. Judas Maccabeus is honored as the sole leader of the resistance. The narrative concludes with his defeat of Nicanor, the Syrian governor of Judea (14:12), ending a major threat to the sanctity of the rededicated temple, and Judas is even described at one point as a leader of the Hasideans (*Hasidim*), in curious contrast to their role in 1 Maccabees. The period covered by 2 Maccabees is about 180–161 B.C.

While 1 Maccabees is generally considered historically more reliable where the two are parallel, 2 Maccabees is of value because it describes in greater detail the Hellenistic reform and the origin of the revolt prior to the emergence of the Maccabees, and because it provides greater insight into the history of the Jewish religion. It represents an epitome, or condensation, of a five-volume history written by an otherwise unknown Jason of Cyrene probably sometime after 110 B.C. The original language was Greek, and the condensation has survived as a part of the Septuagint, or Greek

OUTLINE OF CONTENTS

The Second Book of the Maccabees

I. Two letters from Jews in Jerusalem to the Egyptian Jewish community concerning the new festival of Hanukkah (1:1–2:18)
II. The preface to the epitome (2:19–32)
III. The epitome, or summary, of Jason's history (3:1–15:36)
   A. A threat to the Temple during the high-priesthood of Onias III is thwarted by a supernatural manifestation (3:1–4:6)
   B. The Hellenistic "reforms" (4:7–50)
   C. The desecration of the Temple by Antiochus IV Epiphanes, here pictured as a response to a revolt against the Hellenistic reforms rather than, as in 1 Maccabees, an effort to impose a state religion on the Jews (chap. 5)
   D. Tales of martyrdom (chaps. 6–7; cf. 4 Macc.; *T. Moses* 9; and Wisd. of Sol. 2:12–5:23)
   E. Judas defeats Nicanor's first invasion (chap. 9)
   F. Antiochus is struck by God and repents upon his deathbed, leading to the purification and rededication of the Temple by Judas (9:1–10:9)
   G. Judas defeats Timothy and Lysias under Antiochus V Eupator (10:10–11:38)
   H. Judas defends Jews in Palestine (chap. 12)
   I. Judas rebuffs an effort by Antiochus V to reinstall Menelaus, high priest during the Hellenistic reforms (chap. 13)
   J. Judas defeats and kills Nicanor (who has undertaken a second campaign) following a vision of the martyred Onias III, the pious high priest, in which Judas receives a sword to defeat his adversaries (14:1–15:36)
IV. The epitomist's conclusion (15:37–39)

version of the OT. Protestants treat it as a part of the Apocrypha, while Catholics classify it as one of the deuterocanonical books.

2 Maccabees is generally termed a "pathetic" history (from Gk. *pathos*, "emotion" or "feeling") because of the way in which it dwells upon the deaths of the righteous martyrs or the wicked king in a manner designed to evoke compassionate or contemptuous pity in the reader. The writer develops a theology of history in 6:12–17 that echoes the point of view of the Deuteronomistic school (see Judg. 2:11–23). Because the Jews themselves have profaned the Temple when the Hellenizers Jason and Menelaus used its treasure and vessels to buy the high-priesthood from Antiochus, God disciplines them by permitting Antiochus to desecrate the Temple (throughout the book God's punishment tends to fit the crime—see 4:38; 9:5–6; 13:8). Repentance, however, ensures that God will protect the Jews from their enemies by sending a leader like Judas and by responding from heaven with a manifestation of supernatural power in defense of Temple or people (2:21; 3:22–40; 5:18; 9:5; 10:29–31; 15:22–27). The righteous who perish in the process can expect the resurrection of the dead (7:9–11; 12:44; 14:46) and are able to intercede to heaven on behalf of the living (15:12). Sin offerings on the part of the dead are also possible (12:39–45). 2 Maccabees is thus an important piece of evidence for the development of the idea of the resurrection of the dead in the period between the composition of Isa. 26:19 and Dan. 12:2 (in the fourth or third and the second centuries respectively) and the origin of Christianity. ***See also*** Apocrypha, Old Testament; Judith; Maccabees, The First Book of the; Resurrection; Temple, The. D.W.S.

Macedonia (mas-e-doh'nee-uh), a region in the northeastern part of the Greek peninsula.

Originally the name designated only the great river plain at the head of the Thermaic Gulf. Here invaders of Dorian extraction established a united kingdom about 640 B.C. In the following three centuries this kingdom contended against its immediate neighbors (Illyrians, Thracians, and northern tribal groups) and against outside powers such as Persia, Athens, and Sparta. Although strongly influenced by Hellenic culture especially after 450 B.C., it retained its independence and slowly expanded, especially into the mountainous north. In the fourth century B.C. Philip II (359–336) annexed these contested northern areas and added the Strymon Valley and the Chalcidicean Peninsula to his kingdom to form the most powerful state in Greece. His son, Alexander III ("the Great") used this in turn as a base from which to conquer a vast empire stretching to Egypt and India. After Alexander's death (323 B.C.) this empire broke apart, and Macedonia itself experienced considerable dynastic strife during the next century and a half. Rome decisively defeated the Macedonian army at Pydna (168 B.C.) and in 148 B.C. established Macedonia as a province with its capital at Thessalonica. Roman engineers began immediately (146 B.C.) to construct an arterial military and commercial road, the Via Egnatia, from the Adriatic coast through Pella, Thessalonica, Amphipolis, Philippi, and Neapolis in Macedonia to Byzantium in Asia Minor; portions of this still survive. The apostle Paul probably traveled the Neapolis-Thessalonica segment (Acts 16:11–17:1). During the struggle for power at the end of the Roman Republic Macedonia suffered much devastation from the armies that traversed it, and major battles were fought at nearby Pharsalus (48 B.C.) and at Philippi (42 B.C.). Economic recovery began under Emperor Augustus (27 B.C.–A.D. 14) and by A.D. 44 Macedonia no longer required direct imperial rule. It was then governed by a senatorial proconsul.

Alexander the Great's exploits are noted in 1 Macc. 1:1 and 6:2. Haman's identification as a "Macedonian" in the LXX version of Esther 9:24 (see also LXX Addition E, v. 10) probably serves to link this archetypal anti-Semite with the Greek archenemy of the Jews, Antiochus IV. Paul made his first European converts to Christianity in Macedonia (Acts 16:9–17:14). He himself recalls his initial journey (ca. A.D. 50) from Philippi to Thessalonica and then to Athens (1 Thess. 2:2; 2:17–3:2; Phil. 4:15–16) and says that he preached the gospel "as far round as Illyricum" (Rom. 15:19). He also mentions a second visit to Macedonia (ca. A.D. 55; 2 Cor. 2:13; 7:5; see also Acts 20:1–6). 1 Thess. 4:10 seems to presuppose the existence of other early Christian communities in Macedonia besides Philippi and Thessalonica; on the founding of the church at Beroea see Acts 17:10–12. ***See also*** Alexander; Illyricum; Paul; Philippi; Thessalonica. R.A.W.

Machaerus (muh-kee'ruhs), a fortress-palace some thirty-six hundred feet above the Dead Sea, about fifteen miles southeast of the mouth of the Jordan River. A fortress built on the site by Alexander Jannaeus (103–76 B.C.) was destroyed by Pompey's general Gabinius; it was then extensively rebuilt by Herod the Great to include a palace within the fortress. Because of its proximity to Arabia and its location above the north-south road from the Red Sea to Damascus, the site was regarded as strategically important by Herod Antipas, tetrarch of Galilee and Perea (4 B.C.–A.D. 39). According to the Jewish historian Josephus, Machaerus was the scene of the imprisonment and death of John the Baptist. Another account of John's imprisonment and death is found in Matt. 14:3–12 and Mark 6: 17–29. ***See also*** John the Baptist. M.K.M.

Machir (may'keer; possibly Heb., "hireling" or "property [of God]"), a name held by two biblical personages. **1** The son of Ammiel from Lo Debar who harbored Mephibosheth, Saul's grandson (2 Sam. 9:4–5), and was an ally of David (2 Sam. 17:27). **2** Either the oldest (Josh. 17: 1–2) or only (Num. 26:29) son of Manasseh. His mother was Aramean (1 Chron. 7:16) and his wife was named Maacah (1 Chron. 7:16). Some traditions claim that his sons conquered the Transjordan region of Gilead (Num. 32:39–40; Deut. 3:15) or even both Gilead and Bashan (Josh. 17:1), while other traditions suggest that they lived west of the Jordan (Judg. 5:14, 17). M.Z.B.

Machpelah (makh-pee'lah; Heb., "double"?), the burial place of Sarah, Abraham, Isaac, Rebekah, Jacob, and Leah. It is identified both as "the cave of Machpelah" (Gen. 23:9; 25:9) and "the field of Machpelah" (Gen. 23:17, 19; 49:30; 50:13); Abraham purchased it from Ephron the Hittite for four hundred shekels of silver. The account of the purchase is given in meticulous detail in Genesis 23 (Priestly document), emphasizing that their burial place was the only land that the patriarchs owned in Canaan. According to the biblical tradition, the field with its cave was located east of Mamre (Gen. 23:17), a city identified with Hebron (Gen. 23:19).

There is a long history of reverence for the place among Jews, Christians, and Moslems. The tradition concerning the site is mentioned in *The Testaments of the Twelve Patriarchs, Jubilees* (46:4–10), and in Josephus' *Antiquities* (1.21.1; 2.8.2). Acts 7:15–16, on the other hand, places the tomb "that Abraham had bought" not in Hebron, but in Shechem. Josephus (*War* 4.9.7) reports that there were in his time impressive monuments of Abraham and the other ancestors in the town of Hebron. Herod had built a wall around the traditional burial place and probably had set up the monuments that Josephus describes. The Bordeaux Pilgrim (A.D. 333) describes a beautiful stone wall surrounding the cave in which the patriarchs were entombed. Other early travelers report seeing a church, and later ones, such as Muqsaddasi (A.D. 985), give accounts of the mosque and the cenotaphs. The Crusaders occupied the site and either converted the mosque to a church or constructed a new building. In the present day the site of ancient Machpelah is in the town of Hebron itself, and the walls enclose both a mosque and a synagogue. The surrounding walls, some 8 to 9 feet thick, are 197 feet long and 111 feet wide. Most authorities are convinced that this wall—except for the upper courses—is the one built by Herod. ***See also*** Hebron; Patriarch. G.M.T.

Madeba. ***See*** Medeba.

madness, a state of irrationality. In biblical times it was generally attributed to some other spirit or power taking over a person's mind. Saul is the primary example of someone afflicted with madness in the OT. When God's spirit left King Saul to rest on David, Saul was invaded by an "evil spirit" (1 Sam. 16:14–17). This spirit caused outbreaks of violence against David in which Saul attempted to kill him (1 Sam. 18: 10–11; 19:9). However, God's favor toward David was shown in that no matter what Saul did, David continued to prosper. Psychologists might be tempted to diagnose Saul as manifesting symptoms of paranoia and manic depression. However, the biblical writer is interested in the story as evidence of the powerful, though sometimes dark and frightening, work of God's plan for Israel. God's hand was behind the evil spirit that invaded Saul much as it was behind the outbreak of Saul's prophetic ecstasy (1 Sam. 10:6, 10).

This biblical picture of "madness" has some features in common with the frenzied personalities of Greek tragedy. There madness is also a mysterious combination of divine powers turned against the hero and internal forces that he or she cannot control or account for. Some physical symptoms of madness are roving about, wild rolling of the eyes, sweating, and foaming at the mouth. Madness is accompanied by terrifying visions. Mad persons do things that are contrary to all "good" human behavior, such as harming their friends and aiding their enemies. Stoning appears to have been the archaic response to the mad person. Perhaps the response was based in a magical attempt to heal the "contagion" brought into society by such unnatural behavior.

In the NT madness takes the form of demonic possession (e.g., Mark 5:1–13; 9:14–29). However, it was also brought up as a charge against Jesus by those who objected to his violation of their social or religious standards (e.g., Mark 3: 21–22, because of his activity as an exorcist; John 8:48; in Matt. 11:18 it is also an accusation against John the Baptist). ***See also*** Devil; Magic and Divination; Saul. P.P.

Magadan (mag'ah-dan). ***See*** Magdala.

Magdala (mahg'dah-lah), a thriving rural community (modern Tarichaeae) on the western shore of the Sea of Galilee between Capernaum to the north and Tiberias to the south. It appears to have been more romanized than Capernaum and to have contained a small synagogue. Mary "from Magdala" figures among Jesus' women disciples (Luke 8:2) and was among the first witnesses to his resurrection (John 19:25; 20:1, 18; Matt. 27:56, 61; 28:1; Mark 15:40, 47; 16:1; Luke 24:10).

Magdalene, Mary. ***See*** Mary.

magi. ***See*** Wise Men.

magic and divination, means by which humans attempt to secure for themselves some action or information from superhuman powers. Magic is an attempt by human beings to compel a divinity, by the use of physical means, to do what they wish that divinity to do. Divination is an attempt to secure information, also by the use of physical means, about matters and events that are currently hidden or that lie in the future. The word "magus," from which the word "magic" is derived, came originally from Persia, where it designated a priestly class. From there, it spread to all nations in the Mediterranean world. Magical practices are as old as the written records of humanity, and, in the world of the Bible, they can be found in ancient Mesopotamian, Egyptian, and Greek documents. Although a systematic presentation of the theory of magic did not appear in the Greco-Roman literature until the third and fourth centuries of the Christian era, the general principles upon which the practice of magic was based were more or less accepted by all. These principles may be summarized briefly as follows:

A host of intermediary beings called demons exist between gods and humans. Depending on their proximity to the gods, demons possess divine power in diminishing measures. Those closest to the gods have bodies of air; those closest to humans, bodies of steam or water. Because of this descending order, the unity of the cosmos can be preserved. Otherwise, human and divine would be irreparably separated and no communication between the two would be possible. Everything is connected through the demons who mediate between the divine and the material. Magic rests upon the belief that by getting hold of demons in physical objects, the divinity can be influenced. The magician's art is to find out which material (metal, herb, animal, etc.) contains which divinity and

Daniel kneels before the angel Gabriel, who interprets a vision (Dan. 8); woodcut from the Cologne Bible (1478–80). Divination and the practice of magic are mentioned in the Bible but are also strongly opposed in both OT and NT.

to what degree. By using the element or combinations of elements containing a particular divinity in its purest form, a sympathetic relationship with the divinity will be established. If, however, elements offensive to a divinity are used, the result will be antipathetic. Thus magic can achieve either blessing or curse. The magician knows the secret and knows how to use it in the correct way with the best results.

Magic and the Biblical World: Because of the pervasive presence in the biblical world of magical beliefs and practices, one should not be surprised that such practices seeped into the lives of the Israelites and the early Christians. Even where magic was not intended, the need to speak about divine-human contact inevitably made use of the same vocabulary and concepts used in magic.

The most awesome power seemed to rest in the name of a divinity, because the name and its bearer were in the closest relationship to each other. The name of God, *YHWH,* was, therefore, never pronounced (Exod. 3:13–15). Jesus "has a name inscribed which no one knows but himself" (Rev. 19:12). The divine name could invoke blessing and drive away evil, so baptism in the early church was administered "in the name" of God and Jesus (Matt. 28:19), and healings were in Jesus' name (Acts 3:6).

It was believed that great power rested in those holy men who were in close proximity to God. Physical contact with such a person would have beneficial consequences. Thus Elijah could heal the son of the widow of Zarephath by stretching "himself upon the child three times" (1 Kings 17:17–24). The same miracle was repeated by Elisha with the son of the Shunamite (2 Kings 4:31–37). Jesus touched the hand of Peter's mother-in-law and she was healed (Matt. 8:14–15); he touched the eyes of the blind men and they received their sight (Matt. 9:29). The Holy Spirit was given through the laying on of the apostles' hands; this was the secret the magician Simon wished to learn (Acts 8:9–24). Anything in connection with such holy men absorbed and transmitted a portion of their power. Elijah's mantle parted the waters of the Jordan, and when Elisha put it on, Elijah's spirit rested on him (2 Kings 2:8–15). The garment of Jesus radiated and transmitted healing power (Mark 5:28–29), as did the handkerchiefs and aprons that people carried away from the body of Paul (Acts 19:11–12). Some believers even attributed beneficial properties to the shadow of Peter (Acts 5:15).

Of course, contact with "unclean" objects would have a negative effect; hence the many purificatory rites. Purification was achieved by the use of the correct rites and materials, among which particular power was attributed to blood (Lev. 14:25), water (Lev. 15:5), fire (Num. 31:23), but also to hyssop, scarlet thread, and many other agents (Ps. 51:7; Num. 19:18; Lev. 14:4). Since demonology is integral to the theory of magic, the biblical references to demons and exorcisms reflect this kind of understanding.

Magic could be practiced on various levels. Accordingly, the Bible uses several words to refer to this occupation. On the highest level were the "Magi," the "wise men," of Matthew 2 and the "Chaldeans" of Daniel 1 and 2 who had priestly functions. Daniel was made "chief of the magicians" because "the spirit of the holy gods . . . light and understanding and wisdom, like the wisdom of the gods, were found in him. . ." (Dan. 5:11). On the lowest level were the "imposters" (2 Tim. 3:13) who played their tricks as do circus magicians today. Between these were the sorcerers, enchanters, and charmers who could cast spells and knew how to use herbs, potions, and drugs.

One of the earliest references to magic is the confrontation between Moses and the Egyptian magicians (Exod. 8:5–9:12). In the plains of Moab, Balak offered a great amount of money to Balaam to put a curse on the Israelites (Num. 22); curse and blessing are also in Deborah's song (Judg. 5). In the scapegoat ritual, by laying his hands upon the head of the goat, Aaron transmitted the people's sins to the animal (Lev. 16:2–22). Near the land of Edom, a bronze serpent made by Moses and placed on a pole was instrumental in saving the lives of the people (Num. 21:4–9; 2 Kings 18:4; cf. John 3:14–15).

Methods of Divination: With divination, in contrast to magic, one does not seek to alter the course of events, only to learn about them. The ancient world developed many devices by which the veil of secrecy covering future events could be lifted. Oracles, such as the Pythia in Delphi, the oak trees of Dodona, or the Memnon of Thebes, were media chosen by the gods through which direct messages came. The future could also be divined by interpreting the signs that the gods sent, such as the flight of birds, eating habits of chickens, and the condition of the entrails, especially the liver, of sacrificial animals (such divination was practiced in the recently excavated city of Mari on the upper Euphrates, but see also Ezek. 21:21). Calling up the dead (necromancy) has survived to our day, as has the interpretation of dreams, which were believed to be major vehicles by which the gods sent messages. The casting of lots to determine the will of the gods was practiced all through the recorded history of humankind. So we read that God appeared to Abraham at the oak tree of Moreh (Gen. 12:6–7) and that the flight of arrows foretold a victory to King Joash (2 Kings 13:14–19). Saul resorted to necromancy when "the Lord did not answer him, either by dreams, or by Urim, or by prophets," and he had to consult the medium of Endor to bring up Samuel for him (1 Sam. 28). Joseph interpreted the dreams of Pharaoh (Gen. 41); Daniel those of Nebuchadnezzar (Dan. 2, 4). Joseph, husband of Mary, received messages in dreams (Matt. 1:20–21; 2:13), as did the wise men (Matt. 2:12), and Pilate's wife (Matt. 27:13).

This selection of references does not exhaust the importance of dreams, to which we may add visions (e.g., the vision of Samuel in the Temple, 1 Sam. 3; Peter's vision in Acts 10) which were so widespread that the word is used in the RSV more than one hundred times. During the early history of Israel, it was an accepted practice to "inquire of the Lord" (Judg. 1:1–2; 1 Sam. 10:22). This expression implies an oracle (similar to Delphi in Greece) where a question could be asked and a reply given by God through a medium. The Urim and Thummim (or ephod) were also oracular media, but answers were restricted to "yes" or "no" (1 Sam. 23:9–12; 30:7–8; Num. 27:21). The same results could be gained by casting lots (Lev. 16:8; Num. 26:55–56), and the OT preserves stories that show the same thing was done by Phoenicians (Jon. 1:7), Persians (Esther 9:24–26), and Romans (Matt. 27:35). The last reference to this sort of divination in the NT comes from the time when the eleven apostles replaced Judas with Matthias by praying and casting lots (Acts 1:26).

In spite of this seeming popularity, however, both magic and divination were strongly opposed in both OT and NT (Isa. 8:19; 44:25; 47:12–15; Deut. 18:10–12; Acts 8:9–24; 13:6–11; 19:13–20; Rev. 21:8; 22:15). The Bible teaches that humans have direct access to God, and the NT especially emphasizes that the role of demons and other intermediaries was made superfluous by Jesus Christ. ***See also*** Amulet; Dreams; Elijah; Miracles; Oracle; Simon Magus; Urim and Thummim. S.B.

magicians. ***See*** Magic and Divination.

magistrate, an official who exercised ordinary administration of the Roman Empire's cities. Magistrates quieted sedition (Luke 12:11), settled property disputes (Acts 16:20–22) and debts (Luke 12:58), and policed and jailed felons (Acts 16:35–38).

Magnificat (mag-nif'i-kaht; from the Lat. for "magnify"), the name of the best known of the several psalms that are incorporated into the birth narrative in Luke's Gospel (chaps. 1–2). The psalm (Luke 1:46–55), spoken by Mary, begins "My soul magnifies the Lord, and my spirit rejoices in God my Savior." In some early traditions of the text and from the witness of several of the early church fathers, Elizabeth, the mother of John the Baptist, is reported to have been the one who uttered this beautiful poem. Because the poem is obviously modeled after the song of Hannah (1 Sam. 2:1–10), many interpreters have argued that it was originally intended to be understood as Elizabeth's and that it originated among followers of John the Baptist. In all of the extant Greek manuscripts, however, and in most of the traditions of the church, the poem has been understood to belong to Mary, the mother of Jesus. Within the setting of the Lucan structure, it appears most likely that Mary is the one to whom it should be attributed.

The poem consists basically of praise to God: for selecting her (Mary) to be a participant in the mighty divine act; for God's care for the lowly, poor, and powerless (a strong Lucan theme and emphasis); and for God's bringing to fulfillment the promise made to Abraham in and through the coming of Mary's son.

The poem is quite beautiful and has been used in various settings in the liturgies of the Christian churches. ***See also*** Elizabeth; Hannah; Hymn; John the Baptist; Mary, The Virgin; Music. J.M.E.

Magog (may'gahg). ***See*** Gog.

Magus, Simon. ***See*** Simon Magus.

Mahalalel (mah-hah'luh-lel; Heb., "praise of El [God]"). **1** The son of Kenan and descendant of Seth (Gen. 5:12); the Greek form of the name is Mahalaleel (Luke 3:37). **2** A descendant of Judah of the clan of Perez (Neh. 11:4).

Mahalath (mah-hah'luhth; Heb., "mild"). **1** The granddaughter of Abraham, the daughter of Ishmael, and one of the wives of Esau (Gen. 28:9). **2** The wife of King Rehoboam of Judah (924–907 B.C.) and the granddaughter of David (2 Chron. 11:18). **3** A term of unknown significance that occurs in the titles of Psalms 53 and 88. It may be a musical notation, referring to a melody or rhythm pattern, although even that remains speculation. ***See also*** Psalms, The.

Mahanaim (mah-hah-nah'im; Heb., "the camp"), a city in Gilead, in the tribal territory of Gad near its border with Manasseh (Josh. 13:26, 30). It was also a levitical city assigned to the family of Merari (Josh. 21:38; 1 Chron. 6:80) and the capital of a Solomonic district (1 Kings 4:14). Strategically situated near the confluence of the Jordan and the Jabbok, Mahanaim was the city in which Ishbosheth and his supporters were based when David became king of Judah after Saul's death (2 Sam. 2:8, 12, 29). Ironically, David himself fled there during Absalom's revolt (2 Sam. 17:24, 27; 19:33; 1 Kings 2:18). Mahanaim's history thus shows it to have been a place of refuge, and this motif probably underlies its mention in Gen. 32:2 as the place where Jacob stayed before his encounter with Esau; when the "messengers of God" met him there Jacob said, "This is the [military] camp *[maḥanēh]* of God" (RSV: "This is God's army!"; cf. also 32:10). The exact location of the site is uncertain. ***See also*** Jabbok. M.D.C.

Mahaneh-dan (may'heh-neh-dan; Heb., "camp of Dan"), the location in Judah where the Spirit of the Lord began to stir Samson (Judg. 13: 25), and where the Danites encamped when they were en route to Ephraim (18:12). The exact location is unknown, but it was in the area of Zorah and Eshtaol (Judg. 13:25), west of Kiriath-jearim.

Mahath (may'hath), a Levite, the father (and grandson?) of Elkanah. He participated in the cleansing of the Temple during Hezekiah's reforms (2 Chron. 29:12) and later shared the responsibility of collecting the Temple offerings (2 Chron. 31:13). He may be the same Levite who belonged to the clan of Kohath (1 Chron. 6:35). Some writers suggest that he is identical with Ahimoth, the son of Elkanah (1 Chron. 6:25), but several different men called Elkanah are apparently grouped together here (1 Chron. 6:23–26; see vv. 34, 35, 36), confusing the proper relationships. ***See also*** Elkanah.

Maher-shalal-hash-baz (may'uhr-shal'al-hash'bahz; Heb., "The spoil speeds, the prey hastens"), the second or third son of Isaiah to receive a symbolic name. His name assured Judah that it need not fear Damascus and Samaria, since they would soon be plundered (Isa. 8:1–4).

Mahlah (mah'luh). **1** One of the daughters of Zelophehad of the tribe of Manasseh. She and her sisters appealed to Moses and won the right to inherit their father's property since he had died with no male heirs (Num. 27:1–5; Josh. 17: 3). Their appeal led to a statutory ordinance that allowed women the right of inheritance (Num. 7:7–11). A later appeal by other Manassehites who feared the dispersal of tribal lands under such a law brought a modification of the law that required the daughters to marry only within the family group of their tribe to be eligible for the inheritance (Num. 36:1–12). **2** A descendant of Manasseh (1 Chron. 7:18). ***See also*** Zelophehad.

D.R.B.

Mahli (mah'lee). **1** A Levite mentioned in the Priestly genealogy of Exod. 6:19 as well as in various lists of levitical families (cf. 1 Chron. 6: 19, 29; 23:21; 24:26; Ezra 8:18). Num. 3:20, 33–36 reports that the Mahlites, together with the descendants of Mushi's brother, had specific responsibilities in the operation of the tabernacle. **2** Mahli's nephew, the son of Mushi, who was named after Mahli (if the notices in 1 Chron. 6: 47; 23:23; and 24:30 are accurate).

Mahlon (mah'lawn), the son of Elimelech and Naomi, Ephrathites from Bethlehem of Judah, with whom he emigrated to Moab "when the judges ruled Israel" (Ruth 1:1–2, 5; 4:9–10). He married Ruth, a Moabitess, but died childless. The book named after his widow, Ruth, tells how she ultimately bore a son who was regarded not only as heir to Mahlon's estate but also heir to that of Boaz, Ruth's new husband. The name may mean "sickly, diseased" in Hebrew.

Mahol (may'huhl; Heb., "dance"), the father of the wise men Heman, Calcol, and Darda (1 Kings 4:31, Hebrew text 5:11). Some understand the phrase "sons of Mahol" to be a title meaning "members of the orchestra (guild)."

maid, a female of indeterminate age, sexual experience, and social status (Gen. 16:2; 24:16; Deut. 5:14; 22:14–17; Matt. 9:24; Mark 5:41–42; Acts 16:16). The word is also used by a woman as a humble self-designation before a superior (1 Sam. 1:11, 16; Ruth 3:9) and metaphorically of cities or countries and their inhabitants (Isa. 47: 1; Jer. 31:4, 21; Amos 5:2).

mail. ***See*** Dress.

Makkedah (mah-kay'dah), one of sixteen cities in the Shephelah (an area southwest of Jerusalem) assigned to the tribe of Judah (Josh. 15:41). Its precise location is not known. Mentioned alongside Azekah (about twelve miles west of Jerusalem) as the end of Joshua's rout of the five kings attacking Gibeon, Makkedah is the place where those kings were found hiding in a cave and then slain. Joshua subsequently took the city of Makkedah and killed its king (Josh. 10:16–28). ***See also*** Azekah; Gibeon.

Malachi (mal'uh-kī), **the Book of,** the last book of the prophetic corpus and of the Christian OT, and one of the twelve Minor Prophets. The name of the book (Heb. "my messenger") derives from 3:1 where an eschatological precursor is announced: "Behold, I am about to send *my messenger*" (cf. 1:1; 2:7). The Septuagint (LXX) as well as other versions do not take the title as a personal name and most scholars regard the author as anonymous. The brevity of the book and its subtitle "oracle" provide an analogy with the similarly subtitled collections at the end of the book of Zechariah (9:1; 12:1), which are roughly of the same length.

The content of the book places its date in the early Persian period between the reestablishment of the Temple in 515 B.C. and the mission of Nehemiah in 445, possibly in the reign of Xerxes (486–464). The Persian governor is mentioned in 1:8 and the Temple sacrificial system that had fallen into disrepute when sick and useless animals were offered in violation of normal practice is presupposed (1:7–10; 3:8). The author's preoccupation with worship practices and his disappointment at the community's loss of religious devotion demonstrate a great change merely two generations after the rededication of the Second Temple.

Most significant of the new conditions was the lax attitude of the Judeans toward intermarriage (2:10–16), a major concern of the missions of Ezra and Nehemiah. The persistence of so much wrongdoing evokes in Malachi the question regarding the reality of God's justice (2:17). The prophet responds by announcing the imminence of the coming of a "messenger of the covenant" (3:1) who would prepare the community for a final judgment, which is the subject of the last verses of the book (4:4–6, Hebrew 3:22–24).

OUTLINE OF CONTENTS

The Book of Malachi

Traditionally, the book has been divided into eight sections, the first a superscription and the last a concluding coda.

I. Introductory oracle on behalf of Israel-Jacob and against Edom-Esau (1:2–5)
II. Condemnation of the priests for corrupting worship and not properly teaching the Torah and covenant prescriptions to the people (1:6–2:9)
III. A critique of the covenant faithlessness of Judah, who married the daughters of foreign gods; the prophet exhorts the people to remain faithful to their Jewish wives and, having done so, promises them a godly offspring (2:10–16)
IV. Israel has wearied God, and so God will soon come in judgment (2:17–3:5)
V. Prophetic appeal for repentance and against the people's false testing of God by withholding tithes (3:6–12)
VI. A rebuke directed at those who spoke against God and his faithlessness, and a promise that the God-fearers shall be remembered for righteousness while the evildoers shall be destroyed (3:13–4:3)
VII. An appeal to remember the Torah of Moses before the day of judgment, a day to be preceded by the advent of Elijah and his acts of love and restoration (coda; 4:4–6)

These concluding verses serve as capstones not only to the prophetic corpus but possibly also the Pentateuch and Prophets together. The Deuteronomic character of the conclusion (cf. Deut. 18:15–18), modeled after Exod. 23:20, as well as the book as a whole, now identifies the eschatological precursor as Elijah, who is to return from heaven to reunite all Israel before the end time. These verses and ideas have left an indelible imprint on later Jewish and Christian messianic views (e.g., Matt. 17:10–13).

Malachi provides an important glimpse of life in Jerusalem in the first half of the fifth century B.C. The rebuilding of the Temple had not occasioned the kind of good life Haggai had predicted. As individuals lapsed in their performance of religious obligations the prophet exhorts people back to their moral stance by asking for true ritual obedience and abstinence from mixed marriages. The hopeful ending enables all to anticipate better times. Jewish tradition numbers Malachi the last of the Prophets and a member of the Great Synagogue. E.M.M.

Malchiah (mal-kī'uh; also Malchijah; Heb., "my king is Yahweh"). **1** A descendant of Gershom (1 Chron. 6:40). **2** A priest (1 Chron. 9:12). **3** The head of the fifth course of priests at Jerusalem (1 Chron. 24:9). **4** Three men listed as having married foreign women (Ezra 10:25, 31). **5** One who repaired the Jerusalem Dung Gate (Neh. 3:14). **6** A jeweler who helped rebuild the Jerusalem wall (Neh. 3:31). **7** One who accompanied Ezra during the reading of the law (Neh. 8:4). **8** A man who sealed the Covenant (Neh. 10:3). **9** A priest who participated in the ceremony of the wall dedication (Neh. 12:42). Some of these individuals may have been one and the same (cf. 2, 9). M.A.F.

Malchus (mal'kuhs), in John 18:10, the high priest's slave (perhaps a Nabatean) whose right ear was severed by Peter when Jesus was arrested; he is not named in the other Gospels.

malefactor, a term in the KJV for "evil doer" (John 18:30; Prov. 24:19), "wrong doer" (1 Pet. 2:12; 4:14), and "criminal" (Luke 23:32–33; 2 Tim. 2:9).

mallow (mal'loh), any plant of the family *Mal-*

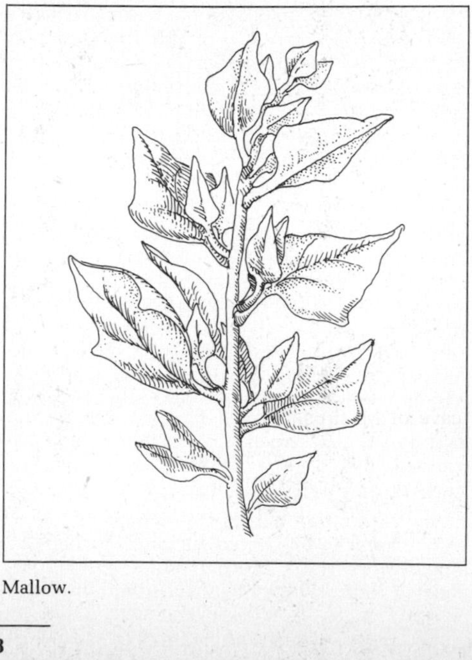

Mallow.

vaceae. Biblical usage cites its characteristic fading (Job 24:24) and its relatively unpleasant nature as a food source (Job 30:4); it was used for food only in desperate circumstances.

Malluch (mal'uhk). **1** An ancestor of the levitical Temple musician Ethan (1 Chron. 6:44). **2** The son of Bani who married a foreigner (Ezra 10:29). **3** The son of Harim who did the same (Ezra 10:32). **4** A signer of the postexilic covenant (Neh. 10:4). **5** A priestly signer of the postexilic covenant (Neh. 10:27). **6** A priest who accompanied Zerubbabel (Neh. 12:2) in the return from Babylonian exile (ca. 530 B.C.).

Malta (mawl'tuh), ancient Melita, an island sixty miles south of Sicily, today comprising, with two smaller islands to the northwest, the nation of Malta. First occupied in Neolithic times (ca. 8000–4500 B.C.), it began to be colonized by Phoenicians in the early first millennium B.C. and passed under the control of Carthage from the sixth to the third centuries B.C. Although taken by the Romans in 218 B.C., Maltese culture retained its Punic identity, so that Acts 28:2 refers to the people as "natives" (RSV: Gk. *barbaroi*, "barbarians").

According to Acts 27:27–28:11, Paul was shipwrecked in a bay of Malta en route to Rome, spending the three winter months there. Roman inscriptions mention the principal local official as "first man" or "chief man" (RSV), just as Publius is called in Acts 28:7. The traditional site of Paul's landing is today called St. Paul's Bay, on the northeast coast of Malta. ***See also*** Paul; Publius. C.H.M.

mammon (from Aramaic *mamôn*, "wealth"), a term used in warnings against preoccupation with wealth (Matt. 6:24; Luke 16:9, 11, 13). ***See also*** Wealth.

Mamre (mahm'reh), an ancient Semitic name. **1** An Amorite ally of Abraham in his battle against Chedorlaomer and the coalition of four eastern kings (Gen. 14:13–24). Mamre was the brother of Eshcol and Aner (Gen. 14:13, 24). **2** A focal place in Abraham's movements about southern Palestine. Mamre is usually identified with modern Ramet el-Khalil, just north of Hebron. According to biblical tradition, Abraham built an altar at Mamre (Gen. 13:18). Such a shrine would explain Abraham's repeated return to Mamre and his many theophanic experiences there. Abraham purchased the nearby cave of Machpelah for a family tomb. Mamre was apparently named for Abraham's ally in battle (see 1 above). Perhaps this Mamre owned the land or had previously had a shrine there. At Mamre God told Abraham that Sarah would have a son (Gen. 18:1–15). There Abraham pleaded for Sodom and Gomorrah to be spared (Gen. 18:16–33). In the nearby cave of Machpelah the patriarchs and their wives were buried (Gen. 23:17–20; 25:7–10; 35:27–29; 49:28–33; 50:12–13). ***See also*** Machpelah. J.F.D.

man (as generic term). ***See*** Human Being.

Manaen (man'ee-uhn), an intimate friend or member of the court of Herod Antipas who was converted to Christianity and became a prophet and teacher in the church at Antioch (Acts 13:1). ***See also*** Antioch; Herod; Prophet.

Manasseh (muh-na'suh), the son of Hezekiah and king of Judah (698–642 B.C.); he reigned longer than any other king of the house of David, fifty-five years. Manasseh is roundly condemned for his aberrant ways by the author of the book of Kings. He is accused of cancelling the altar reform of his father, allowing local "high places" to be rebuilt, and fostering the reintroduction of foreign cultic practices: "For he rebuilt the high places which Hezekiah his father had destroyed; and he erected altars for Baal, and made an Asherah, as Ahab king of Israel had done, and worshiped all the host of heaven, and served them. And he built altars in the house of the Lord, . . . And he built altars for all the host of heaven in the two courts of the house of the Lord. And he burned his son as an offering, and practiced soothsaying and augury, and dealt with mediums and with wizards" (2 Kings 21:3–6). This abandonment of Israel's law was not limited to the royal court; through Manasseh's example, idolatry spread abroad to the people of Judah and Jerusalem (2 Kings 21:9). Furthermore, according to the historiographic outlook of the book of Kings, whereby loyalty to the Lord is rewarded and apostasy punished, Manasseh was directly to blame for the destruction of Jerusalem and the exile of Judah, so great was his sin (2 Kings 21:12–15; 22:16–17).

As for the political history of Manasseh's age, little is reported in biblical sources. Assyrian sources refer to Manasseh as a loyal vassal for the better part of his reign. Thus the Assyrian king Esarhaddon reports that "the 22 kings of the western countries, the seashore and the islands," among them "Manasseh of Judah" did corvée work and furnished building materials for the reconstruction of the royal palace in Nineveh. This same monarch called upon his western vassals to construct the port town of Kar-Esarhaddon on the Phoenician coast after the destruction of Sidon in 676 B.C.

Some years later, during an early campaign of Ashurbanipal of Assyria to Egypt, Manasseh mobilized a Judean contingent to fight alongside of other national units who had been enlisted for service in the Assyrian army. Vassal dues included military service as well as steep payments in money and in kind. A fragmentary biblical tradition preserves references to Manasseh's imprisonment by the king of Assyria, who took him captive "with hooks and bound him with fetters of bronze and brought him to Babylon." There, Manasseh prayed to the Lord and was subsequently returned to his former position (2 Chron. 33:10–13). That Manasseh was suspected of disloyalty at least once during his long reign is very likely and this episode may be related to the unrest in the west in 671 B.C. at the end of Esarhaddon's rule in Assyria. (Some scholars think that Manasseh was implicated in the rebellion against Assyria of Shamash-shum-ukin in Babylon in 652–648 B.C.)

Judah's vassaldom to the Assyrian Empire, which in the seventh century B.C. stretched from the Nile to the Taurus Mountains and eastward to the Iranian plateau, can best account for the rampant idolatry recorded in the book of Kings for the reign of Manasseh. It is often put forward that Assyria required the adoption of imperial cults as part of the vassal service due the overlord. But Assyrian imperial policy made no such demands; on the contrary, foreign local cults flourished and were sometimes encouraged by the conqueror. Note the account of the "restoration" of the Israelite cult in Bethel by the king of Assyria for the well-being of the settlers of the province (2 Kings 17:24–34). The repeated commercial and military contacts by Judeans with the admixture of peoples in the empire was the seedbed out of which grew the cultic entanglements decried by biblical writers. Thus, the diminutive kingdom of Judah succumbed to the wave of a new general culture composed of Aramaic and Canaanite elements that united the entire Near East.

The story of Manasseh's repentance in 2 Chron. 33:10–16 is evidently historical fiction, for, if true, it obviates the need for the reform of King Josiah (2 Kings 22–23; 2 Chron. 34–35). The Chronicler has rationalized Manasseh's lengthy reign in terms that recall Ezekiel's doctrine of personal accountability (cf. Ezek. 18) and so does not impute Judah's fall to Manasseh. ***See also*** Hezekiah; Idol; Kings, The First and Second Books of the. M.C.

Manasseh, the Prayer of. ***See*** Prayer of Manasseh, The.

Manasses (muh-nas'ez), the Greek form of the Hebrew *Manasseh*, a tribe (Rev. 7:6) and son of King Hezekiah in Jesus' genealogy (Matt. 1:10). ***See also*** Apocrypha, Old Testament; Manasseh.

mandrake *(Mandragora officinarium)*, a plant of the nightshade family that spreads large spinach-shaped leaves in a rosette pattern. The flowers that form in the middle of the rosettes later become yellow-red fruits resembling tomatoes. Although considered a delicacy, it has an unusual smell and taste (Song of Sol. 7:13). The fruit of the mandrake may have produced

Mandrake.

strange effects since it was used medicinally as a narcotic or purgative. The woody root, resembling a human figure, supposedly indicated the plant's magical properties. Sometimes called a "love apple," it was purported to be an aphrodisiac and enhancer of fertility. Mandrakes were found in the wheat fields by Reuben and were the indirect cause of the birth of Zebulun (Gen. 30:14–20). P.L.C.

maneh (mah'neh, KJV; RSV: mina). ***See*** Weights and Measures.

manger, a box or trough, usually carved from stone, used for the feeding of animals (cf. Luke 13:15). Mangers could be found wherever animals were kept, either in a lower portion of a house or in a cave near a house or even beneath a house. In caves, the manger was frequently carved out of the wall. According to Luke 2:7, 12, 16, a manger was used as the bed for the infant Jesus after his birth in Bethlehem.

In the early traditions, the place of Jesus' birth was thought to have been a cave, although the Lucan account does not supply such information. Later (early fourth century A.D.), the Emperor Constantine erected a basilica over a cave in Bethlehem believed to be Jesus' birthplace, and this basilica evolved into the present Church of the Nativity. ***See also*** Bethlehem. J.M.E.

manna (man'nah, from Heb. *man*, Gk. *manna)*, a food God provided for the Hebrews in the wilderness (Exod. 16:1–36; Num. 11:4–9). The manna was found each morning on the ground and is described as "a fine, flake-like thing, fine as hoarfrost" (Exod. 16:14). It is further described as being white (Exod. 16:31), like coriander seed (a small, globular, grayish-colored seed, Exod. 16:31), and like bdellium (a sticky resinous gum, Num. 11:7). Each Hebrew was to gather one omer (approximately two quarts) of manna each day, but two omers on the day preceding the Sabbath (Exod. 16:16, 22). The manna could be boiled in pots or ground into a meal and baked into cakes (Num. 11:8).

Manna that was left on the ground after the sun warmed the earth quickly disappeared. The Hebrews interpreted this as meaning that it melted (Exod. 16:21). The disappearance is more likely the work of ants, which remove any manna once the ground warms. Likewise, the description of worms in any excess manna (Exod. 16:20) is probably a description of the ants that would seek out and remove manna stored in the tents of the Hebrews. A jar of manna was kept, along with Aaron's budding almond branch, in the Holy of Holies beside the Ark of the Covenant (Exod. 16:33–34).

F. S. Bodenheimer has suggested that manna was the honeydew secretion of two kinds of scale insects feeding on the sap of the tamarisk. These insects ingest large amounts of plant sap, which is rich in carbohydrates but poor in nitrogen. The excess carbohydrate ingested in order to obtain the needed nitrogen is then excreted as honeydew. This honeydew is rich in three basic sugars and pectin. In the dry desert air most of the moisture quickly evaporates from the honeydew, leaving sticky droplets on the plants or ground.

Bodenheimer notes that the geographical area where manna was found according to the earliest writings of Scripture, from Elim to Rephidim, agrees well with his own observation of the limits of manna production. Bodenheimer also notes that the season of manna production begins in late May or early June, precisely the time indicated by the biblical account.

In the NT, Jesus is challenged to do great signs like the provision of manna in the wilderness. He responds that the manna, bread of heaven, came as a gift from God, and that he (Jesus) was the bread of life (John 6:25–35). Similarly in Rev. 2:17, the faithful are promised some of the hidden manna, a reference to Jesus' offering the bread of life. ***See also*** Wilderness.

Bibliography

Bodenheimer, F. S. "The Manna of Sinai." *The Biblical Archaeologist* 10 (1947):2–6. J.F.D.

Manoah (mah-noh'ahkh), Samson's father, a Danite from Zorah. The narrative of the events surrounding Samson's birth (Judg. 13:2–25) depicts Manoah as incredulous and slow-witted in comparison to his wife: he wants the angel's revelation repeated (v. 8), he questions the angel to test his wife's truthfulness (v. 11), and when he finally realizes that the man is an angel, he is afraid that he and his wife will die—prompting her reassuring reasoning (vv. 20–23). According to Scripture, Manoah's tomb lies between Zorah and Eshtaol (Judg. 16:31), some fifteen miles east of Jerusalem. J.U.

man of lawlessness, an enigmatic phrase found in 2 Thess. 2:3. Of the many possible interpretations given in the scholarly literature, one plausible suggestion is that the man of "lawlessness" (or "rebellion") is an eschatological and representational figure who is to be manifested in the future and whose arrival will signify the culmination of the past, present, and future hostile forces standing in opposition to the apostolic ministry of the church, and, thus, of God. His appearance will climax the process the author of 2 Thessalonians refers to as "the mystery of rebellion" (2 Thess. 2:7). But since this moment has not yet arrived and the Lord Jesus has not yet destroyed him (2:8), those who argue that "the day of the Lord has come" (2:2) are in error. ***See also*** Antichrist, The; Thessalonians, The Second Letter of Paul to the. K.P.D.

manservant. ***See*** Servant.

mansions (KJV), rooms or home. Jesus, in view of his ascension, comforted his disciples by means of an analogy: "In my father's house are many rooms" (John 14:2; KJV: "mansions," NEB: "dwelling-places"). Since, in biblical thought, the earth is roofed by seven domelike heavens, there would be sufficient space for the divine householder's human family. Furthermore, the deity's earthly "house" (temple) had various compartments, and thus it seemed logical that its heavenly counterpart would have them as well. Extravagance ("mansions") is not intended by the Greek original, as is clear from the only other instance where this word is used in the NT: "We will . . . make our *home* with him (John 14:23; KJV: "abode," NEB: "dwelling"). ***See also*** Heaven. L.R.B.

mantle. ***See*** Dress; Tunic.

manuscript. ***See*** Texts, Versions, Manuscripts, Editions.

Maon (may-ohn; Heb., "dwelling," "refuge"), a personal and a place name. As is often the case in Scripture, a name that in one passage is used as a personal name in another passage is used as a place name. That is the case with Maon (1 Chron. 2:45; Josh. 15:55; 1 Sam. 25:2). He is one of a number of descendants of Caleb, all of whose names are also place names: Mareshah, Ziph, Hebron, and Bethzur (1 Chron. 2:42–50). Each of these places has been located by historical geographers with a six to twelve mile radius from Hebron. Some scholars identify biblical Maon with modern Khirbet el Ma'in, located twenty-five miles west-northwest of Beersheba, but the majority identify it with Tel Ma'in, which is located eight and a half miles south of Hebron. Nabal the Calebite was Maon's most celebrated OT resident (1 Sam. 25:2–42).

J.G.G.

Mara (mahr'uh; Heb., "bitter"), the name Naomi applied to herself to describe her fate (Ruth 1:19–21). ***See also*** Naomi; Ruth.

Marah (mah'rah; Heb., "bitterness"), the unpalatably bitter pools of water (whence the name) reached by the Israelites after they crossed the Red Sea and entered the Wilderness of Shur (Exod. 15:22; the Wilderness of Etham according to Num. 33:8). Thirsty and angry, the

Three Israelites complain to Moses that the water at Marah is bitter; Moses then turns to God who shows him a tree that will sweeten the water; detail from a thirteenth-century French illuminated Bible.

Israelites slandered Moses who, upon God's orders, turned the waters sweet by throwing wood into the brackish pools. Occurring so soon after the great miracle at the Red Sea, this incident not only gave evidence of Israel's tendency to doubt God (Exod. 15:24), but God's own propensity to test his chosen people (v. 25). Despite the many locations proposed as the site of Marah, none has gained the complete confidence of scholars; as a result, the location remains in doubt. ***See also*** Exodus.

J.M.S.

maranatha (mah-rah-nah-thah'), an Aramaic expression transliterated into Greek (1 Cor. 16:22; *Didache* 10:6) meaning "Our Lord has come" (*maran atha*) or "Our Lord, come" (*marana tha*). The prayer, "Come, Lord Jesus" (Rev. 22:20), which is a Greek translation of this expression, favors the latter. The use of *maranatha* in 1 Cor. 16:22 indicates that this was an early prayer originating in the Palestinian church and that Jesus already in earliest times was probably referred to as *Mar* or "Lord."

marble, a metamorphic rock, composed of extremely compact crystallized limestone. Its veined and varicolored appearance made it highly desirable for architectural decoration and artistic use. Biblical use attests its functions in architecture ("marble pillars" in the palace of Ahasuerus, Esther 1:6, and marble floors there as well) and decoration (material gathered by David for use in the Temple, 1 Chron. 29:2). As part of the seer's vision of the destruction of "Babylon" (Rev. 18:12) marble was part of the precious goods no longer salable by merchants. In archaeological evidence, marble fragments attest its use in statuary during the Greco-Roman period (333 B.C.–A.D. 324) in addition to the more common uses in architectural decoration and construction from various periods.

R.S.B.

Marcus (mahr'kuhs), the Latin form of the name Mark; it appears in the KJV in Col. 4:10; Philem. 24; and 1 Pet. 5:13. ***See also*** Mark.

Marduk (mahr'do͞ok). ***See*** Merodach.

Mareshah (mah-ree'shah). **1** An important town in one of Judah's Shephelah (western) districts (Josh. 15:44); it was located approximately one mile south of Beit Jibrin, and is identified with modern Tel Sandahannah. Mareshah was among the towns fortified by King Rehoboam ca. 920 B.C. (2 Chron. 11:5–12). Near the end of the tenth century B.C., the armies of King Asa and Zerah the Ethiopian "drew up their lines of battle in the valley of Zephathah at Mareshah," a struggle that resulted in victory for the Judeans (2 Chron. 15:9–15). Eliezer, the prophet who spoke against the alliance between Jehoshaphat and Ahaziah, was from Mareshah (2 Chron. 20:37). This town's destruction was prophesied by Micah (1:15). During the exilic and postexilic periods (sixth–fourth centuries B.C.), southern Judah was absorbed into Edomite (or Idumean) territory; Marisa (Mareshah's Greek name) was a leading commercial and cultural center in this region. Its cosmopolitan population came under the control of Seleucid, Ptolemaic, Hasmonean, and Roman conquerors, and Marisa's history ended with the Parthian destruction in 40 B.C. (cf. 1 Macc. 5:66; 2 Macc. 12:35; Josephus).

While the environs of Mareshah/Marisa have

been investigated in recent years by Israeli archaeologists, Tell Sandahannah was originally excavated by Bliss and Macalister in 1900. They recovered some material from the Iron Age (1200–1000 B.C.) but their major efforts focused upon exposing the architectural remains and layout of the Hellenistic city, whose final phase measured ca. 500 feet on each side. In addition to a full repertoire of Hellenistic pottery, coins, and inscriptions, some of the world's finest examples of rock-cut, elaborately painted tombs have been found at Marisa.

2 The firstborn son of Caleb, and the father of Ziph and Hebron (1 Chron. 2:42, Septuagint). In the Hebrew text, Caleb's son is called Mesha first, then Mareshah.

3 A son of Laadah, a descendant of Judah (1 Chron. 4:21). G.L.M.

Mari (mah'ree), the name of an ancient city uncovered by French archaeologists at modern Tell el-hariri, located on the right bank of the Euphrates River, just north of the modern Syro-Iraqi frontier. Since the first expedition of 1933–34, some thirty campaigns have unearthed major palaces and temples dating from the mid-third millennium to the early eighteenth century B.C. Mari was destroyed by Hammurabi of Babylon around 1765 B.C., and it never again rose to prominence.

History: Mari's location midway between the great powers of Sumer (Kish, Uruk, Eridu, Agade, Ur) and those of Syria (Ebla) allowed it to be a center for manufacture and trade during the third millennium. References to Mari as a major political power are therefore found in the archives recovered from these city-states. The documents from Mari of this period have not been fully published.

When, at the turn of the millennium, Sumerian culture began to give way to that of the West Semitic Amorites, Mari was ruled by *shakkanakku*, "governors." These brought prosperity to the city, and it was during their time that the foundation of the great palace was laid that was to last until Mari's fall. A chronology for these "governors" as well as a transition to the later so-called Lim dynasty have yet to be firmly established.

The Lim dynasty is better known to us, since its history can be reconstructed from the thousands of texts that date from 1825 to 1765 B.C. They tell of Yakhdun-Lim, who fortified cities all along the Middle Euphrates and who even led a military expedition to the Mediterranean; of his son (?) Sumu-Yamam, who was assassinated in a harem conspiracy, leaving Mari to the mercy of an ever scheming king of Assyria, Shamshi-Adad; of Yasmakh-Adad, son of the latter, who stayed in power for about twenty years, losing it approximately four years after his father's death; and of Zimri-Lim, son of Yakhdun-Lim, who came back to occupy his father's throne. Defeated by Hammurabi of Babylon, Zimri-Lim was the last major king of Mari.

Palace Life and Government: The twenty-year rule of Zimri-Lim is probably the most heavily documented of any king of ancient times, not only because we have hundreds of letters from him, his family, and his administrators, but also because we have dozens of documents dated to each month of his reign. Since we know the sequence of at least twelve years of Zimri-Lim's rule, we can reconstruct life in the palace of a major city-state during peace and war. During those years, the king and his retainers had two meals a day, consisting of a variety of breads, legumes, meats, fish, wine spiked with honey, beer, and sweets. Seasonal food included truffles and a variety of fruits. Ice was available, year-round, stored in underground buildings.

For entertainment, the king hunted lions and watched elaborate ballets. The king himself played a role in selecting the female dancers, since these were to enter his harem. It is likely that the courtiers listened to the reading of literary texts, but the examples recovered from Mari have not been published as yet. We can reconstruct a voyage that Zimri-Lim took when visiting Halab (Aleppo), where lived his father-in-law, king Yarim-Lim of Yamkhad. Very likely, he also went to Ugarit. The trip took at least four months and was punctuated by many stops at the courts of allies and vassals as well as by visits to local shrines.

The king had many wives and concubines at each of his four palaces along the Euphrates and Khabur rivers. First among these wives was Shiptu of Yamkhad, whom Zimri-Lim married late in his reign. We cannot be sure whether Shiptu bore him children, but Zimri-Lim had many daughters from other women. We can reconstruct the fate of at least a dozen of these daughters. Some married prominent court functionaries, others became priestesses—in Mari itself as well as in Sippar where they became "daughters-in-law" of the god Shamash. But most were given as wives to allies and vassals. Especially dramatic were the fates of Shimatum and Kirum. Both these sisters were married to the king of Ilansura, with tragic consequences for Kirum who seems to have lost her mind and had to be brought back home.

The king was the main administrator of Mari and its territories. He was helped by a private secretary, who accompanied him on his frequent trips, but above all by countless bureaucrats, male as well as female, in the palace and in the provinces. The more highly placed a functionary, the more diverse were the assigned duties. In fact, each major functionary seems to have been in control of a *bitum*—literally "a house"—wherein were to be found various artisans' quarters, supply storehouses, living quarters, and the like. In the provinces, the

Inscribed statue of Ishtup-ilum, "governor" of Mari, second millennium B.C.

king's authority was communicated among others by the *shapitum*, "governor," the *merkhum*, "military representative (?)," the *suqaqum* and the *khazannum*, the king's delegates to tribal communities. Nonsettled elements constantly needed the king's attention, for some of these, in particular the Benjaminites, were constantly fomenting troubles.

Wars could take place at any time of the year although the more civilized ones were launched in the spring. The king usually delegated responsibility to a *rab amurrim*, "general," but he also went to the front. Armies could reach large numbers, with some engagements pitting fifty thousand men, raised from among all levels of the citizenry. Allies were expected to bring their troops to battle. Heavy weaponry included battering rams, towers, breach-mines, but the common soldiers used bows, javelins, swords, knives, and throw-sticks. They were protected by helmets, shields, codpieces, and in some cases, hauberks. The defeated were parceled out among the victors, with the king receiving the major share. Prisoners could be redeemed by their own communities or else they served at the victor's pleasure. The harem of a defeated king was simply taken over by the winning ruler.

Religion: As befits a major political power with ample resources to care and feed the gods, Mari worshiped many gods. Its temples also housed the gods of surrounding cities; these were released to their own shrines, seasonally or by appeal to the king, in order to gain the favor of the provincial population. We cannot state that in Mari one god dominated the others, but we can say that certain personnel gravitated to the worship of one deity and that certain deities were better approached for specific requests than others. It is certain that the goddess *Belet-ekallim*, for example, was favored by the females of the palace. On the other hand, when Zimri-Lim asked a favor from heaven, he wrote a brief but poignant letter to the river god Naru. Sacrifices took place daily; and although we have documentation for only a brief period during the reign of Zimri-Lim, we can recognize that the outlay of sacrificial animals was heavy. But in this way, sanctified meat was made available to members of the palace. (One recently published text is exceptional for establishing a ratio between animals that were to be slaughtered and those that were to be "released" upon making a vow *[ikribum]* to a deity.)

Gods were unpredictable in choosing a channel by which to communicate their message to the king. They could approach priestly as well as "secular" figures; they could choose male as well as female, young or old. They could relay their message through a trance, a dream, or a vision. The king never received that message directly, but rather through an intermediary who wrote the gist of the message on a clay tablet, but who also probably dispatched orally a more complete account. The king may have had as many as three different accounts from as many intermediaries. In order to verify the authorship of the message as well as the reliability of the medium, the king's diviners turned to various examinations of the entrails of sacrificial animals.

Mari and the Bible: Mari's direct bearing on Hebrew society as reconstructed from the Bible is slight. It is possible that some clans from the tribes, which are better known thanks to the Mari documents, eventually found their way to the area around Jericho; but the links for such a migration are broken. Mari does give us a rich repertoire of West Semitic names; it does inform us on the procedures for census taking, on the way prophetic pronouncements reached the king, and on the legal procedures required for adoption and for registering inheritance. But this information is available, albeit in poorer fashion, from Mesopotamian documents of many and differing periods. It is no longer prudent, therefore, to rely on Mari in order to formulate dates for the Hebrews' patriarchal period (ca. 2000–1750 B.C.). However, Mari's archives do allow us to reconstruct an ancient Near Eastern society in all its diverse aspects as well as in its uniqueness better than has heretofore been possible. We can therefore turn to Mari, rather than to contemporary paradigms, in search of models by which to evaluate and judge the social experiment that came to be known as Israel. ***See also*** Archaeology, History, and the Bible; Patriarch.

Bibliography

The *Biblical Archaeologist* issue 47/2 (1984), pp. 65–120, is devoted to Mari and its legacy.

J.M.S.

Mark (Lat. *Marcus;* Gk. *Markos*), a popular Latin name borne by prominent Romans from Cicero to the emperor Marcus Aurelius. Mentioned eight times in the NT (Acts and several Letters; never in the Gospels), it customarily names one who accompanied the apostles Paul and Peter. In the account in Acts, a Mark, surnamed John, was the son of a woman (Mary) in whose house in Jerusalem Christians from the earliest period met for prayer, and to which Peter went, apparently as a matter of course, on his miraculous release from prison (Acts 12:12). Mark accompanied Saul (Paul) and Barnabas on a journey from Antioch to Jerusalem with famine relief aid (Acts 12:25), but his untimely abandonment of a later missionary journey on which he accompanied Barnabas and Paul (Acts 13:5, 13) precipitated a dispute when Barnabas proposed taking Mark on another such journey. Paul's opposition to that course of action led to independent missionary journeys undertaken by Barnabas with Mark, and Paul with Silas (Acts 15:36–40). That is the last mention of John Mark in Acts. A Mark is mentioned by Paul, however, as one of five Christians who sent greetings to Philemon and some other recipients of that Letter (Philem. 24). If this is the same Mark, it indicates a later reconciliation with Paul. The same five Christians are also among the group that sends greetings to Christians in Colossae (Col. 4:10), where Mark is identified as the "cousin of Barnabas," an apparent reference to the Mark mentioned in Acts. A Mark is also identified by the author of 2 Timothy (4:11) as "very useful in serving me," and as "my son" in a Letter whose author is identified as the apostle Peter (1 Pet. 5:13).

Later traditions, assuming that all NT references were to the same person, identified this Mark as the author of the second Gospel, who, serving as Peter's interpreter in Rome, recorded, at the urging of Christians there, what he could remember of that apostle's preaching. Still later traditions claim that the Gospel, originally reported as written after Peter's death, was written during the apostle's life, and eventually it was claimed that it was written at Peter's urging. Other traditions make a "stub-fingered" Mark the first to preach in Egypt and the founder of Alexandrian Christianity. Sixth-century legends identify Mark as one of the seventy disciples of Jesus (Luke 10:1), the one who bore the jar of water (Mark 14:13), and the one in whose house the events of Pentecost occurred (Acts 2:1–4). Later legends portray his martyr's death and his reburial in Venice. That Mark 14:51–52 refers to the author of the Gospel is a modern conjecture.

P.J.A.

mark, an artificially inflicted sign on the body in the form of incision, tattoo, brand, or stamp. In the OT several kinds of distinguishing marks are mentioned. **1** The mark of Cain (Gen. 4:15), given as a protection, making the person of Cain inviolable. **2** The mark of the prophet (1 Kings 20:41), possibly an incision on the forehead. **3** Circumcision (Gen. 17:14; 1 Cor. 7:18), the most prominent mark identifying the Jew as belonging to God (cf. Isa. 44:5; 49:16). **4** The mark of a slave who did not wish to leave his master, whose earlobe was pierced by an awl (Exod. 21:6; Deut. 15:17).

In the NT only two instances can be mentioned. **5** The "marks of Jesus" that Paul bore (Gal. 6:17); these could have been scars from his sufferings for Christ (Acts 14:19; 2 Cor. 11:23–27). Paul, who called himself a "slave of Jesus" (Rom. 1:1), may also have had in mind the custom of branding a slave. **6** The "mark of the beast" (Rev. 13:16–18; 14:9–11; 16:2). The number 666 is thought to conceal the emperor Nero's name and the "mark" of the official imperial seal, necessary to conduct business. Accepting this mark was apostasy, as true Christians were marked with God's name upon their forehead (Rev. 3:12; 7:3; 14:1; 22:4; cf. Ezek. 9:4).

S.B.

Mark, the Gospel According to, the Bible book believed by most (not all) scholars to be the earliest of the four NT Gospels. Thus, it was probably one of the sources used by the author of the Gospel of Luke (Luke 1:1) and was also used by the author of Matthew. Although the author remains unidentified in the Gospel itself, early tradition assigned it to Mark, a companion of the disciple Peter, who reportedly wrote down, in Rome, what he had heard Peter preach. The nature of the material in Mark, however, points to a period when it was circulated in oral form before the author collected it and wrote it down, so it is doubtful that Mark simply wrote down what he had heard Peter preach. Another early tradition identifies Alexandria in Egypt as the place of origin. Attempts to identify this Mark with person(s) who bore the name in other NT writings (Acts 12:12, 25; 15:37, 39; Col. 4:10; 2 Tim. 4:11; Philem. 24; 1 Pet. 5:13) are rendered less sure by the popularity of that name in Roman culture.

Date and Origin: Because of reference to the destruction of the Temple in Jerusalem (Mark 13:2), the date of composition may be around

MARK, THE GOSPEL ACCORDING TO

the time this event occurred, A.D. 70. Because it was written in Greek and interprets phrases in Aramaic (5:41; 7:34; 15:34), the language of Palestine, the original readers were not Palestinians. Explanation of Jewish customs (7:3–4) makes it equally likely that the original readers were Gentiles. Mark's faulty knowledge of Palestinian geography (7:31) puts the place of origin outside Palestine as well. Beyond that, it is difficult to be precise about the origins of the Gospel. By failing to include any self-identification in the text, the author indicated that such information was unnecessary to understand the story contained in it.

The impetus that caused the author to assemble and order the individual traditions about Jesus for the first time may have been furnished by the (imminent) fall of Jerusalem, which some interpreted wrongly as signaling the return of Christ (13:6, 22). Increasing opposition to believers may also have played a role in prompting its composition (8:34–38; 13:9–13). Misinterpretation of individual traditions about what Jesus said and did, something which did occur in Paul's congregations (see 1 Cor. 11:17–27), as well as popular misinterpretation of Jesus as head of a group of magicians (Mark 9:38; Acts 8:9–19) or of philosophers (Acts 17:16–20), may also have shown the need to place those traditions within an interpretative framework.

Jesus' Identity: Whatever the motivation was for composing this Gospel, the author shaped the traditions in such a way that they told the story of a Jesus who could only be recognized for what he truly was, God's own Son, after he had died on the cross. While the reader is informed of Jesus' identity at the very outset of the narrative (1:1), an identity confirmed by a voice from Heaven (1:11; 9:7) and the outcry of demons (1:24; 5:7), that identity is kept secret until the moment of Jesus' death. The crowds, the religious authorities, and even the disciples fail to comprehend Jesus' true identity during his earthly career, despite the preaching and teaching he did and the miracles he performed. While Mark includes many traditions of miracles of Jesus, surprisingly enough they have little effect in leading people to a correct judgment about him. While trust in Jesus caused some to seek his miraculous help (5:23, 28; 10:47, 52), there is no indication that anyone was led to see Jesus as Son of God because of his miracles. The crowds, despite their enthusiasm for his miracles (1:33; 3:7–8) and teaching (4:1; 6:34), failed to identify him correctly, seeing in him a prophet (6:15) or a miracle worker (9:38) rather than God's Son, the Messiah (Christ). The religious authorities, despite their acquaintance with the religious traditions that allowed them to comprehend the meaning of what Jesus did and said (12:1–12, esp. v. 12) and thus to identify correctly who he was (14:61), nevertheless

The Evangelist page of the Gospel According to Mark from the *Lindisfarne Gospels* (ca. 700) depicts Mark holding his writings. Over his head is his symbol, the winged lion.

refused to accept their own conclusions as valid and saw in Jesus rather a blasphemer deserving of death (14:63–64). The disciples, who accompanied Jesus, heard him teach, and saw his mighty acts, in the end failed to understand who Jesus was and, despite occasional flashes of insight (8:29) and pledges of undying loyalty (14:29–31), in the end deserted and actively denied him (14:50, 66–72), thus leaving him to face the taunts of his enemies (14:65; 15:29–32) and his painful death (15:34, 37) alone and deserted.

Because it is this death and the ensuing resurrection, however, that provide the key to understanding Jesus, the inability to understand who he is prior to those events is not accidental in the view of the author of Mark. To those apart from his twelve disciples and others who followed him closely, things occur in riddles, which they are unable to comprehend, despite what they see and hear (4:10–12). Those who have known Jesus from his youth—his family and close acquaintances—are similarly unable to understand him. His family regards him as unbalanced (3:21), and those with whom he grew up take offense at him (6:3). Religious authorities, whose murderous intent is clear from the outset (3:6), oppose him at every turn, thus demonstrating the religious system they represent to be unfruitful (11:13). If lack of understanding from such quarters might ordinarily be expected and hence would not prove divine intent, one would not expect it from the disciples; yet it was precisely the disciples who not only do not understand (4:

13; 8:21; 9:6), but who are prevented from understanding (6:52; 8:17–18). Before his death on the cross, therefore, even those who are in daily association with Jesus are unable to comprehend him. Indeed, even their apparently correct confession is demonically tainted and does not share the divine intent for Jesus (8:29, 32–33). Only after his death on the cross can a human being understand Jesus as the Son of God (15:39). Only after his resurrection will the disciples finally understand Jesus against the background of his divine glory (see 9:9 in relation to 9:2–8).

All of this means that for Mark's understanding of Jesus, the death on the cross was not a historical accident, but the direct will of God. Thus Jesus predicts three times the divine destiny that awaits him ("the Son of man must suffer") as well as the divine vindication ("and after three days rise again"; 8:31; 9:31; 10:33–34). Therefore despite the lack of any record in Mark of appearances of the risen Jesus (16:9–20, absent from the oldest manuscripts, is a later addition compiled from information in the other Gospels), it is clear that Jesus' prediction of his resurrection, like his predictions of his death, would surely be fulfilled (cf. 14:28; 16:7). Perhaps the absence of appearances of the risen Christ is Mark's way of saying that until the return of Christ in glory (13:26–27; 14:62), an event that will come only after cosmic imbalances have occurred (13:24–25—hence the impossibility of predicting its occurrence on the basis of human events, even for Jesus himself; 13:32), life will continue to be marked by persecutions and suffering for Jesus' followers (13: 9–13), causing some to fall away (4:16–17).

Cross and Resurrection: Since for Mark the key to making sense of Jesus is his destiny of cross and resurrection, Mark's Christology (i.e., his understanding of Jesus) is shaped by that same key point. While Jesus is clearly the royal Son whom God anointed ("Christ" means "anointed") to be King (1:1, 11; 9:7; cf. Ps. 2:2–9), such titles cannot be understood apart from Jesus' destiny in the cross and resurrection. Rather, the title the author has Jesus use to describe himself in terms of his destiny in this narrative is "Son of man." This title, which also has royal overtones (see Dan. 7:13–14), is nevertheless defined in Mark as being tied to Jesus' destiny on the cross. It is used when Jesus predicts his Passion (8:31; 9:31; 10:33–34), his coming glory (14:62), and the purpose of his life (10:45). Because no human being can understand Jesus in that way before his crucifixion, no one uses the title except Jesus himself. While true estimates of Jesus may be given, they are not intended in an accurate sense by those who give them (Peter in 8: 29–33; Pilate's inscription in 15:26; the religious authorities in 15:32). Only after the cross, which for Mark is Jesus' enthronement (the chief priests' acknowledgment in 15:32 is ironic; they speak the truth without intending to), is it possible to recognize in him the Son of God (15:39). Thus Mark's Christology stands also under the same interpretative rubric of cross and resurrection as does the rest of his narrative.

The author of Mark thus created a theologically rich narrative by combining earlier traditions about Jesus into a story for which he provided occasional summary statements (1:32–34; 3:7–12; 6:53–56). Sometimes the author placed similar traditions together (conflict stories, 2:1–3:6; parables, 4:1–34), sometimes he sandwiched one inside another (5:21–43; 11:12–25), and sometimes he combined them into repeated cycles (8:31–9:8; 9:30–41; 10:33–52, which contain a prediction of Jesus' fate, the failure of disciples to understand, instructions on discipleship, and a proof of Jesus' exceptional nature). In that way, the author made his points more by the way in which he positioned the earlier traditions than by writing his own narrative material. Perhaps he felt constrained to use the earlier traditions in such a way that his readers would recognize in his narrative familiar elements of the career of Jesus and so would be more inclined to accept this narrative. The result nevertheless shows the composer to have been a person of powerful theological understanding who told the story of

The earliest extant manuscript fragment of the Gospel According to Mark (8:34–9:1); Chester Beatty papyrus fragment, third century A.D.

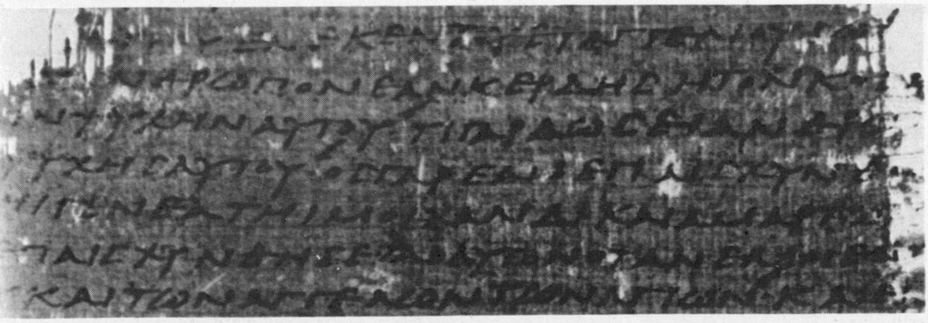

Jesus in the light of Jesus' fate in the cross and resurrection. ***See also*** Gospel, Gospels; Mark; Synoptic Problem, The.

OUTLINE OF CONTENTS

The Gospel According to Mark

I. Jesus appears, preaching the Kingdom of God with power (1:1–3:6)
  A. Beginnings—John the Baptist (1:1–13)
  B. Jesus' ministry introduced (1:14–45)
  C. Conflict with religious authorities (2:1–3:6)
II. Jesus' ministry in Galilee (3:7–6:6)
  A. True followers of Jesus (3:7–35)
  B. Teaching in parables (4:1–34)
  C. Working miracles (4:35–5:43)
  D. Conflict with his own (6:1–6)
III. Jesus begins his final journey to Jerusalem (6:7–8:21)
  A. Mission of the Twelve and John's death (6:7–29)
  B. Feeding and healing miracles (6:30–56)
  C. Teaching about the law (7:1–23)
  D. Healing and feeding miracles (7:24–8:10)
  E. Foes and friends misunderstand (8:11–21)
IV. Jesus heals blind eyes—teaching on discipleship (8:22–10:52)
  A. Blind eyes opened (3:22–26)
  B. First passion prediction and attendant events (8:27–9:29)
  C. Second passion prediction and attendant events (9:30–10:31)
  D. Third passion prediction and attendant events (10:32–45)
  E. Blind eyes opened (10:46–52)
V. Final week in Jerusalem (11:1–16:8)
  A. Jesus teaches in the Temple (11:1–12:44)
  B. On times before the end (13:1–37)
  C. Final acts of Jesus (14:1–42)
  D. Jesus tried and condemned (14:43–15:47)
  E. The empty tomb (16:1–8)
VI. Later epilogue: Jesus appears (16:9–20)

Bibliography

Achtemeier, Paul J. *Mark. Proclamation Commentaries.* Edited by G. Krodel. Philadelphia: Fortress, 1975.

Eusebius. *The Ecclesiastical History*. Translated by K. Lake. Loeb Classical Library. Cambridge: Harvard University Press, 1965 (see index for references to "Mark").

Kingsbury, Jack D. *The Christology of Mark's Gospel*. Philadelphia: Fortress, 1983. P.J.A.

marketplace. ***See*** Agora; Architecture; Athens; Corinth; Stoa.

marriage, the physical and spiritual union of a man and a woman. Gen. 2:21–24, in which God fashions one wife for Adam, expresses the biblical ideal of monogamous marriage (see Mark 10:6–9). However, the patriarchs practiced polygamy (Gen. 29:15–30). They also took concubines, especially in cases in which the wife had difficulty in conceiving children (Gen. 16:1–2). In the legislation of the Torah, it is taken for granted that a man may have two wives and that relationships were not always harmonious between them (Deut. 21:15). The kings of Israel were known to have had large harems, although the prevailing form of marriage was monogamy.

The unmarried woman, living in her father's house, was transferred into her husband's jurisdiction by his payment of the "bride price" (Heb. *mohar*) to her father (Gen. 34:12). If a man seduced a girl, he had to pay the bride price as a penalty and make her his legal wife (Exod. 22:16).

It is clear from Gen. 34:12 that the bride price was separate from the other gifts presented by the groom's family to the bride's. When the family of Rebekah accepted the terms of her marriage, Abraham's servant responded by presenting costly gifts to her, her mother, and brother (Gen. 24:53).

Marriages were generally contracted at a young age and arranged by the parents or at least arranged with their consent. It was common to marry within the clan, and first cousins were suitable partners (Gen. 24:4; 28:2). The Bible prohibits consanguineous marriage (Lev. 18). Priests were subject to even more stringent marriage regulations than ordinary Israelites, such as the prohibition of marriage with a divorcée (Lev. 21:7).

There was usually a betrothal period after which the marriage was celebrated (Deut. 22:23). David was promised the oldest daughter of Saul, Merab, but when the time of the marriage came, she was given to Adriel (1 Sam. 18:17–19). It is not certain if written contracts were in use, as they are not mentioned until Tob. 7:14.

The central ritual of the marriage ceremony itself was the symbolic bringing of the bride into the groom's house, followed by great rejoicing. Song of Sol. 3:11 describes the bridegroom as wearing a special crown given to him by his mother, and in Isa. 61:10 he wears a garland. A later description relates that the bride was escorted to meet the groom, and the groom came out with his friends accompanied by musicians and the sound of tambourines (1 Macc. 9:37–39). The bride wore her finest clothes, many jewels (Isa. 61:10), and a veil (Gen. 29:23–25; Song of Sol. 4:1). There followed a lengthy celebration with merrymaking, singing (Jer. 16:9), and feasting often lasting a week or two (Judg. 14:12).

Marital faithfulness was the ideal (Prov. 5: 18–29). The prohibition of adultery is one of the Ten Commandments central to the moral code of the Torah (Exod. 20:14; Deut. 5:18). While it was certainly considered a wrong against one's neighbor, it was also a sin against God. Marriage, therefore, became the metaphor with which to describe the relationship between God and Israel (Hosea 3). Prostitution was strongly condemned and often appears as a metaphor for grave sins associated with idolatry (e.g., Exod. 34:15; Deut. 31:16; Judg. 2:17; Hos. 9:1). The married couple was expected to develop a bond of mutual love and respect, which they, in turn, would pass on to their children.

A marriage could always be ended by the husband upon the presentation of a written bill of divorce permitting the wife to remarry (Deut. 24: 1–2). However, it is not stated specifically what constituted grounds for divorce. The *tannaim* (early rabbinic sages) argued over whether adultery alone constituted sufficient grounds, or whether the husband could divorce his wife for any reason. The latter view was accepted in later Judaism. Mark 10:2–9, however, totally rejects divorce.

If a man had intercourse with a virgin, he was compelled to marry her and could never divorce her (Deut. 22:29). Similarly, he could not divorce a wife whom he falsely accused of not being a virgin when he married her (Deut. 22:19). A woman who was married to a man, divorced, and married to another, could never remarry the first (Deut. 24:3–4).

There was no law among biblical Israelites that allowed the woman to initiate divorce. Although it is not mentioned, it is probable that a husband who divorced his wife forfeited the bride price and was no longer able to make use of the property the wife brought into the marriage.

The levirate law is specified in Deut. 25:5–10. The brother of a man who dies without a son had an obligation to marry the wife who was left, and "the first son whom she bears shall succeed to the name of his brother who is dead." Tamar, daughter-in-law of Judah, tried to force Judah to fulfill his obligation to provide a levirate marriage for her (Gen. 38), and the marriage of Boaz to Ruth was intended in some way to fulfill this same custom (Ruth 4: 10).

Some of the sectarians of the Second Commonwealth period, including the Essenes, practiced celibacy by separating from their wives after fulfilling the commandment of procreation. While, according to many scholars, members of the Dead Sea sect appear to have been celibate, they also seem to have been married, and a marriage ritual is presented in their scrolls.

In the NT, marriage is often used figuratively in connection with the Kingdom of God (e.g., Matt. 25:1–13; Luke 14:16–24; Rev. 19:7, 9), but it is an institution for the present rather than the future age (cf. Mark 12:25; 1 Cor. 7:8). It is nevertheless not to be taken lightly (Mark 10:9; 1 Cor. 7:10–11; Heb. 13:4); divorce (which in the NT world the wife could also initiate; Mark 10:12; 1 Cor. 7:13), if permitted at all, is only for the gravest of reasons (Matt. 19:9). The negative view of marriage found in Paul's first Letter to Corinth is due to his expectation of the end of the present age, rather than to a negative view of the institution as such (e.g., 1 Cor. 7:26–31). ***See also*** Priests.

Bibliography

Burrows, M. *The Basis of Israelite Marriage.* New Haven, CT: American Oriental Society, 1938.

Neufeld, E. *Ancient Hebrew Marriage Laws.* London: Longmans, Green, 1944.

Patai, R. *Sex and Family in the Bible and the Middle East.* Garden City, NY: Doubleday, 1959.

L.H.S./P.J.A.

Mars Hill, the term used in the KJV for the Areopagus, an outcropping of stone in Athens near the Acropolis (Acts 17:22). ***See also*** Areopagus.

Martha (Aramaic, "lady" or "mistress"; feminine of "lord"), a close friend and follower of Jesus as attested by Luke and John. According to Luke 10:38–42 she invites Jesus into her home, apparently as head of the household. She is described as "busy with much service" (Gk. *diakonia*), presumably meal preparation, while her sister Mary sits at Jesus' feet and listens to his teaching. Martha asks Jesus to tell Mary to help her, but Jesus replies that while Martha is troubled about "many things," only "one thing is needful" (or "a few things, indeed only one" in some ancient versions). The reference to "many things" may be to dishes for the meal, or perhaps to different kinds of service as in Acts 6:1–6, with Martha's kind corresponding with the office of deacon in the church as known to Luke.

This story may have influenced the account of Jesus' anointing in a home in Bethany in John 12:1–8. Here Martha serves while her brother Lazarus sits at table with Jesus, and her sister Mary anoints his feet. That John's Gospel sees Martha as an important disciple of Jesus is clear from the story of the raising of Lazarus in Bethany (11:1–44). Martha is named first, before Mary and Lazarus, as loved by Jesus (11:5). Going out to meet him, she receives teaching concerning the resurrection, acknowledges him as Lord, and confesses faith in him as "the Christ, the Son of God" (11:20–27). Although she expresses confidence in Jesus and his ability to receive from God whatever he asks (John 11:22–27), she expresses doubt at the tomb of Lazarus (11:39). ***See also*** Bethany; Mary.

W.M.

martyr (Gk. *martys*), a technical term in second-century Christianity for those who showed allegiance to Christ by their death. In the NT, the death of Stephen (Acts 22:20) and references to Christians who suffered death (Rev. 2:13; 17:6) carry some of the nuances of this later meaning. The earlier Greek term, however, is generally translated "witness" (see Acts 7:54–58; Rev. 11:2–11, which emphasize the prophetic witness rather than the death itself). ***See also*** Witness.

Mary (Gk. *Maria* or *Mariam;* Heb. *Marah,* "bitter" or "grieved," or *Miryam,* "rebellion"), a name borne by seven women in the NT, unless two or more are identical. **1** Mary, the mother of Jesus. ***See*** Mary, The Virgin. **2** Mary of Bethany, the sister of Martha and Lazarus (Luke 10:38–39; John 11:1). She appears once in Luke, sitting at Jesus' feet and listening as a disciple to his teaching (10:38–42). Martha objects that Mary has left her to serve alone, but Jesus commends Mary's choice as that "which shall not be taken away from her" (10:42). In John's version Mary anoints Jesus' feet with costly ointment and wipes them with her hair while Martha serves (12:1–3). Jesus defends her against Judas Iscariot's objection that the ointment could have been sold and the money given to the poor (12:4–8). John also mentions her as present with Martha at the death and raising of Lazarus (11:19, 20, 28–32). Others follow her when she goes out to Jesus (11:31), and her grief moves him deeply (11:33). **3** Mary Magdalene, or "of Magdala," mentioned first in every listing of Jesus' female disciples (Mark 15:40–41, 47; 16:1; Matt. 27:55–56, 61; 28:1; Luke 8:2–3; 24:10). She therefore seems to have been the leader of a group of women who "followed" and "served" Jesus constantly from the outset of his ministry in Galilee to his death and beyond. Matthew and Mark acknowledge them only immediately after Jesus' death, but Luke mentions their presence with the Twelve in Jesus' ministry in Galilee (8:1–3). Here Mary is included among the many women who provided for Jesus' ministry from their own means and among a smaller number "healed of evil spirits and infirmities." That she was healed of some serious affliction is expressed by describing her as one "from whom seven demons had gone out" (v. 2). She is foremost as a witness to Jesus' death according to all four Gospels (Mark 15:40–41, 47; Matt. 27:55–56, 61; Luke 23:49, 55–56; John 19:25), to the empty tomb (Mark 16:1–6; Matt. 28:1, 6; Luke 24:1–3, 10; John 20:1–2), and in receiving the news or appearance of the risen Christ to tell to the disciples (Mark 16:6–7; Matt. 28:5–9; Luke 24:4–10). According to Luke the women's testimony was not believed but was later vindicated (24:11, 22–48). According to John 20:11–18 the risen Jesus appeared first to her and talked with her about his coming ascension (v. 17). She is characterized as an apostle in some apocryphal NT writings (e.g., *The Gospel of Philip*). She rivals Peter in that she receives revelations from the risen Christ to pass on to the rest of the apostles. **4** Mary, the mother of James, or of James and Joses or Joseph, or "the other Mary," among the women disciples at the cross (Mark

Martha and her sister, Mary of Bethany; from a fifth-century ivory of the two watching the raising of their brother Lazarus from the dead (cf. John 11:17–44).

15:40; Matt. 27:55–56), with Mary Magdalene at the burial, empty tomb (Mark 15:47; 16:1; Matt. 27:61; 28:1), and first appearance of the risen Christ (Matt. 28:9). **5** Mary, the wife of Clopas, one of the women at the cross in John 19:25, often taken to be the same as Mary the mother of James and Joses. **6** Mary of Jerusalem, whose home was used as a meeting place for Jesus' followers after his death. Many were praying there when Peter arrived after his escape from prison to leave a message for James and the brothers and sisters (Acts 12:11–17). That no husband is mentioned may mean that she is the widowed head of the household and so perhaps leader of one of the house-churches mentioned in Acts 2:46. Rhoda, the "maid" or "little girl" who went to the door (v. 13), could be a slave member of the household, pointing to it as substantial. Mary's son John, also known as Mark, accompanied her nephew Barnabas (Col. 4:10) and also Paul on some of their missionary travels (Acts 12:25; 13:5, 13; 15:37–39). **7** Mary, one among many greeted by Paul in Rom. 16:1–16 and described as having "worked hard among you" (16:6), perhaps as a teacher or administrator (see 1 Cor. 12:28).

Bibliography

Swidler, L. *Biblical Affirmations of Women*. Philadelphia: Westminster, 1979. W.M.

Mary, the Virgin, the wife of Joseph, known as "the Virgin" because of her reported virginal conception of Jesus and perpetual virginity according to post-NT Mariology.

Paul refers to her obliquely in describing Jesus as "born of a woman, born under the law" (Gal. 4:4). "James the Lord's brother" in Gal. 1:19 suggests another son of Mary (but see below).

She is negatively portrayed in Mark, less so in Matthew, and positively in Luke. In Mark 3:21 Jesus' family seemingly accepts the verdict of the crowd that he is deranged and of the Jerusalem scribes that he is possessed by demons (3: 21–30). When his mother and brothers come to seize him and ask for him, he characterizes those about him and those who do God's will as his family (Mark 3:33–35). Matt. 12:46–50 and Luke 8:19–21 contain the same story, but unconnected with the accusations and attempted seizure. Luke's wording in 8:21, "My mother and brothers are those who hear the word of God and do it," includes them in Jesus' true family.

In Mark 6:1–6 people of "his own country" take offense at him as "the carpenter, the son of Mary and brother of James and Joses and Judas and Simon" and unnamed sisters (6:3; taken to be relatives, not siblings, by those holding to Mary's perpetual virginity). Jesus' response, "A prophet is not without honor, except in his own country, and among his own kin, and in his own house" (6:4), evidently includes his mother. Luke's version (4:16–30) excludes the reference to his mother, brothers, and sisters and identifies Jesus as "Joseph's son" (4:22).

Matt. 1:18–25 and Luke 1:26–56; 2:1–38 give differing birth stories, but both include the virginal conception, announced to Joseph in a dream in Matt. 1:18, 25, to Mary by the angel Gabriel in Luke 1:26–38. Mary accepts as God's servant the angel's announcement (Luke 1:38) and travels from Nazareth to Judea, to her pregnant kinswoman Elizabeth, who hails her as "blessed among women" and "the mother of my Lord" (1:39–45). Mary responds with a hymn of praise (1:46–55, the Magnificat). In Matthew Mary and Joseph are in Bethlehem at the birth, in a home where Mary and the child are found by wise men from the east, bringing precious gifts (2:1–13). Joseph takes Mary and Jesus to Egypt to escape Herod's slaughter of male children, eventually to settle in Nazareth (2:12–23). In Luke the couple travel from Nazareth to Bethlehem for a Roman census, where Mary gives birth (2:1–7), and angels and shepherds pay homage (2:8–20).

In Luke the scene moves to the Temple for after-birth purification and consecration of the firstborn (2:21–24). Here the aged Simeon and Anna acknowledge the Messiah's birth (2:25–38), with Simeon telling Mary, "a sword will pierce through your soul also" (2:35), perhaps characterizing her as hearing and doing God's word (cf. 1:38; 8:21 with Heb. 4:12). Luke also has a blessing on Jesus' mother from a woman in the crowd, which he applies to those who hear and keep God's word (11:27–28).

Luke tells of an exchange between the boy Jesus and his mother in the Temple, in which he places God above his parents (2:21–40). Luke also includes her among the women disciples praying in the upper room with the Twelve (Acts 1:41), and so also as one who received the Holy Spirit at Pentecost, as she did at Jesus' conception (Luke 1:35; Acts 2:1–4).

Jesus' mother is unnamed in John's Gospel. Her belief in Jesus' power is demonstrated at the wedding in Cana (2:1–11), though he initially resists her appeal (v. 4). She and his brothers accompany him to Capernaum (2:13). Later she is excluded from the brothers' unbelief (7:1–10), appearing at the cross with her sister, Mary (wife of) Clopas, Mary Magdalene, and the beloved disciple, whom Jesus commends to his mother as her son, and this "son" to her as "mother." She is then taken into his home (19:25–27).

The woman who gives birth to the Messiah in Rev. 12:2, 5 is not taken to be Mary, but as a symbol of God's people (Israel and the church) who bring forth the Christ. ***See also*** Magnificat; Virgin Birth.

Bibliography

Brown, R. E., K. A. Donfried, J. A. Fitzmyer, and J. Reumann, eds. *Mary in the New Testament*. Philadelphia: Fortress, 1978. W.M.

Maskil, a Hebrew word of uncertain significance that appears in the headings of some thirteen psalms, Psalms 32, 42, 44, 45, 52, 53, 54, 55, 74, 78, 88, 89, and 142. Some current versions of the Bible leave the word untranslated, while others, in accordance with its apparent root meaning of "understand" or "ponder," translate it as "instruction" or the like. Scholars have suggested that *maskil* is possibly a technical term relating to the manner of a psalm's performance, and/or a class of composition. The latter hypothesis is supported by the Psalter's use of other apparent class names in parallel fashion, as well as by the appearance of the word in Amos 5:13, where it may designate such a class. ***See also*** Psalms, The. J.L.K.

masons, craftsmen who build with stone. They along with stonecutters and carpenters were brought from Tyre to build David "a house" (2 Sam. 5:11; 1 Chron. 14:1), Solomon the Jerusalem Temple (1 Chron. 22:15), to repair it (2 Kings 12:12; 22:6; 2 Chron. 24:12), and rebuild it (Ezra 3:7). It is unclear precisely when local talent could fully displace the imported expertise.

It is unclear just how such a technician functioned in ancient times. Worked stone was presumably the province of the stonecutters, as may have been the quarrying of the supply. Whether the division of labor came at the point where prepared stone was put in place, with or without mortar, is unspecified. The term may also have applied to brickmasons, although the common use of mudbrick throughout the Near East for superstructures of defense walls as well as common housing walls would suggest broadly available skills for that task. It is also possible that the term applied to well or cistern cutters, those who engineered underground water tunnels such as those found at Jerusalem, Megiddo, and Gezer; builders of subterranean kilns such as that found at Hesban; cutters of tombs, whether shaft or chamber type; and builders of bridges, levelers of roadbeds through rocky terrain, and builders of stairs, layers of cantilevered rock roofs, and other tasks requiring some sort of special knowledge and skill.

Reuse of stone from earlier buildings is frequently evident in the archaeological material, and knowledge of the quality of the product was essential to a builder (note a metaphorical reference to this in Ps. 118:22).

Whatever the precise division of labor, the easy access to stone supply in Palestine (contrary to the situations in Mesopotamia and the lower Nile valley) and the successful craftsmanship in stonework are amply evident in the archaeological remains in the country. Elaborate stone gateways are a hallmark of Solomonic achievement at Hazor, Megiddo, Shechem, and Gezer. The improved tools developed once iron technology was mastered are evident in the superior accuracy of stonecutting and joints fitted in this period, although the Early Bronze Age (3000–2000 B.C.) temple remains at Ai (modern et Tell) bespeak the remarkable skill of earlier generations. Header-stretcher walls were especially characteristic of Iron Age II period constructions (such as the defense wall at Samaria), and marginally drafted stones of the walls of Herod's Temple at Jerusalem stand to this day. The Neolithic defense tower at Jericho was the precursor of a series of stone defense systems that because of their size, stability, and cost were most frequently reused by successive occupants. The large rock-cut access to water, such as at Gibeon (modern el-Jib), attests the long, patient application to a common social need in which such craftsmen participated. R.S.B.

Masorah (mah-soh'rah; Heb., "transmission"), the traditional Hebrew text of the Bible, preserved in rabbinic circles, with detailed notes and annotations added in order to maintain it intact. The siglum MT ("Masoretic Text") refers to this form of the text of the OT.

Massa (mas'ah), the seventh son of Ishmael (Gen. 25:14; 1 Chron. 1:30) and an ancestor of a north Arabian tribe (associated with Tema). The attribution of the words of Agur (Prov. 30:1) and Lemuel (Prov. 31:1) to the region of Massa suggests Arabian sources for that material.

Massah (mah'sah), according to tradition the spring in the wilderness where Israel tested the Lord. Following the gift of manna to the people in the wilderness, the people of Israel complained against Moses about the need for water. The Lord instructed Moses to strike a rock with his rod in order to provide for their needs. Moses named the place Massah (and Meribah) because of the Hebrew word that means "testing" or "trial" (Exod. 17:7; Deut. 6:16; 9:22; 33:8; Ps. 95:8).

master, one who owns property or exercises authority. **1** An owner of property (Exod. 21:4, 28; Luke 16:13; Acts 16:16; 1 Tim. 6:1). **2** One who exercises political authority (Gen. 45:8–9; 1 Sam. 26:19). **3** The husband of a wife (Deut. 24:4; 2 Sam. 11:26). **4** A polite form of address (Gen. 24:18; 33:8; 1 Kings 18:7). The word is also used of God (Deut. 10:17; Ps. 136:3; Eph. 6:9) and of Jesus Christ (Luke 5:5; 2 Pet. 2:1). Christians are admonished to call no one master but Christ (Matt. 23:10).

Mattaniah (mat-ah-nī'uh; Heb., "Yahweh's gift"). **1** A levitical musician from the sons of Heman who was appointed to the Temple by David (1 Chron. 25:4). **2** An Asaphite Levite who participated in Hezekiah's reform (2 Chron. 29:13). **3** The last king of Judah, renamed Zedekiah by Nebuchadnezzar, who appointed him to succeed his exiled uncle (or brother; 2 Kings 24:17–25:7). **4** A Levite, son of Mica, who returned to Jerusalem after the Exile (1 Chron. 9:15). **5** Four postexilic Israelites who divorced their foreign wives in response to Ezra's proclamation (Ezra 10:26, 27, 30, 37). **6** A name also used for other postexilic figures whose relationship to one another cannot be determined with certainty; a Levite who came back to Palestine from Babylonian exile with Zerubbabel (Neh. 12:8), a guard of the gates (Neh.12:25), a priest (Neh. 12:35), and the father of Zaccur (Neh. 13:13). ***See also*** Zedekiah. F.E.G.

Mattathias (mat-uh-thī'uhs; Heb., "gift of Yahweh"), a common name, particularly in the Maccabean period. **1** A priest of the family of Joarib (1 Macc. 2:1) or Jehoiarib (see 1 Chron. 24:7) who, with his five sons, called "Maccabees," began the revolt against Seleucid rule in 167 B.C. in their Judean village of Modein. **2** His grandson, Mattathias the son of Simon, who was murdered at the same time as his father (1 Macc. 16:14–17). **3** Mattathias the son of Absalom, one of the army commanders under Jonathan (1 Macc. 11:70). **4** One of the envoys sent by Nicanor to Judas Maccabeus (2 Macc. 14:19). **5** A name included twice in Luke's genealogy of Jesus (Luke 3:25–26). ***See also*** Maccabees. F.O.G.

Matthew, one of the original twelve disciples called by Jesus. Matthew appears in all four of the apostolic lists (Matt. 10:2–4; Mark 3:16–19; Luke 6:14–16; Acts 1:13). The tradition of the "call" of Matthew is found in Matt. 9:9, where his occupation at the time of the call is identified as that of tax collector (cf. Matt. 10:3). In the parallel accounts (Mark 2:13–14; Luke 5:27–28), however, the name of the tax collector called is Levi (the son or brother of Alphaeus according to Mark). The use of different names in these parallel passages has given rise to long-standing debate as to whether "Matthew" and "Levi" refer to the same person. The absence of "Levi" in the apostolic lists of Mark and Luke-Acts (as well as in Matthew) causes some to argue for two persons. Most, however, have maintained that "Matthew" and "Levi" constitute a double name (as, for example, "Simon" and "Peter," "Saul" and "Paul") and thus have argued that the reference is to the same person. If Matthew and Levi are the same person, then Matthew is "the son (or brother) of Alphaeus" (Mark 2:14) and thus perhaps the brother of James (not James the brother of John and son of Zebedee), also one of the Twelve (Matt. 10:3; Mark 3:18; Luke 6:15; Acts 1:13). Tradition credits Matthew with having composed the Gospel bearing that name, but this is questionable. ***See also*** Alphaeus; Apostle; Disciple; James; Levi; Matthew, The Gospel According to; Publicans; Twelve, The.

P.L.S.

Matthew, the Gospel According to, a Gospel most likely written about A.D. 90 by an unknown Christian who was most probably at home in a church located in or near Antioch of Syria. The date of A.D. 90 commends itself because the destruction of Jerusalem appears to be an event that was rapidly receding into the past (22:7). Although the apostle Matthew may have been active in founding the church in which this Gospel originated (9:9; 10:3), the author exhibits a theological outlook, command of Greek, and rabbinic training that suggest that he was a Jewish Christian of the second generation (cf. 13:52). Antioch of Syria is most likely the place of writing (cf. 4:24) because the social conditions reflected in Matthew correspond with those that seem to have prevailed there: the church of Matthew was resident in a prosperous, urban, Greek-speaking area and subject to persecution from the side of a seemingly large population of both Jews and Gentiles (5:10–12; 10:17–18; 24:9–14).

Composition: For most scholars, the Two-Source Hypothesis still explains best the composition of Matthew. Apparently, the author drew upon two written sources: Mark, and a collection of sayings of Jesus called Q. In addition, he used traditions available only to him (M). From these, he fashioned a theologically sophisticated story of the life and ministry of Jesus. The formula at 4:17 and at 16:21 divides

The Evangelist page of the Gospel According to Matthew from the *Lindisfarne Gospels* (ca. 700) depicts Matthew seated, writing in a codex. His symbol, an angel, is behind him.

this story into three main parts: the figure of Jesus Messiah (1:1–4:16); the public ministry of Jesus Messiah and Israel's repudiation of him (4:17–16:20); and the journey of Jesus Messiah to Jerusalem and his suffering, death, and resurrection (16:21–28:20).

The context of this story of Jesus is the history of salvation. It extends from Abraham (1:1, 17) to the consummation of the age (25:31–46) and comprises two epochs. The first epoch is the time of the OT, which is the time of prophecy (11:13). The second epoch is the time of fulfillment (cf. 1:22; 26:56), which is the time of the earthly-exalted Jesus (1:23; 28:20). The time of Jesus encompasses the ministries to Israel of John the Baptist (3:1–2), of Jesus (4:17), and of the earthly disciples (10:7), as well as the ministry to the nations of the post-Easter church (24:14; 28:18–20). Still, central to this time is the ministry of Jesus himself, for the ministry of John prepares for it and the ministries of the pre-Easter and post-Easter disciples are an extension of it (10:1–8; 28:18–20).

Major Themes: Matthew's story of Jesus proclaims a central message. It comes to the fore in 1:23 and 28:20, passages that "enclose" the story (cf. 18:20). The message is that in Jesus, Son of God, God has drawn near with his eschatological Rule to dwell to the end of time with his people, the church. This message summons the reader to perceive that God is uniquely present and at work in Jesus and that, in becoming Jesus' disciple, one becomes a child of God, lives in the sphere of his end-time rule, and engages in mission to the end that all people may find God in Jesus and become Jesus' disciples.

In the first part of his story (1:1–4:16), the author presents Jesus to the readers. Initially, he describes him as the Messiah, Son of David, and Son of Abraham (1:1). Jesus is the Messiah because he is the Anointed One, Israel's long-awaited King (1:17; 2:2, 4; 11:2–3). He is the Son of David because Joseph adopts him into the line of David (1:16, 18–25) and he fulfills the eschatological expectations associated with David (9:27–31; 12:22–23; 15:21–28; 20:29–21:17). He is the Son of Abraham because in him the entire history of Israel attains to its culmination and the Gentiles, too, find blessing (1:17; 8:11).

Upon Jesus' birth, the Magi arrive in Jerusalem and ask where they may find the King of the Jews (2:1–2). To Herod and, later, to Pilate as well, the title King of the Jews denotes that Jesus is a throne-pretender or insurrectionist. The result is that Herod plots to have Jesus found and killed (2:13) and Pilate, later, hands him over to be crucified (27:26, 37). In Matthew's perspective, Jesus is in truth the King of the Jews, not, however, because he aspires to the throne of Israel or foments rebellion against Rome but because he saves his people by submitting to suffering and death (27:27–31, 37, 42).

John the Baptist is Elijah brought back to life, the forerunner of Jesus (3:1–12; 11:12). He readies Israel for Jesus' coming by calling Israel to repentance in view of the nearness of God's end-time Kingdom and the final judgment (3:2, 10–12).

The baptismal scene constitutes the climax of the first part of Matthew's story (3:13–17). After John has baptized Jesus, God empowers Jesus with his Spirit and declares him to be his unique Son whom he has chosen for messianic ministry (3:16–17). This declaration by God reveals that Jesus is preeminently the Son of God in Matthew's story. The significance of this title is that it points to the unique filial relationship that Jesus has to God; conceived and empowered by God's Spirit (1:18, 20; 3:16–17), Jesus is "God with us" (1:23), the one through whom God reveals himself to humankind (11:25–27) and who is God's supreme agent of salvation (1:21; 26:28).

Guided by the Spirit, Jesus submits to testing by Satan (4:1–11). Three times Satan endeavors to get Jesus to break faith with God. Jesus, however, resists Satan's temptations and shows himself to be the Son who knows and does his Father's will. Returning to Galilee, Jesus is poised to begin his public activity (4:12–16).

In the second part of his story (4:17–16:20), the author tells of Jesus' ministry to Israel (4:17–11:1) and of Israel's repudiation of him (11:2–16:20). Through his ministry of teaching, preaching, and healing (4:23; 9:35; 11:1), Jesus summons Israel to repentance (4:17; 11:20–21). Israel, however, repudiates Jesus (chaps. 11–12), yet wonders and speculates about his identity (11:3; 12:23; 13:55–56; 14:2; 16:14). Against the background of Israel's false views about Jesus' identity (16:14), the disciples correctly confess him to be the Son of God (14:33; 16:16).

In the third part of his story (16:21–28:20), the author depicts Jesus' journey to Jerusalem and his suffering, death, and resurrection. The passion predictions sound the theme (16:21; 17:22–23; 20:17–19), and the motif of the journey binds together disparate materials (16:21–21:11). In Jerusalem, Jesus makes the Temple the site of his activity, where he teaches, debates, and speaks in parables (21:12–23:39). Addressing the parable of the wicked husbandmen to the Jewish officials, Jesus raises the claim that he is the Son of God whom the officials will kill (21:37–39). In wanting to arrest Jesus for telling the parable (21:45–46), the Jewish officials show that they reject Jesus' claim.

At his trial, it is the claim of Jesus' parable to be the Son of God that the high priest puts to Jesus to secure his condemnation (26:63–66). When Jesus replies to the high priest's question in the affirmative (26:64), he is sentenced to death for blaspheming God. The irony is that God has indeed affirmed Jesus to be his Son (3:17; 17:5).

Upon Jesus' death, the Roman soldiers also affirm Jesus to be the Son of God (27:54). What the readers know that the soldiers do not is that the death of Jesus Son of God constitutes the climax of his earthly ministry and the act whereby he atones for the sins of humankind (1:21; 26:28). Atop the mountain in Galilee, Jesus appears to the disciples as the resurrected Son of God who remains the crucified Son of God (28:5, 16–20). Seeing Jesus as such, the disciples at last perceive not only who he is (16:16) but also what he has accomplished (26:28), and they consequently receive his commission to go and to make of all nations his disciples (28:18–20). Matthew's story ends, therefore, with both the disciples and the readers sharing the same perception of Jesus and receiving his commission.

Entwined with the story line of Jesus in Matthew is that of the disciples. Called by Jesus, his followers live in the sphere of God's end-time Rule and form a "family" (12:48–50) of the "sons of God" (5:9, 45) and of Jesus' "disciples" (10:24–25). This new family becomes the church (16:18; 18:17). The quality of life that characterizes the disciples is that of the greater righteousness (5:20). The disciples exhibit this quality when they are perfect (5:48), that is, when they are wholehearted in doing the will of God as explicated by Jesus (7:21). At the center of doing the will of God is the exercise of love (22:34–40). Loving as God loves, therefore, is of the essence of Christian existence (5:44–45). ***See also*** Abraham; Antioch; Baptism; David; Disciple; Gospel, Gospels; John the Baptist; Kingdom of God; M; Messiah; Q; Son of God; Synoptic Problem, The; Temptation. J.D.K.

OUTLINE OF CONTENTS

The Gospel According to Matthew

I. Jesus presented (1:1–4:16)
  A. Jesus as fullfillment of end-time expectations (1:1–25)
    1. Jesus' ancestors recalled (1:1–17)
    2. Jesus' birth announced (1:18–25)
  B. Birth of Jesus (2:1–23)
    1. Appearance of the Magi (2:1–12)
    2. Jesus taken to Egypt (2:13–15)
    3. Slaughter of the innocents (2:16–23)
  C. Jesus and John the Baptist (3:1–4:11)
    1. John baptizes in Judea (3:1–12)
    2. John baptizes Jesus (3:12–17)
    3. Jesus tempted by Satan (4:1–11)
    4. Jesus in Galilee (4:12–)
II. Jesus' ministry (4:17–16:20)
  A. Jesus' ministry to Israel (4:17–11:1)
    1. Jesus calls disciples (4:17–22)
    2. Jesus teaches (4:23–7:29)
    3. Jesus does mighty deeds (8:1–9:34)
    4. Jesus commissions the Twelve (9:35–11:1)
  B. Israel's repudiation of Jesus (11:2–16:20)
    1. Israel repudiates Jesus (11:2–12:50)
    2. Jesus speaks in parables (13:1–52)
    3. Rejection of Jesus and the death of John the Baptist (13:53–14:12)
    4. Jesus feeds, heals, and teaches (14:13–16:12)
    5. Disciples confess Jesus as Son of God (16:13–20)
III. Jesus in Jerusalem (16:21–28:20)
  A. Jesus predicts his passion in Jerusalem and journeys to it (16:21–21:11)
  B. Jesus in the Temple (21:12–23:39)
  C. Jesus speaks about end times (24:1–25:46)
  D. Jesus' trial and crucifixion (26:1–27:66)
  E. Jesus risen from the dead (28:1–20)

Matthew's Bible. ***See*** English Bible, The.

Matthias (muh-thī'uhs), according to Acts 1:15–26, the successor among the Twelve Apostles to Judas Iscariot. After prayer, Matthias was chosen by lot over another candidate, Joseph called Barsabbas. According to Acts, both men had been with Jesus from the beginning of his ministry until his ascension. The NT contains no other reference to Matthias. ***See also*** Apostle; Barsabbas; Twelve, The.

Mattithiah (mat-ti-thī'uh; Heb., "gift of Yah [God]"). **1** A Levite who was in charge of baked goods in the Temple (1 Chron. 9:31). **2** A Levite gatekeeper of the clan of Merari during the reign of King David (1 Chron. 15:18). **3** A Levite musician during the time of David (1 Chron. 15:21); he is probably the same musician chosen to help celebrate the transfer of the Ark of the Covenant to Jerusalem (1 Chron. 16:5); and he is possibly also the same Levite of the clan of Jeduthan who was head of the fourteenth course of musicians (1 Chron. 25:3; 21). **4** A postexilic member of the clan of Nebo who took a foreign wife (Ezra 10:43). **5** One, probably a Levite, who was with Ezra at the reading of the law (Neh. 8:4). D.R.B.

mattock, an agricultural tool with a double-bladed metal head, often made with one blade attached at a hoelike angle and the other in an axelike position. Farmers used the mattock to loosen soil and dig weeds in fields and terraced vineyards (cf. Isa. 5:6; 7:5).

While the KJV uses "mattock" to translate three Hebrew words in three passages (1 Sam. 13:20–21; 2 Chron. 34:6; Isa. 7:25), the RSV uses mattock only in 1 Sam. 13:20–21, a passage that says the Hebrews were obliged to take their farm implements to the Philistines for sharpening. ***See also*** Farming; Metals; Tools.

maul, the term used in the KJV for the RSV's "war club" in Prov. 25:18, suggesting a mace or heavy stick used as a common infantry weapon in antiquity. It may have been topped by a heavy knob or hafted to a stone for increased efficiency. Some mace heads were inscribed or decorated with ceremonial or royal insignia.

Maundy Thursday, the Thursday before Easter on which Christians memorialize the last supper Jesus ate with his disciples. "Maundy" comes from Latin "mandatum (novum)," the words in John 13:34 (Vg) used in the service of foot washing observed in the Catholic Church on the Thursday before Easter. According to an ancient agricultural calendar evidently observed by Jesus, this was the date of Passover. According to the Roman Calendar, Passover occurred the following night.

meadow, a flat open portion of pasture or field. Suitable for grazing (Ps. 65:13; KJV: "pastures"), it also serves as a symbol for desolation in a prophetic curse on a seacoast population (Zeph. 2:6), its isolation and overgrown state compared to its former thriving life.

meal offering. ***See*** Worship.

meals, food taken at regular intervals, often in the presence of others. The ancient Israelite usually ate two meals a day, a light meal in late morning or at midday and a more substantial meal in the evening, around sunset. In ancient Palestine the normal diet might include the following foods: bread, cooked or parched grain (wheat, barley, millet), wine, cheese and curds (primarily from goats' milk), figs or fig cakes, grapes and raisins, dates, olives, wild honey, beans and lentils, melons, and cucumbers. Onions, leeks, and garlic supplied seasoning; olive oil was used for cooking. Poultry and eggs became common only relatively late in Israelite history. The NT indicates that fish was a common food in the first century. Except among the wealthy, meat was not part of the daily diet but was reserved for special occasions such as feasts or sacrifices (see Lev. 7:11–18). The Torah emphatically distinguishes between living creatures that may be eaten and those that may not (Lev. 11; Deut. 14). The Torah also stresses that meat to be eaten must be entirely drained of blood, for "the blood is the life" (Deut. 12:23; see Gen. 9:4; Lev. 17:14). Sheep and goats were the main sources of meat, and the tail of the sheep was considered a special delicacy.

Significance of Meals in Ancient Israel: In Israel, meals were much more than occasions for satisfying hunger, for it was understood that persons who ate and drank together were bound to one another by friendship and mutual obligation. Moreover, the meal could be intensely symbolic when it was eaten in conjunction with the making of a covenant between persons (e.g., Gen. 26:28–30; 31:43–54) or between God and his people (Exod. 24:9–11). The Israelite experience of eating "before the Lord" when one brought sacrifices and offerings (e.g., Deut. 12:6–7; 14:22–26) perhaps reflects the ancient view that through a sacred meal human beings can commune with the deity.

Especially when accompanied by wine and the entertainment of music and dancing (Isa. 5:12; Ecclus. 32:3–6; Luke 15:22–25), meals were fitting occasions for celebration and rejoicing (cf. Amos 8:10), and feasts often marked events of special significance, such as a sheep-shearing (2 Sam. 13:23–28), a wedding (Judg. 14:10), or the return of an absent family member (Luke 15:22–24). The "appointed feasts" prescribed by Torah (e.g., Weeks) or tradition (e.g., Purim) were celebrations of God's beneficence on behalf of his people, the most important festal meal in Israel being, of course, Passover. The Passover meal proper came to be celebrated on the first evening of the seven-day Feast of Unleavened Bread, a feast tied closely with Passover in the Pentateuch and, with it, Israel's primary commemoration of the Exodus from Egypt (Exod. 12; Num. 28:16–25; Deut. 16:1–8).

Among the Jewish sectarians at Qumran on the western shore of the Dead Sea, the daily communal meal, which began with a priestly blessing of the bread and wine, bore special religious significance—perhaps because it anticipated the banquet of the new age when the two messiahs, priestly and royal, would be present (1QS 6:2–5; 1QSa 2:11–22). This expectation is reminiscent of Isa. 25:6–8, where a "feast of fat things" symbolizes God's eschatological salvation.

In NT Times: From scattered clues we can glimpse something of the etiquette that prevailed at banquets given by the well-to-do in NT times. It prescribed, for example, the proper kind of clothes to be worn by guests (Matt. 22:11–12), the obligations of the host to greet his guests with a kiss and provide for the washing of their feet (Luke 7:44–45; cf. Judg. 19:21), and the responsibilities of the banquetmaster (Ecclus. 32:1–2). In the Palestine of Jesus' day it was apparently customary to issue two invitations to a banquet—the first some days ahead of time and the second when the meal was ready (Luke 14:16–17). Once arrived, the guests were seated according to age or rank (cf. Luke 14:7–11).

In describing meals that Jesus participated in, the Gospels state that he reclined (at table). This expression indicates that in the Palestine of Jesus' day the Greco-Roman custom of reclining at formal meals had become widespread. (Amos 6:4–6 would seem to show that the practice of reclining at meals, perhaps of Mesopotamian origin, is even older.) On couches placed around a large table (or three tables placed to form an open-ended rectangle), guests and host reclined on the left elbow and ate with the right hand, body diagonal to the couch and feet extending off the back. Usually three persons reclined on one couch. The reclining posture at table explains how Luke could describe the woman with the ointment as standing behind Jesus while anointing his feet (Luke 7:36–38). It also explains how, in the Gospel of John, Jesus could wash the disciples' feet as they ate (13:5) and how the beloved disciple could recline on Jesus' breast (13:23).

By NT times the blessing of the food at the beginning of a meal had become standard practice in Judaism; when wine was drunk, a prayer of thanksgiving over the cup concluded the meal. The Pharisees, in addition, insisted on the ritual washing of hands. Although Jesus blessed the food before eating, he and his disciples did not adopt the practice of handwashing (Mark 7: 1–5; Luke 11:37–38).

In Jesus' Ministry: Jesus' table fellowship with his followers was an important feature of his ministry, and according to the Gospels his eating with "tax collectors and sinners" drew criticism from his detractors. Their accusation that he was a "glutton and a drunkard" (Matt. 11: 18–19; Luke 7:33–34) suggests that, unlike John the Baptist, Jesus took pleasure in eating and drinking. His table fellowship was intended to symbolize for his companions the blessing of joyous fellowship in God's presence that would characterize the new age (cf. Matt. 8:11 with 11: 18–19). According to one interpretation, in the Lord's Prayer Jesus taught his disciples to pray, "Give us this day tomorrow's bread"; so understood, this petition was a plea that God would allow a foretaste of future blessedness amid the afflictions and failures of the present age. It may be in light of the bread/banquet image of future blessedness that we should understand the Gospel stories about Jesus' feeding of the multitudes (Mark 6:30–44 and parallels; Mark 8:1–9 and parallels; John 6:1–14).

Several times in the gospels, especially in Luke, a meal is the setting for important teachings of Jesus (Matt. 9:10–13; Luke 7; 11:37–52; 14:1–24), and some of Jesus' parables have to do with a feast or feasting (Matt. 22:1–10; Luke 14:16–24; Matt. 22:11–13; Luke 15:11–32; cf. Matt. 25:10; Luke 16:19–21). As Matthew and Luke understand it, the parable of the great banquet (Matt. 22:1–13; Luke 14:16–24) is a story about the salvation that God offers the world.

Several appearances of the risen Jesus to his disciples occur in the setting of a meal. It was only when Jesus blessed and broke the bread that the eyes of Cleopas and his companion were opened so that they recognized him (Luke 24: 30–31). In John 21 the Risen One gives his disciples bread and fish to eat beside the Sea of Galilee (vv. 9–13; see also Luke 24:41–43).

In Early Christianity: Meals continued to be crucially important in early Christianity. The book of Acts describes the Christians in Jerusalem after Pentecost as attending the Temple, breaking bread in their homes, and partaking of food "with glad and generous hearts" (2:46). The reference here may be to one of the two early Christian sacraments, the Lord's Supper, which was originally a full hunger-satisfying meal (note the phrase "after supper" in Luke 22:20 and 1 Cor. 11:25, implying a full meal). Having its origin in Jesus' last meal with his disciples before his death (itself to be viewed in the context of his regular table fellowship), the Supper was a commemoration of the crucified Lord and a means by which the risen Lord was present among each community of believers. By at least the middle of the second century the sacrament of bread and wine had been separated from the communal Christian meals, which in the letter of Jude are now called "love feasts" (12).

In the Revelation to John believers are invited to "the marriage supper of the Lamb" (19: 9), but at the "great supper of God" the birds of the air will feed on the flesh of the world's kings, captains, and mighty men (19:17–18; cf. Ezek. 39:17–20). Thus in the last book of the Bible the banquet is an image of both God's greatest reward and his most awful punishment. ***See also*** Feasts, Festivals, and Fasts; Food; Lord's Supper, The; Passover. S.K.W.

measure. ***See*** Weights and Measures.

meat. ***See*** Food; Meals; Worship.

meat offered to idols. ***See*** Food Offered to Idols.

Medan (mee'dan), the third son of Abraham by Keturah (Gen. 25:2; 1 Chron. 1:32); the term may possibly also be a reference to the inhabitants of Midian.

Medeba (med'e-bah), a city and surrounding territory located on a fertile plateau approximately six miles south of Heshbon and twenty-five miles south of Amman.

It is mentioned along with Heshbon and Dibon (Num. 21:30) in the account of the land taken by the Israelites from Sihon. The tableland of Medeba is part of the inheritance of Reuben (Josh. 13:9, 16). In a battle between Joab and an Ammonite-Syrian coalition, the Syrians encamped before Medeba (1 Chron. 19: 7). In the Moabite Stone the Israelites are said to have occupied the land of Medeba for forty years. Mesha, king of Moab, claims to have recaptured and rebuilt it. It is included in

Isaiah's oracle against Moab (Isa. 15:2). John, the oldest son of Mattathias, was ambushed by the sons of Jambri from Medeba during the Maccabean revolt against Syria, begun in 167 B.C. (1 Macc. 9:36). Jonathan and Simon, his brothers, took revenge by annihilating a wedding party of their enemies (1 Macc. 9:37–42). The Jewish historian Josephus relates that John Hyrcanus, Simon's son, captured Medeba after a six-month siege. He also says that Alexander Jannaeus took it along with other towns and that Hyrcanus II promised to restore them to Aretas, king of the Nabateans.

The Romans made Medeba a provincial town. It continued to flourish until the end of the Byzantine period (A.D. 640). During this period it was the seat of a bishopric and it is mentioned in the articles of the Council of Chalcedon (A.D. 451). The most impressive archaeological remains at Medeba are the mosaics, which date from the Byzantine period. The chief mosaic, the Medeba Map, dates from the sixth century A.D. It is now housed in the Greek Orthodox church in the town. ***See also*** Dibon; Heshbon; Mesha; Moabite Stone, The; Nabatea, Nabateans; Reuben. B.M.

Media (mee'dee-ah), **Medes** (meeds), the names of a place and people often associated with that of Persia (especially in the books of Esther and Daniel). Media became a province of the Persian Empire in 549 B.C. when the Medan overlord was conquered by Cyrus the Great. The area of Media appears as one to which deportees from the Northern Kingdom were taken in 722 B.C. (2 Kings 17:6; 18:11). Ecbatana (Agbatana), the Medan capital, located some four hundred map miles north of the Persian Gulf, became one of the administrative centers of the Persian Empire (Ezra 6:2). In the stories related in the book of Esther and in Daniel 5 and 6, the laws of Medes and Persians are described as unalterable (e.g., Esther 1:19; Dan. 5:28), a description that is evidently a folk-tale motif, related to the prohibition on altering laws found in numerous ancient legal texts (cf. Deut. 4:2; 12:32; Ezra 6:11). The Medes appear as the divine instrument of judgment on Babylon in Isa. 13:17; Jer. 51:11, 28; also with Elam in Isa. 21:2 (cf. Jer. 25:25 in a picture of total judgment on Babylon at the hands of all the nations).

Medan nobles march up a stairway at Persepolis, bringing gifts to the Persian king Darius I (521–486 B.C.)

Dan. 5:31; 9:1; and 11:1 introduce a "kingdom of the Medes" that existed between the fall of the Babylonians and the rise of the Persians. This has no historical basis. It may perhaps best be understood as expressing the fulfillment of those prophetic texts that envisage the overthrow of Babylon by the Medes. Acts 2:9 includes Media as one of the areas from which Jewish pilgrims have come to Jerusalem.

The history of the Medes before their empire was taken over by Cyrus is obscure at many points. They appear in numerous Assyrian inscriptions from the mid-ninth century B.C. onwards, established in the area of modern Iran and penetrating the Zagros mountains. Herodotus, the fifth-century B.C. Greek historian, has an account of their history, but appears to have no real knowledge of the chronology. The extent of their empire is a matter of debate; it was evidently fully developed in the seventh century B.C. The Medes took a major part in the eventual overthrow of the Assyrians, capturing Nineveh in 612 B.C. and sacking Harran in 610. In the early sixth century, the Medes came into conflict with the Lydians in Asia Minor, a conflict that was to be brought to a successful conclusion by Cyrus. Under the Persians, Media was a large province. It appears probable that the administrative title "satrap," associated particularly with the organization of the Persian Empire by Darius I, was of Medan origin. ***See also*** Cyrus II; Darius; Persia.

Bibliography

Cook, J. M. *The Persian Empire*. London: Dent, 1983.

P.R.A.

mediation, mediator, the activity and person performing it of functioning as a go-between or intermediary between two people or parties, in order to initiate a relationship, promote mutual understanding or activity, or effect a reconciliation after a dispute. In the study of religion mediation usually refers to a person who represents the community in worship and other contacts with divine beings. In the OT various figures in Israel's history mediate between God and humans and in the NT Jesus is the unique mediator who reconciles sinful humans to God.

In the OT: In the OT the priests are religious mediators between humans and God. Their functions include offering community and private sacrifices, praying and singing in the Temple, protecting the integrity of the holy places and rituals, and maintaining themselves in a state of ritual purity. All the religious regulations concerning priests, holy places, worship, and the Temple were designed to render humans holy so that they could relate to a God who is holy. The priests themselves were consecrated to their special office (Exod. 29; Lev. 8) as mediators between the profane and the holy. Priests also blessed the people (Num. 6:22–27) and offered the first fruits brought to the Temple by the people (Deut. 26:1–10). The mediating function of the priesthood can be seen most clearly on the Day of Atonement, when the high priest alone entered the Holy of Holies, the inner chamber of the Temple, to offer incense in atonement for all the sins of the people during the past year (Num. 16).

Major OT leaders also mediated between God and Israel. Abraham sacrificed and prayed to God in the name of his clan (Gen. 12:7–8) and he also interceded on behalf of Sodom and Gomorrah (Gen. 18:22–33). Jacob sacrificed to God and received God's blessing on all his descendants in Israel (Gen. 35:1–15). Moses mediated between God and the Hebrews in Egypt, during the wandering in the desert, at Sinai, and when Israel sinned by worshiping the golden calf (Exod. 32:30–34). Joshua mediated between God and the people in the making of the covenant in Israel (Josh. 24:14–28), Samuel mediated the appointment of the first king (1 Sam. 8–12), and Solomon prayed in the people's name at the dedication of the Temple (1 Kings 8:22–53). The prophets who acted as God's messengers in bringing his word to the people also acted as mediators in effecting reconciliation between the people and God (Jer. 14:1–9). Finally, the Suffering Servant found in Second Isaiah 53, whatever his identity, atones for the sins of Israel and effects a reconciliation between God and Israel.

In the NT: In the NT Jesus is explicitly called a mediator in only four passages, one from the Pauline literature and three from Hebrews. "For there is one God, and there is one mediator between God and men, the man Christ Jesus, who gave himself as a ransom for all" (1 Tim. 2:5–6). In Hebrews Christ is three times said to mediate the new covenant between God and humans (Heb. 8:6; 9:15; 12:24). Hebrews also develops a notion that is found in the passage from 1 Timothy, namely, that Jesus redeems humans. All these statements in Hebrews are set in the context of the new temple in heaven where Christ is the high priest and the one perfect sacrifice. Jesus also mediates by praying for his disciples (John 17; Matt. 11:25–27), by healing, by teaching God's word, and by forgiving people their sins. All of Jesus' activities to save humans can be looked on as mediation between God and humanity (though the NT does not use that category to characterize Jesus' work and words). Consequently, believers are instructed to pray in Jesus' name to God (John 14:13). Many Pauline and Gospel passages say or imply that contact with God is through Jesus Christ and this implies mediation by Jesus. A.J.S.

Mediterranean Sea, the large sea enclosed by the coasts of Europe, North Africa, Asia Minor, and Syro-Palestine. Its islands and coastal borders formed the basis for trade and the exchange of cultures as well as colonization and conquest from the second millennium B.C. on. Although there are occasional references to the Mediterranean Sea in the OT (e.g., Pss. 29:3; 104:25–26) lack of seaports kept the Hebrews from becoming seafarers. It remained a mysterious and forbidding part of their world.

Greek culture spread along the coastal areas of the eastern half of the Mediterranean. The coast of Spain and of Africa in the vicinity of Carthage and its colonies was romanized. People in these areas spoke Latin and adopted a Roman way of life.

Surveys of shipwrecks in the Mediterranean show that the major period of trade extended from 300 B.C. to A.D. 300, with its peak in the middle of this period. Ships hugged the coast of the Mediterranean in sailing from one place to another. Roman ships could carry as many as three thousand amphorae (large jars used for storing grain, etc.). Ignoring risks from storms, it was possible to ship grain from one end of the Mediterranean to another for less than it would cost to cart the same amount seventy-five miles over land. Hence bulk goods were generally transported by sea. The apostle Paul frequently traveled on such ships (Acts 16:11; 20:6; 21:1–3) and was on one that was wrecked by a storm (Acts 27:13–44). ***See also*** Sea. P.P.

meek, the quality characteristic of humility when coupled with gentleness. The meek person not only does not threaten or challenge others but accepts others openly and confidently, e.g., Moses (Num. 12:3) and Jesus as teacher (Matt. 11:29). God promises his Holy Land to such persons (Ps. 37:11; Matt. 5:5). ***See also*** Humility.

Megiddo

AN IMPORTANT CITY in antiquity in the Plain of Esdraelon located in northwestern Palestine, Megiddo (me-gid′doh) is identified with modern Tell el-Mutesellim, about twenty miles southeast of Haifa and ten miles northwest of Jenin.

Strategic Location: Megiddo owes its importance to its strategic location and good water supply. Two important routes for armies and trade passed at its foot. The one from the south came from Jerusalem, through Shechem, then from Megiddo alongside the Carmel range to the Plain of Acco on the coast and then north to Phoenicia. The second linked Egypt with the Fertile Crescent, from the coast of Palestine by way of the Philistine and Sharon plains, passing through the Carmel range east of Megiddo, then through the Plain of Esdraelon (or Megiddo Plain) east to Damascus and Mesopotamia. This is the best pass through the

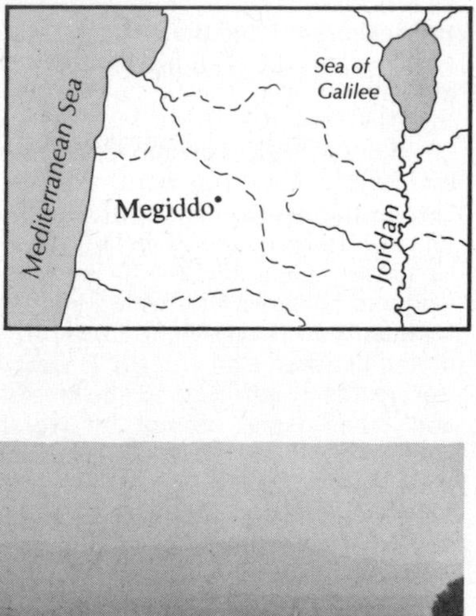

(*Below*) Part of the defensive wall overlooking the Jezreel Valley built by Jeroboam II at Megiddo in the eighth century B.C.

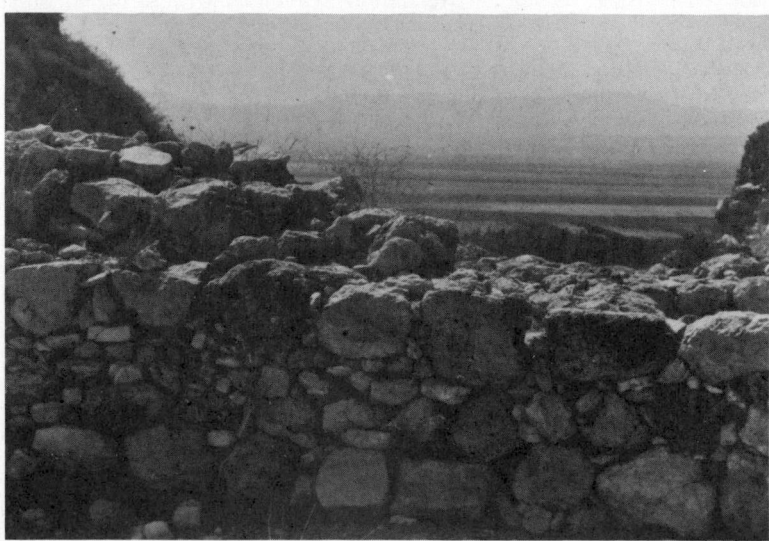

Carmel ridge and Megiddo's location has throughout history made direct control a matter of singular strategic importance, from the armies of Thutmose III in the fifteenth century B.C. to General Allenby's in World War I. When the mound was no longer occupied in Roman times a Roman camp at modern el-Lajjun, about a half-mile south, controlled the pass. Travelers and traders have passed through Megiddo from the Stone Age to the present.

In the Bible and Other Ancient Texts: Megiddo is mentioned in a number of Egyptian and Assyrian texts as well as in the Bible. The earliest reference is in the fifteenth-century B.C. annals of Thutmose III on the walls of the Temple of Karnak in Upper Egypt. Megiddo's defeat is described in detail, elaborating the battle plan, the booty of prisoners, chariots, and household goods, and the tribute of gold, silver, grain, and wine. The Barkal Stele erected at the Fourth Cataract of the Nile further describes this campaign.

Megiddo is mentioned in the city lists of Thutmose III, and according to his annals the second campaign of Amenhotep II (about 1430 B.C.) ended near Megiddo. In one of the Taanach Letters the king was ordered to send tribute to Megiddo. Amarna Letter 244 was written by the prince of Megiddo concerning the threats to his town, and five other letters from Prince Biridiya to the pharaoh are known. An Egyptian letter of the nineteenth dynasty (and of the thirteenth century B.C.) describes the road from Megiddo to the coastal plain.

According to the OT Joshua defeated a king of Megiddo (Josh. 12:21), and although the town was given to the tribe of Manasseh (Josh. 17:11; 1 Chron. 7:29), the Canaanites were not driven out (Josh. 17:12; Judg. 1:27). At Taanach by the waters of Megiddo Deborah and Barak met the Canaanites (Judg. 5:19), but it may have been the time of David before the city was firmly in Israelite hands. It was in one of Solomon's administrative districts (1 Kings 4:12), and he fortified Megiddo along with Jerusalem, Hazor, and Gezer (1 Kings 9:15).

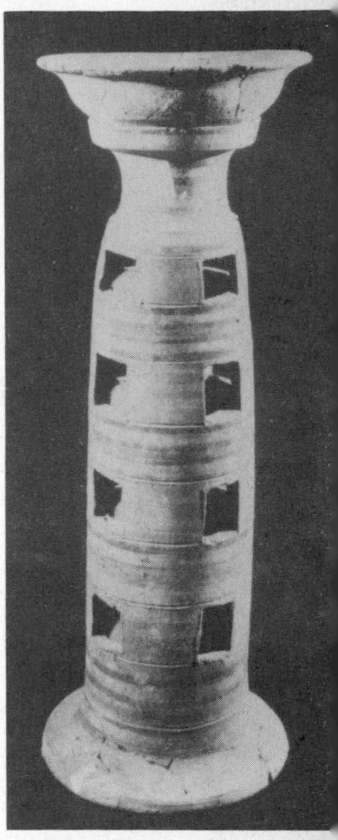

A painted cult stand with bowl from Megiddo, ca. 1200–1000 B.C.

A Canaanite "high place" at Megiddo, ca. 2600–2300 B.C.

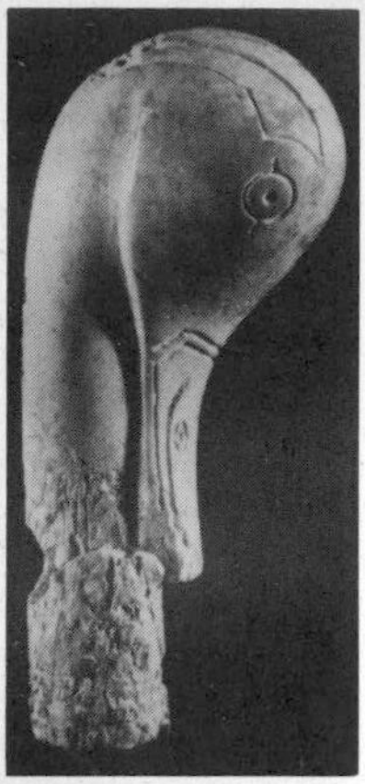

Ivory duck's head; fourteenth century B.C.

Although Megiddo is not mentioned in the Bible's description of Pharaoh Shishak's conquest in 918 B.C. (1 Kings 14:25, 26), it is listed among his conquests on the walls of the Amun Temple at Karnak, and a fragment of a stele bearing Shishak's name was found at Megiddo. Ahaziah, the king of Judah, died at Megiddo during Jehu's revolt (2 Kings 9:27). According to the annals of Tiglath-pileser III the northern part of Israel was captured in 733/32 B.C. and Megiddo was made the capital of one of the three Assyrian provinces. Finally, Josiah met his death at the hands of Pharaoh Neco near Megiddo in 609 B.C. (2 Kings 23:29; 2 Chron. 35:22). This was probably the end of Megiddo's prosperity as the town is not mentioned again in ancient texts. But its importance as a battleground is remembered in the NT as Armageddon (Heb. *Har Megiddon,* "The Mound of Megiddo"), the place of the final victory of God over all the forces of the world (Rev. 16:16).

Archaeological Excavations: Megiddo was first excavated by G. Schumacher for the German Oriental Society from 1903 to 1905. In a 20–25 meter-wide trench he excavated the entire north-south length of the mound. He distinguished eight strata going back to Middle Bronze II (from the nineteenth century B.C.) and uncovered two large buildings dating to that time, the *Mittelburg* (German, "middle stronghold") and the *Nordburg* (German, "north stronghold"), as well as an Israelite palace. Extensive excavations on the east revealed a large Israelite building he called a sanctuary because of its stone pillars, and he made a number of soundings on other parts of the mound.

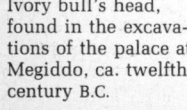

In 1925 the Oriental Institute of the University of Chicago undertook the most extensive excavations ever attempted in Palestine. Continuing until 1939, then interrupted because of World War II, the original plan was to excavate the complete mound layer by layer down to bedrock. The enormous task had to be abandoned after the removal of the first four strata, and work continued largely in two areas, in the north in the vicinity of the city gates, and in the east where bedrock was reached. In all, twenty strata were delineated.

Ivory bull's head, found in the excavations of the palace at Megiddo, ca. twelfth century B.C.

In addition to the limitations of time and money, the work of the University of Chicago expedition was hindered by change of leadership, successively from C. S. Fisher, to P. L. O. Guy, to G. Loud. Their work has only been partially published in three large volumes (*Megid-*

Egyptian pharaoh Shishak I listed the names of vanquished towns in Palestine—including Megiddo—within the "walls" depicted below the torso of each fettered prisoner on these reliefs at Karnak, tenth century, B.C.

do I, Megiddo II, and Megiddo Tombs) and several smaller monographs on the pottery, water system, ivories, and cult remains. Incomplete and inadequate publication led others, particularly W. F. Albright and G. E. Wright, to attempt to correct aspects of the chronology. Then from 1960 to 1971 the Israeli archaeologist Y. Yadin returned to the site to investigate the stratigraphy of the early monarchy, and in 1965 I. Dunayevski examined the stratigraphy in the sacred area. The occupational history of the site is still distinguished by the twenty strata of the University of Chicago expedition, but there are some major subdivisions, and various combinations must be made.

Evidence of Occupation, Strata XX–VII-B: Flint tools and bones may indicate a prepottery stage of the Neolithic period, and scattered potsherds testify to later Neolithic habitation. Segments of mud-brick dwellings, pits, ovens, and mixed pottery date various Chalcolithic settlements from the early fourth millennium to about 3200 B.C. (Stratum XX).

Strata XIX–XV belong to the Early Bronze age (3000–2000 B.C.). To Stratum XIX (EB I) belongs the first of several sanctuaries in the eastern area of the town where there was a sacred area for hundreds of years. The temple was of the usual Early Bronze type, rectangular with the entrance on the long wall and an altar directly opposite. A courtyard to the east was paved with flagstones, several layers of which had incised figures, mainly of hunting scenes, which are some of the earliest examples of local art in Palestine. The largest city wall in Megiddo's history belongs to Stratum XVIII (EB II); it was 8 meters thick with stone foundations preserved to a height of 4 meters. During Early Bronze III (Strata XVII–XVI) a large round altar, more than 8 meters in diameter and 1.4 meters high, was erected in the area of the earlier shrine. A flight of steps ascended the altar on the east and it was surrounded by a wall, within which were found a great quantity of animal bones indicating cultic sacrifice. Later in Early Bronze III (Stratum XV), three new temples were erected, all of the broad-room type with the entrance in the long south side and the square altar opposite.

Strata XIV–X belong to the Middle Bronze age (nineteenth–sixteenth centuries B.C.), with indications of Hyksos (rulers, perhaps Canaanite, who extended their control to Egypt, ca. 1720–1550 B.C.) dominance in Strata XII–X. In the sacred area stelae and bronze statuettes of Strata XIII–IX and large buildings of Stratum XII suggest a *bāmâh* (Heb., "high place") with nearby temples. The earliest city gate comes from Stratum XIII, and the typical Hyksos city gate with three sets of piers belongs to Stratum XI. The city wall was strengthened in Stratum XII, and modifications in this and the next stratum are of the usual Hyksos rampart and glacis type.

The first of a series of palaces near the gate area belongs to Stratum X. The relative continuity in plan from Strata XII to VII-A indicates rather peaceful and prosperous times extending through the Late Bronze age. With the expulsion of the Hyksos Megiddo came under Egyptian domination, and even Thutmose III's destruction of it about 1468 B.C. (end of Stratum IX) did not lead to decline. Stratum VIII (second half of the fifteenth century B.C. to the first half of the fourteenth) shows great material wealth with the expansion of the palace and its rich treasures of ivory plaques, jewelry, and beads. A fortified

Horn-shaped ivory vessel encircled with a gold band; fourteenth century B.C.

A Philistine pottery "pilgrim flask" found at Megiddo dating to 1100 B.C. may indicate Philistine presence during that period.

This box carved from a single piece of ivory and decorated with lions and sphinxes represents part of a hoard found in a twelfth-century B.C. palace.

temple is now on the site of the earlier altars. This is the Amarna Age and the tablets portray the weak control exercised by Egypt. A fragment of a clay tablet containing part of the Gilgamesh Epic (a Babylonian story concerning the origins of the cosmos) found in the vicinity of the gate probably belongs to this time. The last period of the Late Bronze age (Stratum VII-B) was separated from Stratum VII-A by destruction, but the same or very similar inhabitants reoccupied the site and reused the public buildings.

Stairs leading up the side of a storage pit, which had a capacity of approximately 12,800 bushels, from the eighth century B.C.

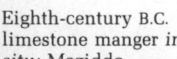

Evidence of Occupation, Strata VII-A–I: Stratum VII-A marks the beginning of the Iron Age (twelfth century B.C.), determined especially by a cartouche of Rameses III found on one of the carved plaques from a great cache of ivories, originally used as inlay decorations for palace furniture. This occupation ended in a great destruction, probably about 1130 B.C. The following settlement (Stratum VI-B) was much poorer; extensive new building activity in Stratum VI-A and Late Philistine pottery may indicate Philistine presence. The destruction at the end of the eleventh century may be attributed to David's conquests.

The V-B occupation was again a period of decline, and its haphazard constructions may belong to the Israelites under David before the centralized planning of the royal cities of Solomon (tenth century B.C.). The recent excavations have done much to clarify the confused results of the early excavations for the Solomonic and later periods. Stratum V-A/IV-B is Solomonic, to which may be assigned the six-chamber gateway and casemate city walls similar to those at Hazor and Gezer (1 Kings 9:15). These were contemporary with a palace or fortress that lay beneath the north stables and the offset-inset wall formerly attributed to Solomon, as well as a "palace" in the south and a nearby building beneath the south stables. In addition, the gallery (which was the earliest part of the city's water system, a narrow passageway lined with ashlar masonry leading down the southwest slope of the mound to a spring), was shown stratigraphically to belong to the Solomonic constructions. Solomon's city met destruction at the hands of Pharaoh Shishak in 918 B.C..

Prosperity continued during the Omride dynasty in the first part of the ninth century B.C. (Stratum IV-A). To it belong the offset-inset wall with the four-chamber gate, the stable complexes (more probably storerooms than stables), and the subterranean water system with a vertical shaft and horizontal tunnel to the spring at the foot of the mound. Alterations and additions to the building complexes indicate rather continual occupation down to the time of the Assyrian conquest in 733 B.C.

Eighth-century B.C. limestone manger *in situ*; Megiddo.

Stratum III belongs to the Assyrian dominance, with numerous and spacious private dwellings showing Eastern influence. The city gate now had two chambers. Stratum II, dating probably to the time of Josiah (639–609 B.C.), and Stratum I of the Persian period (ca. 538–333 B.C.) were unfortified.

See also Esdraelon; Hazor; Taanach.

Bibliography

"Megiddo." In the *Encyclopedia of Archaeological Excavations in the Holy Land*. Englewood Cliffs, NJ: Prentice-Hall, 1977. Vol. 3, pp. 830–856.

Yadin, Y. "Megiddo of the Kings of Israel." *Biblical Archaeologist* 33 (Sept., 1970): 66–96.

N.L.L.

Melchizedek (mel-kiz'uh-dek; Heb., "king of righteousness"), the king of Salem (Jerusalem) and priest of God Most High who blesses Abraham as the latter returns from battle (Gen. 14: 17–20). In Ps. 110:4, the incident is recalled, as God addresses the Hebrew king as "priest for ever after the order of Melchizedek." In later literature, Melchizedek is regarded as an ideal priest-king and, in the Dead Sea Scrolls, as a heavenly judge. In the Letter to the Hebrews, Melchizedek is a supernatural figure whose miraculous origin and indestructible life foreshadow the eternity of the Son of God (Heb. 5:6, 10; 6:20–7:22). ***See also*** Abraham; Jerusalem; King; Priests. J.W.T.

Melita. ***See*** Malta.

mem (maym), the thirteenth letter of the Hebrew alphabet; its numerical value is forty. In proto-Sinaitic inscriptions it was drawn as a pictograph of wavy water. This vertical zigzag is preserved in later forms of the letter, as in Phoenician and early Hebrew scripts. The old form can still be recognized in Latin "M" and in archaic and early Greek mu. In the late fifth century B.C. the form changed with the cursive Aramaic script. Medial and final forms evolved; these are the prototypes of the forms found in the classical Hebrew square script. ***See also*** Writing.

מ

memorials, various physical and abstract entities in the Bible such as stones, words, and days intended to serve as reminders to people and to God of some word or event. Theophanies (Gen. 28:18–22; cf. Exod. 24:4), God's splitting the Jordan River (Josh. 4:4–24), and serious sins (Num. 16:40) are commemorated through physical memorials. The celebration of the Passover day memorializes God's salvation of Israel (Exod. 12:14). In secular life, memorials mark gravesites (Gen. 35:20), especially when someone dies childless (2 Sam. 18:18; Isa. 56:5). Written words serve as memorials in the phylacteries (Exod. 13:9) and in the narrative of Amalek's defeat (Exod. 17:14). God is also reminded of his covenant with Israel by the written word (Mal. 3:16), though visual cues, such as the shoulder pieces of the ephod of the priestly breastplate (Exod. 28:12, 29) and the aural cue of the blasting trumpet (Num. 10:10), are also used. In the NT, prayer and alms can serve as a memorial (Acts 10:4), and Luke and Paul claim that the Last Supper is a meal intended to be repeated as a remembrance of Jesus (Luke 22:19; 1 Cor. 11: 24). M.Z.B.

Memphis (mem'fis; KJV: "Noph"), an ancient (Old Kingdom, ca. 2700–2200 B.C.) capital of Egypt, located on the west bank of the Nile about fifteen miles south of modern Cairo, and a prominent political and religious city throughout the Pharaonic period (to 605 B.C.). The Hebrew form of the name is *Nōf* (once *Mōf*), from Egyptian *Mennufer*. Traditionally, Memphis was founded by Menes, the first king, as the political center of a united Egypt. Memphis served also as a cult center of Ptah, a creator and artificer god; he not only created the world and all other gods, he also made things useful for human beings, such as shrines, cities, arts, and crafts. The Memphite theology, known from a relatively late text (ca. 700 B.C.), emphasizes Ptah's creative word. Memphis is mentioned in the prophetic books as symbolic of Egyptian power and idolatry, to be overthrown (Isa. 19:13; Ezek. 30:13), and as a place of exile or retreat for Israel (Jer. 2:16–18; Hos. 9:6). Indeed, the Egyptians settled many foreigners there. Although extensive remains existed as late as the medieval period, very little survives today. ***See also*** Egypt; Pyramid Texts, The. H.B.H.

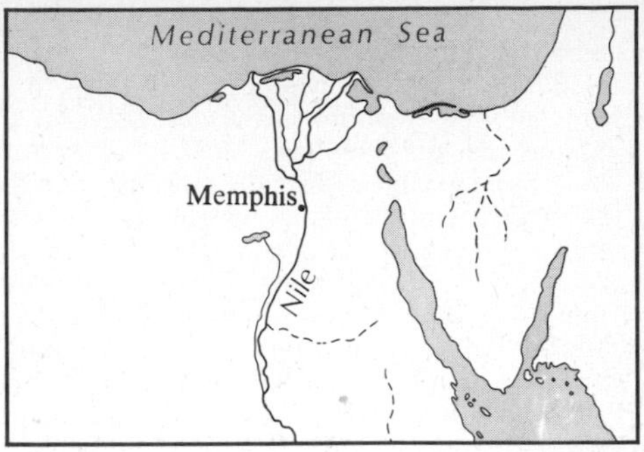

Menahem (me-nah'hem), a king of Israel in the third quarter of the eighth century B.C. Menahem son of Gadi was a usurper from the former capital, Tirzah (2 Kings 15:14). He assassinated Shallum, who had slain his own predecessor one month earlier, and ruled in Samaria for ten years. The Assyrian annals indicate that "Menahem of Samaria" paid tribute to King Tiglath-pileser III during his first western campaign (743 –738). The same incident is described in 2 Kings 15:19–20, where Tiglath-pileser is called by his Babylonian throne name, "Pul." There we are told that Menahem raised "a thousand talents of silver" by imposing a levy on the wealthy citizens of Israel. His purpose was to win the favor of Tiglath-pileser "that he might help him to confirm his hold of the royal power." The tax must have been resented, however. Menahem died soon afterward, and his son, Pekahiah, fell victim to a conspiracy within two years (2 Kings 15:25). P.K.M.

mene, mene, tekel, upharsin (men'ay te'kel o͞o-fahr'sin), the mysterious words written on the wall in Dan. 5:25. These words confound the Babylonian wise men but are interpreted by Daniel (vv. 26–28), who takes them as the

Aramaic verbs *mn'*, "to number" (God has numbered your days), *tkl*, "to weigh" (you have been weighed and found wanting), and *prs*, "to divide" (your kingdom is divided between the Medes and the Persians). Most scholars think that the original text had only one *mene* and that the reference is to three weights or monetary units—the mina, the shekel (one fiftieth of a mina), and the half-mina. These in turn may have been intended as a slighting evaluation of successive Babylonian kings with Nabonidus and Belshazzar as the half-minas. Such references are lost in the present text of Daniel, which retains, however, the punning tendency inherent in the riddle (e.g., *parsin* is taken both as "divided" and as a reference to the Persians: see v. 28). ***See also*** Belshazzar; Daniel, The Book of. J.J.C.

Menorah (me-nohr'uh). ***See*** Lampstand.

Mephibosheth (mi-fib'o͞o-sheth), an intentionally distorted form of the original name Mippibaal (Heb., "out of the mouth of Baal"). Baal, which means "lord," was earlier used as a simple epithet for God, but because the epithet was also used for a major Canaanite deity, later scribes often replaced this element in proper names with the word *bosheth*, "shame."

Two men in the Bible bear this name. **1** A son of Saul whom David handed over to the Gibeonites for execution (2 Sam. 21:8–9). **2** Jonathan's son, the grandson of Saul, whom David spared because of his covenant with Jonathan (2 Sam. 4:4; 21:7). The names of the two individuals appear to have been confused, however, since according to 1 Chronicles, the real name of Jonathan's son was Meribbaal (8:34; 9:40).

David treated Mephibosheth with kindness (2 Sam. 9:6–13), but Mephibosheth's apparent disloyalty during Absalom's revolt angered David (2 Sam. 16:1–4). Only partly appeased by Mephibosheth's explanation, David divided Saul's property between Mephibosheth and his servant Ziba (2 Sam. 19:24–30). ***See also*** David; Jonathan; Saul. J.J.M.R.

Merab (mee'rab; Heb., "growth, increase"), the elder of Saul's two daughters (1 Sam. 14:49) whom Saul promised to David for fighting the Philistines, expecting that he would be killed in battle. When David returned, Merab had already been given to Adriel. Several Hebrew manuscripts and ancient translations mention that David gave Merab's sons to the Gibeonites for execution as an act of appeasement (2 Sam. 21: 8–9; other texts read "Michal's," but see 2 Sam. 6:23).

Merari (me-rah'ree). **1** The third son of Levi (Gen. 46:11; Exod. 6:16; Num. 3:17; 1 Chron. 6: 1; 6:16; 23:6) and through his sons, Mahli and Mushi (Exod. 6:19; Num. 3:20; 1 Chron. 6:19; 23: 21; 24:26), the eponymous ancestor of the levitical clan of the Merarites (Num. 3:33–37; 4:29–33; 1 Chron. 6:29; 6:44). The cities and territories allocated to the Merarites appear in Josh. 21: 7, 34–40 and 1 Chron. 6:77–81. Prominent Merarites included Asaiah, who supervised the two hundred and twenty Merarites that David selected to help bring the Ark to Jerusalem (1 Chron. 15:6); Ethan, who was appointed as a musician for the occasion (1 Chron. 15:17, 19); Kish and Azariah, who assisted in Hezekiah's reform (2 Chron. 29:12); Jahath and Obadiah, who helped supervise Josiah's repair of the Temple (2 Chron. 34:12); and Sherebiah, Hashabiah, and Jeshaiah, who led Merarite contingents in the time of Ezra (Ezra 8:18–19). Merarites also served as gatekeepers for the Temple (1 Chron. 26:10, 19). **2** The father of Judith (Jth. 8:1; 16:7). M.A.S.

merchant. ***See*** Agora; Trade and Transportation.

Mercurius (mair-kyo͞or'ee-uhs; Lat.; Gk. *Hermes*), a god who functioned variously as messenger of the gods; deity of thieves, tricksters, travelers, and athletes; and the god of science, eloquence, and the arts. Often he is represented as a young man wearing a winged hat and sandals and carrying a herald's staff. At Lystra, Paul is called Hermes (KJV: "Mercurius"), meaning the god of eloquence (Acts 14:12).

mercy, an attribute of both God and the good human being. Hebrew uses several words for "mercy," of which the most frequent is *ḥesed*, which means loving-kindness, mercy, love, loyalty, and faithfulness. Another Hebrew word and the Greek word for mercy in the NT refer to the emotion aroused by contact with undeserved suffering, that is, compassion and a deeply felt love for a fellow human being. In the OT mercy/loving-kindness is associated with the covenant obligation between God and humans. Humans must be faithful to the covenant and God binds himself to fidelity to the covenant by mercy and by grace (another Hebrew word used to mean mercy). Divine and human mercy are closely associated with justice and righteousness because all refer to behavior appropriate to a relationship.

In the NT God's merciful faithfulness is attributed to his sending of Jesus and saving his people (Luke 1:58; Eph. 2:4; Rom. 11:30–32). God's mercy toward the faithful will manifest itself at the final judgment (2 Tim. 1:18; Luke 16:24; James 2:13). Mercy is also recommended in human relationships through reference to the OT (Matt. 9:13), the promise of divine mercy (Matt. 5:7), and human example (Luke 10:37). Jesus shows mercy to the needy (Luke 17:13; 18:38) and mercy was incorporated into early Christian benedictions (1 Tim. 1:2). ***See also*** Justice; Love. A.J.S.

mercy-seat. ***See*** Ark.

Meremoth (mair'uh-mohth), a name occurring several times in postexilic writings. It is difficult to tell whether these are different people or various references to the same person. **1** A Levite who returned from the Babylonian captivity with Zerubbabel (Neh. 12:3). **2** A Levite, the son of Uriah the priest; he inventoried the valuables brought back by exiles returning with Ezra (Ezra 8:33) and helped repair the walls of Jerusalem under Nehemiah (Neh. 3:4, 21). **3** A member of the clan of Bani who took a foreign wife (Ezra 10:36). **4** One who signed the covenant to keep the law (Neh. 10:5). D.R.B.

Meribah (mair'ee-bah). ***See*** Massah.

Meribbaal (mair-i-bay'uhl; Heb., meaning uncertain, perhaps "Baal [deity] is an advocate" or "hero of Baal"), the crippled son of Jonathan and grandson of King Saul (1 Chron. 8:34). The name usually occurs as Mephibosheth, an alteration of Meribaal where the name Baal, often associated with the Semitic fertility god, was replaced with the word "shame" (Heb. *bosheth;* 2 Sam. 4:4; 9:3–13). ***See also*** Mephibosheth.

Merneptah (muhr-nep'tah), the son and successor of the long-lived Ramesses II. He ruled Egypt ca. 1213–1204 B.C. A victory hymn relative to his brief campaign in Canaan and southern Syria between 1212 and 1209, the "Israel Stele," has the earliest known reference to Israel. Israel, classified as a people, is boastfully described as laid waste, without survivor. Merneptah successfully withstood a major invasion by a joint force of Libyans and Sea Peoples and a rebellion in Nubia. ***See also*** Ramesses.

Merodach (mair'oh-dahk), also known as Marduk (mahr'dook), a Mesopotamian god. Merodach is mentioned in Jer. 50:2, where he is also referred to as Bel (cf. Isa. 46:1; Jer. 51:44). Several Babylonian names with Merodach as the theophoric element appear in the Bible: Evil-merodach, Merodach-baladan, and Mordechai. Merodach was the chief god of the city of Babylon and eventually of Babylonia. It appears that originally Merodach was a storm deity, the name Mar.udu.ak probably meaning "Son of the Storm." The biblical reading Merodach seems to be a more correct pronunciation than the conventional Marduk.

When in the Old Babylonian period Hammurabi managed to unite northern and southern Babylonia (albeit temporarily), Merodach was elected to the office of ruler of mankind by the gods An and Enlil (Codex Hammurabi 1.1). This election is a continuation of an old Mesopotamian practice whereby the god of the politically dominant city ruled the land for a time, ultimate power, however, residing with and reverting to the divine assembly and its leaders. Merodach, however, did eventually become the chief god of Babylonia, a ruler whose rule was absolute and not dependent upon the agreement of the divine council, some time in the latter half of the second millennium. He was thus transformed from a local god into a national or, more properly, a universal god. Merodach's cult spread to Assyria, though the Assyrians understandably had some difficulty assimilating it and defining an efficacious and stable relationship with Merodach and his city. Apparent threats to the prerogatives of the Merodach cult led the priests of Babylon to welcome and justify Cyrus's conquest (late sixth century B.C.).

Merodach's rise to absolute kingship of the gods is described in the *Enuma elish*, the Babylonian epic of creation. This work has been connected with Genesis 1 and other acts of, or allusions to, creation and God's conflicts with dragon/sea/chaos as well as to an assumed enthronement festival in Israel. The date of composition of *Enuma elish* has some bearing on its interpretation and its putative relationship to the Bible. Until recently an Old Babylonian date was assumed. More recently, dates in the latter half of the second millennium have been proposed. Thus the modern scholar W. G. Lambert argues that the work was composed after Nebuchadnezzar I restored the status of Merodach from Elam, while T. Jacobsen thinks that the conquest of the Sealand (the south) and its unification with Babylon and the north under Ulamburiash (fifteenth century B.C.) provide the background. However T. Abusch is now of the opinion that it is a mistake to ascribe the work to, and explain it as a consequence of, a period of Babylonian political ascendancy and would suggest that it was composed some time during the early first millennium in a period of political weakness of the city Babylon. ***See also*** Merodach-baladan. I.T.A.

Merodach-baladan (mair'oh-dahk-buh-lah'duhn), the biblical form of Marduk-apla-iddina II, twice king of Babylonia (721–710 B.C.) and leader of the Chaldean tribe Bit-Yakin in southern Babylonia. The tribal area of Bit-Yakin was in the southeast of Babylonia around the great swamp; this tribe lived close to Elam and during the period of activity of Merodach-baladan, alliances between Bit-Yakin and Elam were forged and stood in opposition to the Assyrians.

Merodach-baladan was already active in the final years of Tiglath-pileser III and even then appears as an important Chaldean chief. Merodach-baladan seems to have been an able political and military strategist and leader. At the death of Shalmaneser V and the accession of Sargon II, Assyria faced serious problems in the west and in Babylonia. Merodach-baladan gained control of the Babylonian throne (721

The Babylonian king Merodach-baladan, 721–710 B.C., investing one of his officials with a grant of land; inscribed boundary stone.

B.C.) and detached Babylonia from the empire. The Assyrians did not achieve victory against the Elamites, allies of Merodach-baladan, at the Battle of Der, 720, and Merodach-baladan retained the Babylonian throne until 710.

During his reign he held sway over the Babylonian cities along the Euphrates and the Chaldean settlements in the south. He seems to have ruled Babylonia in a relatively efficacious and sympathetic manner and to have created some unity among the Chaldean tribes. Still, in 710 the Assyrian king Sargon was able to defeat Merodach-baladan and conquer Babylonia. Merodach-baladan retreated to the south and the citizens of Babylonia welcomed Sargon. He continued fighting in the south at Dur-Yakin; even here he was defeated but again escaped. After the accession of Sennacherib to the Assyrian throne, Merodach-baladan again took Babylon in 703 for nine months. The Assyrians under Sennacherib routed Merodach-baladan, though the Chaldean had drawn the support and assistance of Elamites, Chaldeans, and Babylonians from a number of cities. Merodach-baladan took refuge in the southern swamps. In 700, Sennacherib directed a campaign against Bit-Yakin. Merodach-baladan fled to Elam, dying there before 694. Under Sargon and Sennacherib, Merodach-baladan's tribe Bit-Yakin suffered mass deportations by the Assyrians.

In 2 Kings 20:12–19 and Isa. 39:1–8 (cf. 2 Chron. 32:31), we are told of an embassy sent by Merodach-baladan to King Hezekiah of Judah in order to establish some sort of alliance and coordinate actions against Assyria. Although this text tells of the embassy after recounting events of Sennacherib's campaign against Hezekiah in 701, the embassy should be dated either to 705, the year when Sennacherib ascended the Assyrian throne, or even more probably to 714–713, at the time of the anti-Assyrian rebellion in Ashdod. ***See also*** Assyria, Empire of; Babylon; Merodach. I.T.A.

Merom (mee'rohm; Heb., "height"), a city in Galilee that was the site of a defeat of the Canaanites by the Israelites (Josh. 11:5, 7). Merom is included in late second-millennium Egyptian lists of captured cities and was taken by Tiglath-pileser III in 733 B.C. Its exact location is not certain; suggestions include such modern sites as Tell el-Khureibeh and Meiron; in medieval tradition Joshua's victory is associated with the latter. (Madon [Josh. 11:1; 12:19] is often corrected to Merom, following the Septuagint.)

M.D.C.

Merom (mee'rohm; Heb., "height"), **the Waters of,** a major water source or stream near the city of Merom in Galilee. ***See also*** Merom.

Meroz (mihr'awz), a town cursed in the Song of Deborah (Judg. 5:23) for failing to join the Israelites' fight against Sisera. Of uncertain identity, it was most likely somewhere in the Plain of Esdraelon or in the adjacent hills near the battle site.

Mesha (mee'shah; Heb., "savior"). **1** A son of Caleb (1 Chron. 2:42; however, LXX: "Maresha"). **2** The ninth-century B.C. king of Moab who also bred sheep. After a long period of being subject to Israel, as was his father Chemosh-(yat?), and paying tribute to Ahab (2 Kings 3:4), he led a revolt (2 Kings 3); a Moabite inscription found at Dibon also describes an extensive building program. Although the accounts differ somewhat, it would appear that Israel's king Jehoram was unable to suppress the revolt, despite assistance from the kings of Judah (Jehoshaphat) and Edom. The Bible ascribes some of Mesha's success to his willingness to sacrifice his son, the crown prince (2 Kings 3: 27). **3** A Benjaminite born in Moab (1 Chron. 8: 9). **4** A place (Gen. 10:30). F.E.G.

Meshach (mee'shak), the Babylonian name given to Mishael, one of Daniel's three companions (Dan. 1:7). The etymology is uncertain, but a relation to Marduk, the god of Babylon has been suggested. ***See also*** Abednego; Daniel; Shadrach.

Meshech (mee'shek). **1** The sixth son of Japheth (Gen. 10:2). His name, like the names of the fourth son (Javan) and fifth son (Tubal), is also the name for an area. **2** A region in Asia Minor. Meshech appears in Assyrian texts as Muski or Musku from 1200 B.C. onwards. The people of Musku were noted metallurgists and aligned with Tubal. There is little doubt that the frequent biblical association of Meshech and Tubal (Gen. 10:2; Ezek. 27:13; 32:26; 38:2–3; 39:1; 1 Chron. 1:5) reflects this ancient political alliance in mountainous, central Asia Minor. Midas, king of Musku, was an enemy of Sargon II of Assyria. J.G.G.

Meshelemiah (me-shel-uh-mī'uh), a Korahite Levite who was the head of a family of gatekeepers in the time of David (1 Chron. 9:21; 26:1–2). He is probably the same person elsewhere called Shallum (1 Chron. 9:17, 19; possibly also v. 31) and Shelemiah (1 Chron. 26:14). A postexilic family group of gatekeepers were called "sons of Shallum" and are assumed to be descendants of Meshelemiah (Ezra 2:42; Neh. 7:45). However, the names Shallum and Meshallum were so common, especially after the Exile, that care is necessary in identifications. ***See also*** Shallum.

Meshullam (me-sho͞o'luhm; Heb., "reconciled, perfected"). **1** The grandfather of the scribe Shaphan during the reign of Josiah (2 Kings 22:3). **2** The son of Zerubbabel (1 Chron. 3:19). **3** A Gadite who lived in Bashan (1 Chron. 5:13). **4** A Benjaminite, son of Elpaal (1 Chron. 8:17). **5** A Benjaminite, son of Shephatiah (1 Chron. 9:8). **6** A Benjaminite, father of Sallu (1 Chron. 9:7; Neh. 11:7). **7** A priest, son of Zadok, and father of Hilkiah (1 Chron. 9:11). **8** A priest, son of Meshillemith, and father of Jahzerah (1 Chron. 9:12). **9** A Levite of the Kohathite clan who assisted in Josiah's repair of the Temple (2 Chron. 34:12). **10** The son of Bani, a man who married a foreign woman in the time of Ezra (Ezra 10:29). He is perhaps the same Meshullam who opposed Ezra's marriage policy (Ezra 10:15) and sought Levites for Temple service (Ezra 8:6). **11** The son of Berechiah, who helped build the wall of Jerusalem under Nehemiah (Neh. 3:4, 30). His daughter married Jehohanan (Neh. 6:18). **12** The son of Besodeiah who helped repair the Old Gate in Jerusalem under Nehemiah (Neh. 3:6). **13** One who stood on Ezra's left hand when he read the Torah (Neh. 8:4). **14** A priest who set his seal to the covenant in Neh. 10:7. **15** A chief of the people who set his seal to the covenant in Neh. 10:20. **16** The head of the priestly house of Ezra in the days of Joiakim (Neh. 12:13). **17** The head of the priestly house of Ginnethon in the days of Joiakim (Neh. 12:16). **18** A gatekeeper (Neh. 12:25). **19** A prince of Judah who took part in the procession dedicating the rebuilt wall of Jerusalem in the time of Nehemiah (Neh. 12:33). M.A.S.

Mesopotamia (mes-uh-puh-tay'mee-uh; Gk., "between the rivers"), the region bounded on the east by the Tigris River and on the west by the Euphrates River. The biblical term for Mesopotamia, Aram-naharaim, refers to the land east of the Middle Euphrates. Other terms in the Bible referring to regions of Mesopotamia include: Shinar, Kashdim (Chaldea), Ashur, and Bavel. Modern Iraq encompasses much of Mesopotamia.

Geographic conditions range from desert in the central region to forests in the surrounding high country. The combination of natural river levees and seasonally inundated alluvial flats creates the floodplain of the Tigris and Euphrates rivers, a region known as Babylonia in the second millennium B.C. This region supported woodland environment, comprised predominantly of the date palm. Scarce rainfall and erratic, violent flooding of the rivers made farmers in the region almost entirely dependent upon irrigation for crops.

The region is noticeably lacking in natural resources such as stone, wood, and metal ores. Trade for these items developed, with routes following the rivers. The route up the Euphrates would have been the one Abraham's family followed in their travels from Ur to Haran. Control of the river crossings reflected military and political power.

Mesopotamia was home to several population groups. The Sumerians entered the southern reaches of the alluvial plain, probably from the east and north. A Semitic group, the Akkadians, developed the first empire in Mesopotamia in the late third millennium B.C. Western Mesopotamia was home to the Amorites, another Semitic population that appears in the Bible.

The political divisions, Babylonia and Assyria, correspond to the southern and northern regions of Mesopotamia, respectively. The peripheral regions, particularly sites such as Mari and Ebla in the west and Nuzi in the north, contributed significantly to cultural and social developments in Mesopotamia proper.

Cultural developments originating in Mesopotamia are numerous. The Neolithic revolution (ca. 8000–4500 B.C.), which evidenced the domestication of plants and animals, took place in the eastern, upland reaches of Mesopotamia as well as in the uplands of Anatolia and the Levant. Writing originated in Mesopotamia, as evidenced by pictographic tablets from the southern city of Uruk, which date to the middle of the fourth millennium

B.C. Its outgrowth, the cuneiform system of writing the Sumerian and Akkadian languages, flourished in Mesopotamia for three millennia and was adopted for writing Hittite and the West Semitic dialect Ugaritic. Mesopotamia also produced the first compilations of legal writings, including those of Hammurabi, Eshnunna, and Lipit-Ishtar.

The literary developments include works such as the Gilgamesh Epic. Numerous historical inscriptions found at sites in ancient Mesopotamia corroborate biblical accounts. The influence of Mesopotamian hymns and prayers can be felt in the later biblical literature. Artistic developments include sculpture, bas-reliefs, monumental architecture, glyptic art (engraving on fine stones), and fine textiles, which were traded as far away as Anatolia (modern Turkey).

L.E.P.

messiah (from the Heb. *mashiaḥ*, "anointed one"), a term that could be applied to any person "anointed" and sent by God.

Early Usage: In the political sphere, it referred to the kings who would come to continue the Davidic dynasty (Pss. 18:50; 89:20, 38, 51; 132:10, 17). "Anointed" might also refer to a priest (cf. Lev. 4:3, 5). "Messiah" could refer to anyone divinely appointed to a task that affected the destiny of the chosen people. Since the Davidic king is the chosen ruler of God (2 Sam. 7:8–16), "messiah" is often associated with the prophetic expectation that God would raise up an ideal Davidic ruler to occupy the throne of Israel (e.g., Jer. 33:15; Ezek. 37:23–24). However, none of the prophetic books use "messiah" for the future king. In Isa. 45:1 "anointed" refers to Cyrus as God's agent. In Hab. 3:13 "messiah" refers either to the reigning king or to Israel as a nation.

Dan. 9:25 associates the renewal of Jerusalem with a coming "anointed one," a prince. However, Daniel does not contain any further speculation about "the anointed." Similar caution must be exercised in regard to the claim that the "king from the sun" in *Sib. Or.* 3:652–56 represents a future "messianic king" of Israel. The author appears to be referring to the seventh king in the Ptolemaic line as one who would bring great peace. Such expectations are similar to those associated with Cyrus. We find a more firmly established expectation of a future Davidic king, described as God's "anointed," in the *Psalms of Solomon* 17–18. This "ideal king" reflects opposition to the non-Davidic Hasmonean dynasty. He is a human ruler, though endowed with special gifts of wisdom and righteousness (17:23, 35, 41–42, 46–47).

A more complex picture of the "anointed one" emerges in the *Testaments of the Twelve Patriarchs* and the Dead Sea Scrolls. Christian editing of the *Testaments of the Twelve Patriarchs* makes it difficult to trace the development of its images of the "messiah." Levi and Judah are the priestly and kingly rulers of the people (*T. Simeon* 7:2; *T. Joseph* 19:6). *T. Judah* 21:2 states that God made kingship subordinate to priesthood, a reflection of the predominate role of the chief priest in the postexilic period. Since royal characteristics are also attributed to Levi, some scholars hold that the dual "messiahship" was a later development, perhaps in opposition to the combination of priestly and kingly power by the Hasmonean kings. The Dead Sea Scrolls also contain passages referring to the coming of two figures, a priestly "anointed" of Aaron, and a kingly "anointed" of Israel (e.g., 1QS 9:11; 1QSa 2:14, 20; CD 20:1; 4QPBless 2:4; 4QFlor 1:11–13). The material so far published shows little interest in the persons of the "anointed ones" as though they were "savior figures." Parallels between the conduct of the "messianic meal" eaten by the community with the "messiahs" (1QSa 2:11–22), and the meal celebrated by the sect (1QS 6:4) suggest that what is said of the future "messiahs" can also be experienced as part of the daily life of the community.

The Similitudes of Enoch (*1 Enoch* 37–71), probably from the mid-first century A.D., link the day of judgment with a heavenly figure, the "Son of man," who is also referred to as "messiah" (*1 Enoch* 48:10; 52:4). However, exploration of the Danielic image "Son of man" is the real focus of attention in this work. These examples are sufficient to show that "messiah" had no fixed, technical meaning in Jesus' time. In some circles, it denoted a political or priestly agent sent from God as part of the triumphant establishment of God's power.

Jesus as Messiah: Similar ambiguities surround the application in the NT of the expression "anointed" (Gk. *christos*) to Jesus. "Messiah" was evidently not a role that a person might simply assume by identifying himself with it. "Messiah" is missing from the sayings of Jesus in "Q," an early source used by Matthew and Luke. The Gospels consistently show Jesus' reluctance to accept the designation "messiah" without qualification. Peter's confession (Mark 8:29; an independent version of this tradition is preserved in John 6:67–69) is immediately "corrected" by the announcement that Jesus is the suffering Son of man (8:30–31). In Mark 14:62 Jesus admits to being "messiah" before the Sanhedrin, although in Matt. 26:64 and Luke 22:67 the wording of this passage is changed. Evidently, the possibility of misunderstanding the Christian use of "anointed" for Jesus still had to be avoided. Such misinterpretation would seem to have been linked to the use of "messiah" in connection with a future king of Israel.

Although "messiah" did not unambiguously denote a person who would claim the political position of "king of Israel," Jesus' execution as "King of the Jews" (Mark 15:2, 26) makes that association with the title probable (see the mockery scene, Mark 15:32). Luke preserves the Jewish expression "God's anointed" at several points (Luke 2:26; 9:20; 23:35; Acts 3:18). In other places "messiah/christ" is provided with some explication using other phrases or titles, especially "Son of God" (Matt. 16:16; 26:63; Mark 14:61; Luke 23:35). Matt. 1:16 and 27:17, 22 refer to Jesus "who is called 'the Christ.'" Such passages may represent an early tradition that Jesus was at first "called 'messiah'" by others. That designation might well have been more like an epithet than a formal title or designation of political or religious office. It could easily have emerged in response to those words and deeds of Jesus that were seen to carry with them the authority of divine commissioning. John 6:15 preserves a tradition in which the people react to the feeding of the multitude by seeking to make Jesus "king." In John 6:14 the miracle is treated as a sign that Jesus was the Mosaic prophet of the last days (cf. Deut. 18:15, 18). In the Dead Sea Scrolls an anointed "prophet" is to accompany the "messiahs" though his function is not clear (1QS 9:10–11; 4QTestim 5–8). The Johannine trial narrative takes great pains to explain that the "kingship" attributed to Jesus is not to be defined in political terms (John 18:33–37; 19:12–15). Other episodes in which Jesus arouses expectations that he is to be identified with a future "deliverer" of the people are the entry into Jerusalem (Mark 11:1–10 and parallels) and the cleansing of the Temple (Mark 11:15–19 and parallels). In the Gospel tradition both episodes have been explicated as the fulfillment of prophecies (cf. Matt. 21:4; John 12:15–16; Matt. 21:10–17; John 2:13–22). Matt. 21:10–11 links the two episodes with the crowd's identification of Jesus as "the prophet from Galilee." Such "prophetic" actions may have provided the foundation for some to refer to Jesus as "anointed of God" without presuming that Jesus, himself, sought a political revolution in which he would be established as the "anointed" Davidic "king of Israel."

Christian Usage: After the death and resurrection of Jesus, "messiah" takes on a specifically Christian meaning as a "title" that refers only to Jesus. The "messiah" Jesus is the crucified agent of God, who has died "for our sins" (1 Cor. 15:3). Acts 2:36 speaks of God having made Jesus "both Lord and Christ" at his resurrection/exaltation into heaven. In such a context "messiah" denotes Jesus' vindication and exaltation by God. Luke 2:11 links "messiah" with the christological titles "Lord," commonly associated with the risen/exalted Jesus (cf. Rom. 1:4b; Phil. 2:11), and "Savior" in the announcement of Jesus' birth. Acts 3:19–22 preserves yet another early Christian use of "messiah" for Jesus. It describes his return at the Parousia, a function elsewhere ascribed to him as "Lord" (1 Thess. 4:17; 1 Cor. 11:26; 16:22).

None of the uses of "messiah" in Jewish writings of the period points toward the suffering or death of the person so designated. The juxtaposition of the confession that Jesus is "messiah" with the prediction of the suffering Son of man in Mark 8:27–33 brings out this difficulty. The "suffering servant" of God (Isa. 52:13–53:12) provided Christians with powerful images of Jesus' vocation to suffering. However, the "servant" is not "the anointed of God." Explicit acknowledgment of the theme of the "suffering messiah" occurs in the Lucan writings. The messiah, according to Scripture, was to suffer before entering his glory (Luke 24:26, 46; also see Acts 3:18; 17:3; 26:23). Paul can also speak of the paradox of "Christ" crucified (1 Cor. 1:23; 2:2; Gal. 3:1), but concern with the expression "messiah/christ" is not part of that reflection. In Paul, as in much of the rest of the NT, "Christ" is frequently used as part of Jesus' name (see also such passages as Acts 4:10; 8:12).

The Christian confession that Jesus is "messiah" played its primary role in Christian debates with Judaism. This role is evident in the speeches of Acts (Acts 2:31–32; 3:18; 5:42; 8:5; 17:3; 18:5, 28). It is also evident in the Fourth Gospel. John 1:41 preserves the Aramaic "messiah," with a translation for the Greek-speaking reader, in Andrew's summons to Peter. Other passages in the Fourth Gospel represent debates between Johannine Christians and their Jewish opponents over the claim that Jesus is messiah. Jesus' origins are said to disqualify him by those who do not recognize that his true origin is "from God" (John 7:41–42). Jesus' death is said to disqualify him because the messiah was to have "remained forever" (John 12:34). An uncertain crowd wonders whether Jesus might be "messiah" (7:26–31; 10:24). Finally, "messiah" is spoken as a confession of faith in Jesus as Son of God and Savior by those who are believers (4:29; 11:27; 17:3; 20:31). When Johannine Christians were excommunicated from the Jewish synagogue for their faith in Jesus, the confession "Jesus is messiah" became an identifying mark of the true Christian (9:22). It retains this function in the struggle against dissident Christians reflected in the Johannine Letters (1 John 2:22; 5:1). Justin Martyr's *Dialogue with Trypho* provides a mid-second-century example of the use of "messiah" in Christian debate with Judaism (35.7; 39.6; 43.8; 47.4; 48.4; 108.2). ***See also*** Jesus Christ; Son of God; Son of Man.

Bibliography

Collins, J.J. *The Apocalyptic Imagination*. New York: Crossroad, 1984.

Dunn, J.D.G. *Unity and Diversity in the New Testament*. Philadelphia: Westminster, 1977.

Schürer, E. *The History of the Jewish People in the Age of Jesus Christ*. Revised and edited by G. Vermes, F. Millar, M. Black. Vol. 2. Edinburgh: T. & T. Clark, 1979.

P.P.

metals, malleable materials of varying degrees of strength, hardness, and value. Biblical references to metals are frequent but allusive. Tubal-cain (Gen. 4:22) is known as a metalsmith. Palestine is described as "a land whose stones are iron, and out of whose hills you can dig copper" (Deut. 8:9; cf. Ezra 1:9–11). Tablets from excavations at Ebla in Syria report the transfer of gold and silver in large quantities (ca. 3200 B.C.). Hab. 2:18 has the RSV's only use of the word "metal" describing an idol made with human hands. Jerusalem's Temple reputedly housed 5,469 articles of gold and silver (Ezra 1:11). Palestinian metalworking sites included numerous mines, smelting and forging operations, and artifacts. ***See also*** Brass; Copper; Gold; Iron; Lead; Refining; Silver. R.A.C.

Methuselah (me-tho͞o'zuh-luh), the eighth member of the Sethite line from Adam to Noah: the son of Enoch, the father of Lamech, and the grandfather of Noah (Gen. 5:21–27; 1 Chron. 1: 3). Methuselah lived for 969 years, the longest lived person in the Bible. The genealogy of Cain records that Methushael was the father of Lamech (Gen. 4:18); according to this genealogy Methushael was the great-grandson of Enoch.

mezuzah (muh-zo͞o'zah), the doorpost of a city gate, sanctuary, or private house. The Israelites sprinkled the blood of the Passover sacrifice on their doorposts to avoid the killing of their firstborn (Exod. 12:7, 22–23). Samson pulled out the gate and gateposts of Gaza (Judg. 16:3). The Israelites were enjoined to write divine exhortations upon their doorposts, in addition to reciting and teaching them, and binding them to the hand and forehead (Deut. 6:9; 11:20). In Judaism, *mezuzah* came to indicate the container affixed to a doorpost in which scriptural passages were placed.

Mezuzah in an ivory case; Italian, fifteenth century.

Mica (mī'kuh; Heb., "who is like Yah [God]?"), a shortened form of Micaiah. **1** The son of Mephibosheth (Meribbaal) and Saul's great-grandson by Jonathan (2 Sam. 9:12); he is also called Micah (1 Chron. 8:34–35). **2** A Levite, the son of Zichri and father of Mattaniah, a postexilic inhabitant of Jerusalem (1 Chron. 9:15; Neh. 11: 22); he is probably the same Levite who is elsewhere called the son of Zabdiel and father of Mattaniah (1 Chron. 11:17). He may also be the same Levite called Micaiah and the son of Zaccur and father of Mattaniah (Neh. 12:35). It is possible that these represent three different persons. **3** A Levite who signed the covenant to keep the law (Neh. 10:11); possibly the same as 2 above. ***See also*** Micah; Micaiah. D.R.B.

Micah (mī'kah), a shortened form of the name Micaiah (Heb., "who is like Yahweh?"). Etymologically the name is an expression of praise to the God who is incomparable. The name is given to several different individuals in the Hebrew Bible:

1 The prophet Micah of Moresheth, a town some twenty-five miles southwest of Jerusalem, to whom the book of Micah is attributed. In addition to the information in Mic. 1:1, Jer. 26:18 reports that Micah came to Jerusalem in the time of Hezekiah, that is, during the last decade or so of the eighth century B.C., and announced the destruction of the city (cf. Mic. 3:12). His exact dates are unknown, but he would have been a contemporary of Isaiah of Jerusalem.

2 A man in the hill country of Ephraim, a central but mainly passive figure in the story of the migration of the tribe of Dan (Judg. 17–18). His mother consecrated eleven hundred pieces of silver "to the Lord" (Judg. 17:3) to make a graven image and a molten image, a strange act in light of the OT prohibitions against images and idols. He established a shrine, made an ephod and teraphim, and set up one of his sons as priest. When a Levite from Bethlehem ("of the family of Judah," Judg. 17:7) appeared, Micah hired him as priest at the shrine. When the tribe of Dan, seeking a place to live, sent spies into the hill country of Ephraim, they stayed with Micah, asking the Levite to consult the Lord concerning their journey. Hearing his good report, they completed their exploration to the north and returned to lead the Danites to their new territory. When the five spies, along with six hundred armed Danites, returned through the hill country of Ephraim they stole Micah's "graven image, the ephod, the molten image" (Judg. 18:17) and took the Levite with them to their new territory in the north. The story is thus basically a negative account of how the shrine in Dan was established.

3 According to the genealogy in 1 Chron. 5:5, one of the descendants of Reuben.

4 The son of Meribbaal who was the son of Jonathan (1 Chron. 8:34–35; 9:40), the same as Mica the son of Mephibosheth in 2 Sam. 9:12.

5 A Levite in the time of David, one of the sons of Uzziel (1 Chron. 23:20; 24:24–25).

6 The father of Abdon in the time of Joaiah (2 Chron. 34:20), named Michiah in 2 Kings 22:12. ***See also*** Micah, The Book of. G.M.T.

Micah (mī'kah), **the Book of,** one of the books of the twelve Minor Prophets in the Bible. The title comes from the name of the prophet to whom the book is attributed (Mic. 1:1). The book is a collection of prophetic addresses.

In terms of both form and content the book has two major sections, each organized thematically to move from prophecies of punishment to prophecies of salvation. The first section, Mic. 1:2–5:15, contains prophecies of punishment against the two capital cities of Samaria and Jerusalem in chaps. 1–3, followed in chaps. 4–5 by prophecies of salvation that see Mount Zion in Jerusalem as the center of the coming reign of peace. The second section, Micah 6–7, has announcements of judgment in 6:1–7:6 and of salvation in 7:7–20. It begins with the Lord's trial proceedings against Israel (6:1–5) and focuses upon the ruptured relationship between God and his people. The concluding speeches (7:8–20) announce reconciliation and renewal.

Mic. 1:1 dates the prophet in the reign of three kings of Judah: Jotham, Ahaz, and Hezekiah. The single external reference to Micah, in Jer. 26:18, reports that the prophet came to Jerusalem in the reign of Hezekiah. Other allusions within the book are consistent with a date in the time of Hezekiah, that is, the last decades of the eighth century B.C. Micah went from his home in the small town of Moresheth, about twenty-five miles southwest of Jerusalem, to speak the word of the Lord in Jerusalem.

It is highly unlikely that all the addresses in the book were first delivered by Micah in the eighth century, though there has been considerable disagreement about how much stems from the original prophet. Some commentators argue that Micah was exclusively a prophet of doom and that all hopeful expressions come from a later time. How, for example, could the prophet who expected Zion to be a ruin (Mic. 3:9–12) also promise that it would one day be the highest of the mountains of the earth (4:1–4)? But it is by no means certain that Micah had no positive vision for the future. Nevertheless, there is clear evidence that the style, content, and historical perspective of some of the speeches reflect not the period of the Assyrian threat in the eighth century but the Babylonian exile in the sixth century B.C. and later. The style of 7:1–7 in particular is quite different from the first chapters of the book. Mic. 7:8–10 assumes the destruction of the nation by the Babylonians, and 7:11–13 has in view the rebuilding of the walls of Jerusalem after the return from Exile during the Persian period in the late sixth or early fifth century B.C. Moreover, 7:14–20 seems to assume the existence of the Second Temple in the postexilic period.

Though the book is the product of centuries of tradition, its message can be summarized in a relatively consistent fashion: because of their sins, and particularly those of people in powerful places, God is about to punish his people by means of military defeat and exile. Later those people will be brought back to their land, and God will establish perpetual peace.

Micah may be outlined briefly in the following way:

I. Superscription (1:1)
II. First collection of speeches (1:2–5:15)
  A. Prophecies of punishment (1:2–3:12)
  B. Prophecies of salvation (4:1–5:15)
III. Second collection of speeches (6:1–7:20)
  A. Prophecies of punishment (6:1–7:6)
  B. Prophecies of salvation (7:7–20).

See also Prophet. G.M.T.

Micaiah (mi-kī'yah). **1** King Abijah's mother (2 Chron. 13:2), elsewhere called Maacah. **2** The son of Imlah, a prophet at Ahab's court (1 Kings 22). Ahab and Jehoshaphat, king of Judah, wanted to liberate Ramoth-gilead from the Arameans. Before going to war they consulted some four hundred prophets, all of whom assured them that God would grant victory. When Micaiah was summoned, however, he reported a vision of the Israelites wandering about the hills like sheep without a shepherd. He described a meeting of the divine council at which God had commissioned "a lying spirit in the mouth of all [the] prophets" (v. 22) to "entice Ahab, that he may go up and fall of Ramoth-gilead" (v. 20). Ahab ordered Micaiah cast into prison and proceeded with his plan for war. Although he took the precaution of disguising himself before going into battle, he was fatally wounded when "a certain man drew his bow at a venture" (v. 34), and the Israelites left the battlefield in disarray, as Micaiah had predicted. **3** One of the princes sent by Jehoshaphat to instruct the cities of Judah in religious matters (2 Chron. 17:7). **4** The father of Achbor, a member of Josiah's delegation to Huldah the prophetess (2 Kings 22:12). **5** The son of Gemariah and grandson of Shaphan, both friends of Jeremiah. When Micaiah heard

Baruch read the scroll of Jeremiah's oracles, he reported it to his father and other court officials (Jer. 36:11–13), and they arranged to have it read to King Jehoiakim. **6** The forebear of certain postexilic priests (Neh. 12:35), elsewhere called Mica (Neh. 11:17, 22). **7** A priest in the time of Nehemiah (Neh. 12:41). P.K.M.

Michael (Heb., "who is like God?"), patron angel of Israel, first mentioned by name in Dan. 10:13, 21; 12:1. In the NT he is mentioned in Jude 9, where he contends with the devil for the body of Moses, and in Rev. 12:7, where he is at war with the dragon. He figures prominently in Jewish writings of the intertestamental period, including the Qumran War Scroll. It is also used as a human name in 2 Chron. 21:2.

Michal (mī'kahl; short form of Heb. *Michael*, "who is like God?"), Saul's younger daughter (1 Sam. 14:49), who became David's wife. Her love for David was exploited by Saul, who hoped to dispose of David by asking an unusual and difficult bridal price (1 Sam. 18:20–29). Like her brother Jonathan, she saved David from Saul's attempt to kill him, cleverly covering up his escape (1 Sam. 19:11–17). Saul later gave Michal to Palti (1 Sam. 25:44) but she was returned to David as part of a political bargain (2 Sam. 3:12–16). Michal and David quarreled over his behavior before the Ark (2 Sam. 6:12–23; cf. 1 Chron. 15:29) with tragic consequences for Michal. She died childless. ***See also*** David; Saul. J.C.E.

Michmash (mik'mash), a village located in the rugged hills of the territory of the tribe of Benjamin, about seven miles north of Jerusalem. It was on the north bank of the Wadi Suweinet opposite Geba, and together they guarded the pass to the Jordan Valley. Michmash stood almost 2,000 feet above sea level, and two rocky outcrops called Bozez and Seneh stood nearby on either side of the valley (1 Sam. 14:4, 5).

In this pass the Philistine power in the eastern hill country was broken (1 Sam. 13, 14). Saul had gathered troops in the hill country of Bethel (1 Sam. 13:2) when Jonathan killed the Philistine governor at Geba. The Philistines rallied their forces at Michmash with greatly superior numbers (the actual number is exaggerated; thirty thousand, or even three thousand [Septuagint] chariots could not possibly function in the terrain [1 Sam. 13:5]) and dispersed raiding parties to the west, north, and east (1 Sam. 13:5, 17). But then Jonathan led a surprise attack across the wadi and terrified the Philistines (1 Sam. 14:13–15). Saul and Jonathan pursued the Philistines who had been thrown into confusion (14:15), and drove them from the hill country (14:31). The account can be vividly followed, and although the text is sometimes unclear (for example, there is confusion between Gibeah of Saul and Geba), it is obviously told by someone familiar with the rugged terrain.

A northern attack on Jerusalem by the Assyrians is suggested by a poem in Isaiah 10 and Michmash is mentioned (v. 28). General Allenby is said to have driven the Turks from the area in 1917 by following the topography of 1 Samuel 13 and 14.

Michmash was inhabited after the Exile according to the lists in Ezra (2:27) and Nehemiah (7:31; 11:31). ***See also*** Philistines. N.L.L.

Michtam (mik'tam), a technical term of uncertain meaning introducing Pss. 16, 56–60, and probably Isa. 38:9. Although designated *miktab*, "letter," Isa. 38:9 closely resembles an individual lament or thanksgiving psalm and may be a late reflection of Sumerian letter-prayers. The LXX renders *michtam* as *stelographia*, "inscription on a stela." Possible etymologies include Hebrew *ketem*, "gold," and Akkadian *katamu*, "to cover" (by extension, "to expiate").

Midianites (mid'ee-uhn-īts), descendants of Midian, a son of Abraham and his concubine Keturah (Gen. 25:1–2). When Abraham expelled Isaac's rivals "to the east country," Midian was included (Gen. 25:6). Thus, the Midianites were counted among the "people of the East" (Judg. 6:3, 33; 7:12), a general designation for the nomadic inhabitants of the Syrian and Arabian deserts. The "land of Midian" (Exod. 2:15) probably refers to the center of Midianite territory, that part of northwestern Arabia bordering the Gulf of Aqaba's eastern shore (cf. 1 Kings 11:18). The term "Midianite" probably identified a confederation of tribes that roamed far beyond this ancestral homeland, a usage that explains the biblical references to Midianites in Sinai, Canaan, the Jordan Valley, Moab, and Transjordan's eastern desert. Apart from the OT, sources of information on the Midianites are few; nonbiblical texts are ambiguous, and it is difficult to associate any archaeological artifacts with this elusive people.

The first significant reference to the Midianites is a record of their involvement in the sale of Joseph into slavery, an account in which Midianites are closely associated or equated with Ishmaelites (Gen. 37:25–28, 36; 39:1; cf. Judg. 8:24).

Of great importance to Exodus is Moses' sojourn in Midian. Moses went there as a fugitive from Egyptian justice (2:15), was befriended by Jethro, the priest of Midian (2:16; 3:1), and married Jethro's daughter Zipporah (2:21). While still in the general region of Midian, Moses was commissioned to lead the Hebrews out of Egypt (3:1–15; 4:19). Later, Moses' Midianite brother-in-law, Hobab, guided the Israelites in the wilderness (Num. 10:29–32).

When the Hebrews were encamped in the

plains of Moab, the "elders of Midian" and the Moabite king Balak hired Balaam to curse their new enemies (Num. 22:1–7; cf. Josh. 13:21). Since the Midianites led Israel into idolatry and immorality at Shittim (Num. 25:1–7, 16–18), Moses was commanded to seek revenge by destroying the Midianite population in this region (Num. 31:1–12).

Following seven years of oppression by the people of the East, the Hebrew warrior Gideon soundly defeated the camel-riding Midianites. Many years later, Gideon's victory was recounted in Ps. 83:9, 11; Isa. 9:4; and 10:26. ***See also*** Amalekites; Camel; Horeb, Mount; Ishmaelites; Jethro; Keturah. G.L.M.

midrash (from the Heb., "to search, inquire, and interpret"), the type of biblical interpretation found in rabbinic literature, especially the Talmuds and the midrashic collections, such as Midrash Genesis, Midrash Qohole. Midrashic interpretation pays close attention to the meanings of individual words and grammatical forms, elucidates one verse by another verse, and relates the teachings of rabbinic Judaism to the biblical text. Midrash assumes that the biblical text has an inexhaustible fund of meaning that is relevant to and adequate for every question and situation. In a wider sense, the word midrash is used for any interpretation which has such characteristics. ***See also*** Haggadah.

migdal (mig'dahl; Heb., "tower"), a military defensive tower within a city (Judg. 8:17; 9:51), on its walls (2 Chron. 32:5), or projecting outward from them (Neh. 3:25–27). A *migdal* might guard a gateway (2 Chron. 26:9) or stand isolated in front of a gate as a forward defense post (2 Chron. 14:7). The word also applies to observation towers, often connected with towns and located in strategic positions along highways or borders (2 Kings 17:9). Nonmilitary towers protected fields, vineyards (Isa. 5:2) or pasturage (Gen. 35:21). Metaphorically, *migdal* stands for shelter and protection (Ps. 61:3; Prov. 18:10), or for anything tall and graceful, as a speaker's wooden rostrum (Neh. 8:4), or a woman's nose, neck, or breasts (Song of Sol. 4:4; 7:4; 8:10). ***See also*** Cities; Defense; Tower; Walls. L.E.T.

A *migdal*, or defensive tower at Arad, ca. 2500 B.C.

Migdol (mig'dawl; Heb., "tower" or "fortress"), a city in northern Egypt cited in different biblical contexts. **1** An Israelite campsite landmark on the way out of Egypt (Exod. 14:2; Num. 33:7), in the eastern delta, possibly near modern Tell el-Maskhutah. **2** The location of a Jewish settlement in the time of Jeremiah (late seventh–early sixth century B.C.; Jer. 44:1; 46:14), possibly modern Tell el-Heir near or identical with 1 above. **3** The northern extremity of Egypt, used with Syene (modern Aswan) to designate all of Egypt (Ezek. 29:10; 30:6); it is probably the same as 2 above.

Migron (mig'rohn; Heb., "steep"?), a town in the hill country of Judah. In 1 Sam. 14:2 Saul was at Migron "on the outskirts of Gibeah." Gibeah is probably a misreading for Geba across the valley from Michmash (see 1 Sam. 13:16). In Isa. 10:28 Migron is mentioned in association with Geba and Michmash as a point on the route of the invading Assyrians. The site is probably to be identified with modern Tell Miriam near Michmash. ***See also*** Geba; Michmash.

Mijamin (mij'uh-min). **1** The ancestral head of the sixth course of priests (1 Chron. 24:9). **2** A Levite who returned with Zerubbabel from the Babylonian captivity (Neh. 12:5); he is possibly the same Levite who took a foreign wife (Ezra 10:25) and signed the covenant to keep the law (Neh. 10:7). Some scholars think Miniamin refers to the same person (Neh. 12:17, 41), although the connection is not clear.

Mikloth (mik'luth). **1** A Benjaminite, the father of Shimeah (Shimeam) and son of Gibeon (1 Chron. 8:32; 9:37–38). **2** The chief officer under Dodai who was commander of twenty-four thousand men in King David's army (1 Chron. 27:4). This reference to Mikloth is not in some manuscripts and is omitted by some versions.

Milcah (mil'kah). **1** The daughter of Haran, the wife of Abraham's brother Nahor (Gen. 11:29). She bore eight children, one of whom was Bethuel, father of Rebekah (Gen. 22:20–23) who became Isaac's wife. **2** One of the five daughters of Zelophehad belonging to the tribe of Manasseh (Num. 26:33) who claimed before Moses that, since their father had no sons, his inheritance should belong to her and her sisters. Their claim was sustained by the Lord (Num. 27:1–7), so long as they married within the tribe (Num. 36:1–12). ***See also*** Bethuel; Haran; Zelophehad. F.R.M.

Milcom (mil'kohm; from the Semitic root *mlk*, "king"), the Ammonite form of Baal, the northwest Semitic god of fertility and the storm. He was closely related to the Phoenician Baals, Melcart and Molech, to whom human sacrifices, particularly children, were offered. The worship of Milcom was introduced into Jerusalem by Solomon (1 Kings 11:5, 33) and abolished by Josiah (2 Kings 23:13). ***See also*** Baal; Molech.

mildew (Heb., "yellow" or "pale"), generally a superficial growth on organic matter or plants by fungi of the *Erysiphaceae* or *Peronosporaceae* families. Viewed consistently as divine punishment (Deut. 28:22), its association with "blasting" and "fiery heat" suggests damage in the wake of destructive east winds (Sirocco). It is a tool of God's judgment (Hag. 2:17; Amos 4:9), and relief from it is a divine grace (1 Kings 8:37; 2 Chron. 6:28).

mile. ***See*** Weights and Measures.

Miletus (mī-lee'tuhs), a large port and commercial center at the ancient mouth of the Meander River on the west coast of Asia Minor. The city was originally founded by the Ionians about the eleventh century B.C. The Persians controlled the port at least twice, but it was freed by Alexander the Great in 334 B.C. The city flourished during the Hellenistic and Roman periods (324 B.C.–A.D. 325), with four harbors and three market areas, of which one is the largest known market of the ancient Greek world. The enormous gate to this market has been removed to the Pergamum Museum in Berlin and rebuilt there. The Roman theater of Miletus, with a seating capacity of fifteen thousand, was situated on a peninsula between two bays and was known as one of the best in all Asia Minor. The temple of Apollo, the principal deity of the city, stood in front of the northern harbor. Paul stopped here on his way to Jerusalem for the last time and summoned the elders of Ephesus to come for a farewell address (Acts 20:15–38). A reference to another possible visit of Paul to the city can be found in 2 Tim. 4:20. M.K.M.

The Aegean Sea from the site of ancient Miletus.

mill, any of a variety of installations for grinding food grains (Isa. 47:2; Matt. 24:41) or other foodstuffs (Num. 11:8). The normal domestic form of a mill was a saddle quern of limestone or basalt and a hand-held grinding stone. The grain was placed on the saddle and rubbed by

An olive press, or mill, from Capernaum.

back and forth motions of the hand grinder until it reached the desired fineness. Larger communal or industrial installations comprised an upper (movable) and a lower (stable) millstone between which the grain would be placed or fed through a hollow in the upper stone. The upper stone was rotated by human (Lam. 5:13), prison (Judg. 16:21), or animal labor. It pivoted on a small anchoring protrusion of the lower stone's upper surface, working the grain outward toward the edges of the stones as grinding proceeded. Because of the importance of this equipment for everyday survival, Deuteronomic law prevented taking it as collateral (Deut. 24:6). Its commonplace role in life was such that absence of the sound of milling was a symbol of destruction (Rev. 18:22; Jer. 25:10). The everyday household grinding might be done by servants (Exod. 11:5), and the portability of an upper millstone is evident in its use as a weapon on occasion (Judg. 9:53; 2 Sam. 11:21). That it could function as a device for execution is reflected in Jesus' comment (Mark 9:42; Matt. 18:6; Luke 17:2). The necessary quality of hardness for good function is used symbolically in Job 41:24 concerning Leviathan, and its weight and size figure in its use in Rev. 18:21.

In addition to the countless examples of

household grinders found in archaeological sites, Roman sugar mills have been identified in Transjordan both in the Jordan Valley and at the Roman installations of Khirbet Iskander. R.S.B.

millennium, a thousand-year period or, generally, an era of permanent peace, joy, and blessings on earth or elsewhere. Psalm 90, praising the everlasting God, declares that a thousand years in his sight "are but as yesterday" (v. 4). Possibly on this basis, the author of *Jubilees* (4:30) concluded that Adam died on the "day" he ate the forbidden fruit after all, i.e., within the first thousand years. Following this clue, the writer of *2 Enoch* speculated that history consisted of a week lasting seven thousand years, after which the eighth "day" (i.e., thousand years) would be "endless" (33:1–2).

Early in the second century A.D., a Christian writer, concerned to explain to other Christians why the promised coming of Jesus and the new age had not yet occurred, suggested that with God (or Jesus) a thousand years is the same as a day (2 Pet. 3:8). This writer thought people were then living in "the last days" (3:3) so probably did not contemplate a continuous thousand-year period; rather he meant simply that God reckons time differently than humans do.

The writer of Revelation, vividly portraying the defeat of cosmic evil powers (and of Rome, Rev. 17:1–18:24), which, toward the end of the first century A.D., he expected soon to take place, looked for a thousand-year epoch within the framework of the coming eschatological events. During this time, Satan would be bound and sealed "in the pit," while those Christians who had withstood persecution and refused to worship the image of the beast (probably the Roman emperor) would reign with Christ for a thousand years (Rev. 20:1–6; cf. 2 Esd. 7:28, which anticipates a four-hundred-year period of messianic reign or rejoicing). After that, Satan would be loosed for a final onslaught, but then, with Death and Hades, he would forever be banished "to the lake of fire and brimstone" (20:7–14).

In Persian Zoroastrianism, time was visualized in three periods of one thousand years each, but such beliefs do not appear to have influenced biblical thought. Commonly, the term "millennium" is used to refer to that age when, at last, God's reign is to be established forever (or, in secular circles, to some sort of utopian era). ***See also*** Apocalyptic Literature; Eschatology; Kingdom of God; Messiah; Parousia; Satan. R.H.H.

millet, a small-seeded annual grass (*Panicum miliaceum*) grown for both grain and stalks. In Ezek. 4:9 it is mixed with other grains and used in making bread. Millet was used for food for both humans and animals.

millo (mil'loh; Heb., "earthen fill"), a type of construction in which a building, a section of a city, or an entire site was elevated on an artificial platform of earth held in place by one or more walls. The earthen platform is the "millo" and the structure built on the platform is the "house of the millo" (Heb. *bêth-millô*). The fortress temple at Shechem was built on an earth filling obtained by cutting down the embankment fortification of the Middle Bronze Age city. This temple is probably the *bêth-millô* mentioned in Judg. 9:6, 20. Kathleen Kenyon's excavations on the eastern slope of the City of David indicate that during the Canaanite period the hill on which Jerusalem stood was too narrow to accommodate a growing population. It was extended by a "millo" construction. Stone walls were built parallel to the line of the hill, and the spaces between them were filled with earth, creating a platform that extended the hill eastward. After his capture of Jerusalem David rebuilt the interior of the city "from the Millo inward" (2 Sam. 5:9). The Jerusalem millo and the walls associated with it required frequent maintenance. Repairs by Solomon (1 Kings 9:15, 24; 11:27) and by Hezekiah (2 Chron. 32:5) are recorded. King Joash was assassinated in one of the structures built on the Jerusalem millo (2 Kings 12:20). ***See also*** Jerusalem; Shechem. L.E.T.

mina. ***See*** Money; Weights and Measures.

Minaeans (min-ee'uhnz), ancient people of Arabia in the region of Main in modern North Yemen. Like the Sabeans, they conducted trade throughout the Levant. Numerous Minaean inscriptions, some dated to the early first millennium B.C., have been found, mostly in Arabia but also as distantly as Memphis in Egypt and Delos. The Meunim or Meinim in 1 Chron. 4:41 and 2 Chron. 26:7 are identified in the Septuagint as Minaeans, as are the Ammonites in 2 Chron. 20:1 and 26:8, and Zophar in Job 2:11; these identifications are problematic and may be the substitution of a more familiar for a less familiar name. In Ezra 2:50 (see Neh. 7:52) the Meunim or Meinim are Temple servants. ***See also*** Seba, Sabeans. M.D.C.

mind, the English translation of various Hebrew and Greek words denoting the human capacity for contemplation, judgment, and intention. As intellect, mind makes possible the critical appraisal and selection of differing opinions. In this sense, mind may also describe one's own mind-set, attitude, or characteristic point of view (e.g., Phil. 2:2–5). In both the OT and the NT, "heart" is often used as the equivalent of "mind" and, indeed, is sometimes translated as "mind" (e.g., Isa. 65:17; Jer. 19:5). In the NT, Paul is especially concerned that the Christian's mind be transformed by a renewed dedication to the will of God (Rom. 12:2). ***See also*** Conscience; Heart. R.A.B.

minerals, inorganic substances often obtained by mining. The Bible knows both precious and common minerals such as iron (e.g., Deut. 8:9; cf. Gen. 4:22; Josh. 6:19; Jer. 28:13; Acts 12:10) and copper (e.g., Job 28:2; Ezek. 24:11; Matt. 10:9) ores, beryl (e.g., Exod. 28:20; Ezek. 28:13; Rev. 21:20), onyx (e.g., Gen. 2:2; Exod. 36:9; Job 28:6; Rev. 21:20), and chrysolite (e.g., Ezek. 1:16; Rev. 21:20). ***See also*** Flint; Jewelry; Marble; Metals; Refining.

mines, excavations for the extracting of mineral ores. Job 28:1–11 has the most detailed description of mining in the Bible where terms are of a general rather than technical character. The subject is the inaccessibility of wisdom. By analogy wisdom is hidden as precious metals are hidden in the mountains. There is a "source" (RSV: "mine") for silver and a "place" for gold; iron is "taken" out of the earth; men (not miners) search underground for "stone" (RSV: "ore"), "cut" channels, "open shafts" in uninhabited valleys, "overturn" mountains, and "put [their] hand[s]" to flinty rock. As descriptive as the procedures are, they show a basic unfamiliarity with technical terms connected with mines and mining. In Deut. 8:9 the verb used for the mining of copper is the same word used elsewhere for digging a cistern or well. The term for a miner is simply "digger." Thus, the verbs "take" or "dig" reveal nothing of the process. Zech. 6:1 refers to "mountains of copper."

The lack of specificity about mines and mining is due likely to the paucity of mineral resources in Palestine. Geological explorations have shown adequate sources of materials for construction purposes generally underlying much of the land, but ore sources are concentrated in a few locations.

The semicircular area extending from the base of the hill marks the perimeter of a fourteenth–twelfth century B.C. smelting camp at Timna.

Five centers of ancient mining and metal production have been discovered in Israel and Jordan. **1** The Timna Valley region in the Wadi Arabah at the southern end of the Dead Sea down to the Gulf of Aqabah, where archaeologist Nelson Glueck discovered copper smelting furnaces at modern Tell-el-Kheleifeh. Beno Rothenberg (1960–83) discovered more than three hundred sites of ancient mining and smelting in the Arabah. Glueck assigned his findings to King Solomon and later (tenth–sixth centuries B.C.). Rothenberg's researches specifically deny Solomonic use, showing instead copper mining and metallurgy from three periods: the fourth millennium B.C. (Chalcolithic, i.e., Copper-Stone Age); Egyptian workings of the fourteenth to the twelfth centuries B.C.; and the Roman period (second century A.D.). Most recently (1983) Rothenberg discovered a copper smelter, a workshop with crushing implements, mining hammers, crushed ore, and pottery from the Middle Bronze I period (just before the time of Abraham in the Bible, ca. 2000 B.C.). This is the first time extractive metallurgy of this period has been found in the Near East. In 1981 John J. Bimson wrote a defense of Glueck's dating of the Timna finds to the Solomonic period. **2** The 'Amram Valley, south of Timna in the Arabah; it has copper mines and industrial installations. **3** The Wadi Feinan and modern Khirbet e-Nahaš at the foot of the Edom mountains in southern Jordan; these have copper and iron mines as well as evidence of smelting sites. **4** Wadi es-Sabra in what is now Southern Jordan (Edom) about four and a half miles southwest of Petra, the northern capital of the ancient Nabatean kingdom. Here copper and iron mines were discovered by Glueck. Deposits of copper and veins of rich iron ore (tested to ca. 63.2 percent iron) were noted. **5** Mugharat Wardeh, about two miles from the Jabbok (Zerqa) River in southern Gilead (Ajlun region of modern Jordan), where the largest iron mine in Palestine was found. Evidence at the mine and an associated smelting site is from the Ayyubid-Mamluk period of Islamic history (ca. A.D. 1185–1250). Roman evidence on the site cannot be linked to the mining activity. While some think an earlier Philistine or Davidic use of the mine is likely, no evidence has yet been found to prove the early dates.

Bibliography

Glueck, N. *The Other Side of Jordan*. New Haven, CT: American Schools of Oriental Research, 1970.

Rothenberg, B. *Timna*. London: Thames & Hudson, 1972. R.A.C.

minister, a person who serves. In the basic

meaning of the term, there is no indication as to the arena or nature of the service. It might involve ministering as an assistant, as the young Samuel was to Eli (1 Sam. 3:1), as Joshua to Moses (Josh. 1:1), or as John Mark to Paul and Barnabas (Acts 13:5). Priests at the altar were ministers (Ezek. 45:4), but so was Onesimus when he cared for the needs of the imprisoned Paul (Philem. 13). Political leaders were viewed by Paul as ministers of God (Rom. 13:4), but Peter's mother-in-law, by attending to domestic chores, was also a minister (Mark 1:31). Those chosen to serve tables in the Jerusalem church were ministers (Acts 6:2), as was Paul when he collected relief funds for the poor (Rom. 15:25). A minister serves the need, whatever it is; to that end, in the NT, the whole church was to be equipped (Eph. 4:12), and by the standard of ministering to the hungry, naked, lonely, sick, or imprisoned all are judged (Matt. 25:44). Jesus not only taught that the great were those who ministered (Mark 10:43–44) but was a model of one who came not to be ministered to but to minister (Mark 10:45). The basic words translated "minister" all carry the idea of humble service: bondservant or slave (Rom. 1:1), one who pulls the oars (1 Cor. 4:1), worker (1 Cor. 9:13), and servant (Exod. 24:13; 2 Cor. 3:6). This last word, *diakonos* (Gk., "deacon"), is the most common term for minister in the NT.

While ministry was an obligation of all, certain persons were ministers in special ways. Priests were ministers in the Temple (Joel 1:13), and a synagogue had at least one minister (Luke 4:20). The NT contains lists of ministers including apostles, prophets, teachers, evangelists, and pastors (1 Cor. 12:28; Eph. 4:11), but precise definitions of duties are not clear. Likewise, bishops, elders, and deacons ministered in the churches (Phil. 1:1; Acts 20:17, 28; 1 Tim. 3:1, 8; Titus 1:5, 7), but lines of authority were not yet developed. The one thing clear in the NT is that all followers of Christ were to be ministers according to the teaching and example of Christ. ***See also*** Bishop; Church; Elders; Ordain, Ordination; Priests; Servant; Slavery.

F.B.C.

Minni (min'ī), a state and people known as *Mannaya* (or *Mannay*) from Assyrian royal inscriptions beginning with Shalmaneser III (858–824 B.C.) and called Manneans. They lived in the eastern Turkish mountain territory south of Lake Urmia, part of modern northern Iraq. In Jer. 51:27 they were part of a coalition with Ararat (Urartu) and Ashkenaz (probably Scythians) from the same region that opposed Babylon.

Minnith (min'ith), one of the twenty cities taken from the Ammonites by Jephthah (Judg. 11:33). Its pairing with a southern tribal city, Aroer, as the opposite boundary would suggest a location somewhere in the northern sector, near modern Amman. The precise location is unknown but probably lies somewhere northeast of modern Hesban.

mint, a strongly scented herb used in cooking, medicinally as a carminative and stomachic, and on floors of synagogues as an air-freshener. In Matt. 23:23 and Luke 11:42, paying tithes on inexpensive mint symbolizes attention to details of ritual law as opposed to the "weightier matters . . . justice and mercy and faith."

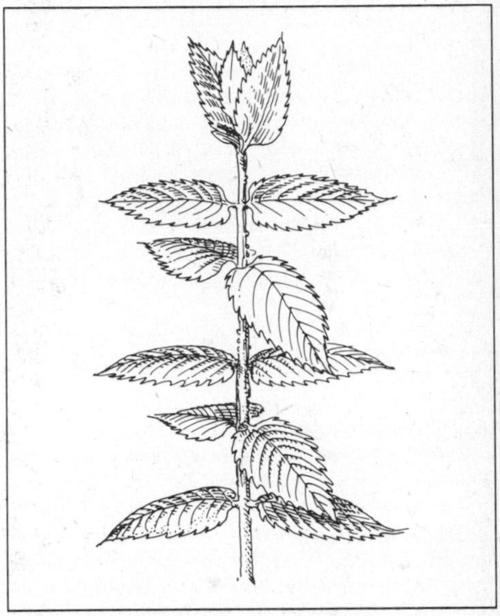

Mint.

miracles, special interventions by God on behalf of his people. Miracles are closely associated with the creative and salvific deeds of God throughout OT tradition. These "powerful," "mighty" or "miraculous" deeds of salvation and creation take place through the action of God's Spirit and power. This mighty power of God, manifested throughout the history of Israel, is understood to be unique (Josh. 4:23–24; Pss. 77:14–15; 145:10–12; Jer. 16:21). It was especially evident in the Exodus event. God often executed his salvific will through the deeds of individuals specially gifted with his Spirit and power. These "miracle workers" of the OT, men such as Moses, Joshua, Elijah, and Elisha, were empowered with this Spirit to act as agents of God on behalf of his people.

Background: The miracle worker Jesus stands in this OT tradition as a Spirit-equipped agent of God. But a full understanding of the miracles of Jesus does not come from the OT alone. It is

The miracle of the healing of the leper by Jesus (cf. Mark 1:40–42) from the *Four Gospels*, a late twelfth-century illuminated manuscript.

necessary to consider certain characteristics and thought patterns from the apocalyptic-eschatological milieu in which the NT took shape. After the Babylonian exile, certain developments occurred in Jewish thinking about God and the problem of suffering and evil. As ideas of the transcendence of God became more and more pronounced, the belief in angels as intermediaries between God and his universe strengthened. One of the explanations of the origin of evil was that sin can be traced back to the "fall" or rebellion of some of the angels against the rule and authority of God. The world of spirits was divided in two: Satan and his demons versus God and his faithful angels. These evil spirits not only tempt people to sin but also make them suffer from sickness and diseases. Both sin and sickness, then, have a common demonic origin. Human lives could be controlled by Satan and his demons. But in Jewish apocalyptic thought God's permission of the rule of Satan and demons was considered only temporary. There was the hope that God's reign, perhaps through the agency of a messiah, would suddenly break into history and overcome the control of evil powers. The "end time" to be brought about by God would have cosmic repercussions extending to the evils affecting human lives.

Since there is a very close relationship between the creative and salvific activity of God, both would be involved in the coming of the End. People would be saved from the grip of evil powers and the created world would be transformed or "re-created." The end time would in some way correspond to the beginning of time. What God had originally planned and willed when he created the universe would be restored and reach its fulfillment in the last days. Whatever had gone wrong in the lives of human beings would be rectified, restored, and brought to perfection.

The Miracles of Jesus: In the NT, the miracles of Jesus, mighty deeds of God's salvific and creative power, are understood to be one of the ways in which the final, decisive reign of God has come into history. Jesus' miraculous healing and exorcistic activity freed broken human lives from the bonds of demonic possession and restored diseased and corrupted human bodies to their intended state. Jesus' miracles demonstrated that the end-time Kingdom of God, in which God would overthrow the power of Satan, has now arrived in his person (Matt. 12:28; Luke 11:20). Likewise, the miracles performed by the disciples of Jesus served as signs of God's overthrow of Satan (Luke 10:17–18). The healing and exorcistic miracles of Jesus, then, contributed toward the actual bringing about of the Kingdom of God.

The miraculous activity of Jesus was the activity of a Spirit-equipped eschatological agent of God. The miracles of Jesus flowed from the creative and salvific Spirit of God. Jesus was equipped with this Spirit at his baptism (Matt. 3:16–17; Mark 1:9–11; Luke 3:21–22). This same Spirit led and accompanied Jesus into his testing by Satan (Matt. 4:1–11; Mark 1:12–13; Luke 4:1–13). The victory of the Spirit-equipped Jesus over Satan in this testing indicated that a new, eschatological situation had arrived. His overcoming of Satan, the leader of demons, in these temptations prepared and made possible his later healing and exorcistic ministry.

Characteristics of Accounts: The literary genre of the account of a miraculous healing exhibits the same essential characteristics wherever it is found: (1) The presence of a person (or representative of that person) in need of healing. This characteristic often includes various details that serve to heighten the miraculous deed: the great length of the illness, previous failures at being healed, the horrible, terrifying condition of the afflicted person, doubt about the ability of the healer, various effects the sickness has on members of the community or household, etc. (2) The words or actions of the healer. This sometimes includes various bodily manipulations: touching the ears, washing the eyes, commands to walk, dialogue with demons, etc. (3) The fact or confirmation of the healing. This often includes such details as a raised person eating again, the praise of those witnessing the event, a visible sign that demons have left a person, a return to previously impossible activity, etc.

Although both the healings and the exorcisms of Jesus belong to this same literary genre, there are some slight differences. In an exorcism Jesus encounters and expels personified evil, a demon or demons, from a person held in demonic possession. The person has no control over the sickness, which has overcome that person as an extrinsic force. While the sickness involved in a healing can be considered demonic in origin, the healings were the result of Jesus' direct encounter with the sick persons (or their representatives) and not directly with the demon or evil power involved. The evil is intrinsic to the person and moral responsibility of some kind is involved, since sin and sickness were reciprocally related in the Jewish thought of the time (Matt. 9: 1–8; John 9:1–2). Both healings and exorcisms thus concerned the overcoming of the demonic effects of sin and sickness. Jesus authorized his disciples to continue and extend his miraculous healing and exorcistic ministry (Matt. 10: 1–8; Mark 3:13–15; 6:7–13; Luke 9:1–6; 10:9, 17–20).

The miraculous healings and exorcisms, then, were unique personal experiences of the salvation brought by Jesus. They were the means by which the eschatological reign of God became a reality in peoples' lives. They were events in which people of faith personally received the Kingdom which has come in the person of Jesus. They are meant to bring others to faith in Jesus as the eschatological Savior sent by God.

Jesus' miracles of healing and exorcism have a variety of functions within the Gospel compositions. An example of this variety can be seen in the healing of the man with the withered hand (Matt. 12:9–14; Mark 3:1–6; Luke 6: 6–11), which serves as both a healing and a "controversy" story involving Sabbath observance. The various summaries of Jesus' healing and exorcistic activity show how essential and extensive these miracles were in the ministry of Jesus.

There are significant differences in literary genre among what are commonly grouped together as "miracle stories." The healings and exorcisms of Jesus, for example, are not of the same literary genre as some of the other "nature" miracle stories—the miraculous multiplication of the loaves and fishes, the stilling of the storm, the walking on the sea, etc. Some of these other types of miracle stories are actually "epiphanies," which reveal something about the hidden and more profound character of Jesus (cf. Mark 4:41). ***See also*** Apocalyptic Literature; Devil; Eschatology; Magic and Divination.

Bibliography

Russell, D. S. *The Method and Message of Jewish Apocalyptic 200 B.C.–A.D. 200*. Philadelphia: Westminster, 1964.

Theissen, G. *The Miracle Stories of the Early Christian Tradition*. Philadelphia: Fortress, 1983.

J.P.H.

Miriam plays a timbrel and sings as other women dance before Moses and the Israelites (Exod. 15:20–21); thirteenth-century French miniature.

Miriam (meer'ee-uhm), the sister of Moses and Aaron. We first hear of her when the infant Moses was placed in a basket on the Nile and his sister (not named here) watched from a distance; when the baby was discovered by Pharaoh's daughter, the sister offered to find a Hebrew wetnurse and fetched Moses' mother (Exod. 2: 4–8). After the Exodus, Miriam had a prominent position among the women, for Exod. 15:20–21 records her leading the women in the victory song after the events at the Red Sea. Miriam is called a prophetess in this passage. She later considered her prophecy equal to that of Moses when she and Aaron complained about the marriage of Moses to the Cushite woman (Num. 12); for that, she was struck with leprosy and was healed a week later after Aaron asked Moses to intercede for her. Miriam died and was buried at Kadesh. In later biblical tradition the leprosy of Miriam was presented as a caution to Israel (Deut. 24:9), and Miriam was remembered together with Moses and Aaron as leaders sent by God (Mic. 6:4). In postbiblical Jewish legends the prophecy of Miriam is stressed, and she was considered to have foretold the birth of Moses as savior of his people. T.S.F.

mirrors, reflective devices used primarily to

view one's face. Archaeological discoveries throughout the Near East attest that during the biblical period mirrors were made not of glass but of highly polished metal, e.g., silver, gold, copper, or bronze. The KJV erroneously translates the Greek and Hebrew words for mirror as "molten looking glass" (Job 37:18) or "glasses" (Isa. 3:23). Other textual references would seem to demand the translation "metal mirror" since mirrors were even melted down (Exod. 38:8). The poor quality of the mirror, used metaphorically by Paul to denote a cloudy reflection (1 Cor. 13:12), seems also to suggest metal, rather than glass. Excavation has shown a wealthy woman's assemblage of toiletries to include a mirror, garment pins, bead and gold jewelry, fine perfume, and cosmetic dishes. In the Roman period, mirrors became more commonplace. Metal mirrors were round in shape, either of one piece or with a handle of bone, wood, or ivory. Often the handle was cast or carved in the form of the Egyptian goddess Hathor. S.L.R.

Mishael (mish'uh-el; Heb., "who is what El [God] is?"). **1** The son of Uzziel of the Kohathite clan of Levites (Exod. 6:22; Lev. 10:4). **2** One, probably a Levite, who stood with Ezra as he read the law (Neh. 8:4). **3** The Hebrew name of one of the young men taken captive to Babylon by Nebuchadnezzer along with Daniel; he was given the Babylonian name Meshach (Dan. 1: 6–7; 2:17). ***See also*** Meshach.

Mishma (mish'muh; Heb., "a sound"). **1** The fifth of the twelve sons of Ishmael (Gen. 25:14). **2** A descendant of Simeon (1 Chron. 4:25–26).

Mishnah (from the Heb., "to repeat and to study"), a collection of rabbinic laws arranged in sixty-three tractates and six orders which cover agricultural tithes, public feasts, marriage (especially economic arrangements), torts, sacrifices at the Temple. and ritual purity. Created about A.D. 200 in Palestine under Rabbi Judah the Prince, the text underwent some evolution and was interpreted and its teachings modified by the Palestinian and Babylonian Talmuds. ***See also*** Halakah; Talmud.

mist, subterranean streams said to water the earth in Gen. 2:6. Storm-driven mist or fog is used as an image for those who are led astray into sin (2 Pet. 2:17); coupled with darkness it is used as a description of a person going blind (Acts 13:11).

Mitanni (mi-tan'nee), an important empire in northern Mesopotamia from about 1600 to 1330 B.C. It was also called Hanigalbat, Hurri, and Naharina. Its rulers came from a small Indo-Iranian aristocracy, though the population was largely Hurrian. They seem to have been responsible for the introduction of chariot warfare in the Near East.

From ca. 1520 to 1420 B.C., Mitanni struggled with Egypt for hegemony over Syria. At one point Mitanni's influence spread as far south as Palestine, contributing to the feudal structure of Canaanite society. Peace came in 1420 B.C., but despite the ensuing good relations with Egypt, Mitanni could not resist the new Hittite power to its west. After a prolonged struggle, the Hittite king Suppiluliuma (ca. 1380–1346 B.C.) defeated Tushratta, Mitanni's last great ruler; a century later Assyria destroyed what remained of the once great state. J.J.M.R.

mite. ***See*** Money.

miter, headdress of the high priest. ***See also*** Dress.

Mithredath (mith're-dath; Persian, "gift of Mithra"; also Mithridates, 1 Esd. 2:11, 16). **1** An official at the Persian court, "the treasurer," acting as Cyrus's agent in returning the Temple vessels to Sheshbazzar for restoration to Jerusalem (Ezra 1:8). **2** One of a group who sent a letter to Artaxerxes (Ezra 4:17). This letter appears to be distinct from the one that follows in 4:8–16.

Mitylene (mit-i-lee'nee), the main city and harbor on the east side of the large island of Lesbos in the Aegean Sea, just off the northwest coast of Asia Minor. Paul and his companions stopped at Mitylene on their return trip to Jerusalem during the third journey as recorded in Acts 20:14. ***See also*** Lesbos.

mixed multitude (Heb. *'erev rav*, "great crowd"), those who left Egypt with the Israelites (Exod. 12:38). The similarity in sound to *'arov*, "swarms of flies" (Exod. 8:21–31), emphasizes the turmoil of the departure. In the postexilic period, Neh. 13:3 used *'erev* in a restricted sense for "those of foreign descent" who must be separated from the people.

Mizar (mi'zahr; Heb., "small"), a hill (KJV) or small mountain (Ps. 42:6), probably in the region of Mount Hermon and the water sources of the Jordan River. Its precise identity is unknown.

Mizpah (miz'pah; also Mizpeh; Heb., "watchtower"), the name of at least five places in Palestine. The name Mizpah occurs frequently with the definite article, "the watchtower, the Mizpah." "Watchtower," like the word "fort," must have been applied to many different sites. One help in differentiating the biblical references to Mizpah is the addition of a regional designation: Mizpah of Judah, Mizpah of Gilead, Mizpah of Moab.

1 The land of Mizpah (Josh. 11:3, 8); this was in the north of Palestine near Mt. Hermon. After Jabin, king of Hazor, was defeated by Joshua, he fled eastward to the valley of Mizpah. This same Mizpah is defined a few verses earlier as the dwelling place of the Hivites, under Mt. Hermon.

2 Mizpah of Gilead, the name given to the site of the covenant between Laban and Jacob when Jacob returned to Palestine (Gen. 31:49). The popularly named "Mizpah Benediction" derives from Laban's request that God keep Jacob honest while Laban was absent and could not. The location was in Gilead, north of the Jabbok River. At this same Mizpah, the Israelites entered into covenant with Jephthah to be their leader (Judg. 11:11).

3 Mizpeh of Judah, one of the cities in the Shephelah assigned to Judah in the tribal division of the land (Josh. 15:38).

4 Mizpeh of Moab, an unknown site in Moab where David placed his parents under the protection of the king of Moab when Saul was pursuing him (1 Sam. 22:3).

5 Mizpah of Benjamin, a town on the border of Judah and Israel. It was the assembly point for the Israelite tribes going against Gibeah of Benjamin (Judg. 20:1–48). Mizpah was also on the circuit made annually by Samuel when he was judging Israel (1 Sam. 7:16–17). King Asa made Mizpah a fortified city after the heavy fighting between Israel and Judah (1 Kings 15:17–22). After the fall of Jerusalem at the Exile (587 B.C.), Mizpah became the Babylonian provincial capital. Gedaliah was made provincial governor but was assassinated at Mizpah by Ishmael and a band of nationalistic zealots.

This Mizpah has been identified with two modern sites, Nebi Samwil, about five miles north of Jerusalem, and Tell en-Nasbeh, about eight miles north of Jerusalem. Nebi Samwil has not been excavated, but all pottery remains from the area come from periods later than the monarchy (1025–924 B.C.).

Although no conclusive evidence proves that Tell en-Nasbeh is Mizpah, the site does fit well with the biblical and occupational history of Mizpah. Tell en-Nasbeh was excavated from 1926 to 1935 by W. F. Bade. The mound covers about 7 acres. Its occupation layers extend from the beginning of the Iron Age (1200 B.C.) to the Persian period (539–333 B.C.) with only slight evidence for permanent settlement outside these time periods.

One of the most important finds from Tell en-Nasbeh was the city wall. The entire length of about 2,165 feet was excavated. The wall was of the offset-inset type. It had nine or ten towers protecting it. The outer face of the wall ranged up to 40 feet high and averaged 16 feet thick. A fosse (i.e., a ditch) existed along portions of the outside of the wall, the only fosse known from the Iron Age in Palestine. The wall was also protected by a glacis, material forming an outer downward-sloping abutment at the base of the wall. This wall probably belonged to the fortified city of Asa's time (ca. 905–874).

The city gate belonging to this period was also well preserved. It had an opening nearly 14 feet wide. The massive wooden doors no longer remained; however, the door sockets and the door stop in the middle were found in place. On the inside and outside of the gate were open squares. Stone benches lined the outside of the gate and the inner rooms of the gate complex. Perhaps these benches were used by the elders as they decided the legal matters of the town.

Tell en-Nasbeh is one of the few Israelite towns to have been excavated almost completely. It thus provides a good picture of the fortifications, houses, public structures, tools, and utensils of Israel during the monarchy.

J.F.D.

Mizraim (miz'rī-em), one spelling of the Hebrew word for Egypt (in the KJV where the RSV has "Egypt" in Gen. 10:6, 13; 1 Chron. 1:8, 11). In some passages (1 Kings 10:28; 2 Kings 7:6; 2 Chron. 1:16–17) it may designate a region in southern Turkey (called "Musri" in Assyrian royal records of Shalmaneser III and others) from which horses were bred and exported. It was probably the region of Cilicia at the northeast corner of the Mediterranean Sea because of the mention of Kue (Cilicia; RSV) in the same connection.

Mnason (nay'suhn), "an early disciple" from Cyprus in whose home (either near or in Jerusalem) Paul and his companions lodged at the time of Paul's final visit to Jerusalem (Acts 21:16).

Moab (moh'ab). **1** Lot's son born from an incestuous relationship with his elder daughter. A similar relationship between Lot and his younger daughter produced Moab's half-brother, Ben-ammi (Ammon; Gen. 19:30–38).

2 The people descended from Moab, Lot's son. They were closely linked with their northern neighbors, the Ammonites (descended from Ben-ammi), with whom they later shared a border, and through Lot, Abraham's nephew, with the Israelites as well.

Moab is known from several ancient sources. According to the OT, contacts between Moab and Israel came in the attempt by Moses to negotiate a safe passage for the Israelites through Moabite territory, i.e., the plateau east of the Dead Sea bordered on the north by the Arnon River and on the south by the Zered (Judg. 11:17). Other sources note that Moab's land was given it by God (Deut. 2:9), yet the Moabite king Balak hired a prophet named Balaam to serve the Israelites (Num. 22–24). Israel camped in the plains of Moab before entering the promised land, territory north of the Arnon River extending as far north as "opposite Jericho" (Num. 35:1; Deut. 1:5). This brief sojourn proved detrimental to Israelite religion (Num. 25).

Contact between Moab and Israel is mentioned in Judges where a Moabite king named Eglon had extended his control over Benjaminites in the hill country and valley near the City of Palms (probably Jericho). A left-handed Benjaminite assassinated Eglon, providing a period of peace for the region (Judg. 3:12–30). The story of Ruth is also set in the period of the Judges and concerns the manner in which this Moabite woman came to Bethlehem and ultimately married and became King David's great-grandmother. Both Saul and David fought with the Moabites, the latter subduing them (1 Sam. 14:47; 2 Sam. 8:2). Moab's history remains somewhat obscure in the accounts of the Divided Monarchy, Moab being mentioned only occasionally (2 Kings 3; 13:20; 24:2). Prophets often spoke against Moab (Isa. 15–16; Jer. 48; Zeph. 2:8–11).

The discovery of the Moabite Stone in 1868 helped illumine Moab's history during the ninth century B.C. It was written at the behest of the Moabite king Mesha who is mentioned in 2 Kings 3:4. The inscription reveals that Moab had fallen under the control of the Omride dynasty in Israel but managed to free itself through armed struggle and the providential care of the national deity Chemosh. Mesha's capital was Dibon, modern Dhiban, a few miles north of the Arnon.

Moab is also known from Assyrian records which reveal that Moab paid tribute in the eighth century and that during the reign of Assurbanipal in the seventh century a Moabite king led a campaign against Arab tribes who opposed Assyrian control of the Transjordan. These records presuppose a subservient but working relationship between the kingdom of Moab and the Assyrian Empire. According to the Jewish historian Josephus, the Babylonian Empire under Nebuchadnezzar ended what little autonomy Moab possessed (sixth century B.C.), and while there are no other records from the Persian period to assist historians, it seems probable that the Babylonian campaign put a decisive end to any political entity named Moab. Of course, the land was still known as Moab for centuries and many inhabitants were called Moabites.

Something of Moab's language and culture is known from the Bible and Mesha's inscription. The chief Moabite deity was named Chemosh, a god known from other texts to have been venerated in northern Syria. Mesha describes Chemosh as angry with Moab and responsible for the nation's subjugation to Israel; however, Chemosh was also responsible for the victory over Israel. A religious rite of sacrificial dedication, the ban (Heb. *ḥerem*), was practiced by the Moabites as it was in Israel. The language of Moab was similar to that of its neighbors. Mesha's inscription has many parallels to classical Hebrew in orthography and vocabulary, though strong dialectical differences remain.

The land of Moab is comparatively high in elevation, reaching points over 3,000 feet above sea level, and is also comparatively well watered. Archaeological investigations suggest few large towns in ancient Moab, and the economy was based on cultivating wheat and barley and above all on raising sheep and goats. Several cities are mentioned in either the Bible or the Mesha inscription, some of which can be identified with reasonable certainty. These include Madeba (modern Medeba), Dibon (modern Dhiban), and Kir (modern Kerak). ***See also*** Lot; Moabite Stone, The. J.A.D.

Moabite Stone, the, a black basalt stele found at Dhiban, Jordan (biblical Dhibon), bearing a thirty-four-line inscription of Mesha, the ninth-century B.C. king of Moab mentioned in 2 Kings 3:4. After its discovery in 1868 by the Alsatian priest F. A. Klein, the stone was shattered by the local Bedouin, but in subsequent years approximately two-thirds of the fragments were recovered by the French orientalist C. Clermont-Ganneau, who, with the help of an impression taken before the stone was broken, was able to reconstruct the monument, which is now in the

The Moabite Stone: Stele of Mesha, king of Moab (ninth century B.C.), containing an inscription important for study of the language and history of ancient Israel.

MOABITE STONE, THE

Louvre. Because its language is closely related to biblical Hebrew and its script belongs to the same tradition as the earliest Hebrew documents, the inscription is an important source for the study of the language and writing system of ancient Israel as well as the history of the ninth century B.C.

The stele is dedicated to Chemosh, the god of Moab, in gratitude for Mesha's triumph over his enemies. Speaking in the first person, the king recounts his successes and achievements, beginning with the liberation of Moab from Israelite domination. He boasts of the recovery and rebuilding of the region of Medeba, which had been conquered by Omri, and the capture of nearby Israelite cities. Among the building projects recorded are those in Karhoh, the district of Dibon in which the monument was erected.

A small fragment of a second Moabite stone was found in Kerak, Jordan, in 1958. Its three incomplete lines show that it, too, was a royal inscription of the mid-ninth century B.C., probably another monument left by Mesha. The text reads: (1) [I, Mesha, son of Che]moshyat, king of Moab, the [Dibonite. . . .] (2) Chemosh *for grazing land*, because [. . .] (3) [. . .] him. And behold, I made the [. . .]. P.K.M.

THE MOABITE STONE:
A TRANSLATION OF ITS TEXT

(line 1) I, Mesha, son of Chemosh[yat], king of Moab, the
(2) Dibonite (my father reigned over Moab for thirty years and I reigned
(3) after my father)—I made this high place for Chemosh in Karhoh [. . .]
(4) because he saved me from all the kings and caused me to triumph over all who opposed me.
(5) Omri, king of Israel, oppressed Moab for many years, because Chemosh was angry with his land.
(6) When his son succeeded him, he too said, "I shall oppress Moab." In my days he spoke *this way*,
(7) but I triumphed over him and his house, and Israel was utterly destroyed forever. Omri took possession of the entire land
(8) of Medeba, and [Israel] lived there during his days and half the days of his son—forty years; but
(9) Chemosh restored it in my days. I built Baal-meon, making a cistern in it, and I built
(10) Kiryathaim. The men of Gad had lived in the land of Ataroth since ancient times, and the king of Israel had built
(11) Ataroth for them; but I fought against the city and captured it, slaying all the people of
(12) the city *for the satisfaction of* Chemosh and Moab. I brought back from there *the altar-hearth of its beloved [god]*,
(13) dragging it before Chemosh in Kerioth, and I settled men of Sharon and men of
(14) Maharith there. Then Chemosh said to me, "Go capture Nebo from Israel!"
(15) So I went by night and fought against it from the break of dawn until noon. I captured
(16) it and slew them all—seven thousand men, boys, women, girls,
(17) and maidservants—for I had devoted it to Ashtar-Chemosh. I took from there *the utensils*
(18) of Yahweh, dragging them before Chemosh. The king of Israel had built
(19) Jahaz, and he lived there while he was fighting against me. But Chemosh drove him out before me.
(20) I took from Moab two hundred men, all its poor citizens, and exalted them in Jahaz; I took possession of it in order
(21) to annex it to Dibon. It was I who built Karhoh, both the forest wall and
(22) the summit wall; it was I who built its gates and I who built its towers;
(23) it was I who built the palace and I who made both the reservoirs for water inside
(24) the town. There were no cisterns inside the town at Karhoh, so I said to the people, "Each of you make
(25) a cistern for himself and his house!" Also, it was I who cut *beams* for Karhoh using
(26) Israelite captives. It was I who built Aroer; it was I who made the highway in the Arnon;
(27) and it was I who built the high-place temple, for it had been torn down. It was I who built Bezer—for it was in ruins.
(28) [. . .] the men of Dibon armed for battle, for all Dibon is (my) bodyguard. I made
(29) one hundred [. . .] reign as kings in the towns that I annexed to the land. It was I who built
(30) [. . .] Medeba, Beth-diblathaim, and Beth-baal-meon, where I exalted *the herdsmen*
(31) [. . .] *the sheep* of the land. As for Horonaim, [. . .] was living there [. . .]
(32) [. . .]. Then Chemosh said to me, "Go down and fight against Horonaim!" So I went down and [fought against it.
(33) I captured it, and] Chemosh restored it in my days [. . .]
(34) [. . .].

***Key-** [ ]: restored material at break in the stone; [. . .]: text missing; italic: translation of text uncertain; ( ): additions for English sense.*

Modein (moh'deen), the home of the Hasmonean family, about twenty-three miles northwest of Jerusalem (1 Macc. 2:1), where the Maccabean revolt began (1 Macc. 2:15, 24–35). ***See also*** Hasmoneans; Maccabees.

Modin (moh'deen). ***See*** Modein.

Moladah (moh'luh-duh), a city in southern Judah, mentioned with Beer-sheba (Josh. 19:2). It is listed as belonging to both the tribes of Judah (Josh. 15:26) and Simeon (1 Chron. 4:28). It probably originally belonged to Simeon and was then occupied by Judah as the tribe of Simeon was absorbed into Judah and lost its identity (see Gen. 49:7). The city was later occupied by Judahites returning from exile in Babylon (Neh. 11:26). The site is unknown.

mole, the term in the KJV for the RSV's "chameleon" in Lev. 11:30 but used in Isa. 2:20 for a burrowing rodent symbolic of a desolate habitat (with bats). The term designates burrowing animals of the family *Talpidae,* and the word in Isa. 2:20 may be the mole-rat, *Spalax typhlus,* a molelike burrowing rodent 6 to 9 inches long. It lives in darkness, like bats, but apart from the verse in Isaiah, the two are not usually associated.

Molech (moh'lek), the epithet of a deity to whom children were offered as sacrifices. That Molech is a deity, not the name of a type of offering, is clearly indicated by Lev. 20:5. Isa. 30:33 reveals that the word was originally "king" (Heb. *melech)* but was later given a pejorative vocalization *(molech)* from "shame" *(boshet).* Molech should not be identified with Milcom, an Ammonite god (Molech in 1 Kings 11:7 should probably be emended to "Milcom"; cf. vv. 5, 33 and 2 Kings 23:13). What god is intended by Molech is unclear since the title "king" *(melech)* can be used in many divine names. The names of the gods Adrammelech and Anammelech (2 Kings 17:31) to whom the Sepharvites offered their children by fire contain the element *melech* and may show more specifically what divinities were intended by Molech.

Children were dedicated ("passed over") and burned to Molech at the Tophet in the Valley of Hinnom near Jerusalem. This practice with Molech specifically mentioned is found in only four passages (Lev. 18:21; 20:2–5; 2 Kings 23:10; Jer. 32:35). This type of offering without mention of Molech is found abundantly elsewhere (Deut 12:31; 18:10; 2 Kings 16:3; 17:17, 31; 21:6; Jer. 7:31; 19:5; Ezek. 16:21; 20:26, 31; 23:37; 2 Chron. 28:3; 33:6).

Some scholars have suggested that the terms "passing over" children to Molech and "burning in fire" indicate a dedication of the children to the god's service rather than actual sacrifice. Jer. 19:5, however, calls such dedications "burnt offerings" and Ezek. 23:37–39 calls the act "slaughter" and says the children were given to the deity as food. Hence, offerings to Molech must be considered actual sacrifices (cf. Ps. 106:37–38).

This worship may be of Phoenician origin, but the connection is not entirely certain. Deuteronomy explains it as the custom of the indigenous population of Canaan. The Israelites practiced this type of worship from about 735 B.C. until about 575 B.C. The references to it in Jeremiah and Ezekiel show that Josiah's reforms did not entirely eradicate it. ***See also*** Cults; Syncretism; Worship. D.P.W.

molten metal, metal cast by being poured over a form or into a mold. The process was used for several components of Solomon's temple built by Hiram of Tyre, including the pillars, capitals, and basin known as the "molten sea" (1 Kings 7:15, 16, 23). The Bible describes several molten images used as idols (see Judg. 17:3–4; Isa. 40:19; Hos. 13:2), including most prominently the golden calf (Exod. 32). Worship of such objects, which the Bible associates particularly with Canaanite and Assyrian religions (Num. 33:52; Nah. 1:14), is prohibited to Israel (Exod. 20:4; Lev. 19:4; Deut. 27:15).

Money

A COMMODITY used as a medium of exchange or a designation of value. In the OT money took different forms including metals, goods, and livestock. In the Apocrypha and the NT coined money, legally authorized by governing bodies, became the standard of exchange for goods and services.

Money in the Ancient Near East: In Gen. 47:14–17 Joseph "gathered up all the money that was found in the land of Egypt and in the land of Canaan, for the grain" that was bought in time of famine. This "money" included metals in the form of wire, rings, ingots, or lumps and also cattle, horses, and other animals when metallic money was unavailable. Barter in commodities was just as acceptable as payment in precious metals.

The archaeological record in Israel shows that strata at most sites from the period ca. 1200–587 B.C. contain little evidence of metal coins used as money. Excavated metal objects from this period include armor, weapons, and jewelry. In this society, however, each piece of precious metal had monetary value, so that earrings, pins, and other adornments also functioned as money. Money took on many forms, moreover, including bar ingots, pieces of cut metal, wire, coils of wire, foil, and rings, as excavations throughout the entire Near East have shown.

Standards for weighing money varied from place to place. In Gen. 23:16, Abraham purchased a burying place from Ephron the Hittite for 400 shekels of silver, "according to the weights current among the merchants." The Babylonian standard was probably used in this transaction, because it was most commonly employed throughout the Near East in commerce between Mesopotamia, Syro-Palestine, and Egypt. This standard set 1 silver shekel equal to 8.25 grams and the following ratio was used: 1 talent = 60 minas = 3,600 shekels. This denominational division lasted into the Hellenistic period.

Ancient texts include receipts for goods sold in local and international commerce. For example, an ox would commonly cost 1 gold shekel, which was equal to 15 silver shekels or approximately 2 tons of grain. Solomon dealt in horses and chariots with the kings of the Hittites (Kue) and the kings of Aram (1 Kings 10:28–29); the horses were priced at 150 silver shekels and the chariots at 600 silver shekels. At this rate, four horses would purchase one chariot.

Origins of Coinage: Croesus, king of Lydia in the seventh century B.C., was probably the first to coin silver, gold, and electrum (an alloy of silver and gold) in weights recognized as legal tender. The earliest coins bore no inscriptions and did not circulate widely. Their use, however, spread to Persia by the mid-sixth century B.C. The silver *sigloi* of Darius the Great, which copied coins of east Greek manufacture, were used throughout Persian realms in the eastern Mediterranean.

Bronze coin with the name of Agrippa (I); minted in Jerusalem ca. A.D. 37–44, obverse.

A Babylonian *minna* from the reign of Nebuchadnezzar II.

A bronze coin minted by the Roman emperor Titus ca. A.D. 79–81 to commemorate the ending of the Jewish revolt; reverse. At the bottom left a mourning Jewish woman is depicted.

Persian gold *darics* were struck by the central government, while silver *sigloi* were struck by local satrapies.

Still, neighbors of the Greeks were slow to grasp the use of coinage. Weighed amounts of metal continued to facilitate trade in most of the large commercial centers. Minted metals initially benefited governing authorities rather than financiers or merchants. As trade increased and more wealth was attained, the functions of government changed and became more complex, requiring a greater number and kind of official transactions with the populace. Payment in coin greatly facilitated receipt of taxes, temple maintenance, payment of mercenaries and soldiers, and expenditures on public works. A conversion from bullion to coin, was, therefore, a conscious effort by local communities to simplify monetary transactions. Thus, coined metal at first remained near its origin and was used for particular governmental purposes. Soon, however, coins were traded like any other valuable objects. Differing weight standards among Babylonians, Persians, Phoenicians, and Greeks slowly merged in the fifth and fourth centuries B.C., until Alexander the Great established a single standard for all coinage used from Greece to India. Foreign trade and internal commerce were greatly enhanced by coined money but had little to do with its origins.

Money in the Old Testament: Biblical references to money include prices paid for land, prophetic injunctions against corruption in the marketplace, and obligations to the Temple. For example, after a woman gave birth to a child, there followed a purification period with the offering of "a lamb a year old . . . and a young pigeon or a turtledove . . . and [the priest making] atonement for her . . ." (Lev. 2:6–8). Such "temple taxes" were common in ancient Israel and elsewhere; the animals could be purchased with metals or in kind. Elaborate tariffs covered the range of services rendered by religious institutions; for instance, the Marseille Tariff inscription details costs in a Punic (Canaanite) setting of the fourth century B.C., which probably corresponded to an analogous Hebrew custom. The monies were used for priestly maintenance and upkeep of temples and related institutions.

Jehoash, king of Israel in the late ninth century B.C., institutionalized support for the temple using monies assessed to individuals and monies a man's heart prompted him "to bring into the house of the Lord." The priests were instructed (2 Kings 12:4–5) to use this money to repair the temple. The uncoined metals were probably collected, weighed, melted down into small ingots and measured according to royal standards. The ingots were used to pay the workmen.

From the time of the United Monarchy (ca. 1000 B.C.), the Israelites were assessed for government service in the army or in public works (1 Kings 5:13). There were also public taxes to pay the costs of government and foreign tribute exacted against the nation (2 Kings 23:35).

The Hebrew word usually used for "money" *(kesef)* literally means "silver." Silver was more common than gold, which had to be imported from Egypt or Anatolia, so most biblical transactions used silver. Achan reported to Joshua on spoils taken from Jericho (Josh. 7:21) including money in the form of rings and bars. The gold Job received from his family when his riches were restored (Job 42:11) also included

From left to right: Double shekel from Sidon, late fifth or early fourth century B.C., obverse; gold shekel from Tyre, early fourth century B.C., obverse and reverse; gold coin from Egypt, during the reign of Ptolemy IV, reverse.

rings. The use of coins in Syro-Palestine probably began under Persian influence after 539 B.C., when Babylon fell to the Persians. At the same time contact with coinage from Greek realms increased. Hebrew weights already carried denominational markings that were regulated by religious authorities to ensure against corruption and fraud (see Prov. 16:11; 11:1). It was only a short step then to the production of locally made coins as well.

By the late fifth century, more and more foreign currency appeared in markets in Gaza, Tyre, Sidon, and Jerusalem. When authorities struck coins, merchants found that they no longer had to weigh the "shekel" because the royal stamp verified its weight. Coins made trade simpler and more efficient. The Phoenician cities of Aradus, Byblos, Sidon, and Tyre struck coins before 400 B.C., while Gaza produced coins imitating Athenian issues by the early fourth century. As Persian control of the western provinces waned through the fourth century, Jewish authorities in Jerusalem and Samaria also began to strike small coins.

Silver drachma minted during Persian control of Palestine, fourth century B.C. The reverse (bottom) bears the Aramaic inscription *Yehud*, the name of the Persian satrapy of Judea.

No coins found in Palestine predate the late sixth century B.C. The necessity to coin money was resisted, especially inland from the port cities, where conservative usage of metal rings and bars persisted. In Ezra 2:68–69 the Israelites had not only rebuilt Jerusalem, but families made freewill offerings for the rebuilding of the Temple, giving the Treasury "sixty-one thousand darics of gold, five thousand minas of silver, and one hundred priests' garments." The daric was then the principal gold coin weighing 8.4 grams and punched with a die depicting the Persian king shooting a bow.

Before the end of the fourth century, Jewish authorities struck small silver coins with the approval of the Persian government. The coins read in Hebrew *yehud*, "Judah." Persian authorities later issued some similar coins themselves. The period 375–332 B.C. was a time of political upheaval; the Phoenician city-states led two abortive revolts that brought severe sanctions upon local rulers, including the revocation of minting privileges. That necessitated the issue of coins with "ethnics" (i.e., phrases that indicate which country minted the coin) in Aramaic—the Persian diplomatic language—rather than Phoenician or Hebrew, since Persian satrapy officials assumed mint functions.

Most of the *yehud* coins were bronzes, struck between 360 and 332 B.C. One example bears the name of *yehizqiyyah*, high priest when Alexander the Great came to Jerusalem in 332 B.C. Another silver coin bears the name of *yohanan*, high priest in Samaria, a coin that may have

A bronze shekel of Tyre from the Hellenistic period; obverse.

been struck in defiance of Persia ca. 340 B.C. during the last revolt.

Money in the Apocrypha: After 332/331 B.C., no coins were struck in Palestine, except in official mints of Alexander the Great at Akko and Tyre, until the Maccabean revolt, when in 168 B.C. Jews again won minting rights. Under Alexander Yannai (Gk., Ioanaeus), Maccabean leader 103–76 B.C., coins were struck in Jerusalem with the obverse showing a flower (probably a lily) and the "ethnic" *yehonatan hammelek,* "Jonathan the King"; on the reverse was an anchor with the Greek inscription, *basileos alexandrou,* "belonging to Alexander the King." These coins, struck in lead and bronze, functioned as small change, with larger coins produced in other Hellenistic mints. Jonathan later overstruck his coins, altering the title "king" to "high priest and friend of the Jews," for he was not of David's line and some argued that

COINS OF THE BIBLICAL WORLD

Name	*Approximate Date*	*Metal*	*Weight in Grams**	*Equivalent*
Double-*shekel* of Sidon	400 B.C.	silver	27.50	
Shekel of Tyre	370 B.C.	silver	13.90	
Persian *daric*	500–340 B.C.	gold	8.42	
Hebrew *shekel* (light standard)	550–350 B.C.	silver	8.25	
Yehud coin	350–250 B.C.	silver	0.70–0.10	
Hebrew *shekel*	A.D. 30	gold	16.36	15 silver *shekels*
Jewish *shekel*	A.D. 67	silver	14.54	
Jewish *mina*		silver	727.00	50 *shekels*
Jewish talent		silver	43,620.00	60 *minas*
Roman *denarius*	A.D. 30	silver	3.64	
Quadrans of Roman procurators	A.D. 30	bronze	2.10	
Jewish *peruta*	A.D. 30	bronze	1.05	
Greek *lepton*	A.D. 30	bronze	0.57	
Judea Capta didrachm (Roman issue from mint of Caesarea)	A.D. 70	silver	7.27	

*Weights often vary from coin to coin of the same type.

A bronze coin minted at Jerusalem ca. 37–34 B.C. during the reign of Herod the Great; obverse (top) and reverse.

he had no right to the throne. The other Hasmonean rulers continued to issue coins in bronze supplementing Alexandrine issues until Rome seized power in 37 B.C.

Money in the New Testament: Herod the Great issued coins on Roman standards with the inscription (in Greek) *herodou basileos,* "belonging to Herod the king." He began the practice of dating his coins, which were made in Jerusalem and Tiberias. Concurrently, Roman procurators coined money locally to supplement imperial coinage, which came principally from Rome, Alexandria, and Antiochia. Local coins were the small change. Their types depicted neutral symbols like grapes or a cornucopia, nonreligious symbols that would not anger the Jewish populace, even though Romans preferred religious emblems on coins. Antiochia and Caesarea in Cappadocia supplied Judea with their large silver coins, including the denarius mentioned in the NT. It was the usual salary paid to a laborer for one day's work (Matt. 20:2). It was also the Temple tax in Jesus' time and was probably the coin referred to in Matt. 22:21, "Render therefore to Caesar the things that are Caesar's," since a likeness of the emperor appeared on the obverse. The Temple tax increased to a half-shekel (2 denarii) following the revolt of A.D. 66–70.

A shekel of the Bar Kochba revolt, ca. A.D. 132–135; reverse.

It is impossible to estimate in modern terms the value of these ancient coins. The KJV translators used English designations such as "farthing" and "penny," but these are misleading and provide only a relative guide to the coins' values. The coins paid to Judas Iscariot (Matt. 26:15) were probably silver shekels from Tyre or Antiochia. Thirty pieces (approximately equal to 120 denarii) were considered compensation ("blood money") for an accidentally slain servant in Exod. 21:32. The "widow's mite" was a Greek *lepton* (Mark 12:42), the coin of least value then in circulation. It was half a Roman *quadrans* or Jewish *peruta*, and would have been smaller than a U.S. dime. Any of these coins, ranging in size from 8 to 40 millimeters in diameter, could have been used in Jerusalem in A.D. 30. The cosmopolitan nature of the city rendered exchange of funds a complex matter.

The money changer's role was significant because he served as financier and banker, often sitting at the gate of the city or a building (like the Temple) to perform the exchanges required for commerce. When a money changer exchanged Antiochian tetradrachms for local shekels, a fee of 4 to 8 percent was exacted. When adult males came to the Temple to pay their half-shekel Temple tax, rabbinic instruction insisted that it be paid in silver didrachms of Tyre. The money changers were needed to complete the transaction. According to the Mishnah (*Šeqal.* 1:3) this tax was collected in the month preceding Passover and for twenty days immediately before the feast in the Temple precincts themselves. When Jesus "cleansed the Temple" (Matt. 21: 12–13; Mark 11:15; Luke 19:45–46), money changers may have been collecting this tax for the public welfare. Money changers sometimes cheated when assisting in transactions selling sacrificial animals. Rabbi Simeon reduced the number of obligatory sacrifices (*Ker.* 1:7) in an attempt to eliminate this fraud in the mid-first century A.D. Money changers also functioned as bankers, paying interest on held deposits, even when contrary to Jewish laws against usury (*Šeqal. 1:6.)*.

Silver shekel from the revolt against Rome, with Hebrew inscription. *Top:* "Jerusalem the Holy." *Bottom:* "Shekel of Israel sh[nat] g[imel]" ("year three," i.e., A.D. 68).

In the later first century, Roman coinage was interrupted by a Jewish revolt from A.D. 66 to 70. Coins were struck with the Hebrew legend *shekel israel*, "shekel of Israel." Issued on the Athenian standard, the reverse depicted three pomegranates and the words *yerushalayim qadesha*, "Jerusalem is holy." When the Romans put down the revolt, Vespasian and Titus authorized commemorative coins with the Latin inscription *judaea capta*, "Judah is captured."

Coins found today by archaeologists are very helpful in dating levels at a site because of the "ethnics" and dates on the coins. Each coin has its own history, which illuminates biblical history and life in Jewish and early Christian communities.

See also Weights and Measures. J.W.B.

money-changers. ***See*** Money.

monogamy. ***See*** Marriage.

monotheism, the belief that there is only one deity. Most major religions of the biblical world were polytheistic: they had many deities. Israel was exceptional for its emphatic recognition of one God only. This was an essential affirmation of Judaism and part of the foundation of Christianity.

In Ancient Israel: It is not clear how Israel's monotheism originated. Certain trends in Egyptian religion of the second millennium B.C. tended to universalize one single deity, and theoretically these could have influenced Moses; but the wide difference in character between these phenomena and the God of Israel counts against their relevance. It is not intrinsically probable that external religious developments inspired this aspect of Israelite faith. Nor is it easy to see how monotheism could have evolved out of an earlier polytheism by some process of selection and rejection; there are not really enough texts to demonstrate this. It has often been argued that some historical experience, such as deliverance from Egypt, led Israel to recognize Yahweh as the uniquely active and saving deity. Yet no texts depict this event as a sudden or cataclysmic passage from faith in many gods to faith in one.

It seems more natural to consider Hebrew monotheism as primitive but originally tribal. From the earliest relevant times there were Israelite groups for whom it was natural or axiomatic that a people had one deity who was their special god. This may not have been unique; the Moabites may have been similar. The groups in Israel that early insisted zealously on one God may have been small; traditions of the early Levites and the Kenites are a probable trace. Eventually the logic of monotheism succeeded in imposing itself upon the nation through dominant religious traditions. It came to be hardly thinkable that a Jew would be other than a monotheist.

Biblical monotheism was group-centered and practical rather than theoretical. It did not prevent the occasional speaking of other gods as if they existed or had control of other lands or peoples (e.g., Exod 12:12; Num. 33:4; Josh. 24:15; Judg. 10:6). Elements of their mythology continued to be used. Names used for them were used for the true God also; but the proper and most used term for Israel's God was his personal name, Yahweh. Monotheism had an element of zealotry, insisting fiercely on the oneness of God and his name. And, considered seriously, this reduced other gods to nonentities, with no power or reality.

Polytheism of some kind, especially perhaps in the form of a female consort for Yahweh, continued to attract many in Israel, and polemic against it in the Bible was continual (e.g., Judg. 6:30–32; Isa. 27:9). It was attacked as being foreign (Jer. 5:19), as a return to the old Canaanite gods (Judg. 10:6–9), as being linked with repellent ritual, sexual, and moral practices (Hos. 4:12–13), as being associated with the worship of objects of wood and stone (Isa. 44:9–17), and as having brought historical disaster on the people (Mic. 1:2–7). Above all, the ethical demands of Yahwistic religion were made to depend on the requirement of monotheism. These elements are especially interlinked in Deuteronomy, probably a reform document that unites the oneness of God (cf. the all-essential *Shema* of Deut. 6:4) with the insistence on the one and only holy place. Isaiah 40–55 combines a strong emphasis on monotheism with a stress on the role of the one God as creator of the world and ruler of all its parts. Polytheism is continually ridiculed, but in a way that suggests it is no longer deeply understood or felt as a serious temptation. After the return from Exile monotheism was scarcely challenged in Israel.

In the NT: In the NT the monotheistic convictions of Judaism are taken for granted. The "first of all the commandments" according to Jesus is the *Shema*, the affirmation of the oneness of God (Mark 12:29). The NT Letters also emphasize the oneness of God (1 Cor. 8:6; Eph. 4:6; 1 Tim. 2:5) and correlate it with the one Lord or mediator and the one faith and baptism. The term "God" is applied to Jesus only rarely and with reserve; in the synoptic Gospels this is true also of "Son of God." Jewish opponents are not represented as criticizing Christianity for abandoning monotheism. Nevertheless the close association of Jesus with God seems to lead toward the seeing of monotheism in a different way, wherein deity has inner distinction as well as unity. The implications of this are not yet worked out within the NT and only beginnings toward an answer are presented. ***See also*** Polytheism. J.B.

months. ***See*** Time.

moon, the earth's natural satellite. In the Bible, the moon is perceived in several ways. Gen. 1:16 records that the moon, called the lesser light, was created to shine at night as a counterpart to the greater light, the sun, which shines during the day. Pss. 8:3 and 136:9 describe the moon as part of God's handiwork. As a marker of the night sky, it is described in Jer. 31:35. It is viewed as a symbol of permanence in Pss. 72:5; 89:38; 121:6; and Heb. 3:11. Along with the sun and the stars, the moon bows down to Joseph in his dream in Gen. 37:9. Joshua commands the sun and moon to stop in their courses during his encounter with the Amorites (Josh. 10:12, 13).

Apocalyptic references to the moon are numerous and speak of it as an object that will darken because God's light, a metaphor for his rule, will be everlasting (Isa. 60:19, 20; Job 25:5; Eccles. 12:2; Ezek. 32:7). Joel (3:4) prophesies that the moon will turn to blood before the coming of the Messiah. Similarly, in the Mesopotamian conception, an eclipse of the moon was taken as a portent of evil.

In the NT, the moon is also viewed as a herald of the Messiah (Mark 13:24; Luke 21:25; Acts 2:16–21). In Rev. 21:23, the moon is seen as superfluous since the Lamb will light Jerusalem.

Terms: Hebrew has two terms for moon: *yareakh* and *levonah*. The first is a common Semitic term, appearing as *yrkh* in Phoenician and as *arkhu* in Akkadian, where it is also the usual word for "month" or one lunation. *Yerakh* also means month in Hebrew.

Levonah is a derivative of "white." In most biblical references, *levonah* is used in parallelism to *shemesh*, "sun," to describe the brilliant luminosity of the moon (Song of Sol. 6:10; Isa. 30:26). But in Isa. 24:23, *levonah* is used in parallelism to *bosh*, "shame," to evoke an image of colorlessness accompanying embarrassment.

In referring to the new month, the biblical author uses the term "new, renewal" (Heb. *khodesh*) rather than either of the standard terms for moon. Terms for the lunar crescent refer specifically to the first and fourth crescents.

Calendar: The calendar employed by the Hebrews of the OT was based entirely on observation. The determination of years was based on solar observations, whereas months were determined by lunar observations. Only the festivals Passover and Sukkoth are celebrated at the approach of the full moon. These holidays come as close as is possible in the luni-solar system to marking the vernal and autumnal equinoxes, respectively. Of all the months, only the beginning of Tishri (Sept.–Oct.) was singled out as a special day. The biblical text does not use the term "head of the year" (Heb. *rosh hashanah*) for it. Tashritu, the corresponding month in the Babylonian calendar, was similarly treated.

According to early rabbinic sources, the new moon was originally fixed by proclamation of witnesses regarding the reappearance of the moon's crescent. If the crescent had not been sighted on the thirtieth day of the month, the new moon was proclaimed for the thirty-first day. Beacons were kindled on the Mount of Olives to mark the arrival of the new moon crescent. This system was extended throughout the Diaspora until the Samaritans began to light misleading beacons to confuse the calendar and the observance of the new moon. The high court countered this attack on rabbinic authority by sending messengers to remote communities with the announcement of the new moon.

Worship: Pronouncements against worshiping the moon, decried as pagan practice, are issued in Deut. 4:19 and 17:3. 2 Kings 23:5 records Josiah's command to the high priest, Hilkiah, to eliminate worship of the moon. Isa. 1:14 ("your new moons and your appointed feasts my soul hates") condemns misuse of the cult, including new moon rituals; though it is possible that specific paganizing practices are alluded to.

In spite of these denunciations, evidence for cultic celebration of lunar phases is found in the biblical text. Num. 28:11–15 preserves a ritual calendar that details monthly offerings for the moon. This passage is still read in traditional synagogues on the Sabbath when the new moon is pronounced. Num. 10:10 and Ps. 81:4 instruct the population to sound the horn at the new moon as a way of offering praise to God. The new moon is celebrated by David and Jonathan (1 Sam. 20). Remnants of lunar celebration are evidenced in the celebrations and gatherings in the historical passages in 1 Chron. 23:31; 2 Chron. 8:13; 31:3; Ezra 3:5; and Neh. 10:33. Most of these include mention of the Sabbath. It appears that at the time of the new moon, all commerce was halted (Amos 8:5) and the prophet was not consulted (2 Kings 4:23).

The importance of the moon in worship in the ancient world varied in degree and by location. In Mesopotamia, lunar worship was already firmly established by the beginning of recorded history. Records from lunar cult observances taking place in the chapel of the *ur-sakar*, "new moon crescent," date to 2400 B.C. New moon festival offerings are attested at pre-Sargonic Lagash and Sargonic Nippur. In the Neo-Sumerian period (2100–2000 B.C.), lunar festivals were regularized with observances marking the first, second, and fourth quarters of the moon. A fourth festival occurring on the twenty-fifth day of the month, and not corresponding to a lunar phase, was added in the early second millennium B.C. The lunar festivals survived well into the first millennium B.C., when as many as eight festivals were observed in the course of one lunation.

Two important Mesopotamian centers for moon worship, Ur and Harran, figure prominently in the patriarchal narratives. Ur was the homeland of Abraham's father, Terah. After leaving Ur, the family went to Harran, where Terah died (Gen. 11:31, 32). The city god of both Ur and Harran was called Nanna in Sumerian, Sin (Su'en) in Akkadian. His headdress consisted of four pairs of horns topped by a crescent moon. The crescent resembled a boat, and Nanna was sometimes called the "shining boat of Heaven." His sphere of activity is hard to define. He is seen as a wise god, the originator of life, the leader and guardian of humankind and the lord of destinies. He is considered the father of the sun god. His consort is known as Ningal, "great lady" in Sumerian, and as Nikkal in Aramaic and Phoenician. The text "Nikkal and the Kathirat" relates the marriage of Nikkal to Yarikh, as the moon god was known in Ugaritic.

The names of two ancient Israelite cities, Beth Yerakh and Jericho (Heb. *Yerikho*) are derived from a word for moon and probably indicate the existence of lunar worship at those sites at some early—presumably Canaanite (cf. the god Yarikh)—period. ***See also*** Feasts, Festivals, and Fasts. L.E.P.

Mordecai (mohr'duh-kī; from Akkadian *Marduk, Merodach*). **1** One of the exiles who returned to Jerusalem with Zerubbabel (Ezra 2:2; Neh. 7:7; 1 Esd. 5:8). **2** The hero of the book of Esther. Mordecai raised his orphaned cousin Esther and enabled her to become the queen of King Ahasuerus of Persia. But Mordecai aroused the anger of the king's vizier, Haman, by refusing to bow down to him. Haman therefore plotted to have Mordecai and all the Jews of Persia killed in revenge. Mordecai prompted Esther to appeal to Ahasuerus to spare her people. Ahasuerus, who had belatedly honored Mordecai for saving his life, was outraged to learn of the plot. He ordered Haman's execution and allowed the Jews to destroy their enemies. This deliverance is now celebrated in the Jewish festival of Purim, called the "Day of Mordecai" in 2 Macc. 15:36. Noting the historical problems the book raises, scholars consider the story of Esther to be fictitious. While this view is undoubtedly correct, the identification of an official named Marduka in the court of King Xerxes I (485–465 B.C., generally identified as Ahasuerus) suggests to some a potential historical basis for the existence of Mordecai. ***See also*** Esther; Haman; Purim, The Feast of. M.A.S.

Mordecai, astride a horse, being conducted by Haman through the open square of the city as told in Esther 6:1–11; panel at the third-century A.D. synagogue at Dura-Europos.

Moreh (moh'ruh; Heb., "teacher, oracle-giver"; in positive sense, sometimes of God), a place name, suggesting a location for divine instruction—an activity often connected to prominent trees. **1** The terebinth (a large tree resembling an oak) at the sacred site near Shechem where Abram built an altar commemorating God's appearance to him (Gen. 12:6–7; note a fine wordplay between *moreh* and *nir'eh*, "appear"). Deut. 11:30 uses it as a landmark for the Gerizim-Ebal pass; in Gen. 35:4 (here: "oak"), it is probably where Jacob buried idols near Shechem. The Diviners' Oak in Judg. 9:37 may also designate this tree, here with a negative connotation ("divining" was forbidden in Israel, Deut. 18:10, 14, and elsewhere). Trees in Josh. 24:26 and Judg. 9:6 were inside Shechem; the Moreh tree lay outside. **2** Moreh Hill—again suggesting a place to receive oracles—the extinct volcano opposite Mount Gilboa at the east extremity of the Jezreel plain, where Midian encamped against Gideon's forces (Judg. 7:1). ***See also*** Ebal; Gerizim; Oak; Terebinth. E.F.C.

Moriah (moh-rī'ah). **1** An unidentified site in rugged terrain three days' travel from Beer-sheba where Abraham was to sacrifice Isaac (Gen. 22:2). **2** The rocky hill in Jerusalem where Solomon built the Temple (2 Chron. 3:1), a possibly deliberate cross-identification by the Chronicler with David's purchased threshing floor (2 Sam. 24:18–25). In that way the Temple, built on land belonging to David, could be associated with him, even if he was not allowed to build it (2 Sam. 7).

morsel (KJV: "sop"), a fragment or piece, usually of bread. In lieu of eating utensils small pieces of bread were the primary means of conveying food from bowl to mouth. Eating from the same bowl involved the participants in a covenant-like friendship. To "break bread together" and then betray the friendship was universally acknowledged as contemptible (Ps. 41:9; Matt. 26:23; Mark 14:18–20; John 13:18–30). That is why Judas's betrayal of Jesus was an especially grievous offense. Whether Jesus offered to Judas a special morsel ("this morsel," John 13:26) or simply a morsel is uncertain.

mortar. **1** The grinding vessel in which a pestle was the crushing instrument (Prov. 27:22; Num. 11:8). Archaeological examples of stone mortars range from large grain grinders to delicate spice and cosmetic versions. **2** The sealer between courses of stone or brick, whether a natural material like bitumen (Gen. 11:3) or a prepared compound (Exod. 1:14). A hint of the preparatory process as trampling is reflected in Isaiah's metaphoric reference (Isa. 41:25), and Jeremiah's oracle against Egypt used stones buried under mortar as a figure for the successful Babylonian conquest of the land (Jer. 43:9). Nahum 3:14 sees treading mortar as a preparation for defense, and Zephaniah uses it as a proper noun for a location in Jerusalem where silver traders functioned (1:11). Its precise location is uncertain, though the upper Tyropoeon Valley has been suggested. Archaeological evidence for mortar includes examples of mud, bitumen, and plaster compounds. R.S.B.

mortgage. ***See*** Loan.

mosaic (moh-zay'ik), a decoration made by inlaying small pieces of different colored materials (such as tile, stone, glass, or marble) to form patterns or pictures. Mosaic inlays from ancient times can be found on floors, walls, and even furniture.

The earliest known mosaics have been found in lower Mesopotamia and date to the fourth millennium B.C. These patterns, called cone mosaics, were formed by placing small painted

A mosaic dating to ca. 400 on the floor of the church at Tabgha commemorates the miracle of Jesus feeding the multitude (Matt. 15:32–38).

cone-shaped tiles into mud plaster on walls. Designs of triangles, diagonals, chevrons, and zigzags were formed. These early mosaics may well have been intended to imitate carpets and wall tapestries. The Sumerians from this same region used mosaics also to decorate musical instruments, game boards, and furniture.

Apparently the Hebrews of the OT era made very little use of mosaics, although some ivory inlay pieces that might be considered mosaics have been recovered from the excavation of Samaria. In Palestine mosaics became more prominent during the Roman-Herodian period (40 B.C.–A.D. 44). Beautiful examples of Herodian mosaics have been uncovered at Masada and in recent excavations of the old Jewish quarter of Jerusalem.

Mosaics reached their peak as an art form during the Byzantine period (A.D. 324–632). Both Jewish synagogues and Christian churches were richly decorated with mosaics during this era. The Madeba map, a map of the Holy Land found in Madeba, Jordan, originally contained one and a half million cubes.

In Ravenna, Italy, the churches of St. Apollinarius and St. Vitalis preserve magnificent sixth-century Byzantine mosaics. The Dome of the Rock, built by the Ummayad conquerors of Jerusalem in A.D. 691, is covered with mosaics inside and outside. It is an excellent example of early Arab mosaic art. J.F.D.

Moses, the first and preeminent leader of the Israelites, who led the people out of Egypt to the threshold of the promised land; he is also the lawgiver and the archetypical prophet. He is the dominant individual character in the OT narrative from Exodus through Deuteronomy. The text speaks of him in superlatives: "And there has not arisen a prophet since in Israel like Moses, whom the Lord knew face to face" (Deut. 34:10). For all his greatness, however, Moses never loses his humanness, displaying anger, frustration, and lack of self-confidence in addition to his leadership abilities, humility, and perseverance.

Birth and Family Background: The first information readers are given about Moses concerns his birth, in secret, to an unnamed Levite couple (Exod. 2:1–10). Because of the Egyptian decree to kill all newborn Hebrew males, the child was first hidden by his mother and then cast adrift on the Nile in a watertight container. As his sister watched a short distance away, Pharaoh's daughter found him, whereupon the sister stepped forward to suggest an appropriate nurse for the infant—none other than his natural mother. Thus the child was raised by his own mother and then returned to Pharaoh's daughter who adopted him and named him Moses (Heb. *mosheh),* which the Bible explains as meaning "Because I drew [from the root *mashah,* 'to draw'] him out of the water" (Exod. 2:10). (But the name may actually be an Egyptian one meaning "is born"; cf. the last component of Egyptian names like Thutmose, Ahmose, etc.)

This story resembles folktales found throughout the world of babies who averted ordained death, were hidden or raised by surrogate parents, and returned or emerged to play a major role in their societies. The closest analogy is "The Legend of Sargon," an Akkadian text that recounts the birth of Sargon of Agade. According to this text Sargon's mother bore him in secret, placed him in a basket of rushes sealed with pitch, and floated it down the Euphrates.

Moses leading the Israelites safely across the Red Sea and the Egyptians caught in the water; page from the tenth-century *Paris Psalter*.

It was found by Akki, the drawer of water, who raised the child as his own. The goddess Ishtar protected the child and he grew up to become a great king. The existence of such a story suggests that Exod. 2:1–10 is not to be regarded as historical, but rather as a conventional motif—a story of a special birth. The Bible's more usual special-birth motif involves a "barren mother," i.e., a woman who had difficulty conceiving but finally gave birth to a special child (cf. the birth stories of Isaac, Jacob, Joseph, and Samuel). But since Exodus 1–2 stresses the fertility of the Israelite women and the increase of the Israelite population, a "barren mother" story would have been out of place here. So instead a different type of special-birth story occurs.

The legendary quality of the story is further emphasized by the fact that none of the characters is named (except Moses). It is from Exod. 6:20 (cf. Num. 26:59; 1 Chron. 6:3; 1 Chron. 23:13) that we know that Moses' father was Amram, his mother Jochebed. His brother Aaron, older by three years, is first mentioned in Exod. 4:14, then in Exod. 6:20, and his age is given in Exod. 7:7. Miriam, the sister, is omitted from the genealogy in Exod. 6:20 but is named in the ones in Num. 26:59 and 1 Chron. 6:3.

Nothing is known of Moses' childhood. He reemerges as a young man who identified himself with his brethren, the enslaved Israelites. In an attempt to protect one of them he killed an Egyptian and was forced to flee Egypt. He sojourned in Midian, married Zipporah, a daughter of Jethro (also called Jether, Reuel, and Hobab), a Midianite priest. Their first son was Gershom (Exod. 2:22); a second son, Eliezer, is mentioned in Exod. 18:3–4 (cf. 1 Chron. 23:15).

Moses as Prophet: It is in his role as prophet that Moses stands out above all others. The verse cited in the opening paragraph, Deut. 34:10, refers to this aspect of him, as does Num. 12:7 and others. The contact between God and Moses was closer and more direct than between God and any other prophet.

Moses' Call: Apparently unprepared for his prophetic mission, Moses' attention was caught by a burning bush. Slowly his reaction changed from curiosity to awe as he realized that he was in God's presence (Exod. 3:1–6). Yet Moses was reluctant to accept the task of bringing the Israelites out of Egypt and gave a series of excuses for which God provided retorts ranging from assurances of God's help to the appointing of Aaron as Moses' assistant. Although initial reluctance is typical of a number of prophets, e.g., Jeremiah, and in an extreme form, Jonah, the picture we get of Moses here is a combination of humbleness and stubbornness.

Signs and Wonders: In addition to words of encouragement and the foretelling of future events, God gave Moses a sign to convince him that he was truly being commissioned (Exod. 3:12). Moses also received proofs for the Israelites and for the Egyptians that God had indeed sent him. To convince the Israelites Moses was told the name of God in the famous and difficult phrase "I am that I am" (Exod. 3:14; cf. also 6:3), and shown a series of wonders he will perform for them: changing a rod into a serpent and back to a rod again; making leprosy appear and disappear from his hand; and changing water into blood. The first of these wonders was also performed before Pharaoh; the last was transformed into the first of the ten plagues.

The plagues themselves (Exod. 7–11) can be construed as signs—proof to the Egyptians of God's superior power. They also served as a form of punishment to Pharaoh and his people for having dealt harshly with the Israelites. It is not only Moses who performed wonders; Aaron was sometimes the one to set the plague in motion through his action, as in the first, second, and third plagues. Both Moses and Aaron threw soot towards the sky, bringing the plague of boils. Moses himself brought the hail, the locusts, and the darkness by stretching his hand or rod upward. Even the Egyptian magicians were credited with some power to work wonders; they could duplicate some of the early wonders but apparently could not undo them. They could cause a rod to become a serpent, make water turn to blood, and produce frogs; but their serpent was swallowed by Aaron's, never to revert to a rod, and they could not remove the blood or the frogs. They recognized God's power, however, only when they were unable to duplicate his wonder—in the plague of gnats (or lice; Exod. 8:16–19).

Wonders may be harmful or beneficial. On the wilderness journey for the Israelites' benefit Moses divided the sea (Exod. 14:21–15:21), turned brackish water into sweet water (Exod. 15:22–25), and produced water from a rock (Exod. 17:1–7). His raised hands ensured victory over the Amalekites (Exod. 17:11–12). In the book of Numbers it is recounted that Moses provided the people with meat (11:1–35) and with fresh water (20:2–11).

Many of these wonders resemble the wonders of other prophets, e.g., Elijah and Elisha. It should be stressed that in all of these cases the power to perform wonders does not originate with the individual, nor is it the result of magical manipulations (as in the case of the Egyptian magicians); the power to work wonders comes from God. It is he who causes the wonder through his human agent. Thus it is God who dictates the action and God who enables it to be accomplished. Some of the plagues and the provisioning of Israel in the wilderness are achieved by God directly, without any actions on the part of Moses or Aaron (e.g., the swarm of flies in Exod. 8:20; the quails and the manna in Exod. 16:13); others are initiated by a specific human gesture. But even in the latter case God is at work behind the scenes, as is evident from Exod. 9:23: "Then Moses stretched forth his rod toward heaven; and the Lord sent thunder and hail . . ." (cf. also Exod. 10:13; 14:21).

Spokesman and Intercessor: A prophet functions mainly as a spokesman, a "forthteller." Ironically it is the power to speak well that Moses initially claimed to lack, so he could therefore not be effective as a spokesman before Pharaoh. As a concession, God appointed Aaron to be a spokesman for Moses, even as Moses was a spokesman for God (Exod. 4:14–16; 7:1). Yet the man who was "slow of speech" is credited with the magnificent speeches of Deuteronomy as well as with all manner of discourse in the Exodus–Numbers narrative. At times it becomes difficult to distinguish between the roles of Moses and Aaron, as both speak and perform actions. We will, therefore, refer to Moses in the following discussion even though it is sometimes Aaron who actually does the talking.

Moses spoke for God to the Israelites and to Pharaoh. His first task was to persuade the Israelites that he was truly God's representative, and it is to this end that Aaron performed the signs that God had provided to Moses. The brothers were successful; the people believed them. Yet later, after the Egyptians had increased their workload and made conditions harsher, the people lost confidence in their leader and Moses complained to God that he would never be able to convince Pharaoh to do what he requested if he could not convince even the Israelites (Exod. 6:12). Despite this weak beginning, Moses and Aaron went again and again to Pharaoh to deliver God's message. And, since the channel of communication operated in both directions, Moses relayed Pharaoh's wishes to God. When Pharaoh pleaded for the removal of the frog plague, Moses entreated God and the frogs were removed. The same occurred in the case of the flies, the hail, and the locusts.

It is, of course, to the Israelites that Moses was sent as prophetic spokesman, and it is to them that he continually conveyed God's commands. These ranged from information about the journey, encouragement, and chastisement, to instructions on how to collect the manna. In fact, everything that Moses said can be viewed as emanating from God. This applies to Moses' most important discourse: the giving of the law. The giving of the law is an aspect of Moses' prophetic function.

As he did in the case of Pharaoh, Moses served as the link between the Israelites and God; he interceded with God on behalf of the people. The first occurrence is in Exod. 5:22–23 after the Israelites' suffering had increased. A crucial intercession took place in the golden calf episode. Here Moses assuaged God's anger by suggesting that if God punished his people it would be construed by the Egyptians as a weakness on God's part—his inability to protect the Israelites in the wilderness. This, and a reminder of the promise made to Abraham, convinced God to withdraw his anger (Exod. 32:11–14). On another occasion when God's anger was manifest, the people cried to Moses to plead for them. When he prayed on their behalf they were spared (Num. 11:2). Even when Moses' own position was threatened—when the people wanted to stone him and appoint a new leader—Moses still reacted to God's anger at this by reminding him, as he had before, that the other nations would perceive the destruction of Israel as a weakness of God. Here, too, Moses was successful in obtaining at least a partial pardon (Num. 14). Other instances occur in Miriam's leprosy (Num. 12); Korah's rebellion (Num. 16); and the copper serpent incident (Num. 21).

Intercession is part of the prophetic aspect of Moses; he is a link between God and human beings. The most dramatic evidence of Moses as an intermediary occurred at Sinai. Moses had, already long before, been commissioned by God to represent him, but in Exod. 20:19 the people, fearing direct contact with the divine, commissioned Moses to represent them before God.

Moses indeed fulfilled his task as spokesman well, working to the benefit of God and the people. In fact, he is so often a spokesman for someone else that very often we lose sight of his own personal needs and desires. So apparently it must be with a prophet and a national leader.

Lawgiver and Judge: The law is a central feature of the Pentateuch and so the lawgiver assumes importance. It is Moses who gives the law, which originates from God, to Israel. As we have suggested above, the giving of the law need not be considered a separate function of Moses, but rather part of his prophetic function. Thus Moses brought the law engraved on tablets and proclaimed the laws and ordinances that constitute a significant part of Exodus, Leviticus, Numbers, and Deuteronomy. Even before the revelation at Sinai Moses instructed the people about the celebration of the Passover and the observance of the Sabbath.

On a more practical level, Moses served as judge and arbiter (this being a function of his role as national leader as well as interpreter of God's law). At first he was the sole judge, but at the suggestion of his father-in-law, Jethro, he instituted a system of lower judges for lesser matters; the difficult cases were brought to Moses (Exod. 18).

One such case involved the inheritance rights of Zelophehad's daughters. Since there was no precedent for daughters to inherit land, Moses consulted God. The response was that in the event that a man had no sons, his daughters should inherit his land so that his name and holdings might be perpetuated. God thus ruled in favor of the claim of Zelophehad's daughters (Num. 27). But in the sequel (Num. 36) the leaders of the tribe of Manasseh (Zelophehad's tribe) approached Moses with their concern: if the daughters were to marry men from other tribes, then the land would eventually be passed on to their children and thereby lost to the tribe of Manasseh. Thus the purpose of the original ruling would be thwarted; the land would be alienated from its original owner and tribe. Moses acknowledged the legitimacy of the concern of the Manasseh representatives and ruled that, while the daughters could inherit their father's land, they had to marry within their own tribe. Here we see the development of legal application in action. We also get some insight into the sensitivity with which Moses dealt with all parties concerned.

National Leader: Moses was sent to lead the people out of Egypt, and there is no question that he was a successful leader. He took a mixed multitude and under his guidance they were shaped into a national entity. Moses led the people from encampment to encampment and directed them when conflicts with other nations arose. Like most leaders, he was subjected to complaints and grumblings and even rebellions (e.g., Exod. 16), and he was called upon to provide solutions to problems and psychological encouragement.

Moses before the burning bush, loosening his sandal in response to God's command in Exod. 3:5; from the mosaics at the Monastery of St. Catherine, Sinai, sixth century A.D.

At times Moses himself appears discouraged, and this allows us to see him in a more human light. For instance, in Exod. 17:4, after complaints about water, Moses sought help from God saying, "What shall I do with this people?" Even more vivid is the portrayal of Moses' frame of mind in Numbers 11. Displeased with the people's actions and with God's anger, Moses felt that he had been made to appear at fault, and that his burden was too heavy for him. At this point God allowed the burden of leadership to be shared by seventy elders who received a measure of God's spirit.

It often happens that attacks on a leader come from those closest to him, and so it was with Moses. Resentment of his special bond with God was voiced by his own brother and sister (Num. 12), and a major rebellion was instigated by Korah, a member of Moses' own tribe (Num. 16). But with God's help Moses was able to weather these attacks on his position.

Death and Burial: Ironically, although Moses must certainly be judged successful in his mission, he himself was not permitted to partake of this success; he was not granted the privilege of entering the promised land but could only glimpse it from across the Jordan. At this crucial juncture a new leader, Joshua, was appointed by

God. When it was time for Moses to die, he ascended Mt. Nebo, in Moab, and, after viewing the future home of the Israelites, expired. The text records that "he," that is, God, buried Moses and that no person knows his burial place (Deut. 34:6). So, like his birth, Moses' death has a specialness attached to it. This is emphasized by the ideal lifespan, 120 years, and his lack of any signs of aging. In death, as in life, Moses was superior yet modest, singled out by God for special closeness yet never totally removed from his human context.

The Historicity of Moses: Our only source of knowledge about an individual named Moses is the Bible. Archaeology has not unearthed objects bearing his name, nor do ancient Near Eastern documents contain references to him. Therefore, judging his historicity, like the historicity of other early biblical figures, depends on one's view of the historicity of the Bible, especially the Pentateuch where the preponderance of Mosaic references are found. The historicity of the Pentateuch is a vexed question in biblical scholarship. Based on inconsistencies and doublets, scholars have isolated separate sources dating from different periods. Because some of the Moses stories show inconsistencies (e.g., in some of the wilderness narratives) or occur in doublets (e.g., intercessions in Exodus and Numbers), it is difficult to know which material is historically authentic, if any. Most scholars think that the most reliable references to Moses come from the J and E sources, the two earliest.

Some scholars have gone further and isolated four different themes or traditions connected with Moses: the exodus from Egypt, the revelation at Sinai, the wandering in the wilderness, and the entrance into the Promised Land. These themes, according to modern scholars like M. Noth and G. von Rad, originated in separate settings among various tribes and preserve different historical experiences. It would then seem doubtful that the same leader could have figured in all of them. According to this view there is a gap between the original themes/traditions and the picture presented even in the earliest sources of J and E.

This difficulty is refuted by those who suggest that even if the traditions developed independently, it is not impossible that Moses originally had a place in all of them. Each tradition developed differently, and so each developed a different view of Moses as well. Thus different aspects of the same person are preserved in different traditions.

Another problem is posed by some: in one of the earliest references to the Exodus, the poem in Exodus 15, Moses is not mentioned. By the same token, references to Moses outside of the Pentateuch (especially in prophetic and hymnic literature), even in connection with exodus or Sinai motifs, are relatively few. Thus the historicity of the man, as opposed to the events, is called into question. But this does not mean that Moses was actually a negligible or nonexistent person; it results simply from the fact that prophetic and hymnic literature is concerned with God and Israel, not with individuals, and therefore it highlights very few historical personages.

It is unlikely that a quick consensus will be reached concerning the historicity of the Pentateuch. Indeed, it might be better if this concern were replaced by concern for its literary and religious aspects. Here there is no need to rely on the hypothetical reconstruction of sources or traditions. The Pentateuch makes abundantly clear (and it is not contradicted by references elsewhere in the Bible), that there was one person who, at least from the point of view of Israel's literary-religious tradition, played a major role at the crucial point when the nation was born and its religious norms established. The importance of Moses, like the importance of all great national heroes, transcends his historicity.

Moses in the NT: Because of the towering significance of Moses as the mediator of God's law to the chosen people, it is not surprising that in the NT Moses is mentioned principally in connection with the law. That is true both in the Gospels (Matt. 19:7; Mark 7:10; Luke 16:31; John 1:17) and in the Letters of Paul (Rom. 9:15; 10:19; 1 Cor. 9:9; 2 Cor. 3:13). He is also citied as exemplary for his faith in God (Heb. 3:2; 11:24) and is regarded as having announced beforehand the coming of Jesus as Messiah (Acts 3:22; 26:22). Indeed, the traditions contained in the writings of the NT are unanimous in the estimation of Moses as one specially chosen by God to free God's people and give them God's law. ***See also*** Biblical Criticism; Exodus; Law; Sources of the Pentateuch; Prophet; Torah.

Bibliography

Buber, M. *Moses*. Oxford: East and West Library, 1946.

Childs, B. *The Book of Exodus*. Philadelphia: Westminster, 1974.

Neher, A. *Moses and the Vocation of the Jewish People*. New York: Harper & Row, Torchbooks, 1959.

A.B.

Moses, Assumption of. ***See*** Apocalyptic Literature; Pseudepigrapha.

Most High, the usual translation of a Hebrew adjective meaning "high" or "exalted" when applied to God. Taken from Canaanite culture (cf. Gen. 14:19–20), it became a popular name for God in the OT (e.g., Pss. 7:17; 21:7; 91:1), and, in Greek translation, appears also in the NT (e.g., Mark 5:7; Luke 1:32; Acts 7:48). ***See also*** God.

mote. ***See*** Speck.

moth, a term denoting any small, winged butterfly-like insect; in the Bible it always refers to the insects that eat clothes. As such, it is a symbol of decay and human frailty (Job 4:19; 13:28; Ps. 39:11; Isa. 50:9; 51:8; Hos. 5:12). In the NT, it is a symbol of the transitory nature of earthly riches (Matt. 6:19, 20; Luke 12:33; James 5:2).

mother. *See* Family, The; Marriage; and such individual entries as Athaliah; Deborah; Elizabeth; Hagar; Hannah; Mary; Rachel; Rebekah; Ruth; Sarah.

mount, mountain, a high land mass projecting above the surrounding area. Mountains are a dominant feature of the biblical landscape and accordingly have influenced greatly the way of life and beliefs of the ancient peoples inhabiting this land. Mountains have important effects upon the climate, population, economic life, and state of civilization of the region in which they occur, e.g., regions on their windward side have greater rainfall, while those on the leeward side are arid.

Mountain Chains in Palestine: In Palestine there are two formidable mountain chains. West of the Jordan River lie the great western highlands. This chain, running north-south, is an extension of the mountains of Lebanon and comprises three distinct ranges separated by plains and valleys: the Galilee, Ephraim and Judah, and in the south, the Negev. The Carmel mountains near Haifa are an east-west spur of this chain. East of the Jordan River, the eastern highlands rise even more precipitously above the Rift Valley, extending from Mt. Hermon in the north through biblical Gilead, Amman, and Moab to Edom in the south.

The north-south orientation of these mountains dictated the major routes of communication, i.e., the road system, which likewise, to a large extent, determined settlement patterns. Major trade routes spanned the country north-south forming a land bridge between the great empires of Egypt to the south and Syro-Mesopotamia to the north. This bridge facilitated the movement of trading caravans and of invading armies. East-west communication was limited to gaps between the mountain ranges.

Mountains are frequently referred to in the biblical text as dwelling places (Gen. 36:8), places of refuge (Gen.14:10; Judg. 6:2; Matt. 24:16), lookouts (Matt. 4:8), landmarks (Num. 34:7), assembly sites (Josh. 8:30–33; Judg. 9:7), military camps (1 Sam. 17:3), cemeteries (2 Kings 23:16), geographical boundaries (Josh. 15:8), places of ambush (Judg. 9:25), scenes of battle (1 Sam. 23:26), sanctuaries for the animal world (Ps. 11:1), pastures (Luke 8:32), and the habitat of goats (Ps. 104:18) and birds (1 Sam. 26:20).

The term "mount" is applied to an isolated mountain or a notable peak or specialized summit within a range, e.g., Mounts Ebal, Seir, Gerizim, Gilboa, Hermon, Nebo, Tabor, Sinai or Horeb, Carmel, Olives, Zion, and others. That

Mount Gilboa, 1696 feet above sea level, overlooks the Jezreel Valley.

each of these mounts has religious associations should come as no surprise, for throughout the ancient world mounts or mountains were imbued with religious significance and symbolism.

Sinai and Zion: Despite the injunctions against deifying mountains in Hebrew religion (Ezek. 18:6, 11, 15; Jer. 3:2, 6; Hos. 4:13)—God was to be worshiped exclusively without restriction to any specific location—sacred mountains are attested in the biblical text. Two mountains inextricably associated with God are Mount Sinai or Horeb and Mount Zion. It is on Mount Sinai where the covenant between God and Israel was sealed (Exod. 19:24), where Moses spoke to God (Exod. 19:3, 10; 24:9), and where God revealed his presence (19:16, 18). Mount Zion was another favored abode of God (Pss. 68:16; 84:5). These traditions clearly demonstrate the influence of Near Eastern mountain myth and specifically Canaanite mythology on Hebrew religion. Prior to the discovery of Ugaritic texts where Mount Zaphon, the sacred mountain of the Canaanite god Baal, is mentioned, the Hebrew word *Zaphon* was always translated "north." Now that we know the correct meaning of the word, we find that Mount Zion in Jerusalem is equated with Mount Zaphon: "Mount Zion in the far north" (Ps. 48:2, RSV) should read "Mount Zion is the heights of Zaphon." The use of Zaphon as a proper name clarifies other passages as well where sacred mountains are referred to, e.g., "Zaphon and Amana, thou has created, Tabor and Hermon joyously praise thy name" (Ps. 89:12). References to the "mountain of the Lord" and to the sacredness of mountains are extremely numerous (Gen. 22:14; Exod. 3:1; Deut. 11:29; Josh. 8:30; 2 Kings 4:25; Isa. 2:2; Isa. 8:18; Ezek. 28:14).

In the NT: In the NT, Jesus makes it clear that the worship of God was not restricted to any particular mountain (John 4:2–24). Yet, mountains figure prominently in contexts of worship, prayer, and events of great religious significance. The Sermon on the Mount exemplifies this continuing tradition (Matt. 5:1–7:29). Jesus' temptation occurred on a very high mountain (Matt 4:8) as did his transfiguration (Mark 9:2); for his own prayer and devotion, Jesus sought the mountains (Matt. 14:23; Mark 6:46; Luke 6:12; 9:28; John 6:15). The Mount of Olives was the setting for Jesus' entry into Jerusalem (Mark 11:1; Luke 19:29); his betrayal occurred on the lower slopes at Gethsemane (Matt. 26:30–56; Mark 14:26–50); and it is reported that the Mount of Olives was the site of his ascension (Luke 24:50; Acts 1:9–12). S.L.R.

Mount, Sermon on the. ***See*** Sermon on the Mount, The.

mourning rites, the rituals practiced upon the death of a relative or national figure or in times of national crisis. Death was acknowledged by rending the clothes and dressing in sackcloth. These practices were followed by Jacob when he was presented with the bloody coat of his son Joseph (Gen. 38:34). When Job was informed of the death of his children, he "rent his robe, shaved his head, and fell upon the ground, and worshiped" (Job 1:20), and his friends wept, rent their robes, sprinkled dust upon their heads, and sat on the ground with him for seven days and seven nights (Job 2:12–13; cf. 2 Sam. 13:31). In Micah we find mention of lamentations while naked (1:8) and the cutting off of one's hair (1:16; cf. Ezek. 27:30–31). Jeremiah expects the mourners to make themselves bald and cut themselves (Jer. 16:16), while Leviticus specifically prohibits shaving, cutting the hair, tattooing, or the making of gashes in the skin on account of the dead (Lev. 19:27–28).

Ezekiel was commanded by God not to mourn the death of his wife. "Bind on your turban, and put your shoes on your feet; do not cover your lips, nor eat the bread of mourners" (Ezek. 24:17). A contrast between times of mourning and times of joy (Isa. 61:3) enumerates the wearing of ashes and the abstention from anointing oil as signs of mourning. Further, no ornaments were to be worn (Exod. 33:4). Friends of the mourner sat in grief with him (Job 2:12–13) and gave him a meal of bread and wine to console him (Jer. 16:7). Formal lamentations or elegies (Heb. *kinot)* were recited, as at the death of Josiah when "singing men and singing women" performed as professional mourners (2 Chron. 35:25).

Mourning rites are also attested in the Bible in times of national calamity. After the defeat of Ai, Joshua rent his clothes and put dust upon his head (Josh. 7:6) as did Mordecai when he received the news that Haman was planning to exterminate the Jewish people (Esther 4:1–3). In addition, Mordecai went out into the city "wailing with a loud and bitter cry," and the Jews of the city fasted as well. Psalms 74, 79, and the book of Lamentations are elegies (Heb. *kinot)* for the destruction of Jerusalem and the Temple.

Various mourning periods are specified in the narratives ranging from seven days (Gen. 50:10), to three weeks (Dan. 10:2), to "many days" (Gen. 37:34). Although a captive woman must mourn for a month (Deut. 21:13), a definite period of mourning is not commanded anywhere else in the Bible. The Talmud legislated several periods of mourning, each less intense than the previous one, to bring mourners gradually out of their grief lest they mourn excessively. The period of *aninut* lasted from the announcement of death until the burial. Mourners were forbidden to take meat or wine and to perform certain commandments, both as a sign of grief and as a way of giving full attention to the burial preparations. After the burial, the period of *shiv'ah* lasted for seven days. Mourners rent their clothes, sat upon the ground, and did not labor, receiving condolences from the community. During the period of *sheloshim*, the first thirty days, mourners did not cut their hair or attend social or festive gatherings. The entire year following the death of a parent was marked by the abstention from joyous events.

There are no specific instructions for mourning in the NT, although the custom of communal mourning for the dead did continue (Mark 5:38; John 11:33). ***See also*** Sackcloth. L.H.S.

Mughara, Wadi el (mōō-gah'rah; Arabic, "Caves, Valley of the"), caves also known as the Carmel Caves, lying on the western slope of the Carmel promontory, just eighteen miles south of Haifa. Within this valley, which opens upon the vast coastal plain, there are three major caves of interest for prehistoric research: Mugharet el-Wad ("Cave of the Valley"), Mugharet et-Tabun ("Cave of the Oven"), and Mugharet es-Sukhul ("Cave of the Kid"). The site became famous as a result of British excavations carried out by Dorothy Garrod in 1929–34. Discoveries of prehistoric cultural materials show a continuous development from a hunter-gatherer society (Tayacian), ca. 150,000 B.C., to a society of incipient agriculturalists (Natufian), ca. 10,000 B.C.

The largest cave, Cave of the Valley, is 71 meters long. Early human skeletal and cultural remains dating from the Mousterian to the Natufian periods were encountered inside the cave, while Natufian occupation extended to the wide terrace in front. This important Natufian site included architectural remains, burials with bodies in flexed position with necklaces of dentalia on the skulls, and the first art objects to appear in Palestine. The Cave of the Oven and the Cave of the Kid both revealed important human skeletal remains bearing on the relative chronological position of Neanderthal and modern human forms. In the Cave of the Kid, the expedition uncovered eleven skeletons evincing characteristics of both Neanderthal and modern *(Homo sapiens)* forms. The evidence from Carmel raises the question whether in the Near East *Homo sapiens* evolved from, or was contemporary with, Neanderthal forms. S.L.R.

The Carmel Caves (Wadi el Mughara), where excavations have revealed cultural remains from ca. 150,000–10,000 B.C.

mulberry *(Morus nigra)*, a long-lived tree whose heart-shaped leaves and dense, spreading branches provide shade. The small blackberry-like fruit produces a dark red juice which is referred to as the "blood" (RSV: "juice") of the mulberry in 1 Macc. 6:34. The white mulberry, the leaves of which are used to feed the silkworm, is a more recent import from China and Persia. The references to the mulberry (KJV; RSV: "balsam") in 2 Sam. 5:23–24 and 1 Chron. 14: 14–15 are thought to apply instead to aspens, trees whose leaves stir noisily in the slightest breeze. The mulberry is also identified as the sycamine of Luke 17:6, which is not to be confused with the sycamore, or mulberry fig. ***See also*** Sycamine; Sycamore P.L.C.

mule, the hybrid offspring of a donkey and a horse, normally a jackass and a mare. While its lack of understanding was proverbial (Ps. 32:9), the mule's strength, endurance, and docility made it ideal for transporting goods (2 Kings 5: 17; 1 Chron. 12:40) and riding (Isa. 66:20). From their earliest appearance in the OT (2 Sam. 13: 29), mules are usually associated with royalty (2 Sam. 18:9; 1 Kings 1:33, 38, 44). Since the law prohibited the breeding of hybrids (Lev. 19:19), it is likely that mules were imported into Israel (1 Kings 10:25; Ezra 2:66; Neh. 7:38; cf. Ezek. 27: 14). Mules are not mentioned in the NT. ***See also*** Animals; Horse; Trade and Transportation. G.L.M.

mummification, an elaborate embalming technique practiced in ancient Egypt, which spread to some extent south and east to Nubia. Early in Egypt's history people observed that bodies buried in the warm, dry sand, and thus dried out, were often well preserved. This experience, coupled with the Egyptian belief in bodily resurrection, prompted the development of intentional, careful means to preserve the body. For that matter, burial in the sand prior to proper interment remained a practice in Egypt for many centuries, especially for the poor. By the later Old Kingdom (ca. 2300–2200 B.C.) there was a well-developed mummification process for wealthy burials, and the techniques were significantly improved by the time of the New Kingdom (sixteenth century B.C.).

The expensive, protracted process took about seventy days and involved removing the brain tissue (usually through the nostrils), taking out the major organs, preparing the body interior, and covering the body with natron to help dry it out prior to the final cleansing, padding, and wrapping with many layers of cloth. (The primary organs were separately preserved in special jars or boxes.) There were also less elaborate alternatives. One more modest process involved injecting the body with oil and treating it with natron. The oil was subsequently drained out, bringing with it the dissolved interior organs. In the cheapest style, the embalmers merely cleansed the body and treated it with natron prior to the wrapping. The precise embalming practices varied with time and place as well as in expense. The fully treated body was then placed in a coffin, often rather elaborate, and transported to the tomb for the "Opening of the Mouth" ritual by which the body regained the powers of speech, hearing, and sight, making it ready for new life. Mummification was extended to include the embalming of various animals sacred to particular deities. Sacred animal cemeteries with literally thousands of burials are known from many sites.

Genesis reports that Israel (Jacob), who died in Egypt, was embalmed by the physicians, a process requiring forty days (50:1–4), and that Joseph, who also died in Egypt, was embalmed and placed in a coffin (50:26). The Genesis references reflect the more elaborate process described above. Mummification was not practiced by the Israelites, although it continued among the Coptic Christians of Egypt to a limited extent. ***See also*** Burial; Embalming; Jacob; Joseph. H.B.H.

Muppim (muhp'im). ***See*** Shephupham.

murder, the taking of another human being's life illegally. Protection from killing is a central part of God's covenantal blessing to Noah after the Flood; God himself will seek blood for a human being's blood, whether the latter is shed by an animal or another human being (Gen. 9: 4–6), for human beings were created in God's image. In the Decalogue, God prohibits killing (Exod. 20:13; Deut. 5:17), the sanction here too being understood as divine.

Forms of Legal Liability: Whereas such moral condemnations are widely drawn, the forms of legal liability were carefully defined. Causing death by direct physical contact in principle rendered the killer liable to death (Exod. 21:12), but the possibility of asylum was available in cases of accident (Exod. 21:13, the origin of our notion of "an act of God"; Deut. 19:15 exemplifies this with the case of the flying axehead) but not cases of premeditation, such as ambush (Exod. 21:13) or previous hatred (Exod. 21:14; Deut. 4:42; 19:4, 6, 11; Josh. 20:5; Num. 35:20). Direct killing with an instrument liable to cause death also took the offender outside the protection of the asylum laws (Num. 35:17–19). Homicide in the course of a sudden quarrel was viewed as comparable to accidental homicide (Num. 35:22–23). But the protection afforded by the asylum was limited. According to one understanding of Deut. 19:6, it commenced only when the offender reached one of the designated cities of refuge, but Num. 35:12 and Josh. 20:9 seek to protect the accused en route, which accords with the motive of avoiding the shedding of innocent blood (Deut. 19:10). Once the offender reached the city of refuge, there would be an adjudication (Num. 35:24); according to Josh. 20:4, it took place at the city gate, and the fugitive would not be admitted to the city in advance of it. If the offender was found to have acted without premeditation, the avenging kinsman (Heb. *go' ayl hadam*, interpreted by some as a public official) would be turned away from the city (Josh. 20:5); if not, the offender would be handed over (Deut. 19:12), to be executed by the kinsman. Where protection was granted, it extended only within the boundaries of the city of refuge (Num. 35:26–27). On the death of the high priest, the offender was free to return home (Num. 35:28).

It is likely that this system was designed to monitor and control customary practices whereunder the kin of the deceased were free to exact blood vengeance or accept a ransom (Exod. 21:30), subject to the offender's recourse to temple sanctuary, probably at the local shrine (Exod. 21:13). Even then, offenders might be dragged from the altar to their death (Exod. 21:14), at this stage apparently without any legal proceedings. The later system restricted the rights of the kin, not only by requiring formal adjudication when the accused sought asylum, but also by banning the acceptance of ransom (Num. 35:31–32) and requiring the evidence of two witnesses (Num. 35:30). The residual role of the kinsman as executioner might still lead to abuse (including the acceptance of ransom).

At least by the time of Ezra (mid- to late sixth century B.C.), with the loss of autonomy and the territory of most of the cities of refuge, the adjudication of murder became entirely a matter of state regulation, to be administered by judges appointed by Ezra under the authority of the Persian king (Ezra 7:25–26). Capital jurisdiction apparently was removed from Jewish courts under the Romans, one rabbinic tradition dating this to A.D. 30 (*y. Sanh.* 1:1; but see *b. Sanh.* 37b). Nevertheless, the Mishnah dealt with the law of murder largely on the basis of the biblical texts. But where the court found the accused parties guilty, after they had fled to the city of refuge, they were to be beheaded under authority of the court, rather than be handed over to the kin for execution (*m. Mak.* 2:6; *m. Sanh.* 9:1). The biblical tests of intention were replaced in the Mishnah by a requirement that those accused be warned by witnesses immediately before they commit the offense, and that they acknowledge such warning—a clear indication of the rabbinic distaste for capital punishment, explicitly found elsewhere. The alternative for the rabbis was a system of imprisonment (*m. Sanh.* 9:5), perhaps with a hint of divine judgment as to the ultimate fate of the accused, who was placed on a diet of "the bread of adversity and the water of affliction" (Isa. 30:20).

Special Situations: The "Covenant Code" considers a number of situations that fall outside the paradigm case of murder and that in modern law would be treated as presenting problems of causation, manslaughter, or justification. When death occurs after the victim has risen from the sick-bed and walked outside, the offender is not regarded as the cause of death (Exod. 21:18–19). Where death has been caused by an ox and the owner is blameworthy because he had been warned of previous incidents but did not keep the animal in, the owner is responsible for the death (Exod. 21:29). Homicide is justified where a thief is caught breaking in at night (Exod. 22: 2–3). A master is not entitled to kill his slave outright, but if disciplinary measures lead to the slave's death a day or so later, the master is exempt (Exod. 21:20–21). By contrast, David was held morally, if not legally, accountable for the death of Uriah, although David's personal role was restricted to the giving of the orders that led to Uriah's death (2 Sam. 11–12).

There is little trace of collective responsibility in the biblical sources on murder. The elders of the nearest city were required to deny participation and knowledge, as part of a ceremony of expiation, where the victim of an unknown killer was found in the country. The denial is sufficient to rebut the prima facie suspicion; the expiation removes the pollution of the land by the innocent blood. Despite the RSV translation (Deut. 21:1–9), there is no suggestion of "guilt" on the city for the killing. The same rationale underlies the case of the householder who fails to furnish his roof with a parapet (Deut. 22:8): if someone falls from it, there will be innocent blood in the house. There is no suggestion here of legal liability (unlike the case of the ox owner), nor even of moral liability that may occasion divine punishment (again despite the RSV use of "guilt of blood").

In the NT, Jesus reiterates the prohibition against murder (Matt. 19:18), whose source is Satan himself (John 8:44). Indeed, to hate another human being is reckoned as murder by Jesus (Matt. 5:21–22; cf. 1 John 3:15). ***See also*** Law; Robbery.

B.S.J./P.J.A.

murrain (muhr'en; KJV; RSV: "plague" in Exod. 9:3), an obsolete term for infectious diseases afflicting animals and plants.

Mushi (mōō'shī), the son of Merari and grandson of Levi. He was the ancestral head of a major subdivision of the Merarite clan of Levites, the Mushites (Exod. 6:19; Num. 3:20; 26:58).

Mushites. ***See*** Mushi.

Music

INSTRUMENTAL AND VOCAL SOUNDS having rhythm, melody, or harmony. Secular and sacred music played no less a role in the lives of the people of biblical times than it does in our own day. It added to the pomp of national celebrations, bolstered the soldier's courage, enlivened work and play, lent comfort in times of sadness, and provided inspiration in religious expression. The sound of early Near Eastern music would seem less strange to the modern ear than previously thought. Though we are not informed about ancient rhythms and tempos, we do know that heptatonic, diatonic scales, familiar to us from Western music, also existed in antiquity. A number of stringed instruments would have produced sounds similar to modern small harps, lyres, and lutes. Other instruments, notably woodwind, percussion, and the simpler stringed instruments, were merely less sophisticated forms of modern orchestral or folk instruments, and some are still in use in the traditional cultures of the contemporary Near East.

Round-bottomed, silver, stringed harplike instrument found in the royal graves at Ur, ca. 1339 B.C. (It may be incorrectly reconstructed from two different instruments. The sound box from an even earlier lyre is shown in the section of color photographs.)

Mesopotamian and Egyptian Music: On the earliest Sumerian clay tablets from Uruk (ca. 3000 B.C.) appears the pictographic sign for the typical boat-shaped Sumerian harp; and the earliest depiction of this instrument is found on a seal impression from Chogha Mish (modern southwest Iran) dating ca. 3200 B.C. An actual example of such a harp, together with nine ornamented lyres and a set of silver pipes, was found at Ur—the traditional home of Abraham—in the royal graves of Queen Pu-Abi and her retinue (ca. 2650 B.C.). An inlaid panel that once decorated one of the lyres shows an animal orchestra, a common early folk theme, that included a lyre-playing donkey, a clapping and singing bear, and a jackel keeping time with a sistrum and a percussion instrument. By the end of the third millennium, textual evidence, including collections of divine hymns, hymns to temples, and hymns to and for the kings of the third dynasty of Ur—featuring many musical terms—attests even more directly to a well-developed Sumerian musical tradition.

Statue of a singer discovered at the royal palace at Mari; third millennium B.C.

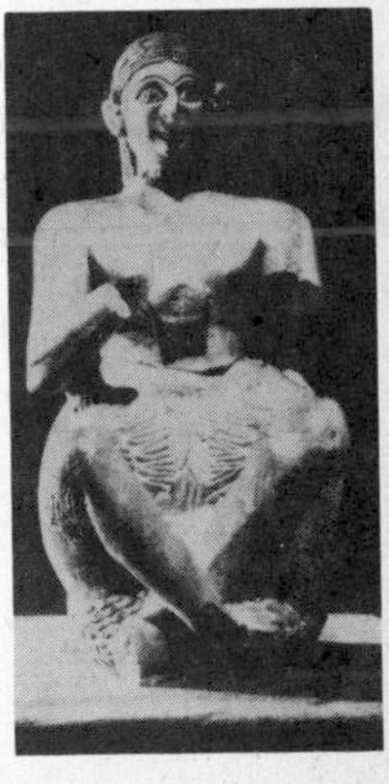

Even more is known about Assyrian and Babylonian music in the second and first millennia. Illustrations, particularly first millennium Assyrian reliefs, depict a varied assortment of instruments, and encyclopedic lists of names of instruments were compiled in the scribal schools. A large repertoire of hymns, laments, and liturgical litanies gives some notion of the use of song in religious ritual, especially those that were provided with labels indicating their type or purpose or the nature of their accompaniment or manner of performance.

Mesopotamian sacred and courtly music was apparently performed or directed by families of professional musicians, perhaps not unlike David's levitical guilds of musicians. Professional musicians were trained in the temple schools, and it was probably such musician-scribes who set down on cuneiform tablets dating from ca. 1800 to ca.

A man dances to the music of clappers, pipe, and lute; limestone relief from Carchemish, ninth–eighth century B.C.

500 B.C. the Mesopotamian theory of music, whose details have gradually come to light over the last several decades. Assyriological and musicological research has shown that the Mesopotamian musical system knew seven different heptatonic-diatonic scales, one of them like our own major scale; the Mesopotamian material therefore provides evidence for the antiquity of Western music some fourteen hundred years before the earliest Greek sources. One complete piece of music whose explicit notation uses technical Akkadian interval names followed by number signs was found at ancient Ugarit in Syria; the piece is a Hurrian cult hymn to the moon goddess Nikkal and dates to ca. 1400 B.C.

Egyptian music also has a long history, with graphic and written remains stretching from ca. 3000 B.C. to Roman times. More importantly, many instruments depicted in illustrations or mentioned in written documents have actually survived intact and serve as a valuable source of comparative data for the study of both Mesopotamian and biblical instruments. These include several types of lyres, harps, and lutes, a copper and a bronze trumpet from the tomb of Tutankhamen (1347–1338 B.C.), true end-blown flutes as well as double reedpipes of both the clarinet and oboe varieties, and many percussion instruments such as drums, cymbals, sistrums, bells, rattles, and clappers.

A blind harpist playing his instrument; detail of a relief from the tomb of Paätenemheb Saqqara, ca. 1212 B.C.

Hebrew Secular Music: Biblical references to music begin with the mention of Jubal, "the father of all those who play the lyre and pipe" (Gen. 4:21). It is no coincidence that his name is related to the Hebrew word for "ram" *(yobel)*, from whose horns the primitive signal-horn *(shophar)* was made.

References to the popular enjoyment of music are common in early biblical history. It was always a part of celebrations, whether a farewell party complete with "mirth and songs, with tambourine and

A pair of bronze cymbals from Megiddo, ca. 1200–1000 B.C.

lyre" (Gen. 31:27); a joyous homecoming (Judg. 11:34); or the feasts of the idle rich, who spend their days with "lyre and harp, timbrel and flute and wine" (Isa. 5:12). Singing accompanied work as well as play, and many work songs or chants have been recorded, e.g., those of the well diggers (Num. 21:17–18), the watchman (Isa. 21:12), and the pressers of grapes (Jer. 25:30; 48:33).

Warfare gave rise to martial songs. Such heroic ballads were probably set down in the lost "Book of the Wars of the Lord" (Num. 21:14) and the "Book of Jashar" (Josh. 10:13; 2 Sam. 1:18), and were no doubt sung by itinerant minstrels and bards (cf. Num. 21:27–30). Miriam sang of Moses' final defeat of Pharaoh (Exod. 15:20–21); and Deborah celebrated Israel's victory over Jabin with a song of triumph (Judg. 5). Samson exulted over his slaying of the Philistines (Judg. 15:16) in a rhythmic victory chant like the one the women sang back and forth at Saul's homecoming (1 Sam. 18:6–7). But Israel was not always victorious, and songs were also composed for fallen heroes, such as David's moving lament for Saul and Jonathan (2 Sam. 1:19–27).

A seated harpist playing; Mesopotamian terra-cotta plaque, 1800–1500 B.C.

Hebrew Sacred Music: Music was not apparently an important part of Israelite religion in the early days of biblical history. With the monarchy (after ca. 1040 B.C.), however, and the growth of the Temple came professional musicianship both at court (1 Kings 1:34, 39–40; 10:2; Eccles. 2:8) and in religious ritual. Some have expressed doubts that the organization of Temple ritual and liturgy, as described in 1 Chronicles 15 and 16, was the sole handiwork of David; and doubt has also been cast on his role in the composition of the Psalter. Certainly the David reported in the OT is a larger than life figure, and the levitical guilds of musicians established by him may have attempted to enhance their own prestige and prerogatives by attaching his name to some of the works of others. But there are too many indications of David's skill as a musician to discount his traditional accomplishments without

A lyre with twelve strings connected by an oblique crossbar decorates a brown jasper seal (seventh century B.C.) from Jerusalem.

more solid evidence. He was a composer of songs and lamentations, a skilled lyre player (1 Sam. 16:16–18), an inventor of instruments (Amos 6:5), a valued court musician (1 Sam. 19:9), and even a dancer (2 Sam. 6:14–15). The literary record of his many abilities is foreshadowed only by that of the Sumerian king Shulgi of Ur (2093–2045 B.C.), who celebrated his own remarkable talents in music, athletics, and statesmanship in a number of finely crafted hymns. In any event, Temple music doubtless featured both trumpet calls (cf. Num. 10:10; Ps. 98:6) and the singing of songs of thanksgiving, praise, and petition following the sacrifices (2 Chron. 29:20–30). At the reestablishment of the Second Temple (late sixth century B.C.), the descendants of the original levitical musicians (Ezra 2:41) reassumed responsibility for the music of the liturgy, and the influence of those hereditary guilds can be seen in the references to their founders in the psalm headings. Some idea of how the vocal music may have been performed may be gotten from the structure of many psalms. Refrains and acclamations (e.g., "Hallelujah"), divisions into strophes, and above all the common devices of poetic parallelism all strongly suggest types of responsorial or antiphonal performance.

Musical Instruments: Much of what is known about the instruments of the Bible comes from literary evidence: the Scriptures and their earliest translations, and the descriptions and comments of the rabbis, church fathers, and classical authors. Additional evidence has come from archaeological discoveries, both the remains of actual instruments and the abundant pictorial representations of instruments and musical scenes from throughout the entire Near Eastern and Mediter-

A bronze flute player from Byblos dates to the second millennium B.C.

Egyptian crescent-shaped harp (fourth century B.C.) with a sphinx head wearing the crowns of Upper and Lower Egypt.

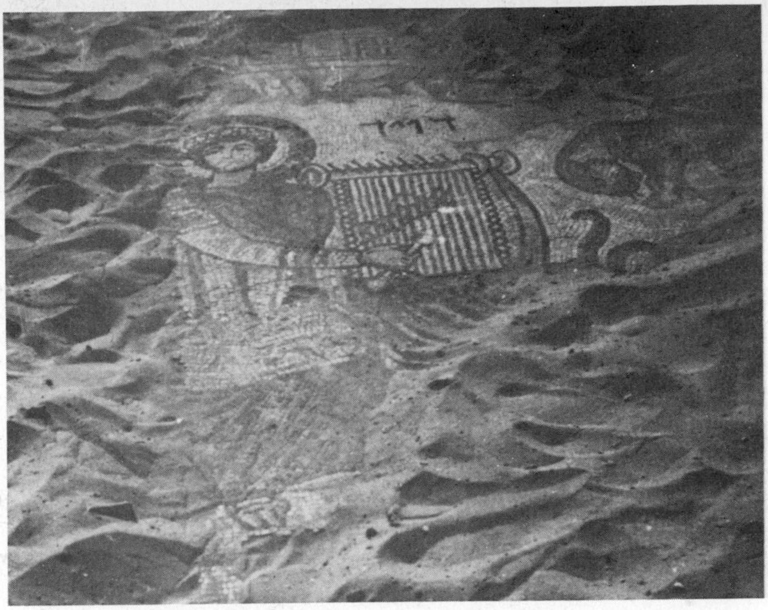

David, the "sweet psalmist of Israel," depicted playing a lyre in a sixth-century floor mosaic at the synagogue at Gaza.

ranean world. Even so, identifications are difficult and usually represent merely the best guesses that biblical scholarship presently has to offer.

The *shophar*, or ram's horn, is the most frequently mentioned biblical instrument, and the only ancient instrument still in use in the synagogue. The word may ultimately come from the Akkadian name for the ibex, or wild goat, but the instrument was usually made from the horn of a ram, sometimes softened with heat and straightened or shaped. It was a simple instrument that could only produce two or three notes, and it was used mostly for signaling, especially in times of war (Judg. 3:27; 6:34; Neh. 4:18–20) or of national celebration (1 Kings 1:34; 2 Kings 9:13).

A bronze figurine of a woman playing a long-necked lute (twelfth century B.C.); found at Beth-shan.

The trumpet (Heb. *khatsotsrah*) was made of metal, either bronze or silver. It was probably a short, straight instrument, with a high, bright tone and a range of only four or five notes. Its early uses are well summarized in Num. 10:2–10. It was played by the priests, usually in pairs, but occasionally in large choirs (2 Chron. 5:12–13), and it numbered among the sacred gold and silver utensils of the Temple (2 Kings 12:14; cf. Num. 31:6).

The *kinnor*, David's "harp," was actually a lyre, a portable rectangular or trapezoid-shaped instrument with two arms, often of unequal length and curved, joined at the top by a cross-piece; the strings were of roughly the same length (unlike a harp's). This instrument was popular all throughout the ancient Near East, and the word itself appears in the cuneiform vocabularies of ancient Ebla in Syria (ca. 2400 B.C.), and in Assyrian, Hurrian, Hittite, Ugaritic, and Egyptian texts. It was an instrument of joyful celebration, generally used to accompany singing.

A trumpeter from Carchemish, ninth century B.C.

Another stringed instrument, always mentioned together with the lyre, was the *nebel*, either a kind of angular harp with a vertical resonator such as is often depicted on first millennium Assyrian reliefs, or another kind of lyre with an unusual waterskin-shaped sound-box known only from depictions on coins from the Bar-Kochba period (A.D. 132–135). The RSV usually translates it "harp" (but also "lute" in Ps. 150:3).

The principal biblical wind instrument was the *khalil* (RSV: "flute" or "pipe"), which consisted of two separate pipes of reed, metal, or ivory, each with its own mouthpiece containing either a single (clarinet-type) or double (oboe-type) reed. The pipes were played together, one probably acting as a drone accompaniment. The *khalil* was primarily a secular instrument, generally used on joyful occasions (1 Kings 1:39–40; Isa. 5:12), but it was also suitable for mourning (Jer. 48:36; Matt. 9:23).

The *ugab* is usually considered another kind of pipe, perhaps a true flute, though the Septuagint considers it a stringed instrument. It is mentioned together with other stringed instruments in Gen. 4:21 and Ps. 150:4.

Percussion instruments included the *toph*, a small tambourine without jingles (also called a "timbrel," "tabor," or "tabret"), small bronze cymbals 4 to 6 inches in diameter, which may have been played with an up-and-down motion, and a kind of noisemaker (2 Sam. 6:5), variously translated as "castanets," "rattles," "sistrums," or "clappers." The bells attached to the high priest's robe (Exod. 28:33–34; 39: 25–26) are better translated as "metal jingles," since true bells with clappers were unknown in Israel before the ninth century B.C. They served a protective rather than musical function.

In Dan. 3:5, 7, 10, and 15 appears a list of instruments reportedly played by the court musicians of the Babylonian king Nebuchadnezzar (604–562 B.C.). They are either Aramaic terms or Aramaic forms of Greek words, and the identification of most of them is still not entirely certain. They probably included a curved horn, a flute or, less likely, a Panpipe, a lyre, a small boat-shaped harp, and a second kind of lyre or possibly an early type of zither. The last term (RSV: "bagpipes") is an Aramaic form of the Greek word *symphonia*, which may

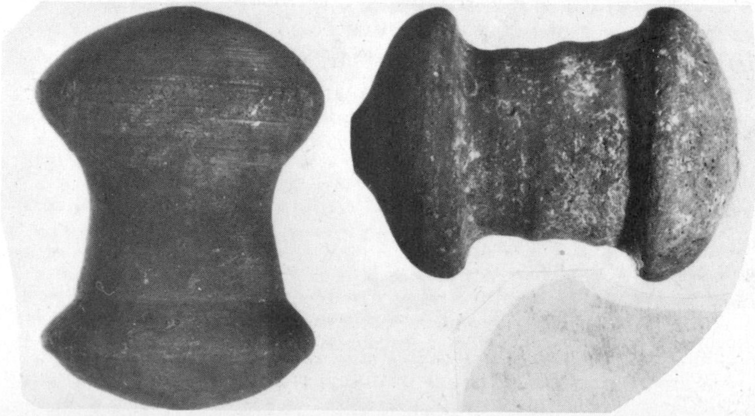

Pottery rattles found at Tell Beit Mirsim typify those used from the second millennium to the ninth century B.C. They were filled with one or more small pellets to make noise.

simply mean several instruments "sounding together," and therefore "music."

Four different instruments are mentioned in the NT, the double-pipe (RSV: "flute"), the lyre (RSV: "harp"), the trumpet, and the cymbals. The "noisy gong" mentioned by Paul in 1 Cor. 13:1 probably refers to the large brass vases that were placed at the rear of Greek theaters to help amplify the actors' voices.

The Psalm Headings: About two-thirds of the psalms designate their authorship in their headings: either David, the "sweet psalmist of Israel" (2 Sam. 23:1), or, with only a few exceptions, founders of families of levitical musicians connected with the original establishment of the Temple liturgy. Other terms and expressions in the headings refer more directly to musical matters, the nature, purpose, or manner of performance of individual compositions.

Some songs are called "psalms," from the Greek translation of Hebrew *mizmor;* both terms refer to a song with instrumental accompaniment. Other titles include "song" (Heb. *shir,* a word ultimately derived from Akkadian and Sumerian), "song of praise," and the common word for "prayer" (also applied to the misplaced psalm Hab. 3). The meanings of the untranslated terms *Maskil* and *Miktam* are unknown; they come from roots meaning "to have insight" and "to cover, conceal." *Shiggaion* in Ps. 7 (and Hab. 3) is related to the Akkadian word for a kind of lament or cry of woe.

Some comments refer to the manner of a psalm's performance, e.g., "upon stringed instruments *[neginoth]*" or "for the flutes *[nehiloth]*"—although these translations are not entirely certain. *Alamoth* (Ps. 46) and *Sheminith* (Pss. 6; 12) may refer to a type of harp tuning and the playing of a melody an octave higher. *Mahalath* (Pss. 53; 88) may refer to a type of dance, perhaps to a rhythm.

Also found in the headings are song cues, the titles or opening words of popular older songs to whose tunes the psalms were to be sung, e.g., "Hind of the Dawn" (Ps. 21), or "Lilies" (Ps. 45).

The frequently occurring word *Selah,* which appears within or at the ends of certain psalms, is probably also a kind of performance indication. The word's meaning is unknown, but based upon the translation of the Septuagint it is thought to indicate a pause in the singing, possibly signaled by the sounding of cymbals. At such points musical interludes may have occurred, or a different group of performers may have taken up the singing.

Music in the NT: In addition to the names of several instruments (see above, "Musical Instruments"), there are some references in the NT to singing in the context of worship (Eph. 5:19; Col. 3:16b), although there is no indication of who did the singing or when in the worship service it occurred. The references to singing by the inhabitants of heaven in Revelation (e.g., 4:10) and the hymnic fragments cited (e.g., 4:11; 5:9; 7:15–17; 11:17–18) may provide an insight into the kind of music that was used in early Christian worship.

See also Asaph; David; Psalms, The.

Bibliography

Sendry, Alfred. *Music in Ancient Israel.* New York: Philosophical Press, 1969.

A.D.K./D.A.F.

Mustard.

Myrrh.

musical instruments. ***See*** Music.

mustard, a common plant used for oil, as a condiment, and as a pot-herb. While it is hyperbole that mustard is "the smallest of seeds . . . the greatest of shrubs" (Matt. 13:31; Mark 4:31; Luke 13:19), in both the parable of the mustard seed and in the statement about faith (Matt. 17: 20; Luke 17:6) the mustard seed's significance lies in its size relative to the mature plant or to a mountain. The Kingdom of God has small beginnings, but it blossoms manyfold. For faith however small, nothing is impossible.

Muth-labben (mo͞oth'lah-buhn), a word in the heading of Psalm 9 that may have served as some sort of notation for its musical performance. ***See also*** Psalms, The.

Myra (mī'ruh), a principal city of Lycia in southwestern Asia Minor, where Paul's company changed ships on the way to Rome (Acts 27:5–6), probably at its port of Andriaca. The apocryphal *Acts of Paul and Thecla* recounts that Paul preached in Myra. A later bishop of Myra, St. Nicholas, was the origin of the Santa Claus legend and remains today the patron saint of Greek sailors. The site, occupied by modern Dembre, has ruins of a theater, tombs, and inscriptions, all from Roman times, attesting to Myra's importance for commercial navigation in antiquity. ***See also*** Lycia; Paul.

myrrh (muhr; from Heb. *mor* and Gk. *murra, samodendron*, or *smurna)*, an aromatic gum that grows in Arabia, Abyssinia, and India. Highly prized from earliest times (Gen. 37:25), it was used in incense (Exod. 30:23) and as a perfume for garments (Ps. 45:9) or for a lover's couch (Prov. 7:17). It was part of the cosmetic treatment used to purify young girls for the king's bed (Esther 2:13), and it was also used in embalming (Mark 15:23; John 19:39). Myrrh appears among the items of luxury trade flowing into Babylon (Rome) as it meets its doom (Rev. 18:13). Along with gold and frankincense it exemplifies the rich gifts brought to the infant Christ by the Magi from the East (Matt. 2:11).

P.P.

myrtle *(Myrtus communis)*, a large ornamental evergreen shrub that grows in dense copses along rivers and streams. Its greens were used to adorn the booths at the Feast of Tabernacles (Neh. 8:15). The fragrant leaves were also used in perfume manufacture. The myrtle is a symbol of peace, joy, generosity, and justice. The name "Hadassah" is derived from the Hebrew word for myrtle, *hadas* (Esther 2:7).

Mysia (mish'ee-uh), the region of northwestern Asia Minor along the Hellespont and the Aegean Sea. Paul passed through two towns in the area, Troas (Acts 16:8, 11) and Assos (Acts 20:13). Pergamum was also in this region (Rev. 1:11; 2: 12).

mystery, that which is secret, hidden, or beyond normal human understanding, although it may be revealed or disclosed to certain people.

In the OT and Judaism: God, "the Lord," had

Myrtle.

secret knowledge he revealed when he chose (Isa. 48:3, 6; Amos 3:7). God's knowledge was a "mystery" because some of it was not known, and even when known, was not always understood. God delivered it in person (Gen. 17:1), or through an angel (from heaven, Gen. 22:11; on earth, Num. 22:23), through dreams (Gen. 20:3), or through "the Spirit of the Lord"(2 Sam. 23:2). To the OT prophets, revelation occurred when "the word of the Lord" came to them (Jon. 1:1) and/or they had visions (Ezek. 1:1; Dan. 2:19); even with visions, the Spirit could be the source (Ezek. 2:2). In Daniel and some of the books of the Pseudepigrapha, divine mysteries are sealed in books in heaven, but God will make known the contents at the end of this age.

The Israelites believed that divine knowledge was needed to solve human problems; it

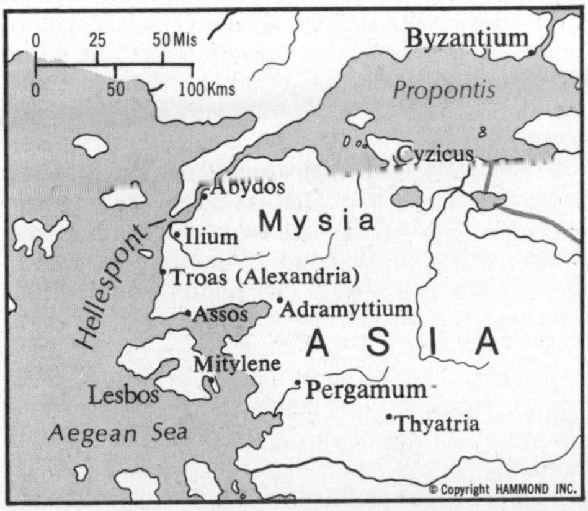

provided laws for relations with God and among humans, rules for priestly ritual, and explanations of sin, injustice, and foreign domination. Early prophets explained evil as God's punishment of Israel for its sins. In the eschatology (beliefs about the end of this age) in Daniel and later books, the secret, divine plan is that a new age will come, at which time the wicked will be punished, righteous Jews rewarded, and God will rule permanently over a perfect earth. Even misfortunes fit God's purposes, for they purify the sufferers and ensure their inclusion among the happy righteous. The wicked are blinded to these mysteries of God (Wisd. of Sol. 2:21–22). The Essenes at Qumran believed that God was still revealing his mysterious knowledge to them. Numerous Jewish writers retold history to make it fit God's plan.

Several aspects point to a literary development of the traditions about God's "mystery." "The word of the Lord" contains divergent views (e.g., the content and interpretation of the Law and the proper attitude toward Gentiles); often the visions follow a standard literary pattern and contain literary sources. Some Jewish (and Christian) "revelations" consist of reinterpretation of OT prophecy.

In Christianity: In the NT, the use of the Greek word for "mystery" or "secret" New Testament *(mysterion)* is founded on Jewish eschatology. To the Jewish concept of God's secret plan are added the Christian beliefs that the time is fulfilled and that the Messiah or Christ is Jesus. Evidence of the Jewish connection is the idea that God kept his mystery hidden for ages but revealed it to the ancient prophets and the Christian apostles (Rom. 16:25–26; 1 Cor. 2:7; 4: 1; Eph. 3:9; Heb. 1:1–2; 1 Pet. 1:10–12; Rev. 10: 7). Often the mystery was the heart of the Christian gospel under various names: "mystery of God" (Col. 2:2; Rev. 10:7); "mystery of his will" (Eph. 1:9); "mystery of Christ" (Eph. 3:4; Col. 4: 3); "mystery of the gospel" (Eph. 6:19); "mystery of the faith" (1 Tim. 3:9); "mystery of our religion" (1 Tim. 3:16); "word of God" (Col. 1:25–26; cf. 1 Cor. 2:7 [literal translation]: "we speak the hidden wisdom of God in a mystery").

Some Christian problems were explained as mysteries, e.g., the question of whether Jesus was the Christ. Mark 4:11–12, which is placed between the parable of the sower and its interpretation, tries to explain why so few people understand "the secret [literally, mystery] of the Kingdom of God"; the reason given is that Jesus preached to them in parables (here understood as "mysteries") to prevent them from understanding! Actually, parables were used to clarify, not obscure, teaching (Matt. 13:51; cf. Mark 4:33). Elsewhere, NT authors give the cause of Jewish disbelief as God's hardening their hearts, claiming this as a fulfillment of Isa. 6:9–10 (see Matt. 13:14–15; John 12:40).

The birth of Mithra, god of light and obedience, whose cult was a major rival in popularity to early Christianity.

Paul explained the nonbelief of Jews as "a mystery": God has hardened part of Israel "until the full number of the Gentiles come in [believe]" (Rom. 11:25–26).

Other Christian problems, too, were treated as mysteries: the nature of the general resurrection (1 Cor. 15:51–55); the time of Jesus' return and the disbelief of many (2 Thess. 2:1–12); the question of whether salvation is also intended for Gentiles (Eph. 3:4–6; Col. 1:25–27). The meaning of a passage in the OT can be a mystery, as is Gen. 2:24 in Eph. 5:31–32. Speaking in tongues is uttering "mysteries in the Spirit" (1 Cor. 14:2). The revelation of mysteries (except in the synoptic Gospels) is ascribed to the Spirit, not to Jesus' teaching (1 Cor. 2:7–10; Eph. 3:4–5).

In Mystery Religions: "Mystery" had a very different sense in pagan mystery religions, which were prevalent around the Mediterranean in the late Hellenistic age (ca. 100 B.C.–A.D. 300). They were called "the mysteries" because of their secret initiation rites, which united new members with the deity so that they would live forever. The Eleusinian and Samothracian mysteries were Greek in origin. Orphism and the cult of Dionysus probably came to Greece from Thrace. The cults of Isis, Mithra, Cybele/Attis, Adonis, and the Syrian goddess originated in the Near East; they became mystery religions after contact with the Greek mysteries.

Similarities between Christianity and the mysteries have raised the question of how much the latter influenced the former. Some argue that they had no influence, while others claim that Christianity was another mystery religion. Gentiles from the mysteries may have joined Christianity in large numbers, for it offered personal, eternal salvation, and added the threat of an imminent judgment day. Such new members would have tended to bring in features from their former religions.

Some similarities, however, have entirely independent origins. Adonis and Osiris were said to have died and returned to life, but such beliefs were not the cause of the faith in Jesus' resurrection. The belief in Jesus' ascension did not arise from the tradition that Mithra ascended into the heavens in a chariot with the god Sun. Although some mysteries practiced a type of baptism, Christian baptism originated in the Jewish-Christian environment.

In post-NT times, however, some entirely new features were contributed to Christianity by the mysteries. In art, Mary was on occasion portrayed like the nursing Isis, and pictures of Jesus as the Good Shepherd often showed stylistic elements that also appear in representations of Attis and Hermes. Jesus is also on occasion portrayed as the god Sun. Some historians even speculate that Jesus, trained in the synagogue, would not have commanded drinking blood and eating human flesh, even symbolically, and that the Lord's Supper ritual must therefore have been introduced by Gentile converts. Justin Martyr (ca. A.D. 150) remarked on its similarities to rituals in Mithraism. A later, Christianized Gnosticism also used and reinterpreted some aspects of the mystery cults. ***See also*** Angel; Apocalyptic Literature; Dreams; Eschatology; Essenes; Gnosticism; Prophet; Pseudepigrapha; Resurrection; Revelation; Tongues, Speaking with; Vision.

Bibliography

Bianchi, Ugo. *The Greek Mysteries*. Leiden: E.J. Brill, 1976.

Godwin, Joscelyn. *Mystery Religions in the Ancient World*. San Francisco: Harper & Row, 1981.

Vermaseren, Maarten J. *Cybele and Attis*. London: Thames and Hudson, 1977.

H.M.T.

mystic, one who has a direct experience of the divine presence, an intimate and transforming communion or union with God. OT prophets, especially Ezekiel, seem rooted in this experience, which is also suggested by several psalms (e.g., Ps. 73:23–26). Traces of mysticism are sometimes identified in the Pauline Letters (2 Cor. 12:2–4; Gal. 2:20), especially where Paul speaks of union with Christ.

Opposite: An example of Nabatean architecture, carved into a sandstone mountain at Petra. Originally used as a temple to Dushara, the structure was reused by early Christians as a chapel.

N

Naamah (nay'uh-muh). **1** A daughter of Lamech and his wife Zillah, and the sister of Tubal-Cain (Gen. 4:22). **2** One of the cities that was included in Judah's "inheritance," i.e., its portion of the promised land (1 Kings 14:21, 31). **3** An Ammonite wife of Solomon and the mother of Rehoboam, who succeeded Solomon to the throne of Judah (1 Kings 14:21, 31; 2 Chron. 12:13).

Naaman (nay'uh-muhn). **1** A son (Gen. 46:21) or grandson (Num. 26:40) of Benjamin; the ancestor of the Naamites. **2** A leper cured by the prophet Elisha (2 Kings 5). Naaman was the commander of the army of the king of Syria or Aram (Damascus) in the time of Elisha. Having learned of the reputation of the Samarian holy man from a captured Israelite girl who waited on his wife, Naaman resolved to go to Israel to seek a cure for his leprosy. He obtained permission from his king, who gave him a letter for the king of Israel asking that Naaman be healed. The letter, however, alarmed the Israelite king. Knowing that he lacked the power to heal Naaman, he suspected that the Aramaean king was trying to provoke a quarrel. Eventually, however, Elisha heard of the king's concern and summoned Naaman to his house. When he arrived, he sent instructions that he should dip himself in the Jordan seven times. At first Naaman, who had expected the prophet to heal him in person, was angry and disappointed, retorting that Damascus had its own rivers, the Abana and Pharpar, that were better than any in Israel. Finally, however, his servants persuaded him to follow Elisha's instructions. He washed in the Jordan and was healed, whereupon he returned to Elisha and vowed to sacrifice to no god but Yahweh from that time on, requesting a load of the local soil so that he could worship the Israelite god in Damascus. Although Elisha explicitly refused any reward from Naaman, his servant Gehazi pursued the departing Aramaean and deceitfully procured a gift in his master's name. Elisha, however, was aware of his servant's deceit and proclaimed that Naaman's leprosy would be transferred to Gehazi and his descendants forever.

The healing of Naaman's leprosy is mentioned in Luke 4:27 in the context of a controversy between Jesus and the people of Nazareth. Jesus, who is regarded with suspicion because he has done great things in Capernaum but not in his home town, cites "Naaman the Syrian" as an example of a foreigner who received divine help even when lepers in Israel did not. P.K.M.

Naarah (nay'uh-ruh). **1** A city on the border of Ephraim near Jericho (Josh. 16:7); it is probably the same as Naaran (1 Chron. 7:28). It is tentatively identified as modern Tel el-Jisr, about three and a half miles northwest of Jericho. **2** One of the wives of Ashhur, a descendant of Judah (1 Chron. 4:5–6).

Nabal (nay'bahl; Heb., "fool"), a Calebite who acquired much wealth from raising sheep and goats in Carmel and who was married to a beautiful woman named Abigail. Shortly after the death of Samuel when David and his men were encamped in the Wilderness of Paran, David sent messengers to Nabal requesting food for his soldiers. Even though David's men had done no harm to Nabal's sheepshearers, Nabal (true to the meaning of his name) responded to the request with insults. As David gathered his men to avenge this impropriety, Abigail went out to meet David with provisions and with a plea for mercy. When Abigail reported David's favorable response to her husband the morning after a drunken feast, Nabal became ill and died ten days later. His death not only prevented David from committing an evil act of revenge but also provided him with Abigail to be his wife and the mother of his son Chileab (1 Sam. 25:1–42; 2 Sam. 3:3). ***See also*** Abigail. F.R.M.

Nabatea, Nabateans (nab-uh-tee'uh, nab-uh-tee'uhns), a region and a people east and southwest of the Dead Sea that played a significant role in the politics and economics of the intertestamental and NT periods of Palestine and Transjordan. Attempts to identify the Nabateans with Nebaioth, the eldest son of Ishmael (Gen. 25:13; 28:9; 36:3; 1 Chron. 1:29; Isa. 60:7) or with the Nabaiateans of Ashurbanipal's records are at best inconclusive.

Origin and Language: Apparently originating in the northwestern Arabian Desert, the Nabateans seem to have moved into Edom about the sixth century B.C., as the Edomites themselves (later to become known as Idumeans) were migrating into Judah and the Negev. By the fourth century B.C., the Nabateans had occupied the southern

Finely decorated Nabatean "eggshell" pottery found at Moa in the Aravah Valley in modern Israel, first century A.D.

NABATEA, NABATEANS

part of Transjordan, the Wadi Arabah, and the southern Negev, nominally subject to Persian rule, but asserting their independence after the defeat of Persia by Alexander the Great and warding off a Greek attempt at conquest in 312 B.C.

Although apparently Arabic by blood, the Nabateans soon came to speak a dialect of Aramaic, the *lingua franca* of the Persian Empire, and developed their own elongated cursive version of the Aramaic uncial (i.e., capital letter) block script. The cursive version is known primarily from funerary and votive inscriptions. Apparently nomadic tribespeople originally, they developed a sedentary lifestyle as they settled into the region that came to be called Nabatea. They built new cities in the desert, including Petra, Acdat, Shivta, and Mamshit, and developed older Edomite and Moabite towns as fortresses to protect their far-flung caravan routes, the principal source of their wealth. To support the population of these desert cities, highly sophisticated water-gathering systems were invented, which allowed the agricultural exploitation of the Negev, in particular, on a scale unmatched until modern times. Only the Islamic invasion of the seventh century A.D. brought an end to this desert heritage of the Nabateans.

Religion and Art: Nabatean religion was dominated by a supreme god, Dushara (perhaps meaning "He of Seir"), later identified with the Hellenistic Dionysus or Zeus, and by el-Uzza, later identified with the mother goddess Atargatis, symbolized by a dolphin. The most significant Nabatean temples have been found at Petra, Khirbet el-Tannur, and in the Wadi Ram in Jordan.

Artistically, the Nabateans excelled in the production of exquisitely painted "eggshell" pottery, the most beautiful of their time in the Levant. Their monumental architecture, a melange of Greek and Roman classical styles more remarkable for its scale and feats of carving in the living rock of Petra than for genuinely original creativity, is nonetheless profoundly impressive in the middle of the Edomite desert.

Political History: Little is known of Nabatean political history from the end of the fourth century B.C. until the reign of the first known king, Aretas I (ca. 169 B.C.). One of the pretenders to the high-priesthood of Jerusalem, Jason, fled after a revolt by the Jews against the Seleucid (Syrian) king Antiochus IV eastward across the Jordan, where he was imprisoned by "Aretas the ruler of the Arabs" (2 Macc. 5:8). Aretas I is also mentioned in an inscription found at Elousa in the Negev along the Petra-Gaza road. The Nabateans also appear in 1 Macc. 5:25 and 9:35 as friendly to Judas Maccabeus and his brother Jonathan.

The names, numbers, and times of reign of the following kings are disputed by scholars, but a possible reconstruction of the series is as follows: civil war among the Seleucids following the death of Antiochus VII (129 B.C.) appears to have allowed the expansion of Nabatean control. A Nabatean Malichus I is known only from coins, but an Erotimus (ca. 110–100 B.C.) seems to have warred against both Egypt and Syria. In 96 B.C., Aretas II appears as an ally of Gaza against Alexander Jannaeus of Judea. Obodas I, son of Aretas, and then Rabel I continued hostilities against the Hasmonean and wrested control of parts of Moab and Gilead from him. Aretas III (87?–62 B.C.), by defeating and killing the Seleucid Antiochus XII in battle, gained a considerable reputation throughout the area and was invited to become ruler of Coelesyria, the first Nabatean to rule over Damascus, where he added to his name the title "Philhellene." In the civil conflict that followed the death of Queen Alexandra in Judah in 68 B.C., Aretas III, at the urging of the Idumean Antipater, entered the fray on behalf of her elder son, Hyrcanus II. Pompey's envoy Scaurus, however, negotiated a solution that sent Aretas back to Nabatea and gave Syria to Rome and Jerusalem to Aristobulus II, Alexandra's younger son, for the moment. In 62 B.C., Scaurus invaded Nabatea, but through Antipater's negotiations, retreated after Aretas' payment of three hundred talents in tribute.

Malichus II (47–30 B.C.; or Malichus I, 62–30, by another reckoning) was involved by Antipater on the side of Julius Caesar against Pompey's supporters in 47 B.C. in Egypt. Antipater married a Nabatean woman, Kufra or Kypros, who bore him Phasael, Joseph, Pheroras, Herod (the Great), and Salome.

When Herod took over Judea in 40 B.C., he appealed to Malichus for help against the invading Parthians but was turned down. The Romans did help him and also forced Malichus to pay a tribute to Herod for favoring the Parthians. Cleopatra VII of Egypt, ever conniving, managed to set Herod and Malichus against each other, but in such a way as to weaken both so that their mutual hostility continued until Malichus' death.

Obodas II (or III; 30–9 B.C.) was almost completely overshadowed by his brother Syllaeus, a plotter of the first rank. After Herod turned down Syllaeus' request for the hand of Herod's sister Salome, Syllaeus was sent by Obodas as guide for a disastrous Roman expedition under Aelius Gallus into Arabia and Ethiopia in 25–24 B.C. Later, in 9 B.C., Syllaeus afforded protection for bandits from Trachonitis who raided Herod's kingdom, and refused to repay a loan of fifty talents he owed Herod. When Syllaeus departed for Rome, Herod attacked the robbers' stronghold, winning Caesar's disfavor. When Obodas died, Syllaeus tried in Rome to overturn the succession of Aretas IV in his own favor and simultaneously plotted the assassination of Herod. Herod discovered the plot, sent Nicolaus of Damascus to Rome to plead his case, and Syllaeus finished by losing his head.

Aretas IV (9 B.C.–A.D. 40) gave his daughter in marriage to Herod's son Antipas in a mutual effort to heal Jewish-Nabatean relations. It was under the reign of this Aretas that Nabatean commerce and influence attained its peak, with Aretas himself even visiting Rome. About A.D. 28, Antipas divorced his Nabatean wife to marry Herodias, eventually occasioning the execution of John the Baptist according to Matt. 14:1–12 and Mark 6:17–29. Aretas attacked Antipas' forces, defeating them in a skirmish, but bringing on the threat of Roman intervention in A.D. 37. It was also under this Aretas that Paul's life was endangered in Damascus ca. A.D. 34–35 (2 Cor. 11:32–33; cf. Acts 9:23–25).

Another Malichus (III?; A.D. 40–70) aided Titus against the Jews with a thousand cavalry and five thousand archers. Rabel II (A.D. 70–106) brought a period of peace, but Nabatea was incorporated into the Roman province of Arabia by the Roman governor of Syria, Palma, under the emperor Trajan in A.D. 106, ending Nabatean independence.

Nabatean culture continued to exist, however, contributing significantly to Roman and later Byzantine civilization in the area, particularly in desert agriculture, even after caravan routes had shifted away from the area. Petra itself suffered a series of disastrous earthquakes in A.D. 110, 303, 363, 555, and 750, and was gradually forgotten by the civilized world (except for a short-lived Crusader fortress) until its rediscovery in the nineteenth century. Excavations at Petra have been carried out sporadically since 1965 by British and American expeditions. ***See also*** Antipater; Arabia; Aretas IV; Herod; Maccabees; Petra; Seleucids, The.

Bibliography

Browning, I. *Petra*. Park Ridge: Noyes, 1973.

Hammond, P. "New Light on the Nabateans." *Biblical Archaeology Review* 7, 2 (March/April 1981): 22–41.

Lawlor, J. I. *The Nabataeans in Historical Perspective*. Grand Rapids, MI: Baker, 1974.

M.K.M.

Nablus (nab'luhs). ***See*** Neapolis.

Nabonidus (nab-oh-nī'duhs), the last of the Chaldean monarchs and last native king to rule Mesopotamia in antiquity. He held the throne from 556 to 539 B.C. until displaced by the Achaemenid Cyrus II. Though the cuneiform documentation for Nabonidus is rich, the reconstruction of his personality and rule still lacks many details. He seems to have been at once a military leader of no small merit, a "learned antiquary" interested in the past of his country, and a religiously dedicated person (though not a fanatic). Nabonidus was born in Harran, in northern Mesopotamia. His name, Nabu-na'id, which in Babylonian means "the god Nabû is extolled," is remarkable when one observes that he was a passionate devotee of the moon god, Sin, whose sanctuary, Ehulhul in Harran, was restored by himself and his mother, Adad-guppi'. A strange fact of his life is his ten-year sojourn in the desert town of Teima, in the Arabian peninsula, while his son, Belshazzar, ruled in his stead in Babylon. Nabonidus is not mentioned in the Bible, but Daniel 4, which speaks of the madness of Nebuchadnezzar, is possibly a reflex of a Babylonian propaganda piece against Nabonidus by the priests of Marduk in the city of Babylon objecting to the elevation of Sin of Harran at the expense of their deity. Aramaic scroll fragments from Qumran record a tale of a Jewish advisor to Nabondius who encouraged him to worship the one Deity rather than the gods fashioned from metal and wood. ***See also*** Daniel; Daniel, The Book of; Nabopolassar. D.B.W.

Nabopolassar (na'boh-poh-las'uhr), the Babylonian founder of the Chaldean dynasty (626–539 B.C.). Most of the twenty-one years of his rule (626–605 B.C.) are attested in the *Chronicles of Chaldaean Kings* by D. J. Wiseman (London: British Museum, 1956). Nabopolassar (Babylonian *Nabû-apli-uṣur*, "O Nabû, preserve the heir!") does not mention his father's name, which indicates he was not originally of royal blood. The early years of his reign saw him battling the Assyrian occupiers of Babylonia. Later, in league with the Medes and possibly the Scythians, his efforts culminated in the fall of Nineveh in 612 B.C. Though Nabopolassar's name is not mentioned in the Bible, this defeat of the Assyrians is celebrated in the book of Nahum. Nabopolassar's son, Nebuchadnezzar II, defeated the Egyptians at Carchemish shortly before the death of his father (see Jer. 46:2; 2 Chron. 35:20). ***See also*** Nebuchadnezzar. D.B.W.

Naboth (nay'buhth), the owner of a vineyard adjacent to a royal estate in Jezreel (1 Kings 21). Ahab the king wanted to buy the vineyard, but it was patrimonial property and Naboth refused to sell it. Seeing that Ahab was despondent, Jezebel, his wife, wrote to the elders of Naboth's village demanding that Naboth be charged with cursing "God and the king" (cf. Exod. 22:28) by two witnesses (cf. Deut. 17:6; 19:15). In accordance with the prescribed penalty for blasphemy (Lev. 24:16; cf. Deut. 17:2–7), therefore, Naboth was stoned to death by the villagers. Ahab hurried to Jezreel to confiscate Naboth's property, but there he encountered the prophet Elijah, who pronounced God's judgment on him. Every male in Ahab's house would perish, and his dynasty would come to an end. As for Jezebel, she would be eaten by dogs in the territory of Jezreel.

The biblical narrative interprets the fall of Ahab's dynasty as divine punishment for the crimes committed against Naboth. Ahab himself responded to his condemnation with penitence and was spared (1 Kings 21:27–29), but his son Joram was slain by the usurper Jehu, who cast his body on the plot that had belonged to Naboth and proclaimed Elijah's oracle fulfilled (2 Kings 9:24–26). Shortly afterwards Jezebel also perished in the predicted manner (2 Kings 9:30–37). P.K.M.

Nadab (nay'dab), the firstborn son of Aaron and Elisheba and the brother of Abihu, Eleazar, and Ithamar (Exod. 6:23). As sons of the priest descended from Levi, the four were trained and ordained to be priests as well (Exod. 28:1).

Nadab and his brother Abihu seem to comprise a pair somewhat distinct from their brothers. On one occasion, these two eldest sons of Aaron were invited to accompany Moses and their father Aaron to the summit of Mount Sinai where, along with seventy elders representing the people, they saw God and ate and drank in God's presence (Exod. 24:1, 9–11). At another time, the two sealed their doom when they offered "unholy fire" to the Lord during the sojourn at the foot of Mount Sinai. For offering what the Lord did not command, the brothers were consumed by divine fire (Lev. 10:1–2), leaving Eleazar and Ithamar to serve as priests with their father (Num. 3:4). ***See also*** Aaron; Abihu. F.R.M.

Nag Hammadi (nahg hahm-mah'dee), a town in Upper Egypt near ancient Chenoboskion, near which was discovered in December 1945 a collection of texts that have shed important light on the religious history of the first Christian centuries. The find consists of thirteen papyrus volumes or codices, which are bound like modern books. Two of these codices, XII and XIII, are only partially preserved. The remaining codices are complete, although the texts within them are often fragmentary; the copyists evidently did not possess the complete text of the material they were copying.

Language and Dates of the Texts: The forty-five works in the collection are in Coptic, the form of late Egyptian written in Greek characters and used in early Christian Egypt. Most of the texts are written in the Sahidic dialect, although there are frequent deviations from the standard literary form of that dialect. Two codices, I and X, as well as part of Codex XI, are written in another dialect, Subachmimic. The works of which these Coptic texts are translations were originally composed in Greek. Papyrus fragments in Greek of some texts, such as *The Gospel of Thomas* and *The Sophia of Jesus Christ*, have been discovered at Oxyrhynchus in Egypt.

Bound papyrus codices found at Nag Hammadi in 1945.

The codices were probably copied in their final form sometime in the fourth century. Dates from this century are preserved on some of the fragmentary papyrus documents used as backing for the leather covers of the codices. The original Greek texts were written earlier, many in the second and third centuries, and some possibly in the first.

Content: The contents of the collection are diverse in genre. The codices contain sayings collections (*The Gospel of Thomas* and *The Sentences of Sextus*); homilies (*The Gospel of Truth*); letters (*The Epistle of Peter to Philip* and *The Treatise on the Resurrection*); acts (*The Acts of Peter and the Twelve Apostles*); expository treatises (*The Tripartite Tractate, Marsanes, Allogenes,* and *The Valentinian Exposition*); prayers (*The Prayer of the Apostle Paul, The Prayer of Thanksgiving,* and *The Three Steles of Seth*); apocalypses (*The Apocalypse of Paul, The Apocalypse of Adam, The Apocalypse of Peter,* and *The First and Second Apocalypses of James*); revelatory proclamations (*The Thunder*); dialogues between Jesus and his disciples (*The Apocryphon of John, The Sophia of Jesus Christ, The Dialogue of the Savior*); and one exegetical work (*The Exegesis on the Soul*).

Diversity also characterizes the theological orientation of the collection. Many of the works provide important primary evidence for Gnosticism. Some of the texts, such as *The Gospel of Truth, The Tripartite Tractate,* and *The Valentinian Exposition*, are associated with the Christian Gnostic school named after the influential second-century teacher Valentinus. Many other works are more difficult to place in the history of Gnosticism. The speculative system of *The Apocryphon of John*, which is preserved in three copies at Nag Hammadi, resembles the system of the so-called Barbeloites mentioned by Irenaeus (*Adversus Haereses* 1.29), but it is impossible to correlate the bulk of the texts with the numerous Gnostic sects listed by Irenaeus and the other church fathers. Many texts (e.g., *Eugnostos, The Apocalypse of Adam, The Thunder*) are clearly Gnostic, but non-Christian. Others have only a superficial Christian veneer (e.g., *The Sophia of Jesus Christ*, which is clearly a Christian reworking of the tractate *Eugnostos*). The hypothesis has been advanced that many of these works with little or no Christian content represent an early form of Gnosticism called by modern scholars "Sethian," after the prominence of Seth, the son of Adam, in some of them. Still other tractates are not directly related to Gnosticism. There are, for example, Hermetic works (*Asclepius 21–29, The Discourse on the Eighth and the Ninth*), pagan sayings collections (*The Sentences of Sextus*), and even a short selection from Plato's *Republic*. There are also some works that are Christian and non-Gnostic, such as *The Teachings of Silvanus* and possibly *The Authentic Teaching*.

Thus the collection does not represent any single Christian or non-Christian school or sect. Why the texts were assembled remains unclear. The library may have been collected for the purpose of combating heresies, although it is more likely that the tractates represent the pious reading of somewhat heterodox monks in Upper Egypt. A connection with the Pachomian monastery at Chenoboskion has been conjectured but not definitely proven. It is perhaps significant that the texts generally display an ascetic ethos, with none of the "libertinism" attributed to some Gnostic groups by the church fathers. This orientation may indicate some connection with a monastic environment. Nor is it clear why the collection was hidden, although ecclesiastical pressures to enforce doctrinal orthodoxy in the late fourth century were probably a factor.

Significance: The texts from the discovery have already made important contributions to the study of early Christianity. Works such as *The Gospel of Thomas* provide new data for the exploration of early traditions of the sayings of Jesus. Isolation of the "Sethian" texts has stimulated a reassessment of the categories in which the Gnostic movement is understood. Earlier Sethian texts (e.g., *The Hypostasis of the Archons, On the Origin of the World*) afford new information about the roots and sources of the Gnostic movement in Judaism. Later Sethian texts (*Allogenes, Marsanes*) display significant affinities with third-century Neo-Platonic circles. The Valentinian texts provide new materials for understanding the history of this influential school of Christian Gnostics in the second and third centuries. One of these texts, *The Gospel of Truth*, may be a work of Valentinus himself. Other Valentinian texts (e.g., *The Tripartite Tractate*, dating from the third century) display both sensitivity to orthodox criticism of Gnostic theology and growing philosophical sophistication in elaborating Gnostic ideas. The collection as a whole has not permitted a definitive resolution of the controversial issue of the relationship between Gnosticism and earliest Christianity, but the texts clearly demonstrate the existence of a non-Christian Gnosticism in the first two centuries of the Christian era.

At present the entire Nag Hammadi collection is available in facsimile form and in English translation. Critical editions with translations and commentaries are available for most of the tractates, but much detailed work remains to be done in analyzing the texts and integrating them into the history of early Christianity. ***See also*** Gnosticism; Gospel of Thomas.

Bibliography

Jonas, Hans. *The Gnostic Religion*. Boston: Beacon Press, 1958.

Robinson, James M., ed. *The Nag Hammadi Library in English*. San Francisco: Harper & Row, 1977.

Rudolph, Kurt. *Gnosis*. San Francisco: Harper & Row, 1983.

H.W.A.

Nahalal (nay'he-lal), a town of Zebulun (Josh. 19:15) assigned to the Levites (Josh. 21:35), but shared by Canaanite inhabitants (Judg. 1:30; "Nahalol") whom Zebulun was unable to expel. The location is uncertain, but it may be modern Tell en-Nahl on the Kishon River near modern Haifa.

Nahaliel (nuh-hay'lee-el; Heb., "torrent valley of God"), a stopping point of the Israelites (Num. 21:19) during the wilderness wandering in the Transjordan, probably modern Wadi Zerqa Ma'in which discharges into the Dead Sea north of the Arnon River.

Nahash (nay'hash; Heb., "serpent"), a name occurring several times in the narratives dealing with Saul and David. An Ammonite king named Nahash besieged Jabesh-gilead and thus provided the Benjaminite Saul an opportunity to solidify his kingship over Israel (1 Sam. 11). Perhaps this is the same Ammonite king who was kind to David (2 Sam. 10:2) and whose sons Hanun (2 Sam. 10:4) and Shobi (2 Sam. 17:27–29) had contact with David. The name is also given to a relative of David, though the relationship is not clear (see 2 Sam. 17:25).

Nahath (nay'hath; Heb., "descent"). **1** The son of Ruel and grandson of Esau; he was a chieftain of the Edomites (Gen. 36:13, 17). **2** A Levite of the clan of Kohath and grandson of Elkanah (1 Chron. 6:26). While some scholars take Elkanah here (v. 26) to be the same as the one listed in the genealogy of Samuel (v. 35) and then equate Nahath with the Toah mentioned there (v. 34; or Tohu, 1 Sam. 1:1), the verses where Nahath occurs (1 Chron. 6:22–27) are an abbreviated genealogy that is not at all clear. Such an identification of Nahath with Toah is thus questionable, although possible. **3** A Levite who shared the responsibility of collecting the Temple offering during the reign of Hezekiah (2 Chron. 31:13). ***See also*** Elkanah. D.R.B.

Nahor (nay'hohr; KJV: "Nachor" in Josh. 24:2 and Luke 3:34). **1** A descendant of Shem, and the son of Serug and father of Terah (Gen. 11:22–25; 1 Chron. 1:26; Luke 3:34). **2** The son of Terah and the brother of Abraham (Gen. 11:26–27; Josh. 24:2) who married Milcah (Gen. 11:29). This Nahor, grandson of 1 above, was the parent of twelve sons (equivalent to tribes) by his wife Milcah and a concubine, Reumah (Gen. 22:20–24). Of these, the tribes born to Milcah were probably the subsequent Aramaean tribes living north and east of Palestine. The tribes born to Reumah were considered less closely tied to Israel, and probably lived north of Damascus. It may have been to this territory that Abraham subsequently sent his servant ("to the city of Nahor," Gen. 24:10) to obtain a wife for Isaac. In addition to the marriage of Isaac to Nahor's granddaughter Rebekah (Gen. 14:15, 24), the relationship of these tribes is further indicated by their worship of a common God (Gen. 31:53). **3** A city ("the city of Nahor," Gen. 24:10) mentioned frequently in the Mari texts that was located east of the upper reaches of the Balikh River, a northern tributary of the Euphrates. This would put the location in modern southern Turkey or northern Syria, probably south and east of Haran (Gen. 29:4–5). R.S.B.

Nahshon (nah'shuhn), the son of Amminadad and the leader of the tribe of Judah during the wilderness wandering (Exod. 6:23; Num. 1:7; 10:14). He is also an ancestor of David and stands in the lineage of Jesus through Joseph (Ruth 4:20; Matt. 1:4; Luke 3:32).

Nahum (nay'hem; Heb., "consolation, compassion"), **the Book of,** the seventh book in the OT in "The Book of the Twelve" (the so-called minor prophets). Nothing is known about the prophet other than his name and the place of his birth, Elkosh, a town in southwest Judah. The book was written in the half century between 663 and 612 B.C. These dates are fixed by the reference in 3:8 to the fall of Thebes (663) and the fact that Nineveh was destroyed in 612. A date for the book close to the actual fall of Nineveh is frequently assumed, though an earlier date is certainly possible. If the revolt of Manasseh is not to be dismissed as a figment of the imagination of the author of Chronicles, the situation as it existed in Judah ca. 652–648 fits the occasion rather well. The basis for such a revolt on Manasseh's part would have been the conviction that Assyria's days were numbered. The book of Nahum presents precisely that message and may have been used to persuade the Judean king to take part in such a revolt—the assurance that Assyria's fall was certain, in fact that it was ordained of God the Divine Warrior. The book would then have taken on deeper meaning as part of the theological basis for the subsequent resurgence of Judean independence under Josiah, especially after the death of Asshurbanapal in ca. 630. The final destruction of Nineveh in 612 would have been the ultimate fulfillment of this prophecy and would thus explain its inclusion in the canon.

It is likely that Nahum was a central prophet functioning within the Temple cult in Jerusalem. The book belongs to the so-called oracles against the nations and as such was probably motivated by political aims. In its present canonical form it is closely related to the book of Habakkuk. In fact the two books may be outlined as a single literary unit as follows:

I. Hymn of theophany (Nah. 1)
II. Taunt song against Nineveh (Nah. 2–3)
III. The problem of theodicy (Hab. 1)
IV. Taunt song against the "wicked one" (Hab. 2)
V. Hymn of theophany (Hab. 3).

The opening hymn of theophany (Nah. 1: 2–8) is in the form of an acrostic on the first half of the Hebrew alphabet (cf. Ps. 9), which presents the two sides of God's character: he is slow to anger but he will vent his wrath against those who defy him. The appearance of the Divine Warrior is presented in mythic imagery with the cosmos returning to chaos in the day of God's wrath.

In the taunt song (Nah. 2–3), sometimes described as an ode on the fall of Nineveh, the language is graphic, depicting in vivid form scenes of horror and vengeful rejoicing because Assyria is finally experiencing the atrocities she had inflicted on others.

In its poetic form the book of Nahum has no superior within the prophetic literature of the OT. The vivid and rapid succession of images gives it a peculiar power. It delineates the swift and unerring execution of God's fury against his merciless foes and those of his people. At the same time it also points rather sharply to God as the sure refuge and security for those who obey and trust him. ***See also*** Habakkuk, The Book of; Nineveh. D.L.C.

nails. **1** The small horny plates covering the fingertips (Deut. 21:12; Dan. 4:33). **2** Devices for fastening construction materials together (1 Chron. 22:3). In construction history, early wooden pegs as fasteners were replaced by copper and bronze nails (ca. 3000 B.C.), but the introduction of iron technology (ca. 1200 B.C.) made much harder nails available and opened the possibility of multistoried buildings. Proverbial fastening strength was used metaphorically for wisdom (Eccles. 12:11), for permanence (Isa. 41:7), or for futile confidence (Jer. 10:4). Crucifixion was carried out sometimes using nails to fasten the condemned to the posts, graphic evidence of which was found north of Jerusalem in an ossuary containing foot bones fastened to wood with iron nails. While the synoptic Gospels do not mention nailing Jesus to the cross, such an understanding of Jesus' crucifixion underlies the request of "doubting Thomas" (John 20:25) when he was informed that Jesus had risen from the dead. R.S.B.

Nain (nay'in), a village identified with modern Nein six miles southeast of Nazareth at the foot of Givat ha-Moreh in the Valley of Jezreel (cf. Judg. 7:1). In later Jewish sources, the town was called Naim (Heb., "pleasant"). Here Jesus resuscitated the widow's only son (Luke 7:11–17). Ruins of a medieval church remain in the village, and to the southeast are ancient rock-cut tombs.

Naioth (nay'oth), a place in or near Ramah in the tribal area of Benjamin, a short distance north of Jerusalem, where David, fleeing Saul, took refuge with Samuel and the prophets associated with him (1 Sam. 19:18). Saul's messengers, sent to Naioth to take David, became imbued with the prophetic spirit, as did Saul himself when he followed (1 Sam. 19:20–24).

names, nouns by which entities are identified. The Bible is the main source for the proper names of ancient Israel. Biblical narratives preserve a wide variety of personal and geographical names (PNs and GNs, respectively). These are augmented by geographical and genealogical lists in early and late sources which, when handled critically, can provide much accurate information.

Another valuable source of Israelite proper names is the corpus of ancient Israelite inscriptions, preserving hundreds of names, some not attested in the Bible. Most important for the OT period are the ostraca and stamp seals. An increasing number of names from the intertestamental and NT periods are being discovered in Aramaic, Hebrew, and Greek inscriptions on seals, tombs, ossuaries, ostraca, and papyrus documents. These augment the names attested in the NT and contemporary Jewish writings. Israelite PNs and GNs are also sporadically attested in non-Israelite ancient Near Eastern inscriptions.

Productive comparative study is possible due to the large quantity of proper names available in ancient Semitic languages related to Hebrew, such as Eblaite, Amorite, Ugaritic, Phoenician, Ammonite, Moabite, Edomite, Aramaic, and later Arabian dialects. Akkadian (Semitic) and Egyptian names, although preserved in great numbers, are less similar in style and form, but along with names in Hurrian, Hittite, Persian, and later Greek and Latin sources, they have proven beneficial in understanding difficult and foreign names in the Bible.

Personal Names: The majority of Israelite names, and ancient Semitic names in general, had a readily understandable meaning. That parents consciously chose a child's name is implied by the content of these names, many of which are translatable sentences.

Compound names, usually consisting of two elements, are attested in a variety of grammatical constructions, especially statements, which occur in nominal, adjectival, and verbal forms. Interrogative and imperative constructions are infrequent. Most compound PNs are theophoric, containing a divine name (DN) or title. The most common DN in Israelite PNs was Yahweh (Jehovah is an anglicized, hybrid form of this), appearing as Jo-/Jeho- or -iah/-jah. The next most attested element was the generic *el*, meaning "god" (El was also the DN of the head of the Canaanite pantheon). Titles such as *adon* ("lord"), *baal* ("master," also a Canaanite DN), *melek* ("king"), *zur* ("rock") as well as kinship terms like *ab* ("father"), *ah* ("brother"), and *am* ("kinsman/[paternal] uncle") were sometimes used instead of a DN. Confusion can arise, however, regarding elements used both generically and as DNs, such as *baal*, *el*, and several others; or with kinship terms, which might be associated with a deceased relative rather than a deity.

Different types of compound PNs include: names expressing parents' recognition of divine assistance, such as Mattaniah ("gift of Yahweh"), Elnathan/Nathanael ("God has given [this child]"), and Shemaiah ("Yahweh has heard [the parents' prayer]"); names expressing parental desires for the child, such as Jeberechiah ("may Yahweh bless [this child]"), Ezekiel ("may God strengthen [this child]"), and Jehiel ("may God preserve [this child]"); names expressing parents' convictions, such as Elijah/Joel ("Yahweh is [my] God"), Uzziel ("God is my strength"), Adoniram ("my lord is exalted"), and Ahimelek ("my [divine] brother is king"); and names reflecting circumstances at the child's birth, such as Ben-oni ("son of my sorrow," Gen. 35:16–20), and Ichabod ("where is the glory?" 1 Sam. 4:19–22). Names like Menachem ("comforter") and Eliashub ("God restores") may suggest that a newborn was regarded as a substitute for a deceased family member.

The elements of a compound name could also be employed singly, making a shortened, or hypocoristic form, as in Mattan, Nathan, Uzzi, and so on. There were other types of simple or one-element PNs too. Some were originally animal or plant names like Caleb ("dog"), Deborah ("bee"), Jonah ("dove"), Tamar ("palm tree"), and Allon ("oak"). Others reflected circumstances at birth, such as Haggai ("[born on] a festival day") and Becorath ("firstborn"); physical characteristics, like Zuar ("little one") and Laban ("white [fair-skinned]"); or qualities hoped for, as in Amon ("reliable"). Evidence available from the NT and contemporary Jewish writings indicates that these types of simple and compound PNs continued in use, but with a trend towards hypocoristic forms of the latter. There was also a greater tendency toward adopting a foreign name or a name showing foreign influence.

Geographical Names: Although many of the features discussed in relation to PNs apply to GNs as well, GNs are in certain ways more difficult to treat. Some are very old and their meanings are obscure (true of a few PNs too). Also, many of the names of cities, rivers, and mountains preserved in the Bible, Semitic for the most part, were in existence before the Israelites entered Canaan and were merely adopted by them, as with Jerusalem, Megiddo, Mt. Hermon, and the Jordan River. Other GNs were changed by the Israelites, as in the case of Laish becoming Dan (Judg. 18:29), while new sites received new GNs. Inferences from biblical GNs concerning Israelite religion are limited since Israelite GNs follow the basic typology of pre-Israelite Caananite GNs, making it impossible to discern whether many names were Israelite creations or merely adoptions. The NT similarly reflects the continuation of many GNs, the replacement of others, such as Herod's renaming of Samaria as Sebaste, and the formation of new ones. It is possible to trace many of these ancient GNs into Arabic forms today.

As with PNs, GNs of both simple and compound form existed. However "sentence" GNs are attested in the Bible infrequently, as are theophoric GNs. Examples of the latter include Beth-el ("house/temple of God/El"), Beth-dagon ("house/temple of Dagon"), and Baal Hazor ("lord/Baal of Hazor"; this latter type was usually short for a fuller form with "beth" in the first position). "Beth," with the meaning "house/place," also occurred in nontheophoric GNs, as in Beth-marcaboth ("house/place of chariots") and Bethlehem ("house/place of bread/food"). Other compound GNs contain an element referring to the environment, such as *beer* ("well"), as in Beer-sheba; *en* ("spring") as in En-gedi; *abel* ("meadow") as in Abel-meholah; and *emeq* ("valley") as in Beth-emeq.

Many simple GNs also referred to natural features, including Ramah and Ramoth ("height[s]"), Gibeah and Gibeon ("hill"), Horeb and Negeb ("dry"). Names based on structures include Mizpah ("watchtower"), Succoth ("booths"), Geder ("wall/enclosure"), and Gath ("wine press").

GNs were also named after people, as with Nobah (Num. 32:42) and Dan (Judg. 18:29), or in relation to an event, as with Bochim ("weepers," Judg. 2:4–5) and Ebenezer ("stone of help," 1 Sam. 7:12). Plant and animal names were employed as GNs too, such as Tamar ("palm tree"), Shimir ("thorn"), En-rimmon ("spring of the pomegranate"), Ephron ("gazelle"), Akrabbim ("scorpions"), and En-gedi ("spring of the goat").

Value of Names: The value of these ancient names for biblical studies is found in the variety of cultural clues they provide. For example, theophoric PNs indicate which deities were important to various societies in the polytheistic ancient Near East. The majority of Israelite theophoric PNs contained either a form of the DN Yahweh, or to a somewhat lesser extent, the generic term *el*. Names of Israelites in the Bible living between the Exodus and the Babylonian exile (thirteenth through early sixth centuries B.C., excluding those whose sole attestation occurs in Chronicles, Ezra, or Nehemiah), reveal that only a small percentage of the population of ancient Israel had PNs containing a foreign DN, even during times of proclaimed apostasy. PNs in Israelite epigraphic sources corroborate this point with similar evidence.

Theophoric PNs are also a valuable guide to qualities associated with a given deity. PNs containing the DN Yahweh depict him as: strong, glorious, noble, righteous, gracious; king, father, brother, light; someone who creates, gives, strengthens, remembers, knows, blesses, protects, saves, judges, restores, and so on.

Name studies help chart various cultural trends, such as: preferred grammatical forms of names in different periods; similar categories of GNs used by pre-Israelite Canaanites and Israelites; the small number of theophoric PNs attested for women in the Bible; more frequent use of kinship terms and certain divine titles in PNs through the time of the United Monarchy (ca. 1004–926 B.C.); fads in the popularity of some PNs; the increased foreign influence on names by the NT period; and the increased practice of papponymy, naming a child after its grandfather. Papponymy was part of a growing tendency evident from the Persian period (late sixth century B.C.) onward, to select PNs previously borne by relatives or well-known biblical characters, rather than ones that "meant" something.

The use of patronyms, common among ancient Semites, is amply attested in the Bible and in Israelite inscriptions. Well-known biblical examples include Joshua the son of Nun and Simon Bar-Jona ("son of Jonah"). Other forms of identification included GNs, as in Goliath of Gath and Jesus of Nazareth, and professions, as in Simon the tanner and Shimshai the scribe.

The Bible also illustrates the significance and power associated with certain names and with

NAMES OF GOD IN THE NT

the act of naming. Obedient Israelites would be "called by the name of the Lord" (Deut. 28:10). God's messengers spoke in God's name (2 Sam. 12:7; Acts 4:18). Representatives of a human authority similarly spoke in his name (1 Sam. 25:5; Esther 3:12). Changing another's name displayed the power of the changer and the allegiance owed by the one whose name was changed. Names changed by God include Abram, changed to Abraham (Gen. 17:5); Sarai, to Sarah (Gen. 17:15); and Jacob, to Israel (Gen. 32:28). According to Mark 3:16 Jesus gave the name Peter (Gk., "rock-like") to Simon. PNs changed by a human authority include Eliakim, to Jehoiakim (2 Kings 23:34); Mattaniah, to Zedekiah (2 Kings 24:17); and Daniel, to Belteshazzar (Dan. 1:6, 7). D.M.P.

names of God in the New Testament. The names used by NT authors to refer to God reflect the fact that the NT was written in a Greek-speaking culture primarily on the basis of a tradition and terminology inherited from the OT and Judaism as mediated by the Septuagint (LXX). This tradition was significantly modified both by the early church's understanding of the teaching of Jesus and by its understanding of the person of Jesus as the definitive expression of God.

God: The most common word for God in the NT (1,318 times) is the Greek word *theos* ("god"), used often by the LXX (more than 4,000 times) primarily as the translation of the usual Hebrew word for God, *elohim*. This word was also used by the LXX for the pagan gods, just as it was the standard word for the gods of the Greeks and Romans of NT times. Although the NT writers sometimes use "god" for the pagan gods (e.g., 1 Cor. 8:5) and on rare occasions apparently apply it theologically to the glorified Christ (e.g., John 20:28), the vast majority of cases refers to the God revealed in the history of Israel and in the person of Jesus. Thus, "the God and Father of our Lord Jesus Christ" is a frequent designation (e.g., Rom. 15:6).

Lord: In the OT, the chief title and representative name for God was the individual and personal name "Yahweh," translated *kyrios* (Gk., "Lord") in the LXX and "the LORD" by several English versions. This name was used by OT authors more than 6,000 times, compared to about 2,500 times for *elohim*, "God." The NT continues to use "Lord" for God (about 100 times), primarily in quotations from the LXX (e.g., Mark 1:3; 12:11; Acts 2:34) and in set phrases such as "hand of the Lord" (Luke 1:66). The vast majority of the 719 occurrences of *kyrios* ("Lord") in the NT refers to Jesus, however, usually as the exalted Christ (e.g., Acts 2:36; John 20:28). Thus, the two most common OT names for deity, "God" and "Lord," are used in the NT not only for God but also (though rarely in the case of the word "God") for Jesus as the exalted Lord of the church's faith. A much less common word for "Lord" in the LXX, *despotēs* (Gk., "lord," "sovereign," "master") is also used in the NT both for God (Luke 2:29; Acts 4:24; Rev. 6:10) and for Christ (Jude 4; 2 Pet. 2:1).

Father: The common ancient Near Eastern idea that the deity is the father of the clan or nation was appropriated sparingly by Israel, which understood it in an adoptive, not biological, sense (Exod. 4:22–23; Hos. 11:1–4). Although "Father" never became a common name for God in the OT, it was used more freely in the later OT period (e.g., Isa. 63:16) and especially in post-OT Judaism. "Father" was also a common name for deity among the Greeks, being applied to Zeus, for example, not only because of his rulership among the gods, but because of his love and care. This general designation of God as "Father" is found only rarely in the NT: e.g., Heb. 12:9 ("Father of spirits") and James 1:17 ("Father of lights," i.e., the heavenly bodies).

It was the person and teaching of Jesus that played the formative role in the NT's language about God as "Father." For Jesus, "Father" was the principal and most frequent designation for God. He used not only the common Jewish "our [or your] Father" (e.g., Matt. 5:45; 6:9) but also the intimate family word for "father" in his native Aramaic language, *abba*, which was also appropriated in the later liturgical practice of the church (Mark 14:36; Rom. 8:15; Gal. 4:6). Not only did the concept of God as "Father" express the personal relationship to God affirmed by Jesus and the church (e.g., Matt. 11:25–27), but in that cultural setting the term included especially the connotations of obedience, agency, and inheritance. Those who address God as "Father" acknowledge God as the one to whom absolute obedience is due (Matt. 7:21; 26:42) and themselves as the agents who represent God and through whom God works (Matt. 11:25–27; John 10:32) and as God's heirs (Rom. 8:16–17).

"The God of the Fathers": This significant OT title for God, as well as the more particular phrase of the same meaning, "the God of Abraham, Isaac, and Jacob," is found in the NT only in two Gospels (Mark 12:26; Matt. 22:32) and in the book of Acts. As in the OT, it emphasizes the continuity of Israel and the church's faith, that the God of present experience is the same as the God revealed to the ancient patriarchs. Luke-Acts, which is especially interested in pointing out this continuity, thus uses the title four times (Acts 3:13; 5:30; 7:32; 22:14). In Paul and the literature dependent upon him, this title is replaced by "the God and Father of our Lord Jesus Christ" (Rom. 15:6; 2 Cor. 11:31; Eph. 1:3, 17; Col. 1:3; 1 Pet. 1:3).

The Almighty: The LXX had translated two of the Hebrew expressions for God in the OT, which probably meant "God, the one of the mountains" (RSV: "God Almighty") and "Yahweh of Hosts," with the more philosophical and formal *pantokratōr* (Gk., "Almighty"), which the Greeks had also used for their gods. Jesus and the NT authors seem to avoid this appellation, which is found only in 2 Cor. 6:18 and nine times in Revelation, mostly in self-designations of God or in ascriptions of praise in a liturgical context.

Alpha and Omega: These are the first and last letters of the Greek alphabet and thus represent God as the Beginning and the End, the source and goal of all creation, and thus the *only* God. The phrase itself is not found in the OT, but the basic formula from which it is derived is found in Isa. 44:6 and 48:12. In the NT, only the author of Revelation uses this name for God (1:8; 21:6); he also applies it explicitly to Jesus Christ (22: 13; cf. 1:17; 2:8).

The Holy One: This OT title for God, especially in Isaiah, explicitly refers to God only once in the NT (Rev. 16:5). It is used of Jesus in Mark 1: 24; Luke 4:34; and John 6:69. In 1 John 2:20, the reference may be either to God or to the exalted Christ.

General Terms: The common impersonal words for "deity" in Greek are absent from those LXX books that are derived from the Hebrew canon of the OT and appear only once in the remainder of the LXX (Wisd. of Sol. 18:9). Correspondingly, "Deity" as a term for God is found in the NT only in Paul's address to the Athenians in Acts 17:29, and in Col. 2:9.

The line between explicit names for God and more general designations is sometimes difficult to draw. Among the more common general designations used in the OT that are adopted in significant ways by NT authors are "King" (e.g., Matt. 5:35; 1 Tim. 1:17; 6:15), "Judge" (e.g., John 8:50; Heb. 12:23), and "Savior" (e.g., Luke 1:47; 1 Tim. 1:1; 2:3; 4:10), all of which are applied more frequently to Jesus Christ than to God.

In the NT period, many Jews expressed their reverence for the explicit names for God by substituting periphrastic ways of speaking of God. This practice is reflected to some extent in the NT, especially in the sayings of Jesus (though Jesus did not hesitate to make use of explicit names for God). Among such periphrastic and reverential terms for God are "the Blessed" (Mark 14:61), "Power" (Mark 14:62), "Heaven" (Luke 15:18 and often in the Matthean phrase "Kingdom of Heaven" as a substitute for "Kingdom of God"), and the "Majestic Glory" (2 Pet. 1:17). In addition, God is sometimes referred to by using the passive voice (the so-called "divine passive," e.g., Matt. 5:4, 6, 7, 9) and the impersonal "they" (e.g., Luke 16:9; also Luke 6:38; 12: 20; and 12:48 are such in Greek but not in the English translation). ***See also*** Abba; Alpha; Father; God; Lord; Omega. M.E.B.

names of God in the Old Testament. The names, titles, and metaphors for God in the OT reflect Israel's setting in the ancient Near East, the theological richness of OT traditions, and the social contexts that shaped religious life. What unites the many appellations, which are a central feature of Israel's dynamic religion, is not monotheism in a strict sense. While there were pre-exilic trajectories such as the emerging wisdom tradition in which monotheistic tendencies were present, the articulation of the existence of one God found clear expression for the first time in Second Isaiah during the crisis of the exile (sixth century B.C.). Yet even before the exile, Israelites believed that the God who had encountered them and shaped their destiny demanded their undivided devotion and loyalty. It was this conviction that led OT theologians (priests, prophets, court historians, and sages) to transform the variety of appellations and their religious traditions into descriptions of the God of Israel.

The Personal Name for God: In the ancient Near East, great significance was attached to personal names, for they revealed character and identity and signified existence. The revelation of a divine name and its continued use were of substantial importance for a people.

Yahweh. The most important name for God in the OT is the tetragrammaton YHWH (occurs about 6,800 times), usually pronounced "Yahweh," though the known pronunciation was lost in the postexilic period. Due to the increasing sanctity attached to the name and the consequent desire to avoid misuse, the title *'Adonai* (Heb., "My Great Lord") was pronounced in place of the tetragrammaton. In written texts the vowels of *'Adonai* were combined with the consonants YHWH to remind readers to pronounce *'Adonai* instead of Yahweh. The incorrect hybrid, "Jehovah," arose from Christian misunderstanding in the late Middle Ages. The respect for the sanctity of the personal name of God is reflected in modern Judaism.

The origin of the name Yahweh (usually translated "LORD" in English Bibles) remains uncertain. Even the biblical sources are divided at this point. The Yahwist *(J)* traces the revelation of the name Yahweh to the primeval period (Gen. 4:26), while the Priestly Source *(P)* honors Moses as the first to know this name (Exod. 6:2–3). The meaning of the name most probably derives from the imperfect form of the Hebrew verb "to be." In Exod. 3:14 (the Elohist Source, *E*), God responds to Moses' question about his identity with the ambiguous statement, "I am who [what] I am," or "I will be who [what] I will be." In *E*'s connection of the name with the Hebrew Qal (simple) stem of the "to be" verb, the meaning appears to connote divine mystery (cf. Gen. 32:22–32) and freedom. A variation of this same interpretation understood the name to signify God's presence. Another interpretation connects Yahweh with the Hebrew

Hiphil (causative) verbal stem and thus understands God's name to mean: "He causes to be what exists [happens]"; i.e., Yahweh is creator and ruler of history. It is this latter meaning that is more likely. Through Israel's encounter with God in nature and history, faith in God as the one who created the world, shaped human destiny, and elected Israel to be the covenant people was actualized. Each pronouncement of the name Yahweh was a succinct expression of this faith.

Yahweh Sabaoth. This compound name, "Lord of Hosts," which occurs 279 times in the OT, depicts God as the commander of armies. Originating in holy war, the expression became a polemic against astral cults: Yahweh rules the heavenly armies. The name was eventually understood as a plural of intensity, "Lord Almighty," thus neutralizing the existence of the celestial gods. The Septuagint (LXX) translates this name "Lord Almighty."

Generic Names for God: *Elohim*. Occurring about twenty-five hundred times in the OT, Elohim is one of three common generic names for deity in the OT. The term is plural and on occasion means "gods" (e.g., Exod. 20:3), but most often it is a plural of majesty for Israel's "God" (e.g., Gen. 1:1). Unlike the term El, Elohim is not found in other Semitic languages. While originally possessing polytheistic associations, Israelite theologians transformed the meaning of the term and used it to refer to God. While the name was used in most traditions, periods, and regions, it was especially favored in Northern Israel.

Eloah. The second generic name for deity in the OT is Eloah (Heb., "God"), though it is found only fifty-seven times, the great majority of which occur in Job. The poet of Job may have used this generic word for God to avoid the specific Israelite conceptions of covenant and salvation history associated with the name Yahweh. Job, a part of wisdom literature, prefers to speak of the universal dominion of creation theology.

El. Occurring more than two hundred times in the OT (including compounds), El (Heb., "god") is the common Semitic name for deity in ancient Near Eastern cultures. Every divine being was properly designated by this generic name. El is also the name of the head of the pantheon of Ugarit, however. As creator and father of the gods, El possessed the authority of the divine decree that ordered the world of gods and humans. Polytheism and the worship of El were major components of both Canaanite and Israel's ancestral religions. In the settlement of Canaan, the tribes of Israel began to assimilate Canaanite religious centers and associate those religious traditions with Yahweh, the one who liberated them from Egypt.

El Shaddai. According to *P* (Exod. 6:3), El Shaddai (Heb., "God, the One of the Mountain [s]") was worshiped by the patriarchs Abraham, Isaac, and Jacob. In the mythologies of the ancient Near East, gods often resided on a cosmic mountain that was the center of the earth. Shaddai came to be identified with El, the head of the Canaanite pantheon, and then with Yahweh (Exod. 6:3; Ezek. 1:24). The LXX translated Shaddai "Almighty." Thus many English Bibles translate El Shaddai as "God Almighty."

El Elyon. El Elyon (Heb., "God Most High"), originally a compound for the high god El, was worshiped in Jerusalem before David's conquest (ca. 1000 B.C.). In Genesis 14, Melchizedek is the priest-king of Jerusalem who blesses Abraham in the name of "God Most High, Maker of Heaven and Earth," the "God who gave Abraham's enemies into his power. In *J*'s rendition of this story, El Elyon is identified with Yahweh. After the Israelite takeover of Jerusalem, the El Elyon tradition is associated with Yahweh (Ps. 47:2–3).

El Olam. El Olam (Heb., "God of Eternity") was the Canaanite god of Beersheba. After this religious center was incorporated into Israelite religion, the title came to designate Yahweh (Gen. 21:33).

El Berith. El Berith (Heb., "God of the Covenant") was the Canaanite god of Shechem (Judg. 9:46). In Joshua 24 the Deuteronomic historians placed the covenant renewal ceremony at Shechem following the conquest of Canaan. In the *D* history the covenant became the basis for the tribal league during the period of the Judges (eleventh century B.C.).

El Roi. El Roi (Heb., "The God of Seeing/Divination") was a localized deity of a sacred spring (Beer-la-hai-roi) whose water sustained Hagar in the desert and inspired her to see a divine vision (Gen. 16:13–14). *J* connects this story with Yahweh, who promises Hagar a son (Ishmael) who will have many descendants.

In summary, the local Canaanite gods and El, the head of the pantheon, were worshiped in sanctuaries eventually taken over by Israel. Canaanite religious traditions were eventually applied to Yahweh. In this theological process, Yahweh, the God of liberation from Egyptian slavery, merged with Canaanite gods, including the high god El, who legitimated a stratified social system of city-states ruled by local dynasts. This combination provided the critical tension that characterized Israelite religious expression throughout the OT.

Social Titles for God: The changing social constructions of Israel also provided important titles for God.

'Adonai. 'Adonai (Heb., "My Great Lord") is a plural of majesty derived from the singular Adon (Heb., "lord"), a title of respect used to address a social superior (e.g., king, husband, slave owner). In the postexilic period, 'Adonai

came to replace the name Yahweh in common worship because of the increasing sanctity associated with the latter name (e.g., Job 28:28).

Baal. Baal (Heb., "lord") is a title designating a social superior (e.g., leader, owner, husband). In Canaanite religion, Baal is the name of the storm god of fertility who brought rain and military victory. This god rivaled Yahweh for Israel's devotion, as especially noted in prophetic literature (e.g., Hosea). While certain theomorphic names may indicate that some Israelites identified Baal with Yahweh (e.g., Meribbaal, the son of Jonathan), the term was generally avoided because of strong pagan associations (cf. Hos. 2:16–17).

Royal Titles. The political matrix of Israel and other ancient Near Eastern cultures provided a host of titles and images for God. Among the more important are royal titles: king (Ps. 95:3), judge (Gen. 18:25), and shepherd (Ps. 23). These titles signified God's position and function as ruler over Israel.

Family Titles. Other important titles derived from the Israelite family, including father (Deut. 32:6), brother (Ahijah: Heb., "brother of Yahweh," 1 Sam. 14:3), kinsman ("kinsman [fear] of Isaac," Gen. 31:42), and redeemer (Ps. 19:14). These titles may have originated in patriarchal religion where the personal deity of the head of the clan became the protector of the group ("The God of My Father," Exod. 3:6). The "redeemer" was the next of kin responsible for delivering the relative from hard times (Lev. 25:25). While God is not explicitly called "mother" or "sister," the OT does use female images to speak of God. God is depicted as mother who conceives, bears, and gives birth to Israel (Num. 11:12; Deut. 32:18) and as midwife (Ps. 22:9–10). These images demonstrate that the OT does not limit and confine God to the masculine gender. ***See also*** Baal; El; El Bethel; El Shaddai; Father; God; King; Lord of Hosts; Shepherd; Sources of the Pentateuch. L.G.P.

Nannar (nan'er; Heb., "lightgiver" from Sumerian *Nar-nar*), a term for the Sumerian god Sin, identified as the moon. Sin was worshiped at Ur in south Mesopotamia. ***See also*** Sumer.

Naomi (nay-oh'mee; Heb., "my pleasantness"), one of the major characters in the book of Ruth. Naomi, her husband Elimelech of Bethlehem, and their two sons went to Moab in a time of famine (Ruth 1:1–2). The sons married Moabite women but both sons and Elimelech died (1: 4–5). Naomi decided to return to Bethlehem and urged her daughters-in-law to remain with their families in Moab (1:8–14). Ruth refused, vowed loyalty to Naomi, and returned with her to Bethlehem (1:16–17). There, Naomi encouraged Ruth to ask protection of Boaz, a kinsman of Elimelech (chap. 3). Boaz redeemed Elimelech's property and married Ruth in accordance with levirate law (chap. 4; cf. Deut. 25:5–10). Their son, Obed, preserved Elimelech's line and later became the grandfather of King David. ***See also*** Ruth. M.A.S.

Naphtali (naf'tuh-lee; Heb., meaning uncertain), second son of Jacob and Bilhah (Gen. 30: 7–8) and eponymous ancestor of the Israelite tribe of that name. Naphtali's territory was bounded on the west by Asher, on the south by Zebulun and Issachar, and on the east by the river Jordan and the Sea of Galilee. This territory Naphtali shared with Canaanites (Judg. 1:33). Its northern location is reflected in the position it occupied along with Dan and Asher on the north side of the Tent of Meeting (Num. 2:25–31).

In the period of the Judges, Barak, son of Abinoam, from Qedesh in Naphtali, successfully led a force of ten thousand against the army of Sisera (Judg. 4:6–10, 12–16) and twice the tribe of Naphtali answered the call of Gideon to battle invading Midianites (Judg. 6:35; 7:23). During Solomon's reign, the administrative officer in charge of Naphtali was son-in-law to the king; and Hiram of Tyre, the son of a widow from the tribe of Naphtali, is credited with the manufacture of the bronze/copper work commissioned by Solomon for the Temple (1 Kings 7:13–47; but according to 2 Chron. 2:13–14 it was Huramabi of the tribe of Dan). The only craftsman designated by name in the account of Solomon's building activity, Hiram's skill is described in terms reminiscent of those employed to describe the abilities of Bezalel, the master craftsman of the tabernacle in the wilderness (Exod. 31:3; 35:31) and the "shoot from the stump of Jesse" (Isa. 11:2). In the period of the Divided Monarchy, Naphtali was invaded by Ben-hadad of Syria at the request of Asa of Judah during the course of the war between the latter and Baasha of Israel (1 Kings 15:16–20). Later, during the reign of Pekah of Israel, Tiglath-pileser III invaded Naphtali and deported its population to Assyria (2 Kings 15:29). In the course of the Maccabean wars, forces of Demetrius of Syria, intent upon removing Jonathan from office, reached Qedesh (Naphtali) in Galilee and were met by Jonathan, who managed to turn a near defeat into victory (1 Macc. 11:63–64, 67–74).

Naphtali in Poetic Sources: 1 The Blessing of Jacob (Gen. 49:21). As it stands, the text is obscure, but if one changes certain vowels in the final word it yields the following translation: "Naphtali (though) born a mountain-ewe, gives birth to lambs of the fold." The poet thus contrasts Naphtali's prior state of independence with its state of political dependence in the period of the poet. **2** The Blessing of Moses (Deut. 33:23). "Naphtali, sated with favor, and filled with Yahweh's blessing, possess the sea and the south(?)!" The final word, *darom*, translated "south," is suspect in so early a poem, for it is found otherwise only in the late books of Ezekiel, Job, and Ecclesiastes. If, with the alteration of its first letter, it may originally have read *marom*, "highland" (cf. Judg. 5:18), then the blessing has reference to the tribe's well-favored territory from the Sea of Galilee to the Galilean highlands. **3** The Song of Deborah (Judg. 5:18). Along with Zebulun, Naphtali is lauded for its participation in the war against Sisera. ***See also*** Tribes, The. S.G.

napkin, cloth used for wiping perspiration from the face (Acts 19:12, "handkerchief") or to wrap an object (Luke 19:20). John 11:44 and 20:7 mention the custom of wrapping the head of a corpse. Its position in John 20:7 may be an indication that Jesus' body had not been stolen from the tomb (see v. 2b; Matt. 28:11–15).

Narcissus (nahr-sis'uhs), person mentioned in Rom. 16:11 as one whose "family" included Christians. Perhaps a house-church met in his home but not all of the family were Christians. It is unlikely that the reference is to a freedman of the Emperor Claudius by this name.

nard. ***See*** Spikenard.

Nash Papyrus, the. ***See*** Texts, Versions, Manuscripts, Editions.

Nathan (nay'thuhn; Heb., "gift [of God]"). **1** A prophet in the court of David. Three significant events are recorded about him. In 2 Samuel 7 (and 1 Chron. 17) it says that David consulted with him on his intention to build a temple to house the Ark of the Covenant (v. 2). In a revealing statement on the prophet's knowledge of God's will, Nathan at first assumed that God approved of this plan (v. 3) but then was told by God that David's wish would be fulfilled only by his son (vv. 4–5, 12–13). The reason for the postponement of the erection of the Temple is indicated in vv. 6–16. In the past, God's presence in a tent was appropriate to accompany the children of Israel on their wanderings. However, now that the Israelites were settled (v. 10), and God had initiated with David a permanent human rulership over Israel (vv. 11, 16), the proof of the establishment of this permanence and security—the reign of David's heir—would be the proper symbolic time for the building of a house to the Deity (v. 13). Additionally, peace obviates the necessity for God (and the Ark) to lead the Israelites into battle (v. 9; cf. 1 Chron. 22:7–10). The assurance in this prophecy of the unconditional eternality of the Davidic dynasty (vv. 12–16) captured the popular imagination during First Temple times (ca. 950–586 B.C.) and obstructed the attempts of the later prophets to affirm the primacy of the conditional Sinai covenant in order to bring the people to repentance.

After David committed adultery with Bathsheba and arranged Uriah's death (2 Sam. 11), God sent Nathan to rebuke David (2 Sam. 12). Nathan, through the parable of the poor man's ewe lamb (vv. 1–4), trapped David into accusing himself and acknowledging his own guilt (vv. 5–6, 13). David's "measure for measure" punishment is threefold (vv. 10–14): violence will be a constant family companion (witness Amnon, Tamar, and Absalom); his wives will have public intercourse with another (2 Sam. 16:22); and the son of the illicit union must die (2 Sam. 12:18). Like the episode of Naboth's vineyard (1 Kings 21), this story illustrates the unique ability of Israel's prophets to confront the monarch with moral crimes. Unlike other royalty in the ancient Near East, who ruled absolutely and often capriciously, the Israelite king was subservient to the Torah of God (note that the sentence pronounced by David upon the rich man in 2 Sam. 12:6 is identical with Exod. 22:1).

In 1 Kings 1, readers are afforded a rare behind-the-scenes view of the machinations of royal succession. Here, Nathan, without hint of divine instruction, is the king-maker, setting the stage and directing dialogue (vv. 13–14), manipulating David to crown Solomon his successor. Not that Nathan is acting immorally; rather, David is too feeble to act on his own and must be led onto the proper path.

The Chronicler mentions the writings of Nathan as part of his source (1 Chron. 29:29; 2 Chron. 9:29) and partly attributes to his authority the musical role of the Levites in the Temple (2 Chron. 29:25).

2 A son of David (2 Sam. 5:14; Zech. 12:12; 1 Chron. 3:5; 14:4), and Jesus' ancestor in Luke 3:31.

3 The father of one of David's warriors (2 Sam. 23:26).

4 The brother of another of David's warriors (1 Chron. 11:38).

5 The father (sometimes identified with the prophet) of one of Solomon's officers (1 Kings 4:5).

6 The father of one of Solomon's priests (1 Kings 4:5; but see 1 Chron. 2:34–36 where the same [?] Nathan is a descendant of an Egyptian servant).

7 Two men at the time of Ezra (Ezra 8:16; 10:39). ***See also*** Bathsheba; David; Prophet; Solomon. J.U.

Nathanael (nuh-than'ee-uhl). **1** A priest required by Ezra to put away his foreign wife (1 Esd. 9:22). **2** An ancestor of Judith (Jth. 8:1). **3** One of the chosen disciples of Jesus mentioned only in John's Gospel; brought to Jesus by Philip (John 1:43–51; cf. 21:2). Described by Jesus as "an Israelite indeed, in whom is no guile," Nathanael is characterized as resolute in his devotion and piety to God. Nathanael's confession is exemplary: "Rabbi, you are the Son of God! You are the King of Israel!" Nathanael is also noted, however, for his earlier scornful question, "Can anything good come out of Nazareth?" Because his name is absent from the apostolic lists in the other Gospels and Acts, many scholars have identified him with one or another of those listed, most commonly Bartholomew. ***See also*** Apostle; Bartholomew; Disciple; Philip; Twelve, The. P.L.S.

nations, large political divisions, normally of homogeneous ethnic populations. Both the OT and the NT teach God's sovereignty over the nations. God appointed them (Deut. 32:8); before him they are nothing (Isa. 40:7) and to them He will be a light (Isa. 42:6; Luke 2:32). The chief snare of "the nations" is their gods (Deut. 7:22–26), which are accounted as mere idols (Ps. 96:5) and not true gods (Isa. 44:12–20; 45:14). Non-Israelite peoples are often grouped together under the rubric "nations" (e.g. Exod. 34:24; Deut. 11:23; Josh. 23:13).

Natufian (na-tōōf'yan), an archaeological designation for a people or period at the upper edge of the Paleolithic Age, 10,000–8,000 B.C. The Natufians are named after the Wadi en-Natuf near Jerusalem where excavation first revealed their distinctive tool forms. Since that time numerous manifestations of this culture have been found throughout Palestine and even in Syria. It is these peoples who, following the final retreat of the last glaciers of the Ice Age, first began to intensify their collection of wild grains, i.e, took the first tentative steps toward the domestication of plants and animals. Their sickle blades and food-grinding equipment reflect this greater awareness and exploitation of the environment. Besides rock shelters, they occupied open-air, apparently permanent dwelling places, as evidenced by the settlement of Mallaha. The first art also appeared at this time. They are the earliest people known to have occupied the Holy Land. S.L.R.

Nazarene (naz'uh-reen), a term applied to Jesus in all four of the Gospels and in Acts and, in one passage, also applied to the early Christians. The Greek word has two different spellings, perhaps deriving from different roots in Hebrew or Aramaic, but both are apparently understood, perhaps erroneously, as references to Nazareth, the home of Jesus. In most instances, the RSV translates the term by the English phrase "of Nazareth" (but cf. Matt. 2:23; Mark 14:67, where it is rendered as "Nazarene"). In Acts 24:5, the word, in the plural, is applied to the early Christians, and it apparently continued in use for some time as one of several designations for Christians. ***See also*** Christian; Jesus Christ; Nazareth; Way. J.M.E.

Nazareth (naz'uh-reth), the place from which Jesus' mother came (Luke 1:26) or the place in which he grew up (Matt. 13:54; Luke 4:16; Luke 2:4, 51; Matt. 2:23). Nazareth was an insignificant agricultural village not far from a major trade route to Egypt, the *Via Maris*. It is not mentioned in the OT, Josephus, or rabbinic writings. Not surprisingly, Jesus' Nazareth origins are held up to scorn by those skeptical of his mission (John 1:46).

A Hebrew inscription found at Caesarea lists Nazareth as one of the villages in which the priestly divisions (cf. Luke 1:8–9) were resident after the Jewish revolt. Some scholars think that this notice attests to the piety attributed to Nazareth, which has not produced any remains with pagan symbolism.

The village appears to have occupied 40,000 square meters and to have had a population of 1,600 to 2,000 persons in Jesus' time. The major settlement in the area appears to have occurred in the second century B.C. No layout of the village or its houses has been discovered, although the typical dwelling would probably have consisted of a small group of rooms around a central courtyard, and some houses may have had a second story.

According to legend, there was a Jewish-Christian community in Nazareth during the second and third centuries A.D. However, the early pilgrims were not much interested in Nazareth. In the sixth century A.D. legends about Mary sparked interest in the site, where one now finds the Church of the Annunciation and a well designated as "Mary's Well or Fountain." P.P.

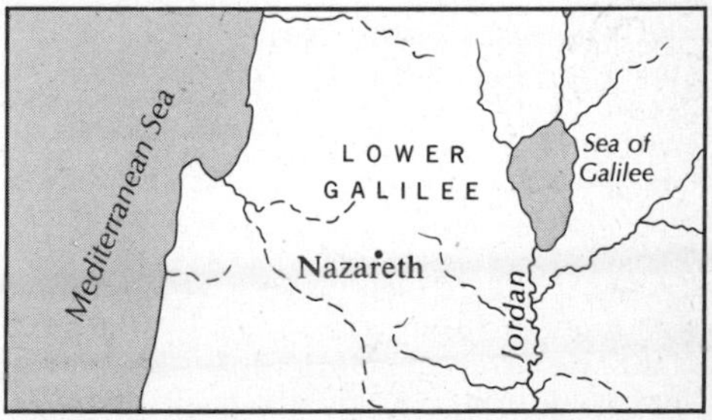

Nazirites (na'zuh-rīts; Heb., "dedicated" or "consecrated [ones]"), men or women who entered a consecrated state upon their own or a parent's vow (Num. 6:1–21; 1 Sam. 1:1–11; Judg. 13:1–7). There were three main conditions for entering and remaining in this holy state: refrain from the fruit of the vine and other intoxicants, not allow a razor to touch one's hair for one's term as a Nazirite, not go near a dead body—not even that of one's own father or mother (Num. 6:1–7). In the last condition the rigor is comparable to that required elsewhere only of the high priest (cf. Lev. 21:10–12 and 21:1–4). The first condition was also a distinguishing feature of the Rechabites (Jer. 35). Upon completion of a term the Nazirite could drink wine (Num. 6:20), and some were tempted to do so before (Amos 2:10–11).

The Bible sets forth an elaborate ritual for reconsecration, should a Nazirite become unclean through contact with a dead body (Num. 6:9–12), and for bringing the period of consecration to an end (vv. 13–20). The Mishnah in the tractate named *Nazir* puts the minimum term at thirty days.

Joseph is called a *nazir* (Gen. 49:26; Deut. 33:16). Samuel is not explicitly named one but the wording of the vow made by his barren mother, Hannah (1 Sam. 1:11), strongly suggests he should be counted a Nazirite. Samson is the most famous, explicitly named Nazirite; and much of the irony and pathos of the narrative cycle lies in Samson's gradual loss or deprivation of his special God-given status (Judg. 13:7; 16:17). Both Samuel and Samson were consecrated by vows uttered when they were still in their mothers' wombs. In the NT it is likely that one of the significances attached to Jesus' being called a "Nazarene" (Matt. 2:23) is that he too should be viewed as a Nazirite in the sense of being consecrated to God from the womb.

J.G.G.

Neapolis (nee-ap'uh-lis; Gk., "New City"), the name of many Greco-Roman towns founded near ancient sites, e.g., Naples, Italy. Neapolis in the NT is the seaport, modern Kavalla, for Philippi, ten miles inland (Acts 16:11). Noteworthy also is Flavia Neapolis, modern Nablus, founded about A.D. 72 by Vespasian just west of ruined Shechem in the Gerizim-Ebal pass; Justin Martyr was born near there in A.D. 100. Early Neapolis coins depict a colonnade, a stairway up Gerizim, and temples on the summits. Remains of Roman and Byzantine times are encountered frequently in Nablus, including water works, tombs, and a small theater. The Samaritan community that reveres Mt. Gerizim still lives there. ***See also*** Gerizim; Philippi; Samaritans. E.F.C.

Nebaioth (ne-bay'uth), the firstborn son of Ishmael (Gen. 25:13; KJV: "Nebajoth"; 1 Chron. 1:29) and Esau's brother-in-law (Gen. 28:9; 36:3). As a tribe Nebaioth's descendants were as famous for their herds of sheep (Isa. 60:7) as was the tribe of Kedar, and they may have been the *Nabaiati* mentioned in the records of the Assyrian kings Tiglath-pileser III and Ashurbanipal in the eighth and seventh centuries B.C.

Nebat (nee'bat), the name of the father of Israel's king Jeroboam I (ca. 924–903 B.C.; 1 Kings 11:26). He is identified as an Ephraimite from Zeredah, modern Deir Ghassaneh, about ten miles west of Shiloh. He is mentioned several times in 1 and 2 Kings and 2 Chronicles.

Nebi Samwil (ne'bee sam-weel'; Heb., "the prophet Samuel"), a settlement on a high promontory (2,935 feet above sea level) commanding a direct visual surveillance of the main road from the coast up to Jerusalem on the west and the main north-south hill country route that lay just east of it. It was five miles northwest of Jerusalem and according to late tradition was the site of Samuel's burial.

Nebo (nee'boh). **1** A Babylonian god (Isa. 46:1) considered the son of Marduk. His statue was paraded with Marduk's in Babylon at the New Year Festival, setting the context for Isaiah's taunt (Isa. 15:1–9). He was associated with water, writing, and speech. Of the last six kings of Babylon, three carried his name in their personal names, *Nabo*polassar, *Nebu*chadnezzar, and *Nabo*nidus. **2** A Moabite city (Num. 32:3, 38), probably modern Khirbet Mekhayyet, about five miles southwest of Hesban. It was part of Sihon's kingdom (Num. 21:26–30). Assigned to the tribes Reuben and Gad (Num. 32:3), it was Moabite under Mesha (mid-ninth century B.C.) and it figured in the prophecies of both Isaiah (15:2) and Jeremiah (48:1, 22). **3** A mountain promontory (Deut. 32:49) from which Moses was called to view Canaan at the time of his death, modern Jebel en-Nebu, 2,740 feet above sea level, and about 4,030 feet above the Dead Sea whose north edge lies below it to the west. As part of the Abarim range (Num. 33:47), the promontory is conspicuously visible from Hesban but is accessible most easily from Medeba five miles southeast. The most panoramic view of the Jordan Valley and land to the west is from a lower promontory across a saddle to the northwest, modern Ras es-Siyaghah. Byzantine churches and other installations continue to be excavated by Franciscan teams in this area. **4** The ancestor of some returning exiles (Ezra 2:29; 10:43; and possibly Neh. 7:33) who may have been associated with a town in Judah, Nuba, six miles northwest of Hebron. R.S.B.

Nebuchadnezzar (ne'buh-kuhd-nez'uhr), the name of four kings now known to us from ancient Mesopotamia. The first was the king of the Second Dynasty of Isin (southern Mesopotamia), who ruled 1124–1103 B.C. He is known as Nebuchadnezzar I. The king mentioned in the Bible is known as Nebuchadnezzar II by modern scholars. The Behistun inscription (western Iran) of Darius I (522–486 B.C.) tells of two contenders for the throne (522 and 521 B.C.) who bore the name Nebuchadnezzar (called by moderns III and IV, though some doubt has been raised concerning the existence of the last).

Bulls alternating with serpent-dragons adorn the walls of the Ishtar Gate, built in Babylon by Nebuchadnezzar II (ruled 605–562 B.C.) and now reconstructed in the Staatliche Museum, East Berlin.

Nebuchadnezzar II ruled Babylonia from 605 to 562 B.C. He was the son of Nabopolassar, founder of the Chaldean dynasty. Nebuchadnezzar II was the most powerful and longest reigning king of the Neo-Babylonian (625–539 B.C.) period. He brought the city of Babylon and the southern Mesopotamian state of Babylonia to the pinnacle of their power and prosperity.

The name *Nabû-kudurri-uṣur* means "O Nabu, preserve the offspring [lit., 'boundary-stone']." From this Babylonian form, the alternate biblical spelling Nebuchadrezzar is taken.

The major competitors for power in the days of Nebuchadnezzar II were Media (northwest Iran) and Egypt, always with great-power ambitions for ports and trade in the Levant (Syria, Lebanon, Israel). Nebuchadnezzar's marriage to a daughter of the king of the Medes held the alliance with that power secure until after Nebuchadnezzar's death. As for Egypt, Pharaoh Neco suffered a defeat at the hands of Nebuchadnezzar at the city of Carchemish in 605 B.C., from which he did not recover (2 Kings 24: 7).

Much information about the early rule of Nebuchadnezzar II comes from the *Chronicles of Chaldaean Kings* (D. J. Wiseman; London: British Museum, 1956). However, of the forty-three years of the reign of Nebuchadnezzar II, only those up to 594 B.C. are preserved. Other records tell of the conquest of Tyre (571 B.C.; cf. Ezek. 27: 12) and the invasion of Egypt in Nebuchadnezzar's thirty-seventh year (reported by a fragmentary British Museum tablet; see Ezek. 29:19–21). Accounts indicate that Nebuchadnezzar was an able but cruel ruler (cf. 2 Kings 25:7) who stopped at nothing to subdue peoples who stood in his path of conquest.

Amēl-Marduk (Evil-Merodach), Nebuchadnezzar's son, ruled from 562 to 560 B.C. According to accounts in 2 Kings 25:27–30 and Jer. 52: 31–34 he recognized King Jehoiachin and allocated an allowance for him "all the days of his life." Babylonian clay tablets mentioning the disbursement of oil to Jehoiachin, five sons of the king of Judea and other Judeans confirm in a dramatic manner this Scriptural statement.

Building projects sponsored by Nebuchadnezzar included the beautification of Babylon, his capital, the construction of fortification walls in addition to those already in place, and the improvement of Marduk's temple in Babylon, Esagila. There is extant a list of the personnel of the court of Nebuchadnezzar II, showing the complex infrastructure of the royal palace.

From the perspective of biblical Israel, the events associated with the reign of Nebuchadnezzar II that had the most lasting effect upon their destiny were the destruction of Judea, the conquest of Jerusalem, the setting to the torch of the Temple of Solomon, and the exile to Babylonia (597–581 B.C.). The reflection of these events and the events that led up to them can be seen in the biblical materials in 2 Kings and 1 and 2 Chronicles, taken with Jeremiah. Related materials may be found in Ezra, Nehemiah, and Esther. Daniel 1–5 represents an account of Jews in the court of Nebuchadnezzar, along with apocalyptic visions.

Jeremiah, the great prophet who was an eyewitness to the destruction of the Temple, counseled submission to Nebuchadnezzar, whom he viewed as the instrument of the Lord's wrath. In time, Jeremiah wisely foresaw, Nebuchadnezzar's own land would face its day of reckoning as well (Jer. 27).

It is thought by some scholars that Daniel 4, which records the madness of Nebuchadnezzar, may have incorporated accounts pertaining to the less well-known Babylonian monarch of this same dynasty, Nabonidus. ***See also*** Daniel; Daniel, The Book of; Jeremiah, The Book of; Nabonidus.
D.B.W.

Nebuzaradan (neb-o͞o-zah-rad'uhn), a Babylonian high official who, in 586 B.C., oversaw the destruction of Jerusalem and its Temple (2 Kings 5:8–22). He supervised personally the disposition of the captured property and population in Judah: vessels used in worship and appurtenances of precious metals were carried off as spoil to Babylon. The poorest people of the land, the refugees behind Jerusalem's walls, were permitted to resume their pursuits as "vinedressers and fieldworkers." The leaders of the rebellion against Babylon, the high priest and the surviving royal officials, were transferred to Riblah where they were summarily executed. Nebuzaradan exiled the remainder of the city's populace; an exception was made in the case of the prophet Jeremiah who was permitted to stay behind as counselor to the new governor Gedaliah (Jer. 40:1–6).

Nebuzaradan's official title, "chief cook" (often incorrectly rendered "chief executioner"), is attested both in Hebrew *(rab ṭabbāḥîm)* and in Akkadian *(rab nuḫatimmu)*. Nebuzaradan is listed second among the courtiers of King Nebuchadnezzar on a Neo-Babylonian administrative document. ***See also*** Gedaliah; Jeremiah, The Book of.
M.C.

Neco (nee'koh; KJV: "Necho[h]") **II** (610–595 B.C.), king of Egypt during the twenty-sixth (Saite) dynasty (ca. 664–525 B.C.), and successor to the very successful Psammetichus I (664–610 B.C.) who established Egyptian control in Philistia during part of his reign. Neco became pharaoh during the last days of the Assyrian Empire when it was precariously clinging to life in north Syria. As a former Assyrian vassal with expansionist ideas and concerned to limit Babylonia (Chaldea) as a possible successor to Assyrian dominance, Egypt sent a major sea and land expedition to north Syria in 609 B.C. to aid Assyria against the Babylonian forces. In doing so Neco encountered King Josiah of Judah at Megiddo (2 Kings 23:29); Josiah was presumably acting either for Judean independence and thus against Egypt, which was seeking to become dominant in the area, or in the interest of Babylonia against Assyria. Josiah died as a result of that encounter, but the Egyptian forces were not successful in the attempt to install the Assyrian remnant in Haran. Yet with Assyria no longer a factor, Egypt was, for the moment, the dominant power in southern Syria and Palestine.

On his return from north Syria about three months later, Neco summoned Jehoahaz (Shallum), king of Judah, whom the Hebrew people had anointed as successor to his father, Josiah, to Riblah, deposed him, put him in bonds, and carried him off to Egypt. Neco assigned Judah a heavy tribute and installed Jehoiakim (formerly Eliakim) as successor to his younger brother. In 605 B.C. Neco again battled Babylonia in north Syria, at Carchemish, losing decisively. Shortly thereafter Jehoiakim switched his allegiance to Babylonia, who came to control all of Syro-Palestine.

Apart from his ambitious undertakings in Syro-Palestine, Neco, building on his father's foundation, expanded the Red Sea trade and tried to reestablish commercial contacts with Punt (Somalia). Although he stayed out of Syro-Palestine after 605, he sent a major expedition into Nubia, initiated an extensive canal project in the eastern Nile delta, and successfully resisted the Babylonian attempt to invade Egypt in 601–600 B.C. ***See also*** Jehoahaz; Jehoiakim; Josiah.
H.B.H.

necromancy. ***See*** Magic and Divination.

needle's eye, a hyperbolic reference (Mark 10:25 and parallels) in a saying of Jesus on the difficulty of a rich man entering the Kingdom of God. There is no evidence for the view that it referred to a narrow gate in the walls of Jerusalem.

needlework, embroidery or other fine sewing. Needlework was used on the screen for the entrance to the tabernacle (Exod. 26:36) on blue, purple, and scarlet material with fine twisted linen. The same combination was specified for the screen at the gate of the court (Exod. 27:16) and Aaron's girdle (Exod. 28:39; see also Exod.

36:37; 38:18; 39:29). Knowledge and skill of fine needlework was found throughout the ancient Near East and still marks the dress garments of women in villages where distinctive patterns distinguish regions and sometimes specific towns. Fine needles of bone, copper, and bronze have been found in various archaeological contexts, confirming the widespread use of the skill.
R.S.B.

neesings (from "neeze," a Scottish term for "sneeze"), a term in the KJV where the RSV has "sneezings" in Job 41:18.

Negeb, the (nay'geb; Heb. *negev*, "dry, parched, south country"), the southern part of Judah, and the largest region in the modern state of Israel. The Negeb forms an inverted triangle with its base roughly following a line from Gaza past Beer-sheba to the Dead Sea. The line then runs south from the Dead Sea through the Wadi Arabah to the Gulf of Aqabah at Elath/Aqabah. The border then runs northwest to Gaza. The Negeb is a hot, dry region with less than 8 inches of rainfall annually.

Some evidence of settlement in the Negeb dates back as early as the Paleolithic period (100,000–10,000 B.C.). Scattered settlements are found from the Neolithic (10,000–4000 B.C.) and Chalcolithic (4000–3000 B.C.) periods. Several factors seem to have led to the establishment of permanent settlements in the harsh climate of the Negeb. First, the presence of sufficient water for settlement from springs, wells, oases, or cisterns of sufficient capacity. Second, the proximity of important trade routes also led to permanent settlement. Towns would be established to meet the needs of travelers and to protect the route. Third, many of the towns on the northern border of the Negeb were established, or at least maintained, as border fortresses. Beer-sheba, Hormah, and Arad fall into this category.

Several highways went through the Negeb. The most important was the Via Maris (Lat., "coastal road"), which connected Egypt through Palestine with Mesopotamia and Anatolia. The Via Maris skirted along the western edge of the Negeb near Gaza. Three other north-south roads went through the Negeb. One ran from Jerusalem and Hebron to Beer-sheba and Nissana and then connected with the Via Maris. Another road came from Hebron to Arad, Hormah, and then to the oasis at Kadesh-barnea. The third

The Negeb, the "dry, parched, south country;" where the Israelites spent much of the wilderness wandering period.

road followed the Wadi Arabah from the Dead Sea to Elath/Aqaba. The main east-west road was the Way to the Arabah, from Kadesh-barnea to Bozrah in Edom (modern Buseirah). Just west of Kadesh, it connected with the Way to Shur, another route to Egypt. A minor road connected Elath with Kadesh; another connected Arad, Hormah, and Beer-sheba with the Dead Sea eastward, and the Via Maris westward.

The Hebrews spent much of the wilderness wandering period (ca. 1290–1250 B.C.) around the oasis of Kadesh-barnea in the southern Negeb (Deut. 1:19, 46). The Amalekites, a seminomadic people, also lived in the Negeb (Num. 13:29).

During the period of the monarchy (1025–587 B.C.), many small villages and fortresses were established in the Negeb. The fortresses guarded the southern borders of Judah. The many villages and more intensive agriculture in the region suggest an expanding population during the monarchy so that marginal land had to be farmed. These farmers knew the technique of terrace farming.

After the fall of Judah at the Exile (587 B.C.), the Edomites gained control of the Negeb. However, the area had limited population until the arrival of the Nabateans in the last two centuries B.C. The Nabateans resettled many sites and built additional villages. They were very adept at farming and pasturing the dry region by careful water conservation. Only during the Byzantine period (A.D. 334–632) did the Negeb support a larger population. After the Arab conquest (A.D. 632), the Negeb declined and has supported only a limited population until modern times. ***See also*** Kadesh; Wilderness.

J.F.D.

Neginah (ne-geen'uh), apparently a term for a stringed instrument (cf. 1 Sam. 16:16, 23; Isa. 23:16). *Neginah* appears in various Psalm headings (Pss. 4; 6; 54; 55; 61; 67; 76) as well as at the end of the "Psalm of Habakkuk" (Hab. 3:19). Presumably it designates in these instances the manner of performance or accompaniment.

Nehemiah (nee-uh-mī'uh; Heb., "Yahweh comforts"), **the Book of,** the eleventh book in the OT and the last of the historical books called the Former Prophets. In the Hebrew Bible, Nehemiah forms the second part of Ezra-Nehemiah. Chaps. 8 and 9 continue the story of Ezra from Ezra 7–10; this section is now enclosed within the Nehemiah narrative, though it is not entirely clear where the division is to be made. Thus, the book consists of several sections: chaps. 1–7, Nehemiah's commission and first governorship; chaps. 8–9, Ezra's reading of the law and a psalm of distress; chap. 10, a new covenant; and chaps. 11–13, the repopulation of the city of Jerusalem, dedication of the walls, and Nehemiah's second governorship. Various lists also appear whose relationship to their contexts is not entirely clear.

Dating Nehemiah's Activity: Nehemiah's activity is set in the reign of a Persian ruler Artaxerxes. It appears probable that this is Artaxerxes I (465–424 B.C.). If so, Nehemiah's first governorship began about 445 and lasted until 433 (Neh. 2:1; 13:6); his second began at an unspecified date after this. The decision for Artaxerxes I depends largely on the correlation with Sanballat of Samaria, whose sons were active in the later years of the fifth century B.C., as is shown by the Elephantine papyri. Since there were probably three governors of Samaria named Sanballat, however, the possibility that Nehemiah belongs to the reign of Artaxerxes II (405/4–359/58) cannot be ruled out. Josephus, the first-century A.D. Jewish historian, relates

OUTLINE OF CONTENTS

The Book of Nehemiah

I. Nehemiah's commission and first governorship (1:1–7:73)
   A. Nehemiah receives commission from Persian king to rebuild walls of Jerusalem (1:1–2:8)
   B. Initial steps: opposition from non-Jews, secret survey of walls, organization of Jews for rebuilding (2:9–3:32)
   C. Opposition from non-Jews and defensive tactics of Nehemiah (4:1–23)
   D. Nehemiah's economic reforms among Jews (5:1–19)
   E. Walls completed despite plots against Nehemiah by non-Jews (6:1–7:3)
   F. Concern for repopulating Jerusalem: census of returned exiles (7:4–73)

II. Religious observances in response to the law (8:1–10:39)
   A. Ezra reads the book of the law to the people (8:1–12)
   B. Resulting celebration of Feast of Booths (8:13–17)
   C. A psalm of distress: public confession of sin (9:1–37)
   D. A new covenant to keep the law and support the Temple (9:38–10:39)

III. Further organization of the Jewish community (11:1–13:31)
   A. Repopulation: lists of people and officials living in Jerusalem (11:1–12:26)
   B. Dedication of city walls and arrangements for Temple revenues (12:27–13:3)
   C. Nehemiah's second governorship: reforms in keeping with the law (13:4–31)

the story of Nehemiah separately from and after that of Ezra.

The Narrative: The book of Nehemiah is narrated in the first person. This is evidently a stylized form, like some royal inscriptions, designed to glorify this national hero. The passages that invite a blessed memory for Nehemiah (5:19; 6:14; 13:14, 22, 29, 31) are akin to votive texts, requesting divine blessing on particular individuals.

The narrative that Nehemiah tells can be summarized in the following way. Nehemiah, cupbearer to the king, is distressed at the ruined condition of Jerusalem. As a result he prays to God and then appeals to the Persian king who grants him a commission and support to rebuild the walls of Jerusalem (1:1–2:8). Nehemiah's encounter with opposition and his survey of the walls and organizing of the rebuilding (2:9–3:2) are followed by opposition narratives involving Sanballat of Samaria, Tobiah of Ammon, Geshem of Arabia, and others (chaps. 4; 6). The reason for the opposition is not clear, nor is it entirely evident that the three main opponents really worked in concert. Indeed, Tobiah even appears to have had substantial support for his opposition to Nehemiah from within Jerusalem (6:17–19). Nevertheless, Nehemiah is shown as a governor engaged in reform and protection of the distressed (chap. 5). The account of the completion of the walls (7:1–3) has its real sequel in the narrative of their dedication (12:27–13:3). This narrative sequence is interrupted by an account of the repopulation of the city, introducing a list of the restored community (7:6–73), which is found also in Ezra 2. The story of Ezra in chaps. 8–9 further interrupts the narrative sequence of the book of Nehemiah. Chap. 10 lists the subscribers to a new covenant and lays out its requirements. The repopulation theme is then resumed in 11:1–12:26, a passage that incorporates various lists of officials. 13:4–31 describes Nehemiah's second period as governor, noting the further opposition of Tobiah and his associates in Samaria, Nehemiah's reorganization of tithing, his insistence on Sabbath observance, and his action against foreign marriages.

There are many problems of interpretation in the Nehemiah narrative; among them are the sequence of events, the reasons for opposition, and the relationship of his activity to that of Ezra. The material concerning Ezra clearly constitutes a separate source, now partly integrated into the larger work.

Later traditions (Ecclus. 49:13; 2 Macc. 1–2) show further glorification of Nehemiah; in the latter he becomes the restorer of Temple and city after the Exile, and the collector of the Hebrew Scriptures. This shows considerable overlap with the development of the Ezra tradition. In some circles Nehemiah was seen as a great patriotic hero. The presentation in the book of Nehemiah attributes to him royal and prophetic characteristics: prophetic action (5:13) and royal-style activity in legal and religious reform (chaps. 10; 13). A historical assessment is difficult to make. ***See also*** Chronicles, The First and Second Books of the; Ezra; Sanballat; Tobiah.

Bibliography

Fensham, F. C. *The Books of Ezra and Nehemiah.* New International Commentary on the Old Testament. Grand Rapids, MI: Eerdmans, 1982.

Myers, J. M. *Ezra-Nehemiah.* Anchor Bible. Vol. 14. Garden City, NY: Doubleday, 1965. P.R.A.

Nehiloth (ne-hee'lohth), an instrument named in the KJV heading of Psalm 5; the RSV renders it "flute."

Nehushta (nee-hōōsh'tah), wife of king Jehoiakim of Judah and mother of king Jehoiachin (2 Kings 24:8). As queen mother she played an important role in the royal court; therefore she was exiled to Babylon along with her son (2 Kings 24:12) and the members of other prominent families.

Nehushtan (ne-hōōsh'tan), the name of the copper serpent destroyed during the religious reforms of King Hezekiah (727–698 B.C.; 2 Kings 18:4). It was a cult symbol that stood, most likely, in the Temple court in Jerusalem for the people who assembled there. The account in Num. 21:8–9 states that its form was that of a (Heb.) *saraf,* or "fiery serpent." It appears to have been an apotropaic object, protecting those bitten by serpents (cf. Num. 21:4–9; John 3:14). Many modern scholars assume that it entered the Jerusalem cult from the Canaanite heritage.

neighbor, in the OT one who lives nearby (Exod. 12:4; Jer. 12:14; Prov. 27:10) or, figuratively, one who is a fellow Israelite (Exod. 2:13; 1 Sam. 28:17). In the latter sense, one is also termed "brother" (Lev. 25:25; Deut. 15:2–3; Neh. 5:1).

As members of a community united by divine covenant, law, and teaching, the Israelites' obligations to God were reflected in their moral obligations to each other. They were to be "a kingdom of priests and a holy nation" (Exod. 19:6). Thus, they were commanded concerning each other not to covet their neighbor's wife or possessions (Exod. 20:16–17; Deut. 5:20–21); not to hold a neighbor's garment for pledge past sunset (Exod. 22:25–26); not to steal, deal deceitfully, swear falsely (Lev. 19:11), or defraud (v. 13); not to gossip, or to be passive while injustice is being done to another (v. 16); not to hate one another (v. 17), to avenge or bear a grudge (v. 18), to take usury (Lev. 25: 36–37), or to enslave (v. 39); not to oppress (vv. 43, 46), to withhold loans or charity (Deut. 15: 7–11), or to ignore a neighbor's stray animal or lost property (Deut. 22:1–4). The Israelites were obligated to each other for the property placed in one's care (Exod. 22:6–14), "to love your neighbor as yourself" (Lev. 19:18), to help the poor through free loans (Lev. 25:35), or hiring the poor for pay (vv. 39–40), and the like. One who has harmed his neighbor will be punished in kind (Lev. 24:19–20, 22). God will destroy those who slander their neighbors (Ps. 101:5; cf. Prov. 11:9). To despise one's neighbor is to be devoid of wisdom (Prov. 11:12) and to sin (14:21). According to Zechariah 3:10, in the messianic age neighbors shall dwell together in peace.

When Jesus quoted Lev. 19:18, he broadened it beyond the bounds of fellow Israelites, as he made clear in the parable of the good Samaritan (Luke 10:27–37). For that reason, references in the NT to loving one's neighbor are to be understood as referring to any human being (e.g., Rom. 13:8–9; Gal. 5:14; James 2:8). ***See also*** Ethics.

J.U.

Nekoda (ne-koh'duh). **1** A family group ("sons of Nekoda") of Temple slaves (Nethinim) who returned from the Babylonian captivity with Zerubbabel (Ezra 2:48; Neh. 7:50). **2** Another family group who also returned but who could not prove their ancestry (Ezra 2:60; Neh. 7:62). ***See also*** Nethinim.

Nemuel (nem'yo͞o-el). **1** A descendant of Reuben of the clan of Pallu (Num. 26:9). **2** A son of Simeon and head of the clan of the Nemuelites (Num. 26:12; 1 Chron. 4:24). He is also called Jemuel (Gen. 46:10; Exod. 6:15).

Neolithic Age (Gk., "new stone"), the latest of the three subdivisions of the Stone Age (beginning about 500,000–200,000 B.C.; cf. Paleolithic [ending ca. 25,000–12,000 B.C.]; Mesolithic [ca. 12,000–8000 B.C.]), during which pottery was invented and villages were formed. In Palestine it comprises generally the years 8000–4500 B.C. It was followed by the Chalcolithic period (4500–3000 B.C.) and the Bronze Age (3000–1200 B.C.).

Nephilim (nef'i-leem), people of the pre-Flood generation, the offspring of daughters of men and divine beings (Gen. 6:1–4). Their generation and their conduct seem to have provoked the Flood as punishment (Gen. 6:5–8:22). In Num. 13:33 the Israelite spies describe the inhabitants of Hebron as Nephilim, so large and powerful that "we seemed like grasshoppers." The name could mean "fallen ones" and allude to stories in related cultures of rebellious giants defeated by the gods in olden times (cf. Isa. 14:12). ***See also*** Giant.

Nephtoah (nef-toh'ah), a water source on the boundary of Judah (Josh. 15:9) with Benjamin (Josh. 18:15). It is identified as modern Lifta with its spring three miles northwest of Jerusalem.

Ner (nuhr; Heb., "light"), the name of the Benjaminite father of Abner, Saul's military commander (1 Sam. 14:50–51; 26:5, 14). Nothing else is known of his life, and his relation to Saul is unclear. Suggestions include that he was Saul's uncle (1 Sam. 14:50, derived by textual adjustment there and at 1 Chron. 8:33) or that he was Saul's grandfather (by considering Kish to be a son of Ner in 1 Sam. 9:1; see also 1 Sam. 10:14–15).

Nereus (nee'ro͞os), a Christian who, with his sister, is greeted by Paul in Rom. 16:15. Possibly they are children of Philologus and Julia. ***See also*** Julia.

Nergal-sharezer (neer'gahl-shahr-ee'zuhr), a Babylonian official. The name occurs three times in Scripture (Jer. 39:3 [twice], 13) as being among the officers present in Jerusalem during and after the siege of 587 B.C. The first occurrence is followed by what may be his official title; in the second and third, he is designated "Rabmag." A Rabmag official is mentioned in contemporary Neo-Assyrian and Babylonian documents as *rab-mugi* (meaning unknown). The Babylonian *Nergal-šar-uṣur* means "O Nergal, preserve the king!" Neriglissar is the anglicized form of the name taken from the Greek Nargalasar, with variants in the Septuagint at Jer. 46:3 and in the Masoretic Text at Jer. 39:3. Caution is advised regarding the proposed identification of the Nergal-sharezer of the Jeremiah passages with the future king of Babylonia (ruled 559–556 B.C.) of the same name since the name is borne by persons other than the king and no patronymic is given here. D.B.W.

Neri (nay'ree), an ancestor of Jesus (Luke 3:27).

Neriah (ne-rī'uh; Heb., "light of Yah [God]" or "Yah is light"), the father of Baruch, the scribe and associate of Jeremiah (Jer. 32:12; 36:4–32), and also the father of Seraiah, an officer of King Zedekiah (Jer. 51:59). ***See also*** Baruch.

Neriglissar (ne-re-gli'sahr). ***See*** Nergal-sharezer.

Nero (neer'oh; A.D. 37–68), Roman emperor (ruled A.D. 54–68), the son of the fourth wife of the emperor Claudius, Agrippina. Nero would eventually murder his mother and wife Octavia in order to marry the beautiful Poppea, whom he also later murdered. The early part of Nero's reign, while Nero was under the influence of the

The profile of the Roman emperor Nero portrayed on bronze sestertus (ca. A.D. 65).

philosopher Seneca, promised a rule of moderation in which the senate would have restored to it the powers usurped by Claudius. A change in Nero's conduct occurred in A.D. 62 and he tended toward public brutality and sexual licentiousness and demanded public adulation as a god. The handsome young emperor of the early coins changed into a somber figure, mouth shrinking into fat cheeks and an increasingly protruding chin.

Nero came under increasing criticism for his preoccupation with artistic activities such as drawing, painting, participating in musical and theatrical contests and for his preoccupation with chariot races. He mounted an artistic tour of the Greek East and also portrayed himself as following in the footsteps of Alexander the Great. However, Nero had none of the latter's interest in the conduct of war. He used the wealth of the empire to buy popularity with gifts of money to the praetorians and later to the populace of Rome, who were also pacified with cheap or free corn. A fire in Rome in A.D. 64 enabled Nero to use the land to build a grand palace, "the gold house." When Nero needed a scapegoat for the fire, he ordered the brutal execution of a number of Christians. Both the apostles Peter and Paul probably lost their lives in this persecution.

Faced with revolts in Britain, Gaul, and Spain and increasing unpopularity at home, especially among the army, which disliked this effeminate emperor, a despairing Nero fled Rome and took his own life. However, legends later circulated in the eastern provinces that Nero would return. Christian hostility to Nero as the epitome of excessive Roman power and brutality is evident in Revelation 13. The number of the beast, "666," forms an acronym for his name (Rev. 13: 18). ***See also*** Revelation to John, The. P.P.

nests, the abode of birds. The term is used frequently in OT passages in both a literal and a metaphorical sense. The theme of birds and their nests or making nests reflects the awareness and deep appreciation of the natural world commonly found in the literature of the ancient Near East, e.g., it is forbidden to harm a hen by taking her from her nest (Deut. 22:6). Assyria is likened to one robbing a nest (Isa. 10:14). Numerous species and their nests are referred to: an eagle stirring up her old nest (Deut. 32:11); doves building nests on the sides of the mouth of the gorge (Jer. 48:28); nests of the great owl and vulture on deserted sites (Isa. 34:15); nests of swallows on altars (Ps. 84:3).

Metaphorically the term "nests" is often used to refer to the abode of human beings: the people of Lebanon make their nests in the cedars (Jer. 22:23); the cautious man strives to set his nest on high (Hab. 2:9); and in a nest one shall grow old (Job 29:18). S.L.R.

Nethanel (neth-ahn'el; sometimes Nethaneel; Heb. *natanel,* "God gives"). **1** The son of Zuar (Num. 1:8) and commander of 54,400 men (2:5; 10:15) who took part in the dedication of the altar of the tabernacle (7:18–23). **2** The fourth son of Jesse, and a brother of David (1 Chron. 2: 14). **3** A priest who was to blow the trumpets before the Ark (1 Chron. 15:24). **4** A prince of Judah sent by King Jehoshaphat (ca. 874–850 B.C.) to instruct all the cities of Judah in the "book of the law of the Lord" (2 Chron. 17:7–9). **5** A Levite, the father of Shemaiah (1 Chron. 24: 6). **6** A Levite, the son of Obed-edom, a gatekeeper in the Temple (1 Chron. 26:4). **7** One of the Levites who contributed to the Passover offering in the time of Josiah (late seventh century B.C.; 2 Chron. 35:9; 1 Esd. 1:9). **8** The son of Pashhur, and a priest who married a foreign wife while in exile (Ezra 10:22; 1 Esd. 9:22). **9** The head of the priestly house of Jedaiah in the days of the high priest Joiakim (late sixth–early fifth century B.C.; Neh. 12:21). **10** A priest who took part in the dedication of the rebuilt wall of Jerusalem (Neh. 12:36). S.L.R.

Nethaniah (neth-uh-nī'ah; Heb., "God gives"). **1** The father of the man Ishmael who first joined, then attacked and killed Gedaliah, the ruler of Judah appointed by Babylonia (2 Kings 25:23, 25; Jer. 40:8–41:18). **2** A Temple musician, the son of Asaph (1 Chron. 25:2, 12). **3** A Levite sent by King Jehoshaphat to teach in Judah (12 Chron. 17:8). **4** The father of Jehudi, a messenger for Jeremiah (Jer. 36:14).

Nethinim (neth-ee-neem'), a class of Temple servitors known from the books of Ezra, Nehemiah, and Chronicles. The term is derived from the Hebrew root *ntn* in the sense of "to give someone over into Temple service." Later traditions identified the Nethinim with the Gibeonites who tricked Joshua into sparing them (cf. Josh. 9). When their ruse was discovered it was decreed (Josh. 9:27) that they serve as hewers of wood and drawers of water for the community and the altar. Ezra 8:20 mentions the Nethinim "whom David and his officials had set apart to attend the Levites." Either the service of the Nethinim was organized in David's time, or he provided captives or other foreigners who joined this class. Jewish tradition mentions that 538 Nethinim returned from the Babylonian Exile. Scholars are divided as to whether the Nethinim were actually slaves, property of the Temple, or simply servitors like the Levites (cf. 1 Chron. 9:1–2). The mention of "the Kerosite" in the Arad ostraca may indicate the presence of Nethinim in the pre-exilic period (cf. Ezra 2:44; Neh. 7:47). At Ugarit there was a class of cultic servitors called *ytnm*, one of whom has a name that appears in the list in Ezra 2:45–46. It is therefore possible that the Nethinim were an international guild skilled in cultic arts who attached themselves to Israel in an early period. Similar also to the Nethinim in function are the *shirku*, known from Neo-Babylonian documents. According to the Mishnah (*Qidd.* 4:1), Nethinim could marry priests, Levites, or Israelites. Most likely, the Nethinim had been assimilated into Israel by Second Temple times (ca. 530 B.C.–A.D. 70) and they were no longer recognizable as a distinct class. L.H.S.

Netophah (ne-toh'fah), a Judean hill village near Bethlehem (1 Chron. 2:54; Ezra 2:21–22; Neh. 7:26). It was the home of two of David's mighty men, Maharai and Heleb (2 Sam. 23:28–29; 1 Chron. 11:30). It was also the home of Gedaliah's supporter Seraiah, after Jerusalem's fall to Babylon (586 B.C.; 2 Kings 25:23; Jer. 40:8–9). Various levitical and other returnees from exile in Babylon counted it their home (Ezra 2:22; Neh. 7:26; 1 Chron. 9:16). It may be modern Khirbet Bedd Faluh some three and a half miles southeast of Bethlehem. The modern spring 'Ain en-Natuf may reflect the name.

nets. ***See*** Fish.

nettle, any of a group of stinging or thorny plants, usually of the genus *Urtica*. It is a symbol of desolation and inaccessibility (Prov. 24:31; Isa. 34:13; Hos. 9:6; Zeph. 2:9). In Job 30:7 nettles serve as protection for Job's opponents.

new birth. ***See*** Conversion.

new covenant, the term given by Jeremiah to a new arrangement between God and human beings in which the law would be written in their hearts rather than on tablets of stone (Jer. 31:31–33). It is also an alternate translation of the Greek words (*kainē diathēkē*) that are normally translated "New Testament." Christians see in Christ the beginning of the new covenant between God and human beings of which Jeremiah spoke. ***See also*** New Testament.

new moon. ***See*** Feasts, Festivals, and Fasts; Moon.

New Testament, the collection of writings comprising the second portion of the Christian Scriptures, the first part being the OT.

Origin of the Name: "New Testament" (NT) is a variant translation of "new covenant." The background of the concept is Jer. 31:31–34, a passage influential in both the Qumran community and early Christianity (1 Cor. 11:25; 2 Cor. 3:6; Heb. 8:8–13; 9:15; 12:24; cf. Luke 22:20 in some manuscripts). In the latter, the term new covenant is used of a new declaration of God's will in Jesus, not, at this early period, of Christian writings.

The transfer of the terminology to a collection of Christian writings was a natural extension, however, given Paul's use of "old covenant" to refer to the writings of the Mosaic covenant (2 Cor. 3:14), usage followed in the second century by the Christian writer Melito of Sardis. The transition may be tracked in an unnamed anti-Montanist writer of A.D. 160–180, quoted by the fourth-century church historian Eusebius, who speaks of not wanting to add to "the word of the new covenant of the gospel"; in Tertullian (second and third centuries A.D.), who says, "If I fail in resolving this article [of our faith] by passages which may admit of dispute out of the Old Testament, I will take out of the New Testament a confirmation of our view . . . both in the gospels and in the [writings of the] apostles"; and the great Christian scholar Origen's contention, "we take in addition, for the proof of our statements, testimonies from what are believed by us to be divine writings, that is, from that which is called the Old Testament and that which is called the New." By the fourth century, it was common practice to refer to the then canonical Christian writings as the NT.

Contents of the Canon: Although disagreements among Christians about the contents of the NT are fewer than about the OT, unanimity has not been reached (e.g., some branches of the Syriac church do not include 2 Peter, 2 and 3 John, Jude, and Revelation; certain Protestant scholars, following Martin Luther, who would not accept Hebrews, James, Jude, and Revelation as of equal authority with the rest, argue for a "canon within the canon," a smaller core that is truly normative within the larger twenty-seven–book whole). Roman Catholics by virtue of the Council of Trent (April 8, 1546) and most Protestants

NEW TESTAMENT

by virtue of custom (e.g., Anglican Articles 6: "All the books of the New Testament as they are commonly received, we do receive") accept a twenty-seven–book NT that corresponds to the list of Bishop Athanasius of Alexandria in A.D. 367.

The NT writings, when classified according to type, fall into three groups: biographical/historical (four Gospels, Acts), epistolary (Pauline Letters, Hebrews, general or "catholic" Letters), and apocalyptic (Revelation). When classified according to subject matter, the NT writings are grouped in terms of those that give accounts of the life of Jesus (four Gospels), the one that tells of the origins of the church (Acts), and those that represent the beginnings of Christian theology (Letters, Revelation). When classified as by the early church fathers, the NT consists of the Gospel (the four) and the Apostles (Acts through Revelation).

Order of the NT Writings: The NT writings are not arranged in the order of their composition. No certainty attaches to the chronology of NT writings, and opinions differ widely. At most, one can say that they fall into two groups: (1) the genuine Letters of Paul (here opinions range from the seven undisputed letters—Romans, 1 and 2 Corinthians, Galatians, Philippians, 1 Thessalonians, Philemon—to as many as ten, only the Pastorals [1, 2 Tim., Titus] being almost universally regarded as non-Pauline), which fall between the late forties and the early sixties, and (2) the remainder of the NT books, which fall between 65 and 150. If the NT's order was that in which the writings were penned, Paul's Letters would come first.

The present order of the NT is roughly chronological insofar as the subject matter is concerned. The life of Jesus (Gospels) precedes the history of the early church (Acts); the Letters reflect the life of the early Christians; and Revelation closes the canon with a grand vision of the ultimate future, paradise regained. Within this overall arrangement, the Gospels come first in the order Matthew, Mark, Luke, and John. Although this is only one of the seven orders in use in the ancient church, it was adopted by the Council of Laodicea (A.D. 363) and reflects an early tradition preserved by Origen that this was believed to be the order of the composition of the Gospels. This opinion was not that shared by all the fathers (e.g., Clement of Alexandria, according to Eusebius, who places Mark after Matthew and Luke). The Pauline Letters follow Acts and are arranged according to two principles. First, the Letters to the seven churches are separated from those to the three individuals. Then, within each category, the order is generally in terms of descending length. The one exception is that Galatians precedes Ephesians, although the latter is slightly longer. This arrangement of Jerome and Athanasius is but one of six ancient orders. The general or "catholic" Letters (James; 1, 2 Pet.; 1, 2, 3 John; Jude) circulated in antiquity in half a dozen different orders. Our order possibly reflects Gal. 2:9 (James, Cephas/Peter, John).

The arrangement of the whole (Gospels, Acts, Paul, general Letters, Revelation), one of seven orders in the ancient church, is that of the Council of Carthage in 397 and was adopted by the Council of Trent (mid-sixteenth century). It places the historical books first, using Acts as an introduction to the apostolic Letters (Paul, Hebrews, general Letters) in order to emphasize the unity of the church, with Revelation last as the Christian's vision of the future hope. The various component parts of what later became the NT were associated with the parts of the OT (2 Pet. 3:16; all Paul's Letters and the other scriptures; First Apology of Justin Martyr: memoirs of the apostles or the writings of the prophets), and the NT as a whole was patterned after the Law and the Prophets (Tertullian: "the law and the prophets she [i.e., the church] unites in one volume with the writings of the evangelists and apostles"; similarly Irenaeus).

The different divisions of the material within the NT books are not ancient. The chapter divisions are usually attributed to Cardinal Hugo de San Caro, who in A.D. 1248 used them in preparing a Bible index, but he may have borrowed them from the earlier archbishop of Canterbury, Stephen Langton. The modern verses derive from Robert Estienne (Stephanus), who, according to his son Henry, made the divisions while on a journey on horseback from Paris to Lyons. They were first published in Stephanus' Greek Testament of 1551 and first appeared in an English translation of the NT in William Whittingham's version of 1557. The first complete Bible in English with our verses was the Geneva Bible of 1560. The punctuation in the modern text is an editorial decision, there having been almost no punctuation in the ancient manuscripts. Likewise, the paragraphs in some versions are a modern editorial decision. Sometimes these divisions are an aid to understanding; sometimes they are a hindrance.

The Language of the NT: The NT books were all written in Greek, not classical Greek but Hellenistic Greek, with kinship both to the literary and to the unliterary *koine* (i.e., the Greek spoken in the Mediterranean basin ca. 300 B.C.–A.D. 300), as well as openness to influences from the Greek OT, the Septuagint. Although Jesus and his earliest followers probably spoke Aramaic, in their present form in the Gospels even the words of Jesus are given in a Greek form. The writings that comprise the NT are products, then, not of original Aramaic-speaking Christianity but of later Greek-speaking Christians. The original readers/hearers were Greek-speaking peoples, mostly Christians, some Jewish Christians and some Gentile Christians, with thought worlds that differed greatly from one another. The idioms through which Matthew, John, Paul, Hebrews, James, and Revelation communicate are as different as daylight and darkness, even if the words of all are Greek.

Authorship: The authors of most NT books are unknown except in the most general terms. At least seven Letters can be linked with the apostle Paul. The others associated with his name are usually attributed to his disciples who followed the common Mediterranean practice of writing in the name of a revered teacher. Of the two Letters claiming to be from Peter, only one (1 Peter) has any chance of being linked to the apostle; the other (2 Peter) is perhaps the latest writing in the NT, often dated as late as A.D. 100–150. The four Gospels, Acts, Hebrew, and the three Johannine Letters make no claim as to their authorship. Second-century Christians, beginning with Papias (A.D. 140), linked the First Gospel with Matthew, one of the Twelve, and the Second Gospel with Mark, a disciple of Peter. Irenaeus (ca. A.D. 180) continued Papias's views about Matthew and Mark and added his belief that Luke, the follower of Paul, put down in a book the gospel preached by that apostle, and that John, the Beloved Disciple, published his Gospel while residing in Asia. By the time of Irenaeus, Acts was also linked with Luke, the companion of Paul.

Clement of Alexandria (ca. A.D. 190–202) expresses the Egyptian view that Hebrews was by Paul in Hebrew and that Luke translated it into Greek. Origen (early third century) is aware of the claim that 1 John was written by the apostle John and of the problems with linking 2 and 3 John with the apostle. Although the Letters of James and Jude and the Revelation to John claim to come from James, Jude, and John, the unanswered question is: which James, which Jude, and which John? As early as Justin Martyr (mid-second century), Revelation was attributed to the apostle John. As late as the fourth century, James and Jude were treated among the disputed books, something unlikely if the writings were apostolic in origin. On the basis of the evidence supplied by the writings themselves, as opposed to that offered by the church fathers, little can be said about the identities of the authors of most of the NT writings. From the point of view of authority for the church, however, authorship is irrelevant. It is a document's presence in the canon that is decisive.

Authority: None of the authors of NT books wrote with any thought that his contribution to early Christian life would be something that would eventually be collected into a body of Scripture that would be authoritative for all Christians in all times and places. Each wrote with specific recipients and a specific situation in mind. In this sense, all of the NT documents are occasional literature. At the same time, in many cases it is clear that the authors wrote with a definite sense of the authority of their contributions. In 1 Cor. 9:9, 14, the words of Jesus are regarded as authoritative alongside the Law. Paul wrote with a sense of setting forth an authoritative teaching, one applicable for all his churches (1 Cor. 4:17; 7:17; 11:16; 14:33). Rev. 22:18–19 is the clearest statement claiming divine authority in the NT. Luke-Acts, in setting forth the true tradition of Jesus as passed down through the apostles to the Ephesian elders (Acts 20:17–35), implies the normative status of this tradition (and in a Gospel-Apostle form). Later canonization merely functioned as ecclesiastical confirmation of the individual author's conviction.

The NT writings were not immediately gathered into a canon of Scripture. From our vantage point, they are only the cream selected from a much larger body of Christian literature of antiquity that included what we know as the Apostolic Fathers, the Apocryphal NT, and the Apologists. The selection process was gradual. Sometime near A.D. 100, Paul's Letters were probably collected and published for the larger church. This collection would have possessed authority for the circles in which it was used.

By the middle of the second century, a collection of the four Gospels was made. At this time, Luke was separated from Acts so that thereafter Acts had a life of its own. If one takes seriously the claim of Tertullian, some type of Christian canon existed before Marcion—a canon that the heretic cut down to his own canon of an expurgated version of Luke and ten "corrected" Letters of Paul. If one does not accept Tertullian's claim, then by the end of the second century, partially in reaction to Marcion, a NT canon of some sort existed. This canon was a collection of collections (the four-fold Gospel, the Pauline Letters, and Revelation, which was itself a collection of seven letters and seven visions), with the Pauline Letters introduced by Acts and supplemented by several general Letters to counter Marcion's exclusive focus on Paul. The Christian writings that were produced within a period of seventy-five to one hundred years, in contrast to the period of nearly one thousand years for the production of the OT documents, were now on the road toward acceptance in a twenty-seven–book NT canon normally used by Western Christians today. The first time that we know of a list containing precisely these twenty-seven books is in Athanasius' Easter letter of A.D. 367.

Early Manuscripts and Later Editions: We do not possess any autographs (originals) of NT writings. We have only copies of copies of copies. There are about five thousand Greek manuscripts of the NT that exist in part or in whole. The earliest are the papyri (e.g., P^{46}, an early-third-century copy of most of Paul's Letters and Hebrews; P^{66}, a copy of parts of John from A.D. 200; P^{72}, a third-century copy that includes

Jude, 1 and 2 Peter; P^{75}, a copy of much of Luke and John from about A.D. 200). The next oldest are the uncials, written on vellum (leather scraped smooth). They are called uncials because of the block capital letters in which they are written. The uncial manuscripts include Codex Vaticanus, or B, a fourth-century manuscript originally containing the entire Bible, and Codex Sinaiticus, or א, another fourth-century manuscript of the entire Bible. The latest manuscripts are the minuscules, dating usually from the ninth century and later, so called because they are written in a cursive script. On the basis of these handwritten manuscripts, modern Greek NTs are made, and from the modern Greek NTs translations are made into English and other languages. The first printed edition of the Greek NT was that of Erasmus in 1516. Today, the two most widely used Greek NTs are those of Nestle-Aland and the United Bible Societies, which in their twenty-sixth and third editions, respectively, agree in their text of the NT.

The New Covenant: The NT speaks about the new covenant God established with his people (as foretold in Jer. 31:31–34). Whereas the covenant instituted through Moses at Sinai was based on the gracious initiative of God in the Exodus (Exod. 20:2; Deut. 5:6) and was broken by a faithless people (Jer. 31:32), the new covenant is rooted in God's grace in and through Jesus the Christ (1 Cor. 11:25) and is enabled by a new ingredient. In the new covenant, God not only graciously set people in relationship with himself but also acted at Calvary, on Easter, and at Pentecost so as to assume responsibility for his people's faithfulness to the relationship. This good news is variously expressed in the Christian Bible: for example, God puts his law within his people, writing it on their hearts (Jer. 31:33); there is a new covenant, not in a written code but in the Spirit (2 Cor. 3:6); the Christians' righteousness or faithfulness to the relationship is enabled by the indwelling Christ whose faithfulness to God in the days of his flesh is now lived out in and through the believers (Phil. 3:9; Col. 1:27); life in the new covenant is an abiding in Christ in which he abides in the believers, enabling them thereby to bear fruit (John 15:4–5). ***See also*** Aramaic; Bible; Biblical Criticism; Canon; Chronology, New Testament; Covenant; Gospel, Gospels; Greek, New Testament; Letter; Septuagint; Texts, Versions, Manuscripts, Editions; Theology, New Testament.

Bibliography

Kee, Howard Clark. *Understanding the New Testament.* 4th ed. Englewood Cliffs, NJ: Prentice-Hall, 1983.

Moffatt, James. *An Introduction to the Literature of the New Testament.* 3d ed. Edinburgh: T. & T. Clark, 1918.

Neill, Stephen. *The Interpretation of the New Testament 1861–1961.* London: Oxford University Press, 1964.

C.H.T.

New Testament, names of God in the. ***See*** Names of God in the New Testament.

New Testament, Old Testament quotations in the. ***See*** Old Testament Quotations in the New Testament.

New Testament, sociology of the. ***See*** Sociology of the New Testament.

New Testament as Literature. ***See*** Literature, New Testament as.

New Testament chronology. ***See*** Chronology, New Testament.

New Testament quotations in patristic authors. The use of the NT by the early Christian writers (up to the fifth century) is important to the study of the NT in three major ways: first, their allusions to or citations of the NT documents (and other early Christian literature) provide vital information for the study of the development of the NT canon; second, they provide crucial data for NT textual criticism (the study of the transmission of the text of the NT and the search for its original form); and, third, they elucidate the history of interpretation, both of the science of interpretation as a whole as well as of individual passages.

The NT Canon: The most difficult period for the reconstruction of the history of the NT canon is that from the writing of the documents themselves (ca. A.D. 50–95) up to the latter part of the second century (ca. A.D. 180). This is also the period of the greatest flexibility in the use of these documents in the church. The reason for this is due mostly to the fact that the need for such specifically Christian authority was a developing process, and therefore the use of the documents as authority for the church reflects this development.

The earliest writers outside the NT (Clement of Rome [A.D. 96]; Ignatius of Antioch [ca. A.D. 115]; the author(s) of the *Didache* [ca. A.D. 100?]) regularly cite the OT as Scripture, inspired of the Holy Spirit, but they merely mention, or allude to the content of, the documents that are later to become the NT. Thus Clement tells the Corinthian church at the end of the first century to "pick up the letter of the blessed apostle Paul. . . . Under the Spirit's guidance, he wrote to you about himself and Cephas and Apollos" (*1 Clem.* 47:2–3). This is a clear reference to our 1 Corinthians, which means that at the end of the first century this Letter of Paul was being read by the churches both in Rome and Corinth. Clement also cites the teaching of Jesus as authoritative. For example, he cites some sayings (*1 Clem.* 13:2) that have clear affinities with Luke 6:36–38; however, the differences are so noteworthy that it seems clear that he is not citing Luke but rather still has access to similar (probably oral) traditions that had earlier been available to Luke as well. Thus Clement is clear evidence that Jesus and Paul had continuing authority in the church at the end of the first Christian century; however, it is likewise clear that the author of Clement did not yet think in terms of a *New* Testament.

This same attitude generally prevails in the available writings throughout the first half of the second century. However, at the same time one can see some developments in attitude toward these documents that would eventually become the NT. For example, Polycarp of Smyrna, in his Letter to the Philippians (ca. A.D. 135), alludes to, or loosely quotes from, several of the NT documents (Matthew, Mark, Luke, Acts, the Pauline Letters, Hebrews, and esp. 1 Peter); and these are so thoroughly interwoven throughout the whole Letter, in precisely the same manner as citations from the OT, that there can be no question that his spiritual life had been deeply nourished by these books. This is also true of Justin Martyr (ca. A.D. 155), who cites profusely from an apparently harmonized version of the first three Gospels.

By the time one comes to Irenaeus of Lyons and Clement of Alexandria toward the end of the second century, the concept of canonicity has now clearly emerged. Both Irenaeus and Clement cite the NT documents in such a way as to make it clear that for them they held authority in the same way as the OT, and Irenaeus in particular specifically argues for the "canonicity" of the fourfold Gospel. In the next generation, Tertullian in North Africa and Origen in Alexandria (and later Caesarea) both cite and use the NT as the documents that form the fountainhead of the Christian faith. Indeed a part of Origen's legacy to the church are his commentaries and homilies on most of the NT books, a few of which are still extant. (It should be noted that there will be yet another century and a half before the final shape of the NT canon has been determined.)

NT Textual Criticism: The quotations of the NT by the early Christian authors is an especially valuable source for the science that attempts to reconstruct the original text of the NT. Such quotations are a third line of evidence for this task, along with the Greek manuscripts themselves (actual copies of the Greek NT) and the early versions (the earliest translations of the NT into such languages as Latin, Syriac, and Coptic). The value of the patristic citations is that they give us datable evidence from specific points of geography, so that one may have a fairly good idea of the nature of the NT text in that region at a given time in history.

There are also some difficulties with this evidence, however, especially in evaluating it. First, there is a problem with the writers themselves: one cannot always be sure whether an author is copying from his Bible or citing from memory. Furthermore, the citing habits of authors are about as diverse as one meets in contemporary sermons. Some quotations are very precise: others are close, but reflect lack of concern for exactness; still others are notoriously loose. Second, there is the fact that the writings of these authors have themselves also gone through a long process of transmission, so that one cannot always be sure that our extant copies now represent exactly what the author wrote or whether the biblical citations were modified by the copyists to conform to later texts.

Nonetheless, after all of these factors are taken into consideration, there still remains enough certain evidence to help put some pieces into place. During the second century the citing of the NT tended to be more relaxed, quite in keeping with the development of the canon itself. That is, although in this early period the documents were clearly authoritative, they had not yet attained a full canonical status, so an author, who may have tended to cite the OT rather exactly, cited the NT documents much more loosely. In fact, it is this phenomenon that is partly responsible for a large number of the variant readings that exist in the textual tradition. But by the time of Irenaeus, Tertullian, and Origen all of this had changed. Origen, in particular, cites his NT generally with great precision and is a significant witness for the text as it circulated in Alexandria in the first half of the third century, and later in Caesarea, where he moved in A.D. 230 and lived out the rest of his life (he died ca. 255). And even among the later writers with the loosest kinds of citing habits, such as Epiphanius of Salamis (ca. 310–403), who cites some texts in as many as seven different ways and seldom ever cites precisely, one can still determine the general character of the NT they used.

What we learn from this evidence is that two distinct forms of the NT text existed in the East and West. The last authors in the West to write in Greek (Hippolytus of Rome and Irenaeus) both used Greek texts that looked very much like those that lay behind the earliest Latin versions. Tertullian, and all subsequent writers in Latin, are clearly dependent on these Latin versions.

A different picture emerges in the East. A distinct text emerged in Egypt that looks very much like a good preservation of the original texts themselves. This text is found in Origen, as well as in the earliest Greek manuscripts from this area. However, when Origen moved to Caesarea, he began to use a NT there that differed considerably from that in Alexandria. A similar, somewhat mixed text can also be found in other early writers from this area (Eusebius of Caesara [265–340], Epiphanius [ca. 310–403], Basil [ca. 330–379], the Gregorys [fourth century]). At a still later date a text was being used by Chrysostom in Antioch (A.D. 347–407) and then in Constantinople that looked much like that of Basil and the Gregorys, but had been modified considerably, so that it was about seventy-five percent along the way to the text that would eventually dominate in the Greek church and that lay behind the King James Version of the NT.

The History of Interpretation: The actual use of the NT for theology and church practices is a vast area of research in its own right. Most writers used their Bibles in a variety of ways, depending on the kind of circumstances to which they were addressing themselves.

There had in fact been a long tradition in Judaism that had learned to accommodate Scripture to culture and contemporary thought forms by allegorizing the biblical text. Philo of Alexandria (first century B.C.–first century A.D.) had especially paved the way for this in the Diaspora, and methods like his were also in vogue among the influential Christian teachers from this city (Clement and Origen). The result was that much of the church, with the notable exception of the school at Antioch beginning in the third century, learned to interpret Scripture in this fashion.

Thus, in the learned Origen, for example, one can find this remarkable interpretation of Jesus' "going down to Capernaum" in John 2:12, based partly on a desire to harmonize John with Matthew and Luke and partly on his "spiritual" reading of the Fourth Gospel: since this word seems to stand in contradiction to the accounts of Jesus' movements in Matthew and Luke, one must look for a meaning different from the literal one. The answer is to be found in the meaning of the name "Capernaum," which means "field of consolation." Therefore, what John meant was that after the wedding in Cana Jesus went down to "console those whom he was training to become disciples."

But far more often common sense tended to prevail, and Scripture was appealed to, and quoted, because of what appeared to be its plain meaning. This is especially true of quotations in the form of exhortations (e.g., Polycarp, *Phil.* 2:3: ". . . remembering what the Lord said as he taught: 'Judge not that you be not judged,' " citing Matt. 7:1), or in appeals to the events of Christ's life and ministry, or to the basic theological statements of the Christian faith. Such common sense also prevails in the course of controversy, especially among Christians, where the plain meaning of the text is frequently appealed to over against what is believed to be the distorting of the text by one's opponents.

Patristic writers were as capable of citing texts out of context as are moderns and therefore often seemed to miss their original point; but overall the citation of the NT among the church fathers was an expression of good sense. The most useful of all these citations for modern study of the NT are to be found in John Chrysostom (d. A.D. 407), who was schooled in Antioch and later became appointed preacher in Antioch and then patriarch in Constantinople. His homilies are models of diligent search for the intended meaning of the text and of courageous application of that meaning to his contemporaries. Because of this his comments on the NT found in his many homilies of most of the NT books are still worth reading, and often he provides keys to the meaning of the Greek text that might otherwise have been lost to history.

A Bibliographic Note: Because of the importance of these early citations of the NT both for the study of the NT text and for the history of interpretation, an index of several volumes is currently being prepared under the auspices of the Centre d'Analyse et de Documentation Patristiques (Paris, 1975–), entitled *Biblia Patristica, Index des Citations et Allusions Bibliques dans la Littérature Patristique.* This index is particularly thorough and includes every imaginable allusion to a NT passage, as well as citations and adaptations of various kinds. For the complete indexes of the patristic writers and their works, one should consult the *Clavis Patrum Graecorum* (for the Greek writers; 3 volumes; Turnhout [Belgium]: Brepols, 1976–1984) and the *Clavis Patrum Latinorum* (for the Latin writers; Brugge [Holland]: Beyaert, 1961). For further information on the church fathers themselves, their lives, works, and theology, see J. Quasten, *Patrology* (3 vols.; Westminster, MD: Newman Press, n.d.). ***See also*** Canon; Texts, Versions, Manuscripts, Editions. G.D.F.

New Testament theology. ***See*** Theology, New Testament.

New Year Festival (Heb. *Rosh Hashanah,* "the beginning [lit. 'head'] of the year"), the festival celebrated on the first day of the month of Tishri (Sept.-Oct.), the seventh month of the Jewish calendar. Basic regulations for the observance of the New Year Festival appear in Lev. 23:23–25 and Num. 29:1–6. These texts refer to the festival as "a holy convocation" or "the day of trumpet blasts." It is a day of rest on which no work is to be done. Sacrificial offerings include one young bull, one ram, and seven male lambs together with their respective cereal offerings. In addition, a male goat is to be sacrificed as a sin offering.

There is some confusion in the biblical tradition concerning the New Year Festival. The first of Tishri is nowhere designated as New Year's Day in the Bible. The term *Rosh Hashanah* appears only in Ezek. 40:1 where it refers to the general time of the year, but not specifically to the New Year Festival. According to Exod. 12:2, the month of Abib, later known as Nisan (March-April), is the first month of the year, but no New Year Festival is prescribed for the first of Nisan. The first of Nisan, however, is the beginning of the eleven-day Babylonian New Year Festival. This has prompted some scholars to suggest that the biblical New Year originally fell on the first of Tishri but at some time, probably during the Babylonian exile, the observance shifted to the first of Nisan to conform with Babylonian practice. Others argue that the original New Year was in the spring and later shifted to the autumn. A third position distinguishes two types of New Years. The first of Nisan was the regnal New Year, by which the reigns of kings were reckoned, and the first of Tishri was the religious or agricultural New Year for reckoning the liturgical calendar. In this respect, it is noteworthy that the Mishnah (*Rosh. Hash.* 1:1) identifies four New Years, including the first of Nisan, the New Year for kings and festivals, and the first of Tishri, the New Year for agriculture and reckoning the reigns of foreign kings.

Another issue concerns the relation of the biblical New Year Festival to the Babylonian New Year or *akitu* festival. This festival, held in the spring from the first to the eleventh of Nisan, emphasized the renewal of creation and kingship. The celebration featured a liturgical recitation and reënactment of the Babylonian creation epic in which Marduk, the city god of Babylon, defeated the chaos monster Tiamat and set the cosmos in order. The festivities also included a ritual procession around the city, a ritual humiliation of the king, and a ritual marriage of Marduk atop the ziggurat of Babylon. At the end of the festival, the king received the tablets of destiny that assured his rule for another year. Some scholars have attempted to argue that a similar New Year Festival was observed in Jerusalem during the monarchical period, but the evidence does not support such a claim. It is more likely that the biblical New Year Festival was a harvest celebration associated with the Day of Atonement (Lev. 23:26–32; Num. 29:7–11) and the Festival of Booths (Lev. 23:33–43; Num. 29:12–38; Deut. 16:13–15; cf. Exod. 23:16; 34:22). ***See also*** Babylon; Nisan; Tiamat; Time; Tishri. M.A.S.

Nicanor (nī-kay'nuhr). **1** Son of Patroclus, one of the king's friends (1 Macc. 3:38; 2 Macc. 8:9), a Syrian general assigned by the Seleucid king Antiochus IV Epiphanes to suppress the Maccabean uprising in Judea. He was associated with two other high officers, Ptolemy (the son of Dorymenes) and Gorgias. Both 1 Maccabees 4 and 2 Maccabees 8 tell, although with somewhat different details, the story of Judas Maccabeus' rout of their forces near Emmaus in 166 B.C. Nicanor returned later with another army but was decisively defeated in the battle of Beth-horon on 13 Adar (March), 161 B.C. Judas Maccabeus' triumph on what came to be known as "Nicanor Day" and the mutilation and exposure of Nicanor's remains end the account in 2 Maccabees victoriously; in fact, however, swift retaliation by the Syrian commander Bacchides a few months later at Beroea brought Judas's life to an end. ***See also*** Maccabees; Seleucids. **2** According to Acts 6:1–6, one of the seven appointed by the Jerusalem church to administer the daily distribution of food. F.O.G.

Nicodemus (nik-oh-dee'muhs), a Pharisee, a teacher of Israel, and a ruler of the Jews as described in the Gospel of John. Nicodemus questions Jesus (John 3), later defends him (7:50–52), and finally appears with Joseph of Arimathea to prepare his body for burial (19:39).

Mentioned only in the Fourth Gospel, Nicodemus plays a significant role in that he apparently personifies a learned Jewish constituency that was well disposed toward Jesus but did not understand him adequately (John 3) and had not reached the point of confessing him publicly as the Christ. Perhaps Nicodemus and Joseph of Arimathea, who is said to be a disciple of Jesus secretly "for fear of the Jews" (19:38), represent exactly the kind of timid disciple the author of John wished to persuade to come out openly for Jesus. Yet, the initial confusion of Nicodemus, who could not comprehend Jesus' talk about being born anew or from above (3:4, 9), was never explicitly overcome. At most, the Evangelist allowed for the possibility that it would be. ***See also*** Joseph; Regeneration. D.M.S.

Nicolaitans (ni-koh-lay'i-tahns), a religious sect in Ephesus and Pergamum whose members were denounced in Rev. 2:6, 15 for eating food sacrificed to idols and for sexual license. The church fathers considered them followers of Nicolaus of Antioch mentioned in Acts 6:5 and founders of libertine Gnosticism, which remained active beyond the second century. Though this suggestion is possible, not many scholars would regard it as historically reliable. ***See also*** Revelation to John, The; Ephesus; Pergamum.

Nicolaus (nik'uh-lay'uhs; KJV: "Nicolas"), one of the seven men selected in the early days of the Jerusalem church to administer the distribution of food to the poor, including the widows, under the supervision of the apostles (Acts 6:1–6). His designation as a "proselyte" indicates that he was a Gentile. ***See also*** Hellenists; Proselyte.

Nicopolis (ni-kah'poh-lis; Gk., "city of victory"), according to Titus 3:12, the place Paul hoped to winter in and where he asked Titus to join him. The request is strange, however, in a letter instructing Titus concerning his ministry in Crete (Titus 1:5). Several towns were named Nicopolis, but this reference is almost certainly to the town founded in Epirus (west-by-northwest of Corinth) by Octavian in 31 B.C. commemorating his victory over Antony at nearby Actium. 2 Tim. 4:10 may indicate that Titus joined Paul in Nicopolis and then went to Dalmatia, but this notice (see also 1 Tim. 3:14) can hardly be harmonized with itineraries of Paul or Titus suggested by Acts and Paul's acknowledged letters. ***See also*** Titus. J.L.P.

Niger (nī'juhr), another name for Simeon, a leading prophet or teacher in the church at Antioch (Acts 13:1). ***See also*** Prophet; Simeon.

night, the period between the darkness that falls after the sun has set and the beginning of the light that precedes the dawn. It is a metaphor in the Bible for a time of danger (Ps. 91:5) and of sadness (Ps. 30:5); of the absence of God (John 9:10; cf. 13:30) and the presence of death (Luke 12:20); of visions (Dan. 7:7) and of dreams (Matt. 2:12) that communicate divine things. For that reason, in the description of the new Jerusalem, the seer affirms that there will be no more night (Rev. 21:25; 22:5), since God will be present with his people, to protect and communicate with them. ***See also*** Time. P.J.A.

nighthawk, one of a number of birds regarded in the OT as unclean and thus unfit for human consumption (Lev. 11:13–19; Deut. 14:12–18). Its exact identity is unknown; some have conjectured it designates some species of owl.

Nile (nīl), the great river of Egypt flowing north from its sources in Lake Victoria in Uganda and in the highlands of Ethiopia, a distance of 4,037 miles, the entire length of the Sudan and Egypt, to the Mediterranean. The two major branches, the White Nile (from Lake Victoria) and the Blue Nile (from Ethiopia), merge at Khartoum, with one modest tributary somewhat farther to the north and none at all in Egypt itself. Beyond Khartoum the Nile flows through several cataracts, inhibiting navigation but not preventing it. The last cataract is at Aswan, the beginning of the Nile Valley proper. (Because the Nile flows from south to north, the southern Nile valley is referred to as Upper Egypt.) From here on the Nile flows north in a well-developed valley with cliffs on either side almost as far as Cairo, and the river becomes important for its overflow and the hydraulic irrigation of the adjoining floodplain. Within the Nile Valley the river is fairly constant at about six-tenths of a mile in width, whereas the valley varies from six to nine miles across.

Most of the agricultural land is on the west bank, since the river generally flows closer to the eastern cliffs. The wider western floodplain benefits, in a number of areas, from secondary channels of the river. The best known of these is the Bahr Yusuf, which formerly flowed into the Faiyum, a large, well-watered area with a permanent lake somewhat south of Cairo, extending about fifty miles into the western desert. From Cairo (the area of ancient Memphis and On) the river fans out into a great delta, ultimately over one hundred and fifty miles wide. (The delta is referred to as Lower Egypt.) Here the ancient branches were rather more numerous than today, as several are dried up, including the Pelusiac branch, that were first encountered by travelers from Palestine into Egypt.

Today the delta has a high water table and extensive areas occupied by lakes and swamps. Presumably the situation was similar in antiquity. Following the spring rainfall in the highlands of East Africa, the Nile at Aswan rises over 18 feet and reaches its peak flow in mid-September, with the low point coming in late April. Prior to the building of the modern dams the Nile overflow brought a tremendous amount of new sediment and minerals each year (about 185 million tons) and therewith renewal for the agricultural land. But an inundation that was too high, too low, or unseasonal could mean disaster. Nonetheless, almost all the people lived in the Nile Valley or the delta and owed their very existence to the Nile. Even in the delta the yearly rainfall is 8 inches or less, and in the southern Nile valley there is virtually no rain.

The Nile is also the major highway of Egypt. Movement north and south along the floodplain was certainly possible, but on any extensive journey frequent crossings of the Nile were required. Heavy goods of course were transported on the river. Indeed, the great building projects of Pharaonic Egypt were dependent on easy movement of massive loads by Nile barges. During the inundation the Nile could deliver great loads to virtually any site along the valley. The importance of Nile transport is indicated by the representations of boats in tombs, the burial of special boats alongside the pyramids, and the provision in the temples of storage places for the boats used by the gods in their journeys. It was the Nile that bound Egypt together.

In biblical times the sources of the Nile were unknown. The Egyptians themselves had practical knowledge of the Nile well into the Sudan, but the Nile was so essential to them and so mysterious that it was also seen in special ways. In some texts the floodwaters of the Nile are described as rising out of caverns at the Aswan cataract. Even the Nile in the delta area was thought to have a special origin near On (Heliopolis). Special nilometers were maintained at strategic points, such as near Memphis in the north and on the island of Elephantine at Aswan, so as to estimate in advance the height of the inundation. As Egyptian power expanded

Sailing boats in a contemporary photograph of the Nile in front of the Elephantine Island near Aswan, Egypt, the beginning of the Nile Valley proper.

southward into Nubia, additional observation points were established at the second and even the fourth cataracts. But even with advance warning a high Nile might prove destructive and a low Nile remain insufficient.

The Nile inundation, the river's dynamic essence, was personified in the god Hapy. Hapy, the Nile's fecundity, was represented as a well-fed figure apparently both male and female, often colored green or blue, the colors of life. Hapy is a representative of Nun, the primeval water itself. But it is striking that although Hapy is depicted in most of the temples, Hapy had no special temple. The seasonal festivals recognizing the Nile took place at a number of points along the river, with various offerings, amulets, and figurines. At times there was even human sacrifice to the Nile.

The Nile was well known in biblical tradition and to the biblical writers. There are many references to the Nile and its impressive flooding, unlike any rivers of Palestine (e.g., Jer. 46:7–8; Amos 8:8). Punishment of Egypt might mean that God would dry up the Nile (Isa. 19:5), and the ultimate arrogance of the Pharaoh was his claim that "my Nile is my own; I made it" (Ezek. 29:3). In the time preceding the Exodus, Pharaoh commanded that every Hebrew male child should be cast into the Nile (Exod. 1:22), though Moses was providentially rescued by being placed in a basket of bulrushes (Exod. 2). The signs and wonders, including turning Nile water into blood (Exod. 4:9; 7:14–22), struck at the very lifeline of Egypt. ***See also*** Egypt. H.B.H.

Nimrim, a desert stream. The waters of Nimrim (Heb., perhaps "leopards") are said to be desolate (Isa. 15:6; Jer. 48:34). They are identified as those of either Wadi en-Numeira on the east side of the Dead Sea near its southern end or the Wadi Shu'eib seven miles north of the Dead Sea. Based on the context, however, the former would seem to be the more plausible location. ***See also*** Dead Sea.

Nimrod, an ancient Mesopotamian king and conqueror mentioned in Gen. 10:8–12 (cf. 1 Chron. 1:10) and Mic. 5:6 (cf. Heb. 5:5). In the latter passage, the "land of Nimrod" is a poetic term for Assyria. Nimrod is the son of Cush, which in Gen. 10:8 seems to mean Cossea, the country of the Kassites in Mesopotamia. Nimrud is the name of several places in Mesopotamia, including Nimrud, ancient Calah. The biblical Nimrod is the first powerful king on earth; the first cities of his kingdom were the famous Babylon, Erech, and Accad in Babylonia, and Nineveh and Calah in Assyria (v. 10). Like another fabled figure of the ancient Near East, Gilgamesh, he was a mighty hunter "by the favor of the Lord" (Heb., "before the Lord"). Nimrod appears in the Yahwist source in Genesis, a source interested in "culture heroes" and founders of cultural and political institutions (see Gen. 4:

17–26). Nimrod would then be the hero-founder of the great Eastern empires that threatened Israel during much of its existence.

Whether Nimrod reflects a single historical person, and if so, who that person was, is debated by scholars. Some suggest that Nimrod is derived from the god Ninurta, but the Bible portrays him as flesh and blood. More plausible is the suggested derivation from Tukulti-Ninurta I of the thirteenth century B.C., the first Mesopotamian to rule effectively both Babylonia and Assyria. Certainty is impossible. The Bible may have intended only a corporate figure of a great king. R.J.C.

Nimrud (nim'ro͞od). ***See*** Calah.

Nimshi (nim'shī), the grandfather of Jehu, king of Israel (i.e., the Northern Kingdom; 2 Kings 9: 2, 14). While Nimshi seems in some places to be designated as the father of Jehu ("Jehu the son of Nimshi," 1 Kings 19:16; 2 Kings 9:20), the word "son" is most likely used more broadly in these passages to mean "descendant." ***See also*** Jehu.

Nineveh (nin'e-ve; from Assyrian *Nina* or *Ninua*), one of the oldest and greatest cities of Mesopotamia. Ninevah was the capital of Assyria at its height from the time of Sennacherib, who assumed the throne in 705 B.C. to its fall in 612 B.C. and subsequently a symbol of Assyria's utter collapse. The city was located on the east bank of the Tigris River opposite Mosul. Its ruins consist of a number of small mounds and two large tells in an 1800-acre enclosure surrounded by a brick wall almost eight miles in circumference. The main focus of excavations has been the larger of the tells, Quyunjik ("little lamb"). The smaller tell, Nebi Yunus ("the prophet Jonah"), marks the traditional site of the tomb of the prophet Jonah and is occupied by a modern settlement.

Name and History: The *Ninua* of cuneiform sources goes back to an earlier form, *Ninuwa*, which would seem to underlie the received biblical writing. In addition to the syllabic spelling, the cuneiform texts also occasionally use a pseudologographic form, *Nina*, which is the combination of two signs (AB + HA) that represent an enclosure with a fish inside. This reading is of particular interest in light of the prophet Jonah being swallowed by a large fish (Jon. 1: 17). Another line of folk interpretation is found in Greek literature where the city is called *Ninos*, after a legendary hero by that name. It has been suggested that the name of the city was connected in some way with a goddess associated with fish. From the Akkadian period on, the city was dedicated to the "Ishtar of Nineveh."

Though the city was occupied from prehistoric times and rebuilt repeatedly by kings of the Middle Assyrian period, the city reached the height of its fame at the turn of the eighth century B.C., when Sennacherib made Nineveh the capital of the expanding Assyrian Empire. When Assyria subsequently held sway over Egypt, under Esarhaddon and Ashurbanipal, Nineveh was the most powerful city in the world. Nonetheless, its end was but decades away. In 612 B.C. the city fell to the combined forces of the Babylonians and the Medes. Some twenty-five centuries later the discovery of the great library of Ashurbanipal in the ruins of Nineveh would furnish the clues for the recovery of the intellectual and spiritual treasures of ancient Mesopotamia.

In the Bible: The earliest biblical mention of Nineveh is in the Table of Nations (Gen. 10:11), which claims Nimrod as the city's founder. Parallel passages in 2 Kings 19:36 and Isa. 37:37 mention Nineveh in conjunction with the assassination of Sennacherib by his two sons. The end of Nineveh is proclaimed by two contemporary biblical prophets, Zephaniah and Nahum. Though Zephaniah's prophecy is brief and incidental (Zeph. 2:13–15), the book of Nahum in its entirety is directed against the city, under the title "An Oracle Concerning Nineveh." Nahum's poetic work describes the fall of Nineveh in unexcelled imagery and power.

Another biblical work centering on Nineveh is the book of Jonah, but here historical facts are reshaped in the interests of a remarkable narrative story with an unforgettable moral lesson. Such literary touches as the "king of Nineveh" (3:6) and the city being so large that "a

Plan of the site of ancient Nineveh; a modern mapmaker's reconstruction based on available evidence.

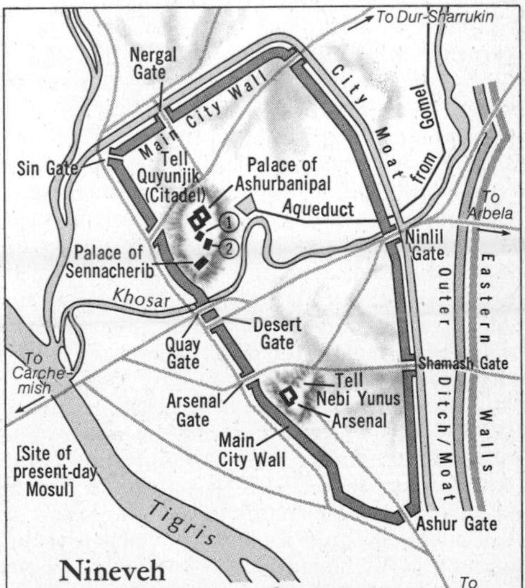

journey of three days" (3:3) was required to cross it belong to the narrative world of that particular story. Nonetheless, in its own way the book of Jonah, too, witnesses to the glory that once was Nineveh. Here, curiously, the people of Nineveh are unusually responsive to the message of God's prophet. They proclaimed a fast and put on sackcloth, "from the greatest of them to the least of them" (3:5), before the news had even reached the "king of Nineveh," who then followed suit (3:6). These Ninevites would arise again at the Last Judgment to condemn the generation of Jesus (Matt. 12:41; Luke 11:30–32). ***See also*** Assyria, Empire of; Jonah, The Book of; Nahum. D.L.C.

Ninlil (nin'lil), a Mesopotamian mother goddess, the wife of Enlil and goddess of Nippur. Ninlil was originally a grain goddess. An original form of Ninlil was Sud, daughter of Nisaba and Haia; Sud was associated with the Sumerian cities Shuruppak and Eresh. An important Sumerian historiographic document, the Tummal inscription, lists the various kings who restored the Tummal, a Ninlil sanctuary near Nippur, and brought the goddess there. In Assyria, Ninlil became a wife of the national god, Assur. The marriage of the goddess to Enlil is recounted in the Sumerian compositions "Enlil and Ninlil" and "The Marriage of Sud." In her new role as wife of Enlil, she assumed the Sumerian name Nin.lil, "Lady Wind." An Akkadian form of Ninlil was Mulliltu; in the Assyrian dialect of Akkadian, Mullitu appears as Mulishshu, and this form reappears as the theophoric element in the name Adrammelech (2 Kings 19:37; Isa. 37:38), the murderer of the Assyrian king Sennacherib. ***See also*** Enlil; Nippur. I.T.A.

Nippur (nip'po͞or; Sumerian Nibru), a city in central Babylonia. The city occupied a special place in the political and religious life of Mesopotamia, especially in the period prior to 1500 B.C. Its god was Enlil. The god, his priests, the temple, and the city possessed special political prerogatives; a set of mythological and theological images and forms developed around the god and temple, and this Nippur tradition influenced the cultural life of the Babylonians and Assyrians. In the sixth century B.C., Nippur served as a major area of settlement for the exiled Judeans.

The core city consists of two main sections: the eastern section (containing the sacred areas of the Enlil complex, Inana temple, and North temple) and Tablet Hill. Based on the finding of Ubaid pottery remains in soundings and on the surface, Nippur seems to have been settled already in the Ubaid period. Certainly the city can be traced back almost to the beginning of the Uruk period (Uruk XIV), ca. 3500 B.C.

Sometime in the early third millennium B.C., Nippur was the central meeting place of a league of cities. Here, under the aegis of Enlil and his priesthood, representatives of major cities met in assembly and decided upon joint actions and offices of the alliance of cities. Located between the cities of the north and south, Nippur was regarded as the seat of the chief god of the Babylonian pantheon, Enlil, and it became an important religious and political center. From this evolved its later role in the monarchy. Thus, for example, during the later Ur III–Isin periods, the ruler of the country was legitimated and charged by Enlil. Regular ritual journeys to Nippur by god (e.g., Nanna) and king were carried out in order to induce Enlil to bestow yearly blessings of abundance and prosperity upon the ruler and the land. The control of Nippur often amounted to legitimacy for a claim of rule over all of Babylonia (Sumer and Akkad).

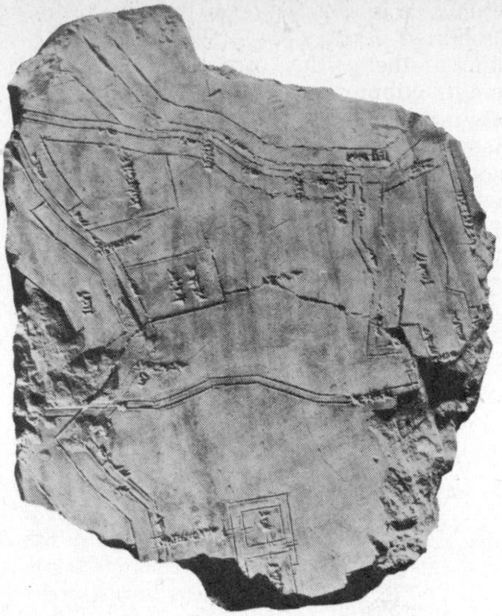

This plan of ancient Nippur, which indicates the locations of the temple, city walls, gates, and canals, appears on a clay tablet fragment.

Nippur was a major scribal center. Much of Sumerian literature known to us comes from the remains of scribal schools from the Old Babylonian period. Eventually Babylon attained first political and then religious preeminence, thus replacing Nippur. In the attempt to attain legitimacy and to create connection with earlier traditions, Babylon incorporated and built upon the traditions of Eridu. Assyria, on the other hand, linked up more directly with Nippur; thus the god Assur is identified with Enlil, Ninlil becomes one of his wives, and Enlil's son Ninurta takes on a significant role in Assyria.

In the late eighth and seventh centuries B.C.,

Nippur was generally pro-Assyrian (Nippur supported Assyria even when Babylon and other northern cities were antagonistic or indifferent). Nippur served as an Assyrian garrison city in Babylonia during the wars between the Assyrians and Babylonians. It remained loyal even during the ascendancy of Nabopolassar. Eventually taken, the city and region were largely destroyed. Hence the Babylonians settled the Judean exiles in the region of Nippur in order to repopulate and rebuild the area. Autonomous settlement allowed the exiles to retain their ethnic identity and resist assimilation. In the Achaemenid period (seventh to fourth centuries B.C.) the business records of the Murashû family found in Nippur mention a considerable number of Jews participating in various economic activities. ***See also*** Enlil.

Bibliography

Kramer, S. N. *The Sumerians*. Chicago: University of Chicago Press, 1963.

Tadmor, H. *A History of the Jewish People*. Ed. H. H. Ben-Sasson. Cambridge: Harvard University Press, 1976. Pp. 160–164, 173. I.T.A.

Nisan (nī'sahn), the first month of the OT year (Esther 3:7; Neh. 2:1). Nisan is an Akkadian loan word and forms part of the Babylonian system of lunar month names taken over by the Jews some time after the Exile. Akkadian *nisannu*, itself a Sumerian loan word, corresponds to the Sumerian month name Bára.zag.gar, the first month in the Nippur system that became standard for Babylonia during the Old Babylonian period. Nisan falls in the spring (March–April) and corresponds to the earlier Hebrew designation *'abib* (Exod. 13:4; 23:15; 34:18; Deut. 16:1). The festival of Passover is celebrated in mid-Nisan, and it also marks the time of Jesus' crucifixion (cf. Matt. 26:17–19).

No (noh), the Hebrew name for Thebes, Egypt's magnificent capital city during much of the second and first millennia B.C. Located in Upper Egypt some 330 miles south of modern Cairo, the metropolis included vast monumental temple and palace complexes along both banks of the Nile, much of which is still visible today in the ruins of Luxor, Karnak, Qurneh, and Medinet Habu. After its zenith in the Middle and Late Kingdoms (ca. 1570–1085 B.C.) the city continued to enjoy periods of ascendancy until its violent and bloody conquest by the Assyrians in ca. 663 B.C. Nahum (3:8–10) alludes to Thebes's conquest, and both Jeremiah (46:25) and Ezekiel (30:14–16) pronounced doom upon the city during their day. D.A.D.

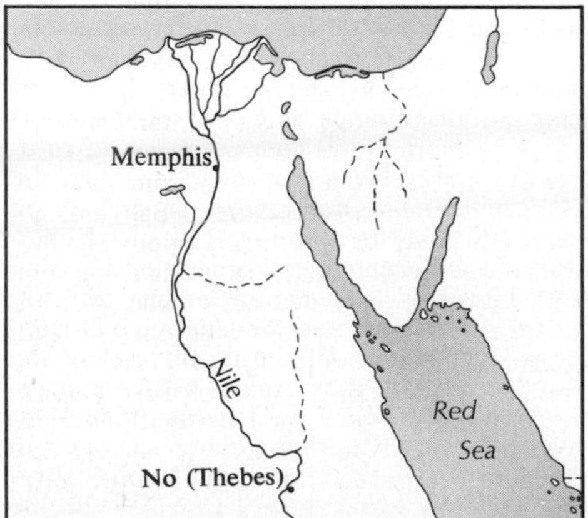

Noah (noh'uh), the son of Lamech (Gen. 5:28–29); the grandson of Methuselah; and the ninth descendant from Adam via Seth. The story of Noah is found in Gen. 6–9. His birth is the first recorded after Adam's death. Noah and his household are the sole human survivors of the Flood, which God brought upon the world to punish human sin. Noah, sole righteous man of his era (5:9; 7:6; cf. 6:8), was chosen, with his entourage, to perpetuate life on earth.

According to the account attributed to the Priestly author (P), Noah was commanded to build an ark and take along male and female pairs of every terrestrial and flying species (6:19–20), while according to the so-called Yahwistic account (J), Noah was commanded to take along seven pairs of clean animals and flying species, but only two pairs of unclean animals (7:2–3). All remaining nonaquatic life perished when God loosed heavenly and subterranean waters for forty days and forty nights (7:11–23). Noah's ark floated for ten months, alighting atop the Armenian mountains of Ararat—Babylonian Urartu (7:14–8:5). After sending a raven (unsuccessfully) and a dove (successfully) to scout the area, Noah emerged with his family onto land, performed sacrifices, and received God's (here Yahweh's) promise not to send more floods (8:15–22). A rainbow appeared as sign of God's new covenant with humankind, and Noah received laws prohibiting bloodshed and consuming of lifeblood (9:1–17 [P]). As the first man to plan a vineyard, Noah grew drunk one day and was seen naked by his son Ham. Ham's brothers Shem and Japheth averted their eyes and covered their father. Noah cursed Ham's son Canaan for his indiscretion, condemning him to serve his brothers (9:18–27). The transfer of the curse to Canaan presumably reflects a later attempt to justify the dominion over the Canaanite sphere by the Hebrew descendants of Shem. Remarkably, the blessing and curse in 9:26–27 is Noah's sole utterance throughout the story.

The story is skillfully woven from two sources. The Yahwistic (J) source prefers the divine name "Yahweh," a ready-made ark, a forty-day flood (with forty days between the ark's

Noah building the ark; ivory plaque from Salerno, Italy.

alighting and its unsealing), and an emotionally expressive deity. The Priestly (P) source prefers the name "God," shows Noah commanded to build the ark to specific dimensions, depicts a 150-day flood (and 150-day ebbing) and a dispassionate, legally minded deity. The vineyard episode is a tradition originally unrelated to the Flood. The overall story is symmetrical, centering on expansion and recession of the waters. Noah, shown midway between nomadic and agriculturalist existence, echoes the thematic concerns and biases of the Cain and Abel story (Gen. 4:2–16), among others.

Noah's nearest ancient Near Eastern parallel is the Babylonian Utanapishtim, who recounts to Gilgamesh (*Gilgamesh* Tab. 11) experiences of a great flood that remarkably resemble Noah's. Unlike Noah, Utanapishtim obtains immortality. Noah is mentioned alongside Job and Daniel in Ezek. 14:14 as one famed for righteousness.

Noah is mentioned several times in the NT (e.g., Matt. 24:27–28; Luke 3:36; Heb. 11:7). 1 Peter compares Noah's deliverance from flood waters to the deliverance from sin through Christian baptism (3:20–21). ***See also*** Flood, The; Genesis. J.W.R.

Nob (nahb), a city in the territory of Benjamin (Neh. 11:31–35; Isa. 10:27–32) known as "the city of the priests" (1 Sam. 22:19). Nob developed as a religious center following the destruction (late eleventh century B.C.) of the sanctuary at Shiloh. David is said to have sought assistance from Ahimelech and the priests of Nob when he was outlawed from Saul's court, receiving some of the holy "Bread of the Presence" for his soldiers and the sword of Goliath for himself (1 Sam. 21:1–9; cf. Matt.12:1–8; Mark 2:23–28; Luke 6:1–5). When King Saul learned through an informer, Doeg the Edomite, that Ahimelech had "inquired of the Lord" for David, he ordered the death of the priest and his clergy. The king's guard refused to carry out the order, but Doeg the Edomite complied, slaughtering eighty-five priests and putting all of the city of Nob to the sword (1 Sam. 22:6–23). Abiathar, the son of Ahimelech, was a survivor of this massacre, thereafter being the recipient of David's favor (hence the confusion of priest's names in Mark 2:26). It is evident from Isa. 10:27–32 that Nob was located not far from Jerusalem on the north and within eyesight of that city. ***See also*** Benjamin; David; Saul. J.D.P.

Nod (nahd), the land of Cain's self-imposed exile, "east of Eden" (Gen. 4:16), otherwise unknown. The Hebrew etymology suggests a "homeless" or "aimless" place.

nomads, a word derived through Latin from a Greek term meaning "to pasture, distribute," referring to those who remain unsettled in place, preferring rather to wander freely about without permanent residence. Nomadic life is sometimes imposed by the limitations of climate on people. This is still true in parts of Africa as well as the Near East and in other parts of the world as well, particularly in central Asia and the outback of Australia. Excessively romantic views of nomads obtain in modern minds partly because their life is distant from centers of observation, and partly because early theories on the nomadic background of certain biblical characters and events were poorly informed.

Nomadism as seen in the Bible is largely pastoral, that is, people traveled with flocks of sheep and herds of goats, asses (for transport, if not for trade), and (after about 1200 B.C., the beginning of the Iron Age in Syro-Palestine) camels in search of food and water. By contrast, references to oxen or cattle show clear agricultural settings, where both water and forage were more ample, neither being in sufficient supply for such animals in true nomadic conditions. Even the groups dependent on sheep and goats for life support may have operated in a dimorphic social order, that is, using settled villages with normal village facilities for part of the year and foraging more broadly for pasture and water during the rest of the year. In most territory inhabited by nomads there is sparse water and sparse pasture for year-round survival, thus forcing occupants to forage widely to keep flocks and families alive. The tendency was to take the family with the flock for ease of security to both, and living conditions in such times required mobile housing, minimal amounts of baggage limited to necessities, and usually grouping of travelers for mutual assistance and security from attack. Knowledge of where water and pastures were available was vital to survival, and since tribal territorialism frequently extended to such outlying nomadic circuits it was also necessary to know which tribes were friendly and which were not. The degree to which real transhumance (the alternation of agricultural and pastoral nomadic life by a portion of the population of a site) functioned has only begun to be studied in Near East archaeological research. Clear evidence of a variety of arrangements is still observable among modern inhabitants of the Near East, where bedouin visitors often move into a neighborhood of stable water supply for short periods of time, arranging to graze their herds over recently cut grainfields belonging to the local farmers for the duration of their stay. Presumably the farmers get their return in the locally distributed manure from the nomad flocks.

The portrait of Israelites in the wilderness, grazing flocks in and around Kadesh-barnea (Num. 20–33), was no doubt nourished by the agriculture and social structures around the oasis. Pure nomadism, therefore, is difficult to find in biblical history. The debate about the nomadic life of the patriarchs is surely offset by their frequent settlements for longer or shorter periods of time in the agricultural and urban centers of Canaan (note Abraham at Shechem [Gen. 12:6] and Hebron [Gen. 13:8], Isaac at Gerar [Gen. 26:6], Jacob with Laban's family [Gen. 29–31], and the move from Canaan to Egypt [Gen. 46:1–7]). Moses' sojourn with the Midianites (Gen. 2:16–22; 3:1) comes close to presenting nomadic life, except that there is such sparse information that the impression may derive from the simple absence of evidence. Recent studies of tribal life have indicated that tribes function in urban as well as in agricultural societies, suggesting that tribal identities portrayed in connection with Israelite settlement in Canaan had little or nothing to do with nomadism as such.

The study of relations between settled and nomadic biblical populations has also only begun. New archaeological data on traditionally nomadic periods such as Early Bronze IV (ca. 2500–2000 B.C.) from sites in the Sinai, the Jordan Valley, and the Transjordan (such as Khirbet Iskander) may clarify the matter in the future, but for the present, modern claims about the strong moral, religious, military, and social role of nomads in biblical history ought to be held in cautious and modest reserve.

R.S.B.

Noph (nof; KJV; RSV: "Memphis"), a city in Egypt (Isa. 19:13; Jer. 2:16; 44:1; 46:14, 19; Ezek. 30:13, and, following the Hebrew text, Ezek. 30: 16). ***See also*** Memphis.

northeaster, the. ***See*** Euroclydon.

numbers, symbols used to designate quantity. The Egyptians and the Sumerians had advanced number systems and mathematics by the beginning of the third millennium B.C. The Egyptian system was decimal. The Sumerian system was a combination of a decimal and a duodecimal (12) or sexagesimal (60) system. Remnants of the duodecimal and sexagesimal systems are evident in our time system (24 hours, 60 minutes, and 60 seconds), degrees of a circle (360), and our units of dozen (12) and gross (144). The same system originally lay behind our calendar with 12 months, each with basically 30 days, for a 360-day year.

The Hebrews used the decimal system but did not develop their own symbols until the postexilic period (539 B.C. on). In all pre-exilic inscriptions, numbers are either represented by Egyptian symbols or are written out. The Arad inscriptions regularly used Egyptian symbols for numbers. The Samaria ostraca (fragments of pottery) more frequently had the number written out. Letters of the Hebrew alphabet were first used for numbers on coins in the Maccabean period (168–40 B.C.).

Symbolism and Significance: Some numbers in biblical usage had symbolic meaning. Seven probably represented completeness and perfection, as seen in the seven days of creation and the corresponding seven-day week, climaxing with the Sabbath (Gen. 1:1–2:4). Even the land was to have a Sabbath, lying fallow in the seventh year (Lev. 25:2–7). In Pharaoh's dream, there were seven good years followed by seven years of famine (Gen. 41:1–36). Jacob worked seven years for Rachel; then, when he was given Leah instead, he worked an additional seven (Gen. 29:15–30). The finest quality silver was described as having been refined seven times (Ps. 12:6).

A similar use of the number seven can be seen in the NT. There are seven churches mentioned in Revelation 2–3 and seven deacons in Acts 6:1–6. To Peter's question concerning forgiveness, Jesus responds that we are to forgive not seven times, but seventy times seven (Matt. 18:21–22).

Multiples of seven were also important. After forty-nine years came a Jubilee year, when all Jewish bond-servants were released and land that had been sold reverted to its former owner (Lev. 25:8–55). The OT speaks of seventy elders (Exod. 24:1, 9). Also, Jesus sent out the seventy (Luke 10:1–17). Seventy years was to be the length of the Exile (Jer. 25:12; 29:10; Dan. 9:2). A period of seventy weeks of years was to culminate in the coming of the messianic kingdom (Dan. 9:24).

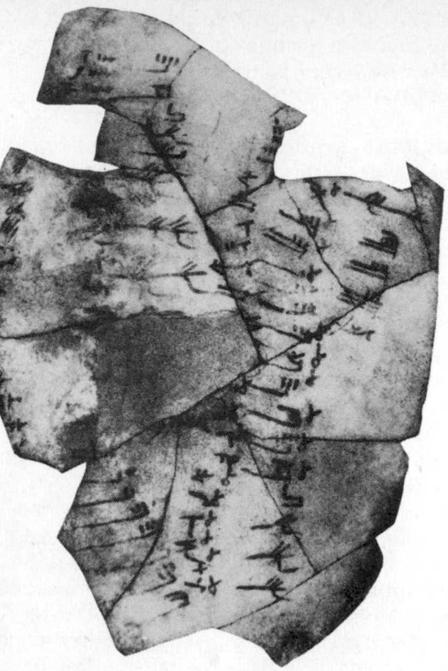

An ostracon with numbers written in both Egyptian hieratic script and Hebrew; pieced together from fragments found at the fortress at Kadesh-barnea.

Three also indicated completeness. The created order has three parts: heaven, earth, and underworld. The godhead is composed of three beings: Father, Son, and Holy Spirit. Three major feasts appear in the religious calendar (Exod. 23:14–19). Also prayer was urged three times daily (Dan. 6:10; Ps. 55:17). The sanctuary was divided into three parts: vestibule, nave, and inner sanctuary (1 Kings 6:2–22). Three-year-old animals were prized for special sacrifices (1 Sam. 1:24; Gen. 15:9). Jesus said the Son of man would be in the grave for three days and three nights (Matt. 12:40).

Four was also a significant number. There were four cardinal directions, four corners of the earth (Isa. 11:12), and the four winds (Jer. 49:36). Four rivers flowed out of Eden to water the world (Gen. 2:10–14). Surrounding God were four living creatures (Ezek. 1:10; Rev. 4:6–7).

Forty, a frequently occurring multiple of four, represented a large number or a long period of time. Forty days and nights of rain (Gen. 7:12) flooded the earth. Likewise, Jesus was tempted in the wilderness for forty days (Mark 1:12). Forty years represented approximately two generations. During the forty years of Israel's wilderness wandering, all the adults who had rebelled against God died (cf. Num. 14:20–23). At age forty, a person reached maturity (Exod. 2:11; Acts 7:23). No more than forty lashes could be imposed on an offender (Deut. 25:3).

In the Talmud, Midrashim, and the Cabala, a system of numerology called *gematria* developed. *Gematria* attempted to discover hidden meaning for words based on the numerical values of the letters. The Hebrew letters of the name Eliezer, Abraham's servant, have a numerical value of 318. Gen. 14:14 says that Abraham took 318 trained men to pursue the kings from the east. The Midrash notes that Abraham had but one helper, Eliezer, since Eliezer has the numerical value of 318. In a similar pattern, the number 666 in Revelation is often taken as a *gematria* for the emperor Nero.

Not all number usage in the Bible was symbolic. The pattern x, x + 1 appears frequently as a device of emphasis in parallelism. A good example may be seen in Prov. 30:18–19 with three and four:

Three things are too wonderful for me;
  four I do not understand:
the way of an eagle in the sky,
  the way of a serpent on a rock,
the way of a ship on the high seas,
  and the way of a man with a maiden.

J.F.D.

Numbers, the Book of, the fourth book in the Pentateuch. The designation "Numbers" comes from the name of the book in the Septuagint (LXX) and is reflected in the name for the book in the Talmud. The title is probably drawn from the account of the census with which the book begins (1:2). The book is unique in the Pentateuch, being composed of diverse literary types such as historical narrative (cf. 10:11–14; 16–17; 20–25; 31–32), statistical information (1, 3, 4, 7, 26), itinerary (33), poetry (20:14–18, 27–30; 23:7–10, 18–24; 24:4–9, 15–24), ritual prescription (5, 6, 8, 9, 15, 18, 19, 28–29), and other legal material (5, 15, 27, 30, 36). The framework of the book is a historical narrative describing preparations in the Wilderness of Sinai for the journey to Canaan (1–10:10), the wilderness journey from Sinai to Transjordan (10:11–21:9), and conquests in Transjordan and preparations for entering into Canaan (21:10–36:13). The various components of the book come from diverse traditions and ages in Israel's history and several stages of editing are evident. The book in its present form comes from a date much later than the events described and thus cannot be taken at face value as entirely historical. Nevertheless, much of its content is demonstrably quite ancient and preserves early traditions about the wilderness period and information about the early history and culture of Israel in Canaan. ***See also*** Hexateuch; Sources of the Pentateuch.

D.P.W.

Nun (no͞on), Joshua's father, thus an Ephraimite

(e.g., Exod. 33:11; "Non" in 1 Chron. 7:27). The extra-biblically attested name means "fish."

nun (nōōn), the fourteenth consonant of the Hebrew alphabet, used by the KJV to head the fourteenth section of the acrostic Psalm 119, vv. 105–12.

Nunc Dimittis (nuhnk di-mit'is), one of several poetical pieces or psalms included in Luke's account of the birth of Jesus (chaps. 1–2) in order to emphasize the significance and joy that surrounded Jesus' coming. The Nunc Dimittis (Luke 2:29–32) is a hymn of joy and praise attributed to Simeon, a truly pious man who had been waiting to see God's great act of deliverance on behalf of all people. The poem receives its name from the first words of the Latin version (English: "Now let . . . depart"). This poem centers upon one of the major emphases of Luke-Acts, that is, God's salvation for all people, Gentiles as well as Jews. It has found a significant place in the liturgies of the Christian churches. ***See also*** Hymn; Music; Simeon. J.M.E.

nurse, a woman who breastfeeds a child or one who takes care of another. Hebrew mothers usually nursed their own children (Gen. 21:7; 1 Sam. 1:23; 1 Kings 3:21; 2 Macc. 2:27; cf. Song of Sol. 8:1). Moses' mother was hired to nurse her child (Exod. 1:15–2:10, esp. 2:7–9). Weaning usually occurred about age three and was sometimes accompanied by festivities (Gen. 21:8; 1 Sam. 1:23–24). Occasionally wet nurses were employed. They served in royal families (Exod. 2:7–9; 2 Kings 11:2; 2 Chron. 22:11), and Rebekah had a wet nurse, Deborah, who remained with her all her life (Gen. 24:59; 35:8). Distinguishable from the wet nurse (Heb. *meineqet)* is the attendant to whose care the child was entrusted *('omenet)*. A nurse had charge of Mephibosheth, Saul's five-year-old grandson (2

OUTLINE OF CONTENTS

The Book of Numbers

I. Preparations for the journey to Canaan (1:1–9:23)
  A. Israelites numbered (1:1–4:49)
    1. Census of the Israelites (1:1–54)
    2. The arrangement of the wilderness camp (2:1–34)
    3. The census of the Levites (3:1–4:49)
  B. Final preparations (5:1–9:23)
    1. Various laws and offerings (5:1–7:89)
    2. Dedication of the Levites (8:1–26)
    3. Passover and the fire cloud (9:1–23)
II. The wilderness journey (10:1–21:20)
  A. Departure (10:1–14:45)
    1. Marching orders (10:1–35)
    2. Complaints in the desert (11:1–12:16)
    3. Spies sent to Canaan (13:1–33)
    4. The people rebel and must wander an additional forty years (14:1–45)
  B. Events in the desert (15:1–21:20)
    1. Laws for the Promised Land (15:1–41)
    2. Rebellion in the desert (16:1–16)
    3. Miracle in the desert (17:1–12)
    4. More laws for the Promised Land (18:1–19:23)
    5. More miracles in the desert (20:1–13)
    6. Setbacks in the desert (20:14–21:20)
      a. Edom refuses passage (20:14–21)
      b. Rebellion and attack by serpents (21:1–20)
III. Conquests and preparations (21:21–36:13)
  A. Conquests (21:31–31:53)
    1. Sihon and Og defeated (21:21–35)
    2. Balaam's prophecies and Balak's defeat (22:1–24:25)
    3. False worship and punishment (25:1–18)
    4. A second numbering (26:1–65)
    5. Daughters of Zelophehad (27:1–11)
    6. Joshua chosen as Moses' successor (27:12–23)
    7. Festivals, offerings, and laws (28:1–30:16)
    8. War against Midian (31:1–54)
  B. Preparations for life in the Promised Land (32:1–36:13)
    1. Reuben, Gad, and half of Manasseh allowed to settle in Transjordan (32:1–42)
    2. Summary of travels (33:1–49)
    3. Boundaries of Israel's land (33:50–34:29)
    4. Levitical cities and cities of refuge (35:1–34)
    5. Marriage of Zelophehad's daughters (36:1–13)

Sam. 4:4). Naomi became Obed's nurse (Ruth 4:16). This role could also be filled by a man (*'omen*, 2 Kings 10:1, 5; Esther 2:7; metaphorically of kings, Isa. 49:23). The nurse is a symbol of nurture, care, and protection. Thus it is not surprising to find Moses and, by implication, God spoken of as a nurse (Num. 11:12). Moses' rhetorical questions there point to Yahweh as the one who conceived the people and is responsible for their nurture (cf. Deut. 32:13–14). Paul refers to himself as a nurse to the Thessalonians (Gk., *trophos*, 1 Thess. 2:7). J.C.E.

nuts, the fruits of various trees both native and exotic to Palestine. The "garden of nuts" (KJV) referred to in the Song of Sol. 6:11 is probably a walnut orchard (*Juglans regia*). The nuts presented as gifts in Gen. 43:11 are pistachios (*Pistachia vera*), still a favorite food in the Near East today. The almond (*Amygdalis communis*) is another popular nut mentioned by name in the same passage. ***See also*** Almond.

Nuzi (nōō'zee), an ancient city in what is now northeastern Iraq, situated about ten miles southwest of Kirkuk. The site, modern Yoghlan Tepe, had been occupied from prehistoric times but experienced a rapid decline after the fall of the Mitanni Empire. A small body of texts was found in the Old Akkadian, Ur III, and Old Assyrian levels (late second, early first millennium B.C.) at which time the city was named Gasur. Several thousand tablets were found in the later levels of the Nuzi period when the site was dominated by Hurrians. These tablets span a period of four generations and can be dated to the second half of the fifteenth century B.C. Additional Nuzi-type tablets have been unearthed recently at Tel al-Fahhar (ancient Kurruhanni) located about nineteen miles southwest of Nuzi. These Nuzi tablets are one of the primary sources of knowledge of Hurrian customs and practices, and aid scholars in understanding the cultural situation of early biblical history. Since the homeland of the biblical patriarchs in the middle Euphrates Valley was the object of substantial Hurrian penetration but little pertinent epigraphic material has come to light from this region, scholars look to Nuzi for data that would be valid by extension for the Hurrian areas of Haran and Nahor. However, since the Nuzi texts constitute one of the rare private archives from Mesopotamia, especially distinguished in its quantitative representation of family law, it is often difficult to discern whether the Nuzi sociolegal institutions are uniquely Hurrian or reflect common Mesopotamian practice. ***See also*** Mesopotamia. B.L.E.

One of the Nuzi tablets from ca. second half of fifteenth century B.C., which help reconstruct Hurrian cultural life during the early biblical period.

Nympha (nim'fuh). ***See*** Nymphas.

Nymphas (nim'fuhs; KJV; RSV: "Nympha"), a Christian member from Laodicea to whom Paul extends greetings (Col. 4:15). Ancient manuscripts vary as to whether Nympha (feminine) or Nymphas (masculine) is the correct reading. House-churches such as the one that met in the home of Nympha(s) were a common phenomenon in the early stages of Christianity (Philem. 2; Rom. 16:23).

Opposite: The Black Obelisk of the Assyrian king Shalmaneser III (ruled 858–824 B.C.). Although its shape is inspired by Egyptian obelisks, it does not taper to a pyramid. The second row depicts "Jehu, son of Omri." A detail of this appears with the color photographs.

O

oak, an acorn-bearing tree noted for its great size. The oak has been revered and has both historical and mythological associations as a symbol of strength. Among the more than three hundred species worldwide are the Palestinian and Tabor oak trees, as they are popularly known in biblical lands. The evergreen Palestinian oak has small leathery leaves edged with tiny thorns. It is in the hill country at an elevation of 1,000 feet where forests of oak at one time dominated the biblical landscape. In northern Transjordan stood the luxurious forests of biblical Bashan; "of oaks of Bashan they made your oars" (Ezek. 27:6), and "Wail, oaks of Bashan, for the thick forest has been felled!" (Zech. 11: 2). Oak forests likewise carpeted Gilead and parts of Edom, upper Galilee, and Carmel.

At lower altitudes, in the coastal plain, lower Galilee, and interior valleys, the Tabor oak represented the climax vegetation. It is a deciduous, high-outbranching tree with large leaves. The Plain of Sharon was at one time covered with an impenetrable oak forest which was compared with the lush forests of Carmel and the Lebanon (Isa. 33:9; 35:2).

Although much of the forest land was cleared in antiquity, today one still sees stands of oaks in the hill country and the occasional lone oak or terebinth, "sacred tree," still preserved. As a sacred, venerable, mighty tree, the oak is associated with worship (Gen. 13:18), with sacrificial offerings (Hos. 4:13), long life (Isa. 6:13), death (the Absalom passage, 2 Sam. 18:9–10, 14), and sanctuaries ("the oak in the sanctuary of the Lord" at Shechem, Josh. 24:26).

S.L.R.

oath, a statement by which people give assurance that they have spoken the truth or by which they obligate themselves to perform certain actions. God is usually invoked as guarantor of the oath, with the expectation that a broken or false oath will be punished. Oaths thus are a holy ritual and to swear falsely is to profane God's name (Exod. 20:7; Lev. 19:12). Swearing by God's name was most solemn (Matt. 26:63), but people also swore by holy things (Matt. 5:36; 23: 16–22) and by raising their right hands (Rev. 10: 5–6). Covenant ceremonies demanded the swearing of oaths (Gen. 26:28).

The Hebrew word for "oath" comes from the number seven, the sacred and magical number in Hebrew culture. In Genesis 21 seven lambs are used as witnesses to a covenant. Oaths and curses (a related type of statement) are often indicated in the Bible by abbreviated formulae, such as "May the Lord do thus and so if . . ." (1 Sam. 3:17; 14:44) and "As the Lord lives . . ." (1 Sam. 19:6). A full oath ritual for the wife suspected of adultery is found in Numbers 5. Peter responds to the inquiries of people in the high priest's courtyard with a simple denial, an oath and a curse (Matt. 26:69–74). The NT also contains a tradition, similar to one found among the Essenes, that one should not swear oaths (Matt. 5:34; James 5:12). ***See also*** Covenant; Curse and Blessing; Witness.

A.J.S.

Obadiah (oh-buh-dī'uh; Heb., "worshiper" or "servant of Yah[weh]"), a common biblical name used of at least eleven biblical personages including the prophet Obadiah and a high royal official allied with the prophets during Ahab's reign (1 Kings 18:3). The name is used of premonarchical, monarchical, and postexilic people (i.e., the entire time span of the OT). Its popularity is also indicated by its use in five seals, a Samaria ostracon, and in three Hellenistic Egyptian papyri. Any faithful worshiper could be called God's servant (Ps. 113:1), though the title is usually used of special personages such as Moses (Num. 12:7) or David (1 Kings 11:34). The name thus expresses the parents' hope that the child would be loyal to God. Names expressing the same sentiment are common in the ancient Near East and are found in Phoenicia, Ugarit, and Mesopotamia. ***See also*** Obadiah, The Book of.

M.Z.B.

Obadiah (oh-buh-dī'uh), **the Book of,** an OT book, the fourth of the twelve Minor Prophets. It is the shortest book in the OT with only twenty-one verses. Its prophecy is directed against the Edomites, whose punishment is predicted for their participation in the sack of Israel. It is thus similar to the Book of Nahum, which predicts Assyria's downfall.

Obadiah is difficult and abounds in philological problems. It opens with the words "The vision of Obadiah" (v. 1) and gives no further historical or biographical information about the prophet. Many scholars question the book's unity since vv. 1–6 are partially shared with Jer. 49:14–16, 9–10, the book incorporates several styles, and it equivocates about whether the destruction is only against Edom or includes all the nations. However, the book is best interpreted as a unity; its inconsistencies may have been caused by the author's reuse in vv. 1–6 (or 1–11) of the same early anti-Edom material that was also used in Jeremiah 49.

The book has three sections:

I. The inevitable destruction of Edom (1–9)
II. The misdeeds perpetrated by Edom against Israel (10–14)
III. The future restoration of Israel at the expense of the other nations (15–21).

The first section is unusually full of vivid imagery and describes Edom's pride in terms reminiscent of Ezekiel's oracle against Tyre (Ezek. 28). The second section emphasizes the severed kinship between the brothers Jacob and Edom/Esau (10, 12) and ends with a string of eight prohibitions recalling Edom's hostile acts of

587/6 B.C. Verse 15 acts as a bridge between Edom's destruction and the general destruction of the nations, thus introducing the third section, which is very rich in references to earlier prophetic images. The nations drink poison (v. 16; cf. Jer. 25:15–16 and elsewhere), a remnant remains on Mt. Zion (Isa. 37:32), and Israel is a destructive fire (Isa. 10:12–19). Finally, Israel repossesses its land (19) and the exiles far ("Sepharad" is Sardis) and near ("Zarephath" is in Phoenicia) return (20); God's dominion in ultimate victory is portrayed through the common image of God as king (21).

The composition of this book was probably motivated by Edom's participation in the sack of Jerusalem in 587/6. Edom's participation is not recounted in the biblical historical books but is hinted at in Lam. 4:21–22 and Ps. 137:7, and is explicit in the extrabiblical 1 Esdras 4: 45. Edom's participation in this destruction was particularly resented because Israel felt a kinship relationship to Edom, considering them brothers (Gen. 25:24–26). The book was probably composed soon after the destruction of the Temple and before Edom's destruction in the fifth century B.C. (cf. Mal. 1:2–4). A date of composition in the sixth or fifth century B.C. also fits the author's extensive familiarity with prophetic motifs. M.Z.B.

Obed (oh'bed; Heb., "worshiper"). **1** A man about whom there is no story in the Bible apart from the record of his birth to Ruth and Boaz (Ruth 4:13–22). Obed nevertheless assumes significance in both OT and NT for his genealogical role as the father of Jesse and grandfather of David (1 Chron. 2:12) and hence an ancestor of Jesus (Matt. 1:5; Luke 3:32). **2** The son of Ephlal and the father of Jehu, mentioned in the genealogy of the tribe of Judah (1 Chron. 2:37–38). **3** One of the mighty men in the list of King David's armies (1 Chron. 11:47). ***See also*** Boaz; David; Jesse; Ruth. F.R.M.

Obed-edom (oh'bed ee'duhm; Heb., "worshiper of Edom"). **1** The name of a Gittite in whose house David stored the Ark of God for three months. During the transport of the Ark from Baale-judah (or Kiriath-jearim) to Jerusalem, Uzzah, one of David's men, touched the Ark and died. Unwilling to continue with the Ark into Jerusalem, David left it in the house of Obed-edom, who was then blessed because of its presence (2 Sam. 6:6–12; 1 Chron. 13:13–14). **2** One of the Levite gatekeepers at the tent of meeting who, along with others, led with lyres the procession that brought the Ark of God from the home of Obed-edom the Gittite to Jerusalem (1 Chron. 15:18, 21). When the Ark was set inside the tent in Jerusalem, Obed-edom the Levite was appointed one of the ministers of the Ark (1 Chron. 16:5). ***See also*** Ark; Kiriath-jearim; Uzzah. F.R.M.

obedience, submitting to the will or authority of another. The OT has no separate word meaning "obey." "Obey" translates the Hebrew "to hear" (Gen. 22:18; Isa. 42:24). The concept is also expressed as "keeping" or "observing" the commandments (Exod. 16:28; 34:11) and "walking" in God's ways (1 Kings 11:33). God punishes disobedience by exile, e.g., from the Garden of Eden (Gen. 3:22–24) or from the Promised Land (Deut. 4:25–28), but God forgives and restores (Deut. 30:1–5).

In the NT Christ is obedient to God (Rom. 5: 19; Phil. 2:8; Heb. 5:8), and Christians are called to obedience of faith (Rom. 1:5; 16:26), obedience to Christ (John 3:36; Heb. 5:9), and obedience to the gospel (Rom. 10:16; 1 Pet. 4: 17). The NT also reflects Roman social-political order in calling for obedience to the state (Rom. 13:1–5) and, in later writings, obedience of slaves, children, and wives within the household (Eph. 5:21–6:9; 1 Pet. 2:13–3:7). ***See also*** Commandment; Law. J.D.

obeisance, a gesture made by kneeling and placing one's face to the ground (cf. Josh. 5:14); it may be repeated several times for emphasis (Gen. 33:3; 1 Sam. 20:41). The gesture indicates submission, servitude, and respect to one's superior (1 Sam. 25:41; 2 Sam. 24:20); it can also express gratitude (2 Kings 4:37) and is thus appropriate as an act of worship (2 Sam. 12:20). The verb for obeisance can be used as a metonym for the worship of God and is found in this sense in prohibitions against idolatry (Exod. 20: 5; 1 Kings 9:6).

obelisk, a four-sided free-standing pillar, normally monolithic, tapering inward as it rises, terminating in a small pyramid. Obelisks were produced in Egypt from at least the latter part of the Old Kingdom (fifth dynasty, late third millennium B.C.) until the Ptolemaic period (late fourth century B.C.). Associated especially with the cult of the sun god Re, whose primary worship center was On (Heliopolis), obelisks were apparently seen as resembling the rays of the sun, the podium being the primeval hill over which the sun rose, and became symbolic of royal rejuvenation. Jer. 43:13 refers to the obelisks of Heliopolis, literally "the pillars of the sun temple which is in Egypt." As a pair flanking a temple entrance, two obelisks represented the rising and setting sun; as models in tombs they related to resurrection. On, Thebes (center of the cult of Amun-Re), and Pi-Ramesse (a capital of Ramesses II) had major obelisks, products of the eighteenth–twentieth dynasties (ca. 1546 –1085 B.C.), the tallest of which exceeds 105 feet. The obelisks elsewhere were generally shorter. Some obelisks were themselves, as divine symbols, objects of a cult. Obelisk-type pillars, inspired by Egyptian models, were erected at Byblos (Phoenicia) and at other Syro-Palestinian sites. There are now more major Egyptian obelisks in Rome than in Egypt; one was even moved to New York's Central Park. ***See also*** Egypt; On; Re. H.B.H.

oblation, an offering presented to God, usually consisting of a nonliving object in contrast to an animal sacrifice, e.g., meal (Lev. 2:4), first fruits (v. 12), or land for the sanctuary (Ezek. 48: 9). The prophet Isaiah denounces vain oblations (Isa. 1:13, 16–17). ***See also*** Worship.

occupations, activities by which people earned their livelihood. ***See*** individual entries.

Oded (oh'ded; meaning uncertain). **1** The father of the prophet Azariah (2 Chron. 15:1). **2** A prophet of Israel in the reign of Pekah (735–732 B.C.). He persuaded the army of Israel to treat the captives from Judah kindly and to return them to their countrymen (2 Chron. 28:9–15).

offering for the saints. ***See*** Contribution for the Saints.

offerings. ***See*** Worship.

Og (ahg), the king of Bashan whose territory lay north of the river Jabbok. He was defeated by the Israelites at Edrei before they crossed the Jordan River to enter the land of Canaan (Num. 21:33–35; Deut. 1:4; 3:1–13). Israelite tradition identifies him as the last remnant of the Rephaim, a race of giants who inhabited Canaan prior to the Israelite settlement. This tradition is supported by mention of his great bed of iron located in Rabbah of the Ammonites (Deut. 3:11). This was probably a tomb, a dolmen constructed with basalt blocks. His territory was occupied by the tribe of Manasseh. ***See also*** Rephaim. M.A.S.

Oholah (oh-hoh'lah), **Oholibah** (oh-hohl'i-bah; Heb., "she of the tent" and "my tent is in her"), the names of the allegorical sisters spoken of by the prophet Ezekiel (Ezek. 23); Oholah represents Samaria and Oholibah represents Jerusalem. After a youth of prostitution with the Egyptians, Oholah turned her lust upon the Assyrians and was eventually taken advantage of and destroyed by them. Oholibah surpassed the harlotries of her sister, defiling herself with the Assyrian and Babylonian lords. She, too, will suffer punishment for her lewd ways, for God will not ignore the faithless idolatry of Samaria and Jerusalem. A.B.

Oholiab (oh-hoh'lee-ahb; Heb., "the father's tent"), a Danite craftsman and fabric artisan who worked with Bezalel in the design and construction of the tabernacle (Exod. 31:6; 38:23).

Oholibamah (oh-hahl-i-bay'muh; Heb., "the tent of the high place"). **1** The daughter of Anah and wife of Esau (Gen. 36:2, 5). **2** A descendant of Esau and a clan chieftain of the Edomites (Gen. 36:41; 1 Chron. 1:52).

oil, in the Bible, olive oil. Oil of varying qualities was produced by different stages of production. The best oil—beaten oil (cf. 1 Kings 4: 11)—was produced by placing olives that had been crushed (for example, by treading on them, Mic. 6:15) in baskets and letting the oil drip through. An oil of a lesser quality was obtained by beating the olive pulp and applying pressure. The pulp could be ground again and squeezed another time to obtain still more oil.

Oil was a basic part of the diet. That the widow at Zarephath had only a jar of flour and a jar of oil indicates this (1 Kings 17:12–16). It was a basic component in bread making. As an extension of its use in foods, oil was a basic component in cereal offerings (cf. Lev. 2). Any type of oil could be used for these, except for the cereal offering that accompanied the daily burnt offering. In this beaten oil had to be used (Exod. 29:40; Num. 28:5). Cereal offerings in which the element of joy was missing lacked oil and incense (Lev. 5:11; Num. 5:15).

Oil was also used for cosmetic purposes. Oil could be compounded with perfumes to make aromatic ointments (cf. Esther 2:12; Song of Sol. 1:3; 4:10). Mourners did not use oil on their bodies during their period of sadness (2 Sam. 14: 2; Isa. 61:3; Dan. 10:2–3). It was an expression of gladness, refreshment, and pleasure (Pss. 23:5; 104:15). Oil was used as an emollient to soften skin of wounds (Isa. 1:6) or to treat leather shields (Isa. 21:5).

Oil was used in the religious anointing of objects and persons. Jacob anointed sacred pillars

A man crushes olives, source of oil in the biblical world, using a restored ancient stone press. Once crushed, the olives were placed in special baskets for the oil to drip through.

(Gen. 28:18; 31:13; 35:14). The special anointing oil was applied to Aaron, his sons, and various pieces of tabernacle furniture (cf. Exod. 29; 30:22–33). Oil was put on the right ear, thumb, and toe of a healed leper as part of his purification (Lev. 14:10, 12, 15–18). Kings were anointed (1 Sam. 10:1; 16:13; 1 Kings 1:39). Prophets, too, apparently received an anointing (1 Kings 19:16). A recipe for the composition of the priestly anointing oil is given in Exod. 30: 22–25.

Oil was employed as fuel for lamps. The oil for the lamp in the tabernacle was to be beaten oil (Exod. 27:20; Lev. 24:2). In the NT oil is used in healing rites (Mark 6:13; James 5:14).

Oil is used to indicate fertility of land (Deut. 33:24; Job 29:6) and with wheat and new wine to indicate agricultural blessing and abundance (Deut. 7:13; 11:14). ***See also*** Anoint; Food; King; Lamp; Ointments and Perfumes; Priests; Prophet.

D.P.W.

oil tree, the term used by the KJV in Isa. 41:19 where the RSV has "olive." Various terms used in the Septuagint indicate an unclear or at least inconsistent identification of what the Hebrew word used in Isa. 41:19 designated. The true olive *Olea europaea* is most likely, but species of pine and cypress have been suggested by other scholars. The Hebrew is literally "tree of oil," but pine or cypress would lend itself better to the Temple carvings than "olivewood" (cf. 1 Kings 6:23, 31–33).

ointments and perfumes, soft unguents or salves and aromatic scents commonly used in the ancient Near East for anointing, for medicinal purposes, for beautification, in incense, and in Egypt, for embalming. Most ointments contained a base of olive oil, to which aromatic spices, especially myrrh, were added (Exod. 30: 23–25). Archaeological excavation has brought to light a great variety of small delicate flasks and jars that undoubtedly served as containers for cosmetics, ointments, and perfumes. The most precious containers were of alabaster (Matt. 26:7) and were often small jars with a lid and pedestal base, or vials with a sealed neck. Anointing the head with oil was a common form of hospitality (Pss. 23:5; 92:10; 133:2), though Mary Magdalene anointed Christ's feet (Luke 7: 40). Ointments were a precious commodity and symbolized a sacred consecration. Kings were anointed (1 Sam. 10:1; 2 Kings 9:1; 1 Kings 1:39), as was the tabernacle (Exod. 30:26–29). Similarly well attested are the uses of ointments for healing (Isa. 1:6; Luke 10:34; Jer. 8:22) and for perfume (Ruth 3:3; 2 Sam. 12:20; Song of Sol. 1: 3).

Perfumes were likewise regarded as precious and served not only cosmetic uses but were also a main ingredient of incense and the sacred anointing oil. Often referred to as spices (Exod. 25:6; 35:28), aromatic sources derive from plants such as frankincense, myrrh, cinnamon, and saffron. The spice trade was an extremely profitable one and caravans plied the routes between Africa, India, Arabia, and Near Eastern ports (Ezek. 27:22; Gen. 37:25; 1 Kings 10:10). Fragrances made women attractive (Esther 2:12), provided a pleasing scent to clothes and furniture (Song of Sol. 4:11; Ps. 45:8), and flavored wine (Song of Sol. 8:2). The blending of several perfumes was an important component of formulas for the sacred incense and anointing oil (Exod. 30:22–25, 34–35).

S.L.R.

Old Gate, the, a gate in the wall of Jerusalem restored by Nehemiah (Neh. 3:6; 12:39), probably in the west, possibly in the north wall. Its precise location and identification remain unclear.

old prophet, the, an unnamed prophet (1 Kings 13:11) who lived in Bethel during the reign of Jeroboam I (ca. 926–907 B.C.). Hearing of a Judean prophet, also unnamed, who had uttered a prophecy against an altar in Bethel, the old prophet went in search of him. When he found him and heard that God had forbidden the Judean prophet from delaying in Israel, the old prophet lied to him about a word of the Lord that had come to him, brought the unnamed Judean prophet to his own dwelling, and thus caused the Judean prophet's death because of disobedience to God's word (1 Kings 13).

Old Stone Age. ***See*** Paleolithic Age.

Old Testament (from Gk. *diatheke*, "testament" or "covenant"), the first section of the Christian Bible, in its Protestant form identical in contents but not in order to the Hebrew Scriptures that constitute the Bible of Judaism. It is remarkable that the Bible of Christianity includes the Scriptures of another religion, Judaism. This was the case from the very beginning. Christianity, arising from within Judaism and affirming the acceptance of a Jewish Messiah, took it for granted that the sacred books of Judaism were authoritative. In fact, the earliest Christian writers, whose books became the NT, regularly appealed to those Scriptures to establish the truth of their new faith. This was the case even though the limits of the Jewish Bible were not finally established until the end of the first century A.D.

While some of the earliest Christians thought in terms of an old and a new covenant (2 Cor. 3:14; Heb. 8:7), it was the church fathers Tertullian (ca. A.D. 160–230) and Origen (A.D. 185? –254?) who first used the term "Old Testament" for the pre-Christian Scriptures as a whole. On the basis of the contrast between old and new, then, the Old Testament is conceptu-

OLD TESTAMENT

"Nash Papyrus": Oldest OT manuscript, prior to the discovery of the Dead Sea Scrolls, ca. 150 B.C. It contains the Ten Commandments and the *Shema* (Deut. 6:4).

ally—if not in size—the first half of the Christian Bible.

OT Canons: The simplest definition of the OT is that it is part of the Christian canon, or formally recognized list of sacred books. However, while all Christian communities accept that definition, its precise application is by no means simple, because various churches include different books in their OT canons. The Protestant OT includes the same thirty-nine books as the Bible of Judaism, but in a different order. In addition to these thirty-nine books, the Roman Catholic OT includes several other books and additions to books. These are Tobit, Judith, Wisdom of Solomon, Ecclesiasticus, Baruch, Prayer of Manasseh, 1 and 2 Maccabees, 1 Esdras, three additions to the book of Daniel and one to Esther. Sometimes the Letter of Jeremiah is listed separately and sometimes as part of Baruch, and the book of 2 Esdras was also included in the Latin Vulgate. The OT of the Eastern Churches is slightly different still. In the Protestant Bible, the books that are in the other Christian OTs but not in the Bible of Judaism are identified as the Apocrypha and printed in a separate section.

The differences between the OT canons can be explained by the history of the Bible in the different religious communities. The foundation for the development of all of the canons is the Bible of Judaism. It consists of three parts, corresponding to the stages of their acceptance as sacred Scripture. They are in Hebrew the *Torah*, the *Nebiim*, and the *Kethubim*, or, in English, the Law, the Prophets (Former and Latter), and the Writings. With the exception of a few chapters in Aramaic, all the books were written in Hebrew. In the Hellenistic age (325–63 B.C.) the Jewish communities outside of Palestine, especially in Alexandria, began to translate first the Torah and then the other books into Greek. It was the Greek version of the Hebrew Scriptures, along with the additional books in the Catholic Bible, that became the OT of the Christian Church.

As a comparison of the tables of contents of Jewish and Christian Bibles shows, not only was the early Christian Bible larger than that of Judaism, the order of the books was different. The Greek and subsequent versions begin with the Pentateuch, which corresponds to the Hebrew Torah. Then follow the historical books, including those such as 1 and 2 Chronicles which are at the end of the Hebrew Bible. Next come the wisdom books and finally the prophetical books. The organization appears to be a chronological one: listed first are books that treat the past, then those concerned with the present, and concluding with those focused upon the future. It may also be observed that the Greek version has much greater consistency of genres in each of its parts—presumably a Hellenistic influence—than does the Hebrew Bible.

The three-part Protestant Bible is the result of the work of the reformers Martin Luther and John Calvin. During the Reformation of the sixteenth century, as the Reformers called for reliance upon Scripture over church tradition, they returned to what they considered the earlier form of the OT, the books held sacred in Judaism. They retained the order of the books established in the early church, but separated out the books not in the Hebrew Bible and identified them as the Apocrypha. Protestants have continued to be ambivalent about the authority of this part of the Bible.

Authority: The OT is a religious book both in terms of its origin and its continued use in communities of faith. Its various parts deal with matters of human life and experience in the context of ultimate and transcendent meaning, that is, in terms of the ways and will of God.

It is important to keep in mind that to identify this document as "Old Testament" is to consider such religious meaning within a Christian context. That is to say, for the Christian churches the OT does not stand alone but only as part of the Bible as a whole. That is not true, of course, when Judaism considers the

OLD TESTAMENT

same books as the Bible, or when the writings are read and studied only for their historical or literary contents. But for communities and individuals of faith, these books comprise religious documents.

The question of the authority and meaning of the OT—as a particular aspect of the issue of the authority of the Bible—has been treated variously over the centuries. The earliest Christians and their Jewish contemporaries assumed that it contained the word of God and took its authority for granted. In the first few Christian centuries, the OT came to be read more and more spiritually and christologically through the lens of the NT: the Israelite figures and texts were seen as types of promises of what was to happen with the coming of Christ. Realizing that the ancient words had to be interpreted and applied in ever-new situations, the church before the Reformation came more and more to understand the Bible through tradition, including the creeds and the decisions of church councils. The Reformation intended that all matters of Christian faith and practice should be authorized by the Bible alone.

That the Bible, including the OT, is the word of God may be understood in very different ways. It was only in the nineteenth century that a doctrine of verbal inspiration developed. This view, that every word of the Bible was directly inspired by God, arose in part as a reaction against biblical criticism, which in its study of the human origins of the Bible seemed to understand the Bible's authority in terms of its power to inspire and guide in the context of everyday as well as religious experience. Some have serious doubts about the importance of the OT in relation to the NT, thus keeping alive a debate as old as the second century A.D.

The influence and importance of the OT, as part of the Bible, are both deep and wide. Translations of the Bible have helped to shape the development of languages, from the English of the Authorized or King James Version to those in new nations of the twentieth century. The art, literature, and even world-view of a great many cultures are deeply indebted to this ancient document.

Literature: The OT is not a single, unified document of a single type or by a single author, nor does it claim to be. Instead, it is a veritable library of ancient Israelite literature. If as a whole it is to be identified by a single category, it would have to be called an anthology, a collection of diverse literary works. One way to better understand that anthology is to classify its parts according to literary genre or type.

In broad terms, the various books and their parts may be identified as narratives, law, poetry, wisdom reflections and proverbs, corporate and personal prayers, and apocalypses. While many of the works are quite distinctive, none of these types is unique to the OT; examples of all can be found among other ancient Near Eastern literature. Some books consist entirely or almost entirely of one type while others include several.

The Pentateuch and the historical Books are mainly narrative, though other types of literature will be found within them. Genesis includes poetry and Exodus both poetry and law. A narrative, broadly defined, reports past events. Narratives that include a plot, description of a setting, and characterization are stories. Whatever their specific point or purpose, stories mean to create interest and hold the attention by the creation of tension.

Many of the OT narratives must be identified as histories, though not without some qualification. Accounts such as those in the books of Samuel and Kings report and interpret the public events of the past, and in that sense they are history. But in addition to being guided by the facts, so far as they could be determined, the writers relied on oral tradition, only some of which would have been historically reliable. Even more important, they interpreted all events theologically. Thus they tended to write theological or salvation history, not history in the modern sense. Moreover, the accessibility to and the interest in accurate and detailed information varied considerably. One of the tasks of modern historical study of the OT is to determine to what extent such documents can be used to reconstruct the events of the past.

Among the other narrative works are short stories, tales, and stories with a lesson, such as Ruth, Esther, Judith, Tobit, and Jonah. Contained within the narrative books are individual stories of different types, such as family sagas,

David (bottom center) slaying Goliath (cf. 1 Sam. 17); illuminated manuscript, twelfth century.

and narratives that explain places, names, or practices in terms of their origins.

Its first five books and even the OT as a whole have been identified as "the law," but as a type of literature the term must be used more precisely. As the story from creation to the entrance into the promised land is told, virtually all of ancient Israel's laws were understood to have been given at Mount Sinai. This means that they are understood in the framework of the covenant between God and Israel, as the stipulations by which the people continued to be God's people. Laws are found in collections, such as the Decalogues in Exodus 20, 34, and Deuteronomy 5, the Book of the Covenant in Exodus 21–24, or the Holiness Code in Leviticus 17–26. For the most part, the individual laws are of two kinds, casuistic and apodictic. The casuistic is case law in two parts, the statement of a condition and then its legal results: "If a man borrows anything of his neighbor, and it is hurt or dies, . . . he shall make full restitution [to its owner]" (Exod. 22:14). Such formulations are found in all other ancient Near Eastern laws, such as the Code of Hammurabi. Apodictic laws are different in their inclusive and absolute character. They consist of a single short sentence, either a command or prohibition: "Honor your father and your mother" (Exod. 20:12); "You shall not steal" (Exod. 20:15).

The OT poetic books include Psalms, Job, Proverbs, Ecclesiastes, Song of Songs, Ecclesiasticus, and the Prayer of Manasseh. Most of the prophetic books are in poetry as well, but in other respects they are quite different from the ones listed here.

Most modern translations enable readers to recognize and better understand texts that originated in Hebrew poetry by printing the lines in verse form. The most important mark of Hebrew poetry, parallelism of lines or other parts, can then be noted:

Why do the nations conspire,
and the peoples plot in vain? (Ps. 2:1)

This is an example of synonymous parallelism, with "nations" in the first line paralleled by "peoples" in the second, and "conspire" paralleled by "plot in vain."

Another characteristic of Hebrew poetry is its meter or rhythm, which appears to be based not on the length of syllables but upon patterns of accented syllables. The most easily recognizable meter is that used for the dirge, which alternates lines of three and two accents. Israelite poetry also made use of wordplays, assonance, and other rhetorical devices.

Wisdom literature, whether in the form of short sayings such as those found in Proverbs 10–30 or longer compositions such as Job, was written mainly in poetry. One also finds lyrical poetry, that is, lines meant to be sung, ranging from the love poetry of the Song of Songs to the liturgical songs of the Psalms. Among the liturgical songs are individual and communal laments or complaints, thanksgiving songs, hymns, and royal psalms.

The prophetic books, Isaiah, Jeremiah, Ezekiel, and the twelve Minor Prophets, contain some of the most distinctively Israelite literature, though prophets and prophecies were known in the ancient Near East generally. Behind the development of the books stand the prophetic figures themselves, individuals who announced the word of God concerning the immediate future, whether that future contained disaster or salvation.

The most common genres in the prophetic books are speeches. As a rule they are short, poetic addresses to the people as a whole, a group, or even an individual. When the prophets announce judgment they indicate the reasons in terms of the sins of those addressed. Remarkably, the prophets ordinarily present these speeches as the direct word of God that has been revealed to them. In addition to speeches, most prophetic books also contain shorter or longer narratives and sometimes prayers.

The apocalypse is a distinctive type of literature that arose in the late OT period. It is represented in the OT only in the book of Daniel, though there are somewhat similar materials in Isaiah 24–27 and Zechariah 9–14. An apocalypse is a long and elaborate report of a vision of the course of history and of its end. It generally is marked by a strong sense of the struggle between the powers of good and evil, belief in angels and demons, and in the resurrection of the dead. Such literature was widespread in the last two centuries B.C. and the first century A.D.

Origin and Growth of the OT: Relatively few of the books of the OT contain direct information concerning their time and place of origin or their author. Church and synagogue tradition remember Moses as the author of the Pentateuch, but the books themselves contain no such claim. Most of the works are anonymous and undated. Consequently, if we wish to understand the literature better by placing it in historical context, we must investigate all of the evidence at hand.

Such investigation shows that in most cases it was a long and often complicated road from the first oral or written stages in the growth of a book, through its use in the ancient community of faith, to its subsequent acceptance as sacred Scripture. Many books, such as those of the Pentateuch, are composite works; that is, the words of more than one author have been combined to form the present book. Most of these writers or editors are anonymous, though in many cases their work can be dated. In a great many instances, what we have now in writing once was passed on as oral tradition. This would have been the case with many of the in-

Moses (center), *The Well of Moses*, by Claus Sluter at Dijon, France, 1395–1406.

dividual stories in the book of Genesis, many of the individual laws, and most of the short prophetic speeches. Moreover, works such as the Psalms arose for use in public worship, including group singing. On the other hand, some books such as Job and probably Isaiah 40–55 arose as written compositions.

The development of the written literature of the OT spanned more than a thousand years, and even more if one includes the oral traditions. Some of the oldest works, most likely poetry such as Exodus 15:21, probably arose before 1000 B.C., and the latest ones, such as the Book of Daniel, in the last century or two B.C.

But even that was not the end of the story. What originated in Hebrew was translated first into Greek and then into other languages such as Latin. Then in the modern age, beginning in the sixteenth century, a variety of new translations rendered into the vernacular of most peoples has been produced and printed. ***See also*** Apocalyptic Literature; Bible; Canon; Law; Poetry; Prophet; Sources of the Pentateuch; Texts, Versions, Manuscripts, Editions. G.M.T.

Old Testament, names of God in the. ***See*** Names of God in the Old Testament.

Old Testament, sociology of the. ***See*** Sociology of the Old Testament.

Old Testament as Literature, the. ***See*** Literature, The Old Testament as.

Old Testament chronology. ***See*** Chronology, Old Testament.

Old Testament quotations in the New Testament.

Introduction: The OT is quoted or alluded to in every book of the NT except Philemon and 2 and 3 John. It is used in Christian moral teaching, both in the preaching of Jesus and in the Letters. It played an especially important part in the formulation of the church's faith. The sacred books of the Jews were equally sacred to the first Christians, who were themselves Jews or Gentiles in close contact with Judaism. Paul refers to the books of the OT as "the oracles of God" (Rom. 3:2). Those most frequently cited are the Pentateuch, the Prophets, and the Psalms. Occasionally, reference is made to books of the Apocrypha (e.g., clear allusions to the Wisdom of Solomon in Rom. 5:12 and Heb. 1:3) and even the Pseudepigrapha (e.g., direct quotation of *1 Enoch* 1:9 in Jude 14–15).

Reference to the OT is made by means of quotations, allusions, and themes. Quotations are adduced by a writer for a particular purpose and often have a formula of introduction (e.g., "as it is written," Mark 7:6). A fulfillment formula is a special feature of Matthew (e.g., 1:23) and is found also in John (e.g., 12:38). Where an OT passage or theme is the subject of a sustained argument, a writer may include allusions to the passage or its context in the course of the exposition. A good example of this is found in Paul's argument on Abraham in Romans 4. Very often, however, allusions are merely verbal, as a writer whose mind is well stocked with biblical phrases makes use of them in an original composition (e.g., Luke 1:25, alluding to Gen. 30:23). The writer of Revelation draws constantly on the OT, creating a new composition out of a wealth of biblical allusions. OT themes may be adduced with very little allusion to the actual text (e.g., Cain as an example of hatred in 1 John 3:12). Usually, however, themes and allusions go together, as in Romans 4 on the faith of Abraham and in Hebrews 7 on Melchizedek.

Jewish Background: Although the use of the OT in the NT has distinctive features, it is comparable in many ways to the use of Scripture in Judaism at the time. Paul uses rabbinic techniques of interpretation, notably *khahrahz* (Heb., "to string beads," i.e., to explain one biblical passage by adducing another, e.g., Rom. 10:18–21) and *kal wahkhohmer* (the *a fortiori* argument, e.g., 2 Cor. 3:11, "For *if* what faded away came with splendor, what is permanent must have *much more* splendor"). An example of the latter is ascribed to Jesus in John 7:23. The

OT QUOTATIONS IN THE NT

NT also has examples of *midrash*, i.e., the exposition of a biblical text. Thus, the discourse on the Bread of Life in John 6:25–59 is an exposition of the text quoted in 6:31, "He gave them bread from heaven to eat" (cf. Exod. 16:4, 15; Ps. 78:24; John's text is not an exact quotation).

Some quotations show features found in the Targums, the Aramaic translations of the Scriptures used in synagogues where Aramaic was the language of the people. As the translation, originally given orally, followed the reading of the lesson in Hebrew, it is often paraphrastic and explanatory, sometimes modernizing the ideas to make them more relevant to the congregation. Paul has examples of this in 1 Cor. 10:1–4 (the theme of Israel in the wilderness applied to temptations of Christians) and Rom. 10:6–8 (Deut. 30:12–14 adapted and applied to Christ).

More Jewish precedents can be seen in the Dead Sea Scrolls (DSS). These writings have illuminated the NT interpretation of the OT and also the techniques used to achieve it. According to the *Damascus Document* (CD) 6:19, the community regarded itself as the people of the New Covenant, and according to the *Manual of Discipline* (1QS), this was specifically to "prepare the way of the Lord" (8:14, quoting Isa. 40:3). Messianic prophecies are applied not only to the Messiah of Israel, who is the legitimate king of the line of David, but also to the community as a whole. Thus, Amos 9:11 is applied to the Messiah in the *Florilegium* or *Eschatological Midrashim* from Qumran Cave 4 (4QFlor 1:12), but is referred to the "congregation" in CD 7:16–17. The Psalms are treated as prophecy and so are given an eschatological interpretation. Thus, Ps. 2:1–2, on the raging of the nations against God's anointed one, is interpreted in 4QFlor 1:19 as follows: "Interpreted, this saying concerns [the kings of the nations] who shall [rage against] the elect of Israel in the last days." Here again, "the elect" is plural, meaning the whole community, not just the Messiah as the Psalm ("his anointed one") implies. Behind this method of interpretation is the idea of God's plan, kept secret in past ages, but revealed in a "mystery" (Heb. *rahz)* to the prophets, and now coming to pass in the last times. There is also a Christian expression of this idea (Col. 1:26). The biblical commentaries of the DSS expound the Prophets and Psalms in this way, giving a verse-by-verse exposition of the text in relation to the history and eschatological expectations of the community. Similarly, many of the quotations of the Prophets and Psalms in the NT are applied to Jesus and the church in relation to the eschatological plan of God.

A special refinement of these commentaries is the use of textual variants to aid the interpretation. The most striking example is in the *Habakkuk Commentary* (1QpHab) on Hab. 2:16 (1QpHab 11:8–15), where the Hebrew (Masoretic) text (MT), "Drink, yourself, and be uncircumcised *[heahrayl]!*" is read as "Drink, yourself, and stagger *[hayrahayl]!*" This is clearly correct, and is supported by the Septuagint (LXX) against the MT. However, in the comment following the text, the writer says, "He did not circumcise the foreskin of his heart," which shows knowledge of the faulty reading of the MT. We shall see that selective use of variant readings is a feature of some of the quotations in the NT.

Quotations in Moral Teaching: Jesus taught the people "as one who had authority, and not as the scribes" (Mark 1:22). This seems to mean that he did not appeal to precedents set by earlier teachers, or even to the Scriptures, to back up his teaching. In the teaching that has come down to us in the synoptic Gospels, his quotations of the OT occur either in matters of controversy or in order to confirm the Law. In Mark 2:25–26, he defends the disciples when they are accused of breaking the Sabbath by direct appeal to 1 Sam. 21:1–6. In the dispute on divorce in Mark 10:2–9, he goes behind the permission for divorce in Deut. 24:1–4 to the more fundamental principles concerning marriage in Gen. 1:27 and 2:24. The same material is rearranged in Matt. 19:3–9 to emphasize the continuing validity of the Deuteronomic permission. In Mark 7:1–13, Jesus opposes casuistic devices that frustrate the intention of the Law, quoting Isa. 29:13 and Exod. 20:12. He confirms the Law when he gives the two commandments of Deut. 6:4 and Lev. 19:18 in Mark 12:28–31. On the other hand, the quotations from the Law in the Sermon on the Mount, where the Law is contrasted with the teaching of Jesus in a series of antitheses (Matt. 5:21–48), may well belong to Matthew's editing rather than the underlying tradition, as they do not appear in the parallels in Luke. The Beatitudes (Matt. 5:3–12) incorporate OT allusions, but these are not formal quotations. Naturally, verbal reminiscences of Scripture occur fairly often in Jesus' teaching (e.g., Mark 9:48, alluding to Isa. 66:24).

The parenetic sections (i.e., moral teaching) of the Letters show familiarity with Jewish moral teaching. This explains why the same quotation sometimes appears in the work of two different authors. Thus, Prov. 10:12 ("love covers all offenses") is found, somewhat revised, in both 1 Pet. 4:8 and James 5:20. Deut. 32:35 ("Vengeance is mine") occurs in Rom. 12:19 and Heb. 10:30. In 1 Pet. 3:10–12, there is an extended quotation of Ps. 34:12–16, which provides the basis for the surrounding exhortation. Paul, in Rom. 12:20, makes similar use of Prov. 25:21–22. Paul also appears to know Jesus' use of Lev. 19:18 to summarize the Law (Rom. 13:8–10; cf. James 2:8, where it is quoted with allusions to the wider context of Lev. 19).

The moral teaching of the Letters also includes quotations that became current in the primitive church primarily for other reasons.

OT QUOTATIONS IN THE NT

Words from the Suffering Servant passage (Isa. 53) are used in a description of Christ in 1 Pet. 2:21–25, not to prove that his sufferings accord with God's plan as revealed in Scripture, but for the sake of moral example. Both Paul (Rom. 10:6) and John (12:38) quote from Isa. 53:1 in connection with the unbelief of the Jews. The reverse procedure appears when Paul takes up Hab. 2:4 ("the righteous shall live by his faith"). This is quoted in Heb. 10:38 in connection with the moral quality of faithfulness (just as in 1QpHab 8:2–3 it is applied to the Qumran community's "faith in the Teacher of Righteousness," i.e., fidelity to his interpretation of the Law). In Gal. 3:11 and Rom. 1:17, however, Paul applies it to the "righteous by faith" (omitting the pronoun "his"), as opposed to the "righteous by Law," thus using it as the key text in his argument on justification by faith.

Fulfillment Quotations: The essential message of Jesus according to Mark 1:15 is, "The time is fulfilled, and the kingdom of God is at hand; repent, and believe in the gospel." This indicates that the present time is the era of fulfillment of prophecy, as in the DSS. Moreover, the word "gospel" corresponds with the expression used for "herald of good tidings" in the LXX of Isa. 40:9 (the Greek root is the same). Direct allusion to the same passage is probable in Mark 9:1, where "before they see the kingdom of God come with power" echoes Isa. 40:10 and to some extent corresponds with the Targum.

From the first, the church proclaimed Jesus, risen and exalted, to be the Messiah in fulfillment of Scripture, and this was proved from messianic texts. The basic exaltation text is Ps. 110:1, which is quoted in the Gospels, Acts, the Pauline Letters, and Hebrews. Resurrection on the third day may have been supported from Hos. 6:2, which is applied to the resurrection of the dead in Jewish sources, but is not actually quoted in the NT. Jonah's three days' sojourn in the belly of the fish (Jon. 1:17; MT, 2:1), also used of the resurrection of the dead in Jewish sources, is applied to Jesus in Matt. 12:40. Jesus' resurrection as Messiah fulfills Ps. 2:7, quoted in Acts 13:33; Heb. 1:5; and 5:5 and alluded to in a probably pre-Pauline formula in Rom. 1:4. The same text may lie behind the divine words at the baptism of Jesus in Mark 1:11, though they mainly reflect Isa. 42:1. Thus, the divine declaration of the messiahship of Jesus is pushed back from the resurrection to the baptism. Passages from the messianic Psalm 118 are also applied to the christological significance of the resurrection in Acts 4:11 and 1 Pet. 2:7, and also in Matt. 21:42; Mark 12:10–11; and Luke 20:17, and the application is made to Jesus' entry into Jerusalem in Matt. 21:9; Mark 11:9; and John 12:13. Jesus' future function as the exalted Messiah is expressed in terms of the "one like a son of man" (Dan. 7:13) in Matt. 24:30; Mark 13:26; and Luke 21:27, and the text from Daniel is alluded to frequently in Matthew. In Matt. 26:64; Mark 14:62; and Luke 22:69, Dan. 7:13 is conflated (combined) with Ps. 110:1; in Rev. 1:7, it is conflated with Zech. 12:10. It is not too much to say that the resurrection, interpreted in the light of messianic texts, is the starting point of Christology.

That Jesus died as Messiah (contrary to current expectation) is proved from passages in Isaiah and Zechariah and certain Psalms. This shows a creative use of the OT theme of the righteous sufferer, which may have had its starting point in Jesus' own approach to his death. Almost every verse of Isaiah 53 is quoted or alluded to in connection with Jesus' sufferings. It is probably the chief warrant behind the pre-Pauline statement in 1 Cor. 15:3 that "Christ died for our sins in accordance with the scriptures," and may lie behind the Passion predictions in Mark 8:31, etc. Zech. 9:9 is applied to Jesus' entry into Jerusalem in Matt. 21:5 and John 12:15, and Zech. 12:10 is applied to the crucifixion in John 19:37. The latter is also placed alongside Dan. 7:13 in Matt. 24:30 and conflated with Dan. 7:13 in Rev. 1:7. Jesus quotes Zech. 13:7 in Matt. 26:31 and Mark 14:27. Ps. 41:9 is alluded to in Mark 14:18 and actually quoted in John 13:18 to account for the treachery of Judas. Ps. 22:1 provides Jesus' cry of dereliction in Matt. 27:46 and Mark 15:34, and v. 18 is applied to the parting of Jesus' garments in all four Gospels (fully quoted in John 19:24). Psalm 69 is also widely used in connection with the Passion, principally in John 2:17; Acts 1:20; and Rom. 15:3 (cf. also Rom. 11:9–10).

That the message of the gospel would meet with unbelief is proved from further passages in Isaiah. Isa. 6:9–10 is quoted in Matt. 13:14–15; Mark 4:12; John 12:40; and Acts 28:26–27. Similar words in Isa. 29:10, perhaps originally adduced as a commentary on Isa. 6:9–10, are quoted by Paul in Rom. 11:8 along with words from Deut. 29:3. Paul also quotes Isa. 29:14 in 1 Cor. 1:19. From the point of view of faith, Jesus is both the precious cornerstone (Isa. 28:16, quoted in 1 Pet. 2:6) and the rock of offense (Isa. 8:14, quoted in 1 Pet. 2:8). These two quotations are conflated by Paul in Rom. 9:33 and may be alluded to in Matt. 16:18 and 16:23. We may note further the use of Hab. 1:5 in connection with this issue in Acts 13:41 (it is applied to the opponents of the Qumran commentary in 1 QpHab 2:1–9).

Other quotations are concerned with qualifications for messiahship, e.g., the Bethlehem passage in Mic. 5:2, quoted in Matt. 2:6 and perhaps alluded to in John 7:42, and Isa. 9:1–2, quoted in Matt. 4:15 and perhaps alluded to in John 7:52 and 8:12. Matt 2:23 ("He shall be called a Nazarene") also belongs here, but the source of the quotation is uncertain. A special concern is the position of John the Baptist in relation to Jesus. He is assigned the role of the

OT QUOTATIONS IN THE NT

forerunner of the Messiah and identified with Elijah, who was expected to return before the judgment, with the aid of quotations from Mal. 3:1 (Mark 1:2; also Matt. 11:10; Luke 7:27); Mal. 4:5 (Matt. 17:10); and Isa. 40:3 (Matt. 3:3; Mark 1:3; Luke 3:4–6; John 1:23).

The distribution of the quotations mentioned above shows the use of the same Scriptures in different parts of the NT. This suggests that they were selected in the first instance in connection with the explication of the Christian message and the defense of it against unbelievers. Speeches in Acts that are addressed to Jewish audiences (e.g., 2:14–36; 7:2–53; 13:16–41) are much richer in OT quotations and allusions than are those addressed to Gentiles and probably preserve many features of the apologetic use of Scripture in the primitive church. These also appear in Romans 9–11, where Paul is concerned with the unbelief of the Jews, and again in 1 Peter 2. It is necessary to show that this unbelief is not a count against the Christian proclamation, because it is part of the fulfillment of what God has made known in Scripture.

A fulfillment formula to introduce quotations is a special feature of Matthew (ten times) and John (five times, but John also uses the simple "as it is written" or a similar formula another five times). These are very frequently, though not exclusively, used in connection with quotations that belong to the more primitive stratum just mentioned. Both Matthew and John apparently were written in situations of dialogue and hostility between Christians and unbelieving Jews. Nearly all these quotations are drawn from the Prophets and the Psalms. The later collections of anti-Judaic testimonies have suggested to some that the earliest Christian writing was a testimony book, or collection of proof-texts, from which these formula quotations were taken. It seems more likely, however, that such a collection belongs to a later stage.

The use of Scripture in the early church was a dynamic process. Texts already current in one connection were sometimes given a secondary application to another issue (cf. above on quotations used in moral teaching that had become current primarily for other reasons). Further texts were also adduced in connection with those already established. Thus, Ps. 8:6 is used in 1 Cor. 15:27 and in Heb. 2:7–8 to express a particular facet of the exaltation of Jesus, for which the foundation text is Ps. 110:1. Hebrews exploits Psalm 110 further by deducing from Ps. 110:4 the high-priesthood of Jesus (Heb. 5:5–10; 7:15–17). In Rom. 10:11–13, Paul draws together the "faith" text, Isa. 28:16, and Joel 2:32. Moreover, the development of Christology was carried forward by applying to Jesus as the exalted agent of God texts that properly apply to God (e.g., Phil. 2:10–11; cf. Isa. 45:23).

It is not clear to what extent the fulfillment texts go back to Jesus himself. It seems that, like his followers, he thought of his own time as the period of eschatological fulfillment, but he was reticent about personal claims to messiahship. If Mark 12:35–37 (embodying a quotation of Ps. 110:1) has an authentic basis, it may be evidence that he discouraged such ideas, though the interpretation of this passage is disputed. The self-designation "Son of man" carries allusion to Dan. 7:13 only when other features of the text occur in the context, and the authenticity of these sayings is doubtful. Thus, messianic texts belong to the church's interpretation of Jesus in the light of the resurrection and cannot with certainty be ascribed to Jesus himself. It is also disputed whether he was influenced by Isaiah 53 in facing his own betrayal and death. These were certainly interpreted with the aid of this prophecy from the earliest days, however.

Arguments Based on Scripture: Besides the use of Scripture as proof-texts, the NT contains examples of arguments conducted entirely in terms of scriptural interpretation, notably in the major Pauline Letters and in Hebrews. Thus, Paul argues justification by faith in Galatians and Romans on the basis of Scripture, because his opponents share his respect for it and must be defeated on their own ground. In Galatians 3 and Romans 4, direct quotations from Genesis are subjected to detailed analysis, and further allusions are adduced in the process. An important distinction is made in Gal. 3:16 by pressing the exact meaning of the words quoted in a manner reminiscent of rabbinic discussions. Another example is the allegory of Hagar and Sarah in Gal. 4:21–31, where the main argument depends on allusions to Genesis 16 and 21, but Isa. 54:1 is adduced to support the interpretation. Other instances are the allusions to Israel in the wilderness (1 Cor. 10:1–13) and the highly complex exposition of Exodus 33 and 34 in 2 Corinthians 3, contrasting the old and new dispensations by means of the *a fortiori* argument (see above). In Hebrews, the argument of the whole Letter depends on the contrast between old and new. Quotations and allusions are taken up with regard to Moses (chap. 3), the promised land (chap. 4), Melchizedek (chap. 7), the covenant (chap. 8), and the sacrificial system (chaps. 9 and 10). This procedure in Hebrews has its basis in the prophetic view of Scripture discussed above and perhaps also to some extent in a Platonic understanding of the dualistic nature of reality.

Such arguments from Scripture should be distinguished from the use of Scripture in apocalyptic passages (e.g., Mark 13; Revelation), in which images and phrases from the OT are used as the vehicle of a new symbolic presentation of the plan of eschatology on a cosmic scale. Many of the biblical images used in Revelation can be paralleled in Jewish apocalyptic writings. The central new feature is the "Lamb . . . as though it had been slain" (Rev. 5: 6) as the image of Christ, derived from imaginative use of Isa. 53:7, and other sacrificial passages currently used in connection with the death of Christ.

Liturgical Formulas: Jewish liturgy included not only the reading of Psalms and lessons from the OT but also the use of hymns and prayers that incorporate scriptural phrases and allusions. It can be safely assumed that from the earliest days Christian worship carried over many of these forms. In the NT, this influence is seen chiefly in the doxologies (e.g., Rom. 1:25; 9:5; 11:36; Rev. 4:8, 11; 5:9–10, 12, 13). The hymn of the four living creatures in Rev. 4:8 is based on the *Sanctus* (Isa. 6:3) and includes allusion to Exod. 3:14.

Text Form: The Greek text of the quotations in the NT often differs from that of the LXX and sometimes is closer to the MT. This is especially true of the fulfillment quotations, which were employed before the church became predominantly Greek-speaking, and this explains why non-LXX forms are found in Paul and 1 Peter. In some cases, the text has been carefully selected to assist the application (note the similar feature in the DSS discussed above). Thus, Matt. 12: 18–21 is a quotation of the passage on the Servant of the Lord in Isa. 42:1–4, but it has been modified to fit the details of the ministry and death and resurrection of Jesus. As the first verse of the text has already been used in connection with the baptism of Jesus (Matt. 3:17), it is probable that the baptism is also in view. Thus, the whole of Jesus' ministry is messianic, from his baptism, through his quiet preaching and suffering and death, to the spread of the gospel to the Gentiles which followed the resurrection. To secure this interpretation, Matthew has worked from the Hebrew text, but there is perhaps a debt to the Targum in v. 19, where "wrangle" appears to be a mistranslation of the Aramaic "lift up [i.e., his voice]." The final words in v. 21, however, take advantage of the LXX, which reads "and in his name will the Gentiles hope," in place of the Hebrew text's "and the coastlands will wait for his law," thus securing the application to the Gentile mission of the early church.

Abbreviation of the text is another very frequent feature. A text may be telescoped so as to concentrate attention on the particular point at issue or to leave out matter that appears unsuitable to the interpretation. Thus, in the above mentioned example of Matt. 12:18–21, part of Isa. 42:3–4 is omitted from v. 20 because it seems to contradict the quietness of Jesus' ministry. The versions of Isa. 6:9–10 in both Mark 4:12 and John 12:40 are greatly abbreviated in different ways.

Conflation (combination and mixture) of texts achieves a similar purpose. This usually involves some adaptation of the text to make the quotations fit together. We have seen examples of this in the earlier discussion of Paul. Matthew's account of the death of Judas Iscariot includes a composite quotation of Zech. 11:12–13 that involves phrases from Jer. 32:6–15 and 18:2–3 (Matt. 27:9). This seems to be the reason that it is attributed to Jeremiah in the fulfillment formula.

Though it is sometimes claimed that gospel episodes have been conjured up out of OT quotations, these features of adaptation of the text point in the opposite direction. The apostolic message and the traditions about Jesus are primary, and the OT comes into use for the defense and explication of the faith. ***See also*** Messiah; New Testament; Old Testament.

Bibliography

Lindars, Barnabas. *New Testament Apologetic: The Doctrinal Significance of the Old Testament Quotations.* Philadelphia: Westminster, 1961.

B.L.

Old Testament theology. ***See*** Theology, Old Testament.

olive, an evergreen tree and its fruit, an oval-shaped oil-bearing drupe. As today in Mediterranean regions, the olive in antiquity was the fruit par excellence; either the fresh fruit or its oil found a place at every meal. The olive tree was so highly regarded in antiquity—its fruit was a mainstay of the diet, it was ubiquitous to the biblical landscape (Deut. 8:8), even clinging to rocky hillsides, and it was long-lived and venerable—that it is no wonder it assumed an almost mythical character. The tree became a

Olive.

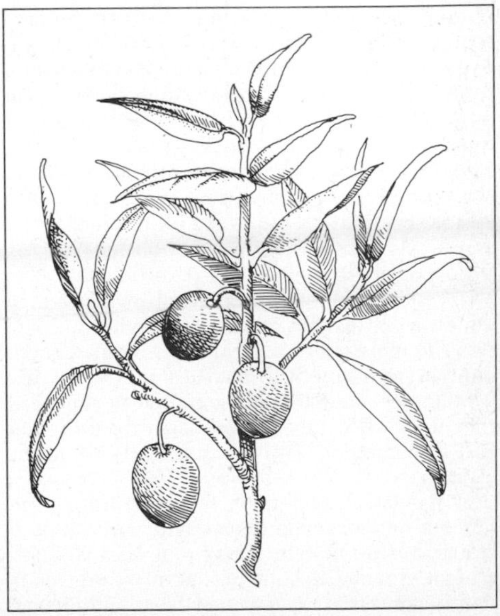

symbol of fertility (Ps. 128:3), beauty (Jer. 11:16; Hos. 14:6), divine blessing (Deut. 7:13), peace and bountifulness (Gen. 8:11), and it was inextricably associated with Jesus (the Mount of Olives [Mark 14:26; John 8:1]).

With an increased awareness among archaeologists of the necessity to collect paleobotanical specimens, we now know a great deal more about the origins of agriculture in the Near East. It has long been known that cereal cultivation (generally equated with a surge toward settled life in the Neolithic period, ca. 8000–4500 B.C.) preceded fruit tree husbandry. It is now evident that olive cultivation, well established in the Early Bronze Age (third millennium B.C.), had its origins in the preceding proto-urban age. The earliest known domesticated olives have been recovered from fourth-millennium B.C. Chalcolithic sites, e.g., at modern Teleilat Ghassul near the northern tip of the Dead Sea. Fruit tree cultivation in this area would necessarily have involved irrigation, a relevant fact supporting domestication. The olive pit is easily identifiable and, despite some overlap, domestic varieties are generally larger than their wild relatives. Besides actual floral remains, evidence for an established olive oil industry in the Early Bronze Age appears in the form of Egyptian texts that mention imports from Canaan and in the large basins and jars probably used as containers and transport vessels. At Ras-Shamra, ancient Ugarit, similar basins have been found in association with an oil-pressing installation, dated to the Late Bronze Age (ca. 1500–1200 B.C.).

Numerous olive oil installations have been found throughout the biblical lands. The basic technology, with some variation, involved two separate processes: the olives were crushed, then subsequently squeezed. The first process required a huge stone crushing wheel, which was set on edge, pivoted on a vertical beam, and rolled on top of a circular stone basin upon which the olives were placed. A few rotations of the wheel were sufficient to crush the olives. Treading the olives was another method (Mic. 6:15). The crushed olives were then placed into special baskets and set so the oil drained into a basin; this was the "first oil" or "beaten oil," the oil used for lighting lamps (Exod. 27:20). The oil-pressing operation consisted of a beam to which stone weights (average weight: 300 kg.) were attached and a vat that included a deeper depression beside it to collect the oil. Pressure from the beam on the olives in the vat squeezed the oil out of the olives. Eventually the sediment and water settled while the pure oil rose to the surface.

With its characteristic gnarled trunk and lancelet bluish green leaves and white undersides, the olive tree thrives in the Mediterranean climate of hot, dry summers and cool, damp winters. It can survive for a thousand years; some specimens are said to date from the Roman period. The tree was propagated through grafting (Rom. 11:17–24). These shoots at the base of the parent tree are compared to a family blessed with many children (Ps. 128:3).

There was hardly a phase of life not touched by the olive tree. It was used for food (Num. 11:8), for fuel for lamps, as a medicine (Isa. 1:6; Luke 10:34), as an anointing oil (1 Sam. 10:1; 2 Kings 9:3; Isa. 61:1), in sacrifice (Lev. 2:4; Gen. 28:18), and its wood was used for furniture (1 Kings 6:23, 31–33). The olive branch was the first vegetation seen by Noah after the Flood (Gen. 8:11); in Greek mythology the olive was a gift from the goddess Athena to humankind. Today the olive branch remains an emblem of peace and bountifulness. S.L.R.

Olives, Mount of, a high hill to the east of Jerusalem. It is a comparatively good area for growing olives in the poor land surrounding Jerusalem. Rabbinic tradition claimed the olive branch was brought to Noah from this mount, which escaped the flood (*Midr.* XXX *Gen.* III, 6). An area of the mount was appropriately called Gethsemane (Heb., "Oil Press"), probably being a garden area where the fruit of the mount was processed (John 18:1). Jesus often prayed here (Matt. 26:36; Mark 14:32; Luke 22:39–46).

Pilgrims, like Jesus, who could not find lodging in the city stayed on the mount (John 18:1; Luke 22:39). Jesus preferred the Bethany area of the mount (Matt. 21:17).

The mile-long Mount of Olives dominates Jerusalem, rising 230 feet above the Temple Mount. It is part of a Senonian limestone range of hills protecting Jerusalem that resulted from a bifurcation of the highland ridge dividing two miles north of the city and uniting again just south of it. The Mount of Olives is the central section of the ridge's eastern branch, being separated from the city by the Kidron Valley. The section north of it is called Scopus, "lookout." The southern section begins after the Mount of Olives descends to the level of the Temple Mount. This is known as the Mount of Offense because Solomon built pagan shrines here (1 Kings 11:7).

The Mount of Olives was Jerusalem's watchtower. Every approach from Transjordan as well as from the north and south is visible from it. Some have suggested that the mountain to which Jesus was taken from Jerusalem (Matt. 4:8) and "led up" from the Judean desert (Luke 4:5) to view the kingdoms of the earth may have been this mount.

Jerusalem also communicated to the world from here by signal fires, as when the beginning of each month was announced. Isaiah may have had this mount in mind as the place for announcing the king's coming (Isa. 40:9). This "high place" was a natural location for the first sanctuary in the Jerusalem area, Nob (1 Sam. 21:

1; 2 Sam. 15:32). This probably was in the area of the present-day Augusta Victoria Hospital.

This natural bulwark against attack from the east was further strengthened by two villages at the base of its slope facing the Judean desert, Bahurim at the junctions of Mount Scopus and Mount of Olives on the north, and Anania or Bethany near the descent to the Mount of Offense on the south.

Bethphage fortified the center of the mount. This was the terminal of the Jericho road. From this strategic location Jesus entered Jerusalem at the completion of his ministry (Matt. 21:1; Mark 11:1; Luke 19:29).

Because the Temple was totally open to view from the mount, people were to be mindful of their conduct there. The red heifer was slaughtered on the mount as the high priest looked into the Holy of Holies. A bridge linked the eastern gate of the Temple Mount with the Mount of Olives. Because burial inside the city was forbidden, the mount gradually filled with tombs, in part due to the belief that on the last day the dead would rise to gaze on the Holy Place. The author of Revelation may refer to this mount as the place from which the descent of heavenly Jerusalem is observed (Rev. 20:10).

As a bulwark whose penetration meant the destruction of Jerusalem it became a symbol of the way of defeat. David climbed the mount in humiliation as he fled from Absalom (2 Sam. 15:13–30). The description of Jesus' coming to the mount on the night of his betrayal may echo this story (John 18:1). Isaiah pictures the Assyrians advancing to Nob, whence the city was cursed (Isa. 10:32). The way to exile across the mount established this as the way of defeat. Ezekiel pictured Jerusalem's departed glory resting here before it disappeared (Ezek. 11:23). *The Testament of Naphtali* uses the mount as the place of the vision that showed the various conquests of the city until the Hellenistic period (325–63 B.C.; *T. Naph.* 5:1–8). Jesus also used the mount as his podium for pronouncing judgment over the city (Luke 19:37–44; Matt. 24:3; Mark 13:3). Some have seen the stationing of the Tenth Legion of Rome on the mount in A.D. 70 as part of the fulfillment of his prophecy (Josephus *War* 5:69–70).

Hope rose that the defeat of Jerusalem would be reversed and that the Lord would return to his city (Ezek. 43:2; Isa. 40). Zechariah pictures God on that day standing on the mount, which will be divided as he enters the city. Following his entry, this now useless defense work will be leveled (Zech. 14:4, 10). The geographic outline of the synoptic Gospels is influenced by this vision, as Jesus travels from Jericho to the Mount of Olives on his way to cleanse the Temple.

The association of the mount with the departure and return of God's glory provides the natural setting for the ascension of Jesus and of his promised return (Luke 24:50; Acts 1:12). ***See also*** Bahurim; Bethany; Bethphage; Gethsemane; Jericho; Jerusalem; Kidron; Nob. B.E.S.

Olivet. ***See*** Olives, Mount of.

Olympas (oh-lim'puhs), a man in Rome whom Paul greets along with other members who may be in the same household (Rom. 16:15).

omega (oh-may'guh), the long "O" sound and the last letter in the Greek alphabet. It thus came to mean "last." It is used symbolically with alpha (the first letter in the Greek alphabet) in Revelation to refer to God and Christ (1:8; 21:6; 22:13). ***See also*** Alpha.

The letters *alpha* (left) and *omega*.

omer. 1 A dry measure equaling one-tenth of an *ephah* (ca. three-fifths of a bushel; Exod. 16:36). **2** The first sheaf (Heb. *'omer)* of barley harvested in the spring which was to be brought to the priest who performed an elevations offering with it at the sanctuary on the "day after the Sabbath" (Lev. 23:9–15). Originally, "Sabbath" may have referred to the first Saturday after the initial harvest, although there is no certainty on that. Later, the *'omer* ritual became dependent on the fixed date of the Feast of Unleavened Bread. ***See also*** Feasts, Festivals, and Fasts; Weights and Measures.

Omri (ohm'ree; Heb., meaning uncertain; possibly, "worshiper of Yahweh"), the sixth king of Israel (ca. 876–869 B.C.), a contemporary of King Asa of Judah and founder of a dynasty that included his son Ahab (ca. 869–850), Ahaziah (ca. 850–849), and Joram (ca. 849–842). According to 1 Kings 16:23, Omri ruled Israel for twelve years, six of them in Tirzah. The background to his ascent to the throne in Tirzah was the extinction of Baasha's dynasty and the subsequent power struggle among the high officers of the army. When Zimri, an army officer, assassinated Elah, son of Baasha, "all Israel" made Omri "the captain of the host," king of Israel. Omri and "all Israel" with him captured Tirzah, with Zimri taking his own life. The power struggle continued between Omri and Tibni, son of Ginath (1 Kings 16:21–22), each supported by "half of the people," and ended with the latter's death.

Of all Omri's deeds after he became king of Israel, the only one mentioned in the Bible is the founding of a new capital at Samaria, which marked a new chapter in the history of the Israelite kingdom. From a historical point of view, Omri was to the kingdom of Israel what David before him was to the United Kingdom. Both brought stability and prosperity to a troubled land by establishing a dynasty in a neutral political center. Archaeology has demonstrated the fact that Samaria was unoccupied until Omri's time and has revealed a high quality of workmanship under the reigns of both Omri and Ahab. The name "Omri" became an established term in Assyrian documents to indicate the Israelite kings even after the death of Omri and his descendants. Jehu, who founded a new dynasty in Israel, is called by Shalmaneser III "the son of Omri"; and Assyrian annalists continue to refer to Israel as the "land of (the house of) Omri" for a hundred years after the end of his dynasty.

According to the stele of Mesha, king of Moab, Omri gained possession of Madaba in Transjordan. Such successes were the result of a policy of mending quarrels and establishing peaceful relations with his neighbors. The prolonged war between Judah and Israel was terminated with the kings of the Davidic line accepting (at least temporarily) the existence of the Northern Kingdom. Omri entered into an alliance with Ethbaal, king of Sidon, which was sealed by the marriage between Ahab, Omri's son, and Jezebel, Ethbaal's daughter. The triple alliance between Israel, Judah, and Phoenicia served as a counterweight to the threat of Aram-Damascus, which continued to influence affairs even in Samaria. There were "bazaars" in Samaria belonging to Damascus already in Omri's time (1 Kings 20:34), and Israel was forced to grant special privileges to Aramean merchants.

Ostraca (fragments of pottery on which people have written) of this period, unearthed at the "ostraca house" in Samaria, include both Yahweh and Baal names, indicating syncretism and apostasy in line with the negative assessment of Omri on the part of the Deuteronomic historian (1 Kings 16:25–26). ***See also*** Ahab; Jehu; Mesha; Samaria, City of; Shalmaneser.

D.L.C.

On (ohn; Egyptian, "city of the pillar"). **1** An ancient city and religious center in northern Egypt whose ruins (modern Tell Hisn and Matariyeh) are located in the suburbs of modern Cairo, 7 miles northeast of the center of the city. On, called in Greek Heliopolis ("city of the sun"), was Egypt's center of sun worship, where the solar god Re (Atum) was venerated. The Temple of Re in On was the next largest temple in all Egypt, surpassed only by that of Amun in Thebes. The city was famous for its obelisks (thus its name), one of which still stands there

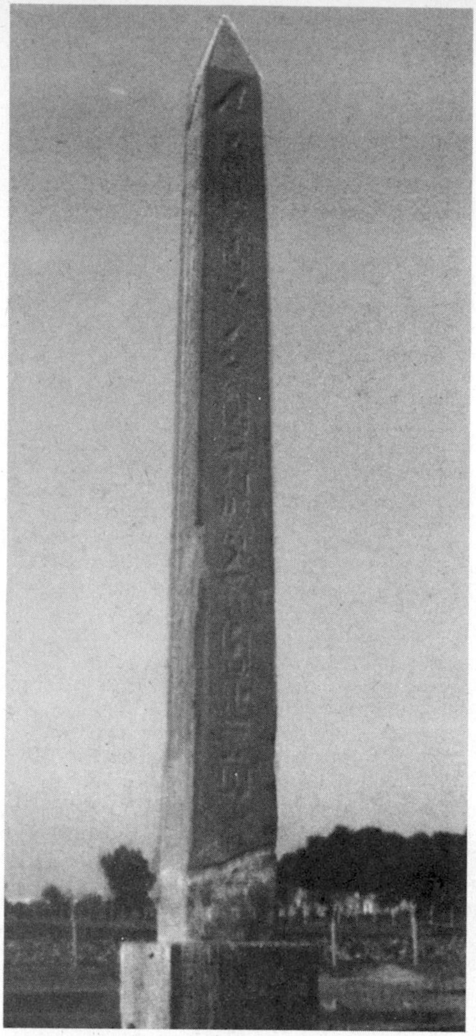

Obelisk of Pharaoh Senwosret I (1971–1926 B.C.) at modern Tell Hisn, near Cairo, and site of biblical On.

today, almost four thousand years old. Two of On's obelisks, erected there by Thutmose III in the sixteenth century B.C., now stand in Western countries, one in Central Park of New York City, the other on the Thames embankment in London.

In the Bible, Joseph married an Egyptian girl named Asenath, the daughter of Potiphera, priest of On (possibly the high priest there; Gen. 41:45, 50; 46:20). According to the Septuagint, On (Heliopolis) was one of the cities in Egypt built by the Israelites (Exod. 1:11). Isa. 19:18 may contain a reference to On in its prediction that the "City of the Sun" (according to some Hebrew manuscripts) will be one of the five cities in Egypt where Hebrew-speaking worshipers of Yahweh will dwell. (In the second century B.C. there was a community of Jews and a Jewish temple in Leontopolis, just north of Heliopolis.) In his oracle concerning Egypt, Jeremiah predicts that Nebuchadnezzar will destroy the temples of Egypt and will demolish the "pillars" (i.e., obelisks) of the "Temple of the Sun," probably referring to the Temple of Re in On (Jer. 43:13). Ezekiel predicts that judgment will befall the city of On (written *'awen*, perhaps as a pun; *'awen* in Hebrew meaning "trouble, wickedness") and that the inhabitants will be taken into captivity (Ezek. 30:17). According to later Christian tradition the Holy Family lived in Heliopolis during their sojourn in Egypt, and an ancient well and a sycamore tree at the site are associated by local tradition with events of the family's visit.

2 The son of Peleth, a leader of the tribe of Reuben who joined the rebellion of Korah against Moses in the wilderness (Num. 16:1). ***See also*** Egypt; Joseph. D.A.D.

Onam (oh'nuhm; Heb., "vigorous"). **1** The son of Shobal and grandson of Seir the Horite (Gen. 36:23). **2** The son of Jerahmeel, a descendant of Judah (1 Chron. 2:26, 28).

Onan (oh'nuhn; Heb., "power," "wealth"), the second son of Judah and the daughter of a Canaanite named Shua (Gen. 38:4; 46:12; Num. 26:19). After the death of Er, Judah's firstborn, Judah instructed Onan to perform the levirate marriage rite with Er's wife, Tamar. Onan failed in this duty and apparently let his semen go to waste (presumably by *coitus interruptus*), an act displeasing to God and for which he was slain (Gen. 38:8–10). The Judahite genealogy in 1 Chron. 2:3 does not mention the death of Onan. ***See also*** Marriage.

Onesimus (oh-nes'i-muhs; Gk., "useful"), Philemon's slave for whom Paul appeals in his Letter to Philemon. Apparently, Onesimus had run away from his master, met Paul (probably in Ephesus), and been converted to Christianity (Philem. 10). Though he had formerly been "useless" to his master, he now has become "useful" (Philem. 11)—a wordplay on his name. The theory that Onesimus was Archippus' slave (Philem. 2; Col. 4:17), not Philemon's, lacks evidence. The conclusion that Onesimus was released for service to Paul's mission and became an important leader in the church is confirmed by the description of him as "the faithful and beloved brother, who is one of yourselves" (Col. 4:9). The identification of him with the Onesimus who was bishop of Ephesus some sixty years later and the notion that he collected Paul's letters and wrote Ephesians represent speculation. More likely, the prominence of Onesimus led to the use of his name by later church leaders. A tradition identifies him as the bishop of Beroea, and Melito of Sardis (mid-second century) wrote to his "brother Onesimus." In the fourth century, two other bishops bear the name "Onesimus." ***See also*** Paul; Philemon; Philemon, The Letter of Paul to. W.R.B.

Onesiphorus (ohn-uh-sif'uh-ruhs), a Christian who is commended for special kindnesses to Paul, both in Ephesus and during Paul's Roman imprisonment (2 Tim. 1:16–18), and whose "household" is twice mentioned (2 Tim. 1:16; 4:19). These references may imply that Onesiphorus had died (cf. 2 Tim. 1:18).

Ono (oh'noh), a town near the southern end of the Plain of Sharon. It was built by Benjaminites (1 Chron. 8:12), is to be identified with modern Kefr Ana, and is mentioned in the Karnak list of Pharaoh Thutmose III. Along with Lod it was reoccupied after the Exile (Neh. 11:35) and Nehemiah's enemies waited to meet him in the plain of Ono (Neh. 6:2).

onycha (ahn'i-kah; Heb., "nail," "claw," "husk," or "flap"), an ingredient for incense (Exod. 30:34), probably from a marine shellfish.

onyx, a type of quartz with varicolored bands. Onyx is the usual RSV translation of a Hebrew word (*shoham*) that designates a precious stone, found in the land of Havilah, according to Gen. 2:12, and ranked with gold of Ophir (Job 28:16). It heads the list of precious stones provided by David for the Temple (1 Chron. 29:2). The two stones on the shoulders of the high priest's ephod were onyx (Exod. 28:9–12) and so was the eleventh stone on his breastpiece (Exod. 28:20). In Ezek. 28:13 "onyx" translates a different word (Heb. *yashepeh*, called "jasper" in Exod. 28:20), while *shoham* is translated "beryl." Onyx appears in Rev. 21:20 (Gk. *sardonyx*) as one of the twelve jewels adorning the wall of the heavenly Jerusalem. P.A.B.

Ophel (oh'fel; Heb., "hill"), the ridge extending south between the Kidron and Tyropoeon valleys that was fortified by David after his capture of Jerusalem (2 Chron. 27:3; 33:14). Repaired by Nehemiah after the Exile (Neh. 3:26–27), it was also the dwelling of some Temple personnel (Neh. 11:21). It has been most recently excavated by Yigal Shiloh.

Ophir (oh'fuhr), a people descended from Shem (Gen. 10:29; 1 Chron. 1:23). The land of these people is designated by the same name (1 Kings 9:28; 10:11) and was a famous source of gold (Job 22:24; 28:16; Ps. 45:9; Isa. 13:12).

The location of Ophir is uncertain. Suggestions have ranged from Africa to India and Arabia. It could be reached most easily by ship (1 Kings 9:28; 10:11), and speculations about cargo sources have led to associate Ophir with

Punt in Africa. The association with some other names has been used in support of an Arabian identification. ***See also*** Tarshish.

R.S.B.

Ophrah (ohf'ruh). **1** A town belonging to the Abiezrite clan of the tribe of Manasseh (Judg. 6: 11, 15), the home of Gideon (Judg. 6–8), and the scene of Abimelech's slaughter of his seventy brothers (Judg. 9:5). Its location is disputed. Proposed identifications include: modern et Taiyiba, in the territory of Issachar, east of Mt. Moreh; Affula, on the western flank of Mt. Moreh; and the Iron Age site of et Taiyiba, in the hills of Manasseh, ca. four and a half miles south of Megiddo. **2** A town of Benjamin (Josh. 18:23; cf. 1 Sam. 13:17), identified with modern Taiyiba, four miles northeast of Bethel; it is evidently the Ephron of 2 Chron. 13:19, Aphairema of 1 Macc. 11:34, and Ephraim of 2 Sam. 13:23 and John 11:54. **3** A descendant of Judah (1 Chron. 4:14).

D.A.D.

oracle, a message from a god, usually in response to an inquiry; also the sacred precincts whose powers made it possible for the oracle-prophet to consult the god. The Greco-Roman world knew three types of oracles: the oracle obtained through the casting of lots; the dream oracle obtained by sleeping in the sacred precincts, usually connected with healing; and the inspired oracle by which an oracle-prophet responded to inquiries. Though oracles were associated with a place, other prophets, diviners, and soothsayers might be employed by the state to give advice and to travel with the army, or they might set up practice in the local marketplace.

The lot type of oracle occurs in the OT as *urim* and *thummim* (1 Sam. 14:41; 28:6; Exod. 28:29; Deut. 33:8; Lev. 8:7; Num. 27:21). Acts 1: 26 reports that lots were cast to decide who would replace Judas, who committed suicide after betraying Jesus. Dream oracles are reflected in Saul's attempt to consult Samuel before a battle (1 Sam. 28:7–25) and the interpretation of dreams by "the wise" (Gen. 40:8; 41:25, 39; Dan. 2:19–47; 5:11–12). They guide Joseph (Matt. 1: 20; 2:13, 19) and the early community (Acts 10: 10, 30; 9:10). Inspired oracles could either respond to inquiries or be unsolicited prophecies. Some Israelite prophets were attached to the Temple. Other "free prophets" pronounced oracles of salvation and judgment in a cultic setting (cf. Jer. 4:10–12; Ezek. 18:9–13). Paul relates a healing oracle (2 Cor. 12:9) and oracles about the last days (1 Cor. 15:51–52; 1 Thess. 4:16–17a). Other oracles predict suffering (1 Thess. 3:4; Acts 21:11; 11:28; 18:9–10; 23:11; 27:23–24). ***See also*** Lot, Lots; Magic and Divination; Prophet; Urim and Thummim.

P.P.

oral materials, sources, and traditions, stories, songs, poetry, and other materials of varying types and lengths that circulated in oral or written form and on which the final texts of the OT and NT are based. In ancient Israel stories about Abraham, Isaac, Jacob, Moses, the Exodus,

Ancient site at Delphi, Greece, of one of the best-known oracles of the Greco-Roman world.

the wilderness wanderings, and the conquest of the land of Canaan were told again and again by parents to their children (see Exod. 12:26–27; 13:14–15; Josh. 4:6–7) and by skilled storytellers to larger gatherings of the community. Later stories dealt with judges (such as Deborah, Gideon, and Samson), kings (Saul, David, Solomon, and their successors), prophets (such as Samuel, Nathan, Elijah, and Elisha), and other key figures and events.

Also many songs (e.g., Gen. 4:23–24; Exod. 15:1–18, 21; Num. 21:17–18; Judg. 5), laws, proverbs, psalms, and especially most prophetic utterances arose orally. Remembering such traditions was a valued skill.

As these materials were handed down from generation to generation, they underwent change by becoming embellished, refined, and reinterpreted. Traditions that had similar content or style were brought together into, for instance, a cycle of stories about Abraham, a collection of laws (e.g., the Covenant Code in Exod. 20:22–23:19 or the Holiness Code in Lev. 17–26), or a series of prophetic utterances about a certain theme (e.g., those in Mic. 1–3 or in Mic. 4–5).

Such collections of traditions could in turn become sources for the later writings that we have in our present OT. Four great sources probably lie behind our Pentateuch: about the time of Solomon (latter half of the tenth century B.C.) the Yahwistic source (commonly called J), beginning with Gen. 2:4b and continuing through Genesis, Exodus, and Numbers, was probably compiled out of many of the early oral traditions; the Elohistic source (called E), also in Genesis, Exodus, and Numbers, emerged perhaps a century later and drew more on traditions from the Northern Kingdom than did the southern J; D, the source for much of Deuteronomy, brought together mostly the northern laws during the seventh century; and P, the Priestly source to be found from Genesis 1 through Deuteronomy 34, was a postexilic (late sixth–early fifth century B.C.) combination of both narratives and laws. Each of these sources has a distinctive point of view and style. They all eventually became combined into the Pentateuch as we know it.

Many other sources existed for other parts of the OT. A few times they are even mentioned: the Book of the Wars of the Lord (Num. 21:14); the Book of Jashar (Josh. 10:13; 2 Sam. 1:18); the book intended for Joshua (Exod. 17:14). In Isa. 8:16 the prophet orders preservation: "Bind up the testimony, seal the teaching among my disciples." Jeremiah 36 recounts an interesting story of the gathering of some of his utterances. There is also a striking incident described in 2 Kings 22–23 about a written source—often thought to be the source D—that is found and then is used in King Josiah's religious reformation.

Oral traditions and written sources preceded the final form of much of the NT as well, although this process was only decades long in contrast to the centuries during which some of the OT grew. After the death of Jesus the early believers spoke repeatedly about his life, ministry, and death. They recounted many of his sayings, including terse paradoxes (e.g., Mark 10:31), proverbs (e.g., Matt. 6:27), prophetic statements (e.g., Mark 1:15), and comments about law and piety (e.g., Mark 3:4). Equally important were the numerous parables and miracle stories.

Such materials, originally oral, became collected into various sources on which the writers of the Gospels later drew (Luke 1:1–4). A careful comparison of the similarities and differences among Matthew, Mark, and Luke suggests at least the following sources: various short writings about Jesus to aid in the preaching and teaching ministry of the early church, serving as the primary sources for Mark, certainly the first Gospel to be written; a sayings source commonly called Q (for German *Quelle*, "source") with some two hundred verses that Matthew and Luke have in common but that are not in Mark; another source on which only Matthew drew; and also one distinctive to Luke. The Gospel of Mark itself served as one of the primary sources for Matthew and Luke. However, the Gospel of John, although written after the other three, did not seem to use them as sources but rather drew directly on older oral traditions. Paul probably wrote his Letters without benefit of many sources other than some sayings of Jesus (e.g., 1 Cor. 7:10–11) and some church formulations, such as the christological hymns in Phil. 2:6–11 and Col. 1:15–20.

Oral tradition was handed down among Jewish scribes and rabbis after the close of the OT era. This occurred mainly in the form of interpretations of the Torah—expositions of its legal stipulations (*halakah*) and sermonic expansions of its narrative parts (*haggadah*). These were transmitted orally for centuries and finally achieved written form in compilations known as the Mishnah and the midrashim. ***See also*** Sources of the Pentateuch. D.A.K.

ordain, ordination, to establish, determine, or appoint by one with authority to do so. As primary authority, God ordains in the sense of establishing the moon and stars (Ps. 8:3), appointing creatures for special purposes (Jon. 1:17; 4:6–8), setting geographical boundaries (1 Chron. 17:9; Acts 17:26), establishing governments (Rom. 13:1), and fixing the time of judgment (Acts 17:31). God is sometimes portrayed as so totally sovereign that events are described as foreordained, such as the salvation of the faithful (Rom. 8:29–30; Acts 13:48) and the damnation of the wicked (Jude 4). Within God's sovereign purpose, according to the NT, Christ's special place is ordained in the sense of appointed (Acts 3:20; Heb. 1:2) and designated (Rom. 1:4).

Those with authority derived from God also ordain. Angels ordained the law (Gal. 3:19), Moses (the law) appointed priests (Heb. 7:28), and David and Samuel appointed gatekeepers (1 Chron. 9:22).

Persons who received authority to perform special religious duties were ordained for those tasks. Jeremiah was appointed a prophet (Jer. 1:5), priests in Israel were ordained (Heb. 5:1), the Twelve were appointed by Jesus to preach and heal (Mark 3:14–15), elders were appointed by Paul and Barnabas (Acts 14:23) and by Titus (Titus 1:5), and persons were appointed by churches to various other duties (Acts 6:3; 13:2–3; 15:2). Paul not only understood himself ordained to be an apostle (Gal. 1:15) but that all who ministered in the Church were appointed to that service by God (1 Cor. 12:28). In the NT, acts of ordination involved laying on hands (Acts 6:6; 13:3; 1 Tim. 4:14), prayer (Acts 6:6; 13:3), and fasting (Acts 13:3). In time, as ministry became more institutionalized, so did rites of ordination. ***See also*** Minister. F.B.C.

ordeal. ***See*** Magic and Divination.

Oreb and Zeeb (aw'reb, zee'eb), two Midianite princes whose names in Hebrew mean "raven" and "wolf." They were killed by the Ephraimites in Gideon's battle against the Midianites (Judg. 7:24–8:3). Their death was commemorated by "the rock of Oreb" and "the press of Zeeb," and their crushing defeat was invoked by the psalmist in Ps. 83:11.

Orion, a constellation thought in ancient times to resemble the mythological hunter for whom it is named; it contains two stars of the first magnitude, Betelgeuse and Rigel. The constellation lies south of Gemini and Taurus. God's creation of Orion is cited by Amos (5:8) and Job (9:9; 38:31) as evidence of God's overwhelming majesty. ***See also*** Pleiades.

ornaments. ***See*** Amulet; Breastpiece; Dress; Jewelry; Magic and Divination.

Ornan (awr'nan). ***See*** Araunah.

Orontes (oh-rahn'teez), the principal river of western Syria (modern Nahr el-'Asi, "the rebellious river"), which originates on the eastern side of the Lebanon range and flows for two hundred fifty miles north through Syria into southern Turkey, where it turns southwest and enters the Mediterranean below Antioch-on-the-Orontes (modern Antakya). It thus forms the northern part of the great Rift Valley which continues south through the Jordan Valley, the Dead Sea, and the Arabah into the Red Sea and east Africa. The Orontes Valley is extremely fertile, and together with its strategically important geography this accounts for the number of major cities situated in it. These include: Riblah (see 2 Kings 23:33; 25:6, 21); Kadesh-on-the-Orontes (modern Tell Nebi Mend), the site of a battle

The Orontes River with Tell Nebi Mend, biblical Kadesh-on-the-Orontes, in the background.

between Egyptians and Hittites in ca. 1286 B.C.; Emessa (modern Homs); Hamath (modern Hama); Qarqar, where in 853 B.C. a coalition of Syrian kings together with Ahab of Israel fought with the Assyrian King Shalmaneser III; Alalakh (Tell 'Atshana); Antioch (Acts 11:19; 13:1); and Seleucia, Antioch's port. ***See also*** Antioch; Hamath; Riblah. M.D.C.

Orpah (awr'pah). ***See*** Ruth.

Osee (oh'zee). ***See*** Hosea, The Book of.

Oshea (oh-shee'ah). ***See*** Joshua.

Osnappar (ahz-nap'uhr), an Assyrian noble who resettled non-Jewish people in the cities of Samaria (Ezra 4:10) after the fall of Israel in 722 B.C. He may be the same as the Esarhaddon of Ezra 4:2, or it may be his son, Ashurbanipal, both of whom were kings of Assyria in the seventh century B.C.

ossifrage (aws'e-fraj; Lat., "bone breaker"; KJV; RSV: "vulture"), an unclean bird (Lev. 11:13; Deut. 14:12) associated with other birds of prey.

ossuaries (from Lat. *os* or *ossum*, "bone"), small chests used for gathering human bones after the corpse had rotted. Ossuaries are usually made from limestone with average dimensions of 20–30 inches by 12–20 inches by 10–16 inches. Ossuaries became popular in Palestine in the first century B.C. and were used at least until the fourth century A.D. Corpses were placed in the wall niches of burial caves. After the corpse had disintegrated, the bones were gathered into an ossuary, which was placed either in a smaller niche or on the floor. Ossuaries, many of which were found at the site of ancient Beth-shearim, were often decorated with engravings and identified with the name of the deceased and a warning not to disturb the bones. Not all persons were subject to secondary burial in ossuaries. Some were placed in the ground and others in permanent coffins. The diversity in burial practices may reflect both practical questions of space and changes in the views of afterlife. ***See also*** Burial. A.J.S.

Limestone ossuaries engraved with decorative motifs, such as these, were sometimes used for "second burials" in ancient Palestine.

Ostia (awst'ee-uh), a Roman city at the mouth of the Tiber River. It was the principal harbor for Rome during the first and second centuries A.D. Alexandria in Egypt, the source of the grain supply for Rome, was three weeks away by sea. Until the harbor was made deep enough for seagoing ships, they had docked at Puteoli, 138 miles from Rome. Grain then had to be carted overland, an expensive undertaking. The natural harbor at Ostia had been filled with silt so that a large ship there would have had to anchor outside and transfer cargo to barges, a considerable risk in stormy weather. Julius Caesar (100–44 B.C.) planned to enlarge Ostia, but the actual project was not undertaken until Claudius (emperor A.D. 41–54) constructed a large artificial harbor three miles north at Portus. Trajan (emperor A.D. 98–117) completed a second harbor in A.D. 104 beside that constructed by Claudius and the following years marked the peak of Ostia's prosperity. Because those harbors were not completed when Paul was taken to Rome, he landed at Puteoli (Acts 28:13).

Construction of the artificial harbor required dredging 200 acres and constructing concrete breakwaters, lighthouses, wharves, and unloading facilities. In the ancient city itself one could find warehouses, granaries, offices for the imperial administration, banks, stores, eating places, bakeries, bars, and brick apartment buildings. The imports coming into the harbor were grain, fruits, fish, meat, hides, oil, wine, minerals, jewelry, lumber, glass, paper, dyes, clothing, spices, ointment, and perfumes. Shipowners complained that the lack of exports to carry out cost them money. They were provided with incentives in the form of special insurance against shipwreck, tax exemptions, and citizenship for anyone who had been in the grain-carrying service for six years.

As befits a city with a polyglot population from all over the world, a number of shrines and temples were located there, the remains of which have been found in addition to those that served the imperial cult. A Serapis temple served sailors from the Levant. The first-century

Remains of the fourth-century A.D. synagogue at Ostia.

A.D. synagogue was redone in the second century and some eighteen Mithras shrines dating from A.D. 160 to 250 have been found. The Mithras cult appealed to the merchants, freedmen, and sailors in this city of approximately one hundred thousand persons. P.P.

ostraca (ahs′truh-kuh), plural of the Greek *ostrakon,* "potsherd." Potsherds provided a readily available medium on which to make hasty or informal notations in pen and ink during biblical times. Many prophetic oracles may have been preserved originally in the form of ostraca, written by disciples of the prophets. Since ostraca are virtually indestructible, numerous examples have been found by archaeologists. Several hundred ostraca were found at Masada, and over two hundred at Arad. The Samaria ostraca are receipts for taxes paid to the governor of Samaria during the eighth century B.C. The eighteen Lachish Letters from the time of Jeremiah (sixth century B.C.) are military correspondence between Yaoush, the commander at Lachish, and a junior officer, Hoshaiah, in charge of a nearby garrison town. Numerous other sites have produced smaller numbers of ostraca. ***See also*** Arad; Lachish. L.E.T.

This ostracon, one of two hundred ostraca found at Arad (ca. 600 B.C.), reads in part "to Nahum."

ostrich, the largest living bird, but one incapable of flight. Of the four biblical words that have traditionally been translated as "ostrich," one (Heb. *bet-ya'anah*) is better translated as "owl" and another (Heb. *ḥasidah*) as "stork." The remaining two (Heb. *ya'ana* and *renamin*) are universally accepted as referring to the ostrich.

Although the ostrich used to inhabit the open steppes of Mesopotamia and Arabia, excessive hunting for plumes and sport caused it to become extinct in these areas; the last living bird was seen in 1941. Today it occurs in the wild only in Africa, where it is also bred for its leather on special farms.

The ostrich *(Struthio camelus)* stands up to 8-1/2 feet high. Although it has only rudimentary wings and is unable to fly, its elongated neck, long legs, and two-toed feet make it especially adapted to running and it can reach a speed of forty miles per hour. The cocks are taller than the hens and have a better developed plumage; the feathers were a much sought-for item. In antiquity ostrich eggs were eaten and the eggshells used to manufacture containers and ornaments. Its meat, however, was forbidden to the Hebrews (Lev. 11:16; Deut. 14:15).

Though living mostly on plant food, the ostrich can be considered an omnivore because it also eats insects and other small animals. The cocks are polygamous and their hens share for their eggs a communal nest, which is nothing more than a shallow pit dug into the sand. While the cock takes over the incubation of the eggs at night, the hens take turns during the day.

These peculiar habits have apparently puzzled people for a long time. A detailed description is given in Job 39:13–18, where the ostrich's characteristic way of waving its plumage is alluded to and it is reported to know no motherly love (v. 13). Its way of nest building is referred to (v. 14) and it is wrongly alleged that ostrich eggs are easily crushed (v. 15). The ostrich hen is supposed to be indifferent to her young (v. 16; this is repeated in Lam. 4:3). The ostrich is accused of stupidity (v. 17) and justifiably acclaimed to be quicker than a horse (v. 18).

I.U.K.

Othniel (ahth'nee-el), one of the minor judges mentioned in Joshua and Judges. The son of Kenaz and brother of Caleb, Othniel won his niece's hand in marriage by capturing the city of Debir (formerly called Kiriath-sepher). This young woman, Achsah, proceeded to request that her father give her a field with ample springs of water. According to the story in Josh. 15:15–19, Caleb gave his daughter the upper springs and the lower springs (cf. Judg. 1:11–15). The other valiant deed attributed to Othniel was the defeat of Cushan-rishathaim, king of Mesopotamia (Judg. 3:7–11). This account is preserved in the usual Deuteronomistic framework (Israel sinned; God sent an enemy against it; repentance followed, as did deliverance). Likewise the standard formula concludes the story, specifically that the land had rest forty years.

J.L.C.

ouch, an obsolete term for "clasp," "bezel," or other "settings" for precious stones. It is used by the KJV for the RSV's "settings" (Exod. 28:11), "settings of filigree" (Exod. 28:25; 39:13, 16), or "filigree" (Exod. 39:13).

oven, a device in which retained heat is used to prepare food. Used mainly for baking bread (Lev. 2:4), an oven could also serve as a stove when a large cooking pot was placed upon it. The *tannur* (Heb.) consisted of a cylindrical clay structure seldom more than 2.5 feet in diameter and open at the top. A hole could be scraped out in the middle, and potsherds were sometimes plastered around the outside to retain the heat. When bread was baked a potsherd or stone could be placed over the top to enclose the oven. Ovens are commonly uncovered in Palestine when excavating domestic structures. Ovens were fired with any available fuel (cf. Matt. 6:30) and were used metaphorically to designate great heat (Ps. 21:9; Lam. 5:10; Hos. 7:6, 7). ***See also*** Bread.

N.L.L.

owl, a member of the Strigidae family of birds. Several species of owl occur in Palestine but their correlation with the biblical terms is problematic. The Hebrew word *(bet-ya'anah)* often interpreted as referring to the ostrich might more correctly be translated as "eagle owl" *(Bubo bubo)*, the largest of owls. The Hebrew word in Ps. 102:6 *(kos)* is difficult to identify more closely but might be the "little owl" *(Athene noctua)* or the "tawny owl" *(Strix aluco)*. The Hebrew term in Isa. 34:11 *(yansup)* probably refers to the "barn owl" *(Tyto alba)*, though it is sometimes translated as "ibis." All three are included in the list of unclean birds (Lev. 11:16; Deut. 14:15).

I.U.K.

ownership, the legal right of possession, which allows the one possessing it complete dominion over property to the exclusion of all others. The concept of ownership varies in different legal systems. In ancient Near Eastern law, this concept seems to have been defined in terms of varying degrees of possession and control. Thus, for example, scholars argue that the ancient pledge was purchased or owned by the creditor by virtue of the loan that represented a purchase price. This ownership of the pledge, however, was subject to the debtor's right of redemption upon repayment of the loan. The highest degree of ownership is the one that bestows upon the possessor the legal power to voluntarily relinquish control over the property to a third party. This degree of ownership was achieved only after the owner had been induced to sever all connection with the property and to relinquish all claims on it by gifts and money. Thus the purchase price did not serve merely as an objective sum of money whereby one acquired title to the property but primarily served as the inducement by which the seller's heart was fully satisfied to relinquish rights to the property. Echoes of this necessity to satisfy the seller's heart in order to obtain complete ownership may be found in the biblical account of Abraham's purchase of the Machpelah cave

(Gen. 23). Although Ephron pretended to prefer presenting the land to Abraham as a gift, Abraham insisted on a final sale transaction, albeit at an exorbitant price, so that Ephron would be fully satisfied and thereby relinquish all claims to the cave.

Biblical Law: Biblical law does not restrict the transfer of ownership of movable property. It strongly disapproves, however, of the sale of land that would undermine the socioeconomic structure of ancient Israel's tribal and familial holdings, fixed at the time of the settlement of Canaan (thirteenth century B.C. and later). In Lev. 25:23, the irrevocable transfer of ownership of land is prohibited. This law is rooted in the religious concept of the divine ownership of the land, and it is safeguarded by the institution of the Jubilee Year and the law of redemption.

The Jubilee Year was the final year in a fifty-year cycle, consisting of seven Sabbatical Year periods. It effected the automatic release of sold land to the original owner of the patrimony. Accordingly, every sale of land was considered to be leased for the number of years remaining until the onset of the Jubilee Year. Hence the sale price was computed by the number of years for which the land would be leased (Lev. 25:13–17). According to the law of redemption, even before the Jubilee Year, the seller had the right to redeem the land from the purchaser whenever he could afford to do so. If the seller did not have the means, his next of kin could redeem the land (Lev. 25:25–28). Hence an impoverished man would often offer his land first to a relative (Jer. 32:9).

This right of redemption and automatic release in the Jubilee Year also extended to houses in unwalled villages. Houses in walled cities had only a one-year redemption period and were not subject to release in the Jubilee Year (Lev. 25:29–31). Thus, both the law of the Jubilee and the law of redemption limited severely the transfer of ownership of patrimonial land. This attitude against alienation of one's patrimony is expressed strongly in the monarchical period by Naboth, who refused to sell his vineyard to King Ahab (873–851 B.C.; 1 Kings 21:3). From this narrative, however, it may be learned that the crown had the right to confiscate and thereby acquire ownership of the property of one who had committed treason (1 Kings 21:16).

The nonlegal literature of the Bible records examples of land acquisition by purchase. The patriarchal narratives detail Abraham's purchase of the field and cave of Machpelah from Ephron in language that reflects ancient Near Eastern sale contracts (Gen. 23). Mention is also made of Jacob's purchase of land from Hamor (Gen. 33:18–20). The legal procedure for the transfer of property in pre-exilic Judah (pre-586 B.C.) is described in Jer. 32:6–16 and included the witnessed signing of a deed of purchase that was then placed in an earthenware jar for safekeeping. In Ruth 4:7–8, there is a terse reference to the symbolic act of removing one's shoe in the ratification of redemption and exchange transactions.

In the NT: There are no comparable regulations concerning ownership in the NT, where possession of goods and real property was simply taken for granted, as was their purchase (cf. Matt. 13:34–35) or selling (cf. Acts 4:34–37). The attempt of hired hands to gain property by eliminating the heir (Mark 12:7) seems to presume legal arrangements, but aside from some speculation, no evidence to explain such a practice has been found. It was also assumed that persons had the right to dispose of their possessions as they saw fit (cf. Matt. 20:15). Jesus did stress the need to use possessions for the benefit of those in need (e.g., Matt. 5:42), although that was not always the highest priority (cf. Mark 14:5–7). ***See also*** Freeman, Freewoman; Redemption of Land; Sabbatical Year; Slavery. B.L.E.

ox. ***See*** Bull.

Oxyrhyncus (ahk'si-ring'kuhs), an ancient Egyptian town (modern Behnesa) situated on the edge of the western desert, 120 miles south of Cairo. Excavated at the end of the nineteenth and the beginning of the twentieth century by B. P. Grenfell and A. S. Hunt, the site has provided literally bushels of Greek papyri, both documentary (i.e., official documents and correspondence) and nonliterary (i.e., personal letters, informal notes, etc.). By 1983, nearly fifty volumes of the Oxyrhyncus Papyri series had been published, presenting the Greek text, with introduction and notes, of more than 3,400 separate items. Among those that preserve fragments of biblical texts dating from the third and fourth centuries are a leaf containing part of Matthew 1, now at the University of Pennsylvania; parts of Romans 1 and 1 John 4, both at the Semitic Museum, Harvard University; parts of 1 Corinthians and Philippians, now in Cairo; and a leaf from Revelation, now at Princeton Theological Seminary. Also found at Oxyrhyncus were fragments of a papyrus codex preserving several logia (sayings) of Jesus now known to be part of the apocryphal *Gospel of Thomas*. ***See also*** Codex; Papyrus; Texts, Versions, Manuscripts, Editions. B.M.M.

Opposite: Philistine captives pictured on reliefs at Medinet Habu that celebrate the successful repulsion of the Philistine invasion of Egypt by Pharaoh Ramesses III, ca. 1190 B.C. The Philistines were one of the "Sea Peoples"; they eventually settled on the southern coastal plain of Canaan where they became one of Israel's principal rivals.

P

P, the siglum for the Priestly source, one of the four sources scholars believe they have found in the Pentateuch. It is concerned with religious ritual and exact specifications of time and measurement. ***See also*** Priestly Writer(s); Sources of the Pentateuch.

Paddan-aram (pad'en-air'em; KJV: "Padan-aram"), the name used by Priestly tradition for the northwest region of Mesopotamia, between the Khabur and Euphrates rivers. It is called Aram-naharaim (Heb., "Aram between two rivers") by the early J source (Gen. 24:10, RSV: "Mesopotamia"). In Assyrian *padana* was a road or garden; Aram refers to the people or land of the Arameans. Haran and perhaps Ur were located in Paddan-aram. Isaac's wife Rebekah was from there (Gen. 25:20), and Isaac sent Jacob back there to Rebekah's brother, Laban, to obtain a wife (Gen. 28:2–7).

Pagiel (pay'gi-el; Heb., "El [God] has met"), the leader of the tribe of Asher during the wilderness wandering (Num. 1:13; 10:26).

Pahath-moab (pay'hath-moh'ab). **1** A leader of the postexilic community who signed the covenant to keep the law (Neh. 10:14); he is probably understood as the head of the family groups below. He may also be the father of Hassub, one who worked to repair the walls of Jerusalem under Nehemiah (Neh. 3:11). **2** A large family group with two branches (the "sons of Jeshua" and the "sons of Joab") who returned with Zerubbabel from the Babylonian captivity (Ezra 2:6; Neh. 7:11). **3** A much smaller family group who returned with Ezra (Ezra 8:4). **4** A family group of which eight members took foreign wives. All of these family groups may be parts of the same clan. D.R.B.

paint, painting, a medium for and a means of applying color to surfaces, formed with various pigments in a liquid or paste matrix. In biblical usage it applied to cosmetic decoration of the eye (Jer. 4:30; 2 Kings 9:30; Ezek. 23:40) as well as to the normal modern practice of decorating a home (Jer. 22:14). Archaeological evidence shows it was used on pottery and on building interiors and exteriors. Israelite mention of it is sparse, however, possibly due to the legal prohibition against making images (Exod. 20:4; Deut. 5:8).

palace, the residence of a king or other dignitary. The frequent biblical references are to such royal residences (2 Chron. 2:1, 2), to their staffs (1 Kings 4:6; 2 Kings 20:18; 24:12;), their facilities (Esther 1:5; 5:1; Dan. 4:29; 5:5), or their security forces (Luke 11:21). The examples available in the Near East from archaeological work (Luxor, Knossos, Mycenae, Persepolis, Boghazkoy) illustrate amply that palaces were elaborate, richly decorated, and heavily fortified.

Paleolithic (Gk., "old stone") **Age,** the archaeological period dating from ca. 2,000,000–10,000 B.C. This period witnessed the cultural and technological development of humans from their first handmade tools to their arrival at the threshold of the domestication of plants and animals. The Paleolithic falls within the geological era known as the Pleistocene or Ice Age. The earliest human remains discovered in the Near East, probably *Homo erectus,* come from this period, from the site of Ubeidiya near the southern tip of the Sea of Galilee. Important Neanderthal and *Homo sapiens* remains have come to light in the caves of Mt. Carmel.

Palestine, the territory along the eastern coast of the Mediterranean Sea traditionally known as the land of the Bible. (Refer to map 1 in the section of color maps.)

Name: Besides "Palestine" there are several other designations for this area: the Holy Land, the Promised Land, the land of Canaan, and the land of Israel (Heb. *eretz ysrael).* Ironically the name "Palestine" is derived from the Philistines, the archenemies of the Israelites. Originally a designation for the southern coastal strip where the Philistines had settled in the twelfth century B.C., Palestine became the name for the entire region. The ancient Greek historian Herodotus was the first to use *Palaistinē,* the Hellenistic form of Philistia, in the inclusive sense.

After the suppression of the Bar-Kochba revolt in A.D. 135 the Roman emperor Hadrian expunged the name *Provincia Judea* and substituted *Provincia Syria Palaestina* or simply *Palaestina* (Palestine). By A.D. 400 three provinces had been established with the designations *Palaestina prima* and *secunda,* west of the Jordan River, and *Palaestina tertia,* east of the Jordan and north of the Arnon River. The main part of the province of Palestine was in Cisjordan, meaning west of the Jordan, but sections of Transjordan, meaning east of the Jordan, also belonged to the province of Palestine.

After World War I when the British ruled Palestine by mandate, they revived "Palestine" as the official title of the land west of the Jordan. In 1923 the British government divided Transjordan from Cisjordan, making Transjordan an emirate under British sovereignty.

Archaeologists often use the title "Palestine" as a geographical, not a political, designation for the region including modern Israel and the western sector of modern Jordan. Despite perennial disputes over boundaries in the Near East, the areas west and east of the Jordan have much in common with respect to history, geography, and archaeology. "Palestine" serves as a convenient term for all the archaeological periods of the biblical land, while the geographical term "Israel" would be inaccurate; this latter designation did not come into existence until the tenth century B.C.

Geography: Throughout history the political boundaries of Palestine have fluctuated considerably. Broadly described, Palestine is bounded on the north by the foothills of the Anatolian plateau, on the south by the Sinai desert, on the east by the Euphrates ("the great river" in the Bible), and on the west by the Mediterranean ("the great sea" in the Bible). These boundaries include the modern states of Israel, Jordan, Syria, and Lebanon. In round figures Palestine was no more than five hundred miles long and ninety-five miles wide. In accord with the traditional biblical formula "from Dan to Beersheba" Palestine would have been much smaller, about the size of Vermont. Natural boundaries surrounded Palestine on three sides: the desert on the east and south, the Mediterranean on the west. In biblical times the cities were more like villages, small in size and population. The population of either of the two capitals, Samaria and Jerusalem, probably never exceeded thirty thousand inhabitants. According to scholarly estimates, in the first half of the eighth century B.C. the population of the Northern Kingdom was about eight hundred thousand and of the Southern Kingdom about three hundred thousand.

Although Palestine was insignificant in size and poor in natural resources, its strategic location made it a vital region; it was a land bridge for two continents and a crossroad for several nations. Armies and caravans traversed Palestine for centuries. Its geographical position immersed it in the political, commercial, cultural, and military activities of the whole region. Its strategic location also made it vulnerable: Palestine was ruled by a succession of conquerors: Egypt, Assyria, Babylonia, Persia, Greece, Rome, Byzantium, the Moslem caliphates, the Crusaders, the Ottoman Turks, and the British.

Aerial view of the Jordan River, which meanders for two hundred miles between the Sea of Galilee and the Dead Sea, three times the distance as the crow flies.

Physical and historical geography cannot be separated; they go hand in hand. The former is concerned with the configuration of the terrain; the latter deals with people's use of the land and the impact of its geography on the life of the people. A country's geography determines to some degree its history and helps to explain the history. Related phenomena, such as topography, climate, soil, and natural resources, affect a country's internal history and may influence its international relations.

Palestine's geographical position between the sea and the desert had a distinct bearing on its history. The unbroken Mediterranean coast's lack of adequate harbors for anchorage discouraged maritime pursuits. The wilderness on the east made the people of Palestine vulnerable to the incursions of desert raiders.

Climate: Climate influenced the daily life of the people. Palestine is situated in a zone of subtropical climate, characterized by dry summers and rainy winters. Seventy percent of the annual rainfall occurs between November and February. Precipitation varies greatly in different parts of the country; most of the rain falls along the coastal plain. The annual rainfall in Upper Galilee to the north is about 45 inches; in the Negeb to the south about 8 inches. Palestine's vegetation depends upon the rainfall, but not entirely; dew also plays an important part. Abundant along the coastal plain, especially on Mount Carmel, the dew is a great help to the summer vegetation.

Westerly winds prevail in Palestine, but there is also an unpleasant east wind from the desert to the south and southeast of Palestine; known as the *sirocco* (Italian), the *hamsin* (Arabic), and the *sharab* (Hebrew), it is the "east wind" of the OT (e.g., Gen. 41:6; Exod. 14:21; Isa. 27:8). This oppressive, dust-laden wind blows in the early autumn and late spring and often persists for several days.

Economy: Deuteronomy describes Palestine as "a land of wheat and barley, of vines and fig trees and pomegranates, . . . a land whose stones are iron, and out of whose hills you can dig copper" (8:8–9). The economy of Palestine was basically agricultural and pastoral. Agriculture was conducted primarily in the north where the chief crops were wheat, barley, olives, grapes, and figs; the breeding of sheep and goats was done mostly in the south. In addition to domestic animals, there were foxes, jackals, hyenas, lizards, snakes, and scorpions. The lions and bears of biblical times are now extinct.

Palestine is not rich in raw materials, except for the iron mines in Transjordan and the copper mines of the Arabah in the south. The mineral products of Palestine are limestone, basalt, and clay. There is gypsum in the mountains of Galilee, sulphur in the environs of Gaza, and glass sand is dug near Beer-sheba.

Geology also had its part to play in the life of the people. The rocks in Palestine are basically limestone, chalk, basalt, and sandstone. The hard limestone makes excellent building stone; the porous limestone, which is the base of soil in Palestine, traps water. The resultant wells and springs are excellent for agriculture.

Five Natural Zones: Between the Mediterranean Sea to the west and the Syrian desert to the east, Palestine is divided into five natural zones running longitudinally, clearly evident on a relief map; they are, from west to east, the coastal plain, the Shephelah, the central mountain range, the Jordan Valley, and the Transjordan plateau.

The Coastal Plain. The coastal plain is divided into the northern, central, and southern sections, a strip a hundred and thirty miles long, with Phoenician Tyre in the north and Philistine Gaza in the south. The main features of the coastal plain, narrow in the north and wider in the south, are (from north to south) the Plain of Acco, the Jezreel Valley, the Sharon, the Philistine coast, and the western Negeb. There are two coastal streams: the Kishon enters the sea just north of Mount Carmel; the Yarkon serves as a border between the Sharon and the Shephelah. The great international highway, the *Via Maris* (Lat., "the way of the sea"), runs the length of the coastline.

Jezreel or Esdraelon ("Esdraelon" is the Greek form of "Jezreel") is the broad and inviting valley connecting the coastal area and the Jordan Valley. This rich agricultural region is excellent for farming. The Plain of Sharon, the central portion of the coastal plain, extends for a distance of about forty-five miles from the Carmel range to Joppa. Forested in antiquity, the Sharon was not heavily inhabited in biblical times. The Philistine coast encompasses the fertile land between Joppa and the Wadi Ghazzeh (located about six miles south of Gaza). The Philistine pentapolis consisted of Gaza, Ashkelon, and Ashdod along the coast, Gath in the Shephelah, and Ekron six miles inland. Although natural harbors were lacking in this area, Ashkelon served as the main Philistine port.

The western Negeb lies at the southern end of the coastal plain. Usually translated "south" from its position, "Negeb" means "dry land"; it designates the rugged territory between Beer-sheba and the Gulf of Aqabah. The biblical Negeb is the east-west zone from Gaza to the Dead Sea, known today as the northern Negeb. The Bible identifies the southernmost area of Palestine as the Wilderness of Zin (Josh. 15:1). The two prominent biblical sites located in the Negeb are Kadesh-barnea, where Moses and the Israelites spent thirty-eight years on their trek from Sinai to Transjordan, and Beer-sheba, where the patriarchs worshiped.

The Shephelah. The Shephelah, meaning "lowlands," is the range of limestone hills between the Philistine plain and the Judean mountains. There narrow foothills are "lowlands" from the vantage point of the Israelites living in the higher hill country to the east. Thickly settled in biblical times, the Shephelah is a fertile region. As a buffer zone between the coastal plain and the mountains, the Shephelah was strategic in the defense of Palestine; fortified towns like Lachish were situated in the Shephelah.

The Central Mountain Range. The next geographical zone is the central mountain range, also called the hill country. Situated between the Shephelah and the Jordan Valley, it is the geographical backbone of Palestine. The principal regions of the hill country are Galilee, Samaria, and Judah. Galilee, which figures prominently in the NT, is divided into Upper and Lower Galilee. The highest mountain regions in Palestine are in Upper Galilee; Lower Galilee has rolling hills and fertile soil.

In the OT the most famous and prosperous part of the country was the Northern Kingdom, known as Samaria; it is the geographical center of Palestine. The valley of Jezreel separates Samaria from Galilee. Deriving its name from the capital city of Israel, Samaria is rich in agriculture, especially grain, olives, and vines. Mount Ebal and Mount Gerizim are the two most conspicuous peaks among the hills of Samaria. In biblical times these mountains had both military importance and religious significance.

Judah designated the Southern Kingdom ruled by the Davidic kings; it was the least desirable region of western Palestine. In Greek and Roman times (ca. 333 B.C.–A.D. 324) this southern region of Palestine was called Judea, the Greek form of Judah. The boundaries of both Judah and Judea fluctuated throughout history. Jerusalem, "the holy mountain," was the capital city of the southern region. With an elevation of about 2,460 feet above sea level, Jerusalem is secured on three sides by valleys: on the east by the Kidron Valley, on the west by the Valley of Hinnom; the Tyropoeon is a central valley dividing the mount of Jerusalem into the Upper City (the western hill) and the Lower City (the city of David and the Temple Mount).

The Jordan Valley. The unique feature of Palestine's geography is the Rift Valley, splitting the country down the middle. Palestine strad-

To the north, past the summit of Mount Gerizim in the central foreground, lies Mount Ebal, across the Shechem-Neapolis pass. The site of ancient Shechem lies in the center of the photograph.

dles this fissure, the largest geological fault on earth. Beginning in northern Syria, the Rift extends to easternmost Africa. The Rift, as well as Palestine's hilly topography and wadi system, militated against political unity; they fragmented the country into separate tribes or other political units.

The Jordan River flows down the middle of the Rift, whose average width is about ten miles. The Rift is composed of the Huleh Valley, the Sea of Galilee (Chinnereth), the Jordan Valley, the Dead Sea, the Arabah plain and the Gulf of Aqabah (Elath).

Ten miles north of the Sea of Galilee is the Huleh Valley; lying between the Litani River and Mount Hermon, it is mostly within modern Lebanon. The Sea of Galilee (it is a fresh-water lake) figured prominently in the ministry of Jesus. The earliest name for this harp-shaped body of water was Chinnereth, derived perhaps from a fortified city at the northwest corner of the Sea of Galilee. Thirteen miles long and seven miles wide, the Sea of Galilee is 630 feet below sea level.

The Jordan, the largest river in Palestine, meanders for two hundred miles between the Sea of Galilee and the Dead Sea, three times the distance as the crow flies. In its southerly course between the Sea of Galilee and the Dead Sea the Jordan drops about 600 feet. The Yarmuk and Jabbok rivers are important tributaries of the Jordan from the east; there are no significant tributaries from the west.

The Dead Sea is another unusual geographical feature of Palestine. It is so called because its high mineral content prevents the survival of marine life. In view of its high concentration of sodium chloride (six times the oceans' salt content) the Bible refers to this body of water as the Salt Sea. On the other hand, the Dead Sea contains such useful minerals and natural resources as potash, bromine, phosphate, magnesium, calcium, and potassium. The Dead Sea measures fifty-five miles from north to south and is about ten miles wide. Thirteen hundred feet below sea level at its surface, the Dead Sea is the lowest depression on earth.

"Arabah" in the Bible designates the Rift Valley from the Sea of Galilee to the Dead Sea; today the term refers only to the continuation of the Rift between the Dead Sea and the Gulf of Aqabah (Elath), a distance of about a hun-

To the east, from the caves at Qumran, ancient home of the Essenes, lies the northern end of the Dead Sea, the lowest depression on earth.

dred and ten miles. Covered with alluvial sand and gravel, the Arabah is rich in copper deposits.

The Transjordan Plateau. The final self-contained zone is the Transjordan highlands. The term "Transjordan" embraces the whole easterly region between the Rift and the Syrian desert. Four main east-west tributaries cut the Transjordan highlands: the Yarmuk, the largest river in Jordan, the Jabbok, the Arnon, and the Zered. These bodies of water also serve as boundaries for the various geopolitical sections of Transjordan: Bashan (north of the Yarmuk), Gilead (south of the Yarmuk), Ammon (between the Jabbok and Arnon), Moab (between the Arnon and the Zered), and Edom (south of the Zered).

The Jabbok is the modern Nahr ez-Zerqa, "the blue river"; Jacob wrestled with an "angel" at the ford of the Jabbok near Penuel (Gen. 32:24–30). Wadi Mojib, the modern name of the Arnon, is a precipitous canyon associated with Moab. The Zered is identified with the Wadi el-Hesa, which divided Moab and Edom. On their way to Jericho the Israelites crossed the deep Wadi Zered.

Transjordan is divided into three main sections: Bashan in the north; Gilead, Ammon, and Moab in the center; and Edom in the south. The King's Highway, a well-known international caravan route, extends from Damascus to the Gulf of Aqabah; it runs the length of Transjordan, passing through Bashan, Gilead, Ammon, Moab, and Edom. Transjordan has been the subject of intensive regional archaeological surveys during the past decade.

Bashan in the northern district of Transjordan parallels the Sea of Galilee; it is good pasture land. Several biblical authors commented on natural features of Bashan, suggesting prosperity and luxury (1 Chron. 6:71; Ezek. 39:18; Mic. 7:14). The black basalt so abundantly available in Bashan is used for building stones today as in biblical times.

The mountainous region of Gilead is most pleasant and is well known for its excellent pasture. Gilead was forested in antiquity, and its trees may have produced the balm to which Jeremiah alluded (Jer. 8:22). David fled to Gilead when Absalom attempted to usurp his throne (2 Sam. 17:21–26). The prophet Elijah was a native of Gilead (1 Kings 17:1).

The boundaries of Ammon in the north-central part of the country were never clearly defined. The citadel in modern Amman is the site of the ancient capital of Ammon. The territory of Moab in central Transjordan lies east of the Dead Sea. Both Kerak and Dhiban (Dibon) served as the capital cities of Moab. This region is known for wheat, barley, sheep, goats, and camels. The Israelites had a strong antipathy toward the Moabites, with whom they often contended.

Edom is the region in the highland of Seir, located in southern Transjordan. The characteristic shrub forests covering the mountains of Edom may account for the name "Mount Seir," meaning "hairy mountain" in Hebrew. The Edomite territory extended south of the Dead Sea on both sides of the Arabah, as far as the Gulf of Aqabah. Controlling the King's Highway, which brought trade from India and South Arabia to Egypt, the Edomites acquired great wealth.

After the fall of Jerusalem in 586 B.C. the Edomites incurred the fury of the Judahites by occupying their land. Their encroachment on the land of Judah may have been occasioned by the invading Nabateans, an Arabic-speaking people from the desert who settled in Edom, making Petra their capital. The Edomites of south Judah became the Idumaeans of Hellenistic and Roman times. Herod the Great (Luke 1:5) was an Idumaean.

Archaeological History: The advent of written records is one of the great dividers between the prehistorical and historical periods; it dates to about 3000 B.C. in the Near East. Current field surveys are producing abundant material from the prehistorical period to supplement earlier studies.

Old, Middle, and New Stone Ages. Artifacts from the Paleolithic period (Old Stone Age, ca. 400,000–14,000 B.C.) have been found on the surface of the ground at a number of sites in Palestine. In this period, humans were hunters and gatherers of wild plants. The Paleolithic period is represented in Palestine by the Mount Carmel man; caves on the western edge of the Carmel range have produced stratified evidence of Paleolithic and Mesolithic occupation.

The Mesolithic period (Middle Stone Age) began about 14,000 B.C. Several pertinent sites containing evidence of a microlithic flint industry are scattered throughout Palestine. The Natufian is a Mesolithic culture. It is so called from the valley of Natuf, about ten miles northwest of Jerusalem, where an important flint deposit was found. The Natufians lived in caves, hunted, and harvested wild grain. A number of Natufian sites are known, notably Beidha, near Petra in Transjordan.

The Neolithic period (New Stone Age, ca. 8000–4200 B.C.) is well represented in the Levant; the study of several hundred sites has just begun. Beidha is also an important Early Neolithic site; its earliest Neolithic levels date to about 7000 B.C.

Jericho is a key site for Neolithic culture. The earliest occupation at Jericho dates to about 8000 B.C. A clear distinction is made between Prepottery Neolithic A and B. Lasting during most of the eighth millennium, Prepottery Neolithic A is characterized by circular house structures, a lithic industry, and the domestication of wheat and barley. No longer nomads, the people lived in huts; agriculture was responsible for a sedentary form of life in Palestine. A remarkable stone tower associated with the town wall in Prepottery Neolithic A came to light at Jericho. Prepottery Neolithic A ended abruptly; then followed Prepottery Neolithic B, from the late eighth to the seventh millennium; it, too, came to an abrupt end. Sites of this period existed all over Palestine. Characteristic of Prepottery B were the domestication of wheat and barley, domestic goats, and architecture consisting of more elaborate houses with multiple rooms of rectangular form grouped around courtyards.

One of the major Neolithic sites in the Near East was discovered recently at Ain Ghazal, a Prepottery Neolithic B village in the northeastern suburbs of Amman (Jordan). This site is three times larger than Jericho. A collection of modeled clay human statues and figures made of clay or plaster came to light at Ain Ghazal. These statues, dating to about 6200–6000 B.C., certainly bear a relationship to the remarkable find at Jericho of human skulls with features restored by plaster and shell incrustations.

Pottery first appeared toward the end of the Neolithic period. The earliest pottery in Transjordan dates to Late Neolithic (ca. 4700–4200 B.C.); it came from the site of Dhra, east of the Dead Sea. In the coastal region of Palestine ceramic vessels fired in a kiln date to the first half of the fifth millennium.

Chalcolithic Age. Evidence from the Chalcolithic Age (Copper–Stone Age, 4200–3300 B.C.) was first recognized at Teleilat Ghassul, near the northeastern end of the Dead Sea. Occupied in the Early Chalcolithic, Ghassul was a fully developed village site. Because of the discovery of Chalcolithic at Teleilat Ghassul, the culture is often referred to as Ghassulian.

The transition between the Chalcolithic and the Early Bronze periods is sometimes referred to as the "Proto Urban" phase. In this period people lived in villages; they also introduced new pottery as well as new methods of burial in the form of rock-cut tombs with multiple burials.

Early, Middle, and Late Bronze Ages. The Early Bronze Age (ca. 3300–2300 B.C.) is well represented at sites such as Arad, Megiddo, and Jericho west of the Jordan, and at Bab-edh-Dhra east of the Jordan. Bab-edh-Dhra is well known for its large cemetery consisting of shaft tombs with multiple chambers in Early Bronze Age I, and of charnel houses of mud-brick in Early Bronze Age II–III. The Early Bronze Age III (2700–2300 B.C.) saw the full urban development of Palestine.

When the Early Bronze Age came to an end in 2300 B.C, an Intermediate Early Bronze–Middle Bronze period (ca. 2300–1900 B.C.), sometimes referred to as Early Bronze IV, followed. The material culture was seminomadic, nonurban, perhaps to be attributed in part to the incursions of pastoralists from Syria and Mesopotamia. They may have been the invading Amorites, a Northwest Semitic–speaking people who were present in Palestine by 1900 B.C.

The Middle Bronze Age (ca. 1900–1550 B.C.) was a period of prosperity marked by the reappearance of urban civilization and characterized by well-built houses, massive fortifications, and walled towns. Dan, Hazor, Shechem, and Gezer are typical Middle Bronze sites. Egyptian and Mesopotamian written records from this period contain references to Palestine.

The Late Bronze Age (1550–1200 B.C.) was a time of Egyptian hegemony over Palestine; the quality of the material culture declined in this period. The year 1200 B.C. marked the advent of the Iron Age and the entry of the Israelites and their archenemies, the Philistines, into Palestine. The remaining periods are the proper subject of biblical history.

Mapping Biblical Sites: The beginning of the nineteenth century marked the reawakening of scientific interest in Palestine. In 1799 when Napoleon Bonaparte invaded Palestine, he brought with him geographers and engineers to prepare maps of the land. Foremost among the explorers of this era was the American Edward Robinson, whose historic travels in the Holy Land in 1838 and 1852 signaled the beginning of a new era in the geographical study of Palestine. While investigating the physical and historical geography of Palestine, Robinson also succeeded in identifying over a hundred biblical sites.

Robinson's contribution to the geography of Palestine inspired other explorers, among them Titus Tobler of Germany, Victor Guérin of France, and Claude Conder of England. Influenced by Robinson the British in 1865 established the Palestine Exploration Fund for the systematic and scientific exploration of Palestine. The Fund's geographical Survey of Western Palestine (1872–1878) accomplished the mapping of more than ten thousand sites; the resultant Map of Western Palestine still serves as the basis for the cartography of Cisjordan.

The work begun by the nineteenth-century explorers continues relentlessly today, as scholars from many lands make their contribution. P.J.K.

palm *(Phoenix dactylifera)*, a tall, slender tree whose leaves fan out at the top like a plume. The date is its much-consumed fruit. The palm is especially hardy in arid environments since it has deep tap roots that effectively seek out the water table. This enables it to live a long life, bearing fruit for many years (Ps. 92:12–14). Palms are therefore especially characteristic of water sources and oases, thus the reference to them at the springs of Elim (Num. 33:9) and at Jericho, the oasis city of palms (Deut. 34:3). The botanical name, *Phoenix*, is derived from Phoenicia, the ancient land of palms.

Many parts of the tree were used. The fruit was consumed as a sweet. A fermented drink was made from the sap. The leaves were used as roofing for houses and for weaving mats and baskets. According to tradition, the leaves were also gathered and displayed as a symbol of joy and celebration on the arrival of Jesus into Jerusalem (John 12:13).

The upright and stately form of the palm suggests justice and nobility. The attractive array of leaves provided a decorative motif in Solomon's Temple (1 Kings 6:29, 32).

The Hebrew word for date palm, *tamar*, is used as a proper name in the Bible. As a place name, Tamar is referred to in Ezek. 47:18–19 and 48:28. Absalom's sister (2 Sam. 13:1) and daughter (2 Sam. 14:27) were both named Tamar. ***See also*** Date. P.L.C.

Palm Sunday, the Sunday before Easter, commemorating Jesus' entry into Jerusalem (Mark 11:8; Matt. 21:8; John 12:12 identifies the branches as palm).

Pamphylia (pam-fil'ee-uh), a district about eighty miles long and thirty miles wide in southern Asia Minor, bounded on the north by the Taurus Mountains, on the east by Cilicia, and on the west by Lycia. The Kestros River, which was navigable in the first century, flows through the district to the southern coast of Asia Minor. The climate along the coastal plain was uncomfortable and malaria was prevalent in that region. During the Maccabean period, Jews were apparently living in the area (1 Macc. 15:23), and Jews from there were reported in Jerusalem at Pentecost (Acts 2:10). In A.D. 74, the district became a Roman province and expanded its boundaries to include the northern highland region (Pisidia). Two cities in Pamphylia, Perga and Attalia, were visited by Paul and his companions during their first journey. At Perga, just five

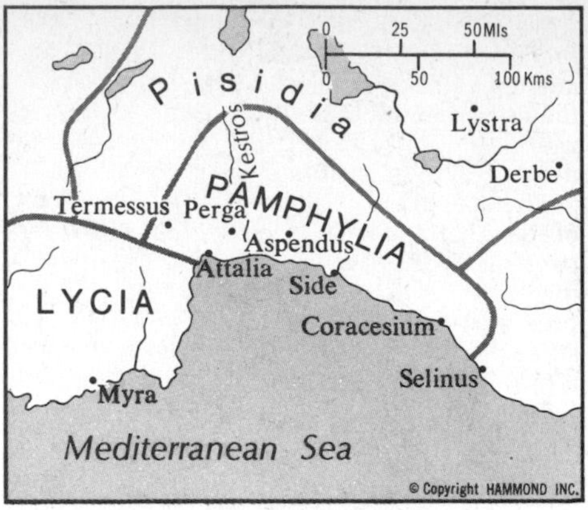

miles from the Kestros River, John Mark left Paul and Barnabas and returned to Jerusalem (Acts 13:13). A Roman road through the district connected Perga with the main port of Attalia, which Paul and Barnabas used to board a ship bound for Antioch (Acts 14:24–26). Paul sailed past Pamphylia en route to Rome (Acts 27:5). ***See also*** Attalia; Perga. M.K.M.

Pannag, the KJV transliteration of an otherwise unknown word as a place name (Ezek. 27:17). According to its context it may also be a commodity the Israelites sold to Tyre.

paper, material upon which writing was done (2 John 12), in antiquity made from the pith of the papyrus plant. ***See also*** Papyrus; Writing.

Paphos (pay'fohs), a city located on a rocky plateau along the southwestern coast of Cyprus. In antiquity, "old Paphos" was the seat of the kingdom of Paphos and, in the city, possessed the principal temple of the Greek world for the cult of Aphrodite, who, according to legend, had been born of the sea foam along the nearby coast. At the end of the fourth century B.C., Nikokles, the last king of Paphos, founded a new city as his political and commercial capital eleven miles west on the coast. "New Paphos" continued to grow in importance as a capital during both the Ptolemaic and Roman periods. When Saul and Barnabas came to Cyprus on their first journey, it was in this capital city that they met the Roman proconsul, Sergius Paulus, and the Jewish prophet, Elymas (Bar-Jesus), associated with him (Acts 13:6–12). ***See also*** Cyprus; Elymas; Paulus, Sergius. M.K.M.

Papyri, Oxyrhyncus. ***See*** Oxyrhyncus.

papyrus, an aquatic plant of the sedge family (*Cyperus papyrus*) that grew abundantly in the shallow waters of the Nile in the vicinity of the delta (Job 8:11). Resembling a stalk of corn (maize), the plant was used in a great variety of ways, not only in making "paper," but also for fuel, food, medicine, clothes, rugs, sails, ropes, and even a kind of chewing gum. According to the Roman antiquarian Pliny the Elder, "Civilization—or at the very least, human history—depends on the use of papyrus."

To manufacture a sheet of "paper," the stem of the mature plant was cut into sections about twelve to fifteen inches in length. After each of these was split open lengthwise, the core of pith was removed and sliced into very thin strips. These were laid lengthwise on a flat surface just overlapping each other and all facing the same direction; then a second layer, placed at right angles, was laid on top. The two layers were pressed or pounded together until they formed one fabric. The resultant sheet, when dried and smoothed with pumice, was light in color, strong, and flexible. If the sheet had been well made, there would be little difference in the smoothness and finish of the two sides. The size and character of these papyrus sheets naturally varied considerably with the quality of the papyrus. About twenty individual sheets would be joined together end to end to form a roll. From such a roll, pieces could be cut to the size needed for writing a letter, a bill of sale, a deed, or any other record. For a book of some considerable length, several rolls would be glued together; the Gospel of Luke, for example, would have required about thirty feet in length. Early in the second century, however, Christians came to prefer the format of the codex, or leaf-book, for their sacred books.

The price paid for a sheet or roll of papyrus was, of course, determined by its size and quality. In general, papyrus was relatively expensive, and economy-minded people would sometimes write on the back of a sheet or roll already used for other purposes.

Papyrus.

Preserved by the dry climate of Egypt, literally hundreds of thousands of papyrus documents of all kinds have been found. Among papyrus copies of the books of the Greek Bible, some of the most noteworthy are those in the collections acquired by Chester Beatty (Dublin) and Martin Bodmer (Geneva). The former collection includes a fragmentary codex from the second century containing the Greek text of the books of Numbers and Deuteronomy and a codex of ten letters of Paul from about A.D. 200; the latter collection includes a codex of the Gospel of John from about A.D. 200, and another, dating from the third century, contains the Gospels of Luke and John. ***See also*** Codex; Oxyrhyncus; Texts, Versions, Manuscripts, Editions; Writing. B.M.M.

Papyrus, Nash. ***See*** Texts, Versions, Manuscripts, Editions.

parables, very short stories with a double meaning. In the biblical tradition, the terms translated from Hebrew, Aramaic, or Greek by the narrower term "parable" should more accurately be translated by the wider term "metaphor." The basic distinction that the biblical tradition finds worthy of emphasis is that between literal and metaphorical language. In the context, the term "parable," therefore, must cover both aphorisms and stories, proverbs and riddles, dialogues and discourses, as long as these are metaphorical or figurative. In this understanding, the parables of Jesus range from metaphorical aphorisms, such as that on the kingdom and house divided in Mark 3:24–25, to metaphorical narratives, such as the one on the prodigal son in Luke 15:11–22, to metaphorical discourses, such as John 10. The biblical tradition's wide interpretation of parable in the sense of metaphor makes it possible to say with Mark 4:34 that all of Jesus' words are parables.

In the Aristotelian tradition, however, the distinctions are more detailed and more precise. In *The Art of Rhetoric* (2.20) Aristotle divides rhetorical proofs into general statements that can be used for deductive purposes, such as maxims and proverbs, and specific stories that can be used for inductive purposes. These latter stories can be either historical or fictional, and the fictional ones may be either possible, such as parables, or impossible, such as fables. For the Aristotelian tradition, then, parables are a very specific type of metaphor. They are realistic but metaphorical narratives.

The contemporary understanding of the parabolic genre is closer to the Aristotelian than the biblical tradition. For moderns, the three elements in a parable are narrativity, metaphoricity, and brevity; it is a very short story with a double meaning. On the surface level it speaks, say, of sowing or fishing, but on a deeper level it points to something else and it challenges one to discover that something else by close interpretation.

While the OT abounds in metaphors, aphorisms, proverbs, riddles, and other figurative discourse, it also contains parables in the narrower sense of a short story with a double meaning. The "Song of the Vineyard," found in Isaiah 5:1–2, is one such example. Its parabolic nature was recognized by Jesus when he fashioned his parable of the wicked husbandmen after it (Mark 12:1–11). Another example is the story Nathan tells David about the theft of a prized lamb (1 Sam. 12:1–4). In the Song of the Vineyard, the hearers are explicitly invited to participate in the story (Isa. 5:3–4), and David's reaction to Nathan's parable shows David's participation in that story as well. In each instance, the parable has attached to it its interpretation (Isa. 5:7; 2 Sam. 12:7–9), a feature also found in some NT parables (e.g., Mark 4:14–20 for Mark 4:3–9; Matt. 13:36–43 for Matt. 13:24–30). Despite the appearance of parables in the OT, however, it is with the sayings of Jesus that the biblical parable achieves its most widespread use.

PARABLES OF JESUS

Mustard Seed (Mark 4:30–32; Matt. 13:31, 32; Luke 13:18–19; Q/Matt. 13:31; Q/Luke 13:18–19; *Gos. Thom.* 20)
Sower (Mark 4:3–8; Matt. 13:3–8; Luke 8: 5–8; *Gos. Thom.* 9a)
Evil Tenants (Mark 12:1–11; Matt. 21:33–42; Luke 20:9–18; *Gos. Thom.* 65a [see also 66])
Harvest Time (Mark 4:26–29; *Gos. Thom.* 21d)
Leaven (Q/Matt. 13:33; Q/Luke 13:20–21; *Gos. Thom.* 96)
Great Supper (Q/Matt. 22:1–4; Q/Luke14: 16–24; *Gos. Thom.* 64a)
Lost Sheep (Q/Matt 18:12–13; Q/Luke 15: 4–6; *Gos. Thom.* 107)
Talents (Q?/Matt 25:14–30; Q?/Luke 19:11–27)
Wheat and Weeds (Matt. 13:24–30; *Gos. Thom.* 57)
Treasure (Matt. 13:44; *Gos. Thom.* 109)
Pearl (Matt. 13:45–46; *Gos. Thom.* 76a)
Net (Matt. 13:47–48; *Gos. Thom.* 8a)
Rich Fool (Luke 12:16–20; *Gos. Thom.* 63a)
Unmerciful Servant (Matt. 18:23–24)
Laborers in the Vineyard (Matt. 20:1–15)
Ten Bridesmaids (Matt. 25:1–12)
Good Samaritan (Luke 10:30–35)
Barren Fig Tree (Luke 13:6–9)
Tower Builder (Luke 14:28–30)
King at War (Luke 14:31–32)
Lost Coin (Luke 15:8–9)
Prodigal Son (Luke 15:11–32)
Unjust Steward (Luke 16:1–7 [or 8a])
Rich Man and Lazarus (Luke 16:9–31)
Unjust Judge (Luke 18:2–5)
Pharisee and Publican (Luke 18:10–13)
Children in the Field (*Gos. Thom.* 21ab)
Empty Jar (*Gos. Thom.* 97)
Assassin (*Gos. Thom.* 98)

Parables of Jesus: When the parables of Jesus are understood in the biblical tradition as including the full spectrum from metaphorical aphorism through metaphorical narrative to metaphorical discourse, the listing includes almost everything Jesus said. When they are understood in the Aristotelian and contemporary traditions as including only metaphorical narratives, the list on the accompanying table is the basic corpus. The list is given in terms of the number of independent sources for each parable; in those cases where the parable may have appeared in more than one source, that is also indicated (e.g., the parable of the mustard seed, which apparently appeared in Mark and in Q).

The distinction between metaphorical aphorism and metaphorical narrative is usually quite evident. The aphorism is a one-liner, such as Mark 10:25, while the narrative has, as it were, three acts: a beginning, a middle, and an end. But the narrative should also have a middle and end not absolutely and irrevocably contained in its beginning. This is a significant criterion in those intermediate cases where we have what looks like a metaphorical narrative but is really just a developed metaphorical aphorism, and some of these may even be present in the list in the accompanying table. They are quite common in Q (a source, posited by scholars, containing sayings of Jesus), where they reflect the theology of Wisdom offering herself, being either accepted or rejected, and rewarding or punishing accordingly. A classic example is the three successive acts of building, storming, and staying/falling in Q/Matt. 7: 24–27 and Q/Luke 6:47–49. This is not a narrative but an explicit development of what is already implicit in the aphorism of Matt. 7:24 and Luke 6:47.

In the basic parabolic corpus given in the table there are excluded not only metaphorical aphorisms and discourses but also those extended or developed metaphorical aphorisms that come closest in appearance to the metaphorical narratives so peculiarly characteristic of Jesus. Certain cases might still be argued one way or another, but, in general, the table lists Jesus' parables in the sense of figurative stories whose plot is not just the inevitable unfolding of the opening sentence.

Interpretation: Parables provoke interpretation. They do this by making one wonder how they apply to their referent. They also do it by making one wonder what their referent is.

In some cases the referent is quite clear from

The Roman road from Jericho to Jerusalem. The parable of the Good Samaritan is set in this region (Luke 10:29–37).

the context. This may be given before and/or after the parable, and the parable may even be applied to its referent in specific detail. This often happens, for example, in rabbinical parables exemplifying the answers to exegetical difficulties or moral problems. The insertion of Jesus' parables into their present Gospel positions often clarifies the referent by context in similar if less detailed fashion. Thus Luke connects the parables of the lost sheep, the lost coin, and the prodigal son, both to each other in 15:3–32 and to their present referent in 15: 1–2.

If one asks, however, about the original referent of the parables in the life of the historical Jesus, the question is much more difficult. One plausible working hypothesis is to connect all of the parables to his dominant theme of the Kingdom of God, to its gracious advent, its disturbing presence, and its challenging implications. This conjunction of Kingdom and parable is underlined by the parable of the mustard seed, for example (Mark 4:30–32; Matt. 13:31; Luke 13: 18–19). We have three independent versions of this story and it appears as a Kingdom parable in all three. But even if one accepts the Kingdom as the original referent of Jesus' parables, one can still ask whether the Kingdom for Jesus is a future and apocalyptic event or a present and mysterious reality. The answer must take into account the serene and everyday normalcy of Jesus' parabolic imagery as against the necessarily extraordinary and unique imagery of apocalyptic discourse.

In their present Gospel locations, parables may be interpreted not only by general context but also by specific commentary from Jesus himself. Thus, on the one hand, Mark 4:13–20; Matt. 13:18–23; and Luke 8:11–15 interpret the parable of the sower, but the *Gospel of Thomas* does not; Matt. 13:37–43 interprets the wheat and weeds, but the *Gospel of Thomas* does not; and, on the other, *Gos. Thom.* 64b interprets the great supper, but Matthew and Luke do not. Those interpretations are most likely from the tradition rather than from Jesus himself, but their presence and especially their diversity sound an important warning. Parables demand interpretation, and multiple, diverse, and successive commentary is their destiny. The sower, a parable of parabling the Kingdom, reminds us that misinterpretation is always possible but also that even faithful interpretation will be plural rather than univocal. The parable risks losing control over the hearer in the interest of participation by the hearer because the Kingdom of God is an interaction between the divine and the human. The parable is a most appropriate form for such a process. ***See also*** Good Samaritan; Gospel of Thomas; Jesus Christ; Kingdom of God; Prodigal Son.

Bibliography

Crossan, J. D. *In Parables*. New York: Harper & Row, 1973.

Jeremias, J. *The Parables of Jesus*. Rev. ed. New York: Scribner, 1963.

Via, D. O. *The Parables*. Philadelphia: Fortress, 1967.

J.D.C.

Paraclete (pair'uh-kleet), the transliteration of a Greek term meaning "called to the side of" and hence "advocate" (cf. 1 John 2:1). Its importance derives from its use in the Gospel of John (14: 16–17, 26; 15:26; 16:7–11; cf. 16:13–15), where Jesus promises his disciples that when he departs he will send them another Paraclete (RSV and NIV: "Counselor"; KJV: "Comforter"; JB and NEB: "Advocate") to remain with them. As the Fourth Gospel makes clear, the Paraclete is the Holy Spirit, or Spirit of Truth (14:17, 26). In fact, the Fourth Gospel's teaching about the Holy Spirit is set forth in terms of the Paraclete, who continues the work of Jesus himself (14:16–17), recalling things the earthly Jesus taught or revealing things he was unable to convey (14:26; 16:12–14). In John's view, this spiritual knowledge or insight, unavailable until after Jesus' death and resurrection, makes for the first time Christian faith and understanding fully possible. ***See also*** Holy Spirit, The; John, The Gospel According to.

D.M.S.

paradise, a location or status of uninterrupted bliss. Some groups within Judaism had come to believe in life after death by the early second century B.C. They sought concrete images with which to express that new faith as an extension of traditional ideas. Since God had placed the first couple in an idyllic park (the Garden of Eden), it was plausible to assume that a similar location awaited the righteous after death. The Greek Bible referred to the Garden of Eden as "Paradise," and hence the term came to be used for the destination of the righteous. The word "paradise" is ultimately of Persian origin, and denotes a "park" or "forest." Since the Bible lands were often barren, it is not surprising that such an image would be meaningful.

Once this particular image was established, questions arose in the minds of the pious: where is paradise located? Is it an intermediate state prior to the resurrection, or is it the eternal home of the righteous thereafter? Various suggestions were made. For some thinkers, paradise was located in the remotest part of the earth, and for others it was in the lower part of the sky above.

NT writers generally accept the paradise image. Paul speaks of it in connection with his vision of the "third heaven" (2 Cor. 12:1–4), and Jesus suggested to the thief that both of them were destined for paradise at the moment of death (Luke 23:43).

Some passages, instead, suggest that the martyrs are immediately taken to the highest of seven heavens where they await the resurrection at "the altar" (Rev. 6:9–11; 7:9–17). Other passages imply that the dead, righteous and wicked alike, descend to the underworld and await the resurrection in a sleeplike state (Matt. 12:40; 1 Thess. 4:13–16). This is more in accordance with older biblical thought. Some writers suggest that, following the resurrection, the righteous will live in a paradise on earth and will feast from the "tree of life" (Rev. 2:7; 22:1–2). ***See also*** Death; Heaven; Resurrection; Sheol. L.R.B.

parallelism, a rhetorical device involving one or more linguistic repetitions or correspondences (grammatical, lexical, semantic, or phonetic) in adjacent lines or phrases. While present in prose, parallelism is more prominent in biblical poetry, where it often appears to be a basic structuring device. An example is Ps. 103:10: "He does not deal with us according to our sins, nor requite us according to our iniquities." In this verse the syntactic, semantic, and lexical correspondences between the two phrases are many and obvious (e.g., "deal with"/"requite"; "sins"/"iniquities"; "according to"/"according to"). Other verses may have fewer correspondences but may still be considered parallel.

paralysis, one of the diseases Jesus heals (Matt. 8:5–13; 9:1–8; 12:9–14; Mark 2:1–12; 3:1–6; Luke 5:17–26; 6:6–11) to illustrate the arrival of the Kingdom of God and fulfill the expectation that in the eschatological age such defects in God's creation would be eliminated (see Isa. 35: 5–6).

Paran (pay'ruhn), the wilderness site where the Israelites camped after they left Mount Sinai (Num. 10:11–12; 12:16), and from which spies were sent to reconnoiter Canaan (Num. 13:3–26). The return of the spies to Kadesh suggests that the location was south of Canaan along the north edge of the Sinai triangle. The association of Kadesh with the Wilderness of Zin (Num. 33: 36) and Paran (LXX) reinforces the identification.

Gen. 21:21 designates it as Ishmael's home after his banishment. If 1 Sam. 25:1 accurately reports David's visiting the place after Samuel's death, it suggests territory at the south edge of Judah. Similarly, if 1 Kings 11:18 accurately reflects the flight of Edomite Hadad from Midian through Paran to Egypt, it would confirm a location west of Edom and Midian in the same region.

References to Paran in Deut. 33:2 and Hab. 3: 3 speak poetically of a mountain in which divine manifestation occurred. In those passages "Paran" refers to Mount Sinai. R.S.B.

parchment. ***See*** Writing.

pardon, the act by an empowered authority of reversing a sentence rendered under a verdict of guilty. This context of the legal system is not unrelated to the biblical understanding of pardon. At the heart of the matter for the biblical writers, however, is not the mere history of an idea or concept from the OT to the NT but the event and experience of a crucial reality. From the biblical perspective, the human creature is subject to the created order and accountable to the Creator for violations of this order. Human inability to perceive this is regarded as blindness and self-deception. The condition would be hopeless if the Creator were not mercifully disposed toward his creatures.

The OT believes that God is eager to pardon (e.g., Neh. 9:17; Jer. 36:3; Pss. 86:5; 130:4; Dan. 9:9), to find humility and repentance (2 Chron. 7:14; Ps. 86:5) and the will to change (Deut. 30; Num. 14:18; Josh. 24:19–21; 1 Kings 8:36; Ps. 51:12; Jer. 5:1–9). The provision for pardon as atonement/expiation has been made by God himself to remedy the condition of sin. Ezek. 33:10–16 is typical of the prophetic voice urging people to turn back to God for pardon (cf. also, e.g., Isa. 55:6–7). For both OT and NT, pardon and forgiveness are virtually synonymous.

In the NT Gospels, Jesus preaches a message of pardon (e.g., Luke 15), and the intercession of Jesus—especially his death (1 Cor. 15:3; Luke 23:34)—is proclaimed as the basis for seeking and receiving pardon. The community of faith is conscious of the intercession of its resurrected Lord (John 17) and prays for forgiveness (Matt. 6:12; Luke 11:4). There is no sin that cannot be pardoned (Mark 3:28–29 and parallels speak of that which is tantamount to the willful rejection of pardon; cf., however, 1 John 5:16–17; Heb. 6: 4–8; 10:26–31). John the Baptist understood himself to be in the final hour of God's judgment; his baptism of repentance was the last hope for forgiveness and that quite apart from all sacrificial rites (Mark 1:4; cf. Matt. 3 and Luke

3; John 1:29–34). In the cup of the Lord's Supper, the new covenant in Jesus' blood is for the forgiveness of sins (Mark 14:24; 1 Cor. 11:25). Paul's theology of the cross sees forgiveness as the basis for a new beginning (2 Cor. 5:17; Gal. 1:4; 2:20; 6:15; Rom. 8:9–11). For John's Gospel, this forgiveness is carried out in the life of the community of faith (John 20:23). Finally, God's pardon is experienced through the work of his Spirit (1 Cor. 2:12–16; cf. Col. 2:12; Acts 2:38). The experience of pardon is also known as reconciliation (2 Cor. 5:18–21; Rom. 5:10–11; Col. 1:20) and peace with God (Rom. 5:1; 1 Thess. 1:1; 5:23). ***See also*** Atonement; Covenant; Expiation; Forgiveness; Guilt; Reconciliation; Redemption; Salvation; Sin. J.E.A.

parent. ***See*** Family, The; Father; Marriage; and such individual entries as Athaliah; Deborah; Elizabeth; Hagar; Hannah; Mary; Rachel; Rebekah; Ruth; Sarah.

parental blessing, the blessing given by a father to his children, especially that given to his firstborn son. Normally given when the father is an old man nearing death (Gen. 27:2; 48:21; 49:1), this blessing forms part of his testamentary farewell to his children. A prime example of this in the OT is the blessing of the younger son Jacob by Isaac. In the Yahwist narrative, the blessing comes to Jacob by deception (Gen. 27), a motif that is absent from the Priestly version of the blessing (Gen. 28:1–5). In Israel's blessing of Joseph's sons, the motif of the choice of the younger son (Ephraim) over his older brother (Manasseh) reappears (Gen. 48:15–20). The parental blessings given to Jacob and Ephraim in Genesis are an element of the theology of blessing in the patriarchal narratives (cf. Gen. 12:2–3 to Gen. 27:29 and 48:19–20). An example from the Apocrypha of the parental blessing is Tobit's blessing of his son Tobiah (Tob. 5:17; 11:27). J.S.K.

Parmenas (pahr'muh-nuhs), one of the seven selected in the Jerusalem church to care for the widows and distribute food to the poor (Acts 6:1–6). He was probably a Hellenistic Jew. ***See also*** Hellenists.

Parousia (pah-ro͞o-see'uh), a Greek term meaning "arrival," "coming," or "being present." The Gospel of Matthew has three sayings of Jesus concerning the future Parousia of the Son of man (24:27, 37, 39) and one in which the disciples ask Jesus what the "sign" of his own Parousia will be (24:3). Paul refers to the future Parousia of Christ five times (1 Cor. 15:23; 1 Thess. 2:19; 3:13; 4:15; 5:23). James encourages belief that the Parousia of "the Lord" is near (5:7–8). The author of 2 Thessalonians, perhaps Paul, refers to the Parousia of "our Lord Jesus Christ" (2:1, 8). 2 Peter speaks of Jesus' previous Parousia, possibly at the transfiguration (1:16), but also of "his" (probably Jesus') future Parousia (3:4) and of the future Parousia of "the day of God" (3:12; cf. "the day of the Lord," 3:10, and "the day of eternity," 3:18). 1 John refers once to "his" (probably Jesus') Parousia (2:28), expected very soon (2:18).

Judgment: Several of these sayings link the coming of the Son of man, Lord, or Christ with the prospect of judgment. The sayings in Matt. 24:37, 39 compare the Parousia of the Son of man to the unexpected and disastrous coming of the flood in the days of Noah. Paul twice expresses the hope that his Thessalonian congregation will be found *blameless* at the Parousia (1 Thess. 3:13; 5:23). James characterizes the Lord whose coming is at hand as "the Judge" (5:8–9). In 2 Peter, the Parousia (3:4) is directly associated with the coming "day of judgment" (3:7), and 1 John uses similar language, referring both to the prospective Parousia ("that . . . we may have confidence and not shrink from him in shame"; 2:28) and the prospective day of judgment (4:17). In the synoptic Gospels, Jesus frequently intimates that the coming of the Son of man will be the time when people will be judged (Matt. 13:41–43; 16:27; 25:31–46; Luke 18:8; 21:36; cf. Matt. 7:21–23, where Jesus is to be the Judge). Generally, the Synoptics portray the Son of man as Judge, though in Matt. 19:28 and Luke 22:30, the twelve disciples are to judge the tribes of Israel. In Luke 12:8–9, the angels of God appear to be the judges (but cf. 1 Cor. 6:3, where Paul writes that Christians are to judge angels!). In Matthew, angels appear as attendants or bailiffs (13:41; 24:31) of the kingdom of the Son of man, a term evidently equivalent to his court of judgment (Matt. 13:41; 16:28). References to Jesus' prospective kingdom often have a similar meaning (e.g., Matt. 20:21; Luke 22:30). Jesus is expected as Judge in other NT writings as well (e.g., 2 Tim. 4:1; James 5:8–9; 1 Pet. 4:5).

A few synoptic passages link the coming of the Kingdom of God with that of the Son of man (Matt. 10:5–23; 19:23–28; Mark 8:38–9:1; Luke 9:26–27; Luke 17:20–24). It is likely that Jesus and the early Christians expected both to come at the same time. Thus, the term "Parousia" may refer more broadly to several occurrences expected at the end of the present and beginning of the new age: the coming of the Son of man and Kingdom of God, the last judgment, and the resurrection of the dead.

Signs: Various sayings indicate that certain clues or signs would reveal that the Parousia events were near: the series of apocalyptic occurrences set out in Matt. 24:4–33; Mark 13:5–26; and Luke 21:8–26 and the coming of the Antichrist or false messiah(s) (1 John 2:18) or the "man of lawlessness" (2 Thess. 2:3). Yet some sayings of Jesus deny that there will be any preliminary signs (Mark 8:12; Luke 17:20–21), and on several occasions he urged his hearers to "watch" or be ready at all times (Matt. 24:42; 25:13; Mark 13:33–37) since the Son of man will come unexpectedly "like a thief in the night" (Matt. 24:43–44; Luke 12:39–40), a saying that finds echoes in later NT writings (1 Thess. 5:2; 2 Pet. 3:10; Rev. 3:3; 16:15).

Delay: The delay of the Parousia troubled early Christians. According to Matt. 10:23, the Son of man should have come before the Twelve had finished their initial preaching mission in Judea. According to Mark 9:1 and 13:30, at least some of Jesus' contemporaries should have lived to see the Parousia. John 21:20–23 awkwardly tries to account for the fact that, contrary to expectation, "the beloved disciple" did die before Jesus' coming. As time passed, many Christians died, and doubt arose as to whether there would be a resurrection of the dead (1 Cor. 15:12–19). Paul explained that Christ was the "first fruits" of the resurrection and that at his Parousia the dead would be made alive (1 Cor. 15:20–23; cf. 1 Thess. 3:13, where Paul seems to say that at Christ's Parousia he will bring "his saints" with him). 2 Peter proposes several reasons for the apparent delay (3:3–9) but insists that the day of the Lord may still come at any time (3:10; cf. Ezek. 12:21–28). The writer of Revelation likewise believed and promised that Jesus would come "soon" (e.g., 1:1, 3; 22:6–7, 10, 20).

No NT passage refers to Jesus' *second* Parousia or coming as such. In John 14:3, Jesus says that he will come again, and the writer of Hebrews declares (9:28) that Christ will appear a second time. Usually, however, reference is simply to the *coming* of the Son of man or Christ as Lord, which, like the coming of the Kingdom of God, the day of judgment, and the resurrection of the dead, was expected in the not distant future, at the end of the present age. ***See also*** Eschatology; Jesus Christ; Judgment, Day of; Judgment, The Last; Kingdom of God; Messiah; Millennium; Resurrection; Son of Man. R.H.H.

Parthians (pahr'thee-uhnz), an Iranian people. The northeastern region of Iran, known as Parthava since at least the seventh century B.C., became prominent when the Parni tribe of central Asia wrested it from the Seleucids. By the second century B.C., the Parni dynasty, traced to Arsaces I, had expanded throughout the Iranian plateau and beyond. They were strong enough to stop Roman expansion at the Euphrates in 53 B.C., although Trajan did later briefly occupy their capital at Ctesiphon. As a result of their rivalry with western powers, the Parthians became involved in Judean affairs, supporting Antigonus II as king in Jerusalem until Roman assistance enabled Herod to displace him. Luke reports some Parthians were present in Jerusalem at Pentecost (Acts 2:9). The Parthian Empire fell to the Sasanians early in the third century A.D. F.E.G.

partridge, a medium-sized, stout-bodied gamebird. The most frequent species of the partridge is the chukar partridge *(Alectoris chukar)*, a medium-sized gamebird with red legs and red beak that lives in rocky terrain. Its typical cackling voice is similar to that of a clucking hen. When chased, it prefers to run, and only flies short distances.

In 1 Sam. 26:20 Saul's pursuit of David is compared to a partridge hunt. In Jer. 17:11, the partridge is wrongly accused of stealing other birds' young.

pascal (pas'kuhl; sometimes spelled paschal), "pertaining to Passover," a term usually applied to the lamb slaughtered for the Passover feast. According to the Gospel of John, Jesus was crucified the day the pascal lamb was slain (cf. 1 Cor. 5:7).

Pashhur (pahsh'huhr; KJV: "Pashur" from Egyptian *pš-ḥr*, "Portion of [the god] Horus"). **1** A priest, son of Immer, and chief officer in the Temple; he opposed Jeremiah's prophecy, beat him, and put him in stocks. Jeremiah renamed him "Terror on Every Side," reaffirmed his own word of destruction, and prophesied personal exile to Babylon for Pashhur and his family (Jer. 20). **2** The son of Malchiah, who apparently was King Zedekiah's son. Zedekiah sent Pashhur to inquire of the Lord through Jeremiah (Jer. 21) while Nebuchadnezzar was making war against Judah. Jeremiah repeated God's word of destruction. The same Pashhur, a high official, accused Jeremiah of treason and recommended his death (Jer. 38). Later, among the priests who returned from exile was Gedaliah, a descendant of Pashhur, son of Malchiah (1 Chron. 9:12; Neh. 11:12, though of different generations). The descendants of Pashhur, distinct from the descendants of Immer, made up one of the important priestly families who returned from the Exile (Ezra 2:38; 10:22; Neh. 7:41). **3** The father of the Gedaliah who joined Pashhur, son of Malchiah, in the action against Jeremiah (Jer. 38:1); he was per-

The name "Pashhur" written in Hebrew on an ostracon from Arad, ninth–sixth century B.C.

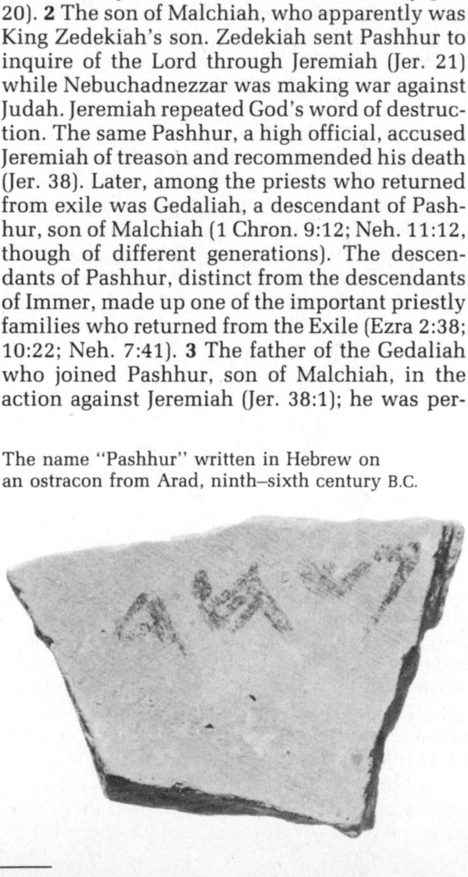

haps the same Pashhur as 1 above. **4** A high official who was contemporary with Nehemiah (Neh. 10:3). ***See also*** Jeremiah, The Book of.
H.B.H.

passion, aroused or inflamed emotions. Apart from this normal meaning (Prov. 14:30; 1 Cor. 7: 9; 1 Thess. 4:5) the term is also used to refer to the suffering and death of Jesus. Hence the expression "Passion narrative" is often used today to cover the whole account of Jesus' arrest, trial, and crucifixion in the four Gospels. Acts 1: 3 is the only passage to speak of "his Passion." A number of other passages speak of the "necessity" that the "Messiah" suffer (Mark 8:31; Luke 17:25; 24:26, 46; 3:18; 17:3; Heb. 9:26). ***See also*** Cross; Trial of Jesus, The. P.P.

Passion Sunday, in the liturgical year the second Sunday prior to Easter and the Sunday that begins the Lenten season of Passiontide. With the reforms of the Second Vatican Council (1962–65), the period of Lent was simplified for the Roman Catholic church, and the Sunday prior to Easter, formerly known as Palm Sunday, was renamed Passion Sunday. Other churches have also made this change, and on occasion both names are retained as Passion Sunday (Palm Sunday), or Sunday of the Passion: Palm Sunday.

Passover, the, a religious festival commemorating God's deliverance of the Jews from bondage. The English term translates the Hebrew word *pesach* as used in Exod. 12:13, "*I will pass over you,* and no plague shall fall upon you to destroy you, when I smite the land of Egypt" (see also vv. 23, 27). The verb also may have the connotation "protect" in Isa. 31:5, although such a sense is probably already reflective of the Exodus (Isa. 31:3). Elsewhere in the Hebrew the verb means "hop, skip" (1 Kings 18:21, 26; RSV: "limp") or "limp" (2 Sam. 4:4; RSV: "lame," and see the noun form "lame" from the same root in Lev. 21:18; 2 Sam. 9:13; Isa. 35:6). Unconvincing attempts have been made by scholars to derive the etymology of *pesach* from Akkadian, Egyptian, and Arabic loan words. In the Bible, the noun *pesach* always refers to the sacrifice (Exod. 12:27) or the attendant festival (2 Kings 23:22).

Scholars have difficulty reconstructing the origins and historical development of the Passover festival due to the relative paucity of information in the Bible and elsewhere and the differing perceptions of the literary sources and traditions that marshal the evidence. The Bible contains eight chronological references to the Passover.

Biblical References: The first is to the Passover of the Exodus (Exod. 12:1–13:16), generally seen to be a pastiche of sources, the dominant one being P, the Priestly source. Since Exod. 12 starts out with a reference to the partaking of the paschal lamb in the first month of the year (vv. 2–10), Abib (March–April; 13:4), some scholars think that the Passover was originally a spring New Year festival, similar to the autumnal Feast of Tabernacles. On the 10th of the month each family was to choose a lamb (v. 3) to be slaughtered at twilight on the 14th (v. 6). The blood was to be smeared on the doorposts and lintel of the house (v. 7), which God would see and thus spare the inhabitants from the destruction of the Egyptian firstborn (vv. 12–13). The apotropaic (protective) nature of the rite is thus indicated. After roasting, all of the flesh of the animal was to be eaten in the house that night, but only by the Israelites and their circumcised slaves; the remnants were to be burned in the morning (vv. 8–10, 43–47). The people were to eat the sacrifice hurriedly, dressed to flee Egypt (v. 11). This day would be a memorial feast in perpetuity (v. 14). From the evening of the 14th until that of the 21st the Israelite houses would be clean of leaven, and only unleavened bread, *matzot,* would be eaten (vv. 14, 18–20). These days too would be celebrated yearly, although there is confusion on whether it would be celebrated already in the desert (implied in v. 17?), or only upon entering Canaan (13:5–7[E], and v. 10). The 1st and 7th days of eating the *matzot* would be shared assemblies, with no work allowed (12: 16). The festival of *matzot* was also conceived as a memorial to the Exodus (12:17; 13:3, 9). It is incumbent upon parents to explain the significance of these feast days to children (12:26–27; 13:8; cf. 13:14).

The next reference is to the second year of the Exodus (Num. 9:1–14, identified as P and therefore late by most scholars): the Passover sacrifice and its attendant rites are kept in the wilderness of Sinai (vv. 3, 5). Those who were defiled by a corpse (vv. 6, 10) or too far away (vv. 10, 13) would keep the Passover with *matzot* and bitter herbs on the 14th day of the second month. A non-Israelite who dwelled among the tribes would also be required to observe the Passover (v. 14). The lateness of this passage is evidenced by the reference to the "too distant way" (v. 10), which assumes a central sanctuary (cf. Deut. 12:21; 14:24).

After entering Canaan in the days of Joshua (Josh. 5:10–12), at Gilgal on the plains of Jericho the Israelites performed the Passover sacrifice (v. 10), and on the following day they ate *matzot* and parched corn (v. 11; cf. Lev. 2:12). There is controversy over the dating of this passage. Those who see it as early contend that here is evidence of the unification of the Passover sacrifice with the eating of *matzot* within an historicized memorial to the Exodus already at Israel's incursion into Canaan. Those who see this passage as late (influenced by Deuteronomy) understand the reference as anachronistic.

A fourth reference is to the time of the judges

and Samuel. In the midst of a description of Joshua's Passover, 2 Kings 23:22 and 2 Chron. 35:18 allude to an exemplary Passover of earlier times.

Another refers to the time of Solomon, implied by 1 Kings 9:25 and stated in 2 Chron. 8: 13 (the feast of *matzot*) and 31:26.

A sixth reference is to the days of Hezekiah (727–698 B.C.; 2 Chron. 30:1–27, not recorded by Kings): a Passover kept by royal decree in the second month due to impurity of the priests (v. 3), which was kept by Judah and some of the remnants of the northern tribes in Jerusalem (vv. 11–13). The priests purified the people (v. 16), and the Levites oversaw the slaughter of the paschal lamb (v. 17). The Passover was succeeded by the seven-day *matzot* festival accompanied by praise of God and music (v. 21). Three facts have convinced some scholars of the unhistorical nature of this passage: first, Kings records no such event; second, it appears to contain elements of Solomon's dedication and Josiah's Passover (2 Chron. 35: 1–18); and, third, Hezekiah, like Josiah later, is seen to be concerned to make reforms in the north (2 Kings 23:15–20; 2 Chron. 34:33). However, 2 Kings 18:4 does depict Hezekiah's broad religious reforms, which would be consistent with an attempt at a proper Passover celebration.

A seventh reference is to the days of Josiah (639–609 B.C.; 2 Kings 23:21–23; 2 Chron. 35: 1–19). In the eighteenth year of Josiah's reign, as part of his reforms based upon the newly found book of the covenant (2 Kings 23:21; cf. 22:8, 11; 23:2–3), he decreed the observance of the Passover in Jerusalem (cf. Deut. 16:2, 5–6), which is viewed by the historian as extraordinary (2 Kings 23:22–23). The author of Chronicles' expanded account (2 Chron. 35:1–19) adds that the Levites slaughtered and flayed the thirty thousand lambs and kids for the *pesach* given by the king and the twenty-six hundred given by the princes, as well as the cattle for the sacrifices (vv. 6–11). The priests purified the people with the sprinkling of the blood (v. 11). The *pesach* was roasted, but the other animals destined for the sacrifices were boiled (v. 13). Thus, Chronicles reconciles the discrepancies between Exod. 12:8–9, which commands roasting, and Deut. 16:7, which states that the *pesach* should be boiled. The seven-day feast of *matzot* accompanied the *pesach* (2 Chron. 35: 17). The uniqueness of the event is reemphasized (v. 18).

A final reference is to the days of Zerubbabel (Ezra 6:19–22). After the dedication of the rebuilt Temple, during the sixth year of Darius (515 B.C.; Ezra 6:15–17), the returned exiles from Babylon observed the Passover. The purity of the community is emphasized (Ezra 6: 20–21), in keeping with the concern for reinstituting proper worship after the Exile. As in 2 Chronicles 35, the Levites slaughter the *pesach* (v. 20). The seven-day feast of *matzot* was kept with great joy (v. 22).

Although dates are not adduced, it is apparent that the command in Deut. 16:2, 5–7 to observe the *pesach* "at the place which the Lord your God will choose, to make his name dwell in it" indicates a transition from the house ceremony (Exod. 12:46) to that of the Temple. Unfortunately, it is impossible to know the date of this transition, scholarly conjecture notwithstanding.

Extrabiblical References: In addition to the evidence from the Hebrew Bible, two ostraca and a papyrus refer to the meticulous celebration of the Passover in the Jewish community of Elephantine in Egypt in the fifth century B.C.

Origin and Significance: Much ink has been spilled concerning the nonhistorical prebiblical origins of the Passover. The most accepted position is that the *pesach* sacrifice originated in a seminomadic ceremony held in spring and fall when feeding grounds for the flock were alternated due to change of seasons. The ceremony thus would have been a petition for the deity's protection and favor during the time of migration. Another view ties the Passover in with a spring New Year's festival. There is considerable difference of opinion as to when the sacrifice from the flock was joined in ceremony with the offering of the first fruits of the barley harvest. The fact is, however, that the Bible knows of no such disparate origins. The historical aspects always appear together with these of agriculture and sheepherding, just as the feast of *matzot* is always joined to the *pesach*. This reality alone is evidence that all these elements came together at a very early stage of Israelite history.

The ultimate significance of the Passover, though, is not in its sociology or history, but in its unique role in the life of the Jewish people. It was and is the festival of freedom and redemption par excellence. Representative of God's love and saving acts, it always gave the people hope in the face of physical and spiritual oppression. As a family celebration, it served as a unifying bond from generation to generation. Its strength is seen in its emergence as the most important of Jewish festivals, in its three-thousand-year continuity, and in its continuing relevance to the needs of the people, whether it be freedom from social discrimination or the acquisition of religious liberty.

The traditions of God's love and of his saving acts prompted the nascent Christian community, according to the Gospels at the command of Jesus, to celebrate a thanksgiving (Gk. *eucharistia)* festival commemorating the Passover he celebrated with his disciples the night before his crucifixion (1 Cor. 11:23–26) and the saving effects of that death and subsequent resurrection (Matt. 26:17, 26–28). The centrality of that observance for the Christian faith, drawing on the Passover as the central observance of the Jewish faith, clearly shows how deeply rooted Christianity is in the historic life and faith of the people of Israel. ***See also*** Exodus; Feasts, Festivals, and Fasts; Temple, The; Worship.

Bibliography

Childs, B. S. *The Book of Exodus*. Philadelphia: Westminster, 1974. Pp. 178–214.

Schauss, H. *The Jewish Festivals*. New York: Schocken, 1977. Pp. 38–85.

Segal, J. B. *The Hebrew Passover*. London: Oxford, 1963.

J.U.

pastoral Epistles. ***See*** Timothy, The First and Second Letters of Paul to and Titus, The Letter of Paul to. These three letters are called "pastoral" since they express a pastoral concern for the addressees, and because they exhibit a concern for the orderly pastoral care of Christian congregations.

Pathros (path'ruhs), Upper Egypt, the region south of Memphis and the Nile delta. There were Israelite exiles in Pathros (Isa. 11:11); Jeremiah and Ezekiel cried out against them (Jer. 44: 1, 15; Ezek. 29:14; 30:14).

The Pathrusim were the people of Pathros and were described as descendants of Egypt (Gen. 10:14; 1 Chron. 1:12).

Patmos (pat'muhs), one of the Sporades Islands in the Aegean Sea. It lies about thirty-seven miles southwest of Miletus, a city on the coast of western Asia Minor. It is a small island, about ten miles long from north to south and six miles wide at its broadest point. In Rev. 1:9 John says that he was on Patmos "on account of the word of God and the testimony of Jesus." Early Christian tradition says that John was banished to Patmos by the Roman authorities. This tradition is credible because banishment was a common punishment used during the Imperial period for a variety of offenses. Among such offenses were the practices of magic and astrology. Prophecy was viewed by the Romans as belonging to the same category, whether pagan, Jewish, or Christian. Prophecy with political implications, like that expressed by John in the book of Revelation, would have been perceived as a threat to Roman political power and order. Three of the islands in the Sporades were places where political offenders were banished (Pliny *Natural History* 4.69–70; Tacitus *Annals* 4.30).

The island of Patmos, where early Christian tradition says that John of the book of Revelation was banished by the Roman authorities.

Patmos was the scene of at least some of John's visionary experiences and was probably the place where he wrote the book of Revelation. His banishment made communication in written form with Christians in Asia Minor a necessity. ***See also*** Miletus. A.Y.C.

patriarch, the male head of a family or a clan. In the OT the term conventionally and specifically refers to the key figures in the Genesis narrative, Abraham (Gen. 12–24), Isaac (Gen. 25–36), and Jacob (Gen. 25–36), who are reckoned as the progenitors and pioneers of biblical faith. The figure of Joseph (Gen. 37–50), set in a different literary mode from the other three, is not treated in the same sense in the development of the tradition and so is not included among the patriarchs.

Historical Persons: Whether the patriarchs were specific historical persons is a difficult question. Scholarly consensus maintains that these persons, their movements, and families are well rooted in the cultural, political, and economic fabric of the Near East. There is, however, a dissenting opinion from this consensus which holds the patriarchs to be literary fictions, but this is a distinctly minority judgment. American archaeological study has proposed a high degree of correlation between the patriarchal figures and the data of Mesopotamian culture. That synthesis has linked the patriarchs to various peoples of the Middle Bronze (2000–1500 B.C.) and/or Late Bronze (1500–1200 B.C.) period, with special reference to the Amorite, Hurrian, and Aramean movements. These correlations, however, are increasingly regarded as problematic. A most general connection seems reasonable, but precise correlations are eschewed by scholars.

Literary Tradition: The patriarchs are embedded in a complicated literary tradition. The materials of the book of Genesis have undergone an extensive evolution and/or editing process. That process seems to move from quite early tribal narrative memories to sophisticated and disciplined theological reflection. As a part of the process, there is no doubt that the patriarchal memories and persons have been subjected to stylization, imagination, and literary construction. The result is that the historical persons of the patriarchs cannot be separated from the narrative presentation in which they are cast. The patriarchs are therefore participants in a narrative memory that tends to minimize if not exclude the appropriateness of the historical question. In contemporary discussions, these literary questions tend to override the older historical questions.

Religious Discernment: The patriarchs are carriers of a distinctive religious discernment. They are the vehicle through which a peculiar revelation of God is made available to the community. Following the modern scholar Albrecht Alt, scholars view the "religion of the patriarchs" as a religion of God's guiding promise. This religion, sharply contrasted to the animistic religion (also hinted at in the book of Genesis), presents a God who goes with the designated community to lead, guard, and protect.

Theological Claim: Following such contemporary scholars as G. von Rad and W. Zimmerli, it is widely held that the promissory character of the patriarchal narratives marks the decisive theological claim of the OT. This promissory character is the decisive mark of Yahweh who is the God who makes promises and keeps them. This promissory character is the decisive mark of Israel who is a people summoned to hope and to depart toward the promise. The subsequent theological use made of the memory of such promises goes well beyond the initial disclosure. See, for example, the uses made of it in the portions of the book of Isaiah written during the period of the Exile (41:8–10; 43:1–2; 51:2–3; 54:1–8) and in various texts of the NT (Rom. 4; Gal. 3–4; Heb. 11:8–22).

Wives of the Patriarchs: While we have used the conventional rubric "patriarch," such a designation is not without problem. It rightly focuses upon the three key actors in the Genesis narrative, but at the same time it neglects in each the primary wife—Sarah, Rebekah, Rachel—who figures prominently in the narrative. In each case, it is the "barren wife" (11:30; 25:21; 29:31) who becomes the pivotal point of interest in the narrative. In each, the gift of a child to the barren woman is the key turn that permits the story to advance and history to continue. The wives of the patriarchs emerge as important theological referents in the derivative tradition (cf., e.g., Jer. 31:15; Isa. 54:1–3; Matt. 2:18; Gal. 4:27; Heb. 11:11). They become the vehicles through which God does "impossible things" against the possibilities of the day (e.g., Rom. 4:17–21). Thus in the future it may be preferable to use the term "the ancestors" to include both the key male figures and the "barren" women who become mothers of faith. ***See also*** Abraham; Genesis; Isaac; Jacob; Pentateuch.

Bibliography

Gunkel, Hermann. *The Legends of Genesis*. New York: Schocken, 1964.

Hunt, Ignatius. *The World of the Patriarchs*. Englewood Cliffs, NJ: Prentice-Hall, 1967.

von Rad, Gerhard. *Old Testament Theology I*. New York: Harper & Row, 1962. Pp. 165–75.

Westermann, Claus. *The Promises to the Fathers*. Philadelphia: Fortress, 1980. W.B.

Paul

PAUL THE APOSTLE was the most effective missionary of early Christianity and the church's first theologian. He is sometimes called the "second founder" of Christianity. Known as "Saul" within the Aramaic-speaking community, the apostle was usually called "Paul," the Roman form of his name. More than one-fourth of the writings of the NT are attributed to him.

Primary sources for Paul's life and thought are his Letters. Acts, which includes much biographical material about him, should be seen as secondary. Although tradition attributes it to a travel companion of Paul, Acts sometimes conflicts with the Letters and presents the particular theological perspectives of its author. Thirteen Letters in the NT are ascribed to Paul, but modern scholarship believes some of these were written by later followers of the apostle (especially Ephesians, 1 and 2 Timothy, and Titus). As fully reliable sources, the scholar depends on Romans, 1 and 2 Corinthians, Galatians, Philippians, 1 Thessalonians, and Philemon.

Third-century papyrus fragment of the book of Acts from Oxyrhynchus, Egypt.

Early Life: According to Acts (21:39; 22:3), Paul was born and reared a Jew in Tarsus, an important city of Cilicia. The date of his birth is uncertain but is usually estimated at about A.D. 10. In a statement reported in Acts 22:28, Paul claimed that he had been born a Roman citizen (see 21:39). This would mean that he had inherited citizenship from his father (or some other ancestor) who had done meritorious service for the Romans. Paul's use of Greek confirms his origin as a Hellenistic Jew of the Dispersion, at home in the Greco-Roman world.

Paul's earliest education would have been in the home, with his father as instructor. The loyalty of Paul's parentage to the ancestral faith remains a mark of pride. Of himself Paul boasts, "circumcised on the eighth day, of the people of Israel, of the tribe of Benjamin, a Hebrew born of Hebrews" (Phil. 3:5). At about age six, Paul would have attended the synagogue school for instruction in the Scriptures and Hebrew. Paul, according to Acts 22:3, was educated in Jerusalem "at the feet of Gamaliel." This teacher would have been the important Rabban Gamaliel, noted for his spirit of tolerance (Acts 5:34–39). Although his Letters never mention a rabbinic teacher, Paul's arguments reflect methods of biblical interpretation used by the rabbis. Paul, like most rabbis, was a member of the Pharisaic party (Phil. 3:5).

Acts 26:10 is sometimes read to imply that Paul had been a member of the Sanhedrin. This seems unlikely, since Paul could scarcely have omitted such an achievement from his list in Phil. 3:5–6. Similarly unlikely is the possibility that Paul, as a young student in Jerusalem, had seen Jesus. Nowhere does Paul mention such an encounter, and his Letters evidence little knowledge of the life and teachings of Jesus. Early in life, Paul learned a trade, probably from his father. The trade was tentmaking and other leatherwork (Acts 18:3). Practice of this trade provided Paul later with means to support his missionary activity (1 Thess. 2:9; 1 Cor. 9:6).

Prior to his conversion, Paul had been a persecutor of Christians. Acts reports that he "laid waste the church" and "dragged off men and women and committed them to prison" (8:3). He "persecuted them even to foreign cities" (26:11), receiving authority from the high priest to extradite Christians from Damascus (9:1–2; 22:5). What jurisdiction the Jerusalem hierarchy might have had over inhabitants of distant cities is problematic, and Paul's assertion that he was "still

A medieval depiction of the dramatic conversion of Paul according to Acts 9: *(Top register, left to right)* The Lord calls Saul, who falls to the ground blinded and then is led to Damascus; *(center)* Ananias, instructed in a vision, then heals Saul's blindness; *(bottom)* Saul preaches in the synagogue; illuminated page from the First Bible of Charles the Bald (846).

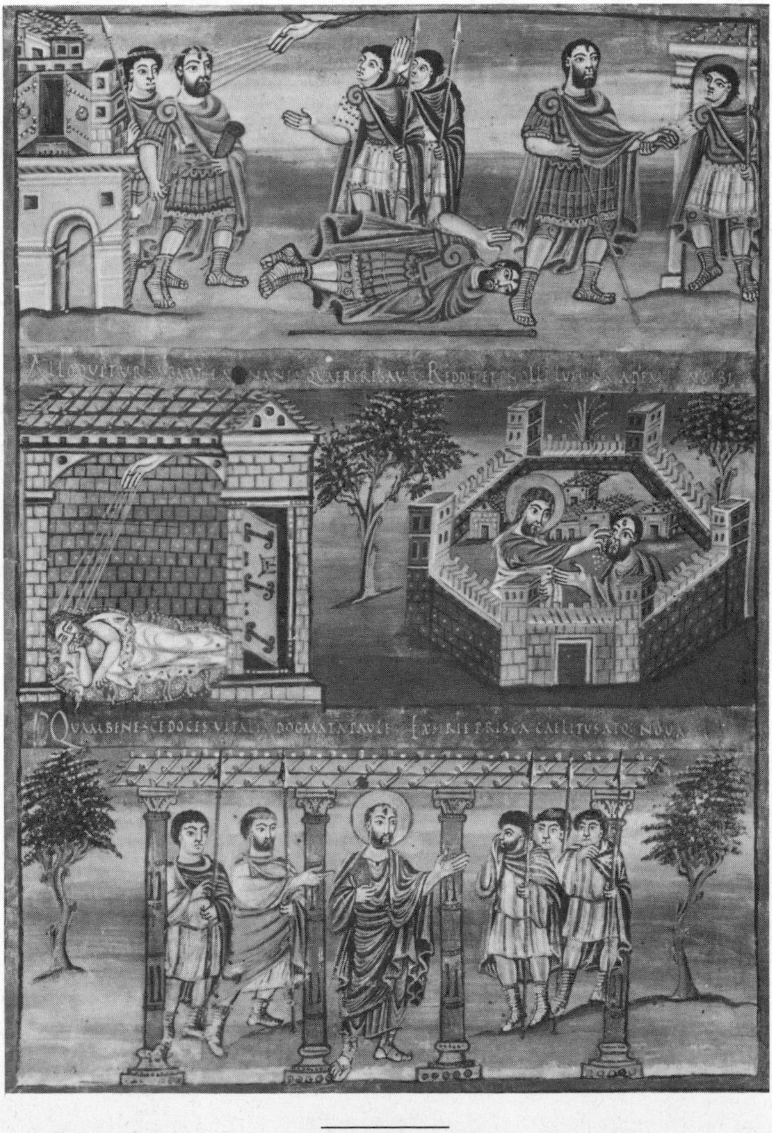

not known by sight to the churches of Christ in Judea" (Gal. 1:22) raises questions about his persecuting activity in Jerusalem. That Paul had been a persecutor, however, is confirmed by his Letters: "I persecuted the church of God violently and tried to destroy it" (Gal. 1:13; see Gal. 1:23; 1 Cor. 15:9). As a Pharisee, Paul may have been angered by the failure of the followers of Jesus to live strictly by the requirements of the law (see Gal. 1:14). He was no doubt enraged by the Christian identification of the crucified Jesus as Messiah (Christ). Paul had expected a triumphant messiah, not one who bore the curse of the cross (Gal. 3:13). For Paul, the crucified Christ had been a stumbling block (1 Cor. 1:23).

The late-second-century apocryphal *Acts of Paul and Thecla* describes the apostle as "a man small of stature, with bald head and crooked legs . . . with eyebrows meeting and nose somewhat hooked." Paul himself reports that his critics say "his bodily presence is weak, and his speech of no account" (2 Cor. 10:10). Paul's physical weakness is epitomized by his "thorn in the flesh" (2 Cor. 12:7). The report of the thorn, together with references from Galatians (4:13, 15; 6:11), has been variously interpreted to imply that Paul was afflicted by such disorders as malaria, eye trouble, or migraine headaches. In spite of this unidentifiable malady, Paul had the strength to overcome serious physical obstacles (2 Cor. 11:24–28). Paul was a person of strong emotional expression: once a persecutor of Christians, later a bitter foe of opponents (Gal. 5:12; 2 Cor. 11:13).

A portrait of Paul by the Lombard artist Vincenzo Foppa, ca. 1490.

Conversion: Paul's conversion was not without preparation. As a Jew influenced by speculation about the future, Paul had looked forward to the coming of the Messiah. As a persecutor, Paul had heard the message of the disciples and had been impressed by their perseverance. His conversion did not involve turning to a new God (see 1 Thess. 1:9); before and after, Paul worshiped the God of the OT. Moreover, Paul's conversion did not involve a serious moral trauma. Paul claimed that, before he accepted Jesus as Christ, "as to righteousness under the law" he had been "blameless" (Phil. 3:6).

Paul's conversion is presented in the form of a call narrative, like

EVENTS IN PAUL'S LIFE

Birth	A.D. 10
Reared in Tarsus	
Conversion	34–35
Spends three years in Arabia (i.e., Nabatea; Gal. 1:17)	
First visit to Jerusalem after his conversion	37
Writes *1 Thessalonians*	49–50
Encounters Gallio in Corinth (Acts 18:12–17)	50–51
Jerusalem Conference (Gal. 2:1–10; Acts 15:1–21)	50–51
In Ephesus	52–54
Writes *Galatians, 1 Corinthians, Philemon, Philippians*	53–55
In Corinth	55–56
Writes *Romans*	55–58
Executed at end of imprisonment in Rome	A.D. 62

All dates are approximations and take Paul's Letters as the primary evidence.

that of the prophets (see Jer. 1:4–10). This is clear from his most extensive account (Gal. 1:11–17), where the experience is seen to involve two main elements: the revelation of Jesus as God's Son and the commission to preach him to the Gentiles. In Acts, the conversion of Paul is recounted three times (9:1–19; 22:3–16; 26:4–18). These accounts stress supernatural details: light and voices from heaven, Paul's blindness and recovery. They also observe that Paul's conversion was facilitated by a religious leader (9:10–18; 22:12–16) and that Paul was baptized (9:18; 22:16)—events nowhere mentioned in Paul's Letters. For Paul, one feature was crucial: he had seen the Lord (1 Cor. 9:1); the risen Christ had appeared to him (1 Cor. 15:8). This vision led to the conviction that the crucified Jesus was the Messiah. It also showed that the events of the end of history had started to unfold, that in these last days God was accomplishing his divine purpose through the crucified Christ, as power working in weakness (2 Cor. 12:9).

Missionary Activity: The balance of Paul's life is devoted to responding to God's commission. The attempt to chronicle that life involves a number of problems. For example, scholars note that Acts presents Paul as making five trips to Jerusalem after his conversion (9:26; 11:30; 15:4; 18:22; 21:15), while the Letters record only three (Gal. 1:18; 2:1; Rom. 15:25). Scholars also note that the Jerusalem conference is described in Acts 15:6–21 as if it had occurred early in Paul's missionary career, while in Gal. 2:1–10 it is said to have taken place fourteen (or perhaps seventeen) years after his conversion, and when, later in his career, Christians in Jerusalem describe the conference to Paul, they assume he was ignorant of its decisions (Acts 21:25; cf. 15:22–29). The offering that Paul at the conference agreed to collect (Gal. 2:10) is scarcely mentioned in Acts (24:17, 26), but in the Letters it is seen to be a major concern of the latter part of Paul's missionary endeavor (1 Cor. 16:1–4; 2 Cor. 8–9; Rom. 15:25–28).

In response to these problems, most scholars conclude that the conference was held relatively late in Paul's career. Acts, in turn, is seen to present too many trips to Jerusalem. Its author depicts the movement of the mission from Jerusalem to Rome as a symbol of Paul's repeated turning from Jews to the Gentiles (13:46; 18:6) and consequently constructs Paul's activity into three missionary journeys, all beginning in the east and moving west. Some scholars believe Paul engaged in missionary work farther west (in Macedonia and Achaia) prior to the conference. For them, the fourteen years of silence (Gal. 1:21–2:1) were filled with activity.

Taking the Letters as primary (but not ignoring evidence from Acts), Paul's career can be summarized in the following way. After his conversion in about A.D. 34 or 35, Paul spent three years in Arabia (i.e., Nabatea; Gal. 1:17). No doubt some of that time was spent in religious reflection, but probably Paul began to preach relatively soon. Unless he had been doing more than meditating, Paul would scarcely have had to flee from Damascus (2 Cor. 11:32–33; Acts 9:23–25). His first visit to Jerusalem after his conversion occurred around 37. Although the account in Acts presents him as "preaching boldly" (9:29), Paul's own testimony is that he saw only Cephas and James (Gal. 1:18–20).

After this fifteen-day visit to Jerusalem, Paul engaged in missionary activity in Syria and Cilicia (Gal. 1:21). Acts 13 and 14 describe a mission to Cyprus and central Asia Minor (Antioch of Pisidia, Iconium, Lystra, and Derbe). At Lystra, Paul is reported to have been stoned (Acts 14:19), an incident confirmed by 2 Cor. 11:25. During this fourteen-year period, Paul may have engaged in missionary work in north Galatia (founding the churches addressed in Galatians), Macedonia (Philippi and Thessalonica; see 1 Thess. 1:2–3:10), and Achaia (Corinth). Acts, of course, places the missionary activity in these provinces after the Jerusalem conference (16:11–18:21). Acts and the Letters agree that Paul was accompanied on this mission by Silvanus (Silas) and Timothy (1 Thess. 1:1; 2 Cor. 1:19). At Philippi, Paul is said to have been beaten with rods (Acts 16:22), one of the three times he suffered this punishment (2 Cor. 11:25). At Corinth (2 Cor. 10:14), where he labored for a year and a half (Acts 18:11), Paul probably wrote 1 Thessalonians—the earliest book in the NT. There he also appeared for trial before Gallio (Acts 18:12–17), the newly appointed governor, whose accession to power can be dated at around 50 or 51. According to Paul's strategy, the mission was begun in a large urban center, after which fellow workers were enlisted to help in spreading the gospel into the surrounding areas (2 Cor. 1:1).

The Jerusalem conference (Gal. 2:1–10; Acts 15:1–21) was probably convened in 50 or 51. According to both accounts, the primary issue was the question of requiring circumcision for Gentile converts, i.e., requiring Gentiles to become Jews before they could become Christians. Both accounts agree, too, in regard to the decision: circumcision should not be required. According to Galatians, the leaders of the Jerusalem church (Peter, James, and John) approved Paul's mission, but requested him to collect an offering for the poor of the Jerusalem congregation (1 Cor. 16:1–4; 2 Cor. 8–9; Rom. 15:26).

The Cilician Gates, a pass through the Taurus Mountains, linked the Roman provinces of Cilicia and Cappadocia in Asia Minor. Acts records that Paul passed through this area on two journeys.

Paul discoursing with bystanders who become intent listeners; eleventh-century enamel plaque.

After the conference, Paul traveled to Antioch (see Acts 15:30; 18:22). Cephas (Peter) arrived shortly thereafter (Gal. 2:11). At first, Cephas ate with the Gentile members of the church. When emissaries from James, the leader of the Jerusalem church, came to Antioch, Cephas withdrew from table fellowship with the Gentiles. Apparently, the "circumcision party" (Gal. 2:12), asserting its power in Jerusalem, had insisted that Gentile Christians observe Jewish food laws (see Acts 15:22–29; 21:25). Paul, upset by Cephas's failure to recognize that the fellowship of the Lord's table depended solely on faith, "opposed him to his face" (Gal. 2:11).

After the conference, Paul carried on an extensive mission in Ephesus (ca. A.D. 52–54). There Paul wrote most of his correspondence to the Corinthians. An early letter mentioned in 1 Cor. 5:9, 11 was probably lost. Paul wrote 1 Corinthians in response to problems in Corinth reported by Chloe's people (1 Cor. 1:11) and by a letter from the Corinthian church (1 Cor. 7:1). When relations between Paul and the Corinthians deteriorated, Paul seems to have made a quick visit from Ephesus to Corinth—a journey scholars call the "painful" or "sorrowful" visit (implied by 2 Cor. 2:1; 12:14; 13:1). This visit aggravated the conflict, and provoked Paul to write the "severe" or "tearful" letter (2 Cor. 2:2–4; 7:8), part of which may be preserved in what we now have as 2 Corinthians 10–13. Galatians also comes from this period, being written after the Jerusalem conference (Gal. 2:1–10). In Galatia, as in Corinth, the church had been invaded by opponents who preached a "different gospel" (Gal. 1:6) and/or "another Jesus" (2 Cor. 11:4).

During the Ephesian ministry Paul was probably imprisoned (see 2 Cor. 1:8–11). Although the account in Acts 19 mentions no prison, Paul says that he had suffered "far more imprisonments" (2 Cor. 11:23) at a time when Acts has reported only the imprisonment at Philippi (16:23–39). During this probable Ephesian imprisonment, Paul seems to have written Philippians and Philemon (Phil. 1:7, 13, 14, 17; Philem. 1, 9, 10, 13). Imprisonment in Ephesus (rather than Caesarea or Rome) would help explain how the extensive exchange of information between Paul's prison and the church at Philippi (Phil. 2:25–30; 4:18) was possible. It would also make more feasible Paul's plan to visit the Philippians after his release (Phil. 1:26; 2:24). Similarly, a runaway slave from Colossae (Onesimus) would much more likely have met Paul in Ephesus than in the more distant Caesarea or Rome, and Paul's plan to visit the owner of the slave (Philem. 22) is more plausible if Paul is imprisoned in nearby Ephesus. If Colossians is an authentic Letter of Paul, it too would have been written from the Ephesian imprisonment (see Col. 4:3, 10), since the situation from which it was written is closely related to that of Philemon (see Col. 4:10–17; Philem. 2, 23–24).

After leaving Ephesus, Paul moved on to Troas, and eventually to Macedonia (2 Cor. 2:12–13). There he met Titus, who brought him good news from Corinth (2 Cor. 7:5–7). In response, Paul apparently wrote 2 Corinthians 1–9, the "reconciliation letter." He then left Macedonia for Corinth where he spent three months (probably the winter of 55 or 56; see Acts 20:2–3) and wrote Romans. From Corinth, Paul departed for Jerusalem with the offering, anticipating trouble from the Jews and

Ships in a storm on a third-century Roman relief. Acts 27 recounts a tumultuous storm and shipwreck on Paul's journey to Rome.

Jewish Christians (Rom. 15:31). Biographical information from the Letters ceases at this point. Acts, however, describes in detail Paul's final trip to Jerusalem (20:3–21:16), his imprisonment (21:27–23:30), his transfer to Caesarea (23:31–26:32), and his voyage to Rome (27:1–28:31).

Those who accept the pastoral Epistles (1 and 2 Timothy, Titus) as genuine believe Paul was released from his first imprisonment in Rome (2 Tim. 4:16–17) and made another journey in the East. During this hypothetical journey, he is supposed to have visited such places as Troas (2 Tim. 4:13), Ephesus (1 Tim. 1:3), Miletus (2 Tim. 4:20), and Crete (Titus 1:5). According to 2 Tim. 4:6–8, Paul is back in prison, anticipating martyrdom. This reconstruction, built on data which the pastorals have derived from the authentic Letters, is unconvincing. Although a tradition suggests that Paul had been released from Rome and visited Spain (*1 Clement* 5:7), this tradition probably rests on Rom. 15:24, 28. More likely, Paul was executed at the end of his original Roman imprisonment, probably in A.D. 62.

Letters: Paul's writings are not literary epistles, but occasional letters, written to particular churches about particular problems. They were intended to be read to the assembled congregation (1 Thess. 5:27). Paul constructed his Letters according to the epistolary conventions of the day. The letter begins with an introductory salutation followed by a paragraph of thanksgiving. Then comes the body of the letter where the major concerns are addressed. Usually the earlier part of the letter deals with doctrine while the later sections present ethical exhortation. Toward the end of the letter, Paul frequently discloses his travel plans. The letter ends with greetings and a benediction.

Within the Letters Paul employs various rhetorical forms. His style is influenced by the diatribe—the Hellenistic form of discourse where the speaker raises questions and then proceeds to answer them (see Rom. 3:27–31). From time to time, formulas like "I appeal to you" (Rom. 12:1; 1 Cor. 1:10) are introduced. Paul also includes traditional material: hymns (Phil. 2:5–11), confessions (1 Cor. 8:6), and liturgical expressions (1 Cor. 11:23–25). Paul dictated his Letters (Rom. 16:22), and his oral style sometimes results in awkward or incomplete expressions (see Rom. 2:17–21).

In interpreting Paul's Letters, attention is given to various problems.

A question can be raised, for example, about the integrity or unity of the Letters. Most scholars believe 2 Corinthians to be a composite of at least two letters, and some doubt the unity of Philippians. The Letters were arranged in their present form by an editor who collected them around the end of the first century. They are arranged according to length with longest first. Attention has also been given to the identification of the opponents Paul faced. Although efforts have been made to identify them as Judaizers or Gnostics, different foes—representing the variety of early Christianity—were probably encountered in different situations. Recently, some forms of sociological analysis have been applied to the Letters. By this method, Paul's churches are investigated within their cultural and social settings. For example, Paul's notorious restriction of women (1 Cor. 14:33–36; 11:2–16; regarded by some scholars as later interpolations) may have resulted from disturbances caused by some women in Corinthian society—problems that did not exist in other situations where Paul's more typical Christological perspective was affirmed (Gal. 3:28).

Theology: Paul was not a dogmatic or systematic theologian. Romans, which is a summary of his gospel, is something of an exception. Although some interpreters suppose Paul's thought underwent gradual evolution, most agree that the central features of his theology took shape early and remained consistent. The background of Paul's thought is also debated. In general, his debt to Judaism is acknowledged. Paul's theological method owes much to the rabbis, and his concept of righteousness is anticipated in the Dead Sea Scrolls. On the other hand, his view of the world is influenced by Hellenistic cosmology, and his Christological expressions (see Phil. 2:5–11) reflect the imagery of the descent and ascent of heavenly redeemers. Paul's belief that baptism accomplishes unity with Christ (Gal. 3:27) and that improper participation in the Lord's Supper causes sickness and death (1 Cor. 11:30) is reminiscent of ideas prevalent in the Hellenistic cults. Above all, however, Paul is a biblical theologian; his primary purpose is to interpret the revelation of the righteous God—the God of the OT.

Various attempts have been made to locate the center of Paul's thought. According to traditional Protestant interpretation, the center is found in Paul's doctrine of justification by faith. Actually, the terminology that presents this doctrine is limited in large measure to Romans and Galatians. The view of Albert Schweitzer—that the center of Paul's thought is his apocalyptic mysticism—has recently been revived in a new way. Apocalyptic thought, according to the new view, emphasizes a real end of history. Paul, in adopting apocalyptic categories, intends to affirm the ultimate triumph of God.

Fundamental to Paul's theology is his acceptance of Jesus as Christ and Lord. Since the Messiah has come, the end is at hand (Rom. 13:11; 1 Cor. 10:11). The decisive event has already occurred in history (Gal. 4:4) in the death and resurrection of Christ (1 Cor. 15:20). Since the Messiah is the crucified one (1 Cor. 1:23), the cross is crucial to Paul's Christology (1 Cor. 2:2). Through the crucified one, the love of God is revealed (Rom. 5:8)—a revelation of the Creator in the person of Jesus Christ (2 Cor. 4:6).

The other side of this revelation of love is the disclosure of God's wrath (Rom. 1:18). For Paul, wrath means judgment or alienation from God. Paul argues that efforts by Gentiles and Jews to get right with God have failed (Rom. 1:18–3:20). As alienated from God, people are under the control of sin, which enslaves humanity (Rom. 5:21; 6:6) and results finally in death (Rom. 5:12–21; 6:23). The law that reveals God's righteous demands (Rom. 7:12) also shows people to be sinners (Rom. 7:13). Moreover, the law is helpless as an instrument for salvation (Gal. 3:21); it even encourages people to seek to establish their own righteousness by self-centered effort (Rom. 10:3).

The new revelation of God's righteousness (or justification; one Greek word underlies both translations) is disclosed in Christ (Rom. 3: 21–22). This revelation is a gift of God's grace (Rom. 3:24). It shows both that God is righteous and that God gives righteousness to people (Rom. 3:26). As a gift of grace, righteousness is conveyed even to sinners and Gentiles. This forgiving grace of God does not compromise God's moral integrity. The revelation in Christ shows that God's gracious mercy and God's righteousness are consistent. This saving action of God is announced in the gospel—the powerful proclamation (Rom. 1:16) in which Christ is re-presented (Gal. 3:1). The response by which God's action is claimed by people is faith (Rom. 3:22, 25; 10:17)—a venturesome commitment to the Crucified One (Phil. 3:9–11). To persons who respond in faith, God grants a new relationship that is variously characterized as justification (Rom. 3:24, 26; Gal. 2:16), redemption (Gal. 4:5; 1 Cor. 1:30), and reconciliation (2 Cor. 5:18–19; Rom. 5:10).

The new situation can be characterized as a life of freedom and responsibility. The person of faith is free from wrath (Rom. 5), sin (Rom. 6), law (Rom. 7), and death (Rom. 8). In response to God's grace, the person of faith is called to ethical obedience. Ethics is central to Paul's thought; he believes the whole law is summed up in the command of love (Rom. 13:9; Gal. 5:14). The demand of love has its norm in Christ (2 Cor. 5:14); the law of love is the law of Christ (1 Cor. 9:21; Gal. 6:2). In the ethical struggle, the follower of Christ is aided by the Spirit which God in the last days has given (Rom. 8:4, 9–11; Gal. 5:25). The response of faith creates a community—the people of God (Gal. 6:16). Their central act of worship is the Lord's Supper—a common meal in which the community celebrates the presence of Christ and anticipates his coming (1 Cor. 11:23–26). In depicting the church as the body of Christ (1 Cor. 12:12–27; Rom. 12:4–5), Paul stresses the unity of the community and the interdependence of its members in doing the work of God.

See also Acts of the Apostles, The; Antioch; Caesarea; Corinth; Ephesus; Epistle; Faith; Gallio; Gamaliel; Gentile; Justification; Letter; Lord's Supper, The; Messiah; Onesimus; Pharisees; Philippi; Pseudonym; Synagogue; Tarsus; and individual articles on the Letters of Paul.

Bibliography

Beker, J. Christiaan. *Paul the Apostle: The Triumph of God in Life and Thought.* Philadelphia: Fortress, 1980.

Bornkamm, Günther. *Paul.* New York: Harper & Row, 1971.

Jewett, Robert. *A Chronology of Paul's Life.* Philadelphia: Fortress, 1979.

Keck, Leander E. *Paul and His Letters.* Proclamation Commentaries. Philadelphia: Fortress, 1979.

Meeks, Wayne A. *The First Urban Christians: The Social World of the Apostle Paul.* New Haven: Yale University Press, 1983.

W.R.B.

Paulus, Sergius (paw'luhs, suhr'ji-uhs), the Roman proconsul when Paul and Barnabas visited Cyprus (Acts 13:5–12). He is pictured as an intelligent Gentile, sympathetic to the Christian gospel. According to Acts, he became a Christian after Paul caused the blindness of the hostile Jewish magician Elymas or Bar-Jesus. ***See also*** Cyprus; Elymas; Proconsul.

pavement. ***See*** Gabbatha.

pe (pay), the seventeenth letter of the Hebrew alphabet; its numerical value is eighty. In proto-Sinaitic inscriptions this letter was represented by a pictograph of either a mouth or a corner. The form developed in early Phoenician and Hebrew scripts, which are the prototypes of Latin "P" and Greek gamma. The Aramaic cursive script developed medial and final forms, and these are the ancestors of the classical Hebrew square forms of the letter. ***See also*** Writing.

פ

peace, a word with a wide range of meanings in both the OT and the NT. Its root meaning in the OT (Heb. *shalom*) is wholeness or well-being, and it can be used in both religious and secular contexts. It is used as a general greeting (Judg. 6:23; Ezra 5:7; Dan. 4:1) and as a farewell (Exod. 4:18; 2 Sam. 15:9). In these uses, it seems to indicate good wishes for the people addressed and friendly intentions on the part of the speaker. It is also used to indicate peace between nations as opposed to war (Josh. 10:1, 4; 1 Sam. 7:14; 1 Kings 5:12).

Peace is often associated with other terms. The OT speaks of "peace and security," usually from invasion (2 Kings 20:19; Ps. 122:7) and "peace and prosperity" (Deut. 23:6; Ezra 9:12). Here, peace is associated with material well-being, good harvests and safety from wild beasts and enemies (Lev. 26:6–10; Zech. 8:12). Peace is also found in conjunction with moral concepts. It is associated with truth in the sense of faithfulness (Esther 9:30; Zech. 8:16, 19). Above all, it is found in parallel with righteousness (Ps. 85:10; Isa. 60:17). Righteousness will bring peace (Isa. 32:17), but there is no peace for the wicked (Isa. 48:22; 57:21).

Peace is the gift of God (Lev. 26:6; 1 Kings 2:33; Pss. 29:11; 85:8; Isa. 26:12). The false prophets cry, "Peace, peace," at times when the true prophets know that God is not sending peace (Jer. 6:14; 8:11; Ezek. 13:10, 16). The OT speaks of God's covenant of peace in connection with priests (Num. 25:12–13; Mal. 2:4–6) and in connection with God's promises to Israel (Isa. 54:10). In Ezekiel, God's peace is the future or eschatological blessing (Ezek. 34:25–31; 37:26), and, in Isaiah, the Messiah will be a Prince of Peace (Isa. 9:6).

Throughout the various OT uses of peace as material well-being, righteousness, and as having its source in God, the emphasis tends to be relational: peace exists between people or between people and God. The idea of peace as individual spiritual peace with God or internal peace of mind is not an OT notion.

The Greek word for "peace" normally means simply the absence of war or conflict. In the NT, however, the word also acquires much of the range of *shalom* and some new, specifically Christian understandings. As in the OT, it is used in the Gospels as a greeting and farewell (John 20:19, 21, 26; Mark 5:34; Luke 7:50). This peace appears to be a concrete blessing which the disciples can give to others, but, if the others are unworthy, it returns to the disciples (Matt. 10:13; Luke 10:5, 6). Virtually all of the NT Letters include "peace" in their opening greeting, usually paired with "grace" (e.g., Rom. 1:7; 1 Cor. 1:3; 2 Cor. 1:2; Gal. 1:3).

The term is used in the NT to mean absence of strife among individuals or nations (Luke 11:21; 14:32; Rev. 6:4). It is also used for order and concord within the Christian congregation: Paul frequently exhorts Christians to be at peace with one another (Rom. 14:19; 1 Cor. 14:33; 2 Cor. 13:11; 1 Thess. 5:13; cf. also Mark 9:50). Christians should strive for peace with all people, Christian or not (Heb. 12:14). Paul writes, "If possible, so far as it depends upon you, live peaceably with all. Beloved, never avenge yourselves, but leave it to the wrath of God" (Rom. 12:18–19). Here and in Jesus' commands on not resisting evil and on loving one's enemies (Matt. 5:38–48; Luke 6:27–36), the NT advocates a nonaggressive stance.

The association between peace and material prosperity found in the OT is not stressed in the NT; rather, the connection between peace and spiritual blessing is emphasized. Peace occurs in association with righteousness (Rom. 14:17; Heb. 12:11; James 3:18), grace (Phil. 1:2; Rev. 1:4), mercy (Gal. 6:16; 1 Tim. 1:2), love (Jude 2), joy (Rom. 14:17; 15:13), and life (Rom. 8:6).

The spiritual blessings are from God. God is a God of peace (Rom. 15:33; Phil. 4:9; 1 Thess. 5:23; Heb. 13:20). The gospel can be described as the gospel of peace (Acts 10:36; Eph. 6:15). Christ's work is to bring peace. Christ's death has accomplished peace between God and humanity (Rom. 5:1; Col. 1:20) and peace between Jew and Gentile (Eph. 2:14, 17). Yet of greater value than peace is obedience to God's will. That is why in the Gospels Jesus also speaks of bringing not peace but a sword, creating division in families where some obey God's will by following Jesus, and others do not (Matt. 10:34–36; Luke 12:51–53).

Finally, in the NT, the notion of individual spiritual peace or peace of mind is found in a few passages. The peace of God (Phil. 4:7) or the peace of Christ (Col. 3:15) may rule people's hearts; a mind set on the Spirit is life and peace (Rom. 8:6). The God of hope may fill one with joy and peace (Rom. 15:13). ***See also*** Reconciliation. J.D.

peace offering. ***See*** Worship.

pearl, a lustrous concretion formed by a mollusk consisting of the same material as its shell. It is the only gem produced by a living process.

Its association with gold and costly attire (1 Tim. 2:9), gold and precious stones (Rev. 17:4; 18:16), and other precious materials (Rev. 18: 12) indicates that pearls were very valuable and highly esteemed in the Hellenistic world. As a result the twelve gates of the new Jerusalem are described as twelve individual pearls (Rev. 21:21) and entering the Kingdom of God is portrayed as finding a pearl of great price that is worth all one has (Matt. 13:45–46).

There are no clear references to pearls in the OT. R.H.S.

Pedahzur (pe-dah'zuhr; Heb., "the Rock [divine title] has redeemed"), the father of Gamaliel who was the leader of the tribe of Manasseh during the wilderness wandering (Num. 1:10; 10:23).

Pedaiah (pe-dah'yah; Heb., "the Lord has ransomed"). **1** The father of Joel, an officer of King David in charge of the western territory of Manasseh (1 Chron. 27:20). **2** The father of Zebidah, the mother of King Jehoiakim (2 Kings 23:26). **3** The third son of King Jehoiachin (Jeconiah) and father of Zerubbabel and Shimei (1 Chron. 3: 18–19). According to Hag. 1:1, 12, 14; 2:2, 23; Ezra 3:2, 8; 5:2; and Neh. 12:1, Shealtiel, the brother of Pedaiah, was the father of Zerubbabel. **4** One of the men who assisted Nehemiah in rebuilding the wall of Jerusalem (Neh. 3:25). He was a son of Parosh, an important postexilic clan (Ezra 8:3; Neh. 7:8). **5** The grandfather of Sallu, a Benjaminite resident of postexilic Jerusalem (Neh. 11:7; cf. 1 Chron. 9:7). **6** A Levite appointed by Nehemiah as treasurer in the storehouse to distribute food to Levites (Neh. 13: 13). **7** One of the men who stood at the left hand of Ezra during the reading of the Torah in Jerusalem (Neh. 8:4). M.A.S.

peg. ***See*** Pin.

Pekah (pee'kah, a shortened form of the name Pekahiah, Heb., "Yahweh opened [the eyes]"). The two forms are distinguished in the Bible, however, since two successive kings of Israel had the same name. Pekah, the son of Remaliah, seized the Northern Kingdom's throne by murdering king Pekahiah, the son of Menahem.

2 Kings 15:27 assigns a twenty-year reign to Pekah, but he could hardly have ruled in Samaria longer than three years (735–732 B.C.), since contemporary Assyrian records show that Menahem was still on the throne in 737 B.C. One solution is to assume that Pekah had already begun to rule independently in Gilead prior to the murder of Pekahiah.

Pekah was the ally of King Rezin of Damascus, who may have supported Pekah's usurpation of the throne. In contrast to Menahem and his son Pekahiah, who had been submissive vassals of Assyria, Pekah supported Rezin's attempt to establish an anti-Assyrian coalition. Tyre and Philistia joined them, but Ahaz of Judah refused. A combined Aramean-Israelite army attacked Jerusalem in an attempt to replace Ahaz with a certain Tabeel, but the attempt failed (Isa. 7: 1–10), and Assyria soon crushed the allies. Pekah himself was murdered by Hoshea, who managed to secure Assyrian confirmation to rule over what remained of Israel. ***See also*** Ahaz; Isaiah, The Book of; Rezin. J.J.M.R.

Pekahiah (pek-ah-hī'ah; Heb., "God opened [his eyes]," i.e., looked protectingly upon the child), the son of Menaham and king of Israel, the northern state, from 738 to 737 B.C. in its last, unstable period prior to the destruction of the capital, Samaria, in 722 B.C. After a brief reign he was assassinated by one of his officers of the same name, Pekah ben Remaliah, who then took the throne (2 Kings 15:23–26). It is possible that Pekah usurped both the throne and throne name of his predecessor. Pekahiah and his father were pro-Assyrian. With his death an anti-Assyrian policy was implemented, leading to war with Judah. R.J.C.

Pelaiah (pe-lay'ee-uh; Heb., "Yah [God] has performed a wonder"). **1** The son of Elioenai, descendant of David and in the royal lineage of the kings of Judah through Zerubbabel (1 Chron. 3:24). **2** One, probably a Levite, who explained to the people the law read by Ezra (Neh. 8:7). **3** A Levite who signed the postexilic covenant to keep the law (Neh. 10:10); perhaps the same as 2 above.

Pelatiah (pel-uh-tī'uh; Heb., "Yah [God] has rescued"). **1** A descendant of David and in the royal lineage of the kings of Judah through Zerubbabel (1 Chron. 3:21). **2** One of the leaders of the Simeonite clan of Ishi who drove out the Amalekites and settled on Mount Seir (Edom; 1 Chron. 4:42). **3** A leader of the people in postexilic Jerusalem who signed the covenant to keep the law (Neh. 10:22). **4** A corrupt leader in Jerusalem during the Exile seen by Ezekiel in a vision; he symbolized an attitude of arrogant false security and a misunderstanding of God's purposes in the Exile. His death represented God's judgment on such a distorted perspective (Ezek. 11:1–13). D.R.B.

Peleg (pe'leg), the ancestor of the Mesopotamian branch of the sons of Eber ("Hebrews")—those who lived by irrigation (cf. Heb. *peleg*, "canal")—through whom Abram was descended from Shem (Gen. 11:16–26). "In his days the earth was divided" (Gen. 10:25), an allusion to the tower of Babel story, plays on a word meaning "divide" *(palag)*. As an ancestor of Abraham (Gen. 11:16–26), he was also an ancestor of Jesus (Luke 3:35).

Peleth (pe'leth). **1** The father of one of the conspirators in Korah's rebellion (Num. 16:1). "Peleth," however, is probably a mistake for "Pallu" (cf. Num. 25:6, 8). **2** A Jerahmeelite (1 Chron. 2:33).

Pelethites (pe'le-thīts), a group of mercenaries who, along with the Cherethites, constituted David's bodyguard (2 Sam. 8:18; 23:23). Though their origins are obscure, the Pelethites probably had Aegean or Anatolian forebears, who, like the ancestors of the Cherethites and Philistines, settled on the coastal plain of Palestine at the time of the invasions of the Peoples of the Sea. David may have won their allegiance while he was in the service of the Philistine king of Gath (1 Sam. 27).

Pelge (pel'guh). ***See*** Peleg.

pelican, a large web-footed bird with a large bill and pouch beneath it for catching fish. Two species of pelicans can be seen seasonally in Israel today: *Pelecanus onocrotalus* and *Pelecanus crispus*. While the word "pelican" appears in lists of unclean birds (Lev. 11:18; Deut. 14:17), it is questionable whether that is a good translation. The Hebrew word so translated *(ga'ath)* means "one who vomits" and it seemed to fit the pelican well, since it was assumed (falsely) to regurgitate food for its young. "Scops-owl" has been suggested as a more appropriate translation.

Pella (pel'ah). **1** A city in Macedonia that was the home of its kings. **2** A major site in the Transjordan prominent as a city of the Decapolis (Matt. 4:25; Mark 5:20) in Roman times. Modern Khirbet Fahil, it stands in the lower foothills of the eastern edge of the Jordan Valley about eighteen miles south of the Sea of Galilee and about seven miles southeast of Beth-shan. Nourished by a strong spring at the south foot of the 100-foot-high, 400-yard-long tell, the site has been inhabited at least since Chalcolithic times (3000 B.C.). The site is currently under archaeological exploration by a combination of Australian and American excavators, and its history can only be sketched tentatively. It flourished in Canaanite occupation (Middle and Late Bronze Ages, 2000–1200 B.C.) and drew mention in the Tell el-Amarna letters (as Pehel, 1400 B.C.). Excavations in 1958 and 1967 brought evidence of occupation in the Iron Age I and Iron Age II periods (1200–600 B.C.). It was expanded and revitalized

Columns stand at the site of ancient Pella of the Decapolis. In the background is the 400-yard-long, 100-foot-high tell.

in Hellenistic times (334–63 B.C.), being taken from the Ptolemies by the Seleucids in 218 B.C. That trade flourished in this period is evident from recovered Rhodian jar handles. Capture by the Hasmonean Alexander Janneus (83–82 B.C.) may have inflamed anti-Jewish sentiment in the people. The Roman general Pompey took it in 63 B.C., launching another period of prosperous expansion. Evidence of Christian use of the city as refuge during the first Jewish revolt (A.D. 66–70) is still inconclusive. Byzantine occupation saw considerable expansion, as elsewhere in the period (Hesban, for example), reaching its greatest extent in the fifth and sixth centuries. Islamic occupation began in A.D. 635 and continued through the Middle Ages. Decline in the last few centuries led to its loss until rediscovered in the nineteenth century. ***See also*** Maccabees.

Bibliography

Smith, R. H. *Pella of the Decapolis, Vol. I: The 1967 Season of The College of Wooster Expedition to Pella.* Wooster, OH: College of Wooster, 1973.

R.S.B.

Pelusium (pel-o͞o'see-uhm). ***See*** Sin.

pen. ***See*** Writing.

pendant. ***See*** Amulet; Jewelry.

Peninnah (pe-nin'uh), one of the wives of Elkanah and the rival of Hannah (1 Sam. 1:2, 4).

penknife. ***See*** Writing.

penny. ***See*** Denarius.

Pentapolis (Gk., "five cities"), in Philistia a league of five cities ruled by five lords (Josh. 13:3; 1 Sam. 7:7). In Wisd. of Sol. 10:6 Pentapolis refers to the five cities of the plain (Gen. 14:2). Cyrene was part of a Pentapolis in Cyrenaica. ***See also*** Philistia.

Pentateuch (pen'tah-to͞ok), the first five books of the OT, traditionally called the Law of Moses. ***See also*** Hexateuch.

Pentateuch, Sources of. ***See*** Sources of the Pentateuch.

Pentateuch, the Samaritan. ***See*** Samaritans; Texts, Versions, Manuscripts, Editions.

Pentecost (pen'tuh-kawst; from the Gk., "fiftieth"), a religious observance that has roots in the OT and continues to be observed in both Judaism and Christianity.

As a designation for a particular religious observance, the Greek word appears only twice in the LXX, namely, in Tob. 2:1, and 2 Macc. 12: 32. In the Hebrew OT, the customary name for the observance is the Feast of Weeks (Heb. *Shavuot*). It is regarded as the second of three obligatory observances, coming between Passover and Tabernacles (cf. Exod. 23:14–17; 34: 18–24; Deut. 16:16; 2 Chron. 8:13). In Exod. 23: 16, it is called "the feast of harvest, of the first fruits of your labor, of what you sow in the field." In Exod. 34:22, the Feast of Weeks is further defined as "the first fruits of wheat harvest." These phrases indicate that the Feast of Weeks was originally an agricultural festival, an occasion on which the community was expected to show gratitude to God for the first fruits, i.e., the early harvest.

Dating: The dating of this festival also suggests its original agricultural context. Deut. 16:9 says that it is to be dated seven weeks "from the time you first put the sickle to the standing grain." Lev. 23:15–16 directs: "And you shall count from the morrow after the sabbath, from the day that you brought the sheaf of the wave offering; seven full weeks shall they be, counting fifty days to the morrow after the seventh sabbath." Josephus calculated the date of Pentecost as the fiftieth day after the first day of Passover, and, in time, this manner of calculation became standard.

According to OT regulations, one was not allowed to work on the day of Pentecost. The sacrifice of various animals and of bread made from newly harvested grain was required (cf. Lev. 23:15–21; Num. 28:26–31).

In the Hellenistic period, (300 B.C.–A.D. 300) Pentecost began to lose its association with agriculture and came increasingly to be associated with the religious history of the Hebrew people. The book of *Jubilees*, continuing to refer to it as "first fruits" (22:1), identifies it with the covenant between God and Noah (Jub. 6:1–21; cf. Gen. 8:20–22; 9:8–17). It was probably after the destruction of the Temple in A.D. 70 that Pentecost was finally transformed into an observance of the giving of Torah on Mount Sinai. Exod. 19:1 was interpreted to mean that the interval between Passover and the arrival at Sinai was fifty days. Thus, in Judaism, *Shavuot* continues to be an observance of thanksgiving for Torah.

The NT shows clearly that Pentecost was celebrated in the first century and that it came to have a special Christian significance. In writing to the Corinthians, Paul says that he plans to stay in Ephesus until Pentecost (1 Cor. 16:8). Apparently, he expects his readers to understand his meaning, a fact that has led some interpreters to suggest that Pentecost had become a Christian observance as early as Paul's time. Paul does not make another explicit reference to Pentecost, but in Rom. 11:16 he appears to have the observance in mind when he speaks of offering a lump of dough as first fruits.

Pentecost in Acts: The book of Acts also speaks of Pentecost in connection with Paul's travels (20:16), but of greatest interest is the description of the first Pentecost after the death and resurrection of Jesus (Acts 2:1–42). In this passage, the apostles and others have convened in Jerusalem on the day of Pentecost. The author of Acts reports that there was a sudden sound "like the rush of a mighty wind" (v. 2) from heaven, followed by "tongues as of fire, distributed and resting on each one of them" (v. 3). As a result, the apostles began to speak in tongues, i.e., in languages that were understood by Jews and proselytes from many nations. The apostle Peter then interpreted the event as a fulfillment of the prophecy of Joel 2:8–32. He proclaimed that the last days had arrived and that Jesus had been raised from the dead, and he called for repentance. As a result, about three thousand persons were added to the group of believers.

Within the literary context of Acts, the events associated with Pentecost constitute the fulfillment not only of the prophecy of Joel but also of the promise of Jesus. In Acts 1:8, just prior to his ascension, the risen Jesus had said, "You shall receive power when the Holy Spirit has come upon you; and you shall be my witnesses in Jerusalem and in all Judea and Samaria and to the end of the earth." Thus, events of Pentecost are presented in Acts as the fulfillment of this promise: on that day, the Holy Spirit did indeed come upon the apostles and empowered them to witness to Jesus the Christ. The event is celebrated in many Christian bodies on Pentecost Sunday, which is the seventh Sunday after Easter in the church calendar. ***See also*** Acts of the Apostles, The; Feasts, Festivals, and Fasts; Spiritual Gifts; Tongues as of Fire; Tongues, Speaking with. J.B.T.

Penuel (pen-yo͞o'el; or Peniel; Heb., "face of God"), a city located on the Jabbok (modern River Zerqa), east of the Jordan. Here Jacob wrestled with a "man" (Gen. 32:24–31). Gideon was refused food by its inhabitants (Judg. 8:8–9) and later took revenge (Judg. 8:25). It was "built" by Jeroboam (ca. 924–903 B.C.; 1 Kings 12:25) and is probably listed as one of the cities conquered by Pharaoh Shishak (ca. 922 B.C.). Commentators locate it at modern Tulūl edh-Dhahab, particularly the eastern mound. In 1 Chron. 4:4 and 8:25 it is probably used as a personal name. ***See also*** Gideon; Jacob; Jeroboam I; Shishak.

people, peoples, terms used to translate a number of Hebrew and Greek terms referring to different kinds of social, ethnic, or cultural collectivities (the KJV does not use the plural "peoples" except in Rev. 10:11 and 17:15, causing some confusion cleared up by the RSV, which uses both "people" and "peoples"; see esp. Ps. 67:4; Isa. 55:4; 60:2). Interest in the origins of the various peoples of the world is evident in genealogies (Gen. 5, 10) and in the Tower of Babel story about the development of different languages (Gen. 11). In neither of these instances, however, are there careful distinctions drawn between geography and ethnography. Genesis 10 reflects an important division between peoples based on language groups. Semitic (from Shem) peoples (speaking Hebrew and Aramaic) were prominent in Palestine. Other Semitic peoples spoke Akkadian (Assyro-Babylonian) and dialects of Arabic (Minaean, Sabaean, and Ethiopic). The Egyptians, for the most part, constituted a Hamitic (from Ham) group. Indo-Aryans (from Japheth) constituted a third major division.

The most important use of the term "people" (Heb. *'am*) in the OT is as a sociocultural designation for the social entirety of Israel, in contrast to the term "nation" (Heb. *gôy*), which is used chiefly as a political term. This distinction is evident in Num. 23:9. "Lo, [Israel is] a people *['am]* dwelling alone, and not reckoning itself among the nations *[gôyim]*." Israel is often simply called "the people" (Heb. *ha 'am*) or "the people of Yahweh" (Heb. *'am yĕhwâh;* Judg. 5: 11, 13; 1 Sam. 2:24). In the NT "the people of God" is sometimes used to describe the "old Israel" (Heb. 11:25; Matt. 1:21; Luke 1:68; Rom. 11:1–2) but is more importantly used as a designation of the church (Rom. 9:25–26; 2 Cor. 6:14; Titus 2:14).

In several instances in the OT "the people" refers to the community acting with authority in making covenants or declaring war (Judg. 5: 2; 21:2, 15; 1 Sam. 4:4; 14:45). "The people" also designates a juridical community (Exod. 22:28; 23:11). Primary subgroups within Israel are also called "a people" (*'am;* Joseph in Josh. 17:14–17; Zebulun in Judg. 5:18).

The phrase "people of the land" occurs frequently in the OT, especially in Jeremiah, Ezekiel, 2 Kings, and 2 Chronicles, where it is probably a term designating the qualified male citizenry as opposed to the ruling class. In Ezra and Nehemiah (Ezra 10:2, 11; Neh. 10:30) it becomes a derogatory term aimed at those who were ignorant and nonobservant Jews by the standards of Ezra and Nehemiah. ***See also*** Amorites; Canaan, Canaanites; Hittites; Horites; Nations; Semites. F.S.F.

Peor (pee'ohr; Heb., "opening"), a mountain in Moab to which Balak took Balaam (Num. 23:28). It was apparently the site of a shrine to Baal (Num. 25:3, 5) with which Israelites were involved to their subsequent detriment (Num. 25: 18; Josh. 22:17; Ps. 106:28). Its precise location is unknown.

perdition (from the Lat. for "destruction"), a term referring to the origin or goal of those who are condemned to destruction in the final judgment. It is used of Judas (John 17:12) and of the Antichrist and his followers (2 Thess. 2:3; Rev. 17:8, 11). It is also used to translate the Greek "destruction" elsewhere in the KJV (Phil. 1:28; 1 Tim. 6:9; 2 Pet. 3:7).

Perea (puh-ree'uh; from the Gk. for "beyond"), area east of the Jordan River, i.e., "beyond the Jordan" (cf. Isa. 9:1). The name occurs nowhere in the Bible except once in a few manuscripts of Luke 6:17, but is frequent in the writings of the first-century historian Josephus. The biblical expressions "beyond the Jordan" and "across the Jordan" appear to be the equivalent of Perea in Matt. 4:15, 25; 19:1; Mark 3:8; 10:1; John 1:28; 3:26; and 10:40. The area was the scene of John's baptizing, and its people flocked to hear Jesus. Jesus and his disciples apparently used the Jordan Valley route from Galilee to Judea through Perea to avoid passing through Samaria.

Located on the eastern slopes of the Transjordanian plateau, Perea's northern boundary was just south of Pella. Its southern frontier ran from the Dead Sea to Machaerus, the fortress where John the Baptist died, up to the edge of the Moabite Plateau. The eastern boundary ran north–south about fifteen miles east of the Jordan River.

In OT times, parts of Perea belonged to Gilead, Ammon, and Moab. The region was conquered and Jewish laws and customs were introduced by the Hasmonean (Maccabean) kings in the second century B.C. but reorganized by Gabinius, the Roman proconsul of Syria, in 57 B.C. At the time of Jesus, Perea was predominantly Jewish and belonged, with Galilee, to the tetrarchy of Herod Antipas, whose administrative capital for Perea was named first Livias (after the wife of Caesar Augustus) and then Julias (after their daughter, the spouse of Tiberius). Nero gave the region to Herod Agrippa II, but at the latter's death ca. A.D. 100 it was absorbed by the province of Syria. ***See also*** Agrippa II; Antipas; John the Baptist. C.H.M.

Perez (pay'rez; Heb., "a breach"; KJV: "Pharez"), a son of Judah and Tamar; his twin brother was Zerah (Gen. 38:29). From him descended the Perezite branch of the Judah tribe (Num. 26:20; 1 Chron. 2:4–5). David was a Perezite and brought prestige to the group (Ruth 4: 12, 18–19), and through this line Perez was an ancestor of Jesus, according to the genealogy found in Matt. 1:3.

perfect, perfection, the English translation of words signifying, respectively, "being complete, sound, upright, or blameless" and "the attainment of maturity." In the OT, the most common Hebrew term for "perfect" can be applied to God as perfect in knowledge, justice, fidelity, and promise keeping (Job 37:16; Deut. 32:4; 2 Sam. 22:31; Ps. 18:30); his law is perfect (Ps. 19:7). Applied to persons, the same term means "blameless" (Gen. 6:9; Deut. 18:13), "upright" (Prov. 2:21), and observant of the law (Ps. 119:1). The NT Greek term for "perfect" can mean "mature" (1 Cor. 2:6; 14:20; Heb. 5:14), and the noun means "maturity" (Heb. 6:1). The command to be "perfect"in Matt. 5:48 ("merciful" in Luke 6:36) means to be complete or inclusive in love. Christ became perfect through his sufferings (Heb. 2:10; 5:9; 7:28). Nowhere are humans considered perfect, but readers are exhorted to be perfect (or whole) by steadfast faith (James 1:4). Paul says that he has not yet attained perfection (Phil. 3:12); that will be realized only in the life to come (Phil. 3:8–21). Perfection is a gift bestowed by Christ (Heb. 10:14). ***See also*** Justification; Righteousness; Sanctification.
A.J.H.

perfume. ***See*** Cosmetics; Incense; Ointments and Perfumes.

perfumers (KJV: "apothecaries"), traders who compounded and dispensed a variety of aromatic substances. Perfumers played an important role in ancient Israel, where the aromatic oils and incense they compounded were required for religious as well as cosmetic and medicinal use, including embalming (2 Chron. 16:14). The holy anointing oil and the incense used in the tabernacle were the work of such perfumers (Exod. 30:25, 35; 37:29), who constituted a recognized guild in postexilic times (Neh. 3:8; TEV: "a maker of perfumes"), drawn from priestly families (1 Chron. 9:30). Perfumers are also mentioned in the royal household, as a class of female servants alongside cooks and bakers (1 Sam. 8:13). ***See also*** Incense; Ointments and Perfumes; Spices. P.A.B.

Perga (puhr'guh), a city near the Kestros River in the district of Pamphylia, about twelve miles inland from the southern coast of Asia Minor. Excavations at the site have brought to light an inscription indicating that the inhabitants considered Greek heroes of the Trojan War to be the founders of their city. Second-century coins minted in Perga depict a statue of Artemis Pergaia standing in a temple, evidence that the city must have been a cult site. It was at Perga that John Mark left Paul and Barnabas, on their first journey, to return to Jerusalem (Acts 13:13), and Paul and Barnabas preached here at the end of that journey as well (Acts 14:24). ***See also*** Mark; Pamphylia. M.K.M.

Pergamum (puhr'guh-muhm), an ancient city in the region of Mysia in western Asia Minor. The modern village of Bergama, Turkey, now covers part of the ancient site. One of the seven messages of the book of Revelation was addressed to Pergamum (Rev. 1:11; 2:12).

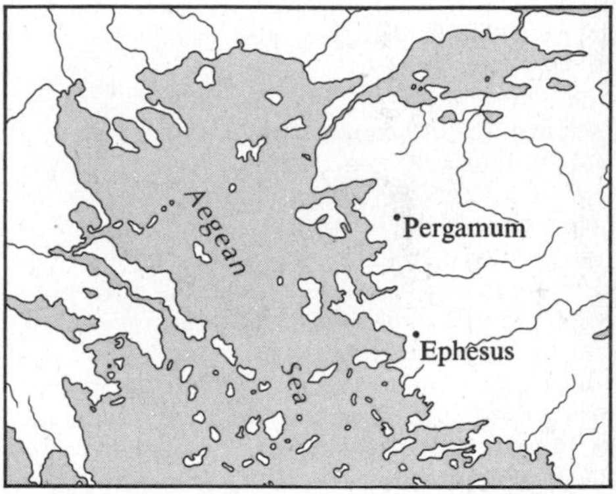

The site was occupied from prehistoric times but became famous in the Hellenistic period. In the third century B.C., Pergamum became the center of an independent kingdom. Its cultural achievements were notable. King Eumenes II (197–159 B.C.) founded a library second only to that of Ptolemy Philadelphus in Alexandria. Pergamum also had a famous school of sculpture. Its wealth was based on agricultural surplus, silver mines, stock breeding, woolen textiles, and the making of parchment.

Pergamum was one of the most beautiful of Greek cities. Its public buildings were built on terraces on a steep mountain and culminated in the palace and fortifications at the acropolis. The whole is a magnificent example of Hellenistic city planning. In 133 B.C. the last king to reign in Pergamum, Attalus III, bequeathed his kingdom which comprised parts of Phrygia, Ionia, and Caria as well as Lydia and Mysia in his will to the Romans. After his death it was constituted as the Roman province of Asia with Pergamum as its capital. Under Augustus, the province was reconstituted as a senatorial province with a governor of consular rank who governed as proconsul. The capital was probably changed at this time to Ephesus; that is, the governor landed and resided there.

During the Roman period, a shrine of Asclepius, the Greek god of healing, was built in the lower city. It was a kind of spa at which

Remains of the ancient Temple of Asclepius at Pergamum.

both natural and supernatural modes of healing were employed.

In Rev. 2:13 Pergamum is described as the place where Satan's throne is. Revelation 12–13 suggests that Satan is linked with Rome. Even though Pergamum was no longer the governor's residence when the Revelation to John was written sometime late in the first century A.D., it was one of the cities in which he regularly held court. The governor alone held the right of capital punishment. The sharp two-edged sword of Christ mentioned in the greeting (2:12) and in the threat (2:16) is contrasted implicitly with the "sword" of the governor. Another connotation of "Satan's throne" may be that Pergamum was one of the oldest and most prominent centers of the imperial cult, i.e., the worship of the Roman emperor as a divine being, in the province.

A.Y.C.

Perizzites (pair'i-zīts), one of the older population groups of the land of Canaan, usually listed as one of the six or seven inhabiting the land (Exod. 3:8, 17; 23:23; 33:2; 34:11; Deut. 7:1; 20:17; Josh. 3:10; 9:1; 11:3; 12:8; 24:11; Judg. 3:5; 1 Kings 9:20; cf. Gen. 15:20). Occasionally they are mentioned with the Canaanites as the two native peoples of Canaan (Gen. 13:7; 34:30; Judg. 1:4–5). They evidently lived in the central highlands, particularly the forested hill country of Ephraim (cf. Josh. 17:15; Judg. 1:4–5). Their identity is uncertain. Some have connected them with the Hurrians; others with the Amorites. ***See also*** Canaan, Canaanites. D.A.D.

perjury, the utterance of a false statement under oath or affirmation. The Decalogue (Ten Commandments; Exod. 20:1–17) forbids both the swearing of false oaths and the bearing of false testimony (Exod. 20:7, 16; Deut. 5:11, 20; cf. Lev. 19:12; Jer. 7:9). False witnesses are to suffer the same punishment that they had hoped to inflict upon the others (Deut. 19:16–21). In the biblical law, there is no reference to witnesses' use of an oath to substantiate their testimony. Mention is made only of the assertory oath of litigants to establish their innocence in the case. For example, bailees will pronounce an oath to prove that they did not misappropriate the property given to them for safekeeping (Exod. 22:10). Should they have sworn falsely, the law allows them to rectify their wrongdoing by making full restitution, paying a fine, and bringing a sin offering (Lev. 5:21–26). In the NT, perjured witness against Jesus is reported (Mark 14:56–59). 1 Timothy notes that perjurers are among those for whom "the law" was laid down (1:10). ***See also*** Oath. B.L.E.

persecution, a term restricted to describing formal hostile activity against a specific group. Mob action against an individual (Acts 7:57–58) or clandestine plots (Acts 23:12–15) are not persecution. While Stephen's claim that all of God's prophets were persecuted (Acts 7:52) may be an exaggeration, there is evidence of severe harassment against them in pre-exilic Israel (Isa. 28:9–10; 50:5–6; Ezek. 33:32–33; Jer. 26:20–23; cf. 11:8–23; 1 Kings 19:10; 22:26–27). Yet the fact that a prophet like Nathan, despite his unpopular message, was respected (2 Sam. 12:1–15) shows that such harassment was sporadic and not part of official policy. Only when Antiochus IV Epiphanes (175–164 B.C.) tried to suppress customs necessary for Jewish religious identity can we speak of formal hostile activity against a specific group. Both Daniel and 1 Maccabees record his policy directed against Jewish dietary rules, circumcision, and other central practices. Those who refused to give them up were "condemned to death," i.e., persecuted (1 Macc. 1:41–61).

Jesus spoke of "persecutions" coming upon his followers (Matt. 5:10–12; 10:23). This is best understood as the domestic hostility in family and synagogue caused by conversion to a new faith. Jesus did "not come to bring peace, but a sword" (Matt. 10:34), dividing households and causing financial and social loss to his followers. Because of their distinctive faith, Jesus' followers might lose "house, brothers, sisters, mother, father, children, and lands" (Mark 10:29). The problem is domestic: "a man's foes will be those of his household" (Matt. 10:36).

Paul claims that he "persecuted" the church (1 Cor. 15:9; Gal. 1:13; Phil. 3:6). Acts 8 may be an exaggerated interpretation of this, for it is doubtful if Jerusalem Jews could force the imprisonment of unorthodox Jews in Galilee, much less in Damascus. Paul's harassment was probably on the order of a Pharisaic purist stirring up local synagogues to expel deviants or to report them to local magistrates as troublemakers (as was done against Paul the Christian; cf. Acts 14:19; 17:5–7; 2 Cor. 11:23–24). Jewish hostility to Christians became formal policy after the Roman-Jewish war (66–70). Johannine Christians tell of a formal synagogue policy to expel those who confessed Jesus as the Christ (John 9:22; 12:42–43; 16:1–2). Some scholars identify this with the *Birkath ha-minim*, the ban of excommunication on heretics whose imposition is associated with the Jamnia academy.

Little is known of Nero's alleged persecution of Christians after the fire in Rome in A.D. 64. Tacitus' account (*Annales* 15.44) is heavily biased against Nero and hence unreliable. 1 Peter does not speak of a formal Roman persecution of Christians. It is only in the second century (ca. 110), at the time of Pliny the Younger (*Letters* 10.96–97), that we learn of a formal Roman policy to root out Christian beliefs. Pliny's letters to Trajan discuss imperial policy toward those who refuse to worship the emperor, less a religious than a political issue. This may be the background for the view of Roman hostility to Christians in Rev. 13–14, 17–18.

J.H.N.

Persepolis (puhr-sep'uh-lis), Persian city mentioned in 2 Macc. 9:2 as a place whose temples Antiochus IV attempted to rob. This incident demonstrated the impiety evident in Antiochus' attack on the Jewish Temple at Jerusalem (ca. 175 B.C.), an impiety that resulted in his death in 2 Macc. (2 Macc. 5:21; 7:19).

Excavations have yielded two collections of tablets in Elamite from 509–494 B.C. and 492–457 B.C. These records deal with supplies and payments and suggest that Persepolis served as an administrative center by 509 B.C. at the latest. The massive terrace on which palatial buildings stand along with the fortifications stem from the reign of Darius I (the palace was begun about 520 B.C.). Darius, Xerxes, and other Persian kings are buried in the vicinity. However, the city was unknown in the western part of the empire. The Greeks only came to know of the city when it was taken by Alexander the Great (331–330 B.C.). Though the city had offered no resistance, Alexander ordered the great palace of Xerxes destroyed. This act may have been in revenge for Xerxes' burning the temples on the Acropolis at Athens.

The great palace at Persepolis shows no signs of having been inhabited. The only objects revealed by excavators are trophies such as might be captured in war. Nor does the complex contain sanitation facilities. Therefore, it would appear that the palace complex was used for ceremonial purposes. There may have been royal dwellings below the palace on the plain. Diodorus, a historian who wrote in the first century B.C., records a later complaint that the palaces at Persepolis had been built with spoils taken from Egypt (*History* 1.146).

Overview of Persepolis; construction was begun by the Persian king Darius in the sixth century B.C.

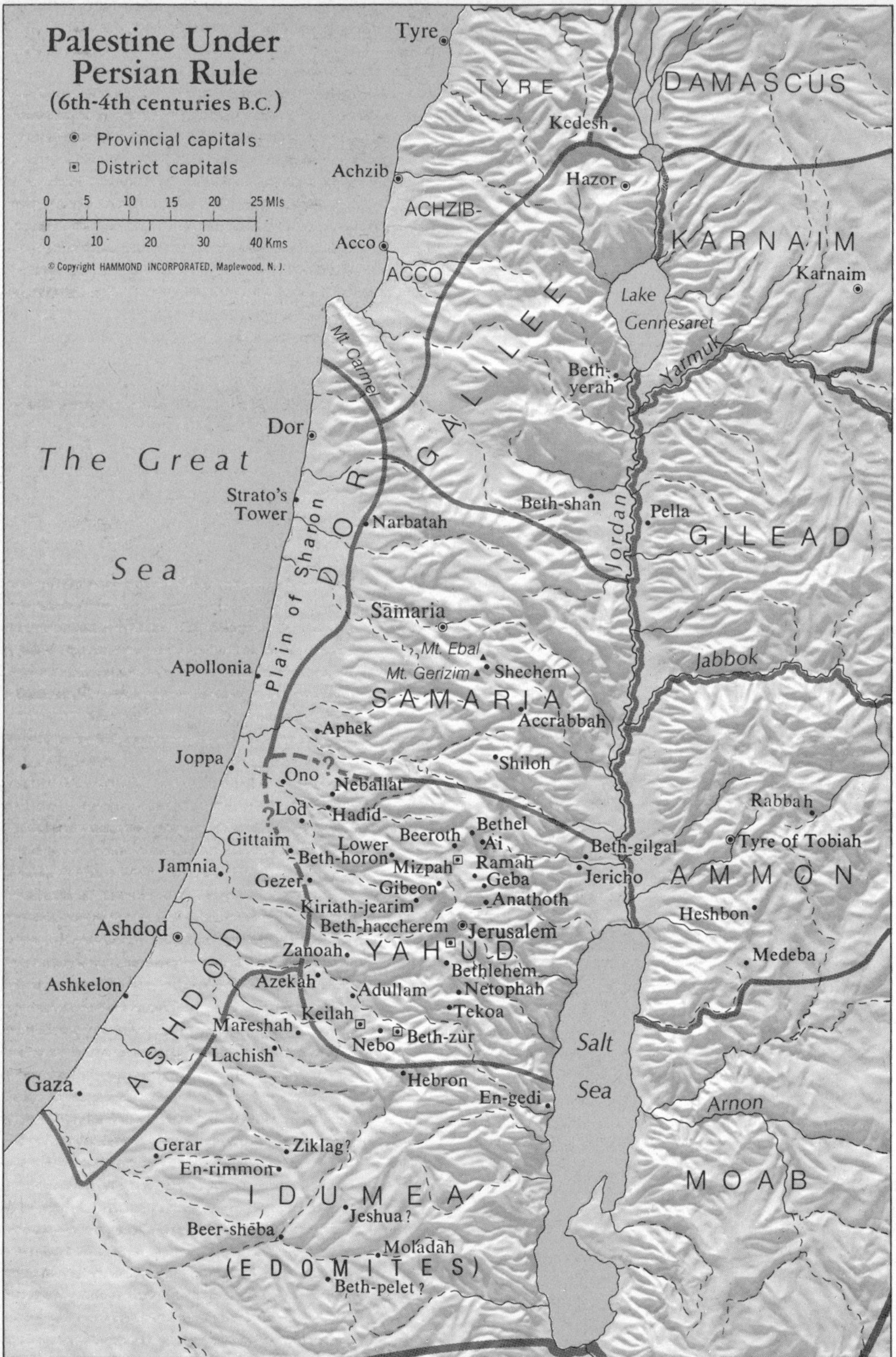
Palestine Under Persian Rule
(6th-4th centuries B.C.)
Provincial capitals
District capitals
0 5 10 15 20 25 Mls
0 10 20 30 40 Kms
© Copyright HAMMOND INCORPORATED, Maplewood, N. J.
Tyre
TYRE
DAMASCUS
Kedesh
Hazor
Achzib
ACHZIB
KARNAIM
Karnaim
Acco
ACCO
Lake Gennesaret
Yarmuk
Mt. Carmel
GALILEE
Beth-yerah
Dor
The Great Sea
DOR
Strato's Tower
Narbatah
Beth-shan
Jordan
Pella
GILEAD
Plain of Sharon
Samaria
Mt. Ebal
Mt. Gerizim
Shechem
Jabbok
Apollonia
SAMARIA
Accrabbah
Aphek
Shiloh
Joppa
Ono
Neballat
Lod
Hadid
Rabbah
Gittaim
Lower Beth-horon
Beeroth
Bethel
Ai
Beth-gilgal
Tyre of Tobiah
Jamnia
Mizpah
Ramah
Jericho
AMMON
Gezer
Gibeon
Geba
Kiriath-jearim
Anathoth
Heshbon
Ashdod
Beth-haccherem
Jerusalem
Zanoah
YAHUD
Bethlehem
Medeba
Ashkelon
Azekah
Adullam
Netophah
ASHDOD
Keilah
Tekoa
Mareshah
Nebo
Beth-zur
Salt Sea
Lachish
Hebron
Gaza
En-gedi
Arnon
Gerar
Ziklag?
En-rimmon
MOAB
IDUMEA
Jeshua?
Beer-sheba
Moladah
(EDOMITES)
Beth-pelet?
NABATEANS

Though the tablets record the presence of magi and offerings to the god Ahura-Mazada, there is no indication that the buildings constituted a cult center. The great treasury at Persepolis may have given rise to the story in 2 Maccabees. A number of sources do suggest that there was a temple of Anahita near Persepolis. Susa was the capital of the region. The king may have come to Persepolis for some form of New Year festival. A report made to Darius shows that he was there during the winter of 495/94 B.C. The city was not rebuilt after its destruction by Alexander the Great.

P.P.

Persia, an empire that at its height stretched from Greece in the west to India in the east. The Persian Empire came into being with the victories of Cyrus the Great over his Medan overlord (ca. 550 B.C.) and lasted until the conquests of Alexander the Great (ca. 330 B.C.). The origin and original locality of the ancestors of the Persians remain uncertain; links with Parsua, south of Lake Urmia (some 175 miles west of the southern end of the Caspian Sea), are possible, but more probable are those with Persis, east of the Persian Gulf, where Pasargadai and Persepolis, great centers of the Empire, were situated.

Rulers: The rulers of the Empire were: Cyrus (king of Anshan ca. 560 B.C., d. 530); Cambyses (530–522); Darius I (522–486); Xerxes I (486–465); Artaxerxes I (465–424); Xerxes II (424); Sogdianos (424–423); Darius II (423–405/4); Artaxerxes II (405/4–359/8); Artaxerxes III (359/58–338/37); Artaxerxes IV (338/37–336); and Darius III (336–330). Of these, Cyrus is hailed as the chosen deliverer of the Jews from Babylon (Isa. 44:28, "my shepherd"; 45:1, "my anointed") and as stirred up by God to rebuild the Jerusalem Temple (2 Chron. 36:22–23; Ezra 1:1–2; 3:7; 4:3). Cyrus's decree authorizing this was rediscovered in the archives by Darius I and reaffirmed (Ezra 5:1–6:15). The analogy of the Cyrus cylinder, which claims the Babylonian god Marduk chose Cyrus to restore his shrine in Babylon, suggests that the Persians asserted their rights to be royal successors in both Babylon and Jerusalem, and no doubt elsewhere.

The reign of Darius I provides the dating framework for the books of Haggai and Zechariah. Artaxerxes is mentioned in Ezra 6:14; 7:1; and 9:9 and in Neh. 2:1; 5:14; and 13:6. The story of Esther is set in the reign of Ahasuerus (Xerxes, 1:1–2). A later Darius (II or III) is named in Neh. 12:22.

Both Esther and Daniel refer to Medes and Persians together (Esther 1:3, 18–19; Dan. 5:8; 6:28), particularly to stress the unalterability of their laws. Dan. 5:31 and 6:28 distinguish a Medan from a Persian empire (cf. 10:1), but 8:20 treats the two as one. Dan. 10:13, 20–21, dealing with the conflicts of the empires, speaks of a "prince of Persia" against whom the angel Michael represents divine power on behalf of the Jews (cf. also 11:2). In a list of officials in Ezra 4:9–10, Persians and other peoples appear among those who were settled in Samaria and elsewhere by Osnappar (probably Ashurbanipal).

Lack of precision in statements about Persia suggests limited knowledge among the Jews of the background history. The impression of benevolent Persian protection is clear in some passages (e.g., Ezra 1:11; 5:5; 7:6, 9, 27; Neh. 2:8) but is not borne out by hostile material in Ezra 4:8–23 or by distress under Persian rule indicated in Ezra 9:9 and Neh. 9:36–37. Persia, like other ancient empires, taxed local populations heavily; imperial policy was dictated by strategic and economic needs, especially in wars against Egypt, which necessarily affected Judah, and against Greece. The Empire was skillfully administered, but rebellions were frequent, including those of satraps in the province Beyond the River to which Judah belonged.

Religion: The nature of Persian religion in this period remains a matter of debate. Although Zoroaster seems to have lived in the seventh century B.C., no certain date can be given for the activity of this great religious leader and hence for the time when his influence might be expected to appear; how far and when the particular emphases and practices of Zoroastrianism spread remains unclear. Influences from Zoroastrianism on Judaism and Christianity are often claimed; the emphasis on the supreme deity of light, Ahura Mazda, and on conflict with darkness, Ahriman, could provide stimulus to the belief in conflict against evil forces in which the God of Israel was engaged, perhaps influencing its expression. Biblical thought about God, while stressing that conflict, does not give to the power of darkness the degree of independence that seems to appear in Zoroastrianism. Nevertheless, in both religious systems, the triumph of light is affirmed. Other points of influence, especially in angelology, have often been proposed. ***See also*** Artaxerxes; Cyrus II; Darius; Ezra; Media, Medes; Nehemiah, The Book of.

Bibliography

Boyce, M. *Zoroastrians: Their Religious Beliefs and Practices*. London: Routledge and Kegan Paul, 1979.

Cook, J. M. *The Persian Empire*. London: J. M. Dent & Sons, 1983.

P.R.A.

Map opposite: The territory of the ancient Israelites became part of the Persian Empire when it was established in the sixth century B.C. As part of the Persian Empire, Judah was known as "Yahud."

Persis (puhr'sis), a woman greeted by Paul as "beloved" and "one who has worked hard in the Lord" (Rom. 16:12).

Person of Christ, the. *See* Jesus Christ.

Peshitta (puh-shi'tah), a Syriac text of the Bible. ***See also*** Texts, Versions, Manuscripts, Editions.

pestle, a crushing instrument used in a vessel (mortar) to grind grain, spices, or condiments; it was usually short, hand-held, and made of wood or stone. It is used metaphorically in Prov. 27:22 for the impossibility of eliminating a fool's weakness, since it belongs irreducibly to his nature.

Peter, one of Jesus' twelve disciples. Originally named Simon, Peter was a Galilean fisherman (Mark 1:16; Luke 5:2; John 21:3), the son of John (Matt. 16:17; John 1:42; 21:15–17) and brother of Andrew. According to a tradition preserved in John 1:35–43, the brothers came from the village of Bethsaida (John 1:43; 12:21) and had been disciples of John the Baptist before they became disciples of Jesus. Peter was married (Mark 1:29–31; 1 Cor. 9:5). He is said to have owned a house in Capernaum (Mark 1:29). The traditional site of "Peter's house" has been excavated, though most of the structure on the site is from a later period.

The name "Peter" is the Greek word for "rock" *(petra)* and translates an Aramaic nickname *(Cepha')* that also means "rock." The Greek rendering of the Aramaic name, *Cephas*, is also used for Peter in the NT (John 1:42; 1 Cor. 1:12; 3:22; 9:5; 15:5; Gal. 1:18; 2:9, 11, 14). Peter's emergence as a leader among Jesus' disciples is reflected in the story found in Matt. 16:18–19 that Jesus bestowed the nickname "rock" on Simon as a sign of his future role as upholder and interpreter of the traditions established by Jesus.

Calling: All of the Gospel traditions place Peter among the first disciples to be called, frequently along with his brother Andrew and the sons of Zebedee (cf. Mark 1:16–20; Matt. 4:18–22; in John 1:40–42 Peter is summoned by Andrew and given his "name" as part of his calling). Luke 5:1–11 preserves a longer, independent story about the calling of Peter and the sons of Zebedee, which may be related to the Johannine tradition in which the risen Jesus calls the disciples away from their fishing (John 21:1–11). In its present form, this story exemplifies the ideal response to the call for discipleship. Confronted with Jesus' divine power evident in the large catch, Peter confessed his own sinfulness (Luke 5:6–8). When summoned to change his life and become a "fisher of human beings," Peter and his companions left everything in order to follow Jesus (vv. 9–11). Peter's possessions were always at Jesus' disposal. Jesus stayed at Peter's house at Capernaum, where he is said to have healed Peter's mother-in-law (Mark 1:29–31; Matt. 8:14–15; Luke 4:38–39). He used Peter's boat as a place from which to speak to the crowd (Luke 5:1–3). Matt. 14:28–33 recounts a story of Peter's attempt to walk on water as instruction to the church that it must learn to have faith in Jesus' power during its own "troubled times." Behind this story, we also see the somewhat rash and impetuous Peter who appears in all the stories handed down about him. In John 21:7, as soon as Peter hears that the Lord is on the shore, he throws on his clothes and jumps into the water.

Peter represented dictating to Mark, following an early Christian tradition; ivory relief.

Role as Leading Disciple: Peter is credited with being a leader among the disciples during Jesus' ministry. Frequently, he was their spokesman. His name always occurs first in lists of the disciples (Mark 3:16; Luke 16:14; Matt. 10:2; in Matthew "first" is added to Peter's name). Along with James and John, he is singled out for special revelations of Jesus' divinity (Mark 5:37; Luke 8:51, the healing of Jairus' daughter; Mark 9:2; Matt. 17:1; Luke 9:28, the transfiguration). He is singled out as a spokesman for the disciples in three ways: first, he is credited with special insight into Jesus' identity as God's Messiah (Mark 8:29; Luke 9:20; Matt. 16:16–17; in Matthew Jesus responds with a beatitude proclaiming that Peter's insight is a revelation of God). Second, he voices views that represent opinions of "the world," views that are rejected, as in his opposition to Jesus' prediction that it is his messianic role to suffer and die (Mark 8:31–33; Matt. 16:22–23; in keeping with his policy of omitting episodes that place Jesus' disciples in an unfavorable light, Luke omits the story of Jesus rebuking Peter). Finally, Peter requests information, as in the question to Jesus about the reward for those who have "left all" to follow him (Mark 10:28; Matt. 19:27; Luke 18: 28).

Peter's role as spokesman is expanded in the special material from which Matthew drew the information about Peter in his Gospel. As the one who is to function as a "Christian rabbi," interpreting the traditions of Jesus, Peter must have special understanding of that teaching. He is the one who requests clarification about the saying by which Jesus declared "all things clean" (Matt. 15:15; in Mark 7:17 it is simply "the disciples" who ask). In Acts 10:9–16 God reveals to Peter in a heavenly vision that "all things are clean" and thus paves the way for Peter to baptize the first Gentiles. Peter deals with the authorities on the question of paying the Temple tax and then receives further instruction from Jesus, who significantly provides for both himself and Peter (Matt. 17: 24–27). Peter also receives special instruction on forgiveness within the Christian community (Matt. 18:21–22). In the Johannine tradition there is a variant of Peter's confession of Jesus: when others have deserted Jesus, Peter confesses Jesus as "the Holy One of God" who has the words of eternal life (John 6:68–69). The impetuous Peter, acting as a "proper disciple," misunderstands the gesture of footwashing (John 13:1–10) and elicits information about the meaning of what Jesus has done. Peter is also the one who asks about the identity of Jesus' betrayer (John 13:24–25).

All the Gospels agree that Peter had impetuously promised that he would follow Jesus even to death, only to be answered with Jesus' prophecy that he would in fact deny him (Mark 14: 29–31; Luke 22:33–34; Matt. 26:33–35; John 13: 37–38). The accounts of Jesus' Passion then contain scenes in which Peter denies being one of Jesus' disciples (Mark 14:53–72 and parallels) interlocked with the scenes of Jesus being interrogated by the Jewish authorities. Peter's denial provides a foil for Jesus' faithfulness.

Luke 22:31–32 "rehabilitates" Peter through Jesus' prayer that "your faith may not fail; and when you have turned again, strengthen your brothers." In John 21:15–17 the risen Jesus elicits a threefold protestation of love, corresponding to the threefold denial, from Peter before commissioning him to feed Jesus' sheep. These passages suggest that Peter's leadership among the disciples in the post-Easter church was based on his having been the first disciple to see the risen Lord (e.g., Luke 24:34; Mark 16: 7?). Our earliest testimony to the resurrection, the creedal passage in 1 Cor. 15:3–5, places an appearance to Peter before all the others. It may also have been the occasion for a reassembling of the disciples who had scattered at the time of Jesus' arrest. However, none of the Gospel narratives recounts the circumstances of such an appearance.

Mission: Paul tells us that Peter was one of the leaders of the Jerusalem community he went to "visit" two or three years after his conversion (Gal. 1:18–19). Paul's own rhetorical agenda in Galatians would keep him from ascribing any "official" purpose to the visit. However, many scholars think that at this time Paul's gospel and mission were subject to some authority from the Jerusalem community. The overall picture of Peter as one of the chief leaders responsible for an expanding Christian mission, first to Jews, then to interested Gentiles, is confirmed by the picture of Peter in Acts 1–15. Peter may, indeed, as Acts 10–11 suggests, have been responsible for some form of compromise by which Gentiles were considered "clean" and acceptable members of the Christian community. The story of Stephen, the "Hellenists," and their mission in Acts 6–8 suggests that there were different forms of preaching to the Gentiles. The "Hellenists" preached a rejection of Jewish cult and Mosaic authority considerably more radical than that of other Christians, including Peter. Acts 8:14–17 brings this independent Samaritan mission under the aegis of the Jerusalem church by having Peter and John confer the Spirit on the converts. The dispute at the Jerusalem council over whether circumcision is to be required of Christians showed that Peter's support of a circumcision-free mission was not enough to decide the practice of the whole church (Gal. 2:1–10; Acts 15:1–29). It appears from the account in Acts 15 that leadership of the church in Jerusalem had passed over to James (esp. vv. 13–21).

Although Gal. 2:7–8 speaks of Peter as missionary "to the circumcised," he appears also to have converted Gentiles (Acts 10; 11:1–18). Castigating Peter for encouraging Jewish Christians at Antioch to separate from their Gentile brothers and sisters lest visiting Jewish Christians be scandalized by associating with Gentiles, Paul admits that Peter, himself, was willing to "live like a Gentile" (Gal. 2:11–14). Peter's attitude of compromising with the visitors may have won out, since Paul leaves Antioch at about this time (Acts 15:36–41 gives a different reason for Paul's departure, however). Peter's influence at Antioch is reflected in the Petrine traditions of Matthew (e.g., 16: 17–19), which may have originated there.

We have only very sketchy information about the rest of Peter's missionary career (1 Cor. 9:5 mentions his traveling as a missionary). Peter enjoyed considerable prestige among the Corinthians, some of whom claimed special allegiance to him (1 Cor. 1:12; 3:22). Since only Paul and Apollos are explicitly mentioned as working in Corinth, some scholars argue that Peter had gained this reputation through persons he had converted elsewhere rather than having

Peter's threefold denial of Jesus as the cock crows (cf. Matt. 26:69–75); fifth-century ivory detail.

preached in Corinth. A letter from Rome, 1 Peter, is directed to churches in rural Asia Minor, reflecting Peter's reputation there, even if, as some scholars think, he was not the author of that letter. These churches were predominately Gentile and were probably the fruit of Petrine missionary work in that area. (2 Peter, a much later writing, uses Petrine authority to counter rejection of Christian preaching about the Parousia that was in part based on false interpretations of Paul's Letters.)

Death: We know that Peter died as a martyr in Rome (1 Pet. 5:1, 13; John 21:18–19; *1 Clem.* 5: 1–6:1). But we have no early traditions about how he came there, whether he ever served as "presbyter-bishop" in Rome—a possibility that seems somewhat unlikely since apostles played a unique role superior to that of the supervisors of local churches—or what led to his martyrdom, perhaps under Nero in A.D. 64. Nor have archaeologists been convinced that excavations under St. Peter's basilica in modern-day Vatican City have uncovered the remains of the apostle. Indeed, it may not have been possible to recover the body if Peter died in the arena during Nero's persecution. Therefore, some scholars think that the original monument was a simple marker of the place where Peter died. Later development of a cult of saints and relics converted that monument into a "tomb" of the apostle. ***See also*** Acts of the Apostles, The; Antioch; Capernaum; Galatians, The Letter of Paul to the; Matthew, The Gospel According to; Peter, The First Letter of; Peter, The Second Letter of; Resurrection.

Bibliography

Brown, R., K. Donfried, and J. Reumann, eds. *Peter in the New Testament*. Minneapolis, MN: Augsburg, New York: Paulist, 1973.

Brown, R., and J. Meier. *Antioch and Rome: New Testament Cradles of Catholic Christianity*. Ramsey, NJ: Paulist, 1983.

O'Connor, D. *Peter in Rome: The Literary, Liturgical and Archaeological Evidence*. New York: Columbia University Press, 1969. P.P.

Peter, the First Letter of, first Letter attributed to the apostle Peter in the NT canon and one of the seven catholic or general Letters in the NT. Interpretations of 1 Peter have traditionally focused on three topics: baptism, suffering, and traditional exhortation. Although baptism is important (1:3, 23; 3:20–21), 1 Peter does not record a baptismal liturgy; despite the many references to suffering (1:6–7; 2:18–25; 3:8–17; 4: 12–19), it does not reflect a Roman persecution of Christians. Rather the Letter is a summary of Christian exhortation, telling newly baptized converts of their new dignity in Christ, detailing the new way of life befitting this holy conversion, and situating the new Christian life in terms of the pattern of Jesus' suffering and resurrection. The Letter aims at socializing new converts by presenting a coherent view of their new life in terms of the Christian story and symbols.

Conversion as "a New Birth": 1 Peter highlights conversion as "a new birth." By numerous contrasts, the author stresses that a radical change has taken place in the lives of converts by joining God's covenant. They have moved from

no hope to true hope (1:21)
impurity to purity (1:18; 4:3)
slavery to freedom (1:18)
perishability to imperishability (1:4, 23)
ignorance to knowledge (1:14)
flesh to spirit (4:6)
death to life (1:3)
disobedience to obedience (1:2, 22)

1

2

3

4

5

1 Painted ceramic horse from a tomb near the Philistine city of Gaza, sixth century B.C. **2** Marble sarcophagus of the Roman prefect Junius Bassus, Rome, A.D. 359. The subject matter, depicting scenes from the OT and the NT, represents a newfound freedom of expression for Christians under the emperor Constantine and the Edict of 325. **3** Sumerian bull-lyre, an ancient musical instrument found in a royal burial pit at Ur from the third millennium B.C.. This detail shows the bull's head with its original gold overlay and lapis lazuli beard and hair. **4** Head of an ancient Near Eastern man as depicted on a glazed terra-cotta tile from the Temple of Ramesses III, twelfth century B.C. **5** Statues, from left to right, of Melchizedek, Abraham holding Isaac, Moses, Samuel, and David line the jambs of the Royal Portal at Chartres Cathedral (ca. 1145–1155).

1

2

3

4

1 Carpet page with a double-armed cross and eight medallions from the *Book of Kells*, an illuminated Bible manuscript from the eighth century. **2** Initial B from the *Windmill Psalter*, thirteenth century. Within this letter is a depiction of the Tree of Jesse showing Jesse reclining in the lower loop, David crowned in the middle, and the Virgin and Child in the upper loop. Also shown are the figure of God at the very top, the creation story interwoven in the foliage, the four major and twelve minor prophets, and the symbols of the four Evangelists in the corner medallions. **3** Prism of Sennacherib. It records Sennacherib's conquest of Judah in 701 B.C. and reads in part, "[Hezekiah] I shut up like a caged bird in his royal city of Jerusalem." **4** The so-called Marzeah Tablet, showing the wedge-shaped marks of cuneiform script, in this case Ugaritic from the fourteenth century B.C.

1

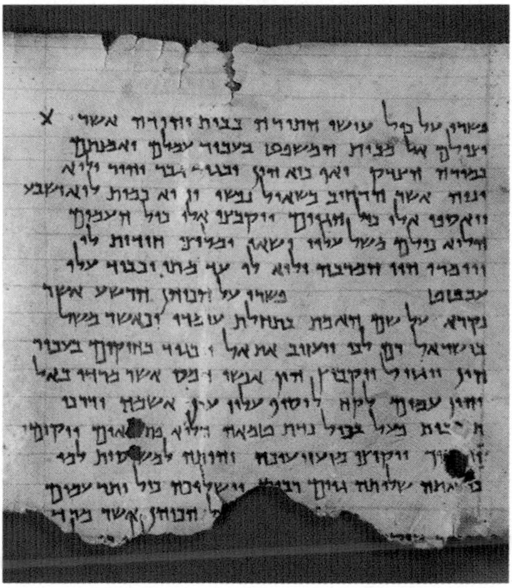

2

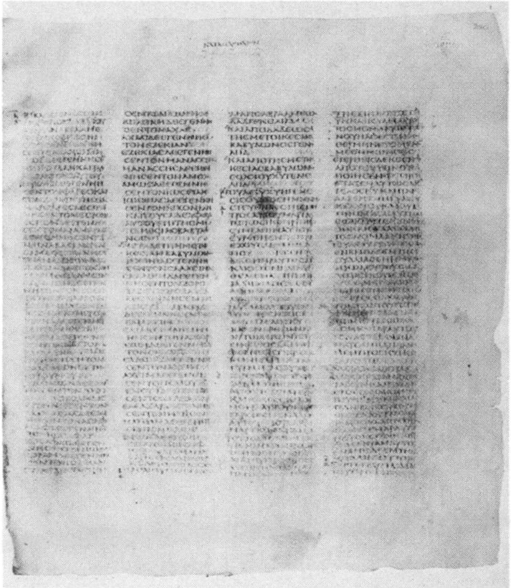

3

1 Isaiah Scroll "A," one of the Dead Sea Scrolls from the Qumran caves, open to columns 32 (right) and 33, Isa. 38:8–40:28. The Hebrew is in a Hasmonean script, ca. 100 B.C. The break in the second line of the left-hand column may have been to emphasize what follows: "A voice cries: 'In the wilderness prepare the way of the LORD, make straight in the desert a highway for our God' " (Isa. 40:3). **2** A section of the *Pesher* or commentary on the book of Habakkuk found at Qumran. It is written in Hebrew using the Jewish square script, probably of the Herodian type (50 B.C.–A.D. 40). **3** A facsimile of a page from Codex Sinaiticus, showing the opening of the Gospel According to Matthew. This parchment manuscript of the Bible, written in Greek and dating from the fourth century A.D., was found at the Monastery of St. Catherine, Sinai, in the nineteenth century.

1

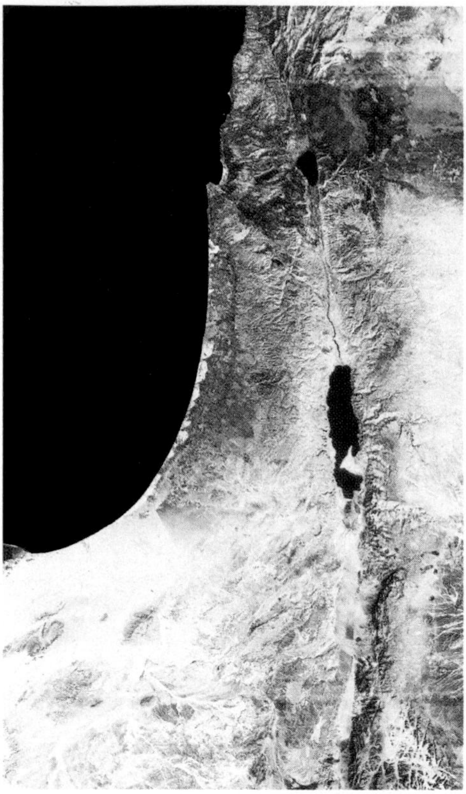

2

3

4

5

1 Columns that lined a main street in Herod's city of Caesarea, first century B.C., lie in ruins at the edge of the Mediterranean Sea. **2** Aerial view, from 570 miles above the earth, of Israel and surrounding area shows the Dead Sea, the Sea of Galilee, mountains, deserts, and (at upper left) the Mediterranean Sea. **3** The Sea of Galilee, variously referred to in the Bible as the Sea of Tiberias, Lake of Genessaret, or the Sea of Chinnereth, is a harp-shaped freshwater lake about thirty-two miles around, located in northern Palestine. **4** The Dead Sea—also called by various names in the OT and not mentioned in the NT—is actually a lake into which the river Jordan flows. Because of its high mineral content (25 percent) the Dead Sea does not support marine life. **5** The Wilderness of Judea, west of the Dead Sea, was not traversed by major trade routes due to its inimical terrain. This is the kind of countryside envisioned by the Evangelists when they describe the temptations of Jesus (e.g., Luke 4:1–2).

1

2

3

4

5

1 Ancient Egyptians winnowing with wooden scoops, much as the ancient Israelites did with shallow baskets and as is still done in many places in the Near East. A mural from the Tomb of Mennah, scribe of Thutmose IV (fourteenth century B.C.). **2** Ceramic "pilgrim flasks" from the cemetery of Deir el-Ballah, thirteenth century B.C. **3** A Hellenistic terra-cotta lamp dates to the Maccabean era (167–63 B.C.). Its typical Greek form, with a long nozzle for the wick and a broad opening in the cover to receive the oil, indicates it was probably imported into ancient Israel. **4** Flowers blossoming in the countryside of Galilee along the way to Safed. **5** Terraced rows of olive trees near Antipatris along the road from Jerusalem to Caesarea. Hardy enough to grow almost anywhere, the olive tree was ubiquitous in the biblical landscape. Its fruit was eaten and the oil derived from it had many uses: in cooking, for lamps, as a medicine, for anointing, and in sacrifices.

1

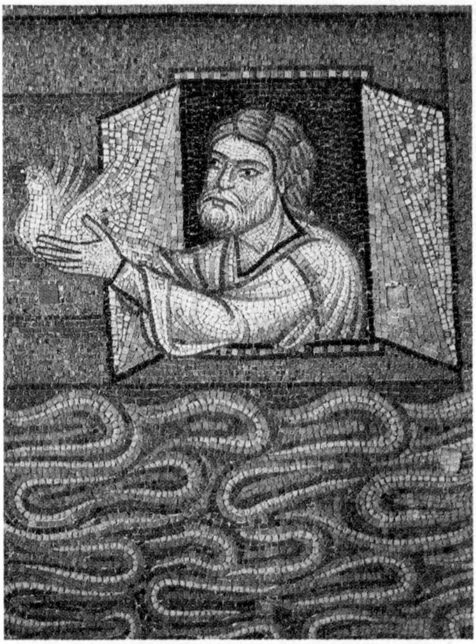

2

3

4

1 The paralytic brought by his friends to Jesus to be healed (Luke 5:18). Crowds around the house prevented them from entering, so they went up on the roof and lowered the man on his mat into the room. Manuscript page from *The Four Gospels*, twelfth century. **2** Noah, who according to Gen. 8:8–12 released a dove on three occasions "to see if the waters had subsided from the face of the ground." A detail from the mosaics, begun in the eleventh century, in St. Mark's Cathedral in Venice. **3** Jonah being cast overboard into the mouth of a great fish. Detail of an altarpiece triptych with fifty-one enamel and gold scenes from the OT and NT that was originally part of an ambo, or raised pulpit; from 1181, by Nicholas of Verdun. **4** Stained glass windows at Reims Cathedral depicting the crucifixion were designed by the twentieth-century Russian Jewish artist Marc Chagall in 1974, to replace those destroyed by bombs during World War II.

1

2

3

1 Interior of Hagia Sophia in present-day Istanbul. One of the most imposing structures in the history of architecture, the building was constructed in the sixth century as a Christian church by the Byzantine emperor Justinian. With the Turkish conquest of Constantinople (the older name of the city) in 1453, Hagia Sophia became a mosque; today it is a museum. **2** Elijah. Detail of the Transfiguration mosaic pictured below. **3** Christ rises above the figures of Moses on the right, Elijah on the left, and John, Peter, and James below. Medallions surrounding the scene depict the other nine apostles and major and minor prophets of the OT. The prominence of Moses and Elijah, along with Peter, James, and John, suggests the mosaic takes its theme from Christ's transfiguration (Matt. 17:1–8). The mosaic is in the apse of the Church of St. Catherine, Sinai, also built by Justinian in the sixth century.

1

2

3

1 The annunciation to Mary by the angel Gabriel. The book in Mary's hand is open to the passage from Isaiah, "Behold, a young woman shall conceive and bear a son" (7:14). Detail of a painting by Masolino da Panicale ca. 1430. **2** Sarah and Abraham. Sarah's remarkable conception of a son in her old age (Gen. 17:15–19) was a continuation of God's promise to Abraham, regarded as the father of the Israelite people, that his descendants would be a blessing for the world. Detail of a Russian icon. **3** Abigail intercepts King David and persuades him not to harm her husband, Nabal, whom he has come to kill for refusing to recognize his authority (1 Sam. 25). Detail from a thirteenth-century French miniature.

"not my people" to "my people" (2:10)
"no mercy shown" to "mercy shown" (2:10).
Their conversion was both radical and beneficial. How fortunate they are!

Yet this conversion entailed considerable suffering. For with the new allegiance to the Christian God, old allegiances to local family or city gods were abandoned. This shift in loyalties signaled to outsiders that old ties to family, clan, and municipality were weakened. As a result Christianity and its converts were suspected of destroying the social fabric. After all, conversion could result in loss of family ties, family wealth, and social position (see Mark 10:29). This is the context for understanding the references to suffering in 1 Peter.

If Christians are "aliens" in terms of family or municipality (1:1, 17), they are nevertheless members of a new commonwealth (1:2), even

OUTLINE OF CONTENTS

The First Letter of Peter

1 Peter is formally shaped as a typical letter, with an opening greeting and address (1:1–2) and a thanksgiving (1:3–9). The letter body contains the central exhortation (chaps. 2–5). It concludes with notice of a secretary (5:12) and with final greetings (5:13–14).

- I. Letter introduction (1:1–9)
  - A. Address (1:1–2)
  - B. Greeting (1:2)
  - C. Thanksgiving (1:3–9)
- II. Christian identity (1:10–2:4)
  - A. Place in salvation history (1:10–12)
  - B. Call to holiness (1:13–21)
  - C. New birth (1:22–2:4)
- III. As Christ, so Christian (2:5–10)
  - A. Chosen
  - B. Precious/rejected stone
- IV. Christian table of household duties (2:11–3:22)
  - A. To all (2:11–17)
  - B. To slaves (2:18–25)
  - C. To wives (3:1–6)
  - D. To husbands (3:7)
  - E. To all (3:8–22)
- V. Christian future (4:1–19)
  - A. Dead to flesh, alive in Spirit (4:1–6)
  - B. The end is at hand (4:7–11)
  - C. Purification of the church (4:12–19)
- VI. Household duties continued (5:1–11)
  - A. To elders (5:1–5)
  - B. To all (5:6–11)
- VII. Letter conclusion (5:12–14)
  - A. Secretary (5:12)
  - B. Greetings (5:13–14)
  - C. Farewell (5:14)

1 PETER

God's own household (1:3–5). The new identity of converts is given special attention in 2:1–10, verses describing the new Christian order of things and the Christian's place in that order. Two parallel stories are told, that of Jesus and that of the church. Jesus is described as a Chosen Stone: God chose Jesus (2:6) and established him as the cornerstone of a new temple (2:7). This stone is precious to God, yet rejected by humans (2:8). Likewise, Christians are "a chosen race, a royal priesthood, a holy nation" (2:9). Like Jesus, they are "living stones ... built into a [new] spiritual house" (2:5). Like Jesus, they are precious to God, even if hated by their neighbors. Jesus' story socializes converts in terms of their new identity and history.

Jesus' story continues in chaps. 2–3 as the pattern for interpreting the lives of converts. Slaves may be a "royal priesthood" in the church, but they could still suffer from their old masters. They should find the true meaning of their negative experience by looking to Jesus and imitating him (2:21). Suffering comes even to the elect. They should not return evil for evil (3:9), but call this a "blessing" (3:15). If converts have to suffer, they should suffer as innocent persons (3:16–17). The basis for all this is the foundation story of Jesus in 3:18–22, which tells of his suffering as well as his resurrection and enthronement in heaven. Jesus' story is model and pattern for the lives and destinies of all converts.

Finally, converts are exhorted to be a new and loyal household. Typical of NT exhortations is a code of household duties for masters and slaves, parents and children, and husbands and wives (Eph. 5:21–6:9; Col. 3:18–4:1). 1 Peter expands this to cover the whole household of God's church; all Christians are exhorted (2:11–17; 3:8–22); then slaves (2:18–25), wives (3:1–6), husbands (3:7), and elders (5:1–6). In substance the converts are told to "be holy, for I [God] am holy" (1:16), that is, to live a holy life worthy of one "born anew to a living hope through the resurrection of Jesus" (1:3). They are to conform their lives and values according to the basic Jesus story as it is told in 3:18–22.

Authorship and Date: While the Letter claims to come from the apostle Peter, the Greek style bespeaks an education a fisherman like Peter would be unlikely to have had. The similarity of language and phrases in 1 Peter and the Letters of Paul do not argue for dependence of 1 Peter on them, but rather is to be accounted for by understanding that both authors drew from a common stock of early Christian traditions. While 1 Peter thus stands in the mainstream of early Christian thought, it was probably written in the late years of the first century by a follower of Peter who wished to address a new situation in Asia Minor in the spirit of the Peter he had followed. The suggestion that Peter gave authority to Silvanus (5:12) to write the Letter in Peter's name may also merit consideration, although the situation presumed in Asia Minor (see 1:12 and 4:12, which presume a time late in the first century) would argue for a date subsequent to the traditional date of Peter's martyrdom in 64. The "Babylon" mentioned in 5:13 may be the place of origin, and is probably to be understood as a cryptic reference to Rome (see also Rev. 17:5–6).

Bibliography

Elliott, John H. *A Home for the Homeless: A Sociological Exegesis of 1 Peter*. Philadelphia: Fortress, 1981. J.H.N.

Peter, the Second Letter of, second Letter attributed to the apostle Peter in the NT canon and one of the seven catholic or general NT Letters. Although 2 Peter claims to be a second letter from Peter (3:1), it is judged today as a pseudonymous letter. "Peter," its alleged author, is the recipient of several revelations (Matt. 16:17; Mark 9:2–8; 13:3–37; Acts 10:11–16), which serves to augment the present claim to have received a special revelation about the Parousia (i.e., the return of Christ; 1:16–18). The Letter is remarkable for the diverse traditions it alludes to: biblical materials (2:4–8), some of Paul's letters (3:15–16), the gospel tradition about the transfiguration (1:16–18), and traditions about the Parousia (3:10). In addition, 2 Peter is generally agreed to have incorporated the Letter of Jude as the central part of the present work. Although written in the form of a letter, 2 Peter is best seen as a last will and testament to the church: it is written on the occasion of the death of the author (1:12–14), who predicts the coming of heretics to disturb God's church (3:3–4) and who leaves as a legacy the correct interpretation of important issues (1:15).

Content and Purpose: 2 Peter is a piece of apology and polemic, responding to a crisis in the church over God's theodicy and the eschatological doctrine of the Parousia as the end of the world and its judgment. First, 2 Peter claims that heretics are already in the church: "false prophets" who speak peace when doom is coming (2:1–3) and "scoffers" who mock "the promise of his coming" (3:3–4). They argue from the delay of the day of judgment that God will not judge; from the eternity of the world they argue against its predicted end.

Second, in response to this heresy, 2 Peter defends God's coming judgment, appealing to images intelligible to pagans and Christians alike. The author affirms that "God did *not* spare" the evil angels (2:4), Noah's world (2:5), or Sodom and Gomorrah (2:6–8). As God once destroyed the world by water, so he can end it by fire (3:5–7). The biblical allusions are clear, but these examples could also be understood by pagans as references to their traditional myths of the Titans cast into Tartarus, the flood of Deucalion and Phyrra, and the fiery destruction of Phaethon. From these examples, 2 Peter concludes with the principle that God both rewards and punishes: "God knows how to rescue the godly . . . and to keep the unrighteous under punishment until the day of judgment" (2:9–10). Third, he defends God's alleged "slowness" in judging. God's time is mysterious, as the psalmist noted (3:8). God's "slowness" is really God's long-suffering, giving sinners time to repent (3:9). Even Paul, notoriously difficult to understand, agrees with 2 Peter on God's slowness to judge as God's gift of long-suffering (3:15–16; see Rom. 2:4–6).

Besides defending God's coming judgment, 2 Peter mounts an apology for the Christian prophecy of Jesus' Parousia as a time when the world will end and judgment will be meted out. The scoffers have no use for any prophecy whatever, especially for the Parousia prophecy. They consider it a "myth" invented to terrify and so control people. The author denies, however, that the Parousia prophecy is a "cleverly devised myth" (1:16). He was an eyewitness when the prediction was given. The key here is to understand Jesus' transfiguration as the early Christians did, namely, as a prophecy of Jesus' glory at his return and his judgment on sinners. The author claims to have been inspired to see and hear the prophecy (1:16–18) and to be its official interpreter (1:20–21). Therefore, the author claims, he is not fabricating the notion of Christ's return in glory.

This prophecy contains a summary of the Christian eschatological doctrine. The world will come to an end on the day of the Lord (3:10–12), when a new heaven and earth will be formed (3:13). That day will be a day of judgment (3:10; 3:7). This doctrine in turn calls for a high standard of ethical conduct, for on the day of judgment the wicked will be punished

OUTLINE OF CONTENTS

The Second Letter of Peter

I. Letter introduction (1:1–2)
II. Eschatology and ethics (1:3–11)
III. Letter setting: Peter's death (1:12–15)
IV. First apology: Prophecy of the Parousia (1:16–21)
V. Polemic against heretics (2:1–22)
    A. God's sure judgment (2:4–10)
    B. Crime and punishment (2:11–16)
    C. Denial of judgment—rejected (2:17–22)
VI. Second apology: End of the world (3:1–7)
VII. Third apology: "Delay" as gift (3:8–10)
VIII. Eschatology and ethics again (3:11–14)
IX. Even Paul agrees (3:15–16)
X. Letter conclusion (3:17–18)

and the godly rewarded. As a result, great attention is given to praising the ideal moral behavior of orthodox Christians (1:1–11) and exposing the follies of sinfulness (2:11–22).

Date: Unlike the first letter attributed to the apostle Peter, this one gives no indication of its place of origin, and any attempt to determine one would be pure speculation. Its date of composition is likely to be late first or early second century because of its mounting concern with the delay of Christ's return (3:8–9), its dependence on Stoic physics (3:10; the dissolution of all things into their original fire is the Stoic idea of *ekpyrrosis* [lit., Gk. "conflagration"]), and the inclusion of much of the Letter of Jude into its second chapter.

Bibliography

Fornberg, Tord. *An Early Church in a Pluralistic Society*. Uppsala: C.W.K. Gleerup, 1977.

Neyrey, Jerome H. "The Form and Background of the Polemic in 2 Peter." *Journal of Biblical Literature* 99 (1980): 407–431.

J.H.N.

Pethahiah (pe-thuh-hī'yah). **1** The head of the family to which the nineteenth division of the priesthood was assigned in the time of David (1 Chron. 24:16). **2** A Levite who participated in Ezra's penitential service (Neh. 9:5). He was among those who agreed to divorce foreign wives (Ezra 10:23). **3** A Judahite of the time of Nehemiah, who was "at the king's hand in all matters concerning the people" (Neh. 11:24), which may mean that he served as an advisor on Jewish affairs at the Persian court.

Pethor (pee'thawr), a place in Mesopotamia from which Balaam was called by Barak, king of Moab, to curse Israel (Num. 22:5; Deut. 23:4). Mentioned in the annals of Pharaoh Thutmose III of Egypt and King Shalmanezzar III of Assyria, it was a little south of Carchemish, on the other side (that is, the west side) of the Euphrates on the Sagur River. It may be modern Tell Ahmar.

Petra (pee'truh), capital of the Nabatean kingdom, forty-seven miles south-by-southeast of the Dead Sea. ***See also*** Nabatea, Nabateans.

Phalec (fay'lek, KJV; RSV: Peleg). ***See*** Peleg.

Phanuel (fuh-nōō'uhl), the father of Anna, the aged Jewish prophetess who spoke of the future greatness of Jesus (Luke 2:36–38). ***See also*** Anna.

pharaoh (fair'oh), the Hebrew word for the title held by the king of Egypt. This word was used in the Bible either by itself or attached to the king's name (e.g., "Pharaoh Hophra," Jer. 44:30). It comes from two Egyptian words, *per* and *aa*. This Egyptian combination originally meant "great house," which was the name given to the royal palace in the third and the first half of the second millennia B.C. Starting in the reign of Thutmose III (1504–1450 B.C.) in the eighteenth dynasty, *per-aa* came to refer to the king himself, and from the reign of the twenty-second-dynasty ruler Shoshenq I (945–924 B.C.) on, the term can be found, just as in the Bible, prefixed to the king's name, e.g., "Pharaoh Shoshenq."

One of the Colossi of Memnon representing Amenophis III, 1403–1365 B.C. (New Kingdom Period); west bank of the Nile at Thebes.

The king of Egypt was considered a god by his subjects. He was the embodiment of the royal falcon god Horus, and from at least the fifth dynasty (ca. 2494–2345 B.C.) on, he was looked upon as the son of the great sun god, Re. When he died, he became the god Osiris and joined the other divinities in the afterworld. Theoretically, all of the land of Egypt and its products belonged to the pharaoh (see Gen. 47: 20), and his word was the law of the land. Throughout most of the third millennium B.C., the king ran the government with the aid of members of the royal family. Toward the end of the third millennium and into the early second millennium, more and more governmental authority became distributed among the nobles, and with the rise of the Egyptian empire in the eighteenth dynasty an enormous bureaucracy had to be established to handle the affairs of government. The chief officer in this bureaucracy was the vizier (Egyptian *tjaty*). The description given in Genesis 41–47 of Joseph's responsibilities under Pharaoh reflects the duties of a vizier.

Egyptian kings had five names, two of which

were written within the elongated oval loops called cartouches by modern scholars. The second of these two names, e.g., Thutmose or Ramesses, is approximately equivalent to our modern family names. The first one was given to him at his enthronement; the throne name for Thutmose III, for example, was *Menkheperre*, "Established is the form of Re [the sun god]."

The king wore one of several crowns. The "White Crown" symbolized his dominance of Upper (southern) Egypt, while the "Red Crown" symbolized his rulership of Lower (northern) Egypt, and the "Double Crown" reflected his control over both Upper and Lower Egypt. The "Blue Crown," or war crown, was worn by the king when he went into battle. The king is often depicted holding a shepherd's crook and a flail across his chest as symbols of authority, while in battle scenes he usually holds a mace or a short, curved sword (the scimitar).

At least four, possibly five, pharaohs are mentioned by name in the OT. There are also many other references to unnamed Egyptian kings, a few of whom can be identified with more or less probability. The pharaohs mentioned by name are:

1 Shishak, the twenty-second (Libyan) dynasty king Shoshenq I (945–924 B.C.), who gave asylum to Jeroboam (1 Kings 11:40) and later invaded Palestine (1 Kings 14:25–26; 2 Chron. 12:1–9).

2 Tirhakah, the twenty-fifth (Kushite) dynasty king Taharqa (690–664 B.C.), who is mentioned in 2 Kings 19:9 and Isa. 37:9 as the "king of Ethiopia." Before he became king, he fought unsuccessfully against the Assyrian king Sennacherib in 701 B.C.

3 Pharaoh Neco, the twenty-sixth (Saite) dynasty king Neco II (610–595 B.C.), who defeated and killed Josiah at Megiddo in 609 B.C. (2 Kings 23:29; 2 Chron. 35:20–24), removed Josiah's son and successor, Jehoahaz, from the throne, and put Jehoiakim in his place (2 Kings 23:30–35; 2 Chron. 36:1–4). Neco ultimately lost all of Egypt's west Asiatic possessions to the Babylonian king Nebuchadnezzar (2 Kings 24: 7).

4 Pharaoh Hophra, the twenty-sixth (Saite) dynasty king Waibre (Gk., "Apries"; 589–570 B.C.), whom Jeremiah said would be delivered into the hands of his enemies, just as Zedekiah, king of Judah, had been to the Babylonian king Nebuchadnezzar (Jer. 44:30).

5 So, the "king of Egypt" (2 Kings 17:4) to whom King Hoshea sent messengers just before he revolted against the Assyrians. This word may refer to the twenty-second-dynasty king Osorkon IV (ca. 727–720 B.C.), or it could come from an Egyptian epithet meaning "the Saite" and thus refer to the kings of the twenty-sixth (Saite) dynasty (664–525 B.C.).

Other, unnamed Egyptian kings who are prominently mentioned in the Bible include: **6** The pharaoh from the time of Abram (Gen. 12: 15–20). **7** The pharaoh of the Joseph story (Gen. 39–50). **8** The "Pharaoh of the Oppression" (Exod. 1–2), whom many biblical scholars equate with Sety I (1291–1279 B.C.) or Ramesses II (1279–1212 B.C.). **9** The "Pharaoh of the Exodus" (Exod. 5–12), often identified by biblical scholars as Ramesses II (1279–1212 B.C.) or, somewhat less likely, his son and successor Merenptah (1212–1202 B.C.). **10** The pharaoh(s) who granted asylum to Hadad of Edom and gave Hadad his wife's sister in marriage (1 Kings 11: 14–22). The first king may be the twenty-first-dynasty pharaoh Amenemope (993–984 B.C.), while the pharaoh responsible for the second action may be Siamun (978–959 B.C.). **11** The pharaoh who took Gezer and presented the city as a dowry to his daughter when she married Solomon (1 Kings 9:16). This diplomatic marriage is also mentioned in 1 Kings 3:1; 7:8; 9:24; and 11:1. This pharaoh is probably the twenty-first-dynasty king Siamun rather than his successor Psusennes II (959–945 B.C.). ***See also*** Neco II; Ramesses; Shishak; So; Tirhakah.

Bibliography

Frankfort, H. *Kingship and the Gods*. Chicago: University of Chicago Press, 1948.

Gardiner, A. H. *Egypt of the Pharaohs*. Oxford: Clarendon, 1961.

Montet, P. *Eternal Egypt*. Trans. D. Weightman. London: Weidenfeld and Nicholson, 1964.

J.M.W.

Phares, Pharez. ***See*** Perez.

Pharisees (fair'i-seez), a group of specially observant and influential Jews, mainly in Palestine, from the second century B.C. to the first century A.D. The name is obscure. It may mean "separate ones" in Hebrew, referring to their observance of ritual purity and tithing, or less probably "the interpreters," referring to their unique interpretations of biblical law. The Pharisees are described by two first-century sources, the NT and the historian Josephus, and also by rabbinic literature, which covers a broader period of time. Each literature gives a different account of the Pharisees and modern descriptions differ widely depending on which sources are accepted and how conflicts are resolved. The picture of the Pharisees derived only from the Gospels and formerly accepted as historical, that they were little more than legalists and hypocrites and were culpably blind to Jesus' message, has largely been discredited as early Christian polemic against Jewish and rabbinic leadership. The interpretation of the Pharisees as religious liberals emanated from modern Jewish apologetics and is ill suited to antiquity. Though a comprehensive and secure description of the Pharisees eludes us, some insight can be gained from each of the ancient sources.

According to Josephus: Josephus, a Jewish historian of the first century who wrote for non-Jews in Greek, calls the Pharisees a "choice [of life]" and a "philosophy." He gives some general characteristics of the Pharisees in contrast to the Sadducees and Essenes; he recounts some of the activities and influence of this group; and he mentions occasional influential Pharisees. According to Josephus, the Pharisees were the group most influential with the people, were noted for their accurate and therefore authoritative interpretations of Jewish law, and had their own traditions and way of life to which they were faithful. They had a simple standard of living and cultivated harmonious relations with others. On the issue of free will, a distinguishing factor among Greek philosophies, Josephus places the Pharisees between the Essenes and Sadducees because they accepted the influence of both fate (or providence) and free will on human actions. They believed that the soul survives death and is punished or rewarded with another life. Though Josephus acknowledges the Pharisees' prominence and even claims to be one in his *Life*, he criticizes their total power over Queen Alexandra (76–67 B.C.), their opposition to other rulers, and their attacks on their enemies. He often refers to their reputation as accurate interpreters of the law, without affirming it himself. Some Pharisees incited opposition to the government, though others worked with the chief priests to keep order. In the first century Josephus says they numbered six thousand.

At no time do we learn how one "joined" this group and what was required to stay in it. It may have been like a Hellenistic school, teaching a way of life, or a political, social faction competing for recognition and power within Judaism, or a sect separating itself from the parent body. The Pharisees exhibited various tendencies at different times, so they probably changed over the two centuries of their existence as different persons and groups from the Pharisees exercised diverse roles in society.

In the NT: In the NT the Pharisees play the role of Jesus' opponents and are almost always cast in a negative light, because they are presented as proponents of a way of living Jewish life that differed from Jesus' way. They are associated with the scribes alone (in Matt. and Luke) but seldom with the elders, chief priests, *and* scribes, who are the leaders in Jerusalem. The Pharisees were zealous observers of the law, prominent among the people and especially concerned with ritual purity, tithing food according to OT law, and correct observance of Sabbath. These are typical sectarian interests. They were learned in the law and sometimes contrasted with the Sadducees from whom they differed especially on resurrection (Acts 23:1–8; in Mark 11:18–26 Jesus agrees with the Pharisees against the Sadducees). When Paul wishes to identify his own place in Judaism, he says he is a Pharisee (Phil. 3:5; Acts 23:6). Yet, in the Gospels the Pharisees are condemned as hypocrites (Matt. 23) because they are used as opponents of Jesus. In general, the Gospel writers, who wrote several decades after Jesus, manifest little accurate and consistent knowledge of Jewish leadership and groups from the period before the destruction of the Temple in A.D. 70.

In Rabbinic Literature: Rabbinic literature, which in its present form dates from A.D. 200 and later, contains three types of data. The laws associated with the names of pre-70 Pharisees and with the schools of Shammai and Hillel, first-century Pharisaic leaders, concern ritual purity, tithing, and Sabbath observance, sectarian concerns that also surfaced in the Gospels. These laws may be accurately attributed to them, according to the contemporary scholar J. Neusner. Stories about these Pharisaic leaders present them as authoritative and dominant figures in Jewish society, religion, and politics. But since the rabbis who wrote these stories traced their lineage to the Pharisees, it is likely that they portrayed the Pharisees in their own image two or three centuries later. Another group of rabbinic texts speak of the "separatists" (Heb. *perushim)*, often presumed to be the Pharisees. But sometimes this term refers to dissidents who are clearly not Pharisees, and sometimes it refers to ascetics. In passages where the Pharisees are contrasted to Sadducees, the Pharisees are scholars who accept the written and oral law. They are the leaders who set the law for Jewish society and the judges who enforce it. Yet this portrait fits the rabbis after A.D. 70 rather than the Pharisees in the Temple period.

Though a full history and description of the Pharisees is impossible, some characteristics are probable. The Pharisees had their own traditions on how to live a life faithful to the Judaism to which they were devoted. Their internal rules were sectarian with an emphasis on ritual purity, food tithes, and Sabbath observances. They were admired by the people and functioned at least some of the time as a social and political force against foreign and hellenized Jewish leaders (i.e., those Jewish leaders who were sympathetic to Greek language and culture). Some or all were learned in the law and some were politically powerful. ***See also*** Essenes; Josephus; Parables; Rabbi, Rabboni; Sabbath; Sadducees.

Bibliography

Bowker, J. *Jesus and the Pharisees*. Cambridge: Cambridge University, 1973.

Neusner, Jacob. *From Politics to Piety*. Englewood Cliffs, NJ: Prentice-Hall, 1973.

Rivkin, E. *The Hidden Revolution*. Nashville, TN: Abingdon, 1978.

A.J.S.

Pharpar (fahr'pahr), one of the two rivers of Damascus according to 2 Kings 5:12. It is probably to be identified with the modern Nahr el-Awaj, which flows from Mount Hermon in an easterly direction and passes about ten miles south of Damascus. Together with the Abana (modern Nahr el-Barada) it waters the fertile Damascus oasis. ***See also*** Abana; Damascus.

Phasael (fah'suh-el), the largest of three towers built by Herod the Great north of his palace in Jerusalem, named for his eldest brother, Phasaelus (or Phasael), who had died heroically in the Parthian War. Herod constructed this fortification into the Hasmonean wall defending the west side of Jerusalem.

When Titus razed Jerusalem in A.D. 70, according to the historian Josephus, he allowed to remain standing part of the west wall (to stand as a protection for the Roman garrison) and the three towers (to show later generations what a proud city had been overcome by the valiant soldiers of Rome). It appears to have been the remains of Phasael that were known in Byzantine times as the "Tower of David," although in more recent centuries that name passed to the Turkish minaret of the Citadel over the site of Herod's palace.

The base of the Phasael tower, as it stands today, is of Herodian ashlar masonry up to about twenty meters, with higher courses dating only from much later times. ***See also*** Herod; Phasaelis; Phasaelus. C.H.M.

Phasaelis (fah-suh-ee'lis), a town (modern Khirbet el-Fasayil) ten miles north of Jericho in the Jordan Valley. Built by Herod the Great in memory of his brother Phasael (Phasaelus), it was bequeathed by him to his sister Salome (4 B.C.), who left it to the Empress Livia, wife of the Roman emperor Augustus (A.D. 10). It appears on a sixth-century mosaic floor map from Madeba, Jordan.

Phasaelis should not be confused with Phaselis (fah-see'lis), a Lycian port and recipient of the Roman consular letter concerning Jews, ca. 139 B.C. (1 Macc. 15:23). ***See also*** Herod; Lycia; Phasael; Phasaelus.

Phasaelus (fah-suh-ee'luhs), also Phasael. **1** Son of Antipater and elder brother of Herod the Great, governor of Judea from 43 until 40 B.C., when, having been treacherously delivered by the Parthians to Antigonus the Hasmonean, he killed himself in captivity. **2** His son, father of Cypros, wife of Agrippa I. ***See also*** Antipater; Herod; Maccabees.

Phaselis (fah-see'lis). ***See*** Phasaelis.

Phicol (fī'kuhl), the commander of Abimelech's army. Phicol witnessed the agreements between Abimelech and Abraham and between Abimelech and Isaac (Gen. 21:22; 26:26). The meaning of the name is not certain; various Egyptian etymologies have been proposed. ***See also*** Abimelech.

Philadelphia, an ancient city (modern Alashehir, Turkey) in the region of Lydia in western Asia Minor. Philadelphia is one of the seven cities mentioned in the book of Revelation. It was founded by Attalus II, king of Pergamum (159–138 B.C.). Because of its strategic location, it served as a vital link in communication and trade between Sardis and Pergamum to the west and Laodicea and Hierapolis to the east. It was a center of agriculture, leather production, and textile industry. ***See also*** Hierapolis; Laodicea; Lydia; Pergamum; Revelation to John, The; Sardis.

Philemon (fī-lee'muhn), resident of Colossae and owner of the slave Onesimus, for whom Paul appeals in his Letter to Philemon. He was converted to Christianity by Paul (Philem. 19), probably at Ephesus. He had been associated with Paul's mission, for he is described as "our beloved fellow worker" (Philem. 1). Since he was able to host a congregation (Philem. 2) and prepare a guest room for Paul (Philem. 22), Philemon was an individual of substance. Paul observes that Philemon was recognized as a person of faith and love toward Christ and the church (Philem. 4–7). ***See also*** Onesimus; Paul; Philemon, The Letter of Paul to. W.R.B.

Philemon, the Letter of Paul to, the shortest of Paul's Letters. It is a personal but not a private letter. Written primarily to Philemon, it is also addressed to Apphia (perhaps his wife), Archippus, and the congregation that meets in Philemon's house (1–2) in Colossae (Col. 4:9, 17). The Letter appeals on behalf of Onesimus (10), Philemon's slave, who has apparently run away after defrauding his master (18–19). Since fugitive slaves were subject to severe penalty (usually burning the legs or arms with hot iron or branding the forehead), Onesimus may have come to Paul for asylum. Runaway slaves could flee to shrines or altars (even one in a private residence) for sanctuary. Onesimus knew of Paul through his master's association with the apostle (1, 19). Paul is in prison (1, 9, 10, 13, 23), probably in Ephesus—a location that would make feasible his projected visit to Philemon (22). While enjoying Paul's protection, Onesimus has been converted to Christianity (10).

Paul sends the slave back to his master (12) bearing this Letter. According to Roman law, fugitive slaves were to be returned to their owners; anyone harboring a runaway was subject to a fine. However, if the slave was seeking protection from a maltreating master, he would not legally be a fugitive. Roman laws regarding slaves would apply to this situation only if Philemon was a Roman citizen—a matter about which we have no information. The exact nature of Paul's appeal, which is composed with rhetorical skill, is not certain. Paul may simply be asking Philemon to receive the slave back without punishment. However, his recommendation to accept Onesimus "no longer as a slave, but ... as a beloved brother" (16) may imply the freeing of the slave and his acceptance into the Christian community. According to many interpreters, Paul is seeking the release of Onesimus for service in his, Paul's, mission. Paul says that he would like to have kept Onesimus with him "in order that he might serve me" (13) and that he expects Philemon will do "even more than I say" (21).

The ingenious theory of John Knox that Onesimus is the slave of Archippus and that the Letter to Philemon is the letter "from Laodicea" (Col. 4:16) rests on insufficient evidence. If Colossians is a genuine letter of Paul, it was written at the same time and place as Philemon (Col. 4: 10–14; Philem. 23–24). Knox's belief that Onesimus was released and became an important leader in the church is supported by the preservation of the Letter to Philemon and the reference to Onesimus in Col. 4:9.

Although Paul does not attack the institution of slavery (see 1 Cor. 7:20–24), his Letter to Philemon has important ethical implications. He urges the slave owner not to treat Onesimus (in accord with Roman law) as property but as a person in Christ (see Gal. 3:28; 1 Cor. 12:13), who should be received as though he were Paul himself (17). Philemon is free to make his decision (14) in response to the command of love (4–7). ***See also*** Colossians, The Letter of Paul to the; Onesimus; Paul; Philemon. W.R.B.

Philetus (fī-lee'tuhs), a man accused, with Hymenaeus, of upsetting the faith of some by teaching that "the resurrection is past already" (2 Tim. 2:16–18), evidently a false reading of Paul's eschatology. ***See also*** Hymenaeus.

Philip, a name borne by important people in 1 and 2 Macc. and the NT. **1** Philip II, king of Macedonia (359–336 B.C.) and father of Alexander the Great (1 Macc. 1:1; 6:2). **2** Philip V, king of Macedonia (220–179 B.C.), mentioned in 1 Macc. 8:5. **3** Philip, governor of Jerusalem, appointed by Antiochus Epiphanes ca. 179 B.C. (2 Macc. 5:22; 6:11; 8:8). **4** Philip, a close associate and foster brother of Antiochus Epiphanes (1 Macc. 6:14–15; 2 Macc. 9:29). **5** Philip, mentioned in Matt. 14:3 and Mark 6:17 (cf. Luke 3: 19) as the "brother" of Herod (Antipas) and first husband of Herodias; perhaps Herod (Philip), son of Herod the Great and Mariamne II and half-brother of Antipas. **6** Philip the Tetrarch, son of Herod the Great and Cleopatra of Jerusalem, not to be confused with 5. According to the historian Josephus, he was granted rule over a portion of his father's kingdom following the latter's death in 4 B.C. His rule over this non-Jewish territory, stretching from the Sea of Galilee north and east toward Damascus, was apparently a benevolent and prosperous one. He built Caesarea Philippi, named in honor of the emperor (and himself), and rebuilt the city of Bethsaida on the Sea of Galilee. He died ca. A.D. 33–34, and his territory became part of the Roman province of Syria. **7** Philip the Apostle, one of the Twelve whose name appears in the four apostolic lists (Matt. 10:3; Mark 3:18; Luke 6:14; Acts 1:13). John's Gospel contains most of the references to Philip. According to John 1:43–51, Philip was from Bethsaida in Galilee, the home also of Andrew and Peter. When called by Jesus, Philip sought out a skeptical Nathanael, who also responded to Jesus' messianic identity. Philip's pragmatism is perhaps suggested in his response to Jesus' direct question concerning feeding the multitude: he observed that it would take a large amount of money to feed so many (John 6:1–14). Later, it was Philip whom Greeks approached with their request to meet Jesus (John 12:20–22). How much can be made of Philip's association with Gentiles in this episode is not clear. In John 14:8–11, it is Philip who said to Jesus, "Lord, show us the Father, and we shall be satisfied." Philip appeared with the other apostles in Jerusalem after Jesus' ascension (Acts 1:13). Later tradition surrounding his activities is legendary and uncertain. The Gnostic *Gospel of Philip* is attributed to Philip, and the *Acts of Philip* purports to recount his activities. **8** Philip the Evangelist, not to be confused with 7. This Philip first appears in the NT when he is appointed (along with Stephen and others) to supervise the daily distribution of food to the widows following the dispute between the "Hellenists" and the "Hebrews" (Acts 6:1–6). Later, Philip carried the gospel to Samaria (Acts 8:5–13), and he subsequently baptized the Ethiopian eunuch (Acts 8:26–39). For the author of Acts, this latter is the first of three conversion stories (with Saul/Paul in 9:1–19 and Cornelius in chap. 10) that demonstrate God's role in originating the mission to the Gentiles. The final NT reference to Philip is in Acts 21: 8–9, where he and his four unmarried daughters, residing in Caesarea, are visited by Paul on his way to Jerusalem. ***See also*** Alexander; Andrew; Antiochus; Apostle; Bethsaida; Caesarea Philippi; Cornelius; Disciple; Ethiopia; Eunuch; Herod; Herodias; Macedonia; Nathanael; Stephen; Twelve, The. P.L.S.

Philippi (fil'uh-pī), an ancient city in northeastern Greece. Its site, dominated by a high acropolis and surrounded by mountains on three sides, lies ten miles inland from the modern port city of Kavalla (ancient Neapolis).

The history of Philippi before the fourth century B.C. remains obscure, although there are reports of two older settlements on or near the

site, Krenides and Datum. Philip II of Macedonia, particularly interested in the nearby gold and silver mines of Mount Pangaeus, annexed the entire region and in 356 B.C. formally established Philippi as a city bearing his own name. Although the extensive city wall which still survives perhaps originated at this time, Philippi remained insignificant until after the Roman conquest of Macedonia in 168–167 B.C. Included by Aemilius Paulus in the first of the four districts into which Macedonia was then divided (Livy, *Roman History* 45.29; see Acts 16:12), it became a major stopping place on the Via Egnatia, the newly constructed road connecting Byzantium with the Adriatic ports that led to Italy.

In October of 42 B.C. Mark Antony and Octavian defeated Roman Republican forces led by Brutus and Cassius in two separate battles just west of Philippi. Brutus committed suicide immediately after the defeat, and the poet Horace, also a soldier on the losing side, recalled how Brutus threw away his shield as he ran in retreat (*Odes* 2.7.9–12). Shortly afterward, Mark Antony settled many veterans from his army here and refounded Philippi as a Roman colony; its territory included the towns of Neapolis, Oisyme, and Apollonia. After the battle of Actium (31 B.C.) more settlers came here from Italy by order of Octavian (Augustus), and Philippi was again refounded, receiving the formal name that it thenceforth retained, Colonia Julia Augusta Philippensis. These settlers along with some of the previous inhabitants constituted the legal citizen body; and Philippi was governed by "Italian law" (*ius Italicum*), the highest privilege attainable by a Roman provincial municipality.

Despite such strong Roman influence, the variety of Philippi's religious life suggests that its inhabitants, noncitizens included, were more mixed in their backgrounds. Roman gods such as Jupiter and Mars had their cults, but the Thracian goddess Bendis remained very popular, and sanctuaries to gods from Egypt and to Cybele, a Phrygian goddess, are also known. A Jewish synagogue was apparently located just outside the city walls (Acts 16:13). The apostle Paul came to Philippi ca. A.D. 50 and founded here his first European Christian community (Acts 16:12–40; 1 Thess. 2:2). This church, always one of Paul's favorites, received his Letter to the Philippians ca. A.D. 54 and one or more further visits from him ca. A.D. 55 (1 Cor. 16:5–6; 2 Cor. 2:13; 7:5; Acts 20:1–6). A letter of Polycarp of Smyrna written to the Philippian Christians ca. A.D. 125 still survives, and Philippi enjoyed considerable ecclesiastical prominence even in medieval times.

Excavations, which still continue, have uncovered extensive remains on the now uninhabited ancient site: a portion of the Via Egnatia, the forum area, and surrounding porticoes (as rebuilt ca. A.D. 175), numerous rock reliefs of various divinities, temples, and the ruins of several Byzantine churches. A Roman-period crypt that may still be seen became known after the fifth century as "The Prison of St. Paul." This attribution, however, is extremely dubious. ***See also*** Macedonia; Paul; Philippians, The Letter of Paul to the. R.A.W.

Philippians (fi-lip'ee-uhnz), **the Letter of Paul to the,** a letter or possibly an edited collection of letters written by the apostle Paul to the Christians in the Macedonian city of Philippi and subsequently included in the NT canon.

Despite certain problems and growing pains, the Philippian Christian community had been especially responsive to and supportive of Paul, and he in turn reveals in this document a special affection for them as he urges them to greater unity among themselves and to a more profound reliance on Christ's saving power. With this community he could freely share his own varied feelings as he sat in chains, facing a possible death sentence (Phil. 1:12–26), and in one of his most moving passages he could offer them a veritable spiritual last will and testament (3:1–4:1). In recounting his own situation Paul invites the Philippians to observe how Christ's power has been at work in him and to imitate this in their own lives. Paul also urges his audience to imitate the total self-surrender of Christ himself (2:1–13). Using (and possibly editing) an older Christian poetic composition or "hymn" that recalled Christ's descent into the physical world, his death, and his exaltation by God (2:6–11), a text that itself provides important evidence for beliefs about Christ held by certain groups within earliest Christianity, Paul challenges the Philippians to turn from self-centeredness to a giving of themselves for others.

Composition: While almost no one doubts the Pauline authorship of Philippians, many argue that the present canonical text actually combines two or three shorter letters. At Phil. 3:1 there is a very harsh transition: 3:1a seems to begin the concluding words of a letter (cf. 2 Cor. 13:11; Gal. 6:17) while 3:1b (or certainly 3:2) begins a strongly worded condemnation of advocates of circumcision, probably, given the language of 3:2, Jews rather than Jewish Christians. The first three words of Phil. 4:4 exactly repeat the last three words of 3:1a, a feature that can signal the later insertion of material into a prior textual unit. Further, it is somewhat strange that Paul would have failed to acknowledge the Philippians' gift until the end of a relatively long letter. Phil. 4:10–20 may therefore originally have been a separate brief thank-you note.

Those who divide Philippians into three separate fragments believe that Phil. 4:10–20 (4:10–23?) was written first by Paul while in prison and before Epaphroditus' illness (2:26–27); that 1:1–3:1a (3:1a and b?) and 4:4–7 (4:2–9?) and 4:21–23(?) formed a second letter from prison; and that 3:1b(3:2?)–4:3(4:1?) and 4:8–9(?) derived from a third letter written probably when Paul was no longer a prisoner. The proponents of a two-letter hypothesis combine 4:10–20 with the second prison letter. Following either hypothesis, the editing (certainly before A.D. 90) of these shorter letters into a single document was part of a more general and widespread effort to collect and prepare Paul's writings for use in community worship and instruction.

OUTLINE OF CONTENTS

The Letter of Paul to the Philippians

I. Salutation (1:1–2)
II. Thanksgiving for the community's unity and fellowship (1:3–8)
III. Prayer that this love may grow (1:9–11)
IV. Reassuring news about Paul's situation in prison (1:12–26)
V. Exhortation: preserve unity and love within the community and show yourselves fearless and without reproach before non-Christians (1:27–2:18)
VI. Timothy and Epaphroditus are to be sent to Philippi (2:19–30)
VII. Exhortation: rely on God's justification and avoid the teachings of Jews who demand circumcision (3:1–4:1)
VIII. Two co-workers of Paul require reconciliation (4:2–3)
IX. General exhortations (4:4–9)
X. Thanksgiving for the community's monetary gift (4:10–20)
XI. Closing greetings and blessing (4:21–23)

However, a multiple-letter theory has not yet been as clearly demonstrated for Philippians as for 2 Corinthians. No agreement exists on how Phil. 4 is to be divided, and even the sharp break at 3:1 is not altogether unparalleled in Paul's writings (see Rom. 16:17). In addition, the supposedly separate fragments share common vocabulary to some degree, even words found rarely or not at all in Paul's other Letters.

Date: References to Paul's imprisonment serve as the best clue for determining when Philippians or its relevant fragments were written. Earlier investigators thought that Paul's mention of the "praetorium" (1:13) and of "Caesar's household" (4:22) clearly indicated a Roman origin for the Letter, but in fact these entities existed in any Roman provincial capital. Since Paul makes reference to much traveling back and forth between Philippi and his own place of imprisonment (1:26; 2:19; 2:23–24; 2:25–30; 4:18), it is unlikely that he was in Rome or, as others have proposed, at Caesarea, since these cities are quite distant from Philippi. Probably Paul also was a prisoner at Ephesus ca. A.D. 55 (see 1 Cor. 15:32; 2 Cor. 1:8–10), and it is much more likely that he wrote from here or from some other place of incarceration (see 2 Cor. 11:23) closer to Philippi. If 3:1b–4:3 plus 4:8–9 was indeed originally part of a separate letter, its testamentary form (cf. Acts 20:18–35) may well point to a period closer to the end of Paul's life for its composition. ***See also*** Epaphroditus; Ephesus; Paul; Philippi; Prison.

Bibliography

Beare, F. W. *Commentary on the Epistle to the Philippians*. Black's New Testament Commentaries. 2d ed. London: Adam & Charles Black, 1969.

Houlden, J. L. *Paul's Letters from Prison*. Pelican New Testament Commentaries. Baltimore, MD: Penguin, 1970. Pp. 31–116.

Kümmel, Werner. *Introduction to the New Testament*. 2d ed. Nashville, TN: Abingdon, 1975. Pp. 320–35.

R.A.W.

Philistia (fi-lis'tya; Heb. *peleshet*), the territory controlled by the Philistines, the fertile coastal plain of Palestine that stretches from the "River of Egypt" northward to Ekron. ***See also*** Philistines.

Philistines (fil'is-teens), a warlike people who, with the other Sea Peoples, migrated from the Aegean basin to the southern coast of Palestine in the early twelfth century B.C. and became one of Israel's principal rivals.

Name: The Hebrew name for the Philistines is *pelishtim;* the OT usually refers to their territory as *'eretz pelishtim* ("land of the Philistines") or *peleshet* ("Philistia"). The modern term "Palestine" is derived from *Palaistinoi*, a Greek name given to the descendants of the Philistines.

Origin: Although the exact origin of the Philistines remains uncertain, there is no doubt that they were part of a great ethnic upheaval that occurred in the Aegean area in the final decades of the thirteenth century B.C. During this unsettled period, an unknown combination of social, political, and economic factors caused the displacement of various peoples on the Greek mainland and Aegean islands and in eastern Anatolia. The so-called Sea Peoples emerged from this hodgepodge of refugees, and their military advance across the eastern Mediterranean brought an end to the Hittite empire and the city-state of Ugarit. Ultimately, the Sea Peoples reached the coasts of Phoenicia, Palestine, and Egypt. In the eighth year of his reign (ca. 1190 B.C.), Ramesses III fought two groups of the Sea Peoples, the Tjekker and the Philistines. Though the battle was fought on land and sea, the Egyptians prevailed; a written and pictorial description of this episode was carved on the walls of Ramesses' funerary temple at Medinet Habu. Following his victory, Ramesses settled the Philistines along the southern coast of Canaan, and this Aegean people claimed a new homeland—Philistia.

In agreement with the external sources, the Bible points to an Aegean origin for the Philistines by linking them with Caphtor (Jer. 47:4; Amos 9:7; cf. Gen. 10:14; Deut. 2:23; 1 Chron. 1:12). Caphtor is almost certainly to be identified with Crete (cf. Cherethites; Pelethites; Caphtorim).

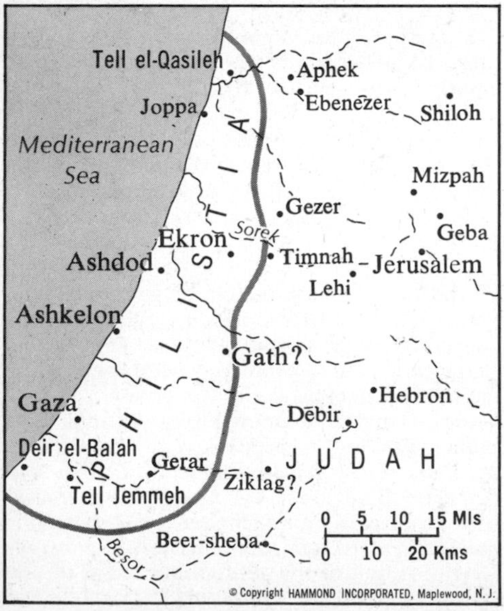

The Philistines began settling along the coast of Palestine in the early twelfth century B.C. When they consolidated their claim to the area, their principal cities were Ashdod, Ashkelon, Ekron, Gath, and Gaza.

History: Since nonbiblical texts do not use the term "Philistines" before ca. 1200 B.C., most scholars assume that the appearance of this name in Gen. 21:32, 34 and 26:1, 8, 14–18 is anachronistic. While it is quite possible that there were peoples of Aegean origin in Canaan during the patriarchal period, it seems likely that a later editor "updated" their ethnic designation by calling them Philistines. If the name "Philistine" was not used until the twelfth century B.C., a similar explanation must be given for its appearance in Gen. 10:14; Exod. 13:17; 23:31; and Josh. 13:2–3.

As the Philistines consolidated their claim to Palestine's southern coast, roughly in the area between Gaza and modern Tel Aviv, they organized themselves into a league of city-states. The "Philistine pentapolis" was composed of Gaza, Ashdod, Ashkelon, Gath, and Ekron; these five cities remained important throughout Philistine history. Although this region was rich in agricultural and commercial potential, the Philistines were not satisfied with such a narrow strip of land. Their expansion into the hinterland eventually brought them into conflict with the Israelites, who were expanding their territory at about the same time from the opposite side of Canaan. This competition for land and political control produced a fierce rivalry that lasted from the middle of the twelfth century B.C. until ca. 965 B.C. (i.e., from the time of the Philistine expansion into Israelite territory until their defeat by David).

In agreement with Josh. 13:2–3, Judg. 3:1–3 says that the Philistines were among the nations that the Lord left in Canaan "to test" Israel. Beginning with the book of Judges, the OT records numerous encounters between the Hebrews and Philistines. The first reference to hostility between these two rivals is Judg. 3:31, a single verse that praises Shamgar for delivering Israel by killing six hundred Philistines with an oxgoad. Strength and military prowess are acclaimed in the well-known story of Samson (chaps. 13–16), but this account also serves to illustrate the Philistine encroachment into Hebrew territory. Indeed, during some forty years of Philistine domination over Israel (13:1; 14:4), the tribes of Dan and Judah fought for their very existence. The Samson narratives document the eastward expansion of Israel's rival by mentioning the Philistine presence in Timnah and Lehi, both in the strategic Valley of Sorek. This Philistine expansion worsened the land shortage that eventually forced the Danites to migrate northwards (cf. chap. 18).

Shortly after the call of Samuel, Israelite-Philistine tension erupted into all-out war. Israel was defeated at Ebenezer, the Ark was captured, and Shiloh was destroyed (1 Sam. 4–6; cf. Ps. 78:56–66; Jer. 7:12–14). After rededicating themselves to God, Israel defeated the Philistines at Mizpah (1 Sam. 7:3–14). The balance

Ashdoda, a Philistine cultic object in the shape of a seated woman, from Ashdod, twelfth century B.C.

of power fluctuated, but the establishment of the monarchy and a regular army enabled Saul to defeat his foes (chaps. 13–14), in spite of the Philistine superiority in weaponry (cf. 13:19–22). While Saul fought a variety of enemies on all fronts (cf. 14:47–48), "there was hard fighting against the Philistines all the days of Saul" (14:52). The acclaim that David received after his victory over Goliath and the resultant rout of the Philistines (17:41–54) led to Saul's jealousy and David's flight. David took refuge with the Philistine king of Gath, Achish, and became one of his vassals (27:1–28:2), but David was not present when the Philistines killed Saul and his sons on Mt. Gilboa (chap. 31). This Philistine victory led to an even greater expansion of their holdings (cf. 31:7).

The death of Saul caused David to break his alliance with the Philistines and establish his kingship in Hebron (2 Sam. 1:1–2:11). In an effort to crush David's independent state, the Philistines attacked, but David "smote the Philistines from Geba to Gezer" (2 Sam. 5:17–25). Ultimately, David's opposition to the Philistines broke their power (2 Sam. 8:1; cf. 1 Chron. 18:1). Although the Philistines continued to resist Israel's expansion (cf. 2 Sam. 21:15–22; 23:8–39), they were no longer a major threat to the Hebrews.

When Solomon came to the throne, he received tribute from subordinate kingdoms on the Israelite frontiers, including the city-states of Philistia (1 Kings 4:21). Solomon allied himself with the Egyptian pharaoh by taking an Egyptian wife and receiving the city of Gezer as dowry (1 Kings 9:16). The passing of this important city from Egyptian to Israelite hands is a good indication of the low ebb of Philistine power at this time.

This does not mean that Philistine hostility toward the ancient Hebrews had disappeared; indeed, intermittent fighting between these two peoples continued throughout the history of the Divided Monarchy. Judah received tribute from the Philistines during the reign of Jehoshaphat (2 Chron. 17:11), but the Philistines were among those who raided Judah in Jehoram's day (2 Chron. 21:16–17). While Uzziah made successful incursions into Philistia (2 Chron. 26:6–7), Ahaz lost territory to the Philistines (2 Chron. 28:18). According to the biblical record, the last Israelite king who had contact with the Philistines was Hezekiah; he directed successful campaigns against this traditional rival (2 Kings 18:8).

Since much of this fighting took place during the eighth century B.C., reference should be made to oracles of two Hebrew prophets from this era. Amos (1:6–8) leveled a severe indictment against Gaza, Ashdod, Ashkelon, and Ekron because of the Philistine involvement in slavery (cf. Zeph. 2:4–7; Joel 3:4–8). Isa. 9:12 says that the Lord used the Philistines to punish Israel, but the prophet also warned Philistia about an approaching enemy who would come "out of the north"—the Assyrians (14:28–31).

Isaiah's warning in 715 B.C. (i.e., the year Ahaz died) came long after the Assyrians began interfering with the internal affairs of Philistia. At the end of the ninth century B.C., Adad-nirari III mentioned tribute payments from the Philistines. The military power of Tiglath-pileser III, Sargon II, Sennacherib, and Esarhaddon was felt by the often rebellious cities of Philistia between 734 B.C. and 676 B.C. (cf. Isa. 20). Although the Assyrians exacted tribute from the Philistines and set pro-Assyrian rulers on the thrones of Philistia's city-states, the Assyrian kings allowed this coastal region to retain a measure of autonomy because Philistia acted as a buffer zone on the Egyptian frontier.

Following the collapse of Assyria, the cities along Palestine's southern coast were controlled by Egypt and, when the Philistines joined Egypt in an anti-Babylonian alliance, Nebuchadnezzar deported the rulers and populace of Philistia (cf. Jer. 25:20; 47:2–7; Zech. 9:5–6). While some of the Philistine cities continued into the Byzantine period (and beyond), the Babylonian exile brought an end to the political unit known as Philistia.

Archaeology: Our knowledge of the Philistines is based not only on the Bible and extrabiblical historical sources (including the temple reliefs at Medinet Habu), but on excavated material from numerous archaeological sites. Evidence from these sites, most of which are located in the coastal plain and foothills of southern Palestine, agrees with the written sources in placing the Philistine arrival, expansion, and decline between ca. 1200 B.C. and 1000 B.C. Even the distinctive, Aegean-influenced Philistine pottery, which is commonly found in strata dating to the twelfth–eleventh centuries B.C., disappears after ca. 1000 B.C., a clear indication of the Philistines' adoption of local culture.

The locations of three cities of the Philistine pentapolis are certain—Gaza, Ashkelon, and Ashdod. Current excavations at modern Khirbet Muqanna (Tel Miqneh) may identify this site as ancient Ekron, but the location of Philistine Gath is still uncertain (modern Tell es-Safi?). Major excavations have been conducted at Ashdod, with the recovery of significant data, while the Philistine evidence from Gaza and Ashkelon is meager. Recent investigations at other sites (e.g., Deir el-Balah, Tell el-Batashi, Tell Gezer, Tell Jemmeh, Tel Qasile) have shed new light on Philistine architecture, burials, pottery, metallurgy, religion, and commerce. For example, Tell Jemmeh, located ca. seven miles south of Gaza, yielded artifacts from Arabia, Egypt, Phoenicia, Assyria, Cyprus, and Greece; such evidence demonstrates that Philistia was a crossroads for international trade.

Religion: The OT refers to three Philistine deities—Dagon, Ashtaroth, and Baal-zebub—all of whom had Semitic names; this indicates that the Philistines assimilated the divinities or the names used in local Canaanite religion, a common phenomenon in ancient times. Dagon had temples in Gaza (Judg. 16:21, 23–30), Ashdod (1 Sam. 5:1–7), and probably in Beth-shan (1 Chron. 10:10; cf. 1 Sam. 31:10). Ashtaroth had temples in Ashkelon (Herodotus 1.105) and probably in Beth-shan (1 Sam. 31:10); and Baal-zebub had a temple in Ekron (2 Kings 1:1–16).

Like other ancient peoples, the Philistines offered sacrifices to their gods (Judg. 16:23), sought counsel from priests and diviners (1 Sam. 6:2–9), and developed the art of soothsaying (Isa. 2:6). Apparently, Philistine warriors carried portable idols into battle (2 Sam. 5:21) and had respect for other national deities (cf. 1 Sam. 5:1–6:21).

Prior to the excavations at Tell Qasile, virtually all information about Philistine religion was derived from the biblical passages mentioned above. This situation changed when three superimposed Philistine temples were uncovered at this important site, which is located within the city limits of Tel Aviv. The layout of the latest temple includes both Canaanite and Cypriot-Greek features. Also important was the recovery of a number of cultic vessels from this complex, some of which have Aegean antecedents.

A Philistine pottery sarcophagus from Deir el-Balah, twelfth century B.C.

Language: Strangely enough, not one written text can be attributed to the Philistines with certainty. There are several inscriptions in Cypro-Minoan or Cypro-Mycenaean script that might be Philistine (e.g., seals from Ashdod and tablets from Tell Deir Alla), but none of them can be deciphered. While most Philistine names are Semitic, the names Achish and Goliath find their parallels in Crete and western Anatolia, respectively. Several Hebrew words were probably borrowed from the Philistine language, e.g., *seren*, "lord" (cf. 1 Sam. 5:8); *kôba'*, "helmet" (cf. 1 Sam. 17:5); and *'argaz*, "box" (cf. 1 Sam. 6:8). Like the rest of Philistine culture, their language ultimately disappeared and a local Semitic dialect was adopted. The isolation of Philistia's cities, even in postexilic times, produced a language barrier between the Ashdodites and the Judeans (Neh. 13:23–24). ***See also*** Cherethites; Pelethites; Philistia.

Bibliography

Dothan, T. *The Philistines and Their Material Culture*. New Haven, CT: Yale University Press, 1982.

Hindson, E. *The Philistines and the Old Testament*. Grand Rapids, MI: Baker, 1971.

Kitchen, K. A. "The Philistines," in D. T. Wiseman, ed., *Peoples of Old Testament Times*. Oxford: Clarendon, 1973. Pp. 53–78. G.L.M.

Philo (fī'loh; ca. 20 B.C.–A.D. 50), a wealthy Alexandrian Jew, both statesman and philosopher, the most prolific author of Hellenistic Judaism (i.e., the non-Palestinian branch of Judaism most influenced by Hellenistic culture). Although stemming from the period of the rabbinic sages Hillel, Shammai, and Gamaliel, as well as Jesus and Paul, Philo's writings are remarkably free of rabbinic concerns and betray no awareness of any Christian person or event. Rather, Philo combined a fierce loyalty to Judaism with a profound love of Greek philosophy to present a literary defense of Judaism to his racially troubled city and an extensive allegorical interpretation of Scripture that made Jewish law consonant with the ideals of Stoic, Pythagorean, and especially Platonic thought.

No NT writing owes a direct debt to Philo, but the Gospel of John (especially the *Logos* doctrine of its prologue), the Pauline Letters, and the Letter to the Hebrews reflect to some extent Philo's philosophical terminology and milieu. His writings were preserved by Christians, and later his philosophical ideas and allegorical method had a direct impact on Christian theology through the writings of Clement of Alexandria and Origen. ***See also*** Alexandria; Logos. J.M.B.

Phinehas (fin'ee-uhs). **1** A priest, son of Eleazar, grandson of Aaron (Exod. 6:25; 1 Chron. 6:4, 20), and ancestor of Ezra (Ezra 8:2). Phinehas demonstrated his zeal for God during the wilderness period. Seeing an Israelite man having intercourse with a Midianite woman as part of the rites of Baal of Peor, Phinehas killed them both with one thrust of a spear. This stayed the wrath of God against the people and earned a covenant of eternal priesthood for Phinehas and his descendants (Num. 25:1; cf. Ps. 106:30–31; Ecclus. 45:23–24; 1 Macc. 2:26, 54). Phinehas accompanied Israelite soldiers in a holy war against Midian (Num. 31:6), successfully negotiated a religious dispute between Israel and the Transjordanian tribes (Josh. 22:10–34), and advised the Israelite tribes to attack Benjamin (Judg. 20:27–28). 1 Chron. 9:20 states that he was in charge of the Temple gatekeepers. His home was in Gibeah (Josh. 24:33). **2** A priest, the son of Eli (1 Sam. 1:3). He and his brother Hophni abused their priestly office at Shiloh for which they were condemned (1 Sam. 2:12–36). Both were killed in battle at Aphek by the Philistines who captured the Ark (1 Sam. 4:11). On hearing the tragic news, Phinehas's wife gave birth to Ichabod. **3** The father of the priest Eleazar (Ezra 8:33; 1 Esd. 8:63). ***See also*** Eli; Hophni; Priests. M.A.S.

Phlegon (fleg'ahn), a Christian greeted by Paul in Rom. 16:14; perhaps a member of a house-church.

Phoebe (fee'bee; KJV: "Phebe"), a leading woman of the church in Cenchreae near Corinth in Greece, commended by Paul in Rom. 16:1–2 as worthy of special hospitality. Indeed, Romans 16 may be a letter of recommendation for Phoebe as she moved from Cenchreae, perhaps to Ephesus (Paul's long list of greetings that follows the recommendation in vv. 3–16 appears to suggest Ephesus as the destination). Three special terms are used by Paul to describe Phoebe. She is called "sister," a familial term derived from households and often used in the early Christian communities. She is referred to as a "deacon" (in the Greek, there is no distinction between the masculine and feminine forms) of the church in Cenchreae. Despite Phil. 1:1, it is unlikely that this term designates any official position, as in modern ecclesiastical organizations; it may be paraphrased as "co-worker in the missionary enterprise." Finally, Phoebe is described as a "helper" of Paul and many others; this apparently indicates that she was a "patroness" of the house-church in Cenchreae. As in the case of Jason in Thessalonica (Acts 17:6–9), this probably meant that she owned the house in which the church met and took legal responsibility for the activities there. A possible indication of her importance to Paul is the fact that he speaks of her before giving his long list of greetings. ***See also*** Cenchreae; Church; Paul; Romans, The Letter of Paul to the; Women. A.J.M.

Phoenicia (foh-nee'shee-uh), the name given to a strip of the coastal Levant during the first millennium B.C. It was in that period that the city-states of Tyre, Sidon, Arvad, Byblos, and others engaged in long-distance navigation, maritime commerce, and colonization with Cyprus, North Africa, Sicily, Sardinia, and Iberia. **Name and Origin:** The geographical and chronological boundaries for Phoenicia are imprecise, in part because neither the Phoenicians themselves nor their Near Eastern neighbors used the term "Phoenician." It is in Homer, probably in a milieu of the ninth to eighth centuries B.C., that the inhabitants of Sidon are called Phoenician, although the term may first occur in Mycenaean Linear B texts of the thirteenth century B.C. The Phoenicians were famous for their costly purple dye produced from crushed mollusks; it has long been suggested that the name "Phoenicia" is derived from the Greek word for red-purple, *phoinix*. By the same token "Canaan," a name for parts of the Levant, may come from a Hurrian word for red-purple, *kinahhu*.

In fact the Phoenicians of the Iron Age (first millennium B.C.) descended from the original Canaanites who dwelt in the region during the earlier Bronze Age (3000–1200 B.C.), despite classical tradition to the contrary. There is archaeological evidence for a continuous cultural tradition from the Bronze to the Iron Age (1200–333 B.C.) at the cities of Tyre and Zaraphath. In the Amarna age (fourteenth century B.C.) many letters to Egypt emanated from kings Rib-Addi of Byblos, Abi-Milki of Tyre, and Zimrida of Sidon, and in other New Kingdom Egyptian texts there are references to the cities of Beirut, Sidon, Zaraphath, Ushu, Tyre, and Byblos. Additionally there is a thirteenth-century B.C. letter from the king of Tyre to Ugarit, and a Ugaritic inscription has turned up at Zaraphath. Despite these facts showing that the coastal cities were occupied without interruption or change in population, the term "Phoenician" is now normally applied to them in the Iron Age (beginning about the twelfth century B.C.) onward when the traits that characterize Phoenician culture evolved: long-distance seafaring, trade and colonization, and distinctive elements of their material culture, language, and script.

Principal Cities and Sites: The heartland of Phoenician city-states was the coastal area from Acco in the south to Arvad in the north, which in the main constitutes modern Lebanon where the Lebanon mountain range is an imposing barrier to communications between coastal cities and the inland. The most important cities and sites are the island-city Tyre, with its mainland counterpart Ushu (Old Tyre), and Sidon and its neighbors, Zaraphath and the religious center Eshmun, followed by the other island-city, Arvad, with its mainland settlement of Amrit/Marathus, the ancient port of Byblos that was famous long before the Phoenician period, and Beirut with the small burial ground at Khalde. The roster of Phoenician cities changed during the near millennium-long period beginning in 1200 B.C., reflecting the waxing and waning of their individual fortunes and the impinging historical events of the Near East.

Phoenician silver coin showing a Phoenician ship and hippocampus monster—part horse, part fish.

At the beginning of the Iron Age, as part of the invasion of the Sea Peoples (groups from the Greek islands, especially Crete), the Philistines occupied the coastal area south of Mt. Carmel, including Dor, Ashdod, Ashkelon, and Gaza. By the eighth century B.C., however, the material culture of the Phoenicians extended southward, and Sidon controlled Dor and Joppa during the Persian period (539–333 B.C.). There were no major Phoenician cities north of Arvad, but Phoenician influence extended into Cilicia in the ninth and eighth centuries B.C.

Culture and Influence: Obscurity surrounds the emergence of Phoenician culture during the twelfth and eleventh centuries B.C. In a foray, the Assyrian king Tiglath-pileser I (1114–1076 B.C.) sojourned at Arvad and received tribute from Byblos and Sidon, and there are archaeological data from Tyre and Zaraphath for this period. The Egyptian *Tale of Wenamun*, dating to the mid-eleventh century B.C., graphically portrays the decline of Egyptian prestige and power in the Levant. This was due in part to the invasions of the Sea Peoples and the general disruptions of Late Bronze Age cultures throughout the eastern Mediterranean, with the collapse of Mycenaean and Hittite cultures and the destruction of city-states in the Levant. Trade was severely affected. During the fourteenth and thirteenth centuries B.C. Mycenaean and Cypriot imports flowed into the Levant but they were only a trickle from the twelfth century B.C. onward.

In the aftermath of the disruptions and the power vacuum a new order emerged in which flourishing Phoenician settlements replaced such destroyed centers as Ugarit on the coast of northern Syria. Instead of the Levant being the recipient of Aegean wares, Phoenician cities began exporting goods and services to Cyprus and Palestine.

The history of Tyre and Sidon is intertwined (indeed they were only twenty-two miles [35 km.] apart). Classical tradition suggests that Sidon was the more powerful at first but by the tenth century B.C. Tyre dominated. Tyre's kings ruled a stretch of the coast that included Sidon, and often they were referred to as kings of the Sidonians (1 Kings 16:31).

By the tenth century B.C. Phoenician craftsmen were sent to Israel to assist Solomon in the construction of the Temple at Jerusalem. In return Solomon sent grain and olive oil to Hiram, king of Tyre, and even Galilean territory was given to him (1 Kings 5), although it was not to his liking. Tyre's colonization of Cyprus in the

Phoenician porters, in pointed caps and unfringed robes, carry tribute to the Assyrian ruler Shalmaneser III; ninth-century B.C. engraved bronze gates.

tenth century B.C. was established and it controlled the southern coastal city of Kition where Phoenicians constructed temples for their goddess Astarte.

In the ninth century B.C. Tyre strengthened its influence over the northern kingdom of Israel. Phoenician influence is also to be seen in the region of Cilicia at Zinjirli where King Kilamuwa, probably Aramaean in origin, chose the Phoenician language and script for a long inscription at the front of his palace. Other Phoenician inscriptions come from the same region in the following centuries; Azitiwada marked the rebuilding of his city with bilingual inscriptions in Phoenician and hieroglyphic Hittite at Karatepe. The strong Phoenician influence in Cilicia may be due to trading activities in a network including Urartu, the northern rival of Assyria in the ninth and eighth centuries B.C. Phoenician trade and colonization of the western Mediterranean became strong in this period. Classical tradition places the date of foundation of Carthage at 814 B.C. by Tyrians.

During the earlier centuries Phoenician cities were autonomous for the most part and free from interference from outside political forces, although Assyrian monarchs from time to time demanded tribute. The pace of Assyrian activity in Phoenicia quickened in the ninth century B.C. when Ashurnasirpal II, Shalmaneser III, and Adadnirari III exacted tribute and taxes from Sidon, Tyre, and other Phoenician cities. Assyria was gradually extending its control over the Levant. As a result of the far-reaching reorganization of the Assyrian Empire by Tiglath-pileser III (744–727 B.C.), the nature of the impact on Phoenicia changed from one of occasional demands by raiding armies to incorporation as vassals into the empire. Many cities lost their autonomy altogether and became part of Assyrian provinces administered by governors; for example, an Assyrian province of Simyra was established by Tiglath-pileser III.

During Sennacherib's reign (705–681 B.C.) he crushed a serious revolt by coastal cities in 701 B.C. and forced Luli (Elulaeus), king of Tyre, to flee to Cyprus, where he died. Later Sidon revolted against the Assyrian ruler Esarhaddon (681–669 B.C.) who in 676 B.C. sacked and destroyed it and in its place built a governor's residence, called Kar-Esarhaddon, for a new Assyrian province. He also made a treaty with Baal, king of Tyre. Ashurbanipal (668–627 B.C.) laid siege to Tyre and Nebuchadnezzar besieged it for thirteen years (586–573 B.C.; Ezek. 26–28: 19).

Sidon reemerged as the dominant city of Phoenicia in the Persian period (539–333 B.C.) and led a Phoenician contingent in the Persian wars of the early fifth century B.C., helping bridge the Hellespont and fighting at Salamis. In Phoenicia itself, remains of this period are best represented at a sanctuary near Sidon dedicated to the god Eshmun, at Byblos, and at Amrit (Marathus). In 332 B.C. Tyre finally yielded to military attack when Alexander built a mole between the island-city and the mainland during his seven-month siege.

Phoenicians expanded into the western Mediterranean during the ninth and eighth centuries B.C. in Sardinia, Sicily, North Africa, and Iberia. Their trading stations and colonies on the Atlantic and Mediterranean sides of Gibraltar (Tartessos region) exploited the rich silver mines and other raw materials of Iberia. Many causes have been put forward for the impetus of Phoenician expansion: the geographical setting of an inland mountain barrier naturally turned them seaward; depletion of natural resources (timber); overpopulation; development of a craft industry that demanded raw materials and foreign markets (Ezek. 27–28); and the influence of Assyria. It is debatable whether Phoenician expansion developed internally or was in reaction to growing Assyrian imperialism. If it was in response to Assyrians and Chaldaeans, did the Phoenicians flee their homeland to escape oppression (Isa. 23) or did they prosper economically as key middlemen in the empire's trade network (Isa. 23; Ezek. 27–28), which extended the length of the Mediterranean? The greater economic threat came from competing Greek expansion during the eighth century B.C. and later. The Phoenicians extracted from the mollusk *Murex trunculus* a rare and costly purple dye for textiles and garments. Heaps of crushed *murex* shells have been found at Zaraphath, Sidon, and Tyre.

Solomon turned to skilled Phoenician builders, who helped cut and assemble stone and wood for the Temple at Jerusalem (1 Kings 5). Today the best examples of Phoenician sacred architecture are the temple of Astarte at Kition, the sanctuary at Eshmun, and a small shrine at Zaraphath. Phoenicians often constructed stone walls with vertical piers of ashlar blocks laid in an alternating pattern of header and stretcher. The area between the piers was filled with irregular field stones. Ivory carving was another Phoenician craft. Their ivories, which were often inlays for furniture, date to the eighth and seventh centuries B.C. and have been found at Megiddo, Samaria, and elsewhere in Palestine, in Assyrian cities, on Cyprus and in the western Mediterranean, and in the homeland at Zaraphath and Byblos. The ornate Levantine style exhibits a strong Egyptian influence with motifs of winged sphinxes, lotus flowers, and human figures with Egyptian headdress. Metal bowls with embossed and engraved designs of a central medallion and concentric bands were produced by skilled Cypro-Phoenician craftsmen in bronze, silver, and gold.

Phoenicians spoke a Northwest Semitic language closely related to Ugaritic, Hebrew, and Aramaic. According to the ancient Greek historian Herodotus the Phoenicians introduced the alphabet to Greece. Alphabetic writing was already well established in the Late Bronze Age at Ugarit where a cuneiform script was used. The Phoenician alphabetic script is similar to early Hebrew and Aramaic scripts of the first millennium B.C.

Religion: Phoenician religion shared elements with other Canaanite cultures of the Levant in which the pantheon (i.e., the gods who were worshiped) differed from city to city and from one age to the next. Nature and fertility deities predominated. Baal, Astarte, Eshmun, Adonis, and Melqart were the chief deities, while Tanit, most popular in North Africa, was also known in Phoenicia. Baal, the chief god of Tyre and Sidon, was the leading rival to Yahweh worship in the northern Israelite kingdom (1 Kings 16: 29–32:18). Baal's consort was the goddess Astarte. At Byblos the deities El and Baalat took the place of Baal and Astarte, and nearby the young god Adonis was worshiped at a country shrine of Aphka at the source of the river Nahr Ibrahim. Lucian (second century A.D.) relates that the death of Adonis was marked by annual rites of mourning when the river became red with the god's blood. At Sidon the god Eshmun was also worshiped at an important country sanctuary near springs for the river Nahr el-Awali. Eshmun, whom the Greeks identified with the healing god Asclepius, was most popular in the Chaldaean and Persian periods. Melqart, whose relationship to Baal is ambiguous, was worshiped at Tyre and in the western Mediterranean. At Carthage the goddess Tanit was propitiated by infamous child immolation by fire. Sacrificial precincts (Heb. *tophet*; 2 Kings 23:10; Jer. 7:31) containing cremation urns have been found at Carthage and on Sicily and Sardinia but none have turned up in Iberia or Phoenicia. However, a dedicatory inscription from Zaraphath for Tanit-Astarte makes it clear that Tanit was worshiped in Phoenicia as early as the seventh century B.C. In the NT, Jesus journeyed into this region (Mark 7:24; cf. v. 26), and the area was visited by various Christian missionaries (Acts 11:19; 15:3; 21:2). ***See also*** Hiram; Philistines; Sidon; Solomon; Tyre.

Bibliography

Harden, D. *The Phoenicians.* New York: Praeger, 1962.

Moscati, S. *The World of the Phoenicians.* London: Weidenfeld & Nicolson, 1968.

Pritchard, J. B. *Recovering Sarepta, A Phoenician City.* Princeton, NJ: Princeton University Press, 1978.

T.L.M.

Phoenix, a seaport (possibly modern Port Loutro) on the southeastern coast of Crete. It was while on board an Alexandrian ship en route from Fair Haven to Phoenix for winter harborage that Paul and his captors were shipwrecked (Acts 27:12).

Phrygia (free'jee-ah), a large region of interior western Asia Minor, during the NT period divided by the Romans into the provinces Asia and Galatia. The Phrygians, apparently of Thracian stock, were renowned for fanatical worship of the mother-goddess Cybele and her consort Attis. Jews too inhabited the region as early as the second century B.C., according to the historian Josephus. Acts 2:10 mentions Phrygian Jewish pilgrims among those who heard the apostles speaking in tongues at Pentecost.

Even though Paul never explicitly mentions his ministry there, it is likely he and his fellow missionaries were primarily responsible for evangelizing Phrygia. Philemon, whom Paul knew personally and whom he intended to revisit, probably lived in or near Colossae. Paul's silence concerning Phrygia most likely is due to his habit of referring to Asia Minor areas by their provincial names; if so, references to Galatia and especially to Asia may in fact pertain to Phrygia. Be that as it may, Acts says he preached in Antioch of Pisidia (not actually in Pisidia; 13:14–51), and again later passed

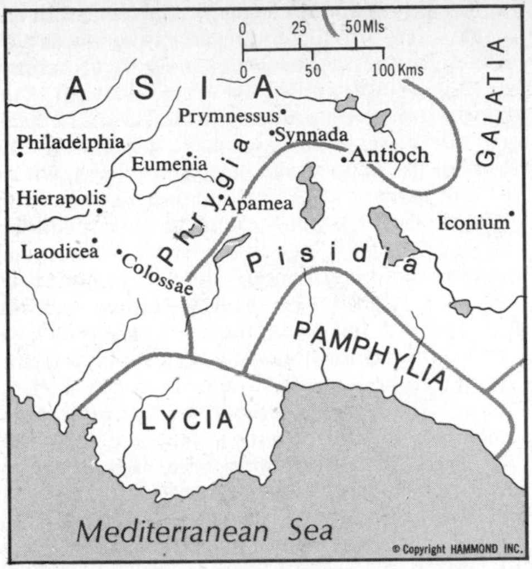

through Phrygia twice (16:6; 18:23). According to pseudo-Pauline letters, he or his companions worked in Antioch, Laodicea, Hierapolis, Colossae, and Iconium (Col. 1:2; 2:1; 4:13, 15–16; 2 Tim. 3:11). The second-century apocryphal *Acts of Paul*, which is almost certainly dependent on earlier tradition, tells of his ministry to Antioch and to Iconium, where allegedly he converted a woman named Thecla, later long venerated in the region as a prophetess, teacher, and healer.

The itinerant author of the Revelation to John also worked in this area, as one can see from his comments concerning Laodicea (3:14–22). Papias, bishop of Hierapolis early in the second century, tells of missionaries who still traveled through the area, and of the prophesying virgin daughters of Philip (see Acts 21:8–9), two of whom lived in Hierapolis. Our primary witnesses to Christianity in Phrygia—Paul, Revelation to John, Papias, and *The Acts of Paul*—all suggest it was characteristically apocalyptic, sectarian, and socially disruptive. The New Prophecy that sprang up in Phrygia during the mid-second century with the appearance of the prophets Montanus, Maximilla, and Priscilla seems to have been rooted in this distinctively Phrygian form of Christianity. ***See also*** Colossae; Hierapolis; Laodicea. D.R.M.

Phygelus (fī'juh-luhs), an Asian Christian who, with Hermogenes and others, abandoned Paul the prisoner (2 Tim. 1:15). This and the following three verses are sometimes thought to create a vivid impression of authenticity and thus to pose difficulties for the theory that 2 Timothy is pseudonymous; oral tradition may, however, have preserved such references. ***See also*** Hermogenes; Timothy, The First and Second Letters of Paul to, and Titus, The Letter of Paul to.

phylacteries (Heb. *tephillin*), a pair of small black boxes containing passages from Scripture written on parchment. According to ancient Jewish tradition, the *tephillin* are fastened by black straps to the upper left arm and above the forehead. The tradition is based on Exod. 13:9, 16; Deut. 6:8; and 11:18. The paragraphs in which these verses appear are the very ones placed inside the phylacteries.

There is no evidence as to when the practice of wearing phylacteries originated. The verses from which the practice is derived appear to carry a metaphorical meaning, namely, that the acceptance of God's laws and the recognition of his power be on one's mind and body. Exod. 13:9 in particular is suited to such an interpretation, as it is speaking within the context of the annual observance of the Passover service without reference to a daily practice. A nonliteral understanding of these verses is further strengthened in light of the widespread metaphorical use of ornaments to indicate something carefully remembered and held dear (Isa. 62:3; Jer. 2:32; Prov. 1:9; Song of Sol. 8:6; *Gilgamesh Epic* XI, 164–165). Nevertheless, Deut. 6:8 and 11:18 may intend the practice to be followed literally (there it is words that are to be bound to the body, and the context also refers to the literal writing of these words on doorposts and gates).

A "silver phylactery" is mentioned in an Aramaic papyrus from Elephantine, Egypt, dating from the beginning of the third century B.C. Phylacteries found at Qumran, along with statements in Matt. 23:5 and in rabbinic literature (e.g., *M. Meg.* 4:8), show that the practice was widely observed toward the end of the Second Temple period. While the wearing of phylacteries was not universally accepted during the rabbinic period (post–A.D. 200), the celebrated Bar-Kochba phylacteries from Wadi Murabbaat attest to the steadfast adherence to the practice, even under trying circumstances, of those who did keep it.

Like many religious objects, phylacteries were often conceived of by the masses as possessing apotropaic (i.e., protective) powers. This association was deepened by the outward resemblance of the phylacteries to a type of amulet known as *qemia* which was also thought to possess protective powers. However, the edifying contents of the phylacteries as well as the laws forbidding their use by certain people thought to be most susceptible to demonic power show that the phylacteries were originally intended as a spiritual and educational device. The official understanding of phylacteries is brought out in many rabbinic sources, most notably in the Babylonian Talmud, tractate *Berakot* 14b–15a: "Whoever wishes to take the yoke of the kingship of heaven upon himself completely should [first] relieve himself and wash his hands, and [then] don *tephillin* and recite the *Shema* and the *Tefillah;* this is the complete [acceptance of the] kingship of heaven."

Like other religious objects, phylacteries could be used to flaunt piety. Such a show is criticized in Matt. 23:5 and in Talmudic sources (e.g., *Midr. Eccles. Rab.* 4:1). ***See also*** Frontlet.

Bibliography

Rabinowitz, L. I. "Tefillin." *Encyclopaedia Judaica.* Vol. 15. Pp. 898–904.

Tigay, J. H. "On the Term Phylacteries (Matt. 23: 5)." *Harvard Theological Review* 72 (1979): 45–52.

Yadin, Y. *Tefillin from Qumran.* Jerusalem: Israel Exploration Society, 1969. D.A.G./J.H.T.

physicians, those healing illnesses by profession. The OT text does not provide a representative sample of the illnesses and therapies obtaining in ancient Israel. The physician healer (Heb. *rofe'*, "healer," Jer. 8:22; 2 Chron. 16:12) and midwife (e.g., Gen. 35:17; 38:28; Exod. 1: 15–22 [following the Masoretic Text vocalization]) come under the category of medical personnel. In addition, priests and prophets or miracle workers (e.g., 1 Kings 17:17–24; 2 Kings 4:14–37; 5) are shown providing medical services; prophet (Isa. 38; 2 Kings 20:1–11) and patriarch (Gen. 20:7, 17–18) at times served as intermediary between God and king on the occasion of illness. Information regarding modes of healing may even be inferred from divine attributions (e.g., Ps. 147:3).

As with other ancient cultures, there was in Israel no necessary conflict between belief in divine, demonic, and/or human causation of illness or between requests for divine assistance and the application of practical therapy. Prayer played a role in some treatments. Certainly, miraculous cures are occasionally described (1 Kings 17:17–24; 2 Kings 5:1–14). It is unnecessary to seek scientific explanations for such cures. Here and there we may be dealing with natural remission or psychogenic illness amenable to certain therapies, but on the whole, the stories are intended to demonstrate the supernatural powers of God and/or of the miracle worker. Yet it must be assumed that belief in natural causes of illness existed and that rational diagnoses seeking autonomous causes of illness co-existed with other approaches. Practical aids included: bandages, salves, poultices, bone setting (e.g., Isa. 1:6; Jer. 8:22; Ezek. 34:4, 16). A good perspective on biblical medicine is provided in Ecclus. 38:1–15. The general absence of incantations and magical therapies (exorcism) from the Hebrew Bible should not lead us to conclude that they did not exist in ancient Israel.

Worthy of special mention are the different kinds of medical personnel and types of documentation in ancient Mesopotamia, because of its general influence on the culture of Israel. Professional handbooks and correspondence of royal courts provide detailed and reliable information on the approach to illness of and types of therapeutic activities undertaken by the *āshipu* (exorcist) and *asû* (doctor).

While many healing miracles are reported of Jesus in the NT Gospels (e.g., Matt. 8:1–4; Mark 5:1–20; Luke 13:10–13; John 9:1–7), the term "physician" is never applied to him. Jesus assumed that such healing activity would also characterize his followers, something the Gospels (e.g., Mark 6:13) and Acts (e.g., 3:1–8; 14: 8–10) record, but again, the title "physician" is never applied to them either. Physicians were known in the NT world, however, even though their skills were not held in high esteem (e.g., Mark 5:26), and a physician named Luke, whom tradition has identified as the author of the Third Gospel, is mentioned as a companion of Paul (Col. 4:14). I.T.A.

Pi-beseth (pī-bee'zith), a city in the delta in Egypt. Ezek. 30:17 includes it as part of the prophet's oracle against Egypt. Known in Greek as Bubastis, it is modern Tell Basta on an eastern branch of the delta flow. Its name reflects its identification with the Egyptian cat goddess, Bastet.

Pi-hahiroth (pī-hah-hī'rawth), a town mentioned in Exod. 14:2, 9 as an Israelite stopping place on the route from Egypt (see also Num. 33: 7). Its associations with Baal-zephon and Migdol suggest an eastern Nile delta location, but the site is not precisely known.

Pilate, Pontius (pī'luht, pon'shuhs), Roman prefect of Judea, the fifth governor of the province and the second-longest holder of the office (A.D. 26–36). His term included the time of John the Baptist's activity, as well as that of the public ministry and crucifixion of Jesus (see Luke 3:1). In addition to the NT references, where Pilate plays a central role in the events surrounding the trial and crucifixion of Jesus (Matt. 27:1–2, 11–26; Mark 15:1–15; Luke 23:1–25; John 18: 28–19:16; Acts 3:13; 4:27; 13:28; 1 Tim. 6:13), we have information about Pilate and his rule in the historical writings of Philo Judaeus and Flavius Josephus. An important piece of archaeological evidence is a dedication inscription, found in Caesarea Maritima in 1961, where Pilate is given his correct title of prefect (not procurator).

In the Jewish Sources: Pilate's character is represented very negatively in the Jewish sources: he is presented as insensitive to Jewish religious scruples and all too ready to use brutal force to repress any dissent. He is also charged with incompetence and venality. Since, however, we hear only one side on Pilate (the only extant Roman mention is a brief reference in the historian Tacitus to the crucifixion of Jesus), and

PILATE, PONTIUS

Pilate washing his hands at the trial of Jesus (cf. Matt. 27:24); from a fifth-century ivory.

since Pilate governed Judea for an unusually long term, which may indicate that the Roman government was not displeased with his performance, it appears best to withhold judgment on his character.

Josephus reports that, when Pilate first brought Roman troops to Jerusalem from Caesarea, he committed an unprecedented violation of Jewish sensibilities by allowing the troops to bring into the city their military standards with the busts of the emperor, which were considered idolatrous images by the Jews; and this was done in an underhanded manner, the troops bringing in and setting up the images by night. A massive protest demonstration in Caesarea's stadium forced the removal of the standards, but only after the Jews used tactics of nonviolent mass resistance, lying down and baring their necks when Pilate's soldiers, swords in hand, surrounded and attempted to disperse them.

Philo tells of an incident where Jewish letters of protest to Rome brought the intervention of the emperor himself, who commanded Pilate to remove golden shields with the emperor's name on them that he had placed in his residence in Jerusalem. Similar incidents were not always resolved without bloodshed, however. Josephus again speaks of protests that broke out when Pilate appropriated Temple funds to build an aqueduct for Jerusalem. On this occasion, Pilate had Roman soldiers, dressed as Jewish civilians and armed with hidden clubs, mingle with the shouting crowd and attack the people at a prearranged signal. Many were killed or hurt.

There is no extrabiblical account of the incident mentioned in Luke 13:1, "of the Galileans whose blood Pilate had mingled with their sacrifices," but it does not appear out of character with the other incidents or with the slaughter of Samaritans in A.D. 35, mentioned by Josephus, which apparently brought about Pilate's recall. A Samaritan prophet (Josephus calls him a liar) gathered large numbers of his people to Mount Gerizim with the promise of showing them the holy vessels supposedly hidden there by Moses. Pilate treated the event as an insurrection and attacked the crowd with cavalry and heavy infantry, killing many in the battle and executing the leaders among the captured. Vitellius, the imperial legate to Syria, felt compelled to remove Pilate from office and sent him to Rome to render account of his conduct.

In the Gospel Accounts: Pilate's part in the trial and execution of Jesus is, of course, the focus of most later interest in him. His role is presented somewhat differently in each of the Gospels, reflecting the diversity of theological agendas of the various authors as well as a growing tendency, as time passed, for Christians to exonerate the Romans and to lay blame for Jesus' crucifixion on "the Jews."

Mark's account (15:1–15) presents Pilate in the most ambiguous light: he "wonders" at Jesus' silence when questioned and accused of calling himself "King of the Jews" and bends to the will of the mob (stirred up by the chief priests) in sending Jesus to the cross and setting Barabbas free, even though he sees no good reason for this (15:14–15). Matthew's account (27:1–2, 11–26) introduces Pilate's wife (not named in the Gospel but called Procla or Procula in later tradition), who warns Pilate to have nothing to do with "that righteous man," about whom she has had a dream; also introduced is the hand-washing incident, in which Pilate claims, unchallenged, his own innocence and "all the people" cry, "His blood be on us and on our children!" (27:24–25). Luke's version (23:1–25) has Pilate send Jesus, accused of perverting the nation, forbidding payment of tribute to Caesar, and claiming his own kingship, to Herod Antipas, whose soldiers (not the Romans) mock him. John (18:28–19:16), in an elaborate scheme of "inside" and "outside" scenes, carries even further the idea that Pilate, who did not wish to condemn Jesus, was a helpless pawn (not only of the Jewish people but also of God; see 19:11). John also has Jesus emphasize the otherworldly character of his kingship.

Later Christian tradition went even further than the Gospels in the direction of exonerating Pilate, in some cases even suggesting his eventual repentance and conversion to Christianity. ***See also*** Barabbas; Judea; Procurator; Trial of Jesus, The. F.O.G.

pilgrimage, a journey to a shrine, holy place, or sanctuary for a religious reason. Such journeys are a common feature of religious devotion and are not confined to any particular religious tradition, period of time, or group of people. In the ancient Near East, shrines or cultic (worship) centers were often established at sites connected with divine activity, such as an extraordinary event (e.g., Josh. 4:1–7) or unusual natural phenomena, or at sites revered by tradition as holy (e.g., Gen. 13:18). The shrine often became the goal of pilgrimages, and worshipers would bring offerings to the shrine for petition or thanksgiving. Archaeological excavations in various parts of the world have uncovered such shrines, altars, and temples containing pottery jars or other objects used for the offerings.

The earliest pilgrimages recorded in the Bible were to the shrines or cultic centers that existed throughout Israel before the reforms of King Josiah (ca. 622 B.C.). At a critical point in Jacob's life (the changing of his name to Israel) he made a pilgrimage in ritual purity to Bethel, the place where he had earlier erected an altar after seeing God in a dream (Gen. 35:1–15; cf. 28:10–22; 12:8). Shiloh was also the goal of an early annual pilgrimage (Judg. 21:19–21; 1 Sam. 1:3–7, 21), and other early cultic centers in Israel also attracted worshipers, including Gibeon (1 Kings 3:4), Beer-sheba (Amos 5:5; 8:14), and Gilgal (Hos. 4:15; Amos 4:4–5; 5:5), as well as numerous "high places" (1 Sam. 9:12–19, 25). Although the provisions concerning pilgrimage in Deuteronomy are connected with Jerusalem in their present context, they may reflect an earlier tradition of pilgrimage to these local shrines (e.g., Deut. 26:1–11).

To Jerusalem: In the time of David (ca. 1000 B.C.), Jerusalem was established as a religious center (2 Sam. 6:12–19), and following the completion of the Temple under Solomon (1 Kings 8; 2 Chron. 7:8–10) it increasingly became the goal of pilgrimage, a place to which the people could bring their offerings and a place they could celebrate the feasts and offer sacrifice to God (Deut. 12:6–7, 11–12, 17–18). After the division of the nation (ca. 924 B.C.), Jeroboam I of the Northern Kingdom, in an attempt to prevent the people from traveling to the Temple in Jerusalem (in the Southern Kingdom), established sanctuaries at the ancient shrine of Bethel and at Dan (1 Kings 12:26–30). The reforms of Hezekiah and Josiah attempted to eliminate the outlying shrines and high places because of the threat of corruption by Baal worship (2 Kings 18:4; 23:4–20), but they continued to exist until the period of the Exile (587 B.C.).

The old Israelite religious legislation required pilgrimage to Jerusalem three times a year: at Passover (the Feast of Unleavened Bread), the Feast of Weeks (Pentecost), and the Feast of Booths (Deut. 16:16; cf. Exod. 23:13–17; 34:18–23), although it is unlikely that the entire male population attended all of these feasts. In any case, in NT times there were large crowds of pilgrims in Jerusalem for the feasts from widely scattered places (Luke 2:41–45; John 12:20; Acts 2:1–10). According to the Fourth Gospel, Jesus made several pilgrimages to Jerusalem to celebrate the feasts (John 2:13; 5:1; 7:2–10).

Those on pilgrimage often traveled in groups (Pss. 42:4; 55:14; Luke 2:44) and the joy of the occasion would be marked by singing and rejoicing (Isa. 30:29). Several of these songs are preserved in the "Songs of Ascent" (or "degrees" in some older versions) or "Pilgrim Songs" sung by the pilgrims as they approached Jerusalem (Pss. 24, 84, 118, 120–134).

Jews continued to make pilgrimages to Jerusalem after the destruction of the Temple (A.D. 70) as well as to the tomb of Samuel at Nabi Samwil (Ramah). The western retaining wall of the Temple Mount known as the "Wailing Wall" is still the goal of Jewish pilgrims who bemoan the loss of the Temple and pray for the peace of Jerusalem.

In Christian Tradition: Christian pilgrimages to the Holy Land began as early as A.D. 100 although they did not become popular until the time of Emperor Constantine I (A.D. 306–337). After his conversion to Christianity, he and his mother, Helena, attempted to locate places in the Holy Land associated with the life of Jesus and in so doing stimulated the construction of shrines and churches on the sites. These locations drew pilgrims whose piety and devotion were expressed in a veneration of the sacred places. By the end of the fourth century A.D. pilgrimages to the Holy Land, as well as to Rome, Egypt, and numerous other local shrines associated with relics, miracles, visitations, or martyrs, were commonplace and an accepted part of Christian devotion.

In a figurative sense, the NT portrays the Christian life as a journey toward a heavenly city (Heb. 11:13–16; cf. 1 Pet. 1:17; 2:11). The allegory in *The Pilgrim's Progress* by John Bunyan is a popular expression of this concept. ***See also*** Bethel; Feasts, Festivals, and Fasts; High Place; Passover, The; Shiloh; Via Dolorosa; Zarephath. D.R.B.

pillars. **1** Vertical columns of wood or stone used as architectural members to hold up roof supports, whether in temples (1 Kings 7; Judg. 16:25–29), palaces (Esther 1:6), or houses, as archaeological evidence abundantly shows. They were set on firm bases or in sockets for stability and were capped by capitals sometimes elaborately decorated or carved. The two nonsupporting pillars erected at the front entrance of the Temple (1 Kings 7:15–22) were lavishly finished both in material and motifs. One possible function for these named items was that they were a Hebrew adaptation of Canaanite symbolism (see 3 below). Pillars could be solid, single-block columns, sometimes fluted, or composite columns built of drum cylinders fitted together in vertical alignment.

2 Memorials marking individual burials (Gen. 35:20, Jacob's memorial to Rachel at her grave), self-commemorations (2 Sam. 18:18, Absalom's monument to himself), or significant events (Gen. 28:22, 31:45; 35:14, aspects of Jacob's life), in some cases leading to shrine locations. Inscribed stelae commemorating historical events were used by Egyptian, Assyrian, Greek, and Roman forces and have been recovered at numerous locations in the Near East, e.g., the Nahr el-Kelb north of Beirut in Lebanon.

3 Sacred objects. The stone pillar representing the male deity and the lush tree or wooden post representing the female deity were standard parts of Canaanite Baalist shrine equipment. Their presence symbolized the sexual union of the gods necessary to allow agricultural fertility to continue from one year to the next. Israelite religion opposed this point of view vigorously in law (Exod. 23:24; Deut. 7:5; Lev. 26:1) and prophetic warning (Hos. 3:4; 10:2; Mic. 5:13), despite its somewhat popular appeal among the ordinary folk (Amos 2:7–8). The mysterious and uncertain nature of the two pillars in front of the Temple is due in part to the fact that such bisexual symbols would have had no place in a monotheistic theology.

Additional sacred pillars include the sacred tree at the shrine at Shechem (Judg. 9:6), parts of the tabernacle (Exod. 26:32), the altar at Bethel (Gen. 35:14), a special shrine in Egypt (Isa. 19:19), numerous sacred pillars in Egypt (Jer. 43:13, "obelisks"), and possibly the twelve-stone center at Gilgal (Josh. 4:129–24) and the one placed by Moses (Exod. 24:4) somewhere in the wilderness.

4 Meteorological or volcanic phenomena, such as the pillars of cloud or fire (Exod. 13:21) that guided Israel in the wilderness and marked the door of the tent of meeting (Exod. 33:9, 10; Deut. 31:15), experiences long remembered as acts of God's gracious love (Neh. 9:12–19; Ps. 99:7).

5 Symbols, often of strength or support. They supported the earth (1 Sam. 2:8; Ps. 75:3) or the heavens (Job 26:11). It was wished that daughters would be strong as corner pillars (Ps. 144:12). They supported the "house" of wisdom (Prov. 9:1), and Isaiah could describe people as mainstays of society with the term (Isa. 19:10), as Paul could similarly describe James, Cephas, and John in the reputations they enjoyed in the Church (Gal. 2:9). The church was the pillar of truth (1 Tim. 3:15). As an angel's legs could be described as "pillars of fire" (Rev. 10:1), so the pillar of salt could be remembered as a symbol of the folly of Lot's wife (Gen. 19:26).

6 Markers of various sorts. According to archaeological evidence from Palestine, pillars were used as boundary stones, menhirs, and milestones. The function of the still enigmatic dolmens (usually two slabs of rock capped by a horizontal slab) scattered in fields is still debated. R.S.B.

pillow, a headrest, whether made out of goat's hair (conjectural translation in 1 Sam. 19:13, 16) or another material such as stone (Gen. 28:11, 18). The KJV uses the term in Ezek. 13:18, 20 where the RSV has "magic bands," and the pillow (RSV: "cushion") on which Jesus slept in the boat (Mark 4:38) was probably a seat pad.

pim, a weight averaging 7.8 grams in samples found. This makes it equal to three-fifths of a heavy shekel or seven-eighths of a light shekel. In 1 Sam. 13:21 it was the Philistine price for sharpening iron implements. ***See also*** Weights and Measures.

pin, a short, pointed shaft. A pin (Heb. *yathad*) is mentioned in Judg. 16:13–14, where it apparently designates the short, pointed stick used to beat up the weft in a loom (the Masoretic text is unclear and the Septuagint understands the term as a peg driven into the wall to secure the loom). The same Hebrew word is used elsewhere for a tent stake or peg (Judg. 4:21), including those used in erecting the tabernacle (Exod. 27:19, KJV: "pins"), a peg for hanging objects (Ezek. 15:3, KJV: "pin"), and a digging stick or spade (Deut. 23:13).

pine, a word used as both noun and verb in the OT. **1** A tree of the genus *Pinus* with straight-grained highly resinous wood, good for construction (Song of Sol. 1:17), shipfitting (Ezek. 27:6), reclamation (Isa. 41:19), decoration (Isa. 60:13), aromatics, and other products. **2** A verb meaning to fade away or dwindle (Lev. 26:16; 26:39; Isa. 24:16; Ezek. 24:23).

pipe. *See* Music.

Piram (pī'rem; Heb., "wild ass"?), the king of Jarmuth and one of the Amorite allies who attempted to stop Joshua at Gibeon (Josh. 10:3–11), only to be killed and hung (Josh. 10:22–26). Jarmuth is probably modern Khirbet Yarmuk about fifteen miles southwest of Jerusalem.

Pirathon (pihr'uh-thawn), a town considered the home of Abdon, who was buried there (Judg. 12:15), and Benaiah, one of David's guards (2 Sam. 23:30; 1 Chron. 11:31; 27:14). It is probably modern Far'ata about five miles west and slightly south of Shechem.

Pisgah (piz'gah), a mountain in the area east of the Dead Sea. In the Bible "the top of Pisgah" is mentioned four times. In Num. 21:20, Pisgah, which looks down upon the desert, is located in the region of Moab. In Num. 23:14, Balak took Balaam to the field of Zophim, to the top of Pisgah, in the land of Moab. In Deut. 3:27 and 34:1 Moses went up from the plain of Moab to Mount Nebo, to the top of Pisgah, which is opposite Jericho, to view the land.

The "slopes of Pisgah" are also mentioned four times. In Deut. 3:17 and 4:49 the Sea of the Arabah, the Salt Sea, is "under the slopes of Pisgah" to the east. In Josh. 12:3 the territory of the Israelites, beyond the Jordan, is described in part as extending "to the sea of the Arabah, the Salt Sea, southward to the foot of the slopes of Pisgah," while in Josh. 13:20 the Reubenite territory includes "the slopes of Pisgah."

Most commentators identify Mount Pisgah with modern Ras es-Siyaghah, which is located to the east of the Dead Sea and northwest of Mount Nebo and separated from the latter by a saddle. ***See also*** Arabah; Balaam; Balak; Dead Sea; Jericho; Moab; Moses; Nebo. B.M.

Pishon (pī'shawn), one of the rivers in the Garden of Eden (Gen. 2:11), but a minor one in the company of the Tigris and the Euphrates. There is no scholarly agreement on whether the reference in Genesis is to a river, or to a larger body of water, such as the Persian Gulf.

Pisidia (pi-sid'ee-uh), a mountainous region just north of Pamphylia in south-central Asia Minor which, in 25 B.C., became part of the Roman province of Galatia. Paul and Barnabas passed through this region twice during their first journey (Acts 13:14–51; 14:24) and were persecuted in its principal city, Antioch, where there was apparently a sizable Jewish community (Acts 13:14–15, 43–45). The inhabitants of these rugged mountain ranges, like the people in the plateau region of Lycaonia, were perhaps unaccustomed to innovative religious ideas, a fact that might account for their violent reactions to Paul and Barnabas (Acts 13:50; 14:5–20). ***See also*** Antioch, Galatia. M.K.M.

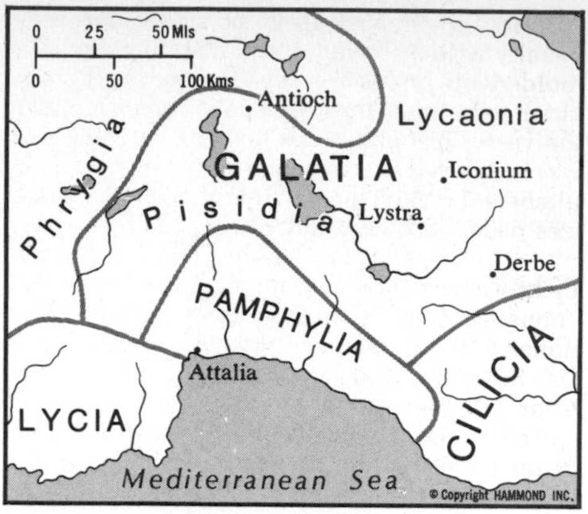

pit, a term that translates a variety of Hebrew and Greek words for natural, crafted, or symbolic depressions in the earth. Included are bitumen pits (Gen. 14:10), traps used to kill deliberately (Gen. 37:22) or accidentally (Ps. 7:15), public hazards (Exod. 21:33), burials (2 Sam. 18:17), animal traps (or lairs? 2 Sam. 23:20), landmarks (2 Kings 10:14), the abode of the dead (Job 33:18), foundation trenches for construction (Mark 12:1), or a bottomless source of scourges and plagues (Rev. 9:1, 2; 11:7) and the destination of the Devil (Rev. 20:2).

Archaeological evidence of pits is frequently found. They include wells, cisterns, lined and unlined storage vaults, graves and shafts dug in soil or cut in rock, and modifications of natural caves for use as cisterns, dry storage, or animal and human shelter. Chalcolithic and some Early Bronze Age houses are partially pits in earth or stone built up with surrounding walls and roofs for shelter. R.S.B.

pitch, a brown-black, gummy, resinous, tarlike substance used for waterproofing and as an adhesive. Resinous pitches are derived from conifers such as pine. Tarlike mineral pitches can be derived from natural asphalt or bitumen deposits or as by-products of petroleum processing. The Dead Sea area provides natural deposits of asphalts. Moses' mother waterproofed the rush basket that she put him in and set upon the Nile by smearing it with pitch (Exod. 2:3). Pitches were used to waterproof boats as well, and in the Bible they provided caulking for Noah's ark (Gen. 6:14). The burning streams of pitch in Isa. 34:9 refer to the flammable properties of asphalt and bitumen. Pitches were also commonly used as adhesives for hafting tools and weapons, as well as for securing inlays. P.L.C.

pitcher, a ceramic, glass, or stone container, usually with a single vertical loop handle and a molded lip or inserted spout for pouring, the latter sometimes through a set of sieve holes in the vessel just above the pouring lip. Jeremiah was instructed to bring wine to the Rechabites in pitchers (Jer. 35:5) and a broken pitcher symbolizes death (Eccles. 12:6).

Pithom (pee'thōōm; from Egyptian *per-atum*, "house of Atum"), an Egyptian store city mentioned in Exod. 1:11 together with Raamses (and On, Septuagint). It was built by Israelite slave labor not long before the Exodus. Apparently the city contained a temple center of the creator god, Atum, of On-Heliopolis. The modern identification is uncertain. Many scholars locate Pithom at modern Tell el-Maskhuta in the eastern delta along the Wadi Tumilat, but confirmation is lacking. A location in the general area is likely because Ramesses II (1279–1213 B.C.), the pharaoh of the Exodus, and his predecessors undertook major building projects in the eastern delta and many people from the biblical lands were located there. ***See also*** Exodus; On; Raamses, Rameses. H.B.H.

pity, a quality due to which a person does some significant kindness to another in need, notably when that other has no right to the kindness and cannot repay it. The quality inheres in a person's eyes and/or heart (Deut. 7:16; 19:13, 21; Ps. 17:10) and is revealed by what a person does in behalf of others in need (e.g., Ps. 111: 4–9; Mark 1:41; 8:2). One who acts out of pity is said to be compassionate or gracious. Such pity is a quality of God (Exod. 34:19; Rom. 9:15; Jon. 4:2; Pss. 103:8, 13; 111:4; James 5:11); its withdrawal is a sign of God's judgment (e.g., Jer. 13: 14; Ezek. 5:11; 7:4, 9). It normally marks the behavior of fathers toward their children (Ps. 103:13; but see Ezek. 5:10). Prophets expect it of God's people in dealing with their less fortunate fellows and resident aliens (e.g., Zech. 7:8), and Jesus uses it as the touchstone of his picture of the final judgment (in Matt. 24:31–46). Pity is undoubtedly part and parcel of the care and concern for neighbor that Jesus sought (Matt. 5:43–47; Luke 6:27–28). ***See also*** Loving-kindness; Mercy. B.J.M.

plagues, infectious diseases occurring naturally or in punishment for sin, other calamities sent by God, or the ten plagues of Egypt. In Gen. 12: 17, God strikes Pharaoh "with great plagues" because of Abram's wife. This isolated J (Yahwist source) usage foreshadows the punishments inflicted on Pharaoh and his country at the time of Moses. Rarely called plagues in Exodus (see 9:3, 14–15; 11:1, all attributed to the J source), they are mentioned only occasionally elsewhere (Deut. 28:60; 1 Sam. 4:8; Pss. 78:43–51; 105:27–36; 135:8–9; 136:10; cf. Amos 4:10; Hab. 3:5). In the Pentateuch, plague terms often describe punishment for Israel (Exod. 5:3; 30:12; Lev. 26:25; Num. 8:19; 14:12, 37; 17:11–15; 25: 8–9, 18–19; 31:6; Deut. 28:21; 32:24; cf. Exod. 12:13). In Leviticus 13–14, Hebrew *nega'* describes skin disease or rot in a house. Jeremiah and Ezekiel regularly threaten pestilence, sword, and famine as a threefold divine punishment. Elsewhere, plague terms occasionally describe disease or punishment for sin.

The ten plagues of Egypt (Exod. 7–12) represent a complex tradition whose origins can only be glimpsed. Popular retelling before and after the settlement in Canaan has given the stories a lively narrative force, as well as some duplication and exaggeration. The source division is disputed. J and P (Priestly source) shaped the narratives, and there were later additions; E (Elohist source) is not clearly represented in the plague stories, however, and may have had only the death of the firstborn (cf. Exod. 4:22–23). Also, a tradition of peaceful departure from Egypt (without plagues, but with gifts from the local populace) may underlie Exod. 3:21; 11:2–3; and 12:35–36.

As reconstructed, the J cycle may be seen to include eight episodes: Nile water turning foul (Exod. 7:14–17a, 18, 20a, 21a, 23–24); frogs swarming out of the Nile into living quarters (7: 25–29; 8:4–11a; RSV, 7:25–8:4, 8–15a); flies on the Egyptians and their land, but not on the Israelites (8:20–32); a plague on the cattle of the Egyptians, but not on the cattle of the Israelites (9:1–7); thunder and hail to harm cattle in the fields (9:13–21, 23–25a, 26–30, 33–34); locusts to devour crops left after the hail (10:1–11, 13–19); darkness over the land of Egypt for three days, except where the Israelites lived (10:21–26, 28–29); and the death of all the Egyptian firstborn (11:1, 4–8; 12:29–32). If the plague on cattle is secondary within J (since it harmonizes awkwardly with the hail on cattle in the fields), the original J cycle would have had seven episodes.

The P cycle is now primarily a supplement that recasts J as a contest between Pharaoh and God. The staff that turned into a serpent, originally a sign to authenticate Moses before the people (4:1–5, from J), now begins a contest between Aaron and Pharaoh's magicians (7:8–13, from P), and the contest theme recurs several times. As reconstructed, P's contributions are: all Egypt's water, not just that in the Nile, is turned to blood, and the magicians produce the same effect (7:17bg, 19–20a*a*, 21b–22); frogs come up out of all Egypt's waters, not just the Nile, and the magicians also equal that (8:1–3, 11b; RSV vv. 5–7, 15b); the dust of the earth is turned to gnats on humans and animals in all the land, the magicians fail to reproduce that, and they acknowledge God's "finger" at work (8:16–

Moses (right) turns Egypt's water into blood, the first of the ten plagues (Exod. 7: 14–19), while Aaron (center) performs miracles; woodcut from the fifteenth-century Cologne Bible.

19); ashes from the kiln are thrown into the air and cause boils breaking out in sores on humans and animals throughout all the land, and the magicians cannot stand before Moses because of the boils (9:8–12); hail is brought on all the land, upon humans and animals and plants, and the magicians are not even mentioned (9:22, 25b, 35); and characteristic formulae are added to the episodes of locusts (10:12, 20) and darkness (10: 27), as well as in conclusion (11:9–10). The death of the firstborn is moved outside P's contest cycle to come within the Passover description (12:12–13; cf. 12:17). Thus it inaugurates the actual deliverance from Egyptian bondage.

Outside of the Pentateuch, different versions of the plagues may be found in Psalms 78 and 105; and different traditions have also been preserved in such postbiblical authors as Josephus and Pseudo-Philo. ***See also*** Sources of the Pentateuch. K.G.O.

plains, areas of level land. In Palestine, a land of geographical contrasts, a plain takes on special significance. Fertility, possibilities of trade and conquest, and ease of travel are particular characteristics associated with broad valleys and tablelands.

The Plain of Megiddo or Esdraelon Plain is a fertile valley (Heb. *biq'âh,* 2 Chron. 35:22; Zech. 12:11) linking the coastal plain with the Jordan Valley; this was the main land route from Egypt to Damascus and the east. Megiddo guarded its western entrance and Taanach and Jezreel were other towns on the plain that were the scenes of biblical events. The Song of Deborah places the defeat of the Canaanites near Taanach (Judg. 5:19), Jezreel was a royal residence during Ahab's kingship (1 Kings 21:1), and Josiah was killed in battle at Megiddo (2 Kings 23:29).

The Plain of Sharon was only eight to twelve miles wide along the Mediterranean coast, but during biblical times it was thick with forests of oak and swampy marshes; it was not fertile or productive.

North of the Plain of Sharon were several smaller plains along the coast: the Plain of Dor south of Mount Carmel, the Plain of Acco north of Carmel, and the Phoenician plain with its natural harbors at Tyre, Sidon, and Byblos. South of Sharon was the broad Philistine plain, which often defied Israelite control. The cities of the Philistine pentapolis were Ashdod, Askelon, Gaza, Gath, and Ekron, and their characteristic material culture can be traced eastward. Valleys in the hill country formed small plains such as those around Shechem and Dothan.

The Jordan Valley broadens out into a plain particularly around Jericho (Josh. 5:10; 2 Kings

25:5). The Hebrew word most often used to describe the Jordan plain is *'arābâh*, meaning "wilderness" or "desert plain." *'Arābâh* also describes the area east of the Dead Sea opposite Jericho, usually in reference to the "plain of Moab" (Num. 22:1; 33:48–50; Deut. 34:1; Josh. 13:32). These desolate areas were important in the desert wanderings and conquest narratives (Josh. 4:13) and for armies to pass through in their conquests (Jer. 39:5). The RSV often translates *'arābâh* as a proper name for the plain west of the Jordan River (Josh. 12:8; 2 Sam. 2:29), east of the river (Josh. 12:1), and on both sides (Josh. 11:2).

Five cities believed to be on the southeast shore of the Dead Sea (Sodom, Gomorrah, Admah, Zeboiim, and Zoar) have been known as the "Cities of the Plain" from the narratives of Lot (Gen. 13, 19) and the battle of the four kings against five in Genesis 14. The Hebrew word translated "plain" in the KJV is *kikkār*, meaning basically "round" or a "circle"; it probably refers in these passages to a round area or district. The RSV translates *kikkār* as "valley" (Gen. 13:10–12; 19:17, 25, 28). Recently excavations have been carried out near the southeast shores of the Dead Sea and the Bronze Age (after 3000 B.C.) occupation seems to be in the first ridge of foothills rather than down in the plain; "Cities of the Plain" or even "of the Valley" may be inaccurate translations. Perhaps *kikkār* refers to the cities around (but not in) the Dead Sea plain.

In the OT the Hebrew word *mîshôr* is used for plain or level place both literally (1 Kings 20:24; 2 Chron. 26:10) and figuratively (Ps. 27:11; Jer. 21:13; 28:8). When *mîshôr* refers to a particular plain, the RSV and NEB translate it "tableland" (the Medeba plain, Josh. 13:9, 16). Sharon, the name for the plain, may be derived from this Hebrew root. ***See also*** Esdraelon; Philistines; Sharon, The Plain of. N.L.L.

plaister, an archaic variant of the word "plaster" (KJV, Isa. 38:21).

plane, a tree of the genus *Platanus*. Biblical usage associates it with pine (Isa. 41:19; 60:13) and describes its use to control the appearance of offspring of animals (Gen. 30:37–39). Its symbolic value as beauty is also mentioned (Ezek. 31:8). *Platanus orientalis* is most likely a correct identification.

plants, trees, vines, shrubs, herbs, vegetables, flowers, fruits, or ornamental forms of life characterized by roots, a stem, and leaves or foliage equivalent. "To plant" identifies the action of placing either seeds, cuttings, or small samples of plants into soil so as to bring them to growth. Biblical usage includes both the noun and the verb in extended degree. This review does not exhaust the biblical uses but points to representative texts. Readers are referred to articles on specific trees, flowers, fruits, herbs, and other items for more exhaustive treatment.

The general disposition reflected in the Bible is that plants, like animal, marine, and other forms of life, are God's good gifts. As such they are to be cherished, used, enjoyed, shared, and processed for the good of all people (Gen. 1:29, 30; 2:8; 3:18). There are some plants that are special messengers of this blessing, such as a tree growing by water (Jer. 17:8; Ps. 1:3) or a rich vineyard (2 Kings 19:29; Prov. 31:16; Amos 9:14). Conversely, there are forms of judgment and curse that are described as deprivation of the normal benefits from plant life.

> . . . though you plant pleasant plants
> and set out slips of an alien god,
> though you make them grow on the day that you plant them,
> and make them blossom in the morning that you sow;
> yet the harvest will flee away
> in a day of grief and incurable pain.
> Isa. 17:10b–11

Overgrown, barren, and deserted sites are also used as metaphorical expressions of divine displeasure or judgment (Amos 4:9; 5:11).

Levitical law forbade early exploitation of fruit-bearing trees (Lev. 19:23), and it was forbidden to plant a tree as the religious symbol of the Canaanite fertility goddess Asherah (Deut. 16:21). Plants can symbolize weakness (2 Kings 19:26) or strength (Ps. 144:12), God's nourishment (Ps. 104:14) or his destruction (Isa. 40:24). A plant can symbolize the persistence of life (Job 14:7–9) or its temporary and unstable character (Job 8:12; Eccles. 2:4–7). Planting is seasonal action (Eccles. 3:2) but plants need sustained care to be productive (Isa. 5:1–4).

In the NT, various plants are used as metaphors for God's proper action (Matt. 15:13), all else being futile. They are a metaphor for life which tests the conduct of humans (Matt. 23:33–41). Planting is just one stage in the growth of the church (1 Cor. 3:6–8) whose life, as all of life, is a gift of God. R.S.B.

play. ***See*** Games.

pledges. ***See*** Loan.

Pleiades (plee'uh-deez), a constellation that in the Bible is always mentioned with Orion. Astral phenomena played a large role in ancient knowledge and practice, constituting the unchanging cosmic order and governing times for human action. Orion and Pleiades are mentioned in two OT passages. In Amos 5:8, those who overturn the moral order (5:7; following astral cults?) will encounter One who, having ordered the times and seasons of light and darkness (5:8; cf. Gen. 1:3), but who caused water to flood the earth (5:8; cf. Gen. 6–9), will shine forth to destroy the strong wicked (5:9). Job 9:9 reflects Job's conviction, in view of his undeserved suffering, that the divine creation and manipulation of the order of the cosmos is unfathomably arbitrary and devoid of justice. In Job 38:31–33 God answers Job, challenging his interpretation of astral phenomena and reasserting the divine wisdom intrinsic to the divine governance of times and seasons of human experience. J.G.J.

plow, a farming implement used for breaking up the earth. Biblical texts include both literal and figurative use of the term. In the agricultural cycle of Palestine, plowing was a seasonal activity geared to preparation of the soil prior to planting. Practically, it could occur any time in the rainy season (October–April) or in the dry season before soil hardened too severely, the setting for some wry humor (Prov. 20:4; Isa. 28: 24). While Israel's acquaintance with agriculture is attested early (Gen. 45:6), it was life in Canaan that forced them to adapt to local practices (1 Sam. 13:20) for the care and maintenance of plows and other equipment. The local charge of one pim for sharpening a plowshare indicates Israel's dependence on Canaanite neighbors to practice the craft. Primitive plows made of forked tree branches with metal points to dig into the earth are still sometimes used.

Figurative use of plowing includes its standing for marital abuse (Judg. 14:18), cultivating sin (Job 4:8), a national fate (Hos. 10:11), straightforward dedication (Luke 9:62), legitimate hope for compensation (1 Cor. 9:10), the absurdity of injustice (Amos 6:12), the aggravation of enemies (Ps. 129:3), destruction (Jer. 26: 18; Mic. 3:12), and the hoped-for time of peace (Isa. 2:4; Joel 3:10; Mic. 4:3). Except for recognition of uneven (therefore unfair and certainly awkward) pulling power, it is not clear why Israel's law prohibited plowing with mixed teams (Deut. 22:10). In some texts the "plowman" is teamed with vinedressers as a euphemism for farmers (2 Kings 25:12; Isa. 61:5; Jer. 52:16). ***See also*** Pim. R.S.B.

plowshare, a sharp iron blade attached to the beam of a plow. Lacking rudimentary iron technology, Israelites of the early monarchical period (ca. 1020–1000 B.C.) took plowshares for sharpening to the Philistines (1 Sam. 13:19–23). As instruments that can only be used in times of peace, they are contrasted to swords, also made of iron, which are instruments of war; turning swords into plowshares demonstrates peace (Isa. 2:4; Mic. 4:3). In Joel 3:10 the process is reversed, however.

plumb line, a length of string or light rope with a weight (Lat. *plumbum*, "lead") attached at one end that, when suspended by the other end, will show a true vertical line. It is used in the construction of any object that needs to be vertically true, such as a wall of a building or a fence. Amos sees the Lord with a plumb line in his hand, which he is using to test Israel. As a result of that test, Israel, for failing to be "plumb" with God, will be destroyed (Amos 7:7–9).

pods (KJV: "husks"), probably the fruit of the carob or locust tree, common in Syria, Palestine, and Egypt. When ripe, these pods are filled with a dark honeylike syrup. They were then collected, ground up, and fed to animals. They were also eaten by the very poor (cf. Luke 15:16). Since it is possible that the locusts eaten by John the Baptist (Matt. 3:4) refer to this plant rather than to the insect, these pods are also called St. John's Bread.

poetry, evocative compositions that communicate more by connotation than denotation. Songs, prayers, proverbs, speeches, and other lofty pronouncements in the Hebrew Bible are usually written in a particular style, one that has traditionally been equated with the "poetry" of the Bible.

Form: The characteristic feature of this style is a brief, two-part sentence whose second part typically reasserts, strengthens, or otherwise completes what was said in the first: "Happy the man who fears the Lord, who greatly delights in his commandments" (Ps. 112:1). The effect of this sentence form is to provide the whole with a feeling of closure and completeness: just as, in poetry, a rhyme can pull things together and give a couplet a final "click," so the second part of such a sentence, strengthening and finishing off the first, marks it as complete and polished. The sentence gains an elegant and sometimes emphatic or epigrammatic quality.

While speaking or writing in this sentence form is certainly less demanding than, say, composing rhymed couplets in English or dactyllic hexameter in Latin, there is nonetheless much room for artistry and skill in meeting its requirements. Great variety is observable in the relationship between the two (or, rarely, three) parts of these sentences. Sometimes the second part seems little more than saying the same thing twice in different words, an emphatic restatement ("let me praise the Lord in my life, let me sing of my God while I live," Ps. 146:2); more often, it carries the first part further, completes it, supplies some grammatically or semantically necessary conclusion ("Since *X* . . . then *Y* . . ." "By day . . . by night . . ."), or otherwise seems to polish things off. Especially in wise sayings such as those in the book of Proverbs, this two-part sentence can function almost like a riddle: the listener is invited to figure out the relation between the first and second parts. Such, for example, is the statement in

Eccles. 7:1: "Better a name than precious oil, and the day of death, than the day of one's birth." Everyone would agree that a person's good name is a more precious commodity than any actual possession, even precious oil; but the day of birth is almost always a happy occasion, and death almost always a time for mourning—so in what sense is the latter "better"? The point of this saying seems to be that the human body, like precious oil, is perishable; eventually it must spoil and die. A good name, however, is quite the opposite: it takes a lifetime to build, but once completed, i.e., on the day of a person's death, it is immutable, imperishable. Thus, the proverb seems to be arguing, just as a name is better than precious oil, so is the day of one's death, when the building of a name is finally complete, better than the day of one's birth, when that process is only beginning.

Effects of the Two-Part Form: Although scholars have long been aware of the feeling of regularity and heightened eloquence created by this style, they have had some difficulty in describing its workings. In antiquity, Josephus, and later Eusebius, Jerome, and others, asserted that biblical songs were written in quantitative meters, just like Greek or Latin verse—in fact, in the same meters as these! It was not until the Renaissance that Western scholars began to realize that this assertion was false (and of apologetic intent); yet even afterward, scholars have intermittently continued to search for some other sort of metrical system underlying these sentences—accentual, syllabic, "word rhythm," and so forth. In truth none of the systems proposed can be made to work consistently, for the regularity is only approximate—they are usually two or three or four words per part, but there is some room for exceptions. It seems that an approximate and intermittent regularity was all that this style demanded.

One contributing factor to the regularity is the extraordinary terseness and compression characteristic of this style. Utterances framed in it frequently dispense with such features as the Hebrew definite article *ha-*, the relative *asher* ("which" or "that"), and other common signposts of ordinary discourse. More generally, it is this same principle of terseness that holds clauses down to three or four words, allowing complex thoughts and images to develop only within the confines of these brief, two-part assertions strung one after the next. Thus, where an English-speaking orator might have said, "Listen, O Heaven and Earth, as I speak words which, like the rain and dew sent from above to nourish fertile fields, may prove fructifying to those whom I hereby admonish. . . ," Moses begins his farewell in Deut. 32 in these balancing clauses:

> Give ear, Heaven, as I speak, and let the Earth hear my words. Let my speech flow down like rain, my discourse distil like dew—like showers upon grain-fields, or raindrops on the grass.

Parallelism: The attempt to pin down the workings of this style eventually led the eighteenth-century biblical scholar Robert Lowth to coin the term *parallelismus membrorum* ("the parallelism of the clauses"), and since then "parallelism" generally has enjoyed wide popularity as an explanation of the principle underlying this style. Of late, however, this approach has been seriously questioned. For while some form of paralleling, in meaning or syntax, can be shown to characterize quite a few of the two-part sentences involved, far too many exceptions exist to allow paralleling to be accepted as the generative force behind all such sentences. Moreover, it is clear that the term "parallelism" has been used extremely loosely by biblical scholars. Almost no series of consecutive sentences (in the Bible or anywhere else) can be shown to be utterly devoid of some form of parallelism, so that finding instances of parallelism in this style, in whatever muted or obscure form, proves very little. Moreover, the notion of "parallelism" has occasionally served to group together various very different features and thus cover over important distinctions. Surprisingly, "parallelism" has been used to label such phenomena as actual repetition, for example, or numerical ("Three things . . . four things . . .") or other sequences.

Contemporary scholars have shown that the "principle of parallelism" is really a bit of shorthand for a complex group of phenomena: various forms of ellipsis, especially of subject or verb in the second part (called "gapping" by one writer), and a whole range of semantic equivalences and associations. The basic principle underlying this style in the Hebrew Bible might thus better be described simply as "seconding" or "extending," the process of following up the typically short, spare assertion of Part A with another, subjoined one in Part B: "A is so, and what's more, B"; "Not only A, but B"; "Not A, and certainly not B"; "First A happened, then B"; "If A . . . , then B . . ."; and so forth. This form, so frequently emphatic (as many of the above examples imply), was sometimes abstracted to include almost any sequence of two or three short clauses. The basic requirement seems only to have been that parts A and B be (syntactically) separated, so that the pause between them be maintained; and that B identify itself, semantically and/or syntactically, as A's completion rather than the start of a wholly new thought. It is the necessity of maintaining this delicate balance, i.e., of keeping A and B divided yet related, that generates the frequent recourse to repetition, apposition, ellipsis of subject or verb, word pairs, and other manifestations of "parallelism."

Poetry Versus Prose: A particularly vexing problem for scholars has been that of distinguishing biblical "poetry" from "prose." Neither of these terms, derived from other literary traditions, has an equivalent in biblical Hebrew, and there is no evidence that ancient Israelites divided their literary corpus into these two camps. Obviously, these terse, two-part sentences were favored for some types of compositions (songs, proverbs, etc.), where they were used with great consistency; but the same sentence form can frequently be found here and there in ordinary narratives, particularly in dialogue, as well as in legal material, blessings and curses, oracles and prayers. Moreover, in various prophetic books, this terse, binary style seems now and again to slip into a looser and less easily identified idiom; it is often hard to say where "poetry" ends and "prose" begins. Even in the Psalms, the contrast between the clipped, binary style of, say, Psalm 94 and the looser style of Psalms 23, 35, and 122 is striking. Some scholars have used statistical analyses (for example, of the relative presence or absence of the definite article and other signs of a lack of terseness) in order to help distinguish poetry from prose in the Bible. But at present this remains a crude tool (the Song of Solomon, for example, ends up in the "prose" camp by such a measurement!), perhaps inevitably so. As one recent writer remarked, "the distinction is often quantitative rather than qualitative, and in terms of degree rather than kind."

Historically, this distinction between biblical poetry and prose was at first wholly dependent on literary genre: those compositions that, if they had been written in Latin or Greek, would have been composed in verse were declared by early biblical commentators to be the Bible's "poetry"—the Psalms, for example, or various songs such as the hymn of the Israelites at the Red Sea (Exod. 15), or the songs of Moses (Deut. 32), Deborah (Judg. 5), and David (2 Sam. 22), as well as Job, Lamentations, and other books. Prophetic books were held to be "prose," at least until the scholar Robert Lowth forcefully argued their structural similarity to psalms and songs on the basis of their "parallelism." Nowadays the term "poetry" is still used to refer to those parts of the Bible in which the terse, "seconding" style is most apparent (especially Psalms, Proverbs, Job, Song of Solomon, Lamentations, Ecclesiastes, much of the prophetic corpus, and individual songs, oracles, etc., found in biblical narrative); but there is an increasing awareness that in biblical Hebrew even more than in other languages, the precise distinction between poetry and prose is difficult to draw.

The only formal poetry in the NT consists of fragments of poetic lines quoted by various authors (Acts 17:28, from Aratus, *Phaenomena* 5; 1 Cor. 15:33, perhaps from Menander, *Thais;* Titus 1:12, from Callimachus, *Hymn to Zeus).* Poetic intention, if not formal expression, however, is evidenced in such NT passages as the Magnificat (Luke 1:46–55), the prophecy of Zechariah (Luke 1:68–79), the Nunc Dimittis (Luke 2:29–32), and some other passages which may reflect early Christian hymns (e.g., Phil. 2: 6–11; 1 Tim. 3:16).

Bibliography

Kugel, J. L. *The Idea of Biblical Poetry.* New Haven, CT: Yale University Press, 1981.

O'Connor, M. *Hebrew Verse Structure.* Winona Lake: Eisenbrauns, 1980. J.L.K.

police (KJV: "sergeants"), a term that translates a Greek word meaning "those who hold a staff" and refers to the officers commanded by the magistrates (Acts 16:35, 38). ***See also*** Magistrate.

polygamy. ***See*** Adultery; Family, The; Fornication; Marriage.

Polyglot, the Complutensian. ***See*** Texts, Versions, Manuscripts, Editions.

polytheism, the belief in the existence of numerous gods. In the environment of the Bible most societies were polytheistic: there were "many gods and many lords" (1 Cor. 8:5). Different deities had different functions, associations, characters, and mythologies. Some were male, some female, and they had individual personal names. They might be grouped in families and generations; the younger gods might overcome and displace the older. Theomachy, war among the gods, could have an important role, not least in creation stories: a younger god defeated an older, monstrous deity and from its body fashioned the world. The variety among the gods did not exclude elements of rank and leadership; but leadership did not always mean complete supremacy.

Polytheistic religions are known in detail from ancient Egypt, Mesopotamia, Greece, and Rome; particularly relevant for the OT is the Canaanite polytheism of Ugarit (cf. also the later evidence of Philo of Byblos [ca. A.D. 63–141]), in which occur divine names known also from the Bible: El, Elyon, Baal, Anath, Athirat (cf. Heb. *Asherah),* Dagon. This Canaanite mythology stressed the elements of conflict, sexuality, fecundity, the mountain of the gods, and the building of the palace.

The OT from early times opposed the entire ethos of polytheism and its mythologies. Certain echoes of it continue in the various names for God, perhaps in the plural form *Elohim* (Heb., "God"), in the concept of the "sons of God" or court of heavenly beings, in the imagery of battles with hostile superhuman powers, in the occasional recognition that another land is the sphere of another god. But for Israel there was only one God, and sole devotion to this one God was a paramount essential: to follow or serve "other gods" was a cardinal offense, emphasized particularly in Deuteronomy and in Isaiah 40–55. It is repeatedly stated, however, that large groups of Israelites committed this offense; perhaps not so many really did so. Polemic against polytheism was partly an internal argument among the Israelites: it reinforced the theology and the ethical demands of the God of Israel. Finally hostility to polytheism tends to become caricature and ridicule: it ceases to include any real analysis of polytheism or any profound understanding of its workings or its attractions. Rejection of it became a standard constituent of Jewish life and it ceased to form a real temptation for many Jews.

The NT follows this tradition in taking for granted the established monotheism of Judaism. Its reserve in using the term "God" or even "Son of God" of Jesus is part of this; later sources and later text forms use "God" of him rather more. The NT does not depict Jewish opponents as criticizing Christianity for reintroducing polytheism. In the Greco-Roman world Christianity largely followed the lines of established Jewish apologetic, dismissing the absurdities of polytheism, linking it with moral depravities, and affirming the oneness of true deity as background to the Christian affirmations. In all the ancient world the primary choice was not that between a God and no God, but that between one God and many gods. ***See also*** Monotheism. J.B.

Pomegranate.

pomegranate *(Punica granatum)*, a small tree whose bright red fruit resembles an apple. Its hard shiny rind encloses a pulp of fleshy seeds, the juice of which is especially refreshing in a hot environment (Song of Sol. 8:2; Deut. 8:8). The beautiful round fruit was a common decorative motif used on the hems of the robes of the Temple priests (Exod. 28:33–34) and carved into the timbers and beams of Solomon's Temple (1 Kings 7:18, 20). Extract of the rind was used medicinally and as a red dye, as well as in tanning leather. The pomegranate was regarded as a symbol of fertility and eternal life. P.L.C.

Pontius Pilate. ***See*** Pilate, Pontius.

Pontus (pahn'tuhs), a Greek word meaning "sea," often used without further modification to identify the Black Sea. In NT times it commonly referred to a province of Asia Minor stretching along the south shore of the Black Sea from Bithynia to Armenia. According to Philo, a first-century Jewish author, Jews lived throughout Pontus. Acts says Jewish pilgrims from that province heard speaking in tongues at Pentecost (2:9). Acts 18:2 mentions a Jewish native of Pontus named Aquila who, with his wife Priscilla, left Rome during Claudius' eviction of Jews, and met Paul in Corinth. The NT mentions no mission to Pontus, though 1 Pet. 1:1 addresses Christians there. Later traditions attribute its evangelization to Peter or Andrew. By A.D. 100 the Christian movement had caused social unrest throughout the province. The father of Marcion, a second-century sectarian leader, apparently was bishop of the Pontic city Sinope. D.R.M.

pool. ***See*** Cisterns; Reservoir; Solomon's Pools; Water.

poor, lacking in material or spiritual goods. Poverty, the state of being poor, is mentioned in two ways in Scripture. In the secondary way, encountered primarily in Proverbs, poverty is the consequence of moral lassitude, especially laziness (Prov. 13:18; 20:13). In the primary sense, however, when the poor are encountered in their need or treated as a group, their situation is understood not as a consequence of personal failings but as a result of social factors, particularly injustice (Prov. 13:23).

The view of the poor is revealed in the chief Hebrew terms for the poor, which address them as needy, without power, and abused by those with greater power. Leviticus defines the poor as those who are lowly because their "power [lit., hand] wavers" (25:35) or is insufficient (14:21). They do not have the capacity to provide for themselves the essentials of life. Their deficiency in life-supporting power is understood to exist in relation to the rest of the community, represented by the phrase "with you," repeated twice in 25:35 (cf. "beside you" in v. 36); that is, their crisis is based in the network of power relationships that form society.

Behind such poverty lies economic conflict (Eccles. 4:1). The intensity of the conflict is reflected in the prevalence of slavery (Neh. 7:66–67; Exod. 20:17), since slavery was the lot of the losers in the economic struggle (2 Kings 4:1; Amos 2:6–7; 8:4–6). The condition of the wage earners, vulnerable because they were cut off from a reliable relationship to the land, was as bad (Job 7:1–2) or worse (Deut. 15:16–17).

The extent of poverty increased to a new level in the time of the eighth-century B.C. prophets Amos, Isaiah, and Micah. Economic conditions in the preceding two centuries had produced a commercial and landed aristocracy. Inequities increased and the new elite was able to exploit the poor through sharecropping arrangements (Isa. 3:14–15). Through foreclosures, land became concentrated in fewer hands (Isa. 5:8). The peasants lost their patrimonies in the land (Mic. 2:1–2). From the standpoint of one of the prophets, a whole class was being wiped out (Amos 8:4).

Responsibility to the Poor: The responsibility of redressing the plight of the poor is fundamental to biblical faith. At the basis is the nature of God as one who hears the cries of the poor (Ps. 12:5). The deliverance from Egypt is presented as the great exemplar of God's justice to the needy (Ps. 68:5–10; Exod. 2:23–24). As their dilemma is grounded in injustice, their need is for justice (Isa. 10:2). As their condition is loss of power, the response required is empowerment. A literal rendering of "you shall maintain him" in Lev. 25:35 is, "you shall make them strong." This demand is extended outside the chosen people, for almost the same wording is used in condemning Sodom, which did not "make strong the power [hand] of the poor and needy" (Ezek. 16:49).

In the law attention is given to social structures that affect the poor. The land is to be left fallow every seventh year "that the poor ... may eat" (Exod. 23:11). In this year the landed means of production are to be given over in their entirety to the poor and the debts of the poor are to be cancelled (Deut. 15:2). That the landless poor have rights in the land is also supported in their claim to immediate sustenance from the fields (Deut. 23:24–25) and in restrictions on reaping and gleaning so that some harvest is left to them (Lev. 19:9–10). The law also restricts the processes that tear people down. The empowering in Lev. 25 includes a proscription of interest on loans intended to relieve the distress of the recipient (23:36–37). A collateral (pledge) is prohibited if it were one that would further weaken the debtor (Deut. 24:6) or cause the debtor to suffer (Exod. 22:26).

Finally, there is to be open-handed sharing with the poor. Jesus' statement that "You always have the poor with you" (Mark 14:7) is a citation of the strong command on giving to the poor in Deut. 15:11 and a reminder of the permanence of this obligation, one also commanded by Jesus (Luke 12:33).

The ideal for the ruler is to be one who fully assumes the responsibility of delivering the poor and crushing their oppressors (Ps. 72:4). It is part of the messianic expectation (Isa. 11:4) seen fulfilled in Jesus (Luke 1:52–53; 4:18–21). The hope for "good news proclaimed to the poor" (Luke 4:18; 7:22) was ancient (Ps. 68:10–11; Isa. 29:18–19; 35:4–6). The beatitude concerning the poor in Luke emphasizes God's siding with the poor against their afflictors (6:20, 24). In Matt. 5:3 "the poor in spirit" are those who have the attitude of dependence upon God associated with poverty (cf. Zeph. 2:3; 3:11–13).

A major concern of Paul was to make a collection for the poor (Rom. 15:26) in Jerusalem (2 Cor. 8–9). His purpose was "that there may be equality" (2 Cor. 8:13–15). ***See also*** Justice; Ownership; Wealth.

Bibliography

Batey, Richard. *Jesus and the Poor*. New York: Harper & Row, 1972.

Boerma, Conrad. *The Rich, the Poor—and the Bible*. Philadelphia: Westminster, 1980.

de Vaux, Roland. *Ancient Israel*. New York: McGraw-Hill, 1965. Pp. 65–90, 164–77. S.C.M.

poplar, a tree of the genus *Populus*. Probably the white poplar *(Populus alba)* or the storax

Poplar *(Populus alba)*.

(Styrax officinalis) is the tree mentioned in Gen. 30:37, where its color is of consequence. It grew in groves with other trees (Hos. 4:13) and symbolized solid life (Hos. 14:5).

porch, or vestibule. **1** A forecourt or central court of a house (1 Kings 7:6; Mark 14:68) or the pillared hall on a flat roof (Judg. 3:23). Private homes during the Greco-Roman period often had porches that opened onto the street just outside the front door. **2** A colonnaded portico or passageway, often part of a public building or temple (e.g., the stoa at Athens; Solomon's portico). These frequently provided shelter for travelers or those in ill health (John 5:2) and a forum for religious and philosophical discussions (Acts 17:16–32). **3** An area of the throne from which the king of Israel pronounced judgment (1 Kings 7:6–7).

Porch, Solomon's. ***See*** Solomon's Portico.

Porcius (por'shee-uhs) **Festus.** ***See*** Festus, Porcius.

porcupine. ***See*** Hedgehog.

porter (gatekeeper, doorkeeper, watchman), term used in the KJV for various officers: guardians of city gates (e.g., 2 Sam. 18:26; Ezra 7:24); of private houses (Mark 13:34); and of a sheepfold (John 10:3). The Temple officers so described appear as a subgroup of the Levites (1 Chron. 23:3–5; cf. Ezra 2:40–42; Neh. 7:43–5).

Portico, Solomon's. ***See*** Solomon's Portico.

post. **1** A vertical beam, usually of wood, that served as part of a frame from which a door or a gate was hung. When Samson took revenge on the Gazites he carried off not only the gate but the posts as well (Judg. 16:3), thus leaving the town defenseless until they could be replaced. One not permitted entry could stand at the gatepost and observe what occurred inside (Ezek. 46:2). **2** The position occupied by persons in pursuit of their duties, whether king (1 Kings 20:24), priest (2 Chron. 7:6), or watchman (Isa. 21:8).

Postexilic Period, the time following the Babylonian exile of Israel (587–539 B.C.). The period began with the conquering of Babylon by the Persians and Cyrus's toleration of diverse religions. This moderate and enlightened practice led to the restoration of the Jewish community in Palestine (cf. Ezra 1:2–4; 6:3–5). Among the most prominent literature from this period is Isaiah 40–66, Haggai, Zechariah 1–8, Ezra, and Nehemiah. While the term "postexilic" can refer more generally to the time up until the end of the "OT period" when contrasted with "preexilic" and "exilic," it may best be limited to the restoration extending through the fifth century B.C. The current tendency to discuss the Exile and restoration together presents a more enriching understanding. ***See also*** Exile. K.H.R.

Potiphar (pah'tuh-fuhr; Egyptian, "he whom Re has given"), an official of Pharaoh and captain of the guard who purchased the patriarch Joseph in Egypt from some Midianite (Ishmaelite) merchants who had themselves purchased him from his brothers (Gen. 37:36; 39:1). Potiphar recognized Joseph's special talents but cast him into prison because of a false accusation by Potiphar's wife (Gen. 39:6–20). ***See also*** Joseph; Potiphera.

Potiphera (poh-tif'uh-ruh; KJV: "Potipherah"; Egyptian, "he whom Re has given"), a priest of On whose daughter, Asenath, was given in marriage to Joseph by Pharaoh (Gen. 41:45, 50; 46:20). As priest of On, center of the cult of the sun god Re, Potiphera would have been an important person. The priests of On engaged in a wide variety of commercial, political, and cultic duties. ***See also*** Asenath; Joseph; On; Re.

potsherd. ***See*** Pottery.

pottage (lit., "boiled thing"), a soup or stew made with lentils (Gen. 25:34) or herbs (2 Kings 4:39), sometimes with meat. It was used to nurture Elisha (2 Kings 4:38–41) and was used by Jacob to get Esau's birthright (Gen. 25:29–34). When eaten with bread (Gen. 25:34) and beverage it comprised a full meal.

potter. ***See*** Pottery.

Potter's Field, a tract of land near Jerusalem, used to bury strangers. It is identified in Matt. 27:1–10 with the Field of Blood (Akeldama in Acts 1:18–19), a term associated with the money paid to Judas for betraying Jesus. The quotation erroneously attributed to Jeremiah in Matt. 27:9–10 is from Zech. 11:12–13 (cf. however, Jer. 18:1–3; 32:6–15), but altered to fit Christian legends concerning Judas's end.

Since the fourth century, the field has been identified with a location near the confluence of the Hinnom and Kidron valleys. Early pilgrims located Akeldama south of Mount Zion on the far side of the Hinnom Valley, corresponding to the site today just north of St. Onuphrius' Monastery. Still visible are tombs from a Jewish necropolis and ruins of a medieval burial vault for pilgrims. ***See also*** Akeldama; Judas. C.H.M.

potter's wheel. ***See*** Pottery.

Pottery

OBJECTS MADE FROM CLAY and hardened by fire. One who makes such objects is a potter, and the art of pottery making is ceramics.

The Significance of Pottery for Biblical History: Clay has two distinctive traits: it can be fashioned into a particular shape, which it can retain; and when it is fired at a temperature of 700–900 degrees Fahrenheit, it undergoes chemical changes that harden the shape and render it almost impervious to decay or corrosion (although it can be broken by impact).

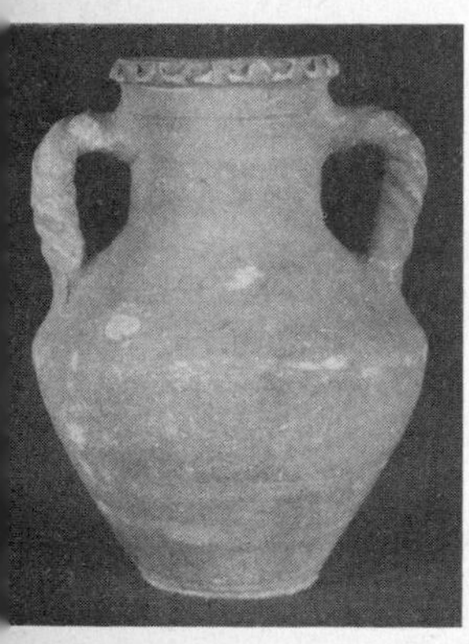

Parthian twisted-handled amphora (second–fourth century A.D.)

Because of these characteristics pottery has become an indispensable tool of archaeologists as they seek to reconstruct the history of the biblical lands. In contrast to Egypt and Mesopotamia, Palestine has preserved few stone monuments that record its past and relatively few inscriptions. On the other hand, potsherds, broken bits of ancient pottery, are found in abundance wherever biblical peoples and their predecessors settled. The usual pattern of settlement was to build a new city on the ruins of one that had been destroyed. A *tell*, the mound that results from the accumulated layers of the remains of cities, is eloquently described in Joshua 8:28; "So Joshua burned Ai, and made it for ever a heap of ruins, as it is to this day." Buried within the tells of Palestine, the broken remnants of the everyday utensils and objects of each successive generation lay unnoticed for their historical importance until 1890, when William Flinders Petrie conducted the first excavation of a tell in Palestine at Tell el-Hesi.

Petrie recognized that pottery unearthed and understood in the light of its proper sequence had enormous value for dating successive occupation layers. This is because the styles and methods of the manufacture of pots changed over the centuries, sometimes rapidly, sometimes very slowly. Bases were rounded, flattened, or elongated; handles altered their shape and their point or manner of attachment; variations on rims—wide, narrow, turned in, turned out—were almost limitless. If the form of the pottery associated with a particular period could be established, then a simple piece of rim, base, or handle made in this form could be dated. Thousands of whole pots have been found in the tombs of various periods, contributing greatly to the identification of pottery forms. Petrie was able to use his knowledge of pottery from dated Egyptian tombs to suggest dates for comparable wares at Hesi, thus introducing the principle of cross-dating to turn a relative chronology into an approximate absolute chronology. Since this pioneer contribution, the pottery unearthed in the course of every excavation has been the object of critical examination and study, resulting in continuous progress in the identification and dating of pottery forms.

In recent times this emphasis on the changing shape of pottery as a

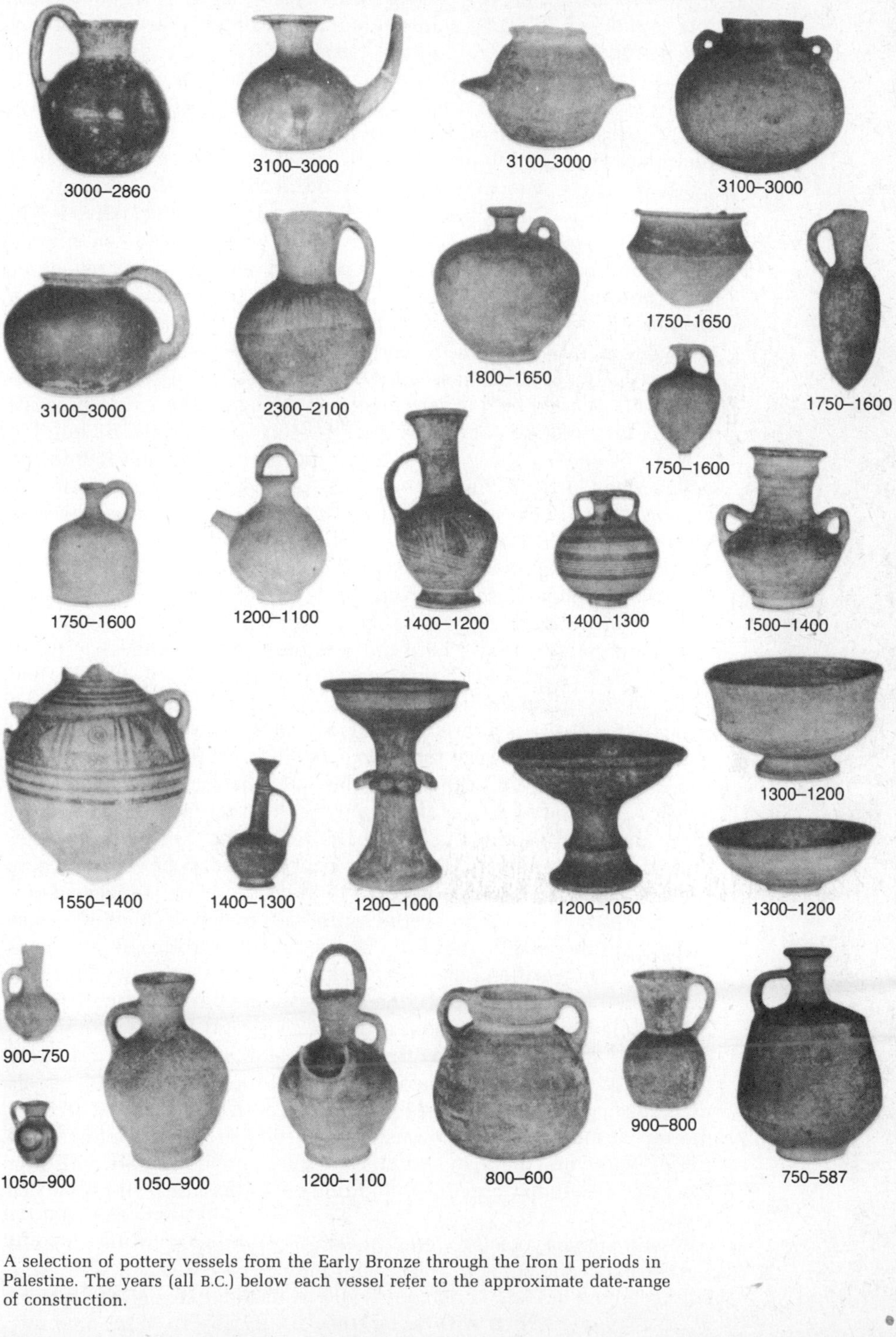

A selection of pottery vessels from the Early Bronze through the Iron II periods in Palestine. The years (all B.C.) below each vessel refer to the approximate date-range of construction.

gauge of passing time or new developments has been broadened so as to exploit more fully the cultural significance of the ceramic evidence. Pottery industries are now being studied carefully as excellent indicators of the technological achievement and economic structure of any one period. Scientific techniques of examination, such as petrographic and spectographic analysis, are being applied to thin sections of potsherds to determine the mineral content and composition of the clays and, if possible, their geological source.

Manufacturing Techniques: The clay used by potters in the biblical lands was an earthen clay usually found in the immediate vicinity. It was combined with nonplastic grit and mixed with water. When it had attained the desired consistency, the water was removed, leaving the clay bed or batch. It then had to be de-aired or wedged to prevent air pockets from building up and shattering the fired ware. A common method employed was treading by the feet (cf. Isa. 41:25).

Evidence indicates that the earliest vessels were shaped by hand in a variety of ways. One was by molding. Clay was pressed around the inside of a basket which was then consumed in the firing process, leaving the finished pot. Some small vessels were formed by holding a lump of clay in the palm of one hand while pinching it into the desired shape with the other—the "pinch-pot." Large square or oblong vessels were fashioned from flat slabs of clay joined together with slip (clay diluted with water). Sometimes long rolls of clay were coiled in a circle around a base, layer upon layer, until the desired height and shape were achieved; the walls of the vessel were then thinned and smoothed.

Early Bronze Age (3200–2100 B.C.) pottery from Tell Halif has distinctive markings made by the potter, perhaps a personal signature or designation of the customer.

It is impossible to say where and when the potter's wheel was introduced, but it clearly revolutionized the pottery industry. All pots had to be turned or moved in the making, and a wheel greatly facilitated this effort. The earliest form was the tournette or slow wheel, of which many examples have been found in Palestine. A typical tournette consisted of a lower, thick-walled stone bowl that had a conical depression in the center and an upper stone bowl with a flat upper surface and a lower conical projection that fit into the depression. This type of wheel, topped by a turntable, was rotated either by hand or foot and was probably lubricated with olive oil. On the basis of archaeological evidence, we can conclude that the tournette probably remained in use throughout the Israelite period. The fast wheel, introduced later, consisted of a shaft with a horizontal disk on top, and a heavy wheel that was turned with the feet until the proper momentum was achieved. A lump of clay was thrown onto the disk with great force so that it would stick, the form was opened with the hand, and the sidewalls drawn up to the desired height, thickness, and shape. A number of small vessels might be made from one large lump of clay, each one being cut off from the top of the column as it was finished. Larger, more sophisticated pieces were often made in sections and later joined together with slip. This was a common practice for adding necks, handles, and spouts as well.

Newly shaped articles were allowed to dry slowly in the air until they reached the stage of leather hardness. The earliest vessels were sun-dried but not fired and could only be used for storing dry materials. If they were filled with water, they would absorb it, become soft, and eventually collapse. In the early 1960s excavations at a Neolithic settlement at Catal Hüyük in Turkey revealed a variety of such unbaked earthenware estimated to date to ca. 6750 B.C. The earliest examples of true pottery, fired clay, in Palestine appeared in Jericho in the late sixth millennium. Although there is no precise evidence concerning the firing techniques in ancient Israel, extrapolation from contemporary Near Eastern methods has proved helpful. In early times pots were simply stacked in a shallow hole in the ground and a heap of combustible material was burned over them. At a later stage the pottery was separated from the fuel by a perforated clay partition, and finally the closed kiln was developed. Firing probably took from two to three days, since the temperature had to be raised and lowered slowly to avoid cracking the vessels. The amount of air in the kiln at the time of firing as well as the composition of the clay body determined the color of the pot. Particularly well-preserved examples of ancient kilns have been found at Serafand in modern Lebanon.

Israelite pottery differs from modern pottery in that it was not glazed. The preferred mode of decoration was to coat the whole pot or parts of it with a liquid clay or slip. After the pot had dried but before it was baked, it would then be burnished or polished with a rubbing tool of bone, stone, or wood. During the tenth and ninth centuries B.C. burnishing was generally done by hand; afterward as it was turned on the wheel. Some ware was painted although this was not a common practice except for an occasional line of red or black around the shoulder or middle of the pot. A third type of decoration seen on much early pottery was incision or puncture along the rim and neck.

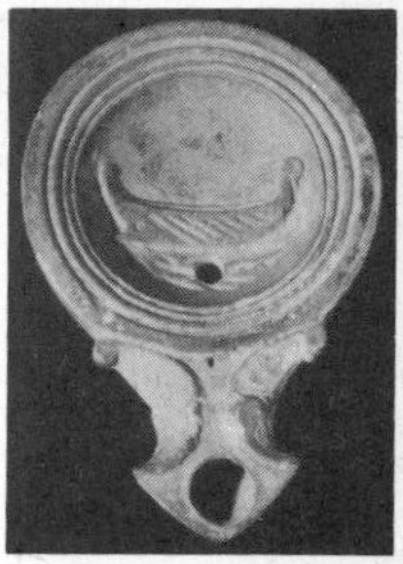

An oil lamp from the first century B.C.–first century A.D. depicts a Roman galley.

The art of the potter was a difficult one to master. It required knowledge of finding the right raw materials and of the best method of preparing the batch and shaping, decorating, and firing the ware. Traditions of pot making were passed on from generation to generation, an abrupt change in the tradition indicating newcomers on the scene. Potters and their workshops were familiar scenes in every village and town (cf. Jer. 18:3–4). Eventually, as cities became larger, guilds of potters were established to meet the needs of increased production (cf. 1 Chron. 4:23).

Most Palestinian pottery was made for utilitarian purposes. Articles in the home included bowls, cups, cooking pots, lamps, jars, pitchers, and juglets, as well as the household oven and huge storage jars. Other items like spindle whorls, buttons, figurines, and toys were also made of pottery. Although essentially functional, the pottery of the biblical period frequently displays excellent craftsmanship and high artistic accomplishment.

Even broken vessels had their use. Potsherds were used as notepaper on which important messages, such as the Lachish letters, were written. Larger sherds were used as braziers to take fire from the hearth, or as ladles (cf. Isa. 30:14). Potsherds may also have been used to scrape oil or dirt from the skin (cf. Job 2:8). Broken vessels were occasionally repaired in antiquity by drilling holes at the edges of sherds and joining them together with some sort of string. Most potsherds, however, were simply discarded and forgotten, providing archaeologists of today with invaluable historical clues.

Some Distinctive Features of Palestinian Pottery: The pottery of the

Storage jar from the Jordan Valley; Chalcolithic Period (4300–3200 B.C.).

"Syrian bottle" from a burial cave at Gezer, fourteenth century B.C.

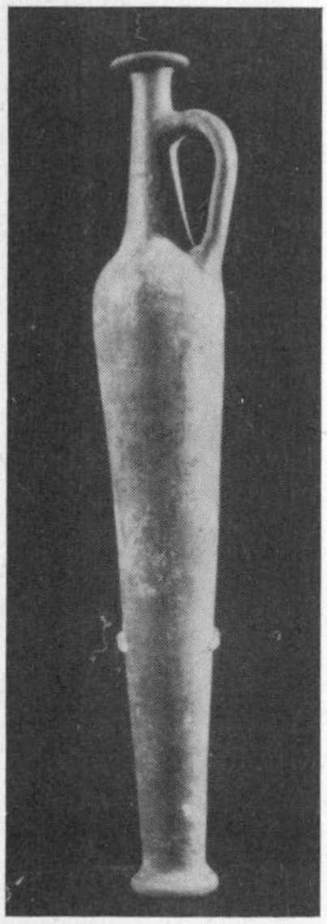

late Neolithic period (8000–4300 B.C.) was handmade, of coarse ware, and poorly fired. Its types include saucers, bowls, and storage jars decorated with a burnished red slip, painted triangular designs, or incisions. Pottery continued to be handmade in the Chalcolithic period (4300–3200 B.C.), but the ware is finer and better fired and the forms more advanced. These include V-shaped bowls, goblets, cornet cups, and "churns," decorated by incision or paint. The largest collection of Chalcolithic pottery has been found in Ghassulian and Beer-sheba cultures. In the Early Bronze Age (3200–2100 B.C.) typical of the first phase (EB I) are forms with ledge handles, high loop handles, or vertical pierced lug handles and wares with gray or red burnish, or band slip or line-group paint. The key diagnostic pottery of the second phase (EB II) is called "Abydos" ware after the site in Egypt where it was first found in first-dynasty tombs and identified as non-Egyptian. The subsequent association of this pottery with Canaan has been very important for correlating the pottery of Egypt and Palestine. Characteristic vessels are pitchers and jars with burnished red slip on the lower half and brown painted triangles and dots on the upper half. Typical of the third phase (EB III) is Khirbet Kerak ware, red- or black-burnished vessels decorated with incised lines. New pottery forms, indicating a new culture, appear in the Middle Bronze Age (2100–1500 B.C.). By 1900 B.C. all pottery was produced on the wheel, which allowed for the development of homogeneous and pleasing forms. Distinctive are the carinated bowls, often burnished over rich dark or cream slip, and graceful large jar forms. The single-spouted, open oil lamp came into widespread use at this time. In the Late Bronze Age (1550–1200 B.C.) Palestine was under Egyptian control, and its pottery was influenced both by Egypt and by trade connections with Aegean and eastern Mediterranean civilizations. Bichrome painted ware with friezes of birds, fish, and geometric designs appeared. Imports, mainly from Cypriot and Mycenaean origin, became common and were widely imitated.

There is marked continuity between the Canaanite pottery of the Late Bronze Age and the pottery of the Iron Age (1200–600 B.C.), including both Israelite pottery and the pottery of other groups. On the other hand, the profound changes brought about in Canaan by the settlement of the Israelite tribes are reflected in some new ceramic elements that eventually developed into a distinctive Israelite pottery. This reached its highest expression in the days of the Divided Kingdom (ca. 926–587 B.C.) when standardization of ware through mass production resulted in shapes that remained virtually unchanged for three hundred years.

The typical Israelite bowl was covered with slip, usually red, inside and over the rim, and on that a band of burnish was rubbed in spiral fashion, beginning in the center and extending over the rim. This is the well-known "ring-burnished" bowl. Evidence of the high standard of the potter's art is nowhere better seen than in the beautiful shape of the ring-burnished water decanter from the eighth and seventh centuries. A popular perfume juglet with one handle is distinctive because of its black color, which contrasts with the usual Palestinian red. The large storage jars that could hold about ten gallons each also testify to the expertise of the potter. In the eighth century under the Judean kings royal stamps were pressed into the wet clay of the handles reading *lmlk*, "Belonging to the king." The "Samarian thin bowls" are noteworthy for their egg-shell-thin ware and their striking decoration. They had red slip inside and outside or red and yellow slip alternating in bands and were highly burnished.

In marked contrast to the generally unpainted Israelite pottery was the elaborately decorated Philistine pottery of the early Iron Age. The most characteristic features in the decoration are metopes enclosing stylized birds or geometric patterns like friezes of spirals and groups of interlocking circles. The distribution of sites at which considerable quantities of this distinctive pottery appear provides an indication of the main areas of Philistine occupation.

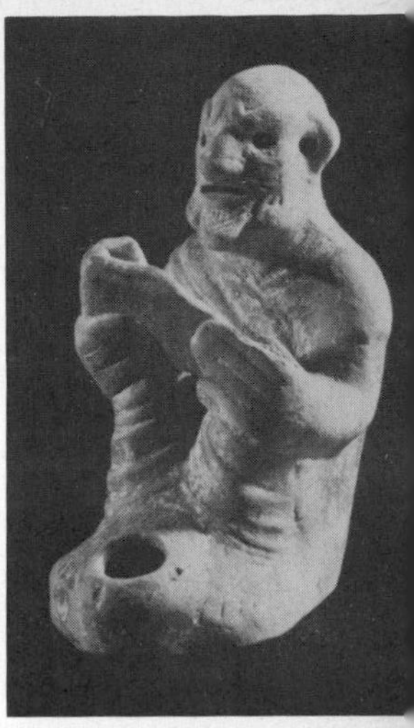

A clay oil lamp from Amka, a town northeast of Acre, is shaped like a schoolmaster unrolling a scroll as he reads; third–second century B.C.

The conditions of hardship and privation that followed the Babylonian destruction of Judah in 587 B.C. are reflected in the marked decline in the quality of local pottery made during the Persian period (587–332 B.C.). This is also true of the Hellenistic period (332–63 B.C.), characterized as it was by almost constant warfare. In these periods finer wares were imported from the highly specialized workshops of the Greek world. Most notable were the black-figure, red-figure, and black-glazed vessels. The pottery imported from the West was widely imitated, although the Palestinian pottery did not succeed in duplicating the superb quality and carefully wrought decoration of the Hellenistic models. During the early Roman period (63 B.C.–A.D. 135) pottery manufacturing centers all over the Mediterranean began to produce vessels with the same distinctive shapes and glossy red surface treatment. This *terra sigillata* ware is found in abundance in Palestine. Local potters under the Herods also developed some very fine ware of their own. Recent excavations in Jerusalem have uncovered thin-walled bowls of excellent quality, painted on the inside in stylized floral patterns in red and sometimes in brown or black.

Symbolic Use of Pottery in the Bible: The potter's art provided the biblical writers with many symbols. Perhaps best known is the creation story of Gen. 2:7, which depicts God as a potter fashioning a man from clay. The theme of God, the Master Potter, molding people and nations is a common one (Jer. 18:1–6; Isa. 29:16; 64:8; Rom. 9:20–24). One who argues with God is as foolish as the potsherd who argues with the potter (Isa. 45:9). The smashed vessel symbolizes utter and permanent destruction (Jer. 19:10–11). Human frailty is that of the earthen jar (Lam. 4:2). The pottery-made oil lamp is a favorite biblical symbol that is used in a variety of contexts.

See also Archaeology, Methods of; Lamp.

Bibliography

Amiran, Ruth. *Ancient Pottery of the Holy Land*. Jerusalem: Masada Press, 1969.

Johnston, Robert H. "The Biblical Potter." *Biblical Archaeologist* 37, no. 4 (1974): 86–106.

M.M.S.

pound. ***See*** Money.

poverty. ***See*** Poor.

power, the actual or potential capacity to effect something by virtue of inherent excellence or rightful authority. Power is manifested in the reproductive forces of nature (Gen. 4:12; 49:3), in the physical strength and vitality of human beings (Judg. 16:6; Prov. 20:29), as well as animals (Job 39:11; Prov. 14:4), and in the military prowess of men (1 Sam. 14:52; 2 Sam. 23:8–10). Natural forces exhibit power (Exod. 14:21; Isa. 43:16), as do emotions like love and greed (Song of Sol. 8:6; Isa. 56:11). Various forms of political authority are also a manifestation of power (Luke 7:8; Acts 26:10, 12; Rom. 13:1).

More mighty than any of these, however, is God, who is the ultimate source of all power (Pss. 66:7; 147:5; Jer. 10:6; Job 36:22). God's power is manifested in nature (Ps. 65:6–7; Jer. 10:12) and history, especially in God's act of redemption at the Exodus (Exod. 15:6, 13; 32: 11; Deut. 3:23). Compared to God's power, human power pales into insignificance (Pss. 33: 16–17; 147:10–11). God gives power to the faint (Isa. 40:29), and human beings may take refuge in God's strength (Ps. 28:7–8; Jer. 16:19; Luke 1:49). According to the NT, the power of God was made manifest in the life and deeds of Jesus (Mark 6:2, 5; Luke 4:14, 36; 5:17; 6:19). His followers were empowered by the Holy Spirit (Acts 1:8; 4:33; Rom. 15:19). Even the proclamation of the gospel of Jesus Christ was seen by Paul as a manifestation of divine power (Rom. 1:16; 1 Cor. 1:18). Finally, the NT also speaks of cosmic powers at work in the world, who stand in opposition to God, but whose power has already been broken and subordinated to the power of God made manifest in Christ (Rom. 8:38; 1 Cor. 15:24; Eph. 1:21; Col. 2:15; 1 Pet. 3:22). ***See also*** Dominion. W.E.L.

praetor (pray'tohr), a senior Roman magistrate of senatorial rank. Praetors served as judges, commanders in the army, managers of the senate treasury, supervisors of the roads, of grain distribution, or of public works, or as governors of provinces. A person was eligible for praetorship at age thirty if he had served in the lower offices of the *cursus honorum* (Lat., "career of honors," i.e., a public career). It was usual for an individual to have held three appointments as praetor before becoming a consul. Jesus was scourged in the praetor's residence ("Praetorium") by Roman soldiers (Mark 15:16–20).

Praetorian Guard, the (KJV: "palace"), the probable meaning of "praetorium" in Phil. 1:13 (cf. also "those of Caesar's household" in Phil. 4:22). It refers either to a select unit of the Roman army that served as imperial bodyguards or simply to the military (and other) personnel attached to a praetorium (the official residence of a Roman official). ***See also*** Architecture; Gabbatha.

praetorium. ***See*** Architecture; Gabbatha.

praise, to glorify, or the act of glorifying God, frequently in communal worship (Ps. 113; Luke 1:64; Acts 2:47; Rev. 19:5). The Hebrew term for the Psalms translates as "Praises." ***See also*** Hallelujah; Psalms, The; Worship.

prayer, the act of petitioning, praising, giving thanks, or confessing to God; it is expressed by several different words in both the OT and the NT. Prayer can be individual or corporate, audible or silent. It is conditioned by the biblical understanding of God as a personal being who hears the prayers of his people (1 Kings 9:3; Pss. 34:15; 65:2; Matt. 7:11; 1 John 5:15).

In the OT: The earliest instances of prayer in the OT are conversations between persons and God. Such conversations take place between God and Adam (Gen. 3:9–12), Abraham (Gen. 15:1–6), and Moses (Exod. 3:1–4:17). It is said that God spoke to Moses "face to face, as a man speaks to his friend" (Exod. 33:11). Kings (1 Sam. 23:2–4; 1 Kings 3:5–14) and prophets (1 Sam. 3:4–9; Isa. 6:1–13; Jer. 1:4–19) are portrayed as conversation partners with God (frequently the divine presence is by way of visions or dreams).

The forms of prayer in the OT include petitions for guidance, requests for divine help, intercessions, praise and thanksgiving, and confession. Prayers for guidance are offered by Isaac (Gen. 24:12–14), Moses (Num. 11:11–15), and most notably by Solomon, who asks for wisdom (1 Kings 3:5–14). Requests include prayers for the necessities of life (1 Kings 8: 22–53; Prov. 30:8), deliverance from enemies (Gen. 32:11; Pss. 31:15; 59:1), and retribution (Judg. 16:28; Ps. 137:7; Jer. 17:18). Intercessions are offered by the patriarchs and Moses (Gen. 18:22–32; Exod. 5:22–23; 32:11–13), David (2 Sam. 12:16–17), and various prophets (Amos 7: 1–6; Ezek. 9:8; 11:13). While such intercessions are generally for the whole people, there are instances of intercessions for individuals (1 Kings 17:20–21; 2 Kings 4:32–33) and Gentile governmental authority as well (Jer. 29:7; Ezra 6:10). Praise and thanksgiving are offered to God for his steadfast love (Pss. 100:4–5; 108: 3–4), his creation of the world, his rule over it, and his benevolent care for all that he has made (Pss. 145–150). Confession is prescribed for the annual Day of Atonement (Lev. 16:21), but it can be made whenever an offense against God has occurred. Confession is usually made by the confessor on behalf of the people (Exod. 32:31–32; Neh. 9:16–37; Dan. 9:20) or by the community (Judg. 10:10), but there are instances of individual confession (2 Sam. 24:17; Ps. 51). Confession is made in the certainty of

Jesus praying in the garden at Gethsemane (Luke 22:39–46); sixth-century mosaic at San Apollinare in Classe, Ravenna, Italy.

God's promises to forgive (Lev. 26:40–45; Isa. 1:18; Mic. 7:18–19).

The OT assumes that prayer can be offered at any time and place. There are, however, prescribed times: confession is made on the Day of Atonement; hours are set for daily prayer (Dan. 6:10); and the Sabbath and other festivals are days for prayer. The Temple was a place of prayer, as were the synagogue and home in the postexilic era. The prophets taught that prayer is more than a matter of ritual; it must be offered with integrity, pure motives, and only within the context of having attended to ethical concerns (Isa. 1:15–17; Hos. 6:6; Amos 5:21–24; Mic. 6:8; cf. Ps. 24:3–6).

In the NT: Jesus is portrayed as a model and instructor in prayer in the NT, especially in Luke's Gospel, where he prays at decisive moments: his baptism (3:21), the calling of his disciples (6:12), transfiguration (9:29), Gethsemane (22:39–46), and crucifixion (23:46). The major prayers attributed to Jesus, however, are in Matthew (6:9–13, the Lord's Prayer; cf. Luke 11:2–4) and John (chap. 17, the High Priestly Prayer). Jesus teaches that prayer should not be ostentatious and verbose but in private and with brevity (Matt. 6:5–8), earnest (Luke 11:5–13), in faith (Mark 11:23–24), and in a forgiving spirit (Mark 11:25). God is to be addressed as "Father" (Matt. 6:9; 7:11).

Within the early church, prayer was addressed directly to God (1 Cor. 1:4; Col. 1:3) or "through" Christ (Rom. 1:8). That prayer should be "through" Christ is based on the prior concept that God's grace and love come "through" Christ (Rom. 1:5; 5:1; 8:39) and that the reigning Christ is Lord and is accessible as mediator (Rom. 10:9–13; 1 Cor. 1:9).

As in the OT, the prayers of the NT are of several kinds. Paul frequently gives thanks for the faith and witness of those to whom he writes (Rom. 1:8–9; 1 Cor. 1:4; Phil. 1:3–5), and worship regularly includes prayers of thanksgiving (1 Cor. 14:16–17) and praise (Acts 2:47). Prayers are to be offered for daily needs (Matt. 6:11; 7:11; Phil. 4:6) and for the healing of the sick (James 5:13–16). Intercessions are made by Paul for his congregations (Rom. 15:13; Phil. 1:9–11), and he asks for their intercessions (Rom. 15:30–32; 2 Cor. 1:11; 1 Thess. 5:25). Intercessions are to be made for all persons, including rulers, that a peaceable life may be enjoyed by all (1 Tim. 2:1–2). There are prayers for forgiveness (Luke 18:13; cf. Matt. 6:12) and guidance (Acts 1:24–25; 6:6; 13:2–3).

Christ and the Spirit take on special roles in the prayers of the NT. Prayers are offered directly to Christ (Acts 7:59; 1 Cor. 1:2), although not frequently. The language of the "Kyrie" ("Lord, have mercy") is found at Matt. 17:15 and 20:30–31 (cf. 8:25), and the prayer "Maranatha" ("Our Lord, come!") appears at 1 Cor. 16:22 (cf. Rev. 22:20); both are addressed to Christ. Not only, however, are prayers offered "through" Christ or to him; Christ also prays as intercessor for the saints (Rom. 8:34; Heb. 7:25). Likewise, the Spirit's role in prayer is manifold. Prayer is "in the Spirit" (1 Cor. 14:15; Gal. 4:6; Phil. 3:3), who prompts and guides believers in prayer. On the other hand, the Spirit intercedes for believers (Rom. 8:26–27), because the Spirit knows their weaknesses and the mind and will of God (Rom. 8:27; 1 Cor. 2:10–11).

Prayer is not always answered in the way expected (see 2 Cor. 12:7–9). The picture that emerges from a survey of the biblical materials is that prayer is to be made to God in faith and expectation, but, in the NT, through Christ and in the Spirit. Prayer is not an act of attempting to manipulate God but a means of giving God thanks and praise, calling upon him for one's daily needs and the care of others, and asking that his will be done and that his kingdom come.

See also Atonement, Day of; Feasts, Festivals, and Fasts; Holy Spirit, The; Lord's Prayer, The; Maranatha; Psalms, The; Sabbath; Synagogue; Temple, The; Worship.

Bibliography

Fisher, Fred L. *Prayer in the New Testament.* Philadelphia: Westminster, 1964.

Harrington, Wilfrid. *The Bible's Ways of Prayer.* Wilmington, DE: Michael Glazier, 1980.

McFadyen, John E. *The Prayers of the Bible.* London: Hodder & Stoughton, 1906. A.J.H.

Prayer, the Lord's. ***See*** Lord's Prayer, The.

Prayer of Manasseh, the, a penitential prayer composed by a pious Jew sometime during the second or first century B.C. It is typical of Jewish prayer during the intertestamental period (ca. 160 B.C.–A.D. 45; cf. Tob. 3:2–6, 11–15; Jth. 9:2–14; Rest of Esther 13:9–11; 14:3–19; Song of the Three Children 3–22), yet goes beyond the typical to provide perhaps the finest example of the genre. Its parts include:

I. Invocation of God (v. 1)
II. Ascription of praise, mentioning both God's wrath and his mercy to sinners (vv. 2–8)
III. Confession of sin (vv. 9–10)
IV. Supplication for God's pardon (vv. 11–15a)
V. Doxology (v. 15b).

The prayer was suggested by 2 Chron. 33:12–13, 18–19, where the idolatrous king, Manasseh, is said to have prayed to God for forgiveness, and its intended audience may have been Jews who had broken the first or second commandment (Exod. 20:1–6) in responding to the lure of Hellenistic culture. The theme is the efficacy of repentance in securing God's pardon for the wicked. In speaking of guilt as a weight or burden (v. 10), the work contains perhaps a hint of the Hellenistic theme of the psychological self-punishment of the guilty (cf. Wisd. of Sol. 17: 1–21; Philo *Flaccus* 162–80). The metaphors for this experience seem also to reflect the details of the punishment of the fallen angels in *1 Enoch* 9:4, 11–12; 13:5; 54:1–5; 56:1–4—the petitioner is weighed down by iron fetters, cannot lift his face to heaven, and asks God not to condemn him to the depths of the earth (vv. 9–10, 13).

Because of its brevity, the Prayer of Manasseh cannot be dated with any certainty, nor can its place of composition or original language be easily fixed. It is not found in the Hebrew Bible, and is attested only in the third century A.D. in Christian sources. Appearing in only a few Septuagint (LXX) manuscripts, generally appended to the Psalms, the Prayer of Manasseh was apparently unknown to the Bible scholar Jerome in the fourth century B.C. Protestants include it among the Apocrypha. It was not present in the edition of the Vulgate declared canonical by the Council of Trent and, when printed in Catholic Bibles, it is placed with 1 and 2 Esdras in an appendix to the NT. It is considered canonical in Eastern Orthodoxy. ***See also*** Apocrypha, Old Testament; Prayer. D.W.S.

preaching. **1** As a mode of communication, the translation of a number of Hebrew and Greek words. In the OT, "preaching" refers to an announcement, the content of which is supplied by the context (Jon. 3:2; Neh. 6:7), but it also translates a word meaning to announce *good news* (Isa. 40:9; 52:7; 61:1). This latter word, in its Greek form, became a favorite of the early Christian community. But the act of preaching cannot be confined to the occurrence of certain words. The prophets were those who spoke for God, and their oracles are sermonic. In 2 Pet. 2: 5, Noah is called a preacher of righteousness. In the NT, preaching is explicitly or implicitly conveyed by many terms. The two most commonly used are the word from which we get "evangelize," meaning "to announce good news" or "to preach the gospel" (Matt. 11:5; Rom. 1:15), a term that carries within it both mode and content, and the word meaning "to herald" or "to make an authoritative proclamation" (Matt. 3:1; Acts 10:42; 2 Cor. 4:5). Preaching is also described by more modest words, such as announcing (Luke 9:60), speaking (Acts 20:7), or simply telling (Mark 2:2). In addition, there are terms that carry a special emphasis: witnessing (Acts 2:40), exhorting (Rom. 12:8), and prophesying (1 Cor. 12:28).

The Christian movement was launched and nourished by preaching. In the tradition of the prophets, both John the Baptist (Mark 1:7) and Jesus (Luke 4:18) came preaching. The Twelve continued this function (Acts 5:42), and Paul understood his primary task was to preach the gospel (1 Cor. 1:17). While certain persons were designated as evangelists (Acts 21:8; Eph. 4:11), the whole church shared in the proclamation of the gospel (Acts 8:4).

2 As a term designating content in early Christianity, the good news, the gospel. At times, the content of the good news is spelled out. According to Luke 4:18–19, Jesus preached good news to the poor, release to captives, sight to the blind, liberty to the oppressed, and the acceptable year of the Lord. Paul's gospel consisted of the death, burial, resurrection, and appearance of Jesus Christ according to the Scriptures (1 Cor. 15:3–8). Portions of sermons in Acts (2: 16–36; 3:12–26; 13:16–41; 17:22–31) reveal the content of preaching in some early churches. In the opinion of many scholars, the four Gospels contain the core of the content not only of the preaching of Jesus but also of the Christian communities. The Letter to the Hebrews, called by the writer a "word of exhortation" (13:22), is a sermon and represents a style of preaching (citing a text, interpreting and applying it) that became widespread after the second century. In the NT, however, most references to preaching do not elaborate but refer to the content simply by such terms as the gospel (Mark 1:14), the proclamation (Rom. 16:25), the kingdom of God (Luke 9:2), Christ (Phil. 1:15), Christ crucified (1 Cor. 1:23), or the word of God (Acts 13:5).

3 An act whose purpose in the NT is "repentance and forgiveness of sins" (Luke 24:47), for God does not desire that any should perish (2 Pet. 3:9). This word of God's love for all peoples had been in the preaching of the great prophets (Isa. 2:1–4). Preaching also served to edify and instruct the believers. While distinctions between preaching and teaching are made (Matt. 9: 35; Rom. 12:6–8), they can be exaggerated by modern interpreters to the detriment of both. ***See also*** Gospel; Gospels; Teaching. F.B.C.

precious stones. ***See*** Breastpiece; Jewelry.

predestination, a theological affirmation that takes up and extends the affirmations of election, providence, and covenant. Throughout the centuries of religious reflection and debate, the notion of predestination has tended to become a questionable category. To some, it suggests a God who is unfair, capricious, and arbitrary (cf. the handbooks of dogmatic theology). But its use in the Bible as a whole does not support the (mistaken) notion that God plays favorites, blessing certain of his creatures while cursing others. Whereas providence emphasizes a divine ordering and regulation of the world and history toward a positive goal, predestination emphasizes a divine predetermination of human destiny in conformity with an eternal plan. God "foreordains" according to his "design and purpose"; he "chooses" and "elects" according to his "counsel" and "will" (e.g., 2 Chron. 19:7; cf. Rom. 11:15; Prov. 16:4; Rom. 9:18, 20–24; Gen. 50:20).

Sovereignty of God: For all such terms, the notion of the sovereignty of God is a key starting point. God alone is the Creator and sustainer of all that is; God is the sovereign Lord who designed the standards for life and directs all things toward their appointed destiny; God alone is wise enough, righteous enough, and loving enough to determine what shall become of his creation. God does what he wills (e.g., Ps. 115:3; Isa. 45:5–7; 46:8–11; Rom. 9:11, 15; Eph. 1:11).

In the OT, God chooses the Hebrew people as his own covenant people (e.g., Deut. 7:6–10); he chooses individuals to carry out his will and purpose (e.g., Judg. 2:16; 1 Kings 18:1); he raises up prophets to proclaim his word (Isa. 6:1–13; Jer. 1:1–2; Amos 3:6–8); he uses nations and events of history to execute his judgment and accomplish his goals (Isa. 7:18–19; 45:1–4). The worlds of nature and of history are under God's control (Isa. 45:5–7; Gen. 3:17–18; Rev. 21:1).

In the NT, God alone decides when the time has reached its fullness or is ripe (e.g., Acts 1:7; Eph. 1:10; Col. 1:26; 2 Tim. 1:9; Rom. 3:25–26; 9:11; John 2:4; 7:30; 12:27; 13:1; 17:1; this same idea is also found among the Dead Sea Scrolls). Divine necessity is connected with the destiny of the Son of man figure in the Gospels (Mark 8:31; 9:31; 10:33–34 and parallels; cf. also Luke 24:25–27, 44–46). God has appointed a day of his choosing for fulfillment of his plan (e.g., Heb. 4:7; Acts 17:26–31; 2 Tim. 4:8; 1 Thess. 4:13–5:11; 2 Pet. 3:8–10), which he determined before the foundation of the world (Eph. 1:4; 1 Cor. 2:7; 1 Pet. 1:20). God decides what is to be granted (e.g., Mark 10:40 and parallels; Eph. 1:6; Rom. 9:11) in accord with his purposes in Christ (1 Pet. 1:2; Eph. 1:9; 3:11; Acts 10:42; 2 Thess. 2:13). His gifts and call are irrevocable (e.g., Rom. 11:29); his counsels are beyond human scrutiny (e.g., 1 Cor. 2:6–13; Rom. 11:33–36); and his will is that all should choose life (e.g., 1 Tim. 2:4; 2 Pet. 3:9). God is all-powerful to carry out his will and promises (e.g., Luke 1–2).

For many people today, the notion of the sovereignty of God is difficult to accept. It is questionable, however, that the notion has been easy to accept for people of any age. Empirical realities seem to throw the idea of God's sovereign predestination into doubt. The problem of ubiquitous evil appears to be its greatest rival. The Bible does not pretend that the concept of predestination resolves all paradoxes or detoxifies the bitterness of disappointments, contradictions, and injustices in life. The affirmations of predestination belong to those ultimate dimensions of life on the extreme outer limits of what humans can perceive and talk about. Humans enter these outer limits by permission, as it were, where faith is mingled with mystery. Knowledge and assurance of predestination are vague at best; to lay claim to either is to venture the risk of faith and to invite contradiction. Yet, predestination remains in the biblical understanding of reality and human destiny.

The Bible's Focus: The Bible does not develop abstract theories of predestination applied speculatively and generally to all phenomena. Rather, it concentrates on God's predetermined plan to redeem and to rescue his creatures from destruction. Human beings are on a destructive course, but God has determined to alter this course "from of old" and to see the alteration through to its redemptive conclusion (an important theological consideration in a nuclear age). In contrast to ancient mythology, which speculated on the cosmic struggles of various divine and suprahuman powers as the background to all that happens on earth, the Bible concentrates on the history-shaping, personal decisions of the one God. In the OT, God maintains fidelity to his people chosen in covenant. To understand and appropriate this opened up a future of confidence and trust (Pss. 33:11; 115:3; Prov. 21:1). Even suffering could thus be regarded as part of the divine plan to save, although mere mortals were unable to understand such matters (e.g., Job 11:7; Ps. 92:6–8).

In keeping with this OT emphasis on God's unfolding, predestined plan to rescue and to deliver, the NT concentrates on Christ as the means to this end. His suffering unto death was determined within God's plan of salvation. His death was determined by divine counsel to be the foundational necessity (Mark 8:31); indeed, Christ was the "lamb" sacrificed before the foundation of the world (Rev. 13:8). The NT does not ask why his death should have been divinely necessary; to speculate would be impious. Nevertheless, in his suffering unto death, Christ saves people who believe and who were themselves "chosen before the foundation of the world" (Eph. 1:4; Matt. 25:34).

Free Will and Faith: This sense of predestination in the NT is not exclusive, at least as far as humans can speak about its relationship to them. God chooses faith and those who believe; he does not predestine that some may not believe (known as "double predestination" in the handbooks of dogmatic theology). That God's choice of Christ's suffering unto death and faith becomes for some a stumbling block and folly (1 Cor. 1:18–25) is a reality but not subject to human scrutiny and reflection on the basis of a view of predestination. The choice to become a participant in God's predestined plan to deliver humankind from sin is generally the free-will option of all human beings. Special cases such as those people who lived before Christ or those not having the option for whatever reason do not point to automatic exclusion from God's grace and love (e.g., Rom. 3:25–26). God does not withhold his care from anyone. Wherever the NT speaks of predestination, it does so with the intent of underscoring God's will to embrace all his creation in the saving help predestined for it. And this does not limit human free will and initiative (e.g., Phil. 2:12).

Not special cases but disbelief became the major problem for biblical writers when wrestling with the affirmations of predestination. That people refuse their appointed predestiny was a perplexing dilemma and a disturbing reality for these writers. When contemplating the end-time consequences of this reality, they saw an awful conclusion to time and history that included "weeping and gnashing of teeth" (Matt. 8:12; 13:41–42). It is a frightful moment for any human reflection upon the outer limits of ultimate possibilities; certainly, no human can talk of this judgment easily and casually.

God's Covenant Promise: Among the NT writers, the apostle Paul takes an unparalleled step of boldness when pondering the promise connected with God's predestined plan for salvation. In the face of unbelief among his contemporaries in Israel, he maintains (Rom. 9–11) that God will not allow his plan to be thwarted by such unbelief. Paul does not come to this conclusion by reasoned deduction, as though he were privy to special disclosures from on high; he does not figure out, as it were, what God is up to through generations. Rather, he links predestination to God's covenant promise to Israel and affirms that God does not break his promises. He wills and is able to keep his promises of old. This is a crucial moment in Paul's thought, because for him the gospel is also by nature promise. If God changes his mind and goes back on former promises, what guarantee is there that he will not also do so as regards the gospel promise? Of course, Paul does not "know" that he will not, but his fundamental theological understanding is that God maintains fidelity as Promiser. And what Paul claims for God's promise to Israel he claims for the whole human race, because this covenant promise was to be a blessing for all the families of earth.

At the key junctures of Paul's development of this line of thinking, he chooses forms of expression that are doxological/prophetic declarations rather than rational deductions unveiling some detailed road map of history (e.g., Rom. 8:31–39; 11:33–36). These declarations do not convince in the style of debate, but rest on the common experience of God's grace for all who call upon him. God's predestined final hour in time and space is not equated with Paul's own personal history or with the experience of some other individual, but it is not independent of them either. No other NT writer goes so far in the deep struggle to understand the far-reaching implications of predestination for human freedom and unbelief. ***See also*** Election; Providence; Salvation. J.E.A.

Pre-exilic Period, a general historical term usually referring to the period of time prior to the Babylonian exile (586 B.C.). It is usually limited to the time of the United Monarchy and the Divided Kingdom (ca. 1000–586 B.C.), although some might also include the period of the judges (thus extending the period back to ca. 1175 B.C.). Scholars assume narrative, historical, prophetic, legal, and gnomic literature was produced during this period of over five hundred years. ***See also*** Divided Kingdom, Divided Monarchy; Exile; United Monarchy.

Premonarchical Period, in the ancient history of Israel the period of the judges, the thirteenth and twelfth centuries B.C. It represented a time of transitions: the Israelites moved from a seminomadic population to a farming nation, from a highly diverse people to one with common purposes, and from a confederacy to a monarchy. While the book of Judges illustrates the problems in these transitions, it also demonstrates the birthing of a determined and resilient people. ***See also*** Judges, The Book of.

presbyter, presbytery (Gk. *presbyteros,* "elder"; *presbyterion,* "council" or "assembly of elders"), a group of (usually older) men appointed to oversee the life of a congregation. The early Christian office of elder doubtless originated from OT and Jewish models (see, e.g., Num. 11:16–17, 24–25). In NT times, each Jewish community had its council of elders (note the Sanhedrin in Jerusalem and "the elders" at Qumran). Paul and Barnabas appointed elders "in every church" (Acts 14:23; cf. 20:17–38; 1 Pet. 5:1–4; James 5:14; Rev. 4:4). In some instances, elder and "bishop" were apparently equated (Titus 1:5–9). For reference to a council of elders (presbytery), see 1 Tim. 4:14. ***See also*** Bishop.

press, a device for crushing olives or grapes. ***See also*** Olive; Vine.

priesthood. ***See*** Priests.

Priestly writer(s), the name given to the author(s) of one of the sources found in the books of Genesis through Numbers. The siglum given the source is "P," because the authors appear to have come from priestly circles during the sixth century B.C. Some scholars do not think of the P source as an independent narrative like the Yahwist source. The focus of the Priestly materials is upon God's regulations, with little colorful reflection on the human wrestling with those words. The style with few exceptions (such as Gen. 1:1–2:4a) tends to be ponderous, pedantic, and prolix. Many cultic practices are rationalized (Gen. 2:1–3; 17:1–27; Lev. 17:10–14). The major purpose of P is the revitalization of the Sinai covenant and related institutions for Israel in a time of anticipated restoration. The final shape of Genesis through Numbers can be attributed to the Priestly writers. ***See also*** Levites; Priests; Sinai; Sources of the Pentateuch.

K.H.R.

Hittite priestesses holding ritual vessels; relief from Carchemish (ca. 1400–1200 B.C.).

priests, the specially designated officials who served in the Temple performing ritual functions and conducting the sacrificial services. The Hebrew word *kohen,* also attested in Phoenician, Punic, Ugaritic, Arabic, and Aramaic, designates not only Jewish priests but also those who served in temples dedicated to other gods. Melchizedek, the king of Salem, was also a Canaanite priest (Gen. 14:18); Asenath, the wife of Joseph, was the daughter of an Egyptian priest (Gen. 41:45); Jehu assembled the priests of Baal (2 Kings 10:19–20), and the like. A term that appears only three times in the Bible, *kemarim,* always designates idolatrous priests such as those who worshiped the gods of the Canaanites, Ammonites, and Assyrians (Zeph. 1:4). There is no feminine form of *kohen. Bat kohen* (daughter of a priest) refers to a woman of a priestly family.

Identity: The priesthood was limited by Pentateuchal law to the Levites, that is, members of the family of Levi, the son of Jacob. According to Deuteronomy, all the levitical families had a right to the priesthood since they did not receive an inheritance of land like the other tribes (Deut. 10:8–9). Aaron and his sons exclusively received the anointing oil and were attired in special clothing of the priesthood (Exod. 28–29). The families of Eli at the temple of Shiloh (1 Sam. 14:3), Zadok in Jerusalem (Ezek. 40:46), and Amaziah at Bethel (Amos 7:10–17) were not specified as Aaronides but were of levitical descent.

History: In the patriarchal period (ca. 2000–1700 B.C.) there was no official priesthood. The head of the family performed sacrifices in various holy places (Gen. 31:54). The only priests mentioned at this time are of nations that were not nomadic and had fixed sanctuaries (e.g., Gen. 41:50; Exod. 3:1). As the Israelites developed a more structured society, a special class came to preside over the more and more complex rituals that their religion entailed.

After the conquest of Canaan (probably late thirteenth to early twelfth centuries), ordinary Israelites often sacrificed at altars (Judg. 13:19–20) or high places (Heb. *bamot;* 1 Kings 3:3–4), but in the temples, the "houses of God," only priests of levitical lineage were allowed to perform the rites. These temples were constructed from Dan to Beer-sheba. The Ark of the desert period (ca. 1300–1250 B.C.), under the care of the family of Aaron, came to rest at Shiloh, and the Aaronides then became the officiators at this temple. In the time of Josiah (ca. 639–609 B.C.; 2 Kings 23:8), all the priests were brought to serve in the Jerusalem Temple, and the outlying temples and cult sites were abolished. This centralization gave control of the entire cult to the priests serving in the Jerusalem Temple.

Ezekiel typifies the desire of the Israelites in the Babylonian exile (after 586 B.C.) to reconstitute the priesthood in all its glory. The building of the Second Temple (begun late sixth century B.C.) allowed the priests to return to duty. The actual cultic functions were discharged by the descendants of Aaron, while the other Levites held subsidiary roles. The Second Temple did not, however, match the glory of its predecessor. One of the most significant things missing was the Ark itself; the anointing oil was no longer in use, and other customs of the First Temple were not practiced. At this time, the ranks of the priesthood swelled, and the Temple dues were not sufficient to support them. Many priests, therefore, turned to agriculture. Nehemiah often chastises the people for not bringing their obligations (Neh. 12:44–47), and the priests for deserting the house of God (13: 10–11). According to many scholars, it was decided at this time that the priests would be called upon to officiate for only a short period of time each. The various duties were divided to give all the households an opportunity to serve while none were completely dependent on Temple duties for their livelihoods. The first-century historian Josephus knew of these priestly divisions in his day (see also Luke 1: 8–9).

During the Hellenistic period (ca. 333 B.C.–A.D. 70), the priesthood dominated the nation. The priests were many in number and had a great deal of prestige. The head of the Temple, the high priest, was *de facto* the head of government of Judea. He represented Judea in dealing with the ruling powers, collected taxes, and was responsible for the spiritual welfare of the people. A large number of aristocrats were of priestly lineage. Many priests were scattered throughout the country and came to Jerusalem only to officiate during their terms of Temple service. Until the time of Antiochus Epiphanes (175–163 B.C.), the high priest held his position for life.

The priestly households attained their greatest power during the Hasmonean period (ca. 165–63 B.C.), although there was often conflict between them regarding the extent to which they would become hellenized. The priests were leaders of the Sadducees and the Sanhedrin. At this time, the Pharisees began to loosen the hold of the priests on the spiritual leadership of the people. When Herod became king (37 B.C.), the rule of the nation shifted from the priests to the secular monarchy. He appointed a high priest, not necessarily from any particular family, reduced him to a ceremonial role, and deprived the office of its political powers.

In other sects, such as the one at Qumran near the Dead Sea, the Zadokite priests were accorded an extra measure of respect, such as being the first to bless the food and receive a portion. It was anticipated that a priestly messiah would take an exalted role in the reestablished independent state, alongside the Davidic messiah.

Christians transferred the role of the priest as mediator between God and humans onto Jesus whom they saw as both God and man. He became eternal High Priest by God's appointment (Heb. 5:1–6) and supplanted the ancient sacrificial system by his own sacrifice (Heb. 7: 27–28; 9:23–26).

The Roman procurators (A.D. 6–41, 44–66) appointed the high priests, many of whom bought the office through their great wealth. These wealthy families created an oligarchy of power and prestige and were regarded by the Pharisees as tyrannical to the peasants and sympathizers with the Romans. This aristocracy came to an end with the destruction of the Temple and the ascendancy of the Pharisees.

After the destruction of the Temple in A.D. 70, the priestly descendants of Aaron continued to maintain certain privileges, such as the recitation of the priestly benediction. Certain restrictions remained in force, such as the prohibitions of contact with the dead and marriage with a divorced or widowed woman.

Functions: The concept of the service of the priest in the ancient Near East was that he ministered to the god by fulfilling all his needs and worshiping in the house wherein his presence dwelt. In Israelite religion, these images eventually became relegated to technical or literary language. Thus, in Ezekiel, the service of God is expressed in terms of taking care of his needs, feeding him from the sacrifices upon his altar (table). The tribe of Levi is enjoined to "come near to me to minister to me; and they shall attend on me to offer me the fat and the blood, says the Lord God; they shall enter my sanctuary and they shall approach my table, to minister to me . . ." (Ezek. 44:15–16).

Chief among the duties of the priests was the performance of sacrifices. Only they were allowed to approach the altar, and then only within the context of a complex series of rituals and while wearing specific vestments that symbolized their holiness. The blood of an animal was often sprinkled, and certain portions of meat were burnt, depending upon the type of sacrifice. While ordinary priests performed these daily functions, the high priest was entrusted with the sin offerings, especially that of the Day of Atonement. Priests also pronounced the priestly blessing (Num. 6:22–26) over the people, blew trumpets on festive occasions such as holidays and new moons, and blew the shophar (trumpet made from a ram's horn) on the Day of Atonement to announce the Sabbatical Year (Lev. 25:9). The Levites who worked in the Temple alongside the Aaronide priests were the musicians, gatekeepers, singers, and the like.

In addition to preparing the sacrifices, the priests also were in charge of the maintenance of the Temple. They conducted routine inspections of the Temple grounds, noting what had to be repaired, and they solicited funds to carry out the work. In connection with donations to the Temple, they were often called upon to evaluate property and fix the type of sacrifice permitted to those of limited means by evaluating the ability of a worshiper to pay for a sacrifice (Lev. 12: 6–8; cf. Luke 2:22–24). The collection of tithes

Stone table found in a priest's home in Jerusalem in the Upper City, facing the Temple Mount; ca. A.D. 70.

and other obligatory Temple donations was administered by the priests, who were expected to eat their emoluments in a state of ritual purity.

When a person suffered a disease or physical sign of impurity, the purification rites were performed by a priest. The methods of purification included things like waiting a specific amount of time, bathing, washing one's clothes, being sprinkled with water by the priest, and bringing a sacrifice the blood of which would be sprinkled on one's behalf by the priest. The priests were charged with diagnosing the disease *tsaraat* (usually translated "leprosy," it was used to designate a number of disorders of the skin; cf. Lev. 13–14) as well as purifying the persons or objects affected by it (Lev. 14; see Mark 1:44). Contact with the dead (Num. 19:11–19), emissions (Lev. 15), the carcass of an unclean animal (Lev. 11:24–40), even contact with the red heifer, the means by which impurity of the dead was removed (Num. 19: 1–10), required these rites of purification.

In First Temple times (ca. 950–586 B.C.) the high priest had the Urim and Thummim attached to his breastplate which he consulted for a divine reply to an inquiry (Num. 27:21). Lots were often cast, as was the case in the division of the land among the tribes (Num. 26: 55–56) and the choosing of Saul as king (1 Sam. 10:20–21).

Among the functions of the priests was that of judging (Deut. 17:9; 12; Ezek. 15:1, 24). The priests administered the ordeal of the suspected adulteress (Num. 5:11–31). In the blessing of Moses before his death, Levi is charged with teaching the law to the people of Israel as well as offering incense and sacrifices upon the altar (Deut. 33:10).

As a prestigious, elite class the priests were also expected to preserve the holiness of the sanctuary and the uniqueness of the people of Israel. Therefore, they were subject to added restrictions not incumbent upon the average Israelite. A priest was forbidden to officiate if he had a physical defect (Lev. 21:17–24), was ritually impure, was under the influence of alcohol, or had married a woman forbidden to a priest. A priest was allowed to marry only a virgin of Israel, not a divorcee, prostitute, convert, or, in the case of the high priest, a widow (Lev. 21:14). Ezekiel makes an exception of the widow of a priest (Ezek. 44:22).

A priest could not defile himself by attending the cemetery except for the burial of a close relative (parent, sibling, child, or wife; Lev. 21: 1–3). The high priest could not have contact with the dead even if they were his parents (Lev. 21:11). Upon the death of Aaron's sons, Moses forbade Aaron and his remaining sons to manifest the signs of mourning during the week of their consecration (Lev. 10:6). Although Israel is said to be "a kingdom of priests and a holy nation" (Exod. 19:6), it was the priesthood that embodied the highest levels of sanctity in ancient Israel. ***See also*** Josiah; Purity; Temple, The; Tithe; Worship.

Bibliography

Cody, A. *A History of the Old Testament Priesthood.* Rome: Pontifical Biblical Institute, 1969.

de Vaux, R. *Ancient Israel.* New York, Toronto: McGraw-Hill, 1965. Vol. 2, pp. 345–405.

Gray, G. B. *Sacrifice in the Old Testament.* With a Prolegomenon by B. A. Levine. New York: Ktav Publishing, 1971. Pp. 179–270.

L.H.S.

prince, a person of high rank. The Hebrew terms for "prince" are multiple, but they invariably refer to a person of extraordinary power and authority. The word may emphasize an individual's prowess in battle, or it may suggest an office one has attained, whether chief of a tribe, head of a family, satrap, or king. The heir to the throne is also called a prince, as are the chief rulers of a kingdom who answer only to the king (so the seven princes of Persia and Media whose names are given in Esther 1:14). In messianic expectation there was room for a prince of peace (Isa. 9:6). At the opposite end of the spectrum, the devil received the title "prince of this world" (John 12:31). This chief official is thought to have ruled over lesser beings who endeavored to lead good people astray (cf. Mark 3:22).

J.L.C.

Prisca, Priscilla (pris'kuh, pri-sil'uh), a prominent woman in the early Christian church, always mentioned in connection with Aquila, her husband. Paul calls her Prisca (a common Latin name), but Acts prefers Priscilla. Prisca's husband was a leatherworker and normally would not be expected to travel extensively with his wife and to purchase property, as is suggested in the NT references (Acts 18:2–28; cf.

Rom. 16:3; 1 Cor. 16:19). The fact that Prisca is mentioned before Aquila (unusual for the ancients) both by Paul and by the writer of Acts may indicate that Prisca had a higher social status (perhaps through inherited wealth) than her husband and that this was the source of their means. Driven from Rome by Claudius' edict (A.D. 49/50) that expelled Jews from that city, they moved to Corinth, where they came into contact with Paul; then, leaving Corinth with Paul, they settled in Ephesus. Paul greets them in Rom. 16:3 and 1 Cor. 16:19 (cf. also 2 Tim. 4:19). ***See also*** Aquila; Claudius; Decrees; Paul; Women. A.J.M.

Priscilla. ***See*** Aquila; Prisca, Priscilla.

prison, a building or other facility used for holding individuals in judicial confinement.

Types of Imprisonment: Various types of imprisonment were known in biblical times. Accused persons were often imprisoned either while their cases were being investigated or to assure their appearance for trial. The OT contains several examples: Gen. 39:19–41:14; 1 Kings 22:26–27; Num. 15:34 (see also Lev. 24:12, "until the will of the Lord should be declared"). In NT times Roman magistrates had the right either to remand accused persons to civil or military prisons or to release them on bail or on personal recognizance. Provincial magistrates often chose to imprison accused persons, and defendants of lower social status were everywhere particularly vulnerable. The NT offers many examples of pretrial imprisonment: Acts 4:3; 12:3–4; 16:23–24; 23:35; Phil. 1:7–26. The binding or chaining of Jesus before bringing him to Pilate may reflect some sort of formal arrest procedures (Matt. 27:2; Mark 15:1).

Some accused, particularly those of higher status, were held under more relaxed custody, sometimes without being chained. They could receive visitors and transact business (e.g., Paul at Rome [Acts 28:16–31]). Another type of imprisonment was for those condemned to death, a penalty common in antiquity. Debtors unable to pay their creditors were also imprisoned, sometimes in special debtors' prisons, until their debts were paid. Luke 12:58 makes precise reference to the "officers" who in Roman times had charge of such prisons (see also Matt. 5:25; 18:30). The asylum granted under Israel's law to those who had accidentally killed someone in fact constituted a form of imprisonment since the individual who left the city of refuge could be slain by the victim's next of kin (Num. 35:9–34; see also Deut. 4:41–43; 19:1–10; Josh. 20:1–9). Solomon's confinement of Shimei ben Gera to Jerusalem can be compared to this practice (1 Kings 2:8, 36–46).

Although the use of imprisonment as a legal penalty remained uncommon, such practice was known in Greece, in Rome, and also in Israel. While some of the prophet Jeremiah's various imprisonments (sixth century B.C.) resulted from lawless violence (Jer. 37:15–16; 38:5–7), his retention in "the court of the guard" may reflect somewhat more orderly judicial processes (Jer. 32:2–3; 37:21; 38:13). Ezra 7:26 lists imprisonment as one of several recognized forms of legal punishment. The NT offers no clear examples of imprisonment used in this fashion. Paul's imprisoning of Christians (Acts 8:3) probably refers to his handing them over to the custody of synagogue authorities who would then administer the penalty provided for in Israel's law, a flogging of up to forty lashes (Deut. 25:1–3; 2 Cor. 11:24; Acts 22:19). However, the pretrial retention of an individual could easily be abused and become in fact a means of punishment (e.g., John the Baptist [Mark 6:17–20]).

Prison Conditions: Despite various efforts to promote reforms, conditions in ancient prisons were often harsh. Most prisoners wore chains; their feet might be shackled, their hands manacled or even attached to their neck by another chain, and their movements further restricted by a chain fastened to a post. The existence of laws prohibiting chains that were too short or too restrictive indicates that jailers sometimes employed such practices. The very word "chains" became a synonym for imprisonment. Some prisoners were also kept in wooden stocks, devices to restrain the feet, hands, or even the neck of an individual (see Acts 16:24). Prisons often were very dark (see Isa. 42:7); the inner area of the prison mentioned in Acts 16:24 was probably without windows. Although solitary confinement was known, prisoners generally were kept grouped together, accused and condemned, men and women alike. Overcrowding was not infrequent (Isa. 24:22). Prisons often had poor air circulation, a lack of hygienic facilities, rats and vermin, and food of poor quality. Unscrupulous guards might at times use the withholding of food or even outright torture to extort money from prisoners or their relatives. Although various rulers, especially in Roman Imperial times, struggled to prevent such abuses, the quality of prison life largely remained the responsibility of local officials, and conditions undoubtedly varied considerably from place to place.

Numerous early Christians encountered prison at first hand, and NT exhortations such as Matt. 25:36 and Heb. 13:3 to visit those in prison clearly had immediacy. The best known prisoner in the NT is the apostle Paul; he himself refers to the many times he was imprisoned (2 Cor. 6:5; 11:23), and the phrase "the prisoner of Christ Jesus" is almost a Pauline title (Philem. 1, 9; Eph. 3:1; 4:1; 2 Tim. 1:8). This designation is in part ironic—if Paul is *Jesus'* prisoner, in reality he is free! The accounts of miraculous deliverances from prison found in Acts 12:6–10 and 16:25–26 also serve to stress that God's power is greater than all the chains and prisons that humanity can devise. ***See also*** Cities; John the Baptist; Joseph; Paul.

Bibliography

Sherwin-White, A. N. *Roman Society and Roman Law in the New Testament.* Oxford: Clarendon, 1963. R.A.W.

prize, either the spoils of war (as in Jer. 21:9) or something won in an athletic contest. Paul employs the latter as a metaphor for salvation (Phil. 3:14), the imperishable nature of which he contrasts with the perishable wreaths (made of parsley, celery, etc.) coveted by the athletes of Greece and Rome (1 Cor. 9:24–25). ***See also*** Battle; Crown; Games; War.

Prochorus (prah'kuh-ruhs), one of the seven in the Jerusalem church appointed by the apostles to take care of the widows and the poor (Acts 6: 1–6). ***See also*** Hellenists.

proconsul, a former Roman consul who served in consular rank as the governor of a province or in command of an army. Asia and Africa were always governed by former consuls. Other senatorial provinces might be governed by praetors. The proconsul Sergius Paulus became a Christian when he heard and saw what Paul and Barnabas were about (Acts 13:7–10), and it was when Gallio assumed his duties as proconsul of that Roman province of Achaia (modern Greece) that some of Paul's opponents leveled charges against him before that Roman official (Acts 18: 12–17).

procurator, an agent who looked after a person's affairs in that person's absence. During the Imperial period (after 31 B.C.), the procurator was an agent of the Roman emperor who was either a freedman or member of the equestrian class. Such agents might administer departments such as the mint, gladiatorial schools, or mines. The primary function of such agents was to look after the provincial interests of the emperor. In imperial provinces the procurator was under the legate. In senatorial provinces the procurator was more independent and might even serve as a check on the governor of the province. An equestrian procurator might also be assigned to govern minor provinces such as Thrace and Judea, which had no troops garrisoned in them. He would sometimes be dependent upon the governor of a larger, neighboring province. Contrary to some translations, Pontius Pilate (Matt. 27:11), Felix (Acts 23:24), and Festus (Acts 24:27) are designated as "governor" rather than "procurator" in the NT. P.P.

prodigal son, the younger son, who wastes

Return of the Prodigal Son, detail, Rembrandt, ca. 1668.

his inheritance in Jesus' parable (Luke 15:11–32). He experiences his father's forgiveness while his dutiful elder brother protests the father's actions.

professions and trades. ***See*** such individual entries as: Baker; Carpenter; Embalming; Farming; Fuller; Magic and Divination; Masons; Mines; Music; Perfumers; Pottery; Publicans; Rabbi, Rabboni; Scribe; Shepherd; Soldier; Spinning and Weaving; Town Clerk.

prognosticators, the archaic KJV translation of those who "predict what shall befall you" (Isa. 47:13). The prophet castigates faith in astrology, which is at issue in this verse.

promise, an assurance of some future act. Although absent as a specific term in the OT, the concept of promise runs throughout its narrative. The prediction of innumerable offspring to childless Abraham and Sarah (Gen. 15:5; 17: 6–7; 22:17–18), of a land for Israel (Gen. 15: 18–21; 50:22–25), of the perpetual rule of David's descendants (2 Sam. 7:16), and of a future world to God's liking (e.g., Isa. 11:1–9) all function implicitly as promise. Later Jewish traditions explicitly link God's promises to the future world, giving it an eschatological character. The Syrian *Apocalypse of Baruch* says that already in Abraham "the promise of future life was planted" (57:2) and will be harvested in the future world promised by God (14:13).

In the NT, the word "promise," both as noun and verb, is used extensively. Paul found scriptural authority for his Gentile mission in God's promise to Abraham through whom all nations (i.e., Gentiles) would be blessed (Rom. 4:9–25; Gal. 3:6–29). Through faith in Christ, God's promise was being fulfilled, and Gentiles were becoming Abraham's offspring (Rom. 4:16), members of the children of promise (Rom. 15: 8–12) without reference to the law. The inclusion of the Gentiles, however, does not nullify God's promises to the Jews (Rom. 9:4). Ultimately, Jews and Gentiles will gather as one people of God (Rom. 11:25–26).

The author of Hebrews sees in Jesus the realization of the promises given to but not realized by the ancients (11:39–40). Even though the new promises surpass the old, the inheritance even of the new is uncertain without obedience (4:1; 6:11–15; 10:36). The continuity forged by Paul between the promise to Israel and fulfillment in Christ is, however, missing in Hebrews. ***See also*** Abraham; Covenant; Eschatology; Gentile; Law; Torah. C.J.R.

property. ***See*** Inheritance; Ownership; Trade and Transportation.

prophet (Heb. *nabi'*, Gk. *prophētēs*), a person who serves as a channel of communication between the human and divine worlds. The biblical prophets played a crucial role in the development of Judaism and Christianity and influenced later Western thought by becoming the paradigm for identifying authentic divine messengers. Since their appearance in ancient Israel, the prophets have been understood in a number of different ways, both by scholars and by general readers of the Bible. Particularly in Christian tradition, the prophets have been regarded as predictors of the future, whose words pointed to the coming of Jesus and to the future course of world history. More generally, the prophets have been considered moral and ethical innovators, who brought Israelite religion to a higher level of development than it had previously achieved. In the twentieth century, many of the traditional understandings of the prophets have been questioned, and they have been variously portrayed as great preachers, as moral philosophers, as raving ecstatics, or merely as Israelite traditions.

The great variety of ways in which the OT prophets have been described suggests that they were multifaceted figures and that Israelite prophecy itself was a complex phenomenon. While it is possible to support any given

A prophet, as depicted in a sixth-century mosaic at San Apollinare in Classe, Ravenna, Italy.

picture of the prophets by appealing to the OT evidence, no single picture can incorporate all of the biblical data. Various types of prophets existed in Israel, and individual prophets also had unique characteristics they did not share with other prophets. However, once this diversity is recognized, it is possible to make some broad generalizations about the OT prophets and the roles that they played in Israelite religion and society.

Titles: The most common prophetic title used in the OT is *nabi'*, a word usually translated in the Septuagint (LXX) by the Greek word *prophētēs* and in English versions by the general term "prophet." The etymology of the title is uncertain, but it may mean "one who calls" or "one who is called." Although this title was used throughout Israel in all historical periods, it did not have the same connotations for all OT writers. In the Deuteronomistic history and the literature influenced by it (Deuteronomy, Joshua, Judges, Samuel, Kings, Hosea, Jeremiah), "prophet" is the preferred title for people who were considered legitimate links between the human and divine worlds, while other titles were used for figures who were not thought to be legitimate. In this literature prophets were accorded high status and played an authoritative role in Israel's religious life (Deut. 18:9–22).

On the other hand, OT writings from Judah and Jerusalem (Amos, Micah, Isaiah, Chronicles) use the title "prophet" less frequently, and it often appears in negative contexts. In this literature the preferred designation for prophetic figures is "visionary" (Heb. *ḥozeh*), a title that refers to the distinctive means by which these individuals received their revelations. Visionaries seem to have been active primarily during the monarchical period (ca. 1004–586 B.C.), when some of them were members of the royal establishment in Jerusalem (1 Chron. 21:9; 25:5; 29:29; 2 Chron. 9:29; 12:15; 19:2; 29:25, 30).

In addition to the titles "prophet" and "visionary," the OT mentions three other titles that were not in common use. In 1 Samuel 9, Samuel is called a "seer" *(ro'eh)*, a title that was already archaic in the time of the OT writers (1 Sam. 9:9). A seer appears to have been a specialist in communicating with God through visions, dreams, or divination, a function that was later taken over either by prophets (Deut. 18: 9–22) or by various diviners and priests. Although there are some late references to seers (2 Chron. 16:7, 10), it is likely that the seer disappeared from Israel early in the monarchical period. More frequently used is the title "man of God," which appears particularly in the prophetic stories set in the time of Elijah and Elisha (1 Kings 17–2 Kings 10). A "man of God" may have originally been someone able to use divine power in miraculous ways, but it is likely that the title was eventually given to anyone who enjoyed a special relationship to God. During the same period, the writers of Kings speak of prophetic groups called "sons of the prophets." These groups were clearly hierarchically structured prophetic guilds that flourished for a brief time in northern Israel (ca. 869–842 B.C.) and played an important role in the overthrow of the dynasty of Omri (1 Kings 17–2 Kings 10).

Origins and Development: For many years historians assumed that prophecy was a uniquely Israelite religious phenomenon that had no parallels elsewhere in the ancient Near East. However, during the past century several archaeological discoveries have shown this assumption to be false. The most important of these finds occurred at the Mesopotamian city of Mari, where excavators uncovered letters written in the eighteenth century B.C. Several of these texts describe the activities and messages of various types of oracle givers whose words and actions resemble those of the later OT prophets. Some of these early figures bear special titles, such as "answerer," "ecstatic," and "speaker," although to date no Israelite prophetic title has come to light. Archaeologists have also discovered Assyrian texts from the OT period itself (ca. 680–627 B.C.) that contain collections of oracles from "ecstatics," "shouters," "revealers," and "votaries." From Palestine have come inscriptions mentioning various kinds of oracle givers, including the visionary, a title that is given to some of the OT prophets.

All of this extrabiblical evidence indicates that prophetic activity existed elsewhere in the ancient Near East both before and during the biblical period, and some scholars have therefore suggested that prophecy originated on the periphery of Mesopotamia, in Canaan, or even in Egypt, and then was borrowed by the Israelites. At the moment there is no way to prove or disprove this hypothesis, although it is important to note that there is no biblical evidence to indicate that Israel recognized prophecy as an import. In addition, anthropological studies of prophetic phenomena show that prophecy can arise spontaneously in any society where the necessary social and religious conditions are present. There is therefore no reason to assume that prophets could not have appeared in Israel without outside cultural influences.

Although the OT locates most prophetic activity during the period of the monarchy, some biblical traditions place the origins of prophecy at the very beginning of Israel's history. Even if the references to the prophetic activities of Abraham and Moses are treated as retrojections from later times (Gen. 20:7; Num.12; Deut. 18: 9–22), the fact that Miriam, Deborah, and others are identified as prophets may indicate that prophecy had important religious and social functions in some early Israelite groups (Exod. 15:20–21; Judg. 4:4–10; 6:1–10). It is at least clear that in the period just before the rise of the monarchy (eleventh century B.C.) prophets were well established at some of Israel's sanctuaries. Samuel played important religious and governmental roles at several Israelite cult centers and was involved in the creation of the new central government (1 Sam. 3–16). Thereafter, prophets were a regular part of Israel's public life, both in Judah in the south and in Israel in the north. They related to the government and to the Temple in various ways, some supporting the royal establishment or working inside it and some standing outside and advocating radical change. Although prophetic attitudes changed during the monarchical period, it is difficult to detect major changes in the institution of prophecy itself. Those relatively late prophets who wrote books (e.g., Jeremiah) do not seem to have been markedly different from the earlier ones who did not (e.g., Elijah). There is no evidence to suggest that the growth of prophecy followed an evolutionary pattern.

Just as it is difficult to determine when prophecy began in Israel, so also it is difficult to identify the point at which prophecy ceased. Prophetic activity did continue after the Exile (sixth century B.C.), and prophets such as Zechariah and Haggai helped to shape the restored community in Jerusalem. However, after the Exile prophecy seems to have lost much of its influence, and prophets became much less visible. In spite of the later rabbinic claim that prophecy ceased in the early postexilic period (after Haggai, Zechariah, and Malachi), it is likely that prophets had minor official duties

The angel carries the prophet "Habakkuk" by the hair from Judea to Babylon, an incident in the deuterocanonical Bel and the Dragon (33–39); seventh-century A.D. relief.

in the worship practices of the Second Temple (1 Chron. 25). Outside of this officially sanctioned activity, prophecy seems to have continued only in peripheral groups that left no imprint on the OT record.

Personal Experiences: The prophet's experiences with the divine world were essentially private and were difficult to communicate even in the best of circumstances. It is therefore not surprising that the prophets said little about their encounters with God and concentrated instead on the visual or aural messages they received on these occasions. Only a few of the prophets even described their initial "calls" to prophesy (Amos 7:15; Isa. 6; Jer. 1:4–10; Ezek. 1–3), and still fewer spoke in detail of the experience that gave rise to a particular oracle (1 Kings 19:9–18; 22:17–23).

Nevertheless, enough clues have been preserved in the OT to suggest that Israelites thought of the prophetic experience as one that occurred when people were possessed by the spirit of God. "The hand of the Lord" fell upon them (1 Kings 18:46; 2 Kings 3:15; Jer. 15:17; Ezek. 1:3); the spirit of God "rested on them" (Num. 11:25–26) or "clothed itself" with them (Judg. 6:34). In this situation they were no longer in control of their own actions and words but were completely dominated by God. They felt compelled to speak the divine message that had been given to them (Amos 3:8; Jer. 20:9). Because of the feelings of helplessness and terror that accompanied possession by God's spirit, many prophets viewed the experience negatively and tried unsuccessfully to avoid it (Jer. 1:6; 11:18–12:6; 15:15–21; Ezek. 2:1–3:15; cf. Jon. 1:1–10).

Behavior and Speech: During their possession experiences, the OT prophets seem to have exhibited characteristic patterns of behavior and speech which allowed them to be identified as prophets. The details of these patterns are unclear, and they may have varied somewhat according to the historical, geographical, and social settings of the prophets' activities. However, the existence of characteristic prophetic behavior is suggested by the fact that the Hebrew verb "to prophesy" sometimes actually means "to act like a prophet" or "to exhibit the behavior that is typical of prophets." Such behavior could be recognized by all Israelites, although some groups evaluated it positively while others did not. In some instances it was understood as a sign of divine legitimation and favor (Num. 11: 11–29; 1 Sam. 10:1–13), while in other cases it was thought to be an indication of madness or of possession by an evil spirit (1 Sam. 18:10–11; 19:18–24; 1 Kings 18:26–29; Jer. 29:24–28).

Some of the OT prophets were probably ecstatics whose possession behavior was marked by psychological and physiological symptoms such as reduced sensitivity to outside stimuli, hallucinations or visions, loss of control over speech and actions, and a sense of being out of touch with reality. The intensity of these symptoms and the degree to which the prophets could control them probably varied, and it is unwise to generalize about the degree to which ecstasy influenced the prophets' messages. Sometimes ecstasy was incapacitating and dangerous (1 Sam. 19:18–24; 1 Kings 18:26–29), but among the writing prophets, if ecstasy existed at all, it was accompanied by controlled actions and intelligible speech (Jer. 4:19; 23:9; Ezek. 1:1–3:15).

As part of their characteristic behavior, some prophets wore distinctive clothing or bore a special mark that identified them as a prophet or as a member of a prophetic guild (1 Kings 20: 35–41; 2 Kings 1:8; Zech. 13:4). Others sometimes performed symbolic acts, either as dramatic reinforcement for an oracle (Hos. 1:4–9; Isa. 7:3; 8:1–4; 20:1–6; Jer. 19:1–15; 27:1–28:17) or as a way of actually bringing into existence the state of affairs being described in the oracle (2 Kings 13:14–19; Ezek. 4:1–8).

One of the clearest marks of prophetic behavior was the stereotypical way in which the prophets constructed their oracles. Oracles often began with an account of the commissioning of the prophetic messenger, an account that was followed by an accusation against an individual who had violated Israel's covenant law. After the accusation, the prophets delivered an announcement of judgment directly to the accused. The announcement usually began with the "messenger formula" ("thus says the Lord"), which identified the sender of the message and gave the authority for the oracle of judgment (1 Sam. 2:27–36; 13:11–14; 15:10–31; 2 Sam. 12; 1 Kings 11:29–40; 13:1–3; 14:7–14; 17:1; 20:35–43; 21:17–22; 22:13–23; 2 Kings 1: 3–4, 6; 20:14–19; 21:10–15; Jer. 20:1–6; 22:10–12, 13–19, 24–27; 28:12–16; 29:24–32; 36:29–30; 31:17). A variation on this speech pattern was used by prophets in Judah and Jerusalem, who sometimes began their oracles with the cry "alas," followed by one or more participles describing the addressee and indicating the crime. This introduction was followed by an announcement of judgment (Amos 5:18–20; 6: 1–7; Isa. 5:8–10, 11–14, 18–19, 20, 21, 22–24; 10:1–3; 28:1–4; 29:1–4, 15; 30;1–3; 31:1–4; Mic. 2:1–4).

Social Context and Functions: The OT prophets did not carry out their activities in isolation but were an integral part of their society. Because divine possession was not a continuous experience for any of the prophets, they played various social roles in addition to carrying out their prophetic activities. Prophets like Amos prophesied only occasionally and were normally involved in secular occupations (Amos 1:1; 7: 14–15). Others, such as Jeremiah and Ezekiel, were priests who were occasionally transformed into prophets (Jer. 1:1; Ezek. 1:3). While some prophets may have had full-time responsibilities in the Temple or the royal court, others carried out religious tasks that did not always involve prophecy (1 Chron. 25:1–8; 2 Chron. 20: 1–23; 34:30).

In addition to being involved in normal community activities, the prophets also received from their societies support and legitimation. Anyone could claim to have received a message from God, but that person could become a prophet only when a group of people recognized the prophetic claim as genuine and accepted the prophet's authority. Social support was sometimes provided by an organized group of disciples (Isa. 8:16), but usually the process was more informal (Jer. 26). Prophets who could not obtain at least a minimal amount of social support were unable to influence their societies and were in danger of being branded false prophets or lunatics. On the other hand, prophets who were considered authoritative by at least one group were usually tolerated by the rest of Israelite society. The prophets seem to have had unrestricted access to the king, the royal court, and the Temple and were not harassed unless their messages became too strident and threatening to the society (Jer. 26:1–24; 38:1–13). Normally prophets were not held responsible for their words or actions because they were under the direct control of God (Jer. 26:12–16).

All OT prophets shared the common task of delivering to individuals or groups the divine messages that they received during their prophetic experiences. However, the prophets had various social and religious functions depending on their social locations. Those prophets who were part of the royal court or who had regular roles in the Temple worship were usually concerned to preserve and strengthen the social structure. They were certainly capable of criticizing current institutions and advocating change, but they wanted to be sure that change took place in an orderly way. On the other hand, prophets who had no regular involvement with Israel's powerful social institutions were more likely to advocate radical change, even at the expense of social stability.

Theology: The OT prophets were firmly rooted in history, and this fact has important implications for understanding their theology. Because the prophets were not all members of the same social or religious group, they inherited different historical and theological traditions. All of the prophets knew the basic facts of Israel's history and shared the major elements of Israelite faith, but they understood these things in somewhat different ways and used different words to speak about them. In addition, the prophets spoke to specific groups of people and directed oracles to particular historical and social situations. The historical dimensions of prophecy make it difficult to talk about prophetic theology in general. Instead it is necessary to examine the theologies of individual prophets and to appreciate the unique shape that each of them gave to divine revelation. However, once the particularity of OT prophecy has been recognized, it is possibly to abstract some general theological beliefs that were held by all of the prophets.

All of the prophets held the fundamental belief that Israel had been elected by God and enjoyed a special relationship with God by virtue of that election. The mutual obligations involved in this relationship were spelled out in various covenants, particularly the covenant at Sinai (Exod. 19–Num. 10; Deuteronomy) and the covenant made with the house of David (2 Sam. 7). However, most of the prophets whose words have been preserved in the OT also agreed that the people of Israel and Judah had refused to fulfill their obligations and had rebelled against God. The prophets described this rebellion in various ways (cf. Isa. 1:2–6; Jer. 2:2–37; Ezek. 16), but they seem to have been concerned with all breaches in the divine-human relationship. Deviations in ethical behavior, social injustice, the worship of other gods, and religious abuses were all condemned equally because they were considered symptoms of Israel's general religious illness (Isa. 1: 9–17).

The prophets also agreed that Israel's rebelliousness would be punished, although they did not always agree on the nature of the punishment or its severity (cf. Isa. 1:7–8; Jer. 7:1–15; 14: 1–15:4; Amos 4:6–12). Some, such as Isaiah and

Ezekiel, believed that God would punish Israel but would remain faithful to the promises that had been made to David; Israel would remain the elect people of God. Others, such as Jeremiah, at least considered the possibility that God's punishment would terminate the divine-human relationship. Prophetic disagreements on this point became particularly sharp during the Exile, when the very existence of Israel was in question.

However, God's final word through the prophets was one of hope and promise. No matter what the people did, God would remain faithful and would return the people to their land, where they would enter into a new relationship with God.

Early Christian Prophets: Prophecy played an important role in Christianity from the very beginning (Acts 2:14–21). The early church used OT prophecy to interpret the life and teachings of Jesus, who himself was recognized as a prophet (Matt. 13:57; 21:11; Luke 4:24; John 4: 19; 9:17). After the resurrection, prophecy beame one of the gifts of the Spirit and at least in some congregations was a normal part of worship (1 Thess. 5:20; 1 Cor. 12:28–29; 14:26–32). However, prophecy soon became the province of a specialized office in the church, and prophets were ranked with apostles and teachers as church leaders (Acts 11:27; 13:1; 15:32; Eph. 2: 20; 3:5; 4:11; James 5:10; 1 Pet. 1:10; Rev. 22: 6–9). The presence of so many prophets caused major problems with false prophecy and made it necessary to devise tests to determine the validity of prophetic oracles (Matt. 7:15; 24:11, 24; Mark 13:22; Acts 13:6; 2 Pet. 2:1; 1 John 4:1; Rev. 2:20; 19:20; 20:10). Difficulties in recognizing false prophets may have led church leaders to try to suppress prophecy altogether and probably hastened the disappearance of prophets from the Christian community.

Bibliography

Aune, David E. *Prophecy in Early Christianity.* Grand Rapids, MI: Eerdmans, 1983.

Blenkinsopp, Joseph. *A History of Prophecy in Israel.* Philadelphia: Westminster, 1983.

Heschel, Abraham J. *The Prophets.* New York: Harper & Row, 1962.

von Rad, Gerhard. *Old Testament Theology.* Vol. 2. New York: Harper & Row, 1965.

Wilson, Robert R. *Prophecy and Society in Ancient Israel.* Philadelphia: Fortress, 1980.

R.R.W.

prophetess (Heb. *nebi'ah*), a woman who serves as a channel of communication between the human and divine worlds. In their prophetic behavior and religious functions they are not distinguished from their male counterparts.

According to some traditions, prophetesses played a central role in Israel's early history. The prophetess Miriam is said to have composed a song to celebrate Israel's crossing of the sea (Exod. 15:20–21), while the prophetess Deborah "judged" Israel and helped to lead the people in battle (Judg. 4:1–10). In a much later period, the prophetess Huldah appears as an important religious official to whom King Josiah sent messengers to inquire of God (2 Kings 22:14–20). In Nehemiah's account of the reconstruction of Jerusalem, he reports opposition from several prophets and the prophetess Noadiah (Neh. 6:10–14).

In NT times, the prophetess Anna was one of the first to recognize Jesus as the Messiah (Luke 2:36–38). Prophetesses were also found in some early churches, where they occasionally became involved in disputes over the direction of the church (Rev. 2:20). ***See also*** Prophet. R.R.W.

propitiation. ***See*** Expiation.

proselyte, a convert from one religious faith or group to another. In biblical studies this term refers especially to Gentiles who became Jews. In the OT many laws recognize the rights and place of resident aliens, non-Israelites living permanently in Israel. They had to observe certain laws, could offer sacrifice and, if circumcised, could take part in Passover. Such open association with Israelites probably led to their constant assimilation into Israel. In NT times proselytes to Judaism were required to accept one God and Jewish ethical and religious observances; males had to be circumcised (though a few Hellenistic Jewish authors do not mention this painful requirement). Later rabbinic sources also speak of a ritual immersion (not baptism in the Christian sense) and a sacrifice at the Temple as part of the conversion rite, but firm evidence for these practices in the first century is lacking (*b. Yebam.* 46–47).

From the second century B.C. through the fourth century A.D. some evidence suggests that many Gentiles were attracted to Judaism because of its monotheism, sexual ethics, and Sabbath observance. In addition, Jews may have actively sought converts during this period (see Matt. 23:15; Josephus *Against Apion* 2.39), in contrast to later centuries when converts were discouraged because of sanctions by Christian civil authorities and developments internal to Judaism.

Acts mentions proselytes among those listening to Peter (Acts 2:10) and Paul (13:43) and a proselyte, Nicolaus, as one of the seven deacons (6:5). Acts also mentions those who "fear God" or "reverence God." These expressions may simply indicate someone with a proper attitude toward God whether Jew or non-Jew, but some usages (e.g., 13:16, 26) have suggested to commentators that the Jewish community recognized a class of members who did not fully embrace Judaism, especially circumcision, but who kept some of the fundamentals of the law. Except for one third-century A.D. inscription from Asia Minor, no direct evidence exists for such an institutional class of "God-fearers." However, it is probable that many Gentiles were friendly to and interested in Judaism and had some association with the synagogues. This same fluid group may have been open to Christian as well as Jewish proselytism. ***See also*** Conversion. A.J.S.

prostitute. ***See*** Harlot.

proto-Sinaitic script. ***See*** Writing.

proverb, a short, popular saying that communicates a familiar truth or observation in an expressive and easily remembered form. The term is applied to a variety of sayings in the Bible. The most common example is the folk saying drawn from human experience and characterized by picturesque, insightful, witty, or even amusing comment on human behavior or experience (e.g., Prov. 16:18, 27:15; 29:2; Luke 4: 23). The majority of these proverbs are composed of two lines in a poetic form that closely links the first line with the second (a couplet). They occur in several distinct forms: those based on direct correspondence or association (Judg. 8:21; Prov. 9:10; Gal. 6:7), on contrast (Prov. 11–13, 18:23; Jer. 23:28; John 1:46), on comparison (Gen. 10:9; Prov. 20:2; Ezek. 16:44; Hos. 4:9), on what is futile or absurd (Prov. 1:17; Amos 6:12; Jer. 13:23), on the characterization of certain persons (the fool, Prov. 1:7, 32; the adulteress, Prov. 7:6–27; the lazy, Prov. 6:6–11; 24: 30–34; 26:15), on proper priorities (1 Sam. 25: 22; Prov. 22:1; 25:4; 27:5), and on the consequences of actions (Jer. 31:29; Hos. 8:7; Prov. 26: 27) or character (Prov. 15:13; 30:32–33; 2 Pet. 2: 22). However, many of the biblical proverbs are not simply maxims or truisms but express religious and ethical interpretations of Israelite faith (e.g., Prov. 3:1–12, 27–35; 6:16–19; 14:12), and even the more humanistic of the proverbs were collected not simply for their practical value but to provide instruction in the proper ordering of one's life under God (note Prov. 1: 2–7).

The term "proverb" can also refer to a variety of speech and literary forms: a figurative saying that was not easily understood, similar to a parable or allegory (so translated in many versions; Ezek. 17:2; 20:49; cf. John 10:6; 16:25, 29); poetry in ode or ballad form (Num. 21:27–30); a teaching psalm, used with riddle, dealing with a perplexing moral problem (Ps. 49:4); a wisdom discourse (Job 13:12; cf. 27:1); a byword used to taunt or jeer (Deut. 28:37; Jer. 24: 9; cf. Isa. 14:4); or a lament (often translated "taunt song" in newer versions; Mic. 2:4; Hab. 2:6). ***See also*** Parables; Parallelism; Proverbs, The; Riddle; Wisdom. D.R.B.

Proverbs, the, an OT book bearing a traditional title, "Proverbs of Solomon," which disguises the fact that this work is made up of several collections of sayings and poems, as indicated by the presence of other subtitles.

Chaps. 1–9, subtitled "The Proverbs of Solomon, Son of David, King of Israel," are basically wisdom poems on various topics: the value of wisdom, evils the wise person should avoid, the discourses of personified wisdom, etc. These chapters open with a statement of purpose (1:1–6) and contain fully developed poems (e.g., 2:1–22, on the benefits of wisdom), in contrast to the disparate and separate sayings that dominate the rest of the book. The subtitle "The Proverbs of Solomon" in 10:1 introduces a collection of sayings in antithetic parallelism (chaps. 10–15) and synonymous parallelism (chaps. 16–22). These are pithy sayings drawn from experience and traditional teachings that usually inculcate a moral value (honesty, diligence, self-control, etc.). The subtitle "Words of the Wise" may have originally stood at 22:17 (as in the Septuagint) to introduce a series of admonitions, usually with motive clauses, that extends down to 24:22. This section betrays an awareness of the "teaching" of the famous Egyptian sage Amenemopet. Another subtitle, "These Also Are the Sayings of the Wise," introduces a short collection, 24:23–34. Chaps. 25–29 are introduced by the subtitle "The Proverbs of Solomon Which the Men of Hezekiah King of Judah Copied"; these sayings resemble those in chaps. 10–22. A subtitle in 30:1, "The Words of Agur Son of Jakeh of Massa," attributes the following words to Agur, presumably a non-Israelite; several numerical sayings (x, x + 1; cf. 30:18–19) complete this chapter. A subtitle in 31:1 describes the following sayings (vv. 2–9) as "the words of Lemuel, king of Massa," another non-Israelite. The compilation concludes with an acrostic poem in praise of the virtuous wife (31:10–31).

In its present form the book is probably to be dated in the postexilic period (late sixth cen-

OUTLINE OF CONTENTS

The Proverbs

The book is best outlined as a series of collections:

I. Wisdom poems (1:1–9:18)
II. Wisdom sayings (10:1–22:16)
III. Admonitions (22:17–24:22)
IV. "Sayings of the wise" (24:23–34)
V. "Proverbs of Solomon": wisdom sayings (25:1–29:27)
VI. "The words of Agur" (30:1–33)
VII. "The words of Lemuel" (31:1–9)
VIII. Poem on the ideal wife (31:10–31)

tury B.C. on), but many of the sayings in chaps. 10–29 doubtless originated in the period of the monarchy (ca. 1004–926 B.C.), or perhaps even before. The origins of this wisdom are to be sought both in the Israelite clan and the wise men at the Jerusalem court. The ascription of the work (along with Ecclesiastes and the Song of Solomon) to Solomon derives from the Israelite view of that monarch as the wise man par excellence (cf. 1 Kings 4:29–34).

The book intends to teach the youth how to cope with life through observation, docility, self-control, and fear of the Lord (1:6). The perspective is optimistic: wisdom (equated with righteousness) brings life; folly (equated with wickedness) leads to destruction. R.E.M.

providence, one of the most commonly held and most vigorously debated beliefs in both ancient and modern times: that there is a benevolent and purposeful ordering of all events of history. Nothing happens by chance; though not always perceptible to human understanding, there is a divine or cosmic plan to the universe, a reason for everything.

One philosophical version of this concept is "determinism" or (its negative expression) "fatalism": everything is determined by a higher power, destiny is a matter of fate, one can do nothing to shape one's own destiny, what will be will be. Such a view results in human resignation (quietism/do-nothing-ism).

Another, somewhat more positive, version was the Stoic view that "world-reason" permeated the cosmos and could be recognized in all natural and historical phenomena. Stoic philosophy was designed to put one in harmony with this principle of world-reason. The end result was the achievement of perfect serenity through oneness with what is and shall be.

Even less philosophical people have always asked "Why?" when seeking to understand life and history. Reading the stars or the entrails of sacrificial animals or consulting the Delphic oracle were favorite means among ancients for determining the relationship of what is to what shall be. Such techniques provided a measure of reconciliation between learned response from normal cause and effect relationships and the bizarre, the paradoxical, the unexpected.

The communities of faith reflected in the documents of the Bible also held to a view of providence. In contrast to the foregoing, however, God the Creator was held to be personally responsible for preserving and regulating the created order. In this context, providence is related to the notions of "election" and "predestination." This God has a plan and purpose for his world. Providence is not a principle of orderliness or reason; rather, providence is the will of the Creator who is actively involved in moving his creation to a goal. History is not a cyclical process of endless repetition; history is being moved toward the predetermined end.

In the OT and Jewish literature, the Book of Job and the Wisdom of Solomon represent two classical locations for this confidence regarding providence. Here, as in other texts, the key terms often translated "providence" are really "foreknowledge" or "foresight" (which, indeed, is the etymological Latin meaning of "providence"). While humans see and judge from the limitations of time and space, even when able to lean on the recorded wisdom of prior generations, God sees the end from the beginning. In spite of evil and all that is perplexingly enigmatic in life, the message of the OT and subsequent Jewish literature is to trust in the providential care and good will of the Creator (Deut. 32:7–43; Job 10:12; Pss. 74:12–17; 104:27–30; cf. Wisd. of Sol. 14:3; 17:2; 3 Macc. 4:21; 5:30; 4 Macc. 9:24; 17:22).

In the NT, the basis for such an invitation to trust providence is Jesus Christ. He becomes, through his life, death, and resurrection, the guarantor that God's providential goal is salvation rather than destruction. The belief that history has a saving goal is grounded in his coming. The earliest Christians believed and preached this understanding of providence in a great variety of verbal expressions and human situations (e.g., Matt. 6:25–33; 10:29–31; Rom. 8:28–39; 2 Cor. 4:11–18; 1 Pet. 1:3–9). ***See also*** Astrologer; Election; God; Grace; Magic and Divination; Oracle; Predestination; Salvation; Stoics. J.E.A.

provinces, administrative areas set up within the Roman Empire. The Latin term, *provincia*, originally referred to a definite sphere of action. In the late Republic it was applied to territories, Asia, Gallia, and Narbonensis. Under Augustus (27 B.C.–A.D. 14) the empire was made up of twenty-eight provinces, some created by dividing larger provinces like Gaul, Spain, and Macedonia. They also included a number of allied states ruled by client kings. Many of the provinces consisted of territory that had been directly annexed through conquest: Sicily, Sardinia, Corsica, Spain, Macedonia, Cyprus, Illyricum, Cilicia (southeast Asia Minor), Syria, Gaul, Egypt, and most of the Danube and German territories. The conquest of Britain and Dacia (modern Romania) was completed by later emperors. Other provinces came into being as bequests from native kings, who sought to ensure a safe transition for their supporters: Asia, Bithynia (northwest Asia Minor), and Cyrene. Judea became a Roman province when Herod the Great's son proved unable to govern. The corn-producing area of the Bosporus was unusual in remaining a client kingdom.

In 27 B.C. the senate's grant of *provincia* to Augustus made the emperor responsible for those provinces that were not entirely pacified (hence "imperial provinces"). As *princeps* (Lat., "prince") Augustus had supreme command of the army. The senate retained control of provinces (hence "senatorial provinces") in which military presence was not required: Sicily, Sardinia and Corsica, Illyricum, Macedonia, Greece, Asia, Bithynia, Crete and Cyrene, and Africa. However, legions were stationed in Africa, Illyricum, and Macedonia during the early principate. Proconsuls or propraetors were sent to govern senatorial provinces for a year term. However, the emperor could always overrule a senatorial governor. The emperor also had financial agents in those provinces who took care of the imperial estates and served as a watch on the governor. Since the agents could bring harsh retribution on rapacious officials, these agents might be more powerful than the governor. The imperial provinces were governed by legates of consular or praetorian rank. Their appointments lasted as long as the emperor chose to retain them in office. They were responsible only to the emperor. Egypt, whose grain supply was crucial to the city of Rome, remained the private possession of the emperor. It was governed by a prefect.

A province was essentially the network of cities within its boundaries. Those cities formed the political and social nucleus of each province and were concentrated along the coasts or major rivers. In the eastern provinces urbanization had resulted from the hellenization of the area after Alexander's conquest. The Romans inherited a dense and ready-made network of cities. In the western provinces the only cities were those of Phoenician and Greek foundation. Under Augustus urbanization was extended in Gaul and Spain. Towns and cities served to diffuse Greco-Roman culture. In areas such as Germany where Rome could not build an administrative structure based on cities, its rule was a failure.

Most of the thousand or so cities of the empire were on the order of ten to fifteen thousand persons. Only a few, Alexandria, Antioch, and Carthage, had several hundred thousand. Inland there might be great stretches with no cities at all.

While the areas to which 1 Peter is addressed are the names of Roman provinces (1 Pet. 1:1), scholars are not agreed on whether or not the author of Acts consistently used them, or on occasion also used ethnic designations for various areas. Macedonia and Achaia (Acts 19:21) are surely meant as provinces, but there is question whether the reference to "Galatia" in Acts 16:6 means the province of that name, or the older, more limited area occupied by the Gauls, and hence ethnic Galatia. The same problem occurs in trying to determine to whom Paul addressed his Letter to the Galatians; one does not know whether that referred to the Roman province, or to the ethnic area. ***See also*** Roman Empire.

P.P.

pruning. ***See*** Vine.

Psalms, the, collection of some hundred and fifty songs, prayers, and various other less easily classified compositions that forms the nineteenth book of the OT. Ascribed by tradition to King David, the Psalms have, since late antiquity, played a central role in synagogues and churches; not only have they figured prominently in Jewish and Christian liturgies, but they have, by their style and their words, inspired later writers to compose psalmlike prayers and hymns, both for public worship and private piety. Probably no book of the Bible was known so well to medieval Christendom as the Psalms, and even today this book enjoys a unique place in the hearts of all readers of the Bible.

Diversity: By any standard, these prayers and songs are a heterogeneous lot, differing widely in such matters as date of composition, style, literary form, and original purpose and life-setting. This great variety was, for centuries, obscured not only by their collective attribution to David, but by the very fact of their having been grouped together in a single book and unified under a single name. "Psalm" goes back to the Greek *psalmos*, used by translators to render the Hebrew *mizmor*, "song," a word that appears in the titles of some psalms. In Hebrew the book is known most commonly as *sefer tehillim*, "book of praises," a convenient catchall. Another name for the book, "Psalter," goes back to the Greek *psalterion*, a stringed instrument. As modern scholarship has continued to study the Psalms, however, the differences between them have more and more become the focus of inquiry.

To be sure, some differences had always been apparent. On the most basic level, some psalms have a clearly celebrative quality, glorifying God's powers or historic deeds or offering thanksgiving for a particular intervention (recovery from illness [e.g., Ps. 30], for example, or triumph over "enemies" [e.g., Pss. 30, 54]). Others are, equally clearly, of a petitionary character, lamenting the speaker's dire straits and appealing for divine help (e.g., Pss. 6, 140). Some psalms seem to be intended for recitation by an individual, a particular "I" who appears in the text (e.g., Pss. 23, 130), while in others the words are apparently to be sung or recited by a group, a choir, or the community as a whole (e.g., Pss. 113, 132). But so long as the Psalms were attributed to David (or occasionally to other ancient figures), these differences—to the extent that they were noticed—were ascribed to circumstances in the author's own life: one psalm was composed upon a happy occasion, another in time of distress;

in one David speaks on his own behalf, in another on behalf of his people, etc. In fact, early, anonymous scribes apparently sometimes added a brief phrase at the beginning of a psalm, seeking in that way to connect it to some event in the life of its presumed author (see, e.g., Pss. 34:1; 51:2).

Authorship and Date: This approach to the Psalms as personal, occasional lyrics showed remarkable resilience even after the mid-nineteenth century, when the tradition of Davidic authorship came to be widely questioned. With the steady advance of biblical scholarship, however, and especially with the availability of comparative material from ancient Egyptian and Babylonian literature, such notions eventually began to be abandoned. Not only did scholars now hesitate or refuse to date psalms to the time of David (in general they were dated much later, some writers at the turn of the twentieth century even denying the possibility that any of the psalms predated the Babylonian exile), but they began increasingly to treat the Psalms as "stock" compositions, composed by anonymous bards to be recited again and again by individuals or communal choirs either as part of community worship or in times of private joy or distress.

The general lines of this approach have continued to be pursued by contemporary scholars, albeit with some revision. In particular, the matter of dating has undergone another radical shift, due in part to certain striking resemblances discovered between the language of some psalms and that found in the ancient literature of Ugarit, a city somewhat to the north of biblical Israel. On this basis, compositions such as Psalms 29 and 68 have not only been dated far earlier than before but are now believed by some to be among the oldest parts of the Hebrew Bible. By contrast, certain other parts of the Psalter (e.g., Pss. 1, 119) bespeak an entirely different age and mentality: some have dated them among the youngest parts of Hebrew Scripture.

Types: The Psalter is thus a heterogeneous collection or, more likely, a collection of subcollections spanning many centuries. The editorial note at Ps. 72:20 is one visible seam, perhaps indicating the existence of an earlier smaller "psalter" called "the Prayers of David son of Jesse." More fundamentally, the fifteen "Songs of Ascents" (Pss. 120–34) present a discernible subgroup, as do the psalms attributed to the "sons of Korah" (Pss. 42, 44, 47, 48, 49, 84, 87), Asaph (Pss. 50, 73–83), and the like. Moreover, the predominance of reference to God by the word "Elohim" in Psalms 42–83 has led scholars to view this group as being of distinct provenance or editing, especially in view of the overlap between some of its psalms and those that precede it in our Psalter (thus, Ps. 53 is a doublet of Ps. 14; Ps. 70:2–6 = Ps. 40:14–18; Ps. 71:1–3 = Ps. 31:2–4; cf. Ps. 108, which is a doublet of Pss. 57:8–12 and 60:7–14). It has been theorized that all these materials, which had originally been written at different times and for different purposes, were gradually gathered together into collections by various groups in several locations and were still later combined into a single Psalter.

Besides considering the evolution of the Psalter as a book, modern scholars have especially concerned themselves with classifying the Psalms into different types, largely on the basis of the distinctions listed above (i.e., communal vs. individual psalms; "praise" vs "petition/lament"), and with trying to pin down particular conventions, characteristic forms, phrases, or themes associated with each type.

Purpose or Use: Of special concern has been the question of how various types might have fit into the daily life of ancient Israel. Because of the frequent mention of God's "house" or "palace" and sanctuary appurtenances, as well as of the psalmist's appearing or bowing down "before God," many psalms have been thought to have been composed for one of Israel's ancient religious sites and especially the Jerusalem Temple. Indeed, some scholars have asserted that virtually all the psalms in our Psalter were composed for worship at a religious site and constituted nothing less than the verbal equivalent or accompaniment to the offerings of incense and sacrificial animals that comprised Israel's regular service of God. Objections have been advanced to this claim; nonetheless, the "liturgical connection" is now widely accepted for many psalms. Numerous hymns, for example, appear by their wording intended for recitation at annual religious festivals (though the precise character of some of these observances is still in dispute). Similarly, it has been argued that some "psalms of the individual," both petitions and thanksgivings, were intended specifically to be recited at a sanctuary, the thanksgivings presumably accompanying an actual offering.

This, in turn, has caused critics to reassess the language of the Psalms. In the light of the proposed religious milieu of many of them, references to the "presence," "face," "protection," "wings," and the like of the Deity take on a new concreteness. So, more generally, the practice of many critics in approaching the words of particular psalms has been to seek to concretize them, to tie them down to processionals, priestly blessings, and other cultic regalia, or to link the requests for divine "goodness" or "blessing" to the somewhat mundane but vital concerns for adequate rainfall, a good harvest, and other necessities that might have shaped Israel's communal worship. This approach has often proven quite convincing.

For much the same reason, the very vagueness of many petitions has aroused the suspicion of some critics: who, for example, are the otherwise unspecified "enemies" from whom the psalmist seeks to be protected? And why is his salvation in psalms of thanksgiving so often presented in floridly metaphorical but hardly specific language? It has been argued that the language of many praises and complaints is left purposely vague so as to allow the composition to be reused by a variety of different speakers, each making reference to his particular case, but in language that gives more the illusion than the substance of specificity.

All this in turn has tarnished, at least in the eyes of some, the "spirituality" of the Psalter, since many of its most sublime passages have had to be reunderstood (and in some cases retranslated) in somewhat less lofty terms. Part of this "de-spiritualization" is an illusion created by the gap between worship in ancient Israel and worship in modern-day settings. The latter seems predicated on the very distance or elusiveness separating Deity and worshiper; the former, at least in its liturgical setting, was, on the contrary, based on the fact of divine presence, an absolute reality. What to moderns may seem mechanical and hopelessly concrete takes on quite a different aspect when restored to such a setting and mentality. Moreover, declarations of fealty, dependence, and so forth acquire a solemn significance when uttered publicly at the very "dwelling place" of the Deity: they are indeed what many psalms seem to represent them as, verbal offerings, thus wholly comparable to sacrifices, tributes in the most concrete sense.

This notwithstanding, a liturgical setting cannot be posited for all the Psalms—many, especially those whose language suggests a late date of composition, seem clearly to belong elsewhere, to private piety or possibly to noncultic yet communal worship. Indeed, it has been argued that much material in the Psalter originally tied to public worship came gradually to have a life outside of it as well. Political events may have had a role in such an evolution. The destruction of old religious sites as well as the centralization of worship may have encouraged the establishment of nonsacrificial rites in the former places of sacrifice, with psalmody taking on an increased importance. Similarly, the Babylonian exile may have served to give the verbal component of worship a new independence. Whatever its causes, such a gradual shift might not only explain the scarcity of worship references in late psalms but would suggest that even originally cultic material may later have come to be "reread," understood in new ways and used in new circumstances.

Such a "rereading" tendency seems amply attested not only in the latest parts of the Psalter but in such extrabiblical documents as the writings of the Qumran community that were found among the Dead Sea Scrolls. Indeed, the very existence of our present Psalter, with its integration of diverse materials, may be due to just this process: festive hymns, prayers, and songs that had once been designed for the sanctuary all eventually became "praises" *(tehillim)* suitable for worship in any setting. In fact the Psalms were, in the apparent view of one manuscript from Qumran (11QPsa), now nothing less than revealed Scripture, "praises" and songs spoken by David through divinely sent wisdom and even "in prophecy." And so they have remained.

David depicted composing psalms, a role that tradition ascribes to him; page from the *Paris Psalter* (900).

Bibliography

Childs, B. S. *Introduction to the Old Testament as Scripture*. Philadelphia: Fortress, 1979. Pp. 504–25.

Gerstenberger, E. "The Psalms." In J. H. Hayes, *Old Testament Form Criticism*. San Antonio, TX: Trinity University Press, 1974. Pp. 179–223.

Miller, P. D., Jr. "Trouble and Woe: Interpreting the Biblical Laments." *Interpretation* Jan. 1983: pp. 32–45.

J.L.K.

Psalms of Solomon, a group of eighteen pseudepigraphical psalms, extant only in Greek and Syriac but possibly composed originally in Hebrew. According to the commonly accepted view, the psalms were compiled around the middle of the first century B.C. The political allusions in them seem to reflect the conquest of Judea by the Roman general Pompey (63 B.C.).

The psalms themselves treat various topics. Notable is a lament on Israel's troubles, a hymn of messianic hope, and various others that deal with religious and political themes. ***See also*** Pseudepigrapha.

Psalter. **1** A name designating the biblical book of Psalms. **2** A name for a collection of biblical psalms used in worship. A number of such collections have survived from the early Middle Ages, often combined with portions of the Gospels. ***See also*** Psalms, The.

Pseudepigrapha (sōō-duh-pig'ruh-fuh; Gk., "writings with false superscriptions"), a collection of some sixty-five documents connected with but not part of the OT and written by Jews or Christians, for the most part during the three centuries before and the two centuries after the beginning of the Christian era. They are called "pseudepigrapha" because, in many cases, the person with whom they are identified was not the author. By the time of Jesus of Nazareth and the Jewish rabbi Hillel, the religious person in early Judaism (ca. 250 B.C.–A.D. 200) had a collection of writings that were regarded as paradigmatic for all aspects of life. This collection was the Hebrew Bible, or the Christian OT. By the first century A.D., almost all the writings in this collection were perceived as divinely inspired; by the middle of the second century, the OT canon was considered closed.

So powerful was the influence of the OT that contemporary religious writings were almost always the result of reflections and meditations on these Scriptures or expansions of them; all language, symbols, and metaphors were shaped by these texts in a way virtually unparalleled in the history of ideas. For example, when the author of *The Testament of Judah* (chaps. 3–7) describes the Maccabean wars, he refers to them in OT forms and paradigms: Dan and Judah pretend to be "Amorites" and they fight against the "Canaanites." Indeed, a great hindrance in perceiving the dates of these early Jewish writings is the penchant for referring to contemporary events in terms of past cataclysms; for example, the Roman destruction of Jerusalem in A.D. 70 is described with prose and poetry borrowed from old descriptions of the sixth-century B.C. conquest of Jerusalem by the Babylonians. Thus, the author of *4 Ezra* laments over Rome's conquest of Jerusalem with the words: "Are the deeds of those who inhabit Babylon any better? Is that why she has gained dominion over Zion?" (4 Ezra 3:28).

The sixty-five documents of the OT Pseudepigrapha are often attributed to one or another of the Hebrew patriarchs. They were written by Jews or Christians during the three centuries before and the two centuries after the beginning of the Christian era. One writing, *Ahiqar*, predates this period and is included because of its importance for the study of early Judaism and the origins of Christianity. Some writings postdate A.D. 200. These are included because they provide valuable information regarding the development of Jewish traditions and cycles, contain perhaps an edited version of an otherwise lost early Jewish document, or preserve much earlier Jewish traditions. Hence, some writings in the OT Pseudepigrapha clearly predate the destruction of Jerusalem in A.D. 70; others certainly date from that cataclysmic event until the defeat of the proclaimed messianic warrior Simon Bar Kokhba in 135; others probably can be dated prior to 135 or 200, when the Mishnah (i.e., Jewish oral traditions) was codified; other Jewish writings are extant only in later Christian versions. One must be careful to distinguish, for example, between a book like *Jubilees*, which certainly dates from the second century B.C., and a work like *The Ascension of Isaiah*, which is a composite of Jewish and Christian lore. Guidance regarding the dates, origin, and theological importance of each document in the Pseudepigrapha is now provided in a new edition: James H. Charlesworth (ed.), *The Old Testament Pseudepigrapha*. 2 vols. (Garden City, NY: Doubleday, 1983, 1985); all quotations from the Pseudepigrapha are taken from this collection of translations.

It must be emphasized that the term "Pseudepigrapha" is used because of custom, tradition, and wide international acceptance. In no way does this term indicate what the Greek original denotes: "writings with false superscriptions." No longer do scholars use the term in its etymological sense, even though many of the documents are incorrectly assigned (sometimes, perhaps, by much later scribes) to such figures as Enoch, Abraham, Moses, Solomon, Elijah, and Ezra.

The documents in the Pseudepigrapha can be arranged under five loosely defined genres.

Apocalyptic Literature and Related Works: This category includes nineteen documents:

1 (Ethiopic Apocalypse of) Enoch
2 (Slavonic Apocalypse of) Enoch
3 (Hebrew Apocalypse of) Enoch
Sibylline Oracles
Treatise of Shem
Apocryphon of Ezekiel
Apocalypse of Zephaniah
4 Ezra
Greek Apocalypse of Ezra
Vision of Ezra
Questions of Ezra
Revelation of Ezra
Apocalypse of Sedrach
2 (Syriac Apocalypse of) Baruch
3 (Greek Apocalypse of) Baruch
Apocalypse of Abraham
Apocalypse of Adam
Apocalypse of Elijah
Apocalypse of Daniel

Either the author or a subsequent scribe gave these titles to the documents now preserved almost always in late manuscripts, although fragments of some documents in the Pseudepigrapha have been discovered among the Qumran literature (Dead Sea Scrolls). The noun "Apocalypse" comes from the Greek word meaning a "revelation" or "disclosure." Thus, these documents contain a revelation of what is occurring in the heavens above the earth or what is to happen in the impending future. Such disclosures are usually graphically illustrated with visions and auditions, and there are often cosmic trips by Enoch or other "holy ones" into the hidden reaches of our universe.

Yet, the reason for these descriptions is not so much cosmology as theology; the concern is not so much with the distant world or future age as it is with the ramifications of these disclosures for the choices to be made in the present, earthly world. Hence, an ethical dimension is often implicit, even at times explicit, as in *1 Enoch* 101:1: "Examine the heaven, you sons of heaven, and all the works of the Most High; and be afraid to do evil in his presence." The moral import of apocalyptic thought is emphasized, for example, in *2 Enoch* 39–66, where Enoch returns to the earth and instructs his sons regarding righteousness, and in *The Testaments of the Twelve Patriarchs* (see below), where each of the twelve sons of Jacob instructs and admonishes his sons. At least one apocalyptic writing laments the present state of the world and is pessimistic; note, for example, *4 Ezra* 7:48–49 [118–119]:

> O Adam, what have you done? For though it was you who sinned, the fall was not yours alone, but ours also who are your descendants. For what good is it to us, if an eternal age has been promised to us, but we have done deeds that bring death?

Other apocalypses contain a yearning for a new, glorious age, which seems to be dawning; note, for example, *2 Baruch* 73:1–2:

> And it will happen that after he has brought down everything which is in the world, and has sat down in eternal peace on the throne of the kingdom, then joy will be revealed and rest will appear. And then health will descend in dew, and illness will vanish, and fear and tribulation and lamentation will pass away from among men, and joy will encompass the earth.

The character and date of the apocalyptic works already listed may be succinctly suggested. *1 Enoch*, a most important apocalypse replete with divine information about the world and history, is a Jewish composition; it is composite and dates from the third century B.C. to the first century A.D. (probably the first half). *2 Enoch*, also a brilliant apocalypse with penetrating insights into our universe and humanity, is extant only in Slavonic; the original Jewish core probably dates from the end of the first century A.D. *3 Enoch* is Jewish and in its present form dates from the fifth or sixth century A.D. It is not the work of one author, but rather the deposit of many traditions; portions of the writing probably date from the first or second century A.D.

Leather manuscript fragment in Greek of the *Sibylline Oracles*, ca. the fourteenth century A.D.

The Sibylline Oracles, which predict future woes and calamities, comprise both early Jewish and later Christian writings, dating from the second century B.C. to the seventh century A.D. They usually served as political propaganda. *The Treatise of Shem* clarifies the features of a year according to the house of the zodiac in which the year begins; although difficult to date, the document seems to be an Alexandrian composition from the end of the first century B.C. *The Apocryphon of Ezekiel* is lost, except for quotations and an excerpt in both the writings of the fourth century church father Epiphanius and the Babylonian Talmud. The original Jewish document dates from sometime around the turn of the era. *The Apocalypse of Zephaniah* is only partly preserved; the original Jewish work probably describes Zephaniah's travels to heaven and Hades and was written around the turn of the era.

The fourth book of Ezra (*4 Ezra*) is a Jewish work that postdates the destruction of the Temple in A.D. 70; a later Christian altered its pessimistic tone by prefixing two chapters and affixing two others. *The Greek Apocalypse of Ezra* records Ezra's visions of heaven, hell, and the Antichrist; in its present form, this apocalypse is Christian, is rather late (perhaps as late as the ninth century), and is a mixture of Jewish and Christian sources. *The Vision of Ezra* is Christian but is clearly in the cycle of Ezra writings like *4 Ezra* and *The Greek Apocalypse of*

PSEUDEPIGRAPHA

Ezra; it dates from between the fourth and the seventh centuries. *The Questions of Ezra* is Christian and like *The Vision of Ezra* is placed within the Ezra cycle; its date has not yet been determined. *The Revelation of Ezra* concludes the Ezra cycle; somewhat like *The Treatise of Shem,* it describes the nature of the year according to the week day in which it begins. It is Christian and difficult to date, certainly predating the ninth century, the date of the extant manuscript. *The Apocalypse of Sedrach,* in its present form, is Christian and perhaps as late as the fifth century, but it obviously preserves material from the early centuries of the present era.

The Syriac Apocalypse of Baruch (2 Baruch), a Jewish work that is far more optimistic than 4 *Ezra* and probably a later reaction to it, dates from around A.D. 100. *3 Baruch* is either a Christian work that utilized Jewish traditions or a Jewish work that has been edited by a Christian. The latter possibility seems more probable. The Jewish writing would date from the first or second century A.D.

The Apocalypse of Abraham is extant only in Slavonic; the early Jewish core is dated by most scholars between A.D. 70 and 150. *The Apocalypse of Adam,* in its present form, is Gnostic, but not Christian Gnostic, and several scholars have argued or suggested that it derives from Jewish traditions or sources that are from the first century A.D. *The Apocalypse of Elijah,* a composite work of Jewish and Christian materials, was probably written between A.D. 150 and 275; the Jewish material is obviously even older than the earliest date of the composite work. *The Apocalypse of Daniel,* according to some scholars, contains very early, perhaps fourth-century A.D. sections; the present work clearly dates from the beginning of the ninth century but contains Jewish traditions that may be centuries earlier.

Testaments: The second genre of documents in the OT Pseudepigrapha is "Testaments" (often with apocalyptic sections); this group contains the following documents:

- Testaments of the Twelve Patriarchs
- Testament of Job
- Testaments of the Three Patriarchs
  - Testament of Abraham
  - Testament of Isaac
  - Testament of Jacob
- Testament of Moses
- Testament of Solomon
- Testament of Adam

OT narratives usually provide the setting for these "Testaments." Although there was no concrete genre to bind the authors, there is a shared structure or format to most of these writings. The OT patriarch, on his death bed, calls his sons and followers around him in order to convey his last words of instruction and perception. These testaments (or last wills) contain moral instruction and are often dramatized by visions into the future. In a certain sense, this genre was influenced by Jacob's testament to his sons (Gen. 49).

The Testaments of the Twelve Patriarchs, in its present form, is a Christian work that probably dates from the second half of the second century A.D. Most scholars are convinced, however, thanks to the recovery of the Testaments of *Levi, Judah,* and *Naphtali* (from *The Testaments of the Twelve Patriarchs)* among the Qumran scrolls (and thus their clearly pre–A.D. 70 dates), that the work is originally a Jewish composition that dates from the second or first century B.C. This extremely important document is a depository of Jewish ethics, but there are also apocalyptic sections and a significant belief in two Messiahs (found also in the Qumran literature): "And there shall arise for you from the tribe of Judah and [the tribe of] Levi the Lord's salvation" *(T. Dan* 5:10).

The Testament of Job is a Jewish work that urges the embodiment of an endurance like Job's; it was written around the turn of the era. *The Testaments of the Three Patriarchs* (or the Testaments of *Abraham, Isaac,* and *Jacob)* are three works organically linked, with two Christian writings, the Testaments of *Isaac* and *Jacob,* successively evolving from *The Testament of Abraham,* originally a Jewish work that probably dates from around A.D. 100. *The Testament of Moses,* which purports to be Moses' farewell exhortation to Joshua, is a Jewish composition that obtained its present form shortly after the turn of the era; it is only partly preserved in one Latin palimpsest.

The Testament of Solomon is a folk story about how Solomon built the Temple using magic and demons but fell from God's favor because of his love for an idolatrous Shummanite woman. As extant, it dates from around the third century A.D. While it is possible, as some scholars have argued, that an underlying Jewish writing dates from the first century, it is clear that portions of the Testament represent first-century Palestinian Jewish ideas. *The Testament of*

Ethiopic text of 1 Enoch 48.

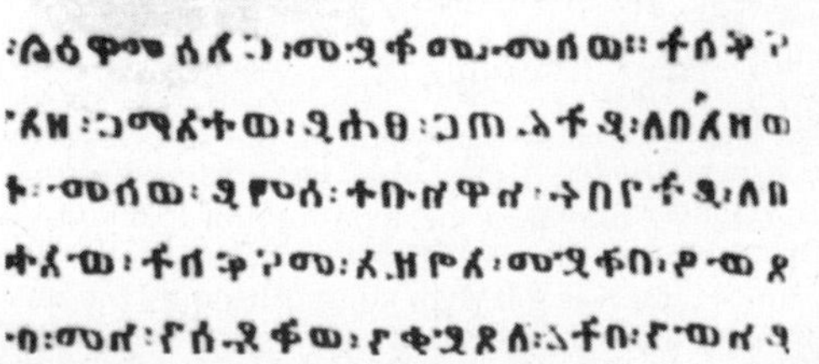

Adam is a composite work containing the Horarium (Hours of the Day), the Prophecy, and the Hierarchy (of the Heavenly Powers); it reached its present Christian form before the end of the third century A.D. In their original form, however, the Jewish portions may be at least a century earlier.

Expansions of the OT and Other Legends: The third genre of documents in the OT Pseudepigrapha contains the following documents:

The Letter of Aristeas
Jubilees
Martyrdom and Ascension of Isaiah
Joseph and Asenath
Life of Adam and Eve
Pseudo-Philo
Lives of the Prophets
Ladder of Jacob
4 Baruch
Jannes and Jambres
History of the Rechabites
Eldad and Modad
History of Joseph

These documents especially demonstrate the creative force of the OT; with only one exception, they expand upon and embellish the narratives and stories of the OT.

The Letter of Aristeas—the exception just mentioned—is an apology primarily for the Septuagint but also for the Temple; it dates from the first half of the second century B.C. *Jubilees* is a conservative writing that celebrates the supremacy of the Law and the Sabbath, directs polemics against a lunar calendar, and extols Jewish exclusiveness. It is a rewriting of Gen. 1:1 through Exod. 12:50 and is ostensibly a revelation to Moses by the Angel of the Presence. It was written during the second century B.C., probably not long before 150 B.C. *The Martyrdom and Ascension of Isaiah* (chaps. 1–5) is Jewish and was composed certainly long before the end of the first century A.D. and probably around 100 B.C. Joined to the *Martyrdom* is the "Vision of Isaiah" (chaps. 6–11), a Christian work, which predates the third century A.D. Later interpolated into the *Martyrdom* is another Christian work, the so-called *Testament of Hezekiah* (3:13–4:22), which dates perhaps from the end of the first century A.D. The three sections were combined before the fourth century.

Joseph and Asenath, a romance between Joseph and Pentephres' daughter, is an expansion of Gen. 41:45. The leading scholars today see this work as dating from around A.D. 100, if not earlier. *The Life of Adam and Eve*, an expansion of Genesis 1–4, dates from the first century A.D., perhaps the first half. *Pseudo-Philo*, a rewriting of Genesis through 2 Samuel, with legendary expansions, was written either between A.D. 70 and 135 or just before 70. In it (40:5) a memorable lament attributed to Seila, Jephthah's daughter (cf. Judg. 11:30–40), includes the following lines:

> May my words go forth in the heavens,
> and my tears be written in the firmament!
> That a father did not refuse the daughter
> whom he had sworn to sacrifice, . . .

The Lives of the Prophets, devoid of some Christian accretions, is a deposit of folklore regarding the lives and deaths of twenty-three prophets; the account is enriched with folklore and legends, many undoubtedly popular in and around Jerusalem. It was written in or just before the first century A.D. *The Ladder of Jacob*, preserved only in the *Explanatory Palaia*, a medieval Slavonic text, is an expansion on Jacob's dream at Bethel (Gen. 28:11–22). Some scholars have seen behind chaps. 1–6 an early Jewish document, dating perhaps from the late first century A.D.; chap. 7 is a Christian work, once independent, but now an appendix to the pseudepigraphon. *4 Baruch*, an expansion on Jeremiah, was written shortly after A.D. 100; it is a Jewish writing edited by a Christian. *Jannes and Jambres*, a tale about the Pharaonic magicians who opposed Moses (Exod. 7–8; cf. 2 Tim. 3:8–9), derives from many diverse, very early legends. As a book, it is Christian in its present edited form, but it certainly goes back to Jewish traditions that predate the first century A.D.

The History of the Rechabites, a legendary expansion of Jeremiah 35, as extant, is a Christian work that predates at least the sixth century, but there are reasons to speculate that portions preserve early Jewish traditions. The core chapters may derive from a Jewish writing that predates A.D. 100. *Eldad and Modad* is lost, except for one quotation in *The Shepherd of Hermas;* if a Jewish pseudepigraphon, it is very early and is an expansion of Num. 11:24–30. *The History of Joseph*, an elaborate legend based on Gen. 41:39–42:38, is difficult to date, but originally it may be both early and Jewish. It certainly predates the extant sixth-century papyrus.

Wisdom and Philosophical Literature: The fourth genre of documents in the OT Pseudepigrapha contains the following works:

Ahiqar
3 Maccabees
4 Maccabees
Pseudo-Phocylides
The Sentences of the Syriac Menander

These writings preserve some of the insights of ancient wisdom, not only within early Judaism but also in surrounding cultures. Here, we confront the universalistic truths so essential for sophisticated and enlightened conduct and behavior in all facets of life, secular and religious. Jews tended to borrow philosophical truths from other cultures, frequently but not always recasting them in light of the Torah.

Ahiqar, an Assyrian composition of the late

seventh or sixth century B.C., predates the period covered by the OT Pseudepigrapha; it is included among the Pseudepigrapha, however, because it is important for an understanding of the thought of early Judaism, is cited by the author of Tobit (1:21–22), and is not found in other collections of ancient literature. *3 Maccabees*, primarily a humorous account of divine intervention that saved the Jews from persecution by Ptolemy IV Philopator, was written near the turn of the era, perhaps even as early as the early decades of the first century B.C. *4 Maccabees*, a philosophical diatribe influenced by Stoicism and Greek rhetoric, was composed probably sometime in the century preceding the destruction of Jerusalem in A.D. 70. *Pseudo-Phocylides*, Jewish maxims attributed to an Ionic poet who lived in the sixth century B.C., was compiled perhaps between 50 B.C. and A.D. 100. *The Sentences of the Syriac Menander* is a florilegium (collection) of old wisdom sayings probably compiled by a Jew around the third century A.D. The work is at times strikingly similar to *Ahiqar* and to Ecclesiasticus (The Wisdom of Jesus the Son of Sirach).

Prayers, Psalms, and Odes: The fifth, and final, genre of documents in the OT Pseudepigrapha contains the following writings:

- More Psalms of David
- Prayer of Manasseh
- Psalms of Solomon
- Hellenistic Synagogal Prayers
- Prayer of Joseph
- Prayer of Jacob
- Odes of Solomon

Some of these poetic compositions are influenced by the thought and style of the Davidic Psalms, while others show the more free developments of poetic style characteristic of early Jewish hymns.

More Psalms of David contains five additional psalms of David and some verses of a sixth; these were composed over a wide period of time. One dates from the third century B.C., while others date from the second century B.C. to the first century A.D. Sometimes the reference to David is palpable; note, for example, Psalm 151A, v. 1:

> I was the smallest among my brothers,
> and the youngest among the sons of my father;
> and he made me shepherd of his flocks,
> and the ruler over his kids.

The Prayer of Manasseh, often included in the Apocrypha, a beautiful and penetrating penitential prayer, was composed by a Jew around the turn of the era. *The Psalms of Solomon* preserves eighteen psalms written by pious Jews near or in Jerusalem during the last half of the first century B.C. *The Hellenistic Synagogal Prayers*, Jewish prayers identified behind books seven and eight of the *Apostolic Constitutions*, are difficult to date. They were probably com-

Aramaic fragment of 1 Enoch 22 found among the Dead Sea Scrolls.

posed during the second and third centuries A.D., if not earlier. *The Prayer of Joseph*, as extant, is more typical of the works collected under the category "Expansions of the Old Testament"; it is only partially preserved, but there are reasons to date it to the period between A.D. 70 and 135. *The Prayer of Jacob* is lost, except for twenty-six lines preserved in a papyrus fragment. It is a Jewish prayer that is difficult to date, but it must predate the extant fourth-century papyrus. *The Odes of Solomon*, a Christian collection of forty-two odes significantly influenced by the literature of early Judaism, especially the Qumran scrolls, was composed around A.D. 100 and is strikingly similar to the Gospel of John.

The new edition of the OT Pseudepigrapha (see above) also contains a supplement of thirteen Jewish works preserved primarily or only in quotations by the fourth century bishop and church historian Eusebius, who found them almost always in a now lost work by Alexander Polyhistor, who lived in the first century B.C. Some of the excerpts are fascinating. For example, Aristobulus, a brilliant Jewish philosopher influenced by Pythagorean, Platonic, and Stoic ideas, argued that Pythagoras, Socrates, and Plato heard God's voice. Artapanus, a Jewish historian who lived in the second century B.C., even suggested that all the greatness of Egyptian culture, including idolatry and polytheism, was to be attributed to the work of Abraham, Joseph, and Moses. ***See also*** Apocalyptic Literature; Apocrypha, Old Testament; Bible; Canon; Josephus; Mishnah; Music; New Testament; Old Testament; Philo; Prayer; Pseudonym; Rabbi, Rabboni; Scrolls, The Dead Sea; Septuagint; Talmud; Wisdom. J.H.C.

pseudonym, a fictitious or assumed name. As a matter of convention in the intertestamental period, many writers assumed the names of various persons mentioned in the OT, including Adam, Enoch, Moses, Job, Ezra, and the twelve sons of Jacob, to draw upon that individual's authority or symbolic importance. The book of Daniel is pseudonymous, while, in the NT, such Letters are attributed to James, Peter, Jude, and, in some cases, to Paul. ***See also*** Apocrypha, Old Testament; Pseudepigrapha.

Ptolemais (toh-luh-may'uhs). ***See*** Acco.

Ptolemy (tahl'uh-mee), the dynastic name of the kings who ruled Egypt after the death of Alexander the Great. **1** Ptolemy I, "Soter" (d. 283/2 B.C.), founder of the dynasty. He established the administrative and military structure of Egypt. He also created a hellenized Egyptian cult around the god Serapis for the Greek populace and established the "museum," the library at Alexandria that would make the city the center of learning and research throughout the Hellenistic period. **2** Ptolemy II, "Philadelphus" (ruled 283–246 B.C.), who adopted the Egyptian custom of marrying his full sister, which scandalized his Greek subjects. Under his reign the hellenization of Egypt and the ascent of Alexandria to intellectual prominence continued. During his reign the Greek translation of the Hebrew OT, the Septuagint (LXX), was begun. **3** Ptolemy III, "Euergetes," who ruled from 246 to 222/21 B.C. **4** Ptolemy IV, "Philopater," who ruled from 221 to 204 B.C. **5** Ptolemy V, "Epiphanes" (ruled 204–180 B.C.), who was crowned according to ancient Egyptian rites in 197 B.C., an event commemorated on the Rosetta Stone. **6** Ptolemy VI, "Philometor" (ruled 180–145 B.C.), who shared rule with his brother, Ptolemy VII. **7** Ptolemy VII, "Neos Philopator" (145–144 B.C.). **8** Ptolemy VIII, "Euergetes II," who ruled from 140 B.C. to 116 B.C. The second half of the second century was characterized by considerable strife between the brothers and constant wars with various factions in Syria. **9** The children of Ptolemy IX, Cleopatra Bernice (81–80 B.C.) and sons Ptolemy X and XI (80 B.C.), with whose deaths Ptolemaic rule ended. **10** The illegitimate Ptolemy XII, who took the throne and ruled until 51 B.C. His two sons were killed fighting Julius Caesar and were followed on the throne by their sister Cleopatra VII, who had a child by Julius Caesar and was later married to Mark Antony from whom she received territory in Syria and Palestine. She committed suicide when she and Antony were defeated by Octavian (Augustus) in 31 B.C. ***See also*** Egypt; Rosetta Stone. P.P.

Ptolemy IV on a gold coin; on his head is a crown formed of the sun's rays.

Puah (po͞o'uh), a name derived from two Hebrew words in the OT. **1** Derived from Hebrew *pu'āh*, one of the Hebrew midwives who cleverly disobeyed the Pharaoh's orders and spared the Hebrews' male children (Exod. 1:15). Derived from Hebrew *pu'āh* it refers to the following: **2** The son of Issachar and head of the clan of the Punites (1 Chron. 7:1). The name also occurs as Puvvah (Gen. 46:13) and Puvah (Num. 26:23). **3** The father of Tola, one of the judges of Israel (Judg. 10:1).

publicans, tax and toll collectors in the Roman Empire. Contracts for collecting taxes in a region were farmed out, usually to wealthy foreigners. They in turn hired local inhabitants to collect the taxes, such as Zacchaeus, who was a chief tax collector in Jericho (Luke 19:1). Farmers who tried to move their goods to a market outside their immediate territory were subject to tolls which ate up any monetary profit. Goods sold in certain markets were also subject to taxes and farmers were generally destitute or in debt to moneylenders and tax collectors. Sometimes community leaders were forced to collect taxes in their districts. The publicans were personally responsible for paying the taxes to the government, but they were in turn free to collect extra taxes from the people in order to make a profit. Opportunities for theft, fraud, and corruption abounded and tax collectors were generally despised in Greco-Roman literature, including the NT. Among Jews they were also rejected because they had contact with Gentiles and were ritually unclean. "Publicans and sinners" are cited together as examples of undesirable types (Matt. 9:11; 11:19; Luke 15:1). In a surprising reversal of cultural norms, Jesus compares tax collectors and harlots favorably with the Jewish leaders because the tax collectors and harlots are believing in Jesus and entering the kingdom and the leaders are not (Matt. 21:31). Zacchaeus believes in Jesus and says that he will repay fourfold those whom he has defrauded (Luke 19:8). ***See also*** Tribute, Tax, Toll. A.J.S.

Publius (po͞ob'lee-uhs), the chief magistrate of the Island of Malta when Paul was cast ashore there by a shipwreck (Acts 28:1). Because Paul healed Publius' father of fever and dysentery, the people of Malta showed Paul and his companions much kindness (Acts 28:7–10).

Pudens (pyo͞o'denz), known only as a greeter of

Timothy (2 Tim. 4:21), unless he was Pudens the friend of the Latin poet Martial. ***See also*** Claudia; Eubulus; Linus.

Pul (po͞ol), the name by which Tiglath-pileser III, king of Assyria, was known in the Babylonian King List A and the Ptolemaic Canon. Pul may be a shortened and familiar form of the second element, *-pileser*, a wordplay on the Akkadian word *pulu*, "limestone block." This nickname was not used in contemporary documents and never served as a royal name. Late biblical writers learned the name in Babylonia and were confused as to the king's true identity (2 Kings 15:19; 1 Chron. 5:26).

Tiglath-pileser III, king of Assyria 745–727 B.C., is also called "Pul" in the Bible; relief from Susa, eighth century B.C.

pulse, a porridge of meal and legumes. It is a term in the KJV where the RSV has "vegetables" in Dan. 1:12, 16; it was food for Daniel and his companions at their request, so they could avoid defilement with unclean foods.

punishment, everlasting, the concept that after death an individual can be subjected to ongoing retribution for evil acts committed during life. The idea developed slowly over a long period of time. The ancient Hebrews, like the other Semitic peoples of the ancient Near East, believed that at death the human person lost earthly life but did not go out of existence entirely. They had no notion of an immortal soul separable from the body. Rather, they believed that the dead had a shadowlike or phantomlike existence in the realm of the dead. The realm of the dead was usually located under the earth. It was called by various names, most commonly Sheol. This name is related to the verb "to inquire" in Hebrew and probably reflects the practice of seeking oracles from the dead. In the OT Sheol is not particularly a place of punishment. Existence there is characterized by weariness and forgetfulness.

The notion of eternal punishment does appear a few times in the OT, though not particularly associated with Sheol. In Isa. 66:24 it is said of the wicked that "their worm shall not die, their fire shall not be quenched, and they shall be an abhorrence to all flesh" (RSV). In Daniel 12:2 it is said that some will rise from the dead to shame and everlasting contempt.

In 2 Kings 23:10 the Valley of Hinnom, a ravine south of Jerusalem, is mentioned as a place where children were burned as sacrifices to the god Molech. Perhaps as early as the third century B.C., this valley came to represent the place of eternal punishment (*1 Enoch* 27; 90:26–27; 2 Esdr. 7:36). This notion appears in the NT, where the valley is called Gehenna (e.g., Matt. 5:22). In Jewish literature of the Greco-Roman period and in the NT, the punishment envisaged in this valley is a fiery one. The book of Revelation does not use the term Gehenna but speaks of a lake of fire in which the wicked will be punished (Rev. 20:14–15).

The notion of eternal punishment was greatly elaborated in the early Christian apocalypses that came to be called apocryphal (to the NT). In *The Apocalypse of Peter,* for example, various places of punishment are revealed. In each case the mode of punishment suits the sins for which the lost souls are being punished. It is this later tradition that Dante incorporated in his *Inferno.*

Today there is a range of interpretations of this tradition among Christians. Fundamentalists and some conservative evangelicals believe that hell is an actually existing, physical place and that various horrible physical afflictions will be visited there upon sinners in eternity. A moderate view holds that hell is not a specific place and that God is not preparing physical punishments for the wicked. Hell is rather the state of eternal separation from God. It is the conscious loss of the presence of God and of heavenly bliss. Some liberals understand language about everlasting punishment symbolically. From this point of view, these symbols express something about earthly life, not about an afterlife. Hell may be interpreted as the state in this life of hardened rebellion against God, a state of disobedience beyond forgiveness and redemption. Support for this view is found in the Gospel of John. There the opposite of everlasting punishment, eternal life, is presented primarily as a quality of life in the present: real

life, abundant life. *See also* Apocalyptic Literature; Eschatology; Heaven; Hell; Judgment, Day of.
A.Y.C.

pur. *See* Purim.

purge, to cleanse of impurities. The term appears in a variety of contexts: to cleanse a land of idolatry (2 Chron. 34:3, 8); to atone for sin or purify from iniquity (1 Sam. 3:14; Pss. 65:3; 79:9; Isa. 6:7; Heb. 1:3; 10:2; 2 Tim. 2:21); and to prepare a new altar for use in Temple sacrifice (Ezek. 43:20, 26). The purging or refining of metal was used as a metaphor for expiating sin (Isa. 1:25; Mal. 3:3). The removal of undesirable persons could be expressed as an explicit purging of rebels from the land (Ezek. 20:38) or metaphorically as the purging of a threshing floor (Matt. 3:12; Luke 3:17) or the purging of a lump of leaven (1 Cor. 5:7).

purify, purification. *See* Purity.

Purim, the Feast of, a minor holiday of the Jewish calendar based upon the account in the book of Esther. King Ahasuerus of Persia was persuaded by his minister, Haman, to destroy all the Jews in his kingdom on a day chosen by the drawing of lots (Heb. *purim*). The king's Jewish wife, Queen Esther, along with her cousin, Mordecai, foiled the plot and saved her people. The holiday is preceded by the Fast of Esther, commemorating the period of assembly and fasting before the deliverance. On Purim, according to Talmudic practice, the Megillah (Scroll of Esther) is read in the synagogue, charity is distributed, gifts of food are exchanged, and a festive meal is eaten. *See also* Esther. L.H.S.

purity, the condition of being free from any physical, moral, or ritual contamination. In the Hebrew Bible people may contract impurity by contact with a corpse, certain dead animals, the involuntary flow of fluids from the sexual organs, a disease such as *tsara'at* (usually mistranslated as "leprosy"), or the eating of prohibited foods. Certain objects are regarded as pure (*tahor*) but may be rendered impure (*tame'*) as a result of contact with an impure person who has not undergone purification rites. While impure, a person is enjoined from certain actions, primarily contact with the Temple or its religious practices.

Although aspects of the demonic may have been present in the earliest conceptions of ritual impurity, the Hebrew Bible understands moral impurity (i.e., sinfulness) to be the underlying cause of physical impurity. Both were seen as defilement of the individual and, therefore, in need of purification. The moral imperfection represented a defilement from within, a rebellion against God's law. The physical signs of impurity were seen as the symptoms of this moral or religious imperfection. In all cases, this impurity, being contagious, had to be gotten rid of. This necessitated the complex system of purificatory rituals.

Specific rites of purification were enjoined for the various forms of ritual impurity. The process of purification consisted of several stages: a waiting period of from one day to several months, depending upon the nature of the impurity, counting from the time of the cessation of the cause of pollution; a cleansing agent such as water (Lev. 15:16), fire (Num. 31:23), or blood (Lev. 14:25); and the offering of a sacrifice.

The duty of the priest was to maintain the ritual purity of Israel and its sanctuary. Thus, the laws of purity are found mainly in the priestly documents in such biblical books as Leviticus and Numbers. At the same time, the purificatory rites were not automatically efficacious. Purification only worked if the person was free of immorality and repentant of the evil that caused impurity. Hence, the role of the priest was to administer the rites that removed the last vestiges of impurity from the conscience of the worshiper. This was the case not only for the individual but for the nation as a whole. Once a year, on the Day of Atonement, Israel had to atone as a community, the priestly house had to be atoned for, the altar had to be cleansed, and the sanctuary itself purified. In this way the priests preserved the purity of the nation, and the presence of God continued to dwell among Israel.

Ritual purity and impurity were particularly important in the literature of the Dead Sea Scrolls. The sect of Qumran was itself extremely strict and maintained the standards of priestly purity even in its everyday life. The *Temple Scroll* envisaged a society in which the Torah's laws of purity would be strictly observed. The sect emphasized repeatedly that purification rites were only efficacious if undertaken after repentance and with a pure heart. Very similar practices were part of the religious life of the Pharisees and the early Tannaim (those who handed on traditions).

Christian doctrine likewise states that impurity is a spiritual or moral quality that comes from within. The blood of Jesus is understood as the agent that has purified all people once and for all. Jesus is believed to serve simultaneously as the last sacrifice necessary as well as the intercessor high priest (see the Letter to the Hebrews). Thus, in Christian theology the elaborate system of biblical purity is abrogated.

The Jewish tradition, although forced to give up the sacrificial ritual due to the destruction of the Jerusalem Temple, retained the laws of ritual purity wherever possible. Therefore, the immersion of a woman in the *miqweh* (ritual bath) after menstruation remained a requirement of Jewish law. The ritual washing of the hands is an example of a rabbinic enactment that extended the laws of purity from the Temple to the home. ***See also*** Priests; Worship. L.H.S.

purple, a distinctive dye color associated with royal garb. Such dye was a product of the Syrian and Phoenician coastal zone whose people maintained a monopoly on the item through much of history. It derived from a distinctive combination of colors acquired from gastropods of the Muricidae family that lived in Mediterranean waters of the region. Various shades were mixed, primarily red to purple. "The purple" came to stand for the color, cloth dyed in it, people who wore it, and classes rich enough to afford it, like royalty.

Specifically, the dye was extracted from the secretion of the hypobranchial gland of the mollusks, and the most popular shades were produced by a double-dyeing treatment. From the middens of shells along the north Mediterranean coast of Lebanon and Syria, the *Murex brandaris* and *Murex trunculus* were the most frequently used sources. The limited habitat and the small amount of dye extractable from each shell made the product especially valuable.

Biblical references to blue and scarlet together with purple are extensive (Exod. 25:4; 36:35), and the colors were prized for priestly vestments in Israel's tradition. A good wife was clothed in purple (Prov. 31:22), Solomon's palanquin seat was purple (Song of Sol. 3:10), Jesus was temporarily cloaked in purple during his pre-execution incarceration (Mark 15:17–20; John 19:2–5), the rich man's clothes included purple in the parable of the rich man and Lazarus (Luke 16:19), Lydia of Thyatira was a trader of purple goods when she became Christian (Acts 16:14), and purple figured in the eschatological vision of the harlot condemned, meaning Rome (Rev. 17:4; 18:12, 16).

While Israel imported its purple, as did others, Solomon specified that men skilled to work in "purple, crimson, and blue fabrics" be included in the Phoenician work force he obtained from Hiram, king of Tyre (2 Chron. 2:7), in response to which Hiram sent one Huramabi (2:14), and the work was done (3:14). R.S.B.

purse (KJV: "girdle"), a leather pouch in which money was carried (Prov. 7:20; Hag. 1:6; Luke 22:35–36). Jesus forbade his disciples to carry money in their purses, as evidence of their trust that God would provide for them through the generosity of others (Matt. 10:9). The Gospel of John reports that Judas Iscariot was in charge of the common funds used by Jesus and his disciples (John 12:6; 13:29).

Put (po͞ot). **1** The third son of Ham (Gen. 10:6; 1 Chron. 1:8). **2** A region in Africa, probably located in Libya. Warriors from Put fought on the side of the Ethiopians and Egyptians when the Assyrians captured No-amon (Thebes) in 663 B.C. (Nah. 3:9; Ezek. 30:5).

Puteoli (pyo͞o-tee'oh-lee; from the Lat. either for "small wells" or for "stink"), the seaport (modern Pozzuoli) just west of Naples where, according to Acts 28:13–14, Paul landed on his way to Rome and stayed seven days with the local Christian community. The apocryphal *Acts of Peter* has Peter also landing at Puteoli en route to Rome after Paul had departed for Spain.

Founded probably in the sixth century B.C. by Greek colonists from Samos, Puteoli was originally a port of Cumae named Dicaearchia. In 215 B.C., the Romans garrisoned the town against the Carthaginian general Hannibal and renamed it Puteoli. In 194 B.C., it became a Roman colony. During the first century A.D., Puteoli was the major port of Italy, where Alexandrian grain ships (like Paul's) docked to unload cargo for Rome. ***See also*** Paul. C.H.M.

pygarg (pī'gahrg), an obsolete term for a white-rumped ungulate; the KJV uses this term where the RSV has "ibex" in Deut. 14:5.

Pyramid Texts, the, a collection of magical spells relating to the rebirth and eternal glory of the king of Egypt. The texts occur in several pyramids of kings and queens from the end of the fifth dynasty to the eighth dynasty (ca. 2350–2160 B.C.). The texts are not found in the earlier, great pyramids of Giza. First discovered by scholars in 1881, the texts are carved on the walls of the burial complex inside the pyramid. Each pyramid has its own particular collection of spells. The intent of the spells was to affirm—even bring about—the resurrection and ascent to the sky of the deceased ruler. The spells generally predate the pyramids in which they are inscribed and are often quite archaic. They represent the oldest corpus of religious texts from Egypt and underlie the later Coffin Texts and Book of the Dead, in which the afterlife is no longer a royal prerogative. ***See also*** Egypt; Pharaoh; Resurrection. H.B.H.

pyramids. ***See*** Burial.

Pyrrhus (pihr'uhs), the father of Sopater of Beroea, who accompanied Paul on his last journey to Jerusalem (Acts 20:4).

Opposite: Ancient Romans as depicted in the "Imperial Procession" portion of a frieze of the *Ara Pacis Augustae* (altar of the peace of Augustus), 13–9 B.C.

QR

Q

Q, a symbol (probably from the German *Quelle*, meaning "source") designating material common to the Gospels of Matthew and Luke, but not found also in the Gospel of Mark (e.g., Matt. 3:7–10; Luke 3:7–9). Scholars who favor the Two-Source Hypothesis (Mark and Q are sources for Matthew and Luke) as the solution to the Synoptic Problem also frequently use the symbol to designate the hypothetical source or sources from which this material came. The Q material consists almost entirely of Jesus' teachings and has nothing about his birth, death, or resurrection. Q plays no role in the Griesbach Hypothesis, which affirms that Matthew was the earliest gospel. ***See also*** Synoptic Problem, The.

Qadisha (kah-dee'shah; Heb., "the holy [river]"), modern Nahr Abu 'Ali, a river that flows from the upper slopes of the Lebanon range northwest to the Mediterranean which it enters at the city of Tripoli. The modern park containing the few remaining cedars of Lebanon is in the upper gorge of the river, but there is no evidence for the conjecture that it was the route used for transporting the cedars sent by Hiram of Tyre to Solomon for the construction of the Temple (cf. 1 Kings 5:1–12).

qesita. ***See*** Kesitah.

quail, a small plump gamebird. It is generally agreed that the Hebrew word translated "quail" in the OT *(selaw)* denotes the common quail *(Coturnix coturnix)*. Its plumage is of a sandy brown base color with black and pale streaks. The quail breeds in Europe and western Asia and passes through Palestine and Sinai on its way to its winter quarters in Africa.

During the Exodus large flocks of quail provided the Israelites with the food God had promised them (Exod. 16:13; Num. 11:31; Ps. 105:40). The large numbers so easily collected by the Hebrews (over a hundred bushels per person) can be explained by the fact that the quail, though a strong flyer over short stretches, is dependent on the wind to cover large distances. Changes in the wind direction force it to the ground and make it easy prey. In ancient Egypt quails were potted and pickled in large quantities, but excessive hunting has now considerably decreased their numbers.

I.U.K.

quarries, sources of construction stone, whether cut from the sides of outcrops or dug from beneath soil layers.

The labor involved was immense (1 Kings 5: 13–18) for large projects, and sometimes proverbially dangerous (Eccles. 10:9). In prosperous times the products were commercially available (2 Kings 12:12; 22:6; 2 Chron. 34:11). Finishing the product was sometimes done at the quarry site (1 Kings 6:7), whether for economic, religious, or aesthetic reasons, and the labor could be under royal project command as well (2 Chron. 2:2, 18).

Quarrying techniques were extensively developed in ancient Egypt, where the blocks for the Old Kingdom pyramids were cut from quarries far up the Nile and floated downstream on barges, sometimes guided by two or three pilot boats to keep the load under way and navigable. Aswan was the site of famous granite quarries, and the techniques were similar in quarrying sandstone or limestone in Palestine. Cuts outlining the blocks were made with picks. Wedges of wood were then inserted and wetted, and the swelling forced the block loose from its setting. Ledges created by the removal of stone blocks were found beneath the Byzantine church at modern Tell Hesban in 1971, adding another to the large registry of quarry sites in the archaeological record. Evidence of informal quarrying for previously used stone is found at almost every large archaeological site. The economy of trimming an already available block versus having to quarry a new one was nearly irresistible to ancient builders, as it is also to modern builders.

R.S.B.

Quail; Coptic tapestry, third or fourth century A.D.

Quartus (kwahr'tuhs), a companion of Paul who joins him in sending greetings in Rom. 16: 23.

quaternion. ***See*** Squad.

queen, a woman sovereign, consort or wife of a king, or a mother of a king. Israel, unlike other nations around it, knew no legitimate female sovereigns. Two such foreign queens are mentioned in the Bible, the queen of Sheba (1 Kings 10; 2 Chron. 9) and Candace, queen of the Ethiopians (Acts 8:27). Although not mentioned in the OT, Hatshepsut of Egypt was one of the important pharaohs in the eighteenth dynasty (ca. 1500 B.C.). Athaliah (2 Kings 8:26; 11:1–4) was queen mother who usurped the throne of Israel for seven years upon the death of her son, Ahaziah. A king's wife in ancient Israel apparently had no official function. Marriages were often contracted to cement alliances with other nations (2 Sam. 3:3; 1 Kings 3:1; 16:31; 2 Kings 8: 25–27). The queen mother had a more important role than the queen consort in both Israel and surrounding nations (1 Kings 2:19; 15:13). ***See also*** Athaliah; Candace; Esther; Jezebel; Sheba, Queen of. F.S.F.

Queen of Heaven, a high goddess worshiped by some Jews living in Jerusalem and Egypt in the time of Jeremiah (late seventh–early sixth centuries B.C.; Jer. 7:18; 44:17–19, 25). Jeremiah rejected this worship as idolatry and interpreted the fall of Jerusalem as punishment for such worship. In the first century A.D., the mother goddess of Ephesus, called Artemis by the Greeks, the Syrian goddess Atargatis, and the Egyptian Isis were all worshiped as Queen of Heaven. In the book of Revelation, this high goddess worshiped under many names is Christianized, so to speak, and presented as the Heavenly Israel (Rev. 12).

quern (kuhrn), a stone with a flat or slightly concave surface used for grinding grain into meal by hand. Most samples are basalt or limestone in Palestine, and the grain was pulverized by being crushed with a hand-held grinding stone repeatedly kneaded over the grain against the quern surface. Such an activity is probably presumed in Jesus' saying in Matt. 24:21.

quicksands. ***See*** Syrtis.

Quirinius (kwi-rin'ee-uhs), **P. Sulpicius,** Roman consul who held the position of governor (legate) of Syria for several years, beginning in A.D. 6. He is the "Quirinius" (KJV: "Cyrenius") of Luke 2:2, during whose administration the "enrollment" took place and Jesus was born in Bethlehem. The historian Josephus tells of a census carried out under Quirinius' authority in A.D. 6 or 7, after the banishment of Archelaus, the ethnarch of Judea, Samaria, and Idumea. The property of Judea's Roman subjects, now to be governed directly by a Roman prefect, was assessed for the purpose of levying taxes. Apparently this is the census ("enrollment") of Luke 2:1–3. Two problems, however, await resolution. The first and most serious is the discrepancy of at least ten years between Luke's dating of the events surrounding Jesus' birth to the time of Herod the Great (Luke 1:5; cf. Matt. 2:1–22), who died in 4 B.C., and Josephus' dating of Quirinius' census. The second is the difference between Luke's reference to "all the world" being enrolled and Josephus' limitation of the census to the former territory of Archelaus. Various possible solutions to these problems have been proposed, but none has received general acceptance. The problems simply underscore the uncertainty of the historical information available to Luke regarding the circumstances surrounding the birth of Jesus. ***See also*** Archelaus; Enrollment; Herod. F.O.G.

quiver, a container for carrying arrows, usually made of leather and carried on the back or over the shoulder. The quiver was standard equipment for archers, both hunters (Gen. 27:3) and soldiers (Job 39:23; Isa. 22:6). Figuratively speaking, Lam. 3:13 attributes the distress that accompanied Jerusalem's fall to the arrows of God's quiver (Heb. *benê ashpâh,* "sons of the quiver"). This connection between arrows and quivers was so well known that biblical writers used these objects as symbols for the relationship between children and parents (Ps. 127:5), the servant and God (Isa. 49:2), and war and death (Jer. 5:16). ***See also*** Archers; Arms, Armor; Weapons. G.L.M.

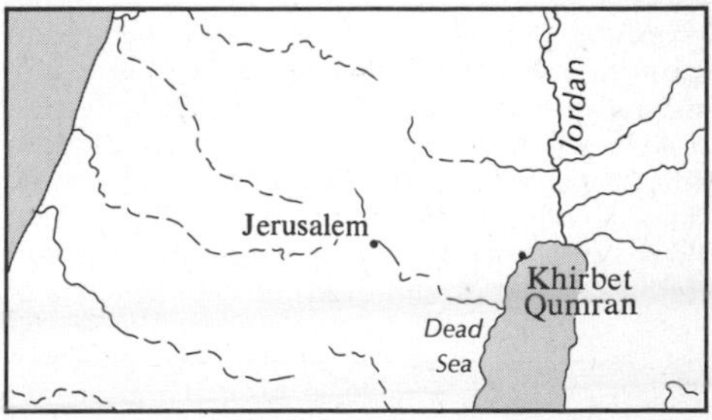

Qumran (ko͞om'rahn), **Khirbet** (kihr'bet), the site of the settlement, probably Essene, that produced the Dead Sea Scrolls. It lies eight and a half miles south of Jericho on the first shelf of hills above the west shore of the Dead Sea. ***See also*** Scrolls, The Dead Sea.

Qurun Hattin (ko͞o'ro͞on haht-teen'). ***See*** Hattin, Horns of.

R

Ra. *See* Re.

Raamah (ray'uh-mah; also Raama, 1 Chron. 1:9), the Cushite father of Sheba and Dedan (Gen. 10:7), hence an Arabian locale and people. Famous as a spice trading source (Ezek. 27:22), its location is, while uncertain, probably in southwest Arabia near modern Ma'in.

Raamses, Rameses (ram'ee-seez), one of two store-cities (KJV: "treasure-cities," the other was Pithom) built by the Hebrews for Pharaoh (Exod. 1:11). The reference in Gen. 47:11 to the "land of Rameses," an area where Joseph settled for his father and brothers at the order of an earlier pharaoh, is anachronistic. It was from Raamses that the Israelites departed on the Exodus (Exod. 12:37; Num. 33:3, 5). The Egyptian name of this city was *Per-Ramessu*, Piramesse, "House of Ramesses." Named after Ramesses II (1279–1212 B.C.), who is often considered the pharaoh of the Exodus, Raamses served as the delta residence for the succeeding kings of the nineteenth and twentieth dynasties (ca. 1212–1070 B.C.). For many years, scholars identified Raamses with Tanis (Heb. *Zoan*), modern San el-Hagar in the Egyptian delta, where many monuments inscribed with the name of Ramesses II and his successors were discovered. However, it was determined that all of these Ramesside period monuments were moved to Tanis from somewhere else. It is therefore most probable that Raamses is to be placed in the area of modern Khatana-Qantir on the Pelusiac branch of the Nile, about fifteen miles south of Tanis. Evidence for a palace of Sety I (1291–1279 B.C.) and Ramesses II and the houses of high officials of the Ramesside period was found there, within an enormous city stretching more than a mile from Qantir south to Tell el-Dabaa (which is the site of the earlier Hyksos capital of Avaris). ***See also*** Pithom; Rameses; Zoan. J.M.W.

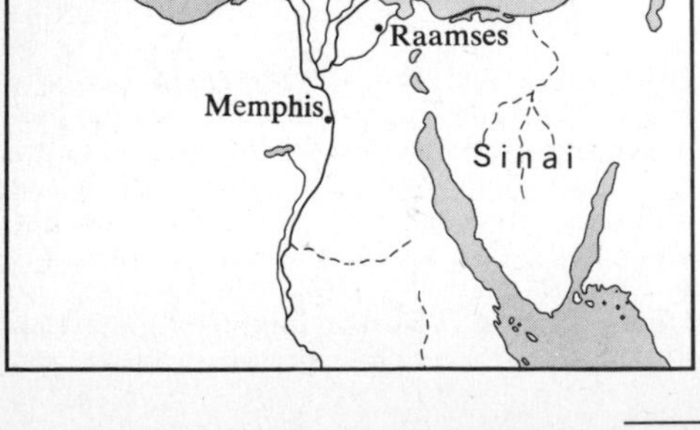

Rabbah (rahb'bah). **1** A city of Judah (Josh. 15:60) in the district with Kiriath-jearim, identified tentatively with modern Khirbet Hamideh. It appears as Rubute in several ancient extrabiblical sources: Tell Amarna Letters, nos. 287, 289, 290; Taanach Tablet no. 1; Thutmose IV's topographical list, town no. 105; and Shishak's list, town no. 13.

2 The only town (alternately Rabbat of the Ammonites or Rabath-Ammon, meaning the "great" or "capital' of the Ammonites) mentioned in the Bible as specifically Ammonite. It is modern Amman, located about twenty-four miles east of the Jordan River and twenty-three miles northeast of the Dead Sea.

Recent excavations on Jebel el-Qalah, the citadel of the ancient city, indicate at least sporadic occupation throughout the Bronze Age and a fairly heavily fortified town of about 1750–1550 B.C. Salvage excavations at the old Amman Civil Airport have uncovered a structure believed to be a mortuary dating to the thirteenth century B.C. The citadel excavations reveal tenth–ninth-century B.C. phases of a defense wall, quite possibly related to David's siege of the city and the later rebuilding (2 Sam. 11:1; 12:26–31). Iron Age II remains date to the eighth and seventh centuries B.C., with evidences of destruction that recall the rebukes of Amos (Amos 1:14), Jeremiah (Jer. 49:2, 3), and Ezekiel (Ezek. 25:5) against Rabbah and the Ammonites.

Rabbah was renamed Philadelphia after it was captured by Ptolemy Philadelphus (third century B.C.), and it flourished as a Hellenistic city, as fortified walls and structural remains testify. Architecturally, the second-century A.D. Roman remains are what are prominent today, especially the Nymphaeum, columned street, and large amphitheater in downtown Amman. ***See also*** Ammonites. N.L.L.

Rabbi, Rabboni (Heb., "My Great One"), a title that took on the meaning "My Master" or "My Teacher" and eventually became used in the absolute sense. *Rab,* without the possessive article, is used in the OT as a title meaning "chief" or "officer" (2 Kings 18:17). By the time of the Mishnah (A.D. 200) *rab* had come to mean a master as opposed to slave and a master or teacher of students. The NT has two forms of the title, *rabbi* and *rabbounei* (these Greek words are sometimes translated, as "master," or simply transliterated, as "rabboni"). These probably reflect the pronunciations in Hebrew and Aramaic in the first century. Later pronunciations attested in the Targums (translations of Hebrew

Scriptures into Aramaic) and inscriptions are *rebbi, ribbi, rib*, and *ribboni*. In the second and third centuries *rabbi* began to designate someone authorized to teach and judge matters of Jewish law.

In the NT Rabbi is used only in direct address of Jesus, not as a title. The Gospel of John (end of the first century) offers a translation of the term as "teacher" (1:38). The Gospel of Matthew implies that rabbis are teachers among the Jews (23:7–8). The Gospel of John uses the address "Rabbi" of Jesus often in chaps. 1–12. The address "Rabboni" in John 20:16 is probably employed to express familiarity and devotion. The Gospel of Matthew has only outsiders address Jesus as Rabbi; the disciples use titles with more christological weight such as "Lord." In the Gospel of Luke only Judas Iscariot calls Jesus "Rabbi." A.J.S.

Rabmag (rab'mag). ***See*** Nergal-Sharezer.

Rabsaris (rahb-sahr'is), a title of Assyrian and Babylonian officials. **1** An official who appears as one of three Assyrian officials sent by Sennacherib to convince King Hezekiah to surrender (2 Kings 18:17–37). **2** Two Babylonian officials who appear in Jerusalem in the time of Nebuchadnezzar's destruction of it (586 B.C.; Jer. 39:3, 13). **3** An official mentioned as being in charge of the youths in Nebuchadnezzar's palace (Dan. 1:3).

The term Rabsaris should be translated "Chief [of the] Eunuch[s]"—the element *saris* derives from Akkadian *sha-rēshi*, "eunuch"—and the title should be treated literally. The Akkadian term *Rab-sha-rēhi* is the reading of the logograms LÚ.GAL.LÚ.SAG as well as LÚ.GAL. SAG and is the origin of the Aramaic *rbsrs* attested on a docket from Nineveh as well as of *Rab-saris* in Hebrew. Because of the important governmental role of the *Rab-sha-rēshi* and many *sha-rēshis*, scholars have sometimes been loath to take the term at face value and to acknowledge that all such officials were necessarily castrates; instead, they have assumed that only those *sha-rēshis* who were palace and harem officials were eunuchs and that otherwise the term was simply a designation for a type of governmental official. Since some *sha-rēshis* were undoubtedly eunuchs, and given the usual meaning of the Akkadian loan word *sha-rēshi* (*saris* in West Semitic), it is more reasonable to assume that all such officials—*sha-rēshi* and *Rab-sha-rēshi*—were castrates (unless there is compelling evidence to the contrary in a specific instance). The eunuch's lack of a familial support group, absence of descendants to whom he might wish to transfer wealth and office, and perhaps the contempt of other sectors of the society directed his loyalty and devotion to the crown and its interests. Accordingly, while the *Rabsaris* might be a high harem or court official (Dan. 1:8), he would normally serve in the imperial and military administration in a high-ranking and powerful position. The *Rab-sha-rēshi* was dispatched on military missions, and the term may even denote the commander-in-chief. I.T.A.

Rabshakeh (rab'shah-ke), one of the emissaries sent by the Assyrian king Sennacherib (705–681 B.C.) to Hezekiah, the king of Judah (727–698 B.C.), with a demand for a ransom, which Hezekiah paid out of the Temple treasures. When a further demand for surrender was relayed by Rabshakeh, the prophet Isaiah promised Hezekiah that God would prevent Jerusalem from falling into Sennacherib's hands. A plague subsequently visited on the Assyrian army caused Sennacherib to withdraw from Judah. He was subsequently slain by two of his sons (2 Kings 18:13–19:37; cf. Isa. 36–37). ***See also*** Sennacherib.

raca (rah'kah; KJV, Matt. 5:22), an obscure term of abuse, probably from the Aramaic meaning "empty one," which then takes on the meaning "empty-headed" or "fool." The RSV translates "whoever says 'Raca' " as "whoever insults."

race, racing, contest of speed or endurance. The metaphor of the footrace seldom occurs in the OT (Ps. 19:5; Jer.12:5; Eccles. 9:11), probably because competitive sports had no significant place in the social life of ancient Israel. When a gymnasium was erected in Jerusalem by the hellenizing high priest Jason early in the second century B.C., the devout Jews declared that "new customs" were being introduced "contrary to the law" (2 Macc. 4:7–17). From prehistoric times, however, the Greeks had promoted athletic contests in association with their religion: e.g., the Olympic games were held in honor of Zeus, the Isthmian games in honor of Poseidon. Competitive sports included boxing, wrestling, jumping, discus and javelin throwing, and, above all, the chariot, horse, and foot races.

Metaphorical allusions to the footrace are numerous in the NT, particularly in the Pauline corpus (see, however, Heb. 12:1–2, 12–14). In his travels among the Greeks, Paul was able to observe some of the pan-Hellenic contests (e.g., at Corinth and Ephesus). This probably accounts for the several uses that he makes of the Greek root referring to the place of sporting combat, the contest itself, and any kind of strenuous combat or contest (1 Thess. 2:2; 1 Cor. 9:25; Phil. 1:30). From one perspective, Paul viewed the Christian's life as an intense striving, a combat requiring self-discipline and strenuous training. In running this race, one must exert one's energies to the full, throwing off clinging sin, contending for the faith, and persisting in the race to the finish line (1 Cor. 9:24–27; Phil. 1:27–30; 3:13–14; 1 Thess. 2:2;

cf. Col. 1:28–29; 1 Tim. 4:7–10; 2 Tim. 4:7–8; Jude 3). In a similar vein, the writer of the Letter to the Hebrews exhorts his Christian readers to run their "course" unencumbered in any way, cheered onward by many witnesses including the martyrs of the past, with eyes fixed upon Jesus "on whom faith depends from start to finish" (Heb. 12:1–2, NEB). The victors in the race "in which we are entered" are to receive "the crown of righteousness"—"an imperishable wreath," not woven of fading leaves like those so proudly worn by winners in the Greek games (2 Tim. 4:8; 1 Cor. 9:25; Phil. 3:12–16; 1 Tim. 6:11–12). Other NT passages probably also allude to the footrace or athletic contest (Rom. 9:16; 15:30; Gal. 2:2; 5:7; Phil. 2:16; Col. 2:1; Acts 13:25; 20:24; 2 Tim. 2:5). ***See also*** Crown; Games. J.L.P.

Rachel (ray'chuhl), the more favored of the two wives of Jacob. While looking for Laban his kinsman, Jacob met Rachel at a well; he entered Laban's household, fell in love with Rachel, and agreed to serve Laban for seven years as a bride-price for her. When her elder sister Leah was substituted for Rachel at the bridal feast, Jacob married Rachel a week later and agreed to serve another seven years for her (Gen. 28:9–20). Rachel was barren in the early years of her marriage, during which time Leah bore Jacob four sons. To maintain her position vis-à-vis her co-wife Leah, Rachel offered her handmaiden Bilhah to Jacob as a surrogate mother, a custom known from Near Eastern sources (Gen. 30:1–8). These children fulfilled Rachel's wifely responsibility; when Bilhah bore sons, Rachel named the first Dan, "God has vindicated me [Heb. *danni]* . . . and given me a son" (Gen. 30:6) and the second Naphtali after the fateful contest she waged (Heb. *niphtalti)* and won from her sister (Gen. 30:8). Rachel was clearly the dominant wife in the marriage. When Leah's son Reuben found mandrakes (a fertility symbol), Rachel was able to offer a night with Jacob in trade (Gen. 30:14–16).

Jacob meets Rachel at the well (left) and then bargains to serve her father, Laban, for seven years in exchange for her hand in marriage (Gen. 29:10–20); detail from a thirteenth-century French miniature.

Rachel finally bore a son, Joseph. Her favored position among the wives continued, and during their return to Canaan, Jacob placed Rachel and Joseph (Gen. 33:1–2) in the least exposed position. Leah supported Jacob's decision to leave Laban's household and Rachel took with her the family teraphim (household images). When Laban searched for them, Rachel hid them in her camel cushion and sat on them, pretending that she was menstruating (Gen. 31:32–35). The images apparently were buried under the terebinth near Shechem (Gen. 35:4). Rachel died bearing Benjamin and was buried in the later tribal territory of Benjamin (Gen. 35:16–21). She and Leah are mentioned as the matriarchs of Israel in Ruth 4:11. She is also remembered in a poetic passage in Jer. 31:15, in which the voice that the prophet hears is the voice of Rachel weeping for her children; in this passage Rachel is the personification of the land and nation as the bride of God who is weeping for her exiled son Ephraim. The historicity of Rachel and Leah is a matter of speculation. They are considered the matriarchs of the tribes that formed the tribal federation (amphictyony) of the period of the judges. Joseph had two tribes, Ephraim and Manasseh. The former was the dominant tribe of the Northern Kingdom; moreover, the tribe of Benjamin was the object of civil war and was later the home of Saul, first monarch of the United Kingdom. The fact that Leah means "cow" and Rachel means "ewe" has led to speculation that the rivalry between the two reflected rivalry between sheep herders and cattle herders, or that they were projections of totemic symbols of early groups of tribes (the Leah tribes and the Rachel tribes) that joined the tribal federation. T.S.F.

Raguel (rag'wel), the name in the KJV for Reuel, the father-in-law of Moses (Num. 10:29). ***See also*** Jethro; Reuel.

Rahab (ray'hab). **1** The harlot who sheltered Joshua's men when they came to spy Jericho (Josh. 2). She defied the orders of the king of Jericho, misdirected the king's men, and then helped Joshua's men escape from Jericho by climbing down a rope from her home which was built against the city wall. Rahab is portrayed as motivated by a genuine fear of God and a belief that he would conquer the city; she asked in return that the men swear to her that they would spare Rahab and her family when they returned to conquer. Rahab was to signal the invaders by tying a length of crimson cord to her window (Josh. 2:18). When the Israelites did conquer Jericho, only Rahab and her father's family were saved (Josh. 6:25). According to later Jewish legend, Rahab was one of the four most beautiful women in history. She became a righteous convert, married Joshua, and was the ancestor of eight prophets (including Jeremiah), and of Huldah the prophetess (*b. Meg.* 15a). In the NT, Rahab is cited as a heroine of faith (Heb. 11:31) and of righteous works (James 2:25), and is included in Jesus' ancestry by Matthew (1:5). **2** The mythical chaos dragon whom God killed in battle and thus made an orderly creation possible (Isa. 51:9; Ps. 89:10). **3** A pejorative name for Egypt (Ps. 87:4; Isa. 30:7). T.S.F.

raiment. ***See*** Dress; Gestures.

rain. ***See*** Farming; Palestine.

rainbow, a multicolored arc in the sky caused by refraction of sunlight through droplets of water. First mentioned in Gen. 9:12–13, the rainbow appears as sign of God's covenant promise not to destroy the world by flood again. The Hebrew word *qeshet* means both "bow" and "rainbow." Lam. 2:4 and Hab. 3:9–11 depict it as instrument of divine wrath, its arrows (e.g., lightning, thunderbolts, rains) released earthward (cf. Ecclus. 43:11–21). An ancient illustration of the god Ashur depicts him drawing a rainbow as a weapon. Gen. 9:12–13 thus suggests a *spent* bow. Ezek. 1:28 associates the rainbow with a manifestation of divine glory (cf. Rev. 10:1). ***See also*** Covenant; Flood, The; Noah; Sign. J.W.R.

The god Ashur using a rainbow as a bow; fragment from a glazed brick, Assyrian, ninth century B.C.

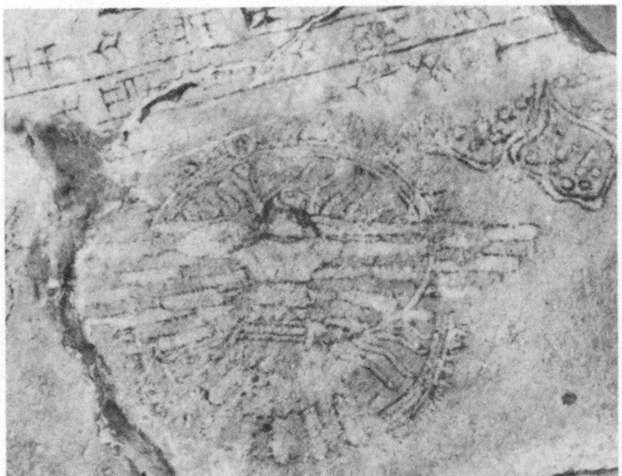

raisins, sun-dried grapes used for food (Song of Sol. 2:5), gifts (1 Sam. 25:18–31; 2 Sam. 16: 1–4), military rations (1 Chron. 12:40), or religious offerings (Hos. 3:1; Isa. 16:7; Jer. 7:18). They were nourishing and traveled well both unprocessed and pressed into cakes.

Ram (Heb., "God [is] high, exalted"; cf. Ab*ram*, Ahi*ram*, Am*ram*, Adoni*ram*, Jo*ram*). **1** The son of Hezron, an ancestor of David according to Ruth 4:19 (Greek versions read "Aram"; cf. Matt. 1:3, 4) and 1 Chron. 2:9 (brother of Jerahmeel). **2** The son of Jerahmeel, who was the son of Hezron (1 Chron. 2:25, 27). **3** An ancestor of Elihu's "family" (tribal division; Job 32:2).

ram, a male sheep (Heb. *'ayil*), frequently mentioned as a sacrificial offering in OT priestly legislation (Lev. 5:15; 8:18–29; Num. 7:15). God provided a ram as a substitute for the sacrifice of Isaac (Gen. 22:13). Rams' skins were used for the covering of the tabernacle (Exod. 36:19), and a ram's horn (Heb. *shophar*) was used to call Israel to battle and to worship. Ps. 114:4 describes the earth's agitation at God's appearing as mountains "skipping" like rams. The two-horned ram of Daniel's vision (Dan. 8) represented the kings of Media and Persia. There is no equivalent word in the NT. P.A.B.

The "Ram in a thicket" from a royal grave at Ur, third millennium B.C.

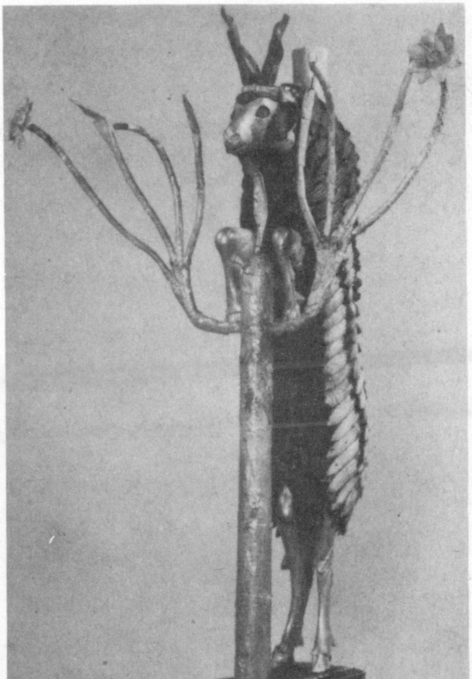

Ramah (rah'muh; Heb., "height"), a name given alone and in combination with other words to several places in Palestine.

1 Ramah of Benjamin, which is identified with modern er-Ram, about five miles north of Jerusalem and west of Geba and Michmash on the border of Israel and Judah. It is unexcavated but surface exploration indicates occupation begins about the twelfth century B.C., and it can be associated with a number of OT passages.

Deborah judged between Ramah and Bethel (Judg. 4:5). Baasha, King of Israel (ca. 902–886 B.C.), fortified Ramah, but, by an alliance with Ben-hadad of Damascus, Asa of Judah (ca. 908–872) tore it down (1 Kings 15:17–22). According to Isa. 10:29 the Assyrians advanced toward Jerusalem through Ramah. Ramah is mentioned in Hosea's cry against Israel (Hos. 5:8), and Jeremiah was set free there (Jer. 40:1). Ramah is among those towns listed with inhabitants following the Exile (Ezra 2:26; Neh. 7:30). Rachel was associated with this town (Jer. 31:15; Matt. 2:18).

2 Ramah of Ephraim. The Ramathaim-zophim of 1 Sam. 1:1 in the RSV would be better translated "a man of Ramathaim, a Zuphite from the hill country of Ephraim" (NEB). It is thereafter called Ramah in the story of Samuel, but it is probably to be distinguished from Ramah of Benjamin. Samuel's hometown was Ramah; he returned there periodically, and he was buried there (1 Sam. 7:17; 25:1). David was pursued by Saul to Ramah (1 Sam. 19:18–24).

This may be the Arimathea of the NT (Matt. 27:57; John 19:38) and may be identified with modern Rentis, about eighteen miles east of Joppa.

3 A border town in Asher (Josh. 19:29); a location to the north in the vicinity of Tyre seems to be indicated. Its identification is unknown, but it is usually associated with modern Ramieh near the south border of Lebanon.

4 A fortified town in Naphtali (Josh. 19:36), probably located at modern er-Ramah in the Valley of Beth-kerem about twenty miles east of Acco.

5 Ramah of the Negeb or Ramath-negeb (Josh. 19:8) in the lands of the tribe of Simeon. Here David sent some of his spoil from the Philistines (1 Sam. 30:27). Ramath-negeb is mentioned in Arad ostraca no. 24, and its context suggests it was an outpost facing the Edomite threat; therefore it has been identified with modern Khirbet Ghazzah southeast of Arad and on the southeast edge of the Negeb. ***See also*** Samuel; Samuel, The First and Second Books of. N.L.L.

Rameses (ram'e-seez). ***See*** Raamses, Rameses.

Ramesses (ram'e-seez; Egyptian, "Re [the sun god] is born"; also Ramses, Rameses), the family name of eleven kings of Egypt during the nineteenth and twentieth dynasties (ca. 1293–1070 B.C.). This era is often referred to as the Ramesside period. The Ramesside pharaohs were buried in the Valley of the Kings in western Thebes, but they lived in the eastern delta at Piramesse (see below). The principal kings of the Ramesside period are the following.

1 Ramesses I (1293–1291 B.C.), an army general who founded the nineteenth dynasty. His son was Sety I (1291–1279 B.C.), whose reign included military campaigns into western Asia in which the Hittites were defeated and various Palestinian cities were conquered.

2 Ramesses II (1279–1212 B.C.), son of Sety I, sometimes called "the Great" by early scholars. In the fifth year of his reign, he fought a great battle against the Hittites at Kadesh in Syria. This king was a very active builder throughout Egypt and Nubia; he also liked to have his name inscribed on the monuments of earlier kings. He founded the city of Piramesse (the biblical Raamses) in the eastern delta as the new royal residence. Many biblical scholars consider Ramesses II the pharaoh of the Exodus.

3 Merenptah (1212–1202 B.C.), a son of Ramesses II. A stele set up to record some of this king's victories includes the words "Israel is desolated and has no seed"; this is the first documented mention of Israel in the ancient Near East and has led some scholars to suggest that Merenptah was the pharaoh of the Exodus (which would make Ramesses II the pharaoh of the oppression).

4 Ramesses III (1182–1151 B.C.), the son of the first king of the twentieth dynasty, Setnakht. He successfully fought off an invasion of Egypt by the Sea Peoples from the northern Mediterranean region in the eighth year of his reign. One tribe included among the Sea Peoples was the Peleset (the biblical Philistines), who subsequently settled in southwest Palestine.

5 The later Ramesside kings, Ramesses IV–XI (1151–1070 B.C.), ruled over a country decaying economically, politically, and militarily. The Egyptian Empire in Palestine probably ended in about the reign of Ramesses VI (1141–1134 B.C.). ***See also*** Exodus; Pharaoh. J.M.W.

Ramoth (ram'ohth). ***See*** Ramoth-gilead.

Ramoth-gilead (ray'mahth-gil'ee-ad), a levitical city of the tribe of Gad. In the tribal inheritance, Ramoth-gilead was assigned to Gad and became both a levitical city and a city of refuge (Josh. 21:38; 1 Chron. 6:80; Deut. 4:43; Josh. 20:8). It was located east of the Jordan River in an area that later became the shifting border between Syria and Israel. During Solomon's reign it was a chief town of a tax district (1 Kings 4:13). King Ahab of Israel was killed there (1 Kings 22) and there the prophet Elisha anointed Jehu king of Israel (2 Kings 9:1–16). The precise location is unknown although two major possibilities are Tell el Husn near Irbid and Tell Ramith.

The latter is the more likely location and is situated further east near the current Jordanian-Syrian border. J.A.D.

ransom. ***See*** Redemption.

Rapha (ray'fuh; Heb., "he [God] has healed"), a clan head, the son of Benjamin (1 Chron. 8:2).

Ras-Shamra (rahs-shahm'rah), the modern Arabic name of the site of the ancient city of Ugarit. Ras-Shamra lies beside the Syrian coast of the Mediterranean Sea at roughly the northern latitude of Cyprus. Inscriptions from the site establish its identification as Ugarit. The name "Ugarit" perhaps means "field" (Ugaritic *ugar*) or the like. The existence of Ugarit was known prior to excavations at Ras-Shamra from reference to the city in an Amarna letter, but the importance of the site could not have been guessed apart from the work of archaeologists.

The site attracted the attention of archaeologists in 1928 when a peasant happened upon a thirteenth-century B.C. tomb. This discovery occurred at coastal Minet el-Beida (Arabic, "White Harbor"; Gk. *leukos limēn*) close to Ras-Shamra. The excavation of both sites began in 1929 under the direction of the French archaeologist C. F. A. Schaeffer. The excavation of Ras-Shamra has continued throughout this century, interrupted by World War II (1939–1947) and occasionally during the 1970s (by the Yom Kippur War, 1973). The *tell* or mound of Ras-Shamra is trapezoidal, with a maximum length of approximately 3,300 feet (1,000 m.) and a width of 1,650 feet (500 m.). A fresh-water stream flows to the Mediterranean Sea by Minet el-Beida.

Five Phases: The excavators of Ras-Shamra have divided its material remains into five major phases. A level of the remains of the site corresponds to each phase.

The earliest level is assigned the number V. According to radiocarbon data, its material belongs to the seventh and sixth millennia B.C. The first inhabitants of the location did not use pottery, although they possessed crude clay figurines of a sort usually associated with primitive fertility religion. Stone tools and weapons have been found in this level, and the site may have been surrounded by a crude wall.

Level IV at Ras-Shamra represents what archaeologists call the Chalcolithic Age (in the fifth millennium). The pottery from this level is similar to pottery found elsewhere in the Mediterranean, at first to the pottery of Cyprus, later to the pottery of Tell Halaf on the frontier between Syria and Turkey.

Level III begins with the decline of the Chalcolithic Age (ca. 3500 B.C.) and is followed by an intrusion of Ubaid culture. The intrusion ends abruptly. Ubaid culture seems to have spread from Mesopotamia. This level continues into the Early Bronze Age (ca. 3000 B.C.) and terminates after the appearance of "Khirbet Kerek" pottery, a type of pottery known also from ancient Palestine (ca. 2500 B.C.).

Level II encompasses remains dated to ca. 2100–1600 B.C. Egyptian artifacts are relatively common for this period; city life flourished at

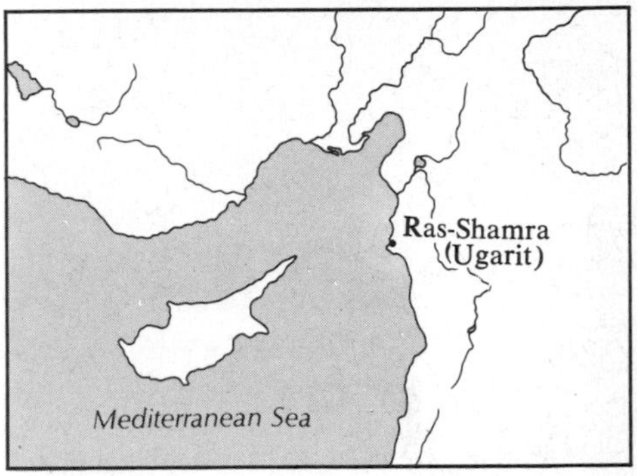

Ugarit, and two monumental temples, for Baal and Dagon, were built, perhaps on the site of earlier sanctuaries. In the latter part of this phase Ugarit suffered a decline associated with the era of the Hyksos in Egypt (ca. 1750–1550).

The final level of the tell (I) includes material from the Late Bronze Age (1500–1200 B.C.). To this level belong the cuneiform texts of Ras-Shamra as well as the imposing royal palace of Ugarit. The royal palace was one of the largest palaces of its day. This was the "golden" age of the city. It ended abruptly ca. 1200 B.C. in conjunction with the general movements of the Sea Peoples, invaders from Crete and other Greek islands (the Philistines among them), into the ancient Near East. No significant habitation occurred at Ras-Shamra after this period.

Cuneiform Texts: By far the most important discoveries at Ras-Shamra have been the deposits of cuneiform texts recovered from a number of locations on the tell. "Cuneiform" texts are so called because they are produced by impressing wedge-shaped marks (Lat. *cuneus*, "wedge") on clay. Allowed to harden or baked, these clay texts are durable and survive long after papyrus and other writing materials decay. At Ras-Shamra, a large number of cuneiform texts were written with symbols for syllables (syllabic cuneiform) in the Akkadian language. A second variety of text displayed a previously unknown script that proved to be alphabetic (alphabetic cuneiform). Quickly deciphered, thanks to the labors of linguists Charles Virrolleaud, Hans Bauer, and Eduard Dhorme, these alphabetic texts revealed a previously unknown Semitic language having affinities with biblical Hebrew. This language is now called Ugaritic.

Syllabic cuneiform texts have come primar-

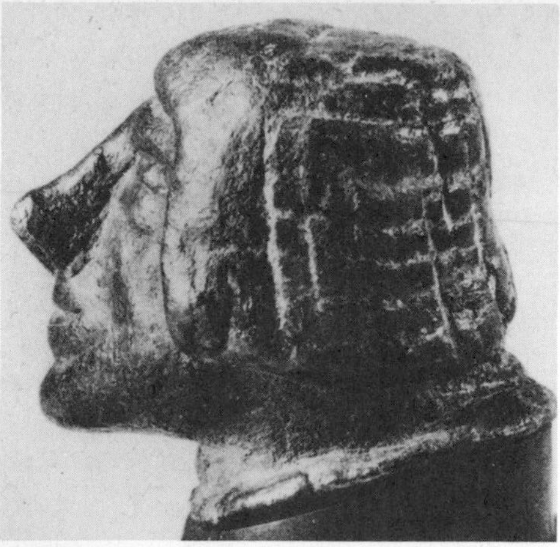

Weight in the form of a human head found at Ras-Shamra; thirteenth century B.C.

ily from the royal palace of Ugarit. They reveal the history, economy, society, and religion of the ancient city. Alphabetic texts have come from scattered spots on the tell including not only the royal palace, but also a priestly "library" in the vicinity of the Dagon and Baal temples. These texts sometimes treat daily matters, but among the alphabetic texts have been found fine literary works divisible roughly into the categories "myths" and "legends." The most important Ugaritic texts come from the fourteenth century B.C., although many scholars assume that a period of oral transmission preceded commitment of the literary works to writing. The Ugaritic texts have thrown extraordinary light on the OT. Composed as poetry, they exhibit stylistic devices known from the Hebrew Bible with a vocabulary cognate with that of the OT. They tell of the deeds of gods worshiped in Israel's environment (El, Baal, Asherah, Anat) and even reveal for the first time a legendary patriarch Danel known also in the OT ("Daniel"; Ezek. 14:14, 20; 28:3).

Ugarit at Its Height: At its height, Ugarit was a thriving city. The metropolis was the administrative center of a small kingdom that followed political tides and was subject at times to Egypt, at times to the Hittite Empire. Personal names reveal a diverse population in the kingdom, with a large Hurrian element. The countryside produced a variety of agricultural products—olive oil, grain, wines. Seafaring was important to the city; votive anchors have been recovered from its Baal temple.

Baal Zaphon was the chief god of the city, although in lists of gods he ranks below others. Alongside El, Baal plays an important role in the myths of Ugarit. Nonmythic texts reveal the veneration of a host of gods and goddesses. Of public ritual, very little is known directly. It is widely assumed that the affairs of the cult at Ugarit were coordinated with the concerns of the farmer. Private religion is still more difficult to reconstruct, although the existence at Ugarit of an institution called the *marzeah*, a type of funerary observance, is of interest because of a biblical reflection of it (Jer. 16:5). Mortuary concerns may have played an important role in the piety of ancient Ugarit's people. ***See also*** Amarna, Tell el-; Anat; Asherah; Baal; Dagon; Daniel; El; Writing.

Bibliography

Gray, John. *The Legacy of Canaan*. Leiden: E. J. Brill, 1957. R.M.G.

raven, a glossy black corvine bird. The Hebrew word translated "raven" *(orebh)* in the OT probably refers to the true raven *(Corvus corax)* as well as to other members of the crow family *(Corvidae)*, which includes the rook, the jay, the fan-tailed raven, the jackdaw, and the hooded crow. Although an object of God's care (Job 38: 41; Ps. 147:9; Luke 12:24), the raven is an unclean bird (Lev. 11:15; Deut. 14:14) mentioned for its habit of picking at the eyes of its prey (Prov. 30:17) and for its tendency to live in ruins (Isa. 34:11). In Gen. 8:7 Noah sends a raven out to look for land, and in 1 Kings 17:4 Elijah is fed by ravens. I.U.K.

Re (ray), or Ra (rah), the Egyptian sun god in his manifestation as the sun at its zenith. In Egyptian mythology Re was the son of the earth god Geb and the sky goddess Nut; his two children were the god of light, Shu, and the goddess of dew and moisture, Tefnut. Re journeyed across the sky each day in his solar bark (boat). The principal center of worship for Re was Heliopolis. Re is usually depicted as a man with a falcon's head surmounted by a sun disk. The cult of Re was sometimes combined with that of other deities to produce composite deities, e.g., Amun-Re or Re-Horakhty.

The worship of Re was intimately bound up with that of the pharaoh, who was considered the son of Re. The first king we know to have been officially called "son of Re" was Khafre (Gk. *Chephren*) in the fourth dynasty (ca. 2613–2494 B.C.); from the fifth dynasty (ca. 2494–2345 B.C.) on, Egyptian kings regularly claimed to be the son of this god. The throne name (also called the *prenomen*) of many pharaohs included the name of this god; e.g., *Nebmaatre*, "Re [is] the lord of truth," was the *prenomen* of Amenhotep III, while *Menkheperre*, "Established is the form of Re," was the *prenomen* of Thutmose III. The family name *Ramesses*, "Ramesses" meaning "Re is born," was held by no less than eleven kings of the nineteenth and twentieth dynasties (ca. 1293–1070 B.C.).

Although Re is not mentioned in the Bible, references to, or influences associated with, the cult of the sun god can be seen in several

The Egyptian sun god Re; bronze statue, Egypt, first millennium B.C.

places. For example, in Gen. 41:50 and 46:20, Joseph's wife, Asenath, is described as the daughter of Potipherah, a priest of On (Heliopolis; Gk., "City of the Sun"). In Mal. 4:2, the mention of a winged sun recalls the Egyptian motif of the winged sun disk, although this motif also occurs elsewhere in the ancient Near East. The biblical view that human beings were created in God's image (e.g., Gen. 1:26–27; 5:1) recalls a passage in a late third-millennium B.C. Egyptian text in which humankind is described as being created in the likeness of Re. Many scholars also think that certain words and phrases in Psalm 104 derive from the Hymn to Aton (a hymn of praise directed to the sun disk worshiped as a deity by the heretic pharaoh Akhenaton, who ruled Egypt in 1350–1334 B.C.); such parallels are probably due to concepts and motifs being passed on down through the years rather than to any direct relationship between these chronologically distinct texts. ***See also*** Akhenaton; Asenath.

J.M.W.

Reaiah (ree-ī'uh; Heb., "Yah [God] has seen"). **1** A descendant of Judah of the clan of the Zorathites (1 Chron. 4:2). **2** A descendant of Reuben (1 Chron. 5:5). **3** A family group ("sons of Reaiah") of Temple servants (Nethinim) who returned from the Babylonian captivity with Zerubbabel (Ezra 2:47; Neh. 7:50).

reaping, the harvesting of grain. The term is used figuratively for the final judgment (Matt. 13:24–30, 36–43; Rev. 14:15–16), evangelism (Matt. 9:37–38; Luke 10:2; John 4:35–36; Rom. 1:13), and recompense for good (Hos. 10:12; 2 Cor. 9:6; Gal. 6:7–8) or evil (Job 4:8; Prov. 22:8; Hos. 8:7; 10:13; Gal. 6:7–8). ***See also*** Farming.

Reba (ree'buh), one of the five kings of Midian killed by the Israelites (Num. 31:8). His territory was assigned later to the tribe of Reuben (Josh. 13:21).

Rebekah (re-bek'uh), the wife of Isaac, the daughter of Bethuel (Abraham's nephew), the sister of Laban, and the mother of Jacob and Esau. Genesis 24 recounts how Abraham's servant came to his homeland to find a wife for Isaac, and how (in response to prayer) he found Rebekah at the well and she brought him home. Similar stories about Rachel (Gen. 29:9–12) and Zipporah (Exod. 2:16–20) indicate that girls could be found at the wells and were not enjoined from talking to strange men. The negotiations for Rebekah's marriage were carried out by her brother Laban, an indication that Bethuel was old or infirm. Because of this and the curious episode in Gen. 26:6–11, in which Isaac claimed that Rebekah was his sister, some scholars have suggested that Rebekah entered into a special type of marriage, the "wife-sister" marriage, which conferred special status on the wife; others have contested this interpretation.

Rebekah was barren for twenty years, but conceived the twins Jacob and Esau after Isaac interceded with God. During her pregnancy she received an oracle that the twins would beget separate nations, and that Jacob would be dominant despite Esau's status as firstborn (Gen. 25:20–26; cf. Rom. 9:10–13). Jacob was clearly Rebekah's favorite, and she instigated the plot by which she covered Jacob's arms and neck with goatskins and sent him in to impersonate the firstborn Esau so that he would get Isaac's blessing (Gen. 27:1–29); she then convinced Isaac to send Jacob to his kinspeople to find a wife in order to take him out of the path of Esau's anger (Gen. 27:41–28:5). Nothing more is known about Rebekah other than the fact that she was buried in the Cave of Machpelah (Gen. 49:31). The only story about Rebekah and Isaac that does not deal with the succession of the patriarchs is the tale about Isaac pretending that Rebekah was his sister in the land of Abimelech, the king of Gerar (Gen. 26:6–11), which is a doublet of the story of Abraham and Sarah in Gerar (Gen. 20).

T.S.F.

rebirth. ***See*** Conversion; Regeneration.

receipt of custom, ASV translation for revenue or tax office, the place where tolls or customs taxes were paid (Matt. 9:9; Mark 2:14; Luke 5: 27). ***See also*** Tribute, Tax, Toll.

Rechab (ree'kab). **1** The son of Rimmon who, with his brother Baanah, was a captain of Ishbosheth's bands. After Abner's death, the two brothers murdered Ishbosheth and brought his head to David, whom they expected to be pleased; instead, he had them executed (2 Sam. 4). **2** An ancestor of Jehonadab (Jonadab), a Kenite (1 Chron. 2:55) who supported Jehu's coup (2 Kings 10:15). Toward the end of Jehu's monarchy (ca. 816 B.C.), a group of his followers called "Rechabites" came to Jerusalem to escape Nebuchadnezzar's invasion. They apparently lived in tents, avoided agriculture, and drank no wine in accordance with the principles of Jehonadab. Jeremiah cited them as an example of fidelity to prior commitments, in contrast to the unfaithful Judeans. Although Judah had therefore to be punished for her infidelity, Jeremiah assured the Rechabites that there would always be a descendant of Jonadab (Jer. 35). ***See also*** Abner; Ishbosheth; Nazirites. F.E.G.

reconciliation (Gk. *katallagē*), a term indicating the changed relationship for the better between persons or groups who formerly were at enmity with each other. The NT encourages reconciliation between estranged parties (Matt. 5:24; Luke 12:58) and spouses (1 Cor. 7:11). But the noun and its corresponding verb most often refer to the new relationship between God and humanity effected by Christ's redemptive work (Rom. 5:10–11; 11:15; 2 Cor. 5:17–20; Eph. 2:16; Col. 1:20, 22).

For Paul the subject of the reconciling activity is always God "who through Christ reconciled us to himself" (2 Cor. 5:18). There is no need for God to be reconciled to humanity as appears in 2 Macc. 1:5; 7:33; and 8:29. To the contrary, humanity stands in need of reconciliation with God. Paul describes the human condition prior to reconciliation as weak, ungodly, and sinful (Rom. 5:6–8; cf. Eph. 2:12). But it was precisely when we were enemies that God reconciled us to himself (Rom. 5:10).

God effected this reconciliation through the death of his Son upon the cross (Rom 5:10; 2 Cor. 5:19; Col. 1:22). At other times Paul specifies this further by speaking of the "blood of Christ" (Eph. 2:13) and the "blood of the cross" (Col. 1: 20). The immediate effect of reconciliation is "peace with God" (Rom. 5:1; Eph. 2:14) so that Christians can view themselves as a "new creation" (2 Cor. 5:17). The scope of reconciliation, however, goes beyond God and the individual. The world is also affected by Christ's redemptive work (2 Cor. 5:19; Rom. 11:15). In Colossians this reconciliation takes on cosmic proportions (1:20), and in Eph. 2:11 it results in a new relationship between Jew and Gentile. Although the work of reconciliation belongs to God, Paul views his ministry as one of reconciliation and himself as an ambassador for Christ inviting others to receive this reconciliation (2 Cor. 5:18–20). ***See also*** Justification; Peace; Redemption; Salvation. F.J.M.

red, the color of healthy blood or a ruby stone. In biblical usage it is the color of the earth from which Adam was made (Gen. 2:7; the letters for "Adam" in Hebrew can also mean "ruby," and "dust" can also mean "reddish in color"), the color of Esau at birth (Gen. 25:25), the color of pottage (Gen. 25:30), of drunken eyes (Gen. 49: 12), of cattle (Num. 19:2), of blood (2 Kings 3: 22), of weeping faces (Job 16:16), of wine (Prov. 23:31), of sin (Isa. 1:18), of clothing (Isa. 63:1–2), of horses (Zech. 1:8; 6:2), of threatening skies (Matt. 16:3), and of the apocalyptic dragon (Rev. 12:3). In Christian liturgical practice, red is the color of martyrs and festivals. ***See also*** Scarlet. R.S.B.

redaction criticism. ***See*** Biblical Criticism.

redeemer, one who buys back a property or house that has been sold; or, a kinsman who buys back a family member who has fallen into slavery (Lev. 25:25–34, 47–55). In the OT, the term is applied in its latter meaning to God (Job 19:25; Pss. 19:14; 78:35; Prov. 23:11; Isa. 41:14; 43:14; 54:5; 60:16; Jer. 50:34). It is never used of Jesus Christ, although the term "redemption" is applied to him (e.g., 1 Cor. 1:30). ***See also*** Redemption.

redemption, a term associated in current English usage with a transaction involving the release of an item (or person) in exchange for some type of payment. This association is not at all foreign to biblical understandings of redemption. The contexts of usage in the OT and the NT, however, add important dimensions that help in grasping the theological implications of the concept.

In the OT: In the OT, three different Hebrew roots are used to express the idea of redemption. The first is a technical legal term and is applied to the redemption of inheritance, of family members from servitude or difficulties, of tithes, or of various objects and property (e.g., Lev. 25:25, 47–49; 27:15–20; Ruth 4:1–6; Ps. 72:4, 14; Jer. 32:1–15). Often without great distinction from the first, a second root is used of the redemption of the firstborn among male children (or even of animals) by means of some payment or offering (e.g., Num. 3:45–51; 18:15–16). Where offenses and conflicts are involved, redemption can also be achieved through payment of money (e.g., Exod. 21:8, 30). Specialized usage in cases of the shedding of blood (e.g., Num. 35:12, 19) and of God acting in a redemptive manner toward his people (e.g., Exod. 6:6; 15:13; Deut. 7:8; 1 Chron. 17:21; Pss. 19:14; 25:22; 106:10; Isa. 41:14; 43: 1–4; 44:21–23; 24–28; Hos. 13:14) or toward individuals in difficult or life-threatening situations (e.g., Gen. 48:16; 2 Sam. 4:9; Job 19:25; Pss. 26:11; 49:15; 69:18; 103:4) can also be found. These first two Hebrew roots are therefore somewhat synonymous, although the former is favored by certain writers (the authors of some of the psalms and Isa. 40–55, sometimes called Second Isaiah), while the latter is preferred, it would seem, by others (the authors of Deuteronomy and certain other psalms).

The specialized theological notion of redemption tends to gravitate around the third root, which is frequently used where God's relationship to his people as a whole is reestablished or restored after acts of rebellion, disobedience, or infidelity. This third root is often translated as "ransom" (e.g., Ps. 49:7–8; Exod. 21:30) or "redeem" (Ps. 130:8; in Amos 5:12, it is "bribe") and carries the sense of "atonement."

In the NT: This theological sense is the one reflected in Christian traditions and appropriated somewhat differently by NT writers. Here, the center of gravity for the notion is the profound human need for deliverance and freedom in matters of ultimate destiny and the meaning of life (e.g., Rom. 5:9; 6:6; 7:6; 8:2; cf. also 1 Cor. 2: 6; Gal. 5:4; Heb. 2:14–15). Presupposed is the idea that alienation and bondage (i.e., sin) are endemic to the human condition and have far-reaching consequences. The frame of reference and goal of redemption is the salvation of God's creation. Here, the Creator becomes the Redeemer of his creatures. The redemption is represented as having been accomplished exclusively in the sacrificial death of Jesus of Nazareth (e.g., Rom. 3:23–25a; 8:23; 1 Cor. 1:30; Eph. 1:7, 14; 4: 30; Col. 1:14; Heb. 9:15; 1 Cor. 6:20; 7:23; Gal. 3: 13; 4:5; 1 Pet. 1:18–19; Rev. 5:9; 14:4). The proclamation of this redemption is based on Jesus' own reported understanding of the significance of the impending death of the Son of man (Mark 10:45; Matt. 20:28; cf. also Mark 8:31 and parallels), the verification of that understanding in his resurrection from the dead (1 Cor. 15:3–7; 1 Pet. 1:18–21), and the assurance expressed in the phrase "on our behalf" and related formulas of early Christian reflection, missionary preaching, and worship (e.g., Mark 10:45; 1 Tim. 2:6; Titus 2:14; Matt. 26:28; Mark 14:24; 1 Cor. 11:24; also 1 Cor. 15:3–7).

While the origins of the notion of redemption in the NT are to be traced to OT theological concepts, it would be a mistake to see the relationship strictly in terms of the history of ideas. In the NT, the starting point is the stark reality of Jesus' death; to this are added interpretive features from OT traditions (cf. Luke 1:68, 74; 24:21) and from the earliest strata of the traditions about Jesus' ministry. That writers such as Paul were also influenced by considerations from life in the first century (e.g., human bondage and the manumission of slaves) is extremely likely. ***See also*** Atonement; Expiation; Forgiveness; Liberty; Pardon; Reconciliation; Regeneration; Salvation; Sin; Slavery. J.E.A.

redemption of land, in the Israelite legal codes (Lev. 25:23–34) the right of Israelite landowners to regain property that had been sold. The land was considered as belonging to God and therefore the inheritances granted to the tribes divinely ordained; the laws of redemption were designed to protect the poor by keeping family inheritances intact. Provisions were made for various means through which the land could be reclaimed: the kinsman-redeemer could purchase the land (cf. Jer. 32:6–15; Ruth 4:1–4), the original owner could buy it back (Lev. 25:26–27; cf. vv. 14–16), or it would automatically revert to the previous owner every fifty years (the Jubilee Year; Lev. 25:10, 13, 28). ***See also*** Feasts, Festivals, and Fasts; Ownership; Redemption. D.R.B.

Red Sea, the narrow sea between Africa and Arabia, part of the Great Rift Valley system, about 1,450 miles (2,330 km.) long and averaging about 150 miles (240 km.) wide. The constricted southern exit through the straits of Bab el-Mandeb opens into the Indian Ocean, and the northern end divides around the Sinai peninsula, with the Gulf of Aqabah on the east and the Gulf of Suez on the west. Enclosed between hot deserts, the summer water temperature reaches eighty-five degrees Fahrenheit (29° C.).

Dangerous coral reefs and powerful north winds make navigation difficult, but trade along it was important from a very early date. How early is unknown, but the Egyptian queen Hatshepsut certainly used it for her expedition to Punt in the mid-fifteenth century B.C. Whether the Edomites utilized it to supplement their important land trade is uncertain, but King Solomon undoubtedly maintained a

The Red Sea, with the tip of the Sinai peninsula at bottom.

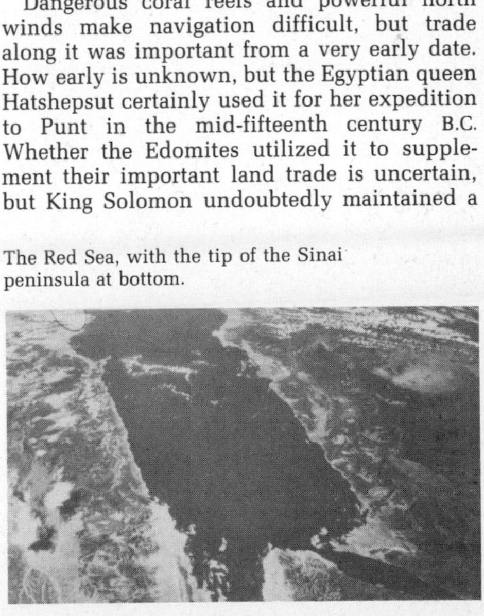

fleet at Ezion-geber on the Gulf of Aqabah, a fleet that made triennial journeys to south Arabia and east Africa (1 Kings 9:26–28; 10:11, 22). Jehoshaphat of Judah later attempted to do likewise, but his ships were destroyed (1 Kings 22:48).

A major problem concerns the meaning of "Red Sea" in the Exodus story, since we cannot identify the various places mentioned in that account. The Hebrew term for the Red Sea is always *yam suph,* literally "Sea of Reeds," but the Hebrews did not distinguish between "sea" and "lake." Three possible routes for the Exodus have been suggested: the southern route at, or close to, the Gulf of Suez; the central route across the marshes of Lake Timsah, now part of the Suez Canal; and the northern route, identifying *yam suph* with Lake Bardawil and assuming the Israelites followed the narrow spit of land dividing the lake from the Mediterranean. No one of these suggestions, however, has won general acceptance. ***See also*** Edom; Exodus; Jehoshaphat; Sinai; Solomon. D.B.

reed, a general term referring to tall hollow grasses growing in shallow water by streams, rivers, lakes, and marshes throughout the Holy Land. It may be identified as any one of several common plants. The giant reed *(Arundo donax)* grows to over 10 feet high forming dense thickets along lake margins (Job 40:21). Reed mace or cattail (genus *Typha),* topped by a cylindrical brown spike, is often depicted as the mock scepter of Jesus in Matt. 27:29–30. The common reed *(Phragmites communis)* sports dense purple plumes atop its tall stems which move gracefully in the wind (Matt. 11:7).

Common reed.

The tall, sturdy stems of these grasses had diverse uses. The jagged edges of the broken stems were capable of piercing flesh (2 Kings 18:21) and may have been used as fishing spears. They are sturdy enough to have been used as a walking stick (Ezek. 29:7). Reeds were also effective as makeshift flutes, pens (3 John 13; 3 Macc. 4:20), and even as a form of measuring rod (Ezek. 40:3). ***See also*** Flags; Rush. P.L.C.

refining, the process of removing impurities from metal ore. Two verbs in Hebrew are employed metaphorically for the cleansing or purifying of persons or things either by filtering or washing, or by burning or smelting. When referring to metalworking, the process is that of melting a solid to a liquid in order to remove the dross (Isa. 1:25; Mal. 3:3), or to a process of burning in which the fire helps in the extraction of metal from an ore by enhancing chemical reactions (Isa. 48:10; Jer. 6:29; 9:6; Ps. 12:6). Copper smelting was practiced early by the Hebrews using pottery crucibles or by heating ore with charcoal in a furnace. Refining by smelting is known from Timna in the Arabah and other sites, e.g., Gerar, Rumeileh, Tel Qasile near Tel Aviv, Abu Matar near Beer-sheba. In 1 Peter, the refining of gold is used as a metaphor for the stronger faith that emerges after persecution (1: 7). ***See also*** Furnace; Mines; Smith. R.A.C.

refuge, a place of safety or protection from enemies. Six of the levitical cities were designated as cities of refuge (Josh. 20:7–9) where one who accidently caused a death might seek asylum from avengers until his case could be judged by the elders of the city. If he was found to be innocent of deliberate murder, he could continue to live in sanctuary in the city of refuge (Num. 35:6–28; Deut. 19:1–13). God is often portrayed as a refuge or shelter for humanity, most frequently in psalms (Pss. 7:1; 11:1; 46:1; 2 Sam. 22:3; Isa. 25:4; Jer. 16:19; Heb. 6:18). ***See also*** Avenger; Cities; Priests. D.R.B.

regeneration (Lat., "rebirth"), a term associated with human hopes and longings for the dawn of a new day, the establishment of a better world, and the creation of a new humanity. The term and concept were prominent in the Hellenistic world of the first century A.D. For biblical writers, the hope of regeneration is linked to faith in the Creator, who is understood as the source of new creation through the power of his word and the work of his Spirit. These writers have very little confidence in human potential for self-regeneration.

Although the term "regeneration" does not occur in the OT, the OT prophets focused attention on an appointed hour in the future when God would make all things new, reconstitute human disposition, make resistant hearts supple, renew his covenant, and refresh spirits through the outpouring of his Spirit (e.g., Isa. 65:17–25; 66:22; Jer. 31:31–34; 32:38–41; Ezek. 36:25–28; 37:1–14; Hos. 6:1–2; Joel 2:26–32; Zech. 13:1; cf. also Ps. 51:10–12). With this appointed day, the radical renewal of God's people would dawn; God's promises of judgment and blessing/salvation would be fulfilled.

NT writers declare that this day has dawned in the life (e.g., Matt. 10:7–8; 11:4–6; 12:28; 18:3; Luke 4:18–19), death, and resurrection of Jesus. The technical terms for "regeneration" are found in a few key texts, all of which are relatively late. God causes us to be "born anew," we are "born anew [by God]" (1 Pet. 1:3, 23; cf. 2:2); God "saved us . . . by the washing of regeneration" (Titus 3:5); it is necessary to be "born from above" (John 3:3, 7; cf. also 1:13; 3:5–6, 8; 1 John 3:9; 5:1–12; James 1:18, 21; for the translation "above" rather than "anew," cf. John 3:31; 19:11, 23). These are the classical locations for this terminology, but the scope of importance of regeneration in the NT is not limited to them.

Language regarding new creation and a new eschatological (promised end-time) existence dominates the fundamental orientation of all NT preaching and writing. The locus of this orientation is the resurrection of Jesus; the new creation has dawned with the dawn of Easter (e.g., Rom. 6:3–14; 8:10–17; 12:2; 1 Cor. 12:13–14; 2 Cor. 1:20–22; 3:18; 4:16; 5:17; 6:16–18; 13:3, 5; Gal. 2:19–21; 3:27–29; 6:15; Eph. 2:10, 15–16; 4:24; Col. 2:12–15; 3:1–12; Heb. 10:22; 1 Pet. 1:3–5; Rev. 1:5–6). The means through which this new reality becomes the new existence for human beings is articulated variously and with different emphases. It is imparted through the power of God's word and his Spirit, received through faith, experienced sacramentally (baptism and the Eucharist), is lived out in the obedience of responsible living, and is in constant conflict with the old existence (a future resolution of this conflict is a dimension of hope; e.g., Rom. 7:14–25; 8:21–25; cf. also Matt. 19:28–30).

Here, as elsewhere, early Christianity conducted an earnest conversation not only with its OT heritage but also with the popular religion and philosophy of its environment. Then, as now, the hope for regeneration and renewal cut a deep and wide furrow in the hearts and minds of people everywhere. ***See also*** Conversion; Eschatology; Holy Spirit, The; Mystery; Redemption; Salvation; Word. J.E.A.

Rehabiah (ree-huh-bī'uh; Heb., "Yah [God] has enlarged"), the son of Eliezer and grandson of Moses and the head of a large family group (1 Chron. 23:17; 24:21).

Rehob (ree'hohb; Heb., "broad, wide." Rehob in personal names is shortened from something like "[God] made room, saved"). **1** The father of Hadadezer, king of Zobah, an Aramaean city-state north of Damascus (2 Sam. 8:3, 12). **2** A Levite of the time of Nehemiah (Neh. 10:11). **3** A site in upper Galilee (Num. 13:21). **4** A place in the plain of Accho of the tribe of Asher (Josh. 19:28, 30; 21:31; Judg. 1:31; 1 Chron. 6:75). **5** A place in Beth-shean (2 Sam. 10:8).

Rehoboam (ree-huh-boh'uhm; KJV and NT: "Roboam"), the son of Solomon by Naamah, an Ammonite princess (1 Kings 14:31). He was successor to his father as the last king of the United Monarchy and the first king of Judah after the northern tribes revolted against his rule under Jeroboam I, who was made their king. There is some uncertainty about the chronology for Rehoboam's reign. He is said to have become king when he was forty-one and to have ruled for seventeen years (1 Kings 14:21; 2 Chron. 13:7). His reign has been variously dated as starting in 937, 933, or 926 B.C., the last of which would date Rehoboam's reign as 926–910 B.C. The basic biblical narratives concerning Rehoboam are found in 1 Kings 11:43; 12:1–24; 14:21–31; and 2 Chron. 9:31–12:16.

Rehoboam's accession to the throne came under very difficult political circumstances. Solomon's policies of forced labor and high taxation to support his greatly expanded court and administrative apparatus had created a good deal of popular unrest. Added to this was his attempt at breaking up tribal loyalties by the creation, in order to facilitate tax collection, of twelve administrative districts that basically disregarded the old tribal borders. The growing resentment against such policies erupted after Solomon's death, on the occasion of Rehoboam's aborted coronation at Shechem. Rehoboam rejected the counsel of his older mentors who advised easing the people's tax burden and went instead with the guidance of his contemporaries who counseled the continuance of the policies of his father. Upon hearing this message from Rehoboam, the northern tribes revolted and instituted their own monarchy. Rehoboam unsuccessfully attempted to put down the revolt (1 Kings 12:18, 21, 24).

After the division, Rehoboam instigated border warfare against Israel (1 Kings 12:21–24; 14:30; 2 Chron. 12:15), apparently in an attempt to clear the approaches to his capital city. The threatened nature of Rehoboam's kingdom is reflected in his construction of a line of fortresses around Judah (2 Chron. 11:5–10), which may have been built either before Pharaoh Shishak's invasion or in response to it. The line ran south of Jerusalem along the central ridge, turning west south of Hebron, continued northward through the Shephelah to Aijalon, where it turned back toward Jerusalem. The sixteen stations in the line are little more than three miles apart, and the area enclosed does not include the coastal plain, with its trade routes and access to the Mediterranean, nor the plain of Beer-sheba.

Rehoboam's reign saw the Palestinian campaign of Pharaoh Shishak I ("Sheshonk," 1 Kings 14:25–28; 2 Chron. 12:2–9), founder of the twenty-second dynasty in Egypt. This invasion, which occurred in ca. 920 B.C., in Jeroboam's fifth year, included the hill country, the coastal plain, and the Negeb. The biblical account only mentions the pharaoh's assault upon Judah, but Shishak's version, on the wall of the temple at Karnak, shows 156 captives, each representing a Palestinian city, most in Israel. The section of the inscription that apparently lists sites in Judah, however, is very poorly preserved. This raid illustrates the military weakness caused by the division of the Hebrew kingdom, which resulted in such widespread destruction only five years after the death of Solomon. This destruction has been confirmed to some extent by the results of archaeology, especially at Tell Beit Mirsim, Lachish, and Beer-sheba. According to 1 Kings 14:25–28, Shishak came up against Jerusalem, and many of the treasures of the Temple and palace had to be handed over as ransom.

From the perspective of the Chronicler (2 Chron. 12:5), Shishak's invasion came as retribution for Rehoboam's infidelity to God. 1 Kings 14:22–24 provides a list of his apostasies, many of which reflect the pagan influences introduced by Solomon. The author of Chronicles (2 Chron. 11:18–22) includes a section on Rehoboam's family, somewhat problematic material without parallel in Kings, which says that he had eighteen wives, sixty concubines, twenty-eight sons, and sixty daughters. ***See also*** Jeroboam I; Shishak.

Bibliography

Malamat, A. "Origins of Statecraft in the Israelite Monarchy." *The Biblical Archaeologist* 28 (1965):34–65.

F.S.F.

Rehoboth (ray'hoh-bohth), a place name in the OT. Isaac's servants dug a well and called it Rehoboth (Heb., "broad places"), because they found respite from their quarrels over water rights with the herdsmen of Gerar (Gen. 26:22). The site is most often identified with modern Ruheibeh, southwest of Beer-sheba. Rehoboth-on-the-River is the home of Shaul (Gen. 36:37; 1 Chron. 1:48), one of the early kings of Edom (Gen. 36:31). The River is possibly the Brook Zered (modern Wadi el-Ḥasā) rather than the Euphrates. The site itself is unidentified. Rehoboth-Ir (Gen. 10:11) is probably not the name of a city in northern Mesopotamia but a description of Nineveh. ***See also*** Beer-sheba; Gerar; Isaac; Nineveh; Zered, The Brook. B.M.

Rehoboth-ir (re-hoh'bohth-eer'; Heb., "[the] open places of [the] city," or "city-plazas," as, e.g., in Lam. 2:12). A place built by Nimrod (in Gen. 10:11). It is thus to be interpreted either as an otherwise unknown city between Nineveh and Calah or as a district of Nineveh. There are similar Akkadian expressions that support the latter interpretation.

Rehum (ree'huhm). **1** Apparently one of eleven leaders of groups returning from Exile (Ezra 2:2; Neh. 7:7 has "Nehum"). **2** "Commander," "high commissioner" (NEB), one of the officials sending accusation against the Jews rebuilding Jerusalem (Ezra 4:8–23). This led Artaxerxes to stop the work. This narrative cannot be dated; it is often assumed to precede the activity of Nehemiah. **3** A Levite, son of Bani, sharing in the repair of the wall under Nehemiah (Neh. 3:17; perhaps also Neh. 10:25), a "chief of the people" and signatory to the Covenant (Neh. 9:38). **4** A priest or priestly clan associated with Zerubbabel and Jeshua, perhaps an error for Harim (Neh. 12:3; cf. 12:15). ***See also*** Artaxerxes; Nehemiah, The Book of; Zerubbabel. P.R.A.

Rei (ray'ee; Heb., probably "the Lord is a friend"), a member of David's court who remained loyal during the conspiracy of Adonijah (1 Kings 1:8).

Rekem (ray'kuhm). **1** A Midianite king slain with four others by the Israelites on their way to Canaan (Num. 31:8; Josh. 13:21). **2** An eponymous ancestor of a Calebite family that was associated with the man Hebron (1 Chron. 2:43–44). **3** An eponymous ancestor (Rakem) of one of the Machir clans in Gilead (1 Chron. 7:16). **4** A town in the territory of the tribe of Benjamin (Josh. 18:27).

Release, Year of, an ancient Israelite institution by which Hebrew slaves would be released in the seventh year after their purchase (Exod. 21:2–6; Jer. 34:8–15). According to the legal tradition in Lev. 25:47–55, the Hebrew slave could be redeemed through payments by relations or released during the Jubilee Year. ***See also*** Hebrews; Jubilee; Sabbatical Year.

religion, religious, the English translations of various Greek terms appearing only in Acts, Colossians, the Gospel of John, the pastoral Letters, James, and 2 Peter (i.e., in the later writings of the NT). The root occurring in Acts 17:22 (RSV: "very religious") and Acts 25:19 (RSV: "superstition") was commonly used in Hellenistic culture for observances offered to a deity. A second root is used in Acts 26:5 of Jewish observances and customs (RSV: "religion"), in Col. 2:18 of the "worship" of angels, and in James 1:26–27 of proper conduct toward others. The third root is found most frequently in the pastoral Letters and is variously translated in the RSV as "religion" (1 Tim. 3:16; 5:4; 2 Tim. 3:5; Titus 2:10), "godliness" or "godly" (1 Tim. 2:2; 4:7, 8; 6:3,

5, 6; Tit. 1:1; 2:12; 2 Pet. 1:3, 6; 2:9; 3:11), "piety" (Acts 3:12), "devout" (Acts 10:2, 7), or "worship" or "worshiper" (Acts 10:23; John 9:31); this root refers both to the Christian message and to proper conduct. ***See also*** Godliness, Godly; Worship. J.W.T.

Remaliah (rem-uh-lī'uh), the father of Pekah, an official of King Pekahiah of Israel (i.e., Northern Kingdom) who assassinated the king and took the throne (2 Kings 15:25; Isa. 7:1).

remnant, the portion left over after a part has been removed. Thus, it may refer to vegetation (Exod. 10:5) or human and animal life (Gen. 7:23). It often refers to that element of a community that has escaped death or exile (Jer. 24:8; Ezra 9:13–15).

In biblical thought, the remnant has been or will be saved and redeemed by God. This concept is frequently mentioned in prophetic writings since it is the obverse of the idea that God will punish the sinning people with near total destruction (cf. 1 Kings 19:15–18). Thus, Amos speaks of a nonviable or pitiful remnant in his prophecies of rebuke (3:12; 5:3; 6:9; 7:1–6; 9:1; cf. 1:8), although if the people repent, destruction of "the remnant of Joseph" may be avoided (5:14–15). This concept becomes significant in Isaiah, where a "remnant will return" to both God in repentance and the land in redemption (Isa. 7:3; 10:20–22; 11:10–16; 17:5–8; 28:5; 30:17–19; 37:4, 31–32; cf. 6:13). In Micah, "remnant" is already a term meaning "those who will be redeemed" (4:6–7; 5:2–8; cf. 2:12; 7:18–20). This understanding is evident also in Joel 3:5 (cf. Obad. 17). In Zephaniah, the righteous remnant of Israel will be redeemed (3:11–20; cf. 2:3, 7, 9).

Jeremiah's prophecies of rebuke are very harsh—they depict no surviving remnant (Jer. 6:9; 11:21–23; 15:9) or a terrible destiny for the survivors (8:3; 24:8–10). However, in his prophecies of hope, Jeremiah assures redemption to the "remnant of my flock" (23:3–4) who were led astray by their rulers (vv. 1–2). Also, God will save the "remnant of Israel" (31:7), but if the "remnant of Judah" after the Babylonian destruction emigrates to Egypt, they will forfeit God's mercies and be destroyed (42:9–22).

Similarly, Ezekiel, too, portrays the destruction of even the remnant of Judah (5:1–4, 8–17; 9:4–10). However, his cry "Ah, Lord God! Will you make a complete end of the remnant of Israel" (11:13) evokes a prophecy of redemption (vv. 14–22). The postexilic community identified themselves as the remnant (Hag. 1:12, 14; 2:2; Ezra 9:13–15; Neh. 1:2–3; 7:72). Zechariah promises the remnant a life of peace and prosperity (8:1–15), but they must adhere to moral behavior (vv. 16–17).

It is not surprising that the Qumran community, which saw themselves as the last wave of the returning exiles from Babylon, identified themselves as the "remnant" (CD 1:4–5; 1QH 6:8). So too the apostle Paul, citing prophecies from Hosea and Isaiah (Rom. 9:25–29), finally concludes that those Jews who follow Christ constitute the true remnant, "chosen by grace" (11:5). ***See also*** Prophet. J.U.

repentance, a word covering several biblical ideas that range from regret to changing one's mind or behavior so as to bring about a moral or ethical conversion. Thus in the OT God can repent (Heb. *naham*) in the sense of regret that he has made Saul king (1 Sam. 15:11). The most important aspect of OT repentance, however, is contained in the Hebrew word *shub*, which expresses the idea of turning back, retracing one's steps in order to return to the right way.

In the early stages of Israelite history, the nation was more conscious of its collective guilt than of its individual guilt. In times of national catastrophe, therefore, it celebrated cultic liturgies of repentance that included an assembly of the people, fasting, lamentation, and the confession of sin. The prophets of the eighth century B.C., however, and those who followed, leveled a strong criticism against merely cultic and liturgical repentance. Amos complains that the people did not turn to the Lord (4:6, 8, 9, 10, 11). Hosea, after describing a liturgy of repentance (6:1–3), says that Israel's love "is like a morning cloud, like the dew that goes early away" (6:4). Isaiah pleads for social justice rather than empty ritual (1:10–17; cf. 58:5–7; Amos 5:21–24). The prophets, therefore, insist upon an interior conversion manifested in justice, kindness, and humility (Mic. 6:6–8). Jeremiah calls upon Israel to acknowledge its guilt (3:11–14) and Ezekiel brings the notion of individual responsibility to a climax (3:16–21; 18; 33:10–20). For all of their harshness, however, the prophets also hold out hope to Israel. Jeremiah and Ezekiel look to a day when God will place a new heart within his people (Jer. 24:7; Ezek. 36:26–31) and Isaiah promises forgiveness to those who will repent (1:18–19).

In the NT the notion of repentance as turning to the Lord (Heb. *shub*) is expressed in the Greek verb *metanoein*. The idea is slightly modified, however, inasmuch as the Greek includes the concept of changing one's mind, coming to a new way of thinking. John the Baptist is the immediate successor of the prophets. Like them he calls the people to repentance and demands proof of authentic conversion (Matt. 3:9–10); his preaching leads to forgiveness of sins (Mark 1:4; Luke 3:3). Yet John's message also differs from that of the prophets inasmuch as his call for repentance is intimately connected to the imminent arrival of God's Kingdom and the coming of the Messiah (Matt. 3:2, 11–12; Luke 3:15–17). Moreover, John seals this repentance with a baptism of water.

Jesus' call to repentance is also closely linked to the arrival of the Kingdom (Mark 1: 14–15). The summons to conversion, moreover, is associated with his own person so that a decision for or against him signifies a choice for or against repentance (Matt. 11:20–24; 12: 41–42). In the eyes of Jesus all are sinners and in need of repentance (13:1–5). He comes to call sinners and not the just (Luke 5:32), and he tells parables that promise God's forgiveness to those who recognize their sinfulness (Luke 15; 18:9–14).

Paul rarely employs the term repentance (Rom. 2:4; 2 Cor. 7:9, 10) and John never does. Both authors presuppose it, however, in their concepts of faith, which demand a turning away from sin. Although the author of Hebrews seems to suggest that there cannot be a second repentance (6:4–6), the author of Revelation calls the seven churches to repentance (2:5, 16; 3:3, 19). The general tradition of the NT, therefore, is that repentance is an ongoing affair. ***See also*** Faith; Jesus Christ; John the Baptist; Justice; Kingdom of God; Prophet.

Bibliography

Eichrodt, Walter. *Theology of the Old Testament*, vol. 2. Philadelphia: Fortress, 1967.

Jeremias, Joachim. *New Testament Theology: The Proclamation of Jesus*. New York: Scribner, 1971.

Von Rad, Gerhard. *The Message of the Prophets*. New York: Harper & Row, 1967.

F.J.M.

Rephaiah (ref-ay'yuh; Heb., "Yah [God] heals"). **1** A descendant of Judah in the royal lineage of the kings of Judah (1 Chron. 3:21); the text is not clear whether this is an individual or a family group. **2** One of the leaders of the Simeonite clan of Ishi who drove out the Amalekites and settled on Mount Seir (Edom; 1 Chron. 4: 42). **3** The grandson of Issachar and a leader in the clan of Tola (1 Chron. 7:2). **4** A Benjaminite descendant of Saul (1 Chron. 9:43); he is also called Raphah (1 Chron. 8:37). **5** An official of postexilic Jerusalem who helped repair the city walls (Neh. 3:9). D.R.B.

Rephaim (ref'ay-im), a noun appearing in three contexts in the Bible. **1** Those who are dead and inhabit Sheol, "shades" (Ps. 88:10), "dead" (Prov. 9:18). **2** Pre-Israelite inhabitants of Transjordan (Gen. 14:5; Deut. 2:10–11). **3** "Giants" from Philistia (1 Chron. 20:4, 6, 8; 2 Sam. 21:16,18, 20). The relationship between these three uses is obscure.

Rephaim (ref'ay-im), **Valley of,** the broad valley or plain southwest of Jerusalem, modern Baqa. It was named after some early inhabitants of Palestine: thus "Valley of Giants" in the KJV (Josh. 15:8; 18:16; cf. Septuagint and Josephus [*Antiquities* 7.4.1]).

The boundary between the tribal lands of Judah and Benjamin went up the Hinnom Valley from Jerusalem, passing the northern end of the Valley of Rephaim, to the Waters of Nephtoah (springs of Lifta today), northwest of Jerusalem (Josh. 15:8; 18:16). The Philistines encamped in the Valley of Rephaim and David met them there in battle (2 Sam. 5:18, 22; 23: 13). It was known for its fertility (Isa. 17:5). N.L.L.

Rephidim (re'fi-dim), a stopping place for the Israelites after they left the Wilderness of Sin but before they reached the Wilderness of Sinai (Exod. 17:1; 19:2; Num. 33:14–15). The people complained because there was no water there, so Moses struck a rock and water flowed miraculously (Exod. 17:1–7). Afterward the Israelites fought there against the Amalekites and were victorious after Moses, aided by Aaron and Hur, held out his rod (Exod. 17:8–16). The location of Rephidim is uncertain; some identify it with the Wadi Refayid in southwest Sinai. ***See also*** Exodus.

The miracle at Rephidim, where, according to Exod. 17:1–7, Moses struck a rock and caused water to flow out; wall painting from the catacomb of St. Callixtus, Rome, fourth century A.D.

Resen (ree'zen), a yet unidentified city in Assyria lying "between Nineveh and Calah" (Gen. 10:12) whose construction is ascribed to Nimrod.

reservoir, a natural or artificial rock-cut storage container for the collection of rainwater. Such installations, variously called reservoirs, pools, or cisterns, were essential for settlements relying almost totally on winter rains for their water source. Even sites located close to a spring augmented their water supply by such collection methods. Early Bronze Age exploitation of water resources is attested to at Jawa, Arad, and 'Ai, but it was not until the second and first millennia B.C. that public and private reservoirs multiplied greatly as the use of plaster for waterproofing became widespread. Kings constructed cisterns to hold water for times of siege (2 Kings 20:20) and for agriculture (2 Chron. 26:10), and great rock-cut pools are referred to at Hebron (2 Sam. 4:12), Samaria (1 Kings 22:38), and Gibeon (2 Sam. 2:13). Early Israelite settlement in the less fertile hill country was in large part made possible by means of plastered cisterns.

S.L.R.

resh (raysh), the twentieth letter of the Hebrew alphabet; its numerical value is two hundred. ר In the early proto-Canaanite and proto-Sinaitic inscriptions the letter is represented by a pictograph of a head. The Greek rho suggests that the Hebrew form was *rosh* ("head") and that *resh* is the Aramaic name. The Greek ρ preserves the archaic form. In later times the form developed under the influence of Phoenician and Aramaic cursive scripts. The classical Hebrew square form of the letter is related to this development. ***See also*** Writing.

Resheph (ree'shef), a Canaanite god of pestilence, equated in antiquity with Mesopotamian Nergal and Greek Apollo. The name "Resheph" has some connection with flame, perhaps because of the heat of fever accompanying sickness.

The cult of Resheph is attested from earliest times in Mesopotamian sources (third millennium B.C.), later at Ras-Shamra. It penetrated Egypt, especially during the eighteenth dynasty (ca. 1546–1319), where Resheph was thought a warrior. The Israelite personal name Resheph (1 Chron. 7:25) shows that Resheph had a following in the Holy Land. In the OT, Resheph comes to mean "pestilence" (Deut. 32:24; Ps. 78:48). ***See also*** Ras-Shamra.

residue. ***See*** Remnant.

rest. 1 Remainder (the most frequent meaning of the term; Gen. 14:10; 44:10; 1 Kings 11:41; 1 Chron. 11:8; Luke 12:26; Acts 15:17; Rev. 2:24).

2 The condition of repose, cessation of motion, and peaceful restoration. This meaning of the term occurs in a wide variety of biblical applications, translating several Hebrew words. The model of God's resting on the seventh day (Gen. 2:2) conditioned the Sabbath as a day of rest (Lev. 16:31), the Sabbatical Year (Lev. 25:3–6) as a year of rest for land under cultivation, and the Jubilee Year as a periodic social restoration of wealth and property (Lev. 25:8–17). The reality of needed daily rest was recognized for animals (Ezek. 34:14) as well as for humans (2 Sam. 4:5), the latter requiring peace of mind for best effect (Ps. 116:7). A special rest was sensed as a journey ended (Deut. 12:10; Rev. 14:13), and the promise of the Christian life is named as rest provided by God (Heb. 4:1) on the model of the rest promised to the Israelites in the time of Moses (Heb. 3:10–11). The quality of peace of mind or contentment is also described as rest, whether of the earth (Isa. 14:7), of individuals (Job 3:13), or of communities (Jer. 6:16). The lack of peace of mind due to disturbance (Ps. 22:2), pain, or work (Eccles. 2:23) disrupts or destroys rest.

A particular aspect of rest is that of cessation of war, a time of peace (Josh. 11:23; Judg. 3:11, 30; 5:31). 2 Chron. 14:5 describes a peaceful rule under a king as a rest for the kingdom. Lack of international disturbance was viewed as a time of rest for the monarch (2 Chron. 20:30). Deliverance from oppression of enemies even during a siege was viewed as rest (2 Chron. 32:22).

There is a special quality of rest viewed as that given by God to those in close harmony and fellowship with their Lord. For the Israelites, it derived from fulfillment of covenant life. " 'Yet thou hast said, "I know you by name, and you have also found favor in my sight." Now therefore, I pray thee, if I have found favor in thy sight, show me now thy ways, that I may know thee and find favor in thy sight. Consider too that this nation is thy people.' And he said, 'My presence will go with you, and I will give you rest' " (Exod. 33:12–14). Christian writers saw this fulfilled in the Christ for all people (Rom. 4:16; Heb. 3:1–2), and the goal of life was put as the achievement of the rest only God could thus give (Rev. 14:13).

R.S.B.

restitution, a biblical concept closely related to the idea of restoration. Both, of course, are involved with sins committed against persons and/or property, either deliberately or inadvertently. Restoration appears to indicate replacement for whatever was taken or destroyed, whereas restitution seems to be repayment over and above the actual loss, analogous to what is today called "punitive" damages (e.g., Exod. 22:1–15; Lev. 6:1–7; Num. 5:5–7). For example, the ancient law found in Exod. 22:1, 4 clearly stipulates that anyone who steals an ox or a sheep must pay restitution to the owner of the animal(s). If the thief kills or sells the ox, he is required to pay restitution of five oxen; if he kills or sells the sheep, he is required to pay restitution of four sheep (cf. also 2 Sam. 12:6). If, however, the animal has not been harmed and is found safe in the possession of the thief, the culprit is required to pay double. Interestingly enough, if the thief has no means to pay this fine, he is to be sold for his theft.

In Leviticus, it is commanded that if someone robs or cheats a neighbor, that person is to restore the amount in full and add a fifth to it (Lev. 6:1–7). In addition, the guilty party was required to offer a guilt offering. This principle is reflected in the NT story of Zacchaeus, who, as a tax collector, had cheated and "gouged" the people from whom he had collected the taxes (Luke 19:1–10). After his encounter with Jesus, he voluntarily agreed to give half of his goods to the poor and to restore fourfold to anyone he had defrauded. The principle of restitution is clearly part of this episode, but Zacchaeus went far beyond the requirement of the law in this matter.

In most of the NT writings, the word group used to designate the idea of restitution or restoration has a rather different meaning, namely, that of restoring in the sense of reestablishing (Matt. 17:11; Mark 9:12; Acts 1:6; 3:21) or even healing (Matt. 12:13; Mark 3:5; Luke 6:10; Mark 8:25; but cf. Heb. 13:19, where it is somewhat closer to the OT idea but not in any "legal" sense). This probably is a result of the NT movement away from legalism. Clearly, however, the notion of restitution is continued, as was seen in the Zacchaeus story (the verb translated "restore" in this story is elsewhere used, however, to refer in a much more general sense to "paying," "repaying," or simply "giving back"). Such a principle would be an integral feature of a new community founded upon the idea of loving one's neighbor as oneself. ***See also*** Forgiveness; Law; Reconciliation. J.M.E.

Rest of Esther, the. ***See*** Esther, The Rest of the Book of.

restoration. ***See*** Regeneration; Restitution.

resurrection, a rising to life from death. The concept of resurrection is derived from Jewish apocalyptic literature. In earlier OT writings there is no belief in life after death (Ps. 115:17). When eventually this belief developed it was in the form of the resurrection of the dead, rather than of the immortality of the soul (Isa. 26:19; Dan. 12:2). Resurrection is to be distinguished from resuscitation or reanimation of the physical body. It denotes a complete transformation of the human being in his or her psychosomatic totality (1 Cor. 15:53–55). This is expressed in a number of metaphors. The resurrected will shine like stars (Dan. 12:3). They will be like the angels (Mark 12:25). Resurrection was thought of not as an event for each individual at death but as a corporate event. God would raise all of the elect at the end of history.

The Resurrection of Jesus: The post-Easter proclamation of the resurrection of Jesus is to be seen in the context of this apocalyptic hope. Jesus' resurrection is an act of God. God raised the Son from the dead as the first fruits in anticipation of the general resurrection (1 Cor. 15:20). The resurrection of the believers would follow as a result of Christ's resurrection (1 Cor. 15:22).

Earliest Traditions: The earliest traditions about the Easter event are not to be found in the appearance stories at the ends of the Gospels (Mark 16:9–20, though part of the canonical text, is not part of the original Mark). They are all

The general resurrection at the end of history as depicted in a panel of the Verdun Altar, 1180.

later developed traditions emanating from subapostolic times. The earliest witness we have of the Easter event is to be found in 1 Cor. 15:3–8. Paul wrote this account around A.D. 55 and was quoting what he delivered to the Corinthians when he founded that community ca. A.D. 50. But, vv. 3–7 were already a tradition Paul had received from others who were Christians before him (v. 1). This takes us back to the time of his call to be an apostle (ca. A.D. 33) or at the latest Paul's visit to Jerusalem ca. A.D. 35 (note that the two persons mentioned in vv. 5 and 7 are the same persons Paul saw on that visit, Gal. 1:18–19).

From 1 Cor. 15:3–8 we learn that faith in the resurrection was based not on the empty tomb, which Paul does not mention, but on the appearances of the Lord. The word used for "appeared" is the same Greek word used elsewhere for visionary experiences. We may today characterize these experiences as revelatory disclosures from the transcendent realm. No distinction was drawn between the resurrection and ascension. The appearances are manifestations of the resurrected and already ascended Christ from heaven.

The impact of these disclosures is: first, the conviction that God raised Jesus from the dead (note that the language used here is derived from Jewish apocalyptic literature; we might say today that God took Jesus into his own eternity); second, the consolidation of the disciples into a community, later designated "church" (Gk.

ekklēsia), i.e., the end-time people of God; and third, the inauguration of the community's mission to Israel and later to the gentile world.

In the Gospels: The story of the empty tomb as found in the Gospels, though in its present forms belonging to the later tradition, nevertheless appears to rest on an early report of Mary Magdalene and other women that on visiting the tomb after the burial they discovered it empty. In itself this discovery does not establish a resurrection and might conceivably suggest a mere resuscitation. It is also susceptible of other explanations, some of which are mentioned in the Gospels themselves (cf. Mark 15:47; Matt. 28:13; John 20:15). The disciples after the appearances welcomed the women's report as congruous with their faith in the resurrection and developed the empty-tomb narrative as a vehicle for the Easter proclamation.

Later the Gospels developed appearance narratives. The effect of this attempt at narration is the growing materialization of the appearances and of the understanding of the resurrection. Jesus now walks on earth as he had walked before (Luke 24:15). He talks, eats, drinks, and invites people to touch him. The theological motivation for this materialization is often held to be anti-docetic (i.e. against the idea that Jesus was nonmaterial) but that would probably be an anachronism. More likely it originated in a profound conviction of the identity of the risen Lord with the earthly Jesus. A further effect is a growing desire to separate the ascension from the resurrection (Luke 24:51; John 20:17). This tendency culminates in Acts 1: 9–10 in a period of forty days between the resurrection and ascension (a period lengthened in later apocryphal, Gnostic revelations about the risen Jesus). As treated by Luke-Acts the ascension has a double effect on the understanding of resurrection. In Luke's Gospel it forms a conclusion to the earthly life of Jesus while in Acts it inaugurates his heavenly reign.

See also Ascension of Christ, The; Death; Eternal Life; Hades; Immortality; Soul; Tomb, Jesus'.

Bibliography

Fuller, R. H. *The Formation of the Resurrection Narratives*. Philadelphia: Fortress, 1980.

Perkins, P. *Resurrection, New Testament Witness and Contemporary Reflection*. Garden City, NY: Doubleday, 1984.

R.H.F.

retribution, the concept of repaying persons in kind, according to their just deserts. The idea of retribution is pervasive in the Bible, and yet the term "retribution" as such occurs only twice in the RSV (Rom. 11:9; Heb. 2:12). The burden of the concept is carried by synonymous terminology ("recompense," "vengeance," "wages," "requital," "reward") and by larger legal, narrative, or oracular texts.

Retribution as a principle of human law was well established in antiquity, and biblical Israel was no exception. The most famous expression of this principle is the "law of retaliation" (Lat. *lex talionis)*, which is stated very succinctly in Deuteronomy: "It shall be life for life, eye for eye, tooth for tooth, hand for hand, foot for foot" (19:21; cf. Exod. 21:23–25; Lev. 24: 19–20; Matt. 5:38–42). Interpreters are widely agreed that this formula, so brutal on the face of it, actually represented an advance over earlier legal thinking both because it allowed no favoritism and because it guaranteed that the punishment could not exceed the crime. Nevertheless, the bleak harshness of the *lex talionis* was always subject to control by the community. In Exod. 21:22 it is not the aggrieved individual who decides how the principle is to be applied in a specific case, but rather the "judges" make the determination. In Matt. 5:38–42, Jesus specifically opposes to the principle of "an eye for an eye" an ethic of nonresistance to personal insult. Paul echoes the same theme in Rom. 12: 17.

A Prerogative of God: In fact, retribution in the Bible is primarily a prerogative of God. Even in the single narrative instance in which the law was literally applied by humans to a human (Judg. 1:7), the Canaanite victim attributed to God ultimate responsibility for the mutilation Israel had inflicted upon him. The prophets spoke frequently of God's just punishments for injustice and idolatry, both upon Israel's enemies and upon Israel and Judah themselves. Under the direct influence of the preaching of Jeremiah, the writers of Deuteronomy raised the retributional scheme to its most elaborate OT expression. The whole of Deuteronomy is cast in the form of a treaty between God the sovereign and the servant people Israel. Near the end of it, Moses sums up the meaning of this great covenant scheme: "See, I have set before you this day life and good, death and evil. If you obey the commandments of the Lord your God . . . then you shall live and multiply. . . . But if your heart turns away . . . I declare to you this day, that you shall perish; . . ." (Deut. 30:15–18). Here the certain connection between obedience to the will of God and blessing and life is juxtaposed to the curses and death that follow upon disobedience. God will repay his people in a manner exactly appropriate to their degree of faithfulness.

The picture of God the retributor in those texts that deal with the end of time can be summed up for the OT in Dan. 12:1–3. To those who had ceased to hope for justice in the events of human history, the late apocalyptic writer promised that at the end of time "many of those who sleep in the dust of the earth shall awake, some to everlasting life, and some to shame and everlasting contempt" (12:2). This motif becomes a strong one in the many NT texts that present the end of the age as The Retribution. Those who have been faithful will be separated from those who have not and all will receive their appropriate reward (Matt. 25:31–46).

Divine retribution as a magnificent heavenly model for human justice is well established in the Bible, and it serves as a bulwark against any underestimation of the seriousness with which God deals with human evil and sin. However, the Bible suggests that the relationship of God to human sin and suffering can be understood in other ways as well. Three deserve brief mention here.

The book of Job is a sustained polemic against the rather simple reward-and-punishment ideology of the popular religion of the day, such as that reflected in the "Psalms of the Two Ways" (e.g., Pss. 1, 37). The entire case of Job is absurd because a completely righteous man suffers what appear to be the punishments announced in Deuteronomy 28 as coming upon the ungodly. But God is not the author of Job's sufferings, so his sufferings cannot be explained in some retributional scheme. The conclusion of the book (42:5–6) suggests that God's comforting and saving presence more truly reflects God's nature than does the unwarranted and inexplicable suffering of the righteous.

Rather widespread in the wisdom tradition of Israel is the acknowledgment of what has come to be called "the destiny-producing deed." When a sage remarked that "he who digs a pit will fall into it, and a stone will come back upon him who starts it rolling" (Prov. 26:27; cf. Ps. 7:14–18; Eccles. 10:8–11; Ecclus. 27:25–26), he was making the rather commonsensical observation that human beings are capable of launching cause-and-effect sequences that can bring disastrous results upon themselves and upon other people. God plays no role in these chains of events and is not responsible for these results.

The Larger Framework: Most important, however, is the import of the larger framework within which the biblical notion of retribution is nested. The Bible can be viewed as a drama that begins with God and human beings living in right relationships with each other. Those relationships are then broken from the human side, and the human community consequently must endure many vicissitudes until at last God restores the original right relationships in the new age. Viewed this way, the story of the Bible is not finally the story of reward and punishment but rather of God's success in restoring the original harmony of the good world. In such a larger context, divine retribution is embraced by divine redemption; biblical writers can therefore speak of a divine determination not to destroy that which deserves destruction (Hos. 11:8–9). Even on the cosmic scale, promises Paul, the day will come when "the creation itself will be set free from its bondage to decay and obtain the glorious liberty of the children of God" (Rom. 8:21; see other expressions of this hope in Phil. 2:10–11; 1 Cor. 15:22–28). ***See also*** Law; Vengeance.

Bibliography

Koch, Klaus. "Is There a Doctrine of Retribution in the OT?" In *Theodicy in the OT*. Edited by J. L. Crenshaw. Philadelphia: Fortress, 1983. Pp. 57–87.

Kushner, Harold S. *When Bad Things Happen to Good People*. New York: Schocken, 1981.

Towner, W. Sibley. *How God Deals with Evil*. Philadelphia: Westminster, 1976.

W.S.T.

Return, the, a term used by scholars for the homecoming of the exiles from Babylonian captivity to the areas of Judea and Samaria in the sixth century B.C.

Return of Christ. ***See*** Eschatology; Millennium; Parousia.

Reu (ree'o͞o), the son of Peleg; a descendant of Shem and an ancestor of Abraham (Gen. 11:18–21). He figures in the ancestry of Jesus through Joseph (Luke 3:35).

Reuben, the firstborn son of Jacob by his wife Leah and the ancestor of the tribe that bears his name (Gen. 29:32; 35:23; 46:8; 49:2–3; Exod. 1:1–2; 6:14; Num. 26:5; 1 Chron. 2:1; 5:1, 3). Gen. 29:32 explains the name as meaning that God had seen Leah's affliction, but the name explains itself as an exclamation in Hebrew by the parents upon the birth of a boy—"Look, a son!"

Gen. 30:14–15 depicts Reuben as a child devoted to his mother who gathers mandrakes (an aphrodisiac?) and presents them to her. This leads to Jacob's returning to Leah's bed and, thus, to Leah's giving birth to Issachar (vv. 16–18). In a perhaps not unconnected episode, Reuben has intercourse with his father's concubine Bilhah, Rachel's handmaiden, after Rachel's death (35:19–22). Although for a son to lie with his father's concubine is a rebellious act indicating usurpation of authority (2 Sam. 16:21–22), in this case the story may be indicating Reuben's intention to cause his father to return to Leah's tent by "spoiling" Rachel's handmaiden, i.e., the last remaining connection to Rachel (cf. Homer *Iliad* 9.443–455). However, Reuben's act leads ultimately to his disenfranchisement as firstborn (Gen. 49:3–4; 1 Chron. 5:1–2). Nonetheless, Reuben's behavior in the Joseph story reflects the role of responsibility that belongs to the firstborn (Gen. 37:21–29; 42:22, 37).

Many scholars interpret the information about Reuben in Genesis as reflective of the fortune of the tribe: once the Reubenites had a prominent role among the Israelites and thus Reuben is the "firstborn," "the first fruits of the strength" of Jacob (Gen. 49:3; cf. Deut. 21:17). However, in the course of time, the tribe weakened (Gen. 49:4, "you shall not have pre-eminence"; cf. Deut. 33:6, "Let Reuben live, and not die"), and Reuben's intercourse with Bilhah is viewed as the etiological explanation for the fact that the power and right of the firstborn passed to the tribes of Judah and Joseph (as indicated by the superior influence of Judah and Joseph in the Joseph story; see also Gen. 49:8–12, 22–26; Deut. 33:13–17; 1 Chron. 5:1–2). ***See also*** Bilhah; Jacob; Leah; Reubenites.

J.U.

Reubenites, the tribe that carried the name of the firstborn of Jacob and Leah, Reuben (Gen. 29:32). As such the tribe is mentioned first in the list of those who leave Egypt (Exod. 6:14), in the list of the tribal leaders in the desert (Num. 1:5), and the census there (1:20–21; 26:5–10), in the blessing of Moses (Deut. 33:6), and in the apportionment of the land by Joshua (Josh. 13:15–23; see also Num. 2:10, 16; 7:30; 18:18; Deut. 13:4; Ezek. 48:31). This placement is not followed by the Chronicler, however, whose emphasis is on the Davidic dynasty and therefore Judah. Thus, Chronicles introduces Reuben as the first of Israel's sons (1 Chron. 2:1; see also 27:16), but proceeds to list the genealogy of the tribe of Judah first (2:1–4:19). The most complete genealogy of Reuben is in 1 Chron. 5:3–8.

According to Numbers 32, the Reubenites and the Gadites were granted by Moses their request to dwell in Gilead due to the pastureland available there for their cattle. The one agreed condition was that they spearhead the capture of western Canaan (see also Josh. 1:12–18). After Joshua's victories they were permitted to return to Gilead (Josh. 22:1–9). The sources (Num. 32:33–38; Josh. 13:15–23; 1 Chron. 5:8–10; 6:63–64), although not always consistent, indicate that the Reubenites settled south of Gad in Gilead, north of the Arnon River (but see Josh. 15:6; 18:17, which might indicate a Reubenite settlement west of the Jordan).

Due to the paucity of material, the history of the tribe is difficult to reconstruct. Scholarly conjecture holds that the biblical viewpoint of Reuben as Jacob's firstborn indicates that Reuben was once a powerful tribe. However, Jacob's rebuke (Gen. 49:4; cf. 1 Chron. 5:1) and Moses' blessing (Deut. 33:6) indicate that Reuben became weak. Perhaps the destruction of the Reubenite families of Dathan and Abiram due to their rebellion against Moses (an attempt to reassert the firstborn's authority? Num. 16) is a biblical attempt to explain the reason for the decline of the tribe.

The Song of Deborah (Judg. 5:15–16) testifies to the tribe's (selfish) refusal to join the battle against Sisera, but 1 Chron. 5:10 witnesses to the Reubenites' strength during the days of Saul (late eleventh century B.C.). The captivity of Reubenite families by Tiglath-pileser III of Assyria in 732 B.C. (1 Chron. 5:6) is the last historical mention of the tribe. The prophet Ezekiel (48:6–7, 31) predicts the ultimate resettlement of the tribe alongside its brethren. ***See also*** Gilead; Reuben.

J.U.

Reuel (rōō'ayl; KJV: "Raguel," Num. 10:29; Heb., "friend of God"). **1** The son of Esau and Basemath, the daughter of Ishmael, whose descendants show Esau's ties with Edom (Gen. 36). **2** The priest of Midian, father (?) of Hobab, who gave his daughter Zipporah in marriage to Moses (Exod. 2; Num. 10:29). Perhaps he was the same as Jethro, the priest of Midian, also identified as Moses' father-in-law (Exod. 4:18; the Heb. term means a male relative by marriage). Through Reuel Midianite (Kenite) influence on Moses is conceivable. **3** A Gadite, father of Eliasaph (Num. 2:14), also cited as "Deuel" (Septuagint: "Reuel"). **4** A Benjaminite (1 Chron. 9:8). ***See also*** Hobab; Jethro; Midianites; Moses; Zipporah.

H.B.H.

revelation, the English translation of Hebrew and Greek terms originally referring to "uncovering" or "disclosing." The act of revelation is also frequently expressed by other terms in Scripture, particularly word groups dealing with speaking and showing. Two essential features of the idea of revelation emerge from these observations: first, revelation is conceived as an unveiling of what was already true, whether as enduring reality, as past event, or as foreordained future; second, although whatever is being revealed was true all along, it was previously concealed or unknown. Thus, for knowledge to be understood as "revelation," it has to be the knowledge of the few, as contrasted with the ignorance of the many, or new knowledge, as contrasted with the ignorance of the past (e.g., 1 Cor. 2:9–10).

Human beings may, of course, reveal human secrets (Prov. 11:13), and one may speak of revelation in connection with supernatural powers opposed to God (e.g., 2 Thess. 2:3, 8). When the object of revelation, however, is fundamental truth, God is the revealer, and the knowledge that results is a gift rather than a product of human or demonic ingenuity. Thus, for example, God is said to reveal Torah (i.e., teachings of the law; Deut. 29:29), himself (1 Sam. 3:21), secrets (Amos 3:7; Dan. 2:29), power (Isa. 53:1), prophecies (1 Cor. 14:29–30), righteousness (Rom. 1:17), anger (Rom. 1:18), or the Son (Gal. 1:16).

Such revelations begin with one or a few persons, for what is commonly known does not need to be revealed. The prophet, apostle, or other agent who receives such revelations may be obliged to transmit them to others, as, for example, Amos (3:7–8) or Paul (Gal. 1:15–17). On the other hand, they may be instructed to keep some revelations hidden, whether because it would be altogether wrong to utter them (2 Cor. 12:1–4) or because they are intended for another era (Dan. 12:9; 2 Esd. 14) or even without a reason being offered (Rev. 10:4).

The principal modes by which human beings receive revelations in the biblical documents

REVELATION TO JOHN, THE

are visions (e.g., Jer. 1:11–13) and auditions (e.g., Isa. 22:14). These may come while one is awake or in dreams. God may speak directly to a human being or through an angelic intermediary, and sometimes the two modes are difficult to distinguish, as in Moses' encounter with the burning bush (Exod. 3:2–4) or Abraham's meeting with the three travelers (Gen. 18:1–19:1). Revelation may also be made available in the created order itself (Rom. 1:18–23). Revelation is not limited to extraordinary experiences; some texts seem to treat it more as a matter of inner conviction (e.g., Ps. 16:7) or the interpretation of historical events (Ps. 111: 6).

From the early third century B.C. onward, the language of revelatory experience became an important element in the developing genre that we now call "apocalyptic," that is, "revelatory" literature. In such works as Daniel, 2 Esdras, Revelation, and *1 Enoch*, we meet a prophet or seer who is given access in ecstatic experiences to secrets of various kinds—about the past, the structure of the universe (e.g., *1 Enoch* 41), the heavenly court, or the future. A particular interest was the transition from the present age to the world to come. The description of such experiences evokes prophetic visions such as those of Ezekiel and also ecstatic experience such as that of Paul (2 Cor. 12:1–7). We do not know, however, to what extent the language of apocalyptic reflects actual experience or to what extent it had become purely a literary formula.

In later Christian theology, the idea of revelation underwent a broadening, so that it came to mean something very close to "the distinctive content of Christian faith" as opposed to any other form of human knowledge or thought. Scholastic and later theology from the early Middle Ages to the Renaissance came to treat reason and revelation as two antithetical modes of knowing, of which the latter must be considered superior for theological purposes. It is not clear that such a sharp distinction can be made in Scripture itself, where specifically revelatory works stand side by side with other documents (e.g., Proverbs) that claim an origin in human wisdom. ***See also*** Apocalyptic Literature; Dreams; Inspiration; Vision. L.W.C.

Revelation to John, the, the last book of the NT, also called the Apocalypse. The term "apocalypse" comes from the Greek word for revelation, which is used in the preface to characterize the work (1:1).

In modern times, the word "apocalypse" has come to designate a particular literary form. An apocalypse is a narrative account of the reception of revelation by a human individual from one or more heavenly beings. The revelation includes descriptions of the heavenly world and of a qualitatively new future. The book of Daniel in the OT is also an apocalypse, as is 2 Esdras in the Apocrypha. Revelation is the only apocalypse in the NT, although other books contain passages of similar content, e.g., Mark 13 and parallels, 1 Thess. 4:13–18.

Author: Although the author never claims directly to be a prophet, several passages suggest such was his self-understanding (e.g., 22:9). He calls himself John (1:4). Nothing in the work links the author to John the son of Zebedee or John the Elder. Sound judgment requires the conclusion that he is a John otherwise unknown to us. His work was preserved because he was recognized as a prophet in the early church and because the work itself was accepted as a valid revelation of God's will.

Date: According to Irenaeus, a leader of the church in the second century, John saw his revelation near the end of the reign of the Roman emperor Domitian. No good reason for doubting Irenaeus' testimony has been brought forward. The book in its present form should therefore be dated to A.D. 95 or 96. Earlier traditions have certainly been incorporated. In some cases,

The end of the Revelation to John in the Codex Sinaiticus, an outstanding fourth-century A.D. manuscript of the Greek Bible.

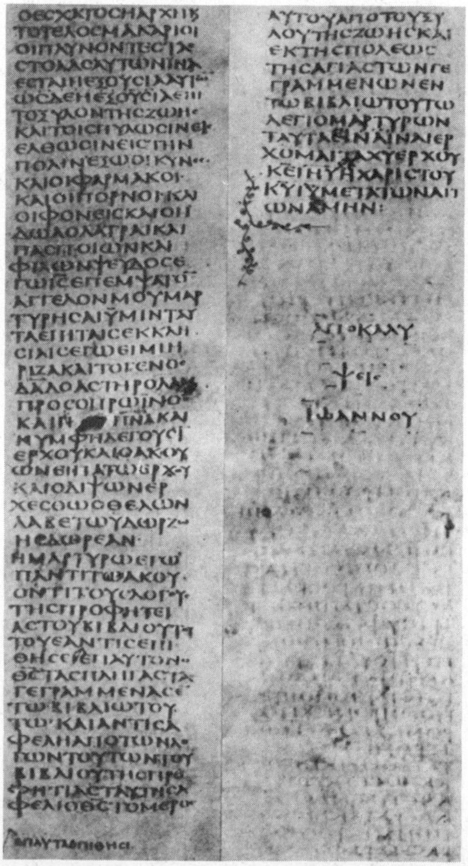

sources with relatively fixed wording were used, in, e.g., chaps. 11, 12, and 17:10.

Occasion: The occasion of the book has often been seen as the persecution that Christian tradition says Domitian initiated against the church. Recent research has called the existence of such a persecution seriously into question. The hard evidence supports only the conclusion that under Domitian Christians were subject to the same sporadic repression they experienced under other emperors of the late first and early second centuries. Another theory is that Domitian escalated the ruler cult by insisting on new divine honors of his person. The evidence for this theory is not very strong. It seems best to conclude that John was not simply reacting to objective changes in the situation of Christians, but that with prophetic insight he interpreted the typical situation in a new way.

Content and Purpose: In Revelation John tells how he received revelatory visions from Christ and describes those visions. Most of them concern the future, but John tells them in order to interpret the experience of the first readers and to evoke a particular response to that experience. In decribing his visions, he uses traditional images. The result is that the book has two levels of meaning. The traditional images call to mind the "old story" of the conflict between the creator-god or God and a rebellious beast of chaos. The various versions of this story express in a vivid and concrete way the perennial struggle between order and chaos, life and death.

John uses these traditional images to interpret his situation. The bestial, chaotic images are applied to the Roman Empire, its leaders and friends, and the very culture related to it. The "new story," which is the second level of meaning, uses the story of conflict to interpret the relationship between the followers of Jesus and the Roman Empire. The hostility of Rome to the Christian message and way of life is revealed as a renewed rebellion of chaos against order, of creature against Creator.

The Christ of the messages exhorts the readers to remain faithful, especially in the face of hostility from their non-Christian neighbors. Another important theme is the warning not to practice immorality (i.e., idolatry) and to avoid meat sacrificed to pagan gods. These warnings teach that the faithful Christians must often be critical of their culture.

The woman clothed with the sun in chap. 12 represents the faithful people of God who will be protected by divine power in situations of adversity. Chaps. 13 and 17 allude to the emperor Nero, who slaughtered Christians in Rome ca. A.D. 64, as a symbol of political power that abuses its God-given authority. In chaps. 17 and 18 Rome is portrayed as (the new) Babylon, because the armies of Rome, like those of Babylon at an earlier date, destroyed Jerusalem and the Temple in A.D. 70.

Beginning with the seven seals, the visions focus upon the future. The five series of visions, beginning with the seals and ending with the second unnumbered series, all have the same plot. Their common underlying pattern is threefold: (1) persecution (e.g., 6:9–11; 12–13), (2) punishment of the nations, or judgment (e.g., 6:12–17; 14:14–20), and (3) triumph of God, the Lamb, and his followers or salvation (e.g., 7:9–17; 15:2–4). By repeating this pattern, Revelation expresses the insight that reality in general and Christian life in particular are characterized by conflict and struggle. A further insight is that death is only a phase in that struggle, not the end. The new and old stories of conflict are reinforced by the example of Jesus. They are models for understanding and coming to terms with powerlessness, suffering, and death. Readers are given hope within struggle and challenged to distinguish God's cause from Satan's cause in their everyday life.

Interpretation: Revelation has always been interpreted in various ways; the twentieth century is no exception. Today fundamentalist and conservative evangelical Christians believe the book was written to predict the end of the world in our own time. Some of them expect, for example, a world war to occur in the Middle East that will involve

OUTLINE OF CONTENTS

The Revelation to John

- I. Prologue (1:1–8)
  - A. Preface (1:1–3)
  - B. Opening of a letter (1:4–6)
  - C. Prophetic sayings (1:7–8)
- II. Vision of Christ with seven messages (1:9–3:22)
  - A. Vision of Christ (1:9–20)
  - B. Seven messages (2:1–3:22)
- III. Visions of heaven and seven seals (4:1–8:5)
  - A. Vision of God (4:1–11)
  - B. Vision of the Lamb (5:1–14)
  - C. Seven seals (6:1–8:5)
- IV. The seven trumpets (8:2–11:19)
- V. Seven unnumbered visions (12:1–15:4)
- VI. The seven bowls and Babylon (15:1–19:10)
  - A. Seven bowls (15:1–16:20)
  - B. Babylon (17:1–19:10)
- VII. Seven unnumbered visions and Jerusalem (19:11–22:5)
  - A. Seven unnumbered visions (19:11–21:8)
  - B. Jerusalem (21:9–22:5)
- VIII. Epilogue (22:6–21)
  - A. Sayings (22:6–20)
  - B. Benediction (22:21)

nuclear weapons and will fulfill the prophecy of a battle at Armageddon (Rev. 16:12–16).

More liberal Christians recognize that the prophecies of Revelation were addressed to the late first century and that most of them were not fulfilled in a literal, historical way. Such Christians do not understand prophecy to be primarily a matter of prediction. John's prophetic role consisted in exposing and denouncing idolatry and the abuse of power in his day. His expression of hope for a new heaven and a new earth reminds us that the Kingdom of God is not just a matter of the salvation of the individual or even the maintenance of the faithful church. The rule of God ought to encompass all of creation. Only when all are faithful and the world-order is characterized by peace and justice will God's work be complete. The readers of Revelation today are challenged by it to discern and distinguish divine and satanic forces at work in our world. ***See also*** Apocalyptic Literature; Apocrypha, Old Testament; Daniel; Nero; Roman Empire.

Bibliography

Caird, G. B. *A Commentary on the Revelation of St. John the Divine*. New York: Harper & Row, 1966.

Collins, Adela Yarbro. *The Apocalypse*. Wilmington, DE: Michael Glazier, 1979.

Fiorenza, Elisabeth Schuessler. *Invitation to the Book of Revelation*. Garden City, NY: Doubleday, 1981.

A.Y.C.

revenge. ***See*** Avenger.

Revised Standard Version (RSV), a mid-twentieth-century English translation of the Bible. ***See*** English Bible, The.

Revised Versions. ***See*** English Bible, The; Texts, Versions, Manuscripts, Editions.

Rezeph (ree'zef), a town cited as having fallen to Assyria (2 Kings 19:12; Isa. 37:12) and symbolizing in part the unstoppable Assyrian force. From Assyrian royal records it is known as *Rasappa* and had served as an Assyrian provincial capital after its capture, probably by Shalmaneser III about 838 B.C. Possibly it is modern Rezzafeh about a hundred miles southeast of Aleppo, off the south bank of the Euphrates.

Rezin (ree'zin), an Aramaic name whose original Hebrew vocalization, to judge from Greek and Assyrian transcriptions, was *raz-yohn* (Heb., "pleasant, agreeable").

1 The king of Damascus. Rezin was among those who paid tribute to the Assyrian king Tiglath-pileser III in 738 B.C., but within three years Rezin had organized an anti-Assyrian coalition consisting of Damascus, Tyre, Philistia, Israel, some Arab tribes, and perhaps Edom. When King Ahaz of Judah refused to join, the allies seized part of his territory, including Elath on the Red Sea. Rezin's attempt to take Jerusalem and depose Ahaz failed (Isa. 7:1–10), however, and Tiglath-pileser soon crushed the allies. After neutralizing Phoenicia and Philistia in 734 B.C., he devastated Rezin's territory in 733. Damascus survived, but the following year, bereft of its allies, the city fell, and Rezin was executed (2 Kings 16:5–9).

2 The ancestor of a group of Temple servants in the postexilic period (Ezra 2:48; Neh. 7:50). ***See also*** Ahaz; Isaiah, The Book of; Pekah.

J.J.M.R.

Rezon (ree'zuhn; Heb., "potentate"), the son of Eliadah (1 Kings 11:23), one of two foreign and one Israelite adversaries raised by God against Solomon. In this context, they are raised up against Solomon on account of Solomon's sin in taking foreign wives. Rezon was an Aramean, and is sometimes identified with Hezion (1 Kings 15:18). Rezon mutinied against Hadadezer and established in Damascus an independent fiefdom that broke free of Israelite hegemony.

Rhegium (ray'ji-uhm), a Greek colony (modern Reggio di Calabria) located at the southwestern tip of the Italian boot, opposite Messana in Sicily. Although a Roman ally as early as the Punic Wars, Rhegium maintained a Greek character into the time of the Roman Empire. In spite of numerous earthquakes, it remained well populated throughout the first century A.D. and was a center for Pythagorean philosophy. Unfavorable winds hindered navigation between the narrow straits, perhaps explaining Paul's delay there (Acts 28:13).

Rhoda (roh' duh), a slave, servant, family member, or follower of Jesus in the home of Mary, the mother of John Mark, in Jerusalem. When Peter was miraculously released from prison and came to the house, she answered his knock but was so overcome with joy that she ran and announced his presence to the others assembled in prayer without first letting him in (Acts 12:12–16). ***See also*** Mark; Mary; Peter.

Rhodes (rohds), an island off the southwest tip of Asia Minor (1 Macc. 15:23; Acts 21:1). In biblical times this small island republic was a cultural center and a center of higher education. It was also known for its healthful climate. Caesar and Cicero both went there to study rhetoric and philosophy. Tiberias retired there from the turmoil at Augustus' court from 6 B.C. until A.D. 2.

In the third century B.C. the Rhodian navy guarded seaborne trade in the Mediterranean. Its famed colossal statue of Apollo was destroyed by an earthquake in 227/26 B.C.

Roman conquest of Greek territories after the conclusion of the third Macedonian war in 167 B.C. ended the island's prosperity as a commercial center. Rhodes was stripped of her territories in Asia Minor and saw her banking and shipping revenues drop by ninety percent. With Rhodes no longer able to support a navy, the pirates and slave traders of Cilicia and Crete preyed on Mediterranean trade until Pompey rid the area of pirates in the 60s B.C. Rhodes was pillaged by Cassius in 43 B.C., but the island returned to a modicum of prosperity under Roman rule. Paul passed Rhodes on his sea journey from Ephesus to Tyre (Acts 21:1). P.P.

Riblah (rib'luh), a city in the Lebanese Beqaa Valley that guarded the important international thoroughfare connecting Egypt with northern Syria and Mesopotamia. Situated about seven miles south of Kedesh on the Orontes at a crossing place of the river, Riblah functioned as a strategic military base during the seventh and sixth centuries B.C. Here Pharaoh Neco II established the Egyptian headquarters following his defeat of Josiah at Megiddo and the capture of Kedesh in 609 B.C. In the same year Neco summoned Jehoahaz to Riblah, deposed him, put him in chains, and appointed Jehoiakim as Judah's king in his stead (2 Kings 23:31–35). Two decades later, after the Babylonian conquest of Jerusalem, Nebuchadnezzar brought King Zedekiah to Riblah, killed his sons before his eyes, then blinded him and carried him off in chains to Babylon (2 Kings 25:5–7; Jer. 52: 9–11). Many of Judah's leading officials were also brought to Riblah and executed at that time (2 Kings 25:19–21). The ruins of the ancient site are near the modern village of Ribleh.

According to Num. 34:11, a town named Riblah was a border city on the northeast corner of the promised land (cf. KJV: "Diblath," RSV: "Riblah," Ezek. 6:14); but it is uncertain whether this is the same city as Riblah on the Orontes. D.A.D.

riddle, in the Bible, a saying whose meaning is not immediately clear or is purposely veiled. It requires careful thought or interpretation to be understood. This encompasses a variety of sayings. The clearest example of a riddle is Samson's riddle of the lion and the honey whose answer was to be guessed by his groomsmen (Judg. 14:12–19). The queen of Sheba questioned Solomon with "hard questions" (1 Kings 10:1; 1 Chron. 9:1), and the mark of a wise person was the ability to understand riddles (Prov. 1:6; cf. Dan. 5:11–12). However, a riddle could refer more broadly to an allegory in which the meaning was deliberately veiled behind symbolic objects (Ezek. 17:2–24; cf. 24:1–15) and could also include "dark speech" that required interpretation (Num. 12:8; cf. John 10:6; 16:25, 29). A perplexing moral problem could be termed a riddle (Ps. 49:4), and the numerical sayings of Proverbs 30 (vv. 15–31) illustrate a riddle form in which is described things "too wonderful" to be easily understood (vv. 18–20). The element of "hiddenness" implied in the riddle allowed the term to be used in a negative sense to describe the shrewdness and deceit of the insolent king in Daniel's vision (Dan. 8:23–25). ***See also*** Proverb; Wisdom. D.R.B.

righteousness, the state of being in the right, or being vindicated. "Righteousness" renders an important Hebrew root, *ṣdq*, that appears over five hundred times in the OT and a Greek root, *dikaio-*, that appears over two hundred and twenty-five times in the NT. The KJV and RSV employ "righteousness" terms about three times as often as "justification" words, but both must be considered in grasping what is a single biblical concept. English has two possible translations: "right, righteous, righteousness, be or declare (or make) righteous," from an Anglo-Saxon root *rightwise;* and "just, justice, justification, justify," from the Latin *justitia*. The interrelatedness of the two concepts is seen in Rom. 3:21–24: "the righteousness of God has been manifested . . . for all who believe. . . . they are justified by his grace."

In the OT: In the OT, righteousness is used of God (Pss. 119:137–38, 144; Isa. 24:16), the king (Pss. 45:4, 7; 72:1–7), the people (Pss. 32:11; 92:11), and individuals (Ezek. 18:5–9) like Noah (Gen. 6:9; cf. 2 Pet. 2:5). Some interpreters stress righteousness as conforming to a norm, the law, or "what is right" (Deut. 16:20). Others see it as relational, fitting the situation (Gen. 38:26; 1 Sam. 24:17). Often a law-court setting is involved: the guilty are condemned, the innocent acquitted (Deut. 25:1; Isa. 5:23; Deut. 16:18). This forensic (i.e., legal) use extends to God's judgment too (Ps. 7:7–11; Jer. 2:4–13; 12:1; Mic. 6:1–8). God's loyalty to (covenant) promises is likewise part of God's righteousness (Neh. 9: 7–8, 33; Dan. 9:14–16). There is a strong ethical component of "upright conduct" throughout the OT (Pss. 1:6; 23:3; Prov. 8:20; 13:6; 16:13; 21: 3; Lev. 19:36).

Most surprising is the way righteousness also refers to God's saving actions: in the RSV "vindication" (Isa. 61:1–2). This "salvation" side appears especially in Second Isaiah, as "deliverance" (46:12–13; 51:5, 6, 8) or "victory" (41: 2). In Judg. 5:11 the plural is rendered as "triumphs of the Lord." "The Lord our righteousness" means God as savior (Jer. 23:6). God is "justified" (Ps. 51:4) in judging and as righteous . . . Savior" (Isa. 45:21). Hence "the righteous" become those who trust in God's vindication (Ps. 37:12–13; Jer. 20:12). In the Dead Sea Scrolls and its "teacher of righteousness," God's righteousness offers hope for redemption from sin.

In the NT: Jesus sought "sinners," not "the righteous" of the day (Mark 2:17). Not the Pharisee but the tax collector went home "vindicated" (Luke 18:14). Jesus called for righteousness (Matt. 5:20) but also spoke of it, like the Kingdom, as God's gift (Matt. 5:6; 6:33).

After Easter, OT "righteousness" language was employed to express the meaning of Jesus' death. Jesus is "the Righteous One" (Acts 3:14; 7:52) whose suffering and resurrection bring the unrighteous to God (1 Pet. 3:18; Rom. 4:25). This saving righteousness means forgiveness (Rom. 3:24–26); justification, sanctification, "washing" from sins (1 Cor. 6:11; cf. 1 Cor. 1: 30 ["Christ . . . our righteousness"]; 2 Cor. 5: 21).

Paul develops the forensic (1 Cor. 4:4) and ethical aspects (1 Thess. 2:10) in a salvation context (2 Cor. 3:9). How one attains righteousness comes to new prominence in Paul's Letter to the Galatians, written against the Judaizers (2:12–21). Righteousness comes by faith, not "works of the law" (3:5). Paul appeals to the OT (Hab. 2:4) and Abraham (Gen. 15:6); God's promise, fulfilled in Christ, is received by faith (Gal. 3:6–18). These two ways to righteousness—one's own based on the law, and from God through faith in Christ—are contrasted in Phil. 3:9–11 and Rom. 10:3–13. The saving righteousness of God becomes the theme of Romans (1:16–17), a righteousness received through Christ's cross (3:21–31) and exemplified by Abraham (chap. 4). Its meaning is freedom (cf. Gal. 5:1, 13) and life in the Spirit (Rom. 5–8, esp. 5:16–21). While reading Israel's history in terms of (un)righteousness (Rom. 9–11, esp. 9:30–31), yet with hope (10:1; 11:26), Paul presents the ethical demand for Christians as well as the gift character of righteousness (Rom. 14:17; Gal. 5:5; Phil. 1:11; 2 Cor. 9:10).

Ephesians speaks of grace and faith but uses the verb "save" instead of the OT "declare righteous" (2:4–10; cf. Titus 3:3–7; 2 Tim. 1: 9–10). Hebrews cites Hab. 2:4 (in 10:36–39; cf. also 1:9; 7:2) in its "word of righteousness" (5: 13). It stresses faith in chap. 11 and righteousness (11:4, 7; cf. 33) and speaks of "the just made perfect" (12:23) through Christ's sacrifice (cf. 9:26–28; 10:19–20). 1 Peter teaches that God judges justly (2:23) and that the righteous Christ died for our sins (3:18) so that we might "live to righteousness" (2:24). Matthew emphasizes righteousness as a gift (5:6; 6:33) within salvation history (3:15; 21:32) and as a disciple's response (5:10, 20; 6:1, RSV: "piety"). Acts has a vivid passage about being "freed" (Gk. *dikaioō)* from what the law could not free one from (13:38–39). John 16:8–11 sees the Paraclete's role as setting the world straight about righteousness, and 1 John insists that Jesus Christ the righteous (2:1) cleanses from unrighteousness (1:9) so that believers can "do right [eousness]" (3:7, 10).

James 2:14–26 cites Gen. 15:6 to show, against those who took faith as mere acknowledgment about God (2:18–19), that faith must include works (of love; 2:22). The passage attempts thus to defend the view of righteousness by faith (alone, 2:24) but with a strong ethical side. James 1:20, along with Matt. 6:33 and 2 Pet. 1:1, uses the expression found in Paul, "the righteousness *of God*." Perhaps deriving from Deut. 33:21 (RSV: "just decrees") and apocalyptic (cf. Dan. 9:7), the phrase has been taken to refer to an attribute or quality of God (Rom. 3:5, RSV: "justice") expressed as power (Rom. 1:16–17). It is thus understood to be the righteousness that comes from God as a gift (Phil. 3:9), or the righteousness valid before God at the judgment (Rom. 10:3). ***See also*** Justice; Justification.

Bibliography

Reumann, J., J. Fitzmyer, and J. Quinn. *Righteousness in the New Testament.* Philadelphia: Fortress; New York: Paulist, 1982. J.H.P.R.

Righteous One, the, a term applied to Jesus by Stephen in Acts 7:52 (KJV: "the Just One"). ***See also*** Stephen.

Rimmon (rim'ahn; Akkadian, "thunderer"; Heb., "pomegranate"). **1** A title borne by the Syrian storm god Hadad, who was worshiped in his temple in Damascus by Naaman, the Syrian army commander (2 Kings 5:18). After Naaman was cured of leprosy by the God of Israel, he asked the prophet Elisha for "two mules' burden of earth" from Israel to take back to Syria; he intended to set up an altar to the God of Israel on the earth in the temple of Rimmon. This temple is thought to have been on the site of the later Roman temple to Zeus and the present Umayyad mosque. **2** A Benjaminite from Beeroth, father of Baanah and Rechab, the men who killed Ishbosheth and brought his head to David (2 Sam. 4:2, 5, 9). **3** En-rimmon, a town in the south of Judah given to the tribe of Simeon (Josh. 19:7); in Josh 15:32 and 1 Chron. 4:32 the name appears as "Ain, and Rimmon." It was occupied by Jews returning from the Exile (Neh. 11:29). According to Zechariah (14:10), Rimmon was south of Jerusalem. Its exact location is uncertain. Often associated with Khirbet Umm er-Ramamin, about nine miles north of Beersheba, Rimmon has recently been connected with the site of Tell Halif (Arabic, *Tell Khuweilifeh*) a few miles to the northwest. **4** A rock to which six

A pomegranate-shaped ceramic bowl found at Tell Halif suggests the site may be biblical Rimmon (Heb. *rimmon* means "pomegranate").

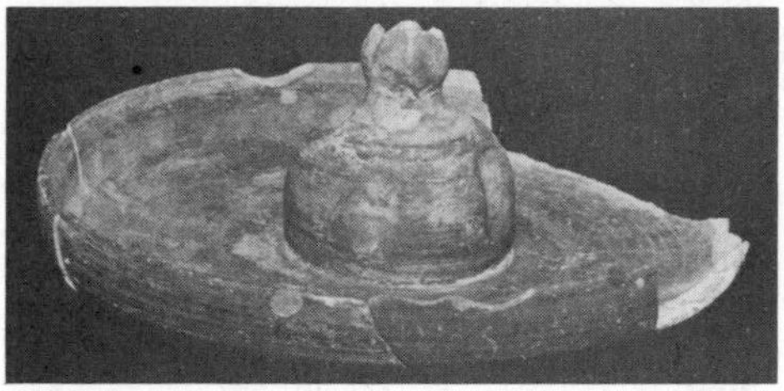

hundred Benjaminites fled to escape from the Israelites (Judg. 20:45–47; 21:13); it is identified with a limestone hill about three miles east of Bethel, on which is the modern village of Ramun. **5** A town in Zebulun, given to the Levites (Josh. 19:13; KJV: "Remmon-methoar"). Written Rimmono in 1 Chron. 6:77 and Dimnah in Josh. 21:35, it is identified with modern Rummaneh, about six miles north-northeast of Nazareth. J.M.W.

rings. **1** Circular rings attached to various furnishings of the tabernacle through which staves were placed in order to carry them during the wilderness journey: the Ark (Exod. 25:12–15; 37:3–4); the table (Exod. 25:26–28; 37:13–15); the altar of burnt offerings (Exod. 27:4–7; 38: 5–7); and the altar of incense (Exod. 30:4; 37:27). Such rings were also used to secure the frames of the tabernacle (Exod. 26:24–30; 36:29–34). **2** Circular rings attached to the breastplate of the high priest which secured the ephod, a decorative linen garment (Exod. 28:23–28). **3** Rings as jewelry either for adornment and worn on the fingers (Job 42:11; James 2:2), ears (Gen. 35:4; Exod. 32:2, 3), or nose (Gen. 24:47; Isa. 3:21; Prov. 11:22) or as a symbol of authority, i.e., as a signet ring of a king (Gen. 41:42; Esther 3:10; Jer. 22:24; cf. Luke 15:22). Such rings were frequently used as official seals (Esther 8:8, 10). ***See also*** Breastpiece; Ephod; Jewelry; Tabernacle. R.H.S.

rise. ***See*** Resurrection.

River of Egypt. ***See*** Egypt, Brook of.

rivers, watercourses on which virtually all major cities in the ancient world were located, because they made transportation and commerce possible and provided irrigation for farming. Metaphorically, rivers or streams of flowing (living) water symbolize salvation or the Spirit of God (Ezek. 47:1–12; Zech. 14:8; Rev. 22:1; John 7:38). ***See also*** entries under the names of individual rivers.

Rizpah (riz'pah), the daughter of Aiah and concubine of Saul (2 Sam. 3:7). After Saul's death Abner took her as a claim to the throne (cf. 1 Kings 2:22). An objection from Ishbosheth, Saul's son, offered an excuse for Abner's negotiations with David (2 Sam. 3:6–10). When God sent a famine because Saul had broken the oath with the Gibeonites (2 Sam. 21:1), David agreed to hand over seven sons of Saul for expiation. Two were the sons of Rizpah. Her devotion led to a long vigil over the bodies, keeping off the birds by day and the beasts by night, from the beginning of the barley harvest (April-May) until the rains came (October). Finally David's attention was drawn to the matter (2 Sam. 21: 1–11). ***See also*** Abner. N.L.L.

road, a KJV term for the RSV's "raid" (1 Sam. 27:10). For road as a travel route, ***see*** Trade and Transportation.

robbery, stealing the property of others. The precise ambit of the Decalogue prohibition "You shall not steal" (Exod. 20:15) is difficult to determine. The verb used there for "steal" (Heb. *ganav*) is narrower in its usage than the word "rob" (Heb. *gazal*), but it nevertheless can be used with persons as the object to denote kidnapping. This has led some scholars (anticipated by rabbinic interpretation) to see the Decalogue prohibition as directed originally against kidnapping, so as to parallel murder and adultery as part of a series of capital offenses. For those who regard the Decalogue as a moral rather than a legal code, such a restrictive interpretation is unnecessary.

The "Covenant Code" contains rules regarding various forms of theft of domestic animals (Exod. 22:1–4), imposing penalties of multiple restitution in kind. Both the evidence required and the nature of the sanctions suggest the setting of an agricultural community that sought to avoid getting tied up in court proceedings. This is reflected also in the provision for self-defense: if the owner kills a thief who intrudes by night, he is exempt; if he kills a daytime intruder, he is liable. The rabbis later reinterpreted the test in terms of the owner's knowledge of the intruder's intentions.

In the code of the Babylonian king Hammurabi (eighteenth century B.C.), we find a more complex set of rules regarding theft (§§6–10, 14, 253–56, 259–60, 265), with more widespread use of the death penalty. The Bible reserves the latter for cases of brigandage (dealt with under the law of war), kidnapping, and deliberate sacrilege. But the capital cases in the code of Hammurabi are also all special in some respect or other, so that attempts to generalize the differences in terms of the underlying values of the cultures should be treated with some caution.

The predominant image of the thief is one who comes suddenly, by night (Job 24:14, 16), making his entry by tunneling through the walls of a sheepfold or a house. But neither secrecy nor nocturnal activity was legally significant. Nor is the modern distinction between theft and robbery (the latter being a form of theft aggravated by violence) evidenced in the Bible. Highway robbery was a quite different phenomenon, representing a form of political opposition that stretched from the period of Abimelech (twelfth century B.C.; Judg. 9:25) to the *sicarii* (Lat. "assassins") and Zealots of the NT period (first century A.D.). The threat from such organized bands was to the central authority's control of the communications network rather than to property; hence, brigandage was treated by military rather than judicial means. But the term for such robbery (Heb. *gazal*) came to be used by the prophets for a wide range of economic exploitation (robbing the fatherless, Isa. 10:2; Ezek. 39:10; robbing the poor, Isa. 3: 14–15; Prov. 22:22; the context is often that of excessive credit terms and execution of debt, Ezek. 18:7–9; 33:15); this too represented the offense of the powerful against the powerless, implying here a rejection of the moral authority of God (Lev. 19:11–13). The priestly legislation deals with such matters in the context of its own concerns: the property offense compounded by a false oath requires restoration, a fine, and a guilt offering (Lev. 6:1–7); the same applies in the case of inadvertent use of sacred property (Lev. 5:14–16).

Where the offender was known, theft might be followed by immediate pursuit with a view to repossession (Gen. 31:23; Judg. 18:22). Early rabbinic sources urge that any such repossession be performed openly, under claim of right, rather than furtively, but ultimately the practice was discouraged (*M. B. Qam.* 10:38). In the absence of a strong police force, repossession was both easier and more satisfactory than securing the attendance of the suspect in court. Similarly, the Mishnah's authorization of lynching in cases of deliberate sacrilege (*m. Sanh.* 9:6) was disapproved by later rabbinic sources (*y. Sanh.* 9:7).

Rabbinic sources continue the prophetic tradition of moral condemnation of "robbery" (*Eccles. Rab.* 1:13; *Deut. Rab.* 2:25*b*; *Sanh.* 108a), and its prohibition is included in the laws given by God to the descendants of Noah (i.e., all humankind; *b. Sanh.* 57a).

The NT continues the condemnation of robbery (1 Cor. 6:10; cf. 1 Pet. 4:15), yet Jesus used the sudden and unexpected intrusion of the robber as a metaphor for the sudden inbreaking of God's kingdom and the consequent need to stay alert (Luke 12:39–40; cf. 1 Thess. 5:2; 2 Pet. 3:10; Rev. 16:15). ***See also*** Law. B.S.J./P.J.A.

robe. ***See*** Dress.

Robinson's Arch, part of a spring or support for a descending staircase of the complex of buildings built on the Temple Mount in Jerusalem by Herod. The remnants of this arch can still be seen today near the southwestern corner of the Temple Mount in the Old City of Jerusalem. During the Herodian period (late first century B.C. to early first century A.D.) a stairway descended from the top of the temple complex to the ground, allowing access to this high point of the city for persons who approached from the south. When it was discovered in 1838, this arch and its associated stairway were thought to extend across the Tyropoeon Valley to the western hill of the city. Subsequent excavations have shown this assumption to be false and that the stairway turned southward. The arch is named after E. Robinson, an American clergyman, who surmised its ancient function during his investigations of Jerusalem in 1838. J.A.D.

rock, a large chunk of stone. In lands such as those of the Mediterranean basin, rocks are plentiful. They are a danger to ships when storms drive them near shore (Acts 27:29), but on land they can be used as places of refuge for both animals (Prov. 30:26) and human beings, either to hide from other human beings (1 Sam. 24:2) or from God himself (Isa. 2:19, 21). Yet even rocks could not withstand God's power (1 Kings 19:11). Moses used the cleft in a rock to protect himself from seeing God's face, which would have cost him his life (Exod. 33:20–23). Israelite faith spoke figuratively of God as a rock, signifying the permanence and stability of divine protection (Deut. 32:4; 2 Sam. 22:2; Pss. 18:2; 71:3).

It was by striking a rock at God's bidding that Moses provided water for the Israelites in the desert (Exod. 17:6). Paul later identified that rock with Christ to show that the Israelites had also been favored with participation in the sacraments (1 Cor. 10:4). Jesus spoke of rocks that hindered agriculture (Mark 4:5–6) and of a rock whose firmness resembled the foundation upon which those people built who accepted what he said (Matt. 7:24–25). He resisted Satan's temptation to turn rocks into bread to satisfy his own hunger (Matt. 4:2–3) and identified Peter (Gk. *Petros,* "rocklike") as the rock upon which his church would be built (Matt. 16:18). J.A.D.

rod, a term representing several different words in Hebrew and Greek and referring to several functions in antiquity. The beloved Twenty-third Psalm contains the famous reference to "thy [God's] rod and thy staff, they comfort me" (v. 4). The imagery is that of a shepherd caring for a flock. The rod refers in this particular instance to a type of club with which to defend the flock, and the staff is a longer rod or pole upon which the shepherd could lean or with which he could guide the flock.

The following references give some idea of the range of meanings associated with the term in the Bible: **1** A staff for travelers (Gen. 32:10; Mark 6:8). **2** An instrument for punishment; it was used by a father to punish his son (Prov. 13: 24; 22:15) or an officer to beat a prisoner (Matt. 27:26; see 2 Cor. 11:25). **3** A symbol of authority (Judg. 5:14; Gen. 49:10). Moses' rod was a symbol of his office and evidence of the divine authority for his actions. With this rod Moses performed wonders in Egypt and even instructed Aaron to use his for similar purposes (Exod. 4:1–5; 7:8–24; 14:16). By striking the rock at Horeb with his rod Moses provided water for the Israelites in the wilderness (Exod. 17:1–7). When there was a dispute over the authority to lead the people, Moses took Aaron's rod and placed it in the tabernacle along with others representing the leading families of the nation. Aaron's rod budded and produced almonds, signifying the authority vested in his line (and that of Moses) by God. **4** Something used to measure distances (Ezek. 40:3, KJV; RSV: "reed").

J.A.D.

Rodanim (roh'dah-neem), probably the people of Rhodes (i.e., Rhodians). The Masoretic Text (MT) of 1 Chron. 1:7 lists the Rodanim among the descendants of Javan, but the MT of Gen. 10:4 uses the name Dodanim for the same people. The Septuagint reads *Rodioi* in both passages. Since Javan's other descendants lived in the Aegean region, the connection between the Rodanim and the island of Rhodes is acceptable. In Ezek. 27:15, the name Rodan is also preferred over Dedan. ***See also*** Dedan; Dodanim; Javan; Rhodes.

roe, roebuck, the roe deer *Capreolus capreolus;* it was considered clean by the Hebrews and therefore edible (Deut. 14:5 [KJV: "fallow deer"]). It was a delicacy suitable for the royal table of Solomon (1 Kings 4:23).

roll, a word used as both noun and verb in the Bible. Aside from its common verbal use, biblical texts employ it as a noun meaning a list (Ps. 40:7), a record of performance (Heb. 10:7), and simply as the rolled form (scroll) of a book (Isa. 34:4).

Roman Empire, the lands around the Mediterranean Sea and in Europe ruled by Rome. While events recorded in the books of the OT took place prior to the emergence of Rome as the sole power in the Mediterranean basin, Rome's influence was already strong at the time of the Maccabean revolt (begun 167 B.C.), and from that point until Rome assumed control over Palestine in 63 B.C. its power influenced events throughout the eastern Mediterranean world. The spread of that influence had begun much earlier, however.

The Expansion of Rome: From the mid-third century B.C. through the early second century A.D. the Romans expanded their power over an enormous variety of peoples outside Italy. The granaries of Sicily came under Roman control in 241 B.C., Sardinia in 231 B.C. Large areas of Spain were added after the second Punic war (ca. 201 B.C.), though the Roman conquest of Spain would take another two centuries to complete. Macedonia (northern Greece) finally fell to the Romans in 148 B.C. and Achaia (southern Greece) in 146 B.C., at which time Corinth was entirely destroyed. The Corinth of the NT was a city built by Julius Caesar. In the same year (146 B.C.) the destruction of Carthage gave Rome the province of Africa, another grain-growing region. In 133 B.C. the last ruler of the Attalid dynasty of Pergamum, which had broken away from the Seleucids (rulers of Syria), bequeathed the heavily populated province of Asia Minor to the Romans. It provided growing cities with textile and other industries as well as agricultural resources. Pergamum, the former royal capital, was a free city under Roman control.

Pompey's campaigns in the east in the 60s B.C. abolished the Seleucid monarchy. Judea was annexed to heavily populated Syria, which was to serve as a buffer against the Parthians across the Euphrates. As a result all the lands in this part of Asia looked toward Rome and not Parthia for leadership.

Augustus: In the 50s Julius Caesar was given command of an army to subdue Illyricum (modern Yugoslavia) and Gaul (modern France and Belgium) on both sides of the Alps. Caesar conquered tribes in France and Belgium and invaded Britain as well. The new territories of north and central France to the Rhine border became a new province, *Gallia Comata,* "long-haired Gaul." It had a vigorous provincial culture and resources in agriculture, stock breeding, mining, pottery, and glass making. Following these successes, Caesar invaded Italy, where he assumed dictatorial powers. The civil wars that followed his death ended when Augustus defeated Antony and Cleopatra (31 B.C.) and established himself as sole ruler of the empire. In Augustus' time the population of the empire is estimated to have been between seventy and ninety million, with thirty to fifty million in Europe, slightly fewer in Asia Minor, and somewhat less than twenty million in Africa.

The official transfer of command to Augustus in 27 B.C. was an implicit acknowledgment that the Republican system was not able to deal with the problems of such a vast rule without Augustus and his personal and material resources. Augustus, in turn, was constrained by the limited number of persons he could call upon to administer the empire. Consequently, as much as possible was left in the hands of the Senate. In addition, Rome was reluctant to intervene in the governing structures of the prov-

ROMAN EMPERORS
IN THE FIRST CENTURY A.D.

	Years of Rule
Augustus	27 B.C.–A.D. 14
Tiberius	A.D. 14–37
Caligula	37–41
Claudius	41–54
Nero	54–68
Galba; Otho; Vitellius	68–69
Vespasian	69–79
Titus	79–81
Domitian	81–96
Nerva	96–98
Trajan	98–117

The *Ara Pacis Augustae* (altar of the peace of Augustus), dedicated by the emperor Augustus in 9 B.C. to proclaim a new era of peace in the Roman Empire.

inces at the local level. However, Augustus did evolve a separate financial system that made the procurators of the provinces responsible directly to the emperor for collecting taxes and other revenues.

The Romans saw themselves as the legitimate rulers of the civilized world. This vast empire had been gained, Cicero wrote, only through just wars: "Our people by defensive wars in support of its allies has taken possession of the whole world" (*De Re Publica* 3.35). After the aristocratic misrule in the provinces and the bloody civil wars at home, the imperial order seemed to usher in a new age of peace. It provided permanent military security and high standards of administrative, judicial, and fiscal efficiency. The new era of peace was widely proclaimed in Augustan literature. Augustus' return from campaigns in Gaul and Spain was celebrated by dedication of the *Ara Pacis Augustae* (altar of the peace of Augustus), in January, 9 B.C. Augustus had had the doors of the temple of Janus closed in 29 B.C., signifying the end of warfare. Imperial coinage also celebrated the new age of peace. Even for many of the subject peoples the new Roman order presented an effective and stable rule that stood above local and regional disputes.

The Birth of Christianity: It was in the time of Augustus that Jesus was born (Luke 2:1), and that the events recorded in the NT began. Rome was thus the dominant political and military force of the world of the NT. According to the Gospel records, Jesus was born in Bethlehem as the result of a Roman census (Luke 2:1–4), drew illustrations in his teaching from the ever present occupying forces (Matt. 5:41, a service a Roman soldier could demand of a civilian), lived his life in a land under Roman domination, and was put to death by a Roman governor on a Roman means of execution, the cross.

Paul carried out his entire mission within the bounds of the eastern portion of the Roman Empire, wrote his most carefully reasoned letter to Christians who lived in its capital, took advantage of his Roman citizenship (Acts 16:37–38), was arrested by Romans in Jerusalem (Acts 21:31–33), escorted by them (23:24) to the Roman governor's residence in Caesarea (23:33), and when he exercised the citizen's right to appeal to Caesar (25:11) they took him to Rome itself (Acts 27–28).

The apostle Peter is remembered to have written a letter sent to Christians in the Roman provinces in Asia Minor (1 Pet. 1:1), and tradition has it that he was martyred in Rome, the capital city of the empire. In trying times, the author of the Revelation to John denounced bitter persecutions of Christians (Rev. 17), persecutions that came to an official end only when the emperor Constantine in A.D. 313 issued his edict of toleration and subsequently gave his official favor to Christianity as his own religion. Thus the entire career of the early church, as well as the events recorded in the NT and the writing of the NT books themselves, took place in a world dominated by the Roman Empire. ***See also*** Provinces.

Bibliography

Millar, F., ed. *The Roman Empire and Its Neighbors*. New York: Delacorte, 1967.

Wells, C. *The Roman Empire*. Stanford, CA: Stanford University Press, 1984. P.P./P.J.A.

Romans, the Letter of Paul to the, the longest and generally regarded as the most important of Paul's extant Letters.

The Original Letter: There is manuscript evidence for three versions of Paul's Letter to the

ROMANS, THE LETTER

Romans: a long, a short, and a middle-sized version. Most scholars agree that an abbreviated edition (chaps. 1–14 plus the benediction, 16: 25–27) was not the original letter. Those who argue that it is unlikely that our present, long version (chaps. 1–16) went to Rome usually cite the following four reasons: First, Paul probably did not know twenty-six believers in Rome whom he could greet by name (16:3–15). Second, Paul elsewhere greets no addressee by name in the letter closing. Third, since Paul had not yet been to Rome, the greetings presume that twenty-six of Paul's co-workers and Christian friends recently with him in the east have migrated to Rome, and such a mass movement to Rome in that time seems improbable. Finally, the erroneous doctrine and false teachers Paul attacks in 16:17–19 sound more like those in the eastern churches (e.g., 2 Cor. 11:13; Phil. 3:18–19) than those mentioned in Romans; nowhere else in this Letter does Paul so rigorously attack his opponents. Thus, it is argued, the middle-sized version (chaps. 1–15 plus the benediction) remains as Paul's most likely letter to Rome. On that basis, chap. 16 was an appendix to the original (perhaps originally intended for Ephesus) and tells us nothing about the situation in Rome. On the other hand, no ancient manuscript copy of Romans exists without chap. 16; hence its exclusion from Paul's original letter to Rome remains speculation.

The Founding of the Roman Church: The founder of the Roman church is unknown. Gal. 2:7 appears to rule out Peter, and Paul had neither established nor visited the church, although when he wrote he hoped to visit it soon. While the precise date of the founding of the Roman church is also uncertain, a congregation apparently existed in Rome before A.D. 49 when the Emperor Claudius banned Jews, including Jewish Christians, from Rome for internal squabbling (see Acts 18:2).

Date: The presence of Jewish Christians in the Roman church (7:1) suggests that Paul wrote the Letter after 54 when Nero lifted Claudius' ban. Paul's prolonged exchange with the Corinthian church probably began in 51 when Gallio was proconsul (Acts 18:12), but when he wrote Romans he had left Corinth for the last time. In the intervening period came (according to Acts) an eighteen-month stay in Corinth and a prolonged period in Ephesus, from which Paul wrote four letters to Corinth and made two additional visits. The time required for this prolonged exchange suggests a date between 55 and 58 for the writing of Romans.

Purpose: Scholars disagree over why Paul wrote Romans. Did Paul, realizing he was near the end of his career, write Romans as a summary of his mature thought? With his mission in the east complete (15:19), did he write seeking support for his projected Spanish mission (15:24, 28)? Uncertain of his reception in Rome and still smarting from charges brought to Corinth and Galatia, did he write to defend himself and his gospel? With the lifting of the ban of Claudius and the return of Jewish Christians to Rome, had tensions arisen between Jewish and Gentile Christians requiring Paul's mediation (14:1–15: 13)? Each of these positions has its advocates. Paul probably wrote for many reasons, however. Although the controversies in Galatia and Corinth did influence Romans, this Letter is no systematic summary of Paul's theology given elsewhere. Romans is clearly distinct from Paul's other Letters: it has the structure of a letter, conveys the warmth of personal correspondence, addresses real concerns of the Roman church, and deals with uncertainties about the apostle's imminent visit.

Content: Into the unusually short, stereotyped greeting (1:1–7), Paul crams the tradition undergirding his gospel and supporting his apostleship. Appealing to tradition, the apostle authenticates his apostleship and legitimates his gospel, thus countering the charge of being a dangerous innovator.

The thanksgiving (1:8–15) underscores the importance of Paul's commission to Gentiles. He intends to visit the Roman church to reap some harvest there as among "the rest of the Gentiles" (1:13). He announces his obligation to "Greeks and barbarians" (1:14). The summary of his gospel (1:16–17) speaks of God's power to "everyone," Jew and now Greek.

From 1:18 forward, Paul explains his Gentile gospel and defends it against challengers. He argues that Jews and Gentiles have historically failed to honor the Creator or do his will and thus need God's grace (3:23). Nevertheless, Paul's gospel of grace appears to some as a pernicious provocation. If it erases every distinction between Jews and Gentiles, why be a Jew (3:1)? If human sin elicits divine favor, why not sin with abandon to multiply God's grace (3:8)? Before dealing with these objections (6:1–11:36), Paul treats related concerns. Recalling how God counted Abraham righteous on account of his faith (Gen. 15:6) rather than by circumcision (Gen. 17:10), Paul argues that Gentiles may now become children of Abraham by faith. Through faith in Christ they are counted righteous (chap. 4) and receive access to and reconciliation with God (5:1–11).

For those who question how Jesus' act of obedience can benefit others, Paul recalls a familiar example (5:12–19). Because of his disobedience, Adam was exiled from Eden to a life marked by toil and want, fratricide and fear, pain and death. Ever since, through repeated acts of disobedience (not by biological inheritance!), humankind has shared in his frustration and futility. The first Adam and the last (i.e., Jesus) correspond in the way the action of each influences the destiny of all. They differ in the result they effect. Through the first

Adam, "many were made sinners" (5:19); through the last Adam came "acquittal" for all. Paul contends that those understanding humankind's solidarity with the first Adam should comprehend how Christ can unite all peoples.

In 6:1–7:6, Paul answers the charges (see 3:8) that his gospel of grace encourages sinning. The behavior of believers in Corinth, where some took salvation to mean all things were lawful (1 Cor. 10:23; see Rom. 14:14), gave the charge substance. Drawing on three examples (baptism, slavery, and marriage), Paul refutes the charge. In baptism, the believer symbolically dies to sin and becomes alive to God. How, Paul wonders, can one making this transition continue living in sin's bondage (6:1–14)? In 6:15–23, Paul asks how those redeemed from slavery to sin for service in Christ can still behave like slaves of the old master. In 7:1–6, he notes how the death of a husband frees his wife to remarry. Similarly, believers who have died to the law belong to Christ. How, therefore, can they act as if they were still in the prior marriage? Through these examples, Paul means to correct the mistaken impression that his gospel encourages libertinism.

While Paul's last example solved one problem, it raised another. Any pious Jew would bristle at Paul's suggestion that the law, God's gift to Israel, inflicted bondage. If the law is evil, then questions arise: is God so sinister as to give malevolent gifts? Is the law indeed evil? Paul immediately retorts, "Absolutely not!" (7:7, author's translation). Later, Paul adds, "The law is holy, and the commandment is holy and just and good" (7:12). The defect is not in the law but in the human heart. Corrupted by sin, the heart twists the law, a good thing, into an ugly distortion. While the law forbids one to "covet" (7:7), all persons crave most what is explicitly forbidden. The flaw is not in the law or its Giver but in the person. (Note: Sin, not flesh is the offender. When Paul says, "nothing good dwells . . . in my flesh," 7:18, he does not mean that flesh as such is evil, but flesh taken over by sin. Flesh can be corrupted by sin, but it is not itself inherently corrupting.)

Paul's "I" language in 7:7–25 is autobiographical only in a general sense. Paul speaks here not as a guilt-ridden Pharisee, anxious over his failure to keep the law. Instead, he tells the universal story of the corruption of the good law by the power of sin.

In chap. 8, the new age breaks into view. The law of the Spirit, Paul affirms, sets believers free from "the principle [law] of sin and death" (8:2, author's translation). Paul knows God's words to Jeremiah, "I will put my law within them, and I will write it upon their hearts" (Jer. 31:33). Through Christ, the law of the Spirit has been inscribed on the heart, eliminating resistance to God. Thus, Paul argues, the charge that his gospel repudiates the law is false. In the light of God's final Day, Paul does not reject the law but revalues it.

Chaps. 9–11 answer urgent questions raised by Jewish objections to Paul's Gentile mission: God promised to be Israel's God and to make Israel his people. In offering the gospel to the Gentiles, has God rescinded this promise? Paul's reply—that God has always chosen to bless some over others (e.g., Jacob over Esau) and is, therefore, free to turn away from Israel to the Gentiles—raises another objection: is God fair to choose the rejected (Gentiles) and reject the chosen (Jews; 9:14)? If God chooses Gentiles, how can Jews be condemned for rejecting the gospel (9:19)? If Gentiles who did not pursue righteousness now achieve it by faith, and Jews who did seek righteousness are denied salvation, can God be just? Paul's reply is that God is free to turn to Gentiles but has not forsaken Israel. In the future, God will join Jews with Gentiles in one community (11:25–32). Fearing Gentile arrogance over their salvation, Paul warns, "if God did not spare the natural branches [Jews], neither will he spare you [Gentiles]" (11:21; cf. 11:13–24).

Sensitive to the charge that his gospel encourages immorality, Paul earlier argued that moral license and Christian freedom are incompatible (6:1–7:6). Chaps. 12–15 give instances of the work of the gospel in everyday life. First, concerning insiders, Paul exhorts all with charismatic gifts—prophecy, teaching, administration, and benevolence—to use the charisms for the church's nurture (12:3–13). Toward outsiders, Paul encourages love: bless the persecutors, care for the lowly, eschew revenge, and feed the hungry (12:14–21). Christian love also dictates respect for "governing authorities" and payment of Roman taxes (13:1–7). The state serves God, Paul argues, when it preserves order (13:3–4) and provides an arena for witness until the end (13:12). Moreover, God's care for and claim on the world allow no Christian to abandon it. While Paul offers no advice for occasions when loyalty to God conflicts with loyalty to the state, it is nevertheless mistaken to base a blind allegiance to the state on Romans 13. Paul's opening argument against idolatry (1:21–22) would preclude such deification of the state.

In 14:1–15:13, Paul encourages church factions to "welcome one another . . . as Christ has welcomed you" (15:7). The identity of the quarreling weak and strong is disputed. Yet in view of the return of Jewish Christians to Rome in A.D. 54, the reference to Jewish and Gentile Christians in 15:8–9, to purity laws in 14:14, 20, and to both Jewish and Gentile Christians elsewhere in the Letter, the bickering may have been between conscientious Jewish Christians and "liberated" Gentile believers. Yet there were no Jewish regulations that forbade all meat (14:2) or the consumption of wine (14:21). Whatever the issue in dispute may have been, Paul gently pushes both factions toward reconciliation.

In the Letter closing, Paul shares his travel plans. His eastern mission complete (15:19, 23), he intends to deliver the offering to Jerusalem (15:25–28), then travel via Rome to Spain. Questions flood his mind: will the Roman church endorse his gospel? Will it support his mission to Spain as did the Macedonian church his work in Greece (2 Cor. 11:9)? Will the "unbelievers in Judea" frustrate his plans (15:31)? Will his offering "be acceptable to the saints" (15:31)? The Acts of the Apostles (21:17–28:31) gives substance to Paul's premonition of failure. While Paul tells us nothing more, Acts reports that once in Jerusalem, Paul was arrested and charged with speaking against the Temple, the law, and Judaism. His appeal to Caesar eventually took him to Rome, and there, tradition holds, he died a martyr's death. ***See also*** Acts of the Apostles, The; Baptism; Contribution for the Saints; Election; Expiation; Faith; Fall, The; Flesh and Spirit; Gentile; Grace; Justification; Law; Paul; Predestination; Promise; Reconciliation; Redemption; Rome; Sin; Spain; Spiritual Gifts.

OUTLINE OF CONTENTS

The Letter of Paul to the Romans

- I. Introduction (1:1–17)
  - A. Salutation (1:1–7)
  - B. Thanksgiving (1:8–15)
  - C. Summary of Paul's gospel (1:16–17)
- II. Wrath now revealed on all (1:18–3:20)
  - A. Gentiles under the power of sin (1:18–32)
  - B. Jews under the power of sin (2:1–29)
  - C. Objection (3:1–8)
  - D. Judgment on both Jews and Greeks (3:9–20)
- III. Righteousness now revealed to all (3:21–4:25)
  - A. Righteousness by faith to all, Jews and Gentiles (3:21–31)
  - B. Scripture proof: Abraham made righteous by faith (4:1–25)
- IV. The life of righteousness by faith (5:1–8:39)
  - A. God's righteousness through Jesus Christ (5:1–11)
  - B. The way Jesus mediates God's righteousness (5:12–21)
    - 1. Sin and death through first Adam (5:12–14)
    - 2. Acquittal, life, and grace through Christ (5:15–21)
  - C. Replies to objections that grace fosters immorality (6:1–8:39)
    - 1. If grace overcomes sin, why not sin more to receive more grace? (6:1–7:6)
      - a. Response: can the baptized behave in the ways of the old life? (6:1–14)
      - b. Response: can a freed slave still serve an old master? (6:15–23)
      - c. Response: can a widow who remarries return to her deceased husband? (7:1–6)
    - 2. Objection: if a believer is liberated from the law, is the law therefore sinful? (7:7) Response: a heart corrupted by sin, not the law, is sinful (7:7–25)
    - 3. The believer is not lawless but walks by the Spirit in love (8:1–39)
- V. Objection: why be a Jew? and Paul's answer (9:1–11:36)
  - A. To Israel belong special privileges (9:1–5)
  - B. Israel's rejection, even if final, is not a failure on God's part (9:6–13)
  - C. God's selection of Gentiles, even if arbitrary, is not unjust (9:14–29)
  - D. God's selection is not arbitrary: everyone, Jew or Gentile, who turns to God will be saved (9:30–10:21)
  - E. The Jewish rejection is not final (11:1–32)
    - 1. A remnant has accepted the gospel (11:1–6)
    - 2. God uses the rejection of Jews (11:7–24)
    - 3. All Israel will be saved (11:25–32)
  - F. Doxology of praise to God (11:33–36)
- VI. God's righteousness in the daily life of the believer (12:1–15:13)
  - A. Introduction (12:1–2)
  - B. Response to insiders (12:3–13)
  - C. Response to outsiders (12:14–13:17)
    - 1. Persecutors (12:14–21)
    - 2. Governing authorities and state (13:1–7)
  - D. Response to all: love (13:8–10)
  - E. Urgency imposed by the approaching end (13:11–14)
  - F. Weak and strong in Rome (14:1–15:13)
- VII. Paul's travel plans (15:14–29)
- VIII. Conclusion (15:30–33)
- IX. Appendix: recommendation, greetings, warning against false teachers (16:1–23)
- X. Letter closing (16:25–27)

Bibliography

Achtemeier, P. J. *Romans.* Atlanta: John Knox, 1984.

Barrett, C. K. *A Commentary on the Epistle to the Romans.* New York: Harper & Brothers, 1957.

Donfried, Karl P., ed. *The Romans Debate.* Minneapolis, MN: Augsburg, 1977.

Käsemann, Ernst. *Commentary on Romans.* Grand Rapids, MI: Eerdmans, 1980. C.J.R.

Head of the emperor Augustus (ruled 27 B.C.–A.D. 14) on a bronze sestertius minted toward the end of his reign, ca. A.D. 10–14.

Rome, the chief city of the Roman empire. The traditional date for the founding of the city is 753 B.C., though there is evidence of earlier settlement. From such evidence, the following bits of information can be gleaned. 1. Around 650 B.C. the swamp, which would later be drained to provide an area for the forum, was being used as a necropolis, or cemetery. 2. A few references to the time when Rome was ruled by kings remain on stelae. 3. We read of tending the flame of a sacred hearth, the task that in historical times would fall to the vestal virgins, in a shrine at the east end of the forum.

The Early City: Until the end of the third century B.C. Rome was not at all the impressive city that we know. Temples had patched roofs. The streets were winding, narrow, and unpaved. A number of new temples were built during Republican times (from about the fifth century to 31 B.C.), including two to Greek divinities: one to Aesculapius (Asclepius) on Tiber Island and another to the Great Mother *(Magna Mater)* on the Palatine hill. *Magna Mater* was the Roman name for Cybele, a fertility goddess from Anatolia (modern Turkey). These developments foreshadow the plethora of foreign gods to be found in Rome during Imperial times (beginning with Augustus in 31 B.C.). Imperial Rome would harbor a sizable Jewish population that served as the foundation for the spread of Christianity into the city.

Toward the end of the Republic (ca. 83 B.C.), the Roman general Sulla sought to imitate what he had seen in the Greek east by building a great, terraced sanctuary to the goddess Fortuna. The wall paintings in the sanctuary as well as those in the houses of Pompeii show the great interest in Egyptian style and motifs that existed in the late Republic and early Imperial periods. The ships that sailed between Alexandria in Egypt to Rome also brought with them the intellectual ferment of that Egyptian city. A narrow gate to the sanctuary dedicated to Fortuna suggests that pilgrims paid admission to this temple and bought the votive offerings sold in the stalls on the fifth terrace. The seventh and final terrace contained the most holy place in the sanctuary. The priests offered sacrifices in view of the worshipers assembled on the semicircular steps. This temple used the fundamentals of Roman architectural innovation: concrete, arches, and vaults. It was faced with limestone. No marble was used except in the statuary. With their discovery of concrete and the principles of arches and vaults, the Romans were able to create massive structures and buildings that could enclose any space. At the end of the first century A.D. the architect who designed Trajan's forum was influenced by the great temple to create terraces and concrete-framed arches within the marketplace.

Expansion: In 52 B.C. Pompey dedicated Rome's first stone theater in the Campus Martius. Julius Caesar (100–44 B.C.) built a two-story basilica north of the old Roman forum. A balcony around the second story provided a place to overlook the events below. Caesar also initiated the practice of emperors building their own forums within the city. Like the Greek agora, the Roman forum was the political and social center of the city. Its temples expressed the relationship between the community and the gods. At the back of Caesar's forum a temple to his supposed ancestor Venus stood on a high podium. Both Domitian (A.D. 81–96) and Trajan (A.D. 98–117) did restoration work on that temple. The forums contained market halls (basilicas) and places for the people to assemble as well as memorials and triumphal arches commemorating the victories of the emperors. Augustus (27 B.C.–A.D. 14), Vespasian (A.D. 69–79), Trajan, and Nerva (A.D. 96–98) each added forums to the city. Trajan's overshadowed the others as it was over a thousand feet long.

The visitor to Rome was also impressed by the great amphitheaters and the Circus Maximus. The invention of concrete and use of the arch enabled the Romans to build in the round

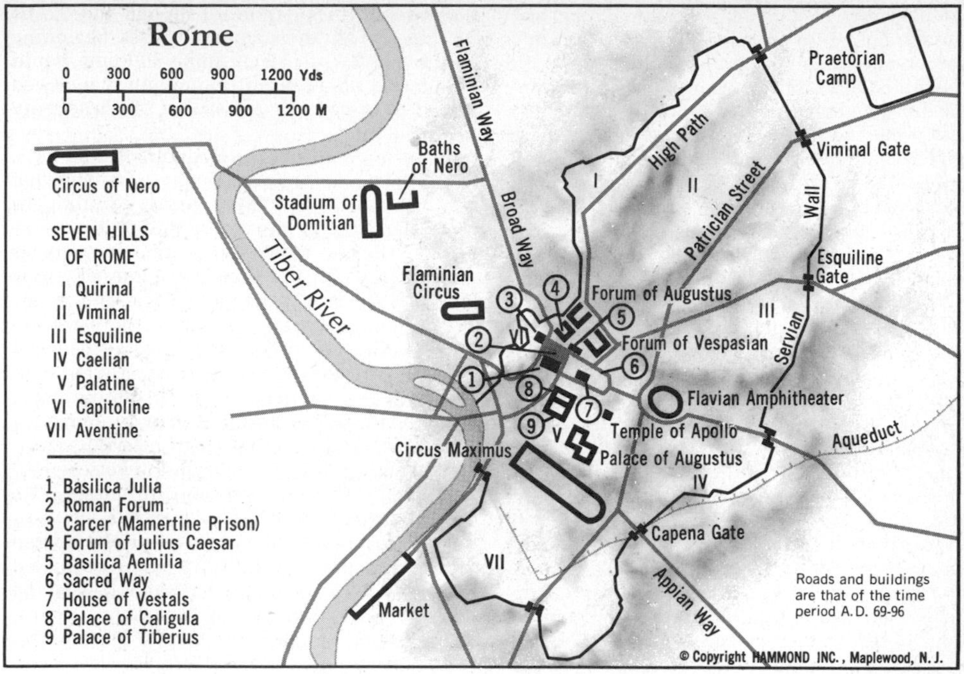

in open spaces. They did not require a natural hillside as the Greeks did. In the valley between the Argentine and Palatine hills where chariot races were conducted, Caesar and Augustus constructed the Circus Maximus. After successive enlargements it could accommodate 110,000 to 180,000 spectators. The most famous amphitheater is the Colosseum, which was not built until the end of the first century A.D. It was constructed over the area that once contained Nero's famous "Golden House." The Colosseum could contain 50,000 spectators. It contains four stories and eighty great arches. This structure is 160 feet high.

Great height was a common feature of Roman Imperial architecture. The emperor Hadrian built a mausoleum over 130 feet high. The Romans set up obelisks (tall, four-sided pillars) that they brought from Egypt. Roman emperors copied the obelisk idea in their own style by erecting monumental pillars. Trajan's hundred-foot column of Parian marble contains 155 scenes on twenty-three spirals. If the scroll carved on the column were unrolled, it would be 650 feet long. The scroll was made wider as it moved up the column so that people could read it to a great height, especially from the balconies of libraries in the forum. The scroll shows the events of Trajan's campaigns against the Dacians, scenes from army and navy life, and pictures of native customs. Some of its scenes are said to have influenced Dante's *Purgatorio.*

Life in Rome: The Romans also prided themselves on more utilitarian building accomplishments such as paving roads, constructing systems of bridges for them, and especially using aqueducts to deliver running water to the city. The availability of water encouraged the construction of fountains and numerous public baths. Augustus' friend Agrippa restored and enlarged four existing aqueducts. He was also able to use concrete to build two more. Agrippa was the first to have several water channels run over a single series of stones. Another element in his overhaul of the city's drainage system was repairing the retaining walls along the Tiber.

The public baths were just as much centers of social life as the forum, the Circus Maximus, or the amphitheaters. The largest bath remains are those of Caracalla (A.D. 211–217) and Diocletian (A.D. 289–305). They cover some 30 acres and consist of a conglomeration of rooms and courtyards. Baths of all types were available: cold, warm, hot, steam, air, and sun. There were facilities for exercise, gymnastics, and massage. In addition the garden parks, the library, and the museum provided places for conversation and study. The admission fee and the cost of oil for anointing the body may have kept many from using these baths too often. The city also boasted numerous smaller baths. There were some hundred and seventy such under Augustus and the number swells to over nine hundred in late antiquity (fourth century A.D.).

The wealthier Romans lived in villas, an atrium style of house with a peristyle section and a garden area in the back around which one found the dining room and bedrooms. Lead pipes were used to connect individual homes to the sewage and water systems. Heaters created warm air under the floors of the houses. The slaves occupied the second floor. The emperor Augustus still lived in a modest home on the Palatine, but Tiberius built the first palace and Nero the famous "Golden House." Later centuries would see the wealthy also building palaces as homes.

Most of the approximately one million inhabitants of the city, however, were crowded into the brick and wooden tenements, *insulae* (Lat., "islands"), which are well known from excavations at Ostia. Such buildings could be as large as 4,000 square feet and rise five to six stories. They had no water supply or latrines. The ground floors contained shops, workshops, and storerooms. A typical ground-floor unit contained three to five rooms. As one went higher in the building the units became smaller and darker. The *insulae* were crowded, noisy, and very public. Not surprisingly many shopkeepers moved out onto the streets to conduct their business, thereby contributing to the general congestion. Vehicular traffic along the Appian Way was banned during the day. Consequently the uproar of carts along its stones made for an equally noisy night. These tenement buildings were also perpetual fire traps and burned rapidly in the great fire under Nero in A.D. 64, which was blamed on the Christians.

Augustus: Augustus boasted that he had found Rome a city of brick and left it a city of marble. Much of this building also sought to impress on spectators the religious foundations of the new imperial order. Rome, it was said, owed its prosperity and worldwide rule to its piety. The civil wars of the late Republic had seen a decline in the state religion. Augustus restored some eighty-two ruined temples within the city of Rome. The Temple of Mars, the Avenger, was a symbol of Roman supremacy over the world. It was constructed of marble from all over the empire; colored marble came from Africa, Greece, and Asia Minor to complement the white Caeraca marble from Italy.

The most stunning Augustan accomplishment was the great altar of the Augustan peace built between 13 and 9 B.C. A square enclosure surrounded this monumental altar. Friezes on the enclosure wall and the altar itself depicted the imperial family and its associates. It was one of the artistic masterpieces of the age. In the figured upper panels of the north and south sides the procession moves westward. Turning the corner of the enclosure one entered the door to sacrifice at the altar. An enormous calendar sundial stood next to the altar. The signs of the zodiac were labeled in Greek and the months in Latin. The dial's pointer was a one-hundred-foot obelisk that was oriented so that the shadow of the obelisk fell across the altar of peace on Augustus' birthday, a striking reminder of the birth of the Roman emperor as the birth of peace! (The obelisk has since been removed and set up on the banks of the Tiber next to Augustus' mausoleum.)

We get some sense of the size of the city that had become the capital of such a great empire from a fourth-century A.D. listing of the buildings in Rome: 1,797 villas; 46,602 tenement buildings; 254 mills; 190 grain silos; 8 bridges; 8 great squares; 11 forums; 36 triumphal arches; 1,152 fountains; 28 public libraries; 2 circuses; 2 amphitheaters; 3 theaters; 11 hot spring baths; and 865 private bath houses. This city contained almost a million people in its 265 precincts. They had long since ceased to be purely of old Roman stock. Persons from all over the empire with their different languages, customs, and gods could be found in the streets of Rome. The religious themes of Imperial architecture sought to impress upon the inhabitants and visitors from throughout the great empire the theme of peace. Roman greatness had transformed the world. The warlike past of Rome had issued in the peace, order, and tranquility of the later Hellenistic times.

It was into that peace and tranquility that Jesus was born, in a Roman province, and in a town to which, as Luke reports, his mother had gone as the direct result of an edict from Rome (see Luke 2:1–4). It was within that same world that the apostles carried out their mission of spreading the Christian faith.

Jews and Christians in Rome: While Roman power was making itself felt in the Mediterranean world already at the time of the later writings of the OT (e.g., Daniel) and the Apocrypha (e.g., 1, 2 Maccabees), it did not dominate the world then as it did during the time the NT was being written. Because Rome was the principal city of the empire, it was inevitable that both Christians and Jews should eventually be attracted to it.

It is difficult to know when the first Jews located in Rome, although their presence in other major cities of the Mediterranean world would make it likely they were present for a length of time before the Christian movement reached the city. We also have no information about when the Christian faith arrived in Rome. By the time Paul wrote his Letter to Christians there (mid-first century A.D.), it had already become an important church (Rom. 1:8). Perhaps the presence of a Jewish settlement in Rome was the point of entry for Jewish Christians coming there.

About the year A.D. 49, the emperor Claudius issued an edict expelling Jews from Rome. The fact that Christians as well were expelled (see Acts 18:2) indicates that at that time Roman officials did not differentiate between Christians

Panorama of the Roman forum.

and Jews, perhaps because the Christian community was not large enough to be significant. Some fifteen years later, however, they were numerous enough to attract the blame from Nero for a fire that devastated Rome (A.D. 64). There is an early tradition that puts the martyrdom of both Paul and Peter in Rome about this time. While we have a record of Paul's arrival and two-year stay in Rome (Acts 28:16–31), there is no mention in the NT of when Peter got there or how long he remained.

The Christian community in Rome continued to exercise influence on other churches. That is shown by the likelihood that 1 Peter and Hebrews originated there. 1 Clement, a letter from Rome sometime in the early second century, shows how that interest continued, in this instance interest in the church in Corinth. ***See also*** Augustus; Jupiter; Ostia; Roman Empire; Triumphal Arch.

Bibliography

Cornell, T., and J. Matthews. *Atlas of the Roman World.* New York: Facts on File, 1982.

MacKendrick, P. *The Mute Stones Speak.* 2d ed. New York: Norton, 1983. P.P.

roofs, the usually horizontal but sometimes angled constructions covering rooms or buildings. Roofs appear in literal and figurative senses in biblical texts. As the covering of a building, a roof served primarily to give shade, to keep out rain or other foul weather, and to support a variety of activities carried out on rooftops, from sleeping to storage to sounding alarms.

The roof of the ark (Gen. 6:16) was primarily for weather protection, but a roof stood for the protection of the host for his guests as well (Gen. 19:8). In the common model of a flat house roof lay the hazard of falling from it, subject of the law to provide a parapet around such a hazard (Deut. 22:8). Roofs provided storage as well as hiding space (Josh. 2:6–8), resting room usable as latrine or murder site (Judg. 3:20–25), or, in a public building, as an observation platform (Judg. 16:27). From his roof David saw Bathsheba's bath (2 Sam. 11:2) and a roof was used for a guest room for Elisha (2 Kings 4:10). The palace roof was suitable for various shrines to foreign gods (2 Kings 23:12), and a house roof could serve as a platform from which to lower a sick man's bed to a room inside (Mark 2:4; Luke 5:19). Roofs needed regular restoration (Eccles. 10:18). On the battlefield, shields formed as a roof could protect against arrows (Ezek. 26:8).

Symbolically, a tongue stuck to the roof of the mouth meant silence (Job 29:10) or the condemnation of the unfaithful (Ps. 137:6). Extreme thirst made the tongue stick to the roof of the mouth (Lam. 4:4), and God could silence a prophet in the same way (Ezek. 3:26).

Simple roof construction usually comprised a horizontal bed of branches or beams, sometimes supported by columns, on which layers of earth or limestone plaster were laid. They weathered into decay in rainy season conditions and needed to be restored in dry season weather to endure. Large public buildings had roofs suspended from the side walls or supported by columns or a combination of both, especially where balconies were part of an interior structure. R.S.B.

room, a space bounded by three or more walls.

Biblical references include dwelling spaces (the "upper room" of Mark 14:15), guest rooms (Mark 14:14; Philem. 1:22), Temple rooms (Ezek. 40:10; 1 Kings 6:29–30), and royal chambers (Jer. 35:4).

rope, a twisted or braided line. Rope could be made of cloth, string, leather, vine, or any other strong material. It could be used as a belt (Isa. 3: 24), as a means of escape (Josh. 2:15), as a device to trap someone or something (Job 18:10), to lead a beast (Job 41:2), to tie a prisoner (Judg. 15:13), to destroy a city (2 Sam. 17:13), to symbolize submission (1 Kings 20:31–32), to guide a domestic animal (Job 39:10), to pull a vehicle (Isa. 5:18), to lower someone into a pit or cistern (Jer. 38:6, 11) or raise him up (Jer. 38:12–13), and as marine rigging (Acts 27:32, 40).

The archaeological evidence for rope tends to be sparse because of its vulnerability to decay. String-cut bases on small jars are common in several periods, and the potters used a "rope" molding for decorative purposes, frequently incising or marking it with fingers. Lug handles were intended to be carried by cord or rope suspension. R.S.B.

rose, a general term for a colorful flower, the specific identification of which is often dependent on context. The Phoenician rose *(Rosa phoenicia)* is one of the true roses growing wild in the Holy Land. A thorny bush bearing many blossoms, it grows well at higher altitudes and therefore is probably the rose of the mountains in 2 Esd. 2:19.

Rose of Sharon.

The rose by the brook (Ecclus. 39:13) and the rose plants of Jericho (Ecclus. 24:14) most likely refer to the oleander bush *(Nerium oleander)*, a plant with shiny, leathery evergreen leaves and large deep pink or white flowers. Growing along *wadis* (dry riverbeds) and other watercourses, the oleander is an outstanding feature of the otherwise arid countryside all over the Holy Land. It is also widely cultivated today in city parks and gardens.

The rose of Sharon (Song of Sol. 2:1) is probably not a true rose, but a bright red tulip-like flower *(Tulipa montana)*, today prolific in the hills of Sharon. It displays a dramatic deep red mat of color in the grass with the beginning of spring, after the winter rains. Another plant of the lily family, *Narcissus tazetta*, grows wild in the more arid regions of the Holy Land and therefore may be the rose (KJV; RSV: "crocus") of Isa. 35:1, "and the desert shall rejoice, and blossom as the rose." P.L.C.

Rosetta Stone, a granite block bearing an inscription in Egyptian and Greek found by Napoleon's soldiers digging near Rashid (Rosetta) in Egypt in 1799. The stone was ceded to the British in 1801. This stone played a critical role in the deciphering of ancient Egyptian hieroglyphics, since it provided a bilingual inscription issued in Memphis by Pharaoh Ptolemy V (ca. 203–180 B.C.). The top version, with some lines and the beginning and end of each line missing, is in old hieroglyphics. The middle version in demotic script is also Egyptian and the bottom version is in Greek. By matching Greek and de-

The Rosetta Stone, written on in both hieroglyphic and demotic Egyptian and Greek; ca. 203–180 B.C.

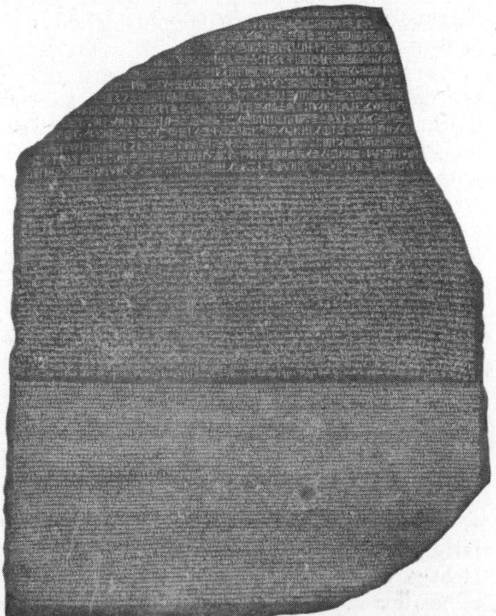

motic words and discovering that the royal name, Ptolemy, occurred within a cartouche, it was possible to attach phonetic values to some of the hieroglyphic signs. Further work on other examples of royal names by the linguist Champollion demonstrated the phonetic nature of the hieroglyphic script in both Hellenistic and earlier Pharaonic times. P.P.

Rosh (Heb., "head"). A son of Benjamin, he is listed as one of those who descended to the Egyptian delta with the Jacob tribes (Gen. 46:21).

Rosh Hashannah (rohsh hah-shahn'ah). ***See*** New Year Festival.

royal cities. ***See*** Cities.

RSV, abbreviation for the Revised Standard Version of the Bible. ***See*** English Bible, The; Revised Standard Version.

ruby, a precious stone of a deep red color. The KJV translates as "ruby" a Hebrew term (*peninim*) now thought to designate pearls (Job 28:18; Prov. 3:15 ["jewels"]; 8:11; 20:15; 31:10) or coral (Lam. 4:7). The true ruby, a transparent red variety of corundum, is not found in ancient Near Eastern sites before the third century B.C. The RSV uses "ruby" in the Apocrypha to translate two Greek terms (*smaragados*, Tob. 13:17; *anthrakos*, Ecclus. 32:5). ***See also*** Pearl.

rue (ro͞o), an herb, *Ruta graveolens*, used as condiment, medicinal ingredient, and charm component. It is specified in Luke 11:42 as subject to tithing by Pharisees.

Rufus (ro͞o'fuhs), a common name in the Greco-Roman world of the first century. **1** The brother of Alexander and son of Simon of Cyrene who was compelled to carry Jesus' cross (Mark 15:21; neither Rufus nor Alexander appears in parallels, Matt. 27:32; Luke 23:26). **2** A recipient, with his mother, of Paul's greeting in Rom. 16:13. The probability of 1 and 2 being the same person depends upon a Roman origin for the Gospel of Mark and the original inclusion of chapter 16 in Paul's letter to the Romans. If those two places where a "Rufus" is mentioned do not have a point of connection in Rome, it is unlikely that the two references designate the same person. ***See also*** Alexander; Mark, The Gospel According to; Romans, The Letter of Paul to the; Simon.

Rule, Golden. ***See*** Golden Rule.

ruler, a word used to translate several terms in Hebrew and Greek that represent various kinds of leadership positions in society. "Ruler" is used, without much precision, to designate the leader or chieftain of some segment of the social structure, be it family, clan, or tribal unit (Exod. 18:25; Judg. 11:8, in which cases "ruler" translates the Heb. *ro'sh*, "head"). In the NT the leader or president of a synagogue is called the "ruler (Gk., *archon*) of the synagogue" (Matt. 9:18; Mark 5:22–43; Luke 13:10–17).

Similarly there are rulers who were apparently the chief overseers of livestock (Gen. 47:6), of David's public works projects (1 Chron. 29:6), of Persian satrapies ("rulers of the provinces," Esther 8:9), and of cities under Hezekiah (2 Chron. 29:20). In all of these instances, the Hebrew term *sar*, which is sometimes translated "prince," is used.

In the NT, there are also "rulers of the city" where the reference is to the local Greek magistrates, rather than to the Roman authorities (Acts 16:19, *archon;* 17:6, *politarch).*

David is called the "ruler over all Israel" (1 Sam. 25:30) and Solomon is termed the "ruler over Israel and Judah" (1 Kings 1:35). In both cases, the term translated is *nagid*, which is sometimes used as a title of some of the kings of Israel and Judah and appears to point to God or a prophet of God as the designator of the *nagid*. ***See also*** David; Satrap; Solomon. F.S.F.

Ruler of the Synagogue (Mark 5:35–38), the title of an office known from inscriptions and from analogy with Greco-Roman religion. The head or ruler of the synagogue was usually a wealthy and prominent member of the congregation who was charged especially with providing for the material needs of the congregation. ***See also*** Synagogue.

run, runners, words that are used with different shades of meaning in the OT and the NT. The usual meaning of "run" is, of course, moving quickly from one place to another (cf. 2 Sam. 2:18–23; John 20:2, 4), but it is also used figuratively to denote the struggle of the person of faith to stay the course against evil and remain committed to God in this world (cf. 1 Cor. 9:24–26; Gal. 2:2; 5:7; Heb. 12:1).

The meaning of the term "runners" is more varied. These persons could be messengers who relayed news (cf. Jer. 51:31; 2 Chron. 30:6, 10; Esther 3:13; Job 9:25); a group of persons around a king assigned to run errands and do his bidding (cf. 1 Sam. 8:11; 2 Sam. 15:1); or a group that served as a bodyguard for the king (cf. 1 Sam. 22:17; 2 Kings 10:25; 11:4) and ran in front of the king's chariot (cf. 2 Sam. 15:1; 1 Kings 1:5). Runners were foot soldiers, as contrasted with cavalry and chariot warriors. ***See also*** Arms, Armor; Army; Battle; Chariots; Defense; Guard, Bodyguard; Race, Racing; Soldier; War; Weapons. J.M.E.

rush (or bulrush), a grasslike member of the sedge family with a pithy or hollow stem that grows in marshy or wet areas (Job 8:11). Various species of rushes and reeds are common along the rivers of the Middle East, including the Nile and the Jordan, and the Huleh Basin of northern Israel. Since there are several species of this type of plant it is not immediately clear which is referred to in the Bible; however, scholars generally agree that papyrus was ordinarily meant. The "bulrushes" of which the infant Moses' basket was woven were probably papyrus (Exod. 2:3) since Isaiah (18:2) mentions "papyrus vessels" used by the Ethiopians. The plants were used as fuel (Job 41:20) and woven into ropes (Job 41:2). Because of their fragile stems and their requirement for a specific environment they became a symbol of weakness and vulnerability (Job 8:11–14; Isa. 19:6–7; cf. 2 Kings 18:21; Matt. 11:7) or represented the lowly and insignificant (Isa. 9:14; 19:15; cf. 58:5). But in the same manner the flourishing of rushes could also be used as a symbol of abundance and blessing (Isa. 35:7). Various English versions often interchange the translation of "rushes" (or "bulrushes") and "reeds" from several Hebrew and Greek words. ***See also*** Flags; Papyrus; Reed.

D.R.B.

Rush.

Ruth (Heb., probably "satiation"), a Moabite who married Mahlon of the Judahite family of Elimelech. Widowed and childless, she abandoned her family, country, and faith to accompany her mother-in-law Naomi to Bethlehem. Her radical actions continued as she secured food for herself and Naomi and summoned the relative Boaz to be their redeemer. Boaz married her. She bore a son who became the grandfather of David. The women of Bethlehem exalted Ruth as the loving daughter-in-law who meant more to Naomi than seven sons, the ideal number (Ruth 4:15). Her name appears later in the Matthean genealogy of Jesus (1:5). P.T.

Ruth, the Book of, the eighth book of the OT. It is a beautifully crafted historical short story about how the lovingly loyal behavior of Ruth, a Moabite widow in a Jewish family from Bethlehem, brought back fullness of life to her widowed mother-in-law, Naomi, aided by Naomi's worthy relative Boaz. The result was security for Ruth as well, through the birth of her child, Obed, David's grandfather. The story thus offers a bridge from the time of the judges (Ruth 1:1) to the monarchy. It resembles in style and content stories in Genesis 22, 24, and 38; the Joseph cycle; the frame of Job (1; 42:7–17); and episodes in 2 Samuel 9–20. Most of these pertain to David and his antecedents; all share with Ruth dramatic tension in confronting human predicaments and problems of injustice. Scholars now tend to date the composition of Ruth early (tenth–eighth centuries B.C.), rather than around 400 B.C. as previously maintained (thought to be composed as a protest against the dissolution of mixed marriages in Nehemiah 13 and Ezra 10). The story represents the stream of openness to the world, a stream running deep and wide in the OT. E.F.C./P.J.A.

OUTLINE OF CONTENTS

The Book of Ruth

I. Ruth and Naomi (1:1–22)
   A. Ruth is married and widowed (1:1–5)
   B. Ruth returns with Naomi to Bethlehem (1:6–22)
II. Ruth and Boaz (2:1–4:22)
   A. Ruth gleans in Boaz's fields (2:1–23)
   B. Ruth and Boaz at the threshing floor (3:1–18)
   C. Boaz marries Ruth when her next of kin refuses to marry her (4:1–12)
   D. A son is born to Ruth and Boaz who will become grandfather of David (4:13–22)

rye (KJV; RSV: "spelt"), a food grain (Isa. 28:25; Exod. 9:32). ***See also*** Spelt.

Opposite: Sarah, fragment of Genesis 16 from the late fourth-century *Cotton Genesis.*

S

sabachthani (sah-bakh'thah-nee), Aramaic word, part of Jesus' cry from the cross in Matt. 27:46 and Mark 15:34. ***See also*** Eli, Eli, Lema Sabachthani.

Sabaoth, Lord of. ***See*** Lord of Hosts.

Sabbaias (suh-bay'uhs; KJV; RSV: "Sabbeus"; 1 Esd. 9:32), a man who married a foreign woman; he is the same as Shemaiah in Ezra 10:31.

Sabbath (from Heb. *shabbat*, "to cease, desist"), the weekly day of rest and abstention from work enjoined upon the Israelites.

Origin: An etiological origin for the Sabbath is supplied in Gen. 2:1–3, which speaks of God ceasing from the work of creation on the seventh day, blessing the day, and declaring it holy. Scholarly explanations of the Sabbath's origins have focused on certain days in the Babylonian monthly calendar on which normal activities of the king and certain professions were restricted. These days, known as "evil days," were determined by the lunar cycle, corresponding with the quarters of the moon. While the postulating of a dependence on the Babylonian calendar is tempting, it cannot be objectively sustained. The biblical Sabbath was ordained as a weekly institution with no relation whatsoever to the lunar cycle. Moreover, the somber nature of the Babylonian "evil days" stands in stark contrast to the joyous nature of the Sabbath.

Of uncertain relation to the lunar "evil days" was the day of the full moon on the fifteenth of the month, known as *shapattu*, a term possibly related to *sabbath*. This day was described as a "day of pacifying the heart [of the god]" by certain ceremonies. No significant similarities between this day and the Sabbath are known, however. The closest analogy between the biblical Sabbath and Babylonian culture is the shared literary motif of the god(s) resting after having created humans (see *Enuma elish* 7.8, 34). Even here, the parallel is distant: the biblical God rests at the conclusion of his creative efforts, while the Babylonian gods are freed from the labors required to feed themselves since humans were created to relieve them of that task.

Observance: The Sabbath was a cornerstone of Israelite religious practice from earliest times. This can be seen from the consistent mention of the Sabbath throughout all the strata of Pentateuchal and extra-Pentateuchal sources, with the exception of wisdom literature. In the Pentateuch, Sabbath observance is legislated repeatedly in general terms (Exod. 20:8–11; 23:12; 31:12–17; Lev. 23:3; Deut. 5:12–15), though the types of work prohibited are relatively limited; those mentioned include gathering food, plowing and reaping, kindling a fire, and chopping wood (Exod. 16:29–30; 34:21; 35:3; Num. 15:32–36). The positive specifications of Sabbath observance include giving rest to one's servants and animals (Exod. 20:10; 23:12; Deut. 5:14).

Outside the Pentateuch, evidence relating to the practical observance of the Sabbath is not overabundant, but it is more extensive than that found for most laws. During the monarchial period (ca. 1050–586 B.C.), the Sabbath (as well as the New Moon) was marked by visits to prophet and Temple (2 Kings 4:23; Isa. 1:13). Business activity came to a halt (Amos 8:5). The Sabbath was a joyous day, much like the festivals (Hos. 2:13; Lam. 2:6). Its desecration was severely attacked by Jeremiah, who lashed out against those who carried burdens from their houses or through the gates of Jerusalem (Jer. 17:19–27). During the period of the restoration, Nehemiah enforced observance of the Sabbath by locking the city gates of Jerusalem in order to prevent traders from selling their wares (Neh. 13:15–22). Contemporary documents from a Jewish colony in Elephantine, Egypt, likewise mention the Sabbath, attesting to its recognition by Diaspora (i.e., non-Palestinian) Jews in the fifth century B.C.

In addition to these features of popular observance of the Sabbath, one can also piece together a picture of Sabbath observance in the Temple. The Pentateuchal prescriptions of additional sacrifices and changing of the showbread on the Sabbath (Lev. 24:8; Num. 28:9–10) apparently reflect accepted practice (cf. Ezek. 45:17; 46:4–5; 1 Chron. 9:32; 23:31; 2 Chron. 2:3; 8:13; 31:3). The sacrificial service may have been accompanied by a special psalm (Ps. 92:1). There is also a somewhat cryptic reference to the changing of the royal guards at the Temple on the Sabbath (2 Kings 11:4–12).

Purpose: Two major rationales for Sabbath observance are presented in the Pentateuch. The concept of the Sabbath as a memorial of God's resting from the work of creation is expressed in Gen. 2:1–3 and repeated in Exod. 20:11 and 31:17. The latter passage broadens the concept in defining the Sabbath as "a sign forever between me and the people of Israel." Although God had already sanctified the seventh day at the time of creation, he did not reveal its special status to humankind at large, but only to his people Israel. Thus, Israel's observance of the Sabbath underscored its special relationship with God. This rationale was emphasized by Priestly writers.

Along with the theological rationale, a distinctly humanistic approach is to be found in Exod. 23:12 and Deut. 5:14–15, both of which ground the observance of the Sabbath on the need to give servants, strangers, and work animals an opportunity to rest. The added reminder in Deut. 5:15 of Israel's experience in Egypt most likely intends to bolster the owner's feeling of compassion for the weak and destitute (cf. Deut. 15:15; 16:12).

Sabbath observance took on an added significance with the prophets active shortly before and during the exilic period. Jeremiah attaches the very fate of Jerusalem to the observance of the Sabbath, thereby expressing a radical new conception (Jer. 17:19–27; cf. Neh. 13:17–18). Ezekiel subscribes to the same line of thought in equating the Sabbath with all the other commandments (Ezek. 20:11–24). The prophecies in Isaiah 56:2–7 and 58:13–14 likewise single out the Sabbath as the primary commandment, observance of which will bring personal as well as national salvation. The mention of the Sabbath in the Elephantine papyri and the appearance of the personal name Shabbetai, meaning "born on the Sabbath" (Ezra 10:15) likewise attest to its importance in this period.

This unique prophetic idea may stem from the ever-growing need for Israel to preserve its own identity in the face of a hostile pagan world. To this end, Ezekiel significantly draws from the Priestly formulation in describing the Sabbath as a "sign" between God and Israel (Ezek. 20:12), though his stress on the national consequences of Sabbath desecration represents a new application of the Priestly concept. Another explanation for the prominence of the Sabbath in the exilic literature is the fact that observance of the Sabbath was not dependent on the Temple cult. Although some of the old Sabbath practices, such as the additional sacrifices, became impossible with the destruction of the Temple, the continued observance of the Sabbath on the lay level would ensure Israel steadfastness to its faith.

In addition to the weekly seventh day of rest, the term "Sabbath" and its related form *Shabbaton* occur elsewhere in the Pentateuch referring to some of the festival days and to the seventh "Sabbatical" Year, on which the land was to lie fallow (Lev. 16:31; 23:24, 32, 39; 25:2–6; 26:34, 35, 43). Each of these occasions shares the chief characteristic of the weekly Sabbath, namely, the restricting of work. It has been suggested that the Sabbath day and the Sabbatical Year express the belief that Israel's time and land belong ultimately to God.

In the earliest Christian community, observance of Sabbath regulations fell into disuse among Christians of Jewish descent, principally because Jesus himself had been lax in his obedience to them (e.g., Matt. 12:1–8; Mark 3: 1–5; Luke 13:10–17; John 5:1–10) even though he continued to take part in synagogue services held on the Sabbath (e.g., Luke 4:16). Jesus' claim to lordship over the Sabbath (Mark 2:28) was an important element in the hostility he aroused in those who felt that Sabbath traditions were incumbent on all Jews (e.g., Mark 3: 6; John 5:18). Jesus' attitude toward the Sabbath, coupled with the tradition that his resurrection occurred on the first day of the week (Sunday; cf. Matt. 28:1), meant that Sunday rather than the Sabbath (Saturday) became the chief liturgical day for Christians.

Bibliography

Greenberg, M. "Sabbath." *Encyclopaedia Judaica*. Vol. 14. Pp. 557–62.

Porten, B. *Archives from Elephantine*. Berkeley and Los Angeles: University of California Press, 1965. Pp. 122–33, 150, 173.

D.A.G./J.H.T.

Sabbath day's journey, the distance one is allowed to walk on the Sabbath. Exod. 16:29 legislates: "Let no man go out of his place on the seventh day." Num. 35:5 defines the Levitical pasture lands as extending 2,000 cubits in each direction from the city center. Tannaitic law defined the Sabbath day's journey as 2,000 cubits. Acts 1:12 mentions that Jerusalem is a Sabbath day's journey from the Mt. of Olives. The Zadokite Fragments (Damascus Document) also counted 2,000 cubits from the city as a Sabbath limit for walking after one's animals. Boundary stones marking the Sabbath limits (Heb. *tekhum shabbat*) of the city were found in the excavation of Gezer. ***See also*** Sabbath. L.H.S.

Sabbatical Year, the biblical prescription that every seventh year the land must lie uncultivated, based on the assumption that the land does not actually belong to any one person to dispose of at will, but to God himself. Fruit that grows on its own in the Sabbatical Year was to be left for the poor and the wild animals (Exod. 23:10–11; Lev. 25:1–7). In addition, "every creditor shall release what he has lent to his neighbor" (Deut. 15:2). This remission of debts is designed to provide the means to correct social inequities. It was an Old Babylonian custom for kings to declare a remission of debts and obligations.

The observance of the Sabbatical Year in Second Temple times (late fifth century B.C.–A.D. 70) is attested in Neh. 10:32 and 1 Macc. 6: 49, 53, and Julius Caesar confirmed the Jews' exemption from taxes in the Sabbatical Year (Josephus *Antiquities* 14.202). Hillel instituted the *prozbul* (a decree of exemption or exception) to allow debts to carry through the Sabbatical Year. After the Jewish revolt (A.D. 66–74) and the Bar-Kochba war (A.D. 132–135), the tax exemption was cancelled and rabbinic legislation became more lenient. Rabbinic law still requires the observance of the Sabbatical Year in modern Israel. ***See also*** Jubilee. L.H.S.

Sabbeus (suh-bee'uhs). ***See*** Sabbaias.

Sabeans. ***See*** Seba, Sabeans.

Sabta (sab'tah; also Sabtah), a son of Cush (1 Chron. 1:9; Gen. 10:7) and a tribe in southwestern Arabia of uncertain location.

Sabtecha (sab'te-kah; KJV: "Sabteca"), a son of Cush (Gen. 10:7; 1 Chron. 1:9) and a tribal locality in Arabia still unidentified.

Sachar (say'kahr; KJV: "Sacar"). **1** One of David's elite guards, a Hararite (1 Chron. 11:35). **2** A levitical gatekeeper (1 Chron. 26:4) of Korahite descent.

sackbut (sak'buht, KJV; RSV: trigon), a small three-cornered, four-stringed musical instrument (e.g., Dan. 3:5), not to be confused with a later medieval wind instrument of the same name. ***See also*** Trigon.

sackcloth, a dark-colored material of goat or camel hair used for making grain bags and garments. English "sack" is derived from the Hebrew *saq,* via Latin *saccus* and Greek *sakkos.* Joseph's brothers carried their money and their grain in sacks (Gen. 42:25), and the men of Gibeon met Joshua with worn-out sacks upon their sack animals (Josh. 9:4). A garment of sackcloth was uncomfortable and was therefore worn by those in mourning. Jacob "put sackcloth upon his loins" when mourning for Joseph (Gen. 37: 34). When national calamity threatened the destruction of the Jewish people in the book of Esther, the Jews lay in sackcloth and ashes, fasting, weeping, and lamenting (Esther 4:3). This material must have been inexpensive or of poor quality for "no one might enter the king's gate clothed with sackcloth" (Esther 4:1–3). The use of sackcloth continued for a very long time as it is still mentioned in 1 Macc. 2:14, 3:47 and in the NT (Matt. 11:21) as a sign of distress and repentance. ***See also*** Mourning Rites. L.H.S.

sacraments, religious rites that confer special graces. Before the word "sacrament" came to have religious connotations, it was used in a secular sense in the Roman world to refer to money deposited in a lawsuit by both parties. The party who lost the suit forfeited the money to sacred purposes. It was also used in a military context to describe the oath of allegiance taken by a new recruit into the army. The early church father Tertullian referred to conversion to Christianity as a sacrament, the admitting of the new recruit into the warfare of the living God *(Ad Martyras* 3). The term "sacrament" was associated with Christian worship services by the time of Pliny (ca. A.D. 112), because when he reported on Christian worship services, he explained the sacramental nature of the services by deducing that Christians bound themselves by an oath *(sacramentum)* not to commit some kind of crime *(Epistles 10.–96).* Pliny misunderstood the significance of sacraments for Christian worship, but he was aware of the fact that sacraments were part of their religious activity, and he understood sacraments to mean "oaths," as in Roman military usage.

In the Latin Vulgate, Jerome translated the Greek word *mysterion* by the Latin *sacramentum.* Christian practices such as baptism and the Eucharist were called mysteries in the early church, and they continue to be called mysteries in the Greek Orthodox church to this day. Because of Jerome's translation, however, it was natural for the Latin church to refer to these ceremonies as "sacraments."

Jesus and the disciples at the Last Supper, which is regarded by Christians as the basis for the sacrament of the Eucharist; embroidered gold wire on purple silk, fourteenth-century.

Over a period of time, baptism and the Eucharist acquired in the popular mind a quasi-magical significance, partly from the influence of pagan mystery cults, and partly from Jewish influences related to ritualistic and initiatory ablutions, as well as from the Passover. While it is anachronistic to speak of "sacraments" in the OT, since the development of the notion of sacrament occurred in the post-NT church, sacramental thought did appropriate terminology from various OT religious observances to show the continuity between Israel and the church. Thus baptism was related to the act of circumcision, the sign that indicated the child's membership in the chosen people, and the Passover terminology employed in the Gospel accounts of the Last Supper was used to help explain the significance of the Eucharist.

Varied in Number: Although baptism and the Eucharist were considered the primary sacraments, the term "sacrament" was used in the early church to describe many kinds of religious ceremonies and practices. By the twelfth century Hugo of St. Victor listed some thirty sacraments. This was probably the result of Augustine's definition of sacraments as signs pertaining to things divine, or visible forms of an invisible grace. Since there is no limit to the number of ways God's grace can be expressed, the number of sacraments increased with Christian sensitivity and imagination, but this made administrative control difficult. Therefore the Council of Trent (A.D. 1545) decreed that not all signs of sacred things had sacramental value. Visible signs become sacraments only if they represent an invisible grace and become its channels.

At a later council, the Roman Catholic church limited the number of sacraments to seven: baptism, confirmation, the Eucharist, penance, extreme unction, orders, and matrimony. Part of the need for exact definition came during the sixteenth century in response to the Reformation. The Reformers, in turn, responded to the conclusions of the Roman Catholic church as it was redefined at the Council of Trent.

The Reformers held that the number seven was chosen arbitrarily, so they defined "sacrament" still more sharply, claiming that "sacrament" should apply not to all visible means of an invisible grace but only to those means which Jesus himself commanded to be practiced. This limited the number to two—baptism and the Eucharist. At the Last Supper, Jesus ordered the disciples to partake of the bread and wine in remembrance of him (1 Cor. 11:23–25), and after the resurrection he commanded his following to make disciples of all the nations, baptizing them (Matt 28:19). Luther, who had been an Augustinian monk, may also have been influenced by Augustine's belief that baptism and the Eucharist constituted sacraments "in an eminent sense."

Varied Significance: The significance of sacraments varies among denominations and believers today. Some believe the sacraments are the only means of salvation and that they have a special force that guarantees forgiveness of sins. Others think they represent God's grace, which can be received in many ways; they are traditionally practiced but not required for salvation.

For the Roman Catholic church validity of the sacraments depends on a qualified priest and willing recipients, except for infants, mentally incompetent people, and extraordinary cases. In an emergency any Christian may baptize someone before death, and the mentally incompetent may receive extreme unction without conscious consent. Most Protestants limit the performance of sacraments to ordained clergy leaders and think sacramental effectiveness depends upon the faith of the recipient. ***See also*** Baptism; Lord's Supper, The.

G.W.B.

sacrifice. ***See*** Worship.

Sadducees (sad′yo͞o-seez), a group in Judaism from the second century B.C. to the first century A.D. Their name in Hebrew *(tsaddiqim)* means the "righteous ones" and may be descriptive, or it may be derived from the name of Zadok, the high priest under David (1 Kings 1:26). The Sadducees are mentioned in the writings of the Jewish historian Josephus, the NT and rabbinic literature, but no consistent picture emerges. None of their own literature has survived.

According to Josephus: In Josephus they, along with the Pharisees and Essenes, are enumerated as the oldest Jewish philosophies or ways of life. In contrast to the other two groups the Sadducees are said to reject the immortality of the soul, to attribute all human activity to free will and none to fate (or providence), and to reject other traditions, especially those of the Pharisees. Josephus also says that the Sadducees were influential with only a few wealthy families and not with the people, who followed the Pharisees' interpretation of the law. Josephus also says that the Sadducees were boorish in their social interaction, that they encouraged conflict with rather than respect for their teachers, were more stern than the Pharisees in recommending punishments for crimes, and that they aroused Herod's suspicions because they supported the Hasmoneans against him. From this data many commentators have surmised that the Sadducees were mostly priests and wealthy, powerful community leaders who sat in the Sanhedrin, were greatly hellenized (i.e., influenced by Greek culture), and cultivated good relationships with the Romans. But Josephus gives varying attributes to the Sadducees in different passages of his writings and presents neither their full program nor the nature of their group.

In the NT: The NT mentions the Sadducees occasionally, often in conjunction with the Pharisees, but does not present a coherent picture. The Sadducees, in contrast to the Pharisees, do not believe in life after death (Mark 12:18 and parallels; Acts 23:8) or in angels and spirits (Acts 23:8). But the Sadducees are lumped with the Pharisees as opponents of Jesus (Matt. 3:7; 16:6). In Acts (4:1; 5:17; 23:6) Sadducees are active in the Temple, associated with the priests and members of the Sanhedrin. The NT assumes the presence of the Sadducees but does not describe them fully nor differentiate them fully from the Pharisees.

In Rabbinic Literature: In rabbinic literature the Sadducees are treated as opponents of the Pharisees and their heirs, the rabbis. The items on which they disagree in the Mishnah and Tosefta are purity laws, civil law, Temple ritual and Sabbath observance, all matters of great interest for the rabbis. The Babylonian Talmud also mentions their denial of resurrection. Some texts treat the Sadducees as heretics; in other texts in the Babylonian Talmud "Sadducees" has been substituted for "heretics" under the influence of later Christian censors. A few passages suggest that the Sadducees totally rejected rabbinic interpretations of the law. In all cases the Sadducees are set against the rabbinic interpretation of the tradition and used as foils.

A coherent picture of the beliefs and practices of the Sadducees cannot be fully recovered from the sources at our disposal. They had a group of characteristic beliefs and interpretations of Judaism but were not in conflict with the leadership. Consequently, they are not a sect but resemble an ancient school of thought. According to Josephus they competed with the Pharisees and other political and social groups for power and influence, so they appear to have been a faction or interest group within Judaism. Since some priests are identified as Pharisees in Josephus and many priests are associated with neither the Sadducees nor Pharisees, the Sadducees cannot be identified as exclusively priestly nor can the chief priests be assumed in all cases to be Sadducees. ***See also*** Essenes; Josephus; Pharisees; Zadok.

A.J.S.

Sadoc (say'dahk). ***See*** Zadok.

saffron *(Crocus sativus)*, the dried styles and stigmas of the crocus used as a flavoring and as a yellow coloring in foods and textiles (Song of Sol. 4:14). Highly valued, it was originally imported from the Far East.

Saffron.

saints, persons distinct because of their relationship to God. In the OT, two different Hebrew terms are commonly rendered by this English expression. One, derived from the word meaning "covenant faithfulness," suggests that those who are so designated are bound closely to their God in love (e.g., Pss. 31:23; 148:14). The other, derived from the word for "holy," identifies those so described as set apart and dedicated to the service of God (e.g., Dan. 7:27). In both cases, the faithful of Israel are in view, and their "sainthood" consists in the relationship they bear to the God who has destined them for righteousness and salvation (Pss. 16:3; 132:9, 16).

The same associations are present in the NT, where "saints" always translates the Greek term for "[the] holy ones" and where it refers to Christians in distinction from nonbelievers (e.g., 1 Cor. 6:2). Thus, in Rom. 1:6–7, the phrases "called to belong to Jesus Christ," "God's beloved," and "called to be saints" are virtually synonymous. In Acts and the Pauline Letters, the term most often refers to Christians resident in particular places, such as Jerusalem (e.g., Acts 9:13; Rom. 15:25, 26, 31), Lydda (Acts 9:32), and Corinth (e.g., 1 Cor. 1:2); occasionally, however, Paul gives it a broader reference (e.g., Rom. 16:2), the normal usage of later writers (e.g., Heb. 6:10; Jude 3). In Revelation, it is a frequent term for the Christian martyrs (e.g., 17:6). ***See also*** Holiness; Love; Mercy; Sanctification.

V.P.F.

Salamis (sal'uh-mis), a city on the eastern coast of Cyprus, which, according to Greek mythology, was founded at the end of the Trojan War. Named after the island of Salamis, it eventually developed around the excellent natural harbor, becoming the main port of Cyprus and a commercial center for the Roman Empire. After leaving Antioch and sailing from the port of Seleucia, Saul, Barnabas, and John Mark stopped in Salamis (Acts 13:1–5). ***See also*** Cyprus.

Salecah (sal'kah; KJV: "Salchah"), a city of Og in Bashan (Deut. 3:10) captured by Israel and assigned to Gad (Josh. 12:5–6; 13:11; 1 Chron. 5:11). Modern Salkhad in the Jebel Druze in Syria is a likely identification.

Salem (say'luhm; Heb. "peace"), the locality over which Melchizedek was king (Gen. 14:18) and that was frequently identified with Jerusalem. This identification is specifically made in Ps. 76:2, where Salem is used in parallelism with Zion as the dwelling place of God. Later writers, including Josephus, also connected Salem with Jerusalem, but other ancient writers identified it with alternative sites. In the Letter to the Hebrews, the author recalls that the root meaning of Salem is "peace" (7:2); thus, Melchizedek is identified as "king of peace." ***See also*** Jerusalem; Melchizedek; Peace; Zion.

Salim (say'lim), a place near Aenon, possibly in the Beth-shean Valley near the northern end of the Jordan River, where John was baptizing (John 3:23). ***See also*** Aenon.

Sallai (sal'ī). **1** A postexilic Benjaminite resident in Jerusalem (Neh. 11:8). **2** A priest in Jerusalem under the high priest Joiakim, possibly of the family Sallu (Neh. 12:20; see 12:7).

Sallu (sal'oo). **1** A postexilic Benjaminite resident of Jerusalem (1 Chron. 9:7; Neh. 11:7). **2** A postexilic levitical family in Jerusalem (Neh. 12:7).

Salma (sal'muh). **1** A descendant of Judah and father of Boaz; an ancestor of King David and in the ancestry of Jesus through Joseph (1 Chron. 2:11; Matt. 1:4). He is also called Salmon (Ruth 4:20–21; Matt. 1:4–5) and Sala (Luke 3:32). **2** A descendant of Judah and the father of Bethlehem (1 Chron. 2:51, 54). However, this passage represents more geographical and historical relationships than actual family genealogies (note v. 54). ***See also*** Salmon.

Salmon (sal'muhn), the son of Nahshon and the father of Boaz (Ruth 4:20–21), and therefore ancestor of David and Jesus (Ruth 4:22; Matt. 1:4–5; Luke 3:32).

Salmone (sal-moh'nee), modern Cape Sidero at Ermoupolis (ancient Itanos) on the northeast extremity of Crete, site of a temple to Athena Salmonia. Paul sailed past here en route to Rome (Acts 27:7).

Salome (suh-loh'mee). **1** Daughter of Herod (not Philip as in Matt. 14:3; Mark 6:17), son of Herod the Great, and of Herodias. Matt. 14:3–11 and Mark 6:17–28 tell the story of her dance before her uncle and now step-father, Herod Antipas, and her request, at the instigation of her mother, for the head of John the Baptist. Josephus, who does not recount this incident, gives the location of John's imprisonment and death as the grim Herodian fortress of Machaerus; he also gives Salome's name (in the Gospels she is identified only as the daughter of Herodias). Salome later married her uncle Herod Philip the tetrarch. ***See also*** Herod; Herodias; John the Baptist. **2** According to Mark 15:40 and 16:1, one of the Galilean women at Jesus' crucifixion and later at the empty tomb, perhaps the wife of Zebedee and thus the mother of James and John (cf. Matt. 27:56). F.O.G.

Salome dancing before Herod, twelfth-century illuminated manuscript.

salt, the most commonly used seasoning in antiquity: "Can that which is tasteless be eaten without salt?" (Job 6:6). Its preservative powers made it an absolute necessity of life and a virtual synonym for essential life-giving forces and, not surprisingly, endowed it with religious significance. In the Sermon on the Mount, Jesus calls the people who listen to him the "salt of the earth" (Matt. 5:13). In Israelite worship, salt was used to season incense (Exod. 30:35) and all offerings had to be seasoned with salt (Lev. 2:13; Ezek. 43:24). A related usage finds salt symbolizing the making of a covenant (Num. 18:19; 2 Chron. 13:5).

Numerous references to "the Salt Sea" (Josh. 15:5; Deut. 3:17) and the Valley of Salt (2 Kings 14:7; 2 Chron. 25:11) clearly identify the Dead Sea area as the place where supplies of salt were procured. Salt could either be mined in the rock formations along the Dead Sea (Lot's wife was turned into a "pillar" of salt, Gen. 19:26), or be obtained by letting water evaporate from pans. Once the salt was removed from sediment, it was rinsed, purified, and crushed until fine.

Ironically, salt also became associated with the destruction of life, a land gone to waste (Deut. 29:23; Job. 39:6; Ps. 107:34; Jer. 17:6; Zeph. 2:9). In a common practice of conquest, Abimelech "razed the city and sowed it with salt" (Judg. 9:45). S.L.R.

Salt, City of, a town assigned to the tribe of Judah (Josh. 15:62) in the wilderness and in association with En-gedi, along the Dead Sea. It is now identified as Khirbet Qumran, the location of the community that produced the Dead Sea Scrolls.

Salt, Hill of, a place to which tradition has attached the locus of Lot's wife's turning to salt (Gen. 19:26). One suggestion for its location is modern Jebel Usdum ("mountain of Sodom") at the southwest end of the Dead Sea.

Salt Sea, the. *See* Dead Sea.

Salt Valley, the valley where David defeated the Edomites (2 Sam. 8:13; Abishai in 1 Chron. 18:12) and, later, Amaziah defeated the same enemy and took Sela (2 Kings 14:7; parallel in 2 Chron. 25:11). Wadi el-Milk (Arabic, "salt") in southern Judah carries its name today, but most scholars would place it in Edom near the southern end of the Dead Sea.

saltwort, a plant of the genus *Salsola*. In biblical terminology it was formerly translated as "mallow" (for instance, in Job 30:4). It represents poor food sought in desperation.

salutations, oral expressions of good wishes. Salutations have long been important in the Near East. Social status determined the form of the greeting: subjects prostrated themselves before their oriental kings and invoked eternal life for them (cf. Neh. 2:3; Dan. 2:4); clients or inferiors acknowledged their patrons or superiors by similar means.

Hebrew and Aramaic greetings invoked peace, well-being, or blessing (cf. 1 Sam. 17:22; 2 Kings 4:29). The same sentiments were expressed as the initial greetings of letters. The Greek equivalent was the spoken "Hail!" or "Greetings!" *(chaire)*, which was also used in letters as the writer's initial greeting to the recipient (cf. Acts 15:23). Greetings to or from a third party were conveyed in the letter closing with the Greek word *aspazomai* ("I greet"). Paul and other NT writers used this Greek formula in the Letter closing (e.g., 1 Cor. 16:19–20; Heb. 13: 24; 1 Pet. 5:13) but preferred the fuller, oriental form of the peace wish in the initial greetings (e.g., Gal. 1:3–4; 1 Pet. 1:2; 2 John 1:3). ***See also*** Gestures; Letter. J.L.W.

salvation, a term that has lost much of its original meaning in current English usage. In part, this may be due to overuse in former times, compounded by popular but imprecise application among various religious groups. Because of this, it is important to exercise care in exploring its range of meaning for the biblical writers. It is an extremely important term in the Bible; thus, further neglect can only lead to considerable theological loss.

The term for salvation in the OT can connote, in keeping with its root meaning of "broadening" or "enlarging," the creation of space in the community for life and conduct. More often than not, this is created with divine help, particularly in circumstances where God's people face an adversary (e.g., Exod. 14:13–14, 30; 15: 2; 1 Sam. 7:8; 2 Sam. 22:28; 1 Chron. 16:35; Neh. 9:27; Pss. 7:1; 17:7; 18:1–3; 54:1; 59:1–2; 106:43–48; 116:1–6; 118:5–14). God rescues and delivers from the situation of opposition and peril to one of recovered spaciousness, prosperity, and well-being. This meaning of the term is expanded to include deliverance from other forms of conflict, particularly in matters of the people's relationship to God. Such a field of reference draws on other terms such as "redemption," "atonement," "reconciliation," "pardon," "expiation" (cf. also "peace" and "righteousness"). The goal of such deliverance is the establishment of God's reign among his people and the other nations of the world (e.g., Isa. 49:25–26; 52:6–10; 55:1–5; Jer. 31:31–34; Ezek. 36:22–32; 37:23–28). Particularly the apocalyptic writings anticipate the arrival of this reign (e.g., Isa. 24–27).

The NT writers, apparently following the lead of Jesus himself, appropriate this specialized usage of salvation to designate the establishment of God's end-time Reign. In doing so, they identify God's intent to "save"/"rescue" (the meaning of the Greek root) with the person and ministry of Jesus of Nazareth (e.g., Luke 19:10; also 14:16–24; 15:3–10; 18:10–14; Matt. 10:6–8; 15:22–28; 18:12–14; 21:28–32). Jesus' name comes from the Hebrew root meaning "salvation," and thus God the Savior and Jesus the Savior become (as in other ways) inextricably linked (e.g., Matt. 1:21; Luke 2:11; also John 4: 42; Acts 5:31; 13:23; Phil. 3:20; 2 Tim. 1:10; Titus 1:4; 2:13; 3:6; 2 Pet. 1:1, 11; 2:20; 3:2, 18; 1 John 4:14).

The meaning of the term "gospel" ("good tidings") is the essence of salvation (Rom. 1:16–17; 10:9–10). The traditions about Jesus record various accounts of Jesus' acts of delivering people from forms of physical, spiritual/psychic, and demonic/cosmic bondage to a condition of restored wholeness and soundness (e.g., Mark 1:40–45; 2:1–12; 5:1–20, 34; 10:52; Luke 7:50; 17:19; John 9; 12:3–7). "Saved" life is thereby seen in the context of a life that is "redeemed" in relation to God, oneself, and others in community.

For these NT writers, the death and resurrection of Jesus is the ultimate focal moment for the dawn of salvation (e.g., 1 Cor. 15). Drawing on the sacrificial images and institutions of ancient Israel, early Christians associate Jesus' death with that of the Passover lamb as "atonement" (John 1:29, 36; 6:51; 1 Cor. 5:7; Heb. 9:24–26). The "on our behalf" formula appropriates the efficacious significance of Jesus' death for those who receive it by faith as a gift of grace (e.g., Mark 10:45; 1 Tim. 2:6; Titus 2:14; Mark 14:24 and parallels; 1 Cor. 15:3–7; Eph. 2:5, 8). It means "reconciliation" (Rom. 5:1–11; 2 Cor. 5: 18–20). It brings "regeneration" and a new conscience/consciousness. It encompasses the whole cosmos (Rom. 8:19–23; Eph. 1:10; Col. 1: 19–20). The resurrection points, moreover, not only to present significance (Rom. 13:11–14; 1 Cor. 15:1–2) but also to future deliverance from

SAMARIA, CITY OF

impending judgment and wrath (1 Thess. 1:9–10; also Mark 13 and parallels; Rom. 1:18–2:11; 5:9–11; Phil. 3:20; Titus 2:13).

The apocalyptic vision mentioned above (e.g., Isa. 24–27) is appropriated with certain qualifications to underscore the deliverance motif and that of life and well-being in the future Kingdom of God (e.g., Luke 13:28–30; 22:29–30; 23:43; 1 Cor. 2:9–10; 11:26; 1 Thess. 4:16–17; Rev. 21:1–22:5). Other traditions stress more the language of inheritance and the certainty of sharing the eternal life of Jesus' resurrection (e.g., Rom. 8:12–17; 1 Thess. 5:9; Heb. 1:14; 5:9; 9:28; 1 Pet. 1:5, 9; also John 4:14; 7:37–38; 10:10). The emphasis remains throughout the NT on the exclusive nature of the connection between Jesus' destiny and the promise of salvation (e.g., Acts 4:11–12; 5:31; Heb. 2:3). The consummation of salvation exceeds human ability to grasp it (1 Cor. 2:9–10); in the present, the gift of the Spirit is a foretaste of what is promised and hoped for (Rom. 8:23; 2 Cor. 1:22; 5:5; Eph. 1:14). ***See also*** Apocalyptic Literature; Atonement; Conscience; Conversion; Eschatology; Eternal Life; Expiation; Forgiveness; Grace; Holy Spirit, The; Justification; Kingdom of God; Liberty; Pardon; Peace; Reconciliation; Redemption; Regeneration; Righteousness; Sin.

J.E.A.

Samaria, city of, the capital of the northern kingdom of Israel for the greater part of the history of that independent state. Omri built the city in the early ninth century B.C. and moved his administrative center there from Tirzah (1 Kings 16:24). It remained the capital until the demise of the kingdom in 721 B.C., when the city was taken by the Assyrians after a long seige (1 Kings 17:1–6, which credits Shalmaneser V with taking the city; compare the Assyrian annals, in which credit is claimed by Shalmaneser's successor, Sargon II). According to the folk etymology preserved in 1 Kings 16:24, the place name (Heb. *Shomron*) was derived from Shemer, from whom Omri is said to have purchased the hill on which the city was built. The name was also used for the administrative district of which Samaria was the capital and the gentilic form (Samaritan) was used for the residents of

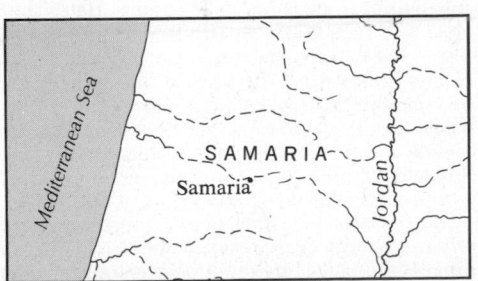

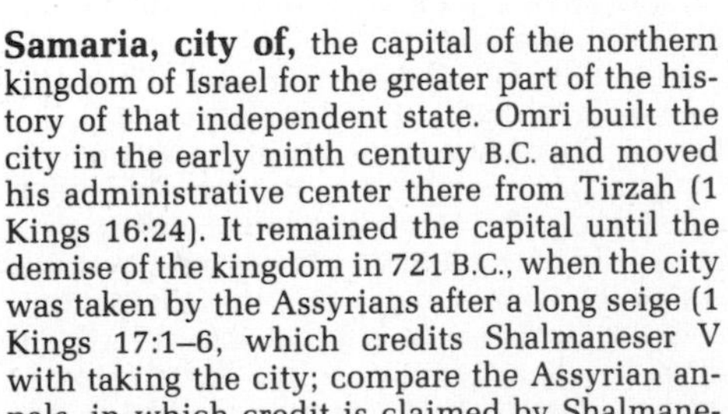

A bronze figurine of a young bull, found at a cult center in the province of Samaria from ca. 1200 B.C.

the area. Both usages came into vogue only after the Assyrian conquest, following the Assyrian practice of naming a province after its capital city.

The city was well situated defensively on a hill rising about 300 feet above the valleys on the north, west, and south, with a long, sloping ridge to the east. Strategically located beside major roadways, the city gave access to Jerusalem on the south, Megiddo and the Jezreel Valley on the north, the sea and coastal plain on the west, and Shechem and the Jordan Valley on the east. The city did lack, however, an adequate water supply. Thus, in addition to practical considerations, the building of the new capital was clearly a symbolic statement for Omri, expressing the dominance and power of his developing state.

In the OT: Samaria is mentioned frequently in the OT, as would be expected of the seat of political power and, from the perspective of biblical historians and the prophets, the source of corruption. In addition to the mere chronicling of events that took place there, such as the tenure record of the kings who ruled the city, we are told that Ahab built an altar and temple for Baal in Samaria (1 Kings 16:32), a shrine later destroyed by Jehu in the Yahwistic reform that accompanied his coup d'état (ca. 834 B.C.). The royal city of the north, Bethel, did not become a cultic pilgrimage center after the model of Jerusalem in the south. Bethel remained "the king's sanctuary" (Amos. 7:13). The reference to "your calf, O Samaria"/"the calf of Samaria" in Hos. 8:4–6 is to the calf (or calves) of Bethel, venerated by the kings of Samaria, as is clear from the parallel oracle in Hos. 10:3–6 (Beth-aven in v. 5 [Heb., "house of falsehood"] being a term of contempt for Bethel). That Bethel was the site of pilgrimage and worship by the nobles of Samaria is seen also in the juxtaposition of oracles against Samaria and Bethel in Amos 4: 1–3 and 4–5. But Samaria was not exempt from prophetic criticism of its idolatry (Amos 8:14), being compared in this respect to both pagan cities and Jerusalem (Isa. 10:10–11; Ezek. 16: 46–55; 23:1–49). Elsewhere in the prophetic oracles, the people of Samaria are condemned for their pride (Isa. 9:8–17), wickedness (Hos. 7:1–7), rebellion (Hos. 13:16), oppression and exploitation of the poor (Amos 3:9–12; 4:1–3), and for the indolence and spiritual insensitivity engendered by their wealth (Amos 6:1–7).

Archaeological Evidence: The affluence of the people of Samaria so graphically portrayed by Amos (6:4–6: "those who lie upon beds of ivory . . .") is revealed also in the material remains excavated at the site, including over five hundred ivory fragments used, mostly, as inlays for wooden paneling, furniture, boxes, and toilet articles. The site has been extensively excavated by numerous institutions and by some of the foremost Palestinian archaeologists: by Harvard University early in the century (G. A. Reisner and C. S. Fisher), by Harvard, the Palestine Exploration Fund, the British Academy, the British School of Archaeology, and the Hebrew University in the 1930s (J. W. and G. M. Crowfoot, E. L. Sukenik, K. Kenyon, N. Avigad, J. Pinkerfeld), by the Department of Antiquities of Jordan in 1965, and by the British School of Archaeology in 1968 (J. B. Hennessy). The excavations revealed that the city was built in the ninth century B.C., although pottery remains from the Early Bronze period (3000–2000 B.C.) indicated earlier, informal settlements. Six periods from the ninth century to the Assyrian conquest were distinguished and ascribed to the otherwise known activities of Omri, Ahab, Jehu, Jeroboam II, and the Assyrian conquerors. However, the various excavators and the subsequent interpreters of their publications have not agreed on the ascription of particular periods to specific kings. The interpretation of the excavations has been hampered by the fact that the city was destroyed several times and rebuilders deepened previous cuts in the bedrock for the foundations of their stone structures or cut new foundations rather than superimposing them on the other ones.

During the Assyrian and Persian periods Samaria was the capital of the province of the same name. Following conquest by the Macedonians (332 B.C.) the city was rebuilt as a Greek *polis* (city). It was destroyed by John Hyrcanus in 108 B.C. and rebuilt magnificently by Herod the Great (ca. 30 B.C.), who renamed it Sebaste in honor of Augustus (Gk. *Sebastos).* The Greek name is still preserved in the name of the modern Arab village, Sebastiyeh.

The Gospel of John records a journey of Jesus through Samaria, his conversation with a woman there, and the many who believed in him "from that city," which may refer to Samaria (4:4–42). ***See also*** Samaria, District of; Samaritans.

Bibliography

Crowfoot, J. W. and G. M., and K. Kenyon. *The Objects from Samaria.* London: Palestine Exploration Fund, 1957.

Crowfoot, J. W., K. M. Kenyon, and E. L. Sukenik. *The Buildings of Samaria.* London: Palestine Exploration Fund, 1942.

Reisner, G. A., C. S. Fisher, and D. G. Lyon. *Harvard Excavations at Samaria.* Cambridge, MA: Harvard University Press, 1924. J.D.P.

Samaria, district of, the central hill country of Palestine, the natural borders of which were defined by the sea on the west, the Valley of Jezreel or Plain of Esdraelon on the north (with Mt. Carmel to the west and Mt. Gilboa to the east), the Jordan River on the east, and the Valley of Aijalon on the south. This was the region settled by the Joseph tribes, with the half-tribe of Manasseh settled in the northern half of the area and the tribe of Ephraim in the southern half or to the north and south of the twin mountains Gerizim and Ebal, respectively. The geographical centrality of these peaks (on the north-south axis) assured a prominent role for the city of Shechem, nestled on the lower slope of Mt. Gerizim. But the influence of Shechem came to be usurped by Samaria, after which the region was named. Other important cities of the region were Dothan, Megiddo, Taanach, Beth-shean, Bethel, and Tirzah. The area was comparatively more fertile than the southern portion of Canaan in which the tribe of Judah and its clans settled. Soil and rainfall were conducive to viticulture, the cultivation of fruit and olive trees, vegetable gardening, and wheat farming. It would appear that the use of the name "Samaria" for the region dates from the time of the Assyrian conquest (post 722 B.C.), following the Assyrian practice of naming a province after its capital city, rather than to the earlier period of the Israelite monarchy (924–722 B.C.).

In the Bible: References to Samaria in biblical literature predating the Assyrian conquest of the Israelite capital are to the city and not the political district (e.g., Amos 3:9, 12; 4:1; 6:1; 8:14; Hos. 8:6; 10:5–7; 13:16; Isa. 7:9; 8:4; 10:9–11; Mic. 1:5–6). But the later oracle of Jer. 31:5–6 is clearly a reference to the region ("the mountains of Samaria"/"the hill country of Ephraim"). The use of the term "Ephraim" for the region and its people was popular with the prophets both before and after the Assyrian conquest of Samaria —especially with the earlier prophets Hosea (ca. thirty-six times) and Isaiah (ca. twelve times), where the term is often synonymous with the kingdom of Israel, of which this region was the political and cultural heart. That the region was

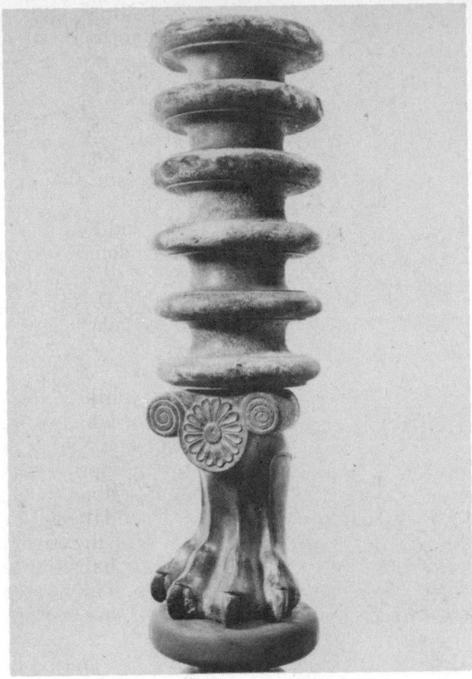

Fragment of an Achaemenid throne found at Samaria, probably from the Persian period (fourth century B.C.). The throne may have belonged to a governor of Samaria.

not known as Samaria during the time of the northern Israelite monarchy is further indicated by the formulaic expression in 1 and 2 Kings, "X reigned (or began to reign) over Israel *in* Samaria" (e.g., 1 Kings 16:29; 22:51; 2 Kings 3:1; 10:36; 13:1, 10; 14:23; 15:8, 23, 27; 17:1). The Deuteronomic historians were themselves active after the time when the region came to be known as Samaria, and this is reflected in their use of the term "cities of Samaria" in the account of the settlement of Mesopotamian colonists in the regions by the Assyrians (2 Kings 17: 24–28). But they did not generally refer to the region or to the kingdom of Israel as Samaria, except for two anachronistic slips: one in 1 Kings 21:1, where Ahab is called king of Samaria, the other in 1 Kings 13:32, where "cities of Samaria" is truly an anachronism, inasmuch as the city of Samaria itself had not yet been built at that point in the narrative.

In addition to Samaria (Assyrian *Sa-me-ri-na),* Assyrian texts also refer to the region as the land of the House of Omri (Assyrian *Bit Hu-um-ri-a),* a term used not only after the fall of that dynasty but also after the fall of that kingdom (722 B.C.)

History: Following the Assyrian conquest, the character of the local population of Samaria was altered due to the loss of some native Israelites by deportation (2 Kings 17:6; Assyrian records indicate ca. twenty-seven thousand) and evacuation (many of the evacuees settled in Jerusalem, expanding that city to about four times its previous size) and by the concurrent settlement of foreign colonists in the region (2 Kings 17:24–41). This is said to have resulted in the paganization of the area, of which the judgment in 2 Kings 17:34–41 appears to be an overstatement (cf. Jer. 41:5).

During the time of Josiah (late seventh century B.C.) attempts were made by Judah to bring Samaria under political and cultural domination, but this was short-lived. Following the destruction of Jerusalem (586 B.C.), the Babylonians incorporated that city and the northern part of Judah into the province of Samaria. But the Persians later separated Jerusalem from Samaria and restored the Judean province, accounting for the hostility of Sanballat, governor of Samaria, who with his allies, Tobiah of Ammon and Geshem of Arabia, harassed the rebuilders of the Jewish state (Neh. 2:9–20; 4:1–9; 6:1–14). Antipathy between Judah and Samaria was also abetted by the refusal of the leaders of the Jewish community to allow the Yahwists of Samaria to assist in the reconstruction of the Jerusalem Temple (Ezra 4:8–24; 1 Esd. 5:64–73).

At the beginning of the Hellenistic period (325–63 B.C.), a revolt against Macedonian rule broke out in Samaria and the local population was forced to flee. Samaria was rebuilt as a Hellenistic city and the ancient city of Shechem was rebuilt by the disenfranchised Samaritans. It was this segment of the Samaritan people who built a Temple to the Hebrew God on Mt. Gerizim and whose descendants are encountered in the NT and the writings of the first-century historian Josephus as "the Samaritans." During the Hasmonean period (ca. 166–63 B.C.), both Samaria and Shechem were destroyed by John Hyrcanus and the territory passed to Judaean control. But in 63 B.C. Pompey assigned the area to the province of Syria. It was later granted to Herod the Great (30 B.C.) and subsequently to Herod's son Archelaus (4 B.C.–A.D. 6). The Romans understood the cultural relationship between Judah and Samaria and did not divide the two into separate governances. Both were ruled by Roman procurators (and by Herod Agrippa, from A.D. 41–44) after Archelaus was deposed. In the NT, Samaria is mentioned as the region of members of the Samaritan religious community (Matt. 10:5; Luke 9:52; John 4:1–42), as a territory of early evangelization (Acts 1:8; 8:4–25), as the home of the arch heretic Simon Magus (Acts 8:9–24), and as an area whose churches were supportive of the theological position of Paul (Acts 15:1–3). ***See also*** Samaria, City of; Samaritans.

J.D.P.

Samaritan, the Good. ***See*** Good Samaritan.

Ruins of a Roman basilica constructed at the hilltop site of the ancient city of Samaria.

Samaritan Pentateuch, the. *See* Samaritans; Texts, Versions, Manuscripts, Editions.

Samaritans, in the OT an ethnic term for the residents of the district of Samaria. The term appears only once (2 Kings 17:29) in the account of the settlement of Mesopotamian colonists in the region by the Assyrians, in the comment that these foreign people made gods of their own which they placed "in the shrines of the high places which the Samaritans had made." In the NT, however, the term is used exclusively for the members of a particular ethno-religious community based in the area, living for the most part around Mt. Gerizim (John 4:1–42) but residing also in their own villages throughout the region (Matt. 10:5; Luke 9:52), who might be encountered in villages neighboring on Samaria (Luke 17:11–19) or even on the roadway between Jerusalem and Jericho (Luke 10:29–37).

From these texts one learns that the Jews and Samaritans shared a common heritage ("our father Jacob," John 4:12) but differed from one another radically in regard to the relative sanctity of Jerusalem/Zion and Mt. Gerizim ("Our fathers worshiped on this mountain; and you say that in Jerusalem is the place where men ought to worship," John 4:20). They also had different legal traditions regarding the cleanliness of vessels and, in general, they avoided contact with one another (John 4:7–10). The negative attitude of the Jews towards the Samaritans is reflected in Jesus' statement in Matt. 10:5, in which Samaritans are linked with Gentiles in contrast to "the house of Israel" (cf. Acts 1:8, in which Samaria occupies a median position between Jerusalem/Judea and the gentile world) and in John 8:48, in which the adversaries of Jesus refer to him contemptuously as "a Samaritan"—and demon-possessed as well. The itinerary of Jesus in Mark (10:1; it is followed in Matt. 19:1 but altered somewhat in Luke) seems to reflect a standard Jewish practice of avoiding Samaria in pilgrimages to Jerusalem.

Basically, the Jews regarded the Samaritans as a people foreign to themselves, in spite of an obviously shared heritage: the term "foreigner" used by Jesus of the thankful Samaritan leper in Luke 17:18 (Gk. *allogenēs*) is the term used in the Jerusalem Temple inscription excluding non-Jews from the court of Israel. (The historian Josephus relates that the Samaritans were excluded from the Jerusalem Temple by formal edict, not because of nationality but due to acts of mischief they allegedly perpetrated there.) It was the alien nature of the Samaritans, as commonly perceived, that gave the ironic sting to the story of the grateful leper and to the parable of the good Samaritan: only one out of ten returned to express thanks, and "he was a Samaritan"; the Samaritan stranger was the good neighbor, not the priest or the Levite!

From the few references to Samaria and the Samaritans in the NT, one might be left with the impression that all of the residents of Samaria were members of this community. This is not so. There were, in fact, people of various

 SAMARITANS

cultural backgrounds living in the area. Nonetheless, the Samaritan community (i.e., the particular group with which this article is concerned) was quite large and had throughout the Roman and Byzantine periods (63 B.C. to fifteenth century A.D.) a diaspora of considerable size. There were communities scattered along the Mediterranean coast (notably at Gaza and Caesarea), in Lebanon, in Egypt and Syria, and as far away as Byzantium, Thessalonica, Rome, and Babylon. Today the community numbers only about five hundred but is characterized by vitality after centuries of decline. The main part of the community still resides in the shadow of Mt. Gerizim, in present-day Nablus. It is now, as in antiquity, a community led by priests. Unlike the situation in Judaism, the Samaritan priests remained active and in control of religious affairs after the destruction of their temple. There was, however, during the Roman and Byzantium periods, an active lay-led synagogue party, with which the Samaritan sect of the Dositheans had some connection.

Religious Heritage: As a religious sect, the Samaritans are a strict, Torah-observing party with a resolute pride in their religious heritage. They maintain that they and not the Jews are the bearers of the true faith of ancient Israel as expounded by Moses and as practiced at Mt. Gerizim in ancient times. The name by which they call themselves is *Shamerim*, "observers [of the Torah]." They understand themselves to be the descendants of the Joseph tribes of ancient Israel, as Jews are descendants of the tribe of Judah. Judaism as a heresy is traced to the priest Eli, who is said to have established a rival sanctuary at Shiloh. Thus, for them, the history of the Israelite faith as traced in the second and third divisions of the Jewish Bible is not of sacred but of apostate history. The Samaritans have for Scripture only the Pentateuch, and that in their own distinctive redaction. The chief error of the Jews, according to the Samaritans, is in having edited the Torah to minimize the importance of Gerizim and in having erected a Temple in Jerusalem. In addition to Eli and Solomon, Samaritans cite also Ezra and Hillel for having led the Jews astray: Ezra for having corrupted the text of the Pentateuch and Hillel for having introduced deviant legal and calendrical interpretations. As a priestly dominated community at odds with Pharisaic interpretations, the Samaritans invite comparison with the Sadducees of NT times and with the Karaites of later times. Comparisons have also been made with the Essenes and with the type of early Christianity represented in the Gospel of John. Indeed, recent studies of early Samaritan traditions reveal early Samaritanism as but one of a greater complex of disparate religious movements and ideologies within Judaism (broadly defined) prior to the destruction of the Jerusalem Temple in A.D. 70.

Origin: As for the origin of the sect, most scholars have rejected the Samaritan claim of being the remnant of the Israelite people who have always worshiped the Hebrew God at Shechem and have turned instead to the claims of their detractors, notably Josephus, whose personal animus against the Samaritans was intense. Josephus claimed that the Samaritans were descendants of the foreign colonists from Cutha mentioned in 2 Kings 17:24, an opinion shared by some rabbinic authorities who called the Samaritans *Kutim*. They came to have an independent cultic life, he said, as the result of a schism that occurred in the time of Sanballat (i.e., Sanballat II, not the contemporary of Nehemiah) and Alexander the Great (late fourth century B.C.), when a temple was built on Mt. Gerizim and staffed with renegade and disenfranchised priests from Jerusalem. This cultus was corrupted by hellenization in the time of Antiochus IV (ca. 175 B.C.), a datum with which 2 Macc. 6:1 agrees, and later destroyed by John Hyrcanus in 128 B.C. Although there seems little doubt that the Samaritan sect of NT times (and of today) was derived from the Gerizim cultic establishment of the Hellenic period and developed subsequently through Samaritan Torah teachers who produced their own redaction of the sacred text, the account of Josephus presents difficulties in the reconstruction of early Samaritan history (or prehistory). Because it is highly biased and denegrating in its intent, one must view with suspicion his claim that the

Inscription from a fourth-century A.D. Samaritan synagogue at Shaalbim reads, "The Lord shall reign for ever and ever" (Exod. 15:18 preserved in the Samaritan version).

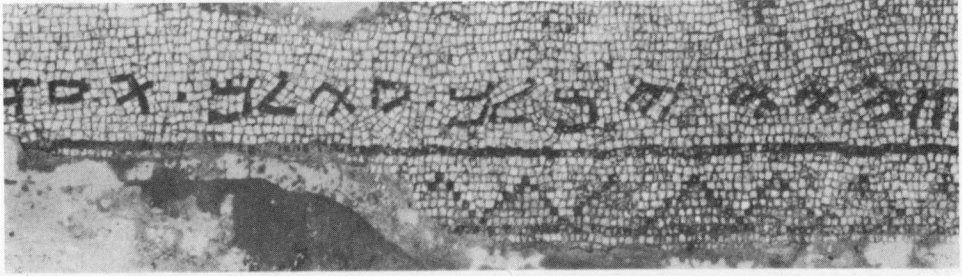

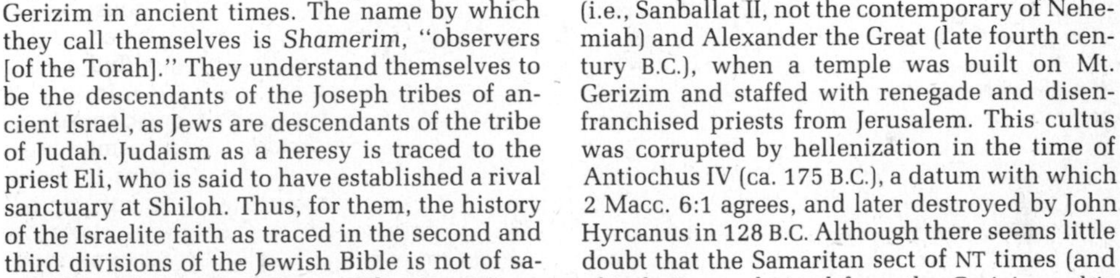

Archaeological remains on Mount Gerizim, where the Samaritan ethno-religious community was centered.

Samaritan priestly caste derived its sacerdotal authority from the Zadokite line of the Jerusalem Temple. Moreover, the story Josephus gives to explain the reason for the exodus of the priests from Jerusalem to Shechem—expulsion due to intermarriage with the family of Sanballat—is problematical (although not impossible). The story is remarkably similar to an earlier incident mentioned in the memoirs of Nehemiah (Neh. 13:28–29). This has prompted some scholars to postulate a Samaritan schism as early as the Persian period (sixth century B.C.), even though the Bible makes no reference to such and Josephus himself dated the alleged "schism" to the early Greek period (fourth century B.C.). It seems most appropriate to regard the Samaritans as a religious community that developed independently of the spiritual leadership of Jerusalem among a people who were, for cultural and historical reasons, alienated from the Jews and who, in time, found it impossible to maintain fraternal relations. ***See also*** Samaria, City of; Samaria, District of.

Bibliography

Coggins, R. J. *Samaritans and Jews.* Oxford: Blackwell, 1975.

Montgomery, J. A. *The Samaritans.* New York: KTAV, 1968.

Purvis, J. D. "The Samaritan Problem." In B. Halpern and J. Levenson, eds. *Traditions in Transformation: Turning Points in Biblical Faith.* Winona Lake, IN: Eisenbrauns, 1982. Pp. 323–350.

J.D.P.

ס

samech (sah'mik), the fifteenth letter of the Hebrew alphabet; its numerical value is sixty. No proto-Canaanite formis attested. By the early tenth century B.C. the form was three horizontal strokes crossed by a vertical one. The Aramaic cursive script transformed the letter considerably in the direction of the classical Hebrew square script form, which is similar in form to an oval. ***See also*** Writing.

Samgarnebo (sam-gahr-nee'boh), a Babylonian mentioned among Nebuchadnezzar II's officials who took their seats in the Middle Gate of Jerusalem during the siege of 587 B.C. (Jer. 39: 3). The name Samgarnebo (Bab. *Sîn-māgir*) is a Babylonian title that can also connote a district; it can be used as a personal name as well.

Samlah (sam'luh), a pre-Israelite king of Edom (Gen. 36:36; 1 Chron. 1:47).

Samos (say'mohs), a mountainous island twenty-eight miles long and twelve and one-half miles wide, located about one and one-half miles from the western coast of Asia Minor, opposite Trogyllium. Greek settlers arrived on Samos ca. 1000 B.C. The Samian fleet was famous throughout the various periods of history. In the third century B.C., the Ptolemies of Egypt used the island as a naval base. During the Maccabean period, there were apparently Jews living on the island (1 Macc. 15:23). In 129 B.C., Samos became part of the Roman province of Asia. Paul and his companions stopped at Samos prior to sailing for the city of Miletus during their final trip to Jerusalem (Acts 20:15).

M.K.M.

Samothrace (sam'oh-thrays), a mountainous island, elliptical in shape, in the northeastern extremity of the Aegean Sea, about twenty miles south of the mainland of Thrace. The rugged coastline leaves the island without a harbor. Before arriving at Neapolis on the second journey, Paul's ship dropped anchor off Samothrace (Acts 16:11).

Samson, an early Israelite hero. The traditions about Samson depict him as a judge who assisted his tribe, the Danites, in their struggle against the Philistines, although most of his heroic exploits were personally motivated and resemble a private vendetta. The stories present him as a Nazirite from birth, but his passion for foreign women compromised the Nazirite vow, which required him to refrain from cutting his hair and to avoid wine and any unclean food. The tales also attribute his extraordinary power to momentary seizure by the divine spirit, and they thereby point beyond the human hero to the true source of superhuman strength.

A religious spirit colors the stories from first to last, despite their racy theme and legendary character. This exalted tone is greatest in the birth announcement and its sequel, an account of the marvelous disappearance of the revealing angel in the fire of an altar (Judg. 13:1–25). Although the name of Samson's father is given (Manoah), no comparable information is supplied about his mother. Nevertheless, she stands out in the story as the real heroine, and Manoah receives instruction from her.

Mighty Exploits: Samson's mighty exploits were occasioned by his erotic involvement with three women. The first object of his affection was an unnamed woman from Timnah, a few miles southeast of Beth-shemesh (located between Jerusalem and Ashdod). At their wedding festivities a riddle contest had grave consequences. Furious that her countrymen had secured the answer to his riddle by threatening his bride, Samson took revenge on local Askelonites from whom he stole garments to cover his wager. Since Samson then returned alone to his home in Zorah, his bride was given to the best man. This act in turn precipitated further revenge on Samson's part, the destroying of grain fields by catching three hundred foxes and setting fire to their tails, then releasing them in the fields. Angry Philistines retaliated by burning Samson's bride and her father, whereupon Samson smote a large number of them. Naturally, the Philistines sought revenge, and by threatening the local tribe of Judah, obtained its assistance in locating a hiding Samson. Bound by his countrymen, he was turned over to the enemy; but the spirit came upon him and he slew a thousand Philistines with the jawbone of an ass. Samson then composed a victory song and prayed for water to quench his thirst. Appropriate names are given for the sites of battle and prayer: Hill of the Jawbone and Partridge Spring (14:1–15:20).

The second woman with whom Samson became entangled was a harlot in the Philistine city of Gaza (located near the Mediterranean seacoast). The local residents learned of his presence and surrounded her house, anticipating victory over an exhausted Samson. But he arose early and walked off with the doors of the city gate on his shoulders, depositing them some distance away on a hill opposite Hebron (16:1–3).

Page from a 1310 Pentateuch portrays Samson grappling with the lion (Judg. 14).

Samson's downfall came when he fell in love with Delilah, presumably a Philistine. Their innocent flirtation quickly became a serious matter, and she toyed with Samson until he finally divulged the secret of his strength. Delilah's motivation is said to have been greed, and she summoned the Philistine lords to come for a shorn Samson. They put out his eyes and set him to work grinding at a mill in Gaza. In due time they celebrated their good fortune with a victory song and made sport of Samson during a sacrifice to their god, Dagon. Resolving to get revenge once more, Samson asked to be situated by the two pillars holding up the house and prayed for renewed strength just once more. God granted his wish, and Samson died with the multitude of Philistines (16:4–31).

Traditions and Stories: The traditions about Samson have been brought together with great skill; they probably circulated orally for some time before achieving written form. Various motifs combine to enhance their popularity: the barren wife, a helpless hero in the arms of a woman, the quest for a deity's hidden name, a hero's death wish, loss of charisma, and terror accompanying a theophany (i.e., the appearance of the divine). The stories also make use of many different literary forms, for example, three prayers, three riddles, two aetiologies, two victory songs, and five heroic deeds, a birth story, and a recognition scene. The stories reflect the period described in Judges, a period when tribal jealousies divided Israelites and when rivalry existed between the Philistine population and Israelite clans.

The figure of Samson presented a problem to many later interpreters, who found it difficult to condone his behavior. Nevertheless, comparisons with Jesus and Heracles became common, and Samson was viewed as a type of Christ. The English poet John Milton's *Samson Agonistes* (1671) transforms Samson into a tragic hero and gives a psychological analysis of suffering. The exploits of this biblical strong man have thus entertained and inspired others throughout the ages, despite Samson's weakness where women were concerned.

Bibliography

Crenshaw, James L. *Samson: A Secret Betrayed, a Vow Ignored*. Atlanta, GA: John Knox, 1978.

J.L.C.

Samuel, a prophet who ruled Israel at the end of the period of the judges and anointed the first two kings. He is the dominant figure at the beginning of the first of the two books of the Bible that bear his name.

Samuel's father, Elkanah, was an Ephraimite from the village of Ramathaim-zophim. Samuel's mother, Hannah, who was barren before his birth, had prayed for a child during a visit to the temple at Shiloh, promising to devote him to the service of Yahweh (1 Sam. 1). The young Samuel, therefore, grew up in Shiloh under the tutelage of Eli, the chief priest. The first oracle he uttered (1 Sam. 3:11–14) was a renunciation of the house of Eli, whose sons had corrupted the cult of Yahweh (cf. 1 Sam. 2:12–17). This marked the beginning of Samuel's career as a prophet (cf. 1 Sam. 3:19–4:1).

Samuel assumed national leadership after a disastrous battle in which the Israelites were routed by the Philistines (1 Sam. 4). Having driven out the enemy and pacified the entire land (1 Sam. 7:13–14), he began periodic visits to a circuit of cities where he passed judgment on cases brought before him (1 Sam. 7:15–17). This pattern continued for most of Samuel's life, but in his old age the men of Israel approached him to request a king (1 Sam. 8). Though angered, he acted on God's instructions and, after warning the people of the burdens a king would impose on them (1 Sam. 8:11–18), he acceded to the request.

Samuel anointed Saul king during a private audience in Samuel's home town (1 Sam. 9:1–10:16). Subsequently, however, he presided over a public ceremony in which Saul was chosen king by casting lots (1 Sam. 10:17–27). After Saul's victorious campaign against the Ammonites (1 Sam. 11) the kingship was ratified in yet another ceremony conducted by Samuel (1 Sam. 11:15). Then in a final public appearance (1 Sam. 12) the prophet admonished the people and their new king to obey the commands of God and promised to continue to act on their behalf.

The men of Israel approach Samuel to request a king (cf. 1 Sam. 8); thirteenth-century French miniature.

Samuel was also the agent of Saul's rejection as king. Because he did not carry out God's instructions as conveyed by Samuel, Saul's kingship was condemned. Samuel prophesied that he would be removed from office in favor of a new king (1 Sam. 13:7–14; 15:10–29). Then God sent Samuel to Bethlehem, where he anointed David (1 Sam. 16:1–13).

Although Samuel's death is reported in 1 Sam. 25:1, he makes one further appearance in the story. In 1 Samuel 28 we are told that Saul invoked Samuel's ghost before his final battle with the Philistines, hoping for a favorable oracle. The ghost, however, reminded Saul of the divine rejection of his kingship and predicted a Philistine victory in the battle.

The biblical narrative presents Samuel as the last of the heroes of the premonarchical age and the first of the prophets who stand alongside the kings. It is tempting to think of him as having played such a transitional role historically—the last judge and the first prophet. He appears in the story, however, as a typical figure rather than as a historically accessible personality. The account of the rise of kingship in 1 Samuel 1–15 is told from a point of view that is suspicious of the institution of monarchy, to which the direct rule of Israel by God acting through a prophet is preferred. In 1 Samuel 7, Samuel is presented as the ideal prophetic leader, in whom all types of authority—military, judicial, and sacerdotal—are combined. In subsequent chapters, after the reality of kingship has been acknowledged, the portrayal of Samuel amounts to a paradigm for the prophetic office under the monarchy: the prophet will anoint and reject kings, intercede with God on Israel's behalf, and guide the conscience of the people (cf. 1 Sam. 12:23). ***See also*** David; Eli; Hannah; King; Prophet; Saul; Shiloh. P.K.M.

Samuel, the First and Second Books of, the eighth and ninth books of the Hebrew Bible, ninth and tenth in most English Bibles. Originally Samuel was one book, deriving its name from the great prophet who dominates the early chapters, but when it was translated into Greek, the book was divided into two with the curious result that Samuel does not appear in the second book that bears his name. Together 1 and 2 Samuel describe the rise of kingship in Israel (eleventh century B.C.) and give an account of the life of David.

Text: The Hebrew text of Samuel that has come down to us is filled with small defects, the result of copyists' errors over the centuries. Scholars attempt to repair these by study of other witnesses to the original text, especially the ancient translations of Samuel into Greek and other languages. Of special importance for this process are three fragmentary copies of Samuel found

1 AND 2 SAMUEL

among the so-called Dead Sea Scrolls at Qumran.

The Deuteronomistic History: 1 and 2 Samuel are part of the so-called Deuteronomistic History that extends from Deuteronomy through 2 Kings. This long narrative, deriving from the Exile (sixth century B.C.) or slightly earlier, contains a variety of ancient materials brought together and evaluated by editors whose criteria for judgment are drawn from the laws of Deuteronomy. Although Deuteronomistic revision and expansion seem to be less extensive in Samuel than in Judges or Kings, the stories told here have special importance for the larger history because they introduce David, the ideal against whom subsequent kings will be judged, and Jerusalem, the city where God chooses to be worshiped (cf. Deut. 12). Key passages include the oracle against the house of Eli in 1 Sam. 2: 27–36, which justifies the subordination of priests from outlying districts to the descendants of Zadok of Jerusalem; the historical review in Samuel's farewell address in 1 Sam. 12:6–25, which belongs to a series of such speeches uttered by major figures in the Deuteronomistic History; and especially the oracle of Nathan in 2 Samuel 7, which asserts the divine election of the Davidic dynasty and warrants the erection of Solomon's Temple.

The Prophetic History: Prior to their incorporation into the Deuteronomistic History many of the materials in 1 and 2 Samuel seem to have been part of an extended narrative reflecting a point of view that stressed the importance of the role of the prophets in Israel, often at the expense of the kings. Some of the ideas expressed in this narrative anticipate aspects of Deuteronomistic thought, and its distinctive ideas are sometimes thought of as belonging to the Deuteronomistic component of Samuel. Some scholars think of this prophetic editing as having taken place after the composition of the primary edition of the Deuteronomistic History.

In much of 1 and 2 Samuel, especially where the leadership of Israel is at issue, the prophetic history has given preliminary structure to the larger stories. It is most apparent in the story of Samuel's birth and childhood (1 Sam. 1–3), the account of the people's demand for a king (1 Sam. 8), the reports of the rejection of Saul (1 Sam. 15) and anointing of David (1 Sam. 16), and Nathan's condemnation of the house of David (2 Sam. 12).

Original Narrative Sources: Certain early narratives upon which the prophetic and Deuteronomistic editors of Samuel drew can be identified. These include the Ark narrative, the Saul cycle, the story of David's rise, and the succession narrative.

The Ark narrative, an account of the capture and return of God's Ark found in 1 Sam. 4:1–7: 1, is sometimes thought to include parts of 2 Samuel 6. The story shows that the Ark was lost to the Philistines in battle because the corruption of the cult at Shiloh (cf. 1 Sam. 2:12–17, 22–25) had provoked God, who used the occasion to afflict the Philistines with plague.

The Saul cycle, a loose collection of materials about Saul's early career, is most visible now in the tale of the lost asses of Kish (1 Sam. 9–10) and the stories about Saul's wars with the Ammonites (1 Sam. 11) and Philistines (1 Sam. 13–14).

The story of David's rise, an extended account of David's rise from court musician to king (1 Sam. 16:14–2 Sam. 5:10), places special emphasis on David's innocence of wrongdoing in the suspicious circumstances of his alienation from Saul, his career as an outlaw and Philistine mercenary, and his acquisition of power after the violent deaths of those who stood in his way. It may have been composed during the reign of David as a court apology,

OUTLINE OF CONTENTS

The First and Second Books of Samuel

I. The story of Samuel (1 Sam. 1:1–7:17)
   A. Samuel's birth and childhood (1 Sam. 1:1–3:21)
   B. The Ark narrative (1 Sam. 4:1–7:1)
   C. Samuel judges Israel (1 Sam. 7:2–17)
II. The election and rejection of Saul (1 Sam. 8:1–16:13)
   A. The demand for a king (1 Sam. 8:1–22)
   B. Saul's election (1 Sam. 9:1–11:15)
   C. The farewell of Samuel (1 Sam. 12:1–25)
   D. Saul's rejection (1 Sam. 13:1–15:35)
   E. The anointing of David (1 Sam. 16:1–13)
III. The rise of David (1 Sam. 16:14–2 Sam. 5:10)
   A. At the court of Saul (1 Sam. 16:14–21:1)
   B. In the wilderness of Judah (1 Sam. 21:2–26:25)
   C. In the service of the king of Gath (1 Sam. 27:1–30:31)
   D. The death of Saul (1 Sam. 31:1–13)
   E. David becomes king (1 Sam. 31:1–2 Sam. 5:10)
IV. The reign of David (2 Sam. 5:11–20:22)
   A. David's achievements (2 Sam. 5:11–9:13)
   B. David's crimes (2 Sam. 10:1–12:31)
   C. Strife in the house of David (2 Sam. 13:1–14:33)
   D. The civil war (2 Sam. 15:1–20:22)
V. Miscellaneous materials (2 Sam. 20:23–24:25)

defending David and his throne against the charges of his enemies. Some scholars, however, think of the apologetic material as secondary, part of a late redaction favorable to David.

The succession narrative is a long narrative explaining Solomon's acquisition of his father's throne after the demise of his older brothers (2 Sam. 9–1 Kings 2). Until recently scholars regarded this material as a unified history composed by an eyewitness who impartially reported events both favorable and unfavorable to the royal family. The current tendency, however, is to question both the unity and objectivity of the succession narrative. The story of David's crimes involving Bathsheba and Uriah in 2 Samuel 11 and his subsequent condemnation by Nathan in chap. 12 are reminiscent of the prophetic stories about Saul and Samuel in 1 Samuel. 1 Kings 1–2 is concerned with the justification of the bloodbath that accompanied Solomon's accession, but Solomon appears only as an infant in 2 Samuel, and it may be that the oldest materials in the succession narrative, including the account of Absalom's revolt in 2 Sam. 13–20 and the story of the execution of the family of Saul in 21:1–14 and 9:1–13, derive from the time of David.

Bibliography

Ackroyd, Peter R. *The First Book of Samuel* and *The Second Book of Samuel*. Cambridge Bible Commentary: New English Bible. Cambridge: University Press, 1971, 1977.

Hertzberg, H. W. *I & II Samuel: A Commentary*. Translated by J. S. Bowden. Old Testament Library. London: SCM, 1964.

McCarter, P. Kyle, Jr. *I Samuel* and *II Samuel*. Vols. 8 and 9 of the Anchor Bible. Garden City, NY: Doubleday, 1980, 1984.

P.K.M.

Sanballat (san-ba'lat), governor of Samaria in the latter half of the fifth century B.C. and one of the chief opponents of Nehemiah's plan to rebuild Jerusalem. Sanballat conspired with Tobiah, governor of Ammon, and Geshem, king of Kedar, to intimidate the Jews and interrupt the work (Neh. 2:10, 19). As the walls neared completion, they authorized raids on the city (Neh. 4:1–2) and, accusing Nehemiah of planning a rebellion against Persian rule, repeatedly summoned him to account for his actions (Neh. 6: 1–7).

Sanballat's name was Babylonian (Sinuballit), but the names of his sons, Delaiah and Shelemiah, mentioned in the Elephantine papyri, show that he was a worshipper of Yahweh. In Neh. 2:10 he is called "the Horonite," i.e., a native of Beth-horon. The founder of a dynasty was sometimes referred to this way, and there is evidence that five of Sanballat's descendants governed Samaria, including Sanballat II early in the fourth century and Sanballat III at the time of Alexander the Great. *See also* Nehemiah, The Book of; Samaria, District of.

P.K.M.

sanctification, "making holy" or "consecrating" a place, thing, or person to God. Since holiness is primarily the attribute of God, what is "sanctified" is removed from "profane" or "secular" use and reserved to the Lord. However, created beings never attain the unique holiness that distinguishes God. In the OT, rites such as sprinkling with blood sanctify places, objects, and persons. The people must consecrate themselves before they can approach the Lord (Exod. 19:22–24).

Religious purification may also be accomplished by sprinkling with water (Num. 19:9–22). As a "holy" day, the Sabbath is not to be profaned (Ezek. 20:12–24). Since the holiness or sanctity of God is to be reflected in the life of the people, obedience to the Torah is said to keep God's name "holy." Through the Torah, God "sanctifies" the people (Lev. 22:31–32). They are called to be "holy" just as God is "holy" (Lev. 19:2; 20:26; cf. also 1 Pet. 1:15–16, and the related call to manifest divine "perfection" in Matt. 5:48).

In postexilic times, the persistent sinfulness of the people led to the image of an eschatological purification of the people (Dan. 7:18–22; Ps. 34:10). God would "sanctify" them and in so doing "sanctify" his own "name," which had been profaned among the nations by Israel's sinfulness. Ezek. 36:22–27 describes this process in three steps: first, the people are purified from their old sinfulness and idolatry by being sprinkled with clear water; second, the Lord gives them a "new heart" (cf. Ezek. 11:19; Jer. 31: 31–34); and, third, the Spirit of the Lord is put in the human heart. The result of this divine sanctification is a person freed from the "evil inclination" of the human heart and obedient to the will of God.

NT writers can speak of the eschatological sanctification as in the future (Matt. 6:9; "hallow" and "sanctify" are translations of the same Greek word) or as being accomplished for the Christian by the salvation received in Christ (2 Thess. 2:13). Christians, or their communities, are "sanctified" as temples of the Lord (1 Cor. 6:11, 20; Eph. 2:21; 1 Pet. 2:9). They have been "made holy" by anointing (1 Cor. 1:30; Eph. 5:26; 1 John 2:20). They benefit from the "once for all" sacrifice of Christ, which is able to affect the inner reality of the person and not just the externals (Heb. 9:11–14). Therefore, Jesus' sacrifice was said to "sanctify" the Christian (Heb. 10:10; John 17: 19). A person might be "consecrated" to a particular mission or service as a prophet (Jer. 1:5; Eccles. 49:7). The Father "consecrated" the Son, sending him to the world (John 10:36). Similarly, the Son "consecrates" the disciples who are to take up that mission in the world

(John 17:17–18). However, "sanctification" is not merely a "passive gift." Christians must live out their lives in a holiness that reflects what they have received (Rom. 6:19; 1 Thess. 4:3, 4:7; 1 Tim. 2:15; Heb. 12:14). ***See also*** Holiness. P.P.

sanctuary, the holy place where Hebrews believed the Lord was present. In the wilderness, this was the tent of meeting; in the time of Solomon, this was at the Temple at Jerusalem. In both places, the Lord's presence was made visible by the fire, which could be seen as a pillar of smoke during the daytime and a pillar of fire at night. The Lord's presence is still indicated in the sanctuary of some churches by a burning candle or lamp over the altar.

There were degrees of holiness in the Temple. A few steps up from the court was the holy place, which was separated from the court by a hanging curtain. Only priests were allowed in the holy place. A few more steps and a curtain separated the holy place from the Holy of Holies, where only the high priest was allowed. Sometimes the entire Temple was called the sanctuary; at other times the sanctuary meant only the Holy of Holies. G.W.B.

sand, a collection of fine particles of stone, particularly siliceous stone. As is common throughout ancient Near Eastern literature, biblical writings include many references to the natural world, for which there was a deep appreciation. The vast deserts of sand as well as the long stretch of sandy coastal land along the Mediterranean Sea became the source of powerful metaphors. Most often the numerical quality of sand was alluded to: "make your descendants as the sand of the sea, which cannot be numbered for multitude" (Gen. 32:12); "Joseph stored up grain in great abundance like the sand of the sea" (Gen. 41:49); "I shall multiply my days as the sand" (Job 29:18). Sand is also known to be heavy (Prov. 27:3) and it served as a hiding place for the Egyptian killed by Moses (Exod. 2:12), as well as for buried treasure (Deut. 33:19). NT writers also used the metaphor of sand to symbolize great quantities (Rom. 9:27; Heb. 11:12). The shifting, unstable qualities of sand provided the image of one of the most memorable parables, "a house built upon the sand" (Matt. 7:26). S.L.R.

Sandahanna, Tell (san'dah-hahn'nah). ***See*** Mareshah.

sandal, a shoe fastened to the foot with thongs or straps. ***See also*** Shoes.

Sanhedrin (Gk. *synedrion*), a council of leaders. The term is used in Greek literature in connection with councils of political and military leaders, federated states, and various trade and private associations. It is usually distinct from the town council of a Greek city (Gk. *boulē*) or the senate of elders (Gk. *gerousia*). The Gospels, Acts, and the first-century historian Josephus mention various Jewish bodies identified as sanhedrins, and rabbinic literature has a series of rules in the Mishnaic and Talmudic tractates *Sanhedrin* that describe the Sanhedrin's composition and function. In rabbinic literature the Sanhedrin functions as a court to decide major cases and to interpret disputed points of law, but the word "sanhedrin" is used seldom because this body is usually referred to by its Hebrew name, which means court (*bet din*). The NT occasionally uses "sanhedrin" for local councils of leaders and elders (Matt. 5:22; 10:17; Mark 13:9; Acts 22:5) and most often for the supreme court of chief priests and elders in Jerusalem which, according to the Passion narratives in the Gospels, judged Jesus (Matt. 26:59 and parallels), and according to the account in Acts, examined and punished the teaching and activity of Jesus' early followers (Acts 4–6; 23–24). Joseph of Arimathea was said to be a councilor (Mark 15:43; literally, a member of the *boulē*; it is unclear whether the Sanhedrin is meant). In Josephus both Jewish and Roman sanhedrins abound as ruling councils (*Antiquities* 14.5.4; *War* 1.8.5) and as courts (*Antiquities* 14.9.4–5; 15.6.2), often with a king presiding.

The Sanhedrin in Jerusalem: A variety of theories have developed concerning the Sanhedrin of Jewish leaders in Jerusalem. The three most prevalent are that the Sanhedrin was composed of political leaders, including some priests and aristocrats; that the Sanhedrin was composed of religious leaders knowledgeable in the law, including priests, Pharisees, and scribes; and that there were two Sanhedrins, one political and the other religious. All these theories try to reconcile and harmonize a diverse body of data into a coherent description of Jewish institutional

Leather sandal, almost two thousand years old, found at Masada.

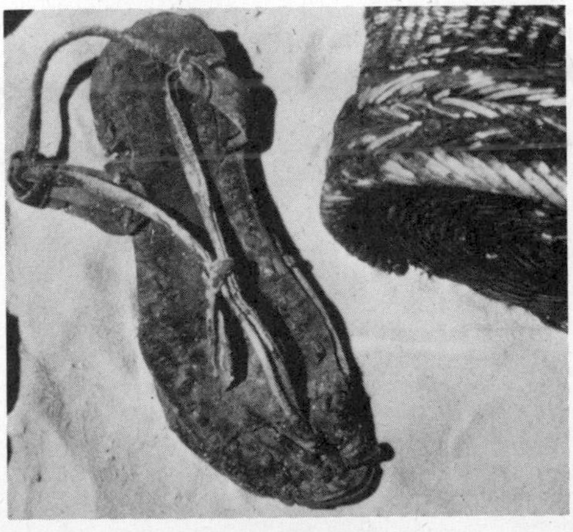

leadership from the second century B.C. to the second century A.D. In addition, the first and third theories address a major issue of anti-Semitism by attributing the trial of Jesus to political leaders rather than to Jewish religious leaders. It seems that the attempt to produce a coherent account from diverse and incomplete sources is doomed to failure. The word "sanhedrin" refers to a series of councils and courts spread over several centuries, composed of whoever was powerful and influential at the time and entrusted with variable powers. Because religion and politics were so intertwined in the community structure, two separate sanhedrins, religious and political, seem unlikely and no direct evidence exists for a dual installation.

In the Gospels: The Gospels attest that some Jewish leaders were opposed to Jesus (e.g., Mark 3:6; John 7:32) but they do not give accurate first-hand information and vary in their usage and characterization of scribes, Pharisees, elders, and chief priests. They refer to the Sanhedrin without giving its precise composition and powers. In Mark the high priest, chief priests, elders, and scribes (14:54–55; 15:1) are explicitly associated with the Sanhedrin in Jesus' trial. In John the chief priests and Pharisees gathered to discuss Jesus (11:47). In Acts the Sanhedrin sat in judgment on the preaching of Peter and John (chap. 4) and was composed of the high priest, the high-priestly family, rulers, elders, and scribes. Gamaliel, a Pharisee and "teacher of the law held in honor by all the people" was a member of the Sanhedrin (5:34). According to Acts 23 both Pharisees and Sadducees sat on the Sanhedrin. In evaluating and disciplining Jesus, Peter, John, and Paul the Sanhedrin sat as a judicial court interpreting and guarding Jewish life, custom, and law.

In Rabbinic Writings: Rabbinic writings, especially the Mishnah *Sanhedrin*, speak of a great Sanhedrin of seventy-one that met in the Temple and was headed by the high priest, of three courts of twenty-three, and of other courts of three. These courts were assigned specific powers over crimes and legal decisions and were composed of scholars. The Mishnah's portrait of the Sanhedrin is set in the Second Temple period (ca. fifth–fourth centuries B.C.), but it is most probably an intellectual construct of the second century A.D. whose historical underpinnings are virtually impossible to determine because of the thorough editing of the Mishnah and Talmudic sources. The Qumran community had its council (Heb. *'eṣah)* and it is likely that Jewish factions, schools and movements, such as the Pharisees, had their own councils of leaders. The rabbinic accounts of the Pharisees before A.D. 70 and of the rabbis after 70 speak of various courts of scholars with legislative and judicial powers. While the rabbinic accounts of the Pharisees are heavily influenced by later ideas, the existence of a council at the head of an organization was very common in the Roman Empire, and a Sanhedrin, whatever its membership and responsibilities, must have existed in NT times. ***See also*** Council; Gamaliel; Senate of Israel, The.

Bibliography

Mantel, H. *Studies in the History of the Sanhedrin.* Cambridge, MA: Harvard University Press, 1961.

A.J.S.

Sansannah (san-san'nah), a town in the Negeb belonging to the tribe of Judah iisted in Josh. 15:31. It has been identified by scholars as Khirbet esh-Shamsaniyat, about three miles northwest of Beersheba, in southern Judea.

Saph (saf), one of the four Philistines identified as "descendants of the giants" slain by David's soldiers (2 Sam. 21:18). In 1 Chron. 20:4 he is identified as "Sippai."

Sapphira (suh-fī'ruh), wife of Ananias who, like him, died after misrepresenting a gift to the apostles (Acts 5:1–11). ***See also*** Ananias.

sapphire, a gem composed of corundum, blue in color. The references in Exod. 24:10; Ezek. 1:26; and 10:1 may be to lapis lazuli. ***See also*** Breastpiece; Jewelry.

Sarah (sair'uh). **1** Abraham's wife, who shared his journey to the Promised Land and his sojournings there. God promised to Abraham numerous descendants, to whom the land of Canaan would belong. For this promise to be fulfilled, the patriarch's wife had a necessary and crucial role. But no sooner was the divine promise given than Abraham jeopardized everything by going to Egypt, where he passed Sarah off as his sister and she was taken into the harem of Pharaoh (Gen. 12). A variant of this story appears in Genesis 20, where Sarah, here Abraham's half-sister, was taken by Abimelech, king of Gerar (cf. also Gen. 26). In both versions, Abraham practiced this deception for fear of being killed on Sarah's account (Genesis 12 stresses her great beauty, though if the placement of these chapters is taken into account, Sarah should be quite old).

Another obstacle to the fulfillment of the promise of numerous progeny was Sarah's barrenness (Gen. 11:30; 16:1). Sarah's solution to the problem was to give her Egyptian maid Hagar to Abraham, a custom according to which Hagar's child would be considered Sarah's (Gen. 16). But the plan backfired when Hagar became pregnant and regarded Sarah with contempt. Asserting her superior status, Sarah dealt harshly with Hagar. Hagar fled to the desert, but the Lord instructed her to return and submit to Sarah.

When Abraham and Sarah were too old for

childbearing, God reiterated the promise, changing Sarai's name to Sarah. Sarah is a variant of Sarai, both forms having the same meaning, "princess," but as with Abraham (Gen. 17: 5), the name change is symbolic, representing a special destiny: "I will bless her, . . . and she shall be a mother of nations; kings of peoples shall come from her" (Gen. 17:16). Not surprisingly, Abraham's reaction to this news was laughter (Gen. 17:17). Sarah also laughed to herself when she overheard their mysterious visitor(s) inform Abraham that she would bear a son (Gen. 18:1–15). She denied laughing, however, when confronted by the Lord. Finally (Gen. 21) the long-awaited heir was born to Sarah and Abraham and, appropriately, was named Isaac, meaning "laughter." Sarah protected Isaac's inheritance by having Hagar and her son Ishmael sent away. Though Abraham was displeased, God supported Sarah's decision, instructing Abraham, "Whatever Sarah says to you, do as she tells you, for through Isaac shall your descendants be named" (Gen. 21:12).

Sarah died at the age of 127, and Abraham purchased the cave of Machpelah from the Hittites for her burial place. Later Abraham (25: 9–10), Isaac (35:27–29), Rebekah (49:31), Jacob (50:13), and Leah (49:31) were also buried there. After Sarah's death, Abraham took another wife, Keturah (Gen. 25:1). Isaac was comforted after his mother's death when he married Rebekah (24:67).

Sarah is mentioned in the NT in Rom. 4:19; 9: 9; Heb. 11:11; 1 Pet. 3:6; and the allegory of Gal. 4:21–31.

2 Daughter of Raguel who, after many difficulties, became the wife of Tobias in the book of Tobit. ***See also*** Abimelech; Abraham; Hagar; Isaac; Ishmael. J.C.E.

sarcophagus. ***See*** Burial.

Sardis (sahr'dis), the regional capital of Lydia in the province of Asia Minor and one of the seven churches addressed in Revelation (Rev. 1: 11; 3:1, 4). The city was founded in Seleucid times (third century B.C.) and Greek was as widely used as the native dialect. The Lydian kings revered the Greek gods, were benefactors of Hellenic sanctuaries, and consulted the oracle at Delphi.

In the sixth century B.C. the Lydians controlled most of the coast of Asia Minor and the islands offshore. Its wealth, especially that of Croesus, was legendary. The influence of Lydian dress, turbans and soft leather boots, and musical innovations based on the seven-stringed lyre could be seen in Athens at the end of the sixth century. However, Croesus challenged the might of the Persian Empire and was defeated. Sardis was made the center of the regional satrapy.

In Roman times Sardis was the center of the imperial cult in the region. The cult was administered by a provincial council. ***See also*** Revelation to John, the. P.P.

sardius (sahr'dee-uhs), a deep orange-red chalcedony considered by some to be a variety of carnelian. It was used as decoration on the high priest's breastplate (Exod. 28:17; 39:10). It appears in the KJV in Ezek. 28:13 where the RSV has "carnelian"; it represents Tyre's lost perfection. In Rev. 21:20 the same terms reflect the incomparable glory of the new Jerusalem.

Sarepta (sah-rep'tah; Heb., "smelting place"; KJV: "Zarephath"), a Phoenician city midway between Tyre and Sidon, where Elijah lodged with a widow during a famine and restored her son to life (1 Kings 17:8–24; cf. Luke 4:26). It is probably present-day Sarfend (Surafend). ***See also*** Zarephath.

Sargon (sahr'gahn) **II,** king of Assyria, 722–705 B.C. In the original Akkadian, *Sharru-kīn* means "the king is legitimate." Sargon succeeded Shalmaneser V, apparently his brother, whose sudden death may have been due to court intrigue. The death provoked massive disruptions in the empire, which took Sargon two years to quell. His first year (721) focused on appeasing various groups at home, particularly those in the city of Ashur. In his second (720), he attacked the two main rebellious clients: Babylonia, under its new leader, the Aramaean Marduk-apla-iddina II (biblical name: Merodach-baladan); and a Syro-Palestinian coalition, led by the cities of Hamath and Gaza, with Egyptian support (2 Kings 17:4). The battle against Merodach-baladan and his Elamite ally ended in stalemate at

Cuneiform inscription on a fragment of a stele erected by Sargon II at Ashdod after his conquest in 712 B.C.

Sargon II (left) and his vizier on a bas-relief at his Khorsabad palace, eighth century B.C.

the Mesopotamian city of Der, leaving Merodach-baladan as Babylonian king for the next decade.

The campaign against Syro-Palestine, however, crushed all resistance (Isa. 10:9–11), even pushing the Egyptians back to their Sinai frontier at Raphia, which was destroyed. In the process, Israelite Samaria was retaken—it had joined the rebellion after an earlier conquest by Shalmaneser V in 722 (2 Kings 17:3–6)—and this time, it suffered conversion to a province and large-scale deportation and replacement of its population. This event effectively marked the end of the Northern Kingdom of Israel as a distinct community (2 Kings 17). Judah, the Southern Kingdom, by contrast, was spared, having remained loyal to Assyria throughout.

These wars of 720, far from providing a permanent peace, set a pattern for the rest of Sargon's reign of almost continuous fighting to maintain the empire. Thus, in Syro-Palestine, two further, and successful, campaigns were undertaken: in 717–716, to conquer Carchemish (Isa. 10:9), and then to force the Arabs and Egypt to yield control of the trade routes south of Palestine (Isa. 19:23); and in 712–711, when Sargon sent his commander-in-chief (Akkadian *turtānu*) to suppress a Palestinian rebellion led by the Philistine city Ashod. Judah, however, was again spared, because it again refused to oppose the mighty Assyrian Empire (Isa. 20).

In the same period, Sargon was also active in the north, against Urartu and its allies, and between 714 and 711 he decisively eliminated the Urartian menace, even as he strengthened the Assyrian presence in southeastern Turkey. With the north and Syro-Palestine relatively stable, Sargon returned, finally, in 710 to Babylonia, intent on removing Merodach-baladan from power and making himself king of Babylonia, like his predecessors Tiglath-pileser III and Shalmaneser V. By 709, these goals were achieved, and by 707, Merodach-baladan's capital was destroyed, although the Aramaean himself remained safe with his ally, the Elamites.

Sargon's Babylonian triumph, nonetheless, was real, acknowledged by kings far and wide and nearly coinciding with his completion, in 706, of a lavish new capital, where all his triumphs could be celebrated. The new city, Dur-Sharrukin (modern Khorsabad), existed only a year, for in 705 Sargon lost his life campaigning against Tabal in southeastern Turkey, where trouble had stirred again; and in the wake of his shocking death (cf. perhaps Isa. 14:4b–21), his successors abandoned Dur-Sharrukin, never to return. ***See also*** Ashdod; Assyria, Empire of; Babylon; Samaria, District of. P.B.M.

Sarid (sair'id), a town on the south border of Zebulun (Josh. 19:10, 12), most likely modern Tell Shadud in the Esdraelon Plain about six miles north and slightly east of Megiddo.

Sarsechim (sahr'se-kim), the name (title?) of one of the Babylonian princes who took Jerusalem (Jer. 39:3). If it is a title it means "chief of slaves."

Satan, the English transliteration of a Hebrew word whose literal meaning is "adversary." This is the basic idea associated with Satan in the OT. The figure of Satan is found in only three places in the OT, and all of these are postexilic in date (i.e., after 538 B.C.): Job 1–2; Zech. 3:1–2; and 1 Chron. 21:1.

In the first two instances (Job 1–2; Zech. 3: 1–2), Satan is depicted as a member of God's court whose basic duty it was to "accuse" human beings before God. He is clearly not at this point an enemy of God and the leader of the demonic forces of evil, as he becomes later. There is some question as to whether, in 1 Chron. 21:1, a specific personality is being described as in Job and Zechariah, or whether the "adversary" is to be understood here as a general tendency toward evil. In the Hebrew text, there is no definite article with the noun "Satan," and the word is probably best translated simply as "an adversary." In either case, the figure in 1 Chronicles is not yet *the* embodiment of evil. It should be noted that "the serpent" of Genesis 3 is never in the OT identified as Satan.

It is during the late postexilic period (after ca. 200 B.C.) and in the intertestamental literature that one first finds the development of the idea of Satan that is assumed in the NT writings. Probably under the influence of Persian ideology, there developed in Hebrew thought the idea of a dualism rampant in the created order—a dualism of good versus evil. There existed already the idea that God had a heavenly host, a group of messengers to carry out his work and orders. The Persians also believed in a ruler over the powers of evil, who had many servants in this realm known as demons. The Hebrews could easily understand and assimilate such thinking into their already existing ideas, but they had not yet developed any idea of a major being as a leader of the forces of evil. Thus, in the development of the religious thinking of the Jewish people, several different names were used to designate the leader of those forces hostile to God: the devil, Belial (also Beliar), Mastemah, Apollyon (meaning the "Destroyer"), Sammael, Asmodeus, or Beelzebub. Satan, however, came to be the most usual designation (in Greek, Satan was translated as "the devil"). Another interesting development took place during this period: the figure of the devil or Satan came to be identified with "the serpent" of Genesis 3.

Satan and his cohorts then came to represent the powers of evil in the universe and were even known in Jesus' time as the Kingdom of Satan, against which Jesus had come to fight and to establish the Kingdom of God (e.g., Mark 3:23–26). The demons were considered to be the cause of sickness, both physical and mental, and of many calamities of nature (e.g., storms, earthquakes); in general, they were the forces responsible for much of human sin (and therefore misery), and they were always opposed to God's purposes and God's people.

In the NT writings, Satan appears frequently, especially in the Gospels. The figure is also known by numerous other designations, among which are the devil (e.g., Matt. 4:1), the tempter (e.g., Matt. 4:3), the accuser (e.g., Rev. 12:10), the prince of demons (e.g., Luke 11:15), the ruler of this world (e.g., John 12:31), as well as certain of the proper names listed above. One of the most interesting designations is "the evil one." In fact, it is quite possible that, in the Lord's Prayer, the original meaning of the petition, "deliver us from evil," may have been, "deliver us from the evil one" (Matt. 6:13b).

In both Jewish and Christian apocalyptic writings, it is clearly affirmed that, no matter how powerful Satan may appear to be, his final overthrow by the power of God is certain (e.g., Rev. 20:1–10, where "the dragon, that ancient serpent, who is the Devil and Satan" is to be "thrown into the lake of fire and brimstone . . . and tormented day and night for ever and ever").

Much modern thought about the figure of Satan, particularly at the popular level, owes its origin to John Milton's *Paradise Lost* (1667), not to the biblical writings (e.g., the application of Isa. 14:12–15 to Satan and his "fall" from heaven). While the figure of Satan is powerful and even heroic in Milton's work, it should be remembered that Milton's Satan and the biblical figure are not always the same. ***See also*** Adversary; Angel; Apocalyptic Literature; Baal-zebub; Belial; Demon; Devil; Eschatology; Evil; Fall, The; Lucifer; Serpent; Sin. J.M.E.

satrap (sa'trap), a provincial governor among the Achaemenid Persians. The word, originally Persian and taken over by the Hebrews and Greeks, occurs in the Bible only in the plural (Esther 3:12; Dan. 3:2). According to Dan. 6:1 (RSV), "It pleased Darius to set over the kingdom a hundred and twenty satraps," whereas the Greek historian Herodotus speaks of only twenty (3.89).

satyr, an imprecise translation of the Hebrew *sa'ir,* which generally means "he-goat" but sometimes has the connotation of "goat-demon" (Lev. 17:7; 2 Chron. 11:15, both in a pejorative sense; see also Isa. 13:21; 34:14).

Saul, a Benjaminite from the mountain village of Gibeah who became Israel's first king. According to biblical tradition Saul was divinely appointed in response to a popular demand for a king, but he was not long in favor with God, who rejected him for disobedience. He spent much of his reign in conflict with David, whom God had chosen as his successor.

The chief reason that Saul became king was probably his prowess as a military leader (cf. 1 Sam. 14:47–48). He seems first to have achieved regional prominence by leading a successful march against Nahash, an Ammonite king who had laid siege to the fortress of Jabesh-gilead (1 Sam. 11). This victory won Saul a base of power extending beyond Benjamin and across the Jordan into Gilead. The summary of his wars in 1 Sam. 14:47–48 also mentions campaigns against Moab, Edom, the Aramean state of Zobah, and Amalek (cf. 1 Sam. 15). Israel's primary enemy at this time, however, was Philistia. Although Saul never achieved any permanent advantage over the Philistines (cf. 1 Sam. 14:52), he did enjoy some success against them, and his kingdom offered the Israelites an alternative to Philistine sovereignty. His son Jonathan attacked the Philistine garrison in Gibeah, provoking an

Saul being presented by Samuel to the people, who proclaim him king (1 Sam. 10: 17–24); detail from a thirteenth-century French illuminated manuscript.

open revolt (1 Sam. 13:3–4). The result was a decisive Israelite victory at Michmash (1 Sam. 14), and the Philistines were temporarily excluded from the central hill country. It is difficult to determine how much territory Saul actually controlled, but it is unlikely that his kingdom extended beyond the central hills and parts of Gilead. The incorporation of Judah and the outlying territories into Israel was probably the achievement of David.

The designation of Israel's first king is the subject of an old folktale underlying 1 Samuel 9–10, where Saul is introduced as the handsome and unusually tall son of a prominent Benjaminite named Kish. One day, while searching for some asses that belonged to his father, he entered a village in the Ephraimite hills to seek the assistance of the local seer. The man turned out to be the prophet Samuel, who anointed his surprised guest as prince, or king-designate, over Israel (1 Sam. 10:1). After this private ceremony Saul was selected in a public lottery and acclaimed king by the people (1 Sam. 10: 17–27). His kingship was renewed or confirmed after his victory over the Ammonites (1 Sam. 11: 14–15).

The biblical account of the origin of monarchy in Israel reflects a point of view that is suspicious of kingship. The office of king is shown to be subordinate to the divine will as mediated through the office of prophet. Thus we are told that Samuel supervised all the events that brought Saul to the throne. Moreover, when Saul failed to carry out instructions given him by Samuel, he was rejected by God (1 Sam. 13:7–14; 15:10–29), who sent Samuel to Bethlehem to anoint a new king (1 Sam. 16: 1–13).

The biblical account of the latter years of Saul's reign (1 Sam. 16:14–31:13) derives for the most part from an old story of David's rise to power. Saul serves as a foil, the divinely rejected king in contrast to whom the chosen successor is eulogized. Thus we are told that when David came to the court in Gibeah, he soon surpassed the king in military prowess (cf. 1 Sam. 18:6–7) and won the loyalty of all Israel, including Saul's eldest son, Jonathan (1 Sam. 18:1–4), and his daughter Michal, who became David's wife (1 Sam. 18:20–27). Saul, now tormented by "an evil spirit from the Lord" (1 Sam. 16:14), became increasingly obsessed with jealousy and suspicion. He persecuted David relentlessly, drove him into hiding in the desert, and even pursued him there. The conflict was not resolved until Saul, defeated in a battle with the Philistines on Mount Gilboa, killed himself by falling on his own sword (1 Sam. 31:4), thus leaving the way open for David to come to the throne. ***See also*** Benjamin; David; Jonathan; King; Samuel.

P.K.M.

savior, one who delivers from a present and/or future danger. The primary usage of the word "savior" in the OT is in reference to judges and other leaders raised up by God to bring deliverance to Israel in times of national crisis (e.g., Neh. 9:27). It was also used of God, who, of course, used these human saviors as his agents. In Second Isaiah it became a recognized title for God (e.g., Isa. 43:3) in connection with the deliverance brought to Israel in the return from the

Exile. This usage represents a turning point in the history of the word, since from then on salvation by God acquired more than purely political or military significance and prepared the way for its NT use in reference to the end-time salvation brought by Christ.

Surprisingly, the word is rarely found in the earlier NT writings (Phil 3:20; Luke 1:24; 2:11; 5:31; 13:23), where it is used in the OT sense of end-time deliverer. The other instances all occur in later NT writings; once in the deutero-Paulines (Eph. 5:23), six times in Jude and 2 Peter (Jude 25; 2 Pet. 1:1, 11; 2:20; 3:2, 18), and twice in the Johannine literature (John 4:42; 1 John 4:14) in the unique phrase "savior of the world." The term also occurs twelve times in the Pastorals (1 Tim. 1:1; 2:3; 4:10; 2 Tim. 1:10; Titus 1:3, 4; 2:10, 13; 3:4, 6).

In the Greco-Roman world the title "savior" was frequently used of gods, not in the OT sense of historical or end-time deliverer, but as the source of present, material benefits such as health, peace, and prosperity. The combined title "god and savior," or "god-savior," was very common.

"Savior" also had political connotations. Ptolemy I was called "savior" in the same sense as people used another title, "benefactor" (cf. Luke 22:25). With the adoption of the imperial cultus in the eastern Roman Empire, the emperors assumed the title "god and savior." This imperial usage may explain why the title "savior" only became common in second-century Christianity. The true savior is not Caesar but Christ (four times in the Pastorals). Here it is no longer used in the sense of end-time deliverer but to refer to Christ as the bringer of present, personal benefits such as cleansing from sin. R.H.F.

savory, pleasing to the taste. Isaac asked his son, Esau, to make for him "savory food" from game so that he could give him a blessing (Gen. 27:3–4). Jacob, however, urged by his mother, Rebekah, went to his father disguised as Esau, offered him a substitute savory dish made of goat meat and received the blessing (27:8–14, 17, 25). This meal should not be understood as a meal that confirms a covenant (cf. 31:54), but simply as a family meal deriving from Isaac's taste for game (25:28).

savour (KJV), in the OT, a pleasing odor. Offerings burned on the altar are often described as being a "pleasing odor to the Lord." This terminology occurs specifically with the burnt offering (which was entirely burned on the altar; cf. Lev. 1:9, 13, 17), the cereal offering (2:2, 9, 12), the fat parts of the well-being offering (3:5, 16), and the fat parts of the consecration offering and accompanying bread which was burned on the altar (Exod. 29:25). It is used once of the fat parts of the purification offering (Lev. 4:31). Num. 15:24, however, when describing a burnt offering and purification offering does not apply the term to the fat parts. This indicates that calling the burning of fat pieces of the purification offering a "pleasing odor" was not originally part of the way that sacrifice was understood. In a few cases "a pleasing odor" is used of the burnt offering plus the cereal offering and libation that accompany it (cf. Num. 15:7; 28:8).

Ezekiel uses the phrase "a pleasing odor" regarding illicit offerings the Israelites make to idols (6:13; 16:19; 20:28). Once he uses it of God's accepting the people as "a pleasing odor," perhaps meaning accepting them when they make proper offerings to him (20:41). ***See also*** Savory; Worship. D.P.W.

scall, a term in the KJV where the RSV has "itch," in Lev. 12:30 and numerous verses that follow.

scapegoat. ***See*** Atonement, Day of; Azazel.

scarlet, bright red color extracted from an insect, the *Caccus ilicis*, and used for dyeing fabric and leather. The Hebrew for scarlet was *senî* or *tola'ath*, used separately or in combination; the latter's basic meaning is "worm," referring to the insect producing the color. In Isa. 1:11 the two Hebrew words are used in parallelism, "scarlet" and "crimson," in this case referring to the blood-red guilt of the sinner as opposed to whiteness of innocence.

Symbolic of honor and riches, scarlet was used extensively for the tabernacle furnishings (Num. 4:8), often in combination with blue and purple (Exod. 26:1). To be clothed in scarlet was prized (2 Sam. 1:24; Prov. 31:21), and, mockingly, Jesus was clothed in scarlet at his trial (Matt. 27:28). The scarlet thread (Gen. 38: 28) and the cord (Josh. 2:18) drew particular attention to the firstborn of Tamar and the home of the harlot. N.L.L.

scepter, a king's elaborate ceremonial staff (Ps. 45:6). Originally a club that could also be used for digging (Num. 21:18), the scepter appeared frequently in ancient art and scripture as royal regalia with an established role in protocol (Amos 1:5, 8; Isa. 14:5; Esther 4:11; 5:2; 8:4). Israel in the wilderness period was the scepter (i.e., constituted the sovereignty) of God (Num. 24:17). Judah acquired similar status (Gen. 49: 10; Ps. 60:7; Ezek. 19:11), as the origin of the Davidic king, the mighty scepter God sends forth from Zion. By metonymy, "scepter" might stand for any national sovereignty: e.g., Moab (Jer. 48:17), or Egypt (Zech. 10:11). The single NT reference to scepter (Heb. 1:8) is a variation of Ps. 45:6. R.B.

Sceva (see'vuh), a Jewish high priest and the father of seven Jewish exorcists who attempted to imitate Paul's use of the name of Jesus in their exorcising of evil spirits, according to Acts 19: 11–20. This unauthorized use of the name had unanticipated negative consequences when, rather than exorcising a spirit, the exorcists themselves were overcome by the spirit-possessed man. The name Sceva does not appear in known lists of the Jewish high priests of the era. The story must be seen in the context of first-century beliefs in demon possession and as an indication of the triumph of the Christian gospel (see Acts 19:17–20). ***See also*** Magic and Divination. A.J.M.

schism (from the Gk. for "tear" or "rip"), a formal division within a religious body. The word occurs once in the NT (1 Cor. 12:25) where Paul is speaking of the body of Christ and says that God has given greater honor to the inferior part "that there may be no discord [lit. 'schism'] in the body." The word is first used in its technical sense of a separation from the unity of the church in the writings of the second century church father Irenaeus. In current theology Roman Catholics use schism for groups out of communion with the pope, in contrast to heresy which involves doctrinal differences. Protestants and Anglicans tend to use it of all divisions among Christian groups. ***See also*** Heresy.
A.J.S.

school, an institution outside the home in which teachers instruct students. In antiquity many wealthy families provided tutors at home for their children and all families passed on occupational skills, cultural information, and values to their children, but these wider educational processes must be distinguished from school. In antiquity school also referred to the groups who had a way of thought and life derived from a philosopher or religious leader and who promoted their way of life by gathering and training disciples.

Schooling in the OT: The OT gives little direct information about schools, but the existence of schools may be deduced from the activities of the monarchy and priests and from Near Eastern parallels. The priests had to preside over a complex ritual, teach Israel's traditions, and instruct the people who came to the Temple, so it is highly likely that priests were trained at the Temple. Even at an early date (twelfth century B.C.), Samuel goes to Eli for an apprenticeship at Shiloh (1 Sam 1:24–28). In a later period Jehoshaphat is pictured as sending the Levites and priests to teach the book of the Law of the Lord in the cities (2 Chron. 17:7–9). The kings, nobles, and high officials of the complex state under the monarchy (1025–587 B.C.) also needed training. When Solomon's son Rehoboam became king he consulted with the young men who had grown up with him (1 Kings 12:8–10) and one of Solomon's enemies, Hadad, married

Lintel from a third-century school at El-Al, near Golan, with the inscription, "This is the school of Eliezer Ha-Rapad."

an Egyptian and had his son Genubath raised in Pharaoh's house among the sons of Pharaoh (1 Kings 11:20). The seventy sons of Ahab were raised by elders who were their guardians (2 Kings 10:6). Chronicles attributes to Jonathan, David's uncle, and to Jehiel the care of the king's sons. Though none of these texts speaks directly of an institutional school, they demonstrate the need for organized training of the leaders of Israel.

Israel's position as an active participant in diplomacy and trade in the first millennium B.C. demanded that the leaders and numerous officials and bureaucrats be educated to read, write, and carry on business according to law and accepted form. Israel's calendar, taxes, and economics demanded a knowledge of mathematics and the numerous traditions that were handed on demanded written records, even in a society that still had a strong oral base. In addition, the OT often refers to writing, to the chronicles that lie behind the books of Kings, to the duty of reading the Law yearly (Deut. 31: 12–13), and to the duty to write the law on doorposts of the house (Deut. 6:9). At least some people were assumed to be able to read and write, from Moses on Sinai to an anonymous boy from Succoth (Judg. 8:14) to the king's Scribe, a high official during the monarchy (2 Kings 22:3). Prophets (Elisha, Isaiah, Jeremiah) also had disciples who preserved their traditions orally and in writing; these schools of prophets may have been more like schools of thought and ways of life than institutional schools, but at some point literary training and activity took place. Finally, the OT itself bears witness to intense literary activity and reflection on previous written traditions from the Exile (586 B.C.) on.

Possible Methods of Instruction: The OT reveals almost nothing about the content of instruction in school. Isaiah 28:10 and 13 have a pattern that may match the memorization that went on in school ("precept upon precept . . . line upon line . . . here a little . . .") and some claim that the book of Proverbs is a school text. Archaeological discoveries in Palestine and the rest of the Near East reveal that students learning how to write copied exercises. (A calendar found at Gezer with the agricultural seasons on it may be a student's exercise.) More advanced students copied classics and documents such as letters and contracts. Students being trained for high office learned diplomacy, economics, and government because the scribal class in the OT and the Near East was the bureaucracy of government. On the local level scribes wrote documents and kept records; on the higher level they were responsible officials of the government, working for the king. Such officials had to be recruited and trained in schools. It is a reasonable hypothesis that fortified cities and regional capitals had either scribes or priests able to teach the young. We know nothing specific about such schools, but following the Canaanite example, they were probably simple rooms in a building. Proverbs speaks of wisdom calling out to students in the city gate (Prov. 8:3), but this is not a clear reference to a school. Most probably the king's palace and the Temple saw to the education of the top officials and chief priests.

Ezra the scribe (fifth century B.C.) was a high official of the Persian government charged to see that the law of God was known and observed. Though the law was read and explained to the people in Nehemiah 8, we have no evidence for schools. The book of Ecclesiasticus (early second century B.C.) has praise for the scribe (38:24–39:11) who knows God's law and is an advisor to rulers. It mentions a school in the concluding hymn (51:23), though it is unclear whether the speaker is Wisdom referring to her school metaphorically, or Ben Sira, the author, referring to his school in Jerusalem. Ecclesiasticus also mentions paying for instruction (51:28). The Ptolemaic and Syriac empires, of which Israel was a part from 332 B.C., and the Roman Empire, which succeeded it in 63 B.C., were highly literate and had well-developed institutions for instruction of youth. It is very probable that Jews of this period were influenced by this cultural milieu and had comparable educational institutions. The Essene community at Qumran, which had a strong priestly component and which produced the Dead Sea Scrolls, was highly literate, and Josephus, who was a first-century priest, describes his education, but not the schools he had contact with.

The rabbis who emerged as the leaders of Judaism after A.D. 70 and who valued oral tradition were nevertheless highly literate because they read and studied the text of the Bible and eventually produced a massive corpus of written traditions in the Talmuds and midrashim (i.e., commentaries). A late tradition in the Babylonian Talmud (*b. B. Bat.* 21a) ascribes the founding of schools throughout Israel to Joshua ben Gamala, a first-century figure known also from Josephus. The Palestinian Talmud claims that there were 480 synagogues in Jerusalem, each with a school attached to it. *Abot* 5:21, a tractate in the Mishnah, gives a schematized and ideal curriculum of study with the ages at which students should progress from reading and writing through studying Scripture, Mishnah, and Talmud. None of these texts provides historical data for OT or NT times, but they show where Jewish instruction arrived in later centuries. The study of the Torah became the center not only of education, but of Jewish piety.

NT Evidence: The NT tells us nothing directly about schools. In Luke Jesus is portrayed as reading from Scripture in the synagogue (4:16–20) but it is not certain that Luke gives a historically reliable portrait. We have no evidence that Jesus wrote anything as part of his teaching. He is portrayed as the oral teacher par excellence. John 8:6 says that Jesus wrote on the ground as part of his interaction with the crowd that wished him to condemn an adulteress, but it does not say that he wrote letters or words. Paul wrote letters to his churches and had been educated in Jerusalem with Gamaliel but he does not describe the nature of his schooling. The early Christian community quickly set its traditions in writing in a variety of works inside and outside the NT. Sociological studies of the Christian community show that Christians were drawn from all classes of society, including the higher classes of the Roman Empire who received an excellent education in a variety of literary and philosophical schools. The majority of people in ancient society, including the majority of Christians, were illiterate, but schools existed for those who had opportunity to attend and the effect of the literate class on society at large as well as Judaism and Christianity was significant. ***See also*** Education; Mishnah; Scribe; Talmud; Teaching. A.J.S.

science, an organized body of knowledge. The word is found in the KJV to denote "knowledge," though not in the modern sense of "science" (Dan. 1:4; 1 Tim. 6:20).

scorpion, any arachnid of the order *Scorpionida* of which a dozen species are known in Palestine, most of which are the yellow variety *Buthus quinquestriatus*. They are mainly nocturnal and carry a stinger at the end of the tail by which they paralyze food and defend themselves. They are symbols of desolate danger (Deut. 8:15), of extremely severe treatment (1 Kings 12:11, 14; 2 Chron. 10:11, 14), of the most hazardous surroundings (Ezek. 2:6), and of excessive pain and torture (Rev. 9:3, 5, 10). They symbolize the powers of evil (Luke 10:19) and Jesus uses them as a symbol of the paternal mistreatment no caring father would do to his child (Luke 11:12). R.S.B.

scourge, whip or lash made of leather thongs attached to a handle (John 2:15). As a metaphor, it refers to any punishment (at the hands of enemies or natural disaster) visited on the people by God (Josh. 23:13; Isa. 10:26; 28:15, 18; Job 9:23).

The word often refers to the use of scourging to punish criminals. Legally, a "milder" form of flogging was used by magistrates as a warning to those responsible for disorder. Josephus (*War* 2.13.7) reports that authorities in Caesarea quelled rioting between Jews and Greeks by catching those responsible and punishing them "with stripes and bonds." Paul faced such punishment on several occasions at the hands of both Jewish and Roman authorities (2 Cor. 11: 24–25; Acts 16:22–25; 21:24).

A more severe beating was administered in connection with other punishments. It could sometimes lead to the death of the condemned person. Livy reports that such lashing preceded crucifixion (*History* 22.13.9; 28.37.3). In Luke 23:14–22 Pilate suggests that Jesus be given the lighter beating as a warning. Mark 15:15 and Matt. 27:26 report that Jesus received the severe beating as one who had been condemned to death. ***See also*** Cross; Trial of Jesus, The.

P.P.

scribe, one capable of reading and writing, usually with competence in some area such as law, economics, or the like. The word derives from the Latin root for "write" and translates Hebrew and Greek words with similar etymologies. In the ancient Near East the designation "scribe" covered a variety of offices from that of the local scribe who copied documents and contracts for the people to government officials invested with serious responsibilities. Like the modern secretary, the scribe was generally concerned with written records, bureaucracy, and administration. Scribes were common to Egypt, Mesopotamia, Israel, and other countries of the Near East. The book of Proverbs contains international wisdom traditions that were developed by the scribal class in many countries; literature from other countries shows that the scribal class engaged in a vigorous and complex educational effort to continue its functions.

In the OT the scribe first appears as a muster officer (Judg. 5:14). In the monarchical period (eleventh to tenth centuries B.C.) the scribe was a high cabinet officer concerned with finance, policy, and administration (2 Kings 22; Jer. 36: 10). Jeremiah's associate, Baruch, who recorded his words, was also a scribe (Jer. 36:32). In postexilic times (sixth century B.C.) Ezra the scribe was sent by the Persian king to instruct and guide the inhabitants of Judea. He was both an official of the Persian Empire and learned in the laws and customs of Israel (Ezra 7). In the early second century B.C. Ben Sira praises the scribe for his learning and also his involvement in affairs of government (Ecclus. 38:24–39:11). In the Maccabean period (167–63 B.C.) the learned Hasideans who sued Alcimus and Bacchides for peace (1 Macc. 7:12–13) and Eleazar, the prominent leader who was martyred (2 Macc. 6:18), are all called scribes, with the probable implication that they were learned in the Mosaic law. The term does not seem to denote a group with particular beliefs or a set political program, but rather learned men of whatever party or persuasion.

Ancient Egyptian royal scribes, New Kingdom period.

In the NT the scribes appear alone occasionally and along with other Jewish groups often. In almost all cases they are opponents of Jesus (but see Mark 12:28–34). In Mark the scribes most often appear in association with the high priests and elders (11:27) and the bulk of their appearances are in conjunction with the death of Jesus. Similarly, in the early chapters of Acts the scribes and elders are opponents of Christianity (4:5; 6:12). In Matthew and Luke the scribes are also paired with the Pharisees in questioning Jesus. Thus the scribes are seen both as part of the leadership and also as a learned class. Two passages (Mark 2:16; Acts 23:9) speak of scribes of the Pharisees, indicating that scribes could belong to other groups within Judaism.

Scribal traditions continued on into rabbinic Judaism, where the emphasis on study, knowledge of the law, and learned argument probably derived from the earlier learned class. Our sources tell us little about scribal training, but literacy and knowledge of the law demanded education, active teaching, the ability to interpret Scripture, and experience in judging individual cases. The scope of scribal authority at different periods and locations remains unclear, but they were probably influential in the Temple and at many levels of government. ***See also*** Education; School; Teaching; Town Clerk.

A.J.S.

scrip. ***See*** Bag.

scripts. ***See*** Writing.

scripture (from the Lat., "writing"), a document or collection of documents containing material that is highly esteemed in the religious community accepting the document(s). Such documents do not stand by themselves but are preserved and interpreted within ongoing religious communities that also have living traditions about worship, belief, and behavior. In late antiquity, Jews and Christians were not alone in esteeming written records of their religion. Greeks, Romans, Persians, and Egyptians all preserved and valued written documents such as hymns, oracles, myths, and revelations. In Judaism and Christianity, the term "Scripture" eventually came to be restricted to those writings listed in an approved canon. It is not always clear whether references in the NT speak of "Scripture" in the technical sense or simply of "writings" (see, e.g., Matt. 21:42; John 2:22; 19:24; Acts 8:32; Rom. 1:2; 1 Cor. 15:3–4; Gal. 4:30; 2 Tim. 3:16; James 2:23; 1 Pet. 2:6; 2 Pet. 3:16). ***See also*** Bible; Canon; Inspiration; New Testament; Old Testament; Revelation. L.W.C.

scroll (Heb. *megillah),* a roll of papyrus or specially prepared leather used for writing on in antiquity (see Jer. 36). Papyrus scrolls were imported from Egypt, where they had been manufactured since at least 3000 B.C. To make a papyrus scroll even strips cut from the pith of the papyrus plant were laid side by side in horizontal and vertical rows, forming the front and back side of the sheet, respectively. Water and pressure were applied to make the strips adhere. After drying, the sheets were rubbed smooth with shells or stones. Leather scrolls were made of sheep, goat, or calf skin that had been dehaired, scraped, washed, stretched on a frame, and dried. The hair side, on which the writing was done, was scraped smooth and rubbed with a pumice stone. Rectangles of prepared leather were stitched together to make a scroll. Vertical and horizontal guide lines were traced with a dry point and a straight edge. Black ink was made from carbon soot mixed with water and gum, red ink from red ocher or iron oxide. While writing could be erased from papyrus with water (Num. 5:23), errors on leather had to be marked out or scraped off. Scribes wrote with pens made from rushes, frayed at the end, and from the Hellenistic period on (after 63 B.C.), with pointed reed pens split at the end. Equipment was carried in a case tied to the scribe's waist (Ezek. 9:2). Whether papyrus or leather scrolls were customarily used for writing biblical books in the pre-exilic period (prior to 586 B.C.) is disputed, but at least by the Hellenistic period leather was the preferred material (e.g., the Dead Sea Scrolls), and was required by rabbinic tradition *(Sop.* 1:1–4). References to scrolls and writing in the Bible include Deut. 28:58; Josh. 1:8; Ps. 45:1; Isa. 8:1; Jer. 8:8; 25:13; Ezek. 2:9–10; Rev. 5:1. ***See also*** Scrolls, The Dead Sea; Writing. C.A.N.

Scrolls, the Dead Sea (DSS), broadly, scrolls and fragments discovered roughly between 1947 and 1960 at seven sites along the northwest shore of the Dead Sea (eleven caves near Wadi Qumran, three caves of Wadi Murabba'at, caves of Naḥal Ḥever, Naḥal Ṣe'elim, and Naḥal Mihras, and at Khirbet Mird and Masada); related to the DSS in this sense are medieval copies of Qumran texts found in 1896 in the Cairo, Egypt, Genizah. More specifically, however, DSS is restricted to the Qumran scrolls and fragments, which are the most important of the finds.

Specific finds are the following: *Qumran Cave One:* seven major scrolls (two copies of Isaiah, one complete and one fragmentary; *Manual of Discipline; War Scroll; Thanksgiving Hymns; Genesis Apocryphon; Pesher* [or "commentary"] *on Habakkuk*) and fragments of seventy-two other texts. *Qumran Cave Two:* thirty-three fragmentary texts (eighteen biblical, fifteen nonbiblical). *Qumran Cave Three:* fourteen fragmentary texts (three biblical, eleven nonbiblical) and the Copper Scroll. *Qumran Cave Four:* the most important, no complete scrolls, but a heap of fragments (between 15,000 and 40,000), which have constituted a giant jigsaw puzzle for scholars; to date, 520 texts have been identified (157 biblical texts, thirteen *pesharim* or "commentaries" on quoted parts of

The first page of the *Thanksgiving Hymns* scroll, which is a copy of the Essene community's prayer book; Qumran Cave One.

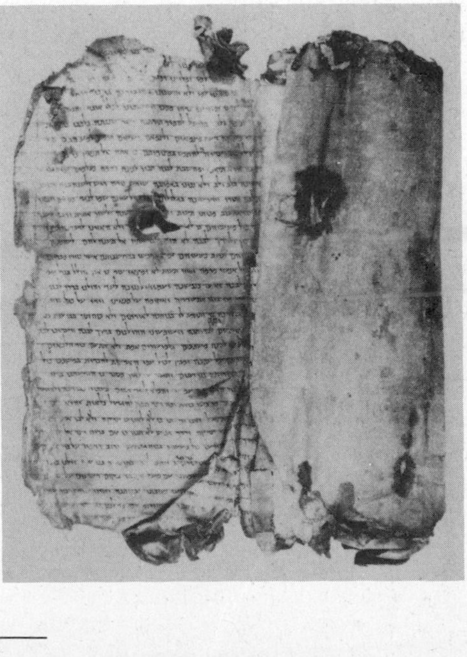

SCROLLS, THE DEAD SEA

the Jewish Bible, and 350 nonbiblical documents including sectarian texts, Semitic originals of previously known intertestamental literature, and many previously unknown Hebrew and Aramaic texts). *Qumran Cave Five:* twenty-five fragmentary texts (eight biblical, seventeen nonbiblical). *Qumran Cave Six:* thirty-one fragmentary texts (seven biblical, twenty-four nonbiblical). *Qumran Cave Seven:* nineteen fragmentary texts, all written in Greek (two have been identified: Exod. 28:4–7; Let. Jer. 43–44; the others are tiny and unidentified); despite claims to the contrary, none of these is from the NT. *Qumran Cave Eight:* five fragmentary texts (four biblical, one nonbiblical). *Qumran Cave Nine:* a lone papyrus fragment. *Qumran Cave Ten:* an inscribed potsherd. The total number of texts found in *Qumran Cave Eleven* is not known, but sixteen have been published in whole or in part. The texts from Caves One through Three and Five through Ten have been fully published, as have the majority from Cave Eleven, but approximately seventy percent of those from Cave Four still await publication (since 1952!).

The texts from Qumran are dated roughly between the end of the third century B.C. and A.D. 70. The Hebrew and Aramaic documents were written in four basic scripts, which permit their palaeographic dating (within a fifty-year margin of error): Archaic Script (end of the third century to 150 B.C.); Hasmonean (150–50 B.C.); Herodian (50 B.C. to A.D. 40); and Ornamental (mid-first century A.D. on), a form also used in the Murabbaʻat texts. The majority of the Qumran texts are in the Hasmonean and Herodian scripts, as are those of Masada. The Hebrew, Aramaic, and Greek texts of Murabbaʻat date roughly from between the two Jewish revolts against Rome (A.D. 66–70 and 132–135). According to preliminary reports, the texts from Ḥever, Ṣe'elim, and Mihras apparently come from that same period, but they have not yet been published. The texts from Khirbet Mird are of later date (roughly fifth to eighth centuries A.D.); the Arabic texts and a few Christian Palestinian Aramaic fragments found there have been published.

The Qumran texts, "the greatest manuscript discovery in modern times" (W. F. Albright), are important for the light they shed on three areas: Palestinian Judaism before and at the beginning of the Christian era; the transmission of the OT text in the same period; and the Palestinian background of the NT.

Palestinian Judaism: Josephus mentions three kinds or "sects" of Palestinian Jews in his day: Pharisees, Sadducees, and Essenes. He devotes his longest description to the Essenes, and, even though what is learned from the DSS about the Qumran community does not agree in every detail with this description, most modern scholars have accepted the identification of the Qumran community with the Essenes (or some branch of them). Thus, the Qumran scrolls would represent the library of this sect. The sectarian writings in the Qumran literature provide an almost complete copy of the Essene rule book *(Manual of Discipline)* and ten fragmentary copies of it from Cave Four (not yet published). This text differs from another, previously known rule book of the sect, the Damascus Document, found in the Cairo Genizah, extensive copies of which came to light in Caves Four, Five, and Six. How to relate these two rule books is a major problem of interpretation and of understanding the sect. From Cave One have also come a copy of the community's prayer book *(Thanksgiving Hymns)* and a text describing an eschatological war in which God and his angels will join the "sons of light" (the sect) in wiping out all evil and their enemies *(War Scroll)*. Further fragmentary copies of both texts were found in Cave Four but are only partially published. From Cave Eleven have come the community's psalter (or possibly another form of prayer book), containing biblical psalms in a different order mixed with nonbiblical writings; and the lengthy Temple Scroll, which recasts much of the pentateuchal legislation in a new form put on the lips of God himself and gives elaborate details about the building of the Jerusalem Temple. Lastly, light has been shed on this sect's mode of interpreting Scripture, not only in their *pesharim* (verse-by-verse "commentaries" on passages from the Prophets and Psalms) but also in isolated quotations from the OT in their sectarian writings. This mode is quite different from anything in the later writings of the rabbis (third to fifth centuries A.D.). We also learn of the messianic expectations of this sect: their expectation of a prophet like Moses (cf. Deut. 18:15–18), a Messiah of Israel (Davidic), and a Messiah of Aaron (priestly).

Transmission of OT Text: Prior to the discovery

Fragment of a scroll found at Qumran (1 Q *Dan.*[a]); it preserves portions of Daniel 1 and 2.

of the DSS, the oldest copy of any extended portion of the Hebrew Bible was dated A.D. 895 (a codex of the Former and Latter Prophets, from the Cairo Genizah). In Cave One, however, a full text of Isaiah was found, dated palaeographically to 100 B.C. The differences between the Qumran text and the Masoretic Text (MT), the Hebrew text preserved from medieval manuscripts, separated in date by a thousand years, amounted to thirteen significant variants and a host of insignificant spelling differences, which have proved a gold mine for the study of first-century B.C. Palestinian Hebrew. This illustrated the care with which the text of Isaiah had been transmitted over the centuries. When Cave Four was discovered, however, a different picture appeared. For certain books of the OT, especially 1 and 2 Samuel, Jeremiah, and Exodus, there were copies of the Hebrew text, from pre-Christian times, in forms differing from the medieval MT. In some cases, the Qumran biblical texts were closer to the Greek Septuagint (LXX); in others, closer to the Samaritan Pentateuch. It is now apparent that these differing ancient text forms of the OT deserve far greater care and attention than they received in the past. The LXX, for example, is now seen not just as a poor, tendentious translation of the Hebrew, but rather as a witness to a different pre-Christian Hebrew text form. Moreover, there appear to have been three local text types in pre-Christian times: a form of the Pentateuch known in Babylon, close to the MT; a form known in Palestine, close to the Samaritan Pentateuch; and a form of OT books known in Egypt, related to the LXX. Eventually (probably between A.D. 70 and 132 in Palestine), a process of standardization apparently set in, preferring one form of text, a set spelling, and even a definitive shape of writing.

Palestinian Background of NT: So far, no mention has been found in these thoroughly Jewish writings of Jesus, John the Baptist, or early Christians. Many of the tenets and practices of the Essene community, however, as seen in the DSS, provide a new and interesting background for aspects of NT writings. The use of isolated OT quotations in the NT resembles many of the similar quotations of the OT in the DSS; the formulas introducing such quotations in the NT are far closer to Qumran introductory formulas than to those in the Mishnah (the earliest part of the rabbinic writings). The "sons of light," a designation for Christians (Luke 16:8; John 12:36; 1 Thess. 5:5), has no OT background and is not found in rabbinic writings, but it occurs, with its counterpart "sons of darkness," in the *Manual of Discipline* and the *War Scroll*. Light has been shed from various Qumran texts on several titles applied to Jesus in the NT ("Son of God," "Son of man," "Lord," "Prophet," "Christ"); thus, these titles apparently were not the product of the hellenization of the Christian gospel as it was carried by early missionaries from Palestine

Hebrew scrolls inscribed on copper sheets found at Qumran Cave Three.

into the Greco-Roman world, as some have maintained. Parallels have been found for many items and expressions in the Gospels of Matthew and John, in the Pauline corpus, and in the Letter to the Hebrews. Lastly, whereas the origins of Christian monasticism were formerly traced to the Christian fathers of the Egyptian desert, the DSS, in agreement with Josephus' description of the Essenes, reveal Qumran as an ascetic community, at least partially celibate, living a strict communal life, and thus, in the judgment of some, a far more intelligible matrix for early Christian monasticism than the Egyptian fathers. ***See also*** Essenes; Messiah; Mishnah; Qumran, Khirbet; Samaritans; Septuagint; Teacher of Righteousness; Texts, Versions, Manuscripts, Editions.

Bibliography

Dupont-Sommer, A. *The Essene Writings from Qumran*. Gloucester: Peter Smith, 1971. The best English translation, though incomplete.

Fitzmyer, J. A. *The Dead Sea Scrolls: Major Publications and Tools for Study*. Missoula, MT: Scholars Press, 1977. An almost complete listing of texts and conventional abbreviations.

Vermes, G. *The Dead Sea Scrolls: Qumran in Perspective*. Cleveland, OH: World, 1978.

J.A.F.

sculpture, the art of carving or modeling in relief or in the round. The second commandment's prohibition of graven (carved) images (Exod. 20:4) is thought to have inhibited development of this art among the Hebrews. The sculpture known to us from OT Scriptures and from archaeology attests dependence on foreign (especially Phoenician) models and artisans, e.g., the carved cedar beams and panels of Solomon's Temple, with their motifs of palms, pomegranates, and cherubim, and the carved ivory inlays discovered in Samaria (cf. Amos 6:4). While most standing images were understood as idols representing foreign gods (including Aaron's golden calf [Exod. 32] and Jeroboam's calves [1 Kings 12:28–30]), the cherubim in the inner sanctuary of the Temple (1 Kings 6:23–28) were a notable exception. The "sculptured stones" near Gilgal (Judg. 3:19, 26) may represent memorial stones or carved images in an open-air sanctuary (cf. Josh. 2:20). ***See also*** Cherub; Idol; Ivory; Temple, The. P.A.B.

Scythians (sith'ee-enz), a nomadic people from the Caucasus who threatened the Assyrian Empire and later the Persian Empire from the north. In the OT they are called Ashkenaz (Gen. 10:3; 1 Chron. 1:6; Jer. 51:27). The fifth-century B.C. Greek historian Herodotus describes an unsuccessful campaign by the Scythians against Egypt in the course of which they looted a temple of Aphrodite in Ashkelon; on the basis of this account the Scythians have been identified as the unnamed enemy from the north in Jer. 1:14 (cf. Zeph. 1:10), but this seems unlikely. The Scythians' cruelty was proverbial in later antiquity (see 2 Macc. 4:47; 3 Macc. 7:5; 4 Macc. 10:7; and also perhaps Col. 3:11). ***See also*** Ashkenaz. M.D.C.

Scythopolis (skī-tahp'uh-lis). ***See*** Beth-shan.

sea (Heb., *yam*, a common Semitic root), a term denoting any large body of water, salt or fresh; "the sea" can designate the Mediterranean Sea and also the direction west (directions being reckoned from the standpoint of a person facing east). The bronze sea, sometimes simply "the sea," was a great basin in the forecourt of the Temple (2 Kings 25:13; Jer. 27:19). In the Ugaritic texts from Ras-shamra, Sea is the enemy of Baal Haddu, the storm god. The storm god uses his weapons of wind, lightning, and thunder to beat back Sea; their battles apparently interpret the alternation of fertile seasons in the world. Vestiges of the battle between Sea and Baal can be seen in the Bible, where God often is depicted with traits of the storm god (Isa. 27:1; 51:10; Job 7:12; 26:12; Pss. 74:16–20; 89:9–10; 93:3–4; 114, among other places). The personification of Sea, however, is much weaker in the Bible than in the Ugaritic texts. ***See also*** Creation. R.J.C.

seah (see'ah), a unit of dry volume measure of uncertain size, probably about one-third of a bushel. It is translated simply as "measure" in both OT (Gen. 18:6) and NT (Matt. 13:33) texts. ***See also*** Weights and Measures.

seal, a device by means of which ownership of objects or origin of documents could be designated. The term is used in two primary senses in the Bible, with secondary meanings developing from them through the use of metaphor. The primary references are to an object, usually a small, semiprecious stone with writing cut into its surface, that makes an impression on clay or wax; and the second primary sense refers to the impression itself made by the seal.

Use and Manufacture: Seals were widely used throughout the ancient Near East from the fourth millennium B.C. through the Roman period because they provided both identification and prestige to the owner. The majority of seals from the OT period identify the owner and often these have a title and an emblem or engraved scene as well. Those persons who possessed seals were usually members of the upper classes and often associated with the workings of government (see below). Their seals performed important functions in their professional activities.

Cylinder seals were popular in antiquity though less so among Israelites and early Christians. Such seals could be rolled by hand across wet clay in order to produce an intricate scene once the cylinder had made a complete revolution. Scenes of religious activities and depictions of deities or royalty could be executed easily in this fashion and then made public through the distribution of impressions.

The question of a seal's manufacture is an intriguing one, especially because so many of them are quite small (oval in shape, with some less than an inch long) yet possessed of exquisite design. Apparently copper and iron were used for drilling, sometimes with an abrasive glued to the implement. That diamonds were occasionally used is a recent conjecture, but the evidence is not conclusive. Water and olive oil were probable lubricants. The lapidary must have possessed keen hand and eye coordination, artistic talent, and the ability to write in reverse so that the impression made by the seal could be read correctly. Some seals are bored through at one end so that they might be fastened to a cord and worn around the neck (see Gen. 38:18). Others were set in a frame and used for rings or necklaces.

There are approximately sixty references to seals and sealing in the Bible. Representative examples of the use of seals are to render something secure against tampering (Jer. 32:10; Matt. 27:66), to demonstrate authority (1 Kings 21:8; John 6:27), to seal a letter (1 Kings 21:81; 1 Cor. 9:2), to seal a covenant (Neh. 9:38), to delegate authority (Esther 8:8; John 6:27), and to seal documents (Isa. 8:16; Jer. 32:10; Rev. 5:

Seal from the reign of Nebuchadnezzar II (605–562 B.C.) portrays a man, a woman, and a snake beneath the tree of life.

1). Archaeological research suggests some additional uses for seals among the Israelites known also among other peoples: as amulets, heirlooms, gifts, deposits in a temple, burial deposits, and as tools used to imprint pottery vessels.

As Archaeological Evidence: Seals can be of great benefit to the reconstruction of past history and cultures, as the following illustrations make clear. On numerous occasions Egyptian scarab seals (so named because they resemble the sacred beetle) or cartouches (name-rings used to produce seals) have been found in excavations in Palestine. Not only does this illustrate the cultural influence of Egypt on Palestine during the third and second millennia B.C., but when a seal is found by an archaeologist in a stratified deposit it can be very helpful in dating the stratum. Excavations at Tel Lachish, for example, have uncovered a seal on one of the ancient gate systems bearing the name of Ramses III (ca. 1183–1152 B.C.). The gate is part of a stratum destroyed by fire. The destruction, therefore, is most probably dated to the reign of Ramses III and is taken by some scholars to be evidence of early Israelite incursion as they settled in the promised land (Josh. 10:31–32.).

Recently discovered clay *bullae* (hardened seal impressions) from the postexilic era (i.e., after late sixth century B.C.) in Palestine have shed additional light on an obscure period in biblical history. They have provided names with the title "governor" that supplement the meager evidence of the Bible for reconstructing the succession of leaders for the community. Furthermore, various impressions bear the stamp *yehud*, "Judah," supporting the conclusion that Judah was administered as a separate province in the Persian Empire.

Over a thousand seal impressions on jars have been discovered dating to the late eighth and early seventh centuries B.C. These impressions have in common the inscription "to" or "belonging to the king" (Heb. *lmlk*); a scarab figure with either two or four wings; and the name of one of four towns in Judah: Hebron, Ziph, Socoh, or an unknown location (Heb. *mmsht*). Recent investigation has dated these impressions to the reign of Hezekiah (ca. 715–687 B.C.) and perhaps to his preparations for war with Assyria. The stamped jars were containers for commodities that may have come from taxation and/or royal landholdings.

Personal Seals: A number of personal seals have been discovered that may shed light on the structure of Israelite society in the pre-exilic period. They range in date from the ninth to the sixth centuries B.C., with the vast majority coming from the eighth and seventh centuries. Among the titles following the personal name are:

"Who is over the house," probably a title synonymous with major-domo or royal steward. The office is known from several references in the OT.

"Scribe." A recently discovered impression reads: "Barakiah son of Neriah the Scribe." This name and title should be compared with that of Jeremiah's faithful friend of the same name and title in Jer. 36:32 ("Baruch" and "Barakiah" are the shorter and longer forms respectively of the same name).

"Servant of the King." A number of seals have been found with this title.

"Son" or "Daughter of the King." Several examples have been discovered belonging to men. Recently one example was found that belonged to a woman; it read: "daughter of the King" (Heb. *Mah adanah*). A beautiful lyre was engraved on the seal.

While the NT uses the terms "seal" and "sealing" in their primary senses (e.g., Rev. 5: 1), metaphorical use is made of the terms as well. Paul refers to the circumcision of Abraham as a "seal of the righteousness which he had by faith" (Rom. 4:11). Christians are "sealed with the promised Holy Spirit" (Eph. 1:13). Perhaps most striking of all is the reference in Heb. 1:3 to Christ as the "stamp" of God's nature, where the single Greek word *(charaktar)* refers to the impression made by a seal.

Bibliography

Gorelick, L., and E. Williams-Forte. *Ancient Seals and the Bible*. Malibu, CA: Udena Press, 1983.

J.A.D.

Seal of Solomon, the, a late medieval and modern form of reference to the five-pointed star or pentagram. It is first found in ancient Palestine on Judean seals. It occurs in a pagan Hellenistic tomb from Marissa and appears in ancient Jewish synagogue art, frequently together with the six-pointed hexagram later known as the "Star of David." Its origins are in pagan art.

sea monster (Heb., *tannin*) a term that can mean simply "serpent" (Exod. 7:9–12; Deut. 32: 33; Ps. 91:13) but more commonly a monster of the deep (Gen. 1:21; Ps. 148:7) or even a dangerous sea dragon, one of the foes of God (Jer. 51: 34; Isa. 27:1; 51:9; Ps. 74:13; Job 7:12). "Sea monster" can also stand for Egypt, the great foe of God's people (Ezek. 29:3; 32:2).

Sea Peoples, the name given to a group of peoples, apparently from the Greek island of Crete, who began to invade the eastern coastlands of the Mediterranean Sea sometime around the thirteenth century B.C. Their attempt to invade Egypt was repulsed by Ramesses III (ca. 1190 B.C.), a victory he commemorated on a monumental frieze. There the Sea Peoples, called in Egyptian the Perasata (probably the source of the biblical term "Philistines," which designates these people), are depicted as slender warriors wearing tasseled kilts and magnificent helmets. Their subsequent invasion of the plains of Canaan sometime later was more successful, and, since their invasion from the west coincided with the invasion of Canaan by the Israelites from the east, a collision between them was inevitable. That collision, which lasted for many years, is reflected in the conflicts between the Israelites and the Philistines recorded in the books of Judges and 1 and 2 Samuel. ***See also*** Amarna, Tell el-; Ashdod; Caphtor; Crete; Gaza; Philistines. K.H.R.

season, a period of the year marked off by prevalent climatic conditions. There are only two seasons in Palestine, the dry (April-September) and the wet (October-March). The amount and duration of rainfall and the temperatures vary from year to year and place to place. Generally as one goes south or east rainfall is lighter and the temperatures are warmer. In Hebrew or Greek no particular word designates season, but several words are used for a specific period of time described by such things as weather: the time of rain (Deut. 11:14), heat of summer (Ps. 32:4); features of the agricultural year: threshing and sowing (Lev. 26:5), blossoming of the fig tree (Matt. 24:32); or annual festivals: the Feast of Unleavened Bread or Passover (Exod. 23:15; Luke 2:41; 22:1).

In the Gezer Calendar, a schoolboy's ditty written during the period of the early Israelite monarchy (tenth century B.C.) on a potsherd, the months of the year are described by agricultural activity: "His two months are olive harvest, His two months are planting grain . . ." ***See also*** Weather. N.L.L.

seat, judgment. ***See*** Judgment Seat.

Seba (see'bah), **Sabeans** (sah-bee'uhnz; KJV: "Saba," "Sabeans"), a place mentioned four times and a people mentioned three times in the biblical text. Job 1:15 identifies the destroyers of his family as Sabeans. Isaiah sees the Sabeans as one of several nations God gave as a ransom for Israel (43:3). They were also a source of wealth (45:14), together with Egypt and Ethiopia. In Joel 3:8 they are described as a "nation far off" in Joel's threat that they will buy Phoenician and Philistine slaves from Judah. Gen. 10:7 catalogs Seba as a son of Cush, together with Havilah, Sabtah, Raamah, and Sabteca, as does 1 Chron. 1:9. Kings from Seba were mentioned together with those of Sheba and Tarshish as bringing tribute and gifts (Ps. 72:10) to Israel's king. Their definition as a distant wealthy source of riches seems clear. The precise location is not evident from biblical sources.

From the evidence of archaeological work begun in 1762 and continuing to this day, with studies not only of sites, but of inscriptions coming to light in increasing numbers, it is clear that the Sabeans occupied the portion of southwest Arabia that is today the land of Yemen. It was comparatively well watered and fertile but the resources were augmented by extensive irrigation facilities (as at Marib). The Sabeans' location was also fortunate for trade development. They could capitalize on traffic in myrrh and frankincense through the land caravan route running north up the Hijaz, the coastal plain that lies at the eastern shore of the Red Sea. Their extensive trade in gold and precious stones was known to the biblical writers (see also Isa. 60:6; Jer. 6:20; Ezek. 27:22–23, where Sheba occurs as the Hebrew spelling of the South Arabic name Saba). Their territorial controls fluctuated, but included at times the port of Aden where contacts with shipments of goods from India as well as Africa were made. Sabean ships ranged to Africa and India, contributing both to the variety of trade goods and to the wealth of the exchanges flowing into Sabean resources.

While Sabean history is only sketchily known, its Semitic inhabitants successfully developed caravan trade by the tenth century B.C. as evidenced by the visit of the queen of Sheba to Solomon (1 Kings 10:1–13; 2 Chron. 9:1–12). Sabean colonization apparently included parts of the adjacent Ethiopian coast. From the ninth to fifth centuries, Sabean kings numbered over twenty, from which archaeological evidence survives in the form of temples, dams, and sluices for irrigation, bronze statues, and inscriptions. Saba weakened thereafter, but its successful defense against Rome's initial efforts to subdue it led to importation of Hellenistic art and pottery soon locally imitated. Abyssinian occupation in the fourth century A.D. was accompanied by conversion of the leaders to Christianity, and subsequent Jewish leadership dominated the territory until the Persian conquest about 575 and its later capture by Islamic forces in 628. ***See also*** Sheba; Sheba, Queen of. R.S.B.

Sebat (se-bat'). ***See*** Shebat.

Secacah (si-kay'kah; Heb., "thicket, cover"), a city of Judah (Josh. 15:61), probably modern Khirbet es-Samrah, located three and a third miles southwest of Khirbet Qumran in the Valley of Achor.

Second Coming of Christ, the. ***See*** Eschatology; Millennium; Parousia.

second death, the death of the soul or spirit, the death of the resurrected person, or eternal damnation. In Matt. 10:28 a saying attributed to Jesus alludes to God as one who has the power to destroy both soul and body. A Jewish text written in the second century B.C. describes a chaotic wilderness in which fire blazes brightly. In this place the spirits of the wicked will be killed during the last days (*1 Enoch* 108:3–4). According to the book of Revelation, all the dead will rise on the day of judgment. Then the wicked will be cast into the lake of fire to suffer their second death (Rev. 20:11–15; 21:8). ***See also*** Abyss; Hades; Hell; Punishment, Everlasting. A.Y.C.

Second Quarter, a part of the city of Jerusalem (2 Kings 22:14). ***See also*** College.

sect, a sociological category usually referring to a religious group protesting against a parent body. Some characteristics common in sects are voluntary association, exclusiveness toward outsiders, equality of members, a low degree of internal organization and differentiation, total commitment, appropriation of the parent body's ideology and status, and rejection of the parent body as corrupt. Sectarian analysis was developed by the modern German historian Troeltsch in connection with Christian church history. If the category is applied to first-century Judaism with appropriate caution, the Qumran and early Jewish Christian communities may be understood as sects. Pharisees, Sadducees, and Zealots cannot be identified as sects in any proper sense of the term; they were rather "parties" within Judaism. ***See also*** Essenes; Pharisees; Sadducees; Zealot. A.J.S.

Secundus (se-kuhn'duhs), a Christian from Thessalonica who accompanied Paul from Macedonia on Paul's last trip to Jerusalem (Acts 20:4–5). He probably helped Paul gather money for his contribution from the Gentile churches to the poor in Jerusalem (see 2 Cor. 8:23). ***See also*** Contribution for the Saints.

security, a term found in the biblical writings primarily in contexts where the people are said to be able to dwell in their land "in peace and security." In such instances, security has the connotation of safety, protection from harm or enemies, often with the added idea that God is providing this protection (cf. Judg. 18:7; 2 Kings 20:19; Ps. 37:3; Jer. 33:6; 1 Thess. 5:3). In two instances, however, security appears to carry different connotations: that of collateral for a loan (Lev. 6:2) or bail for the release of someone from prison (Acts 17:9).

seed. 1 The productive unit of a plant in contrast to trees, i.e., grain (Gen. 1:11, 12, 29; Deut. 11:10; 14:22). **2** Human semen (Lev. 15:16–18; 22:4; Heb. 11:11). **3** Human offspring or descendants in general (Gen. 9:9; Lev. 22:4; Mark 12: 19–22). **4** The physical (Gen. 12:7; 17:7) and spiritual (Gal. 3:29; Rom. 4:11–12, 16) descendants of Abraham. **5** Jesus Christ as the seed of Abraham (Gal. 3:15–18) and David (2 Tim. 2:8). **6** The divine nature implanted in the believer (1 John 3:9).

Jesus used seeds as examples in four of his parables: the seed and weeds (Matt. 31:24–30); the sower, seed, and soils (Matt. 13:3–9); the seed growing secretly (Mark 4:26–29); and the mustard seed (Mark 4:30–32). R.H.S.

seer (Heb. *ḥozeh,* "visionary"; *ro'eh,* "seer"), a person who received divine messages in visions or dreams. Visionaries existed in Israel throughout the history of the nation and were found particularly in Judah, where they may have been connected with the royal court (2 Sam. 24:11; Amos 7:12; Mic. 3:7; Isa. 29:10; 30:10; 1 Chron. 21:9; 25:5; 29:29; 2 Chron. 9:29; 12:15; 19:2; 29: 25, 30). The title "seer" is given primarily to Samuel (1 Sam. 9:5–21). ***See also*** Prophet.

Segub (say'guhb). **1** The youngest son of a Bethelite named Hiel. He died (possibly as a human sacrifice) when his father rebuilt the Jericho gates (1 Kings 16:34), fulfilling the word of Joshua (Josh. 6:26). **2** The son of Hezron and a daughter of Machir (1 Chron. 2:21, 22).

Seir (see'eer; Heb. "hairy"). **1** The mountainous region southeast of the land of Canaan inhabited by the Edomites. Also called "Mt. Seir," the region may have encompassed not only the mountains east of the Arabah (the Rift Valley), but those on the west side as well. This is suggested by such passages as Num. 20:16, where Kadesh-barnea (modern Ain el Qudeirat) is said to be a town on the edge of Edom's territory (cf. Num. 20:23; Deut.1:44; 33:2; Judg. 5:4). The eastern highlands, built mainly of red Nubian sandstone, rise up to over 5000 feet above sea level and receive enough rainfall for some cultivation and animal husbandry. Perhaps the most important physical advantage of Seir in ancient times was its location, positioned to control the trade routes from Arabia and the Red Sea. The two centers of power in the land were Bozrah and Teman, both of which guarded important caravan routes.

According to Deut. 2:22, the Horites (Hurrians) had inhabited Seir before they were driven out by the Edomites; these Horite clans are enumerated in Gen. 36:20–29. The Edomites, descendants of Jacob's brother Esau, eventually established a kingdom in the region (Gen. 36: 9–19, 31–43; Josh. 24:4). On Israel's journey from Kadesh-barnea to the Plains of Moab it was denied passage through Seir by the Edomites (Num. 20:14–21; Deut. 2:1–8). Subsequently the region continued to play a significant role in Israel's history (cf. 2 Sam. 8:13–14; 2 Kings 14:7, 22).

2 A hill on the northern border of the tribe of

Judah, located west of Jerusalem on the western slopes of the Judean highlands, between Kiriath-jearim (modern Deir el Azar) and Chesalon (modern Kesla; Josh. 15:10). Its exact identification is uncertain. ***See also*** Edom. D.A.D.

Seirah (see'rah; KJV: "Seirath"), the haven to which Ehud fled (Judg. 3:26). The location is unknown, as is the nature of the place, that is, whether it was a town, region, cave, or some other feature.

Sela (see'lah; Heb., "crag"). **1** The fortress city of Edom (2 Kings 14:7) stormed and renamed Sela by King Amaziah of Judah. This Sela is modern Umm el-Bayyarah just above Petra in south Transjordan and excavated by C. M. Bennett. **2** An Amorite border town (Judg. 1:36) whose location is unknown. An unidentified location mentioned in Isa. 16:1.

selah (see'lah), a word of uncertain derivation and unknown origin and meaning found in certain psalms in the OT (e.g., Pss. 3, 4, 52, 88, 143). It appears additionally in Hab. 3:3, 9, 13, verses that are part of a psalm preserved in that prophetic book. There has been much speculation about its meaning—a musical notation, a pause in singing for narration, instructions on dynamics to the choir or to instrumental accompaniment—but there is no agreement among scholars about its function or significance. Absent new evidence, any attempt to define it must remain speculative.

Seleucia (seh-lo͞o'shuh), the ancient port city of Antioch in Syria (modern Samandag, Turkey), founded by Seleucus I Nicator in 301 B.C., apparently on an older site called Pieria. In the mid-third century B.C., Ptolemy III Euergetes of Egypt took the city ("fortress" in Dan. 11:7), but it was regained by Antiochus III in 219. According to 1 Macc. 11:8, Ptolemy VI Philometor again captured Seleucia for Egypt in his coastal campaign of 146, but the city reverted to Seleucid control in 138. Granted the status of a free city by Pompey in 63 B.C., Seleucia remained such throughout NT times.

According to Acts 13:4, Barnabas and Saul (Paul), accompanied by John Mark, sailed from Seleucia to Cyprus at the beginning of their first missionary journey (ca. A.D. 49). Other references to voyages to and from Antioch probably imply embarkation and landing at Seleucia (Acts 14:26; 15:39).

Other cities also named Seleucia were in Cilicia, Mesopotamia, and Bashan. ***See also*** Antioch; Paul; Ptolemy; Seleucids, The. C.H.M.

Seleucids (se-lo͞o'sidz), **the,** a dynasty of Hellenistic kings that ruled an area including, at various times, Bactria, Persia, Babylonia, Syria, and southern Asia Minor after the death of Alexander the Great and until the Roman takeover of the region in the first century B.C.. The name originates from Seleucus I Nicator, son of Antiochus, one of the generals of Alexander. In the struggle for power following Alexander's death in 323 B.C., Seleucus was eventually successful in carrying out a series of moves that made him one of the most powerful of the successor kings (Diadochi). The rule of the Seleucid dynasty dates from 312 B.C., when Seleucus and Ptolemy I of Egypt joined to defeat Antigonus of Phrygia at the battle of Gaza, thus regaining for Seleucus the satrapy of Babylonia, earlier lost to Antigonus. At the battle of Ipsus in 301 B.C., Seleucus gained much of Asia Minor and Syria, but Coele-Syria and Palestine, which Seleucus regarded as rightfully his, were appropriated by Ptolemy, his former ally. The struggle for Coele-Syria and Palestine was finally settled in 198 B.C., when Antiochus III ("the Great") defeated the Egyptian general Scopus at the battle of Paneas, and Seleucid rule of Palestine began.

Of all the Seleucid rulers, Antiochus IV Epiphanes is most important as far as the biblical literature is concerned. His eleven-year reign was marked by an aggressive attempt to hellenize the Jews, an attempt that led to the Maccabean war and eventually to Jewish independence from Syria. The two books of Maccabees reflect this struggle, detailing the offensive actions of Antiochus, who meddled in the appointment of high priests, forced Greek customs upon the Jews, looted the Temple, defiled the altar, and cruelly persecuted the pious Jews who wished to observe their religious laws and customs (see 1 Macc. 1:10–62; 2 Macc. 4:7–7:42). The book of Daniel also reflects the impact of Antiochus Epiphanes upon the Jews. In chaps. 7–12, Antiochus plays a major role (he is the "little horn" of 7:8, 20–27; 8: 9–14, 23–25 and the oppressor of the "saints of the Most High"; the "abomination that makes desolate" of 11:31 is almost certainly a refer-

THE SELEUCID DYNASTY

Seleucus I Nicator	312–281 B.C.
Antiochus I Soter	281–261
Antiochus II Theos	261–246
Seleucus II Callinicus	246–226
Seleucus III Soter (Ceraunus)	226–223
Antiochus III ("The Great")	223–187
Seleucus IV Philopator	187–175
Antiochus IV Epiphanes	175–164
Antiochus V Eupator	164–162
Demetrius I Soter	162–150
Alexander Balas	150–145
Demetrius II Nicator	145–139
(Antiochus VI Epiphanes Dionysus	145–142)
Antiochus VII Sidetes	138–129

(Hereafter, much internal strife and frequently rival claimants.)

ence to an altar to Zeus that Antiochus caused to be erected on the altar of the Jerusalem Temple).

The latter years of the dynasty saw much internal strife among princes of the Seleucid house and a conquest of their weakened kingdom by Tigranes of Armenia (83–69 B.C.). Eventually, the Romans put an end to the Seleucid reign when Pompey made Syria a Roman province in 64 B.C.

The Seleucids founded Antioch in Syria as their capital, as well as many other cities that were to become centers for the spread of Hellenism (e.g., Antioch of Pisidia, Apamea, Laodicea, Edessa, Beroea, Seleucia, and Dura-Europos). Hellenized Jews lived in these cities, in large part because of the Seleucid practice of rewarding veterans with land in newly colonized areas (Jewish soldiers had fought in the army of Seleucus I, just as other Jews had fought with Ptolemy). Hellenism influenced Judaism in many ways, and this influence can be seen in some of the later OT writings, in the intertestamental literature, and in the NT. The Seleucid dynasty played an important role in developing this influence. ***See also*** Alexander; Antiochus; Daniel, The Book of; Maccabees; Maccabees, The First Book of the; Maccabees, The Second Book of the; Ptolemy; Seleucia.

F.O.G.

self-control, the English translation of a Greek term common in the Greek, especially the later Stoic, philosophical tradition but seldom appearing in the Greek OT (LXX) or the NT, probably because biblical faith sees human beings not as autonomous but as responsible to and directed by the will of God. Felix was alarmed when Paul "argued about justice and self-control and future judgment" (Acts 24:25). Paul knew that it was difficult for Corinthian Christians to exercise self-control in sexual matters (1 Cor. 7:9). He compared himself with an athlete who "exercises self-control in all things" for the Gospel's sake (1 Cor. 9:25). For Paul, self-control was not really a human achievement but was linked with love, joy, peace, etc., as "the fruit of the spirit" (Gal. 5:22–23). 2 Pet. 1:6 links self-control with such characteristics as faith, knowledge, and steadfastness. Again, "God did not give us a spirit of timidity but a spirit of power and love and self-control" (2 Tim. 1:7). A bishop must not be arrogant or quick-tempered or a drunkard but "a lover of goodness, master of himself, upright, holy, and self-controlled" (Titus 1:7–8).

J.F.J.

Semites, a term used to describe various peoples of the Fertile Crescent in antiquity (i.e., Arabs, Arameans, Assyrians, Babylonians, Canaanites, Hebrews and Phoenicians). It originated in the eighteenth century A.D. among Western scholars to describe observable tendencies in language and culture within the peoples of the region from Persia in the east to Africa in the west. The term itself reflects the name Shem, one of Noah's three sons born after the Flood. In Gen. 10:21–31 there is a description of Shem's descendants according to the names of nations known to the biblical writer(s). The whole of Genesis 10 has been called by scholars the "table of nations," because it presents the then-known world of nations in three categories, each one tracing its lineage back to one of Noah's three sons, Shem, Ham, and Japheth (Gen. 10:1).

It must be stressed that this is not an ethnic term and that unanswered questions remain regarding the origins of the Semitic peoples. Older historians somewhat romantically portrayed the Arabian, Sinai, and Syrian deserts as the original homes of the Semites and suggested that repeated waves of these nomads moved from the desert to the more fertile areas. This view is largely rejected today by scholars who find instead a very complex but often supportive relationship between the "nomadic" and the more settled, agrarian societies. Several elements of the oldest civilizations known to have left records of commerce and a spoken language in the Middle East show Semitic influence, and perhaps that is all that can justifiably be said about their origins.

Linguists and philologists do use the term "Semitic" with regard to groups of languages. There is some disagreement among them concerning the interrelationships among the various Semitic languages, but there is general agreement among scholars on the following classifications: *East Semitic* includes various dialects of Assyrian and Babylonian. The term "Akkadian" is sometimes used as a reference to these languages. They are written in cuneiform, a type of writing impressed on wet clay with a wedge-shaped pen. *Northwest Semitic* includes the various Aramaic and Canaanite dialects. Classical Hebrew, Moabite, and perhaps Ugaritic are some examples of the latter. *South Semitic* includes Arabic and Ethiopic.

The advance of archaeological work in the last two centuries has made available to scholars for the first time a number of texts written in these languages. This situation has allowed the student of comparative Semitics to place the study of classical Hebrew on firmer historical ground as far as its relationship to other ancient Semitic languages is concerned.

The development of an alphabetic language and script among ancient Semites was transmitted by the Phoenicians to the Greek Isles, ultimately to influence many of the world's most widely used languages including English. While many details of this transmission remain obscure, the contribution of the alphabet is one of the enduring legacies of Semitic culture.

Religion appears in great variety among the Semites as evidenced by surviving texts. Some scholars point to the early narratives in the book of Genesis concerning Israel's ancestors as one illustration. Yet another example can be found in the texts discovered in Syria at the site called Ras-Shamra (ancient Ugarit). Sacrifice and polytheism are characteristic of Semitic religions; however, such a milieu produced the three great monotheistic religions of the modern era: Judaism, Christianity, and Islam. Interestingly, the scriptures of each of these religions was written in a Semitic language. While the NT of Christianity was written in ancient Greek, its OT was written in Semitic languages (Hebrew and Aramaic).

The term "anti-Semitic" is often used to describe those views prejudicial against Jews or Judaism. While such prejudice is to be deplored, the use of the term anti-Semitic to describe this bigotry is unfortunate because there is nothing about the definition of Semitic that should limit it to Judaism. J.A.D.

Senaah (se-nay'ah), a city whose people are listed among those returning from exile in Babylon (Ezra 2:35; Neh. 7:38). It may be modern Khirbet 'Auja el-Foqa about three miles north of Jericho. Its location parallels its identification with Magdalsenna (Heb., "Tower of Sena'a"), a fortress that guarded the road from the Jordan valley to Baal-hazor in earlier times.

Senate of Israel, the, a body called together by the high priest, along with the Sanhedrin, to assess and judge the apostles in Acts 5:21. "Senate," Greek *gerousia*, means literally a council of elders and was often the ruling council of a Greek city. In the Greek of Exod. 12:21 it translates the Hebrew "elders of Israel." It is likely that Senate and Sanhedrin are used interchangeably in this verse in Acts.

Seneh (sen'nuh), the name of one of two rocky crags flanking the pass at Michmash which Jonathan used in approaching the Philistines (1 Sam. 14:4). Identity of the crags remains uncertain, but they are probably to be located in the Wadi es-Suweinit about seven miles northeast of Jerusalem.

Senir (see'nuhr), the Amorite name for Mount Hermon, according to an editorial note in Deut. 3:9. In Ezek. 27:5, Senir supplied fir planking and Lebanon a cedar mast for the metaphorical ship, Tyre—here Senir probably designates the entire Anti-Lebanon mountain range. Hermon and Senir appear together, as separate parts of a whole, in Song of Sol. 4:8 and 1 Chron. 5:23. ***See also*** Hermon; Lebanon; Tyre.

Sennacherib (sen-ak'uhr-ib), king of Assyria (705–681 B.C). He assumed the throne of the vast Assyrian Empire convulsed by uprisings on both its southern and western flanks following

Sennacherib seated on his throne, receiving booty from Lachish, which he conquered in 701 B.C.; Nineveh reliefs.

the death of his father Sargon II. Babylon and its sometime ally Elam were perceived as the most immediate threat to his rule, so that Sennacherib undertook a two-year campaign (704–702) to restore Assyrian suzerainty over the south.

In 701, he turned to the troubled west. Details of this military undertaking are known from two major sources: an Assyrian royal inscription of Sennacherib's "third campaign" and 2 Kings 18:7–8, 13–16; 18:17–19:37, a patchwork of chronistic and prophetic material arranged and edited by the author of the book of Kings. These sources complement each other and are in agreement as to the main outline of the rebellion and its suppression by the superior Assyrian forces. Only the biblical source reports the miraculous salvation of Jerusalem. The following outline is based on a critical reading of both sources and on the assumption that Sennacherib campaigned only once in the west, in 701.

King Hezekiah of Judah spearheaded an anti-Assyrian coalition of Phoenician, Philistine, and south Syrian states. Though there were several years to prepare for the inevitable Assyrian response—note the drilling of the Siloam tunnel in Jerusalem to supply water to the city in case of siege (2 Kings 20:20; 2 Chron. 32:3–4)—the coalition was no match for Sennacherib. The coastal cities succumbed quickly, so that the full brunt of reprisal was soon directed against Judah. An Egyptian relief force under the command of Tirhakah engaged Sennacherib at Eltekeh in the Judean Shephelah (cf. 2 Kings 18: 21; 19:9); but it suffered heavy losses and withdrew.

During the attack upon Judah's border fortresses, Sennacherib sent a negotiating team, led by top Assyrian officers—their titles are recorded in 2 Kings 18:17 (Tartan, Rabsaris, Rabshakeh)—to solicit Hezekiah's surrender. The counsel of the prophet Isaiah not to surrender strengthened Hezekiah's determination to hold out (2 Kings 19:5–7; 2–34). But "when all the fortified cities of Judah" had fallen to Sennacherib, Hezekiah capitulated. He agreed to pay a heavy indemnity of "three hundred talents of silver and thirty talents of gold" (2 Kings 18:14–16), which together with other valuables he sent to Nineveh. Thus, the siege of Jerusalem was lifted and the city spared destruction. The other territories of the kingdom of Judah were ceded to loyal Assyrian subjects, namely, the rulers of Ashdod, Ekron, Gaza, and Ashkelon. Thus Hezekiah resumed his former status as Assyrian vassal. Sennacherib commemorated his victories in Judah with a wall relief in his palace at Nineveh depicting the attack and capture of Lachish.

Assyrian historical inscriptions indicate that for most of the next twelve years Babylonian affairs engaged Sennacherib's attention. Other areas of the empire remained pacified; the fear of Assyrian military might sustained a *pax Assyria*. But at least three campaigns to Babylon were undertaken (700, 694–693, and 691–689). Apparently it was this seemingly intractable situation that led to the unprecedented decision to destroy Babylon and put an end to the problem once and for all.

Sennacherib designated his son Esarhaddon as his heir, though he was not in the direct line of succession. Two of his other sons, Adrammelech and Sarezer, murdered their father and led an unsuccessful rebellion against Esarhaddon (2 Kings 19:37). ***See also*** Assyria, Empire of; Hezekiah. M.C.

Sephar (sef'uhr), one of the limits of the territory inhabited by the family of Joktan (Gen. 10: 30). It may be either a region, a boundary, or a town. The identity remains uncertain, although most suggestions place it somewhere in southern Arabia.

Sepharad (sef'uh-rad), the residence of some exiles from Jerusalem mentioned in Obadiah 20. It is identified with Sardis (modern Sart) in east central Turkey, the capital city of the ancient Lydian Empire. Its standing as a major commercial center is reflected in the archaeological materials uncovered at the site, including a large Jewish synagogue from the later stages of settlement.

Sepharvaim (sef-ahr-vay'yim), a city from which the Assyrian government drew settlers to place on Israelite territory after Israel's fall to Assyria in 721 B.C. (2 Kings 17:24, 31). Later references to the city of the same name (2 Kings 18:34; 19:33), whose kings and gods are impotent, may refer to the identical location, but that remains uncertain. Isa. 36:19 and 37:13 contain the same name but do not clarify the identification.

Sepphoris (sef'oh-ris), a Jewish town in Lower Galilee, about three miles northwest of Nazareth. During the Hasmonean period (152–37 B.C.), the town probably became the administrative center for the Galilee area. Sepphoris submitted to Herod the Great, but, after his death in 4 B.C., it was sacked by Varus. While tetrarch of Galilee and Perea, Herod Antipas rebuilt the city and resided there prior to making the city of Tiberias his capital. After the destruction of Jerusalem in A.D. 70, Sepphoris was the seat of the Sanhedrin until it moved to Tiberias. There is no reference to Sepphoris in the Bible, but the inhabitants of nearby Nazareth most certainly would have been acquainted with it. It was probably during the second century A.D., under Hadrian's reign, that the city's name was changed to Diocaesarea, meaning "City of Zeus and the Emperor"; it was still referred to by this name in the fourth century. M.K.M.

Septuagint (sep'tōō-uh-jint), the Greek translation of the Hebrew OT that began in the third century B.C. in Alexandria, Egypt. The name Septuagint comes from the Greek word for "seventy" (hence the symbol LXX, 70 in Roman numerals) and refers to the seventy-two Jewish translators brought to Egypt by Ptolemy II Philadelphus (285–246 B.C.) to translate the Pentateuch, according to the legendary account in the *Letter of Aristeas*. The translations of the books of the OT differ in style, accuracy, and substance, indicating that there was no single original translation into Greek. Manuscripts found at Qumran among the Dead Sea Scrolls and other early manuscripts and quotations from the Septuagint in ancient writings all indicate that revisions were constantly being made to the Septuagint. In addition, Hebrew manuscripts found at Qumran differ from the standard Hebrew text (the Masoretic Text) but agree with some of the Greek renderings in the Septuagint. Thus the Septuagint often witnesses to a Hebrew manuscript tradition different from and earlier than the Masoretic Text and so is valuable in solving textual difficulties. The Septuagint sometimes has a different order within books and a shorter or longer version of a book. For example, Jeremiah is one-eighth shorter in Greek and may derive from a Hebrew version earlier than the one presently in the Hebrew Bible; the order of the materials in Psalms and Proverbs differs from the Hebrew texts; and Joshua has many additions, omissions, and changes. Finally, several later Greek translations were made (Aquila, Theodotion, Lucian) and parts of these have found their way into the Septuagint. ***See also*** Masorah; Scrolls, The Dead Sea. A.J.S.

Sepulchre, Church of the Holy, church located in Jerusalem dating from Byzantine times (after sixth century A.D.) and thought to contain the location of Jesus' tomb. The present edifice

View toward the apse in the Church of the Holy Sepulchre, Jerusalem.

is based on the church built by the Crusaders (A.D. 1149). It is controlled by six groups, Latin Catholics, Greek Orthodox, Armenians, Syrians, Copts, and Ethiopians, and contains twenty-two chapels.

In the first century A.D. this location lay outside the walls of Jerusalem in an unused quarry. Tombs of the first century have been found elsewhere in the area cut into the vertical surfaces left by the quarrying operations. Thus, the site fits the description of the place of crucifixion as "place of the skull" with nearby graves (John 19:17).

Some scholars think that until A.D. 66, the outbreak of the revolt against Rome, the Jewish Christian community in Jerusalem assembled at the tomb for prayer. The Roman emperor Hadrian later filled in the area and constructed a temple to Aphrodite (A.D. 135).

Some tradition may have led Constantine to choose this site for a church of the Holy Sepulchre (dedicated in A.D. 335). The caliph Hakim systematically destroyed the Byzantine structure in A.D. 1009. The present tomb monument only dates from the nineteenth century. A small section of the base of the original fourth-century tomb can be seen in the base of the Coptic shrine. Through a hole in the wall of the Syrian chapel one can see remains of a Jewish tomb, burial shafts, and ossuary pits from the first century. Part of this formation had been cut away by Constantine's builders. The fourth-century church was bigger than the present structure. Parts of it are hidden in and under neighboring buildings. ***See also*** Cross; Via Dolorosa. P.P.

Serabit el-Khadem (ser-ah'bit el-kah'dem; Arabic, meaning uncertain), a sandstone plateau about 2,600 feet above sea level in the mountainous region of southwest Sinai. The Egyptians came to Serabit el-Khadem and the nearby Wadi Magharah to mine turquoise. This blue or greenish-blue semiprecious stone, called *mefkat* in Egyptian, occurs in a single stratum of rock running through the region and was easily mined by cutting shafts and galleries down from the top of the plateau or along the sides of the surrounding wadis (dry stream beds that flow only during the rainy season). Turquoise was frequently used by the ancient Egyptians for jewelry, amulets, and inlays.

The mining expeditions sent to Serabit el-Khadem left many inscriptions, which allow scholars to trace the history of Egyptian activity in this area. Some texts were carved on stelae and other objects, some were incised in the mine faces, and still others were carved in the rock on the hillsides. The earliest inscriptions are in the Wadi Magharah and belong to several kings of the third dynasty (ca. 2686–2613 B.C.). Egyptian expeditions worked in this wadi until the early part of the eighteenth dynasty (ca. 1490 B.C.). Beginning in the late twentieth century B.C., Egyptian expeditions also started mining at Serabit el-Khadem, and activity continued here until the reign of Rameses VI (1141–1134 B.C.) in the late twentieth dynasty, when the Egyptians ceased operations at the turquoise mines.

The Egyptians built a temple at Serabit el-Khadem to the goddess Hathor, "Mistress of Turquoise." Many of the Egyptian inscriptions were found in and around this sanctuary. A number of short inscriptions written in a Semitic language known as "Proto-Sinaitic" were found in the temple area and some of the nearby

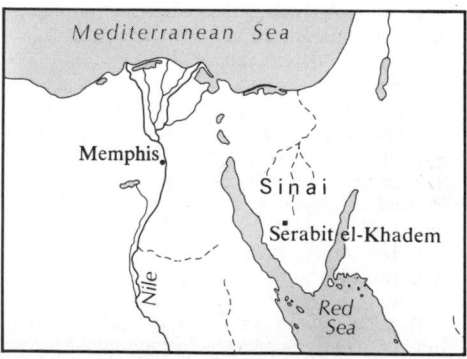

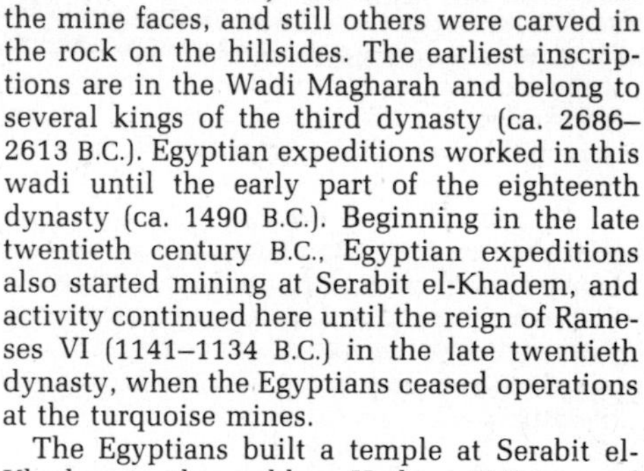

Egyptian temple of the goddess Hathor at Serabit el-Khadem, fourteenth century B.C.

mines. These texts may date to the sixteenth and fifteenth centuries B.C. They are important because they were written in a linear alphabetic script containing about thirty different signs. This is the earliest alphabet ever found. It provides a crucial link between the Egyptian pictorial script and the Phoenician alphabet, from which the Greek and ultimately our own alphabet are derived. ***See also*** Writing. J.M.W.

Serah (ser'ah), a daughter (or perhaps a family or clan) of the Hebrew tribe of Asher (Gen. 46:17) who reportedly moved to Egypt. She is subsequently included in the census (Num. 26:46 [KJV: "Sarah"]; 1 Chron. 7:30) of settlers in Palestine. This prominence spawned heroine status in later nonbiblical stories.

Seraiah (see-rah'yah; Heb., probably "Yah [weh] persists"), the name of as many as twelve men in the OT. **1** David's scribe (2 Sam. 8:17). The attestation is, however, unreliable, for the same man's name is given in 20:25 as Sheva, in 1 Chron. 18:16 as Shavsha, and in 1 Kings 4:3 as Shisha. **2** The chief priest who had the misfortune of witnessing the burning of the first Temple in Jerusalem in 587 B.C. before he was personally executed by Nebuchadnezzar (2 Kings 25:18–21; Jer. 52:24–27). **3** The son of Tankhumeth who survived the same crisis, however, and brought his militia to swear allegiance to Gedaliah, the Judean governor installed by the Babylonians (2 Kings 25:23; Jer. 40:8). **4** The "quartermaster" who accompanied the defeated Judean king Zedekiah to Babylon, bearing with him the prophet Jeremiah's written curse against that enemy kingdom (Jer. 51:59–64). **5** The son of Azriel, whom King Jehoiakim had earlier sent to arrest Jeremiah and his scribe, Baruch (Jer. 36:26). Without giving us biographical details, the postexilic historian simply mentions another seven men by the same name (namely, 1 Chron. 4:13–14; 4:35; 6:14 [possibly to be identified with Seraiah no. 2]; Ezra 2:2; 7:1; Neh. 10:2; and Neh. 11:11; 12:1, 12).

W.S.T.

seraphim (sair'uh-fim), fiery beings of supernatural origin. Seraphim appear in Isaiah's vision of God where they are attendants or guardians before the divine throne, analogous to the cherubim (Isa. 6:1–7). They praise God, calling "Holy, holy, holy is the Lord of Hosts," and one touches Isaiah's lips with a hot coal from the altar, cleansing him from sin. Seraphim have six wings. Two cover their faces, two cover their feet (a euphemism for genitals), and they fly with the remaining two. The etymology of the Hebrew word *seraphim* (singular: *saraph*) suggests a translation of "fiery ones" and probably stems from the fiery imagery often associated with the Presence of God (cf. Ezek. 1:27). "Flying saraphs" (RSV: "serpent") appear in Isa. 14:29 and 30:6 together with "adders" and "vipers." These examples call to mind the use of *saraph* to describe the "fiery serpents" that afflicted Israel in the wilderness (Num. 21:6–9; Deut. 8:15). This suggests a serpentine form for the seraphim. If this association is correct, seraphim serve not only as guardians of the divine throne, but also as emissaries of divine judgment. ***See also*** Cherub. M.A.S.

Serapis (suh-ra'pis), the deity of a cult established by Ptolemy I (d. 383/2 B.C.) to serve as a focal point for the Greek population in Egypt. The god was derived from Osor-Hapi, the deified Apis bull, and Osiris, the god of the underworld and consort of the goddess Isis. The cult mixed Egyptian and Greek features and was centered in Alexandria. The temple, called a Serapeum, contained a great cult statue with a gold head and jeweled eyes. Artistic representations of Serapis often present him with a head like Zeus. He is represented as ruler of the fertile earth and was thought, like Isis, to overrule fate. He was also a healing god known for curing blindness. As one of the many deities worshiped in the Roman Empire, Serapis would have stood under the ban of "idolatry" which Paul denounced (Rom. 1:22–23; 1 Cor. 8, 10). P.P.

sergeants. ***See*** Police.

Sergius Paulus (suhr'ji-us paw'luhs), proconsul of Cyprus. He is mentioned in Acts 13:7. ***See also*** Paulus, Sergius.

Sermon on the Mount, the, the first of five discourses of Jesus which are found only in Matthew's Gospel (chaps. 5–7, 10, 13, 18, 24–25). It is a compilation of sayings of Jesus, drawn, according to the Two-Source Hypothesis, mainly from Q but also from a source peculiar to Matthew (M). It has as its counterpart in Luke the Sermon on the Plain (Luke 6:20–49). The Sermon on the Mount may be outlined as follows:

5:1–2	The setting
5:3–12	The Beatitudes
5:13–16	The new community
5:17–20	The abiding validity of the law
5:21–48	On practicing righteousness toward others in matters of:
	Murder (5:21–26)
	Adultery (5:27–30)
	Divorce (5:31–32)
	Oaths (5:33–37)
	Retribution (5:38–42)
	Love of enemy (5:43–48)
6:1–7:12	On practicing righteousness toward God:
	Almsgiving (6:1–4)
	Prayer (6:5–15)
	Fasting (6:16–18)
	On not laying up false treasure (6:19–24)
	On not being anxious (6:25–34)
	On not judging (7:1–5)
	On not squandering what is precious (7:6)
	On resting assured that God hears prayer (7:7–12)
7:13–27	Concluding warnings and exhortations

Jesus delivers this discourse as the Son of God (3:16–17) whose authority is greater than that of the scribes (7:28–29) or even Moses (5:21–48). It is the example par excellence of his teaching (4: 23; 5:2; 7:28–29; 9:35; 11:1). The setting is an unnamed mountain in Galilee, and the audience is the crowds and the disciples (5:1–2; 7:28–29).

The Beatitudes ("blessings"; 5:3–12) describe the reversal of conditions that will take place in the future when the end-time Rule of God becomes a consummated reality. Because God's end-time Rule is already a present, though hidden, reality in Jesus, the Beatitudes are pronouncements that bespeak the inestimable joy that attends the certainty that the events prophesied are in the process of coming to pass.

The persons whom the Beatitudes envisage form the new community of Jesus' disciples, which is the "salt of the earth" and the "light of the world" (5:13–16). Through the lives they lead, disciples summon others to glorify God, that is, to live in the sphere of his end-time Rule by becoming disciples of Jesus.

Jesus teaches that the law has abiding validity and that what distinguishes the lives of the disciples is the greater righteousness (5:17–20). The greater righteousness, in turn, has a double focus: it involves behavior toward others (5:21–48) and toward God (6:1–7:12). The essential mark of all such behavior is love (5:44–45; 7: 12). In fact, for disciples to love as God loves is for them to be perfect (5:48), that is, to be wholehearted in doing God's will as interpreted by Jesus (7:21). Wise disciples are those who both hear and do what Jesus has taught (7: 24–27). ***See also*** Beatitudes; Kingdom of God; Law; Love; M; Matthew, The Gospel According to; Q; Torah.

J.D.K.

serpent, a reptile, in the Bible another term for snake. In the ancient world, there was general respect for, revulsion at, and fear of serpents, most being assumed to be poisonous and therefore dangerous. The serpent thus came to be understood symbolically with both positive and negative connotations. In some ancient cultures, the serpent was associated with deity and was depicted in statues and paintings with various gods and goddesses. Serpents also played various roles in ancient mythological stories (e.g., the Babylonian *Gilgamesh Epic*). Some even linked the serpent with the process of healing, as in the case of the Greek god Asclepius. In Canaanite religion, which the early Hebrew people encountered upon their arrival in the area, the serpent was associated with the fertility worship of Baal, his consort Astarte (also known as Anath or Asherah) being depicted with a serpent.

Against this general background, one is not surprised to find many references to serpents in the biblical writings. In the OT literature, serpents usually have a negative connotation. The older story of creation (Gen. 2:4–3:24), which explains the sinfulness of the human race, has as its villain the serpent (note, however, that not until much later is the serpent in this story identified with Satan or the devil). In ancient mythology, particularly in Mesopotamia, the great sea serpent was another symbol for evil and chaos, the great enemy of order and the gods. In the OT, references to Leviathan and Rahab (e.g., Isa. 27:1; 51:9b–10a; Pss. 74: 14; 104:26; Job 26:12) are vestiges of this idea, and these creatures were understood to be the enemy of God and God's people.

In the NT writings, the same negative attitude toward serpents is evident. The religious leaders were called "a brood of vipers" by John the Baptizer (Matt. 3:7) and by Jesus (Matt. 23:33). In Luke 3:7, even the people in general are so labeled by John.

In a few instances in the Bible, there are references to positive qualities associated with serpents, however. The attribute seen as most desirable was that of "cunning" (Gen. 3:1; Matt. 10:16). There is also the story of the bronze serpent that Moses made in the wilderness and that was believed to have healing properties (Num. 21:4–9; cf. John 3:14–15; note, however, that Moses made the serpent only after an attack upon the people by deadly serpents). A story regarding Paul's harmless en-

Aaron turning his staff into a serpent in an attempt to persuade Pharoah to let the Israelites go (cf. Exod. 7:10); from the Alba Bible.

counter with a poisonous serpent is reported in Acts 28:1–6.

There are several passages in the Bible where the ultimate victory of God and God's people over the evil of this age are depicted using serpent imagery (e.g., Luke 10:19; Rev. 20:2–10). One must remember, however, that such materials are symbolic and metaphorical, and not to be taken literally as some have done. ***See also*** Asp; Dragon; Leviathan; Nehushtan; Rahab; Viper.

J.M.E.

Serpent's Stone (KJV: "Zoheleth"), the place where Adonijah celebrated his self-established coronation in David's old age (1 Kings 1:9). It was reportedly near En-rogel, a spring south of the Old City (Ophel) of Jerusalem.

Serug (see'ruhg), the son of Reu; he was a descendant of Shem and ancestor of Abraham (Gen. 11:20–23) and he is in the ancestry of Jesus through Joseph (Luke 3:35).

servant, a term in the English Bible often meaning slave as well as a hired attendant, since the English translates several Greek and Hebrew words that range in meaning from a hired servant to a slave bought or taken in war. In the OT "servant" is a frequent translation of the Hebrew *ebed*, the literal meaning of which is "slave." In the NT it translates the Greek *doulos*, which also has the literal meaning "slave." The English reader, therefore, must bear in mind that the notion of slave often lies behind the translation "servant."

In the OT: The chief characteristic of the servant, understood as slave, is that the servant belongs to another and so has no legal rights. Nonetheless, the servant-slave does share in Israel's cultic life in terms of circumcision (Gen. 17:12), the Sabbath (Exod. 20:10), sacrifice (Deut. 12:18), and the Passover (Exod. 12:44). In this way Israel recalled her own history of bondage (Exod. 20:2). "Servant" is also used as a term of humble self-designation (2 Kings 8:13) and as a way of expressing political submission (Josh. 9:11). Even the soldiers of the king's army referred to themselves as his servants (2 Sam. 11:24).

It was against this background that a religious sense of the term developed that was applied to several categories of people. The OT calls the righteous person (Ps. 119) and the patriarchs Abraham, Isaac, and Jacob (Exod. 32:13) servants of the Lord. Likewise it applies the term to other important figures such as Moses (Deut. 34:5), Joshua (Judg. 2:8), Samuel (1 Sam. 3:9), David (2 Sam. 7:5), Solomon (1 Kings 3:7), and Job (Job 1:8). In addition, the term becomes a way of identifying the prophets Abijah (1 Kings 14:18), Elijah (2 Kings 9:36) and Jonah ben Amittai (2 Kings 14:25), so that the phrase "my [thy, his] servants the prophets" becomes a frequent formula (2 Kings 17:13, 23).

The most striking usage, however, occurs in the four servant songs found in the latter half of Isaiah. These are usually identified as Isa. 42:1–4; 49:1–6; 50:4–9; and 52:13–53:12. The last is the longest and the most puzzling of the poems; it speaks of redemption through suffering. While Christians have seen a prophecy of the suffering Messiah in it, many Jewish scholars identify the servant with Israel, especially the ideal Israel whose mission it is to redeem the nations. Others have identified the servant with some historical figure, either a king such as Hezekiah or a prophet such as Isaiah or Jeremiah. Whoever the servant represents, the figure portrayed in these songs brings the religious aspect of servant in the OT to a climax.

In the NT: In the NT servants frequently appear in the Gospels, especially in the parables (Matt. 18:23–35; 21:33–44). For Jesus the concept becomes a way of expressing humankind's relationship to God. God is the Lord to whom the believer owes unreserved service. "No one can serve two masters" (Matt. 6:24). Nor is a servant above the master (Matt. 10:24). Rather, the faithful servant does the master's will (Matt. 24:45–46) and realizes that in the presence of God even the best disciple is only an unprofitable servant (Luke 17:10).

Jesus presents himself as a servant when he washes his disciples' feet at the Last Supper (John 13:1–20). He tells his disciples that he came "not to be served but to serve" (Mark 10:45), and Matthew (12:18–21) quotes from the first servant song (Isa. 42:1–4) to describe Jesus. Likewise, Paul, quoting from an early Christian hymn, says that although Jesus was in the form of God, he "emptied himself, taking the form of a servant" (Phil. 2:7). On the basis of his own example, then, Jesus encourages his disciples to be servants to each other (Mark 10:44; John 13:14).

Obedient to this exhortation, Christians refer to themselves as "servants of God" (1 Pet. 2:16) and "servants of Christ" (1 Cor. 7:22; Eph. 6:6). The latter, however, is the most frequent. Paul describes himself as a "servant of Jesus Christ" (Rom. 1:1; Gal. 1:10; Phil. 1:1), as do the authors of James (1:1), 2 Peter (1:1), and Jude (1). Service to God and Jesus Christ, however, implies a change of allegiance from one lord to another. Paul makes this clear when he writes that Christians were once enslaved to other masters such as sin (Rom. 6:16–19) and the elemental spirits of the universe (Gal. 4:3). But with the coming of Christ this servitude is ended (Gal. 4:4–7). A similar idea is expressed in John when Jesus says "everyone who commits sin is a slave to sin" (8:34).

In this regard, the NT is dramatically different from its milieu. For the Greek the highest ideal was self-determination expressed in freedom. Thus the Greek looked upon the slave as an inferior kind of person. It would have been contradictory to the Greek ideal to speak of becoming a servant to another, even to God. Christianity stood this ideal upon its head, but did not challenge the institution of slavery as such. Paul encourages slaves to be obedient (Eph. 6:5; Col. 3:22) and he sends the runaway slave Onesimus back to his master (Philem.). Nonetheless the NT undermines the institution of slavery inasmuch as it proclaims a radical equality in Christ (1 Cor. 7:21–22; Gal. 3:28; Col. 3:11). ***See also*** Isaiah, The Book of; Jesus Christ; Prophet.

Bibliography

Cullmann, Oscar. *The Christology of the New Testament.* Philadelphia: Westminster, 1963.

Mowinckel, Sigmund. *He That Cometh.* New York: Abingdon, 1954.

de Vaux, Roland. *Ancient Israel.* Vol. 1. New York: McGraw-Hill, 1965.

F.J.M.

service, in the Bible, normally something to be done by a slave, i.e., servile work. Servile work was servile because slave and nonslave belonged to two different species, so to speak, just as humans differ from God. Service referred to tasks performed by lesser persons for those who controlled their existence. Relative to God service looked to Temple worship and its rituals (e.g., Exod. 31:10; 35:19; Esd. 6:18; Luke 1:23), while relative to humans it pertained to forms of bondage (e.g., Gen. 30:26; Exod. 1:14). It is noteworthy that for Paul, the slave service a person owed God in temple worship is now to be displayed in the Christian's service to neighbor, which is service to Christ (Rom. 12:1–2; 14:17–18; Gal. 5:13; see also 1 Cor. 9:19; 2 Cor. 4:5).

B.J.M.

Seth, the third son of Adam, according to the Yahwist's genealogy in Gen. 4:25 (the Priestly genealogy of 5:3 makes Seth Adam's firstborn). Seth's birth in 4:25 seems intended to contrast with the debauched and violent line of Cain. When Seth was born, the Hebrew text notes, "then began [the custom of] calling on Yahweh's name (4:26)." ***See also*** Sources of the Pentateuch.

seven, seventy. ***See*** Numbers.

Seveneh (se-vee'nuh), an alternate reading for Syene, a city on the southern border of Egypt, toward Ethiopia (Ezek. 29:10; 30:6). ***See also*** Svene.

seven words from the cross, the seven sentences spoken by Jesus from the cross in the passion stories. Mark 15:34 and Matt. 27:46 have the Hebrew/Aramaic phrase *"Eli, Eli, lema sabachthani,"* alluding to Ps. 22. Lucan themes of forgiveness and repentance appear as Jesus forgives his enemies (Luke 23:34; "Father, forgive them; for they know not what they do") and promises salvation to the repentant criminal (23:43; "Truly, I say to you, today you will be with me in Paradise"). In John 19:26–27 Jesus entrusts his mother to the beloved disciple. John 19:28, "I thirst," fulfills Ps. 69:21. Luke 23:46 ("Father, into thy hands I commit my spirit!") and John 19:30 ("It is finished") indicate the completion of Jesus' mission as he entrusts himself to God. ***See also*** Eli, Eli, Lema Sabachthani; Vinegar.

Shaalbim (shay-al'bim; Heb., "place of foxes"), an Amorite city dominated by Dan (Josh. 19:42 [Shaalabin]; Judg. 1:35) and in the jurisdiction of Ben-deker, one of twelve administrative officers under Solomon's administration (1 Kings 4:9). The site is probably modern Selbit, three miles northwest of Aijalon and about five miles northeast of Gezer.

Shaalim (shay'uh-lim; KJV: "Shalim"), an area scouted by Saul while he hunted the lost asses of his father, Kish (1 Sam. 9:4). The precise location is unknown, but it was likely in Benjaminite territory.

Shaaraim (shay-ah-ray'im; Heb., "double gate"). **1** A town of Judah in the Shephelah (Josh. 15:36 [KJV: "Sharaim"]; it was somewhere near Azekah in or near the Wadi es-Sant (1 Sam. 17:52). **2** The Simeonite city of 1 Chron. 4:31. It may be the Sharuhen (modern Tell Fa'ra) of Josh. 19:6.

Shaashgaz (shay-ash'gaz), the royal eunuch in charge of concubines at the second harem of King Ahasuerus (Esther 2:14).

Shabbethai (shab'e-thī). **1** A Levite opposed to Ezra's reform policy of separating from foreign wives (Ezra 10:15). **2** A Levite who helped explain the law (Neh. 8:7). **3** A Levite who conducted external business in the Temple of Jerusalem (Neh. 11:16). All three definitions may refer to the same person, or 2 and 3 may be identical. The name also appears in 1 Esd. 9:14, 48.

Shaddai (shad'ī). ***See*** El Shaddai.

Shadrach (shad'rak), the Babylonian name given to Hananiah, one of Daniel's three companions (Dan. 1:7), subsequently thrown into the fiery furnace. The etymology is uncertain. It has been taken as a deliberate pejorative variation of Marduk, god of Babylon. ***See also*** Abednego; Daniel; Meshach.

Shadrach, Meshach, and Abednego in the "burning fiery furnace" of Nebuchadnezzar; third-century A.D. fresco from the catacombs of Saint Priscilla, Rome.

Shaharaim (shay-huh-ray'im), a descendant of Benjamin (1 Chron. 8:8). He banished two of his three wives, although the reason for that action is not mentioned.

Shalem (shay'lem; Heb., "peace"), a town near Shechem (KJV, Gen. 33:18). The RSV on the other hand translates the word not as a place name but as an adverb, to describe Jacob's arrival at Shechem—"safely," in other words, "in peace."

Shalisha (sha-lī'sha), one of the regions scouted by Saul while searching for his father's lost asses (1 Sam. 9:4). It was probably located in the region of the tribal lands of Ephraim or Benjamin.

Shallum (shal'uhm). **1** The son of Jabesh, who made himself king of Israel by assassinating Zechariah, son of Jeroboam II, and so ending the dynasty of Jehu. He was himself assassinated a month later (2 Kings 15:10–15). **2** The husband of the prophetess Huldah (2 Kings 22:14; 2 Chron. 34:22). **3** Jehoahaz, the fourth son of King Josiah (1 Chron. 3:15). He was proclaimed king of Judah after his father had been killed by Necho of Egypt. Three months later Necho made Eliakim (= Jehoiackim) king, deporting Shallum to Egypt, where he died (2 Kings 23:30–34), as announced in Jer. 22:10–12. **4** The father of Hanameel, a relative from whom Jeremiah bought family land (Jer. 32:6–10). **5** The father of Maaseiah, a Temple official (Jer. 35:4). **6** The chief gatekeeper in the Levites' area of the Temple (1 Chron. 9:17–18), whose descendants were also gatekeepers (Ezra. 2:42; Neh. 7:45; 1 Esd. 5:28). He was one of those who divorced foreigners they had married (Ezra 10:24; 1 Esd. 9:25). He may be the same person as the Korahite official (1 Chron. 9:19), the father of Mattithiah (1 Chron. 9:31). **7** Another who divorced a foreign wife (Ezra 10:42). **8** A levitical priest (1 Chron. 6:1–15), ancestor of Ezra (Ezra 7:1–2; 1 Esd. 8:1; 2 Esd. 1:1). **9** The son of Hallohesh, governor of half of the district of Jerusalem. With his daughters he rebuilt part of the city wall (Neh. 3:12). **10** A Judahite of the Jerahmeel branch (1 Chron. 2:40–41). **11** A Simeonite (1 Chron. 4:25). **12** A son of Naphtali (1 Chron. 7:13). **13** The father of an Ephraimite leader (2 Chron. 28:12). S.B.P.

Shalmai (shal'mī), a family of Temple servants resettled in Jerusalem after the Exile (Neh. 7:48). In Ezra 2:46 it is the term used by the KJV for the RSV's "Shamlai," probably designating the same people; see also 1 Esd. 5:30.

Shalman (shal'muhn), perhaps an abbreviation for Assyria's king Shalmaneser (IV or V). It may, on the other hand, refer to the Moabite monarch Shalmanu whose invasion of Gilead (late eighth century B.C.) would have been news close at hand for those whom the prophet Hosea addressed (Hos. 10:14).

Shalmaneser (shal'muhn-ee'zuhr), the name of two Assyrian kings important for the history of ancient Israel. **1** Shalmaneser III, the son of Ashurnasirpal II and king of Assyria (858–824 B.C.). Though not mentioned in the Bible, two contacts with kings of Israel are recorded in his royal inscriptions. In 853, Shalmaneser's advance into north Syria was halted at Qarqar on the Orontes River by a coalition of twelve Phoenician and Syrian states, among them "Ahab of Israel," who had sent a contingent of "2,000 chariots and 10,000 foot-soldiers" (although some scholars question the reliability of these figures). In 841, following Shalmaneser's defeat

The Assyrian king Shalmaneser III (left), armed with a bow and arrows and accompanied by an attendant and a soldier, receives Sua, the Gilzanite; from the Black Obelisk of Shalmaneser, ninth century B.C.

of Hazael of Damascus, King Jehu, who had seized the throne in Samaria in a bloody coup the year before (2 Kings 9–10), acknowledged Assyrian hegemony and rendered tribute. A relief on the Black Obelisk of Shalmaneser memorializes this act of submission. **2** Shalmaneser V, the son of Tiglath-pileser III, king of Assyria (727–722 B.C.). Though no contemporary royal inscriptions are extant, a picture of his short five-year reign is reconstructable on the basis of 2 Kings 17:1–6 and some passages in the writings of the first-century historian Josephus (*Antiquities* 9.283–87). Shalmaneser undertook two military campaigns to the Mediterranean coast, the area that had been under his governance while he was crown prince. In 726, Hosea of Israel recognized him as overlord and rendered tribute (2 Kings 17:3). Shortly thereafter, a rebellion against Assyria, with the backing of a Delta chieftain of Egypt, broke out in Phoenicia and Israel; this prompted the second appearance of Shalmaneser in the West. Hosea was imprisoned in 724, in his ninth and last year as king (for this calculation, cf. 2 Kings 17:5; 18: 9–10). Shalmaneser laid siege to Samaria, then ruled by army officers and/or city elders; the city held out for two years, until the autumn of 722. Samaria fell to Shalmaneser (2 Kings 17:6a); this event is recorded in the Babylonian Chronicle (col.1, line 28): "He destroyed the city of Samaria." Because of Shalmaneser's death, the fate of Samaria was left undetermined; the usual punishments meted out to defeated cities were postponed. The "King of Assyria" who exiled Israelites from Samaria (2 Kings 17:6b) was Sargon II, who reconquered the city in 720 B.C. ***See also*** Assyria, Empire of. M.C.

Shama (shay'muh), the son of Hotham, and one of David's mighty men (1 Chron. 11:44).

shame, a concept that is expressed in the biblical writings by a variety of Hebrew and Greek terms. Most frequently, it denotes the guilt a person feels or should feel for having sinned against God (e.g., Jer. 2:26), but it can also connote the disgrace one finds in failure, either by actively having done something wrong or by having failed to do something right (e.g., Prov. 14:34). While the OT writers did not really have an idea of "conscience," they did believe that there should be a natural sense of disgrace and unworthiness when one sins against God or one's companions. It was considered appalling when people no longer had any sense of shame (cf. Jer. 6:15; also Job 19:3). In the NT, it is possible to be ashamed (or not ashamed) of Christ and his gospel (e.g., Mark 8:38; Rom. 1:16; cf. Heb. 2:11; 11:16). ***See also*** Conscience; Guilt; Repentance; Sin. J.M.E.

Shamed. ***See*** Shemed.

Shamgar (sham'gahr), a mighty warrior in Israel in the premonarchical period. He was famed for killing a total of six hundred Philistines with an oxgoad (Judg. 3:31). Bearing a non-Semitic name he is identified as the "Anathite" (lit. "a son of [the goddess] Anath"). He was probably a mercenary who changed sides in the era of Deborah, collaborating with Jael (Judg. 5: 6–7) in disruption of caravan trade, to Israel's great advantage.

Shamir (shay'muhr; Heb., "thorn"). **1** A Levite, the son of Micah (1 Chron. 24:24). **2** The home town of Tola, one of the minor judges (Judg. 10: 1–2). **3** A hill country village assigned to the territory of the tribe of Judah (Josh. 15:48), probably modern el-Bireh about twelve miles southwest of Hebron.

Shamma (sham'ah), the name of a family of the tribe of Asher (1 Chron. 7:37).

Shammah (shah'mah), a Hebrew proper noun. **1** The son of Reuel who was born to Esau and Basemath. Along with his brothers Nahath, Zerah, and Mizzah, Shammah was a chief of Reuel in the land of Edom (Gen. 36:13, 17; see also Isaac's genealogy in 1 Chron. 1:37). **2** The third of Jesse's eight sons who passed before Samuel in order to determine who was the Lord's anointed (1 Sam. 16:6–10). He was one of the three eldest sons who followed Saul into battle against the Philistines, and to whom his younger brother David took provisions from Jesse in Bethlehem to the valley of Elah (1 Sam. 17:12–54). **3** The son of Agee the Haraite who is listed as one of three mighty men in the army of David. While others fled from the Philistines at Lehi, Shammah took his stand in a plot of lentils and slew the enemy (2 Sam. 23:11–12). ***See also*** Basemath; Esau; Jesse. F.R.M.

Shammai (sham'ī). **1** The son of Onam (1 Chron. 2:28, 32). **2** The son of Rekem (1 Chron. 2:44, 45). **3** The son of Mered and the Egyptian woman Bithiah (1 Chron. 4:17). All three were Judeans.

Shammua (sham-mo͞o'uh; Heb., "heard"). **1** The son of Zaccur; he was one of the twelve spies, a representative of the tribe of Reuben, who was sent by Moses into Canaan (Num. 13:4). **2** One of David's sons born in Jerusalem (2 Sam. 5:14; 1 Chron. 14:4); he is also called Shimea (1 Chron. 3:5). **3** A Levite whose son Abda (Obadiah) was a postexilic inhabitant of Jerusalem (Neh. 11:17); he is elsewhere (erroneously?) called Shemaiah (1 Chron. 9:16). **4** The head of the clan of Bilgah during the period of restoration (Neh. 12:18); he is possibly the same as 3 above, although since this person lived in the time of the second high priest after the return from the Exile, it is probably a different person (see v. 12). ***See also*** Shemaiah; Shimea. D.R.B.

Shaphan (shay'fan; Heb., "rock badger, coney"). **1** The head of a family of Judeans serving the court at the time of King Josiah (ca. 639–609 B.C.; 2 Kings 22:3–20; 2 Chron. 34:8–20). He was involved in relaying the "book" found in the Temple to the king, on the basis of which the Josianic reforms were presumably shaped. He was sent to consult the prophetess Huldah as part of a royal embassy. His sons and grandsons continued to play roles in the life of the court at the time of the prophet Jeremiah, saving Jeremiah from the court's desire for his death (Jer. 26:24), relaying Jeremiah's letter to the exiles in Babylon (29:3), and providing the house in which Baruch could read Jeremiah's dictated scroll (36:10–12). **2** The grandfather of the Gedaliah in whose custody Jeremiah was placed after the fall of Jerusalem to Babylonian forces (39:14; 40:5), to assure that Jeremiah was cared for properly. Some scholars think that this Shaphan may be the same person described in 1 above, however. **3** The father of Jaazaniah (Ezek. 8:11) whose apostasy is reviewed in Ezekiel's vision. R.S.B.

Shaphat (shay'fat; Heb., "judged"). **1** A Simeonite member of the group sent by Moses to spy out the land of Canaan (Num. 13:5). **2** The father of the prophet Elisha (1 Kings 19:16, 19; 2 Kings 3:11; 6:31). **3** A Davidic descendant and a grandson of Zerubbabel (1 Chron. 3:22). **4** A Gadite chief living in Bashan (1 Chron. 5:12). **5** A herdsman of David, and a son of Adlai (1 Chron. 27:29).

Sharai (shah'rī), one of the returned Judean exiles who had married foreign women (Ezra 10:40).

Sharezer (shah-ree'zuhr). **1** A son of the Assyrian monarch Sennacherib who reportedly helped murder his father (2 Kings 19:37; Isa. 37:38). **2** In Zech. 7:2 a name that appears in a very confused text, possibly as part of the name of a god, possibly the name of an emissary from Bethel.

Sharon, the Plain of, the area where the coastal plain widens south of the slopes of Mt. Carmel and the crocodile marshes (the modern Nahr Zerqa), extending about thirty miles south to the Yarkon River north of Joppa. It varies from about eight to twelve miles in width. The streams from the well-watered hills to the east must avoid a central mass of Mousterian Red Sand. They move sluggishly south and north of the mass, spreading into broad areas of swamps and flooding in wet seasons.

In Israelite times the dunes supported an impenetrable oak forest (compared to the thick forests of Lebanon and Carmel in Isa. 35:2) rather than the citrus groves seen today. Pastureland would have been on the fringe of the forest (1 Chron. 27:29). The rose of Sharon is a kind of crocus growing as a "lily among brambles" (Song of Sol. 2:1–2). "Sharon is like a desert" (Isa. 33:9) and "Sharon shall become a pasture for flocks" as the barren slopes above Jericho will become a place for cattle to feed (Isa. 65:10). Thus the biblical picture of Sharon is a forbidding jungle of oaks and swampy marshes rather than a fertile or productive plain.

The sand dunes and marshes meant the main land route, "The Way of the Sea" (Lat. *Via Maris*), hugged the drier foothills of the highland on the east. Along this road were the more permanent settlements, Socoh (1 Sam. 17:1) lying above the Iskanderun River (modern Wadi Zeimar) and Aphek (Josh. 13:4) (modern Ras el-Ain) at the source of the Yarkon.

The coast was without good natural harbors. It was the Romans under Herod the Great who developed the imposing city of Caesarea with its artificial harbor, its aqueducts bringing fresh water from Mt. Carmel, and a network of roads to the interior. ***See also*** Plains. N.L.L.

Sharuhen (shah-rōō'hen), an important Hyksos stronghold in southwest Palestine in the seventeenth and early sixteenth centuries B.C., captured by the Egyptian king Ahmose (ca. 1560 B.C.) after a siege lasting three years. Sharuhen was held by an Egyptian garrison at the time of Thutmose III's great victory at Megiddo in 1482 B.C. In Josh. 19:6 it appears in a list of cities allotted to the tribe of Simeon at the time of the Israelite conquest; parallel lists give its name as Shilhim (Josh. 15:32) and Shaaraim (1 Chron. 4:31).

Sharuhen is probably to be identified with Tell el-'Ajjul, the largest mound in southern Palestine, which is located about four miles southwest of modern Gaza near the principal ancient highway leading up from Egypt. This site was excavated by the British Egyptologist W. M. Flinders Petrie in 1930–34 and by members of his staff in 1938. Excavations indicate that the mound was initially used as a cemetery at the end of the third and beginning of the second millennium B.C. It became a rich and powerful city in the latter part of the Middle Bronze Age (ca. 1750–1550 B.C.), when it was protected on three sides by an enormous ditch set in front of a steep slope (glacis). Within this enclosure, Petrie found several stratified city levels belonging to the Middle Bronze Age and beginning of the Late Bronze Age (ca. 1550–1200 B.C.), as well as evidence for a major destruction (probably due to Ahmose). He also discovered a series of five superimposed "palaces": two belonged to the Middle Bronze Age, while the final three were evidently Egyptian fortresses dating to the Late Bronze Age. The great wealth of the Hyksos city is attested by the fact that more gold objects were found at Tell el-'Ajjul than at any other Bronze Age site in Palestine. The end of the Egyptian Empire in the twelfth century B.C. resulted in the abandonment of the garrison at Sharuhen. There is little evidence of later occupation other than some burials on the mound that belong to the tenth century B.C. ***See also*** Hyksos. J.M.W.

Shaul (shohl; Heb., "dedicated" or "asked for"). **1** An Edomite king from Rehoboth (Gen. 36:37–38). **2** The Israelite head of the Shaulite clan (Gen. 46:10; Exod. 6:15; 1 Chron. 4:24; Num. 26:13). **3** A son of the Levite Kohath (1 Chron. 6:24).

Shaveh (shay've), **Valley of,** the valley where the king of Sodom and Melchizedek, king of Jerusalem, met Abraham as he returned from his battle with the kings of the north (Gen. 14:17). This valley, also called the King's Valley, was presumably the same as that in which Absalom erected his monument (2 Sam. 18:18). Suggestions as to its identity include the Kidron, the western Hinnom, and the Wadi Joz, all valleys in the Jerusalem area.

Shaveh-kiriathaim (shay've-kihr-ee-ah-thay'uhm; Heb., "plain of Kiriathaim"), the plain where the Elamite king Chedorlaomer fought and subdued the Emim (Gen. 14:5). On the basis of the location in Kiriathaim the plain should be somewhere near el-Qereiyat, northwest of Dibon in what is now Jordan.

shaving, the act of removing facial hair, in the Bible particularly the beard. As a sign of mourning and as part of several purification rituals, shaving had religious significance in Israelite society.

As Assyrian reliefs show, Israelite men of the pre-exilic period wore full beards and shoulder-length hair. (The short hair that Paul commended to men as natural [1 Cor. 11:14] was a later Greek or Roman fashion.) The beards were trimmed (2 Sam. 19:24), but under normal circumstances men were ashamed to appear in public without them (2 Sam. 10:4–5). When in mourning, however, they shaved their heads and beards (Job 1:20; Jer. 41:5; 48:37). Priests were prohibited from this practice (Lev. 21:5), and Deut. 14:1 extends the prohibition to all Israelites, but this law seems little known prior to the Exile (Isa. 22:12).

The men or women who consecrated themselves to God as Nazirites could not cut their hair until they fulfilled their vow; then they shaved their heads and offered the hair on the altar for their purification (Num. 6:5–19). The most famous Nazirite was Samson (Judg. 13–16), and Samuel may have been one, though priests were later prohibited from such vows (Ezek. 44:20). Acts reports that even as a Christian Paul continued to observe such vows (Acts 18:18; 21:24).

Shaving also played an important role in other purification rituals, whether for the patient who had recovered from serious skin disease (Lev. 13:33; 14:8–9), or for the female prisoner of war whom an Israelite desired to marry (Deut. 21:12). ***See also*** Nazirites. J.J.M.R.

Shavsha (shav'shah), a scribe in David's court (1 Chron. 18:16). Other forms of the name may include "Seraiah" (2 Sam. 8:17), "Sheva" (2 Sam. 20:25), or even "Shisha" (1 Kings 4:3). Because of its non-Hebrew origin, the name may indicate use of foreign scholars at the royal court.

Sheal (shee'uhl; KJV, "Jasael"), a returning exile who had married a foreign woman (Ezra 10:29; see also 1 Esdras 9:30).

Shealtiel (shee-al'tee-el; Heb., "God is a shield" or "God is victor"), a son of the Judean King Jeconiah (Jehoiachin; 1 Chron. 3:17; Matt. 1:12, not Neri as in Luke 3:27). He was the father of Zerubbabel, the leader of postexilic returnees (but 1 Chron. 3:17–19 calls him Zerubbabel's uncle). Shealtiel thus connected the royal family of King Jeconiah with postexilic Judean developments under Zerubbabel.

Sheariah (shee-uh-rī'uh), one of the Benjaminite sons of Azel (1 Chron. 8:38; 9:44), and a descendant of Saul.

Shearjashub (shee'ahr-yay'shuhb; Heb., "a remnant will return"), the eldest of Isaiah's sons (Isa. 7:3). By giving his child this unusual name, Isaiah made Shearjashub a living symbol of the prophet's early message concerning the Northern Kingdom of Israel (Isa. 10:21–22). Only a remnant of it would survive.

Sheba (shee'buh). **1** A town included in Simeon's inheritance, along with Beer-sheba and Moladah (Josh. 19:2). **2** A Benjaminite, the son of Bichri, who led a revolt against David after Absalom's rebellion was put down. Hoping to seize northern Israel, he was pursued by Joab and his army and was decapitated at the instigation of a "wise woman" of the town of Abel-beth-maacah (2 Sam. 20). **3** A man of the tribe of Gad (1 Chron. 5:13). **4** The Hebrew spelling of the South Arabic name Saba, an area of great wealth (Isa. 60:6; Jer. 6:20; Ezek. 27:22–25). ***See also*** Seba, Sabeans.

Sheba, Queen of, a ruler of the Sabeans contemporary with King Solomon (tenth century B.C.) whom she visited to test his wisdom. Impressed with his wealth as well as his wisdom, she blessed both Solomon and the God of Israel for such splendor. She gave Solomon 120 talents of gold in addition to other precious items, and Solomon in his turn bestowed rich presents upon her, prior to her return to her own land. Her appearance in the narrative of 1 Kings is intended to glorify the figure of Solomon rather than give information about this wealthy queen, who is otherwise unknown in the OT (1 Kings 10:1–10, 13; cf. 2 Chron. 9:1–9, 12). ***See also*** Seba, Sabeans.

Shebah (shee'bah). ***See*** Shibah.

Shebaniah (sheb'uh-nī-uh; Heb., "Yahweh has restored"?). **1** A trumpeter in the Temple (1 Chron. 15:24). **2** A Levite from Jerusalem who joined in exclamations exalting God in Ezra's time (Neh. 9:4). **3** A priest who sealed the covenant between Israel and God at Jerusalem after the Exile (Neh. 10:4; 12:14); "Shechaniah," Neh. 12:3). **4** A Levite, possibly Shechaniah (Neh. 10:10).

Shebat (she-bat'), the eleventh month of the Hebrew year, corresponding to January-February (Zech. 1:7; 1 Macc. 16:14).

Shebnah (sheb'nah), the state secretary of King Hezekiah at the time of Sennacherib's campaign against Judah (2 Kings 18:18–19:2; Isa. 36:3–37:2). Apparently he had been demoted to this position from the higher office of royal steward following a bitter critique of Isaiah (Isa. 22:15–25).

Shebuel (she-byōō'el). **1** A Levite son of Gershom, hence a descendant of Moses (1 Chron. 23:14–16; 26:24). His duties (assisting the priests in Temple services, managing the treasuries, and dividing Temple duties) reflect late rather than early Temple practice, however. **2** A Levite musician (1 Chron. 25:4) also called Shubael (25:20).

Shecaniah (shek'uh-nī'uh; Heb., "God has taken up abode"), a frequent name in Chronicles, Ezra, and Nehemiah. **1** A descendant of David and Zerubbabel (1 Chron. 3:21–22) and head of a family that returned with Ezra from Babylon (Ezra 8:3). **2** The chief of the tenth division of priests in the Davidic order (1 Chron. 24:11). **3** One of the priests in Hezekiah's time who distributed the Temple offering to the priests in outlying cities (2 Chron. 31:15). **4** One who returned with Ezra (Ezra 8:5). **5** A man who had married a foreigner and repented, and who then proposed a covenant to put away foreign wives and children (Ezra 10:2–4). **6** The father of one who helped repair the wall of Jerusalem (Neh. 3:29). **7** The father-in-law of Tobiah the Ammonite (Neh. 6:18). **8** A priest who returned with Zerubbabel (Neh. 12:3). P.A.B.

Shechem (shek'em), a city located forty-one miles north of Jerusalem in the pass between Mount Ebal and Mount Gerizim. It dominated an important trade route and controlled a fertile valley to the east where Jacob's sons pastured their flocks (Gen. 37:12, 13, 14). Shechem was a

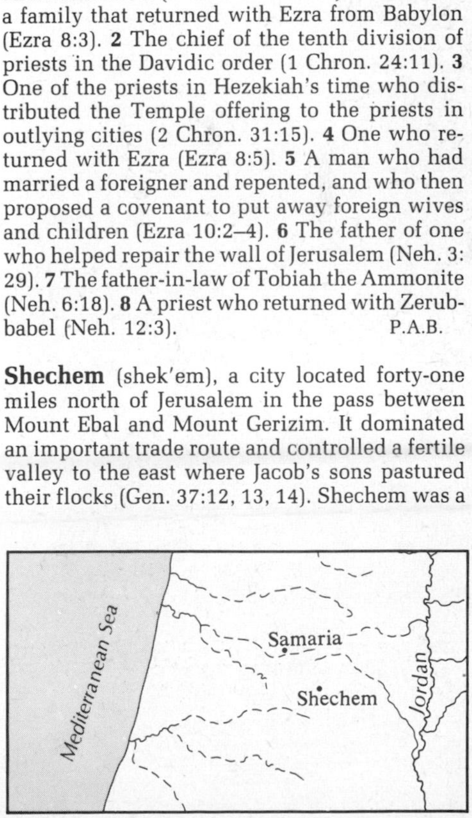

SHECHEM

Korathite levitical city of refuge in the territory of Manasseh (Josh. 17:2, 7), although it is also described as being "in the hill country of Ephraim" (Josh. 20:7). The city was excavated by a German expedition under the direction of E. Sellin between 1913 and 1934. More recently the Joint Expedition, directed by G. E. Wright, worked at the site for eight seasons between 1956 and 1969.

The Patriarchal Period: Shechem was the first city visited by Abraham in his migration from Haran (Gen. 12:6), but it figures most prominently in the traditions associated with Jacob. It was the scene of the rape of Dinah by Shechem, the son of Hamor, king of Shechem (Gen. 34). In the narrative the prince and the city have the same name. The father's name, Hamor, means "ass" in Hebrew. During excavation in the east gate, the decapitated skeleton of a donkey was found, with what appeared to be the bones of an animal sacrifice nearby. The ass was probably the sacred animal of the city, and the names of father and son may symbolize the city itself. The city was "Shechem, the son of the ass [its sacred animal]." When the Hebrews returned to Canaan from Egyptian slavery, they brought Jacob's mummified body with them and buried it in a tomb near the city (Josh. 23:32).

Egyptian texts of the nineteenth century B.C. indicate that Shechem was an important urban center during the patriarchal period. Archaeological evidence shows that during the nineteenth and eighteenth centuries B.C. the city was surrounded by a massive embankment of earth, topped by walls of mudbrick on stone foundations. The highest ground within the walls was occupied by a multiroom palace-temple complex, set off from the rest of the city by a stone wall. In the seventeenth century B.C. the embankment was replaced by a wall composed of huge stones and entered by impressive gates on the north and east sides. The royal palace was moved to a position directly against the inner face of the new wall, and the palace-temple complex was replaced by a rectangular "fortress temple" with walls 17 feet thick.

Silver coin depicting a temple and altar at the top of a stairway leading up Mount Gerizim, ca. A.D. 198–217.

While the Israelites were in slavery in Egypt, Shechem continued to flourish. Its king, Lab'ayu, is described in the Amarna Letters (fourteenth century B.C.) as the most important ruler in central Palestine, controlling a small empire and making inroads on the territory of his neighbors. During this period the fortress-temple was rebuilt and continued in use into the Israelite period. It is the temple of the Lord of the Covenant mentioned in Judges 9.

The Israelite Period: When the Israelites entered Canaan (thirteenth century B.C.) Shechem passed peacefully into their hands and became the earliest religious center of the tribes. At Shechem Joshua renewed the Sinai covenant with Israel's tribal leaders, probably at the temple of the Lord of the Covenant (Josh. 24). Abimelech, a son of Gideon by a concubine who lived at Shechem, roused the Shechemites to his support and had himself declared king (Judg. 9:1–6), against the spirit and traditions of the old tribal confederacy, which held that the Lord was the only king in Israel (Judg. 8:22–23). Shechem soon revolted against Abimelech's rule and in reprisal he destroyed the city (Judg. 9:45).

After a time when the site was occupied only by crude huts and grain storage pits, the city was rebuilt. The old Canaanite royal tradition, which had long been associated with Shechem, continued to be attached to the rebuilt city. Rehoboam went there to be crowned king (924 B.C.) in the northern part of his kingdom (1 Kings 12:1). After the revolt of the northern tribes Jeroboam I rebuilt the city (1 Kings 12:25). Traces of his work survive at the tower of the east gate. For a time Shechem served as Jeroboam's capital, but its population had too many local loyalties and he moved his capital to Tirzah. Shechem then settled down to a fairly prosperous existence as a provincial center. Typical Israelite four-room houses were built on a series of terraces rising from the east gate to the former sacred area, which was now transformed into a granary, probably for the collection of taxes. The fortifications of the Israelite city followed the plan of its Canaanite predecessor. Israelite Shechem was destroyed by the Assyrian armies in 722 B.C. The walls of the houses were covered by over 4 feet of destruction debris.

Shechem was rebuilt about 350 B.C. as the religious center of the Samaritans. Their temple

Remains of a high place at the site of ancient Shechem.

stood on Mount Gerizim, and at the foot of the mountain they constructed a city designed to rival Jerusalem. A strong defensive wall enclosed solidly constructed houses and at least one luxurious villa near the old sacred area. The city was destroyed, probably by John Hyrcanus during his conquest of Samaria, in 107 B.C. It was razed to the ground. Its walls were buried beneath deep layers of fill and it was never rebuilt. ***See also*** Abimelech; Amarna, Tell el-; Dinah; Rehoboam; Samaritans.

Bibliography

Wright, G. E. *Shechem: The Biography of a Biblical City*. New York: Doubleday, 1962. L.E.T.

Shedeur (shed'ee-uhr; Heb., "Shaddai is light" or "Shaddai is fire"), the father of the Reubenite Elizur who was chosen to help Moses as tribal head (Num. 1:5; 2:10; 7:30, 35; 10:18).

sheep, a ruminant mammal related to the goat. Sheep are mentioned in the Bible more than five hundred times and a large variety of terms are employed to describe the different breeds, age, and sex types. While most of the references in the OT are literal, practically all references in the NT are metaphors comparing the relationship of Christ and his followers to that of the shepherd and his flock.

The earliest evidence for the domestication of the sheep comes from Zawi Chemi Shanidar in northern Iraq and dates back to about 9000 B.C. Until recently it was believed that the sheep was imported to Palestine as an already domesticated animal, but recent finds from southern Jordan suggest that wild sheep were once living in the area and might have given rise to independent domestication. Sheep were originally domesticated to provide a steady supply of meat. Wild sheep do not have real wool, just a woolly undercoat, and it was probably not until 4000 B.C. that the animal's potential in this respect was discovered and they were bred especially for wool production. Another domestic trait is the fat tail, which is common to most breeds in the Near East, including the Awassi sheep, which is raised today in Israel. The fat tail is considered a delicacy and was sometimes required as a sacrifice (Exod. 29:22–25).

In contrast to the goat, the sheep prefers flat or gently rolling grazing grounds and eats plants down to the root, thriving on the stubble left over from the barley and wheat harvest. The Bible provides several references to the skill of the shepherd, who knows each of his animals by name, whose voice is recognized by his sheep (John 10:3–4), and who take care of them in illness (Ezek. 34:15–16). The constant search for greener pastures is a regular task for those who tend sheep (1 Chron. 4:39–40). The importance of finding adequate shelter for the night is often alluded to (Luke 2:8; Num. 32:24). Sometimes natural caves were used for this purpose (1 Sam. 24:3), a practice that continues to the present day. A very moving picture of the relationship between a lamb and its owner is painted in 2 Sam. 12 (cf. Ps. 23:2, 5).

Like goats, sheep provided most necessities of life: milk (Deut. 32:14; Isa. 7:21, 22), meat (1 Sam. 14:32), hides (Exod. 25:5; Heb. 11:37), and wool (Lev. 13:47–48; Job 31:20). Even their horns were used as containers for oil (1 Sam. 16:1) or as musical instruments (Josh. 6:4). The skins were usually made into clothing and the inner covering of the tabernacle was made from skins that had been dyed red (Exod. 26:14).

Wool especially was a precious good and trade object. The Moabite king Mesha had to pay to the king of Israel an annual tribute of the wool of a hundred thousand rams (2 Kings 3:4). The shearing always was a special occasion and

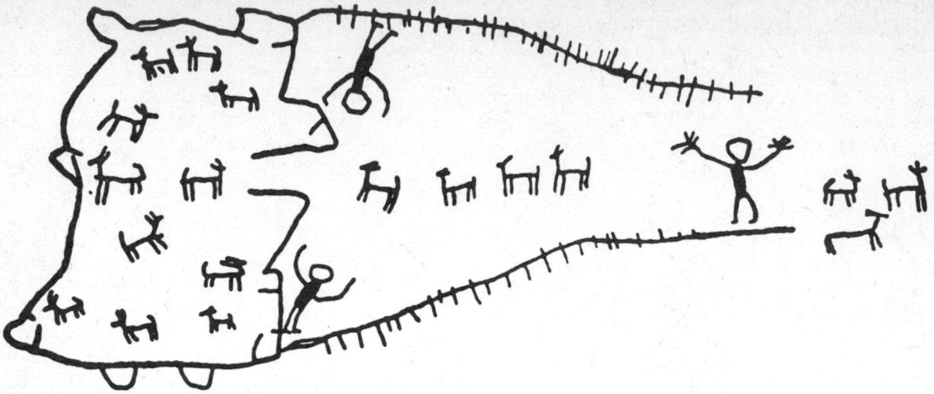

Shepherds driving their flock into a fortified sheepfold erected to protect the animals from marauders. Extended walls shield the narrow entrance; a Safaite rock drawing found in the desert east of Amman, Jordan.

Jacob used it to escape from his uncle Laban, whose attention was on the shearing (Gen. 31:19).

Jacob can be considered the first systematic animal breeder in the Bible. Genesis 30 tells how he tried to manipulate the quality of his flock by selecting the strong individuals for reproduction (vv. 41–42). He also attempted to induce his ewes to produce offspring of a certain color by placing a similar color in front of them (vv. 37–39).

Throughout the NT the sheep is used in a figurative sense for human beings. Jesus compared Israel to sheep lost (Matt. 10:6; cf. Isa. 53:6) and without a shepherd (Matt. 9:36). Sheep also play a role in several parables of Jesus (Matt. 12:11; 18:12; 25:33) and the Gospel of John pictures Jesus as a protecting shepherd, willing to give his life for his sheep (10:7–9; cf. Ezek. 37:24; Ps. 23:1; Heb. 13:20). The people whom Jesus fed he compared to sheep without a shepherd (Mark 6:34) and he is himself compared to a sheep led to slaughter (Acts 8:32; cf. Isa. 53:7).
I.U.K.

Sheep Gate, the, a gate probably located in the north city wall of Jerusalem, on the north side of the Temple area. This gate was built after the return from Exile by Eliashib and his brothers (Neh. 3:1) as part of Nehemiah's reconstruction of the Jerusalem walls (Neh. 12:39). Because of its proximity to the Temple area and pool of Bethzatha (Bethesda) (John 5:2), it has been surmised that sheep to be sacrificed were brought into the city through this gate.

Sheerah (shee'ruh; KJV: "Sherah"), the daughter of Ephraim (1 Chron. 7:24) who was credited with building up both Upper and Lower Beth-horon.

Shehariah (she-hah-rī'uh), a Benjaminite chief, and the son of Jehoram (1 Chron. 8:26).

shekel (shek'uhl), in OT times a standard unit of weight, approximately 14.5 grams of silver; in intertestamental and NT times, a common silver coin of the same weight, struck by Jewish authorities. In Matt. 17:27, the RSV translates Gk. *statēr* as "shekel." ***See also*** Money; Weights and Measures.

Shekinah (she-kī'nuh), a Hebrew word from the root "to dwell" that is translated as the "Presence" of God. God's *Shekinah* is not a being or reality separate from God (despite the positions of Philo [late first century B.C. to first century A.D.] and Maimonides [A.D. 1135–1204]) but a title for and designation of God in post-OT writings, especially in his presence among humans and in the world. The Targums (Aramaic translation of the Hebrew OT) often avoid anthropomorphisms and substitute *Shekinah* for "God." Rabbinic literature refers to God's *Shekinah* in a variety of contexts. God's presence was seen in the cloud that led the Israelites in the desert and in the tent of meeting in the desert. The Priestly writer's word for the tent of meeting, the *mishkan* or "tabernacle," comes from the same root as *Shekinah*. The glory of God, which filled the Temple, was his *Shekinah* and when the Temple was destroyed, God's *Shekinah* left the Temple. In one tradition the *Shekinah* returns to heaven, but in another it remains in the Western (or Wailing) Wall of the Temple Mount. Rabbinic traditions conceive of God's *Shekinah* as omnipresent, but as especially present in Israel, and in the post-Temple period, in synagogues and houses of study. ***See also*** Tabernacle.
A.J.S.

Shelah (shee'lah; Heb., "javelin"). **1** A Shemite son of Arpachshad (Gen. 10:24) who was the father of Eber (1 Chron. 1:18, 24; Gen. 11: 12–15; but see Luke 3:35–36 where he is identified as a son of Cainan). **2** The third son of Judah who is a Shelanite ancestor (Gen. 38:5, 11, 14, 26; 46:12; 1 Chron. 2:3; see also Num. 26:20; 1 Chron. 4:21).

Shelemiah (shel'uh-mī'uh; Heb., "God has recompensed," or "restored"). **1** The father of Nethaniah (Jer. 36:14). **2** One of Jehoiakim's men sent to seize Baruch (Jer. 36:26). **3** The father of Jehucal (Jer. 37:3; 38:1). **4** The father of Irijah (Jer. 37:13). **5** Two men who had married foreign women (Ezra 10:39, 41). **6** The father of Hananiah who helped repair the Jerusalem wall (Neh. 3:30). **7** A priest in charge of the storehouses (Neh. 13:13). **8** A gatekeeper (1 Chron. 26:14); this Shelemiah appears to be the same person called Meshelemiah in v. 1 and Shallum in 1 Chron. 9:17, 19, and 31. ***See also*** Shallum.

P.A.B.

Sheleph (shee'lef), a son of Joktan (Gen. 10:26; 1 Chron. 1:20). The names of Joktan's other sons indicate that Sheleph designated not an individual but more likely an Arabian tribe. The association with Hazarmaweth (i.e., the Hadramaut region in southwest Arabia) suggests a location in modern Yemen.

Shelesh (shee'lish; Heb., "third" or "triplet'), a man who headed an Asherite tribe (1 Chron. 7: 35).

Shelomi (she-loh'mee; Heb., "peace"?), the son of an Asherite chief, Ahihud (Num. 34:27).

Shelomith (she-loh'mith), a name that occurs both as a woman's and a man's; it is sometimes confused with Shelomoth. **1** The Danite mother of a sojourner in the Israelite camp who blasphemed the name of God (Lev. 24:11). **2** A daughter of Zerubbabel (1 Chron. 3:19). **3** A son (daughter?) of Rehoboam by Maacah, daughter of Absalom (2 Chron. 11:20). **4** A Levite, the chief son of Izhar (1 Chron. 23:18), called Shelomoth in 1 Chron. 24:22. **5** A Gershonite Levite who was a son of Shimei, according to the traditional reading of 1 Chron. 23:9 (written Shelomoth). **6** The head of a family group that returned with Ezra from Babylon (Ezra 8:10).

P.A.B.

Shelomoth. ***See*** Shelomith.

Shelumiel (she-lo͞o'mee-el; Heb., "God is peace"?), the Simeonite son of Zurishaddai (Num. 1:6; 2:12; 7:36–41; 10:19) who assisted Moses with the census. Judith's ancestry is traced to Salamiel, son of Sarasadai (Judg. 8:1), who is probably the same person as Shelumiel.

Shem (Heb., "name," "renown"), one of the three sons of Noah. Shem occupies a special place among the sons of Noah because he was the eldest (Gen. 5:32; 9:18), the recipient of special blessing (Gen. 9:26, RSV), and the ancestor of a group of peoples that included the Hebrews (Eber, Gen. 10:21, 24). The term "Semite" ("Shemite") has been applied in modern times to peoples speaking the Semitic languages. It has also been used as a racial designation. However, the list of Shem's descendants in Gen. 10:21–30 includes non-Semitic peoples (e.g., the Elamites, v. 22), showing that the basis for the grouping was geographical or political rather than linguistic or racial. In Gen. 9:20–27, Shem is the ancestor of Israel and is located in Palestine together with his two brothers, Ham (father of Canaan, representing the original inhabitants of the land) and Japheth (ancestor of the Philistines and other "Sea Peoples"). Canaan is cursed for dishonoring his father in the latter's drunken stupor and is made the slave of his brothers, who "covered their father's nakedness." Shem is rewarded by a special relationship with God (Gen. 9:26, RSV) and Japheth with an enlarged dwelling place "in the tents of Shem" (i.e., in the territory of Israel).

P.A.B.

Shema (shee'muh), an OT town (Josh. 15:26) that may be named after the clan of Shimei (1 Chron 4:26–27). It is associated with the Hebron area and the four Calebite clans (1 Chron. 2:43; as often in the OT, names of persons and places are used interchangeably).

Shema (shuh-mah'; Heb., "Hear you . . ."), the name of and first Hebrew word of the classical Jewish declaration of faith found in Deut. 6:4, which reads (literally), "Hear you, Israel, Yahweh our God, Yahweh is one"—although some have translated the last clause "Yahweh alone." The last letters of the first and last words of this verse are written in Hebrew Bibles in oversized script, thereby forming the Hebrew word "witness" to indicate that by this verse Jews testify to the oneness and uniqueness of their God—a difference in both quantity and quality from polytheism.

By the second century A.D. the *Shema* prayer consisted of Deut. 6:4–9; 11:13–21; and Num. 15:37–41 together with special benedictions to be recited every morning and evening (based upon Deut. 6:7). In traditional Jewish practice, the *Shema* is written in the phylacteries and mezuzah. As a watchword of faith and faithfulness the *Shema* constitutes the climax of the saying recited before death. This declaration was also recited during martyrdom. Jesus identified the *Shema* as the first commandment in the law (Mark 12:29).

J.U.

Shemaah (she-may'ah), the father of the Benjaminite bowmen Ahiezer and Joash, both of whom joined David to assist him in his battles (1 Chron. 12:1–3).

Shemaiah (she-may'uh; Heb., "Yahweh has heard"), a popular biblical name; the popularity of the name is also confirmed by extrabiblical sources (it appears in several of the ostraca found in the excavations at Arad in the northern Negeb [nos. 27, 31, 39]). **1** A late tenth century B.C. prophet who warned Rehoboam against fighting Israel (1 Kings 12:22; 2 Chron. 11:2) and called Rehoboam and his princes to repent before Pharaoh Shishak invaded Judah from Egypt (2 Chron. 12:5, 7). His prophecies were one of the sources for the Chronicler's history of Rehoboam's times (2 Chron. 12:15). **2** A false prophet in the days of Jeremiah who wrote from Babylonia denouncing Jeremiah and who in turn was denounced by God (Jer. 29:24–32). **3** A common name among the Levites (e.g., 1 Chron. 9:14; 15:8; 2 Chron. 17:8; 29:14; Neh. 11:15). **4** Several of those who served with Ezra and Nehemiah in the return from Exile (Neh. 3:29; 10:8; 12:6; Ezra 8:13). **5** A descendant of David (1 Chron. 3:22). **6** A descendant of Simeon (1 Chron. 4:37). **7** A descendant of Reuben (1 Chron. 5:4). **8** The father, from Kiriath-jearim, of Uriah, a prophet whom King Jehoiakim put to death for his prophecies (Jer. 26:20–23). **9** The father of one of the princes of the court of Jehoiakim who listened to the scroll Baruch read to them (Jer. 26:12–15). N.L.L.

Shemariah (shem-ah-rī'ah; Heb., "God has kept"). **1** One of the Benjaminite men who joined David at Ziklag (1 Chron. 12:5). **2** A son of Judah's King Rehoboam (2 Chron. 11:19). **3** A son of Pahath-moab who had married a foreign woman (Ezra 10:32). **4** A son of Binnui, one among the returnees from exile who had also married a foreign woman (Ezra 10:41).

Shemeber (shem-ee'buhr), a king of Zeboiim (Gen. 14:2) who was defeated by an alliance of eastern kings.

Shemed (shee'med; KJV: "Shamed"), a Benjaminite who, with Eber and Misham, built (founded) the cities of Ono and Lod (1 Chron. 8:12).

Shemer (shee'muhr; Heb., "watch"?; also Shomer [1 Chron. 7:32] and Shamer [KJV, 1 Chron. 6:46; 7:34]). **1** The owner (or owning clan) of the hill Omri bought and used for his capital city Samaria (1 Kings 16:24). **2** The father of Bani in the lineage of Temple musicians (1 Chron. 6:46). **3** An Asherite descendant (1 Chron. 7:32, 34).

Shemida (she-mī'dah; Heb., "Eshmun [the Phoenician God] has known"?), the Gileadite who headed the family of Shemidaite descendants of Manasseh (Num. 26:32; Josh. 17:2; 1 Chron. 7:19). The name appears on an ostracon from Samaria from the eighth century B.C.

Sheminith (shem'in-ith), a term used by musical groups (with lyres in 1 Chron. 15:21). It designates the eighth mode (in titles of Pss. 6, 12), one of several melodic patterns.

Shemiramoth (she-mihr'uh-moth; Heb., "name of heights"?). **1** A Levite harpist in the group David commanded to accompany the Ark and continue the worship (1 Chron. 15:18, 20; 16:5). **2** A Levite, a commissioned teacher in Judah (2 Chron. 17:8) during Jehoshaphat's reign (ca. 874–850 B.C.).

Shemuel (shem'yo͞o-el; Heb., "name of God" or "his name is God"). **1** A Simeonite land-divider, the son of Ammihud (Num. 34:20). **2** A clan chief, the son of Tola, who served in David's forces (1 Chron. 7:2). It appears in the KJV for "Samuel" in 1 Chron. 6:33.

Shen, the term in the KJV (following the Hebrew text) for the RSV's "Jeshanah" (following Greek and Syriac texts) in 1 Sam. 7:12. ***See also*** Jeshanah.

Shenazar (she-naz'uhr), the fourth son of the exiled Judean king Jehoiachin (Jeconiah; 1 Chron. 3:18), possibly the same person known as Sheshbazzar in postexilic days.

Sheol (shay'ohl), a biblical term for the netherworld. In some sources, particularly poetic and prophetic ones (cf. Deut. 32:22; Amos 9:2), the reference is simply to the deep depths of the earth. More commonly, Sheol is the underworld where departed spirits go (Prov. 9:18). Some of the biblical texts preserve a distinct mythological flavor, where Sheol is a power that can destroy the living (cf. Isa. 5:14). The etymology of the word is still in question. As a gloomy netherworld for departed spirits Sheol is the counterpart of Hades and Tartarus. M.A.F.

Shepham (sheef'uhm), a place on the eastern border of Israelite land (Num. 34:10–11) presumably near modern Riblah, but of still unknown location.

Shephatiah (shef'ah-tī'uh; Heb., "God has judged"). **1** The fifth son of David, by Abital (2 Sam. 3:4). **2** The father of a Benjaminite who resettled Jerusalem after the Exile (1 Chron. 9:8). **3** One of the Benjaminite warriors who went over to David while he was at Ziklag (1 Chron. 12:5). **4** The chief officer of the Simeonites in David's tribal administration (1 Chron. 27:16). **5** One of Jehoshaphat's sons who were slain by their brother Jehoram when he ascended the throne (2 Chron. 21:2). **6** The head of a lineage whose members returned from Babylon with

Zerubbabel (Ezra 2:4) and Ezra (Ezra 8:8). **7** An ancestor of a division of "Solomon's servants" who returned with Ezra (Ezra 2:57). **8** An ancestor of a Judahite living in Jerusalem in Nehemiah's time (Neh. 11:4). **9** One of the princes who sought the death of Jeremiah for his prophecies during the siege of Jerusalem and who cast him into a cistern to die (Jer. 38:1–6).
P.A.B.

Shephelah (shef-ay'lah), **the,** a noun that in Hebrew is always used with the definite article. It refers to the low hills in western Palestine separating the coastal plains from the central mountain ridge to the east. The overwhelming number of references are to the Shephelah of Judah. These hills provided a buffer between Judah and Philistia, and both parties sought control of the Shephelah because of its strategic value (Jer. 17:26).

Shepher (shee'fuhr), one of the camp stops of the Israelites (Num. 33:23–24) during their wanderings after the Exodus from Egypt. It is called "Mount" Shepher (KJV: "Shaphar") but is of unknown location.

shepherd, one who pastures or tends a flock of sheep and/or goats. Since these were the most important domestic animals in Palestine, there are many references to sheep and shepherds throughout the Bible. Many important figures in Hebrew history were pastoralists, including Abraham, Isaac, Jacob, Jacob's sons, Moses, and David. The occupation first appears in Gen. 4:2, when Abel, "a keeper of sheep," comes into conflict with Cain, "a tiller of the ground." While there has always been competition between shepherds and farmers, these two lifestyles actually exist symbiotically. Indeed, in one way or another, nearly everyone in ancient Palestine was involved in pastoral activity, from the lowly herdsman (cf. Amos 7:14–15) to the master breeder (cf. 2 Kings 3:4). The shepherd's humble status can be seen in the contrast drawn between David's pastoral and royal careers (2 Sam. 7:8; cf. Ps. 78:70–71). Nomadic peoples like the Amalekites and Midianites were shepherds, but the economic importance of sheep meant that many villagers and townspeople also tended flocks on a part-time or full-time basis. In addition to being a major sacrificial animal, sheep provided the ancients with meat, milk, fat, wool, skins, and horns.

The economic value of sheep stands in direct proportion to the amount of supervision (i.e., guidance and protection) these beasts require. Sheep become lost easily; once lost, they are defenseless (Ezek. 34:5–6; Matt. 18:12). The unaggressive behavior of sheep is emphasized in Matt. 7:15: "Beware of false prophets, who come to you in sheep's clothing but inwardly are ravenous wolves." Perhaps most famous are the sheep's submissiveness (Isa. 53:7; Jer. 11:19) and its trust in the shepherd (John 10:3–5).

The "Good Shepherd" depicted on the ceiling of the crypt of Lucina in Rome, second or third century A.D.

Although the shepherd's work was often boring, it was undoubtedly a livelihood that called for diligence and endurance. The search for pasturage and water sometimes took the herdsman and his flock far from home. This meant that shepherds put up with simple food, harsh weather (cf. Gen. 31:40), and primitive lodging (Song of Sol. 1:8; Isa. 38:12). Such routine hardships were occasionally accompanied by danger from wild animals, e.g., lions, bears, and wolves (1 Sam. 17:34–35; Isa. 31:4; Amos 3:12; Mic. 5:8; John 10:12). Shepherds also had to be on guard against thieves (Gen. 31:39; John 10:1, 8, 10).

Most of the shepherd's work involved a routine of leading the sheep to food and water and returning them to the safety of the fold. Because sheep are highly gregarious, the shepherd had to keep alert for strays and check his effort by counting the sheep as they entered their enclosure for the night (Lev. 27:32; Jer. 33:13; Ezek. 20:37). If animals were missing, the herdsman's duty was to rescue the lost (Ezek. 34:11–12; Matt. 18:11–14). Special attention was given to expectant ewes, newborn lambs, and sick animals (Isa. 40:11; Ezek. 34:16).

In addition to fieldstone or brush sheepfolds,

shepherds used simple but functionally sound equipment. Protection from the elements was provided by a heavy cloak (cf. Jer. 43:12). A staff was used to control the movement of the flock, and a rod was used to ward off enemies (Ps. 23: 4). Also important were a bag for food and a sling (1 Sam. 14:40). Shepherds played reed flutes to calm the flocks and while away the hours (cf. Judg. 5:16). Reference should also be made to the use of dogs to help manage the movement of the sheep (Job 30:1).

Shepherd Imagery in the Bible: Pastoral language was used in a figurative way throughout the ancient Near East and in the Hellenistic world; it is, therefore, quite natural that the OT and NT should also use shepherd imagery. In numerous passages the customs of shepherds are used to illustrate spiritual principles; e.g., sheep without a shepherd are like those who have strayed from God (Matt. 9:36; Mark 6:34), and shepherds are compared to spiritual overseers (Num. 27:16–17; Eccles. 12:11; John 21: 15–17).

Many ancient peoples affirmed the sovereignty of their deities by referring to them as shepherds (cf. Gen. 48:15; 49:24). Descriptions of the shepherd's work are often used to describe Yahweh's activity. The most extended allegories of the shepherd are found in Psalm 23 and Ezekiel 34; both passages portray God as one who protects and cares for a helpless flock. In addition to these two chapters, this analogy appears in Psalms quite frequently (e.g., 28:9; 74:1; 77:20; 78:52–53; 80:1; 95:7; 100:3; 121:3–8), and it is a favorite literary device of the prophets (e.g., Isa. 40:11; 49:9–10; Jer. 23:1–4; 31:10; 49:19–20; 50:17–19; Mic. 4: 6–8; 7:14).

While kings and princes were called shepherds in other ancient Near Eastern literature (cf. Nah. 3:18), the OT normally applies this title to political leaders in a negative way. Since God was the true shepherd of Israel, the subordinate herdsmen (i.e., rulers) often fell short of God's standards; as such, they were condemned for their stupidity and mismanagement (e.g., Jer. 10: 21; 22:22; 23:1–4; 25:34–38; Ezek. 34:1–10; Zech. 10:3; 11:4–17).

Of course, there are exceptions to this negative use of pastoral imagery. David was a shepherd who ruled his people with an "upright heart" and a "skillful hand" (Ps. 78:70–72), and Cyrus was referred to as God's shepherd (Isa. 44:28). Most important was the promise that God would raise up new shepherds (Jer. 3: 15; 23:4), a promise that eventually took on messianic significance (Ezek. 34:23; 37:22, 24). Not only would God's shepherd be from the Davidic lineage, but he would also suffer on behalf of the sheep (Zech. 13:7; cf. 12:10).

The only literal reference to shepherds in the NT is found in Luke 2:8–20; elsewhere they appear in parables and figures of speech, most often in the Gospels. Jesus claimed that his mission was "to the lost sheep of the house of Israel" (Matt. 10:6; 15:24). The parable of the lost sheep was told to exemplify God's love (Matt. 18:12–14; Luke 15:3–7), while the shepherd's separation of sheep and goats was compared to judgment (Matt. 25:32–33). In a well-known allegory, Jesus refers to himself as the "good shepherd" who "lays down his life for the sheep" (John 10:1–29; cf. the quotation of Zech. 13:7 in Matt. 26:31 and Mark 14:27). Jesus is called "the great shepherd of the sheep" (Heb. 13:20), "the Shepherd and Guardian of your souls" (1 Pet. 2: 25), and "the chief Shepherd" (1 Pet. 5:4).

While issuing a warning about fierce wolves (i.e., false teachers), Paul admonishes the Ephesian elders to oversee and care for the flock, which he equates with "the church of God" (Acts 20:28–30). This same function is encompassed by the English word "pastor," which is the normal translation given in Eph. 4:11, although the Greek term used there is the same one that is usually rendered "shepherd" (cf. 1 Pet. 5:1–4). ***See also*** Sheep. G.L.M.

Shephi (shee'fī), an Edomite, the son of the clan chief Shobal (1 Chron. 1:40). The name also appears as "Shepho" (Gen. 36:23).

Shephupham (she-fōō'fuhm; KJV: "Shupham"), the name of a Benjaminite clan (Num. 26:39); "Shephuphan" (1 Chron. 8:5) and "Muppim" (Gen. 46:21) may be other names for the same clan.

Sherebiah (shair-uh-bī'uh; Heb., "God has sent severe heat"?). **1** The "discreet" Levite among the postexilic Judeans working with Ezra (Ezra 8:18, 24). **2** A Levite teacher of law (Neh. 8:7; 9:4, 5; 10:12). **3** A Levite chief who returned from exile with Zerubbabel (Neh. 12:8, 24).

Sheshach (shee'shak), a cryptogram for Babylon (Heb. *bābel;* Jer. 25:26; 51:41), obtained by using a rabbinical cipher called Athbash in which the last letter of the alphabet is used for the first (tav[t] = aleph[a]), the second from the last is used for the second (shin[sh] = beth[b]), etc. Many versions replace the word with "Babylon."

Sheshai (shee'shī), a descendant of Anak (Num. 13:22; Josh. 15:14; Judg. 1:10), who lived in Canaan when the spying Israelites entered. He was defeated by Joshua's forces, presumably near his residence, Hebron.

Sheshan (shee'shan), the head of a Jerahmeelite family of Judah (1 Chron. 2:31, 34, 35).

Sheshbazzar (shesh-baz'uhr), the "prince of

Judah" (Ezra 1:8, 11; 5:14, 16, RSV) to whom Cyrus (538 B.C.) entrusted the "gold and silver vessels" of the Temple to be restored to Jerusalem. The name derives from Babylonian *Šamaš-* or *Sîn-ab-utṣur* and means "O Shamash/Sîn preserve the father" (the versions allow for either). Identifications with Zerubbabel (Ezra 3:2) are circumstantial and thus questionable. Sheshbazzar may be identical with Shenazzar, a son of Jeconiah (1 Chron. 3:18).

Sheth **1** A form of Seth, the third son of Adam (Gen. 4:25). **2** A word usually taken as a proper noun, a group of people ("sons of Sheth") associated with the Moabites (Num. 24:17). However, it is likely that the word is a (deliberately?) corrupted form of the word "tumult" (Heb. *sha-'ōn)* used to describe the warlike nature of the Moabites ("Sons of [battle] tumult"; cf. Jer. 48: 45). Since Sheth is a form of Seth (1 above), this may be a wordplay that identifies the Moabites as distant kinsmen of the Israelites but at the same time condemns their aggression against the Israelites (see Num. 22:1–4). ***See also*** Moab; Seth. D.R.B.

Shetharbozenai (shee'thahr-bahz'uh-nī), a Persian provincial official who, along with the provincial governor Tattenai, challenged Zerubbabel's right to rebuild the Temple (mid-sixth century B.C.). He sent an official protest to the Persian king Darius. After a search of the archives in Ecbatana, a copy of the decree of Cyrus allowing the Jews to return and rebuild the Temple was found and Darius ordered Shetharbozenai and Tattenai not only to cease harassing the Jews but also to lend financial assistance from the provincial treasury (Ezra 5:3, 6; 6:6, 13). ***See also*** Darius.

Sheva (shee'vuh). **1** The chief scribe or secretary of King David (2 Sam. 20:25), elsewhere called Shavsha (1 Chron. 18:16) and Seraiah (2 Sam. 8:17). He is probably also the same person called Shisha, the father of two scribes in the time of Solomon (1 Kings 4:3). Some scholars suggest that he was a non-Israelite, probably Egyptian, which would account for the variation of the name. **2** A Judahite descendant of Caleb (1 Chron. 2:49). ***See also*** Seraiah; Shavsha.

shewbread. ***See*** Showbread.

Shibah (shī'bah; Heb., "oath"), the well dug by Isaac's servants during his time with Abimelech of Gerar (Gen. 26:26–33). It is probably the source for the city name "Beer-sheba."

shibboleth (shib'boh-leth; Heb., either "ear of grain" or "flood, torrent"), the password required by Jephthah's Gileadite sentries (Judg. 12:6). Ephraimites retreating across the Jordan could only say "sibboleth," and forty-two units (hardly 42,000) were slain. Apparently three sounds are involved, two of which merged earlier in west Palestine, where the Ephraimites lived, than in Transjordan, where the Gileadites resided. ***See also*** Judges, The Book of.

shield. ***See*** Spear.

Shiggaion (shi-gay'yuhn), a Hebrew word of uncertain meaning that appears in the heading of Psalm 7. Its plural form appears in Hab. 3:1, also in connection with poetic materials.

Shihor (shī'hohr), a body of water "east of Egypt" (Josh. 13:3) or near the Nile (Isa. 23:3) that served as a reference for the south edge of Israel (1 Chron. 13:5). The northern parts of the Pelusiac or Bubastite branches of the Nile in the eastern delta are most likely meant.

Shihor-libnath (shī'hohr-lib'nath), a boundary of Asher where it adjoined Carmel (Josh. 19: 26). It may be modern Wadi Zerqa which drains the western slope south of Dor.

Shiloah (shi-loh'ah). ***See*** Siloam Inscription.

Shiloh (shī'loh), an ancient religious center of Israel. Located about ten miles north of Bethel to the east of the Jerusalem-Nablus road (Judg. 21: 19), it is identified with modern Khirbet Seilun. Shiloh was the administrative and religious center for the Israelite tribes during the early settlement period (twelfth century B.C.). There the tabernacle was set up (Josh. 18:1), the distribution of the land by lot took place (Josh. 18, 19), the Levites were assigned their cities (Judg. 21), and the ten tribes gathered to consider the apostasy of the east Jordan tribes (Josh. 22).

Shiloh was the central sanctuary and seat of the priesthood (Eleazar, Josh. 21:1, 2; Eli and his sons, 1 Sam. 1:3, 9; Samuel, 1 Sam. 1:24; 3: 21) until the Ark was captured in the battle with the Philistines at Ebenezer (1 Sam. 4). The Ark was not returned to Shiloh and the city never regained its prestige. Shiloh's destruction by the Philistines is not related in the OT, but Jeremiah cites its fate in his prophecies (Jer.

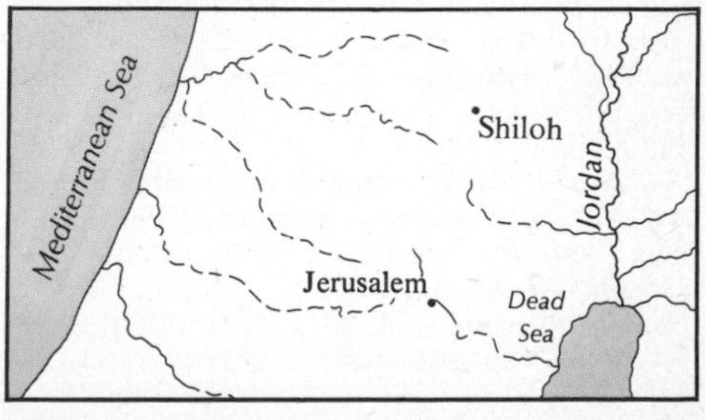

7:12–14; 26:6–9). It did continue as a town to some extent as is shown by the fact that the wife of Jeroboam sought Ahijah the prophet at Shiloh (1 Kings 14:2–4) and that men of Shiloh came to Mizpah after the murder of Gedaliah (Jer. 4, 5).

Shiloh has been the scene of several excavations and there have been scattered publications of the results, but the evidence presented has been insufficient and debatable. The excavations of the Danish under H. Kjaer in 1926, 1929, and 1932 were cut short by his death. Only preliminary reports were published. Thirty years later, in preparing for the final publication, a short campaign was conducted by S. Holm-Nielson. The publication that resulted advocated different conclusions than the earlier work. In 1981 excavation was resumed by Bar-Ilan University under the direction of I. Finkelstein and excavations have continued at the site.

As a result of the early campaigns, archaeological evidence was cited for Israelite settlement of Shiloh (Iron Age I remains) and for the destruction of Shiloh by the Philistines after the battle of Ebenezer (widespread Iron Age I destruction believed to date to 1050 B.C.), and then occupation ceasing for centuries (no Iron Age II remains were recognized). As a result of the 1963 campaign, M-L. Buhl and S. Holm-Nielson, authors of the final publication, denied a Philistine (Iron Age I) destruction, maintained occupation continued into Iron Age II, and considered the fate of Shiloh to which Jeremiah alludes to be the result of Sargon's campaign of 722 B.C., with a final disaster and deportation by Nebuchadnezzar in the early sixth century.

The renewed excavations are attempting to clarify the problems raised. Excavation areas were chosen in an attempt to avoid the widespread Roman-Byzantine occupation. As earlier, a heavily fortified Middle Bronze II (mid-eighteenth century B.C.) town is indicated. After extensive destruction, limited Late Bronze I occupation followed. A period of abandonment preceded the relatively small Iron Age I settlement of at least two phases, ending in an intensive conflagration. Some Iron Age II occupation has been noted, as well as Hellenistic. Roman fortification walls are evident, as is the Byzantine occupation. Two Byzantine churches were uncovered in the early excavations. ***See also*** Ark; Priests; Samuel; Samuel, The First and Second Books of.

Bibliography

Buhl, M-L., and S. Holm-Nielson. *Shiloh, The Danish Excavations at Tell Sailun, Palestine, in 1926, 1929, 1932 and 1963*. Copenhagen: National Museum of Denmark, 1969.

Israel Exploration Journal 32 (1982): 148–150; 33 (1983): 123–126, 267–268.

N.L.L.

Shilshah (shil'shah), a member of the tribe of Asher and the son of Zophah (1 Chron. 7:37).

Shimea (shim'ee-ah; Heb., "God has heard"). **1** The third son of Jesse (1 Chron. 2:13). **2** One of David's sons born in Jerusalem (1 Chron. 3:5). **3** A Merarite Levite (1 Chron. 6:30). **4** A Gershomite Levite (1 Chron. 6:39).

Shimeath (shim'ee-ath), the mother of one of the murderers of King Joash of Judah (2 Kings 12:21; 2 Chron. 24:26).

Shimeathites (shim'ee-uh-thīts), a scribal family living at Jabez (1 Chron. 2:55). Neither the place nor people can be precisely identified.

Shimei (shim'e-ī; Heb., "[God] has heard"), the name of at least eighteen men in the OT, some of which follow. **1** A Benjaminite of Saul's house, who cursed David as David fled Jerusalem during Absalom's revolt. When David returned, Shimei met him at the Jordan with a thousand Benjaminites, confessing his sin and pledging his allegiance. David spared Shimei's life on oath but on his deathbed instructed Solomon to put him to death. Solomon accordingly contrived to execute Shimei for breaking an agreement. **2** A member of David's court (1 Kings 1:8), perhaps the same Shimei who wielded authority over Solomon's Benjaminite district (1 Kings 4:18). **3** A Ramathite overseer of David's vineyards (1 Chron. 27:27). **4** The head of a levitical family (Exod. 6:17; Num. 3:18). **5** Several Levites in various types of Temple service (1 Chron. 6:17; 25:17; 2 Chron. 29:14; 31:13). **6** The brother of Zerubbabel (1 Chron. 3:19). **7** A Benjaminite ancestor of Mordecai (Esther 2:5). **8** Three men who had married foreign women (Ezra 10:23, 33, 38). P.A.B.

Shimeon (shim'ee-uhn), a son of Harim who had married a foreign woman (Ezra 10:31).

Shimon (shī'muhn), a family or clan of the tribe of Judah (1 Chron. 4:20).

Shimrath (shim'rath), the son of Shimei, a Benjaminite (1 Chron. 8:21).

Shimri (shim'rī). **1** A Simeonite ancestor of Ziza (1 Chron. 4:37). **2** The father of David's mighty man Jediael (1 Chron. 11:45). **3** A Levite working in the Temple during the reign of King Hezekiah of Judah (2 Chron. 29:13).

Shimrith (shim'rith; Heb., "God has protected"), a Moabite woman who was the mother of Jehozabad, one of the murderers of King Joash of Judah (2 Chron. 24:26).

Shimron (shim'rahn). **1** The fourth son of Issachar and the head of the Shimronites (Gen. 46: 13; Num. 26:24; 1 Chron. 7:1). **2** A Canaanite royal town (Josh. 11:1) assigned to the tribe of Zebulun (Josh. 19:15).

Shimshai (shim'shī; Heb., "sun"), an officer of the Persian court on duty in Palestine (Ezra 4:8, 9, 17 and 23). He endorsed a letter to Artaxerxes, the king of Persia, complaining about Judean postexilic reconstruction work and received official support for its cessation. The work in Jerusalem was resumed later.

shin, the name of the twenty-first letter of the Hebrew alphabet. It had a numerical value of three hundred and had the phonetic value of *sh*. A variant took the sound s. Both were written in a rough equivalent of the English letter "W."

ש

Shinab (shī'nab; Heb., "[the god] Sin is my father"), the king of Admah, one of the five monarchs in a coalition against the eastern alliance of four other kings (Gen. 14:2). Defeated initially, the alliance of five kings was rescued by Abram (Gen. 14:13–16).

Shinar (shī'nahr), **Plain of,** a district of Babylonia in southern Iraq. According to Gen. 10: 10, the Plain of Shinar included Babel (Babylon), Erech (Warka), and Accad or Akkade in central Mesopotamia close to Baghdad. The Tower of Babel is said to have been built in "a plain in the land of Shinar" (Gen. 11:2). "Amraphel king of Shinar" was one of the four kings who, according to Genesis 14, invaded the Dead Sea region and were subsequently pursued and defeated by Abraham at "Horbah, north of Damascus" (Gen. 14:1–16). Many scholars, however, believe this tradition to be legendary. In later times "Shinar" was equated with Babylon, from which, among other places, the exiles would one day be rescued (Isa. 11:11). Dan. 1:2 says that Nebuchadnezzar took "Jehoiakim king of Judah ... with some of the vessels of the house of God" to Shinar. Zech. 5:11 predicts the ephah of wickedness will be taken to a house built for it in Shinar. ***See also*** Babylon; Nebuchadnezzar. D.B.

Shion (shī'uhn), a border post of the lands of Issachar (Josh. 19:19). Its location is uncertain.

Shiphi (shī'fī; Heb., "abundance" or "overflow"), a member of the tribe of Simeon who was the father of Ziza (1 Chron. 4:37).

Shiphrah (shif'ruh), a woman who was one of two midwives approached by Pharaoh to carry out his plan to destroy all Israelite boys when they were born (Exod. 1:15).

Shiphtan (shif'tan; Heb., "the god has judged"?), the father of Kemuel, of the tribe of Ephraim (Num. 34:24). Shiphtan was one of the men assigned to divide the land among the tribes of Israel.

ships. ***See*** Boats.

Shishak (shī'shak; Heb.), a king of Egypt, whose Egyptian name was Shoshenq I (945–924 B.C.). Born in Egypt but descended from a line of Libyan nobles, he was the founder of the twenty-second (Libyan) dynasty (ca. 945–715 B.C.), whose capital was at Tanis (Heb. *Zoan*) in the northeast part of the delta. A contemporary of Solomon, he gave asylum to Jeroboam (1 Kings 11:40) until the latter returned to take over the northern kingdom of Israel after Solomon's death (1 Kings 12:2–3). When the country was divided between Rehoboam and Jeroboam, Shishak, for reasons still unclear, launched a major invasion of Palestine. This campaign, which took place in the fifth year of Rehoboam's reign (probably equivalent to a year late in Shishak's reign), is described in 1 Kings 14:25–26 and 2 Chron. 12:1–9. According to the biblical narrative, Shishak's large army took the fortified cities of Judah and "came up against Jerusalem." A list of cities captured by the king was carved on a wall in the temple of Amun-Re at Karnak. This list, which is in badly damaged condition today, originally contained the names of over 150 Palestinian cities. The absence of Jerusalem from this list is explained by Rehoboam's decision to pay tribute to Shishak, which included the treasures of the Temple and royal palace, to avoid an Egyptian conquest of the city (2 Chron. 12:5–9). ***See also*** Rehoboam; Zoan. J.M.W.

Shitrai (shit'rah-ee). A Sharonite, one of David's servants. He handled the livestock in the Sharon plain (1 Chron. 27:29).

shittah (shi'tuh; "acacia" tree or wood), a transliterated Hebrew term (*šiṭṭâ*) that identified the tree or wood *Acacia nilotica* or the more substantial *Acacia tortilis*. In the plural form, *shittim* (Exod. 25, 26, 27, 30, 35, 36, 37, 38), it is designated as the proper wood to be used in constructing the Ark of the Covenant (Exod. 25: 10) and the accompanying items like the carrying poles (Exod. 25:28), bars (Exod. 26:26), pillars (Exod. 26:32), tables (Exod. 25:23), and altars (Exod. 37:25; see also Deut. 10:3). In Isa. 41:19 it symbolizes the revival of lush life as part of a growth with other substantial trees. It was highly resistant to insects and other decay and was suitable for cabinet-making, being both hard and durable. R.S.B.

Shittim (shi'tim), a place in the territory of Moab north of Mt. Nebo and Heshbon and across the border from Jericho (Num. 33:48–49). Here, according to the various narratives, the Israelite men sinned with Moabite women (Num. 25) and the Israelites were numbered in a census (Num. 26). At Shittim Joshua was commissioned to succeed Moses (Num. 27:23) and from there men were sent as spies to the promised land (Josh. 2:1). Shittim may be identified with the modern Tell el-Hamman in Jordan.

Shiza (shī'zah), a member of the tribe of Reuben. He was the father of Adina and a member of David's armies (1 Chron. 11:42).

Shoa (shoh'uh), a people named in association with Babylonians, Assyrians, and probably Aramaeans who would threaten Judah, according to Ezekiel's warning (Ezek. 23:23). The people have not been precisely identified, although they were probably located north of Judah, given the known locations of the associated groups. In this section of Ezekiel, Judah appears as one of two sisters and is named Oholibah. ***See also*** Oholah, Oholibah.

Shobab (shoh'bab). **1** One of David's sons born in Jerusalem (2 Sam. 5:14; 1 Chron. 3:5; 14:4). **2** A son of Caleb and Azuba (1 Chron. 2:18).

Shobach (shoh'bak), commander of the eastern Aramaean forces of Hadadezer, who marshaled troops to assault David. In the subsequent fight at Helam in the Transjordan Shobach's forces were beaten decisively and Shobach himself was mortally wounded. The defeat stymied further Aramaean-Ammonite action against David (2 Sam. 10:15–19; 1 Chron. 19:16–19, where the name is spelled "Shophach").

Shobai (shoh'bī), one of the families of returning exiles who served as gatekeepers in Jerusalem (Ezra 2:42; Neh. 7:45; 1 Esd. 5:28).

Shobal (shoh'bal; Heb., "basket"). **1** The second son of Seir, a Horite clan chief who lived probably in Edom (Gen. 36:20, 23, 29; 1 Chron. 1:38, 40). **2** An ancestor of a Calebite tribe in Kiriath-jearim (1 Chron. 2:50, 52), which was considered part of Judah (1 Chron. 4:1–2).

Shobek (shoh'bek), one of the men sealing the covenant in Jerusalem under Nehemiah (Neh. 10:24).

Shobi (shoh'bī), the Ammonite prince, son of King Nahash, who supplied David during David's stay at Mahanaim in the Transjordan while he was in conflict with his son Absalom (2 Sam. 17:27–29). Shobi may have served as successor to his brother Hanun following the latter's insolent treatment of David's servants and the subsequent military disaster. Such conduct on Hanun's part was all the more inappropriate because the Ammonites were then strictly a tributary people to David's throne (2 Sam. 10:1–11:1; 12:26–31; 1 Chron. 19:1–20:3).

shoes, coverings for the feet, used for decoration as well as protection. Sandals were the common form of foot covering in biblical times, although laced or strapped boots were worn by Assyrian and Roman soldiers and Palestinian women in ankle-high shoes are depicted in an Egyptian tomb painting (cf. Ezek. 16:10). Most people, however, appear barefoot in ancient Egyptian and Mesopotamian art, with sandals shown on soldiers, travelers, and persons of rank. Footwear may have been more common in northern regions. Sandals consisted basically of a leather, wood, or fiber sole attached to the foot by thongs (Gen. 14:23). Assyrian sandals were characterized by a heel cap.

Putting on sandals was a sign of preparation for a journey (Exod. 12:11; Deut. 29:5; Josh. 9:5, 13) or for warfare (Isa. 5:27). Jesus' instructions in sending out the Twelve, that they should go barefoot (Matt. 10:10; Luke 10:4), countered normal practice. Sandals belonged to fine dress (Luke 15:22) and full dress (Acts 12:8). Footwear was removed indoors, in sacred precincts (Exod. 3:5; Josh. 5:15), and during mourning (Ezek. 24:17). Removing or carrying a master's shoes was a slave's task in NT times (cf. Mark 1:7; Matt. 3:11).

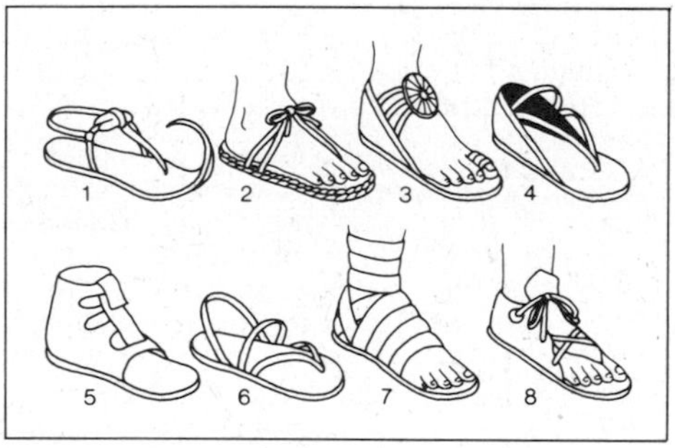

Shoes: 1. Egyptian (1200 B.C.), 2. Egyptian, 3. Babylonian, 4. Assyrian (900 B.C.), 5. Greek *krepis*, 6. Greek *pediba*, 7. Roman *calceus*, 8. Roman *crepeda*.

Transfer of property was confirmed in Hebrew custom by the symbolic exchange of a sandal (Ruth 4:7, 8; Amos 2:6), arising, probably, from the practice of claiming title to land by walking its boundaries or casting a shoe upon it (Ps. 60:8). The public removal of a man's shoe by the woman he has refused to take in levirate marriage was a humiliating gesture with sexual innuendo (Deut. 25:9–10). ***See also*** Marriage.

P.A.B.

Shoham (shoh'ham), a Merarite Levite, the son of Jaaziah (1 Chron. 24:27).

Shomer (shoh'muhr; Heb., "keeper, watcher"). **1** The parent of Jehozabad, one of the murderers of Judah's king Joash (2 Kings 12:21). **2** A son of the Asherite Heber (1 Chron. 7:32; in v. 34 it appears as "Shemer").

shoot. ***See*** Branch.

shophar (shoh'fahr), the horn of an animal formed into a musical instrument. The biblical shophar was a ram's horn (Josh. 6:4–13). Although it was possible to fashion a shophar from the horn of a sheep or goat, later Jewish tradition preferred that it be made from a ram's, the animal Abraham substituted for the sacrifice of his son Isaac (Gen. 22:1–14). The shophar is mentioned many times in the Bible, beginning with Exod. 19:16, the revelation at Mt. Sinai, where the loud blast of the horn caused the people to tremble in fear. The Israelites were commanded that when they entered the land God would give them, they were to proclaim the Jubilee Year with a blast of the shophar (Lev. 25:9).

In the Bible, the shophar most often signifies an important announcement or a call to arms (Judg. 3:27) and was the means by which Joshua conquered the city of Jericho (Josh. 6: 4–5). As an instrument, the shophar was also used as part of a musical ensemble (Ps. 98:6). In the Jerusalem Temple, the ram's horn was an integral part of the rituals.

The book of Numbers describes the first day of the seventh month as the "Day of the blowing of the shophar" (Num. 29:1). Postbiblical Judaism termed this day *Rosh Ha-Shanah* (cf. Ezek. 40: 1) and a prescribed sequence of notes are to be blown as a call to repentance with a long blast at the conclusion of the Day of Atonement. Jewish tradition, based on Isa. 27:13, maintains that the shophar will be sounded to usher in the final messianic redemption (cf. Rev. 8–9). The shophar plays a prominent role in the eschatological battle described in the *War Scroll* from Qumran. L.H.S.

Shoshannim (shoh-shan'im; RSV: "lilies"), a term in the KJV that appears in the titles of Psalms 45, 69, and 80. It seems to have been a type of instruction concerning performance, perhaps referring to the melody to be used. ***See also*** Music.

shovel, an implement for clearing away ashes from the tabernacle's outer altar. The altar shovels were made of copper (Exod. 27:3; 38:3). The ashes were scooped up in them and apparently placed in copper pots (see Exod. 27:3), which were then carried outside the camp and emptied at the cultic ash dump (Lev. 6:10–11). Solomon's Temple also had copper shovels for its burnt offering altar (1 Kings 7:40, 45; 2 Chron. 4: 11, 16). When Jerusalem fell, the Babylonians took these as spoil (2 Kings 25:14; Jer. 52:18).

showbread (in older English translations, "shewbread"), twelve loaves of unleavened bread that were placed on a specially constructed table in the holy place of the tabernacle and Temple as an offering to God. They were to be baked of fine flour and arranged in two rows of six with frankincense in each row. The bread was to be replaced with freshly baked bread every Sabbath day and the old loaves were to be eaten by the priests (Lev. 24:5–9; Exod. 25:23–30; 1 Sam. 21:5–6; cf. Matt. 12:3–4). The showbread is variously referred to as the Bread of the Presence (Num. 4:7), holy bread (1 Sam. 21:6), or simply the bread (Exod. 40:23). ***See also*** Worship. D.R.B.

shrine, specifically a box or container in which sacred objects are placed. In a general sense a shrine is any place in which sacred objects are housed or at which such objects are placed, or any sacred place at which worship is performed. Thus, the Ark of the Covenant was a shrine since it contained the tablets of the testimony (Exod. 25:16). The most holy place of the tabernacle or Temple in which the Ark was housed can also be termed a shrine (Exod. 26:33; 1 Kings 6:19; 8:6). In the broad sense, the tabernacle and Temple can be called shrines since they were places of worship. Similarly, non-Hebrew cult places that housed idols or other sacred objects (cf. 2 Kings 23:4–20) or at which worship was performed can be called shrines. ***See also*** Ark; Cults; Tabernacle; Temple, The; Temples; Worship. D.P.W.

Reconstructed shrine house with snake and animal decorative motifs; from Beth-shan, 1000–850 B.C.

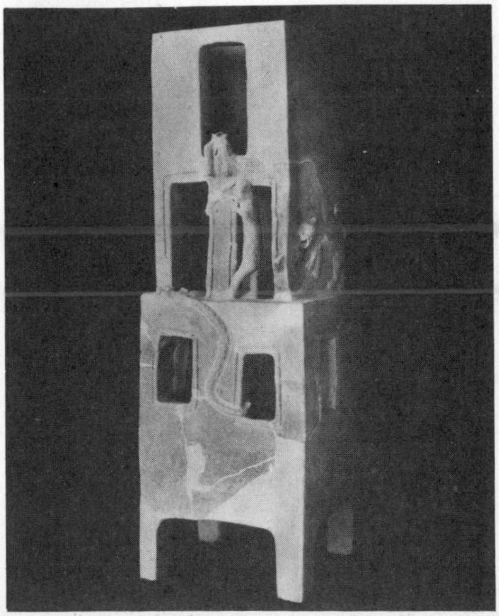

shroud, the cloth used to wrap a corpse. One such piece of material was used to wrap the body of Jesus after the crucifixion (Matt. 27:59; but see John 20:6–7). That piece of cloth has never been confidently identified, although some claim the shroud kept at Turin, Italy, is the one used for Jesus.

The shroud at Turin, which appears to bear the image of a human body, was first discovered in France in the fourteenth century. It has no known history before that. It is 14 feet long and 3-1/2 feet wide. It seems to have been used for a corpse that was 5 feet, 11 inches tall and weighed about 170 pounds, but that proves nothing, because no one knows how tall or heavy Jesus was.

Many scientific tests have been applied to the shroud of Turin. These show that the body it contained had been crucified. Marks on the cloth in the area of hands and feet are evidently blood stains, but that does not prove the body was that of Jesus. Thousands of people were crucified in antiquity. Alexander Jannaeus (second century B.C.) crucified eight hundred prominent Jews on one day—all of whom were probably wrapped in shrouds and buried. Some of these were probably the same size as the body held by the shroud of Turin.

No test has been made to show how old the cloth is, but even if it were proved to have been woven during the first century, that would still only reduce the odds to several thousand possibilities. G.W.B.

Shuah (sho͞o'ah), a term akin to an Assyrian term for an Aramaean land on the Euphrates. The biblical word identifies three people. **1** A Canaanite father of Judah's wife (RSV: "Shua" in Gen. 38:2, 12; KJV: "Shua" in 1 Chron. 2:3). **2** An Asherite, a child of Heber (1 Chron. 7:32, "Shua"). **3** A son of Abraham and Keturah (Gen. 25:2), possibly a reference to an Arab or Aramaean tribe inhabiting the Upper Euphrates region. This would link with references to Shuhites, a tribe thought to have lived either there or in Edom.

Shual (sho͞o'uhl; Heb., "fox" or "jackal"?). **1** A territory (one of three) against which Philistine raiders moved in the time of King Saul (eleventh century B.C.; 1 Sam. 13:17). Its association with Ophrah suggests a northerly location for the Philistine camp at Michmash. **2** A portion of the Asherite clan of Zophah (1 Chron. 7:36).

Shuham (sho͞o'ham), a clan ancestor of a group of people from the Hebrew tribe of Dan (Num. 26:42–43).

Shulamite. ***See*** Shunem; Shuni.

Shunammite (sho͞o'nuh-mīt), a native of the town of Shunem. **1** Abishag, who nursed David in his old age (1 Kings 1:3). **2** A woman whose dead son was revived by Elisha (2 Kings 4:8–37). ***See also*** Abishag.

Shunem (sho͞o'nem), town on the southern border of Issachar (Josh. 19:18) guarding the pass to the Valley of Jezreel on the north, opposite the town of Jezreel at the foot of Mt. Gilboa. It is identified with modern Solem.

Shunem is mentioned in the fifteenth-century B.C. conquest lists of the Egyptian pharaoh Thutmose III, the fourteenth-century Amarna letters, and the tenth-century inscription of Pharaoh Shishak at Karnak. The Philistines camped at Shunem before defeating the Israelites at Mt. Gilboa (1 Sam. 28:4), and David's nurse in his old age, Abishag, was from Shunem (1 Kings 1:3). Elisha frequently stopped at this town in his travels and a woman there provided him with quarters; in return Elisha's promise of a son was fulfilled and later Elisha revived him from death (2 Kings 4). ***See also*** Gilboa; Jezreel. N.L.L.

Shuni (sho͞o'nī), the third son of Gad, and the ancestor of the Shunites (Gen. 46:16; Num. 26:15).

Shupham. (sho͞o'fuhm). ***See*** Shephupham.

Shur (sho͞or), **Wilderness of,** a desert region somewhere in the Sinai Peninsula, east of the present Suez Canal. It was inhabited by Ishmaelites (Gen. 25:18) and was for a period the home of Abraham (Gen. 20:1). The Israelites during the Exodus entered it immediately after leaving the Red Sea (Exod. 15:22). "The way to Shur," where the angel met Hagar (Gen. 16:7), is probably the desert track leading southward from Beer-sheba, along which Saul, and later David, pursued the Amalekites "as far as Shur" (1 Sam. 15:7; 27:8). No suggestion for the meaning of the name "Shur" has so far won general acceptance among scholars. ***See also*** Abraham; Amalekites; Beer-sheba; Exodus; Hagar; Ishmaelites. D.B.

Shushan (sho͞o'shahn), the ancient capital of Elam (the southwestern area of modern Iran), which reached its height of importance as the residence and especially the winter capital of the kings of Persia. Called "Susa the capital" in Esther 1:2 (and Neh. 1:1), it provides the setting for the story of Esther and Mordecai. Daniel is also placed in Shushan during the reign of Belshazzar (Dan. 8:2).

Archaeological work has determined the outlines of the history of Shushan from the fourth millennium B.C. until after its capture by Arabian armies in the seventh century A.D. Excavation has centered on the impressive remains of the royal palace and city as well as the acropolis. Shiite Muslim tradition later located Daniel's tomb there. The city was also the site of a huge marriage ceremony of about ten thousand men from the army of Alexander the Great with Persian women in 324 B.C. ***See also*** Esther; Persia. W.L.H.

Shushan Eduth (shōō'shan ee'duth; Heb., "Lily of Testimony"), a part of the title of Psalm 60 that referred performers to a melody or song patterns to be used. Such song patterns and melodies have since been lost.

Shuthelah (shōō'thuh-luh), the founder of an Ephraimite clan, the Shuthelahites (Num. 26: 35–36). The Ephraimite mentioned in 1 Chron. 7:21–22 may be the same person, although on the other hand different generations may be indicated.

shuttle. ***See*** Spinning and Weaving.

Sia (sī'ah), a family of Temple servants who returned from exile in Babylonia who worked at the reconstruction of the city of Jerusalem (Neh. 7:47). They are probably identical to the "Siaha" of Ezra 2:44 (cf. 1 Esd. 5:29).

Sibbecai (sib'uh-kī), a Hushamite who killed a giant named Saph (2 Sam. 21:18) in the battles against the Philistines at Gob (Gezer in 1 and 2 Chronicles). Identified as a Zerahite (1 Chron. 27:11), he commanded David's forces in the eighth month and was among the elite of the thirty mighty men (1 Chron. 11:29; the same person may be named "Mebunnai" in 2 Sam. 23: 27).

Sibmah (sib'muh), a place in the rich Moabite plateau allocated to the tribe of Reuben (Num. 32:38; "Sebam" in 32:3; Josh. 13:19). In later prophetic oracles it was described as Moabite territory (Isa. 16:6–9; Jer. 48:31–32) known for vineyards. It may be modern Qurn el-Kibsh some five miles southwest of Hesban.

sickle, an instrument with a simple or compound blade set as a small curve and rigged with a handle to allow short horizontal strokes for cutting grass, weeds, or grains. Early models recovered are compound blades of serrated flint segments fastened in a wooden frame with bitumen. Later models include metal blades, but the use of flint continued long into the Bronze and Iron ages. A quick sweeping arc at the stems held by the other hand would be an efficient use of the tool. Biblical references to its use in harvest are numerous (Deut. 16:9; 23:25; Jer. 50:16; Joel 3:13; Mark 4:29) and it appears metaphorically as a tool of the harvest of human life at the Last Judgment (Rev. 14:14–20). R.S.B.

Iron sickle, which represents the type of tools the Philistines manufactured and supplied to the Israelites.

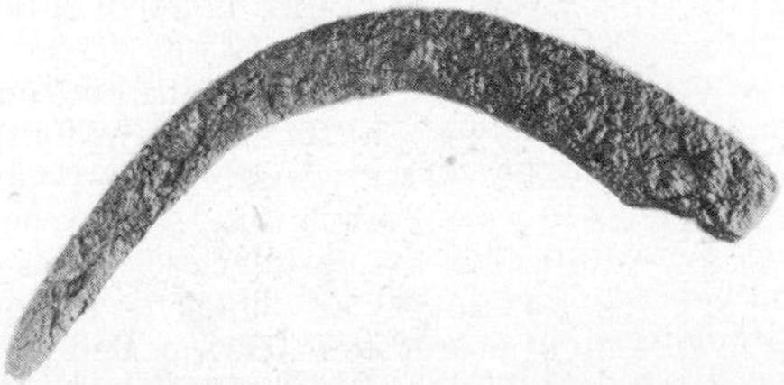

Siddim (sid'im), **Valley of,** depression at the south end of the Dead Sea (Gen. 14:3, 8, 10) that was the scene of a war between four eastern kings and the monarchs of five local cities. The location is most likely the eastern shore of the Lisan projection, from modern Bab edh-Dhra south.

side locks, hair alongside the temples which, like the corner of a beard, was not to be cut in a prohibition of what was apparently a pagan mourning practice (Lev. 19:27; see also 21:5).

Sidon (sī'duhn), one of the two leading cities (with Tyre) of ancient Phoenicia. Sidon is located twenty-two miles north of Tyre on the Mediterranean coast of modern Lebanon. Substantial archaeological investigation is not possible because of the modern city on the site, but a Crusader sea castle lies some meters offshore on the north side of Sidon while the ruins of a medieval land castle and an ancient heap of murex shells are on the south side of the town. It possesses a port with an inner and outer harbor on the north side and another on the south. Immediately outside Sidon stone round houses of the Chalcolithic period (4000–3000 B.C.) have been found, and the neighborhood cemeteries of the Babylonian to Late Roman periods (ca. 625 B.C.–A.D. 324) have produced numerous sarcophagi, the most famous of which (now in Istanbul) depicts Alexander the Great in battle and hunting scenes carved in marble.

In the Amarna Age (fourteenth century B.C.) King Zimrida of Sidon wrote two letters to the pharaoh of Egypt. In one he professed his loyalty and requested Egyptian aid in regaining territory that had fallen to *Habiru* rebels. But in other correspondence the kings of Byblos and Tyre portrayed Zimrida as having joined the rebellion and allied himself with Aziru, king of Amurru, against them and Egypt. At the beginning of the Iron Age (ca. 1200 B.C.) Sidonian colonists refounded Tyre, according to classical tradition. The Egyptian *Tale of Wenamun,* dated to the mid-eleventh century B.C., mentions the presence of fifty ships in the port of Sidon. It may have outclassed Tyre during the first centuries (1200–1000 B.C.) of the Iron Age, but during most of the Phoenician period Tyre led or controlled Sidon despite the fact that from the Greek perspective of the Homeric poems the term Phoenician was synonymous with Sidon. For example, the Assyrian king Sennacherib in 701 B.C. defeated Luli, whom he called king of Sidon but who is almost certainly the same as Elulaeus, king of Tyre. In the seventh century B.C. Sidon was besieged by King Esarhaddon of Assyria who razed the city (677 B.C.) and built in its place an Assyrian residence nearby called Kar-Esarhaddon.

Sidon's fortunes improved during the Persian period (539–332 B.C.), due in part to the decline of Tyre following a thirteen-year siege (586–573 B.C.) by the Babylonian king Nebuchadnezzar and in part to the favor bestowed upon Sidon by Persian monarchs. The mainland settlement of Sidon may have been more tractable than island Tyre, which submitted but remained unconquered. Phoenician refusal to support the Persian king Cambyses' planned attack on North Africa, where Tyre's chief colonies were located, may have been led by Tyre.

Cambyses conquered Egypt in 526 B.C. with the aid of the Phoenicians. King Tabnit of Sidon ruled about this time and it may be no accident that he was buried in an Egyptian general's reused stone sarcophagus upon which Tabnit left his own inscription. His mummified body in it revealed him to be a strong man, 5 feet 5 inches tall, with wavy reddish-brown hair tinted with henna. The sarcophagus of his son, King Eshmunazar II, possessed a Phoenician inscription of twenty-two lines from which we learn that he built several temples for Astarte at Sidon and for Eshmun at a mountain spring and that Sidon was given possession of Dor and Joppa south of Tyre. His father, King Tabnit, was a priest of Astarte and his mother, Amo'ashtart, was priestess of Astarte and both were offspring of Eshmunazar I, king of Sidon. The sanctuary of Eshmun on a hillside a few miles away at the river Nahr el-Awali has been excavated by M. Dunand and others, revealing important buildings, inscriptions, and statuary of the Babylonian, Persian, and Hellenistic periods dedicated to Eshmun. He was the god of healing and was equated with the Greek deity Asclepius. In the Persian Wars, when Darius and Xerxes attacked Greek city-states, King Tetramnestus and his fleet of three hundred Sidonian triremes (warships with three banks of oars) led the Persian navy.

In 351 B.C., on the enthronement of Artaxerxes III Ochus in Persia, Sidon revolted. King Tennes led Sidon in rebellion, but when the Persians reacted and the cause looked hopeless Tennes treacherously betrayed Sidon in order to save himself. The city was burned and, although rebuilt, did not regain its former position. Sidon quickly submitted to Alexander the Great in 332 B.C. and assisted him in the siege of Tyre. During the Hellenistic and Roman periods Sidon was a prosperous center for commerce and learning.

Sidon is mentioned frequently in the OT prophetic books, often in conjunction with Tyre (e.g., Isa. 23:2, 4, 12; Jer. 25:22; Ezek. 28:21–22; Joel 3:4; Zech. 9:2) and the area was visited by Jesus (Matt. 15:21; Mark 7:24) and Paul (Acts 27:3).

Bibliography

Jidejian, N. *Sidon Through the Ages.* Beirut: Dar el-Machreq, 1971.

Katzenstein, H. J. "Tyre in the Early Persian Period (539–486 B.C.E.). *Biblical Archeologist* 42:1 (1979):23–34.

T.L.M.

siege, the military tactic of surrounding a community, cutting off its supplies and rescue aid, and reducing its resistance to the point of surrender or destruction. It can also refer to any prolonged distress or suffering.

Biblical references to siegeworks, siege towers, and siege mounds indicate common experience with the process. Only unfruitful trees were permitted to be cut for preparing siegeworks against an enemy city (Deut. 20:20). Babylon built siegeworks against Jerusalem under Nebuchadnezzar (2 Kings 25:1). Metaphorically, Job speaks of God's treating him that way (Job 19:12) and the helplessness of siegeworks in the face of a wise man is touted by Ecclesiastes (9:14–15). Isaiah sees God besieging Jerusalem (Ariel) with towers and siegeworks (29:3), as does Ezekiel (4:2), and Daniel (11:15) sees it used against the king of the south (the Ptolemies). Ezekiel's description is quite graphic and accurate, combining a siege wall (the Romans in a later period built one entirely surrounding Masada, remains of which are still visible from the summit as well as ground level), a mound (the ramp is still visible also at Masada), camps (also visible at Masada), and battering rams (most graphically presented in the bas-reliefs from the palace of Sennacherib at Nineveh showing the Assyrian conquest of Lachish, but known also from Nimrud).

Siege tactics also included sapping under the defender's walls, ramming the gates, storming the gates and walls with ladders or towers, or setting fire to the wooden materials in the defense system. One of the longest sieges in biblical history occurred at Samaria; the city held out for three years against the Assyrians before capitulating in 722 B.C. ***See also*** War; Weapons.

R.S.B.

sieve, a perforated plate or screen used for separating grain from chaff or various sized grains from each other. Earlier models used woven hair, grass, or small reeds set in flat, round rims or held in a concave basin form to allow shaking motions that would agitate the contents and separate them. Biblical usage is mainly metaphorical for the discipline of God (Amos 9:9) or his judgment (Isa. 30:28; Luke 22:31).

sign, a significant event, act, or other manifestation that betokens God's presence or intention. Signs may be miraculous and spectacular, as in the case of those performed by Moses before the people of Israel to demonstrate that God had sent him to them (Exod. 4:1–9, 17, 30) or before Pharaoh for the same purpose (Exod. 7–11). On the other hand, a natural phenomenon such as a rainbow or a sunset may be called a sign (Gen. 9:13; Ps. 65:8), as may an identifying mark such as circumcision (Gen. 17:11) or even a prophet and his children (Isa. 8:18).

In the NT, signs tend to be apocalyptic or miraculous, but the shepherds are told that the infant Jesus "wrapped in swaddling cloths and lying in a manger" (Luke 2:12) will be a sign of God's salvation. When Jesus is asked about a sign indicating the coming destruction of the Temple (Mark 13:4), he responds in terms of natural, if catastrophic, events (Mark 13:5–13). These phenomena are usually described as apocalyptic and merge with more distinctly supernatural events predicted later on in the same discourse (Mark 13:24–27).

In the synoptic Gospels, when Jesus is asked to perform or manifest a sign, he refuses (Mark 8:11–12; Matt. 12:38–39) and denounces the quest for signs (cf. John 4:48). Yet Paul speaks of miraculous apostolic signs (2 Cor. 12:12), and Jesus is characterized in Acts 2:22 as "a man attested to you by God with mighty works and wonders and signs which God did through him in your midst." In the Gospel of John, Jesus repeatedly performs signs that are intended to evoke faith in him (2:11), although they also cause offense (11:47–48), and the Evangelist seems to be aware of the inadequacies of miracle faith (i.e., faith based on signs) except as the beginning point for a more adequate perception and understanding of Jesus (2:23–25; but cf. 20: 30–31). ***See also*** Miracles. D.M.S.

signet. ***See*** Seal.

Sihon (sī'hahn), a king of the Amorites whose capital was Heshbon, a city lying east of the northern tip of the Dead Sea. The etymology of his name is obscure, as are the circumstances of his origins. According to the OT Sihon opposed the Israelites as they sought to move from the south through Transjordan. The two forces clashed at Jahaz, resulting in the defeat of Sihon and the incorporation of his territory into the Israelite tribal holdings (Num. 21:21–30; Deut. 2:24–37; Judg. 11:18–22). While the Israelites were not to inherit Moabite or Ammonite territory, the area attributed to Sihon's kingdom and claimed by Israel seems to have included some territory also claimed by Ammon and Moab.

Recent archaeological work in the general area attributed to Sihon—essentially the area between the headwaters of the Jabbok and the Arnon—has shown some occupational evidence dating to the Late Bronze Age and earliest Iron Age (fifteenth to twelfth centuries B.C.). None of this evidence relates directly to Sihon with the exception of the excavations at Tell Hesban, north of Madeba. Only scattered twelfth-century B.C. artifacts have been found there, and they give indication of a very small settlement during the end of the period assigned to Sihon. Nevertheless the memory of this defeat lived on in Israelite consciousness (1 Kings 4:19; Ps. 135:11; 136:19; Neh. 9:22). J.A.D.

Silas, Silvanus (sī'luhs, sil-vay'nuhs), generally regarded as alternate names for the same person, a leader in the early church and an associate of Paul. The Letters of Paul and 1 Peter refer to him as Silvanus (a Latinization), but Acts prefers Silas (either a Semitic or a shortened Greek form). According to Acts 15:22–35, Silas and Judas Barsabbas, prophets in the Jerusalem church, were sent along with Paul and Barnabas to take the apostolic decrees from the Jerusalem conference to the church in Antioch. Silas's background was probably similar to that of Barnabas and John Mark, and it was thus perhaps no accident that they encountered one another more than once in early Christian history. For example, when Paul and Barnabas at Antioch quarreled over Mark (Acts 15:36–41), Paul chose Silas to accompany him on a mission tour in Asia Minor and ultimately into Macedonia and Achaia (Acts 15:41–18:5).

Silvanus (Silas) is mentioned in the Letters of Paul (1 Thess. 1:1; 2 Thess. 1:1; 2 Cor. 1:19) and in 1 Peter (5:12). Except in 2 Cor. 1:19, he is connected with the writing of the Letters. He is either a co-author (in the case of Paul) or a secretary or courier (in the case of 1 Peter).

Certainly Silas was an important figure in the churches in Macedonia (Acts 18:18 suggests that he may have remained in Macedonia when Paul left) and may have been regarded as an apostle (1 Thess. 2:6; cf. 2 Cor. 1:19). His early connections with the church in Jerusalem were no doubt helpful in giving added theological legitimacy to the Pauline mission. Silas's Roman citizenship, reported in Acts 16:37–38, would also have been of considerable personal help to Paul on his travels. ***See also*** Barnabas; Barsabbas; Mark; Paul; Peter, The First Letter of. A.J.M.

Siloam (sī-loh'uhm) **Inscription,** a Hebrew inscription recovered from the Siloam tunnel in Jerusalem. The text commemorates the excavation of the tunnel, which connected the spring of Gihon, the principal source of water for ancient Jerusalem, with a reservoir within the city known as the pool of Siloam.

The Gihon arises on the eastern slope of the

Cast of the Siloam Inscription originally carved on the wall of Hezekiah's tunnel, Jerusalem, describing the construction and completion of the tunnel, which connected the Gihon spring to the Pool of Siloam; eighth century B.C.

Ophel, the southeastern hill of Jerusalem, upon which the City of David was located. Originally, therefore, it emptied into the Kidron Valley. After the occupation of the site, however, an open basin was dug at the mouth of the spring to collect the waters. From this basin, known as "the upper pool," the waters were conveyed south along the slope of the city mound by an aqueduct called "the conduit of the upper pool" (2 Kings 18:17; Isa. 7:3). Recent excavation has shown that this aqueduct was in part a tunnel and in part an open canal, so that in addition to receiving the flow from the upper pool it collected rainwater from the slope of the mound. It contained a number of "windows," through which water could be released for the irrigation of the valley below. The reference in Isa. 8:6 to "the waters of Shiloah that flow gently" probably reveals the name for this water system that was in use during the reign of Ahaz. "Siloam" is a later, Greek form of "Shiloah." At the mouth of the aqueduct was another reservoir called "the lower pool" (Isa. 22:9). "The Pool of Shelah" (Neh. 3:15) and "King's Pool" (Neh. 2:14) are probably other names for this second reservoir.

Because the original Shiloah or Siloam channel lay outside the fortifications of the city, it was difficult to protect during a siege. As part of his preparations for Sennacherib's attack on Jerusalem, therefore, Hezekiah sealed the old outlet of the upper pool (2 Chron. 32:2–4, 30; cf. Isa. 22:8–11) and devised an underground passage to divert the flow of the Gihon to a reservoir within the fortified precincts of the city (2 Kings 20:20), evidently the "reservoir between the two walls" of Isa. 22:11. The shaft of Hezekiah's tunnel followed a sinuous path through 1,749 feet of bedrock under the City of David to a new pool on the western slope of the Ophel in the valley later known as Tyropoeon. The name of the older aqueduct was transferred to the new system. The first century Jewish historian Josephus knew the western reservoir as Siloam, and in John 9:7 Jesus refers to it as "the pool of Siloam." However, the modern village of Silwan, which also preserves a form of the ancient name, is located across the Kidron to the east of the Gihon spring.

The Inscription, now in the Museum of the Ancient Orient in Istanbul, was found in 1880 by two boys wading inside the tunnel some 20 feet above the western reservoir. It consists of six lines incised on the lower part of a prepared surface on the rock wall of the shaft. The blank upper surface has led some scholars to suppose that part of the inscription is missing; others believe that the text was originally intended to be surmounted by a relief. The Inscription cannot be dated long before 701 B.C., the year of Sennacherib's siege of Jerusalem. The script is the Hebrew lapidary hand of the eighth century B.C., and the language is comparable to the standard Hebrew prose of the Bible. The text describes the completion of Hezekiah's tunnel by two crews who, having set to work from opposite directions, dug until only three cubits (ca. 4.5 feet) of rock separated them at a point one hundred cubits (ca. 150 feet) beneath the streets of the city. From there they were able to guide each other through the remaining rock by shouting. This was possible, we are told, because of something extending north and south in the rock. Perhaps this was a fissure, as the translation below suggests, but the Hebrew word is obscure.

The Inscription may be translated as follows:

1. The [ ] of the penetration. This is how the penetration took place. While [the diggers were] still [wielding]

2. their axes towards each other, with three cubits still to be pen[etrated, they could he]ar each other sho-

3. uting, for there was a *fissure* in the rock running to the south [and to the nor]th. So at the moment of pene-

4. tration, the diggers struck towards each other, axe against axe. Then the waters flowed

5. from the spring to the pool—one thousand two hundred cubits. And one h[un-]

6. dred cubits was the height of the rock above the heads of the digger[s]. P.K.M.

Silvanus (sil-vay'nuhs). ***See*** Silas, Silvanus.

silver (Heb. *kesep*), a pale, precious metal capable of being hammered or drawn out thin, known to people of Bible lands as early as 3000 B.C.

Silver mining and metallurgy were known and practiced by craftsmen at Ebla (Tell Mardikh in Syria). Some Ebla texts show the value of cattle in silver, and list silver as tribute from Mari, recording once as much as 2188 minas of silver (1 mina equals 47 grams). Silver bars, daggers, adze-heads, and small ceremonial shovels are in evidence from biblical times, as are pieces of jewelry and amulets. Silver was used as a standard for business transactions and as a measure of wealth. Excavations at Ur of artifacts from ca. 2500 B.C. show Sumerian use of silver for musical instruments, pipes, statuettes, and filigree jewelry.

The source of silver in antiquity for the Bible lands was likely western Asia Minor and particularly the islands of the Aegean. The 1984 explorations by H. G. Bachmann may be able to pin the source specifically to the island of Sifnos, one of the Aegean Cyclades group. The Laurion mine near Athens was in use by 1000 B.C. as a source of silver. Spain's Rio Tinto silver mines were likely the source of silver for Phoenician and Roman coinage.

Among the most recent archaeological findings in Jerusalem are two little silver scrolls bearing texts that include God's name in Hebrew. While the divine name Yahweh has been found on inscriptions in other parts of the country, this is the first time this name has appeared on an archaeological find in Jerusalem. The scroll dates to the sixth century B.C.

The first biblical reference to silver from among the approximately four hundred OT passages from Genesis to Malachi is Gen. 13:2, where Abraham's possession of silver along with his cattle and gold mark him as a wealthy man. He purchased the burial cave at Machpelah from Ephron the Hittite for four hundred shekels of weighed silver (Gen. 23:16). Joseph, the Hebrew in Pharaoh's court (ca. 1750 B.C.), had a silver cup which he placed in his brother Benjamin's sack (Gen. 44:2, 5, 12, 16). Later he gave Benjamin "three hundred shekels of silver" (Gen. 45:22). As early as the period of the judges (ca. 1200–1000 B.C.), the Israelites knew of silver craftsmanship, as reported in Judges where Micah's mother took eleven hundred pieces of silver to a silversmith for fashioning an idol (Judg. 17:1–6).

Other OT references include silver used for foundations, decorations, vessels for worship, and trumpets for the tabernacle (Exod. 26:19; 27:10, 17; 36:24, 26; Num. 7:13, 14; 10:2), and the Jerusalem Temple with its treasury (1 Kings 7:51; 1 Chron. 28:15, 16; 2 Chron. 2:7; Ezra 8: 26, 28; Neh. 7:71). Figuratively, silver and the refining process are used to show the testing of people's hearts (Ps. 66:10; Isa. 48:10), great abundance (Zech. 9:3; Isa. 60:17; Job 3:15; 22: 25; 27:16), and either positively the brightness of a dove's wings (Ps. 68:13) and the purity of God's word (Ps. 12:6) or negatively the corrosive deterioration of God's people (Jer. 6:30; Isa. 1:22). Silver was known in the raw state (1 Kings 15:15; Exod. 31:4; 35:24, 32) as well as mined (Job 28:1) and well refined (Prov. 10:20; 1 Chron. 29:4; Mal. 3:2, 3; Ezek. 22:20). Long before coinage silver was known as a standard of wealth (Gen. 13:2; 24:35; Exod. 25:3; Num. 22:18) and was weighed out for payment of an obligation by measures such as the shekel, talent, or mina (Gen. 20:16; Exod. 21:32; Lev. 27: 16; Josh. 24:32). Silver was used for special articles of value or prestige such as Joseph's drinking cup (Gen. 44:2), a royal crown of silver and gold (Zech. 6:11), and as jewelry given to Rebekah (Gen. 24:53); as booty received from Egyptian women (Exod. 3:22); and as silver-studded ornaments for Solomon's bride (Song of Sol. 1:11). Oppositely, silver was often a material for idols as early as the Exodus and Judges and as decried in the prophets (Exod. 20:23; Judg. 17:4; Isa. 2:20; Jer. 10:4; Dan. 2:32, 33; Hos. 13:2).

The NT mentions silver vessels (2 Tim. 2:20), idols (Rev. 9:20), and shrines to Artemis of Ephesus made by Demetrius the silversmith who feared Paul's preaching (Acts 19:23–27). Money had no ransoming power (1 Pet. 1:18). Peter had no silver (Acts 3:6) and Paul earned none for preaching (Acts 20:33). Books on magic arts burned by new Christians at Ephesus were valued at fifty thousand pieces of silver (Acts 19: 19). Judas received thirty pieces of silver for his betrayal of Jesus (Matt. 26:15; 27:3, 5, 6, 9). Generally belittled in the NT, silver cannot be compared to the Deity (Acts 17:29) or Christ (1 Cor. 3:12). Wealth measured in silver corrodes and corrupts (James 5:3) and brings only weeping instead of joy (Rev. 18:22). Disciples of Jesus take no silver on their missionary ventures (Matt. 10:9). R.A.C.

Simeon (sim'ee-uhn; Heb., "to hear"). **1** The second son of Jacob and Leah (Gen. 29:33). Simeon and his brother Levi massacred the men of Shechem to avenge the rape of their sister Dinah (Gen. 34). Simeon was later held hostage in Egypt when Joseph sent the other brothers back to Canaan for Benjamin (Gen. 42:24). Subsequently Simeon and his six sons migrated to Egypt with the entire family of Jacob (Gen. 46: 10; Num. 26:12–14; 1 Chron. 4:24). In Jacob's blessing, Simeon was rebuked because of his actions at Shechem and was told his descendants would be divided and scattered (Gen. 49: 5–7).

The tribe of Simeon was given an allotment within the tribal territory of Judah in the southernmost region of Canaan. Their cities included Beer-sheba, in the center of the Negev; Ziklag (possibly modern Tell Sheri'ah) and Sharuhen (modern Tell el Far'ah?) in the western Negev; and Hormah (modern Tell Malhata?) in the eastern Negev (Josh. 19:1–9). Simeon joined forces with the tribe of Judah during the early phase of the Israelite conquest of Canaan (Judg. 1:3–17). Simeon's subsequent history is shrouded in silence. In the days of Hezekiah (727–698 B.C.) the tribe achieved a military victory over the Amalekites, the perennial enemy of the inhabitants of the Negev (1 Chron. 4:41–43). During the Divided Monarchy (tenth to eighth centuries B.C.) Simeon seems to have been reckoned as one of the ten tribes belonging to the Northern Kingdom (cf. 1 Kings 11:30–32; 12:20–23; 2 Chron. 15:9). Little else is known of its fate; it is not mentioned after the Exile (586 B.C.). **2** An ancestor of Jesus according to Luke's genealogy (Luke 3:30). **3** An early, devout man of Jerusalem during the days of Herod who was looking for "the consolation of Israel" (Luke 2:25–35). He had been promised by the Holy Spirit that he would see the Messiah before he died. Simeon recognized the infant Jesus as the Messiah when Jesus' parents presented him at the Temple. He held the infant in his arms and praised God, "For mine eyes have seen thy salvation" (v. 30). He declared, "This child is set for the fall and rising of many in Israel" (v. 34). **4** The Hebrew name of Simon Peter ("Symeon"; 2 Pet. 1:1 in Greek; Acts 15:14, although the Symeon there may be Symeon Niger mentioned in Acts 13:1; see 5). **5** A Christian at Antioch with prophetic and teaching gifts, who served the church there together with Barnabas and Saul prior to the latter's first missionary journey (Acts 13:1). His surname, Niger (Lat., "black"), suggests that he was an African. D.A.D.

Simon. **1** Simon Maccabeus, the son of Mattathias Hashmon, a ruler in Palestine (142–134 B.C.). **2** Simon Peter, one of the twelve apostles (Matt. 10:2; Mark 3:16; Luke 6:14). **3** The second "Simon" among the Twelve, otherwise called Simon "the Zealot" (Luke 6:15; Acts 1:13) or "the Cananaean" (Matt. 10:4; Mark 3:18). **4** Judas Iscariot's father (John 6:71; 13:2, 26). **5** One of Jesus' brothers (Matt. 13:55; Mark 6:3). **6** The leper of Bethany in whose house Jesus was anointed with "very expensive ointment" (Matt. 26:6–13; Mark 14:3–9). **7** The Pharisee whose house was the scene of Jesus' anointing by a "sinful" woman (Luke 7:36–50, likely a variant verison of 6). **8** "A man of Cyrene" (North Africa) identified by Mark as father of Alexander and Rufus, who was compelled to carry Jesus' cross (Matt. 27:32; Mark 15:21; Luke 23:26). **9** The leatherworker (tanner) in Joppa with whom Peter remained "for many days"; during this stay Peter had his vision of the clean and unclean animals (Acts 9:43; 10:5–6, 32). **10** Simon Magus, a magician from Samaria (Acts 8:9–24); ***see*** Simon Magus. ***See also*** Alexander; Apostle; Bethany; Brothers; Cananaean; Cyrene; Disciple; Joppa; Judas; Peter; Pharisees; Rufus; Tanning; Twelve, The; Zealot. P.L.S.

Simon Magus (sī'muhn may'guhs), a magician ("Magus" is from the Gk. for "magic," cf. Acts 8:11) in Samaria who became a Christian believer and was baptized as a result of the preaching of Philip, according to Acts 8:9–24. Subsequently, however, he was excoriated by Peter for attempting to purchase the power of the Holy Spirit. Thus, in Acts, he becomes both a negative model for the superiority of the Spirit of Christ over magic and, like Ananias and Sapphira, of the folly of greed (cf. Acts 5:1–11).

Acts, which calls him simply Simon, tells us nothing about his origins. Perhaps he was not a Samaritan but lived among the strictly Gentile population of the area. The name Magus appears in later legends about him in the Clementine literature (a series of writings that deal with St. Clement of Rome and name him as author) and the church fathers, where he is either an opponent of Peter or an early Gnostic. Although in Acts Simon apparently repents (8: 24), some later Christian writers regarded him as the veritable father of heresy (cf. Acts 8:10: "This man is that power of God which is called Great"). ***See also*** Ananias; Gnosticism; Holy Spirit, The; Magic and Divination; Peter; Philip; Samaria, District of; Sapphira. A.J.M.

simple, term with the connotation of "unsuspecting" (Heb. *tom;* 2 Sam. 15:11) referring to someone who is naive, foolish, easily deceived, and led into evil (Heb. *pethi*; Job 5:2; translated by different expression in Deut. 11:16; Hos. 7:11; Prov. 20:19). It is also used to refer to persons whose innocence makes them an easy target for deceit (Rom. 16:18).

Sin (KJV; RSV: "Pelusium"), the "strength of Egypt" (RSV: "stronghold of Egypt") which, according to Ezek. 30:15, is one of the places destroyed by the Babylonian king Nebuchadnezzar. The Hebrew word comes directly from the Egyptian *sin*, "fortress." Sin was an important stronghold protecting Egypt's northeast frontier. The Pyramid Texts of the Old Kingdom mention Sin as the provenience of good wine. A prince of Sin is mentioned in the Assyrian Annals of Ashurbanipal. Called Pelusium by the Greeks, Sin has been identified with modern Tell Farama, situated in the northeast corner of the Nile delta about twenty-four miles southeast of Port Said. This site has never been systematically excavated. ***See also*** Nebuchadnezzar. J.M.W.

sin, that which is in opposition to God's benevolent purposes for his creation. According to the biblical writers, sin is an ever-present reality that enslaves the human race and has corrupted God's created order. The concept of sin is first and foremost a religious concept, because all sin is ultimately against God, God's laws, God's creation, God's covenant, and God's purposes. It is the basic corrupting agent in the entire universe.

There are numerous Hebrew and Greek words used to designate sin in the biblical writings. Perhaps the most basic is a Hebrew word meaning "revolt" or "transgression" and indicating a deliberate act of defiance against God. This idea lies at the heart of the Genesis account of the beginning of sin (Gen. 3:1–7), where the essential problem lies in the desire of the humans to "be like God." All sin is an act of idolatry, the attempt to replace the Creator with someone or something else, usually one's own self or one's own creation. Paul understood this very well, as he indicates in Rom. 1:18–3:20: all humankind lies under condemnation because all are idolators of one type or another.

Manifestations: From this basic idea derive most of the other ideas connected with the attempt to describe the many different manifestations of sin. There is sin that is characterized by falling short of God's requirements or "missing the mark"; there are cultic sins (failure to observe the ritual requirements), political and social sins, and "spiritual" sins (e.g., envy, hate, etc.). In the NT, there is the "unforgiveable" sin (against the Holy Spirit), which, in modern terms, might be paraphrased as an attitude or mind-set wherein a person willfully refuses to accept the forgiveness of sin offered by God through his Son (Matt. 12:22–32; Mark 3:19b–30; Luke 12:8–10; cf. also 1 John 5:16–17). There is sin implicit in the failure of a person to do right, especially toward one's fellow human beings (e.g., Matt. 25:31–46; Luke 16:19–31), the failure of a person to use God-given ability (e.g., Matt. 25:14–30; Luke 19:12–26), and there is sin even in ignorance, where one commits unconscious or inadvertent sin (e.g., Lev. 5). Perhaps the most heinous sins are those done "with a high hand" (i.e., deliberately and arrogantly; e.g., Num. 15:30–31) and the sin of hypocrisy, especially among "religious" persons (e.g., Matt. 23; Acts 5:1–11).

Universality: Because sin is such an integral feature of human experience, both individual and corporate, many people have argued for a doctrine of "original sin," i.e., sin that is "born into" persons as human beings. There is no passage in the Bible that directly teaches such a doctrine, but there are many that certainly point to the universality and even inevitability of sin in human life. The OT prophets, for example, located the source of sin in the "heart," i.e., in the very depth of one's being, the seat of volition and action (e.g., especially Jer. 5:23; 17:9–10; cf. Ezek. 36:26; Isa. 29:13). In the NT, Paul insists that "all people, both Jews and Greeks, are under the power of sin" (Rom. 3:9; cf. 1:18–3:20; 5:12–21). The words of the author of 1 John rise up in the face of any notion that sin can be totally overcome and avoided in this world: "If we say we have no sin, we deceive ourselves, and the truth is not in us. . . . If we say we have not sinned, we make him a liar, and his word is not in us" (1:8–10).

Origin: As for the origin of sin, the OT writings have very little to say about the matter, the story in Genesis 3 being the only passage to speak directly to this issue. During the intertestamental period (ca. the last three centuries B.C.), however, many ideas were prevalent about the origin of sin. Most of the speculation focused on the story in Genesis 3 and the additional story in Gen. 6:1–4 about divine creatures having intercourse with human women. As a result of the development of later religious thinking regarding demons and Satan, many linked sin to an outside power that forced its way into the human situation. Others believed that humans were born with conflicting "inclinations," one toward good and one toward evil. These inclinations were constantly struggling to obtain controlling influence in each person's life. In the NT, Paul related the sinful condition of the human race to the original transgression of Adam, insisting at the same time, however, that the result of sin (death) "spread to all people" not simply because of Adam's sin but "because all people sinned" (Rom. 5:12).

God's Activity: Whatever the origin of sin, the

cumulative testimony of the biblical writers is that sin is universal, something that enslaves every person individually and that corrupts society collectively. Further, the enslavement of sin is something from which the human race cannot extricate itself by its own efforts. Perhaps the most persistent motif permeating the pages of the Bible is that of human sin and God's activity in dealing with it. In the OT writings, the emphasis is upon God's covenant with the Hebrew people, the establishment of a new relationship between God and the people such that all people could somehow learn about and enter into the proper divine–human relationship. In the NT writings, the emphasis is upon an even closer relationship between God and humankind through the new covenant in Jesus of Nazareth. Through Jesus, the Kingdom of God has been proclaimed and inaugurated, sinners have been forgiven and reconciled to God, and a new relationship has been established that will bring the hopes, dreams, and aspirations of all the biblical writers to fulfillment. This is to be accomplished through the work of God in Christ to break the enslaving power of sin and liberate people from its sway. People must, however, participate in the process and in the struggle (e.g., Rom. 7). ***See also*** Atonement; Demon; Devil; Evil; Expiation; Fall, The; Forgiveness; Grace; Guilt; Holiness; Justification; Pardon; Reconciliation; Redemption; Regeneration; Salvation; Sanctification; Satan. J.M.E.

Sin, Wilderness of, an area distinct from the "Wilderness of Zin." The Wilderness of Sin was a desert area "between Elim and Sinai" (Exod. 16:1), where the Israelites "murmured against Moses and Aaron" (Exod. 16:2–3), and where manna was first given to satisfy their hunger (Exod. 16:13–36). The Exodus is said to have continued to Rephidim via Dophkah and Alush (Exod. 17:1; Num. 33:11–12). Unfortunately, none of the places can be identified exactly, although it is possible that Dophkah is near the ancient Egyptian turquoise and copper mines at modern Serabit el-Khadim. If so, the Wilderness of Sin would be at the western foot of the Sinai massif. ***See also*** Elim; Rephidim; Sinai; Zin, Wilderness of. D.B.

Sinai (sī'nī; derivation uncertain, perhaps related to the Mesopotamian moon god Sin). **1** The Sinai Peninsula, a large, wedge-shaped block of territory that forms a land bridge between Africa and Asia. Sinai is bounded on the west by the Suez Canal and Gulf of Suez, while the Negeb and Gulf of Aqaba form the peninsula's eastern border. Sinai's northern and southern limits are clearly defined by the Mediterranean Sea and the Red Sea, respectively. Its total area is ca. twenty-four thousand square miles. The southern apex of this inverted triangle is ca. two hundred and forty miles from the Mediterranean shore; the northern base extends from Rapha to the Suez Canal, a distance of ca. one hundred and twenty-five miles.

Since it is actually part of the Saharo-Arabian desert, Sinai's climate is arid. The peninsula's extensive wadi system drains an annual rainfall that seldom exceeds 2.5 inches, except along the Mediterranean coast. More diversity is found in the geology and topography of Sinai's three major regions. The northern region consists of a low, sandy plateau and includes large tracts of sand dunes and some oases; this coastal zone has served as a thoroughfare for many ancient and modern armies. Sinai's central region is a high, limestone plateau that has little water and sparse vegetation. The peninsula's southern region is covered by rugged, granite mountains, some of whose peaks exceed 8,000 feet in elevation and are snow-capped in winter.

Although the Sinai Peninsula may appear to be inhospitable to human occupation, a number of settlements dot modern maps of this territory. The bedouin population alone numbers ca. fifty thousand. Recent archaeological research demonstrates that this wilderness has been occupied by sedentary and/or nomadic peoples, albeit intermittently and sparsely, for ca. thirty thousand years.

Naturally, the prehistoric inhabitants of Sinai had contacts with neighboring regions, but the earliest significant evidence of such connections dates to ca. 2650 B.C. At this early date, the Egyptians began mining Sinai's turquoise, an enterprise that led to later Egyptian activities in the peninsula. Most famous are the turquoise and copper mines at modern Serabit el-Khadem, a site in west-central Sinai that was worked throughout most of the second millennium B.C. The proto-Sinaitic inscriptions from Serabit el-Khadem date to ca. 1500 B.C. and represent the earliest stages in the development of a Semitic alphabet.

This script also serves as an example of the kinds of cultural exchanges that occurred in the Sinaitic corridor. Other contacts came through commercial and military activities in this region and, while the Bible notes that Sinai's environment was hostile (Deut. 1:19; 8:15), it also observes that Sinai was not impassable. When Abraham, Jacob, and the family of Jacob made their way between Canaan and Egypt, the trade routes across the peninsula were already well established. Many centuries later, Saul and David fought the Amalekites in northwestern Sinai (1 Sam. 15:7; 27:8), and Elijah made a pilgrimage to this region's famous mountain (1 Kings 19:8). Still later, Joseph, Mary, and Jesus entered the Sinai as they fled from Herod (Matt. 2:13).

Throughout its history, Sinai was crossed or occupied by many other peoples—Assyrians, Babylonians, Persians, Greeks, Nabateans, and Romans—but the most famous sojourn in this

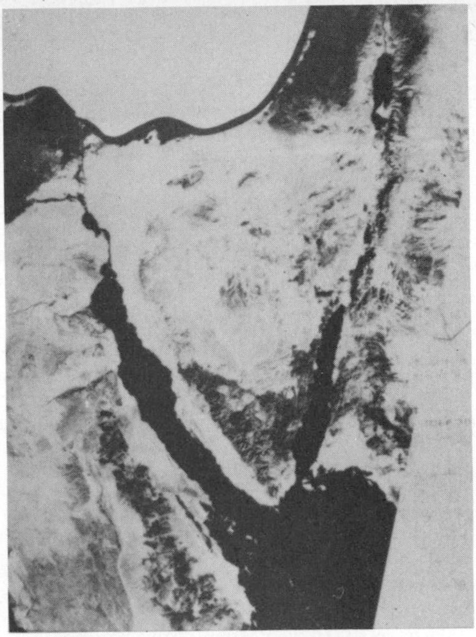

The Sinai Peninsula appears as an inverted triangle in this photo taken from an orbiting satellite.

wilderness was made by the Hebrews after the Exodus. Indeed, Sinai was the setting for some of the most important events in Israelite history. The OT does not, however, refer to the entire peninsula when it uses the word "Sinai." Instead, the OT mentions five smaller, distinct tracts of wilderness in this large territory (i.e., Shur, Sin, Sinai, Paran, and Zin).

2 The Wilderness of Sinai, the biblical name for the small, distinct wilderness region in which Mount Sinai was located. Its exact location cannot be ascertained, since its limits are defined in relation to other place names that also defy accurate pinpointing. In general, the Bible locates this tract of wasteland in between the wildernesses of Sin and Paran and in the vicinity of Elim, Rephidim, and Kibroth-hattaavah (Exod. 16:1; 19:1–2; Num. 10:12; 33:15–16). The traditional location of the wilderness of Sinai is in the south-central part of the peninsula. It was in this wilderness that the Israelites were encamped when they received the law (e.g., Exod. 19:1–2; Lev. 7:38), were numbered (Num. 1:19; 3:14; 26:64), and celebrated the Passover (Num. 9:5). It was also in the wilderness of Mount Sinai that Moses encountered the burning bush (Exod. 3:1–2; Acts 7:30, 38).

3 Mount Sinai, the mountain on which the law was delivered to Moses (Exod. 31:18; 34:29, 32; Lev. 26:46; 27:34; Neh. 9:13). The biblical writers refer to Mount Sinai by various names (e.g., "the mountain," "the mountain of God," "Mount Horeb," "the mountain of Horeb," and "the mountain of God in Horeb"). This mountain played a significant role in the spiritual development of Moses (Exod. 3:1–12), and its sacred character was magnified when Sinai became the locus of divine revelation par excellence (Exod. 19:18, 20, 23; 24:16; Deut. 33:2; Judg. 5:5; Ps. 68:8). Indeed, the Lord's presence on this peak came to symbolize divine protection (Judg. 5:4–5; Ps. 68:8). In his allegory of the two covenants, Paul uses Sinai to symbolize the old system (Gal. 4:24–25; see Heb. 12:19–21).

Although Exodus and Numbers provide many details concerning the itinerary followed by the Israelites in their trek from Egypt to the plains of Moab, few of these places can be identified with any certainty. In fact, the general direction of the wanderings in Sinai is still debated, although scholars usually choose between three alternate routes (i.e., a northern, central, or southern route). Consequently, the location of Mount Sinai is also disputed. As many as a dozen mountains in Sinai and northwestern Arabia have been identified with this sacred spot, but none of them has been accepted by all scholars. Since none of the theories concerning Mount Sinai's location is supported by archaeological evidence, consideration must be given to the Jewish, Christian, and Muslim traditions that relate to the proposed sites. Once this word of caution has been stated, one can safely say that Jebel Musa, or another mountain in its immediate vicinity, remains the most likely candidate. This identification assumes that the Israelites followed a southern route across the peninsula and places the wilderness of Sinai and its fabled mountain in south-central Sinai. ***See also*** Exodus; Horeb, Mount; Sin, Wilderness of.

Bibliography

Arden, Harvey. "Eternal Sinai." *National Geographic* April 1982: 90–102.

Beit-Arieh, Itzhaq. "Fifteen Years in Sinai." *Biblical Archaeology Review*. July/August 1984: 26–54.

Bernstein, Burton. *Sinai: The Great and Terrible Wilderness*. New York: Viking, 1979. G.L.M.

Sinaiticus, Codex. ***See*** Aleph.

sinew, a word that in biblical usage appears to cover a variety of anatomical elements including tendons, ligaments, and possibly muscle and other tissues. In Gen. 32:32 it may even refer to nerve tissue. It is used figuratively in Isa. 48:4 for stubbornness. In Job 10:11 and Ezek. 37:6, 8 the actual connective human tissues seem to be involved. "The sinews of his thighs" in Job 40:17 in the description of an animal in sexual arousal or anger may refer to the penis or related organs.

Sinim (sin'eem, KJV; RSV: "Syene"). ***See*** Syene.

Sinites (sī'nīts), a Canaanite tribe (Gen. 10:17; 1 Chron. 1:15). They have usually been associated with Lebanon or Phoenicia, but nothing about such a location is certain.

sin offering. ***See*** Worship.

Sion (sī'uhn), the term in the KJV where the RSV has "Sirion" (Deut. 4:48) or "Zion" (Matt. 21:5 and other NT texts). ***See also*** Sirion.

Sirach (sī'rak), **Son of** (Heb. *Ben Sirach*), the author of Ecclesiasticus, also known as The Wisdom of Sirach. ***See also*** Apocrypha, Old Testament; Ecclesiasticus.

Sirah (sī'rah), **the cistern of** (KJV: "the Well of Sirah"), the location from which the rebellious Absalom was called by Joab who subsequently killed him (2 Sam. 3:26–27). It is probably near Hebron, but its location is not precisely known. ***See also*** Absalom; Joab.

Sirion (sihr'ee-uhn), the name used for Mt. Hermon by the people of Sidon (Deut. 3:9; 4:48). Ps. 29:6 employs the word in parallel poetic construction with Lebanon, as does Jer. 18:14, reinforcing the reference to Mt. Hermon despite some variations in the Hebrew text.

Siron (sī'rahn). ***See*** Senir; Sion.

Sisera (si'se-ruh), the commander of nine-hundred chariots opposing Israel for control of Esdraelon (Judg. 4–5). Sisera's name is of non-Semitic origin; he is possibly connected with the early Sea Peoples (the biblical designation of this group as "Philistines" is generic). His headquarters at Harosheth "of the nations" (possibly *Muhrashti* of the Amarna Letters) lay somewhere in the Sharon Plain. In Judg. 4 his overlord was "Jabin king of Canaan" at Hazor (4: 2; 23–24; 1 Sam. 12:9 LXX; Ps. 83:9). If not anachronistic, the name evokes a memory of a peaceful settlement by Kenites near the northern Kedesh (and thus near Hazor) in the preceding era (Judg. 4:11, 17 as flashback). Sisera headed forces of the "kings of Canaan" in the far older poem (Judg. 5:19). With Israelite strength in the hill country (4:5) and Galilee, Barak at Kedesh in south Naphtali summoned ten units (hardly 10,000) from Zebulun and Naphtali to muster at Mt. Tabor. Judg. 5 lauds four more tribes. Battle was joined "at Taanach, by the waters of Megiddo." A cloudburst and an ensuing flash flood gave the advantage to Israel. Sisera's forces were destroyed in retreat, while he fled on foot to the tent of the Kenite woman Jael. Feigning hospitality she received him into her tent and then killed him (Judg. 4:17–22). The war may be dated ca. 1125–1100 B.C., when Megiddo was abandoned and Taanach was violently destroyed.

"Sons of Sisera" are listed among Temple slaves (Ezra 2:53; Neh. 7:55; 1 Esd. 5:32). ***See also*** Barak; Judges, The Book of. R.B.

Sismai (sis'mī; KJV: "Sisamai"), the Jerhameelite son of Eleasah and the father of Shallum (1 Chron. 2:40).

sister, a term referring to physical or spiritual kinship. We know of Moses' sister (Exod. 2:4) and Aaron's sister (Exod. 15:20). Marriages were prohibited with one's full or half sister (Lev. 18). Yet "sister" is used for the beloved in Song of Songs 4:9–11, perhaps referring to fictive kinship ties. Members of Jesus' circle were "brother, sister, and mother" (Matt. 12:50). The co-worker Phoebe was Paul's "sister" (Rom. 16: 1); young women in the churches of the pastoral Letters of the NT were also called "sisters" (1 Tim. 5:2). ***See also*** Brothers.

sit. ***See*** Gestures.

Sitnah (sit'nah; Heb., "hostility"), a well dug by Isaac's servants, water rights for which were contested by the servants of Gerar's king Abimelech (Gen. 26:19–21). It may be near Rehoboth in south-central Judah but it has not yet been precisely located.

Sivan (si-vahn'), a word taken into Hebrew from the Akkadian language *(simannu)*, it is used in Esther 8:9 as a synonym for the third month, which largely falls in May or June.

six, a number that appears occasionally in the Bible without apparent symbolic significance. The mysterious number of the beast in Rev. 13: 18—666—is the number of its name (v. 17). In Hebrew and Greek, letters were used also as numerals. Each name thus had a numerical value, calculated by adding the numerical values of the letters. 666 is the numerical value of "Nero Caesar" in Hebrew. ***See also*** Beasts; Numbers; Revelation to John, The.

skirt, a word that in biblical usage designates three aspects of clothing. **1** A loose corner of a garment (1 Sam. 15:27; 24:4–5) like the one David removed from Saul's robe. **2** Both literally and figuratively the edge of a garment. For a literal description of the decoration to be put on the edge of the ephod, see Exod. 28:33–34; 39: 24–26. Jer. 13:22, 26; Lam. 1:9; and Nah. 3:5 use the term figuratively as the sign of Jerusalem's shame. **3** The KJV uses the term for the "mouth" of a garment (RSV: "collar"; Ps. 133:2).

Skull, Place of the. ***See*** Calvary.

Skythopolis (skī-tahp'uh-lis). ***See*** Beth-shan.

slave. ***See*** Servant; Slavery.

Terra-cotta tablet inscribed with a contract concerning the purchase of a slave by Lugal-Ushumgal, prince of Lagash; Tello, ca. 2300 B.C.

slavery, the total subjection of one person to another. Aside from crown and temple slavery, slave labor played a minor economic role in the ancient Near East, for privately owned slaves functioned more as domestic servants than as an agricultural or industrial labor force. The chief source of crown and temple slaves was captives of war (1 Kings 9:21; Num. 31:25–47; Josh. 9:23), while that of private slaves was defaulting debtors and their families (Exod. 22:2; 2 Kings 4:1) or indigents who resorted to voluntary self-sale (Lev. 25:39; Exod. 21:5–6; Deut.15:16–17).

Ancient Near Eastern law collections deal mostly with the slave in relation to an injuring third party, thus emphasizing the slave's status as chattel. However, most biblical legislation focuses upon the relationship of slaves to their own masters, thus emphasizing the slaves' humanity. Although the Bible acknowledges the slave's status as the property of the master (Exod. 21:32; Lev. 25:46), it seeks to restrict the master's power over the slave. The master was punished for excessive use of authorized force leading to the immediate death or permanent maiming of the slave (Exod. 21:20, 25–26). The slave was part of the master's household (Lev. 22:11) and was required to rest on the Sabbath (Exod. 20:10; Deut. 5:14) and to participate in religious observances (Gen. 17:13; Exod. 12:44; Lev. 22:11; Deut. 12:12, 18; 16:11, 14).

In contrast to ancient Near Eastern treaties providing for the mutual extradition of fugitive slaves, biblical law prohibited such extradition and granted them asylum (Deut. 23:16–17; but cf. 1 Kings 2:39–40). The servitude of a Hebrew debt-slave was limited to six years (Exod. 21:2; Deut. 15:12; Jer. 34:14). Upon manumission, slaves were to receive gifts (Deut. 15:14) to enable them economically to maintain their new freedom. The servitude of voluntarily self-enslaved Hebrews ended with the onset of the Jubilee Year and their return to their patrimonies (Lev. 25:13, 40).

Slavery continued in the Roman Empire in NT times, and many slaves became Christians (e.g., Col. 3:22–24; 1 Tim. 6:1–2). While the institution of slavery as such is not condemned in the NT, Paul urged Philemon to treat his slave Onesimus as a brother rather than as a slave (Philem. 15–16). ***See also*** Law. B.L.E.

sledge, an instrument used for threshing grain. It was made of long, flat pieces of wood, turned up in the front, on which would be placed stones for weight. The underside was studded with sharp stones or pieces of metal (Isa. 41:15; Amos 1:3; Job 41:30). ***See also*** Threshing.

slime, a moist, slippery substance of moderate viscosity. In the OT it is used to symbolize something that has no taste (Job 6:6), or something that is impermanent, as the trail left by a snail (Ps. 58:8). The KJV often uses the word "slime" for the RSV's "bitumen." ***See also*** Bitumen.

sling, a weapon used to hurl small projectiles at an enemy, human or animal. This simple device was made of a cloth pad (i.e., "the hollow of a sling," 1 Sam. 25:29) and two cords, one attached to each side of the pad. Ammunition consisted of smooth brook pebbles (1 Sam. 17:40), hammer-worked stones, or, in the Greco-Roman period, lead pellets. To "load" the weapon, the warrior placed a projectile on the pad, which was held with one hand; a small pouch was created when the slinger pulled the cords taut with the other hand. While holding the ends of the cords, the sling was whirled in the air, thereby building up centrifugal force. At the proper instant, one cord was released, and the missile was fired at its target.

While the sling was long used by shepherds to protect their flocks from predatory animals, this weapon was also used at an early date in warfare. Indeed, the story of David's victory over the heavily armed Goliath illustrates the military value of slings (1 Sam. 17). The accuracy of the left-handed slingers from the tribe of Benjamin was famous (Judg. 20:16; 1 Chron. 12:2). From at least the tenth century B.C. onward, many ancient Near Eastern armies had regular units of slingmen (2 Kings 3:25; 2 Chron. 26:14). The sling was so well known in ancient Hebrew society that biblical writers referred to this weapon in symbolic ways (1 Sam.

25:29; Job 41:28; Prov. 26:8; Jer. 10:18; Zech. 9: 15). *See also* Weapons. G.L.M.

smith, one who works metal. The first-named smith of the Bible is Tubal-cain in Gen. 4:22. He is the son of Lamech and Zillah, a brother of Naamah of the eighth generation from Adam. Described as the hammerer of crafts, thus associated with the arts and crafts of earliest humankind, Tubal-cain is known traditionally as the father of metallurgy.

Descriptions of the smith's craft are found in Isa. 44:12 and in Ecclus. 38:28. In Isaiah the term refers to an ironworker laboring over the coals of his forge, shaping the metal with hammers, powered by his strong arm. The passage in Ecclesiasticus pictures the smith seated at an anvil intent on the pattern of the iron object and its decoration. These descriptions serve as analogies demonstrating the power, diligence, and skill of the smith's work. Of all such craftsmen, not known for their counsel or discipline, it is said that they "keep stable the fabric of the world" (Ecclus. 38:33, 34).

The Bible knows of smiths for silver (Judg. 7: 14; Acts 19:24), gold (Isa. 40:19; 41:7; 46:6), iron (Isa. 44:12), and bronze (1 Kings 7:14). The name also describes a thousand men taken to Babylon during the second wave of exile under Jehoiachin. A significantly large proportion of the exiles (one-tenth of all captives) were smiths (2 Kings 24:14, 16; Jer. 24:1; 29:2).

A more general term for a craftsman or artisan is sometimes translated as smith (Heb. *horesh*). The activities described by the term include the sharpening of plow points (1 Sam. 13:19), bronze working such as that of Hiram of Tyre's father (1 Kings 7:14) and, in Isaiah, workmen who make idols and weapons (Isa. 40:19; 41:7; 54:16). Deut. 27:15 tells of a curse laid upon such idol makers and Hos. 13:2 reports that Ephraim is condemned for perpetuating the sin of idolatry.

The earliest archaeological finds related to the smith's craft come from Tell Mardikh (Ebla) in Syria dating to the early bronze age (ca. 3200 B.C.) where excavators found a ceremonial hammer of gold and silver and pictures in bas-relief attached to wooden frames with copper pegs. A few of the frames had been overlaid with gold. Texts from Ebla indicate a guild or caste of smiths and one burial site contained evidences of the goldsmith's art.

Many processes and techniques of the smith's craft are mentioned in the Bible including forging, casting, beating, overlaying, furnishing, whetting, cutting, and soldering. R.A.C.

Smyrna (smuhr'nuh), an ancient city (modern Izmir, Turkey) on the west coast of Asia Minor. It is one of the seven cities mentioned in the book of Revelation (1:11). It lay at the end of a major east-west road, possessed an excellent harbor, and was surrounded by rich farmland. The city's leadership was consistently loyal to Rome. A temple dedicated to the worship of Rome (*dea Roma;* Lat., "the goddess Rome") was built there in 195 B.C.

The message addressed to Smyrna reflects

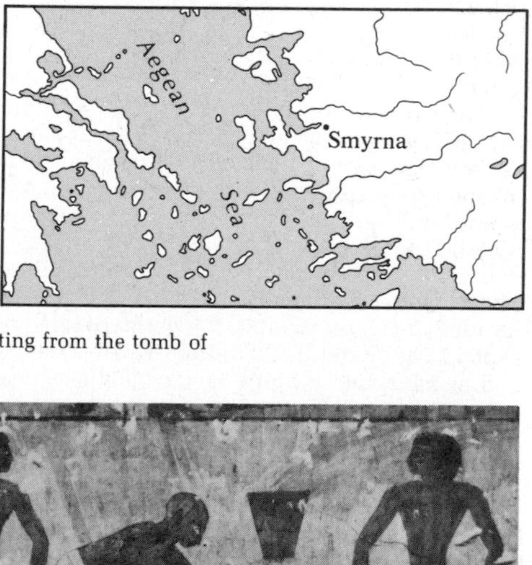

Copper foundry workers; detail of an Egyptian wall painting from the tomb of Vizier Rekhmire, fifteenth century B.C.

conflict between Christians and Jews (Rev. 2: 9–10). It may be that local Jewish leaders were appearing before the city authorities or the Roman governor (cf. Acts 17:5–8) and accusing their Christian neighbors of crimes. Polycarp, bishop of Smyrna, was martyred in A.D. 156. The account of the martyrdom makes clear that there was great hostility between the local Jewish and Christian communities at that time.

Information about the Christians in Smyrna between the time of the composition of the book of Revelation and the martyrdom of Polycarp is available in the letters of Ignatius, bishop of Antioch, written early in the second century. ***See also*** Revelation to John, The. A.Y.C.

snail, a gastropod mollusk. Its sole biblical appearance in Ps. 58:8 is symbolic of impermanence by reference to its slimy trail. The KJV also uses the term for some unclean food (RSV: "sand lizard" in Lev. 11:30).

snake. ***See*** Serpent.

snare, a trap; technically, it is a slip-knotted cord or wire pulled tight to wrap and hold the leg(s) of an animal or bird when it steps into the loop to get the bait or by accident. Biblical usage includes reference to its use in catching birds (Ps. 91:3) and animals (Amos 3:5), but it is more frequently used symbolically for death (2 Sam. 22:6; Ps. 116:3), the actions of wicked people (Ps. 119:110), or the devil (1 Tim. 3:7). It capitalized on surprise, a feature often noted (Luke 21: 34), and caused its victims to enmesh themselves while struggling to get free (Prov. 22:25). It depended on deceit to be successful (Prov. 21: 6) and was camouflaged by hunters to take the prey by surprise (Ps. 64:5). R.S.B.

snow, cystallized water formed when moisture-laden air is chilled. It is relatively rare except in the northern reaches of biblical lands and at higher elevations. It is common in the mountains of Lebanon, northern Syria and Turkey, but it is rare in Jerusalem or the Transjordan. It was known well enough for biblical writers to refer to it literally (Ps. 148:8; Prov. 25: 13; Isa. 55:10; Jer. 18:14; 2 Sam. 23:20). It also served as a common standard for whiteness, whether as symptomatic of illness like leprosy (Exod. 4:6; Num. 12:10; 2 Kings 5:27) or in its own right (Ps. 51:7; Isa. 1:18; Dan. 7:9; Matt. 28: 3; Rev. 1:14). It was recognized to be properly seasonal (Ps. 26:1) and its control lay in the hand of God, as with all of nature (Job 37:6; 38:22). Its whiteness symbolized the ultimate in purity (Lam. 4:7). R.S.B.

snuffer. ***See*** Temple, The.

So, the "king of Egypt" (2 Kings 17:4) to whom King Hoshea sent messengers just before the latter revolted against the Assyrians. The Assyrians under King Shalmaneser then attacked Samaria (725 B.C.). The identification of "So" is uncertain since no name similar to this one appears anywhere in the Egyptian records. "So" may refer to the twenty-second dynasty king Osorkon IV, who ruled Egypt ca. 727–720 B.C., or it may be derived from an Egyptian term *pa Saw(w)*, which means "the Saite" and indicates an individual from the city of Sais in the Egyptian Delta. ***See also*** Pharaoh.

soap, a cleansing agent formed by the hydrolysis of fat with an alkali. In the Bible it refers to cleaning both the body (Jer. 2:22) and clothes (Mal. 3:2). The composition of such soap in biblical times probably used olive oil as the fat and some salt-bearing plants as the alkali source.

sobriety. ***See*** Drunkenness; Vine.

sociology of the New Testament. Beginning in the 1970s, biblical scholars turned in increasing numbers to the social sciences as methodological aids in the analysis of the NT and the reconstruction of the historical development of early Christianity. In academic circles, this was spurred by broad interests among political and social scientists in the dynamics of social and cultural change. In religious circles and on the fringes of modern society, there were those who were raising fundamental questions about prevailing values in contemporary life and who were seeking like-minded groups that could provide mutual understanding and support. The anthropologist Clifford Geertz sees the role of religion in culture as a response to chaos, an attempt to form symbols and an image of order that accounts for the ambiguities, puzzles, and paradoxes in human experience.

This depiction of the role of religion is exemplified admirably in the situation in Judaism at the time of the rise of Christianity. The Temple and its priestly establishment had become a colossal commercial enterprise, with its hierarchy maintaining control through cooperation with the Roman imperial authorities. The Essenes had retreated in despair to the Judean desert to maintain their purity as the faithful remnant of God's people, while awaiting God's intervention and their own vindication. The Pharisees had shifted the focus of their religious life from the Temple cult to the family and voluntary gatherings in homes or public halls (synagogues). Clearly, there was a series of competing schemes to bring divine order out of the chaos of Jewish life under Roman rule, and to do so in a way that would confirm God's control of the history of the covenant people and of the created order.

The foundations of the socio-historical approach to the study of Christian origins were laid in the early decades of the twentieth century, primarily through Max Weber's monumental studies in the sociology of religion, in which he demonstrates the importance of religion for social and economic development in various world cultures. One of his most influential basic insights was that religious movements begin with the appearance of charismatic figures (persons without formal authorization and training who by the power of word and act attract devoted followers) and then begin to shift to institutional forms in which power is hierarchically structured and questions of stability, order, and conformity assume major importance. Figures from Judaism in the century before and after the birth of Jesus who fit well the charismatic description include the Teacher of Righteousness (at Qumran), John the Baptist, and Jesus himself. In each case, the charismatic stands over against the religious and political establishment and summons a community of followers who are persuaded by his message. In each case, the movement he launched also took on institutional forms, including standards for behavior and rules for membership.

Strongly influenced by Weber was Alfred Schutz, who turned his attention to analysis of the view of the world that binds together the members of such groups throughout human history. He points out that individuals are born into a world that consists of a tightly knit web of relationships, signs and symbols with particular meaning, social institutions, and systems of status and prestige; all of these elements and the pattern they form are taken for granted by those living within them. Tensions arise and out-groups form when the accepted elements of the social world are challenged or repudiated, however. This is precisely what happened when the Essenes denounced the established priesthood as corrupt and unfit for the role it had assumed, or when John the Baptist called his supposedly pious contemporaries a "generation of snakes" (Matt. 3:7), or when Jesus dismissed as irrelevant the Pharisaic efforts to gain and maintain special relationship with God through ritual observance (Mark 7:1–23).

Interest in the social background of early Christianity and in the dynamics of the new movement was evident already in the nineteenth century, but the assumption among the historians of religion who devoted themselves to discovering parallels between what was going on in the Greco-Roman world and what happened in early Christianity seems to have been that one could explain beliefs or practices in the early church if one could find similar examples in the non-Christian world of that time. Thus, for example, the myths of such dying and rising gods as the Egyptian deity Osiris were pointed to as an explanation for the Christian belief in the death and resurrection of Jesus; the story of Apollonius of Tyana, an intinerant philosopher and wonder worker, was considered as accounting for the NT stories about the miracles of Jesus. What was ignored by these scholars, as well as by their more recent adherents, is twofold: much of the evidence that is adduced to make the case for the "parallels" is far too late to have influenced the NT writers, and similarities are noted without attention to the basically different view of the world adhered to by the various reporters of these events. For example, the exorcisms that Jesus performs are declared to be signs of the establishment of God's Rule in the world (e.g., Luke 11:20), while the healings in the shrines of the god Asclepius and the goddess Isis in the first century and earlier were depicted as the benefactions of the deity in behalf of ailing individual devotees.

What the insights from the sociology-of-knowledge methods outlined by Schutz and others require is that one seek to reconstruct in as specific detail as the evidence allows what was the encompassing view of the world, of human nature and destiny, that is both explicit and implicit in any document, including the writings of the NT. An essential tool in this undertaking is what Weber called the "ideal type." The ideal type is a purely conceptual construct with which a real situation or action is compared for explication of its individual components. For example, if an ideal type for charismatic groups is posited, specific historical examples can be compared to it. While the Teacher of Righteousness and Jesus can both properly be called "charismatics," the groups that arose around them were fundamentally different in that the Qumran community was rigidly exclusive, while the Jesus movement was radically inclusive ("a friend of tax collectors and sinners," Luke 7:34). Of equal importance in this type of analysis are the degrees of conformity to the ideal type and the distinctive points of divergence from it as well. But the historical questions about the origins of Christianity cannot be answered through theological ideas or concepts alone; they must be addressed by pointing up the issues of the social forms and patterns evident in the various facets of first-century Judaism and in the ways Jesus and the early Christians challenged those traditions.

Social Structures: Since Christianity made an astonishingly rapid and effective shift from the Palestinian Jewish matrix in which it arose to the wider Roman world, penetrating the societies of so many Mediterranean cities, it is obvious that attention must be given to the structures of Roman society if one is to understand both the successes and the hostility the movement fostered. An important beginning in this type of analysis was made by E. A. Judge, who noted that the basic conviction the Romans inherited from the Greeks was that it was precisely from membership in an ordered community that one's humanity sprang. The basic decisions of the state were made in public assemblies, and the wealthy contributed the funds for essential public works. The Romans sought to preserve these mechanisms for local autonomy, so long as the interests of Rome itself were not thereby threatened. Thus, the NT's assignment of responsibility in cities from Athens to Jerusalem to make decisions about Jesus and Paul respectively is in keeping with Greco-Roman political policy. The idea of a local commonwealth, or network of responsibilities shared by community members (Gk. *politeia*), began to give way in the second century to the theory of universal citizenship—a trend fostered by an increasingly powerful central government in Rome, beginning with the second-century emperors Trajan and Hadrian. Not surprisingly, it is in this period that we have the first clear evidence of pressure on the Christians to take part in the divine honors to the Roman gods and the emperor (documented by Pliny's letter to Trajan concerning the rapid spread of Christianity in Asia Minor and its consequences for splintering loyalties to the Roman state).

A second social structure after the community was at the domestic level: the family. Order within families was central to the structure and function of Roman society, with great powers assigned to the husband/father, while wives, children, and slaves stood in clearly defined lesser roles. Personal identity was established through the family structure. Thus, Jesus' call to leave father, mother, and family to devote oneself to the service of the coming Kingdom of God (e.g., Mark 10:29) would appear as a social revolution, whether among Jews or among Romans.

A third type of social structure was the unofficial association (Gk. *koinōnia);* these were informal groups that gathered in the interests of common goals or concerns, which might be religious, ethnic, commercial, or aesthetic in nature. These clubs or informal organizations were suspect in the eyes of the Roman authorities, especially if they had political aims or employed political rhetoric. Obviously, to speak of the coming of a new kingdom, as the Christians did, would arouse suspicions.

The church as *koinōnia* seems to have transcended from the beginning the normal stratification of society in the Roman period, especially where the gospel took hold in urban areas. Judge's preliminary investigation has been greatly expanded and deepened by the work of Wayne A. Meeks and Gerd Theissen. Building on the clues to the social roles of the constituents of the churches founded by Paul, especially in Corinth, these scholars show how the church simultaneously broke down the social barriers that characterized life in the Roman world and penetrated the upper strata of power within the Roman political structure. The upward mobility of the Christian movement is attested by the inclusion of the city treasurer of Corinth among those who send greetings to the Christians in Rome (Rom. 16:23).

The tension between charismatic authority and the necessity to move toward institutionalization in the Pauline churches is another area of investigation. How were the Roman authorities to react to this *koinōnia* already turning institutional? The seriousness with which Rome viewed the church, or any other threat to its imperial order, is well attested. Raising these kinds of questions and utilizing sociological avenues to explore for answers make it clear that the early church was by no means an intellectual group debating theological views and theories. Rather, it was deeply involved in the life of its time, and its surrounding culture contributed profoundly to the way in which hopes and fears were articulated.

Similarly, raising questions of social structure within the Judaism of Jesus' time has made it evident that one should not read back into the early first century the more or less closed system of rabbinic interpretation of the Law of Moses that became dominant after the Romans destroyed the Jerusalem Temple (A.D. 70) and gave to the Pharisees the right to structure Judaism in a way that would be politically safe for the Romans and personally authoritative among Jews. Especially through the studies of the modern scholar Jacob Neusner, there has become evident the pattern of conflicting claims to be the true interpreters of the biblical heritage of Judaism that was underway between Pharisees and followers of Jesus throughout the first century. Most clearly, this is reflected in the Gospel of Matthew, where the recriminations against the Pharisees are intensified from the apparently older version in Mark (e.g., Matt. 23). At stake between these conflicting groups is the definition of God's covenant people.

Sociology of Religion: The analyses offered earlier in the twentieth century of the patterns and forms adopted by religious movements in the writings of Max Weber and Émile Durkheim have had a renewed impact on biblical studies in the past decade. Similarly, the distinction that Ernst Troeltsch offered in 1912 between "church" (established institution) and "sect" (voluntary gathering of the like-minded, standing over against the church) has continued to influence the study of early Christianity, although his specific definition of terms has been significantly altered. Christianity began and flourished initially as a sect within Judaism: it started as a protest—not primarily an economic one, but one against the dehumanization by the establishment; it rejected the view of reality held by the establishment, offering love and acceptance within a voluntary community, while calling for the total commitment of its members and awaiting vindication by God in the near future. The early Christians included those who were economically marginal, those who were excluded from the religious community by reason of personal or occupational impurity, as well as those who were accepted by the establishment but discontented with it (e.g., wealthy women [Luke 8:2–3], a ruler of a synagogue [Mark 5:22], a tax collector [Matt. 9:9], a woman with a bloody flux [Mark 5:25–34]). There was no hierarchy in this movement initially, but the community was bound by the common experience of love and acceptance, by the promise of divine reconciliation, and by the hope of renewal of God's world.

Recent studies of millenarian movements by anthropologists such as Kenelm Burridge and Bryan R. Wilson have described the dynamics by which such movements arise, including the sense of deprivation of power that pervades a society and that therefore predisposes its members to identify with the promise of transformation of the world and the reward of the faithful. This dynamic is evident in the apocalyptic book of Daniel in the OT, which seems to have been written when there was a growing despair of the renewal of Israel, ruled as it was by an increasingly secular Jewish family, the Hasmoneans (Maccabees), which entered into diplomatic relations with a pagan power (Rome) in order to assure the preservation of the Jewish people.

The Roman takeover of Palestine in the first century B.C. brought intensified domination and heightened economic difficulties, with the heavy tax burden under the Herodian family and with the control of the land by absentee owners (cf. Mark 12:1–12 and parallels). Theissen has pointed up four factors that prepare people for responding to apocalyptic messengers with promises of a New Age of vindication. The socioeconomic factor includes social rootlessness, the appearance of charismatic figures, the dispossession of the poor by the wealthy landowners, the loss of local identity, and the obvious gap between the native poor and the secularized aristocracy. The sociopolitical factor focuses on the tension between the theoretical divine rule and the actual domination by the priestly artistocracy, intensified by the presence of prophetic and nationalistic figures, fanning flames of discontent. The socioecological factor takes into account the Jesus movement, with its ties to simple workers and small-town systems and hostility toward the Hellenistic cities of the area with their display of secular culture and entertainments. And the sociocultural factor represents the problem of maintaining Jewish identity as the covenant people, which leads to the sharp alternative of intensifying the norms, as the Pharisees did, or of setting them aside, which is the alternative Jesus encouraged his followers to take.

The miracles of Jesus were interpreted as signs of divine approval and as assurances of the fulfillment of the promise of the Kingdom of God. The Gospel of Mark and the Q strand of the Jesus tradition (largely sayings material common to Matthew and Luke but not found in Mark) attest to the appeal and the effectiveness of the charismatic movement with its apocalyptic message in Palestine and Syria, but when the movement spread to the Hellenistic cities of the Mediterranean world it shifted its authority center from charisma to local leadership. This led to the establishment of resident authority figures, who ultimately became the monarchic episcopacy of the second and subsequent centuries. Elaine Pagels claims that a major factor in this authority shift was the antifeminist urge of a male-dominated leadership group that resented and soon destroyed the significant role that women had played in the charismatic period of the church. Howard Clark Kee traces the social links between the Jesus tradition and the way in which it was ordered and adapted by Mark in the service of that segment of the early Christian community that he was addressing and representing in his Gospel. The dependence upon spontaneous local support for the movement, the absence of any hierarchic roles among the disciples, the voluntary, inclusive nature of the participation in the movement, and the expectation of an imminent end of the age all point to the apocalyptic orientation and the charismatic leadership style of the Markan community.

Anthropology: Two major insights from the anthropological studies of primitive cultures by Mary Douglas have made a deep and enduring contribution to NT interpretation. The first is her theory about the centrality of language as the instrument for creating and sustaining an individual's sense of belonging to a particular society. She observes that what one regards as "the real world" is to a large extent built up on the language habits of one's fundamental group, so that what we see and experience occurs as it does and is understood as it is largely because the language habits of our community predispose certain choices of interpretation. Similarly, ritual forms, like speech forms, are transmitters of culture and reinforce the patterns of behavior as well as the limits by which the identity of the members of the group is established and maintained.

Douglas proposes a graphic scheme on the basis of which various groups can be analyzed and compared. The vertical scale of the graph she calls *grid*, by which she refers to the degree to which certain criteria for group membership are consciously shared by the group ("high grid") or are matters of private persuasion ("low grid"). The horizontal scale she calls *group*, by which she means the scale ranging from the freedom of the individual member of the group

 SOCIOLOGY OF THE NEW TESTAMENT

("low group") to supreme control by the group over the individual ego ("high group"). Various religious movements may be positioned in a variety of places in relation to these intersecting scales. For example, a system of strong-grid/strong-group will tend toward a routinized piety and its symbols, beliefs in a punishing moral universe, and a category of rejects. With a high classification system, as in first-century Essenism, there are strong boundaries between purity and impurity, so that all moral failings are sins against the religious tradition and violations of the integrity of the community. What Douglas calls "small group" arises in a situation where there is a sense that justice does not prevail, where demonic powers are in control of the universe, and the world has become a battleground between the forces of good and evil. The small group defines its own rights, for the present and the future. The apocalyptic movements of Judaism in the second century B.C. and the community self-understanding implicit in Mark and the Q tradition exemplify this way of understanding the world and the place of the New Covenant people within it.

This leads to the other central insight of Douglas that has bearing on the origins of Christianity: purity as the demarcator of boundaries between the holy people and the rest of humanity. The questions of purity and defilement are not isolated human phenomena but occur in the context of a systematic ordering of ideas in which the primary concern is the holiness of the god and of the people who stand in a special relationship to deity. In the tradition of Israel, the words associated with holiness connote "set apart," and the importance attached to this concept and to the practice of sanctification are basic to Israel's belief in Yahweh as the God who has ordered the universe and to their obligation to maintain their special relationship to God by keeping the covenant and observing all God's commandments (cf. Deut. 28:1–14). Since the divine order is central to this understanding of the world, any deformity or violation of that order or any transgression of the categories of creation violates the sacred boundaries. The system of feasts and annual ceremonies not only celebrates the divine ordering of creation but also helps to maintain that order. Ritual and purity are, therefore, essential to the ordering of life; they are by no means dispensable decorations imposed on the basics of human existence. The ground of the ordered life is in the divinely ordered cosmos, so that ritual creates one single, symbolically consistent universe.

Douglas notes that the idea of society is a powerful image that serves to control or arouse human action. The image has a form with external boundaries and margins that can repulse attacks or reward conformity. It is more appropriately pictured in organic rather than architectural features, so that the human body is its most apt symbol. Accordingly, bodily contact, intake, and discharge represent the margins that threaten the integrity of the society, whether by threatening external boundaries or by confusing internal ones. Such threats symbolize, especially among minority groups, a loss of political or cultural unity. Therefore, the preparation and eating of food become of paramount importance, as does the maintenance of sexual and ethnic purity. To deal with these threats to societal integrity, there develop within certain cultures systems of purity that attempt to force experience into logical categories, even though there are always ambiguities between theory and actual practice. The observance of ritual purity is not optional, however; it is essential to the preservation of the divinely intended cosmic order.

In addition to her studies of African and Indian tribes in which these systems are evident, Douglas discusses at length the ritual code of Israel as preserved especially in Leviticus. Her hypotheses serve extremely well for the assessment of the struggles among Jews in the Hellenistic and Roman epochs, when they were seeking to define the basis of group identity. For the priestly group and its Sadducaic supporters, the essential basis of Israelite identity was the Temple ritual itself, with its annual cycle of ceremonies by which the appropriate sacrifices were offered, the people of Israel cleansed, and the cycles of agricultural fertility celebrated and thereby maintained. For the Essenes, as noted above, the secularization of the priesthood was so complete as to move certain dissidents to withdraw to a place where purity could be maintained totally and for all the true members of the covenant people, in their monastic settlement by the Dead Sea. The Pharisees, however, sought to appropriate purity for themselves personally, rather than to have its requirements be performed on their behalf by the priests. The observance of ritual purity was transferred to the home and to the voluntary gatherings in what was later to develop into the institution of the synagogue. The rite of circumcision was central to identity within the covenant people from remote antiquity; to it were added the dietary regulations. These may have been applicable earlier only for the priests, but they became universally binding in the Pharisaic tradition and therefore reinforced the experience of the holiness of God's people in the very epoch when the political and cultural pressures—first from the Hellenistic and then from the Roman authorities—were threatening the Jewish sense of special identity within the divine cosmic order.

It is because of this powerful significance of purity that the move on the part of both Jesus and Paul to dismiss ritual requirements as not only unimportant but also inappropriate for covenantal identity aroused such antipathy on the part of the Jewish leaders. What was at stake was not merely another alternative interpretation of the Jewish heritage but the integrity of the people of God as it was understood by the Pharisees, Sadducees, and Essenes, in spite of their basic disagreements on details. We can understand better the conflict between Paul and the Jerusalem-based apostles on the issue of whether Christians should be circumcized, and why Paul was so annoyed with Peter for having withdrawn from eating with those Christians who did not observe kosher laws (Gal. 2:11–14). The central importance of community identity to which Douglas has drawn attention points up the importance of these issues in early Christianity, and why so much space is devoted in the Gospel of Mark (regarded by most as the earliest Gospel) to questions of purity in Jesus' physical contacts, healing activity, eating, and acceptance of hospitality.

Sociology of Knowledge: In the writings of Schutz mentioned above, and of Thomas Luckmann, there is set forth a theory that knowledge is socially acquired, so that human beings participate in the world of everyday life in ways at once inevitable and patterned. The normal adult simply takes this world for granted and assumes that others, including ancestors and parents, experienced it in the same way. It is the area of thought and action that sets the limits for what we do and think. As a coherent scheme of thought and knowledge, it provides a stable reference point for decisions and evaluations in relation to action and understanding. When experiences do not fit the given patterns, the structure is called into question and modified appropriately "until further notice." Both the description of the world and the valuing of various aspects of it derive from this socially given process, and it serves as the basis for our expectations about the future. It is the experience and the assumptions that humans share with others in their society that give the structure to the world as they perceive it. The transmission of this knowledge leads to objectifications and symbols that serve as the basis of the individual's understanding of his or her place in the cosmic scheme of things, conditioning both present experience and future expectation. Creative individuals appear from time to time who challenge or even modify in significant ways this body of knowledge that has been taken for granted and thus has provided the basis of personal and group identity for those who share it.

The story of the challenge embodied in Jesus' words and actions and the tragic response that it elicited from the religious and political leadership can best be understood in terms of conflicting "life-worlds." For those who assume the centrality of the Temple as the dwelling place of God in the midst of his people and as the means of their maintaining right relationship with the one who called them as covenant people, Jesus' action in driving out officials essential to the Temple's efficient operation (money-changers needed by pilgrims from distant lands; Mark 11:15) and his announcement of its impending destruction could only be regarded as audacious and subversive. For those who, like the Maccabees two centuries earlier, regarded the essence of Jewish existence as the establishment and maintenance of an independent state of Israel, Jesus' encouragement of payment of taxes and his refusal to lead a popular uprising would be perceived as infidelity to patriotic aspirations. For those like the Pharisees and Essenes, for whom personal purity was a paramount requirement for the enjoyment of divine favor, Jesus was a despicable violator of the integrity of the sacred people.

For the Romans, with their expectation of a balance between limited local autonomy of subject people and ultimate submission to Roman imperial authority, Jesus' mix of political rhetoric ("Kingdom of God") and disparaging remarks about Roman-authorized rulers (Herod as "that fox," Luke 13:32), coupled with his refusal under pressure to disclose his plans or his own role, could only lead to the decision of Pilate to have him executed as a threat to peace and stability. While his own "life-world" shared with that of other Jews the conviction about the centrality of the covenant relationship between God and his people, as well as about the Scriptures as the primary sources in which the divine purpose was to be discerned, he differed radically from his coreligionists in his removal of the ethnic and cultic boundaries of Israel and in his inviting participation on the part of outcasts, sinners, traitors, and Gentiles.

There was, however, no single view of the world found among the early Christians, as the range of perspectives within the NT shows. Among the Gospel writers, for example, different aspects of the new reality that Jesus is seen as bringing are depicted. Mark emphasizes the break with the old age and the imminent coming of the new age in which God's people will be vindicated (Mark 13:24–37) once they have carried out their roles of preaching, healing, and perhaps of martyrdom in his name. Matthew lays stress on the new community as the True Israel, with Jesus as the New Moses (speaking from the mountain to instruct God's people) and the apostles exercising authority in his name within the church (Matt. 16:16–19). Luke emphasizes the inclusive nature of the community of faith, beginning with the lowly shepherds in Bethlehem and the initial preaching of the good news to the poor, and moving through the stories of the prodigal son, the good Samaritan, the conversion of a Pharisee bent on the destruction of the church (Paul), of an Ethiopian eunuch, an Athenian sophisticate, a Roman military officer, devotees of pagan deities in Ephesus, until the good news is preached in the capital city of Rome itself. The values and strategies of these different facets of the early Christian communities are evident in the elements of tradition that the writers include and in the nuances that they give to speech and narrative accounts. The interpreter must not only consider what is being said explicitly in these documents but also look beneath the surface to the assumptions and values and aspirations that are implicit in the texts.

The method called for by the sociology of knowledge illuminates distinctions that might otherwise be overlooked in a NT phenomenon such as miracles. For example, in neither the pagan world of the early centuries A.D. nor early Christianity were miracles understood in a uniform way. Rather, a miracle was perceived at one point to be the direct response of a divinity to a request from a person or in behalf of a person in need (as in the earlier phases of the cults of Isis and Asclepius). Later on, the miracle was represented as a sign of a special ongoing relationship between the god or goddess and the devout person, for whom the miracle was not merely an act of divine mercy but a symbol of a special relationship between the human and the divine. This is the case in the story of Lucius Apuleius (*Metamorphoses*), whose experience of change from the form of an ass back into that of a human being symbolizes his transformation from a pointless, difficult life into the office of priest of Isis, whose kindness gave meaning and purpose to his life. Similarly, in the Gospel of John, the miracles of Jesus are represented as "signs" (John 20:30–31) of new life, of divine light, of heavenly food, of new understanding that comes when one is brought into the community of the faithful. There, Jesus addresses his own in the first person: "I am the light, the bread, the way, the resurrection, the life." The miracle has become the sign of participation in the life of the new people of God with the new resources that God has provided through Jesus.

In Mark and the Q tradition, on the other hand, the miracle is an act that points ahead to the defeat of the powers of evil and to the coming of God's Rule. It is the assurance of the vindication of God's people, in keeping with the expectations and experiences of Jewish apocalyptic groups, as attested in Daniel, for example, where God preserves his own when they stand faithful in defiance of the threats and commands of the pagan ruler (Dan. 1–5). The fact that there are rough parallels between miracles reportedly performed by Jesus and those attributed to pagan deities points to the widespread longing for direct divine action in the Roman world during the period of Christianity's rise, but the interpreter must always look behind the superficial similarities to ask about the distinctive world of meaning in which the NT writers understand these events to have occurred.

Sociology of Literature: In addition to the age-old efforts to classify literature by literary form, there has appeared in recent decades an analytical method that seeks to determine what the social function of a document was. In some instances, this function seems quite obvious: a history, an entertaining narrative, a letter conveying information or requesting it, a biography about a notable figure, etc. A deeper question raised by the sociology of literature, however, is: what was the underlying purpose for which a given work was written? For example, the novels or romances that were written in the first century B.C. down to the third century A.D. are ostensibly entertaining, even exciting, accounts of travels and adventures of colorful figures of the eastern Mediterranean world. Yet, it has been recognized by some scholars that they often served as subtle propaganda for a cult of a god or goddess. Thus, Chariton's romance attracts sympathy for the cult of Aphrodite, while Xenophon's *Ephesiaca* is written in praise of Isis for her guidance and protection of a pair of her devotees.

In the domain of Jewish writings from this period, the Dead Sea document *The Scroll of the Rule* (or *Manual of Discipline*) includes items as seemingly disparate as a few narrative details about the experience of the founder of the Essene sect and then extensive regulations for the common life of the community. Its function is not merely archival; rather, it serves as the foundation document for the group, in that it explains how the sect arose, while setting forth the courage of its founder who broke with his priestly tradition, and it gives detailed advice about how the group is to prepare for the divine vindication that is soon to come.

What insights will inquiries into the social function of ancient writings provide students of the NT? The model of the foundation document helps us to understand the aim of the writer of the Gospel of Mark. It is not simply a biography; indeed, it omits such characteristic features as the birth and family upbringing of Jesus. It does tell us enough about him, however, to inform us how the movement began and how he stands as the model for his followers in terms of his insight concerning and his total commitment to the outworking of God's purpose for his people. It also provides detailed instructions on such issues as marriage and divorce, taxes, ritual and Temple participation, and the nature of and preparation for the coming of God's Rule. All the features fit this model, while to regard Mark as a loose expansion of Paul's gospel (as some interpreters do) makes no sense of the details that have in fact been included.

Another kind of model, which mingles features of history and the romance, seems appropriate for an analysis of Luke and Acts, although Luke's Gospel comes closest of all the Gospels to the features of a biography (infancy, childhood, launching the career, etc.). The historical dimensions of the two-volume work, as well as the romantic features of Acts (sea voyages of the faithful, confrontations with local authorities, miracles of deliverance and punishment), point up how skillfully the author has understood his potential readership, how he has emphasized those aspects of the tradition that would evoke interest on the part of pagan readers, even while making two important points: that God took care of his messengers and that none of the political rulers was ever able to establish a charge of political insurrection against Jesus, Paul, or other apostles. The author was able to communicate with his readers in a style and medium that were very likely to gain and hold their attention, even while propagandizing for the new understanding of the church as the potentially inclusive people of God.

If one makes the functional distinction between a true letter (as written for a specific occasion to consider matters of mutual concern with a specific reader or readers) and a letter as a formal document in which the sender is conveying official pronouncements to a wider community over which he or she has or claims responsibility, then the distinction to be made between the authentic Letters of Paul and later documents written in his name becomes clear and significant. Although intellectual differences between, for example, the Letters to Timothy and Galatians or 1 Corinthians are important, the sociology of literature requires us to distinguish the respective functions of these two types of literature. In Galatians, Paul is addressing a specific issue: the ambivalence of the churches of Galatia on the issue of Paul's apostolic authority and the freedom of Christians from Jewish legal obligations. In 1 Corinthians, he is confronting behavior problems within the church there ranging from incest to sexual asceticism and from divisiveness to despair of sharing in the resurrection. The issues in the authentic Letters are concrete and are addressed in strictly personal terms. In the later writings attributed to Paul, on the other hand (e.g., the Letters to Timothy), the weight falls on the acceptance of one's assigned place within a structured community, with the bishops in charge. In Weber's terms, the church has moved from charismatic to institutional form, and the sociological analysis of the literary form of these two types of literature confirms this assessment.

Analogously, the apocalyptic style of parts of Mark and especially of the book of Revelation is indicative of the self-understanding of the Christian communities that are reflected in these documents: sectarian groups that see themselves as, humanly speaking, helpless before the prevailing powers, but that have been granted insight and hope to look beyond the present difficulty, through the time of unprecedented struggle that will precede the end of the age to the time of divine deliverance. Once more, a sociological analysis of the style of the literature enhances one's understanding of its message.

Conclusions: There are difficulties inherent in this approach to the NT. The tendency is inevitable that the use of sociological methods will emphasize the diversity rather than the unity of the NT. Yet, if the gospel was to reach such a range of societies as comprised the Roman world, it had to speak many different languages; or, more accurately, it had to address persons in the social and cultural models and forms that were constitutive for their self-understanding if they were to hear and heed the new message. Another peril is that of reducing the Christian story to its supposedly social essentials. This has been undertaken by writers who reduce Jesus' message to calling people to return to the early egalitarianism of ancient Israel under God —that is, to social and especially economic reform of a Christian Marxist variety. Just as older Protestant liberalism and more recent forms of existentialist interpretation reduced the message of Jesus to one of individual moral renewal, so the social reform approach reduces the gospel to economic factors. Rightly employed, however, the sociological methods sketched above can open dimensions and depths of meaning in the NT that take more fully into account the fact that human wholeness involves social history, renewal of the created order, transcendence of the day-to-day world through symbolic insights, and hope of future renewal in the purpose of God. ***See also*** Apocalyptic Literature; Covenant; Daniel, The Book of; Essenes; Galatians, The Letter of Paul to the; Jesus Christ; John the Baptist; Magic and Divination.

Bibliography

Judge, E. A. *The Social Pattern of the Christian Groups in the First Century: Some Prolegomena to the Study of New Testament Ideas of Social Obligation*. London: Tyndale, 1960.

Kee, H. C. *Community of the New Age: Studies in Mark's Gospel*. 2d ed. Macon, GA: Mercer University Press, 1983.

______. *Miracle in the Early Christian World*. New Haven and London: Yale University Press, 1984.

Meeks, W. A. *The First Urban Christians: The Social World of the Apostle Paul*. New Haven and London: Yale University Press, 1983.

Thiessen, G. *The Social Setting of Pauline Christianity: Essays on Corinth*. Philadelphia: Fortress, 1982.

H.C.K.

sociology of the Old Testament. Interest in the sociology of the OT, that is, all aspects of ancient Israelite society and the social changes

SOCIOLOGY OF THE OLD TESTAMENT

that took place in Israel during the biblical period, is part of a more general concern with uncovering the historical setting of the biblical literature, a concern that is already reflected in the OT itself. Thus, for example, the editors of the book of Psalms sought to understand some of the Davidic Psalms more clearly by identifying the occasions in David's life that prompted him to compose them. This historical information was then added to the Psalms' superscriptions as an aid to readers (e.g., Pss. 3; 18; 51; 54; 60). In a similar way, general historical information has been added to some of the prophetic books in order to make their oracles more comprehensible (e.g., Isa. 1:1; Jer. 1:1–3; Amos 1:1).

Interest in the sociology of the OT intensified after the end of the biblical period. Readers of the OT began to recognize that an ever-growing gap separated them from the world of the biblical writers, and this gap sometimes obscured the meaning of the text. The OT authors lived in a particular historical society and participated fully in its culture. Their language included idioms and images that were current in their own time, and they referred to events and social customs that were known by their contemporary readers and hearers. When ancient Israelite society ceased to exist, however, some of these references became unintelligible, and some of the richness of the text's meaning was lost. The more the language and cultural experiences of the OT readers diverged from those of the biblical writers, the less clear the text became.

Early Studies: At least by the Middle Ages, Jewish and Christian interpreters began to try to reconstruct aspects of Israelite society in order to better understand the OT's message. Explorations into OT sociology in this period were usually unsystematic and employed a variety of investigative techniques. Unusual Hebrew words and idioms in the Bible were compared with similar constructions in rabbinic Hebrew and in Arabic, and some attempt was made to analyze the literary conventions that governed OT poetry. Social and cultural customs were explained by referring to the works of authors who were closer historically and culturally to the biblical period, and some medieval interpreters even drew on their own experiences to throw light on Israelite society.

The use of contemporary comparative material became even more common in the eighteenth and nineteenth centuries, when the social sciences began to establish themselves in universities throughout Europe. Sociologists such as Herbert Spencer (1820–1903), Karl Marx (1818–1883), Max Weber (1864–1920), and Émile Durkheim (1858–1917) studied social phenomena in their own time and described the regularities and overall patterns that were thought to exist in all societies, both ancient and modern. At the same time, anthropologists began to collect information on a variety of cultures, most of which were thought at the time to be "primitive" societies totally untouched by Western civilization. Some anthropologists, such as Sir Edward B. Tylor (1832–1917) and Sir James George Frazer (1854–1941), tried to organize these new data in such a way as to demonstrate the gradual evolution of human culture from primitive beginnings to the advanced state that it had reached in Western Europe. Later anthropologists such as Bronislaw Malinowski (1884–1942) and A. R. Radcliffe-Brown (1881–1955), however, rejected this comprehensive approach and stressed instead the necessity of studying cultural data thoroughly in their own social context and then describing the complex interaction of the parts of the society as a whole. This view of the task of social anthropology led to the production of a number of detailed studies of individual societies. Modern social anthropologists continue this type of research, although they are more interested in the process of social change than were their scholarly ancestors.

From the very beginning of their establishment as academic disciplines, sociology and anthropology attracted the attention of biblical interpreters interested in reconstructing ancient Israelite society. By the middle of the nineteenth century, archaeologists were beginning to uncover large amounts of textual and cultural material from the ancient Near Eastern societies that surrounded Israel, and this comparative evidence added new depth to the scholarly understanding of Israelite history. This understanding was further enriched when biblical interpreters began to apply the results of sociological research to the Bible and to the ancient Near Eastern evidence.

One of the early attempts at a sociological interpretation was made by the sociologist Max Weber, who tested his theories of the origins of capitalism by reconstructing a social history of biblical Israel. Weber concluded that Israel was originally a conglomeration of seminomadic and settled agricultural groups that were unified through their common allegiance to a covenant and governed periodically by "charismatic" leaders. This early social structure changed with the rise of the monarchy, when a strong central government robbed the individual tribes of their power. The monarchy helped to create a class of wealthy landowners, and the society was soon divided economically into two distinct social classes. The oppression of the poor provoked the judgment oracles of the prophets, who advocated a return to the earlier egalitarian society and stressed the necessity for ethical behavior in response to the demands of the covenant. Weber's reconstruction was quickly taken up and amplified by biblical scholars, and Adolphe Lods (1867–1948) and Antonin Causse (1877–1947), among others, produced histories of Israel based on Weberian principles. Less influential at the time were the sociological theories of Marx, Durkheim, and Tylor, although the latter's work did convince important biblical scholars, including W. Robertson Smith (1846–1894) and Julius Wellhausen (1844–1918), that contemporary cultural data could safely be used to reconstruct the religion and society of ancient Israel.

In contrast to the way in which biblical interpreters used nineteenth-century sociological research, the new anthropological data were generally used less systematically. Frazer tried to apply his enormous collection of material to specific biblical passages, and others invoked anthropological parallels to explain particular "primitive" features of Israelite society. More responsible was the use that biblical scholars made of anthropologists' comparative studies of folklore. Beginning with the pioneering work of Hermann Gunkel (1862–1932), interpreters re-examined the OT literature in order to uncover signs of its original oral form. Taking a cue from folklore studies, Gunkel argued that distinctive literary genres could be isolated in the OT and that their preliterary structures could be recovered. Each of these genres had a particular social setting in Israel's national life, and Gunkel thought that these settings could be reconstructed with the aid of cultural data drawn from modern societies. Gunkel's approach, with its stress on the sociological dimensions of Israelite literature, has had a profound influence on OT research, and his method continues to be used today, although in a somewhat modified form.

Current Research: In spite of early enthusiasm for the application of sociological research to the OT, this sort of comparative approach was soon rejected by biblical interpreters, and by the middle of the twentieth century interest in the sociology of the OT had almost disappeared in the scholarly community. The primary reason for this rejection was the recognition by biblical scholars that the sociological and anthropological research they were using contained serious flaws. Some of the overarching sociological theories were based on unsound data, while others had difficulty dealing with unique social phenomena that could not be made to fit general sociological patterns. In the case of anthropology, material had sometimes been collected unsystematically and had been presented as part of a general theory of culture, the validity of which could not easily be supported. Comparative material of this sort was then imposed on the biblical evidence, and the result was a distorted picture of early Israelite society. Biblical interpreters therefore turned away from sociological studies and occupied themselves with the theology, literary genres, and traditions of the text.

In recent years, however, OT interpreters have again recognized the important role that social factors play in shaping any piece of literature and have begun to do research on the sociology of the OT. At the same time, new developments in the social sciences have provided researchers with more sophisticated tools and have helped them to avoid the problems associated with earlier comparative studies.

Several major approaches to the study of ancient Israelite society are now being employed. Using revised versions of the theories of Weber and Marx, some scholars have analyzed Israel's social structure in the period of the judges and have given coherent descriptions of the changes that occurred when Israel made the transition from being a tribal society to being a monarchical state. Others have collected the detailed studies of individual societies provided by social anthropologists and have then used this comparative material to study the nature and function of particular religious and social phenomena in ancient Israel. This sort of approach has been used to explore Israel's tribal organization and to analyze prophecy and apocalyptic. Finally, archaeologists working in the land of Israel have begun to apply more sophisticated techniques of analysis to their material and have succeeded in reconstructing the social setting of some of the cultural remains they have found. Detailed work of this sort throws important light on the way that ancient Israelites lived and thus aids in understanding the texts that they produced.

Much of the new research on the sociology of the OT has not yet been tested and integrated into a comprehensive picture of the nature and development of Israelite society. As a result, there is no commonly accepted account of Israel's social history. Enough work has been done, however, to permit a general outline of such a history. Details can be filled in only when additional studies have been done, and new archaeological discoveries can always modify what was previously thought to be true.

Early Israelite Society, a Lineage-Based System: Most archaeologists now trace the origins of biblical Israel to the movements of West Semitic (mostly Amorite) peoples that took place in Mesopotamia during the second millennium B.C. When the OT accounts of Israel's ancestors are compared with Mesopotamian archaeological evidence and the picture of Amorite tribal life gleaned from cuneiform texts, enough similarities emerge to permit a sketchy reconstruction of early Israelite social structure. Like most Amorite groups, early Israel seems to have based its social structure on the idea of kinship. In such systems the basic social unit is the nuclear family (parents and their children), and this family model is extended throughout the rest of the social structure. Two nuclear families can be related to each other by tracing common descent from a single figure in the third generation, a grandparent. The nuclear families related in this way constitute an extended family, whose head is the ancestor from whom all of the family members are descended. Extended families can, in turn, be related to each other by tracing their descent to an earlier ancestor, usually not living, and the resulting group can be seen as a single social unit, sometimes, though inaccurately, called a clan. Clans can in turn form tribes by claiming to be descendants of a single person, and in theory the process can be continued indefinitely until the whole society is united as one massive kinship unit. The society or any of its parts can then be described by employing a segmented or branched genealogy, a family tree. Kinship organizations of this sort are usually called "lineages" by anthropologists.

Although a lineage-based society can, in theory, include any number of people, in fact lineage genealogies usually include no more than ten generations of ancestors, and the normal practice is to mention only five or six generations. This limit on genealogical depth means that the actual number of people in the society is also limited. There are two major reasons for this limitation. First, lineages tend to become socially unstable as they grow larger. Social and political authority in a lineage is vested in the lineage head, the oldest living member of the lineage and the person from whom all of the remaining members are descended. In small lineages, such as the nuclear or extended family, this person is capable of enforcing lineage decisions and maintaining social unity. In larger lineages, however, the lineage head named in the lineage genealogy is likely to be no longer living, and no one person can exercise authority in the lineage. This means that disputes must be settled by negotiations between the living heads of the smaller constituent lineages. As more people become involved in this process, there is more likelihood of disagreement and of a permanent split in the lineage. Second, most of the affairs of everyday life involve only the nuclear or perhaps the extended family. These groups therefore have a greater degree of social reality than do larger lineage groups, which may become important only on ritual occasions or in times of war, when individual families are incapable of defending themselves.

Israelite society was organized as a hierarchical lineage system at least as early as the period of the Judges (twelfth century B.C.; Josh. 7), and the frequent use of branched genealogies in Genesis suggests that Israel's ancestors were similarly organized (Gen. 22:20–24; 25:12–16; 35:22–26; 36:1–43; 46:8–27). If so, then early Israelite lineages of various sizes presumably lived on the edges of established towns and entered into a symbiotic relationship with the local inhabitants (Gen. 12:6–9; 13:12–18; 33:18–20; 35:16–21; 37:12–17). The Israelites occasionally practiced farming (Gen. 26:12–16), but they were primarily sheep breeders, who periodically left their camps in search of pasture for their animals. In return for supplying the townspeople with wool and meat, the Israelites received from the towns agricultural products and some manufactured goods. Although there is no direct evidence on this point, it is likely that individuals occasionally left the lineage and took up residence in a town, either because they were driven out of the lineage for some reason or because they sought better economic opportunities.

Israel's lineage-based social system survived more or less intact into the period of the judges and, after the conquest, provided a basis for the unity of Israelite society. Israel's largest lineage groups, however, seem to have become progressively more unstable as time passed. Although all Israelites may have shared common religious beliefs, this religious unity did not always translate into social harmony. It was sometimes difficult to get all of the tribes to participate in defending individual groups (Judg. 5:15–17), and occasionally local disputes led to intertribal war (Judg. 19–21). There are several likely reasons for the progressive disintegration of the lineage system. First, after the Israelites settled in Canaan, their economy became more complex. Some groups moved into recently captured towns and took up occupations there. Others became successful farmers. The population began to grow, both because of the strong economy and because non-Israelites were incorporated into the Israelite lineages. The increase in population forced farmers to put new land under cultivation and pushed them into areas where Israelites had not previously lived. It is thus likely that some of the lineages became too large to function efficiently, and as a result they fragmented and made group unity difficult to achieve. Second, a number of Israel's smaller lineages seem to have been isolated geographically by the mountainous terrain, and this made their participation in larger lineage groups more difficult. Finally, outside of the lineage heads, Israel seems to have had no leaders capable of getting the small lineages to act together as a group. Prophets such as Deborah occasionally played such a central role, particularly in time of war (Judg. 4:4–10), and Levites may have served as itinerant priests and administrators, but the nature of the lineage structure prevented a single person from exercising political control over several tribes at the same time.

In an attempt to solve the problem of social unity that is inherent in any lineage system, some Israelite lineages, mostly in the north, adopted the practice of delegating political authority to individual chiefs for a particular purpose and for a limited period of time. These "judges" were believed to have been chosen directly by God in times of danger and served primarily as military leaders (Judg. 2:11–23). Some groups apparently wanted to make the office of judge hereditary and to move Israel in the direction of a genuine monarchy, but this would have altered the traditional social structure and was resisted (Judg. 8:22–9:57).

The Effects of the Monarchy: The line between lineage-based society and monarchical state was finally crossed decisively with the election of Saul as Israel's ruler, but the change did not take place without considerable opposition from some of the lineages, which feared the loss of their political power. The OT narratives of Saul's rise reflect several different attitudes toward the idea of kingship, and it is difficult to know to what extent the stories reflect historical reality. It is probably safe to assume, however, that the strongest opposition to the monarchy came from the powerful northern tribe of Ephraim, whose point of view was represented by the prophet Samuel. As a prophet, Samuel gave divine legitimation to the idea of an extremely limited monarchy, and he sought to retain control over Israelite worship, to prevent the establishment of a principle of dynastic succession, and to ensure Saul's continued dependence on the lineage militias. When Samuel did not completely succeed in his attempt, he anointed David in Saul's place and thereafter opposed Saul with all of the power of his important office (1 Sam. 7–16).

David (late eleventh–early tenth centuries B.C.) was more successful in consolidating the power of the monarchy, but he still experienced some limits to his authority. After Saul's death, the northern tribes rejected David and unsuccessfully tried to maintain their own monarchy. David, however, had political support from his own southern tribe of Judah and from a heterogeneous group of supporters that had no allegiance to the lineage system (1 Sam. 22:2). With this political base, he became king of Judah at Hebron, and his authority was later recognized by the north. Although he was successful in bringing the remaining Canaanite cities (including Jerusalem) under Israelite control and in extending his power across the Jordan, he does not seem to have made serious attempts to break the power of the old lineage system, and the economy did not improve radically during his time. The nuclear and extended families apparently remained the basis of the social system, and the rebellions that took place during his reign attest to the continued life of the lineage system (2 Sam. 16; 20). David did, however, install a central bureaucracy in his new capital of Jerusalem and included in it members of his own family and some of his Judahite supporters. He may also have used forced labor for some of his building projects, but his attempt at systematic taxation does not seem to have been successful.

Royal power was further centralized under Solomon (ca. 965–924), who increased Israel's foreign trade, particularly with Tyre, and engaged in extensive building projects. This must have led to the creation of a large class of merchants, although there is not much archaeological evidence of economic growth, and it may be that Solomon's trading ventures were not as successful as the biblical texts indicate. It is certain, however, that the central government increased its power enormously during Solomon's reign. The building projects required both money and labor, and to obtain these Solomon reorganized his kingdom to facilitate tax collection and the recruitment of forced labor. In the process he broke down some of the old tribal boundaries, thus further weakening the lineage structure, and created a complex hierarchy of royal officials. As is typical with monarchies, political, religious, and economic power began to be drawn toward the central government and toward those involved in government-supported economic enterprises.

Solomon's harsh imposition of royal authority provoked a revolt in the north, and after the king's death the northern tribes withdrew to set up their own state under Jeroboam (1 Kings 11–12). This revolt was originally supported by northern prophets, such as Ahijah of Shiloh, who opposed Solomon on both religious and political grounds. Ahijah and the groups he represented may have originally thought that the new monarchy in the north would restore them to the central roles in the religious establishment that they had enjoyed in the time of Samuel, but if so, their hopes were dashed when Jeroboam set up a state that simply duplicated the abuses of Solomon's kingdom. Ahijah therefore condemned the Northern Kingdom and became the first of a chain of prophets who opposed the religious and political policies of the crown (1 Kings 12–14). Only during the time of the prophet Elisha did this critique succeed in bringing about a change in the government's point of view, but this prophetic victory was short-lived, and the Northern Kingdom soon returned to its former ways (2 Kings 1–10).

Although the prophets described in the books of Kings had nothing good to say about the religious practices of the northern state of Israel, in economic terms the north was relatively successful. Beginning with Jeroboam, Israel (also called Ephraim) enjoyed slow but steady economic growth and under the Omrid dynasty (881–842 B.C.) became a major military and commercial power. The archaeological record contains evidence of expanding agricultural production and trade. Important industries were developed in pottery, textiles, wine, olive oil, and metal products. Given the hierarchical organization of the state, however, the growing economy primarily benefited those at the top of the social structure, such as merchants and government officials. Those in the lower classes became the victims of the system, losing income and often hereditary land. This situation was condemned by the prophets Amos and Hosea, who saw economic oppression as a symptom of a greater religious illness. The prophets' oracles of doom were eventually fulfilled when the Northern Kingdom was destroyed by the Assyrians in 722 B.C.

In the Southern Kingdom, Judah, the economic and political situation was rather similar. Political power was fully centralized in Jerusalem, which was also the country's major economic and religious center. Distinct classes of priests and bureaucrats grew up around the capital, and because of the continuity of the Davidic dynasty, members of the royal family were more influential than was the case in the north. After the fall of the Northern Kingdom, a series of disastrous political moves by the Judean kings made it necessary for them to pay heavy tribute, first to the Assyrians and later to the Babylonians. These bills were paid primarily at the expense of the lower classes, and the resulting poverty and oppression were condemned even by prophets such as Isaiah, who basically supported the ideals of the Jerusalemite establishment.

The Exile: The destruction of Jerusalem and the Temple in 586 B.C. was a turning point in Israel's social history. Although the period of the Exile and the reconstruction still requires more study before a complete history can be written, several trends in the development of Israelite society can be noted. First, the Exile effectively ended the existence of an Israelite central government in Jerusalem. Although some of those who returned from Babylon may have tried to re-establish the Davidic dynasty, the real political power in Jerusalem was held by a succession of foreign rulers, first the Babylonians, then the Persians, Greeks, and Romans. Thus, after the Exile anyone who wanted to exercise political power had to first come to an understanding with a foreign government. Second, with the monarchical form of government destroyed by the Babylonians, the older lineage system seems to have reasserted itself, at least at the levels of the extended family and the nuclear family. Cuneiform texts from Babylon show that family ties were maintained by the exiles, and a renewed interest in genealogies in the postexilic OT literature suggests that the lineage may have again become an important social group (1 Chron. 1–9). Third, at least some of the exiles prospered economically during their stay in Babylon and were tempted to integrate themselves completely into the surrounding culture. Finally, the Exile saw the development of numerous conflicting religious, political, and social groups, each advocating different explanations for the disaster and suggesting different ways in which a new Israel could be built.

The Postexilic Period: The intergroup conflicts that began in the Exile became more serious when the Persian government actually allowed the exiles to return (sixth–fifth centuries B.C.). Issues that were previously theoretical then became real, and the exiles had to decide how the new government would be structured and how the new Temple would be built. The postexilic OT books all reflect these debates and suggest that Israelite society became more fragmented as the reconstruction progressed. Priestly groups who did not return to power in the Temple opposed those who did. Advocates of cooperation with the Persians came into conflict with those who supported renewed Israelite independence. Those who returned from exile despised those who did not, and the builders of the new Temple excluded from the religious community Israelites who had remained in Judah during the Exile.

As the postexilic period (late sixth century B.C. on) continued and more groups were deprived of social, political, and religious power, apocalyptic religion took on new life. Groups that considered themselves excluded from their rightful place in society increasingly looked for a solution to their problems at some future time when God would directly intervene in history in order to realize their expectations. Apocalyptic literature, such as that found in the latter parts of the books of Daniel and Zechariah, was produced by a number of these groups, although only a few such writings have found their way into the OT. The apocalyptic programs that these groups created varied depending on the composition of the group, but all of the scenarios reflected a feeling that the social structure was out of alignment and required major reform. Only in a few cases were these hopes fulfilled during the OT period, and most apocalyptic groups remained a minority voice in the midst of a hostile culture. ***See also*** Amorites; Apocalyptic Literature; Biblical Criticism; Covenant; David; Exile; Family, The; Jerusalem; Judges, The Book of; King; Priests; Prophet; Samuel; Saul; Semites; Sociology of the New Testament; Solomon; Temple, The; Tribes, The.

Bibliography

Rogerson, J. W. *Anthropology and the Old Testament*. Atlanta, GA: John Knox, 1979.

Silver, M. *Prophets and Markets*. Boston: Kluwer-Nijhoff, 1983.

Wilson, R. *Sociological Approaches to the Old Testament*. Philadelphia: Fortress, 1984.

R.R.W.

Soco (soh'koh; Heb., "thorny"; KJV: "Socho").

1 A town in Judah between Adullam and Azekah (Josh. 15:35). It was used later by Philistines (1 Sam. 17:1), fortified by King Rehoboam of Judah (2 Chron. 11:7), and then used again by the Philistines (2 Chron. 28:18). It was probably modern Khirbet ʻAbbad about two miles south of Azekah. **2** A second town in Judah (Josh. 15: 48), probably the modern Khirbet Shuweikeh about ten miles southwest of Hebron. **3** A town in Solomon's third district (1 Kings 4:10). It was probably modern Tell er-Ras located about ten miles northwest of Samaria. **4** A descendant of Judah and a son of Heber (1 Chron. 4:18). Even in this case it may be a place name, possibly the one in Josh. 15:48 above. R.S.B.

sod, an archaic term used in the KJV for boiled food (Gen. 25:29; 2 Chron. 35:13; Lam. 4:10).

Sodom (sah'duhm), perhaps the best remembered of the five cities of the valley (Gen. 19:29). The city's inhabitants joined with neighbors in fighting the marauding Chedorlaomer, the king of Elam (Gen. 14:1). Abraham's nephew, Lot, chose Sodom for his residence (Gen. 13:8–13).

A precise location is not given for the city though the general area is associated with the Dead Sea. Archaeological research early in the twentieth century suggested to some that Sodom, along with other cities of the valley, is located under what is now the shallow, southern end of the Dead Sea. Furthermore, this research assigned a date for Sodom early in the second millennium B.C. on the basis of observable settlement patterns in the general area and the assumption that the chronological reckoning of the patriarchal narratives implied such a date. There is no positive evidence that ancient Sodom is submerged under the Dead Sea, however. More recent investigation has shown in detail that there were urban areas just to the east and south of the Dead Sea during most of the third millennium and in places perhaps into the early second millennium as well. Indeed, on the basis of the excavations of the Bab ed-Dhra (located on the tongue of land extending into the Dead Sea from its eastern shore) and at Numeira (further south on the eastern shore), some have proposed that to these two sites belong the valley cities of the Genesis narrative. Both of these cities were inhabited during most of the third millennium.

Sodom is remembered as a wicked city that brought divine wrath upon it. The Genesis narrative records both attempted sexual perversity and gross inhospitality (Gen. 19:1–11). Other writers use Sodom as an example of warning (Deut. 29:16–28) and sometimes as an accusation against the covenant people (Amos 4:11; Isa. 1:9–11). This principle extends into the NT period, where references to the wickedness of Sodom may still be found (Matt. 10:15; Luke 10: 12; Rom. 9:29, quoting Isaiah; 2 Pet. 2:6; Jude 7).

There is also an interesting reference to the "Sea of Sodom" (i.e., the Dead Sea) in 2 Esd. 5: 7, where it is stated that in the days to come this "dead" sea will produce fish as a miraculous sign. ***See also*** Abraham; Lot. J.A.D.

sodomy, a generic term for copulation that is not "natural" and heterosexual, derived from the story of Sodom whose inhabitants sought to have sexual relations with Lot's visitors (Gen. 19:1–11). The Bible frequently condemns male homosexuality (Lev. 18:22; 20:13; Rom. 1:27; 1 Cor. 6:9) as well as bestiality (Exod. 22:19; Lev. 18:23; 20:15–16; Deut. 27:21), presumably because it considered male and female to be natural correlates (see Gen. 1:27; 2:18–24). Lesbianism along with male homosexuality is condemned by Paul (Rom. 1:26–27).

sojourn, a noun that derives its meaning from the meaning of the verb "to live among for an extended time." Therefore it is applied to the stay of a people (particularly Israel's tribes) in a place for any length of time, such as Jacob's tribes in Egypt (Gen. 47:4), the man of Judah (Elimelech) in Moab (Ruth 1:1), or Jacob and Isaac at Hebron (Gen. 35:27).

sojourner. ***See*** Foreigner; Gentile; Stranger.

soldier, a person involved in military activity, one who is trained for war. The word "soldier" appears in the Bible quite frequently, along with a number of synonymous terms (see 1 Chron. 12: 23–38 for an extensive list of examples). Special attention should be drawn to the phrase "men who drew the sword," since this action identifies the soldier's primary function (i.e., combat) and symbolizes warfare in general (Judg. 8:10; see Ezek. 21:3). During the biblical period, warriors were equipped with a variety of offensive and defensive weapons; fully armed soldiers from two distinct eras are described in 1 Sam. 17:5–7 and Eph. 6:11–17, with the latter reference comparing the panoply of a Roman soldier to the Christian's spiritual armor. Distinction was made between infantrymen, horsemen, and charioteers (Ezek. 26:7; Acts 23:23).

Although other ancient Near Eastern peoples had standing armies at an early date, the Hebrews had no professional soldiers until the establishment of the monarchy (eleventh century B.C.). Abraham's "trained men" were obviously skilled warriors, but they were recruited from his household (Gen. 14:14). The Hebrew conquest of Canaan (thirteenth–twelfth centuries B.C.) was accomplished by tribal militias of adult males (Num. 1:1–46). Since combat entailed great risk and called for courage and strength, some men were exempt from military service (Deut. 20:5–8). The Levites were not counted among those who were "able to go forth to war," but they offered reassurance to

Assyrian infantry and cavalry equipped with spears and bows pursuing fleeing desert raiders; from a relief at the palace of the Assyrian king Ashurbanipal at Nineveh, seventh century B.C.

soldiers before battles (Num. 1:47–50; Deut. 20: 1–4). In the period of the judges and the early reign of Saul (twelfth–eleventh centuries B.C.), soldiers were mustered to battle by trumpet call or messengers (Judg. 6:34–35; 1 Sam. 11: 7–8).

The beginning of a standing army in Israel may be seen in the special force that Saul gathered together (1 Sam. 13:1–2; 14:52). David continued this process by developing his famous bodyguard of "mighty men" (1 Sam. 22:2; 2 Sam. 10:7) and by making a census of the Israelites, a necessary step in the establishment of a national army (2 Sam. 24). Thereafter, the professional soldier was the norm. Mercenaries were also a part of this early Israelite army (2 Sam. 20:23; 2 Chron. 25:6).

Soldiers usually shared in the loot captured in battle (Num. 31:27; Deut. 21:11; Josh. 22:8), and their return from war was a cause for celebration (Judg. 11:34; 1 Sam. 18:6–7). As in modern armies, the soldier's routine included guard duty (Judg. 7:19).

Because the Roman Empire was maintained by military power, the Roman soldier was a common sight in NT times. Soldiers were involved in the arrest and crucifixion of Jesus (John 18:3, 12; 19:2, 23–25, 32, 34). After Paul was arrested in Jerusalem, he was frequently in the company of soldiers; the apostle used the word "soldier" to describe his co-workers (Phil. 2:25; Philem. 1:2; see the figurative use of "soldier" in 1 Cor. 9:7 and 2 Tim. 2:3–4). ***See also*** Army; War. G.L.M.

solemn assembly, the translation generally used for the Hebrew terms *atzeret* and *atzarah*. These terms refer to gatherings of the people, in a state of ritual purity, for sacred, religious purposes. These purposes include set festivals, such as the seventh day of the Festival of Unleavened Bread (Deut. 16:8) or the eighth day of the Festival of Booths (Lev. 23:36; Num. 29:35; 2 Chron. 7:9; Neh. 8:18). They might also include special assemblies such as that called by Jehu for Baal (2 Kings 10:20) or for times of emergency (Joel 1:14; 2:15–16). Such assemblies were sometimes criticized by prophets when the people acted unjustly in their everyday lives (Isa. 1:13; Amos 5:21). ***See also*** Worship.

Solomon (sahl'uh-muhn; also known as Jedidiah, Heb., "Yahweh's beloved," 2 Sam. 12:25), David's son by Bathsheba and his successor, who reigned for forty years in the second third of the tenth century B.C. Although 1 Samuel 12 implies that Solomon was Bathsheba's second child by David, born after the child conceived during their adulterous affair had died, 1 Chron. 3:5 may indicate that there were intervening children.

As David grew old, his son Adonijah began to take steps to succeed his father with the support of several court officials, including the

Solomon is portrayed as a wise teacher in this late fourteenth-century illustration for the book of Proverbs.

general Joab and the priest Abiathar. Another faction gained the support of Bathsheba in approaching David on the basis of a previous promise, not recorded in the Bible, that Solomon would be his successor. David affirmed his commitment to Solomon, who was immediately installed by the priest Zadok with the assistance of Nathan, the prophet, and Benaiah from the royal guard. Solomon served as coregent until David's death, at which time Adonijah, who had previously agreed to accept Solomon's succession, sought Bathsheba's support in his request to marry Abishag, who had served David in his old age. Solomon saw the request as a threat and had Adonijah executed along with his supporter Joab. The priest Abiathar was expelled from Jerusalem and Shimei, a Benjaminite who had caused problems for David, was restricted from leaving Jerusalem on pain of death, a threat that was later carried out (1 Kings 2).

Reign: Solomon appears to have been responsible for a political consolidation, demonstrated by his creation of administrative districts cutting across the old tribal boundaries (1 Kings 4: 7–19). His priestly activities also suggest a substantial expansion of the king's role (1 Kings 8; contrast 1 Sam. 13). Solomon's reign was also characterized by vigorous activity in the international sphere. His empire included trade routes linking Africa, Asia, Arabia, and Asia Minor, thus generating substantial revenue while supporting widespread commercial activities, including, apparently, participation in the horse trade based in Asia Minor. His fleet sailed from Ezion-geber in the Gulf of Aqaba to Ophir on the coast of the Red Sea (either in eastern Africa or western Arabia). The Bible ascribes to him seven hundred wives, including Moabite, Edomite, Phoenician, and Hittite women (1 Kings 11:1), at least some of whom he doubtless married as part of political alliances. Among these were an Egyptian princess, whose father (probably Pharaoh Siamon) gave Solomon the city of Gezer, and an Ammonite woman, whose son Rehoboam eventually succeeded to the throne. Solomon's extensive building program included store cities as well as fortifications. In Jerusalem, he built an elaborate palace complex, which took thirteen years to complete, and a temple, which took seven, with the assistance of King Hiram of Tyre. The Bible's description strongly suggests Canaanite influence, as one would expect under the circumstances. Solomon also gave Hiram twenty cities in Galilee.

Wisdom: Such activities brought wealth and a cosmopolitan atmosphere to Solomon's kingdom. His wisdom is said to have "surpassed the wisdom of all the people of the east, and all the wisdom of Egypt" (1 Kings 4:30, Hebrew 5:10), reflecting the kind of international intellectual activity Solomon's political accomplishments would suggest. According to the OT, this wisdom was God's response to Solomon's request, when offered whatever he might choose, for an understanding mind (1 Kings 3:5–9; Solomon is already called wise in 2:9). The OT makes much of his wisdom, describing his ability to determine which of two prostitutes was a disputed child's true mother (1 Kings 3:16–27), to answer difficult questions posed by the queen of Sheba (1 Kings 10:1–3), and to tell fables and sing songs (1 Kings 4:32–33, Hebrew 5:12–13). This tradition is reflected also in the ascription of several sections of the book of Proverbs to him (see Prov. 1:1; 10:1) along with the book of Ecclesiastes (see Eccles. 1:1), where his wealth and wives no doubt served as a useful backdrop for the author's own purposes. Solomon's many wives and internal references to his wealth (e.g., Song of Sol. 3:8) probably played a role in the traditional ascriptions of Song of Songs to him (Song of Sol. 1:1), just as the tradition that he wrote poetry was doubtless important in the ascriptions of Psalms 72 and 127. His impact, in part as the last Davidic king to rule over a united kingdom, seems also to have served as an inspiration for the activities of Judah's eighth-century B.C. King Hezekiah (see 2 Chron. 30:26; Prov. 25:1).

Policy: The OT does not find all of Solomon's activities praiseworthy. The cosmopolitanism resulting from his participation in international affairs brought many foreign religious practices to Jerusalem along with a less stringent attitude than some biblical authors, at least, found acceptable. Whereas Solomon's policies about worship at some high places prior to the Temple's construction may have been countenanced, he is later condemned for building such shrines and for having married foreign women (e.g., Neh. 13:26). The book of Kings (e.g., 1 Kings 11:9–25) regards these as causing God's decision, announced by the Shilonite prophet Ahijah, to split the kingdom, removing ten of the twelve tribes from Davidic control.

Solomon's policies were not only religiously offensive. The OT explicitly mentions three political enemies—Hadad, an Edomite prince (1 Kings 11:14), Rezon of Zobah (v. 24), and Jeroboam of Israel (v. 26), each of whom sought refuge in Egypt, adding an international dimension to his opposition. Moreover, Solomon's building activities were expensive in both economic and human resources. (Some scholars consider the warning against royal behavior in 1 Sam. 8:11–17 to have been based on Solomon.) Later complaints suggest a high level of taxation, while the Bible mentions the use of forced labor, limited to non-Israelites according to some sources (1 Kings 9:20–22), but not according to others (1 Kings 5:13). The schism that followed Solomon's death is implicitly ascribed to his policies (1 Kings 12:4). To what extent the invasion by Pharaoh Shishak, which took place five years after Solomon's death, fits into this is less clear (see 1 Kings 11:40).

The OT's view of Solomon is thus ambivalent. On the one hand, his reign clearly marks the peak of Israelite success, both politically and religiously (although Chronicles suggests and Kings implies that some credit for initiating the building of a temple should be given to David). It is in Solomon's reign that the promises made to the patriarchs come to their fulfillment (1 Kings 4:20). On the other hand, syncretism and the influx of foreign practices under Solomon mark the beginning of religious decay, accompanied by growth in internal dissent and the emergence of external enemies.

The proverbial nature of Solomon's glory and his wisdom is reflected in sayings of Jesus (Matt. 6:29; 12:42). Matthew also lists Solomon as one of Jesus' ancestors (Matt. 1:6–7). ***See also*** David; Wisdom. F.E.G.

Solomon, the Song of. ***See*** Song of Solomon, The.

Solomon, Wisdom of. ***See*** Wisdom of Solomon, The.

Solomon's Pools, three reservoirs, one above another, 714 feet (217 m.), 441 feet (134 m.), and 390 feet (120 m.) long respectively, about twelve miles (19 km.) south of Bethlehem, below Qala't el-Burak, a seventeenth-century Turkish fort later used as a caravanserai. Constructed no later than the second century B.C. and repaired by Pontius Pilate, as well as more than once subsequently, these supply water along two aqueducts to Jerusalem. The identification with Solomon is derived from Josephus, a Jewish historian of the first century A.D. ***See also*** Pilate, Pontius.

Solomon's Porch. ***See*** Solomon's Portico.

Solomon's Portico, a colonnade thought to have been situated along the east side of the Temple enclosure built by Herod the Great as part of his restoration of the Temple of Jerusalem. If so, the portico would have been directly above the Kidron Valley, facing the Mount of Olives. With the destruction of the Temple in A.D. 70, nothing from this colonnade remained standing, and there have been no excavations along the east side of the Temple Mount. Jesus was familiar with this porch (John 10:23), and, after his resurrection, the apostles gathered there with the people (Acts 3:11; 5:12). ***See also*** Temple, The. M.K.M.

Solomon's Seal. ***See*** Seal of Solomon, The.

Solomon's servants, foreign slaves used for menial tasks in Solomon's Temple (Ezra 2:55, 58; Neh. 7:57, 60; 11:3). They were similar in function to the Nethinim (Ezra 8:20) who helped the Levites after the Exile (586 B.C.). ***See also*** Nethinim.

Solomon's Temple. ***See*** Temple, The.

son, a male offspring. The Hebrew word *ben* (Aramaic *bar*, Gk. *auios*) enjoyed a rich semantic range, although it is used most often in the Bible with reference to actual physical lineage. In the plural it frequently combines with the word Israel to designate a specific group of people, male and female (the Israelites). An adopted son was also referred to by this word. In polite address persons with no actual kinship to the speaker were afforded this title; the one addressed was ordinarily an inferior (cf. the aged priest Eli's use of "my son" in speaking to the child Samuel, 1 Sam. 3:16). The expression "son of" came to describe a characteristic feature of something. For example, "son of fatness" with reference to the land suggests fertile soil (Isa. 5:1), and "son of strength" connotes might. A similar use of "daughter" occurs (cf. "daughters of song," Eccles. 12:4) and "daughter of Zion" really means the sister city, Jerusalem. When used with a place, as in "sons of Zion," the meaning is "inhabitants." In Proverbs and Ecclesiastes "my son" develops into a technical form for a student, although it seems also to retain its literal sense in many instances. This designation of students as sons was also the practice in Egyptian and in Mesopotamian wisdom literature. The biblical prophetic tradition uses the expression "sons of prophets" to describe professional membership in the prophetic guild (cf. Amos 7:14). Likewise, allegiance to a particular deity was expressed in this way (sons of Chemosh, Num. 21:29; cf. sons of Belial, KJV Deut. 13:13), and "sons of God" alludes to divine beings (godlike creatures). Satan belonged to this select group, according to Job 1:6. The singular "son of man" simply meant "human" at first (e.g., Ezek. 2:1) but eventually signified a heavenly being who descended to earth (Dan. 7:13–14; cf. Mark 8:38), whereas "son of God" was merely an exalted way of referring to a great man.

In the NT, the use of the word "son" to designate a physical descendant (e.g., Matt. 21:28; Mark 13:12; Luke 15:31) is also common. In addition, the apostle Paul uses the word to denote a close and affectionate relationship in the Christian faith, both of individuals (1 Cor. 4:17; Phil. 2:22; Philem. 10) and of groups (1 Cor. 4:14). Because the term "son" was used to denote the unique filial relationship of Jesus to God (Matt. 3:17; Mark 1:1; Luke 9:35; Acts 3:26), it also came to be applied to those who through trust in Jesus attained the same relationship with God (John 1:12; 1 John 3:1–2). ***See also*** Son of God; Son of Man. J.L.C.

song. ***See*** Music.

Song of Ascent (KJV: "Song of Degress"), a musical piece sung by pilgrims as they climbed the hill to Jerusalem at the time of festivals such as the Feast of Booths, the Festival of Weeks, and the Passover, which were celebrated in the Temple. A number of such songs are preserved as Psalms 120–134. ***See also*** Music; Psalms, The.

Song of Solomon, the (Heb. *Shir Hashshirim*, "Song of Songs," which means the best or greatest song), a poetic OT book known also as "Song of Songs" or "Canticle (of Canticles)." The attribution of the work to Solomon probably derives from that monarch's renowned marriages (1 Kings 11:3) as well as from the mention of his name in the Song (1:5; 4:6–11; 8:11–12). There is no agreement about the date, although the prevalent opinion is inclined to the postexilic period (post mid-sixth century B.C.).

The Song consists of from about five to fifty love poems, the number depending upon the interpretation of transitions within the eight chapters. However, a dialogue between a man and a woman runs throughout the work and gives it a certain unity. The characters in the work are a man (idealized as a king and a shepherd), a woman, and the Daughters of Jerusalem. These latter function as a foil for the woman's statements. It is not likely that the book was conceived as a drama with three characters, wherein a king and shepherd vie for the hand of a peasant maiden.

The poems are of several kinds: songs of yearning, admiration, self-description, description of the physical charms of the beloved (similar to the Arabic love poem called a *wasf*). There may even be a proverbial saying in 8:6, where the power of love is compared to that of death.

The literal historical interpretation of the

OUTLINE OF CONTENTS

The Song of Solomon

I. Title and introduction (1:1–6)
II. Dialogue between the man and woman (1:7–2:7)
III. Reflections (2:8–3:11)
 A. Reminiscence by the woman (2:8–17)
 B. Loss and recovery (3:1–5)
 C. Description of Solomon's wedding procession (3:6–11)
IV. Dialogues (4:1–8:4)
 A. Dialogue between the man and woman (4:1–5:1)
 B. Dialogue between the woman and the daughters (5:2–6:3)
 C. Address of the man to the woman (6:4–12)
 D. Dialogue between the man and woman (7:1–8:4)
V. Appendices (8:5–14)

Song understands it as an exchange of love between a man and a woman. It is not clear that the setting is a marriage celebration. The two lovers express their feelings for one another in extraordinarily vivid and exotic imagery (animals, flowers, spices, etc.). The religious interpretation, which was popular at one time, understands the poem as originally (although not in its present form) deriving from the religious celebrations of divine marriage (e.g., Tammuz to Ishtar). There are many examples of this kind of literature in ancient Mesopotamia, but the Song does not really fit here; it is rather to the love songs of Egypt (dealing with human love) that it bears closer resemblance.

The traditional interpretation by both the synagogue and church found in the Song another level of meaning: the love between God and his people, i.e., the Lord and Israel, Christ and the Church or the individual person. Such an interpretation can become arbitrary when individual details are interpreted in allegorical fashion. But if the work as a whole is interpreted in the light of the prophetic understanding of the covenant as a marriage relationship (e.g., Hos. 1–3; Isa. 62:5), this level of meaning can be defended. R.E.M.

Song of Songs, the. ***See*** Song of Solomon, The.

Song of the Three Children, the, one of the Additions to Daniel found between Dan. 3:23 and 3:24 in the Septuagint (LXX) and Theodotion. It includes:

I. The Prayer of Azariah, the Hebrew name of Abednego (vv. 1–22)

II. Additional narrative material describing the intensity of the flames (vv. 23–27)

III. A hymn sung by the three youths while in the furnace (vv. 28–68).

The prayer and the hymn are probably independent liturgical compositions done in Hebrew and later adapted sometime during the second century B.C. to fit the story in Daniel 3. The addition follows the practice of supplying prayers and songs at appropriate places in stories, but it may also have been intended to shift the emphasis of Daniel 3 from the tyranny of the king to the piety of the three youths. The prayer is penitential in character and seems to reflect the desecration of the Temple by the Syrian king Antiochus IV Epiphanes in 167 B.C. It treats the catastrophe as the consequence of "our sins," begs God's mercy for the sake of his promise to Abraham (cf. Gen. 12:1–3), Isaac, and Israel (Jacob), and, in the absence of a "place to make an offering before thee" (v. 15), it presents the sacrifice of "a contrite heart and a humble spirit" (v. 16). The last suggestion echoes Psalm 51 but also anticipates the ultimate transformation of Judaism under the Pharisees and rabbis from a religion centered around the Temple to one concerned with prayer, acts of mercy, and the way of Torah.

The hymn calls upon God's creatures to bless him, moving from heavenly to earthly things, then from animals to humanity, and finally to Israel. While its order is related to Psalm 148, it is possible that both the psalm and the hymn are dependent upon a system of cosmic order present in speculative wisdom. In contrast to the prayer, in which the Temple seems to be desecrated, the hymn places God in his temple (v. 31), although it may well be that the heavenly rather than the earthly temple is intended —an idea from the conceptual world of postbiblical Judaism (cf. Rev. 11:19).

Protestants include the Song of the Three Children among the Apocrypha, while Catholics retain it as part of the book of Daniel. ***See also*** Apocrypha, Old Testament; Daniel, The Additions to. D.W.S.

Son of God, a person or a people with a special relationship to God.

In the OT: In the OT and pre-Christian Judaism there are four notable uses of the term "Son of God." First, it is predicated of Israel constituted as a nation through the Exodus (e.g., Hos. 11:1). Second, it is a title given to the monarch at the time of enthronement (e.g., Ps. 2:7, a coronation psalm). Third, the angels are called "sons of God" (e.g., Job 38:7). Fourth, in the deuterocanonical book The Wisdom of Solomon it is applied to the righteous individual (Wisd. of Sol. 2:18). Primarily, it denotes not physical filiation but a divine call to obedience in a predestined role in salvation history.

It is a matter of dispute whether the term "Son of God" was already current in pre-Christian Judaism as a messianic title as Mark 14:61 would seem to suggest. But in view of the discovery of Psalm 2:7 in a messianic application in the Dead Sea Scrolls (4QFlor. 10–14), it is probably safe to conclude that it was just coming into use in this context during the period of Christian origins.

In the NT: The pre-Easter Jesus undoubtedly had a unique experience of God as his *Abba* ("Father"). He addressed God with this intimate appellation, normally reserved for an earthly father (e.g., Mark 14:36). Although the synoptic tradition contains two sayings in which Jesus refers to himself as "son" in relation to God as his Father (Mark 13:32; Matt. 11:27 [Q]), the authenticity of these sayings is widely questioned, and it remains uncertain whether Jesus actually called himself "son" in relation to God as Father. The most we can be certain of is that, since his use of *Abba* implies a unique filial consciousness, it implies the idea that he is "son."

The use of "Son of God" as a christological title should be clearly distinguished from the Father/Son language. The evidence suggests that in spite of its presence in the synoptic Gospels, the title did not come into use until after Easter. At his resurrection/exaltation Jesus was *appointed* "Son of God" (Rom. 1:4). This belief seems to have arisen through the application of the coronation psalm, already interpreted messianically at Qumran, to the Risen One (Acts 13: 33; cf. Heb. 5:5). The use of the word "appointed" in Rom. 1:4 indicates that "Son of God" at this stage in the history of Christian thought denoted an office or function, rather than a metaphysical quality as in later dogmatics. This usage is in accord with OT and Jewish practice. Christology of this type is sometimes designated "adoptionist," but it is not adoptionism in the later, heretical sense, according to which Jesus, having been initially purely human, later became divine. It means that at his resurrection/exaltation Jesus embarked upon a new role in salvation history as the mediator of God's final offer of salvation.

In the course of time the moment at which Jesus was appointed "Son of God" in this functional sense was pushed back to his baptism as is indicated by the voice from heaven (Mark 1: 11). At that moment Jesus was marked out for his messianic role. This process of retrojection does not entail the christologizing of a life that had been previously unmessianic, for from the earliest time after Easter the community had recognized that God had been at work in Jesus (Acts 2:22; 10:38) and such terms as "prophet" or "servant" were used to indicate that in his earthly lifetime Jesus had appeared as God's agent (prophet, Luke 24:19; servant, Acts 3:13). "Son of God" simply takes over the duty of these earlier titles. It has also been suggested that the Son of God christology was first pushed back only to the moment of the transfiguration (Mark 9:7), but this is unlikely for the voice at the transfiguration seems rather to have been modeled on the voice at the baptism. Once this process of retrojection had shifted the crucial christological moment to baptism, the title "Son of God" could be used occasionally by others, e.g., the demons (Mark 3:11). It is noteworthy, however, that Jesus never claims for himself the title "Son of God." While he is represented as accepting it in Mark 14:61–62, both Matthew (27:64) and Luke (22: 67) are at pains to tone down Jesus' acceptance of the title as though what he says to the High Priest is, "It—like the title 'messiah'—is your word, not mine." The ejaculation of the crowd, "For he said he was the son of God" (Matt. 27: 43), is clearly secondary, as a comparison with the Markan parallel shows.

A connected development with the foregoing process of retrojection is the idea of the sending of the Son. This appears in a formula exhibiting a constant pattern: God as subject; a verb of sending or its equivalent; the Son as object; and a statement of God's saving purpose in sending the Son (see Gal. 4:4–5; Rom. 8:3–4; John 3:17). In the parable of the wicked husbandmen (Mark 12:6) a similar image occurs, though without an explicit statement of the saving purpose. The roots of this sending formula probably lie in the earlier designation of Jesus as "prophet," which in turn originates in his own self-understanding. Jesus had a strong consciousness of his sending (cf. Mark 9:37), a consciousness that was shared by the OT prophets, on whom it was patterned (e.g., Isa. 6:8). When "Son of God" took over from "prophet" the sending of the Son formula was born.

A related formula is the "handing over" formula (Mark 14:21; Rom. 4:25; John 3:16). This in turn could have its roots in the earlier designation of Jesus as "servant of God," for the term "handed over" or "delivered" occurs in the Servant Song of Isaiah 53 (as found in the Septuagint version).

It is sometimes held that the sending formula was designed to express a preexistence Christology, according to which sending refers to the incarnation of the preexistent Son. The origin of the preexistence Christology is probably to be dated later than the sending formulas, for the latter almost certainly antedate the writings in which they occur. Thus, Gal. 4:4 is widely held to be pre-Pauline and John 3:16–17 to be pre-Johannine. However, Paul may have understood and John certainly understood these formulas in light of their own preexistence theologies.

In the birth narratives of Matthew and Luke the title "Son of God"is shifted back to the conception, birth, or infancy of Jesus (Mat. 2:15; Luke 1:35). However, this also does not imply a preexistence and incarnational Christology or a divine sonship in the metaphysical sense. Rather, it implies his predestination from the womb for a messianic role in salvation history. This functional sense of the divine sonship is made particularly clear in Luke 1:32–33.

There is a growing consensus among scholars that the preexistence Christology originated not with the title "Son of God," but with the identification of Jesus as the personal incarnation of the divine Wisdom. This identification underlies the development of preexistence Christology in the wisdom hymns of the NT (Phil. 2: 6–11, though the presence of preexistence in this hymn is sometimes questioned; Col. 1:15–20; Heb. 1:2–3; John 1:1–18). This identification leads to an expansion of the meaning of "Son of God." The preexistent Wisdom or Word of God is as such also the eternal Son of God, who was with God from all eternity as the agent of creation, revelation, and redemption. That identification has already taken place in the Logos hymn of John 1 (see v. 14; also v. 18, if "Son" rather than "God" is the correct text).

The traditional, dogmatic Christology of Nicea (A.D. 325) and Chalcedon (A.D. 451) and of Christian orthodoxy since that time rests upon the Johannine development from a functional to a metaphysical Christology. ***See also*** Incarnation; Jesus Christ; Wisdom.

Bibliography

Dunn, J. D. G. *Christology in the Making: A New Testament Inquiry into the Origins of the Doctrine of the Incarnation.* Philadelphia: Westminster, 1980. Pp. 12–64, 163–250.

Fuller, R., and P. Perkins. *Who Is This Christ? Gospel Christology and Contemporary Faith.* Philadelphia: Fortress, 1983. Pp. 41–66, 96–108, 121–34.

Hengel, M. *The Son of God.* Philadelphia: Fortress, 1976. R.H.F.

Son of man, a term with a variety of meanings in the Bible. The NT usage of the term "Son of man" is at first sight simple enough. With one exception (Acts 7:56) and apart from the citation of Ps. 8:4 in Heb. 2:6 and an allusion to Dan. 7:13 in Rev. 2:13, the term is used exclusively by the earthly Jesus in reference to himself. It is usual to classify these occurrences in the synoptic Gospels under three headings: sayings in which Jesus refers to his present activity during his earthly ministry (e.g., Mark 2:12 and parallels; 2:24 and parallels; also Matt. 8:20 [Q] and 11:19 [Q]); sayings in which Jesus refers to his impending passion and/or resurrection (Mark 8:31 and parallels; 9:9 and parallels; 9:31 and parallels; 10:33 and parallels); and sayings in which he refers to his future activity as judge and Savior at the end (e.g., Mark 8:38; cf. Luke 12:8 [Q]; Mark 13:26 and parallels; 14:62 and parallels). In John "Son of man" as a self-referent of Jesus has a more varied usage, the most characteristic being those sayings that speak of the exaltation of the Son of man, an expression that makes a double allusion to the cross and exaltation (John 3:14; 8:28;12:34). John 1:51 looks like an original Parousia saying (third category above) transferred to the present ministry (first category). John 6:53 speaks of eating the flesh and drinking the blood of the Son of man, and John 9:35 (if the text is correct) of believing in the Son of man.

The difficulties begin when one asks the origin of the term. Is it authentic to Jesus? If so, in what sense did he use it? Regarding the origin of the term, it is widely held, especially among German scholars, that the term "Son of man" was already current in pre-Christian, Jewish apocalyptic writings (Dan 7:14; *The Similitudes of Enoch*). Here already the Son of man appears as God's end-time agent of salvation and judgment. British scholars, in particular, often argue that the only pre-Christian example is Daniel, but that there the "Son of man" stands for Israel as a corporate entity. *The Similitudes of Enoch (1 Enoch* 37–71) do not appear in early versions of *Enoch*.

It has therefore been argued by some British scholars that there was no pre-Christian, apocalyptic concept of a "Son of man," and that therefore no light is cast by such sources on the way Jesus used that phrase. Jesus must have used "Son of man" as a simple self-designation, perhaps as a self-effacing way of referring to himself simply as a human being (cf. Ps. 8:4). This usage could account for both the present and suffering references. Sometimes, in this view, the future sayings are explained as post-Easter developments under the influence of Dan. 7:14.

Those who accept the view that there was a pre-Christian apocalyptic concept of a "Son of man" sometimes argue that Jesus used it of a transcendental figure other than himself (see esp. Mark 8:38; Luke 12:8 [Q], where Jesus appears to distinguish between himself and the coming Son of man). This coming Son of man will vindicate Jesus' present offer of final salvation to his contemporaries. After Easter and the rise of an explicit christological faith in Jesus, it is held, his followers saw in him his own vindicator and therefore identified him with the apocalyptic Son of man.

Yet another current view is that Jesus did not use the term "Son of man" at all, either as a self-designation or in reference to a coming figure distinct from himself. It was, in this view, the post-Easter community that first introduced the term "Son of man" to the Jesus tradition in the apocalyptic sense. In both the last mentioned views the present and suffering sayings must have developed out of the future sayings by retrojecting the title into Jesus' earthly life. As this survey indicates, there is no unanimity among scholars at present either as to the origin or the exact meaning of the title "Son of man."

Bibliography

Dunn, J. D. G. *Christology in the Making: A New Testament Inquiry into the Origins of the Doctrine of the Incarnation.* Philadelphia: Westminster, 1980. Pp. 65–97.

Fitzmyer, J. A. "The New Testament Title 'Son of Man' Philologically Considered." In *A Wandering Aramean: Collected Aramaic Essays.* Missoula, MT: Scholars Press, 1979. Pp. 143–60. R.H.F.

sons of God, children of God, phrases denoting superhuman beings. The words "sons of" (Heb. *bene)* in this phrase indicate the members of a people, tribe, or group, just as "sons/children of Israel" (Heb. *bene ysrael)* means "Israelites." The "sons" or "children of God" in the OT refer to different beings, the main alternatives being reflected in two prominent groups of texts.

In the first group is the enigmatic passage in Gen. 6:1–4, which gives an account of how the union of "the sons of God" with "the daughters of men" produced a race of "mighty men that were of old." Here the expression clearly refers to divine beings, and male divine beings at that, given their union with human women. The passage is a remnant of ancient Near Eastern mythological tradition. In the Ugaritic texts, for example, the pantheon or the gods as a whole are identified as the children of the chief god, "the totality of the sons/children of El."

There are other OT texts in which "sons/children of God" refers to divine beings. In Job 38:7 the phrase occurs in parallel with "the morning stars" (RSV), and in Ps. 89:6, a heavily mythological hymn, God is beyond comparison with other deities, the "sons of God" (RSV fn.). In Ps. 29:1 the "heavenly beings" (RSV fn., "sons of God") are called to praise God. The expression also appears in Deut. 32:8 (RSV reading with 40 from the Dead Sea Scrolls and similar to LXX; MT reads "sons of Israel"). The phrase is closely related to the idea of a heavenly court as in Psalm 82 (see also, e.g., Isa. 6; Ezek. 1–3).

The other prominent context, reflecting a somewhat different use of the term, is Job 1–2, in which "the satan" is one of "the sons of God" (1:6; 2:1). Here the LXX translates the phrase "angels" (Gk. *angeloi*). That seems to be an accurate interpretation, for the "sons of God" here certainly are not deities as such. They are subordinate to God and function primarily as messengers. Similar in force is the reference in Dan. 3:25 to the fourth figure in the furnace whose appearance was like "a son of the gods." In later, mainly apocalyptic, reflection such ideas provided the basis for accounts of the rebellion or fall of the angels (*1 Enoch* 6–36; *Jubilees* 5:1–10). In the NT, the two phrases "sons of God" and "children of God" are synonymous, and refer to those who accept Jesus Christ as God's gift of reconciling grace (Gal. 3:26; see also Rom. 8:14, 16, 19, 21). While Jesus specifically identified those who make peace as God's sons (Matt. 5:9), for the most part the two phrases came to mean what we express with the word "Christian" (e.g., John 1:12; Phil. 2:15; Heb. 12:7; 1 John 3:1; 5:2). In all cases, "sons" means both men and women. ***See also*** Angel.

G.M.T.

sons of prophets, a term probably denoting a group of professional prophets (e.g., 1 Sam. 10:5). When Amos asserts he is neither a prophet nor a prophet's son, he is probably disclaiming any identification with such a group (Amos 7:14). ***See also*** Prophet.

Sons of Thunder. ***See*** Boanerges.

soothsayer, one who foretells events. The word has a negative connotation in the OT, where soothsayers are classed with sorcerers (Jer. 27:9) and with magical practices (Deut. 18:10, 14) and are forbidden to Israel (Mic. 5:12).

sop. ***See*** Morsel.

Sopater (soh'pah-tuhr). ***See*** Sosipater.

Sophereth (sof'uhr-eth; Heb., "scribe"), a family of Temple servants who returned to Jerusalem in postexilic times (Neh. 7:57; RSV: "Hassophereth," Heb., "the scribe," Ezra 2:55; 1 Esd. 5:33).

sorcery. ***See*** Magic and Divination.

Sorek (soh'rek), the name of the valley (and brook) where Delilah, Samson's lover who betrayed him, lived; it is mentioned only once in the Bible (Judg. 16:4). There Samson was captured by the Philistines and taken to their city Gaza, where he destroyed the temple of Dagon. The story, along with other evidence, indicates that the area, once inhabited by the tribe of Dan and serving as the boundary between Dan and Simeon, was under Philistine control during the period of the judges (1200–1000 B.C.).

The valley extends between Ashkelon and Gaza in southwestern Palestine, and the brook that bears its name runs westward and then northward into the Mediterranean Sea from the area near Beer-shemesh. In biblical times this city served as the guardian of the Sorek Valley, which is known in modern times as Wadi es-Sarar. ***See also*** Delilah; Samson. F.R.M.

Sosipater (so-sip'uh-tuhr), a Jewish Christian who, with Timothy, Lucius, and Jason (all except Timothy are referred to as "my kinsmen"), joins Paul in sending greetings in Rom. 16:21. Perhaps he was the same person as Sopater of Beroea, who accompanied Paul through Macedonia as he prepared for his last trip to Jerusalem (Acts 20:4).

Sosthenes (sahs'thuh-neez). **1** The "ruler" of a Jewish synagogue in Corinth while Paul was there, according to Acts 18:17. He either replaced Crispus as synagogue leader when the latter became a Christian or had shared the office with him (Acts 18:8). Sosthenes was beaten by a local mob in the presence of Gallio the proconsul, who chose not to intervene in what he regarded as a religious dispute (Acts 18:12–17). **2** The co-author with Paul of 1 Corinthians (1:1). If he is the same person described in 1, he became a Christian and possibly went from Corinth to Ephesus to visit Paul with the delegation of Stephanas, Fortunatus, and Achaicus (1 Cor. 16:17–18). Otherwise, nothing further is known about him. ***See also*** Corinth; Crispus; Gallio; Paul; Synagogue. A.J.M.

soul, a word in the Hebrew Bible with a wide range of meanings. God "breathed the breath of life" into Adam and he became a "living soul" (Gen. 2:7); Adam is *living* clay, as opposed to ordinary clay (Gen. 3:19). This life principle can ebb and flow; one may fear for one's soul (Ezek. 32:10), risk one's soul (Judg. 5:18), or take one's soul (1 Kings 19:4). "Soul" may refer to an individual person: Leah bore sixteen "souls" (children) to Jacob (Gen. 46:18). For a Hebrew, "soul" indicated the unity of a human person; Hebrews *were* living bodies, they did not *have* bodies. This Hebrew field of meaning is breached in the Wisdom of Solomon by explicit introduction of Greek ideas of soul. A dualism of soul and body is present: "a perishable body weighs down the soul" (9:15). This perishable body is opposed by an immortal soul (3:1–3). Such dualism might imply that soul is superior to body.

In the NT, "soul" retains its basic Hebrew field of meaning. Soul refers to one's life: Herod sought Jesus' soul (Matt. 2:20); one might save a soul or take it (Mark 3:4). Death occurs when God "requires your soul" (Luke 12:20). "Soul" may refer to the whole person, the self: "three thousand souls" were converted in Acts 2:41 (see Acts 3:23). Although the Greek idea of an immortal soul different in kind from the mortal body is not evident, "soul" denotes the existence of a person after death (see Luke 9:25; 12:4; 21:19); yet Greek influence may be found in 1 Peter's remark about "the salvation of souls" (1:9). A moderate dualism exists in the contrast of spirit with body and even soul, where "soul" means life that is not yet caught up in grace. ***See also*** Flesh and Spirit; Human Being. J.H.N.

source criticism. ***See*** Biblical Criticism; Synoptic Problem, The; Sources of the Pentateuch.

sources of the Pentateuch, the materials from which the first five books of the OT were composed. As a very extensive composition that incorporates many diverse genres and discrete units of material, the Pentateuch (Genesis through Deuteronomy) is without parallel in ancient Near Eastern literature. The question of how this unique composition was produced has occupied biblical scholarship for four centuries, and various models accounting for the composition of the Pentateuch have been propounded. No single model satisfies the evidence conclusively.

There are two broad types of models. One views the Pentateuch as the product of an author who worked earlier traditions and sources into a new, independent composition. The other sees the Pentateuch as a composite, produced by a redactor who edited parallel literary documents into a single text. Some envision a longer history of oral tradition and literary sources behind the documents the redactor used, some a shorter history. Some reconstruct a series of redactions prior to the final one; others imagine a single redaction. It is also possible to mix the two models.

Critics of all schools agree that behind the text of the Pentateuch lie earlier sources. They exist, however, only as a result of scholarly hypothesis; we have no actual texts. The theory that the text was not written as a single original creation entails developing procedures for finding the components of the text. It should be borne in mind that the process of discovering sources reflects some model of textual composition in the mind of the critic.

Identifying the Sources: The Pentateuch quotes one source. It cites "The Book of the Wars of the Lord [Heb. *Yahweh*]" as the source for a border description in Num. 21:14–15. The excerpt appears to be in verse form, and the term for "book" (Heb. *sefer*) refers to a written record (e.g., Exod. 32:32; Num. 5:23; Deut. 17:18; 24:13). Apart from its intriguing title, that is all we know about this book. Num. 21:27 attributes a song about the fall of Moab to unidentified "ballad singers" (Heb. *moshelim*), which does not necessarily imply a written source. One may, however, compare this source to "The Book of Jashar," a written source from which the song at Gibeon (Josh. 10:13), David's lament (2 Sam. 1:18), and Solomon's hymn (Greek version of 1 Kings 8:13) were excerpted, and suggest that songs, like that in Num. 21:27–30, too, were excerpted from a written source.

The Pentateuch further implies discrete written sources when it delineates specific records that Moses was to have written down: the indictment of Amalek (Exod. 17:14), the laws of Exodus 20–23 (Exod. 24:4), the cultic laws of Exodus 34 (Exod. 34:27–28), the Israelites' itinerary (Num. 33:2), the Deuteronomic law code (Deut. 31:9, 24), and the poem in Deuteronomy 32 (Deut. 31:22). Exod. 24:12 and Deut. 9:10 attribute a written form of the Decalogue to God, suggesting that it, too, had been a discrete source. It would also seem that the genealogy of ten generations from Adam to Noah in Genesis 5 once enjoyed independent written existence as it is introduced as a "book" (v. 1).

Identifications of other sources in the Pentateuch are based on less explicit evidence or more subtle discriminations. The clearest cases are those in which the source of one passage is another text within the Pentateuch. Exod. 1:1–5 seems to draw directly on, and abridge, the family tree of Jacob in Gen. 46:8–27. The narrative outline of the Israelites' journey from Egypt to Moab, extending from Exodus 12 through Numbers, directly excerpts the itinerary in Numbers 33 (see, e.g., Exod. 12:37; 13:20; 14:1, 8, 22; 15:22–23, 27; 16:1; 17:1; 19:2). One could infer that an author or editor used material from written sources to frame the narrative or provide it with continuity.

On the basis of the distinctive character of genealogical and other lists, and the inference that such lists were excerpted and inserted in passages like Exod. 1:1–5 and the narrative of the wilderness journey, one might also deduce that other lists were incorporated into the Pentateuch from elsewhere. Further support may be found in lists that abruptly break off before their anticipated end. An example is the gene-

SOURCES OF THE PENTATEUCH

alogy of the Israelites in Exod. 6:14–27, which stops at Levi because the text's interest is in tracing the lineage of Moses and Aaron, as the conclusion of the passage states. An even more abrupt case is Gen. 37:2: "This is the history [lit., generations] of the family of Jacob." The expected genealogy of Jacob's twelve sons jumps ahead to Joseph, the focus of the ensuing narrative.

Lists such as the Numbers 33 itinerary, genealogies, and the list of the kings of Edom (Gen. 36:31–39) display distinct beginnings and closings and a distinctive style. When critics observe distinct beginnings and closings and a distinctive style in other passages in the Pentateuch, they tend to conclude that these, too, were incorporated into the present text, or its sources, from earlier sources.

Gen. 2:4a, for example, says: "These are the generations of the heavens and the earth when they were created." Verse 4b then says: "In the day that the Lord God made the earth and the heavens . . ."—another beginning. There follows an account of creation different from the one in Gen. 1:1–2:3 in both content (e.g., man was created before vegetation and the other animals) and style (e.g., the former account names God *Elohim* only, the latter *Yahweh;* the former denotes the act of creation by "create" [Heb. *bara'*], the latter by "form" [Heb. *yatsar*]). It tells a story with a beginning, middle, and end (3:24). One could deduce that Gen. 2:4a closes the preceding story and that Gen. 2:4b begins another, partly parallel one, and that each derives from a different source.

Collections of law (especially Exod. 20:22–23:19; 34:10–27; Lev. 17–26; Deut. 12–26) and archaic poems (e.g., Gen. 4:23–24; 27:27–29, 39–40; 49:2–27; Exod. 15:1–18; Num. 21:14–15, 17–18, 27–30; 23:7–10, 18–24; 24:3–9, 15–24; Deut. 32:1–43; 33:2–29) also stand out in genre, structure, and style and are attributed to independent sources. Most of these law collections and poems are set off by introductory and/or closing formulas.

In passages where divergence in content and style is not accompanied by some explicit indication of a distinct source, identifying sources is less certain. We shall consider two such types of sources: those that are discerned within the text of the Pentateuch, and those that are hypothesized to have existed outside the text.

Source-Critical Analysis: Critics have attempted to analyze passages into their components by segregating units that diverge in content and style. Repetitive duplication, substantive inconsistency or contradiction, abrupt digression, and sustained difference in terminology have been taken to suggest boundaries between sources. Although none of these features would in and of itself indicate different sources, the coincidence of a number of these features in the same place suggests such distinctions.

A case in point is the Flood story in Gen. 6:5–9:19. Here we encounter repetitions, contradictions, and consistent divergences in style and terminology from passage to passage. The text fluctuates between passages in which God is called "the Lord" (Heb. *Yahweh*): "the Lord" commands Noah to take seven pairs of all pure animals and one pair of the impure animals into the ark, and it rains for forty days and nights; and passages in which God is always called "God" (Heb. *Elohim*): God commands Noah to take only one pair of each animal, and the Flood rises for a hundred and fifty days. In addition, the former passages are characterized by a more personal "Lord" who "grieved to his heart" (6:6) about human behavior and "shut [Noah] in" the ark (7:6). The latter passages feature a genealogy (6:9–10), details of age and date (7:6, 11; 8:4–5, 13–14), and the covenant (6:18; 9:8–17).

The former passages, which we shall follow scholarly convention and call "J" for its use of the Hebrew tetragrammaton *J(Y)HWH*, and the latter passages, which we call "P" ("Priestly") for reasons to be explained below, also employ distinctive vocabulary. Contrast these two descriptions of destruction of life by the Flood:

J: "Everything on the dry land in whose nostrils was the breath of life died" (7:22).

P: "And all flesh died that moved upon the earth, birds, cattle, beasts, all swarming creatures that swarm upon the earth, and every man" (7:21).

Critics are impressed by the fact that the stylistic difference here corresponds to the two accounts of creation, which likewise employ different names for God. Compare J here to J in Gen. 2:7: "Then the Lord God formed man of dust from the ground, and breathed into his nostrils the breath of life . . ."; and P here to P in 1:28: "And God said to [the humans], 'Be fruitful and multiply, and fill the earth and subdue it; and have dominion over the fish of the sea and over the birds of the air and over every living thing that moves upon the earth.' " This last verse also resembles 9:1–3 and other passages attributed to P in the Flood story.

It has been hypothesized that behind the Flood story lie two written sources, which extend beyond this story to include a creation account and many other units. The present text has been produced by intersplicing these two sources. A source-critical analysis is:

J: 6:5–8; 7:1–5, 12, 16b–17, 22–23; 8:6–12, 13b, 20–22; 9:18–19.

P: 6:9–22; 7:6–11, 13–16a, 18–21; 7:21–8:5; 8:13a, 14–19; 9:1–17.

Using similar criteria, critics isolate another source, "E," as it refers to God as *Elohim*, dis-

SOURCES OF THE PENTATEUCH

tinct from both J and P. Although E is difficult to identify outside Genesis, critics assign to it chapters that seem to present an alternate version of an episode that occurs in J: Gen. 20:1–17 (E), which doubles Gen. 12:10–20 (J); Gen. 21:8–20 (E), which doubles Gen. 16:1–16 (J); and Gen. 21:22–34 (E), which doubles Gen. 26:17–33 (J). Characteristic of E is that God appears less immanently than in J, through a messenger (angel) or dream. Commonly, J and E are understood to be combined in several narratives, for example, the story of Joseph (Gen. 37–50). In J Judah tries to save Joseph, the father is called Israel, the Ishmaelites buy Joseph and take him down to Egypt. In E Reuben tries to save Joseph, the father is called Jacob, and the Midianites kidnap Joseph. Style and vocabulary are also adduced to identify the two sources.

Once separated, the hypothetical sources in the Flood story, the Joseph narrative, and other texts do not appear complete. Some narrative material was probably omitted (e.g., J's description of the ark). More crucially, we have no idea what or how much material of these sources is not in the Pentateuch. We cannot be sure of the full extent and shape of the sources.

Hypothesizing Sources Outside the Text: Because many cultures transmit epics and other literary forms orally, and because the Bible frequently refers to oral performance or transmission of its texts or traditions (e.g., Exod. 13:8; 15:1, 21), oral sources may lie behind the Pentateuch and its written sources.

Oral traditions, of course, leave no record and their postulation is entirely speculative. Deut. 26:5–10, however, presents a formula summarizing Israel's story from the descent of the ancestors from Canaan to Egypt through God's deliverance of Israel from Egypt and guidance to the land of Canaan. This "credo," as it has been called, was to be recited by Israelites bringing first-fruit offerings to God. Perhaps, it has been suggested, this credo is a miniature of a large epic, verse in form and oral in medium, stretching from the patriarchal promises to the arrival of Israel at the promised land. Fragments of what looks like ancient verse (e.g., Exod. 19:3) dot the Pentateuch; they could be vestiges of the epic.

That prose texts in the Pentateuch may have been transformed from earlier epic verse can be argued in two further ways. First, the prose account of crossing the Reed Sea in Exodus 14 seems to adapt parts of the archaic song in Exodus 15. Second, several of the prose episodes in Genesis 1–11 include occasional bursts of archaic verse (e.g., 1:27; 2:23; 3:14–19; 7:11b) and exhibit poetic patterns or diction (e.g., "the deep" [Heb. *tehom*], and "beasts of the earth" [Heb. *ḥayeto-'erets*], in Gen. 1). The written sources, or the redactors or authors of the Pentateuch, then, may have employed an extensive oral epic, or a number of smaller works in verse, in composing the present text, just as they drew upon "The Book of the Wars of the Lord" and the "ballad singers."

More remote, and for the most part indirect, sources of sections of the Pentateuch are narratives and laws attested in other works of ancient Near Eastern literature. Among the many possible interrelations are: the Mesopotamian flood story (note the episode of the birds in the *Epic of Gilgamesh* Tablet 11) and the Flood story in Genesis; the Egyptian "Tale of Two Brothers" and Genesis 39; the Akkadian legend of Sargon and the birth story of Moses in Exodus 2; various law codes and Exodus 21–23; the Assyrian vassal treaties and the curses in Deuteronomy. Compare, e.g., Deut. 28:23–24 with this excerpt from the Vassal Treaties of Esarhaddon: "May all the gods . . . turn your soil into iron. . . . Just as rain does not fall from a copper sky, so may there come neither rain nor dew . . ., but let it rain burning coals in your land . . ." (James B. Pritchard, ed., *Ancient Near Eastern Texts Relating to the Old Testament*, 3d ed. [Princeton: Princeton University Press, 1969], p. 539). Since the correspondences go much further, a literary dependence of Deuteronomy 28 on Assyrian or Aramaean vassal treaties of about the eighth century B.C. seems likely.

The Documentary Hypothesis: The prevailing account of the composition of the Pentateuch in modern scholarship is the "Documentary Hypothesis." In most versions of the theory four documents are hypothesized to have been redacted in forming the Pentateuch: J, a Judean source of about the tenth century B.C.; E, a north Israelite source of about the eighth century B.C.; D, the core of Deuteronomy, which is identified with the "book of the law *(torah)*" that was promulgated by King Josiah in 622 B.C. (see 2 Kings 22–23); and P, which is variously dated before, during, or after the Babylonian exile of the sixth century B.C. The redaction is generally understood to have taken place in stages: first JE, then JED, then JEDP. In each stage of redaction editorial adaptation and reshaping of the prior material is assumed. Most of Exodus 25–Numbers 36 is assigned to P, as are the first and last chapters of the Pentateuch, giving the impression that partisans of P were the final redactors. The final redaction occurred by the fifth century B.C.

The chronological sequence of the documents is reconstructed by relating the other sources to D. Laws in JE seem to precede Deuteronomy. JE (e.g., Exod. 23:19) allows Israelites to bring offerings to God to any sanctuary, but D (e.g., Deut. 12:13–14) restricts offerings to a single site. Several laws in D appear to revise laws in JE. For example, Deut. 15:12–28 follows the structure and uses some of the phraseology of the slave law of Exod. 21:2–6 (JE). D, however, treats women the same as men, unlike JE, and exhorts the Israelites to be generous toward manumitted slaves. The law concerning rape in Deut. 22:23–27 could be regarded as an expansion of the less comprehensive law in Exod. 22:15–16. Alternatively, JE and D could in both cases be drawing on a common source.

The position of P is even more problematic. Its laws focus on the rituals of the sanctuary, the priesthood, and ritual purity, hence its label, "Priestly." P does not abide offerings made by anyone but an anointed priest of the Levite tribe. Thus, whereas in J's Flood narrative Noah offered the excess pure animals he took into the ark as thanksgiving to God after the Flood, in P's version Noah took no extra animals and made no offering as he was not a proper priest. P does not, however, explicitly forbid offerings at any but a single sanctuary, as D does. If P were later than D, P might presuppose the centralization of sacrificial worship in D and feel no need to legislate it. On the other hand, once ritual slaughter is centralized, as in D, it means any Israelite who wants to eat meat must travel to the one sanctuary. D makes allowance for profane slaughter of animals so that Israelites need not travel to the sanctuary for this purpose (Deut. 15:22–23); P forbids it (Lev. 17:3–4). Perhaps, then, P does not assume centralization of worship and is not later than D.

All that is clear is that JE, D, and P differ in the substance of many of their laws and differ in their terminology as well. Favorite idioms of D and P can be readily identified.

Content and style also serve to associate the legal portions of P with narratives attributed to P (see above on P and the Flood story and compare, e.g., Exod. 39:32 with Gen. 2:1–3, and Lev. 11:46 with Gen. 1:21, 24).

Whether the material attributed to J, E, and P ever existed in single, long, parallel documents that covered the extent of the Pentateuch cannot be deduced merely from the identification of fragments of sources with affinities to one another throughout the text. Prior to redaction, J, E, and P may have existed as collections of small units. From the variety of sources we have identified above, it would also seem that the Pentateuch embodies many materials besides J, E, P, and D.

Conclusion: Although the Pentateuch may allude to prior sources in certain passages, for the most part the final text does not call attention to its diverse sources. Had some of the sources circulated independently, the Pentateuch may at one time have been recognized as a composite. It does seem, however, that the process that constituted the Pentateuch, in each of its stages, tended to blend and integrate its material into a new entity, a text to be read as a continuous whole. ***See also*** Bible; Old Testament.

Bibliography

Cross, Frank M. *Canaanite Myth and Hebrew Epic*. Cambridge: Harvard University Press, 1973.

Hahn, Herbert F. *The Old Testament in Modern Research*. Philadelphia: Fortress, 1966.

Sellin, Ernst, and Georg Fohrer. *Introduction to the Old Testament*. Translated by David E. Green. Nashville, TN: Abingdon, 1968. Pp. 103–95.

E.L.G.

South, the; Southland, the. ***See*** Negeb, The.

sowing, the act of scattering seeds as part of the cultivation of food grains. While the seeds of some crops were planted more carefully than Near Eastern cereals, "sowing" typically refers to the wholesale scattering of wheat and barley. Unlike their Mesopotamian counterparts, who sometimes used a seeding device that was attached to the plow, Egyptian or Palestinian farmers simply carried a container full of seed and broadcast this seed with their free hand.

In contrast to Western practice, the Palestinian farmer often plows after sowing, thereby working seeds into the soil for protection and germination; this practice is apparently presumed in Jesus' parable of the sower (Matt. 13: 3–8). If plowing precedes sowing, livestock may be driven across a field to harrow the seed.

The Mosaic law contains regulations on sowing (Lev. 11:37–38; 19:19; Deut. 22:9). Eventually, sowing attained metaphorical significance (Ps. 126:6; Prov. 11:18; Matt. 13:3–43; 2 Cor. 9: 6; Gal. 6:7–8). ***See also*** Farming; Plow; Seed.

G.L.M.

Spain, a large peninsula in southwestern Europe known since Roman times as Hispania; it first received the Ligurerians from Italy, then the Celts (sixth century B.C.), who were then challenged by the Iberians (fifth century B.C.). Known by the Phoenicians and the Greeks, Spain was invaded by Carthage in 237 B.C. but lost to Rome in 206 B.C. After some two hundred years of stubborn resistance, a "pacified" Spain gave Rome three emperors and many of her best soldiers. Although Spain appears in Rom. 15:24, 28 as the intended western horizon of Paul's mission, this hope was probably cut short in Rome by Paul's martyrdom. C.J.R.

span. ***See*** Weights and Measures.

sparrow, a term that may refer to any small, brown bird that flits and twitters. Both the Greek and Hebrew words are frequently translated "bird" in the RSV (Pss. 11:1; 102:7; 104:17; 124: 7; Eccles. 12:4; Lam. 3:52). Sparrows (Old World "sparrows" are members of the weaver family) are mentioned as nesting near the Temple altar (Ps. 84:3). They were sold in the marketplaces of the Middle East as inexpensive food for the poor, and Jesus used them as a symbol for something of minimal value (Matt. 10:29, 31; Luke 12: 6, 7).

speaking with tongues. ***See*** Tongues, Speaking with.

spear, a close-range weapon composed of a long wooden shaft on which was mounted a shorter, pointed blade (i.e., spearhead). During the biblical period, the spearhead was usually made of bronze or iron, and it was attached to the shaft in various ways. Through most of the spear's early history, a tanged blade was inserted into the end of a split shaft, and the juncture was tightly bound. By the middle of the second millennium B.C., the socketed spearhead became almost universal. Artistic representations and excavated examples demonstrate that spearheads were made in different sizes and shapes, and among them were leaf-shaped, triangular, and barbed blades. Since the spear was a major weapon in most ancient armies, metallurgical advancements were quickly adapted for the production of stronger and more effective spearheads.

The RSV uses "spear" to translate several words in the Hebrew OT; some distinction is made, however, since one of these Hebrew terms *(kîdôn)* is more frequently rendered "javelin" in the English text (see passages where both weapons are named, e.g., 1 Sam. 17:6–7, 45; Job 39:23; 41:16; Ps. 35:3). Although these two weapons were similar in form, they served different functions in combat. The spear was used primarily for thrusting or stabbing (Num. 25:7–8; 1 Sam. 26:8; 2 Sam. 23:8, 18, 21, as opposed to 1 Sam. 18:11; 19:10; 20:33), but the lighter, shorter javelin was a medium-range weapon designed for throwing. Apart from a disputed reading in Matt. 27:49, the spear's only appearance in the NT is in John 19:34. The two hundred "spearmen" who escorted Paul to Antipatris (Acts 23:23) might have been javelin throwers.

Warrior holding a spear with a triangular spearhead; from a Moabite stele, second millennium B.C.

Although it is not as frequently mentioned as the sword, the spear was a well-known weapon in the biblical period. Deborah lamented the lack of spears in her army (Judg. 5:8; cf. 1 Sam. 13:19–22), thereby acknowledging their importance. To emphasize his trust in the Lord, David belittled Goliath's dependence upon sword, spear, and javelin (1 Sam. 17:45–47). Since spear and shield complemented each other in hand-to-hand combat, they are often mentioned together (2 Kings 11:10; 1 Chron. 12:8; 2 Chron. 11:12; 14:8). Indeed, one's ability "to handle spear and shield" made one "fit for war" (2 Chron. 25:5). Naturally, giants carried very large spears (1 Sam. 17:7; 2 Sam. 21: 16).

Figurative references to the spear are rare but potent (Pss. 35:3; 46:9; 57:4). The prophets speak about the future age of peace as a day in which spears would be converted into pruning hooks (Isa. 2:4; Mic. 4:3; see Joel 3:10, where the opposite process was envisioned). ***See also*** Soldier; War; Weapons. G.L.M.

speck (KJV: "mote"), a small fragment of chaff, fiber, wood, etc. Jesus criticized the judgmental tendency when he said that we see such specks in the eyes of others but not the logs (note the hyperbole) in our own (Matt. 7:3–5; Luke 6:41–42).

spelt, a variety of wheat generally known as *Triticum dicoccoides* or more specifically *Triticum aestivum spelta*. In biblical usage it refers to a crop that survived the hail plague because of late germination (Exod. 9:32), a crop used to border the field (Isa. 28:25), and an ingredient for bread (Ezek. 4:9).

sphinx, the Greek name for a creature having a lion's body and human head. In Greek legend, this mythical beast posed a riddle that only Oedipus could answer. The sphinx was a common artistic motif in ancient Egypt. Stone sphinxes served as guardians in front of tem-

Ivory and gold winged sphinx from Nimrud, eighth–seventh century B.C.

ples; sometimes a row of sphinxes was placed along each side of the temple's avenue of approach. The most famous sphinx is the enormous recumbent example (240 feet in length) cut out of the living rock alongside the causeway leading up to the pyramid of King Khafre (Gk. *Chephren*) at Giza (ca. 2550 B.C.). The head of this creature is thought to be a representation of the king himself. The Sphinx may represent Khafre in the guise of the sun god Aton who guards the Giza necropolis.

In Mesopotamian art, the sphinx was shown with wings and either a male or female head. Hittite sphinxes always had female heads. Later on, in Greek art, the sphinx was represented with female breasts and wings. The cherubs mentioned in the Bible may have been sphinx-like creatures with a human head, lion's body, and wings (e.g., Exod. 25). ***See also*** Cherub. J.M.W.

spices, salves, perfumes, or aromatic oils. Spices were part of the luxury trade of the ancient world; a "balm," resin of *Pistacia mutica*, was among the gifts sent to Joseph (Gen. 43:11). Balsam oil or perfume in general appears in the catalogue of wealth that flows through Tyre (Ezek. 27:22). Spices were used in the anointing oil, perhaps a balsam oil (Exod. 35:28; 1 Kings 10:2). "Spices" may also refer to a sweet-smelling cinnamon or a sweet cane (Exod. 30:23). Aromatic oils and perfumes were used for embalming and anointing a corpse (Mark 16:1; Luke 23:56; John 19:40). P.P.

spies, those who seek to obtain privileged information secretly. In the OT, spies are involved in three complexes of material: the dispatch of twelve spies by Moses to reconnoiter the land of Canaan (Num. 13–14; Deut. 1:19–46); the sending of two spies to Jericho by Joshua (Josh. 2); and the mission of the five spies sent to Laish as part of the Danite migration to the North (Judg. 18). The usual form of the spy story includes the selection and dispatch of the spies, their return and report, the announcement that God has given the reconnoitered land to Israel, and the report of the subsequent invasion and conquest. J.S.K.

spikenard (KJV; RSV: "nard"), a scented ointment or perfume imported from the Himalayas in alabaster boxes and opened on special occasions (Song of Sol. 1:12; 4:13, 14). In the NT it is its expense (approximately one year's wages) that is emphasized (Mark 14:3–5; John 12:3–5).

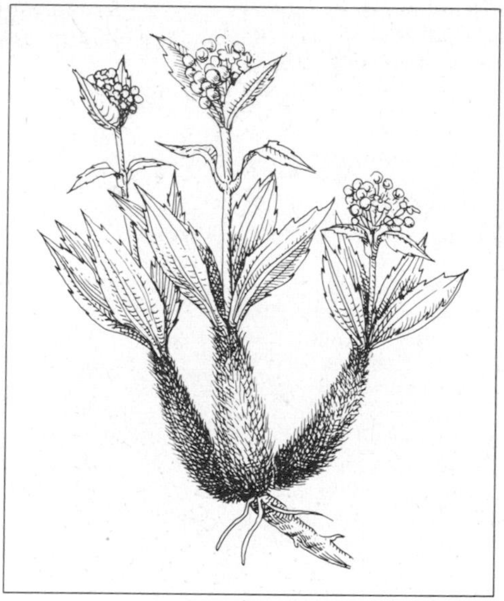

Spikenard.

spinning and weaving, the arts of producing yarn and cloth from fibers of various kinds. Spinning and weaving were traditionally women's arts in the ancient Near East and Greco-Roman world, and they remained a common household occupation even when weaving became a male profession or profession shared by men (among them perhaps Paul, Acts 18: 1–3). The distaff represented the female domain, and portraits of noblewomen with spindle in hand show that spinning was common to all classes of women. The woman praised in Proverbs 31 "seeks wool and flax . . . puts her hands to the distaff, and . . . hold[s] the spindle" (vv.

13, 19). She clothed her family, but also produced for the market (vv. 21–24). The women of Israel spun the wool, flax, and goats' hair for the tabernacle hangings and coverings (Exod. 35: 25–26), though the weaving was done, or directed, by men (v. 35). Before Josiah's reforms women wove vestments in the Temple for the Asherah cult figure (2 Kings 23:7). Delilah wove Samson's locks in her loom (Judg. 16:13–14).

Textile production was an important industry of the palace and temple in ancient Syria and Mesopotamia, often employing slave labor. Ebla (in modern Syria) was the center of a far-reaching textile trade (ca. 2300 B.C.), and Phoenician weaving and dyeing were renowned. Early Egyptian models recovered from tombs show workrooms with women engaged in various operations of cloth production. Men appear as weavers in later texts, working in government factories or at home looms under contract.

Wool and flax were the common textile fibers of Palestine, Mesopotamia, and Greece, while goats' hair was used for tent fabrics, coarse mantles, and sackcloth. Wool was often dyed to produce patterned weaves, including intricate tapestries. Linen, the main textile of Egypt, was usually left white, since it was difficult to dye. Cotton was not used in Palestine until Hellenistic times.

The fiber was prepared for spinning by washing, retting (soaking to separate out the flax), and carding to produce a fluffy mass. This was secured on a hooked stick (distaff) held under the spinner's left arm, and wisps of fiber were drawn out in a continuous strand as they were spun—or a lightly twisted rope (rove) was formed with the fingers and coiled in a pot or basket. The drawn-out fibers were attached to a spindle, with which they were twisted and attenuated into a strong thin yarn. The spindle was a rod, 9 to 15 inches long and tapered at both ends, with a notch or hook at one end to catch the yarn and a perforated disk (whorl) of stone, bone, or pottery to weight it and steady its rotation. The spindle was twirled in the hand or hands, rolled against the thigh, or suspended after being set in motion. As a length of thread was formed it was wound onto the spindle and the process was repeated.

Woman spinning; stone relief, seventh century B.C.

Weaving was done by intersecting one set of threads (the warp), attached to a loom, with a running thread or threads (the weft or woof). Several types of looms were used in biblical times. The common loom of early Palestine and Greece consisted of two vertical beams fixed into the ground with a horizontal beam attached at the top (cf. Goliath's spear "like a weaver's beam," 1 Sam. 17:7). The warp threads were hung from the crossbeam and weighted in bunches with small clay or stone weights (common objects in excavation sites). In later times, a lower crossbeam was introduced, and the web was woven up, rather than down as in the warp-weighted loom. The ancient Egyptians used a horizontal loom consisting of two beams held by pegs in the ground, with the warp stretched between them. Similar looms are used by bedouins today.

The weft was drawn by a shuttle through a "shed" created by separating the warp threads into two series by means of a heddle (today called a warping stick). After each passage of the shuttle the new thread was pressed firmly into the growing fabric with a sword-shaped beater (batten), pin, or (later) comb. Patterns were made by adding or alternating different colors of yarn and by changing the interlacing of warp and weft. Gold and silver "thread" was also used (Exod. 39:3). Simple garments were commonly woven in one piece, as Jesus' seamless tunic (John 19:23). Tassels were formed at the lower corners (Num. 15:38) from the free warps left when the garment was cut from the loom (Isa. 38:12). ***See also*** Asherah; Linen; Pin; Tabernacle; Wool. P.A.B.

spirit. ***See*** Flesh and Spirit; Holy Spirit, The; Soul.

Spirit, the Holy. ***See*** Holy Spirit, The.

Spirit of God. ***See*** Holy Spirit, The.

spirits, evil. ***See*** Demon; Devil.

spiritual gifts, a concept present only in the NT, primarily in the Pauline Letters, although the idea of being empowered by the Holy Spirit for particular tasks is by no means alien to the OT (e.g., Judg. 3:10; Num. 11:29). Various Greek terms are employed when these are in mind, but most notably *ta pneumatika*, which emphasizes the spiritual origin of the gifts (*pneuma* means "spirit"; see 1 Cor. 14:1), and, more often, *ta charismata*, which emphasizes that they are bestowed as an act of divine grace (*charis* means "grace"; see Rom. 12:6). In distinction from "the fruit of the Spirit," which all Christians are to manifest without variation (Gal. 5:22–23), the gifts of the Spirit are understood to vary from one believer to another (Rom. 12:6; 1 Cor. 12: 4–11; cf. 1 Pet. 4:10).

In the Letters of undisputed Pauline authorship, there are four separate listings of the Spirit's gifts (Rom. 12:6–8; 1 Cor. 12:8–10; 12: 28; 12:29–30), but since no two of the lists are identical it seems clear that no one list is intended to be definitive. The various gifts may be grouped under three general headings:

The *gifts of utterance* include prophecy (Rom. 12:6; 1 Cor. 12:10, 28; cf. 1 Cor. 12:8; 14:6), with which the ability to distinguish between true and false prophecy is closely associated (1 Cor. 12:10; cf. 14:29 and 1 Thess. 5:19–21); instruction (Rom. 12:7; 1 Cor. 12:28; cf. 1 Cor. 14:6); speaking in tongues (1 Cor. 12:10, 28; cf. 14: 1–19); and the ability to interpret speaking in tongues (1 Cor. 12:10, 30; cf. 14:5, 13).

The *gifts of practical ministry* are caring for the needy (Rom. 12:7–8): serving, encouraging (TEV), contributing, performing acts of mercy, and perhaps giving aid (1 Cor.12:28: helping); and administration (1 Cor. 12:28; perhaps giving aid in Rom. 12:8).

Healing (1 Cor. 12:9, 28) and performing miracles (1 Cor. 12:10, 28) are *gifts of wonder-working faith*, this "faith" (1 Cor. 12:9; cf. 13:2) being distinguishable from the faith "reckoned as righteousness" (Rom. 4:5) of which Paul usually writes.

The gift of apostleship, ranked first in 1 Cor. 12:28, is active in all three ways: in the ministry of the word (e.g., 1 Cor. 1:17; 4:17), in pastoral care (e.g., Rom. 15:25–29; Philemon), and in the working of miracles (e.g., 2 Cor. 12:12; Gal. 3:5). It is notable, however, that the lists in Eph. 4:11 and 1 Pet. 4:10–11 include only gifts of intelligible utterance and of practical ministry; there are no references to speaking in tongues or miracle working.

Responding to disruptions caused by speaking in tongues in his Corinthian congregation, Paul emphasized that every believer is graced by some gift and that all gifts are bestowed by "the same Spirit" (1 Cor. 12:4–11). Nevertheless, since their purpose is to serve "the common good" (12:7), he concluded that prophecy, intelligible to all, is to be preferred to speaking in tongues, intelligible only to God (unless there is an interpreter; 1 Cor. 14:1–5). ***See also*** Apostle; Corinthians, The First Letter of Paul to the; Holy Spirit, The; Miracles; Paul; Prophet; Teaching; Tongues, Speaking with. V.P.F.

spitting. ***See*** Gestures.

sponge, the porous skeleton of marine animals, whose fibrous connective structure has water-retaining properties that make it useful for bathing. The Gospels report that Jesus was offered a sponge soaked in wine vinegar to drink on the cross (Mark 15:36; Matt. 27:48; John 19:29).

springs. ***See*** En-gannim; En-gedi; En-rogel; Gihon; Jericho; Siloam Inscription; Water.

squad (KJV: "quaternion"), the English translation of a Greek word designating a group of four soldiers. It is found in Acts 12:4 (cf. also John 19: 23), where Peter was placed in the custody of four such groups, one for each of the three-hour-long night watches. Normally, one squad would be sufficient, one person standing guard on each of the watches while the other three slept. Apparently Peter was thought to need especially careful guarding. ***See also*** Guard, Bodyguard; Prison; Soldier.

square, a rectangle with sides of equal length. **1** A shape required for many of the appurtenances of the Temple described in Exodus (e.g., 27:1; 28:16) and Ezekiel (e.g., 43:16, 17). **2** A level area near the city gate in ancient cities used for various public assemblies (e.g., 2 Sam. 21:12; Job 28:7).

stable, a shelter for animals, usually donkeys, horses, or other draft animals. The tradition of Jesus' being born in a stable derives from Luke's reference to Mary's putting the baby "in a manger" (Luke 2:7), a feeding trough usually found where animals are corralled. Caves used for such shelter are common even in modern times in the Near East. The KJV's "stable" in Ezek. 25: 5 is rendered more correctly by the RSV as "pasture."

Stachys (stay'kis), a Christian who received a special greeting from Paul (Rom. 16:9).

stacte (stak'tee), an ingredient to be used in preparing incense (Exod. 30:34). The meaning of the Hebrew root *nāṭāp*, "to drip" or "ooze," has led some to identify it as the sap of the storax tree, *Styrax officinalis*, or the opobalsamum tree, *Commiphora opobalsamum*.

staff. ***See*** Rod.

stairs, stepped ledges providing access up or down that are integrated into the construction of a building or other facility. Stairs were most common as a device for reaching the second floor or roof of a house. Biblical usage is somewhat diverse. The Temple built by Solomon had stairs to both the second and third stories (1 Kings 6:8). Repairs were made in Jerusalem in postexilic times, using the stairs down from the "City of David" as a zone marker for repair responsibility (Neh. 3:15; see also 12:37). Special stairs for Levites are mentioned in Neh. 9:4. In Ezekiel's vision of the Temple the inner court vestibule facing the outer court had a stairway of eight steps on the south, east, and north sides (40:31, 34, 37). In this description access to second and third stories was by a single stairway on the side (41:7).

Stairs were part of normal temple access in Roman architecture, in many instances using the foundation platform as a step or steps (Jerash, Baalbek, Petra, Pergamum). The same was true of the earlier Greek temples. Cities frequently cut elaborate stairways to ensure access to the water supply (Gezer, Megiddo, Gibeon). Some fascinating inside and outside stairways were built in both public and private buildings by the Nabataeans (modern Umm al-Jimal has some of the best preserved of both types). Ramps, rather than stairways, characterized some Egyptian construction (Hatshepsut's tomb at modern Deir el-Bahri), but the interior stairs in the great pyramid of Cheops at Giza are still spectacular. R.S.B.

stall, a space for one animal within a stable or barn. The biblical usage betrays less precision, using the term for what would now be called a pen. In Amos 6:4 the "calves from the midst of the stall" reflects the still-used practice of isolating animals for special preslaughter fattening or "finishing." Mal. 4:2 reports the typical exuberance of young animals released from their pen into open pasture. More traditional individual pens may be specified in 1 Kings 4:20, citing Solomon's forty thousand stalls of horses (2 Chron. 9:25), but 2 Chron. 32:28 and Hab. 3:17 may have indicated the group pens again.
R.S.B.

stars, Star of Bethlehem, respectively, the self-luminous bodies in the sky (except meteors, comets, and nebulae) and the star that guided the Wise Men to the infant Jesus at Bethlehem (Matt. 2:1–12). In modern times, the sun is considered a star; in ancient times, however, and in the Bible, the sun, moon, and stars are distinguished (Gen. 1:16). Moreover, while planets are not considered stars today, biblical writers considered them such, for the "Day star, son of Dawn" (Isa. 14:12), was most likely Venus, and "the star of the god Rephan" (Acts 7:43) was probably Saturn.

In the ancient Near East, the stars were regarded as supernatural beings (divinities) affecting human destiny. The same was true in Greek and Roman culture, particularly after the time of Alexander the Great (fourth century B.C.). Astrology sought to predict coming events through observing the courses of the stars and planets. A lament over Babylonia refers to Babylonian astrologers "who divide the heavens, who gaze at the stars, who at the new moons predict what shall befall you" (Isa. 47:13).

In the OT, the stars are not thought of as divinities, although certain passages imply that stars and planets influence human events (Job 38:33; cf. Judg. 5:20), and astrology is rejected as a foreign influence (Jer. 10:2). The stars and constellations have been created by God (Gen. 1:16; Pss. 8:3; 136:9; Job 9:9; Amos 5:8). God has named them (Ps. 147:4; Isa. 40:26) and has set them in their courses (Jer. 31:35; Job 9:7). No one can count them (Gen. 15:5; 22:17; 26:4).

There is evidence that star worship was introduced in both the Northern and the Southern Kingdoms. Amos (eighth century B.C.) condemned it in the Northern Kingdom (Amos 5:26). Introduced in the Southern Kingdom during the reign of Manasseh (687–642 B.C.; 2 Kings 21:3–5), star worship was suppressed by Josiah (640–609 B.C.; 2 Kings 23:4–14). The book of Deuteronomy, which played a major role in Josiah's reform of 621 B.C., condemns star worship (4:19; 17:2–5). Instances of star worship were thus anomalies in the history of Israel; it was generally condemned as a form of idolatry.

The Star of Bethlehem, according to Matt. 2:1–12, led the Wise Men from the East to Jerusalem (2:1–2) and Bethlehem (2:9) during the reign of Herod the Great (37–4 B.C.). Although there have been different theories concerning the identity of this star, the prevailing consensus in modern times has been that the so-called Bethlehem Star would not have been a star at all but rather a conjunction of the planets Jupiter and Saturn in the constellation Pisces in 7 B.C., having the appearance of a great star. Moreover, Pisces was considered in astrological traditions a constellation of the Jews. Matthew's account is probably a blend of astrological lore and midrashic interpretation of OT texts: "a star shall come forth out of Jacob, and a scepter shall rise out of Israel" (Num. 24:17) and "nations shall come to your light, and kings to the brightness of your rising" (Isa 60:3). The tradition of a heavenly sign appearing about the time of Jesus' birth was seen by Matthew as a fulfillment of the OT texts, understood as messianic promises, and he related the story to show both the fulfillment of prophecy and the universal significance of Jesus. ***See also*** Astrologer; Midrash; Moon; Sun; Wise Men. A.J.H.

stater (stay'tuhr), a Greek silver coin worth about four drachmas, the wages for four days' work. The stater in Matt. 17:27 was probably the heavier stater from the mint at Tyre accepted by Jews as a holy shekel. ***See also*** Money.

stealing. ***See*** Robbery.

stele, stela (stee'lee, stee'luh; Gk., "standing stone"; pl. stelae), an upright stone slab, usually inscribed, used to commemorate an event, mark a grave, or give a dedication to a deity. Egyptian stelae have been found at several sites in Palestine, such as Beth-shan, Timna, and Deir el-

Black limestone stele of Melishipak II, the Cassite king of Babylon; 1200 B.C.

Balah. Canaanite stelae are known from Beth-shan, Hazor, and Tell Beit Mirsim. A small piece of an inscribed Hebrew stele was found at Samaria; this fragment contains only a single word, *asher* ("who, which"). Several uninscribed stelae were discovered in the Israelite sanctuary at Arad. The most famous stele from Palestine is the Moabite Stone, written ca. 850 B.C. on behalf of Mesha, king of Moab, in a language close to Hebrew. This stele, found at Dhiban (biblical Dibon) in 1868, records Mesha's victory over Israel and his building activities at various Moabite sites. ***See also*** Mesha; Moabite Stone, The; Writing. J.M.W.

Stephanas (stef'uh-nuhs), Paul's first convert, together with his household, in Corinth (1 Cor. 16:15; cf. 1:16). Apparently he remained loyal to Paul, and when trouble broke out in the Corinthian church he accompanied Fortunatus and Achaicus on a visit to Paul in Ephesus with information about the problems (1 Cor. 16:17–18). Some of these problems were also detailed by a letter (1 Cor. 7:1), which may have been carried by the trio. They may also have carried the letter known to us as 1 Corinthians back to Corinth. Stephanas is strongly commended by Paul as one worthy of exercising authority in the church (1 Cor. 16:16). ***See also*** Achaicus; Corinth; Corinthians, The First Letter of Paul to the; Fortunatus; Paul. A.J.M.

Stephen, a leader in the early Jerusalem church whose story appears in Acts 6:1–8:2. The other references to Stephen in the NT refer to this story (Acts 11:19; 22:20).

According to Acts 6:1–6, a dispute had developed in the Jerusalem church between the "Hellenists" (probably Jewish Christians from the Diaspora whose first language was Greek) and the "Hebrews" (Palestinian Jewish Christians who spoke Aramaic). In order to resolve the dispute, seven Hellenists were chosen for positions of leadership, one of whom was Stephen. Thus, Stephen functions in Acts as the key representative figure for the very significant Hellenistic Jewish element in the primitive Jerusalem church.

Stephen is portrayed in Acts as a bold man, wise, full of faith, and possessed of the Holy Spirit (Acts 6:5, 8, 10). The ecstatic aspect of Stephen's short Christian career is highlighted in the account. It was by the power of the Spirit that Stephen confronted his fellow Hellenists who did not believe in Jesus as Messiah. They, in turn, brought Stephen's activities to the attention of a wider audience: the Sanhedrin (Acts 6:11–15).

Apparently, the opposition to Stephen was based primarily on a deduction he had made from his messianic faith in Jesus: that, with the vindication of Jesus as Messiah, the religion of the Temple had outlived its usefulness and the Mosaic law should now be seen in a new and different light (Acts 6:11–14; cf. Matt. 24:2; Mark 13:2; Luke 21:6). Stephen's opponents understood that this deduction would undermine the basic legitimacy of the religious practice associated with the Temple.

The speech of Stephen in Acts 7:2–53 is presented as Stephen's defense of his position. It also functions, however, as a model of early Christian apologetic to Hellenistic Judaism. The essential point is that Israel has always been slow to accept a dramatic new activity of God in fulfilling his promises. After the promises were given to Abraham (vv. 2–8), Israel systematically rebelled against the call of its inspired leaders (vv. 9–43) and was too prone to isolate the presence and activity of God to local places such as the Temple rather than see God in crucial historical events such as the recent case of Jesus' exaltation in Jerusalem (vv. 44–53). Once again, Israel was in danger of misperceiving a new expression of God's activity. According to Acts, this message angered Stephen's audience and he was stoned to death without judicial hearing before either Jewish or Roman authorities (vv. 54–58).

It is clear that the writer of Acts wished to draw a close parallel between Stephen's death and that of Jesus (see Luke 23:34; Acts 7:60). Stephen and Jesus, both filled with the Spirit, died unjustly with a word of forgiveness on their lips.

As Stephen, especially in his death, is linked

to Jesus, so also Acts links him to the future with the mention of Saul's (i.e., Paul's) consenting presence at the martyrdom (Acts 7:58; 8:1; 22: 20). Stephen's death and the subsequent scattering of his fellow messianic Hellenists led to the mission of Philip in Samaria and elsewhere (Acts 8:4–40) and ultimately to the wider mission spearheaded by Paul throughout the eastern part of the Roman Empire (see Acts 11:19).

Thus, although Stephen appears in only one episode in Acts, the author of Acts was conscious of the immense theological and historical significance of the early Hellenistic Jewish Christians in Jerusalem of whom Stephen is the exemplary figure. ***See also*** Hebrews; Hellenists; Law; Martyr; Paul; Persecution; Sanhedrin; Temple, The; Torah. A.J.M.

steward, a word used to translate a number of terms and expressions in the Bible common to all of which is the idea of "overseeing" the possessions, business affairs, property, servants, the training of children, etc., of an owner or master. A steward is one who is placed "over the house" (Gen. 43:19; 44:1, 4; 1 Kings 16:9; 18:3; etc.). That "house" can be a private household and its function (Gen. 44:1; Luke 12:42; Gal. 4: 2), a specific task (1 Chron. 29:6), a palace (Esther 1:8; 1 Kings 18:3; Isa. 36:3; Luke 8:3), business affairs (Matt. 20:8; Luke 16:1–8), a city treasury (Rom. 16:23), and in the NT in a metaphorical sense of the divine mysteries, i.e., the gospel revelation (1 Cor. 4:1), a divine commission (1 Cor. 9:17), or a divine gift (1 Pet. 4:10).

Bishops/elders are called stewards (Titus 1: 5–9) and are expected to possess holy qualities as they manage the household of God. The apostle Paul also saw himself as a steward (1 Cor. 4:1–2) who would have to give an account of his stewardship (1 Cor. 4:3–4; cf. 2 Tim. 4: 7–8) as the Apostle to the Gentiles (Eph. 3:2; Gal. 2:7–8; Rom. 1:5–6; 13–15). There is also a sense in which every Christian is a steward entrusted with a divine gift (1 Pet. 4:10). Faithful and wise stewardship of this gift or "talent" will result in blessing and reward but unfaithfulness will result in judgment (Luke 12:42–43; Matt. 25:14–30). R.H.S.

stoa (Gk., "colonnade"), an open colonnade with a back wall to which columns were joined by the roof. A stoa might be used as an independent architectural unit, used as an entrance porch, or placed on one or more sides of a court. Large stoas have inner rows of columns or sections of solid wall that make the stoa more like an enclosed hall. Shallow projecting wings with gables on either end give the free-standing stoa a more balanced appearance. In Hellenistic times stoas of two or more stories were developed. Those built on hills might have several stories or substructures. The upper story often served as a gallery over the lower section of the stoa.

A stoa served many purposes: it was a place for council meetings, for law courts, or for magistrates' headquarters; a repository for public documents; a building housing offices, shops, and storerooms; or a meeting place for a school. A school of philosophy took its name from such a meeting place (Stoics), and when Paul was in Athens, he was confronted by them in the marketplace around which the stoas in Athens were ranged (Acts 17:17–18). ***See also*** Agora; Athens; Stoics.

P.P.

Stoics (stoh'iks), members of a philosophical school founded in Athens by Zeno (335–263 B.C.). Although the scholars of the school developed theories of physics, cosmology, and logic, it was best known for its emphasis on moral conduct. The school was named for the "Painted Porch," a colonnade (Gk. *stoa*), in which it met at Athens. The Stoics held that the entire universe was a living creature animated by the divine Logos (reason or mind). This Logos was identified with Zeus. Every person was a slave of the ruling Logos.

Since the Logos pervaded everything, whatever happened in the universe was governed by this universal law of nature or providence. All human beings were brothers and sisters in this universal, living body. This imagery was well suited to the cosmopolitan empires of the period. Since everything that happens to people was determined, the only way in which individuals could control their lives was to control the passions governing how external events affected them. Control of oneself was the avenue by which humans showed their freedom and superiority to fortune.

In the turbulent world of Roman politics, many leading Romans found the Stoic philosophy a consolation and guide for life. One frequently faced sharp, sudden reversals of fortune that called for the resources of inner discipline expounded by the Stoics. One of the most famous Stoic teachers and writers of the first century, Epictetus, was a lame Phrygian from Hierapolis, who had been slave to Nero's freedman Ephaphroditus. After gaining freedom, Epictetus lectured to large audiences that they should only be concerned about what was under their control. Another famous Stoic teacher was Nero's tutor and advisor, Seneca, who retired from the court when Nero's career turned bad and was later forced to commit suicide by the suspicious emperor. In the second century, the emperor Marcus Aurelius, who had studied Epictetus, recorded his meditations while in the field with the army. Stoicism did not hold out hope for life after death but sought to call people to identify with the divine reason immanent in the cosmos. Some Stoic philosophers in Athens discussed Paul's religious views with him (Acts 17:18). P.P.

stone, any of a large variety of hardened natural inorganic, often mineral, substances. Occurring frequently in Syro-Palestine and Anatolia, largely absent in Mesopotamia, and available only up the Nile in ancient Egypt, stone forms the most stable construction material provided in nature. Found in Palestine largely as limestone mixed with some chert, or sandstone, or the volcanically produced and very hard basalt, it provided amply for everyday construction needs. Precious and semiprecious stones were another matter. They were frequently imported from various supply points, as with turquoise from the Sinai peninsula. Ore-bearing stone carrying copper and iron was located in the southern reaches of both Palestine and the Transjordan.

Biblical references provide examples of the wide spectrum of uses to which stone was put. It could serve as a memorial, shrine, and pledge (Gen. 28:18–22). It could cover wells (Gen. 29:2–10) and doorways to tombs (Mark 15:46; Matt. 27:60; Luke 11:39). It could be worked into bowls, mortars, pestles, sockets for doors, and other implements (Exod. 7:19). It served as a weapon, whether thrown by hand (Exod. 8:26), sling (1 Sam. 17:49), or catapult. It symbolized immediate destruction by its action of sinking rapidly in water (Exod. 15:5), and its immobility could symbolize death (Exod. 15:16). It could give the weary rest (Exod. 17:12), serve as construction material for altars (Exod. 20:25), or be a public record of binding law (Exod. 24:12), the accomplishments of persons (Exod. 28:10), or noteworthy events, as with royal stelae. It could serve as a device of public execution (Lev. 24:14) or private anger (Exod. 21:18). Used as an object of worship (Lev. 26:1) it could be conducive to sexual excess (Jer. 3:9, in probable reference to ritual prostitution as part of Canaanite religion) or other idolatry (Ezek. 20:32; Deut. 28:36, 64; 29:17). It could serve as a memorial of significant events (Josh. 4:1–10), or of covenant renewal (Josh. 24:26–27), or as a named boundary point (Josh. 15:6; 18:17). It served as a platform for executions (Judg. 9:5, 18), and as a weapon it could be honed to fine accuracy (Judg. 20:16). It stood as the measure of hardness (Job 38:30, for ice; 41:24, for the human heart). It could cause accidental stumbling (Ps. 91:12) or serve as a device of magic (Prov. 17:8). Stone of special quality served as cornerstones for walls or buildings (Isa. 28:16), but it could symbolize ultimate ruin (Hos. 12:11). It symbolized the opposite of nourishing bread (Matt. 7:9) but could in properly fashioned form hold water or wine (John 2:6–11).

Use of stone for tools like axes, knives, scrapers, hammers, and grinders, which began in prehistoric times, has continued in some respects to the present day in the biblical lands, especially in rural life. When boys get into a fight, the first weapon likely is a quickly grabbed rock. Stoning remains part of the punitive procedures used in some parts of orthodox Judaism. ***See also*** Limestone. R.S.B.

stoning, a form of capital punishment. Most of the offenses punished by stoning were crimes against the sovereignty of God. They included blasphemy (Lev. 24:15–16; cf. 1 Kings 21:13; Acts 7:11, 58), incitement to worship other gods (Deut. 13:6–10), worship of other gods (Deut. 17:2–7), worship of Molech by child sacrifice (Lev. 20:2–5), divination by mediums (Lev. 20:27), violation of the Sabbath (Num. 15:32–36), and violation of the taboo of devoted objects (Josh. 7:25). Stoning is specified also in cases of adultery (Deut. 22:21; 24; cf. John 8:3–7), filial insubordination (Deut. 21:18–21), and homicide by a goring ox (Exod. 21:28–29).

A description of the procedure in judicial stoning may be gleaned from various references. The stoning usually took place outside the city (Lev. 24:14; Num. 15:35; Deut. 17:5; 22:24; 1 Kings 21:13; but cf. Deut.22:21). The criminal probably was stripped (Ezek. 16:39). The witnesses were the first to cast stones, followed by the entire community (Deut. 13:10; 17:7; cf. John 8:7). Accounts of nonjudicial stoning are recorded in 1 Kings 12:18; 2 Chron. 24:21.

The custom continued into NT times, as attested by the stoning of Stephen (Acts 14:19; cf. John 8:5,7). The fact that Jesus died by crucifixion rather than stoning shows it was a punishment inflicted not by Jews but by the Romans. ***See also*** Law. B.L.E.

storage, the laying up of supplies for future use. Biblical references to storage focus on the special accommodations of store-cities and storehouses in addition to the routine acts of saving material or, metaphorically, emotions and other human traits.

Store-cities were used in Egypt (Exod. 1:11) where Israelites helped build them. Solomon's construction program included store-cities (1 Kings 9:19; 2 Chron. 8:4–6) in addition to fortifications and other facilities. Store-cities in Naphtali were captured by Ben-hadad of Syria during his invasion of Israel at the time of King Baasha (902–886 B.C.; 2 Chron. 16:4). Jehoshaphat built store-cities in Judah during his rule (874–850 B.C.; 2 Chron.17:12). In each of these cases it is likely that the facilities were intended to cache military goods in addition to economic supplies.

Storehouses required assigned gatekeepers and watchmen (1 Chron. 26:15) and were regular parts of the postexilic Temple facility (Neh. 10:38). Royal storehouses could provide equipment for rescuing a person in trouble (Jer. 38:11–13). The Temple storehouse retained the tithes of the people (Mal. 3:10), and storehouses were coupled with barns as routine equipment for rich humans (Luke 12:16–19) but were not found among nature's inhabitants (Luke 12:24). Royal storehouses served to supply people in times of famine (Gen. 41:56), and empty storehouses at such times were a disaster (Joel 1:17).

As for materials kept in storage, references include edible food (Gen. 6:21); crops (Luke 12:17) elsewhere specified as grain (Gen. 41:49), wine (2 Chron. 11:11, 32:28), wheat, barley, and oil (Jer. 41:8); and iron (1 Chron. 22:3). People also stored documents (Ezra 6:1); silver, gold, and sacred vessels (2 Chron. 5:1); and baggage (Isa. 10:28).

In popular cosmology God's storehouses held the wind (Ps. 135:7; Jer. 10:13; 51:16), snow and hail (Job 38:22), and the ocean (Ps. 33:7). People could store up sin (Hos. 13:12) and violence (Amos 3:10) and wrath for days to come (Rom. 2:5) as well as wisdom (Prov. 2:7). Stores could be carried off as booty of war (Isa. 39:6) and the very heavens and earth could be stored for the eschatological fire that would judge "ungodly men" (2 Pet. 3:7).

Archaeological evidence shows that storage containers ranged from modest jars, bowls, and perfume juglets (silver tetradrachmas were found in a jug at Shechem and Islamic coins in a lamp at Hesban) to large store jars, to dry and wet storage pits and cisterns, to caves, to elaborate buildings such as those found at the Hittite capital of Boghazkoi or Masada or Shechem (where the Late Bronze Age temple was adapted for storage in the Iron Age). Jars held some of the Dead Sea Scrolls and a small juglet retained some dried ink in the desk of the scriptorium at Qumran. Some storage chambers could be entered only by ladders over the walls, and subterranean storage pits were frequently sealed with stone lids. Material could be stored on house roofs as well. R.S.B.

stork, a large wading bird. The Hebrew word usually translated as "stork" *(ḥasīdâh)* could also appropriately be translated "heron," which should perhaps be included in the term. Two species of stork migrate through Palestine in spring: the white stork *(Ciconia ciconia)* and, less frequently to be seen, the black stork *(Ciconia nigra)*. Jer. 8:7 probably refers to the seasonal appearance of the stork, whereas Ps. 104:17 ("has her home in the fir trees") enigmatically refers to storks once nesting in Palestine. Zech. 5:9 compares the wings of angels to those of a stork, although it was considered an unclean animal (Lev. 11:19; Deut. 14:18).

I.U.K.

stove. ***See*** Oven.

stranger ("sojourner" or "alien" in some translations), in the Bible one who is not a member of a particular social group. Accordingly, Abraham was a stranger among the Hittites at Hebron (Gen. 23:4) as were Moses in Midian (Exod. 2:22) and the Israelites in Egypt (Deut. 23:7; cf. Ruth 1:1). After the settlement in Canaan, the term not only designated a temporary guest but also acquired the more specialized meaning of a resident alien who lived permanently within Israel. No doubt because the Israelites were keenly aware of their own heritage as strangers without rights in a foreign land, they developed specific laws governing the treatment of strangers (Exod. 22:21; 23:9; Deut. 10:19). Since the temporary guest was protected by the rather strict conventions of Near Eastern hospitality (e.g., Gen. 18:1–8; cf. Heb. 13:2), the laws more directly affected the resident alien who had no inherited political rights. Strangers were to be treated with kindness and generosity (Lev. 19:10, 33–34; 23:22; Deut. 14:29). They were included in the Israelite legal system (Lev. 24:16, 22; Num. 35:15; Deut. 1:16) and were subject to most of the religious requirements, such as the laws of ritual cleanliness (Lev. 17:8–13; but cf. Deut. 14:21) and the keeping of the Sabbath and fast days (Exod. 20:8–10; Lev. 16:29). They could celebrate Passover if they were circumcised (Exod. 12:48–49) and could offer sacrifices (Num. 15:14–16, 29). Ezekiel even envisioned a time when they would be granted an inheritance in the land as a sign of full citizenship (Ezek. 47:22–23). In later Judaism, the laws concerning strangers developed into the regulations governing the acceptance of Gentile proselytes into Judaism. In the NT "stranger" usually means simply someone who is not known (Matt. 25:34–40; John 10:5) or, in some older translations, a foreigner (Luke 17:18; Acts 17:21).

The term "stranger" also appears in a figurative sense, usually in appealing to the generosity and mercy of God in dealing with his undeserving people (Ps. 39:12; 119:19; 1 Chron. 29:15). The idea of dwelling in a land owned by someone else is also applied theologically to the relationship of the people Israel to the land; it belonged to God and they were the strangers in it (Lev. 25:23).

The NT picks up this concept in two different ways. On one level, the Gentiles, who were excluded by Judaism from being the people of God, are no longer aliens and strangers in the new Christian community but are counted as full citizens of God's own household (Eph. 2:11–21). On another level, the Christian is not a citizen of this present world but a citizen of the heavenly kingdom and is therefore only a stranger or a pilgrim in this world (1 Pet. 1:1, 17; 2:11; cf. Heb. 11:13). ***See also*** Foreigner; Hospitality; Proselyte. D.R.B.

strangled animals, animals that have not been slaughtered according to Jewish law, which calls for slitting the throat and draining the blood. This law also applied to Gentiles living among Jews (Lev. 17:10–14). In Acts 15:20, Gentile Christians were asked not to eat strangled meat, so that they could share table fellowship with Jewish Christians.

straw, the dried parts of grasses or herbaceous plants often used as fodder for animals (1 Kings 4:28; Gen. 24:25, 32). It is also the by-product of the processing of cultivated cereals, either the stubble of the cut grain left in the fields for the herds to graze over or the chaff separated by winnowing from the threshed grain (Pss. 1:4; 83: 13). Straw was used as a binder for mud bricks (Exod. 5:7–18) or, when mixed with animal dung, as an efficient fuel for kitchen hearths (Isa. 25:10). ***See also*** Chaff.

stripes, wounds inflicted by beating with a whip or rods (Exod. 21:25; Isa. 53:5; 1 Pet. 2:24 where Isa. 53:5 is applied to Jesus). Deut. 25:2–3 prohibits a judge from condemning a person to more than forty lashes, so Paul speaks of receiving "forty lashes less one" at the hands of Jewish authorities (2 Cor. 11:23). ***See also*** Scourge.

stumbling block, any obstacle that may cause someone's downfall, whether literal (Lev. 19:14) or figurative (as elsewhere in the Bible). In Ezekiel it is idolatry (e.g., 14:3–4, 7), while in Jer. 6:21 it is left unspecified. According to Isa. 8:14–15, the disobedient stumble over their God, and in the NT this thought is applied to the unbelievers and Christ (Rom. 9:32–33; 1 Pet. 2: 8). Paul specifically calls Christ's death a stumbling block or offense (Gk. *skandalon*) to the world (1 Cor. 1:23; Gal. 5:11), but he also warns that believers who flaunt their new-found freedom in Christ may place a stumbling block *(proskomma)* or hindrance *(skandalon)* in the way of others who do not share their knowledge (Rom. 14:13; 1 Cor. 8:9). ***See also*** Liberty; Rock; Snare; Stone. V.P.F.

suburbs, the term in the KJV for the RSV's "common land" (Lev. 25:34) or "pasture lands" (Num. 35:2). The term designates open grazing terrain around villages or cities. Such plots are referred to as associated assets when cities are assigned (Num. 35:7; Josh. 14:4; Ezek. 45:2 [RSV: "open space"]; and others). The word is not used in the Bible in its modern sense of residential areas surrounding a metropolis.

Succoth (suhk'uhth; Heb., "booths," "tents," or "temporary dwellings"). **1** A town in the Jordan Valley on the OT "Way of the Plain" (2 Sam. 18:23), which connected it with such towns as Adam, Zarethan, and Pella, and on a major route from central Palestine to Transjordan. Jacob returned from the East to Shechem by this route after his meeting with Esau (Gen. 33:17). Josh. 13:27 places it in Gad, although its previous control by Sihon, king of Heshbon (Hesban), would locate it farther south, near Madeba on the plateau. When Gideon was driving the Midianites out of Esdraelon to their homeland in eastern Transjordan, he asked the inhabitants of Succoth to give nourishment to his three hundred warriors. Perhaps because they feared reprisals from the Midianites, they refused him scornfully, for which after his victory he meted out brutal punishment (Judg. 8:5–16).

The final biblical mention of Succoth concerns the bronze vessels to be used in the Temple, which Solomon had cast "in the clay ground between Succoth and Zarethan" (1 Kings 7:46; 2 Chron. 4:17, which has "Zeredah" in place of "Zarethan"). Two parallel passages in the Psalms (60:6; 108:7) celebrate the conquest of the "Vale of Succoth" as well as the territory of Shechem, and, in the following verses, the whole of Transjordan. This celebration evidently belongs to the period of the United Monarchy (ca. 1025–922 B.C.), and probably to the reign of Solomon rather than that of David, who would have discouraged any idea of "conquering" Shechem.

All these passages put together indicate that Succoth was a place of considerable importance, fairly close to the east bank of the Jordan, where there was a ford giving access both to Shechem and to Esdraelon, and with easy access to the Transjordan plateau. Unfortunately, neither Succoth itself nor the neighboring towns of Zarethan and Penuel can be identified with any certainty. At present the weight of scholarly opinion seems to favor Tell Deir 'Alla for Succoth, about two miles (3 km.) north of the Jabbok (modern Zerqa), with Zarethan perhaps at Tell es-Sa'idiyah about two miles (3 km.) farther north, and Penuel at Tulul edh-Dhahab one and a half miles (2.5 km.) up the Jabbok.

Tell Deir 'Alla was apparently first occupied in the Late Bronze Age (ca. 1500 B.C.) and was evidently at that time an important sanctuary, but it was destroyed by an earthquake at the beginning of the twelfth century. The contemporary scholar Yohanan Aharoni suggests that the "officials of Succoth" in the Gideon story were priests of this sanctuary, and that its destruction belongs to the same occasion.

Subsequently itinerant metalworkers occupied the tell in the twelfth century, and they were followed in the period of the United Monarchy by new immigrants from further east, who built a small walled town on the tell. This was captured by the pharaoh Shishak of Egypt during the reign of Jeroboam I of Israel (ca. 926–907 B.C.). Deserted for a considerable period, it was reoccupied and the sanctuary rebuilt in the seventh century B.C., but it was once more destroyed at some point in the Persian period and not reoccupied until the Middle Ages. H. J. Franken, who excavated the site in 1960–64, seriously doubts the identification of Tell Deir 'Alla with Succoth and suggests that it may have been Gilgal. The nearby, but much smaller, Tell Ekhsas, "Hill of Booths" and Tell es-Sa'idiyeh have also been proposed, and the question still remains a very open one.

2 The first stopping place on the Exodus route (Exod. 12:37; Num. 33:5–6), often identified with Tel el-Mashkutah on the eastern edge of the Nile Delta; but this now seems very dubious. The name may perhaps indicate a merely temporary encampment. ***See also*** Adam; Gideon; Heshbon; Midianites; Pella; Penuel; Shechem; Shishak; Sihon; Transjordan; Zarethan. D.B.

Succoth-benoth (suhk'uth-bee'nuhth; Heb., "booths of girls"), the name of a god (perhaps Sarpanitu, although it is not certain) worshiped in Samaria by the Babylonians (2 Kings 17:30) brought there under Assyria's population displacement policy. In order to keep conquered areas pacified, Assyria deported native populations and replaced them with foreigners. That policy was implemented in the Northern Kingdom, Israel (Samaria), when it fell to Assyria in 721 B.C.

suffering, pain or distress, one of the most persistent of all human problems. Even those who experience relatively minor suffering in their own lives are constantly confronted with the suffering of others—within their own families, among their acquaintances, or even in distant lands. Suffering takes many forms: physical pain, frustrated hopes, depression, isolation, loneliness, grief, anxiety, spiritual crisis, and more. Such unpleasantness comes to good religious people, too. Certainly, the biblical peoples struggled with the presence of suffering in their lives and sought ways to understand it and cope with it that could include their belief in both God's power and God's goodness. The biblical responses to suffering can be divided into five categories.

Suffering as the Result of Human Sin: The most common way to understand the presence of suffering in the world is to say that it is the fault of human beings. The first three chapters of Genesis state that the world was intended to be a good place but that the disobedience of the man and woman (with a little help from the snake) introduced suffering into the world (as demonstrated by the curses in Gen. 3:14–19). No longer is the world the way God wanted it to be. All descendants of the first parents are now born into a sinful world where there is the potential for disaster. All are vulnerable to the possibility of suffering in their lives. The mere fact of being human and living in a world where people hurt each other and themselves can account for much of what is called suffering.

Other OT texts push the idea of cause and effect between human sin and human suffering a bit further. Historians and prophets interpret the meaning of specific calamities in Israel's history. In the time of the judges, all went well for the people when they were obedient to God, but when they turned against God, the Almighty would raise up an enemy to punish them. When they finally cried to God in desperation, God would raise up a judge to fight on their side and restore their good fortunes. Thus, the ups and downs of Israel's history can be explained (says the Deuteronomic historian in Judges, Samuel, and Kings) as rewards for fidelity or punishment for idolatry. Similarly, the greatest catastrophe, the Exile, is seen as fit retribution for all of Israel's and Judah's failings (see esp. 2 Kings 17). Such a calamity would not have occurred if God did not will it (God has the power), and God would not have allowed it if it were not just (the people deserve it).

This is not yet, however, a belief in just retribution in each individual life. Good people as well as evil people suffered and died in the defeat by the Babylonians. When a whole nation is destroyed, it is impossible to make such fine distinctions. When a city is destroyed, good and bad alike are affected. Nevertheless, it is still possible to say, as these texts do, that the suffering is retribution for wicked behavior.

Other OT texts, however, do speak as if just retribution even for individuals is possible. Ezekiel 18 argues that God will deal with each individual, rewarding or punishing all persons according to their own deeds and not because of what their parents have done. Many of the Proverbs imply that the one who leads a good life will be more successful and less likely to suffer than one who defies God. Job's counselors were convinced that a good God who works in the world would never do such horrible things to Job if Job had not done something to deserve it. Though Job seemed to be innocent, he must have had a secret sin of which he needed to repent before his good fortunes would return.

This theory about the origin of suffering may work fairly well as a general statement about the state of the human race or even to account for the suffering of a decadent society. It becomes more and more suspect, however, as a way to differentiate why one individual suffers and another does not. There are too many examples of innocent sufferers and wicked people who prosper for this to be pushed as a universal explanation for an individual's suffering. Many sufferers who have read the texts that see suffering as punishment need to know that other biblical passages argue against a simple-minded and heavy-handed universalizing of the retribution doctrine. The book of Job shows that the counselors are wrong and Job, as he said, was an innocent sufferer. In Luke 13:1–5 and in John 9, Jesus indicates the mistake of interpreting each example of suffering as if it is the consequence of someone's sins. In the apocalyptic frame of mind of many NT books, it is actually more likely that the good people will suffer rather than the evil ones. Jesus warns his listeners that if they follow him, they should be prepared to take up their crosses (Mark 8:34–35). Following Jesus is no guarantee that one will avoid suffering.

Suffering Leading to Some Greater Good: Although suffering is by definition a very undesirable experience, it may lead to some greater good. As terrible as it seems at the time, one may look back on it from a distance and realize that some good has come from it. Many have found this to be a helpful way to find meaning in their suffering. It avoids preoccupation with suffering as punishment, with God as the Judge, and turns the sufferer toward the future and the possibilities that God will work something good from what seems so bad.

Suffering may be of benefit to other people. Joseph suffered greatly at the hands of his brothers, who sold him into slavery. At the end of his life, however, Joseph looked back at his life and saw that many people had benefited because of his suffering (Gen. 50:15–21). He was in the right place to prepare for the famine. He would not have been there if his brothers had not done evil toward him. They are indeed guilty of a hostile act toward him, but God used their wickedness and Joseph's suffering to bring about a greater good. It was, however, only with considerable hindsight that Joseph was able to come to this conclusion. Similarly, it is hard for most sufferers to believe this until enough time has elapsed that the trauma of suffering has been put into a larger perspective.

Christians believe that the suffering of Jesus Christ is somehow of benefit to all humanity. His death, brought about by human beings acting out of wicked motives, has been turned by God into the Christians' most central saving act. The suffering of one has benefited the many.

Another variation of this biblical understanding of suffering is the idea that a person's own suffering is of benefit to him or her. Many have attested that they are better people after being tested by the fires of adversity. Eliphaz (Job 5:17) and Elihu (Job 33:15–18; 36:8–12) suggest this possibility to Job. Prov. 3:11–12 describes suffering as the discipline of a loving parent, an idea picked up and expanded by the author of Hebrews (12:3–11). In Rom. 5:1–5, Paul tells his readers to rejoice in their suffering because it will help produce endurance and character and hope in them. Such words as these have often been comforting to sufferers, though only if this is a conclusion of their own and not an "answer" imposed on them by someone who seems callous to the reality of their present pain.

Suffering Caused by Cosmic Evil Forces: The first view discussed blames humans for suffering, either collectively or individually. The second view hedges a bit on the blame but sees God's role as one of turning what is bad into something that, if not good, at least can be of some benefit. Another possibility is that the cause of suffering is neither human beings nor God but supernatural forces for evil, hostile to both God and humans, too powerful for humans to withstand on their own but no match for the Almighty. Most of the OT does not personify this power for evil as the Devil or Satan. The Devil is never mentioned, and Satan as a cosmic figure occurs in only three places—Job 1–2; 1 Chron. 21:1; and Zech. 3:1–2. The snake in the Garden of Eden is never called Satan, though later generations of interpreters surely made the connection. Other poetic passages in the OT refer to the Sea or a sea monster as a personification of superhuman powers of evil (e.g., Isa. 27:1; 51:9–10; Job 7:12; 26:12).

In the NT, suffering is often ascribed to the presence of demons (Luke 9:38–39), evil spirits (Acts 19:11–12), Satan (Luke 13:16), or the Devil (Acts 10:38). Psychological, physical, and spiritual suffering may be caused by these evil forces and are not due to human sin or God's execution of justice.

In modern times, many people are uncomfortable with these images as a way of identifying the origin of suffering. On the other hand, many find that there is no better way to talk about some forms of suffering. Some experiences of suffering are so terrible, so enormous in scale or depravity, that it is difficult to believe that humans are bad enough or that God is cruel enough to cause them. If one believes in a third force that is a common enemy of both God and humans, it is possible to join forces with God, not needing to blame either God or self, knowing that God will ultimately triumph over anything that can hurt humankind (see, e.g., Rom. 8:35–39).

The Mystery of Suffering: Human efforts to explain with satisfaction all experiences of suffering are doomed to frustration. Answers may be found that are partially satisfying, that may work in some cases, or that may provide some help for the need to find meaning. No matter how hard one tries, however, unanswered questions remain. At some point, one is finally confronted with the necessity of giving up the intellectual search and leaving the unknown in the care of God.

For chapter after chapter, Job and his friends try out all the best explanations for suffering that their tradition has to offer. Every interpretation offered up by the counselors is promptly rejected by Job. None of their answers fits. He wants a word directly from God, an explanation that will either acquit him or bring out into the open God's indictment against him. When God finally speaks in chaps. 38–41, it is not what Job has anticipated at all. Job cannot get in a word to force his own agenda. God overwhelms him with a comparison between the power and wisdom of the Almighty on the one hand and the weakness and ignorance of human beings on the other. Human beings cannot even begin to comprehend the complex wonders of the created order, let alone the mysteries of human suffering. There is an enormous gap between what God knows and what people know. Humans should be content to be human, leaving to God those matters that are, and will always be (at least this side of the grave), beyond human comprehension. God's presence apparently gives Job the confidence to trust God with those things that he cannot find out for himself. His relationship with God is now secure enough that he can live with unanswered questions.

Permission to Lament: This final category is of a different sort than the others. Whether or not humans can find answers to their questions about suffering, they still need some ways to cope with the immediate experience. The biblical laments provide some help, not with the "why" questions, but with the "how" questions. How can one survive? How can one get through the long nights of pain, the months of loneliness without the loved one, the weeks and months when despair hangs like a heavy weight around one's neck? "How long, O Lord?" The laments (e.g., Psalms 3; 5; 10; 17; 38) provide a biblical resource that helps sufferers to keep praying to God even when they are angry with God, doubtful of God's good intentions, uncertain even where God might be found. They give them permission to express negative emotions without fear of reprisal from God. They remove the isolation, letting people know that others who have traveled this way before, even great heroes of the faith like David and Jeremiah, have had thoughts and feelings similar to their own. They are not the only ones who have ever lived who have felt like this. Perhaps they are not losing their minds or their faith.

In modern culture, there is an enormous pressure to stifle lament, to take one's pain with a "stiff upper lip," to smile on the outside and conceal the pain on the inside. The response of biblical peoples to the suffering in their lives can be helpful to all who seek ways to deal with unpleasant thoughts and emotions that intrude into their existence in times of great trial.

There is no single biblical answer, then, to human questions about suffering. Rather, several possibilities are explored and presented. Some answers will be helpful to those who search for understanding; some will not. Some will ring true at one time in a person's life, but not at another. There will be times when no solution is forthcoming and one can only pray for the faith that is able to turn unanswered questions over to God. Throughout one's pilgrimage of suffering, however, there is assurance from the biblical writers that God will hear the prayers of those who cry out for help and comfort (e.g., Pss. 65:2; 66:16–20; 102:1–2, 17; Mk.11:24; 2 Cor. 1:8–11; Phil. 1:19–20). ***See also*** Apocalyptic Literature; Demon; Devil; Evil; Job, The Book of; Prayer; Providence; Satan; Sin.

Bibliography

Crenshaw, James L., ed. *Theodicy in the Old Testament.* Philadelphia: Fortress, 1983.

Gerstenberger, E. S., and W. Schrage. *Suffering.* Nashville, TN: Abingdon, 1980.

Simundson, Daniel J. *Faith Under Fire: Biblical Interpretations of Suffering.* Minneapolis, MN: Augsburg, 1980. D.J.S.

Sukkoth (so͞ok'uhth). ***See*** Tabernacles, Festival of.

Sumer (so͞o'mair), an ancient civilization situated in the alluvial plain between the Tigris and Euphrates rivers in the southern part of what is now Iraq. The Sumerians developed the first major civilization of the ancient Near East. Together with Akkad, its neighbor to the north, the country was later known as Babylonia. Major cities of Sumer included Ur (the birthplace of Abraham, Gen. 11:26–32), Uruk (biblical Erech), Lagash, Nippur, Shuruppak, Eridu, Kish, and Eshnunna. Archaeological excavation of these cities and others in the past century has yielded a wealth of information on the culture, history, literature, and religion of Sumer, providing important material for understanding the cultural context of the ancient Near East and the Hebrew Bible.

The Sumerians were not the original inhabitants of the Tigris-Euphrates plain. They entered the plain approximately 3300 B.C., displacing the native population known to scholars as Ubayids. The Sumerians' original homeland is uncertain, although their non-Semitic, agglutinative language, like that of the Turkic peoples, suggests south-central Asia as a possibility.

Originally, Sumer consisted of a number of city-states, each with its own protective god. Political power was held by the free citizens of the city and a governor, called *ensi*. But as the city-states vied with one another for power and as pressures from outside invaders increased, the institution of kingship (Sumerian *lugal*, "big man") emerged, whereby the ruler of one city-state dominated others.

Kings: The first known king of Sumer is Etana of Kish (ca. 3000 B.C.). He is described as the "man who stabilized all the lands." His descendant, Enmebarragesi, built a temple in Nippur to Enlil, god of the air and chief of the Sumerian pantheon. This established Nippur as the leading cultural and religious center of all Sumer.

Kish eventually lost its power as the kings of Uruk, Lagash, and other cities established their hegemony over the region. Conflict among the city-states so weakened the country that by 2360 B.C., a Semitic king, Sargon I of Agade (biblical Akkad), was able to conquer Sumer. During the rule of the kings of Agade (2360–2180 B.C.), the region became known as Sumer-Akkad and Akkadian, the Semitic language of Akkad, began to replace the Sumerian language. Sargon's grandson, Naram-sin, plundered the temple of Enlil at Nippur. Later Sumerian writers saw Enlil's anger as the cause of an invasion by the Gutians, who overran Naram-sin's empire and destroyed Agade.

After several generations, Sumer began to recover under the leadership of King Gudea of Lagash. After the last of the Gutians were overcome, Ur-nammu founded the third dynasty of Ur (2050–1950 B.C.), which saw a renaissance of Sumerian culture. The famed ziggurat of Ur, a stepped-pyramid structure with a temple dedicated to the moon god, Nanna-sin, was built during this period. The law code of Ur-nammu is the earliest law code known in history. Later invasion by Amorites and Elamites resulted in the destruction of Ur and the following centuries saw continuing struggle between the Sumerian city-states. Finally, around 1750 B.C., the Semitic king Hammurabi of Babylon defeated King Rin-sin of Larsa and became the sole ruler of Sumer-Akkad. This marks the end of Sumer and the beginning of Babylonia.

Invention of Cuneiform Writing: Nevertheless, much of Sumerian culture continued to thrive in Babylonia. Perhaps the most important Sumerian contribution to civilization was the invention of cuneiform writing, a wedge-shaped script formed by pressing a reed stylus into wet clay tablets, which were later dried, baked, and stored in libraries. The Babylonians and other surrounding peoples adapted the cuneiform script to their own languages so that for centuries cuneiform was the dominant mode of writing in ancient Mesopotamia. Most Sumerian tablets contain economic and administrative records but others include mythology, history, hymns, wisdom texts, law, and much more. Of special interest to students of the Bible are the aforementioned law code of Ur-nammu, the Sumerian King List, the Flood Story of Ziusudra, the Paradise Myth of Enki and Ninhursag, early forms of the Gilgamesh Epic, and the Descent of Inanna to the Underworld.

Sumerian religion included a large number of gods and goddesses identified with the forces of nature. Prominent among them were the four creating gods who controlled the major elements of the universe: An, the sky god; Ki, the earth goddess later known as Ninhursag; Enlil, the air god and chief of the Sumerian pantheon; and Enki, the god of water and wisdom. Other important deities included Nanna, the moon god; Utu, the sun god; and Utu's daughter Inanna, the evening star, known to the Babylonians as Ishtar. Inanna's husband was the vegetation god, Dumuzi (Babylonian Tammuz). Dumuzi was conceived as a dying and rising god. During the dry season when nothing grew, he was in the world of the dead. But in Sumerian mythology, Inanna rescues him for six months of the year during which time the rains come and the earth blooms. Their reunion was celebrated at the New Year Festival when the king and a priestess assumed the roles of Dumuzi and Inanna in a sexual sacred marriage rite, thus assuring continued fertility and prosperity for the coming year. ***See also*** Babylon; Mesopotamia.

Bibliography

Kramer, Samuel Noah. *Sumerian Mythology*. Rev. ed. Philadelphia: University of Pennsylvania Press, 1972.

______. *The Sumerians: Their History, Culture, and Character*. Chicago: University of Chicago Press, 1963.

Pritchard, James B. *Ancient Near Eastern Texts Relating to the Old Testament*. 3d ed. Princeton, NJ: Princeton University Press, 1969.

M.A.S.

sun, the star around which the earth orbits. The sun was recognized in the Bible as a beneficent source of light and heat (Deut. 33:14) upon which all life depended, but its power to smite was also known and feared (Isa. 49:10; James 1:11). Created and appointed by God to "rule over the day" (Ps. 136:8), it marked the hours and seasons by its movements (Gen. 1:14–16), and it marked directions by its rising and setting (Isa. 45:6; Deut. 11:30). It surveyed the whole earth from its heavenly course (Ps. 19:6), marking all that occurred below as existence "under the sun" (Eccles. 1:3, 9). It traversed its course like a runner (Ps. 19:4–5), or as drawn by horses and chariot (2 Kings 23:11). It was resplendent as a bridegroom (Ps. 19:5), as enduring as the ages (Ps. 72:17). Surrounding peoples worshiped the sun (Babylonian Shamash; Egyptian Re, Aton) and place names like Beth-shamesh (Heb., "House or Sanctuary of the Sun") attest such worship in pre-Israelite Canaan. Illicit sun worship was also found in Israel (2 Kings 23:5, 11; Ezek. 8:16). The sun's radiance and restorative power served as figures of God's eschatological reign (Mal. 4:2: "the sun . . . with healing in its wings"; Isa. 30:26; cf. Rev. 21:23), and divine intervention in history was signaled by miraculous changes in the sun's course or appearance (darkening, Isa. 13:10; Mark 13:24; premature setting, Amos 8:9; advance or retreat, Josh. 10:12; Isa. 38:7–8). P.A.B.

superscription, title, what is written above or on something, providing concise information. **1** The traditional names ("The Gospel according to Matthew," etc.) of biblical books. **2** The KJV rendering (RSV: "inscription") for what is written on a coin (Matt. 22:20; Mark 12:16; Luke 20:24). **3** The words ("the King of the Jews") written on the sign placed by Pilate on the cross of Jesus; at John 19:19 this is called a

Shamash, the Akkadian sun god, stepping through the mountains at dawn with rays springing from his shoulders; cylinder seal impression, ca. 2400 B.C.

"title," while at Luke 23:38 it is an "inscription" (KJV: "superscription"), at Matt. 27:37 a "charge" (KJV: "accusation"), and at Mark 15:26 an "inscription of the charge" (KJV: "superscription of his accusation"). ***See also*** Cross.

A.J.H.

Supper, the Lord's. ***See*** Lord's Supper, The; Sacraments.

surety. ***See*** Loan.

Susa (sōō′sah). ***See*** Shushan.

Susanna 1 The heroine of the deuterocanonical book who is falsely accused of adultery by two elders whose advances she refused. In the story she is successfully defended by a wise youth, Daniel. The story precedes the book of Daniel in the Septuagint and follows it in the Vulgate. **2** One of the group of women who traveled with Jesus and his disciples and provided for them (Luke 8:3). ***See also*** Apocrypha, Old Testament; Susanna (one of the Additions to Daniel).

Susanna, one of the Additions to Daniel in the Greek translations of the Hebrew OT, found after chap. 12 in the Septuagint (LXX) version and at the beginning of Daniel in Theodotion. It was probably composed in Hebrew and appended to some manuscripts of the Hebrew-Aramaic version of Daniel sometime prior to 100 B.C. Susanna is the story of Daniel's rescue of a young and beautiful woman, condemned to death for adultery as a consequence of a plot by two magistrates to blackmail her into having intercourse with them.

The story opens with the marriage of Susanna to Joakim, in whose house the local court sits (vv. 1–6). Two of the elders or magistrates of the court desire Susanna and look for an opportunity to find her alone (vv. 7–14). As she takes a bath in her garden, they hide and then give her the choice of submitting to them or having them accuse her falsely of adultery (vv. 15–21). Susanna refuses their demands (vv. 22–23). She is accused, tried, and condemned to death (vv. 24–41). In response to her prayer for help, God sends the youth Daniel to aid her (vv. 42–46). He interrogates the two elders separately, proving their guilt, and the court sentences them to death in Susanna's place (vv. 47–62). The story concludes with Susanna's parents and husband praising God and the note that this case first established Daniel's reputation among the Jewish people (vv. 63–64).

The story is a masterpiece of the art of Jewish narrative. Like Tobit, Judith, the Rest of Esther, and the stories in Daniel 1–6, it illustrates how God defends the righteous who call upon him. The difference in the case of Susanna is that the threat comes from within the Jewish community rather than from outside it. Susanna also reflects the isolation of upper-class Jewish women in postbiblical times through virtual confinement to the home and the use of the veil in public. Protestants include the book among the Apocrypha, while Catholics consider it part of the canonical text of Daniel. ***See also*** Apocrypha, Old Testament; Daniel, The Additions to; Women.

D.W.S.

swaddling, the practice of wrapping newborn infants in strips of cloth to keep their limbs straight. Ezek. 16:4 indicates the procedure that was followed in the birth of a child: the umbilical cord was severed, the infant was washed and then rubbed with salt, and then it was wrapped in cloths. According to Luke 2:7, 12, Jesus was wrapped in swaddling cloths after his birth. The Hebrew word of which "swaddling" is the English translation could also denote cloths used in the binding of broken limbs (cf. Ezek. 30:21) and was sometimes used figuratively (cf. Job 38: 9). ***See also*** Child, Children. J.M.E.

swallow, a small bird of the family Hirundinidae. It is not certain that either of the two Hebrew words *(deror, sis)* translated "swallow" (RSV) represents the bird we know by that name. The first term *(deror)* appears twice in the OT; once in Ps. 84:3 along with a general term for "bird" to portray the peace and tranquility of the Jerusalem Temple, and once in Prov. 26:2 where it is used to compare an unfounded curse to the flight of a bird. The second term *(sis)* is likewise used twice; once as a simile to describe the sound of clamor from the sick Hezekiah (Isa. 38: 14), and once as an example of habit in contrast to the fickleness of God's people (Jer. 8:7). F.R.M.

swan. ***See*** Water Hen.

swearing. ***See*** Oath.

swine, or pig, a stout-bodied, short-legged omnivorous mammal, family Suidae. Swine are "unclean animals" in the OT, because they have cloven hooves but no ruminant stomach (Lev. 11:7; Deut. 14:8). The prohibition against the pig as a food animal for Jews is probably rooted in religious prohibitions against animals sacred to other peoples. The modern fear of a trichinosis infection, a parasitic and often lethal disease transmitted to humans by consumption of insufficiently cooked pork, is valid but unlikely to be the original reason for regarding swine as ritually unclean (Isa. 65:4; 66:3).

The pig was domesticated in Neolithic times (ca. 9000–4500 B.C.) from the wild boar *(Sus scrofa)*, which still roams the Jordan Valley and the Jordanian highlands in great numbers today. Pigs were useful animals, because they converted all kinds of otherwise unusable food, such as leftovers, rodents, acorns, and roots, into meat. But they also required careful herding to keep them away from cultivated areas.

The low estate to which the prodigal son fell is signified by his occupation as a swineherd (Luke 15:15, 16). Pigs also figure in the story in Matt. 8:28–34, where Jesus heals two men by allowing their demons to occupy a herd of swine that then rushes headlong into the Gadarene Lake. The proverbial foolishness of "casting pearls before swine" has its origin in Matt. 7:6, while the saying "like a gold ring in a swine's snout" stems from Prov. 11:22. I.U.K.

sword, a close-range weapon composed of a metal blade, which was usually bronze or iron in the biblical period, and a wood or bone handle (Judg. 3:22). The sword is distinguished from the dagger on the basis of length; the former designation is normally applied to weapons that are over one foot long. Depending upon its function (i.e., slashing or stabbing), the blade was single- or double-edged (Judg. 3:16; Ps. 149:6), curved or straight, pointed or blunt. Since swords were so common in the ancient world, the biblical writers provided few descriptive details about these weapons. Fortunately, archaeologists have recovered many swords and daggers from virtually every period of antiquity; this makes it possible for readers of the Bible to obtain some understanding of the weapons mentioned in particular biblical episodes.

Between the third millennium B.C. and the Greco-Roman period (333 B.C.–A.D. 324), the sword evolved through a variety of shapes, lengths, and levels of durability. The earliest swords were made of bronze and averaged only about 10 inches in length; blades were double-edged, straight, and pointed. While this dagger-like weapon was used primarily for stabbing, the longer sickle-sword was made for slashing. Through the centuries, numerous changes were made in blade production and in the method of attaching the blade to its hilt, but the major change in the development of swords took place when iron-working became widespread. Archaeological and biblical evidence points to the Philistines' early monopoly on the military use of this superior metal (1 Sam. 13:19–22). With the arrival of the Iron Age ca. 1200 B.C., the straight, long sword was developed as a formidable weapon for the first time in history. Since iron possesses greater hardness and strength than bronze, iron was ideal for the forging of longer blades and more durable cutting edges. The double-edged, pointed sword reached a length of 30 inches, and this weapon was strong enough for thrusting and slashing. Although the long sword was improved and used throughout the Mediterranean region until relatively modern times, Greek and Roman soldiers also used shorter swords. The typical sword of Roman soldiers in NT times was the *gladius*, a lightweight, well-balanced weapon

Curved sword from the excavations at Byblos, eighteenth century B.C.

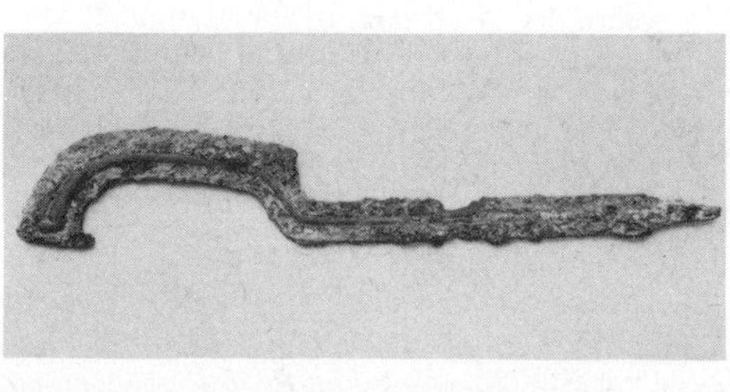

with a blade about 2 feet long (see Eph. 6:17: "sword of the Spirit," Lat. *spiritus gladius*).

Between the first biblical reference to the sword, the mysterious "flaming sword" in Gen. 3:24, and the final mention of this weapon, the sword of judgment in Rev. 19:21, the term "sword" appears in the Bible well over four hundred times, making the sword the most frequently mentioned weapon in Scripture. References to swords occur in accounts from every biblical period. Most passages refer to the literal weapon of war, but the sword also symbolizes aggression (Jer. 2:30; Matt. 26:52), disharmony (2 Sam. 2:26; Matt. 10:34), deceit (Ps. 55:21), divine assistance (Ezek. 30:21–25), God's word (Eph. 6:17; Heb. 4:12), and divine wrath (Isa. 34:5–6; Jer. 50:35–37; Ezek. 21:9–20; Hos. 11:6). Since the sword was normally kept in a sheath (1 Sam. 17:51), the drawn sword signified war (Judg. 8:10). The prophets allude to the drawn and sheathed sword to symbolize the threat of God's judgment (Jer. 47:6; Ezek. 21:3–5, 28–30). Highly figurative are the book of Revelation's references to the sword of judgment that protrudes from the Lord's mouth, a probable reference to the power of his words of judgment (1:16; 2:12, 16; 19:15, 21). Above all of this military terminology stands the hope that an age of peace will eventually eliminate the need for swords (Isa. 2:4; Mic. 4:3; see Joel 3:10, where this situation is reversed). ***See also*** Soldier; War; Weapons. G.L.M.

sycamine (sik'ah-mīn), a tree used in an example by Jesus (Luke 17:6). Most authorities believe it to be black mulberry.

Sycamine (black mulberry).

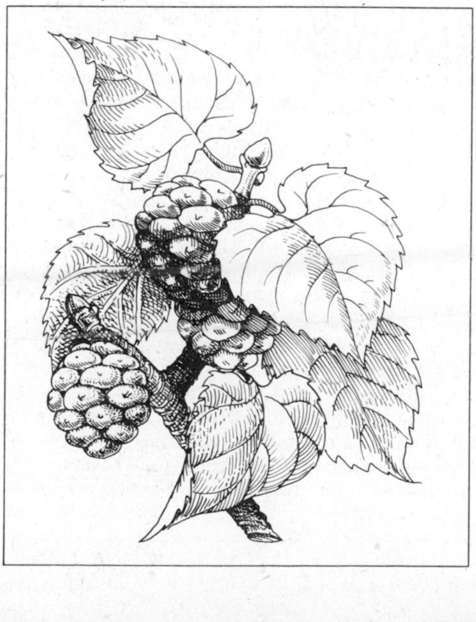

sycamore *(Ficus sycomorus)*, the biblical sycamore, or mulberry fig, that thrives in warm lowland areas of the Holy Land, a tree not to be confused with the sycamore of more temperate regions. Although its fruit is smaller than and not as tasty as that of the regular fig, it is a popular food, especially for the desert bedouins, who often pause in the shade of its low, spreading branches. The wood, though soft and porous, is quite durable and is therefore often used in the manufacture of furniture and for the construction of buildings (1 Kings 10:27; 1 Chron. 27:28; Isa. 9:10; Amos 7:14; Luke 19:4). P.L.C.

Sychar (sī'kahr), according to John 4:5, a village in Samaria where Jesus spoke with the Samaritan women (John 4:5–42). John 4:5 locates the village near a field reputedly given by Jacob to his son Joseph, with a well still active in Jesus' time (4:6). The actual site of the village is disputed, most scholars holding for Tel Balata, ancient Shechem (Lat. and Gk., "Sychem"; cf. Acts 7:16), but some for the nearby village of Askar. Both are near what is called today "Jacob's Well," some thirty miles due north of Jerusalem. The solution depends in part on the accuracy of the site of Jacob's Well. ***See also*** Jacob; Jacob's Well; Joseph; Samaria, District of; Samaritans. C.H.M.

Sychem (sī'kem). ***See*** Shechem.

Syene (sī-een'nee; KJV: "Seveneh"), a town on the east bank of the Nile just north of the First Cataract. Called *Swn* (modern Aswan) by the Egyptians, it was at the southern border of Egypt; Ezekiel's pronouncement on the forthcoming fate of all Egypt at the hands of the Babylonians speaks of "from Migdol to Syene" (Ezek. 29:10; 30:6). On the island of Elephantine (Heb. *Yeb*), across from Syene, there was a late sixth- and fifth-century B.C. military colony in the service of the Persians. The Elephantine Papyri, several groups of Aramaic documents found on the island, show that this colony included many Jews, who had their own temple to God, were permitted to celebrate the Passover festival, and lived both on the island and in Syene. ***See also*** Passover, The; Temples. J.M.W.

symbol, a term derived from a Greek noun meaning a "contract," "tally," or "mark" by which something is inferred, which, in turn, is derived from a verb meaning "to bring together" or "compare." The word is not found in either the OT or the NT, though symbolic language and actions are common throughout the Bible. A *sign* is chosen or devised for its aptnesss and can be neither equivocal nor arbitrary. A *symbol*, in contrast, bridges two realities, bringing them

Loaves of bread and a fish, which were symbolic in early Christian art of the Eucharist; wall painting from the catacomb of St. Callixtus, Rome.

into relationship with one another, but since it connotes a reality that is not directly knowable and about which only indirect discourse or reference is possible, the symbol may not only reveal but also veil the reality it represents.

Natural Symbols in the OT: Natural symbols such as dawn, rain torrents, or the stars (Job 38: 4–41; cf. Pss. 65:5–8; 103:19; 104:1–4; 19:1) reveal the splendor and power of God. Since everything that God has made is good (Gen. 1: 31), creation itself makes possible a covenant relationship with the Creator that even human sin does not annul. The covenant that was manifested in the "bow in the cloud" (Gen. 9:8–27) remains as a reminder of God's promise not to destroy the natural order and is therefore also a reminder of the grace and mercy of the Creator towards all living creatures.

Symbolism in Israel's History: For Israel, the Law (Torah) was the supreme manifestation of the will of God and the foundation of its existence as a people. The structure of the Torah took its shape within the frame of Israel's awareness of a divine intention that has to do with revelation and reconciliation as symbolized in the events described in Exodus 19–24: the theophany manifested in fire, smoke, and earthquake; the rehearsal of the stipulations of the covenant before the people to the accompaniment of awesome natural signs; and finally the sealing of the covenant in blood, sprinkled on the people, with their promise to obey.

The symbolism of fire and cloud is found earlier in the narrative in Exodus in the appearance of the angel of the Lord to Moses in the burning bush (Exod. 3:1–6) and in the pillars of cloud and fire that accompanied the people on their journey (Exod. 13:21–22). The cloud on Sinai (Exod. 16:10; 19:9; 24:15–18), denoting the presence of God, is associated also with the tent (characteristic of the E tradition) or tabernacle (P tradition) as a materialization of the divine glory, or *Shekinah* as it is known in later Judaism.

The incident of the golden calf (Exod. 32) or, more properly, the young bull, may be an expression of the fight against the invasion of the Canaanite cult into Israel's worship. At any rate, the "sin of Jeroboam" in the later Northern Kingdom was to allow images of Yahweh to be set up at Bethel and Dan in the form of young bulls (1 Kings 12:26–33), as though they were the gods who brought Israel out of Egypt. When the prophets denounced syncretism in Israel's worship, they symbolized the corruption as the offering of sacrifice to bulls (e.g., Hos. 12:11; 13:2).

Two symbols identified with the covenant are the Sabbath (Exod. 20:8–11; 23:12; Deut. 5:12–15) and circumcision. The whole life of Israel depended on the maintenance of the Sabbath (Jer. 17:24–27; Ezek. 20:19–20; 44:24). The Sabbath was to be a day of rest, for God rested on the seventh day and sanctified it (Gen. 2:1–3), and even in the wilderness when God sent manna, it did not fall on the Sabbath (Exod. 16:22–30). In the Deuteronomic code, the Israelites were to remember the Sabbath by refraining from oppressing subject peoples, since they themselves had been in bondage (Deut. 5:12–15).

In the P tradition, circumcision was the sign of the covenant made with Abraham (Gen. 17: 1–14) and was performed as early as eight days after birth. In Ezekiel, it is a mark or token of initiation into the covenant community (Ezek. 28:10; 31:18; 32:19). Jeremiah called for a deeper circumcision of the heart (Jer. 4:4).

Symbolic Words and Actions: Revelation in the OT is characteristically expressed in the mode of word or speech. Since it communicates the reality of God, a reality that is not directly knowable, the word that comes to the prophets (Isa. 1:2; Jer. 1:2; Ezek. 1:3; Mic. 1:1; etc.) constitutes as such the supreme symbol of God's self-disclosure. The word of God denotes God's presence, call, or power to create or heal (1 Sam. 15:10; Ps. 119: 105; Isa. 55:11; Jer. 37:17; Ps. 33:6; Ezek. 37:4; Ps. 107:20). The God so revealed is described throughout the OT in predominantly masculine imagery (King, Lord, and so on), but feminine imagery is also frequent (Num. 11:12; Hos. 11:1, 3, 4, 8; Jer. 31:20; Isa. 42:14; 46:3–4; 49:14–15; 66:12–13; Pss. 22:9; 131:1–2).

The Feast of the Passover symbolized different events connected with the Exodus: the eating of unleavened bread, for example, because time was lacking to procure sufficient food for the journey (Exod. 12:33–34, 39). Each subsequent commemoration of the Passover was a re-living of the original experience. For other actions with symbolic meaning, see also Exod. 21:1–6; Ruth 4:7; 1 Kings 22:11; and 1 Sam. 16: 13. The prophets often conveyed a message in such enacted parables as Isaiah's walking barefoot and naked (Isa. 20), the spoiled waistcloth of Jeremiah (Jer. 13:1–11), and Hosea's experience through his marriage of God's displeasure with Israel's corrupt and syncretistic worship. The names of Hosea's children ("Not pitied" and "Not my people"; Hos. 1:6, 9) continue the

Menorah, shophar, and other traditional Jewish sacred objects; third-century pottery sherd from Beit Natif.

symbolism (see also Ezek. 4:1–3; 1 Sam. 15:27–28; Jer. 19:1–11; 28:10–11).

Symbolic Persons, Names, and Places: Particular persons might symbolize a group, as David was worth ten thousand of the army (2 Sam. 18:3), or even embody the presence or power of God: Moses was "as God" to Pharaoh (Exod. 7:1; cf. 4:16; 17:9). Elisha had healing power because the divine spirit dwelt in him as a "man of God" (2 Kings 4:9, 35).

The giving of a name is frequently associated with the honor or character of its bearer or with good or painful events surrounding the bearer's birth: Hosea's children, for example (see above) or Ichabod (meaning "Inglorious"), born prematurely to the wife of Phinehas, one of the two priests accompanying the Ark who were killed by the Philistines (1 Sam. 4:19–22). Isaiah gave his son the name Shearjashub ("A remnant shall return") to signify the return of the remnant to carry on the history of Israel (Isa. 7:3). A new name was often given to express an alteration in a person's character or circumstance, for instance, Abram (Gen. 17:1–8) or Jacob (Gen. 32:24–28). The divine name, Yahweh (Exod. 3:14), sometimes called the tetragrammaton because it consists of four Hebrew consonants, is of obscure origin. It seems not to have been pronounced in later Judaism, perhaps for the sake of reverence, yet the name of Yahweh was to be remembered (Exod. 20:24; cf. Jer. 23:26–27), especially in holy places.

Certain place names are symbolic of rebellion against God (e.g., Babel; Gen. 11:1–9) or of religious deviance (e.g., Samaria; Mic. 1:6–7). In contrast, Canaan supremely symbolized the land of the covenant because its cities and people were God's heritage (2 Sam. 10:12; 21:3); above all, this was true of Jerusalem, the place of the Temple and God's dwelling place (Ps. 48:1–3; cf. Psalm 84).

Sacred Symbols: From the time of the entry into Canaan, holy places commemorated ancestors, kings, or heroes for the Israelites: for example, Abraham (Gen. 12:8) or Jeroboam (1 Kings 12:26–31). Their significance diminished, however, when the Temple became the one holy place for the Hebrews. While evidence varies from the pre- to the postexilic period, the symbolism of the Temple and its furnishings generally remains constant. In the Temple erected by Solomon, the idea of a portable sanctuary had not been wholly lost, even though the God of Israel had acquired a fixed dwelling place. Two cherubim covered the Ark in the Holy of Holies and appear to have carried a throne, as is suggested in passages such as 1 Sam. 4:4; 2 Sam. 6:2; Pss. 80:1; 99:1; Ezek. 43:6–7; 9:3; and 10:19. The ephod or priestly garment and the breastplate (Exod. 28–29) symbolized the spiritual dignity of the priest. The robe of the high priest, adorned with pomegranates and bells, the miter with its inscription, "Holy to the Lord" (Exod. 28:36–38), and all the sanctuary furnishings were sacrosanct: altar, utensils, and even the water used there (Exod. 29:37; 30:10, 27–29, 34–38). Kneeling as an attitude of prayer (1 Kings 8:54; Ps. 95:6) is symbolic of reverence or humility (2 Kings 1:13), just as standing (Ps. 33:8; Ezek. 2:1) symbolizes awe or attentiveness.

Other Symbols: Certain numbers have particular associations in the OT, the number one often suggesting wholeness or indivisibility (Deut. 6:4), and four (Exod. 25–27; Ezek. 10:21), seven, ten, one hundred, and one thousand (all frequent) indicating completeness or fullness of some kind. Forty is a moderate round number (as in Gen. 7:12). Sacred objects such as amulets, made of various materials, were worn for protection against evil or for blessing and may have been fashioned in the form of crescents, pendants, etc. (perhaps referred to in Isa. 3:18–21). In the form of a capsule, they were at times fixed to a doorpost (Deut. 6:9). The color white symbolized purity (Isa. 1:18; Dan. 11:35); black, death or mourning (Job 30:30; Jer. 4:28); and red, guilt, bloodshed, or warfare (Isa. 1:18; Nah. 2:3; Zech. 6:2). Blue was associated with sacred places or vestments (Exod. 26–28).

Jesus Christ as the True Image of God: Salvation in the NT is characteristically the result of a historical and essentially new act, the incarnation of the Word (John 1:14). Various writers in the NT agree in emphasizing that God assumed flesh in Jesus (John 1:14; Col. 1:19). When the Word of God became flesh, he made the image of God visible. He is truly God, not a symbol of God. He is also truly human and not merely a symbol of humanity, for he assumed the form of those who are created in God's image, entering into the very creation that is subject to death, in order to renew it through his own death and resurrection (Phil. 2:6–11). Paul can summarize the content of his preaching as "the word of the cross" (1 Cor. 1:18), indicating the inherent power of a new symbol to denote the salvation that is proclaimed by the church's preachers.

In expressing the imperfection and incompleteness of the institutions of Judaism, the Letter to the Hebrews gives prominence to the idea of perfection (Heb. 7:11; cf. 6:1), that is, of Christ's completion or fulfillment of the symbols of the former economy of grace, given "in many and various ways" (Heb. 1:1). These foreshadowed the revelation given in Christ and are all now superseded by the one who reflects the glory of God and bears the very stamp of his nature (Heb. 1:1–3). Christ is mediator in that his death was the sacrificial act by which the covenant of Sinai was replaced by a new or better covenant (Heb. 8:6–7; 9:15; 12:24), effected by the shedding of his blood (Heb. 10:19; 13: 12, 20). The new covenant is better because in it the eternal world has become actual. The law was a shadow of good things to come (Heb. 10: 1) but not the reality.

In the dualistic universe of Hellenism, there is a "beyond" that is inaccessible from the material world below, except by symbols (such as Plato's shadows on the cave). In the NT, the eschatological future that is not yet present—the Reign or Kingdom of God—has become a reality in Christ, of which life in the Spirit is a guarantee (2 Cor. 1:22; 5:5; Eph. 1:14). In John's Gospel, the miracles of Jesus are distinct both from the "signs and wonders" (John 4:48) of the Hellenistic world and even from the miracles of the synoptic Gospels. John frequently uses the Greek word usually translated "sign" (John 2: 11, 18, 23; 3:2; 4:48, 54; 6:2, 14, 26, 30; 7:31; 9: 16; 10:41; 11:47; 12:18, 37; 20:30), though the translation "characteristic" or "distinguishing mark" is also possible, since the miracles in John are intended to point to the messianic age Jesus announces also in his preaching. In John, Jesus' signs are typically followed by or associated with a teaching related to them: the feeding of the multitude and the discourse on the bread of life (John 6); the healing of the blind man and the teaching of Jesus as the light of the world (John 8–9); and the raising of Lazarus and the "I am" saying about Jesus as the resurrection and the life (John 11). Many are brought to faith by means of the signs, and for those who believe they are proof of his glory, which is to be seen supremely in his death and resurrection, the greatest of his signs (John 12:33; 18:32, both using the Greek verb meaning "to show by a sign").

The special significance of the parables may be mentioned as symbolizing in their own way the character of God's Reign, the eschatological nature of Jesus' preaching, and the seriousness of his call to decision for God and his salvation (see esp. the so-called kingdom of heaven parables, Matt. 13:44, 45, 47; 18:23; 20:1; 22:2; 25:1, with their characteristic introduction, "The kingdom of heaven is like . . ."). Mark 4:10–12 expresses the ambiguity and openness to misunderstanding of the parables, an ambiguity they have in common with symbols. For the disciples, the parables have done their work in disclosing the secret of God's Rule. Those outside do not perceive its presence in Jesus.

In his preaching and ministry, Jesus laid the foundation of the church of the post-Easter period. Since his followers saw themselves as the true Israel, the NT language about the church uses much of the religious and cultic symbolism of the OT. The church is "a chosen race, a royal priesthood, a holy nation, God's own people" (1 Pet. 2:9), phrases derived from Exod. 19:6. But the early church also had certain forms that denoted its distinctiveness. Baptism, the universal symbol of incorporation into the church (as distinct from circumcision), symbolized dying to sin and rising to newness of life (Rom. 6:3–6; Col. 2:12) through the physical actions of descent into the water, immersion, and ascent from the water. The evidently simple rite reflected in the NT came to acquire a complex visual, auditory, and kinetic symbolism in the later classical rites of baptism. The Lord's Supper, as a visible sign of the death of Christ, and therefore to be proclaimed until he comes (1 Cor. 11: 26), is a remembrance of Jesus' last supper with the disciples (and other meals in his ministry), a participation or communion in his risen life (1 Cor. 10:16), and a foretaste or pledge of his completed work of salvation. The so-called fourfold action of the Eucharist—taking bread, blessing, breaking, and giving (Matt. 26:26–29; Mark 14: 22–25; Luke 22:17–20)—also acquired in later liturgical practice a developed and stylized symbolism.

The symbolism of the book of Revelation, unique in Christian apocalyptic literature, is largely drawn from OT sources, particularly Daniel. The eschatological hope of the church is grounded on the certainty of God's salvation in Christ, despite the apparently irretrievable domination of Satan. The symbolism of Revelation includes various spirits, angels, battles, cities, bizarre creatures, human figures, and numbers; perhaps most famous are the number of the beast, 666 (Rev. 13:18), and the four horsemen (Rev. 6:1–8). ***See also*** Amulet; Ark; Baptism; Breastpiece; Bull; Calf; Cherub; Circumcision; Covenant; Ephod; Fire; Kingdom of God; Logos; Lord's Supper, The; Manna; Miracles; Parables; Passover, The; Pillars; Rainbow; Revelation to John, The; Shekinah; Sign; Tabernacle; Temple, The; Theophany; Word.

Bibliography

Eliade, Mircea. *Images and Symbols: Studies in Religious Symbolism*. New York: Sheed and Ward, 1969.

Johnson, Frederick E., ed. *Religious Symbolism.* New York/London: Harper & Row, 1955.

Pedersen, Johannes. *Israel, Its Life and Culture.* 2 vols. London: Oxford University Press, 1926–1940. J.A.R.M.

Symeon (sim'ee-yuhn). ***See*** Simeon.

synagogue, a Greek word meaning a "gathering of things" or an "assembly of people." The Jewish synagogue is both a congregation of Jews who pray, read Scripture, and hear teaching and exhortation based on Scripture and the place where the congregation assembles. As the synagogue developed in rabbinic Judaism, it also became a place for study of the Bible, its commentaries, and Talmudic materials. The origin of the synagogue is obscure, but it certainly existed by the first century A.D. in both Palestine and the Diaspora.

First-century A.D. synagogues in Palestine are attested by the Gospels. Jesus preached and discussed with Jewish leaders and congregations in synagogues (e.g., Matt. 4:23; 9:25; Mark 1:21; 3:1–6; Luke 4:16–28; 13:10). The synagogue was a place of prayer, reading of Scripture, preaching, and teaching. It is uncertain whether the many references to synagogues in the Gospels reflect the situation during Jesus' lifetime or the period after the destruction of the Temple (A.D. 70) when the Gospels were finally written. Josephus, the Jewish historian of the late first century, speaks of a few synagogues in the north of the Holy Land. Synagogues were certainly common in the Diaspora. Philo, the first-century Egyptian Jewish writer, attests to the presence of numerous synagogues in Alexandria. Inscriptions found at various places in the Roman Empire show that Jewish congregations were found in many places. Acts portrays Paul as teaching in synagogues wherever he goes (e.g., Acts 18:4; 19:8).

Origin: The origin of the synagogue remains unknown, but the question has produced a number of theories. Many have suggested that the synagogue arose in the Babylonian exile as a response to the loss of the Temple as the center of Jewish religious life. Though the suggestion is reasonable, no direct evidence exists for its presence and the biblical passages cited (Ezek. 11:16; 14:1) are far from convincing. In addition, no mention of the synagogue is made in Ezra and Nehemiah, nor is any destruction of synagogues mentioned during the Maccabean revolt. The public reading of Torah is described in Nehemiah 8 and mentioned in 1 Macc. 3:48, but these assemblies are extraordinary public gatherings; we do not know whether these practices were regularly done. Some scholars suggest that the Hellenistic crisis during the second century B.C., in which there was a conflict among Jews over acculturation and fidelity to tradition, produced the synagogue as a mode of resistance to Hellenism, i.e., Greek culture and custom. Since the synagogue existed in developed form in the first century A.D., it is likely that it came into being in the two centuries preceding, but no direct evidence for it then exists. In the Diaspora, some Egyptian inscriptions from the third and second centuries B.C. mention a "place of prayer" (Gk. *proseuchē*), but we do not know what went on in the houses of prayer and it is not certain that these refer to synagogues.

A building has been found on the island of Delos in the Nile that has been identified as a Jewish synagogue, but the building has no clear Jewish symbols or characteristics to identify it unambiguously as a synagogue. It is likely that Jews often met in a large room in a house. A building set aside for special religious purposes had to await a certain level of material prosperity and community development. In only four recently dug sites in Palestine have rooms or buildings been identified as synagogues: Masada, Herodium, Magdala (Migdal, Tarichaeae), and Gamala. The results of these excavations are preliminary and the identifications are not certain in all cases, especially for Masada and Herodium. Existing structures were transformed into assembly halls, but that they were specifically synagogues is not certain. In all cases the buildings or rooms are relatively small and unadorned and vary greatly in plan.

Physical Structure: Buildings that can be clearly identified as synagogues become plentiful both in Palestine and the Diaspora during the third century A.D. This is consistent with the development of rabbinic Judaism, which gradually asserted control over Judaism after the Temple was destroyed in A.D. 70 and which stressed synagogue- and school-centered prayer and study. Synagogue buildings were often decorated with mosaics and reliefs and were built in three styles, the basilica, the broadhouse, and the apsidal. The basilica was borrowed from Greco-Roman architecture and often had the entrance facing Jerusalem. The inside was rectangular and divided lengthwise by two rows of columns into nave and two side aisles. When the congregation faced Jerusalem to pray, they had to face the entrance; consequently a permanent Torah shrine, where the scrolls of Scripture were kept, and a *bema* (Gk., "platform"; a raised platform where the leaders of the congregation stood or sat) were difficult to establish. Contemporaneously the broadhouse design developed, in which one of the long walls of the rectangle faced Jerusalem and so a permanent Torah shrine and *bema* were possible. Later the apsidal synagogue developed, in which the entrance was on the side away from Jerusalem and the side facing Jerusalem had an apse (a large semicircular niche) for the Torah shrine and *bema*. Synagogues in the Diaspora followed similar designs, though sometimes Jews took over buildings built earlier and adapted them to their purposes. In all cases, the floor plan, orientation, and architecture varied considerably. Some Diaspora synagogues are notable for their size or beauty, e.g., the ones in Sardis in Turkey, Dura in Syria, Stobi in Macedonia, and Ostia in Italy.

Function: The function of the synagogue, how the congregation was organized, and what went on in the synagogue can only be surmised. In Palestine before the destruction of the Temple the synagogue would have been one of many indigenous organizations in Jewish villages and cities. People may have met to read Scripture and pray either in a house or outside, without any elaborate organization. In the Diaspora where Jews were a minority in the cities they inhabited, the synagogue probably functioned as the center of the community and its leaders may have been community leaders recognized by the civil authorities. Synagogues were used to teach the young, to house visitors, and for communal meals.

Liturgy: The versions of Jewish prayers that have been transmitted in the tradition show that the synagogue liturgy did not have a fixed text but varied both in content and wording over time and from place to place. It is certain that Scripture was read, though probably not according to the later three-year and one-year fixed cycles of readings. Primacy was given to the Pentateuch, but readings from the Prophets were also included. The existence of many Targums (translation of the Hebrew Bible into the vernacular, Aramaic) and versions of the Septuagint (the Greek translation of the Bible) testifies to the importance of understanding the ancient text. Philo, Josephus, and the NT show that the Bible was interpreted to the people in the synagogues. It is also likely that the two most important prayers in Judaism were in use, though not according to a fixed text. The first is the *Shema*, consisting of three biblical passages (Deut. 6:4–9; 11:13–21; Num. 15:37–41) with attendant blessings. The second is the "Prayer," also called the *Amidah* or Eighteen Benedictions. This series of blessings has varied in text and number over time, but it is treated as very old in rabbinic tradition. ***See also*** Prayer.

Bibliography

Levine, Lee I., ed. *Ancient Synagogues Revealed.* Detroit, MI, and Jerusalem: Wayne State University, Israel Exploration Society, 1982.

A.J.S.

syncretism, either a conscious combining of two or more religions over a short period of time, or a process of absorption by one religion of elements of another over a long period of time. In both types the absorbed elements are usually transformed and given new meaning by the fresh context. The borrowed item may remain outwardly the same but its new context signifies something quite new.

The religion of Israel as it emerged and developed in the late second and first millennia B.C. constantly reacted to the religions of the West Semitic ("Canaanite") world in which it lived. The Bible itself acknowledges the impact of neighboring religions through its constant polemic against some of their aspects and through its reinterpretation of other aspects. What is known about Canaanite religion (directly from the Ugaritic tablets of the late second millennium and indirectly from the Bible) and about the other religions of the ancient Near East suggests that Israel did its heaviest borrowing in its worship and legal systems, in its royal ceremonial, and in its wisdom literature. The portrayals of deities in the religion attested in the Ugaritic tablets influenced the depiction of Yahweh. The God of Israel combines traits of the prominent Canaanite god, El, the ancient patriarch who lives in a tent, and of Baal, the young god of the storm, mighty in war. Paucity of comparative evidence, however, makes it difficult to judge the exact extent of borrowing and transformation especially where institutions are concerned.

Some elements of Israelite religion are not attested in comparable literature; these elements seem rather to be derived from the uniquely biblical affirmation that Yahweh alone is God. Belief in one God meant that Yahweh had no consort and did not therefore create by sexual generation. It implied further than no statue could represent him to the worshiper since the prohibition against statues in the first commandment is part of the command to worship Yahweh alone. The conventional ancient depiction of the gods, the divine assembly, is in the Bible shadowy and utterly subservient to the Most High. Monotheistic faith informs the peculiarly Israelite phenomenon of prophecy; the prophets speak in the conviction that the people's conduct affects the entire course of history because all that happens on earth is in the hands of one God. Other biblical themes are related to the distinctively biblical confession: the extraordinary interest in world history as revelatory of the one God, the avoidance of conventional narrative about the gods acting in heaven, and the emphasis upon divine and human justice.

Though syncretism in the gradual sense noted above was always operative in Israel's history, the Bible sees certain periods as critical with regard to foreign influence. We prescind here from the popular narratives in Genesis about Israel's beginnings in which the ancestors are always different from the nations in the person of "the Canaanites," the local king, and Pharaoh. The conquest of Canaan, generally dated to the thirteenth century B.C., is accompanied in Deuteronomy, Joshua, and Judges by warnings not to intermarry with the Canaanites or to follow their ways. The reign of Solomon in the tenth century was a time of subversion of Israelite values by foreign wives (1 Kings 3–11). The ninth century in Israel and the early seventh in Judah were both periods of apostasy, to judge from the abundant literary record of apostasies for these periods. In the sixth century B.C., largely as the result of the Exile, the Jewish community defined itself against an alien environment through written Scripture and specific practices. These strong measures helped the Jewish community clearly to differentiate itself from its neighbors in the postexilic period. The next crisis of which there is record was the hellenization of many Jews in the wake of Alexander's conquest of the East in the late fourth century. The book of Daniel in the second century vehemently defends the ancient tradition against the new ways.

In the first century A.D., Christianity developed from Judaism, a development that was caused not by the influence of foreign ideas upon the Jewish community but by an emphasis given by some Jews to the belief in Jesus as the Messiah, a belief interpreted in light of the apocalyptic tradition that already existed within early Judaism. Neither Judaism nor Christianity can therefore be adequately explained as purely syncretistic phenomena. R.J.C.

synoptic problem, the, the problem of determining the relationships among the Gospels of Matthew, Mark, and Luke, which are called "synoptic" because they present similar portraits of Jesus and share a great deal of material. They are similar in outline, contents, order, and wording. Most impressive are the verbal agreements, which are almost total in some passages.

Most scholars explain such similarities by assuming literary relationships among these Gospels (that is, use of common source material and/or use of each other as sources). Most also think that Mark was the earliest Gospel and was used independently as a source for both Matthew and Luke. This explains Matthew's and Luke's similarities with Mark. But there are also similarities between Matthew and Luke in material not found in Mark. To explain this phenomenon, many scholars have assumed that Matthew and Luke also independently used a hypothetical source, now called "Q." This widely held theory is called the Two-Source Hypothesis, because it states that there were two major sources used in the composition of Matthew and Luke, namely, Mark and Q. The unique material found, respectively, in Matthew and Luke, which came from neither Mark nor Q, is designated by the symbols "M" (for Matthew) and "L" (for Luke). Thus, according to the Two-Source Hypothesis,

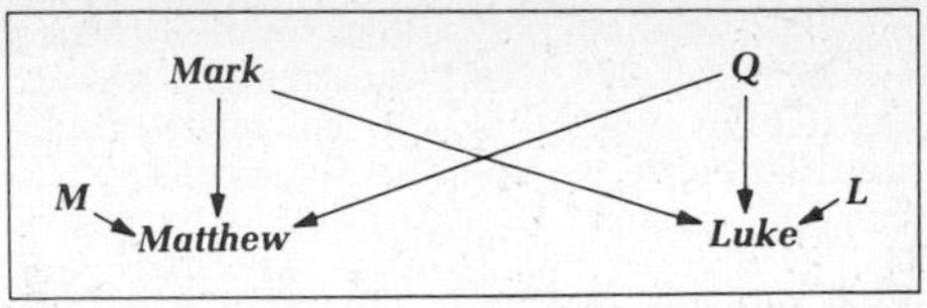

Relationships among the Synoptic Gospels according to the Two-Source Hypothesis.

Mark was written first; Mark, Q, and M were sources for Matthew; and Mark, Q, and L were sources for Luke.

Some scholars reject the Two-Source Hypothesis. The leading alternative is probably the Griesbach Hypothesis (for J. J. Griesbach, 1745–1812), which dates Matthew first, sees it as a source for Luke, and regards both Matthew and Luke as sources for Mark. Other theories are more complex, appealing to the continuing influence of oral tradition and/or successive revisions of one or more of the Gospels to account for the similarities. ***See also*** L; M; Q. J.B.T.

Syntyche (sin'ti-kee), a Christian woman in Philippi who received urgent exhortations from Paul to resolve her dispute with Euodia, a fellow Christian (Phil. 4:2–3). ***See also*** Euodia.

Syracuse (sihr'uh-kyo͞oz), a Greek colony on the southeast coast of Sicily, founded by Corinth ca. 734 B.C. It developed into the principal city of the island, with a fifth-century B.C. temple of Athena. Phoenician settlers were expelled in 234 B.C., but the city was taken by Rome in 212 B.C. On his voyage to Rome, Paul spent three days there (Acts 28:12).

Syria, an indeterminate regional term, sometimes signifying all the Levant (i.e., eastern Mediterranean shore) between Turkey and Egypt, sometimes the northern section, and sometimes only part of it. For ancient history the term "Syria" should be confined to the area surrounding Damascus, the Aram of the OT, which varied in size according to the strength of the rulers.

Geography: Damascus lies in a great oasis east of the Anti-Lebanon mountains, fed by the river Barada ("Abana," 2 Kings 5:12), which also provides a route westward into the elevated rift valley of the Beqa'a. Eastward the folds of the Anti-Lebanon spread fanwise toward the northeast, and southeastward lie the great basalt outflows, extending far into Arabia. These barriers to movement direct all routes toward the rich oasis, making Damascus a city of major commercial importance. The rainfall is everywhere scanty, however, with Damascus having only an average annual total of 8.6 inches (215 mm.). The whole area is therefore essentially desert, with settlements confined to the areas surrounding the rare springs. Further south Syria includes the better watered region of Bashan, which lies east of Galilee and which in NT times was divided into three areas: Gaulanitis on the west (OT "Geshur" and "Maacah"; modern Golan Heights), characterized by volcanic cones rising sometimes 1,500 feet (450 m.) above the plateau; the tableland of Batanea (OT "Argob," Deut. 3:4, or "Bashan"); and the wild volcanic area of Trachonitis, part of the territory of Philip (Luke 3:1). Bashan was famous in the OT for fertility and livestock (Ps. 22:12; Ezek. 39:18; Amos 4:1), and in NT times it exported grain to Rome.

Northward from Damascus the corrugated landscape created by the fanlike alignment of the mountains is still dry steppe with only minor settlements, although pasturage improves. The northern limit of this "nuclear Syria" is reached at the broad Homs-Palmyra Depression cutting inland from the coast north of Tripoli. An evident cultural divide, this marks the southern limit of the richer northern steppeland controlled by Hamath (modern Hama), and earlier, from 2400 to 2250 B.C., by Ebla (Tell Mardikh). It was the limit also of Israelite imperial ambitions (Num. 34:7–9; 2 Kings 14:25; Ezek. 47:15–17). West of the Anti-Lebanon, in the Beqa'a area, known to the Romans as Coele-Syria, the northward flowing river Orontes and the southward flowing Litani both rise, not far from Baalbek, about 3,000 feet (915 m.) above sea level. This valley provides an obvious access for invaders from both north and south, but it is not an easy route and the great trading caravans all went through Damascus. Unquestionably Damascus considered the Beqa'a as Syrian, but its control was intermittent.

Relations with Israel and Surrounding Empires: Israelite-Syrian relations were often antagonistic, but at times the two combined for mutual defense, as when King Ahab of Israel joined with Ben-hadad of Damascus and other rulers to resist the Assyrian Shalmaneser III at Qarqar (Tell Qurqur) in 853 B.C. Normally Syria dominated Israel, but David apparently conquered and garrisoned Damascus (2 Sam. 8:3–6), and Ahab gained commercial rights there (1 Kings 20:34). Jeroboam II of Israel (786–746 B.C.) is said to have conquered Damascus (2 Kings 14:28) and restored the empire of David and Solomon. The text is unfortunately obscure, but evidently Syria for a time paid tribute to Israel. Later (753–733 B.C.) King Pekah of Israel sought the help of Rezin of Syria against King Ahaz of Judah, but he achieved nothing (Isa. 7:1–17). Ahaz appealed for help to Tiglath-pileser III of Assyria, who conquered and ravaged Damascus in 732, making it part of his empire. Later, in 720, Sargon II overwhelmed Hamath. Thereafter Syria was a vassal, passing from Assyrian control to Babylonian, and becoming in 333 part of the empire of Alexander the Great. After Alexander's death in 323 Syria was governed by the Seleucids, who in ca. 300 made Antioch their imperial capital. From 64 B.C. and throughout the NT period Syria was under Roman control, forming part of a much larger province of that name.

Jesus never visited Syria, but after Pentecost Christianity spread rapidly into the region, and according to Acts Paul's conversion occurred as he traveled to Damascus to arrest the Christians there (Acts 9:1–25). The Nabatean king Aretas in distant Petra is said to have governed Damascus at the time (2 Cor. 11:32–33), but this seems doubtful. Perhaps the Nabatean ambassador had considerable authority in the city because of the importance of the Nabatean trade. ***See also*** Antioch, Aretas IV; Bashan; Damascus; Hamath; Trachonitis. D.B.

Syriac versions. ***See*** Texts, Versions, Manuscripts, Editions.

Syrophoenician (sī'roh-fuh-nee'shuhn), **a,** the woman who, having heard of Jesus' ministry, sought healing for her daughter (Mark 7:26). She is also referred to as a Greek, i.e., as a Gentile, or, as some would say, a "pagan." The term "Syrophoenician" indicates that this woman was from Phoenicia, located in the Roman province of Syria, or, more specifically, from the area of the old cities of Tyre and Sidon. In the parallel passage (Matt. 15:22), the woman is called a "Canaanite," an ancient geographical designation that would have included this area. ***See also*** Canaan, Canaanites; Gentile; Greeks; Phoenicia; Sidon; Syria; Tyre. P.L.S.

Syrtis (sihr'tis), ancient name of two bays on the northern coast of Africa south of Sicily, between Cyrene and Carthage. The Greater Syrtis, now the Gulf of Sidra off Libya, was to the east; the Lesser Syrtis, now the Gulf of Gabes, to the west. Both held navigational dangers dreaded by sailors in antiquity (Acts 27:17), the Greater Syrtis being shallow and full of shifting banks of quicksand, the Lesser because of its winds and surf.

Opposite: The reading of the Torah, perhaps by Ezra; panel from the third-century A.D. synagogue at Dura-Europos.

T

Taanach (tah'nek), a site in Palestine occupied for over three thousand years. Ancient Taanach is located at Tel Ta'annak next to the modern village that still bears the ancient name. It is situated on the southern edge of the Esdraelon Plain five miles southeast of Megiddo. The main route from the southern hill country to Megiddo and the Plain of Acco, and a route linking the Plain of Esdraelon with the Sharon Plain through the Carmel Range both passed by Taanach.

The earliest historical text mentioning Taanach is the relief at the Temple of Karnak in Upper Egypt of Pharaoh Thutmose III's first Asian campaign in 1468 B.C. The Akkadian tablets found in the excavations at Taanach, some of which are letters to the local king, are dated to about 1450 B.C. According to the biblical tradition Joshua defeated the king of Taanach (Josh. 12:21), and although the town was allotted to Manasseh (Josh. 17:11; 1 Chron. 7:29) and named a levitical city (Josh. 21:25), the Canaanites were not driven out (Judg. 1:27). Taanach is mentioned as the place where Deborah and Barak defeated the Canaanites, and the victory is celebrated in the Song of Deborah (Judg. 5:19). The town may not have been controlled by the Israelites until the period of the monarchy (late eleventh century B.C.); it is listed in one of Solomon's administrative districts (1 Kings 4:12). Taanach is mentioned in another Karnak relief describing Pharaoh Shishak's victorious campaign in Palestine in 918 B.C. It does not appear again in a historical source until Eusebius' *Onomasticon* of the fourth century A.D.

Taanach was one of the first sites to be excavated in Palestine in campaigns between 1902 and 1904 directed by Ernst Sellin. Spectacular finds included a Bronze Age patrician's house, a large incense stand with reliefs, and several Akkadian cuneiform tablets.

Between 1963 and 1968 excavations were undertaken by the Graduate School of Concordia Seminary, St. Louis, Missouri, and the American Schools of Oriental Research under the direction of Paul W. Lapp. The results represent the occupational history of the site.

Taanach was first inhabited in the Early Bronze Age about 2700–2400 B.C. (EB II–III). It was a typical city-state of the period as attested by its fortifications, their rebuilds, and the intricate stratigraphy. The site was then unoccupied for about seven hundred years except for campsite occupation near the beginning of the second millennium B.C. In the Hyksos period of the seventeenth and sixteenth centuries B.C. (Middle Bronze II C) it prospered again. There were massive fortifications of the Hyksos type and one of the earliest casemate constructions found in Palestine. The fine patrician house of the earlier excavation belonged to this period, and about sixty subfloor burials re-

Taanach cultic stand with reliefs of animals and a winged sun disk in the top row; tenth century B.C.

vealed a great variety of intramural burial practices. At the end of the sixteenth century the city suffered a substantial destruction but revived quickly for a flourishing era in the next half century, attested by a large Late Bronze I building complex with an adjacent cobbled street. This occupation came to an end near the middle of the fifteenth century, probably at the hands of Thutmose III in 1468 B.C.

A modest occupation followed, and it is to this period that the Akkadian tablets may belong, including another found in the later excavations. There is little evidence of occupation from the late fifteenth to the late thirteenth century B.C., which suggests that the place name in Amarna tablet no. 248 does not refer to Taanach.

Several substantial structures belong to the twelfth century B.C. and a Canaanite cuneiform tablet concerning a shipment of grain was uncovered in one of these. The occupation ended in a violent destruction about 1125 B.C. which may be associated with the victory celebrated in the Song of Deborah (Judg. 5). The light eleventh-century settlement was followed by an important tenth-century occupation revealing an area that contained a mass of cultic material including iron blades, pig astragali (bones), loom weights, three small stelae, about eighty reconstructable vessels, a unique cultic stand, and a complete figurine mold. This ended in a major destruction with ceramic evidence suggesting it was a result of Shishak's campaign of 918 B.C.

Later occupation was limited to a few Iron Age II remains, a number of stone-lined pits and a building of the Persian period (ca. 538–333 B.C.), and scattered Hellenistic shards. An impressive fortress was constructed on the highest part of the mound in the Abbasid period (ca. 750–969 A.D.). ***See also*** Deborah; Esdraelon; Megiddo.

Bibliography

Lapp, P. W. "Taanach by the Waters of Megiddo." *Biblical Archaeologist* 30 (1967): 2–27. Preliminary reports in *Bulletin of the American Schools of Oriental Research* 173: 4–44; 185: 2–39; 195: 2–49.

N.L.L.

Tabeel (tay'bee-el; Heb., "El [God] is good"). **1** The father of an unnamed person whom Pekah, the king of Israel (Northern Kingdom), and Rezin, the king of Syria, conspired to make king over Judah (Southern Kingdom) should they succeed in overthrowing Ahaz (Isa. 7:6). In some versions the name is Tabeal. **2** A Persian official residing in Samaria; he was one of those who wrote to the Persian king Artaxerxes protesting the rebuilding of the Temple in Jerusalem by the returned exiles (Ezra 4:7).

tabernacle, the portable sanctuary of the Israelites during the wilderness period, according to the Priestly sources of the Pentateuch and related texts. The directions for building it are given in Exodus 25–30 and the account of its actual construction follows in Exodus 35–40. It consisted of a rectangular enclosure, hung with curtains supported on poles, some 145 feet (44 m.) long, 72 feet (22 m.) wide, and 7 feet (2.2 m.) high (Exod. 27:18). Within this, there was another building, also curtained, divided in two by a veil, behind which was the Holy of Holies containing the Ark; before the veil stood the altar of incense, the seven-branched lampstand, and the table for the bread of the Presence (Exod. 25:30). In the courtyard outside this building stood the altar of burnt offering and the laver (Exod. 30:18). When the Israelites moved about during their wilderness wanderings, the whole tabernacle was dismantled by the Levites and re-erected by them wherever the tribes pitched camp (Num. 1:51). While it was stationary, the twelve tribes camped around it in a defined order (Num. 2:1–31), with the Levites in its immediate vicinity (Num. 1:52–53). The furnishings of the tabernacle were made of the finest and costliest materials (Exod. 25:3–7).

This picture raises doubts as to what extent the tabernacle can be considered an actual fact during the wilderness period. The constant movement of so large a structure is difficult to envisage in desert conditions, nor is it likely that wilderness Israel had the craftsmen, materials, or wealth to erect it. Above all, the Priestly account records a structure that, in its shape and the cultic objects it contains, resembles Solomon's Temple. What it presents is a description of the Temple under the guise of a portable sanctuary. It is thus a retrojection of

An ark with draped curtain *(parokhet)* and flanked by seven-branched lampstands *(menoroth)*, *lulavim*, shofars, and incense shovels; mosaic from the fourth-century synagogue at Hammath-Tiberias.

the Jerusalem Temple to the wilderness epoch, in accordance with the Priestly view that all Israel's religious institutions originated at that time, but with the knowledge that a permanent building did not exist before the settlement in Canaan.

Tent of Meeting: But the Priestly account is not therefore a mere fiction. As well as using the word "tabernacle" (Heb. *mishkan)* for its structure, it also employs, some 130 times, the expression "tent of meeting" (Heb. *ohel mo'ed).* This refers to a much simpler type of shrine that is much more likely to have existed during the wilderness wanderings. It is described in an early passage, Exod. 33:7–11. From this we see that the tent of meeting was a simple tent that one man could pitch, it was outside the camp, unlike the tabernacle, which was in the middle, and it was looked after by a single officiant. It was not a place of sacrifice nor is there any real evidence that it sheltered the Ark. Rather it was a shrine for the receiving of oracles, and the divine presence did not reside permanently there but was manifested, in the form of a pillar of cloud, whenever Moses entered the tent to inquire of God. As such, it had a different function from a temple or tabernacle and there is nothing improbable in its existing later alongside a temple at Shiloh (1 Sam. 2:22) or alongside a high place as at Gibeon (2 Chron. 1:3) or, because it was easily portable, its being brought into Solomon's Temple (1 Kings 8:4). What the Priestly authors do is to build upon their knowledge of this ancient institution and transfer its most significant features to their picture of the tabernacle. So the divine cloud descends on the tabernacle (Exod. 40:34–35) and the "meeting" with God takes place over the Ark in the tabernacle (Exod. 25:22). The two are also brought together by the odd feature of a tent on top of the tabernacle (Exod. 36:14); the materials from which it was made, tanned ramskins and goatskins (Exod. 36:19), retain a genuine desert tradition, being those of a bedouin tent, and particularly the *qubba* (portable tent-shrine).

For the NT writers, the significance of the tabernacle is found in Exod. 25:40, which they interpret as meaning that the earthly tabernacle had a heavenly counterpart, which is the true tabernacle (Heb. 8:2, 5; 9:22). In Acts 7:44–50, the wilderness tabernacle, made according to the pattern of the one in heaven, is contrasted with Solomon's Temple made with hands, while in Rev. 13:6; 15:5; and 21:3 the only tabernacle envisaged is that in heaven. ***See also*** Ark; High Place; Levites; Temple, The.

Bibliography

Clements, R. E. *God and Temple*. Philadelphia: Fortress, 1965. Chaps. 3, 7.

Wright, G. E., and D. N. Freedman, eds. *The Biblical Archaeologist Reader I*. Garden City, NY: Doubleday (Anchor Books), 1961. Pp. 201–228.

J.R.P.

The "tent of meeting" may have been a simple portable shrine similar to the one depicted in this drawing from the Temple of Bel at Palmyra and known from Egypt, Mesopotamia, and Canaan.

Tabernacles, Festival of (or Booths, Ingathering, Heb. *Sukkoth*), along with Passover and the Festival of Weeks, one of three major pilgrimage festivals of Judaism. Celebrated for eight days (from the 15th of Tishri [late September or early October]), it was Israel's joyous, thanksgiving, autumnal harvest festival for the ingathering from the threshing floor and the winepress (Exod. 23:16; 34:22; Deut. 16:13–15). Its main distinctive ritual is the requirement to "dwell in booths" in commemoration of God's protection of Israel during the wilderness wanderings (Lev. 23:39–43; Neh. 8:13–18). The preeminent annual festival, called "the feast of God" (Lev. 23:39; Judg. 21:19) or "*the* feast" (1 Kings 8:2, 65; 12:32; Isa. 30:29; Ezek. 45:23, 25; Neh. 8:14; 2 Chron. 5:3, 7–8; John 7:10; cf. John 7:2), it was the occasion of the dedication of Solomon's Temple (1 Kings 8), the public reading of the Torah (every seven years, Deut. 31: 10–11), and the future ingathering of all nations to Jerusalem to worship God (Zech. 14:16). ***See also*** Feasts, Festivals, and Fasts; Time. J.U.

Tabitha (tab'i-thuh), another name for Dorcas, a highly regarded Christian in Joppa (Acts 9: 36–42). ***See also*** Dorcas.

tablets of the Law, the two stone tablets of the Ten Commandments inscribed by God on Mt. Sinai (Exod. 24:12; 31:18; 32:15–16; Deut. 9:10–11; 10:1–6; Exod. 34:28 is ambiguous). The first set was broken by Moses in his anger at the sight of the Golden Calf (Exod. 32:19). The second set was placed in the Ark of the Covenant.

Tabor (tay'buhr). **1** An isolated mountain rising to a height of 1,843 feet in the northeast portion of the Plain of Esdraelon. Its relative height and steep ascent from the plain below give one standing on it a commanding view of the valley and of the heights of Mt. Carmel to the west and Mt. Hermon to the north. The slopes drain into the Jordan River on the east. Until recently the mountain was forested.

On the border of the tribal lands of Issachar (Josh. 19:22), Zebulun (Chisloth-tabor in Josh. 19:12, cf. 1 Chron. 6:77), and Naphtali (Josh. 19:34), it was the central place for Barak to gather his forces (Judg. 4:6, 12) and from there he descended for his battle with the Canaanites (Judg. 4:14). The north-south road from Hazor and Damascus to the pass of Megiddo and the Coastal plain passed around its foot, and the east-west route from the Megiddo Plain went between Mt. Tabor and the Hill of Moreh to the Sea of Galilee. Here Gideon's brothers were killed by the Midianite kings, Zebah and Zalmunna (Judg. 8:18).

Although not actually very high, Tabor's isolation in the plain led the Psalmist (Ps. 89:12) and the prophets (Jer. 46:18) to compare it to Mt. Carmel and Mt. Hermon. It may have been a sacred mountain from early times (cf. Deut. 33: 18–19). It is not mentioned in the NT, but since the fourth century A.D. it has been celebrated as the site of the transfiguration. The date of the first church on the mountain is uncertain but pilgrim sources mention one in the sixth century. A crusader monastery fell to Saladin in 1187 and Melek el-Adel of Damascus fortified the mountain in the thirteenth century. On the summit today the Greek Orthodox have a monastery and the Franciscans have constructed a basilica over the ancient remains.

2 Tabor, Oaks of. They were located near Bethel (1 Sam. 10:3), but the exact location is unknown. ***See also*** Esdraelon; Transfiguration, The. N.L.L.

tabret (tab'rit), a term in the KJV that the RSV renders "tambourine" (Gen. 31:27; 1 Sam. 10:5), "timbrel" (1 Sam. 18:6; Isa. 5:12; 24:8; 30:32; Jer. 31:4), or "one before whom men spit" (Job 17:6). ***See also*** Music; Timbrel.

tache (tach), a term in the KJV that RSV renders "clasp" or "hook," a term that appears primarily in texts regarding the tabernacle (Exod. 26:6; 36: 13; and others).

Tadmor (tad'mohr), a city (modern Tadmur) in Syria located in a fertile oasis in the Syrian desert a hundred and forty miles northeast of Damascus. Because of its location midway between Mesopotamia and the western arm of the Fertile Crescent it was an important caravan city from the second millennium B.C. to the early Islamic period (seventh–eighth centuries A.D.). During the height of its prosperity in the Roman period it was called Palmyra (from the Lat. for "the city of palms"). The well-preserved ruins from this era give a remarkably detailed picture of a wealthy Syrian metropolis. Its monumental architecture includes temples Semitic in plan but with classical decorative motifs dedicated to such gods as Bel, Nebo, and Baal Shamin, a theater, an agora, baths, and other typical elements

Aerial view of the well-preserved ruins at Palmyra (Tadmor).

of a Roman city, along with a large number of ornate tombs with elaborate sarcophagi and statuary. The large number of inscriptions from Palmyra in Greek and Palmyrene, the local Aramaic dialect, reveal its syncretistic religious traditions.

Tadmor is mentioned only once in the Bible: in 2 Chron. 8:4 Solomon is said to have built "Tadmor in the wilderness." The related but not identical passage in 1 Kings 9:18 reports that Solomon built "Tamar in the wilderness, in the land of Judah." Tamar (Heb., "palm") is known from Ezek. 47:19 and 48:28 as a town south of the Dead Sea. Masoretic tradition interprets the received text's reading "Tamar" as "Tadmor." It is not impossible that Solomon engaged in some building activity in Syria, especially in light of David's defeat of the king of Zobah (2 Sam. 8:3–6), but it is more likely that the text of Chronicles (and the Masoretic reinterpretation of Kings) is due to the enhancement (by the Chronicler or one of his sources) of Solomon's prestige by attributing to him construction or at least reconstruction of one of the more famous Syrian centers. ***See also*** Solomon. M.D.C.

Tahath (tay'hath; Heb., "beneath" or "low"). **1** One of the encampments of the Israelites during the journey in the wilderness (Num. 33:26–27); the site is unknown. **2** The son of Assir; he was a Levite of the clan of Kohath (1 Chron. 6:24, 37). **3** A descendant of Ephraim and grandfather of 4 below (1 Chron. 7:20). Some scholars understand Tahan (Num. 26:35) to be the same person (or the same as 4), although Tahan could be another son (descendant) of Ephraim (see 1 Chron. 7:25). **4** A descendant of Ephraim (1 Chron. 7:20).

Tahpanhes (tah'pan-heez; KJV: "Tahapanes," Jer. 2:16), Tehaphnehes (Ezek. 30:18), the equivalent of Greek Daphnai, modern Tell Defenneh, situated on the Pelusiac branch of the Nile in the northeast delta. According to

Herodotus (*History* 2:30), the twenty-sixth-dynasty king Psammetichus I (664–610 B.C.) established a garrison of Greek mercenaries at Daphnai to guard against the Assyrians; later on the Persian king Darius I (522–486 B.C.) also kept guards there. In about 586 B.C., the prophet Jeremiah and other Jews sought refuge at Tahpanhes from the Babylonian king Nebuchadnezzar (Jer. 43:7; 44:1; 46:14). The British Egyptologist W. M. Flinders Petrie excavated Tell Defenneh in 1887 and discovered what are probably the remains of the fortress of Psammetichus. ***See also*** Jeremiah, The Book of. J.M.W.

Tahpenes (tah'pee-neez), the wife of an unnamed twenty-first dynasty pharaoh; her sister was given in marriage to Hadad of Edom at the time of David (1 Kings 11:19–20). The name Tahpenes is not attested in any Egyptian source. It is probably a Hebrew transcription either of an Egyptian title meaning "the king's wife" or an Egyptian proper name. ***See also*** Hadad.

Tahtim-hodshi (tah'tim-hawd'shee), a place name found in the KJV for an area visited by David's census takers (2 Sam. 24:6; RSV: "Kadesh . . . of the Hittites"). If the RSV is correct, it referred to Kadesh in modern Syria, located at Tell Nebi Mend on the Oronte River south of Homs. It represented the northern limit of David's kingdom.

tale, a story that often contains imagined or exaggerated elements. To call something a tale implies it is an account unworthy of belief (Luke 24:11). In some older translations the word meant "tally," "total," or "number." More modern translations use other words: "number" (Exod.5:18), "full number" (1 Sam. 18:27), or "count" (1 Chron. 9:28).

talebearing, gossiping; it is closely connected to slander in the Bible, which condemns both. Lev. 19:15–16 lumps slander together with legal injustice and even false testimony in a capital case, but Proverbs uses the same word to condemn the talebearer and to warn the wise not to associate with gossips (11:13; 20:19). The NT also lists both as sins (Rom. 1:29–30).

talent. ***See*** Money; Weights and Measures.

talitha cumi (tah-leeth'ah ko͞o'mee), an Aramaic sentence that means "young girl, arise," spoken by Jesus when he raised the daughter of Jairus from the dead. Mark translates it into Greek as "Little girl, I say to you, arise" (5:41). Many manuscripts have an eastern Aramaic form of the verb, "cum," instead of the Palestinian "cumi."

Talmai (tahl'mī). **1** One of the sons of Anak (descended from the Nephilim, Gen. 6:4) who lived at Hebron when spies sent by Moses into that region of the Negeb returned with reports of giants in the land. The sons of Anak were finally driven away by the military commander Caleb (Josh. 15:14) or by Judahites (Judg. 1:10). **2** The king of Geshur whose daughter, Maacah, was one of David's wives and the mother of Absalom (2 Sam. 3:3; 1 Chron. 3:2). It was to Talmai that Absalom fled after killing his half-brother Amnon (2 Sam. 13:37). ***See also*** Caleb; Geshur; Maacah; Nephilim. F.R.M.

Talmon (tal'muhn). **1** A Levite gatekeeper (1 Chron. 9:17). Scholars are divided over whether this passage (1 Chron. 9:17–34) should be seen as a record of postexilic Jerusalem (after 586 B.C.; cf. Ezra 2:42; Neh. 11:19) or of a much earlier time used as an introduction to the narratives of Saul and David that follow. In either case, Talmon was probably seen as the ancestral head of a clan of gatekeepers (see Neh. 7:45; 2 below). If the passage is postexilic, he is probably the same as 3 below. **2** A levitical family group of gatekeepers ("sons of Talmon") who returned from the Babylonian captivity with Zerubbabel (Ezra 2:42; Neh. 7:45). **3** A Levite gatekeeper in postexilic Jerusalem (Neh. 11:19; 12:25). D.R.B.

Talmud (tahl'mo͝od; Heb., "teaching, study, learning, a lesson"), two long collections of Jewish religious literature, one called the Palestinian Talmud, and the other called the Babylonian Talmud. The Talmuds are commentaries on the Mishnah, the Hebrew code of laws that emerged about A.D. 200 under Rabbi Judah the Prince. The part of the Talmud that is commentary is called the *Gemara* (from the Aramaic word "to learn") and consists of atomistic analysis of the words and sentences of the Mishnah, comparison of one Mishnah with another, a selection of traditions related to the Mishnah, interpretations of Scripture, stories about rabbis and others, and long digressions on various topics. The bulk of the *Gemara* is written in Aramaic, the vernacular of the Jewish community of the time, but some traditions such as the *Baraitot* ("outside" traditions), which claim to be tannaitic (before A.D. 200), are in Hebrew. The Palestinian Talmud covers the first four orders of the Mishnah which are concerned with agriculture, feasts, women, and damages. It was completed in the mid-fifth century A.D: The Babylonian Talmud covers the Mishnaic orders of feasts, women, damages, and sacrifices and was completed in the mid-sixth century A.D., with many additions and modifications being made in the succeeding few centuries. The Babylonian Talmud was more fully edited than the Palestinian and became authoritative for most of Judaism because of the dominance of the Babylonian community well into the Islamic period. ***See also*** Mishnah. A.J.S.

Tamar (tay'mer; Heb., "date palm"), a woman's name and a place name. **1** The Canaanite daughter-in-law of Judah, whom Judah promised successively to each of his three sons as each older one died without issue (Gen. 38:1–30). When Judah withheld Shelah, his youngest, fearing to lose him also, Tamar disguised herself as a prostitute and offered herself to her father-in-law. When she was exposed by her pregnancy, she identified her partner, who confessed that she had acted "more righteously" than he (Gen. 38:26). Tamar bore twins to Judah, Perez and Zerah. Through Perez she is reckoned to the ancestry of David (Ruth 4:12, 18–22; 1 Chron. 2:4) and Jesus (Matt. 1:3). **2** The daughter of David who was raped by her half-brother Amnon (2 Sam. 13:1–29). Her brother Absalom, to whom she fled, avenged her by having Amnon murdered. **3** Absalom's only daughter, "a beautiful woman" (2 Sam. 14:27), and his sister's namesake. **4** A city "in the wilderness," according to the RSV and the earliest form of the Hebrew text; the KJV and the traditional Hebrew vocalization read "Tadmor." **5** A city marking the southeast border point in Ezekiel's description of the restored territory of Israel (Ezek. 47: 18–19; 48:28). The site remains unidentified (cf. Hazazon-tamar, Gen. 14:7). ***See also*** Absalom.
P.A.B.

tamarisk (genus *Tamarix*), a tree or shrub referred to in Hebrew as *eshel*. Tolerating sandy and even saline soils, this drought-resistant tree grows in deserts as well as in watered places, near streams and marshes. The tamarisk is a graceful evergreen with tiny, jointed, grey-green, needlelike leaves which give it a feathery appearance. It provides year-round food for goats. Its wood is used for construction and is a good source of charcoal. Its common occurrence in desolate places makes tamarisk an ideal shade tree and a revered spot for burials (1 Sam. 31:13). ***See also*** Trees; Woods.

Tammuz (tahm'uhz), the Hebrew form of *Dumuzi* (Sumerian, "proper son"), a god widely honored from the third millennium B.C. in Mesopotamia. The vast and complex Mesopotamian literature about this god shows three essential aspects of him: as lover and consort of Inanna; as one held in the underworld and mourned because of his absence; as the embodiment of spring vegetation and then of vegetation in general. Many laments are preserved that bewail the "far one" who has disappeared, detained in the underworld. The laments reflect the aspect of Tammuz as god of vegetation; his disappearance is connected to the drying up of the steppe in summer. His cult may have been brought to Israel by the Assyrians in the ninth and eighth centuries B.C. Aspects of Tammuz became synthesized with West Semitic gods of similar characteristics. Baal Haddu, for example, went down into the underworld, died, rose, and was mourned during his absence. Some of Dumuzi's traits also appear in Adonis, a god first attested in Greece in the fifth century B.C. In Ezekiel's vision of four sins being committed in the Jerusalem Temple, the third is a group of women weeping for Tammuz in the north gate (8:14). The women in Ezekiel are mourning this dying and rising god. The action is an abomination to Ezekiel who believes that God does not die and cannot be mourned. ***See also*** Ezekiel, The Book of; Sources of the Pentateuch. R.J.C.

Tanis (tan'is). ***See*** Raamses, Rameses.

tanning, the process of rendering leather permanently soft and pliable. Literally the Greek and Hebrew words for tanning translate as "reddened" or "to dye red." When skins or hides are transformed into leather, the skin darkens or "reddens" as a result of the process employed. The process of tanning is undoubtedly a very ancient form of technology whose practice is documented in ancient Egyptian texts and paintings. Once the hides were cleaned of all hair and foreign matter, they were ready for treatment in a special solution. The mixture consisted of plant juices, lime, and perhaps bark or leaves.

Due to the nature of the work, the population did not hold the tanner in high regard. The odors accompanying the process as well as the tanning of unclean animals were repugnant to townspeople. Thus we read that tanners were consigned to live outside of the town: Simon the tanner, for example, lived by the seaside, at Joppa (Acts 10:16). Nonetheless, Peter and a devout soldier displayed a more tolerant attitude by lodging with Simon (Acts 9:43; 10:7). Because of the many uses to which it could be put, leather was a valuable commodity. "Tanned rams' skins" were offerings given by the people of Israel at Mount Sinai (Exod. 25:5; 35:7, 23). These skins were fashioned into the coverings for the tent of meeting which housed the tabernacle (Exod. 36:14; 36:19; 39:34). Skins were also used for many products besides clothing: leather buckets, waterskins, wineskins, and butter churns (Gen. 21:14; Judg. 4:19; Matt. 9:17). S.L.R.

Taphath (tay'fath), Solomon's daughter who was married to Ben-abinadab, Solomon's administrator of Naphath-Dor (1 Kings 4:11).

Tappuah (tap'pōō-uh). **1** A town of the Shephelah (Josh. 15:34), perhaps modern Beit Nettif, west of Bethlehem. **2** A northern town on the border of Ephraim and Manasseh (Josh. 16:8), probably Tell Sheik Abu Zarad, south of Shechem. Ephraim possessed the town but the territory of Tappuah was occupied by Manasseh (17: 8). Menahem sacked Tappuah (2 Kings 15:16). A king of Tappuah was beaten by Joshua (Josh.12: 17); probably one of the sites above is indicated.

tares. ***See*** Weeds.

target, the mark toward which something is delivered. Job depicts himself as the target of God's archers (16:12). The word is used in the KJV for two types of weaponry: 1 Kings 10:16 (RSV: "shields") and 1 Sam. 17:6 (RSV: "javelin").

Targums, translations of the books of the Hebrew Bible into Aramaic, made when Aramaic was the common spoken language in Palestine. They were produced between about 250 B.C. and A.D. 300 and were usually read in the synagogues. ***See also*** Synagogue; Texts, Versions, Manuscripts, Editions.

Tarshish (tahr'shish). **1** A Benjaminite son of Bilhan (1 Chron. 7:10). **2** One of seven princes of the Medes and the Persians (Esther 1:14). **3** An unknown location famous for associations with sea traffic (1 Kings 10:22; 2 Chron. 9:21; Isa. 23: 1; 23:14; 60:9; Ezek. 27:25; Jon. 1:3). The Jonah association suggests a location in the Mediterranean, and sites suggested have included Tarsus, and Tartessus in Spain. Isa. 23:1 rather suggests Cyprus or the Aegean, but 1 Kings 10: 22 cites a Solomonic expedition that in other associations has suggested a route eastward to Arabia, India, or the coast of Africa. 1 Kings 22: 48 cites ships of Jehoshaphat bound out from Ezion-geber, reinforcing the eastern route and eliminating a Mediterranean option. Whether because of its rich gold resources or some other reason, it tended to be idealized (Isa. 2:16). ***See also*** Ophir. R.S.B.

Tarsus (tahr'suhs), a large, prosperous commercial city located on the Cydnus River, about ten miles from the Mediterranean Sea at the foothills of the Taurus Mountains on the southeastern coast of Asia Minor. Situated 79 feet above sea level in the fertile eastern plain of the region of Cilicia, Tarsus became the capital of the region under the Romans.

According to the Greek geographer Strabo (ca. 63 B.C.–A.D. 23), the Cydnus River had its source from the melting snows of the mountains above the city. The river flowed through the ancient capital into a lake some five miles to the south which served as a naval station and harbor for Tarsus. It was because of the river that inland Tarsus had the opportunity to develop into a thriving maritime center.

This feature, combined with the fact that the main trade routes passed north through Tarsus to central Asia Minor via the Cilician Gates in the Taurus Mountain pass, or east via the Syrian Gates of the Amanus Mountains to Syria, gave Tarsus a cosmopolitan nature. Paul's boast, recorded in Acts, that Tarsus was "no mean city" (Acts 21:39) was certainly warranted. It was the meeting place of West and East, of the Greek culture with its oriental counterpart.

The date of the foundation of the city is uncertain, but archaeological evidence shows habitation dated back to the Neolithic Period (ca. 5000 B.C.), and several Bronze Age (ca. 3000–1200 B.C.) cities were built successively on the site. In the middle of the tenth century B.C., the Assyrian king Shalmaneser III conquered Tarsus. When the city rebelled during the reign of Sennacherib a century later, it was destroyed. Rebuilt, Tarsus was under Persian control until it was taken in 333 B.C. by Alexander the Great, who resided there for a short period. The city passed into the hands of the Seleucid dynasty (312–65 B.C.), whose efforts to hellenize the inhabitants provoked an insurrection against Antiochus IV Epiphanes (2 Macc. 4:30). With the advent of the Romans, the region of Cilicia was organized into a Roman province with Tarsus as its capital.

Cicero, the Roman orator and statesman, was governor of Tarsus in 50 B.C. Mark Antony gave Tarsus the status of a free city, and it was here that he met Cleopatra in 41 B.C. It was under the rule of Augustus (27 B.C.–A.D. 14) that the city came to its golden age and was renowned as a center of intellectual life, surpassing even Alexandria and Athens. Tarsus had long been a center of Stoic philosophy, and several of its citizens were famous Stoic philosophers: Zeno, Antipater, Athenodorus, and Nestor. One of the basic tenets of Stoicism states that virtue is the only good as well as the means of fortification against all the pressures of life. This concept seems to be reflected in some of Paul's writings (e.g. Phil. 4:11–12).

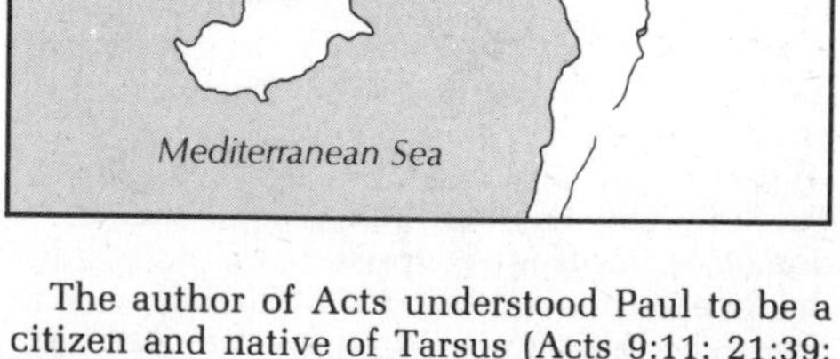

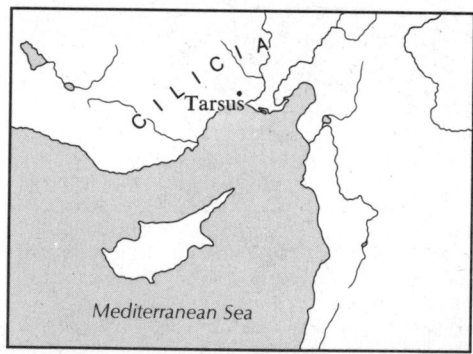

The author of Acts understood Paul to be a citizen and native of Tarsus (Acts 9:11; 21:39; 22:3) and thus a Jew of the Dispersion (i.e., who lived outside Palestine). As a Jew of Tarsus, Paul would have been reared in a non-Jewish environment and would have spoken the common language of the Roman Empire, Greek. His knowledge of the Jewish Scriptures would have been from the Septuagint, the Greek translation from the original Hebrew. His Jewish name appears as "Saul" (only in Acts), along with the Roman "Paul." ***See also*** Cilicia; Paul; Stoics. M.K.M.

Tartan (tahr'tuhn), an official title of rank within the Assyrian military, the commander-in-chief or field marshal second only to the king. An officer of this rank led Sargon's assault against Ashdod (ca. 712 B.C.; Isa. 20:1). Another officer of this rank was sent by Sennacherib along with two other officials, the Rab-shakeh and the Rabsaris, to demand Hezekiah's surrender of Jerusalem (ca. 701 B.C.; 2 Kings 18:17). In some versions the title is understood as a proper name; in others it is translated as "commander" or something similar. ***See also*** Rabsaris; Rab-shakeh.

Taurus Mountains. ***See*** Tarsus.

Taverns, the Three, a way station on the Appian Way, about thirty miles south of Rome, ten miles north of the Forum of Appius, where Paul was met by members of the Christian community of Rome, as he journeyed there from Puteoli (Acts 28:15). ***See also*** Appius, Forum of.

tax. ***See*** Money; Publicans; Treasures; Tribute, Tax, Toll; Worship.

Teacher of Righteousness, the leader of the Essenes when they withdrew from Jerusalem to Qumran about 150 B.C.; his real identity is unknown. He was a priest who was prominent in the Temple; one hypothesis suggests that he had been high priest during the period from the death of Alcimus in 159 B.C. to the accession of Jonathan Maccabee in 152 B.C. He may have been associated with the Hasideans (the "pious") who supported the Maccabees in their wars against the Hellenizers who wanted to introduce Greek customs among the Jews. He and his followers most probably rejected Jonathan as high priest because he was not from a high-priestly family.

The title "Teacher of Righteousness" may mean both the righteous teacher and the one who teaches righteousness. The title is in contrast to the Teacher's opponents: the preacher of lies who split from the community and the wicked priest in Jerusalem who persecuted the Teacher. The Teacher of Righteousness functioned as the true interpreter of Scripture for the community (1QpHab 7). The Thanksgiving Hymns (1QH) also found among the Dead Sea Scrolls stress God's mercy toward the community, the true knowledge of God, salvation, and the trials undergone by the teacher. ***See also*** Essenes; Qumran, Khirbet. A.J.S.

teaching, the process of instruction and the content of instruction. Little is known of the modes of teaching used in Israel during OT and NT times. Cultural parallels suggest that some schools were established to teach reading and writing to the small percentage of the population who were literate. Occupational, cultural and moral instruction took place within the family, clan, and village. Education for higher office probably took place within the king's court by scribes, and instruction in religious law was probably carried on by priests in the Temple. The books of Proverbs and Ecclesiasticus reflect some of the contents of higher education. The book of Deuteronomy stresses that the law of Israel must be taught and learned and this conviction continued into the rabbinic period.

In the NT Jesus is presented as the oral teacher par excellence (John 3:2; 13:13). In the Gospel of Matthew Jesus is presented as a teacher and large blocks of his teachings are spaced throughout the Gospel (chaps. 5–7, 10, 13, 18, 24–25). Little is said about how Christianity was taught in the early church. In Acts Paul is pictured as going to the synagogues to preach about Jesus and then withdrawing into the homes of believers to continue his ministry (Acts 18:4–7; 19:8–9). The Pauline and post-Pauline Letters speak of an office of teacher (1 Cor. 12:28–29; Eph. 4:11) but do not say how it was carried out. Emphasis is also put on the content of the message, which according to Paul must be the gospel (Gal. 1:6–9). Faithful teaching of the message is emphasized more and more in the later books of the NT, such as in the pastoral Letters (1 Tim. 4:6, 11, 16; 6:2, 3). ***See also*** Education; School; Scribe. A.J.S.

teeth, a word used of both humans and animals, in both literal and figurative ways in the Bible. It is used as a symbol to denote predators or agents of devastation. God breaks the teeth of young lions (Job 4:10) but can also send the teeth of beasts (Deut. 32:24) as a punishment for turning to others who are no gods (v. 21). In the prophet Joel the devastation wrought by the teeth of locusts is taken as a judgment sent by God, calling the people to repentance (Joel 1:2–2:27; cf. Rev. 9:8). In addition to actual animals or insects, "teeth" is used of symbolic (Dan. 7:5, 7, 19) or mythic (Job 41:14) beasts and of human beings. The psalmist prays God will break the teeth of the predatory and impious (Ps. 58:3–6), and God is praised for not having delivered up the psalmist as a prey into the teeth of rampageous foes (Ps. 124:1–7; see also Ps. 3:7; Prov. 30:11–14).

"To gnash the teeth at or against" expresses deep hostility and intention of harm (Job 16:9; Pss. 35:16; 37:12; 112:10; Lam. 2:16; Acts 7:52). "To have white teeth" (Gen. 49:12) or "teeth like ewes" (Song of Sol. 4:2; 6:6) is a sign, respectively, of blessing and beauty. "An eye for an eye, a tooth for a tooth" expresses the requirement of a physical punishment equivalent to—but not exceeding—the injury received (Exod. 21:24; Lev. 24:20; Deut. 19:21). "Weeping and gnashing of teeth" is a characteristic response among those excluded from the Kingdom of God (Matt. 8:12; 13:42; Luke 13:28). "Cleanness of teeth" is synonymous with famine (Amos 4:6). "With" (KJV) or "by" (RSV) "the skin of my teeth" (Job 19:20) suggests, respectively, that only the gums are left in the mouth or that the escape was as narrow as the film on teeth. One can "have one's teeth set on edge" by vinegar (Prov. 10:26) or sour grapes (Jer. 31:30; Ezek. 18:2). J.G.G.

Tekoa (te-koh'ah), a name used in reference to a wilderness (2 Chron. 20:20) and to a town. Two persons known to David came from the settlement (2 Sam. 14:1–17; 23:26), and according to the author of Chronicles, Rehoboam fortified the site (2 Chron. 11:6). The settlement is located on a ridge about ten kilometers south of Bethlehem. Because of its vantage point warnings could be given if an enemy threatened Jerusalem from the south (Jer. 6:1). Most likely this site is the home of the prophet Amos (Amos 1:1) despite the claim of some scholars that Amos's home must be a Tekoa in Galilee, a site known in postbiblical times. J.A.D.

tell, the Arabic word for a natural hill or an artificial hill of accumulated debris from human occupation, the latter being its normal meaning in archaeological usage. Such *tell* formation was due to fundamental factors involving human settlement patterns as well as to weather and the peculiar nature of construction materials common in the Near East.

Settlement by communities was bound by the necessities of a stable fresh water supply, an economic base of support, and the defense potential of a site. A good combination of all three drew people to a location century after century, and each culture left its physical remains, whether by design or accident.

Weather in the Near East tends to be dry and hot, allowing unusually good preservation even of organic remains, in contrast to a temperate or jungle climate. Thus physical material left by a culture tends to be well preserved.

Construction material and building habits involved the extensive use of mudbrick, because of its ease of production everywhere, and the economic fact that it was cheaper and safer to tear down and rebuild a mudbrick wall than to try to repair its structural damage or fault. Remains of such mudbrick covered all material lost or discarded when it was mashed flat, thus preserving over the centuries layer after layer of human occupation debris. The catch-basin effect of major city walls surrounding a town simply increased the cumulative pace.

Tells, then, are the physical record of human occupancy starting with the first inhabitants of the site over bedrock or virgin soil and proceeding to the most recent inhabitants' deposits at the uppermost layer. Reading that record is the archaeological task called stratigraphy. The value of a tell is unpredictable. Huge formations like that at Beth-shan (over 100 feet high before excavation) are not necessarily most helpful. Tell el-Harmal in Iraq, a major administrative center, rose only four feet over the plain but contained much useful information. R.S.B.

Tell Beit Mirsim (tel bīt meer'sim; also Kiriath-sepher). *See* Debir.

Tell el-Amarna. *See* Amarna, Tell el-.

temperance. *See* Self-control.

Tell el-Milh, located in the Negeb near Arad, is typical of the artificial hills of accumulated debris from human occupation common in Palestine.

The Temple

THE RELIGIOUS STRUCTURE in Jerusalem that was the center of Israelite national life in the biblical period, beginning with the monarchy (tenth century B.C.) and continuing until its final destruction by the Roman legions in A.D. 70. Even in the sixth century B.C., when the Temple lay in ruins for about seventy years as the result of the Babylonian conquest of the kingdom of Judah (586 B.C.), sacrifice took place in the Temple courtyard. The Temple Mount (Mt. Zion in Jerusalem) continued to symbolize, in prophecy and tradition, God's relationship with his people. Despite the fact that the Temple's existence for over a millennium was nearly continuous, it did undergo two major reconstructions, one following the Exile, beginning in 520 B.C., and the other as part of the enormous building projects carried out by King Herod, who reigned in Palestine from 37 to 4 B.C.

Because of these two rebuilding projects, it is customary to consider the Jerusalem Temple as having had three distinct stages of existence. The First Temple, also known as Solomon's Temple, is the product of Israel's United Monarchy in the tenth century B.C. The Second Temple was rebuilt on the site of its destroyed predecessor at the end of the sixth century; it is sometimes known as Zerubbabel's Temple because Zerubbabel was the chief political officer in the Persian subprovince of Yehud (Judah) at the time of the restoration of the Temple. The third stage of the Jerusalem Temple is known as Herod's Temple and consisted of Herod's enlargement and embellishment of the Second Temple.

Although three major architectural periods for the Temple can be identified, many other changes in its ground plan, appurtenances, and decoration took place during the centuries when it stood in the administrative center of the nation in Jerusalem. Some of those changes are recorded in the biblical account of the monarchy; other alterations perhaps were made but were not included in the biblical record. Because of the continued refurbishing to which the Temple was subjected, the ancient sources that provide the bulk of the information about the Temple's appearance and function are sometimes confusing and contradictory. The building was one in its conceptualization but was many in its execution. Hence the sources from different periods would reflect the different appearances of what was, in concept, the same structure. These sources include twenty-three of the books of the OT and eleven NT books. In addition, many extrabiblical literary works, such as the Apocrypha and Pseudepigrapha, the Dead Sea Scrolls (especially the Temple Scroll), the works of Philo and Josephus, and the Mishnah, contribute to our knowledge of the Temple, particularly in its final form before the fall of Jerusalem in A.D. 70.

For many years, biblical scholars have tended to project back upon the ancient Temple their experience with contemporary religious edifices. Yet sacrificial practices were carried out in Jerusalem, and that dimension of the Temple alone sets it apart from postbiblical religious buildings. Furthermore, temples in the ancient world functioned in many ways fundamentally different from the manner in which synagogues and churches operate in Western civilization. The Temple was not simply a religious or cultic building. Its very name—its most common designation in the Bible is "House of Yahweh"—indicates that it was conceived of as a residence for God and not as a place of public worship and prayer. In fact, the general populace had access only to the Temple courts and not to the inside of the structure itself. Even the clergy did not circulate freely within the building, the inner sanctum being off limits to all but the chief priest and to him only on one occasion annually (the Day of Atonement). Although the Temple was not a public building in the sense of its interior being open to the public, it was very much a public building in a political and economic sense. Because ancient Israel, even during the monarchy, was not a secular state, the Temple played an integral role in the organization, legitimation, and administration of the national community.

First Temple: The First Temple is known chiefly from the description in 1 Kings 6–8 and the parallel account in 2 Chronicles 2–4. Ezekiel also has an extensive Temple section (chaps. 40–46). However, because of the visionary nature of Ezekiel's description and because it probably dates from after the destruction of the Temple in 587/6 B.C., its reliability as a witness to the First Temple, at least as it appeared at the beginning of its history, is minimal. Not a trace of the first Jerusalem Temple is available archaeologically; and even if it were, it is doubtful that a razed building of the early first millennium could supply the kind of detail that exists in the biblical sources. Nonetheless, the archaeological recovery of other ancient temples in Syro-Palestine provides an important corpus of comparative material.

The basic shape of the Jerusalem Temple was a rectangle, which was subdivided laterally into three sections, all of the same interior width, 20 cubits. The building measured 60 cubits long and was 30 cubits high. (For the Temple, the royal cubit, 20.9 inches, is probably the intended unit of linear measure; that would make it about 105 feet

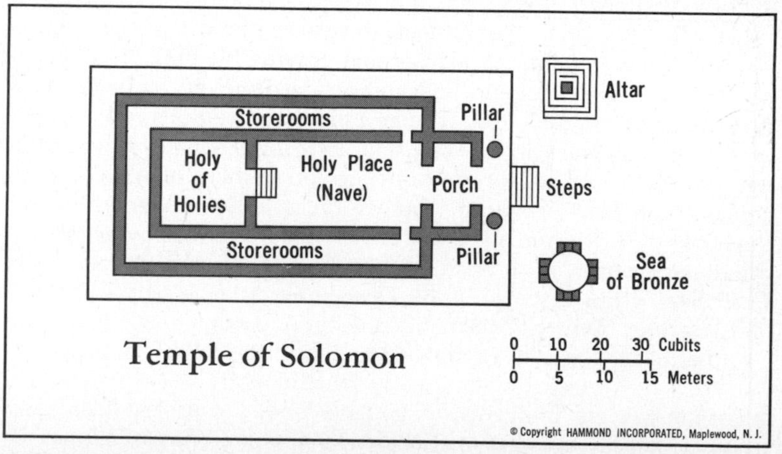

In this plan of the Temple of Solomon, the "Sea of Bronze" is placed according to 1 Kings 7:39.

long, 35 feet wide, and 52 feet high.) These are internal measurements based on the information in 1 Kings 6:2. The dimensions provided in Ezekiel (41:13–14) are for a 100 by 50 cubit structure. Ezekiel's data may reflect the external measurements of the Temple and include the subsidiary rooms built around it; they also may have been influenced by the proportions of the tabernacle, which was situated within a 100 by 50 cubit precinct. Although the interior decorations of the Temple are described in great detail (1 Kings 6), no information is given about its external appearance aside from the specifications about the hewn stone used for the walls. From the outside, the building probably presented a rather stark, formidable appearance.

Entrance to the Temple interior was gained by passing through the first of its three sections, the *'ulam*, which is related to an Akkadian word meaning "front" and which is translated "vestibule" by the RSV (1 Kings 7:19; 2 Chron. 3:4). Other versions render it as "porch," "portico," or "entrance hall." None of these translations reflect accurately the function of this 10-cubit-deep section of the Temple. The *'ulam*, unlike the two other sections, was not flanked by the side chambers of the Temple. Directions for paneling its internal walls do not appear, in contrast with the instructions for the inner two rooms, making it questionable whether its walls were paneled or decorated at all. Instead, its manner of construction (1 Kings 7:12; cf. 1 Kings 6:36) is identical to the technique described for the construction of both the public court of the Temple and also the great court of the adjacent palace area. Furthermore, the doorways to the inner two sections are described in detail, but no doorway to the *'ulam* is specified; it apparently had none. The account in the book of Kings also gives no height for the *'ulam*. This series of contrasts between the information about the two inner rooms and the details of the first room suggest that it was not an enclosed room at all but rather was an open-air forecourt through which the divine dwelling was entered in much the same way that every Near Eastern house was entered through its private courtyard.

The presence of Jachin and Boaz (two bronze pillars) at the entrance to the Temple further suggests that the *'ulam* was a forecourt. These great bronzed columns were situated at the top of the ten stairs

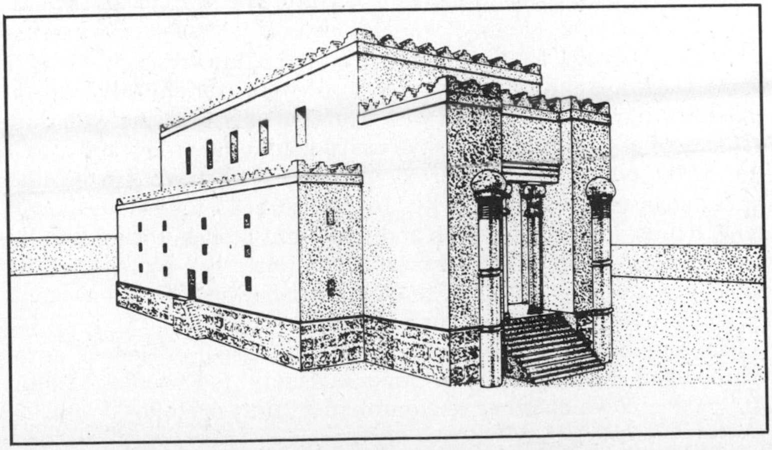

A depiction of the Temple of Solomon by T. A. Busink, an authority on ancient architecture.

that, according to Ezekiel (41:8), led up to the 6-cubit-high platform on which the Temple stood. Each stood 18 cubits high (1 Kings 7:15; cf. 2 Chron. 3:35 and Jeremiah in the Septuagint, which record 35 cubits) and was surmounted by an elaborate capital or double capital of at least 5 additional cubits. The pair of Jerusalem pillars loomed large at the entrance to the Temple. They were highly visible elements of the Temple's architecture, and consequently they were the visual link for the general public to the unseen grandeur within the building. Furthermore, they were probably free-standing and as such represented the gateposts that were part of the entryway to the Temple's private forecourt.

The second section of the Temple was its main or largest room, measuring 40 by 20 cubits and reaching a height of 30 cubits. Its name in Hebrew, *hikhal*, is related to Akkadian and Ugaritic terms, and ultimately to a Sumerian word, meaning "great house" and referring to a palace or any large and imposing dwelling (as in Hos. 8:14; 2 Kings 20:18). The residence of a deity would qualify as a "great house," and in fact this term for the largest chamber of the Temple is occasionally used to designate the Temple as a whole (e.g., Jer. 7:4; Zech. 8:9). The RSV calls it the "nave" (1 Kings 7:50; 2 Chron. 3:4–5); other translations include "main room," "temple proper," "holy place." Like the more common name for the Temple, "house of the Lord," this term also signifies the conceptualization of a temple as an earthly dwelling place of the deity. A large and elaborate cypresswood doorway carved with cherubim and palm trees and overlaid with gold provided entry to the central room.

The size of the *hikhal* and also the fact that it had windows indicate that this was the chamber in which most of the cultic activity associated with the building's interior took place. The windows were probably clerestory windows, set in the upper part of the walls above the flanking series of external subsidiary rooms. In addition, the internal Temple furniture was situated in this room and required regular attending to. A small altar for incense, made of cedar and overlaid with gold, stood in front of the entrance to the third room. Ten golden lampstands, which probably consisted of cylindrical stands surmounted by multispouted lamps (1 Kings 7:49), were situated in two groupings, five on the north and five on the south. The third major appurtenance placed in this chamber was also made of gold, or at least overlaid with gold: the table for the enigmatic "bread of the Presence" (1 Kings 7:48). The floors and walls of cypresswood were overlaid with gold, the latter first having been carved with figures of cherubim and with flowers and palm trees. The extensive use of gold in this room and also in the third room is to be contrasted with the use of bronze for the other appurtenances: the huge "molten (or bronze) sea," the ten lavers with their stands, the pillars Jachin and Boaz, and probably the great altar for sacrifice. Made of the less valuable metal, they represented the lower order of sanctity of the outside courtyard in which they stood, to which nonpriests as well as priests had access.

The innermost chamber of the Temple is known in Hebrew as the *debir*, which the RSV translates "inner sanctuary" (1 Kings 6:5; 2 Chron. 4:20; 5:9) and which other versions render "Holy of Holies," "oracle," "shrine," "adytum," or "most holy place." The Hebrew word may be related to the ordinary verb meaning "to speak," in which case the inner chamber would be the place where God speaks, or the "oracle." Entrance to the innermost room was gained through olivewood doors; like the doors to the *hikhal*, they were carved with flowers, palm trees, and cherubim and were overlaid with gold. The carved walls and the floors, also like those of the central chamber, were covered with gold. The internal measurements of the inner chamber, 20 by 20 by 20 cubits, made it a perfect cube. Its height was 10 cubits less than that of the adjacent central chamber, with which it was otherwise so closely associated in construction and decoration. Perhaps a slightly elevated floor and lowered roof accounted for the difference and helped to create an architectural focus on the contents of the inner room.

The darkness of the *debir* was filled with two enormous olivewood cherubim, overlaid with gold, each with a 10-cubit spread to its outstretched wings and each 10 cubits high. Under the adjacent wings of the cherubim, which commonly represented the protective quality of supernatural beings (cf. Gen. 3:24) in ancient Near Eastern iconography, stood the "ark of the covenant of the Lord" (1 Kings 6:19). The Ark was the most important object in the Temple. If the building as a whole was conceived of as the earthly dwelling place of God, with the rich furnishings and decorations suitable for a microcosmic replication of the heavenly abode of the Lord, then the Ark was the object within that building that represented both the divine presence itself and also the binding covenantal relationship between God and Israel. Although the Israelites did not believe that God's presence could be localized or confined to a particular building, they shared with all peoples the psychological and emotional need for a visible and material indication that God was nearby. Because God was seen as the source of material blessing and national protection for the Israelites, affirmation of God's availability to provide those essentials was communicated by the physical structure that, with all its splendor, symbolized a divine dwelling and assured the people of ready access to their God.

The symbolic nature of the Temple as a residence for God went beyond the function of providing assurance to the Israelites that God was with them. Construction of the Temple was anticipated by David, who brought the Ark to Jerusalem and who, at least according to the Chronicler (1 Chron. 22:2–5), began the task of assembling the raw materials—stone, metal, and wood—from which the Temple would be built. Within four years of ascending to the throne, Solomon began the actual construction. Although the biblical sources may exaggerate the scope of the project, it is clear that Solomon gave great priority to its completion. An enormous workforce was assigned to the task (1 Kings 5:13–17; cf. 2 Chron. 2:17–18). Within seven years, a remarkably short span of time for a project of this nature, the work was completed. An elaborate, fourteen-day-long ceremony of dedication, with a guest list that included international as well as national dignitaries (1 Kings 8:1–2, 65), was held.

The decision to build the Temple coincided with the formation of the monarchy and the emergence of Israel, for the only time in its long history, as a political power that was not only independent but that also was the dominant force in the Levant for almost a century. During the reigns of David and Solomon, Jerusalem was the capital of a small empire that reached from "the entrance of Hamath to the Brook of Egypt" (1 Kings 8:65). The construction of the Temple was integrally related to the formation of the Israelite state and to the imperial status of its capital in Jerusalem.

The formation of nation-states or city-states in the ancient world involved the concept that the nation's or city's chief deity approved and would support the concentration of power in the hands of the few who controlled the administrative structure of a state. Consequently, the building of a temple nearly always accompanied the establishment of a dynastic power. A temple building, as the visible symbol of a god's presence, was the most effective way for the leaders of a country to communicate, in the days before mass literacy and broadcast media, the fact that their god favored the political organization that was being established. The building of a temple added the essential note of absolute legitimacy to the formation of a new system of governance. The Davidic monarchy depended upon the existence of the Temple, as well as upon the skill and charisma of the monarchy's leaders, to secure the support and loyalty of the populace.

The legitimizing function of the Temple also operated on an international level. Its existence in Jerusalem demonstrated to non-Israelites—ambassadors and foreign wives, merchants and visitors—who had come to Jerusalem, especially during Solomon's long reign, that the God of Israel was present and had granted to the king his right to exercise dominion over Israel and over all the conquered territories. David had established imperial control through his brilliant use of military force; Solomon sustained that control through diplomacy. The Temple as part of the administrative center in Jerusalem bore the message that the Israelite domination of subject states had divine sanction.

Comparative archaeology contributes to this understanding of the political role of the Temple. The situation of Jachin and Boaz as gateposts to the Temple's inner court (*'ulam*) made them highly visible symbols of the entrance of the invisible God into the Temple, just as stone-carved reliefs from ancient Near Eastern sites marked the important event of the bringing of the cultic image of a city's god into its dwelling place. That the Jerusalem pillars surpassed in size analogous entry columns of other Syro-Palestinian temples suggests that the status of the Jerusalem Temple was greater than that of the temples of any other contemporary city-state or nation-state. The very size of the Temple as a whole presents a similar situation. The interior space of the Jerusalem sanctuary was considerably greater than that of the excavated temples of Syria and Palestine from the centuries closest to the existence of the Israelite empire. The Jerusalem Temple with its tripartite plan was part of Near Eastern architectural traditions for temples; but it surpassed similar buildings in size, as befitting its location in a city of international status.

A further indication of the political role of the Temple can be seen in the way it incorporated imported materials and workmanship into its decoration. Israel's lack of skilled workers and suitable raw materials led Solomon to enlist Phoenician aid. However, with Jerusalem conceived of by the Israelites as the theological center of the ancient world, the use of materials from all parts of that world also helped establish Jerusalem's cosmic centrality. The greatest influence upon the embellishment of the Temple can be found in the artistic traditions uncovered in the ruins of the major Syro-Hittite cities of the early Iron Age. Solomon used the visual embellishments best known to those populations to whom he most needed to communicate the divinely chartered rule and dominance of Jerusalem.

The international role of the Temple can also be seen in the elaborate, three-tiered complex of storerooms, thirty rooms to a story, which surrounded the Temple on three sides. The storage capacity of these rooms exceeded the needs of the Temple's rituals and personnel. Known as the *yatsi'a* (rendered "galleries," "side rooms," or "side chambers"), this structure housed the Temple treasury. It was a storehouse for religious objects as well as for precious items sent to Jerusalem as gifts and tribute or secured as booty or taxes. The fortress-like architecture of the Temple is a feature of its economic function, along with the palace, as a repository for the national wealth and even weaponry (cf. 1 Kings 7:51; 14:25–26; 15:18; 2 Kings 11:10; 12:4).

Second Temple: The Second Temple was built between 520 and 515 B.C. to replace the Temple built by Solomon, which had remained at the center of national life in the southern kingdom of Judah after Solomon's death until the Babylonians conquered Jerusalem. Renovations, repairs, and refurbishings may have altered the First Temple somewhat during the course of the centuries of the Judean monarchy (924–586 B.C.), but the basic structure had remained the same. The Babylonians destroyed the First Temple by carrying away all its precious items and furnishings, in the process dismantling those too large to transport easily, and then burning it (2 Kings 25:8–17). However, since only the roofing and internal paneling of the Temple were wooden and could be burned, the stone foundation and much of the superstructure probably remained. There is no indication that the walls were razed. With the prodding of the postexilic prophets Haggai and Zechariah and through the leadership of the high priest Joshua and the Persian appointed governor Zerubbabel, who was also a Davidic descendant, the work of restoration was carried out. Concern about the lack of splendor in the postexilic building (Hag. 2:3; Ezra 3:12) probably reflects the dearth of precious metals in its decoration rather than any diminution in its size.

Although the restored Temple was crucial in representing continuity with both the appearance and the role of the pre-exilic building and institution, a radical change took place in its traditional balance of religious and political-economic functions. Without a king to sit on the throne of David, the legitimizing role of the Temple in national life shifted to the priestly administrators of Judah, which had become the postexilic Persian province of Yehud. The priests had always been important in national life, but their responsibilities were enlarged after the Exile as they stepped in to fill the gap left by the absence of the civil authority of kingship. The Persians evidently allowed the high priest and his staff to assume much of the internal governance, fiscally and legally, of Yehud. Zechariah's Temple visions, particularly in chaps. 3 and 4, continue the age-old concept of the Temple as a legitimizing factor for the administrative structure of the community. For Zechariah, the priesthood's role is expanded and the monarchic role becomes a matter of future expectation. The Temple stood alone, without the palace, as the center of semi-autonomous national life and as the focus of the dispersed community still in exile.

Hebrew inscription (shown here in part) from the outer wall of the Temple Mount reads, "of the place of trumpeting"; first century B.C.

Third Temple: Herod's Temple comes at the end of the sequence of Jerusalem temples and is best known to us physically because of the extensive excavations along its western retaining wall and at many other buildings dating from the rule of Herod the Great (37 B.C.–A.D. 4). The Second Temple had undergone desecration and despoliation after the Greeks (325 B.C.) and then the Romans (63 B.C.) replaced the Persians as the imperial masters of Palestine. Yet Herod's temple-building project, described in considerable detail by the first-century historian Josephus and referred to extensively in other Jewish sources (especially the mishnaic tractate *Middoth*) and in the NT, went far beyond any simple task of refurbishing or repairing the sixth-century structure. Herod's struggle to take over the Judean kingdom and his monumental efforts to make it a significant part of the Roman Empire are reflected in the magnitude of his building projects.

Herod, probably the descendant of an Idumean, was in essence a usurper of the throne in Jerusalem. He did not enjoy the traditional Jewish support that had been held by the Hasmonean (Maccabean) rulers who preceded him and who had combined the office of high priest with the kingship acquired as the result of their revolt against the Seleucids in the second century B.C. His grandiose building projects included the construction of an entirely new, gold-covered Temple, although with the sanctuary itself corresponding approximately to the Solomonic dimensions, on an enormous platform (ca. 169,000 sq. yds.) and within a broad public area (see Matt. 21:12; Mark 11:15). The Temple and its courts were surrounded by a Roman-style double colonnade and entered through monumental gates. Both the literary sources and the archaeological discoveries affirm that the builders of this vast complex sought to incorporate the current Greco-Roman architectural fashion. It is questionable that He-

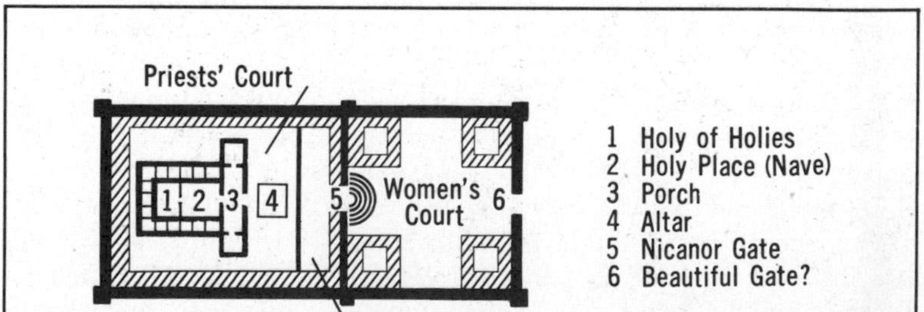

rod's intentions arose from religious sensibilities or allegiance to the God of Israel. The political dimension that had always been present in temple building came to dominate Herod's plans. His attention to the Temple would win over, he hoped, dissident Jewish elements within his kingdom. Furthermore, the scale and style of the Temple, as of the other buildings of Herodian conception, were meant to make a visual statement to Rome about the importance of the Jewish kingdom.

Jesus driving the money changers from the Temple (Mark 11: 15–19); alabaster relief at the Basilica of St. Mark, Venice, sixth century A.D.

The importance of the Temple in the religious life of Jews at this time is evident in the NT. The birth of John the Baptist was announced in the Temple (Luke 1:11–20), and the sacrificial offering for every Jewish male child was offered there for Jesus (Luke 2:22–24). The Temple was also the place his future prominence was announced by Simeon (Luke 2:25–35) and Anna (2:36–38). Jesus' religious significance was first seen in the Temple (Luke 2:42–51), and he taught in its precincts when he went to Jerusalem (Mark 12:35; John 7:14, 28). His later purging of its worship practices (Mark 11:15–19) figured prominently in the charges that brought about his death (Mark 14:58; 15:29; cf. 13:1–2). Early Christians continued to gather in the Temple (Acts 2:46; cf. 3:3; 4:1–2), and Acts records that Paul was arrested there at the instigation of his opponents (Acts 21:27).

The largest and grandest of the Jerusalem temples was also the shortest lived. The Roman siege of Jerusalem had the Temple as its focus, and Titus and his legions set fire to the edifice in A.D. 70. Today, the Muslim shrine called the "Dome of the Rock" or the Mosque of Omar stands on the Temple site.

See also Altar; David; Herod; Jachin and Boaz; Lampstand; Priests; Solomon; Tabernacle; Temples; Worship; Zerubbabel.

Bibliography

Haran, M. *Temples and Temple Service in Ancient Israel.* Oxford: Clarendon, 1978.

Meyers, C. "The Elusive Temple." *Biblical Archeologist* 45 (1981): 31–42.

Parrot, A. *The Temple of Jerusalem.* Studies in Biblical Archaeology, no. 5. London: SCM, 1957.

C.L.M.

Romans carrying spoil, including a menorah and trumpets, from the Temple; relief on the Arch of Titus, Rome, A.D. 81.

temples, religious structures which were probably the most important and most visible institutions in the biblical world. Their prominence as architectural structures on the ancient landscape is a reflection of their integral role in the political and economic structure of ancient society. While we think of temples primarily in terms of their religious dimension, i.e., as relating specifically to deities, temples were in fact basic components in the political organization and administration of territorial units, from city-states to nation-states or empires, in the ancient Near East.

The English word "temple" is misleading in its usage as a translation of certain terms in the Hebrew Bible. Derived from the Latin word *templum*, which strictly speaking denotes separated or marked-off space, or a holy place, it could theoretically denote any of a number of types of worship places known in the biblical world, including altars, high places, and stelae. English parlance, however, normally uses "temple" to indicate an actual building or structure that partakes of the sacred.

The essential nature of such a building in OT times is revealed in the two Hebrew terms translated "temple": *bayit*, "house [of God]," and *hikhal*, "[Yahweh's] palace." These words differ from the two NT (Greek) terms for temple: *naos*, which denotes a sacred building, and *hieron*, which refers to a sacred area or place.

Both Hebrew terms are essentially secular in origin, both refer to a structure rather than to a holy place or precinct, and both conceptualize such a structure as a residence or dwelling for the deity. While neither the Israelites nor their Canaanite neighbors may have adhered to the literal notion of a deity inhabiting an earthly building, that idea undoubtedly underlies the origins of all ancient Near Eastern temples and continued to function symbolically throughout the biblical period. Indeed, the plan, furnishings, personnel, and service associated with temples can be reconstructed rather well on the basis of both archaeological and textual sources. All this information depicts the functioning of an institution intended to provide amply and royally for the needs of its divine inhabitant, even if the earthly house was only a pale copy of the deity's real and splendid residence in heaven.

Archaeological Data: The archaeological investigation of temples is not quite so simple a matter as it might seem. Since the organizing principle of temple building was the construction of a dwelling place for a god, the designs for temples were drawn, at least in the earlier stages of their architectural history, from the typical plans for larger human houses or palaces. Identification of excavated buildings as temples is thus problematic.

Nonetheless, a number of features usually allow certain buildings to be identified as temples. Temples tend to be located in prominent places within a city. As part of the administration of the political unit in which they existed, they were often adjacent to similar, and often larger, royal buildings. Together, the royal and divine residences, which we call palace and temple, constituted a separate precinct in an ancient city. At least in some cases, the temple-palace complex was set off as an acropolis or as a raised and/or walled section of the city. Even if a palace was not included, the temple by itself, since it was technically sacred space, would normally have been separated from the rest of the city by surrounding courtyards and walls, although the dwellings of the city's inhabitants were often built up against the courtyard walls.

In addition to the prominence of their location, temples can often be identified as residences for deities by some architectural divergence from the secular monumental buildings of their time. Size alone is not a criterion since, as we have noted, palaces might exceed temples in size. However, the thickness of a temple's walls matched or even surpassed that of the walls of adjacent palaces. The temple was in a sense like a fortress, protecting the sanctity of the god, the lavish furnishings of the god's dwelling, and also the precious commodities brought into and stored in the temple storerooms.

Perhaps the most indicative feature of a temple is that its ground plan typically includes, in its innermost part, a special recess or distinct small room meant for the statue of the resident deity. Furthermore, the artifacts recovered in buildings that might be classified as temples include a repertoire of pottery forms and other objects not found in normal domestic settings. Superior workmanship, religious symbolism in the decoration, and costly materials characterize such artifacts and allow them to be designated "cultic objects." They constitute the furnishings of the deity's house and the vessels for the provision of all the god's needs. Finally, the courtyard of a temple if it can be fully excavated would be expected to reveal an altar. As a place for burnt offerings of all kinds and for animal sacrifice, altars had to be outside the roofed temple building, although small altars might exist inside the building for the burning of incense.

Types of Temples: With these criteria in mind, the existence of temples in many of the major cities occupied by the Canaanites or Philistines, either prior to or contemporary with ancient Israelite origins in Palestine, can be established with reasonable certainty. Two major types of temples have been recognized. The oldest is called the *broad-room*, which was basically a rectangular or roughly square room with the entrance on one of the long sides and a niche or platform for the god opposite the entrance. The orientation is thus along the short axis. Some of the earliest examples, as in Early Bronze Age (3000–2000 B.C.) Ai and Megiddo and possibly also at Arad, are clearly derived from typical Early Bronze Age house architecture. It is to be noted that some scholarly dispute regarding their identification as temples persists. The basic broad-room was expanded in various ways: by the addition of ancillary rooms around the associated courtyard, by the development of the niche into a discrete cella (shrine-room), or by the construction of a portico at the entrance.

The last two mentioned features extend the short axis of the building and so relate the broad-room sanctuary at least in some instances to the other major temple type, the *long-house* buildings, in which the orientation is along the long axis. In their more developed forms, they consisted of a series of rooms, usually two or three, along an axis so that an officiant would have to pass through each room in succession to reach the innermost room. Usually, the second or middle room in a long-house temple was largest, with the first room constituting an anteroom and the third room being a cella. Such a tripartite arrangement is evident in several Megiddo and Hazor structures as well as, according to the biblical description, in the Jerusalem Temple. This type emerged in the Middle Bronze Age (2000–1500 B.C.), with the earliest examples perhaps being the extremely thick-walled fortress temples of Shechem, Hazor, and Megiddo.

This typology does not exhaust the kinds of temples excavated in Palestine. The Philistines, as at Tel Qasile, evidently had their own variation; and so did those Canaanites strongly influenced by Egyptian (as at Beth-shan) or northern (Syrian) traditions. In addition the so-called square temples, such as the one from the beginning of the Late Bronze Age (1500–1200 B.C.) at Amman, are set apart from urban areas and may, if indeed they are temples, represent the worship sites of seminomadic groups. In short, there is no dominant form. Each example adhering roughly to one of the major types nonetheless exhibits its own unique characteristics. Similarly, no dominant pattern of orientation can be discerned, except that orientation tends to remain constant at a given temple site over the duration, often many hundreds of years, of its existence. This may indicate that the principle of orientation relates to the layout of the city in which the temple is built and not to any theological concerns.

Further developments in temple architecture appeared, beginning in the Hellenistic period (300 B.C.–300 A.D.), with the introduction of Greco-Roman temples into Palestine. These imposing structures along with the older Semitic sanctuaries helped determine the architectural

TEMPLES

Early Bronze Age (3000–2000 B.C.) "broad-room" at Ai, which may have been a temple.

form of the synagogues and churches that emerged in the early centuries A.D. While early Christians continued to participate in Temple worship in Jerusalem (Acts 2:46), after its destruction in A.D. 70, a destruction predicted by Jesus in word (Mark 13:2) and act (Mark 11: 15–16), the Christian community did not build its own temple. Worship was held in houses, which owed more to the synagogue than to the Temple in Jerusalem.

Biblical Information: The archaeological recovery of Palestinian temples is supplemented by biblical references to temples, or residences for non-Israelite gods, at various places. 1 Samuel mentions the "House of Dagon" (5:2, 5) and the "House of Ashtaroth" (31:10). Judges refers to the "House of Baal-berith" (9:4) and the "House of El-berith" (9:46). Although the latter two temples are at Shechem, they cannot with certitude be related to any of the excavated buildings at that site. Neither can the "House of El" of the patriarchal stories be linked with any remains from Bethel.

The Bible also records the existence of a number of Israelite temples in addition to the major one in Jerusalem. While the terminology associated with such buildings does not usually include the designation "House," other information indicates that a temple building or an equivalent tent shrine, rather than simply an altar or high place, is to be understood. Except for the Northern Kingdom sites of Dan and Bethel, these possible Israelite temples (Shiloh, Gilgal, Mizpah, Hebron, Bethlehem, Nob, Michah's Shrine in Ephraim, Ophrah, and Gibeah) are mentioned in sources describing the premonarchical or early monarchical periods. None of them have been recovered archaeologically. Furthermore, it is not clear that any of them continued to function once the Jerusalem Temple was built. The only Israelite (i.e., Northern Kingdom) temple apparently existing during the monarchy, a cultic building at Arad, is not mentioned in the Bible. It is known only from excavations, and its very identity as a temple has been questioned.

The apparent disappearance of non-Jerusalem

temples from Israelite territory once the Jerusalem Temple was built by Solomon is evidence in part of the administrative nature and political role of temples, which served to legitimize the political power responsible for their construction and maintenance. The non-Jerusalem buildings were regional centers servicing the tribal groups. With the centralization of political power in a monarchy, the location of the mechanisms of statecraft in one capital city meant that the complementary cultic institutions likewise shifted to that place, although altars and high places continued to exist throughout Israel. The close connection of the god's dwelling with political administration is further indicated by the fact that temples were not public houses of worship. They were entered only by priests, although the laity could enter the courtyard and worship there. The archaeological evidence of temple size and layout, along with the information from both the Bible and Near Eastern temple texts about temple personnel and ritual, allows for such a conclusion. ***See also*** Temple, The; Worship.

Bibliography

Ahlström, G. W. *Royal Administration and National Religion in Ancient Palestine.* Studies in the History of the Near East. Vol. 1. Leiden: E. J. Brill, 1982.

Biran, Avraham, ed. *Temples and High Places in Biblical Times.* Jerusalem: Hebrew Union College, 1981.

Haran, Menahem. *Temples and Temple Service in Ancient Israel.* Oxford: Clarendon, 1978.

C.L.M.

temple servants. ***See*** Nethinim.

temptation, generally an enticement to do evil, the term is used in the Bible to convey two somewhat different ideas. The first is that of "testing" or "proving by testing," to determine the depth and integrity of one's commitment to God (see, e.g., God's command to Abraham to offer his son Isaac as a sacrifice in Gen. 22:1–19; also the testing of Job in Job 1–2). In the NT, some of the writers thought of persecution as a "testing" in this manner (e.g., 1 Pet. 1:3–9). The intent of this testing is ultimately to strengthen the person's faith and devotion to God.

The second nuance of temptation is more in line with modern popular understandings of the term, namely, an enticement toward sin leading to a deliberate act of evil against God or one's neighbor. The biblical writers are careful, however, to make it clear that God does not "tempt" humans to do evil (e.g., James 1:12–15) and in fact makes available the resources necessary to resist temptation (e.g., 1 Cor. 10:13). The familiar petition in the Lord's Prayer dealing with temptation probably should be understood as "Do not allow us to go into temptation" (Matt. 6:13a), as the original Aramaic likely would have read. It is quite possible, moreover, that the reference is to "testing" rather than to "temptation" as this is popularly understood.

A quite different aspect of "temptation" or "testing" in the biblical writings is that of human beings attempting to put God to a test, usually for the purpose of testing God's plans or purposes (e.g., Judg. 6; cf. Matt. 12:39) or, even more, to determine whether they can manipulate God (e.g., Ps. 95:8–11; cf. Matt. 4:5–7; Luke 4:9–12). Such activities stem from a lack of trust in God and his promises. This understanding seems to be involved in the most famous of all temptation accounts, the temptation of Jesus by Satan (Matt. 4:1–11; Mark 1:12–13; Luke 4:1–13).

All of the synoptic Gospels (Matthew, Mark, and Luke) have accounts of Jesus' temptation, although only Matthew and Luke give any details (John's Gospel has no such account). In each Gospel, the temptation takes place immediately after Jesus' baptism, which is interpreted as his commissioning for the messianic ministry, a ministry to be characterized by servanthood (Matt. 3:13–17; Mark 1:9–11; Luke 3:21–22; cf., e.g., Mark 10:45). The temptation is not for Jesus to prove his divine Sonship to himself. Such Sonship is never questioned in the NT. Rather, the temptation or "testing" is implicitly presented as Jesus' struggle over whether to obey God's call to be a servant-messiah or to interpret messiahship in the traditional terms of power, strength, and conquest. Such a struggle can be detected throughout the Gospel accounts of Jesus' ministry, where it is

Jesus tempted by the devil to throw himself from the pinnacle of the Temple in Jerusalem (cf. Luke 4:9–12); fourteenth-century mosaic depiction at the Kariye Church, Istanbul.

made clear that the disciples never really understood Jesus' commitment to a servant ministry.

In the biblical writings, therefore, temptation or testing has these two nuances: the strong inclination of humankind toward evil when it is known that God wills good and testing situations that may demonstrate one's commitment to God and God's ways and even strengthen one's faith. In each, if people overcome temptation, i.e., pass the test, their faith has been enhanced and their character strengthened (e.g., Rom. 5:3–5). ***See also*** Persecution; Sin; Suffering.

J.M.E.

ten. *See* Numbers.

Ten Commandments, the, a series of commands from God to the chosen people, mediated by Moses. The text of the Decalogue (Gk., "ten words") or Ten Commandments is given in its entirety twice in the OT with only slight variations. In Exod. 20:1–17 the setting is Mount Sinai; Moses brings down to the people the two tablets of the law written by the very hand of God (Exod. 24:12). In Deut. 5:6–21 the text is part of Moses' recitation of the history of salvation with which he prefaces his last will and testament.

Origin and Setting: Everything about the Ten Commandments suggests that it was a text intended to be memorized and publicly recited by the covenant community. Not only are the commandments in number equal to the fingers of both hands, but a similarity of form also pervades most of the list: "you shall not" is followed by a verb. Placed at the very beginning of the lengthy block of legal materials known as the Sinai passage (Exod. 19:11–Num. 10:10), the Decalogue functions as a summary of the covenant tradition suitable for recitation on public occasions of national reaffirmation of loyalty to the sovereign God. Although the OT makes no specific mention of a regular "feast of covenant renewal," the events recalled in Deuteronomy 27 and in Joshua 24 appear to be such occasions: the people gather at Shechem, swear their allegiance to the law, and watch as inscribed stones are set up to preserve the terms of the covenant. We may even suppose that certain religious officials were responsible to lead the recitation of the law on these occasions, and that these "covenant mediators" may have interpreted the Ten Commandments for their own generation. Prophetic preaching may have its origins in this task of proclamation (see Hos. 4:1–2).

Function: Israelite law can be separated into two large categories: case law and categorical law. The former, represented, for example, in the "Book of the Covenant" (Exod. 20:22–23:33), preserves decisions about actual cases reached through the judicial processes of a settled agricultural community. Biblical case law is roughly equivalent to our common law. Categorical law, on the other hand, does not seem to emerge from actual cases but sets forth the broad principles of community life. The Ten Commandments and similar lists of legal sentences (see Deut. 27:15–26; Lev. 19:13–18) amount to something like the constitutional law of ancient Israel. In function the Ten Commandments can be compared to ten posts supporting the fence separating the viable community of Israel from the marauding beasts of disorder, confusion, and bloodshed howling outside the pale. Of all the statutes needed to regulate the life of the community, these ten were deemed essential beyond all others. Should any one of these ten fenceposts collapse, chaos could break in and wreak havoc in the community. For Israel, survival itself was at stake with every one of these ten categorical imperatives.

The Commandments in Brief: The commandment reckoned to be the first one by most Protestants and Eastern Orthodox Christians, "you shall have no other gods before me" (Exod. 20:3; Deut. 5:7) is considered the first half of the second commandment in Jewish tradition. In Lutheran and Roman Catholic tradition, this commandment is combined with the prohibition against graven images to form the first commandment; Exod. 20:17 is then divided into two commandments to make up the ten. This commandment does not deny the existence of other gods, but it demands total allegiance on the part of Israel to its own God, the covenant-giver. The prohibition against graven images (Exod. 20:4–6; Deut. 5:8–10) may in the first instance have been aimed at images of Israel's own God, Yahweh. God will not be localized in an object such as a golden calf (see Exod. 20:4–6; 1 Kings 12:28), because to permit this to happen would make God an object of manipulation. God has images in the world (Gen. 1:26), but they walk on two feet and they love God and keep the commandments (Exod. 20:6). The prohibition against the misuse of the name of God (Exod. 20:7; Deut. 5:11) is directed at another form of manipulation of the deity for personal interest. Magical, imprecatory, and other trivial cultic uses of the sacred name are forestalled.

The commandment to rest on the Sabbath is motivated in Exod. 20:11 by the Creator's own Sabbath rest. In Deut. 5:12–15 the Sabbath is a day of remembrance of liberation from Egyptian slavery. The commandment to set one day apart from all others ("to keep it holy") stands as a bulwark against endless self-destructive human greed, and spares Israel the horror of being a Sabbathless culture. The command to honor father and mother (Exod. 20:12; Deut. 5:16), the only one accompanied with a promise, promotes a community climate in which the chances of survival are enhanced by a tradition of tender solicitude shown by the young toward the older generations. The uninterrupted flow of community tradition from one generation to the next is also ensured by the "honor" shown to the father and—in a perfectly equal way—to the mother. Technically speaking, "You shall not kill" (Exod. 20:13; Deut. 5:17) prohibits only that kind of antisocial killing, done in vulgar self-interest, that poses a threat to the very existence of the community. Jesus' radicalization of this commandment in Matt. 5:21–26 suggests that the definition of antisocial murderousness could evolve and that the commandment could come to mean more than it originally meant.

"You shall not commit adultery" (Exod. 20: 14; Deut. 5:18) guards marriage and family against the intrusion of third parties and the socially disruptive questions of the legitimacy of children and the transfer of the family legacy. "You shall not steal" (Exod. 20:15; Deut. 5:19) may originally have included, as the object of the verb, the term "a man" (see Exod. 21:16). As it stands, however, this commandment protects private property from illegal attachment. The prohibition against bearing false witness (Exod. 2:16; Deut. 5:20) is aimed not so much at lying in general as it is at perjury in court. The very survival of a community is threatened when the weak, disadvantaged, and falsely accused can find no remedy before impartial judges informed by credible witnesses. Finally, the commandment against covetousness (Exod. 20:17; Deut. 5:21) points for the first time beyond public and overt acts to private attitudes. Like all Hebrew verbs of mental activity, however, "to covet" also includes an element of enactment. It is action in rehearsal. Unenforceable as it may be, in its attack upon inordinate desire this final commandment seeks to forestall the conspiracies that lead to illegal, ruthless seizure of persons and property. ***See also*** Law. W.S.T.

tent, a portable shelter made of cloth or skins, used by shepherds (Isa. 38:12), nomads, and soldiers. In Israel's experience it covered a shrine (2 Sam. 7:2) and served as storage space (1 Sam. 17:54, armor; 1 Kings 8:4, holy vessels), but it was primarily used as living quarters (Gen. 4:20, 25:27; 2 Sam. 20:1).

Dark in color (Song of Sol. 1:5), tents were likely woven of goat hair (Exod. 36:14) and required purification on occasion (Num. 31:20). Large tents could be constructed piecemeal and fastened by clasping loops at the edges (Exod. 36:15–18). Entrances could be covered by a screen (Exod. 36:37) or be arranged by simply raising the side or a flap of the side. The anchorage to the ground was by pegs (Judg. 4:21) or by tying the line to a large stable boulder when camped on rock. Unless supported by poles and raised by tightly anchoring the fabric over the poles on all sides, a tent would collapse and lie flat (Judg. 7:13). The stability of a tent depended on well-placed stakes or pegs (Isa. 33:20) and strong and durable cords or anchoring lines (Isa. 33:20). The work of raising a tent involved unpacking and unrolling the fabric, anchoring the corner lines, then raising the poles in place, work requiring the spreading of the fabric to place corners, anchorages, and poles (Jer. 10:20). Only when it was erected could the curtain(s) dividing the interior space be rigged (Jer. 10:20). Failure of the cords to hold provided a metaphor for death (Job 4:21).

As a Dwelling: Households might live in a single tent (Exod. 33:8) or have a group of tents for individuals and servants (Gen. 31:33) of the family. Because of the relatively expensive nature of tents and the need for several animals to transport a group of them, multiple tents signified wealth above average. Tents could also be used to store or hide precious or forbidden material (Josh. 7:21). Thus guards could be posted at tents (1 Chron. 9:23), but they could not stop the destruction of the tent of the wicked (Job 8: 22). Like cities, tents could be besieged (Job 19: 12). Care was needed in selecting sites to pitch one's tents (Deut. 1:33) because unwise selection would bring hazards (Hos. 9:6). Royal tents could be palatial (Dan. 11:45), but life in tents could also symbolize the purer style of a nomadic past (Jer. 35:6–10, the Rechabite ideal).

Contact with such a past is most vividly given in Genesis 18, describing Abraham's hosting some visitors at his tent camp at Hebron. Set in a grove of trees, the tent was used for shady rest in the hot part of the day. When the visitors approached, Abraham ran out to greet them and extended the hospitality of shade, food, drink, and conversation. Inquiry about Abraham's wife elicited the fact that she was "in the tent" (either her own nearby [Gen. 31: 33] or in the divided portion of the tent reserved for women), close enough to overhear the conversation (Gen. 18:10). Implied in the actions of the hospitality was a variety of equipment normal to any household. Some kind of storage and carrying vessel for water to wash the feet of the travelers was available. Bread was provided, implying a facility to grind meal and bake over an open fire or in a small oven (possible in a long-term campsite). Meal storage, a kneading quern, and the necessary metal sheet or rock for baking the cakes was involved. There were tools for butchering the calf and vessels for the curds and milk, for cooking the meat, and for serving the food to the guests. Rest under the tree may have been on the ground, but it would not have been strange for relatively wealthy persons to provide reed mats or cloth pads for guests in that situation. In addition, a tent was normally furnished with some kind of oil lamp for night light.

Where Located and Situated: Tents, like houses, were preferably located close to a good supply of fresh water, on terrain that by being high and affording good visibility or by being hidden was secure from unexpected intrusion. The ground needed to be reasonably smooth and flat for comfort and stability. A small stone circle or depression in the earth could serve as the cookfire location. Given the prevailing wind and weather patterns, tents in Syro-Palestine are almost always set with one long side to the east, allowing early warmth from the morning sun. The opposite long side facing west could be kept anchored low to keep out the chilling wind or raised in the heat of the day to allow cooling breezes to enter. In modern bedouin practice, the women's side of the tent is for storage and cooking equipment, whereas the men's side is kept relatively free of gear for easy hospitality. Domestic animals would have been corralled nearby, but dogs, uncooped chickens, or other small livestock would be allowed to roam the tent and its environs at will.

Biblical usage includes metaphoric references to tents in addition to the long, detailed descriptions of the sacred tents (e.g., Exod. 26). God was portrayed as living in a tent (Ps. 15:1), as he had provided a tent for the sun (Ps. 19:4). God's tent provided secure hiding for his people (Ps. 27:5) and he stretched out the heavens like a tent (Ps. 104:2) when it is pitched. A tent is a metaphor for life for the righteous person (Prov. 14:11). The tent could figure the transitory nature of human life (2 Cor. 5:1, 4), and the writer of Hebrews could contrast the earthly shrine-tent with the "true tent" available in Christ (Heb. 8:1–6). Some tents could accommodate wickedness (Job 11:14; Ps. 84:10) and should in such cases be avoided.

The apostle Paul while in Corinth stayed with Aquila and Priscilla, recent victims of the Roman emperor Claudius' ban on Jews in Rome, because they, like he, were tentmakers. It is said that he worked at his trade while in Corinth, presumably engaging in missionary effort and pastoral work as time and opportunity afforded. As a native of Tarsus in Cilicia, he may have learned about *cilicium*, a goat's hair cloth used especially by seamen and soldiers, or he may have been a leatherworker, since in Hellenistic times many tents were constructed of leather.

Tent campsites are notoriously difficult to locate archaeologically because the occupants seldom stayed long in one place. The result is that little physical evidence remains from their occupation. A small area swept clear of pebbles and stones, a small hearth or fire pit, possibly a broken pot, a lost scraper blade or a broken grinding stone would be all that was left in archaeological terms. Recent studies have focused on the dimorphic communities where people used houses in settled towns for part of the year, moving into tents for wider pasturage or simply for cooler accommodation for the other part of the year. These studies may develop better techniques for learning the archaeology of tent sites. R.S.B.

Tent of meeting. ***See*** Tabernacle.

Terah (tair'uh), a descendant of Shem, the son of Nahor, the father of Abraham, Haran, and Nahor. The name has alternatively been associated with Akkadian *turahu* ("ibex") and Aramaic *yerakh* ("moon"), but a final determination is not at hand. All three of Terah's sons were born when he was seventy (Gen. 12:26). The repeated formula "These are the generations of . . ." (Heb. *'eleh toledot)*, which marks divisions between narrative cycles in Genesis (cf. 2:4; 5:1; 25:12, 19; 36:1; 37:2), is associated with Terah (11:27), thus commencing the Abraham cycle. Terah's son Haran died during his father's lifetime, having fathered one child, Lot. After Haran's surviving brothers married, Terah endeavored to move the entire clan from Ur-of-the-Chaldees to Canaan, but he got only as far as the north Syrian locale Haran (the name is unrelated to the person Haran), where he settled and died at the age of two hundred and five. Ancient rabbinic interpreters portrayed Terah as a manufacturer and worshiper of idols, in partial explanation of God's command to Abram in 12:1 to leave his father's house. ***See also*** Abraham; Ur. J.W.R.

teraphim (tair'uh-fim), statues or figurines representing household gods. They were common in Syria and Palestine, even among Israelites, throughout the pre-exilic period (to 586 B.C.). In Gen. 31:19, Rachel stole her father's teraphim. Laban's angry reaction suggests their importance. According to many ancient and modern interpreters, talismanic, cultic, and legal significance accrued to their possession. Their function as title to Laban's estate cannot be ruled out.

In Judg. 17:5 and 18:4, 17, 20, teraphim are cultic objects, mentioned as symbols of a private priesthood. The Ephraimite Micaiah had established his own shrine, furnished with a hired Levite, ephod, teraphim, and a silver statue donated by his mother (Micaiah had earlier robbed her but then confessed and repaid the theft). Some Danites migrating from Judah encountered the Levite and persuaded him to serve at their intended shrine in Laish, taking along Micaiah's teraphim. Micaiah's desolation over the loss (18:24) again shows the symbolic importance of teraphim.

In 1 Sam. 19:13–16, Michal aided David's escape from Saul by filling a bed with large teraphim, disguised as David bedridden. Prophets inveighed against teraphim as wanton superstition (1 Sam. 15:23; Zech. 10:2). Hos. 3:4 depicts them as integral to Israel's royal and priestly institutions. Josiah's reform banned them (2 Kings 23:23). Ezek. 21:21 portrays the king of Babylon divining by them before his attack on Jerusalem. ***See also*** Idol; Jacob; Laban; Micaiah; Priests. J.W.R.

terebinth *(Pistachia terebinthus,* variety *palaestina),* a tree common to the lower regions of the hills of the Holy Land. Its broad, spreading branches, great size, and long life make it a tree much venerated. The term for terebinth is often translated as oak, another sacred tree. The shade of the terebinth was a location preferred for burials (1 Chron. 10:12; RSV: "oak") and for the safekeeping of treasured objects (Gen. 35:4). It is called the turpentine tree (Ecclus. 24:16; KJV) since turpentine is made from its resinous sap. In Isa. 6:13 (KJV) it is also called the teil tree.

Tertius (tuhr'shi-uhs), Paul's amanuensis or "secretary" who, in Rom. 16:22, sent his own greetings along with those of Paul. ***See also*** Epistle; Letter.

Tertullus (tuhr-tuhl'uhs), the prosecutor, according to Acts 24:1–8, who represented the Jewish leaders from Jerusalem before the Roman procurator Felix when charges were brought against Paul in Caesarea. The author of Acts, in good classical style, produces a speech in which Tertullus makes the charges. Tertullus may have been a Jew or he may have been a professional Roman advocate (the name is Roman). A reading in Codex Bezae (the important "Western" text of Acts) presumes that he was Jewish and that it was only the Romans who stood in the way of Paul getting what Tertullus regarded as his just deserts from the Jews (Acts 24:6b–7, which is missing from many ancient manuscripts and thus also from the RSV). The fact that Felix postponed Paul's trial suggests that Tertullus was not entirely successful in his plea (Acts 24:22–23). ***See also*** Felix, Antonius; Paul. A.J.M.

testament (Gk. *diathekē*), a will or an agreement. **1** The last will and testament of a person, disposing of the person's property. **2** A convenant in the sense of the Sinai convenant and of the OT and NT. Paul presumes meanings 1 and 2 in his discussion in Gal. 3:15–18. **3** A literary genre common in Jewish literature in the intertestamental period (ca. 200 B.C.–A.D. 50) and also found in the Bible. In a literary Testament a famous figure delivers a speech or gives a blessing to his descendants or followers. Usually the speech contains predictions of their future destiny, moral exhortations, or blessings. Jacob's blessing on his twelve sons (Gen. 49) is the model for many Testaments, especially *The Testament of the Twelve Patriarchs.* Moses' blessing on Israel (Deut. 33) and Jesus' last discourse (John 13–17) are other examples. Nonbiblical Testaments are the Aramaic *Testament of Levi* from Qumran, *The Testament of Abraham, The Testament of Moses,* and many others. ***See also*** Pseudepigrapha. A.J.S.

Testament, New. ***See*** New Testament.

Testament, Old. ***See*** Old Testament.

Testaments of the Twelve Patriarchs. ***See*** Pseudepigrapha.

testimony, evidence recalling particular events or deeds. **1** The tablets containing the law given by God to Moses (Exod. 31:18; Num. 17:4). **2** The laws of God as a directive for one's life (1 Kings 2:13; Ps. 119:36, 88). **3** The statutes and ordinances received from Moses (Deut. 4:45; Rev. 15:5, RSV: "witness"). **4** The attestation of a contractual agreement (Ruth 4:7, RSV: "manner of attesting"). **5** In the NT God's activity through Jesus in word and deed (John 3:32; 5:32; Rev. 1:2), the presentation of God's revelation in Jesus Christ (Matt. 10:18; Luke 21:13; Acts 22:18; 2 Tim. 1:8) and a symbolic rebuff directed toward those who reject the disciple's witness (Mark 6:11).

testing. ***See*** Temptation.

teth (teth), the ninth letter of the Hebrew alphabet. It was early written as crossed lines within a circle, from which developed the Greek letter *theta.* Teth stands at the beginning of the ninth section of Psalm 119 and, in the Hebrew, is the first letter of each verse (Ps. 119:57–64).

Tetragrammaton (tet'rah-gram'ah-tahn; Gk., "four letters"), **the Sacred,** the designation for the four Hebrew consonants YHWH that comprise the name of Israel's God (Exod. 3:15; 7:2). The name itself was considered by the Hebrews as too holy to utter so the word "Lord" (Heb. *adonai)* was substituted when the text was read. The hybrid word "Jehovah" is a combination of the vowels of "Adonai" with the consonants of the tetragrammaton; its appearance in the KJV was the result of the translators' ignorance of the Hebrew language and customs.

tetrarch (te'trahrk), originally the title for "a ruler of a fourth" or "one of four rulers." In Hellenistic and Roman times, however, it is applied somewhat loosely to petty rulers of dependent states; a tetrarch is lower in status than an ethnarch, who, in turn, is lower than a king. The term occurs seven times in the NT, with three of these occurrences in Luke 3:1, where not only Philip and Herod Antipas, sons of Herod the Great, are mentioned but also the problematic Lysanias, tetrarch of Abilene. The other four occurrences refer to Herod Antipas (Matt. 14:1; Luke 3:19; 9:7; Acts 13:1). On the other hand, Herod Antipas is called "king" in Mark 6:14, 26, suggesting that some equivalence may have existed between the two titles. ***See also*** Ethnarch; Governor.

F.O.G.

Texts, Versions, Manuscripts, Editions

THE ORIGINALS of the books that comprise the Hebrew OT and the books of the Greek NT have not survived. We do, however, have very old copies of the original books, which are called "manuscripts" (MSS) because they were hand-written. Moreover, both OT and NT books were translated into other languages of the ancient Near East and copies of these early translations, called "versions" (VSS), are available to us. Through the science of textual criticism, biblical scholars have been able to establish rather accurate texts for both the OT and the NT books. These are available to us today in printed editions.

The Hebrew Text of the Old Testament

The Writing of the OT Books: An example of how an OT book came to be written can be found in Jeremiah 36. Baruch, the scribe of Jeremiah, recorded the spoken messages of the prophet (v. 4). When the king destroyed the original scroll (vv. 20–23), Baruch produced another scroll and added other prophetic messages to the original (v. 32).

The language spoken in Judah at the time was Hebrew, and with the exception of portions of Daniel and Ezra, which are in Aramaic, the books of the OT were written in Hebrew.

Hebrew, together with Canaanite, Moabite, Phoenician, and Ugaritic, belongs to the Northwest Semitic family of languages. The Hebrew alphabet, consisting of twenty-two consonants, can be traced back to about 1000 B.C. The shape of the letters underwent a process of change from the earlier cursive form to the boxlike shape called the "square script," which is known from pre-Christian times. This Northwest Semitic alphabet was taken over from the Phoenicians by the Greeks and with some adaptations is the alphabet of the Greek NT. This Greek alphabet became the progenitor of all European alphabets that have spread the world over.

Although other writing materials were known, parchment (made of leather) and papyrus (from the papyrus plant) were in wide use hundreds of years before the biblical books came to be written. Reed pens were used to write on these materials with ink made of soot mixed with a solution of gum.

The Transmission of the Hebrew Text: Until the discovery of the Dead Sea Scrolls (DSS) in 1947, the Hebrew MSS (other than the Nash Papyrus fragment) were dated no earlier than the ninth century A.D. The discoveries at Qumran, however, have pushed the MS tradition of the Hebrew Bible back a thousand years. One reason for the scarcity of early Hebrew MSS was the reverence with which the scrolls were held in Judaism. When MSS showed signs of wear and tear, they were disposed of. And since Jewish scribes exercised great care in copying the sacred books, they did not think that older copies had any advantage over new ones.

An example of writing in Aramaic, a language spoken from the ninth century B.C. and in common use during the first century A.D.; in the mosaic floor at Naaran synagogue.

Variant readings, however, did creep into the copies of the Hebrew books; this became a growing concern to Jewish rabbis, and by the end of the first century of the Christian era a kind of standard text emerged. At the end of the fifth century A.D., the scribal tradition, popularly traced back to Ezra, was continued by scholars known as Masoretes (literally Heb., "transmitters"), and because of their work on the text of the OT, our Hebrew Bible today is said to have the Masoretic Text (MT).

Scribes in the pre-Masoretic period had already made word and paragraph divisions in the Hebrew text (not to be confused with the chapter divisions of our Bibles today, which were introduced as late as the fourteenth century A.D.). The Masoretes, whose centers of activity were Babylonia and Tiberias, were bent on preserving the most accurate consonantal text possible. To prevent the misreading of the original consonantal text, they introduced vowel signs into the Hebrew Bible and thereby fixed the pronunciation of words. They left the original consonantal text unchanged, except for corrections and improvements, which they placed in the margin. The textual notes supplied by the Masoretes are called Masorah. After the Masoretic schools of Babylonia became defunct (prior to the tenth century A.D.), the Tiberian school continued its textual studies. Two families, Ben Asher and Ben Naphthali, vied with each other in transcribing and preserving the best Hebrew text on which the printed editions of the Hebrew Bible were later based. The Ben Asher tradition has generally been preferred by scholars.

MSS of the Hebrew Bible: Before the discovery of the DSS, the chief extant MSS of the Hebrew OT were: the Cairo Codex of the Prophets (A.D. 894); the Aleppo Codex of the entire OT (ca. A.D. 930); the Leningrad Codex (ca. A.D. 1008), which formed the basis of Rudolf Kittel's third edition of the Hebrew Bible; the British Museum Codex of the Pentateuch (first five books of the OT = Torah) (ca. A.D. 950); the Leningrad Codex of the Prophets (A.D. 1016); and the Reuchlin Codex of the Prophets (ca. A.D. 1105), which, unlike the others mentioned here, stands in the Ben Naphthali rather than the Ben Asher tradition. There are other MSS, some of them quite fragmentary, but these are the most important MSS of the OT in the Masoretic tradition. With the discovery of the DSS in the Judean desert in 1947 and following, we now have MSS a thousand years older than those just mentioned. The largest copies of OT books found in the caves at Qumran are two Isaiah scrolls (one complete, one incomplete). Fragments of over a hundred scrolls of OT books have been discovered at Qumran and Murraba'at on the western shore of the Dead Sea. The texts reflect some diversity of readings, but they also show a trend toward a standard Hebrew text.

The Printed Hebrew Bible: Jewish scholars faithfully transcribed the MT during the Middle Ages. With the invention of printing in the fifteenth century, however, Jewish printers in Italy began putting portions of the Hebrew OT into print. The entire OT was first published in Soncino in 1488. Rabbinic Bibles, which contained not only the biblical text but also Targums (translations of Hebrew OT books into Aramaic) and commentaries, were also put into print. The first such Bible was published by Daniel Bomberg of Venice, in 1416–17. This served as a base for the rabbinic Bible edited by Jacob ben Chayyim in 1524–25.

About 1520, Christian scholars began to publish the so-called polyglot Bibles, in which the Hebrew text was included as one column beside others in other languages. The Complutensian Polyglot, published in 1522, was prepared by Cardinal Ximenes and published in Spain. Other polyglots followed. The most massive was the London Polyglot (1654–57), which had not only the Hebrew text but the Samaritan Pentateuch, a Targum (Aramaic), the Septuagint (LXX; Greek), the Vulgate (Latin), the Peshitta (Syriac), and other versions.

A page from one of the OT volumes of the Complutensian Polyglot, 1522.

Bomberg's printed Bible enjoyed almost canonical status up to the twentieth century. Although other editions were published, it was only in 1937, when Rudolf Kittel published his third edition, that the ben Chayyim tradition was abandoned. Kittel's *Biblia Hebraica*, which became a kind of international standard, was based on the Leningrad Codex. Recently the *Biblia Hebraica Stuttgartensis* was published. It has made few changes in the text itself as Kittel published it but has improved the textual apparatus. Other printed editions of the Hebrew Bible are in the process of preparation.

The Versions of the OT

The Samaritan Pentateuch: This is, strictly speaking, not a version, but simply the Hebrew Pentateuch written in Samaritan letters. It arose out of the conflict between the Samaritan and the Jewish communities in the fifth century B.C. The Samaritans established their own place of worship at Shechem (now Nablus) and accepted the Pentateuch as their Bible. Since this Pentateuch was prepared long before the Hebrew text became standardized, it is an important witness to the early form of the OT text.

The Samaritan text differs from the MT in about six thousand places, but most of the variations are trifling, having to do with grammar and spelling. In some places it is closer to the DSS; in about sixteen hundred places it agrees with the Greek LXX. Although the Samaritan Pentateuch was known to some church fathers, it was not until A.D. 1616 that European scholars were able to obtain a copy of it. It was published for the first time in the Paris Polyglot Bible in 1632.

The most important copy of the Samaritan Pentateuch is the Nablus Scroll, still in the hands of the Samaritans. It probably dates from the early centuries of the Christian era. The standard printed edition of the Samaritan Pentateuch was published at Giessen, Germany, by A. von Gall in 1914–18 and is based on some eighty MSS. It was reprinted in Berlin in 1963. The Samaritan Pentateuch is an independent witness to the Hebrew text.

The Aramaic Targums: By the time the Jews returned from Babylon in the fifth century B.C., they had pretty nearly made the switch from Hebrew to Aramaic as their spoken language. The ancient Hebrew, however, remained the language of the sacred books. It became necessary, therefore, to translate the biblical text into Aramaic for those who attended the synagogue. These oral paraphrases were eventually put into writing and are called Targums (*targum* meaning "translation" or "paraphrase"). The Targums that have survived show either a Palestinian or a Babylonian provenance.

A complete MS of an Old Palestinian Targum of the Pentateuch

(Codex Neofiti I) was discovered in the Vatican Library as recently as 1957. In addition, there are the Jerusalem I and II Targums of the Pentateuch, wrongly ascribed to Jonathan and known, therefore, also as the Pseudo-Jonathan Targums. The official Targum of the Pentateuch took shape in Babylonia and is called Targum Onkelos. It dates from the second or third century A.D.

Several Targums of the Prophets are also available. The official Babylonian Targum of the Prophets is known as Targum Jonathan bar Uzziel. It was published in Leiden, the Netherlands, by A. Sperber (the Former Prophets, 1959; the Latter, 1962). The Targums of the third division of the Hebrew Bible, the Writings, reflect a greater diversity in style. There are Targums for most of the books in this division with the exception of Ezra, Nehemiah, and Daniel (parts of Ezra and Daniel are already in Aramaic). A Targum of the book of Job was discovered at Qumran. Some of the Targums of the Writings can hardly be called paraphrases, let alone translations; they are more like commentaries.

Some of the OT quotations in the NT are closer to the Targums than to the Hebrew original (see, e.g., Mark 4:12; Eph. 4:8).

The Greek Translations of the OT: *The Septuagint* VS. Greek-speaking Jews in the Diaspora (Dispersion) were in need of a Bible in Greek. In Alexandria, which had a large Jewish community, efforts were made to translate the Hebrew Scriptures into Greek. According to a tradition preserved in the Letter of Aristeas, the Egyptian Ptolemy Philadelphus, who ruled 285–246 B.C., sent a delegation to the high priest in Jerusalem who, in response, chose six men from each of the twelve tribes and sent them to Alexandria with a copy of the Hebrew Torah (the first five books of the OT). These men translated the Hebrew Pentateuch into Greek in seventy-two days. Other versions of this story add interesting details, but there is considerable doubt about the trustworthiness of some of these traditions. In any case, the translation got the name Septuagint, meaning "seventy." Perhaps because seventy elders accompanied Moses up the mountain to receive the Law it was only appropriate that the number should be rounded off to seventy (the symbol for the Septuagint, LXX, is seventy in Latin numerals).

As time went on, the Prophets and also the Writings were translated into Greek, and since different translators were involved, the style of the LXX is not uniform. By the time of Jesus ben Sirach (late second century B.C.), the LXX was completed.

The LXX contains not only the books of the Hebrew Bible but also the Apocrypha. Also, there are a number of passages that have been transposed by the LXX translators. The Psalms, for example, are rather scrambled. Job is considerably shorter in the LXX than in Hebrew. The unevenness of the style of the LXX may be due not only to the different translators but also to the fact that the Hebrew text they used differed somewhat from the later standardized text.

The LXX became the Bible not only of Greek-speaking Jews but also of the early Greek-speaking Christians. However, due to the controversies between church and synagogue and the emergence of a standardized Hebrew text about A.D. 100, the LXX lost its popularity in the Jewish community. The preservation of the LXX must then be credited to the Christian church. It is available in the great codices from the fourth and fifth centuries A.D.—Sinaiticus, Vaticanus, Alexandrinus, and others (see below under NT). The first printed edition of the LXX was published in 1522 in the Complutensian Polyglot Bible. In the English-speaking world, the edition of H. B. Swete, published at Cambridge (1887–94), became popular. Alfred Rahlfs, who edited the LXX published by the Württemberg Bible Society in 1935, knew of fifteen hundred complete and fragmentary MSS of the LXX. Several more have been discovered since. At present, a new edition of the LXX is being published in stages, known as the Goettingen Septuagint.

Revisions and Rival Versions of the LXX. Once the LXX had been renounced by the Jewish community, other translations emerged. Aquila of Sinope produced a slavishly literal translation of the Hebrew text into Greek (ca. A.D. 130). At the end of the second century A.D., Theodotion produced a very free translation of the Hebrew books into Greek. It became so popular that the church preferred his version of Daniel to that of the LXX. About A.D. 170 Symmachus prepared a Greek version of the OT. He tried to produce an idiomatic and accurate translation.

A revision of the LXX was undertaken by the famous Christian scholar Origen at the beginning of the third century. His monumental work is known as the Hexapla—a sixfold version of the OT. It was completed about A.D. 245. This massive work had the Hebrew text in the first column, the Hebrew text written in Greek letters in the second, Aquila's Greek version in the third, Symmachus' version in the fourth, a revision of the LXX in the fifth, and the Greek translation of Theodotion in the sixth column. The whole work ran to nearly seven thousand pages. Only fragments of the entire work are available in MS form. Fortunately, Origen's fifth column (i.e., the LXX) was recopied several times and is available in extant MSS. Moreover, his revised LXX was translated into Syriac before the Hexapla was lost in the Moslem conquests of the seventh century.

In the century following Origen, three editions of the LXX were published. Eusebius of Caesarea supplied Constantine with copies of the Bible that contained the fifth column of Origen's Hexapla. Also, Lucian of Samosata, who died a martyr's death in A.D. 311, undertook a revision of the LXX. A third edition of the LXX was prepared by Hesychius of Egypt. These different versions of the LXX tended to intermingle, and so it is somewhat difficult to establish the original form of the LXX.

No version of the OT has been so significant in the history of Bible translation as the LXX. Also, it was the text from which the NT writers, who wrote in Greek, quoted most often. Moreover, the translation of Hebrew words into Greek resulted in Greek words taking on Hebraic meanings, a fact of great significance for the interpretation of the NT. Thus, for example, "grace" came to mean God's benevolence, not simply human charm or pleasantness.

Other Ancient VSS: The OT was translated into many other languages in the early centuries of the Christian era. Since most of these VSS contain both OT and NT, they are discussed under the NT section. Suffice it to say here that the OT was translated into Latin, Syriac, Coptic, Ethiopic, Armenian, Georgian, and Gothic by the fifth century A.D., and into Slavonic and Arabic by the tenth.

Papyrus fragment from Egypt containing verses from John 18, the oldest extant manuscript of any part of the NT; early second century A.D.

The New Testament: Formation and Language

About the time when the text of the OT books was assuming standard form (first century A.D.), the books that were to constitute the NT were being written. Before the NT books were written, the teachings of Jesus circulated in oral form. It was standard practice in the ancient Near East to pass on traditions in oral form. With the expansion of the church into the Mediterranean world, the need for written material arose. By the end of the first century, most of the books of the NT had been written, and eventually twenty-seven such books comprised what Christians call the NT.

The copying of the original writings must have begun very early, for a fragment of John's Gospel circulated in Egypt early in the second century (P^{52}). Copying was done for both private and public use. In the process, errors tended to slip in, as can be seen from extant MSS.

By the time the NT books came to be written, Greek was the principal language of the Mediterranean world, although Latin was the official language of the Roman government. Greek is one of a number of languages that constitute the Indo-European family. Different dialects had been absorbed into the Greek language spread by the conquests of Alexander, producing a widespread dialect called Koine (Gk., "common"). The NT books were written in Koine Greek, the language of that day. There are also some Latinisms in the NT, since Latin was the official language of the government. Also, the vocabulary and style of the Greek NT have been strongly influenced by its Hebrew and Aramaic backgrounds.

The Character of the NT MSS

Scrolls and Codices: Some of our earliest copies of the NT are papyrus MSS. From the third century on, however, parchment became the standard writing material up to the age of printing (fifteenth century), when paper replaced both papyrus and parchment. Writing on papyrus or parchment was done "with pen and ink" (3 John 13). The ink was normally black or brown, although deluxe codices were at times written in silver or gold on fine parchment, called vellum. Red ink was not uncommon for titles, headings, and initial letters or lines.

The form of the NT books originally was that of a roll. The writing on these rolls was arranged in a series of columns. Finding passages

Mark 5:18–24 from the fifth-century Gothic Codex Argentius ("the Silver Codex") written on purple vellum in large letters of silver ink.

in rolls was not very convenient and so about the beginning of the second century the codex (the leaf-form of a book) came into use in the church.

Styles of Writing: Two basic types of writing style were in use: the cursive or "running" hand, which could be written more rapidly, and the more formal style, somewhat resembling our capital letters. MSS in this more literary style are called "uncials," those in the flowing hand are called "minuscules." NT MSS from the third to the sixth centuries are generally uncial; the minuscules are generally from a later period.

Palimpsests: Since parchment was costly, the original writing was at times scraped and washed off, the surface resmoothed and then used again. Such copies are called palimpsests (from two Greek words meaning "rescraped"). Of the 252 uncial MSS of the NT extant, 52 are palimpsests.

Helps for Readers: Some MSS of the NT provide helps for readers. There are, for example, chapter divisions (these divisions bear little relation to our present chapter divisions). These divisions often have headings (called *titloi* in Greek). Some scribes supplied information about the life of the author of the NT book or explained difficult words in the margins and between the lines. Some MSS are rich in Christian art. Since the NT books were read in worship, some have the beginning and end of the lessons clearly marked. In fact, a great many MSS are called "lectionaries," since they contain the lessons to be read during the church year.

Classification of NT MSS

Their Number: There are some five thousand complete or partial MSS of NT books available. To these must be added the thousands of copies of VSS of the Greek NT, which date from the early centuries of the Christian era. Also, there are numerous quotations of NT passages in the writings of the church fathers. Compared with the relatively small number of MSS of nonbiblical books from the ancient world, the NT is extremely well documented. The antiquity of some of the NT MSS is as impressive as the number.

Listing NT MSS: Before standard lists were universally accepted, it was often difficult to know where some of the MSS were located. Different systems of labeling or numbering added to the confusion. The standard list of Greek NT MSS was begun by C. R. Gregory, 1908, and his work has been superseded by the work of K. Aland, 1963.

MSS are classified on the basis of writing material. Papyrus MSS are listed separately from those made of parchment and are identified by a "P," followed by a superior number (P^{45}, for example, is a codex belonging to the Chester Beatty Papyri). Uncial MSS are commonly designated by the capital letters of the Latin and Greek alphabets. Since, however, the number of uncials exceeds the number of letters of the Latin and Greek alphabets, they also have an Arabic numeral assigned to them, preceded by a zero (the Vaticanus, for example, has the designation "B, 03"). Several uncial MSS are so important they also have names (Vaticanus, Alexandrinus, etc.). The minuscule MSS are referred to simply by Arabic numerals. Lectionaries are designated by the letter "l," followed by an Arabic numeral.

Significant Uncial MSS: Heading the list is the *Sinaiticus*. This codex was discovered after other uncials had already been assigned their

John 5:37–6:23 from the late fourth- (or early fifth-) century Codex Sinaiticus, discovered at the Monastery of St. Catherine, Sinai, by Constantine von Tischendorf.

letters of the alphabet, and since it was thought unwise to renumber the MSS, the Sinaiticus received the first letter of the Hebrew alphabet *(aleph)*. Where publishers do not use Hebrew characters, the letter "S" (Sinaiticus) is at times used to indicate this MS. It was discovered by the German scholar Constantine von Tischendorf in the middle of the nineteenth century in the monastery of St. Catherine at Mount Sinai and was eventually given to the Russian Czar Alexander II, patron of the Greek Orthodox Church. The British Museum purchased the MS in 1933. It contains both the OT and the NT in Greek. In addition to the twenty-seven books of the NT, it has two other early Christian writings, *The Shepherd of Hermas* and *The Epistle of Barnabas*. The text is written on vellum with four columns to the page. The date is late fourth (or early fifth) century.

The *Alexandrinus* dates from the middle of the fifth century. Evidently it came from Alexandria to Constantinople. In 1627, it came to England from Constantinople, and it lies next to the Sinaiticus in the British Museum. Originally it contained all of the OT (in Greek) and the NT, together with *1–2 Clement* and *The Psalms of Solomon*. However, most of Matthew is missing. It has two columns per page and is written on vellum with black ink. It was the first great uncial made accessible to scholars and so got the letter "A."

The *Vaticanus* comes from the fourth century and originally contained all the books of the Bible. Today some parts are missing. Missing are the NT books from Hebrews 9:14 onwards (including the Pastorals). Each page has three columns of text, written on fine vellum. Unfortunately a corrector has spoiled it somewhat by going over the original copy. It is in the Vatican library.

Codex *Ephraemi* is a fifth-century palimpsest. Someone erased the text of the NT in the twelfth century and wrote the sermons of Ephraim, the Syrian church father, over it. Tischendorf deciphered the biblical text behind the sermons and published his findings in 1845. Only 64 leaves of the OT (in Greek) are left. Of the NT, there are 145 leaves, containing portions of every book of the NT, except 2 Thessalonians and 2 John. The codex has only one column of text per page. It is in the National Library in Paris.

Codex *Bezae* is a bilingual MS of uncertain provenance, with the Greek page on the left facing the Latin page on the right. It contains only the Gospels (in the Western order: Matthew, John, Luke, Mark) and Acts. The text is written in "sense lines," which means that some are short and others are long. The first three lines of each NT book are in red ink. It was presented to Cambridge University by Theodore Beza, successor of John Calvin at Geneva, and so it is also called "Codex Cantabrigiensis." It comes from the fifth (possibly sixth) century and has a remarkable number of unique readings.

Minuscules: The minuscules are generally of a later date, but the date alone does not determine the value of a MS. When a copy is made from an early parent MS, the date of the parent MS rather than the date of the copy is what counts. There are almost three thousand minuscules (complete or partial) known to scholars today. Whereas most of them reflect a kind of fourth-century standard text, called Byzantine, some minuscules are in the Western or Alexandrian tradition.

Ancient Papyrus MSS: A great many secular papyri had been discovered in the sands of Egypt before any biblical texts on papyrus came to light. In 1931, Chester Beatty, an American who lived in Dublin, was able to purchase twelve MSS discovered in a graveyard in Egypt. These Chester Beatty Papyri, as they are now called, pushed the date of the earliest MS of the NT back to about A.D. 200 or 250.

Among the Chester Beatty papyri, P^{45} comprises portions of 30 leaves of a papyrus book that originally had about 220 leaves and contained all four Gospels and Acts. P^{46} comprises 86 leaves of the Pauline Letters. Portions of several Letters are lacking, and the pastoral Letters apparently were not included in the first place. P^{47} comprises 10 leaves of the book of Revelation.

Portions of Romans 15 and 16 from the Chester Beatty Biblical Papyrus II, from ca. A.D. 200–250.

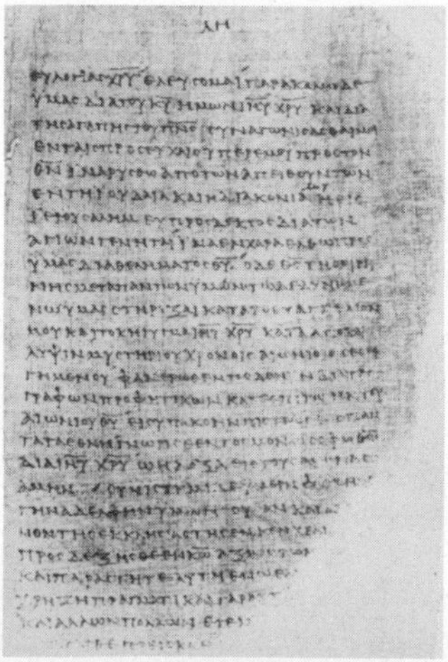

Since the purchase of the Chester Beatty Papyri, the most important addition to the collection of papyrus MSS was made by M. Martin Bodmer, of Geneva. In 1956, the discovery of Bodmer II, written about A.D. 200, was announced. This MS (P^{66}) contains a major portion of the Gospel of John. P^{72} was edited in 1959 and contains, among other things, the Letter of Jude and the two Letters of Peter, providing us with the oldest text of these writings. P^{75} is another early MS of Luke and John, dated between A.D. 175 and 225. This is our earliest copy of Luke's Gospel and one of the earliest of John.

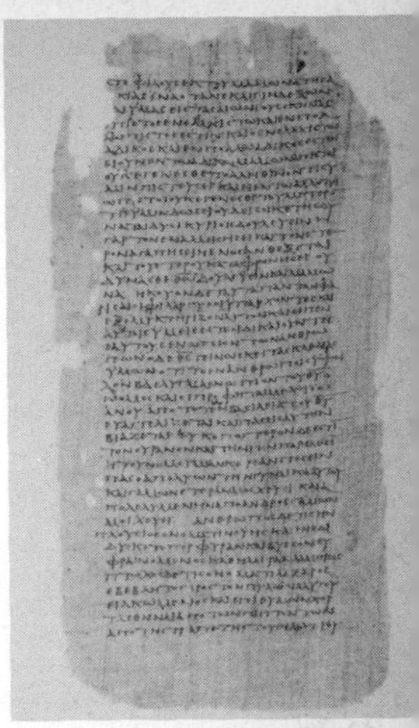

Luke 16:9–21 from Bodmer papyrus XIV (P^{75}), ca. A.D. 175–225.

Translations of the Greek NT

Early Eastern Versions: *The Syriac VSS.* One of the first efforts to render the Greek Gospels into Syriac was that of Tatian, who produced what has come to be called the *Diatessaron* (literally "through four," but in the sense of a "harmony of four parts"). Either before he left Rome, where he was a student of Justin Martyr, or after his return to his homeland in the Land of the Two Rivers (second century), he wove the four Gospels together into one continuous account. It came to be known in the East as the "mixed" Gospel. The whole work had some fifty-five chapters, and that suggests that the Diatessaron was designed to be read in the churches. The Diatessaron became very popular and was translated into a number of other languages (Persian, Arabic, Latin, Dutch, Medieval German, Old Italian, and Middle English). In 1933, a fragment of the Diatessaron in Greek was discovered and so there has been some debate on whether the "harmony" was made first in Greek and then translated into Syriac or whether it was made in Syriac to begin with.

For some time, the Diatessaron circulated side by side with other Syriac translations of the Gospels, known as the *Old Syriac VSS.* Little was known about ancient Syriac VSS until 1842, when a fragmentary codex of the four Gospels from the fifth century came to the British Museum with a mass of Syriac MS material. Dr. Cureton of the museum edited this codex and found it to be an Old Syriac VS of the Gospels. It is now called the "Curetonian Syriac." In 1892, a palimpsest MS of the four Gospels in Syriac was discovered in the Monastery of St. Catherine. It is now called the "Sinaitic Syriac." These Syriac texts take us back to the late second or early third century. Unfortunately, no MS of the Old Syriac VS for Acts and the Letters has yet been discovered, although we have quotations from these books in the Syriac church fathers. As time went on, the Old Syriac VS was superseded by the Peshitta.

The *Peshitta* (Syriac, "simple") was prepared in the early part of the fifth century and became the standard version of the Syriac church. It contains also the OT. The Pentateuch seems to have been translated in the second or third century A.D. Whether Jewish scholars were involved in the first attempts to translate the OT into Syriac is not altogether certain. In contrast to the LXX and the Latin Vulgate, the Peshitta originally omitted the Apocrypha. These books were added later. In its official form, the Peshitta included only twenty-two books of the NT. More than three hundred and fifty Peshitta MSS of the NT are available to scholars today.

In A.D. 509, Philoxenus, bishop in eastern Syria, asked a certain Polycarp to revise the Peshitta. His effort was in turn revised again in

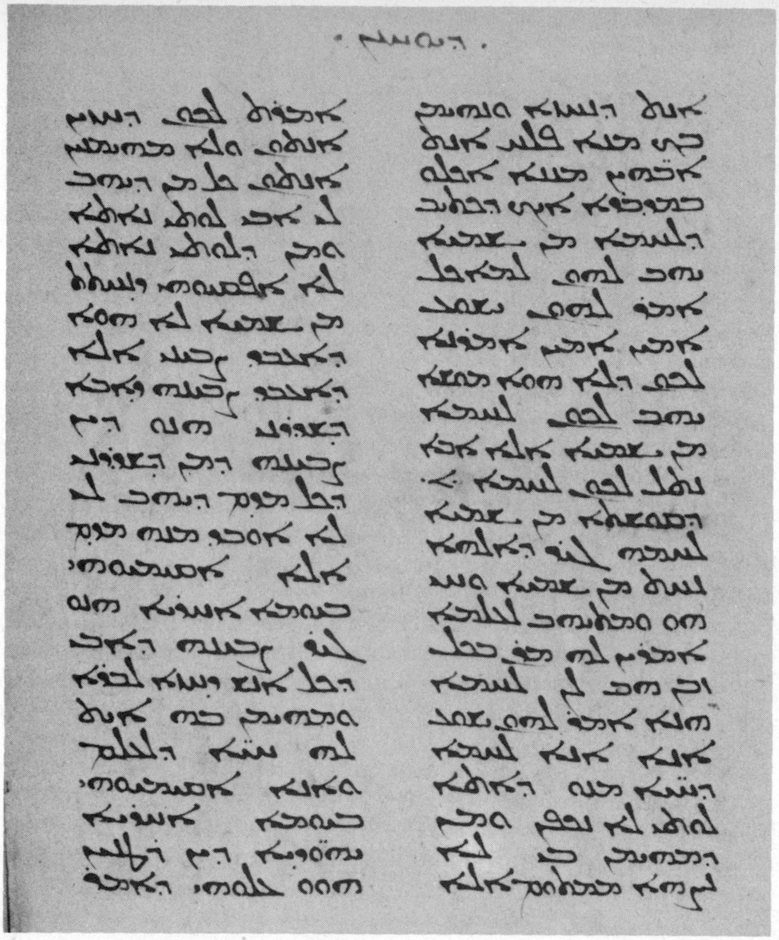

"Curetonian Syriac" version of John 6:30–41, fifth century A.D.

616 by Thomas of Harkel. These revised VSS include also the five books of the NT absent from the Peshitta. There is also the Palestinian Syriac VS in the Aramaic dialect of Christians in Palestine. It dates from the fifth century and is known chiefly from lectionaries of the Gospels, preserved in several MSS from the eleventh or twelfth centuries.

The Coptic VSS. Various dialects were spoken in Egypt in the early centuries of the Christian era. Outside of Greek-speaking Alexandria, Bohairic was the tongue of the common people. Farther up the Nile, Sahidic was spoken. Bohairic is the language of the Coptic church's liturgy to this day. About the beginning of the third century, portions of the NT were translated into Sahidic. The Bohairic VS appears to be somewhat later. Both VSS preserve some very interesting readings and are important witnesses to the NT text.

The Armenian VS. Since it is one of the most beautiful and accurate translations, it is sometimes called "the Queen of the Versions." With the exception of the Latin Vulgate, more MSS of this VS are extant than of any other early VS. Christianity came to Armenia in the third century and eventually the entire country became officially Christian. In the early part of the fifth century, an Armenian alphabet had been devised by Mesrop. Whether the translation was made from the Greek or from the Syriac is still a question of debate. The early Armenian VS seems to have undergone a revision in the eighth century.

The Georgian VS. Georgia lies between the Black Sea and the Caspian Sea, north of Armenia. Christianity came here in the fourth century. Again, an alphabet had to be devised before the NT could be translated into Georgian. The Gospels at least were translated as early as the middle of the fifth century. The majority view seems to be that the translation was made from the Armenian VS. Later it was revised and brought into closer conformity with the Greek text. The oldest Gospel MS in Georgian is the Adysh MS of A.D. 897.

The Ethiopic VS. There is some debate among scholars whether the Ethiopic VS dates as early as the fourth century or whether it comes from the sixth or seventh. Ethiopia had an alphabet long before the time of Christ. Christianity came to Ethiopia by the end of the fourth century and eventually the entire country became officially Christian. Whether the Old Ethiopic (known as Ge'ez) VS was based on a Greek or a Syriac original is not clear. It was revised later in the light of the Greek. The earliest MS available is a codex of the four Gospels from the thirteenth century.

Other Eastern VSS. The Bible was also translated into Arabic, Persian, and other Eastern languages, but they are too far removed from the first-century Greek NT to be of great help in establishing the text of the NT.

Early Western VSS: *Old Latin* VSS. As Latin came to be adopted as the language of the West, the need for a Latin Bible arose. It appears that the first attempts to render the Bible into Latin were made in the Roman province of Africa. During the third century, several Old Latin VSS circulated not only in North Africa but also in Europe. No codex of the entire Bible is extant, but a goodly number of MSS of the Gospels and Acts are available. The rest of the NT is not represented that well. Representing the African family, there is Codex Palatinus, a fifth-century MS of the Gospels, now at Trent. More important is Codex Bobiensis, now at Turin, containing about half of Matthew and Mark, representing a text that goes back to the second century.

Of the European family, the most outstanding is the fourth-century Codex Vercellensis, now at Vercelli in northern Italy. It is the most important MS of the Gospels in Old Latin next to Bobiensis. Codex Veronensis, stored at Verona, Italy, is a fifth-century codex, written in silver and occasionally gold letters on purple parchment. Codex Colbertinus comes from the twelfth century but has the Gospels in Old Latin. One of the largest MSS in the world is appropriately called "Gigas" (giant). Its pages are 20 × 36 inches. It was in Prague until it was moved to Stockholm in 1648. It contains the whole Bible in Latin, but only Acts and the book of Revelation are in Old Latin; the other books are from the Vulgate.

The Old Latin Bible was printed in several volumes at Oxford, beginning in 1883, and another series was begun in Rome in 1912. At the moment, an ambitious project is under way at the Monastery of

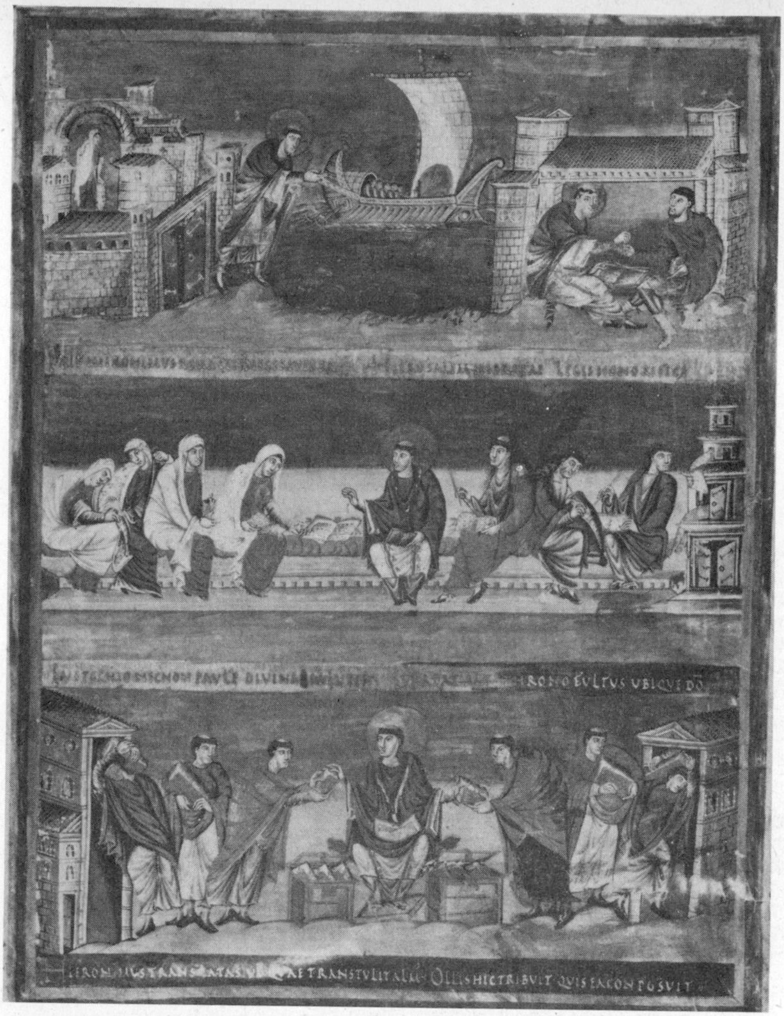

Jerome (ca. 331–420), translator of the Vulgate, leaves Rome for Jerusalem (top), works among scribes and students (middle), and distributes copies of his translation (bottom); from the ninth-century First Bible of Charles the Bald.

Beuron in Württemberg, Germany, to publish the most trustworthy Old Latin Bible to date.

The Latin Vulgate. Several forms of the Old Latin VS were in circulation in the fourth century. In A.D. 382, Pope Damasus asked the scholar Jerome to bring some order out of the chaos. Jerome began his work in Rome but later moved to Bethlehem. His revised Latin VS was not immediately accepted and for some time Old Latin and Vulgate VSS circulated side by side. Eventually, however, Jerome's version won out and got the name "Vulgate" (in the sense of "common" or "popular"). More than eight thousand MSS of the Vulgate are extant today.

It was inevitable, in the course of time, that Jerome's original Vulgate should be corrupted by errors in transmission. Several attempts were made, therefore, to purify the Vulgate text. About A.D. 800, Charlemagne engaged the famous British monk Alcuin to carry out a revision. In the thirteenth century, scholars at the University of Paris revised it, and this became the basis for the first printed Bible, produced by Gutenberg in 1456. When the Council of Trent decreed (1546) that the Latin Vulgate was to be regarded as the authoritative version, it was quickly recognized that the Vulgate had no one standard form and required a thorough revision once again. Out of such efforts emerged the Sixto-Clementine Vulgate in 1592, which became a kind of "authorized version" of the Roman Catholic church. A critical edition of the NT was published at Oxford beginning in 1890. Since 1907, Benedictine scholars have been working on a revision of the Latin Vulgate.

Among the most trustworthy MSS of the Vulgate are Codex Amiatinus (Florence), Codex Cavensis (Salerno), Codex Dublinensis (Book of Armagh, at Dublin), Codex Fuldensis (Fulda), the Lindisfarne Gospels (British Museum), Codex Sangallensis (St. Gall), and others.

The Gothic VS. Shortly after the middle of the fourth century, Ulfilas (meaning "Little Wolf"), a missionary among the Goths of the lower Danube, translated the Bible from Greek into Gothic. For this purpose he had to create an alphabet—primarily from Greek and Latin characters but also from Gothic runes—and reduce the language to a written form. He translated the OT from the standard Greek VS; for the NT Ulfilas used the Greek text that had established itself at Byzantium. It was a rather literal translation and is the earliest known literary monument in a Germanic dialect. Several fragmentary MSS of the Gothic Bible are available. The most complete is Codex Argentius ("the Silver Codex") from the fifth century, which is now in Uppsala, Sweden.

The Old Slavonic VS. About the middle of the ninth century, a Moravian Empire was formed in eastern Europe that professed Christianity. King Rostislav, in order to check the growth of Frankish influence from the West, in 863 asked that Slavonic-speaking priests be sent from Byzantium. Two brothers, Constantine (who later assumed the name Cyril) and Methodius, responded to the invitation. They devised a Slavonic alphabet and translated the Scriptures from Greek into Slavonic.

The Printed Greek NT

The First Printings: With the invention of printing, a new era dawned in the history of the transmission of the biblical text. The practice of copying MSS was discontinued and paper replaced parchment as writing and printing material. With the Renaissance and the Reformation, interest in the biblical languages was revived and this led to the printing of the Greek NT.

Cardinal Ximenes was the first to put the Greek NT into print in the Complutensian Polyglot Bible. This massive four-volume work came off the press in Spain in 1514, but ecclesiastical authorities delayed its publication. So it happened that Erasmus of Rotterdam was the first to publish a printed Greek NT in 1516. His first edition was a diglot, with the Greek column alongside his own translation of the Greek into Latin. Erasmus' Greek NT had a poor MS base, for he had only few MSS at his disposal and most of them were of a late date. He published five editions of the Greek NT. With minor changes, this text was published again and again during the next three hundred years. It came to be known as the Textus Receptus because of the claim in the

Greek NT published by the Elzevir brothers of Leiden in 1633 that this was the text received by all. It was essentially the text that had become a kind of standard in Antioch of Syria in the fourth century. For that reason, it is also known as the Anthiochian or Syrian text. And since this text became common in the Eastern church with its seat at Byzantium, it is also called the Byzantine text. It is this text that underlies the KJV.

The Search for a More Trustworthy Text: For the next two centuries, scholars put forth serious efforts to collect variant readings from the Greek MSS, the VSS, and the church fathers. With the discovery of new MS material in the nineteenth century, it became obvious that the Byzantine text did not represent the best and earliest form of the Greek NT. Through hundreds of years of copying, a great many variant readings had crept in. Some of these errors were made unintentionally, but others were made deliberately. Fortunately, no major doctrine is affected by these variant readings.

Copyists at times made mistakes because they wrote from dictation and the ear could not always distinguish clearly between some of the vowels and diphthongs. Other mistakes were made because the eye did not clearly distinguish between letters that looked alike or because a word or line was missed. Sometimes errors were made when the scribes carried over words or phrases from parallel passages they had stored away in their memory.

Occasionally, scribes tried to improve upon the text and wrote comments in the margins and these were at times incorporated into the text at a later stage. Scholars call them "glosses." Some changes involved the spelling of words; others reflect the tendency to bring one Gospel in line with another, or to bring OT quotations in the NT in line with their OT form. At times, copyists wanted to clear up a difficulty in the text for the reader or even altered a reading out of doctrinal or liturgical considerations.

The science of textual criticism began when scholars became aware of the multitude of variant readings in the MSS of the Greek NT. A number of seventeenth-century scholars did the spade work in the field of textual criticism. Important names to be mentioned in connection with this endeavor include John Fell (1625–86), John Mill

The scribe Ezra copying into a codex; from the Codex Amiatinus, A.D. 716.

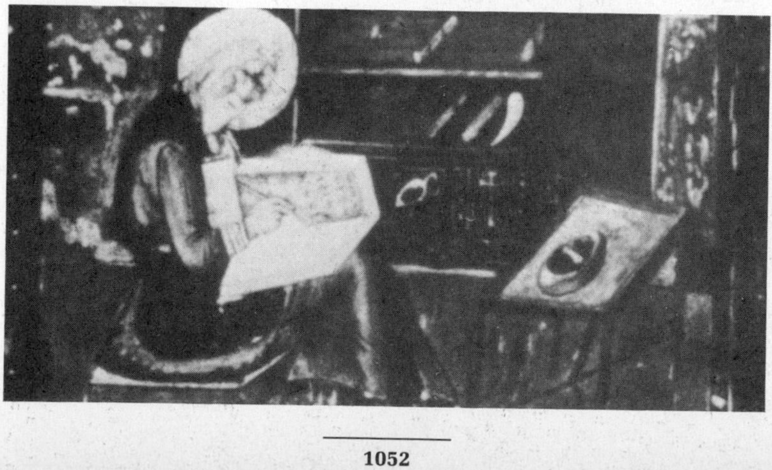

(1645–1707), Edward Wells (1667–1727)—all of Oxford; Richard Bentley (1662–1742) of Cambridge; J. A. Bengel (1687–1752), of Tübingen; and Jakob Wettstein (1693–1754), a native of Basel. The foundations of a more scientific approach in textual criticism were laid by J. J. Griesbach (1745–1812) who, on the basis of his study of the Greek MSS, the VSS, and the church fathers, isolated three larger families (i.e., texts related to one another) in the textual transmission of the NT: Alexandrian, Western, and Byzantine. Also, he laid down some fifteen rules of textual criticism, many of which hold even today.

In the nineteenth century, scholars like Charles Lachmann (1793–1851), Constantine von Tischendorf (1815–74), and S. P. Tregelles (1813–75) helped to overthrow the rule of the Textus Receptus. The most noteworthy edition of the Greek NT at the end of the nineteenth century (1881) was published by the Cambridge scholars B. F. Westcott and F. J. A. Hort. One weakness in their approach was that they put too much stock in the Sinaiticus and Vaticanus, which they called the "neutral text" (in the sense of "uncontaminated by error"). Conversely, they had too negative a view of the Byzantine text. As scholarly studies continued and new MS material came to light (even as late as the middle of the twentieth century), Westcott and Hort's approach had to be modified.

Today, many scholars argue that one cannot simply follow the readings of those Greek MSS, VSS, and church fathers that belong to one or the other textual family, whether this be Alexandrian, Western, Byzantine, or Caesarean (not all accept the latter as a distinct family). Every reading has to be weighed and considered on its own merits. This is sometimes called the "eclectic" method. In studying variant readings, the age of the text is more important than the age of the MS. Readings supported by ancient witnesses, especially when these come from a wide geographical area, are generally preferred. The quality, not the quantity, of MSS is the determining factor in choosing a reading. Also, the shorter reading is usually preferred, for scribes tended to add or expand. Moreover, the more difficult reading is usually correct, since copyists tended to ease difficult readings. In parallel texts (i.e., the Gospels), differences in readings are generally preferred, for there was a tendency to harmonize parallel passages. The reading from which the other variant readings seem to be derived is likely to be correct. These rules (and others) help the textual critic to weigh the evidence and to determine what seems to be the correct reading.

In 1966, after a decade of work by an international committee, the United Bible Societies published an edition of the Greek NT for Bible translators and students. The third edition of this text was published in 1975, and is at present the best text available.

See also A; Aleph; Aramaic; B; Canon; Codex; Dispersion; Greek, New Testament; Hebrew; Ink; Latin; Oxyrhyncus; Paper; Papyrus; Samaritans; Scroll; Scrolls, The Dead Sea; Semites; Septuagint; Sources of the Pentateuch; Writing.

Bibliography

Metzger, Bruce M. *The Early Versions of the New Testament.* Oxford: Clarendon, 1977.

______. *The Text of the New Testament.* 2d ed. New York: Oxford University Press, 1968.

Wuerthwein, E. *The Text of the Old Testament.* Grand Rapids, MI: Eerdmans, 1979.

D.E.

textual criticism. ***See*** Biblical Criticism; Texts, Versions, Manuscripts, Editions.

Thaddaeus (thad'ee-uhs), one of the twelve apostles as identified in two of the apostolic lists (Matt. 10:3; Mark 3:18). In the other lists, however, "Judas, the son (or brother) of James," appears instead of "Thaddaeus" (Luke 6:16; Acts 1:13). Variant readings in Matthew have "Lebbaeus," and the KJV reads "Lebbaeus, whose surname was Thaddaeus." "Lebbaeus," however, does not appear in the best texts and is omitted in most translations. Resulting explanations include: (1) Thaddaeus, Judas, and Lebbaeus are the same person; (2) the lists in Luke and Acts reflect a change in the apostles; and (3) tradition has preserved the fact that Jesus had an inner group of trusted followers (the Twelve) and has retained the names of most of the members of this group but not without slight variations. The second explanation appears unlikely. The third is plausible in light of the fact that the Gospel traditions were transmitted within different communities, making some variation far from surprising. Those who argue that Thaddaeus and Judas are the same person still question his identification with the author of the Letter of Jude. Post-biblical traditions supply additional information about Thaddaeus, but this is of questionable value. ***See also*** Apostle; Disciple; Judas; Jude, The Letter of; Twelve, The. P.L.S.

thank offering. ***See*** Worship.

Tharshish. ***See*** Tarshish.

theater (Gk. *theatron,* a "place for seeing"), an area suited to public presentations. The theater developed out of ancient Greek religious rituals involving song and dance. Its heart was a circular section of flat, hard earth, the orchestra, on which the dancing took place. The theater was located on a convenient hillside, in many Greek cities on the hill upon which the acropolis (Gk., "high city") was built. If necessary the flat space for the orchestra could be created by terracing into the hill. Sometimes the site was one traditionally sacred to the god Dionysus in whose honor the theatrical competitions were held.

Until Hellenistic times the scene building (Gk. *skēnē*) was a simple tent, booth, or hut that served as a background for the performance. If a stage was added it was a simple platform. The orchestra might be marked by stone slabs or a water channel. Seating, which went somewhat farther around the orchestra than a semicircle, was created by hollowing out the slope in the middle and banking it up at the ends, which widened out to give those seated there a better view and to make it easier to exit from the theater. The ends were held up by retaining walls above the passages on either side that led to the auditorium. The seating area was divided by one or two horizontal passages and cut by radiating stairways. Seats were cut out of native rock or made of stone slabs. One or two rows of specially ornamented and carved seats in the front of the theater were reserved for priests and public officials. The audience probably brought cushions to the theater to sit on.

Nothing separated the audience from the or-

The remains of the Greek theater at Gebal, modern Jebail, on the Mediterranean coast of Lebanon.

chestra so that the audience might feel itself included in the action of the tragic drama. In comedy the actors or the chorus could approach the audience across the orchestra and speak directly to individuals.

In Hellenistic times more permanent scene buildings with a stage added were constructed. Pillars or columns and panels might be used in the front of the stage building. The Romans joined the ends of the auditorium to the scene building, which thereby reduced the shape of the auditorium to a semicircle. They also began to replace the hard, flat earth with ornamental stone paving. Having mastered the technique of vaults and arches, the Romans were able to build theaters just about anywhere.

Romans preferred gladiator shows, beast fights, and other spectacles to drama. They added walls around the orchestra in Greek theaters to accommodate such entertainments. Popular performances consisted of comedies or farces with stock characters and mimes or clown burlesques. The more serious comedies and tragedies written during the Roman period, such as those by Nero's mentor Seneca, were not written to be performed but to be read.

Theaters in Hellenistic cities also served as gathering places for political events or criminal prosecutions. In the riot in Ephesus caused by Paul's Christian preaching, two of his companions were dragged into the theater to be dealt with (Acts 19:28–41). P.P.

Thebes. ***See*** No.

Thebez (thee'biz), a city near Shechem, part of the sphere of control of Abimelech, the son of Gideon (Judg. 9). Like Shechem, Thebez had a *migdal*, often translated "strong tower," but better "fortress-temple of the Strong One" (i.e., the deity El). Here Abimelech met his death (Judg. 9:50–54, remembered in 2 Sam. 11:21). Thebez is often associated with modern Tubas, twelve miles by road north-northeast of Shechem; archaeological evidence would then commend Khirbet edh-Dhuq a mile north of Tubas. Also plausible is an identification with Tirsah, four miles nearer Shechem. Certainty about the location is not yet possible, however. ***See also*** Abimelech; Migdal; Shechem; Tirzah.

theft. ***See*** Robbery.

Theodotus (thee-ah'duh-tuhs). ***See*** Synagogue.

theology, New Testament, the study of the theological views expressed or presupposed in the various writings in the NT.

Early History of the Discipline: NT theology as a discipline originated in German Lutheranism, and NT theologies have been produced mainly by Germans. After the Reformation, Protestant dogmaticians had been accustomed to draw up lists of proof texts from Scripture to support their dogmatic statements. With the rise of Pietism toward the end of the seventeenth century and with the accompanying revolt against the use of nonbiblical and philosophical concepts in dogmatic theology, theologians began to produce theologies based directly and solely on Scripture ("biblical theology").

At first, biblical theologies were organized under doctrinal topics as in dogmatic theology (e.g., God, creation, incarnation, redemption, Holy Spirit, church, and last things). But the rise of the historical-critical method in the study of the Bible had far-reaching consequences both for the organization of NT theologies and for the conception of the task. First, biblical theology was divided into "biblical theology of the OT" and biblical theology of the NT." Second, NT theologies came to be separated from OT theologies and were organized according to the historial development of NT thought and to the (critically established) chronological order of the NT writings and groups of writings. Thus a NT theology would begin with Jesus, then go on to Paul, to John, and to the later NT writings. Third, a growing realization that the NT documents were conditioned by the times and circumstances in which they were written led to an increasing historicization of the discipline. Instead of setting out a normative theology for contemporary preaching, NT theologies became more and more descriptions of the history of NT religion and thought. Fourth, this led to inclusion of other early Christian writings within the treatment, such as the Apostolic Fathers. The full development of this process was reached in an essay on the task and methods of NT theology by William Wrede in 1897.

In 1909 Adolph Schlatter published a programmatic essay in which he sought to restore NT theology as a theological discipline. Schlatter advocated the restoration of the link between thought and life, and intended NT theology not to be merely descriptive but to have a normative relation to the church's contemporary faith and proclamation.

The Bultmann Thesis: Rudolf Bultmann published a monumental two-volume NT theology in 1951–54 in which he sought to combine the concerns of Wrede and Schlatter. Bultmann presented parts of the NT, like Wrede, in a purely historical and descriptive manner. These parts were: Jesus' message, the earliest church, the Hellenistic community aside from Paul, and the later NT writings aside from John. Then, like Schlatter, Bultmann presented the theologies of Paul and the Johannine writings as normative for faith, interpreting them anthropologically and existentially, i.e., as expressions of human self-understanding. This self-understanding of faith Bultmann intended to be appropriated in the proclamation of the Christian message today.

The Post-Bultmannians: In the hands of Bultmann's pupils, the Bultmannian synthesis has progressively disintegrated. Dissatisfaction was felt with Bultmann's handling of the historical or earthly Jesus. In some thirty pages he had presented Jesus' message merely as *one* of the presuppositions of the NT proclamation rather than as a constitutive part of it. He had emphasized the gap between Jesus and the earliest preaching after Easter. The Proclaimer became the Proclaimed: Jesus had preached the Kingdom of God; the early church preached him. This appeared to expose the early Christian message to the danger of becoming a mythology or at best a myth hung upon the "mathematical point" of the cross.

What made the cross the saving event it appeared to the post-Bultmannians was the prior career and intention of Jesus himself, and therefore an enquiry into Jesus was seen to be crucial and integral to NT theology. That enquiry, of course, was to be critically conducted, using rigorously all the methods of source, form, and redaction criticism. But enough could be known of the historical Jesus (his preaching of the Kingdom, his teaching about God's demand and about God as Father, his conduct in performing exorcisms, and his eating with the outcasts) to provide adequate continuity between Jesus and the post-Easter church. None of Bultmann's pupils who have taken this line has written a NT theology. The only NT theology to emanate from the post-Bultmannian school (Hans Conzelmann, English translation 1968) went to the other extreme and subsumed the historical Jesus under the synoptic Gospels, as the first layer of the synoptic tradition.

Herbert Braun went to a different extreme in a discussion of the problems of a NT theology. Taking off from Bultmann's anthropological interpretation of Paul and John, Braun reduced the whole Christian message as given in the NT to a human sense of obligation and enablement ("I ought" and "I can"), providing thereby a German version of the "Death of God" theology. For Braun, the Christology of the NT was variable, the anthropology constant. This was a laudable attempt to secure the unity of the NT, but it eliminated the Christ event as a saving act of God from its central place in the NT and turned NT theology upside down.

Bultmann has also been criticized by others within his own school and outside it for narrowing the scope of the Pauline message by an exclusive emphasis on its anthropological-existential aspect. This is to ignore the apocalyptic framework of early Christianity, continued by Paul, which gives the early Christian message a social, historical, and cosmic dimension. Paul was not exclusively concerned with individual salvation. These insights have provided contemporary relevance to the Pauline message in the current theologies of hope and of liberation.

Yet another important issue within NT theology, which was first put forward by Bultmann and which has received discussion within the post-Bultmann school, is the problem of "early catholicism" in the NT. By early catholicism is meant the development of institutional features in the subapostolic age (i.e., A.D. 70–125) such as an incipient canon of Scripture, creedal formulae, an ordained as opposed to a charismatic form of ministry, liturgical and catechetical forms. This institutionalization was a response to the delay of the Parousia (i.e., Christ's second coming) and a consequent realization that the church was here to stay, and also to the death of the original apostolic witnesses. Among the post-Bultmannians, Ernst Käsemann, in a series of essays (English translation 1964, 1967) has offered a negative assessment to these developments, thus posing the question of a "canon within the canon." The canon within the canon is here held to be the Pauline message of justification through faith alone. Judged by this, at least some of the early catholic developments are seen to be questionable.

Alternatives to Bultmann: Outside the Bultmann school, one German Catholic scholar (Karl Schelke, 1968–70) and one Anglican (Alan Richardson, 1958) have published NT theologies organized on the old dogmatic concept principle. The dangers are that the varieties within the NT theology will be minimized and that premature harmonization may occur. Richardson has laid particular stress on church, ministry, and sacraments.

A more viable alternative to Bultmann is the "salvation-historical" approach. In a series of works (English translation 1946–65), Oscar Cullmann presented a salvation-historical interpretation of NT theology as a deliberate alternative to Bultmann's anthropological-existential interpretation. For Cullmann, Christ was the mid-point in time (time is here conceived as a linear process—a view that is really characteristic of Luke-Acts and that is questionably extended to the whole of the NT). Joachim Jeremias (English translation 1971) structured his NT theology in terms of call and response, the message of Jesus being the call, the message of the early church the response. Unfortunately, Jeremias lived to complete only the first volume, the call, and never completed the second volume, which was to have contained the response.

The difficulty with this organization is that it gives too much weight to the historical Jesus. In the bulk of the NT writings, the message of Jesus as such plays only a minor role (cf. the small number of direct quotations of Jesus' sayings in the Pauline Letters). Rather, the NT writings are for the most part a response to the death and resurrection of Jesus. Werner Georg Kümmel (English translation 1973) dealt selectively with the "chief witnesses" of NT theology, namely Jesus, Paul, and John. It is curious to find Jesus included among the "witnesses" to NT theology. Jesus, at least his cross and resurrection, would seem to be rather its primary datum.

The fourth representative of the German-speaking salvation-historical school was Leonhard Goppelt, whose two-volume NT theology appeared posthumously (English translation 1981, 1982). Unlike Bultmann but like Jeremias, Goppelt devoted his first volume exclusively to the historical Jesus. But Jesus was dealt with not as one of the presuppositions, nor as the call, nor as one of the principal witnesses, but as *the essential* presupposition of NT theology. NT theology proper comes in Goppelt's second volume, which dealt with the variety and unity of the apostolic witness. Here the apostolic message of the death and resurrection of Jesus was seen to be the central focus of NT theology.

Among the few American NT theologies, mention should be made of that by George Eldon Ladd (1974), a conservative evangelical. This work was notable for the fact that it treated the Gospels (including the Fourth Gospel) as sources for the historical Jesus and had no section on the theology of the Evangelists—the opposite procedure to that of Conzelmann.

The Problems of NT Theology: Since the rise of the historical-critical method, NT theologies are best organized on historical rather than dogmatic lines; otherwise the diversity of the NT is obscured. This, however, raises the problem of the unity behind the diversity. To find it, as Bultmann did, in the self-understanding of the believer is to subjectivize and individualize the NT message and to shortcut its historical, social, and cosmic dimensions.

Rather, the center of unity must be found in the apostolic proclamation of the salvation-historical event of Jesus Christ, specifically his death and resurrection. That death and resurrection acquire their significance, however, from the message and intention of Jesus himself; thus a continuity between Jesus' preaching of the Kingdom of God and the post-Easter kerygma (proclamation) has to be established—otherwise the kerygma is in danger of becoming a mere myth.

The nature and role of the Easter event also requires thorough explanation. If it is merely the disciples coming to faith in the redemptive significance of the cross (Bultmann), or if it is merely the continuation of the historical Jesus' offer of salvation (Willi Marxsen, E. Schillebeeckx), it is in danger of being evacuated of its positive NT content, which is the proclamation that God raised Jesus from the dead. The synoptic, Pauline, and Johannine theologies all require separate treatment and have to be demonstrated as legitimate variations on the central apostolic kerygma. For this reason, it would seem inappropriate to designate the Pauline message of justification as *the* center of NT theology (Käsemann), for it is only *one* of the contingent expressions of the NT and even of Pauline theology, devised for the concrete situations that confronted Paul in Galatians, Romans, and Philippians 3.

The subapostolic writings of the NT (deutero-Paulines, i.e., 2 Thessalonians, Colossians, Ephesians, and the pastoral Letters; plus 1 and 2 Peter, James, and Jude, and possibly, though debatably, Acts and Hebrews) require special handling as writings that in various degrees reflect features of early catholicism. It must be asked: to what extent and in what way are these documents and their institutional features normative for the proclamation, confession, and practice of the contemporary church? Are we to postulate, as Käsemann did, a canon within the canon, rejecting these later NT documents as degenerations from earlier NT and especially from original Pauline Christianity? Another problem area with the canon is the restriction of NT theology to these particular books and the exclusion of other early Christian literature, e.g., the *Didache*, *1 Clement*, and the Letters of Ignatius. Some of these writings may be earlier than some of the later writings within the NT canon (e.g., 2 Peter). How then can we claim that these writings and only these writings (i.e., the canon) enshrine the normative apostolic witness? The answers to these various questions will determine what kind of NT theology will be written in the future. ***See also*** Biblical Criticism; Church; Gospel, Gospels; Hermeneutics; Jesus Christ; John, The Gospel According to; Luke, The Gospel According to; Mark, The Gospel According to; Matthew, The Gospel According to; Paul; Resurrection.

Bibliography

Dunn, J. D. G. *Unity and Diversity in the New Testament*. Philadelphia: Westminister, 1977.

Hasel, G. F. *New Testament Theology: Basic Issues in the Current Debate*. Grand Rapids, MI: Eerdmans, 1978.

Neill, S. C. *The Interpretation of the New Testament 1861–1961*. London: Oxford University Press, 1964.

Morgan, R. *The Nature of New Testament Theology*. London: SCM, 1973.

R.H.F.

theology, Old Testament.

Defining the Task of OT Theology: The rise of OT theology as a discipline distinct from dogmatic theology did not occur until the eighteenth century A.D. Until then, all theology was considered to be biblical, or, stated somewhat differently, the distinction between dogmatic theology and biblical theology was not grasped. The Bible was understood as the repository of the very truth that the theologians sought to delineate in a systematic manner. The Bible was thus the basis for the theological enterprise, and no tension was perceived between biblical faith and contemporary formulations.

The Enlightenment introduced an important change. In applying the same literary and historical tools that had been used since the Renaissance in the study of the ancient Greek and Latin classics, biblical scholars began to discover characteristics in the biblical writings that seemed distinct or even quite alien in relation to the doctrines of the church. Some of them began to insist on freedom from ecclesiastical authorities in their attempts to bring to light the true nature of the biblical writings. On the basis of this new perspective, most university-trained biblical scholars of the nineteenth century preferred to write histories of the religion of Israel rather than OT theologies. Adding further impetus to this development was a series of very important archaeological discoveries (e.g., Code of Hammurabi, the *Enuma elish*, and the Tell el-Amarna tablets) that drew attention to the place of Israelite religion within the cultural horizon of the ancient Near East.

The twentieth century has witnessed renewed interest in biblical theology and the concern to delineate the qualities that are unique to the faith of Israel, without denying, to be sure, the important connections established by the previous generations of scholars between Israelite religion and the religions of neighboring nations. What is most important to recognize, however, is that the legacy of the Enlightenment is evident in all contemporary endeavors to describe the theology of the OT: the OT does not present a systematic theology, but rather a rich diversity of writings addressing various historical, ethical, and social problems from theological perspectives often quite different from one another. These writings arose over a period of more than one thousand years, and in many cases subsequent generations altered and amplified the received material so as to apply it to their changed circumstances. The task of OT theology is to present the origin, nature, and history of transmission of these writings as accurately as possible so as to give a clear delineation of the beliefs to which they give witness and of the communities within which they arose.

Given the complexity of the data, it is not surprising to discover that unanimity does not prevail among OT theologians on the question of methodology. Some insist that it is the task of the biblical theologian to give as objective a description of the theological views of the biblical writings and the communities within which they were produced as possible, so as not to obscure the unique contribution of the Bible to contemporary faith. The task of translating those views into contemporary statements of faith is kept quite distinct and normally assigned to another discipline, carried on especially by the systematic theologian. Others protest that the theological meaning of the biblical writings cannot be grasped by such a dispassionate approach; the depths and subtleties of Israelite religion can be understood and represented only by one personally acquainted with the language of faith and involved in the decisions and actions arising out of faith. They accordingly do not distinguish as rigidly between "descriptive" and "constructive" or "normative" aspects of biblical study.

It is well and good that scholars differ in the extent to which they move in their theological treatment of the OT toward the task of translating the meaning of the ancient texts into contemporary language and concerns, for the task of elucidating the theological meaning of the biblical writings is multifaceted and complex. In fact, it is not unusual for the same scholar to weigh the descriptive and normative aspects of theological study differently in different works. While it would be counterproductive to try to define the extent to which contemporary concerns are legitimate in a work of OT theology, two lessons from past scholarship should not be forgotten.

The first lesson is that the deep grounding of Israelite faith in historical events establishes as an essential facet of OT theology a thorough delineation of the specific context within which each of those writings arose and the light shed by that context on its meaning. The contribution of this descriptive task to the meaning of biblical theology is too great to justify any tendency to move back to a preliterary critical or historical method of study. And it is a fallacy to assume that we are somehow immune to the type of prejudices that led previous generations of scholars to interpret Moses or Jesus in such a way as to produce a reflection of their own cultural values or political ideologies. Careful linguistic, historical, and comparative study must provide the foundation upon which all responsible biblical theology is built, for unless the biblical writings are appreciated in their cultural and historical specificity, no matter how alien that specificity strikes our modern senses, it is difficult to see how they will be freed to address us and to challenge our perception of reality.

The second lesson acts as a counterbalance for the first and arises from the justifiable criticism that the nineteenth-century works on the history of the religion of Israel, while contributing much to our understanding of the background of the Israelite cult, did not give an adequate picture of the theological beliefs of the communities and individual writers coming to expression in the OT. It seems fair to observe that a full treatment of the theology of the OT requires more than detached objectivity.

While indeed requiring the restraints on subjectivity to which scientific methodology is dedicated, the very nature of the subject calls for the kind of in-depth understanding that is best fostered by personal theological concern and commitment. To this defense of commitment as compatible with honest scholarship may be added the now universally recognized fact that no scientific investigation is without presuppositions; indeed, investigations in every field are guided by assumptions and hypotheses that structure the inquiry or experiment. It therefore seems advisable to apply the term "history of the religion of Israel" to studies that are defined as strictly descriptive in nature, recognizing that studies falling under the rubric of biblical theology, while based upon careful description and critical assessment of all available data, will also be engaged in understanding the inner theological dynamics of the biblical writings, with an eye to their contemporary applications.

This distinction should not imply antagonism or competitiveness between the two disciplines but can be appreciated as a way of clarifying the specific tasks of each as well of the nature of their interrelationship. While biblical theology will be guided by the kinds of criteria proper to any theological endeavor, it will draw deeply on the results of the history of the religion of Israel, especially in light of the fact that the attribution of religious significance to the historical realm is one of the hallmarks of biblical faith. In like manner, the primarily theological orientation of OT theology will not inhibit the utilization of yet other disciplines, such as the archaeology of the biblical lands, sociology, and anthropology. For example, valuable light has been shed on the earliest period of the Israelite religion by social anthropology, even as aspects of the prophetic and apocalyptic movements coming to expression in the Bible are now more clearly understood through the application of tools derived from the sociology of knowledge. The relation of biblical theology to such disciplines can be summed up thus: since it is a basic claim of biblical faith that God is known through the events of history and the experiences of the community of faith, any discipline capable of advancing our understanding of the historical and social contexts within which the writings of the Bible arose will be regarded as a valued ally.

The Starting Point of Biblical Theology: We have already observed that every scholarly endeavor inevitably is based upon presuppositions. This is already true on the level of the descriptive task with which OT theology begins. For example, a scholar who accepts Ernst Troeltsch's "analogy principle" (i.e., to be credible, a happening recorded in a historical source must have parallels in modern experience) will dismiss all reconstructions of the Exodus from Egypt or the resurrection of Jesus, which defy explanation within the nexus of cause and effect as understood by modern science, whereas others may not be thus bound. What is to be expected of every scholar, however, is that the presuppositions operative in his or her methodology be stated as honestly and as clearly as possible.

When the biblical theologian moves toward the exposition of the contemporary meaning of the biblical writings, the role of presuppositions takes on an even greater significance, determining both the questions brought to the text and to a large extent the nature of the answers found in the text. A contrast between two approaches will illustrate how determinative is the role of presuppositions in the interpretation of biblical texts.

On the one hand, there are some biblical theologians who insist that the basic data of biblical theology is what actually happened in antiquity, the so-called *bruta facta* observable to any witness, regardless of that witness's religion or world-view. They can be quite insistent that the special faith perspective of the biblical writers is to be set aside in the endeavor to establish the data base of biblical theology. On the other hand, many argue that the most significant history for the theologian is Israel's account of God's saving acts, that is to say, interpreted history, or history seen by the "eyes of faith." Clearly, the assessment of the biblical documents and the relative weight ascribed to disciplines like Near Eastern archaeology will differ on the two sides of this question. Once again, any biblical theologian should state clearly for her or his audience or readership the presuppositions guiding the particular study.

The study of the history of biblical theology readily illustrates how OT theologians, like their contemporaries in other fields of thought, have been influenced by the dominant ideas of their historical and cultural setting. Throughout the nineteenth century, for example, the imprint of Hegelian idealism can be seen on the pages of German biblical works. In our own century, the thought of the philosopher Martin Heidegger has been a strong factor in a whole school of NT scholarship. Foremost in that school is Rudolf Bultmann, who found in existential philosophy the means by which the essential message of the NT could be ascertained, namely, in terms of the self-understanding coming to expression in the Christ of faith and in human history. Because the basic this-worldly orientation of the OT did not seem to offer vivid illustrations of the turning away from the material world to the world of the spirit, Bultmann viewed the OT largely in a negative light as exemplifying a "miscarriage" of the divine promise. We can also detect here the influence of the law/gospel dichotomy that has played a major role in much Lutheran biblical theology.

What lessons can be learned from the history of the relationship between contemporary philosophy and the biblical theologian? Since presuppositions are inevitable and philosophy is in part the attempt to identify and describe presuppositions, it would be naive to claim that what may be perceived as excessive influence of certain philosophical movements upon theology could be corrected by an approach to biblical theology that rejects all input from philosophy. Rather, it seems that the proper attitude should be analogous to that described above in relation to historical criticism or the social sciences: philosophy should be regarded as a source of conceptual tools enabling the biblical theologian to gain a more adequate understanding of the meaning of the biblical writings. But again here a balance must be struck, lest the tools begin to generate their own meaning. The Bible, in other words, should not become a resource for illustrating the tenets of a given philosophical system. On the other hand, philosophical ideas may legitimately aid in the task of clarifying the intrinsic meaning of the biblical writings. This intricate balance can be illustrated in relation to the philosophical notions originating with Alfred North Whitehead. Especially as they have been developed by Charles Hartshorne, process ideas in many cases can be shown to have such close affinities with notions found at the center of OT thought that the former become a useful means of probing the theological meaning of the latter. On the other hand, when the primary commitment of a scholar is centered in process philosophy, the danger that biblical notions will be forced into an interpretation at the cost of their intrinsic meaning becomes so great as to disqualify the exercise from belonging to the discipline of OT theology.

The ideal relationship exists where philosophical and biblical theological studies develop in dialogue with one another, for then the chances are enhanced that tools and concepts can be developed that will be useful to both. Since it is a given that the various disciplines within a particular historical-cultural setting are inevitably under the influence of a broadly pervasive set of cultural influences, it seems highly desirable that the checks and balances contributed by such interdisciplinary dialogue be utilized. This is especially true in the case of disciplines like biblical theology and philosophy, which are dedicated to many of the same goals.

Recent Issues in OT Theology: One recent issue in OT theology is the canonical or final shape of the OT. In 1938 Gerhard von Rad argued that biblical scholars had become so preoccupied with small units of tradition within the OT as to neglect the significance of larger literary compositions such as the so-called Yahwistic document (one of the literary strata integrated into the present form of the first four books of the Bible). In the past decade this concern has been revived, enlarged, and connected explicitly to the area of OT theology by a number of scholars, preeminent among whom is Brevard Childs. In this case objections have been raised to the fascination of many biblical scholars with the earliest stages of biblical compositons, reconstructed often with the help of a high degree of speculation. Instead, they argue, the stage of the OT writings that must be regarded as authoritative is the final canonical stage, inasmuch as it alone represents the form of Scripture historically held as authoritative by both the synagogue and the church.

This emphasis on the canon has come as a necessary corrective to an atomizing tendency within biblical scholarship that has not paid sufficient attention to the larger theological themes that often come to expression most clearly in the final shape of the canon. But it should be noted that the problem has not arisen primarily as the result of preoccupation with earlier stages of the tradition per se, but as the result of an approach taken by many scholars that simply has been disinterested in theological questions. When guided by theological sensitivity, careful attention to all recoverable stages of a composition's history can contribute to an understanding of that composition's theological significance that is not possible if attention is devoted exclusively to one stage, be it early or late.

It is necessary, of course, to recognize the bearing of theological presuppositions on this question. For those accepting a doctrine of verbal inspiration or infallibility as the starting point of biblical theology, the final form of the canon will be authoritative to the exclusion of earlier stages (of course, the existence of different canons within the various confessional groups complicates this position, as does the fact that the various ancient versions preserve text types that in many cases differ significantly from one another in length and readings). On the other hand, those recognizing God's word as arising within the relationship characterized by divine initiative and human response will seek to understand all stages of the biblical tradition for the light they shed on the divine-human relationship, for it is this relationship that supplies the essential ingredients of biblical theology.

Another recent concern has been the hermeneutics of liberation movements. The field of biblical hermeneutics, as the one that defines the presuppositions and the techniques of interpretation used in the theological study of the Bible, traditionally has been one addressed by church bodies. In recent decades, there has been a marked tendency for specific movements to define the hermeneutic appropriate to their perception of the Bible's relation to social change. Pioneering in this endeavor were black theologians like James Cone, who pointed to the experiences of blacks as an interpretative key to the meaning of central themes in the Bible, like the Exodus from Egypt. Impressive results also have been produced in Latin America by "liberation theologians" such as Gustavo Gutierrez. Their emphasis has been on the crucial importance of the disenfranchised and the poor in both the NT and the OT and on the mandate this holds before the contemporary church, given the growing gap between rich and poor and between oppressors and oppressed in our world. Feminist theologians in turn have produced various definitions of the hermeneutic appropriate for their concerns, a notable example being Elisabeth Schussler Fiorenza's *In Memory of Her*. These efforts have contributed significantly to the creativity of contemporary biblical theology by drawing attention to presuppositions uncritically accepted by generations of biblical scholars that were actually bound up with the interests of elitist groups, and by presenting the perspectives of excluded groups as a valuable point of entry into neglected aspects of the biblical message. Those not belonging to these movements can avail themselves of the contribution they make by scrutinizing their own presuppositions and methods of interpretation in the light of these new works, and by encouraging dialogue among the protagonists of various perspectives, old and new, motivated by commitment to a more inclusive and honest approach to biblical theology.

Another topic concerns the relation between the OT and the NT. Though some OT theologians continue to interpret the Hebrew Bible on the basis of a christological hermeneutic, an increasing number, while not questioning the central importance of the NT for Christian faith, feel that the integrity of both the OT and the NT is best respected by interpreting the OT first on its own terms. One of the major contributions OT theology can offer is a clear statement of the message of the OT that makes that message in its specificity and integrity available to people of all confessions. It thus stands guard against an overly hasty movement into the NT that overlooks the message of the Hebrew Bible, both in its own right witness to a foundational period in God's dealing with the human community of faith and as essential background for understanding the specific meaning of the NT writings. By following the development of the historical faith of Israel and by tracing the development of the different streams within Judaism in the Second Temple Period, the theologian lays the basis for a far more adequate understanding of the circumstances that led to the rise of rabbinical Judaism and early Christianity than is possible by more hasty readings of the pre-Tannaitic and pre-Christian writings.

The Study of the Bible and Jewish-Christian Relations: As we look back on the previous generation of biblical scholarship, the revitalization of biblical studies within the Roman Catholic confession resulting in large part from the decisions of the Second Vatican Council stands out. It may be that one of the aspects of the present generation that will be remembered will be the increased cooperation between Jewish and Christian scholars in the study of both the Hebrew Bible (OT) and the NT. Among a significant number of Christian biblical scholars there has grown a keen sense of the indispensability of a thorough, historical understanding of Judaism for a proper understanding of the growth of biblical faith. This sense has grown in intimate connection with a renewed interest in the Jewish writing of the second and first centuries B.C. and of the first centuries A.D., a field badly neglected since the turn of the century.

Clarification of the Dynamic Historical Character of Biblical Theology: The contributions of biblical scholars utilizing historical, critical methods have often been judged by people of faith in largely negative terms. Often this response was justified, inasmuch as many biblical scholars defined their task in arrogant indifference to the theological concerns of communities of faith. Though many biblical scholars continue to define their tasks apart from commitment to any religious group (and their many important contributions to the biblical field should not be overlooked), there is a growing number of critically trained biblical theologians who find their historical approach the most appropriate one for grasping the theological meaning of Scripture. Here we shall note several characteristics that can be observed among such OT theologians as Bernhard W. Anderson, Walter Brueggemann, and Paul D. Hanson.

The individuals and the communities that produced the writings of the OT are valued for the model of the faithful life that they hold up before contemporary individuals and communities. Basic to that model is the pattern of divine initiative and human response, with God's presence discerned as the creative and redemptive reality at the heart of human history and community experience to which the faithful seek to give their assent through confession and action. As God was present to heal and restore creation and the human family in biblical times, God is believed to be present now, and as an extension of the people of God in biblical times communities of faith today are called to participate in God's universal plan of justice, compassion, and peace.

Within this approach, the wide diversity of theological traditions found in the Bible and even the themes and practices that seem alien to modern sensitivities are regarded not as an embarrassment but as a challenge. The diversity represented by historical, prophetic, priestly, royal, sapiental, and apocalyptic traditions is assessed as perfectly appropriate within a historical process dedicated to understanding the mystery of God's purpose in human experience. And the alien elements, like mythological portraits of God as a divine warrior defeating the chaos dragon and the patriarchal bias found in language dealing both with the deity and with human society, are seen as evidence of the authentically historical character of God's relation to humans. Such elements are eliminated neither through tendentious translations nor by rationalizing arguments but are valued as indications of the specific historical setting within which God was active on behalf of the Jewish people and the many families of the earth, and as evidence of the dynamic ongoing character of biblical revelation.

The rich diversity of traditions found in the OT does not yield a chaotic theological picture, but one which is both dynamic and unified. The reason is that this approach goes beyond analysis of individual periods or traditions to grasp the overall development of biblical theology, by paying attention to all levels of tradition and all periods. The unifying factor is the divine-human relationship, which is traced throughout the span of biblical history, guided by the belief that God is true to God's purpose for creation and humanity and that a trustworthy human witness to that purpose is found in the confessions of God's people that arose over the centuries. The presence of diverse perspectives and of divergent theologies functions positively both in preserving the complexity of the issues addressed within the Bible and as an authentic basis for addressing equally complex issues in the modern world.

Refusing to reduce biblical theology to a strictly descriptive discipline or to an attempt to proceed in a positivistic manner does not preclude a deep appreciation for all that can be known of ancient Israel from such sources as archaeology and extrabiblical mythological and historical texts, for the historical nature of God's involvement with the human community underlines the significance of every detail that can be recovered from the concrete historical settings within which that involvement was experienced. In similar manner, the OT theologian is open to the contributions of contemporary philosophy and the social sciences, for they offer concepts and tools that both aid in interpreting the ancient events and in drawing out the contemporary significance of those events in a manner understandable to modern individuals and communities. The approach outlined here can make use, for example, of H. G. Gadamer's understanding of the key role played by tradition in a community's efforts to relate literary monuments of the past such as are found in Scripture to the life of religious communities today.

In this approach, it seems most natural to move dialectically between descriptive and normative aspects of interpretation. It does not seem advisable to leave the latter strictly to systematic theologians, for though the biblical theologian's task should not be construed as building complete theological systems for today's religious communities, it encompasses more than a disinterested description of an ancient religion. Indeed, the meaning that reaches out from the specific biblical writings in a way that spans bridges over diverse cultures and vast centuries is one the biblical theologians are able to grasp precisely because of their specialized knowledge of the concrete settings within which those writings originated. It has been the nature of biblical faith in all ages that a life-enhancing perspective has been gained through the remembrance of the sacred stories, a perspective that in turn gives the basis for an understanding of contemporary events as the setting of God's ongoing salvation drama. Though contemporary experiences and the insights of other disciplines will help shape the questions brought to the text and will contribute clarity to the conclusions drawn, the final contribution that the theology of the OT can make is an accurate and reflective understanding of the theological meaning of the biblical writings, a meaning that can help break old habits of mind and afford fresh angles of vision for modern communities and individuals. ***See also*** Biblical Criticism; Hermeneutics; Sociology of the Old Testament; Theology, New Testament.

Bibliography

Childs, B. S. *An Introduction to the Old Testament as Scripture.* Philadelphia: Fortress, 1979.

Hanson, P. D. *The People Called: The Growth of Community in the Bible.* San Francisco: Harper & Row, 1985.

von Rad, G. *Old Testament Theology.* 2 vols. New York: Harper & Row, 1965. P.D.H.

theophany, the manifestation of God. The OT contains a number of narratives of or poetic allusions to God revealing himself to men and women. Theophanies frequently are associated with particular holy places, representing the foundation legend of a sanctuary (Gen. 12:6–7; 13:18; 18:1; 28:1–17; Exod. 40:34–38) or the call of a prophet within it (Isa. 6:1–8). They tend to follow a literary pattern with Canaanite roots: God appears, frequently as divine warrior or king, surrounded by fire or in splendor (Deut. 33:2; Pss. 18:8; 104:2; Ezek. 1:27–28; Hab. 3:4), and sometimes riding like Baal upon the wind and clouds (Pss. 18:10; 68:33; 104:3); nature trembles (Exod. 19:18; Judg. 5:4–5; Pss. 18:7; 68:8; Hab. 3:6, 10) or the recipient responds with dread (Gen. 15:12; 28:17; Exod. 3:6; Job 42:5–6; Isa. 6:5; Hab. 3:16); and, as a result, nature becomes fertile (Pss. 68:8–10; 104:10–23; Isa. 35:2, 6–7), or God saves and rules (Deut. 33:5; Judges 5; Pss. 18:16–19; 29:10; 68:19–20; Isa. 35:4–6; Hab. 3:13), or the recipient is given a revelation or call (Gen. 15:12–16; Exod. 3; Isa. 6:8–13; Jer. 1:4–19; Ezek. 1:1–3:15). Elijah's encounter with God in a "still small voice" rather than in earthquake, wind, and fire (1 Kings 19:9–18) may represent a rejection of Canaanite imagery associating God with the forces of nature. Common to many of these passages is the combined experience of dread and fascination that is characteristic of awe before the holy. In the extreme, to see God's face brings death (Gen. 32:30; Exod. 33:20; Isa. 6:5).

Intertestamental usage stems from Ezekiel 1, a central text for the Jewish apocalyptic and mystical tradition, but now the manifestation of God takes place in heaven rather than upon earth, as the culmination of the seer's ascent to heaven (see *1 Enoch* 14:8–25). This is also the case in Rev. 4:1–11. Elsewhere in the NT, more traditional echoes of the language of theophany are heard in the narratives of Jesus' baptism (Matt. 3:17) and transfiguration (Matt. 17:1–8; cf. Exod. 34:35) and Paul's conversion (Acts 9: 1–9). ***See also*** Apocalyptic Literature; Call; Holiness; Prophet; Sanctuary; Transfiguration, The.

D.W.S.

Theophilus (thee-ahf'uh-luhs; Gk., "lover of God" or "friend of God"), the person to whom the Gospel of Luke and the book of Acts are addressed (Luke 1:3; Acts 1:1). The common address supports the theory that both documents were written by the same author. Hellenistic authors sometimes dedicated their books to patrons, benefactors, or persons who had an interest in the subject matter, and it is probable that the author of Luke-Acts so dedicated his writings. In Luke 1:3, Theophilus is given an honorific title ("most excellent" or "your excellency") that would appear appropriate for a high-ranking government official but may also have been used for a benefactor or patron. Various suggestions have been made about the identity of Theophilus, but no information about him is available outside the prologues to Luke and Acts.

J.B.T.

Thessalonians, the First Letter of Paul to the, the thirteenth book of the NT. Most scholars are agreed that 1 Thessalonians is the first Pauline Letter, written about A.D. 50, and therefore the oldest extant NT writing. While the literary unity and integrity of the letter have been questioned from time to time, these proposals have not found scholarly consensus.

Paul, Timothy, and Silvanus are co-authors of this letter to the Christian community at Thessalonica, a fact supported by the predominant use of the first person plural ("we"). Paul and his co-workers arrived there after having experienced much conflict in Philippi (Acts 16:11–40; 1 Thess. 2:2). Thessalonica, so named by Cassander (one of Alexander's generals) after his wife who was the daughter of Philip and the sister of Alexander the Great, was founded about 316 B.C. When Macedonia became a Roman province in 148 B.C., Thessalonica became the most important city of the province and the center of Roman administration.

Background: Both 1 Thessalonians (1:9–10) and Acts (17:4) suggest that the Thessalonian church was composed of Jews and Gentiles. Further, according to the account in Acts, Paul and his co-workers (Timothy and Silvanus), encountered sharp opposition instigated by the Jews and were eventually forced to leave Thessalonica because of this conflict. This polemical situation between the Jews and Paul appears to be reflected in the pointed comments found in 1 Thess. 2:13–16.

In addition to a strong Jewish presence in Thessalonica, we know that several religious cults of the Greco-Roman world were active in this leading city of the province and seat of Roman administration, including the cult of Serapis and the cult of the Cabiri. Paul's description of his apostolic practice in 2:1–12, his ethical advice in 4:1–8, as well as his teaching about the return of Christ (Gk. *parousia)* in 4:13–5:11 may be better understood with this background in mind, a background in which Paul's missionary style and teaching would have differed enormously from that of his competitors, with their ecstatic orgies and their varied expectations of the afterlife.

Content: Paul's affectionate letter to the church of the Thessalonians begins with his remembering their "work of faith and labor of love and steadfastness of hope in our Lord Jesus Christ" (1:3). This same trilogy occurs again in 5:8: ". . . put on the breastplate of faith and love, and for a helmet the hope of salvation." In chap. 3 we learn that Paul, who is probably writing this letter from Corinth, is anxious about the current status of the Thessalonian church. He hopes that they are not "moved by these afflictions" (3:3) and is apprehensive lest "somehow the tempter had tempted you and that our labor would be in vain" (3:5). As a result he sent Timothy from Corinth both to inquire and to encourage. Upon his return to Paul he brought the "good news of your faith and love" (3:6). This section concludes with the apostle's prayer "that we may see you face to face and supply what is lacking in your faith" (3:10). The overall context of the Letter, as well as this specific section, suggests that hope is precisely the element that is deficient and needs to be strengthened. When this is recognized, then the sustained eschatological emphasis of the Letter, especially at key transition points, makes sense. One should note especially 1:10; 2:19; 3:13; 4:13–18; and 5:1–10, 23.

Despite Paul's affection and high regard for these Christians whose faith served as "an example to all the believers in Macedonia and in Achaia" (1:7), he must correct and clarify one major area of misunderstanding: the status of those who have already died in Christ since the end has not yet come. In 4:13 Paul shifts from the repetitious "you know" language (1:5; 2:1, 2, 5, 9, 10, 11; 3:3b–4; 4:1, 2, 6, 10, 11; 5:2) to the phrase "we would not have you ignorant . . . ." These "you know" phrases are not superfluous rehearsals, but Paul's method of reminding this Christian church that they are *already now* sharing in the new life in Christ, which has hope as an essential ingredient. Thus their past and present participation in hope, as well as the integrity of the apostolic office of Paul and his co-workers over against those spurious claims of Paul's competitors, allows him to deal with the key issue in 4:13–18, namely, that the Thessalonian Christian should not grieve as others do who have no hope "concerning those who are asleep." This problem surfaced when some in the community died prior to the eagerly expected imminent Parousia and this anxiety may well have been fueled by those outside the church who mocked what seemed to them the absurdity of Christian eschatological claims. Paul assures his audience that the dead in Christ will not suffer disadvantage, they will not be overlooked, and that they "will rise first" (1:16) on the last day. Paul then reiterates the imminence of the Parousia (5:1–3) and then only in 5:10 does he give his final answer concerning the dead in Christ: "our Lord Jesus Christ . . . died for us so that whether we wake or sleep we might live with him."

Two final observations: first, it is noteworthy that "justification language," used predominately in Galatians and Romans, is absent in 1 Thessalonians, although Paul does use here, as in Romans, the terms "sanctification" and "salvation." In 1 Thess. 4:3, 4, 7 and 5:23, sanctification refers to the quality of new life in Christ, which will culminate in salvation (5:8, 9). This observation may support those scholars who suggest that justification language only appears at a later stage in Paul's thought, provoked originally by an intense battle with judaizing opponents, as in Galatia. At any rate what is constant from 1 Thessalonians through Romans, with different nuances, of course, is Paul's apocalyptic interpretation of the death and resurrection of Jesus in view of God's impending triumph. Second, it is significant for the study of the development of the ecclesiastical structure in the NT that already in 1 Thessalonians there is a reference to an organizational pattern: "But we beseech you, brethren, to respect those who labor among you and are over you in the Lord and admonish you, and to esteem them very highly in love because of their work" (5:12–13). ***See also*** Faith; Hope; Love; Paul; Serapis; Thessalonica. K.P.D.

OUTLINE OF CONTENTS

The First Letter of Paul to the Thessalonians

I. Greeting (1:1)
II. Thanksgiving (1:2–10)
III. Apostolic behavior (2:1–12)
IV. Reception of the Gospel (2:13–16)
V. The apostle's continuing concern for the church (2:17–3:13)
VI. Ethical exhortations (4:1–12)
VII. Instructions about the Parousia (4:13–5:11)
VIII. Exhortations about life in the church (5:12–24)
IX. Letter closing (5:25–28)

Thessalonians, the Second Letter of Paul to the, the fourteenth book in the NT.

Content: Much of the content in 2 Thessalonians is similar to that of 1 Thessalonians. Major new information appears in 1:5–12, where it is promised that those who are causing the suffering among the Thessalonian Christians will be punished at the last day and that the believers will be granted rest. This apocalyptic language is intensified in 2:1–12 in response to the basic issue confronting the author of 2 Thessalonians: "we beg you, brethren, not to be quickly shaken in mind or excited, either by spirit or by word, or by letter purporting to be from us, to the effect that the day of the Lord has come" (2:1–2). In order to persuade his readers that the day of the Lord has not yet come, our writer indicates that the "man of lawlessness" (2:3) must first appear.

The prayer with which the letter begins assures the readers that despite their present suffering, God will finally avenge them, and thus they are encouraged to hold fast to their faith (chap. 1). Chap. 2 warns them not to be overeager in getting ready to meet Christ returning from heaven, since other events must occur before Christ will return, and they have not yet occurred. The letter concludes (chap. 3) with a warning that anticipating Christ's return is not to be used as an excuse for laziness or not working to earn a living. Christians have no ob-

OUTLINE OF CONTENTS

The Second Letter of Paul to the Thessalonians

I. Greeting (1:1–2)
II. Thanksgiving (1:3–12)
III. Instruction about the man of lawlessness (2:1–17)
IV. Exhortations (3:1–16)
V. Letter closing (3:17–18)

ligation to feed people who refuse to work on such grounds.

Authorship: The scholarly discussion concerning the authenticity of 2 Thessalonians as a genuine letter of Paul is intense. At least three specific facts require explanation: the extremely close literary relationship between 1 and 2 Thessalonians; the apparently non-Pauline character of the key text, 2 Thess. 2:1–12; and the unique characteristics of 2 Thessalonians. This last category includes such phenomena as the transformation of the thanksgiving in 1:3–12 into a didactic passage dealing with future judgment; the different nuance of the final greetings in 3: 17–18, which no longer serve as a sign of intimacy but intend to demonstrate authenticity; the use of the term "hope" to mean simply "patience" in 1:3–4; the experience of salvation as primarily a future phenomenon in 1:7–12; the absence of the use of the titles "Jesus Christ" or "Jesus" without the consistent qualification of the title "Lord"; the un-Pauline use of "retribution" in 1:11–12; the fact that 2 Thess. 1:1–2 would be the only Pauline greeting that is statically repeated without the variation we find in his other Letters; the term "calling" in 1:11, which is used in non-Pauline manner, as is the term "possession" in 2:14 (note how differently it is used in 1 Thess. 2:12b; 5:9); and the stress on the term "tradition" in 2:15 (an obvious reference to 2:2) and 3:6. The second use of the term "tradition" in this brief document is significant since Paul only uses the term twice elsewhere (1 Cor. 11:2; Gal. 1:14); here its use to introduce 3: 6–12 is the clearest example of literary dependence in the form of the transformation of material from 1 Thessalonians (cf. 5:14).

How are these and other factors evaluated? Some scholars continue to insist on Pauline authorship, while others would argue that it is a pseudepigraphic letter. Still others are of the opinion that one of Paul's co-workers (both letters claim to be written by Paul, Silvanus, and Timothy) wrote 2 Thessalonians. ***See also*** Man of Lawlessness; Thessalonians, The First Letter of Paul to the. K.P.D.

Thessalonica (thes-uh-luh-nī'kuh), a city in Macedonia, located at the head of the Thermaic Gulf (modern Thessaloniki). In the NT Thessalonica is referred to exclusively in connection with the apostle Paul's missionary activities (cf. Acts 17:1–13; 20:4; 27:2; 1 Thess.; 2 Thess.; Phil. 4:16; 2 Tim. 4:10). The political and religious history of the city are important for a proper understanding of these NT references. The city was founded in 316 B.C. by Cassander, a general in Alexander's army, who gave the city its name in honor of his wife, Thessalonikeia, the daughter of Philip II and the half-sister of Alexander. The new city included the ancient Therme and some thirty-five other towns. When Macedonia became a Roman province in 146 B.C., Thessalonica was made the capital and thus the center of Roman administration. The city supported the victorious Antony and Octavian prior to the battle of Philippi in 42 B.C., an event that ushered in a prosperous new era for Thessalonica. Additionally we know that the Roman statesman and orator Cicero spent part of his exile in Thessalonica in 58 B.C., that the Roman general Pompey took refuge from Julius Caesar in the city in 49 B.C., and also that such prominent literary figures as Lucian and Polyaenus visited the city. The extensive coinage of Thessalonica underscores its prosperity, certainly due to its status as a free city (i.e., one granted certain tax concessions and some other privileges) and its location as a main station on the famous Via Egnatia, which ran through the city on an east/west axis from the Balkans to Asia Minor.

Religious Life: The religious life of Thessalonica included a Jewish as well as a Samaritan synagogue (attested to on a recently found marble inscription). According to Acts 17, Paul encountered unusually bitter opposition from the Jews of the city. There is also evidence for the cult of the Cabiri, the cult of the god Serapis, and the closely associated cult of the goddess Isis. Zeus (extensively represented in the city's coinage) was worshiped, as were Asclepius, Aphrodite, Dionysus, and Demeter. Many of the extant artifacts can be seen in the new archaeological museum in Thessaloniki. A further word needs to be said about the presence of the Cabiri in Thessalonica, for which we have both literary and numismatic evidence. They are also given the name "great gods" (Gk. *megaloi theoi*) and it is possible that the archaeological results in Samothrace may shed new light on these perhaps originally Phrygian deities who promoted fertility and protected sailors, a not unimportant fact for a city located at the head of the Thermaic Gulf. The Cabiri are often confused with and identified with the Dioscuri (Castor and Pollux, sons of Zeus) who also appear on a coin of Thessalonica dated 89 B.C. So deeply revered were these Cabiri/Dioscuri in Thessalonica that they are portrayed on two pilaster reliefs on the face of the arched western gate (built not later than the first century B.C.) as guardians of that gate. The steady growth of their influence is evidenced by coins from the Flavian Age (last third of the first century A.D.) which depict them as the city's tutelary powers.

In addition to these religious expressions there was also a very strong civic cult in the Roman period that regularly expressed gratitude to Roman patrons and Roman client rulers (such as, for example, a Thracian dynast) in recognition of the fact that the city's well-being was dependent on Roman benefaction. There is also evidence for the granting of divine honors to the goddess Roma in connection with honors bestowed on other Roman benefactors, for a temple dedicated to Julius Caesar, whom the Thessalonians acclaimed as a god (it appears that Augustus was also seen as divine by the Thessalonians), and for a group known as "priests of the gods." An interrelationship between the civic cult and the Cabiri/Dioscuri is probable.

Remains of the Ancient City: In the center of modern Thessaloniki one can see the ruins of the ancient Roman forum, which may also have been the site of the Hellenistic forum. It is possible that there was a second agora to the south and close to the harbor as, for example, in Pirene. It has been suggested that the Jewish synagogue may have been located in proximity to this agora. In the Hellenistic period there was a stadium, a gymnasium, and to the west a serapeum (i.e., a temple of Serapis), which was part of a larger sacred area. From the remains of the Vardar Arch at the western entrance to the city a broken inscription reading "In the time of the politarchs" has been found. This term is identical to the unusual description (not attested to in other extant Greek texts) given in Acts 17:6 for the rulers *(politarchas)* of Thessalonica. ***See also*** Thessalonians, The First Letter of Paul to the; Thessalonians, The Second Letter of Paul to the. K.P.D.

Theudas (thyōō'duhs), the leader of a messianic movement in Judah. According to the Jewish historian Josephus (born ca. A.D. 37), Theudas saw himself as a new Joshua figure who would lead his men by God's power across the Jordan and into the Holy Land to commence a new era for Israel. He was killed by the Romans ca. A.D. 44 (*Ant.* XX, 97–98). Theudas is also mentioned in the NT (Acts 5:36–37), but he is there placed prior to another revolutionary, one Judas, who led his doomed rebellion about A.D. 6 (both Acts and Josephus apparently agree on this date).

This discrepancy in the date for Theudas (NT: prior to A.D. 6; Josephus, A.D. 44) remains unresolved. Either Acts or Josephus had serious problems with sources at this point or, less likely, the references are to two different figures. ***See also*** Judas.

thigh, the upper portion of the leg. **1** The right thigh of the animal that constituted the Israelites' well-being offerings given to priests as a stipend in addition to the animal's breast (Lev. 7:32–34). These portions could be eaten by both the priests and their households outside the sanctuary area (10:14). The custom of giving the thigh to a sacrificial officiant is quite ancient (cf. 1 Sam. 9:24). **2** Where one placed a hand during an oath. Oaths were made by placing one's hand "under the thigh" (probably euphemistically meaning on the reproductive organ) of another who makes a request (Gen. 24:2, 9; 47:29). Punishment from God for breaking such an oath might include the death of one's offspring or the fate of dying childless. ***See also*** Gestures; Heave Offering; Oath. D.P.W.

thistle. ***See*** Thorns.

Thomas, one of the twelve disciples or apostles of Jesus, called "Didymus" ("twin") in the Gospel of John (John 11:16; 20:24; 21:2). He appears in each of the apostolic lists (Matt. 10:3; Mark 3:18; Luke 6:15; Acts 1:13). Receiving little mention in the synoptic Gospels, Thomas becomes important in the later portions of the Fourth Gospel. He alone appears to be a tower of strength when he encourages the disciples to accompany Jesus into a hostile Judea even if it means death (John 11:16). He appears to be without understanding when, in John 14:5, he confesses his ignorance about where Jesus is going and therefore finds it difficult to follow him. He is most commonly remembered as the "doubting Thomas" who refused to believe in Jesus' resurrection until he saw the scars and was invited to place his fingers where the nails were driven and his hand into Jesus' side (John 20:24–29). The story stands as a paradigm for all Christians who are called to believe in Christ without having seen him or having been granted tangible proof of his existence (v. 29). Thomas's response is that of all who later believe: "My Lord and my God!" (v. 28). In John 21:1–14, Thomas is one of the small group of disciples who go fishing and then see the risen Lord.

Little is known about Thomas's activities after the crucifixion of Jesus. He is recorded as among those gathered in the upper room after the ascension (Acts 1:13). Thereafter, tradition preserves only legendary stories of little apparent historical value. A Gnostic apocryphal gospel known as the *Gospel of Thomas* is attributed to this Thomas. ***See also*** Apostle; Disciple; Gospel of Thomas; Twelve, The. P.L.S.

thorns, spiny plants normally of little economic or cultural value. Thorns are referred to in the Bible by several different terms such as brambles, briers, thistles, and nettles. They are usually mentioned in a negative sense as irritants, impediments, noxious plants, or indica-

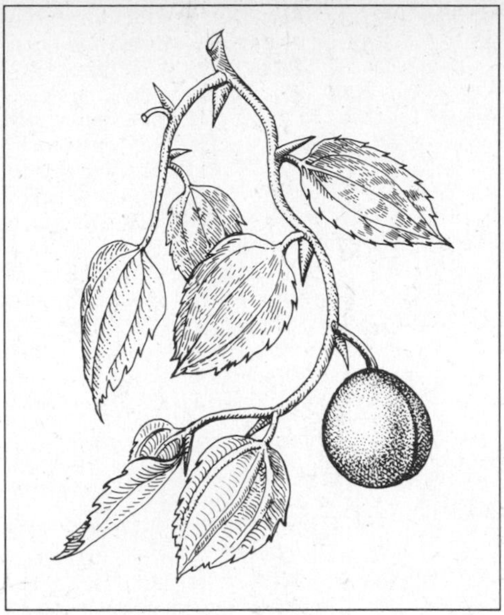

Thorns *(Zizyphus spina-cristi).*

tors of desolate areas. Collectively, the term "thorns" refers to the spine-bearing plants that are especially common in the wastes and arid regions of the Near East. The prickly armor of these plants not only protects them from being destroyed by the indiscriminate grazing of goats, camels, and donkeys, but also reduces transpiration and loss of water during dry periods.

The crown of thorns that was placed on Jesus' head (Matt. 27:29) has been variously identified as Christ thorn *(Zizyphus spina-cristi* or *Zizyphus lotus),* thorny burnet *(Poterium spinosum),* or paliurus *(Paliurus spina-cristi),* all of which are shrubs common in the plains and hill regions of the Levant. Brambles (Luke 6:44) may refer to the fruit-bearing blackberry or raspberry plants (genus *Rubus)* growing on moist stream banks or the spiny burnet dominating the limestone soils. Both plants form impenetrable thickets. Briers, like thorns and brambles, also form woody thickets and spiny hedges (Mic. 7:4; Ezek. 28:24). Many such woody, thorn-bearing shrubs are placed in piles as fencing to keep in animals and to keep out intruders or are used as fuel when dried (Prov.15:19; Hos. 2:6). ***See also*** Brambles.

P.L.C.

thousand, in the OT a Hebrew word used in several related senses. **1** A literal number. This is the most frequent use of the noun in spite of scholars' reservations about the accuracy of such high numbers (e.g., 2 Kings 19:35; Jon. 4:11). **2** A noun referring to a clan or element of a tribe (Judg. 6:15; Num. 10:4). **3** Term used to express a long time or used figuratively (Ps. 90:4; Ps. 84:10; cf. 2 Pet 3:8; Rev. 20:3). **4** A noun used to refer to a military unit (1 Sam. 8:12; 1 Chron. 13:1).

Some scholars posit that in the OT some numbers now read as referring to individuals were originally references to tent or family groupings.

In the NT, one thousand years are reckoned in God's time as but a day (2 Pet. 3:8), and multiples of thousands are used to describe large numbers (e.g., Mark 6:44; 8:9; Acts 2:41; 4:4; Rev. 7:4–8; 21:16).

J.A.D.

Thrace, the region east of Macedonia, west of the Black Sea, populated by independent tribes sometimes considered savage. The NT records no mission or church there, though Samothrace, Neapolis, and Philippi lay nearby.

three. ***See*** Numbers; Trinity, The.

threshing, the process by which the seed coverings of ripe cereals such as wheat and barley are removed. After the harvest, the cut grain is spread to dry on flat, open surfaces, or threshing floors (1 Chron. 21:20–23). The dried stalks are then either beaten with flails or crushed by a heavy board in which sharp stones have been imbedded. The board is dragged across the threshing floor by an ox or a donkey (Deut. 25:4; 1 Cor. 9:9). The husks may also be loosened from the grain by slow heating, or parching, in an oven. The loosened husks, or chaff, are then separated from the grain by winnowing before the grain is ground into flour or stored in jars or granaries (see Matt. 3:12). ***See also*** Granary; Winnowing.

P.L.C.

threshold, the bottom part of a door frame, over which one steps in entering a building or the gateway to a city. Guards were posted at the threshold (i.e., the entrance) of the Temple; these were priests (2 Kings 12:10) or Levites (2 Chron. 34:9). One of their duties was to receive donations from the people entering the Temple (2 Kings 22:4). In Ezekiel's visionary temple, the laity were not permitted to enter the gates to the temple; even the lay ruler was allowed to come only as far as the inner threshold of the gate to worship (Ezek. 46:2). Zephaniah condemns those who jump over the threshold of the temple (Zeph. 1:9), possibly because it was an idolatrous practice. The priests of Dagon in Ashdod would not tread on the threshold to Dagon's temple, since the image of Dagon had fallen on it when the captured Ark of the Lord had been placed in the temple (see 1 Sam. 5:4–5).

S.R.

throne, a word with a variety of meanings in the Bible. **1** The seat of an earthly king (Exod. 11:5). **2** A symbol of earthly royal power (2 Sam. 3:10). **3** A symbol of the seat of earthly judgment

Monarch on his throne wagon surrounded by courtiers; Neo-Assyrian cylinder seal, ninth century B.C.

(1 Kings 7:7). **4** The seat of God as king over the earth (Ps. 47:8). **5** The seat of God as judge of the nations (Ps. 9:4). **6** The seats of those who sit with God in judgment (Dan. 7:9). **7** The Roman governor's seat of judgment or a temple dedicated to the worship of Rome and the emperor in Pergamum, a symbol of Satan's power (Rev. 2: 13). **8** A symbol of Satan's power in which the Roman Empire shared (Rev. 13:2). **9** The seat of the Roman emperor or of the Antichrist (Rev. 16: 10).

Prophets, visionaries, and Jewish mystics saw or ascended to God's throne, sometimes portrayed as a chariot (Isa. 6:1; Ezek. 1:26; Dan. 7:9; *1 Enoch* 14:18; Dss 4QS1; Rev. 4:2; *3 Enoch*).

Jesus as Messiah inherits the throne of David in a figurative sense (Luke 1:32). After the resurrection Jesus is seated at the right hand of God's throne (Heb. 8:1) or with God on the throne (Rev. 3:21). Final judgment will be carried out by God (Rev. 20:11) or by the Son of man with his disciples (Matt. 19:28). ***See also*** Antichrist; Judgment; Messiah; Pergamum; Vision.
A.Y.C.

thumb, the large opposing digit on the hand. The right thumb, big toe, and right ear lobe were daubed with sacrificial blood in the priests' ordination (Exod. 29:20; Lev. 8:23, 24). The healed leper who is being cleansed was likewise daubed with blood and then oil on the same members (Lev. 14:14, 17, 25, 28). The purpose was primarily to provide protection from forces of evil on the most vulnerable parts of the body—its extremities. Loss of the toes and thumbs was humiliating and disabling. In the book of Judges, King Adoni-bezek thus mutilated some seventy defeated enemy rulers and was so treated himself by the conquering Israelites (Judg. 1: 6–7).
S.R.

thummim. ***See*** Breastpiece; Urim and Thummim.

thunder, the noise of clashing air masses expanding from a lightning flash. In biblical perspectives it was most often associated with heights (2 Sam. 22:14; Ps. 18:13; Job 36:29), storms (Exod. 9:23; 1 Sam. 12:17; Job 38:25), and other violent natural phenomena (Isa. 29:6; Rev. 11:19). Used metaphorically it describes the sound of the sea (Isa. 17:12) or roaring streams (Ps. 42:7) and the power and authority of the voice of God (Job 37:2, 5; Ps. 29:3; Exod. 19:19; John 12:28–29). Prophets use it both to express the presence (Ezek. 1:24) and awesomeness of God (Isa. 33:3). In Canaanite religion it was the sign of Baal's presence.
R.S.B.

Thunder, Sons of. ***See*** Boanerges.

Thutmose (tuht'moh-zeh; Gk. *Tuthmosis*; Egyptian, "Thoth [The moon god] is born"), the name held by four kings of the Egyptian eighteenth dynasty (1570–1293 B.C.). The time when these four pharaohs ruled, the late sixteenth and fifteenth centuries B.C., is sometimes referred to as the Thutmoside period. Some of the kings and major events of their individual reigns are listed below:

1 Thutmose I (1524–1518 B.C.), a military man

of nonroyal birth who reached the throne by marrying the daughter of his predecessor (Amenhotep I). He conducted a raid deep into Syria, crossing the Euphrates River and setting up a victory stele on the river bank near Carchemish.

2 Thutmose II (1518–1504 B.C.), a son of Thutmose I, husband of Queen Hatshepsut. His only campaign into Palestine was a minor raid undertaken against a group of bedouins.

3 Thutmose III (1504–1450 B.C.), initially coruler of Egypt with his stepmother, Queen Hatshepsut, then sole ruler of Egypt from 1483 B.C. on. In the twenty-second year of his reign he led an Egyptian army up to Megiddo, where the prince of the Syrian city of Kadesh had brought together a large army of Syrians and Palestinians under his leadership. Thutmose III's capture of Megiddo in 1482 B.C. resulted in the establishment of the great Egyptian Empire in western Asia. This king conducted a total of seventeen campaigns in the Levant; his army reached the Euphrates River in the eighth campaign. Thutmose III is considered the greatest military leader in Egyptian history. Egypt became wealthy and prosperous as a result of all the tribute and trade that reached the Nile Valley from its empire in western Asia and Nubia.

4 Thutmose IV (1419–1386 B.C.), a son of Amenhotep II (who was in turn a son of Thutmose III); he sealed Egypt's diplomatic relations with the north Syrian kingdom of Mitanni by marrying the daughter of the Mitannian king. On a stele found in western Thebes, Thutmose II claims to have conquered the city of Gezer. ***See also*** Gezer; Megiddo. J.M.W.

Thyatira (thī'uh-tī'ruh), a city (modern Akhisar) about fifty-five miles northeast of Izmir (Smyrna), Turkey. It lay on the road between Pergamum and Sardis in Lydia (or at times in Mysia) on the Lycus River. Founded as a Hellenistic city by Seleucus I Nicator in 300 B.C., it had developed many industrial and commercial guilds by the first century A.D..

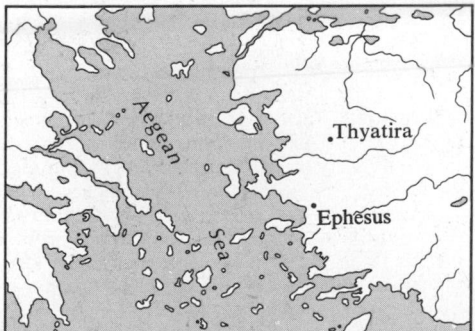

According to Acts 16:14–15, Paul's first convert at Philippi was Lydia, "a seller of purple goods" from Thyatira. She is described as a "worshiper of God," which may mean that she had come into contact with a community of Jews in Thyatira.

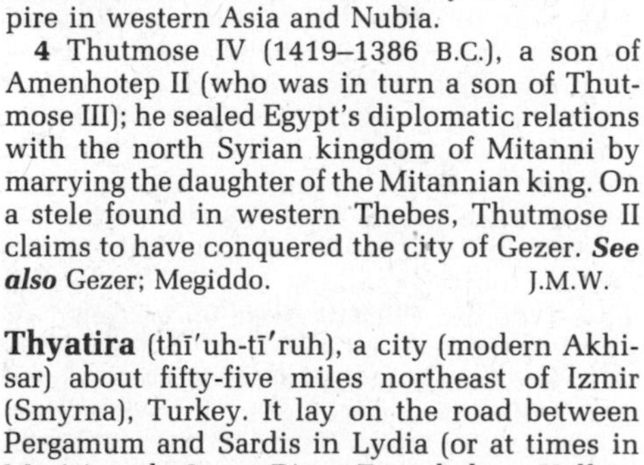

By the late first century, a sufficiently significant Christian community existed in Thyatira to merit the fourth and longest of the seven letters of Revelation (Rev. 2:18–29). The "eyes like a flame of fire" and "feet ... like burnished bronze" (Rev. 2:18) may allude to attributes of the local god Tyrimnos, identified with the Greek sun gods Helios and Apollo. ***See also*** Lydia; Mysia. C.H.M.

thyine (thīn), wood from the citron tree valued for its pleasant scent (Rev. 18:12).

Tiamat (tee'ah-maht), the watery source of life and, finally, Marduk's defeated opponent in *Enuma elish*, the Babylonian account of the emergence of the gods, the formation of the physical world, and the organization of the pantheon under the rulership of Marduk at Babylon. Tiamat is a form of the Akkadian word *tâmtu*, "sea," and is grammatically feminine. It is possible that she is the sea (Persian Gulf, Mediterranean Sea) in the *Enuma elish;* it is equally possible that she is the subterranean waters and is thus a variant of her spouse *apsû/abzu*. She is the mother who begot everything and is presented both sympathetically and hostilely in *Enuma elish*. She is imagined as a cow or goat, a human female, a dragon, and a sea-form. Her slayer, Marduk, divides her body and creates heaven and earth out of its two halves (cf. Gen. 1:6). Tiamat in the form *tehom* (Heb., "deeps") appears in Gen. 1:2; 7:11; and 8:2. ***See also*** Babylon. I.T.A.

Tiberias (tī-bihr'ee-uhs), a city named for Tiberius Caesar on the west shore of the Sea of Galilee. Herod Antipas, tetrarch of Galilee and Perea (Matt. 14:1–6; Luke 3:19), founded it (ca. A.D. 18) to replace Sepphoris as the capital of Galilee. Desirous of a site not full of those opposed to his rule or too close to the powerful cities of the Decapolis, he placed it on a major trade route linking Syria with Egypt. Administration, trade, and fishing became its major industries while nearby hot springs made Tiberias a popular health resort. Herod Antipas built a fortress around which a wall was later added. A stadium, forum, Hadrianem, and ancient synagogues have also been discovered.

Established upon a necropolis (possibly the cemetery for the ancient city of Hammoth [Josh. 19:35]), it was ritually unclean according to Jewish law. While pious Jews certainly refused to live there, well-to-do classes were drawn to the site because government offices and banks were located there. The promise of land and housing attracted the poorer classes. Jesus is not mentioned as having visited Ti-

Remains of walls at Tiberias (founded ca. A.D. 18), on the west shore of the Sea of Galilee.

berias although much of his ministry was spent in surrounding towns (John 6:23 records the only biblical reference to the city). Its influence is evident in that its name was transferred at an early date to the Sea of Galilee, which became the "Sea of Tiberias" (John 6:1; 21:1).

Tiberias was the first Jewish *polis* (Gk., "city"), making it sovereign in internal and external matters (e.g., waging war, negotiating treaties, establishing religious practices, taxation). It had an elected ruler (Gk. *archōn*), assisted by a committee of ten and a town council of six hundred. It was entitled to date its records from the day it was founded and to mint coins.

The Jewish historian Josephus led the forces that captured Tiberias during the Jewish revolt (A.D. 66–70) and destroyed the Herodian palace. Supported by the lower classes but opposed by the rich, he surrendered to Vespasian's forces in A.D. 67. This averted destruction of the city and was no doubt influential in the city remaining under Jewish rule until A.D. 100. Hadrian repopulated the city with a large number of non-Jewish settlers but it later became thoroughly Jewish in character.

By the second century A.D., it was recognized as one of four sacred Jewish sites (along with Jerusalem, Hebron, and Sepphoris). It was the seat of a rabbinical school influenced by Judah the Prince (Judah ha-Nasi, ca. A.D. 135–220) which was responsible for writing the Mishnah (a collection of oral laws). The Palestinian Talmud was completed around the fifth century A.D., shortly before the Tiberian Academy was closed. Tiberian vowel pointing (the preservation by means of vowel points of the pronunciation of Hebrew words) took place in Tiberias. Maimonides (A.D. 1135–1204), the famous Jewish philosopher and physician, who was born in Spain, is buried at Tiberias. D.R.E.

Tiberias (tī-bihr'ee-uhs), **Sea of,** better known as the Sea of Galilee (John 6:1; 21:1). ***See also*** Galilee, Sea of.

Tiberius (tī-bihr'ee-uhs), Claudius Caesar Augustus, Roman emperor from A.D. 14, when he succeeded Augustus, until A.D. 37, when he died in Capri, reportedly the victim of his many years of dissipation. He was the reigning emperor during Jesus' public ministry and thus (except in Luke 2:1) is the "Caesar" of the NT Gospels. Luke 3:1 uses his name in fixing the date for John's preaching and the baptism of Jesus ("in the fifteenth year of the reign of Tiberius Caesar," i.e., in A.D. 29). Matthew, Mark, and Luke contain the incident of the questioning of Jesus concerning the payment of taxes to Caesar (Matt. 22:15–23; Mark 12:13–17; Luke 20:20–26). Jesus' well-known answer centered on his display of a coin of Tiberius, bearing the emperor's portrait. In about A.D. 18, Herod Antipas, tetrarch of Galilee, founded the city of Tiberias, named in honor of the emperor, as his

Silver denarius of Tiberius, Roman emperor from A.D. 14 to 37, during Jesus' public ministry.

capital on the western shore of Lake Chinnereth (the Sea of Galilee). Ironically, Tiberias, whose namesake had once expelled Jews from Rome and had possessed anything but a saintly reputation, was, in time, to become one of the four holy cities of Israel and a center of Jewish learning. ***See also*** Tiberias. F.O.G.

Tibni (tib'nī), the son of Ginath and leader of a faction in the Northern Kingdom who struggled with Omri for control of the throne following the suicide of Zimri (ca. 876 B.C.). However, he was unsuccessful and died soon after, although the reason for his death is unknown (1 Kings 16: 21–22). ***See also*** Omri.

Tidal (tī'duhl), the king of Goiim (some versions read 'the nations") who, in alliance with the kings of Shinar, Ellasar, and Elam, raided the area around the Dead Sea, including Sodom and the Cities of the Plain, and took Lot prisoner. He and the other kings were defeated by Abram and his allies (Gen. 14:1–16).

Tiglath-pileser (tig'lath-pī-lee'suhr) **III,** the king of Assyria from 745 to 727 B.C., also known as Pul. He reorganized and revitalized the Neo-Assyrian empire after decades of internal disintegration. He campaigned vigorously in the West, reaching as far as the Brook of Egypt in the northern Sinai peninsula. The hegemony of Tiglath-pileser was recognized by the kings of Israel and Judah. Menahem of Israel bought the political support of Assyria for his illegitimate rule with "a thousand talents of silver" (2 Kings 15: 19); in Tiglath-pileser's annals at least two tribute payments by Menahem, in 740 and 738, are recorded. The rebellion of Tyre, Aram-Damascus, and Israel against Assyria was crushed during the three years of war, 734–732. Tiglath-pileser captured Galilee and Gilead, exiled its populace, and organized the areas as Assyrian provinces (2 Kings 15:29; 1 Chron. 5: 26). He installed Hosea as vassal king of a greatly reduced Israel.

Tiglath-pileser III (king of Assyria, 745–727 B.C.) wearing his royal cap with a pointed top; from the palace at Nimrud.

Ahaz of Judah came under attack for refusing to join the anti-Assyrian coalition; in order to save his kingdom, he turned to Tiglath-pileser and undertook the obligations of Assyrian vassaldom (2 Kings 16:5, 7–9). Ahaz is mentioned in an Assyrian list of tributaries dated to 734. His onerous tax payments required stripping the palace and the Temple of their treasures (2 Kings 16:17–18). The victorious Tiglath-pileser held court in Damascus in 732; Ahaz was in attendance as befitting a loyal vassal (2 Kings 16:10). ***See also*** Assyria, Empire of. M.C.

Tigris (tī'gris) **River,** one of the two major rivers (the other is the Euphrates) that nourished an extensive floodplain providing the physical basis for the rise of civilization in the ancient Near East. Its name is derived from Old Persian *Tigra*. In Assyrian-Babylonian it was known as *Idiglat*, and the Hebrew *Hiddekel* is preserved in Gen. 2: 14 where it is identified as the third river "which flows east of Assyria" running out of Eden. It was designated also as the site where Daniel perceived a major vision (Dan. 10:4).

The headwaters of the river lie in the mountains of southern Armenia, modern eastern Turkey and northern Iraq, just west and south of Lake Van. It runs generally southeastward along the base of the western foothills of the Zagros Mountains. It is joined en route by three major tributaries and several minor ones draining the western slopes of the hills to the northeast. The main tributaries are the Upper Zab, the Lower Zab, and the Diyala.

Important ancient cities built on the Tigris include Assyria's Nineveh (opposite modern Mosul) and Asshur (the original Assyrian capital), modern Qal'at Shergat. Near modern Baghdad lay the Neo-Babylonian commercial center Opis, and farther south at modern Sulman Pak was the Parthian and Sassanian city named Ctesiphon. Its location is still marked by a most magnificent brick vaulted arch. Across the river on the west bank at modern Tell Umar are the ruins of the Seleucid capital Seleucia.

Physically the river is fast and rugged in the upper reaches, being navigable only from Mosul southward. Its 1,146-mile length was close enough to the Euphrates from about Baghdad south to allow canals to run irrigation water across from the higher western riverbed toward the Tigris. This 10,000-square-mile basin provided the agricultural sustenance for the earliest city-state and empire building of which we have record. The lower reaches of the river were slow flowing, meandering, and ended in salt marshes in antiquity. Now the bed joins that of the Euphrates to form the Shatt al-Arab before emptying into the Persian Gulf. This ancient setting provided the physical context for some of our most ancient literature, in which the survival of life depended on the constantly flexing battle between the forces of the fresh and salt waters. ***See also*** Assur; Euphrates River; Fertile Crescent; Nineveh. R.S.B.

Tilgath-pilneser (til'gath pil-nee'zer). ***See*** Tiglath-Pileser III.

Timaeus (tim-ay'uhs). ***See*** Bartimaeus.

timbrel (tim'brel), a hand-carried percussion instrument, popularly used by women, and forbidden in the Temple. It was associated with religious hymns (Exod. 15:20 [Miriam]; Pss. 68: 25 [maidens]; 89:2; 149:3; 150:4; Jer. 31:4 [virgin Israel]). Usually reflecting joyous occasions (Isa. 24:8; Judg. 11:34), it may have carried unfortunate connotations from its female symbolism at fertility rites. It is closely associated with the tambourine.

time. There is no general word for "time" in the OT, nor are there specific words for the categories of "past," "present," or "future." The Hebrew word most commonly translated as "time" is *ayt*, which really refers to the instant or duration of time during which something occurs (1 Sam. 9:16; Eccles. 3:1–8; Ezra 10:13; 2 Chron. 24:11). Another word, *'olam*, refers to immeasurable time, whether past (Eccles. 1:10) or future (Mic. 4:7). While it does not mean "eternal" in the sense of without end, it does point to a length of time beyond human comprehension. Another common word, *mo'ed*, means "fixed time," i.e., a time designated for a specific occurrence like a festival (Lev. 23:2, 4). In other words, time in ancient Israel was not conceived as an abstract dimension but primarily as related to specific happenings whether of short or long duration.

God is the creator and master of time (Gen. 1: 14) and time begins at creation (v. 5), but there is a conception of eternity (Gen. 9:15–16; Isa. 34:10). The smallest amount of time is called a "moment" (Exod. 33:5; Isa. 54:7–8; Jer. 4:20).

The Hebrew Bible does use the terms "day," "week," "month," and "year." "Day" could either mean the term between sunrise and sunset or from sunset to sunset (Gen. 1:5). Ps. 55:17 speaks of three divisions of daylight, "evening, morning, and noon," while Neh. 9:3 refers to four parts of the daylight. The night was divided into three "watches" (Exod. 14:24; Judg. 7:19; Lam. 2:19). That the day started with sunset is probably due to Israel's calendrical system, which was based on the moon. Used loosely, "day" can mean "at the time" or "when" (Gen. 2:4; Jer. 31:32).

"Week" means literally in Hebrew "a seven" *(shevu'aḥ)*. Ancient Israel is the first known society to have a seven-day week (Gen. 1:1–2:3). The days are not named, but numbered one through six, except for the seventh day, which is called the "Sabbath"—from the Hebrew meaning "rest" in reference to God's rest after creation (Gen. 2:2–3; Exod. 20:10–11).

Like English, the Hebrew name for "month" is related to the word for moon, *yereaḥ*, or the "new [moon]," *ḥodesh*. The lunar month had thirty days (Gen. 7:11; 8:3–4; Num. 20:29; Deut. 21:13). The New Moon was a festival day (1 Sam. 20:5, 18, 24; 2 Kings 4:23; Isa. 1:13–14), and important holidays fell mid-month, on the full moon (Passover, the Feast of Tabernacles; Ps. 81:4). Four apparently Canaanite names for months are mentioned: Abib (Exod. 13:4); Ziv (1 Kings 6:1, 37), Ethanim (8:2), and Bul (6:38). Postexilic texts mention seven Babylonian-derived names: Nisan (Neh. 2:1; Esther 3:7), Sivan (Esther 8:9), Elul (Neh. 6:15), Chislev (Neh. 1:1; Zech. 7:1), Tebeth (Esther, 2:16), Shebat (Zech. 1:7), and Adar (Ezra 6:15; Esther 3:7, 13; 8:12; 9:1, 15, 17, 19, 21). These texts are the earliest evidence of the Jewish adoption of the twelve Babylonian names of the months.

Although 30 days are alluded to in the Bible as a month's duration, the lunar calendar averaged out to 29 1/2 days a month. Since the calendar was also tied to the agricultural-seasonal year, it also had a solar element. The Hebrews apparently had two New Year dates, one at the spring equinox and one at the autumnal equinox (Exod. 12:2, 18; 23:16; 34:22). The tenth-century B.C. inscription known as the Gezer Calendar describes the months by their particular harvests and also commences in the fall. The necessity of intercalating the lunar calen-

The "Gezer Calendar," which describes the months by their particular harvests; cast from a tenth-century B.C. inscription.

dar of 354 1/2 days a year with the seasonal year resulted in the Babylonians' adding a month every two or three years. This system was eventually adopted in Judaism, also—seven out of every nineteen years included an additional month (a "second Adar").

In the NT, three words refer to time in its various dimensions. Two words, sometimes translated "times" (Gk. *chronos)* and "seasons" (Gk. *kairos;* Acts 1:7; 1 Thess. 5:1), can refer to time under two different aspects. The first word is used when time is thought of as a quantity (e.g., "a little time," John 7:33; cf. also 1 Cor. 7:39); the second when it is thought of in terms of its quality, i.e., as "time for" something (e.g., Mark 1:15; John 7:8). That distinction is not always maintained, however (e.g., *chronos* can mean a specific time, Luke 1:57; Acts 7:17; Gal. 4:4; *kairos* can refer broadly to "the present," Rom. 11:5). A third word, "eon" (Gk. *aion),* can refer to a broad sweep of time and is probably drawn from apocalyptic speculation that divided the world into the present, evil eon and the future eon when God would redeem and transform evil reality into good (Matt. 12:32; Eph. 1:21; cf. Luke 20:34; Rom. 12:2; 1 Cor. 2:6 for "present age"; Mark 10:30; Eph 2:7; Heb. 6:2 for "coming age"). The plural "eons" is often translated "forever," although as in the OT, there is a question whether that means unending time or rather time of unimaginable duration (e.g., Matt. 21:19; John 12:34; Rom. 16:27; Heb. 1:8).

The Gospels presume the Jewish reckoning of time in terms of a seven-day week, although Christians revered the first day in the week (modern Sunday) because it was the day of Christ's resurrection (Matt. 28:1; Mark 16:2; cf. Acts 20:7; 1 Cor. 16:2), rather than the last day of the week (Sabbath), when God rested from creation (Gen. 2:2–3; cf. Exod. 20:8–11). There are no names for months cited in the NT, and if, as seems likely, the figures in Revelation mentioning a specific duration of time refer to the same three and one-half years (Rev. 12:14; 1260 days, 11:3; 12:6; 42 months, 13:5), a year was generally thought to have twelve months of thirty days each. The Jewish practice of reckoning days as beginning with sunset is presumed in some places (e.g., Mark 1:32, where people waited until the Sabbath mentioned in v. 21 came to an end), but in other places the Roman method of dividing the night into four rather than three watches is assumed (e.g., Mark 6: 48). A day divided into twelve hours, beginning at daybreak, and with the sixth hour as noon, is presumed in the Gospel accounts (e.g., John 11:9; Mark 15:35), but there is no scholarly consensus about how days were reckoned in the account of the last days of Jesus in Jerusalem (Mark 11–16): whether by the Jewish custom (sunset to sunset) or Roman practice (midnight to midnight). Since by the time of Paul the Julian calendar was in effect in the Roman Empire, one may assume that was the way he also reckoned time during his travels, but he gives no indication on that matter. ***See also*** Farming; Feasts, Festivals, and Fasts; New Year Festival; Sabbath. J.U./P.J.A.

THE HEBREW LUNAR CALENDAR

Name of Month	*Approximate Gregorian Equivalent*
1. Nisan* (*Abib***)	March/April
2. Iyyar (*Ziv***)	April/May
3. Sivan*	May/June
4. Tammuz	June/July
5. Ab	July/August
6. Elul*	August/September
7. Tishri† (*Ethanim***)	September/October
8. Marchesvan (*Bul***)	October/November
9. Chislev*	November/December
10. Tebeth*	December/January
11. Shebat*	January/February
12. Adar*	February/March

**Babylonian-derived name used in the Bible*
***An apparently Canaanite name of the month also preserved in the Bible*
†First month of the "civil year"

Timna (tim'nah; KJV: "Timnah"). **1** A sister of the Horite clan chief, Lotan (Gen. 36:22; 1 Chron. 1:39); she was given as concubine to Eliphaz and became mother of Amelek (Gen. 36: 12). **2** A clan chief of Esau (Gen. 36:40). He is designated as a son of Eliphaz in 1 Chron. 1:36, but the name may designate the Edomite territory inhabited by the clan.

Timnah (tim'nah; alternately Timnath, Timnatha; Gk. *Thamnath*). **1** A town in the southern hill country where Judah pastured sheep (Gen. 38:12–14); perhaps to be identified with the Timnah in the seventh district of Judah (Josh. 15:57). **2** A town on the northern border of Judah, between Beth-shemesh and Ekron (Josh. 15:10), now generally identified with modern Tell-el-Batashi in the Sorek Valley in the western part of southcentral Palestine. Once assigned to Dan (Josh. 19:43), it was Philistine territory at the time Samson married a woman from there (Judg. 14:1–5). It fell again to the Philistines in the time of Ahaz (2 Chron. 28:18) and was captured by Sennacherib in 701 B.C. **3** A town in the hill country of Ephraim, fortified in 160 B.C. by the Seleucid general Bacchides (1 Macc. 9:50). P.A.B.

Timnath-serah (tim'nath sihr'ah), Joshua's inherited city (Josh. 19:50) in which he was buried (Josh. 24:30). It is probably modern Khirbet Tibneh, about eleven miles southwest of Shiloh.

Timon (tī'muhn), one of the seven appointed by the apostles to help in the distribution of food to the poor and widows in the early Jerusalem church (Acts 6:1–6). ***See also*** Hellenists.

Timotheus. ***See*** Timothy.

Timothy. 1 A military officer of the Ammonites who joined forces with the Syrians to oppose Judas Maccabeus and Judea's freedom fighters (ca. 164 B.C.); the Ammonites were crushed in several battles and Timothy was slain (1 Macc. 5:6–8; 2 Macc. 8:30–33; 9:1–4; 10:24–38; 12:1–25, the last passage being misplaced in the narrative). **2** Paul's "beloved and faithful child in the Lord" (1 Cor. 4:17; cf. 1 Tim. 1:2). Timothy is associated with Paul in the prescripts of at least four of the apostle's Letters (1 Thess. 1:1; 2 Cor. 1:1; Phil. 1:1; Philem. 1; cf. Rom. 16:21; cf. also 2 Thess. 1:1; Col. 1:1), an indication of the extent of their joint endeavors. He is otherwise mentioned as an associate and helper of Paul in four of the Letters (1 Thess. 3:2, 6; 1 Cor. 4:17; 16:10; 2 Cor. 1:19; Phil. 2:19) and appears in the Acts of the Apostles, a narrative independent of Paul's Letters (Acts 16:1–3; 17:14–15; 18:5; 19:22; 20:4), in a similar role. Finally, he is the addressee of two of the pastoral Letters, 1 and 2 Timothy (1 Tim. 1:2, 18; 6:20; 2 Tim. 1:2).

According to Paul's earlier Letters, Timothy was a colleague with Paul and Silvanus (Silas) in missions to the Thessalonians and the Corinthians (1 Thess. 1:1; 3:2, 6; 1 Cor. 4:17; 16:10; 2 Cor. 1:1, 19). The ministries of these three in Macedonia are also reported in Acts (17:14–15; 18:5; cf. 19:22). From both sources, we learn that shortly after leaving Thessalonica Paul's anxiety concerning the effects of persecution led him to send emissaries to encourage the Macedonian church in its faith. Paul, himself, was left alone in Athens (1 Thess. 3:1–5; cf. Acts 17:13–16, a slightly more detailed account). From 1 Thess. 3:2–3 we learn that a special responsibility for ministry to the beleaguered Thessalonians was entrusted to Timothy, "our brother and God's servant in the gospel of Christ." When, with Silvanus (Silas), Timothy joined Paul in Corinth, he was the bearer of good news: the Thessalonians remained steadfast in "faith and love," and they longed to see Paul (1 Thess. 3:6).

According to Acts, Paul's next major campaign in the East was located at Ephesus (Acts 18:18–20:1). During the course of this ministry, several occasions arose in Paul's dealings with the Corinthian church that led him to send colleagues to act on his behalf. It is not clear that Timothy was the bearer of 1 Corinthians, or that a firm decision had been reached to send him to Corinth, but disturbances there made such a trip likely (1 Cor. 16:10: note NEB, which reads "if" —not "when"—Timothy comes"; cf. 1 Cor. 4:17). Some have surmised that Paul's plea concerning the church's reception of Timothy, should he come, indicates that the apostle had some doubts regarding his young colleague's effectiveness in a leadership capacity (1 Cor. 16:10–11). More likely, Paul feared that the Corinthians would complain that they merited the attention of the apostle in person, not the ministrations of an "underling," and that their anger would lead them to slight Timothy. A picture of Timothy as Paul's inexperienced, youthful protégé, intimidated by an aggressive opposition and needing the encouragement of his battle-hardened mentor, has sometimes been drawn from hortatory passages in 1 and 2 Timothy (e.g., 1 Tim. 3:14–15; 4:12–16; 2 Tim. 1:8; 2:1–7). It is doubtful, however, that this image of Timothy is supported by references in the Letters generally acknowledged as authentically Pauline, and, in view of the probable origin and purpose of the pastoral Letters (1, 2 Tim., Titus), it is unlikely that the material describing "Timothy" there is strictly biographical.

In the prescript to 2 Corinthians, Timothy is again included, as Paul's "brother" (1:1). It is therefore unlikely that Timothy's usefulness in dealing with the unruly Corinthians was at an end. It is true that it was Titus, not Timothy, who served as Paul's emissary when a serious crisis arose as a result of Paul's "painful visit" and his "severe letter" (2 Cor. 1:23–2:13; 7:5–16), but it is a dubious argument from silence to conclude, as some have done, that Timothy would have been unequal to the task. The frequent references to Titus in connection with the collection for the saints in Jerusalem may only mean that he had been given special responsibility for this project from the start and thus was assigned to deal with obstacles to its completion (2 Cor. 8:6).

The later Letters of Paul continue to portray Timothy as a trusted associate and useful emissary of the apostle (see Phil. 1:1; Philem. 1; cf. Col. 1:1). According to Phil. 2:19–24, Paul plans to send Timothy to Philippi and writes: "I have no one like him, who will be genuinely anxious for your welfare. . . . Timothy's worth you know, how as a son with a father he has served with me in the gospel."

In none of Paul's Letters does he refer to his first meeting with Timothy. Acts 16:1–3 reports that Timothy was already "a disciple" when Paul met him at Lystra (cf., however, 1 Cor. 4:17; 1 Tim. 1:2; 2 Tim. 2:2). According to Acts, Timothy's home life had been unlike that of the apostle (Phil. 3:4–6). Timothy's Jewish mother had married a Gentile, and their son had not been circumcised. This information would explain Paul's action in circumcising Timothy (Acts 16:3) after having so recently withstood the insistence of the Judaizers that Titus be circumcised (Gal. 2:1–5).

While the pastoral Letters are of little help in reconstructing the personal history of Paul's

1 AND 2 TIMOTHY, TITUS

younger colleague, there is no reason to doubt that their author knew the names of Timothy's mother and grandmother, Eunice and Lois (2 Tim. 1:5). ***See also*** Corinthians, The First Letter of Paul to the; Corinthians, The Second Letter of Paul to the; Eunice; Lois; Paul; Silas, Silvanus; Thessalonians, The First Letter of Paul to the; Timothy, The First and Second Letters of Paul to, and Titus, The Letter of Paul to; Titus. J.L.P.

Timothy, the First and Second Letters of Paul to, and Titus, the Letter of Paul to, three NT Letters purporting to have been written by the apostle Paul to two of his associates in Christian missions. Because of their common concerns with congregational matters, these writings are called the "pastoral Letters" and are often read together.

Origin and Authorship: Questions concerning the origin of the Pastorals remain in debate. Are they to be ascribed to Paul directly, or were they perhaps written by a secretary? Alternatively, are they pseudonymous writings composed in the name of the great apostle and containing personal notes that are either fragments of genuine letters or are introduced to give the writer's communication a conventional "letter" form, naming persons known to have been related to Paul's missions in one way or another? Ancient church tradition concerning the origin of the Pastorals is inconclusive. Decisions must therefore be based on internal evidence, which is, on no single point, decisive.

Two major approaches to the Pastorals proceed from different assumptions and lead to possibly different conclusions. As long as questions concerning Pauline authorship predominate, attention focuses upon the personal notes in the Pastorals, especially in 2 Timothy, and their bearing upon data concerning the course of the apostle's ministry, as such are disclosed in the acknowledged Letters of Paul and in Acts. Was Paul released from his Roman imprisonment and able to resume his missions in the provinces of Asia and Macedonia, perhaps to establish a Christian community on the isle of Crete? Was he arrested again, tried, and put to death? If the Pastorals are letters from Paul, then some such scenario would seem to be required. Moreover, it must be argued that new and different circumstances led to a "development" in Paul's theology and ethical teaching which was needed to take the new situation into account. Nevertheless, Pauline authorship is possible.

The alternative approach assumes at the outset that there are sufficient problems relative to traditional views respecting Pauline authorship to suggest that a clarification should first be sought of the historical setting of the Pastorals, a determination of the nature of the "heresy" to which the author constantly alludes, and some understanding of the writer's theological emphases and of the situations prompting certain household and congregational rules urged upon the readers. Here, the conclusion reached by the great majority of scholars is that the Pastorals are to be ascribed to a pseudonymous Christian writer of the early second century, who was convinced that Paul's teaching was normative for the church, and that Paul would have addressed existing conditions in the same way, were he alive and able to guide the work of other apostolic delegates, the successors of Paul's own coworkers of an earlier period.

Major Concerns: The contents of the pastoral Letters reveal two major concerns: the threat of serious heresy; and the urgency of preventive measures, which will give stability to the church and render effective its witness in the world. The author does not debate the heretics, but rather strongly criticizes their behavior. Neither does he prescribe the content of the "sound doctrine" that officers of the church are to use in defense of "the faith"; his concern is that these "apt teachers" of the church exhibit impeccable rectitude. A few features of the heresy are, however, noted. An asceticism was being taught that opposed marriage (1 Tim. 2:15; 4:3; 5:14) and prescribed abstinence from certain foods (1 Tim. 4:3; 5:23; Titus 1:15). Two heretics were teaching that "the resurrection is past already," which implies a spiritualism in which the heavenly life was experienced in the present (2 Tim. 2:18). References to "myths and genealogies" (1 Tim. 1:4; cf. Titus 3:9) may imply the influence of a gnosticizing Judaism (a view that is supported by references to Jewish elements in the heresy; 1 Tim. 1:7–11; Titus 3:9).

The writer's concern for the various ministries of the church seems to reflect a need to clarify their respective functions, a situation similar to that disclosed in early second-century texts, such as the *Didache* and the Letters of Ignatius.

These and other considerations support the widely held opinion that the pastoral Letters belong to the postapostolic age and are addressed to the concerns of second-generation Christianity. No longer were Christians convinced that the world-order would soon pass away with the glorious return of the Christ. The spiritual vigor that characterized the Pauline missions was replaced by an equally serious mandate: to establish the church as "the pillar and bulwark of the truth" (1 Tim. 3:15). To this end, true successors of Paul and his apostolic delegates had to be found who, by virtue of their offices, authority, and personal examples, would be able to defend "the deposit" of the faith of the apostle, entrusted to them, and be ready like Paul to take their share of suffering for the gospel. ***See also*** Bishop; Church; Crete; Ephesus; Epistle; Gnosticism; Heresy; Law; Letter; Paul; Presbyter, Presbytery; Pseudonym; Timothy; Titus.

Bibliography

Dibelius, Martin, and Hans Conzelmann. *The Pastoral Epistles: A Commentary on the Pastoral Epistles. Hermeneia.* Philadelphia: Fortress, 1972. In defense of pseudonymity.

Kelly, J. N. D. *The Pastoral Epistles: I Timothy. II Timothy. Titus.* New York and Evanston: Harper & Row, 1964. In defense of Pauline authorship.

J.L.P.

Tiphsah (tif'sah). **1** A city that marked a northern extremity of Solomon's kingdom (1 Kings 4:24). It is probably modern Dibseh on the west bank of the Euphrates River where it turns east after coming south from Carchemish. It was called Thapsacus by the fifth- and fourth-century B.C. Greek historian Xenophon (1.4.11) and was known as Amphipolis in the third century B.C. **2** A place the RSV translates "Tappuah," the site of a brutal destruction by Menahem, eighth-century B.C. king of Israel (2 Kings 15:16). Modern Sheikh Abu Zarad about eight miles northwest of Shiloh is the likely identification.

OUTLINE OF CONTENTS

The Pastoral Letters

1 Timothy

I. Introduction (1:1–20)
   A. Prescript (1:1–2)
   B. Purpose of Timothy's present ministry in Ephesus: to combat heretical teaching (1:3–11)
   C. Thanksgiving for God's mercy to Paul; an example (1:12–17)
   D. Timothy to maintain a good conscience, something rejected by others (1:18–20)
II. Charge to Timothy (2:1–6:19)
   A. Prayers for all, especially rulers (2:1–7)
   B. Man's worship and woman's (relating to her praiseworthy public image) (2:8–15)
   C. Qualifications for office of bishop (3:1–7)
   D. Qualifications for deacons (and deaconesses?) (3:8–13)
   E. Word to Timothy concerning church (3:14–16)
   F. Asceticism of heretics to be counteracted by Timothy's instruction, example, and care of special persons (4:1–5:2)
   G. Procedures for enrolling widows; how to deal with too many (5:3–16)
   H. Maintaining integrity of office of elder (5:17–25)
   I. Behavior of Christian slaves (6:1–2)
   J. Deplorable conduct of heretics; special warning against avarice (6:3–10)
   K. Exhortations to Timothy (6:11–16; see also 5:21–25)
   L. Word to the wealthy (6:17–19)
III. Conclusion: final warning against teachers of "false knowledge" (6:20–21)

2 Timothy

I. Introduction (1:1–7)
   A. Prescript (1:1–2)
   B. Thankful remembrance for Christian heritage of Paul and Timothy (1:3–7)
II. Exhortations (1:8–4:5)
   A. Experience of suffering as authentication of elect (1:8–2:26)
   B. Presence of heresy as authentication of prophecy; great value of tradition (3:1–4:5)
III. Conclusion (4:6–22)
   A. Personal notes concerning Paul's situation; final instructions (4:6–18)
   B. Greetings (4:19–21)
   C. Grace, offered on behalf of church (4:22)

Titus

I. Prescript, with summary of Paul's calling "to further the faith of the elect" (1:1–4)
II. Instructions (1:5–3:8a)
   A. Concerning elders, and office of bishop (1:5–9)
   B. Warning concerning "circumcision party"; comment on Cretans' celebrated notoriety (1:10–16)
   C. Rules for household: church members of both sexes and all ages, also slaves; example of Titus (2:1–10)
   D. Sanctions for instructions: God's grace manifested in salvation-history; former lives of many believers (2:11–3:8a)
III. Conclusion (3:8b–15)
   A. Titus to avoid "stupid controversies"; heretics to receive special treatment (3:8b–11)
   B. Assignments; greetings; grace (3:12–15)

Tiras (tī'rahs), a son of Japheth (Gen. 10:2; 1 Chron. 1:5) whose clan name appears to be akin to both Egyptian and Greek references to a group of Aegean sea raiders. ***See also*** Sea Peoples.

Tirhakah (tir-hah'kah; Taharka in the Egyptian records), a pharaoh of Egypt's twenty-fifth ("Ethiopian") dynasty, who reigned ca. 690–664 B.C. According to 2 Kings 19:9 (Isa. 37:9), Sennacherib received a report that the "Ethiopian king" Tirhakah was marching out against him. At that moment the Assyrian army was engaged in a military campaign against Judah and was attacking Libnah in the Judean Shephelah (lowlands). According to the Assyrian annals Sennacherib met and defeated the Egyptian force in the Plain of Eltekeh (modern Tell esh-Shallaf?). Some scholars have argued that Tirhakah would have been only nine years old at the time of this campaign (ca. 701 B.C.), and therefore portions of the biblical account must refer to an otherwise unattested second campaign of Sennacherib in ca. 688 B.C. Others maintain, perhaps more cogently, that Tirhakah was twenty years old or more in 701 B.C., and that he led Egypt's troops as army commander; the designation "Ethiopian king" in the Bible is based on a source dating from 690 B.C. or after. ***See also*** Egypt. D.A.D.

Tirzah (teer'zuh; Heb., "pleasantness"), the name of a person (and clan), a region, and a city. **1** One of the five daughters of Zelophahad, descendants through Hepher of Manasseh, who appealed to Moses for adjustment of the inheritance custom. This incident gives a glimpse of Israelite attention to issues of justice and of land tenure (Num. 26:33; 27:1–11; 36:5–12; cf. Josh. 17:3–6). **2** The region belonging to the clan of Tirzah. The names of Zelophahad's five daughters also designated clan holdings as indicated by the Samaria ostraca, ceramic shards recording deliveries from estates within a ten-mile radius of Samaria which date ca. 775–750 B.C. Tirzah is not named, but two "sisters," Noah and Hoglah, are. Taking all the evidence together, the general region of these clan holdings was north and east of Samaria. **3** A city listed as one whose king was defeated by Joshua (Josh. 12:24), so it was probably a Canaanite city-state in the thirteenth century B.C. Three hundred years later, it emerged as Jeroboam's capital (1 Kings 14:17; cf. v. 12). Baasha, who usurped control from Jeroboam's family, reigned from Tirzah (1 Kings 15:21, 33; 16:6); when Zimri displaced Baasha's family, the coup occurred at Tirzah (16:8–9). When Omri besieged Zimri at Tirzah, Zimri burned its citadel and palace down upon himself; Omri then consolidated his reign at Tirzah before moving the capital to Samaria (16:15–23). All this took place within a half century (922–870 B.C.). Tirzah's brief life as Israel's capital apparently accounts for its appearance in a couplet in Song of Sol. 6:4, paired with Jerusalem. Around 745 B.C. Tirzah reappeared as the base of operations for Menahem, still another usurper of the throne (2 Kings 15: 14, 16).

The extensive mound today called Tell el-Far'ah, seven miles northeast of Shechem, is almost certainly the site of Tirzah. It oversees the head of the Wadi Far'ah, a direct route to the Jordan. Travelers going east-west in the central hills would come north-northeast from the Shechem pass around Mount Ebal and turn southeast below Tell el-Far'ah. Between 1947 and 1960, Roland de Vaux and the École Biblique of Jerusalem excavated here. The city was at its largest dimensions in Early Bronze I–II (ca. 3150–2600 B.C.); its fortifications on the western, unprotected side became the foundations for all subsequent defenses, though succeeding towns were smaller in extent eastward and northward. Occupation resumed in Middle Bronze II (ca. 1900–1550), continuing into Late Bronze until roughly 1300. Evidence of destruction ending this period of the city's life is skimpy and of inconclusive date; correlation with a presumed destruction by Joshua is far from certain.

Correlation with biblical information is much firmer in the period 1000–600 B.C. There are four phases: the tenth century, ending with a destruction, probably that of Zimri; a partial rebuild, early ninth century; the eighth century, ending with destruction, probably by the Assyrians in 724–21; and a recovery, down to 600 B.C. Sturdy, roomy tenth-century housing of a uniform character is spread throughout a well-planned city layout. By contrast, the eighth century town had excellently constructed, spacious houses in one sector but makeshift homes in another, across a dividing wall. It suggests increasing social and economic stratification (cf. Amos 5:11). In the phase between these two well-preserved towns, set down into the destruction debris of the tenth century, were walls of unfinished buildings. De Vaux proposed that his interim phase represents Omri's short stay at Tirzah. Basins and a memorial stone, along with other evidence, suggest that there was a gateside sanctuary in continual use from Middle Bronze to the site's final destruction, perhaps attesting Israelite adoption of Canaanite religious equipment and practices. **4** The uppermost stratum reflects recovery after the Assyrian destruction. Distinctive Assyrian-style pottery indicates strong influence, perhaps even the presence of an Assyrian garrison. ***See also*** Baasha; Jeroboam I; Menahem; Omri; Samaria, City of; Samaria, District of; Zimri.

Bibliography

de Vaux, Roland. "Tirzah." In *Archaeology and Old Testament Study*. Edited by D. W. Thomas. Oxford: Oxford University Press: 1967. Pp. 371–83.

———. "El-far'a, Tel, North." In *Encyclopedia of Archaeological Excavations in the Holy Land.* Edited by M. Avi-Yonah. Vol. 2. Englewood Cliffs: Prentice-Hall, 1976. Pp. 395–404. E.F.C.

Tishbite, an adjective applied six times in the Hebrew Bible to the prophet Elijah (1 Kings 17:1; 21:17, 28; 2 Kings 1:3, 8; 9:36). The Septuagint translators understood Tishbite as a reference to Elijah's home town of Tishbe. Tishbe was identified with the site of Listib in the mountains of north Gilead. Since this supposed site of Tishbe was not settled during the Israelite period, the modern biblical scholar N. Glueck changes 1 Kings 17:1 to read "Elijah the Jabeshite of Jabesh-gilead." Glueck supports his identification of Elijah as a Jabeshite by claiming that the brook Cherith, where Elijah lived for a time according to 1 Kings 17:3–7, might be a branch of the river Jabesh. ***See also*** Elijah. M.A.S.

Tishri (tish'ree), the postexilic Babylonian name for the seventh Hebrew month Ethanim (1 Kings 8:2), a thirty-day period roughly corresponding to the latter half of September and the first half of October. It marked the beginning of the religious year with the New Year Festival (Heb. *Rosh Hashanah)* celebrated on the first day of the month (originally on the tenth day; Lev. 23:23–25; Num. 29:1–6) followed by the Day of Atonement (Heb. *Yom Kippur)* on the tenth day (Lev. 16; 23:26–32; Num. 29:7–11) and the eight-day Feast of Tabernacles (or Booths; Heb. *Sukkoth)* beginning on the fifteenth day (Lev. 23:33–44). ***See also*** Atonement, Day of; Feasts, Festivals, and Fasts; New Year Festival; Tabernacles, Festival of; Time. D.R.B.

tithe, a tenth part of one's yearly income set aside for sacral purposes. Tithing was very common throughout the ancient Near East, especially in Mesopotamia where Neo-Babylonian texts from the sixth century B.C. discuss the collection of tithes as a means of supporting a sanctuary. Other documents indicate that tithing could serve nonsacral purposes as well. Fourteenth-century B.C. tablets from Ugarit portray the tithe as a royal tax the king collected and distributed to his officials. The Seleucid kings of Syria likewise viewed the tithe as a source for royal income (1 Macc. 10:31; 11:35), whereas Jews at that time viewed it as a sacral tax (1 Macc. 3:49).

Nature and Function: Reconstructing a clear picture of the nature and function of tithing in biblical times is extremely difficult due to the conflicting accounts concerning tithes in the biblical traditions and the problems in identifying the dates and provenance of the texts. Apparently, tithing was understood and practiced differently at different times and localities throughout the Biblical period. Most biblical texts concerning the tithe agree that it serves some sacral purpose and presuppose that it was mandatory, but they differ as to how it was expended and by whom.

In the time of Ezra and Nehemiah, the tithe was a tax collected at the Temple to support the priests and Levites (Neh. 10:37–38; 12:44; 13:5, 12), although the requirement was not always observed or enforced (Mal. 3:8, 10). Pentateuchal regulations likewise emphasize the sacral and mandatory character of the tithe. Lev. 27:30–33 states that all the tithe of the land, whether of the seed of the land or of the fruit of the trees, belongs to God and that one-tenth of all that passes under the herdsman's staff is also included. Num. 18:21–32 assigns the tithe offerings of the people as the inheritance of the Levites and they in turn must give one-tenth of what they receive to the priests. Deut. 14:22–29 states that the people shall tithe their grain, wine, and oil together with the firstlings of their herds and flocks and that they shall eat their tithe in the Temple. But every third year, the tithe shall go to the Levite, the sojourner, the orphan, and the widow, as these people have little means of support. In the case of the Levites, their poverty was due to Deuteronomy's requirement that all sanctuaries but one be closed, leaving the Levites who served in these sanctuaries unemployed (cf. Deut. 12). If one lived far from the Temple so that transporting the actual tithe was impractical, then it could be converted to cash and replacement food could be bought for consumption at the Temple, but the requirement to eat the tithe in the Temple still stood. Lev. 27:31 states, however, that if a man redeemed his tithe with cash, he should add one-fifth of the actual cash value of the tithe.

Tax or offering: Other texts raise questions about the sacral or obligatory nature of the tithe. When the prophet Samuel warns the people about the dangers of appointing a king, he mentions that the king will exact a tithe from their grain, vineyards, and flocks to give to his officers and servants (1 Sam. 8:15, 17). Here, the tithe is a mandatory royal tax, but no mention of sacral use appears. In the patriarchal traditions, the tithe is freely given at the site of a sanctuary. Abraham gives a tenth of his war booty to Melchizedek, the priest-king of Salem (i.e., Jerusalem) after receiving his blessing (Gen. 14:20; cf. Heb. 7:1–10). Jacob vows to offer a tithe of all his income to God at Bethel after his dream of the ladder to heaven (Gen. 28:22). An interesting attempt to reconcile the conception of the tithe as a royal tax with that of a sacral offering notes that both Jerusalem and Bethel were the sites of royal sanctuaries founded by kings (2 Sam. 6; 1 Kings 6–8; Amos 7:13; 1 Kings 12:25–33). In this view, the patriarchal stories are etiological legends for the later practice of channeling sacral tithes for the Temple through the kings who maintained the Temple (Ezek. 45:17) and controlled its treasury. According to 2 Chron. 31:5, 6, 12, King Hezekiah collected and stored offerings for the Temple, including the tithe.

Later Judaism maintained the tithe, stipulating that all things used for food, which were watched and grew from the earth, were subject to tithing (*m. Ma'aś.* 1:1; cf. Luke 18:12). But discrepancies between the regulations on tithing in Lev. 27:30–33; Num. 18:21–32; and Deut. 14:22–29 resulted in the Mishnah's adopting two tithes. The first was for the Levites and the second was to be eaten by the people. The zeal of some who tithed even their spices was noted by Jesus, who criticized such people for also neglecting more important religious and ethical demands (Matt. 23:23). He did not condemn such tithing practices, however. ***See also*** Levites; Temple, The; Worship.

Bibliography

de Vaux, Roland. *Ancient Israel.* New York: McGraw-Hill, 1965. Pp. 140–141, 380–382, 403–405.

Kaufman, Yehezkel. *The Religion of Israel.* Chicago: University of Chicago Press, 1960. Pp. 189–193.

Weinfeld, Moshe. "Tithe." *Encyclopedia Judaica.* Vol. 14. New York: Macmillan, 1971. cols. 1156–1162.

M.A.S.

title. ***See*** Superscription, Title.

tittle. ***See*** Jot.

Titus. A Gentile "partner and fellow worker" with Paul (2 Cor. 8:23); the named addressee of a short letter in the NT. Information about Titus appears principally in Galatians and 2 Corinthians. The pastoral Letters (1, 2 Tim., Titus), which refer to missions of Titus in Crete and Dalmatia, are likely pseudonymous writings of the postapostolic age; nevertheless, the references to Titus may reflect authentic traditions (2 Tim. 4:10; Titus 1:4–5). Titus is almost certainly not to be identified with Titius Justus (Acts 18:7); indeed, Titus is nowhere mentioned in Acts.

According to Gal. 2:1–10 (cf. 1:15–18), Paul was accompanied, on his second visit to Jerusalem following his call to be an apostle to the Gentiles, by Barnabas and by a Greek named Titus. Some Jewish Christians insisted that Titus be circumcised, but Paul, doubtless aware of the precedent this would set, refused to comply. An alternative reading supports an opposite result (see NEB marginal reading and cf. Acts 16:1–3), but the RSV translation of Gal. 2:5 is to be preferred as alone making sense in the context of the Letter's overall argument.

It is probable that Titus was Paul's associate throughout his extended ministry in Ephesus, although Acts does not report this (19:1–20:1). Possibly Titus was the bearer of 1 Corinthians for, in 2 Cor. 8:6, Paul notes that Titus is resuming work he began at Corinth, namely the collection for Jewish Christians in Jerusalem (cf. 1 Cor. 16:1–4; 16:10 suggests that Timothy was not the bearer of this letter). With greater probability, it was Titus who delivered to the Corinthians another letter, the so-called "severe" or "tearful letter" (cf. 2 Cor. 2:3–9). Personal attacks against Paul threatened the loss of his leadership in Corinth, but Paul, wishing to avoid "another painful visit" (2 Cor. 2:1), placed his fate in the hands of Titus. Paul would travel from Ephesus to Macedonia; Titus would report to him the situation in Corinth as soon as possible (2 Cor. 2:13; 7:5–16). The failure of Titus to meet him at Troas troubled Paul greatly, but a reunion in Macedonia greatly relieved the apostle. Taking advantage of the improved situation, Paul sent Titus back to Corinth. Perhaps not wishing to detract from the crucial role of Titus in the collection, Paul refers to two unnamed companions (2 Cor. 8:6, 16–24). Later in the same Letter, Paul expresses his confidence that Titus will take no advantage of the Corinthians—that, like Paul, he has their best interests at heart (2 Cor. 12:17–18).

The person instructed in the canonical Letter to Titus is sufficiently unlike the resourceful, competent person who commanded the respect of both Paul and the unruly Corinthians to support the view that the writer of the letter was less interested in Titus as a real person than as a type of leader needed in churches of the writer's own time and circumstances. ***See also*** Circumcision; Contribution for the Saints; Corinthians, The First Letter of Paul to the; Corinthians, The Second Letter of Paul to the; Galatians, The Letter of Paul to the; Timothy; Timothy, The First and Second Letters of Paul to, and Titus, The Letter of Paul to. J.L.P.

Titus, the Letter of Paul to. ***See*** Timothy, The First and Second Letters of Paul to, and Titus, The Letter of Paul to.

Titus Flavius Sabinus Vespasianus (A.D. 39–81), the son of Vespasian and Roman emperor from A.D. 79 to 81. After serving in the army in Germany and Britain, he became the commander of a legion under his father in the Jewish war (66–70). When Vespasian was proclaimed emperor, Titus led the forces that captured Jerusalem and destroyed the Temple. The Arch of Titus, which still stands at the Roman Forum, commemorates this victory and displays treasures taken from the Temple. Titus shared Vespasian's rule until his father's death, whereupon Titus was declared emperor. The aid he provided to victims of the eruption of Mt. Vesuvius (79) and of a fire and plague that devastated part of Rome (80) contributed to his popularity. His long-standing affair with the Jewish princess Bernice (the daughter of Agrippa I, great-granddaughter of Herod the Great) was unpopular in Rome, and he ended it when he became emperor. Upon his death the Senate immediately deified him. D.R.E.

Titus Justus. ***See*** Justus.

Tob (tahb), the hometown of a group of "worthless fellows" who associated with Jephthah (Judg. 11:3–5) after he fled from his half-brothers. The town also supplied mercenaries to the Ammonites in their wars with David (2 Sam. 10: 6–13). Jews who had settled there were rescued from neighbors' attacks by Judas Maccabeus (1 Macc. 5:13; 2 Macc. 12:17). The location is probably modern et-Taiyibeh, about twelve miles east and slightly north of Ramoth-gilead.

Tobiah (toh-bī'ah; Heb., "Yahweh is good"; cf. Tobijah, also Tobias in the book of Tobit, Tabeel, Tobiads). **1** The head of a priestly clan whose genealogy was in doubt (Ezra 2:60; Neh. 7:62). **2** An opponent of Nehemiah (Neh. 2:10, 19; 4:3, 7; 6:1–19; 13:4–8) with Sanballat and Geshem. He is described as "the Ammonite" and also (Neh. 2:10, 19) as "the servant." These descriptions suggest a derogatory attitude, but "servant," which has royal connotations in the OT, may indicate high office (i.e., "servant of the [Persian] king"; cf. 2 Kings 22:12). "Ammonite" may indicate his origin or be a nickname; more probably it indicates his responsibility for that area, placing him alongside Sanballat, who was governor of Samaria, and Geshem, who could have been the Arab ruler of Qedar. All three would then occupy important positions under Persian authority. They appear together (Neh. 2:19; 4:7) but there are indications of harmonization in the text, suggesting that they were not really so closely linked. They show general opposition to the restoration of Jerusalem in the late sixth–early fifth centuries B.C. (Neh. 2:10–20; 4:19). Tobiah and Sanballat are associated with an attempt to get Nehemiah to act sacrilegiously (Neh. 6:10–14); Tobiah is shown as in high favor with leading men in Jerusalem, bound to him by marriage relationships (Neh. 6:15–19). During Nehemiah's absence in Babylon, Eliashib the priest gave Tobiah a special room in the Temple, from which Nehemiah ejected him (Neh. 13:4–9). It is clear that Tobiah was a man of considerable influence. It is possible that he was of the same family as the later Tobiads, prominent in the second century B.C. (cf. 2 Macc. 5:10–13). ***See also*** Nehemiah, The Book of; Sanballat.

P.R.A.

Tobijah (toh-bī'juh). **1** A Levite sent by the pious and prosperous Judean king Jehoshaphat (874–850 B.C.) to teach the people of Judah from the "book of the Law of the Lord" (2 Chron. 17: 8–9). **2** One of the men who was memorialized for bringing back gifts of gold from Babylon to Jerusalem (Zech. 6:10, 14).

Tobit (toh'bit), a book found in the Apocrypha. Tobit is a tale of the tribulations of life in the Diaspora (i.e., non-Palestinian areas inhabited by Jews), with the message that God will protect and heal those who are pious and compassionate. The story is set in eighth-century B.C. Nineveh among the exiles from the destruction of the Northern Kingdom of Israel, although the numerous anachronisms make it clear that the narrative is intended as fiction. It revolves around Tobit, an exile of the tribe of Naphtali, his wife Anna, their son Tobias, his bride and relative, Sarah, and the archangel Raphael, the angel of healing, who appears in disguise as Tobit's relative Azarias (Heb., "God helps").

Tobit has been blinded and reduced to poverty as a consequence of his efforts to bury Jews killed by the oppressive Assyrian king. Sarah is plagued by a demon-lover who has killed her seven grooms on their wedding nights. Both pray to God for death, but God responds by sending Raphael, an angel in disguise, who accompanies Tobias on the way to Rages in Media to recover funds Tobit has left in trust. In Ecbatana, they lodge with Sarah's family, and Tobias marries her. The bridal couple defeat the demon with Raphael's aid and return to Tobit and Anna in Nineveh, where the angel helps Tobias restore his father's sight. In addition to a good bit of sound moral instruction derived from the wisdom tradition, the tale advocates the marriage of relatives to preserve Jewish identity in the Diaspora, and it antici-

OUTLINE OF CONTENTS

Tobit

I. Tobit loses his eyesight in his concern for the burial of Jewish victims of Assyrian oppression (1:1–3:6)
II. The story of Sarah and the demon-lover (3:7–17)
III. Tobit's moral instruction to his son, Tobias (chap. 4)
IV. Tobias and Raphael prepare to set out on a journey to recover Tobit's funds (chap. 5)
V. The journey: Tobias catches a fish whose liver, heart, and gall will be used to help Sarah and heal Tobit (chap. 6)
VI. The wedding (chap. 7)
VII. The defeat of the demon (chap. 8)
VIII. Raphael recovers the funds (chap. 9)
IX. The anxiety of Tobit and Anna, and the departure of the young couple from Sarah's home (chap. 10)
X. The return and restoration of Tobit's sight (chap. 11)
XI. Raphael's true identity revealed (chap. 12)
XII. Tobit's prayer (chap. 13)
XIII. The testament of Tobit (chap. 14).

pates the end of the Diaspora and the restoration of the full Israelite community in Jerusalem.

The story is one of the two apocryphal books with sufficient popularity in the West to have convinced Jerome to include it in his Vulgate translation of the Bible. The motifs of the demon-lover and the angel in disguise are common in folklore. Tobit may predate the second century B.C. and is probably contemporary with the stories in Daniel 1–6, which are also concerned with the problems of maintaining Jewish identity and integrity in the Diaspora. The original language was probably Aramaic, although both Aramaic and Hebrew versions are found in the Dead Sea Scrolls. Protestants include it among the Apocrypha, while for Catholics it is one of the deuterocanonical books. ***See also*** Angel; Apocrypha, Old Testament; Demons; Dispersion; Testament. D.W.S.

Togarmah (toh-gahr'mah), the third son of Gomer and brother of Ashkenaz and Riphath (Gen. 10:3; I Chron. 1:6). (Beth-)togarmah is mentioned in Ezek. 27:14 as a city that traded horses and mules to Tyre. This city was called Til-Garimmu in Assyrian texts. It may be the classical Gauraena, modern Gürün, located about seventy miles west of Malatya in Asia Minor.

Tola (toh'lah; Heb., "crimson worm"). **1** The first of the four sons of Issachar (Gen. 46:13; Num. 26:23; 1 Chron. 7:1–2; *Jub.* 44:16) and the chief of the clans of Tolaites, Punites, Jashubites, and Shimronites. Nothing further is known of the four sons of Tola listed in 1 Chron. 7:2. **2** A judge (Judg. 10:1) described as a son of Puah.

tomb, Jesus', the place where Jesus was buried after his crucifixion. Although many Babylonians, Greeks, and Romans burned the bodies of their dead during the funeral services, Hebrews, Israelites, and later Jews, following the customs of Canaanites, Moabites, and other Near Eastern peoples, buried their dead in the ground. For some this was probably just a hole with no markings. Others, like those buried at Qumran, were placed in shallow graves and marked by piles of rocks, with no inscriptions to indicate the inhabitants of the graves. Wealthier people expanded caves and dug into the soft limestone rock to make shelves to hold stone coffins together with their contents. A few built large monuments, like those attributed to the Absalom family and to St. James on the eastern bank of the Kidron Valley.

Many of the tombs that were carved into the limestone hills were closed by doors that looked like stone wheels. Each wheel fit into a groove or track to keep it in place. When the tomb was opened, the wheel was rolled up a sloping track and held in place with some object. To close the door, it was necessary only to remove the block and let the wheel roll downhill in front of the opening of the tomb. This was evidently the kind of tomb in which Jesus was buried, because the Gospel writers tell about a stone that needed to be rolled away from the opening before one could enter the tomb (Mark 16:3; Matt. 28:2; Luke 24:2; John 20:1).

Christians have tried for centuries to find and identify the tomb into which the body of Jesus was laid. One of the conjectured places is the Church of the Holy Sepulchre in Jerusalem. Another place is a white cliff that looks something like a skull (John 19:17), just outside the walls of Jerusalem north of the city, but there is no specific tomb there.

Even if the tomb in which Jesus was placed were discovered, however, there would be no way to identify it. It would contain no stone coffin with his name carved in it; there would be no identifying seals, vessels, or jewelry. His body was hastily placed in a tomb that was not originally prepared for it (Matt. 27:57–60). Furthermore, it could not even be identified as a tomb belonging to the Arimathea family, because it was reportedly new and therefore would not have had the identifying marks of an ancient tomb where many family bodies had been laid (Matt. 27:60). The tomb remains unidentified. ***See also*** Sepulchre, Church of the Holy. G.W.B.

tombs. ***See*** Architecture; Burial; Mareshah; Nabatea, Nabateans; Ossuaries; Sidon; Tadmor; Tomb, Jesus'.

tongue, a word that often has a biological meaning as a part of the body, namely, the organ of taste and speech. It may become parched and cleave to the roof of the mouth, thus leaving one mute (Ps. 137:6). As the organ of speech, it can produce words of praise (cf. Ps. 51:14, 119:172), deceit (cf. Pss. 10:7, 78:36; Prov. 21:6; Mic. 6:12; Jer. 9:3, 5, 8), or mischief (cf. Prov. 17:4). The Letter of James condemns the tongue as unrighteous, untamable, and evil (James 3:6–12). The word "tongue" also frequently designates language (cf. Isa. 45:23; Phil. 2:11; Rom. 14:11), especially a foreign or incomprehensible language, as in the phrases "alien tongue" (Isa. 28:11; cf. 33:19) and "other tongues" (Acts 2:4). ***See also*** Tongues as of Fire; Tongues, Speaking with. J.B.T.

tongues, speaking with, "glossolalia," the act of speaking in a language either unknown to the speaker or incomprehensible (in both OT and NT, the word "tongue" sometimes refers to a language, frequently an alien or incomprehensible language). Apparently, the phenomenon of glossolalia played a prominent role in the life of at least some early Christian communities.

Paul addresses the matter of "speaking in tongues" as a possible problem in the church at Corinth. Although he acknowledges that the ability to speak in "various kinds of tongues" and the ability to interpret these tongues are "spiritual gifts" (1 Cor. 12:10), he is aware not all are to speak in tongues (1 Cor. 12:30), and advises his readers to seek "the higher gifts" (1 Cor. 12:31). In 1 Corinthians 13, he makes it clear that he thinks of love as the greatest spiritual gift. Love is contrasted with speaking "in the tongues of men and of angels" (1 Cor. 13:1); love endures, while tongues will cease (v. 8). Thus, in 1 Cor. 14:1, Paul directs that his readers make love their aim "and earnestly desire the spiritual gifts, especially that you may prophesy." In 1 Corinthians 14, Paul gives a number of directions about the use of glossolalia. Speaking in tongues is not helpful to the community, he says, because it is incomprehensible (14:2). Only when there is interpretation is there edification (v. 5). When the community convenes, no more than three should speak in tongues, each in turn, and there must be an interpretation (v. 27). Paul feels that uncontrolled and uninterpreted speaking in tongues does not edify the community and that it gives outsiders the impression that believers are mad (v. 23). Yet, he allows this activity to take place, so long as it is done in orderly fashion and is accompanied by interpretation. In 1 Corinthians, it seems clear that "speaking in a tongue" means speaking an incomprehensible language, a language that probably was thought of as the language of angels (1 Cor. 13:1).

Acts 2 contains a narrative about the events of the first Pentecost after Easter. On that day, the apostles gathered together, and, after hearing a sound like wind and seeing tongues like fire, they began "to speak in other tongues, as the Spirit gave them utterance" (Acts 2:4). The author of Acts goes on to list various nationalities of persons who heard the apostles speak, all hearing in their own languages. Although the story may suggest that the apostles spoke an incomprehensible language (v. 13), the dominant idea is that they were speaking known foreign languages. In this respect, the phenomenon described here differs from the glossolalia known to Paul and practiced in Corinth.

The phenomenon of speaking with tongues is mentioned twice more in Acts. After Peter preached in the house of Cornelius, the Gentiles there began to speak in tongues (Acts 10: 46). This was taken as a sign that the Holy Spirit had been poured out among Gentiles and that they should be baptized. In Acts 19, Paul met some disciples of Apollos at Ephesus. These disciples, who had been baptized "into John's baptism" (Acts 19:3), had never heard of the Holy Spirit. Paul instructed them, baptized them in the name of Jesus, and laid his hands on them. Then, "the Holy Spirit came on them; and they spoke with tongues and prophesied" (v. 6). The author of Acts probably thought of these two incidents as similar to the one described in chap. 2.

Both in 1 Corinthians and in Acts, the gift of glossolalia is associated with the Spirit. Paul's treatment of it as ecstatic, incomprehensible speech probably reflects actual practices in his churches. In Acts, the phenomenon is treated as a dramatic sign authenticating various communities of Christian believers: the original Jerusalem Christians in Acts 2; Gentile Christians in Acts 10; and the disciples of Apollos in Acts 19. ***See also*** Acts of the Apostles, The; Pentecost; Tongue; Tongues as of Fire. J.B.T.

tongues as of fire, a phrase used in Acts 2:3 to designate one of the dramatic events of the first Pentecost after Jesus' death and resurrection. The author says that tongues as of fire appeared and rested on each of the apostles. As a result, the apostles began to speak in other tongues (Acts 2:4, 8). The description brings together the association of fire with divine power and the imagery of tongues as languages. ***See also*** Acts of the Apostles, The; Pentecost; Tongue; Tongues, Speaking with.

tools, implements used by humans in crafting something. Use of this generic term in the Bible is sparse, writers preferring to designate specific tools, such as ax, pick, or saw (1 Chron. 20:3).

In Exod. 20:25 the use of tools on the stones for the altar to be built for the worship of God was expressly forbidden, since such use caused profanation of the stones. Aaron used a "graving tool" to fashion the calf from the contributed gold, possibly some sort of stylus or engraving device used on the rough molded form (Exod. 31:4). The same prohibition on working stones for the altar is found in Deuteronomy, reflecting a clear date within the Iron Age by its reference to "iron tool" use (Deut. 27:5). That traditional qualification was recalled when Joshua built an altar on Mount Ebal, just north of Shechem (Josh. 8:31). In the construction of the Temple by Solomon, construction materials were to be prepared and finished at the quarry site so that neither "hammer nor axe nor any tool of iron was heard in the temple" (1 Kings 6:7).

Archaeological evidence shows that tool technology followed the course of improvement in material procurement and processing. Thus from prehistoric stone, bone, and shell tools one moves through the successive developments of copper, bronze, and iron, while earlier materials continued to be used where suited or more cheaply available. Flint continues to be used for scrapers and some knives to this day.

Each craft developed specialized tools for its work. Jewelers' drills, farmers' compound sickles, carpenters' adzes, housewives' saddle querns and hand grinders, stonecutters' hammers and chisels, bronze workers' molds, millers' millstones, olive presses, wine vats, scholars' inkwells, priests' incense burners, and butchers' knives are just the beginning of a list of tools found from the biblical period. R.S.B.

Topheth (toh'feth), a location in the Valley of the Son of Hinnom south of Jerusalem. The name was derived from an Aramaic word meaning "hearth" or "fireplace" but was pronounced by the Masoretes with the vowels of the Hebrew word for "shame." This was due to the practice there of sacrificing children as burnt offerings to Baal and Molech in the times of Isaiah and Jeremiah (Isa. 30:33; Jer. 7:31, 32; 19:6, 11–14; cf. 32:35). Kings Ahaz and Manasseh of Judah are reported to have offered their sons in the Valley of the Son of Hinnom (2 Chron. 28:3; 33:6; cf. 2 Kings 16:3; 21:6). King Josiah attempted to put a stop to the practice by defiling the altar at Topheth (2 Kings 23:10) but it was revived after his death. ***See also*** Hinnom, Valley of; Masorah; Molech. M.A.S.

Torah (toh'rah; Heb., "instruction" or "teaching"), God's instructions to Israel. *Torah* has been commonly translated as "law" following the Greek translation in the Septuagint as *nomos* (Gk., "law") and the subsequent Latin *lex* ("law"). However, even *nomos* in the context of the Hellenistic period (333–63 B.C.) revealed divine legal and doctrinal elements. Thus, to identify torah with some sort of legalism is a complete misunderstanding of the term.

In the Hebrew Bible: In the context of the Hebrew Bible, torah is defined in several ways. In the Pentateuch, in Genesis and Exodus, torah refers to God's instruction (Exod. 13:9; 16:4) and parallels "commandment" and "statute" (Gen. 26:5; Exod. 18:16). In Leviticus and Numbers, torah defines cultic instructions: as an introduction (Lev. 6:14; 7:1; 14:2) and as a summary of previous rules (7:37; 14:54; Num. 5:29–30). The phrase "this is the statute of the Torah" (Num. 19:2; 31:21; cf. 35:29) emphasizes the reference to such cultic instruction. In Lev. 10:11 the causal form of the verbal root *yrh* ("to instruct," "to teach") is used to define the main priestly duties, "to teach the people of Israel all the statutes which the Lord has spoken to them by Moses." This teaching includes sacrificial laws, ethical behavior, holidays, and regulations concerning purity and impurity (10:10; 14:57; chaps. 4–7, 11–15, 23).

In Deuteronomy, the priestly teaching function of Torah is also underscored in 17:8–11 and 33:8–10. Deut. 17:8–9, 11 is particularly noteworthy: "If any case arises requiring decision . . . which is too difficult for you . . . you shall [come] to the Levitical priests, and to the judge . . . according to the Torah which they shall pronounce to you, you shall do." However, in most of the occurrences in Deuteronomy, "this Torah" refers to the composite literary elements of the book—speeches, laws, blessings and curses, etc. (1:5; 4:44; 27:3, 26; 28:58; and see "This book of the Torah," 28:61; 29:20; 30:10; 31:26). The Torah in Deuteronomy is perceived as Israel's cultural and national identity: 4:5, 6, 8: "Behold I have taught you statutes and ordinances . . . keep them and do them; for that will be your wisdom and your understanding in the sight of the peoples . . . for what great nation is there that has statutes and ordinances so righteous as all this Torah . . . ?" These verses and other elements have given rise to the theory that the instructive style and the understanding of Torah in Deuteronomy were influenced by the wisdom traditions of Israel.

The Former Prophets (Joshua through 2 Kings), which are perceived by modern scholarship as having undergone a systematic editing by adherents to the school of Deuteronomy, follow the predominant usage of torah in Deuteronomy as referring to the comprehensive nature of that book (Josh. 1:7–8; 8:31–34; 22:5; 23:6; 1 Kings 2:3; 2 Kings 10:31; 14:6; 17:13, 34; 21:8). It appears that "The book of the Torah" found in the Temple (2 Kings 22:8; 23:25) was a version of Deuteronomy. The only references to torah which are un-Deuteronomistic are "The book of the Torah of God" in Josh. 24:26 in which Joshua records the Shechem covenant and the difficult "This is the Torah of man, Lord God" of 2 Sam. 7:19.

In the Latter Prophets Hosea, Amos, Isaiah son of Amoz, and Micah (eighth century B.C.) torah is used in differing contexts. Torah appears in the sense of cultic rules (Hos. 4:6), as parallel to covenant (8:1), and as written divine instructions known to the northern tribes (8:12). Amos (2:4) and Isaiah (5:24; 30:9) see Torah as including God's moral commands (cf. Amos 2:6–12). Isaiah, also, gives the sense of divine teachings through the prophet (Isa. 1:10; 8:16). In Isaiah (2:3), too, and Micah (4:2), the Torah will be taught by God to all nations in the final times.

Habakkuk (1:4) uses torah in terms of ethics. Criticism of the teaching of the Torah by the priests appears in Micah (3:11), Zephaniah (3:4), Ezekiel (22:26), and Malachi (2:6–9). Jeremiah (2:8; 8:8) may also be criticizing the wisdom groups for their failure to promulgate the Torah correctly.

Jeremiah uses torah in a comprehensive sense (6:19; 9:12; 16:11; 26:4) similar to Deuteronomy (of which he was a student). In the New Covenant to be given at the time of redemption (31:33), the Torah remains the content (only the method of transmission has changed) and all will be naturally obedient to it.

Isaiah also uses the word "torah" in the comprehensive sense (Isa. 42:21, 24, as does Malachi in 3:22) and eschatologically (42:4; 51:4). Ezekiel shows the influence of the Priestly sections of the Pentateuch in his use of torah (43:11; 44:23–24), and also eschatologically in reference to the Temple (43:12). In sum, the prophets use the word "torah" in a broad sense. Even the priestly instruction was not limited to cultic issues as was illustrated by the example of a request for priestly torah given in Haggai 2:11–13, which has a precise structural and linguistic parallel in Jer. 3:1.

In the book of Psalms, there is a tendency to praise the Torah and the righteous who cleave to it, so that it is viewed as the purpose and motivation of existence (Pss. 1:2; 19:8; 37:31; 40:9; 94:12; 112:1; 119:97). These Psalms seem to be influenced by the wisdom traditions, perhaps in conjunction with Deuteronomy (see also Ps. 78). Other Deuteronomistic influence may be found in Ps. 89:31–33 (cf. 2 Sam. 7:14), while Ps. 105:45 may reflect Priestly writings (which elevate the Sinai covenant above that of Abraham).

Proverbs knows of torah as advice of a parent (1:8; 3:1) or a sage (13:14). Torah is paralleled to reproof (1:8), command (3:1), and a good lesson (4:2). Although many of the occurrences of torah here are in the sense of general wisdom, the specific use of torah as religious instruction appears also (28:9; 29:18).

The Chronicler depicts the kings as subservient to God's Torah (1 Chron. 16:40; 22:12–13; 2 Chron. 14:3; 23:18; 30:16; 31:3–4, 21; 34:14–15, 19), which is perceived as a specific book (2 Chron. 12:1; 25:4; 33:2–9; but see the Priestly rule mentioned in 2 Chron. 15:3). In Ezra (3:2; 7:6, 10) and Nehemiah (8:1, 8, 18; 9:3; 10:30; 13:1, 3) a fixed written torah is assumed.

Conclusions: The vast majority of the occurrences of the word "torah" in the Bible refer to God's instructions to Moses at Sinai that were transmitted to Israel. These instructions or commandments (in a narrower or wider sense) became Israelite law and the stipulations of the covenant. They were all-important, since they were the specific manifestations of God's will. Since they were God-given, they were obviously good, and obedience would result in long life, prosperity, health, and happiness. Disobedience would be punished with harm, barrenness, exile, destruction, and death. The Torah is the great democratizing influence on Israelite society—all must obey, especially the kings (Deut. 17:18–20). This teaching was permanent, even if the covenant would be broken (Jer. 31:33). The teaching of the Torah was an essential priestly function, but the greatest joy was to have God answer one's prayers and teach it directly to the individual (Pss. 94:12; 119:33–34, 72–73).

Proverbs, which uses torah in the sense of providing parental guidance for a child, may provide the reason why this term was used in the religious sphere. The Israelites as God's children is a well-known metaphor in the Bible (Exod. 4:22; Deut. 14:1; 32:10–12; Hos. 11:1; Jer. 31:9, 20; Isa. 66:13). Thus, torah in the religious sense may have originally connoted the teachings imparted by God the parent to the child Israel. As such, the giving of the Torah is an act of supreme love.

In later Judaism, torah came to mean not only the Pentateuch (known as the written Torah), but also the Talmud (the oral Torah). Indeed, all of Jewish tradition is referred to as Torah. ***See also*** Covenant; Pentateuch. J.U.

Tosephta (toh-sef'tuh; Aramaic, "addition"), a collection of Hebrew laws and comments arranged in tractates that parallel the sixty-three tractates of the Mishnah. The materials in the Tosephta expand upon or comment on the laws in the Mishnah, present other traditions parallel to and/or contradictory to the Mishnah, or gather stories and scriptural interpretations relevant to the themes of the Mishnah. The Tosephta was probably collected in the third century A.D. as a commentary on and complement to the Mishnah, though some date it in the fourth century. Traditions found in the Tosephta are often found also in one of the Talmuds, but the literary relationship is not always clear. In the Talmudic tradition authorship is attributed to Rabbi Hiyya and Rabbi Oshaia (early third century), but this attribution has not been historically verified. ***See also*** Mishnah; Talmud. A.J.S.

Tou (toh'o͞o), or Toi (toy or toh'ī), the king of Hamath who negotiated with David after his defeat of the Ammonites and their allies, some of whom had been enemies of Tou (2 Sam. 8:9–10; 1 Chron. 18:9–10).

tow (toh), the short broken fibers of flax or hemp. In the biblical view it is relatively useless and easily flammable (Judg. 16:9; Isa. 1:31; 43:17 [RSV: "wick"]).

tower (translation of a variety of Hebrew words, most often *migdal*), a tall stone or mudbrick structure, which was either round, semicircular, square, or rectangular in shape. Towers constructed for military purposes included free-standing outposts that were located in strategic positions (2 Chron. 20:24; 26:10; 2 Kings 17:9; 18:8) and projecting bastions that were part of a city's defense system (2 Chron. 14:7; 26:9; 32:5; Neh. 3:25–27); depending on their purpose and building materials, the dimensions of towers varied. Towers provided elevated positions for sentries or for soldiers repelling enemy attacks (2 Chron. 26:15), and some towers were so massively built that they provided refuge for the population in time of attack (Judg. 9:46–52). Reference to the destruction of a city's towers symbolized its fall (Ezek. 26:4, 9), and Isaiah (13:22) depicted Babylon's demise by predicting that hyenas would inhabit its towers (cf. Isa. 32:14). Siege towers were often used in attacks on cities (Isa. 23:13; 29:3; Ezek. 21:22).

In addition to the military function of towers, farmers built small watchtowers in fields and vineyards (Isa. 5:2; Matt. 21:33). These towers provided elevated positions from which fields were guarded; the ground floor of such structures served as living quarters for fieldworkers or guards, since ripening crops had to be guarded day and night.

In addition to the general references to Jerusalem's defensive towers, the Bible also mentions

An archer shooting from a tower; engraving on an eighth-century B.C. quiver.

a number of this city's towers by name: the Tower of the Hundred (Neh. 3:1; 12:39), the Tower of Hananel (Neh. 3:1; 12:39; Jer. 31:38; Zech. 14:10), the Tower of the Ovens (Neh. 3:11; 12:38), and the tower of David (Song of Sol. 4:4). The biblical writers also referred to other famous towers: the tower of Eder (Gen. 35:21), the tower of Penuel (Judg. 8:17), the Tower of Schechem (Judg. 9:46), and the tower of the flock (Mic. 4:8, where *migdal ēder* refers to Jerusalem). Specific reference is also made to a tower in Thebez (Judg. 9:50–51) and a tower in Siloam (Luke 13:4).

Because of the tower's defensive significance, it symbolized security (Pss. 48:12; 61:3; 122:7; Prov. 18:10), but the towers of God's enemies could not protect them from judgment (Isa. 2:15; 30:25; cf. Prov. 12:12, where the Hebrew is obscure). In the Song of Solomon, the maiden's neck is compared to the tower of David (4:4) and an ivory tower (7:4), and her breasts are compared to towers (8:10).

The tower of Babel (Gen. 11:4–5) is normally understood as a Babylonian temple tower or ziggurat. In Ezek. 29:10 and 30:6, the RSV translates *migdal* as a place name, Migdol. ***See also*** Forts; Migdol; Watchtower. G.L.M.

town clerk (lit. "scribe," as the Greek term is translated everywhere in the NT except at Acts 19:35), an official in the Greco-Roman world who had significant authority and responsibility under the Roman system of government. These officials were responsible for the proper form and wording for decrees that were presented to assemblies of the people, and they appear to have been responsible for keeping order and preventing illegal assemblies. Such a person was one of the chief characters in an account of a riot at Ephesus in which Paul was involved (Acts 19:35–41). ***See also*** Cities; Ephesus; Scribe.

towns, settlements of small but indeterminate size. It is practically impossible to distinguish between town and village as biblical usage treats them. They could be walled with gates, as a city (1 Sam. 23:7; Prov. 8:3) but are spoken of in parallel with villages (Mat. 10:11). Named towns, like Tappuah (Josh. 17:8), Bethlehem (Judg. 17:8), Arimithea (Luke 23:50), or Ephraim (John 11:54), were sometimes called cities (KJV) in earlier translations, and no clues are given as to size or condition to distinguish them from villages or cities. It is probable that cities were larger, more frequently fortified, and more often the location of important government facilities. It appears that "town" is closer to village than to city in meaning.

Towns had officials, as a clerk (Acts 19:35) quieted a crowd in Ephesus, but the men of a town could act for its security (Judg. 6:27) and serve as inhibitors to troublemakers. Towns could be identified with populations or sects (Matt. 10:5) as well as symbolize evil and destruction (note Sodom and Gomorrah as models, Matt. 10:15; Luke 10:12). Cities were frequently identified with their surrounding towns and villages (note Ashdod and Gaza, Josh. 15:47; and numerous references in 1 Chron. 7:28). Deuteronomic law made special provision for the protection of the helpless, such as strangers, widows, and orphans, in the population of the towns (e.g., see Deut. 14:29). The public ministry of Jesus was carried out in towns (Luke 13:22) and early missionary work of the church usually began in synagogues or other public places in towns (Acts 8:40; 14:1, 6). R.S.B.

Trachonitis (trak-uh-nī'tis), a Greek name in the NT for a 370 square mile rocky, yet potentially fertile, lava plateau located northeast of Palestine between Galilee and Damascus (referred to in the OT as the land of Bashan). Originally a part of Herod's kingdom, it became the territory of Philip (Luke 3:1) and later was governed by Herod Agrippa I. Two NT cities in the region were Caesarea Philippi and Bethsaida. ***See also*** Agrippa I; Bashan; Philip.

trade and transportation, the movement and exchange of goods and services that make up commerce. This article will first treat the biblical occurrences of the two terms, and then summarize some major features of trade and transportation in the biblical world.

Biblical References: While the term "trade" is used in a few instances to designate one's occupation in general (Acts 18:3, referring in that context to the trade of tentmakers), or to particular occupations (prophet and priest, Jer. 14:18; silversmiths, Acts 19:27), or to groups of occupations ("all whose trade is on the sea," i.e., shipmasters, sailors, and seafaring men, Rev. 18:17), the major use of the term is for people in commercial trading, either foreign or domestic. It is viewed as a normal part of domestic activity by citizens in pursuit of prosperity (Gen. 34:10, 21) or by visitors to a land not formally their own, but seeking normal relations in it (Gen. 42:34, where Joseph invites his family to Egypt, and trading is invited). Trade could be a means of survival for desperate prisoners or refugees (Lam. 1:11), and it could characterize a place (Ezek. 17:4). Successful trade brought wealth (Ezek. 28:5), but it could breed violence and corruption (Ezek. 28:16) leading to destruction (Ezek. 28:18). It was normal to invest resources (Luke 19:13), but traffic in sacrifice materials was considered by Jesus to be an inappropriate use of the Jerusalem Temple precincts, as John's Gospel reports (John 2:16; see also Zech. 14:21). Trade could be planned in advance (James 4:13), but merchants could use dishonest devices for excessive profit (Hos. 12:7), and it could be done without satisfaction (Job. 20:18). Nevertheless, trade was ignored only at one's own peril (Luke 19:20–26).

Trade was an international matter, and the references include mention of a variety of the trading partners of the biblical world. So one finds, for example, Midianites (Gen. 37:28), Arabians (1 Kings 10:15), Tyre (Isa. 23:8), Sheba, Raamah, Haran, Canneh, Eden, Asshur, Chilmad, Javan, Tarshish, Tubal, Meshech, Beth-togarmah, Rhodes, Edom, Judah, Israel, Damascus, Helbon, Uzal, Dedan, Arabia, Kedar, Cyprus, and Elishah (all in Ezek. 27), as well as Chaldea (Babylon, Ezek. 1:29), Ophir (1 Kings 10:11), Egypt, Kue, Syria and the Hittite royal house (1 Kings 10:28–29), some of which remain imprecisely identified. At times trading was a royal enterprise for official purposes of diplomacy (1 Kings 10:1–13) or profit (1 Kings 10:14–29), a matter in which Solomon was the traditional success model (2 Chron. 1:16; 9:14). But some things were beyond trade, such as mythic demons (Leviathan in Job 41:6) or faithfulness (Zech. 11:4–17).

References to travelers and travel are the simplest index to biblical views of transportation other than the specific terms for devices used to move people or goods. Travel could occur either by day or night (Exod. 13:21), and there were advantages to each. Daytime travel over land reduced the dangers of being waylaid by bandits but subjected one to the worst heat in summer unless one took time out. Night travel over land needed moonlight for safest progress, but eliminated the heat problem both for the humans and the animals involved. Sea travel was limited to daytime voyaging within sight of land until use of celestial navigation allowed direct crossings. In the biblical period sea traffic consisted predominantly of coastal routes, and safe havens at intervals of a day's sail were a hallmark of the Phoenician sea travel development. Land travel used what roads were available (Job 21:29), and the word of travelers was a major link in communications (Job 21:29). In times of stress roads might be avoided, and travelers would take to roundabout routes for safety while commercial transport might suspend operations (Judg. 5:6). International travel was commonplace but was judiciously watched for danger (Job 6:19). Its nature could be trade (Ezek. 27:25), legal business (Acts 9:1–7), casual encounter (2 Sam. 12:4), a deliberate group activity planned (Acts 19:29; 2 Cor. 8:19), or the result of a crisis (Acts 11:19). For a person or place to be forgotten by travelers was a distinctive form of oblivion (Job. 28:4), and it could symbolize an extreme of future desolation (Ezek. 39:11) in a prophet's oracle.

Transportation and Trade: It is likely but unprovable that transportation preceded trade as a human achievement. People probably moved to follow food supplies as hunters and gatherers or moved to safe quarters or to a more dependable water supply before they had the means of accumulating surplus goods with which to begin trade. In the remote reaches of Paleolithic and Mesolithic human life (ca. 250,000–8000 B.C.), transportation is likely to have been overland by foot, although the earliest settlements in Egypt and elsewhere allow the possibility of rivers being used for transport in some locations. Absence of clear archaeological evidence is insufficient grounds to declare that no early ancestors moved by crude rafts, long since decayed and unrecoverable as evidence. Late Pleistocene stone tools (from about forty thousand years ago) illustrate that their makers knew variations in raw materials and traveled or traded to get them. "Luxury" goods such as amber

TRADE AND TRANSPORTATION

or sea shells have been found dozens and even hundreds of miles from their sources. Surely throughout the entire biblical period, trade and transportation were mutually nourishing endeavors. With the Neolithic period (from about 10,000 B.C.) and developments in the domestication of plants and animals, the beginnings of true agriculture, and the economic foundations making cities possible, trade and transportation began to grow in a series of technological developments that continue to this day.

Rivers: There is little doubt that early settlement patterns reflect transportation by river craft in both Egypt and Mesopotamia. The central role of the Nile was its proximity to all cultivatable land, aided by a dominant northwest wind which allowed early sailing craft to maneuver upstream as easily as the current allowed raft and barge traffic to move northward downstream. The long stretch below the cataract at Aswan gave an untrammeled waterway to the Mediterranean Sea that served the entire population of Egypt throughout antiquity.

The same importance of rivers is evident in the earliest settlement patterns of Sumer in lower Mesopotamia. The Tigris and Euphrates were far riskier flood hazards than the Nile, but the city-states of Lagash, Kish, Eridu, and Uruk all grew in proximity to river sources both for ease of moving people and goods and for the water available (as in Egypt) for agricultural development. The earliest literary materials from the region reflect a situation where life's survival was dependent on the successful victory of the river's fresh water over the salty demon of the sea (*Enuma Elish*, Tablet 1). Travel on rivers required some sort of stable vehicles to move goods, however, and the history of water transport devices indicates developments from crude rafts to sailing vessels with sufficient cargo capacity to handle large quantities of timber, copper, and other "heavy freight."

Seas: The use of open salt water for transportation is documented at least by Old Kingdom times in Egypt (2700–2200 B.C.) when transportation and trade were carried out with Byblos on the coast of modern Lebanon. Such travel involved craft called "Byblites" for moving both goods and passengers. It was the Phoenicians who developed maritime trade into substantial proportions, colonizing for their purposes the entire north coast of Africa beyond the Strait of Gibraltar to the western coast of modern Morocco, as well as Cyprus, Greece, Italy, Mediterranean islands such as Sardinia, and even the Spanish coast, Malta, and Crete. Subsequent great seapowers like Persia, Greece, and Rome first absorbed and then followed and expanded the trading routes developed by Phoenicia's maritime transportation network.

It was also to the experts of Tyre that Solomon turned not only for his construction projects, but for his maritime development (1 Kings 9:26–28), both shipbuilding and shiphandling being new skills to the Israelites of the monarchy. Seaworthy craft allowed travel from the upper reaches of the Gulf of Aqaba (Solomon's port there was Ezion-geber) into the Red Sea and from there either up the Gulf of Suez or down the coast of Arabia round the tip of the Arabian peninsula and across the east coast of Africa; or they could sail eastward along the south coast of Arabia to touch points east along the Persian Gulf or the centers of life in India on the Indus River.

Sail power was employable in all of this, although the Greeks and Persians, followed by the Romans, developed human-powered rowing ships that reached their maximum development in triremes (three tiers of rowers on each side of a vessel) used by Persia in unsuccessful attempts to subdue Greece (as at the battle of Salamis, 480 B.C.). Roman ships of course reached north Atlantic points in Britain and the continent as well as dominated the Mediterranean by NT times.

It is in such a maritime network that the report of Paul's journey by ship from Caesarea on the Palestine coast to Italy is set, giving some idea of both the normal routing and the hazards of such transportation. The route taken by the ship of Adramyttium (a port in Mysia, in what is modern northwest Turkey) was north up the coast to Sidon, then across the south coast of Cyprus to Myra in Lycia (in modern southwest Turkey). There Paul and his guards transferred to a ship from Alexandria, Egypt, bound for Italy and headed west along the south shore of Crete. Despite seasonal hazards of storms in winter weather, they struck out from Phoenix on the southwest coast of Crete, running into stormy troubles when they hit the open water exposed to western windy seas. Managing only a temporary relief at an island called Cauda (Acts 27:16–17), they took drastic measures with cargo and gear and managed to drift to shore at Malta, remaining there for the duration of the winter. From Malta they set out for Syracuse on Sicily and Rhegium at the toe of Italy's "boot" and made landfall at Puteoli two-thirds of the way up the Italian west coast, from which point the journey proceeded overland. Acts reports a roster of 276 people aboard that ship with a staff of soldiers under a centurion in charge of the prisoners. Wheat is mentioned as cargo, which would be quite normal inasmuch as Egypt served as the "breadbasket" for Rome. Sea connections with points east continued to bring to the Mediterranean world the more esoteric spices, precious stones, and precious metal throughout the biblical period.

Land Transport: Limited water supplies first determined that land travel could not cross the major stretches of desert in the biblical world, the Sahara and the Arabian desert. It funneled land travel around the quarter-moon-shaped arc

TRADE AND TRANSPORTATION

of land from the Mesopotamian valley, across northern Syria south of the major mountain ranges of eastern Turkey, and down the Syro-Palestine corridor five hundred miles to the eastern Nile delta in Egypt (the "Fertile Crescent"), from where one could go by land or river craft to the upper reaches of southern Egypt.

Foot travel was common in all biblical periods, walking being cheap, convenient, and free of other people's timetables. Walking was made easier with a staff or walking stick, especially when moving through the hilly regions of Syro-Palestine. Animals, after they had been domesticated, were used, especially the ass or donkey, which is still a major vehicle for local rural travel. Oxen provided good draft strength for pulling carts, but required more water and forage than many of the zones afforded. Horses were faster and more maneuverable and were traded extensively by Solomon (1 Kings 10:28–29) together with chariots, making both civilian and military transport more efficient. Horses had been used for cavalry presumably since the time of the Hyksos, but again they required more extensive forage, water, and care than the ubiquitous donkey. Presumably the expense of purchase as well as maintenance of horses kept the ass popular. As a cargo carrier it could be fitted with a carrier saddle, and its capacity was enormous for its size. Its sure-footedness added to its value when covering rocky terrain, and its capacity to survive on seemingly inedible plant life allowed it to thrive where other beasts could not. Only the domestication of the camel about 1200 B.C. brought a serious challenge to the dominant role of the ass. The capacity of the camel for cargo was also enormous for its size, and its ability to go for long desert treks without water for days opened up new routes of both freight and passenger traffic that had previously been impossible. That one still sees camel caravans is testimony to the economic advantages they allow for local delivery to remote regions unblessed by highways or airports.

The use of wheeled vehicles is attested in lower Mesopotamia in the third millennium B.C. The early models were made with solid wheels rigidly attached to their axles, which then were mounted to turn under the bed of the cart. Such carts provided noisy, rough transport, but with the invention of a lighter wheel with spokes to a rim from a hub that would rotate on the axle, major improvement in load capacity, maneuverability, and consequent range was achieved. Pictorial representations in Egypt indicate that such chariots were used with teams of four horses for sport or military purposes. For efficiency of wheeled traffic road development from previous tracks of mounted animals or footpaths was essential.

Certain basic routes were developed prior to roads, some of which were followed when roads were built. Within Palestine there were three major north-south routes as well as commonly used transverse or east-west crossings. Because of the lay of the land and Palestine's location in relation to the "great powers" of the time (Egypt, the Hittites, Mesopotamia) the north-south routes were primarily used for both commercial and military traffic over the centuries. Of first importance was the coastal route. Coming up from the eastern Nile delta in Egypt, it followed the curve of the Mediterranean shore, branching inland at the Mount Carmel mountain range to cross the Esdraelon Plain at Megiddo. This "way of the sea" (Isa. 9:1) was fortified by the Egyptians during their control, thus discouraging the Israelite migrants from using it after the Exodus. North of Megiddo the route went along the west side of the Sea of Galilee to Hazor and Damascus, from where connections north through Syria to both the Hittite and Ugaritic centers and, crossing the arc of the crescent, to Mesopotamia were available. From Megiddo there were also transverse connections north of the Carmel ridge to coastal towns like Acco and points north as well as eastward along the plain to Beth-shan and the Jordan Valley, from which routes continued eastward across the Jordan and southward to Jericho.

The other major north-south route ran from the port on the Gulf of Aqaba up the Transjordan hills of Edom, Moab, and Ammon, continuing northward to Damascus. It was part of the great overland route from Damascus to Arabia but allowed land-sea connections from Damascus to points east as well. An intermediate north-south route serving Israel was that in the hills running southward from Jerusalem to Bethlehem, Hebron, and points south. North of Jerusalem it connected with Shechem and the Esdraelon Plain, allowing both north and transverse connections at Beth-shan.

Additional crossings from east to west were possible through the pass between Mounts Ebal and Gerizim at Shechem, the Valley of Achor and Jerusalem down to Jericho, and across the southern reaches of the Shephelah from Beersheba to the Edomite heights. This was especially prominent during Edomite domination of southern Judah and during the Nabataean ascendance. In Hellenistic and Roman times, travel across the eastern Syrian desert used Palmyra as a major center on the way to the Euphrates.

While the Persians constructed a major new facility for traveling with their development of the route from Susa (in western Persia) to Ephesus (on the southwest coast of Turkey), other remains indicate the supremacy of Rome in building enduring roads for public and military use. By means of carefully spaced stations for fresh mounts and overnight rest stops, Persia cut the travel time from Susa to Ephesus from three

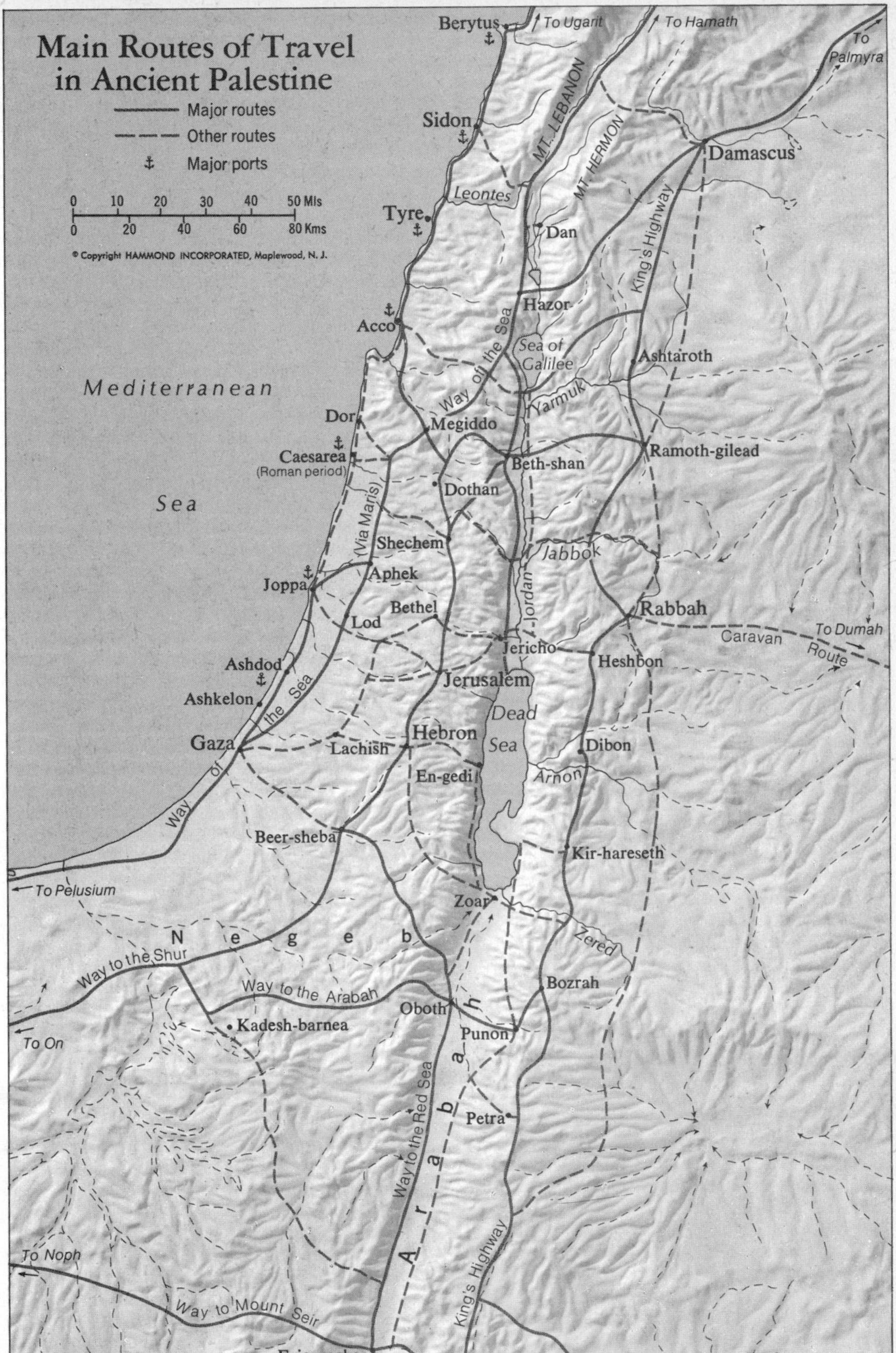
Main Routes of Travel in Ancient Palestine
Major routes
Other routes
Major ports
0 10 20 30 40 50 Mls
0 20 40 60 80 Kms
© Copyright HAMMOND INCORPORATED, Maplewood, N. J.
Mediterranean Sea
Berytus
To Ugarit
To Hamath
To Palmyra
Sidon
MT. LEBANON
MT. HERMON
Damascus
Leontes
Tyre
Dan
King's Highway
Hazor
Acco
Way of the Sea
Sea of Galilee
Ashtaroth
Yarmuk
Dor
Megiddo
Caesarea
(Roman period)
Beth-shan
Ramoth-gilead
Dothan
(Via Maris)
Shechem
Jabbok
Aphek
Joppa
Jordan
Rabbah
Bethel
Lod
To Dumah
Caravan Route
Jericho
Heshbon
Ashdod
Jerusalem
Ashkelon
Way of the Sea
Dead Sea
Gaza
Hebron
Lachish
Dibon
En-gedi
Arnon
Beer-sheba
Kir-hareseth
To Pelusium
Zoar
Negeb
Zered
Way to the Shur
Way to the Arabah
Bozrah
Oboth
Kadesh-barnea
Punon
To On
Arabah
Way to the Red Sea
Petra
King's Highway
To Noph
Way to Mount Seir
Ezion-geber
Gulf of Aqaba
To Tema

TRADE AND TRANSPORTATION

months to a week. Its couriers on royal business would move a message day and night on a road that included ferries and bridges for hazardous terrain or river crossings. Rome built its roads straight and to last. Having seen the legacy from northern Scotland to the eastern Jordanian desert, one cannot help but admire the engineering consistency not only in road plotting and construction, but in tight controls. The writer has only seen one piece of genuinely crooked Roman roadbed. It lies just north of Umm al-Jimal in the eastern Jordan desert. It suggests that the crew was either ill or drunk during construction of that stretch unless the damage has been due to earthquake, evidence of which is not readily apparent. It is unique. Romans marked their roads with milestones, an immense help to archaeologists despite numerous reuses of the stones for other construction. Stone was the primary construction material in Roman road preparation, as well as its paving. The same materials being used for bridge construction has contributed to the longevity of the remains. Biblical stories (such as the parable of the good Samaritan, Luke 10:29–37) indicate both that travel on roads could be dangerous from thieves in ambush and that normal travel facilities in the form of inns were found on most routes. Some of these facilities were extensive in order to accommodate large caravans, both animals and drivers, or at major intersectons, to handle groups of caravans, giving rise to the term "caravanserai" for such installations.

Trade: Trade occurred first whenever a person had an object desired by another person and was willing to exchange it for either some goods or service. As noted above, the evidences of such commerce are rooted in Paleolithic times, given the patterns of raw materials for tools and even luxury goods occurring far from their sources in various locations. That barter moved to formal markets, shops, and government or religious institutions is evident by the dawn of urban civilization in both Mesopotamia and Egypt by 3000 B.C. The earliest forms of writing in Mesopotamia were apparently crude pictographs recording materials contributed to the temples of the city gods. Subsequent cuneiform texts in Sumerian, Akkadian, Eblaite, Hittite, and Ugaritic attest in sheer volume that the economics of life took the lion's share of recordkeeping in all these ancient societies. Similarly in Egypt, the royal records of the dynasties are full of such economic data as the gifts buried with the pharaoh, division of labor for food procurement, records of laborers assigned to projects, and other matters falling in the general category of commerce. While primarily tied to the religious consciousness, whether through temple or the divine pharaoh, ancient Egyptian concerns show abundant interest in the movement of goods and the accounting of such matters.

Goods and Services Exchanged: One might rightly assert that any form of necessary good was subject to trade in circumstances where some were deprived of it but had means of exchange. It is also true that as any society becomes prosperous, it looks on certain goods as desirable, even though they are not "necessary," and develops means of acquiring such goods through trade if they are not immediately accessible in one's property. This is vividly evident both in the story of Solomon's dealings for construction goods, services, and luxury materials (1 Kings 5–10) and in a marvelous vignette on trade in Ezekiel's oracles against Tyre (Ezek. 27–28). Tyre is described as "merchant of the peoples on many coastlands" with good reason, it would seem. In Tyre one found fir from Senir; cedar from Lebanon; oaks from Bashan; pine from Cyprus; ivory; linen from Egypt; blue and purple (cloth) from Elishah; rowers from Sidon and Arvad; pilots from Zemer; caulkers from Gebal (Byblos); soldiers from Persia, Lud, Put, Arvad, Helech, and Gamad; silver, tin, iron, and lead from Tarshish; bronze vessels and manpower from Javan, Tubal, and Meshech; horses, war horses (specially trained?), and mules from Beth-togarmah; ivory tusks and ebony from Rhodes and other ports; emeralds, purple, embroidered work, fine linen, coral, and agate from Edom; wheat, olives, figs, honey, oil, and balm from Israel and Judah; unspecified goods from Damascus; wine from Helbon; white wool and wine from Uzal along with wrought iron, cassia, and calamus; saddlecloths from Dedan; lambs, goats, and rams from Arabia and Kedar; spices, precious stones, and gold from Sheba and Raamah; and choice garments, clothes of blue and embroidered work, and colored carpets from Haran, Canneh, Eden, Asshur, and Chilmad. Among the precious stones specified are carnelian, topaz, jasper, chrysolite, beryl, onyx, sapphire (probably lapis lazuli), carbuncle and emeralds, with worked gold settings. Granting a number of errors in both the items and the ascriptions, it is an impressive index of what crossed as merchandise at a major seventh-century B.C. Mediterranean port, presumably by common knowledge, since Ezekiel was no merchant himself with insider information.

Marketing: From the earliest individual bartering, the steps toward formal market days or market areas in campsites or small village settlements are not clear. What is obvious is that in the earliest city-states of Sumer in Mesopotamia the temple served as a major gathering point for goods if not services. The huge ziggurat and temple constructions, to say nothing of the walls, palaces, canals, and dikes that mark these cities, required extensive acquisition of construction materials and manpower. The democratic nature of earliest Sumerian society suggests that such arrangements required elaborate negotiations and records.

For most of the biblical period in Palestine,

marketing was done through small shops where each specialty product was available from the producer or processor. Even in NT times this style of marketing is reflected in rows of shops lining the edges of the more public Greek agora (as at Corinth) or streets (as at Ephesus). In modern villages and even in sectors of some large cities, this is still the primary mode of selling goods. Traveling merchants were also common in antiquity. Biblical references reinforce the "cottage industry" mode of marketing in such cases as Jeremiah's visit to the house of the potter (Jer. 18:3) or the recruitment of a "scribe" by Paul to write his letters (1 Cor. 16:21). That temples or shrines became places of exchange for those unable to supply their own sacrifice materials was an understandable if not appropriate accommodation (John 2:14–16). It is also understandable that certain products were the result of religious practice and would be economically threatened by beliefs rendering them obsolete (Acts 19:23–41).

Records: Most records of trade that have survived from antiquity have been parts of royal or temple archives. Thus, for instance, economic texts predominated in the finds at Ugarit, Mari, Ebla, and various finds of Sumerian and Akkadian materials. The Dead Sea Scrolls are a kind of exception, where the ritual, theological, and other religious interests superseded attention to economic records. In the vast spectrum of these economic texts one finds, among others, orders and receipts for goods; records of shipments made and received; payment of levies and taxes; inventories of goods received and stored; records of goods required, procured, and consumed; and quantities or weights of materials received. That societies took such matters seriously is indicated by the fact that they were recorded on tablets fired for durability and stored in quarters considered secure. There seem not to have been major banking institutions outside the temple precincts or royal houses, but money changing and lending was a street business readily available. Trade agreements were major portions of diplomatic negotiations, whether in tribal or settled city or national life. Obligations of conquered people to supply both goods, quarters, and services were frequent components in treaties such as the Hittite and Assyrian vassal treaties. Records concerning trade in human resources included bills and receipts of slave purchases, as well as manifests of freedom for slaves.

Means of Exchange: The use of weights and measures fluctuated from country to country and from time to time. The movement from simple trading of goods to the use of some indirect means of exchange is also obscure in many respects. The frequent occurrence of small ceramic disks, sometimes punctured in the center to allow stringing or hanging on a spindle of some sort, has led some archaeologists to suggest their probable use as local tokens of exchange, a sort of voucher system. The introduction of coinage, traditionally regarded as a sixth-century B.C. invention of the Lydians, was made official government practice by the Persians and continues to this day. Coins were usually a government monopoly, with mints sometimes scattered throughout political holdings. Control of the metal value, coin size, design and decoration, and varieties of coins used were thus a means of both economic and political control. The propaganda value of coins should not be underrated. Greeks and Romans brought the art to a high state, and coins are among the most helpful archaeological articles for dating purposes when they are recovered in legible condition.

As in all times and societies, incurring a debt was a common social fact. It appears in biblical stories as an undesirable condition in both OT and NT (see 1 Sam. 22:2; Neh. 10:31; Isa. 24:2; Prov. 22:7, 26; Matt. 18:23–34), and delivery from debt became a metaphor for genuine salvation (Rom. 8:12–17). The value system of exchange of precious goods or monetary equivalents left no mark by which the grace of God could be assessed, yet that grace was more valuable than the most precious pearl a jewel merchant could own (Matt. 14:45–46), and the expectation of the completion of the fulfillment of the Kingdom of God was drawn by apocalyptic writers as the most lavish conceivable Jerusalem, a city whose streets were paved with gold and whose gates were made of a single pearl (Rev. 21:21). For such there could be no adequate rate of exchange. ***See also*** Boats; Money; Ophir; Weights and Measures. R.S.B.

trades. ***See*** such individual entries as Carpenter; Dyeing; Masons; Refining; Smith; Tanning.

Trajan (tray'juhn), Roman emperor A.D. 98–117. Adopted by the emperor Nerva, Trajan came from a family of Roman settlers in Spain. His father had been a senator, and Trajan was the first emperor from outside Italy. Trajan made his reputation as a soldier first under Domitian (A.D. 81–96) when he was commanding a legion in Spain and then under Nerva (96–98) who made him governor of Germanica Superior (part of modern Germany). After a threat against Nerva's life among the praetorian guard, Nerva adopted Trajan as his heir in A.D. 96.

Trajan reduced and annexed Dacia (modern Rumania) as a province in two campaigns. The province provided mineral wealth and a more secure frontier. He campaigned in a large part of Mesopotamia and Assyria, which were proclaimed provinces in A.D. 114 but proved impossible to hold after Trajan's death. Parthia, always troublesome, was made a client kingdom.

In Rome Trajan improved relations with the

The Roman emperor Trajan (98–117); ivory plaque from Ephesus.

Senate and drew upon it for administrative talent. He built public baths and the largest of the imperial forums and erected a huge column celebrating the Dacian campaigns.

While Trajan is not mentioned in the NT, since most if not all of its books had been written by the time he became emperor, we do have some correspondence between him and Pliny the Younger, his ambassador to Asia Minor. Pliny reports some people have been denounced to him as Christians, and he asks Trajan if the accusation is sufficient grounds for execution. Trajan says it is not; only if it can be proved, and the Christians refuse to recant, can they be punished. This correspondence from the first decade of the second century shows that Christians had become numerous enough in Asia Minor to be perceived as a possible threat to local religious belief and Roman administration of the provinces there. ***See also*** Roman Empire; Rome. P.P.

Transfiguration, the, the title given to an event in Jesus' life in which he was "transfigured" (Gk. *metamorphoō*), Moses and Elijah appeared to him, and a Voice spoke from heaven. (See Mark 9:2–8; Matt. 17:1–8; Luke 9:28–36; 2 Pet. 1:16–18.)

The transfiguration is one of the few accounts in Jesus' life outside of the passion narrative that contains a chronological tie—"after six days" (Mark 9:2). The incident is tied both in time and meaning to the preceding account of Peter's confession (Mark 8:27–33). The divine Voice "This is my beloved Son" (Mark 9:7) is both a rebuke of Peter's equation of Jesus with Moses and Elijah (Mark 9:5) and a confirmation of his confession. The words "listen to him" recall Peter's unwillingness to accept Jesus' passion prediction (Mark 8:31–33). The purpose of the transfiguration is primarily for the three disciples. This is clear from the Voice, which is directed to them, and the frequent use of the pronoun "them." What the Voice was for Jesus at his baptism, "Thou art" (Mark 1:11), the Voice at the transfiguration was for Peter, James, and John, "This is" (Mark 9:7).

What actually happened in Jesus' transfiguration has been understood primarily in two ways. The first understands it as a breaking through his humanity of the true form (Gk. *morphē*) of the Son of God (cf. John 1:14); the second as a glimpse of the glory of the Son of God at his Parousia (2 Pet. 1:16–18). Perhaps both are involved. Compare Phil. 2:6–11 where both the pre-existent glory of the Son and the glory resulting from his resurrection/exaltation are mentioned.

The place where this took place is described as a "high mountain." Suggested sites are Mt. Tabor (the traditional site but not a high mountain), Mt. Carmel (out of the way), and Mt. Hermon (a high mountain), but the lack of specificity indicates that what was important for the church was not *where* but *what* occurred. R.H.S.

transgression. ***See*** Evil; Forgiveness; Human Being; Pardon; Repentance; Salvation; Sin.

Transjordan, strictly speaking the area directly east of the Jordan River, but a term normally used today for the high plateau area from the Yarmuq River in the north to the head of the Gulf of Aqabah in the south. The present Kingdom of Jordan represents the first time in history that the area has formed a single united and independent state. Previously it was always either a group of separate states or part of a foreign empire.

The edge of the plateau, overlooking the north-south rift valley of the Ghor, is everywhere higher than its counterpart in the west and consequently receives heavier winter rainfall, which decreases rapidly as the plateau slopes downward toward the Wadi Sirhan and the great basalt barrier in the east. Throughout history, from the pre-pottery Neolithic period (ca. 7000 B.C.) to the present, Transjordan has provided a relatively easy north-south route from Syria to the Red Sea and Midian in northwest Arabia, and vice-versa. There have been two roads, the so-called King's Highway on the plateau edge and the Pilgrim Route along the edge of the desert. The first has the problem of crossing deep and steep-sided valleys, while the second is more level but less well supplied with food and water. Four major valleys cleave the plateau edge: the Yarmuq in the north, the Zerqa (biblical Jabbok), the Mojjib (Arnon), and the Hesa (Zered). These have often served as administrative boundaries, but only the Hesa is a true cultural division. Culturally, and until the Assyrian conquests (ninth-eighth centuries B.C.), tribally and politically, the areas were as follows:

1 Havvoth-jair (Num. 32:41; Deut. 3:14; 1 Kings 4:13), an extension of the Bashan plateau (Josh. 13:30), and a disputed zone between Aram and Israel. In NT times it was part of the Decapolis, including Gadara (Umm Qeis) and Abila (Tell Abil).

2 Gilead, the uplifted highland region of Ajlun, divided by the Zerqa. Still retaining today remnants of its earlier thick forest, this area was incorporated into the tribal lands of Manasseh, being the only area east of the Jordan where the three Israelite crops of grain (wheat or barley), grapes, and olives could be cultivated together. A medicinal balm from this region was proverbial (Jer. 8:22; 46:11) and was exported to Phoenicia (Ezek. 27:17) and to Egypt (Gen. 37:25). The plateau to the east, merging rapidly into semidesert, was Ammonite territory, centering on the upper Jabbok, which rises at Amman (Rabboth Ammon). Gerasa (Jerash) in Gilead and Philadelphia (Amman) were the southernmost Decapolis cities.

3 Moab, east of the Dead Sea; it is divided into two parts by the canyon of the Mojjib. The first, the level tableland of the Mishor to the north (Deut. 3:10; Josh. 13:9), was traditionally the territory of Reuben and Gad (Judg. 5:16; 1 Sam. 13: 7). It was famous for its sheep and was essentially Moabite. The second part is the Moabite heartland between the Mojjib and Hesa. Increasingly pastoral and rising steadily southward, this area was controlled from the great stronghold of Kir-hareseth (Kerak) on the King's Highway (2 Kings 3:21–27).

4 Edom, the high plateau rim south of the Hesa, everywhere well above 4,000 feet (1,220 m.) and touching 5,704 feet (1,738 m.) a little north of Petra. Cultivation is confined to a narrow strip along the plateau edge, and the chief source of wealth was trade with Arabia, perhaps as early as 6000 B.C., and with Anatolia as early as 7000. The region reached its zenith under the Nabateans.

5 The Dissected Plateau in the extreme south, a complicated network of hills and gorges. The entry to the Red Sea and to Midian and Arabia, this may have been the Teman of the OT, though the name (lit. "south") may perhaps signify either southern Edom or northwestern Arabia. ***See also*** Ammonites; Arabia; Arnon, The River; Cities; Gadara; Gilead; Jabbok; Midianites; Moab; Petra; Zered, The Brook. D.B.

translation. ***See*** English Bible, The; Texts, Versions, Manuscripts, Editions.

transportation. ***See*** Trade and Transportation.

travail, the pangs of childbirth (Gen. 35:16; 38: 27; Ps. 48:6; Jer. 4:31; Mic. 4:9; John 16:21). "Travail" is also used metaphorically of Zion bringing forth the new people of God (Isa. 66:7–9; Mic. 4:10). This metaphor may also be applied to the woman clothed with the sun in Rev. 12: 2. Paul speaks of the "labor pains" by which he has brought forth the new Christian converts in Gal. 4:19.

travel. ***See*** Trade and Transportation.

treasures, wealth accumulated and kept primarily in palaces and temples in the ancient world. Treasures were acquired by royal conquest (e.g., 1 Kings 14:25–26; 2 Kings 14:13–14), by trade or taxes on trade (1 Kings 10:11, 15, 22; Ezek. 27:12–27; 28:4–5), or in the form of gifts (e.g., 1 Kings 10:10, 13–15; cf. Matt. 2:2, 11) or tribute (1 Kings 10:14–15). The monarch's treasures would be used to adorn the palace and to purchase military resources (1 Kings 10:16–21, 26–29). Some would be dedicated to the deity for the adornment of the temple (Josh. 6:19). A monarch might use palace or temple treasures to buy off an invader (2 Kings 12:17–18; 18:13–16) or to purchase the assistance of a third party to harass an invader (1 Kings 15:17–21; 2 Kings 16: 5, 7–9). A wealthy individual might buy special favors from a king by a contribution to his treasury (Esther 3:8–11; 4:7). Legendary wealth was attributed to Solomon (1 Kings 10; cf. Eccles. 2: 8) and to Hezekiah (2 Chron. 32:27–29), who, by showing his treasures to Babylonian envoys (2 Kings 20:13; Isa. 39:2), prompted Isaiah's prophecy that they would be carried off to Babylon (2 Kings 20:17; Isa. 39:6). The regular contributions of worshipers also benefitted the temple treasury, and might be designated by the monarch for the materials and labor needed to repair and maintain the temple (2 Kings 12:4–11; 22: 3–7, 9).

The looting of the treasures of Nineveh (Nah. 2:9) is less prominent in the Bible than the despoiling of Jerusalem (Jer. 20:5). Nebuchadnezzar took the treasures of the Jerusalem temple (2 Kings 25:13–17) and palace (2 Kings 24:13; 2 Chron. 36:18; 1 Esd. 1:54) to Babylon where he deposited them in his god's temple treasury (Dan. 1:2). Later Cyrus restored them to the Jewish leaders to be returned to Jerusalem (Ezra 1:8–11), where the leaders volunteered special contributions to fund the rebuilding of the Temple (Ezra 2:68–69). A model for such special contributions appears in the account in Chronicles of the building of the first Temple

(1 Chron. 29:2–8). Artaxerxes authorized Ezra to charge further rebuilding expenses to the Persian imperial treasury (Ezra 7:20–21). Later the treasures of the second Jerusalem Temple were plundered by Antiochus Epiphanes (1 Macc. 1:21–24), who tried unsuccessfully to gain possession of the treasures of another temple by marrying its goddess (2 Macc. 1:11–17).

Moral reflections on wealth are frequent in the OT and subsequent wisdom literature. Treasures accumulate for the wise (Prov. 21:20) and the righteous (Prov. 15:6), those who honor their mothers (Ecclus. 13:4) and those who give alms (Tob. 4:7–9). Wisdom is the source of treasures (Prov. 8:18–21). However, treasures do not last (Prov. 27:24) and may be troublesome (Prov. 15:16). Ill-gotten wealth makes one vulnerable (Prov. 21:6; 10:2; Tob. 12:8–10). Hidden treasure is useless (Ecclus. 20:30; 41:14), but a treasure trove is better than an income (Ecclus. 40:18). Treasure is a metaphor for wisdom (Prov. 2:4; Wisd. of Sol. 7:14), almsgiving (Ecclus. 29:12), a faithful friend (Ecclus. 6:14), and immortality (2 Esd. 8:54). Faithfulness and good works may be accumulated as a treasure deposited with God (2 Esd. 6:5; 7:77).

The NT recognizes the vanity of earthly treasures, the permanence of heavenly treasure, and the way one's life is shaped by what one treasures (Matt. 6:19–21; Luke 12:33–34, cf. 20–21). James 5:1–5 denounces those who live for earthly treasures, while Heb. 11:26 presents Moses, who preferred suffering to the treasures of Egypt, as a model of faith in God's future reward. In the Gospels almsgiving is the way to convert earthly into heavenly treasure (Matt. 19:21–22; Mark 10:21–22; Luke 18:22–23). Buried treasure is an image of the kingdom of heaven (Matt. 13:44); treasure in earthen vessels represents the gospel in Christians (2 Cor. 4:7); and wisdom and knowledge are treasures hidden in Christ (Col. 2:3). S.B.P.

tree of life, the, a well-known image deeply rooted in the mythological and iconographic traditions of the ancient Near East. Widely depicted on seals, reliefs, and other artistic forms, the sacred tree represented fertility, or ongoing life, as well as immortality, or eternal life (Gen. 3:9, 22,24; cf. Ezek. 31:8).

The biblical usage of this motif gives the contemporary imagery another focus, however. The emphasis of the Eden story is not so much on the life-tree though that motif is present, as it is on the rather different aspect of the knowledge-tree.

Although trees in general play a prominent role in the metaphoric vocabulary of the Bible, the phrase "the tree of life" appears in the OT only in Genesis 3. Proverbs (3:18; 11:30; 13:12; 15:4) does refer metaphorically to *a* tree of life; however, such usage lacks the vividness and potency of the life-tree symbolism. Only in noncanonical Jewish literature (1 Enoch 24:4–6; 2 Enoch 8:3–5; 2 Esdras 8:52) and the NT (Rev. 2:7; 22:2, 14, 19) is the richness of the Edenic life-tree imagery utilized by the ancient authors.

Although the verbal designation "tree of life" has an understandably restricted place in biblical tradition, a plastic representation of the life-tree, in the form of the sacred lampstand (*menorah*) described in the tabernacle texts, played a central role in the repertoire of ritual appurtenances of ancient Israel. Its stylized tree shape and the vocabulary of botanical terms that describe it suggest that the cultic lampstand symbolized the fructifying powers of the eternal, unseen God. ***See also*** Lampstand. C.L.M.

trees, prized and sometimes venerated in ancient Palestine. Scrub forests of oak and terebinth covered portions of the central hill country, Galilee and Gilead, while solitary specimens or groves dotted the hills and valleys. Willows formed thickets along the Jordan (Jer. 12:5) and flourished by perennial streams. Tamarisks marked the Negeb and palms the oases. The prized cedar and firs grew only in Lebanon.

Trees were valued for their shade, making them an attractive place to pitch a tent (Gen. 13:18), build a shrine (Gen. 12:6–7), or judge disputes (Judg. 4:4). The ability of the deep-rooted tree to maintain its green foliage through summer heat and drought made it a symbol of life and endurance (Ps. 1:3; Isa. 65:22). The tree was also a symbol of might, especially the towering cedar (Ezek. 31:3; Dan. 4:10–12).

Trees had sacred associations in both Israelite and Canaanite religion, serving as memorial objects (Gen. 21:33) and as symbols of the Canaanite fertility goddess Asherah. They marked the open-air sanctuaries ("high places") honored by the patriarchs (Gen. 12:6–7) but condemned by the prophets for the illegitimate rites held there ("how she [Israel] went up on every high hill and under every green tree, and there played the harlot," Jer. 3:6).

Trees were especially esteemed for their fruit (including olives). The Garden of Eden was stocked with trees for food (Gen. 2:16), and only fruit-bearing trees are mentioned in Gen. 1:11 (cf. v. 29). When the trees seek a ruler, in Jotham's fable, they turn to the fruit trees (Judg. 9:8–13). And Jesus teaches that "the tree is known by its fruit" (Matt. 12:33; cf. 3:10).

Palestinian trees were not suitable for lumber, but they were used for roof beams, furniture, and implements. Large branches also served as gallows or for public display of executed criminals or enemies. Five NT passages use "tree" to designate the cross (Acts 5:30; 10:39; 13:29; Gal. 3:13; 1 Pet. 2:24). ***See also*** Cedar; Fig; Fir Tree; Forest; Olive; Tamarisk; Tree of Life, The; Willow; Woods. P.A.B.

trespasses. ***See*** Punishment, Everlasting; Sin.

trespass offering. ***See*** Worship.

trial. ***See*** Temptation; Trial of Jesus, The.

trial of Jesus, the, the trial of Jesus before the Roman prefect Pontius Pilate (Mark 15:2–5; Matt. 27:11–14; Luke 23:17–25; John 18:28–38). This trial culminated in a sentence of death by crucifixion on the charge of activity that would subvert Roman rule, namely, claiming to be "king of the Jews" (Mark 15:6–15; Matt. 27:15–26; Luke 23:17–25; John 18:38–19:16). The accounts in the four Gospels are not identical, since each has been shaped by its author to instruct the readers of that Gospel about the true significance of Jesus' crucifixion. The accounts show a tendency to shift responsibility for Jesus' death away from Pilate onto the Jews, who are thereby presented as rejecting God's Messiah (e.g., Matt. 27:23–25; Mark 15:14; Luke 23:22–25; John 19:12).

Before Pilate: The basic outline of the trial before Pilate suits known Roman procedures for the trial of a noncitizen. A private accuser could charge someone with a misdeed, which the Roman governor then had considerable freedom in deciding how to treat. In accord with this procedure, Jesus is brought before Pilate's tribunal (Matt. 27:19 mentions the seat on which the judge sat [Gk. *bēma*]) by accusers from among the chief priests and elders (Matt. 27:12; Mark 15:3; Luke 23:1, 4). In practice, there would only have been two or three accusers. Jesus does not appear to have been charged with breaking a particular law but with undesirable actions that could be interpreted as seditious. (For use of the term "king" as an indication of seditious activity, see Josephus *Antiquities* 17.10.8.) The synoptic accounts suggest that Jesus failed to defend himself against the accusations. This motif also fits the early Christian understanding of Jesus as the suffering servant of Isaiah 53, since the servant remains silent before his accusers (Isa. 53:7). In this type of trial, failure to present a defense brought an automatic verdict of guilty. It was also characteristic of Roman court proceedings to subject both innocent and guilty defendants to beating. The severe flogging, which Jesus received, was always combined with some other form of punishment. John 19:12 suggests that Jesus' accusers threatened to denounce Pilate to Rome under the law of treason (as not being a "friend of Caesar") if he failed to condemn Jesus to death. Whatever the pressures brought to bear by those who handed Jesus over to Pilate to be tried, the final responsibility for the sentence in such a case belonged to the Roman governor alone.

Before the Sanhedrin: Mark 15:55–64 (followed by Matt. 26:59–66) presents an unusual night meeting of the Sanhedrin, which is cast as a trial that also culminates in a verdict, guilty of death on the grounds of blasphemy (Mark 14:64). However, Mark also reports that the witnesses brought against Jesus contradicted themselves. Neither Jesus' prophecies about the destruction of the Temple and the coming of the Son of Man, nor the claim that he is messiah, Son of God (Mark 14:58, 61–62), fit the definition of blasphemy, since they do not employ the name of God. There is no secure evidence for some wider definition of blasphemy carrying the death penalty. In addition, the Sanhedrin proceedings do not fit the legal requirements for a trial in a capital case—though these are only known to us from second-century material and might not have been in force in the first century. Luke 22:66–71 presents accusations against Jesus as occurring during a morning meeting of the Council (mentioned in Mark 15:1), which preceded handing Jesus over to Pilate. John 11:45–53 presumes that the decision to remove Jesus from the scene was taken on political grounds before he was arrested. In John 18:19–24 Jesus is questioned by the high priest after his arrest and prior to being turned over to Pilate. Therefore, many scholars think that the proceedings before the Sanhedrin represented an inquiry into possible charges against Jesus that did not produce a legal verdict—perhaps because of the contradictory evidence and divisions between members of the group as to what constituted criminal behavior. Jewish officials then took the step of turning the case over to Pilate, who had broad powers in dealing with potential troublemakers. John in 18:29 may reflect knowledge that no more detailed charge against Jesus was brought before Pilate than that he was a troublemaker.

Before Herod: Luke 23:6–16 contains a notice that Pilate sent Jesus' case to Herod. The scene itself is modeled on elements of the trial before Pilate with a parallel mocking of the victim by soldiers. There is no historical, legal reason for such a move. Offenders were tried where their crime occurred. Josephus (*War* 1.24.2) reports that Herod had an extraordinary privilege of extraditing offenders who had fled his kingdom for other parts of the Empire. Some scholars suggest that memory of that tradition lies behind the Lucan incident. Others think that it may have been a gesture of courtesy on Pilate's part so as not to further offend the Jewish king with whom his relationships were already strained. However, Herod is not said to have taken any action against Jesus. Therefore, the trial before Pilate remains the only legal trial of Jesus that resulted in the death sentence. ***See also*** Barabbas; Cross; Judas; Pilate, Pontius.

Bibliography

Bammel, E., ed. *The Trial of Jesus. Cambridge Studies in honour of C. F. D. Moule.* SBT ser. 2, 13. London: SCM, 1970.

Harvey, A. E. *Jesus and the Constraints of History.* Philadelphia: Westminster, 1982.

Juel, D. *Messiah and Temple. The Trial of Jesus in the Gospel of Mark.* Missoula, MT: Scholars Press, 1977.

Sherwin-White, A. N. *Roman Society and Roman Law in the New Testament.* Oxford: Oxford University Press, 1963. P.P.

tribes, the, territorial groups and primary social organizational units in Israel's social structure before the establishment of the monarchy (pre-late eleventh century B.C.). The tribes can be viewed as distributive parts of one larger entity, Israel, whose identity is traced to an eponymous ancestor, Jacob (Israel; Gen. 33:28; 35:10). The tribe was a kind of corporate personality, a grouping of a varying number of protective associations or "clans," which in turn were associations of extended families. Israel did not have clans, properly speaking, if clans are defined as exogamous; in other words, the Israelite did not have to marry outside his or her "clan." The members of the Israelite "clan" or protective association typically lived in the same or nearby villages, rural neighborhoods, or sections of a larger settlement, provided mutual aid to all the extended families constituting the "clan," and provided troop quotas to the tribal levy. The extended family (which in the OT is called a "father's house"), clusters of which made up the clans, was the primary residential and productive unit in the social structure.

While each tribe had its own proper name, it was a tribe, properly speaking, only by virtue of the fact that it was one of the tribes of Israel. By being a part of Israel, the individual tribe had a place as one of the primary segments of the whole people, and shared in that status equally with all other tribes. Thus it is only in terms of their structure and function within the larger whole that tribes can be understood. The particular identity of a tribe derived from such things as its migration experience, military struggles, and the ways in which it worked out a mixed agricultural and pastoral subsistence strategy dependent upon such things as the rainfall, soil fertility, and other natural resources of its tribal territory, which itself was not fixed either in scope or location but developed over time. A tribe was thus the part of the social structure that dealt with regional needs, provided for its own military self-defense through a tribal militia, and performed religious and legal functions.

The Lists of Tribes: The lists of tribes in the OT, of which there are more than twenty, differ from one another in several respects, notably in the position of the names of tribes and their number. The Song of Deborah (Judg. 5), which is probably the oldest listing (twelfth century B.C.), lists but ten tribes, omitting Judah, Simeon, and Levi. It separates Ephraim and Machir (Manasseh) into two tribes. The Blessing of Moses (Deut. 33) lists eleven tribes, omitting Simeon, but arrives at the number twelve by separating Joseph into Ephraim and Manasseh. The Blessing of Jacob (Gen. 49) lists twelve tribes and does not separate Joseph into two. Even though it lists Reuben as the firstborn of Jacob (by Leah), Reuben is removed from the place of preeminence among the tribes because of his indiscretion with his father's concubine (Gen. 35:22), and that place is assigned to Judah. This list also links Simeon and Levi together in disgrace because of the incident in connection with their sister Dinah (Gen. 34). The two census lists in Numbers (1:20–43; 26:5–50) include twelve tribes, arriving at that number by omitting Levi and listing Ephraim and Manasseh separately. The listing in Genesis 49 is the one maintained in most of the other lists in the OT (Gen. 35:22–26; Deut. 27:12–13; 1 Chron. 2:1–2; Ezek. 48:1–7).

The Ideal of Twelve: The ideal of twelve remained long after the tribal organization disappeared, even into the NT. Ezekiel, in his ideal state, redistributed the land among twelve tribes. A number of individuals in the NT retain their tribal identifications: Jesus from Judah (Matt. 12:6; Heb. 7:14; Rev. 5:5); Paul from Benjamin (Rom. 11:1); and Barnabas from Levi (Acts 4:36). Jesus promised the twelve apostles that they would judge the twelve tribes of Israel (Matt. 19:28; Luke 22:30), Paul refers to the twelve tribes (Acts 26:7), and the book of James is addressed to the twelve tribes in the Dispersion (James 1:1). Thus the number twelve seems to have been settled upon at some time in Israel's history, probably early in the monarchy, and the tribal nomenclature deriving from the names of Jacob's sons by his two wives, Leah and Rachel, and his two concubines, Zilpah and Bilhah, became a part of Jewish traditions. The tribes understood in this way can be charted according to the accompanying diagram.

The variations in the tribal listings, both in the number and position of individual tribes, reflect the fact that the tribes themselves were changing entities when seen in light of the whole of which they were considered to be a part, subject to both increase and decrease with changing situations. Sometimes fusion of formerly separate tribes would take place, as is apparently the case with Caleb, which became part of Judah. Simeon was similarly apparently absorbed into Judah. Sometimes tribes divided, as did Joseph into Ephraim and Manasseh. Reuben apparently lost strength over time and disappeared. Levi seems to have changed its status and become a lineally determined group of priestly specialists rather than a discrete tribe.

Variations in the listings may also derive from the changing nature of tribal confederations and the leadership within those confederations. The Song of Deborah (Judg. 5) suggests an early voluntary coalition of ten tribes. The six sons of Leah may, at one time, have constituted an early tribal confederation. But Reuben

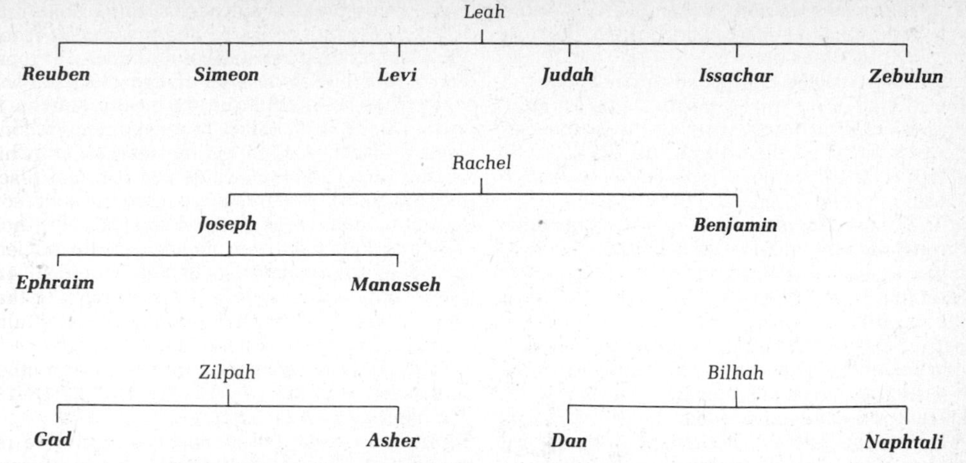

THE TRIBES OF ISRAEL

and Zebulun, although both from Leah, show no geographical, historical, or religious affinities as tribes beyond that of any other pair of Jacob's sons. The concubine tribes, those from Bilhah and Zilpah, are sometimes considered as originally non-Israelite, and thus later additions to the confederation.

Several models of Israel's twelve-tribe confederacy or league have been presented. One such model is that of a religious confederacy called an amphictyony, which has analogues among the Greeks, Old Latins, and Etruscans. An Israelite amphictyony would have been a twelve-tribe confederacy organized around a covenant with God in support of a central shrine, with each member of the confederacy maintaining the shrine one month of the year. Other models suggest that the Israelite confederation was a protective association of autonomous political units, bonded together on the specifically religious grounds of a covenant with God but with many shrines rather than one central sanctuary. This confederacy functioned as the primary legal community and coordinated the national military organization, in such a way that the confederate organization encompassed and subsumed all members of the society and all subgroups within the society. ***See also*** Family, The; Government.

Bibliography

Gottwald, Norman K. *The Tribes of Yahweh.* Maryknoll, NY: Orbis Books, 1979.

Mendenhall, G. *The Tenth Generation.* Baltimore, MD: Johns Hopkins Press, 1973. Chap. 7.

F.S.F.

tribunal, one translation of the Greek word referring to the civil court rostrum or judge's bench in cities of the Roman Empire. According to Acts 18:12–17, Paul was brought by the Jews before the proconsul Gallio at the tribunal in Corinth, but the case was thrown out by the Roman official. Excavations at the site of Corinth in the earlier part of this century turned up, beneath a fourth- or fifth-century Christian church, a large platform in the center of the middle row of shops of the ancient forum or agora. Passages on either side connected the lower and upper areas of the forum. There are benches at the back and sides of the platform, which itself was originally faced with marble. Constructed perhaps ca. A.D. 44, this was probably the site of the trial of Paul and of the subsequent beating of Sosthenes, the ruler of the local synagogue.

According to Acts 25:6–21, Paul was also put on trial before the tribunal in Caesarea after Porcius Festus became governor. The site of this tribunal has not been found.

In Philippi, however, four steps at the north end of the forum have been discovered which are thought to have led up to the local tribunal, perhaps where Paul and Silas were accused by the owners of a slave girl exorcised by Paul (Acts 16:16–24). Similar steps have been found at Veroia, ancient Beroea.

The Greek term is translated "platform" in 1 Esd. 9:42, "public platform" in 2 Macc. 13:26, "throne" in Acts 12:21, and "judgment seat" in Matt. 27:19; John 19:13; Rom. 14:10; and 2 Cor. 5:10 (cf. also Acts 7:5, "a foot's length," literally, "a platform for the foot"). ***See also*** Corinth; Festus, Porcius; Gallio; Judgment Seat; Paul; Philippi; Throne.

C.H.M.

tribute, tax, toll, payment of taxes or of tribute, as a sign of submission or noncitizenship.

The conquered or noncitizens could be conscripted for purposes of labor (Exod. 5; Matt. 5: 41; Josh. 16:10; 2 Chron. 8:7–8). Conquered peoples might also be compelled to pay tribute to the foreign ruler. Royal palaces are regularly decorated with reliefs showing the conquered peoples bringing their tribute to the king (1 Kings 20:1–7; 2 Kings 17:1–6; Neh. 5:4; Esther 10:1).

The most common form of direct taxation throughout antiquity is in the form of direct taxes on agricultural produce (Gen. 41:25–57). Josephus (*Antiquities* 14.203) reports that this tax amounted to 12.5 percent of the crop except in the Sabbatical Year. Increasing independence and political power might enable people to gain a reduction in taxes. Jonathan was able to gain sizable reduction in the land taxes for Judea, Samaria, and Galilee in exchange for his support of the Seleucid kings Demetrius I and II (1 Macc. 10:30–38; 11:28, 34).

Rulers might also derive income from royal estates, interests in other business ventures, and from confiscating the property of those executed as enemies. Herod may have sold or leased the lands of such persons to finance his building projects (Josephus, *Antiquities* 15.5–6). Taxation and confiscation led to the consolidation of landholdings in the hands of the rich, who then leased the land and employed stewards (often slaves) to supervise their property. This division between the wealthy landowner and the peasant is reflected in a number of the parables (Luke 16:1–6; Matt. 28:23–34; Matt. 20: 1–16; Matt. 21:33–41; Luke 12:13–21; Luke 14: 11–27; Luke 12:42–46).

We have little information about other forms of property taxation such as that on slaves, cattle, and the "house tax" (Cicero, *Ad Familiares* 3.8.5; Josephus, *Antiquities* 19.299).

Unlike tribute, which was to be paid by the whole community, a poll tax might be imposed on individuals. This may have been the purpose of the census attempted by David (2 Sam. 24). Solomon succeeded in imposing taxes (1 Kings 4; 2 Chron. 9:13–28; 1 Kings 12:1–3). Quirinius took a census for this purpose in Syria, which apparently also included a census of the newly created province of Judea (Luke 2: 1–2). Creation of the new province is also reported to have been the occasion for an outbreak of resistance to Rome led by Judas the Galilean (Acts 5:37; Josephus, *War* 2.118; *Antiquities* 18.23). Such an ideology of resistance apparently underlies the question about taxation posed to Jesus (Mark 12:13–17), who rejects such violence. Mark 12:15 may indicate that the amount of the imposed tax was a denarius (RSV: "coin").

Indirect taxes were imposed on economic activity. These included market taxes and port fees as well as customs duties (tolls) collected at ports and inland boundaries. While direct taxes were collected by local leaders, the indirect taxes were collected by tax collectors or publicans. Josephus reports that the wealth of one of the Jewish leaders at Caesarea, John, came from taxes collected on business at the port (*War* 2.287). Luke 19:1–10 refers to a wealthy Zacchaeus, collecting taxes at Jericho on the border between Perea and Judea. Tolls had to be paid on the transport of goods from one district to another (Matt. 9:9; Luke 5:27). These taxes appear to have been auctioned to the highest bidder, the "chief toll collector" for a region (Luke 19:2), whose agents manned the toll stations. There is evidence of tariffs as high as 25 percent of value on some items.

Every Israelite male was to pay an annual half-shekel offering toward the costs of the Temple (Matt. 17:24; Josephus, *War* 7.218; *Antiquities* 3.194–6; Philo, *Special Laws* 1.78), though the Essenes appear to have refused to make such an offering (4Q *Ordinances* 11.6–7). After the revolt in A.D. 70, Vespasian imposed the "Jewish tax" on Jews up to age sixty-two. This tax was paid by Jews whether or not they lived in Palestine. It is not clear whether this new tax led Jews outside the Empire to stop paying the half-shekel tax that had gone to the Temple and thus affected the balance of trade or not. The Jewish Tax was paid to the temple of Jupiter Capitolinus in Rome (Josephus *War* 7.218; Suetonius, *Domitian* 12). ***See also*** Tithe.

Bibliography

Freyne, Sean. *Galilee from Alexander the Great to Hadrian 323 B.C.E. to 135 C.E.* Wilmington, DE: Michael Glazier, 1980.

Safrai, S., and M. Stern, eds. *The Jewish People in the First Century*. Vol. 1. (Compendia Rerum Iudaicarum ad Novum Testamentum.) Philadelphia: Fortress, 1974. P.P.

trigon (tri'gahn; KJV: sackbut), a small three-cornered, four-stringed musical instrument mentioned only in Daniel (3:5, 7, 10, 15). ***See also*** Sackbut.

Trinity, the, a term denoting the specifically Christian doctrine that God is a unity of three persons: Father, Son, and Holy Spirit. The word itself does not occur in the Bible. It is generally acknowledged that the church father Tertullian (ca. A.D. 145–220) either coined the term or was the first to use it with reference to God. The explicit doctrine was thus formulated in the postbiblical period, although the early stages of its development can be seen in the NT. Attempts to trace the origins still earlier (to the OT literature) cannot be supported by historical-critical scholarship, and these attempts must be understood as retrospective interpretations of this earlier corpus of Scripture in the light of later theological developments.

For the purpose of analysis, three relevant categories of NT texts may be distinguished (although such sharp lines of demarcation should not be attributed to first-century Christianity): first are references to the incarnation, describing a particularly close relationship between Jesus and God. Although a number of passages make clear distinctions between God and Christ and therefore suggest the subordination of the Son to the Father (e.g., Rom. 8:31–34; 1 Cor. 11:3; 15:20–28; 2 Cor. 4:4–6), there are other texts in which the unity of the Father and the Son is stressed (e.g., Matt. 11:27; John 10:30; 14:9–11; 20:28; Col. 2:9; 1 John 5:20). This emphasis on the unity of the Father and the Son may be understood as a first step in the development of trinitarian thought.

Second are passages in which a similarly close relationship between Jesus and the Holy Spirit is depicted. In the OT, the Holy Spirit (i.e., the Spirit of God) is understood to be the agency of God's power and presence with individuals and communities. In the NT, Jesus is understood to be the recipient of this Spirit in a unique manner (see esp. Luke 3:22, where the Holy Spirit descends in bodily form upon Jesus after his baptism), to be a mediator of the activity of the Spirit (Acts 2:33 and elsewhere), and even to be identified with the Spirit (Rom. 8:26–27, 34; John 14; cf. expressions such as "the Spirit of Christ," "the Spirit of the Lord," "the Spirit of Jesus," and Gal. 4:6, where God sends "the Spirit of his Son"). While one cannot use the creedal formulation that the Holy Spirit "proceeds from the Father and the Son" in its later dogmatic sense, in the NT the Holy Spirit comes to represent both the presence and activity of God and the continuing presence of Jesus Christ in the church.

Finally there are passages in which all three persons of the Trinity are mentioned in the same context. The most important of these are the "Apostolic Benediction" of 2 Cor. 13:14 (the earliest trinitarian formula known) and the baptismal formula of Matt. 28:19 (perhaps a development from the simpler formula reflected in Acts 2:38; 8:16; and elsewhere; see also 1 Cor. 12:4–6; Eph. 4:4–6; 1 Pet. 1:2; Jude 20–21).

The formal doctrine of the Trinity as it was defined by the great church councils of the fourth and fifth centuries is not to be found in the NT. Nevertheless, the discussion above and especially the presence of trinitarian formulas in 2 Cor. 13:14 (which is strikingly early) and Matt. 28:19 indicate that the origin of this mode of thought may be found very early in Christian history. ***See also*** Baptism; Father; God; Holy Spirit, The; Incarnation; Jesus Christ; Monotheism; Son of God; Worship. T.R.W.L.

triumphal arch, a stone monument constructed to commemorate a signal event or achievement. Their mastery of the arch enabled the Romans to construct large free-standing arches for ceremonial purposes. The triumphal arch was built to honor the emperor and carried a dedicatory inscription. It was built with one or three openings and decorated with statuary or bas-reliefs relating the victorious campaigns of the emperor.

The arch of Titus stands near the entrance to the forum in the city of Rome. It combines the traditional Italian style of arch with decorative columns of the post-and-lintel Greek style. The arch includes reliefs celebrating Titus's sack of Jerusalem and destruction of its Temple in A.D. 70, an event that had enormous consequences for both Jews and early Christians. P.P.

Troas, Alexandria (troh'az, al-eks-an'dree-uh), an important seaport city in Mysia on the northwest coast of Asia Minor. Built in 310 B.C. by Antigonus and named Antigonia, its name was changed to Alexandria by Lysimachus, who added Troas, derived from the nearby ancient city of Troy, to distinguish it from other cities named in honor of Alexander the Great. During the NT period, it was referred to simply as Troas. The city became a Roman possession by 133 B.C. Augustus gave it the status of a Roman colony, probably because of its importance as the nearest seaport for travel from Europe into the northwestern area of the Roman province of Asia. In Troas, during his second journey, Paul had a vision of a man from Macedonia inviting him to come to Europe (Acts 16:8–10). Paul and his companions revisited Troas on their final trip to Jerusalem, and Paul raised Eutychus, who had dozed and fallen from a third-story window while Paul was speaking (Acts 20:5–12). ***See also*** Eutychus. M.K.M.

Trogyllium (troh-jil'ee-uhm), a small peninsula jutting out from the west coast of Asia Minor just north of the east end of Samos. The strait thus formed is less than a mile across. Some ancient manuscripts include it in Acts' account of Paul's third missionary journey as a stopover; Acts locates it between Samos and Miletus (Acts 20:15; only in the margin in the RSV).

Trophimus (trahf'uh-muhs), a Christian from Ephesus who, with Tychicus, joined Paul and others for the apostle's final visit to Jerusalem (Acts 20:4–5). Asian Jews mistakenly accused Paul of taking Trophimus, a Gentile, into the Temple's Court of Israel (Acts 21:29), thus provoking mob disturbance that led to Paul's arrest. According to 2 Tim. 4:20, Trophimus (the same man?) remained at Miletus because of illness. Since Paul did not sail past Miletus en route to Rome, this note, if historical, may imply Paul's release from Roman imprisonment, further activity in the East, and a second imprisonment. ***See also*** Temple, The; Tychicus.

trumpet. ***See*** Music; Shophar.

Trumpets, Feast of, a celebration on the first day of the seventh month (Tishri) of the Hebrew religious year. Its name comes from its designation as a "day of (horn-)blasts" (Num. 29:1; cf. Lev. 23:24; Num. 10:10). It was a day of rest. An extra set of new-moon offerings was brought (except for one bull as a burnt offering) because it was the foremost of the new-moon celebrations (Num. 29:2–6; cf. 28:11–15). In the Bible, this day does not appear to have the character of a New Year's celebration. ***See also*** Feasts, Festivals, and Fasts.

trust. ***See*** Faith.

truth, a concept for which the OT has no distinct word. The word generally used means "constant, permanent, faithful, reliable." God above all is true, that is, real and reliable (Isa. 65:16; Jer. 10:10); people are to seek God's truth (Pss. 25:5; 51:6; 86:11). People are admonished to judge truly, and the lack of truth is lamented (Zech. 8:16; Isa. 59:14–15). Reports and prophecies may be true or false (1 Kings 10:6–7). In all these instances, the emphasis is upon reliability; something or someone true will stand up under testing. For the Hebrews, truth was moral and relational, not intellectual.

The Greek word for truth is primarily intellectual: truth is known, not trusted or relied on. NT usage draws on both Greek and OT understandings. The word is found mainly in the Pauline writings and especially the Gospel and Letters of John.

Paul can use the word in the Greek sense (Rom. 1:18), but more often he uses it with OT meanings: truth is to be obeyed (Rom. 2:8; Gal. 5:7); truth proves reliable (2 Cor. 7:14; 11:10); its opposite is malice and evil (1 Cor. 5:8). The Greek idea of truth as correct knowledge appears most clearly in the deutero-Pauline pastoral Letters. One is to know the truth (1 Tim. 4:3; 2 Tim. 2:25) and to avoid false beliefs (2 Tim. 2:18; 4:4).

The Gospel of John builds on the OT understanding that God is true or real (John 3:33; 7:28). Christ reveals God and thus reveals truth (John 8:26, 40; 18:37). Since Christ shares in God's truth, he is himself full of grace and truth (John 1:14, 17). Indeed, he is "the way, and the truth, and the life" (John 14:6); he is the true light and the true vine (John 1:9; 15:1). Christ sends the Counselor, the Spirit of truth (John 15:26). Thus, the OT understanding of God as truth extends to Christ and the Holy Spirit. The believer is guided into truth (John 16:13), to worship God in spirit and truth (John 4:23–24). Doing Christ's word enables one to know the truth and so be free (John 8:32). This Christian freedom is not due to possession of correct knowledge but rather comes from relationship to that which is truly real, namely, God.

J.D.

Tryphaena (trī-fee′nuh), a Christian who, with Tryphosa, receives greetings from Paul in Rom. 16:12. Perhaps the two were sisters; the designation "workers in the Lord," however, allows the possibility that Paul associates them because of their common activity in the church. Evidence from inscriptions indicates that both Tryphaena and Tryphosa were common names in that period.

Tryphosa. ***See*** Tryphaena.

tsade (tsah′de), the eighteenth letter of the Hebrew alphabet. It stands at the beginning of the eighteenth section of Psalm 119 and, in the Hebrew, is the first letter in each verse (Ps. 119:137–144).

Tubal-cain (to͞o′bahl-kayn), the son of Lamech and Zillah, brother of Naamah, half-brother and near-namesake of the herdsman Jabal and the musician Jubal (Gen. 4:22). The Semitic root *(wbl)* suggests "craftsman, forger" (lit., "bringer-forth"), thus the suffix "-cain" (Heb., "-smith") may be a gloss (an early explanatory comment later incorporated into the biblical text). Tubal-cain is known as a forger of all implements of copper and iron. As descendants of the fugitive-wanderer Cain, Tubal-cain and his relatives, and later the Kenites (Cainites), typify nomadic tradesmen associated with the rise of urban life and commerce and with the sin and violence it occasioned (Gen. 4:21–24). Gen. 4:25–26 records the contrasting birth of Adam's third son Seth, a distant ancestor of Israel, who "replaced" the slain Abel and in whose era was begun the custom of calling on Yahweh's name (cf. Gen. 4:26b). *1 Enoch* 6–9 recounts a similar association of civilized arts with sin, by way of amplification on Gen. 6:1–6. Kenites, paradoxically, were associated with the rise of Israel and Yahwism (Judg. 1:13; 4:11; 1 Sam. 15:6). ***See also*** Cain; Kenites.

J.W.R.

tumors, an affliction, similar to boils, with which the Philistines were afflicted while they held the Ark of the Covenant (1 Sam. 5:6–6:17).

tunic, loose-fitting, knee-length garment worn next to the skin by both men and women (Matt. 10:10; Mark 6:9). Another tunic or garment would be worn over the first. ***See also*** Dress.

turban, a cloth draped, wrapped, or wound around the head to give protection or distinctive appearance. The turban functioned as a priestly garment (Exod. 28:4, 37, 39; 29:6; 39:28, 31; Lev. 8:9; 16:4) for Aaron and carried the golden plaque inscribed "Holy to the Lord" (Exod. 28:36–37). Job saw his justice as being "like a robe and turban" (Job 29:14), but Isaiah's indictment of Jerusalem's women included removal of their turbans (Isa. 3:23). Ezekiel saw the humiliation of Judah in similar terms (defiant Jerusalem doting on Babylonians with flowing turbans, 23:15) or bypassing normal mourning by wearing the turbans as usual (Ezek. 24:17, 23). In his vision of the Temple, turbans were part of levitical garb (Ezek. 44:18). Zechariah's vision saw the priestly Joshua fitted with a clean turban to prepare for high-priestly duty (Zech. 3:5). R.S.B.

turtledove, a small wild pigeon *(Streptopelia turtur)*. It migrates through Israel in the spring on the way from its winter quarters in Africa to its breeding areas in Europe. The Hebrew name *(tōr)* reflects its typical "tur-tur-tur" call.

The turtledove is mentioned in the Bible mainly as a sacrifice (Gen. 15:9; Lev. 1:14; 5:7), although Jer. 8:7 alludes to its seasonal appearance (see also Song of Sol. 2:12). In Luke 2:24 Mary sacrifices one after the birth of Jesus.

Twelve, the, a group chosen by Jesus to accompany him and share his ministry (Matt. 10:1–4; Mark 3:13–19; Luke 6:13–16; cf. John 6:70; Acts 1:13). The number apparently refers to the twelve tribes of Israel (Matt. 19:28) and symbolizes the restoration of Israel. As witnesses to his ministry and resurrection, the Twelve authenticate the church's postresurrection proclamation of the traditions about Jesus (cf. the selection of Matthias to replace Judas, Acts 1:15–26). ***See also*** Apostle; Disciple; Matthias.

twin, the. ***See*** Didymus.

Twin Brothers, the, in Greek mythology Castor and Pollux, twin sons of Zeus and Leda. Made into a constellation (Gemini) and thus considered gods, their chief interest was in the safety of mariners (they had been granted power over wind and waves). Many ships of that era had ensigns (or figureheads) on their bows. The ship that brought Paul from Malta to Italy (after the first ship had been wrecked, Acts 27) had as its ensign a replica of the Twin Brothers (Acts 28:11; KJV: "Castor and Pollux"). ***See also*** Boats; Zeus.

Tychicus (tik'uh-kuhs), an Asian Christian who, with Trophimus, joined Paul and others on the apostle's final visit to Jerusalem (Acts 20:4–5). Tychicus (the same man?) is apparently the bearer of Colossians and Ephesians (Col. 4:7–9; Eph. 6:21–22) and possibly of 2 Timothy (4:12). According to Titus 3:12, Paul planned to send either Tychicus or Artemas to Crete, thus freeing Titus to join Paul at Nicopolis. Possibly, Paul sent Artemas to Crete and Tychicus to Ephesus (2 Tim. 4:12). The actual movements of these co-workers of Paul are uncertain. ***See also*** Nicopolis; Trophimus.

Tyrannus (tī-ran'uhs), **hall of,** a place mentioned in Acts 19:9, where it is asserted that Paul withdrew from the synagogue in Ephesus and began instruction in "the hall [Gk., school] of Tyrannus." Codex Bezae (the important "Western" text of Acts) adds that Paul taught from the fifth to the tenth hour (11:00 A.M. to 4:00 P.M.), a time not usually utilized by teachers of morality of this era for systematic instruction. It is not clear whether the hall of Tyrannus was a recognized center for moral instruction by philosophers or some sort of local trade union or guild center. It is highly unlikely that Paul's activity in the hall was systematic enough to be called a "school" in any recognizable sense. ***See also*** Ephesus; Paul. A.J.M.

Tyre (tīr), the leading city of Phoenicia during much of the first millennium B.C. Tyre is located off the coast of southern Lebanon on a small island that has been connected to the mainland since the construction of a siege ramp to it by Alexander the Great (late fourth century B.C.). Of its two harbors the northern (Sidonian) is an excellent natural anchorage while the southern (Egyptian) one was protected by jetties constructed in antiquity. Its mainland settlement, called Ushu by Egyptians and Assyrians, and Old Tyre in classical times, was probably located at Tell Rashidiyeh or Tell Mashouk opposite the island. Fresh water is found in springs on the island and additional water was ferried to it from the mainland in boats.

Sources for Tyre's history are varied; the most reliable are the OT and other contemporary Near Eastern records. Detailed information about the kings of Tyre comes in the first century A.D. from the Jewish historian Josephus who utilized the lost works of the Hellenistic historians Menander of Ephesus and Dius. They claimed access to Tyrian annals. Excavations by M. Chehab have concentrated on the Hellenistic and Roman ruins while a small but important deep sounding in the 1970s by P.

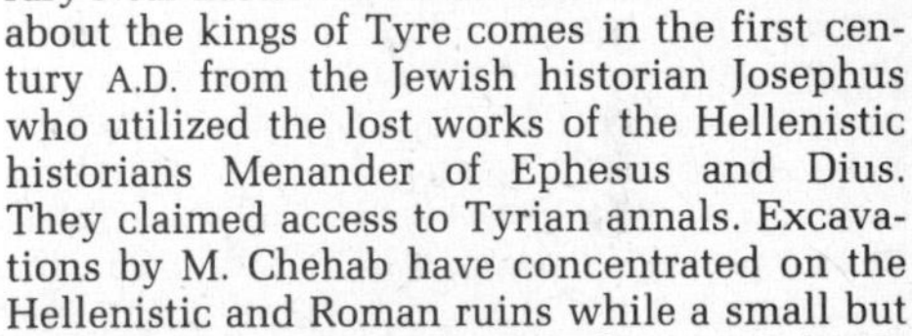

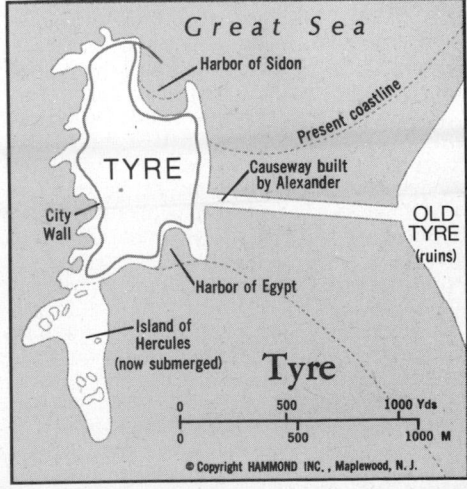

Bikai revealed Phoenician layers. The city has been almost continuously occupied from the third millennium B.C. until the present, except for a major gap from 2000 to 1600 B.C. From the late Bronze Age there are Egyptian, Ugaritic, and Hittite references to Tyre, particularly during the Amarna Age when the Tyrian king Abi-Milki sent ten letters to the pharaoh Akhenaton requesting supplies and military assistance. A classical tradition states that Tyre was refounded by Sidonians around 1200 B.C., possibly in the wake of disturbances by the Sea Peoples, although archaeology shows there was no gap in the occupation of the city at this time.

Tyre emerges as an important Phoenician city in the tenth century B.C. when we learn that King Hiram supplied David with cedars and craftsmen (2 Sam. 5:11; 1 Chron. 14:1; 22:4). Tyre's relations with Israel became much closer when King Solomon turned to Hiram for assistance in building the Temple in Jerusalem. In a trade agreement Hiram responded by felling and transporting cedars and pine wood. Solomon, in return, sent wheat and olive oil to Tyre (1 Kings 5; 2 Chron. 2:3–16). Tyrian craftsmen assisted in the construction of the Temple (1 Kings 7:13–46; 2 Chron. 2:13–15; 4:11–18).

In Tyre Hiram renovated its temples. He also sent his experienced seafarers to join Solomon's fleet at Ezion-geber on the Gulf of Aqaba, whence they sailed to Ophir (1 Kings 9:26–28; 10:11–12; 2 Chron. 8:17–18; 9:10–11). Elsewhere Solomon's "ships of Tarshish" (Tartessos in Iberia?) sailed with Hiram's fleet (1 Kings 10:22; 2 Chron. 9:21–22). Tyre began its sustained program of colonization when it gained control of Kition on Cyprus sometime in the eleventh and tenth centuries B.C.; Hiram may have campaigned there. Ethbaal, a priest of the goddess Astarte, took the throne in the ninth century B.C. after a period of unrest. His daughter Jezebel married King Ahab, ruler of the Northern Kingdom, leading to an increase of Baal worship in Samaria. Tyre's close relations with Samaria, which are also seen in Israel's material culture, continued until Jehu put Jezebel to death (2 Kings 9:30–37).

In North Africa Carthage was founded by Tyre thirty-eight years before the first Olympiad (814 B.C.), an event stemming from a rift between King Pygmalion of Tyre and his sister Elissa (Dido) who led colonists there. In another story the ancient Greek historian Herodotus describes how Cadmus of Tyre led Phoenician colonists to Boeotia where they introduced the alphabet to the Greeks.

Assyrians received tribute in the ninth to seventh centuries B.C. from Tyre. In the campaign of 701 B.C. Sennacherib captured most of the cities of the Phoenician mainland, forcing Luli, king of Sidon, to flee Tyre to Cyprus. The Greek poet Menander (342–291 B.C.) gives a fuller account of the journey of Elulaeus (Luli), king of Tyre, to Cyprus and an unsuccessful five-year siege of the city by the Assyrians. The title "king of Sidon," or "king of the Sidonians," reflects Tyre's control of Sidon and other Phoenician cities. The Assyrian king Esarhaddon (681–668 B.C.) concluded a vassal treaty with King Baal of Tyre stipulating that Tyrian shipwrecks on the coast belonged to Esarhaddon and that an Assyrian official was to advise Baal. In return Esarhaddon granted Tyre trade in most Phoenician ports. The full extent of Tyrian commerce is described in the oracles of the prophets (Ezek. 27; Isa. 23; Amos 1:9–10; Joel 4:4–8; Zech. 9:2–4).

A thirteen-year siege of Tyre (586–573 B.C.) by the Chaldean (Babylonian) monarch Nebuchadnezzar commenced after his destruction of Jerusalem. The siege failed but Tyre submitted to Nebuchadnezzar. Later in the Chaldean period (626–539 B.C.) judges ruled Tyre briefly. In the Persian period (539–333 B.C.) Tyre was surpassed by Sidon as the leading Phoenician city, due to Tyre's loss of its commercial empire in the west to its former colony Carthage and to Persia's preference for Sidon. Tyre's last major act was in 332 B.C. when it impeded Alexander's route to Egypt, forcing him to besiege it seven months. In an epic battle he was the first to conquer the island city.

Although Tyre is mentioned in the NT, it did not play a significant role in the events reported there. The Gospels record that Jesus attracted followers from as far away as Tyre and Sidon (Mark 3:8), and once visited that area (7:24). A saying of Jesus which used Tyre as an example of a Gentile city that will fare better in the last judgment than Palestinian cities that rejected him is also recorded (Matt. 11:21–22). According to Acts, Herod (Herod Agrippa I, king of Judea A.D. 41–44) was struck dead because of blasphemous speech after winning a victory over Tyre (12:20–23), and the apostle Paul landed at Tyre on one of his sea voyages (21:3). ***See also*** Jezebel; Phoenicia; Sidon; Solomon; Temple, The.

Bibliography

Bikai, P. *The Pottery of Tyre*. Warminster: Aris and Phillips, 1979.

Jidejian, N. *Tyre Through the Ages*. Beirut: Dar el-Mashreq, 1969.

Katzenstein, H. J. *The History of Tyre*. Jerusalem: Schocken, 1973. T.L.M.

Tyropoeon (tī'roh-poh-ee'yuhn) **Valley.** ***See*** Jerusalem.

Opposite: Casemate walls—two parallel walls divided by partitions—were widely used in Palestine beginning in the eleventh century B.C. Buildings, such as this synagogue at Masada (aerial view), could be built directly into the wall; in times of war the partitioned areas in the wall could be filled with rubble for reinforcement. In the Bible, Rahab's house was set in the city wall (cf. Josh. 2:15).

U V W

U

Ucal (o͞o'kal), a word understood by many scholars to be a proper name, the pupil or son of the sage Agur (Prov. 30:1). However, the Hebrew of the verse is obscure and some scholars follow the Greek version (Septuagint) and regard the word as a verb meaning "I languish" or something similar.

Uel (o͞o'el; Heb., "will of El [God]"), a postexilic member of the clan of Bani who took a foreign wife (Ezra 10:34).

Ugarit (yo͞o'gahr-it). ***See*** Ras-Shamra.

Ulai (o͞o'lī), a river in the Babylonian province of Elam beside which Daniel saw himself in a vision (Dan. 8:2). Of the three streams near Susa (Shushan), the capital city of Babylonia, the Eulaeus is probably the one referred to. It flows near Susa before joining the Chospes River. ***See also*** Shushan.

Ulam (o͞o'luhm). **1** A descendant of Manasseh of the clan of Gilead (1 Chron. 7:16, 17). **2** The son of Eshek; he was a Benjaminite descendant of King Saul and head of a family of archers (1 Chron. 8:39–40).

unbeliever, a term found almost exclusively in the Letters of Paul, where it apparently denotes any person who is not a member of the Christian community (cf. 1 Cor. 6:6; 7:12–15; 10:27; 14: 22–24; 2 Cor. 4:4; 6:14–15; also Rom. 15:31, where a different Greek word is thus translated). ***See also*** Faith.

uncle, generally the father's brother. There are various persons in Scripture who are obviously uncles, but the term "uncle" (Heb. *dod*) is used rarely. In Leviticus (10:4; 20:20; 25:49) it is used to mean a close kinsman who could function as the "redeemer" (Heb. *go'el*). If an Israelite was forced to sell part of his patrimony, the redeemer purchased it in order to prevent the family's property from being alienated. In Amos 6:10 the reference is to one (KJV: "uncle"; RSV: "kinsman") who must perform the burial of a near kinsman. Elsewhere the term refers to Saul's uncle, Abner (1 Sam. 10:14–16; 14:50); David's uncle, Jonathan (1 Chron. 27:32); Mattaniah, Jechoiachin's uncle (2 Kings 24:17); Abihail, father of Esther and uncle of Mordecai (Esther 2: 7, 15); and Shallum, uncle of Jeremiah (Jer. 32: 7–12). F.S.F.

unclean. ***See*** Animals; Purity.

unction, the act of anointing with oil; one of the seven sacraments of the Roman Catholic Church. ***See also*** Anoint.

United Monarchy, the period when the twelve tribes of Israel were under one king. David's becoming king over Judah (2 Sam. 2:1–7) was largely on the same basis as Saul's kingship; both were military heroes rising to kingship. However, when David became king over Israel (2 Sam. 5:1–5) and then conquered Jerusalem (2 Sam. 5:6–12), he initiated the United Monarchy. As suddenly as the United Monarchy arose around 1000 B.C., it ended with the death of David's son and successor, Solomon, in 922 B.C. Despite all the personal brilliance of David and Solomon, the long-standing traditions of premonarchial tribal alliances continued to haunt the monarchial traditions in succeeding centuries. Nevertheless the power of diverse ideologies and theologies that arose around the house of David persisted in both Judaism and Christianity, serving as a reminder of the period of the United Monarchy. ***See also*** David; Saul; Solomon. K.H.R.

unknown god, an, a designation referred to in an inscription on an altar seen by Paul in Athens (Acts 17:23), which he then used as the basis for his famous Areopagus (or Mars Hill) sermon (Acts 17:22–31). It was apparently a custom in the ancient world for altars to be dedicated to "unknown gods," lest one be forgotten and thus insulted. Such inscriptions have been found, but only in the plural, "gods." ***See also*** Areopagus; Athens.

unleavened, an adjective describing something made without yeast, usually bread (Heb. *matzah*). While unleavened bread could be used for ordinary meals (1 Sam. 28:24–25), it appears most frequently in religious contexts. Lev. 2:4, 11 stipulate that cereal offerings made at the Temple must be unleavened. Both leaven and honey were forbidden due to their association with fermentation and thus, corruption (cf. 1 Cor. 5:8). The unleavened bread not consumed on the sacrificial altar was eaten by the priests (Lev. 10:12–13).

Unleavened bread was also eaten during the Festival of Unleavened Bread, a seven-day festival that originally followed the one-day Passover celebration (Lev. 23:5–8; Num. 28:16–25; cf. Exod. 23:15; 34:18; Deut. 16:1–8; Ezek. 45: 21–25; Mark 14:1; Matt. 26:17; Luke 22:1; Acts 12:3; 20:6). Leavened bread was forbidden dur-

The baking of unleavened bread *(matzah)* illustrated in a fourteenth-century Vogel Kopfhaggada. The artist portrayed humans with birds' heads to "comply" with the second commandment's prohibition against graven images (Deut. 5:8).

ing this festival to mark the beginning of the grain harvest which concluded at the Feast of Weeks (Lev. 23:15–21; Num. 28:26–31; Deut. 16:9–12). The eating of unleavened bread at this festival was also linked to the Exodus from Egypt when, according to the narrative tradition, the Israelites could not wait for the dough to rise because of their haste to escape from Egyptian bondage (Exod. 12:14–20, 34–39). ***See also*** Passover, The. M.A.S.

Unleavened Bread, Feast of the (also called "The Feast of Mazzoth," from Heb. *matsōt*, "unleavened bread"), originally an agricultural festival marking the beginning of harvest; it was celebrated for seven days beginning on the fifteenth day of the month Abib (Nisan, the period March–April; Exod. 23:15; 34:18–20). It was later combined with the Passover (Exod. 12:1–20; Ezek. 45:21–24; Matt. 26:17; Luke 22:1). ***See also*** Feasts, Festivals, and Fasts; Passover, The; Time.

Unni (o͞o'nī). **1** A Levite musician who was appointed to help celebrate the transfer of the Ark of the Covenant to Jerusalem (1 Chron. 15:18, 20). **2** A scribal marginal correction ("Qere") for the name Unno, a Levite who returned with Zerubbabel from the Babylonian captivity (Neh. 12:9); some versions retain the name Unno.

unpardonable sin, an idea based on Mark 3: 28–30. To blaspheme is to slander, defame, revile. The verses must be understood in their context: Jesus healed the sick, evil spirits recognizing him as the Son of God. Yet he was accused of being possessed by Beelzebul and casting out demons "by the prince of demons" (Mark 3:22). But Jesus' power comes from the Holy Spirit. Those who identify the beneficent works of the Holy Spirit with Beelzebul are thus committing an unpardonable sin: they attribute Jesus' power to the devil and thereby deny the saving work of God. S.B.

upharsin (yo͞o-pahr'sin). ***See*** Mene, Mene, Tekel, Upharsin.

Uphaz (o͞o'faz), a word usually understood as a proper noun; it is an otherwise unknown location where gold was obtained (Jer. 10:9; Dan. 10: 5). However, the Hebrew text is uncertain in both references. Many scholars, following some ancient versions (Targums, Syriac, Heb. manuscripts), take Uphaz as a scribal error for Ophir, a near legendary source of gold (cf. 1 Kings 9:28). Other scholars have suggested that Uphaz is a misspelled form of the word "refine" (Heb. *mūphāz*) and should be translated "pure" or "finest" (cf. 1 Kings 10:18; Song of Sol. 5:11). Various English versions translate the word in different ways. ***See also*** Ophir. D.R.B.

upper room, the room in which Jesus is said to have celebrated his last meal with the disciples (Mark 14:15). According to Acts 1:13, the disciples continued to gather there in the days before Pentecost. The much later story of the pilgrimage of the Spanish nun Egeria to the Holy Land (A.D. 384) also claims that Pentecost took place in a building. The present site identified as the Upper Room is in a building that is also claimed to be the tomb of David (though David is buried in his city on the hill, 1 Kings 2:10). The identification of that building as the site of the Upper Room was made no earlier than the tenth century A.D., however. P.P.

Ur, one of the oldest cities of southern Mesopotamia. Ur, modern Tell el-Muqayyar, lies ten miles west of the Euphrates, on whose bank it stood in antiquity, before the river changed course. The site is an oval, about a half-mile at its greatest extent, dominated by an oblong sacred enclosure.

Modern exploration of Ur began in the nineteenth century and resumed at the end of World War I, the most important work being Leonard Woolley's systematic excavations of 1922–1934. Woolley revealed that Ur was occupied already at the earliest known period of settlement in southern Mesopotamia, the Ubaid period (ca. 5500–4000 B.C.). From there it continued, for five thousand years, through all the subsequent periods of Mesopotamian history. In the *Uruk* period (ca. 4000–3000 B.C.), the beginnings of writing and monumental architecture marked the emergence at Ur, as elsewhere in southern Mesopotamia, of complex urban society. In the Early Dynastic period (ca. 3000–2350 B.C.), Ur held a key position in what by then had become a thriving network of southern city-states. During the Akkadian period (2350–2154 B.C.), Ur and the rest of that network fell under the control of the Sargonic dynasty of Agade, with Ur receiving particular attention for the cult of the moon god, its patron deity. In the Post-Akkadian and Ur III periods (2154–2004 B.C.), Ur resumed its independence and then became the focus of a Mesopotamian empire of its own. Most of that political power was lost in the following Isin-Larsa and Old Babylonian periods (2004–1740 B.C.), but Ur managed to retain its importance as a center of international trade and of scribal and religious activity.

Devastated in 1740 B.C., Ur entered a millennium of modest existence (1740–ca. 600 B.C.), as a relatively unimportant city controlled by a succession of Babylonian and Assyrian overlords. This political subservience remained, but was offset by a major rebuilding program under the Neo-Babylonian/Chaldean empire (ca. 600–539 B.C.). When the Neo-Babylonian empire fell to Cyrus the Persian (539 B.C.), the new construction was maintained and even furthered. By the late fourth century B.C., however, as Persian rule gave way to Greek, Ur was fading fast—its decline due especially, it appears, to the beginning of a shift in the Euphrates River bed, which had been so important for transportation and agriculture. By the following century, the end seems to have come, as all evidence for the city ceases.

For this long history, several discoveries of the Woolley expedition have proven especially illuminating or controversial. Thus, in the Ubaid period, a thick layer of clear silt was found, separating occupational levels of the later two phases. Woolley's ascription of this, however, to the Primeval Flood has not won serious support; and most prefer to understand it as the product of local flooding, which was a frequent occurrence in the Euphrates region.

The prize discovery of the Early Dynastic period was the royal cemetery, of phase IIIA (ca. 2600–2450 B.C.). Its sixteen large, vaulted-shaft tombs yielded a wide array of treasures—a gold dagger and helmet, lyres, he-goat statues—and the bodies not only of the principal personages, but, in the major tombs, also of male and female attendants and animals, along with wheeled vehicles. The principals seem to have been Ur's rulers; the animals and other humans were perhaps killed on the rulers' deaths to accompany them to the Netherworld, as certain Mesopotamian texts may suggest.

In the Ur III period, the kings sought to make the city as imposing physically as it was politically. Among their achievements that Woolley's team excavated were a massive brick city wall; a large mausoleum; a number of buildings in the sacred enclosure, including the three-storied

Standard of Ur shows a king at war and triumphant at the defeat of his enemies; Sumerian enameled panel, first half of the third millennium B.C.

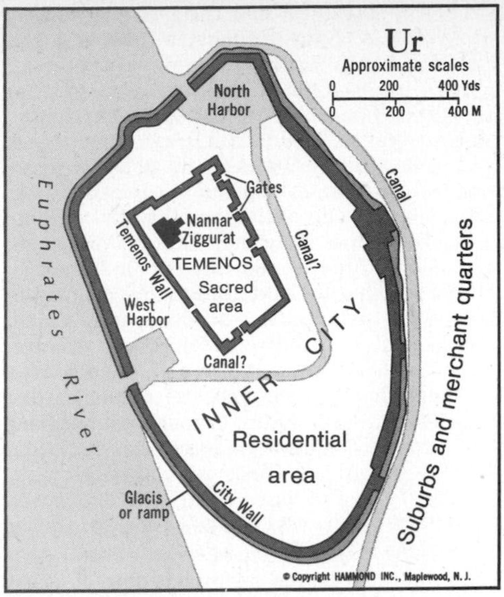

Plan of the site of ancient Ur.

ziggurat, the *giparu*-complex which contained a shrine and rooms for the high priestess of the moon god, and a royal palace. Many of these buildings were enlarged and others added in the Neo-Babylonian/Chaldean revival: for example, a new wall was built around the sacred enclosure; the ziggurat increased from three stories to seven; a new temple and palace were built, the latter ("Palace of Bel-shalti-Nannar") probably for the governor or overlord of the city. Finally, Woolley was able to illuminate the private citizen's life at Ur by excavating several private housing quarters, both from the Isin-Larsa/Old Babylonian periods and from the Neo-Babylonian.

In the Bible: In the OT, Ur is mentioned four times (Gen. 11:28, 31; 15:7; Neh. 9:7), all as the home of the patriarch Abraham before his migration to Canaan and all in the Hebrew phrase *Ur Kasdim*. *Kasdim* here almost certainly refers to the "Chaldeans" (cf. already the Septuagint), so that, if accurate, the phrase as a whole should refer to the southern Mesopotamian Ur of the period of the Neo-Babylonian/Chaldean empire. To be sure, this period is much too late for Abraham, and so most modern scholars agree that the use of the term *Kasdim* here must be considered an anachronism of the biblical editors, who would have worked during the Babylonian exile, precisely the heyday of Chaldean Ur. In light of these difficulties, other suggestions have been proposed. Thus, the fact that elsewhere in the OT the lineage to which Abraham belongs is located only in northern Syria (e.g., Gen. 24) has prompted the modern scholar C. H. Gordon to suggest that *Ur Kasdim* is not the southern Ur, but a northern Syrian one, which he identifies with Ura, north-northeast of Harran. His proposal recalls some earlier traditions which equate Abraham's Ur with Urfa (Edessa), northwest of Harran. Both views, however, are largely rejected today in favor of the southern Ur, which better suits the epithet *Kasdim*—the Chaldeans were never centered in northern Syria—and which was by far the best known Ur in antiquity. ***See also*** Abraham; Babylon; Chaldea; Flood, The; Sargon II.

Bibliography

Moorey, P. R. S. *Ur 'of the Chaldees': A Revised and Updated Edition of Sir Leonard Woolley's Excavations at Ur*. Ithaca, NY: Cornell University Press, 1982. P.B.M.

Uri (yo͞o'rī, a shortened form of Uriah, Heb., "Yah [God] is my light"). **1** A Judahite; the father of Bezalel, the craftsman who supervised the construction of the tabernacle (Exod. 31:2; 2 Chron. 1:5). **2** The father of Geber, a district administrator under King Solomon (1 Kings 4:19). **3** A postexilic levitical gatekeeper who took a foreign wife (Ezra 10:24).

Uriah (yo͞o-ri'uh; Heb., "God is light [or fire]"). **1** A Hittite who was one of David's "heroes" (2 Sam. 23:39; 1 Chron. 11:41). His house was in Jerusalem (2 Sam. 11:9–11). While he was on the battlefield David took Uriah's wife, Bathsheba, ordering him to such an exposed position during the siege of Rabbath-ammon (the present Amman, capital of Jordan) that his death was inevitable (2 Sam. 11:12–17). His name indicates a foreign ancestry. In Hurrian Ariya means "king" or "ruler." It has been suggested that the Hurrian element later received the present Israelite form. **2** The high priest in the reign of Ahar of Judah (ca. 735–715 B.C.). He carried out innovations for his king, like the installation of an altar similar to one seen by Ahaz in Damascus (2 Kings 16:10–16). Apparently he is the priest who was taken by Isaiah (8:2–4) as his witness for the fulfillment of his prophecy against Samaria. **3** A son of Shemaiah, a prophet of Kiriath-jearim. His rebuke of King Jehoiakim (ca. 609–598 B.C.) and prophecies of destruction like those of Jeremiah had necessitated his flight to Egypt, whence he was brought back, slain, and interred in a common grave (Jer. 26:20–23). Over a generation ago, one scholar considered this Uriah to be "the prophet" of the Lachish Letters. Lachish Letter IV seems to have been addressed to a person of this name, though it was never received since the crisis of Babylonian intervention in 598 B.C. prevented its being forwarded. **4** A priest, father of Meremoth, contemporary of Nehemiah (Ezra 8:33; Neh. 3:4, 21). **5** A priest who stood beside Ezra in Jerusalem when he read the Law to the returned exiles (Neh. 8:4). Y.G.

Uriel (yo͞o'ri-el). **1** A prominent Kohathite Levite who helped bring the Ark from the home of Obed-edom to Jerusalem (1 Chron. 6:24; 15:5, 11). **2** A man of Gibeah whose daughter, Michaiah, became the mother of King Abijah of Judah (2 Chron. 13:2). **3** An angel (2 Esd. 4: 1–11). Uriel served as a guide to Enoch in the upper heavens (*1 Enoch* 19–22) and was one of the four angels of the Presence (cf. *1 Enoch* 9:1).

Urijah (yōō-rī'juh; Heb., "my light is Yah [God]" or "Light of Yah"), a variant spelling of Uriah, the chief priest in Jerusalem during the reign of King Ahaz (ca. 735–715 B.C.). He built a new altar at the king's order patterned after an Assyrian altar that Ahaz had seen in Damascus. He apparently did not object to other Assyrian influenced innovations introduced by Ahaz (2 Kings 16:10–16; note also vv. 17–18). He is called by Isaiah as a witness of the prophecy of the Assyrian invasion (Isa. 8:2, here called Uriah). The more proper spelling of the name is Uriah, which some versions use. ***See also*** Uriah. D.R.B.

Urim (ōō'reem) **and Thummim** (thōō'meem), a device consulted by the chief priest (in an unexplained manner) to determine God's response to "yes" or "no" questions asked by the leader of the people (Num. 27:21; 1 Sam. 14:41; 28:6). It was borne in a pouch worn by the priest, over the heart, on the ephod garment (Exod. 28: 30). Apparently, the use of the Urim and Thummim is sometimes indicated by the term ephod (1 Sam. 23:9–12; 30:7–8), by reference to the Ark of the Covenant (Judg. 20:27; 1 Sam. 14:18), and by the phrase "ask of God" (1 Sam. 23:2, 4).

The Urim and Thummim may have been superseded by prophetic oracles after the time of David, and by the period of the return of the Babylonian exiles they were just a memory transmuted into an indefinite future (Ezra 2:63; Neh. 7:65). ***See also*** Ephod. J.U.

Uruk (ōō'ruhk). ***See*** Erech.

usury. ***See*** Loan.

Uthai (ōō'thī). **1** A postexilic inhabitant of Jerusalem, a Judahite of the clan of Perez (1 Chron. 9:4). **2** A member of the clan of Bigvai who returned from the Babylonian captivity with Ezra (Ezra 8:14). The name may be a variant of Athaiah, which, following an Arabic etymology, would mean "pride of Yahweh" or "Yahweh is my pride."

Uz (uhz). **1** The son of Aram and grandson of Shem (Gen. 10:23; see 1 Chron. 1:17, where Uz is listed as a "son" of Shem). **2** The son (RSV: "Huz") of Nahor and Milcah and brother of Buz (Gen. 22:21). **3** The son of Dishan and brother of Aran the Horite (Gen. 36:28; 1 Chron. 1:42). **4** The homeland of the "daughter of Edom" (Lam. 4:21). **5** The homeland of Job (Job 1:1). The location of Uz is uncertain. In Job 1:19 this land is described as a desert area. In Jer. 25:20 Uz is linked inexplicably with the land of the Philistines. In Job 1:15 and 1:17 respectively, Uz is said to have been attacked by Sabeans (from Arabia) and Chaldeans (from Mesopotamia). As noted above, Lam. 4:21 says that Uz was the homeland of the "daughter of Edom." The mention of Job's three friends, Eliphaz the Temanite, Bildad the Shuhite, and Zophar the Naamathite (Job 2:11), also points toward Edom; e.g., in Gen. 36:4 Eliphaz is listed as a descendant of Esau, i.e., Edom (see Gen. 36:1). Overall the evidence indicates that Uz was a desert region east of Palestine, either in Edom or, perhaps, northern Transjordan. ***See also*** Edom; Job, The Book of. J.M.W.

Uzal (yōō'zal), a son of Joktan (Gen. 10:27; 1 Chron. 1:21) and a clan name whose association with other names and locations south of Moab suggests an Arabian location. In Ezek. 27:17 the association of Uzal with other Arabian locations suggests modern San'a in the southwest corner of the peninsula about seventy miles west of Marib.

Uzza (uh'zah). **1** The burial garden of Manasseh (2 Kings 21:18) and Amon (21:26), kings of Judah. **2** A Benjaminite son of Gera (1 Chron. 8: 7). **3** In postexilic Jerusalem a family of Temple servants (Ezra 2:49; Neh. 7:51).

Uzzah (uhz'ah). **1** A son of Abinadab, who assisted in moving the Ark from his father's house. He was killed when the ark threatened to tip, and Uzzah broke the taboo against handling sacred objects by touching it (2 Sam. 6:3–8; 1 Chron. 13:7–11). **2** A Merarite son of Mahli (1 Chron. 6:29).

Uzzen-sheerah (uh'zen-shee'rah; Heb., "ear of Sheerah"; KJV: "Uzzen-sherah"), a village built by the Ephraimite daughter Sheerah (1 Chron. 7:24). While it is presumably near the other villages she is credited with having built, namely, Upper and Lower Beth-horon, the site remains unidentified.

Uzzi (uh'zī; Heb., "strength"). **1** An Aaronite priest descended from Eleazar (1 Chron. 6:5–6). **2** A clan chief of Issachar, and the son of Tola (1 Chron. 7:2–3). **3** A group of Benjaminite families (1 Chron. 9:8). **4** A postexile Benjaminite family (1 Chron. 9:8). **5** A Levite descendant of Asaph (Neh. 11:22). **6** The head of a priestly family of Jedaiah under Joiakim (Neh. 12:19). **7** A Levite musician who participated in dedicating the restored walls of Jerusalem (Neh. 12:41).

Uzziah (yuh-zī'ah; Heb., "Yah is strong"), the name of several people mentioned in the Hebrew Bible. **1** The son of Amaziah and the father of Jotham. All three of these men reigned as kings in Jerusalem during the eighth century B.C. Uzziah (called Azariah in 2 Kings 14:21; 15:1–8, 17–27; 1 Chron. 3:12) ascended the throne at the tender age of sixteen; his father was driven from office, and the son enjoyed popular support. Uzziah had some military success over local enemies, particularly the Philistines, Ammonites, and Meunites (2 Chron. 26:6–8). During his long reign, he seems to have devoted considerable attention to agriculture. To improve the land's yield, Uzziah built towers in the wilderness and dug wells in the Shephelah and in the plain. On his behalf loyal subjects engaged in viticulture and agriculture. Uzziah also paid close attention to equipping an army, according to 2 Chron. 26: 11–15. In later life the king was stricken with leprosy. This illness was interpreted as divine punishment for pride, and the occasion for that pride was the king's attempt to usurp priestly prerogative. Because of this physical defect, Uzziah was forced to abdicate in favor of his son Jotham, who became acting ruler. Perhaps Uzziah's reign was best remembered for something over which he had no control, a devastating earthquake (Amos 1:1; Zech. 14:5). At least two prophets, Amos and Hosea, were active in his time, and Isaiah's well-known vision in 6:1–13 occurred in the year of Uzziah's death. **2** A Levite descended from Kohath (1 Chron. 6:24). **3** The father of Jonathan, an official over the royal treasuries in David's time (1 Chron. 27:25).

J.L.C.

Uzziel (o͞o'zee-uhl; Heb., "God is strong"). **1** The grandson of Levi, son of Kohath, and founder of the Kohathite levitical clan called Uzzielites (Exod. 6:18, 22; Lev. 10:4; Num. 3:19, 30; 1 Chron. 6:2, 18; 23:12, 20; 24:24; cf. Num. 3:27; 1 Chron. 26:23). David appointed Uzzielites to assist in bringing the Ark to Jerusalem (1 Chron. 15:10) and to serve among the Levites in the Temple (1 Chron. 23:12, 20; 24:24). **2** A man of Simeon who settled at Mt. Seir after destroying the Amalekites there (1 Chron. 4:42). **3** The founder of a Benjaminite family (1 Chron. 7:7). **4** One of the sons of Heman, a clan of musicians appointed for Temple service by David (1 Chron. 25:4). **5** A Levite son of Jeduthun who helped cleanse the Temple under Hezekiah (2 Chron. 29:14). **6** A goldsmith, son of Harhaiah, who helped rebuild the wall of Jerusalem under Nehemiah (Neh. 3:8).

M.A.S.

V

vagabond, one who wanders without a fixed place of residence. It is a symbol in the OT for the sudden and unexpected appearance of poverty to the indolent person (Prov. 6:11). The term is also used in the KJV in other places: Gen. 4:12, 14; Ps. 109:10 (RSV: "wanderer"); Acts 19:13 (RSV: "itinerant").

vail. ***See*** Veil.

vale, valley, a depression in the earth's surface. The land of Palestine features a wide variety of valleys, ravines, and gorges due to the presence of the Carmel and Central mountain ranges. The Hebrews used five different words to describe these valleys. In the north (Jezreel)

Animals grazing in the lower Jordan Valley of modern Israel.

and west there are many wide, fertile valleys or plains. The territory between the central ridge and the Jordan Valley is marked by numerous narrow gorges or precipitous canyons called *wadis* by the Arabs. Valleys served as the location for military battles (Gen. 14:8), cities (Gen. 19: 29), crops (1 Sam. 6:13), springs (1 Kings 18:5), and grazing lands (1 Chron. 27:29).

valley, cities of the, the traditional title for the five cities of the Jordan Valley mentioned in Gen. 14:8 (cf. 13:12; 19:29): Admah, Gomorrah, Sodom, Zeboiim, and Zoar (Bela). ***See also*** Cities.

vanity, the English translation of various Hebrew and Greek words, particularly in the KJV. The basic idea appears to have been "that which is empty of meaning, purpose, or content." For example, one of the Hebrew words thus translated means "vapor" or "breath," that is, something devoid of substance or permanence. The worship of idols is vanity (cf. Jer. 10:15; 16:19; Isa. 57:13; Acts 14:15). According to Ecclesiastes, the search for meaning in life is "vanity," that is, elusive and without definite substance. It should be noted that "vanity" is not used in the biblical writings to mean conceit or preoccupation with self. The meanings in the OT and the NT range from "nothingness" to "purposelessness" to "emptiness" to "chaos."

J.M.E.

Vashni (vash'nī), in some translations (e.g., the KJV), the eldest son of Samuel according to 1 Chron. 6:28. Although the present Hebrew text of this verse reads "the firstborn [was] Vashni and Abijah," a parallel passage in 1 Sam. (8:2) reads: "the name of his firstborn was Joel and the name of his second, Abijah" (cf. 1 Chron. 6: 33). Apparently, in the Chronicles passage the name "Joel" was inadvertently omitted and the Hebrew word meaning "and the second" (Heb. *veshēnî* or *vehashēnî)* was corrupted into a proper name.

Vashti (vash'tī), the queen of the Persian king Ahasuerus (Xerxes I); her royal position was taken from her because she refused to obey a summons from the king (Esther 1:9–22). ***See also*** Ahasuerus; Esther.

Vaticanus, Codex. ***See*** B.

vau (vahv), the sixth letter of the Hebrew alphabet; its numerical value is six. In proto-Sinaitic inscriptions it is represented by a pictograph of a peg; later the circular top was open, so that the letter took on a Y-shape. The Aramaic cursive script has a variant of this form, as does the classical Hebrew square script. The old Phoenician *vau* seems to be the prototype of Greek upsilon, which the Romans turned into "U" and "V." ***See also*** Writing.

ו

Veadar (vee'uh-dahr; Heb., "and Adar," also called *Adar Sheni*, "the second Adar"), a thirteenth month that was inserted into the Jewish calendar between the months Adar and Nisan; it is added seven times in a cycle of nineteen years to correlate the Jewish lunar-based calendar, composed of twelve lunar months of 29½ days (a 354-day year), with the solar year (365 days). It falls in late March and early April. ***See also*** Time.

vegetables. ***See*** Food.

veil, a covering, usually of some type of cloth. **1** A piece of fabric worn by a woman to conceal her face or cover her head (Song of Sol. 4:1, 3; 6:7; Isa. 47:2). Apparently, an Israelite woman wore a veil at the time of her wedding. When Rebekah first saw Isaac, she put on her veil and, afterwards, they were married (Gen. 24:65–67). Jacob's inability to recognize that Leah had been substituted for Rachel on his first wedding night can be explained if Leah was veiled. On the other hand, Tamar wore a veil to trick Judah into thinking that she was a prostitute so that he would lie with her and fulfill the levirite duty (Gen. 38:14, 19). According to Paul, women should wear veils when praying or prophesying (1 Cor. 11:4–16). **2** A covering Moses wore to conceal his face after he received the second set of tablets of the testimony at Mt. Sinai (Exod. 34: 29–35). At that time, his face shone, which made the people afraid. Consequently he wore the veil except when he went in to speak with God. Paul claimed that this was to conceal the temporary nature of the old covenant (2 Cor. 3:13). **3** The covering over the entrance to the Holy of Holies in the Temple (2 Chron. 3:14), which also hung before the Ark in the wilderness tabernacle (Exod. 26:33; 35:12; 39:34; Lev. 24:3). Only Aaron and his sons were permitted to pass beyond the veil (Num. 18:7). At a later time, only the high priest could enter the Holy of Holies and only on the Day of Atonement (Lev. 6:2). According to the Gospels, the veil of the Temple tore at Jesus' death, exposing the Holy of Holies (Matt. 27:51; Mark 15:38; Luke 23:45).

M.A.S.

Women covering their faces with veils; first-century A.D. relief from Palmyra.

vengeance, punishment in retribution for injury. God appears as a God of vengeance, particularly in the OT, exacting punishment both upon Israel for infidelity to the Covenant (Lev. 26:25; cf. Luke 21:22) and upon other nations for their treatment of Israel (Deut. 32:35; Isa. 61:2).

In Israelite society, private vengeance by the "avenger of blood" of the injured family was the rule in cases of injury and death (Num. 35: 9–28; cf. Gen. 4:23–24). A tendency to mitigate this practice (cf. Gen. 4:15; 2 Sam. 14:1–24) appears in the institutions of sanctuary (Exod. 21: 12–14) and cities of refuge (Num. 35:9–28), which provided some legal protection for one accused of murder, and in "an eye for an eye" (Exod. 21:23–25), which limited retribution to the extent of the original injury. Lev. 19:18 enjoins one to "love your neighbor as yourself" rather than to seek revenge (cf. Prov. 25:21), while Jesus, in commenting upon "an eye for an eye" (Matt. 5:38–42), and Paul, in appealing to God as a God of vengeance (Rom. 12:19), both eliminate vengeance as a legitimate motive for human behavior. ***See also*** Avenger; Blood; Cities; Judgment, Day of; Law; Murder; Pardon; Punishment, Everlasting; Reconciliation; Retribution. D.W.S.

vermilion, a bright red pigment comprised of mercuric sulphide and varying in color from crimson to nearly orange. It was the color of Jehoiakim's house which was condemned by the prophet Jeremiah (Jer. 14:22). Ezekiel declared it the color of images of Chaldeans in the condemned city of Oholibah (Jerusalem; Ezek. 23:14). In the Wis. of Sol. 13:14 wooden idols were painted this color (RSV: "red paint").

Veronica. ***See*** Woman with a Flow of Blood.

versions. ***See*** Texts, Versions, Manuscripts, Editions.

Vespasian (ves-pay'zhuhn), a Roman general who began the siege of Jerusalem in the first Jewish war of rebellion against Rome (A.D. 66–70). In the midst of the siege, he was named Roman emperor, and he ruled from 69 to 79. His son Titus, who took over the siege in Jerusalem and pursued it to its conclusion, also succeeded him as emperor (79–81). ***See also*** Titus.

vessel, a container, often for liquids. "Vessel" is the usual KJV translation for terms designating a wide variety of containers and implements (Heb. *keli;* Gk. *skeuos);* the RSV translates them "vessel," "bag," "bowl," "utensil" and "instrument." The most common vessels were of earthenware (Jer. 18:4; Rom. 9:21; figuratively, 2 Cor. 4:7), followed by baskets, and vessels of metal, skin, stone, and wood. Pottery vessels included bowls, basins, jars, flasks, pots, and goblets. They were used for storage and transportation (of water, oil, grain, and olives), cooking, eating, drinking, and presenting offerings. They are

Iron Age Philistine vessel decorated with geometric patterns and stylized bird.

found in every domestic excavation site and in graves, where they accompanied the deceased with provisions. Skin vessels were used for drawing and carrying water, storing wine, and churning milk. Vessels of gold, silver, copper, and bronze were employed in the tabernacle and Temple service (Exod. 37:16; Num. 7:85; 2 Kings 25:14; see Mark 11:16; the RSV translates *skeuos* as "anything"), while alabaster vessels held fine perfumes and ointments (e.g., Mark 14:3). ***See also*** Pottery. P.A.B.

vestibule. ***See*** Porch.

vesture, an archaic word for garments or clothes. Garments were made of wool, leather, or linen and were worn for protection and for reasons of modesty (Gen. 3:7, 21; 9:23). Special occasions, such as weddings or funerals, were marked by the wearing of special garments (Gen. 37:34; 38:14; Matt. 22:11). Special vestments were also used to distinguish people in their official functions, such as rulers, priests, and prophets (Gen. 41:42; Exod. 35:19; 2 Kings 2: 13–14). ***See also*** Dress.

Via Dolorosa (Lat., "way of pain"), the traditional pilgrimage route in Jerusalem commemorating Christ's journey to the cross (Mark 15:20–23). The traditional route is not likely to have been historical, since Pilate probably condemned Jesus at the Herodian palace on the opposite side of the city (Matt. 27:19; Luke 23:4; John 18:28; Philo *Delegation to Gaius* 38; Josephus *War* 2.301). A route from there through the city to Golgotha would have led east on David street and then west on Triple Suk to Golgotha.

The present route consists of two devotional stops near the Ecce Homo arch, seven outside leading to the Church of the Holy Sepulchre, and five inside the church itself. Though Byzantine pilgrims followed approximately the present route from Gethsemane to Calvary on Holy Thursday, they made no devotional stops. Numerous routes developed during the Middle Ages. The devotional practice of representing the gospel story in churches around fourteen stations led to the development of the present route. The route itself was fixed in the eighteenth century and all of the stations established in the nineteenth. P.P.

vial, a small container used to hold oil or perfume. A vial was used by Samuel to anoint Saul as king (1 Sam. 10:1). The KJV uses the term in a number of passages in the book of Revelation (5:8; 15:7; 16:1–3, 17; 17:1; 21:9; RSV: "bowl"). Most commonly found in archaeological excavations are globular, piriform, or cylindrical vials in the shape of juglets, generally with a single vertical loop handle, an everted rim, and a button or round base.

villages. *See* Towns.

vine, a plant whose long trunk grows along the ground or fastens itself to other objects by means of tendrils. In biblical usage (Heb. *gefen,* Gk. *ampelos)* "vine" is almost always the grapevine *(Vitis vinifera).* Other vining plants are specifically named (melons, Num. 11:5; cucumbers, Isa. 1:8), while the "wild" vine of 2 Kings 4:39 was probably a type of gourd. The "choice vine" (Heb. *soreq,* Jer. 2:21) was a particular grape variety producing a rich red wine.

The vine was noted for its luxuriant foliage, intertwining branches, and trailing or climbing shoots (Ps. 80:11; Ezek. 19:10–11). Its fragrant blossoms are recalled in love poetry (Song of Sol. 2:13), but it was its fruit, and especially the "wine . . . in the cluster" (Isa. 65:8; cf. Matt. 26:29) that gave it place of honor among the "trees." Its wood, in contrast, was useless, fit only for burning (Ezek. 15:2–8).

Grapes were eaten fresh (Jer. 31:29) and dried into raisin clusters (1 Sam. 25:18), and the juice was boiled down into a thick syrup ("honey"). But wine, or "new wine," was the chief product. The climate and terrain of Syro-Palestine especially favored viticulture, and its wines were renowned from Egypt to Babylon. Biblical tradition associates vine growing with the beginnings of agriculture and civilization, making Noah the first vinedresser and the first drunkard (Gen. 9:20–21). But it identifies the debauchery that accompanied the use of wine more specifically with Canaanite culture (Gen. 9:22–27).

Terms for vine, vineyard, or wine are commonly paired with terms for fields or grain, representing the two main types of agricultural production (Exod. 22:5; Num. 16:14; Deut. 33:28; cf. plows and pruning hooks, Isa. 2:4; threshing floor and winevat, Hos. 9:2, 4). Olives or oil extended the basic pair (1 Sam. 8:14; Deut. 6:11), while vine and fig together described the main fruiting plants.

A vine was a common sight in a Palestinian courtyard, climbing a tree or (in Roman times) a trellis. A peasant ideal of peace and prosperity is expressed in the repeated phrase, everyone "under his vine and under his fig tree" (1 Kings 4:25; Mic. 4:4). Vineyards were commonly planted on hillsides (Isa. 5:1), which were less suitable for grain cultivation, though they were also established in the major valleys and plains. The Hebron area was especially noted for its grapes (Num. 13:22–24; Gen. 49:11–12), as was Sibmah in Transjordan (Isa. 16:8). An annual vintage festival was held at Shiloh (Judg. 21:19–21).

Vineyards required long-term intensive care

Picking grapes from the vine; tomb of Mennah, Thebes, Egypt, ca. 1400 B.C.

(Isa. 5:1–7; Mark 12:1). The soil was first dug and cleared of stones and a wall (or hedge) erected to discourage predators (Ps. 80:12–13; Song of Sol. 2:15). A watchtower and winevat completed the installation, with a booth for lodging during the harvest (Isa. 1:18). Vines required heavy annual pruning (Lev. 25:4; John 15:2), hoeing (Isa. 5:6), thinning and support of fruit clusters, and sometimes irrigation (Isa. 27:3). Intensive labor heightened expectations of the harvest and made loss of the vintage a bitter disappointment (Isa. 5:2; Deut. 28:39). Deuteronomic law exempted from military service the man who had planted a vineyard but not enjoyed its fruit (Deut. 20:6). Flourishing vineyards meant peacetime; war's devastation was represented by a ravaged vineyard: walls broken, vines choked by thorns, branches trampled by wild beasts (Isa. 5:5–6; Ps. 80:12–13). Restoration would be a time of planting vineyards and drinking their wine (Isa. 65:21), a time when the mountains would "drip sweet wine" (Amos 9:13).

Production and Use of Wine: Wine ranked with oil as an important commercial crop, and the royal house played a major role in its production and trade. A large cellar was required to maintain the rich consumption of the court (Esther 1:1–9; Neh. 5:18), but wine was also an important commodity of exchange; Solomon paid Hiram of Tyre for timber and artisans with provisions of grain, wine, and oil (2 Chron. 2:10, 15). The king's storehouses and winepress (Zech. 14:10) were supplied from the produce of royal lands (1 Chron. 27:27) and from taxes in kind. Eighth-century B.C. inscribed potsherds (Gk. *ostraca)* from Samaria record palace receipts of wine and oil from landowners in the region.

Wine was produced by treading the grapes in a large vat connected to a smaller, lower vat by a channel. Fermentation began in the lower vat, where the juice was collected, and continued in jars or skins (Matt. 9:17). The grape harvest was a time of special joy (Isa. 16:10). Singing and shouting accompanied the work (Jer. 48:33) and dancing and feasting celebrated the vintage (Judg. 21:20–21). Worship of the god(s) of the land and sexual rites marked the Canaanite feast of ingathering (Judg. 9:27), later replaced by Israel's Feast of Tabernacles (Deut. 16:13).

Bread and wine represented the basic elements of food and drink (Judg. 19:19; Lam. 2:12), giving rise to metaphorical and symbolical uses (Prov. 4:17), as in the Eucharist (1 Cor. 11:23–26). But wine was especially identified with court dining and feasts (Heb. *mishteh*, from *shatah*, "to drink"; Esther 1:1–9; Dan. 1:5, 8, 16; 1 Sam. 25:36; John 2:1–10), where it was frequently mixed with spices (Song of Sol. 8:2; Prov. 9:5). A special kind of drinking feast was the Canaanite mourning feast *(mirzēah)*, characterized by ritual drunkenness and sexual intercourse, which persisted in Israel despite prophetic condemnation (Amos. 6:4–7; Isa. 28:7–8; see "house of mourning," Jer. 16:5, and "house of banqueting," Song of Sol. 2:4).

Wine was generally viewed as a blessing (Gen. 27:28; Deut. 7:13) that "gladdens the heart" (Ps. 104:15; cf. Eccles. 10:19), suppresses pain, and banishes misery in forgetfulness (1 Tim. 5:23; Prov. 31:6). Its absence on special occasions such as weddings was a misfortune, and on one occasion Jesus remedied such a lack by miraculous means (John 2:1–10). Wine was offered to God in Israelite worship (Lev. 23:13; Num. 28:14) and was employed medicinally to administer drugs (Matt. 27:34) and treat wounds (Luke 10:34). But a glad heart meant a dull mind (Hos. 4:11), making one irresponsible (Prov. 31:4), unwary of danger (2 Sam. 13:28), and easily manipulated (Gen. 19:32–35; Esther 5:4–10; 7:2). The drunkard is depicted as foolish or mad (Jer. 51:7), reeling and vomiting (Isa. 28:7–8), licentious (Rev. 18:3), sprawling in senseless stupor, and babbling incoherently (Acts 2:13). The wise are counseled to avoid strong drink (Prov. 23:29–31). Kings should abstain lest they pervert justice (Prov. 31:4–5); bishops and deacons should be temperate (1 Tim. 3:3, 8). Priests were prohibited from drinking on duty (Lev. 10:9), and Nazirites pledged abstinence for the duration of their vows (Num. 6:3–4, 20; cf. Luke 1:15). The itinerant Rechabites rejected all fruits of the vine as expressions of sedentary life (Jer. 35:7–9).

The vine was a rich source of symbolism in ancient Near Eastern literature, ritual, and art. The twining branch signified life and the grape cluster, or vineyard, fertility (Song of Sol. 7:12). Raisins pressed into cakes were used in the cult of the goddess of love (Hos. 3:1; cf. Song of Sol. 2:5). Wine was the "blood of the grape" (Gen. 49:11; Deut. 32:14), an image recalled in Jesus' words over the cup of the Last Supper (Matt. 26:28). God's judgment of the wicked is like the treading of a winepress (Isa. 63:1–3; Rev. 14:18–20). The Lord's vintage is wine of wrath (Jer. 25:15; Rev. 14:19) and a cup of staggering (Isa. 51:22).

Israel accepted the vine and its fruit as gifts of the Lord, not the land (Hos. 2:8–9, 15). Israel itself was likened to a vine, planted and tended by God (Jer. 2:21; Ps. 80:8–9). The NT applies the image to Jesus and the church: "I am the vine, you are the branches. He who abides in me . . . bears much fruit" (John 15:5). ***See also*** Banquet; Cucumber; Drunkenness; Mourning Rites; Raisins; Rechab. P.A.B.

vinegar, sour wine or wine vinegar, a common drink among the poorer classes (Ruth 2:14). It was forbidden to Nazirites (Num. 6:3). The offer of "vinegar" to Jesus on the cross could be understood as a compassionate gesture in Mark 15:

36 and Matt. 27:48. However, Ps. 69:21 speaks of "poison and vinegar" given to the suffering righteous by enemies. Both the mocking offer of vinegar in Luke 23:36 and the reference to fulfillment of Scripture in John 19:28 suggest this latter context.

vine of Sodom, a plant whose fruit appears tempting yet is inedible (Deut. 32:32). Often identified as the apple of Sodom (*Calotropis procera*), it is a plant of the Dead Sea area that bears a greenish-yellow applelike fruit filled with dry white fibers resembling those of the milkweed.

vineyard, the plot in which grapes are raised. Vineyards are one of the standard signs of agricultural wealth in Palestine in biblical times. While the proper handling of such property was extensively defined in various law codes (Exod. 22:5; 23:11; Lev. 19:10; 25:3, 4; Deut. 20:6; 22:9; 23:24; 24:21; 28:30), breaches of treatment were found even in royalty (1 Kings 21:1–18). Isaiah's "Song of the Vineyard" is a masterful review of standard viticulture applied to the life of a people (Isa. 5:1–7). As vineyards were a sign of divine blessing, their absence was a metaphor of divine judgment (Jer. 35:7, 9). The vineyard as a common scene of labor was used in a parable of Jesus found in all three synoptic Gospels (Mark 12:1–9; Matt. 20:1–41; Luke 20: 9–16). ***See also*** Vine. R.S.B.

viol. ***See*** Music.

viper, a genus of snakes prevalent in the ancient world, some of which were poisonous and some not. Because the bite of the poisonous viper could be fatal, people naturally wanted to avoid any contact with any type. Consequently, the term viper came to be used figuratively as a designation for evil (cf. Isa. 30:6; 59:5; Job 20:16) or for people who were evil (cf. Matt. 3:7; 12:34; 23:33; Luke 3:7).

Paul's encounter with a viper (Acts 28:3–6) caused people to think of him as a god. Some have argued that there were no poisonous snakes on Malta at that period of history and that the snake that attached itself to Paul's hand may have been a type from the constrictor family. ***See also*** Serpent. J.M.E.

virgin (Heb. *bethulah,* lit. "separated"; Gk. *parthenos*), in the OT a woman who has not had sexual intercourse with a man, although the word translated "virgin" (*bethulah*) may also mean simply a young woman of marriageable age, as does the word *almah* (incorrectly translated "virgin" in the RSV). *Bethulah* is also used of Israel in the OT (e.g., Jer. 18:15), and frequently in a figurative way when the fate of cities is at issue (e.g., Isa. 23:10, 12).

The Greek word *parthenos,* used to translate both Hebrew words in the LXX, does not necessarily mean "virgin," but it is so used in the NT. Paul encourages virgins, both male and female, not to marry, but he does permit it (1 Cor. 7: 25–38). The four virgin daughters of Philip who prophesied (Acts 21:9) may be related to the origin of the later order of virgins. Ignatius' letter to the Smyrneans refers to women in the order of widows (see 1 Tim. 5:9) as virgins. The word is also used metaphorically of the church (2 Cor. 11:2–3) and of the morally faithful (Rev. 14:4). ***See also*** Virgin Birth. W.M.

virgin birth, the tradition of Mary's conception of Jesus by the Holy Spirit apart from sexual intercourse, explicitly mentioned in the NT only in the birth stories of Matthew and Luke. In Matt. 1:18–25 it appears as the fulfillment of Isa. 7:14 that a virgin (Gk. *parthenos,* used in the LXX to translate the Heb. *almah,* a young woman of marriageable age) would conceive and bear a son. In Luke 1:26–38 miraculous conception (vv. 34, 37) is linked with the title Son of God applied to Jesus, a title formerly used of Davidic kings (cf. vv. 32, 35 with 2 Sam. 7:12–14, Ps. 2: 6–7).

Suggested allusions to the tradition elsewhere in the NT (e.g., Matt. 13:55; Mark 6:3; Luke 4:22; John 1:13, 14; Gal. 4:4–5; Heb. 7:3) are generally regarded by scholars as uncertain or implausible. The genealogies in Matt. 1:1–16 and Luke 3:28–38 assume Joseph's paternity, as do Luke 2:41–51 and John 1:45, 6:42.

Mary's virginal conception is mentioned in early post-NT writings, some of which show it was contested (see *The Gospel of Philip* 55:23–25). ***See also*** Virgin. W.M.

virtue, the English translation of a Greek term pointing, in the Greek philosophical tradition, to excellence of moral character. OT and NT writers speak more often of righteousness than of virtue because the former points less to human achievement and merits than to God's acts. Paul may have had a list of virtues typical of the late Stoic school of philosophy in mind when he wrote: "whatever is true, whatever is honorable, whatever is just, whatever is pure, whatever is lovely, whatever is gracious, if there is any virtue (RSV: "excellence"), if there is anything worthy of praise, think about these things" (Phil. 4:8). Yet here Paul links virtue and praise within a Christian context of hope and prayer and example. Similarly, 2 Pet. 1:5–7 includes virtue in a list beginning with faith and culminating with love, prefacing this with an appeal to the God who has called us to God's own glory and virtue (2 Pet. 1:3; cf. 1 Pet. 2:9, which also speaks of God's "virtues" [RSV: "wonderful deeds," TEV: "wonderful acts"]). J.F.J.

vision, the sight of things normally hidden from human eyes. Visions, dreams, and heavenly journeys are closely related phenomena through which secrets are thought to be revealed. These media of revelation are especially characteristic of apocalyptic literature. Visions can be distinguished from theophanies and epiphanies of angels or of Jesus. In theophanies and epiphanies the emphasis is on the appearance or presence of a heavenly being and often on the message conveyed by that being. In visions the emphasis is on an object, a scene, or a sequence of events that is enacted.

Accounts of visions have certain typical formal features. They are usually in the first person: the visionary describes his or her experience. The setting is often given near the beginning: the date, place, and time at which the vision occurred. Then follows the content of the vision, usually introduced by the words "I saw." Sometimes the account concludes with remarks about how the visionary reacted to the vision or what he or she did immediately afterward.

Ancient Jewish and Christian visions may be grouped into five types: **1** Visions of the enthroned deity or the divine council (Exod. 24: 9–11; 1 Kings 22:19–23; Isa. 6; Ezek. 1:1–3:15; Rev. 4:2–11). **2** Visions of some other heavenly reality or of an earthly reality: present, threatened, or to come (1 Kings 22:17; Amos 7:1–3, 4–6; Jer. 4:23–26; Ezek. 8–11; 40–48; Zech. 1: 7–17; 3; 6:1–8; *1 Enoch* 57, 66; *T. Levi* 8; *2 Bar.* 6–8; 2 Esd. 13). **3** Visions based on a play on words or a symbol (Amos 7:7–9; 8:1–3; Jer. 1: 11–12, 13–14; Jer. 24; Ezek. 37:1–14; Zech. 2: 5–9; 5:1–4; *1 Enoch* 61:1–5). **4** Allegorical visions, that is, visions in which each object, being, or event represents in a figurative or pictorial way a corresponding entity in reality (Zech. 1:18–21; 4; 5:5–11; Dan. 8; *1 Enoch* 85–90; *2 Bar.* 36–37; 53; Rev. 12, 13, 17; 2 Esd. 9: 38–10:59; 11–12). **5** Visions that combine two or more of the above types (Dan. 7; *1 Enoch* 14: 8–36:4; 40:1–41:7 plus 43–44; 46; 52; 53:1–54:6; 60:1–6; 71; *T. Levi* 2:5–5:7; *2 Bar.* 22–30).

Vision accounts, especially the symbolic and allegorical types, grasp the imagination and evoke feelings in ways that ordinary language cannot. Like poetry they present an interpretation of reality and invite the reader or listener to share it. They combine cognitive insight with emotional response. Although they were originally experienced and recorded to address a particular historical situation of the past, their symbolic character gives them meaning and application beyond their original contexts. ***See also*** Apocalyptic Literature; Dreams; Epiphany; Symbol; Theophany; Throne. A.Y.C.

vow, a promise to abstain from something not ordinarily prohibited (e.g., the vow of the Nazirite, Num. 6), or, more commonly, an offer to pay God for help he gives. The first vow mentioned in the OT is Jacob's, who promised God worship and tithing in return for his protection (Gen. 28: 20; 31:13). Similar vows are the vow of Israel to "devote" (i.e., sacrifice) all of Arad to God (Num. 21:1–3), Jephthah's vow of a living being (Judg. 11:30), Hannah's vow of Samuel's service (1 Sam. 1:11), Absalom's of worship (2 Sam. 15: 7–8), and the unspecified vow of sailors for safety from shipwreck (Jon. 1:6). Apostate Israel is said to have vowed to offer incense to the queen of heaven (Jer. 44:25).

Animals sacrificed in payment of vows must be without blemish (Lev. 22:17–25; Mal. 1:14), must not be firstlings (who already belong to God; Lev. 27:16–28), and are a communion sacrifice that must be eaten in two days (Lev. 7: 16–17; see the sacrificial specifications in Num. 15:1–16). Payment can be made in money with set values for each animal (Lev. 27), with adjustments made for the poor. Payment of vows was ultimately centralized (Deut. 12). Vows did not have to be made (Deut. 23: 22), but once made, they had to be paid (Num. 30; Deut. 21:21–23). A woman's vow could be cancelled by her husband or, if she lived in her father's house, by her father, if the man acted the same day (Num. 30). Psalms such as 56: 12–13 and 66:13–15 mention the individual offering and payment of vows (cf. Pss. 22:26; 61: 9; 116:14, 18). In the NT, Acts records that the apostle Paul, to fulfill a vow, cut his hair (18: 18), but we are given no details about the nature or purpose of that vow. T.S.F.

Vulgate, the authorized Latin version of the Bible. In the late fourth century, Pope Damasus commissioned Jerome to bring order to the existing Latin versions. The resulting translation was called the Vulgate ("common text"). ***See also*** Texts, Versions, Manuscripts, Editions.

vulture, a large carrion-eating bird. The vulture was considered "king of birds" by the Hebrews (see Lam. 4:19), but it was also regarded as unclean (Lev. 11:13). Four species occur in Israel: **1** The griffon vulture *(Gyps fulvus)*, which is probably the biblical *nesher* (Deut. 32:11; Ps. 103:5; Prov. 30:17). **2** The bearded vulture *(Gypatus barbatus)*, which is likely the Ossifrage (Lev. 11:13). **3** The Egyptian eagle *(Neophroon percnopterus)*, probably corresponding to the carrion vulture (Deut. 4:17). **4** The black vulture *(Aegypius monachus)*, which some have correlated with the osprey, although the suggestion is doubtful (see Deut. 14:12).

W

wadi (wah'dee), an Arabic word for stream or stream bed. Many streams in the area inhabited by ancient Israel flow only seasonally. During the dry seasons occasional pools of water may have collected in the stream beds or the beds may have been completely dry. The wadis could be used to advantage in military matters ("ravine," Josh. 8:10–23). They were undependable water sources and could symbolize deceit (Jer. 15:18).

wafers, thin cakes, somewhat like tortillas, made of wheat flour (semolina), baked unleavened and spread with oil. Along with other kinds of bread, wafers had to accompany the thank-offering of the worshiper, the priests' ordination offering, and the Nazirite's peace offering (cf. Lev. 7:12; Num. 6:15; 8:26). They could also be offered independently as a cereal offering.

wages, the compensation paid to a free laborer hired for a fixed period of time or for a specific service. It was apparently common to hire a laborer in ancient Israel for a day's work, for the Torah requires payment of wages at the end of the day (Lev. 19:13; Deut. 24:14; Job 14:6; cf. Matt. 20:1–2, 8). However, there are also references to yearly (Lev. 25:53; Isa. 21:16) and triennial hire (Deut. 15:18; Isa. 16:14; 1 QIsa[a] 21:16).

The Hebrew Bible contains scattered examples of wages paid to laborers: to Jacob when he worked as a shepherd for Laban (Gen. 29:15; 30:32–33; 31:8); to Moses' mother as a nurse, by Pharaoh's daughter (Exod. 2:9); to Tamar for harlotry, by Judah (Gen. 38; cf. Deut. 23:18; Isa. 23:17; Ezek. 16:31; Hos. 9:1; Mic. 1:7); the levitical portion (Num. 18:31); the hiring of Balaam to curse Israel (Deut. 23:5; Neh. 13:2); the hiring of mercenaries (Judg. 9:4; 2 Sam. 10:6; Jer. 46:21; 2 Kings 7:6; 2 Chron. 24:6); the hiring of Shemaiah to prophesy falsely (Neh. 6: 10–13); the hiring of counselors (Ezra 4:5); the hiring of a priest (Judg. 18:4); the hiring of a seer (1 Sam. 9:6–9); the hiring of skilled craftsmen (Isa. 46:6; 2 Chron. 24:12); and the wages to be paid to elders (1 Tim. 5:17–18; cf. Luke 10:7).

Specified fixed wages are not mentioned, although occasionally the Bible relates the price in a given situation (Gen. 30:32–33; 1 Sam. 9:8; 2 Chron. 25:6; Matt. 20:1). This indicates that the wage was agreed upon by the employer and employee. Nonetheless, it appears that hired workers were often either not paid or not paid sufficiently, resulting in a poor labor class who come under the concern of the Torah and Prophets (Deut. 24:14–15; Jer. 22:13; Mal. 3:5; cf. Gen. 31:7, 41; 1 Sam. 2:5; Job 7:2–3; James 5:4).

The term "wage" is also used metaphorically in the religious sense as reward given by God for the "labor" of loyalty, suffering, or right action (Gen. 15:1; Ezek. 29:18–19; Isa. 40:10; 61: 8; 62:11; 1 Cor. 3:8; of children, Gen. 30:18; Jer. 31:16; Ps. 127:3) or as the just recompense of sin (Rom. 6:23). ***See also*** Slavery. J.U.

wagon. ***See*** Cart.

wallet, the bag a shepherd carried. David reportedly carried the pebbles for his sling in a wallet on his way to meet the Philistine champion Goliath (1 Sam. 17:40; KJV: "skrip").

walls, structures that limit areas, whether in building or for defense. This term is used in the Bible to translate a number of Hebrew and Greek words representing various kinds of structures. Ancient literature, art, and archaeological remains provide detailed information on the techniques of wall construction used in the biblical world.

Like their modern counterparts, ancient farmers built low walls around fields and vineyards (Gen. 49:22; Num. 22:24–25; Isa. 5:5). Since these walls were made of unhewn stones, they often called for repair (Prov. 24: 31). Vineyards and orchards were frequently planted on terraced slopes (see Jer. 31:5); these stone-walled terraces are still a common sight in the Middle East. The stones used in these agricultural walls were sometimes set in mud or mortar, though they were often simply stacked on top of each other. All of these simple structures increased the productivity of arable land by helping to prevent soil erosion, discouraging poachers, and preventing animals from grazing in crops; at the same time, the construction of walls aided in the age-old task of clearing the fields of undesirable stones.

House walls were usually built of unhewn or rough-cut stones or mudbricks usually set on stone foundations. These walls were sometimes covered with a thin coating of plaster. Naturally, this plaster improved the appearance of walls, but it also played a significant role in the treatment of houses with "leprosy" (Lev. 14:37–45). More important buildings were normally built of large, hammer-dressed stones. Courses of stone or mudbrick were sometimes separated by a course of wooden beams, a technique that was used in the construction of the Temple (1 Kings 6:36; 7:12).

City Walls: Throughout most of the biblical period, cities were surrounded by a system of for-

Assyrians lay siege to an unidentified town. To the right a siege machine batters the walls, protected by archers, while left and center the Assyrians try to break down the foundations with spikes and tunnel underneath; ninth-century B.C. reliefs.

tifications that consisted of walls, towers, and gates; populations that lived in unwalled settlements were exposed to great risks (Ezek. 38:11; Zech. 2:4). City walls had to be high enough and thick enough and be constructed on such solid foundations that the fortifications and their defenders could deter enemy attacks. There was, in fact, a constant effort made by attackers and defenders to surpass the ingenuity of their opponents; siege warfare was the outgrowth of this competitive effort. The famous bas-reliefs from the Assyrian ruler Sennacherib's (705–681 B.C.) palace at Nineveh graphically portray some of the techniques used in attacking and defending a walled city (see Isa. 36:1–2; 37:33). Indeed, the Bible has frequent references to various aspects of siege warfare (Deut. 20:20; 2 Sam. 20:15; Ps. 89:40; Jer. 6:6; Ezek. 4:1–3; 26:7–10; Joel 2:7–9; see also Luke 19:43; 21:20). This list, which is by no means exhaustive, points to the defensive significance of walls and indicates that large amounts of energy and expertise were poured into the task of destroying the barrier (i.e., the city wall) that separated attackers from defenders. Surprisingly enough, some cities were able to resist besieging forces for a long time (2 Kings 17:5). Perhaps the most efficient way of attacking a city was to trick its defenders into leaving the safety of their walls (Josh. 8:10–17).

Although cities varied in size, the average area enclosed by a city wall in ancient Palestine ranged between 5 and 10 acres. The walls that surrounded these settlements varied in height, width, and design from period to period. The oldest known fortified town in Palestine is Jericho; its earliest walls, which date to ca. 7000 B.C., were made of solid stone and were over 6 feet thick. Between Neolithic Jericho and the next oldest fortifications, there is a gap of about four thousand years, since fortified cities do not appear again until ca. 3000 B.C. The walls of cities like Megiddo and Gezer were erected in this era, and subsequent periods witnessed the modification or rebuilding of the earlier defenses.

From early in the third millennium B.C., until the Roman period (beginning in 63 B.C.), cities in the Middle East were nearly always surrounded by a stone wall. Some of the earliest city walls were over 15 feet thick and were built of solid stone; other walls had stone facings, but wall cores were filled with rubble. These massive walls were frequently reinforced with earthen buttresses and sloping ramparts. Much attention was given to the construction of deep and wide foundations; this protected the walls from undermining and breaching operations. Foundation trenches were dug into the rubble of earlier walls, and some walls were built on bedrock. In most instances, only the walls' lower courses were constructed of stone; most of these massive walls had mudbrick superstructures. The stone courses protected the base of the wall from moisture and enemy attack and made the wall far less costly to build. Until well-dressed (i.e., carefully shaped) masonry was introduced in the Solomonic period (tenth century B.C.), most of the stone used in city defenses was rough-hewn. The building of fortifications flourished during the second quarter of the second millennium B.C., and many city walls that protected Palestine's population during the next five centuries were reused remainders from the earlier period.

During the eleventh century B.C., a type of wall known as the casemate began to be used in Palestine on a regular basis. This construction style consisted of two parallel walls that were separated by five or six feet of open space; these outer walls were joined by short cross walls at regular intervals, thereby creating a series of small rooms within the wall. These chambers were usually filled with rubble to give added strength. Thus, it was possible to build a wall that possessed great strength and required far less labor than would have been necessary for a solid stone wall of comparable width (i.e., ca. 15 feet). The casemate wall is particularly well known because of its appearance at the Solomonic cities of Hazor, Megiddo, and Gezer (see 1 Kings 9:15), where it was found in association with a sophisticated gate complex. Although the casemate wall did not disappear altogether, the methods of siege warfare that were developed by the Assyrians in the ninth century B.C. led to a preference for solid walls with salients and recesses (i.e., offset-inset walls).

Importance in the Bible: Because of the cities they protected or because of a particularly memorable event, the walls of some cities became famous: Jericho (Josh. 6:20), Beth-shan (1 Sam. 31:10, 12), Babylon (Jer. 51:44), Damascus (Jer. 49:27), and Tyre (Ezek. 26:4). Especially frequent are references to Jerusalem's walls (e.g., 2 Sam. 5:9; 1 Kings 3:1; 2 Chron. 36:19; Neh. 1:3; 2:17).

The preceding survey of ancient city walls places a number of biblical passages in sharper focus. For example, the OT agrees with the other sources by acknowledging that city walls were wide enough to serve as elevated platforms for defensive activities (2 Sam. 11:20–21, 24; Isa. 36:11–12). Indeed, Josh. 2:15 notes that Rahab helped the Hebrew spies to escape from Jericho by letting "them down by a rope through the window, for her house was built into the city wall, so that she dwelt in the wall."

Walls were so important in the ancient world that the biblical writers referred to city defenses in some of their most potent figurative expressions. For example, if city walls averaged between 20 and 30 feet in height, David's metaphor in 2 Sam. 22:30 is all the more striking (see Ps. 18:29), and the exaggeration of the Hebrew spies becomes understandable (Num. 13:28; see Deut. 1:28). Other passages that use the imagery of walls to convey their message include Prov. 18:11; 25:28; Isa. 2:15; 22:5; 26:1; 30:13; 60:10, 18; Ezek. 38:20; and Mic. 7:11. Likewise, most of the NT references to walls are figurative. In Acts 23:3, Paul compares Ananias to a "whitewashed wall," while in Eph. 2:14 the hostility between Jew and Gentile is compared to a "dividing wall." Cities in NT times continued to be walled, since the apostle Paul was lowered to safety through a window in the Damascus city wall (Acts 9:25). The most extensive discussion of walls in the NT is found in Rev. 21:12–19, where the seer describes the walls of the heavenly Jerusalem. ***See also*** Defense; House.

Bibliography

Kenyon, Kathleen. *Royal Cities of the Old Testament*. New York: Schocken, 1971.

Paul, Shalom M., and William G. Dever, eds. *Biblical Archaeology*. New York: Quadrangle/New York Times Book Co., 1974.

Yadin, Yigael. *The Art of Warfare in Biblical Lands*. 2 vols. Jerusalem: International Publishing, 1963.

G.L.M.

war, armed conflict between two or more opposing peoples. War was so common in the biblical period that the OT makes specific reference to times of peace (Judg. 3:11; 1 Kings 5:4; 2 Chron. 14:1, 5–7). As in modern times, the wars of antiquity were fought for political, economic, and religious reasons, and Palestine's position near the landbridge between Africa and Asia greatly multiplied the number of wars in which the inhabitants were involved.

The weapons, strategies, and tactics used for war in the ancient Near East and the Greco-Roman world were highly diversified, and the methodology of war varied from people to people and from period to period. Nevertheless, some aspects of warfare were universal. For example, battles were fought on land and/or sea, with land encounters being subdivided into two basic categories: battles in open terrain (1 Sam. 14) and attacks on fortified cities (2 Kings 17:5; 25:1). While only a few ancient peoples developed significant naval forces (e.g., Phoenicians, Greeks, Persians, Romans), most ancient Near Eastern and Greco-Roman armies included two major divisions, foot soldiers and horsemen, and many armies made effective use of chariots (e.g., the Egyptians and Assyrians). Infantrymen were divided into various contingents that specialized in the use of particular weapons (e.g., bows and arrows, slings and slingstones). Although some field campaigns were provisioned "off the land," the great imperial armies counted auxiliary troops within their ranks whose responsibility it was to provision the troops (e.g., the sophisticated logistical system that contributed to the success of Alexander the Great).

Like their modern counterparts, ancient armies poured much human energy and technical skill into the preparation for and waging of war. The number of soldiers involved in a single battle varied from a handful to many thousands, and the death and devastation caused by war was often enormous (2 Kings 8:12; 25:9–10). Finally, students of ancient warfare cannot help but be impressed by the technical skills that were employed in the production of weaponry. A careful examination of the archaeological evidence and artistic representations that relate to military activity allows one to understand that even ancient warfare was an art and a science that involved great learning (see Isa. 2:4; Mic. 4:3).

Ancient cavalryman carrying a shield and weapon; from a tenth- or ninth-century B.C. relief discovered at Tell Halaf (Gozen).

Since the Hebrew conquest and settlement of Canaan was partly accomplished by means of armed conflict with a number of people, Israel's early history (ca. 1225–1025 B.C.) is, to some degree, a history of the wars of Israel. Following these early phases of Israel's history, the Hebrew monarchy (ca. 1025–586 B.C.) was established and maintained by means of war. The biblical literature that describes the period between the Exile and the end of the NT era does not mention war as much as the narratives relating to the earlier history. Nevertheless, the events and thoughts of the later centuries were molded by the wars that brought Israel under the dominion of Egyptian, Assyrian, Babylonian, Persian, Hellenistic, and Roman conquerors. Throughout this history, many of Israel's outstanding leaders were known for their military achievements (e.g., Joshua, Deborah, Gideon, Saul, David, and Uzziah). Special attention should be drawn to the popular revolts led by Judas Maccabeus (ca. 167 B.C.) and Simon Bar-Kochba (A.D. 132).

This emphasis upon war may be seen as a natural development, since one of the fundamental images of God in the OT is that of a warrior (Exod. 15:3; Ps. 24:8; Isa. 42:13). Israel's wars were often based upon an ideology that emerged from this understanding of God's nature—Israel's enemies are the Lord's enemies (Judg. 5:31; 1 Sam. 30:26), and the Lord assists Israel in times of war (Exod. 14:13–14; Josh. 10:11; 24:12; 1 Sam. 17:45). Although "holy war" in the proper sense is not mentioned in the OT, divinely sanctioned wars are mentioned quite frequently (Josh. 8:1; Judg. 4:14–15; 1 Sam. 23:4; 2 Kings 3:18), but this ideology was not unique to Israel (see the Mesha Inscription set up about the middle of the ninth century B.C. to commemorate the victory of Mesha, king of Moab, over Israel). While this so-called divine war creates numerous problems for theologians and ethicists, it must be recognized that war was a common phenomenon, almost a necessary evil, in the ancient world.

Although religion was not called upon to explain every war in which Israel engaged, it is obvious that the disastrous defeat that led to the Exile in 586 B.C. was understood as a withdrawal of God's assistance and the resultant failure of Israel's army to withstand the Babylonian invasion. In fact, the idea that God "used" war to punish an apostate Israel appears again and again in the OT (Isa. 5:26–28; Jer. 5:15–17; Ezek. 21:1–32; 23:22–28). The belief that God disciplined other nations by means of war was also widespread (Isa. 13; Jer. 46:1–10; Nah. 2:1–9); once again, this theological interpretation of history was common in other parts of the ancient Near East. Ultimately, the language of war was employed by the biblical writers to depict judgment (Joel 2:1–11; 3:9–12; Zeph. 1:14–18; Rev. 12:7–8; 17:14; 19:11). Because war was such a well-known phenomenon and such a serious matter, whether in reality or in its literary analogies (Pss. 18:34–42; 55:21; Eccles. 3:8; 9:18), it was also used as an appropriate symbol for the Christian life (2 Cor. 10:3–4; Eph. 6:11–17; 1 Tim. 1:18; 2 Tim. 2:3–4; James 4:1–2; 1 Pet. 2:11). ***See also*** Weapons.

Bibliography

Connolly, Peter. *Greece and Rome at War.* Englewood Cliffs, NJ: Prentice-Hall, 1981.

Warry, John. *Warfare in the Classical World.* New York: St. Martin's, 1980.

Yadin, Yigael. *The Art of Warfare in Biblical Lands.* 2 vols. Jerusalem: International Publishing, 1963. G.L.M.

Wars of the Lord, the Book of the, an otherwise unknown and lost work quoted in Num. 21:14–15. From the context in which the quotation is made, it would seem that the book probably contained poems celebrating the victories of the Israelites over their enemies during the period of the conquest (twelfth century B.C.). It is possible that vv. 17–18 and 27–30 are also quotations from the book. The title emphasizes God's actions in fighting for Israel (cf. 1 Sam. 17:47).

watch. ***See*** Time.

watchman, a sentry stationed on a wall (2 Sam. 18:24; Song of Sol. 5:7) or in a watchtower (2 Chron. 20:24) whose task it was to warn of approaching danger (Ezek. 33:2–6; cf. Ps. 127:1). Watchmen also guarded the fields and vineyards, especially during harvest season (Isa. 5:2; cf. Job 27:18). The term is often used in a figurative or symbolic sense (Isa. 62:6; Ezek. 3:17; 33: 7–9; Mic. 7:4). ***See also*** Tower; Vine; Walls; Watchtower.

watchtower, a high fortified tower located either within a town (Judg. 9:51; 2 Chron. 26:9) or elsewhere (2 Chron. 26:10), presumably at a strategic location. The obvious purpose was military: it was either a position to defend or a location from which to assess enemy troop movements. When erected in fortified towns watchtowers were probably attached to and built into walls of the city and had a separate entrance (Judg. 9:52). In fields towers could serve both as a lookout and as a fieldhouse for owners of large properties. The upper story or roof was utilized for work or sleeping and the lower portion for storage of agricultural tools.

E.M.M.

water, a critical factor in the life of ancient Palestine. Rainfall was its primary source, and on it both crops and springs depended. Perennial streams were few and located mostly in the highland east of the Jordan, while the wadis (dry stream beds) of western Palestine flowed only with the run-off of winter rains ("freshets that pass away," Job 6:15; cf. Jer. 15:18). Mountainous terrain and lack of dependable streams made irrigation unfeasible in most of the area—in contrast to the alluvial plains of Egypt and Mesopotamia—though Roman engineers built impressive water systems on the coastal plain and Transjordanian plateau (e.g., the aqueduct at Caesarea). Deuteronomy marked the contrast between Canaanite and Egyptian water sources by describing the promised land as a "land . . . which drinks water by the rain from heaven" (11:11).

Rain determined settlement patterns as well as modes and patterns of cultivation. The earliest towns were established near permanent springs, and elaborate tunnels and conduits were constructed in some cities (Gezer, Jerusalem, Megiddo) to ensure continuous and safe access to the water supply within the city walls. The increased use of plaster-lined cisterns at the beginning of the Iron Age (ca. 1200 B.C.) permitted settlement in previously unoccupied areas of the hill country where springs were lacking or inadequate. Fluctuation in the amount and timing of the annual rains affected life in the whole land, but especially in the zone of marginal rainfall between the hill country and the desert. In wet years the area under cultivation might be extended well into the wilderness, but a few successive years of light or erratic rainfall would make agriculture impossible, forcing migration to more fertile areas, such as the Nile delta (Gen. 41:57), or conversion to pastoral nomadism.

Water was essential to both human and animal life and was especially critical in the wilderness, where wells and springs were few and often unreliable (Gen. 21:14–19; Exod. 17:1–7). Migrating groups had to purchase water (Deut.

Aerial view of the water system at Hazor. It allowed safe access to the water supply even in times of siege; ninth century B.C.

2:28). A cup of water offered to a guest or stranger was a simple, and expected, sign of hospitality (Job 22:7; Matt. 10:42).

Water was also used for washing and bathing, serving the needs of hygiene, refreshment, and ritual purification. Jews of Jesus' time washed their hands before meals in accordance with religious prescription (Mark 7:3), and guests were offered water for footwashing (Luke 7:44)—a service commonly performed by a servant (cf. John 13:5). OT laws prescribe ablutions for various types of contaminating conditions, including various skin diseases (Lev. 14:8), bodily emissions (Lev. 15:1–21), and contact with dead or "unclean" animals (11:1–39). Pilate declared his innocence through a symbolic act of handwashing (Matt. 27:24).

Some waters were thought to have curative properties (John 5:1–7). Others were "bitter" (Exod. 15:23) or "poisoned" (Jer. 8:14), making them undrinkable or bringing illness to those who drank them (2 Kings 2:19–21).

Water as Symbol: According to ancient Egyptian and Mesopotamian thought, water was the primary cosmic element from which all life emerged. The OT reflects something of this view when it speaks of the "deep" (Heb. *tehom)* as the primeval ocean, divided at creation into upper and lower waters (Gen. 1:2, 6–9). The waters above the firmament are the source of rain, while the waters below form seas, lakes, and underground streams. Babylonian religion deified the power in the sweet- and salt-water sources; the subterranean sweet waters were identified with wisdom, fertility, and life, while the restless, raging sea represented chaotic and destructive power. Creation in Mesopotamian and Canaanite myth involved the subduing (or slaying) of the waters of chaos, often personified as a serpent. Elements of this mythic conception persist in poetic images of the OT, apocalyptic visions, and religious symbolism: God slew the dragon Rahab or Leviathan (Isa. 51:9; Ps. 89: 9–10; Ps. 74:12–14; cf. the "ancient serpent" identified with Satan in Rev. 12:9), founded the earth upon the seas (Pss. 24:1; 136:6), and sits enthroned over the flood (Ps. 29:10). God's voice thunders over "many waters," sometimes identified as "many peoples" or hostile nations (Isa. 17:13; cf. Luke 21:25; Rev. 17:15). The power of the sea is reasserted in apocalyptic writings, but in the final day the beast from the sea will be vanquished and the sea itself will be no more (Rev. 21:1).

Water is employed in numerous biblical similes and metaphors describing instability (Gen. 49:4), loss of strength (being "poured out," Job 3:24; Ps. 22:14), and melting away in fear (Josh. 7:5). It vanishes (Ps. 58:7) and cannot be gathered again when spilled (2 Sam. 14: 14). But water also conveys ideas of refreshment and power. Good news from afar is "like cold water to a thirsty soul" (Prov. 25:25). God is the "fountain of living [i.e., everflowing] waters" for Israel (Jer. 2:13), and Jesus offers water of eternal life (John 4:10–15). Amos calls for justice to "roll down like [the] waters" of a perennial stream (5:24). A person in dire distress feels engulfed by waters, submerged in the deep (Ps. 69:1–2; Lam. 3:54). Salvation is experienced as being drawn up from the waters of death (Ps. 18:16).

Baptism recalls this symbolism of salvation as well as cleansing; those "born of water" (John 3: 5) are likened to those whom God saved through the Flood (1 Pet. 3:20; cf. 1 Cor. 10:1–5). God's cosmic rule was symbolized in Solomon's Temple by the great model of the cosmic sea (1 Kings 7:23–26). Ancient Near Eastern tradition located the source of the great rivers of the world, or the life-giving springs, at the mountain or garden of God (cf. Gen. 2:10–14). Ezekiel envisions water flowing from the threshold of the restored Temple, bringing life to the whole land (47:1–2), and the author of Revelation depicts the river of the water of life flowing from the throne of God (Rev. 22:1–2). ***See also*** Baptism; Cisterns; Leviathan; Rahab; Rivers; Sea; Wadi; Well. P.A.B.

watercourse (Heb. *aphiq)*, a term for a stream bed or channel that is employed in poetic metaphors. Ps. 126:4 likens the restoration of Israel's fortunes to watercourses in the dry Negeb. Ezekiel depicts Pharaoh as a great cedar, felled to earth, its boughs broken in the watercourses (Ezek. 31:12), and as a dragon, whom God will slay, drenching the land with his blood and filling the watercourses with it (Ezek. 32:6).

Water for impurity. ***See*** Water of Purification.

water hen (KJV: "swan"), an unclean fowl, probably an omnivorous water bird (Lev. 11:18; Deut. 14:16). It may refer to a member of the *Rallus* genus, although that is not certain.

water of bitterness, a specially prepared potion given by a priest to a woman whose husband suspects her of committing adultery but can offer no adequate proof (Num. 5:11–31). The potion would distort the womb or cause a miscarriage in a guilty woman but would allow an innocent wife to conceive. The expression "water of bitterness" is derived from one of the two components of the phrase "the water of bitterness" and the "water that brings the curse" (Num. 5:22–24). Because the Semitic root *mr(r)* ("bitter") can also mean "to bless," it is likely that "water of bitterness" is better rendered "water of blessing," with the full phrase regarded as being "water of judgment." J.M.S.

water of purification, the liquid used in an ancient purification ritual to cleanse one from the defilement incurred by coming into close contact with human death, either by touching a human bone, a grave, or a corpse, or by entering a tent where someone had died. An unblemished red heifer that had never been put under the yoke was sacrificed and the blood sprinkled toward the sanctuary. The heifer's body was then burned with cedar wood along with hyssop and scarlet (wool?) and the ashes collected and preserved. They were to be mixed with living (running) water and sprinkled upon the defiled person, using a branch of hyssop, on the third and seventh day after the defilement. After bathing and washing their clothes the individuals would then be considered clean and acceptable in the community again. The mixture of water and ashes would also be sprinkled on the tent and its furnishings if a death had occurred within the tent (Num. 19:1–22; 31:21–24). ***See also*** Heifer; Hyssop; Purity. D.R.B.

Water of separation. ***See*** Water of Purification.

waterpot, a container for water. Several types of clay pots were used for water during biblical times. The largest (Heb. *kad)* was used for storage or carrying a supply of water from the community source, as did Rebekah (Gen. 24:14) and Elijah (1 Kings 18:33). The Samaritan woman carried a water jar (Gk. *hydria,* John 4:28), and those at the Cana wedding feast were made of stone (John 2:6, 7). The pitcher (Heb. *gābîʿa)* held water or wine (Jer. 35:5); the disciples searched for a man with a water pitcher (Gk. *keramos,* Mark 14:13; Luke 22:10). The finer decanter (Heb. *baqbûq)* was what Jeremiah symbolically smashed (19:1–13), and the pilgrim's flask (Heb. *ṣappaḥat)* was used by soldiers (1 Sam. 26:11) or travelers (1 Kings 19:6). ***See also*** Pottery. N.L.L.

wave offering. ***See*** Worship.

waw. ***See*** Vau.

way, the English translation of various Hebrew and Greek words, used with several different meanings in the OT and the NT. The literal meaning of "path," "road," or "journey" evolved into more figurative usages to describe "natural" patterns of behavior observed in the world (e.g., Prov. 30:19), God's patterns of activity (e.g., Ps. 18:30; Isa. 55:8–9), or human lifestyles (e.g., Ps. 1:6). The most important usage centered in the meaning that related to human behavior and whether this behavior was in agreement with God's plans and purposes.

In the NT writings, however, the term took on an even more specific meaning. Jesus was identified as *the* Way to a new relationship with God (John 14:4–6), which issued in a new quality of life, a new way of living (cf. Heb. 10:20). One of the earliest designations for the emerging Christian community appears to have been that of followers of "the Way" (Acts 9:2; 19:9, 23; 24:22; cf. Mark 10:52). ***See also*** Christian.

J.M.E.

wayfarer (KJV: "wayfaring man"), any one of a variety of craftsmen and merchants who traveled regularly for work (smiths), as a mode of life (beggars, musicians), or by historical necessities (exiles, slaves; Judg. 19:17; 2 Sam. 12:4; Jer. 9:2; 14:8). In wartime they disappeared (Judg. 5:6), presumably for safety.

wealth, the abundant possession of various forms of property. In the early period of Middle East culture, wealth consisted of the possession of large and small cattle and slaves, as well as silver and gold (Gen. 24:35). Material goods are esteemed because they are created and ultimately owned by God (Ps. 50:10; Eccles. 3:10–13; 1 Tim. 4:3–5). Likewise, they are received through God's blessing (Deut. 28:1–14). Wealth is attributed to the patriarchs (Gen. 13:2), godly kings (2 Chron. 32:27–29), and Job (Job 42:10–17). They were leaders with significant responsibilities. Some in the early church were also rich (Matt. 27:57; 1 Tim. 6:17–19; but cf. 1 Cor. 1:26–27; James 2:5–7).

In the biblical view, wealth is given by God for definite purposes. God abundantly bestows material blessings for the purpose of meeting the needs of the poor (Deut. 15:10; 2 Cor. 9:8–10). Job defended his integrity with the claim that he had given to them open-handedly (Job 31:16–20). Sodom was condemned for failing to do so (Ezek. 16:49). John the Baptist makes sharing part of the demands of the inbreaking Kingdom of God (Luke 3:11). Provision for the poor is the purpose of work (Eph. 4:28), not the accumulation of wealth (Prov. 23:4), which is not to be sought for its own sake (Prov. 28:20, 22).

Wealth came to be viewed more negatively later in the biblical period. There was a shift in the understanding of the way God's rewards would be received so that God's blessings were increasingly seen as coming at the end of history. Wealth in the present was therefore less likely to be viewed as a divine reward (Mark 10:23–26). There also arose a growing consciousness of massive poverty, and wealth was viewed in relationship to it. In this context the rich could be categorically condemned (Luke 6:20–21, 24–25). When judgments on society were made, wealth was a chief focus of attack. The connotation of wealth tended to change from abundance to excess (Luke 12:15–21). Luxury is described in biting detail and condemned because of the failure of compassion (Amos 6:4–7; Luke 16:19–31) or because of the presence of injustice (Isa. 3:13–26; James 5:1–6). In the teaching of Jesus there is an incompatibility between riches and salvation (Luke 6:24; 16:19–

31; 18:18–30), but repentance is possible for the rich (Luke 18:27; 19:1–10). One chooses between a present material reward and a future heavenly reward (Luke 6:24; 14:14; 16:25; Matt. 6:19–21).

Warnings also are made regarding the danger of wealth to spiritual and moral health (Ezek. 7: 19–20). Wealth is a contrary force competing with God, drawing away one's basic affections (Matt. 6:21, 24; cf. Job 22:23–26). A desire to be wealthy can destroy saving faith itself (1 Tim. 6:9–10). It can lead to trusting oneself rather than God (Prov. 30:8–9). In contrast to poverty or wealth, the ideal is material sufficiency (Prov. 30:8–9; Eccles. 3:12–13 [cf. 2:1–11]; Matt. 6:11, 25–33; 1 Cor. 7:30c–31a; 1 Tim. 6: 8). ***See also*** Mammon; Ownership; Poor. S.C.M.

weaning, the practice of training a child to eat food other than his or her mother's milk. In biblical times it was an occasion to celebrate when a child was weaned (Gen. 21:8). It marked Samuel's departure for special training (1 Sam. 1: 21–28). A weaned child symbolized the peaceable kingdom of the Messiah (Isa. 11:8) or the helpless result of a delinquent leadership (Isa. 28:9).

weapons, offensive and defensive instruments and equipment used by soldiers in combat. Weapons used for hunting and fighting were among humankind's earliest inventions. The extant literature, archaeological remains, and artistic representations from the ancient Near East and Greco-Roman world demonstrate that weaponry in the biblical period was highly diversified and amazingly sophisticated. Not only was the effective use of certain weapons dependent upon training and skill, but the technical production of such instruments was an art, a science, and an industry. Generally speaking, weapons used in field combat and siege warfare were modified and improved over time. Changes in the arsenal of one people necessitated alterations in the weapons among neighboring peoples. In other words, competition to obtain an advantage over one's enemy has always been a significant factor in the evolution of weaponry.

As in the modern world, advancements in ancient technology were quickly adapted for use in instruments of war. One of the most important steps in the history of weapons was the development of carburized iron, a phenomenon that occurred in the eastern Mediterranean toward the end of the second millennium B.C., but earlier improvements in metallurgy (i.e., the production of copper and bronze) had been applied to arms production for nearly two thousand years before the Iron Age. Naturally, the shape, size, and overall durability of dagger and sword blades and spearheads and arrowheads were affected by such improvements in

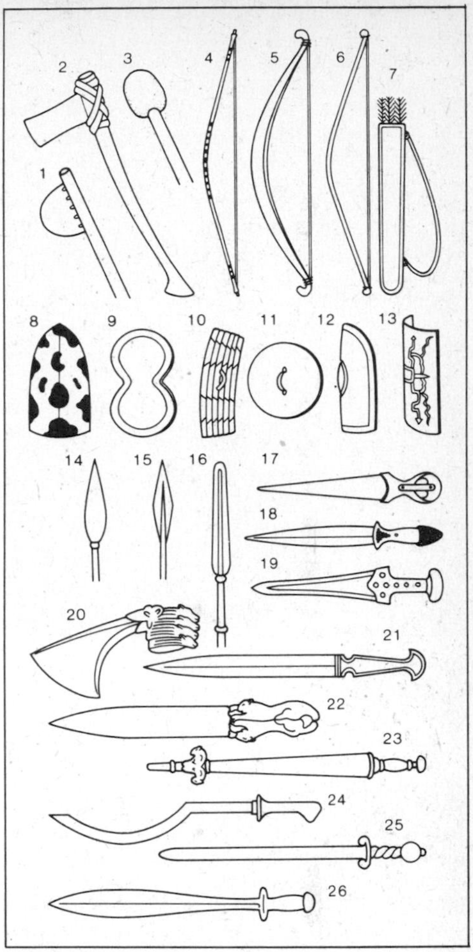

Weapons: 1. Egyptian poleax (ca. 2700 B.C.); 2. Egyptian ax (1580 B.C.); 3. Type of ancient stone mace; 4. Type of Egyptian bow (1430 B.C.); 5. Assyrian bow (1200 B.C.); 6, 7. Assyrian bow and quiver with arrows (850 B.C.); *Ancient shields:* 8. Egyptian (2000 B.C.); 9. Late Minoan (1580–1100 B.C.); 10. Assyrian (700 B.C.); 11. Assyrian (650 B.C.); 12. Roman (100 B.C.); 13. Roman (300 B.C.); 14. Assyrian spear; 15. Syrian spear; 16. Egyptian spear (1600 B.C.); 17. Egyptian dagger (2000 B.C.); 18. Sumerian dagger; 19. Late Minoan dagger (1600–1100 B.C.); 20. Weapon with curved blade coming from mouth of animal (ca. 3000 B.C.); 21. Sword of Marduk-shapik-zeri (1250 B.C.); 22. Sword with straight blade, two lions forming hilt (ca. 3000 B.C.); 23. Assyrian sword (900 B.C.); 24. Ancient sickle sword; 25. Type of Roman sword; 26. Type of Greek sword.

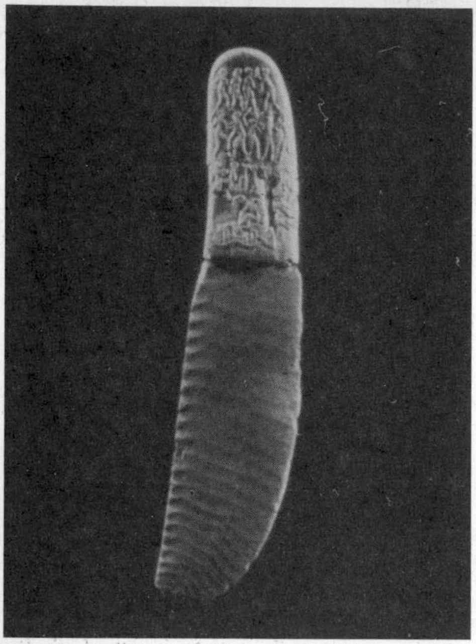

Egyptian knife carved from the tooth of a hippopotamus; the decorated handle shows warriors of different tribes in hand-to-hand combat; fourth millennium B.C.

copper, bronze, and iron technology. Another important weapon that improved over time was the chariot, whose speed and maneuverability were increased by changes in design and construction materials, including metals. Other major steps in the development of ancient weaponry include the invention of the composite bow, piercing battle-ax, "Corinthian" helmet, and siege engines.

Although the Bible does not provide the detailed description of weapons that one finds in the ancient Greek authors Homer and Polybius, 1 Sam. 17:5–7 and Eph. 6:11–17 do list some of the weapons used in the OT and NT periods (see 2 Chron. 26:14–15; Jer. 46:3–4). Moreover, the Bible is replete with references to virtually every offensive and defensive instrument of war used in antiquity. Given the geographical location of the biblical lands and the frequency of war in the biblical period, this is to be expected. Offensive weapons may be divided into categories that correspond to the range at which the weapons were typically used against an enemy (i.e., short-, medium-, and long-range weapons).

Short-range weapons were normally used in hand-to-hand combat; this category has more members than the other two combined. Although the battle-ax was an important short-range weapon in the ancient Near East, it is not mentioned in the Bible. The war club (Prov. 25: 18) and hammer (Jer. 51:20) were probably akin to the mace, another important weapon in antiquity. Frequently mentioned in the Bible are the rod and staff (Ps. 2:9; Isa. 10:5, 15), sword or dagger (Judg. 3:16–22; 1 Sam. 17:51), and spear (Num. 25:7–8; 1 Sam. 17:7).

Medium-range weapons were designed for throwing at enemies who were a fairly short distance away. Although some spears were light enough to be included in this category (1 Sam. 18:11; 19:10; 20:33), the lighter and shorter javelin was more suited for this purpose (1 Sam. 17: 6).

Long-range weapons could be fired at enemies some distance away, enemies on a battlefield or on a city's ramparts. Basically, the ancients had two long-range weapons in their arsenals, the sling (1 Sam. 17:40, 50; 2 Kings 3: 25) and bow (Isa. 21:17; Jer. 50:14).

The relationship between offensive and defensive weapons is obvious, so the latter were also well known in the biblical period. Included in the Bible's references to pieces of armor are the shield and buckler (1 Chron. 12:24; Ps. 35: 2; Eph. 6:16), helmet (1 Sam. 17:38; 2 Chron. 26: 14; Eph. 6:17), scale armor and coats of mail (1 Kings 22:34; Neh. 4:16), breastplate (1 Kings 22: 34; Eph. 6:14), and greaves (1 Sam. 17:6).

Although it was a mobile fighting platform, the chariot should be included in a discussion of ancient weapons; indeed, it was frequently mentioned by the biblical writers (e.g., Exod. 14:17–18; 1 Kings 10:26). Note should also be made of the unclear but intriguing reference to Uzziah's "engines" (2 Chron. 26:15).

The military hardware of foot soldiers, horsemen, and charioteers was so well known in the ancient world that the biblical writers referred to most of the aforementioned weapons in figurative speech. Even the terms "weapon" and "weapons" assumed symbolic meaning in a number of passages (e.g., Ps. 7:12–13; Eccles. 9: 18; Isa. 54:16–17; 2 Cor. 10:4). ***See also*** Chariots; Sling; Spear; Sword; War.

Bibliography

Gonen, Rivka. *Weapons of the Ancient World.* London: Cassell, 1975.

Muhly, James D. "How Iron Technology Changed the Ancient World." *Biblical Archaeology Review*, Nov./Dec., 1982: 40–54.

Yadin, Yigael. *The Art of Warfare in Biblical Lands.* 2 vols. Jerusalem: International Publishing, 1963.

G.L.M.

weasel, any small carnivore of the genus *Mustela.* Certain members of this genus were considered unclean (Lev. 11:29).

weather, climatic conditions, which for Palestine (approximately the same latitude as the state of Georgia or southern Spain) are also influenced by the formation of the land and its nearness to the desert and sea.

There are generally two seasons, a rainy season, which is winter, and the dry and bright summer. The early or "former" rains (cf. Jer. 5: 24, KJV) come in the autumn, usually October or November. The heaviest rains are in December through March, while the "latter" rains are in April or May.

The rains come from the sea, watering mainly the western slopes of the central highlands. In general the rain decreases the closer one comes to the Transjordan desert, increasing only on the mountain slopes. Rainfall also tends to decrease as one moves from north (the Lebanon mountains and the hills of Galilee) to south (the Negeb and Sinai deserts). Rainfall is about the same in the coastal towns in the west as Jerusalem in the highlands, i.e., 20–24 inches a year. In the western hills of Galilee the 35–40 inches a year is close to that of New York City, while the deserts of Transjordan, the Negeb, and Sinai, as well as the Jordan Valley, may have 8 or less.

The seasonal variations in temperature are relative to the amount of rainfall and the altitude. January is usually the coolest month, with temperatures averaging 45 degrees Fahrenheit, in the hills of Galilee, 48 degrees in Jerusalem, 56 degrees at Acco and Gaza on the coast, and 59 degrees at Jericho in the Jordan Valley. In the summer months Jerusalem and towns on the central ridge have some of the most pleasant weather, averaging only about 74 degrees. In the Jordan Valley the temperature reaches unbearable levels, with average temperatures in the upper 80s.

The Bible has no word for weather; rather it speaks of the state and signs of the heavens (Job 37:21, 22; Matt. 16:2, 3), the growing conditions for the crops (Deut. 11:14; Isa. 30:23), and the signs of the seasons (Deut. 28:12; Prov. 26:1; Song of Sol. 2:11). ***See also*** Season. N.L.L.

weaving. ***See*** Spinning and Weaving.

wedding, a ceremony by which a man and a woman enter into matrimony. Within the larger communal transaction known as marriage, a wedding was in biblical times, as it is today, the occasion upon which a woman and a man formally initiated a new household with the blessing of their families. The term itself occurs only once in the OT (Song of Sol. 3:11) and rarely in the NT (Matt. 9:15; Mark 2:19; Luke 5:34; Matt. 22:8–12). Furthermore, wedding customs evolved over the millennium embraced by the biblical witness, and it is therefore impossible to give a definitive description of how a wedding was done in ancient Israel at any specific point in time. However, the evidence warrants certain observations.

No hint is preserved, either in the OT or the NT, that a religious ceremony accompanied the wedding. The occasion was a legal one, and perhaps written contracts were signed, just as written bills of divorce could also be signed (cf.

The wedding feast at Cana, where Jesus, according to John 2:1–11, turned water into wine; fourteenth-century mosaic at the Kariye Church, Istanbul.

Deut. 24:1–3; Jer. 3:8; Mark 10:4). The still-practiced Jewish custom of beginning a wedding with the writing of a marriage contract can be traced back to the first century B.C. The nuptial celebrations consisted of a procession from the house of the bride to the bridegroom's home (cf. Matt. 25:6; the latter may have been symbolized by a tent; cf. Num. 25:8; 2 Sam. 16: 22; Ps. 19:6; Song of Sol. 1:16. The tent is preserved in Judaism and in modern Arab marriage customs in the symbolic canopy of *khuppah* under which the bride and groom conclude their vows.) Both parties were beautifully dressed and ornamented (Isa. 49:18; Jer. 2:32; Ps. 45:14–15), and the bride wore a veil (Song of Sol. 6:7) which she took off only in the nuptial chamber, a custom that may make intelligible Leah's mistaken identity in Gen. 29:21–25.

"The voice of mirth and the voice of gladness" (Jer. 16:9), dancing, the pronouncing of blessings (Ruth 4:11–12), and the recitation of love poetry were contributed by the accompanying villagers, family, and friends. The great nuptial poem celebrating erotic love, the Song of Solomon, identified with the occasion of one of his own royal weddings (cf. 3:6–11), is a lovely and extended example of the lush poetry of such occasions. Psalm 45 is another wedding poem in which all of the above-mentioned steps are followed by a royal couple. After the procession, a week-long feast took place at the bridegroom's house (Matt. 22:2), or in special cases, even at the bride's house (Gen. 29:27; Judg. 14:10–12).

The sexual relationship was consummated on the first night (Gen. 29:23), in the "tent" (Gen. 24:67) or some other bridal chamber. If the mores of Near Eastern villagers down to the present day are admissible evidence, they support the importance that Deut. 22:13–21 places upon the "tokens of virginity." These blood-stained garments of the wedding bed were preserved by the bride's parents as evidence should the groom elect later to slander his wife as having "played the harlot" prior to their marriage. So joyous for the entire community was a wedding and the inauguration of a new family that a newly married groom was free from conscription into the army for one year, "to be happy with his wife whom he has taken" (Deut. 24:5).

Although Jesus' parable of the marriage feast in Matt. 22:1–14 (simply a banquet in Luke 14: 16–24) provides hints about Jewish wedding customs late in the biblical period, its real intention is to teach that "many are called, but few are chosen." Like the wedding guests who refused to come or who came disrespectfully attired, the kingdom of heaven will exclude those who do not accept and prepare for it. Similarly, the reference to the wedding in Matt. 9:14 (and its parallels in Mark 2:19; Luke 5:34) is used to teach that joy and feasting like that of a wedding would be better responses than fasting to the presence of the Lord in the midst of the human community. A similar affirmation of joy in community is present in the account of Jesus' first manifestation of his divine power, at the wedding feast in Cana (John 2: 1–11). Finally, in the apocalyptic vision of Rev. 19:6–21, the heavenly banquet set forth for the birds of prey on the day of God's victory over the powers of evil is described metaphorically as the "marriage supper of the Lamb" (v. 9). ***See also*** Marriage.

Bibliography

de Vaux, Roland, O. P. "Marriage." In *Ancient Israel: Its Life and Institutions*. Translated by John McHugh. New York: McGraw-Hill, 1961. Part I, chap. 2.

Patai, Raphael. *Sex and the Family in the Bible and the Middle East*. New York: Doubleday, 1959.

W.S.T.

wedge. ***See*** Money; Tongue.

weeds (KJV: "tares"), probably darnel *(Lolium tremulentum)*, a somewhat poisonous weed looking very much like wheat during its earliest stages. As a result of the resemblance, early separation from wheat is nearly impossible. This is further complicated by the fact that the roots of the two intertwine (Matt. 13:29).

In the interpretation of the parable of the "tares" (Matt. 13:36–43) weeds represent unbelievers intermixed with believers either within the church (cf. "kingdom" in v. 41) or among the nations of the world (cf. v. 38). The parable teaches that ultimately judgment is a divine prerogative alone. The parable of the net makes the same point (Matt. 13:47–50; cf. Luke 9:51–56; 1 Cor. 4:5; Rom. 12:19). R.H.S.

week. ***See*** Time.

Weeks, Feast of. ***See*** Feasts, Festivals, and Fasts.

weights and measures, methods of determining and providing consistent amounts of mass or distance. The biblical system of weights and measures can be reconstructed, at least tentatively, from three sources: from references in the surviving literature of Egypt and Mesopotamia, from which civilizations the Palestinian systems were borrowed; from scattered references in the OT and NT to local practice; and from archaeological discoveries, whether of actual weights, vessels of measurable capacity, or architectural remains whose dimensions may reveal standard modules.

Weights: All reconstructions of the monetary system in ancient Israel, as well as in NT times, presuppose the use of balances to weigh out fragments of precious metal, principally silver, in payment. The Hebrew word for the basic unit of currency in the OT, the *shekel,* comes from the root *skl,* "to weigh," i.e., to pay. Balances, probably consisting simply of two metal pans suspended from a hand-held beam, are mentioned in several OT passages (Job. 6:2; Ps. 62:9; Isa. 40: 12; Ezek. 5:1; Dan. 5:27). Accurate or "just balances" are commended (Lev. 19:36; Job 31:6; Prov. 16:11; Ezek. 45:10), but several references to "false balances" show that dishonest manipulation was easy and common (Prov. 11:1; 20:23; Hos. 12:7; Amos 8:5; Mic. 6:11, "wicked scales"). Several of the stone balance weights found show clear signs of having been chiseled on the bottom so as to correct or otherwise alter their weight—an ancient practice from which may derive our modern word to "chisel," i.e., to cheat.

Beam balances are pictured in Egyptian reliefs from the second millennium B.C. Several fragments of bronze beams, chains, and pans have been found in second- and first-millennium B.C. sites in Palestine, sometimes with stone weights, and often in the area of the city gate, where biblical references indicate that much commerce was carried out (as in the later Roman *agora,* i.e., marketplace; cf. 2 Kings 7:1, 18).

Many small worked stones recovered in excavations may have been used commonly in ancient Israel as ad hoc balance weights; but many others so employed may have been overlooked by archaeologists. For our knowledge of the "official" system, however, we are depen-

WEIGHTS AND MEASURES

Israelite bronze weights from the ninth–eighth century B.C.

dent on stone weights marked with specific symbols or values that allow us to reconstruct the accepted standard with reasonable assurance.

First of all, it is evident that the Israelite system was largely borrowed from that of greater Canaan, which in turn derived it from Mesopotamia. The names of three of the four principal units are the same in all three languages—*mina*, *shekel*, and *gerah*—and the ratios are similar. The largest unit, the talent, was known to the Babylonians as *biltu* and to the Israelites as *kikkār*, "a round thing" (or standard weight). (Our translation of the latter as "talent" comes from the Greek *talanton*, "weight.") However, there were several systems of weights and measures used in ancient Assyria and Babylonia, including those based on a "light" and a "heavy" standard. Thus, despite the discovery of many actual weights, we can give only an approximation of the system (Table A). Nonetheless, for our purposes it is clear that the Assyrian-Babylonian system was sexagesimal (using the number 60 as a base in computation) instead of decimal (using the number 10), as in the Egyptian and most modern systems. Thus 1 talent equaled 60 minas, and 1 mina equaled 60 shekels; but 1 shekel equaled 24 gerahs.

However, although the Israelite system borrowed the basic Mesopotamian units as noted above, it gave them different values, both in ratios to each other and in absolute weights. It was quinquagesimal, i.e., divisible by 5 or 50, rather than 6 or 60. A number of biblical references (Exod. 38:25–26; cf. Gen. 23:15; Exod. 30:24; 38:29; Num. 31:52; 1 Sam. 17:5) suggest that the talent equaled only 50 shekels. Again, according to the sole helpful biblical passage (Ezek. 45:12), the mina was only 50 shekels. Other passages (Exod. 30:13; Lev. 27:25; Num. 3:47; 18:16; Ezek. 45:12) state that the shekel was reckoned at only 20 gerahs. To calculate the exact weights of each of these units, we must turn now to the only external evidence we have, actual weights that have come to light in chance finds or in controlled excavation.

No inscribed talent or mina weights have been found in Palestine, and very few uninscribed weights have been recognized (except for a probable 8-mina weight from Tell Beit Mirsim). It is likely that the larger weights were rarely in use. We do have, however, a growing number of the smaller shekel and fraction-of-a-shekel weights, so that now for the first time we can reconstruct the Israelite system fully. It appears, however, that there were at least two systems in operation simultaneously (as in Mesopotamia); that there were discrepancies among individual weights even within the same system; and that matters were further complicated late in the OT period, when Egyptian hieratic signs (simplified forms of earlier hieroglyphic pictograms) for numerals were grafted to the Mesopotamian framework. Let us summarize the biblical and archaeological data for each system.

The first we call the "light" or *common shekel* system. Numerous biblical passages refer

Table A

APPROXIMATE EQUIVALENT VALUES OF ANCIENT ASSYRIAN AND BABYLONIAN WEIGHTS

		Heavy Standard		
	Royal Weight		*Common Weight*	
Talent	61.2 kg.	134.6 lb.	60 kg.	132 lb.
Mina	1.05 kg.	2.32 lb.	1 kg.	2.2 lb.
Shekel	16.74 g.	.62 oz.	16.667 g.	.59 oz.
		Light Standard		
	Royal Weight		*Common Weight*	
Talent	30.6 kg.	67.3 lb.	30 kg.	66 lb.
Mina	525 g.	1.16 lb.	500 g.	1.1 lb.
Shekel	8.75 g.	.31 oz.	8.33 g.	.293 oz.

In every case, 1 talent equals 60 minas; 1 mina equals 60 shekels.

WEIGHTS AND MEASURES

to the shekel (e.g., Exod. 38:29; Num. 3:47; 1 Sam. 17:5, 7), making it clear that this was the basic, most commonly used measure of weight and payment. Several dozen inscribed shekel weights have been found from the eighth and seventh centuries B.C., all but one from Judaean sites (a 16-shekel weight is known from Shechem). All bear an open loop sign resembling a "figure 8," which the OT scholar R.B.Y. Scott has convincingly interpreted as meaning "shekel," claiming it is a stylized representation of the small leather pouch (Heb. ṣerōr) in which lump silver, the common medium of exchange, was carried. Among the shekel weights known thus far, we have denominations of 1, 2, 4, 8, 16, and 24. As has long been recognized, however (R.B.Y. Scott, Y. Aharoni, and others), these shekel weights are marked with the Egyptian hieratic symbols for 1, 2—and then for 5, 10, 20, and 30. It seems that late in the monarchical period, probably to facilitate international trade, the Israelites borrowed the convenient Egyptian numerical signs but gave them their own values in part. The Israelites also equated their weights to the Egyptian *deben* (equivalent to 8 shekels), and *qedet* (one-tenth of a *deben*). Thus by this time (late eighth and seventh centuries B.C.), an originally Mesopotamian *sexagesimal* system had been transformed into a *quinquagesimal* system, but with the addition of Egyptian decimal markings!

Although this may be quite confusing to us, the overall shekel system "worked" because it was consistent. It utilized the 8-shekel weight (with the hieratic symbol of the latter) as the basic module, so that below that you had what were essentially fraction weights (the 4-, 2-, and 1-shekel weights), and above it each next weight was larger by 8 shekels (the 16- and 24-shekel weights; none larger are known). The Egyptian signs constituted a kind of "shorthand" that could easily be adapted to the Israelite system, regardless of the original values. Whether the average citizen or merchant read the signs at face value and made the recalculation, or simply understood them as Hebrew symbols, we do not know, but the latter seems more likely.

The chart in Table B lists the denominations and average weights of the shekel weights thus far known, together with the hieratic symbols on them and their equivalencies to the Egyptian system. It will be seen that the average weight of the shekel in this system can be computed as ca. 11.40 grams, probably the "light" shekel.

Recently the discovery of the "missing links" in a series of smaller weights, similarly inscribed, has enabled us to reconstruct the fraction weights, or weights of less than 1 shekel, of this "light" shekel system. Assuming that the shekel contained 20 gerahs, the scholar G. Barkay assembled some thirty-five known examples of smaller weights, many of them heretofore enigmatic, and showed that we can now recognize gerah weights in denominations of 2 through 8, plus 10 (and the others will likely be found in time). Furthermore Barkay's scheme demonstrates that these weights were also marked with Egyptian hieratic symbols, but here they must be read at face value (i.e., not 5=4, 10=8, as on the shekel weights). There was apparently no confusion, since the obvious difference in size kept the two systems distinct.

Table C outlines the gerah system as it presently appears. This table also makes clear that

Table B
SHEKEL AND FRACTION WEIGHTS

"Light" or Common System			*"Heavy" System*		*Hieratic Symbols*	*Egyptian Equivalent*	
*Shekel Weights**		*Fractions*	*Fractions***			*deben*	*qedet*
		2–10 Gerahs (= .565 g.) (Shekel = 20 Gerahs)	Beq'a	6.019 g.			
			Pim	7.825 g.			
			Netseph	9.823 g.			
1	11.40 g.				| = 1		
2	23.19 g.						
4	45.306 g.				|| = 2		
8	91.00 g.				 = 5		
16	188.50 g.				 = 10	1	10
24	268.24 g.				 = 20	2	20
					 = 30	3	30

This table shows the average weight in grams of the known examples, Egyptian hieratic markings, and Egyptian equivalents.

**Shekel average = ca. 11.40 g.*

***No 1–24 shekel weights are known. Shekel average = ca. 12.50 g.*

WEIGHTS AND MEASURES

the average gerah was ca. 0.565 gram, which would yield a shekel of ca. 11.30 grams. This is strikingly close to our previous calculation of 11.40 grams—especially considering that any balances, where tested, have a margin of error of 5 percent or more.

A second, or "heavy," shekel system can be reconstructed from another series of fraction weights, these bearing not numerical signs but Hebrew terms instead, some of them mentioned also in the Bible. The letters are always inscribed in a beautiful lapidary Paleo-Hebrew script of the late eighth and seventh centuries B.C., which may date most of these weights to the time of King Josiah (ca. 639–609 B.C.).

"Beq'a" weights. The Hebrew verbal root *baq-'a* means "to cleave, split," from which it is assumed that the *beq'a* was approximately half a shekel. The term appears in Gen. 24:22; Exod. 30:13, 15; and 38:26, where indeed it can be so understood. The dozen or so weights published thus far inscribed *beq'a* average ca. 6.2 grams; if these are actually half-shekels, we may then have a "heavy" shekel of ca. 12.50 grams alongside the "light" shekel of 11.40 grams.

The word *netseph*, found on some twenty inscribed weights thus far, is obviously Hebrew, but it does not appear in the OT. The Arabic cognate *nusf*, "half," suggests that it may have been approximately a half-shekel, but the average of the known examples, ca. 9.8 grams, comes out nearer to four-fifths of the "heavy" shekel (ca. nine-tenths of the "light" shekel). At present we have no solution for this anomaly.

"Pim" weights. This Hebrew word appears in a famous but long obscure passage in 1 Sam. 13:19–21, which states that the price the Philistines charged the Israelites for sharpening iron implements was "one *pim*." Earlier commentators and translators had tried to relate this term—occurring only here in the Hebrew Bible—to *pê*, "mouth," but the discovery of the first of some dozen or more actual *pim* weights resolved the difficulty. The average of the known examples is ca. 7.8 grams, or a little over three-fifths of the "heavy" shekel (ca. seven-tenths of the "light" shekel).

Table C

KNOWN GERAH WEIGHTS OF THE ISRAELITE "LIGHT" OR COMMON SHEKEL SYSTEM

<table>
<tr><th>Gerah</th><th>Hieratic Symbol</th><th>No. of Examples Found</th><th>Average Weight in Grams</th></tr>
<tr><td>(1)</td><td></td><td></td><td>0.565?</td></tr>
<tr><td>2</td><td>|| = 2</td><td>1</td><td>1.705?</td></tr>
<tr><td>3</td><td>||| = 3</td><td>3</td><td>1.67</td></tr>
<tr><td>4</td><td>|||| = 4</td><td>2</td><td>2.408</td></tr>
<tr><td>5</td><td>ㄱ = 5</td><td>4</td><td>2.60</td></tr>
<tr><td>6</td><td>//ㄴ = 6</td><td>6</td><td>3.534</td></tr>
<tr><td>7</td><td>ℷ = 7</td><td>1</td><td>3.61</td></tr>
<tr><td>8</td><td>⥱ = 8</td><td>11</td><td>4.2875</td></tr>
<tr><td>(9)</td><td></td><td></td><td></td></tr>
<tr><td>10</td><td>ᐸ = 10</td><td>5</td><td>5.303</td></tr>
</table>

The same Egyptian hieratic scripts used on the larger shekel weights are used on these fraction weights but are read instead at face value. One shekel equals 20 gerahs. (After G. Barkay, 1981.)

The discrepancies noted above are really not surprising. The variance within each series (as much as 10 percent or more) can easily be accounted for by the difficulty of shaping these small weights exactly, and also by the fact that the soft limestone wore away slightly with long use. The existence of at least two systems is already hinted at in the Bible, such as in descriptions of "the shekel of the sanctuary" (Exod. 38:25–26; 30:24), shekels "by the king's weight" (2 Sam. 14:26), and shekels of "the weights current among the merchants" (Gen. 23:15). It may be that the "heavy" shekel, possibly following the older Mesopotamian system of a shekel containing 24 (slightly smaller) gerahs, remained the official standard of the royal court and priesthood, while the "light" or 20-gerah shekel was in more common use.

In any case, these discrepancies were not only confusing but invited corrupt practices, calling for frequent rectification. We have already noted the biblical condemnation of "false balances." False weights are also condemned—specifically the practice of switching weights on an unsuspecting customer. Deut. 25:13 states expressly: "You shall not have in your bag two kinds of weights, a large and a small." Among the economic reforms carried out by King Hezekiah (ca. 727–698 B.C.) and King Josiah (ca. 639–609 B.C.) there were probably regulations designed to standardize weights and measures. It is perhaps no coincidence that nearly all of our inscribed weights come from the eighth and seventh centuries B.C., to judge from archaeological context where known, or from paleography (the science of dating scripts) in other examples.

In the NT there are fewer references to weights, but in compensation we have abundant other information on Roman period practices from classical sources. The "talent" (Matt. 18:24; 25:15–28) was probably equivalent to 6,000 drachmas. The "mina" of Luke 19:13–25 is uncertain. The "pound" of ointment (Gk. *litra*, Lat. *libra*, John 12:3; 19:39) was probably equivalent to 12 ounces.

Measuring Area: There is no special terminology for measures of area in the OT. A "yoke" (Heb. *tsemed;* 1 Sam. 14:14) is presumably what a pair of oxen could plow a day, possibly about an acre. The Latin Vulgate, however, translates "yoke" by *jugerum* (related to *jugis*, "yoke"), about five-eighths of an acre. Isa. 5:10 is the only other reference to a "yoke" of land. Another OT term for land area is *ma'ana* (Heb., "ploughing ground"?; only Ps. 129:3), translated by the KJV as "acre" but by the RSV simply as "furrow."

Finally, *seah* in the story of Elijah's digging a trench around his altar on Mt. Carmel (1 Kings 18:32; "measure") denotes the area that "two measures of seed" would plant, but we are uncertain what that is. Later Talmudic sources confirm that land area was ordinarily estimated by the amount of seed required to sow it.

Measuring Length: As it was in Mesopotamia and Egypt, the "cubit" (Heb. *'ammah*, "elbow") was the standard of linear measure in ancient Israel. Like the subordinate measures, the "span" and the "finger," it derived from a natural, convenient point of reference, the approximate length of a man's forearm. The word occurs in the OT more than a hundred times, in descriptions of distances, buildings, furnishings, and the like. No actual cubit measures have been found by archaeologists, doubtless because they were of perishable wood, but Hezekiah's famous water tunnel inscription in Jerusalem, discovered in A.D. 1880, giving the length of the tunnel as "1,200 cubits," may be compared with the actual measured length of 1,749 feet. This would yield a cubit of about 17.5 inches—very close to the average length of a man's forearm from elbow to finger tips. Solomon's Temple would thus have been 90 feet (60 cubits) long, 30 feet (20 cubits) wide, and 45 feet (30 cubits) high (1 Kings 6:2).

There were, however, several cubits in use in ancient Israel, just as there were shekels. In addition to the usual or "short" cubit, there was the "long" cubit implied in Ezekiel's vision of the restored temple (Ezek. 40:5), possibly equivalent to the Egyptian cubit of ca. 20.6 inches. A third cubit may be referred to in the description of the bed of Og, King of Bashan, the "common cubit" (Deut. 3:11).

Smaller units of linear measure were the "span" (Heb. *zeret*), or distance between extended fingertips, about one-half a cubit, or 9 inches on the shorter scale, a little over 10 inches on the longer scale of Ezekiel. A "handsbreadth" (Heb. *ṭepaḥ*), about one-sixth a cubit, would be ca. 3 inches. A "finger" (Heb. *'esba'*) designates one-fourth of a handsbreadth, about three-quarters of an inch.

In the NT the word "cubit" (Gk. *pēchys*) seems to be merely a popular estimate of both length and time. Jesus says to his disciples "Which of you by being anxious can add a cubit to his life?" (Matt. 6:27); and the disciples on the Sea of Galilee started to bring in their boat when they were about "two hundred cubits" off shore (John 21:8). The Greek *stadion* (pl. *stadia;* Luke 24:13; John 6:19; 11:18; Rev. 14:20; 21:16) contained 400 cubits, about 200 yards in either Greek or Roman usage (the KJV regularly translates "furlong"). The "mile" (Matt. 5:41) was probably the standard Roman mile of 1,000 double paces, 5,000 Roman feet, or 1,618 yards.

Measuring Capacity: There are many units of capacity measure in the OT. They are related mostly to the Assyrian-Babylonian rather than the Egyptian system, but they were never finally fixed.

The homer (Heb. *ḥōmer*) was a standard dry measure, the term being derived from the word for "ass" and referring (as the Assyrian *imeru*) to the load of grain a donkey might normally carry. On the basis of Assyrian texts it would have been about 14 bushels, but some calculations make it more like 6.5 bushels. The homer, equal to the cor, contained 10 baths or ephahs (Ezek. 45:11–14).

The cor (Heb. *qōr*) was equal to the homer, but it could be used for liquid measure as well (1 Kings 4:22; 5:11, 25; 2 Chron. 2:10; 27:5; Ezek. 45:14), in which case it would have contained about 35 gallons, and possibly up to 60.

The lethech (Heb. *lētek*), mentioned only in Hos. 3:2, is interpreted by the Mishnah as half a homer or cor, or about 2 to 3.25 bushels.

The ephah (Heb. *'ēpâh*) was equal to one-tenth of a homer or cor, thus about 1.5 to 2.5 pecks, or three-eighths to two-thirds of a bushel. The ephah is mentioned numerous times in the OT, especially with grains and cereals, and must have been the most common dry measure.

The bath (Heb. *bat*) was a liquid measure equal to the ephah (Ezek. 45:14). Storejars from the eighth century B.C. have been found at Tell Beit Mirsim inscribed "bath" and at Lachish inscribed "royal bath." These jars, when reconstructed, would yield ca. 5.5 gallons, corresponding approximately to the ephah.

Top view of dome-shaped weights inscribed with their values. Some of the values, from right to left, are: 18, 8, 4, and 2 shekels.

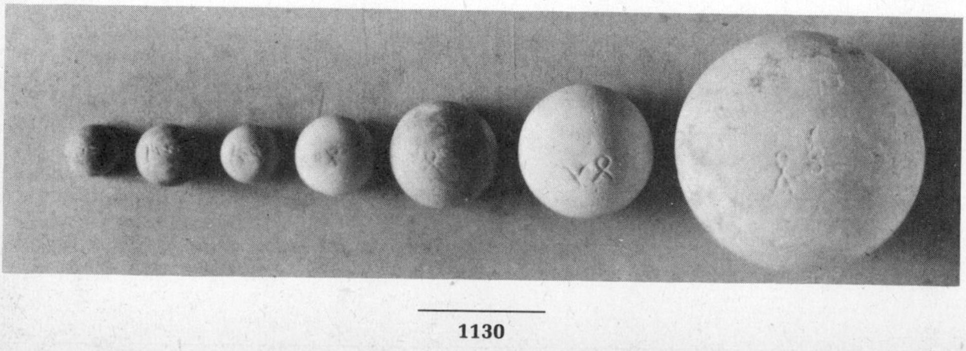

Cattle of Punt (lower left) being weighed against gold weights on a balance; fifteenth-century B.C. reliefs at Thebes.

Quantities of liquid from small to very large were measured with the bath (1 Kings 7:26, 38; 2 Chron. 2:10; 4:5; Isa. 5:10).

The seah (Heb. *se'ah)* was a dry measure of uncertain size. References in Gen. 18:6; 1 Kings 18:32; 2 Kings 7:1, 16, 18; and Isa. 27:8 are rendered by the KJV and RSV as simply "measure," but the Septuagint (LXX) would suggest 1.5 *modii* or about one-third of a bushel.

The hin (Heb. *hin)* is an Egyptian liquid measure that can be shown by actual examples to be 0.46 liter, or about half a quart. But according to calculations based on the writings of the historian Josephus, the Israelite hin was one-sixth of a bath, or a little less than a gallon. Ezek. 4:11 gives a daily ration of water as one-sixth of a hin, or ca. two-thirds of a quart.

The omer (Heb. *'omer)* was one-tenth of an ephah (Exod. 10:36), or a little more than 2 dry quarts. According to Exod. 16:16–18, the omer was a day's ration of grain.

The issaron (Heb. *'issaron*), mentioned only rarely (Exod. 29:40; Lev. 40:10), is evidently one-tenth of some measure, presumably an ephah.

The kab (heb. *qab)* is referred to only in 2 Kings 6:25. In rabbinical sources it was one-eighteenth an ephah, or about 1.6 of a dry quart.

The smallest unit of capacity, the log (Heb. *log;* only Lev. 14:10, 12, 15, 24), was used for oil. It was apparently one-fourth of a kab, or about two-thirds of a pint. Exactly as just balances were demanded by biblical law, so just measures were called for (Lev. 19:36; Ezek. 45:10).

In the NT, capacity is determined by Greek or Roman measures. The *sextarius* is about a pint, the *metrētēs* (John 2:6) is possibly 20 to 30 gallons. *Modios* (Matt. 5:15; Mark 4:21; Luke 1:3) is the Greek term for "bushel," about one-fourth of an American bushel. The ointment Mary poured on Jesus' feet (John 12:3) was a *litra,* the Roman pound of 12 ounces. A *choinix* (Rev. 6:6) was about 1 quart.

It must be observed that our reconstruction of ancient weights and measures, while more extensive and accurate than it was just fifteen or twenty years ago, is still provisional and may change with further archaeological discoveries.

Bibliography

Barkay, G. "Iron Age Gerah Weights." *Eretz-Israel* 15 (1981):288–296 (Hebrew; English summary, p. 85).

Dever, W. G. "Iron Age Epigraphic Material from the Area of Khirbet el-Kôm." *Hebrew Union College Annual* 40–41 (1969–1970):139–204.

Scott, R. B. Y. "Weights and Measures of the Bible." *The Biblical Archaeologist* 22 (1959):22–40.

W.G.D.

well (Heb. *be'er),* a hole or depression dug for the purpose of collecting water. A well was constructed by digging into the ground or by curbing surface springs. Wells, together with cisterns, were the major source of water in ancient Palestine. Digging a well in this semi-arid land was an occasion for rejoicing (Num. 21:17), but also for strife (Gen. 21:25–26; 26:15, 18; Exod. 2:16–17). Wells were located in the wilderness (Gen. 16:7, 14), in fields (Gen. 29:2), and in towns (2 Sam. 23:15) and supplied both human and animal needs. The city well, which was usually located outside the gate (Neh. 2:13; John 4:6–8), served as a meeting place, especially for the women, who had the daily task of drawing water for the household (Gen. 24:11). The well is used figuratively to describe the beloved as a source of pleasure (Prov. 5:15; Song of Sol. 4:15) and to characterize a wicked city that keeps its wickedness "fresh" as a well keeps its water (Jer. 6:7). ***See also*** Beer-sheba; Cisterns.

P.A.B.

"we" source. ***See*** Acts of the Apostles, The.

whale, an aquatic mammal of the order *Cetacea.* It is identified in Matt. 12:40 as the carrier of Jonah after he was cast into the sea, although the book of Jonah identifies it simply as a "great fish" (Jon. 1:17–2:10). "Dragon" (Ezek. 32:2) and "sea monster" (Job 7:12) are rendered as "whale" in the KJV. There is no way at present to determine precisely which species the biblical writers intended.

wheat (genus *Triticum),* one of the principal cereal grasses, along with barley, of the Holy Land. Domesticated originally in the Near East, it has been cultivated since prehistoric times. Several types exist in the present and were known also in the past and are variously referred to as einkorn, emmer, spelt, and possibly rye (KJV, Isa. 28:25). It is often translated as corn or ears of corn (KJV) or grain (RSV; Gen. 41:5; Mark 2:23).

After the harvest in the late spring, the wheat

Wheat, as depicted on bas-reliefs at ancient Hermopolis, Egypt.

was prepared for domestic use as flour by threshing, winnowing, parching, and grinding or milling. The finely ground flour was preferred for baking breads and cakes and was therefore a major dietary component (Exod. 29: 2; Lev. 2:1).

Wheat is less hardy than barley and is more susceptible to drought, frost, and poor soil conditions. Dependence on wheat as the staff of life often led to famine in times of environmental stress (Gen. 43:1–2). In good years, however, production was so great that it was an item of export from the Holy Land. Solomon is said to have sent twenty thousand measures of wheat to Hiram of Tyre in payment for the cedars and cypress sent for the construction of the Temple and palace of Jerusalem (1 Kings 5:10–11). ***See also*** Corn; Rye; Spelt. P.L.C.

wheels, round disks fitted with an axle at their center for supporting a load-carrying device. Early representations of wheels show them to be solid, anchored to the axle, the whole combination turning beneath the bed of the vehicle (Royal Standard of Ur, third millennium B.C.). Subsequent developments freed the wheel to turn on the axle, designed spoked wheels with rims for lighter weight and maneuverability, and adapted the device to other uses than transportation (potter's wheel for shaping the clay [Jer. 18:3] or pulley for use in raising water from a cistern [Eccles. 12:6]). In addition to carts, wagons, and chariots, biblical writers refer to wheels on the Temple court lavers (1 Kings 7: 30–33), four on each. Ezekiel's vision of God's throne includes wheels with eyes (Ezek. 1:4–28) and in Dan. 4:9 and *1 Enoch* 14:18 they are part of the throne support. The crushing effect of a wheel is behind Prov. 20:26 and the rumble of wheels bespoke destruction (Nah. 3:2). R.S.B.

whirlwind, a violent, destructive windstorm, common in Israel during the rainy season. True whirlwinds, i.e., swirling winds or tornadoes, are unusual, but sometimes they appear near the coast during the early winter. Whirlwinds and storms usually accompanied a theophany such as God's appearance to Job (Job 38:1; 40:6) and Ezekiel's vision of God (Ezek. 1:4; cf. Nah. 1:3; Zech. 9:14). According to 2 Kings 2:1, 11, the prophet Elijah did not die, but a whirlwind, accompanied by a chariot and horses of fire, carried him up to heaven. ***See also*** Elijah; Job, The Book of.

whore. ***See*** Harlot.

wickedness. ***See*** Redemption; Regeneration; Restitution; Sin.

widow, a woman whose husband has died. The status of the widow in ancient Israelite society was precarious. Having no inheritance rights and often in want of life's necessities, she was exposed to harsh treatment and exploitation. Widowhood was perceived by some to be a disgrace; death before old age was probably viewed as a judgment upon sin, and the reproach extended to the surviving spouse (Ruth 1:19–21; Isa. 54:4). Israel's legal corpus provided some measure of security for the widow. If a deceased Israelite had brothers, a levirate marriage could be arranged, but this was not always done (Deut. 25:5–10; Gen. 38). A priest's daughter could return to her father's house (Lev. 22:13). Often, however, widows had no respectable recourse but to rely on public charity.

God's concern for the plight of the widow is revealed in the Law, the Prophets, and certain of the Writings of the OT (Deut. 14:29; Jer. 49: 11; Pss. 68:5; 146:9). It was taught that the neglect or oppression of widows provoked the divine wrath (Ps. 94:1–7; Job 22:9–11, 29–30; Isa. 1:16–17, 21–25). Noteworthy in Deuteronomy is the linkage of God's mercies (shown to his people who were sojourners in Egypt) with Israel's obligation to care for "the sojourners, the fatherless, and the widow" (Deut. 10:14–19; 24: 17–22; 27:19).

Stories in the Gospels reveal Jesus' sensitivity to the widow's marginal existence: he restored to life "the only son" of the widow of Nain (Luke 7:11–17); he declared that a certain "poor widow's" copper coins exceeded in value the large gifts of the scribes to the Temple treasury, suggesting that some of their wealth was obtained by "eating up the property of widows" (Mark 12:38–44, NEB).

In the early church, widows were cared for and steps were taken to ensure equal distribution of food (Acts 6:1–6). The writer of the pastoral Letter 1 Timothy urged a just and cost-efficient plan for the use of limited funds, so that "real widows" (those in abject poverty and truly alone) could be provided for (5:3–16). To this end, families were charged to care for their own (5:3–4, 16), and rules of eligibility for the enrollment of widows were prescribed (5: 9–15). This enrollment probably implies the existence of an order of widows who devoted themselves to intercessory prayer and to rendering special services to the church. According to the second-century writers Ignatius (*Smyrnaeans* 13:1) and Polycarp (*Philippians* 4:3), such an order or ministry existed in their time. This order of widows later merged with that of church deaconesses. ***See also*** Family, The; Inheritance; Marriage; Women. J.L.P.

wife. ***See*** Concubine; Family, The; Marriage; Women; and individual entries by name.

wilderness, a desolate or deserted area devoid of civilization. One Hebrew word above all others is used for "wilderness," or "desert," in the OT: *midbar*, indicating both "that which is desolate and deserted" and "that which is beyond," i.e., beyond the limits of settlement and therefore of government control, perceived by both city dwellers and villagers as being essentially disorderly and dangerous, the home of wild beasts and savage wandering tribes. In time of war or repression refugees would flee to the *midbar* (Isa. 21:13–15; cf. Rev. 12:6, 14); "greatly distressed . . . enraged . . . [they] will curse their king and their God" (Isa. 8:21–22). But only too often they would find "no way to a city to dwell in; hungry and thirsty, their soul fainted within them" (Ps. 107:4–5).

Certainly, the primary Israelite experience was that of escaping from Egypt through the desolate wastes of Sinai and of entering there into covenant with Yahweh, but they remembered how they hated the wilderness wanderings and had no desire at all to return (Exod. 15:22–25; 16:3; Pss. 78:40; 95:8). It remained for them always "the great and terrible wilderness, with its fiery serpents and scorpions and thirsty ground where there was no water" (Deut. 8:15). *Midbar* was for them, as "wilderness" was originally in English, the *wild*, alarming wasteland, where men and women find themselves *bewildered* and disoriented.

Although often equated with the drought-stricken desert (Heb. *yeshimon;* Deut. 32:10; Ps. 106:14), the wilderness (*midbar*) included poor steppeland, e.g., the area surrounding the oasis of Damascus (1 Kings 19:15), and could include the marginal cultivated land on the Transjordan plateau (Num. 21:13; Deut. 4:43), as well as the pastureland east of Bethlehem, where in the Christmas story shepherds were "keeping watch over their flock" (Luke 2:8), as David had done centuries before them (1 Sam. 17:28). It could comprise also tangled thickets and scrub, such as the "thorns" and "briers" of the wilderness near Succoth in the Jordan Valley (Judg. 8:7, 16). Wilderness (*midbar*) in fact merged into wooded areas (Heb. *ya'ar*), which is normally translated "forest," and both were perceived by the settled Israelites as dangerous trackless country where one could rapidly become lost or be attacked by wild beasts. In fact, the two are equated in Ezek. 34:25 when God promises, "I will make with them a covenant of peace and banish wild beasts from the land, so that they may dwell securely in the wilderness [*midbar*] and sleep in the woods [*ya'ar*]." An even more impressive parallel may

Desert "wilderness" in the Sinai peninsula near Jebal Musa, a traditional site of Mount Sinai.

be found in Isa. 32:15, where wilderness replaces the thickly forested "Lebanon" of Isa. 29:17. They both belonged to the savage, ill-controlled regions beyond the cultivated farmlands. To the north and west lay the woods; to the south and east the wilderness.

NT writers held similar opinions (Heb. 11:37–38), viewing "waterless places" as the natural habitat of evil spirits (Luke 11:24; see Isa. 34:14). It was therefore appropriate that it was in the desert that Jesus was tempted by Satan to abandon his vocation of suffering Son of God (Matt. 4:1–11; Luke 4:1–13). When Jesus fed the multitudes in the wilderness (e.g., Mark 8:4), he showed he was able to overcome its dangers, both physical and supernatural. Jesus' forerunner, John the Baptist, had also appeared in the wilderness with his message of repentance (Mark 1:4), thus reminding Israel of its first days as chosen people in the desert of Sinai. The fact that John performed a baptism indicates that the wilderness was not a waterless stretch of sand, but rather a desolate area where water was nevertheless available, perhaps somewhere in the Jordan Valley. The remaining NT references to wilderness are principally in contexts where Israel's period of wilderness wandering is at issue (e.g., John 3:14; Acts 7:36; 1 Cor. 10:5). ***See also*** Bethlehem; Desert; Sinai, Succoth. D.B./P.J.A.

willow, any water-loving tree of the genus *Salix* (Ezek. 17:5; Lev. 23:40; Job 40:22; Isa. 44:4). Even when it was a sorrowful symbol of the exile in Babylon, the tree was associated with water (Ps. 137:1–2).

Willows, Brook of the, a stream crossed by Moabite refugees carrying their belongings (Isa. 15:7). The most likely identification is the Seil el-Qurahi, the lower portion of the Wadi el-Hesa southeast of the Dead Sea.

winds, perceptible movements of air masses. Winds were an important determinant of weather in ancient Palestine. In the rainless summer months moisture-laden winds from the Mediterranean (west or northwest) flowed over the land during the daytime, moderating the midday heat and leaving a heavy dew at night. These steady winds enabled threshers to winnow grain (Ps. 1:4). In the winter months the western winds brought thunderstorms (1 Kings 18:45), which were welcomed for their life-giving rain, despite their often violent effects: shaking the forest (Isa. 7:2) and agitating the sea (Ps. 107:25). Unstable weather between the two main seasons spawned the sirocco, the searing east or south wind that descended sporadically from the desert, blasting vegetation (Gen. 41:6; Ps. 103:16; Jon. 4:8), drying up water sources, and wrecking ships at sea (Ezek. 27:26). Striking in violent gusts (Job 1:19) or in a steady blast, it was often laden with suspended dust. God used an east wind to dry up the Flood (Gen. 8:1) and drive back the waters of the sea (Exod. 14:21).

Wind was a mysterious force, moving endlessly from unknown origin to unknown destination (Eccles. 1:6; John 3:8). It was a symbol of transience (Ps. 78:39), fruitless striving (Eccles. 1:14), and empty talk (Jer. 5:13), but also of untamed, irresistible power, whirling, scattering (Jer. 18:17), tossing to and fro (Eph. 4:14). God alone could command the winds (Mark 4:41), sending them forth from his storehouses (Jer. 10:13), riding upon them in the clouds (Ps. 18:10; 104:3; Ezek. 1:4), and commissioning them to do his will (Exod. 15:10; Ps. 104:4). The Holy Spirit at Pentecost was perceived as a mighty wind (Acts 2:2), and the four winds of heaven described the extremities of the universe (Dan. 7:2; Matt. 24:31; Rev. 7:1). ***See also*** Flesh and Spirit; Whirlwind. P.A.B.

wine, fermented grape juice. It was considered luxurious and sometimes dangerous food (1 Sam. 1:14; Neh. 5:18; Prov. 20:1; 23:29–35; Isa. 25:6; 1 Tim. 3:18). ***See also*** Vine.

wine-bibber, a drunkard; drunkards are denounced in Prov. 23:30. Jesus was accused of being a drunkard (Matt. 11:19) by those who rejected his ministry among the outcast.

wine press. ***See*** Vine.

wineskin. ***See*** Bag; Bottles; Vine.

winnowing, the process by which threshed grain is separated from chaff, the extraneous, nonedible stalks and husks (Ruth 3:2). In the ancient Holy Land, the threshed grain and chaff was mounded on a flat open surface, or piled on a cloth, a wide but shallow basket, or a sieve. It was then raked or thrown into the air where the brisk afternoon wind removed the lighter chaff (cf. Ps. 1:4). The heavier grain dropped back to the ground and was gathered. The threshed and winnowed grain was then ready for use or storage in granaries. The same procedures are still used in many places in the Near East today. John the Baptist used the process of winnowing as a metaphor for divine judgment (Luke 3:17). ***See also*** Threshing. P.L.C.

winnowing fork (KJV: "fan," in Matt. 3:12; Luke 3:17), the hand device used by the farmer to throw the mix from his shredded pile of grain and straw into the air to let the wind carry the straw and chaff away and the grain fall back for collection (Isa. 41:16). The winnowing fork needed sufficient tines closely enough spaced to hold nearly clean grain (Isa. 30:24). Such fine separation of straw and chaff from the kernels of wheat became a metaphor for the punishment of Jerusalem by God (Jer. 15:7; cf. Matt. 3:12; Luke

3:17). In the final stages the grain would be thrown up into the breeze by shovel, the breeze carrying off the last of the chaff and leaving the grain ready for sifting and the removing of pebbles by direct hand inspection. Prevalent north and west winds provided a natural fanning mill for Palestine's farmers, as it does to this day. Fanning was done on the threshing floors after the sledges had been driven over the harvested grain sufficiently to cut the straw fine. ***See also*** Sledge; Winnowing. R.S.B.

wisdom, a term in the Hebrew Bible (OT) standing for many things ranging from the technical skill of the artisan (Exod. 36:8) to the art of government (1 Kings 3:12, 28). It also designates simple cleverness (2 Sam. 14:2), especially the practical skill of coping with life (Prov. 1; 5; 11; 14), and the pursuit of a lifestyle of proper ethical conduct (Prov. 2:9–11 and throughout). Wisdom is also seen as belonging properly to God (Job 28), associated with creation (Prov. 8: 22–31), and even identified with the Torah or Law (Ecclus. 24:23).

Wisdom Literature in the OT: In the Hebrew Bible, "wisdom literature" is generally understood to refer to Proverbs, Job, and Ecclesiastes; among the Apocrypha, it includes Ecclesiasticus (The Wisdom of Jesus the Son of Sirach) and The Wisdom of Solomon. The extent to which other parts of the Bible can be described as "wisdom" (e.g., the story of Joseph in Gen. 37–50) is disputed, but certain Psalms seem to betray wisdom influence (e.g., Ps. 37). The relationship between wisdom and apocalyptic and the extent to which the latter was influenced by the former also remains a moot point.

This literature has characteristic traits: (1) There is an absence of reference to the typical salvation beliefs, such as the patriarchal promises, the Exodus, the Sinai covenant, etc. (2) The object of the Hebrew sage is to transmit the lessons of experience, so that one may learn to cope with life. The teaching inculcates certain goals, such as self-control (especially in speech), honesty, diligence, etc. If one follows the counsels of the sage, wisdom will bring life; its opposite, folly—a practical, not merely intellectual folly—brings destruction. (3) A characteristic problem is retribution, the way in which the wise/foolish (i.e., virtuous/wrongdoers) are treated. Proverbs upholds the optimistic view shared by such books as Deuteronomy but disputed by Job and Ecclesiastes. (4) Certain literary forms are cultivated: the discrete, separate saying, which is usually a pithy expression in two parallel lines; the admonition, whether positive or negative, which is often accompanied by a motivation; wisdom poems (typical of Prov. 1–9); and reflections (characteristic of Ecclesiastes). Job is dominated by disputation speeches between the protagonist and the three friends (chaps. 3–31).

Solomon was famous in biblical tradition for his wisdom (1 Kings 4:29–34); hence Proverbs and Ecclesiastes came to be attributed to him. The origins of Israelite wisdom are presumed to lie in the insights, oral and written, of the family and clan and also of the wise men who could have provided training for courtiers in Jerusalem. The existence of some kind of "school" may be inferred from similar institutions in Mesopotamia and Egypt. Wisdom, in fact, is an international possession, cultivated throughout the ancient Near East, and many parallels to Israelite wisdom, both remote and close, have been proposed (e.g., the teaching of the Egyptian sage Amenemopet and Prov. 22:17–24:22).

An outstanding trait of biblical wisdom is the personification of Lady Wisdom in Proverbs 1; 3; and 9 (cf. Job 28; Ecclus. 24). She is described as originating from God and is associated with creation (Prov. 3:19; 8:22–31). According to G. von Rad, she is "the self-revelation of creation" and, one might add, the revelation of God in and through creation (Ps. 19:1). Wisdom theology is a theology of creation, for it was within the area of creation and human experience that the Hebrew sages operated.

The Wisdom Tradition in the NT: The wisdom tradition continues through the intertestamental period (Ecclus., Wisd. of Sol.) and appears in Christianity (NT) and Judaism (Sayings of the Fathers). First of all, Jesus is presented in the synoptic Gospels as a wisdom teacher, a rabbi. The many logia (sayings) attributed to him are cast in the aphoristic style of the sages (e.g., Matt. 6:19–7:27), and comparisons and parables abound. The wisdom of Jesus is "greater than Solomon" (Luke 11:31; cf. Mark 6:2). In Matt. 11:2–19, and Luke 7:18–35 Jesus is implicitly designated as wisdom (cf. Matt. 11:27; Luke 10: 22). What appears as a threat by wisdom in Luke 11:49–51 is a means for Matthew to identify Jesus with wisdom (Matt. 23:34–36). Like wisdom in Proverbs 8, Jesus issues an invitation to all to follow him and take up his yoke (Matt. 11: 28–30).

"Wisdom" does not occur in the Johannine literature, but Jesus is proclaimed as the divine Logos or Word, who has become incarnate (John 1:1–18). This interpretation was served by the personification of wisdom (Prov. 8; Ecclus. 24; Bar. 3:9–4:4; Wisd. of Sol. 7–9). Some would claim that a *sophia* (Gk., "wisdom") myth, which comes to development in later Gnosticism, underlies this portrayal.

Wisdom is a serious concern in Paul's dealings with the Corinthians. Here he contrasts their worldly wisdom with the folly of the cross (1 Cor. 1:17–25; cf. 2:6–16) and affirms that Christ is the "wisdom of God" (1 Cor. 1: 24). The OT personification of wisdom seems to lie behind the christological development in Eph. 3:8–10 and Col. 1:15–20. In Col. 4:5 and

Eph. 5:15 the Christian is to walk in wisdom, and the "spirit of wisdom" (Eph. 1:17) is a gift from the Father.

The Letter of James as a whole bears striking resemblance to traditional wisdom literature because of its hortatory or parenetic nature. Wisdom is a gift to be asked from God, who will grant it (1:5). This is practical wisdom. While it is "from above," in contrast to the wisdom that is "earthly," it expresses itself in exemplary conduct; it is "peaceable, . . . full of mercy and good fruits" (3:13–18).

Many themes of biblical wisdom appear in the writings of the postapostolic age (e.g., *Didache; The Shepherd of Hermas*) and in Gnostic literature (e.g., *The Gospel of Thomas*). ***See also*** Ecclesiastes; Ecclesiasticus; Job, The Book of; Logos; Proverbs, The; Wisdom of Solomon, The.

Bibliography

Murphy, R. E. *Wisdom Literature.* Grand Rapids, MI: Eerdmans, 1981.

von Rad, G. *Wisdom in Israel.* Nashville, TN: Abingdon, 1972.

Wilken, Robert L., ed. *Aspects of Wisdom in Judaism and Early Christianity.* Notre Dame, IN: University of Notre Dame Press, 1975. R.E.M.

wisdom literature. ***See*** Wisdom.

Wisdom of Jesus, the Son of Sirach, the. ***See*** Ecclesiasticus.

Wisdom of Solomon, the, a poetic discourse composed in Greek by a Hellenistic Jew, probably in Alexandria, Egypt. The latest likely occasion for its composition is the persecution of Egyptian Jews under Gaius Caligula in A.D. 38–41, although dates as early as the last half of the first century B.C. have also been suggested. The writer assumes the identity of Solomon (cf. Wisd. of Sol. 7:1–14 and 8:17–9:18 with 1 Kings 3:6–9) to speak in praise of wisdom and righteousness and warn against the folly of oppression and idolatry. While the wicked may seem to prosper in this life, they are not aware, he claims, that they must face a future judgment (4:20) and even at birth in effect cease to be (5:13). Righteousness, on the other hand, is immortal (1:15). The book has survived as a part of the Septuagint, or Greek version of the OT. It is considered a part of the Apocrypha by Protestants and one of the deuterocanonical writings by Catholics. Its parts include:

I. A discourse on the justice of God (chaps. 1–5)
II. In praise of wisdom as a guide for life (chaps. 6–9)
III. Wisdom as a key to history, from Adam to Moses (chaps. 10–12)
IV. The origins and forms of idolatry (13:1–15:17)
V. A case in point: the Egyptians and the Israelites in the Exodus (15:18–19:22).

The initial discourse (chaps. 1–5) proclaims that "Because the Spirit of the Lord has filled the world, . . . no one who utters unrighteous things will escape notice, and justice, when it punishes, will not pass him by" (1:7–8). The ungodly, it argues, have made a covenant with death, and, assuming this life to be the whole of existence, they live as they please and oppress the righteous. With allusions to the Enoch tradition (4:10–15) as well as to Second Isaiah's suffering servant (5:1–8; cf. Isa. 52:13–53:12), the discourse speaks of a righteous one who was persecuted but, to the consternation of his persecutors, comes to be numbered among the heavenly beings (5:5) at the final judgment. A parallel account of martyrdom among Egyptian Jewry—perhaps even related to the same occasion if the Wisdom of Solomon is from the time of Caligula—is the account of the death of the righteous Eleazar in 4 Maccabees. The latter goes beyond the Wisdom of Solomon by appropriating the theme of vicarious atonement found in Isa. 52:13–53:12 (see 4 Macc. 6:27–30).

The second section of the Wisdom of Solomon picks up the story of Solomon, the king who chose wisdom (cf. 1 Kings 3:5–9), and advocates that all rulers should seek wisdom from beside the throne of God in order to rule wisely and justly. Wisdom is defined as God's spirit, intelligent, holy, the fashioner of all things, an emanation of God's glory, a reflection of eternal light, and an image of divine goodness (7:22–26). The passage clearly understands divine wisdom (cf. Prov. 8:22–31) in terms of Hellenistic philosophy, in a manner similar to Philo's *logos* or rationality of God, a subordinate agent responsible for creation. While the Christian idea of the Word *(logos)* of God in John 1:1–5, 14 is similar, neither the Wisdom of Solomon's divine wisdom nor Philo's *logos* are to be thought of as consubstantial or one with God, as in the Christian doctrine of the Trinity. In listing the various topics of natural and cosmological lore—both secret and manifest—taught to Solomon, Wisd. of Sol. 7:17–22 gives us a look into the scope of Jewish speculative wisdom of the age—a form of wisdom also appearing in apocalypses like *1 Enoch*, where an angel reveals cosmological secrets to the seer (see *1 Enoch* 41).

Chaps. 10–12 then use the theme of wisdom as a key to unlock the secrets of history from Adam to Moses. Curiously enough, it pictures wisdom as protecting Adam and delivering him from his transgression. Cain thus becomes the first to perish through folly (10:1–3). At the end of this section, the book shifts its attention from oppression to the idolatry of the Egyptians and Canaanites to demonstrate that "one is punished by the very things by which he sins" (11:16).

The writer then turns to an interesting discussion of the roots of idolatry that goes beyond the polemics found elsewhere to suggest several different theories of its origin (13:1–15:17). Led by the beauty of God's creation to worship the natural phenomena, humanity subsequently assumes that it can fabricate gods and begins to trust in the works of its hands. Another suggestion echoes that of Euhemeros (ca. 300 B.C.), who claimed that the gods were the result of the deification of heroes. The Wisdom of Solomon suggests that parents make statues to remember dead children and kings create images to impose their authority at a distance, so that out of the grief of parents and the vanity of kings spring the cults and secret mysteries of paganism.

The Wisdom of Solomon concludes (15:18–19:22) by turning to the Exodus to demonstrate the theory of poetic justice enunciated earlier (cf. 11:16). The ultimate irony is that the Egyptians, who had imprisoned the people of God, are really themselves captives of the power of darkness. In developing this idea, the writer explores the Hellenistic idea of the psychological self-punishment of the guilty (chap. 17; cf. Philo *Flaccus* 162–80). The radical drama of liberation is symbolized through the image of the transformation of nature, so that fire burns in water and yet has no power over human flesh (19:18–21).

While the Wisdom of Solomon claims to address alien kings in order to teach them how to rule wisely, its real audience is more likely the Hellenistic Jewish community in Alexandria and its purpose to support it in facing persecution and in resisting the dangers of idolatry in a pagan culture. ***See also*** Apocrypha, Old Testament; Ecclesiasticus; Immortality; Judgment, Day of; Persecution; Wisdom. D.W.S.

wise men, sages who appear in the biblical traditions within the context of an international

The three Magi, or Wise Men, of the Matthean account of Jesus' birth (Matt. 2:1–18) as depicted in the mosaics at San Apollinare in Classe, Ravenna, Italy, sixth century.

wisdom movement (on Egyptian, Persian, and Babylonian wise men, see Gen. 41:8; Esther 1:13; Dan. 2:12); the term applies also to the Magi in the infancy narrative of Matt. 2:1–18.

Wise men espoused wisdom in Israel in at least three settings: the tribe, the court, and the school. In each case, the wisdom shared was generally practical, concerned with knowledge about the principles governing the world and the life of the individual. The usual form of instruction was the proverb. Wisdom was based on reason rather than revelation, but reason enlightened by piety, for "the fear of the Lord is the beginning of wisdom" (Prov. 9:10). According to Deut. 1:13–15, wise men were selected for the tribes in the days of Moses to provide instruction in the law and from their own understanding and experience. A professional class of wise men developed (Jer. 18:18; Isa. 29:14) along with priests and prophets. Some served at the royal court to guide rulers and to preserve (as scribes) the sacred traditions (Jer. 8:8–9; 18:18). Finally, professional wise man provided instruction in schools they established (Ecclus. 51:23). Proverbs, Job, Ecclesiastes, Ecclesiasticus, and the Wisdom of Solomon are thought to have been composed by professional sages. The preeminent wise man in Israel's traditions was Solomon, whose "wisdom surpassed the wisdom of all the people of the east" (1 Kings 4:30). Occasionally, the traditions speak of the "wise woman" (2 Sam. 14:2; 20:16).

The Wise Men, or Magi (from the Greek root meaning "magic"), who appear in Matthew are said to be "from the East" (2:1), which could mean Arabia, Mesopotamia, or elsewhere. They are portrayed as astrologers, since they are guided by the star (2:2), and as Gentiles, since they do not know the scriptural prophecy concerning the location of the Messiah's birth (2:2–6). Popular traditions have portrayed them as three in number, although Matthew does not say so, because of the three gifts (2:11), and as kings in light of Isa. 60:3, although for Matthew they are astrologers. Later, postbiblical, traditions have also supplied names (Caspar, Melchior, and Balthasar). Epiphany ("manifestation," January 6) is the annual celebration, based on this account, of the manifestation of Jesus to the Gentiles, of whom the Wise Men are considered the first to pay him homage. ***See also*** Astrologer; Epiphany, Feast of; Proverb; Stars, Star of Bethlehem; Wisdom. A.J.H.

witch, a specialist in the manipulation of intangible powers of evil against people. Witches were commonly held to have existed in the ancient Near East and were doubtless known to the ancient Israelites. The OT contains lists of offenders of various kinds no longer precisely definable, but which probably included witches. The longest such list is found in Deut.

18:10–11, where the practitioners of various acts forbidden to the readers are said to flourish in the nations Israel is dispossessing. A slightly shorter list attributes such offenses to Manasseh (2 Kings 21:6; 2 Chron. 33:6), and several of the same terms are combined with the prophets and dreamers to whom Jeremiah tells the Judeans not to listen (Jer. 27:9). Pairs of such terms are found in Lev. 19:26; Isa. 47:9, 12 (of Babylon); and Mic. 5:11. A woman who practices one of these activities and who may be a witch is proscribed in Exod. 22:18, and Nah. 3:4 designates Nineveh such a woman. The so-called witch of Endor (1 Sam. 28) is a necromancer or medium. ***See also*** Magic and Divination. S.B.P.

withe. ***See*** Bowstring.

withered hand, hand viewed in 1 Kings 13: 1–6 as divine punishment; its restoration is seen as divine mercy. Jesus' healing of an atrophied hand on the Sabbath (Mark 3:1–6; Matt. 12:9–14; Luke 6:6–11) is portrayed as manifesting divine mercy that contrasts with rule-oriented attitudes seen as heartless. ***See also*** Disease and Healing; Miracles; Sabbath.

witness (Heb. *ayd;* Gk. *mahr'tōōs*), in the legal sphere, one who speaks from personal experience about what happened to oneself or another. This may occur at a trial (Deut. 17:6; Prov. 19:28; Mark 14:63) or a legal transaction (Isa. 8:2; Jer. 32:10). It is in this legal sense that two or three witnesses are called upon to corroborate a member's apostasy (Matt. 26:60; 2 Cor 13:1; Heb. 10: 28). Witnesses initiate the death sentence (Deut. 17:7; Acts 7:58). Bearing false witness is roundly condemned (Exod. 20:16; Prov. 12:17; Acts 6:13) and can bring severe reprisal (Deut. 19:16–21; Prov. 21:28). Sometimes a pillar or altar of rocks is built as a visible witness to a convenantal agreement (Gen. 31:44; Josh. 22:27, 34; Isa. 19: 19–20). God is frequently called upon as a witness to confirm a person's or nation's proper or improper conduct (1 Sam. 12:15; Rom. 1:9; Jer. 29:23; Micah 1:2).

The term takes on several specialized meanings in the NT, referring to a person present at the ministry, death, resurrection, and ascension of Jesus (Luke 24:48; Acts 1:22) or to one who attests to the truth about God (John 8:18; Rev. 1:5; 11:3). The "cloud of witnesses" in Heb. 12:1 compares the multitude who have suffered but retained their faith to the great crowd of spectators at a Greco-Roman athletic contest, whose presence spurs the contestants to give their best efforts. "Martyr" is derived from the same Greek word as "witness." ***See also*** Testimony. D.R.E.

wizard, one who practiced such things as magic, sorcery, divination, or necromancy. The word can refer to either a male or female. Israel was forbidden to consult them (Lev. 19:31; Isa. 8:19). They were banned as early as the reign of Saul in the late eleventh century B.C. (1 Sam. 28: 3), although Saul did consult a female diviner to raise up the ghost of Samuel (1 Sam. 28:9). King Josiah (639–609 B.C.) banned them (2 Kings 23: 24) after they had gained a foothold in the reign of Manasseh (697–642 B.C.; 2 Kings 21:6). ***See also*** Magic and Divination.

wolf, a member of the species *Canus lupus*, large members of the dog family. In biblical usage the literal reference to some such animal is found only in Isa. 11:6; 65:25; and John 10:12. All other usages are metaphorical references to the wolf's hunger (Gen. 49:7); destruction (Jer. 5: 6); or vicious, fierce, or ravenous conduct regarding the innocent (Ezek. 22:27; Hab. 1:8; Zeph. 3:3; Matt. 7:15; Matt. 10:16; Luke 10:3; Acts 20:29).

woman with a flow of blood, woman whose healing when she touched Jesus' garment is reported in the Gospels (Mark 5:25–34; Matt. 8: 20–22; Luke 8:43–48). Later tradition identifies her as "Veronica."

women, a topic in the Bible that can be approached in several ways. We can look at the legal status of women and the roles and functions of women in society, and we can look at portrayals of human and divine women.

The Legal Status of Women in the Patriarchal Period: The biblical world was undoubtedly androcentric and dominant actions were undertaken by men. Two separate social systems are portrayed in the Bible. The first, most probably older system is the extended family of the patriarchal period, which was patrilineal and patrifocal. The male head of the family had absolute rights of disposition over his children. A woman left her father's dominion to enter the dominion of the head of the family into which she was marrying. The most important social bond created by marriage was that between the father-in-law and the new daughter-in-law. In the event of the husband's death, the woman stayed in the new family, either as the mother of children, or being passed to another son in the institution of levirate marriage (Gen. 38:7–11; Deut. 25:5–10). In such a system, women had no direct access to power or decision making.

As the stories of the matriarchs of Israel show, the women of this period made their mark either by directly influencing their husbands (Sarah, Gen. 16:5; 21:10) or by trickery (Rebekah, Gen. 27; Rachel, Gen. 31). Although most women may have thrived, the system of patriarchal disposition lent itself to such abuses as the offer of Lot's daughters to the men of Sodom (Gen. 19:8) and of the women in Gibeah (Judg. 19:24), and the sacrifice of the daughter of Jephthah (Judg. 11).

Women in Classical Israel: Apart from the royal family, classical Israel consisted of nuclear rather than extended families. This change, heralded in Gen. 2:24, did not mean "emancipation" for women, who were still considered under the dominion of their husbands (Gen. 3:16). It should be noted, however, that in the family hierarchy, the sons of the family were not considered higher than the mother, and a son who rebelled against father or mother would be stoned (Deut. 21:18–21). Yet according to the formal laws of Israel women were clearly subordinate, although there does seem to have been a considerable diminution in the rights of the head of household to dispose of family members as compared with their rights during the patriarchal period.

Women owed sexual exclusivity to their present or future husbands. A woman was expected to be a virgin when she married. If she was seduced into premarital sex, the seducer had to pay the bride-price to her father, who could then decide whether to grant her to him in marriage (Exod. 22:16–17); if she was raped, the attacker had to pay the bride-price, was given the girl in marriage, and could not divorce her (Deut. 22:28–29). A man could accuse his bride of not being a virgin: if the allegation was "proved" by the lack of blood upon the bedclothes, the girl could be stoned for behaving wantonly while in her father's house (Deut. 22:13–21). Adultery, defined as sex by a married woman with a man not her husband, was punishable by death (Lev. 20:10; cf. John 8:3–7). A man could accuse his wife of adultery and thus cause her to undergo a solemn oath procedure attesting her innocence (Num. 5:11–31).

Divorce was the prerogative of the husband. It was somewhat regulated by Deuteronomy, which provided for a bill of divorce so that women could remarry (24:1), and which did not allow men to divorce wives that they had had to marry after rape (Deut. 22:28–29), or wives that they had unsuccessfully accused of not having been virgins (22:13–21). Although one cannot imagine that it would be pleasant to be married in perpetuity to a man by whom one has been raped or falsely accused, the purpose of these laws was clearly to prevent men from freely divorcing unloved wives in a socioeconomic system in which single divorced women would be at a disadvantage.

Women did not normally hold property, and the male head of the household could annul the vows of his women if he did so on the day he heard of them (Num. 30:5–8). The inferior status of women is indicated in economic terms by the valuation for the purpose of vows of women at thirty shekels and of men at fifty (Lev. 27:3–4). Women were to be isolated during the ritual impurity of their menstrual period (Lev. 15:19–24) and after childbirth (Lev. 12:1–8), when the period of impurity was double if the child was female.

Biblical narratives indicate, however, that the position of women vis-à-vis their husbands was not as weak as the laws envision. The Shunnamite woman was able to entertain Elijah without the prior consent of her husband (2 Kings 4:8–17), and Abigail could commandeer large amounts of her husband's supplies and bring them to David (1 Sam. 25). The biblical laws probably indicate the ideal male-female relations envisioned by their male formulators rather than reflect the social situation as it actually existed.

Nondomestic Roles: Certain women are shown in nondomestic roles, acting on the stage of history. There were two prominent royal women, Jezebel (1 Kings 18–19; 2 Kings 9:30–37) and Athaliah (2 Kings 11). Although these were considered villainesses since they were on the wrong side, they were strong and determined women; and Jezebel, in particular, was a woman of dignity and devotion. The "wise woman" of Tekoa came and convinced David by a parable, much in the manner of Nathan (2 Sam. 14). The "wise woman" of Abel (2 Sam. 20:16–22) negotiated for her town in warfare; the fact that Joab approached the city walls to speak to her and that she could convince the town to deliver Sheba may indicate that "wise woman" was a title of some town official rather than a descriptive adjective. Deborah was a political leader who also coordinated a war and was recognized as a leader both before and after the war (Judg. 4–5). Miriam was acknowledged as the leader of the women, who led the women in the victory song (Exod. 15:20–21). Although her powers could not be compared to those of Moses (Num. 12), she was remembered as one of the triumvirate of Exodus leaders (Mic. 6:4).

Both Deborah and Miriam were remembered as prophetesses and this seems to have been an acceptable, if rare, occupation of women. There was no surprise expressed that the prophet whom Josiah consulted on the occasion of the finding of a scroll of the law was the woman Huldah (2 Kings 22:14–20); the fact that she was a woman is passed in silence, probably an indication that women could be accepted and expected in this role. During the restoration period there is a mention of Nehemiah's opponent Noadiah the prophetess; again, her sex is treated as irrelevant (Neh. 6:14). Women did not have to choose between marriage and prophecy, for Huldah was clearly married, and Deborah may have been. Women also played some role in worship, particularly as singers (2 Chron. 35:25; Neh. 7:67).

The Image of Women: The image of the ideal wife is conveyed in Proverbs 31: she is strong, competent, able to succeed economically, but family-centered, always acting for the provision of her household. She is not sensual, but the woman of Song of Songs (where there is no mention of marriage) is portrayed in a noncondemnatory way as frankly erotic. Jael is portrayed as fierce (Judg. 4:17–21), although normally the ferocity of women is discounted (Isa. 19:16; Jer. 51:30). Above all, women are depicted (and perhaps feared) for being articulate: Abigail convinces David of appropriate action (1 Sam. 25), as does the wise woman of Tekoa (2 Sam. 14: 2–10); the wise woman of Abel convinces her city to follow her counsel (2 Sam. 20:16–20), Tamar attempts unsuccessfully to thwart a rape by logical arguments (2 Sam. 13), and both Samson's wife and Delilah talk him into revealing his secrets by nagging and verbal manipulation (Judg. 14:15–17; 16:4–17).

The Nonhuman Female: There is considerable dispute as to whether a goddess was worshiped in ancient Israel. In the Bible itself, however, there is no indication of a goddess. The most important nonhuman female image is the personification of the land and of the collectivity of the nation as "Lady Israel," which is found throughout the Prophets. The relationship of God to Israel can be depicted as a close marital bond by this image, first expressed by Hosea, and the "holy family" of Israel becomes God, "Lady Israel," and the people (see, e.g., Jer. 31). Furthermore, Israel's lack of faithfulness toward God can be expressed as the waywardness and adultery of a faithless wife (e.g., in Hosea). Sexual imagery becomes a vehicle for the expression of the passionate relationship between God and Israel. At the same time, in the condemnation of the wayward Israel in Ezekiel 16 one might detect misogynistic attitudes that are not proper to express directly: the Bible contains no openly misogynistic statements about the nature of ordinary women.

Another important nonhuman female image is "wisdom" in the book of Proverbs (e.g., 8–9). Wisdom is often found associated with goddesses in pagan cultures. There are several reasons for this. The intellectual's passion for learning is comparable to sexual passion and may even partially supplant it, so that "Lady knowledge" becomes pursued like a human woman. In addition, the woman caretaker seems all-knowing to the very young child, and this may have influenced the portrayal of knowledge as female. In the Bible, wisdom is seen as a creature rather than as a goddess, but as a companion to God.

Whether or not there were goddesses in the popular imagination, there is no doubt that they had no place in the prophetic mentality. Instead, the image of God undergoes a "feminization" from the early "man of war" of Exodus 15, and emphasis is placed on the nurturing, more motherly aspects of God (e.g., Hos. 11:1–4; Jer. 31:20; Isa. 46:3–4).

Women in the NT: While there are indications that patriarchal rules were continued among Christians (e.g., 1 Tim. 2:11–12; but cf. Eph. 5: 22–24, where submission of wives is under the rubric that all are to be subject to one another in Christ, v. 21, including husbands, v. 25, who are to imitate Christ's self-sacrificing love toward their wives), there are also indications that the role of women was influenced by the non-Jewish environment of early Christianity. Thus, in the discussion of divorce in Mark 10:2–12, it is assumed a wife can divorce her husband (v. 12) as was the case in Roman society. The frequent mention of women among the followers of Jesus (e.g., Luke 8:1–3; 23:55–56; 24:10), and the prominence of such women in the early church as Prisca (Rom. 16:3; 1 Cor. 16:19), the deaconess Phoebe (Rom. 16:1), and Mary (Rom. 16:6), among others, indicates they played an important role in the early church. Paul's refusal to let women speak in the Corinthian church (1 Cor. 14:34–36) was thus not universal, despite his claim to the contrary (1 Cor. 14:33b), and his statement that in Christ the religious distinction between the sexes had been eliminated (Gal. 3: 28) was observed in other churches (e.g., Phil. 4: 3).

New Approaches: Part of the feminist approach to the Bible has been to deal with the stories of women in two particular ways: "depatriarchalizing" and "remembering." "Depatriarchalizing" is the attempt to read the Hebrew text without the prism of intervening interpretations; when this is done it is clear that the biblical text is not so "patriarchal" or misogynistic as we would otherwise have believed. An example is the new reading of Eve. It is clear in the biblical text that at the creation, woman was not intended to be subordinate to man, for the Hebrew word *ezer*, normally translated "helper" (Gen. 2:18), is frequently used of God (e.g., Pss. 30:10; 54:4) and does not imply subordination. Eve is portrayed as the spokesperson for the couple, and during her talk with the serpent she presents theological arguments. She is never portrayed as wanton, or as tempting or tempted sexually, nor does the biblical author single her out for greater blame than her partner. This approach also concentrates on such passages as the Song of Songs, in which there is a clear lack of any patriarchal or condemnatory attitude toward women, thus indicating that the Hebrew Bible was not a monolithically patriarchal document.

"Remembering," the retelling the stories of patriarchal abuse of women as a hagiography and martyrology, provides not only documentation of patriarchy, but a sacred history to be remembered and thus overcome. Such female "victims" as Hagar, Jepthah's daughter, the concubine from Gibeah, and Tamar the daughter of David are remembered in this way. ***See also*** Marriage.

Bibliography

Bird, Phyllis. "Images of Women in the Old Testament." In *Religion and Sexism*. Edited by R. Reuther. New York: Simon and Schuster, 1974. Pp. 41–88.

Swidler, Leonard. *Biblical Affirmations of Woman*. Philadelphia: Westminster, 1979.

Trible, Phyllis. *God and the Rhetoric of Sexuality*. Philadelphia: Fortress, 1978. T.S.F.

wonders. ***See*** Sign.

woods, as a collective term, a stand of trees. A highly valued resource of the Holy Land, wood was used for the manufacture of everything from small everyday household items to the palaces of kings and temples and altars of the Lord. It was especially important as fuel for domestic hearths and for industrial installations such as kilns, metal smelters, and forges. It was also used for sacrificial fires (Gen. 22:7; Num. 19:6). Wood was valuable as an export commodity to countries whose timber resources were limited. Luxury woods such as ebony were imported into the Holy Land (Ezek. 27:15). Cedar was preferred for the construction of items meant to last, such as buildings and furniture. Pine, oak, cypress, and sycamore were also popular as construction materials. Noah used gopher wood (cypress) to build the ark (Gen. 6:14). Olivewood was used by Solomon for the cherubim carved on the oracle that housed the Ark of the Covenant (1 Kings 6:23) and the tabernacle was made of acacia wood *(shittah;* Exod. 26:15). Sturdy poplar and oak were favored implement hafts and roofing. The very light wood of the palm also had a broad range of uses. A great variety of woods existed in ancient times. However, these resources have become severely depleted over time as demand has continued to exceed supply. P.L.C.

wool, the fleece of a sheep, used in ancient Palestine for clothing (Lev. 13:47–48; Ezek. 34:3). White wool was one of the principal products traded by Damascus to Tyre (Ezek. 27:18). The wool of a hundred thousand rams had to be paid by Mesha, king of Moab, as tribute to Ahab, king of Israel (2 Kings 3:4). The color of undyed wool became a symbol of purity (Isa. 1:18) and whiteness (Dan. 7:9; Rev. 1:14).

word, that which is spoken, either by a human or by God. In the Bible, God's revelation is characteristically his speaking. Therefore, the expression "word of God" or "word of the Lord" holds an important place in the Bible and biblical religion, usually denoting God's revelation of his will and purpose. The Bible itself is not infrequently referred to as the Word of God by Christians. It is important to note, however, that the expression "word of God" in Scripture does not usually refer to the written word at all, but rather to God's or his emissaries' speaking and inspiration.

In the OT, God's word is central. God speaks and thus creates (Gen. 1:3, 6, 9, 11, 14, 20, 24, 26). He utters the words of the Decalogue (Exod. 20:1). Prophets hear and speak what the Lord has spoken to them (Isa. 1:2; 6:8–10), for they are primarily recipients and transmitters of the word of the Lord (Jer. 1:2). The NT usage of the term is subject to later and extrabiblical influences but can be seen as a development of the OT. Jesus preaches the word (Mark 2:2), and the gospel of Jesus Christ is called the word of God (Acts 4:31). Eventually, Jesus himself is said to be God's Word (John 1:1, 14; cf. Heb. 1:2). Thus, in both the OT and the NT, God's speaking and word are of fundamental importance. ***See also*** Creation; Logos; Prophet.

D.M.S.

world, the, a term used with various meanings in different parts of the Bible. The Bible as a whole has no unitary conception of "world" as such. The concept is somewhat diffuse, if present at all, in the OT, but, under the influence of Greek thought and Christian views of salvation, becomes much more distinct in the NT.

In the OT: In the OT, God is Creator of the heavens and the earth (Gen. 1:1–2:3). There is ample reflection on the Creator's role in establishing the earth and everything in, above, and under it (cf. Job 38), including humankind (cf. Gen. 1:26–28; 2:7, 15–24; Ps. 8:3–8). But an overall concept of the world in the sense of a universe is expressed in no particular term. A Hebrew word for earth or land *(eretz)* is sometimes used in the sense of world, or the world, but it is only rarely translated in this way in English versions (cf. RSV, Jer. 25:26). Another, rarer term *('olam)* is more frequently translated "world," but its meaning cannot always be clearly distinguished (e.g., Ps. 24:1, where the two terms appear in apparently synonymous parallelism). The idea of creation and humanity as God's handiwork is very much a part of OT theology, and indeed quite important, even though there is no single term corresponding to "world." Probably belief in God's fundamental and continuing role as Creator precludes any understanding of the world as an independent entity standing over against God. At the same time, the creation is in no sense an emanation or extension of the Creator so that it could be considered divine.

In Ancient Greek Thought: In ancient Greek thought and language, precisely what is absent in the OT becomes very important. The world or cosmos as an ordered system, the universe, was a phenomenon to be understood and explained as a whole. Far from being the result of God's creation by word or deed, it was conceived as an extention, projection, or at least a reflection of the ultimate principle of reality which, in the Hebrew tradition but also in Greek thought, was called God. The concept of the world in modern Western thought owes more to Greek philosophy than to the OT, as our use of such terms as "cosmic" and "cosmology" attests. The modern negative connotations of "world" (i.e., "worldly," "worldliness") owe something not only to Greek but also to early Christian thought and the NT.

In the NT: The NT employs three terms for world: the one most frequently attested *(kosmos)*, transliterated into English as "cosmos"; a second term meaning "inhabited world" (*oikoumenē*, from which "ecumenical" comes); and a term transliterated as "aeon" that has temporal connotations (*aiōn;* "this world/the world to come"). The most frequently used and most important is the first. Sometimes it is used in a neutral or even positive sense of the universe, as in Acts 17:24 ("God who made the world and everything in it"). In such cases, one is not far from what the psalmist expresses when he speaks of God, "who made heaven and earth, the sea, and all that is in them" (Ps. 146:6). Sometimes, "world" simply refers to humanity or the inhabited world (Rom. 1:8).

Frequently, however, "world" has significant theological connotations, particularly in the Pauline and Johannine literature. When Paul speaks of God in Christ reconciling the world to himself (2 Cor. 5:19), there is no doubt that, in his view, the world is in need of reconciliation.

Apart from God's revelation in the gospel, the world did not, through its wisdom, know God (1 Cor. 1:21). The world is the arena in which sin, which alienates people from God, reigns. Therefore, "the world" is a shorthand way of referring to the totality of humanity in the bondage of sin. This bondage is not a permanent condition, for through God's action in Christ "the form of this world is passing away" (1 Cor. 7:31). Thus Paul can urge the Romans not to be conformed to this world (Rom. 12:2). In this latter case, "world" translates the word that comes into English as "aeon," which can also mean "age." This overlap of terms suggests that, in Paul's thought, this world belongs to an old and transitory age or epoch. Thus the seer of Revelation writes that "the kingdom of the world has become the kingdom of our Lord and of his Christ, and he shall reign for ever and ever" (11:15).

In the Gospel of John, the world is the object of God's salvation in Christ (3:16; 12:47). Moreover, it is his creation through Christ (1:3, 10). Yet the world apart from Christ stands under judgment (16:8–11), hating Jesus' followers, who have been separated from the world and are not of the world (17:16). The dualism between God, Christ, and the disciples, on the one hand, and the world, on the other, is described in terms of a sharp antinomy. Disciples are urged to have nothing to do with the world, especially not to love it (1 John 2:15–17). At the same time, Jesus has explicitly not prayed for disciples to be taken out of the world (John 17:15). Even in the Fourth Gospel, the world continues to be God's, in creation and salvation. It is the same world that Matthew has in view as he portrays the risen Jesus sending his disciples to make disciples of all nations (28:19) or Luke as Jesus informs the disciples that they shall be witnesses from Jerusalem to the end of the earth (Acts 1:8).

The concept of world in the NT maintains roots in the OT, while it is importantly informed by Greek thought, even by the pessimism of late antiquity that was to emerge in Gnosticism. At the same time, the Christian conception of the world of humanity as alienated from God by sin and death is correlated with a view of the world in which it appears as both the arena and the object of God's salvation. In the NT, then, cosmology (the conception of the world) is fundamentally shaped and influenced by anthropology (the conception of humanity) and soteriology (the conception of salvation). ***See also*** Creation; Gnosticism; Salvation; Sin.

D.M.S.

worms, the members of the phylum Annelida as well as the larvae of numerous insects. Most biblical references are probably to larvae or maggots because of their association with death and decay (Job 7:5; 21:26; Isa. 14:11; Acts 12:23; Mark 9:48). Such a creature assaulted the vine of Jonah (4:7), and its appetite for wool is a metaphor for God's destruction visited on those who oppose his people (Isa. 51:8).

wormwood, a shrublike plant that belongs to the aster family and has a bitter taste. Numerous

Wormwood (*Artemisia judaica*).

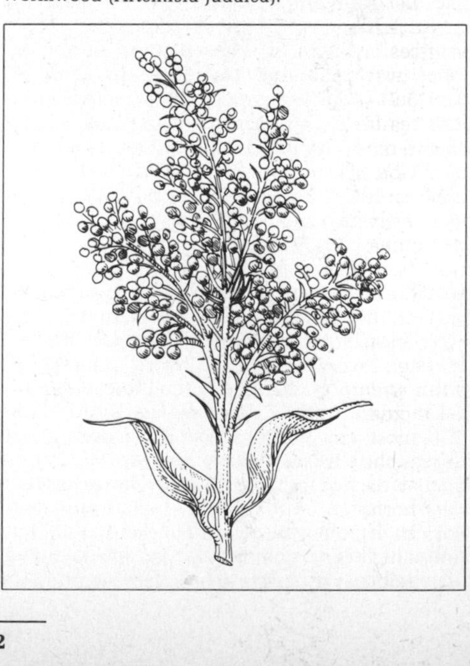

species of wormwood are found in Palestine, the most common being *Artemisia herba-alba*. The plant is often used as a metaphor for bitterness and sorrow (Prov. 5:4; Lam. 3:15, 19; Amos 5:7; 6:12). In Jer. 9:15 and 23:15, God's punishment of the people of Israel is described in terms of wormwood and poisoned water. Rev. 8:11 describes a star called "Wormwood" falling to earth, turning part of the waters into wormwood and killing many people.

worship, the attitude and acts of reverence to a deity. The term "worship" in the OT translates the Hebrew word meaning "to bow down, prostrate oneself," a posture indicating reverence and homage given to a lord, whether human or divine. The concept of worship is expressed by the term "serve." In general, the worship given to God was modeled after the service given to human sovereigns; this was especially prominent in pagan religions. In these the deity's image inhabited a palace (temple) and had servants (priests) who supplied food (offered sacrifices), washed and anointed and clothed it, scented the air with incenses, lit lamps at night, and guarded the doors to the house. Worshipers brought offerings and tithes to the deity, said prayers and bowed down, as one might bring tribute and present petitions to a king. Indeed the very purpose of human existence, in Mesopotamian thought, was to provide the gods with the necessities of life.

Although Israelite worship shared many of these external forms, even to calling sacrifices "the food of God" (e.g., Lev. 21:6), its essence was quite different. As the prophets pointed out, God could not be worshiped only externally. To truly honor God, it was necessary to obey his laws, the moral and ethical ones as well as ritual laws. To appear before God with sacrifices while flouting his demands for justice was to insult him (cf. Isa. 1:11–17; Amos 5:21–22). God certainly did not need the sacrifices for food (Ps. 50:12–13); rather sacrifice and other forms of worship were offered to honor God as king.

Sacrifice: Ideal Israelite worship is depicted in the Priestly instructions of Exodus, Leviticus, and Numbers. Its most prominent feature is sacrifice. Sacrifices were brought as gifts to God; the Hebrew term for cereal offering also means "present" (cf. Gen. 32:19, where Jacob offers a large present to Esau to win his favor) or "tribute" (e.g., 2 Sam. 8:2). In addition, the blood of the sin and guilt offerings was used to cleanse the sanctuary.

The most important part of any animal sacrifice was the disposal of the blood at the altar. Whether dashed against its sides, or smeared on its horns, this ritual act made the sacrifice valid; in fact, it distinguished sacrifice from mere slaughter. Leviticus 17 requires all animals eligible as offerings to be sacrificed, rather than simply slaughtered (see vv. 3–4). In addition, the animal's suet (the hard fat on the entrails) and kidneys belonged to God and therefore had to be burned on the altar (Lev. 3:16). Only a priest could perform these essential acts since only he could officiate at the altar (Lev. 3:5, 11). In exchange for his services, the priest received some portion of the sacrifice.

Cattle, sheep, goats, doves, and pigeons were the only kinds of animals that could be offered, and vegetable offerings used wheat, barley, olive oil, wine, and frankincense. All offerings were salted (Lev. 2:13; cf. Ezek. 43:24). Sacrificial animals had to be unblemished; that is, they could not be diseased or injured or castrated (see Lev. 22:17–25).

The burnt offering (Lev. 1) was the commonest and most general sacrifice. Appropriate for atonement or thanksgiving, its purpose, basically, was to win God's favor. It was probably the oldest kind of sacrifice (mentioned throughout the Bible) and played a major role in public worship (Num. 28–29) and rites of cleansing (Lev. 12:6, 8; 14:19, 22; 15:15, 30; 16:24). The animal offered had to be male (except birds). The animal was entirely burned on the altar, except for the hide, which went to the priest (Lev. 7:8).

The peace offering (Lev. 3) was brought when one wished to eat meat. It could be a bull or a cow, or a sheep or a goat (male or female). The officiating priest received the right thigh, while the animal's breast was shared by all the priests (Lev. 7:31–34). The person bringing the sacrifice received the rest of the animal, which had to be eaten within one or two days (Lev. 7:15; 19:6–8).

The peace offering was further subdivided, according to purpose, into the thank offering, free-will offering, and votive offering (Lev. 7:11–18). Psalm 107 mentions four occasions for which a thank offering would be appropriate: successful passage through the desert, release from prison, recovery from a serious illness, or surviving a storm at sea. The votive offering was given to repay a vow (cf. 2 Sam. 15:7–8), while the free-will offering needed no special occasion. These offerings were distinguished ritually, in that the thank offering required different kinds of breads to accompany it (Lev. 7:12) and had to be eaten in one day, whereas the votive offering and the free-will offering could be left over one night and finished on the following day. Under no circumstances could a sacrifice be eaten after the second day (Lev. 7:15–18).

The ordination offering was a special type of peace offering, whose blood was used as part of the ritual ordaining the high priest. Like the thank offering, it had a bread accompaniment and had to be eaten on the same day that it was offered (Exod. 29:19–28, 31–34; Lev. 8:22–29, 31–32).

The term "sin offering" is somewhat misleading. The purpose of this sacrifice (Lev. 4–5:13) was not to atone for any kind of sin, as the name seems to imply. Crimes against other people were dealt with by appropriate punishments that did not involve sacrifice, while deliberate crimes against God (done "with a high hand") could not be sacrificially atoned for at all (Num. 15:30–31). Rather, the sin offering was used to cleanse the sanctuary of impurity. For this reason it was regularly offered at festivals (Num. 28:15, 22, 30; 29:5, 11, 16, 19). As a private offering, the sin offering (or, more properly, the purification offering) was brought when a person had unwittingly violated a prohibition (Lev. 4:2) or for rites of cleansing (Lev. 12:6; 14:19, 22; 15:15, 30; 16:3, 5; Num. 6:14, 16), or when one had forgotten to cleanse oneself (Lev. 5:2–3), or failed to fulfill a vow (Lev. 5:4), or had not responded to a public adjuration (Lev. 5:1). When both the sin offering and the burnt offering were to be offered, the sin offering always came first; the altar had to be cleansed before other sacrifices could be offered on it (cf. Lev. 9:7–21; 14:19).

The animals used for the private sin offering varied with the status of the offender. The high priest or community as a whole offered a bull; a ruler offered a male goat, while a lay person brought a female goat or a ewe. The ritual also varied: when the community (or the high priest who represented it) had transgressed, the sanctuary itself was defiled; it was cleansed by sprinkling some of the bull's blood in front of the sanctuary veil and smearing it on the horns of the incense altar (Lev. 4:5–7, 16–18). The bull's meat could not be eaten, so it was burned outside the camp (Lev. 4:12, 21). In the case of an individual, whether ruler or commoner, only the outer altar was defiled. It was cleansed by smearing the blood of the goat or ewe on the altar's horns, and the priest received the meat of the animal. In certain cases there was a provision for a less costly sin offering if the person were poor (Lev. 5:7–13; 12:8; 14:21–22).

The guilt offering (Lev. 5:14–6:7) was brought when one had desecrated some holy thing (Lev. 5:14) or perjured oneself (Lev. 6:2–5). Its purpose was the reparation of damages. The sacrifice consisted of a ram, offered in a manner similar to the peace offering (Lev. 7:2–7), but with the necessary addition of the offerer's confession of guilt, and the repayment of damages, plus a twenty percent fine. The priest who offered it received the meat (Lev. 7:7). Uniquely, this sacrifice could even be paid for in money (Lev. 5:18; cf. 2 Kings 12:16). It was always a private sacrifice.

In two special cases, that of the healed leper being cleansed and that of a Nazirite whose vow was desecrated by accidental contact with a corpse (which made one impure), the guilt offering was a male lamb (Lev. 14:12, 21; Num. 6:9, 12). Furthermore, in the leper's case, the blood of the guilt offering was also applied to the person's extremities as part of the cleansing ritual (Lev. 14:12–14, 25).

The cereal offering (Lev. 2) was a vegetable counterpart to the burnt offerings. It could be raw, in which case frankincense was added, or cooked in various ways (baked, boiled, fried), but it could not be leavened or sweetened (Lev. 2:11). Oil was present whether the offering was cooked or raw. The flour used was usually wheat (semolina), but barley flour or parched grain could also be offered (Lev. 2:14). When the cereral offering was a poor person's substitute for the animal sin offering, the flour was offered dry, without oil and incense (Lev. 5:11; cf. also Num. 5:15). Only a handful of the cereal offering (together with all the incense, if present) was burned on the altar; the remainder went to the priest (Lev. 2:2–3; 6:14–16). The sole exception was the priest's cereal offering; it was entirely burned since a priest could not profit from his own offering (Lev. 6:23).

According to Numbers 15 the burnt offering and the peace offering were normally accompanied by cereal offerings (mixed with oil) and wine libations ("drink offerings"). The amount of grain and wine depended on the type of animal being offered: the larger the species, the more grain and wine.

Temple Ritual: The daily ritual was as follows: every morning, the ashes on the sacrificial altar were cleared off and the fire was stoked (Lev. 6:10–13), and the daily burnt offering, a yearling male lamb, plus its accompanying cereal and drink offerings, was offered (Lev. 6:8–13; Exod. 29:38–42; Num. 28:3–8). The high priest, dressed in his priestly garments (Exod. 28:29, 30, 35, 38), entered the sanctuary, trimmed the oil lamps, and offered a specially formulated incense on the incense altar inside (Exod. 30:7–9, 34–36). Outside, he would offer a special cereal offering, composed of wheaten cakes cooked on a griddle (Lev. 6:19–23). In the evening, a second lamb was offered like the morning one, and the high priest again entered the sanctuary to trim the oil lamps (Lev. 24:1–4; cf. 1 Sam. 3:3) and burn incense. He would also offer the second half of the high-priestly cereal offering.

Such was the daily routine. Every Sabbath day two additional lambs were offered, like the daily ones (Num. 28:9–10). Also, the high priest would replace the twelve loaves of bread (the Bread of Presence), which were arranged in two rows on the table inside the sanctuary, with frankincense on top (Lev. 24:5–9; cf. 1 Sam. 21:1–6). At the beginning of each month (the new moon) and at all the festivals the priests blew trumpets (Num. 10:8, 10) and additional sacrifices were offered, both burnt offerings and a sin offering (which was always a male goat; see Num. 28–29). Festival days (or the beginning and end of week-long festivals) were days of rest, like the Sabbath (Lev. 23:7–8, 21, 24, 27, 35, 36).

On the Day of Atonement the people rested and fasted, and the high priest, wearing special garments for the occasion, performed the Day of Atonement ritual (Lev. 16), which cleansed the sanctuary of all impurity. It consisted of two sin offerings, one for the high priest and one for the people, whose blood was brought not only into the sanctuary but into the inner shrine itself, the Holy of Holies, where the Ark of God was kept. The high priest entered the Holy of Holies only after placing a pan of burning incense inside, to make a screen of smoke between him and the Ark (Lev. 16:13). After cleansing the sanctuary, the priest laid his hands on a living goat and confessed the people's sins, thereby transferring those sins to the goat, which was then sent away into the wilderness.

Donations: In addition to these public and private sacrifices, offered at regular seasons or at will, the people donated a tenth portion of their produce to the sanctuary. This tithe was given to the Levites, in exchange for their work in guarding and transporting the tabernacle (Num. 18: 21–24). The Levites themselves gave a tithe of their tithe to the priests (Num. 18:26). Furthermore, the priests received the first fruits of all produce, including a sheaf of grain at the beginning of the harvest and two loaves of leavened bread at its end (Lev. 23:10–11, 17; cf. Num. 18: 11), the firstborn of all livestock (Num. 18:12–13, 15–17), and the first part of the processed produce (flour, wine, oil; cf. Num. 15:17–21; 18: 12).

People might also voluntarily donate items to the sanctuary, which would then belong to the priests. If persons or nonsacrificial animals were donated, only the monetary value was paid (Lev. 27:1–8). Land, tithes of vegetable produce, and nonsacrificial animals could also be redeemed from the sanctuary by the donor, by paying the value plus a twenty percent penalty (Lev. 27:13, 19, 31). An extreme form of dedication was "devotion," which, when applied to cities, involved complete destruction (Num. 21:2–3; cf. Josh. 6:17–21). Anything so devoted could not be redeemed; persons who were devoted had to be killed (Lev. 27:28–29).

A different kind of dedication of a person was the Nazirite vow (Num. 6). People who made this vow could not drink any alcoholic beverage or consume any product of the grapevine; nor could they cut their hair or shave. In fact, the hair was actually consecrated to God (Num. 6:5, 9, 18). The Nazirites were holy and hence were not supposed to become unclean. The vow was of limited duration, and at the end of the term a special ceremony was performed to return the Nazirite to ordinary, common status (Num. 6: 13–20).

Ritual Purity: Persons participating in worship had to be ritually clean. Contact with a corpse (Num. 19) or animal carcasses (Lev. 11:8, 24–25, 31, 39), sexual emissions (Lev. 15), giving birth to a child (Lev. 12), and leprosy (Lev. 13) all caused a person to become unclean in various degrees. An unclean person could not eat sacrificial meat (Lev. 7:20), enter the sanctuary, or even handle tithes or other items belonging to God (Lev. 12:4). Cleansing was effected by bathing and washing one's clothes. Certain more severe states of impurity required additional rites of cleansing and might take several days to complete. Although one was excluded from worship, being unclean was not a crime. Failure to cleanse oneself after the period of impurity had passed, however, was sinful and necessitated bringing a sin offering (Lev. 5:2–3), since (prolonged) impurity defiled the sanctuary (cf. Lev. 16:19; Num. 19:20).

To be eligible to officiate in the sanctuary, priests were required not only to be clean but unblemished (Lev. 21:17–23). Furthermore, they could not officiate while drunk (Lev. 10:9) or mourning (Lev. 10:6). They had to be properly dressed (Exod. 28:40–43); and before officiating at either the altar or inside the sanctuary they were to wash their hands and feet (Exod. 30:18–21; priests did not wear shoes: cf. Exod. 3:5; Josh. 5:15).

Other Versions of Ritual Procedures: The book of Deuteronomy presents a slightly modified (though much less detailed) version of the system described by the Priestly texts. The principal difference lies in Deuteronomy's insistence on a single sanctuary for the entire land of Israel to which all sacrifices were to be brought (cf. Deut. 12:5–14). As a result, Deuteronomy permitted profane slaughter of animals for meat (Deut. 12:15 vs. Lev. 17:2–4), since for many Israelites the distance to the sanctuary was too great (Deut. 12:20–21). There were also other, relatively minor differences in detail in Deuteronomy, regarding the Passover (Deut. 16: 2 vs. Exod. 12:5; Deut. 16:7 vs. Exod. 12:9), tithes (Deut. 14:22–29 vs. Num. 18), and the priests' share of sacrifices (Deut. 18:2 vs. Lev. 7:31–32).

Worship in Ezekiel's visionary temple (Ezek. 40–48) also differs somewhat from the Priestly system. For instance, Ezekiel calls for a purification of the temple on the first and seventh days of the first month, presumably in preparation for the Passover (Ezek. 45:18–20; cf. v. 21). He also mentions only a single daily burnt offering sacrificed each morning (Ezek. 46:13–15). Ezekiel's system was never actually put into effect, but it may reflect the thinking of certain priests of his time, since Ezekiel himself was a priest (Ezek. 1:3).

Patriarchal Period: Actual practice also deviated somewhat from the Priestly system outlined above. The worship practiced by the patriarchs knows nothing of all this. Their worship was simple and informal; they had no priests or temples. Rather, the patriarchs themselves offered burnt offerings at temporary altars they built themselves in the open (cf. Gen. 8:20; 12:7–8; 13:18; 22:13; 26:25). Jacob also worshiped by pouring a drink offering on a pillar he set up and by anointing it with oil (Gen. 28:18; 35:14). In later periods this would probably have been considered idolatrous (Exod. 23:24; Deut. 7:5; 1 Kings 14:22–23).

The Period of the Judges: During the time of the judges this type of worship continued to be practiced, but priests and temples were also known. Levites were considered the proper people to act as priests (Judg. 17:13), but individual Israelites continued to offer their own sacrifices on simple outdoor altars (Judg. 6:24–27; 13:19). There was a temple at Shiloh during this period, where the Ark of the Lord was kept until it was captured by the Philistines. The account in 1 Samuel 1–3 provides a glimpse of temple worship at this time: families such as Samuel's might go there for a yearly feast, where they would offer sacrifice like a peace offering and perhaps pray, as Hannah did. The priests there took a portion of the meat, whatever "the fork brought up" (1 Sam. 2:13–14). As in Leviticus the animal's suet belonged to God. It was to be offered first, after which the priest could take his share. Eli's sons were condemned for disregarding this rule and thereby slighting God (1 Sam. 2:15–17).

First and Second Temple Times: Even after Solomon built the Temple in Jerusalem and installed the Ark there, the people continued to offer sacrifices at local outdoor altars ("high places"). After Solomon's death (924 B.C.), Jeroboam, king of Israel, built two shrines of his own at Bethel and Dan, for fear that the people, by worshiping in Jerusalem, would defect to the Davidic kings there (1 Kings 12:26–29). Jeroboam also appointed non-Levites as priests (1 Kings 12:31) and moved the Feast of Booths to the eighth month (1 Kings 12:32–33). The writers of Kings and Chronicles condemned both Jeroboam's shrines and the "high places" as idolatrous (1 Kings 14:23; 15:14; 2 Kings 12:3; 14:4; 15:4). The "high places" were too often associated with the pillars and other pagan practices (1 Kings 14:23–24; 2 Kings 15:3–4), while Jeroboam's shrines were condemned for the calf images he erected at them (1 Kings 12:31; 14:9). Under Josiah these "high places" were finally eradicated, and worship was centralized at the Jerusalem Temple (2 Kings 23:5–9), as prescribed in Deuteronomy. However, the people continued to offer cereal offerings and incense privately, since there was no blood involved (cf. Jer. 41:4–5, where these offerings are brought to a ruined temple). This practice persisted even in Second Temple times.

An important element of Israelite worship hardly mentioned at all in the Pentateuch is that of prayer and song. Presumably the precise form of prayers or songs was not crucial to orthodox worship; the only recorded prayers are the priestly benediction (Num. 6:24–26) and prayers accompanying the offering of first fruits (Deut. 26:3–11) and tithes (Deut. 26:13–15). The Chronicler records the establishment of levitical singers in the Temple (1 Chron. 16: 4–6), and many of the Psalms were probably composed for use in Temple worship. Individuals would naturally resort to the Temple to pray (cf. 1 Sam. 1:9–18; 1 Kings 8:22; 27–30), but prayer was a private matter and could be done anywhere. Fasting, too, was a private matter (e.g., 2 Sam. 12:16, 21–23), except on the Day of Atonement or when a special day of fasting was proclaimed (Joel 1:14; Ezra 8:21; 2 Chron. 20:3).

It is difficult to ascertain to what extent the rituals performed in Solomon's Temple corresponded to the instructions of the Pentateuch. For instance, there may have been only one daily burnt offering (cf. Ezek. 46:13–15) offered every morning, rather than two, with only a cereal offering presented in the evening (2 Kings 16:15; cf. Ezra 9:5; Ps. 141:2; Dan. 9:21; where the "evening sacrifice" is literally the evening cereal offering). In Second Temple times, the Pentateuchal instructions were followed in detail in Temple worship. In addition, new festivals were added, two of which are mentioned in the Bible: Purim (Esther 9:20–22) and the Feast of Dedication (Hanukkah; cf. John 10:22–23).

A completely new institution of worship was added in the Second Temple period: the synagogue. Its origins are unknown, but it probably began among the exiles, who were otherwise unable to worship, since they were too far from the Temple. The people gathered at the synagogue on the Sabbath to pray and read the Bible, and the Scripture reading was interpreted and expounded in a short sermon (cf. Luke 4: 16–29).

Early Christian Worship: In the NT "worship" still means primarily "bow down" but the word also translates Greek terms signifying service or piety. However, the external form of worship differs radically from that of the OT. Since the death of Christ constituted the perfect sacrifice, no more sacrifices were needed (Heb. 9:11–12, 24–26). Indeed, the entire institution of Temple, priesthood, sacrifice, and cleansing ritual became obsolete. Rather, the church itself, that is, all the believers, was at once temple and priesthood, inhabited by the Holy Spirit (1 Cor. 6:19; Eph. 2:21–22; 1 Pet. 2:9).

As a result, Christian worship was internal rather than external. Only three rituals are known from the NT: baptism, communion, and the laying on of hands. However, for none of these do we have any explicit instructions describing how they are to be performed. Baptism initiated a person into the church; it consisted simply of immersion in water and was probably accompanied by a reference to Jesus, in whose name the person was baptized. The laying on of hands was associated with receiving spiritual gifts (Acts 8:17) or a special commission (Acts 13:2–3). Only communion was celebrated on a regular basis, to commemorate Jesus' death and as a joyous anticipation of the future kingdom feast (cf. Mark 14:25; 1 Cor. 11:26). It consisted of a simple meal of bread and wine over which a blessing was spoken (1 Cor. 10:16).

The first day of the week was a favorite day for Christian assembly (Acts 20:7; cf. 1 Cor. 16:2), though early Christians might also have met daily (Acts 3:46). At these meetings, there would be teaching, exhortation, singing, praying, prophesying, reading letters, and the "breaking of bread" (probably communion; Acts 2:42, 46; 15:30; 1 Cor. 14:26; Col. 4:16). Above all, Christian worship was characterized by great joy and thanksgiving (cf. 1 Thess. 5:16–18). ***See also*** Feasts, Festivals, and Fasts; Patriarch; Priests; Tabernacle; Temple, The; Temples. S.R.

wrath, a word denoting the active feeling of God against sin, expressing in human categories an important attribute of God: that he is holy and righteous and rejects everything that is not. This rejection is real, manifesting itself in actual situations such as the destruction of Sodom and Gomorrah (Deut. 29:23), the chastisement of Moses for his reluctance to obey (Exod. 4:14), and even the death of Uzzah for touching with profane hand the Ark of God (2 Sam. 6:7). The wrath of God is thus a divine reaction to human provocation, not an arbitrary passion or animosity. Even in this reaction God is "slow to anger"; the OT emphasizes that he is "merciful and gracious ... abounding in steadfast love" (Ps. 103:8; Joel 2:13). In the NT, the angry reaction of Jesus against those who desecrated the Temple (John 2:13–17) bears the characteristics of divine wrath. Wrath is also an essential part of Paul's theology: he often mentions that human disobedience and transgression result in the coming of the wrath of God (Rom 1:18; 2:5; 2:8; 5:9; 9:22; Eph. 2:3; 5:6; Col. 3:6; 1 Thess. 1:10). The overpowering theme of the NT, however, is the love of God, not his anger. The NT can say that "God is love" (1 John 4:8); the mission of Jesus was to take the wrath of God upon himself. That is the meaning of salvation in the NT: since the time when Jesus was sent into the world, only those who do not believe and do not obey have to worry about the wrath of God. ***See also*** Judgment, Day of; Mercy. S.B.

wrestle, to vie with someone physically. Jacob wrestled with a messenger of God during the night and emerged triumphant but injured (Gen. 32:24, 25; cf. Hos. 12:5). The idea was not restricted to physical conflict; see, e.g., Rachel's struggle with Leah (Gen. 30:8) and the statement that Christians wrestle against celestial spiritual forces (Eph. 6:12). J.L.C.

writing, the transcribing of human language into visible form. Writing was invented in the ancient Near East sometime before the beginning of the third millennium B.C. It appeared first in southern Mesopotamia and soon afterwards in the Nile Valley. Various systems of writing developed, but all eventually gave way to the alphabet. Alphabetic writing was an important part of the culture of ancient Israel and the early church, and there are numerous references to writing and written documents in the Bible.

Writing Systems of the Ancient Near East: By the latter centuries of the fourth millennium B.C. a pictographic writing system was in use along the lower Euphrates. It evolved into the cuneiform script of the Sumerians, which the Semitic-speaking inhabitants of Mesopotamia inherited. Cuneiform, therefore, became the writing system of both the Babylonians and Assyrians, and from them it was borrowed and adapted to the languages of several other peoples, including the Hurrians, the Hittites, and the Urartians. Characteristically, cuneiform or "wedge writing" was impressed on wet clay tablets using a reed stylus with a wedge-shaped tip. The individual signs, composed of combinations of wedges, included both ideograms (signs representing entire words or ideas) and phonograms (signs representing sounds). The phonograms were syllabic, representing combinations of vowels and consonants. The system as a whole was extremely complex and cumbersome in

Cuneiform tablet from Ebla, ca. 2400 B.C.

SINAITIC SCRIPT
DESCRIPTION OF SIGN
CANAANITE SCRIPT OF 13TH CENT. B.C.
CANAANITE SCRIPT OF ca. 1000 B.C.
SOUTH ARAB SCRIPT OF IRON AGE
MODERN HEBREW SCRIPT
PHONETIC VALUE
OX-HEAD
HOUSE
FISH
MAN PRAYING
FENCE?
DOUBLE LOOP
PALM OF HAND
"OX-GOAD"
WATER
SERPENT
EYE
THROW STICK
BLOSSOM
HUMAN HEAD
BOW
MARK OF CROSS

HEBREW NAME
PHOENICIAN SCRIPT OF 8TH CENT. B.C. BAAL LEBANON KARATEPE
OLD GREEK SCRIPT OF 8TH CEN. B.C.
HEBREW CURSIVE OF ca. 600 B.C.
GREEK NAME
MODERN GREEK SCRIPT
MODERN ROMAN SCRIPT
ALEPH
BETH
GIMEL
DALETH
HE
WAW
ZAYIN
HETH
TETH
YOD
KAPH
LAMED
MEM
NUN
SAMEKH
AYIN
PE
TSADHE
QOPH
RESH
SHIN
TAW
ALPHA
BETA
GAMMA
DELTA
EPSILON
ZETA
ETA
THETA
IOTA
KAPPA
LAMBDA
MU
NU
XI
OMICRON
PI
RHO
SIGMA
TAU

The development of the alphabet, from its origin to modern scripts; from a chart by Frank M. Cross, Jr.

comparison to the alphabetic system that eventually displaced it. A Mesopotamian scribe was obliged to undertake a long and difficult apprenticeship.

Egyptian writing may have emerged under indirect influence from Mesopotamia. In Egypt, however, the pictorial character of the early script was retained. This was true, at least, of hieroglyphic, the pictographic writing used for monumental inscriptions. As in the case of the cuneiform signs, the individual hieroglyphs included both ideograms and phonograms. In this case, however, the phonograms were alphabetic, representing one or more consonantal sounds, rather than syllabic. There were two cursive derivatives of hieroglyphic, called hieratic and demotic. Hieratic seems to have been developed in very early times, but the oldest demotic documents come from the end of the eighth century B.C. Like his Mesopotamian counterpart, an Egyptian scribe had to study for many years to master the complexities of the writing system.

The alphabet was invented somewhere in Syro-Palestine in the first half of the second millennium B.C. It was based on a consonantal principle that suggests an initial Egyptian influence. In contrast to Egyptian hieroglyphic, however, the alphabet employed no ideograms, and each of its phonograms represented a single consonantal sound. The signs were pictographic at first, but they soon evolved into abstract, linear shapes. The earliest undisputed examples of alphabetic writing date to the end of the Middle Bronze Age, ca. 1550 B.C. These are the so-called Proto-Sinaitic inscriptions, graffiti scratched on stone by Asiatic laborers in an Egyptian turquoise-mining community at modern Serabit el-Khadem in the southwestern area of the Sinai Peninsula. The alphabet was in general use in the city-states of Syria and Palestine during the Late Bronze Age (ca. 1550–1200 B.C.), and in the first millennium specialized national or region branches developed. Among these was the Hebrew alphabet, which was used in Israel and Judah until the Exile (586 B.C.). Another branch, which developed in the Aramean states of southern and central Syria, was adopted along with the Aramaic language for the official use of the Assyrian, Babylonian, and Persian empires. The Aramaic alphabet eventually replaced most local systems throughout the imperial region. After the sixth century B.C. most Jewish literature was written with the Aramaic script.

Sometime before the eighth century B.C. the Greeks learned the alphabet from the Phoenicians. By adding vowel signs to the purely consonantal signs of the Phoenicians, they improved the system and produced an alphabet that is the direct ancestor of the one we still use today.

Although the alphabet coexisted for centuries

with the ancient systems of Mesopotamia and Egypt and several other forms of writing, it eventually triumphed over them all. This was at least in part a consequence of its economy and utility. It was much simpler and more flexible than its competitors, and it made widespread literacy possible for the first time. Given the tenacity with which traditional writing systems are maintained, however, it seems unlikely that the obvious advantages of alphabetic writing would have been enough to displace the older systems in the absence of other factors. Of these the most important was probably its selection as the primary medium of international communication for five empires. The Assyrians adopted the Aramaic alphabet for use in the imperial chancelleries, establishing a convention that the Babylonians and Persians inherited, and in the Hellenistic and Roman worlds the Greek and Latin alphabets held sway.

Writing Materials: Various materials served as writing surfaces. Inscriptions intended to be permanent were most often incised in stone. Thus we have stone stelae and monumental inscriptions in Mesopotamian cuneiform—with wedges engraved in stone to imitate those impressed in clay—and Egyptian hieroglyphic. Many alphabetic texts cut in stone have been found in Syria and Palestine, and there are references in the Bible to stone inscriptions (Josh. 8:32) and their imperishability (Job 19:24). Recent discoveries, however, suggest that during the period of the Israelite and Judean monarchies there was a practice of preparing stone surfaces with plaster to receive monumental texts written with ink (cf. Deut. 27:2–3). Such texts survived only in exceptional circumstances, and this may be a chief reason that relatively few public documents from this period have been discovered.

The "tables" Moses brought down from Mount Sinai were made of stone (Exod. 31:18), but the writing tablets mentioned in Isa. 30:8 and Hab. 2:2 were probably incised sheets of wood (covered with wax, cf. Luke 1:63) or metal. Exactly what the "large tablet" of Isa. 8:1 was is disputed. A silver prayer scroll from the First Temple period (tenth–sixth centuries B.C.) has recently come to light in Jerusalem, and the Copper Scroll from Qumran shows that the practice of preserving important documents on sheets of soft metal persisted. Although a chisel was required to execute a stone inscription, metal or waxed wood could be incised with a simple stylus made of iron or tipped with a hard substance like emery (the "point of diamond" of Jer. 17:1). The "iron pen and lead" of Job 19:24 may be a reference to writing on a sheet of lead with an iron stylus or possibly to filling letters engraved in stone with molten lead.

The general needs of correspondence and record keeping in ancient Israel were served by specially prepared leather and papyrus, and their use continued into NT times. The deed of sale executed by Jeremiah in prison, for example, was probably a sheet of papyrus, folded, sealed, and stored in a ceramic jar (Jer. 32:11–14). There is a reference to the use of "paper [i.e., papyrus] and ink" for letter writing in 2 John 12, but during the Roman period papyrus was replaced in many of its uses by parchment, a refined type of leather, because of its greater durability. Leather, moreover, seems to have been the preferred material for sacred documents. The Qumran scrolls suggest that this was the case in Hellenistic and Roman times, although portions of the Bible recorded on papyrus have survived from the same period. According to the Letter of Aristeas (176 B.C.) leather was mandatory for Torah scrolls used in public worship. For both leather and papyrus the writing medium was ink (cf. Jer. 36:18), which was usually black, derived from soot, although both red and yellow ink are also known. The ink was applied with a brush made from a frayed reed and shaped with a penknife, which could also be used to cut leather (cf. Jer. 36:23). In imitation of Egyptian practice these materials were kept in a "writing case," a scribal palette equipped with slots for pens and wells for ink and worn at the belt (Ezek. 9:2, 3, 11).

Notes and informal records were written with ink on broken pieces of pottery. Numerous ostraca, as these texts are called, have survived from biblical times, including such well-known collections as the Samaria ostraca of the ninth century B.C., the Lachish letters of the early sixth century, and a recently discovered group of ostraca from Arad.

The Uses of Writing: Writing was put to numerous uses in ancient Israel. One of these was record keeping. There is mention in the Bible of the collection and preservation of various kinds of information (e.g., Josh. 18:8–9). Surviving inscriptions, such as the Samaria ostraca, show that economic transactions were recorded in writing, and there are references in the Bible to the execution of several kinds of legal documents, such as deeds of purchase (Jer. 32:10), writs of divorce (Deut. 24:1, 3), and so on.

Another common use of writing was correspondence. Letters from several periods of Israelite history have been recovered by archaeologists. The Bible makes frequent reference to the official correspondence of the Israelite and Judean courts, mentioning letters sent by David (2 Sam. 11:14), Jezebel (1 Kings 21:8), Jehu (2 Kings 10:1), and Hezekiah (2 Chron. 30:1), in addition to letters received from the king of Syria (2 Kings 5:5), the Assyrian Rabshakeh (2 Kings 19:14; Isa. 37:14), and Sennacherib himself (2 Chron. 32:17). The fortunes of the Jewish community after the return from Exile are described largely in terms of correspondence with the Persian court (Ezra 4–7). Many of the NT books are themselves letters, written by Paul and others to distant churches.

In addition to its common uses writing served certain ceremonial functions, both secular and religious. These included the erection of victory stelae (1 Sam. 15:12; 1 Chron. 18:3; cf. 2 Sam. 8:3), which in most cases would have borne inscriptions, and public and personal memorials of various kinds (Exod. 17:14; 2 Sam. 18:18). Here, too, belongs the commitment of collections of ritual regulations to writing (Exod. 24:4; Deut. 31:24; Josh. 8:32; etc.) and the recording of prophetic sayings for the instruction of later generations (Isa. 8:1, 16; 30:8; Jer. 30:2). Ritual and magical uses of writing are hinted at by passages like Num. 5:23–24 and Jer. 51:59–64 (cf. Ezek. 2:8–3:3).

Literacy: Although it is difficult to estimate how much of the ancient community could read and write, it seems clear that Israel was a literate society from at least the time of the settlement in Palestine (late twelfth century B.C.). It is surprising to learn that the "young man from Succoth" of Judg. 8:14, apparently a common soldier, was able to write the names of seventy-seven men, but the existence of some degree of literacy in Palestine during the period of the judges is attested by inscriptional remains, including a scribal practice tablet with a crude abecedarium scratched on it. The so-called Gezer calendar, an inscribed limestone plaque from the tenth century B.C., was probably also used for scribal practice.

Isaiah's allusion to a child's ability to "write down" (the number of) a few trees (Isa. 10:19) might be taken to suggest that literacy had become widespread by the eighth century, but this impression is contradicted by the reference in Isa. 29:11 to "one who can read," which shows that such ability was not a general accomplishment. In Isa. 8:1 Isaiah is commanded to write on a tablet, but this does not necessarily mean that the prophet himself could write: Jeremiah, when commanded to write down his oracles, dictated them to Baruch (Jer. 36:2, 4). Note also that when the scroll produced by Baruch was taken to Jehoiakim, the king had it read to him by a member of his court (Jer. 36:20). All of these things suggest a pattern of limited literacy in ancient Israel. In a given generation there may have been many who could read and write, but the general population probably relied on a fairly small number of individuals trained in scribal schools or families (cf. 1 Chron. 2:55).

The situation reflected in the NT is much the same. Paul apparently dictated his letters to a companion (e.g., Rom. 16:22; cf. Gal. 6:11), although he may have concluded them with a benediction in his own hand (2 Thess. 3:17). Such letters were intended to be read aloud to the assembled Christians rather than read individually and were often exchanged among churches (e.g., Col. 4:16). Aside from Luke 1:3, which could also mean the author dictated the text, the Gospels give no indication whether they were written down or dictated by their authors.

Bibliography

Diringer, D. *The Alphabet*. New York, 1948.

Driver, G. R. *Semitic Writing from Pictograph to Alphabet*. 3d ed. London: Oxford: Oxford University Press, 1976.

Gelb, I. J. *A Study of Writing*. 2d ed. Chicago: University of Chicago Press, 1963.

P.K.M.

Writings, the. *See* Hagiographa.

An ostracon from Arad written on in ink (ca. 600 B.C.) mentions "The House of YHWH."

Opposite: Stairway excavated at Tell es-Sa'idiyeh, a proposed site of biblical Zarethan. The stairway was probably roofed and led from the city on top to a water source at the bottom.

XYZ

X

Xerxes (zuhr'ksees), the name of several rulers of the Persian Empire. **1** Xerxes I, who ruled 486–465 B.C. and is known from Greek history for his attempts at conquering the Greek mainland. He is probably the ruler referred to in Ezra 4:6 (there called Ahasuerus, from the Persian form of his name), a passage out of chronological context, who received a complaint against the Jews who had returned to Palestine from the Exile. In Dan. 9:1, an Ahasuerus is mentioned as the father of Darius the Mede (but see 2). The Persian ruler of the book of Esther (1:1, etc., there also called Ahasuerus) is presumably based on Xerxes I, but as presented in Esther he is more a legendary than a historical figure. The Greek translators of the Septuagint (and cf. Josephus *Antiquities* II. 184) consistently render Ahasuerus as Artaxerxes, however. **2** Xerxes II, 425 B.C., who succeeded Artaxerxes I (the son of Xerxes I) but was assassinated almost immediately. He is probably not referred to in the Bible.
P.R.A.

Crown Prince Xerxes (who became Xerxes I) standing behind the Persian ruler Darius I, whom he succeeded in 486 B.C.; Persepolis relief.

Y

Yahweh (yah'way). ***See*** Names of God in the Old Testament.

Yahwist, the name given the earliest literary source underlying the books of Genesis through Numbers. The siglum given the source is "J," which is derived from the German spelling of the name of God, *Jahveh* (in English usually spelled Yahweh), used throughout this source. The Yahwist source is usually dated around 950 B.C. Among its characteristics are bold anthropomorphisms; positive attitudes toward agricultural civilization, the state, and kingship; a mixture of nationalistic and universalistic concerns; and a style that exudes charm, simplicity, and clarity. The anonymous writer wove together the oral and written stories to assist a people in discovering not only the outer history of names and places but also the inner story of God's work among them. Examples of the Yahwist writing are found in Gen. 2:4b–4:26; 32:22–32; Exod. 1–22; and Num. 24:1–25. ***See also*** Sources of the Pentateuch.
K.H.R.

Yam Suph (yahm so͞of), term referring to body of water through which the Israelites escaped at the Exodus, either a marshy area or a body of water south(east) of the Promised Land, perhaps the Gulf of Aqabah. The usual Septuagint equivalent is "Red Sea," but 1 Kings 9:26 has "ultimate sea" (taking Hebrew *swp, suph,* as *soph,* "end"; *yam* means "sea"). The modern translation "reed sea" is possible (since *suph* means "reeds"), but disputed. Apart from the expression *ym swp,* Hebrew *suph* occurs as a place name (Deut. 1:1) and term for "reeds" or "weeds" (Exod. 2:3, 5; Isa. 19:6; Jon. 2:6); it may even imply "final danger" *(soph)* in Jon. 2:6.

The original meaning of the Hebrew *ym swp* is disputed. If it named or described a marshy area across which the Israelites escaped from Egypt, then "reed sea" could have been meant. If it identified a distant sea in the south (the present Red Sea and its extensions on either side of the Sinai peninsula) that came to be regarded as the location of the Exodus, "ultimate sea" may have been intended. The expression may echo Moses' escape from the reeds *(swp)* of the Nile canal in Exod. 2:1–6. First Moses and then the people are rescued from mortal danger, *swp,* by the Lord (cf. the *swp,* "weeds," wrapped around Jonah's head after he sank in the sea, Jon. 2:6).
K.G.O.

Yarmuk (yahr'muhk), **Wadi el-,** the major eastern tributary of the Jordan River, which it enters just south of the Sea of Galilee. Before modern diversion of the water of the Yarmuk and its sources for irrigation it was a perennial stream with an outflow nearly equal to that of the Jordan. Its gorge cuts through basalt of volcanic origin which overlies strata of chalk and limestone. This valley is a natural barrier and was the boundary between Bashan and Gilead in the Iron Age (1200–600 B.C.). Today it forms part of the border between Syria and Jordan. The modern Syrian border town of Deraa just north of the Yarmuk is located on the site of and preserves the ancient name of Edrei, where according to Num. 21:33–35 the Israelites under Moses defeated the forces of Og, king of Bashan. Curiously, the Yarmuk is not mentioned in the Bible, although archaeological surveys have shown that settlements existed in and near it from prehistoric times. In the Neolithic period (10,000–4000 B.C.) the wadi gives its name to a distinctive "Yarmukian culture." In the Roman period several of the cities of the Decapolis were located near the Wadi Yarmuk, including Gadara, Abila, and perhaps Dion. ***See also*** Decapolis; Edrei. M.D.C.

year. ***See*** Time.

yodh (yohd), the tenth consonant of the Semitic alphabet (thus, also "ten" in postbiblical Hebrew) which, like "y" its equivalent, also functions as a semivowel when preceded by a vowel. Both the letter's name and its earliest Phoenician representation derive from *yad,* "hand." When the Aramaic cursive replaced the older Hebrew script, this letter became the smallest in the alphabet; as such, referred to by its Greek name, *iota,* it underlies the famous "jot"of Matt. 5:18 (KJV).

yoke, a wooden or iron frame for joining two oxen or other draft animals so they can pull a plow, cart, or other heavy load. A yoke generally consisted of a single crossbar with leather or rope nooses or wooden rods that were fastened around the animals' necks (cf. Jer. 27:2). The crossbar was attached to a shaft that pulled the load (cf. Deut. 21:3; 1 Sam. 6:7; 11:5; 1 Kings 19:19). A yoke of oxen might refer to a pair of oxen (1 Sam. 11:7; 1 Kings 19:21; Luke 14:19). A "yoke" of land, usually translated "acre," refers to the amount of land a yoke of oxen could plow in one day (1 Sam. 14:14; Isa. 5:10).

Yoke was used figuratively as a symbol of hardship, submission, or servitude. Jeremiah wore a yoke to symbolize his message that Judah should submit to Babylon (Jer. 27–28). When the people of Israel considered whether or not they would accept Rehoboam as king, they asked him to lighten the heavy yoke, i.e., the hard service, that his father, Solomon, imposed on them (1 Kings 12:1–11). Yoke may refer to other burdens or responsibilities, such as sin (Lam. 1:14), service to God (Lam. 3:27; Jer. 2:20; 5:5), slavery (Ecclus. 33:26), or obedience to Torah (Acts 15:10) or Christ (Matt. 11:29–30). M.A.S.

yokefellow (Gk. *syzygos*), either a personal name or an adjective. "Syzygos" is referred to in Phil. 4:3 ("true yokefellow") as one who is to help bring an end to a disagreement between two women in the church at Philippi. The identity of the "yokefellow" has provoked widespread speculation among commentators. Among the more exotic views is that the reference is to Paul's (hypothetical) wife or to an unknown amanuensis. Others regard it as a proper name for one of Paul's co-workers. Perhaps the yokefellow was some unnamed coworker of Paul, possibly even someone elsewhere referred to by name (e.g., Timothy, Titus, possibly even Epaphroditus, see Phil. 2:25–30; 4:18). ***See also*** Epaphroditus; Paul; Philippi; Timothy; Titus. A.J.M.

Yom Kippur (yahm kip'uhr). ***See*** Atonement, Day of.

Y-R-S-L-M, or more properly y-r-sh-l-m, letters that, in Hebrew, indicate Jerusalem. They are found on various artifacts from Palestine, including jar handles and seals. The spelling y-r-sh-l-y-m is found on coins of the first Jewish revolt (ca. A.D. 66–70) and y-r-w-sh-l-m on coins of the second revolt (ca. A.D. 132–135). ***See also*** Money; Seal.

Z

Zaanannim (zay-ah-nah'nim), a point on the southern border of Naphtali with Issachar (Josh. 19:33) where Heber the Kenite pitched his tent (Judg. 4:11) in which the Canaanite king Sisera was subsequently slain (Judg. 4:17–21). It was most likely modern Khan et-Tujjar some five miles west of the Sea of Galilee.

Zabad (zay'bad; a shortened name, Heb., "He [God] has given," or "gift"; cf. the full names Zebadiah, Zabdiel, and related names Zabdi, Zabud, and Zebidah). **1** A descendant of Sheshan in the line of Judah (1 Chron. 2:36–37; cf. v. 31). **2** An Ephraimite of the Shuthelah lineage (1 Chron. 7:21). **3** One of David's "mighty men" (1 Chron. 11:41; cf. 2 Sam. 23:24–39). **4** One of the murderers of King Joash according to 2 Chron. 24:26 (called Jozacar [RSV; MT: "Jozabad"] in 2 Kings 12:21). **5** Three men among the returned exiles who had married foreign women (Ezra 10:27, 33, 43). P.A.B.

Zabbai (zab'ay-ee), a descendant of Bebai, who gave up his foreign wife under the reforms of Ezra (Ezra 10:28). He may be the same individual who is mentioned in Neh. 3:20 as the father of the Baruch who helped to rebuild the walls of Jerusalem. ***See also*** Ezra.

Zabdi (zab'dee). **1** The grandfather of Achan of Judah, who violated Joshua's order not to take the devoted spoil from Jericho (Josh. 7:1). **2** A member of the tribe of Benjamin (1 Chron. 8:19). **3** A Shiphmite who served as an official under David in charge of the "produce of the vineyards for the wine cellars" (1 Chron. 27:27). **4** A Levite in postexilic Jerusalem, the son of Asaph and father of Mica (Neh. 11:17).

Zabdiel (zab'dee-el). **1** The father of Jashobeam, one of David's officers (1 Chron. 27:2). **2** An overseer of priests in the time of Nehemiah and the son of Haggedolim (Neh. 11:14). **3** An Arabian who killed Alexander Balas, a contender for the Syrian throne ca. 150 B.C., and sent the head to the Egyptian king Ptolemy VI (1 Macc. 11:17). ***See also*** Alexander.

Zacchaeus (zuh-kee'uhs). **1** An officer in Judas Maccabeus' army (2 Macc. 10:19). **2** A wealthy tax collector in Jericho (Luke 19:1–10), whose actions belied the meaning of his name ("pure") and warranted the label "sinner" (19:7). Learning that Jesus was to pass by, he, being "small of

Zacchaeus in the tree for a better view of Jesus (Luke 19:3–4); pulpit plaque, Ravenna, Italy.

stature," climbed a tree for a better view. Surprisingly, Jesus summoned him and ate with him. Zacchaeus' promise to contribute to the poor and restore fourfold those wrongfully treated stands in sharp contrast to the response of the rich ruler (Luke 18:18–25). ***See also*** Maccabees; Publicans. P.L.S.

Zaccur (zak'kuhr; Heb., "remembered"). **1** A Reubenite, the father of Shammua, one of the twelve spies sent by Moses into Canaan (Num. 13:4). **2** A descendant of Simeon (1 Chron. 4:26). **3** A Levite of the clan of Merari (1 Chron. 24:27). **4** A Levite musician of the clan of Asaph and head of the third course of musicians in the time of King David (1 Chron. 25:1, 10). He is probably the same person who is listed as the ancestor of a postexilic musician (Neh. 12:35). **5** The son of Imri who helped repair the walls of Jerusalem under Nehemiah (Neh. 3:2). **6** A Levite who signed the postexilic covenant to keep the law (Neh. 10:12); he is possibly the same Levite who was the father of Hanan, a Temple official in the time of Nehemiah (Neh. 13:13). **7** A member of the clan of Bigvai who returned from the Babylonian captivity with Ezra (Ezra 8:14). The Hebrew text reads Zabbud but with a marginal correction (Qere) to Zaccur; however, some versions retain Zabbud. D.R.B.

Zachariah. ***See*** Zechariah.

Zacharias (zak-uh-ri'uhs), KJV for Zechariah the prophet (Matt. 23:35; Luke 11:51), and for

Zechariah the father of John the Baptist (Luke 1: 5–67; 3:2). ***See also*** John the Baptist; Zechariah.

Zadok (zay'dahk), a priest whose descendants served in the high-priesthood for most of the First and Second Temple periods (tenth century B.C. to first century A.D.). Zadok and Abiathar were priests under David (2 Sam. 20:25) and supported him during Absalom's revolt (2 Sam. 15:24–29, 35; 17:15; 19:12). In the succession struggle after David's death, Zadok supported Solomon (1 Kings 1:8, 32), while Abiathar supported Adonijah (1 Kings 1:7). Zadok therefore anointed Solomon (1 Kings 1:39–45) and became his sole priest.

The Bible identifies Zadok's father as Ahitub (2 Sam. 8:17). Confusion regarding the genealogy of Abiathar in this verse caused some scholars to discount its historicity and to claim that Zadok's origins were non-Israelite. This theory has recently been challenged by the OT scholar F. M. Cross, who accepts the Aaronite descent of Zadok. Some have suggested that Zadok originally hailed from Hebron where David had come in contact with him.

1 Chron. 6:8–15 (cf. 9:11; Ezra 7:1–5; Neh. 11: 11) lists the descendants of Zadok, although there are probably gaps in the list. This family controlled the Jerusalem priesthood from the time of Solomon (ca. 965 B.C.) until the Exile (586 B.C.). Ezek. 40:46; 43:19; 44:15; and 48:11 specify that in the rebuilt Temple only Zadokite priests would minister. This line continued to serve in the high-priesthood until 171 B.C. when it passed first to the Hellenizers and then to the Hasmonean house. The sect of the Dead Sea Scrolls, probably founded in the aftermath of the Hasmonean takeover of the high-priesthood, repeatedly emphasizes the sole legitimacy of the Zadokite priests who were the early leaders and probably the founders of the sect. ***See also*** Priests. L.H.S.

Zair (zay'ihr), a location either in or near Edomite territory where Jehoram, the king of Judah (Southern Kingdom), fought the Edomites in an attempt to keep them under Israelite control (2 Kings 8:21). The location is unknown, although some scholars connect it with Zoar (Deut. 34:3) or Zior (Josh. 15:54); other scholars think Zair may be a scribal error for Seir, another name for the whole territory of Edom.

Zalmon (zal'muhn). **1** A member of David's elite group of fighting men (2 Sam. 23:28); he is also called Ilai (1 Chron. 11:29). **2** A mountain near Shechem from which Abimelech cut branches with which to burn the Temple of El-berith (Judg. 9:48); it is usually identified as a promontory or slope of Mount Gerizim or Mount Ebal, which lie on either side of Shechem. **3** An unknown location (Ps. 68:14); possibly the same as 2 above, but probably a much higher elevation east of the Jordan toward Mount Hermon.

Zalmonah (zal-moh'nuh), one of the encampments of the Israelites during the exodus from Egypt (Num. 33:41–42). Although the exact site is not known, it is probably located in the Arabah twenty to thirty miles south of the Dead Sea.

Zalmunna (zal-mo͞on'nuh), a Midianite king who, along with Zebah, was pursued and killed by Gideon (Judg. 8:4–21; Ps. 83:11). ***See also*** Gideon; Zebah.

Zamzummim (zam-zo͞o'mim), the name given by the Ammonites to an ancient race of giants who were the original inhabitants of the area east of the Jordan later occupied by the Ammonites and Moabites; the Israelites called them Rephaim (Deut. 2:20–21). Some scholars identify them with the descendants of Ham who are elsewhere called Zuzim (Gen. 14:5). ***See also*** Rephaim.

Zanoah (zuh-no'ah). **1** A town of Judah in the northern Shephelah (Josh. 15:34; Neh. 11:30), identified with Khirbet Zanu'. **2** A town in the hill country of Judah (Josh. 15:56), possibly to be identified with Khirbet Beit Amra. **3** The grandchild of Mered by his Jewish wife (1 Chron. 4: 18).

Zaphenath-paneah (zaf'en-ath pan-ay'ah; KJV: "Zaphnath-paaneah"), the name Pharaoh gave to Joseph when he appointed him as vizier (Gen. 41:45). It was a common practice in Egypt for Semites to take Egyptian names. However, the Egyptian original behind this particular term is uncertain. Although it has been suggested that it comes from *Djed-pa-netjer-iw.f-ankh* ("The god speaks and he lives"), this name is not attested in Egypt until considerably later than the patriarchal era. It may therefore have been a later addition to the story in Genesis, or it may represent a garbled version of some other Egyptian personal name. According to the Targums, based on a wordplay, the name means "revealer of secrets." ***See also*** Joseph. J.M.W.

Zaphon (zay'fahn), a city east of the Jordan River which was included in the land given to the tribe of Gad (Josh. 13:27). Formerly it belonged to the kingdom of Sihon. The site is mentioned in the Amarna letters and the story of Jephthah (Judg. 12:1–7). The site has been identified with Tell es Sa'idiyeh or Tell el Qos in modern Jordan. ***See also*** Amarna, Tell el-; Sihon.

Zarah. ***See*** Zerah.

Zared (zay'red), the term in the KJV for the RSV's "Zered" in Num. 21:12. ***See also*** Zered, The Brook.

Zarephath (zah're-fath; KJV: "Sarepta"), a port city on the Phoenician coast at modern Sarafand, eight miles south of Sidon and fourteen miles north of Tyre. Phoenician and Hellenistic remains were found at Ras el-Qantara, a promontory overlooking what was a northern harbor and possibly a southern one. Hellenistic, Roman, and later remains cover a wider area along the coast, including a small Roman harbor used from the first to sixth centuries A.D. The modern village of Sarafand is centered some distance inland as are Phoenician rock-cut tombs discovered by villagers.

Occupied from 1600 B.C. onward, Zarephath was most important during the Phoenician period. In the ninth century B.C. the prophet Elijah received the hospitality of a poor widow of Zarephath and miraculously replenished her depleted grain and revived her dying son (1 Kings 17:8–24). Centuries later Jesus referred to Elijah's visit (Luke 4:25–27) and by the fourth century A.D. Christian pilgrims stopped there on their way to the Holy Land. A prosperous town and a church to St. Elijah were mentioned in the sixth century, but by the thirteenth century A.D. only eight houses remained standing.

In an Egyptian text of the thirteenth century B.C. Zarephath is mentioned along with Byblos, Beirut, Sidon, and Tyre. In his campaign of 701 B.C. the Assyrian king Sennacherib included Zarephath in a list of pacified coastal cities, while King Esarhaddon transferred Zarephath to the control of Tyre some twenty years later.

Excavation during 1969–74 by J. Pritchard at Zarephath has provided an archaeological record of Phoenician material culture in its homeland, including a stratigraphic sequence of Phoenician pottery. Continuous occupation at Zarephath from the Late Bronze Age (ca. 1500 B.C.) into the Phoenician Iron Age (ca. 1100 B.C.) demonstrates that Phoenician culture evolved locally. In an industrial quarter dating to several centuries of the Iron Age, twenty-two bilobate-shaped kilns for pottery were found along with settling basins and heaps of misfired pottery, including red-slip ware, mushroom-lip juglets, and other Phoenician ceramic types.

A small one-room shrine with benches along its walls was discovered in the potters' quarter. Near the front of it a cache of objects was found that included terracotta figurines and an ivory plaque with a short dedicatory inscription to Astarte-Tanit. This is the first known syncretism of Astarte, the female deity of the Canaanite Levant, and the other female deity, Tanit, whose center of worship was the western Mediterranean where child sacrifices were made to her. This demonstrates that the worship of Tanit was not entirely restricted to the western Mediterranean. T.L.M.

Zarethan (zayr'e-than), a city in the Jordan Valley whose location has not been firmly established. It was beside the clay ground where Solomon's Phoenician smith cast bronze utensils for the Temple (1 Kings 7:46; 2 Chron. 4:17). When Joshua led the Israelites across the Jordan River, water backed up near Zarethan (Josh. 3:16). In the period of the judges, Gideon pursued the Midianites toward Zarethan (Judg. 7:22). Again during Solomon's reign it is mentioned as belonging to one of his administrative districts (1 Kings 4:12). Several modern sites have been proposed as the location of Zarethan, among them Tell Umm Hamad, Sleihat, Tell el-Merkbere, and Tell es-Sa'idiyeh.

The latter site, one of the most prominent tells in the region, was excavated by J. Pritchard in 1964–67. Tell es-Sa'idiyeh consists of twin (upper and lower) mounds and is on the south bank of the Wadi Kufrinjeh, 1.1 miles west of the Jordan River. Iron Age settlement was concentrated on the upper mound. Its water supply was provided in time of siege by a unique semisubterranean stairway cut into the side of the mound; it linked the walled city with springs at the foot of the tell. A wall of mudbrick running down the center of the staircase supported a roof that hid the system from attackers.

The earliest Iron Age settlement excavated on the upper mound was Level IV, possibly dating to the ninth century B.C. Residential houses in it and the succeeding two strata, Levels III and II, were all made of mudbrick. In Level III one house contained a white-plastered mud platform with associated ashes and incense burners. The settlement in Level II, of the eighth century B.C., exhibits systematic town planning in which standardized houses were constructed in a residential block that, with its flanking streets, was oriented perpendicularly to the defensive wall protecting the perimeter of the settlement. Houses, built back to back, were of a three-room pillar type often found in Palestine. The front room was divided in two by a row of mudbrick pillars. A back room stood on the side opposite the street entrance. Level II was destroyed by a heavy fire, and reoccupation of the area, probably in the seventh century B.C., included scores of circular pits that served as storage facilities for grain. Persian and Hellenistic public buildings were located on the highest point of the upper mound. The large Persian structure was square in shape with a paved central courtyard and a tower built at one of the building's corners.

Early Bronze Age (3000–2000 B.C.) potsherds covered the lower mound, but excavation there also revealed a cemetery dating from the Late Bronze Age to the early Iron Age (ca. 1500–900 B.C.). A number of bronze utensils were found in the graves, including a tripod stand, several

Excavations at Tell es-Sa'idiyeh, an important Iron Age settlement and one of the sites proposed as the biblical city of Zarethan.

bowls, and a strainer in the grave of a female. Also found with her were silver jewelry, beads of gold and carnelian, and ivory cosmetic objects. Another grave contained bronze weapons and skeletal remains wrapped in cloth and covered with bitumen. T.L.M.

Zattu (zah'tōō), the chief of a family of exiles that returned from the Babylonian captivity (Ezra 2:8; Neh. 7:13; 10:14). Some members of this family married foreign women (Ezra 10:27).

zayin (zah'yin), the seventh letter of the Hebrew alphabet. It stands at the beginning of the seventh section of Psalm 119 and, in the Hebrew, is the first letter in each verse (Ps. 119: 49–56).

zealot, a person who opposed the Roman occupation of Palestine which began in 63 B.C. Luke uses the term as an epithet for one of Jesus' disciples, Simon (Luke 6:15; Acts 1:13). Prior to the revolt against Rome (A.D. 66–70) a nationalistic party emerged in Palestine called the Zealots. Some scholars hold that Josephus' reference to a "fourth philosophy," or party, among the Jews established by Judas the Galilean, who led resistance to the Roman incorporation of Judea as a province (A.D. 6), can be used to show that the Zealot party had its origins in a nationalistic movement at the beginning of the first century (Josephus *Antiquities* 18.23).

Most scholars think that it is incorrect to locate organized resistance to Roman rule centered around a particular party leadership and ideology earlier than the decade prior to the outbreak of the revolt. Josephus also admits that a number of parties and groups were associated with the final stages of the revolt (*War* 7.262–70). Disturbances in Galilee occurred throughout Herod's reign, but they do not appear to have been part of an organized resistance movement.

Use of the epithet "Zealot" for one of Jesus' disciples, Jesus' crucifixion by Roman authorities, and the parallel drawn between Jesus and Judas the Galilean in Acts 5:37 have led some to ask whether Jesus was a Zealot. Although unrest was evident in isolated incidents such as Pilate's slaughter of Galileans (Luke 13:1–4) and the border skirmish between Galileans and Samaritans, which was, however, connected more with Jerusalem than Galilee (Josephus *Antiquities* 20.120), such an identification does not seem probable. Unlike John the Baptist's, Jesus' ministry in Galilee does not appear to have caused the Herodian officials in Galilee any concern. Nor is Jesus' call for devotion to the rule of God cast in terms characteristic of Zealot ideology. Mark 12:17 suggests that he was unwilling to align himself with that form of resistance. This view is also embedded in sayings against the disciples' aspirations toward power (Mark 8:33; 10:38–39; Luke 24:21; Acts 1:6).

It would seem then that the epithet "Zealot" used of Simon perhaps refers to the older sense of the word, namely, a person who is devoted to the law, who is "zealous" for God (e.g., Num. 25:13; 2 Kings 10:16; Acts 22:3). ***See also*** Cross; Trial of Jesus, The. P.P.

Zebah (zee'buh; Heb., "sacrifice" or "offering"), a king of Midian who, along with Zalmunna and fifteen thousand survivors of the allied Midianite and Amalekite army, fled from the Israelites led by Gideon. Gideon pursued the kings and the remnant of the army to Karkor east of the Jordan where, in a surprise attack, he routed the army and captured Zebah and Zalmunna. After carrying out reprisals against Succoth and Penuel for failing to lend assistance, Gideon killed Zebah and Zalmunna because he held them responsible for the deaths of his kinsmen at Tabor (Judg. 8:4–21; Ps. 83:11). ***See also*** Gideon.

Zebedee (zeb'uh-dee), a fisherman and the father of Jesus' disciples James and John (Matt. 4: 21–22; Mark 1:19–20; Luke 5:10). His wife, who may perhaps have been named Salome (cf. Mark 15:40), was one of the women ministering to Jesus (Matt. 27:56). The reference to "hired servants" (Mark 1:20) suggests that he was a man of some affluence. ***See also*** James; John the Apostle; Salome.

Zeboim (ze-boy'im). **1** One of five destroyed cities located near the Dead Sea of which Sodom is the best known (Gen. 10:19; 14:2, 8; Deut. 29: 23; Hos. 11:8). The others were Gomorrah, Admah, and Bela (or Zoar). The actual location of Zeboim is unknown despite repeated conjectures that it and Sodom are now submerged beneath the waters of the Dead Sea. **2** A village of Judah inhabited by the Jews in the postexilic period (Neh. 11:34).

Zeboim (ze-boh'im), **Valley of,** a valley in the tribal territory of Benjamin southeast of Michmash to which the Philistines came for battle with Saul and Jonathan (1 Sam. 13:18), probably modern Wadi Abu Daba', a branch of the Wadi Qelt. Both ancient and modern names mean "Valley of the Hyenas."

Zebul (zee'buhl), a city official at Shechem who was loyal to Abimelech, the king, at the time of Gaal's challenge to Abimelech's leadership. Zebul participated in Abimelech's plan for Gaal's defeat (Judg. 9:28–41).

Zebulun (zeb'yo͞o-luhn; Heb., "exalt"), the sixth son of Jacob, his sixth by Leah (Gen. 30: 19–20). Zebulun and his three sons went down to Egypt with the family of Jacob (Gen. 46:14). Jacob's blessing of Zebulun implies that his descendants would live along or near the Mediterranean coast and would maintain close relations with the Phoenicians (Gen. 49:13). The tribe was allotted the territory of south-central Galilee (Josh. 19:10–16). Their southern boundary corresponded roughly with the southern edge of the hills of Lower Galilee and their northern border reached the Beth Netophah Valley. Their allotment extended from just north of Mt. Carmel on the west, to Mt. Tabor on the east. Zebulun was something of a hinterland, almost entirely mountainous, with the exception of the broad valleys on its western and northern edges. Its only towns of note were Hannathon (modern Tell el-Bedeiwiyeh), known from the Tell el-Amarna Letters; Shim'on ("Shimron" in the Masoretic Text and in most English versions), a Canaanite city conquered by Thutmose III and also mentioned in the Tell el-Amarna Letters; and Gath-hepher, hometown of Jonah (2 Kings 14:25). Zebulun, while a hinterland, was not isolated; some of Canaan's most important highways passed along its northern, southern, western, and eastern boundaries, by which the tribe had easy access to the sea (cf. Gen. 49:13; Deut. 33:19). Jesus' hometown, Nazareth, was located in the heart of Zebulun (cf. Isa. 9:1; Matt. 4:15). D.A.D.

Zechariah (zek-uh-rī'uh; KJV: "Zachariah" or "Zacharias"; Heb., "Yahweh remembers"), the name of more than thirty people in the Bible, including a Levite gatekeeper (1 Chron. 26:2, 14), a Levite harpist (1 Chron. 15:18, 20; 16:5), and a trumpet-blowing priest who led David's procession accompanying the Ark of the Covenant into Jerusalem (1 Chron. 15:24). The more important bearers of the name are: **1** A prophet during the reign of Joash (Jehoash) of Judah (ca. 837–800 B.C.). The son of Jehoiada, a priest, he was stoned by the people because of his unpopular preaching (2 Chron. 24:20–23). He is probably the Zechariah mentioned by Jesus in Matt. 23:35 and Luke 11:51 (the addition in Matthew of "the son of Barachiah," a reference to Zechariah the postexilic prophet, is probably a scribal error). **2** The son of Jeroboam II, who succeeded his father to the throne of Israel ca. 746 B.C. He was the last of the family of Jehu. After reigning only six months, he was assassinated by Shallum, evidence of a period of considerable political unrest (2 Kings 14:29; 15: 8–12). **3** One of the "Minor Prophets" after the Exile, associated with the canonical book of Zechariah. **4** The father of John the Baptist. According to Luke 1:5, he was a priest from the line of priests associated with Abijah (cf. 1 Chron. 24:7–19) and was married to Elizabeth, "of the daughters of Aaron." Described as righteous before the law, the couple was childless and "advanced in years" (reminiscent of the OT stories of Abraham and Sarah, Gen. 16:1; 17:1–21; 18:

ZECHARIAH, THE BOOK OF

9–15; 21:1–8, and of Elkanah and Hannah, 1 Sam. 1:1–20). An angel appeared to Zechariah, announcing that his long desire for a son would be fulfilled and the son's name was to be John. Asking for a sign, Zechariah was struck dumb. It was not until after John's birth that Zechariah, filled with the Holy Spirit, was again able to speak, blessing God and prophesying the fulfillment of Israel's hope for the Messiah (Luke 1: 1–25, 57–80). ***See also*** Abijah; Abraham; Ark; Berechiah; Elizabeth; Elkanah; Hannah; Jehoiada; Jehu; Jeroboam II; Joash; John the Baptist; Levites; Sarah; Shallum; Zechariah, The Book of. P.L.S.

Zechariah (zek-uh-rī'uh), **the Book of,** the eleventh of the so-called twelve Minor Prophets. The first eight chapters, nearly in their entirety, can be attributed to Zechariah, son (or grandson) of Iddo. Chaps. 9–11 and 12–14 comprise two separate collections from a later period, and will be discussed separately below.

Historical Setting: The words of Haggai, a contemporary of Zechariah, describe the adverse conditions under which the Jewish community lived during the period after the return of some of the exiles to Judah following the edict of Cyrus in 538 B.C. The economy had suffered as a result of crop failure, there was insufficient food, and the value of personal wealth had been eroded by inflation. Haggai responded to this situation in 520 B.C. with an urgent message: the people were themselves at fault for leaving the Temple—destroyed by the Babylonians in 586—in ruins. But an eschatological turning point was at hand. No sooner would the people take up the task of rebuilding than God would act to restore the kingdom, which would rise to the glory of a messianic age under its Davidic prince Zerubbabel.

Zechariah took up the admonition where Haggai had left off, both chronologically (520–518 B.C.) and thematically (his message is more encompassing). No doubt due in part to his encouragement, the rebuilding of the Temple was carried forward, coming to completion in 516 B.C.

Structure and Message of Zechariah 1–8: The heart of Zechariah's message is formed by a cycle of eight visions in chaps. 1–6, visions received by the prophet in a two-month period in 519. The fourth vision (chap. 3) is distinct from the others in form and theme, and depicts a trial in heaven in which Satan accuses Joshua, and in which God declares the latter free of reproach and then commands that he be consecrated for the high-priestly office. This passage both reflects the exalted position of the Zadokite high priest at this period and hints at the existence of inner-community controversy over his appointment.

The remaining seven visions form an intricate unit giving a symbolic representation of the Jewish community revolving around the rebuilt Temple in a land secured and sanctified by God. Significantly the central vision depicts an elaborate lampstand consisting of seven lamps, on the side of which rise two olive trees. This rich symbolism is interpreted in chap. 4 as representing the all-seeing presence of God (the lamps) and the two anointed emissaries of God on earth, Joshua and Zerubbabel (the olive trees). From this spiritual center of the universe (as indeed the Temple was regarded in the ancient world) the other visions reach out, depicting God's securing the land against foreign oppressors and establishing prosperity (visions 2 and 3), God's purging the community of all who violate the Torah (visions 5 and 6), and finally God's securing the very outer reaches of the universe (visions 1 and 7).

The political setting addressed by this powerful symbolism can be inferred from the plaintive questioning of the angel in 1:12: "O Lord of hosts, how long wilt thou have no mercy on Jerusalem and the cities of Judah, against which thou hast had indignation these seventy years?" The Persian king Darius I (522–486 B.C.) had just crushed the widespread insurrections that had raised nationalistic hopes within many of the Persian vassal states, including Judah. Disappointment threatened the morale of the Jewish community, threatening among other things the Temple rebuilding effort. The visions of Zechariah offered assurance that God remained "exceedingly jealous for Jerusalem and for Zion" (1: 14).

Chap. 1:1–7 and chaps. 7–8 draw various sayings of Zechariah into a framework around the visions. They offer clear evidence of the ethical sensitivity of this prophet, who has sometimes unfairly been described strictly as a cult prophet.

We have noted that the prophetic activity of Zechariah (and Haggai) bore fruit in the completion of the Temple. Are other effects discernible? The enigmatic passage in 6:9–14 offers a tantalizing piece of evidence. It describes the casting of crowns, apparently for the twin members of the Zadokite/Davidic diarchy, Joshua and Zerubbabel. But awkward adjustments to the text have led to the portrayal of a crown being placed solely on the head of Joshua. Zerubbabel has been dropped from the text. Many scholars have taken this as indirect evidence that the messianic fervor engendered by the two prophets had gone so far as to cause the Persians to fear further unrest in Judah, leading to the removal of the Davidic prince. At any rate, this text points to an important development. For the remainder of the Persian period (to 333 B.C.) and on into the Hellenistic (333–63 B.C.), Judah was to be a theocracy under the leadership of a succession of Zadokite high priests.

Zechariah's message grows out of a tradition reaching back to the Temple theology developed by the Zadokite priests in the pre-exilic period and reaching literary culmination in the book of Ezekiel and the so-called Priestly writing. It is a tradition expressing the concerns and theological insights of a guild of priests devoted to maintaining a state of holiness through the proper maintenance of Temple and sacrifice that would be hospitable to the presence of the divine Glory upon which the well-being of the land depended. Along with Ezekiel it gives indication of significant developments in the history of the religion of Israel, including the increasing sense of the transcendence of God which encouraged speculation concerning divine intermediaries, the cultivation of the genre of the vision as a medium of revelation, and the movement toward an elaborate symbolism and a high eschatology anticipating later apocalyptic writings, upon which Zechariah and Ezekiel exercised considerable influence.

The precise chronological notes running through Haggai and Zechariah 1–8 were probably provided by an editor who gave these prophetic collections their final shape, a person with the type of historical concerns discernible behind the Chronicler's history.

Zechariah 9–14: Zechariah 9–11, Zechariah 12–14, and the book of Malachi are three collections of prophetic materials each bearing the heading "An Oracle." It seems likely that at a late stage in the formation of the twelve Minor Prophets, these three collections were added in such a way as to yield the number twelve by attaching two to Zechariah and placing the third as a separate book under the name Malachi (resulting from reading Heb. *mala'ki,* "my messenger," as a personal name in Mal. 1:1). Though containing no explicit evidence for dating, it seems that all three collections consist of materials from the fifth and fourth centuries B.C., written by groups increasingly disillusioned with prevailing conditions, critical of their leaders, and given to apocalytic visions as a means of preserving their hopes for final vindication. ***See also*** Cyrus II; Darius; Exile; Malachi, The Book of. P.D.H.

OUTLINE OF CONTENTS

The Book of Zechariah

I. God's words to Zechariah (1:1–7)
II. Eight visions (1:8–6:15)
   A. First vision: a rider (1:7–17)
   B. Second vision: four horns (1:18–21)
   C. Third vision: a measuring line (2:1–13)
   D. Fourth vision: Joshua (3:1–10)
   E. Fifth vision: lamp and trees (4:1–14)
   F. Sixth vision: a flying scroll (5:1–8)
   G. Seventh vision: winged women (5:9–11)
   H. Eighth vision: chariots (6:1–15)
III. Words of Zechariah (7:1–8:23)
IV. Collections of prophetic oracles (9:1–14:21)
   A. "First oracle" (9:1–11:17)
   B. "Second oracle" (12:1–14:21)

Zedek (ze'dek) **Valley,** a name that does not occur in the Bible. It identifies an artificial valley discovered during excavations in ancient Jerusalem during the early 1920's. It has been determined that the early city of Jerusalem was located on the southeastern ridge extending below the present Temple Mount area. The least defensible aspect of that ridge was its northern border and apparently this valley, which was cut into the hill from the west, was designed for defense purposes. As the city expanded northward under David(?) and Solomon, this valley or moat outlived its usefulness, and was subsequently filled in. The name Zedek is derived from Melchizedek and Adonizedek and was assigned to the valley by the scholar R. A. S. Macalister. J.A.D.

Zedekiah (zed-uh-kī'ah; Heb., "Yahweh is righteousness"). **1** The last king of Judah, who was placed on the throne as a puppet ruler by Nebuchadnezzar after his first conquest of Jerusalem in 597 B.C. (2 Kings 24:17). In spite of the repeated warnings and criticisms of the prophet Jeremiah, reported in the narratives of Jeremiah 37–39 and 52, Zedekiah rebelled against his Babylonian overlords (2 Kings 24:20). As the result, Jerusalem was recaptured and destroyed (586 B.C.) and a bereaved and maimed Zedekiah was taken in fetters to Babylon (2 Kings 25:6–7). **2** A priest of Nehemiah's time (Neh. 10:2). **3** Two nobles of Nehemiah's time (Jer. 36:12; 1 Chron. 3:16). **4** A false prophet opposed by Micaiah, son of Imlah (1 Kings 22:11, 24; 2 Chron. 18:10, 23). **5** A false prophet opposed by Jeremiah (Jer. 29:21–23). W.S.T.

Zeeb, a Midianite prince whom Gideon captured and killed (Judg. 7:25). ***See also*** Oreb and Zeeb.

Zelophehad (ze-loh-fay'had), a man of Manasseh who died in the wilderness leaving no male heir (Num. 26:33; 27:3; 1 Chron. 7:2). His five daughters, Mahlah, Noah, Hoglah, Milcah, and Tirzah, petitioned Moses and Eleazar, the priest, to recognize the right of female inheritance (Num. 27:1–11; cf. Josh. 17:3–6). The petition was granted with the stipulation that female heirs marry within their own tribe to protect the tribal inheritance (Num. 36:1–12).

Zenas (zee'nuhs), person identified as a lawyer (to distinguish him from another Zenas?) whom Titus is asked to speed on his way with Apollos (Titus 3:13). According to post–New Testament tradition, the first bishop of Diospolis (Lydda) was Zenas, author of a life of Titus. ***See also*** Apollos.

Zephaniah (zef-uh-nī'uh; Heb., "God has concealed" or "preserved"). **1** A priest who served as an intermediary between King Zedekiah of Judah and the prophet Jeremiah (Jer. 21:1; 37:3; early sixth century B.C.). He was taken before the king of Babylon at Riblah and was there put to death (Jer. 52:24–27). **2** An ancestor of the prophet Samuel (1 Chron. 6:36). **3** The father of Josia; he was living in Jerusalem in the mid-sixth century B.C. when Darius decreed the rebuilding of the Jerusalem Temple (Zech. 6:10–14). **4** A prophet during the reign of King Josiah of Judah (640–609 B.C.). ***See also*** Zephaniah, The Book of. P.J.A.

Zephaniah (zef-uh-nī'uh), **the Book of,** one of the books of the twelve "Minor Prophets" in the OT. The prophecies of Zephaniah span the reign of King Josiah of Judah (640–609 B.C.). His is the first prophetic voice to be preserved for us in the Bible since the time of Isaiah and Micah (701 B.C.), and his prophecy forms God's radical reaction to the idolatrous results of the reigns of Manasseh (697–642 B.C.) and Amon (642–640 B.C.) in Judah, with their mixing the worship of foreign gods with that of the true God of Israel. It is probable that Zephaniah was a member of that reform group of prophets and Levites who were responsible for Deuteronomy. Chapters 1 and 2 of his book probably date shortly after 640 B.C., while 3:1–17 may come from the period of 612–609 B.C., when it was clear that the reform measures of Deuteronomy had failed. 3:18–20 are probably an exilic, deuteronomic addition to the work.

Zephaniah is the only prophet for whom four generations of ancestors are named, but it is doubtful that "Hezekiah" in 1:1 refers to the Judean king of that name. We know nothing further about the prophet.

OUTLINE OF CONTENTS

The Book of Zephaniah

I. Superscription (1:1)
II. Announcement of universal judgment in the Day of the Lord (1:2–2:4)
  A. Judgment of the earth and of Judah and Jerusalem (1:2–6)
  B. The coming Day proclaimed (1:7–13)
  C. Description of the Day (1:14–18)
III. Picture of the judgment (2:5–3:8)
  A. On foreign nations (2:5–15)
    1. Philistines (west) (2:5–7)
    2. Moab and Ammon (east) (2:8–11)
    3. Egypt (south) (2:12)
    4. Assyria (north) (2:13–14)
  B. On Jerusalem (3:1–8)
IV. Promise of salvation (3:9–20)
  A. For the remnant of Judah and Jerusalem (3:9–13)
  B. The new people of Zion (3:14–17)
  C. For the exiles in Babylonia (Deuteronomic addition; 3:18–20)

Central Message: The central message of Zephaniah is that the fire of God's wrath is about to burn up a creation gone wrong (1:1–2; 3:9), but the announcement is directed principally to Judah and Jerusalem in the effort to call forth their repentance. The sins of the covenant people are four: their idolatry, represented by their worship of such foreign deities as the Canaanite baals (1:4), the Assyrian astral deities (1: 5, 9), and the god Milcom of Ammon (1:5); their accommodation to foreign ways (1:8); their unethical action within their own society (1:9); and, above all, their indifference toward and unbelief in the God of Israel (1:12). This last is characterized as a "thickening upon their lees," a figure drawn from the process of winemaking, in which wine left too long on its sediment becomes thick and syrupy. The Judeans have become thus ruined, proclaims the prophet, because they no longer believe that God does anything in their world (1:12).

The Judeans and foreign peoples, who share their unbelief, will therefore be laid waste on the coming Day of the Lord, a concept rooted in the theology of Israel's Holy Wars and dating from the time of the tribal federation (1220–1020 B.C.). In such theology, God was pictured as a Divine Warrior who fought on his people's behalf to defeat their enemies. Popular theology in Israel therefore believed that the Day of the Lord would be a time when God would finally defeat all of Israel's enemies, inaugurate his kingdom on earth, and exalt his covenant people. The prophets, beginning with Amos, however, announced that God would instead war against his covenant people for their sins against him. Zephaniah portrays this final war against Israel and all unbelievers more fully than does any other prophet.

The coming of the awful Day is described in Zeph. 1:14–16, a passage whose initial words were translated into Latin as *Dies irae*, developed into poetry, and then used in various Latin masses and numerous literary and musical works. The Day will open with a sacrifice, when

God will consecrate his mysterious warriors (1:7), followed by the war cry of God as he wades into the fray (1:14). The battle will begin in Jerusalem's commercial center (1:10–11) and from there spread throughout the earth. God will search out his enemies (1:12), leveling his covenant curses against his own people (1:13), and wasting the lands of foreigners to the west (2:4, 5–7), the east (2:8–11), the south (2:12), and the north (2:13–14), in short, over all the earth. No defense will be adequate against God's war (1:16–18), and he will make a full and sudden end of all unbelievers (1:18).

Only repentance and casting oneself on the mercy of God can save Judah on that Day. Zephaniah therefore calls his compatriots to hold an assembly of fasting and repentance (2:1–3) that will evidence Judah's humility, obedience, and righteousness or trust in the Lord (2:3). If Judah so repents, it may be saved (2:3). However, Judah and Jerusalem, symbolized by their corrupt leaders (3:3–4), refuse Zephaniah's call, as they have always refused God's correction through prophets and the Deuteronomic law (3:2), through military defeat (3:6), and through the evidence of God's work in the natural world (3:5). The judgment upon God's people is therefore inevitable. But a remnant of faithful will be preserved in Judah (2:7, 9) and will spread out over foreign lands. Within Jerusalem there will be left a humble, trusting, and righteous folk (3:9–13) who do no wrong. God will establish his kingdom over all the earth (3:14–17). Jerusalem will rejoice (3:14), and God will exult in the midst of it (3:17).

E.R.A.

Zerah (zee'rah). **1** An Edomite descendant of Esau by Basemath, daughter of Ishmael (Gen. 36:13, 17; 1 Chron. 1:37; cf. Gen. 36:1–4); also the father of an early Edomite king (same person?; Gen. 36:33; 1 Chron. 1:44). **2** A twin son of Judah by Tamar (Gen. 38:30; cf. 46:12; 1 Chron. 2:4, 6), founder of the Zerahites (Num. 26:20) or "sons [descendants] of Zerah" (1 Chron. 9:6; Neh. 11:24). Achan, a warrior who took for personal use some items from Jericho that had been dedicated (lit. "devoted") to God, is identified as a descendant of Zerah (Josh. 7:1, 18, 24; cf. 1 Chron. 2:6–7). **3** The founder of a Simeonite division, the Zerahites (Num. 26:13; 1 Chron. 4:24; called Zohar in Gen. 46:10; Exod. 6:15). **4** Two Levites (1 Chron. 6:21, 41). **5** An Ethiopian (Cushite) leader of a large attacking force whom King Asa of Judah defeated at Mareshah (2 Chron. 14:9–15).

P.A.B.

Zerahiah (zair-uh-hī'uh; Heb., "Yah [God] has dawned" or "Yah has shone forth"). **1** A Levite in the priestly line of Aaron and an ancestor of Ezra (1 Chron. 6:6, 51; Ezra 7:4). **2** A member of the clan of Pahath-moab whose son Eliehoenai returned from the Babylonian captivity with Ezra (Ezra 8:4).

Zerahites (zee'ruh-hīts), the name of two clan groups during the period of the wilderness wanderings, one belonging to the tribe of Simeon (Num. 26:13) and the other to the tribe of Judah (Num. 26:20). The association of the Zerahites with both Judah and Simeon probably reflects the fact that after the settlement in the land the tribe of Simeon was absorbed very quickly into the tribe of Judah and lost its identity (see Gen. 49:7; Josh. 19:1). The same practice of dual identification is seen in the city lists in which cities are named as belonging to both Simeon and Judah (cf. Josh. 15:21–63 with 19:1–9). It is therefore likely that only one group is referred to. It was to the Zerahites that Achan belonged (Josh. 7:17), as did Sibbecai and Maharai, two of David's military commanders (1 Chron. 27:11, 13). ***See also*** Simeon; Zerah; Zohar.

D.R.B.

Zered (zeh'red), **the Brook,** a brook that empties into the Dead Sea at its extreme southeast corner. The crossing of this stream concluded the Israelites' desert wanderings (Num. 21:12; Deut. 2:13–14). Probably the modern Wadi el-Hesa, it cleaves the high eastern plateau to join the southern end of the Dead Sea. It constitutes the frontier between Moab and Edom and is perhaps the "Brook of the Willows" (Isa. 15:7). ***See also*** Edom; Moab.

Zeresh (zee'resh), the wife of Haman (Esther 5:10, 14; 6:13). Various etymologies have been proposed for the name from the Persian, Indian, and Avestan languages, but none of these has won broad consensus. ***See also*** Esther; Haman.

Zerqa (zair'kuh), the modern name for the river that begins at a spring in modern Amman, Jordan, flows north through the village of Zerqa, then turns west to empty into the Jordan River fifteen miles north of the Dead Sea. Joshua probably crossed the Jordan in the area where the Zerqa joins it (Josh. 3:14–17).

Zeruah (ze-rōō'uh), a widow and the mother of King Jeroboam I of Israel (924–903 B.C.; 1 Kings 11:26).

Zerubbabel (zuhr-ruhb'uh-bl; Heb., "shoot of Babylon"), a descendant of the Davidic family. The genealogies differ: 1 Chron. 3:19 gives Pedaiah, a younger son of Jehoiachin, as his father; Hag. 1:1 and Ezra 3:2 (cf. Matt. 1:12; Luke 3:37) give Shealtiel, the eldest son. Zerubbabel appears with Joshua (Jeshua) the high priest as the recipient of Haggai's message (Hag. 1:1; 2:2) to rebuild the Temple. In Hag. 2:20–23 he is to receive royal status as "servant" and "signet ring," executive officer of God. In Zechariah, he is named only in 4:6b–10a, inserted in the vision of the golden lampstand; he alone is the initiator and completer of the restored Temple, not by human power but by divine "spirit." The origin of this passage is uncertain; text and interpretation are difficult. Zech. 2:10 and 6:12 ("the Branch," cf. Jer. 23:5) are generally believed to indicate Zerubbabel. Later reinterpretation may have resulted in his name being removed, perhaps when priestly rulers had superseded governors. These passages also remain problematic.

Zerubbabel appears in Ezra 3:2, 8 and 4:2, 3, usually with Jeshua, as responsible for rebuilding the Temple; in 4:1–3 he refuses the help of "adversaries" who claimed to be true worshipers ever since the Assyrian ruler Esarhaddon brought them to the land—a reference nowhere else attested. They are also mentioned in Ezra 5:2 in the Aramaic account; their names here may be due to the harmonizing of this narrative with that of Ezra 3. In Ezra 2:2; Neh. 7:7; and Neh. 12:1, 47 Zerubbabel appears as leader of one group of returning exiles. These passages reflect various stages of postexilic life in Judah.

Only in Hag. 1:1 and 2:2 is Zerubbabel entitled "governor": the same term appears in seal impressions (bullae) of the official administering the district of Yehud (Judah). He was probably, but not certainly, appointed by Darius I. 1 Esd. 3:1–5:3 has a fictional tale of a contest of wits at the court of Darius; unexpectedly, Zerubbabel is identified as the winner and is granted leave to rebuild Jerusalem and the Temple. ***See also*** Haggai; Zechariah. P.R.A.

Zeruiah (ze-rōō'yah), the mother of Joab, Abishai, and Asahel, three of David's warriors. According to 1 Chron. 2:16 she was David's sister, and perhaps for this reason his three nephews are identified not by their father's name, but by their mother's. If the text of 2 Sam. 17:25 is sound, Zeruiah's own father was a certain Nahash, perhaps an earlier husband of Jesse's wife. The sons of Zeruiah are depicted as impetuous and ruthless men, frequently appearing as foils to the mild-tempered king (cf. 2 Sam. 3:39).

Zeus (zōōs), the chief deity of the Greek pantheon, often described as "the father of gods and men." Zeus as the "sky god," who wielded the thunder bolt and was responsible for weather and rain while enthroned on Mount Olympus, was of Indo-European origin. By Homeric times (ca. 800 B.C.) Zeus was the highest civic god, protector of justice and morals. The circle of twelve gods and goddesses established as a family on Olympus is evident in Homer. Other elements in the Zeus mythology appear to have had a different origin. Zeus's father, Kronos, was said to have swallowed his children until he was given a stone instead of Zeus, which also freed other gods of Zeus's generation, Hera, Poseidon, and Hades. Other features of the Zeus legend include the overthrow of the earlier generation, the Titans, "sons of Earth," and the unions with various goddesses and mortal women.

In Hellenistic times (ca. 300 B.C.–A.D. 300) Zeus was identified with the chief deity of any non-Greek religion. The Stoics spoke of the highest principle, fire or reason, which animates the universe, as "Zeus." Barnabas is taken to be "Zeus" by the people of Lystra (Acts 14:12). P.P.

Ziba (zī'bah), in the OT, a retainer in Saul's household who informed David of a survivor among Saul's people, namely, a grandson in the person of Jonathan's lame son Mephibosheth. David restored Saul's estate to Saul's grandson Mephibosheth, appointing Ziba as overseer (2 Sam. 9:1–12). When David was forced to flee Jerusalem during Absalom's revolt, Ziba met him with provisions and a story of Mephibosheth's designs on the crown. For this information Ziba received in reward the grant of Mephibosheth's estate (2 Sam. 16:1–4). On David's return, Ziba rushed to the Jordan to assist him, while Mephibosheth met him with expressions of loyalty and a story of Ziba's deceit. David thereupon divided the estate between them (2 Sam. 19:17–29). P.A.B.

Zibeon (zib'ee-uhn; Heb., meaning uncertain, perhaps "hyena"), the son of Seir the Horite and a chieftain of the Horites (Gen. 36:20, 29). He is identified as the ancestor of Esau's wife (Gen. 36:2), which reveals a relationship between the Horites and the Edomites. The reference to Zibeon as a Hivite (Gen. 36:2) is a textual error for Horite, since he is always elsewhere connected with the Horites. ***See also*** Edomites; Horites.

Zichri (zik'ree). **1** The head of a levitical family in the time of Moses (Exod. 6:21). **2** The name of three Benjaminites (1 Chron. 8:19, 23, 27). **3** A Levite appointed by David to supervise the dedicated booty (1 Chron. 26:25). **4** The father of the leader of the Reubenites during David's reign (1 Chron. 27:16). **5** The father of a Judahite general in Jehoshaphat's army (2 Chron. 17:16). **6** The father of one of Jehoiada's generals (2 Chron. 23:1). **7** An Ephraimite warrior in the army of Pekah who slew three of Ahaz's officers (2 Chron. 28:7). **8** The grandfather of a Levite who made the return from exile (1 Chron. 9:15; cf. Neh. 11:17). **9** The father of a Benjaminite who lived in Jerusalem after the return from exile (Neh. 11:9). **10** The head of a priestly family in the second generation after the return from exile (Neh. 12:17). P.K.M.

Zidon. ***See*** Sidon.

The Ziggurat at Ur: a view of the southwest face.

ziggurat (zig'uh-raht; from the Akkadian *ziqqurratu*, "temple tower," a noun derived from *zaqāru*, "to build high"), a stepped temple with rectangular or, later, square base built mostly in Mesopotamia. Ziggurats usually had a sanctuary on the ground level, which perhaps was matched by a sanctuary on the ziggurat's summit, where the god was thought to appear. Ziggurats were built from the protoliterate period on. They existed at one time or another in most major Mesopotamian cities, including Babylon, Ashur, Nineveh, Ur, and Eridu, and honored important gods such as Marduk, Ashur, Shamash, Enlil, Anu, and Ishtar. The magnificent ziggurat at Ur, dating from the late third millennium, is well preserved and suggests the great impact that these structures must have had on the ancient Mesopotamians. The first-millennium ziggurat of Marduk in Babylon was called the *Etemenanki*, "the house that is the foundation of heaven and earth," indicating the important place that ziggurats had in antiquity. This is the ziggurat that greatly impressed Herodotus, the fifth-century Greek historian.

Mesopotamian ziggurats influenced the architecture of their neighbors; it is thus not surprising that ziggurats also influenced some of the literary narratives of the Israelites. The construction of the Tower of Babel (Gen. 11:1–9) was probably patterned after the building of a great ziggurat. Indeed, the narrative is set in Mesopotamia (vv. 2, 9) and even reflects Mesopotamian building techniques and phraseology (v. 3). In Gen. 28:12–15, Jacob, on his way to Haran, dreams of angels ascending and descending a staircase (RSV: "ladder"). Possibly, the staircase in this dream is patterned after a ziggurat, whose stairs led to a summit where the god was manifest (cf. v. 17). ***See also*** Babel.

M.Z.B.

Ziha (zī'huh). **1** A family group of Temple servants (Nethinim) who returned from the Babylonian captivity with Zerubbabel (Ezra 2:43; Neh. 7:46). **2** One of the overseers of the Temple servants who lived in Ophel after the return from exile (Neh. 11:21).

Ziklag (zik'lag), a city in the Negev, the wilderness area west and south of the Dead Sea, whose location cannot be determined with certainty. The city was given to David by the Philistine tyrant of Gath, Achish. It was David's base for military operations for a year and four months (1 Sam. 27:5–12), and it was destroyed by the Amalekites at the time of Saul's last stand against the Philistines (1 Sam. 30:1–19). It is listed in the ancestral holdings of both Judah (Josh. 15:31; cf. 1 Sam. 27:6) and Simeon (Josh. 19:5; cf. 1 Chron. 4:30).

Zillah (zil'uh), one of the wives of Lamech and the mother of Tubal-cain (Gen. 4:19–23). The name seems to be derived from the common Hebrew word for "shade," but other, more speculative etymologies have been proposed.

Zillethai (zil'e-tī; Heb., "shadow, protection"). **1** A Benjamite, one of the sons of Shimei (1 Chron. 8:20). **2** A member of the tribe of Manasseh who came to help David while he was taking refuge at Ziklag (1 Chron. 12:20).

A monumental stepped structure, taller than a five-story building, excavated in the city of David—or Zion—from the tenth century B.C. It continues 22 feet beneath the Israelite houses whose remains are located toward the center of the photo.

Zilpah (zil'puh), the handmaiden of Leah, who was given to Jacob as a "surrogate mother" and bore Gad and Asher (Gen. 30:9–13). Even though surrogates were normally given to their husbands by childless wives, Zilpah was given to Jacob after Leah had already borne four sons, apparently in retaliation for the action of the childless Rachel, whose handmaiden Bilhah had borne Dan and Naphtali as a surrogate mother for Rachel. Despite the fact that they bore sons to Jacob, Zilpah and Bilhah are not considered matriarchs of Israel. T.S.F.

Zilthai (zil'tī). ***See*** Zillethai.

Zimran (zim'ruhn), a son of Abraham and Keturah (Gen. 25:2; 1 Chron. 1:32). The name almost certainly refers to a clan living in Arabia, possibly at a place along the east shore of the Red Sea west of Mecca called Zabram by the Hellenistic geographer Ptolemy in the second century A.D.

Zimri (zim'rī; Heb., "[God] is my protection" or "strength"). **1** A Simeonite who lived prior to Israel's entry into Canaan and was killed by the priest Phinehas for bringing a Midianite woman into his home (Num. 25). **2** Commander of half the chariotry in early ninth-century B.C. Israel who led a successful coup against King Elah, as a result of which Zimri became an epithet for one who kills his own master (2 Kings 9:31). He ruled in Tirzah for only one week before another officer (Omri) besieged the city and Zimri committed suicide by entering the royal palace he had set afire (1 Kings 16:8–31). **3** A descendant of Judah (1 Chron. 2:6, perhaps the same as Zabdi in Jos. 7:1). **4** A descendant of Saul's son Jonathan (1 Chron. 8:36; 9:42). **5** A nation, apparently near southern Mesopotamia (Jer. 25:25), although the accuracy and exact reference of the text are uncertain. F.E.G.

Zin, Wilderness of, an area on the southern border of Palestine, including also a place called Zin (Num. 34:3–4; Josh. 15:1–3), within the area of Paran. It included Kadesh-barnea as well as Massah and Meribah (Num. 27:14; Deut. 32:51) and must therefore have been south of the present Israeli border, more or less in the center on an east-west axis. Moses sent spies from here to explore the future homeland (Num. 13:25). It is not the same as the "Wilderness of Sin." ***See also*** Kadesh; Massah; Paran; Sin, Wilderness of.

Zion (zī'uhn), a Hebrew word whose precise meaning is not known. It may mean "citadel" or "fortress," but it has come to refer to at least three different aspects of the city of Jerusalem, as well as "the mountain of Samaria."

According to 2 Sam. 5:6–10, David and his men took Jerusalem from the Jebusites, apparently climbing through a water tunnel or shaft and opening the city gate from the inside. Verse 7 states that "David took the stronghold of Zion, that is the city of David," thus essentially equating the names Jerusalem, Zion, and the city of David. The synonymous use of these terms can be seen elsewhere in the OT.

It is clear both from a close reading of the Bible and from archaeological research that the pre-Israelite fortress of Jerusalem occupied the southeastern ridge, which extends south from the current Temple Mount complex located immediately to its north. This ridge has narrow precipitous valleys on both its eastern and western sides which eventually meet at the southern tip of the ridge.

While this city or fortress can legitimately be called Zion, the Temple Mount area immediately to the north, which was first constructed under Solomon's reign, may also bear the name. This seems implied from a number of Psalms extolling the virtues of Zion and from related themes elsewhere in the OT. Zion is "my [God's] holy hill" (Ps. 2:6), "the holy habitation of the Most High (Ps. 46:4); it is "Mount Zion, which he loves," where God "built his sanctuary like the high heavens" (Ps. 78:68–69).

In Byzantine times the name Zion was erroneously assigned to the hill immediately south of the southwestern corner of the present "old city," and from that time until the present century this site has been proposed as the original Zion. Though it has been shown conclusively that such is not the case, nevertheless two sites of traditional veneration are located there: David's tomb and the upper room of the Last Supper.

There is yet another possibility for the term as suggested by Amos 6:1, where Zion occurs in a phrase that parallels it to "the mountain of Samaria." Perhaps Zion here is equated with Samaria in the sense of a "citadel," although it may be nothing more than a sarcastic comment on the false pride of Samaria's inhabitants.

The descriptive language of Zion is replete with rich imagery. Streams of water come forth from her (Ps. 46:4), although in actuality the city is supplied by two springs, both of which are located off the hill proper. Zion is called "His holy mountain, beautiful in elevation" (Ps. 48: 1–2), adopting language more appropriate to a sacred mountain in north Syria. On numerous occasions Zion is employed as a metaphor for security and protection (e.g., Ps. 125). The NT continues this imagery using the term "heavenly Jerusalem" or Zion metaphorically in reference to the church (Heb. 12:22), the gospel message (1 Pet. 2:6), and the place of God's dwelling (Rev. 14:1). ***See also*** David; Jerusalem.

J.A.D.

Ziph (zif). **1** A descendant of Caleb (1 Chron. 2: 42); however, since this passage reflects more historical and geographical relationships than actual family genealogies, Ziph likely refers to the area settled by the Calebites (see 3 and 4 below). **2** A Judahite member of the Calebite clan (1 Chron. 4:16). **3** A city in the hill country of southern Judah (Josh. 15:55) which gives its name to the portion of the Judean wilderness between the city and the Dead Sea at En-gedi ("the Wilderness of Ziph"; 1 Sam. 23:14–15; 24; 26:2). While David was hiding in this area during his flight from Saul, the Ziphites betrayed his location to Saul (1 Sam. 23:19; 26:1). The city was later fortified and provisioned by King Rehoboam as a defensive garrison (2 Chron. 11: 8). The site is identified as modern Tell ez-Zif, about three miles southwest of Hebron. **4** A city in the far southern territory of the tribe of Judah (Josh. 15:24). Some scholars identify it as modern Khirbet ez-Zeifeh, which lies west of the south end of the Dead Sea in the eastern Negev.

D.R.B.

Zippor (zip'pohr; Heb., "bird"), the father of Balak, the king of Moab who hired Balaam to curse Israel (Num. 22:2, 4; Josh. 24:9).

Zipporah (zip-poh'ruh), the wife of Moses and the mother of Gershom and Eliezer. She was one of the seven daughters of Reuel, priest of Midian (also known as Jethro). Zipporah appears in three narratives. In the first (Exod. 2:16–22), the daughters were drawing water for their sheep, the (male) shepherds chased them away, and Moses (who had just fled Egypt) "saved" them; upon hearing this, Reuel invited him to his home and gave him Zipporah as his wife. In the second narrative (Exod. 4:24–26) God inexplicably attacked Moses, and Zipporah saved him by circumcising her son and touching Moses' feet with the foreskin. Zipporah and her sons stayed with Jethro in Midian when Moses went back to Egypt to lead the Exodus; Jethro brought them to Moses when he came to meet Israel in the desert (Exod. 18:2–5).

T.S.F.

Zoan (zoh'an; Heb.; Egyptian *Djanet*; Gk. *Tanis*), the residence of the kings of Egypt during the twenty-first and twenty-second dynasties (ca. 1070–715 B.C.) and a major commercial and political center down into the Ptolemaic period (ca. 332–30 B.C.), which is located at modern San el-Hagar on the Tanitic branch of the Nile in the northeast delta, about seventy-three miles northeast of Cairo. The "fields of Zoan"—evidently a region around Tanis—are described in Ps. 78:12, 43 as the scene of the wonders associated with the Exodus. According to Num. 13:22, Hebron was built seven years before Zoan. Zoan was still an important city in the days of Isaiah and Ezekiel (Isa. 19:11, 13; 30:4; Ezek. 30:14).

Tanis is one of the largest sites in the Egyptian delta. It has been excavated several times, by W. M. Flinders Petrie (1883–1886), Pierre Montet (intermittently between 1929 and 1956), and most recently by Jean Yoyotte (starting in 1966). The principal feature of Tanis is an enormous mudbrick enclosure wall, inside of which a second wall surrounds a great temple dedicated to the god Amun. This complex was evidently started by the twenty-first-dynasty king Psusennes I (1039–991 B.C.). Elsewhere within the inner enclosure wall are the subterranean tombs of six kings of the twenty-first and twenty-second dynasties.

Because so many monuments inscribed with the names of Ramesses II and his nineteenth- and twentieth-dynasty (ca. 1293–1070 B.C.) successors were found at Tanis, it was thought for a long time that Tanis was the site of ancient Raamses, the store-city (KJV: "treasure-city") where the Hebrews labored for Pharaoh (Exod. 1:11). However, it has now been recognized that these earlier monuments were transferred to Tanis from elsewhere, probably the area of Qantir-Khatana, about fifteen miles south of Tanis, which appears to be the real location of the biblical store-city of Raamses. Therefore, the references to Zoan as the site of the Exodus wonders are anachronistic. ***See also*** Raamses, Rameses.

J.M.W.

Zoar (zoh'uhr), one of the five cities of the plain (along with Sodom, Gomorrah, Admah, and Zeboiim). The four eastern kings led by Chedorlaomer, king of Elam, defeated these five cities in the valley of Siddim (Gen. 14:1–12). God allowed Lot to flee from Sodom to Zoar before he destroyed Sodom and the other three cities with fire and brimstone (Gen. 19:18–23). Zoar is mentioned later in connection with the destruction of Moab (Isa. 15:5; Jer. 48:34). The exact location of Zoar is uncertain; it may be at the site of es-Safi, located about five miles south of the Dead Sea. ***See also*** Cities. J.M.W.

Zobah (zoh'bah), or Aram-zobah, one of the independent city-states the Arameans (Syrians) formed at the beginning of the first millennium B.C. Zobah was situated in the Valley of Lebanon, with Hamath to the north and Damascus to the south. The kingdom of Zobah was extensive, controlling eastern Syria from the Hauran to the Euphrates Valley. So powerful was it that it posed a threat not only to Israel but even to imperial Assyria. 1 Sam. 14:47 mentions Saul's victory over Zobah. Some scholars, however, maintain that the Arameans did not appear on the Israelite stage until the time of David. Aram-zobah was David's arch rival for control of Syria and Transjordan. When David was warring with the Ammonites, Hadadezer ben Rehob, the powerful Aramean king of Zobah, intervened in support of the Ammonites (2 Sam. 8:5; 1 Chron. 18:3–9). As a result, David twice defeated Hadadezer and reduced Zobah to the status of subject.

P.J.K.

Zohar (zoh'hahr). **1** The father of Ephron, the Hittite who sold Abraham the cave of Machpelah in which to bury Sarah (Gen. 23:8; 25:9). **2** A son of Simeon who accompanied Jacob and his family to Egypt (Gen. 46:10) and became the head of a family group there (Exod. 6:15). This is probably the same person who is elsewhere called Zerah (1 Chron. 4:24), the ancestor of the family group called the Zerahites who left Egypt with Moses (Num. 26:13). **3** A descendant of Judah (1 Chron. 4:7); the name occurs as a traditional marginal correction (Qere) for the name Izhar, the form that appears in the Hebrew text. In some versions the name appears as Jezoar. Since this is the only occurrence of this person in the Bible and the text is not clear, the proper form of the name is uncertain. ***See also*** Izhar; Zerah; Zerahites. D.R.B.

Zoheleth (zoh-he'leth). ***See*** Serpent's Stone.

Zophar (zoh'fahr), one of the three friends of Job who offered him comfort and advice (Job 2:11; 11:1; 20:1); their counsel to Job prompts a rebuke from God for its lack of understanding and insight (Job 42:7–9). ***See also*** Job, The Book of.

Zorah (zoh'rah), a town (modern Sar'ah) located in the Valley of Sorek, three miles northeast of Beth-shemesh and fifteen miles west of Jerusalem. The Danite Manoah, father of Samson, came from Zorah, and Samson was raised there (Judg. 13:2, 25). Both he and his father were buried in the region between Zorah and Eshtaol (Judg. 16:31). The Danites were the first tribe to settle in the Zorah area (Josh. 15:33; 19:31). When the neighboring Philistines encroached upon their territory, the Danites migrated north; they settled at Laish and renamed it Dan (Judg. 18). With the departure of the Danites from Zorah the town became Judahite. To protect Judah from the Egyptians, King Rehoboam fortified Zorah and the surrounding towns in the Shephelah region. Upon return from Babylonian exile Jews settled again in Zorah.

P.J.K.

Zoroaster (zawr-oh-as'tuhr), an east Iranian prophet whose followers worshiped the deity Ahura-Mazda. Belief in divine beings, *Ahuras*, was probably part of the older Aryan religion.

Zoroaster appears in a new personal relationship to Ahura-Mazda, whom Zoroaster may have seen as the personification of all of the other divine qualities. A large number of inscriptions from the time of Darius (late sixth century B.C.) show that Ahura-Mazda was considered to be the god of the Iranians, though Zoroastrianism does not appear to have had the formal organization at that time that it would acquire later.

According to Zoroaster, the history of the world was divided into three ages of three thousand years each. The first was the golden age of Ahura-Mazda. The second was a period of warfare with evil that ended with the coming of Zoroaster. The prophet brought a new force enabling humans to participate in separating truth from falsehood. The final period would extend until the renovation of the world.

Some elements of this belief appear to have influenced the development of angelology, dualism, belief in an evil power, Satan, and a periodized story of the world that we find in the Judaism of the Greco-Roman period, especially in Daniel and the apocryphal writings. ***See also*** Apocalyptic Literature; Apocrypha, Old Testament; Pseudepigrapha; Satan. P.P.

Zuar (zoo'uhr), father of Nethanel, the leader of the tribe of Issachar during the wandering of the Israelites through Sinai (Num. 1:8; 2:5; 7:18, 23; 10:15).

Zur (zuhr). **1** A Midianite prince whose daughter, Cozbi, was killed by Phinehas along with her new husband Zimri of Israel (Num. 25:15; see Num. 25:6–8). Zur was slain by the Israelites in the battle in which Moses defeated Sihon, king of the Amorites (Num. 31:8; Josh. 13:21). **2** A Gibeonite, the son of Jeiel (1 Chron. 8:30, 9:36). ***See also*** Sihon.

Zurishaddai (zo͞o-ri-shad'dī; Heb., "Shaddai [divine title translated 'the Almighty'] is my Rock"), the father of Shelumiel, the leader of the tribe of Simeon during the wilderness wandering (Num. 1:6; 10:19).

PHOTOGRAPH AND ILLUSTRATION CREDITS

Aleppo Museum, Syria, *252;* Alinari/Art Resource, N.Y., *117* (upper), *118, 580, 845, 876, 883;* American Bible Society, *266;* American Numismatic Society, N.Y., *647* (upper), *648, 649* (top four), *650* (all), *651* (upper), *697, 841, 880, 1070* (lower); From *Ancient Synagogues Revealed* (Israel Exploration Society), *563, 736* (upper); Denis Baly, *3, 85, 675, 761* (upper), *1070* (upper); Gabriel Barkay, Jerusalem/Israel Exploration Society, *28* (both); Antonia Benedek, *734;* From *The Bible Almanac* (Thomas Nelson Publishers), *755;* Courtesy of the *Biblical Archaeologist* and American Schools of Oriental Research, *234, 421; Biblical Archaeology Review, 638;* Biblioteca Medica-Laurenziana, Florence, *757* (papiro laurenziano PSI 1165), *1052* (Ms. laur. Amat. 1, c. 5 r.); Bibliotheca Bodmeriana, Cologny-Geneve, *1047;* Bibliotheque Municipale, Amiens, *259;* Bibliotheque Nationale, Paris, (Ms. Grec. 74, f. 95 v.) *40,* (Ms. Lat. 1, f. 10 v.) *338,* (Ms. Lat. 1) *656,* (Ms. Grec. 139, f. 419 v.) *758,* (Ms. Grec. 139, f. 1 v.) *835,* (Ms. Lat. 1, f. 3 v.) *1050;* Bilderarchiv Foto Marburg/Art Resource, N.Y., *628;* Photo by permission of Lawrence Blaser, *262;* Roger S. Boraas, *14, 45, 48, 107;* Courtesy of E. J. Brill Publishing, Leiden, *1023;* © British and Foreign Bible Society, London, *263, 594, 802;* By permission of the British Library, *125* (right), *208, 498, 513, 584, 606, 613, 868, 887, 976, 1045, 1048;* Reproduced courtesy of The Trustees of The British Museum, *69* (upper), *76, 78, 88, 92, 98, 142, 145, 151, 191, 206, 209, 224, 236, 332, 412, 429, 451, 538, 564, 647* (lower), *649* (lower two), *651* (lower), *666* (upper), *715, 778, 793, 797, 851* (left), *884, 918, 932, 936, 975, 1071, 1117;* British School of Archaeology in Jerusalem, *460;* Courtesy Ian Browning and Chatto & Windus from *Palmyra* (fig. 130), *1015;* From *The Cambridge History of the Bible,* 3, ed. S. L. Greenslade, © Cambridge University Press, 1963 (plate 12), *1039;* By permission of the Syndics of Cambridge University Library, the Nash Papyrus, photograph courtesy John C. Trever, *720;* L. Cavro, from *The Bible as History in Pictures,* Werner Keller (William Morrow & Co., p. 215), *368* (center right); Courtesy of James Charlesworth/ Biblioteca Medica-Laurenziana, Florence, *837;* Chester Beatty Library and Gallery of Oriental Art, *607, 1046;* Clichees des Musees Nationaux (Musee du Louvre), *83, 95, 253, 392* (upper), *433, 987, 1002;* Dan Cole, *635;* Courtesy of the College of Wooster, Ohio, *768;* Commissioners of Public Works, Ireland, *147;* G. Cornfeld, *427, 467, 772, 823, 1054;* Dagon Collection, Archaeological Museum of Grain Handling, Haifa, *668* (upper); DeRossi, *115* (lower); Deutsches Archaologisches Institut, Abt. Teheran, *368* (center left); W. G. Dever, *140;* Pierre Devinoy, *492;* Moshe Dothan/Israel Exploration Society, *1013;* Ecole Francaise d'Archeologie, Athens, *331;* Courtesy of The Egypt Exploration Society, *137, 261;* Egyptian Museum, Cairo, *435;* Lee C. Ellenberger, *743;* From *Encyclopedia of Archaeological Excavations in the Holy Land* (Israel Exploration Society), *189, 320;* Ron Erickson, *184* (lower), *239, 410, 490, 526;* From *Excavations at Nuzi,* III, T. J. Meek (Harvard University Press © 1935), reprinted by permission, *714;* Jack Finegan, *109;* From Jack Finegan, *The Archaeology of the New Testament* (Princeton University Press, 1969), *397;* E. L. Flynn, *113, 120* (upper), *243;* Courtesy of the Fogg Art Museum, Harvard University, Grenville L. Winthrop Bequest, *125* (left); George Forsythe and Kurt Weitzmann, *The Monastery of St. Catherine at Sinai: The Church and Fortress of Justinian* (University of Michigan Press, 1973), *201, 204* (lower), *475, 548, 658;* Paul Geuthner/Librarie Orientaliste, *854, 1014;* From Nelson Glueck, *The River Jordan* (McGraw Hill, 1968, p. 49), *741;* David Harris, Jerusalem, *718, 735, 898;* © President and Fellows of Harvard College for The Semitic Museum, *1001;* Avraham Hay, Institute of Archaeology, Tel Aviv University, *537, 542;* © Hebrew Union College-Jewish Institute of Religion, Jerusalem, *203;* Hermitage Museum, Leningrad, *825;* Hittite Museum (Museum of Anatolian Civilization), Ankara, *821;* Institute for Antiquity and Christianity, Claremont, Calif., *356, 679;* © Institute of Archaeology, Hebrew University of Jerusalem, *15;* Israel Department of Antiquities and Museums, *89, 108, 134, 321, 459* (lower), *540* (lower), *541* (lower, courtesy *Biblical Archaeology Review*), *669* (upper and lower), *670* (lower), *712, 736* (lower), *752, 907, 917, 947, 949, 1020, 1130;* Israel Exploration Society, *899;* Israel Government Press Office, *41*, *471*, *473* (both), *477*, *660*, *900*; Israel Museum, Jerusalem, *897*, *1072*; From "The Israelite Fortress at Arad," Z. Herog, M. Aharoni, A. Rainey, and S. Moskovit, in the *Bulletin of the American Schools of Oriental Research* (254), *24*; The Jewish Museum of New York/Art Resource, N.Y., *281*, *1105*; D. Johannes, *730*; By permission of the John Rylands University Library, Manchester (Rylands Greek Pap. 457), *1042*; Hermann Junker, from *Giza II*, plate VII b, *914*; Howard Clark Kee, *10*, *184* (upper), *272* (lower), *280*, *340*, *636* (lower), *732*, *744*, *1109*; J. Kenneth Kuntz, *57*, *59*, *61*, *62* (both), *70* (lower), *230*, *385*, *624* (both), *1031*; The Archbishop of Canterbury and the Trustees of Lambeth Palace Library, London, *425*, *444*; Erich Lessing, *11*, *34*, *55*, *58*, *64*, *67*, *114*, *116*, *120* (lower), *172*, *182*, *183*, *270*, *271* (both), *286*, *298*, *301*, *313*, *326*, *342* (lower), *346*, *368* (far left), *390*, *392* (lower), *441*, *463*, *465*, *468*, *477* (upper), *478*, *483*, *485*, *504*, *507*, *517*, *535*, *545*, *551*, *577*, *587*, *620*, *621* (lower), *622* (lower two), *636* (right), *655*, *693*, *706*, *710*, *723*, *739*, *749*, *781*, *817*, *826*, *864*, *912*, *926*, *927*, *931*, *952*, *1029* (both), *1032*, *1068*, *1112*, *1125*, *1131*, *1132*, *1133*, *1137*; Erich Lessing/Aleppo Museum, *417*, *1147*; Erich Lessing/Archaeological Museum, Istanbul, *828*; Erich Lessing/Bibliotheque Nationale, Paris, *721* (Ms. Grec. 139), *893* (Ms. Grec. 139, fol. 5 v.); Erich Lessing/British Museum, *1*, *288*, *539* (all), *851* (right), *924*, *1106*; Erich Lessing/Borowski Collection, Bronfman Archaeological Museum, Jerusalem, *1085*; Erich Lessing/Byzantine Museum, Athens, *890*; Erich Lessing/Egyptian Museum, Cairo, *68* (upper); Erich Lessing/Edith and Reuben Hecht Museum, University of Haifa, *19*, *462*; Erich Lessing/Hessisches Landesmuseum, Darmstadt, *610*; Erich Lessing/Hittite Museum (Museum of Anatolian Civilization), Ankara, *670* (upper); Erich Lessing/Iraq Museum, Baghdad, *68* (lower), *69* (lower), *204* (upper), *352* (lower), *988* (upper); Erich Lessing/Israel Department of Antiquities and Museums, Jerusalem, 23, *324*, *376*, *415*, *423*, *440*, *533*, *540* (upper), *541* (upper), *621* (upper), *622* (upper), *623* (all), *667* (upper), *814* (upper and lower), *815* (upper), *1005*, *1028* (upper), *1127* (upper); Erich Lessing/Israel Museum, *180* (both), *244*, *383*; Erich Lessing/Kunsthistorisches Museum, Vienna, *117* (lower), *249*, *272* (upper), *476*; Erich Lessing/Musee de Cluny, Paris, *484*; Erich Lessing/Musee des Beaux-Arts, Dijon, *525*; Erich Lessing/Musee du Louvre, Paris, *8*, *72* (upper and lower), *122*, *160*, *163*, *185*, *318*, *342* (upper), *370*, *543*, *644*, *667* (lower), *668* (lower left), *842*, *908*, *959*, *989*, *992*, *1124*; Erich Lessing/Musee Lapidaire Chretien, Arles, *446*; Erich Lessing/Museo dell'Arcivescovado, Ravenna, *501*, *1154*; Erich Lessing/Museo della Civilta Romana, Rome, *339*; Erich Lessing/Museo Egizio, Turin, *231*; Erich Lessing/National Library, Athens, *486*, *640*; Erich Lessing/from the collection of the National Maritime Museum, Haifa, *297*, *815* (lower); Erich Lessing/National Museum, Damascus, *235*, *604*, *665* (lower); Erich Lessing/National Museum of Archaeology, Beirut, *792*; Erich Lessing/Selcuk Museum, Turkey, *66*, *1092*; Erich Lessing/Staatliche Museen, East Berlin, *70* (upper), *226*, *691*; Erich Lessing/by courtesy of the Board of Trustees of the Victoria and Albert Museum, London, *761* (lower); Rafi Magnes, *1165*; Metropolitan Museum of Art, New York, gift of J. Pierpont Morgan (1917) *210*, Egyptian Expedition (1933) *334*, Fletcher Fund (1933) *487*, gift of George F. Baker (1890) *846*, photography by the Egyptian Expedition, *960*; Museo delle Terme, Rome, *168*; Museum of Antiquities of the University and the Society of Antiquaries of Newcastle upon Tyne, England, *674*; Courtesy Museum of Fine Arts, Boston, H. L. Pierce Fund 04.736, *20*; Garo Nalbandian, *31*, *162*, *470*, *937*; NASA, *857*, *957*; National Museum, Beirut, *1110*; National Museum, Stockholm, Sweden, *518*, *929*; The Ny Carlsberg Glyptotek, Copenhagen, *763*; Patti O'Connor-Seger/Lahav Research Project, *51*, *53*, *54*, *158*, *812*, *872*; Courtesy of the Oriental Institute, University of Chicago, *177*, *358*, *368* (far right), *618*, *668* (lower right), *773*, *855*, *1152*; From *The Ethiopic Book of Enoch* by Michael A. Knibb and E. Ullendorff © Oxford University Press (1978) *838*; Courtesy of the Pierpont Morgan Library (Ms. 638, f. 33 v.) *4*, (Ms. 638, f. 28 v.) *211*, (Ms. 638, f. 39 v.) *306*, (Ms. 638, f. 13 v.) *455*, (Ms. 638, f. 9 v.) *602*, (Ms. 638, f. 9 v.) *641*, (Ms. 638, f. 4 v.) *850*, (Ms. 638, f. 22 v.) *902*, (Ms. 638, f. 22 v.) *910*; Gene Plaisted, *759*; Pontificia Commissione Di Archeologia Sacra, *862*, *941*, *1004*; Princeton University Press, *654*; James Pritchard/Lemon Bible Lands Museum, *811*; James Pritchard/University Museum, Philadelphia, *1151*, *1157*; Z. Radovan, Jerusalem, *26*, *464*, *522*, *662*, *790*, *905*, *1103*, *1111*, *1120*; Z. Radovan, Jerusalem/Israel Department of Antiquities and Museums, *146*, *352* (upper), *480*, *488*, *578*, *676*, *789*, *1012*, *1038*; Z. Radovan, Jerusalem/Israel Museum, *74*, *895*, *1150*; Rheinisches Landesmuseum, Trier, *247*; Collection of Rijksmuseum van Oudheden, Leiden, *666* (lower); Scala/Art Resource, N.Y., *192*; Reprinted by permission of Schocken Books, Inc., from *Ancient Hebrew Art* by Adolph Reifenberg © 1950 by Schocken Books, Inc., *588*; Hershel Shanks, *303*; Shrine of the Book, Israel Museum, Jerusalem, *840*, *915*; Staatliche Museen, East Berlin, *251*, *363*, *1119*; Staats und Universitatsbibliothek, Hamburg, (Cod. Levy 19, fol. 403^r) *111*, (Cod. Levy 19, fol. 402^v) *901*; Tel Aviv University Archaeological Museum, photo courtesy *Biblical Archaeology Review*, *101*; John C. Trever, *553*, *916*; The Board of Trinity College, Dublin, *325*, *354*; Universitetsbiblioteket, Uppsala, *1043*; © University of Chicago Press, from G. Loud, *The Megiddo Ivories* (1939), *316*; University Museum, University of

Pennsylvania, *71, 139, 665* (upper), *708, 1164;* By courtesy of the Board of Trustees of the Victoria and Albert Museum, London, *776;* From *Views of the Biblical World* (Jerusalem Publishing Co.), *406;* Virginia Museum of Fine Arts, *123;* Walters Art Gallery, Baltimore, *6, 489;* Warburg Institute, photo courtesy Jewish Museum, London, *632;* Wide World Photos, courtesy *Biblical Archaeology Review, 44;* R. B. Wright, *344;* Courtesy of the Yigael Yadin estate, *(Hazor,* p. 116-17) *153, (Israel Exploration Journal,* v. 5, 1955, p. 8) *938;* Yale University Art Gallery/Dura-Europos Collection, *2, 16, 97, 202, 257, 293, 521, 529, 1011;* Bruce Zuckerman/USC Archeological Research Collection, *810.*

Color photographs following page 330. First page: 1, 3. Erich Lessing/British Museum, 2. Avraham Hay, Institute of Archaeology, Tel Aviv University. Second page: 1. Erich Lessing/British Museum, 2. Erich Lessing/Israel Department of Antiquities and Museums, 3. Erich Lessing. Third page: 1, 2. Erich Lessing/Musee du Louvre, 3. Erich Lessing. Fourth page: 1, 2a. Princeton University Press. Fifth page: 1. Zev Radovan, 2b. Princeton University Press. Sixth page: 1. Erich Lessing/Palatine Library, Parma, 2. Garo Nalbandian. Seventh page: 1. Pontificia Commissione Di Archeologia Sacra, 2. Zev Radovan, 3. Roger Boraas. Eighth page: 1, 2. Erich Lessing, 3. Erich Lessing/Monumenti Musei e Gallerie Pontificie, Rome.

Color photographs following page 778. First page: 1. Zev Radovan, 2, 4. Erich Lessing, 3. University Museum, University of Pennsylvania, 5. Elisabeth L. Flynn. Second page: 1. Trinity College Library, Dublin, 2. Pierpont Morgan Library (Ms. 102, f. 1 v.), 3. Erich Lessing/Israel Museum, 4. Bruce Zuckerman/West Semitic Research Project. Third page: 1, 2. Photographs © John C. Trever, 1970, from Shrine of the Book, Israel Museum, Jerusalem, 3. British Library. Fourth page: 1. Garo Nalbandian, 2. National Air Survey Center, Corp., 3, 5. Erich Lessing, 4. Howard Clark Kee. Fifth page: 1, 2, 3, 4, 5. Erich Lessing. Sixth page: 1. Erich Lessing/National Library, Athens, 2, 3. Erich Lessing, 4. Elisabeth L. Flynn. Seventh page: 1. Erich Lessing, 2, 3. George Forsythe and Kurt Weitzman, *The Monastery of St. Catherine at Sinai: The Church and Fortress of Justinian* (University of Michigan Press, 1973). Eighth page: 1. *The Annunciation,* Masolino da Panicale, National Gallery of Art, Washington, D.C., Andrew W. Mellon Collection, 2. Erich Lessing/Open Air Museum, Kizhi Island, 3. Pierpont Morgan Library (Ms. 638, f. 33 v.).

Plant illustrations are based in part on art from *All the Plants of the Bible* by Winifred Walker, copyright © 1957 Winifred Walker, reprinted by permission of Doubleday & Co., Inc.

Diagram, *197,* from *Ancient Times, 2nd Edition,* by James Henry Breasted, copyright 1935, by James Henry Breasted, © copyright renewed, 1963, by Charles Breasted, published by Ginn and Company. Used with permission.

Table, *1148,* adapted from the "Table showing the development of Hebrew, Greek and Roman alphabets" from *The Archaeology of Palestine,* William Foxwell Albright (Pelican Books, 1949, revised 1954, 1956, 1960), copyright © W. F. Albright, 1949, reproduced by permission of Penguin Books, Ltd.

INDEX TO COLOR MAPS

This index lists geographical names found on the color maps at the back of this book. The number(s) of the map(s) on which the name appears is listed first, followed by the key, or grid reference (a letter-figure combination that refers to the letters and figures at the margins of the map). Places whose names changed over time are identified by a "see also" reference. For example, the entry for Azotus indicates it can be found on Map 10 in location B5, and on Map 12 in location A5, and readers are referred to Ashdod, its alternate name.

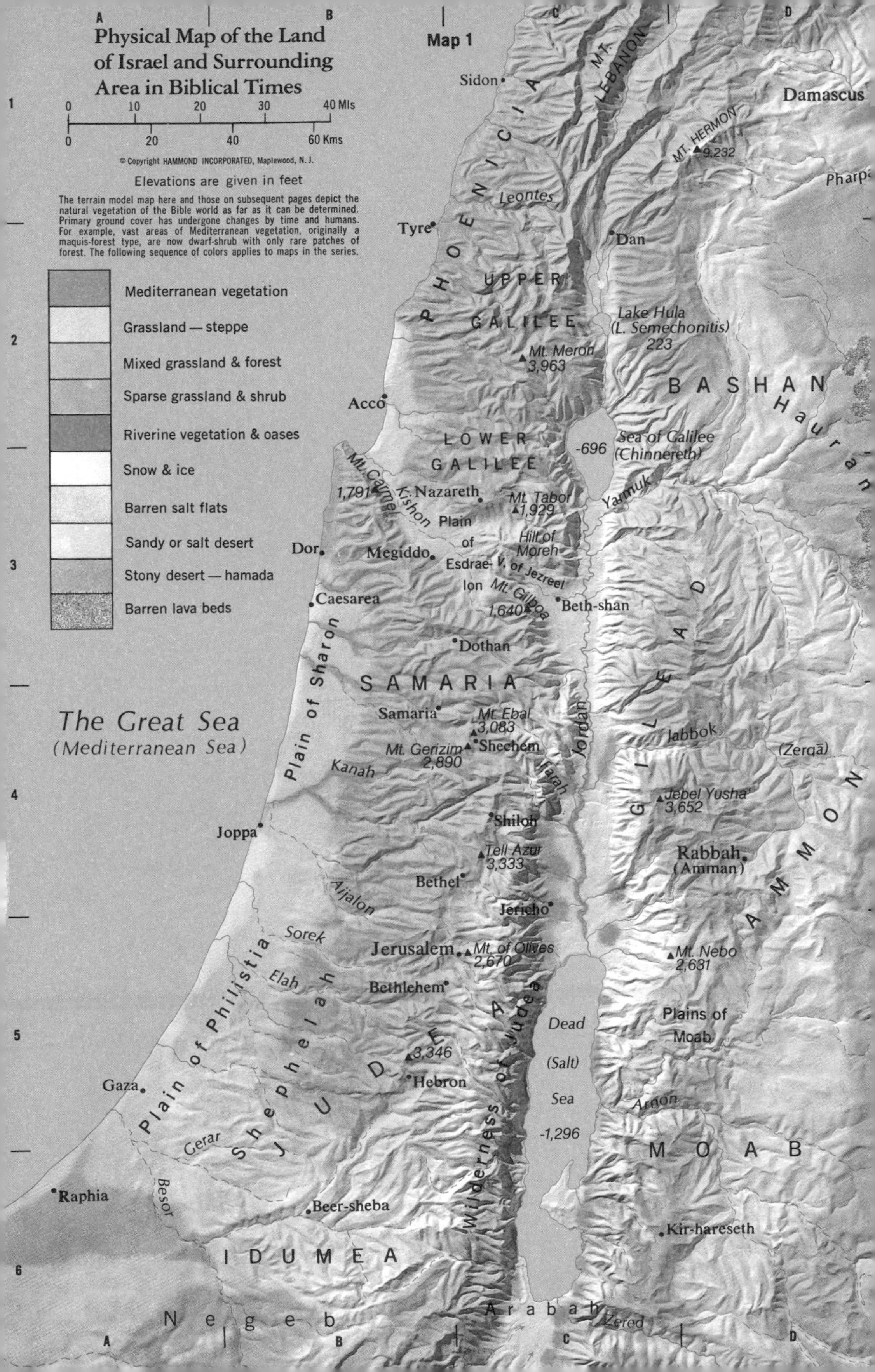
Physical Map of the Land of Israel and Surrounding Area in Biblical Times
Map 1
0 10 20 30 40 Mls
0 20 40 60 Kms
© Copyright HAMMOND INCORPORATED, Maplewood, N. J.
Elevations are given in feet
The terrain model map here and those on subsequent pages depict the natural vegetation of the Bible world as far as it can be determined. Primary ground cover has undergone changes by time and humans. For example, vast areas of Mediterranean vegetation, originally a maquis-forest type, are now dwarf-shrub with only rare patches of forest. The following sequence of colors applies to maps in the series.
Mediterranean vegetation
Grassland — steppe
Mixed grassland & forest
Sparse grassland & shrub
Riverine vegetation & oases
Snow & ice
Barren salt flats
Sandy or salt desert
Stony desert — hamada
Barren lava beds
A
B
C
D
1
2
3
4
5
6
Sidon
PHOENICIA
MT. LEBANON
Damascus
MT. HERMON
9,232
Pharpar
Leontes
Tyre
Dan
UPPER GALILEE
Lake Hula
(L. Semechonitis)
223
Mt. Meron
3,963
BASHAN
Hauran
Acco
LOWER GALILEE
-696
Sea of Galilee
(Chinnereth)
Mt. Carmel
1,791
Kishon
Nazareth
Mt. Tabor
1,929
Yarmuk
Plain of Esdraelon
Hill of Moreh
V. of Jezreel
Dor
Megiddo
Mt. Gilboa
1,640
Beth-shan
Caesarea
GILEAD
Dothan
SAMARIA
Plain of Sharon
The Great Sea
(Mediterranean Sea)
Samaria
Mt. Ebal
3,083
Mt. Gerizim
2,890
Shechem
Jordan
Jabbok
(Zerqā)
Kanah
Farah
Jebel Yusha'
3,652
AMMON
Joppa
Shiloh
Tell Azur
3,333
Rabbah
(Amman)
Bethel
Aijalon
Jericho
Sorek
Jerusalem
Mt. of Olives
2,670
Mt. Nebo
2,631
Plain of Philistia
Elah
Bethlehem
Shephelah
JUDEA
Wilderness of Judea
Dead (Salt) Sea
-1,296
Plains of Moab
3,346
Hebron
Gaza
Arnon
Gerar
MOAB
Raphia
Besor
Beer-sheba
Kir-hareseth
IDUMEA
Negeb
Arabah
Zered

Map 2
The Ancient World in the Late Bronze Age
Areas of influence of major powers about 1350 B.C.E.
0 50 100 150 200 250 Mls
0 100 200 300 400 Kms
© Copyright HAMMOND INCORPORATED, Maplewood, N. J.
Black Sea
Caspian Sea
Mediterranean Sea
(Great or Upper Sea)
Persian Gulf
(Lower Sea)
Red Sea
Libyan Desert
MINOAN-MYCENAEAN DOMAIN
HITTITE EMPIRE
(HATTI)
EGYPTIAN EMPIRE
MITANNI
ASSYRIA
BABYLONIA
KASHKA
URARTU
HURRIANS
(HORITES)
ASSUWA
ARZAWA
LUKKA
Kizzuwatna
TAURUS MTS.
ZAGROS MOUNTAINS
GUTIUM
KASSITES
MEDIA
ELAM
KEDAR
MIDIAN
Sinai
Sumer
Akkad
CAPHTOR
(Crete)
ALASHIYA, KITTIM
(Cyprus)
Lower Egypt
Troy
Karabel
Hermes
Sangarius
Maeander
Beycesultan
Rhodes
Cnossus
Halys
Alaca Huyuk
Hattusas
Ankuwa
Kanish
L. Tuz
Mersin
Carchemish
Malatya
Alalakh
Haleb
Ugarit
Ebla
Hamath
Arvad
Kadesh
Gebal
Sidon
Damascus
Tyre
Hazor
Dor
Megiddo
Shechem
Jericho
Joppa
Jerusalem
Gaza
Hebron
Beer-sheba
Kadesh-barnea
Avaris
(Zoan)
On
Memphis
(Noph)
Heracleopolis
Hermopolis
Akhetaton
(Tell el-Amarna)
Nile
Abydos
Haran
Paddan-aram
Tell Halaf
Tell Leilan
Tell Brak
Nineveh
Tepe Gawra
Arbela
Calah
Jarmo
Asshur
Nuzi
Tadmor
Mari
Euphrates
Tigris
Diyala
Eshnunna
Agade?
Sippar
Cuthah
Babylon
Nippur
Isin
Lagash
Erech
Ur
Eridu
Dumah
Tema
Dedan
Mt. Ararat
Cyrus
Araxes
L. Van
L. Urmia
Ecbatana
Tepe Giyan
Susa
Dilmun?

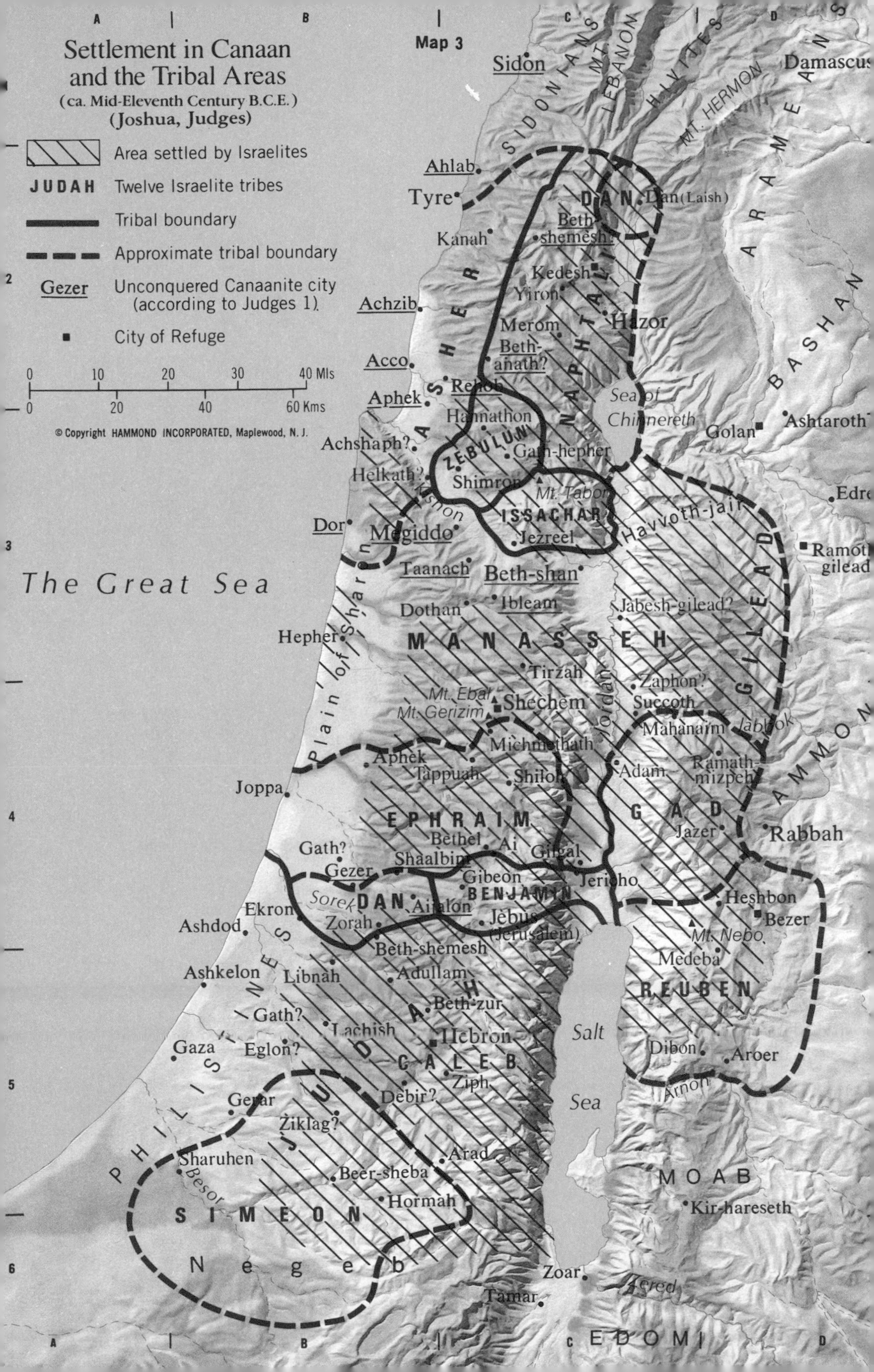

Map 3
Settlement in Canaan and the Tribal Areas
(ca. Mid-Eleventh Century B.C.E.)
(Joshua, Judges)
Area settled by Israelites
JUDAH Twelve Israelite tribes
Tribal boundary
Approximate tribal boundary
Gezer Unconquered Canaanite city (according to Judges 1)
City of Refuge
0 10 20 30 40 Mls
0 20 40 60 Kms
© Copyright HAMMOND INCORPORATED, Maplewood, N. J.
A
B
C
D
1
2
3
4
5
6
The Great Sea
Sidon
SIDONIANS
MT. LEBANON
HIVITES
MT. HERMON
Damascus
ARAMEANS
BASHAN
Ahlab
Tyre
DAN
Dan (Laish)
Beth-shemesh?
Kanah
Kedesh
Yiron
Achzib
ASHER
NAPHTALI
Hazor
Merom
Beth-anath?
Acco
Rehob
Aphek
Sea of Chinnereth
Golan
Ashtaroth
Hannathon
Achshaph?
ZEBULUN
Gath-hepher
Helkath?
Shimron
Mt. Tabor
Kishon
Edrei
ISSACHAR
Havvoth-jair
Dor
Megiddo
Jezreel
Ramoth-gilead
Taanach
Beth-shan
GILEAD
Plain of Sharon
Dothan
Ibleam
Jabesh-gilead?
Hepher
MANASSEH
Tirzah
Jordan
Zaphon?
Mt. Ebal
Mt. Gerizim
Shechem
Succoth
Mahanaim
Jabbok
Michmethath
AMMON
Aphek
Tappuah
Shiloh
Adam
Ramath-mizpeh
Joppa
EPHRAIM
GAD
Bethel
Ai
Jazer
Rabbah
Gath?
Shaalbim
Gilgal
Gezer
Gibeon
Jericho
BENJAMIN
Sorek
DAN
Aijalon
Heshbon
Ekron
Bezer
Ashdod
Zorah
Jebus (Jerusalem)
Mt. Nebo
Beth-shemesh
Medeba
Ashkelon
Libnah
Adullam
PHILISTINES
JUDAH
REUBEN
Beth-zur
Gath?
Lachish
Hebron
Salt Sea
Gaza
Eglon?
Dibon
Aroer
CALEB
Ziph
Arnon
Gerar
Debir?
Ziklag?
Arad
Sharuhen
Besor
Beer-sheba
MOAB
Hormah
Kir-hareseth
SIMEON
Negeb
Zoar
Zered
Tamar
EDOM

Map 4
The Empire of David and Solomon
(ca. 1000-924 B.C.E.)
Boundary of the empire at its greatest extent
Territory conquered by David
Fortified places of Solomon
Copper mining centers
0 10 25 50 75 Mls
0 20 40 60 80 100 120 Kms
© Copyright HAMMOND INCORPORATED, Maplewood, N. J.
The Great Sea
(Mediterranean Sea)
Hamath
Arvad
Kadesh
Zedad
Hazar-enan
ARAM-ZOBAH
Lebo-hamath
Gebal
Berothai
Berytus
PHOENICIA
MT. LEBANON
BETH-REHOB
ARAM-DAMASCUS
Damascus
Sidon
MT. HERMON
Tyre
Abel
Dan
Kedesh
MAACAH
Hazor
Acco
ARGOB
Cabul
Mt. Carmel
GESHUR
Ashtaroth
Dor
TOB
Edrei
Megiddo
Jezreel
Taanach
Beth-shan
Ramoth-gilead
Salecah
Mt. Gilboa
Hepher
Jordan
Shechem
Succoth
Mahanaim
Joppa
ISRAEL
Rabbah
AMMON
Gezer
Beth-horon
Baalath?
Bethel
Jericho
Gibeah
Ashdod
Jerusalem
Heshbon
Beth-shemesh
PHILISTIA
Medeba
Ashkelon
Gath?
Hebron
Gaza
Lachish
Salt Sea
Aroer
Ziklag?
Gerar
Raphia
Beer-sheba
Arad
JUDAH
MOAB
Kir-hareseth
Tamar
AMALEK
Bozrah
Kadesh-barnea
Punon
River of Egypt
EDOM
Sela
Arabah
Sinai
Ezion-geber?

The Kingdoms of Israel and Judah
(ca. 924–722 B.C.E.)
(1 and 2 Kings)
Approximate frontiers
ISRAEL Hebrew kingdoms
AMMON Foreign kingdoms
0 10 20 30 40 Mls
0 20 40 60 Kms
© Copyright HAMMOND INCORPORATED, Maplewood, N. J.
Map 5
Sidon
Damascus
PHOENICIA
MT. HERMON
SYRIA
(ARAM)
Leontes
Ijon
Tyre
Abel-beth-maachah
Dan
Kedesh
Hazor
Merom
Galilee
Bashan
Acco
Chinnereth
Cabul
Sea of Chinnereth
Karnaim
Ashtaroth
Rumah
Hammath
Aphek
Mt. Carmel
Plain of Esdraelon
Mt. Tabor
Yarmuk
Kishon
Havvoth-jair
Edrei
The Great Sea
(Mediterranean Sea)
Dor
Shunem
Megiddo
Jezreel
Mt. Gilboa
Ramoth-gilead
Taanach
Beth-shan
Ibleam
Jabesh-gilead?
Dothan
Abel-meholah?
Tishbe
Plain of Sharon
ISRAEL
Socoh
Tirzah
Jordan
Gilead
Samaria
Mt. Ebal
Penuel
Mt. Gerizim
Shechem
Succoth
Mahanaim
Jabbok
Kanah
AMMON
Aphek
Shiloh
Joppa
Zeredah
Jazer
Rabbah
Lod
Zemaraim
Gath?
Bethel
Gilgal
Mizpah
Jabneel
Gezer
Geba
Jericho
Gibbethon
Aijalon
Gibeon
Ramah
Shittim?
Heshbon
Ekron
Zorah
Jerusalem
Ashdod
Beth-shemesh
Bethlehem
Mt. Nebo
Medeba
Jahaz
Ashkelon
Socoh
Adullam
Etam
Tekoa
Gath?
Mareshah
Beth-zur
Ataroth
Lachish
JUDAH
Salt Sea
Gaza
Adoraim
Hebron
Dibon
En-gedi
Aroer
PHILISTIA
Ziph
Arnon
Debir?
Wilderness of Judah
Desert
Gerar
Ziklag?
Great Arad
Ar?
Raphia
Sharuhen
Beer-sheba
MOAB
Arad of Beth-yeroham
Kir-hareseth
Besor
Zoar
Tamar
Zered
Ziph
Ascent of Akrabbim
Negeb
Arabah
EDOM

Map 6
The Assyrian Empire
Assyrian empire—ca. 824 B.C.E.
Assyrian empire—ca. 640 B.C.E.
Cyrene Greek colonies underlined in red
0 50 100 150 200 250 300 350 Mls
0 100 200 300 400 500 Kms
© Copyright HAMMOND INCORPORATED, Maplewood, N. J.
CIMMERIANS (GOMER)
PHRYGIA
Gordion
Ancyra
Astacus
Cyzicus
Abydos
Aegean Sea
Lesbos
Chios
Euboea
GREEK CITY STATES
Corinth
Athens
Sparta
Samos
Miletus
Sardis
LYDIA
MESHECH
Rhodes
Crete
Phaselis
L. Tuz
TUBAL
Kanish
CILICIA
TAURUS MTS.
Tarsus
URARTU (ARARAT)
Mt. Ararat
L. Sevan
Araxes
Cyrus
Caspian Sea
L. Van
Turushpa
L. Urmia
Minni
Nairi
Melitene
Samal
Haran
Carchemish
Til Barsib
Arpad
Aleppo
Nisibis
Gozan
Habor
ASSYRIA
Dur Sharrukin
Nineveh
Arbela
Calah (Nimrud)
Asshur
ASSYRIAN EMPIRE
MADAI
Ecbatana
ELAM
Susa (Shushan)
Tigris
Diyala
Euphrates
Anat
BABYLONIA
Sippar
Cuthah
Babylon
Borsippa
Nippur
Erech
Larsa
Ur
CHALDEANS
Lower (Eastern) Sea
Upper (Western) Sea
Cyprus
Arvad
Qarqar
Hamath
SYRIA
Tadmor
PHOENICIA
Sidon
Tyre
Damascus
KEDAR
Samaria
AMMON
Eltekeh
Jerusalem
JUDAH trib. to Assyria
MOAB
EDOM
Sela
Raphia
ARIBI (ARABS)
Dumah
Tema
Dedan
Red Sea
Cyrene
LIBYANS
Libyan Desert
Oasis of Siwa
Sais
Tanis
Pelusium
Bubastis
On
Memphis
Nile
Heracleopolis
EGYPT to Assyria 671-651 B.C.E.
Hermopolis
Siut
Abydos
Thebes
Syene

Map 7
Judah After the Fall of Israel
(722–586 B.C.E.)
(2 Kings)
Approximate frontiers
AMMON Independent kingdoms
DU'RU Assyrian provinces
0 10 20 30 40 Mls
0 20 40 60 Kms
© Copyright MCMLXXVIII HAMMOND INCORPORATED, Maplewood, N. J.
A
B
C
D
1
2
3
4
5
6
The Great Sea
(Mediterranean Sea)
Sidon
Damascus
DIMAŠQI
(ARAM)
Phoenicia
MT. HERMON
Leontes
Ijon
Tyre
(free city)
Abel-beth-maachah
Dan
Kedesh
Hazor
Achzib
Nahariyeh
Acco
DŪR-BELḪARRAN
ṢADUA
Chinnereth
QARNINI
Sea of Chinnereth
Karnaim
Ashtaroth
ḪAURINA
Jotbah
Mt. Carmel
MAGIDŪ
Aphek
Yarmuk
Mt. Tabor
Kishon
Shunem
GAL'AZA
Dor
Megiddo
Jezreel
Ramoth-gilead
Taanach
Beth-shan
DU'RU
Ibleam
Dothan
Jabesh-gilead?
Gilead
Tirzah
Jordan
Samaria
Mt. Ebal
Penuel
Shechem
Succoth
Mahanaim
Jabbok
Mt. Gerizim
Kanah
Aphek
SAMERINA
ASSYRIAN EMPIRE
Shiloh
Joppa
Bene-berak
AMMON
Beth-dagon
Jazer
Lod
Rimmon
Rabbah
Gath?
Bethel
Aiath
Eltekah?
Gilgal
Mizpah
Geba
Jabneel
Gezer
Jericho
Shittim?
Gibbethon
Aijalon
Gibeon
Ramah
Elealeh
Gibeah
Anathoth
Heshbon
Ekron
Jerusalem
Sibmah
Ashdod
Nob
Timnah
Beth-shemesh
Mt. Nebo
Bethlehem
Medeba
Azekah
Jahaz
ASDUDU
Ashkelon
Adullam
Moresheth-gath
Tekoa
Gath?
Mareshah
Beth-zur
Ataroth
Lachish
Philistia
Salt Sea
Dibon
Gaza
Adoraim
Hebron
Aroer
Bethel-ezel
En-gedi
Ziph
Arnon
Debir?
Gerar
JUDAH
MOAB
Ziklag?
Great Arad
Ar?
Raphia
Sharuhen
Beer-sheba
EGYPT
Arad of Beth-yeroham?
Kir-hareseth
(Kir, Kir-heres)
Besor
Zoar
Tamar
Zered
Negeb
EDOM

Map 8
Great Empires of the Sixth Century B.C.E.
Political boundaries of major powers ca. 560 B.C.E.
Limits of the Persian empire ca. 500 B.C.E.
Persian royal road
0 100 200 300 400 500 Mls
0 200 400 600 800 Kms
© Copyright HAMMOND INCORPORATED, Maplewood, N. J.
Black Sea
Caspian Sea
Mediterranean Sea
Persian Gulf
Red Sea
Erythraean Sea
Libyan Desert
THRACE
MACEDONIA
GREECE
KINGDOM OF LYDIA (670-546 B.C.E.)
MEDIAN EMPIRE (612-550 B.C.E.)
NEW BABYLONIAN EMPIRE (625-529 B.C.E.)
KINGDOM OF EGYPT (663-525 B.C.E.)
Cyprus (trib. to Egypt 569-525 B.C.E.)
LIBYA
ETHIOPIA (CUSH)
ARABS
CHORASMIA
SAKA
SOGDIANA
MARGUS
BACTRIA
ARIA
PARTHIA
HYRCANIA
ARACHOSIA
DRANGIANA
GEDROSIA (MAKA)
CARMANIA
PERSIS
ELAM (SUSIANA)
MEDIA
BABYLONIA
ASSYRIA
URARTU
MOSCHI
SCYTHIANS
CAUCASUS
CILICIA
KUE
LYCIA
JUDAH
ZALLA
Apollonia
Byzantium
Sinope
Phasis
Trapezus
Chersonesus
Athens
Marathon
Sparta
Sardis
Ephesus
Miletus
Rhodes
Crete
Xanthus
Gordion
Ancyra
Pteria
Iconium
Tarsus
Melitene
Haran
Nisibis
Carchemish
Thapsacus
Hamath
Arvad
Riblah
Gebal
Damascus
Tadmor
Anat
Tyre
Megiddo
Jerusalem
Gaza
Pelusium
Sais
Memphis
Thebes
Syene (Elephantine)
Cyrene
Temple of Amon (Siwa)
Elath
Dumah
Tema
Dedan
Nineveh
Asshur
Arbela
Opis
Sippar
Babylon
Nippur
Erech
Ur
Susa
Behistun
Gerrha
Rhagae
Gabae
Yazd
Persepolis (Parsa)
Pasargadae
Zadrakarta
Damghan
Margiana
Bactra
Cyropolis
Pura
Aral Sea
Danube
Halys
Maeander
Araxes
Cyrus
Tigris
Euphrates
Ulai
Nile
Oxus
Jaxartes
Van
Urmia
A
B
C
D
E
F
1
2
3
4

Map 9
Israel Under Persian Rule (After the Return from Exile)
(539–332 B.C.E.)
(Ezra, Nehemiah)
Satrapy capital
District capitals
Provincial capitals
Towns
0 5 10 15 20 25 30 35 40 Mls
0 10 20 30 40 50 60 Kms
© Copyright HAMMOND INCORPORATED, Maplewood, N. J.
SIDON
MT. HERMON
Damascus
DAMASCUS
Tyre
TYRE
Kedesh
Achzib
Hazor
ACHZIB
Acco
ACCO
KARNAIM
Karnaim
Lake Gennesaret
Mt. Carmel
GALILEE
Beth-yerah
Yarmuk
HAURAN
Dor
The Great Sea
(Mediterranean Sea)
Strato's Tower
Narbatah
Beth-shan
Jordan
Pella
GILEAD
DOR
Plain of Sharon
Samaria
Mt. Ebal
Mt. Gerizim
Shechem
Gerasa
Jabbok
Apollonia
SAMARIA
Accrabbah
Aphek
Joppa
Shiloh
Ono
Neballat
Lod
Hadid
Bethel
Rabbah
Gittaim
Lower Beth-horon
Beeroth
Ai
Beth-gilgal
Tyre of Tobiah
Jamnia
Mizpah
Ramah
Jericho
AMMON
Gezer
Geba
Gibeon
Anathoth
Kiriath-jearim
Heshbon
Beth-haccherem
Jerusalem
Ashdod
Zanoah
JUDAH (YAHUD)
Medeba
Bethlehem
Azekah
Ashkelon
Adullam
Netophah
Keilah
Tekoa
Mareshah
Nebo
Beth-zur
Salt Sea
Lachish
ASHDOD
Gaza
Hebron
En-gedi
Arnon
Gerar
Ziklag?
En-rimmon
MOAB
IDUMEA
Raphia
Jeshua?
Beer-sheba
Moladah
(EDOMITES)
Beth-pelet?
NABATEAN ARABS

The Empire of Alexander
Limits of Alexander's empire 323 B.C.E.
CYPRUS Allied states and client kingdoms dependent on Alexander
Alexander's route
Cities founded by Alexander
Major battles
Nearchus' voyage
0 100 200 300 400 500
0 200 400 600 800
Alexander died at Babylon in June 323 B.C.E.
SCYTHIANS
Olbia
Panticapaeum
Black Sea
Ister (Danube)
ILLYRIA
THRACE
MACEDONIA
Pella
EPIRUS
BITHYNIA
Sinope
Trapezus
CAUCASUS
Caspian Sea
Aral Sea
CHORASMII
MASSAGETAE
Jaxartes
SCYTHIANS (SAKA)
Alexandria Eschata
Maracanda (Samarkand)
SOGDIANA
Oxus
Ilium
Granicus
Aegean Sea
Gordion
Ancyra
(ASIA MINOR)
HELLAS
Athens
Ephesus
Sardis
Sparta
Halicarnassus
Cilician Gates
ARMENIA
Tarsus
Issus
Gaugamela
Arbela
MEDIA
Crete
Mediterranean Sea
Thapsacus
Euphrates
Tigris
CYPRUS
Cyrene
CYRENAICA
Sidon
Tyre
Damascus
SYRIA
LIBYA
Alexandria
Gaza
Jerusalem
Pelusium
Memphis
Oracle of Amon
EGYPT
Nile
Thebes
Syene
Libyan Desert
ETHIOPIA (CUSH)
Red Sea
ARABIA
Babylon
BABYLONIA
SUSIANA
Susa
Ecbatana
Rhagae
Caspian Gates
Hecatompylus
PARTHIA
PERSIS
Persepolis
Persian Gulf
CARMANIA
Alexandria
Harmozia
GEDROSIA
Pura
Bactra
BACTRIA
HINDU KUSH
Indus
ARIA
Alexandria Arion (Herat)
Prophthasia
Alexandria Arachosiorum
ARACHOSIA
Cophen
Taxila
Bucephala
Nicaea
Map 10
Hyphasis (Beas)
INDIA
Indus
Pattala
Probable ancient coastline
Arabian Sea
334
333
332
331
330
329
328
327
326
325
324
323
330-29
325-24
A B C D E F
1 2 3 4

Map 11
Israel's Boundary Under the Maccabees
Boundary of Judea before the uprising, 166 B.C.E.
Maccabean domain at maximum extent
0 5 10 15 20 25 30 35 Mls
0 10 20 30 40 50 Kms
© Copyright HAMMOND INCORPORATED, Maplewood, N. J.
A
B
C
D
1
2
3
4
5
The Great Sea
(Mediterranean Sea)
PHOENICIA
Leontes
Mt. HERMON
Tyre
Ladder of Tyre
Paneas
Cadasa (Kedesh)
Hazor
Seleucia
GAULANITIS
Ptolemais (Acco)
Gamala
Lake Gennesaret
Arbela
Carnaim
Mt. Carmel
GALILEE
Sepphoris
Hippos
Gaba
Plain of Esdraelon
Dion
Philoteria
Yarmuk
Abila
Mt. Tabor
Gadara
Dora
Edrei
Ephron
Scythopolis (Beth-shan)
Strato's Tower
Pella
Narbata
Plain of Sharon
Jordan
SAMARIA
GALAADITIS
Samaria
Gerasa
Amathus
Ragaba
Jabbok
Apollonia
Sichem
Mt. Gerizim
Capharsaba
Pharathon
Alexandrium
Joppa
Ramathaim
Gedor
Timnah
Beth-dagon
Adida (Hadid)
TOBIADS
Gophna
Aphairema
Lydda (Lod)
Modein
Bethel
Philadelphia (Rabbah)
Free city state
Jamnia (Jabneh)
Beth-horon
Elasa
Mizpah
Dok
Tyrus
Caphar-salama
Michmash
Jericho
Gazara (Gezer)
Emmaus
Adasa
Azotus (Ashdod)
Cedron
Heshbon
Samaga
Ekron
Jerusalem
Qumran
JUDEA
Hyrcania
Medeba
Ascalon
Free city state
Beth-zacharias?
Bethbasi
Adullam
Marisa (Mareshah)
Tekoa
Bethzur
Machaerus
Anthedon
Hebron
Salt Sea
Gaza
Adora
En-gedi
PHILISTIA
Arnon
IDUMEA
Masada
Raphia
Arad
Beer-sheba
NABATEANS
Charachmoba
Zoara
AKHRABATTENE
Zered

Map 12
The Roman World
Limits of direct Roman rule or political influence at the birth of Jesus
Provincial or state boundaries
SYRIA Roman provinces
LYCIA Client kingdoms or states
0 100 200 300 400 500 Mls
0 200 400 600 800 Kms
© Copyright HAMMOND INCORPORATED, Maplewood, N. J.
Atlantic Ocean
Britannia
Lutetia
LUGDUNENSIS
BELGICA
Gaul
AQUITANIA
Burdigala
Lugdunum
NARBONENSIS
Narbo
ALPES
ALPS
RAETIA
NORICUM
PANNONIA
Aquileia
Lost by Rome in 9 C.E.
(Elbe)
Rhine
Augusta Treverorum
Germania Magna
Danube
CARPATHIANS
Dacia
Sarmatia
Rha (Volga)
Caspian Sea
TARRACONENSIS
Caesarea Augusta
Tarraco
LUSITANIA
Hispania
Emerita Augusta
BAETICA
Corduba
Tingis
CORSICA AND SARDINIA
Caralis
Rubicon
ITALY
Rome
Tarentum
Sea of Adria
ILLYRICUM
Salonae
MOESIA
Ister (Danube)
THRACE
MACEDONIA
Thessalonica
Byzantium
ACHAIA
Corinth
Athens
Aegean Sea
BOSPORUS KDM.
Black Sea
CAUCASUS
Colchis
Iberia
Albania
Sinope
Trapezus
Artaxata
ARMENIA
BITHYNIA & PONTUS
CAPPADOCIA
Ancyra
COMMAGENE
Pergamum
ASIA
Ephesus
GALATIA
LYCIA
PAMPHYLIA
CILICIA
Tarsus
Antioch
SYRIA
PARTHIAN EMPIRE
Ctesiphon
CYPRUS
KDM. OF HEROD
Jerusalem
NABATEA
Arabia
Red Sea
Mare Internum
(Mediterranean Sea)
CRETA
Cyrene
CYRENAICA
Alexandria
Memphis
EGYPT
Nile
Thebes
Caesarea
MAURETANIA
Cirta
NUMIDIA
Carthage
SICILIA
Syracuse
Leptis Magna
AFRICA

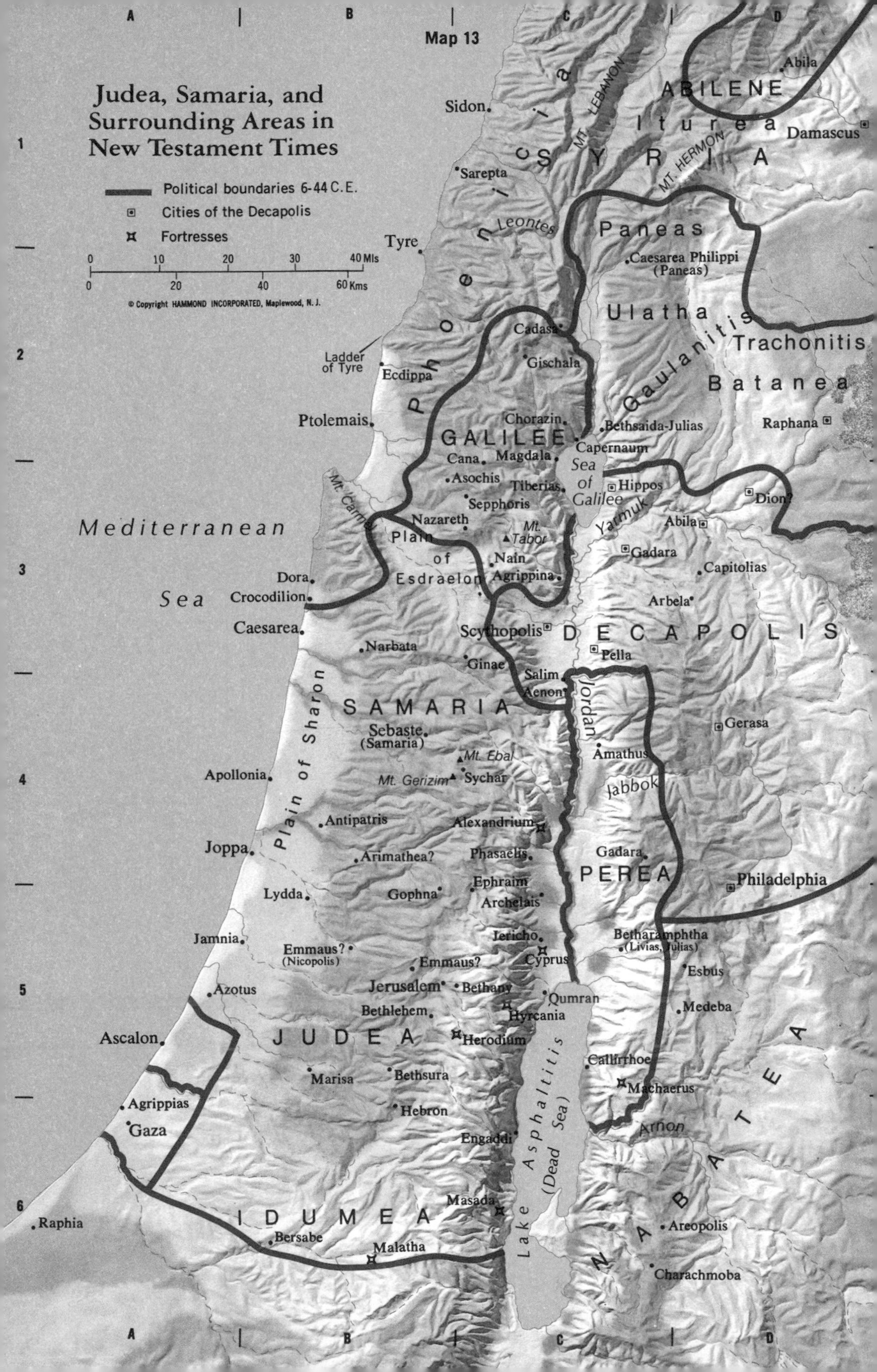
Map 13
Judea, Samaria, and Surrounding Areas in New Testament Times
Political boundaries 6-44 C.E.
Cities of the Decapolis
Fortresses
0 10 20 30 40 Mls
0 20 40 60 Kms
© Copyright HAMMOND INCORPORATED, Maplewood, N. J.
A
B
C
D
1
2
3
4
5
6
Sidon
Sarepta
Tyre
Leontes
Phoenicia
MT. LEBANON
MT. HERMON
ABILENE
Abila
Iturea
Damascus
SYRIA
Paneas
Caesarea Philippi (Paneas)
Ulatha
Gaulanitis
Trachonitis
Batanea
Raphana
Ladder of Tyre
Ecdippa
Cadasa
Gischala
Ptolemais
Chorazin
Bethsaida-Julias
GALILEE
Capernaum
Cana
Magdala
Sea of Galilee
Asochis
Tiberias
Hippos
Dion?
Sepphoris
Yarmuk
Mt. Carmel
Nazareth
Mt. Tabor
Abila
Mediterranean Sea
Plain of Esdraelon
Nain
Gadara
Agrippina
Capitolias
Dora
Crocodilion
Arbela
Caesarea
Scythopolis
DECAPOLIS
Narbata
Pella
Ginae
Salim
Aenon
Jordan
Plain of Sharon
SAMARIA
Sebaste (Samaria)
Gerasa
Mt. Ebal
Amathus
Apollonia
Mt. Gerizim
Sychar
Jabbok
Antipatris
Alexandrium
Joppa
Arimathea?
Phasaelis
Gadara
PEREA
Philadelphia
Lydda
Gophna
Ephraim
Archelais
Jamnia
Jericho
Betharamphtha (Livias, Julias)
Emmaus? (Nicopolis)
Cyprus
Emmaus?
Esbus
Jerusalem
Bethany
Azotus
Qumran
Bethlehem
Hyrcania
Medeba
Ascalon
JUDEA
Herodium
Lake Asphaltitis (Dead Sea)
Callirrhoe
Marisa
Bethsura
Machaerus
Agrippias
Hebron
Gaza
Arnon
Engaddi
NABATEA
Masada
Raphia
IDUMEA
Areopolis
Bersabe
Malatha
Charachmoba

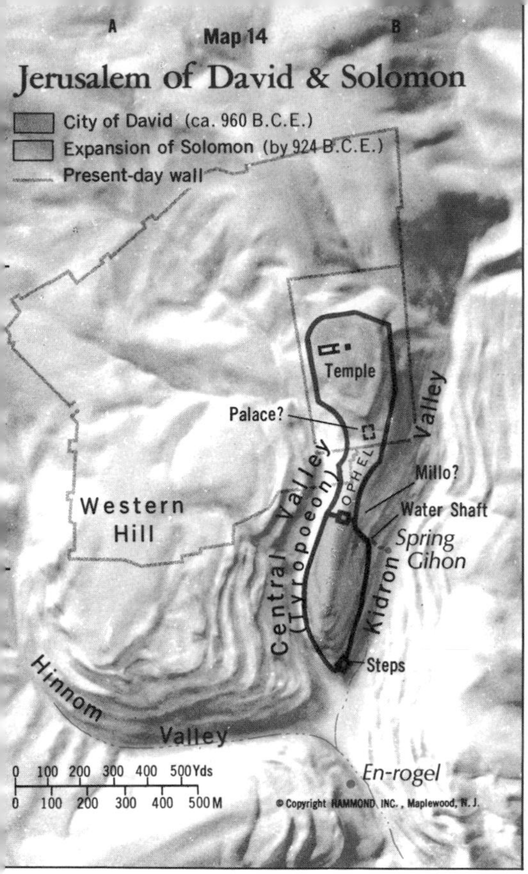
A
Map 14
B
Jerusalem of David & Solomon
City of David (ca. 960 B.C.E.)
Expansion of Solomon (by 924 B.C.E.)
Present-day wall
Temple
Palace?
OPHEL
Valley
Millo?
Water Shaft
Spring Gihon
Western Hill
Central Valley (Tyropoeon)
Kidron
Steps
Hinnom
Valley
En-rogel
0 100 200 300 400 500 Yds
0 100 200 300 400 500 M
© Copyright HAMMOND INC., Maplewood, N.J.

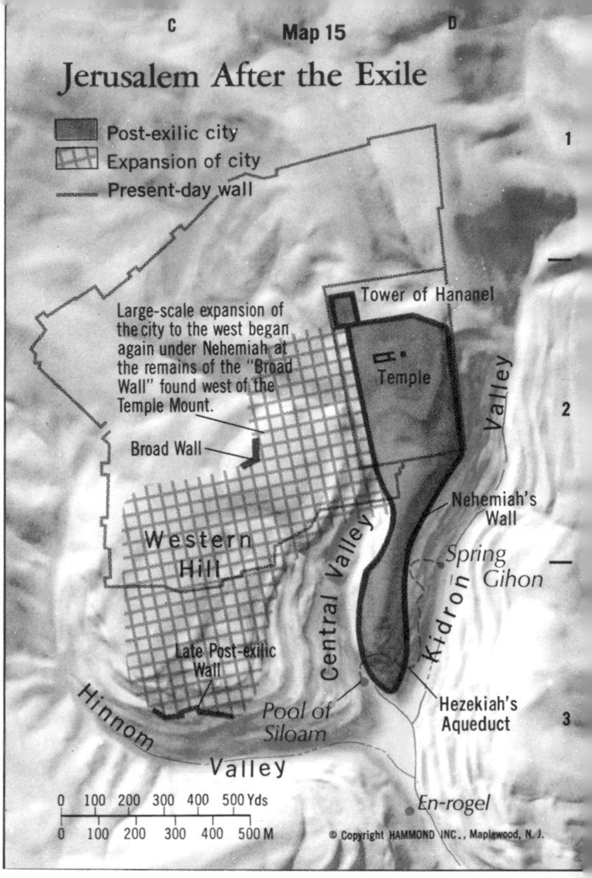
C
Map 15
D
Jerusalem After the Exile
Post-exilic city
Expansion of city
Present-day wall
1
Tower of Hananel
Large-scale expansion of the city to the west began again under Nehemiah at the remains of the "Broad Wall" found west of the Temple Mount.
Temple
Valley
2
Broad Wall
Nehemiah's Wall
Western Hill
Central Valley
Spring Gihon
Kidron
Late Post-exilic Wall
Hezekiah's Aqueduct
3
Hinnom
Pool of Siloam
Valley
En-rogel
0 100 200 300 400 500 Yds
0 100 200 300 400 500 M
© Copyright HAMMOND INC., Maplewood, N.J.

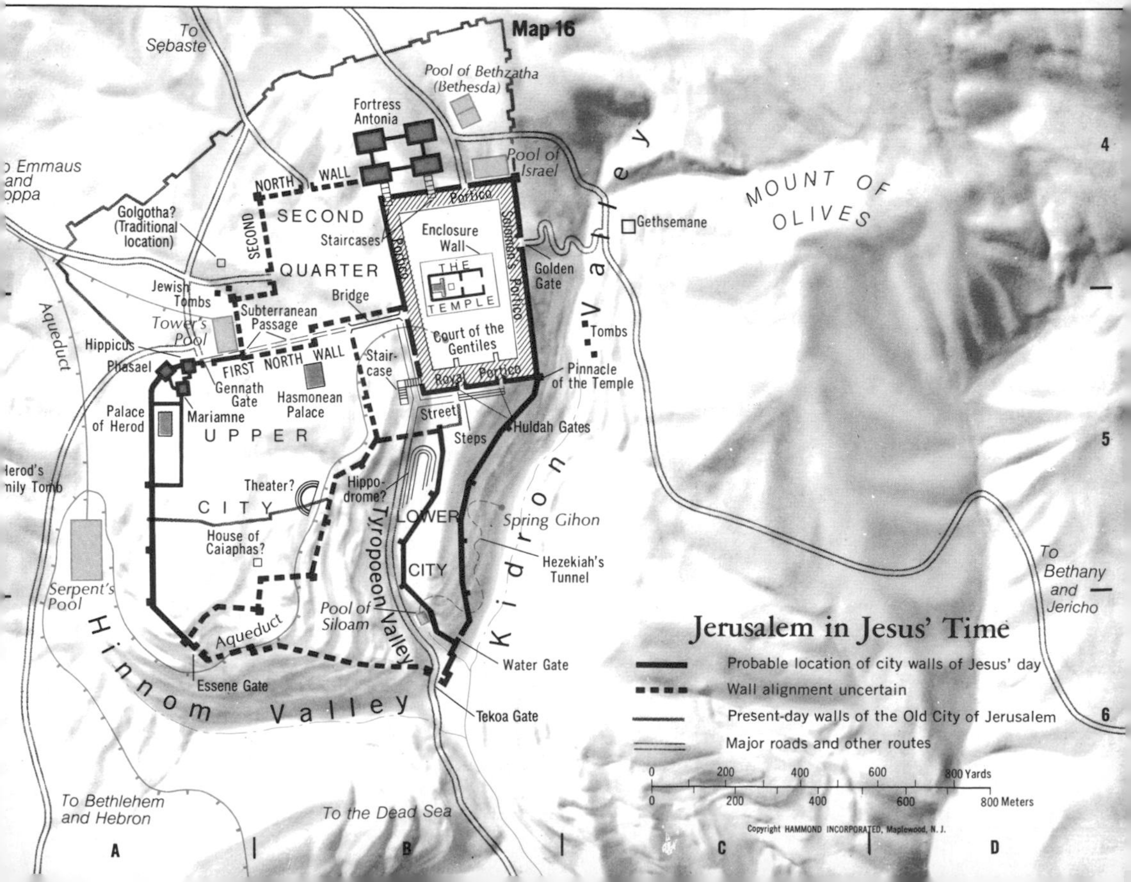
Map 16
To Sebaste
Pool of Bethzatha (Bethesda)
Fortress Antonia
4
Pool of Israel
Valley
o Emmaus and oppa
NORTH WALL
MOUNT OF OLIVES
Portico
Golgotha? (Traditional location)
SECOND
SECOND QUARTER
Enclosure Wall
Solomon's Portico
Gethsemane
Staircases
Portico
THE TEMPLE
Golden Gate
Jewish Tombs
Bridge
Subterranean Passage
Tower's Pool
Court of the Gentiles
Tombs
Aqueduct
Hippicus
Phasael
FIRST NORTH WALL
Staircase
Royal Portico
Pinnacle of the Temple
Gennath Gate
Hasmonean Palace
Palace of Herod
Mariamne
Street
Steps
Huldah Gates
UPPER
5
lerod's nily Tomb
Theater?
Hippodrome?
CITY
LOWER
Spring Gihon
House of Caiaphas?
Tyropoeon Valley
CITY
Hezekiah's Tunnel
To Bethany and Jericho
Serpent's Pool
Pool of Siloam
Kidron
Hinnom Valley
Aqueduct
Water Gate
Essene Gate
Tekoa Gate
6
Jerusalem in Jesus' Time
Probable location of city walls of Jesus' day
Wall alignment uncertain
Present-day walls of the Old City of Jerusalem
Major roads and other routes
0 200 400 600 800 Yards
0 200 400 600 800 Meters
To Bethlehem and Hebron
To the Dead Sea
Copyright HAMMOND INCORPORATED, Maplewood, N.J.
A
B
C
D

Map 17
The Eastern Mediterranean World at the Time of the New Testament (First Century C.E.)
Provincial boundaries in the Roman Empire ca. 60 C.E.
0 100 200 300 Mls
0 100 200 300 400 500 Kms
Black Sea
Mediterranean Sea
Tyrrhenian Sea
Adria
Aegean Sea
ITALY
ILLYRICUM (DALMATIA)
MOESIA
THRACE
MACEDONIA
Epirus
ACHAIA
ASIA
Mysia
Lydia
Caria
Phrygia
Pisidia
BITHYNIA & PONTUS
Paphlagonia
GALATIA
Lycaonia
CAPPADOCIA
KINGDOM OF POLEMON
PAMPHYLIA
LYCIA
CILICIA
SYRIA
CYPRUS
CRETE
SICILY
CYRENAICA (LIBYA)
EGYPT
NABATEANS
Judea
Rome
Ostia
Ortona
Three Taverns
Forum of Appius
Puteoli
Beneventum
Paestum
Tarentum
Croton
Messana
Rhegium
Syracuse
Agrigentum
Malta (Melita)
Scodra
Dyrrhachium
Apollonia
Corcyra
Nicopolis
Larisa
Beroea
Thessalonica
Amphipolis
Philippi
Neapolis
Apollonia
Samothrace
Athens
Corinth
Cenchreae
Sparta
Hebrus
Mesembria
Byzantium
Propontis
Troas
Assos
Lesbos
Mitylene
Adramyttium
Pergamum
Thyatira
Smyrna
Sardis
Chios
Samos
Ephesus
Miletus
Laodicea
Colossae
Cos
Cnidus
Rhodes
Patara
Myra
Attalia
Perga
Nicomedia
Nicaea
Heraclea
Sangarius
Dorylaeum
Pessinus
Ancyra
Halys
Tavium
Sinope
Amisus
Amasia
Comana
Caesarea Mazaca
Lake Tatta
Antioch
Iconium
Lystra
Derbe
Tyana
Tarsus
Seleucia
Antioch
Salamis
Paphos
Phoenix
Cnossus
C. Salmone
Lasea
Fair Havens
Cauda
Cyrene
Alexandria
Pelusium
Heliopolis
Sidon
Damascus
Tyre
Ptolemaïs
Caesarea
Joppa
Jerusalem
Gaza
© Copyright HAMMOND INCORPORATED, Maplewood, N. J.

Archaeological Sites in Israel and Jordan
Principal excavated sites
T, Tel, Tell: city site or mound
Kh, Khirbet: ruin
0 5 10 15 20 25 MIs
0 10 20 30 40 Kms
© Copyright by HAMMOND INC, Maplewood, N.J.
Map 18
Zarephath
Sidon
Damascus
LEBANON
SYRIA
Tyre
Dan
Baniyas (Caesarea Philippi)
T. Anafa
Achzib
Nahariyeh
Kafr Bir'im
Gush Halab
Hazor
Meiron
Nabratein
GOLAN HEIGHTS
Acco
Chorazin
Gamala
Tabgha
Capernaum
T. Shikmona
Kh. Irbid
Sea of Galilee
Kursi
Carmel Caves
T. Abu Hawam
Tiberias
Sepphoris
Hippos
Mediterranean Sea
Atlit
Beth-yerah
Abila
Wadi el-Mughara
Beth Shearim
Nazareth
Jokneam
Umm Qeis (Gadara)
Dor
Megiddo
Bosra
Taanach
Beth Alpha
Caesarea
Ramoth-gilead
Beth-shan
T. Zeror
Pella
T. el-Hayyat
Dothan
T. el-Far'ah (N) (Tirzah)
T. es-Saidiyeh (Zarethan?)
Jerash
Samaria (Sebaste)
Mt. Ebal
ISRAEL
T. Deir 'Allā (Succoth?)
Shechem
T. Mikhal
Mt. Gerizim
Aphek (Antipatris)
T. el-Qasileh
Zarethan?
Izbet Sarta
JORDAN
Joppa
Shiloh
Jordan
WEST BANK
Ain Ghazzal
Mezad Hashavyahu
Bethel
Ai
Kh. el-Mefjir (Gilgal?)
Rabbah-Amman
Araq el-Emir
T. en-Nasbeh (Mizpah?)
Gezer
Jericho O.T.
T. Mor
Tel Miqne (Ekron)
Gibeon
Gibeah
Jericho N.T.
Ashdod Yam
Teleilat el-Ghassul
Heshbon
Timnah
Jerusalem
Ashdod
'Ain Karim
Mt. Nebo
Beth-shemesh
Ramet Rahel
Qumran
'Ain Feshka
Azekah
Madaba
T. es-Safi (Gath?)
Bethlehem
Ashkelon
Herodium
T. el-'Areini
Mareshah
Beth-zur
Lachish
Wadi el-Murabba'at Caves
Kh. Iskander
GAZA STRIP
T. el-Hesi (Eglon?)
Mamre
Dead Sea
Gaza
T. en-Nejileh
T. 'Aitun (Eglon?)
Dibon
T. el-'Ajjul
T. Beit Mirsim
En-gedi
'Aroer
Kh. Rabud (Debir?)
Lehun
T. Jemmeh
T. Halif
T. esh-Shari'ah
T. el-Far'ah (S) (Sharuhen)
Masada
Arad-EB
Beersheba
T. Abu Matar
Bab edh-Drah
Lejjun
Arad
Kh. el-Mishash
Kh. el-Kerak
Khalasa
Kuraub
Zoar
Numeira
Kh. et-Tannur
A
B
C
D
1
2
3
4
5
6

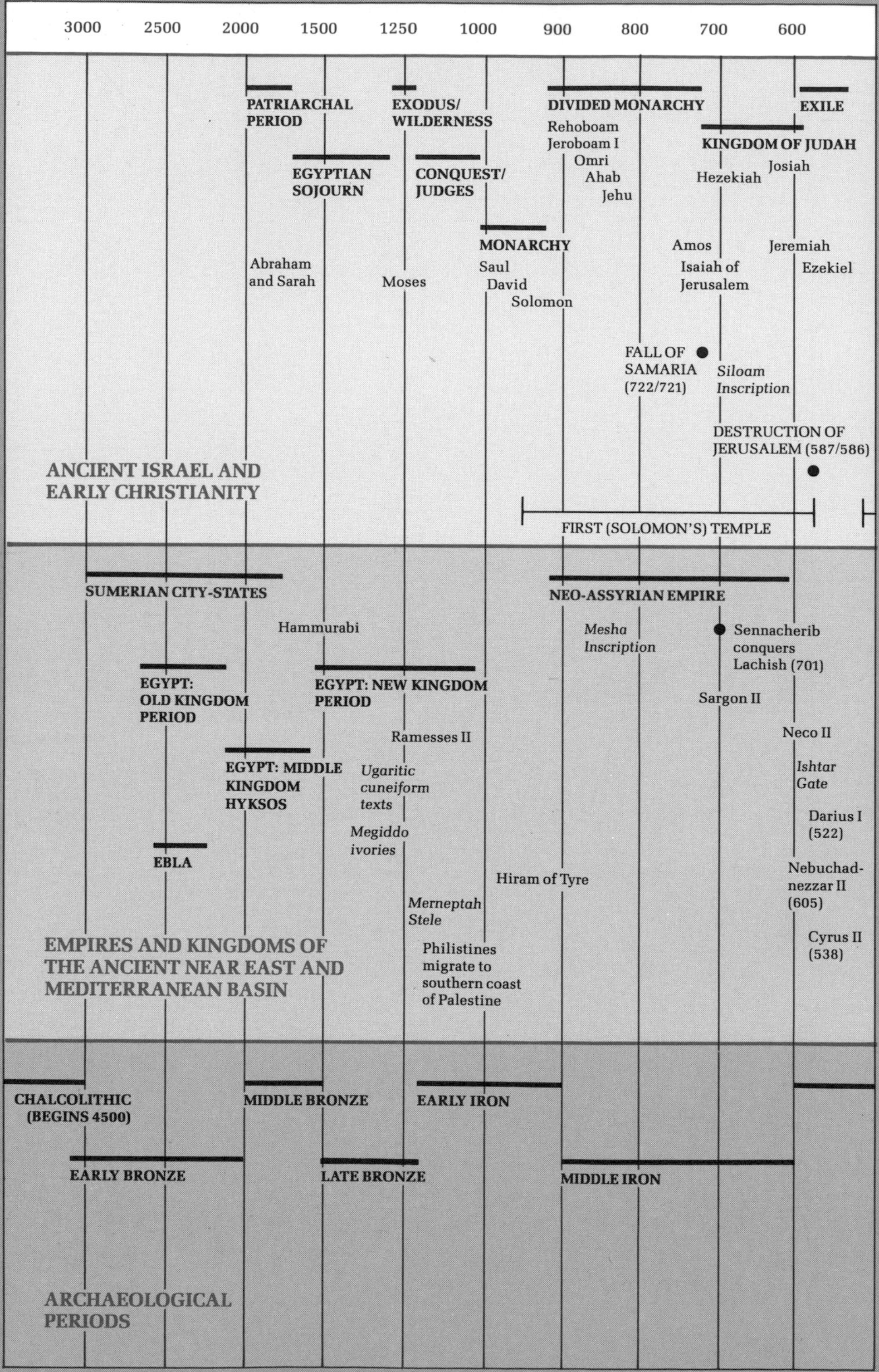

3000
2500
2000
1500
1250
1000
900
800
700
600
PATRIARCHAL PERIOD
EXODUS/ WILDERNESS
DIVIDED MONARCHY
Rehoboam
Jeroboam I
Omri
Ahab
Jehu
EXILE
KINGDOM OF JUDAH
Hezekiah
Josiah
EGYPTIAN SOJOURN
CONQUEST/ JUDGES
MONARCHY
Saul
David
Solomon
Abraham and Sarah
Moses
Amos
Isaiah of Jerusalem
Jeremiah
Ezekiel
FALL OF SAMARIA (722/721)
Siloam Inscription
DESTRUCTION OF JERUSALEM (587/586)
ANCIENT ISRAEL AND EARLY CHRISTIANITY
FIRST (SOLOMON'S) TEMPLE
SUMERIAN CITY-STATES
NEO-ASSYRIAN EMPIRE
Hammurabi
Mesha Inscription
Sennacherib conquers Lachish (701)
EGYPT: OLD KINGDOM PERIOD
EGYPT: NEW KINGDOM PERIOD
Sargon II
Ramesses II
Neco II
EGYPT: MIDDLE KINGDOM HYKSOS
Ugaritic cuneiform texts
Ishtar Gate
Megiddo ivories
Darius I (522)
EBLA
Hiram of Tyre
Nebuchad-nezzar II (605)
Merneptah Stele
Cyrus II (538)
EMPIRES AND KINGDOMS OF THE ANCIENT NEAR EAST AND MEDITERRANEAN BASIN
Philistines migrate to southern coast of Palestine
CHALCOLITHIC (BEGINS 4500)
MIDDLE BRONZE
EARLY IRON
EARLY BRONZE
LATE BRONZE
MIDDLE IRON
ARCHAEOLOGICAL PERIODS